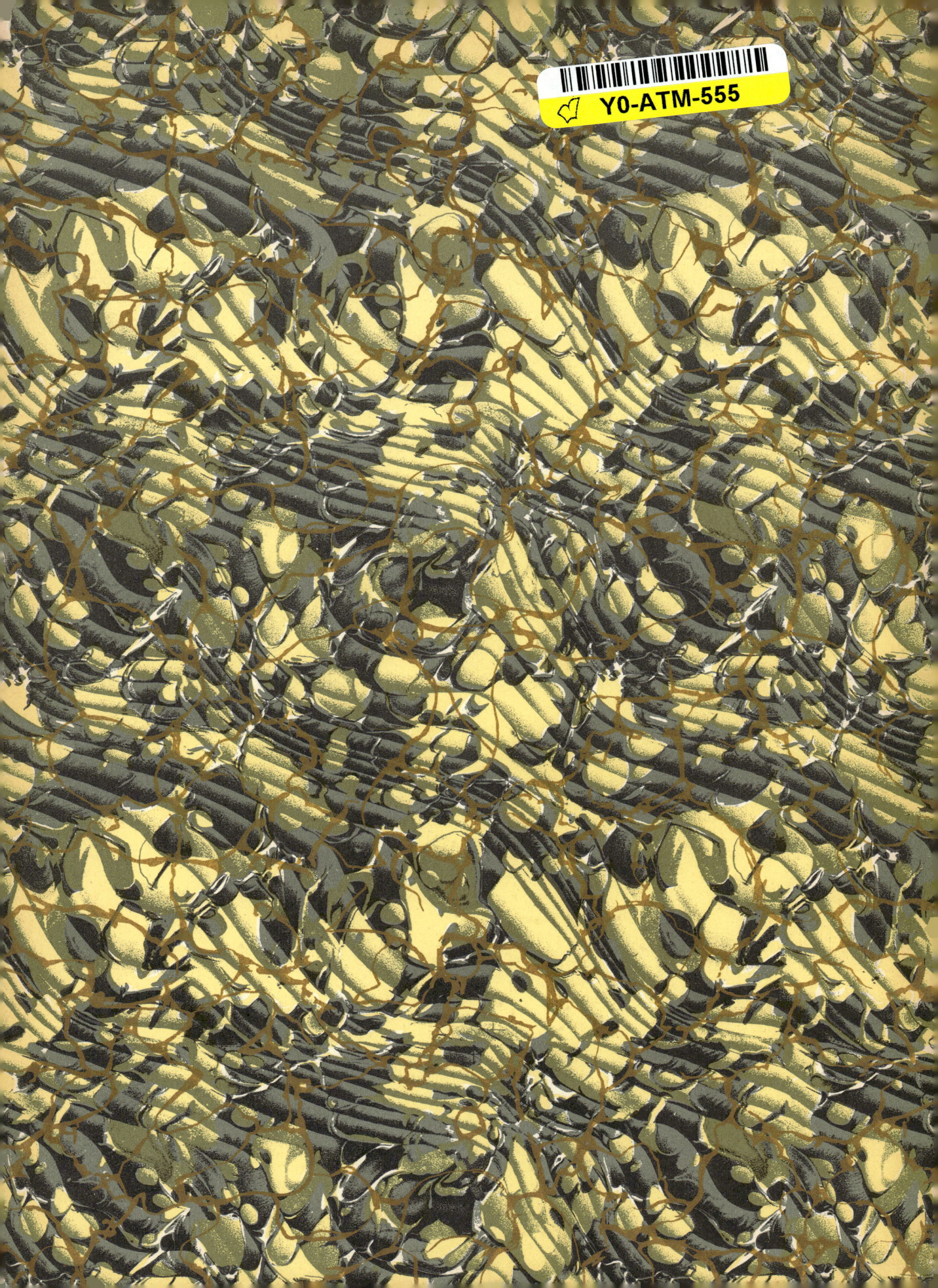

HISTORY
OF
ILLINOIS
AND
HER PEOPLE

BY

PROFESSOR GEORGE W. SMITH, M. A.

Head, Department of History, State Teachers College, Carbondale, Illinois;
Author of a Student's History of Illinois; Member Board
of Directors, State Historical Society

Assisted by an Advisory Board

IN SIX VOLUMES

ILLUSTRATED

Volume V

PUBLISHERS
THE AMERICAN HISTORICAL SOCIETY, Inc.
CHICAGO AND NEW YORK
1927

COPYRIGHT 1927
THE AMERICAN HISTORICAL SOCIETY, INC.

History of Illinois

SAMUEL INSULL. As a resident of Chicago and Illinois since 1892, Mr. Insull's career has been identified with the expression and development of the arts and industries inaugurated by the era of the Columbian Exposition. For nearly twelve years previously he had been a lieutenant of affairs for that master mind of science, Thomas A. Edison. In Chicago he found his life work in the commercial and industrial development of applied electricity. In making Chicago the "capital" of the electrical world, with development and utilization of applied electricity farther advanced in this district than in any comparable area elsewhere, he perfected an organization obviously greater than any individual of its personnel. Yet, as the oft-expressed opinion of associates and subordinates shows, perhaps no organization has ever been more completely permeated by the spirit and force of its chief executive than is true of the staff and army of which Samuel Insull is the head and chief. The hardest individual worker of them all, his important task has been the perfection and maintenance of a system of smooth efficiency adequate for every "peak load" of routine or emergency.

In this he has been obviously one of the busiest of men. Yet for some years the Chicago community has been conscious that it had in Samuel Insull one who could be depended on for leadership, counsel and extraordinary responsibility when the occasion demanded such a man. He proved his sufficiency in this respect during the war period and in civic movements both before and since. It has been a principle of his that: "The materially successful man owes it to the community in which he makes his money to do something for the community—as much as he can—that he does not get paid for."

Samuel Insull was born in London, England, on November 11, 1859, son of Samuel and Emma (Short) Insull. He was educated in private schools, supplemented by study at Reading and Oxford. It was his youthful ambition to sit in the gallery of the House of Commons and report the parliamentary debates for the London newspapers as Charles Dickens had done. As a boy he lived in the Dickens neighborhood and was full of the Dickens history and tradition. From this ambition he was diverted into business channels. While still in his teens he became associated with Col. George E. Gouraud, who was in London as the representative of Thomas A. Edison to organize the Edison Telephone Company of London, the infant telephone industry being then Mr. Edison's major interest. In this employment young Insull helped set up and operate (for demonstration purposes) the first telephone switchboard in Europe, acquired a working knowledge of electrical terms and facts, and evidently revealed out-of-the-ordinary aptitude and industry, since this connection brought him an invitation across the Atlantic.

Mr. Insull came to the United States in 1881, when he was barely twenty-one years old, to be Thomas A. Edison's private secretary. Almost immediately he became much more than a private secretary; he became Mr. Edison's man of business in the fullest sense of the term, handling all of the great inventor's business and financial affairs, which were already large and soon to become much larger, including his personal finances.

The incandescent electric lamp, invented by Mr. Edison in 1879, had been developed in 1881 to the point of commercial practicability. The great electrical industry as it is known today, in all of its wonder working manifestations, dates from that period. In finding and applying the principles that made the incandescent lamp commercially practicable for electrical lighting Mr. Edison had literally "invented" the electrical industry; for those principles as then discovered and applied are still the basis of applied electricity; and the original apparatus for applying them, even the tools and machinery for producing the apparatus, were largely invented and built by Mr. Edison. The first central station in the world for generation and distribution of electrical energy on a commercial scale was built by Mr. Edison in the city of New York and put into service in September, 1882, a year and a half after Mr. Insull arrived in this country. Then followed a period of amazing development and expansion.

During the formative and pioneering period of the electrical industry Mr. Insull had full charge of the business affairs of the "wizard of Menlo Park." He represented Mr. Edison in the organization and management of the Electric Tube Company, the Edison Machine Works, the Edison Lamp Company and Bergmann and Company. He built and operated for Mr. Edison the Edison Machine Works at Schenectady, New York, which was the nucleus of what is now the great Schenectady plant of the General Electric Company. When the various Edison manufacturing concerns, together with the Edison Electric Light Company, were merged in 1889 into the Edison General Electric Company, Mr. Insull became vice president of the new corporation, in charge of its manufacturing and selling departments. This corporation was consolidated in 1892 with the Thomson-Houston Company as the General Electric Company, and Mr. Insull became second vice president of the new corporation.

Meanwhile, Mr. Insull, then only thirty-two years old, had conceived an ambition to make a career for himself in the electric central station business, in generating and marketing electrical energy as distinguished from manufacturing and marketing electrical apparatus. The presidency of the Chicago Edison Company, which had been formed in 1887, was offered to him. Because he preferred Chicago above all other cities for the career he had in mind the offer was accepted and the presidency of the Chicago Edison Company was assumed in May, 1892.

Under Mr. Insull the Chicago Edison Company grew and expanded rapidly, absorbing rivals as large as, or larger than, itself and putting the electric light and power business on the economically sound, "one-city-one-system" basis. In 1907 the Chicago Edison and the Commonwealth Electric Companies of Chicago were consolidated as the Commonwealth Edison Company, which now (1926) generates and distributes directly to the users more electrical energy than any other electricity supply company in the world. It generates (1926) 4.6 per cent of all the electrical energy generated in the United States, although its market contains only 2.6 per cent of the country's population, thus giving Chicago unique distinction in the per capita use of electric light and power.

The Commonwealth Edison Company's development under Mr. Insull is a large part of the history of electrical central station development since 1892. One example to illustrate the point has been the utilization of the steam turbine in the generation of electricity. A turbo-generator of 5,000 kilowatts capacity, installed in the Fisk Street station of the company in 1903, was the largest generator of this type that the General Electric Company could—or would—build at that time. It was an innovation, looked upon with no little skepticism by electrical experts. Mr. Insull, with confidence in its efficiency, assumed the full responsibility for it and inaugurated a veritable revolution in the production of electrical energy. That first 5,000 kilowatt generator eventually became obsolete and was removed to Schenectady, New York, where it is preserved by the General Electric Company as a monument marking the beginning of an era in the economical production of electrical energy. Since the Fisk Street demonstration larger and still larger turbo-generators have been standard central station equipment. Units of 60,000 kilowatts capacity were built in 1924 for the Commonwealth Edison Company's new Crawford Avenue Station, one of 77,000 kilowatts capacity was bought in 1925 and one of 90,000 kilowatts capacity was ordered in 1926.

Mr. Insull's business creed, as it were, in the management of public service companies may be summed up in these words: "Highest possible efficiency in operation to achieve the lowest possible cost of production; best possible service to customers, at the lowest possible rates consistent with fair return to stockholders on their investment, to achieve the largest possible volume of business." His conspicuous success in applying these principles in the Commonwealth Edison Company has led to the utilization of his unusual aptitude for public utility management in other companies. He became chairman of the Board of Directors of The People's Gas Light and Coke Company of Chicago in 1913, but without assuming charge of operating details. During the World war period he gave very little time to private affairs. When the war ended the People's Company had reached the lowest stage of its fortunes. Mr. Insull then took full responsibility for its management and in three years performed what Mr. John J. Mitchell characterized as "the most remarkable example of corporate resurrection" that he had ever seen.

Mr. Insull is (in 1926) president and chairman of the Board of Directors of the Commonwealth Edison Company and The People's Gas Light and Coke Company of Chicago; president and chairman of the Midland Utilities Company and the Northern Indiana Public Service Company and their subsidiaries; chairman of the Middle West Utilities Company; the Public Service Company of Northern Illinois; the Chicago Rapid Transit Company; the Chicago North Shore and Milwaukee Railroad, and of many other public utility enterprises.

The general public found a conspicuous illustration of his genius for organization and administration at the time of the World war, when Governor Frank O. Lowden appointed him chairman of the State Council of Defense of Illinois, which was created by act of the Legislature and clothed with very wide and elastic powers. This body, under Mr. Insull's personal direction, "organized the public mind of the state for every war need." It also organized and guided in detail practically every phase of participation in the war, and in war time activities, by the State of Illinois and its people. The council's interests ranged from soldier and sailor entertainments to soldier and sailor enlistments; from war charities to war industries; from stimulating patriotic thought and action to correcting disloyalties; from conserving energy and resources to raising money, crops and troops. It had 80,000 men and women organized and officered for definite tasks, besides 300,000 enrolled in women's organizations which were under its general supervision. Its record, in respect to work done and cost of getting it done, was unique. No other State Council of Defense accomplished more. While other states made appropriations for this, ranging from $100,000 to $5,000,000, Illinois appropriated only $50,000 and about $5,000 was turned back to the state treasury; so the council's work cost the taxpayers of Illinois only seven-tenths of one cent per capita. There were expenses, of course, amounting to more than that; the total was $270,674 and the figures would have been ten times that but for Mr. Insull's ability to get the council's work done by volunteers, only essential clerical work and printing, postage and the like, being paid for. These expenses, except for about $45,000 of the state appropriation, were met by private subscriptions, plus a small amount of profit from self-supporting patriotic enterprises. The sum of $450,000 was turned back into the United States Treasury as earnings on conservation and exhibition enterprises managed for the federal government.

The limits of this article permit reference to only one among the best known of Mr. Insull's civic activities in time of peace. For some years a group of Chicago men and women of means had financed grand opera in their city, making up large annual deficits. Eventually, when some of the heavier contributors found it inexpedient to continue distribution of the burden over a larger and more general public organization was attempted. The matter was taken in hand by an organization fostered by the Chicago Association of Commerce, which attempted to raise the required guaranty fund of $500,000 a year, and to establish opera as a civic enterprise on a stable financial basis. Mr. Insull was later, in the spring of 1922, drafted into service to complete the guaranty fund and brings the undertaking under proper business and financial control. Under his guidance the required guaranty fund was raised, the annual deficits were reduced, and the continuance of grand opera was assured to Chicago, with control based upon thorough business principle, without the slightest sacrifice of artistic standards.

Union College has conferred upon Mr. Insull the degrees of Doctor of Science; Northwestern University and Notre Dame University, the honorary degree of Doctor of Laws. He holds membership in the American Institute of Electrical Engineers, the British Institute of Electrical Engineers, and other technical organizations. He is on the membership rolls of the Reform, the Devonshire, the City of London, the Royal Automobile and the American Clubs in his native London; the Metropolitan, the Recess, the Bankers and Engineers Clubs of New York; the Chicago, Mid-Day, Chicago Athletic, Casino, Onwentsia, and many other clubs in Chicago and vicinity.

On May 29, 1899, Mr. Insull married Miss Margaret Bird, of New York. They have one son, Samuel Insull, Jr., who is following in his father's footsteps in the public utility industry.

OTTO L. SCHMIDT. A prominent physician, whose recreation and serious avocation has been in the field of historical research, Doctor Schmidt is a native of Chicago, son of one of its old time physicians, and has practiced medicine there. Doctor Schmidt was chairman of the Illinois Centennial Commission, which arranged the celebration of the centennial of the state in 1918.

Doctor Schmidt was born in Chicago, March 21, 1863, one of five children, three still living. His parents were Doctor Ernst and Theresa (Weikard) Schmidt, natives of Germany. Dr. Ernst Schmidt came to the United States in 1857, and became very well known professionally and as a citizen of Chicago. From 1859 to the fall of 1861 his home was in St. Louis, and while there he enlisted for a brief period in the Second Missouri (Union) Regiment as a surgeon. From 1865 for a year he was coroner of Cook County. He was a man of superior education and attainments. He died in Chicago in 1900.

Doctor Otto L. Schmidt has always made Chicago his home. He graduated in 1880 from the Central High School as a member of its last graduating class, and in the same year entered the Chicago Medical College, where he received his degree in 1883. He was an interne in the Cook County Infirmary, later in the Alexian Brothers Hospital, and for two years pursued post-graduate work in Germany and Vienna. In 1887 he established himself in practice at Chicago, specializing in internal medicine. For a time he was physician to Alexian Brothers Hospital, consulting physician to Michael Reese Hospital and Grant Hospital, professor of internal medicine at the Chicago Polyclinic, and for many years has been a member of the Chicago Medical Society, the Chicago Society of Medical History, German Medical Society and the American Medical Association.

Since 1916 Doctor Schmidt has been president of the Illinois Historical Society, and was one of the two officials of that organization selected for membership on the Illinois State Centennial Commission of 1918, being chosen as its chairman. Since 1923 he has been president and since 1911 a member of the Illinois State Library Board, and since 1923 has been president of the Chicago Historical Society. He is president of the German-American Historical Society of Illinois. Doctor Schmidt is a member of the Union League, Chicago Athletic, South Shore Country, Chicago Lincoln and German Clubs.

He married in 1891 Miss Emma Seipp. Their three children are Ernst C., Alma, wife of W. F. Petersen, and C. Tessa.

HON. FRANK TRIMBLE O'HAIR, former congressman from Illinois, has earned a distinguished record in the legal profession and in the civic life of Edgar County, having practiced law at Paris for over thirty years.

He was born in Edgar County, March 12, 1870, son of John Henry and Nancy Eveline (Swango) O'Hair. His father came from Kentucky in 1841 and settled in Edgar County, and the mother came from Kentucky in 1859. Mr. O'Hair is of old American fighting stock. Several of his ancestors came from Great Britain and joined the colonists in their struggle for independence. His great-grandfather, Michael O'Hair, came from County Dawn, Ireland, in 1776, joined the Revolutionary army from Virginia and subsequently moved to Kentucky. Another great-grandfather, Jordan Hardwick, came from Wales at the beginning of the Revolution. The great-grandfather, David Trimble, came from Ireland about 1775. On the maternal side the great-grandfather, Abraham Swango, came from England. Many members of these different families were represented in the Confederate army during the Civil war. There were nine of the Swangos killed from one neighborhood. Mr. O'Hair's father, John Henry O'Hair, served as sheriff of Coles County, Illinois, through the Civil war period. Frank Trimble O'Hair was educated in public schools and graduated A. B. from DePauw University at Greencastle, Indiana, in 1893. In the same year he entered the law business and has practiced steadily at Paris. He served as master in chancery of the Circuit Court at Paris from 1905 to 1912. Mr. O'Hair is a director of the Kansas and Sidell Railway, of the Terre Haute and Western Railway and of the First National Bank of Paris.

For a number of years his abilities have made him one of the ranking figures in the democratic party of Illinois. In 1912 he was elected to represent the Eighteenth Illinois District in Congress, serving in the Sixty-third Congress from 1913 to 1915. Mr. O'Hair is affiliated with Prairie Lodge No. 77 of the Masonic fraternity, belongs to the Elks Lodge No. 8, and to the Knights of Pythias, Improved Order of Red Men, Modern Woodmen of America, the Eastern Star, Pythian Sisters and Daughters of Pocahontas. He is a Rotarian.

He married at Paris, May 10, 1905, Miss Ruth Harding Huston, daughter of David D. and Anna H. Huston. They have two children: Ruth Frances, born October 18, 1907, and Huston Harding, born January 31, 1918.

JAMES JOSEPH BARBOUR during the thirty-five years he has practice law in Chicago has been distinguished by his great ability as an advocate, force and courage in the legal investigation as well as trial of causes, abilities that have drawn him into many engagements where the vital interests of the community have been at stake.

He represents the old New England family of Barbour which was established by Thomas Barbour at Windsor, Connecticut, in 1635. Henry Barbour, the great-grandfather of the Chicago attorney, was born March 12, 1793, and married, in 1817, Naomi Humphrey, a descendant of the Humphrey family that was established at Windsor, Connecticut, in 1640. Heman Humphrey Barbour, Sr., was born July 19, 1820, and married, in 1845, Frances Elizabeth Merrill. They had a large family, one of whom was an eminent attorney and statesman of Connecticut, Joseph Lane Barbour.

Heman Humphrey Barbour, Jr., father of James Joseph Barbour, was born at Hartford, Connecticut, June 22, 1850. He studied law, and practiced from 1871 to 1880, being distinguished by his oratorical gift and his remarkable energy. Becoming convinced of his duty to preach the Gospel, he was ordained to the ministry and held many pastorates in New Jersey, New York, Chicago and elsewhere. He married, in 1869, Frances Emma Luther, of Hardford, Connecticut, and the oldest of their three children was James Joseph Barbour, who was born at Hartford, Connecticut, December 28, 1869.

James Joseph Barbour from earliest boyhood had an ambition to succeed as an advocate. He studied the biographies of many statesmen and lawyers, read the literature of eventful trials, and at every opportunity came in touch with lawyers and work at the courts. He was educated in the high school at Newark, New Jersey, and in 1888 took up the study of law in the office of Judge Frederick A. Smith at Chicago. He attended the Lake Forest University School of Law from 1889 to 1892. For several years he was attorney for the Commercial National Bank at Chicago. From 1904 to 1909 he served as assistant state's attorney. As a member of the firm Knight, Barbour & Adams he was one of the attorneys during the elevated railroad and Yerkes estate litigation. He acted as special council to the attorney general of Illinois in the City of Rock Island vice and graft prosecutions beginning in 1923, and continuing through 1926, and during 1924 served as special assistant state's attorney of Cook County. Mr. Barbour is now a member of the law firm Barbour, Adams & Litsendahl, with law offices at 5 North La Salle Street.

He was elected a member of the Illinois State Senate in 1916, 1920 and 1924, and was a member of the Republican State Central Committee during 1922-24. During the World war he was chairman of the Local Advisory Board, and speaker for various patriotic organizations. He has served as vice president of the American Institute of Criminal Law and Criminology and as president of the Illinois Society. He is the compiler of the third edition of Abbott's Criminal Trial Briefs, published in 1925, and extensively used throughout the United States by lawyers engaged in criminal trials. In 1924 he was president of the New England Society of Chicago. In 1923 he was delegate to the Baptist World's Alliance at Stockholm, Sweden. Mr. Barbour is a Mason, a member of the Evanston Golf Club and the Illini Country Club of Springfield.

He married, September 1, 1891, Miss Lillian Clayton, of Chicago. The three children of their marriage are: Justin Fulton, Heman Humphrey and Elizabeth.

NEWTON ELLSWORTH BELL through an active life of over forty years has been identified with agriculture and in more recent years with manufacturing. He is proprietor of the Bell Machine Works in Paris, Edgar County.

He was born at Talmadge, Ohio, September 18, 1863, son of William and Elizabeth (Ogle) Bell. His ancestor, Richard Ogle, came from England in 1753, and two years later his wife and nine children followed, sailing from Liverpool and landing at Quebec after a voyage of eight weeks. The Ogles and the Bells were pioneers of Ohio. In 1867 the Bell family settled in Clark County, Illinois, and subsequently removed to Edgar County.

Newton E. Bell was educated in public schools and as a youth took up farming, a business he followed long and faithfully and thereby laid the foundation of his business career. Leaving the farm, he founded the Bell Machine Works, a plant located close to the Vandalia Railroad on Main Street in Paris.

Mr. Bell is an independent in politics. He is affiliated with the Paris Lodge No. 268 of the Masonic fraternity, Austin Lodge, Independent Order of Odd Fellows, Eastern Star and the Modern Woodmen of America. He married at Paris, September 16, 1897, Emma Selzer, a daughter of Louis and Catherine Selzer, who came from Germany. Mr. and Mrs. Bell are members of the Presbyterian Church.

JOHN ELBLE. For over forty years John Elble of Alton has been accumulating a reputation as a man peculiarly qualified for prompt and efficient service in public capacities, whether in emergency or routine situations. Mr. Elble has been a successful business man, and has filled nearly every important administrative office in his home city and township. He is the present mayor of Alton.

He was born in that city January 17, 1855, son of Benedict and Margaret (Von Stein) Elble. His father who was born in Baden, Germany, in 1831, came to America in 1848 as a result of some connection with the revolutionary movement in Germany, and at once located in Alton. He was a shoemaker by trade, but for a number of years was in business as a general merchant. He was a steamship agent, and served as city assessor and city treasurer. He was a democrat, a member of the Masonic fraternity, and was a leader in old time musical affairs at Alton. He died in 1872 when only forty-one years of age. His wife was born in St. Louis, Missouri, her people coming from Germany. As a girl in St. Louis she was at one time lost in the underbrush at the foot of Mullanphy Street, and after being absent all night was found the next morning asleep with her little dog. She died in 1867 at the age of about thirty-six. Their six children, all still living, are Amelia, who married George Berner; Mary, who married William Richardson; John; Joseph; Julia, who married William Hopps; and Louise, who became the wife of Wayne Freeman.

John Elble was reared in Alton, attending the public schools, and was continuing his education in Shurtleff College when the death of his father called him to serious responsibilities. He was then about sixteen years of age, and for a time he worked on a farm, in a grocery and fruit store, and for two years was in the Alton plant of the Drummond Tobacco Company and had supervision of the tobacco shipments made by this company to the government to supply the army and navy and the Indian reservations. After his marriage Mr. Elble conducted a bakery for five years, was also in the retail liquor business, and in 1897 became Alton manager of the local plant of the Anheuser-Busch Brewing Company and continued in that business for thirty years.

Mr. Elble made his first campaign for local office in 1882 when he was elected alderman of Alton. He served in the City Council under five mayors and represented three different wards. For sixteen years he was a member of the County Board, and for three terms was chairman of the Board and a member of the Board of Review three times by virtue of this office. He was supervisor of Alton Township when he was elected mayor in April, 1923, being given the largest majority ever paid a candidate for that office. His majority running to 3,302. Mr. Elble was supervisor of Alton Township when the disastrous oil tank explosion occurred at Alton, January 29, 1892, causing the loss of many lives and the injuring of others. At that time Major Moore, who was supervisor of Woodriver Township was away and had asked Mr. Elble to take charge of any emergency in his absence and thus Mr. Elble had the responsibilities devolving upon the official heads of these two townships in handling the situation. Mr. Elble has been a member of a number of county, district and state conventions of the democratic party. He was a member of the local militia company of Alton as a young man, and was a snare drummer of the famous old time Gossrau band. He is a member of the Benevolent Society called the Alton, belonged to the Wigwam Country Club, the fraternal Order of Eagles, and the Evangelical Lutheran Church. He is also affiliated with the B. P. O. Elks and did belong to the Independent Order of Odd Fellows.

On January 29, 1880, Mr. Elble married Miss Anna M. Arens, who was born and reared at Alton, daughter of Theodore and Henrietta (Loeffler) Arens. Five children were born to the marriage of Mr. and Mrs. Elble, two of them, Louise and Fred, dying when young. The daughter Mamie, who died at the age of thirty-two, was the wife of A. J. Woltmade, who lives at Lincoln, Nebraska. The two surviving children are: Benjamin, a resident of Alton, who married Irma Stracke of Warsaw, Illinois; and Nettie, wife of Dr. F. M. Kane, of Alton.

Mr. Elble both in his official capacity and as an individual citizen was one of the leaders in Alton in building up support for the government during the World war, and served on all the local committees to raise funds and promote a united sentiment among the people.

F. J. HERLIHY, president of the Mid-Continent Construction Company, has been an engineer and contractor for many years, and practically his entire experience has been identified with big jobs, the most conspicuous at the present time being the construction of the Wacker Drive in Chicago, one of the notable engineering and construction projects in the middle west. The Mid-Continent Construction Company has handled a number of sections of this project, practically ninety per cent of the entire project.

Mr. Herlihy was born at Bridgeport, a Chicago suburb, in Cook County, in 1881. After his early education he studied engineering, and has given twenty-five years of his life to engineering problems. He has helped plan and build projects running into costs of millions of dollars, and for two years he was vice president and general manager of the White Paving and Construction Company. In 1924 he organized the Mid-Continent Construction Company, and has been president of this company in handling the contracts involved in the construction of the Wacker Drive and other work. Mr. Herlihy's company has accumulated some of the most modern machinery known to the engineering profession in rendering efficient service in jobs involving enormous masses of material such as those involved in the construction of tunnels, subways and streets. The personnel of his organization has been looked after fully as carefully as the material and mechanical facilities. With this organization during the construction of the Wacker Drive some new records were made in the continuous pouring of concrete, more than a thousand cubic yards of structural concrete being poured in one run in two days, and while engineering journals refer to that as a record performance, since then the record has been greatly exceeded, one run giving a total of 3500 cubic yards.

Mr. Herlihy's experience as an engineer and builder has been by no means confined to the Chicago district. He was in charge of the construction of the Montreal Aqueduct leading around the Lachine Rapids of the St. Lawrence River. He had charge of the building of the bridges and viaducts and tunnels for the C. M. & St. P. Railroad between Lewistown and Great Falls, Montana, and also had charge of the construction of the Manheim terminals of the Chicago, Milwaukee & St. Paul at Chicago.

Mr. Herlihy married in 1900 Miss Mary Howard, of Chicago. They are the parents of four children: May, Helen, Frank and Alice. Mr. Herlihy is a member of the Western Society of Civil Engineers. He is independent in politics.

REV. F. B. KEHOE, pastor of St. Patrick's Catholic Church at Alton, has been in the ministry nearly thirty years during which time he has had charge of a number of churches in Southern Illinois. A pastor in Alton for over fifteen years, that community has come to entertain high respect for his consecrated zeal and the influence for good radiating from him and effecting not only his parish but the entire city.

Mr. Kehoe was born at Waverly, Illinois, March 17, 1869. His father Patrick Kehoe, a native of Ireland, came to America in 1849, first living in New York State and in 1854 came to Illinois. He lived in Sangamon and in Morgan Counties, and in 1861 enlisted in the One Hundred and First Illinois Infantry. The greater part of his three years service as a soldier, however, was rendered with the Fourteenth Illinois Infantry. After the war he married Margaret Branick, also a native of Ireland. Both parents are now deceased, and six of their seven children were reared to mature years.

Fourth in the family, Father F. B. Kehoe, grew up at Waverly, graduating from high school there in 1888. He took his classical studies at St. Mary's College in Kansas, began his theological course in St. Mary's Seminary at Cincinnati, and for two years was a student in the Catholic University at Washington, D. C. On June 17, 1896, he was ordained to Cincinnati, and forthwith began the labors that have continued so successfully in Southern Illinois. For about three years he was pastor at St. Mary's Church at Shelbyville, Illinois, was in St. Joseph's Church at Springfield, two years, spent fifteen months at Neoga, and one year at Shipman and four years at Greenfield. In 1907 he took up his duties as pastor of St. Patrick's Church at Alton. His parish within the past fifteen years has more than doubled in membership, its communicants now numbering four hundred families, while there are 249 pupils enrolled in the parochial schools. Father Kehoe administered to this parish alone for several years, but now has two assistants.

He was one of the first members of the great Catholic Order of Knights of Columbus, being a charter member of the second council of the order, that established at Washington. During the World war he was a Four Minute Speaker, and was also active in the Red Cross campaign.

PAUL B. COUSLEY. An unusual experience for a newspaper man has been that of Paul Bliss Cousley. His father was connected with the editorial department of the old Alton Telegraph and the son grew up in the atmosphere of newspaper work and for over thirty years, since leaving high school he has given energies and best abilities to that one newspaper, never having thought change of environment contrary to the usual practice of the members of the press.

Mr. Cousley was born at Alton, October 13, 1876, son of John A. and Anna E. Cousley. His father was managing editor of the Alton Telegraph. Paul B. Cousley was graduated from the Alton High School in June, 1893, at the age of sixteen, and in July of the same year went to work as a reporter for the Alton Telegraph. In 1913, twenty years later he succeeded his father as editor. Father and son have had an important part in making the Alton Telegraph one of the oldest and influential daily papers in Southern Illinois.

Mr. Cousley is also a director in the Piasa Building and Loan Association. He is a Republican in politics, although he has never held any public office. In 1903-5 he was Worshipful Master of Piasa Lodge No. 27, Ancient Free and Accepted Masons, and is a member of the First Presbyterian Church. He married at Alton, May 9, 1906, Miss Mary Esther Sparks, daughter of C. F. Sparks. They have one son, Paul, and five daughters, Mary Esther, Nancy, Catherine, Jean and Ruth.

MATTHEW S. CONNORS, now police magistrate of the City of Alton, is a veteran railroad man, entering the service a third of a century ago, and continuing even after he lost a foot in the service until he was elected to his present post of duty.

Judge Connors was born in Scotland, February 1, 1869, a son of Henry and Sarah (Pollard) Connors. His parents died in Scotland, and Judge Connors in 1879 at the age of ten years came to America with his grandmother Sarah Pollard. They settled in Franklin County, Kansas. His grandmother was a woman of unusual strength of character and has always exerted a strong influence over her grandson in his mature life.

Matthew S. Connors was reared in Kansas, and lived in Franklin County until 1890. Then at the age of twenty-one he went to work for the Santa Fe Railway Company at Topeka, and was with that railroad seven years and subsequently was in other lines of railroad work and for different companies.

In November 1908 he was made general yard master of the Chicago & Alton Railway at Roodhouse, Illinois, and it was while in the performance of duty there that he met with the accident which caused the loss of his right foot. However, after a brief period of disability he resumed the service, and was soon afterward made assistant general yard master of the Chicago & Alton, at Alton, and gave

his time to the duties of this position until 1923 when he was elected police magistrate.

In 1888, Mr. Connors married Miss Maude Edwards of Burlingame, Kansas. They have three sons and two daughters, Leo, Thomas, Charles, Edna and Jane. Judge Connors at one time cast a Presidential vote for Bryan and Debs, but his last vote was for the late President Harding. He is affiliated with the Knights of Columbus, having had his membership for twelve years in Alton Council No. 460. He and his family belong to Sts. Peter and Paul Catholic Church. For many years he has been strongly identified with the railroad union labor movement, and for twenty-five years has been a member of the brotherhood of railway trainmen.

Mr. Connors and his sons have been victims of a most unusual sequence of injuries and accidents. His oldest son Leo lost his foot while a call boy for the Rock Island, Charles suffered an injury that caused the loss of a foot, while Thomas lost his left arm while with the Chicago & Alton. Though all of them have been thus deprived of some useful member while in the performance of duty for the railroad, each and every one is now vigorously engaged in some work or business so that his usefulness to society is scarcely impaired.

J. G. BARDILL, of Highland, merchant and banker, has represented Madison County in both houses of the Illinois Legislature, and his varied activities have brought him a recognized position as one of the outstanding citizens of his home county.

He was born at Grant Fork, Madison County, May 7, 1866, son of Stephen and Eliza (Janett) Bardill. His parents were also natives of Madison County, and all his grandparents were natives of Switzerland and were identified with the pioneer Swiss colony around Highland, Illinois. Stephen Bardill was in the stone quarry and brick manufacturing business for many years. J. G. Bardill was the only son of his parents. The two daughters are Clara, wife of Adolph Meyer, secretary of the Pet Milk Company in St. Louis, and Dora, widow of John Ludwig, of Highland.

Josias G. Bardill secured his early education in the public schools of Grant Fork, and finished a business course in the Bryant and Stratton College at St. Louis. After leaving school he clerked two years in the store at Highland conducted by the firm Ammann & Wildi, beginning his work there at the age of seventeen. For two years he was a clerk in the wholesale dry goods house of Samuel C. Davis & Company at St. Louis, and then for two years conducted a retail grocery store in that city. Returning to Highland, he spent two years in the grocery and bakery business. On the destruction of his establishment by fire in 1891 he became one of the organizers of the Highland Store Company, which was incorporated and succeeded to the business of Ammann and Wildi. Mr. Bardill was made secretary, treasurer and manager of the business, and in 1903 became its president and manager. He remained the active head of this prosperous establishment twenty years, until February, 1923, when he turned over his interest to his sons, Orville and Hubert. Mr. Bardill in 1903 helped organize the State and Trust Bank of Highland, becoming one of its directors and is now vice president. He is secretary and treasurer of the Merchants Oil Company and president of the Highland Water Company and a director in the Worthen Jobbing Company of Chicago. Among other interests he has a cotton plantation of 640 acres in Arkansas.

For a number of years Mr. Bardill has been one of the outstanding leaders in the republican party in this section of the state. He cast his first vote for Harrison in 1888, and has attended many conventions of his party. His first office was that of alderman at Highland, and he also served as city treasurer and in 1901 was elected mayor. In 1908 and in 1910 he was elected a member of the House of Representatives, and in 1914 was elected to the Illinois Senate, being reelected for another four-year term in 1918. He is a thirty-second degree Scottish Rite Mason and Shriner, a member of the Woodmen and Elks, and for the past fifteen years has been president of the Highland Commercial Club. He is known in sporting circles as one of the crack shots, and annually goes on hunting trips. He is also president of the Highland Country Club.

Senator Bardill married in 1887 Elizabeth Harnisch, of Highland. To their marriage were born four sons and two daughters: Herbert, Mildred and Raymond, all deceased, Mildred dying after her marriage to R. K. Tibbetts. The surviving children are Orville and Hubert, who have the active management of the Highland Store Company, now Bardill's Highland Cash Store, and Miss Ruth, who is assistant cashier of the State and Trust Bank.

GEO. E. HART has been a painting and decorating contractor in the City of Chicago for nearly twenty years. Mr. Hart is undoubtedly one of the best known men in his business and partly for that reason was chosen president of the Painters and Decorators Mutual Association, an association of master painters and interior decorators consisting of the more responsible and well known contractors in the City of Chicago and vicinity, brought together in this association for purposes of mutual benefit and the insuring of high class ideals and quality of work.

Mr. Hart was born at Oconto, Wisconsin, but when seven years of age was taken to California, where he finished his schooling at Los Gatos. He learned the painter's trade there and in San Francisco, and followed painting and decorating as a journeyman in California until 1907. On March 7, 1907, he arrived at Chicago and two years later, in 1909, engaged in business for himself as a painting and decorating contractor. His business is now carried on under the name of Geo. E. Hart, Incorporated, with offices at 515 South Crawford Street.

Mr. Hart has enjoyed a high reputation for maintaining business on sound business principles, for promptness in carrying out his contracts, for honesty and efficiency in workmanship, for friendly and amicable relations between employer and employee. He has been one of the leaders in building up a system of ethics in the painting and decorating trade, to the end that all parties concerned, the contractor, the journeyman and the home owner or property owner for whom the work is done shall receive just and honorable service.

It is for the carrying out of these general purposes that the Painters and Decorators Mutual Association was organized, and the selection of Mr. Hart as president of the association is a particular tribute to his individual manner of doing business. The headquarters of this association are at 9 North Franklin Street, Chicago.

Mr. Hart is also active in the West Side Kiwanis Club, being chairman of its Board of Directors. He is a charter member of the new Midwest Athletic Club and serves on its Board of Governors, is a member of the West Town Chamber of Commerce, and has identified himself regularly with civic movements and undertakings on the West Side of Chicago.

CHARLES R. OATMAN, M. D. Now retired from active practice and a resident of Collinsville, Doctor Oatman performed the varied duties of an active physician and surgeon for nearly half a century. He was one of the youngest volunteer soldiers in the Civil war and for a number of years was active in medical education, connected with medical schools in St. Louis.

He was born at Belleville, in St. Clair County, Illinois, October 5, 1846. His father, Dr. Daniel L. Oatman was a native of Germany, born on the River Rhine, was liberally educated there for a notable career, and on coming to America, settled at Lancaster, Pennsylvania, and about 1838, moved to Belleville, Illinois, where he was one of the esteemed early practitioners of medicine. He died in 1849 when about thirty-seven years of age. He married Mary Louisa McLahan, who was born and reared in France. She also died when comparatively young, at the age of about thirty-eight. Doctor Charles R., was the oldest child and is the only survivor. The other two were Dr. Edward Oatman and Julia, who married John Hill.

Charles R. Oatman received his early advantages in district schools, later attended high school, and after the death of his parents he lived in the home of Philip Scott of Shiloh Valley. The Civil war broke out before he had attained his fifteenth birthday, and soon afterward he enlisted as a drummer boy with the One Hundred Seventeen Illinois Infantry under Colonel Risden, and the records at Washington show that he was one of the youngest three-year volunteers in the war. He served from some of the early campaigns until the very close of the great struggle and fought at the siege of Fort Blakeley, one of the defensives of Mobile, Alabama, and one of the last gratifications of the confederates to yield. He was never seriously injured, though enemy bullets three times broke his skin and once his drum was shot from his hand.

Doctor Oatman received his honorable discharge in August, 1865, being then still under nineteen years of age. After that he depended upon his own exertions to get his education, working at manual labor and attending school. In 1867 he entered the old St. Louis Medical College, and was graduated M. D. in 1870. Such was his record in the school that he was appointed demonstrator of anatomy in the school, and also had some experience in general medical practice in St. Louis. Subsequently he assisted in building up two medical schools in St. Louis, and was a lecturer and clinical worker there at intervals for about eighteen years. His name appears on many medical diplomas held by doctors all over the United States.

Doctor Oatman first located in 1870 at O'Fallon, in St. Clair County, Illinois, but since 1875 has been a resident of Collinsville, and performed all the duties of a general physician and surgeon in that community for nearly half a century, finally retiring in 1917. He is a member of the Madison County, the Illinois State and the American Medical Associations, and since boyhood has been a devout member of the Methodist Episcopal Church.

His first wife was Miss Josephine Chilton Lemon, a daughter of James H. Lemon. She died in 1909, the mother of four children. The oldest child was a daughter Olive, now deceased. All three sons took up the medical profession. Dr. Louis J. Oatman, who was a leading physician and surgeon of St. Louis, passed away very suddenly in July, 1925. Olive married Thos. R. Stockett and at her death left an infant son, Lewis Oatman Stockett, who is now married and living in Los Angeles, California, and has a small daughter, Bettie Olive Stockett. Dr. Carl L., is now deceased. Dr. Lorenzo C., is practicing medicine at Collinsville. On February 21, 1910, Doctor Oatman married Miss Frank Bostick, of St. Louis, who was born and reared at Holden, Missouri. Dr. Oatman has grandchildren, Mrs. Ed. Mann of Kansas City; Lewis Oatman Stockett of Los Angeles, California; Miss Isabell Olive Oatman of St. Louis; Charles R., Junior; and Cyrus C.; Josephine Mary; Virginia Olive and James H., of Collinsville, and one great-grandchild, Bettie Olive Stockett of Los Angeles, California.

PALMER E. ANDERSON, United States marshal for the Northern District of Illinois, is one of the able members of the Department of Internal Revenue, and a man whose integrity and courage have never been questioned. He was born and reared at Princeton, Bureau County, Illinois, and comes of Swedish ancestry, of which fact he is very proud, and he takes a great interest in the part those from Sweden have taken in the settlement and development of Illinois, and in the pioneer history of the state. He has been president of the John Erickson League of America.

Princeton gave Marshal Anderson his educational training, and he had the honor of being a student of the Princeton Township High School, which is historical, as it is the first township high school in the United States. For many years he was engaged in the hotel business at Princeton, in this capacity coming into contact with all classes, and gaining a knowledge of men and their motives which is of inestimable value to him in his present high office. He was also president of the Princeton Commercial Club.

As he was winning prestige as a successful business man Mr. Anderson was also becoming an outstanding figure in local politics, and later became active in state affairs. In 1911 he was appointed pastmaster of Princeton by President Taft, his appointment serving to reunite the conservative and progressive wings of the republican party that had been divided in a controversy over the post office following the death of its incumbent.

In 1918 Mr. Anderson became associated with the political fortunes of Senator William B. McKinley, and was one of his most trusted campaign managers. Following Senator McKinley's election to his present office Mr. Anderson was made chief field deputy in the office of the United States Internal Revenue Department at Chicago, and he continued to hold that office until February 28, 1925, the Monday prior to his elevation to the office of United States marshal to succeed Robert R. Levy, who had resigned. On March 2, 1925, Mr. Anderson was officially installed in the Chicago Federal Building at Chicago, as new marshal for the Northern District of Illinois, and entered at once upon his new duties. Marshal Anderson had already made a name for himself in the service because of his outstanding ability as an executive and efficient officer, and in this connection, as in all others which he has maintained, he is a decided leader, and always of the better faction. He was an alternate delegate-at-large to the National Republican Convention in 1916, and received 149,000 votes, the largest vote for any alternate delegate-at-large. For many years he has been an active member of the Hamilton Club of Chicago.

Marshal Anderson married Winnie May Spake, also of Swedish parentage. They have two children: Palmer Spake and Darlene Mae Anderson. While Marshal Anderson's duties require that he maintain his headquarters at Chicago, he still has his residence at Princeton, and his proud fellow citizens trust that they may continue to keep him in their midst.

GEN. W. J. NICHOLSON. No military history of Illinois would be in any way complete that did not contain extended mention of the services rendered by Gen. W. J. Nicholson. Entering the United States army when only nineteen years of age, he saw hardships and hard fighting and the dreary routine of army fort life in the west and active engagements in France, and while he is now retired from the army and devoting his time to business affairs at Chicago, where he is manager of the American Exposition Palace and Furniture Mart, his exploits are still spoken of with reverence and respect by his former military associates and subordinates.

General Nicholson was born in January 16, 1856, at Washington, D. C., and received his education in the schools of the capital. The friendship of his family with that of Gen. U. S. Grant led to his appointment in 1876, when only twenty years of age, to a lieutenancy in the United States army by the great Union leader. The young second lieutenant was soon thereafter assigned to duty in Indian service on the frontier with the famous Seventh Cavalry (General Custer's command), and he remained in this service for about twenty years, stationed at various forts throughout the west. With the Seventh Cavalry he took part in the last battle with the Indians, known as the battle of Wounded Knee, at the Pine Ridge Agency in South Dakota in 1891. He received citation for gallantry at the battle of Canon Creek, Montana in 1877, and at the battle of Wounded Knee, South Dakota, in 1891. With the entry of the United States into the World war early in 1917 General Nicholson had taken part in the preparation for this conflict through his appointment to the command, with the rank of colonel, of the first Citizens' Training Camp at Fort Sheridan, Illinois, in 1916, this camp being modeled along the same lines as the famous First Citizens' Training Camp held at Plattsburg, New York. In the summer of 1916 General Nicholson went with General Pershing's punitive expedition into Mexico, and in April, 1917, at the time the United States formally declared war on Germany, he was appointed to the command of the First Officers' Training Camp at Fort Sheridan, where he made a splendid record, both for his efficiency as an officer and the popularity that gave him a warm place in the hearts of many young Chicagoans and Illinoisans. After he had completed his duties as commander of this first camp at Fort Sheridan he was transferred to Camp Meade, Maryland, to take command of the 157th Brigade, and at this time was advanced to the rank of brigadier general. General Nicholson went overseas in command of the Seventy-ninth Division, which was assigned to duty in the Argonne, on one of the most hotly-contested battlefronts of the war. At Montfoucalm, on this front, his division was subjected to the terrible rain of steel that marked the Germans' last desperate assault in the Verdun sector under the personal observation of the German Crown Prince. General Nicholson's division captured the Montfoucalm stronghold on the morning of the 28th of September, one of the most brilliant exploits of the great war. General Nicholson is one of the few American army officers who received both the Distinguished Service Cross and the Distinguished Service Medal for his services in the World war. Early in 1919 he returned to the United States and for a period was stationed at Camp Upton, Long Island, but formally retired from the army in 1920, and, locating at Chicago, established his home in this city, genuinely welcomed by many who had served under him in France. In business life General Nicholson is general manager of the American Exposition Palace and Furniture Mart in Chicago.

General Nicholson married Miss Harriet Fenlon, of Kansas, and they have a son, Col. W. F. Nicholson, formerly a lieutenant-colonel of cavalry, now in business at Chicago; and a daughter, Mrs. Helen Nicholson Crean, wife of an English professional man, and living at Liverpool, England.

CHARLES H. LUCK, a Chicago business man, president of the Charles H. Luck Envelope Company, is best known in his home section of Chicago, to many thousands of people, on account of his activities and interests he has developed outside of business. One attribute given to Mr. Luck is that of "Mayor of Logan Square," a popular title of which any citizen might well be proud.

Mr. Luck was born in New York City in 1874, and came to Chicago in 1887. He is a son of George J. and Mary (Curry) Luck. His father, now ninety-one years of age, founded the envelope industry in Chicago, and has been an honored and successful business man in that city. The son, Charles H. Luck, took over the active management of the business in 1913, and has built it up from a plant employing a dozen persons to one of the largest of the kind in the city.

Mr. Luck has enduring fame on the North West Side, where practically every one knows him as a man interested in the welfare of his locality, in the prosperity of his friends and acquaintances, and himself willing at all times to use his influence and means to make things easier for the unfortunate. He is an ardent sports enthusiast and is president of the Greater Chicago Amateur Baseball League, said to be the largest amateur baseball league in the world, controlling sixty baseball clubs. Mr. Luck some years ago took charge of the Logan Square Baseball Club as treasurer, and for the first time made that a self supporting institution in local sport. He has also been president of the Liberty Baseball League, vice president of the Chicago Indoor Baseball League, and is a life member of the Logan Square Athletic Club.

Mr. Luck is a member of the Chicago Association of Commerce, the Illinois Manufacturers Association, the North West Side Commercial Association, Chicago Association of Credit Men, Logan Square Athletic Club, and is active in several democratic clubs and organizations. Fraternally he is affiliated with Aerie No. 19, Fraternal Order of Eagles, Golden Rule Lodge No. 726, Free and Accepted Masons, Lincoln Park Chapter, No. 127, Royal Arch Masons, Chicago Commandery, No. 19, Knights Templar, Medinah Temple of the Mystic Shrine, Avondale Council No. 123, R. L., and Chicago Lodge No. 4, Benevolent and Protective Order of Elks.

WILLIAM H. B. MCCORMICK is a substantial and well known citizen who has shown in the passing years the possibilities of successful achievement in connection with the fundamental industries of agriculture and stockgrowing, of which he has been a progressive exponent in his native county of Tazewell during virtually his entire mature life. His well improved farm estate, the old homestead on which he was born, is situated in Hopedale Township, and here his birth occurred June 13, 1861. Aside from his successful alliance with farm industry he has been influential in community affairs, in the Illinois councils of the democratic party, and in the ordering of the policies of the Hopedale National Bank, in the reorganization of which he had much of leadership and of which he has been the president since that time. This well ordered institution, the Hopedale National Bank, bases its operations on a capital stock of $50,000, and its surplus fund aggregates $10,000. In addition to Mr. McCormick, the president, and I. W. Hamilton, who is the vice president, the directorate of the bank includes also Edward Brennemann, Henry Griesmer, C. H. Jingling, Ernest Brennemann and C. W. Sutter.

Mr. McCormick is a son of George B. and Jane E. (Briggs) McCormick, the former of whom was born near Rochester, New York, and the latter in New York City, their marriage having been solemnized in Tazewell County, Illinois. George B. McCormick was reared and educated in the old Empire State, and as a young man he made his way to the west. He remained for a time in Michigan, and thence came to Illinois. After his marriage he continued to maintain his residence in Tazewell County until his death, which occurred in 1880, his widow having survived more than a decade, the son William H. B., of this review, being the only child. Mrs. Jane E. (Briggs) McCormick was a daughter of William H. and Louisa B. (Hoff) Briggs.

William H. Briggs came to Illinois from the State of New York in the year 1837, and became one of the pioneer settlers in Tazewell County, where he secured land and developed a fine farm property, though he had been reared under the metropolitan influences, including business activities, of New York City. He was a leader in civic and industrial development in his township and county, and in the early days he served as township assessor, his work in this connection bringing him only six dollars in remuneration, so few were the settlers then in the township. He was ever a staunch and loyal advocate of the principles of the democratic party, and was one of the honored pioneer citizens of Tazewell County at the time of his death, about 1888, his widow having survived him fourteen years. Their children were Hannah, Jane E., William H., Jr., Cecelia and Phoebe. Hannah never married, and Phoebe became the wife of Jacob H. Hess.

The schools of his native township afforded William H. B. McCormick his youthful education, and he was reared in the home of his maternal grandparents, on the farm which was the place of his birth and of which he is now the owner, he having inherited a part of the property and having purchased the interests of the other heirs. He has been actively identified with agricultural and livestock industry since he was twenty-two years of age, and in his independent operations his success has been on a parity with the energy, good judgment and progressive policies he has ever exemplified. As a youth of twenty years he varied his experiences by going to the Cherokee Nation, in what is now Oklahoma, and closing up the estate of an uncle who lived near Bartelsville, a place then represented by a mill, a store and a blacksmith shop, but now a thriving city of 15,000 population.

Mr. McCormick has shown at all times a loyal spirit of civic stewardship, has served as school director, was township tax collector two years, and he has been almost continuously a member of the Democratic County Committee from the time of attaining to his legal majority, he having been prominent in political affairs in his native county and having served as delegate to a number of the Illinois state conventions of his party, as well as a delegate to its local conventions.

On February 18, 1889, Mr. McCormick was united in marriage with Miss Clara M. Griesemer, who was born in Ohio and who was reared near Hopedale, Illinois, her parents having come to Tazewell County when she was a child. She was born May 13, 1867, was afforded the advantages of the public schools of Tazewell County, and prior to her marriage had been a successful teacher in the rural schools of this county. Mrs. McCormick was the eighth in a family of nine children, and she died January 24, 1922, the mother of no children. On the 30th of December, 1924, was recorded the marriage of Mr. McCormick and Mrs. Salome (Bolliger) Davies, daughter of Lebrecht Bolliger, who was born in Switzerland and who became a prosperous farmer in Deer Creek Township, Tazewell County. Mrs. McCormick received her education in Tazewell County and at the Illinois State Normal University at Normal, Illinois, and she was a teacher in the schools of Tazewell County for six years. By her first marriage Mrs. McCormick has one daughter, Norma Davies. Mrs. McCormick is the popular mistress of one of the attractive and hospitable rural homes of her native county.

FRANK THOMAS DUFFY, M. D. In the recent history of the medical profession of the middle-west there are to be found few records which exceed in the way of rapid advancement and splendid public service that of Dr. Frank Thomas Duffy, of Chicago, a leading member of the medical fraternity, a veteran of the World war and manager of the second largest region of the United States Veterans' Bureau at Chicago. He is a product of the city by birth, education and training, having been born on the South Side of the city where he now lives, at 7424 Calumet Avenue, in 1891, and was educated in the public schools, at Loyola University, and at Loyola Medical School, from which he was graduated with the degree of Doctor of Medicine as a member of the class of 1914.

Doctor Duffy commenced the practice of his profession on the South Side, and by the outbreak of hostilities between Germany and the United States had built up a substantial practice. However, he felt that the cause of country came before personal matters, and in 1917 volunteered in the Medical Corps of the United States Army for service. In August, 1917, he was commissioned a first lieutenant and later in France was promoted to the rank of captain. He was first assigned to duty at Camp Greenleaf, and went overseas with the Seventy-ninth Division in July, 1918. He went into active service with this division on the Argonne front in the latter part of August, 1918, and while in the line of duty was wounded and authorized to wear the wound chevron. He continued in active combat service until the armistice and remained in France with his division until June, 1919, being discharged at Camp Grant June 16, 1919. Although he resumed and still maintains his private practice, Doctor Duffy has been continuously in the service of the Veterans Bureau since the latter part of 1919. He started in as medical examiner in the Chicago office of the Bureau, and was promoted through various positions until 1924, when he was made regional manager of the Bureau at Chicago, the regional office of which he is manager having jurisdiction over the entire State of Illinois and three counties in Northwest Indiana, Lake, Porter and Laporte. This is the second largest regional office in the United States, being exceeded only by New York.

Not long after Doctor Duffy assumed the duties of his new office a reorganization was effected, this being reported in an article which appeared in November, 1924, in the Chicago Daily News, which was substantially as follows: Prior to the reorganization the files pertaining to the claims of all the disabled ex-service men in the three states of Illinois, Wisconsin and Michigan were kept in the Chicago district office and all actions on ratings and awards, payment of compensation, etc., were handled in the district office. Under the reorganization plan the files of all claimants residing in Wisconsin were transferred to Milwaukee and the files of those residing in Michigan were sent to the regional office at Detroit, leaving in the Chicago office only the cases of those men who are residents of the State of Illinois. Payments of compensation, all matters regarding vocational training and all ratings and awards for the men residing in this state are made at the Chicago regional office. The most drastic change instituted by Brig.-Gen. Frank T. Hines, director of the Bureau, was the organization of what is known as claims and ratings boards. Prior to the institution of these boards claimants were examined by the medical examiners, either in the field or in the Chicago subdistrict office, and submitted to the medical rating section of the district office. Regulations in force at that time practically prohibited the medical rating section from ever interviewing or seeing the claimant in the case. This practice, however, has been completely revised and every claimant's case must be considered by the claim and rating board, the doctor who examines the claimant being a member of the board, and the claimant being given an opportunity to present his side of the case in person to the members of the board who rate his case, considering it from every phase of it from a medical, from a compensation and from a vocational training status. The claims and rating boards are also performing another very important work. That is their explaining to the claimant the exact status of his case: Why, if such is the case, compensation cannot be paid: what is lacking in the evidence that he has furnished to establish the fact that his disability was incurred in the service. In plain words the boards endeavor to satisfy the claimant that if his claim is not allowed there is reason therefor in the law affecting disabled ex-service men for this disallowance. One claims and rating board is stationed at the suboffice of the United States Veterans' Bureau in East St. Louis, Illinois, to handle the cases of men in the southern part of Illinois. Two others are kept busy visiting the various hospitals in the state. The files in the cases of the men in the hospitals are taken directly to their beds. As a result of the operation of these boards the percentage of the cases of men in the hospital, upon which the proper action regarding their claims for compensation has not been taken, has been reduced to practically a negligible quantity. In addition to the handling of their claims, the Chicago regional office is also fully equipped to render outpatient treatment to such disabled ex-service men as do not require hospitalization, but whose disabilities have been incurred in the service, except that vocational trainees receive treatment for any disabilities which they may incur. This includes a thoroughly equipped pharmacy, handling as much business in the way of prescriptions as the largest drug store in the City of Chicago; a thoroughly equipped dispensary where treatment either for emergency cases or for minor surgical conditions can be rendered; a physiotherapy department which is one of the most completely equipped, up-to-date institutions of the sort in the city, and a dental clinic to take care of such dental treatment as is authorized; an eye, ear, nose and throat clinic, and, also, a well-equipped orthopedic appliance shop is in operation, where various appliances are manufactured and virtually all the repairs on the orthopedic appliances, such as artificial limbs and braces, are made.

When Doctor Duffy first took up the veterans' work in November, 1919, it was under the jurisdiction of the United States Public Health Service, of which he was first made assistant surgeon, then past assistant surgeon, and now surgeon in the United States Public Health Service, which corresponds to the rank of major in the army. He is still a member of the National Guard, having the rank of captain of the One Hundred Thirty-first Infantry, Thirty-third (Illinois) Division, and is a captain in the Officers Reserve Corps, United States Army. He is a member and fellow of the American Medical Association, and a member of the Illinois Medical Society, the Chicago Medical Society, the Order of Military Surgeons (U. S.) and the American Public Health Association. He is also a member of the Military Order of the World war, American Legion Hyde Park Post No. 34, "Forty and Eight" Society, Midway Athletic Club, Chicago, "High Noon Club." Chicago, Northwestern University Club, of Chicago.

Doctor Duffy married Miss Agnes Mabelle Freeman, of Charleston, Illinois, member of one of the historic families of that city, and a member of Sally Lincoln Chapter, Daughters of the American Revolution, getting her Revolutionary ancestry from both the paternal and maternal sides. They have one son: Frank Thomas, Jr., who was born in 1922.

EMIL JOSEPH VERLIE, general attorney for the Illinois Glass Company, with offices at Alton, is a young lawyer with exceptional qualifications for his profession, and for several years was officially connected with the Legislative Reference Bureau at Springfield.

He was born in Saint Clair County, Illinois, November 7, 1891, son of Jules Albert and Theresa (Grimont) Verlie. His father was born in Saint Louis of Swiss origin and his mother of French stock. Both are still living on their farm in Saint Clair County. Emil J., is the only son, and the one daughter is Blanche Louise.

Emil J. Verlie was reared on his father's farm, and attended the old Jones District School near home. Later he entered the East Saint Louis High School, graduating in 1909, and then attended the law school in the University of Illinois, where he received his LL.B. degree in 1913, and was admitted to the Illinois bar in July of the same year. Mr. Verlie began the practice of law at East Saint Louis, and remained there several years. In 1917 he began giving part of his time to State duties at Springfield, and eventually gave up his practice at East Saint Louis altogether and moved to the capital, where Governor Lowden appointed him Secretary of the Legislative Reference Bureau. This post he held until January 10, 1921, when he came to Alton and engaged in the general practice of law. In 1925 he became general attorney for Illinois Glass Company with offices in Alton. Mr. Verlie married January 14, 1918, Miss Blanch Nan Pew, of Litchfield, Illinois. They have one son, Emil Joseph, Jr., and one daughter, Phyllis Ruth. Mr. Verlie is affiliated with the B. P. O. Elks and other fraternal and social orders, and is a member of the Red Cross Chapter.

JOHN BURKE. As manager of the Congress Hotel, John Burke is one of the notable hotel men of America. He has had a remarkable career, since practically his entire experience has been with one institution, rising from perhaps the lowest paid position in the service to executive head of a hotel that has entertained perhaps as many of the world's celebrities as any institution of the kind in the Middle West.

Mr. Burke was born at Harvard, Illinois, had only a public school education, and in 1900 secured his first position in the Congress Hotel as a package boy. New responsibilities were added to his position very frequently in early years, and he soon became one of the executives on the hotel staff, and for a number of years past has been manager of the hotel. He had completed practically a quarter of a century of continuous service before taking his first real vacation, which came in the summer of 1925, when he went abroad and toured Europe.

Mr. Burke is a member of the Glen Oak Country Club, Midlothian Golf Club and the Lake Shore Athletic Club, the Association of Commerce and a member of the Chicago Hotel Men's Association.

PETER FRANCIS MCNAMEE is a Chicago attorney with offices at 10 South LaSalle Street, and has gained an enviable place in his profession in the ten years since his admission to the bar.

Mr. McNamee is a native of Chicago, born April 20, 1892, son of Peter Francis and Frances (Walsh) McNamee. His father was born in Chicago in 1860, and for many years was well known to the legal profession as a law reporter of the State and Federal Courts. He grew up and was educated in Chicago. He was a democrat in politics and a member of the Law Reporters Association. He died June 25, 1898. He married in Chicago, February 2, 1885. His wife was born in Quebec, Canada,

John F. Eeck

in 1864, and is still living. There were five children: William P., George J., Charles J., Peter Francis and Paul J.

Peter Francis McNamee attended school in Chicago and continued his higher education in Loyola University. He took his law course at Northwestern University, graduating in 1916, and was admitted to the bar October 4, 1916. Mr. McNamee was admitted to practice in the United States District Court May 2, 1921. His practice has been of a general nature. He is a member of the Illinois Bar Association and the Chicago Bar Association and of the legal fraternity Phi Alpha Delta. He is a republican in politics and a member of the Knights of Columbus.

Mr. McNamee married, June 28, 1921, Madeleine Morand, a native of Chicago. They have two children, Margaret and Frances.

COLONEL STUART M. MURDOCH, the present ordinance officer of the Illinois National Guard, has combined his duty and interest in military affairs with a very successful business career. Colonel Murdoch is vice president of the National Plumbing and Heating Supply Company of Chicago.

He was born in that city in 1882, son of Edward and Elizabeth (Agnew) Murdoch. His father was a native of Scotland, while his mother was of Scotch parentage but was born at Belfast, Ireland. They were married in Toronto, Canada, and soon after their marriage located in Chicago.

Stuart M. Murdoch after being educated in public and technical schools entered the plumbing supply business, and has devoted all his active years to that line. For several years he was in business as an individual, and then became associated with the National Plumbing & Heating Supply Company, one of the largest concerns of its kind in the middle west. This company occupies an extensive plant at Sixty-third Street and Prairie Avenue, Chicago. Colonel Murdoch is executive vice president of the company.

He has been connected with the Illinois military establishment for a number of years, beginning with his enlistment as a private in the old First Cavalry of the Illinois National Guard. Later he was in the infantry, then in the Sixth Infantry, then in the One Hundred and Thirty-first Infantry, and was a captain in the Sixty-fifth Infantry Brigade until 1925, when by appointment of Governor Small he was made ordinance officer of the Illinois National Guard with the rank of colonel. During the World war he was with the Illinois Reserve Militia on duty in Chicago. Colonel Murdoch is a member of the Hamilton Club of Chicago, and is a thirty-second degree Scottish Rite Mason and Shriner.

Mrs. Murdoch represents a distinguished family of Illinois. Her maiden name was Marjorie Arthur. She was born at Riverside, near Chicago, daughter of William C. Arthur and granddaughter of Colonel William R. Arthur. Colonel William R. Arthur was one of the builders of the Illinois Central Railroad and for many years one of its executive officers, beginning in the '50s. During the Civil war he was on the staff of General McClellan, with whom he had been previously related in the Illinois Central Railroad. Colonel Arthur owned a fine farm near Champaign, Illinois, and had a home there frequented by many prominent guests. He was a personal friend of Abraham Lincoln, and the Lincoln and Arthur families sometimes met in the old Tremont House in Chicago. Mrs. Murdoch's mother was a Bowles, daughter of Stephen Bradley Bowles, who was a brother of the famous Samuel Bowles, editor of the Springfield, Massachusetts, Republican. The three children of Colonel and Mrs. Murdoch are: William Arthur, a graduate of Morgan Park Military Academy and now attending the University of Wisconsin, Stuart M., Jr., and Miss Marian Arthur.

JOHN FREDERICK EECK has practiced law at Edwardsville since November, 1908, is the present corporation counsel of the city, and in his professional and personal standing is ranked as one of the ablest men of the community.

Mr. Eeck was born of German parentage in Bucks County, Pennsylvania, November 6, 1876, and when he was about two years of age his parents, John H. and Sophia (Ehlers) Eeck, came to Illinois and settled in Fayette County, locating six miles south of Vandalia, near Shobonier, where they engaged in farming and where his mother died in 1912. His father is still alive and active on the farm. John F. grew to manhood at the old homestead. He was the oldest in a household of seven children. He attended the public school at Shobonier. Later he was a student at what was then Austin College at Effingham and in 1904 graduated with the degree of Bachelor of Science from Valparaiso University in Indiana. In addition to the regular scientific course he pursued the study of a number of other subjects, among them being astronomy and a course in surveying. While getting his advanced education he was paying his way by teaching and farming. He taught six terms of school in his home county and in Piatt County. As a teacher he was very successful and for a time was principal of city schools. He speaks both High German and Low German fluently, also reads and writes the former with accuracy.

In 1905 he began the study of law, reading for a time in the law office of Welker & Matheny at Vandalia, and in 1908 completed his course in the Law School at Bloomington, Illinois. He was admitted to the bar in June, 1908, after examination at Chicago, and shortly thereafter located at Edwardsville, where he formed a partnership with Henry B. Eaton, who was later county judge. That partnership was dissolved in September, 1913, and Mr. Eeck was then associated with J. Frank Gillham until the latter was elected to the circuit bench in 1915. Since then he has carried on his large law practice alone.

In 1910 he was the nominee of the democratic party for county judge, but with all the other candidates on his ticket, excepting one, was defeated in the election. During 1913-1915 he served as city attorney, and subsequently was appointed to his present position as corporation counsel, an office he has held since May, 1921. He has offices in the Bank of Edwardsville Building, and is attorney for the Home Building and Loan Association, the largest institution of that kind at Edwardsville.

Mr. Eeck is a member of the Lutheran Church at Vandalia, but at Edwardsville attends the Presbyterian Church, where he is a member of the choir. He is not married. Fraternally he is affiliated with the Knights of Pythias and the Modern Woodmen of America. During the World war he was a member of the Legal Advisory Board and an active participant in the various war activities.

RICHARD S. BARNETT, a past exalted ruler of the Chicago Lodge of Elks, has for many years been a well known figure in real estate circles in and around that city. His work in the real estate field has been of a constructive nature, and he has projected and assisted in carrying out several undertakings in home building programs for people of moderate means.

Mr. Barnett was born at Belleville, New Jersey, September 29, 1869. He grew up in the east, had a public school education, and his early experience in the business field was in insurance. He first located in Chicago in 1898. He was in the insurance business there for a year or so, and then for a time engaged in the lead and zinc mining industry in Jo Daviess County, Illinois, and southwest Wisconsin. From there he returned to Chicago, and since 1912 has been identified with a large and important program in real estate and building. He has opened up and built up a number of prosperous subdivisions in the Chicago metropolitan district. Most notable of these is Villa Park, west of Chicago, now an incorporated village with several thousand population. Mr. Barnett has used his influence and enterprise and organization for the building of moderate priced homes, financing purchases thereof, and has made possible the acquisition of homes by people who otherwise could never hope to be home owners. One phase of his program has been the building of the bare frame work of low priced homes and allowing mechanics and other workers to complete all the interior work after purchase.

Mr. Barnett is also a farmer and stock breeder. He is owner of an 800 acre stock farm with heards of registered Holstein cattle and Duroc Jersey hogs. He also has about three thousand acres of additional land to supplement his main stock farm.

The Elks Lodge, of which Mr. Barnett is a past exalted ruler, is one of the largest and richest in the country. Mr. Barnett was one of the executive committee of the 1926 convention, at which time the Elks Memorial on the North Shore in Chicago was dedicated. This memorial, costing three million dollars, and dedicated in the summer of 1926, has been pronounced by artists and architects as the most beautiful memorial building in the world. It is a permanent memorial to the Elks of the United States who sacrificed their lives in the World war. This Chicago lodge has for a number of years extended about $15,000 each Christmas season for the benefit of the poor of Chicago. It is a great and distinctive honor to be chosen official head of this organization, and of this honor no one was more appreciative, and in the opinion of his fellow members more really deserving than Mr. Barnett. Mr. Barnett is also a Royal Arch Mason, member of the Masonic Grotto, and belongs to the Cook County Real Estate Board and other civic organizations. He married Miss Emma L. Gallette, of New York. His offices are at 17 North LaSalle Street, and his home at Villa Park.

MAJOR FELIX J. STREYCKMANS, member of the Chicago bar for twenty years, has been very successful in private practice, and at different times has rendered notable service in the public side of his profession. His record as an organizer and leader in war activities during the World war is especially notable.

Major Streyckmans was born in Chicago, in 1876, son of Felix and Flora (Gauthier) Streyckmans, and a grandson of John Streyckmans. Both his father and grandfather were born at Walhain in Belgium, in the country of Walloons. John Streyckmans on coming to America was a pioneer settler in Kewaunee County, Wisconsin, in the early '50s. He was one of many thousands who left Europe following the German Revolution of 1848. The town of Walhain, Wisconsin, of which he was the first postmaster, was named by him. His son, Felix Streyckmans, came to this country in 1860. Both Felix and John were soldiers in the Civil war. Felix Streyckmans married after coming to this country, Flora Gauthier, who was born at Jodoigne, Belgium. Soon after their marriage they settled in Chicago.

Felix J. Streyckmans attended public schools in Chicago, studied shorthand, and for a time was court reporter at Joliet. In 1895 he removed to Springfield, entering the office of Attorney General Akin. This was a splendid opportunity for a young man aspiring to success in the legal profession. He had begun his law studies under Mr. Akin while at Joliet. Mr. Streyckmans was admitted to the bar at Springfield. Prior to his admission to the bar he had served as assistant to the attorney general of Illinois, and also as private secretary to Governor John R. Tabner. For a period he was a law partner with Howland J. Hamlin in Springfield. Major Streyckmans in 1906 returned to Chicago, and since then has been successfully engaged in general practice. His offices are at 160 North LaSalle Street. In 1921 he served for a period as special assistant United States district attorney in Chicago.

Having served in the old Illinois National Guard in the Spanish-American war period, Major Streyckmans applied for assignment to military duty at the outbreak of the World war. Instead he was selected by the War Loan authorities at Washington to take charge of and organize the Foreign Language Division of the War Loan Organization for the Seventh Federal District, with headquarters in Chicago. Beginning these duties soon after this country's entrance into the war, after patient and arduous work he organized thirty-six nationalities in Chicago and Illinois into their separate respective groups, each headed by a leading citizen of its own nationality. As each Liberty Loan came on Major Streyck-

Richard S. Barnett

mans directed the activities of these groups with such energy and skill as to bring about the maximum of results in the matter of subscriptions. These results were amazing to those who had misgivings as to the patriotism of Chicago's citizens of foreign races. Their response was quick and generous, and the subscriptions to war loans in Chicago, where seventy-nine percent of the population is foreign born, or with one or both parents of foreign extraction, averaged much higher than in many states and communities, particularly in the South, which boasts of the "pure American" character of their population.

On one occasion, July 4, 1918, under Major Streyckmans' organization, 800,000 people in Chicago of foreign birth or extraction were gathered together in their respective groups for a patriotic war demonstration. He, himself, on that date went to Washington and at the request of the President made the address at a gathering held at Washington's home at Mt. Vernon, as chairman of the American Citizens of Foreign Extraction of the United States.

Just shortly before the close of the war, in October, 1918, Major Streyckmans' associates presented him with an appreciation and tribute, the essential part of which is quoted herewith: "This testimonial is given in grateful recognition of the splendid qualities of their Chief as a harmonizer of racial differences and inherited prejudices; as a leader of Americanization and as an Executive whose wide sympathies and fine leadership contributed to the generous response of thirty-six nationalities to the call of the American government for the support of the Liberty Bond issues and the victory of the allied cause; by his associates of the Foreign Language Division, United States War Loan Organization."

During the Spanish-American War period Major Streyckmans was a member and sergeant major in Company C, Fifth Illinois Volunteer Infantry. Since the World war he has been in the Officers Reserve Corps, being now judge advocate attached to the general staff at Washington, with the rank of major, and is also an instructor in military law.

He is a member of the Chicago and Illinois Bar Associations, the Civic Federation, Foreign Language Information Service, Chicago Foreign Council, Chicago Council of Social Agencies, Association of Commerce, The Hamilton Club and many other civic organizations. He served as secretary of the Citizens Mayoralty Committee that brought about the election of Mayor Dever. Major Streyckmans married Miss Maude M. Brown, of Chicago, and they have one son, Felix.

WILLIAM J. CORBOY is junior member of one of the notable law firms in Chicago, Dunne & Corboy, with offices in The Rookery. The senior partner is former Governor Edward F. Dunne.

Mr. Corboy was born in Cook County, Illinois, June 24, 1888. His father, the late Michael Joseph Corboy, was born in Brooklyn, New York, May 7, 1848, and after a public school education came to Chicago. In 1871 he entered the plumbing business on his own account, and built up one of the largest firms of its kind in Chicago, the M. J. Corboy Company, of which he was president and treasurer when he died in 1920, at the age of seventy-two. He was a member of the Chicago Athletic Club and the South Shore Country Club. He married in Chicago in 1883 Miss Isabel Waller, a native of Chicago. Of their eight children seven are living, William J. being the third in age.

William J. Corboy was educated in Armour Academy, Chicago, and in Yale University, where he graduated in 1911, and subsequently attended the law school of Northwestern University, from which institution he received the degree of Bachelor of Laws. After graduating he became associated with the firm of Dunne & Murphy, and in 1919 became a partner of Governor Dunne. They handle a general practice and Mr. Corboy in addition to his own practice has been since 1922 master in chancery of the Superior Court of Cook County. He is a member of the Chicago Bar Association, Illinois Bar Association, American Bar Association, the Legal Club, the Yale Club of Chicago, the University Club, and the Harvard-Yale-Princeton Club. He served as an officer in the United States Army during the World war.

He married, October 20, 1915, Miss Eileen Dunne, daughter of former Governor Edward F. Dunne, of Illinois. The three sons born to their marriage are William J., Jr., Edward Dunne Corboy and Stuart Daniel Corboy.

JONATHAN KENNICOTT, who came to Chicago with his family from New York State by sailing vessel in 1834, settled on the Des Plaines River, a mile south of the present village of Half Day, in Vernon Township, Lake County, where the home of his son Hiram, "The Mill," became the nucleus of a hamlet known by the Indian name of "Mettawa." A few years later he settled near his sons John and William at "The Grove," where some of his descendants still live, on the Des Plaines Valley Indian trail, now Milwaukee Road, in Northfield Township, Cook County, near the present towns of Glenview and Des Plaines.

His great-grandsons active in Chicago life include among the grandsons of Dr. John A. Kennicott: Frank Kennicott Reilly and Leigh Reilly, members of the publishing firm of Reilly & Lee Company; Ransom Kennicott, chief forester of Cook County, and Walter Kennicott, insurance broker, sons of Captain Amasa Kennicott; and Harold B. Kennicott, wholesale florist, of Kennicott Brothers Company, son of Flint Kennicott, and among the grandsons of Hiram M. L. Kennicott; Cass L. Kennicott, water treatment engineer, and Donald A. Kennicott, associate editor of "Blue Book" and "Green Book" magazines, sons of Colonel Ransom Kennicott, and David R. Kennicott, associated with McKeown Brothers Company, building contractors, and Hiram L. Kennicott, vice president of the insurance firm of James S. Kemper & Company, sons of Captain George Kennicott. Ransom Kennicott attended Northwestern University and is a member of Beta Theta Pi. Cass L. Kennicott attended

Case School of Applied Science, Cleveland, Ohio, and Donald A., David R. and Hiram L. Kennicott attended the University of Chicago. Donald A. Kennicott is a member of Delta Tau Delta and Hiram L. Kennicott is a member of Chi Psi.

Jonathan Kennicott was born in Warren, Rhode Island, April 27, 1775, and was a son of John and Roby (Sherman) Kinnicutt (as the name is spelled in New England), grandson of John and Anne (Eddy) Kinnicutt, great-grandson of John and Elizabeth (Luther) Kinnicutt and great-great-grandson of Roger and Joanna (Shepardson) Kennicott, all of Warren. Roger Kennicott was in Malden, Massachusetts, in 1660 fought in King Philip's war and removed to Warren in 1678. Presumably he came from Devonshire, England, whence sprang the English family of Kennicott, including numerous clergymen and scholars, notably Dr. Benjamin Kennicott (1718-83), of Oxford University, famous for his revision of the Old Testament.

Jonathan Kennicott married Jane McMillan, daughter of Joseph and Avis (Bowen) McMillan, and granddaughter of James McMillan of Perthshire, Scotland, Joseph McMillan was a Revolutionary soldier, and so also apparently was John Kinnicutt, father of Jonathan.

Jonathan and Jane Kennicott had fourteen children, of whom the following ten came to live in Illinois:

Dr. John Albert Kennicott, of "The Grove," widely known as "the Old Doctor," was a pioneer physician and rode his Indian pony, "Pottawatomie," over a broad circuit of the prairies. He was president of the Illinois State Horticultural Society, an officer of the Illinois State Agricultural Society, and the first editor of the "Prairie Farmer." His beautiful place, at "The Grove" is now the home of his granddaughter, Grace Redfield Beck, and her husband, Edward Scott Beck, managing editor of the "Chicago Tribune." One of his sons was Major Robert Kennicott, a founder of the Chicago Academy of Sciences, ornithologist and Arctic explorer, who died in 1866 in Alaska, where his exploits are memorialized by the glacier, town and copper mines bearing his name.

Levi Kennicott settled near "The Grove," but in 1854 migrated to Iowa.

Dr. William Henry Kennicott, of "The Grove" and Chicago, was the second dentist to practice in Chicago. He was a promoter of the Chicago Mechanics' Institute and candidate for mayor of Chicago in 1849.

Hiram Martin Langdon Kennicott was admitted to the bar by act of the New York legislature before he was twenty-one. He was the first justice of the peace, performed the first marriage ceremony and had the first mill and the first store in Lake County. The first election was held in his house, "The Mill." In 1843 he bought a farm in Wheeling Township, Cook County, near the present town of Arlington Heights. His relatives and friends thought that abandoning law for farming was "Hiram's folly," and his place of nearly 1,000 acres, with its large brick house, was ever afterwards called "The Folly." Here he entertained with memorable hospitality and enjoyed his hobbies of croquet, billiards, whist and chess, at which last named game he was at one time a player of national repute. Here grew up twelve children, all of whom lived until the youngest was forty-five.

Joseph Edgar Kennicott, nurseryman, of Arlington Heights, was an ardent member of the Methodist Episcopal Church and one of the founders of the Des Plaines Camp Meeting and of the church at Arlington Heights.

Avis Caroline and Roby Adelia Kennicott, twin sisters, never married and lived out their long lives at the old homestead of their father at "The Grove." Their kindliness, charity and hospitality won for them the name of "The Good Aunts," by which they were known far and wide.

George Augustus Frederick Kennicott died at "The Grove" while still a young man.

Dr. Jonathan Asa Kennicott was for many years one of Chicago's leading dentists. In 1857 he built a house in the woods near the lake south of Chicago and named it "Kenwood," the name afterwards being applied to the surrounding Chicago residence district. He had the family love of flowers and was an enthusiastic horticulturist.

Juan Alonzo Kennicott was a farmer near Barrington. With his brother Levi he was a "forty-niner." A son, Juan A., lives in Arlington Heights, and a son, Ralph R., in Chicago.

Four grandsons of Jonathan Kennicott were in Illinois regiments in the Civil war. Amasa Kennicott, son of Dr. John A. Kennicott, was captain of Company F, Thirty-ninth Volunteer Infantry, Ransom Kennicott and George Kennicott, sons of Hiram M. L. Kennicott, were in the Thirty-seventh Volunteer Infantry, the former as lieutenant-colonel and the latter as captain of Company I. Walter J. Kennicott, son of Joseph E. Kennicott, fell in battle at Falling Water in 1863 and is buried in Antietam National Cemetery, Maryland.

GEORGE MAGNUS RYRIE. Of those who gained honor and esteem as well as financial success in their careers at Alton, one that may be recalled with every degree of fitness was the late George Magnus Ryrie.

The Ryrie family was established at Alton in the fall of 1837. John A. Ryrie was then six years of age. He had been born in Wick, Scotland. His brother, Daniel R. Ryrie, became secretary of the Alton Mutual Savings Company, chartered in 1853, and also organized the banking business which became the First National Bank of Alton in 1865. Daniel R. Ryrie served as cashier of this institution until his death in July, 1877, at the age of sixty-two. He and his brother John A. Ryrie were also associated in the wholesale grocery and commission business. John A. Ryrie in the meantime had engaged in the retail grocery business, and subsequently the George M. Ryrie Wholesale Grocery Company was organized. John A. Ryrie married Elizabeth Stanton.

Their son, George M. Ryrie, who was born at Alton, November 11, 1864, was educated in the grammar and high schools of Alton, and devoted his active career to the wholesale grocery business. He was never an aspirant for political office, and was thoroughly devoted to

home and church. He was a trustee of the First Baptist Church and superintendent of its Sunday School.

In 1887, George Magnus Ryrie married Sophia H. Hopkins, daughter of George K. and Mary B. (Edwards) Hopkins. Her mother, who died January 12, 1924, was a daughter of Cyrus and Sophia (Loomis) Edwards. Cyrus Edwards, a brother of Governor Ninian Edwards, was admitted to the bar at Kaskaskia, Illinois, in 1815, while his brother Ninian was serving as territorial governor. In 1829 he settled at Edwardsville, and had a career of great distinction. He was whig candidate for governor in 1837, and in 1860 was elected on the republican ticket as a member of the Legislature, and was instrumental in securing the election of Lyman Trumbull to the United States Senate. He was one of the founders of and most liberal contributors to Shurtleff College, and was president of its Board of Trustees thirty-five years. He died at Upper Alton August 31, 1877, when eighty-four years of age.

Mrs. Mary Edwards Hopkins' mother was a daughter of Rev. Hubbel Loomis, one of the pioneer ministers of Southern Illinois, who settled at Upper Alton in 1831 and was one of the founders of Shurtleff College. He died in 1872, at the age of ninety-eight years. He was a mathematical scholar and his son, Elias Loomis, held the chair of mathematics in Yale College and was author of mathematical text books that were used by hundreds of schools and colleges.

The father of Mrs. Ryrie, the late George Hopkins, who died in 1901, was a wholesale druggist, being in business at Alton and later in St. Louis.

Mrs. Ryrie became the mother of two children. Her daughter, Helen Claire, lives at home, and her son is John A. Ryrie. John A. Ryrie was educated in the grammar and high schools of Alton, and graduated from Brown University of Providence, Rhode Island, with the class of 1916. He then spent a year in his father's wholesale grocery business, of which he is now president, and soon after America declared war on Germany he joined the army as a private and went overseas, though not called to front line duty. He remained in France until May, 1919, when, returning to Alton, he became vice president of the Ryrie Grocery Company, of which Mrs. Ryrie was president. The business is conducted in a large three-story building with warehouse, and has been one of the substantial institutions in the wholesale district of Alton. John A. Ryrie married Miss Elizabeth Caldwell, of a prominent Alton family, and they have two sons, John A., Jr., and Charles C.

ROBERT H. PARKINSON was admitted to the bar and did his first work as an attorney more than half a century ago. His home for a number of years was in Cincinnati, and he established his residence in Chicago during the World Fair here, and has been known to the profession of that city chiefly through his large practice and exceptional skill in handling patents and trade mark cases. He is a senior member of Parkinson and Lane, one of the best known firms of patent lawyers in the middle west, with offices in the Marquette Building.

Mr. Parkinson was born at Cape Elizabeth, Maine, August 10, 1849. The family of which he is a member is of Scotch-English lineage. His great-great-grandfather Parkinson came from Scotland to the colonies through the north of Ireland, about two centuries ago, founding a home in New England. His son Henry Parkinson, served as a first lieutenant in the Continental army, and among other battles in which he fought for the cause of Independence, was that of Bennington under General Stark. This Henry Parkinson was a graduate of old Nassau, now Princeton University, and as a teacher of classics, who prepared many young men for college, he was widely and popularly known as "Master Parkinson."

The father of the Chicago attorney was Rev. Royal Parkinson, a minister of the Congregational Church, highly educated, of the New England type of character, and in the course of a long ministry, he served a number of churches in New England. He was a chaplain in the Union army during the Civil war. His death occurred at Washington, D. C. Rev. Royal Parkinson married Juanna Griffin. Her ancestors were English and were Colonial settlers of Maine and Massachusetts.

One of six children, four of whom reached mature years, Robert H. Parkinson, was liberally educated, graduating with the Bachelor of Arts degree from Dartmouth College in 1870. He studied law in the office of Converse and French at Woodstock, Vermont, under his father's personal friend Judge James A. Barrett of the Supreme Court of Vermont, and also with the firm of Cross and Burnham, the junior member of which afterwards became United States Senator Burnham, this firm being at Manchester, New Hampshire. Robert H. Parkinson, in the spring of 1872 went to St. Louis, studied law for a time with Judge Adams, who afterwards became a judge of the United States Circuit Court of Appeals, and in June, 1872, was admitted to the bar on examination in open court. In a short time he was in possession of a promising practice at St. Louis, but in 1873 removed from that city to Cincinnati. He practiced there in association with his two brothers, Joseph G. and George B. Parkinson. Their practice was general, but involved an increasing amount of corporation law, and Robert H. Parkinson's abilities were much sought in patents and copyright cases. This practice necessarily was more than local, and his work took him before the Federal Court for extended periods of time in New York City, Philadelphia, Washington, Chicago and other cities.

Mr. Parkinson established a law office in Chicago in 1890, but did not remove his home from Cincinnati until 1893. In this city he has given much attention to patent and trade mark law. He is an honored member of the Chicago, Illinois State and American Bar associations and commands respect for his ability as a lawyer and his character as a citizen.

Mr. Parkinson is a member of the Board of Trustees of the Central Church at Chicago, is a member of the Chicago Club, Union League and University Club, the Illinois State and Chicago Historical Societies, and the Queen City Club of Cincinnati. He is a member of the Honorary Scholarship fraternity, Phi Beta Kappa. He is a member of the bar of the Supreme Court of the United States, and has practiced before it for many years; the same is true of the United States Courts of Appeals and District Courts, of most circuits also Supreme Court of Illinois.

Mr. Parkinson married in 1878, Miss Helen B. McGuffey, of Cincinnati, who died in 1925. Four children were born to their marriage: Elizabeth D., June G., who became the wife of Alfred E. Manierre; Sterling B., and Kelso S. Kelso S., at the age of seventeen, a perfect specimen of physical young manhood, lost his life in Lake Michigan during a storm, when his boat was wrecked while cruising. The other son, Sterling B. Parkinson, is an ex-service man of the World war. He was with the National Guard regiment on the Mexican border, and soon after America entered the World war, he was made a first lieutenant in Colonel Reilly's Forty-ninth Regiment, a part of the famous Rainbow or Forty-second Division. He had a varied service and experience abroad for a time with his regiment, was then transferred to observation work in the air service, then to training men as they arrived in France, and finally was connected with the Intelligence Department. He is now in charge of the Investors Guide of the Chicago Tribune.

DIEBOLD FURRER. While the greatest of interest is taken in everything pertaining to the World war, and the men who are its veterans, there is something particularly appealing about the veterans of an older war, too many of whom have answered to the last roll call on earth, for the battles of the war between the states were fought on American soil, and all of the principles involved were native ones, and not entangled with European problems. The men who went forth in their youth to support what they believed was right are entitled to and must receive the affectionate gratitude of their fellow citizens. The people of Mason County have always kept an especially warm place in their hearts for their union veterans, and one of them who is still enjoying life, and the comforts his industry has provided for him, is Diebold Furrer, of Easton, a retired farmer and business man, a veteran of the war of the '60s, and a member of the Shiloh Association. While America is not his native land, he has made it his own, and sealed it with the sacrifice of his young manhood when he entered its service to preserve its government intact. He was born in Baden, Nunnenweier, Germany, October 17, 1841, a son of John Furrer, also a native of Baden.

When Diebold Furrer was beginning to attend school in his native land his parents left Germany, and set sail from Havre, France, for the United States, their port of call being New Orleans, Louisiana. The mother bore the maiden name of Dietrich. After her death the father married second Barbara Dietrich. By his first marriage John Furrer had the following children: John, who lived and died at Easton; Andrew, who also died at Easton, leaving a family to survive him; Diebold, whose name heads this review; and George, who is a farmer in the vicinity of Easton. By the second marriage there were the following children: Barbara, who married Harmon Ellerbush; Mary, who married D. Dorrel; Louise, who married Frank Day; Sarah, who married Lester Morgan; and Elizabeth, who is deceased. Of this family, Diebold, George and a stepson, John Frank, served in the Union army.

With his wife and eight children John Furrer set forth on the long trip to the New World, hoping to find abroad better conditions than had fallen to his lot in his native land. The sailing vessel in which the little party took passage was forty days on the way across, and when New Orleans was reached all were nearly famished for fresh, sweet water, as what they had on board was not fit for use, and in those days there were no arrangements made for purifying the water on board of these old-time vessels. As soon as they landed at New Orleans the Furrers transferred to a Mississippi river boat which brought them as far as Saint Louis, Missouri, and from there they came up the Illinois River to Havana, Illinois. By the time they reached their destination they had been traveling for two months and glad indeed they were to see the last of water. For a time the family visited at the home of Mose Eckert, and then the father rented a farm. Later, however, he bought a farm near Easton, and there his death occurred during the war, in which several of his sons were serving.

As might have been expected Diebold Furrer had but little educational training, and the greater part of what he knows he learned through his own efforts. He left his father's farm and joined Company A, Twenty-eighth Illinois Volunteer Infantry, and rendezvoused at Camp Butler, Springfield, Illinois. His captain was Richard Ritter, and his colonel, A. K. Johnson. When the regiment left Springfield it was sent to Saint Louis, was there armed with muskets, and transferred to Cape Girardeau. Still later the regiment went into camp at Thebes, Illinois. The first active service of the regiment was at Fort Henry, after which it was sent up the Tennessee River and subsequently participated in the great battle of Shiloh. It is claimed that Henry Probst, a member of Mr. Furrer's company, killer Gen. Albert Sidney Johnston, the famous Confederate commander. Other engagements in which Mr. Furrer participated were: Corinth, Hatchie, the Siege of Vicksburg, and Spanish Fort, Alabama. It was while at the latter place that the mournful news reached the regiment of the assassination of President Lincoln. Mr. Furrer was mustered out of the service at Camp Butler more than a year after the close of the war, as his regiment had been sent into the Rio Grande country to assist in removing Maximilian from Mexico, and were then stationed for some time at Brownsville, Texas. Although he saw no active service and was on guard duty only, Mr. Furrer felt that that period was the worst part of his enlistment, for he wanted to go home with the rest of the soldiers.

When he finally reached Easton after his honorable discharge he farmed for a time, and then built a store at Easton, and sold goods from it for twelve years, when he disposed of the business and began handling grain, in partnership with V. P. Turner, now of Pekin, Illinois. For thirty years Mr. Furrer was connected with the grain business of Mason County, but has been retired for the past few years. He also organized Bank Easton, now the farmers State Bank of Easton, of which he is a stockholder, and of which he was vice president for a long period. He cast his first presidential ballot for Abraham Lincoln in 1864, later, however, joining the democratic ranks. Still later he returned to the republican party. Joining J. Q. Jones Post, G. A. R., of Havana, Illinois, Mr. Furrer has continued to take great interest in it, and also in the Shiloh Association. Each year the veterans of that mighty battle hold a reunion on April 6, on the scene of what is regarded as one of the bloodiest struggles of the war. He also attends very frequently the national encampments, and has covered these reunions of the Grand Army of the Republic from Boston, Massachusetts, to Los Angeles, California, and at many cities in between, including Denver, Colorado, Minneapolis, Minnesota, Indianapolis, Indiana, Columbus, Ohio, and Louisville, Kentucky.

On December 25, 1866, Mr. Furrer married in the country near Easton, Christina Deschler, a daughter of Jacob and Christina (Dietrich) Deschler, the latter being a sister of Mr. Furrer's stepmother. Mrs. Furrer was born in Baden, Germany, February 19, 1851, and died October 18, 1915. Mr. and Mrs. Furrer had the following children born to them: Laura, who married A. W. Barrick, of Saint Louis, Missouri; Edward D., who is cashier of the Farmers State Bank of Easton; Mary, who married Charles Bowman, of Easton; Louis, who is with the North American Construction Company and lives at Chicago; Mrs. Harriet Stevens, who resides at Easton; Mrs. Irene Royston, who resides at Saint Louis; Earl V., who resides at Lincoln, Illinois; Fred J., who resides at Theran, Illinois; and Imogene, who is the wife of Del Overturf, of Saint Louis.

During the many years Mr. Furrer has lived at Easton he has won the confidence and good will of the people of this community, and he is regarded as one of the most representative and highly-respected citizens of Mason County, and one who has done much for his adopted country.

REV. D. J. RYAN, a native of Alton, Illinois, has devoted his entire life to the service of the Catholic Church. His has been a constructive record in various localities of Southern Illinois, and for over thirteen years he has been pastor of St. Joseph's Catholic Church at Granite City.

He was born at Alton, August 5, 1876. son of David and Margaret (Kiely) Ryan. His parents were born in County Limerick, Ireland, and came when young to the United States, being married at Alton. David Ryan was a successful building contractor, erecting many of the buildings, both business and residential, at Alton, Granite City and other towns. He died at the age of seventy-seven, and his widow lives at Alton. They had eight children, D. J. Ryan being fourth in age.

Rev. D. J. Ryan at Alton attended the local schools to the age of fifteen, and then entered St. Joseph's College at Teutopolis, Illinois, where he pursued the classical course, graduating A. B. in 1896. His theological studies were pursued in Niagara University at Niagara Falls, and he was ordained a priest in June, 1901, at the Cathedral at Buffalo by the present Archbishop Quigley of Chicago. Father Ryan for one year was an assistant at St. Joseph's Church at Springfield, Illinois, was then appointed pastor of St. Dennis Church at Shipman, Illinois, following which he spent a year in charge of the Catholic Church at Winchester, Illinois. Then came a postgraduate course in the Catholic University at Washington, D. C., and after a year he was given the title of Bachelor of Sacred Theology.

The late Bishop Ryan of Alton then called him to take charge of the Catholic Church at Auburn, Illinois, and a group of surrounding missions. He had full responsibility for the arduous labors of this charge for eleven years, and in addition to other improvements built a church at Divermon, Illinois. For seven years of this time he also served as a member of the Alton Apostolic Mission Band.

On November 1, 1913, Father Ryan took charge of St. Joseph's Church at Granite City. In the thirteen years of his labors there he has paid off a large debt, remodeled the old buildings and constructed a handsome new modern church that seats over eight hundred people. It is one of the modern churches in the southern part of the state. Each Sunday the average attendance for the different services is over two thousand, and there are over six hundred families on the books of membership, made up of varied nationalities. The parochial school accommodates three hundred and seventy-five children, with a staff of eight teachers. Father Ryan while a student at Niagara University won a gold medal for his composition work on the Holy Scriptures. He is now leader of the Apostolic Mission Band, his assistants residing with him at Granite City being Rev. J. B. Franz and Rev. G. W. Powell. This band has done some notable work throughout the diocese.

FRANCIS CHRISTIAN KING is an attorney at law, with offices in the State Bank Building at East Moline. Mr. King was in the midst of his education when America entered the World war, and for a year or more was in service, after which he completed his law course, and has succeeded in building up a profitable law practice.

He was born in South Moline Township, Rock Island County, January 14, 1895, son of Charles J. and Apollonia (Schneider) King, his father a native of South Moline Township and son of Peter and Margaret King, natives of Germany, who were early settlers in Rock Island County. Apollonia Schneider was born in Bavaria, Germany, and was an infant when her father and mother, John Schneider and wife, came to America and settled in Pennsylvania, and afterwards in Rock Island County. Charles J. King is a farmer and fruit grower in South Moline Township. There were six children: Francis C., Anna, of Lansing, Michigan, Charles J., Bernard, Jula and John.

Francis Christian King was reared on his father's farm in Rock Island County, attending first the rural schools, afterwards the St. Mary Parochial School in Moline, and continued his higher education in St. Bede College at Peru, Illinois. Mr. King was a law student in Notre Dame University in Indiana, graduating from the law school in 1919. For Fifteen months, from October, 1919, to March, 1921, he was in the law office of George Wood at Moline. Then, as a matter of securing additional experience, he spent seven months in New York City as a bond salesman. Returning to Illinois, he opened his law office at Moline in July, 1922.

Mr. King married, June 24, 1925, D. Cleo Day, a native of Wyoming, Illinois, daughter of John and Bridget Day. They are members of St. Ann Catholic Church in Moline.

Mr. King has filled the office of justice of peace, and in politics he is a republican. For two terms he was grand knight of the Knights of Columbus at Moline, and is a member of the American Legion. On September 4, 1917, he entered service with the military police at Camp Dodge, Des Moines, Iowa, being there four months, and was then put in the Second Officers Training School at Camp Dodge, remaining from January 1, to April 15, 1918. He was transferred to Company M of the Three Hundred and Fiftieth Infantry, Eighty-eighth division, and on June 6, 1918, commissioned second lieutenant, and at that date ordered to Camp Pike at Little Rock, Arkansas, and subsequently was at Camp MacArthur, Waco, Texas, being put with the Infantry Replacement and Training Camp in Company L and Company M of the Ninth Battalion. He acted as instructor in training a number of companies for active service. Mr. King was honorably discharged December 6, 1918, with the rank of second lieutenant. Early in the following year he went abroad and spent two months on the battle fields of the west front, and on June 6, 1919, was one of those who represented the United States army in the inter-allied games at Paris.

ALBERT L. WEHMEIER. The claim of Albert L. Wehmeier upon the good will and favor of Minier is based upon many years of effective work as an agriculturist of Tazewell County, and upon his activity in promoting education and kindred accompaniments of advanced civilization, and he is now living in the comfortable retirement his former industry has provided for him. He was born on the county line east of Minier, in Tazewell County, February 13, 1881, a son of August Wehmeier.

A German by birth, having come into the world in Lippe Detmold, August Wehmeier brought with him to the United States when he came to this country after reaching his majority many of the solid virtues of his native land, and here, amid better opportunities and political freedom, he became a man of substance, and was regarded as one of the representative men of his community. His useful life was terminated by death August 17, 1892, when he was only forty-five years old, but during his span of life he increased his original purchase of 120 acres to holdings amounting to 480 acres, although when he died all this land was not completely paid for. When he first came to Tazewell County he had but little capital, and worked for three years as a farm hand, and then was engaged in farming as a tenant. As soon as he had saved a sufficient amount he bought his farm, the property now owned by his youngest son. He was not only a successful grain raiser, but he handled cattle extensively, and made butter and cheese, the latter being of so excellent a quality that people came from miles about to purchase it. In spite of its popularity it sold for ten cents a pound, but it must be remembered that all prices were correspondingly low, including labor. A man of great energy and business astuteness, he made much of his money in cattle buying and trading, and when he died his widow carried on his operations, and when the estate was divided she had not only cleared off what debts had hung over her, but had practically doubled the value of the property, proving that she was as capable as her husband. All of her sons were taught to work, and as soon as old enough each one began to help her in the farm labor.

August Wehmeier married Wilhelmina Fuehring, also born in Lippe Detmold, Germany, and came to the United States with the family of Philip Wehmeier, brother of August Wehmeier. Until her marriage she was employed in the homes of the farmers of Tazewell County, her energy and great capacity for work making her services much valued, and eagerly sought for by those who had need of such assistance. She is now residing at Minier, being now over seventy-four, as she was born March 5, 1851. The following children were born to her and her husband: Alvina, who is the wife of Val. Graff of Minier; Anna, who is the widow of Ed Haning; William, who is engaged in farming near Minier; Albert L., whose name heads this review; Clara, who was married to Frank Thomas, a farmer in the Minier locality; Arthur C., who is engaged in farming in Allen Township, McLean County; George A., who died at Camp Mills, New York City, during the World war, when about to embark for France; and Herbert, who is operating the homestead.

Albert L. Wehmeier attended the local schools and from childhood was taught to make himself useful. He learned every phase of agricultural work through practical experience, and remained at home with his mother until his marriage. Following that he farmed one of his mother's farms as a tenant, and now owns one of the farms secured by the labor of his parents. On it he was engaged in farming until his retirement. Devoting his farm to grain and stock, he found that registered Shorthorns were the most profitable cattle for his purposes, and as he made money he invested the proceeds in land, adding eighty acres to his original farm, for which he paid from $250 to $255 an acre for this property, and holds it at a much higher figure today. In 1923 his fine modern eight-room brick residence at Minier was completed, and he has since occupied it. This is one of the most convenient and attractive homes in the city, and

William R. Moss

he takes great pride in it and his grounds. However, although he has occupied his present residence but two years, he has lived at Minier for a decade, during the period he was still operating his farm, going back and forth each day. He is a stockholder in the companies owning the grain elevators of Minier, and of the Minier State Bank, and he is a member of the Board of Directors of the Little Mackinaw Grain Company. As one of the trustees and treasurer of the Minier Cemetery Association, Mr. Wehmeier is rendering a service in another direction. A quiet man, unobstrusive, he has never sought the bright light of publicity, although he has always given a loyal support to the republican party since casting his first presidential vote for Colonel Roosevelt. While still on the farm he served as a member of the local school board. He belongs to Saint John's Evangelical Church of Minier, and is one of its trustees. During the late war he was active in buying bonds and War Savings Stamps, and working on his farm to raise food for the soldiers. While he was registered in the second draft, he received on questionnaire, the signing of the armistice making a further issuance of them unnecessary.

On December 15, 1903, Albert L. Wehmeier married Rosa Hallstein, born in this locality May 8, 1883, a daughter of John and Maggie (Heisel) Hallstein, the former a German, who was brought to the United States by his parents when still a child, and he died at Minier May 4, 1922, surviving his wife for many years, as she died December 17, 1914. Their children were as follows: Mrs. Elizabeth Graff, Philip J. Hallstein, Mrs. Emma Eisenberger; and Mrs. Wehmeier, the latter receiving her educational training in the country schools. Two children were born to Mr. and Mrs. Wehmeier: Viola May, who is a senior in the Minier High School; and Dale Edward, who died at the age of fifteen years, at the beginning of his high school course.

The record of the Wehmeier family is one that teaches that success and advancement, together with confidence and public esteem accompany honest labor intelligently directed. Many people work hard, but their efforts result in but little good to either themselves or others because they do not know how to make each action result in constructive accomplishment. A great financier once truly said: "Any fool can make money if he will only work; most people can save if they will deny themselves, but it takes brains to profitably invest those savings." The Wehmeiers have known how to work, save and invest, and in this knowledge lies the secret of their success.

WILLIAM R. MOSS, of the firm of Moss, Olds & LaRue, Chicago attorney, is a graduate of the University of Michigan, grew up in the environment of a Michigan farm, and in early life was a teacher. He came to Chicago without means, backing or acquaintance, and for several years was a briefless attorney. Since then he has earned not only a substantial record of attainment and achievement in his profession, but also in various ways has exerted a forceful influence for good citizenship. He has been identified with a number of movements for the suppression of vice and the improvement of civic and social conditions generally. He has been well known as a public speaker. The cause nearest his heart has been Americanization, and much of his time outside of his profession has been given to that movement since the World war.

He was born at Maple Rapids, Michigan, November 3, 1867, son of Myron S. and Mary A. (Price) Moss. His grandfather, Solomon Moss, was born in New York state, and lived there for a number of years. His means and property were lost by security debt. When in 1841 he started west with his family he was a poor man. He traveled by wagon into Canada and into Michigan, becoming one of the pioneers of Clinton County in that state. At the time of this journey Myron S. Moss was three years old, and he grew up in a country just developing out of the wilderness. He spent his active life as a Clinton County farmer, and was known there as a man of rugged character and fine ideals. Myron S. Moss, while not highly educated, exerted a good influence over his son, William R., encouraging him to make the most of his time and talents.

After a boyhood spent at farm work and in attending district schools William R. Moss took up teaching. In 1891 he was graduated from the State Normal School at Ypsilanti, and for a time was superintendent of city schools at Wausau, Wisconsin. After three years in the law department of the University of Michigan he was graduated in 1899, and immediately came to Chicago. For six months he worked without salary in the well known law firm of Herrick, Allen, Boyesen and Martin. Then for several years he accepted the opportunities open to a young attorney without connections or influence, and since 1901 has been engaged in an individual practice, steadily rising in volume and importance. For a number of years he was a trial attorney for the elevated railroads.

Mr. Moss has concerned himself with politics and local government since 1910. A number of organizations have reason to be grateful for his willingness to work for the common good. During 1911-13 he was attorney for the village of Oak Park. During the World war he was chairman in 1917 of the Ways and Means Committee and later of the Americanization Committee of the Chicago Association of Commerce. During 1920-1921 he served as chairman of the Executive Committee of the association. He is now a member of the Senior Council of the association. He is a member of the Union League Club and for four years was a member of its committee on public affairs. He has been identified with practical measures for vice suppression, but more particularly has interested himself in the educational processes that design to convert the large mass of foreign born in Chicago to the ideals and standards of American citizenship. He wrote and published a condensation of Foster's book on syndicalism at the time Foster and his followers were creating so much trouble in Chicago. Perhaps no one in Chicago understands better the unregenerated class of the city's population and the means and methods of nullifying its influence or bringing it into harmony with other classes. Mr. Moss is a former president of the Oak Park Club, is former president of the Michigan Society of Chicago, is a former president of the Executive Club of Chicago and former member and ex-official of the Westward Ho Golf Club. He belongs to the First Congregational Church of Oak Park.

Mr. Moss married, December 21, 1892, Miss Carrie Gauss. She died July 4, 1917, leaving no children. On January 31, 1919, he married Miss Florence Thompson. They have one daughter, Florence Louise, born October 5, 1920.

ALBERT G. MCCALEB, a veteran of the World war, is a native of Chicago and has earned definite success and prestige as a patent attorney, being a member of the firm Williams, Bradbury, McCaleb & Hinkle, patent and trade mark lawyers with offices in the Monadnock Block.

Mr. McCaleb was born in Chicago, December 5, 1893, a son of Harold A. and Harriet (Piper) McCaleb. His mother was a native of Illinois and died in 1895, Albert G. being her only child. Harold A. McCaleb was born in La Salle County, Illinois, in 1860, son of Gilbert B. McCaleb and representative of a family of pioneers in the valley of the Illinois River. They came to Illinois about the time of the Blackhawk Indian war, first settling near Hennepin, the historic old town on the Illinois River. Harold A. McCaleb was for many years engaged in the ice business in Chicago, but is now retired. He is a republican and a member of the Masonic fraternity.

Albert G. McCaleb received a thorough technical education in mechanical and electrical engineering in the Armour Institute of Technology. Subsequently he attended the Chicago Kent College of Law, and was graduated in 1917. He was immediately called to duty as a soldier in the World war, and spent fourteen months as an instructor in the aviation corps, and was also at Fort Sill, Oklahoma, until December, 1918. Since his release from the army he has been engaged in the practice of patent law. The firm of which he is a member comprises a number of able and experienced men in patent and trade mark law, and they look after an immense volume of practice in that specialty.

Mr. McCaleb is a member of the Chicago, Illinois and American Bar Associations, the Chicago Patent Law Association and the American Patent Law Association. He is a Mason, being a Knight Templar and thirty-second degree Scottish Rite, and a member of Medinah Temple of the Mystic Shrine. He belongs to the Delta Chi college fraternity.

Mr. McCaleb married, November 18, 1919, Miss Ruth Fairbanks, of Rochester, New York. They have one son, Malcolm.

ARTHUR F. SELIGMAN, president of the Troy State Bank at Troy, in Madison County, has been one of the most active and public spirited citizens of that locality for many years. He is a native of Troy, and has made his business career of benefit to his home locality in many ways.

He was born at Troy June 1, 1881. His father, David Seligman, was born in Bavaria, Germany, and came to America at the age of fifteen. His mother, Augusta Bethmann, was born at Strassburg, Germany, and came to this country when sixteen. His parents were married in Madison County, Illinois, and David Seligman became a merchant at Troy, dying when his son Arthur was only seven years of age. The widowed mother is still living. All their six children were born in Madison County and four are now living.

The third child of the family, Arthur F. Seligman, grew up at Troy, attended the public schools there, and subsequently had an academic course. His early business career was with the Douk Brothers Coal and Coke Company, an organization having business at many points, and he was with it for seventeen years, becoming chief clerk. For a time Mr. Seligman was located at Springfield, Missouri.

He organized the Troy State Bank in 1918, and has since been president of this prosperous institution, which has capital of $25,000, and surplus and undivided profits of $11,000. He is also president of a lumber company at Troy and sales manager and purchasing agent for the Troy Coal Company.

On October 11, 1903, he married Miss Blanch Isabella Rawson, of Troy. They have two sons and two daughters: Leslie, a student in Milliken University of Decatur, Illinois; David, attending high school; Deering, in high school; and Margaret, in grammar school.

During the World war Mr. Seligman was on the road as a traveling salesman, but assisted in selling Liberty Bonds and was a member of the first registration board of Jarvis Township. He is a thirty-second degree Scottish Rite Mason and Shriner, an Odd Fellow, a member of the Modern Woodmen of America, and is active in the Presbyterian Church and Sunday School. In politics he is a democrat, but is better known as a citizen alert at all times in behalf of worthy objects of community betterment. He served three terms on the Board of County Supervisors, and held that office at the time of the building of the new court house. He was a member of the Town Council at Troy, when the sidewalk construction was undertaken, and has been active on the Board of Education, being a member when the high school building was erected.

TIMOTHY J. SCOFIELD. Throughout his long residence and experience as a lawyer in Chicago Timothy J. Scofield has been chiefly identified with railroad and other transportation interests. He is the second member of the law firm of Loesch, Scofield, Loesch & Richards at 10 South La Salle Street. This firm from its organization has represented the Pennsylvania Railroad Company as its solicitors at Chicago.

Mr. Scofield, who has been a member of the Illinois bar for over forty-five years, was born at Carthage, Illinois, March 20, 1856, son of Charles R. and Elizabeth (Crawford) Scofield. He graduated in the classical course from Carthage College in 1876, was admitted to the bar August 1, 1879, and spent the first eleven years of his professional career at Carthage. During 1890-93 he practiced at Quincy, Illinois, being a member of the firm of Berry, O'Harra and Scofield, general attorneys for

the Quincy, Omaha & Kansas City Railroad and several other corporations. While at Quincy he was appointed first assistant attorney general of Illinois, and in the performance of his duties resided at Springfield from January, 1893, to January, 1897. At the expiration of his term he removed to Chicago and has practiced law in that city since 1897. For a few months in 1899 he was first assistant city attorney. During 1897-99 he was local attorney for the Chicago & Alton Railroad, and in 1901 became the attorney of record for the Chicago Union Traction Company and the Chicago Consolidated Traction Company. In 1906 he became a member of the firm Loesch, Scofield & Loesch, which subsequently became Loesch, Scofield, Loesch & Richards.

Mr. Scofield is a member of the Chicago and Illinois Bar associations, is a democrat, a member of the Illinois Athletic and Iroquois clubs. He married in 1877 Georgia A. Edmunds. The children born to their marriage were Charles J., Jessie J., Veta, Cora K., Junius T., Thomas E. and Edith E.

W. ERNEST MEYER is a native of Madison County, grew up in the rural community around Worden, and for over ten years has been identified with banking in that Southern Illinois town. He is cashier of the First National Bank of Worden.

Mr. Meyer was born on a farm in Omphghent Township of Madison County, April 27, 1890, son of August and Minnie (Zirges) Meyer. His parents were also natives of Madison County, his father born in Moro Township and his mother in Omphghent Township, and she is still living. August Meyer died when past seventy-seven years of age, having spent a long and industrious career as a farmer. There were eleven children, eight of whom are living, and W. Ernest was the sixth in order of age.

Reared on a home farm, attending the district schools, as a youth and young man he found work on the farm, but in 1912 entered Wall & Company, bankers at Worden, as bookkeeper, and has made himself so useful to that institution that he has remained with it in posts of responsibility during its successive changes. It became the Wall National Bank and is now the First National Bank of Worden. Mr. Meyer has been its cashier since 1919. The bank has a capital stock of twenty-five thousand dollars, and is the financial institution for a very prosperous section of Madison County.

Mr. Meyer married in 1914 Miss Julia Koenig. They have three children. Wilber, Lester and Wilma. They are members of the Lutheran Church. During the World war Mr. Meyer acted as treasurer of the United War Fund in his community.

ROY CLIFFORD BERRY, M. D. A native of Southern Illinois, after completing his medical education Doctor Berry engaged in practice there and for the past ten years has been a prominent representative of his profession at Livingston in Madison County. He was born at Harrisburg, Illinois, July 26, 1886, son of A. M. and Ada M. (Ridenhower) Berry, both of whom are natives of Illinois, the former of Scotch-Irish and the latter of German ancestry. Second in a family of four children, three sons and one daughter, Roy Clifford Berry was reared on the old homestead farm, and began his education in district schools.

Later he entered McKendree College at Lebanon, Illinois, finishing his literary education there. He remained at McKendree as a student three years, and in 1910 graduated with the degree Bachelor of Science, and that of Doctor of Medicine from St. Louis University. After serving an internship in the St. Louis Hospitals Doctor Berry practiced medicine one year at Vandalia, Illinois, and for two years was at Lebanon. Since 1914 Livingston has been his home, and in addition to a general practice he acts as surgeon for the New Stanton Coal Company. He is a member of the Madison County, Illinois State and American Medical Associations.

Doctor Berry is also a thirty-second degree Scottish Rite Mason and Shriner, a member of the Independent Order of Odd Fellows and Knights of Pythias. In 1911 he married Miss Cora F. Gedney, of Lebanon. They have one son, James Marion. Doctor and Mrs. Berry are members of the Methodist Episcopal Church.

ATHANASIUS A. PANTELIS claims classical and historic Greece as the land of his nativity, but is an exemplar of the finest ideals of American citizenship. He has been a resident of Chicago since he was a youth of seventeen years, and has gained secure status as a representative member of the bar of the great metropolis of the West, the while his is large influence and recognized leadership among the large contingent of Greek citizens in Chicago, especially along political lines.

Mr. Pantelis, who maintains his law offices at 155 North Clark Street and who has built up a substantial and important law business of general order, was born in Kastrion, Arcadia, Greece, in the year 1887, and in his native land he received excellent educational advantages along academic and classical lines. In 1904, at the age of seventeen years, Mr. Pantelis severed the ties that bound him to his native land and came to the United States. He forthwith established his residence in Chicago, and his personality gained to him associates among the young men of good Chicago families, he having interested himself in the social and athletic affairs of these young men, and having thus not only advanced his rapid acquirement of familiarity with the English language, but also having laid the foundation for enduring friendships among those who have become prominent in connection with civic and business affairs in Chicago. In preparation for his chosen profession Mr. Pantelis completed a course in the John Marshall Law School, in which excellent Chicago institution he was graduated as a member of the class of 1911, his admission to the Illinois bar having been virtually concomitant with his reception of the degree of Bachelor of Laws, and he having since been engaged in the active and successful practice of his profession in the city of his adoption.

Mr. Pantelis is a stanch and well fortified advocate of the principles of the democratic party, and in 1920 he was one of his party's candidates for the office of judge of the Municipal Court, but he was defeated in the general republication landslide of that year.

When the nation entered the World war Mr. Pantelis promptly gave evidence of his loyalty by enlisting, in 1917, for service in the United States army. He received his preliminary training at Camp Grant, and was assigned, as a non-commissioned officer, to the Eighty-sixth (Black Hawk) Division, in which he later gained commission as second lieutenant. He was on duty at various military camps in the United States, but was not called into service overseas. He served two years, and during a part of the time was an instructor in military tactics. After receiving his honorable discharge he resumed the practice of his profession. In Chicago was solemnized the marriage of Mr. Pantelis and Miss Mabel Bingham, and they have three children: Antoinette, Anastasia and Anthony.

R. GUY KNEEDLER, a native of Collinsville, member of a family that has been living in that vicinity for eighty years, has practiced law at Collinsville for over twenty years, and has won many honorable distinctions in the routine work of his profession. Throughout his professional career he has also been active in public affairs, and is one of the recognized leaders in the republican party of Madison County.

He was born on a farm in Collinsville Township in May, 1873. His grandfather, John Kneedler, brought his family from Pennsylvania to Illinois in 1844, and located in Collinsville Township the year of the big flood in the Mississippi River. He died a year later, leaving to his widow the care of ten children and the further improvement of the farm. Christopher D. Kneedler, father of the Collinsville attorney, was born in Pennsylvania, June 30, 1833, and was eleven years of age when brought to Illinois. He attended a log cabin school in the community, worked on the farm for his mother, and in 1852 went west to California, spending four years as a teamster and farmer. On his return to Illinois he married, and spent the rest of his active life as a substantial farmer, finally retiring to a town home in Collinsville. He married Lauretta Penney, of Irish descent, who was born in Collinsville Township. Their six children were Robert, William, Harry, R. Guy, Lauretta, who married Fred Gade and Don, deceased.

R. Guy Kneedler was reared on the homestead farm, attended the country schools to the age of fourteen, then the graded schools at Collinsville. He was graduated from high school in 1889, and then followed several years of farm work and for two years he performed the duties of check weighman at the Collinsville coal mine. About that time he became convinced that the law was the field for which his talents were best qualified, and he entered Valparaiso University in Indiana, graduating from the law department in 1901. He was admitted to the Illinois bar, and before completing his law course was elected city attorney of Collinsville. He held that office from 1901 to 1907, and during 1906-07 was master in chancery of Madison County. In the spring of 1911 he was elected mayor of Collinsville. Along with a busy law practice he has kept up his interest in the republican party and local politics, and late in 1923 announced his candidacy for the republican nomination for Congress to represent the Twenty-second Illinois District.

He has been chairman of the Collinsville Chapter of the American Red Cross since its organization, and participated in all phases of local war work. He is affiliated with Collinsville Lodge No. 712, A. F. and A. M., Mississippi Valley Consistory Thirty-second degree, Ainid Temple at East St. Louis, and the Collinsville Chapter of the Eastern Star. He is also a member of the Knights of Pythias. He married in 1901 Miss Olive Anderson, who was born and reared in Collinsville. Their children are Richard, Josephine and Maud.

CHARLES R. KISER, M. D. For over a quarter of a century Doctor Kiser has performed all the duties involved in an extensive general practice as a physician and surgeon at Madison in Madison County. He is also a banker, and one of the best known men of affairs in that river community.

Doctor Kiser was born at Dayton, Ohio, November 7, 1866, son of Henry Harrison and Mary Ann (Rohrer) Kiser. The Kiser family has been in America for over two centuries, and is probably of Swiss origin. His great-great-grandfather was a soldier in the Revolutionary war and attained the great age of 101 years. The grandfather, Daniel Kiser, was a native of Maryland, and an early settler of Southwestern Ohio. Henry Harrison Kiser was born at Dayton, spent his life as a farmer and manufacturer, and died in 1913, at the age of seventy-five. His wife, Mary Ann Rohrer, died in 1925, at the age of eighty-eight, at Dayton, and was born near Dayton, where her father, Samuel Rohrer, settled about 1820, being then eighteen years of age, and having come out of Lancaster County Pennsylvania. The Rohrers were of Pennsylvania Dutch stock.

Doctor Kiser was the third child and first son of his parents' four children, all of whom are living. He was reared at Dayton, attending the public schools, including two years in high school. He completed his literary education by graduating from Otterbein College at Westerville, Ohio, in 1892, and in 1895 he graduated M. D. from the Medical College of Ohio at Cincinnati. Doctor Kiser served as an interne in the Good Samaritan Hospital one year, and in 1896 located at St. Louis. In 1898 he moved to Madison, Illinois, and has been continuously engaged in practice there. He is now the oldest physician and surgeon in point of continuous service in the Tri Cities of Madison County.

Doctor Kiser is a member of the Madison County, Illinois State and American Medical Associations and served one year as president of the County Society. He was one of the organizers of the Tri-City State Bank, and has been president of that institution from the beginning. The bank has capital of fifty thousand dollars. For a number of years he served as surgeon for the American Car and Foundry Company at Madison, and also acted as phy-

sician for the Alton-Granite City Traction Company and the Illinois Power and Light Corporation. Doctor Kiser is a thirty-second degree Scottish Rite Mason and Shriner, and is a deacon in the First Presbyterian Church. He married, October 19, 1898, Miss Nora M. Taylor, of St. Louis. She is a native of Kansas. They have one daughter, Helen Louise.

SAMUEL WADE, vice president of the Alton National Bank, bears the honored name of his grandfather, who was one of the founders and builders of the City of Alton, and for more than half a century exerted a commanding influence in its civic, social, religious and business life.

Samuel Wade, the pioneer, was born at Ipswich, Massachusetts, April 17, 1806, a descendant of Jonathan Wade, who came to Ipswich from England in 1632. Samuel Wade came to Alton in 1831, and for a time worked at his trade as carpenter and builder. Later he engaged in the packing business with his brother-in-law, Dr. Ebenezer Marsh. Together they established the Alton Bank, the successor of the Alton Marine and Fire Insurance Company, and when Doctor Marsh, the first president of the bank, died in 1877 he was succeeded by Samuel Wade, who held the position until his death on January 1, 1885.

Samuel Wade was a man of the highest integrity, of moral worth and of business enterprise, and his life and influence touched more than the business or financial element of Alton. For a number of years he was a member of the council, being first elected at the first election under the city charter in 1837. He was mayor of Alton for two terms, from 1849 to 1851, and again in 1855 and 1857. He served as a ruling elder in the Presbyterian Church from 1841 to 1870, a period of twenty-nine years, and after the organization of the Congregational Society in 1870 he united with it and became one of its most influential members. Samuel Wade married at Ipswich in November, 1830, Miss Eunice Caldwell, and she followed him to Alton in the spring of 1833. She was a sister of Charles A. Caldwell, who in 1885 succeeded Mr. Wade as president of the Alton National Bank, the successor of the old Alton Bank. On the death of Mr. Caldwell Edward P. Wade, a son of Samuel Wade, the elder, became president.

The present Samuel Wade, a grandson of the pioneer, was born at Alton, September 11, 1873. He is a son of Albert and Mary S. (Sweetser) Wade. Albert Wade, who died in 1912, was for many years an Alton merchant and was also vice president of the Alton National Bank. His wife, Mary S. Sweetser, who died in 1905, was a daughter of Henry Sweetser, another name inexplicably associated with much of the early and later comemrcial history and civic progress of Alton. Henry Sweetser was in the packing business there during the Civil war and later as a prominent lumberman. One daughter of Albert and Mary Wade is Caroline, wife of George D. Duncan, of Alton.

Samuel Wade, third among the four children of his parents, was educated in the grammar and high schools of Alton, and for a few years was associated with the lumber business. For more than thirty years he has been connected with the Alton National Bank, and for the past eleven years has held the office of vice president. He has been identified with a number of other business enterprises in his home city.

In 1895 he married Miss Elen Taylor, of Alton. They have two children: Elizabeth, wife of Harold Boeschenstein, of Alton, and Henry S., a graduate of Cornell University at Ithaca, New York, and now connected with the Illinois Glass Company. Mr. Wade is a staunch republican.

ROBERT H. GREAVES, M. D. One of the able younger physicians and surgeons of Madison County is Dr. Robert H. Greaves of Collinsville, who has achieved a successful place in his work in the few years since he began practice.

He was born in the mining town of Ladd, Illinois, December 26, 1896, son of Walter and Anna (Wolf) Greaves, now residents of Collinsville. His father was born in England and his mother in Germany, and they were married at Ladd, Illinois. His father has been a mining engineer, and for a number of years has made his home at Collinsville.

The older of two sons, Dr. Robert H. Greaves was reared and educated at Collinsville, attending the grammar and high schools. He graduated from the medical department of St. Louis University in June, 1919, and for a year was an interne in the St. Louis City Hospital. Since then he has been building up and attending a general medical practice at Collinsville. He is a member of the Madison, Illinois State and American Medical Associations. He also belongs to a college fraternity and is a Royal Arch Mason. Doctor Greaves married, in 1919, Jesse Groumeyer, of St. Louis. They have one son, Robert H. Jr., and one daughter, Elise.

RAYMOND L. REDHEFFER has been identified with Chicago banking since boyhood, his working experience having covered every detail in a modern city bank from boy clerk to president. Mr. Redheffer is president of the Amalgamated Trust & Savings Bank, Chicago's only labor bank, now located at Clark and Jackson Streets, in the heart of the business district. This bank provides all the service of regular banking institutions, including commercial and savings departments, and real estate, loan, steamship and insurance departments. At the close of the year 1924 its resources were over $2,800,000, an increase from about $500,000 in July, 1922.

Mr. Redheffer was born at Philadelphia, Pennsylvania, December 17, 1880, son of John C. and Anna E. (Freedley) Redheffer, also natives of Pennsylvania, where his father was born in 1838 and his mother on October 1, 1847. She is still living. His father, who died in 1894, was a lawyer by profession and practiced in Philadelphia.

Raymond L. Redheffer was the youngest of eight children. He acquired his primary education in Chicago, but at the age of thirteen, following his father's death, left school and went to work in the First National Bank as bellboy at a salary of thirteen dollars a month. While with that institution he was promoted until he became assistant to the paying teller. In 1906 he entered the service of the Amalgamated Trust & Savings Bank as paying teller, was promoted to assistant cashier, to vice-president and at the same time was made vice-president of the Second Security Bank. In July, 1922, he was elected president of the Amalgamated Trust & Savings Bank, and the remarkable growth of the institution, above noted, has taken place under his able direction as president. This was the first labor bank to be started in New York City. In April, 1923, he was elected president of the Amalgamated Bank of New York City. These two banks have total resources of about $8,000,000. In June, 1925, he was elected vice president of Hitchcock & Company, the well known investment security corporation.

Mr. Redheffer is a member of the Chicago Athletic Club, the Bankers Club, the Exmore Country Club, and in politics is an independent. His home is at Glencoe, Illinois. He has three children: Anna Elizabeth, Joseph Moore and Raymond L., Jr.

WILLIAM H. BOHM. One of the old, substantial and prominent families of Madison County is that of Bohm. Its founder was Frederick Bohm, who was born in Hanover, Germany, January 25, 1815, and died March 5, 1905, when nearly ninety years of age. His parents followed him to this country and spent their last years in Madison County. Frederick Bohm learned the carpenter's trade and in 1836 came to America, landing at New Orleans after a nine weeks' voyage on a sailing vessel. He came up the river to St. Louis and found work on a farm in St. Louis County. For seventeen years he was employed in the government arsenal, getting this employment through Major W. H. Bell, long one of his close friends. When the Civil war broke out he became one of the organizers of the Union League, and was president of that organization. After leaving the arsenal he moved to the farm at Pleasant Ridge in Madison County, the place he had bought for his parents and where both of them spent their last years. From the Pleasant Ridge farm after twelve years he moved to the vicinity of Edwardsville, where he lived the rest of his life.

Frederick Bohm married Sophia Blume, daughter of Rev. Henry Blume, a teacher, preacher and farmer, a leader in the pioneer religious life of Madison County and founder of a family whose membership is still found in Southern Illinois. Mrs. Frederick Bohm died on August 14, 1900. She was the mother of four children. The eldest son, William, died in infancy; Louis F., a graduate of McKendree College, Lebanon, Illinois, and who followed teaching, died when twenty-four years of age; William H. is the subject of this sketch; and Sophia M. married W. C. Stullken, both now deceased. Their three daughters, Malinda, Selma and Elsie, all married and reside in East St. Louis, Illinois, and St. Louis, Missouri, respectively.

When his parents came to this country they also brought his brother Louis and two sisters. They, after the death of their parents, all married and settled in Madison County, Illinois. William F. Bohm, a son of Louis Bohm, lives on a farm near Troy, Illinois. Other descendants are living, mostly all in Madison County, Illinois.

William H. Bohm was a mere boy when his parents moved to Edwardsville Township. He was educated in the little district school which formerly was located on the corner of the Lewis and Poag road. He assisted his father on the farm and took a pride in making his parents' old age pleasant. He developed what was a tract of heavy timber into one of the best farms in Madison County. He has always been identified with the affairs of the county. He served on the Board of Education for years. He has served as supervisor of Edwardsville Township for ten years and was chairman of the Public Building Committee. He took great interest in the construction of the new court house, a structure which is not only a credit to Madison County but to the whole State of Illinois. During the construction period of the new courthouse he was chairman of the Special Courthouse Committee for one year. In politics he has always been a republican. As a farmer he has always been a hard worker, and has handled a great deal of stock of all kinds. He has served as judge of horses and mules at county and state fairs, and has raised as well as bought car loads of choice mules from Missouri and distributed them in Madison County.

On February 8, 1885, William H. Bohm married Miss Emma H. C. Smith, a daughter of the late Christian P. and Frances Smith. The late Christian P. Smith was one of the most influential and substantial men in Madison County. Eleven children were born to William H. Bohm and wife: Louis F., who died at the age of eighteen years; Attorney Alvin C., whose record is given in the following sketch; Bertha Helen and Irma Cecil, who died in infancy; Dr. Wilbert H. S., an osteopathic physician and surgeon; Elmer E., who is married and living on one of his father's farms; Lydia F., wife of Elmer J. Kriege, of Edwardsville, Illinois; Edward W., who died on May 29, 1921, just one day before his eighteenth birthday; E. Dorothea, Frances M. and Clarence W., at home with their parents.

ALVIN C. BOHM, an ex-service man of the World war period, represents one of the old and honored familes of Madison County, and has built up a fine practice as an attorney in Edwardsville.

Alvin Christian Bohm was born on his father's farm about two miles west of Edwardsville, September 16, 1887, son of William H. and Emma H. C. Bohm. A brief sketch of his father precedes this. Alvin C. Bohm acquired his early education in the Edwardsville High School, attended the Salt City Business College at Hutchinson, Kansas, and the Central Wesleyan College at Warrenton, Missouri. Prior to taking up the study of law he assisted his father in the management of the farm, and when the World war came on he answered the call to the colors.

He graduated from the law department of Washington University at St. Louis with the class of 1920, and has since been admitted to the practice of law by the Supreme Courts of Missouri and Illinois and also licensed to practice in the Federal courts. He has offices in the Edwardsville National Bank Building. He has served one term as master in chancery of the Madison County Circuit Court, and at this time holds an appointment under Attorney General Carlstrom as inheritance tax attorney for Madison and St. Clair counties.

Mr. Bohm since early youth has been active in politics, and for six years was secretary of the Madison County Republican Central Committee and has served as a member of the Republican State Committee, representing the Twenty-second Congressional District. He was chairman of the Speakers Committee during the campaign of 1922.

On November 17, 1923, he married Miss Thekla M. Rahn, a daughter of Rev. and Mrs. H. Rahn, the father formerly pastor of the Ellen Evangelical Church at Edwardsville and now stationed at Evansville, Illinois.

Mr. Bohm is also service officer of American Legion Post No. 199, and his associations with fraternal societies include the Masons, Odd Fellows, Knights of Pythias, B. P. O. Elks, Red Men and Moose.

JACK NELSON. The advent of the radio has created a profession practically unknown a decade ago. Its earlier members learned their art not in school, nor from books, but at the instruments, in daily contact with the work they had to do. They had no precedents to guide them, but worked out the problems which their employment brought in the school of experience. They learned professions, as they are recognized by immemorial custom, attached a certain dignity to their practitioners from the nature and difficulty of the subjects with which they deal. The devotees of the radio rise to the level of these professions in the value of the interests which they represent, as well as in the grasp of intellect and varied and high accomplishments which the calling exacts. The outside public accepts the results of the radio experts' genius with little conception of the problems and intricate relations which these results involve. As the radio is the latest and greatest development of science, its conductors, directors and managers are entitled to recognition as leaders of enterprise.

One of the youngest of the men connected with this important industry at Chicago is Jack Nelson, director of Station WJJD, station of the Loyal Order of Moose. He was born at Chicago, April 4, 1897, and is a son of John A. and A. (Johnson) Nelson, the former deceased and the latter still a resident of Chicago. From earliest youth, even in babyhood, Mr. Nelson was attracted by music, and, his mother noting his predilection in this direction, started him taking piano lessons when he was only a small tot. When he was ten years of age his father died, but his mother managed to keep him at school and also interested in music, although she had no idea then of what great value it was to prove to him in the years to come. As the playing at dances, parties, etc., began to be of assistance financially, the study of classical music was gradually abandoned, and Jack started helping himself through high school and college. He wrote "Go, Lane, Go!" when a junior at the Lane Technical High School, and it is still the official high school song and sung lustily by the Lane boys. Also while a student at the same school he founded the Lane Tech Daily (in 1914), the first daily in the United States to be published by a high school. At Northwestern University he wrote or collaborated on the book lyrics and music of five musical comedies produced by Hermit and Crow, the men's dramatic society of that school, and also wrote "The White Star of Sigma Nu," the official national song of the fraternity. During the World war he served as an ensign in the United States Navy.

After he had secured his university degree Mr. Nelson became a jewelry salesman, and subsequently a piano salesman, a capacity in which he was "discovered" by J. Elliott Jenkins, who, with Thorne Donnelly, owned WDAP (Drake Hotel, Chicago.) He began going up to sing and play merely for the pleasure which he derived from it until an opportunity presented itself and he was made program director and announcer of that station, continuing in that capacity through the regime of the Chicago Board of Trade and until after it was taken over by the Chicago Tribune and changed to WGN. Then the Loyal Order of Moose, at Mooseheart, Illinois, presented tempting offers, so he made the change, taking the chief engineer of WGN with him to be chief engineer of WJJD. Mr. Nelson and this chief engineer, Ralph Shugart, make a splendid team, having worked harmoniously through thick and thin, so that now, although they are separated by fifty miles of wire, they seem to sense just what the other is doing. It is Mr. Shugart who handles almost all of the Mooseheart broadcasting, while Mr. Nelson handles the Chicago end, at the "Ideal Radio Studio" in the Palmer House. This nine room suite for radio broadcasting in that magnificent new hostelry of Chicago was designed by Mr. Nelson and is said by experts to be the most practical and complete radio studio in the country. The two actual studios, control room studio parlor, etc., are all arranged so as to obtain the best possible results for broadcasting both for "the air" and the guests of the hotel who are always welcome.

The record of Mr. Nelson is the best proof of his success. When he was directing WDAP it was by far the most popular radio station in Illinois and considered by thousands of "fans" all over the country the best "on the air." He says that it takes two years to build a station to a point where its programs by their quality commanded listeners. In that he has succeeded remarkably well at his present station. In regard to W J J D it can be said that he started with a lot of unassembled equipment and two towers "on a prairie," and has built it to the place where its affiliations are envied by more than one director of another station. Co-operating with the Palmer House in the Chicago Evening Post, and the authority used for educational talks from this station is "Compton's Pictured Encyclopedia." The concerts on the organ from the Geneva Organ Studio of W J J D are another feature.

At few radio stations can be found men like Jack Nelson, with qualifications that make them so well fitted for radio work. His talking voice makes him well suited for announcing and his education in languages and music provides a background for excellence in that field. He has the ability to make friends for the station and hold them, both with the listeners and the artists who sing from his station, which is a great asset in preparing programs. He has that thing called "personality" on the air, and his ability as an entertainer has made him a "radio star," as evidenced by the thousands of letters from radio listeners all over the western hemisphere.

Several of Mr. Nelson's own compositions, notably "Foolish Child," "I've Got a Song for Sale" and "After the Storm," sung by him, have been heard over the radio from New Zealand to Scotland and from the tip end of South America to within ten degrees of the North Pole.

Mrs. Nelson, who was formerly Miss Madelon Mooney, of Toledo, is a great radio fan, and is thoroughly acquainted with all angles of broadcasting.

HENRY J. KREILING. One of the substantial farmers of Forest City Township is Henry J. Kreiling, and his success, especially as a grain and stock raiser, has made him an authority in agricultural matters in Mason County. He was born in his present township, July 6, 1870, and is a son of Harmon Kreiling, and grandson of Gerhardt Bernard Kreiling, a German by birth, who upon coming to the United States, about 1855, established his homestead in Forest City Township, Mason County, Illinois, which property is now owned by his son, John, and here he died. By his first marriage he had the following children: Harmon G., who is mentioned at length below; Henry John; Annie, who married Justus Pfetzing, of Havana, Illinois; and Margaret, who married George Furer, of Easton, Illinois, and has four children. After the death of his first wife Gerhardt Bernard Kreiling married a Miss Witte, and they had the following children: John, who is on the home farm; August, who died at Chicago, and left two children to survive him; Lydia, who married Fred Greenhagen and resides in Mason County; and George, who is the youngest and resides in Forest City Township.

Harmon G. Kreiling was born in Germany, April 27, 1841, and died January 11, 1915. Fourteen years old when he was brought by his parents to Mason County, he was reared in this part of Illinois. Although he had very few educational advantages, as his labor was required in developing the homestead, he learned much through experience and contact with others and was a very well-informed man. Although he wanted to volunteer for service in the war between the states, he was induced by his parents to refrain, but he was very loyal to the Government of his adopted land.

After some years spent as a farmer in the neighborhood of his father's homestead he bought the farm now owned by his son, Henry J. Kreiling. At the time he moved, this property was but little improved and he did much to develop it and make it productive, and he devoted it to grain raising. As he became prosperous he kept on investing in farm land, and at one time owned farms as far away as Mississippi, as well as several farms in Mason County. A man of commanding presence, as he was five feet ten inches in height, and weighed 185 pounds, he attracted attention wherever he went. Very industrious, he worked hard, and was always busy at something constructive. Not only did he exert himself to improve his own condition, but he also accomplished much in behalf of his community, and for years was a member of the local school board. Politically he voted the democratic ticket in national affairs and never missed an election. Long identified with Saint John's Lutheran Church, he was one of its heaviest contributors, and was recognized as one of its pillars.

Harmon G. Kreiling married, in Quiver Township, Mary Budke, a daughter of Gerhardt Budke, a native of Germany, who came to the United States when his daughter was one year old. Mrs. Kreiling died December 4, 1894, having borne her husband the following children: Annie, who is the wife of Charles Himmel, of Quiver Township; Henry J., whose name heads this review; Lizzie, who married August Lussenhopp, of Salt Creek Township, Mason County; Sophie, who married Henry Himmel, of Manito, Illinois; and Chris, who resides at Havana, Illinois.

Henry J. Kreiling attended the country schools of his home community, and had three months' work in the normal school at Valparaiso, Indiana. Remaining at home, he assisted his father in the farm work until he was twenty-six years old, when he was married and began farming for himself, taking charge of his father's homestead, and here he has since remained. While, he, too, has raised grain, he has also been a stockraiser, breeding up Shorthorn cattle until his product rates very high, and occasionally he also feeds and fattens stock for the market.

Like his father, Mr. Kreiling is interested in educational matters, and is a member of the school board. He helped to organize the Farmers Elevator Company of Forest City of which he is a director. His church home is the Pleasant Plains Community Church, and he is one of its trustees. During the late war Mr. Kreiling was very active in stimulating interest among the school children in the War Savings Stamps, and was instrumental in keeping up the purchases to meet the local quota, and he also did much to make successful the drives for all purposes, being in sympathy with the administration's plans for carrying on the war.

On February 24, 1897, Mr. Kreiling married, in Forest City Township, Mason County, Mary B. Zimmerman, a daughter of Henry Zimmerman, a farmer in Pennsylvania as well as in Illinois. He came of Pennsylvania Dutch stock, and was born in Pennsylvania. Following the close of the war between the states Mr. Zimmerman came to Illinois, having rendered gallant service in that war as a Union soldier. After his arrival in Illinois

he married Elizabeth Singley, and Mrs. Kreiling was the only daughter born to them, but they had the following sons; William and Oscar, both of whom are deceased; Elmer, who resides in Fulton County, Illinois; Harvey who is state veterinarian of Illinois and resides at Lincoln; Frank, who is a twin of Harvey, is a veterinarian residing at Havana, Illinois; and Percy, who is dean of the agricultural department of College Park, Maryland.

Mr. and Mrs. Kreiling have had the following children born to them: Mabel, who is a graduate of the Forest City High School, had two years in the Bradley Polytechnic Institute and is now engaged at home on account of ill health; Percy, who is also a graduate of the Community High School of Forest City and took a commercial course in Brown's Business College; Maud, who was graduated from the same high school as her sister and brother, also spent a year in the Normal University at Normal, Illinois, and is now one of the Mason County teachers; and Clarence, who is attending the Community High School at Forest City.

MORTON T. CULVER was admitted to the Illinois bar in 1892, and has since divided his time between his real estate and official duties in his home town of Glencoe and his general law practice in the city. His offices are at 139 North Clark Street.

Mr. Culver belongs to one of the pioneer families of Northern Cook County. His grandfather, John B. Culver, was born at Horseheads, New York, and was a surveyor by profession. Coming west in 1829, he settled at Dutchman's Point in the town of Niles, Cook County. In 1849 he removed to Chicago. One of his ten children was Morton Culver, who was born at Dutchman's Point, August 30, 1841. He attended the Chicago high school, and when the war came on, served a period of 180 days in the One Hundred and Thirty-fourth Illinois Infantry. He worked his way through Northwestern University, completing the four years course in three years. During the early seventies he was principal of the historic Jones School on South Dearborn Street, one of the most historic grammar schools of the City of Chicago. Subsequently he attended the Union College of Law, was admitted to the bar and engaged in practice and in real estate operations. He laid out a number of divisions along the North Shore, at Glencoe, Evanston and Ravenswood. Morton Culver died February 27, 1900, aged fifty-eight. His wife was Eugenia M. Taylor, who was born in New York state in 1843 and has had her home at Glencoe since 1873. She is a daughter of John Taylor and of Revolutionary ancestry.

Morton T. Culver, third in a family of eight children, all but one of whom are living, was born at Chicago, December 2, 1870. He was educated in the public schools at Glencoe, in Northwestern Academy and in 1892 graduated with the LL. B. degree from the Union College of Law. Subsequently he attended the Kent College of Law, and the Chicago Law School conferred upon him the degree Master of Laws in June, 1924. He engaged in practice in 1892, and is known as a specialist in real estate law.

At Glencoe he has had prominent part in local politics and government, serving as village attorney from 1898 to 1900, as village president from 1900 to 1902, as village attorney from 1903 to 1907, police magistrate from 1892 to 1897, and justice of the peace of the town of New Trier from 1897 to 1901. Under Hon. Edward J. Brundage he was an assistant attorney general of the State of Illinois, and for over four years was assigned as assistant counsel to the Public Utilities Commission under Hon. George T. Buckingham.

Mr. Culver was a member of the Illinois National Guard from 1887 to 1896, serving in the coal mining and Pullman strikes in 1894, being sergeant of Company L. He is a member of the Hamilton Club, life member of the Chicago Press Club, the Illinois State and American Bar Associations. He is a past master of the A. O. Fay Lodge No. 677, A. F. and A. M., member of Evanston Chapter No. 144, R. A. M., Oriental Consistory of the Scottish Rite and Medinah Temple of the Mystic Shrine. He belongs to the Lake Shore Athletic Club, the Midland Club, Chicago and Cook County Real Estate Board, the Chicago Association of Commerce and the Medinah Country Club. He married Miss Marion Hawkes at Geneva, Illinois. Their two children are Reginald and Dorothy.

DAVID IVAR SWANSON, representative from the Eleventh District in the 53rd and 54th Illinois General Assemblies, is a Chicago attorney, with offices at 10 South La Salle Street and one of the able men of his generation in the law and in public affairs.

He was born at Chicago, September 14, 1884, son of John and Betty (Jonson) Swanson. His parents came from Sweden. David I. Swanson grew up in Chicago, his early associations training him to take as well as to give hard knocks, and developing in him a character adequate for all the varying responsibilities of life. He attended public schools, and in 1912 received his law degree from the John Marshall Law School at Chicago. Since his admission to the bar in 1913 he has engaged in an extensive independent practice, before the Federal as well as State courts, and he has handled a large volume of litigation in real estate, criminal, commercial and probate law.

Mr. Swanson is a republican, and was first candidate for the Legislature in 1918. In 1922 he was elected one of the representatives from the Eleventh Illinois District and in 1924 was reelected. During the session of the Fifty-fourth Assembly, in the spring of 1925, James O'Donnell Bennett, a veteran journalist, made some interesting studies of the Illinois Legislature. one of them devoted largely to Representative Swanson's personality and methods. In the course of his articles Mr. Bennett said: "Everywhere here I have heard the name David I. Swanson fair spoken in the mouths of careful speaking men. He is chairman of the important judiciary committee and member of the committee on banks, on banking, and building and loan associations and on insurance. The least sophisticated of tax payers will recognize in that list devious, dubious and self aiding opportunities that would unman a young legislator who lacks character. But what you hear on every hand is emphatic comment on Swansons methodical views and tenacity, his patience and industry, his promptness and energy, his honesty. Such comment often winds up with 'he is one of the coming men of Illinois.' When he is home David I. Swanson lives at 7842 Marshfield Avenue, Chicago. He sprang from no downy bed of ease, having had rigorous beginnings in the stock yards area, where boys are hard as nails. His deportment today gives no sign of tough origin."

Mr. Swanson during the World war, served with the Motor Transport Corps at Camp Meigs, Washington, D. C. He is a member of the Chicago and Illinois Bar Associations, the Englewood Business Men's Association, the Kiwanis and Mid-Day Athletic Club, belongs to the Vikings and the Masonic and Odd Fellows fraternities, to the Y. M. C. A., Delta Theta Pi law fraternity, and is a Baptist and member of the Chicago Council, Boy Scouts of America. Mr. Swanson married Mrs. Margaret Carlson, a widow, whose two interesting children, Stanley and Wilbur, he has adopted.

RICHARD S. FOLSOM, who has been a member of the Chicago bar since 1896, has long enjoyed high prestige in his profession, and in a public way is perhaps best known through his service some years ago as corporation counsel of Chicago. He is a son of Charles A. Folsom, who came from New England to Chicago shortly after the close of the Civil war and lived in that city until his death in 1905. His life record is one deserving of more than passing mention. A native of Maine, he was taken to Massachusetts when a small boy, was reared to manhood in that state, and as was the custom at that time, served an apprenticeship with a clothing merchant. He was bookkeeper for a Swedish iron importing house when the Civil war broke out. At Lincoln's first call for 75,000 troops he volunteered, was mustered in as a second lieutenant in the Twenty-fourth Massachusetts Infantry, and subsequently was promoted to first lieutenant and then to captain. At the expiration of his term he reenlisted for the second and also for the third term, and served continuously until just before the close of the war, when he was discharged for disability contracted in the service. Much of his time was spent in North Carolina, where he participated in the sieges of Fort Wagner and Fort Fisher. He was severely wounded at Fort Fisher. After the war he had an experience more or less common in all times with soldiers returned to civilian life, another man in his place of former employment at Boston, and no willingness on the part of the firm to accept the man who for four years had fought the battles of the Union. In the meantime he had married Sarah T. Sweet, daughter of Dr. Richard F. Sweet, of an old New England family. With his wife Captain Folsom moved West to Chicago and for a number of years was identified with the legal profession, chiefly as a counselor. He was held in high regard for his many admirable qualities, and he always took a great personal delight in mingling with his old army comrades. He was a member of the Episcopal Church.

Of the three children of Captain Folsom and wife two survive. Richard S. Folsom was born in Chicago August 5, 1872, was educated in the public schools of the city, attended Racine College in Wisconsin, Columbia College of New York, and was graduated in 1894 with the A. B. degree from Williams College of Massachusetts. He studied law in Northwestern University, was admitted to the bar in 1896, and almost continuously has been identified with a general practice. From 1910 to 1915 he was associated in practice with James Hamilton Lewis and Wallace Streeter of the firm of Lewis, Folsom and Streeter, and is now senior member of Folsom, Affay and Streeter, with offices at 105 West Monroe Street.

By appointment of Judge O. E. Brown, Mr. Folsom served as master in chancery of the Circuit Court of Cook County from 1911 to 1915, and from June, 1912, to April, 1915, was general counsel of the Chicago Board of Education. In 1915 he was appointed corporation counsel of the City of Chicago, and held that office until he voluntarily retired to engage in private practice. While corporation counsel he rendered the important decision on the Sunday closing law for saloons, his opinion being that it applied to the State of Illinois as well as the City of Chicago.

Mr. Folsom has had several business connections, is a member of the Chicago, Illinois State and American Bar Associations, the Law Club, Mid-Day Club and South Shore Country Club. He is a democrat, and a member of the Episcopal Church. During the World war Mr. Folsom was a member of the Legal Advisory Board, Division No. 3. He married, May 30, 1905, Miss Dorothy E. Moulton, daughter of Gen. George E. Moulton, a prominent Illinois citizen.

HENRY E. BUSSE, cashier of the First Trust and Savings Bank of Alton, is a man of mature business experience in Alton, his native city, and has thoroughly earned the responsibilities he now enjoys.

He was born at Alton December 4, 1876, son of Dietrich H. W. and Arnoldena W. A. (Mueller) Busse. The father was born in Prussia, Germany, and his mother in Westphalia, and coming to America, were married in Alton, where the father followed various business lines for many years. He died May 16, 1916, and is survived by the widowed mother. They have seven sons and two daughters, Henry E. being the second child and second son. The names of the family were: William, Henry, Dietrich H. W., deceased, Johanna, deceased, John F., Fred G., Walter, deceased, Rudolph, deceased, Arnoldena, W. A., wife of Frank B. Lenhardt.

Henry E. Busse was educated in the public schools at Alton, and had to start life with nothing beyond a public school training. He worked for some time for the Phinney Wholesale Grocery Company, saving enough money to pay the expenses of a course in the Southwestern Business College at St. Louis. Following that he spent about three years with the Illinois Glass Company, and then en-

Peter J. Angsten

tered the Alton Banking Company as bookkeeper. He served that institution successively in other responsibilities, including the office of cashier. He was with the Alton Banking Company five years, and became cashier of the First Trust and Savings Bank upon its organization.

Mr. Busse married, August 4, 1908, Miss Sophia Louisa Wutzler, of Alton. They have one daughter, Adele Lillian. Mr. Busse has taken an active interest in public affairs, though due to his strong affection for his home he has never joined any secret society. He is a democrat and a member of the Evangelical Church.

JOHN B. MENZ. As a business man and a citizen John B. Menz has been identified with the southern Illinois city of Highland for thirty years. He represents one of the old and substantial families of that community, where Swiss colonists predominated in the founding. Mr. Menz is a banker and merchant.

He was born at Highland, October 19, 1874, son of Jacob and Cecilia (Suppiger) Menz. His mother was born in Highland. His father was a native of Germany, and was about eight years of age when brought to America.

John B. Menz is the oldest of four children, and was reared and educated at Highland, attending the public schools and having a college course at St. Louis. After leaving school he remained in that city working for a time, and then returned to Highland and became interested in the mercantile business with the C. Kinne & Company. Mr. Menz has been with this well known and extensive organization in different capacities, and for more than twenty years has been its secretary and treasurer. He is also well known as a banker, being president of the First National Bank of Highland, and has a number of other commercial interests.

He served as secretary of the Business Men's League for thirteen years. He belongs to the Congregational Church, is a thirty-second degree Scottish Rite Mason, a member of the Highland Country Club, and other local organizations, and has put himself in a position of willing co-operation with all other organizations for social and civic improvement.

Mr. Menz married in 1904 Miss Clara Hendrich, of Highland. They have two sons, Roscoe E. and John Erick, both attending Illinois University at Urbana.

LOUIS EDWARD HART. A member of the bar of Chicago of long and prominent standing, Louis Edward Hart has worked his way to the foremost ranks through individual industry and merit. For thirty years he has been identified with the local fraternity and during this period has at all times shown an appreciation of the highest tenets and ethics of the law.

Mr. Hart was born at Cleveland, Ohio, January 29, 1871, and is a son of Clinton and Olivia N. (Alling) Hart. His father, born in Connecticut, March 3, 1842, was educated in his native state, where he commenced life as a steamfitter. Later he went to Cleveland, where he became a contractor in his special field of endeavor and for many years handled large contracts. His final years were passed as an agriculturist in Ashtabula County, Ohio, where his death occurred in 1914. Politically he was a republican, and as a churchman, a Congregationalist, as was his wife, who, born in Connecticut, September 22, 1843, survived him until 1918, they being the parents of three children: Fred Clinton, Mary Louise and Louis Edward.

On the completion of his primary educational training Louis Edward Hart pursued a course at Grand River Institute, Austinburg, Ohio, from which he was graduated in 1887. He then enrolled as a student at Oberlin College, from which institution he received his degree of Bachelor of Arts in 1893. Admitted to the bar in 1895, he commenced the general practice of his calling in the same year at Chicago, where he has since continued, at present occupying offices at Room 959, 209 South LaSalle Street. He has risen to a high place in his calling, in the confidence of a large clientele and in the esteem of his fellow-practitioners. Mr. Hart belongs to the Chicago Bar Association, the Illinois Bar Association and the American Bar Association. He is also prominent in club life, belonging to the Chicago Club, University Club, Union League Club, Indian Hill Club, Chicago Golf Club and the Law Club. His religious connection is with Wellington Congregational Church, and in political affairs he is a republican. Mr. Hart's pleasant residence is at 322 Belden Avenue.

On December 27, 1899, Mr. Hart was united in marriage with Miss Caroline Wilcox, who was born in Chicago, and they have one son, Louis Edward, Jr.

PETER J. ANGSTEN. While great progress has been made in all lines of business, perhaps none shows such development as does that branch which has for its purpose the protection, through insurance, of the people of loss from all sources. Of course, for many years insurance has been accepted as a legitimate form of business transactions, but it is only within recent years that its scope has been expanded until the present phase has been reached. Actuaries have so tabulated risks, and computed possibilities, that it is now accepted as a duty and a privilege to secure, through the taking out of an adequate amount of insurance, immunity against loss, not only from death or fire, but from all of the chances and changes of this mortal life, and poor and uninformed indeed is the man today who does not carry some form or other of insurance. This development has been brought about, mainly, by an intensive campaign of education, promulgated chiefly by the representatives of the insurance companies and through literature written by experts on the subject. The wonderful increase in the amount of insurance written annually has, naturally, brought into this line of activity, men of superior character and business astuteness, and one who has won distinction in the insurance field is Peter J. Angsten, of Chicago, member of the Angsten-Farrell Company, general insurance, with headquarters at 11 South Lasalle Street.

Peter J. Angsten was born at Chicago, in 1879, a son of Philip and Augusta (Huber)

Angsten, the former also a native of Chicago, was reared in this city. He founded the Angsten cooperage manufacturing plant that was for many years one of the leading industries of its kind at Chicago. In later years he became a builder, and among other structures, erected hundreds of flat and apartment houses in Chicago. He was a member of the Chicago Board of Education for a number of years, and was widely and favorably known as one of the substantial citizens of his native city.

Attending both the grade and high schools of Chicago, Peter J. Angsten had his initial contact with the business world in partnership with his father in the cooperage plant, under the firm name of Philip Angsten & Son. Subsequently he entered the insurance field, in which he has been so eminently successful. He is also a director of the General Re-Insurance Corporation of New York City.

Mr. Angsten has not confined his operations to business circles, but has been active in public affairs in the city and state. For several years he was chairman of the Illinois Industrial Commission, in which capacity he adjusted compensation for thousands of deserving cripples and others having injuries coming under the compensation law. It was he who organized this commission upon its creation under the law passed by the General Assembly, and he remained a member of it for nine years. At present he is a member of the North Shore Park Commission of Chicago. He was one of the organizers and is a member of the Board of Directors of the Broadway National Bank of Chicago. He is president of the Midland Club, which is composed of a large number of business men of Chicago and other cities throughout the country; and belongs to the Bunker Hill Country Club, the German Club, and the Chicago Association of Commerce. For many years his principal hobby was baseball, and he still takes a keen interest in the national game.

Peter J. Angsten married Agnes C. Reiff, and they have four children: Raymond, Philip, Edward and Catherine.

ROBERT I. HUNT, banker and financier, has had many prominent connections with financial affairs in the city of Chicago as well as in Decatur, which city has been his home for many years.

Mr. Hunt was born in Baltimore, Maryland, January 19, 1864. He came west when a child, and after a common school education, began his business experience in Chicago before he was fourteen years of age. After some years of training he was promoted to a responsible position in the credit department of Edson Keith & Company, wholesale millinery and dry goods merchants. Since that time he has been a recognized specialist in matters pertaining to financial management. Only a few of the more important of his business connections can be noted. He helped organize Suffern Hunt & Company and the Decatur Cereal Company, white corn millers; has served as president of the Citizens National Bank at Decatur and for three years was vice-president and treasurer of Morehouse & Wells Company, taking an active part in the erection of their modern store building.

Mr. Hunt assisted in the formation of the Polar Ice Company of Decatur, and for many years acted as its secretary and treasurer. From 1916 to 1921 he was assistant treasurer of the United States, having charge of the subtreasury at Chicago. Upon the absorption of that office by the Federal Reserve Bank at Chicago he turned over to the institution approximately $300,000,000 in cash and government securities. Mr. Hunt is now a director of the Chicago Morris Plan Bank. He is president of the Decatur Water Supply Company, probably the most important public undertaking in this city.

He is a Knight Templar Mason and Shriner, and a member of the Knights of Pythias. Mr. Hunt in 1898 married Annie Packard Sawyer, foster daughter of Mr. and Mrs. Silas Packard, who were two of Macon County's earliest pioneers. Mr. and Mrs. Hunt have three children: Floyd Packard, Virginia and William Orlando Hunt.

CAPT. SAMUEL B. HARTZ had a conspicuous part in the intermediate history of Illinois, and his career was chiefly identified with the City of Peoria, where he died in December, 1891. His son, Irving T. Hartz, has been a manufacturer and business man of Chicago for many years.

Samuel B. Hartz was a native of Pennsylvania, a direct descendant of one of the three Swiss brothers, David, Peter and Conrad, who in 1749 left Europe and on the sailing vessel Phoenix crossed the Atlantic to establish homes in the American colonies. For generations, and to this day, the descendants have resided in Pennsylvania, and have borne an important part in the good citizenship of that commonwealth. At least one of the three original brothers served as an American soldier in the Revolutionary war. Those of the Hartz name in this country have always been honorable, law abiding, industrious and respected, and as such have commanded the wholesome regard of their fellowmen in the various localities called home.

When a young man Capt. Samuel B. Hartz, leaving Pennsylvania, came to Illinois and located at Peoria, where his first employment was as a clerk in a retail store. When Fort Sumter was fired upon by the Confederates in 1861, and when President Lincoln issued his call for 75,000 troops, Samuel B. Hartz not only decided immediate enlistment for himself, but became a leader in arousing sentiments for service in his locality. He recruited two companies, which subsequently became a part of the One Hundred and Eighth Illinois Volunteer Infantry, and of one of these, Company G, he became first lieutenant and with that rank went to the front. He participated in several campaigns of his regiment, and was promoted to captain of his company. At the battle of Island No. 10 he was severely wounded, and as a result was an invalid and eventually sent home. Though incapacitated for military service in the field, he used his voice and influence in furthering the aims of the Federal Government until peace was declared.

Much of the subsequent life of Captain Hartz was spent in mercantile pursuits, and later in the real estate business. He and one other associate built the old Fort Clark Street Railway at Peoria, which later was merged into a general city railway corporation. A man of more than ordinary force of character and of the strictest integrity, he stood deservedly high in the esteem of the people of Peoria. He loved the material things of life, the companionship of his fellows, and his influence was ever on the side of sane, progressive citizenship. The first wife of Captain Hartz was Virginia Emeline Thomas, and his second wife was Stacia Buckner. By the first marriage there were three sons: Irving, Thomas, Alfred Sherman, deceased and Henry Samuel, deceased. Of the second marriage there were two sons, Victor B., deceased, and John W., a resident of Peoria.

Irving T. Hartz, the oldest and only surviving son of Captain Hartz's prosperous marriage, was born at Peoria, March 21, 1861. He acquired his early education in public schools, and his first employment was with the old T. P. and W. Railway Company. For about five years he was engaged in the grain and railroad business in Peoria and then in Chicago. He then went East and had charge of the offices and finances for the contractors of the famous Croton Aqueduct for New York City. Mr. Hartz returned to Chicago in 1888 and from 1889 to 1892 was secretary and manager of the Calumet Iron and Steel Company, was president of the Union Cold Storage Company in 1896-99, and since 1895 has been an executive in the Morden Frog and Crossing Works, with a plant at Chicago Heights, one of the important industries of Chicago, manufacturing equipment and supplies used by railways all over the country. He was vice president of this company from 1895 to 1907 and since then has been its president.

Mr. Hartz is a member of the Loyal Legion, the Chicago Athletic, Midlothian, South Shore Country and Exmoor Golf Clubs, and the New York Club of New York City. He married at Chicago in 1887, Miss Lillian Terhune. The three children born to their marriage were: Homer, Virginia (deceased), and Mildred.

CHARLES WILLIAM HOUGHTON, farmer and stockman of Menard County, occupies the farm in Rock Creek Precinct where he was born and reared, and in the locality where his family has been prominent for four generations.

Mr. Houghton is a descendant of Col. Joab Houghton, who is said to have raised the first company in New Jersey for service in the Revolutionary war. He was granted his commission of captain October 19, 1776. One of the useful soldiers in his company was his son, Aaron Houghton, the pioneer of the family in Southern Illinois. He was only fifteen when he entered the army, and he served through two or three other enlistments. On coming to Illinois he settled on Rock Creek, and his homestead is now owned by J. S. Hurie, who married one of the daughters of the Houghton family. Aaron, the Revolutionary soldier, is buried in the cemetery near Rock Creek Church.

His son, Charles P. Houghton, son of Aaron, came from Mason County, Kentucky, in 1824, and established his home in Menard County. He and his father and mother all died of typhoid fever in 1835, eleven years after they came to Illinois. The wife of Charles P. Houghton was Elizabeth Van Deventer. Their children were: Catherine, Sevigna, William, Phoebe, Mary and Aaron. Aaron Runyan Houghton, father of Charles W., was born at Rock Creek December 7, 1825, and was about ten years of age when his father died. He had a country school education, and was a soldier in the Mexican war, being with General Scott's army in the campaign ending with the capture of the City of Mexico. He was in Company F of the Fourth United States Regiment. While he was being drilled for this war at Springfield he frequently saw Abraham Lincoln, then a prominent Springfield attorney, who came out to camp often to watch the drill. Aaron R. Houghton developed one of the good farms in Menard County and also carried on business as a cattle drover. He began voting as a whig and finally became a republican. His death occurred March 10, 1895. He was a charter member of Petersburg Lodge, Independent Order of Odd Fellows. The wife of Aaron R. Houghton was Elvira Stephenson, daughter of James and Margaret (Clinton) Stephenson, her mother being a daughter of Captain Clinton, an officer in the Revolution. James Stephenson came to Illinois from Kentucky, and after a few years settled in Menard County. He was commissioned a captain by Governor Bond in 1822, and one of his sons was on duty in the Black Hawk war. Elvira Stephenson died February 9, 1893.

Charles William Houghton, only surviving son of his parents, was born October 27, 1859, on the farm which he still occupies, and which during his boyhood had as its residence a building containing at one end a log cabin, had a hall and two rooms at the other end of the frame, a typical specimen of frontier days in Southern Illinois. His own birth occurred in this log building. It was erected by Jesse Combs, a Menard County pioneer, and it now stands on the Chautauqua grounds at Petersburg, having been moved there as a historical relic by Mr. Houghton himself. He was educated in public schools and attended college at Lincoln, Illinois, and his experience in teaching was limited to a single day. Since early manhood he has been a farmer and stock raiser, and has been a regular shipper to the live stock markets. He has been a breeder of Shorthorn cattle. He is a director of the First National Bank of Petersburg, and is president of the Tallula State Bank.

Mr. Houghton has been a member of the local school board, an elder in the Rock Creek Presbyterian Church and a delegate to Presbyteries, synods and general assemblies, and in politics has been a steadfast republican since casting his first vote for James A. Garfield.

He married at Table Grove, Illinois, February 4, 1892, Miss Ada Keach. She was born in McDonough County, Illinois, May 8, 1864, daughter of James and Amanda (Tonner) Keach, and granddaughter of Nathan Tonner. The Tonners and Keaches came from Ohio. Of the children born to Mr. and Mrs. Houghton the oldest son is James Frank, who graduated from James Millikin University at Decatur, Illinois, from the law department of the University of Michigan, and is now practicing law at St. Petersburg, Florida. He married Virginia Sidway. He was a second lieutenant in the World war, and for a time commanded a company, and was on duty at Camp Dodge, Camp Pike, Camp McArthur, and was appointed judge advocate of the court martial at Camp Shelby. The second son, Ralph, like the other children, graduated from the high school of his home community, attended James Millikin University, and during the World war was a storekeeper with the United States Navy, and spent a year in the English Channel in the transport service. Edward William, the third son, was with the Marines in the World war, and after the armistice went to San Domingo and for ten months assisted in the preservation of law and order in that country. He is now a farmer at the home place, and finished his education at the University of Illinois. The older daughter, Marian, is a graduate of James Millikin University and the wife of Ralph Goltra of Evanston, Illinois. The youngest child, Nellora, lives at Evanston.

CHARLES F. MCHATTON, one of the founders and president of the Farmers State Bank of Mt. Sterling, is a native of Brown County, and was a well known and successful stock breeder and farmer before he became a banker.

He was born in Missouri Township, Brown County, September 12, 1863. His father, William McHatton, was a well beloved citizen of Brown County for many years, a man of splendid integrity, generosity and natural nobility. He was born in County Antrim, Ireland, grew up and married there, and was a farmer and merchant near Belfast. Coming to the United States in 1859, he settled in Brown County, Illinois, and lived there until his death in 1903, at the age of seventy-five. He acquired American citizenship as soon as possible, was a democrat, and very active in his church. His wife was Ann Casey, who died in 1916, at the age of ninety. Both are buried in the Mt. Sterling Cemetery. Their children were: Patrick H., a retired farmer at Mount Sterling; William, of Elmo, Washington; Annie, of Mount Sterling; Judge John J., former judge of the Circuit Court of Butte, Montana, now a resident of Los Angeles; Charles Frederick; and Daniel J., of Mount Sterling. Charles F. McHatton never married. His parents came to America on a sailing vessel, being eight weeks on the water and were almost shipwrecked in a severe storm. They landed at New York and came directly west to Brown County, whither friends had preceded them. While they brought little capital and had to put up with the simple comforts of real pioneers, they were never satisfied to provide for themselves and their own family. Their generous instincts reached out over the community. Mrs. McHatton in particular was known as a woman of beautiful charity, and was kindly in thought and prompt to relieve the necessities of those poorer than herself.

When Charles F. McHatton was five years old his parents moved from his native township to Lee Township. He grew up on the farm there, attended a community school, taught in a rural district four years, and completed work in the Northern Illinois Normal College at Dixon. He then resumed teaching, and his last work in the schoolroom was in the new school. Following that he engaged in farming and in the raising of fine stock. His father had done much to stimulate the introduction of pure bred stock into his community. Mr. McHatton took up the business, and for a number of years handled blooded Shorthorn cattle, Percheron horses and Polant China hogs, and in addition to raising such stock for the general market he frequently exhibited them at county fairs and showed a marked genius for success in that line. At the same time he accumulated much farming land, and still owns a farm near Mount Sterling.

In 1914 Mr. McHatton organized the Farmers State Bank of Mount Sterling, his associates being John Murphy, John Briggs, E. E. McCoy, O. T. Patterson and Allen Moody. Allen Moody is the present cashier of the bank. Mr. McHatton has been president from the beginning. The first vice president was Mr. Murphy, and his present successor is Harry Hannant, the second vice president. The bank has been operating on its charter capital of $50,000 and has resources of about $480,000, with deposits of $380,000. Mr. McHatton owns 240 acres of good land three miles west of Mount Sterling on a hard road, also his home in Mount Sterling and stock in the K. of C. Home Building Association. His word in the community in which he lives is regarded as good as any bond.

Mr. McHatton has shown a continuous interest in the welfare and advancement of his home county in Mount Sterling. He has been a member of the town council, the Brown County Farm Bureau, is treasurer of the Mount Sterling Commercial Club, and is chairman of the Brown County Democratic Central Committee, and has attended a number of state and congressional conventions. He is a grand knight of the Knights of Columbus, and during the World war did much to influence patriotic sentiments and financial support for the war by his work as a four minute speaker and as a committeeman in the drives.

DAVID A. WYCKOFF has had thirty-five years of experience in banking in Southern Illinois. For over twenty-five of those years he has been a well known figure in Alton financial circles, where he is president of the First Trust & Savings Bank.

Mr. Wyckoff was born at Jerseyville, Illinois, October 12, 1874, son of Horatio N. and H. Elizabeth (Van Dorne) Wyckoff, both representing families of New York State. His father came to Illinois from New York with his parents when one year old. David A. Wyckoff was reared and educated at Jerseyville, graduating from high school in 1892, and immediately afterward took employment in the State Bank of Jerseyville. He had seven years of training in that institution, and in 1899 took the opportunity for metropolitan bank experience as an employe of the Mississippi Valley Trust Company of St.

Louis, resigning his position there in 1902, after which he helped organize in that year the Alton Bank & Trust Company, of which he acted as cashier. In 1909 he sold out his interest in that bank and in the same year organized the First Trust & Savings Bank of Alton, of which he is president. This bank has a capital of $100,000, and is one of the successful institutions of the kind in Southern Illinois.

Mr. Wyckoff has enjoyed a number of honors in the banking profession and public affairs. He is former chairman of the Madison County Bankers' Association, former treasurer of the Illinois Bankers' Association, and former vice president for Illinois of the Trust Company Section of the American Bankers' Association. He served on the Alton Board of Education, for six years, was treasurer of the Board of Education and since 1912 has been a trustee of Shurtleff College. During the World war he was a member of the County Council of Defense. Fraternally he is affiliated with Franklin Lodge No. 25, A. F. and A. M., at Upper Alton, serving as treasurer for a number of years, and belongs to the Oriental Consistory of the Scottish Rite at Chicago. He and his family are Presbyterians.

At Upper Alton, Illinois, November 1, 1899, Mr. Wyckoff married Miss Mary R. Lemen, daughter of Dr. Edward C. Lemen. Her father was one of the pioneers of the Alton community, a man successful in his professional and business affairs, and the Lemen family has had more than an ordinary share in the development of Southern Illinois. Mr. and Mrs. Wyckoff have three children: Helen M., Rogers L., and Edward H. Wyckoff.

JOHN BENJAMIN ABBOTT. It is a source of satisfaction to any one, as the years pile up, to be able to retire from active participation in life's conflict and enjoy the comforts earned during former periods of industry. When a man is also able to review his life work and realize that his present prosperity has come to him through legitimate sources, then he has added cause for contentment and satisfaction. No one who knows John Benjamin Abbott, retired business man and honored resident of Mason City, would deny him this satisfaction, or fail to accord to him appreciation for what he has done for his community while developing his own private interests.

His father, Henry Abbott, was born in Blackburn, England, February 1, 1819, and married Ann Keen at Southport, England, January 3, 1838. They came to America in 1842, via New Orleans, landing at Beardstown, Illinois. Before leaving England two children were born to them: William and Alice. William, who spent most of his life in Mason County, Illinois, died at Mason City, Illinois, in 1916. Alice, who married Joseph Fletcher, died at Sterling, Illinois, in 1920. Others born in America were: Nancy, who married Richard Campbell, and died at Huron, South Dakota, in 1914; John Benjamin, whose name heads this review; James Henry, who died at Lincoln, Illinois, in 1920; Joseph, who died in Mason County in 1851: and Mary Esther, who married Thomas Pegram and died at Lincoln, Illinois, in 1922. The mother, Ann Keen Abbott, died at Lincoln, Illinois, in 1884, at the age of sixty-five. The father, Henry Abbott, died at Lincoln, Illinois, in 1898, at the age of seventy-nine.

John Benjamin, the only surviving member of his family, was born on his father's farm in Mason County, near Chandlerville, Illinois, June 10, 1847, where he grew to manhood. On October 16, 1869, he married Mary Jane Ainsworth, daughter of Richard and Mary Ann Talbot Ainsworth, natives of Blackburn, England, who came to America in 1842 on the same vessel as did Mr. Abbott's parents.

Mary Jane Ainsworth was born on her father's farm in Mason County, Illinois, July 8, 1849, where she lived until the time of her marriage to John B. Abbott in 1869. In 1871 they moved to Allen's Grove Township, Mason County, where Mr. Abbott continued farming and bought land which he now owns.

Gradually becoming interested in handling grain, in 1876 he went into the grain business, buying the two elevators at Natrona, Illinois, owned by Edwin Nelson and John Cathcart. These he operated for a period of ten years, when he sold them and moved his family to Delavan, Illinois, in order to secure better school privileges for his children. The family remained in Delavan for nearly two years, when they decided to make Mason City, Illinois, their permanent home.

Although out of the active grain business, Mr. Abbott did not lose his interest in it, and in 1902 was instrumental in organizing the Farmers' Grain & Coal Company at Natrona, Illinois, at which time he was elected president of the organization and has held the office continuously up to the present time (1926).

In February, 1903, he was one of thirty-three men, representing seventeen Farmers' Elevators, who met in Springfield, Illinois, to effect the organization of the Illinois Farmers' Grain Dealers Association, of which he was elected treasurer at that time.

To Mr. and Mrs. Abbott were born four children: Richard Henry, born July 17, 1870; Albert Edward, born March 30, 1872: Ira Reed, born April 28, 1874, and Alice Myrtle, born December 11, 1878.

After moving to Mason City in 1889, Mr. Abbott became interested in electric lighting, and purchased the local plant, then in its infancy, and serving only a few street lights. It was poorly equipped and totally inadequate for serving the town. He instituted and installed the alternating system, making an up-to-date plant and furnishing service for the entire city.

His sons early in life developed marked talent for electrical work and decided to make it their life work. After completing their high school course and taking special work in electrical mechanics and business methods, they joined their father in business under the name of J. B. Abbott & Sons. In 1892 the company obtained control of the electric light plant at Petersburg, Illinois, then owned by B. D. Wright, and Richard went there to take up the management and installation of a new system in the plant. This plant, when first purchased, was in the same condition as the original Mason City plant, the service being for only a limited number of street lights. A few years later, when Ira joined Richard in the work at Petersburg, the firm name there was changed from J. B. Abbott & Sons to Abbott Brothers, and the two brothers made Petersburg their permanent home.

Richard married Mabel Wright, of Pekin, Illinois, April 21, 1898, and to them one son was born, Richard, Jr., a graduate of St. John's Military Academy, and now a senior at Washington and Lee University, Virginia (1926).

Ira married Nona P. Watkins, of Petersburg, Illinois, daughter of a prominent stock man and farmer of Menard County, on November 6, 1901, and has resided in Petersburg, acting as secretary to the company and assisting in the management of the business until finally, after the death of the two senior brothers, he took the entire management of the company. He has served his community in various ways through the years, notably in helping secure a grant from the government for a State Park at New Salem, Illinois, the old home of Abraham Lincoln.

Albert always remained in Mason City, having the management of the plant and offices there, and was president of his company at the time of his death, April 20, 1921. He married Sarah Etta Mehan, daughter of Judge and Mrs. Thomas N. Mehan, of Mason City, September 5, 1896, and to them one son was born, Ira Richmond, who after receiving his preparatory education in the Mason City schools and St. John's Military Academy, received his degree at the Illinois State University after taking the electrical engineering course. He is now in the offices of the Illinois Light & Power Company, as assistant manager at Decatur, Illinois.

In 1913 the corporation of the Abbott Light & Power Company was formed, composed of Richard and Ira Abbott of Petersburg and Albert Abbott of Mason City, at which time they took over the Mason City, Greenview and Petersburg plants and located the main plant at Petersburg, gradually extending their service into four counties: Sangamon, Menard, Logan and Mason, with a plant second to none in the state in equipment and efficiency.

While developing and expanding their public service plants the Abbott Brothers were rendering other service to their home towns and communities and becoming foremost citizens and business men.

Richard was a volunteer in the Spanish-American war. He was active in the formation of Company E of the Illinois National Guards at Petersburg in 1894, and was connected with National Guards the remainder of his life, rising from private to lieutenant colonel, which latter office he held at the time of his death, May 3, 1919, being a member of General Dickson's staff, where he rendered great service in the organization and mobilization of the Illinois National Guards during the World war.

He was elected secretary of the Illinois Electric Association in 1914 and served until compelled to resign on account of his war work, but still continued to hold his place on the Executive Committee. He was president of his company at the time of his death.

In 1923, when the Central Illinois Public Service Company was enlarging its territory and desired annexing the territory covered by the Abbott Light & Power Company, the Abbott Company sold their entire interests to them, Ira R. Abbott being retained as manager at Petersburg of the interests formerly held by his company, the two senior brothers having died prior to the sale.

Mr. Abbott's only daughter, Alice Myrtle, is a graduate of the Woman's College, Jacksonville, Illinois. On November 30, 1904, she was married to Rev. Francis Asbury McCarty, a prominent Methodist minister of the Illinois Conference who is now entering upon his sixth year as pastor of the First Methodist Episcopal Church, at Bloomington, Illinois. To them were born three daughters: Mary Helen, now (1926) a freshman in the Illinois Wesleyan University of Bloomington, Illinois; Edith Louise and Alice Jeanette, now in high school at Bloomington.

Beside the five grandchildren mentioned in this sketch Mr. Abbott has two great-grandchildren in the home of Ira Richmond Abbott at Decatur, Illinois. Their mother was formerly Miss Ruth Stone, of Mason City.

Mr. Abbott was made a Mason at San Jose, Illinois, in 1887. He was master of Mason City Lodge No. 403, at Mason City, Illinois, in 1901, 1902 and 1904, and belongs to Mason City Chapter, R. A. M., and Petersburg Commandery, K. T.

Reared in a Christian home, Mr. Abbott was brought up in the church and has been a lifelong member of the Methodist Episcopal Church. Since 1890 he has been president of the Board of Trustees and member of the Official Board of the Mason City Methodist Episcopal Church.

From 1914 to 1923 he held the office of township treasurer of schools at Mason City, as did he also in Allen's Grove Township from 1878 to 1887.

After the death of Mrs. Abbott, May 11, 1914, Mr. Abbott made his home with his daughter, Mrs. McCarty, until April 11, 1916, when he married Miss Lillian Mitchell, of Chicago, daughter of William H. and Harriett E. Mitchell. They have since made their home in the old family home at Mason City, Illinois. Mr. Abbott has wonderful health for his years and expects to spend the remainder of his life in the "old home town," enjoying the fellowship of friends made through the years.

BENJAMIN FRANKLIN KREIDER, member of an old and prominent family of Whiteside County, is a busines sman at Sterling and is an ex-service man, having been one of the volunteers from Whiteside County for duty in the World war.

He was born on a farm in Sterling Township March 28, 1895. His grandfather, John H. Kreider came from Pennsylvania to Illinois in 1854 and lived the rest of his life on a farm two and a half miles north of Sterling. Benjamin F. Kreider is a son of John H. and Anna (Stauffer) Kreider. His father was born in Lancaster County, Pennsylvania, in 1850, and was four years of age when the family moved to Illinois, where he grew up and devoted his active life to farming. He is one of the honored residents of Sterling. He has been a life long republican and in church faith is a Mennonite. Anna Stauffer was his second wife. By his first marriage, to Miss Ebersole, his children were: Tillie, wife of Abe Frey; Harry a farmer in Sterling Township; Abram E., a farmer in Sterling Township; Frank E., a retired farmer at Sterling; John E., a farmer in Sterling Township; and Amos E., a professor in Bluffton College, Ohio, but a resident of Dayton, Indiana.

Benjamin F. Kreider was only two years of age when his parents left the farm and moved to Sterling, where he grew up attending public schools and graduated from high school in 1916. He spent nearly two years in the service of the Hearst newspapers, particularly the Chicago Evening American, being on the road in the interests of the editorial and circulation departments. He then engaged in the office supply business at Sterling.

He was called from business to the scenes of military training, and on April, 30, 1918, was ordered to Jefferson Barracks, Missouri, later to Camp Fremont, California, where he was put with the Thirteenth Infantry but on detached service with a casualty company. Later he was transferred to the Medical Corps with the Eighth Division, and in October, 1918, was ordered with the division to Camp Mills Long Island. Soon afterwards his command embarked for overseas, but after being out three days was ordered to return and at Camp Mills the division was split up, Mr. Kreider accompanying a part of it to Camp Lee, Virginia, and later to Camp Zachary Taylor at Louisville, where he received his honorable discharge February 6, 1919.

On leaving the army Mr. Kreider returned to Sterling, and has since been connected with the well known business firm of that city, the Senneff-Kerr Company, Inc. He is secretary and general manager of the corporation. Mr. Kreider was honored in 1925 with election as commander of Sterling Post No. 296 of the American Legion. He is a Knights Templar and thirty-second degree Scottish Rite Mason, a member of the Mystic Shrine and the B. P. O. Elks. He is active in the work of the Fourth Street Methodist Episcopal Church, and as a republican is serving as precinct committeeman.

He married, June 15, 1918, Miss Neva Mildred Senneff. Her father, Mr. C. W. Senneff, is president of the Senneff-Kerr Company, Inc.

MATHEW L. WELCH, present corporation counsel for Collinsville, finished his law course and was admitted to the bar only a short time before he went into service as a soldier in the World war. Since the war he has made rapid strides towards success and prominence in his profession and as a community leader.

He was born at Sato, Illinois, February 14, 1891, son of Lewis A. and Ella (Fox) Welch. His parents were also born in Illinois. Mathew L. is the only son, and his one sister is Myrtle.

Mathew L. Welch was educated in the public schools of Collinsville, and after graduating from high school entered the law department of Illinois Wesleyan University at Bloomington, Illinois. He was graduated in 1917 and admitted to the Illinois bar the same year.

His service in the World war began on September 4, 1917, when he was inducted into a training camp, and on June 6, 1918, he was commissioned second lieutenant of Company F of the Three Hundred Thirty-third Infantry, on September 23, 1918, he was promoted to first lieutenant, and served until honorably discharged on December 29, 1918. He accepted a commission as first lieutenant in the Reserve Corps in February, 1919.

Soon after beginning the practice of law Mr. Welch was appointed corporation counsel for Collinsville, on May 1, 1919, and by reappointment is now serving his third term. He was appointed assistant state's attorney on December 1, 1924, which position he now holds. He has a good law practice, and takes a commendable part in local affairs. He is a director of the Civic Association, is president of the Lions Club, and is a republican in politics. He is a Knight Templar Mason. Mr. Welch married in 1922 Miss Ruth Taylor, of Fairbury, Illinois, daughter of H. P. Taylor.

CHARLES E. TURNER, state's attorney of Brown County, was born at Mt. Sterling, represents a family long, well and favorably known in banking and other affairs in the county, and was one of this county's representatives in the American Expeditionary Forces, serving with the famous Rainbow Division.

He was born December 1, 1894, in the same house where he still resides. His grandfather, George Turner, was of New England ancestry, a native of Massachusetts, and came West from Brooklyn, New York, bringing his family by river to Illinois, being a pioneer of Brown County. He was a merchant and later for many years was identified with the First National Bank of Mt. Sterling. He died in 1903, when about eighty years of age. His chief interest outside his business and home was the Presbyterian Church. George Turner married Josephine Barrows, who survived him nearly twenty years. They had three children: Arthur; Charles H.; and Minnie, wife of Dr. H. B. Todd, of Houston, Texas.

Charles H. Turner, father of the state's attorney, was born in Brooklyn, New York, in 1863. He grew up and received his early education at Mt. Sterling, and from early manhood was identified with the First National Bank, being its cashier when he died. He was also president of the local school board, was trustee and treasurer of the Presbyterian Church. He married at Brooklyn, New York, Miss Carrie E. Smith, a native of Dwight, Illinois, who had been a teacher before her marriage. Her father, James Smith, came from New York State and was a farmer at Dwight. The children of Charles H. Turner and wife were: Robert R., cashier of the First National Bank of Mt. Sterling; Mary, wife of E. G. Hersman, of Ann Arbor, Michigan; and Charles E.

Charles E. Turner after finishing his course at the high school at Mt. Sterling entered the University of Illinois, graduating with the A. B. degree. However, he was granted his degree and formal graduation while already in training camp for service in the World war. He joined the colors June 2, 1917, attended the Officers Training School at Sheridan, Illinois, and was commissioned a second lieutenant of infantry. Mr. Turner went overseas as a casual in January, 1918, sailing from Hoboken on the U. S. S. Huron and landing at Brest. After one month in the corps training school he was assigned to the One Hundred and Sixty-sixth Infantry of the Rainbow Division. This was the Ohio unit of the Forty-second or Rainbow Division. At different times he served with Companies H and M with Headquarters Company, was with the regiment in the Lorraine Sector, and in July, 1918, participated in the Champaign-Marne defensive, was on the front at Chateau Thierry, and in the great Argonne campaign. He was at the front when the armistice was signed in November, 1918, and subsequently accompanied the Army of Occupation into Germany, his regiment being stationed at Rolandseck on the Rhine River. In May, 1919, he returned to the United States, sailing from Brest on the ship Leviathan. He was honorably discharged from Camp Grant, Rockford, August 27, 1919. Since the war he has been service officer of the local post of the American Legion and is a county judge advocate of the State Legion.

Mr. Turner soon after his discharge entered the University of Michigan Law School and graduated in 1922. He has since built up a successful practice at Mt. Sterling. In November, 1924, he was elected state's attorney of Brown County as a candidate of the republican party, and the only man on that ticket successful in the election. In fact he has the remarkable distinction of being the first republican to hold a county office in Brown County over a period of forty-two years. Mr. Turner was elected by a majority of 360 votes in a county normally democratic by 700. Mr. Turner is unmarried. He is a member of the Phi Delta Phi college fraternity, the Order of the Coif and is a trustee of the Presbyterian Church at Mt. Sterling.

WALTER GOODELL, composer and musical publisher, has become one of the best known and most successful men in his field in the City of Chicago. He is a native of Illinois, and both he and his talented wife were born and reared in the Illinois Valley in LaSalle County.

Walter Goodell was born at Marseilles, in LaSalle County, December 24, 1884, son of Dr. John Hubbard and Clara J. (Simmons) Goodell. Doctor Goodell was born at Syracuse, New York, September 9, 1844, son of Silas Goodell and of remote Huguenot French ancestry. John Hubbard Goodell at the age of seventeen helped drill recruits for the Civil war. In 1864 the Goodell family came to Illinois and first located at Harding. John Hubbard Goodell studied medicine in Rush Medical College in Chicago and was graduated in 1868. He possessed great natural talent in music, and while a student in Chicago sang in the choir of the Holy Name Church. He also had a pronounced mechanical genius, and contrived and invented a number of mechanical devices that ranked him as a first rate mechanical engineer. Among other things he was inventor of the time clock. Doctor Goodell in 1872 engaged in the drug business in connection with the general practice of medicine at Leland, Illinois, and subsequently located at Marseilles. He married in 1874 Clara J. Simmons, of Aurora, niece if Elias Terry, one of the founders of that town. The Simmons and Terry families were pioneer settlers in the Illinois River Valley. Doctor Goodell was active in Masonic organizations, being a Knight Templar Mason.

Mrs. Walter Goodell has a similar interesting ancestry. Her maiden name was Ethel Claire Unland. Her father was Dr. W. G. Unland, of Beardstown, Illinois, whose parents came from Germany and located at Bluff Springs in Cass County, Illinois. Dr. W. G. Unland went abroad for the study of medicine in Europe, also attended the Hahnemann Medical College at Chicago, and had a long and successful career as a physician. He is now living retired. As a boy he heard one of the Lincoln-Douglas debates, and has accumulated a rich fund of memories and recollections of this great Illinois president. Doctor Unland married Emily Minton, who was of Revolutionary ancestry on both sides, and through her mother a descendant of the historic Bleecker family of New York City, for whom Bleecker Street was named. Mrs. Goodell is an accomplished pianist and teacher of voice.

Mr. Goodell has lived in Chicago since 1910. He was self taught in music from the age of five, was graduaed from the Marseilles High School in 1901, and studied theory under Robert H. Just, a pupil of Kistler, studied violin under John H. Stokes and Morey Roberts of Ottawa, Illinois, and S. E. Jacobsohn and Carl Becker of Chicago. Mr. Goodell was first violin with concert and dance orchestras from 1902 to 1910. He was teacher of theory in the Metropolitan Conservatory of Music during 1914-15, and taught theory in the Kankakee Conservatory in 1915. From 1922 to 1926 he was head of the orchestration department of the Balaban-Katz motion picture organization.

Mr. Goodell now conducts a successful music arranging business, and besides arranging music for orchestras and other musical organizations does a large amount of composition. He has published a number of songs of his own composition, and was composer of "Interludium" for the Daily News Contest of Chicago, and winner of three other consecutive prizes for musical composition, besides being winner of the Grand Prize given by the Chicago Daily News in 1925. Mr. Goodell's studio is at 431 South Wabash Avenue, Chicago. His home is at Berwyn. Mr. and Mrs. Goodell have a talented daughter, Claire Louise, aged ten.

WILLIAM J. LAWSON, D. V. S. There is probably no more skilled veterinary surgeon in Menard County that Dr. William J. Lawson of Petersburg, who has been identified with this locality for a third of a century, and who holds the full confidence of his fellow citizens, both professionally and as a private individual. He was born at Cherrywood, Ontario, Canada, on January 26, 1869, a son of James and Isabel (Gilchrist) Lawson, both of whom were born in Scotland, and were children when they were brought to Canada. There they were reared and married, and there their useful lives were spent, the father dying there early in the present century, and the mother

died March 5, 1911, at the age of seventy-nine years. Of the eight children born to them the following survive: David, who is a farmer of Saskatchewan, Canada; Mary, who is the wife of Cuthbert Holmes, of Dunbarton, Ontario, Canada; Isabel, who is a resident of Cherrywood, Ontario, Canada; Alexander, who is a farmer of Cherrywood; Doctor Lawson, whose name heads this review; and Christine, who is the wife of Alfred Stover, of Markham, Ontario, Canada.

Doctor Lawson grew up amid the environment of the parental home, and attended the common schools. His professional training was taken in the Ontario Veterinary College, from which he was graduated in 1892, second of his class in anatomy, for which scholarship he received an award.

Realizing the opportunities of the adjoining republic, Doctor Lawson came to the United States following his graduation and established himself in practice at Petersburg, where he has since remained, and where he now has the distinction of being the dean of his profession. Not long after he came to Petersburg he encountered an epidemic of glanders, a malady that is very dangerous, as it can be communicated by animals to human beings. The neighborhood horses had long been affiliated with it, but Doctor Lawson was the one who properly diagnosed the disease and eradicated it completely. His remarkable success in thus ridding this region of what had been for so long a very serious menace to the health of the entire community won him instant favor, and ever since he has enjoyed a very large practice, which far exceeds local bounds. He is a member of the Illinois Veterinary Association.

Soon after coming to Petersburg Doctor Lawson took out his papers of citizenship, and has always taken a real and constructive interests in local affairs. He was made a Mason in 1908 at Petersburg, and advanced through the different bodies to the Temple, and he is a past high priest of the Chapter. In church work he is a Presbyterian, is one of the deacons of the Petersburg Church, and was one of its trustees. At present he is a member of the City Council, and in November, 1925, was elected a county commissioner, his colleagues on the board being John Crawford and Ira Smith. His first presidential ballot was cast for William McKinley in 1896, and he has since continued a republican.

In November, 1893, Doctor Lawson married Allie M. Conover, a daughter of Lawrence and Helen M. (Thompson) Conover and who was born in Menard County, where her father settled when he came to Illinois from New Jersey. She is one of eight children born to her parents all of whom survive: William A., who is a resident of Los Angeles, California; Sarah, who married William H. Boeker, of Petersburg; Mrs. Lawson, who is the third child; James L., who resides in Texas; Virgie, who is the wife of George Neikirk, of Forest City, Illinois; Nellie, who is the wife of Walter McFadden, of Oakford, Illinois; Dr. F. O. Conover, who is engaged in practice with Doctor Lawson; and Mrs. Lola Huffington, of Oklahoma City, Oklahoma. Doctor and Mrs. Lawson have two children: Dr. Lawrence J., who is a graduate of Rush Medical College, Chicago, Illinois, is engaged in professional work as a specialist in diseases of the eye, ear, nose and throat in Evanston, Illinois. He was in the Medical Corps of the service during the World war, married Ruth Watson, and they have a son, Lawrence J., Junior. Helen, who is a graduate of the Petersburg High School, is a student in Northwestern University, Evanston, Illinois.

PHILIP G. KEMP, who was in the air service of the United States army in the World war period and who now holds the rank of major in the Officers Reserve Corps of the United States army, is chairman of the Chicago Aero Commission, and in the great western metropolis he is successfully established in business as a dealer in building materials, with offices at 133 West Washington Street.

Major Kemp is able to claim the old Blue Grass State as the place of his nativity, he having been born at Middlesboro, Kentucky, but having been reared at Anniston, Alabama, where the family home was established when he was a boy and where his educational advantages included a college course. As a youth Mr. Kemp initiated his business career by taking a position with the Louisville Cement Company, in the metropolis of his native state, and with this corporation he has continued to be actively or indirectly associated during the intervening years. He came from Louisville to Chicago early in 1917, for the special purpose of entering the nation's air service in the World war, and since the termination of his war service he has been successfully engaged in the general building material business in this city, where among the building trades and industries of Chicago he has built up a reputation for efficient service and fair and honorable methods and policies—a reputation that constitutes his most valuable business asset.

After his enlistment in Chicago Major Kemp entred the first air-service ground school established at the University of Illinois, where he gained his initial experience in practical aeronautics. Thence he was eventually sent to Chanute Field, Rantoul, Illinois, where he received his flying training. From that place he was later ordered to Rich Field, Waco, Texas, where he was on constant and active duty for many months while the war was in progress. At these stations he organized and trained fully seventeen different squadrons for the air service, in which department of the United States army he was raised to the rank of major, that which he still holds in the Officers' Reserve Corps, in which he is in command of the Ninth Wing (Attack) Air Service of the United States army.

Recognition of the technical and administrative ability of Major Kemp was given when Mayor Dever appointed him chairman of the newly formed Chicago Aero Commission, his appointment having been approved by the city council. He was thus honored largely by reason of his activities in being the first to suggest and bring together of a group of representative Chicago business and professional men, city officials, and others, for the purpose of forming a permanent air commission in connection with the municipal government.

December 23, 1924, there was introduced in the Chicago city council a resolution that had been prepared by Major Kemp and that provided for the creation of a municipal aero commission, the members of which were to be appointed by the mayor and approved by the city council, with their service to be rendered without compensation. The special work of initial order that has come to this commission has been to formulate and carry forward plans for concerted action on the part of the city and other political divisions of Cook County for the establishing and maintaining of municipal landing fields that shall make Chicago a leading center in connection with air operations, the while the commission is to render also every possible influence and aid in advancing the general air craft industry and service. Major Kemp is an enthusiast in the service thus assigned to him and his associates, and under his vigorous leadership Chicago is assured of continued advancement as the stage of air service activities.

SILAS A. KOCH is a representative of one of the old established and highly esteemed families of Tazewell County, where he was born and reared on the old homestead farm of his father near the Village of Tremont, the date of his nativity having been January 29, 1888, and his youthful education having been acquired in the district school near the family home place. Mr. Koch is a son of the late David Koch, to whom a memoir, with adequate record of the family history, is dedicated on other pages of this work, so that further details are not here demanded.

Mr. Koch continued to be associated with the productive activities of the parental farmstead until after he had attained to his legal majority, and in his independent activities in farm enterprise he has become the owner of a portion of the tract of 220 acres that constitutes the stage of his progressive work as an agriculturist and dairyman. He has resided in his present home in Dillon Township, near Tremont, since the year of his marriage, 1913, and with a fine dairy herd of eighteen head he makes the dairy department of his business one of important and profitable order during the entire course of each successive year.

Popular appreciation of the ability and civic progressiveness of Mr. Koch has been shown in his election to the office of supervisor of Dillon Township and by his retention of this position for what is now (1925) his fourth consecutive term. He has proved a vital and loyal member of the County Board of Supervisors, and in his service he has given careful and effective consideration to the building and operating of the county sanitarium and the tuberculosis sanitarium, besides giving his influence to the movements marking the splendid improvement of the roads of the county. His first election to this office occurred in 1919, and he was elected as candidate of the republican party in the county, his being inflexible allegiance to the cause of this party. In the World war period Mr. Koch aided in the local drives in support of the government war bonds, Red Cross work and other patriotic activities, and made his individual contributions to the cause measure up to the consistent limit of his resources available for this purpose. In registering for military service he was given assignment to class four, and thus was not called into active service.

September 3, 1913, recorded the marriage of Mr. Koch and Miss Nora L. Luft, who likewise was born and reared in the vicinty of Dillon, she being a daughter of Nick Luft, Jr., and likewise a representative of the old and honored Luft family, record of which is given on other pages of this work, in the memoir dedicated to Nicholas Luft, Jr. Mr. and Mrs. Koch have four children: H. Elmore, Clifford Arthur, Lester Donald, and Dorothy Lucile.

HON. GEORGE P. WAGNER. One of the best known citizens of Belleville, universally respected and very highly esteemed, is Hon. George P. Wagner, city police judge, who both officially and personally is exceptionally well qualified for this responsible position. Judge Wagner is a self-made man, and it has been said of this good man and kind, but just, judge that this circumstance has given him a deeper understanding of humanity than might otherwise been his.

Judge Wagner was born August 5, 1865, on a farm six miles distant from Millstadt, St. Clair County, Illinois, son of Philip and Magdeline (Methier) Wagner, and grandson of Philip and Mary Wagner and of Peter Methier. His grandparents and his father were all born in Germany, but his mother was born in the United States and survived until February 5, 1909. The father of Judge Wagner came to America with his parents when six years old and spent his life as a small farmer in St. Clair County, Illinois, near the Monroe County line. He died in Belleville June 3, 1906. Both he and wife were members of the Evangelical Church. Of their family of children George P. was second in order of birth, the others being: John, who married Louise Reispeck; Annie, who married John Cramer; Mary, who married John Lieb; Henry, who married Julia Penepecker; Carl, who married Mary Reispeck; Louis, who married Louisa Hollapach; Katie, who married Edward Hardt; Louisa, who married Fritz Hardt; Peter, deceased, who married Louisa Penepacker; and one who died in infancy, and William Edward, who married Annie Weber of Muscatah, and their children are Irma Virginia, Viola, Pearl and Arthur.

George P. Wagner attended the district schools near his home with some regularity, in the meanwhile helping his father as he was able until he was thirteen years old, when he was hired out by the month to other farmers and worked more or less along this line until he was twenty-one years of age. At that time he came to Belleville and found his first employment in the rolling mills, going then to work for an electric and gas fitting company. In a little less than a year he tried hauling and teaming, but later secured work in a brickyard for the summer months and in the coal mines in the winters.

On January 25, 1904, Mr. Wagner, as a trustworthy custodian, was given charge of the Liederkranz Society Hall at Belleville, where

he continued until 1913, when he became overseers of the Eagles' Home at Belleville, and custodian of the order's property here. In 1915 his responsibilities were increased by his appointment as overseer, for four years, of the Belleville City Poor, during this period, with characteristic energy and industry, finding time to add to his income through work in several of the city's industrial plants. He thus became well and favorably known to all classes, and his appointment to the office of police magistrate on April 4, 1920, met with universal approval, and his subsequent wise administration of his office has shown that no mistake was made.

Judge Wagner married, September 11, 1888, in St. Paul's Evangelical Church at Belleville, Miss Lena Ackerman, daughter of the venerable Jacob Ackermann, a veteran of the Civil war and a member of the Grand Army of the Republic. In early manhood he was an engineer in the Illinois coal mines, and served as a Civil war soldier in the Thirty-sixth Illinois Volunteer Infantry. The following children were born to Judge and Mrs. Wagner: Frank, who married Emma Benger, and they have two children, Olive and Jean; Edward, who married Theresa Carnsmann, and they have one child, Berenice; Julia, who married William Cellmann, and they have one son, Floyd; Louisa, who is the wife of George Wele, and they have three children, Harold, Russell and Katherine; and Florence, who is the wife of Ray Sternsberry.

Judge Wagner united with St. Paul's Evangelical Church in 1905, has been a trustee for many years and is a member of St. Paul's Men's Aid Society. He is prominent in the fraternal Order of Eagles, has filled all the chairs in the local lodge and is now treasurer of the same. He is identified also with other representative organizations, being a charter member of the Order of Moose at Belleville; has been a member of the Germania Bund Society since 1907, of which he is secretary and a trustee; and for twelve years has been a member of the Kronthal Leidertafel Society, one of the oldest established musical organizations of the city, a taste for good music being a German inheritance.

HENRY HAROLD HEWITT has given more than a quarter of a century to his service at the Alton National Bank, of which for the past five years he has been cashier. He is a veteran of the Spanish-American war, and his period of army duty was the only lengthy absence from his work in the bank.

Mr. Hewitt was born at Alton, January 9, 1877, son of George R. and Alice (Billings) Hewitt, his father a native of St. Louis and his mother of Alton. George R. Hewitt located in Alton about 1865, and spent many years in business there. He and his wife had four children.

The oldest of these children, Henry Harold Hewitt, attended the public schools in Alton, and finished his education in the Western Military Academy there. His first employment was as bookkeeper and cashier for the Hapgood Plow Company, but in 1897, at the age of twenty, he became a messenger boy with the Alton National Bank, one of the oldest national banks in Madison County. His period of service has included responsibilities as bookkeeper, teller, assistant cashier, and since 1919 he has been cashier.

In 1902 Mr. Hewitt married Miss Alice Drury, of Alton, where she was born and educated. They have two children, Emily Louise and George Billings. Mr. Hewitt is a member of the Congregational Church, and was chairman of the Alton Chapter of the Red Cross. He was on duty in the Spanish-American war about eight months, being an ensign in the navy and was on the blockading fleet in Cuban waters.

CLIFFORD V. GREGORY. During the last fifteen years one of the best known figures in the field of agricultural journalism has been Clifford V. Gregory, editor of the Prairie Farmer, published at Chicago. The recipient of specialized training, he joined this publication practically upon leaving college halls, and in his editorship has been a constantly increasing influence for the benefit of agriculturists in general, their institutions and organizations.

Mr. Gregory was born on a farm near Mason City, Iowa, where he was reared, and was educated in the public schools and in Iowa State College, the famous agricultural college at Ames, Iowa, from which he was graduated as a member of the class of 1910. On June 1, 1911, he became editor of the Prairie Farmer, a position which he has since held. The Prairie Farmer had its beginning in 1841, although history reports that its ancestry goes back as far as 1839. At that time the Union Agriculturist was established as the official organ of the Union Agricultural Society, and in the following year the Western Prairie Farmer was established at Springfield, Illinois. The two were combined in 1841 under the name of the Union Agriculturist and Western Prairie Farmer under the editorship of John S. Wright, the secretary of the Union Agricultural Society. In 1842 the ownership of the paper passed from the Society, and in January, 1843, the first number under the present name of Prairie Farmer was published with John S. Wright as publisher. In January, 1857, the publication was changed from monthly to weekly. The paper continued under various ownerships until 1882, when it was purchased by Rand-McNally & Company, and in 1908 is was purchased by Burridge D. Butler and is still owned by him and his associates. As noted, Mr. Gregory became editor June 1, 1911, and still occupies this position.

In January, 1916, the Illinois Agricultural Association was organized as a federation of the county farm bureaus of the state. The editor of the Prairie Farmer was elected a member of the executive committee the following year, and was instrumental, at the annual meeting in January, 1919, in securing a reorganization on the basis of individual membership at an annual fee of $5 each, together with plans for a state-wide membership drive. This resulted in two years in a membership of 110,000. At present the organization has a membership of 70,000 and a reserve fund of a quarter of a million dollars. It is generally credited with being the strongest and best financed farm organization in the world. The success of the Illinois Agricultural Association in building up a large, state-wide membership in 1919 and 1920 was generally credited to the strong backing given by the Prairie Farmer. The publication has also done a great work in exposing fraudulent investment schemes and the suppression of blue sky stock salesmen. From its founding it has been constantly a friend of schools and better education.

Mr. Gregory is a member of the Board of Agricultural Advisors of Illinois, which board forms a part of the State Department of Agriculture. His home is located at Wheaton, and he is a member of the Old Colony Club. Mr. Gregory married Miss Edna Springer, of Clear Lake, Iowa, and they have four children: Gwendolyn, Merrill, Howard and Barbara.

LEWIS RICKARD. Among the sterling pioneers of Kendall County who have passed into the Great Unknown, and whose memory formed an indissoluble link between the pioneer past and the present days of opulent prosperity and advanced civilization was Lewis Rickard, who for sixty-eight years was an honored resident of this county. He was for many years identified with agricultural interests in this county, and contributed his quota to the development of the region that then was little more than an untraveled wilderness. He was a native of the Empire State, born at Stone Arabia, Montgomery County, New York, January 10, 1820. The Rickard family were early settlers of Montgomery County, New York, and for a number of generations the name was prominently identified with the best interests of that county. Lewis Rickard was a son of Frederick and Polly (Snell) Rickard, both natives of Montgomery County, New York, born August 5, 1781, and September 6, 1793, respectively. The paternal grandparents of Lewis Rickard were Lodowick and Catherine (Getman) Rickard, who were also natives of Montgomery County, born September 12, 1757, and September 27, 1761, respectively. They were the parents of nine children: Annyeve, John, Catherine, Frederick, George, Lewis, Mary, Delia and Numey.

Frederick Ricard, the father of Lewis Rickard, was a farmer all of his life, and developed into one of the public-spirited and highly respected citizens of his county. A consistent Christian, he was for many years a member and deacon of the Congregational Church. He was twice married, his first wife, who was Polly Snell, died July 2, 1825, and he subsequently married Nancy Shull, who was born February 27, 1796, and died May 29, 1882. He preceded her to the grave several years, dying December 19, 1868. By his first marriage he had the following children: Mary, Josiah, Catherine, Alexander, Caroline, Alma, Almira and Lewis. The children of his second wife were: Emeline and Irene.

Lewis Rickard received his educational training in his native county, and was brought up to an agricultural life. As was but natural in consequence he became a farmer, and was engaged in that line of work all his life. On October 19, 1840, he married, in Montgomery County, New York, Miss Caty Loucks, a native of that same county, born October 9, 1821, a daughter of Peter G. and Nancy (Gray) Loucks. They came of pioneer stock of Montgomery County, and were there born October 10, 1792, and June 20, 1794, respectively. Peter G. Loucks was a son of George and Elizabeth (Bellenger) Loucks, who were parents of twelve children: Lucinda, Mary, Nancy, Charles, Walter, Elizabeth, Caty, Alida, Nathan, George, Orlando and Andrew.

In 1842 Lewis Rickard determined to cast his fortune with the growing West, and migrated with his wife and family to Illinois, first locating at Oswego, Kendall County, but after a short time purchased a farm in Section 22, Bristol Township, where he afterwards made his home for many years. That part of Kendall County was then but sparsely settled, houses being far apart. He cheerfully met and conquered the toil and privations incident to the life of an early settler, and he and his noble wife are classed among the efficient first settlers of this community. When they first came to Illinois they had only about $150 in cash and a very few household goods. He was obliged to haul all his produce by wagon to Chicago, a trip then requiring three days. In his absence his wife attended to all the work at home, taking care of the stock and also going into the fields to help bind the grain by hand, a task that would cause many men of the present day to flinch. With such a wife it was, of course, impossible to fail, and by working hard together they succeeded beyond their combined ambitions, and lived long and healthy lives. This couple reached their sixty-ninth wedding aninversary on October 19, 1909.

Mr. Rickard was a plain-speaking and straight-forward man, and these qualities earned him the reputation of being an honest man and good citizen, and he was respected by all who knew him. He was, too, a well-read man, and after he became infirm and was obliged to refrain from hard work he spent the greater part of his time reading daily papers and magazines. In this way he kept in touch with the outside world and was able to converse intelligently on all current topics. A few years prior to his death his eyesight began to fail, and in a short time he was unable to read. This loss made a great change in him. Up to that time he had been jolly and good-natured, always ready to visit relatives and friends and enjoyed company. After his affliction it was only on rare occasions that he could be induced to leave home, even to call upon near relatives. However, at home he remained the same good-natured, fun-loving man for some time. Then he became practically helpless and gradually wore out because of his years. His wide circle of relatives and friends prefer to remember him as the jolly, ambitious man of his former days. His many excellent qualities live in the memory of all who knew him. His wife loved her home and family and always did all in her power to make things pleasant in the home. She, too, was very ambitious, even in her declining years, and she took the best of care of her aged husband in his affliction, when he was bowed down by his infirmities, and it was only with difficulty that she could be induced to take a rest. The night of January 3, 1910, she retired after a busy day, feeling better than for some time. The next morning she was unable to get out of bed, and it was there she remained for a week, gradually getting weaker until death called her January 11, 1910. Her husband did not long survive after her death, dying March 1, 1910. To this worthy couple four children were born: Arnold, who died at the age of twenty-four years of a disease contracted while in the Union army as a member of the One Hundred and Twenty-seventh Illinois Volunteer Infantry; Lucinda, deceased, who was the wife of Daniel Welsh, of Aurora, Illinois; Lewis L., deceased, and Elmer G., both of whom are farmers of Bristol Township, sketches of whom follow this in this work. In the death of Lewis Rickard and his wife Kendall County lost two of its most worthy people. As a citizen, neighbor and friend Lewis Rickard lived up to the highest ideals, and he was supported and sustained in all that he did by the courage and love of his devoted wife.

ELMER G. RICKARD. Some of the most substantial farmers of Kendall County are those who have spent their entire lives within its boundaries and whose interests are centered here. They have been born and bred on Kendall County soil, and know how to make it produce large harvest in response to their intelligent handling of their industries. One of the men who is distinctively representative of this important class is Elmer G. Rickard. He was born in the home he now occupies in Bristol Township, December 8, 1861, a son of Lewis and Caty (Loucks) Rickard.

Elmer G. Rickard was reared a farmer, and was educated in the district schools and at Oswego. After his marriage he located on the family homestead, and now owns 187 acres of finely improved land. His property is a very valuable one, and his premises show that he is modern in his methods.

On October 10, 1883, Mr. Rickard married, in Montgomery County, New York, Jennie Saltsman, born in that county, November 7, 1865, daughter of Harrison and Matilda K. (Schults) Saltsman, born in the Empire State and farming people. The mother died in Montgomery County, March 9, 1874. The father subsequently married Mary Walrath and is also deceased.

To Harrison Saltsman and wife, Matilda Katherine Saltsman, were born five children: Minnie, born January 28, 1864, wife of Webster Saltsman, now residing at Fort Plain, New York; Jennie, wife of E. G. Rickard; William, born in September, 1868, married Ada Morey, and now residing at Fort Plain, New York; Viola, born in October, 1872, wife of Daniel Nellis and residing at Schenectady, New York; Matilda Katherine, born in March, 1874, wife of William Kelsey and residing at Fort Plain, New York. To the marriage of Harrison Saltsman and Mary Walrath there were born the following children: Florence, wife of Manley Shults, now residing at Fort Plain, New York; Lula, wife of Peter Merkle, and resides in New York City; Nannie, wife of Arthur Shults, and resides at Fort Plain, New York; Blaine, who married Emma Nellis, and resides at St. Johnsville, New York; and Everett, unmarried, and resides at Fort Plain, New York.

Harrison Saltsman was born March 28, 1843, and is a son of John G. Saltsman. His brothers and sisters were: Katherine, born April 10, 1832, wife of Richard Sints; Julian, born December 12, 1833, wife of Frank Munson; Jacob L., born February 11, 1836, married Julia Grey; Harriet, born May 21, 1839, wife of Henry Quackenbush; Reuben, born May 11, 1841, married Violetta Gray; Florence, born September 20, 1852, wife of Fred Von Woert. John G. Saltsman, the father of Harrison, was born September 7, 1805, and died March 1, 1889. In 1830 he married Mary Snell, a daughter of Jacob I. Snell, and she was born July 28, 1810, died January 21, 1887. John G. Saltsman was a son of George Saltsman, who was born January 25, 1783, and married Katherine Coppernoll in the year 1800. George Saltsman was a son of Henry Saltsman, who was born in 1750, and in 1779 married Fannie Cook, who was born November 1, 1763. Matilda Katherine Shults, first wife of Harrison Saltsman and mother of Mrs. Jennie Rickard, was born January 22, 1845, married on February 4, 1863, and died March 9, 1874. She was a daughter of William Henry Shults and was one of four children: Elizabeth, wife of Jacob Saltsman; Priscilla, wife of Ezra Dillenback; and Aletta, wife of Alvin Snell. William Henry Shults died August 18, 1887. He married Mary Margaret Beck October 20, 1830. He was a son of William Shults, who was born September 20, 1788, and died August 7, 1846. The wife of William Shults was Mary Ann Rickard, who was born August 12, 1795, and died June 12, 1850. William Shults was a son of Henry Shults, who was born in April, 1750. Henry was one of three brothers who fought in the Revolutionary war and was the only one of the three who survived the war.

Mary Margaret Beck was a daughter of Benjamin Beck, who was born September 12, 1802, and died December 26, 1886. He married Elizabeth Reese, who was born March 10, 1803 and died April 26, 1885. Benjamin Beck was a son of John Anthony Beck, who was born March 26, 1761, and died April 8, 1847. His wife was Mary Nellis, who was born in August, 1763, and died July 18, 1848. All the foregoing ancestors were born and lived in and about Montgomery County, New York.

Mr. and Mrs. Rickard have three children: Harry L., born February 4, 1888, a lawyer with office No. 1230 Tribune Building, Chicago; Clara M., born June 25, 1891; and Bessie E., born April 14, 1893. Mr. Rickard is a member of the Modern Woodmen of America, also Raven Lodge No. 303, A. F. and A. M., at Oswego. His wife is a member of the Oswego Nineteenth Century Club. They are numbered among the leading people of their locality, and have made creditable records for themselves. Mr. Rickard is a prominent democrat, but has never desired office.

HARRY LEWIS RICKARD, Chicago attorney, with offices at 7 South Dearborn Street, is a native of Kendall County, Illinois, and a member of one of the oldest prominent families in that section of the state.

He was born at Bristol, in Kendall County, February 4, 1888, son of Elmar G. and Jennie (Saltsman) Rickard. His mother was a native of Fort Plain, New York. His father was born at Bristol, in Kendall County, and was a capable and highly respected citizen of that community during most of the years of his life. Harry Lewis Rickard is the oldest of three children. His two sisters are: Clara, wife of Nelson Quinsey, and Bessie, wife of John L. Reddock, Jr.

Harry Lewis Rickard grew up in his native locality, attended public schools, and in 1906 graduated from the high school at Yorkville, Illinois. From high school he entered the University of Illinois College of Law, and was admitted to the bar in October of the same year. Since that date he has been engaged in a growing general law practice in Chicago. He served as government appeal agent for the District of Northern Illinois, at Englewood. He is a member of the Chicago Bar Association, the Illinois State Bar Association, the City Club, and is affiliated with Normal Park Lodge No. 797, A. F. and A. M., and Normal Park Chapter No. 210, R. A. M.

Mr. Rickard married, May 5, 1915, Miss Mabelle B. Northrup. They have two children, Jane Ardis and Harriet Louise.

LEWIS L. RICKARD. A trip through Kendall County will disclose some of the finest farms in this part of the state, for the agriculturists of this section know how to bring forth the best results from their fertile land, and are not backward in buying and using the latest improved appliances in their work. One of these eminently progressive citizens was Lewis L. Rickard, of Bristol Township, born in this township February 1, 1853, and died in March, 1925, a son of Lewis and Caty (Loucks) Rickard, both natives of New York, a complete sketch of whom appears elsewhere in this work.

Lewis L. Rickard grew up on a farm and was always an agriculturist. He received a good common school education, and in 1878 settled on the Rickard homestead, where he lived four years, then moved to his farm on the Fox River, about two and one-quarter miles west of Oswego. On December 24, 1878, Mr. Rickard married, in Aurora, Illinois, Anna M. White, born in Davenport, Iowa, September 9, 1855, daughter of William L. and Maria (Harwood) White. Mr. White was born in Milford, New Jersey, June 14, 1830, and his wife, in London, England, January 16, 1836. In 1849 Mr. White came to Aurora. As a mason contractor he found plenty of work, and constructed many of the important buildings in Aurora. Here he married, November 30, 1854, Maria Harwood, who came with her parents to Aurora in girlhood. In the spring of 1855 Mr. White moved to Davenport, Iowa, where he spent a few months, then returned to Aurora, and there he and his wife passed the remainder of their lives, the latter dying October 7, 1888, and he surviving until December 6, 1903. They were the parents of eight children: Anna M., wife of Lewis L. Rickard; Clara E., wife of Charles G. Pearce, cashier of the Joliet National Bank; George W., of Beardstown, Illinois; William H., deceased; Charles S., deceased; Lewis R., of Aurora; Herbert S., president of the Bradford Steel Mills of Bradford, Pennsylvania; and Ernest B., of Milwaukee. Mr. and Mrs. Rickard have one daughter, Edith M., born March 3, 1880, wife of Charles T. Cherry, Jr., of Oswego. They have one child, Evelyn M., born September 30, 1904. Mr. Rickard was a member of the Modern Woodmen of America, and his wife belongs to the Woman's Club of Oswego. Mr. Rickard was well and widely known, and enjoyed universal confidence, esteem and appreciation, as does his wife. Mr. Rickard was a republican, and held some of the minor offices in his county.

JOHN SCRIPPS LITTLE is president of the Bank of Rushville. He is the third to occupy that position. His father was the first president, and from the founding of the bank more than eighty years ago the Little family has been conspicuous in its management.

The Bank of Rushville has the enviable distinction of being the oldest bank in Illinois with a consecutive record of service. It antedated the national banking system by twenty years. It was organized at a time when there was general distrust of banking institutions of all kinds, even state banks, but the Bank of Rushville, because of the integrity of the men associated with it, has stood the test of time, of war and panics, and today has the largest deposits and largest assets in its history. It was founded in 1844, and the next oldest Illinois bank of consecutive record was established in 1851, this being the Springfield Marine Bank.

The Little family was established in Schuyler County, Illinois, in 1835. George Little, the pioneer, was born in Columbia, Pennsylvania, in 1808, son of James Little, a Pennsylvania merchant. James Little was a Scotch-Irishman and came to the United States, living in Pennsylvania for a number of years, and eventually came to Illinois and is buried at Rushville. George Little had a common school education, had experience in merchandising in Pennsylvania, and came to Illinois alone on horseback. He went back to bring on his parents, and they traveled down the Ohio River and up the Mississippi and Illinois to Schuyler County, probably leaving the steamboat at Frederick, though possibly it was at Erie. They at once located at Rushville, where George Little engaged in merchandising. In 1840 he became associated with William H. Ray in the firm of Little & Ray. This firm was contined until 1880, and afterwards its successors retained the old name of George Little until after his death in 1896 and until 1925. The business is now conducted at the old stand by J. L. and G. H. Scripps, his grandsons.

George Little was also a grain shipper and a packer, having a warehouse at Frederick and sending many boatloads of goods down the Illinois River to market, chiefly to New Orleans. In 1844 the exchange and deposit business of the firm became so great and required so much attention that they segregated it, and thus was first organized the present Bank of Rushville. George Little was president of this bank for over half a century,

W. H. C. Smith M.D.

and at his death was succeeded by S. B. Montgomery, now chairman of the board. When Mr. Montgomery retired from the presidency he was succeeded by John Scripps Little, son of George Little.

George Little was a prominent character in Western Illinois, though not a public man in the sense of being a speaker or politician. He was personally acquainted with all the great figures in the state in his day, including Abraham Lincoln. Grant and Logan were entertained at the Little home, and many of the Illinois governors came there frequently. John Scripps Little for many years has been a collector of Lincoln mementoes, including letters, manuscripts and autographs, and has an amount of data of that kind that could not be duplicated elsewhere and is one of the valuable private collections of Lincoln material. George Little was a very generous contributor to religious matters and had much to do with the erection of the old Methodist Church at Rushville, a building that was burned during the World war. He was president of its Board of Trustees. Physically he was six feet tall, rather slender in build, with deliberate movements and manner of speech. During the Civil war he staunchly upheld the cause of the Union, and thereby aroused the enmity of the Knights of the Golden Circle, who tried to destroy his store.

George Little's first wife was Miss Lloyd. Her children were James and Mary. James never married. Mary became the wife of William H. Scripps, and died in Rushville. The second wife of George Little was Lydia Elizabeth Scripps, daughter of George H. Scripps, who moved from Virginia to Missouri, and from there to Illinois. Lydia Elizabeth Scripps was born at Jackson, Missouri, in 1821, and died in 1906. Her brother, John Locke Scripps, was the first authorized biographer of Abraham Lincoln, and afterwards was appointed postmaster of Chicago by Mr. Lincoln. His sketch of Mr. Lincoln furnished the basis for many subsequent biographies of the great statesman. John L. Scripps was associated with Joseph Medill in founding the Chicago Tribune, and for several years was its chief editor. His cousin, James E. Scripps, received his early training at the Tribune, subsequently went to Detroit and founded the Detroit Evening News, and this branch of the family was responsible for one of the greatest newspaper organizations in the country in recent years, known as the Scripps-McRae News Service and chain of newspapers. The children of George Little by his second wife were: George H., who died and is buried at Rushville; Grace and Virginia E., both of Rushville; and John Scripps.

John Scripps Little was born February 23, 1864. He attended high school at Rushville, early became associated with his father's business, and in 1883 entered the Bank of Rushville as bookkeeper. He has given the bank over forty years of consecutive service, thirty years of that time in the post of cashier, and was then elected president. He has never married.

Like his father, he has kept out of active politics. He was secretary of the first Board of Trustees of the Western Illinois State Normal, and held that office while the location of the school was being determined. He is a Mason, being a member of Medinah Temple of the Mystic Shrine at Chicago, belongs to the Union League and Hamilton Clubs of Chicago, the Arts Club of Chicago, and is a trustee and treasurer of the board of trustees of the Methodist Church. During the World war he was chairman of Liberty Loan drives for Schuyler County, and chairman of the United States Treasury Certificates of Indebtedness. Mr. Little has been an extensive traveler, and during 1899-1900 made a trip around the world, including some of the countries in the Far East.

W. H. C. SMITH, M. D. In point of continuous service Dr. W. H. C. Smith is the oldest professional man in the United States engaged in the care of the feeble-minded. His home has been in Illinois for thirty-five years, and he is a former assistant superintendent of the State School at Lincoln, but for over a quarter of a century has conducted a private school known as Beverly Farm Home and School for Nervous and Backward Children at Godfrey in Madison County. In recognition of his authoritative experience and attainments in the treatment and handling of feeble minded, Doctor Smith has received many appointments and honors. By appointment of former Governor Deneen he served during 1908-09 as president of the Board of Trustees controlling the Illinois State School and colony at Lincoln, and at the same time was president of the Illinois Conference of Charity and Corrections. Through appointment from Illinois governors he served a number of consecutive years as a delegate from the state to the National Conference of Charities and Corrections, and in 1908 was president of the National Association for the Study of the Feeble Minded.

Doctor Smith represents an old New England family that has been in this country for three centuries. Doctor Smith was born at Beverly, Massachusetts, February 6, 1860. He is a descendant of James Smith, who came from Woolwich, England, and settled at Woolwich, Maine, but subsequently in Beverly, Massachusetts, where he married and where he died in 1660. His son, Hasediah, in 1682 built the house at Beverly since known as the oldest building in that town, and the property has been continuously in the Smith family. A later descendant was Francis Smith, who made a distinguished record as a soldier in the war for independence, beginning with the battle of Lexington. He was the great-grandfather of Doctor Smith.

John Groves Smith, father of Doctor Smith, was born at Beverly in 1812, and for many years carried on the business of manufacturing boots and shoes for the fishermen of Gloucester and Marblehead. He married Hannah Choate Cross, who was born October 18, 1816, descendant of Scotch ancestors who settled in Beverly, Massachusetts, in 1750. Her father, Daniel Choate Cross, was a farmer and ship captain, sailed around the world, and his boat was captured by filibusters during the War of 1812.

William Hammond Cross Smith, of Godfrey, Illinois, was the youngest of the twelve children of his parents. He was reared in Beverly, and graduated from high school there in 1877. His father died the same year, and after that he was dependent upon his own exertions and earnings for his higher education. He attended the National College of Commerce at Philadelphia, and in 1889 received his diploma from the Long Island Medical College. He had already become deeply interested in that branch of his profession pertaining to nervous diseases, and prior to coming to Illinois he served five years as business agent for the Pennsylvania State Institute for the Feeble Minded at Elwyn, Pennsylvania. After graduating in medicine he came to Illinois and was appointed assistant superintendent of the Lincoln State Institute for Feeble Minded Children, now known as the Lincoln State School and Colony.

Doctor Smith established Beverly farm at Godfrey September 1, 1897. He has two hundred and twenty acres of land, has an equipment of especially designed and constructed buildings, and has about sixty patients or students in his school, using about twenty-five assistants for their care. The notable efficiency of Beverly Farm is indicated by the fact that it was awarded a gold medal by the Louisiana Purchase Exposition, and at the same time the World's Fair Committee awarded Doctor Smith a gold medal as representative of the American Association for the Study of Feeble Minded. Doctor Smith is a former president of the Madison County Medical Society, and is a member of the Illinois State and American Medical Associations. He is a trustee of the Madison Anti-Tuberculosis Sanatorium.

On September 23, 1891, Doctor Smith married Miss Elizabeth E. Blake, of Clinton, Illinois, daughter of J. S. D. and Susan Blake. Three sons were born to their marriage. Groves Blake was educated in the University of Illinois, is a graduate in medicine from Columbia Medical College, and during the World war had charge of the Transport Surgeons' Department at Hoboken, and also made four trips across the water as transport surgeon. He was president of the American Association for the Study of the Feeble Minded in 1925, and a member of the American Medical Association and the Madison County Medical Society. The second son, Theodore H., is associated with his father at Beverly Farm, and was in the navy during the World war. The youngest child, Leland Cross, is a traveling salesman, with home in California.

Doctor and Mrs. Smith and their son Theodore, in 1923, had a six months' journey around the World, in the course of which they visited twenty-three countries, including Japan, India and Ceylon, as well as many countries around the Mediterranean and in Western Europe.

DANIEL R. PETERS, M. D. A native of Illinois, Doctor Peters has practiced medicine for twenty years, and for the greater part of that time his home has been at Mt. Sterling. Doctor Peters is well qualified as a general practitioner and is becoming increasingly well known as a specialist in eye, ear, nose and throat diseases.

He was born near Barry, Adams County, Illinois. His father, Nathan G. Peters, was born in Tennessee, and settled in Illinois prior to the Civil war, in which he served as a Union soldier. Otherwise his career was devoted to farming. He was a member of the Missionary Baptist Church. Nathan G. Peters, who died at the age of fifty-seven, married Elizabeth Sparks, whose father likewise came from Tennessee. She died at Berry, Illinois, in 1923, at the age of seventy-two. She was a member of the Methodist Church. Her children were: Anna, wife of William Oitker, of Beverly, Illinois; Dr. Daniel Robert; and Lemuel Pinkney, of Clayton, Illinois.

Daniel R. Peters was reared on the farm near Berry, attended the rural schools and the Berry High School, and for three years taught in country districts. Prior to entering medical college he spent two years in a general literary course at Bushnell College, and then entered the Keokuk Medical College. He was graduated M. D. in 1906, doing special work there in eye, ear, nose and throat, and later pursuing a post-graduate course in the same subjects at Chicago. After one year of practice at Keokuk, Doctor Peters removed to Brown County and for seven years was located at Timewell, and since 1913 has practiced at Mt. Sterling. During the World war he had charge of the Four Minute Speakers in Mt. Sterling and volunteered for service in the Medical Corps.

He is one of the prominent Masons of this section, being district deputy grand master of the Sixty-seventh District of Masons. He took his first degrees in Masonry at Kingston and is now a member of Hardin Lodge at Mt. Sterling, the Knights Templar Commandery at Clayton, the Consistory at Quincy and Mohammed Temple of the Mystic Shrine at Peoria. Doctor Peters is serving his first term as county coroner of Brown County, having succeeded Doctor Ash in that office. He is a democrat and a member of the Christian Church.

He married at Pittsfield, Illinois, June 1, 1900, Miss Emma Wells, daughter of Francis and Rena (Bimson) Wells. Her parents were natives of Illinois and spent their lives as farmers in the vicinity of Beverly. Mrs. Peters is the third of four children, the others being: James Wells, of Quincy, Mary, wife of George Stofer, of Baylis, Illinois; and Otis Wells, of Liberty, Illinois. Doctor and Mrs. Peters have two daughters. The older, Roberta, is the wife of Wendell Orr, an electrical engineer at St. Louis. Ruth is a teacher in the public schools at Genoa, Illinois. Both daughters graduated from the Mt. Sterling High School. Mrs. Orr taught in Brown County before her marriage. Miss Ruth is a graduate of the Pestalozzi Kindergarten School at Chicago.

Doctor Peters is a stockholder and director in the Timewell State Bank. A busy professional man, he has taken time to cultivate many of the interests that lie outside of his profession. He is a lover of books, and he and his family have cultivated acquaintance with books in their home. They have also traveled extensively by rail and motor to many sections of their home country.

LAWRENCE A. DAVIS, circuit clerk and recorder of Brown County, represents the third generation of the Davis family in that county, and has for his own part been a useful and popular citizen, well qualified for the post to which the suffrage of his fellow citizens has repeatedly elected him.

He was born at Versailles, November 17, 1886. His grandfather, Caswell Davis, came to Illinois as a pioneer, his ancestors having originated in Virginia, Kentucky and Tennessee. Caswell Davis died when about forty years of age and is buried near Versailles. He married Julia Ann Heflin. They had four sons and one daughter: Howell, James W., Jefferson, John Hampton and Julia. Julia became the wife of Marion Lidgard. Mrs. Caswell Davis after the death of her first husband married Mr. Vaughan, and by that marriage a daughter, Alice, was born and became the wife of William H. Lewis.

James W. Davis, father of the circuit clerk, was born near Versailles, Illinois, followed the career of farming, and died at Versailles November 20, 1920, when almost seventy years of age. He had been educated in the Hall school near Versailles and for many years was a director of that school. He also served as road supervisor, was a staunch democrat and a member of the Christian Church. His wife was Hulda E. Perry, daughter of Fielding Perry, an Illinois farmer. Mrs. James W. Davis, who is still living, was the mother of the following children: Lawrence Alvin; Lewis Caswell, a telegraph operator at Mt. Sterling; Francis Orvil, a farmer at Versailles; Homer Elza, who died in childhood; and Lillie May, of Versailles.

Lawrence A. Davis attended public schools at Versailles, subsequently graduated from the Gem City Business College at Quincy, and for a term was teacher of bookkeeping and penmanship in the Illinois Business College of Chicago. Mr. Davis gave thirteen years of his life to educational work, most of the time in his native county, but also three years in Grant County, Kansas. While there he was elected county superintendent of schools, but resigned and returned to Brown County, where he resumed teaching and subsequently became substitute rural carrier of the mails out of Versailles. A little less than a year later he resigned to enter upon his duties as circuit clerk.

He was first elected clerk in 1920, almost unanimously against his republican opponent, after having won the nomination over three competitors. In the second campaign he was unopposed in the nomination. He succeeded Ernest B. Glaze as circuit clerk. Mr. Davis comes of a democratic family and he cast his first presidential vote for Col. William J. Bryan. He was a resident of Kansas during the World war, and was registered and classified but not called to duty. Mr. Davis is also president of the Mt. Sterling School Board. Fraternally he is affiliated with the Independent Order of Odd Fellows and Modern Woodmen of America.

He married at Versailles June 28, 1911, Miss Anna Mildred Root, daughter of Joseph F. and Laura K. (McCoy) Root. Her mother was a daughter of William McCoy, of a pioneer family of Brown County. Mrs. Davis was born at Versailles July 12, 1891, and finished her high school education there. She was the third in a family of four children, the others being Mrs. Luella F. Gaddis, of Mt. Sterling, Miss Susan V., and Charles H. Root, a farmer at Versailles. Mr. and Mrs. Davis have five children, named Wendell Lawrence, Galen Alvin and Gladys Mildred, twins, Marvin Root and Virginia Ruth.

WILLIAM MERCHANT RICHARDSON VOSE, who died January 19, 1916, was one of the constructive men in the business life of Chicago and vicinity for many years, and to a notable degree impressed his influence on the civic, moral and religious affairs of his home community. As a citizen his record is of particular significance in the city of Evanston, where he had his home for over forty years.

He represented one of the old Colonial families of Massachusetts and in his own life exemplified many of the characteristics of New England integrity. He was born at Lancaster, Massachusetts, January 2, 1847, son of Samuel John Sprague and Mary (Richardson) Vose. His mother was a daughter of William Merchant Richardson, at one time chief justice of the State of New Hampshire. The founder of the Vose family in America was Robert Vose, who was born in Lancashire, England, in 1599, and coming to America in 1630, founded the town of Milton, Massachusetts, where he died in 1683. From him to William M. R. Vose, the direct line of descent included Thomas, Lieutenant Henry, a soldier of the Colonial wars, Robert, Thomas, Peter Thatcher and Samuel John Sprague.

William M. R. Vose grew up in his native town, attended the local academy, and for a time clerked in a dry goods establishment at Boston. In 1868, at the age of twenty-one, he came West to Chicago. For a number of years he was in the service of the Bradstreet Mercantile Reporting Agency, at first as a reporter and then as assistant superintendent. Much time was spent in Texas and Kansas City organizing the service and offices of the Bradstreet Company. He was with the Bradstreet Company until about 1880.

On July 16, 1869, a year after he came to Chicago, Mr. Vose married Patience Elizabeth Watts of Tiverton, Rhode Island. They established a home on the West Side near Robey Street and in 1872 built their home at 733 Forest Avenue, Evanston, occupying it the following year. Since that time the name Vose has been one of unusual prominence in that suburban city of Northern Illinois, the name of which imports character.

Mr. Vose in 1880 became associated with William P. Kimball in the firm of Kimball & Vose, real estate and loans. This firm had much to do with the development of the Evanston subdivisions and planting of elms which today are the pride of that city. The business in time established a banking department, and out of that developed the Western Trust and Savings Bank at the southeast corner of Washington Street and Fifth Avenue in Chicago. After some years the bank was sold, and Mr. Vose then became secretary of the Northwestern Building and Loan Association, serving until this concern was liquidted in 1896.

The home of Mr. Vose was in what for some years, was the separate village of South Evanston, and he was prominent in its affairs, as well as in those of the larger city of Evanston. He served several terms as trustee of the village board of South Evanston, and was instrumental in providing the water and sewerage systems, street paving and lighting of the village. He took a prominent part in organizing in 1883 the Evanston Township High School, and on February 15, 1884, was chairman of the meetings and organized what is now the Second Presbyterian Church of Evanston, of which he was the first elder. During the great railroad strike of 1877 Mr. Vose had charge of law enforcement at South Evanston, and through his vigilance life and property in that vicinity were carefully safeguarded. Mr. Vose was deeply interested in the moral as well as the material development of his community, and he helped organize and became first president of the South Evanston Social Club, which was started in Ducats Block. He was often solicited to hold public office, but declined any office (other than that of village trustee) that would cause his absence from home, of which he was a great lover.

In September, 1903, Mr. Vose became interested in the law firm of Vose and Page, Marquette Building, Chicago, of which his son, Frederic P., was the senior member. Thereafter he devoted much of his time to looking after the correspondence and similar routine of the firm, a work for which his vast experience in banking, real estate and commercial law eminently qualified him. Even during his later years he was usually the last to leave the office in the city. He liked the work, and it was a happy occupation for his years of retirement. His son Frederic, who had a business trip to make to Washington, D. C., called him to bid him good-bye on the afternoon of January 19, 1916, and earlier than usual, found him preparing to go home. The latter said he was perfectly well, "that his work was done." On the same evening he died of cerebral hemorrhage.

The late Mr. Vose came of old New England Congregational stock, strict observers of the Sabbath. However, for many years he worshiped as a Presbyterian, and was one of the old time citizens who kept up family worship as a part of his every day religion. He served the Second Presbyterian Church of Evanston as elder some fifteen years. He was a republican, though he voted for Cleveland in 1884, and in local affairs was inclined to support men and measures rather than party. He was a great reader, had skill as a writer, and contributed a number of articles to the press and trade periodicals. His family and neighbors knew him as the soul of honesty, of friendly disposition and social charm, of judicial temperament, optimistic and inspiring. He was the exemplification of the spirit of the pioneers in constructive community service.

Mrs. W. M. R. Vose lives at Evanston, and her three children are all living: Frederic P., Mary Richardson and Walter Smythe, the sons being associated in the practice of law in Chicago.

Frederic P. Vose has for over thirty years been a Chicago attorney. He was born on the West Side of the city, May 4, 1870, but since 1873 has lived in Evanston, where he attended grammar and high schools. He was a student in Northwestern University from 1890 to 1892 and in 1894 graduated from the Law School of Northwestern University. He was admitted to the bar in 1893, and since 1902 has been senior member of Vose and Page, his younger brother also being a member of the firm. For a number of years Mr. Vose has given special attention in his practice to the electrical industry, and served as general counsel to the National Electrical Credit Association, as editor of its monthly publication, and is general counsel of the Electrical Credit Association, Central Division. His law offices since 1896 have been in the Marquette Building. He has been a contributor to various law and technical journals in the United States and England, and was president of the Electric Club of Chicago from 1908 to 1910. He is a member of the Chicago Illinois State and American Bar Associations, was president of the Commercial Law League of America, 1912-13, and is a director in a number of corporations. He was chairman of the Ways and Means Committee of the Chicago Association of Commerce and presiding officer over its Forum, 1919-1920, and chairman of its Executive Committee, 1922-23.

Mr. Vose married Lucy Beatrice Mason, of Evanston, January 30, 1900. She is a daughter of Thomas and Margaret (Smith) Mason. Mr. Vose served ten years as a member of the Evanston Board of Education, being president of the Board five years. He is a member of the Sigma Chi and Phi Delta Phi fraternities, and has been vice president and director of the Union League Club, a member of the University and Law Clubs of Chicago, is former president of the University Club of Evanston; also is a member of the Westmoreland Country Club and Annandale Golf Club of Pasadena, California.

Mr. Vose is one of the prominent laymen of the Presbyterian Church, serving for more than fifteen years on the Church Extension Board of the Chicago Presbytery, a member of the Board of Christian Education of the Presbyterian Church of the United States of America, and in 1922-24 was president of the Presbyterian Union of Chicago. During the World war he acted as legal examiner for a draft board, and was active in all the Liberty Loan and Red Cross drives.

Mary Richardson Vose was born in Evanston, April 8, 1880. She graduated from the Evanston grammar and high schools and later attended the Music School of Northwestern University, there being made a member of Alpha Chi Omega sorority. She is a graduate of the National Kindergarten and Elementary College of Chicago (now of Evanston). In 1908 she completed a course in the Civics and Philanthropy School, now a department of the University of Chicago.

After working with the United Charities of Chicago she was appointed general secre-

Clarence A. Myers

tary of the Provident Association of Topeka, Kansas, remaining there from February, 1912, till the fall of 1914. On returning to Chicago she became for two years a social worker in The Marcy Home, a settlement house in the Ghetto. In 1917 she enlisted in Red Cross service in Evanston and the year following and until 1922 was field worker in the Home Service Department of Chicago.

She is a member of the Second Presbyterian Church of Evanston, teacher and officer in the Primary Department of the Bible School for many years. She is a member of the Evanston Woman's Club and the Drama Club of Evanston.

Walter Smythe Vose, the younger son of the late William Merchant Richardson Vose, was born in Evanston, March 13, 1882. He was educated in Northwestern University and the University of Virginia, graduated from the Kent College of Law at Chicago in 1911, and since that date has been associated with the law firm of Vose and Page.

He married Alice Owsley in September, 1906. Their two children are Owsley and Elizabeth. Mr. Vose is a Sigma Chi and a former elder in the Second Presbyterian Church of Evanston, and an officer and teacher in the Bible School. He is a member of the Country Club of Evanston.

DICK HOWARD MUDGE, one of the prominent members of the Madison County bar, has been engaged in a general law practice at Edwardsville for over twenty years and is a former mayor of that city.

He was born in Saline Township of Madison County, Illinois, July 9, 1879, fourth among the five children of Elliott W. and Fanny M. (Clark) Mudge. His parents were also born in Madison County, and are now living at Edwardsville. Dick Howard Mudge attended the public schools of Edwardsville, and took his law course in Northwestern University Law School at Chicago, where he was graduated with the class of 1902. After successfully passing the bar examination he was admitted to the bar and at once returned to Edwardsville and opened his office. In his general law practice he has represented many important cases both in Madison and adjoining counties.

On January 17, 1917, he married Miss Ann Louise Gregory, of Alton, Illinois. They have two sons, Dick H., Jr., and John G. Mr. Mudge is a Knight Templar and thirty-second degree Scottish Rite Mason and Shriner, is a democrat in politics, and a member of the Episcopal Church. He gave a thorough efficient and progressive administration as mayor of the City of Edwardsville for two terms, from 1913 to 1917. During the World war he was active in the various campaigns and was chairman of the County Council of Defense.

REV. J. C. MECKEL is pastor emeritus of St. Mary's Catholic Church at Alton. He is one of the oldest Catholic priests in Southern Illinois, and has been continuously in the service of his church in different parts of the state for more than half a century.

Rev. J. C. Meckel was born in Westphalia, Germany, November 10, 1843. He was reared and educated there, and at the age of twenty-five was ordained a priest. Coming to America in 1869, he was assigned arduous responsibilities with headquarters at Olney Illinois, having jurisidiction over four adjoining counties in that section of the state with about eight churches altogether, which he attended consecutively. His service in this laborious pastorate lasted for about five years, and his next location was at Litchfield, Illinois, where he remained about a year, and then for a brief time was made director of the college in Randolph County, remaining there until the school was closed.

Father Meckel for about twenty years was pastor of St. Paul's Church at Highland in Madison County, and left there to remove to Alton and take charge of St. Mary's Parish, where his service of twenty-seven years has brought him a high degree of veneration and esteem. He built up his parish and greatly increased the membership. There are now about five hundred families and the school enrollment is about four hundred pupils. On June 16, 1924, Father Meckel resigned his pastorship. He spent a year traveling in Europe, spending most of his time in Holland and Germany. Upon his return to America August 8, 1925, he came to Alton for a short stay, and has since made his home with the Sisters of the Most Precious Blood, located at Columbia, Pennsylvania, in the diocese of Harrisburg.

CLARENCE A. MYERS, inventor and manufacturer, has been a resident of Chicago for twenty years. His success has been largely built up on the manufacture and sale of a single implement known practically the world over as the Myers Lock Stitch Sewing Awl. This awl is sold and distributed through a mail order organization personally directed by Mr. Myers and located at 6324 Woodlawn Avenue, known as the C. A. Myers Company. The sales total several hundred thousand annually, and the Myers awl is shipped to practically every foreign country. The advertising slogan that has done much to build up the business has been "THE AWL FOR ALL."

Clarence A. Myers was born at Dunkirk, New York, in 1853, son of Alva O. and Elizabeth (Bliss) Myers. When he was a year old his father moved to Novelty, Missouri, and later to Quincy, Illinois, and was a carpenter and contractor in that city until his death at the age of eighty-one.

Clarence A. Myers after attending the public schools in Quincy, Illinois, learned the trade of carpenter under his father, after which followed several years of experience in the candy business. Then went into the manufacture of the Reliable Incubator, one of the first successful plants making Quincy, Illinois, so widely known as a center of incubator and poultry industry. In 1904 he sold out to his brother, who is now owner of the Reliable Incubator and Brooder Company, the Reliable being one of the most widely advertised and largest selling incubators in the country. In 1905 the family moved to Denver, Colorado, where he first patented his lock stitch awl. He then came to Chicago, Illinois, in 1906 where he conducted a mail order business limited to the handling of the sewing awl. The last few years the awl has been placed with the mail order houses and the hardware jobbers. More recently he invented and is now manufacturer of the Myers Electric Iron Cord Holder in connection with the sewing awl. Mr. Myers is a property owner in the Muscle Shoals district of Northern Alabama and has been interested in real estate in and around Chicago. He is a Knight Templar and Scottish Rite Mason and Shriner, being a member of the Woodlawn Commandery, and also the Medinah Athletic Club, which has promoted and is carrying out plans for the construction of one of the finest club houses in the world. Mr. Myers is also a member of the B. P. O. Elks, the Loyal Order of Moose and the Woodlawn Business Men's Association. He married Miss Maria W. Hubert of Beverly, Illinois, in 1875, who became the mother of his five children. His present wife is Olive Bessie Alexander of Gilcrest, Colorado.

J. EDWARD MAASS. Prominent among the men who have contributed to Chicago's prestige in financial matters is J. Edward Maass, vice president of the Illinois Merchants Trust Company. A resident of this city throughout his life, he has been identified with banking matters for thirty-six years, and his standing among the members of his vocation is that of a capable, shrewd and well-informed master of finance.

Mr. Maass was born at Chicago, October 3, 1869, and is a son of Frederick A. E. and Mary (Tesch) Maass. His father, born in Sleswig-Holstein, December 16, 1838, adopted a seafaring life in his youth and rose to the post of first mate of a steamship, a capacity in which he came to the United States. Arriving at New Orleans, he decided to make his future home in this country, and soon thereafter enlisted in a Louisiana infantry regiment for service in the Confederate army during the war between the states. Wounded in battle and therefore disabled for further military duty, he made his way to Chicago, where he met and married Mary Tesch, a native of this city, born in 1849. They had only one child: J. Edward. After his arrival in Chicago in 1864 Frederick A. E. Maass embarked in the wholesale liquor business on the South Side, but lost his business during the great Chicago fire of October 9, 1871. He made a fresh start on the West Side of the city, and continued in the same line of business until his death, which occurred March 29, 1884. He was a good citizen and a member of the school board under Mayor Carter H. Harrison, the elder. Fraternally he was affiliated with the Masons.

J. Edward Maass attended the public schools until reaching the age of fourteen years, at which time he entered the machine shop of the Adams & Westlake Company. Experience taught, however, that he was not mechanically inclined, and when he was sixteen years of age he enrolled as a student at the Metropolitan Business College in order to fit himself for a career in the way of office work. Having completed his course, he became a clerk in the office of W. W. Caldwell, a life insurance agent, with whom he remained one year, and March 28, 1888, entered the American Exchange Bank in the capacity of assistant clearing house clerk. In 1895 he was advanced to assistant cashier, and three years later, when that bank was consolidated with the National Bank of America, he remained in the same capacity. In 1900 a further consolidation was made, with the Corn Exchange Bank, and Mr. Maass was made assistant cashier, and was gradually promoted to cashier and made a vice president. When the consolidation with the Illinois Merchants Trust Company was made he became a vice president. In addition to this bank Mr. Maass is a stockholder in ten other banking institutions. He has numerous other interests that touch the city's life on many sides, being a life member of the Art Institute, the Chicago Historical Society, Field Museum, and a member of the Westmoreland Golf Club, the North Shore Golf Club, Union League Club, Chicago Athletic Club, Illinois Athletic Club, Bankers Club, and Medinah Temple, A. A. O. N. M. S. Politically he is a republican. He is a school trustee of Newtrier Township.

On August 1, 1892, Mr. Maass was united in marriage with Miss Helen Hannah Meyer, and they are the parents of one son: Herbert J.

LLEWELLYN W. MILLER since 1910 has been county superintendent of schools of Lee County. His service as an Illinois educator covers a period of thirty years, with a varied experience from teaching a rural school to his present position.

Mr. Miller was born in Lee County, Illinois, on a farm, February 3, 1870, a twin son of Samuel B. and Sarah (Miller) Miller. His parents were both of Pennsylvania Dutch ancestry but were of unrelated families. The Millers were among the pioneers of Lee County, Illinois. His paternal grandfather, William Miller, came to Illinois from Pennsylvania and lived in Lee County for many years, but spent his last days at Pawnee, Nebraska. The maternal grandfather, Adam Miller, a native of Pennsylvania, was a very early settler of Lee County, but finally moved to Kansas, where he died. The parents of Llewellyn W. Miller were Samuel B. and Sarah (Miller) Miller, natives of Pennsylvania. Samuel B. Miller was born in Lackawanna County, and was a child when brought to Lee County, Illinois, where he grew up and spent his active career as a farmer. He died in 1919, at the age of seventy-six, his wife passing away in 1885. Of their nine children six grew to mature years.

Llewellyn W. Miller had the environment of a farm during his boyhood, and spent such time as he was not in school in the work of the fields. He attended country schools, and at the age of eighteen began teaching in rural districts. Two years later he left the farm to enter Dixon College and in a little more than three years completed the regular four year teacher's professional course, graduating in 1894. In the course of his active experience as an Illinois school man Mr. Miller was principal of the public schools at Putnam, Steward and Compton; was principal of one of the ward schools at Dixon and in 1910 was elected county superintendent of schools of Lee County. His work has been so eminently satisfactory as to bring him reelection for each succeeding term. He was reelected in 1914, 1918, and 1922, and is an unopposed candidate to succeed himself in the 1926 election.

Some of the outstanding points in his administration as county superintendent should be noted. He has given the teachers a definite course of study known as the county manual; has personally held or conducted the examinations of graduates from the rural schools of the county, and directed each year's graduation exercises; has emphasized the comfort of school children and health and sanitary conditions in the schools; and a number of new schools have been erected and old ones remodeled. Mr. Miller is a member of the Illinois State Teachers' Association and the Northern Illinois Teachers' Association, and also belongs to the Lee County Teachers' Association.

Fraternally he is a member of the Masonic Order, Modern Woodmen of America, Mystic Workers, and Modern Brotherhood of America; is a republican and in religion, a Protestant.

He married in 1896 Miss Charlotte Diona Russell, of Granite Falls, Minnesota, a teacher in the rural schools of that state for two years. She is a graduate in voice and piano from the Dixon Conservatory of Music. Mr. and Mrs. Miller have two sons and one daughter. Stanley Russell Miller, who served nearly one year in France with the Expeditionary Forces, is a graduate of the Northern Illinois State Teachers' College at De Kalb, and is now principal of the Junior High School at Aurora, Illinois. The second son, Erman Olcott Miller, is a graduate of the State Teachers' Normal at De Kalb, and has taught manual training in the schools of Dixon and Rochelle. The daughter, Elwyna Diona, is a student in the Dixon High School.

RUDOLPH HENRY ROHLFS. The thriving community of Manito has no more enterprising business man or progressive and public-spirited citizen than Rudolph Henry Rohlfs, senior member of the prosperous general merchandise firm of Brown & Rohlfs. His career is indicative of his energetic and ambitious nature, for he started life with no advantages save those acquired through a public school education, and through his own initiative, resource and sound business judgment has made a place for himself in business activities as well as in the civic, social and musical circles of the community.

Mr. Rohlfs was born November 11, 1879, at Manito, Mason County, Illinois, and is a son of Rohlf and Helena (Knutsen) Rohlfs. His father was born September 25, 1843, at Essen, Germany, the site of the famous Krupp gun works of modern times, and when twenty-seven years of age left the Fatherland for the United States, landing at New York City. There he remained for several days before making his way west to Pekin, Illinois, where he sought and found employment at his trade as a mechanic, which he had learned in his youth in the old country. For a number of years he was employed by the Schmidt Wagon Works, but in 1874 gave up mechanical work and went to Logan County, where he engaged in farming. One year's experience in this field of endeavor, however, convinced him that agricultural work was not his forte and he returned to Pekin, whence, in 1877, he came to Manito and engaged in blacksmithing and wagon and vehicle making. Mr. Rohlfs built wagons and buggies and manufactured plows, employed several skilled mechanics and developed quite a prosperous business, in which he continued to be engaged until 1913. During this time he featured the lister plow, to be used especially in the sandy land, it being particularly fitted for that kind of work. Mr. Rohlfs became noted for his tempering of plow points and other metals with which he worked, his reputation gaining him custom from all over the surrounding countryside, but the wearing and burden of the years caused him to retire from active participation in business in 1913, since which time he has lived quietly at Manito.

During the active years of his life Rohlf Rohlfs was identified prominently with the official affairs of the community, having won the esteem and confidence of his fellow-citizens. He was a member of the town board, an alderman and village treasurer and for many years was a school trustee. As a fraternalist he was a charter member of Manito Camp No. 1094, Modern Woodmen of America, of which for a time he served as banker; and is the next to the oldest surviving member of Manito Lodge No. 476, A. F. and A. M., which he joined in 1883. He became a citizen early and identified himself with the democratic party, but as the years have passed he has become more and more independent as to his political allegiance. At Pekin, Illinois, Mr. Rohlfs was united in marriage with Miss Helena Knutsen, who was born in Oldenburg, Germany, and came to the United States as a woman of twenty-three years, landing alone from the steamer at Galveston, Texas. There she spent two years on her uncle's cotton plantation, and then came north to Illinois, where she had friends and eventually met and married Mr. Rohlfs. Her death occurred at Manito January 23, 1924. They became the parents of four children: Minnie, the wife of M. S. Martins, of Chicago; Rudolph Henry, of this review; Lena, who resides with her father and brother at Manito; and Frank, who is a barber at Manito.

Rudolph Henry Rohlfs has always maintained his home at Manito, where he acquired his education in the public schools. His first employment was with the mercantile firm of Heckman Brothers, and he had not been a clerk long before he had established fixedly in his mind the firm determination that he would one day be an employer instead of an employe. With this end in view he began to conserve his earnings and to accept every honorable opportunity to increase his savings, and at the end of seven years had accumulated sufficient capital to purchase the interest of Mr. Corbett in the general merchandise firm of Corbett & Brown, thus forming the present firm of Brown & Rohlfs, established in August, 1909. There has been no change in the firm since, and the partners have developed a prosperous business which has attracted a large share of patronage not only at Manito but from all over the surrounding locality. As before noted, Mr. Rohlfs possesses initiative. He has always been an advocate of the value of presenting goods attractively, and this caused him to pursue a course in window trimming at the Koester School of Window Trimming and Mercantile Decorations at Chicago, of which he is a graduate. He has made this a prominent feature of the display at the store.

During the World war Mr. Rohlfs was registered but not called to camp or field, although he did his full share as a citizen in assisting in the numerous local drives and campaigns. He is a past master of Manito Lodge No. 476, A. F. and A. M.; served many years as worthy patron of Rebekah Chapter No. 437, O. E. S.; and is a member of Pekin Chapter No. 25, R. A. M.; Damascus Commandery No. 42, K. T., Havana, Illinois; Peoria Consistory, A. A. S. R. M.; Mohammed Temple, A. A. O. N. M. S., Peoria; and Judea Chapter No. 10, White Shrine of Jerusalem. He is also chancellor commander of the Knights of Pythias, Massasoit Lodge No. 261, and a member of the Modern Woodmen of America, in which he has served several terms as banker of the camp. At the age of fourteen years Mr. Rohlfs became a member of the Manito Brass Band, in which he played the b-flat cornet, and when he was only twenty-two years of age was made director of this organization. He had revived the interest in brass bands at Manito on different occasions and twice he has reorganized two later bands, of which he was leader and director. He has been active also in orchestra music for many years, his instrument being the cornet. Mr. Rohlfs is likewise a member of Mohammed Oriental Band of Peoria Shrine, which band has attended the Imperial Council meetings in many prominent cities of the United States.

Mr. Rohlfs is unmarried and resides with his father and sister at their comfortable home at Manito.

PROF. HENRY GALEN SCHMIDT. A school system that is a source of pride to the entire community and one of the best in the State of Illinois is that possessed by Belleville Township in St. Clair County. The superintendent of those schools is Henry Galen Schmidt, one of the most forceful leaders in educational work in southern Illinois.

Mr. Schmidt was born in Gasconade County, Missouri, May 5, 1879, son of Fred and Jane (Robinson) Schmidt. His great-grandfather Schmidt came from Lippe-Detmold, Germany, in 1849, coming to this country as a result of the German revolution of 1848. He landed at New Orleans. His son, Henry Schmidt, grandfather of the school man of Belleville, grew up in New Orleans, learned the trade of tailor and followed it in Louisiana and afterwards in Missouri. He married Martha Hamel, a native of Missouri. Fred Schmidt spent his active life as a general farmer in Missouri and has taken much part in local affairs, serving as township treasurer, and county commissioner and member of the school board twelve years. His wife, Jane Robinson, is a daughter of Galen Robinson, who was born in Virginia and has reached the remarkable age of 105 years. The Robinsons were an old Virginia family. He went as a boy into Kentucky and in 1845 moved to Missouri, where he was a pioneer. On coming west some of the Robinsons settled in Tennessee and others in Kentucky. Galen Robinson married Martha Adams, who was an Ohio woman of Kentucky ancestry. Mr. and Mrs. Fred Schmidt are the parents of seven children, Henry Galen being the oldest living child; Fred, Jr., who married Ida Sutler and has five children; Malinda, who is the wife of Herman Lettman; Ida, wife of Richard Neidhart and the mother of four children; Nora, who married Lewis Uthe and has two children; August, who by his marriage to Alice Stolte has four children; and Viola, who is the wife of Frank Farber has one child.

Henry Galen Schmidt grew up in a country district in southern Missouri, attending country schools through the eighth grade. For two years he was a student at the Owensville High School, spent two years in the Central Wesleyan Normal School and in 1902 graduated from the Central Wesleyan College with the A. B. degree. In the course of his teaching he has been a student not only of his professional technique, but of a broad range of studies, and by work in the summer and other times has gained the Bachelor of Science and Master of Arts degrees from McKendree College of Illinois, and Washington University, and has done work towards his Doctor of Philosophy degree in Illinois University and the University of Chicago.

His record as a teacher includes two years as principal of the grade and high schools at Smithson, Missouri; superintendent of schools two years at Chamois, Missouri, and on coming to Belleville he was for eight years teacher of science in the old Central High School. In 1915 he took up the duties of superintendent of the Belleville Township High School.

Mr. Schmidt was the real leader in the movement to make this township high school one of the most complete in facilities and organization in the state. When he became superintendent work was started on a new group of buildings, including the main building, completed February 12, 1917, the gymnasium, completed in 1919, and the Auditorium, finished in 1924. Superintendent Schmidt threw the first shovelful of dirt when the ground was broken for this imposing group of buildings. At the opening of the new building there were 234 students enrolled, while now the enrollment is 810, and the building facilities are already inadequate. Mr. Schmidt has proved very popular with the student body and has thoroughly organized all the forces working for better educational opportunities in the community. A night school is conducted under him as superintendent, with an enrollment of four hundred students. During the World war he was identified with the war program as a Four Minute Speaker, as chairman of the Boys Farm work in the county, and chairman of the Church Cooperative Committee of the War Camp Community Service Board.

Ellen J. Kincaid. John H. Kincaid

He married at Gasconade, Missouri, August 7, 1902, Miss Anna Wolters, daughter of John and Augusta (Myer) Wolters. Her father, who was a shoemaker, died in 1906 and her mother died in 1922. She is the youngest of four children, the others being: Paul, who married Lena Joachim and has two children; Emma, wife of Daniel Joackisch, and the mother of four children; Hulda, wife of Rudolph Toedaman and the mother of two children. Mr. and Mrs. Schmidt have two sons, Webster, born in 1910, and Blaine, in 1917.

Mr. Schmidt is a member of the Methodist Church. He is a Knights Templar Mason, going by way of the York Rite, and a member of the Modern Woodmen of America and the Modern Brotherhood of America of Mason City, Iowa. He belongs to the County and State Teachers' Association, and the National Education Association. He had an active part in the celebration of Belleville's centennial anniversary in 1916, the chief feature of which was a pageant illustrating the hundred years of history. In that pageant, with five hundred persons participating, he represented the Civil war governor of Illinois in the historic ceremony of presenting a flag to the local regiment on the way to the war. Pictures were taken of this pageant and the flag presentation, these pictures being put in steel cases and placed in a vault to be opened and reproduced one hundred years from 1916.

JOHN HENRY KINCAID, senior member of the reliable firm of J. H. Kincaid & Sons, is one of the most extensive farmers of Menard county, his splendid farm embracing 711 acres of fertile land. He was born in the Indian Point community, Menard County, July 9, 1848, on their farm, a son of John Kennedy Kincaid, and grandson of Andrew Kincaid, the latter having been born near Carlisle, Pennsylvania, December 12, 1784. About 1795 he accompanied his parents to Bath County, Kentucky, and there he was married to Ann P. Caldwell, born in that county, August 8, 1787, a daughter of William Caldwell, born July 31, 1761. On August 17, 1786, William Caldwell was married to Elizabeth Kennedy, whose birth occurred August 2, 1766, and her death, September 8, 1846, and she is interred in the Indian Point Cemetery, being one of the thirteen ancestors of the children of John Henry Kincaid, who lie in this little burial ground of historic moment.

The children of Andrew Kincaid and his wife were as follows: John Kennedy, who was the father of John Henry; Archibald, who was born March 25, 1810, died January 9, 1901, married October 17, 1877, Amelia Milton Brasfield; Eliza J., who was born May 13, 1813, died March 5, 1907, as the wife of Col. Robert L. Wilson, whom she married March 28, 1833, her husband having been a member of the Illinois Legislature together with Abraham Lincoln, and had the distinction of being one of the "long nine," the name applied to the nine very tall members of that session; William Caldwell, who was born November 3, 1815, died February 7, 1882, married Louisa Hale; Mary Ann, who was born January 26, 1818, married December 1, 1836, Alonzo Howe Whitney, and died November 15, 1900; Thomas, who was born October 15, 1822, married Lucinda Patterson, October 18, 1849, and died February 8, 1899; Andrew Edgar, who was born January 27, 1825, married Jane G. Webb, January 1, 1857, and died September 3, 1907; Emily Rachel, who was born December 9, 1831, married first William Berry Moore, December 7, 1848, and October 25, 1858, she was married second to Henry Pendleton Gaines. Her death occurred March 20, 1902.

John Kennedy Kincaid was born in Bath County, Kentucky, June 30, 1808, and resided there until 1832, acquiring a sound educational training that included Greek and Latin, and he continued a classical scholar all his life, his knowledge of these languages giving him prestige and standing. He was apprenticed to the carpenter trade, and worked at it for $12 a month in order to earn the money to continue his studies beyond the common schools.

In 1832 John Kennedy Kincaid left his old home in Sharpsburg, Bath County, Kentucky, and came to Illinois bringing his carpenter tools with him. His route took him down the Ohio River and up the Mississippi and Illinois rivers, leaving the latter at Beardstown, and from there he walked across country to Indian Point, then in Sangamon County, but now in Menard County. At that early day Indian Point was not only the nearest settlement, but the most important one. His carpenter tools followed him from Beardstown and he used them in constructing his own house and barn, but he did not follow his trade in Menard County. For a time after coming here he taught school at Buffalo Hart. His communications with reference to this region which he sent home so interested his father, that in 1833 Andrew Kincaid visited his son, and being pleased with conditions, went back to Kentucky, disposed of his property, and in 1834 drove from Bath County to Menard County, bringing his family, his household effects, his stock and five slaves, the latter of which he set free after his arrival.

John Kennedy Kincaid had not come to Illinois to work as a carpenter or to teach school. He came with the object of securing from the government some of the land then open for settlement, and he selected several tracts near Indian Point, on which his son, John Henry Kincaid is now residing. Some of his land was surveyed for him by Abraham Lincoln in 1835, as deputy under Surveyor J. Calhoun, and the original copy of the notes made by Mr. Lincoln is hanging on the wall of Mr. Kincaid's home, properly framed. It is regarded by the Kincaids as one of their most priceless possessions, and a sacred relic. As the community was in process of building, Mr. Kincaid was induced to lend his assistance as a carpenter, but his farming duties soon became too heavy for him to respond.

In connection with the friendship of the Kincaid family with Abraham Lincoln it may be of interest to know that the two called each other "Abe" and "Ken" and met now and then as the affairs in this locality brought them together. Mr. Kincaid was an abolitionist, and for a long time he was one of those in this region who assisted the runaway Negroes on their flight to Canada to escape from slavery in the South.

While Mr. Kincaid did not help to organize the North Sangamon Presbyterian Church (organized May 20, 1832) that having been carried on just prior to his arrival, but he at once identified himself with it, and continued one of its most useful members the remainder of his life, and he served it as an elder. When it was first organized it was as a branch of what is now the First Presbyterian Church of Springfield, and services were held in a frame building, a portion of which is still standing and is used for residential purposes. It was on what was then a part of the Kincaid holdings, but is now the property of Mrs. Thomas D. Cantrall. In 1860 a substantial brick edifice was erected to replace the original church, and in the work of constructing it Mr. Kincaid played an important part as a member of the building committee. This second church is still used by the congregation of this old religious body.

Another public service rendered by Mr. Kincaid was that connected with the organization of the North Sangamon Academy, and the erection of a suitable building in 1856. The school was built by subscription, on ground donated by Andrew Kincaid and his wife. The object of this school besides educating the children of the community was the training of young men who were preparing themselves for the ministry, and the students from this school were accepted in any of the theological seminaries, so excellent was the preparation. The cost of the building was $3,000. There was a shortage in funds, and Archibald, a brother of John Kennedy Kincaid offered either $100 or eighty acres of land, and the board took the money for it was impossible in those days to realize on farm land.

For about forty years John Kennedy Kincaid served as township trustee, but did not care for any other office. So upright was he that his neighbors used to call upon him to settle estates, and discharge other trusts, and for many years he was the one in this region who was relied upon for all such services. His first presidential ballot was cast in 1832 for a whig candidate and he continued steadfast in his allegiance to that party until the republican party came into existence, when he became a zealous supporter of its principles.

On March 24, 1836, John Kennedy Kincaid and Vienna Williams were married. She was a daughter of James and Hannah (Mappin) Williams. The Williams family also originated in Bath County, Kentucky, but was established in Indian Point some time prior to the advent of the Kincaids, as they came to this region in 1823, accompanied by the Johnson family, William Johnson being a son-in-law of Mr. Williams. The site of the first home of the Johnson family is now marked by a boulder with a bronze tablet. The following children were born to John Kennedy Kincaid and his wife: James Williams, who died in Memphis, Tennessee while serving in the Union army during the war between the states, when he was twenty-five years old; Hannah Elizabeth, who married John Wesley Dalbey, is a widow of Springfield, Illinois, now over eighty-five years old, died February 4, 1926, and is buried in Indian Point Cemetery; Ann Eliza, a twin of Hannah Elizabeth, who married Robert A. Young, is deceased, and her remains are interred in Indian Point Cemetery; Malinda, who married Carlin W. Greene, died at Homewood, Kansas, but is buried in Indian Point Cemetery; John Henry, whose name heads this review; Joseph Howe, who married Mary C. Short, died in San Diego, California, leaving a family; Huldah, who married Charles C. Scott, died at Athens, Illinois, and is buried in Indian Point Cemetery; Julia Etta, who married John K. Kutnewsky, a physician who for twenty-four years was superintendent of the institution for feebleminded at Redfield, South Dakota, and they are both still residents of Redfield.

The North Sangamon Academy and the Springfield Business College gave John Henry Kincaid of this review, an excellent education. Reared on the farm he has spent his life in farming and has developed into one of the leading agriculturists of this region. When he married he established his first home at Irish Grove, and there he spent seven years, and then moved to his present farm, the one on which he was born, and here he has lived for forty years. On it he has erected his residence, several barns and other outbuildings, set out trees and made of it a valuable property. His farming program has been general, including stockraising and feeding, and he has long been a heavy shipper of livestock. He is still active, carrying on his extensive operations in partnership with his sons. Some years ago Mr. Kincaid bred standard-bred horses for road purposes, but is no longer engaged in this industry, but while he was active in it he used to display his product at different fairs and stock expositions.

Like his father, Mr. Kincaid has been closely identified with the North Sangamon Presbyterian Church, in which his children and grandchildren have been christened. Long an officer of the church, he has been an elder for twenty-five years, and in 1925 was a delegate by designation to the general assembly of the church, but could not attend. However he has oftentimes served as delegate to the presbyteries and synods, and has borne his part in upholding the work of this old religious organization.

Nationally Mr. Kincaid is a republican, and cast his first presidential vote for General Grant in 1872, and was a member of the "Tanners' Organization" which participated in the campaign of that year. In local matters he is inclined to support the man he deems best fitted for the office in question.

In 1872 Mr. Kincaid was made a Mason in Greenview, and he is a member of Van Meter Lodge, Ancient Free and Accepted Masons, of Athens; of the Chapter and Commandery of Petersburg, and of the Consistory and Shrine at Springfield.

On February 20, 1878, Mr. Kincaid was married at Indian Point, to Ellen Jane Culver, a daughter of Jonathan S. and Elizabeth Shelton (Brasfield) Culver, and she was born just east of Indian Point, July 31, 1849. Mr. and Mrs. Kincaid have had the following children: James Earle, who was born October 9, 1880, and married, August 7, 1913, Jessie Fay Miller, and their children are, John Edward, Eleanor and Ruth Eloise; John Kennedy, who was born December 29, 1885, and married September 12, 1918, Edith Mae Painter, and they have two children, John Kennedy, Jr., who was born March 9, 1922, and Donald Merle, who was born November 8, 1925. James Earle and John Kennedy Kincaid are associated with their father, under the name of J. H. Kincaid & Sons, in farming their large property and all reside on their property. James Earle Kincaid took up agricultural work in the Illinois State University, and his brother, after completing his high school work in Springfield, entered the same university and was graduated therefrom in 1909, with the degree of Bachelor of Science in Agriculture. They are both Knights Templar and thirty-second degree Masons and Shriners, and both are past eminent commanders of Saint Aldemar Commandery No. 47, Knights Templar of Petersburg.

FRANCIS A. HARPER. One of the forceful and cultured members of the Chicago bar, Francis A. Harper has for a number of years been engaged in a large, lucrative and growing practice, embracing real estate and corporation law. Of late years he has been especially identified with the official life and general progress of Tinley Park, where his pleasant home is the center of much social and intellectual activity.

Mr. Harper was born in the Province of Ontario, Canada, March 28, 1874, and is a son of Marmaduke and Margaret (Thompson) Harper. His father, who was born in 1825, in Yorkshire, England, was a young man when he emigrated to Canada and took up his residence as a pioneer in Ontario. There he continued to be engaged in agricultural pursuits up to 1881, in which year he made removal with his family to Sault Ste. Marie, Michigan, and transferred his interests to the lumber business. He was still later a resident of Marquette County, Michigan, and retired from business in 1900, dying three years later, at the age of seventy-eight years. He was a republican in his political allegiance. Mr. Harper married Miss Margaret Thompson, who was born in Ontario, Canada, in 1839, and survives him, and of their twelve children, eight sons and four daughters, eleven grew to manhood and womanhood, one dying in infancy.

The ninth in order of birth of his parents' children, Francis A. Harper attended the public schools of Michigan, and was graduated from the high school at Champion, Michigan, in 1893. Following this came a course at the Law School of the University of Michigan, from which he was graduated in 1896 with the degree of Bachelor of Laws, being admitted to the bars of Michigan and Illinois during the same year. At that time Mr. Harper located at Chicago, where he accepted a position on the faculty of the Chicago Law School, of which he continued to be a member for seven years. In the meantime he had engaged in the general practice of his profession, although of more recent years he has specialized to some extent in real estate and corporation law. His offices are located in Room 1015 at 11 South LaSalle Street. He is generally recognized as an authority on his specialties, and in a wider sense is one of the successful and progressive lawyers of the Chicago and western bar. He belongs to the Chicago Bar Association, the Illinois Bar Association and the American Bar Association, the Michigan Society of Chicago and the Michigan Alumni Association. He maintains an independent stand as to political affairs. While his offices are at Chicago, Mr. Harper has a lovely home at Tinley Park, Illinois, and as a great lover of flowers spends much of his recreational time working in his well-kept garden. He served four terms as mayor of Tinley Park, from 1911 to 1919.

On October 12, 1898, Mr. Harper married Mary Angela Kennedy, who was born at Calumet, Michigan, a daughter of Judge Cornelius Kennedy, of Michigan, and they have three children: Francis A., Jr., and Ellen and Mary Angela.

KEVIN KANE, while he belongs to the younger element in the legal profession, Kevin Kane has already proved his ability in some very important jurisprudence both at East Saint Louis, his home city, and in Illinois, and is recognized as one of the dependable and resourceful attorneys at the bar. He was born at East Saint Louis, October 23, 1894, a son of Jerre J. and Nellie L. (Lynch) Kane, and grandson of John J. Kane, a leader in politics, and a man of prominence in his part of Illinois. The maternal grandfather of Kevin Kane, Michael Lynch, was born in Ireland, but early came to the New World, and after a stay in Toronto, Canada, settled in New York State, from whence he enlisted in the Union army. Subsequently he became a railroad contractor in Illinois, to which state he moved following the close of the war. While in Toronto he married Margaret Burns.

Jerre J. Kane is very active in democratic politics, a former nominee for sheriff and an ex-city clerk. For many years he has been state committeeman for the Twenty-second District. At present he is sales manager for the Felson Tobacco Company. He and his wife have three children: Lucile, who is unmarried; Kevin, whose name heads this review; and J. J., Junior, who is also unmarried. The father is a member of the Roman Catholic Church, and belongs to the Knights of Columbus.

Kevin Kane attended St. Patrick's Parochial School and after completing his grammar-school courses, he entered Loyola Hall, the Academy of St. Louis University, from which he was graduated in 1912. He was graduated from St. Louis University, St. Louis, Missouri, in 1916, with the degree of Bachelor of Arts, and from Yale University in 1920, with the degree of Bachelor of Laws. In February, 1920, he was admitted to the bar of Illinois, and has been engaged in active practice since April of that year at East Saint Louis.

During the late war, while a student of Yale, he tried for the army and navy, but was rejected owing to the fact that he had to wear glasses. However, he managed to get into the special limited service with the Twenty-second United States Regulars, with whom he remained for two months at Camp Syracuse, when he was transferred to duty at Washington, D. C., and for four months was in the office of General March, chief of staff. In December, 1918, he received his honorable discharge and returned to Yale, where he completed his legal course. For three years while at Yale he was president of the Students' Council, and represented his law class for the same length of time.

Mr. Kane is unmarried. He belongs to the Roman Catholic Church. A Knight of Columbus, he is a past deputy grand master and deputy grand knight of the Knights of Columbus. He was a delegate to the National Democratic Convention held at New York in 1924, which is an honor not usually accorded one of his years, but his experience in politics has been a thorough one, and he inherits his father's ability in such matters, as he does his father's political convictions. Both stand very high in public esteem, and have honorably earned the confidence they inspire.

GEORGE W. BRICHLER, who for thirty years has been responsible for a very splendid service as an undertaker and funeral director in St. Clair County, was born in that county of Southern Illinois, and represents some of the old French stock who settled in this section of the state in pioneer times.

He was born at Belleville, St. Clair County, March 16, 1864, son of John Louis and Magdaline (Munier) Brichler. His grandparents, Christoff and Katherine (Adams) Brichler, were born and married in Lorraine, France, and came to America when John L. Brichler was fourteen years of age, settling on a farm in St. Clair County. The maternal grandparents, Paul and Magdaline (Gross) Munier, were also natives of Lorraine, France, and arrived in this country about twenty years later than the Brichlers. Both families were farming people in St. Clair County. John Louis Brichler devoted his long and industrious life to farming, and died in 1904. He was a very domestic man, devoted to his home and family. His wife died in 1909. They had three children: George W., John and Mary Magdaline. The son John married Tech Gundlacs, and they had a family of twelve children.

George W. Brichler attended the parochial schools at Belleville to the age of twelve, followed that with a course at the college at Teutopolis, Illinois, for a year, and graduated from the Mound City Business College at St. Louis, Missouri. He remained there as a teacher in the college for three years, and for one year was employed in Chicago by the J. Flanders Publishing Company. Subsequently he studied embalming, and in 1892 engaged in the undertaking business, the firm being Benner & Brichler. After ten years Mr. Brichler bought the interest of his partner and since then the business has been a corporation known as the Brichler Undertaking Company, of which Mr. Brichler is the owner. This is one of the oldest and the best equipped undertaking establishments in the city of East St. Louis. Mr. Brichler is also a director in the First National Bank of East St. Louis and the First National Bank of Lebanon, Illinois, and is financially interested in other enterprises.

He married Agnes Gundloch, who died three years after their marriage. On November 16, 1912, he married Esther Wuille. She had three sisters: Eva, who married Robert Traubel; Matilda; and Bettie, who married Ferdinand Weinert. Mr. and Mrs. Brichler are the parents of two children: George W., Jr., and Esther. Mr. Brichler is affiliated with the B. P. O. Elks, the Modern Woodmen of America, Royal Arcanum, the Foresters, Knights of Columbus and the Catholic Church.

DAYTON G. GORDLEY, county clerk of Brown County, an office he has held for several terms, was a successful farmer before he became a county official, and he represents a family that has been in Brown County for three generations, since pioneer times.

He was born in Brown County, February 2, 1877. His grandfather, John Gordley, came from Kentucky, locating east of Hersman, Brown County, where he developed a farm. His life was cut short when he was killed by a falling tree, and he is buried in a private cemetery in that locality. His sons were William, John, Edward and James S. James S. Gordley was also a native of Brown County, and spent his life just east of Mt. Sterling, where he died in 1879, at the age of forty-three. Some of the land owned by him is still part of the family estate. As a young man during Civil war times he went across the plains to California as a gold seeker, and on his return to Illinois engaged in farming. He was a democrat, confined his interest in politics to voting, and was not a member of any church. However, his brother Edward was prominent in politics, serving one or more terms as sheriff.

James S. Gordley married, November 20, 1873, Isabel Brockman, daughter of John R. and Elizabeth E. Brockman, who came to Illinois from Kentucky and were farmers in the Hersman locality. James S. Gordley had two sons, Arthur Clyde and Dayton G., and his widow subsequently married Burrell Badgett and died in 1911.

Dayton G. Gordley and his older brother grew up on the farm. He attended high school at Mt. Sterling and during his vacations worked on the farm and then made farming his regular vocation. His mother was his housekeeper until his marriage. When he engaged in farming for himself he took eighty acres, the property of his mother, land that had depreciated in fertility and improvements. He started there with a capital of three hundred dollars, and had a difficult struggle in making a living and building up the land at the same time. It was, in fact, seven years before he was on a money making basis, and he still owns the old homestead, now a very valuable and productive property.

Mr. Gordley left the farm in 1918 to enter the office of county clerk at Mt. Sterling. While on the farm he had served as road commissioner and as director of the Hazel Dell School. He was also an election official. In the primaries of 1918 he had two competitors for the democratic nomination for county clerk. The following November he was easily

elected, with a plurality of one hundred and sixty-four, and succeeded H. A. Perry in office. In the 1924 election he had no opposition. Mr. Gordley is a member of Hardin Lodge No. 44, Ancient Free and Accepted Masons, at Mt. Sterling, and Unity Lodge No. 310, Independent Order of Odd Fellows, in which he has filled all the chairs, being a past noble grand. During the World war he was registered under the second draft act, but was never called to duty.

In June, 1900, at Springfield, he married Miss Hallie Bloomfield, a native of Brown County, and daughter of Robert and Mary (Bower) Bloomfield. Her mother was a daughter of Doctor Bower, who came from Pennsylvania, while her father's people came from Ohio. Robert Bloomfield was reared in Brown County, and he and his wife are now living retired at Mt. Sterling. Mrs. Gordley has a brother, William, at Quincy. Mrs. Gordley attended high school at Mt. Sterling and Springfield, and was a teacher in Brown County until her marriage. They have three children, Dorothy, James Robert and Richard Glenn. Dorothy after graduating from the Mt. Sterling High School taught four years and is now the wife of C. M. Briggs, of Vincennes, Indiana. The son James Robert graduated from high school, from the Brown Business College at Jacksonville, and is a clerk in the office of the Standard Oil Company at Decatur. He married Dorothy Branch.

GEORGE M. AHLSCHWEDE, JR., as a youth learned the machinist trade, training a natural bent for mechanics, and having in addition talent for executive work and business management. He has for many years been one of the efficiency men with frequent promotions to higher responsibilities in the service of the great corporation known as the International Harvester Company of America. Mr. Ahlschwede is now manager of the corporation in its Southern Illinois territory, with headquarters in East St. Louis.

He was born at Milford, Nebraska, July 18, 1887, son of George M. and Mary Ahlschwede. His maternal grandparents, Jacob and Louise Roller, were born in Alsace-Lorraine, and on coming to America settled at Huntington, Indiana, where their daughter Mary was born. The paternal grandparents were Christ Ahlschwede and wife, who were natives of Prussia, where the Ahlschwedes were at one time a wealthy family, but lost their property and left the old world through political and racial troubles. George M. Ahlschwede, Sr., was about eighteen months old when brought to this country in 1850. He has been a wagon and carriage maker and farmer. The mother died March 1, 1915. There were ten children: Emma; Katherine, who is married and has five children; William, who is the father of one child; Fred, who has a family of five children; Lawrence, who has two children; Miss Louise; George M., Jr.; Christ, who is married and has one child; Bertha, who died leaving three children; and Mary, the mother of two children.

George M. Ahlschwede, Jr., attended the grammar and high schools of Milford, Nebraska, and served an apprenticeship at the machinists and moulders trade. He followed these skilled occupations for five years, and then gave a new direction in his mechanical talents when he became a salesman for the International Harvester Company of America branch at Davenport, Iowa, in February, 1915.

Since then he has spent a decade with the International Harvester Company as salesman and expert. He has the advantage of a thorough technical knowledge of every product manufactured by the corporation, and is also a man of system in business and a thoroughly able salesman and organizer as well. After spending eighteen months at the Davenport branch he was transferred to the Dubuque, Iowa, branch, and in November, 1919, was made assistant manager of the Milwaukee branch, continuing there until November 21, 1922. At the latter date he was made manager of the Southern Illinois branch at East St. Louis. His territory comprises twenty-two counties. Mr. Ahlschwede's record is a remarkable one in a corporation having thousands of employes, and his advancement over many older men has been due solely to merit. He married at Hebron, Nebraska, October 16, 1912, Miss Edna Lindahl, daugher of Charles and Minnie Lindahl. Her father, now deceased, was a contractor and builder. She is one of four children, the others being Roy, Lester and Zola. Mr. and Mrs. Ahlschwede have a daughter, Lois. They are members of the Presbyterian Church, and he is a thirty-second degree Scottish Rite Mason and Shriner.

HARRY A. ROTH is president of Harry A. Roth Company, real estate, an organization directly built up by Harry A. Roth and infused with his ideas, ideals and enthusiasm as one of the master real estate salesmen of his generation.

Mr. Roth is a native of Hungary, came to America in 1905, and for over twenty years has been a resident of Chicago. For several years he was an executive in the Pyle National Company of Chicago. This company first introduced the electric headlight for locomotives, and for many years has been the world's largest manufacturer of this important adjunct to railroad equipment.

It was late in 1923 that Mr. Roth joined the young firm of Krenn & Dato, which had been given the selling agency and management of the extensive property interests of Mrs. Rockefeller McCormick in Chicago and environs. As director of sales for this firm Mr. Roth during 1924 sold six and a half million dollars worth of property, setting perhaps a unique record in the real estate field for a man so new in the business.

On June 1, 1925, Mr. Roth entered the real estate business for himself as senior member of the firm Roth & Gordon. In the fall of the same year he took over all the interests, changing the firm style to Harry A. Roth & Company. During the first five months following the organization of the firm in June it sold over one million dollars worth of property. Mr. Roth personally controls about ten million dollars worth of real estate. Up to and including the winter of 1925-26 he concentrated all his efforts on practically one location—Niles Center, thus carrying out his idea that a successful salesman should concentrate all his energies on one idea at a time. He has a staff of about one hundred and fifty competent and thoroughly experienced salesmen. The personnel department has at its head an able official whose function it is to meet with the salesmen daily, and by this personal contact and lectures prepare the salesman for meeting every exigency that may arise in a transaction. The Roth Company's offices are in the Harris Trust Building at 111 West Monroe Street, occupying one-half of the sixth floor.

Under former conditions in the real estate field in Chicago it was the custom for real estate men to largely discontinue their efforts during the winter months, particularly in the residential sections and subdivisions. While with the Krenn & Dato firm Mr. Roth sold a quarter of a million dollars worth of property in the month of December, including the Christmas holidays. This set the pace, and his own as well as other real estate concerns now continue their efforts all the year through. Mr. Roth is actively associated with various civic organizations and is a Mason and member of the Covenant Club.

MISS MARTHA LYNN CONNOLE on the record of what she has done, and her connections with public and civic affairs, is the leading woman attorney in East St. Louis, where she has practiced law for the past seven years. She is president of the East St. Louis Republican Woman's Club.

She was born at Carrollton, Greene County, Illinois, in 1883, daughter of Anthony and Mary (Markham) Connole. Her paternal grandparents were born and spent their lives in Ireland. Her maternal grandparents were Mathew and Hannah Markham, the Markhams being of English ancestry, while Mathew's wife's people were Irish. They were married in the old country, and their daughter, Mary Markham, was born at Carrolton, Illinois. Anthony Connole was born in Ireland, received his early education there, and at the age of seventeen, came to America, Carrollton, Illinois, to join his older brother, Patrick, who had preceded him several years and had located in Greene County, Illinois. Anthony Connole reached this country about the time the Civil war broke out, he enlisted in the Union army in the first Missouri Cavalry. After serving out his enlistment he came to Illinois and here enlisted in the 63rd Illinois Infantry. He was all through the war and was once slightly wounded. After leaving the army he located at Carrollton in Greene County, and by study and experience perfected a general knowledge of the law. He became clerk of the Circuit Court of Greene County, engaged in the real estate business, and at the time of his death was proprietor of the county abstract office. He was prominent in local democratic politics, was a member of the Grand Army of the Republic and a Methodist. He was killed in an automobile accident in February, 1920. His widow now lives at Carrolton. Their family consisted of eight children: Jennie, who married Edward F. Ford; Henry, who married Mary Rickart and they have two children, Paul and David; Lida, wife of E. A. Thornhill, and mother of a daughter, Mary Virginia; Anna, who is married and has a daughter, Annabelle; Anthony, who married Mabel Hodson, and their five children are Doris, Ruth, Anthony, Thomas and Robert; Miss Martha Lynn; Paul, who married Marie Carrigan and has two children, Roberta and Jack; and Milo, who by his marriage to Edna Hoffinger has two children, Helen and James.

Martha Lynn Connole was an educator before she qualified for the practice of law. She completed her own schooling in the grammar and high schools of Carrollton. Four years of her teaching work was done in the rural districts, four years in grade schools and four years in high school at White Hall, Illinois. She lived with her brother Henry at Madison while studying law at the St. Louis University, and was graduated with the LL. B. degree in 1917 and admitted to the Illinois bar the same year. In January 1918, she located at East St. Louis. During most of the World war period she was employed in the office of the fuel administrator of this district, served on the Woman's Council of Defense, on the draft board, and was a four minute speaker, delivering patriotic addresses all over this part of the state. She was also identified with the Red Cross. Since the close of the war Miss Connole has carried on a general practice, specializing however in probate and chancery cases.

She is a member of the Board of Education of East St. Louis and is president of the Business and Professional Women's State Club as well as chairman of the East St. Louis Republican Women's Club. She belongs to the Illinois State Federation of Women's Clubs, has held all the chairs in the Eastern Star, White Shrine and Rebekahs, and is a member of the Methodist Episcopal Church.

HAROLD A. DONOVAN, except for the eighteen months while he was with the colors during the World war Harold A. Donovan has been engaged in the practice of law at East St. Louis since 1913. He is an attorney with a large practice, largely involving real estate law and real estate transactions, and in this has found a congenial life work.

Mr. Donovan was born at St. Louis, Missouri, September 12, 1888, son of Joseph E. and Mary (Mahoney) Donovan. All his grandparents lived in and around St. Louis, and were prominent people there. His paternal grandfather was Daniel H. Donovan. His maternal grandfather, Mahoney, was one of the founders of the St. Louis Times. Joseph E. Donovan, who died in 1923, had a long and active career at St. Louis and was also well and favorably known in East St. Louis. During the Civil war he was a Confederate soldier with the First Missouri Volunteer regiment. He was wounded and captured, and was held in the Federal prison on Ship Island in the Mississippi River until recovering. On returning to St. Louis he married, took up the real estate business, and removing to East St. Louis, was not only conspicuously successful in his private business but made it an opportunity and medium for a great deal of disinterested public service.

He was the first citizen to sell real estate on the deferred payment plan, and exercised an important influence in bringing about the raising of the street grades and the general improvement of the growing city on the east side of the Mississippi. He was a Catholic and was president of the St. Vincent de Paul Society of his church. His wife, Mary Mahoney, died in 1897. They were the parents of eleven children, the survivors being Frank L., who married Mary Angert; Irwin, who married Laura Edwards; Loras, who married L. H. Walsh and had two children; Loretta, who became the wife of John J. Hogan and has four children; Harold A.; and Norbert J., who married Arline Proctor and has one child.

Harold A. Donovan received practically all his liberal education in various departments of St. Louis University, including his high school course. He graduated in law from the university in 1913 and in the same year engaged in practice at East St. Louis. His practice has been of a general nature, but more and more he has put emphasis on civil law, particularly matters pertaining to real estate titles, transfers, mortgages and special assessment law. The law has fully satisfied his ambition, and while active in politics, has avoided public office.

On January 18, 1918, he enlisted for service in the World war, being assigned to the quartermaster's department of the army at Jacksonville, Florida. On June 6, 1918, he sailed for overseas, landing at Brest and was sent to the headquarters of the quartermaster's department at St. Nazaire, where he did detached work in forwarding supplies to the front. He remained abroad for fully six months after the armistice, and on July 5, 1919, landed in Hoboken, was sent to Camp Merritt, and then to Camp Taylor at Louisville, where he received his honorable discharge July 17. He is a member of the American Legion and the St. Clair Country Club, and is affiliated with the Knights of Columbus and the Catholic Church.

On June 1, 1918, a few days before going overseas, he marired at Newport News, Virginia, Miss Emma Bohn, daughter of Henry and Louise Bohn. Her father was a grocery merchant and director of the Manchester Bank of St. Louis. The children of Henry and Louise Bohn were: Harry M., who married Agnes Young and has three children; Stella, who became the wife of Joseph O. Hoffman and became the mother of five children; Lydia, who married Edward J. Bingle and has one child; Adelaide, who married Marlan H. Stauf and has one child; and Frank. To the marriage of Mr. and Mrs. Donovan were born four children: Louise, Dorothy, Harold A., Jr., and Joseph T.

FRANCIS J. HOULIHAN has been a member of the Chicago bar for over thirty years. The work that has distinguished him among Chicago lawyers has been the skill with which he has handled cases in bankruptcy and involving other commercial issues and problems.

Mr. Houlihan was born at Ogdensburg, New York, July 20, 1865, son of Francis R. and Mary (O'Gorman) Houlihan. His father, who was born at Ogdensburg in 1831, while a boy went on the Great Lakes, becoming a sailor, and in the course of his voyages he and a sailor friend reached the port of Chicago and spent some time in that city. Later he returned to Ogdensburg, where he became a contractor, building up an organization for the unloading and loading of lake ships, with iron ore, lumber, coal and grain. Later he held an office in the customs house and was one of the prominent citizens of Ogdensburg, serving as alderman for several terms, and at the time of his death in 1890 was about to be appointed as American consul at Prescott, Canada, under the administration of President Benjamin Harrison. He was a republican and a member of the Catholic Church. Francis R. Houlihan's wife was born in County Clare, Ireland, in 1835, and died in 1882. She was the mother of five sons and five daughters, Francis J. being the second son and sixth child.

Francis J. Houlihan spent his youth at Ogdensburg and attended school there, including the Ogdensburg Academy, from which he graduated in 1889. In 1890 he arived in Chicago and studied for his profession in the Northwestern University Law School, where he was graduated in 1892. On graduating and being admitted to the bar he was associated with the firm of Byam, Weinschenk & Hirschl, then became a member of the firm O'Hara, Houlihan, Rosenthal, Kurz & Hirschl, later Rosenthal, Kurz & Houlihan, and he is now senior member of the law firm Houlihan & Michels, with offices in the Temple Block at 77 West Washington Street. The firms of which he has been a member have handled an extensive general practice and corporation work. He has been identified with such cases as involve the legal interests or business reorganization of the West Pullman Car Works, the Graham & Sons Bank, the case of Edward W. Morrison and various canal and other bankruptcy cases.

Mr. Houlihan is a member of the Chicago, Illinois and American Bar Associations and of the Law Institute. While living in New York he served as a member of the National Guard. He is a Knight of Columbus, a member of the Alhambra Club, the Catholic Church, and in politics is a republican.

On April 28, 1897, he married Miss Mary J. Conway. a native of Shabanse, Illinois. To their marriage were born two sons and three daughters: Robert A., Mary T., Eileen; Julia (who died in infancy) and Francis J., Jr.

The son Robert A. Houlihan made the supreme sacrifice as a soldier during the World war. He went to France as first class private with Battery F of the One Hundred and Twenty-second Field Artillery, being in action at St. Mihiel and in the Argonne, and on October 31, 1918, died in the United States Evacuation Hospital at Blois. In 1919 Floyd Gibbons, the famous war correspondent of the Chicago Tribune, sent the story narrating the bringing of the first American soldier from the soil of France back to his old home, and relating in brief outline how the father's love for a dead hero had overcome the red tape, the prejudices and positive orders of government and military officials. The father went to

France in the spring of 1919, while the representatives of the great powers were disputing over the treaty, and after weeks of persistent effort secured the body of his dead son and took it back with him to Chicago.

EDWARD EVERETT CLARK, almost a life long resident of Brown County, where he has been known and esteemed as an educator and business man, represents a family of real pioneers in this section of the state.

His grandfather was Abner Clark, who was born in the vicinity of Guilford Court House, North Carolina, February 12, 1777. Four years later he was a boy holding onto his mother's apron strings while she witnessed the battle of Guilford Court House between the American patriots and the army of General Cornwallis. Abner Clark from North Carolina moved west to Kentucky, and in 1835 arrived in Illinois, settling in Pea Ridge Township, in what was then Schuyler, now Brown, County. His oldest son, Calvin Clark, had come to Illinois just before the deep snow of 1830. He resembled somewhat the historic character of "Johnny Appleseed," and as he passed along he scattered blue grass seed brought from Kentucky, some of it falling on the fertile soil of Brown County, and probably from that seed have been propagated many of the blue grass meadows known in the county in modern times. Abner Clark spent the rest of his life as a farmer in Brown County. He married Nancy Gorham. On coming to Illinois with his family he brought two wagons, one pulled by a team of horses and another by a yoke of cattle driven by his son-in-law, George W. Coffman. Among other incidents of the journey was a prairie fire which they encountered and which nearly destroyed the ox team and outfit. Besides Calvin Clark the other children of Abner Clark and wife were: Harrison M., William T., Angell A. and Francis A., all of whom became farmers in Brown County; Perneta, who married Benjamin Adams; Inetta, who married Marion Wilgus; Delilah, who became the wife of George W. Coffman; Perlina, who married William T. Rigg; and Catherine, whose husband was Levin Wilson. His daughters all lived in this section of Illinois and many of their descendants are still there. Three of the grandsons of Abner Clark were Union soldiers in the Civil war; Henry, son of Harrison M., who died of measles at Humboldt, Tennessee, during the war; Harvey Clark, son of Calvin, who survived his military experience and died many years later as a farmer; and Thomas A., son of William T., who was in several battles and was badly wounded but survived and died at his farm home February 1, 1886.

Francis A. Clark, son of Abner and father of Edward E., was born September 11, 1820, the year of the death of Daniel Boone. Practically all his formal education was acquired during one term of three months spent in a log school house. He was fifteen years old when he accompanied his parents from Kentucky to Illinois, and in addition to farming he engaged in cattle trading, being associated with the noted Jacob Strawn of Morgan County and frequently swimming the Illinois River with his cattle. His father, Abner Clark, died August 28, 1849. Francis A. Clark was a man of much native ability, good business judgment, and though he began his career as a farm hand at twelve dollars a month he acquired a considerable landed estate. He was never elected to office, but was a staunch abolitionist and republican. He was never identified with any church or social organization. Francis A. Clark died June 30, 1896, at the age of seventy-six. He married Eliza Rankin, daughter of John Rankin, a Scotch-Irishman. John Rankin and his daughter Eliza were both born near Londonderry, Ireland, and they came to the United State when Eliza was one year old. For a time the Rankins lived in Philadelphia and then moved out to Brown County, Illinois. Eliza Rankin Clark died February 14, 1867, and she and her husband are buried in the cemetery at Mt. Sterling. Her children were: John Harrison, who died in childhood; Catherine McAdoo, wife of Thomas McMurray, a resident of Rocky Ford, Colorado; Alexander Hadden, who died in Brown County in 1917; Abner, a Methodist minister, who has preached in different parts of Illinois and is now a resident of Brown County; William A., a farmer and stock man, who died March 12, 1917; Edmund Knowles, who died in childhood; Lydia, who died in Brown County in 1910, wife of Thomas R. McDannold; Edward Everett; and Benjamin F., a resident of Belle Fourche, South Dakota.

Edward Everett Clark was born in Pea Ridge Township, Brown County, June 28, 1862. At the time of his birth the Union and Confederate armies were fighting the famous peninsular campaign in Virginia. After attending common schools in Brown County he entered Illinois College at Jacksonville, where he was graduated with the class of 1883. Other students in Illinois College at the same time were Richard Yates, Jr., and William Jennings Bryan. Mr. Clark devoted some fifteen years of his life after graduation to teaching. He taught in high schools and for a time was teacher of history in Chaddock College at Quincy. His last work in the school room was at Hersman, Illinois. Since then he has engaged in the real estate and loan business, operating a rental agency, has personally dealt in property in Mt. Sterling and for a number of years represented the Straus Brothers of Fort Wayne, Indiana, in the handling of farm lands. He was one of the three men who organized the Mt. Sterling Telephone Company, his associates being Edwin Pendleton and Alexander H. Clark. Alexander H. Clark operated the first telephone exchange in Brown County. Mr. Clark has been active in church work, and for a score of years was superintendent of the Sunday School of the Christian Church. He is a member of the Modern Woodmen of America. During the World war he aided the recruits in filling out their questionnaires. His own son was registered for the service and put in class four.

Mr. Clark married at Mt. Sterling, Illinois, January 20, 1887, Miss Meribah E. Ritchey. She was born just west of Mt. Sterling, January 8, 1862, daughter of James and Eliza (McKean) Ritchey. Her father came from

Kentucky to Illinois about the same time as the Clark family, and spent his life as a farmer. The Ritchey children were: Alexander, of Mt. Sterling; Robert, who died in Florida; James, who was drowned in Brown County in 1881; Mrs. Clark; and Emma, who died in Brown County in 1891, wife of Clayton Coffman. Mr. and Mrs. Clark had two children. The daughter Meribah E. is a graduate of the Mt. Sterling High School and the University of Illinois, later attended the Teachers College of Columbia University at New York, and has earned distinction in the field of education, being now one of the faculty of the Peabody Demonstration School of Nashville, Tennessee. She has earned two degrees, an A. B. in history and an M. A. in education from Teachers College. The son, James Ritchey Clark, a farmer in Brown County, married Laura Clemmons and has four children, Ruth M., Virginia M., Clemmons E. and Lola G. Edward E. Clark and wife have holdings of 270 acres of good farming land near Mt. Sterling. Also a business block and residence in the city of Mt. Sterling.

HENRY CLINTON EVANS, of Alton, has had an extensive experience in an industry that in recent years has had a phenomenal growth, the manufacture of paper box board. He is now general manager of the Alton Box Board and Paper Company.

Mr. Evans was born at Troy, Indiana, January 4, 1875, son of Hiram and Mary Elizabeth (Harpold) Evans, his father a native of Indiana and his mother of Kentucky, both of old Virginia ancestry. His parents lived out their lives in Indiana, and of their six children Henry C. was the fourth.

Reared and educated in Troy, where he attended the public schools, at the age of twelve he began working during summer vacations in a chair factory. He continued to attend school until he was fifteen, and then became an apprentice in a printing office, and his experience was largely in the printing business until 1897. In that year, after completing a course in the Spencerian Business College at Louisville, Kentucky, he became clerk in the office of the old Air Line Louisville, Evansville and St. Louis Railway at Louisville, now a part of the Southern Railway System.

In 1899 Mr. Evans became bookkeeper for the Southern Straw Board Company at Rockport, Indiana. He also performed the duties of stenographer. While in the office he also familiarized himself with the technical details of manufacture, and in 1902 went to Chillicothe, Illinois, to assist in rebuilding and operating a box board mill. In 1905 he helped move the plant to Pekin, Illinois, remaining there during the reconstruction period. His next service was with the United Box Board Company at Muncie, Indiana, and in 1906 he was transferred to Lockport, New York, where he had charge of the general offices as cashier. In 1908 he was in the service of the American Seating Company at Buffalo, establishing a cost system, but after a year returned to the box board business at Pekin, Illinois, as manager. He was then put in the sales department of the business at Chicago, and had charge of the output of the Central Box Board Company of Rock Falls. He was then in the sales department of the Chicago Coated Board Company until February, 1914, when he was made general manager of the Alton Box Board and Paper Company. He has developed it into one of the important industries of Alton, and has a business with two hundred employes under him. He is also interested in the manufacture of a boiler preservative and is president of the Corrugated Fibre Lath Company of Alton.

Mr. Evans married in 1900 Miss Mary Elizabeth Freehrer. Their three daughters are Mary Elizabeth, Claretta and Joan. Mr. Evans is affiliated with the Masonic Order, the Elks and the Modern Woodmen of America.

DAVID C. BYUS gave a new significance to the old phrase "militant christianity" when, still an active minister of the Gospel, he became a candidate for and was elected sheriff of Cass County, the office he still holds. It is an interesting alliance of the church with the political machinery that has most to do with the enforcement of the law and the preservation of a strict moral standard. Mr. Byus bears the distinction of being the only Ordained Minister serving as sheriff in the United States.

Mr. Byus, who has been in the Methodist ministry in Illinois since 1914, was born at Beech Hill, Mason County, West Virginia, December 16, 1876. His grandfather, Benjamin Byus, was born in what is now West Virginia, and the family were among the pioneers on the western side of the Blue Ridge Mountains. Lieut. William A. Byus, father of Sheriff Byus, was a native of West Virginia, had a rural school education, and at the age of sixteen entered the Union Army as a private, serving in the Army of the Potomac and taking part in the battles of Bull Run and the Lynchburg raid. At the close of the war he was a lieutenant in Company D of the Fourth West Virginia Infantry, and was mustered out at Wheeling. In after years he was commander of Beech Hill Post of the Grand Army of the Republic. He was a farmer, for many years a general merchant at Beech Hill, and is now living retired at the age of eighty-two. He has been a doer of good at all times and for many years a local preacher of the Methodist Church. William A. Byus married Catherine Morris, daughter of Benjamin Morris, who was a native of the Kanawha Valley of West Virginia. The Morris family were early settlers there and were prominent in the Methodist Church, one of them, Thomas Morris, being an early bishop in the Kanawha Valley. Mrs. William A. Byus died in November, 1913, mother of the following children: John, mill superintendent of the American Tin Plate Company at Elwood, Indiana; George E., a merchant near Beech Hill, West Virginia; Sallie M., wife of James Woodyard, of Columbus, Ohio; David C.; Barney, a farmer near Beech Hill; William A., Jr., a Methodist minister at Charleston, West Virginia; and Kate, wife of Thomas McCutcheon, of Wheeling.

David C. Byus acquired most of his education at Point Pleasant, West Virginia, worked in his father's store at Beech Hill, and after his marriage located on a farm near there. From early youth he was interested in religious work, and in 1910 was licensed to preach by the West Virginia Methodist Conference. In 1914 he was transferred to the Illinois Conference, having his first pastorate at Rock Bridge, Greene County. He has been continuously identified with the Jacksonville district, and in 1919 moved to Cass County, serving the Chandlerville Church five years, and is now at Virginia. For two years he was mayor of Chandlerville, using his office to enforce the law. In 1924 he was elected sheriff of Cass County, and nominated again in 1926, being chosen as a republican, though his platform was law and order. He is the second republican ever elected sheriff of Cass County, and his rival for that office was Harold Farrar. During his first year as sheriff Mr. Byus arrested and jailed more violators of the law than in any three year period previously. He also arrested about one hundred men who plead guilty and paid their fines. His administration has confiscated a great number of stills, slot machines and punch boards, and has been responsible for a really impartial enforcement of the law.

Mr. Byus during the World war was preaching in Sangamon County and served as a member of the County Council of Defense. He is a Master Mason, member of the Knights of Pythias, Modern Woodmen of America, and a member of the Kiwanis Club of Virginia. He has always joined actively in the drives for the support of the Red Cross and Salvation Army, in the sale of Christmas seals and in other campaigns that represent the moral and charitable pulses of humanity.

He married at Point Pleasant, West Virginia, September 2, 1896, Miss May First, daughter of Madison and Rena (Fogle) First, her mother a native of Pennsylvania and of Dutch ancestry, while her father was born in Ohio. Mrs. Byus has a sister, Mrs. James McBride, of Indianapolis. The children of Mr. and Mrs. Byus are: Sylvia, wife of R. S. Armstrong, of East Lansing, Michigan, and mother of Estaline and Audry; Guy C., who married February 7, 1926, Bernadine McWilliams, of Virginia, and who served two years in the navy since the World war, being discharged after the disarmament conference and reduction of the naval forces, and is now chief deputy to his father; Morris, a student in Bradley Polytechnic Institute at Peoria; Thelma, attending school at East Lansing, Michigan; Maxwell, attending the Virginia High School; William M., also in high school; while the younger children are John, Paul, Roberta and Virginia Catherine.

WILLIAM D. BERRY has been identified with Roodhouse over forty-five years, and during that time has been a merchant and for many years a banker, connected with the First National Bank, of which he is now president.

Mr. Berry was born at Maysville, Kentucky, February 4, 1862. His grandfather was a native of Maryland and an early settler in Kentucky, becoming a farmer near Maysville. He was the father of sons named Taylor T., Alfred C., Thomas and William H.

William H. Berry was a native of Maysville, Kentucky, acquired a good education, though he never attended college, and for many years was prominent in educational affairs. He was a southerner in sympathy, but was not a soldier in the Civil war. About the close of the war he removed to Illinois, and for a number of years was principal of schools of Petersburg, this state. Leaving Illinois, he went to Kansas City and was principal of one of the schools of that city for twenty years, being a contemporary of the great educator Professor Greenwood. He died at Kansas City in the fall of 1923, at the advanced age of ninety-six. William H. Berry served a number of years as county superintendent of schools of Menard County, Illinois. He was a member of the Christian Church. William H. Berry married Nancy A. Long, who was born at Maysville, Kentucky, in 1840, and died at Petersburg, Illinois, in 1880. Their children were: Albert C., who lived at Lincoln, Nebraska, where he lost his life in an automobile accident in December, 1925; Mary E., who died at Kansas City, wife of Harmon J. Locke; Annie B., who died in Kansas City in February, 1926, wife of Stephen H. VanDoren; William D.; Dr. George F. and Dr. Fred R., both residents of Kansas City.

William D. Berry was about three years of age when the family came to Illinois, and he lived at Petersburg, attending public schools until the age of eighteen. He taught two terms of school in Menard County and in June, 1880, came to Roodhouse, and for five years was a drug clerk for Dr. J. W. Hosman. He then engaged in the drug business as member of the firm Berry & Wolfe, his partner being J. H. Wolfe. After the death of Mr. Wolfe in April, 1897, he carried on the business alone until the fall of 1916, when he sold out, having given his energies continuously to the store for thirty years.

Mr. Berry became one of the organizers of the First National Bank in 1907. He was elected vice president, the president being William H. Ainsworth and the cashier, Charles T. Bates. On the death of Mr. Ainsworth in February, 1921, Mr. Berry was elected president. The vice president is now E. J. VanTuyle, and the other directors are Charles T. Bates, Frank C. Scott and John B. Hunt. The bank still operates on a capital of fifty thousand dollars, and has undivided profits of thirty-five thousand dollars and surplus of ten thousand dollars, after having paid regular dividends all through the years. Mr. Berry is a land owner, has been identified with farming, and for many years has been a feeder of live stock for the market. He has been a member of the town board of Roodhouse, town treasurer, and was assistant postmaster under Ellis Briggs. A democrat, he cast his first presidential vote for Grover Cleveland in 1884. Mr. Berry is affiliated with the Knights of Pythias and Woodmen of the World.

He married at Roodhouse, December 11, 1884, Miss Fannie E. Fisk, daughter of Isaac T. and Elizabeth (Freeto) Fisk. Mrs. Berry was born at Lemont, Illinois, and died in January, 1892. Her daughter, Nellie N., died soon after her mother. The son, George L., now a farmer at Roodhouse, was educated in high school, attended a college of pharmacy in St. Louis, and was associated with his father in the drug business for a number of years. He entered the army under the draft, being the first to go from Greene County, and was assigned to the Medical Corps and went overseas. William D. Berry in March, 1893, married at Kansas City Jennie R. Ash, who was born at Roodhouse, daughter of Jesse and Sarah A. (Gilmore) Ash, a member of a prominent family there. Her mother was a daughter of John Gilmore and a sister of William P. Gilmore, president of the Roodhouse Bank. Mr. and Mrs. Berry's only child, Clifton, died when sixteen months old.

CHARLES T. BATES has been closely identified with the business of Roodhouse for over forty-five years. He came to the town when a boy, has been best known in banking circles here, and is cashier of the First National Bank of Roodhouse.

Charles T. Bates' father, Theron M. Bates, was born in Ashtabula County, Ohio, son of Melzo Bates, who was born and reared at Cambridge, Massachusetts, being one of a family of seven children. As a young man he moved out to northeastern Ohio and spent his life in business as a merchant at Pierpont in Ashtabula County, where he died in 1875, at the age of fifty-six. His wife was Laura Gould, a daughter of Archibald and Sarah (Williams) Gould. She was born in New York State. Theron M. Bates was one of three children, his brother, Osro A. Bates, having spent his active life at Erie, Pennsylvania, and his sister, Vesta, became the wife of Hebert A. Mixer, and she died at Pierpont, Ohio, in 1905.

Theron M. Bates began his railroad career with the Pennsylvania System as a dispatcher, rising to superintendent. On September 1, 1879, he came to Roodhouse and was division superintendent for the Chicago & Alton Railway until 1904. In that year he became general superintendent of the Indiana, Illinois and Iowa Railway Company, but in 1906 resigned and spent the rest of his life as a retired citizen of Coshocton, Ohio, where he died May 27, 1920. During the Civil war he enlisted in a company in Astabula County and was elected its lieutenant. Theron M. Bates married Frances Dutcher, who was born and reared at Batavia, New York, daughter of Daniel and Roena (Wright) Dutcher. She died at East St. Louis in 1914, and both she and her husband are buried at Roodhouse. Their children were: Charles T., F. Roodhouse; Flora F., of Coshocton; Blanche, wife of O. P. Begole, of Coshocton; and Frank A. Bates, of Chicago.

Charles T. Bates was born at Pierpont, Ashtabula County, Ohio, January 10, 1864. He attended school there, also at Erie, Pennsylvania, and was fifteen years of age when his parents moved to Jacksonville, Illinois. He finished his education in the Brown Business College at Jacksonville, Illinois, and his first work was in the offices of the Chicago & Alton Railway at Roodhouse. A few months later, on August 9, 1881, he entered the Roodhouse Bank, being then seventeen years of age. His service and career as a banker covers a period of forty-five years. In May, 1889, he resigned from the Roodhouse Bank to assist in opening the Peoples Bank of Roodhouse. His associates in organizing this institution were his father, T. M. Bates, H. C. Morrow, principal of the Roodhouse High School and Mr. Morrow's father, William M. Morrow, a prominent farmer of Greene county. Theron M. Bates was elected president of the Peoples Bank and his son, cashier. In 1907 the Peoples Bank was reorganized as the First National Bank of Roodhouse, with capital of fifty thousand dollars, and Mr. Bates has continued as cashier of this institution from the beginning.

Mr. Bates for thirteen consecutive years was president of the Roodhouse School Board and has given a great deal of his time to community affairs. He was one of the five commissioners in the organization and forming of the Roodhouse Water Corporation. He is a charter member of E. M. Husted Lodge of Masons, a charter member of the Roodhouse Chapter of Royal Arch Masons, a member of the Knights Templars Commandery at Carrollton, Illinois, and is one of the trustees of the Congregational Church. He has acted upon his convictions that it is the duty of every citizen to vote. He cast his first presidential vote for Benjamin Harrison.

Mr. Bates married at Roodhouse, October 15, 1890, Anna Morrow, daughter of William M. and Emeline (Smith) Morrow. She was born at Roodhouse and died there March 1, 1900, at the age of thirty years. Her daughter, Margaret, is the wife of Ernest B. Smith, of Topeka, Kansas, and has one child, Patricia Ann. Theron Merrell Bates, the second of the family, was educated in the Roodhouse High School, and is now an advertising manufacturer at Coshocton, Ohio. He married May Vinyard, of White Hall, and has a daughter, Anna May. Dr. Charles William Bates, the youngest of the family, graduated from the Roodhouse High School, was a lieutenant of aviation during the World war, and in 1924 graduated from Northwestern University College of Dentistry, and is now practicing his profession in Chicago, Illinois. Mr. Charles T. Bates married at Roodhouse, September 2, 1902, Mrs. Mary Roodhouse Bowlby, daughter of John Roodhouse, founder of the town named after his, and sister of William C. Roodhouse, of the prominent family of that name of Greene County. Mr. and Mrs. Bates are the parents of four children, Helen Gould, Evelin and Frances, twins, and Vesta. The three oldest children are graduates of high school.

CHARLES BENJAMIN ROODHOUSE is a resident of White Hall, and has spent his active career as a Greene County farmer. He has been a very active and substantial citizen, and his name is the more interesting because of the old and prominent family he represents in Greene County. Mr. Roodhouse's wife was a Tunison, and the Tunisons as well as the Roodhouses helped clear away the wilderness and develop the first farms in Greene County.

The old English home of the Roodhouse family was in Yorkshire, England. Benjamin Roodhouse, Sr., the first pioneer of the name in Greene County, Illinois, left Yorkshire and brought his family to America and arrived in Greene County in what has been remembered by the old pioneers as the winter of the deep snow, January, 1831. He died only a few months after settling in Greene County. His sons were Benjamin and John, twins, Peter and James, and a daughter, Jane, who never married. The son Benjamin was born in Yorkshire February 8, 1825. One of his daughters while recently visiting in England was in the old church and examined the church records, finding a notation of the baptism of Benjamin and his twin brother. He was about six years old when the family settled in Illinois, and he grew up with only the advantages of the pioneer schools. The family settled just south of White Hall. In that locality he became a farmer and stock raiser, was also a stockholder and president of the Carrollton Bank, was for many years a county supervisor, and was president of the Fair Association. He cast his ballot for Abraham Lincoln for president, and all his brothers were of the same party in politics, though he was not especially interested in party politics. He belonged to no church, but gave his support to all religious causes, particularly the Methodists. Benjamin Roodhouse married in Greene County, February 22, 1849. The house in which he was married is still standing and is used as a dwelling, just south of White Hall. His wife was Abigail E. Wales, a daughter of Charles Wales, who came from Vergennes, Vermont, as a pioneer to Greene County. She was in the eighth generation from an ancestor who came over on the Mayflower. Benjamin Roodhouse died September 8, 1893, and his wife, November 2, 1898. A brief record of their children is as follows: Ella May, born May 1, 1852, died unmarried November 30, 1900; John M., born February 3, 1854, died at Carrollton June 20, 1883, leaving a son, Orville, who died in Alhambra, California, leaving three sons, Edwin, Thomas and John; Jennie, born May 9, 1858, married J. G. Pope and is a resident of Carrollton; Charles B.; Mary E., born November 23, 1864, was married in Chicago, June 29, 1897, to E. S. Van Arsdale and now resides at Oklahoma City, and has two sons, Stewart and Elliott; Ada, born July 20, 1867, is unmarried and resides at Carrollton; James Peter, born March 4, 1869, a resident of Greenfield, Illinois; and Edward I., born May 1, 1871, married Janie Russell, has two children, Ella and Holyn, and lives with his family at Nampa, Idaho.

Charles Benjamin Roodhouse was born at the home just south of White Hall, May 16, 1860. He attended school at Carrollton, spent one year in a business college at Jacksonville, and throughout his active years has been a farmer and stock man, and is owner of part of the old Roodhouse homestead. He lived on the farm until 1893, and has since directed his varied business interests from his home in White Hall. In politics he is, like his father, a republican, having cast his first vote for James G. Blaine. He is not a member of any church, but his wife is a Presbyterian. He is a member of the White Hall Lodge of Masons.

Mr. Roodhouse married, April 19, 1893, at White Hall, Miss Abbie Tunison, daughter of Henry and Rosetta (Griswold) Tunison. Her mother was a daughter of Cyrus and Abbie (Post) Griswold, thus representing another well known early family of Greene County. Her paternal grandfather was Henry Tunison, Sr., a New Jersey farmer. Henry Tunison, Jr., was born at Bound Brook, New Jersey, March 2, 1828, and on June 14, 1848, he and Rosetta Griswold were married. She was born April 1, 1832. After their marriage they made their first home in a little cabin adjacent to the present Roodhouse farm. Henry Tunison was a man of real leadership in his community, serving as a county supervisor, president of the County Fair Association, was a democrat in politics and late in life took an active part in church. He died February 17, 1897, and after his death his widow lived with her daughter, Mrs. Roodhouse, until she passed away January 6, 1914. The children of Henry Tunison and wife were: George C., born August 13, 1850, and died at the old homestead, May 2, 1911, leaving a son, George Ennis Tunison, who is the present occupant of the Tunison farm; Laura A., born December 17, 1853, married James H. Kirby, of Jerseyville, and died September 4, 1883; Addie E., born September 1, 1859, died in childhood, on February 3, 1870; Mrs. Roodhouse, who was born April 24, 1863; and Harry O., born September 24, 1871, died at Springfield in the State House April 1, 1925.

Mr. and Mrs. Roodhouse are the parents of five children. The oldest, Henry Benjamin, was born April 1, 1894, lives on the farm and in the house where his father was born. He married Avis Moulton, and their children are Dorothy, born February 24, 1917, and Charles Moulton, born June 10, 1919. Charles Edward Roodhouse, the second son, was born October 13, 1895, and is a farmer near White Hall. By his marirage to Louise Gardner he has three children named: James Warren, born November 2, 1917, Mary Rosetta, born December 29, 1919, and Charles Edward, Jr., born July 15, 1923. The third son is Russell Wales Roodhouse, born October 24, 1900. He married Mildred Mosier, and has two daughters, Betty Lou, born April 7, 1922, and Mildred Jane, born August 15, 1923. All these sons live on the parent's farms. Ernest Cornelius Tunison Roodhouse, the fourth son, was born April 14, 1903, and is at home. The youngest of the family is Miss Abbie Lee, born March 7, 1907, now a student in the Woman's College at Jacksonville.

HARRY HODGES GRISWOLD is a White Hall banker, and represents one branch of a very prominent family that has been identified with Greene County since pioneer days.

The Griswolds were early established in New England. The old Colonial home of the family is still standing at Wethersfield, Connecticut, and some of the present day descendants still occupy it. From Connecticut one branch of the family went to Vermont. From Vergennes, Vermont, came the early settler of Greene County, Sylvester Griswold, who subsequently was followed by his brothers, Cyrus, Henry, Edmund, all of whom located in Greene

County, and the Griswolds still living there are descendants of one or the other of the brothers. Sylvester Griswold located on the prairie on what is now called the "Four Corners," and the old farm is still owned by his descendants. He was one of the enterprising men of his day in this agricultural region, and when he retired in 1856 he moved to White Hall and erected the home in which he lived until his death in 1892, when about eighty-four years of age. Sylvester Griswold was perhaps best known in his community because of his wit and humor, a trait more pronounced in him than in most men who came from Colonial New England. He was a republican, had no political aspirations, never joined a fraternity and was not a member of any church, though he supported church causes. His two wives were sisters, of the Hodges family. There were no children by his second marriage. Of the first the two children were Orlando Frank and Emma A. Emma A. is still living.

Orlando Frank Griswold was born at the old Griswold homestead in 1846. He attended local schools, the Jacksonville Business College and the Wisconsin State Normal School at Platteville. As a young man he became cashier of a bank in Platteville, Wisconsin, and was so engaged for a number of years. When he returned to Illinois he lived at White Hall until his death in 1913. He married in Platteville, Wisconsin, Miss Emma Hodges, daughter of Isaac and Lucetta (Crist) Hodges. Her father was a resident of Greene County, Illinois, in early life and went to Wisconsin after the discover of lead in that state. He became a Wisconsin banker. Mrs. O. Frank Griswold died in 1916, at the age of sixty-three. She was the mother of two children: Miss Jessie E., of White Hall, and Harry Hodges. These children attended the State Normal School at Platteville, Wisconsin, and Miss Jessie graduated from the Monticello Seminary at Godfrey, Illinois. Harry H. Griswold attended Illinois College at Jacksonville, and in 1897 graduated Bachelor of Science from the University of Chicago. Harry H. Griswold has never married.

After leaving college he became identified with what was then called the White Hall Bank, now the White Hall National Bank, of which he is assistant cashier. He has always sustained a public spirited part in local affairs. He is a charter member of the Chamber of Commerce and served as treasurer for two years and one term as secretary. During the World war he was preparing to enter the Officers Training School when the armistice was signed. He is a past chancellor of the Knights of Pythias Lodge, and is a member of the Knight Templar Commandery of Masons at Carrollton and of Ansar Temple of the Mystic Shrine at Springfield. He cast his first presidential vote for Major McKinley and has given his support to the national ticket of the republican party. He is chairman of the County Bankers Federation, and is chairman of the Public Library Board. Miss Jessie Griswold is an active worker in the Presbyterian Church and a member of the Eastern Star.

Mr. Griswold has found a constant interest in literature and travel. He is probably one of the best traveled men in Greene County. His journeys have taken him to all parts of the globe. He was once in the Klondike, has been down both coasts of South America, visiting Buenos Ayres on the east, and Valparaiso on the west. He has been in the Mediterranean Sea countries, the Alps and other portions of Europe, in Asia, including China and Japan. He was in Hong Kong during the seaman's strike, when the guests of his ship had to perform manual labor in the absence of the regular employes. During 1923 he was in Southern Europe and the Holy Land, and has traversed practically all the scenes in the life of Jesus and in the history of the ancient civilizations of Asia Minor and the Valley of the Nile, having ascended the Nile as far as the first falls, and visited the Valley of the Kings and the tombs of such ancient monarchs as "King Tut."

JOHN D. GRAY, who recently rounded out thirty years of his career as a lawyer, began his professional work in Mason County, Illinois, where he was born, but for the past twenty years has been in Chicago, and has become one of the leading corporation attorneys practicing in that city. His offices are at 431 South Dearborn Street.

He was born at Havana in Mason County, Illinois, February 6, 1874, son of John A. and Sarah (Henninger) Gray. He represents a pioneer family of Illinois and is also on both sides of American Colonial and Revolutionary stock. His great-grandfather came from England, and in Philadelphia built one of the early state buildings for Pennsylvania. The grandfather of the Chicago attorney was Alexander Gray, who during his early life was a sea captain. In 1842 he and his wife, Sarah, brought their family west to Illinois, traveling by way of the Ohio, Mississippi and Illinois rivers to Havana in Mason County, where they were among the first settlers. Alexander Gray was a wheelwright and cabinet maker, and in pioneer times made coffins and wagons. He established what was known as Gray's Ferry over the river and also owned and operated a line of boats on the Illinois and Mississippi rivers and the Illinois and Michigan Canal between St. Louis and Chicago. At his home in Mason County he erected a two-story house and donated the use of the second story for a school, that being the first school conducted in his locality.

John A. Gray was born at Monticello, New York, in 1841 and was an infant when the family came west to Illinois. He was a farmer, and for over thirty years held the office of justice of the peace, still holding his commission at the time of his death in 1903, at the age of sixty-two. He was a democrat in politics. His wife, Sarah Henninger, was born in Harrisburg, Pennsylvania, and is now seventy-nine years of age. They were married in Peoria and seven children were born to their union, John D. being the third. Four are still living.

John D. Gray acquired his early education in the public schools of Havana, attended the Gem City Business College at Quincy and also the Chaddock College of that city. He took his law course in Northwestern University of

Chicago, graduating in 1894. He was admitted to the bar February 6, 1895, on his twenty-first birthday, and six weeks later was elected city attorney of Havana, being at that time the youngest city attorney in the United States. He held the office two years and was then appointed United States commissioner for the Southern District of Illinois, a position he held about twelve years.

Removing to Chicago in 1904, he engaged in a law practice that for the greater part was identified with corporation law. He looked after the legal interests of a large number of important business concerns, including Croft & Reed, soap manufacturers, the Noble Printing Company, the Independent Plant Company, the White Eagle Bottling Corporation, the Economy Clamp Machine Company, Poehlman Brothers, Nitro Powder Company of New York City, the Great Western Smelting and Refining Company, Sante Fe Oil & Refining Company, the Birkenstein Company, scrap metal dealers, the Carbo Steel Products Company and many others.

Mr. Gray is a member of the Chicago and Illinois Bar Associations, and in the Knights of Pythias was adjutant of the Fourth Brigade of uniformed rank. He is a member of the Sons of the American Revolution, and in politics is an independent voter. Mr. Gray married, September 1, 1901, Miss Eleanor Ashmore, a native of Peoria, Illinois.

CHARLES S. HEATON. A large part of the mercantile activities of the town of Manchester, in Greene County, center around Charles S. Heaton, lumberman, hardware merchant and banker.

Mr. Heaton was born in Greene County, five miles east of Roodhouse, July 30, 1872. His grandfather, Samuel Heaton, came to Illinois from Pennsylvania, founding the family in Greene County. For many years he served as county surveyor. He is buried in the Sanders Cemetery east of Roodhouse. His children were: George; William; Mrs. Sally Chism, a farmer in Greene County; Mark; Mrs. Lila Barrow, who subsequently married a Mr. Duncan; Mrs. Mary Jewett; Bettie, whose first husband was Addison Sullivan, and second, John Henry Graves. The son George was a Union soldier in the Civil war.

Mark Heaton, father of Charles S., was born in Illinois in 1843 and was reared on a farm near Roodhouse. As a youth he volunteered for service in the Union army, being in Company I of the Ninety-first Illinois Infantry. He was made prisoner with other members of that regiment and subsequently exchanged and sent home. Later he resumed service and was in the army when the war closed. After the war he engaged in farming for some years and later became a grocer at Roodhouse, where he died in 1910. Mark Heaton married Lyde Sanders, who was born near Roodhouse and died in 1908, at the age of sixty-four. Her father, Carey Sanders, came to Illinois from Kentucky, and Lyde was the only child of his first wife, a Miss Henderson. He subsequently married Miss Allen, and she became the mother of several children. Mark Heaton and wife were the parents of five sons: Carey, of Roodhouse; George D., of Aurora, Illinois; Harvey; Charles S.; William A., of Elgin, Illinois.

Charles S. Heaton was reared on a farm and in the town of Roodhouse, finished the Junior year of high school and learned merchandising as a clerk in his father's grocery store. He also learned the trade of carpenter and was a journeyman for three years at Roodhouse. Leaving that trade, Mr. Heaton spent seven years as a salaried employee of Hal C. Worcester in the hardware and lumber business. Mr. Worcester established a branch of his business at Manchester and put Mr. Heaton in charge as manager. After five years he and F. L. Knight bought out the business and continued it together for three years. W. A. Heaton succeeded to the Knight interests and the firm for the next four years was Heaton & Brother. Charles S. Heaton subsequently acquired his brother's interest and has since continued the business alone. The old firm of Knight & Heaton acquired the Worcester interest when the firm was located in a building said to be as old as Chicago. Mr. Heaton after becoming sole owner removed the old building and erected in its stead a modern structure, 50 by 66 feet, for the hardware store, while back of that is the implement building, 44 by 50 feet, and further back are the buildings and yards accommodating the lumber and building material. Mr. Heaton also became one of the charter members of the Farmers & Traders State Bank of Manchester and has been on the Board of Directors since the beginning of that institution.

Mr. Heaton took part in the local campaigns for various purposes during the World war. He is a member of the Masonic Lodge, his wife is an Eastern Star, and he has been a member of the official board of the Methodist Church for many years. He married at Roodhouse in May, 1897, Miss Lizzie Drennan, daughter of Jackson and Margaret (Drake) Drennan. Her father who was a veteran of the Civil war, was a tinsmith, and died at Granite City, Illinois. The children of the Drennan family are: William, of Granite City; Maggie, wife of Dr. Walter Kincaid, of Roodhouse; Joseph, of Granite City; Judson, of East St. Louis; Mrs. Heaton; Horace, of Ohio; Theodore and Calvin, of Detroit, Michigan. Mr. and Mrs. Heaton have one son, Charles Jackson, born November 22, 1914.

HON. CHARLES SUMNER STUBBLES, who distinguished himself as a member of the State Legislature of Illinois, was born in Lacon, Marshall County, Illinois, on the 6th of February, 1862, and was the son of Rev. William James and Ann (Holton) Stubbles. The father was no doubt well educated in his youth and given the proper religious training, for he studied theology and in due time was ordained to preach the doctrines of the Methodist Episcopal Church. He was really one of the Illinois pioneer preachers who traveled through the country districts, holding his services in the old rude churches, in the first school houses or in the newly built barns. As the pioneer settlers were the men to establish our present civilization, so the pioneer preachers were the founders of our church systems and our dominant morality, without which anarchy would now rule, or rather unrule, our whole country. Rev. William J. Stubbles bore his part of the trials and hardships of frontier existence, lived a useful and conspicuous life, and finally passed away to his reward.

His son, Charles S., subject of this chronicle, was given a good education by his distinguished parents in his youthful development period, receiving the same at several different places where his father was for a time Methodist circuit rider. Part of his education was received at Henry, Marshall County, and at Abington, Knox County. By the time he had reached early maturity he was well fitted, so far as schooling was concerned, for the active and strenuous duties of existence on earth. This was the time that he decided definitely to study law and became a lawyer. Accordingly he began the study of law in the offices of the well known attorneys McCarthy & Casey at the capital of the state, Springfield, and after about two years was well qualified to pass the required examinations, which he did and was at once admitted to the bar on the 6th of June, 1886.

But instead of beginning the practice of his profession he seemed at first to find an occupation that promised greater remuneration and reward; so for some time he resided at Waltham, Massachusetts, where he learned the watchmaker's trade and in the end, after much study and investigation, became a skilled and proficient electro-metallurgist, with a satisfactory income and a rapidly expanding reputation as an expert in watch making. He made a number of important and valuable discoveries which still further improved his proficiency and widened his reputation and activities. After much study and experimentation he became the inventor of the process by which numerous minerals are successfully spread on and attached to the dials of time instruments of numerous varieties. He made other valuable watch improvements.

While he was a resident of the Bay State he took an active and conspicuous part in worthy public affairs and was finally elected to the position of justice of the peace in Middlesex County. In other ways he distinguished himself in New England and became prominent at Waltham. After a time he again concluded to change his location, and accordingly came west and established himself at Springfield, Illinois, where for some time he was in the employ of the Illinois Watch Factory concern. But this pursuit had its lucrative limitations. as a result Mr. Stubbles finally moved to Peoria, opened his offices and began the practice of law in 1901, and continued the same with much credit and prominence until his death occurred in Peoria at the age of sixty-one years, on the 13th of February, 1923. His health began to fail him early in 1922, soon after he was appointed by Governor Small as a member of the Deep Waterway Commission. At the time of his demise he was senior member of the law firm of Stubbles & Ingram, and had attained much renown as a proficient and satisfactory practioner of the law. His practice was both large and lucrative at his offices in the Peoria Life Building, where clients of all sorts were welcomed and satisfied.

It was while practicing law that he began, as he had in Massachusetts, to take an active and conspicuous part in local politics and in the civic and municipal welfare of the people. Ere long he was brought forward by his party leaders as a candidate for the Lower House of the Legislature, easily won at the polls and in due time took his seat in the House at Springfield. His capacity for important legislative work was revealed in the House, and he was accordingly returned to that body two times, making his election as a member three times. That he served with high distinction is admitted by all his fellow members and by his satisfied constituents. Because of ill health and the approach of death he was unable to assume all the honor granted him. He did not attend any session of the last assembly. He was a member of the Elks, Modern Woodmen, the Rangers of Peoria, the Bar Association and other organizations, in all of which he held offices and took an active and dignified part.

He was twice married and had three sons by his first wife: Roy B., Earl and Russell L. All three reside in the Golden State, where they are actively in business, are prosperous and enjoying the blessings of life. His second wife was formerly Miss Cora B., daughter of Samuel J. and Emma (Fothergill) White. Her father was a native of Arkansas and her mother of Lewiston, Illinois. Both were highly useful and reputable citizens. The father was a farmer by occupation, but was retired at Fulton, Illinois, at the date of his death, which occurred April 24, 1923. His wife died in 1890. They were the parents of five children: Charles J., of Galesburg; Minnie E., a beauty specialist of Peoria; Charity Ann, who is now Mrs. Ringelband; Cora B., widow of subject; and William M., of Minneapolis, Minnesota. Mr. Stubbles had no children by his second wife.

HENRY MINOR HUXLEY, one of the prominent patent lawyers of Chicago, is a scholar in more than one branch of learning.

He was born at Newton, Massachusetts, January 21, 1880, son of Edward Charles and Alice Jane (Haley) Huxley. His father was born at Goshen, Connecticut, and his mother at Cambridge, Massachusetts. His father died in 1908. There were two children, Edward H. and Henry M. Edward Charles Huxley, their father, was educated at Goshen, Connecticut, and in 1862 enlisted in the Nineteenth Connecticut Infantry for service in the Civil war. This regiment subsequently became the Second Heavy Artillery. He was made quartermaster sergeant May 26, 1863, later was promoted to second lieutenant and on April 1, 1864, to first lieutenant. He participated in the Grand Review at Washington in July, 1865, and in after years was identified with the Loyal Legion. Edward C. Huxley was a descendant of Thomas Huxley, who settled at Cambridge, Massachusetts, as early as 1632, and subsequently lived at Suffield, Massachusetts, where he was elected a magistrate.

Henry M. Huxley graduated from high school at Newton, Massachusetts, in 1895. He then entered Harvard University, taking his A. B. degree in 1899, and the Master of Arts degree in 1902. During 1901-02 he spent about a year and a half in Syria and Palestine in exploration work in different sections of Asia Minor and as far east as the Euphrates River. He was appointed Hemminway Fellow in Harvard University, was a teacher there for a time, and devoted considerable study to the language and archaeology of the Holy Land. He compiled Syrian Songs, Proverbs and Stories," published in the Journal of the American Oriental Society.

In 1902 Mr. Huxley became associated with the American Steel & Wire Company at Worcester, Massachusetts, remaining there until 1907. During 1907-08 he was with the Duplex Metals Company of New York, and in 1908-09 started the study of patent law with the firm of Brown and Williams, Chicago. In 1911 he was graduated from the Chicago-Kent College of Law at Chicago, and during 1909-13 was engaged in practice in that city as an employe of the firm Linthicum, Bell & Fuller. During 1913-14 he was one of the firm of Bell & Huxley, was engaged in individual practice during 1914-16, and is now member of the firm Wilkinson, Huxley, Byron & Knight, patent attorneys with offices at 38 South Dearborn Street.

Mr. Huxley is a member of the American Patent Law Association, Chicago Patent Law Association, Law Club, Chicago Bar Association, American Bar Association, the University Clubs of Chicago, Evanston and Washington, the Barrington Hills Country Club, Evanston Country Club, Exmoor Golf Club, and is a republican. He was a member of the Committee on Patent Office Procedure, appointed by Secretary Work of the Department of the Interior, and continued by Secretary Hoover after the Patent Office was transferred to the Department of Commerce.

He is a member of the Loyal Legion, Reserve Officers Association and the Military Order of the World war and American Legion. From August 10 to September 6, 1916, Mr. Huxley attended the Plattsburg Training Camp, and on August 12, 1917, was commissioned captain of Company I of the Eleventh Illinois Infantry. This commission he resigned November 26, 1917, and on December 13 of the same year was commissioned a captain in the Officers Reserve Corps, Ordnance Section, and on January 8, 1918, was ordered to active duty, being stationed at Washington. He was promoted to major, Ordnance Department, United States Army, to rank from October 7, 1918, and served until honorably discharged February 1, 1919. He was commissioned major, Ordnance Section, Officers Reserve Corps, to rank from March 12, 1919, and on September 27, 1922, was commissioned major of infantry in the Officers Reserve Corps, to rank from March 12, 1919. On November 24, 1922, he was assigned to the Three Hundred and Twenty-first Tank Battalion. On August 3, 1920, he was commissioned a first lieutenant of infantry in the Illinois National Guard, and with that rank was federally recognized November 17, 1920, July 15, 1921, he was promoted to captain of infantry, being assigned to Company G Tanks. He was relieved from duty with the Thirty-third Tank Company and transferred to the unassigned list January 1, 1922, and on May 4, 1922, resigned as captain of infantry of the Illinois National Guard.

Mr. Huxley married, April 16, 1913, Carroll Colemage, a native of Winston-Salem, North Carolina. They have one daughter, Margaret Carroll Huxley, born June 10, 1914.

JOHN WILLIAM SANDERS. In manner and disposition one of the quietest and most modest of the working figures around the National Stock Yards of East St. Louis, John William Sanders by those who know is rated as the commission merchant who does more business and is the real expert as a cattle seller at the yards. He has been in that line of business since early youth, and has had about thirty-six years of active experience at the National Stock Yards.

He was born at New Hope in Lincoln County, Missouri, November 17, 1872, son of James Thomas and Olivia Harden (Blakely) Sanders, and grandson of William and Elizabeth (Foley) Sanders. The Foleys were an old Virginia family of Irish ancestry, slave holders, and among the real aristocrats of that state. The maternal grandparents of Mr. Sanders were Samuel Jackson and Susan (Harden) Blakely, Georgia people. Samuel J. Blakely in young manhood married and settled in Howard County, Missouri, later moving to Lincoln County, Missouri, where he lived over fifty years and died. James Thomas Sanders was born in Rappahannock County, Virginia, and moved out to Missouri, serving as a Confederate soldier in the army of Gen. Sterling Price. After the war he engaged in the live stock business, and in 1873 moved to St. Louis, Missouri, where he was associated with his brother-in-law, J. W. Blakely of the old North Pacific stock yards in that city. When those stock yards were abandoned the firm moved to the National Stock Yards at East St. Louis, and he continued his business there until his death on September 6, 1904. He was a man of domestic habits, not interested in politics or public affairs, was a member of the Methodist Church and when not attending to business was invariably to be found at home. He met Miss Blakely after the Blakely family had moved to Lincoln County, Missouri. Mrs. James T. Sanders resides in St. Louis, and celebrated her seventy-fifth birthday in June, 1924. She was the mother of three children, John William and James, twins, the latter dying at the age of sixteen, and the other son, Homer B., is unmarried and lives with his mother at St. Louis, Missouri.

John William Sanders was about one year old when the family moved to St. Louis. He attended public schools there, completed a commercial course in the Perkins & Herpel Business College at St. Louis and remained at school as a teacher for one year and four months after graduating. He then became bookkeeper for the firm of Blakely & Sanders live stock commission merchants, this business being a co-partnership until 1890, when it was incorporated at the Blakely, Sanders, Mann Company. After eight years as a bookkeeper Mr. Sanders took up the work of cattle selling, a line he has since followed and in which he is the acknowledged expert at the

Harry C. Kinne

National Stock Yards and is credited with handling more live stock than any other commission merchant there. The business as Blakely, Sanders, Mann Company was continued until 1917. The original partners having died, it was planned to make a merger of the interests of this firm with the Woodson, Fennewald Live Stock Commission Company. Mr. Sanders entered the employ of the Woodson, Fennewald Live Stock Commission Company for a term of three and a half years, after which said firm was incorporated, Mr. Sanders being elected secretary and treasurer. This is the largest firm in volume of business at the National Stock Yards.

Mr. Sanders married, December 21, 1898, at Paducah, Kentucky, Miss Lena Myrtle Tate, daughter of Jesse and Sallie Tate. Her father, who was a farmer, died in 1884, and her mother passed away in 1901. Mrs. Sanders, one of a family of four sons and four daughters, is a direct descendant of the Daniel Boone family. Mr. and Mrs. Sanders had twin girls who died in infancy, and the son James Lee, who graduated in a scientific and technical course in Purdue University at Lafayette, Indiana. Mr. Sanders is a member of the First Christian Church at East St. Louis. He is a Knight Templar and thirty-second degree Scottish Rite Mason and Shriner. He has given strict attention to business, has had no ambitions for political advancement but was made a member for four years of the school board of East St. Louis.

OTTO H. HERMANN, present city treasurer of Alton, was born in Madison County, and is well known in a number of communities of the county, having made a sterling record as a business man and citizen.

He was born in Foster Township, February 8, 1869, son of Nicholas and Frances (Dickman) Hermann. His father was born in Holstein, Germany, and his mother, in East Freisland. They came to this country before their marriage, were married in Alton, and then located in Foster Township of Madison County, where the father spent his active career as a farmer. Both parents are now deceased, the father passing away at the age of fifty-eight and the mother at seventy-three. They had five sons and three daughters, one of whom died in infancy. The sixth child and third son is Otto H. Hermann.

Mr. Hermann was reared on his father's farm in Foster Township, attended the public schools of that locality and finished his education in Shurtleff College. In his early years he was both a teacher and a farmer, and became known for an intelligent interest and participation in local affairs. His first important office was assessor of Foster Township, and he was twice elected. He was also elected supervisor of the township, and the Board of Supervisors chose him as superintendent of the Madison County Poor Farm. After two years he resigned, and in 1907 located at Alton, where he served eight years on the city police force under Mayor Faulstich, rising to the rank of night captain. He finally resigned from the police force and served four years as deputy sheriff. He was elected city treasurer in April, 1923.

Mr. Hermann married, September 8, 1898, Miss Hannah Burjes, of Foster Township. They have two daughters and one son: Myra, wife of Jerald Gould, of Alton; Eugene, who was a clerk with the Illinois Terminal Railway, and now superintendent of the Bluff City Lime Company of St. Genevieve, Missouri; and Miss Violet, an employe of the Illinois Glass Company. Mr. Hermann is a member of the Modern Woodmen of America and the Court of Honor, and has been a lifelong republican in politics.

HARRY CLARK KINNE, Chicago attorney and professor of law, began his career in that city as a newsboy.

Mr. Kinne was born in Kalamazoo County, Michigan, June 25, 1880. His grandfather, Allison Kinne, a native of Pennsylvania, came West with wagon and team and settled in Kalamazoo County in the early '40s, being one of the pioneers in the development of the agricultural resources of that county. Henry Allison Kinne, father of the attorney, was born on the old homestead farm in Kalamazoo County, April 21, 1848, and until he retired in 1909 was continuously engaged in agriculture. For many years he was a member of the School Board of his home community, and in politics began voting as a republican in early manhood. Henry Allison Kinne married Almeda Gregory, who was born at Medina, Ontario, Canada, March 11, 1849, and died June 26, 1909. In the family were three sons and one daughter, Harry C. being the third in age.

Up to the age of sixteen he attended the grammar and high school at Kalamazoo. He came to Chicago in 1896 and at Englewood began his career as a newsboy, his first wage being fifty cents per week. Later he made as high as one hundred dollars per month in selling and distributing newspapers, and all of this money that he could save was used to complete his education. He attended and in 1898 graduated from Englewood High School. He studied law in the night classes of Illinois College of Law, receiving his LL. B. degree in 1903. He was admitted to practice before the Illinois bar in July of the same year and before the United States Supreme Court in 1913. He has been engaged in general practice in Chicago since 1903, specializing in real estate, probate and chancery practice. He became a teacher in the night classes of Illinois College of Law, in 1909 lecturing on the law of real estate, wills, probate and abstracts. When Illinois College of Law was merged with the DePaul University Law School in 1912 he continued as a teacher in the latter, and has been a member of the law faculty there for seventeen years. Mr. Kinne is also a member of the Chicago Bar Association, Illinois Bar Association, and the Union League Club of Chicago.

His home is at Wilmette, where he is a member of the Methodist Episcopal Church, a member and secretary of the Wilmette Church Federation, and for over twenty years in Englewood and Wilmette has taught a young men's class in Sunday School. He has always been interested in community civic affairs and was president of Wilmette Community Chest Association. He is a member and was secretary of Equity Lodge No. 878, A. F. and A. M., for fifteen years, is a member of Wilmette Chapter No. 253, Royal Arch Masons, Oriental Consistory, Medinah Temple and of Illinois Council No. 115, Royal Arcanum. He is a republican in politics. Mr. Kinne was a member of the Illinois Reserve Militia from 1917 to 1919, and during the war period served as a member of the Advisory Draft Board of the Chicago District.

He married Miss Uella Snider, of Chicago, March 30, 1904. She was born at Waterloo, Ontario, Canada. They have three children, Leah Mildred, Ruth Verle and Harry Clark, Jr.

HUGO E. OTTE, president of the National City Bank of Chicago at 30 South La Salle Street, was born in Chicago, and began his career as a banker in the capacity of a messenger boy with the Union National Bank.

He was born in Chicago May 30, 1872, son of Emil and Catherine (Behrman) Otte. Hugo E. Otte was the youngest of three sons and one daughter, and acquired his early education in the public schools of Chicago. In 1887, at the age of fifteen, he went to work as messenger boy with the Union National Bank. He remained in the service of that institution in different capacities until 1900. Following that he spent four years with the First National Bank in the loan department. Upon the organization in 1904 of the Union Stock Yards State Bank he accepted the post of cashier. This bank was consolidated with the Peoples Trust & Savings Bank and is now known as the Peoples Stockyards State Bank. Mr. Otte in 1905 organized the Lakeview Trust & Savings Bank and served as its president until 1907. In that year he returned to the downtown banking district as cashier of the National City Bank and in 1910 became its vice-president and in 1924, president. In the latter part of 1924 the National City Bank and the National Bank of the Republic consolidated, and he became its president, which position he now holds.

Mr. Otte is affiliated with the Constellation Lodge of Masons, is a member of the Chicago Club, South Shore Country Club, Bankers Club and Knollwood Country Club at Lake Forest. In politics he is a republican. Mr. Otte married in 1894 Miss Annetta Christin. Three children were born to their marriage: Helen, who died at the age of four years; Howard Allen and Milton H.

JAY L. SPAULDING, one of the attorneys practicing at the bar of Princeton, was born on a farm in Bureau County, Illinois, September 24, 1870, a son of Junius P. and Sarah C. (Walker) Spaulding. Junius P. Spaulding was born in Vermont, and when war broke out between the North and the South he enlisted from that state in the Union army. He was captured and held as a prisoner of war at Libbey Prison, Richmond, Virginia. Following his release and the close of the war he came to Illinois, and for several years thereafter was a minister of the Wesleyan Methodist Church, being stationed in the northern part of the state, but the latter portion of his life was devoted to agricultural pursuits, and he owned and resided on a farm in Bureau County, where his death occurred when he was seventy-eight years old. His wife, whom he met and married in Illinois, was born in Ohio, but came with her parents to Illinois, where her father, James Walker, settled.

Owing to the fact that his father was a minister during his youth, Jay L. Spaulding's home was a migratory one, being shifted as his father was transferred from one charge to another, and his early educational training was obtained in the public schools of the several neighborhoods in which his parents resided from time to time. His preliminary training was supplemented by a course in Dover Academy and Wheaton College, after which he prepared himself for the profession he had chosen by reading law at Princeton, and was admitted to the bar in 1893. Since then he has been successfully engaged in a general law practice at Princeton. While he has always supported the principles of the democratic party, he has never sought political honors or accepted office. His life has been an active one in his profession, which has received his full time and energy.

In 1893 Mr. Spaulding married Miss Clara M. Walker, and they have three daughters.

BENJAMIN VOGEL BECKER, prominent Chicago attorney, was born at Warsaw, Indiana, June 20, 1871, son of Leopold and Caroline (Vogel) Becker. He spent some of his boyhood days in his native Indiana town, where he attended public schools, also was in school at Fort Wayne, and in 1887 moved to Chicago and began reading law in the office of Jacob Newman. He was admitted to the Illinois bar in 1892, and to practice in the United States Supreme Court in 1900. In 1898 he became a partner in the firm of Newman, Northrup, Levinson & Becker, and continued in that firm and its successors to the present time. Along with his strictly law business he has gained a number of business responsibilities, being a director of the National Bank of the Republic of Chicago, the Chicago Daily News, Incorporated, the Westinghouse Airbrake Company of Wilmerding, Pennsylvania, the Union Switch & Signal Company of Swissvale, Pennsylvania, and the Fan Steel Products Company of North Chicago. He is a member of the Chicago, Illinois State and American Bar Associations, the Chicago Historical Society, is a republican and belongs to the City, Illinois Athletic, Ravisloe Country, Lake Shore Country Clubs of Chicago, the Bankers Club of New York and the Congressional Club of Washington. He married at Jackson, Michigan, June 20, 1901, Miss Elizabeth Loeb. They have one son, John Leonard.

An estimate of the career of Mr. Becker, written by that eminent and veteran Chicago lawyer, Stephen S. Gregory, may be appropriately used at the conclusion of the above brief biography.

"Mr. Becker is associated with S. O. Levinson, Chester E. Cleveland and Arthur L. Schwartz in the firm of Levinson, Becker, Cleveland and Schwartz, and more recently in the firm of Levinson, Becker, Schwartz & Frank. Mr. Levinson and Mr. Becker are singularly well adapted for professional co-oper-

Henry A Allen

ation. Mr. Becker is a close student of human nature, most sympathetic and considerate of others, and has the rare faculty of getting the best out of other people, a quality of great service to both. He has a mind of great clearness and penetration. He seems to be able to see things as they are, without errors of refraction due to professional bias or blindness, occasioned by looking at one side or aspect of a complicated matter."

REV. JOSEPH O'ROURKE, pastor of St. Mary's Catholic Church at Mt. Sterling, has given thirty-four years to the service of his church in Southern Illinois. His longest pastorate was at Farmersville, and from there he came to Mt. Sterling.

He was born in Ireland, son of Joseph and Catherine (O'Riley) O'Rourke, and of Irish ancestry for many generations back. His people were farmers in County Longford. Father O'Rourke was one of twelve children and the only one to become a priest. He attended the grades of the National School in Ireland, took his classical course at Moyne, and then entered All Hallows College at Dublin, where he was graduated and ordained to the priesthood. He was one of a class of forty-two young priests, and he came to the United States with twelve or fifteen other priests assigned to different parts of the country. Father O'Rourke arrived in the fall of 1892 and first became assistant in the Church of Our Saviour at Jacksonville, in the diocese of Alton, now diocese of Springfield. He was next sent as a priest to a small parish at Dalton City, in Moultree County, and then followed his twenty years of constructive service at Farmersville. While there he built the church and the parsonage, and left a permanent impress on the spiritual and moral life of that community.

He took charge of St. Mary's Church at Mt. Sterling in June, 1919. At Mt. Sterling he has worked diligently to pay off the debt of the church property, maintained both church and school, and has a parochial school running through the grades and high school, with six sisters as teachers.

Father O'Rourke became a naturalized citizen, taking out his papers at Jacksonville. During the World war he helped built sentiment for the government and engaged in all the patriotic activities at Farmersville.

EDWARD L. JOEHL is president of the Walnut Grove Dairy Company of Alton. This is a business that has been in successful existence for seventy years, and Mr. Joehl represents the third successive generation of the family connected with the enterprise.

He was born on a farm in Woodriver Township of Madison County, January 28, 1889. His parents, Mennard and Mary (Grossheim) Joehl, were born in Alton, and are still residents of that city. The grandfather was a native of Switzerland. Edward L. Joehl is the oldest of a family of ten children, nine of whom are still living.

He was educated in public schools and as a youth had practical experience and training in the dairy industry. His grandfather had started the dairy business in St. Louis, and subsequently moved it to Alton, and it has been in the family ever since. At the age of twenty-one Edward L. Joehl took an official part in the business in association with his father, and has since become president. It is a large wholesale and retail milk production and distributing service, requiring twenty-five employes, while the delivery and other departments require the use of four automobile trucks and fourteen head of horses.

Mr. Joehl married, April 30, 1912, Miss Mary Sency. They have two sons, Ralph H. and Edward L., Jr. They are members of St. Mary's Catholic Church and Mr. Joehl is affiliated with the Knights of Columbus, the Eagles and the Elks. He has been interested in the success of the republican party and has served as committeeman of the Tenth Ward. He is treasurer of the Illinois Ice Cream Association and is a director of the Building and Loan Association. Two of his brothers were represented in the World war, A. L. Joehl in the navy and M. J. Joehl in the army.

COL. HENRY A. ALLEN. The limits assigned for this review of the career of an active and distinguished member of the profession of mechanical and civil engineering, Col. Henry A. Allen, are wholly inadequate to give even a cursory sketch of the many brilliant works which he has planned and executed, or of a military record which would alone entitle him to be enrolled among the most skillful and efficient officers who led the United States forces in the World war. It must be sufficient to make allusion to those incidents of a life which will afford the best clue to the character of the man and to his numerous achievements.

Colonel Allen was born at Madison, Wisconsin, in 1867, and is a son of the late Gen. Thomas Scott Allen, one of Wisconsin's distinguished citizens of the Civil war period and succeeding. General Allen began his service in the war of secession as lieutenant-colonel of the Second Wisconsin Regiment of Infantry, a part of the famous Iron Brigade, was later made colonel of the Fifth Wisconsin, which he commanded at the Battle of Mary's Heights, Fredericksburg, Virginia, and at the end of the war was brevetted brigadier-general. Following the war he became secretary of the State of Wisconsin and served as such for four years. Removing then to Oshkosh, he entered the newspaper profession, in which he was engaged for several years. This family is kin to the Ethan Allen family of New England history.

Henry A. Allen was educated in the public schools and the normal school at Oshkosh, following which he received an appointment to the United States Naval Academy at Annapolis, where he was graduated in 1887. His first cruise after his graduation was on the U. S. S. "Constellation," one of the famous sailing frigates of the old Navy; and, by contrast, his next cruise was on the U. S. S. "Boston," the first cruiser in the "new" Navy to put to sea in full fighting trim. Later, Colonel Allen was aide and fleet signal officer under Admiral Stephen B. Luce, commanding the North Atlantic Squadron, U. S. Navy. After about three years' service in the Navy Colonel Allen retired and came to Chicago, where he took up the practice of engineering in 1890. He became electrical engineer with the Western Electric Company of this city, and subsequently was electrical and mechanical engineer with the firm of Eaton & Prince, elevator manufacturers, for which firm he designed the first successful commercial electric elevator. Following this he was consulting engineer for various corporations and engaged on various projects of magnitude, and became mechanical and electrical engineer and manager of various departments for the Fraser & Chalmers Company of Chicago and its successor, the Allis-Chalmers Company, with which concern he remained eleven years. While with this concern Colonel Allen broke several world's records in the designing and construction of pumping and other machinery. After leaving Allis-Chalmers he was with various municipalities and industrial concerns as a consulting engineer, and visited many parts of the world in an engineering capacity, including Alaska, Mexico and the Hawaiian Islands. In the latter he designed and constructed the highest lift pumping irrigation plants in the world. He has also designed filtration plants, garbage reduction plants and incinerators, and made important reports on municipal, hydraulic and electrical installations, in addition to which he has taken out a number of patents on mechanical, electrical and hydraulic devices. He was appointed directly by President Roosevelt as a member of the commission of seven engineers to accompany Hon. William Howard Taft, then president-elect, to Panama for the purpose of making a final decision as to the type of the Panama Canal, and to decide upon other important matters relating to the construction of the Gatum dam. During the administration of Fred Busse as mayor of Chicago Colonel Allen was appointed consulting engineer of Chicago to make examination and reports on municipal tunnels. Later he was asked to accept the position of mechanical engineer-in-charge to rehabilitate the pumping machinery of the city water works system, which position he accepted and still holds. In 1925 Colonel Allen was assigned by Col. A. A. Sprague, commissioner of public works, to still another municipal position, that of chief engineer of the Port Commission of the City of Chicago.

Colonel Allen has a distinguished military record, including his service in the World war as commander of the famous 108th engineers. His connection with the military establishment in Illinois began shortly after the World's Fair in 1893, when he was asked to become a member of the Naval Reserve Force of the state, and was made the first drill officer of that arm of the service, with the commission of ensign. Later he commanded the First Division of the Illinois Naval Reserves, which was one of the crack military organizations of the country, and afterward became the first captain commanding the Naval Militia of Illinois. He served eight years with the Illinois Naval Militia.

After returning from the Panama Canal Colonel Allen was asked by Col. Edward F. Young, then in command of the Illinois National Guard, to accept a position on his staff as chief engineer of the First Division, National Guard of Illinois. While in this position he laid out the brigade camps at Elgin and Dixon, Illinois, and the division camp at Peoria. The experience thus gained was of exceptional value to him in his subsequent service in the World war in France. Prior to the entry of the United States in the great European conflict Colonel Allen was commissioned by Governor Lowden and General Dixon to organize a regiment of engineers, which he did, with the valuable assistance of the Citizens Unit, a patriotic organization of citizens of Chicago. On May 17, 1917, he was commissioned colonel and authorized to organize the First Regiment Illinois Engineers. On July 25, upon the mobilization call of the President, this regiment was mustered into the United States army at war strength and made a part of the Thirty-third Division, Illinois' contingent in the World war. Colonel Allen, in command of his regiment, went overseas with this division, and its splendid record for valor, efficiency and service to the allied cause in the winning of the war forms a most important part of Illinois' history in the great conflict. Colonel Allen has remained in command of the 108th Engineers, and is also an officer in the Organized Reserve Corps, Army of the United States, with the rank of colonel.

Colonel Allen is a member of the Veterans of Foreign Wars, the American Legion, the Western Society of Engineers, the American Society of Mechanical Engineers, the American Society of Military Engineers, the American Society of Naval Engineers and the United States Naval Institute. Colonel Allen is the father of a daughter, Miss Julia C. Allen.

BURT AUSTIN MCDONALD, president of the Commercial Credit Trust Company at Chicago, is a comparatively young man, with a remarkable range of experience in industrial, credit and general banking activities both in Canada, his native country, and in the United States.

Mr. McDonald was born at Listowel, Ontario, Canada, February 11, 1888. As a boy he attended public school at Hamilton, Ontario, continued his education in the Collegiate Institutes of Hamilton and Ontario, and in 1905 entered the University of Toronto. His energies were soon diverted into active commercial channels, and for a time he was employed in the office of the Toronto Bolt & Forging Company, which subsequently became the Steel Company of Canada, Limited. He also studied stenography. Later the McDonald family removed to Regina, Saskatchewan, where Mr. McDonald became assistant to his father, who was with the American-Abell Company, handling threshing machines and engines. Not long afterward Mr. McDonald was appointed accountant of the Regina branch of the American-Abell Company, and in 1910 became assistant treasurer of the city of Regina.

In 1911 Mr. McDonald was made Canadian accountant for the M. Rumely Company of Laporte, Indiana, was promoted to assistant manager of the Calgary branch, and was then given duties in the home office of the company at Laporte.

In June, 1916, Mr. McDonald was appointed Canadian manager for the Guaranty Securities Corporation of New York, with headquarters at Montreal, Quebec. This corporation soon became the Continental Guaranty Corporation, and before the close of 1916 Mr. McDonald was elected a vice president of the company, and in January, 1918, was transferred to the New York headquarters as vice president in charge of new business. Returning again to Canada in October, 1920, he formed the Continental Guaranty Corporation of Canada, Limited, a separate company, all the stock, however, being owned by the Continental Guaranty Corporation of New York. He remained in Montreal as president of the Canadian Company after the Commercial Credit Company of Baltimore took over the Continental Guaranty Corporation. Then, in December, 1922, Mr. McDonald came to Chicago as president of the Commercial Credit Trust. He is a member of the Chicago Chamber of Commerce, of the Westmoreland Country Club, Midday Club and a member of the First Presbyterian Church of Evanston.

Mr. McDonald married, October 30, 1910, Miss Hazel Gibson, a native of St. Catherines, Ontario. They have four children, Lorne, Lola, Elizabeth and Burt Austin, Jr.

MARCUS NORTH. One of the first families to come into Greene County was that of North. Marcus North, of White Hall, represents the third generation of the Illinois branch of the family, and has lived all his life in the county, more than seventy years.

He is in the tenth generation of the family in America. He is therefore one of the true descendants of the original stock of hardy people who first settled in the New England colonies. His American ancestor was John North, who sailed from England in 1635. His descendants have since scattered to practically all sections of the United States.

Asahel North, founder of the Illinois branch of the family, was born at Farmington, Connecticut, September 3, 1782. On August 26, 1819, he married Prudence Swallow, who was born at Windsor, Vermont, September 10, 1799. Their wedding tour was a trip to the west. They left a few days after their marriage, and after a long journey overland in wagon arrived in Illinois, and in the spring of 1821 settled on Apple Creek Prairie in Greene County. They bought the primitive home of a squatter until the public land came into the market. Then Asahel North entered over 800 acres at $1.25 an acre. The rest of his life was spent in that community and in the development of his land. The town site of White Hall includes a portion of the original farm holdings of Asahel North. He died at his home near White Hall March 19, 1846, and both he and his wife were buried on the old North farm. There were twelve children, and those to grow up were: Lucy, who became Mrs. Edward Griswold; Marcus; Sylvia, who married Isaac McCollister; John; and Mrs. Mary Stewart.

Marcus North, Sr., father of the present Marcus North of White Hall, was born in Greene County, December 6, 1824. He was a farmer during his brief career of thirty years. He died November 28, 1854, and is buried in the White Hall Cemetery. He married Elizabeth Wales, who was born at Ferrisburg, Vermont, and was a girl when brought to Illinois. She was a daughter of Charles Wales and a direct descendant of William Brewster of the Mayflower Colony. Mrs. Marcus North lived a widow after her husband's death for fifty-six years. She was the mother of the following children: Edward, for many years a banker at White Hall, who subsequently went to Houston, Texas, and later to Memphis, Tennessee, where he died in 1923; Lucy, who died at White Hall, wife of Charles I. McCollister; and Marcus.

Marcus North, Jr., was born at the old homestead near White Hall, November 1, 1854, and he was less than a month old when his father died. He lived for a time in the home of his maternal grandparents, growing up at Medora in Macoupin County. He attended country schools and finished his education in Blackburn College at Carlinville. He lived with his mother until grown and then took up farming. He was a general farmer, grain and stock raiser, and for many years had an active part in the affairs of the Apple Creek Prairie community. He served as director of schools, and his home for many years was the home for the teachers in that locality. He was actively identified with the community church of the Universalist denomination when it was organized in 1871.

Mr. North married in White Hall Township, April 18, 1876, Miss Martha Baldwin, born March 31, 1858, daughter of Francis and Agnes (Bowman) Baldwin. Her father came to Illinois from Ohio and was a farmer and mill owner. The children of Mr. and Mrs. North are: Walter Francis, a rice grower at Louise, Texas. He married on September 20, 1900, Nellie Richart, and their children are: Irene; Harold M., who married Irma G. Black on January 2, 1925; Russell W., Francis, Arthur R. and Lucy Lea. Ella was married April 20, 1910, to Charles McLaren of Canton, Illinois, and their children are: Irene and Martha J. Miss Minnie E. is at home. Helen was married April 18, 1917, to Frank Weis of White Hall, and their children are Irma and Mary L. Lucy E. was married November 11, 1909, to Henry Shirley, secretary of the tile factory at White Hall, and their children are Irene, Richard H. and Donald N.

WALTER E. BECKWITH. For over forty years the name Beckwith has been prominently associated with the commercial affairs of East St. Louis. During the last twenty years the name has been especially prominent in real estate activities. Walter E. Beckwith is one of a real estate firm that has handled many of the city's largest transactions, the Beckwith Brothers Company, Incorporated.

Walter E. Beckwith was born at Lebanon, Missouri, December 4, 1865, son of Milan Sumner and Flora M. (Putnam) Beckwith. The Beckwiths came from New England. The maternal grandparents, John and Flora (Hawley) Putnam, represented the old Putnam family of New England and on coming west first settled at Rosamond, Illinois. Milan Sumner Beckwith was the first postmaster at

Pana, Illinois, and later a live stock dealer, and from May, 1880, until his death in 1897 was a resident of East St. Louis, and one of the prominent commission men at the stock yards of that city. During the Civil war he was a paymaster in the Quartermaster's Department. His wife died in 1915. They had a family of nine children: Herbert H., who has four children; Flora H., now deceased, mother of four children; Walter E.; Ura V., deceased; Lucy M., who had seven children; Arthur Milan, who has a family of six children; Forest Putnam, whose family consists of two children; Fannie O., who has six children; and Gertrude M., who is the mother of nine children.

Walter E. Beckwith attended public schools in Lebanon, Missouri, and East St. Louis, but after the age of ten his schooling was frequently interrupted while he was working at different things. In time his efforts became concentrated in the real estate business, and in 1903 he and his brother Arthur organized the Beckwith Brothers Company, Incorporated. It is one of the leading firms in the city in point of volume and importance of business done. They have an organization for the building and improving of property and also handle loans and insurance.

Mr. Beckwith married in May, 1891, at Lawrenceville, Illinois, Miss Martha J. Buchanan, daughter of John G. and Martha Buchanan. Her parents both died in 1890. Her father was a farmer, and she was one of thirteen children. Five children have been born to Mr. and Mrs. Beckwith: Ethel, Allen E., Lois, Forest A., and Marjorie. The daughter Ethel is the wife of J. A. Knoerzer, and their children are Jane, Ann and J. A., Jr.

JOHN SMITH YOUNG, M. D. One of the most noted authorities on X-ray diagnosis in Southern Illinois is Dr. John Smith Young, who has the equipment and facilities to handle all the work accomplished by the X-ray and the radiological processes for the medical and surgical profession in East St. Louis.

Doctor Young was born at Dry Fork, Kentucky, July 5, 1888, son of A. E. and Ella (Smith) Young. His great-grandfather Young came from Dundee, Scotland, and was a pioneer in Kentucky. He volunteered at the time of the second war with Great Britain and was a colonel under General Jackson. Aseph Young, grandfather of Doctor Young, was born in Kentucky and married Mary Ellis, a native of the same state. A. E. Young spent his life as a farmer, and died in March, 1917. He married Ella Smith, who is still living, and is a daughter of Ishmael and Margaret (Duncan) Smith, her father a native of Kentucky and of Virginia stock, while her mother was born in Virginia. Ishmael Smith served as a Confederate soldier during the Civil war. John Smith Young was the younger of two living children. His sister, Lillian, is the wife of Herbert Boles, and has two children, and the other sister, Mary, is deceased.

John Smith Young was reared on his father's farm and had to make his own opportunity beyond the advantages of the common district schools. He took some preparatory work in the Nashville Bible School, took a pre-medical course in Vanderbilt University at Nashville, and continued his medical education in Washington University at St. Louis and Barnes Medical School of that city, where he graduated M. D. in 1914. For one year he was resident physician at the Deaconess Hospital in St. Louis, and having shown special skill in X-ray work he was put in charge of the X-ray department of the Barnes Hospital, Washington University Medical School, for eighteen months.

In the meantime he became a member of the United States Medical Reserve Corps, and in December, 1916, joined the Harvard Medical Unit for overseas duty with the British Expeditionary Forces. He had charge of its X-ray department. He sailed in December, 1916, landing at Liverpool, then to London, and on reaching France the Harvard unit was located at General Hospital No. 18 near Etaples, where he remained on duty nine months. He was then transferred to the American Expeditionary Forces with the Johns Hopkins unit at Base Hospital No. 18 at Bazoills, France, in charge of the X-ray department for seven months. His services there were loaned to the French army. After that he was again sent with the British Expeditionary Forces with the Chicago unit, in charge of the X-ray department in Base Hospital No. 12 for four months. He was then transferred to the French Complementare at Evereaux, and was at that position when the armistice was signed. He received the commission of captain in the Army Medical Corps. Doctor Young received his honorable discharge at Camp Taylor, Kentucky, in March, 1919. He then returned to Glasgow, Kentucky, and practiced medicine there about one year. In 1920 he located in East St. Louis, and has since equipped a complete radiological laboratory and handles all the X-ray work for St. Louis physicians and surgeons.

Doctor Young married at St. Louis, Missouri, January 6, 1920, Miss Constance L. Briett, daughter of Fred C. and Lydia (Summers) Briett. Her father is a real estate operator at St. Louis. Mrs. Young has one sister, Miss Florence. The only child of Doctor and Mrs. Young is Marjorie, born in 1923. Doctor Young is a member of the Christian Church, while his wife belongs to the Evangelical denomination. He is a Knight Templar Mason and Shriner, a member of the Knights of Pythias and the American Legion, and his professional connections are with the Missouri State, Kentucky State, Mississippi Valley and Southern Medical Associations, the American Medical Association and the American Radiological Association.

HENRY W. SMITH, M. D. One of the leading professional men of Roodhouse for over thirty years has been Dr. Henry W. Smith, physician and surgeon, whose work and experience entitled him to high rank in his profession.

Doctor Smith was born at Scottville, Macoupin County, Illinois, February 23, 1867. His father, Levi B. Smith, came from Cumberland County, Kentucky, at the age of seventeen and made his home with his uncle, Stephen Smith, in Illinois. He had acquired his

limited education in the schools of Kentucky. Under his uncle he learned the trade of wheelwright, and he followed that several years. He fitted himself for the law by study while engaged in mechanical work, and he continued active in the practice for many years. He was a veteran of the Civil war, being in Company I of the One Hundred and Twenty-second Illinois Infantry, under Capt. Noah Bostick and Col. John I. Renicker. He was in General Grant's army in the campaigns leading up to and through the siege and capture of Vicksburg. He was slightly wounded in the battle of Holly Springs, but soon returned to his regiment and was in the service until the close of the war, taking part in the Grand Review at Washington in the spring of 1865. After the war he was active in the Grand Army of the Republic and attended many of its encampments. A staunch republican, he never sought office for himself. He was a member of the Christian Church of Scottville, was a member of the local school board many years and was affiliated with the Independent Order of Odd Fellows. Levi B. Smith died in March, 1896. He married Lorinda J. Groves. Her father, James Groves, was a native of Germany, coming to the United States in early life, and became a farmer in Morgan County, Illinois. He was a veteran of the Mexican war, serving with General Scott's army in the campaign against the City of Mexico. He married in Illinois Miss Bryan. Mrs. Levi Smith died July 12, 1925, having survived her husband nearly thirty years. Her children were: Florence, wife of John Dugan, of Kansas City; Beatrice, wife of Albert Garner, of Granite City, Illinois; Mary, wife of T. J. Welch, of Granite City; and Dr. Henry W.

Henry W. Smith spent the first nineteen years of his life in Macoupin County, most of the time on a farm, attending the common schools in Scottville. He attended a preparatory school at Bushnell, Illinois, and from there entered the College of Physicians and Surgeons of Chicago, where he was graduated in 1894. Doctor Smith paid all his expenses while in medical school, acting as a nurse, waiter, newspaper carrier, and during part of his senior year was house surgeon of the college. Following his graduation he located at Roodhouse, and has been steadily engaged in practice there since the spring of 1894. He has taken several post-graduate courses, including one in 1920. Doctor Smith in 1923 succeeded Doctor Bates as railroad surgeon of the Chicago & Alton Railway at Roodhouse. During the World war he was a member of the Board of Medical Referee in Jacksonville, but was rejected for active service in the Army Medical Corps.

Outside of his profession he has served as mayor of the town, member of the school board and town treasurer, and for the past twenty years has been republican central committeeman. He has attended State Republican Conventions and was a visitor to the National Convention in St. Louis. Doctor Smith is a member of the Independent Order of Odd Fellows, of several insurance organizations and is president of the Official Board of the Christian Church.

While a student at Bushnell, Illinois, he met Miss Anna M. Welch, of Palmyra. She was born in Macoupin County, only child of Alexander and Martha Ann (Doss) Welch. Her mother was born in Macoupin County, daughter of a pioneer there. Her father was a native of Scotland. Mrs. Smith graduated from the Carlinville High School and from the old Teachers' College at Bushnell, and taught school several years before her marriage. Doctor and Mrs. Smith have one daughter, now Mrs. David E. Thompson. She is a graduate of the Roodhouse High School and of Christian College at Columbia, Missouri. Her husband, David E. Thompson, a brother of Judge Thompson, was an aviator during the World war and is now in the real estate business at Hollywood, California.

SAMUEL H. WYSS. A name that has carried with it all the suggestions of business success and power in the City of Alton for many years is that of Samuel H. Wyss, president of the Alton Banking and Trust Company, but who sold his interest in bank on January 1, 1925. Mr. Wyss has been in business forty years, and has accumulated a wide variety of interests both in commercial and other lines.

He was born at Alton, September 27, 1860, son of Samuel and Caroline (Dietz) Wyss. His father was born in Switzerland, his mother in Germany, and they were married after coming to this country at Alton, where for more than thirty years they were in the hotel business. Both are now deceased. Their family consisted of two sons and one daughter, Samuel H. being the second son and child. The daughter, Bertha, is the widow of William Struble and lives in St. Louis. The other son, William, died at Alton when about fifty years of age.

Samuel H. Wyss was reared in Alton, educated in the local schools, also attended Shurtleff College at upper Alton, and as a young man graduated in pharmacy. He is a registered pharmacist in Illinois, and the drug business claimed his attention in his native city for a period of thirty-five years.

In the meantime he was extending his interest in other directions, and in 1902 he organized the Alton Banking and Trust Company, with capital stock of $100,000. This company now has capital and surplus of $150,000, and as its president Mr. Wyss made it one of the solid financial institutions of the city. Mr. Wyss is the largest stockholder and is treasurer of the Obear Nesten Glass Company, with plants at East St. Louis and Kansas City, Missouri, the offices of the company being in St. Louis. The assets of this company are around a million dollars. As a matter of both profit and personal diversion Mr. Wyss has invested heavily in farming lands, particularly in the rich and fertile district known as the American Bottoms. His largest farm comprises 720 acres, all improved and under cultivation, and a part of this is now being subdivided into acre tracts. Another farm of three hundred acres at Hartford, Illinois, is owned by Mrs. Wyss, who also has 80 acres near Canal.

Mr. Wyss married, August 30, 1893, Miss Dora B. Emert, of Hartford, Illinois. Their children are Pauline D., who married F. L.

Kane, resides in St. Louis and has one son, Paul Wyss; Emert L., a graduate of Law at St. Louis University and assistant cashier of his father's bank; Margaret, Angela and Bertha Helen. Mr. Wyss is affiliated with the Knights of Columbus and the fraternal Orders of Eagles and Elks. A democrat in national politics, he has been active in local affairs and has accepted a number of opportunities to render service in a civic way. For three terms, six years, he was a member of the Alton City Council. He and his family are members of the St. Mary's Catholic Church.

ABNER D. RUCKEL was for many years identified with the community of White Hall and assisted in building up one of that locality's most important industries, pottery works. A business that he started is now continued as the White Hall Pottery Works, with his son Carroll A. Ruckel as president.

Abner D. Ruckel was born in Pennsylvania, in 1835. As a boy he moved with his parents to Michigan and later to Akron, Ohio, where he finished his school education. He learned the machinist's trade, and during the Civil war enlisted at the first call for troops at Elyria. He became sergeant of Company H in the Tenth Ohio Infantry. After his time expired he reenlisted, but being a mechanic, was assigned duty in a government armory at Elyria, Ohio. After the war he was employed in a sewing machine factory at Elyria for a short time, then in a machine shop at Akron, and was also a merchant.

On leaving Ohio he came to Illinois and with M. C. Purdy as a partner formed the firm of Purdy & Ruckel, manufacturing pottery. It was the presence of potter's clay that brought him to White Hall. After leaving the firm he was in the hardware business for a time, was also a flour miller, but eventually resumed the pottery business, building a plant on the site of that now owned by his son and on the site of the original location where he had first engaged in that business.

Abner D. Ruckel died June 7, 1911. He was a member of the Grand Army of the Republic, cast his first presidential vote for John C. Fremont in 1856, and was always a staunch republican. He was a Knight Templar Mason. A. D. Ruckel married at Akron in 1869, Miss Emma Adams, who was born at Warrensville, near Cleveland, in 1841, daughter of Enoch Adams, of Portland, Maine. She died May 13, 1926.

Carroll Adams Ruckel, only child of his parents, was born at White Hall, April 9, 1872. He attended grammar school, worked in a store, but for thirty years or more has been identified with the pottery industry, succeeding his father as head of the business. The firm of A. D. Ruckel & Son is still continued as the proprietors of the White Hall Pottery Works. The owners are C. A. Ruckel, Helen E. Ruckel and T. M. English.

C. A. Ruckel became first president of the Chamber of Commerce upon its organization and is still a director. He represented the Chamber at the Illinois Chamber of Commerce in Chicago. He was a member of the White Hall Council while the sewer system was being installed. He cast his first presidential vote for William McKinley, and has always given his support to the republican party.

He married at White Hall, October 9, 1894, Miss Nora D. Mytinger, whose father was a Union soldier and one of the prominent old-time merchants of White Hall.

EDWARD J. VAN TUYLE. The Van Tuyle family for three generations has been identified with the ownership and working of land in Greene and Scott counties. They have been known as thrifty and energetic farmers and business men, and equally capable good citizens.

Otto Van Tuyle was a resident of New Jersey until he started for the west, bringing his family with wagon and team, and about 1839 established his home along the line of Scott and Greene counties. Some years later he and his brother went back to New Jersey to settle up the family estate, and both died a few days after their return to Illinois. Otto Van Tuyle married Charlotte Bulmer, and both are buried in the Manchester Cemetery of Scott County. Her father, Lieutenant Bulmer, also buried there, was a soldier in the War of 1812. The two children of Otto Van Tuyle born in New Jersey were Robert and Mary, the latter becoming the wife of David B. Hudson. After the family settled in Illinois two daughters were born, Martha Luthera and Julia.

Robert Van Tuyle was born in Somerset County, New Jersey, November 26, 1832, and was about seven years old when the family settled in Illinois. He attended district schools, and on reaching manhood engaged in farming, which was his occupation the rest of his life. He was county commissioner and supervisor, was a democrat, and was known and esteemed for his industry and good judgment, but was never conspicuous, being rather silent and reserved. His wife, born in Scott County, was Margaret A. Clark, daughter of E. J. and Sarah (Smith) Clark. Robert Van Tuyle died October 9, 1903. The children born to him and his wife were: Frederick O., who died in the home community after his marriage to Frances Rawlins; Edward J.; and Charlotte A., of Roodhouse.

Edward J. Van Tuyle was born February 12, 1866, was educated in schools at Roodhouse, in the Brown Business College at Jacksonville, and remained at home to the age of twenty-four. As a farmer he has been a grain and stock raiser, has fed live stock for the market, and has enjoyed the prosperity characteristic of the Van Tuyle family. He owns almost a section of land south of Roodhouse. He has never been active in politics, though he served as a member of the school board in his rural locality. He was one of the first stockholders and is vice president of the First National Bank of Roodhouse.

Mr. Van Tuyle was married at White Hall by Rev. Drake, a Baptist minister, March 18, 1890, to Miss Joanna Morrissey, daughter of John and M. C. (Walker) Morrissey. She was born February 17, 1866, was educated at White Hall and taught in rural districts before her marriage. Mr. and Mrs. Van Tuyle have two talented daughters. Alma May graduated from high school at Roodhouse, at-

tended school at Jacksonville and Peoria, and studied music, taking violin under Hugo Olk in St. Louis. She is now the wife of L. H. Schumann, of St. Louis, and they have two children, Robert and Ada Rosetta. Hilda Lee, the second daughter, graduated from high school at Roodhouse, studied violin and voice at Illinois College at Jacksonville and continued her vocal training in St. Louis. She is the wife of C. E. Hartwein, of St. Louis, and they have a daughter, Martha Jo. Another daughter, Mary Edna, born November 27, 1903, died August 12, 1905.

JOHN FRANCIS MCGINNIS, JR., is a prominent young Alton attorney, associated in practice with his father, John F. McGinnis, Sr. This firm, with offices at Alton, handles a large and important corporation law and loan practice. They are attorneys for the Citizens National Bank of Alton, the Missouri & Illinois Bridge and Belt Railway Company, the Springman Lumber Company, the Western Military Academy, and are local attorneys for the Alton, Granite and St. Louis Traction Company. Mr. McGinnis is also corporation counsel for the city of Alton and master in chancery of the City Court of Alton.

John F. McGinnis, Jr., was born at Alton, October 18, 1893, and was educated in the parochial schools of his native city, subsequently entering St. Mary's College in Kansas, where he was graduated with the A. B. degree in 1913. He studied law in Washington University at St. Louis, taking his LL. B. degree there.

He entered the First Officers Training School at Fort Sheridan, Illinois, on May 12, 1917, and on August 15, was commissioned a first lieutenant. He remained on duty during the rest of the war and when the armistice was signed held the rank of first lieutenant of the Eight Hundred Twelfth Pioneers. He is a member of the American Legion, the Delta Upsilon Phi and Delta Phi fraternities in College, and belongs to the Madison County and Illinois State Bar Associations.

FRANK W. THOMAS, a former president of the Chicago stock exchange and closely identified for many years with the stock and bond business of Chicago.

Mr. Thomas was born at Point Pleasant, Ohio, September 18, 1870, son of Henry and Lucy S. (Sweetland) Thomas, being the youngest of their four children. He was brought to Chicago when a child, attended the Hayes School in that city and the West Division High School. His first employment was as a clerk for a brokerage firm and in 1888, at the age of eighteen, he went to work in a clerical capacity with the American Exchange National Bank. He was there about three years, and then took a position with A. O. Slaughter & Company. He has been with that organization since 1891, gained a partnership in 1903, and since 1916 has been senior partner in the business. He was elected and served one term as president of the Chicago Stock Exchange.

Mr. Thomas is a member of the New York Stock Exchange, the Chicago Board of Trade, the Chicago Athletic Association, the Oak Park Country Club, Midday Club, The Attic, Chicago Literary Society and of a number of other clubs and civic organizations. He is a republican and a member of the Episcopal Church. Mr. Thomas, whose home is in Oak Park, married, June 14, 1900, Miss Susan A. Rogers, a native of Chicago and a daughter of James C. Rogers. They have one child, Lucy Sweetland Rogers.

S. D. ZAPH, M. D., physician and surgeon at Chicago, has achieved a very distinctive record in his profession, particularly in surgery, and is also a young man of varied attainments that have brought him interesting connections outside his working career.

Stamatis Demosthenes Zaph was born at Volo, in Thessaly, Greece, in 1883. He came to America when a youth, and while living in New York became a teacher of Greek in order to pay for his further education. He had attained the equivalent of a high school education before coming to this country. In 1912 he removed to Chicago, and in 1913 entered the medical department of Loyola University, where he was graduated M. D. in 1916. For one year he was an interne in St. John's Hospital at Springfield.

Doctor Zaph in 1918 volunteered for service in the United States Army Medical Corps. He attended the Medical Officers Training Camp at Fort Riley, Kansas, where he was commissioned a captain, and was on duty at various posts and training camps throughout the country. When he received his honorable discharge in 1919 he was located at Fort Benjamin Harrison, Indianapolis. Doctor Zaph for two years after the war was associated in surgery at Springfield with Doctor Compton. In 1921 he returned to Chicago. Prior to his military service Doctor Zaph had supplemented his regular medical education with a full course in the Doctor Still Osteopathic School in Des Moines, and thus was qualified to combine the two schools of medicine in his practice. As a surgeon he has a place of particular high rank in Chicago and Illinois. He is professor of surgery in the Chicago Osteopathic College and Hospital and is a staff surgeon in the hospital. He is a member of the Chicago Medical Society, Illinois State Medical Association, and a fellow of the American Medical Association. Doctor Zaph maintains his offices in the downtown district at 27 East Monroe Street.

For several years he has been high in the councils of "The Ahepa," a national organization of citizens of Greek ancestry in America, one of the main objects of which is to acquaint the American people with the best phases of Greek civilization and Greek culture, and to encourage education and a knowledge of American ideals among Greeks in this country. It has in its membership a large number of leading business and professional men of Greek birth or Greek ancestry, and has become an organization of distinctive influence in national affairs. At the National Convention of The Ahepa held at the Drake Hotel in Chicago in September, 1925, Doctor Zaph was honored by election as supreme governor. He was particularly active in this organization's activities in behalf of relief for the Near East.

Doctor Zaph is also a past president of the Hellenic, Professional Men's Club of Chicago. He is a member of the Kiwanis Club, Medinah Athletic Club, Lake Shore Athletic Club, Medical Arts Club, and belongs to the various bodies of Masonry, including the Mystic Shrine.

Doctor Zaph married a cultured American woman, Miss Frances Dorothy Capps, who after completing her college education carried on extensive study of music. Her great-great-grandfather, Jabez Capps, was very active during the American Revolution and later settled Mount Pulaski, which he named in honor of the Polish patriot, Count Pulaski. The Capps family was very intimately connected with Lincoln in Springfield. She is also related to Major Capps, who served as ambassador to Greece during the Wilson administration. Doctor and Mrs. Zaph have one daughter, Victoria.

FREDERICK CLEMENT ALDRICH was born at Chicago, Illinois, September 12, 1862, son of William and Anna M. (Howard) Aldrich. Mr. Aldrich was educated in the public schools and Chicago Academy, and practically since his eighteenth year has been in the grain business, beginning in the grain commission business in 1880. In March, 1909, he became associated with Finley Barrell & Company, brokers, and January 1, 1911, was admitted to partnership. Mr. Aldrich continued in that relation until December 31, 1915, when he became an active broker on the Chicago stock exchange. For four years, 1913-1915-1918-1920, he was president of the Chicago stock exchange and a member of the board of directors for many years.

Mr. Aldrich married, June 5, 1890, Miss Gertrude Newell, of Kenosha, Wisconsin, and they have two daughters, Anita and Helen. The family home is at Lake Forest, Illinois. He is a member of the Chicago Board of Trade and of the University, Chicago, Saddle and Cycle, Shore Acres and Onwentsia Clubs, and in politics is a republican.

JOHN E. SCHWAAB. A civil engineer by profession, specializing in municipal work, with twenty-four years of experience in railroad work and municipal work, John E. Schwaab represents an old and prominent family of Madison County, Illinois, and is the present city engineer of Alton, and maintains an engineering office, specializing in municipal engineering work under the name of Schwaab and Sheppard.

He was born at Alton, June 30, 1884. His father, George J. Schwaab, was born in the same city, son of John Schwaab, who came from Germany in an early day to Southern Illinois. George J. Schwaab is still living in Alton. The mother of the city engineer was Margaret Elizabeth Dorsett, a native of Alton, and her people were an old Tennessee family. John E. Schwaab is one of a family of two sons and one daughter, and since boyhood he has exercised an independent spirit, making his own way. After attending the public schools of Alton he went to Chicago and paid his way while attending the Chicago Technical School, being a wage worker in the day and attending night classes and shop practice. After completing his training there he returned to Alton and entered the service of the Chicago & Alton Railway. He was with the engineering department of this road altogether for nine years, separated by an interval, and from road man was promoted to resident engineer in charge of construction. One of the important jobs of which he had charge for the Chicago & Alton Railroad was the construction of the freight terminals at Chicago. Mr. Schwaab finally gave up his work with the railroad to engage in private practice at Alton. He has served under five appointments in the office of city engineer, the first time from 1911 to 1915, again from 1920 to 1921, and in 1923 was again called to this important and responsible office, which now holds one where he has supervision over all municipal improvements involving engineering problems. He is a member of the firm of Schwaab and Sheppard, civil engineers.

Mr. Schwaab is a member of the Illinois Society of Engineers, and is affiliated with the B. P. O. Elks and Kiwanis Club of Alton. In politics he is a democrat.

Mr. Schwaab married in 1906 Miss Julia Miller, of Alton. They have two children, John Harold and Irene Louise.

CHARLES K. FOSTER, a resident of Chicago for over thirty years, has in his business activities been identified with the growth and development of one of the largest and most prosperous industrial organizations in the country, and his part in its growth has been reflected in his own increasing responsibilities from minor to higher official positions.

Mr. Foster was born in Detroit, Michigan, October 19, 1867, son of Frederick S. and Adelaide Victoria (Grose) Foster. He was educated in the public schools of Detroit, and in St. Johnsbury Academy in Vermont, and as a youth entered the service of the Merchants and Manufacturers National Bank of his native city. He was employed as a bookkeeper, and learned much of the fundamentals of banking, but preferring a more active career, resigned in 1891 to become a salesman for the Detroit Radiator Company. When that was merged with the American Radiator Company he remained with the larger organization and since 1892, the year the general headquarters of the American Radiator Company were established in Chicago, he has himself had his permanent home in this city. From salesman he was promoted to assistant secretary, then to general manager of sales, then to vice president, and since 1922 has been executive vice president and treasurer. The American Radiator Company is one of the leaders in the group of manufacturing and industrial corporations known nationally and internationally, and Mr. Foster's executive position is corresponding evidence of a very successful career. He is also a director of the Union Trust Company of Chicago.

Through his business activity he has aided most effectively in a service for the common welfare and as a private citizen, has taken a keen interest in public matters, and made

his influence felt. He is a member of the Chicago, Onwentsia, Old Elm Gulf, Saddle and Cycle, Chicago Athletic, Racquet and Industrial clubs, having served as president and secretary of the Industrial Club. Because of his special knowledge and business experience he was called to Washington during the World war, and served as one of the "Dollar a Year" men, rendering a service of special value as vice chairman of the Priority Committee of the War Industries Board for the greater part of two years. It is to men like Charles K. Foster, who freely give of their best, who are proud of their nationality, who continually and unselfishly endeavor to maintain the pre-eminence of America without the expectation of fee or reward for so doing, that our country is indebted.

Mr. Foster married, in 1905, Miss Janet M. Brien. Their home is at 199 Lake Shore Drive.

PERRY H. HILES is head of one of the most successful law firms in Edwardsville, and in professional ability, civic patriotism and public spirit has long stood as one of the abler members of that community. In his career he has been active in politics in Madison County as a worker in the ranks of the republican organization.

Mr. Hiles was born in Jasper County, Illinois, November 29, 1878, son of Jacob F. and Sarah J. (McFadden) Hiles. The Hiles family lived in Pennsylvania, from there went to Eastern Ohio, and John Hiles, grandfather of the Edwardsville attorney, came to Illinois from Ohio about 1840. Jacob F. Hiles was born in Eastern Ohio in 1832, and spent his active career on an Illinois farm. He died in 1899 and his wife, in 1897. Perry H. was the third child and second son in a family consisting of six sons and five daughters, all of whom grew up and ten of whom are still living.

Perry H. Hiles had just reached his majority when his father died. He had attended the public schools of Jasper County, and for about three years he taught there. When his father died he took his seven younger brothers and sisters and as their guardian moved to Normal, Illinois, and established a home while all of them were completing their education. He himself attended the Illinois Normal University, graduating in 1904. After teaching for a time he spent the year 1906 in Alaska as secretary of a gold mining company. On returning to Illinois he entered the Illinois Wesleyan University Law School, and was graduated in 1909. He passed the bar examination in Chicago and in the fall of the same year was admitted to practice and opened his office at Edwardsville, where he has been continuously active in law practice for fifteen years, except the period he was away from home during the World war. He began practice at Edwardsville with Mr. J. L. Simpson in the firm of Hiles & Simpson. They were in partnership for ten years, separating in 1920. After that Mr. Hiles practiced alone a year and then became senior member of the law firm of Hiles, Newell & Brown.

In the early part of the American participation in the great war Mr. Hiles acted as treasurer of the Madison County Chapter of the Red Cross during 1917-18, and in the summer of 1918 was made farm labor administrator for Madison County and also County director of the Boys Working Reserve, with supervision over boys under twenty-one. In September, 1918, he himself enlisted and was sent to the Officers' Training School in the Field Artillery at Camp Taylor, Kentucky. After the armistice he was discharged and then resumed his law practice at Edwardsville. He helped to organize the Edwardsville post of the American Legion, of which he is a member and was its first adjutant.

Mr. Hiles is a Royal Arch Mason and a member of the Eastern Star, Knights of Pythias, Modern Woodmen of America, and St. John's Methodist Episcopal Church. In 1925 he was chairman of the organizing committee which organized the Edwardsville Rotary Club, and served the first year as its president. On November 24, 1914, he married Miss Julia Atwood, of Holland, Michigan. They have one daughter, Marguerite, who was born October 17, 1916. Mrs. Hiles was born at Grand View, South Dakota, April 7, 1890. While she was yet a small girl her parents moved to Holland, Michigan, where she received her early education, later attending Kalamazoo Normal School. She then taught in the public schools of Holland until her marriage. She is a member of the Order of Eastern Star, the Woman's Auxiliary of the American Legion and Edwardsville Monday Club. She is also a member of the St. John's Methodist Episcopal Church of Edwardsville.

JOHN L. MCINERNEY, a Chicago attorney, was born in that city, and has achieved some connections that are of themselves the highest evidence of rating as a lawyer.

He was born in Chicago September 16, 1886, son of Michael F. and Catherine (Heffernan) McInerney, his father and mother being natives of County Limerick, Ireland. His father was born February 2, 1852, and he came to America and reached Chicago in 1872. The parents were married in Chicago, October 20, 1880. Of their eight children five are living, John L. being the fourth in age. His father on coming to Chicago first found employment at the Union Stock Yards, his first work being shutting off the water in the cattle and hog pens. From that menial duty he made his services more important and was promoted to assistant superintendent. In 1879 he engaged in the undertaking and livery business. From that in 1887 he transferred his interests to brick manufacturing, a line he continued until 1893.

In 1879 he was appointed collector for the Town of Lake and was elected to that office in 1881. For nine years he held the office of member of the Board of Education of District No. 2 of the towns of Lake and Hyde Park. In 1890 he was elected and in 1892, re-elected a member of the State Legislature, serving two terms. In 1886 he was appointed township engineer for the Town of Lake, holding the office three months under the administration of Mayor Cregier. He was also alderman from the Twenty-ninth Ward, and the Thirtieth Ward, representing one or the other of these for a period of ten years. He is still active and well known in official affairs in Chicago, and under the Forest Preserve, has supervision of golf clubs on the Forest Preserves of Cook County.

John L. McInerney received a grammar and high school education in the St. Gabriel parochial schools, and from those entered the Chicago Kent College of Law, graduating in 1906 and being admitted to the bar in 1907, at the age of twenty-one. For several years he was an assistant corporation counsel, and on January 1, 1912, engaged in general practice under his own name. He is well known as a corporation attorney. Since 1914 he has been general atorney for the Soo Line Railways, and district attorney for the Minneapolis and St. Louis Railway since 1921.

Mr. McInerney is affiliated with the Knights of Columbus; Catholic Foresters; South Shore Country Club; the Illinois Athletic Club; the Lake Shore Athletic Club, and is a democrat in politics. He married, August 30, 1906, Miss Agnes J. Hoops, who was born in Grand Rapids, Michigan.

HAL C. WORCESTER is a veteran in commercial experience in Greene County, and has devoted over forty-five years of his life to the varied demands of business and community interests at Roodhouse.

He was born at White Hall, November 26, 1858. His father, Judge Linus E. Worcester, came from Windsor, Vermont, to Illinois in 1836. He had been well educated, and at Manchester, Illinois, taught school, after which he became a retail merchant with Simeon Ross at White Hall. The firm of Ross & Worcester continued for many years. He also established a lumber yard at White Hall, and was in the lumber business until a short time before his death. He also erected several residences in that town. Judge Worcester, who died in October, 1892, served several terms as county judge of Greene County and in the late '40s was elected a member of the Legislature. He was not a member of any church or fraternity. Two sons by his first marriage were soldiers in the Civil war. Alfred was a private in the Fourteenth Illinois Infantry and was promoted to lieutenant, married Laney McCollister and left four sons. William P. was in the Ninety-first Illinois Infantry, and after the war for many years was in the government service, being assistant to the surgeon general of the Marine Corps when he died. The second wife of Judge Worcester was Luthera Ladd, who was born on the Ladd homestead near White Hall, daughter of Thomas Ladd. Her sister, Augusta, became the wife of Major E. A. Giller. Her brother, Timothy, spent his life at White Hall. The mother of Hal C. Worcester died in October, 1902. There were two other children: Emma, who became the wife of M. J. Galhuley, of White Hall; and Richard S., of White Hall.

Hal Clay Worcester was reared and educated at White Hall, leaving high school before graduation. He worked in his father's lumber yard, and in 1880 removed to Roodhouse and established a lumber business to which he gave his personal supervision for forty-five years, until August 15, 1925. He made a success by devoting his time and energies to this business. He also served as a director in the Roodhouse Bank, and in 1924 he took the local agency for the Ford car and other Ford products, establishing the Worcester Auto Sales Company, of which he is president, but in which his sons are the active men, his son William L. being manager. Mr. Worcester's business interests have been on a large scale and for some years the total of his sales aggregated a quarter of a million dollars.

For many years he was a director of the Roodhouse schools. He is a democrat in national politics, having cast his first vote for Grover Cleveland in 1884. He is one of the three surviving charter members of the Knights of Pythias Lodge and is a past chancellor. He is a trustee of the Methodist Church.

Mr. Worcester married at Winchester, Illinois, October 7, 1885, Miss Carrie Condit, who was born in Scott County. Her father, William Condit, came to Illinois from New Jersey, was a hat maker by trade and for many years was a merchant at Winchester. The Condit children were: Henry, Thomas, Charles, William, John, Mrs. Worcester, and Maggie, who became the wife of William Keuchler. Mrs. Worcester finished her education in the Woman's College at Jacksonville, and taught school at Winchester before her marriage. The oldest child of Mr. and Mrs. Worcester is Irene, wife of Judge Floyd E. Thompson, of Rock Island, and a man of state-wide reputation as one of the justices of the Illinois Supreme Court. Judge and Mrs. Thompson have a daughter, Mary Ellen Thompson. William Linus Worcester, manager of the Worcester Auto Sales Company, married Chloe Barrow and has two children, Will and Hal. Richard Ladd Worcester graduated from the Roodhouse High School, attended Illinois State University three years, and volunteered when America entered the war, being a first lieutenant in the transportation department at Camp Funston, and was promoted to captain while at Camp Taylor, Louisville, Kentucky. He is now a hardware merchant at Newton, Illinois, and by his marriage to Helen Logler has two children, Dicky and Bob. Paul Condit Worcester, the youngest of the children, graduated from the local high school and has since been associated with his father's business. He was a volunteer during the World war, but was rejected for active duty.

BART R. KENNEDY. That quality of demonstrated efficiency and personal popularity which is the best recommendation for public service has been displayed to preeminent advantage in Bart R. Kennedy, of Alton, who has been elected and re-elected and has served longer as a city official than any other member of the municipal government there. Mr. Kennedy has rounded out eighteen years of consecutive service as city clerk.

He was born at Alton, December 6, 1880, son of Bart and Catherine (Renne) Kennedy. His parents were born and married in Ireland, and after coming to America lived for a time at Stamford, Connecticut, and in 1858 moved to Alton. The father was engaged in the grocery business. Both parents are now deceased, and of their ten children Bart R. was the ninth, and one of three now living.

Mr. Kennedy grew up at Alton, attended grammar and high school, and as a youth began his business career as a bookkeeper in a coal office. For four years he was glassware inspector in the plant of the Illinois Glass Company, and while there he made his first appearance in city politics as candidate for alderman to represent the old Sixth now the Fifth Ward. He was elected, and after two terms he was nominated and elected city clerk, and altogether has been honored with that office by nine elections, at all times running ahead of his ticket, his leadership in this respect on occasions being more than a thousand votes and on two occasions better than four thousand.

Mr. Kennedy was for six years a member of the Alton Board of Education, and was treasurer of the consolidated school districts of Alton. He is a director of the Home Building & Loan Association of Alton. Fraternally he is affiliated with the B. P. O. Elks, the Modern Woodmen of America, is a fourth degree Knight of Columbus, a member of the Alton Chamber of Commerce and the East End Improvement Association. Mr. Kennedy is at present time president of the Alton Fire Department Association of Alton.

In 1910 he married Miss Nellie Alt, of Alton, who was a well known school teacher before her marriage. She died in 1920, leaving two children, George R. and John E. On October 27, 1923, Mr. Kennedy married Miss Rose Mary Garde, of Alton.

CHARLES WILLIAM GREENMAN is a veteran railroad man, his service having covered over thirty-five years, at first with the Michigan Central and for over twenty years with the Wabash Railway. He is now Wabash Railway agent at the Danville freight offices.

Mr. Greenman was born at Ann Arbor, Michigan, March 5, 1868. His grandfather, William B. Greenman, was born in 1810 at Johnstown, Pennsylvania, and when twelve years of age ran away from home and went to Michigan, locating at Ann Arbor. He became a wood turner, and both he and his son John R. were possessed of the old time skill in that honorable occupation. He lived at Ann Arbor until his death in 1864. His wife, Catherine Mann, was born at Ann Arbor. Their son, John Rogers Greenman, was born in Ann Arbor, April 4, 1836; was reared and married there and learned the trade of wood turner. He served during the last two years and eleven months of the Civil war as a Union soldier, and that service greatly impaired his health, so that after the war he went to the vicinity of Traverse City, at Glen Lake, Michigan, living there for many years, but died while visiting his son, Charles W., in Toledo on February 26, 1905. He was a staunch republican in politics, holding various civil offices, a constable for a number of years and at Glen Lake was for a time member of the school board. He was affiliated with the Independent Order of Odd Fellows and the Grand Army of the Republic. John G. Greenman married Mary Elizabeth Crawford, who was born at Albion, in October, 1837, and died January 24, 1920. A brief record of their family of children is as follows: Catherine, who died at Benton, Michigan, wife of Chester Gordon, a lumber contractor, who died near Glen Lake, Michigan; Charles William; David S., who was accidentally killed in 1896 while on duty for the Michigan Central Railway at Ann Arbor; Ida May, wife of Stanley B. Burke, a railroad employe, living at Anacortes, Washington; Ina, who died when seven years old; and Daniel, who died at the age of three years.

Charles William Greenman spent some of his boyhood days in Leelanau County, Michigan, where he attended public schools and finished his public school education in Ann Arbor. He spent three years in the scientific course in the Ann Arbor High School, and was then in the commercial department of the Ann Arbor High School, but left shortly before the time set for his graduation to begin work for the Michigan Central Railway, on March 27, 1889. He was then just a few days past the age of twenty-one. He remained in the service of the Michigan Central as chief clerk, station agent and in other duties until October 1, 1903, finally being chief clerk in the freight office. Leaving the Michigan Central, he went with the Wabash Railway Company, beginning as chief clerk at the Cherry Street Station at Toledo, and on November 7, 1907, was transferred to Attica, Indiana, as Wabash Railway agent, and on March 5, 1913, was appointed agent of the freight office of the Wabash Railway at Danville. The Wabash Railway freight offices at Danville are at 220 East Main Street.

Mr. Greenman is a republican in politics; is a member of the First Baptist Church, and fraternally is affiliated with Anchor Lodge No. 980, A. F. and A. M.; Danville Consistory of the Scottish Rite, and took his first degrees in Masonry with Fraternity Lodge No. 262, at Ann Arbor, Michigan, for eleven years being secretary of that lodge. He belongs to the Railroad Telegraph Operators Association. Since coming to Danville he has acquired considerable property, including five dwelling houses and his own home at 421 North Gilbert Street.

Mr. Greenman married at Ann Arbor, Michigan, June 22, 1892, Miss Lottie A. Murray, daughter of Charles and Mary Jane (Treadwell) Murray. Her father was accidentally killed in a railway accident at Ann Arbor, where her mother still lives. Mrs. Greenman died May 5, 1920, being the mother of five children: Lyleth May, the oldest, is the wife of Chester Daugherty, assistant manager of the National Car Coupler Company at Attica, Indiana. Gladys Vivian is the wife of Roy J. Harrison, works manager of the National Car Coupler Company at Attica. Charles Donald also lives at Attica, where he is foreman in the shipping department of the National Car Coupler Company. He is a veteran of the World war, having trained with the Engineers' Corps at Camp Shelby, Mississippi, and spent twelve months in France. James Meredith, the second son, a clerk with the Wabash Railway Company, lives with his father. John Murray, the youngest, is a student in the Attica High School.

HON. BRUCE A. CAMPBELL, able attorney, capable public official, and a citizen whose Americanism has been conclusively proven on every occasion, is recognized as one of the leaders of his profession at East Saint Louis. He was born at Albion, Edwards County, Illinois, October 28, 1879, a son of Joseph M. and Amabel (Thompson) Campbell, and a grandson of Alexander and Permelia Campbell, natives of Kentucky. In 1812 the Campbell family moved to Wayne County, Illinois, and the first court of the county was held in the home of the great-grandfather of Bruce A. Campbell, and he later, from 1820 to 1824, served in the State Assembly. His son, the grandfather of Bruce A. Campbell, served in the same body during the session of 1853. The maternal grandparents, Dr. Francis B. and Jane (Bowman) Thompson, were also prominent people, he having been born in England, but came to the United States, and settling in Edwards County, continued in practice as a physician until his death in 1885. The father of Mrs. Thompson was one of the very first settlers of Edwards County, and she was born in the county, in 1821, three years after her family settled within its confines.

Joseph M. Campbell, who died in 1918, was for years one of the most prominent men of Edwards County, which he served for thirteen years as county judge, and for about thirty years he was master-in-chancery. As an attorney he had but few equals and no superiors, and he was a leader in community affairs. For many years he served on the local school board, and he was always a friend of the public schools. His wife died April 21, 1925. She and her husband had the following children: Bruce A., who was the first born; Winifred, who is living at Indianapolis, Indiana, married R. C. Craig; Joseph F., who is living in Portland, Oregon, married Essie Zeigler, and they have four children; Jean B., who is living at Carmi, Illinois, married Harry Ziegler, and has three children; Mary A., who married Lloyd D. Bunting, is living in Storrs, Connecticut; Nigel D., who married Jennette Carmichel, lives in Chicago.

Bruce A. Campbell was graduated from the Albion High School in 1894, following which he was a student in the Southern Collegiate Institute, from which he was graduated in 1897. In 1900 he was graduated from the University of Illinois, Urbana, Illinois, with the degree of Bachelor of Arts. Taking up then the study of law in his father's office, he was admitted to the bar in 1901, and began practicing at Albion. During 1903 and 1904 he was city attorney of Albion, and in the latter year was elected to the Forty-fourth Illinois State Assembly from the Forty-eighth District. In 1905 he came to East Saint Louis, becoming here associated with Judge E. C. Kramer, and R. J. Kramer, leading attorneys of St. Clair County, under the firm name of Kramer, Kramer & Campbell. Mr. Campbell was a delegate to the Democratic National Convention that nominated Woodrow Wilson for president, and was delegate-at-large to his party's convention held in New York City in 1924. He has been a delegate to every democratic state convention since 1904, and served as chairman of the state conventions of his party in 1922 and 1926. Mr. Campbell was also the choice of his party for congressman of his district in 1910, but, although he polled a flattering vote, was defeated. He declined an appointment as assistant attorney general of the United States under President Wilson in 1913. During the late war he was very active, participating zealously in war work, and made over fifty speeches and organized the Four-Minute speakers in Southern Illinois; was chief officer of the American Protective League for ten counties of Illinois; was a member of the Elks National War Relief Commission; had charge of over $1,000,000 of the Elks' fund for war relief and rehabilitation work from July, 1918, to July, 1919, and held the office of grand exalted ruler of the Elks during the period of the war.

On June 19, 1906, Mr. Campbell married, at Marissa, Illinois, Miss Beulah Wilson Campbell, a daughter of Dr. J. M. and Lucretia (Wilson) Campbell, the former of whom is living, but the latter died about 1887. The families are not related. Doctor and Mrs. Campbell had the following children: Dr. Joseph A. Campbell, of Marissa, married first Elizabeth Wallingford, by whom he had one son, Joseph, and second, Dixie Wakefield, by whom he has no children; and Beulah. Doctor Campbell was county coroner for years, and is a most highly respected man. One child, Joseph Bruce Campbell, has been born to Mr. and Mrs. Campbell, the date of his birth being March, 1907. He is attending the University of Illinois. Mr. Campbell, while not a member, was reared as an Episcopalian, and his wife is a Baptist. He belongs to the county, state and national bar associations, is president of the East Saint Louis Bar Association, and held the same office with the state association. Fraternally he is a thirty-second degree Knight Templar and Shriner Mason, belongs to the Modern Woodmen of America, and to the Benevolent and Protective Order of Elks, of which he was grand exalted ruler in 1918-1919. During 1911 and 1912 he was president of the Illinois Elks Association, and is now a member of the Elks National Memorial Commission on building the magnificent Elks Memorial at Chicago, and has that work in charge and which also has charge of the publication of the Elks magazine. He was made a Mason at Albion and served that lodge as senior warden. His college fraternities are Sigma Alpha Epsilon and Phi Beta Kappa. In every phase of life Mr. Campbell has displayed those qualities which make for leadership, and he not only is able to accomplish great things himself, but is also able to inspire others to co-operate with him in bringing to a successful conclusion whatever he undertakes.

ALFRED BARTON SCOTT, JR., has been a resident of Danville since 1921, and is treasurer and purchasing agent of the United Electric Coal Companies, probably the largest organization of its kind in Illinois, engaged in "strip mining" operations. Mr. Scott is a young business man with very wide and diversified experience in the financial and executive management of industrial companies.

He was born at Sarnia in the Province of

Ontario, Canada, February 15, 1894. His grandfather, George Scott, was born at Port Elgin, Ontario, and spent most of his life there as a carpenter and builder. In his ninetieth year he moved to Port Huron, Michigan, and lived there until his death, when nearly one hundred years old. His son, Alfred Barton Scott, Sr., now a resident of St. Clair, Michigan, was born at Port Elgin, Ontario, and was widely known during his active career as a trainer and raiser of race horses, having been a familiar figure on turfs and tracks in both the United States and Canada. He was reared and married in Ontario, and in about 1893 removed to Port Huron, Michigan. He is credited with having broken and trained Justice Brooke, the first two year old colt to beat the 2:10 trotting record. He has lived retired at St. Clair, Michigan, since 1911. His wife, Mary Redden, was born at Sarnia, Ontario, and had returned to her old home there for a visit when her first child, Alfred B., was born in 1894. Her other son is George Wellington, a student in the Boston Institute of Technology.

Alfred Barton Scott, Jr., was reared in Port Huron, Michigan, attended public schools there, and for three years was a student in the Detroit University School, where he graduated in 1913. He played with the baseball team of that school and has always been an ardent follower of sports. For eighteen months after leaving school he was on the staff of the Detroit Tribune as boxing critic. Leaving there, he went to Tulsa, Oklahoma, and became a messenger boy in the Central National Bank of Tulsa, but was teller when he resigned a year later. His next experience was in New York City, in the offices of George G. Moore, where he remained from January 1 to May 30, 1917.

Returning to St. Clair, Michigan, he enlisted in the United States Navy, July 10, 1917, and was put in training at Newport, Rhode Island. He received a commission as ensign, but shortly afterwards the armistice was declared and he saw no active service. He received his honorable discharge in December, 1918. At the close of the war Mr. Scott went to Ranger, Texas, during the great oil boom in that section, and had charge of the oil interests of J. E. Crosbie, president of the Central National Bank of Tulsa, Oklahoma, also one of the large individual oil operators in the Ranger field. He was there about a year and then resumed employment with the George G. Moore interests, most of his time being spent in the oil fields of the South.

In July, 1921, Mr. Scott came to Danville, Illinois, and was made assistant top boss for the United Electric Coal Companies and at the end of the year was promoted to purchasing agent, and since May, 1923, has been treasurer of the company as well as purchasing agent. The offices of the company are in the New Meis Building at Danville, these being the main offices. W. G. Hartshorn and Grant Holmes, of Danville, were the originators of the process of coal mine stripping in the United States. The United Electric Coal Companies purchased their interests in 1921, and their operations in the Illinois field produce an enormous volume of coal annually.

Mr. Scott is a republican, member of St. Paul's Catholic Church at Danville, and is affiliated with Danville Lodge No. 332, B. P. O. Elks. Mr. Scott married at Sullivan, Indiana, September 2, 1921, Miss Mary Wilson. She was born at Robinson, Illinois, and was educated in the University of Missouri, and finished her schooling in the noted Finch School of New York City. Mr. and Mrs. Scott have one child: Alfred Barton III.

JACOB FRED AMMANN was born in St. Louis, Missouri, May 15, 1868. His father, David Ammann, was born in Switzerland. The mother, Anna (Merz) Ammann, was born in Germany.

In 1869 the family established their home in Alhambra, Illinois, where the subject of this sketch passed through the grade schools. When he was thirteen years of age his father died and the remaining family again moved to St. Louis. Here the lad worked at odd jobs to help support the mother and a smaller sister, and at the age of eighteen years took a position in a greenhouse, learning the fundamentals of growing flowers. After three years of apprentice work along this line the young man, at the age of twenty-one years, established himself on a small scale in the greenhouse business at Alhambra, Illinois.

In 1890 he entered into wedlock with Bertha C. Gehrig, daughter of Jacob Gehrig, a prominent farmer of Alhambra Township. To this union three girls were born, namely: Alma, who is now Mrs. E. G. Hallquist, of Edwardsville, Illinois; Edna, who is now Mrs. H. N. Wade, of LaGrange, Illinois; and Angeline, who is now Mrs. P. S. Montgomery of Edwardsville, Illinois.

In 1892 Mr. Ammann moved his greenhouse establishment from Alhambra to Edwardsville, Illinois, and here was laid the foundation for the present greenhouse establishment which consists of sixty thousand square feet of glass and which is now devoted entirely to the wholesale growing of roses for cut flowers. Approximately six hundred thousand blooms are shipped annually to the St. Louis market from this establishment.

Mr. Ammann has for many years been active in organization work locally as well as in the organizations of his trade. For several years he served as president of the Commercial Club. He was for several terms a member of the Board of Education; served in the City Council as alderman; and during that time served on many prominent committees which assisted in the general progress of the City of Edwardsville. Mr. Ammann is an elder in the First Presbyterian Church, a republican in politics; and during the World war served as chairman of Madison County Local Board No. 1.

He was twice elected president of the St. Louis Florists' Club, was the first president elect of the Illinois State Florists' Association, which was organized in 1905, and subsequently became its secretary for fifteen years, during which time appropriations were put through the Legislature for the purpose of establishing experimental greenhouses at the University of Urbana, Illinois. Mr. Ammann has since that time served as a member of the Advisory Committee to this station. The experimental work in floriculture carried on at the Illinois station is the largest in scope of any in the country.

In 1918 Mr. Ammann was elected president of the Society of American Florists' and Ornamental Horticulturists, an organization which covers the entire part of North America in the floriculture line. For three years Mr. Ammann served as field manager of the Florist's Telegraph Delivery Association, organizing seventy-six district units of this organization throughout North America.

In 1920 Mr. Ammann was elected president of the Florists' Hail Association of America, a mutual protective insurance for greenhouse establishments. Mr. Ammann is now serving as a member of the Board of Directors of the Society of American Flosists and Ornamental Horticulturists, and is also a member of the National Publicity Committee which committee created the slogan "Say It With Flowers" and through which a national campaign of advertising is continually carried on.

Mr. Ammann has received the above honors without any solicitation whatever on his part and has never held a position in public life or organization work wherein compensation was a consideration.

LAWRENCE W. HELLRUNG. A native son of Alton, Lawrence W. Hellrung has lived there, has prospered in business, has earned the respect and esteem of his fellow citizens, and still has a number of interests and investments, though practically retired from business.

He was born at Alton July 29, 1867, son of Christopher and Mary (Budde) Hellrung. The father, a native of Germany, came to America at the age of sixteen, in 1853, and locating at Alton, became a brick manufacturer. A large amount of building material entering into some of the oldest structures of Alton were made in his plant. He died in the early promise of a very successful career at the age of thirty-three. He was survived by his widow more than half a century. She passed away in January, 1922, the mother of two sons and two daughters.

Lawrence W. Hellrung was only three years old when his father died, and after a brief education in the parochial schools at Alton he went to work at the age of twelve, and ever since has been dependent upon his own exertions for his advancement. For some years he was employed by his uncle, and in 1897 with borrowed capital he engaged in the grocery and saloon business. Six years later he bought out the J. H. Raible wholesale liquor house, and with J. W. Schmidt established the firm of Schmidt and Hellrung, a large and successful business that grew and prospered from 1903 to 1907, when it was incorporated as the Commercial Liquor Company, with Mr. Hellrung as secretary and treasurer. In July, 1919, the firm retired completely from the business. Mr. Hellrung was for a time president of the Commercial Ice and Fuel Company, and his chief connection with business today is as president of the Hellrung Construction Company, though the active man in this business is his son, Herbert C. Hellrung, secretary and treasurer of the company. Mr. Hellrung also has some valuable and important holdings in real estate, and these investments require some of his time.

In 1890 he married Miss Cecelia Schuelle, who died in 1901, the mother of three children, Mary, Herbert and Frances. In 1902 Mr. Hellrung married Mrs. Julianna Ackor Brennfleck, of St. Louis. By this marriage there is one daughter, Julianna. Mr. Hellrung and family are all members of St. Mary's Church at Alton, and he is affiliated with the Western Catholic Union, and is a democrat in national politics.

COLFAX T. MARTIN has been a practicing lawyer at Danville for the past fifteen years. The years of his early manhood were spent largely as a teacher in his native State of Indiana. His reputation is that of an able lawyer and a popular and useful citizen.

He was born near Adams, in Decatur County, Indiana, September 24, 1873. The Martin family is of English ancestry and was established in Virginia before the War of the Revolution. His grandfather, John Martin, was born in Harrison County, Kentucky, lived there until middle life and then moved to the vicinity of Greensburg, Indiana, where he followed farming until his death. He married Nancy Martin, of a distinguished family of that name, also a native of Kentucky. Their son, Ralph Martin, was born near Greensburg in Decatur County, Indiana, in 1834, and spent practically all his life in that section, becoming a substantial farmer. Late in life he retired to Indianapolis, and died in that city in 1914. He was a republican, a member of the Methodist Church and the Masonic fraternity. His wife, Eva Tevis, was born near Moscow, Indiana, in 1849, and died at Lawrence in that state in 1907. Colfax Texis was the oldest of their children. Luther B. is assistant principal of High School at Muncie, Indiana. Charles P. is pastor of the Brookside United Brethren Church at Indianapolis. John E. is a farmer near Carlyle, Montana. Otto T. is a prominent minister of the Methodist Church and is now district superintendent of the Crawfordsville Methodist Church district in Indiana. His twin brother, Otis T., is also a Methodist minister, and pastor of the Kemp M. E. Church at Tipton, Indiana. Eva married Harry Hasewinkle, a resident of Indianapolis, where he is connected with the Atkinson Saw Works. Marcus E., the youngest of the family, died at Cayuga, Indiana, at the age of twenty-three. The father of these children by his first wife, Martha Ferguson, had a son, Ralph E., who was a farmer and died at Rushville, Indiana, in 1918.

Colfax T. Martin spent his early life on a farm in Decatur County, Indiana, attending public schools, graduating from the Clarksburg High School in 1891 and for three years taught in Rush County, in the intervals of his teaching attending the Central Normal College in Indiana, where he was graduated in 1894. For a year he was assistant principal of the high school at Milroy, Indiana, and in 1897 graduated with the degree Bachelor of Pedagogy from the Indiana State Normal School at Terre Haute. Then for a year he was superintendent of schools at La Follette, Tennessee, and for seven years superintendent of schools at Cayuga, Indiana. Teaching supplied him the means to complete his higher education. In 1907 he graduated from the Indiana University at Bloomington, Indiana, with the A. B. degree, and took his law course in the law department of the State University at Indianapolis, graduating LL. B in 1909 and was admitted to the Indiana bar in October of the same year. Mr. Martin opened his office in Danville, Illinois, and has had a growing clientage in general practice, his offices being in the Daniel Building.

Mr. Martin has had a number of congenial and useful relations in his community, both as a citizen and in social circles. From 1915 to 1921 he was a member of the City Council of Danville. He is a republican, is on the official board of St. James Methodist Episcopal Church, and fraternally is affiliated with Olive Branch Lodge No. 38, A. F. and A. M.; Vermilion Chapter No. 82 Royal Arch Masons; Athelstan Commandery No. 45, Knights Templar; is a past chancellor of Damascus Lodge No. 84, Knights of Pythias; member of Paughcaughnaughsinque Tribe No. 73, Improved Order of Red Men; Vermilion Camp No. 254, Modern Woodmen of America, and belongs to the Vermilion County, Illinois State and American Bar Associations. Besides his residence at 35 North Main Street he is interested in some farm property in Indiana. During the World war Mr. Martin was a member of the Legal Advisory Board of Vermilion County, and spent much of his time helping in the local drives.

He married at Cayuga, Indiana, December 25, 1900, Miss Ruth Patrick, daughter of Thamer E. (Stewart) Patrick, now deceased. Her father was a farmer near Cayuga. Mr. and Mrs. Martin have three children: Della F., a student in De Pauw University at Greencastle, Indiana; Thamer E., now taking a post-graduate course in the Danville High School; and Colfax T., Jr.

WILLIAM F. BAUM, for fifty years was actively engaged in the drug business at Danville, and still looks after a wide diversity of interests, including public office. He is one of the senior business men and citizens of Vermilion County.

He was born over the Indiana line in Fountain County, at Covington, February 5, 1848. The Baum family came from Germany and settled in Pennsylvania in Colonial times. His grandfather, Jonas Baum, a native of Ohio, was a soldier in the War of 1812. About 1825 he settled at Covington, Indiana, being one of the pioneers of Fountain County, and helped develop a farm and home out of the wilderness. He lived there until his death. His wife was Elizabeth Steely, a native of Ohio, who also died in the homestead at Covington. Their son, Abner Baum, was born in Ohio, in 1819, was about six years of age when taken to Indiana; was reared and married there, and spent the greater part of his active life as one of the leading farmers in that community. He began voting as a whig and later became a republican, and was a strong and ardent member of the Baptist Church. He finally moved to Nebraska, and died at Rising City, that state, in 1906. His wife, Eliza Hull, was born in Ohio, in 1840, and died at Rising City in 1906. Their children consisted of the following: William F.; Jonas, a druggist who died at Osceola, Nebraska, in 1891; James, a druggist living at Omaha, Nebraska; Daniel, who was a business man and died at Osceola, Nebraska, in 1888; Emma, wife of Frank Scott, a druggist at Rising City, Nebraska; and Oliver S., a minister of the Presbyterian Church at Los Angeles, California.

William F. Baum had a farm rearing at Covington, attending country schools and town schools, and also the Baptist College at Ladoga, Indiana. Leaving college at the age of twenty-two, he had previously taught a term of school in the winter of 1869 in Warren County, Indiana. In 1870 he entered the drug store at Covington, and by a hard working service apprenticeship learned every element in the profession and business of a druggist. In 1872 he acquired at Marshfield, Indiana, a branch store owned by the firm of Board, Gish & Company, and remained in business there until 1875. In the meantime, on November 1, 1874, he had established a drug store at Danville, the fifth store of that kind in the little city, and after 1875, when he sold his Marshfield store, he gave all his attention to the store at Danville. He was the leading druggist in the city for over fifty years, until he retired and sold out his store in 1920. He has had a prominent part in raising the standards of the drug business in Illinois, serving one year as president of the Illinois State Pharmaceutical Association, and in September, 1897, helped organize the National Association of Druggists at St. Louis, being the Illinois delegate at the convention. Mr. Baum during 1897-98 erected one of the first modern office buildings in Danville, known as the Baum Building, a seven-story structure at 41-43 North Vermilion Street. He still owns this building, and has his offices there. He has another business building, occupied by five stores at the corner of Main and North Jackson streets, and a three-story building at 20-22 West Main Street, and much other property, including his attractive home at 318 North Vermilion Street. He is president of the Pioneer Oil, Gas and Refining Company of San Antonio, Texas.

Mr. Baum is serving his tenth consecutive year as a member of the Board of Supervisors in Vermilion County. He was for four years a member of the Board of Aldermen of the City of Danville. Mr. Baum was elected twice to the city council, and while a member of this body introduced a resolution taking into Greater Danville the suburbs of Germantown, South Danville and Rose Lawn, incorporated villages, and three more unincorporated villages, making six altogether, and by this action automatically increased the population of Danville by eight hundred people. Mr. Baum is a republican, a member of St. James Methodist Episcopal Church, and is affiliated with Olive Branch Lodge No. 38, A. F. and A. M.; Vermilion Chapter No. 82, R. A. M.; Athelstan Commandery No. 45, K. T.; Danville Consistory of the Scottish Rite; and is a thirty-second degree Mason. He is also a member of Danville Lodge No. 332, B. P. O. Elks; the Danville Chamber of Commerce and is a member of the Danville Country Club.

Mr. Baum married in September, 1874, at Marshfield, Indiana, Miss Louisa A. Johnson, who was born in that locality. She died at Danville in 1905. The only child of this marriage was Clarence Henry, who graduated from the Danville High School; from the University of Michigan in the pharmacy and chemistry department, and for twenty years was actively associated with his father in the drug business. He is now superintendent of the Lake View Hospital of Danville. Mr. Baum on February 2, 1917, at Sandusky, Ohio, married Miss Bertha L. Levensburger, who was born in that Ohio city. She died at Danville November 22, 1922.

JOHN HARMAN KEITH, one of the prosperous farmers and highway commissioner of Mason County, is a man whose prestige is unquestioned, and whose value to his community is being proved upon every occasion. He has been a resident of Bath during the greater portion of his active years, and he has taken a determining part in its development and improvement. His birth occurred on his father's farm, November 16, 1858, and he is a son of Frederick Keith, Senior, and a brother of L. Frederick Keith, whose history is given elsewhere in this work, together with that of the Keith family. The elder Frederick Keith and his wife were both of German birth, and they were accounted as being among the most desirable people of Mason County, in which they lived for many years.

Growing up on his father's farm, John Harman Keith, the eldest of the children born to his parents, found plenty to keep himself busy on the farm, but he also attended both the public schools and the Lutheran school of the neighborhood, in which he was confirmed. When he commenced life for himself he did it as a farmer, but after a year he sold his property and embarked in the retail liquor business at Bath, and later at Havana. Once more he engaged in farming, but when he was appointed postmaster of Bath he located permanently in the village. He was appointed to that office by President Roosevelt, and again by President Taft, and remained in it for nine years, resigning when President Wilson was inaugurated and the administration became democratic. Upon leaving his office Mr. Keith engaged in handling real estate, being connected with the William Pearson Colonization Company of Winnipeg, Canada, sending out settlers into Last Mountain Valley of Saskatchewan for this company, which was developing that region. Mr. Keith continued this connection for eight years, and did a large amount of business, but the World war interrupted his activities in this line, and he transferred his operations to selling lands in Iowa and Illinois, and is still engaged in this business to some extent. In 1918 he was elected road commissioner for Bath Township, and served for two years, and then, after an interval of two years, was again elected for two years. He is also drainage commissioner for the Farmers Drainage District of Mason and Cass counties; and is chairman of the Legislative Committee of State Highway Association and Town Clerks of Illinois, and is chairman of its Committee on Resolutions.

In the matter of politics Mr. Keith is a republican, and cast his first presidential vote for James A. Garfield, then he voted for James G. Blaine, later for Benjamin Harrison, and has continued to support the presidential candidates of his party ever since. His convention work embraces all of the local, judicial, senatorial, congressional and state conventions, which he has attended as a delegate, and he was a member of the convention which nominated Governor Tanner.

When he was twenty-six years old Mr. Keith married Alice Black, who died, leaving a daughter who subsequently married, and dying, left nine children to survive her, her husband being Allen Clark. Mr. Keith's second wife was Almira Black, a sister of his first wife, and she bore her husband two sons: Harry, who is a resident of Marked Tree, Arkansas; and Arthur, who is a commercial salesman for the Coleman Light Company, and he served during the World war overseas as a member of the Engineer Corps.

On May 16, 1890, Mr. Keith married Miss Arizona Welsh at Marysville, Kansas. Mrs. Keith was born at Jacksonville, Michigan, but was reared at Corning, Iowa, and went to Nebraska with her parents. Her education was obtained in the public schools. She is a daughter of John Newton and Mary Jane (Lount) Welsh, and a great-granddaugher of one of the leaders of the rebellion in Quebec in 1837. He was tried and beheaded for his part in the struggle to secure independence, and within one hour after he was beheaded a mammoth petition was received as large as a wagon, and later a monument to his memory was erected at Quebec. His wife dressed Mrs. Keith at birth. John Newton Welsh was born in Michigan, September 24, 1826, and during the war between the states he served in the Twelfth Michigan Volunteer Infantry, and served for three years in the Union army. A farmer of many years standing, he went to Iowa in 1866, and later to Gage County, Nebraska. From 1890 until his death in 1902 he was a hotel man at Summerfield, Kansas. He was buried at Summerfield, Kansas, and when his widow died, in 1922, her remains were laid by his side. The children born to John Newton Welsh and his wife were as follows: Mrs. Keith, who was born December 9, 1866; Mrs. A. L. Burns, who died at Kansas City, Missouri, leaving a family; Ella, who died unmarried at Summerfield, Kansas; Harvey, who resides at Seattle, Washington; Henry, who is a resident of Summerfield; Ada, who is the wife of True Jordan, and lives at Anthony, Kansas; Susie, who married Orville Hudgens, and resides at Knight, Florida; and Lount, who resides at Longview, Washington. Mr. and Mrs. Keith have had the following children born to them: a daughter who died in infancy; Commodore, who is a fireman on the Missouri Pacific Railroad at Kansas City, Missouri; Mabel, who is the wife of Howard LeTissier, and resides at Jonesville, Louisiana; Ethel, who lives at Shreveport, Louisiana, married to C. B. Thomas;

George W. Miller

Theodore, who resides at Bath; and Herman Newton, who also resides at Bath, and was in the United States Navy after the World war, stationed at Hampton Roads, Virginia, and was honorably discharged at that point. These two sons above mentioned and Mrs. Susie Hudgens, who was a nurse in the service at San Antonio, Texas, represented the family during the World war, and all of them made commendable records for faithfulness and exalted loyalty. At the same time Mr. and Mrs. Keith and their other children and relatives were doing their part at home, assisting in local war work, and making generous contributions of time and money to the great cause. Mr. Keith is a man who is always willing to back any movement he believes to be right, and he has played an important part in the advancement of this region, his work in behalf of good roads being particularly conspicuous for he has always been a zealous advocate of them, and in his present office is given an opportunity to carry out some of the advanced ideas he has had for so many years. He worked hard to keep the C. P. & S. L. branch between Jacksonville and Havana going.

PAUL H. METZGER. Among the careers of important business men which have furnished important news stories to the metropolitan class is that of Paul H. Metzger, whose dramatic progress in Chicago merchandising has been widely commented on in that city.

Mr. Metzger was born on the North Side of Chicago in 1883. His father died leaving a widowed mother with four children. The widowed mother was the first great inspiration to Paul H. Metzger. He became a worker when only eight years old, assisting his mother. At the age of twelve years he found employment in a store at the corner of Washington and Dearborn streets, the Washington Shirt Company, one of the best known stores for men's furnishing goods in that day of comparatively small things. The boy Metzger found in that store the congenial atmosphere and the opportunity for work which his ambition and perseverance craved, and he served successively as stock boy, clerk and salesman. He married when earning the wages of a clerk, and his wife was the second woman after his mother to give him the steady inspiration for success. In 1918 Mr. Metzger was made general manager. In 1920 he became vice president. In February, 1926, he was elected president of the Washington Shirt Company, succeeding Fred L. Rossback, the founder of the company.

Mr. Metzger went to work for the Washington Shirt Company when it occupied only one store, that at the corner of Washington and Dearborn streets. This is now one of the largest companies in the country handling haberdashery and men's furnishing goods. The extent of the business and something of its growth is graphically portrayed by the store numbers and their locations. Stores numbered one to five and fifteen and sixteen are all in Chicago, the first four being in the Loop district. Number five was the first extension of the company to the outlying residential section, the Wilson Avenue district. The sixth store was established at Cleveland, the seventh at Minneapolis, the eighth at St. Paul, and the tenth at Kansas City. In these five cities and suburbs are now conducted a total of eighteen stores, there being at the present time eight stores in Chicago and one in Evanston. Mr. Metzger is a member of the Hamilton Club and the Cooperative Club of Chicago.

Mr. Metzger's wife was Miss Lydia S. Schmidt. They reside at Park Ridge, Illinois, and have one daughter, Dorothea.

GEORGE W. MILLER, attorney, has been a member of the Chicago bar thirty-five years, and his individual attainments and abilities have brought distinction to several well known law firms of that city.

Mr. Miller was born on his father's farm near Gilman, Illinois, January 12, 1869, son of Rufus H. and Ellen M. (Hale) Miller. His father was a native of Ohio and his mother of Massachusetts. He came to Illinois with his parents when a young man, having first attended school in Ohio. In Illinois he was a farmer in his early years. He served as highway commissioner of his township and was a democrat in politics. Rufus H. Miller died in June, 1920, and his wife, in December, 1922. Of their eight children four are living, George W. being the third in age.

George W. Miller attended grammar and high school at Gilman, graduating from high school there in 1887. He taught about a year, and coming to Chicago, was a student in the Union College of Law in 1889-90, and at the same time he clerked in the law office of the late James R. Mann, for many years congressman from the Second Illinois District. He spent some time in Washington, and while there, finished his law course in Columbian University, from which he received his LL. B. in 1891. Returning to Chicago, he was clerk in the law office of James R. Mann from 1891 to 1894, and then became a partner in the firm of Mann, Hayes & Miller. After the death of Mr. Hayes in 1898 the firm was Mann & Miller until January, 1912. Mr. Miller then practiced alone for about a year and a half and in June, 1913, became a member of the firm Busby, Weber & Miller. The present partnership is Busby, Weber, Miller & Donovan, with offices at 38 South Dearborn Street.

Mr. Miller was elected a member of the Illinois Legislature in 1894, and by re-election served in the Thirty-ninth and Fortieth General Assemblies. He was chairman of the committee on judicial department and practice and he introduced and secured in the passage of the first and second Torrens' Bills, introduced and secured the passage of the bill to consolidate the Supreme Court at Springfield, the bill creating the Branch Appellate Court in the First District of Illinois; the Cook County Civil Service Bill, and he took an active part in defeating the Humphrey Bills, which would have given the city traction interests a ninety-nine year lease in Chicago. Mr. Miller was first assistant corporation counsel of Chicago in 1907, under Mayor Busse, and was first assistant state's attorney under John J. Healy for a short time. He is a member of the Chicago, Illinois and American Bar Associations, is a thirty-second degree Scottish Rite Mason, member of Medinah Temple of the Mystic Shrine, Ben Hur, Royal Arcanum, The Maccabees, the Knights of Pythias, Royal League and Independent Order of Foresters. He is a past president and life member of the Hamilton Club, member of the Union League Club, Chicago Golf Club, Chicago Real Estate Board and many other organizations.

Mr. Miller married, August 4, 1892, Miss Carrie E. Sproule. They have one son, James Mann Miller.

MAJOR JOHN S. MILLER was born at Chicago, November 8, 1888, and is a son of John Stocker and Ann (Gross) Miller. His father was an attorney whose broad reputation rested not only on the masterly conduct of great cases,, but on the splendid discharge of his duties as corporation counsel of the City of Chicago under Mayor Washburne in 1891 and 1892. John Stocker Miller was born at Louisville, St. Lawrence County, New York, May 24, 1847, a son of John and Jane (McLeod) Miller. After obtaining a preparatory education in the common schools and academy of his native place he became a student at St. Lawrence University, Canton, New York, from which he was graduated in 1869 with the degree of Bachelor of Arts, and for two years thereafter studiously laid the groundwork for his profession in the law department of that institution. In 1870, after being admitted to the New York bar at Ogensburg, he was appointed to the chair of mathematics by his alma mater, holding that professorship throughout 1871 and 1872, and that of Latin and Greek from 1872 to 1874. In the latter year he resigned his place on the faculty and made his way to Chicago to engage in the practice of his permanent profession. Mr. Miller soon came into prominence, even among the many bright young lawyers who made their home at Chicago immediately following the great fire, which caused the readjustment, through the law, of so many important interests. In 1876 he formed a partnership with George Herbert and John H. S. Quick, under the firm name of Herbert, Quick & Miller. These connections continued unbroken until 1882, when occurred Mr. Herbert's death and the change of style to Quick & Miller. The subsequent changes, preceding the formation of the firm of Peck, Miller & Starr, included an association with Henry W. Leman in 1886, his retirement, the admission of Merritt Starr, later the formation with George R. Peck and Mr. Starr of the firm of Peck, Miller & Starr, and he was with Judge E. O. Brown from 1907 until 1922, the year of his death. During the latter years of Mr. Miller's life his practice was chiefly in the chancery courts, and among his more important cases prior to his identification with the municipal law department were those known as the Flagler litigation, the Riverside, the Phillips and South Park suits. These cases brought him so prominently and favorably before the bar that in 1891 Mayor Hempstead Washburne appointed him corporation counsel. He held the position during the mayoralty term, and won a notable victory for the city in its suit against the Illinois Central Railway over the Lake Front property. The result of the case was firmly to establish the great municipal principle that the bed of navigable waters is the property of the people and is held in trust by the state for their benefit. After retiring from office Mr. Miller continued his private and partnership practice, largely devoted to commercial and corporation law. His high standing in these specialties was greatly advanced by his participation in the Packing House, Standard Oil and John R. Walsh cases, in which he was the leading counsel for the defense. They were acknowledged to be among the most important suits which the government ever prosecuted, and to be professionally identified with them in any capacity was a forcible verification of leadership in the legal fraternity. Involved in the noteworthy litigation were the responsibility of great corporations and leaders of broad interests to the law, and their duties to the public from which they drew the life of their enterprises; and the pressing need of some radical revision of the Inter-State Commerce Law defining the comparative regulating powers of state and national governments.

On December 15, 1887, at Chicago, Mr. Miller was united in marriage with Miss Ann Gross, and from that time forward was a potent factor in social and club life. Branching from his home as a social center, his activities in this direction extended to the Union League Club (of which he was president in 1899), and the Chicago, Hamilton, Chicago Literary, University, Exmoor, South Shore Country and Onwentsia Golf clubs. He was a member of St. Paul's and St. James' Episcopal churches and altogether a typical Chicago citizen who believed that the surest way to advance his own interests and be of benefit to the public was to come into as close contact with as many people and interests as possible.

His son, John S. Miller, of this review, attended Harvard School, Chicago, and then pursued a course in the Harvard Law School, from which he was graduated as a Bachelor of Laws in 1914. He began the practice of his profession at Chicago in the same year, and for the past several years has been a member of the distinguished law firm of Taylor, Miller, Dickinson & Smith, with offices in the Illinois Merchants Trust Building. Prior to the World war Mr. Miller had joined the First Field Artillery of the old Illinois National Guard, enlisting as a private and rising successively to corporal and sergeant. He served with this organization on the Mexican border in 1916, and returning, went early in the spring of 1917 to the Plattsburg training camp. He was later commissioned second lieutenant of Field Artillery. In May, 1917, he was ordered to Fort Sheridan, where he was on duty until August, 1917, being then commissioned major of Field Artillery and assigned to the One Hundred and Sixty-first Brigade, Eight-sixth (Blackhawk) Division. He went overseas with this outfit in September, 1918, and returned to this country in January, 1919, receiving his honorable discharge on the 9th of that month.

Major Miller was among those who were

the original organizers of the American Legion. He was chairman of the temporary committee on organization for Illinois, which met with the general caucus at St. Louis in May, 1919, at which the American Legion was launched. Major Miller is a member of the Chicago Bar Association, the Legal Club of Chicago, the Bar Association of the City of New York, the Chicago Club, Racquet Club, Attic Club and Indian Hills Country Club.

Major Miller married Miss Judith D. Barker, and they are the parents of four children: Judith D., Joan M., Portia A. and John S., III. The pleasant home is located at Winnetka.

ARTHUR EDGAR HAMILTON. A public official of Whiteside County who enjoys an unusual amount of public confidence and esteem is Arthur Edgar Hamilton, serving for the second time as county sheriff. He is yet a young man, has practically spent his life in this county and comes of sturdy old pioneer county stock.

Arthur Edgar Hamilton was born at Lyndon, Whiteside County, Illinois, August 30, 1887, a son of Charles A. and Theora E. (Helms) Hamilton, the old Lyndon homestead being also the birthplace of his father September 13, 1858. Charles A. Hamilton was a son of John M. Hamilton, who was born in Massachusetts, a son of Adam R. Hamilton, a soldier in the War of 1812. John M. Hamilton founded the family here in 1835, acquiring valuable land in Lyndon Township, Whiteside County, Illinois, some of which has never left the possession of the family. He married first Emily Wright who at death left three children: John L., who was a soldier in the Civil war. and two daughters, Caroline and Elvira. His second marriage was with a widow, Mrs. Anna B. Thompson, who was of Scotch ancestry. They had two sons: Charles A. and Frederick E. The Hamiltons were members of the Congregational Church, in which John M. Hamilton was a deacon.

Charles A. Hamilton became one of the leading men of Whiteside County. He had only country school educational advantages and contentedly led a quiet, agricultural life until called to public office by his fellow citizens, who esteemed him for his high personal character and placed high value on his intelligence and sound judgment. In 1906 he was called from his farm pursuits to become sheriff of Whiteside County, and ably performed the duties of that office until the close of his life, before his term had expired. He was a member of the Congregational Church, and for many years had been a Mason and a Knight of Pythias. In 1881 he married Miss Theora E. Helms, who was born in Ustick Township, Whiteside County, Illinois, a daughter of Henry E. and Lucy (Gould) Helms, and a granddaughter of Thomas Gould, a pioneer of the county. Seven children were born to the above marriage: Grace E., Arthur Edgar, Herbert E., Lucy E., John Henry, Cora L., and Donald W., all reaching mature years except Herbert E.

Arthur Edgar Hamilton spent his early years on the home farm, and has always taken more or less interest in agricultural pursuits, although at one time he made some preparation for a professional career. After being most creditably graduated from the Lyndon School and Sterling Township High School he spent two years as a law student in the University of Michigan, from which he was called home by the untimely death of his honored father, and was immediately elected his official successor, bringing about the unusual circumstance of Whiteside County for one and a half years having a sheriff who had just reached his majority. Having capably served out his father's unexpired term Mr. Hamilton turned his attention to farming, and his progressive ideas and practical methods soon proved his adaptability for this line of effort and he continued so engaged until 1922, when he was elected sheriff on his own responsibilty, at that time taking up his residence at Morrison.

Sheriff Hamilton married in 1915 Miss Lillian E. Morris, who was born in Lyndon Township, Whiteside County, October 29, 1886, daughter of Adon S. and Elizabeth (Hazzard) Morris. The Hazzards came to Roxbury, Massachusetts, from England, the progenitor being one Thomas Hazzard, who immigrated in 1630. Both parents of Mrs. Hamilton were born in Lyndon Township. Sheriff and Mrs. Hamilton have four children: Nancy Elizabeth, born July 13, 1916; Charles Arthur, born August 18, 1917; William Henry, born September 21, 1918; and George Williard, born May 11, 1923. They are members of the Congregational Church, the Sheriff being one of the church trustees. He is a member of the Masonic fraternity and belongs also to the Elks.

JOHN HIGGINS HARRISON is one of the widely known successful newspaper publishers of Illinois, and for over a quarter of a century has been identified with the Danville Commercial-News. He served a newspaper apprenticeship during his youth, his father having been a prominent Indiana journalist.

Mr. Harrison was born at Lebanon, Indiana, November 30, 1867. In the paternal line he represents a distinguished American ancestry, being a descendant of Col. Richard Harrison, an officer under Oliver Cromwell during the English Revolution. It is said that he was entrusted with the keeping of King Charles and conducted him to the scaffold. He frustrated the attempt made by the three guardsmen, heroes of the story of Dumas, in their adventure to liberate the king. At the restoration of the monarchy Col. Richard Harrison came to America and became a Virginia planter. At a later date one of the direct ancestors of the Danville newspaper man was John Harrison. a Virginia soldier in the War of the Revolution. His son, Joshua Harrison, lived his life as a farmer in Maryland. A son of Joshua was Joshua, Jr., who was born in Maryland, and was a pioneer over the mountains into Kentucky, where he lived out his life. This Joshua was the great-grandfather of John Higgins Harrison. The grandfather was James Harvey Harrison, who was born in Kentucky, in 1807, but spent most of his life at Ladoga, Indiana, where he owned and operated a large farm. Late in life he moved to Kansas, and died at Norwood, in that state, in 1891. His wife was Elizabeth Watkins.

Thomas H. Harrison, the Indiana newspaper man, was born December 7, 1842, at Ladoga, Indiana, was reared there, was educated in the University of Michigan, and graduated M. D. from the Ohio Medical College of Cincinnati. He served as a surgeon in the Union army, and after the Civil war, practiced for a few years at Lebanon. From medicine he turned his attention to the newspaper profession, and for some years edited the Lebanon Pioneer. In 1888 he bought the Michigan City Dispatch, and after disposing of his paper at Lebanon in 1890, moved to Michigan City and was identified with the Dispatch until his death, which occurred while he was visiting at Battle Ground, Indiana, August 12, 1890. After his death the Michigan City paper was sold. He was a democrat and very active in Indiana politics during his time. For a number of years he was county superintendent of schools of Boone County and for six years was president of the State Benevolent Board of Indiana, this board having control of the institutions for the blind, deaf and dumb and insane. He was an active worker of the Methodist Episcopal Church and a member of the Masonic fraternity. Thomas H. Harrison married Minta Higgins, who was born at Thornton, Indiana, August 21, 1844, and made her home with her only son and child, John Higgins Harrison, until her death in Danville, Illinois, October 24, 1925. She was a descendant of Frederick Landis, who was born March 4, 1739, and was a Revolutionary soldier, being a private in the Fourth Battalion of the Chester County, Pennsylvania, troops.

John Higgins Harrison was educated in public schools in Lebanon, Indiana, graduating from high school there in 1884, and subsequently attended DePauw University at Greencastle, Indiana, where he was graduated with the Master of Arts degree in 1891. While in the University he was a Sigma Chi. Following the death of his father and the end of his college career he had three years of experience in Chicago with various newspapers of the early '90s. Then for two years he acted as press agent for one of the country's big circuses and for a year was press agent for a theatrical syndicate operating houses in Indianapolis, Columbus and Toledo.

Mr. Harrison in December, 1897, came to Danville and acquired a half interest in the old Evening Commercial. In 1902 he became principal proprietor and in 1903 accomplished a consolidation by purchasing the Danville News, since which date his paper has been of the Commercial-News. The life of this newspaper constitutes a notable chapter in newspaper history. Twenty-five years ago its circulation was not over 900, whereas the circulation of The Commercial-News today is 23,000, and it is one of the leading newspapers in influence in Eastern Illinois. Its political complexion is republican. Mr. Harrison is owner of the building and plant, both having been thoroughly remodeled in 1925.

Mr. Harrison has had active connection with republican affairs in Illinois. He was a member of the State Central Committee, 1914-16; delegate to the Republican National Convention, 1916; was chairman of the Republican State Convention and made the keynote speech in 1918.

Mr. Harrison was for eight years chairman of the Board of Commissioners of the state penitentiary at Joliet, serving under Governor Richard Yates and Governor Charles S. Deneen. He is a steward of St. James Methodist Episcopal Church at Danville; member of Olive Branch Lodge No. 38, A. F. and A. M.; Vermilion Chapter No. 82, Royal Arch Masons; a past eminent commander of Athelstan Commandery No. 45, Knights Templar; Danville Consistory of the Scottish Rite and Medinah Temple of the Mystic Shrine at Chicago. He has performed a great deal of service in degree work with all bodies in Masonry. He also belongs to Danville Lodge No. 332, B. P. O. Elks; the Danville Country Club; Danville Chamber of Commerce, and is a director of Lakeview Hospital and trustee of the Danville Y. M. C. A. Mr. Harrison was honored with the office of president in 1923-24 of the Illinois Press Association, and is a member and former president of the Illinois Daily Newspaper Association. During the World war he was a member of the Illinois State Council of Defense. Outside of the newspaper business he has other business interests, being president of the Home Theatre Company, operating the Fischer, Palace and the Terrace Theatres of Danville. He was for five years president of Vein Six Coal Company at Danville. Mr. Harrison is unmarried.

Martin J. Insull, of Chicago, is one of the men who have done most to realize and give practical form to the dream of scientists known as super power, involving the generation in giant central stations of electrical energy and the distribution of such energy over enormous stretches of country and service to thousands of communities that under normal conditions of growth would not attain such service within the expectations of the present century.

Martin J. Insull was born in London, England, and came to the United States in 1887, about six years after his older brother, Samuel Insull, arrived in this country. Martin J. Insull was then eighteen years of age, and had completed a public school education. His first employment was in the Edison Machine Shop at Schenectady, New York. Two years later, in order to equip himself better for his profession and chosen career, he entered Cornell University, and was graduated in 1893 with the degree Mechanical Engineer.

Already in 1892 he had come to Chicago, where he was associated with Frederick Sargent in work on the Columbian Exposition grounds. Frederick Sargent was himself a native of England, and was the eminent engineer who was manager of the mechanical and electrical department at the Chicago Exposition of 1893. During 1893 Martin J. Insull was given the position of a partner in the firm of Sargent and Lundy, engineers, devoting his energies to the commercial feature of the firm's business.

From this partnership he retired in 1898 to organize the Martin J. Insull Company, act-

ing as manufacturer's agent. However, in 1899 Mr. Insull went East to assume the vice presidency and general management of the General Incandescent Arc Light Company of New York City. In 1904 this concern was absorbed by the General Electric Company and its manufacturing plant was moved to the Stanley Electric Manufacturing Company at Pittsfield, Massachusetts, this being one of the units owned and operated by the General Electric Company. Mr. Insull continued with the General Incandescent Arc Light Company as its president until a year later, when the two companies were consolidated as the Stanley General Manufacturing Company and he became one of the vice presidents in charge at Chicago of its Western business.

This position he resigned in 1907 to assume operation and management of electric lighting, railway and other interests in Southern Indiana with which his brother, Samuel Insull, was permanently identified. To these affairs he devoted five years of his time.

On returning to Chicago he assisted in organizing the Middle West Utilities Company, destined to become one of the great commercial institutions in the country. Since its organization Mr. Insull has been vice president and operating executive, the president being his brother, Samuel Insull.

The Middle West Utilities Company was organized in May, 1912, the pioneer company founded on the idea that full electric light and power facilities could be profitably applied to compact groups of smaller cities and towns through closely knit transmission systems. In less than twelve years the company has come to control twenty-two operating companies, which provide utility services directly to nearly two million people in one hundred and ninety-five cities and towns in fifteen states; there being one hundred and thirty-six steam and hydro-electric plants, delivering over seven hundred million kilowatt hours of energy, with over six thousand miles of electric transmission lines, the services including the operation of electric railways, gas plants, ice plants, water works in addition to the great volume of such energy used for manufacturing plants and domestic consumption. The great achievement of the Middle West Utilities organization has consisted in the taking of territory that would otherwise have inadequate service and by linking up the properties, utilizing the most efficient stations and providing new and efficient ones of adequate size, giving to the community service equal to that of the more highly developed commercial and industrial centers. The principal operating companies controlled and owned by the Middle West Utilities Company include the Illinois Northern Utilities Company, McHenry County Light and Power Company and Central Illinois Public Service Company, the facilities of service of one or more of which are known and appreciated by every resident of Illinois; the Central Power Company, operating in Nebraska, the Missouri Gas and Electric Service Company, the Public Service Company of Oklahoma, the Chickashee Gas and Electric Company, also of Oklahoma, Nebraska Utilities Company, Interstate Public Service Company in Indiana, Kentucky Light and Power Company, Electric Transmission Company of Virginia, Twin State Gas and Electric Company, and the Berwick and Salmon Falls Company, in the Northeastern State of Vermont, New Hampshire and Maine, Michigan Gas and Electric Company, Southern Wisconsin Electric Company, American Public Service Company properties in Texas and Oklahoma, Northwest Utilities Company properties in Wisconsin and the Lake Superior District Power Company.

During the progress of the World war Martin J. Insull gave some of his special efforts toward the enlistment of Canadian men and the Canadian Red Cross work. He is a member of the University, Chicago, Mid-Day, Attic, Scarborough, Exmoor Country, Highland Park, and Cornell, New York Clubs. He belongs to a number of engineering and scientific societies and in 1921 was president of the National Electric Light Association.

In 1894 Mr. Insull married Miss Virginia Van Vleet, of New York. They have one daughter, Virginia Cornwell.

JOHN F. BARRETT. One of Chicago's representative and substantial business men is John F. Barrett, head of the grain brokerage firm of John F. Barrett & Company, and one of the pioneers in his line of business on the Chicago grain market.

Mr. Barrett is a native of Chicago and was born in the old family home then standing on the corner of Ohio and Market streets, May 25, 1859. His parents were Anthony and Rose (Collins) Barrett, and he and his brother Anthony are the only survivors of their family of five children. Both parents were born in County Mayo, Ireland. In early manhood his father crossed the ocean in a sailing vessel to Quebec, Canada, and he found work on the Welland Canal. He was a hard-working man, and in hope of providing more comfortably for his family later made his way to Chicago, where he was connected with the firm of Gibbs & Griffen in the grain elevator business. His death occurred in this city in 1872.

John F. Barrett had parochial and public school advantages until he was thirteen years old, when he lost his father and the matter of self support had to be considered. He soon secured a position as messenger boy with the American District Telegraph Company, at a salary of five dollars a week. He proved entirely satisfactory in that position, for the qualities that have made Mr. Barrett a successful and trustworthy business man were evidenced in his youth, and as his years and business knowledge increased he found other opportunities awaiting him. His initiation into the grain business was with the Brown & Fleming Grain Company, and in 1888 his relation along this line became closer as a member of the grain firm of Boyden & Company. In 1895 Mr. Barrett organized the firm of John F. Barrett & Company, and since then this firm has been an important one in the market. Mr. Barrett is a member of the Chicago Stock Exchange, the New York Produce Exchange, the Winnipeg Exchange and the St. Louis Exchange.

Mr. Barrett married, November 9, 1881, Miss Harriet Degan, a native of Chicago, and they have five children: Anthony, who is a resident of Chicago; Harriet, who is the wife of Frank McDonald, and they have three children; Helen, who is the wife of Richard Carey, and they have five children; Thomas F., who married Dollie Murphy, and they have three children; and Margaret, who is the wife of Frank Lavin. Among the many things that are sources of great pride to Mr. Barrett, not the least are his eleven grandchildren.

In political sentiment Mr. Barrett has always been a democrat and has often taken an active part in local campaigns but has always declined political office for himself. He is a member of the Oak Park Lodge of Elks and, an enthusiastic golfer, and is president of the Butterfield Golf Club.

CHARLES ELMER STURTZ. Not only has Charles Elmer Sturtz won a lasting reputation as an able and forceful attorney, but he made a splendid record in the office of state's attorney of Henry County, for his fearlessness and unblemished integrity, made his name one to be feared by evil doers throughout a wide territory. Since 1903 he has been practicing at the bar of Kewanee, and is recognized as one of the leading members of his profession in this part of Illinois. Since 1912 he has been general attorney for the Mystic Workers, and he is connected with some of the most important jurisprudence in the state.

Charles Elmer Sturtz was born in Somerset County, Pennsylvania, November 9, 1862, a son of Charles and Catherine (Kennell) Sturtz, both natives of the same county as their son, and John Sturtz, the paternal grandfather, was also born in Pennsylvania, but his father, Christian Sturtz, the paternal great-grandfather of Charles Elmer Sturtz, was born in Germany, and was the American founder of the Sturtz family. The maternal grandfather, Samuel Kennell, was also a native of Pennsylvania, of English descent.

When war was declared between the states Charles Sturtz enlisted at the first call for ninety-day men, served out his first enlistment and returned to his home in Somerset County, Pennsylvania, but later reenlisted and continued in the service until the close of the war. He had been a teacher and farmer, and in 1868 moved to Whiteside County, Illinois, and settled on a farm four miles south of Sterling, where he continued to live for many years and rear his family. Later on in life he moved to Sterling, where he and his wife both died, he at the age of seventy-eight years, in 1916; and she at a later date, when seventy-nine. He was a republican, and was a member of the Lutheran Church at Sterling. Thirteen children were born to him and his wife; Oscar Lincoln, who died in 1904; Charles E.; Alice; Samuel Wilson; Martin; Herman; Louis J.; Elwin Grant, who died in 1907; Lawrence; Edward; Cora L.; Roy; and Harry Kennell.

Charles E. Sturtz grew to manhood on his father's farm and attended the country schools. In order to earn the money to carry on his own education he taught school for four years, and attended different institutions as he was able to manage his finances. He attended Dixon, Illinois, College. At the same time he was studying law, and in the fall of 1887, entered Knox College, from which he was graduated in 1891, with the degree of Bachelor of Science. He is a member of Phi Delta Theta, a Greek letter fraternity. While at college, especially during his vacation periods, he kept up his law studies, and in the fall of 1891, entered the senior year of the law department of the University of Michigan, Ann Arbor, and was graduated in the spring of 1892, with the degree of Bachelor of Laws, and was admitted to the Michigan bar. In the fall of 1892 he was admitted to the Illinois bar, and for a year was engaged in practice at Chicago. In 1903 he came to Kewanee, where he has since resided, and where he has built up a very desirable connection. Many honors have come to him as a result of his ability and public spirit, and he has served as city attorney and member of the school board, and in 1903 he was elected state's attorney to fill a vacancy, and in 1904 was elected to the same office for the full term of four years. In 1908 he was again elected for another four-year term, and declined the nomination in 1912. It was in the fall of that year that he was elected to his present office with the Mystic Workers. In him the republican party has one of its strongest workers, and he is not only active in the local ranks, but in state matters as well. He belongs to the Masonic fraternity in which he has been advanced to the Temple and Shrine, and he is also a member of the Knights of Pythias and the Benevolent and Protective Order of Elks.

In the fall of 1891 Mr. Sturtz married Miss Alice E. Price, a native of Neponset, Henry County, Illinois, and they have two daughters: Zola May, who is the wife of Albert R. Kays; and Katherine. Mr. Sturtz is one of the best examples of the self-reliant, self-made man Henry County possesses, and his example is an inspiration to others struggling to overcome obstacles and attain to the goal their ambitions have set for them. His ability as an attorney is unquestioned, as is his interest in the welfare and progress of the state, and, if he cares for them, further honors are his for the acceptance, for his fellow citizens recognize his excellent characteristics and his zeal in their behalf.

LEVI DAVIS YAGER, judge of the City Court of Alton, has been a practicing lawyer at the Alton bar for over thirty-five years, and is a son of the late John H. Yager, whose long career was distinguished by important services in the field of constructive statesmanship as well as success as a lawyer.

John H. Yager was born at Eisenach, Germany, November 12, 1833, and when four years of age was brought to New Orleans by his parents and shortly afterward to St. Louis. It is said that he never attended school a day in his life, though for years his personal attainments ranked him as a learned lawyer and scholar. His early education was largely supervised by his mother. In 1854 he began the study of law at Edwardsville under A. W. Metcalf and Judge Gillespie, and in 1857 entered the law office of Judge T. L. Dickey at Chicago and was admitted to the bar from Judge Dickey's office. In 1858 he located at

Alton, during the year that Lincoln and Douglas were engaged in their memorable debate. Mr. Yager became an ardent supporter of Lincoln and ever afterward was a recognized leader in republican councils in Southern Illinois. In April, 1861, President Lincoln appointed him surveyor of customs for the port of Alton, and he served in that office throughout the four-year period of the war.

He was elected to his first term in the Legislature in 1866, and served in both branches. He introduced the bill to establish the Illinois State Reform School. Through his ardent advocacy in Southern Illinois sufficient support was secured to pass the eight-hour law in Illinois, a measure that originated in Chicago. He was also author of the valued insurance policy law, a law subsequently copied by many other states. He was elected counselor for the Illinois Mutual Fire Insurance Company of Alton in May, 1869.

Many important honors were tendered him in public affairs. He was a close friend of General Logan, who frequently visited at the Yager home in Alton. President Grant appointed him collector of internal revenue in 1871, but he declined. In 1873 he was appointed by President Grant a commissioner to the Vienna Exposition. He twice codified the ordinances of the City of Alton.

John H. Yager died January 6, 1911, after more than fifty years of membership at the Madison County bar. He married in 1860 Miss Ida E. Hess, who was born in St. Louis, daughter of George and Elizabeth Hess, who came from Germany. She died at her home in Alton February 26, 1923, at the age of eighty-two. The children of John H. Yager and wife were: Ida E., who married E. W. Sparks; Estelle, who married S. L. Beach; Louis E., Levi D., Edward and Charles M.

Levi Davis Yager was born in Alton, December 29, 1863, and as a youth attended the public schools of his native city. He finished his education in Washington University at St. Louis, graduating in law. He was admitted to the bar August 24, 1886, at Mount Vernon, Illinois, and at once returned to Alton, and became associated with his father in practice. He had an extensive general practice as an attorney until 1917, when he was elected judge of the City Court and has filled that office for the past seven years. In former years he was city attorney and also corporation counsel.

Judge Yager married in 1909 Miss Lucy Francis, of Alton, who died July 27, 1924. They had two children, Levi D., Jr., and Francis. Judge Yager is a member of the Unitarian Church.

CHARLES D. CENTER, M. D., a Quincy physician and surgeon of long service and enviable distinction, was one of the general officers of that city in the World war, attaining the rank of colonel of infantry on December 26, 1917.

Doctor Center was born July 8, 1869, on a farm near Ottawa, Illinois. His grandfather, Nathaniel Center, married Mary Dewey, from Western Massachusetts, a descendant of Thomas Dewey, whose settlement in Massachusetts Colony is fixed in the year of 1646, and one of whose descendants was Admiral Dewey. Nathaniel Center after his marriage lived in Washington County, New York, and subsequently he moved to a farm in Wayne County, that state. He died in 1847. His widow lived to the age of seventy-seven. They were the parents of six children, and all of them with their mother eventually came to Illinois.

Dorr Center, father of Doctor Center, was born in 1838 in New York State, and he and his brother John came to Illinois in about 1858. Dorr Center married in 1866 Harriet Allen, who was born in 1840 in Wayne County, New York, daughter of Solomon and Susan (Westcott) Allen. After their marriage Dorr Center and wife moved to what later became known as Oak Grove Farm near Ottawa, Illinois, his brother John occupying an adjoining farm. Dorr Center had a limited education, but experience was the great school from which he never graduated until death, and his intellectual curiosity brought him a rich and varied knowledge. He was especially characterized by his love of peace, integrity and sense of justice, and in his community he was called upon as an unofficial arbitrator in all sorts and kinds of disputes and disagreements. He and his wife were deeply religious, but in his attitude toward men he was kindly tolerant, and had a belief in the ultimate good of all things. His wife was a very serious minded person, well educated, occasionally spoke fluently and eloquently at church, and was most devoted to her family. She died at the age of sixty-seven, having compressed the love and labor of eighty years or more in those sixty-seven. Their children were four in number: Genevieve, Charles D., Orlo and Ralph, all born in the little farmhouse on Oak Grove Farm.

Dr. Charles D. Center was reared on a farm in Central Illinois, and after the local schools had to acquire his education through his own efforts. He earned part of it by an experience as a book agent, and has regarded that as a valuable contribution of mental resourcefulness and ability to meet and deal with people of all kinds.

After graduating from medical college Doctor Center located at Quincy in April, 1896. He had previously had some experience as an industrial physician in the iron mines of Northern Wisconsin, and was also engaged in private practice at Chicago for a time. Doctor Center became a prominent figure as a member of the staff of the Blessing Hospital at Quincy. He early became identified with the military service, being made assistant surgeon in the Medical Corps of the Illinois National Guard in 1905, and in 1910 was promoted to captain, and two months later to major. In 1912 he was transferred from the Medical Corps to the field and staff as lieutenant colonel of infantry, and at the time of the World war went into the service with that rank.

On September 1, 1896 Doctor Center married Edith Campbell, a native of Prince Edward Island, daughter of James and Rose (Buxton) Campbell, her father a native of Scotland and her mother of England. She had been a nurse in the Presbyterian Hospital at Chicago, and in 1896 was assistant superintendent of the Illinois Training School for Nurses.

Doctor Center on June 1, 1909, married Louise Pecinovski, who had been a nurse in training at the Blessing Hospital in Quincy following her graduation from the St. Mary's School for Girls at Faribault, Minnesota. Her father, John Pecinovski, was a native of Bohemia and an Iowa farmer. Her mother was Louise Converse, of old New England stock. By his first marriage Doctor Center had two sons and by his second marriage two other boys, Charles Converse, born in 1910, and Harry Allen, born in 1912. His son Donald left the University of Illinois in May, 1917, to enlist in the Fifth Illinois Infantry and went overseas with the headquarters company of the One Hundred Twenty-ninth Infantry. In France he was transferred and became battalion sergeant-major of the One Hundred Eighth Trains and Military Police.

THURMAN F. SHOUSE, formerly mayor of the City of Danville, has been identified with that city for many years. He is a Methodist minister, but since leaving the pastorate, on account of ill health, has had a successful experience in several lines of commercial work.

Mr. Shouse was born at Effingham in Effingham County, Illinois, November 9, 1869. The Shouse family has lived in the United States for a number of generations, coming originally from Germany and first settling in Pennsylvania. His father, Thurman F. Shouse, Sr., was born near Logansport, Indiana, in 1823; was reared there, and shortly after his marriage moved to Effingham County, Illinois, where he became well known as a substantial farmer. He died at Effingham in 1885. He also taught school in early life, teaching some of the subscription schools of pioneer days. He served as a school director, in politics was an independent democrat, and was an adherent of the Baptist Church. His wife, Mary Jane Thomison, was born in Tennessee in 1826, and died in Effingham County in 1898. They were the parents of a large family of children: Eliza Jane, who married Thomas Garner, and both are now deceased; Margaret A., wife of Eli R. Renfrow, a farmer at Shumway, Illinois; John H., a farmer who died at Eldorado Springs, Missouri; Columbus S., who died in March, 1926, at the old homestead near Effingham; Rev. Joseph D., a retired minister of the Methodist Episcopal Church, living at Newton, Illinois; Samantha A., wife of Estes Garner, owner and operator of a truck line at Centralia, Illinois; Rhoda A., wife of John A. Riley, a farmer near Effingham; Docia E., wife of William Engle, a farmer near Effingham; Thurman F.; Viola, who died when six years old.

Thurman F. Shouse was reared on his father's farm in Effingham County, attended public schools, graduating from the high school at Altamount in 1892, and for two years continued his higher education in Austin College at Effingham. Having qualified for the Methodist ministry, he joined the Southern Illinois Methodist Conference, and as a pastor in that Conference was located for two years at Johnsonville in Wayne County; at Moccasin for two years; at Coffeen, three years, and from 1901 to 1904 was at Tower Hill. He came to Danville in 1904 as pastor of the Lincoln Methodist Episcopal Church, holding that post of responsibility until 1909. From here he joined the Oklahoma Conference and for two years was pastor of the First Methodist Episcopal Church at Newkirk in that state. Being threatened with a nervous breakdown, he resigned from the ministry and coming to Danville, became a commercial traveler for the Eckert Carriage Company of Auburn, Indiana. A year later he became superintendent and financial secretary of the Springhill Cemetery Association at Danville, and in this position he has found full occupation for his time and energies for fourteen years.

Mr. Shouse on April 3, 1923, was elected mayor of Danville, beginning his official term on the first of May. He was elected on a platform pledging himself to a clean moral city and economical administration, and has lived up to his platform in a way to bring him a high personal credit. Danville when he became mayor was incumbered with a heavy debt, the deficit amounting to approximately $183,000 when he entered office. During his term in office he has reduced the debt over $50,000. In the meantime the essential municipal improvements have not been neglected. A total of about ten miles, comprising one-fifth of the entire paving of the city, has been either constructed new or resurfaced.

Mr. Shouse is a republican in politics, is affiliated with Olive Branch Lodge No. 38, A. F. and A. M.; has taken fourteen degrees in the Scottish Rite and during the World war acted as captain of a district in Danville in all the drives for Liberty Bond sales and other purposes. He is president and a director of a life insurance company at Danville.

Mr. Shouse married at Effingham, Illinois, February 23, 1888, Effie R. Devore, daughter of Daniel A. and Margaret (Miller) Devore, now deceased. Her father was a well known farmer and cattle dealer in Effingham County. The two children born to Mr. and Mrs. Shouse are: Harry E., who died when seventeen years old; and Edna Ruth, wife of Frank M. Fagan, who is general foreman of the Springhill Cemetery Association at Danville. Mr. Shouse also has an adopted son, Jarald E., who was a member of the Danville Fire Department and is now a member of the United States Air Forces, stationed at Selfridge Field, Mount Clemens, Michigan, and has completed the automobile mechanical course at Chunate Field, Rantoul, Illinois.

HARRY B. APKEN. The name of Apken is a well known one at Petersburg and in Menard County, and it has always been synonymous with integrity, good business judgment and public-spirited citizenship, and its present representative, Harry B. Apken, proprietor of the Apken Lumber Company, is living up to the high standards expected of him by his neighbors and associates. He is a native son of Petersburg, where he was born January 30, 1888, and here he received his preliminary educational training, which he subsequently supplemented with a year's work in the commercial department of the University of Illinois between the ages of eighteen and nine-

teen. Upon his return to Petersburg, he entered his father's lumber business, the one he owns today.

The Apken Lumber Company was founded in 1886 by Fred Apken, father of Harry B. Apken. This substantial citizen was born in Germany, February 4, 1852, and was reared by his mother, as his father was a soldier in the German army and very seldom at home. At the age of nineteen years he entered the coasting trade, and continued in it for a couple of years, being first with a Dutch vessel, and later with a British one. When the latter reached Baltimore, Maryland, Fred Apken left it, without leave. At that time he was just twenty-one, and his capital consisted of ten cents. He had youth, however, and the willingness to work, and he found employment as a farm hand in Maryland. As soon as he earned sufficient money to pay his fare to Illinois he came to this state to join relatives living in Menard County. At first he was a farm hand in the vicinity of Petersburg, and later was employed in a greenhouse at Oak Park, Illinois, and drove a truck with vegetables to Chicago. However, city life did not suit him and he returned to Menard County and resumed farm work. During all of this time he had saved his money and, after working for Rourke & Company, lumber merchants, he purchased the business. Still later he established a new yard, forming a partnership under the firm name of Cogdall & Apken. When Mr. Cogdall died in 1895 Mr. Apken bought his interest, and continued the business alone until his son was old enough to come in with him. The business was operated under the name of Fred Apken until the death of the founder, May 27, 1923, when the present name, the Apken Lumber Company, was adopted.

Fred Apken displayed unusual ability in the conduct of his private affairs. He was always progressive and liberal in matters relating to the public welfare. While he never entered politics, he voted the republican ticket and supported its principles. Both as a member of Saint Paul Evangelical Church and as a Master Mason he lived up to the highest ideals of Christian manhood, and no man stood better with his associates than he. Very fond of reading, he kept abreast of current thought through the medium of newly issued literature. During the World war he was a heavy purchaser of securities, and his contributions to war organizations were exceedingly generous.

In 1886 Fred Apken married at Petersburg Anna Hofing, also a native of Germany, who came to the United States in young womanhood with her brother, Jacob Hofing, who subsequently became a hotel man of Petersburg. Mrs. Apken was born in 1850. Harry B. Apken is the only child of his parents.

Not only has Harry B. Apken succeeded to his father's business interests, but he has also inherited the older man's position in public esteem and confidence. He is identified with different local organizations, being a member of the Rotary Club, and of the Christian Church, to which his wife also belongs. Having been advanced through the different bodies of the York Rite in Masonry, he is now en route through those of the Scottish Rite, and is high priest of DeWitt Chapter, R. A. M., of Petersburg; past eminent commander of Saint Aldemar Commandery, and belongs to Ansar Temple, A. A. O. N. M. S., of Springfield. During the late war he was registered and placed in Classification No. 2.

On November 7, 1911, Mr. Apken married at Petersburg Pearl E. Shipley, who was born in this locality, March 30, 1886. She is a daughter of C. W. Shipley and his wife, Evelyn (Houghton) Shipley, and one of a family of four sons and four daughters. Mr. and Mrs. Apken have one son, Robert S., who was born September 6, 1920.

JOHN PEMBERTON, manager of the grain elevator of B. H. McFadden & Son of Forest City, and one of the solid business men of Forest City, was born at Durang in Tazewell County, Illinois, November 10, 1863, and he belongs to one of the pioneer families of this part of Illinois. The paternal grandfather of John Pemberton, Louis Pemberton, came to Mason County from Tennessee, and established his homestead near the old town of Durang in Tazewell County, the site of his home now being opposite the pumping station of the Spring Lake Drainage District. Louis Pemberton was without any capital when he came here, and his first efforts were made as a tenant farmer, but hard work and strict economy produced excellent results, and he died a man of means. When he came to Illinois he brought his family with him in a covered wagon. Twice made a widower in Tennessee, he married a third wife, Kittie Alvin, after coming to Illinois. By his first marriage he had two sons, George and James K., and a daughter, Mrs. James Reagan, who died in the state of Oregon. Both sons served in the war between the states, as did their father, and James K. is still living, making his home at Poteau, Oklahoma, where the greater part of his life has been spent.

George Pemberton was born in Tennessee, in February, 1841, and he died at Forest City August 10, 1899. Although he volunteered for service during the war between the states, he became incapacitated not long after his enlistment, and was honorably discharged for disability at Cairo, Illinois, and returned home, not having been in any engagement. A poor young man, without any adequate training, he had to work hard in spite of his poor health, first at day labor, and later at farming, until he accumulated a little capital. This he used in establishing himself in business in 1871 at Forest City, and there he continued as a merchant until his death, during the last few years having his son, John Pemberton, as his partner. Finally he sold his interest to his son. He was not a man to seek public office, and was not active in community affairs nor fraternal life, except as a member of the Modern Woodmen of America. Never having had a great amount of schooling, he did not feel himself capable of speech making. He never identified himself with the Grand Army of the Republic, nor would he accept a pension from the government.

George Pemberton married Susan Ann Rochester, who was born near Terre Haute,

Indiana, a daughter of James and Martha (Reagan) Rochester. Mrs. Pemberton died in July, 1921, aged seventy-seven years. They had the following children born to their marriage: John, whose name heads this review; Kate, who married Harmon Bishop and lives at Lewiston, Idaho; Effie, who married George Wehmhoff, of Mason county, Illinois, and died at Tacoma, Washington; Allie, who married John Dosier, and lives on a farm near Mason City; Susan, who died at Tacoma, Washington, the wife of Rev. E. J. Snell; and Georgetta, who married O. L. Willett, of Ohio, and resides near Los Angeles, California.

John Pemberton spent his boyhood in Forest City, to which his parents moved in 1871, and what schooling fell to his lot was secured here. In early boyhood he began to make himself useful, assisted his father until after he passed his majority, at which time he was taken into partnership, and subsequently became, by purchase, the owner of the hardware and general merchandise store. Still later Mr. Pemberton had two partners and operated under the firm name of J. Pemberton & Company. In the course of time he sold his business and went into the grain business with McFadden & Company of Havana, Illinois, which concern was later succeeded by B. H. McFadden & Son. Since 1888 Mr. Pemberton has been the Forest City representative of this old house.

In addition to his activities mentioned above Mr. Pemberton aided in the incorporation of Forest City, and was a member of its town board. He was one of the organizers of the Forest City State Bank in 1899, and he was placed on its first Board of Directors, and for two years he has been its vice president. A man of sound convictions and strength of character, he has been able to render valuable assistance both in a public and private capacity, and there are few men in this vicinity who stand any higher in popular esteem and confidence than he.

It was at Manito that Mr. Pemberton was made a Mason, and he has been advanced to the Consistory in that order in the Valley of Peoria. He is a charter member of Forest City Lodge, K. of P., belongs to the local camp of the Modern Woodmen, and is a past consul of the latter. During the late war he was one of the active workers for patriotic purposes, and made an admirable record in the different drives. In December, 1924, Mr. Pemberton was appointed local chairman of the C. P. & St. L. Railroad right of way commission, and continuously held that position for eighteen months or until the Chicago & Illinois Midland Railroad took over that road. He was also treasurer and collected and paid out all the funds of that company.

On October 2, 1890, Mr. Pemberton married, first, at Peoria, Illinois, Kate Graff, a daughter of John and Minnie (Leipold) Graff, natives of Germany and Illinois respectively. Mrs. Pemberton was born at El Paso, Illinois, in 1867, and her education was obtained in the public schools. Being orphaned in early childhood, she was reared by strangers, who gave to the lonely little girl a refuge from the storms of life. She died at Forest City in February, 1901, having borne her husband one daughter, Vera C., who is the wife of William Herman, of Forest City, and Mr. and Mrs. Herman have two daughters, Doris and Fern. In September, 1908, Mr. Pemberton married Margaret E. Kiesling, who was born at Forest City. She was educated in her native city and at Bushnell, and was a public-school teacher for eighteen years prior to her marriage, and is an acknowledged leader in the cultural life of Mason County. She has retained her interest in the public schools of the county, and is proud of the fact that her husband has served as township treasurer of the six school districts of Forest City since January 16, 1902, and that his work in this connection has been of great value to the children of this vicinity. Both of them believe in providing the best of teachers and schoolhouses that the funds will procure, and they are constantly striving to stimulate interest in others so as to do still better each year. No work is more important than that of securing for the rising generation adequate educational advantages, and Mr. and Mrs. Pemberton are rendering a most valuable service in what they are accomplishing.

GEORGE WOOD GOVERT. The name Govert has had many honorable distinctions in the profession of the law and in business affairs at Quincy for more than half a century. The present bearer of the name, George Wood Govert, has practiced law in that city for a quarter of a century.

He was born at Jacksonville, Illinois, June 24, 1874, son of William H. and Rosa F. (Wood) Govert. He was named in honor of his maternal grandfather, a Presbyterian clergyman and graduate of Williams College, who was an early settler and minister of the Gospel in the West, and also for his great-grandfather, a New York merchant who in the earlier years of his life had acted as private secretary to Governor Clinton at New York. The Wood family ancestry is English and the first ancestor in this country was Peter Bulkeley, founder of Concord, Massachusetts, in the early Colonial period. The Govert family is of German ancestry, Mr. Govert's paternal grandparents having come to this country and made settlement at Fort Madison, Iowa. Rose F. (Wood) Govert was born at Jerseyville, Illinois.

William H. Govert, who was born at Fort Madison, Iowa, September 10, 1844, graduated from Illinois College of Jacksonville with the class of 1867, being associated as a classmate with Joseph N. Carter, who later became his law partner. In 1870 he graduated from the Law School of the University of Michigan, and settling at Quincy, formed a partnership with his friend, Joseph N. Carter, making a firm that enjoyed a notable prestige at the bar of Western Illinois until Judge Carter's election to the Supreme bench. William H. Govert served as city attorney for Quincy in his earlier years and for eight years was prosecuting attorney of Adams County. He accepted both of these positions as a means of experience and service in his profession rather than through any political aspirations. He had a large law practice and was also concerned with a number of manufacturing enterprises in Quincy, where he remained an executive until the date of his death, including the Collins Plow Company, J. R. Little Metal Wheel Company, the Gem City Stove Company and others. William H. Govert died December 7, 1921, at the age of seventy-seven, and his wife passed away February 4, 1923. They are survived by three children, all living in Quincy: George Wood, Anna Louise, wife of G. H. Earhart, who is head of the Earhart Motor Company; and Edith W., wife of F. Boyd Castle, of the insurance firm of Bastert, Miller & Castle.

George Wood Govert had a liberal education and thorough preparation for the work of a professional career. He attended the public schools of Quincy, and in the fall of 1891 entered Illinois College at Jacksonville, graduating with the A. B. degree in 1895 and was elected president of his class. After a year of residence he received the A. B. degree in 1896 from Yale University and then entered the Law School which had graduated his father, that of the University of Michigan, taking his LL. B. degree in 1900. In the same year he returned to Quincy and engaged in practice as a member of the firm Govert, Pape & Govert, a firm that continued until William H. Govert retired. Since 1907 Mr. George Wood Govert has been associated in law practice with W. Emery Lancaster.

Since the death of his father he has also succeeded to a number of the executive positions in industrial establishments mentioned above, and is now president of the Collins Plow Company, the J. R. Little Metal Wheel Company and the Gem City Stove Company. He is a director of the State Street Bank & Trust Company, the Modern Iron Works and the Quincy Hotel Company.

Mr. Govert is a loyal alumnus of Illinois College at Jacksonville, serving on its board of trustees. He has never been a seeker for political honors, though he has uniformly been identified with the republican party, and is a member of the Presbyterian Church. Mr. Govert married Lilian Hurt, of Memphis, Tennessee, member of well known Tennessee families of English ancestry. Her mother was of the well known Martin family of Western Tennessee. Mrs. Govert is a Daughter of the American Revolution, being regent of the Quincy Chapter of that patriotic society, and for a number of years was also president of the Young Women's Christian Association of Quincy. Mr. and Mrs. Govert have a son, George Wood Govert, Jr., a graduate of Illinois College at Jacksonville, representing the third generation of the family in that school, and now in his first year in the law department of the University of Michigan.

SOLOMON P. RODERICK is a member of the Chicago bar, and has practiced law for fifteen years. His name is also prominently identified with civic and political affairs in his home city and state. He served several terms in the Illinois Legislature.

Mr. Roderick was born in St. Louis, Missouri, in 1876. His parents, George and Rebecca Roderick, after the great fire of 1871, in which their residence was destroyed, moved from Chicago to St. Louis, but two months after the birth of their son they returned to Chicago. Mr. Roderick grew up and attended school in that city, being educated in the public schools and in DePaul University. He graduated from DePaul University Law School in 1910. His offices are at 105 North Clark Street. Mr. Roderick does a general practice, but his time has been more and more taken up in recent years by corporation and real estate law.

Mr. Roderick was first elected a member of the Legislature in 1914, serving by successive elections in the Lower House in the Forty-ninth, Fiftieth, Fifty-first and Fifty-second General Assemblies. In the Fifty-second Assembly he was chairman of the committee on constitutional convention and helped formulate the measure for holding the Constitional Convention in 1921-22. Mr. Roderick proved his value as a legislator by the wisdom with which he handled many interests committed to his care, and also by the energy with which he combatted ill advised or useless bills.

Mr. Roderick for several years has enjoyed the confidence and high regard of United States Senator Deneen, and regards him as one of the greatest citizens Illinois has ever produced. While in the Legislature he interested himself strenuously in behalf of legislative measures proposed by Mr. Deneen. In the 54th General Assembly, in 1925, although Mr. Roderick was not a member, he was selected by Senator Deneen as his "friend at court" to represent the senator at Springfield, particularly in espousal of the primary election bills which Senator Deneen advocated and which were passsed at that session. One especial result of this legislation is that judges in Cook County are now nominated by primary election instead of the old machine-ruled conventions.

Mr. Roderick is a member of the Illinois Sportsmen's Club, is a Life member of the Chicago Art Institute, life member of the Chicago Historical Society, is a member of the Illinois Jewish Historical Society, belongs to the Chicago, Illinois and American Bar Associations, and fraternally is a Royal Arch Mason, a member of the B. P. O. Elks and Modern Woodmen of America. Mr. Roderick married Miss Lena Lurvey, member of an old time Chicago family. Their home is at 3104 Douglas Boulevard.

LEO H. BORGELT. Among the younger business men of Mason County who are accepting the opportunities presented here for success and are thereby working their way to position and prominence is Leo H. Borgelt. His career, while not so long as some whose biographies appear in this work, has been one of constant activity in various lines of endeavor, and his experience has been broad and varied. Not only has he succeeded in a business way, but has also been known to public life, and since 1922 has served capably in the office of postmaster at Havana. He is generally esteemed, and it is recognized that he is giving the people of Havana and the surrounding vicinity excellent mail service.

Mr. Borgelt was born at Havana, Mason County, Illinois, January 1, 1892, and is a son of William H. and Lutie (Wirth) Borgelt.

His paternal grandfather was Henry Borgelt, a native of Hanover, Germany, who was about twenty years of age when he came to the United States with his parents and became absorbed in farming, a vocation which he followed throughout his life in Illinois. His well-cultivated property, which he improved from year to year, was located three miles south of Havana, and Mr. Borgelt, a sober and industrious citizen of the most reliable character, played his part in bringing this locality under cultivation and in getting the "first things" under way. He died, respected and esteemed by pioneers and later comers, in 1904, at the age of seventy-three years. Henry Borgelt was a stanch republican in his political allegiance, but was purely and simply a tiller of the soil and had no ambitions or inclinations toward a public career. He married Miss Eliza Horstman, a daughter of William Horstman, who, like the Borgelts, was born in Germany and made the trip to the United States via the same route, landing at New York. Mrs. Borgelt died in 1892, the mother of the following children: Henry, of Havana, Illinois; Charlotte, who died as the wife of G. B. Holzgrafe; B. Frank, of Havana; William H., the father of Leo H.; Charles, of Havana; Elizabeth, who died as the wife of John Melhop; Horace, of Havana; Mollie, who married John Vanderveen, of Havana; and Yetta, who died unmarried.

William H. Borgelt was born at Havana, Illinois, in 1860, and received a public school education, following which he applied himself to the blacksmith trade, which he mastered. For many years he was the leading blacksmith of this community and also did a large business in wagon-making, but with the coming of years and the advent of the great automobile industry he retired from business and is now serving as engineer of the Oak Grove school. Mr. Borgelt has always been highly esteemed at Havana and is known as a man of integrity and straightforward dealing as well as good citizenship. He married Miss Lutie Wirth, a daughter of Mrs. George Mack, formerly Ernestina Franslaw. Mrs. Mack was born in Hanover, Germany, and came to the United States as a child of eight years. The Franslaws were unfortunate enough to land from ship in 1849 at New Orleans during a great epidemic of yellow fever, but miraculously escaped that scourge and made their way North. Ernestina Franslaw was first married to Mr. Wirth and bore him four children: Anna, who married Carl Zelle and resides at Lincoln, Illinois; Mary, who married John Ricks, of Jacksonville, Illinois; Lutie, who became Mrs. William H. Borgelt, born September 5, 1865; and Ella, who married Edward McKinley and is now deceased. After the death of her first husband Mrs. Ernestina (Franslaw) Wirth married George Mack, and they became the parents of two children: Margaret, the wife of Carl Rhode, of Columbus, Nebraska; and William, deceased, who left a son, William. To Mr. and Mrs. William H. Borgelt there were born the following children: Erwin, who met death by drowning at the age of fifteen years; Walter, who is engaged in the coal business at Havana, Illinois; Leo H., of this review; Elsie, the wife of Raymond Meyer, of Havana, Illinois; William W., of Bushnell, Illinois; Ralph, who died in infancy; and Zelda and Laura, who reside at Havana.

The educational training of Leo H. Borgelt was acquired in the public schools of Havana, and after he had completed the high school course as a member of the graduating class of 1912 he entered the service of the Chicago, Peoria & St. Louis Railway Company in the capacity of clerk. Subsequently he resigned this position and secured a position with the Havana Metal Wheel Company, being in their general office for four years. Next Mr. Borgelt changed his field of activity radically, becoming a farm manager for F. and C. Borgelt, proprietors of the Borgelt farms, and was so employed when the United States entered the World war and called for its young men to fight for the cause. Mr. Borgelt resigned from his position and went to Springfield, Illinois, where he enlisted, and responding to his wishes he was assigned to the Aviation Corps. He was first sent to Jefferson Barracks, then to Kelly Field, Texas, where he helped to construct this aviation field, then to the University of Texas, where he received instruction for three months, and then went to Kelly Field, San Antonia, Texas, the second time, where he was instructed in flying, securing a pilot's rating. He received his honorable discharge from the service in December, 1918, and returned to Havana to resume the peaceful duties of the civilian. Not long thereafter he was appointed deputy treasurer of Mason County, a capacity in which he served for three years under Treasurer W. J. Shirley. While still active in that capacity he received the appointment as postmaster at Havana and assumed the duties of that office July 31, 1922, as the successor of Mathew M. Bollen. He has given his fellow-townsmen splendid servive and has capably discharged his responsibilities in every way. Mr. Borgelt is a republican in his political allegiance. He has several fraternal connections and was a charter memmer and one of the organizers of Havana Post No. 138, American Legion, of which he is a past commander.

At San Jose, Illinois, June 1, 1920, Mr. Borgelt was united in marriage with Mrs. Kathryn Steinmetz, who was born September 8, 1889, at San Jose, where she graduated from the high school. She is a daughter of George and Lillian (Taylor) Woll, natives of Mason County, where Mr. Woll was a thresherman. He is deceased, but his widow still survives at San Jose, the mother of three children: Kathryn, Edgar and Truman. To Mr. and Mrs. Borgelt there have been born two children: Marcia Adaline and Lois Modelle.

CLARENCE EDWIN WELLMAN, in his third consecutive term as clerk of the Circuit Court of Vermilion County, is a veteran of the Spanish-American war and for many years was active in the Illinois National Guard.

Mr. Wellman was born at Sardinia, Ohio, September 8, 1877. His father, Thomas Wellman, spent all his life in Brown County, Ohio, where he was a farmer. He died at Sardinia in 1878. He was a republican, and was affiliated with the United Brethren Church, of

which his wife was a devout member. She was Sarah Roudenbush, who was born in Brown County in 1850 and died at Sardinia in 1914.

Clarence E. Wellman, only child of his parents, was about a year old when his father died. He attended village schools at Sardinia and in 1893 at the age of sixteen came to Illinois and finished his education in the public schools of Hoopeston in Vermilion County and completed a business course in Greer College there in 1897. For nearly a year he taught school in Woodford County, Illinois, but before the end of the term resigned to enlist in the voluteer forces for service in the Spanish-American war. He entered the army in April, 1898, in Battery A of the First Illinois Volunteer Artillery, and was sent for training to Chickamauga Park, Georgia. From there he went to Porto Rico, and was on that island until September 8, 1898. He received his honorable discharge at Danville, November 25, 1898. After this military service Mr. Wellman had fourteen years of active connection with the Illinois National Guard. He was with Company B of the Third Illinois Infantry at Hoopeston, was commissioned a second lieutenant of the company and from 1912 to 1916 was a member of the Fifth Infantry of the Illinois National Guard at Danville, holding the rank of battalion quartermaster of the commissary department. In 1921 he was elected and served a term as department commander of the Veterans of Foreign Wars of the United States.

Mr. Wellman in January, 1899, soon after his war service, entered the employ of the Sprague Canning Machinery Company of Hoopeston, beginning as mechanic, subsequently was made a draughtsman and then was a road salesman for the company. In January, 1912, having removed to Danville, he was appointed chief deputy in the office of the clerk of the Circuit Court, and has had fourteen years of experience to qualify him in every detail of that department of the county government. In 1916 he was elected for his first term as clerk of the Circuit Court, and was reelected in 1920 and in November, 1924.

Mr. Wellman is a republican, is a member of St. James Methodist Episcopal Church at Danville and is general secretary of its Sunday School, a post he has held for eleven years.

He is a member of several fraternal organizations, Olive Branch No. 38, Ancient Free and Accepted Masons, Danville Consistory Ancient Accepted Scottish Rite, and is Chief Justice of Gao Grotto Mystic Order of Veiled Prophets of the Enchanted Realm, the Knights of Pythias, and is the Adjutant General of the Uniform Rank Knights of Pythias of the Illinois Brigade, the Modern Woodmen of America, the Veterans of Foreign Wars of the United States, and is a past Department Commander.

Mr. Wellman's home is at 1124 Grant Street in Danville. He married at Quincy, Illinois, December 25, 1901, Miss Mary A. Lindahl, daughter of Augustus and Emily Lindahl, her mother a resident of Hoopeston, where her father died. He was a section foreman for the Nickel Plate Railway Company. Mrs. Wellman is a graduate of the East Lynn High School, attended normal schools and taught in Vermilion County five years before her marriage. Mr. and Mrs. Wellman have three children: Earl F., who finished his education in the Danville High School and is now employed by the Allioh Prouty Company of Danville; Gladys M., a senior in high school; and Marion E., a grammar school student.

N. L. PIOTROWSKI. A leading member of Chicago bar, N. L. Piotrowski is also president of the Great Lakes Insurance Company of Chicago, a leader of the Polish people in this country, and a man of broad education and well-developed abilities. His career has been an active, varied and interesting one, during which he has viewed numerous countries, and the extent of his knowledge and the broadening effect of his travels have been combined with good citizenship in a manner greatly beneficial to the city of his adoption.

Mr. Piotrowski was born September 15, 1861, in Poland, and is a son of Simon and Johanna Piotrowski. He received his early education in his native land, and this was supplemented by further preparation at Berlin, Germany, whence he came to the United States in 1882 and continued his studies at Notre Dame and Valparaiso, Indiana. He served as professor of physics and chemistry at St. Thomas Seminary, St. Paul, Minnesota, from 1889 to 1891, and in 1892 came to Chicago, where he established himself in the practice of law, in which he has been engaged successfully to the present. In 1897 he became assistant corporation counsel, holding that office until 1902, and in 1906 was a candidate on the democratic ticket for the office of state treasurer of Illinois. He became city attorney of Chicago in 1911, and acted in that capacity until 1915. In that year he was sent as a special war correspondent by the Chicago Herald, and as such in 1915 and 1916 visited Poland, England, France, Italy, Russia, Austria and the Balkan States, in which countries he interviewed the leading statesmen, contributing numerous interesting and authentic articles to the press. In 1918 he organized the Great Lakes Insurance Company, of which he has since been the president. This is one of the sound and substantial institutions of the city, and has enjoyed success and gratifying growth. Mr. Piotrowski has long been one of the acknowledged leaders of Chicago Poles. From 1918 to April, 1923, he was treasurer of the National Polish Committee of America for the relief of Poland, and in that position raised for the cause $10,000,000.00, in recognition of which service the Republic of Poland conferred on him the order "Polonia Restituta," which is one of the highest honors within the gift of the Republic. During the great war he rendered incalculable services for the Red Cross and in the sale of Liberty Bonds. From 1917 until 1922 he was president of the Polish Catholic Union of America. He belongs to the Union League Club, the North Shore Athletic Club of Chicago and St. Charles Country Club, but finds his chief recreation in travel and in gardening on his estate in St. Charles. He is also a member of Chicago Historical

Society, a life member of Chicago Art Institute and associate member of Field Museum of Natural History.

On September 27, 1893, Mr. Piotrowski married Miss Theresa R. Maag, of Richmond, Indiana, and to this union there have been born two children: Angela, the wife of Eugene C. Lang, who has three children, Elizabeth, Celeste and Nicholas; and Julian, who died in infancy.

ALEXANDER RITCHEY, now living retired at Mount Sterling, was born in Brown County, and for about half a century was actively identified with its agricultural interests.

He was born in Mount Sterling Township April 9, 1845. His grandfather, Samuel Ritchey, probably a native of Virginia, lived in Kentucky and from that state he and his son James and other members of the family came to Illinois, riding horseback. However, Samuel Ritchey subsequently returned and lived out the rest of his life in Kentucky. He married a Miss Irwin. Their sons were John, James, Stephen and Samuel. Their daughters were: Margaret, who married Samuel Stone, and died in Kentucky; Jane, who married Thomas Brockman and came to Brown County; and Betsy, who married William Chapman and subsequently settled in Platte County, Missouri. Of the sons, Stephen became a physician and practiced medicine in Clay County, Missouri; Samuel was a farmer in Clinton County, Missouri, and finally retired and moved to Kansas City; John was a farmer in Hancock County, Illinois.

James Ritchey, father of Alexander Ritchey, was born near Lexington, Fayette County, Kentucky, in 1818, and was about twenty-two years of age when, in 1840, he removed to Illinois. In 1844 he married and established a home, purchasing land from Lewis Brockman and gradually improving his home and making extensions to his landed property. He helped organize the first Christian Church at Mount Sterling and was a man of good influence in his community. He was first a whig and then a republican, and voted for Mr. Lincoln in 1860. James Ritchey, who died in June, 1871, married Eliza McKean, who was born in Ireland and was about a year old when her father, Alexander McKean, came to the United States and established his home in Kentucky. The children of James Ritchey and wife were: Alexander; Robert Samuel, who died at Arcadia, Florida, in May, 1922, leaving one daughter; James William, who with his wife was drowned while crossing Crooked Creek, near Ripley, Illinois; Meribah, wife of E. E. Clark, of Mount Sterling; and Emma Jane, who married Clayton Coffman, and died in Brown County.

Alexander Ritchey attended school at Mount Sterling, grew up on the home farm and remained with his parents until after his marriage. For a year or two he lived in Clay County, Missouri, and purchased a tract of land just across the Missouri River from Kansas City, hauling ties and timbers there to market. He furnished some of the timbers that went into the first bridge over the Missouri River at Kansas City. After improving and cultivating his land he sold it, on the death of his father, and returned to Illinois. For a time he operated the home farm and subsequently purchased a place nearby, and there lived until his retirement. He still owns that property. Mr. Ritchey began with one hundred acres and had an estate of 223 acres when he abandoned farming. He engaged in raising grain and live stock, and for a number of years carried on a program of stock breeding for the market.

Mr. Ritchey has been without political ambitions. He cast his first presidential vote for Horace Greeley in 1872, but since then has been a regular republican. For many years he has been a faithful member of the Christian Church. Mr. Ritchey in 1912 removed to Mount Sterling and occupies one of the substantial homes of that city.

He married at Mount Sterling, December 23, 1875, Miss Lucinda McCaw, who was born in Pike County, Illinois, in 1846, and died in November, 1912. Her people came to Illinois from Kentucky. By this marriage Mr. Ritchey was father of the following children: Frank, who died in childhood; Mary, wife of Charles Dunn, of Williston, North Dakota; Charles a graduate of Yale University and now teacher in a college at St. Paul, Minnesota, married Mary Still and has two children, named Leslie and Mary; George A., a Brown County farmer, married Bertha Cox and has three children, Lois, Naomi and Joanna. Alexander Ritchey married, October 23, 1917, at Mount Sterling, Mrs. Laura (Fuqua) Griffin, daughter of William and Eleanor (Wilson) Fuqua. Her father, who came to Illinois from Kentucky, was a farmer and died about 1864, during the Civil war, while his wife passed away in 1879. Mrs. Ritchey was born in Logan County, Kentucky, November 28, 1860. There were two other children: Paralee, wife of John Wilson, of Los Angeles; and William Fuqua, who died in Brown County in 1911. Mrs. Ritchey attended country schools and school at Mount Sterling. She is a member of the Mount Sterling Baptist Church and is active in several organizations in the church and in her community.

RICHARD A. HILLING. It has been proven conclusively upon many occasions that the elements in an individual's character that are of paramount importance are those which make him of the greatest value to his community. It is practically impossible to gauge a man's worth by the accomplishments which have served to meet his own ends, for it is only by measuring him by the influence which he exerts and the force he wields in assisting progress that a fair and equitable conclusion can be reached. This is particularly true in those communities in which each man is known to his neighbor. One of the men who has been associated with the life of Manito for many years, and who as a contractor and builder has contributed greatly to the growth of this locality, is Richard A. Hilling. While he is interested in various leading enterprises and has held with honor many public offices, his greatest achievement thus far in a career that has not been lacking in accomplishment was the reclamation of various former swamp lands, particularly in the vicinity east of Manito, and near Hennepin, Putnam County.

Mr. Hilling was born in Adams County, Ohio, June 16, 1861, and is a son of John S. and Mary (Postelwait) Hilling. His father was born in Adams County, Ohio, where he passed his life, dying in November, 1867, but a few months after the death of his wife, and being buried at Port William, Ohio. He married Mary Postelwait, a daughter of Jonathan and Sarah (Thompson) Postelwait, the former a native of Virginia and the latter of Adams County, Ohio, where both died and are buried, Mrs. Postelwait being buried at Cherry Fork, Ohio, less than a quarter of a mile from her birthplace. Mr. and Mrs. Hilling had two children: Richard A., of this review; and Clara E., the wife of Charles E. Dwiggens, of Wilmington, Ohio. By a former marriage John S. Hilling had two children: Sarah J., who married George Reed, and died at Port William, Ohio; and William T., of Pekin, Illinois.

Richard A. Hilling was less than six years old at the time of the death of his mother, and when his father died shortly afterward he was taken into the home and hearts of Mr. and Mrs. R. W. Matthews, the former a cousin of his mother. He was reared as their own son and through their affection and kindly training was brought to sturdy and self-reliant manhood. Brought up in the country district of Adams County, Ohio, he received a rural school education, and began to make his own way when he was seventeen years of age, although he continued to live at the home of his foster parents until he was nearly twenty-four years of age. He first identified himself with Illinois in 1886, stopping first at Tremont, where he went to learn the carpenter trade with his half brother. He spent three years there and in February, 1889, took up his residence at Manito, where, as a stranger in the community, he began the erection of the sheds of the Manito Lumber Company, at that time J. Zimmerman & Son, the lumber yard of which stood on the present site of the old livery and sales stable and the chiropractic office. For some years he worked as a carpenter, but in April, 1895, developed into a contractor and builder, his maiden contract calling for the erection of the shed and office of the Manito Lumber Company on its present site. At the same time, it may be noted here, Mr. Hilling secured a financial interest in this concern, and today is one of the heavy stockholders and vice president thereof.

As the years have passed Mr. Hilling has built almost every structure of importance in the way of residences and business buildings at Manito, and many of the country homes, churches and other buildings have been erected under his contract. This includes all of the former swamp region east of Manito which has been built up and improved, the former impassable land now being a flourishing community, including churches and schools. He was one of four men who purchased 400 acres of land near Hennepin, Illinois, which was drained, cleared and tiled by the partners, who turned the dismal swamp into a productive farm. This Mr. Hilling considers his greatest achievement up to this time, and it is agreed that it is a noteworthy one. In addition to his work as a builder Mr. Hilling has been one of the moving spirits of the locality, and has contributed time and money to the welfare of Manito and its institutions. He has served as an alderman, and was an important factor in the movement which prevented the junking of the Chicago, Peoria & St. Louis Railway, thus saving the road for the people along the line. He is a stockholder in the Peoples State Bank of Manito and in Meadow Lawn Cemetery, adjacent to this village. He was actively identified with war movements during 1917 and 1918, and was offered the chairmanship of the Young Men's Christian Association movement, but was forced to decline because of business engagements. Politically a republican, he has been central committeeman for twenty-five years and on numerous occasions has served as delegate to state, judicial and senatorial conventions, but has never found the time to accept political office with the exception of that of alderman. Mr. Hilling was made a Mason at Manito, being a member of the Blue Lodge, and also belongs to the Eastern Star, of which Mrs. Hilling was a member, and in which three of Mr. Hilling's daughters hold membership. He has been twenty times chancellor of the Knights of Pythias, has attended sixteen Grand Lodge meetings, and has been the recipient of every possible honor both in the local and State Grand lodges.

At West Union, Ohio, January 15, 1885, Mr. Hilling was united in marriage with Miss Mary Thompson, who was born at Cherry Fork, Ohio, a daughter of Robert and Mary (Sauers) Thompson. Mrs. Hilling was born August 24, 1861, received a rural school education, was an ideal wife and mother, and was an active woman outside of the home, being a worker in the church and also taking an industrious part in war work, the Hilling home being one of the knitting homes of the locality. She died, widely and sincerely mourned, October 7, 1923, having been the mother of the following children: Robert R., who is associated with his father's business at Manito as a mechanic, married Maud Knollhoff and has a daughter, Mary I. Miss Mary A. is a resident of Chicago. Dickie L. is assistant postmaster at Manito. Bruce E., was in the army training camps, finally in Virginia during the World war, but did not see overseas service, and is now connected with the B. and M. Clothing House at Peoria. He married Bertha Bishop, a daughter of George Bishop and Helen T., who is unmarried, has taken her mother's place as housekeeper for her father. All of the children are graduates of the Manito High School.

JAMES E. DUNNEGAN. In point of years of continuous service James E. Dunnegan is one of the oldest members of the bar of Madison County. He has been practicing law at Alton a half century, and has enjoyed some of the best honors and rewards of professional success.

He was born in Alton, June 10, 1852, son of Lawrence and Margaret (Hoey) Dunnegan. His parents were born in County Langford, Ireland, and his father came to America in 1844, locating at Alton, where in 1851 he married Margaret Hoey. He was one of the earnest and hard working citizens of that community the rest of his life, and died honored and respected January 28, 1902, when past eighty years of age. The mother died in 1895, and of their five children the only one to reach mature years is James E. Dunnegan.

James E. Dunnegan was educated in the public and parochial schools of Alton, also attended Blackburn University and Shurtleff College, and at St. Louis studied law with the firm of Lee and Parmer. He was admitted to the bar at St. Louis in 1873, and two years later returned to Alton to engage in private practice. He still maintains his law office at Third and Piasa streets.

In the course of his professional career he has filled a number of important municipal offices. In 1876 he was elected city attorney and in 1885 was elected city judge, holding that office until March, 1893. In 1905 he was again elected judge of the City Court, and served in that office altogether twenty years. He is an active democrat in politics.

On June 15, 1898, he married Miss Alice O'Connor, of St. Louis, daughter of John and Margaret (Farrell) O'Connor. They have a daughter, Alice Eugenia. Judge Dunnegan and family are members of the Catholic Cathedral at Alton.

FRANK WESLEY MARTIN, a retired farmer of Bath, and one of the directors of the State Bank of Bath, is a man who stands high in the estimation of his fellow citizens, and one who is deserving of considerable praise. He was born in Sherman Township, Mason County, July 17, 1875, a son of the late Charles Martin, and grandson of Elias Martin, the latter of whom was born in New Jersey, and died on the home he established near Bishop in Mason County in the early '80s, when about eighty years old, and he is buried in the cemetery on Pleasant Row. In addition to his farm his chief interest in life was hunting and fishing, and he was an adept in both sports. Of his family three sons and three daughters reached maturity, they being: George; Albert; Charles; Mel, who married Abe Shelebarger; Libbie, who married Joseph Shelebarger; and Mrs. Cornell, but all of them are now deceased.

Charles Martin was born in New Jersey, and was but a boy when he was brought to Illinois, and he died at Hurd's Lake, Illinois, in 1889, when he was about fifty years old. He grew up on his father's farm, and attended the district schools of Mason County. He married, near Topeka, Illinois, Mrs. Charity (Bailey) King, born near Dayton, Ohio. She came to Illinois with her mother and three brothers, the latter being Andrew, Samuel and James Bailey. Mr. and Mrs. Charles Martin had the following children born to them: Frank Wesley, whose name heads this review; and Myrtle, who is the wife of Frank Knuppel, of Poplar City, Illinois. Mrs. Martin subsequently married for her third husband, John Knuppel, and when she died, May 28, 1923, when she was over seventy-eight years of age, she was buried by the side of Mr. Knuppel in Havana Cemetery.

Frank Wesley Martin lived during the first twelve years of his life on the farm where he was born, now the property of Frank Rubencane, and attended the Lake Shore School. The family then moved to Hurd's Lake, Havana Township, near Peterville, and there Mr. Martin reached manhood and completed his country-school work. He began working for wages as a farm hand when still in his teens, but continued to add to his store of knowledge under the direction of Henry Teeney, who was perhaps one of the best educators Mason County has known.

When he had accumulated enough capital to justify him in beginning for himself Mr. Martin married, and became a tenant farmer, his first home being near Bath. For ten years he continued to rent, and then bought the farm he was renting, and this is still a part of his estate. For years he carried on general farming, raising stock and grain, and selling his dairy products. He specialized somewhat in breeding mules and horses, and sometimes fed as many as 100 head of hogs. While living on the farm he erected two barns, an engine house and scales, and kept on adding to his property until he had 235 acres of land. While he was thus active as a farmer he did not neglect his duties as a citizen, and was clerk of Bath Township for sixteen years, when he resigned, and he was then appointed assessor of the township. After he left the farm and moved to Bath he continued as a breeder of stock, and he was in the ice business for a year, and finally became the Ford agent, in connection with Mr. Pewwet of Easton. For eight or nine years he had the agency for the Overland and Chevrolet cars at Bath, but finally sold, and during more recent years has been looking after his private interests. His farm is now principally devoted to sweet clover and alfalfa.

Other interests have engaged Mr. Martin at different periods, and he was also in the elevator business, and did some buying and selling of farm lands. He organized the Farmers Elevator Company of Bath, and first served it as secretary, and later as manager. For a number of years he has been a director of the State Bank of Bath. Casting his first presidential vote for William Jennings Bryan, he has given the democratic party his earnest support ever since, and has been very active in local politics. He served on the village board, and later in the council of Bath, and favored the building of a community high school and the movement to save the Chicago, Peoria & Saint Louis Railroad to the community. At present he is precinct committeeman of his party.

On January 18, 1899, Frank Wesley Martin married near Hurd's Lake Rosetta Rebecca Ermeling, a daughter of Garrett and Mary (Derks) Ermeling. Garrett Ermeling was born in Hanover, Germany, and came to the United States as a child of seven years with his parents, who settled near Havana, and there engaged in farming. There the grandparents of Mrs. Martin died, and they lie side by side in the Havana Cemetery.

Having but a limited education, Garrett Ermeling was, nevertheless, a well-informed man, and a successful farmer. While not a church member, he believed in them, and was a man of high character. He did not care for politics, and never held office. His death took place in 1909, and his widow survived him until 1918. Their children were as follows: Jennie, who is deceased, and was Mrs. William Butler; Emma, who is the wife of Fred Herring, of Bath; John, who is a druggist of Havana; Mrs. Tillie Layman, who was for many years one of the teachers of Mason County, and is now living at Havana; George, who is a resident of Havana; Edward, who is operating the old Ermeling homestead near Kilburn, Illinois; Elizabeth, who is a professional nurse; Esther, who is a dressmaker of Havana; Mrs. Martin, who was born April 12, 1876, and was educated in the local public schools; Clara, who is the wife of William Underbrink, of Archie, Missouri; Eliza, who is the wife of Carl Krebaum, of Havana; and Catherine, who is the wife of Harry Holzgrafe.

Mr. and Mrs. Martin have one son, Raymond Charles, who was born July 7, 1908, and will complete his high-school course at Bath in 1926.

During the World war both Mr. and Mrs. Martin were vitally interested in all of the war activities, and he was one who helped to raise $1,800 for his township. He was registered in the second draft, but was not called because of the signing of the armistice. While he is not a fraternity or church man, he is friendly to all of the churches and all other movements of a moral character.

WILLIAM F. LOELLKE, an ex-service man, has been identified with the Alton Banking & Trust Company since he was seventeen years of age, and is now secretary of that institution.

He was born at St. Louis, Missouri, February 24, 1893, son of Otto H. and Amelia (Schmoellie) Loellke. His parents were natives of Germany, his father coming to the United States at the age of two years and his mother when about seventeen. They were married at Jerseyville, Illinois, then lived in St. Louis, subsequently in Jersey County, Illinois, and since about 1908 have made their home in Alton. Of their two children the only daughter is Mrs. Minnie Harms, of Alton.

William F. Loellke was educated in country schools in Jersey County, also attended high school there and at Alton, and finished a course in Brown's Business College. On November 2, 1910, he went to work in the Alton Banking & Trust Company as a collector, and has held nearly all the minor positions in the service of the bank. He was general bookkeeper, assistant cashier and cashier, and since January 1, 1926, has been secretary of the bank and secretary of real estate and trust departments.

At the polls Mr. Loellke supports the men and measures of the republican party. His services to the government in the World war were on the Mexican border at Fort McIntosh and Fort Brown in district headquarters work until honorably discharged on the 19th day of December, 1918. Mr. Loellke belongs to the American Legion and to the organization known as 40 Homes et 8 Chevaux, also to the Kiwanis Club and to the Benevolent and Protective Order of Elks. His religious faith is that of the Evangelical Church.

On June 6, 1917, Mr. Loellke married Miss Anna Louise Feldwisch, of Alton. They have one daughter, Dorothy Louise.

JOHN SUMNER RUNNELLS. Although not the city of his birth, nor the scene of his early life and achievements, Chicago has claimed John Sumner Runnells as her own for more than thirty years, according him respect, confidence and esteem. Prominent in professional life and long a leader of her bar, he has also been a citizen of force, character and high worth in her business and civic life.

John Sumner Runnells was born at Effingham Falls, Carroll County, New Hampshire, July 30, 1844, son of John and Huldah (Staples) Runnells, and is a descendant in the fourth generation of the last survivor of the Battle of Bunker Hill. Following early educational training in the village schools of Tamworth, Mr. Runnells attended New Hampton Academy, and at the age of sixteen years entered Amherst College, where he completed the full course and from which he was graduated in 1865. During the next couple of years he taught school at Rochester and Dover, in the meanwhile studying law, but in 1868 left New England and went to Iowa, where he became private secretary of Governor Merrill of that state. In the following year, although but twenty-five years old, he was appointed by President Grant, United States consul, to Tunstall, England, and he remained abroad for two years, performing his duties with unusual tact and diplomacy.

Mr. Runnells returned to Iowa in 1871, where he was admitted to the bar and shortly afterward entered upon the practice of his profession at Des Moines, and almost immediately became interested in local politics. In 1875 he was elected reporter of the Supreme Court of Iowa, and edited eighteen volumes of the court's decisions while serving in this office, in addition to attending to a rapidly growing private practice. In 1881 he was appointed by President Arthur, United States district attorney for Iowa, and served four years in that important office. In the meanwhile he had become an active factor in republican politics in the state, serving in 1879-1880 as chairman of the State Central Committee; in 1880 as delegate to the Republican National Convention; and from 1880 to 1884 was a member of the Republican National Committee.

In 1887 John Sumner Runnells came to Chicago with the intention of making this midwest city his future home, and soon afterward founded the law firm of Runnells & Burry, later Runnells, Burry & Johnstone, with which he continued as senior member until 1913, when he retired on account of the pressure of other interests. In 1888 he accepted the position of general counsel, tendered him by the late George M. Pullman, for the Pullman Car Company, and continued in that relation until May, 1911, when he became vice president as well and later was elected president. For eleven years he remained at the head of the company, when, having brought it to a very prosperous condition, he retired, but still serves as chairman of the Board of Directors of this corporation, with which he has been prominently identified for almost forty years. Mr. Runnells has long been recognized as an able, astute business man, and his advice and honorable name have been sought as assets by many of the largest commercial enterprises all over the country. At the present time he is serving as a member of the Board of Directors of the Illinois Merchants Trust Company of Chicago, formerly the old Merchants Loan & Trust Company, of which he was a director for many years before the above merger; is a director of the Pullman Trust & Savings Bank of Chicago, and also a director of the Guaranty Trust Company and of the National Biscuit Company of New York City.

In 1869, at Des Moines, Iowa, Mr. Runnells married Miss Helen R. Baker, daughter of former Gov. Nathaniel B. Baker, of New Hampshire. Mrs. Runnells died in 1918, but their four children all survive.

Mr. Runnells is a member of the Chicago Club, of which he was president from 1906 to 1914; of the Saddle and Cycle Club, of which he was president for a number of years; of the University Club of Chicago and the University Club of New York. He is a valued and interested member of the Chicago Historical Society, and is numbered with the unostentatious philanthropists of this city.

EDWARD H. HANNANT, postmaster of Mount Sterling, has been long and favorably known in agricultural and business circles in Brown County and represents a family that has lived in Southern Illinois for three generations.

Mr. Hannant was born near Perry, in Pike County, Illinois, January 14, 1879. His grandfather, John Hannant, came to the United States from Devonshire, England, bringing his wife and several of his children. He was a farmer in Illinois, and died in Pike County about 1862, being buried in the McCord Cemetery at Perry. His children were: John, who died at Mound City, Kansas; Morisco, a daughter, who died at Los Angeles; Fred, who died at Carlisle, Illinois; Rebecca, who died at Pittsfield, Illinois, in 1907, wife of Henry Wilson; and William A.

William A. Hannant, father of the Mount Sterling postmaster, was born at Jacksonville, Illinois, March 20, 1853. He is now living retired at Perry. His active career was devoted to farming, to feeding and shipping live stock, and his success in that business was an example followed by his son Edward. He married at Perry, Illinois, Ada M. Triplett, daughter of William Triplett. Their children were: Mary Rebecca, who died at New Salem, Illinois, wife of C. T. Beatty; Edward Harry; Adeline, wife of John Vose, of Chambersburg, Illinois; Leroy, who died in infancy; Charles H., of Perry; Floyd D., of Perry; Clyde, who died in childhood; John Ray, of Perry; Olive M., a teacher in the schools of Seattle, Washington; John and Grace, both of whom died in early childhood.

Edward H. Hannant was reared at Perry on the home farm, attended country schools and the Perry High School, and for eight years followed farming, gradually diversifying his enterprise by the buying, selling and shipping of live stock. From Perry he removed to Brown County and for seven years lived on a farm near Mount Sterling, and after his removal to Mount Sterling continued his business as a stock buyer and shipper until he entered upon the duties of postmaster.

Mr. Hannant has been an effective citizen of Mount Sterling for some years. He was a member of the Board of Education in 1917-19, and on the Town Council in 1918-19. While he was on the council occurred an incident that aroused considerable debate and opposition in the community, the council passing and executing an ordinance for the removal of the old wooden awnings over the store fronts. Mr. Hannant for some years has been vice president of the Farmers State Bank. A republican in politics, he cast his first presidential vote for Major McKinley in 1900. He was appointed postmaster March 13, 1922, as successor to William B. Davis. The Mount Sterling office has six rural routes and has a free city delivery.

Mr. Hannant was registered under the second selective service law during the World war. He joined the Masonic fraternity at Perry, where he still retains his lodge and Royal Arch membership, is a member of Quincy Consistory of the Scottish Rite and Ansar Temple of the Mystic Shrine. He belongs to the lodge of Odd Fellows at Mount Sterling.

Mr. Hannant married Miss Celia Jones, daughter of John M. and Mary (Bradbury) Jones. She was born near Perry, Illinois, June 29, 1881, was educated in high school, being the youngest of four children, the others being: Ed Jones, of Rochester, Washington; Nellie, wife of E. E. Taylor, of Perry; and Mrs. Abbie Bickers. Mr. and Mrs. Hannant have one daughter, Veda Norene, who was born in the same house and the same room in which her mother was born. This daughter is a graduate of the Mount Sterling High School and for two years attended James Milliken University at Decatur, Illinois.

OLIVER G. MAXWELL is an attorney by profession but for several years has given his time to a growing practice as an income tax expert at Danville, where he is a member of a firm of accountants and income tax experts.

Mr. Maxwell was born at Oakdale in Washington County, Illinois, August 22, 1882. Three generations of his family have lived in Illinois. The Maxwells were English people who settled in Virginia during Colonial times. Mr. Maxwell has an ancestor who fought in the War of 1812. His grandfather, Frank Maxwell, was a native of Kentucky, and when a young man moved to Oakdale, Illinois, where he acquired and operated an extensive farm. His home was at Oakdale the rest of his life, but he died at Hot Springs, Arkansas. His wife, Catherine Ragland, was born in Illinois.

George W. Maxwell, father of Oliver G., was born at Oakdale in 1858, and has spent all his life in that community, a successful farmer and honored citizen. He has lived retired since 1921. He is a democrat and a Baptist. George W. Maxwell married India M. Bills, who was born at Oakdale in 1858. They had a family of seven children: Mary Catherine, wife of Alfred Kelly, a farmer at Oakdale; Oliver G.; Miss Agnes R., at home; Joseph, superintendent of schools at Hoyleton, Illinois, and who was a sergeant major with the Fourth Division of the American Expeditionary Forces in France for eighteen months, participating in a number of major offensives; John C., a farmer who died in North Dakota at the age of twenty-three; Miss Ruth, a teacher in the public schools at Ellis Grove, Illinois; and James A., a farmer at Oakdale, who was in training as an artilleryman during the World war.

Oliver G. Maxwell grew up on his father's farm, attended common schools in Washington County and graduated in 1907 from the Southern Illinois Normal University at Carbondale. Subsequently he spent three years in the Law School of the University of Illinois at Champaign, leaving the University in 1912 and was admitted to the bar the same year. For eight years he carried on a general law practice at Nashville, Illinois. In 1920, coming to Danville, he took charge of a division of the United States internal revenue office, but in 1921 formed a partnership with Mr. S. E. Aldrich in accounting and income tax work, Mr. Maxwell handling the income tax branch of the business, while Mr. Aldrich supervises the expert accounting and auditing. They have a suite of offices in the Adams Building at Danville. Mr. Maxwell's professional work takes him to the City of Washington several times each year.

He is an independent in politics, attends the First Presbyterian Church, and is a member of the Danville Chamber of Commerce, the Kiwanis Club and the Roselawn Golf Club of Danville. He has an attractive home at 207 Orchard Street in Danville, a farm in Washington County and 160 acres of land in Arkansas.

Mr. Maxwell married, June 11, 1913, at Highland, Illinois, Miss Olga Scrumpf, daughter of Mr. and Mrs. Henry Scrumpf, who reside near Highland, where her father owns three prosperous farms in that section of the state. Mr. and Mrs. Maxwell have four children: Virginia, Margaret R., J. Harvey and Barbara Lou, the first three attending school at Danville.

JOHN CLIFFORD SITTERLY. In John Clifford Sitterly, president of the Spring Valley City Bank, is found one of the foremost business men of this section of Bureau County. Mr. Sitterly has been a resident of Spring Valley for almost forty years, during which time he has largely made her interests his own in the development of her commercial importance and in promoting her civic and social welfare.

John Clifford Sitterly was born in Grundy County, Illinois, August 19, 1860, son of Martin Henry and Isabel (Watson) Sitterly, the former of whom was born at Schenectady, New York, and the latter at Sharon, Pennsylvania, both coming early to Illinois. Martin Henry Sitterly was a gallant soldier in the Union army all through the Civil war, one of the earliest to answer President Lincoln's first call for troops to put down the rebellion. When his first term of enlistment had expired he veteranized and served in the Sixty-first Illinois Volunteer Infantry until the close of the war. In 1870 he removed with his family from Grundy County to Braidwood, Will County, Illinois, where he was occupied as a carpenter contractor until 1889, when he and wife removed to Spring Valley. They were members of the Presbyterian Church. In politics he was an ardent republican and for years was a member of the Grand Army of the Republic. Two of their children reached mature life: John Clifford and Allen W. Sitterly.

John C. Sitterly attended the public schools until he was fourteen years old, and no doubt many an additional lesson has been learned, as is the way of life, in the school of experience. He had been well brought up, was cheerful, honest and industrious, and his services were soon engaged by a local drug store, but as early as 1874 he entered the employ of the Chicago and Vermilion Coal Company and became manager of their dry goods store at Braidwood, in 1883 being engaged in like capacity by the Eureka Coal Company of Braidwood, where he continued until 1887. In that year Mr. Sitterly came to Spring Valley, where he was joined by his parents two years later.

After establishing his home at Spring Valley Mr. Sitterly embarked in business on his own account, engaging in the livery business, which at that time was a very profitable one when well managed. Although changes were brought about with the introduction and increased use of the automobile, for both business and utilitarian purposes, as well as pleasure, he continued to conduct this business up to 1924, when he disposed of it to advantage. In the meanwhile he had become intelligently interested in the sand and gravel business, and since 1909 has been president of the Western Sand & Gravel Company of Spring Valley, one of the largest concerns of its kind in the state. As Mr. Sitterly's business undertakings prospered and he became a large employer of labor and counted as one of the substantial men of the community, he found many additional chances for wise investment at Spring Valley and elsewhere. His reputation as an able financier has long been established here, and his administration of the affairs of the Spring Valley City Bank, as president, has shown business acumen of the highest order. And not alone as a business man has Mr. Sitterly been a useful and valued citizen. Although, like his father, always active in the ranks of the republican party, he has seldom accepted political office, but feeling deeply on the subject of public education and on civic matters in connection with his own ward he has served on the Board of Education and also as a city alderman.

In 1895 Mr. Sitterly married Miss Lizzie L. Nelson, a native of Illinois, who passed out of life on April 22, 1923, survived by three children: Glenn N., Ada M. and Lyle C. Mr. Sitterly has long been active in the Congregational Church. He is a Knight Templar Mason and a Shriner.

Glenn N. Sitterly, of the above family, who is associated with his father in business, served with distinction in the World war. He was born at Spring Valley, Illinois, August 22, 1897, was graduated from the La Salle High School and then entered Beloit College, Wisconsin, where he was a student when, in May, 1917, he went overseas as a member of the American ambulance service, which was an organization entirely independent of military connection with the United States government. He was attached to the French army May 21, 1917, was transferred to the aviation service in June, 1917, and attended aviation schools during the summer of that year. Having finished his training, he was sent to the front as a member of the LaFayette Escadrille. He served with various squadrons at the front attached to the French army throughout the war. He was a pioneer in triplane pursuit work, in piloting and photographing. On July 15, 1918, his plane was brought down on the Marne, one machine gunner being killed and another wounded.

All the time when on the front Mr. Sitterly was active with the Fourth French Army, an army of attack. He was decorated with the military medals the Croix de Guerre, Foraguerre and LaFayette Ribbon. He was one of the Americans who remained with the French army to the close of the war. After the armistice he was sent into Germany with his squadron and was there until March, 1919, when he was honorably discharged, with the final rank of adjutant, and returned home. He is a member of the American Legion and the LaFayette Flying Corps.

JULIAN H. HEBERLING, cashier of the Corn State Bank of Easton, is very popular with all classes, and is recognized as one of Mason County's leading citizens. Every relation of life is met with capable efficiency, and he holds the confidence of his fellow citizens both as a bank official and a man. He was born at Mount Pleasant, Ohio, June 30, 1885, a son of the venerable Henry Heberling.

Henry Heberling was born in Belmont County, Ohio, August 30, 1849, a son of Henry Heberling, a Virginia who accompanied his father to Ohio at a very early day, and they were men of means and slaveholders in the Old Dominion. The younger Henry Heberling did not inherit any slaves, for his father and grandfather had already liberated them, and he grew up in Ohio away from the curse of slavery, and received his educational training in the country schools. Early in life he was a farmer, but later he became a merchant at Mount Pleasant, and when he came to Illinois he embarked in the metal-roofing business. For the past quarter of a century he has been a realtor and banker, being identified with the Corn State Bank of Eaton. He married at Bath, Illinois, Miss Arabella Gatton, a daughter of Maj. Benjamin A. Gatton, a grain merchant of Mason County who came to this region from Kentucky. When gold was discovered in California he went overland to the coast in 1849. Mrs. Heberling died at Easton in 1911, having borne her husband the following children: Harold G., who resides at Chicago; Julian H., whose name heads this review; and Raymond W., who resides at Sawtelle, California.

Three years old at the time he was brought to Illinois, Julian H. Heberling was reared at Havana, this state, and after completing his high-school course, had additional work which he carried on himself, and was graduated from the American Institute of Banking. His business life began with a clerkship in the store of J. W. Bell of Easton, and was continued when he was made bookkeeper of the McFadden Corn Exchange Bank of Easton. At that time B. L. McFadden was president of the bank, as he is now of the Corn State Bank, and the cashier was A. H. Penewitt, while the assistant cashier was Henry Heberling. Julian H. Heberling has risen in the bank until in 1908 he was elected to his present position of cashier.

The McFadden Corn Exchange Bank was founded in 1901 and subsequently the present style was adopted. The present directors are: B. L. McFadden, J. B. Fager, J. G. Knupple, T. K. Behrends, Ira A. Bell and Julian H. Heberling. The bank is capitalized at $50,000, the surplus is $12,500, and the undivided profits are $11,500.

As a citizen Mr. Heberling has served his village as trustee for four years, and for a number of years he has been a school trustee, during which time he assisted in organizing the Community High School of Easton. During the World war he was chairman of several of the Liberty Loan committees, was food administrator, and assisted in other ways to promote all war work. He was registered, submitted his questionnaire, but was not called into the service. As a Mason he has been advanced through all of the bodies of the Scottish and York Rites, and belongs to the Blue Lodge at Mason City, the Commandery at Havana, and the Consistory and Shrine at Springfield. Nationally he is a democrat.

Mr. Heberling married at Easton, a daughter of P. W. Stevens, of Easton, Illinois. Mrs. Heberling was born at Easton in 1887, and she has three brothers, a sister and a half sister. She is a graduate of the high school of the city of her birth. Mr. and Mrs. Heberling have two sons, Richard H. and Julian S.

CHARLES S. KINSEY is a representative of a family that was founded in Tazewell County in the early pioneer days, more than three-fourths of a century ago, and he now has status as one of the successful farmers of Dillon Township, a part of his well improved farm lying within the original townsite of the village of Dillon, which is one of the oldest towns in Illinois and which was a place of no minor importance in pioneer days.

Nathan Kinsey, grandfather of Charles S. of this review, is supposed to have come to Illinois from Ohio, the original home of the family having been in Virginia, where representatives of the name made settlement in the Colonial period of American history. Nathan Kinsey was a bachelor when he arrived in Tazewell County, and it is a family tradition that he made the overland journey with team and covered wagon. He not only became one of the pioneers of this county but also found here a gracious young wife in the person of

Miss Elvira Fisher, a member of a family that was among the first to settle in Tazewell County, shortly after the Dillon family, the first in the Dillon district of the county. The lineage of the Fisher family traces back to German origin, and the pioneer representatives in Tazewell County became active in the development and improvement of farms. Nathan Kinsey finally established his home on a farm one-half mile east of the old town of Dillon, and there he remained until his death, which occurred about twenty years prior to the outbreak of the Civil war, his remains being interred in the old Fisher Cemetery at Dillon, as were also those of both his first and his second wives. Of the children of the first marriage two attained to maturity, John and Louisa, the latter of whom became the first wife of Thomas Alexander and died at Dillon, where her remains rest in the little cemetery previously mentioned. For his second wife Nathan Kinsey wedded Lydia Edwards, and concerning the children of this union it may be recorded that Elias died in Missouri, a bachelor; that the next child was a daughter who became the second wife of Thomas Alexander, whose first wife was her half-sister Louisa, as noted previously, Mrs. Alexander having been a resident of the State of Washington at the time of her death; and that Phoebe, who became the wife of Abram Studyvin, died at Delavan, Tazewell County.

John Kinsey, son of Nathan and Elvira (Fisher) Kinsey, was born on the old homestead farm north of Dillon and the date of his nativity was November 4, 1830. He passed his entire life in this district of his native county, did well his part in upholding the high standard of farm industry in the county, and was influential in advancing communal development and progress along both civic and industrial lines, though he never consented to serve in public office save that of school director, a position that he retained many years. His alert mind and strong individuality enabled him to appreciate and keep in pace with modern developments and ideas, and he represented the best in sterling, useful and honorable citizenship. He was a stalwart advocate and supporter of the cause of the republican party, and he and his wife were earnest members of the Campbellite, or Christian Church.

As a young man John Kinsey was united in marriage to Miss Rebecca Ann Wilson, who was born on the home farm of her father, James Wilson, four miles southeast of Pekin, the county seat. James Wilson was of Scotch and Irish ancestry and is supposed to have come to Illinois from the State of New York. The loved and devoted wife of John Kinsey entered into eternal rest in 1899, and his death occurred in 1907, when he was seventy-six years of age, the mortal remains of both being placed at rest in Antioch Cemetery, near Dillon. Henry, eldest of the children, is now a resident of Van Buren County, Iowa; Seth is a resident of Gridley, McLean County, Illinois; Margaret is the wife of John Manker, and they likewise reside at Gridley; Charles Shirley is the immediate subject of this review; and Moleston resides in Van Buren County, Iowa.

Charles Shirley Kinsey was born at Dillon, November 16, 1866, and in this immediate locality he has continued to maintain his home during the long intervening years—a period marked by his successful activities as one of the representative exponents of farm industry in this section of his native county. His youthful education was acquired in the public schools, and while giving close attention to the affairs of his farm, he has stood exemplar of loyal and public-spirited citizenship, though he has never become active in politics or consented to be a candidate for public office. His first presidential vote was cast in 1888 for General Benjamin Harrison, and he has since continued his unfaltering allegiance to the republican party. He was active and liberal in advancing local patriotic work and service in the World war period, and aided in raising the quota of enlistments in his township, as well as in the drives for subscriptions to the government war bonds, Red Cross work, etc.

March 17, 1891, recorded the marriage of Mr. Kinsey and Miss Eva Ann Luft, who was born and reared in Dillon Township, a daughter of the late Nicholas and Catherine (Horn) Luft, a memoir to her father being entered on other pages of this work, so that further record of the family need not here be given. The birth of Mrs. Kinsey occurred June 1, 1868, and in her native county her circle of friends is coincident with that of her acquaintances. Mr. and Mrs. Kinsey have but one child, Elvira, who was born May 15, 1894, and whose public school advantages included those of the Tremont High School, she being now the wife of Clayton Lord, who likewise is a native of Tazewell County, where he is engaged in farm enterprise in Dillon Township. Mr. and Mrs. Lord have a winsome daughter, Lois.

CHARLES A. PHELPS has practiced law at Chicago for a quarter of a century, and is regarded as an authority on many phases of real estate and building laws. His offices are at 38 South Dearborn Street.

Mr. Phelps was born at Johnstown, New York, December 31, 1873. His grandfather, Charles A. Phelps, was a native of New York State and a pioneer in the glove making industry of that state. Emerson J. Phelps, father of the Chicago attorney, was born at Johnstown, New York, in 1852, was engaged in glove making as a business, and died in 1920. He married Lizzie Belding, who was born at Stratford, New York, in 1853. They became the parents of three children: Charles A.; Florence, wife of Dr. William P. Welch, of Joliet, Illinois; and L. B., a Chicago physician.

Charles A. Phelps had a liberal education, attending the Fairfield Military Academy at Fairfield, New York, and the Frog Conference Academy at Poultney, Vermont, where he was graduated in 1896, and continued his education in Wesleyan University at Middlestown, Connecticut, and in Northwestern University at Evanston. He studied law in the Chicago Kent College of Law, and was admitted to the Illinois bar in 1901. He has handled a great deal of corporation work, and his practice has become more and more specialized in questions involving realty laws and problems affecting building construction.

Mr. Phelps has served as a member of the Chicago Plan Commission. He is a member of the Hamilton Club, Channel Lake Country Club, Oak Park Lodge No. 540, Ancient Free and Accepted Masons, Oak Park Chapter Royal Arch Masons, Siloam Commandery, Knights Templar, and his recreations are motoring, boating and golf.

He married at Chicago, February 14, 1899, Sadie M. Gray. They have two children: Dorothy Louise, now attending normal school, and Gray H., a graduate of the University of Illinois.

ELMER ELSWORTH ETHELL, farmer and banker at Manito, has for a number of years been a conceptive factor in the agricultural and business affairs of Mason County.

He was born near McConnellsville, Morgan County, Ohio, February 27, 1864. His father, Thomas Ethell, was a native of Muskingum County, Ohio. His wife, Jane Tavener, was a daughter of Richard Tavener, who came from Shenendoah County, Virginia. Jane Tavener was born in Morgan County, Ohio, in 1827, and died in July, 1903. When E. E. Ethell was ten years of age the family moved to Illinois, and soon located a mile and three quarters east of McLean, where they lived on a rented place four years, and then bought the land northwest of McLean where Thomas Ethell spent the rest of his industrious career. He died while visiting in Ohio March 15, 1886, at the age of sixty.

Elmer E. Ethell grew up on a farm, attended country schools, and gave his labors to his parents to the age of twenty-two. He started his career with practically no capital and as a tenant farmer in McLean County. From there in 1896 he moved to Bureau County, Illinois, buying land fourteen miles north of Princeton. He was a farmer in that prosperous section of the state for eight years, at the end of which time he sold his property and moved to Mason County, purchasing his present homestead. This is known as the Hickory Grove Farm, the building site being on a high hill overlooking the entire region. Mr. Ethell purchased the half section and has now four hundred and forty acres, two hundred acres being the peat soil, which is ideal for corn. Corn growing has been the chief feature of his agricultural enterprise. He has made many substantial improvements, including the remodeling of his residence and other buildings. In connection with the raising of grain he has a live stock program, made up of horses, cattle, hogs and sheep. Mr. Ethell succeeded the late Dietrich Velde as president of the Peoples State Bank of Manito.

He cast his first presidential vote for Benjamin Harrison in McLean County in 1888, and has been steadfastly identified with that party ever since. Mr. Ethell married in McLean County, October 15, 1885, Miss Margaret A. Tallon, who was born near Circleville in Tazewell County, March 4, 1866, but was reared and educated in McLean County. Her parents were John and Agnes (Ellwood) Tallon, her mother's people coming from England. Mrs. Ethell is one of a family of ten children.

To the marriage of Mr. and Mrs. Ethell were born five children. The son Emmons E. a farmer in Greene County, Illinois, married Bessie Parkins, and has six children, named Lester, Ivan, Bernice, Gladys, Robert and Eldon Lee. The second son, Orin E., a farmer in Sangamon County, married Madge Sparks and has a daughter, Jane. Ralph A., a farmer at the old homestead, married Mabel Clauser and has a son, George Elmer. The fourth son, Vernie, now a farmer near the old home, was overseas in France seven months during the war, being with a machine gun battalion, and was close to the front lines when the armistice was signed. Since the war he has engaged in farming, and by his marriage to Jessie Clauser has a son, Dale. The youngest of the farmer sons of Mr. and Mrs. Ethell is Merlin, who married Ruth Meeker.

EARL L. LONGFELLOW, postmaster of Rock Falls, Whiteside County, is a native of this state, and both he and his father have long been identified with the business life of their community.

He was born at Sterling, Illinois, September 22, 1885, son of Henry Frank and Marcia (Coryell) Longfellow. His grandfather was Nathaniel Longfellow. Henry Frank Longfellow was a native of Maine, lost his father when a boy, and at the age of seventeen came to Illinois. At Rock Falls he was employed as stationary engineer, and there he met and married Marcia Coryell, a native of this state. After several years of residence at Sterling they returned to Rock Falls, where Henry F. Longfellow is foreman in the woodworking department of the Eureka Manufacturing Company, an industry with which he has been identified for many years.

Earl L. Longfellow grew up at Rock Falls, attended common schools there and subsequently took the law course in the La Salle Extension University. However, he never qualified for admission to the bar, though he has found the training valuable to him in a business way. He was a tobacconist at Rock Falls until September, 1923, when he was appointed postmaster, his appointment being confirmed January 8, 1924. He has given a very capable administration of the postoffice.

Mr. Longfellow is a republican and has been active in party affairs since early manhood. He is a Protestant in religion, is a Knights Templar Mason and a member of the Modern Woodmen of America and the Mystic Workers of the World. He married in 1912 Miss Mertie Ebersole. Their four children are Elizabeth, Mabelle, Elsie and Jeanne.

EDWARD N. MONROE is an expert chemist, and even before the great war was interested in the art of dye manufacture. He is the man largely responsible for the founding and upbuilding of one of the leading chemical and dye manufacturing plants in Illinois, the Monroe Drug Company at Quincy, manufacturers of what are known as "Putnam Fadeless Dyes."

Mr. Monroe was born at Chillicothe, Ohio, April 7, 1855, and is of old New England stock. His father, Edward Monroe, a native of Massachusetts, was with the Union forces at Washington during the Civil war, and after

the war went to Missouri, where he improved a farm and lived there until his death. Edward Monroe married Mary Hard, a native of Vermont.

Edward N. Monroe was the only child of his parents. He spent some of his childhood in Putnam County, and grew to manhood on the homestead in Missouri. His early education was confined to public schools, and about 1870 he went to work in a drug store at Unionville, Missouri, and from that time has been an enthusiastic student of everything connected with chemistry and the manufacture of drugs and chemicals. It was in 1876 that he established a business that is now known as the Monroe Drug Company and in 1907 established the manufacturing plant in Quincy. For some years the business manufactured and handled a general line of drugs and chemicals, but after the outbreak of the World war, and the shutting off of imported dyes from Germany, this company was one of those that undertook to supply the deficiency by native processes. The business had a phenomenal growth and has for some years been securely established, being one of the leading plants for the manufacture of the Putnam Fadeless Dyes. Mr. E. N. Monroe is president of the company at Quincy, his son, N. E. Monroe, is vice president and treasurer, and L. P. Bonfoey is vice president and secretary.

Mr. Monroe married Miss Flora Wagner, a native of Pennsylvania. They had three children: Neal E., who was educated for the law, but for some years has been associated with his father in the manufacture of dyes and chemicals; Burk C., now deceased; and Octavia, wife of Lawrence P. Bonfoey.

Mr. Edward N. Monroe has served as a director and vice president of the Stapes Savings, Loan & Trust Company of Quincy, and is a republican in politics.

JESSE R. BROWN, of Alton, is a member of the law firm Hiles, Newell & Brown, one of the best known of Madison County's partnerships, and the only one maintaining offices both at Edwardsville, the county seat, and Alton, the metropolis of the county.

Mr. Brown is a native of Southern Illinois, born at Woburn in Bond County, September 15, 1887. His people have been in Bond County for several generations. His parents, John W. and Mary (Grigg) Brown, were also natives of Bond County. His great-grandfather, William Brown, came to Bond County from North Carolina in early pioneer times. The Brown family is of Scotch origin. The maternal grandfather of the Alton lawyer was Jesse R. Quigg, who came from Virginia with his parents when he was a small boy. Mr. Brown is the second of seven children, six sons and one daughter. All these children are living, and all of them show family characteristics of unusual height, every one being over six feet tall and the three youngest are still in university.

Jesse R. Brown was reared in a rural community of Bond County, attending the district school known as the Grigg School. He also took the course at Greenville College, and for eight years taught school. In the meantime he finished a course in the Charleston Normal, now the Eastern Illinois State Teachers College, and he taught school for eight years. For a time he was principal of the Schram City School and in 1913 he resigned his position as city clerk and city treasurer of Hillsboro, Illinois, to enter the law department of Valparaiso University in Indiana. He was graduated in law in 1915, was admitted to the Illinois bar the same year, and in May, 1916, located at Edwardsville. For about six months he was in the Edwardsville law office of D. G. Williamson, and then formed a partnership with Mr. M. E. Newell in the firm of Newell & Brown.

In September, 1917, Mr. Brown gave up his law practice to enter the Second Officers Training School at Camp Taylor, Kentucky, was commissioned a second lieutenant and later a first lieutenant. He was on duty until his honorable discharge at Camp Shelby, Mississippi, and then returned to Edwardsville, resuming practice with Mr. Newell.

On January 2, 1920, Mr. Brown was called to Chicago to become a member of the legal staff of the Federal department of justice in the prohibition enforcement division, and for about one year he was engaged in the work of formally drawing up the charges for the United States attorneys in law enforcement cases.

Having in the meantime retained his partnership with Mr. Newell, he returned to Edwardsville, and in 1921 Perry H. Hiles became head of the firm, which is now Hiles, Newell & Brown. For several years Mr. Brown had charge of the Alton office, and makes his home in that city. He is a member of the Masonic fraternity, the Knights of Pythias, was formerly worthy patron of the Eastern Star chapter, is a member of Alton Post of the American Legion and a republican in politics. He belongs to the First Presbyterian Church of Alton. He was elected state's attorney of Madison County in 1924 and was married to Elizabeth Miller of Edwardsville the following year.

JOHN F. TYRRELL is a native of Chicago, and was admitted to the practice of law in 1905, and is one of the busy men of his profession in that city. He is senior member of the law firm of Tyrrell, Higgins and Jamieson. He is a man of many interests outside of his profession.

He was born in Chicago, son of Frank P. and Nellie A. (Swift) Tyrrell. His father was born at Dunkirk, New York, and his mother was born at Kenosha, Wisconsin. The grandfather of John F. Tyrrell was a member of the United States secret service under President Lincoln. He was at the Ford Theatre the night Lincoln was shot down by Booth and assisted in pursuit of and capture of Booth. He subsequently prevented the attempt to steal Lincoln's body at Springfield. He lived to the venerable age of ninety years, passing away in 1922.

Frank P. Tyrrell was a captain on the Chicago police force, was chief detective under state's attorney Charles S. Deneen for two terms, and served two years under state's attorney, John J. Healy. Later he was appointed chief of police for the West Park

Board Commissioners by Governor Charles S. Deneen, serving five years before he retired.

John F. Tyrrell was the oldest of four children, and acquired his education in the schools of Chicago, in the Lewis Institute, in Lake Forest University, and in Kent College of Law. In addition to his general practice as an attorney he has served as professor of medical jurisprudence in the Medical School of Loyola University. He is a member of the Chicago, Illinois State and American Bar Associations.

Mr. Tyrrell is affiliated with the Knights of Columbus and the B. P. O. Elks, is a member of the Hamilton Club and the Art Institute. He married Miss Jessie L. Taylor, a native of Chicago. Their four children are Jessie L., John F., Jr., William L. and Robert E. Mr. Tyrrell's offices are at 134 North Lasalle Street.

GEORGE H. STOUTIN. Prominent and efficient in business and a leading force in public affairs, George H. Stoutin, mayor of Sidell, Illinois, has in a comparatively short space of time won public confidence and esteem and made his name known all through this section of Vermilion County.

Mayor Stoutin was born at Colorado Springs, Colorado, December 29, 1889, son of Louis and Ida May (Horner) Stoutin, and a grandson of Samuel Stoutin. The grandfather was born in Germany and came from that country to the United States in early manhood. He settled near Petersburg, Illinois, where he followed farming until he became a soldier in the Union army during the Civil war, during a part of which he was a prisoner of war. Louis Stoutin, father of Mayor Stoutin, was born at Petersburg, Illinois, in 1865, and died at Chicago, Illinois, in 1895. He grew up on the home farm near Petersburg but later moved to Havana, Illinois, there following merchandising until 1887, when he removed to Colorado Springs, and there assisted in putting in the first street car line. In 1892 he removed to Chicago and entered the employ of the Chicago Street Railway Company. He married Miss Ida May Horner, who was born near Havana, Illinois, April 13, 1866, and now resides at Pekin, Illinois. They had two children, George H. and Lois Opal. The latter is a clerk in the offices of the Monon railroad at Pekin and lives with her mother there.

George H. Stoutin was educated in the public schools of Havana, graduating from the high school in the class of 1907. During the next three years he was employed in a drug store at Springfield, a student as well as clerk, and then attended the Chicago College of Pharmacy, from which institution he was graduated in 1912, with his diploma of Registered Pharmacist. Mr. Stoutin for the next six years was with the Owings Drug Company at Mattoon, Illinois.

In 1918 Mr. Stoutin came to Sidell, and finding here the business opening of which he was prepared to take advantage, bought the drug interests of James A. Linder and has continued here ever since. He has a commodious modern drug store and does the largest business in his line in the city. He has additional business interests and is secretary of the Sidell Building & Loan Association, and is a member of the National Association of Retail Druggists.

Mayor Stoutin married, April 1, 1910, at Chicago, Miss Nellie M. Maisel, daughter of Henry and Marie (Weber) Maisel. Her father died at Springfield, where he formerly was a well known carpenter and builder, and her mother still resides in that city. They have two children, Ida Marie and George Edwin Stoutin, both of whom are in school. In addition to his place of business Mayor Stoutin owns a comfortable and attractive residence on Chicago Street. With his family he belongs to the Methodist Episcopal Church, in which religious faith he was reared by Christian parents.

In political life Mayor Stoutin has always been a democrat and a loyal party worker as opportunity has offered, but not as a seeker for office. His election as mayor of Sidell, in 1923, was not altogether a partisan victory, but rather a recognition of his sterling character and appreciation of his marked business capacity. He belongs to the Masonic fraternity, is a member of Sidell Lodge No. 628, A. F. and A. M., and also a member of Dell Lodge No. 422, K. of P.

JOSEPH MANN. To some men nothing is impossible. No matter what manner of disabilities may be theirs, they are able to overcome handicaps and advance further than those to whom nature has been more generous. It is admitted by scientific men that those who are deprived of one faculty have the remaining ones unusually developed; and it is equally true that when there is a physical defect the mental attributes are correspondingly active. In the case of Joseph Mann, county treasurer of Whiteside, the above is abundantly proven. Afflicted from birth by physical weakness, he has faced life with a cheerful efficiency that puts to shame those more active, and not only has strengthened his mental processes, but from the age of eight years has ridden on horseback, and is now an expert horseman, and one of the most skillful in handling these difficult subjects. No one ever hears him complain. In fact so ably has he overcome this handicap that his associates have forgotten it, and accord him a sincere admiration for the energy and ability he constantly exhibits.

Joseph Mann was born at Sterling, Illinois, August 21, 1872, a son of Silas and Mary (Miles) Mann. The father was born in Pennsylvania, coming of solid and honorable Pennsylvania Dutch lineage, and the mother was a native of Illinois, and both are now deceased. She came of Irish descent on her father's side of the house, and of Scotch ancestry through her mother. After their marriage Mr. and Mrs. Mann lived at Sterling, and he was engaged in business as a buyer of poultry, horses and cattle. Their only child, Joseph, was, therefore, though his father's business connections brought into close contact with horses, and, fortunately, being possessed of a fearless courage, early secured a means of locomotion and a livelihood.

After he had secured a common school education, undeterred by his condition, he became self-supporting, and it is a source of great satisfaction to him that he has never asked, or received, any extra consideration on account of his disability. For many years he was a well-known figure in the business life of Sterling as a successful liveryman and also ran the bus line there. Subsequently he sold this business, at an excellent figure, and devoted himself, with adequate returns, to selling life insurance, through this line still further broadening his acquaintanceship and adding to his list of warm, personal friends. In 1922 the republicans placed him on their ticket for county treasurer, recognizing his ability and his character, and knowing that in him, if he were elected, the county would have an honest and efficient official. The returns gave him a very gratifying plurality, and since assuming the duties of office he has justified the wisdom of the voters in electing him.

In 1923 Mr. Mann married Miss Nellie A. Pittman, a native of Whiteside County, and they have one daughter, Josephine N. Mr. Mann belongs to the Benevolent and Protective Order of Elks. He was reared in the faith of the Lutheran Church. In politics he is a republican, and he has always given his party a loyal service.

LAWRENCE BEEKMAN TRAVERS, president of the State Bank of Bath, is one of the leading business men and financiers of Mason County, and one who is attracting attention to himself because of the sagacity he is displaying in his conduct of his financial institution. He was born in the village of Fairview, Fulton County, Illinois, April 7, 1885, a son of the late Thomas H. Travers, the latter of whom was born in Burton Bradstock, Dorsetshire, England, and died at Fairview, Illinois, in June, 1919, at the age of eighty years.

Thomas H. Travers was eleven years old when his parents came to the United States and located at Hazel Dell, Wisconsin. A fisherman in England, when he came to this country the grandfather began working in the lead mines of Wisconsin, and from this employment he secured his financial start. In 1859 he crossed the plains to California, where he remained until 1865, but in that year came to Fairview, where he spent the remainder of his life, and there he is buried. Of his eight children but five accompanied him to the United States, they being: Robert, who was lost in the burning of the ship in the harbor on its return trip from California; Charles, who died in Wisconsin; Thomas H.; Agnes, who married Richard Gould, and is a resident of Fairview; and Jane, who died unmarried at Fairview.

Growing up at Hazel Dell, Wisconsin, Thomas H. Travers secured a limited education, and worked in the lead mines until after the close of the war between the states, when he went to California, and there worked at gold mining. Subsequently, when he came to Illinois, he was a coal miner. Still later he left the mining industry and began handling grain and lumber at Fairview. In 1895 he sold his other interests to devote himself to the Fairview State Bank, of which he was still president at the time of his death. Politics never interested him, although he possessed those qualities which would have made of him an admirable public official had he cared to enter the arena. He was a high Mason and Shriner, and for years was treasurer of his local lodge.

Thomas H. Travers married, at Fairview, Miss Augusta A. Turner, a daughter of Elias Turner, a farmer and former resident of Wisconsin, whose wife, a member of the Morse family of Ohio, who was connected with that of Samuel F. B. Morse, the inventor of the telegraph. A brother of Mrs. Turner was at one time chief justice of Ohio. Mrs. Travers died in November, 1910, at the age of sixty-two years, having borne her husband the following children: Augusta, who resides at Fairview, the wife of T. W. Garrison; Lawrence Beekman, whose name heads this review; S. Morse, who is a resident of Long Beach, California, secretary and treasurer of the Long Beach Ice and Cold Storage Company; and Mary L., who is a resident of Fairview.

Carefully educated, Lawrence Beekman Travers first attended the grammar and high schools of Fairview, and later was a student of the law department of the University of Michigan, from which he was graduated in 1906, with the degree of Bachelor of Laws. The year following he took up special law work at Harvard University, after which he returned to Fairview, and for several years was engaged in looking after his father's interests, which were many and varied.

In 1914 Mr. Travers came to Bath and established the State Bank of Bath, the second financial institution of the village, the former one, the Farmers and Merchants Bank, having liquidated some time previously. The State Bank of Bath was chartered with a capital of $25,000, and associated with Mr. Travers in founding this bank were Moses Morris, F. W. Martin, Carl Heye and Carl Middlekamp. The bank opened its doors for business December 24, 1920, as a state bank, although it has been operated as a private bank from October 1, 1914. Under the new banking law all banks in Illinois had to be under state or national supervision, and Mr. Travers made the change to comply with these regulations, and he was made president; Moses Morris, vice president; and O. E. Lynn, cashier. These officials, with several other prominent business men, compose the directorate of this sound banking house.

Since coming to Bath Mr. Travers has taken a very active part in its progress, and among other far-sighted developments were those which led to the saving of the Chicago, Peoria & Saint Louis Railroad by securing its additional right of way. In this public-spirited movement Mr. Travers was a leader and served on the committee having the matter in charge. He was also a moving spirit in having the Community High School established at Bath, which was opened in 1920, although the building for it was not erected until 1921. During the World war he was the local registrar, served as a member of the Advisory Council, was actively identified with the putting over of the Victory Loan drive, and of boosting the affairs of the Red Cross. Registered in the second draft, he filled his questionnaire, was classified, but was not called.

In addition to these activities he also rendered a valuable service in the operation of his farming properties in Mason and Fulton counties. He is still conducting these farms, on the Fulton County one raising both stock and grain, while on the one in Mason County he is confining himself to grain production.

While he comes from a republican family, he cast his first presidential ballot for Woodrow Wilson, but since that time has given his allegiance to the republican party, but has himself never been willing to hold office, aside from being a member of the County Board of Review for two years when he felt his presence on the board was needed because of his knowledge of finances. Made a Mason at Fairview, he has risen high in his fraternity through all the bodies of both the Scottish and York Rites, and has sat in the Grand Lodge and the Grand Commandery. He is a past master and past commander, and holds membership with the Peoria Consistory and Shrine. While he is not a member of any religious organization, he was reared in the faith of the Dutch Reformed faith.

On February 22, 1913, Mr. Travers married at Chicago, Illinois. Wildred C. Reese, a daughter of George W. Reese. She was born at Canton, Ohio, but was reared at Lewistown, Illinois, and she is one of the five children born to her parents, namely: Edward P., Walter, Philip and Kittie, in addition to herself, and all of them are residents of Illinois. Mrs. Travers was educated at Lewistown, and for thirteen years she was one of the capable and popular educators in the public schools of Fulton County. Mr. and Mrs. Travers have one daughter, Helen Morse, who is now eleven years old. The influence of the Travers family in this part of the state has been felt for a number of years, and as it has always been exerted along constructive lines it has been of great value in community building and advancement, and the people owe a heavy debt to Mr. Travers, his father and other members of the family for what they have accomplished in so thorough a manner.

PAUL W. MOURNING, state's attorney of Schuyler County, is a native son of that county, has been a member of the bar for ten years, and is an ex-service man of the World war. His father has been an Illinois attorney for over forty years.

Mr. Mourning is a great-great-grandson of Roger Mourning, who came from Ireland accompanied by his family, and saw some service in the Continental army during the war of the American Revolution. His son, John Mourning, subsequently established his home in Kentucky, where he married Hannah Ball. Their son, Samuel Mourning, grandfather of the state's attorney, was born in Kentucky and married there Nancy A. Lyon, daughter of John and Martha (Martin) Lyon. Samuel Mourning was an early settler in Hancock County, Illinois. He served as a lieutenant of cavalry in the Union army during the Civil war and was a farmer by occupation.

His son, David L. Mourning, one of the honored members of the Rushville bar, was born in Hancock County, Illinois, March 14, 1857. He was a student in old Carthage College, was a druggist in early life, and studied law privately and also in the office of B. F. Miller & Son at Keokuk, Iowa, supporting himself until he was qualified to practice by teaching. He was admitted to the bar in 1881, and has been a successful attorney since that date. He served one term of four years, 1898-1902, as county judge of Schuyler County. He was the first republican ever chosen to public office in that county. David L. Mourning married Olive Wetzel, daughter of Firman and Nancy Wetzel. The Wetzel family was of German ancestry. Firman Wetzel for many years was a hardware merchant at Hamilton, Illinois. The children of David L. Mourning and wife are: Mabel, Mrs. Esther Palmer, and Paul W.

Paul W. Mourning was born at Rushville, October 21, 1892. He was graduated from high school in 1911, and after four years of work at the University of Illinois was graduated from the Law School in 1915. For one year he was in the law office of his father, and then became secretary of the Farm and Town Building and Loan Association at Rushville, an institution with which he has been identified in that capacity ever since, except for the term he was in the army.

In 1918 he answered the call to the colors, and after thirty days at Camp Grant at Rockford went overseas with Evacuation Hospital No. 37. This unit sailed from Hoboken, New Jersey, on the Northern Pacific, landing at Brest. His vessel was one of five convoyed by French destroyers. He was a private in the hospital service. Of nearly three hundred men composing the hospital unit only twenty were not university graduates. After five days at Brest the unit went to Mars Sur Aliere, on the Marne River, in charge of the hospital tending wounded German and American soldiers. Later the unit was ordered to Toul, where it was assigned similar work, and remained there until after the armistice. The unit was then broken up and Mr. Mourning after some time spent at LeMans was placed in a casual outfit, and from Brest embarked on the U. S. S. Siboney, landing at New York, and was honorably discharged at Camp Grant July 20, 1919.

Mr. Mourning immediately resumed his work at Rushville. In November, 1920, he was elected state's attorney of Schuyler County, on the republican ticket, being the first republican ever to hold that office in that county. He succeeded George B. Steele, and in November, 1924, was re-elected. At his first election he had a majority of 456 and the second time a majority of fifty-five votes, in a county normally democratic by about 700. He comes from a republican family and he cast his first presidential ballot for Charles E. Hughes in 1916. As state's attorney he prosecuted the thirty-one rioters for manslaughter in the killing of Sheriff Lashbrook, and his two deputies, and secured conviction of all of them with sentences to prison of from one to twenty years. This is perhaps the greatest number of persons tried at one time in any state court of Illinois with conviction resulting.

Mr. Mourning is a Commandery Mason, is a member of the Lodge and Encampment of the Independent Order of Odd Fellows, a mem-

ber of the Modern Woodmen of America, and is a charter member of Schuyler Post No. 4 of the American Legion, and for a time was post finance officer. On August 30, 1919, he married Miss Mary Loring, daughter of James B. and Elizabeth (Steele) Loring. Her father was born in Schuyler County and is a farmer there. Mrs. Mourning was born June 19, 1893, on the home farm and finished her education in Rockford College, Illinois. She was teacher of domestic science in the Rushville High School prior to her marriage. The two children of Mr. and Mrs. Mourning are James Paul and Betty Jean.

BENJAMIN W. TILLMAN, who since 1919 has been county agricultural agent for St. Clair County, is a graduate in agricultural science from the University of Missouri, and spent a number of years in the service of the Department of Agriculture of the Federal government and left a position in the University of Missouri Agricultural School to come to his present duties at Belleville.

He was born near Jefferson City, Missouri, in November, 1883, son of Frank and Elizabeth (Hoerschen) Tillman, both his father and grandfather being natives of Missouri, while the maternal grandfather, Michael Hoerschen, came from Germany about 1848. Frank Tillman spent his life as a grain and stock farmer in central Missouri, and during the Civil war was on the Union side with the Missouri regiment of Home Guards. He died in 1910. His widow is still living. There were nine children: Michael, who married Louise Maire; Joseph, who is the father of four children; Maggie, wife of Joseph Maire and the mother of two children; Herman, who married Katie Otto and has two children; Mary, deceased; William, who married Virginia White and has six children; John, who married Miss Schaller and had two children; Benjamin W.; and Frank P., who is married and has two children.

Benjamin W. Tillman was educated in the district schools of Osage County, Missouri, and from early youth had opportunities and encouragement to develop his bent talents towards the scientific side of agriculture. He attended high school at the Columbia Normal Academy and then the University of Missouri, completing his course in the School of Agriculture and graduating with the degree of Bachelor of Science in agriculture in 1907. For three years after graduating Mr. Tillman was instructor in physical culture at one of the oldest and best known preparatory schools in the middle west, the Wentworth Military Academy. From 1910 to 1917 he was with the United States Department of Agriculture as one of the technical field men in soils, and then returned to the University of Missouri, at Columbia, in charge of the Department of Soil Extension work.

In 1919 Mr. Tillman became county agent for St. Clair County, Illinois. This county is the leading county in the state in raising quality and quantity of soft winter wheat, leads in the production of Irish potatoes and has lands especially adapted for fruit, alfalfa and grains. In improving and organizing the agricultural facilities of the county to make the best of these advantages Mr. Tillman has accomplished many important results during his tenure of the office of county agent.

He married in December, 1910, Miss Amy Berrie, who is of Scotch ancestry, a daughter of Robert B. Berrie, who was a contractor and builder at the city of Lexington, Missouri, and died in 1916. Her mother, Mrs. Berrie, represents the Chandler family of Revolutionary stock. Robert B. Berrie was contractor for most of the structures at Lexington, Missouri, and also built some of the best homes in Lafayette County, Missouri. Mrs. Tillman's brothers and sisters were: Bonnel, who married William Mellor and has three children; Mary, wife of Frank Wilson, and has three children; Florence, wife of Ion Gildersleeve; Robert B., who lives with his mother in Kansas City, Missouri. Mr. and Mrs. Tillman have one child, Maryn, now attending the high school at Belleville. The family are members of the Presbyterian Church. He is a Royal Arch Mason, a member of the Grange, and the State and National Agricultural Associations.

WILLIAM A. PROEHL is a general farmer of Mason County, his fine rural property of 240 acres being a mile outside of the limits of Forest City. He is a member of one of the old and substantial families of Illinois, and he was born in Spring Lake Township, Tazewell County, September 29, 1878, a son of Louis Proehl, the latter a native of Pomerania, Germany, who came to the United States and settled in Illinois following the close of the war between the states. After coming here Louis Proehl married, at Pekin, Illinois, Augusta Bodtke, and William A. Proehl was the third child born to their marriage.

Growing up along the banks of the Mackinaw River, William A. Proehl attended the Parkland school, and, although the country schools of his youth were not conducted as they are today, it is a well-known fact that they turned out pupils who have become the leading citizens of the localities in which they settled. Some entered the professions, others became business men, and still others devoted themselves to the important work of cultivating the soil. Even farming, however, has changed, and the modern agriculturist needs knowledge on many subjects, for he must understand his soil, the necessity of fertilization, and the advisibility of drainage or irrigation, according to the climate and natural condition of his land. In other words he must bear his part in the great movement now on foot since the awakening of the world to the necessity for preventing waste by conservation. Natural resources have been wasted in the past, and in nothing has the reclamation work shown greater progress than that which has redeemed the swamp lands in certain sections, just as desert spaces have been made fertile by irrigating systems.

When William A. Proehl left the parental homestead and began life on his own account he went to Washington, Illinois, and farmed eight years and then came to Forest City Township and located on the old John Cross farm that had once been a swamp. In spite of the fact that preliminary drainage work had been commenced by Messrs. Scott and

Pringle, Mr. Proehl took hold of the work with characteristic energy and thoroughness, and has developed a farm second to none in his neighborhood. He raises principally corn, wheat and oats, and raises some hogs for the market. His residence is a comfortable modern frame building, two stories high, and his farm buildings are large and adequate for their several uses, including the accommodation of his stock and the housing of his machinery, of which he has plenty for all the farm work.

While he has been so actively engaged in farming he has not neglected his duties as a citizen, but is serving as a member of the community high school board of Forest City. He was reared in a democratic atmosphere, cast his first presidential ballot for William Jennings Bryan in 1900, and has supported the candidates and principles of the democratic party ever since. He is a director of the Farmers Store at Forest City, and a director of the Forest City Farmers Elevator Company. Both he and his wife belong to Saint Paul's Church, and he is its treasurer and active in its Sunday School work, representing that body in different conventions from time to time.

On December 31, 1901, William A. Proehl married, at Mount Carroll, Illinois, Louisa Goetz, a daughter of George and Elizabeth (Weidmann) Goetz, who were married in Hesse, near Darmstadt, Germany. Arriving in the United States in 1866, they landed at New York City, and after a visit paid to relatives in Ohio they came further west to Mount Carroll, Illinois, where another relative had settled. Mr. Goetz became a farmer in that vicinity, and there he completed his life's span, dying January 27, 1913. His widow survived him until May 31, 1916. Both Mr. and Mrs. Goetz were consistent members of the Evangelical Church. The children born to them were as follows: Philip, who died unmarired at Mount Carroll when he was thirty-four years old; Jacob, who is engaged in operating the homestead; John, who is a resident of Lockwood, Missouri; Elizabeth, who resides near Lanark, Illinois, the widow of George W. Schneider; George, who is a farmer in the Mount Carroll neighborhood; Anna, who is the wife of John Proehl, a farmer of Tazewell County and a brother of William A. Proehl; Lewis, of Carroll County; Louisa, who was born June 7, 1879; Albert, who is now residing at Madison, Wisconsin, in order to give his children better educational advantages; and Lena, who is the wife of Paul R. Becker, of Savannah, Illinois. Mrs. Proehl attended the Mount Carroll High School for two years, and later was a student of the Northern Illinois College, Fulton, Illinois. For five years she was one of the popular teachers of Carroll County, prior to her marriage. Mr. and Mrs. Proehl have had the following children born to them: Pauline, born February 27, 1905, who was graduated from the Forest City High School, became a student of the Bradley Polytechnic Institute, Peoria, Illinois, and later of the Normal University at Normal, Illinois, and is now a teacher in the public schools of Mason County; Wilamina, born September 16, 1907, who was graduated from the community school of Forest City, was later a student of the Normal University and now a teacher in Mason County; Carl William, born August 20, 1909, died at the age of ten years, five months and five days, and is buried in Meadow Lawn Cemetery at Marista, Illinois; and Lillian, born July 25, 1912, and Lucile, born September 11, 1915.

OTTO GNERICH is a business man and banker of Alton who has been distinguished by an unusually rapid progress from minor responsibilities to executive duties in one of the large corporations of Madison County. He is treasurer of the Western Cartridge Company of East Alton.

He was born in Germany, May 17, 1879, was reared and educated in his native land, and acquired the technical education of the German commercial schools. He graduated from a gymnasium or college, and served his apprenticeship in a commercial school, following which he spent six years in various commercial positions in Switzerland, France, Belgium and England.

Coming to America in 1904 he at once located in St. Louis, and in 1905 came to East Alton. His first connection with the Western Cartridge Company was as clerk, and he was advanced to other responsibilities until twelve years later he was made treasurer of the corporation. He is also vice president of the Illinois State Bank of East Alton, and is a director of the German Building & Loan Association.

Mr. Gnerich married, on May 17, 1906, Miss Roberta May Millison, of Alton. They have four children, named Freda, Ernest, Margaret and Roberta. Mr. Gnerich is affiliated with the Elks and is a republican in political views. He took an active part in the local program for the support of the World war, participating with time and means in all the drives.

KENNETH A. ELMORE, ex-chief of police of the Quincy Police Department, is a veteran of the World war, having risen to the rank of captain while on the battle fields of France. He had become well known in local business circles at Quincy before the war.

He was born at Gibbs, Missouri, April 2, 1895, son of Emery and Mamie (Gimbel) Elmore. His father belonged to a family of early settlers in Adams County, Illinois, and both he and his wife were born there. Emery Elmore taught school for a number of years, both in Missouri and Illinois, and then took up the business of carpenter contracting. In 1907, on account of the illness of his wife, he moved to Los Angeles, California, remaining there three years. Subsequently he again returned to California, and for a number of years has been engaged in his business as a carpenter and builder, and also as a dealer in and developer of real estate and properties in and around Los Angeles. He is a member of the Independent Order of Odd Fellows, and the Christian Church, and has been prominent in the Sunday School of the church.

Second in a family of ten children, seven of whom are living, Kenneth Elmore acquired his early education in the common schools at

Louisa E. Proehl

Gibbs, Missouri, and in the country high school. His first active business experience at Quincy was with the Otis Elevator Company and later he was employed by the Irwin Paper Company as superintendent of a warehouse. Subsequently he was employed by the Safe Cabinet Company.

Before the World war he was a lieutenant in Company F, Fifth Illinois Infantry, of the National Guard. He was with the colors two years and six months, rising from lieutenant to captain, most of his active service being with Company B of the One Hundred Twenty-third Machine Gun Battalion in the Thirty-third Division. He participated in the Argonne and other campaigns during the last year of the war.

After leaving the army he resumed his business career at Quincy, and in 1923 was appointed by Mayor Smiley as chief of police of the city. He was well qualified for a vigorous and forceful administration of this department. On April 13, 1926, he was nominated for sheriff on the democratic ticket. Mr. Elmore married Miss Helen Riley, daughter of Robert Riley, of Quincy. They have two children.

WILLIAM ELMER WASHBURN, M. D. Since 1899 Dr. William Elmer Washburn has been engaged in the practice of medicine at Kewanee, and is now recognized as one of the ablest and most resourceful physicians and surgeons of Henry County, and a man who holds the full confidence of the people. He was born at Newtonville, Clermont County, Ohio, May 20, 1870, a son of James Harvey and Martha J. (Kelley) Washburn, natives of Ohio and Illinois, respectively. The Washburn family is one of the oldest in the United States, Martha Washburn having been a passenger on the Mayflower, and from her have descended the Washburns of this country.

James Harvey Washburn served with galantry in the Union army during the war between the states for three years and four months. While he was married in Illinois, he located in Clermont County, Ohio, where he, at the age of eighty-four years, is still residing. They had a family of three daughters and two sons, all of whom were reared on the homestead farm.

Doctor Washburn attended the country schools and later the National Normal School at Lebanon, Ohio. In 1899 he was graduated from the Hospital College of Medicine, Louisville, Kentucky. At different times Doctor Washburn has taken up postgraduate work in the New York Polyclinic and the New York Post-Graduate School of Medicine. Following his graduation he established himself at Kewanee, and here he has since resided, winning approval from the very start of his career because of his faithfulness and capabilities. He is a member of the Henry County Medical Society, the Illinois State Medical Society, the American Medical Association, and the Mississippi Valley Medical Association, and is a member of the staffs of the Saint Francis and the Public Hospitals of Kewanee. Well known in Masonry he has been advanced in that order to the Temple and the Shrine.

On March 7, 1895, Doctor Washburn married Jessie J. Allen, who died in 1923, leaving a son, Raymond A. Washburn. He served as field clerk in the United States army overseas for sixteen months during the World war. At present he is an executive in the office of the Chicago Tribune, located at New York City. On March 10, 1925, Doctor Washburn married Lillian V. Wiley, a daughter of Mr. and Mrs. James Wiley, the latter a pioneer of Henry County.

HARRY F. REAM is a banker by early training and mature experience, and for a number of years has been the executive head and cashier of the Depue State Bank at Depue.

This bank was organized in 1904 and opened for business in January, 1905, and Mr. Ream has been identified with it from the beginning. Mr. Ream was born at Peru in La Salle County, Illinois, May 26, 1879, one of the nine children of Henry and Mary A. (Stockdale) Ream. Both parents were natives of Pennsylvania. His father when a young man moved to Illinois and soon became identified with the Peru National Bank and for many years served as its president.

Harry F. Ream was reared and educated at Peru, attended the St. Bede College near Peru, and at the age of seventeen went to work in the Peru National Bank, getting a complete training in the fundamentals of banking before he took up his duties at Depue. At Depue he served fifteen years as village treasurer. He is a republican in politics, a member of the Catholic Church, and is affiliated with the Woodmen of the World and the Mystic Workers of the World.

On June 6, 1911, he married Miss Helen Weiser Ely, of Colorado Springs, Colorado. They have two children: Marion Louise and Harry F., Jr.

L. FREDERICK KEITH. Although now retired from business pursuits and living in comfort at Bath, L. Frederick Keith was for many years one of the influential figures in commercial circles in Mason County, and accomplished admirable results both in his private ventures and public undertakings. He was born on a farm in Mason County, Illinois, February 15, 1861, a son of Frederick Keith, the latter of whom was born in Wittenburg, Schwabenland, Germany, about 1837.

At the early age of fifteen years Frederick Keith left Germany and came to the United States to join several uncles who had come to this country and settled in Bath Township, Mason County, Illinois. The lad supplemented the education received in his native land with attendance at district school, and worked on the farm for small wages until he reached his majority. Some idea of the perseverance of this youth may be gleaned from the fact that the small amount he had for his trip over gave out by the time he reached Ohio, and so, instead of sending home or to his uncle for funds, he remained in Ohio, working as a farm hand, until he had what he needed to complete his journey. When he became twenty-one he began farming on rented land, his first tenant farm being between Bath and Havana. Within five years, or in 1864, he was able to buy a farm near Saidora, and on it he lived until his death. Adding to his original purchase, he had 300 acres when he died, and on his land he raised grain, and was so successful in his operations that he became a man of considerable means and left a large estate behind him. Politically he was a republican, and was quite active in local affairs, serving as road commissioner and school director, and never missed an election. He was an earnest member of the German Lutheran Church, which was his only affiliation. His wife was a widow, Mrs. Margaret Roloff, when he married her. She was the relict of Louis Roloff, and her maiden name was Baselbeck. By her first marriage she had two children, Louis and Lizzie Roloff, both of whom are deceased. Mrs. Keith was born in Bremen, Germany, and came to the United States with her mother when still a girl, and remained on a farm in Mason County until her first marriage. Mr. and Mrs. Frederick Keith had the following children born to them: J. Herman, who resides at Bath, Illinois; L. Frederick, whose name heads this review; Margaret, who resides at Kilburn, Illinois, was married first to Frank Friend, and after his death she was married to Henry Maselman; and Sophie, who is deceased, was the wife of Allen Clark.

The farm on which L. Frederick Keith was born was the one on which his parents lived as renters, and this property is now owned by Frank Staging. He was taken by his parents to the farm they bought, and there he continued to live until he was twenty-four years old, in the meanwhile securing his education at district schools. Leaving the farm, he went to Bath and for three years worked for his brother in a retail liquor business. Having saved up $225, Mr. Keith bought a stock of groceries and began his career as a merchant. From the beginning he was successful, and so hard did he work and so well did he manage that when he sold the business he was carrying a stock valued at $20,000.

Constant application and confinement had broken his health, and when he sold his store, during the World war, Mr. Keith bought a car and moved to Kansas, where he already owned a Montgomery County farm. It was his idea to start his son as a farmer, but soon discovered that the young man was better fitted for business than for agriculture, so he aided him in getting established at Neodesha, Kansas. He is now manager of the local ice plant and cream station of that community, and making an admirable record. Selling his farm, Mr. Keith returned to Illinois. Increasing illness made necessary hospital treatment, and he spent three months in one of these institutions, and several months of absolute quiet at home. At present he is enjoying life, although he supervises to a certain extent the activities of his Mason County farm.

Casting his first presidential ballot for James G. Blaine, Mr. Keith has continued steadfast in his allegiance to the republican party, and has been very active in local affairs. For twelve years he was president of the village board of Bath, and he served for three years as road commissioner, and while in that office bought the first road-grader in his territory. He has attended the county conventions of his party, and was a delegate to the Deep Waterway Convention held at Saint Louis, Missouri, having been appointed by Governor Small. While he attends the services of the German Lutheran Church, and contributes generously to it and other churches, he is not a member of any religious organization.

In May, 1891, Mr. Keith married, in Bath Township, Miss Lurah Morrow, a daughter of Washington and Mary (Lacy) Morrow. Mrs. Keith was born in Mason County, in 1871, and her parents were also natives of the county, and her father was a hotel man at Bath, the house now occupied by Mr. Keith having been used for hotel purposes. Mrs. Keith died in March, 1895. In May, 1896, Mr. Keith married Miss Hannah Hackman, a daughter of Henry and Eliza (Sager) Hackman. The second Mrs. Keith was born in Havana Township, Mason County, February 22, 1865, and she was educated in the public schools and reared on the farm. She is one of the family of six daughters and two sons born to her parents. Mr. and Mrs. Keith have had the following children born to them: Nelda, who is with the Liberty Trust Company Bank of Saint Louis, Missouri, and is a graduate of Brown's Business College, Jacksonville, Illinois; and Henry F., who has been mentioned before as manager of the Neodesha Ice Cream and Creamery Company. There were no children born of the first marriage.

During the World war Mr. Keith was still engaged in merchandising until near its close, and he rendered some very valuable assistance in putting over the different drives for all purposes.

Henry F. Keith married at Neodesha, Kansas, Miss Lynn Starr.

CHARLES THOMSON ATKINSON, who has been secretary of the Chicago Stock Exchange since 1909, has had a close association with business and financial affairs in that city for over thirty years, beginning his connection with Chicago in a time of great civic enterprise and public spirit during the preparations for the World's Columbian Exposition.

Mr. Atkinson was born in Elmira, New York, November 4, 1864, son of Frank Holway and Helen (Dunn) Atkinson. He acquired a public school education, and as a boy entered the railway service. He was employed by several roads and in different capacities, and from 1889 to 1891 was general agent at Cincinnati for the Chicago, Burlington & Quincy Railway.

Removing to Chicago in 1891, Mr. Atkinson was for some years with some boot and shoe manufacturing houses, at first with Leonard, Atkinson & Company from 1891 to 1897, and from 1897 to 1899 with M. D. Wells & Company. Since then he has been in the stock and bond business, being a stock broker with William H. Colvin & Company from 1900 to 1902, with the Finley Barrell Company from 1902 to 1906, and then for several years manager of the Railway Exchange office of Farson Son & Company. Mr. Atkinson on

December 1, 1909, took up his duties as secretary of the Chicago Stock Exchange. His service in that position has been continuous except from September, 1918, to February, 1919, when he was absent on leave for war work. During 1896-98 Mr. Atkinson was a member of the Illinois Naval Reserve. He belongs to the Sons of the American Revolution, is a republican, and a member of the Chicago, Onwentsia, The Attic and Cliff Dwellers Clubs. His home is in Lake Forest. He married, June 18, 1891, at Chicago, Miss Martha Wells.

FREDERICK DAVID CULBERTSON, M. D. An accomplished physician and surgeon whose practice has been identified with Schuyler County since 1907, Doctor Culbertson is particularly well known and esteemed as the executive head and founder of the Culbertson Hospital at Rushville.

Doctor Culbertson was born at Dubuque, Iowa, October 21, 1882. His grandfather was a Scotchman, married a Miss Donohue from the north of Ireland, and coming to America, was a building contractor in Iowa and in the vicinity of Prairie du Chien, Wisconsin, and finally at Portage, Wisconsin. He and his wife had several sons who were soldiers and officers in the Union army during the Civil war. Joseph M. Culbertson, father of Doctor Culbertson, was born at Portage City, Wisconsin, and in early life took up sawmilling and lumbering. He began as a saw filer, and finally became superintendent of some large lumber companies operating in the North and in the South. He now lives retired at Chicago. He married at Dubuque a native of that city, whose maiden name was Whittier, but who was reared as an adopted child of the Stoltz family of Dubuque. She became the mother of the following children: Dr. Frederick David; Joseph, deceased; Harry, of Chicago; Arthur, of New York City; and Ethel, wife of Harry Turner, of Minneapolis.

Frederick D. Culbertson was reared in Dubuque, attended grammar and high schools there, was a student in Drake University at Des Moines, and took his medical course in Northwestern University at Chicago, where he was graduated in 1906. After getting his diploma he served as an interne in the Englewood Hospital, and for about a year was engaged in industrial practice as physician at a copper mining camp in the vicinity of Baltic in the northern peninsula of Michigan. In 1907 he returned to Illinois and engaged in private practice at Littleton in Schuyler County, and in October, 1910, removed to Rushville. He has done post-graduate work in the Massachusetts General Hospital at Boston, and frequently in Chicago.

At Rushville Doctor Culbertson engaged in a general practice, but soon became known for his special skill in pediatrics, or children's diseases. His successful practice demanded hospital facilities, and he was faced with the alternative of either leaving Rushville or getting a well equipped hospital established there. Eventually, in co-operation with Mrs. Culbertson, he brought about the construction of the Culbertson Hospital, which was opened February 21, 1921, and proved a notable event in the history of Schuyler County. Probably the largest assembly of people ever gathered for any event came to do honor to the institution and its founders. The Culbertson Hospital has accommodations for twenty-five patients and is a general hospital, well equipped for handling all classes of cases.

Doctor Culbertson is a member of the County, Illinois State and American Medical Associations, is a Knight Templar Mason and a Presbyterian.

Mrs. Culbertson before her marriage was Sarah L. DeWitt, who was born at Littleton, Illinois, daughter of Theodore DeWitt. She has two brothers, Fred, of Macomb, Illinois, and Theodore, of Sioux City, Iowa. Mrs. Culbertson was the moving spirit in the planning and erection of the Culbertson Hospital, and she regards its maintenance and service as a very important part of her life work. She finished her education in the high school at Macomb and also took a business course.

WILLIAM F. HANLEY, cashier of the State Bank of Jerseyville, has been identified with banking in his native city since leaving school except for the period of the World war, during which he was in training, in service overseas for upwards of two years.

He was born at Jerseyville, March 9, 1894. His father, William M. Hanley, was a native of Jersey County, and for some years was superintendent of the Otterville schools. Later he engaged in the butchering and retail meat business at Jerseyville, and so continued until his death in 1908, at the age of forty-seven. He served as township supervisor and city treasurer, being on the board of supervisors altogether fifteen years, until his death, when he was succeeded by his brother. William M. Hanley married Theresa Roerig. Her father was well known to a former generation as a stage coach driver between Alton and Jacksonville. Mrs. William M. Hanley continued to reside at Jerseyville. Her children were: William Franklin; C. Thomas, an assistant state's attorney of Cook County, Illinois; Margaret B., assistant cashier of the State Bank of Jerseyville; and Loretta T., a student in the University of Illinois.

William F. Hanley was educated in public schools at Jerseyville. After finishing his first year in high school he went to work for the State Bank, beginning as a clerk, and successive promotions have brought him to the responsible post he now occupies as cashier, in which he succeeded George W. Campbell in 1920.

He left the bank soon after America declared war on Germany, was called to the service under the draft, and after three weeks at Camp Dix, New Jersey, went overseas with the Three Hundred and Third Trench Mortar Battalion, Seventy-eighth Division. Later he was transferred to a field artillery company, and finally was made a musician. He went overseas from Philadelphia on the English ship Mesaba to Liverpool by way of Halifax, being seventeen days in making the voyage. From Liverpool he went to South Hampton, crossed the Channel to LeHavre, and then to camp at Vannes Morbihan, where he was trained with the French Mortar Battery. He was in his first engagement at the St. Mihiel front, taking part in the Preny raid. He spent fourteen days in the trenches and while there volunteered with three others of his outfit for telephone work. He was in the Meuse-Argonne campaign, including the Grand Pre attack, and thence to Sedan, in which locality he was stationed at the time of the armistice.

After the armistice he was with his command at Verdun for several weeks and had many opportunities to witness the great devastation wrought by war on that renowned fortress. He also spent a leave in Southern France, and during the greater part of the winter 1918-19 was at the City of Frense. In the spring he went to Marseilles, taking opportunity in the meantime to visit Paris for a few days, and he also saw something of Spain. He left Marseilles on the Spanish ship Infantile Isabel, passing through Gibraltar, the Azores Islands, and landed at Hoboken, New Jersey, in May, 1919. After several days at Camp Dix he was ordered to Camp Grant, Illinois, and there received his honorable discharge May 22, 1919. At Jerseyville he helped organize Worthy Post of the American Legion, was elected its first treasurer and has since been commander, and he is also chef-de-gare of the Forty and Eight Military Society.

Mr. Hanley is a director of the State Bank of Jerseyville as well as its cashier. He served eight years as city treasurer of Jerseyville, has been township treasurer of schools for five years, is treasurer of the B. P. O. Elks and the Tuberculosis Association. He is a Catholic and a member of the Knights of Columbus.

Mr. Hanley married at Jerseyville, June 9, 1919, Miss Genevieve Bonwell, who was born in McDonough County, Illinois, daughter of J. W. Bonwell. She graduated from the Macomb High School and the Western Illinois State Teachers College, and she and Mr. Hanley met while she was teaching in the grades and high school at Jerseyville. They have a daughter, Genevieve Theresa, born March 6, 1924.

WILLIAM BRUCE DAVIS for over forty years has been a newspaper man in Central Illinois, and is one of the owners of the Democrat-Message of Mt. Sterling, Brown County.

This veteran newspaper man was born in Lexington, Lafayette County, Missouri, July 10, 1865. He belongs to a family that for several generations has been identified with the newspaper business. His grandfather, Samuel H. Davis, was a native of New York and served his apprenticeship as a printer at Albany with Thurlow Weed, in the office of Solomon Southwick. Henry K. Davis, father of William B., was born at Winchester, Virginia, April 11, 1828. While his occupation and profession was printing and publishing, he was also a prominent lay worker in the Presbyterian Church. In 1846 he went to Chicago, worked in a job office three years, and on the death of his father returned to Peoria, Illinois, and with Thomas J. Pickett published the Peoria Register, the first daily newspaper in that city. From the spring of 1850 to 1851 he was employed on the Globe at Washington, D. C. In 1852 he established the Illinois State Bulletin at Bloomington, and was a delegate to the Democratic National Convention at Baltimore in 1852 when Franklin Pierce was nominated for president. During 1853-56 he was a clerk in the treasury department at Washington. For about two years he was foreman of the job department of the old Missouri Democrat of St. Louis. In 1858 he took a position with the Expositor at Lexington, Missouri, but on account of his Union sentiments was obliged to leave that southern community at the outbreak of the war. Returning later, he founded the Lexington Union, which for three or four years was the only newspaper published within three or four counties in that section of Missouri. During the war, while still at Lexington, he was on the staff of Gen. Richard C. Vaughan of the Missouri Enrolled Militia, with the rank of major. In 1867 he invested his means at Kansas City, then just starting up as a town, buying the Daily Commercial Advertiser, a pioneer newspaper there. It was not a financial success and the following year he engaged in job printing. The business he sold in 1872, went to St. Louis, and was connected with the St. Louis Republic, and from there removed to Paris, Texas, where he and F. W. Minor established the Chartist.

After a brief stay in Texas Henry K. Davis arrived at Mt. Sterling, Illinois, about the close of 1874, and purchased the Brown County Democrat, a paper he published until his death in April, 1886.

Henry K. Davis married, March 15, 1860, Mary Davis, who was born at Flintstone, Maryland, daughter of John Davis, of Cumberland, Maryland. She survived her husband many years, passing away in 1918. Her children were: William B.; John Y., of California; Robert Lee, Charles M. and Richard, all residents of Mt. Sterling, Richard being associated with his brother in the Democrat-Message.

William Bruce Davis spent the first ten years of his life in Missouri and at Paris, Texas, and in 1875 arrived at Mt. Sterling, where he finished his education so far as the common schools were concerned. From boyhood he was familiar with the work of a newspaper office, and he learned the printing trade and all the routine of a newspaper office. When his father died in 1886 he was just twenty-one years of age, and succeeded to the proprietorship of the Brown County Democrat. Subsequently the Message was purchased and since then the paper has been the Democrat-Message. For many years it was published weekly, but for a quarter of a century has been a twice a week publication. It is democratic in politics, and has been an influential organ in campaigns. Mr. Davis erected a modern office and shop for his newspaper, and has modern equipment, including two type machines and power for all the work.

Mr. Davis has been a public-spirited citizen of Brown County through all the years. For thirty years or more he has been a member of the local school district board. In 1893 he was appointed postmaster by President Cleveland, serving one term. President Wilson again appointed him to the same office in 1913, and by re-appointment in 1917 he served a little more than eight years, having suc-

ceeded J. F. Regan. He is a member of the local Commercial Club and is a trustee of the Presbyterian Church. During the World war he performed many extraordinary duties as postmaster, and the United States treasury department awarded him a medal for "patriotic service in behalf of the Liberty Loans."

Mr. Davis married at Mt. Sterling, September 25, 1888, Laura Givens, who was born at Mt. Sterling, daughter of John A. and Jane (Putman) Givens. She died at Mt. Sterling in 1906, the mother of two children, Kathryn and George R. Kathryn is the wife of Clifford R. Brooks, of Mt. Sterling, and they have three children, named Mary Virginia, Billie Robert and Patricia. The son, George R., who at present handles the editorial duties of the Democrat-Message, was born at Mt. Sterling in 1894, graduated from high school, spent two years in the University of Illinois, graduated from the Coyle Electrical School in engineering, and for several years was employed by the Central Illinois Public Service Company, until he engaged in the newspaper business with his father. He married Wilma Vermillion and has a daughter, Laura.

William B. Davis married for his second wife Nora Shank, a native of Brown County, where her father, John Shank, was a farmer. John Shank was a captain in the Union Army during the Civil war. Mrs. Davis has a sister, Mrs. J. W. Cartwright, of Burlington, Iowa. By his second marriage Mr. Davis has two children, Susanna and Marilyn.

CHARLES ALBERT CALDWELL is an Illinois banker, and by combining his own and his father's service a continuous record of nearly sixty years has been made in the house of the Alton National Bank.

His father, Charles Augustus Caldwell, one of the citizens and financiers whom the City of Alton held in highest respect, was of New England ancestry and was born at Ipswich, Massachusetts, January 7, 1823. He was a descendant in the seventh generation from John Caldwell, an Englishman who was a resident of Boston, Massachusetts, in 1643, and subsequently lived in the ancestral seat of the Caldwell family in America, Ipswich. His grandson, John Caldwell, an ancestor of the Caldwells of Alton, was killed by the Indians in 1724. A later ancestor, Capt. Ebenezer Caldwell, born in 1745, was in service at the first alarm at the battle of Lexington. Capt. Sylvanus Caldwell, a son of the Revolutionary soldier, was born in 1787, and became a successful business man in the Kennebec Valley of Maine. He was a friend of James G. Blaine. He had twelve children, and two of his daughters became wives of notable citizens of Alton, Illinois, one of them being Mrs. Samuel Wade, and the other the wife of Dr. E. Marsh, Sr.

Charles Augustus Caldwell received his early business training in Augusta, Maine, and on coming to Alton in 1850, entered the office of the Alton Marine and Fire Insurance Company. Out of that company grew the old Alton Bank, of which he became cashier in 1852. In 1865 he was made cashier of the Alton National Bank, and in 1885 was elected its president and served so until his death on October 11, 1890. In 1873 he was elected mayor of Alton, this being the only public office he ever consented to fill. On May 28, 1857, he married Miss Ann Marsh, daughter of Dr. E. Marsh, Sr., and his wife, Ann Cox.

Charles Albert Caldwell, third of the ten children of Charles Augustus Caldwell and wife, was born at Alton in 1863. He was reared and educated in his native city, and as a youth had before him the example of the career of his father. Many years ago he became cashier of the Alton National Bank, and his chief ambition has been to maintain that institution on the same plane of integrity and service at which his father kept it. He has been officially identified with several other business organizations, including a wholesale grocery company and an electric railway company.

Mr. Caldwell married April 15, 1891, Elizabeth Forbes, of Alton. She died in August, 1904, Their one child, Elizabeth R., married John A. Ryrie and they have two sons, George M. and Charles C. Mr. Caldwell has two deceased children, Charles and Albert.

MORTIMER GRANT BARNES, C. E., since 1917 has been a resident of Chicago, holding the position of chief engineer of the Division of Waterways of the State of Illinois. Mr. Barnes' professional experience has made him a notable authority on civil and hydraulic engineering in the United States.

He was born at Reedsburg, Wisconsin, January 17, 1867, son of James B. and Alice (Randall) Barnes. He was educated in the public schools of Nebraska, and acquired his early knowledge of engineering by practical experience in connection with railroad surveys and construction in the State of Nebraska. In November, 1891, he was elected county surveyor of Boone County in that state. He graduated from the University of Michigan with the degree of Bachelor of Science in civil engineering in 1896, and received the degree Civil Engineer from the same institution in 1901, after post-graduate work in hydraulics and masonry. In 1922 he received the degree Master of Engineering from the same institution. While attending the University of Michigan he served a short appointment as assistant city engineer of Ann Arbor, engaged in work on surveys and sewer construction. During four summer vacations he was employed on construction work of the Poe lock and power house at Sault Ste. Marie, Michigan. In 1896-97 he was chief engineer for the Lake Superior Power Company. In 1897-98 he was assistant to Joseph Ripley on surveys and preliminary design of the Birmingham Canal, extending from the City of Birmingham to the Black Warrior River, a distance of about sixty-five miles, an important part in the great Warrior River waterway. Following that he was retained by the Chandler-Dunbar Power Company to design its power plant at Sault Ste. Marie, Michigan, and he was also associated with the improvement of the Brazos and Guadalupe rivers in Texas. In 1899 he was chief of a party assigned to the investigation of the United States deep-waterway project in Northern New York. He was engaged in design and construction work in connection with the Illinois and Mississippi Canal from 1899 to 1905, including the construction of the Moline locks in the Mississippi River. He again became associated with Joseph Ripley as his assistant in charge of designing locks and other structures for the Panama Canal. On completing the preliminary design and report he resigned to accept appointment as engineer with the New York Board of Water Supply. From 1907 to 1911 he was a member of the Advisory Board of Consulting Engineers having in charge the enlargement of the New York State barge canal and improvement of other waterways in that state. From 1911 to 1915 he was a member of the Board of Consulting Engineers of New York canals, and at the same time engaged in private professional practice as consulting civil and hydraulic engineer at Albany, with special service as an authority and expert in the adjustment of disputes in water power litigation.

In October, 1917, he was selected by the Illinois Board of Water Resource Advisors and Officers of the Department of Public Works and Buildings, Division of Waterways of the State of Illinois, as the one outstanding engineer of the country for the position of chief engineer and directing head for the construction of the Illinois waterway project. This selection was confirmed and authorized by Governor Frank O. Lowden, and his services have been continued by Governor Small. For nearly ten years, therefore, he has been the technical expert employed in connection with one of the largest and most vital undertakings in connection with the transportation and commercial expansion of the Middle West. He also practices as a consulting engineer in Chicago.

Mr. Barnes prepared a book on inland waterways, their necessity and importance, published in 1920 under the auspices of the Illinois Department of Public Works. In the introduction, Frank I. Bennett, director of the department, says: "Mortimer G. Barnes, author of this booklet, presents the subject in the dual capacity of an engineer of wide experience and pronounced achievement in the construction and improvement of waterways, and as a successful farmer and live-stock breeder cognizant of the transportation handicaps suffered by the agricultural interest of the country, and the lower costs that will result from the development of navigation on natural waterways in a manner to afford continuing and uninterrupted transportation thereon between important terminal points and popular cities.

"In addition to his engineering work, Mr. Barnes is directing the successful operation of his 3,100 acre ranch in Northern Nebraska. As a farmer and live stock breeder he has been vitally interested in and a close student of economics, and is considered an authority on transportation, advocating the development of waterways not as competitors of railways but in cooperation with them, to the end the great agricultural and business interests of the entire Middle West and other interior sections may enjoy lower freight rates and be on a competitive basis with those parts of the United States enjoying for years direct access to water transportation."

Mr. Barnes is a member of the American Society of Civil Engineers, the Western Society of Engineers, and a member of the Christian, or Disciples Church. His home is at 226 South Maple Avenue, Oak Park. He married in Canada, August 17, 1898, Miss Mina M. Wood. They have three children, Alice E., Florence L. and James M.

MAURICE B. JOHNSTON. A leading member of the bar at Carlyle, and superintendent of the public schools of Clinton County, is Maurice B. Johnston, who is of old pioneer stock in Illinois, a member of a family that has been of consequence here for more than one hundred years.

Maurice B. Johnston was born at Carlyle, Clinton County, Illinois, May 2, 1891, second son of William and Cora L. (Burnside) Johnston, and grandson of William and Elizabeth (Murphy) Johnston, both of whom were born in Illinois and were married at Carlyle. The paternal great-grandfather was born in Ireland and came to Illinois in 1817. The maternal grandfather of Attorney Johnston was William G. Burnside, who was a man of high character and public importance. He was the first settler in Clinton County north of Carlyle, was the first appointed surveyor of this section of the territory of Illinois, and made the first survey of Clinton County.

William Johnston, son of William and father of Maurice B., was a prominent and influential man in Clinton County throughout a long and active life, which came to a close in 1923. He was an able lawyer at Carlyle in his earlier life, and for thirty years served as county superintendent of schools. Politically a democrat, he was active in party affairs all his life, frequently serving officially and at one time was a member of the National Democratic Committee. He was a Shriner Mason, and was a member of the Presbyterian Church.

William Johnston married at Carlyle Miss Cora L. Burnside, who survives, and four children were born to them: Allen G., who married Ella Coulter; Maurice B.; Irl; and Mabel, who is the wife of Dr. W. E. Carter, and they have one daughter, Phyllis.

Maurice B. Johnston attended the public schools at Carlyle and was graduated from the high school in 1908, subsequently entering Cornell University, where he completed his law course and was graduated LL. B. in 1913. In 1914 he entered into the practice of law in his native city and has won high standing at the bar. Since his father's death in 1923 he has been superintendent of schools. On June 14, 1918, Mr. Johnston enlisted for military service in the World war. He was assigned to duty in the legal department of the intelligence branch of the judge advocate's office at Camp Funston, Kansas, where he proved exceedingly efficient. He received his honorable discharge on January 23, 1919, when he returned to Carlyle and resumed his interrupted law practice.

Mr. Johnston married at Carlyle, November 23, 1918, Miss Ruth A. Robinson, and they have one son, William Jerome. Mrs. Johnston is a daughter of John W. and Lydia (Hall) Robinson, the former of whom was in the lumber and steamboat business. Mr. and Mrs. Johnston are members of the Episcopal Church. He is a Mason and Odd Fellow, a member of the American Legion, of the State and County Bar Associations, and of the Phi Delta Phi college fraternity.

NICHOLAS LUFT was a young man when he established his residence in Tazewell County, more than seventy years ago, and he was one of the well known and honored citizens of Dillon, this county, at the time of his death, in July, 1893, his remains having been laid to rest beside those of his wife in the Hampson Cemetery in Sand Prairie Township. Mr. Luft was born and reared in Hesse-Darmstadt, Germany, where he acquired his youthful education, and he had served his allotted time in the German army prior to his coming to the United States, besides which he had learned the blacksmith trade with utmost thoroughness. In 1851 he arrived in Tazewell County, Illinois, and for a time he was employed in the Nichols blacksmith shop at Pekin. Later he followed his trade for a few years in Sand Prairie Township, and he then turned his attention to farm enterprise in that township, his further work at his trade having been only in connection with the operations of his farm. He became the owner of a good farm in section three of the township of Dillon, and on this homestead he continued to reside until he retired from active labor and established his home in the village of Dillon, where he remained until his death, at the age of fifty-seven years. In this county was solemnized his marriage to Catherine Horn, daughter of George Horn, and she survived him a number of years she having been venerable in age at the time of her death.

Here is given brief record concerning the children of Nicholas and Catherine Luft: Margaret became the wife of John Buehler and was a resident of Dillon at the time of her death; Jacob is a farmer in Norton County, Kansas; Nicholas, Jr., will be more specifically mentioned in later paragraphs of this memoir; Peter likewise is a resident of Norton County, Kansas; and Eva Ann is the wife of Charles S. Kinsey, who is the subject of a personal sketch on other pages of this publication.

Nicholas Luft, Jr., son of the subject of this memoir, was born in Sand Prairie Township, January 25, 1863, and was reared principally on the old home farm in Dillon Township. He attended the district school, a German school in Pekin, and that best of all schools, practical experience in connection with man and affairs. He has long been numbered among the progressive representatives of farm industry in Dillon Township, where he owns and occupies a well improved farm, and he is one of the substantial citizens of his native county He was a democrat until the World war period, and has since voted independently. He and his wife are communicants of the Lutheran Church, this faith having been held by the family in Germany. He is loyal and liberal as a citizen, but has had no ambition for political activity in public office. In the period of the nation's participation in the World war Mr. Luft served as one of the solicitors in connection with the Dillon Township drives in support of the government war loans and other patriotic service, and the women of his household busily employed themselves in knitting sweaters, wristlets, hose, etc., and in preparing other needed supplies for the boys of the army and navy.

April 12, 1888, marked the marriage of Nicholas Luft, Jr., and Miss Laura Jane Larimore, who was born in Elm Grove Township, near Dillon, September 21, 1870, a daughter of Thomas and Jane (Reed) Larimore. Mr. Larimore came to Tazewell County from Virginia, and here passed the rest of his life as a farmer. He died in 1906, aged seventy-seven years, his wife having passed away in 1900, at the age of fifty-nine years. Of their children the eldest was Belle, who became the wife of Albert Shay and who died in Sumner County, Kansas; Sarah is the widow of Martin Heisel and resides at Pekin, Tazewell County; Ida is the wife of William Crooks, of Green Valley, this county; Carrie, who became the wife of Frank Myers, is deceased; Mrs. Laura J. Luft was the next in order of birth; Daisy is the wife of Guy Roof, of Medalia; Bertha is the wife of Gilbert Young, of Elm Grove Township; and Benjamin is engaged in farming on the old Larimore homestead near Dillon. In conclusion is given record concerning the children of Mr. and Mrs. Luft: Clell Thomas, of Dillon, married Nellie Watkins, and they have two children, Clell and Marie. Benjamin Nelson, a resident of South Pekin, this county, married Louise Connell, and their children are Willis and Nelson. Nora Lula is the wife of Silas A. Koch, of whom individual mention is made on another page of this work. Guy Albert, now in the employ of the Chicago & Northwestern Railroad Company at South Pekin, was overseas in the World war and arrived at the front three days prior to the signing of the armistice that brought the war to a close. Herman Ludwig resides in Dillon. William Glenn is the active farmer of the Luft estate. Eva May holds a position in the great Morrison Hotel in the city of Chicago. The younger children of the home community are Carrie Hazel, Jesse Lincoln, Flossie Uretta and Sarah Irene.

EDMUND P. NISCHWITZ. Recognized as one of the ablest of the attorneys practicing at the bar of Mason County, Edmund P. Nischwitz has won the appreciation and support to which his talents entitle him, and his practice is a large and constantly augmented one. He was born in Somerset County, New Jersey, August 2, 1872, a son of Philip Nischwitz, born in Hemsbach, Germany. Reaching manhood's estate in his native land, Philip Nischwitz left Germany for the United States, and found employment as a miller in and around Plainfield, New Jersey. As soon as he had saved sufficient money he invested it in a farm, and he completed his life's span upon it, dying in 1897, when about sixty years old.

Philip Nischwitz married Annie Mackey, a native of Ireland, who was brought to the United States by her father when she was a young girl. He was a man of large interests in Ireland, but was killed in a railroad accident between New York City and Buffalo, and she, with two other children, were left orphans, and helpless and friendless. Mrs. Nischwitz died in 1907, having borne her husband the following children: Henry, who died at Plainfield, New Jersey; Kate, who is deceased; Elizabeth E., who resides at Plainfield, New Jersey; Edmund P., whose name heads this review; and Frank, who is also a resident of Plainfield.

Growing up on his father's New Jersey farm, Edmund P. Nischwitz early learned to make himself useful, and he attended the country schools and Stillman High School, named in honor of the New York banker, James Stillman. His literary course was taken in Rutgers College, from which he was graduated with the degree of Bachelor of Arts in 1894, and that same year he came to Illinois and located at Havana, entering the law office of John W. Pitman. Two years later, in 1896, he was admitted to the bar of Illinois before the Supreme Court of the state, and then he and Mr. Pitman formed the law firm of Pitman & Nischwitz. After four years this connection was dissolved, and Mr. Nischwitz has since continued alone. Many honors have been bestowed upon him, and he served as master-in-chancery from 1900 to 1904; has been city attorney of Havana since 1897, with the exception of a few months, and during his occupancy of office an extensive sewerage and paving system has been installed by the city under his direction, and he has backed other substantial improvements. In 1904 he was elected state's attorney of Mason County, and was several times re-elected, serving in that office for sixteen years. As public prosecutor he made a splendid record for his fearlessness and flaming honesty, and firmly established his reputation as a forceful and upright lawyer and convincing speaker. Since 1920 he has been devoting himself to his private practice. In political faith he is a democrat. During the late war he was government appeal agent for Mason County and belonged to its legal advisory board; was a member of the executive staff of the Mason County Chapter, American Red Cross, and was one of the most popular of the Four Minute Speakers of the county. While he was registered in the last draft, the armistice was signed before he received his questionnaire. Fraternally his affiliations are with the college society Beta Theta Pi, Knights of Pythias, Loyal Order of Moose and Modern Woodmen of America. While reared in a religious atmosphere, he is not a church member.

On December 9, 1895, Mr. Nischwitz married, at Havana, Illinois, Miss Annie Heberling, who died December 8, 1925, she was a daughter of Warren and Sarah E. (Vail) Heberling. Mr. Heberling came to Illinois from Mount Pleasant, Ohio, and Mrs. Nischwitz was born in Bath Township, and educated in its schools, those of Havana and the Illinois Woman's College, Jacksonville, Illinois. When Mr. Heberling died at Havana, in 1901, he was a member of the firm of Rice & Heberling, implement dealers. There were three sisters in the Heberling family to reach maturity, of whom one survives, Mrs. May (Heberling) Smith, who resides at Seattle, Washington. Mr. and Mrs. Nischwitz had the following children born to their marriage: Sadie A., who is a graduate of the Havana High School, and later a student of Northwestern University; Edmund P., Junior, who was educated in the Havana public schools and Bradley Institute, Peoria, Illinois, and is in the garage business at Havana; Ruth E., who was graduated from the Havana High School and spent two years in the Illinois Woman's College, Jacksonville, a year in the University of Illinois, and is now a teacher in the public schools of Havana; and Katheryn, who was graduated from the Havana High School in 1925.

HON. ADELBERT H. ROBERTS. The only member of the colored race ever elected to the State Senate of Illinois, Hon Adelbert H. Roberts has been a resident of Chicago since 1891, during a large part of which time he has been the incumbent of public offices, including three terms in the Illinois House of Representatives. His career has been a notable one in numerous ways and the high moral standard that he has always maintained has done much to gain respect for his people at Chicago and elsewhere.

Senator Roberts was born at Decatur, Michigan, in 1867, and is a son of W. G. and Parthenia (Winborn) Roberts. He resided at Decatur until he was seven years of age, when the family removed to Lawrence, Michigan, where he attended school. Still later his parents removed to Ann Arbor, in order to give their son the benefit of schooling in the University of Michigan, where he took the literary courses. Thus equipped, in 1891 he located at Chicago and soon thereafter became attached to the Municipal Court. For several years he acted as a bailiff and in other capacities in several branches of that court, and in the meantime was acquiring property and educating his children. In 1916 he was elected as representative in the State Legislature, representing the Third Representative District, and was re-elected in 1918 and 1920, serving three terms in the House of Representatives. In 1924 he was elected state senator from the Third Senatorial District, this district lying in the Second Ward of Chicago and embracing that part of the city extending from Thirty-second Street on the north to Forty-third Street on the south, and from Lake Michigan on the east to near Halsted Street on the west.

In the session of 1925 at Springfield Senator Roberts made quite a notable record. He was chairman of the committee on criminal procedure and a member of a dozen other important committees. Of him, James O'Donnell Bennett, the famous newspaper correspondent, wrote: "The best diction I have heard in the course of two days of Senate debating was that of the colored senator, Adelbert H. Roberts, of 3405 Calumet Avenue, Chicago, chairman of the committee on criminal procedure and a member of a dozen other important committees. He is one of the few senators who ever quotes from anything but a public document. He has frequent recourse to "the words of Charles Sumner," as he

Lee E. Donley.

puts it, and he quotes them tellingly. That great spirit, who suffered much for the race from which Senator Roberts sprang, would be proud if he could hear this able and dignified legislator quoting him." Senator Roberts' hobby as a lawmaker is the maintenance of the highest possible moral standard, both in public and private life. He was taught by his mother an abhorrence of the drinking evil, and from his earliest days has been an advocate of total prohibition. He was one of the leaders in the Legislature in bringing about the ratification of the Eighteenth Amendment. In the Legislature Senator Roberts has been a strong friend of the University of Illinois and has helped to give the University every possible assistance from the state. He has also taken an active part in legislation favoring the mine-workers of Illinois. One of his accomplishments in the 1925 session of the Senate was the adoption of an amendment to the Fugitive Warrant law, designed to prevent injustice and humiliation to alleged offenders sought to be returned from other states. He introduced and was successful in having passed seven bills in the 1925 session of the Senate. Senator Roberts is a member of Quinn Chapel, African Methodist Episcopal Church. He belongs to a number of secret societies, including the Masons and the Elks, and has always taken an active interest in the Young Men's Christian Association, the Young Women's Christian Association and the Wheatly Home for Colored Girls.

Senator Roberts married Miss Lulu Wiley, a native of Illinois, and they are the parents of two sons: Adelbert H., Jr., a graduate pharmacist of the University of Illinois, and Roscoe L., now a student in the same institution.

PETER F. KIMBLE was one of the venerable residents of Springfield, at the time of his death, January 23, 1925, when past ninety years of age, and his associations with the capital city began on the memorable day that this most eminent citizen, Abraham Lincoln was assassinated. Mr. Kimble at his death resided in the brick home at 1004 South Sixth Street, a house he built in 1868, more than a half century ago.

He was born in Lycoming County, Pennsylvania, March 22, 1833, son of Jacob and Mary (MacLaren) Kimble, his father a native of Pennsylvania and his mother of Scotland. His grandfather, Peter Kimble, served as a soldier in the Revolutionary army under George Washington.

Peter F. Kimble was educated in Pennsylvania, and at the age of twenty-three, in 1856, came west to Illinois, locating in Winchester, where for several years he was in the milling and merchandising business. Then, on the April day of 1865 when Lincoln was assassinated he arrived in Springfield, and for a time continued his connection with the grocery business. In 1867 he was elected city treasurer, and reelected in 1868, serving two terms. After retiring from that office he engaged in the paint and wallpaper business, with his store at 421 Adams Street. He carried a large stock of goods representing his line, and was also a painting and paper hanging contractor, employing a large force of men. Mr. Kimble continued active in business until 1902, when he retired.

Mr. Kimble married, October 13, 1857, Miss Sarah Jane Williams, of Winchester, Illinois. One of her grandfathers was John White, of a prominent Virginia family. Mr. and Mrs. Kimble celebrated their fiftieth or golden wedding anniversary, and she died the following year, 1908. Four children were born to their marriage: Ella, who died in 1907, wife of H. B. Prentice; Maie, who died in 1912; Miss Bertha, who has remained at home; and John M., who died in 1916.

Mr. Kimble until his death was a director of the First National Bank of Springfield, and had a considerable investment in farm lands and city property. As a young man he was affiliated with the Masonic fraternity, was a democrat, served on the county Board of Supervisors two terms, 1874-75, and for many years was a faithful member and trustee of the First Methodist Church.

LEE E. DONLEY, who is serving his second term as circuit clerk of Adams County, was elected to that office about a year after he had returned from overseas duty in the World war.

Mr. Donley is one of the native sons of Adams County who gave service at the time of the great war. He was born in Adams County June 26, 1895, son of William J. and Fannie Marshall Donley. His grandfather, Henry Donley, came from Ireland and was an early settler in Adams County. The maternal grandfather, Thomas Marshall, came from England and was also identified with the pioneer settlement of Adams County, living first at Columbus and later in Houston Township. William J. Donley, a native of Adams County, is a retired farmer now living at Quincy. He and his wife had a family of five children, four of whom are now living. Thomas Marshall was one of the adherents of the republican party in Adams County, and for several years was a member of the County Board of Supervisors.

Lee E. Donley acquired his early education in a country school in Hancock County, subsequently attended the Maplewood High School at Camp Point, and finally the Gem City Business College at Quincy.

He was already a member of the Illinois National Guard when America entered the World war. On March 27, 1917, he enrolled for active duty as a private in Company F of the Fifth Illinois Infantry, which was afterwards made the One Hundred and Twenty-third Machine Gun Battalion. As a machine gunner he served throughout the World war period, getting his discharge with the rank of battalion sergeant major on June 5, 1919. While overseas Mr. Donley participated in the Somme offensive, the Meuse-Argonne offensive, and was on duty in the Vaden Line and Verdun Sector. Mr. Donley was with the colors more than two years, and after getting his honorable discharge he accepted a commission as second lieutenant in the Officers' Reserve Corps, and still holds that commission.

On returning home and released from army duty Mr. Donley entered the Gem City Business College for three months to finish studies begun before the war. For a year after that he held a position in the Camp Point Bank at Camp Point. In 1920 he was nominated as a candidate on the republican ticket for clerk of the Circuit Court of Adams County, and in the election in November was given a large majority. He was the youngest man who ever up to that time had been elected in any county office in Adams County.

Mr. Donley justified his election by a prompt and efficient administration of all the duties of his position, and at the expiration of his term was reelected circuit clerk on November 4, 1924. His term expired November 30, 1924. He has been active in politics and in public matters generally; is a member of the American Legion and Lions Club of Quincy, the Masonic Order, B. P. O. Elks, and is an outdoor man, much interested in hunting and fishing and other sports.

He married, March 16, 1920, Miss Daisy Booth, of Camp Point, daughter of Rolla L. Booth. She was educated in the public schools of Camp Point. They have one child: a son, Roger Booth Donley, born in 1922.

JOSEPH W. MCCARTY. One of the very old and honored families of Illinois is one bearing the name of McCarty, and it was established at Dark Bend, Richland County, Illinois, during the pioneer period of this state, and in America by the great-great-grandfather of Joseph W. McCarty, a general merchant of Bath, when this country was still a colony of England. This ancestor came to the American colonies from Ireland and established himself here, and from him has descended a long line of honorable men and women who have played their part in the development of the country.

Joseph W. McCarty, whose name heads this review, was born in Shelby County, Illinois, March 11, 1869, a son of the venerable Union veteran David A. McCarty of Newton, Illinois, the latter born at South Bend, Illinois, in 1837, the son of an Illinois farmer. Although he received but the ordinary education of a farmer's son of his period, he is a very well-informed man, for he has been a constant reader all his life. When war broke out between the states David A. McCarty enlisted in an Illinois regiment of infantry, was assigned to the Army of the Potomac, and participated in the battle of Gettysburg and other notable engagements of the war. After being several times wounded he was taken prisoner, and had the misfortune to be confined in Andersonville prison for eight months, and when he was released after the close of the war he was so emaciated from the rigors of a war prison that he could scarcely walk. His brother was confined in the same prison with him, and he, too, emerged in bad condition from the same causes. When he went back to civil life David A. McCarty resumed farming, which his military experience had interrupted, and continued this line of endeavor until the death of his wife, about 1876, when he left the farm, and moving to Newton, Illinois, worked at general labor as long as his strength permitted such exertion. He never recovered from the hardships of prison life, and still recalls with horror the days spent under Captain Wirz, commandant of Andersonville prison while he was an inmate of that Confederate bastile.

David A. McCarty married first, in Shelby County, Illinois, Miss Rebecca Cook, whose death, as before stated, occurred in 1876. She left the following children: Mary, who is the widow of W. H. Kibler and lives at Newton, Illinois; Edward F., who also lives at Newton; Sarah, who resides at Fountain Park, New Mexico, the wife of W. A. May; Joseph W., who was the second child in order of birth. David A. McCarty has been four times married, but had no children by his last three marriages.

Joseph W. McCarty lived in Shelby County until he was seven years old, when he was taken by his parents to Newton, and that continued his home until he reached the age of seventeen years, and there he acquired his education. When he left home he went to Findlay, Illinois, and for the following three years worked in that locality as a farm hand. For one year he and a brother conducted a restaurant at Findlay, and then they went to Chicago, and were in that metropolis during the World Columbian Exposition. For several months they were employed in the construction of the Administration Building, and were otherwise employed. Coming back to Findlay, the brothers worked for a year as farm hands, and then Joseph W. McCarty went to Olney and for three years was employed in a hotel, and then for a year he was a farm hand in the vicinity of Odin. Leaving Illinois, he went to Bloomington, Indiana, and for a year was engaged in the construction of the Indianapolis & Evansville Southern Railroad. Coming back to Odin, he worked for a year in a hotel, and then engaged in the restaurant business, which was so satisfactory that he remained in it for three years, and when he sold it was at a profit. Going then to Assumption, Illinois, he embarked in the mercantile business, but after two years sold it and returned once more to Odin, where he worked for a year in the coal mines. Going once more to Assumption, he went into business and was doing well when he was visited by a disastrous fire in 1901, which destroyed his stock. Mr. McCarty then bought a hotel and pleasure resort at the La Grange, Illinois, locks, and remained there for two years, and when he sold he moved to Marion County, Illinois, bought a farm and conducted it for a year, and then exchanged it for a stock of goods at Lis, Illinois. Selling that business after operating it for a year, he went to Peoria, Illinois, and there he was in the retail liquor business for a year. When he sold it he came to Havana, and was here in the walnut log business for two years, and for two years more conducted a restaurant. He then went to Oklahoma, and for a year was in the hotel and restaurant business, but was called back to Illinois by the serious illness of his wife's mother. Buying then the restaurant and hotel business owned by George Merrill at Bath, Illinois, he conducted it for three years, then sold it to Roy O'Leary and went to Tulsa, Oklahoma, and for a year ran a cigar manufacturing business. Once more he sold, returned to Bath, Illinois, and was in a hotel, restaurant and bakery business until 1914, when he disposed of the bakery and embarked as a general merchant, handling dry goods, shoes, notions and similar merchandise, and in this branch has built up a very fine trade. Having been actively engaged in some kind of hard work since he was seventeen years old, Mr. McCarty, although now fifty-seven years old, is as active as he ever was, and still puts in every day out of the six at his store, and these are long days, too. He is six feet four and a half inches in height, and his weight is 315 pounds, so he is a magnificent specimen of vigorous manhood, and a commanding presence at all times. In political faith he is a democrat, but he has never cared for public life.

Joseph W. McCarty married first at Odin, Illinois, in May, 1892, Julia Baker, of Tonti, Illinois, a daughter of Orlando and Malinda (Ray) Baker. The first Mrs. McCarty died at Lis in 1904, having borne her husband the following children: Orville Irwin, who resides at Owosso, Michigan; Nernice Minnie, who resides at Havana, Illinois; Evelun Priscilla, who resides at Chicago; and one who is deceased. Mr. McCarty married at Saint Louis, Missouri, February 13, 1908, Mrs. Dora Allen, of Bath, a daughter of John H. O'Leary, a Union veteran, formerly a farmer, but in later life a rural mail carrier, whose death occurred at Bath, and whose remains lie in the Bath Cemetery. The following children were born to Mr. and Mrs. O'Leary: Willis, Nelson, Roy, George, Mrs. McCarty; and Clara, who was also married. By a former marriage Mr. O'Leary had three children: Charles and Ora, both of whom reside at Peoria, Illinois, and a daughter who is now deceased. Mr. and Mrs. McCarty have no children.

LOUIS ANDREW ZEARING. An old and respected name of Bureau County is that of Zearing, which was founded here almost a century ago by sturdy pioneers from Pennsylvania, in which state their ancestors had for generations been people of worth. The family record reaches back to 1725, when Ludwig or Louis Zearing, a native of Germany, found his way to what were then colonial possessions of other nations. His native industry made accommodation to new conditions easy, and his thrift brought him ample wealth for that time. He prospered in the new land to which, perhaps, his best contribution may have been a vigorous line of worth-while descendants that have ever been a credit to the name. To this old family belongs Louis Andrew Zearing, a prominent member of the bar at Princton, and an overseas veteran of the World war.

Mr. Zearing was born at Brooklyn, New York, October 13, 1888, but from the age of thirteen years was reared in Bureau County. His parents were Louis F. and Emily T. (Hazen) Zearing, who had two other children, Joseph H. and Marilda. His great-grandfather, Martin Zearing, was a son of Henry, a grandson of Henry, and a great-grandson of Ludwig the family founder. Martin Zearing was born in Lebanon County, Pennsylvania, July 4, 1794, in 1819 married Sarah Shafer, of Lancaster County, Pennsylvania, and they became the parents of thirteen children, the fifth in order of birth bearing the name of Louis. In 1835 Martin Zearing came to Bureau County, Illinois, on a prospecting tour, and being pleased with the country, in 1836 came here with his family, settling almost alone upon the wild prairie about one mile east of Dover, establishing here a Christian home in the wilderness, the influence of which spread far and wide.

Louis Zearing, grandfather of Louis Andrew Zearing, was born in Cumberland County, Pennsylvania, September 10, 1827. He grew upon the pioneer farm in Bureau County, sturdy and strong in body, but with meager schooling. In 1850, in company with others, he crossed the plains to the gold fields of California, and returned by way of the Isthmus of Panama, landing at New York City. While there he married Miss Jane Cochran, a native of Scotland, and in 1856 they came to Illinois and settled on a farm in Westfield Township, Bureau County. Four children were born to his first wife, who died in 1868: Louis F., Jessie, Margaret and Martin. In 1869 he married Miss Helen M. Whistler, and they had two children, Susan and John P. The family belonged to the Baptist Church, and in political opinion Mr. Zearing was a decided republican, being opposed to slavery.

Louis F. Zearing was born in Bureau County, Illinois, September 27, 1856, grew up on his father's farm and attended the district schools. After leaving the farm he went to Chicago and for some time was a railroad employe, and later lived for some years in Brooklyn, New York. He developed business capacity in several lines, and for twenty years was prominently identified with the broom-corn industry throughout the United States. In 1901 he returned to Bureau County and now lives comfortably retired at Princeton. He married Miss Emily T. Hazen, who was born May 30, 1856, in Stark County, Illinois, a descendant of early English settlers. They are members of the Methodist Episcopal Church, worthy, respected people in every relation of life.

Louis Andrew Zearing completed his public school education at Princeton and was graduate from high school in 1906. Already having definitely decided upon the law as his profession, his special studies in the University of Illinois were in that direction, and in 1911 he was graduated from the university, with his LL. B. degree. In the same year he was admitted to the Illinois bar, opened a law office at Princeton, and in a very short time demonstrated his legal ability and gained the confidence of many reliable clients. To Mr. Zearing, as to hundreds of other ambitious, hard-working, peacefully inclined young American men, the future at that time seemed all in their own hands and prospects bright.

A marked and serious change came to many, however, when their own beloved country became involved in the World war. Mr. Zearing had been reared in a home atmosphere that counted loyalty to one's native land while enjoying her protection as one of the primitive virtues. On August 27, 1917, he volunteered for service in the United States army, and was sent to the Officers Training Camp at Fort Sheridan, where later he was commissioned a second lieutenant of field artillery, Officers Reserve Corps. In December, 1917, he was sent overseas, and in France was placed in the Fifty-fifth Coast Artillery Corps, which bore so important a part in the operations at Chateau Thierry and Verdun during the memorable days of August and September, 1918, leaving shattered Verdun on December 20, 1918. Mr. Zearing at first was detailed as an instruction officer in field artillery, but later spent sixteen consecutive weeks in the front trenches, and in every emergency bore himself with true soldierly courage. He returned to the United States January 22, 1919, and was honorably discharged at Fort Wright, New York, February 14, 1919.

With but little delay Mr. Zearing resumed his law practice at Princeton, where he has since continued, and at present is serving as master in chancery of the Circuit Court of Bureau County. In political sentiment he has always been a republican. He is a Knight Templar Mason and a Shriner, and is a past commander of Princeton Post, American Legion.

In 1920 Mr. Zearing married Miss Gladys Cummings, daughter of J. W. and Luna (Herrick) Cummings, of Princeton, and they have one daughter, Martha Lou Zearing. Mr. and Mrs. Zearing are members of the Methodist Episcopal Church.

J. CLARKE DEAN. Fortunately situated as it is, Chicago has long been an important business center, and the names of many of its prominent business men have become familiar all over the country. They represent commercial enterprises, business sagacity and personal integrity, valuable assets in every land. A well known member of this group is J. Clarke Dean, senior member of the firm of Dean, Onativia & Co., stock brokers, with offices on South La Salle Street, in the heart of the business and financial district, Chicago.

J. Clarke Dean was born on his father's farm in Winnebago County, Illinois, March 13, 1873, the younger of two sons born to Thomas A. and Anna R. (Horton) Dean. Both parents were born in the State of New York. The father died at the age of eighty-six years. When he first came to Illinois, he was one of the pioneer settlers in Boone County. Later he removed to Winnebago County and acquired many acres of valuable land there, and in the course of time became a heavy stockraiser and substantial farmer. In political sentiment he was a republican, both of his sons, Amos C. and J. Clarke, following in his political footsteps. He attended and brought up his family in the Baptist Church.

After his public school course, J. Clarke Dean attended Bryant & Stratton's Business College, Chicago, and after thorough training in business methods, became identified with the Chicago Trust Company, where for eight years, he was manager of the company's real estate department. Upon retiring from this connection, Mr. Dean was engaged for the next sixteen years with the firm of S. B. Chapin & Co., stock brokers, and upon retiring from this reliable old business house, organized his own firm, Dean, Onativia & Co., stock brokers, the reliability and solidity of which commands high financial and stock exchange standing.

Mr. Dean is recognized as a keen, cautious, far-sighted business man. He is a member of the New York Cotton Exchange, the Chicago Stock Exchange, and the Chicago Board of Trade, the Bankers Club and the New York Stock Exchange Club. His other club memberships include: the Congressional Club, of Washington, D. C.; the Racquet Club, the Chicago Athletic Club, the South Shore Country, the Mid-Day, the Midlothian, the Chicago Yacht, the Lake Shore and the Barrington Country Clubs. For many years he has been a member of the Chicago Benevolent and Protective Order of Elks.

Mr. Dean has two children: Frances A., wife of Harry M. Payne of Chicago and J. Clarke, Jr.

DANIEL J. MURPHY as teacher, public official and banker has impressed his personality and influence strongly on the life and affairs of Jersey County, which has been his home for half a century or more.

Mr. Murphy represents the fourth generation of the Murphy family in America. He is a descendant of Hugh Murphy, who came to America immediately after the signing of the treaty of peace between England and the American colonies. At Philadelphia soon after his arrival he witnessed the review of the Revolutionary forces by George Washington just before they were dismissed to return home. He was the only member of this branch of the Murphy family to see the Father of the Country. He lived in Virginia, Pennsylvania, and finally in Ohio, and died in Highland County, that state, in 1842, and is buried at Dunn's Chapel. His wife was Mary Beatty, and among their children were Samuel, John, Daniel and Elizabeth.

Daniel Murphy was born in Frederick County, Virginia, December 3, 1798, and about 1807 accompanied his parents to Western Pennsylvania, and about ten years later the family moved on to Highland County, Ohio, where he married Cynthia Wildman. Daniel Murphy gave all his active years to farming. He finally accompanied his children to Iowa, and he died and is buried in Jasper County, that state. His children were: John W., James, Townsend, Daniel W., Clarissa, who became the wife of James Zink, and Cynthia, who married John Trevits. All of these children moved out to Iowa and spent their lives in that state except James, who was the founder of the family in Southern Illinois.

James Murphy was born in Highland County, Ohio, November 20, 1826. He grew up a farm boy, acquired an ordinary education, and in 1850 he came to Illinois and located in Pike County. During the rest of his life he followed the trade of carpenter, and he died at Pittsfield when about seventy-seven years of age and is buried there beside his wife. He married, after coming to Illinois, Amy Willett, on July 24, 1853. She was born in Highland County, Ohio, November 10, 1835, daughter of John Willett. She died in 1914. Their children were: Daniel J.; Emmett O.; Della, of Rockford, Illinois; Fila A., who died

Jno. P. Blanc   Mary Ann Blanc

at Couer d'Alene, Idaho; and Nora C., wife of W. Frank Cadwell, of Rockford, Illinois.

Daniel J. Murphy was born at Pittsfield in Pike County, Illinois, June 19, 1854, the oldest child of his parents. He was reared and received his early education in that locality, attending grammar and high schools. After leaving high school he spent two years in engineering service and levee work and then attended for one year the old Chicago University, located on Cottage Grove Avenue in that city. Mr. Murphy then came to Jersey County, and for ten years was a high school teacher, the latter part of that time as principal of the high school at Jerseyville. Mr. Murphy in 1886 gave up teaching, becoming a candidate for county clerk, winning the nomination and being elected to office as successor of James Eads. For seven years prior to that, while engaged in school work, he held the office of county surveyor, resigning it when he became county clerk. He was twice reelected and spent twelve years altogether in the office of county clerk. Mr. Murphy in 1926, twenty-eight years after leaving office, again became a candidate for the office of county clerk.

Since January, 1899, when he retired from office, his talents and energies have been chiefly devoted to banking. He became cashier and a director of the National Bank of Jerseyville and later for nine years he was president of the bank. He left the Jerseyville Bank to become cashier of the Granite City National Bank at Granite City and remained there fourteen years, serving also as a director. Since giving up his active responsibilities as a banker at Granite City Mr. Murphy has made his home at Elsah in Jersey County. He is a democrat, having cast his first presidential vote for Samuel J. Tilden in 1876. He never misses an election, and has always been deeply interested in public affairs and politics.

He maried at Elsah, Illinois, November 24, 1881, Miss Theresa M. Reintges, who was born at Elsah March 15, 1858, and died June 13, 1920. Her parents, Peter and Marie (Hutsch) Reintges, came from Germany to America in 1852 and lived out their lives at Elsah, Illinois. Her father was a stone mason. Mrs. Murphy had two brothers, John B., who died at Elsah, and Jacob C., of Granite City, and a sister, Louise Reintges, of St. Louis, and a half-sister, Lezetta Loehr, who became the wife of Charles P. Welsh of St. Louis.

Emmett L. Murphy, only son and child of Mr. and Mrs. Daniel J. Murphy, was born November 24, 1885. He finished his education in the University of Illinois and is now in the metal brokerage business at Chicago. He married Lucia T. Barrett, and they have a family of three children, Robert M., John B. and Margaret G.

JOHN POWELL BLANE, a retired farmer of Greenview, is one of the outstanding figures of Menard County, has spent his life in this locality, and has been connected with its history for the past sixty years. He was born on his present farm, but in another house, July 25, 1845, a son of George Blane, an Irishman, born in County Down, in the beginning of the last century. He accompanied his parents to the United States when they came to this country, together with another son John and a daughter. Subsequently John Blane returned to Ireland, where he remained until his family was reared, and then he came back to the United States and was connected with the fishing industry on the Atlantic coast. It is believed that the grandparents of John Powell Blane of this review are buried on the Blane homestead, and it is known that they died in this locality.

Liberally educated for his times and opportunities, George Blane when he came to Menard County in 1818 at once began to take a prominent part in local affairs. His first winter was spent in Irish Grove, which was named in honor of his being an Irishman, and he soon acquired several hundred acres of land, entering it from the government at the nominal price then charged, and on it carried on grain-raising and the feeding of stock for the market. On account of his superior education and his good judgment he was made a justice of the peace, and for many years he administered the affairs of his neighbors impartially and satisfactorily. Always a friend of education, he backed every movement for the betterment of the educational facilities, and was long a member of the local school board. Whenever there were any legal papers to be drawn he was called upon to attend to the matter, and his advice was sought and usually taken upon almost every subject. First a whig and later a republican, he led his associates in politics. The Christian Church held his membership, and he was equally prominent in religious affairs. His death occurred during the progress of the war between the states, while two of his sons were serving in the One Hundred and Sixth Illinois Volunteer Infantry.

It was after he located in Menard County that George Blane was married, in the Petersburg locality, to Mary Alkire, a native of Ohio, who was brought to Illinois by her parents, and she outlived her husband a few years and is now buried by his side. Her parents are both dead and are buried near their old home in Sweet Water. Mrs. Blane had three brothers, Leonard, John and George Alkire, all of whom married and reared families in this same neighborhood.

The following children were born to George Blane and his wife: Edward died unmarried in young manhood; Arminda, who married James Bracken, died near Greenview; Maria, who married Gilson Payne, also died near Greenview; George W., who married Harriet Cleveland, is deceased; Abner Peeler, who married Lavicia Knowles, is also deceased; Samuel, who was one of the soldiers of the family, was the father of Judge Frank E. Blane of Petersburg; Mary Ellen, who married Sandy Graham, spent her life in this locality; Melissa, who married Harry Graham, also spent many years of her life here and now lives at Mt. Pulski, Illinois; John P., whose life is here presented; and William F., who was the other soldier of the family, married Margaret Scott and died in Iowa.

John P. Blane laid the foundations of an education in the local district school, and later continued the work by attending Eureka

College. Leaving college about the time he reached his majority, he resumed farming, to which occupation he had been reared, and he continued his operations until about 1917, when he retired. Like his father, he found it profitable to feed stock for the market, and he farmed upon an extensive scale. Like many of the men who have the interest of their community at heart, he has served on the school board, serving as president of the board of the Greenview district for twenty-six years, and for a long period he was president of the local Anti-Horse Thief Association, of which his father was the first president. While he is a republican, he does not adhere strictly to party lines, as he prefers to give his support to all things which give promise of benefiting the public generally. Reared in the faith of the Christian Church, he early united with it and is one of the elders in it. During the World war Mr. Blane was one of the food conservators of his district, and holds the certificate issued by the government for his work in this connection.

On February, 7, 1867, Mr. Blane married Mary Ann Bracken, a daughter of Perry and Nancy (Meadows) Bracken, the former of whom came to Illinois from Kentucky and established his homestead near Sugar Grove, Menard County. Mrs. Blane died March 24, 1910, having borne her husband the following children: Ella, who is Mrs. Jay Goodson, of Los Angeles, California, has two children, Blane and Mabel; Carrie, who resides at Greenview, first married Richard Propst, to whom she bore a daughter, Carol Propst, and she is now the widow of Edwin Logan; Lee E., who is a practicing dentist of Centralia, Illinois, was married first to Calara Propst, by whom he had two children, John and Clara Lee, and after her death he married Minnie Gray, and they have one son, Robert; Edna, who married Harold C. Hiatt, of Greenview, has no children; and Mabel died while attending Northwestern University, Evanston, Illinois. One grandson of Mr. Blane, Blane Goodson, is married and has a daughter, Virginia May, the great-granddaughter of Mr. Blane.

On June 26, 1912, Mr. Blane married Miss Hetty Jenison, a daughter of Luther and Hannah (Estill) Jenison, the former of whom was born in the Spring Creek locality of Sangamon County, Illinois, and the latter was born at Lebanon, Menard County, Illinois, he, March 27, 1832, and she, July 28, 1831. They took up land from the government and on it spent their lives. Six children were born to them, namely: Clara, who died unmarried; Perley, who is also deceased; Puss; Huldah, who married Rev. O. S. Baum, and died in Denver, Colorado; Estill, who is also deceased; and Mrs. Blane. The latter was educated in the Jenison school, Lincoln College and Knox College, and was graduated from the last named. She taught for five years the Jenison school, where she had herself been a pupil. In religious faith she is a Presbyterian, and she is not only active in her church, but in civic matters, for she is a cultured, intelligent woman, and one who realizes her new responsibilities with reference to her citizenship, and is striving to live up to them. Both she and Mr. Blane are very popular, and have friends all over the county.

LEEDS MITCHELL, president of the Chicago Stock Exchange, has been a stock broker of Chicago for a quarter of a century, and has had many prominent connections with the business and social life of the city.

He was born in Chicago, April 26, 1877, son of Joseph Sidney and Helen (Leeds) Mitchell. He was liberally educated, graduating in 1895 from Philips Academy of Andover, Massachusetts; took his Bachelor degree at Yale University in 1899, and returning home, entered the stock and bond firm of Otis, Wilcox & Company. From 1902 to 1904 he was with William H. Colvin & Company, and then became identified with Pringle, Fitch & Rankin, stocks, grain and provisions. In 1905 he was admitted to the firm, which in 1909 became Walter Fitch & Company. Since 1914 he has been a member of the firm Harris Winthrop & Company. Mr. Mitchell besides being president of the Chicago Stock Exchange is a member of the Chicago Board of Trade.

His home is in Chicago, and he is well known in organizations for the promotion of sports. His own recreation are tennis and sailing. He is a composer of music, and two of his songs were recently used by Claire Dux in a program representing the work of Chicago composers. He is a member of the K. O. A. Society of Andover; the Book and Snake Society of Yale; the University Club; The Chicago Club, Casino Club, Racquet Club, Onwentsia Club; Saddle and Cycle Club of Chicago, Shore Acres, The Chicago Golf Club, Sankaty Golf Club, Pacific Club of Nantucket, Massachusetts, and the Yale Club of New York. Mr. Mitchell is a republican. He married, July 7, 1910, Dorothy Day, of Lake Forest, and they have two children, Leeds, Jr., age fourteen, and Margaret Mitchell, aged eight.

WILLIAM L. YELLMAN, retired resident of Rock Island, is a native of Kentucky and for a number of years was in the government service.

He was born at Lexington, Kentucky, in 1860, son of John G. and Sophia Yellman, and was educated in public schools. As a young man he took up work with the revenue service in Kentucky. He married his first wife in that state and by that marriage has a daughter, Frances, now Mrs. Ralph Dimmitt, of Pasadena, California.

In 1905 Mr. Yellman and Ann Delia Power were married. Mrs. Yellman is a native of Maysville, Kentucky, a graduate of Harcourt Place Seminary, Gambier, Ohio, daughter of Hugh and Martha E. (Moore) Power, her father a native of Kentucky and her mother of Ohio. Her paternal grandparents, James and Levisa (Campbell) Power, lived at Aberdeen, Ohio, Levisa Campbell being a daughter of Mathew Campbell, a Revolutionary soldier of Scotch ancestry, and his wife Mary (Shelby) Campbell. Mrs. Yellman comes of a long line of Americans. Her maternal ancestors were among the first in Maryland.

Thomas Harris brought his wife, Mary and

his servant John Hamlington into the Province of Maryland in 1650 from England, acquiring a grant from Lord Baltimore their home was called "Harris Land," and a portion of this land is in the family today.

Nicholas Young, Gent. (archives of Maryland) married Elizabeth Bryan and died 1669, leaving land granted to him by Lord Baltimore. Their home was "Cedar Point." He also received a grant which was called "Bullen."

Robert Yates, born in 1656, of London, Gent, merchant in Charles County, Maryland, married Rebecca Young, daughter of Nucholas and Elizabeth, 1688. Robert Yates, Colonial service: Commissioner and Justice in the "tryall" of the Anacostin King," commissioner for laying out the parishes in Charles County, Maryland, 1694-1697, one of the commissioners appointed for the several counties and of the Quorum, 1694-1696-1697-1698, special commission granted, consisting among others Mr. Robert Yates, gent. to be a justice for the ending of all differences inter Beckford Broadbent. Robert Yates was among the signers of the civil officers and Magistrates of Charles County, Maryland, 1694-97, was vestryman of William and Mary Parish, and in his will remembered his Godsons and Goddaughters "provided they were brought to confirmation." His son, Captain Charles Yates, born 1692, received a grant of land "Yates Meadows" in 1721 and another called "The Adventure" in 1731. He married Jane Bryan and lived in Charles County, Maryland. Proceedings of the Council of Maryland, 1752, ordered that Captain Charles Yates and three others, vestrymen of William and Mary Parish, occupy Pew 7 in said church—Maryland Archives—June, 1852. He died in October, 1752.

Elizabeth Yates, daughter of Charles and Jane, married Joseph Gwinn in 1763, descended from John Gwinn, gent., and his wife, Sarah, who came into the province of Maryland in 1663 and 1668, who received a grant of land "Gwyn's Hope," Charles County, Maryland.

Ann Gwinn, daughter of Joseph and Elizabeth Gwinn married Col. Thomas Harris, born 1741, field officer, 1778, "Militia of all the Counties of Maryland," the fifth generation of Harris in Charles County, Maryland. Their son, Gwinn Harris, was pay master of the U. S. Navy at Annapolis, and at the time of his death was president of the Council of Maryland, 1831. Another son, Joseph Harris, was clerk of St. Marys County for forty-seven years, 1796-1843. John Gwinn, Ann Gwinn's brother, was clerk of the General Court of Maryland from the date of its organization, 1777-1805, when the court was abolished. Another son, Thomas, Jr., was clerk of the Court of Appeals of Maryland from 1801 to 1829, and compiled "Harris Laws," a history of the Courts. John Frances Harris, another son, at the age of twenty-one was intrusted with a cargo of tobacco representing the planters along the Potomac, which he sold abroad, bringing home a cargo of merchandise. He married Ruth Tunstall, of Baltimore, 1807, where he lived. At the age of thirty-six he enlisted as a private, 1812, in Captain Addison's Company Sea Fencibles. He was also "Justice of the Peace for the State of Maryland and County of Baltimore, 1816." His daughter, Ann Delia Harris, educated in a convent in Maryland, married Dr. Thomas Miles Moore in 1832, a graduate of the University of Western Pennsylvania, and Baltimore Medical School. They settled in Maysville, Kentucky, later moving to Aberdeen, Ohio, where Mrs. Yellman's mother, Martha E. Moore, was born. Martha E. (Moore) Power after leaving the careful training in her home of a New England governess attended Washington, Kentucky, Seminary and later the Urbana (Ohio) University. In 1869 she married Hugh Power, a merchant of Maysville, Kentucky. To this union were born Ann Delia and Frederick Moore Power.

Mr. and Mrs. Yellman located at Rock Island in 1909. For some years he continued in business as a salesman for the Proctor & Gamble Company of Cincinnati, but now lives retired at his home, 831 Twenty-third Street. Mr. and Mrs. Yellman are members of the Episcopal Church. He is a democrat, while his wife is a republican, and he is affiliated with the B. P. O. E. Mrs. Yellman is a member of the Woman's Club and has been vice-chairman of the Civic Department, is regent of Fort Armstrong Chapter, Daughters of the Revolution, member of the Board of Bethany Home Protective Association, and during the World war was prominent in war camp community work, and a member of the Board of the Woman's Committee Council of National Defense.

WILLIAM M. C. FOSTER came to Chicago at the age of thirteen and immediately cast his complete energies into the life of the city, working out the problems of his own business destiny. Mr. Foster has made a definite success of his career.

He was born in Pennsylvania. It was in 1889 that he came to Chicago. While his school education did not cease at the time, he was paying his own way, having gone to work in the offices of the Chicago Tribune, being at the time the youngest person on the payroll of the Tribune. After several years in the business office he was made a reporter, and out of this experience of his early years he projected his first independent enterprise, the publishing of the Juvenile Magazine, a boys' paper, which became the largest of its kind in the country. From early years Mr. Foster has been interested in boys' work.

It was largely his knowledge of child psychology that attracted the attention of James L. Mead, founder and president of the Mead Cycle Company. It was on the invitation of Mr. Mead that Mr. Foster became a member of that organization. He is now the vice president and general manager of the Mead Cycle Company of Chicago. Thirty years ago this company occupied a prominent position among the many concerns manufacturing and distributing bicycles in the high tide of the popularity of that vehicle. Mose of those companies have gone or have merged their identity with automobile organizations. The Mead Cycle Company is a familiar name to all who rode bicycles before the dawn of the automobile era. It remains today one of the largest, if not the largest, concern in the world of its kind. The main plant and general headquarters are in Chicago, with a branch manufacturing plant at Birmingham, England.

Mr. Foster has had his home for a number of years at Lake Bluff, in Lake County, one of the most attractive of the North Shore communities. Many wealthy and prominent Chicago men have chosen homes in that section. Mr. Foster for several years has been chairman of the Plan and Zoning Commission of Lake Bluff. Under his leadership this commission has been carrying out a scheme of improvement that will insure for all time the preservation of the natural characteristics of Lake Bluff scenery with the added adornment of scientific planning and landscape engineering. Mr. Foster individually has contributed some particular ideas to the development of Lake Bluff's community beautiful, having made a careful study of modern English village developments for that purpose.

Mr. Foster is a charter member of the Illinois Society of the Sons of the American Revolution. He founded and was the first secretary of the Oak Park Chapter of that organization. He is a member of the Chicago Athletic Club and the Machinery Club of Chicago. He married Miss Gladys Thomson, of Scotch ancestry. They have a family of five children, named, Hunter, Charlotte, Gladys, Margaret and William, Jr.

LORAN E. ORR, M. D. One of the able medical men of Menard County and a veteran of the World war, Dr. Loran E. Orr, of Petersburg, is one of the best representatives of his profession to be found in this locality, as well as a citizen of the highest standing. He was born in Pike County, Illinois, near Hull, January 13, 1883, a son of Norton R. Orr, and grandson of Henry Orr, who was born at Kaskaskia, Illinois, the first capital of the state, came to Pike County, and he died at Hull in that county in 1909, at the extreme old age of ninety-two years. He was of Scotch descent, the family in this country originating with three brothers who came to the American Colonies from Scotland, one of them locating in Virginia, one in Kentucky, and a third in the territory of Illinois. Henry Orr married Ann Hull, for whose father the town of Hull was named. She died in 1907, aged eighty-three years, having been several years his junior. They had a large family of children, all of whom survive save the father of Doctor Orr and one who died in early life. Those surviving are: Thomas A., who resides at Bosworth, Missouri; J. H., who resides at Carthage, Illinois; Charles E., who resides at Hull; Ellis, who resides at Greggsville, Illinois; Mrs. James Bond, who resides at Kansas City, Missouri; Mrs. W. H. Lease, who resides at Hull, Illinois; and Mrs. W. H. Long, who resides at Barry, Illinois.

Norton R. Orr was born on his father's farm in Pike County, and was reared and educated in that district. He was a quiet, unassuming man who lived close to the principles enunciated by the Masonic fraternity and the Methodist Episcopal Church, to both of which he belonged. His wife, Catherine Alford, was born at Southington, Connecticut, and was brought to Pike County when she was seven years old, and she was married in that county. Her father, Rollin W. Alford, married Catherine Woodruff, and they were also farming people. Mrs. Orr died in 1909, and Mr. Orr died October 30, 1925, when he was sixty-eight years old. Three daughters and two sons were born to Norton R. Orr and his wife, namely: Florence, who died in infancy; Doctor Orr, whose name heads this review; Mabel, who is Mrs. Edward Colwell, of Hull; Henry A., who lives at Springfield, Illinois; and Catherine, who is Mrs. T. A. Reynolds, of Baylis, Illinois.

Doctor Orr's boyhood environment until he reached the age of nineteen years was that of the farm, but for twelve years he was in the rural regions of Ralls County, Missouri, where he secured his public school training. Later he was a student of Hannibal High School, and he also studied in the Van Rensselaer Academy in the town of that name in Missouri. For two years he was a clerk of the Chicago, Burlington & Quincy Railroad at Hannibal, after which he matriculated in Keokuk Medical College, Keokuk, Iowa, and was graduated therefrom in 1907, with the degree of Doctor of Medicine. In his vacation periods while he was pursuing his medical education he worked in a drug store in Hull, to which place his parents had returned after their residence in Missouri. It was to Hull he returned after his graduation, but after two years of practice there he went to Tallula, where he also spent two years, and then, in 1911, he located permanently at Petersburg, where he has built up a very large and valuable practice.

On August 26, 1917, Doctor Orr entered the Medical Corps of the United States army for service in the World war, being inducted at Fort Benjamin Harrison, Indianapolis, Indiana, and commissioned a first lieutenant. Later he spent three months in Camp Robinson, Wisconsin, in the Artillery Brigade Hospital, from whence he went to Camp Grant, Rockford, Illinois, where he was in the Base Hospital and Officers Training School. On February 26, 1919, he was honorably discharged, returned to Petersburg, and immediately resumed his practice. He is still an officer, with the rank of captain, in the Medical Reserve Corps.

Doctor Orr belongs to the Petersburg Rotary Club, and is a charter member of Kirby Watkins Post of the American Legion, which he served as commander for two years. High in Masonry, he belongs to Petersburg Lodge Number 19, A. F. and A. M.; DeWitt Chapter Number 119, R. A. M.; Saint Aldemar Commandery Number 47, K. T. of Petersburg; and Ansar Temple, A. A. O. N. M. S., of Springfield. He does not belong to any church, nor has he any political affiliations.

On December 27, 1923, Doctor Orr married, in Petersburg, Bess M. Bergen, a daughter of Thomas H. and Cordia (Terhune) Bergen. The Terhune family is another of the old ones of Menard County, where it was established in the '50s. Mrs. Orr was born in Petersburg, and is a graduate of its high school. Mr. and Mrs. Bergen had the following children: Roy

M., who resides at Boulder, Colorado; Mrs. Orr, who is the second in order of birth; Mrs. L. T. Bentley, who resides at Cheyenne, Wyoming; and Mrs. E. M. Nelson, who resides at Petersburg. Mr. Bergen is one of the prosperous citizens of Petersburg, where he was born, and where he now has extensive interests as a stock dealer.

WALTER L. COHRS, a lawyer by profession, but now assistant manager of the Real Estate Loan Department of the First Trust and Savings Bank of Chicago, is a native of that city and his parents, of German ancestry, were early settlers there.

Mr. Cohrs, a veteran of the World war, grew up in Chicago, attending the public schools, and his advanced education was paid out of his own earnings and efforts. He graduated in law from the John Marshall Law School with the degree of LL. B. in 1916, and was admitted to the practice on his return from the Mexican Border Expedition in 1917.

For eight years Mr. Cohrs was connected with the Chicago Title and Trust Company, part of the time in the legal department. Subsequently he was associated with William N. Marshall, attorney for the New York Life Insurance Company, was an attorney with Libby, McNeil and Libby, packers, and in September, 1919, came to the First Trust and Savings Bank of Chicago, where he is assistant manager of the Real Estate Loan Department, and is also assistant treasurer of the First Trust Joint Stock Land Banks of Chicago and Dallas, Texas, all institutions being affiliated with The First National Bank of Chicago.

Mr. Cohrs was for several years a member of one of Chicago's most famous units, the "Dandy First" Infantry, Illinois National Guard, whose honored commander in the World war was Colonel Joseph B. Sanborn. Mr. Cohrs first enlisted in the Seventh Infantry, National Guard, in 1912, was called out for duty during the Cairo floods of 1913, went with the National Guard to the Mexican Border as sergeant-major of his regiment in 1916, and in 1917 was commissioned a first-lieutenant in the One Hundred and Thirty-first Regiment of Infantry, Thirty-third or Prarie Division, American Expeditionary Forces. This regiment distinguished itself on the battle front, and particularly in the Battle of Chipilly Ridge and Gressaire Woods on August 9-15, 1918. The One Hundred and Thirty-first Infantry, attached as a part of the British Army, was called upon to enact the chief part in capturing Chipilly Ridge, a strategic point which had checked the further advance of the British in the Battle of the Somme. After the desperate but successful feat of the Illinois regiment, the great British offensive was finally launched and did not end until the armistice. The battle engagements of the regiment also included Albert, Hamel, Warloy, the Argonne drive and culminated in the drive on Metz when the Armistice was signed. Mr. Cohrs participated in all of these engagements and was one of the officers chosen to represent the American Army at Metz in December 1918, at ceremonies celebrating the taking over of Alsace-Lorraine by the French Government. While his regiment was part of the Army of Occupation in Germany and Luxembourg, Mr. Cohrs was appointed Judge Advocate of the One Hundred and Thirty-first Infantry. Since the war many of the participants in the battle of Chipilly Ridge and former members of the One Hundred and Thirty-first Infantry organized and have become members of what is known as the Chipilly Post of The American Legion, one of the most active and largest Legion Posts in Illinois. Mr. Cohrs is the present commander of that Post, a distinctive honor which he properly appreciates.

Mr. Cohrs is a member of the Olympia Fields Country Club, is a thirty-second degree Scottish Rite Mason and a member of the Delta Theta Phi law fraternity, Chicago Bar and the Illinois State Bar Associations. Mr. Cohrs married Mary E. Willis of Chicago and has one daughter, Mary Virginia.

NATHAN BLOCK is proprietor of the Fair Store at 150 South East Avenue, Kankakee. It is a splendid and flourishing business, long known and patronized by Kankakee people, and some of the older customers are familiar with its progressive upbuilding from the very modest quarters occupied by Mr. Block some thirty-three years ago.

He was born in Eastern Germany, October 15, 1871, and his parents, Jacob and Esther (Bloomberg) Block, lived out their lives in their native land. Nathan Block was twelve years of age when, in 1883, he came to America. His first home was in Dubuque, Iowa, and while attending public school there he was employed in a grocery store. Going to Chicago, he worked five years in a men's furnishing goods store, and made his first independent start in business as a general merchant at Columbus, Wisconsin. In 1893 he returned to Chicago and established a men's clothing and furnishing store at Fifty-second and Halsted streets. He was in that location from August 1, 1893, until May 1, 1894.

Mr. Block then moved his stock of goods from Chicago to Kankakee and displayed his wares in a small storeroom 14 by 28 feet. He was in that location from May 7th to September 1, 1894, when the growth of his business enabled him to take an adjoining room of the same size. The next May he moved four doors away and remained there three years. In the meantime the owner of the first building he had occupied had erected a new store for Mr. Block, a one-story and basement storeroom 32½ by 85 feet. After eight years Mr. Block purchased the building and remodeled it, giving it a 145-foot depth, with a second floor. Another five years passed and he bought the property adjoining on the south, giving him an additional twenty-two feet of frontage. This building he subsequently tore down and built on the ground a structure connecting and harmonizing with his other building. In the growth of this business there were other additions and changes, all marking the steady development of one of Kankakee's most popular department stores. In 1921 he purchased twenty feet adjoining on the north, and then carried out a complete remodeling of the entire frontage, installing new fixtures and improvements, since which date the Fair Store has been one of the best department stores in this part of the state. It handles a complete line of women's ready-to-wear clothing, dry goods, boots and shoes, and children's and men's clothing. Mr. Block for some years has had as his active associates in the business his sons, George W. and Asa R. Block.

He married, January 10, 1893, Sarah Rosky, a native of Chicago. Her parents, Asa and Aga Rosky, came from Russia. The children of Mr. and Mrs. Block are Asa, George, Elsie, wife of Gilbert Goldstein, of Chicago, and Beatrice, wife of Horace Linheimer, of Chicago. Mr. Block and family reside at 519 South Chicago Avenue. Mr. Block is a member of the B'nai B'rith, is a republican, a thirty-second degree Scottish Rite Mason and Shriner, member of the Independent Order of Odd Fellows, B. P. O. Elks, Chamber of Commerce and Kankakee Country Club.

CHARLES D. HENRY, JR., is one of the capable younger men in the legal profession in Kankakee County. He was born in that section of Illinois, and is one of the ex-service men of the World war.

He was born at Kankakee July 9, 1890, son of Charles and Viola Elizabeth (Linton) Henry, of Kankakee. Growing up in his native city, he attended grammar and high schools there, and in 1916 was graduated from the law department of Northwestern University at Chicago. Mr. Henry for about a year practiced at Kankakee.

On December 15, 1917, he joined the colors with the Quartermaster's Corps, went overseas March 18, 1918, and was first assigned duty at the general headquarters at Chaumont, writing checks for General Pershing and other officers. He was then transferred to the chief quartermaster's office, S. O. S., at Tours, France, and finally was made transport quartermaster on the steamship Rotterdam, attached to the debarking office of New York City. He arrived home August 9, 1919, with the rank of second lieutenant.

Mr. Henry since the war has enjoyed a growing practice as an attorney, with offices in the City Bank Building. He was assistant state's attorney of Kankakee County during 1921-22, and is now vice president of the Kankakee Bar Association. He is a Presbyterian, a republican, a thirty-second degree Scottish Rite Mason, member of the B. P. O. Elks, has filled chairs in the Knights of Pythias and for two years was trustee of the American Legion Post. Mr. Henry married, June 4, 1922, Miss Helen Ogilvie, daughter of Lewis and Anna (Hubbard) Ogilvie, of Bowen, Illinois.

W. W. JARVIS is one of the veteran bankers of Southern Illinois, president of the Troy Exchange Bank, of which he was one of the founders nearly forty years ago. Mr. Jarvis has other distinctions in his home county of Madison, being a surviving veteran of the Civil war, and has been an active participant in the business affairs of his home locality ever since.

His family was identified with the pioneer settlement of Southern Illinois. The Jarvises have been in Madison County since the year following the organization and creation of the county. His grandfather, John Jarvis, came to Illinois territory in 1803, his former home having been near Grafton in what was then old Virginia, now West Virginia. On coming to Illinois he settled in St. Clair County, near Turkey Hill, but in 1813 moved to Madison County and acquired an extensive tract of land, including the present Town of Troy. Jarvis Township of Madison County was named in his honor. In addition to farming he established the Jarvis grist mill, which in the early years was the principal institution of the little village of Columbia, which after 1819 was known as Troy. John Jarvis died there October 29, 1823. He married Sarah Gillham, member of the prominent pioneer Gillham family of Madison County. Some reference to this family is made on other pages of this publication. Sarah Gillham Jarvis died December 24, 1858.

Their son, Wesley Jarvis, was born at Troy, Illinois, August 16, 1812, and devoted his active life to farming. He married Mary A. Kinder, of another pioneer family of Madison County. She was born in Edwardsville Township, October 6, 1813.

William W. Jarvis, the fourth of the five children of Wesley and Mary A. (Kinder) Jarvis, was born at Troy, March 11, 1842, and during his boyhood acquired his education in the Troy public schools. In April, 1861, at the first call for volunteers to check the rebellion, he enlisted in the Ninth Illinois Infantry, in Company I, for three months. At the end of this enlistment he reenlisted for three years, and participated in practically all of the one hundred ten engagements credited to the Ninth Illinois Infantry. He was in the Army of the Tennessee, and was wounded at the battle of Fort Donelson and also at Shiloh, and at the battle of Corinth in 1862 was taken prisoner. He was soon exchanged and rejoined his command, and in May, 1863, was again taken prisoner in Northern Alabama while trying to assist General Strait in his raid. General Strait was afterward captured near Rome, Georgia. For a time Mr. Jarvis was held in Libby prison at Richmond, Virginia. He has been an honored member of the Grand Army of the Republic for many years.

Mr. Jarvis after the war resumed his place on the farm, studied law, but in 1868 he and J. A. Barnsback established the first lumber yard in Troy. The next year he became sole proprietor and continued the business until 1876. Selling out his lumber interest, he opened a commission business at the National Stock Yards at East St. Louis, and continued this business for ten years, until he closed it out in 1886.

In the meantime, on August 1, 1885, he and H. H. Padon opened the Troy Exchange Bank. The following year after disposing of his business at East St. Louis Mr. Jarvis took the active management of the bank and in 1887 became its sole owner. The bank was continued as a private institution until July 1, 1910, when it was incorporated as a state bank. Since incorporation the management has continued with the following officers: W. W. Jarvis, president, John Feldmeier, vice president, D. Genevieve Jarvis, cashier. The directors are Mr. Jarvis and his daughter, John

Feldmeier, Charles E. Molden and John F. Deimling. During the forty years this bank has been in existence it has been practically unaffected by any of the financial panics of the country. His daughter, Miss Genevieve, is one of the prominent women bank executives in the state.

Mr. Jarvis has taken little part in politics, though he served as one of the first commissioners of Madison County before the township system was inaugurated. On December 24, 1867, he and Miss Sarah E. Barnsback were married. She was born in Pin Oak Township, Madison County, October 22, 1846, daughter of Thomas J. and Nancy (Montgomery) Barnsback. Her father was a farmer in Pin Oak until his death in 1880. The Barnsback family came to Southern Illinois in pioneer days from Kentucky. Of the nine children born to Mr. and Mrs. Jarvis, there are four now living: D. Genevieve Jarvis and Miss Elizabeth D. Jarvis, of Troy, and Sarah Jarvis Seele and Mabel Jarvis Seele, of St. Louis.

JONATHAN COLBY BEEKMAN. One of the old families, not only of Illinois but the United States, is that of Beekman, and one of its well-known representatives in this region is Jonathan Colby Beekman, of Petersburg, superintendent of county highways and farms, a man of high character and solid business worth. He was born in Menard County, December 16, 1875, a son of John T. Beekman, grandson of William T. Beekman, and direct descendant of Martin Beekman, who founded the family in Somerville, New Jersey, in 1676, coming to the American Colonies from Grosbrucken, Holland. Nine Beekmans served, as officers or privates, in the American Revolution, and the name is found among the legislators of New Jersey. When William T. Beekman came to Illinois from Somerville, New Jersey, in 1838, he brought with him as a guide through the unchartered wilderness a map that had been printed the preceding year in Philadelphia, Pennsylvania, and this old parchment is still well preserved, and a highly prized possession of Mr. Beekman of this review. Settling at Clary's Grove, William T. Beekman developed a farm, and there he died in September, 1891, and his remains lie in Rose Hill Cemetery, Petersburg. His wife was formerly Mary Spears, and she, too, is deceased, and is buried by the side of her husband. Their children were as follows: John, James, Elizabeth, George, Julia, Tenbrook, Annie, Helen, William and Carrie. He was a fine man and one whose advice was sought by his neighbors upon many subjects.

John T. Beekman was born in Menard County in 1843, and he died in this county in 1888, when he was forty-five years old. The district schools and Jacksonville College educated him. In 1862 he enlisted for service in the war between the states in Company F, One Hundred and Fourteenth Illinois Volunteer Infantry, as a private, and was under the command of General Sherman. His was the brigade that the latter loaned to General Banks when he commenced his Red River expedition, and Mr. Beekman participated in that campaign, and in the one against Vicksburg which resulted in its surrender. Subsequently he was in the battle of Spanish Fort, and took part in the capture of Mobile, Alabama. Still later he was detailed to do police duty at Vicksburg, and he was serving in this capacity when he was mustered out of the service. Following his honorable discharge Mr. Beekman returned to his place on the farm in Menard County, and devoted the remainder of his life to farming. He was a staunch republican, and active in party affairs. The Baptist Church held his membership, and he belonged to the Knights of Pythias and the Grand Army of the Republic.

The wife of John T. Beekman, Sarah Colby, was a distant relative of United States Senator Ingalls of Kansas, and a daughter of Jonathan and Lydia (Ingalls) Colby, of New Hampshire, who came to Illinois, and were farming people of Menard County. One of the Colby sons, William, was a soldier in the Union army. Mr. Colby lost his left arm by accident in a threshing machine, but did not allow his disability to prevent him from continuing his agricultural pursuits. In addition to Mrs. Beekman there were five other children in the Colby family: William, Mary, Henry, Maria and Grosvenor. Mrs. Beekman died in 1917, when she was seventy-five years old. She and her husband had two children: Lucy, the widow of T. M. Robertson, and a resident of Petersburg; and Jonathan Colby Beekman.

After an attendance at the district schools Jonathan Colby Beekman entered the University of Illinois and took up the civil engineering course, but left the university during his junior year, and returning to Menard County, began farming, in which occupation he continued from 1896 to 1920. During that period he established himself on his own farm in his home community, and carried on stock and grain raising, becoming a feeder and fattener, and shipping his own stock to market. In spite of the fact that he was a professional man, for a quarter of a century Mr. Beekman was so occupied with his agricultural activities that he did not make use of the knowledge he had acquired, but when he took over the duties of county superintendent of highways, in July, 1924, he discovered that it was of inestimable value to him, and he is proving himself the right man in the office. Succeeding J. M. Weaver in his present office, Mr. Beekman is the third in the county to hold it. This is not the only public honor bestowed upon him, for he has been highway commissioner, treasurer of his township, a director of the local school board, and one of the three directors of the County High School Board, and he has long been active in the work of the Menard County Farm Bureau, which he served as secretary, and during 1925 as president. Like other members of his family he is a republican, and he cast his first presidential vote for William McKinley in 1896. He has frequented local conventions as a delegate, and was a delegate to the Illinois State Convention of his party that nominated Richard Yates, Junior, for governor. In 1917 Mr. Beekman was commander of the Illinois Division of the Sons of Veterans. Made a Mason at Petersburg, he belongs to the local Blue

Lodge, Chapter, Council, Commandery and to Ansar Temple, A. A. O. N. M. S., of Springfield, and he is a member of the Knights of Pythias.

During the late war Mr. Beekman rendered a valuable service by his strenuous farming and stock raising. Registered in the last call, he filled out his questionnaire, but was not classified.

On September 7, 1898, Mr. Beekman married in Petersburg Kate Golden, a daughter of Abram and Sophie (McKay) Golden. Mrs. Beekman was born, reared and educated at Petersburg. Mr. and Mrs. Beekman have one daughter, Pauline.

HARRY E. BEEKMAN, postmaster of Petersburg, is a man whose life has been devoted to the service of the public, and whose conscientious performance of his official duties has always commended him to the favor of the people whom he has served so capably. His family is an old and honorable one of this neighborhood, having been established here by Postmaster Beekman's grandfather, William T. Beekman, about 1835. A native of Somerville, New Jersey, he came to Illinois in young manhood, and married in Menard County, this state, Mary Speers, a daughter of George Speers, a native of Kentucky who had previously settled in Menard County. Mrs. Beekman was born in 1825, in this county, and in it she and her husband lived out their useful lives, he dying in 1899, and she surviving him until 1905, and both are buried in Rose Hill Cemetery, Petersburg. He was ten years her senior. William T. Beekman was a very prominent man. A builder and contractor, and active in politics, he was also engaged in farming, and was superintendent of the Petersburg & Tonica Railroad, now the Chicago & Alton Railroad, which had secured the right of way through this region through his efforts. Much of the earlier building at Petersburg and in its vicinity was done by him, and so well did he carry out his contracts that some of the buildings he erected are still standing. About 1860 he was sent to the Illinois State Assembly to represent Menard County. The following children were born to William T. Beekman and his wife: John T., who was a farmer and Union veteran of Menard County, now deceased; James B., who spent his life as a farmer of Morgan County, Illinois, and is deceased; Lizzie, who married John M. Zane, a resident of Iowa, where she died; George S., who is a resident of Springfield, Illinois; Cornelius T., who is mentioned below. All of the above mentioned children reached maturity, married and reared families, and the others, now deceased, although they were married, had no children, there having been ten children born to these parents.

Cornelius T. Beekman was born at Petersburg, in 1854, and first attended the country schools of Menard County, but later spent several years at Knox College of Galesburg and in Shurtleff College, Alton, Illinois. For some years thereafter he was engaged in teaching school in Menard County. Always active in the local republican party, he was chosen as a member of the Illinois Reception of Illinois at the World Columbian Exposition. Appointed postmaster of Petersburg by President McKinley, he assumed the duties of that office June 1, 1897, succeeding Rebecca Snape, and continued in office until June 1, 1915, when a democratic appointee succeeded him. For many years he was a member of the Petersburg City Council, and also of the Republican County Committee. Still a resident of Petersburg, he is now living in comfortable retirement. Cornelius T. Beekman married Lula Kuechler, a daughter of Dr. C. F. Kuechler, of Springfield, Illinois, but a native of Germany. Mrs. Beekman was born in Springfield, in 1852. The following children were born to Cornelius T. Beekman and his wife: Carl O., who died unmarried in young manhood; Harry Eugene, who was born June 8, 1883, at Petersburg; Ferdinand K., who is a resident of Enid, Oklahoma, a commercial salesman; Meta L., who is a teacher in the public schools of Havana, Illinois; and William T., who is one of the assistants in the Petersburg postoffice.

Harry E. Beekman attended the public schools of Petersburg, and then took a year's work in the Rockford Business College, Rockford, Illinois. Upon his return to Petersburg he entered the postoffice under his father, and remained there continuously until July 1, 1915, during all of that period being assistant postmaster. At the time of his leaving the postoffice Mr. Beekman entered the office of the circuit clerk of Menard County as deputy clerk, serving until March 1, 1918, under Ross A. Nance and Richard B. Ruh. When he retired from this office he became a member of the Securities Commission, known as the "Blue Sky" Commission, under Louis L. Emmerson, secretary of state, and continued to serve on this commission until he was appointed postmaster of Petersburg, and he assumed the duties of his new office March 1, 1922, succeeding H. M. Levering.

In addition to the above-mentioned valuable service Mr. Beekman has been valuable to Petersburg in local undertakings, having served as secretary of the Menard County Fair Association for a number of years, and for a number of years was secretary of the Petersburg Commercial Club. For six years he was a member of the City Council, and while a member of that body during the administration of Mayor H. M. Levering, the sewerage system was installed. Mr. Beekman has also been a member of the Petersburg Library Board. All his life a republican, Mr. Beekman has been very active in his party, has long been a member of the County Central Committee, and for six years he was its chairman. He has attended county and state conventions many times as a delegate, and, like his father, was also honored by being made a delegate to his party's national convention, his service in this respect being given in 1920. The Menard County delegation was instructed for ex-Governor Lowden, but, with the delegation, he cast his vote finally for Warren G. Harding.

Made a Knight of Pythias in Roland Lodge Number 69 of Petersburg, he has risen to high position in that body, and is a past chancellor commander of that lodge, and is now grand outer guard of the Grand Lodge of Illinois,

and frequently attends the conventions of his fraternity. A member of the Presbyterian Church, he belongs to the same church as that of which the father of United States Senator McKinley was the first pastor. Postmaster Beekman is unmarried. During the late war he was registered and classified as A-1, but was not called into the service, the armistice being signed before he was needed. The above record shows a remarkable similarity between the public life of Postmaster Beekman and his father. Both have been connected with the postoffice, and city council; both have been active in the various conventions of their party, and both are men of exemplary habits and life, and both have always cherished a deep faith in Petersburg and Menard County.

ANTHONY BENOIST CABRILLIAC has been a life long resident of Alton, member of an old family of that city, and many objects have benefited by his liberality, particularly his church.

He was born at Alton in 1848, son of Bernard and Julia (Hubert) Cabrilliac. His father was born in Rocquette, France, and his mother in Belgium. Bernard Cabrilliac was brought to America when a boy, and the family settled in Alton when it was a mere trading post on the Mississippi River. For many years he was in the men's furnishing goods business at Alton, and he died at the age of forty-nine. His widow survived him and passed away in 1913. Their children were Hippelette, Mary, Felix, Theodore, Anthony and George.

Of these children only Anthony and George survive. Anthony was educated in the schools at Alton and in the Christian Brothers College at St. Genevieve, Missouri. He and his brother George have been closely associated in a number of business enterprises, and both are now retired. They live at the old homestead, comprising four square blocks of land at 1502 State Street in Alton. They have a pleasant home, and both are noted for their skill in the art of floral culture. Devout Catholics, they gave the beautiful stations to the Cathedral at Alton, and have also been contributors to the Knights of Columbus Home and many other worthy causes in their home community.

SCOTT WIKE LUCAS, state commander of the American Legion, and an attorney of note, is one of the outstanding figures of Illinois, and one of the most honored professional men of Havana. Many honors have been bestowed upon this young man who has not much more than passed his thirtieth milestone on the highway of life. He was born near Chandlerville, Cass County, Illinois, February 19, 1892, a son of William D. Lucas. His paternal grandfather was one of the pioneers of Cass County, into which neighborhood he came with an ox team, being one of its very first settlers. Entering government land, he developed it, and became one of the prosperous men of his times. At his death he was buried in his home community. It was given him to know Abraham Lincoln, and oftentimes he used to relate that he and the President had cradled wheat in the same field. By birth this pioneer was a Tennesseean. He and his wife had other children in addition to William D. Lucas.

Born on the same farm as his son, William D. Lucas spent his life in Cass County and died at Bath, Illinois, August 31, 1923, when he was seventy-two years old. His life was an uneventful one, and he devoted his energies and abilities to farming, with remunerative results. He married Sarah C. Underbrink, a daughter of Ferdinand Underbrink, a native of Germany who came to the United States. His wife was a member of the Murphy family. Mrs. Lucas survives her husband and resides at Cullom, Illinois. The following children were born to William D. Lucas: Mrs. Cora Gerdes; Allen T., Chandlerville, Illinois; Douglas P., who resides at Ajo, Arizona; Hattie, who is the wife of Hardy Altig, of Cullom, Illinois; Dr. J. W. Lucas, who resides at Abington, Illinois; and Scott Wike, whose name heads this review.

His childhood and youth spent upon the farm seven miles east of Chandlerville, and ten miles from New Salem, where Abraham Lincoln spent his early manhood, and where he met his first love, Ann Rutledge, Commander Lucas was reared amid healthful and patriotic surroundings, and was taught from childhood his duty to his country. After attending the common schools of his home district, those of Chandlerville and Bath, he took his high-school training at Virginia, Illinois, and then became a student of the Illinois State Normal School, Normal, Illinois. For two years thereafter he was engaged in teaching school in the rural districts of Mason County, following which he entered the law department of Illinois Wesleyan University, Bloomington, and was graduated therefrom in 1914, with the degree of Bachelor of Laws.

In 1915 Commander Lucas began the practice of law at Havana, and has continued alone ever since, his first client being one who applied for a divorce, and he won the suit in the first term of court which followed her application. His practice is a general one, but he has been especially successful in the criminal branch of his profession.

One of the most noted of his cases was the one tried at Toulon, Illinois, and entitled the People vs. Rollo Spaulding, a murder case. Rollo Spaulding was charged with the murder of a constable in Peoria County, Illinois. He was suspected of having later on murdered his accomplice in the crime. The evidence against him was purely circumstantial. The skull of one of his victims was introduced, the first time in the history of a criminal case in Illinois or the Nation that such evidence was ever used. Mr. Lucas was one of the prosecutors that secured a conviction of murder in the first degree, and the man was sentenced to life imprisonment, and the Supreme Court of Illinois sustained the verdict. The case is reported in the "309" Illinois: Supreme Court Report. After serving a little more than two years of his term Spaulding committed suicide. The skull used in evidence was that of his accomplice who was with him when he killed the constable, and it was identified by the mother of the young man, who recognized her son's peculiar teeth. The manner in which

Commander Lucas aided in handling this difficult case was commendable and Ernest J. Gailbraith, state's attorney of Peoria County, wrote a letter in which he gave Mr. Lucas the credit for securing the evidence that convicted Spaulding.

In 1920 Commander Lucas was elected state's attorney of Mason County to succeed E. P. Nischwitz, and served four years, during which period he made a most remarkable record for the convictions he secured. Very few of the cases he prosecuted were lost. At the primaries he lost the nomination for re-election by forty-six votes, and his competitor in the primaries lost in the general election by 550 votes. Within a month after the successful candidate was elected he died, and the Board of Supervisors appointed Commander Lucas to the vacancy, he receiving thirteen of the fourteen votes. Accepting the appointment, he served in the office for nine months, but then resigned, August 25, 1925, to make the race for the office of commander of the American Legion for Illinois.

In this race he was successful, the Quincy convention electing him, September 1, 1925, as state commander for Illinois of the American Legion to succeed H. P. Savage, of Chicago. He was elected by a large majority, receiving 580 votes of the 769 in the convention. His program is to continue the rehabilitation of disabled soldiers, child welfare work, to stimulate and inspire real Americanism, and to sell the American Legion to the public and to the veterans who are not yet identified with it. Special attention is to be paid to increasing the membership of the Legion, and Commander Lucas is giving personal service to this part of his program.

Commander Lucas is a veteran of the World war, having entered the service as a private, and assigned to duty in the heavy artillery at Fort Screven, Georgia. For a time he was on special duty, taking charge of all the insurance of that camp, but was later transferred to Fortress Monroe, Virginia, and there he was commissioned a second lieutenant of the Coast Artillery Corps. His service was all on United States soil. Following his honorable discharge he enlisted in the United States Reserve Corps, and is now serving his second period of four years.

Commander Lucas is a democrat, as was his father, so that his political sentiments come to him by inheritance as well as conviction. He belongs to Phi Alpha Delta, the Knights of Pythias, the Modern Woodmen of America and the Loyal Order of Moose. Throughout his life he has been much interested in athletics, and while at college he was a football player of note, and was also active in college and league baseball, in class "B" Bloomington and Peoria.

On January 25, 1923, Commander Lucas married, at Chicago, Edith Biggs, of Havana, a daughter of G. A. and Belle (Randal) Biggs. Mr. Biggs is a native of Ohio, who came to Illinois in 1852, and he and his wife were married in this state. Now he is regarded as one of the largest landowners of Mason County, as well as one of its very prominent citizens. Mrs. Lucas was born at Havana, and she is the only child of her parents. Commander and Mrs. Lucas have no children.

There is no doubt but that the American Legion in Illinois is entering upon an era of great prosperity, usefulness and healthy expansion. With a man of the ability and fearlessness of Commander Lucas at its head progress is certain, and work to which the Legion is dedicated is sure of successful execution. Such men as he are born leaders, and the Legion is fortunate in securing his able services. He brings to his work the enthusiasm of youth, trained knowledge and high ideals, and through it he will develop new avenues of usefulness and constructive service.

SAMUEL ADAMS was admitted to the bar and began practice in Chicago thirty-three years ago, and has enjoyed associations with other eminent members of the Chicago Bar and now is a member of one of the leading law firms of the city, Adams and Hawley.

Mr. Adams was born at Syracuse, New York, November 12, 1871, son of Charles True and Emma S. Adams. He has lived in Chicago since early boyhood, acquiring his preliminary education in the University School of Chicago, graduated from Harvard University summa cum laude with the A. B. degree in 1892, and took his law degree at Northwestern University Law School in 1893. In the same year he was admitted to the Illinois Bar. Some of his earlier associations in practice were with the firm of Bancroft and Adams, and Adams and Candee and from June 1, 1911 to March 7, 1913, he was First Assistant Secretary of the Interior at Washington. From 1913 to 1925 he has been head of the law firm of Adams, Follansbee, Hawley and Shorey at 137 South LaSalle Street.

He was professor of law at Northwestern University Law School from 1901 to 1909 and has been identified with a number of organizations and movements of a professional and civic nature. He is a member of the Chicago Bar Association, the Legal and Law Club, the University Club, Chicago Club, the City Club, Harvard Club, Harvard-Yale-Princeton Club, The Celtic Club of Chicago, the Cosmos Club at Washington and American Bar Association. He was president of the Municipal Voters League for three years. Mr. Adams married Miss Louise Koerner of Belleville, Illinois, May 20, 1899. They have one son, Charles True.

RICHARD V. LINDSEY. The roster of educators who have brought honor to the profession in Tazewell County contains many names of deserved distinction. The place which Richard V. Lindsey occupies among these leaders of the educational profession is one of marked credit. During a career that has been devoted whole-heartedly to his specialized calling, he has made steady advancement, and in his present capacity as principal of the Community High School at Pekin he is accomplishing much for the good of the city and surrounding country.

Mr. Lindsey is a product of the Mississippi Valley country of the Middle West, his birth having occurred in Logan County, Kansas, and his parents being Charles E. and Utie (Whitehair) Lindsey. He comes from a family whose original stock located in Tazewell County during the days of its early settlement. Elder James Lindsey, his great-grandfather, founded the first Christian Church at Mackinaw and also started the branch of the same church at Pekin. This old ancestor came from Kentucky to Illinois and rounded out a long, honorable and useful life in Tazewell County, where he now rests in the old Lindsey Cemetery at Mackinaw. His son, Felix Lindsey, the grandfather of Richard V. Lindsey, was born at Mackinaw, but during the "boom" of 1887 went to Western Kansas. Like his forebears he followed the pursuits of the soil, carrying on agricultural operations until his death which occurred in Logan County, Kansas. His wife was Mary Sparks, a daughter of Richard Sparks, and they became the parents of five children, of whom Charles E. was the third in order of birth.

Charles E. Lindsey acquired a liberal education in the Mackinaw schools, following which he further prepared himself for a career by a course at the Illinois State Normal School, at Normal. At the time of his graduation he took up rural school teaching in Illinois, and when his father moved to Western Kansas he accompanied the family and taught in the Western region for some twelve years, rising to principalship of schools in that state and finishing his principalship in the Chapman Public Schools. He then moved back to Illinois and entered railroad service as traveling passenger agent for the Illinois Central Railway Company, a line with which he is still identified. He has had a useful career and is highly thought of by the many with whom he comes into contact during the course of his regular duties. Mr. Lindsey was united in marriage in Logan County, Kansas, with Miss Utie Whitehair, daughter of Joseph and Laura (Dumy) Whitehair, and to this union there have been born two children: Richard Vernon, of this review; and Lora Marie, of Decatur, Illinois.

The boyhood and part of the youth of Richard Vernon Lindsey were spent in the farming country of Logan County, Kansas, and at Chapman, at which latter place he entered high school. Before his course was completed, his parents returned to Illinois and settled at Normal, where the youth completed his high school education. Following this he pursued a course in the teachers department of the normal school, graduating with the degree of Bachelor of Pedagogy. Prior to this he had entered upon his career as a teacher at Mount Pulaski, Logan County, Illinois, teaching there six years as an instructor. He has since continued his studies, working for the master's degree from the University of Wisconsin. Following his work at Mount Pulaski he went to the Sullivan Township High School as an instructor and remained there two years, subsequently returning to his native State of Kansas, where he was an instructor in the high schools of Kansas City two years. Returning again to Illinois, he became principal of the Millford Township High School, a position he held for a period of four years, and when he left that post it was to locate at Pekin to take up his present work. Here the school facilities have been practically doubled under his regime and the enrollment has increased from 450 students to about 600, while the course of study has been reconstructed so as to place special emphasis upon courses in citizenship. As a teacher Mr. Lindsey is a member of the National Association of Secondary School Principals, the Illinois State Teachers' Association and the National Education Association. He is also a member of the Central Illinois State Teachers Association Executive Board. Mr. Lindsey is a Blue Lodge and Chapter Mason, and was reared in the faith of the Methodist Church, to which he still adheres.

On September 25, 1912, at Granite City, Illinois, Mr. Lindsey was united in marriage with Miss Jessie Mae Bramer, whom he met while a student at Teachers College. She is a daughter of George and Ruth Bramer, residents of Keokuk, Iowa, where Mr. Bramer is superintendent of the Elastic Starch Works. Mrs. Lindsey is the eldest of four children, the others being: Mayme, the wife of Sherman Adsie, of Millford, Illinois; Dr. Max, a graduate of the St. Louis Dental College, who is following his profession at Granite City, Illinois; and Harold, who is preparing for the dental profession at the same college. To Mr. and Mrs. Lindsey there have been born three children: Lorraine Evon, aged eleven years; Richard Vernon, Jr., aged nine years; and Robert James, aged one year.

THOMAS Z. BELL, one of the enterprising business men of Saidora, has established himself in the confidence of the public as a grain buyer, and his operations, which are extensive, form an important factor in the commercial life of this city and county. He was born in Bath Township, Mason County, August 18, 1871, a son of George Bell, and grandson of Thomas Zedic Bell, the founder of the Bell family in Mason County, where he was one of the very early settlers. He came here from Kentucky, and brought his family with him. His wife's maiden name was Finch, and both of them died in this county and are interred in the country cemetery near their old home. Their children were as follows: Mary, who married John Daniels, died in Bath Township; Amanda, who married Thomas L. Goben, died in this county; Robert, who is deceased, spent his life in the Saidora neighborhood; and George was the last-born of the family. Thomas Zedic Bell was formerly married and had children by his first wife, but they were never identified with Mason County.

George Bell was born in Mason County in March, 1843, and he was reared on the farm, and given such educational opportunities as fall to the lot of a farmer's son. He made a great success of farming, to which he devoted his life, and became the owner of 2,000 acres of land around Saidora. Grain raising was his specialty, and he also was successful in marketing it. Although a public-spirited man, he could not be induced to hold office. A man of generous impulses, he was very liberal in his donations to different purposes, especially to the local churches, although he did not belong to any of them. No man stood any higher in popular esteem than he, and when he died, in 1913, his community lost one of its best citizens, and the sense of loss was general. His widow survived him five years. They are buried in Fairview Cemetery near Saidora. Mrs. Bell was Rosa Johnson, a daughter of John and Rosa (Adkins) Johnson. Mr. Johnson came to Illinois from Tennessee, and was a farmer of Lynchburg Township, but Mrs. Bell was born in Bath Township, in 1848. The children born to George Bell and his wife were as follows: Charlotte, who is unmarried, and is operating the old homestead; Clara, who is the wife of A. J. Dadisman, and lives at Denver, Colorado; Thomas Z., whose name heads this review; Jade J., who is a farmer of the Saidora neighborhood; Delbert Cress, a farmer of Kilbourne; Arthur O., a farmer and merchant of Saidora; Ira A., who is a farmer of Mason County, his farm being in the Easton neighborhood; Elizabeth, wife of H. A. Abbott, of Lynchburg Township; Mary A., who is unmarried, a school teacher in the public schools of Denver, Colorado; and Charles Raymond, who is a farmer of the Saidora neighborhood.

Thomas Z. Bell, like his father, was reared amid rural surroundings and attended the local schools, but he supplemented the instruction he received in them with a course in the Jacksonville Business College, from which he was graduated. Mr. Bell began his career as a farmer, but while still a young man commenced buying grain, and out of modest beginnings he has built up a very large enterprise. His elevator at Saidora has a capacity of 20,000 bushels of grain, and for every year for nearly a third of a century he has bought grain over a wide area. For fourteen years he was agent of the Chicago, Peoria & Saint Louis Railroad, but retired from that service some years ago. After many years' connection with the agricultural interests of the county he retired from the farm, and now devotes his entire time to his other enterprises.

As a citizen of the community in other fields he has been identified with the schools as a board member thirty-three years, and he was one of the judges of election when the community high school at Bath was voted upon favorably. For some eighteen years past he has been supervisor of Bath Township, and still holds that office, and while holding it he voted for the bond issue of $55,000 for the construction of the Springfield-Peoria Highway, the state agreeing to pay back this amount to the county, and this has been done. Other matters of moment appearing before the board have received his support, and his influence is recognized as a potent one in county affairs. As chairman of the local committee having in charge the saving of the Chicago, Peoria & Saint Louis Railroad to this section, he rendered a very efficient service, and assisted in raising the $20,000, the quota of the county for the rehabilitating of the road. He has always taken an active part in local politics as a democrat, and in earlier days used to carry the banner of his party in the different state conventions. He was at the convention that nominated Altgelt for governor, and he was also a member of the convention that nominated Judge Jones for governor in 1924. During the World war Mr. Bell was the secret advisor of the exemption board of Mason County, and he was on the registration board of his precinct during the period of the war. In all of the drives for different war purposes he took a determining part. He belongs to Chandlerville Lodge, A. F. and A. M. While he is not a member of any religious organization, his wife belongs to the Methodist Episcopal Church of Jacksonville.

On September 27, 1923, Mr. Bell married at Jacksonville, Illinois, Margaret M. Wolfe, who was born at Pittsburgh, Pennsylvania, in 1892, and was there reared. She accompanied her parents when they came to Illinois and settled at Jacksonville. Entering training for the profession of a nurse at the Passavent Memorial Hospital, she was graduated therefrom, and was engaged in her calling until her marriage. During the war she was in the service, and was stationed at Camp Grant, Rockford, Illinois. She belongs to the local post of the American Legion, being the only woman member in Mason County. Mrs. Bell is one of a family of four children, the others being: Mary, who is married and lives in Pennsylvania; Robert Wolfe, who lives at Ramsey, Illinois; and Lottie, who is the wife of John Jones, and resides at Los Angeles, California. It is a source of great pride to Mr. Bell that he belongs to one of the pioneer families of his native state, and that it has been his privilege to bear his part in the further development and advancement of this great commonwealth.

GEORGE WOODRUFF. In banking circles of Chicago today there is no more forcible, capable or energetic figure than George Woodruff, vice chairman of the National Bank of the Republic. Mr. Woodruff represents the third generation of a family of Illinois bankers, and being trained in every department of finances, he has long held a secure and recognized position among the men who handle and conserve the monied interests of individual and corporation and has contributed immeasurably to the banking history of city and state.

Mr. Woodruff was born at Joliet, Illinois, in 1881, and is a son of Frederick William and Nellie (Davis) Woodruff. His grandfather, George Woodruff, was born at Watertown, New York, and in 1836 made his way overland to Joliet, Illinois, at that time a little settlement containing five log cabins. He immediately became one of the constructive factors in building up the community, growing with its growth and prospering with its prosperity. He organized the Joliet Bank, of which he was president, and in 1864 converted the Joliet Bank into the First National Bank of Joliet, of which he was president up to the time of his death in 1882. He was also the organizer of the Joliet Gaslight Company and of the Union Elevator Company, and in numerous ways contributed to building up what is now one of the state's thriving and enterprising cities.

Frederick William Woodruff was born at Plainfield, Illinois, in 1841, and received his education in the public schools of Joliet and a

preparatory school at Aurora. His early banking experience was gained in the Joliet Bank under his father, and when the First National Bank of Joliet was founded he became its cashier, a position which he held up to his father's death in 1882. At that time he succeeded his father in the presidential position and continued as its incumbent until his own demise in 1906. He was one of the well known bankers of Joliet and had numerous other interests. Mr. Woodruff married Miss Nellie Davis, who was born at Brooklyn, New York, in 1849, their marriage occurring at Rockford, Illinois, in 1880. They became the parents of four children, all living, of whom George is the eldest.

George Woodruff attended the public schools of Joliet, following which he pursued a course at the University of Michigan, at Ann Arbor, and in 1903 completed a law course at Yale. He was admitted to the Illinois bar during the same year, but preferred banking to the legal profession, and accordingly made a trip to Europe, where he made a study of banking methods in England, Germany and France. On his return he was made assistant cashier of the First National Bank of Joliet, of which he became vice president in the following year, and in 1907, when he assumed the presidency after the death of his father, was the youngest national bank president in the United States. Under his administration the assets of the First National Bank of Joliet increased from a few hundred thousand dollars until the institution became the largest bank in Illinois outside of Chicago. In 1909, in the interest of a group of international bankers, Mr. Woodruff inspected all the railroads of China and all of the mileage of the Trans-Siberian Railroad, and in the following year visited every country in South America for a group of American bankers who were interested in establishing branch banks in foreign countries.

The year 1911 saw him rendering further service when he rewrote the constitution of the Illinois Bankers Association, which finally resulted in the abolition by the Legislature of private banks in Illinois, and in 1912 he organized at Joliet the first farm loan bank in America to loan money to farmers on the amortization plan. The year 1913 was a busy one for Mr. Woodruff, as he represented the American Bankers Association and appeared before the Senate Committee in connection with the drafting of the Federal Reserve Law, and having visited the principal European cities and countries as a member of the Rural Credits Commission sent abroad under the Taft administration was called upon to assist in the drafting of the Federal Farm Loan Law. During 1915 and 1916 he was president of the Illinois Bankers Association, and in 1917 served as a member of the Executive Committee of the Liberty Loan organization for the Seventh Federal Reserve District. In 1919 he was the founder of the Illinois State Chamber of Commerce, of which he was elected president for two years, and in the following year visited the principal commercial countries of Europe in behalf of this body, while in 1921 he represented the same body in conference with business leaders in China and Japan.

In 1922 Mr. Woodruff was elected vice president of the National Bank of the Republic of Chicago, and during the following two years the assets of that institution grew from $28,000,000 to approximately $50,000,000. In 1923 Mr. Woodruff was advanced to the presidency, and when the merger of the National City Bank with the National Bank of the Republic was completed in 1924 he became vice chairman of the merged institution, with assets of $100,000,000. He still retains his interests in Joliet as chairman of the board of the First National Bank of Joliet and of the Woodruff Securities Company. For many years Mr. Woodruff has been a contributor to the pages of various financial publications. Despite his numerous business and financial cares Mr. Woodruff appreciates the value and worth of recreation and the companionship of his fellows, and is a popular member of the Union League, City, Mid-Day, Attic, Chicago Yacht, Harvard-Yale-Princeton, Saddle and Cycle, Racquet, University and Bankers Clubs.

On October 21, 1915, Mr. Woodruff was united in marriage with Miss Louise Lentz, who was born at Norfolk, Virginia.

A. U. BARCO is a prominent member of the Madison County bar, with offices in the Citizens Bank Building, Edwardsville, Illinois. He has been a practicing attorney for fourteen years, and is one of the most scholarly men in his profession in Madison County.

Mr. Barco was born in Nameoki Township, Madison County, Illinois, December 25, 1883. His father, Harrison Barco, is the third son of Dempsey Barco and Elizabeth Ann (Stallings) Barco. His grandfather, Dempsey Barco, was born in Bedford County, Tennessee, on December 15, 1828, who was the fifth child of Peter and Clowey (Cooper) Barco, natives of North Carolina. His great-great-grandfather, Abram Stallings, fought in Washington's army from Virginia in the Revolutionary war. Mr. Barco's great-grandfather, Henry Stallings, was born in St. Clair County in 1800, and was one of the early settlers of Madison County, after whom Stallings Station, on the Toledo, St. Louis & Western Railroad, now a part of the N. Y., C. & St. L. Railroad (Nickel Plate System), the Illinois Central and the Litchfield & Madison Railroads.

Mr. A. U. Barco's mother was Anna Marie Mestree (nee Steer), who came to this country in the late '40s as a young lady, when she met William Mestre, one of the officers of the ship in which she crossed the Atlantic Ocean, and later married. His grandfather, William Mestre, came to this country from Spain, owing to his objections to the form of government and the persecutions in that country. His grandmother came from Schleswig-Holstein.

Mr. Barco was educated in the Edwardsville public schools, and subsequently pursued his higher education in McKendree College, in Ohio Wesleyan University, in the University of Chicago, and Northwestern University Law School. He holds the classical degree A. B., and his professional degrees are LL. B. and LL. M. He was admitted to the Illinois bar April 2, 1913, and at once engaged in practice at Edwardsville. In addition to his general practice of the law he has served as master-in-chancery of the Circuit Court of Madison County, and as inheritance tax attorney for the State of Illinois under Attorney General Brundage.

During the World war he served his country in the United States Naval Reserve Forces. By virtue of his ancestry he is a member of the Illinois Society of the Sons of the American Revolution. Mr. Barco was a delegate to the caucus at St. Louis, Missouri, to project the organization of the American Legion. He was organizing adjutant of St. Louis Post No. 4 of the American Legion, and the Honorable Dwight Filey Davis, the present secretary of war, was organizing commander when this post was instituted.

He has been a Master Mason in Edwardsville Lodge No. 99, A. F. and A. M., since August 10, 1914, and is a member of the Phi Gamma Delta college fraternity, the Loyal Order of Moose, a Royal Arch Mason, a Scottish Rite Mason, a member of the Order of Eastern Star, and the Ainad Temple of the Shrine. He is unmarried.

WILL HARTWELL LYFORD, Chicago attorney, whose practice has been chiefly identified with railway corporations, has been a member of the Chicago bar since 1884.

He was born at Waterville, Maine, September 15, 1858, son of Oliver Smith and Lavinia A. (Norris) Lyford. His parents were natives of Maine, his father born in 1822 and his mother in 1825. She died in 1905 and he passed away in 1914, at the age of ninety-two. They had six children, two of whom died very young and the other four are still living. Oliver Smith Lyford was long a prominent figure in railway circles in the Middle West. After getting his education in his native state, he was connected with the Boston Market for a short time and then became baggage master with the Boston & Providence Railway, served as a superintendent with the Erie Railway Company and, coming West, was general superintendent for the Hannibal & St. Joseph Railway and later spent some time with the old Kansas Pacific Railway as general superintendent. In 1877 he located at Chicago as general superintendent for the Chicago & Eastern Illinois Railroad Company. Later he became vice president and general manager of the Chicago & Eastern Illinois, and was active in the service until he retired at the age of ninety years. He was a republican and all his life an active Baptist.

Will Hartwell Lyford finished his education at Colby College, Waterville, Maine, and at the age of twenty began his career in railroad service. He was assistant engineer with the Chicago & Eastern Illinois Railway Company during 1879-80; was stenographer to the general superintendent in 1881-82; was chief clerk to the general manager in 1882-83; was claim agent, 1883-84. In the meantime he studied law, was admitted to the bar in 1884, and at once joined the legal staff of the Chicago & Eastern Illinois Railroad Company. He was assistant general solicitor from 1884 to 1887; attorney in charge of the law department, 1887-89; general solicitor, 1889-92; general counsel from March 15, 1892, to 1913. During the receivership of the road he acted as general counsel for the receivers from 1913 to 1921. Of the new Chicago & Eastern Illinois Railway Company since the discharge of the receivership he has acted as vice president and general counsel since January 1, 1922. Mr. Lyford for a number of years was associated in practice with the law firm of Calhoun, Lyford & Sheean, the senior member of which was William J. Calhoun, one of the most brilliant lawyers of the Middle West and former American minister to China.

Mr. Lyford is a Phi Beta Kappa, Delta Kappa Epsilon, and is a member of the various bar associations; the Chicago, Union League Club, South Shore Country Club and Chicago Golf Club, of Chicago; the Metropolitan Club and Sleepy Hollow Country Club of New York; and Columbia Country Club of Washington. Mr. Lyford's home is at Wheaton, Illinois.

He married, April 28, 1886, Miss Mary Lee MacComas of Nebraska City, Nebraska. They have two children: Gertrude Wells is the wife of Edward R. Boyd and a resident of Ayr, Scotland. Mr. and Mrs. Boyd have two children. The son, Calhoun T. Lyford, graduated from Yale University in 1917, at once entered the Officers Training Camp at Fort Sheridan, was commissioned a first lieutenant in the quartermaster's department and after about a year as an instructor in home camps was sent overseas and was on duty on the front lines up to the armistice. He is now in business in New York City.

HON. HARRY A. LEWIS. A member of the Chicago legal profession since 1890, and for the greater part of the time from 1901 to the present the incumbent of official position, Hon. Harry A. Lewis, judge of the Superior Court of Cook County, is one of the best-known members of the bench. His career has been one in which fine legal abilities, combined with hard work and conscientious devotion to the best interests of the responsibilities which he has been called upon to assume, have resulted in gaining him a position of preference and the general esteem of the community.

Judge Lewis was born August 20, 1869, in the little village of Berwick, Warren County, Illinois, and is a son of John Vorhees and Esther (Huminston) Lewis. His father, who was born in New Jersey, in 1825, left his native state in young manhood and made his way to Cincinnati, where he joined James U. Tyner, who was later attorney general of the United States, with whom he drove through overland by wagon to Chicago, hunting pigeons en route. When they arrived in the small but ambitious and growing community, their team of horses met with the approval of a former settler, who offered to trade for the horses a section of land on the lake front, bounded by what would be now State Street on the east and Van Buren Street on the north. They could not, however, foresee the great growth that was to make this city the great metropolis that it has since become. In fact Mr. Lewis was not favorably impressed with the little city, and in 1852 went to Berwick, Illinois, where he was one of the pioneers in the confectionery business. He served as postmaster of that community for several years, and in politics was originally a whig and later a republican. A life member of the Thousand and One Lodge, A. F. and A. M., when he died in 1897, he was accorded the honor of a Masonic burial. At Hamilton, Ohio, Mr. Lewis was united in marriage with Miss Esther Huminston, who was born in the State of New York, in 1822, and died in 1891, and they became the parents of twelve children, of whom three are living.

The youngest of his parents' children, Harry A. Lewis, attended the public schools of Warren County, and after graduating from the Abingdon High School, entered Elliott College, Burlington, Iowa, from which he was graduated with the class of 1888. He took his degree of Bachelor of Laws from the law department of Northwestern University, and at once took up his residence at Chicago, where he engaged in the practice of law. His talents became formally recognized in 1901, when he was appointed assistant state's attorney, an office which he held until 1904, then becoming county attorney of Cook County. Leaving this office in 1911, he again engaged in general practice with much success until 1919, when he was elected judge of the Superior Court of Cook County, an office which he has since retained. In the prompt and wise performance of his present duties Judge Lewis has demonstrated that he is equal to the responsibilities of any judicial elevation which may come to him. He is a thirty-second degree Mason, belonging to all the bodies of that ancient and honorable order, and also holds membership in the Hamilton Fraternity and Chicago Clubs. His religious membership is in the Englewood Baptist Church, and his political support is given to the republican party.

Judge Lewis married, June 18, 1895, Miss Nellie Fenn, who was born in Ontario, Canada, and they are the parents of three daughters: Ethel M.; Esther Louise, the wife of Charles Howard Fetman; and Alberta F.

HENRY COLLINS HAY for some years has been engaged as a consultant on federal tax matters. He is now member of the firm Snyder & Hay, with offices at 307 North Michigan Boulevard, Chicago, specializing in federal tax problems and reorganization.

Mr. Hay was born at Springfield, Illinois, September 30, 1890, son of Nathaniel and Kate (Ridgely) Hay. His father was born at LaGrange, Missouri, November 3, 1857, and died February 9, 1915. His mother was a native of Springfield, and died in 1895. There were three children, Eleanor, Howard and Henry C. Nathaniel Hay for a number of years acted as purchasing agent for the University of Illinois, and was holding that position at the time of his death. He was a Knight Templar Mason and a republican.

Henry Collins Hay attended public schools in Springfield, including high school, and in 1913 was graduated from the law department of the University of Illinois. In the same year he went West, was admitted to the bar in Colorado, and practiced law at Grand Junction in that state until 1917. He then removed to St. Louis, Missouri, was admitted to the Missouri bar, and practiced in St. Louis until 1921. He then removed to Chicago where he has resided since 1921.

Mr. Hay is a member of the Union League Club, Chicago Yacht Club, Evanston Golf Club and is a member of several fraternities, including the Phi Kappa Psi and Phi Delta Phi. He is a republican in politics. He married February 6, 1915, Miss Josephine Bainbridge, a native of St. Louis, Missouri. They have one son, Collins.

FREDERICK A. HERRING. Probably there is no better-known man or one who is more highly respected throughout Mason County than Frederick A. Herring, one of the retired farmers residing at Bath, in whose environments he finds the surroundings which suit him, and the companionship of warm personal friends. His wealth, which is carefully invested, provides him with all of the comforts and some of the luxuries of life, and affords him the means for generous donations, many of which are not known to the general public. He was born on his father's rented farm in Mason County, May 30, 1864, a son of John Herring.

John Herring was born at Salisbury, Cornwall, England, August 21, 1833, one of a large family of children. One of his brothers immigrated to Australia, accompanied by a sister. Another brother, William, followed John to the New World, settled in southwestern Missouri, and died at Billings, that state, where his descendants are still to be found. In 1857 John Herring, then a young man just entering upon the responsibilities of maturity, a farmer by experience, left England for Canada, and there he married a French-Canadian, and two years after his arrival in Canada he came to the United States and settled in Mason County.

With no capital but a pair of willing hands and the determination to work and save, John Herring first labored as a farm hand for fifty cents a day. In spite of that small wage he and his wife were so thrifty and such good managers that they accumulated a little money, enough to enable him to begin farming on rented land. The last farm on which he worked for wages was the Campbell farm. Even after he secured a farm as a renter the strictest economy was necessary, and the first pair of shoes worn by the eldest child was made by his young mother.

The aim of this young couple was land of their own, and in the course of time the first piece of land was bought from Mr. Whitehead; later more was bought from Mr. Fletcher, but he continued to rent until he had acquired considerable land of his own. At the time he bought it his land was unimproved, chiefly prairie, although there was some semi-timbered acreage, which he cleared. The first home on the farm was a three-room frame house, which was subsequently enlarged to meet the needs of the growing family, but this was finally replaced by the substantial residence, now standing, which is occupied by one of the prosperous farmers of Mason County. On that farm he and his excellent wife completed their life span, and achieved their success, which was represented by 400 acres of valuable land, and other material possessions, and the esteem of their fellow citizens. John Herring was without ambition for public life, and led a quiet existence. His vote was cast for the candidates of the republican party. A Baptist, he became one of the active workers of Mount Zion Baptist Church. His death occurred May 8, 1897, but his widow survived him many years, passing away November 26, 1911. She, too, was zealous as a member of Mount Zion Baptist Church, and left her impress upon the spiritual life of her community. Both she and her husband are buried in Fairview Cemetery near their old home.

The following children were born to John Herring and his wife: Herbert, who is a resident of Iowa City, Iowa; Frederick A., whose name heads this review; Mary, who married Richard Adkins, and resides at Beardstown, Illinois; and John A., who is a resident of Lynchburg Township, Mason County.

Frederick A. Herring was reared on the homestead, and went to school whenever he could do so, but as there was plenty of work on the farm he had but little time for study. After he reached his majority he rented land in his home community, and it was ten years before he invested in land of his own. He then bought 205 acres of land that he still owns, and although there were improvements upon it he has added others, and built a residence that is one of the best in the whole neighborhood, and barns and outbuildings. To his original purchase he kept on adding until he owned 600 acres, on which he carried on mixed farming. In addition to grain he raised hogs and cattle and made butter for the market, selling forty pounds of it each week for years. He raised about every kind of product common to this region, and this diversified farming was very profitable. He and his wife worked early and late in order to achieve success, and their industry and thrift accomplished results which are most satisfactory. During the period of their hardest struggles prices for farm products were very low, twenty cents a pound for butter and seven cents a dozen for eggs prevailing. Even a market was difficult to find, and Mrs. Herring used to walk in Havana from house to house seeking purchases for her chickens at twenty-five cents each. In the course of time, however, better prices were secured, and they were able to take things more easily. Until 1913 they continued actively in control of the farm, but in that year they moved to Bath. However, Mr. Herring still keeps in touch with the farm, where his only son lives, and during rush periods enjoys going into the fields once more and bringing his experience and good judgment into play.

Aside from serving as treasurer of his rural school district, the Patterson, he has declined office. In 1888 he cast his first presidential ballot for Benjamin Harrison, and has clung to the same party faith through life. Reared a Baptist, he joined the Hopewell Baptist Church at Snicarte, Illinois.

On February 4, 1891, Mr. Herring married, in Kilbourne Township, Mason County, Emma C. Ermeling, a daughter of Gerhard and Mary Louisa (Dierks) Ermeling, the latter of whom was a daughter of Peter Napoleon Dierks, who came from Holland to the United States and established himself within three miles of Havana. His wife was a distant relative, and she was born in Hanover, Germany. Mr. Ermeling died April 19, 1909, when he was nearly seventy years old, and his wife died April 1, 1918, when she was nearly seventy-eight, as she was born June 30, 1840. There were fourteen children born to them, of whom twelve reached maturity, namely: Jennie, who married William Butler, and is deceased; Mrs. Herring, who was born February 25, 1864; Rose; Martin, who resides at Bath, Illinois; Mrs. Clara Underbrink, who resides at Archie, Missouri; Elizabeth, who resides at Springfield, Illinois; Mrs. Matilda Layman, who resides at Havana, Illinois; Mrs. Eliza Krebaum, who resides at Havana; Mrs. Catherine Holzgrafe, who resides at Havana; George and Edward, both of whom reside on the home place; John and Esther of Havana.

Mr. and Mrs. Herring have one son, Henry Harrison Herring, who was born November 21, 1891. He was reared on his father's farm, and has always been engaged in agricultural pursuits. His education was obtained at the Patterson school. While he was registered for the World war, he was exempted as he was regarded as being more useful in his work as a farmer than he would have been in the service. He married Ina Bernice Bridgeman, a daughter of Frederick and Mary Bridgeman. There were eight children in the Bridgeman family. Mr. and Mrs. Henry Harrison Herring have four children: Daun Carl, Ava Esther, Howard J. and Betty Francis.

HENRY BOWERS is undoubtedly one of the best known citizens of Pike County. His career there has been one of varied service, including educational work. He held a county office eight years, and during the past decade he has taken up a new line of work and made a splendid success therein, the insurance business. He is one of the representatives in Illinois of the Northwestern Mutual Life Insurance Company of Milwaukee, Wisconsin.

His father, Jacob D. Bowers, was born in Pennsylvania and was left an orphan at an early age. He had two brothers, Henry and John, and a sister, Margaret, who married Rev. Mr. Lucky, of Oconee, Illinois. Jacob D. Bowers came from Shelby County, Ohio, about 1860, crossing the country, and stopped first near Bloomington where his brother John lived. Subsequently he joined a threshing machine outfit which took him into Pike County, and Jacob D. Bowers remained, doing farm work and other manual labor, and finally engaged in farming for himself. At Pleasant Hill, Illinois, he married Nancy J. Stone, daughter of Nathan Stone. She was born in Kentucky and was brought to Illinois when ten years of age. Jacob D. Bowers spent the rest of his life in the Pleasant Hill community, and he and his wife are both buried in the Venable Cemetery. He died in early life, and his wife survived him until July 7, 1897, being sixty-seven years of age when she died. Her last years were spent at the home of her son Henry in Pittsfield. Her children were: Belle, who died in girlhood; Henry; George, of Hammonton, California; Elle, who died in child-

C. H. Keiling,

hood; and James L., who died when a boy, having been poisoned from eating the deadly nightshade.

Henry Bowers, son of Jacob D. Bowers, was born February 13, 1864. He grew up on a farm, was only nine years old when his father died, and as a youth he assisted his mother, working three years as a farm hand at ten dollars a month. He attended school as opportunity offered during the winter months, and at the age of twenty, having made good use of his opportunities, he qualified as a teacher. He taught altogether eleven years. His first school was at Jacobsville, near Pleasant Hill. He taught five terms at wages from $25 to $65 a month. Following that came a year of study in the Illinois Normal University at Normal, and he then resumed teaching for three years at Detroit, Illinois, and for two years at Nebo, and his last school work was done at Oakland, near Pleasant Hill.

In the midst of his teaching Mr. Bowers was urged by his friends to get into county politics and seek the democratic nomination for circuit clerk of Pike County. He won the nomination in 1896 against four competitors, and was elected the following November as successor of George W. Archer. Mr. Bowers served one term of four years and was re-elected his own successor. After eight years in office he was defeated for nomination for a third term. After an interval of four years he again won the nomination and was again elected and re-elected. Thus he spent two periods of eight years in the office of circuit clerk, a service of sixteen years altogether. When he finally retired from the office in December, 1916, he was succeeded by John T. Dinsmore.

Since leaving county office Mr. Bowers has taken up life insurance. He knows both men and affairs, has had a wide experience and has exceptional qualifications of salesmanship and has made a great success of his work with the Northwestern Mutual Life Insurance Company of Milwaukee. Mr. Bowers has kept more or less in close touch with politics in recent years. In 1918 he was elected a member of the Legislature and served in the Fifty-first, Fifty-second and Fifty-third General Assemblies. In his first term he was in the House under Speaker David Shanahan, and received appointment to the committees on roads and bridges, fish and game and congressional apportionment. He was in a republican House all three terms and had no committee chairmanship and was largely a spectator to the business done by the majority party. He retired from the Legislature in 1924. Mr. Bowers cast his first presidential vote for Grover Cleveland in 1888, and has frequently been a delegate to the local, district and state conventions of his party. He joined the Masonic Lodge at Pleasant Hill and served as lodge secretary three years. He is also a member of Nebo Camp of the Modern Woodmen of America.

Mr. Bowers married in October, 1888, at Pittsfield, Miss Printha A. Ruyle, who was born at Pleasant Hill, Pike County, daughter of John A. and Mary Ruyle. She died April 30, 1898. There were three children, Nina E., a graduate of the Springfield Hospital and a trained nurse at Springfield; Jacob R. and Higbee B., both residents of Pittsfield. During the World war Jacob went overseas with the Eighty-fourth Division and was with his command as an ammunition server. The other son was at home waiting to get into the service. On March 15, 1900, Mr. Bowers married for his second wife Mrs. Jessie B. Mack, daughter of Joseph and Paulina Fuson.

CHRISTIAN HERMAN KREILING. In nothing is the spirit of the age more clearly shown than in the interest displayed in the improvement of the roads of the country, and the development of natural resources, particularly through the medium of reclamation projects. These public improvements are generally the outcome of the efforts of trained men who, understanding the situation, devote themselves and their talents to bringing about results which are far-reaching in their scope. One of these men of Mason County who has long been engaged in forwarding the interests of his locality in a very definite manner is Christian Herman Kreiling, of Havana, county surveyor, engineer and farmer, as well as a citizen of the highest standing.

Christian Herman Kreiling was born on a farm at Bishop, Mason County, Illinois, September 26, 1885, a son of the late Herman G. Kreiling, one of the very early settlers of Bishop, where he was very successfully engaged in farming for a long period. He had two sons, the brother of the Mr. Kreiling of this review being Henry J., the elder in order of birth.

When he was about fifteen years old Christian Herman Kreiling left the parental farm, and, entering the University of Illinois, for his first year took special work in agriculture. For the succeeding two years he attended a private normal school at Macomb, Illinois. Returning to the University of Illinois, he completed his high-school and academic courses, following these with work as a civil engineer and scientific subjects, was graduated therefrom in 1909, with the degrees of Bachelor of Science in Civil Engineering. While at the university he was awarded preliminary honors, and his scholarship grades were such as to admit him to membership in the honorary engineering fraternity Tau Beta Pi Greek letter organization.

Having thus equipped himself for professional life, Mr. Kreiling returned to Mason County and began specializing in drainage work, organizing drainage districts, building levees and reclaiming overflowed lands, and this has continued to be one of his leading lines of endeavor ever since. During the disastrous flood of 1922 he was able to save all of the drainage districts from destruction, of which he was the engineer, a feat probably never before, or since, accomplished. Among his various reclamation projects have been the dredging and straightening of the channel of the Sangamon River, which was done in connection with John Goodell of Beardstown; the Lacey Drainage and Levee District; the Langelier Drainage District; the Kerton Valley District; the Seahorn District; the Banner Drainage and Levee District; the Lynchburg and Sangamon Bottom District;

and the Rome View Drainage and Levee District; all of which he had charge as head engineer. In addition to these many important projects he has had charge of much local work including paving and the laying of water mains and sewerage mains in Mason and adjoining counties, including the improvements at Havana, Virginia and Mason City, Illinois. As chairman of the Havana committee for saving to the people of this locality the Jacksonville & Havana Railroad, practically abandoned, he rendered a service that cannot be overestimated, and the results of his successful efforts will live long after the present generation has passed on. For two years he was president of the local Chamber of Commerce, and led his organization into a hearty approval of the movement in favor of building hard surface roads, as well as aiding in the saving of the railroad above mentioned. For a long period Mr. Kreiling has been one of the dominant figures in the Riverside and Havana Clubs. In 1912 he was elected county surveyor on the democratic ticket, and has been successively elected every four years since that time. Registered in the draft, he was classified, but was not called to the colors for service in the World war.

On December 30, 1915, Mr. Kreiling married, at Bloomington, Illinois, Ruby F. Ellenberger, a native of Mason County, where she was born May 26, 1888. She is a daughter of Herman and Amanda (Ellsworth) Ellenberger, of Bishop, Illinois, both of whom were also born in Mason County. Mr. Ellenberger was a farmer, and later a blacksmith at Bishop, but he died at Normal, Illinois, in 1915, and his widow died in the same city in 1923. They had three sons and four daughters born to their marriage, the survivors being: Ray Ellenberger, who is a resident of Chicago, Illinois; Otho, who is a resident of Naperville, Illinois; Myra, who is a resident of Normal, Illinois; Lora, who is also a resident of Normal; and Mrs. Kreiling, who was the second in order of birth. Mr. and Mrs. Kreiling have three children: Dorothy Jane, born July 22, 1917; Harlan Guy, born June 8, 1920; and Carolyn May, born December 10, 1925.

During all of his years of professional work Mr. Kreiling has also been interested in farming, and owns property near Easton and in the Sangamon bottoms near Chandlerville, the latter being reclaimed land. He is a member of the American Society of Engineers, the American Association of Engineers and the Illinois Society of Engineers.

JOHN BRECKENRIDGE GRAGG, present superintendent of schools of Pike County, is a veteran educator, a work he has followed for nearly half a century, not only in Illinois but in other states.

He was born near Lebanon, Russell County, Virginia, April 9, 1852. In 1859 his parents left Virginia and traveled overland to Johnson County, Missouri, and from there the family came to Pike County, Illinois, in 1863. His father, William Hugh Gragg, was born in Russell County, Virginia, in 1817, and was a blacksmith and wagon-maker. After settling in Pike County he operated a shop at El Dara until the fall of 1865, when he started back to Virginia alone, and died at Louisville, Tennessee, and was buried there. He married in Russell County, Cynthia Ann McGraw, who died at Pittsfield, Illinois, in 1897, at the age of seventy-three. Their children were: Elizabeth J., who died at El Dara, wife of E. R. Motley; George R., who died unmarried; John Breckenridge; Florence Margaret, who died at San Antonio, Texas, wife of L. H. Coley; Emma, who died at Pittsfield, wife of J. E. Dutton; and William Hugh, a resident of Lewiston, Idaho.

The death of the father threw upon the widowed mother and her children the necessity of supporting themselves. John B. Gragg was at that time a boy of thirteen. He had attended rural schools in Johnson County, and had gained the equivalent of perhaps the first year in high school when, at the age of fourteen, he gave up his studies altogether and for the next eight years worked for himself and the support of the family. Then at the age of twenty-two he was able to resume his studies at El Dara, Illinois, and when he was twenty-four he began teaching, his first term as teacher being in the Crozier School in Derry Township. After that for fully a quarter of a century he was regularly engaged as a teacher in different schools in this section of the state.

Mr. Gragg in 1904 went out to the State of Washington, expecting to remain there but a few months. However, he was engaged as a teacher and he remained in Washington ten years, his school work being in both eastern and western sections of the state. He taught his last school at Maple Valley, near Seattle. While there he purchased a half section of land in South Adams County, in a semi-arid district, and one of his contributions to the life of that state was the work he did in improving and developing this farm.

On leaving Washington in December, 1914, Mr. Gragg returned to Pike County, Illinois, and was soon again engaged in teaching. He was principal or superintendent of the Milton schools, and while there developed a four-year high school. After four years he gave up teaching, and in the interval of four years at college devoted his attention and energies to the management of his farming interests. Then he became a candidate for nomination for the office of county superintendent of Pike County, was nominated without opposition, and defeated the republican candidate in the election of 1922, succeeding Theodore C. Moore in office. He has had a busy routine in maintaining the excellent efficiency of the schools under his jurisdiction. However, this is not the first time he has held the office of county superintendent. In 1890 he was elected to that office as successor of C. I. Swan. This administration of four years was rather notable, particularly because he carried out a plan for the classification and grading of the rural schools and the adoption of the county superintendent's rural school examination for promotion to the high school. In this work he was a pioneer in this part of Illinois. Again in 1897 he was appointed county superintendent, as successor of W. R. Hatfield, and filled the office fifteen months.

Mr. Gragg is a democrat and cast his first presidential vote for Samuel J. Tilden in 1876. He has never missed an important election in the fifty years since then. During the World war his principal activity was in the Red Cross Chapter. He is an elder of the Christian Church at Pittsfield, is a past noble grand of the Independent Order of Odd Fellows and a member of the Knights of Pythias and Masons.

Mr. Gragg married at Pittsfield, in 1897, Miss Lucy Ellen Benson, who was born at Pittsfield, August 3, 1854, one of the large family of children of Edward Benson and wife. Only four of these Benson children now survive, the other being Charles H. Benson, of Winamac, Indiana, and Alice Jane and Alwilda Elizabeth Benson. Mrs. Gragg was educated in the Pittsfield High School and Illinois State Normal University, and for many years has been associated with her husband in school work, having taught both in Illinois and in Washington.

JAMES FLETCHER. Holding as he does the confidence and respect of a wide circle of acquaintances and friends, James Fletcher, of Bath, is spending his declining years in comfortable retirement after many years of usefulness as a farmer. At one time he was one of the substantial and extensive farmers of Mason County, and in this occupation acquired wealth and prestige, and he is still a very heavy landowner. Mr. Fletcher was born in Greene County, Illinois, January 11, 1847, and came to Lynchburg Township, Mason County, in 1848, a son of John J. Fletcher.

John J. Fletcher was born in Yorkshire, England, April 28, 1820. As youth he was apprenticed to a farmer, and learned his trade thoroughly. In 1844 he came to the United States, and for the first four years thereafter was engaged in farming in the vicinity of Winchester, Illinois, but then moved to Mason County and established himself in Lynchburg Township, and here he died January 7, 1900. He proved his efficiency as a farmer and died owning more than 1,000 acres of land, and other property. For years he was one of the conspicuous stockmen of his locality, and was very successful in other branches of agriculture. He held a number of the township offices, and he was county supervisor and commissioner of navigation for Lynchburg Township. For a long period he was a justice of the peace, and made an admirable record. The democratic party always received his strong support. An excellent judge of stock, he was valuable as a veterinarian, although he never studied that science, obtaining his skill from personal knowledge and experience. A man of unusual capabilities, when he was appointed county surveyor to fill out an unexpired term, he did so very successfully and satisfactorily, although in this, too, he had had no mechanical training. However, he did possess practical common sence and applied it to everything he did throughout life. Very fond of hunting, he became an expert in following wild game, especially deer, and engaged in this form of sport as long as he was able to carry a gun and get into the open.

This most excellent man and good citizen passed away before many of the modern institutions came into being. There was no clubhouse on his farm, or in his neighborhood; no engine pumped water from his well when he used it, and his old mare carried him back and forth between his farm and the nearby town at the rate of five miles an hour. His son and grandson cover the same distance in twenty minutes without exceeding the speed limit. His wife was a widow, Mrs. Anna Briggs, with six children, all of whom are now deceased, the last two having been Mrs. Louisa A. Lindsley, who died recently at Bath, and one who passed away at Wichita, Kansas. Mrs. Briggs came to the United States in 1841, and died in 1883. The only child of her second marriage was James Fletcher, of this review. She was fourteen years older than her husband.

The country school gave James Fletcher his educational training until he was thirteen years old, since which time he has secured his knowledge from experience and association with others. Remaining at home, he worked for his father until he reached his majority, at which time he took over the farm and began growing grain almost exclusively, and made a great success of it, but in 1881 he came to Bath and went into the milling business, buying the mill property of the village, and he continued to operate the plant for fifteen years. When he went out of the business no one else continued it. The building still stands, but its voice has been hushed for many years, and it is one of the landmarks of this section, and a reminder of days forever gone. Inheriting his father's large estate, he increased it until today two sections stand in his name, and on it his son is now carrying on family traditions. He still holds the land his father acquired in Saline County, Nebraska, so that his holdings amount to 1,210 acres. When he went out of the milling business he began handling real estate, for he had too great energy and enthusiasm for work to be content to retire, and he has invested quite heavily in city realty, and still supervises these properties. Mr. Fletcher served Bath Township as supervisor one term, he has been collector and assessor of the township for nearly a quarter of a century, and for as long a period he was a member of the school board. The democratic party exemplifies his ideas with reference to politics, and he has always given it a loyal support. In all of his public life he has displayed the same excellent characteristics which have won him such appreciation as a man, and the village, township and county are indebted to him for his hard work and broad-mindedness. The Methodist Episcopal Church holds his membership, and receives his generous support.

On November 3, 1870, Mr. Fletcher married, in Mason County, Elizabeth H. Patterson, a daughter of William and Sabina (Moore) Patterson. Mrs. Fletcher was born in Monroe County, Ohio, April 24, 1848, and she died August 7, 1925. She united with the Methodist Episcopal Church in her youth, and continued active in the good work of the Fairfield church until the family residence was changed to Bath, and in the church at the latter point she continued her zealous efforts until claimed by death. Her remains were interred in the cemetery at Bath. Five daughters and two sons were born to Mr. and Mrs. Fletcher, and all of them but one reached maturity. Elsie, who is deceased, married C. W. Huffman, of Bath, and they had the following children: William D., Chester S., and Elsie F., who is the wife of John Black of Indianapolis, Indiana. Harriett, who was the twin sister of Elsie, married John P. Van Aukin, and she died near Bath, leaving the following children: Alva, Bessie, Jessie and Beulah. Mrs. Van Aukin died February 17, 1925, and like her mother, was an earnest church worker, and she was also active in the Sunday School work. Jessie A. Fletcher, the third child of James Fletcher and his wife, is the wife of E. F. Hillyard, of Cumberland, Iowa, but she was formerly married, and had a son, Gilbert E. Lacey, by her first marriage. John Clark Fletcher is the only surviving son of James Fletcher, and he is associated with his father, and is the active manager of the rural properties. He married Estelle Bridgeman, and they have two children: John Kenneth and Blanch. The other son, James Gay Fletcher, died in 1918. He married Rosella Koch, but left no issue when he passed away. Elizabeth is the wife of W. G. Hiller, of Peoria, Illinois, a mechanical engineer, and they have two sons: John and Carroll. Ruby M., who was the youngest child in the Fletcher family, died at the age of seven years.

During the late war James Fletcher was very active in local war work, was assigned to the State Council of Defense, and assisted in organizing each school district of the township for war fund purposes. He is a member of the Modern Woodmen o America. His son in 1922 built one of the best equipped club houses for hunters in the state, which will accommodate many hunters.

CARL E. ROBINSON, for two terms state's attorney of Morgan County, has gained honors and success rapidly since beginning his career as a lawyer, his substantial achievements being due in part to the long and steady effort he put forth to acquire an education and fit himself for the vocation of his preference.

Mr. Robinson was born in Sangamon County, Illinois, January 22, 1886, son of George P. and Martha (Atterbury) Robinson, his father having come to Illinois from Indiana when a child. His father now is a resident of Petersburg in Menard County.

Carl E. Robinson was a child when his parents located in Menard County. He could attend the country schools only to the age of fourteen, his father being too poor to give him a high school training. Since then he has been dependent on his own resources and has contrived his own opportunities. He paid his way through the high school at Petersburg, working during vacations and as a coal miner in Morgan County, and sometimes built railroad tracks for the Chicago & Alton line. He learned telegraphy, and after graduating as valedictorian from the Petersburg High School in June, 1904, he went to Chicago and found work as a telegraph operator. He also worked in a packing house at Ottumwa, Iowa, and while there was badly injured in an elevator wreck. His persistence and evident talent brought him to the attention of President Rammelcamp of the Illinois College at Jacksonville. He accepted a scholarship in this school and in September, 1905, entered upon his studies there. He paid his expenses while in college, and while burdened with the responsibility of outside employment, he distinguished himself in college affairs, being twice a member of the Phi Alpha debating team and twice a member of the Illinois College intercollegiate team, and was president of the Phi Alpha Society. When he graduated in June, 1909, he was valedictorian of his class. He obtained the Bachelor of Arts degree, but was again without funds to secure a legal education. For three years he taught school in Morgan County, the first year being principal of the schools at Franklin and for two years principal of the Whipple Academy in Jacksonville. In the fall of 1912 he entered the law department of the University of Chicago, employing his summer vacations as a field agent for the Illinois College. He won notable honors in the law school, and in June, 1915, was graduated with the degree Doctor of Jurisprudence with honor. The following month he was admitted to the Illinois bar, and soon afterwards returned to Jacksonville and opened his law office.

Mr. Robinson was nominated in 1916 as republican candidate for state's attorney, and was elected and has since been reelected. He has given a vigorous enforcement of the law, and to the limit of his ability has upheld the prohibition statutes. He has also secured the active cooperation of the sheriff's office and other officials. In 1920 he was given the largest majority ever given a county official at any election in Morgan County. Mr. Robinson has been a delegate to several republican judicial conventions. He is on the state speakers' campaign bureau. Fraternally he is affiliated with the Masonic fraternity, Independent Order of Odd Fellows, B. P. O. Elks and is an elder in the Presbyterian Church. He has been president of the Jacksonville Kiwanis Club and chairman of the district organization of Kiwanis. In April, 1926, he was nominated in the republican primary for representative in the General Assembly of Illinois from the Forty-fifth Senatorial District, comprising the counties of Morgan and Sangamon.

He married, September 26, 1917, Miss Ruth Leach, daughter of John W. Leach, one of the prosperous farmers living near Jacksonville. They have one son, John Leach Robinson.

EDWIN JOHNSTON, present state's attorney of Pike County, has been a practicing lawyer at Pittsfield over thirty years. He has been a citizen with excellent qualities of leadership, and his name has been identified with several spheres of public service.

His grandfather, Thomas Johnston, was a Pennsylvania farmer and brought his family to Illinois from Beaver County, Pennsylvania, about 1850, traveling down the Ohio River and up the Illinois River to the landing near Pike County, and establishing his home near Milton in that county. Thomas Johnston married Catherine Main, who died not long after

the family came to Illinois. Their children were: Solomon T.; Joseph, who went to Arkansas and died there; William, who died in Pike County; and Elizabeth, who married Peter Mossin.

Solomon T. Johnston was born in Beaver County, Pennsylvania, in the '30s and was a youth when the family came to Illinois. He had a rural school education, and he spent his active career as a farmer near Milton in Pike County. He was a farmer and also handled, fed and shipped cattle. He acquired a large tract of farming land. During the Civil war he enlisted in Company E of the Ninety-ninth Illinois Infantry, and was in service in Missouri and in the Mississippi River Valley. During the Vicksburg campaign he was wounded at the battle of Black River Bridge, just east of Vicksburg, being shot through the body, the ball lodging in his back and remaining there the rest of his life. After being released from the hospital at Memphis he returned home, unfit for further duty as a soldier. As soon as he was able he engaged in farming, and he showed remarkable courage and endurance in spite of his wound, living to be more than eighty years of age. He died on the farm July 23, 1916, and is buried in Green Pond Cemetery. He took an interest in local politics, served as school director and once as township collector.

Solomon Johnston married Susan Heavner, who was born in Pike County, August 3, 1835, and died in January, 1904. Her father came to Illinois from Kentucky. The children of Solomon Johnston and wife were: Thomas J., a farmer in Pike County, Melinda, widow of P. W. Thomas; Louisa, widow of Robert O. Cox; Ellen, wife of Hardin Callendar, of Milton; Allen and Otis, farmers near Milton; Eva, wife of Charles Keys, of Milton; Edwin; and Dr. Frank, of Milton.

Edwin Johnston was born in Pike County, November 13, 1871. He had the experience and training of a farm youth, was educated in district schools, and finished his literary education in Illinois College at Jacksonville. At the age of seventeen he taught his first term of country school. His last school work was done as principal of schools at Pearl, Illinois. While teaching he studied law, and after examination at Mt. Vernon was admitted to the bar in August, 1893. He at once located at Pittsfield, and a general law practice and business has given him ample occupation for his talents and energies through all the years. For a time he was member of the law firm of Mumford and Johnston. For eight years he held the office of city attorney of Pittsfield. Mr. Johnston was elected a member of the House of Representatives in the Forty-second General Assembly, and was a democrat in that republican house, his committee assignments being judiciary, appropriations, education and charitable institutions. He was first elected to the office of state's attorney in 1916, succeeding George C. Weaver. His four year term included the period of the World war and gave him a large assignment of extraordinary duties. Mr. Johnston was elected for his present term as state's attorney in 1924. A democrat, he has attended many conventions of his party, both local and state. He was a spectator in the National Convention at Chicago in 1892 when Grover Cleveland was nominated. Again in 1896 he was a spectator at the famous convention where William J. Bryan was nominated after making his Free Silver speech. Mr. Johnston is a prominent layman of the Christian Church, is a class teacher in the Sunday School and has delivered many addresses and lectures on the Bible and Biblical literature, especially before audiences at Illinois College.

He married at Jacksonville, Illinois, June 3, 1903, Miss Elizabeth Chumley, who was born in Pike County, April 20, 1885, daughter of John T. Chumley. Mr. and Mrs. Johnston have three children, Merrill H., a member of the class of 1926 in the University of Illinois; Helen E., attending Illinois College at Jacksonville; and Glen T., a student in high school.

JOSEPH CLIFTON SNYDER. For over seventy years the name of Snyder has been prominently identified with the business and civic history of Fulton. For more than a quarter of a century the office of postmaster there was held successively by William C. Snyder and son, Joseph C. Snyder. In many other ways the name has been significant of business ability and influence in community affairs.

The pioneer of the family was the late William Cowperthwait Snyder, who was born in Burlington County, New Jersey, July 29, 1821, of Holland Dutch ancestry, a son of James and Sabilla (Cowperthwait) Snyder, who spent all their lives in New Jersey. William C. Snyder in 1845, at the age of twenty-three, came West, first locating at Lyons, Iowa. He brought with him an experience as clerk in a general store, but at Lyons studied medicine and in 1847, when he located at Unionville, just north of Morrison, Illinois, he engaged in the practice of medicine, and was active in his profession there for seven years. When in 1854 he removed to Fulton he conducted a general mercantile store for a year and in 1855 erected a building near the river and engaged in storage and forwarding of freight. He continued actively in this line until 1866, and in 1879 John C. Martindale became associated with him and continued until 1881, when he and his son, Joseph C., resumed somewhat the same enterprise, establishing and conducting storage and warehouse facilities for grain and other merchandise. He remained active in this business until his death in May, 1902.

William C. Snyder was one of the original republicans, a prominent member of his party in north central Illinois and in 1861 was appointed postmaster at Fulton by President Lincoln. He discharged the duties of that office continuously until 1883, in which year he was elected a member of the Illinois State Senate. He was a Royal Arch Mason and was noted for his work in behalf of temperance. William C. Snyder in 1849 married Isyphene Pearce at Clinton, Iowa. She was born at Kingston, Rhode Island, daughter of Jonathan Pearce, who came out to Iowa in 1838, settling on a farm, land which is now included in the City of Clinton. William C. Snyder and wife reared the following children: Kate C., who married Thomas J. Pickett;

Martha, who married Jerome C. Neff; Anna E., who became the wife of Albert L. Stetson; Joseph Clifton; James Justin, who died in 1904; Christopher Henry, now in California; and Lena V.

Joseph Clifton Snyder was born at Fulton, Illinois, November 14, 1857, and is now one of the older living native sons of that locality. As he grew up there he attended the public schools, and had nine years of experience working at the printer's trade. In 1881 he engaged in business with his father, and since 1920 his own son, Earl C., has been associated in the firm of J. C. Snyder & Son. This firm, dealers in fuel, grain and builders' material, is a logical successor of the business established by the grandfather of Earl C. Snyder seventy years ago.

Joseph C. Snyder is a staunch republican, has filled a number of offices of trust and responsibility, having been mayor of Fulton and postmaster from 1883 to 1887, succeeding his father in that position. He was elected township supervisor in 1906, and filled that office eighteen consecutive years.

Mr. Joseph C. Snyder married March 29, 1885, Miss Hattie L. Noble, who was born on Staten Island, New York, during a temporary residence of her parents there, but grew up and has lived nearly all her life in Fulton. They have five children: Ada, wife of E. A. Freeman; Belle, wife of Walter C. Drury; Paul N., of Chicago; Earl C., partner of his father; and Byron Jay, an osteopathic physician, at Fulton.

Earl C. Snyder, representing the third generation of the Snyder family in the business history of Fulton, was born in that Illinois town March 3, 1890. He is a veteran of the World war, having enlisted May 24, 1918. He was trained at Camp Shelby, Mississippi, and on October 3, 1918, went overseas with the Thirty-eighth Division as a corporal in the Machine Gun Company of the One Hundred Fifty-first Infantry. Just before the signing of the armistice he was transferred to Company F of the One Hundred Forty-fourth Infantry. He remained overseas the greater part of the year and on May 24, 1919, sailed from Brest and received his honorable discharge at Camp Bowie, Texas, June 19, 1919. He is a member of the American Legion Post. Earl C. Snyder married, September 23, 1922, Miss Helen McAlvin.

EPHRIAM SUMMERS, of Fulton, and a pioneer of Whiteside County of 1838, was born in the town of Barnet, Caledonia County, Vermont, Sept. 4, 1812, and was the son of William and Emma (Pierce) Summers. He worked at the carpenter and joiner's trade, and was also engaged in farming. He married in February, 1833, in Vermont, Mary L. Dickson, daughter of John and Jane (Lindsey) Dickson.

He came to Illinois in 1838 and made his home at Portland, this county, for a while, but soon located at Sterling, to which place he removed his family from the east in 1840. He learned the blacksmith's trade in the west, and opened a shop in Sterling, which he continued till 1847. He then removed to Fulton, where he worked at blacksmithing till 1850, when he joined a party bound for the gold fields of California. He left Fulton April 9, crossed the plains and arrived in Hangtown, California, early in August following. He spent two years in the Golden State and returned to his home via the Panama and New York route. In 1853 he engaged in the hardware business at Fulton, which he continued till 1857. He was elected justice of the peace several times, and served in all twenty years. In 1873 he was appointed United States gauger, and served as such two years, or until by a change in the law the office was abolished. He also held various local offices.

Mr. and Mrs. Summers had seven children, four sons and three daughters; Cloys, the eldest son, was a soldier of the Civil war and later a merchant of Fulton. He married Margaret Joyce. Morris, another son, died in infancy. Oscar married Elizabeth Exley, and was a business partner with his elder brother, later succeeding him as sole owner. He also served in the War of the Rebellion and attained the rank of captain. Cyrus, the fourth son lived a number of years in Montgomery, Alabama, and was unmarried. Sophia was the wife of Hiram Noble, of Fulton; Orilla was the wife of George Hartford, of Boone, Iowa; and Ida May, the only member of the family living, is the widow of Herman Jordan, of Newton Township, this county, in November, 1925.

Mr. Summers gave up active business several years before his death, and lived in comfortable retirement with several of his children near by, and in the enjoyment of the highest respect and esteem of neighbors and friends. He died in 1898, his wife having preceded him in 1879.

HON. HARRY M. FISHER. For twenty years a member of the Chicago bench and bar, Judge Harry M. Fisher, of the Circuit Court of Cook County, is one of those of foreign birth, but of Chicago training, who have so truly absorbed the best spirit of the city and the times. Prior to taking up his present duties he served several terms as judge of the Municipal Court, and in both offices has demonstrated the possession of splendid legal knowledge and clear judicial temperament.

Judge Fisher was born January 1, 1882, in Lithuania, and is a son of Moses and Fannie (Kauffman) Fisher. His father, a native of the same country, came alone to the United States during the late '80s and secured employment at Chicago, working at his trade of carpenter. When he had sufficient funds he sent for his wife and eight children, of whom Harry M. was the third in order of birth, and they arrived in this city December 24, 1893. The parents are still residents of Chicago, and are highly respected and esteemed citizens of their community.

Harry M. Fisher received his early education in the public schools of his native land and was nearly twelve years old when he arrived in Chicago. Here he readily familiarized himself with English, assisted by attendance at the public schools, and largely through his own efforts secured a professional education. After some preparatory work, accomplished with difficulty, he managed to secure a three-year course at the Kent College of Law, from which he was graduated as a member of the class of 1904, at that time receiving his coveted degree of Bachelor of Laws. Admitted to the bar, he entered at once upon the practice of his calling, and soon had built up a large clientele. His connection with a number of notable cases and his readily recognized ability soon attracted attention, and in November, 1912, he was elected a judge of the Municipal Court. He was re-elected to that office in 1918, and after serving three years of this term was, in June, 1921, elevated to the Circuit Court of Cook County, where he still remains as one of the most impartial, capable and dignified judges who has ever occupied the bench of that court. Judge Fisher is a member of the Iroquois Club, the City Club, the Covenant Club and the Bryn Mawr Country Club, and as a fraternalist holds membership in the Independent Order of B'nai B'rith; Blair Lodge, A. F. and A. M.; Lafayette Chapter, R. A. M.; Chicago Lodge No. 4, B. P. O. Elks, and the Independent Order of Odd Fellows. His political allegiance is given unswervingly to the democratic party.

On June 25, 1905, Judge Fisher married Miss Esta Rodah, a native of Russia, and they are the parents of three children: Beatrice, David and Deverra.

HON. GEORGE PETER CLARY, sheriff of Menard County, is not only one of the ablest men in this office that the county has ever possessed, but he has also won high repute as a poet of unusual parts. It is but seldom that man is given the aggressive qualities that make him a fearless and competent officer, and the other characteristics of temperament which enable him to add to the cultural life of his community, but here and there they are found. Vice President Dawes belongs to the same classification as Sheriff Clary, although his inner life is devoted to music, as that of Sheriff Clary is to the poetic muse.

The Clary family is one of the old ones of Menard County and was founded here in the '20s by John A. Clary, the grandfather of Sheriff Clary. While he had but a limited education, John A. Clary was a man who left his impress upon his time and locality, his personal characteristics being such as to make him an outstanding figure. He came to this region from North Carolina, and the first lived near Tallula, but later he moved to what is now Menard County, but was then included in the northern part of Sangamon County. While he was interested in the progress of his home community, he never was active politically. His farm furnished him with a means of support, and he was successful in what his life work. The Cumberland Presbyterian Church was his religious home and he took a zealous part in its work as a lay member. His death occurred on his farm four miles north of Petersburg, and he and his wife are buried in the cemetery at Concord, Menard County. John A. Clary married Phrona Cogdal, a member of another representative family of the county, and their children were: Ryal, who is mentioned below; Thomas B., who is deceased, having spent his life in Menard County; William P., who is a resident of the county; Enos A., who was in partnership with his brother, William P., in the mercantile business at Petersburg, and is now deceased; Ella, who married Samuel I. Cox; and Elizabeth, who died in girlhood.

Ryal Clary, father of Sheriff Clary, was born north of Petersburg, in 1838, and he died not far from his birthplace when he was thirty-four years old. Like his father, his life was devoted to farming. He married Julia Mattingly, born in Mason County, Kentucky, but brought to Menard County in girlhood, and here she was reared. She has long survived her husband, being seventy-nine years old. The following children were born to Ryal Clary and his wife: Sheriff Clary, who was the eldest; Lizzie, who died in childhood; Dora A., who is unmarried and resides at Petersburg; and Hardin J., who is a resident of Springfield, Illinois. Left a widow with small means, Mrs. Clary found it necessary to exert herself to keep her family intact, and worked hard for them. In those days but few occupations were open to her sex, but she spun, wove, knit and sewed for her neighbors, and her children are a great credit to her and her loving watchfulness. Sheriff Clary feels that too much praise cannot be given to her for her energy, good management and ambition which enabled her to rear the little ones left to her care and give them a sound education.

Sheriff Clary attended the Brush School in his home district until he was seventeen years old, and then began working by the month as a farm hand. His first wages were at the rate of fifty cents a day, but at that time all labor was cheap and poorly paid. Inheriting some of his mother's enterprise, when only eighteen he began handling stock on his own account. From then on during the succeeding thirty-five years he continued in the business of buying and shipping livestock, and became one of the most extensive shippers of his times between Roodhouse and Chicago, and continued in it until he was so occupied by the duties of the office of sheriff that he relinquished his hold on the business so as to give more time to his office. Although a staunch democrat, he had never participated in politics until he was induced to run for the office of sheriff. In his first race he carried every precinct in the county at the primaries against three competitors, and was elected by a large majority, succeeding Sheriff Courtwright. So admirable was his record in the office that had he not been prevented by the Illinois law, which forbids a sheriff to succeed himself, he would have again been the nominee of his party. However, he was deputy under his successor, but resigned after about a year and resumed his stock business. In 1922 he again became a candidate, and was nominated, losing but one precinct in the county in the primaries, and that by only one vote. Once more he was elected by a gratifyingly large majority, and succeeded Sheriff Harry Grandstaff, his old deputy. During his last administration Sheriff Clary has been successful in maintaining law and order to an unusual degree. He broke up a band of arson criminals who were destroying property and endangering lives in Petersburg, and succeeded in having them sent to prison; and he captured a nationally-wanted swindler and turned him over to the Oregon state authorities, and he has made his name one to be feared by evildoers. During the late war Sheriff Clary served as chairman of the local board of Menard County, and was kept busy with the heavy responsibilities of that office.

On May 21, 1907, Sheriff Clary married in Petersburg, Maye Miller, a daughter of Richard and Geske (Dorn) Miller, both of whom were Germans by birth, who came to Menard County, where they were farming people until claimed by death. Mrs. Clary was one of a family of three sons and five daughters, and she was born in Menard County June 24, 1881, being some years younger than her husband, who was also born in Menard County, December 7, 1866. Six children have been born to Sheriff and Mrs. Clary; Mildred and Julia, both of whom are attending the Petersburg High School; and Hazel, John and Phil. One son, George P., is deceased.

As has been previously mentioned, Sheriff Clary is known far and wide as the local poet, whose homely humor directly appeals to his fellow citizens who are well acquainted with the phases of life he portrays. Among some of the best-liked productions are: Concord Church Now and Then, Meditation, Eighteen Years Ago, The Gal of Today and The Butcher Man. The last-mentioned is so excellent an example of his style that it is quoted at length:

"THE BUTCHER MAN.

"The Butcher is the man, you know, who feeds us when we're hungry.
Sometimes he sells us something tough and that sure makes us angry.
And when we take it home to stew, its just like in the navy,
The bloomin' stuff's so awful tough, you can't fork up the gravy.

"He sells us loin steak off the neck, and tells us it's hind quarter,
And when you try to eat the stuff, you need a new self-starter.
He carves you rib-roast off the shank, and round steak off the brisket,
And when you try to swallow it, you're almost 'fraid to risk it.

"He'll sell you soup meat off the hock, and tell you it's so tender,
And when at home you catch the scent, its right back then you send her.
He weighs his hand in with the meat, as he tells you somethin' funny,
We know we ought to own his hand, we've bought it with our money."

RICHARD C. HALL has been a factor in Chicago business life for forty years. In point of years of experience he is one of the oldest men in the rubber goods business in Chicago. He is a former president of the Chicago Association of Commerce.

Mr. Hall was born at Boston, Massachusetts, October 19, 1858, son of Henry Augustus and Susan B. (Cartwright) Hall. His ancestors settled in the Connecticut Valley about two centuries ago. His grandparents were Andrew and Martha (Townsend) Hall, both natives of Boston, Massachusetts. They had a family of seven sons and six daughters, and the next to the youngest was Henry Augustus Hall, who was born in Boston, in 1814, and devoted his active career to the wool business. For many years he was a partner in the firm of John W. and H. A. Hall, wool dealers at Boston. He died in 1893. His wife was born in Shrewsbury, England, in 1824, and died in 1911. They were married at Pittsburgh, Pennsylvania. Of their four sons and three daughters two are now living: Richard C. and Grace.

Richard Cartwright Hall grew up in Boston, where he attended the grammar and high schools. His business career began at the age of seventeen as shipping clerk with the Boston Belting Company. From 1877 to 1883 he was a traveling salesman in western territory for the Eastern Rubber Company of Boston, so that his experience in rubber goods dates back to some of the early processes of manufacture. From 1883 to 1885 he was resident manager for the Eastern Rubber Company at New York. On coming to Chicago Mr. Hall was a member of the firm Elson Hall & Company for two years, and in 1887 became a member of the Duck Brand Rubber Company, wholesale dealers in the Duck Brand of rubber and oil clothing. This business was sold out to the United States Rubber Company, and since 1910 Mr. Hall has been western selling agent for the United States Rubber Company, his offices being at 440 W. Washington Street. He is also a director of the National City Bank and was the first president of the Chicago Credit Men's Association. He was elected president of the Chicago Association of Commerce in 1908.

Mr. Hall for thirty-two years has been a resident of Evanston. He has been interested in many movements and organizations in that city and in Chicago, having served as a vice president of the Sunday Evening Club and the Legislative Voters' League of Chicago; has been president of the Board of Trustees of Boys' Homes and for twenty-five years has been a vestryman of St. Mark's Church of Evanston. He has been a director of the Evanston Y. M. C. A., is a member of the Evanston Club, a republican, and belongs to the Union League Club of Chicago. He married, June 10, 1891, Miss Grace Ellis, of Framingham, Massachusetts. Four children were born to their marriage: Richard E.; Dorothy, wife of George S. Noyes; Edward, who died in infancy; and Elizabeth Grace.

WILLIAM C. ROODHOUSE. One of the best known towns and cities in central Illinois is Roodhouse, division point on the Chicago & Alton Railway. The railroad has been its most important industry. Outside of that the history of the town revolves largely around the family honored in its name, that of Roodhouse. A member of the second generation of this family is William C. Roodhouse, for many years the postmaster of the city.

This Illinois town was named in honor of the late John Roodhouse, who died June 12, 1908, at the venerable age of eighty-two years.

He was born in Yorkshire, England. His parents coming to America, settled near Whitehall in Greene County, Illinois, where his father soon afterward died, leaving the children to be reared by the widowed mother. These children were Peter, James, Benjamin, John and Jane, the latter of whom never married. The four sons all grew up and spent their lives in this section of Illinois, becoming successful farmers, and all of them had families of children. The son James was a captain of cavalry in the Union army, and John himself volunteered but was rejected for physical reasons.

John Roodhouse acquired his education in the schools of Greene County, had the training of a farm boy, and throughout his life his interests were closely tied to the land and its industry. He acquired a large amount of farm land in Greene County, was a dealer and shipper of stock and grain, and for a number of years afforded the primary market for nearly all the stock shipped out of this region. He was one of the organizers of the old Farmers and Traders Bank of Roodhouse, which subsequently became the First National Bank, with him as one of its directors.

On a part of the Roodhouse farm he laid out the town site which bears his name. He and E. M. Housted were the men chiefly responsible for persuading the officials of the Chicago & Alton Railway to locate their division point there. John Roodhouse built up the entire north side of the town square, including the Hotel Roodhouse. His own home was within half a block of the town square, but later he built a new place just south of town. He was president of the Village Board, exercised much political influence, was postmaster of Roodhouse for a time, but was not naturally a politician, and his influence over the community was in consequence of his important business and material interests. He donated the public square to the town and put up the speakers or band stand, and he planted many of the trees which adorn the streets today. In a quiet, unostentatious way he was a source of much benevolence and charity in the community. John Roodhouse was a man of medium height and build, weighing about 160 pounds. He was a charter member of the Roodhouse Lodge of Masons, a liberal supporter and one of the officials of the Methodist Episcopal Church, and his wife joined with him in church affairs and was especially interested in the Sunday School.

At the age of twenty-five John Roodhouse married Sarah E. Baker, a native of Kentucky and daughter of Cuthbert B. Baker, who settled in Greene County, Illinois, and was a farmer by occupation. He was a soldier in the Civil war and was wounded in battle. Mrs. John Roodhouse died April 1, 1902. She and her husband had the following children: John W., a resident of Shawnee, Oklahoma; Edward P., who moved to Missouri and died near Bloomfield, that state; Laura, who became the wife of John B. Bradway, of Roodhouse; William C.; Mary M., wife of Charles T. Bates, of Roodhouse; Evelyn J., who died as the wife of Robert Wallace; and Frank S., present postmaster of Shawnee, Oklahoma.

William C. Roodhouse was born at the old farm home, where he still resides, on July 18, 1867. He grew up there, is a graduate of the Roodhouse High School, and for many years was in business as a merchant. Mr. Roodhouse has served altogether twenty-nine years as postmaster of Roodhouse. He first entered the office during the administration of President Garfield and the subsequent Arthur administration. He was postmaster through all the later republican administrations, his last appointment coming from the late President Harding. He was also for a time city clerk of Roodhouse. He cast his first presidential vote for Benjamin Harrison, and has been a delegate to numerous local, state and national conventions of the party, being at the national convention which nominated Major McKinley for president in St. Louis. He is a York and Scottish Rite Mason, and a member of the Springfield Consistory and Mystic Shrine. He is a trustee of the Methodist Episcopal Church and is active in the Sunday School work.

Mr. Roodhouse married, June 23, 1886, Miss Zila Hosford, daughter of Byron Hosford. Mrs. Roodhouse was born in Galion, Ohio, but attended school in Roodhouse. The oldest of the children of Mr. and Mrs. Roodhouse was Meda, who married D. K. Neal, and died at Roodhouse, leaving two children. Ben O. Roodhouse is a resident of Jacksonville, Illinois, and married Vera Misenbach. George E. Roodhouse is a locomotive fireman with the Chicago & Alton Railway, and married Cecil Taylor. John Roodhouse is assistant postmaster of Roodhouse. Ruth is a student in the Illinois Woman's College at Jacksonville. Evelyn is the present wife of D. K. Neal.

JOSEPH P. STREUBER, state's attorney of Madison County and former judge of the Probate Court, has been practicing law in the county for thirty years, and his professional and public record have made him well known throughout the Third Judicial Circuit.

Judge Streuber was born in Bond County, Illinois, August 10, 1871, son of Rudolph and Catherine (Schwendermann) Streuber, his father a native of Germany and his mother of Bond County, Illinois. Rudolph Streuber was born in 1838, came to this country in 1866, and from 1868 until his death in 1897 lived in Bond County. He was a miller by trade and business, and for many years conducted a mill at Greenville.

Joseph P. Streuber was eight years old when the family located at Greenville, where he attended the grammar and high schools, but at the age of fifteen, he was forced to quit school to assist his father in the Greenville Mill. He began the study of law in the office of Northcott & Fritz in 1890. Judge Streuber was admitted to the bar in February, 1894, and soon afterward established his home and office at Highland in Madison County. He rapidly acquired a successful law practice, and served two terms as city attorney.

When after the census of 1910 Madison County by its population was qualified to establish an independent probate court to handle the probate business of the county, Judge Streuber was nominated and elected on the republican ticket as the first incumbent of the new office, beginning his four year term in December, 1910. He was re-elected in November, 1914, and resigned in July, 1916, to become a candidate for state's attorney was elected in November, 1916, and re-elected in November, 1920. For a number of years has been active in the republican party of the county, serving on the County Central Committee.

Judge Streuber has been a director of the State & Trust Bank of Highland for twenty years when he resigned to accept the directorship and general counsel for the Alton Banking & Trust Company of Alton, Illinois, and is also general counsel for the State and Trust Bank at Highland, Illinois. He is affiliated with the Knights of Pythias, the B. P. O. Elks, the Modern Woodmen of America, the Eagles, and is president of the Alton Kiwanis Club. In June, 1896, he married Miss Katherine Wherli, of Highland. One son was born to their marriage, William J. Streuber, a noted baritone singer.

ALBEN FREDERICK BATES, Chicago attorney, with offices at 160 North LaSalle Street, is a resident of Elmhurst, DuPage County, and is a member of the third generation of the Bates family in what is now one of the most attractive suburban communities in the district west of Chicago.

During the eighteenth century the Bates family had its home in the great maritime center of New Bedford, Massachusetts. The great-great grandfather of the Chicago attorney was owner of whaling vessels that sailed out of that famous port. When the Revolutionary war broke out these vessels were commandeered for the service of the Colonial government. In recompense the Bates family after the war were given a grant of land in the Ohio Western Reserve, and some members of the family located there before the close of the eighteenth century.

The founder of the family in DuPage County, Illinois, was Gerry Bates. He was born in the year 1800. In the early '40s he moved West from Painesville, Ohio, passing through Chicago on his way. Chicago at that time did not make a favorable impression on Gerry Bates. He had the opportunity of purchasing lots on what is now Wacker Drive for $20 each. Instead of locating in Chicago he moved some fifteen miles west to higher ground and purchased a large body of land at what was then known as Cottage Hill, now Elmhurst. This land included the present village of Elmhurst, and part of the property is still in the possession of the Bates family.

Alben Frederick Bates was born at Elmhurst, in 1889, son of Frederick H. and Nellie (Emery) Bates, and a grandson of Gerry Bates, the pioneer. His father, Frederick H. Bates, was born at Elmhurst in 1857 and died in 1920. Alben F. Bates was liberally educated, being a graduate of the Lewis Institute of Chicago, attended Lake Forest University, and was graduated LL. B. from the law department of Northwestern University in 1911. Since that year he has been engaged in a general law practice at Chicago, though many of his legal and business interests are in Elmhurst, DuPage County, where he has his home. He has been city attorney of Elmhurst since 1914, is public administrator for DuPage County, is village attorney for the villages of Roselle and Itasca, is vice president of the Elmhurst State Bank and a director of the Villa Park Trust & Savings Bank and the Westmore Trust & Savings Bank.

Mr. Bates was one of the founders of the Elmhurst Golf Club, a member of the purchasing committee that acquired its grounds. This club has become very wealthy through the great increase in the value of the property since its purchase. Mr. Bates is also a member of the Chicago and Illinois Bar Associations, DuPage County Bar Association, is a Knight Templar Mason and Shriner, member of the Hamilton Club and Medinah Athletic Club. He married Miss Clara Glos, of Elmhurst. Her family were also pioneers of Elmhurst and DuPage County. They have three children, Carol, Alben F., Jr., and Henry.

JOHN WELLS BAIN, president of the Equitable Life & Casualty Insurance Company of Chicago, is one of the younger group of insurance executives in the Middle West. It is a business he has followed most of his active career.

Mr. Bain was born at Schuyler, in Colfax County, Nebraska, March 4, 1886, son of Chauncey and Frances (Samuel) Bain. He was only a small child when his mother died. She was a native of Kentucky. There were three sons, John W. being the second. Chauncey Bain, his father, was a native of Vermont and was president of a milling and elevator corporation which operated eight or ten plants in Nebraska, Iowa and Kansas. He died in 1918. He was a republican in politics.

John Wells Bain attended public schools in Nebraska, and prepared for college in a noted boys' school in Maryland, the Tome Institute. He finished his education in the University of Wisconsin, and took up the insurance business with the Mutual Benefit Insurance Company of Omaha. For seven or eight years he was general manager for this company at Chicago. Mr. Bain spent about four years at Los Angeles, California, engaged in the real estate business. He then became manager of the central division for the Mutual Benefit Insurance Company at Chicago, and in 1923 was elected president of the Equitable Life & Casualty Insurance Company.

Mr. Bain is a republican. He is a member of the Lake Shore Athletic Club of the Episcopal Church. He married, in 1920, Miss Grace Campbell, and they have one son, Wells.

CHARLES BURRALL PIKE, of Chicago, has acquired national distinction through the effective work he has done in promoting the cause of training and preparedness for national defense. He is president of the Military Training Camps Association of the United States and chief civilian aide to the secretary of war.

He was born in Chicago, in 1871, son of Eugene and Mary (Rockwell) Pike. His father came to Chicago in 1867, and became a leading figure in the business and financial world. He was a member of the Board of Directors of the World's Columbian Exposition.

A brother of Charles B. Pike is Eugene R. Pike, for many years prominent in civic and public affairs at Chicago, formerly city comptroller and president of the Lincoln Park Board.

Charles B. Pike graduated from Harvard University in 1893, took his law degree at the Harvard Law School in 1896, and for several years was engaged in law practice. Afterwards he was vice president of the Western State Bank, and then organized and became president of the Hamilton National Bank, and was president of the Merchants Safe Deposit Company. For several years he has given his time chiefly to the management of his father's estate and public affairs. He is managing director of the Eugene S. Pike Estate Land Trust, with offices in the Tower Building at Chicago.

Mr. Pike's home is in Lake Forest. He helped organize and became first president of the Racquet Club of Chicago. He also holds membership in the Chicago Club, the Attic, Mid-Day, University, Saddle and Cycle, Casino, Arts, Shore Acres, Old Elm, the New York Racquet and Tennis and others. He is vice president of the Chicago Historical Society.

Mr. Pike married Frances, youngest daughter of the late Russell A. Alger, secretary of war in the McKinley administration.

Mr. Pike has been president of the Military Training Camps Association of the United States since 1922. He became interested in this form of training when in 1915 he entered the camp for business and professional men at Fort Sheridan, Illinois. Secretary of War Weeks in appointing Mr. Pike chief civilian aide to the secretary of war, in December 19, 1922, wrote, "in recognition of the ability and patriotism of Charles Burrall Pike, president of the Military Training Camps Association of the United States, he is hereby appointed chief civilian aide to the secretary of war, to serve as such for a period of four years unless sooner relieved by resignation or withdrawal of this appointment. He shall cooperate with the War Department and the Army of the United States in such manner as may be deemed expedient."

CHRISTIAN H. KUNNEMAN, who served twelve years as county recorder of Madison County and has long been a leader in the republican party in his section of the state, is a business man of Granite City and was born and reared in the country immediately adjacent to the Mississippi River.

He was born December 3, 1865, on land that thirty years later became part of the site of the industrial city of Granite City. His parents, William and Minne (Wessel) Kunneman, were born in Hanover, Germany, and were married in Madison County. His father was born February 11, 1829, came to southern Illinois in 1854, spent his life as a farmer, and died October 31, 1899. The mother was born in January, 1831, and died December 5, 1896. They reared a family of seven sons and two daughters, six of whom are still living.

Christian H. Kunneman, sixth son of the family, was reared on his father's farm, and attended country schools. As a youth he clerked in a store at Venice and in 1890 engaged in business for himself at Nameoki as a dealer in groceries and farm implements. He sold out five years later and for some time was on the road as a traveling representative of a wholesale fruit and produce house in St. Louis.

Mr. Kunneman in 1900 was elected for his first term as county recorder of Madison County. By re-election he served until the close of 1912, being defeated in the democratic land slide of that year. Since 1913 he has conducted a prosperous real estate and insurance business at Granite City. His home is in the village of Nameoki, where he has business interests. He was elected the first mayor of that town, and is now in his seventh consecutive term. He has also been elected supervisor of the township, was postmaster of the village, and from 1921 to October 15, 1923, served as a member of the Illinois Industrial Commission. In republican politics he has been head of the county and executive committees for a number of years. He is a director of the Granite City National Bank.

Mr. Kunneman is affiliated with the Independent Order of Odd Fellows, Modern Woodmen of America, the Eagles, the Elks and the Moose. He and his family are members of the Evangelical Lutheran Church. He married, October 29, 1891, Miss Ida C. Kahle, who was born in Madison County, in 1871, daughter of Frederick and Catherine (Hatrock) Kahle, natives of Hanover, Germany. Mr. and Mrs. Kunneman have two daughters: Ida and Myrtle.

LEONHARD W. ADLER has had a business career covering a half century. His primary interest has been the milling and grain industry, but his activities have led out into other fields, including banking, and he is now president of the State Bank of St. Jacobs in his home town. He was born in Marine Township, Madison County, Illinois, February 1, 1857. His father, Leonhard Adler, was a native of Germany, and settled at Marine, Illinois, about 1850. Leonhard W. Adler acquired a public school education, confined to the seventh grade, and when he went to work in the flour milling business at the age of seventeen he possessed only this education and the industry and intelligence native to him. He started in the milling business at Marine, Illinois, as a sweeper for 75 cents a day. For many years he has been a power in grain milling circles in Southern Illinois, and is vice president of the Valier Spies Milling Company, owning half a dozen or more elevators and flouring mills. The Valier Spies Company was reorganized and is now the American Milling Company, head office, Kansas City, was consolidated with the Kansas Flour Milling Company of which T. H. Hoffman is president and Charles E. Valier is vice president, incorporated at $15,000,000. Mr. Adler is general manager of the flouring mills at Marine and St. Jacobs. This is a business employing over 300 men. Mr. Adler became one of the original stockholders and a director of the State Bank of St. Jacobs, incorporated in 1903, and since 1916 has been president of that institution, which possesses capital of $25,000, and surplus of $20,000. He has also been a director in the Midland Casualty Company and is interested in other commercial enterprises.

Mr. Adler is a republican, and during his service as mayor of St. Jacobs he was a leader in securing important public improvement. He is a thirty-second degree Scottish Rite Mason and Shriner, a member of the Modern Woodmen and he and his family are active in the Evangelical Church of St. Jacobs. Mr. Adler has been a very busy man in practical affairs, but has also cultivated other interests, and has been an extensive traveler. In 1911 he and his wife made an extended tour of Europe.

He married in 1880 Miss Pauline Peters, a native of St. Louis and daughter of Henry Peters. She died October 25, 1914, the mother of two sons, Leonhard A., born April 17, 1882, and Walter H., born July 21, 1884. Both sons were well educated, Leonhard A. attended the University of Missouri and is now in the grain business in Kansas. Walter H. completed a business college education at St. Louis and is now associated with his father. Leonhard Adler married Margaret Rusco and has one son, Leonhard A.; and Walter married Alice Sohn and has two children, Myra and Allen. Mr. Adler married for his second wife, January 29, 1925, Mrs. Bertha Rueckert, of East St. Louis, Illinois.

GEORGE E. BRANNAN for a quarter of a century has practiced law, but his abilities have brought him a wide range of activities outside the strict limits of his profession. He has been a bank organizer, and is attorney for a number of Chicago's outlying towns and villages.

Mr. Brannan was born at Joliet, Illinois, in 1875, son of Thomas F. and Mary A. (Clarkson) Brannan. His maternal grandfather, John Clarkson, was born in Preston, England, coming to America when a young man and settling at Joliet. He was identified with the pioneer life of that town and is still remembered for his prominence as a citizen there.

George E. Brannan was educated at Joliet, attended the Northern Indiana Normal University at Valparaiso, and he went to Washington as secretary to Congressman John J. Feely, representing the Second District of Illinois. While there he completed his law studies in Georgetown University and was graduated LL. B. in 1902. He had previously studied in the Kent College of Law in Chicago, paying his expenses while there by work as clerk in a law office.

Mr. Brannan first engaged in law practice in Chicago, and his abilities have brought him wide and important connections. Among various towns and villages of Cook County for which he acts as attorney is the village of Niles Center, a position of particular responsibility because of the great developments in and around Niles Center in recent years. Mr. Brannan has engaged in banking and building and development of real estate. He was one of the organizers and is a director of the Broadway National Bank of Chicago, and was one of the organizers and is a director of the Lawrence Avenue National Bank, which began business in January, 1926. He owns some very substantial properties at Niles Center. Early in 1926 he completed and opened for inspection a model electric home in Niles Center. This house attracted much favorable attention from prospective home builders and owners.

Mr. Brannan married Miss Margaret E. Dempsey, of Joliet. Their three children are Mary Loretta, George E. and Margaret.

BENJAMIN F. WEBSTER, Doctor of Veterinary Surgery, who has practiced his profession at Winchester, Scott County, for twenty years, is a native of Pike County and a member of one of the old families of western Illinois.

His grandfather, John T. Webster, was born in Virginia, and married Mary A. Pulliam, a native of Highland County, Ohio. From Ohio he brought his family to Illinois in 1856 and settled in Pike County. They were the parents of six sons, Nathan, Norman, George, Moody, Davy and Galloway. The first four were Union soldiers in the Civil war and two of them were wounded in battle.

George W. Webster, father of Doctor Webster, was born in Highland County, Ohio, September 20, 1845, and was eleven years of age when the family came to Illinois. He grew up and spent his life near Milton in Pike County. During the Civil war he served three and a half years with Company K of the Second Illinois Cavalry, under Col. A. C. Matthews. He participated in the Vicksburg campaign. After the war he became identified with the Grand Army of the Republic and for several years was post commander at Pittsfield, Illinois. He died at Pittsfield August 20, 1925. His wife was Ann Westlake, who died in Pittsfield December 8, 1916. Her father, Benjamin Westlake, came from New York and settled near Pittsfield when a young man and later married Anna Godwin, of Pike County, Illinois. He was a substantial farmer and a citizen, greatly devoted to the cause of the Union both before and after the Civil war. The children of George W. Webster and wife were: Lillian, now of Cincinnati, Ohio; Benjamin F.; Fannie, wife of M. D. King, of Pittsfield; Thomas, of Quincy, Illinois; Harry, of Detroit; Charles, of Ft. Benning, Georgia; Laura, wife of R. A. Brown, of Spokane, Washington; Mrs. Susie Dinnenger, of Lynchburg, Ohio; Wesley, of Quincy; Sadie, wife of Earl Owings, of Winchester, but now residing in Chicago; and Stanley, of Quincy.

Benjamin F. Webster grew up on a farm in Pike County, and farming was the work to which he devoted his early years. He finished his high school education at Milton. On leaving the farm in 1898 he spent five years or so in the west, in western Iowa, Nebraska, Colorado, Idaho and Wyoming. For part of the time he was an office worker with the Union Pacific Railway and later was an auditor for the Pacific Hotel Company, located at Pocatello, Idaho. In September, 1902, he entered the Kansas City Veterinary College, and on March 15, 1905, was graduated with the degree D. V. S. For a short time he practiced in his old home locality of Milton, and since July, 1906, has been established in his profession at Winchester in Scott County.

Doctor Webster has been assistant state's veterinarian under appointment from Doctor

Peters. His work has brought him recognition as one of the leading veterinary authorities in this section of the state.

Doctor Webster was for four years, 1908-12, a member of the Winchester City Council, and in 1923 was elected mayor, as successor of Mayor Carl Miller. While he was mayor efforts were put forth to procure the right of way or otherwise make it possible for the construction of the hard surface road through Winchester. During the same administration a speaker and music stand was erected in the city park, and plans were perfected for the construction of a sewer system. Doctor Webster is a republican, casting his first vote for Benjamin Harrison. He is affiliated with the Independent Order of Odd Fellows and is an elder in the Christian Church.

He married at Winchester, September 22, 1910. Miss Mary Weltha Smithson, a native of Winchester, where she was reared and educated. She is a daughter of Boone and Mary (Leib) Smithson, her mother being a daughter of Nimrod Leib, a pioneer of Scott County who took land direct from the government, part of which land is now the property of Mrs. Webster. Her father, Boone Smithson, was born west of Winchester, in 1846, and his wife was born on the Leib farm in 1848. Boone Smithson died in February, 1922, leaving two daughters, Clara, wife of William Redshaw, of Scott County, and Mrs. Webster. Mrs. Webster has looked after the details of Doctor Websters' office and has been an invaluable aid to him in his professional work. She cast her first presidential vote for Warren G. Harding.

ROBERT B. BROWNE, superintendent of city schools at Pittsfield, comes of a family of educators, and he has been identified with school work as teacher or student practically all his life except for the period of the World war.

He was born at Oshkosh, Wisconsin, July 15, 1894, but has lived in Illinois since he was four years old. The Browne family was established in New England in Colonial times and was represented by soldiers in the Revolution. The grandfather of Mr. Browne was in the United States navy during the Civil war. He was a Massachusetts farmer. George M. Browne, father of Robert C. Browne, was born at Westfield, Massachusetts, in 1857, was educated in public schools, in Harvard College and Tufts College of Massachusetts. Coming out to Illinois, he became an instructor in the Cook County Normal when its head was the late Colonel Parker. He taught science there several years, was then identified with the Oshkosh State Normal in Wisconsin, and for the past twenty-three years has been professor of chemistry in the Southern Illinois Normal University at Carbondale. He married at Austin, Illinois, Addie Gordon, a native of Oil City, Pennsylvania, who is a graduate of the Cook County Normal of Illinois and was a teacher at Austin up to her marriage. The children of George M. Browne and wife are: Lois A., member of the faculty of the Western Illinois Teachers College; Gordon, a teacher at St. Louis; Robert Bell; Myron O., assistant cashier of the First National Bank of Vincennes, Indiana; Margaret, wife of R. W. Karraker, of Jonesboro, Illinois; Arthur, teacher of science at Chenoa, Illinois; and Richard, civic teacher at Chicago Heights.

Robert B. Browne from the age of four to nine lived at Springfield, and the family home was then transferred to Carbondale. He attended the University High School, graduated in 1913 from the Southern Illinois Normal University at Carbondale, and in 1918 received the degree Bachelor of Pedagogy After leaving the Normal in 1913 he spent three years teaching in the Stanley McCormick Academy at Burnsville, North Carolina. Following that came a year of further study at Carbondale, where he was also student instructor in the department of science. He then attended the University of Illinois a year.

During the World war he enlisted as a private, was commissioned second lieutenant and was at Camp Zachary Taylor, Kentucky, a year as an infantry officer in the receiving brigade, where drafted men were started during their training for service. After the armistice he was an adjutant in the convalescent center at Camp Taylor.

After his honorable discharge he came to Pittsfield in 1919, and for two years was principal of the high school, and since then has been superintendent of the city school system. He received the Bachelor of Science degree from the University of Illinois in 1922. Mr. Browne has for several years been an instructor in normal schools, teaching psychology and education one year at Carbondale and two years in the Western Teachers College at Macomb. He is a member of the State Teachers Association, National Education Association, National Society for the Study of Education, and is a member of the American Legion Post and the Forty and Eight Society. In college and university he was a member of the Phi Delta Kappa and Phi Kappa Alpha. He is a Knight Templar Mason, member of the Knights of Pythias and Independent Order of Odd Fellows and is a Presbyterian.

He married at Marion, Illinois, June 18, 1921, Miss Frances Fowler, a native of Marion and daughter of Judge Richmond R. Fowler, who was born in Williamson County, Illinois. Mrs. Browne has a sister, Mrs. John Stone, of Paducah, Kentucky, and a brother, Roe Fowler, now attending the University of Illinois. Mrs. Browne graduated from the University of Illinois in 1919, and taught two years at Champaign before her marriage. She is a member of the Alpha Omicron Pi Sorority and is a Phi Beta Kappa. Her church is the Disciples of Christ. Mr. and Mrs. Browne have two children, Robert Bell, Jr., and Mervin Fowler.

JOHN J. HAWKINS, deputy clerk of Washington County, is a man whose tastes have led him to take a deep interest in the history of his neighborhood, and he, in collaboration with Henry F. Heckert, has compiled and issued several booklets of more than ordinary interest relative to the early events which led to the settlement and development of what is now Washington County. Mr. Hawkins is a native son of the county, having been born here September 26, 1868, a son of Ruben and Mary (Flauaus) Hawkins, and grandson of John

Hawkins, who came with his family to Washington County and entered land from the government in 1848. The maternal grandfather, Philip Flauaus, with his wife, Elizabeth (Rosenberg) Flauaus, natives of Germany, came to the United States about 1843 and settled in Washington County.

Ruben Hawkins was a farmer during his active years, but is now deceased. During the war between the North and the South he served as a corporal in the Eightieth Illinois Volunteer Infantry, Company K, and was captured, but had the good fortune to be exchanged, so was not subjected to the rigors of a military prison. His wife is also deceased. They had the following children: John J., who was the first born; George, who is married, has three children; William, who is married, has one child; Earl, who is unmarried; Louis, who married Anna Lind, and they have six children, Gertie, Elsie, Edna, Louis and two others; Mary, who is deceased, married Frank Reese, and they had four children; Julia, who is deceased, married Herman Nobe, and they had four children; Joseph Otto, who was killed in an accident at Kansas City, Missouri, was married and had children.

The district and graded schools of Washington County furnished John J. Hawkins with his opportunities for securing an education, and he made the most of them, and when he had completed his school days he entered a local store as a clerk. Subsequently he was township clerk of Plumb Hill and Venedy for fourteen years, and then, in 1907 became deputy county clerk, which position he has held ever since, in this capacity proving his reliability and faithfulness.

On May 1, 1888, Mr. Hawkins married in Plumb Hill Township Amanda M. Jones, daughter of James M. and Margaret (Robinson) Jones, pioneers of Washington County, both of whom are deceased, he passing away in 1920 and she in 1921. Their children were as follows: George, who is unmarried; James, who is married and has three children; Albert, who is unmarried; Anna, who is married and has two children; Ellen, who married William Perkins, and has one child, Vera. Mr. and Mrs. Hawkins have one child, Walter A., a farmer. He married Amanda Weihe. They have no children. Mr. and Mrs. Hawkins are members of the Methodist Episcopal Church. For some years he has maintained fraternal relations with the Modern Woodmen of America.

As a result of the investigations of Messrs. Hawkins and Heckert the following facts have been established and given to the public at different intervals.

In 1810 two men, John Lively and David Huggins, brothers-in-law, came to what was then the southeastern part of Saint Clair County, but had formerly been a part of Virginia, and is now Washington County. These men were the very first permanent settlers of the county. They took up land and raised livestock, cattle and horses, their farm being along Crooked Creek, on the east side of Kaskaskia River. In spite of the difficulties incident to pioneer life they were prospering, when the Indians commenced to be troublesome, and Mr. Huggins, the more cautious of the two, Mr. Lively being a very courageous man, moved to the settlement that stood on the present site of Fayetteville, but his partner remained on the farm. The nearest neighbors were on Shoal Creek and at Hill's Station, both about thirty-five miles distant. While he was fearless, Mr. Lively believed in making proper preparations, so he built a stockade enclosure, in which he herded his stock at night. In July, 1818, Mr. Lively saw that his stock was alarmed, although he could not discover the cause. Mrs. Lively, who had shared all her husband's dangers, became so seriously alarmed that she insisted that they leave for the fort, and he, yielding to her entreaties, consented, and prepared for the journey. They were ready to start two hours before sundown, and the hired man and Mr. Lively's boy nephew started for the horses, leaving Mr. and Mrs. Lively and their daughter in the cowpen milking and in good spirits over their proposed trip. Before the man and boy could get back with the horses to hitch them to the wagon they heard the reports of guns. Hastening back, they gazed in horror upon another of the many tragedies which have marked frontier development throughout the history of this country. A band of hostile Indians had crept up, shot and scalped their victims, and the frightened onlookers could hear the feeble voices of the dying pleading for mercy. Powerless to render any aid, they hastened off to the nearest post, on the present site of Fayetteville, with their dire story. This massacre retarded the settlement of this part of the state for a few years, but the pioneers were a sturdy people, and in time they poured in to take up the rich land awaiting them in the valley of the Kaskaskia.

In December, 1807, Henry Dexter and family, John Darter, Barbara Hutchings and Rhoda Smith left eastern Kentucky by way of old Post Vincennes, Indiana, where they obtained supplies, and from whence they journeyed across the wilds. After they had been journeying for many days their supplies were nearly exhausted, and they were glad to meet a post rider carrying mail from Kaskaskia to Vincennes, and asked him for food. He told them of some supplies, principally meat and bread, in a locust tree a mile or two further on. Upon investigation these supplies were discovered, and saved the little party from starvation, and enabled them to reach their destination in Saint Clair County. In gratitude they gave the name of Locust to the nearby creek.

The act creating Washington County was passed one year before Illinois was admitted to the Union, or in 1817, so that this county is a year older than the state itself. The first court in Washington County was called March 9, 1818, and this justices court proceedings was signed by David Pierce as one of the justices. William Rountree, John Kaln and James Gilbreath were the first Board of Commissioners. William H. Bradsby was first clerk of the Circuit Court, first county clerk, county surveyor and probate judge. Daniel S. Swearingen was the first sheriff and first representative. J. Maddox was the first sen-

ator. William H. Clayton was the first county superintendent of schools, while Rufus Recker was the first assessor and treasurer. The first voting precinct then included what is now Clinton County. These and many other equally interesting and important facts are in the booklets of which Mr. Hawkins and Mr. Heckert are co-authors.

BENJAMIN R. BURROUGHS has been a member of the Edwardsville bar since 1876, and in point of service is the oldest attorney in Madison County. His work as a lawyer has been varied by many public services both in his home county and in the state. He is a former judge of the Circuit and Appellate Courts and for many years has been a commissioner of the department of public welfare.

Judge Burroughs was born on a farm in Charles County, Maryland, May 20, 1849, son of John A. and Eliza (Dent) Burroughs. Both the Dent and Burroughs families were represented by soldiers in the Revolutionary army during the war for independence. John A. Burroughs was a Maryland farmer, and two of his sons became identified with Madison County, Illinois.

Benjamin R. Burroughs, the sixth in a family of twelve children, was reared in Maryland, attended a preparatory school in St. Mary's County of that state, and then came west and entered the Union College of Law, now Northwestern University, law department, where he graduated with the class of 1876. One of his classmates was Judge William Farmer, now a justice of the Illinois Supreme Court. Judge Burroughs after graduating came to Edwardsville, and in a few years had earned a high position at the bar.

A distinguishing part of his professional career was his many years of service on the bench. On January 26, 1889, he was elected a judge of the Third Judicial Circuit for the vacancy created by the death of Judge Amos Watts. On June 1, 1891, he was elected for the regular term, and under the new apportionment of 1897 he was elected in June of that year and in June, 1903. In June, 1897, he was assigned to duty as one of the three judges of the Appellate Court of the Third or Springfield District, and in June, 1900, was reassigned to the same court, his associates on the Appellate Bench being John J. Glenn and Oliver A. Harker, later Wright and Harker.

On August 3, 1909, Judge Burroughs was appointed a member of the State Board of Administration, the old department of the state government having in charge the charitable institutions. On July 8, 1912, he was reappointed to the board, and on August 20, 1917, was appointed a member of the newly constituted Board of Public Welfare by Governor Frank O. Lowden. He was reappointed a commissioner of the Board of Public Welfare by Governor Small, and has now rendered continuous service on that board for over fifteen years. Judge Burroughs nominally is a democrat in politics, but he has exercised his independent judgment in casting his vote, and it is noteworthy that he has received public honors from both parties.

He has held chairs in the Masonic fraternity. On January 29, 1873, he married Miss Mary Judy, of Madison County, Illinois. They recently celebrated their fiftieth or Golden Wedding anniversary. Four children were born to their marriage. Mary Maud is the widow of Wilbur M. Warnock, one of Madison County's foremost attorneys; Nora Judy is the wife of I. S. Dillingham, Jr., of Newton, Massachusetts. Clara B., is the widow of Walter Pulsifer, of Edwardsville, Illinois; Wilber G. lives at Detroit, Michigan. Judge Burroughs is a member of the Episcopal Church.

WILLIAM H. KROME. When death claimed William H. Krome, of Edwardsville, he had rounded out a career of nearly half a century of distinguished service as a lawyer, judge, banker and citizen. His associates had long admired his ability, integrity and honor, and a testimonial as to his eminent qualifications for the highest offices opened to the legal mind was found in the unique endorsement of his candidacy for the state supreme bench by the entire bar of Madison County.

Judge Krome was born at Louisville, Kentucky, July 1, 1842, oldest of the twelve children of Charles W. and Anna (Wesseler) Krome. His parents were born in Hanover, Germany, and came to America in 1836, being then young people. They were married at Louisville, Kentucky, in 1841, where he had a large shoemaking establishment, and in 1849 they removed to St. Louis, being embarked there in the wholesale grocery business, and to Madison County in 1851. Charles W. Krome was a farmer for many years.

William H. Krome was reared on a farm, was educated in a district school until the age of sixteen, and then became a student in McKendree College at Lebanon. He was a student of law at the University of Michigan from 1866 until 1868, graduating LL. B. in the latter year. He practiced at first at Collinsville, and then moved to Edwardsville, where he was associated with John G. Irwin until the latter was elected county judge in 1874. Following that he was a law associate of W. F. L. Hadley, and the firm of Krome & Hadley continued until the election of Mr. Hadley to Congress.

His many services and public affairs were rendered at the expense of his heavy law practice. He was elected the first mayor of Edwardsville in April, 1873, and while in office the fire department was established. He was chosen to the State Senate in November, 1874, being one of the youngest members of the body, yet was made chairman of the committee on the judiciary. From 1890 to 1894 he served as county judge of Madison County, and while in that office was frequently called to other counties to hear cases involving municipal improvement assessment. He was chosen a member of the Democratic State Committee in 1880, and was a delegate to the National Convention of 1884.

For many years Judge Krome was also known as an able banker, and had much to do with making the Bank of Edwardsville one of the strongest institutions in Madison

County. He helped organize the old Madison State Bank, serving as a director and president, and when this became the Bank of Edwardsville in 1898 he was made a director and vice president, and subsequently elected its president.

On May 4, 1875, Judge Krome was united in marriage to Lucy Medora Gillham, daughter of Shadrach Bond Gillham, member of one of the oldest and most distinguished families in Madison County. Judge Krome is survived by his wife, one son, and six daughters. William J. Krome, only son, was born February 14, 1876. He is a well known civil engineer, having built Flagler's celebrated Over Sea Railroad across the Florida Keyes.

H. E. WHARFF, M. D. One of the Illinois physicians and surgeons who rendered distinguished service abroad during the war was Dr. Howard R. Wharff, of Edwardsville, who was on duty with the British Army Medical Corps until after the close of the war. Doctor Wharff since his return to Edwardsville has confined his practice to his specialty in eye, ear, nose and throat work.

Doctor Wharff is a son of Dr. Howard T. Wharff who at the time of his death was the oldest practicing physician of Edwardsville. Dr. H. E. Wharff was born at the village of Marine, Madison County, August 23, 1878. His great-grandfather was a native of England, came to the colonies and joined them in the struggle for independence, serving as a captain in the Massachusetts troops. The grandfather of Doctor Wharff was a merchant at Boston and Portland, Maine. Dr. Howard T. Wharff served as a soldier in the Union army three and one-half years, and was once wounded. He practiced medicine at Edwardsville for thirty-three years. The mother of Dr. Howard E. Wharff was born in England and was a child when she crossed the ocean to America, her mother dying and being buried at sea. Howard E. Wharff was the third in a family of six children, three of whom are now living. He finished a public school education in Edwardsville, including the high school, and in 1906 graduated M. D. from the medical department of St. Louis University. For two years he had charge as physician of the Madison County Hospital, and then engaged in private practice with his father.

On June 29, 1917, he was commissioned a lieutenant in the Medical Corps of the United States Army. He was ordered to Washington and was soon loaned to the British forces, and went with the Royal Army Medical Corps, first stationed at Black Pool, England, with the Third Brigade of the Royal Medical Corps. He was next assigned at Barrow in Furness, where he and two other physicians had charge of a military hospital containing five hundred beds. He was also on the British Military Board. For four weeks he was on duty at the Arthur Pudick Hospital at Leads, England, and on September 24, 1918, was sent to France and was with the British front line forces until gassed. He was then ordered back to Boulogne Base and to the Fifty-fourth General Hospital for light duty until recovering.

He was put in charge of two blocks of surgical wards and did special work in ear, nose and throat and continued on duty with the British until March 19, 1919, when he was ordered to report to the American Expeditionary Forces. Soon afterward he entered the Montpelier University in France for three months of special instruction in eye, ear, nose and throat work, and completed his post-graduate course on June 30. He then returned home, landing at New York on July 19, 1919, and was given his honorable discharge at Camp Grant, Illinois, in August, 1919. While overseas Doctor Wharff was promoted to the rank of captain, and he now holds a commission as captain in the Medical Officers Reserve Corps.

He is a member of the Madison County Medical Society, the Illinois State and American Medical Associations. He was formerly assistant surgeon of the Clover Leaf Railroad under his father, who was chief physician of that road. He is affiliated with the Knights of Pythias. In September, 1909, Doctor Wharff married Miss Mary A. Steele, who was born at Aberdeen, Scotland, and was brought to America when a child. They have one son, Duncan Howard, born in 1911 and now deceased. Doctor Wharff married as his second wife Florence Zimmer, of Granite City.

F. A. GARESCHE has for term after term been reelected mayor of Madison, and has also been in consecutive service for twelve years as a member of the Illinois House of Representatives. He was formerly paymaster of the American Car and Foundry Company Works at Madison, and is now a practicing attorney.

Mr. Garesche was born in St. Louis, December 16, 1875, and lived in that city until he moved across the river to the industrial community of Madison. His father, Ferd. L. Garesche, a native of New York, was reared in St. Louis, graduating from St. Louis University with the class of 1849, and lived in that city until his death in 1903. He was prominent in public affairs, serving as commissioner of supplies under Mayor Overstolz. Ferd. L. Garesche married Rosella Hicks, a native of France. She died in January, 1907.

Ferd. A. Garesche, youngest of nine children, was reared in St. Louis, and finished his literary education in St. Louis University, graduating in 1896. Soon afterward he entered the service of the American Car and Foundry Company at Madison, Illinois, and in 1906 was made general paymaster for the company. He held that very important responsibility for about six years. He resigned to take up the study of law in St. Louis University in 1911, and was graduated and admitted to the bar of Illinois in 1913. He has an extensive practice, largely derived from his home community of Madison.

Mr. Garesche was first elected mayor of Madison in 1905, being at that time the youngest mayor in Madison County. He has held the office continuously by reelection for over eighteen years. In 1912 he was elected a member of the House of Representatives, and has been reelected and has served six consecutive terms in the Legislature, being one of the influential members of the House of Representatives.

Mr. Garesche is a former vice president of the Illinois Firemen's Association. During his term as mayor Madison has erected a city hall, has carried out extensive improvements in the way of paving and public utilities, and he took a prominent part in planning and financing what is known in that section of the state as the outlet sewer, a project costing over a quarter of a million dollars.

Mr. Garesche is an active member of the Knights of Columbus, the B. P. O. Elks, the Modern Woodmen and the Eagles. He married, November 14, 1903, Miss Dora E. O'Brien, of St. Louis. Six children were born to their marriage: Dorothy Marie, Ferdinand H., now deceased, John Paul, Robert A., Philip Edward and Richard Louis.

The Chicago Tribune early in 1924 discussed Mr. Garesche as a proposed candidate for the democratic nomination for lieutenant-governor, and among other things said:

"Mr. Garesche is known as the 'permanent mayor' of his home town because he has served in that capacity for twenty-one years, having been elected eleven consecutive times. He also has served six terms in the Legislature as a representative of the Forty-seventh District."

JACOB R. STEGMAN, a veteran of the World war, is one of the prominent young business men of East St. Louis. He has had a wide and successful experience in the lead manufacturing industry, and is the executive head of one of the largest concerns of the kind in the St. Louis industrial district.

He was born at Cincinnati, Ohio, September 14, 1890, son of Adam C. and Viola (Miller) Stegman. The Stegmans and Millers were Ohio families. His grandfather was Adam Stegman. His mother was a daughter of John Miller, and John Miller's wife was a daughter of Jacob Ritter, both of these being soldiers in the Civil war, Jacob Ritter a private in the quartermaster's department, while John Miller was a sergeant in Company H of the Second Ohio Volunteer Infantry and was wounded in battle. Adam C. Stegman spent his life as a carriage manufacturer and died in 1912, while his wife passed away in 1898.

Jacob R. Stegman, one of six children, grew up in Cincinnati, attended public schools, finishing his high school course in 1907. For a short time he worked in a shoe factory, and then for an electric railway company and next found the opening that has brought him his permanent business experience. He became a clerk in the Cincinnati offices of the Eagle Picher Lead Company, and was with that nationally known business from 1908 to 1918, a decade during which he learned every phase of white lead manufacture.

Then, in 1918, he enlisted, being trained at Camp Sherman in Chillicothe, Ohio, with the Eighty-fourth Division in the Three Hundred and Twenty-first Machine Gun Battalion. After ten days at Camp Sherman he went overseas, sailing from Montreal and landing at London, then from Southampton to Cherbourg, France, and was assigned duty with a machine gun battalion in the First Division of the Regulars. He was moved out to the front in the Meuse Argonne sector and was there during the last drive, ending with Armistice Day November 11, 1918. He then went with the Army of Occupation into Germany, and he was transferred to the Intelligence Department at division headquarters at Montabaur. These duties kept him abroad until August 17, 1919, when he sailed from Brest, reaching Hoboken, New Jersey, the same month, and after ten days at Camp Mills was ordered to Camp Meade, where he received his honorable discharge September 26, 1919.

On his release from the army Mr. Stegman rejoined the Eagle Picher Lead Company at Cincinnati and in December, 1919, went to the Chicago offices of the same concern. After two months he came to East St. Louis and has since held the position of manager of the East St. Louis plant of the Hammer Bros. Lead Company, a Missouri corporation, owned mostly by local capital and one of the largest producers of white lead in the middle west.

Since coming to East St. Louis Mr. Stegman has found a number of interesting associations. He is president of the People's Finance & Thrift Company, was a director in the Illinois State Chamber of Commerce and East Side Employers Association, was a director of the local Chamber of Commerce, is a member of the Rotary Club, the St. Clair County Country Club, is a past master of the Masonic Lodge and a thirty-second degree Scottish Rite Mason. Mr. Stegman married, June 12, 1923, Miss Erna Mueller, of East St. Louis, daughter of B. A. and Clara (Sander) Mueller. Her father is an architect of East St. Louis.

WILLIAM HENRY MAY, sheriff of Washington County, is one of the men of Nashville who is rendering a public service, during a most trying period in the county's history, in a manner that reflects great credit upon his courage and efficiency, and he is a well-known figure throughout the county because of his skill as a veterinary surgeon. He was born in Jackson County, West Virginia, October 2, 1861, a son of Jacob May, and grandson of Jacob May, born on the Rhine in Germany. His wife, whose family name was Lawrence, was born in the same neighborhood, and neither of them left their native land, and only two of their children, Jacob and William, did so, both becoming citizens of the United States. William May enlisted in the Union army, and died in a hospital from injuries received as a soldier.

Jacob May, father of Sheriff May, was a farmer and stockman, and built the first silo in Illinois, and was recognized as one of the foremost agriculturists of his times. For years he gave addresses upon subjects pertaining to farming and stockraising in different sections of the state, which were eagerly received, as this was long prior to the organization of Farmers Institutes. When war broke out between the North and the South he commanded Company F, First West Virginia Volunteer Infantry, Union army, served for three years and eight months, and was four times wounded, in the shoulder, thigh, hand and side. Once after being wounded he would have been captured, but he had the presence of mind to pretend he was dead, so that he was overlooked by the enemy, and later he managed to crawl back to his line. For several years in the '70s he was sheriff of Washington County, and later was county commissioner, and he was always very active in the Grand Army of the Republic.

Jacob May married Louisa Aherns, a daughter of Henry and Mary Aherns, natives of Menden, Germany. Mrs. Aherns was a graduate midwife in her native land and also had a license in Illinois. Upon their arrival in the United States they settled at Elmira, New York. It was in Elmira that Mr. and Mrs. May became acquainted, and following their marriage they moved to Powdertown, which later became Haselton, Pennsylvania. It was while the husband and father was serving in the Union army, in 1865, that William Henry May and his mother came to Washington County, and he followed a few months later, as soon as he received his honorable discharge. The first farm was a very small one of forty-six acres, and molasses was the first year's crop. Within a short time Mr. May bought twenty acres more, and when he sold his second farm he acquired ownership of a farm of 125 acres in the neighborhood. In 1871 he sold and bought the Pilot Knob east of Oakdale. For a time he operated a dairy, and still later bought a saw-mill. Jacob May and his wife had the following children: Sheriff May was the eldest, and the only child born outside of Illinois; George Washington married Bell Larkins, and they have five children; Philip Jacob married Frances Rhine, and they had three children, but two died; Charles Theo married twice, first Miss Ryan, who died leaving one child, and second Kattie McCarthy, who bore him a son and a daughter; Mary Louise married Henry Hubba; and Lula married Samuel Kaser. Jacob May died about twenty-two years ago, having survived his wife.

Sheriff May had but limited opportunities for acquiring an education during his boyhood and youth, having to leave school when he had only reached the Fourth Reader. At the age of twenty years, when he was placed by his father in the saw-mill, and made lumber inspector, he recognized the necessity for acquiring an education. This he did by applying himself at night and in his leisure moments, and he advanced to such a degree that in the course of time he was able to take the position of assistant engineer at the Illinois State Prison at Chester. Still later he took up the study of veterinary surgery, and has been following that calling for a number of years. In 1922 he was elected sheriff of Washington County, and is the present incumbent of this office. His son, Paul H. May, is his helper at the jail. Sheriff May belongs to the Evangelical Church. Fraternally he is affiliated with the Knights of Pythias.

On October 19, 1882, Sheriff May married, in Washington County, Minnie Thormann, a daughter of William and Louisa Thormann, the former of whom died thirty years ago, and the latter many years ago. Mr. and Mrs. Thormann had the following children: John, of Princeville; Henry, who is living at Carlyle; William, who is living at Okmulgee, Oklahoma; Fred, who lives at Belleville; Lizzie, who married Herman Hellmeyer; and Minnie May.

Sheriff and Mrs. May have the following children: Jacob, who married Minnie Schorfide; Annie, who married Ollie Boschert, and has two sons; Philip Charles, who married Ada Cobus, or Kobus; Ella, of Washington; William Martin; Rosa, who married Rudolph Fox, and has one child; Irena, who married Ben Meyer, and has a daughter; Daniel Dewey, who is unmarried, and in the employ of the Chicago, Burlington & Quincy Railroad Company; and Paul H., who is the youngest. In his office Sheriff May is proving his worth as an official and good citizen. While he insists upon a fair deal for everyone, he is firm in his enforcement of the laws, and has been very successful in capturing several quite noted criminals. A man of invincible courage, and utter incorruptibility, he is making a record that is likely to sweep him into office once more if he cares to continue to carry the heavy responsibilities of it. Such men as he are difficult to find and once the people do secure them they are slow to relax their hold upon their good services.

MARCELL F. KUEHN, editor and owner of the Progress, the leading independent paper of Saint Clair County, is a man whose efforts, in both a private and public capacity, are directed toward the furtherance of O'Fallon, and the betterment of its people. He was born at Mascoutah, Saint Clair County, Illinois, August 3, 1887, a son of Frank and Martha (Schaeffer) Kuehn, and grandson of Luke and Margaret Kuehn, natives of Germany, who left their native land, after their marriage in 1847, and came to the United States. The maternal grandparents, Dominic and Maggie Schaeffer, were natives of Alsace, France, and Germany, respectively, and came to the United States about 1840.

Frank Kuehn was in business for a number of years as a building contractor, but, sustaining injuries, he was forced to retire from that line, and is now engaged in looking after the Community High School. He and his wife have had the following children born to them: Marcell F., who is the eldest child; Clara, who married P. J. Dougherty; Oscar, who married Anna Reiss, and has two children; Joseph, who married Miss Elsie Albert; William, who married Myrtle Weber; Frank, who is unmarried; Laura, who married Ray Reinhardt; Benjamin, who married Fannie Fay.

His education principally received at the parochial and public schools of Mascoutah, Marcell F. Kuehn entered the printing office of his native town when he was only fourteen years old. Later he was elevated to the foremanship in which capacity he served for seven years. Later went to Saint Louis and worked for the Post-Dispatch, and attended night sessions at McKinley College, taking a commercial course and learning shorthand. Subsequently he spent one year in the employ of the Con P. Curran Printing Company of Saint Louis. In 1915 he became foreman of the Progress at O'Fallon. At that time both the Progress and the Caseyville and Edgemont

O. M. Jones

News were published at O'Fallon, but in February, 1917, the latter went out of business, and Mr. Kuehn bought the former, and since then has been its editor and owner. He conducts his paper independent of party lines, in the interest of the people of O'Fallon, and is making a success of his undertaking. He is an energetic community booster and is credited with the organization of the O'Fallon Business Men's Association and the Rotary Club, in which he has held important offices.

On February 1, 1910, Mr. Kuehn married Mary E. Meyer, a daughter of Joseph and Rose Meyer, the former of whom died in May, 1908, and the latter in 1916. They had the following children: Joseph, who is unmarried; Frank, who is married and has four children; Anthony, Anna, and Katherine, who are all married and have children; and Rose, who is unmarried. For many years prior to his death Mr. Meyer was a prosperous farmer living in the vicinity of Summerfield. Mr. and Mrs. Kuehn have three children: Russell E., Stanley J. and Ethel Katherine. They are Roman Catholics. He belongs to the Knights of Columbus, and to the Loyal Order of Moose. He is also a member of the Rotary Club, the O'Fallon Business Men's Association, a director of the O'Fallon Building and Loan Association and the St. Clair Automobile Club. In addition he is a member of the Board of Directors of the St. Clair-Madison Regional Planning Association, an organization formed for the development of the Great East Side along the Mississippi River.

JOHN A. KNOERZER, a native of southern Illinois, went to work as a boy and by his own unaided efforts has gained a most creditable and useful position in business life. For many years he has been with the Certain-Teed Products Company, one of the largest corporations in America manufacturing paints, prepared roofing, linoleum and a long list of similar products. Mr. Knoerzer is now general superintendent of plant No. 1 of this corporation at St. Louis.

He was born at Carlinville, Illinois, October 16, 1886, son of S. F. and Lillie (Lancaster) Knoerzer. His father was born in Illinois, son of Ferdinand and Anna Knoerzer, natives of Germany, who came to this country about 1830. On the maternal side, Mr. Knoerzer's grandparents were John and Sarah Lancaster, both natives of England, but married in this country. John Lancaster came to the United States in 1834. John A. Knoerzer is one of four children, the others being Everett Charles, Frank F. and Lillie May.

John A. Knoerzer attended public schools at Carlinville, and at the age of fifteen went to work as clerk in the grocery store of his uncle. After two years of this commercial training he came to East St. Louis, and for several years was in the storeroom of the American Steel Foundry Company. It was in 1908 that he joined the Certain-Teed Products Company, and in the service of that corporation for over fifteen years, has had a steady promotion with increased responsibilities. For six months he was a machine operator in the saturating plant, then went into the shipping department, and for two years had charge of all the shipments. He was next made night superintendent of the factory for three years, then superintendent, with a special assignment of duties, and in 1917 became general superintendent, having charge of all the work of this plant, No. 1. During the World war he was classified with an essential industry and in the fourth class.

Mr. Knoerzer married, November 18, 1918, at St. Louis, Missouri, Miss Ethel Beckwith, a daughter of Mr. Walter E. Beckwith, prominently known in East St. Louis as a member of the Beckwith Bros. Real Estate Company. Her mother was Martha J. Buchanan. Mrs. Knoerzer is the oldest of the five children of her parents. The three children of Mr. and Mrs. Knoerzer are Marjorie Anna, Jane Katherine and John A., Jr. Mr. Knoerzer was reared a Catholic, while his wife is a Presbyterian.

OLIVER MORTON JONES has been a practicing lawyer at Danville for over thirty years. An abundant measure of success has attended his professional work, and he has given his time and talents to the law with little participation in politics beyond performing the duty incumbent of every citizen.

Mr. Jones was born at Rob Roy, Indiana, January 18, 1867. In the paternal line he is of Welsh ancestry but of American Colonial stock. His grandfather, Hiram Jones, was born in North Carolina, in 1796, and in 1828 came west and settled in Fountain County, Indiana, where he was one of the pioneers and became a large land owner and farmer. He died at Rob Roy January 16, 1878. His wife was born in Kentucky, in 1804, and died at Rob Roy July 11, 1878. Their son, Henry B. Jones, was born at Rob Roy, October 23, 1840, was reared and married there, and devoted his life to farming in Indiana until 1903, when he removed to Danville and lived retired there until his death on March 29, 1904. In his Indiana community he acted the part of a good citizen, holding a number of local offices, including school trustee, was a republican voter and a devout Methodist. He also belonged to the Masonic fraternity. Henry B. Jones married Joanna Dudley Meeker, who was born near Rob Roy, Indiana, March 18, 1842, and is now eighty-four years of age, a resident of Danville. Her father, Usual H. Meeker, whose ancestors came from England, was born in New York State, October 12, 1811, and as a small boy went with his parents to Ohio, and in 1833 settled in western Indiana, and became a well known farmer there. He died at Rob Roy April 13, 1892. Usual H. Meeker married Sarah Dudley, who was born in the state of Maine in 1910, and died at Rob Roy in August, 1884.

Oliver Morton Jones is one of the two sons, his older brother, Lorenzo E., being a retired farmer at Danville. Oliver M. Jones grew up on his father's farm near Rob Roy, Indiana, attended the public schools there, the high school at Attica, Indiana, and in 1889 graduated with the Bachelor of Science degree from the Purdue University at Lafayette, Indiana. He took his law course in the University of Michigan, graduating with the LL. B. degree in the class of 1891. In that year he was admitted to the Michigan bar, also to the bar of Indiana, and in 1892 was qualified to practice in Illinois, having removed to Danville in 1891. His practice has been in both the civil and criminal law, and has brought him various responsibilities and interests in business and financial affairs. He is a stockholder in and attorney for the Commercial Trust & Savings Bank of Danville and is a director and attorney for the Vermilion County Building Association. He is senior member of the law firm Jones, McIntire & Jones, with offices in the Daniel Building.

Mr. Jones was for ten years a member of the Danville School Board, and for twelve years a member of the Board of Supervisors of Vermilion County. He is a republican; an active Methodist, being on the executive board of St. James Church at Danville; is a member of the Danville Chamber of Commerce; Vermilion County and Illinois State Bar Associations, and Danville Lodge No. 59, Independent Order of Odd Fellows, and Danville Lodge, Knights of Pythias. He has accumulated some real estate interests in Danville, including his residence at 1517 North Vermilion Street.

Mr. Jones married at Deer Creek, Indiana, October 7, 1891, Miss Emma Fouts, daughter of Mr. and Mrs. Solomon Fouts. Her father was a farmer in Carroll County, Indiana. Mrs. Jones likewise finished her education in Purdue University. Mr. and Mrs. Jones have three children: Josephine J., is a graduate of Northwestern University, Evanston, Illinois, and is now the wife of Leon L. Iltis, a professor in the University of Wisconsin at Madison. The daughter Joanna graduated from the Hamilton College in Kentucky, and from the School of Expression at Boston, Massachusetts, and was married to Lewis G. Bishop, a contractor and builder at Danville. The only son, Paul F., graduated from the Danville High School, attended the Northwestern University, and took his law degree at the University of Michigan, now being junior member of the law firm Jones, McIntire & Jones. His son was a volunteer during the World war, being one of the young men selected for duty as instructor in the Students' Army Training Corps at Millikin University at Decatur, Illinois. He was commissioned a second lieutenant of infantry, and was in the service one year.

SIMON P. SCHROEDER, M. D. For many years one of the foremost citizens in the useful life of the community at Nashville, Illinois, has been Dr. Simon P. Schroeder, vice president of the Farmers and Merchants National Bank, formerly coroner of Washington County and for five years county and city physician. While Doctor Schroeder as a physician and surgeon commands respect and enjoys public confidence, he is an educated and broad-minded man who is also acknowledged eminent in other fields of useful effort.

Simon P. Schroeder was born at Freelandville, Knox County, Indiana, January 24, 1861, a son of John K. and Henrietta (Sander) Schroeder. His grandparents, Kurt Schroeder and wife, and Anthony and Louise Sander, were all born in Germany. His father, John K. Schroeder, who died in 1900, was also born in Germany, where he was a cabinetmaker at the time of the revolution of 1848, because of which he came to the United States. He became a farmer near Freelandville, Indiana. To his marriage with Henrietta Sander, who died in 1907, a large family was born. Fred W., the eldest, married Emma Mengedott and they had six children. William was married twice, first to Minnie Grote, who bore one child, and second to Helen Brockschmidt, and they have three children. Herman married Mary Sander, and at death left two children. Sophia married Joseph Kirchhous, and they had twelve children living. Doctor Schroeder is the next in order of birth. Minnie married Charles Kirchhoff and they have four children. Henry married Lena Sander, and they have six children. Dr. Louis married Lydia Mechtemeyer and they have three children. John, the youngest, married a member of the Buchthal family, who, at death, left three children.

Simon P. Schroeder spent his early years on the home farm and attended the district schools in Knox County and later the graded schools at Freelandville and Vincennes, in the meanwhile making such preparation as he could to enter upon the study of medicine. Finally he became a student in the Hospital College of the Medical Department of the University of Kentucky, from which institution he was graduated in 1887 with his degree of M. D., receiving the highest honors in his class and the gold medal. He remained in Louisville, Kentucky, one year longer, serving as interne in the Louisville City Hospital.

Doctor Schroeder came then to Washington County, Illinois, and engaged in the general practice of medicine at Hoyleton for the next fourteen years, and when he then came to Nashville in search of wider opportunity, he left grateful patients and many warm and appreciative friends behind him, a condition that surrounds him at Nashville. Although not particularly active in politics, on numerous occasions he has received political as well as personal support for responsible public offices. For five years he served as city and county physician, from 1899 to 1920 he served as secretary of the Washington County Pension Board, and for the past eight years has been county coroner, an office from which he has but recently retired. For some weeks during this long period he was called upon to serve also as sheriff, on account of a vacancy in that office. During the World war he served as a member of the Medical Reserve Corps, and is still a member of the Council of National Defense.

On September 9, 1888, at Hoyleton, Illinois, Doctor Schroeder married Miss Eunice D. Rohlander, youngest of a family of six children born to Godfried and Louisa (Wagner) Rohlander, the former of whom died in 1898 and the latter in 1863. The other members of the Rohlander family were: John, who married and had two children: Ernest, who is unmarried; Louise, who died young; Hannah, who married August Deppe and they had five children; and Anna, who married Emil Rillenkamp, and they have three children.

The following is the record of the surviving children of Doctor and Mrs. Schroeder: Godfried F., dental surgeon, volunteered for military service in the World war, was commissioned captain and in August, 1918, went to France and remained overseas until July, 1919. He is now stationed at the Edward Hines, Jr., Federal Hospital, Maywood, Illinois. He married Miss Norma Hutchings. Eunice, who is the wife of Dr. Otto Brandhorst, a specialist in dental surgery, who is an instructor in the Medical Department Dental School of Washington University, St. Louis, Missouri. Doctor and Mrs. Brandhorst have two children, William and Helen. Helen H., a graduate nurse, Barnes Hospital, St. Louis, is now the wife of Reynolds Stahl. Paul L., who was physician on the staff of Michael Reese Hospital, Chicago, is now assistant superintendent in Lincoln Hospital, a scientist on research work for the state in the Children's department in psychiatry, Cook County Hospital. The children are brought to him to classify as to their mental condition. He married Miss Mable Moore, and they have three children, Ann Elizabeth, Robert Paul, and Marjorie C. They reside at Oak Park, Illinois. Robert, who is engaged in the practice of medicine at Denver, Colorado, was formerly a member of the medical corps at the Great Lakes, and while there developed a tubercular affection and was sent to Fort Bayard, New Mexico, where his recovery was rapid and he served throughout the World war on the staff of the Bayard Hospital, afterward locating in Denver. He married Miss Helen Truman and has one son, Robert, Jr. Carl, who has preferred an agricultural rather than professional life. He married Wilma Zapp and has one son, Zella D. Fred, the youngest, is a student of dentistry He married Ruth Wilson. Doctor Schroeder, after losing his wife in 1923, married in 1925 Miss Sophie Althoff.

Doctor Schroeder has always taken a deep interest in worthy local enterprises and was one of the organizers of the Farmers and Merchants National Bank at Nashville, of which he is vice president. He is a member of the Evangelical Church and of the American and the Washington County Medical Associations.

WILLIAM ALBERT JOLLEY is one of the proprietors of the Roodhouse Record. His experience makes him a veteran of the newspaper business in Illinois, an occupation and profession he has followed for thirty years or more.

He was born at Piasa village in Macoupin County, Illinois, December 20, 1875. His grandfather, Thomas Jolley, came to Illinois in pioneer times from Tennessee, making the journey overland in ox carts and as part of the colony that migrated to Illinois at that time. Thomas Jolley followed the river traffic, was mate of a steamboat, and died of cholera while in that service and is buried at Helena, Arkansas. He was the father of two sons, Levi Jolley, who spent his life in Piatt County, and Henry Thomas; and three daughters, one of whom, Elizabeth, became the wife of David Allen, and in 1849 crossed the plains to California, but spent her last years at Seattle, Washington.

Henry Thomas Jolley was born near Glasgow, in Scott County, Illinois, in 1842, was reared on a farm and had only the limited opportunities afforded by schools of his day. When the Civil war came on he enlisted as a private in Company E of the Twenty-eighth Illinois Infantry. He was seriously wounded at the battle of Shiloh and disabled for further active duty as a soldier. After leaving the army he engaged in farming, and he spent his last days at Roodhouse, where he died at the age of forty-nine. He married Jane Rogers in Greene County, north of Patterson. She was born near Patterson in 1847, one of the large family of Charles and Miranda (Marsh) Rogers, who came to Illinois from Lexington, Kentucky, representing old families of the Blue Grass district of Kentucky, and of still earlier Colonial ancestry in the United States. Mrs. Henry T. Jolley died in 1918. She was the mother of the following children: Mrs. Ida Cato, of Stuttgart, Arkansas; Mrs. Belle Englehart, of Alton, Illinois; Mrs. May Ferguson, of Stuttgart, Arkansas; and William Albert.

William Albert Jolley was six years of age when his parents moved to Roodhouse and he grew up in that railroad town, finishing his education in high school there. At the age of fourteen he went to work in the mechanical department of the Roodhouse Eye, then edited by W. F. Thompson. By practical experience he learned printing and the various phases of newspaper work. After his training at Roodhouse he became a typical journeyman printer, working in different offices over the country, but spending several years with the Messenger at Medora, Illinois. After an absence of about ten years he returned to Roodhouse and in 1902 bought a half interest in the Record. Since then he has been associated with Frank Merrill in the publishing of that splendid newspaper. Mr. Merrill established the Record in 1898, and it is one of the few newspapers in this section of the state that has been practically under continuous management for over a quarter of a century. For a number of years it was published daily, but since the World war has been a weekly. It is independent democratic in politics and serves well its function of publishing local news pertaining to the county and immediate community.

Mr. Jolley is a member of the Illinois Press Association. For fourteen years he held the office of city clerk at Roodhouse, and during an interval of two years in this time was mayor of the city. He has been master of the local lodge of Masons, is a member of Ansar Temple of the Mystic Shrine, Springfield, is a trustee of the Baptist Church and for some years, superintendent of the Sunday School. Politically he cast his first presidential vote for William J. Bryan in 1896 and supported that candidate three times. He has attended a number of party conventions. He was registered during the World war, but was not called to duty, though he claimed no exemption.

Mr. Jolley married at Medora, Illinois, December 11, 1895, Miss Bessie Ann Pritchett, who was born at Medora, November 13, 1877, daughter of John and Susan (Medley) Pritchett of Jersey County, Illinois. The children in the Pritchett family were: John, Oscar, Albert, Hugh, Mrs. Emma Farrow, now of Lake Worth, Florida, Mrs. Dora Osborne, of Medora, and Mrs. Jolley. Mr. and Mrs. Jolley have three children. The daughter, Irene, graduated from the Roodhouse High School, also attended the Woman's College at Jacksonville, and was organist at the Baptist Church for several years, taught in the schools of that city, and was married to Sidney M. Drake of Roodhouse, now living at Lake Worth, Florida. Mr. and Mrs. Drake have three children, named Sidney M., Jr., Barbara Ann and William Jolley. Mr. Drake is engaged in the real estate business. The second daughter, Vivian M. Jolley, also graduated from the Roodhouse High School, attended Shurtleff College at Alton, Illinois, and is now a teacher of English in the high school at Lake Worth, Florida. The only son, William Albert, Sr., a high school graduate, is now a linotype operator in the Record office. He is a trap drummer and plays in band and orchestra.

WILLIAM D. WEBSTER. Among the business men of White Hall, William D. Webster probably has had the widest range of commercial experience considering territory covered. For many years he was a traveling salesman, covering nearly all the states of the Middle West and Far Northwest. He has been an active business man at White Hall for the past fifteen years.

His father was Richard Webster, who came from the State of Maine to Illinois prior to 1840. He located in Rock Island County, and though a foundryman by trade, he set up in business as a tavern keeper at the village of Hampton. From there he removed to Wisconsin, where he was in the same line of business, and subsequently left that state, starting for Pike's Peak, Colorado, during the mining excitement there. In Missouri he was diverted from his destination, locating in that state, and his place and date of death is unknown to his son, William D. Richard Webster married Mary Palmer. They had three sons and two daughters, the two older sons, Augustus and Frank, enlisting in Missouri for service in the Union army, and Frank dying during his service, while Augustus returned to Missouri and married and reared a large family. The daughters were Elizabeth, who married a Wisconsin man named Hassett, and went to Missouri with her parents; and Lillie, who reared a family in Missouri.

William D. Webster was born at Hampton, Rock Island County, Illinois, November 17, 1849. As a small child he went to live with his father's brother, William Webster, a shoemaker at Hampton, who had no children of his own. He acquired his public school education there, and at the age of fifteen began looking after himself, working as a farm hand on the other side of the Mississippi River in Iowa. His farming experience was concluded when he raised a crop on the shares and made three or four hundred dollars for his season's work. He next became clerk in a Hampton store, was clerk and bookkeeper in a dry goods store at Rock Island for two or three years, and at Cordova, Illinois, followed bookkeeping and eventually became associated in the general merchandise business with John Wynkoop, the firm being Wynkoop & Webster. Mr. Webster subsequently bought out his partner and continued the business alone for several years.

After selling out he went on the road as a traveling representative in Nebraska for Barton Brothers of Kansas City. While in Nebraska he made his home at Lincoln. After two years he became a representative for the American Hand Sewed Shoe Company of Omaha, changing his residence to Omaha, and was on the road for that concern ten years. From there he moved to Minneapolis and for five years sold the output of the O. C. Hansen Manufacturing Company, makers of gloves and mittens, in Minnesota, the Dakotas, Montana, and the Northern Peninsula of Michigan. From Minneapolis he moved to St. Louis for a year, represented a rubber house in Kansas territory, and in 1910 established his permanent home at White Hall.

At White Hall Mr. Webster has conducted a successful variety store business. He bought and remodeled the old building formerly occupied by the Peoples Bank, and has a thoroughly up-to-date store.

Mr. Webster is a loyal and public spirited citizen of White Hall. He is treasurer of the Building Fund of the Baptist Church, a member of the local Chamber of Commerce and was one of the subscribers to the purchase of stock for the local overall factory. He did committee work and subscribed the funds for the successful promotion of the war.

Mr. Webster married in July, 1870, Miss Elizabeth Johnston, a native of New Jersey, who was brought to Illinois by her parents and reared at Cordova. Her father, William Johnston, was a carpenter and is remembered as one of the finest specimens of physical manhood in his generation. He and his wife died at Cordova, and they reared all of their ten children. Those living today are: Joseph, of Marshalltown, Iowa; John, of Portland, Oregon; Charles, of Clinton, Iowa; Mrs. Matilda Wooders, of St. Louis; Mrs. Mary Handell, of Bloomington, Illinois; and Mrs. Webster. Mr. and Mrs. Webster are the parents of two sons and one daughter. The son, Ralph F., lives at White Hall. Charles, a commercial salesman with home at Grand Rapids, Michigan, married Anna Lewis, and they have a daughter, Grace Elizabeth, who is now Mrs. George Papin, of Detroit. The daughter, Hattie, is the wife of Harry C. Cox, of Wyoming, Illinois. The children of Mr. and Mrs. Cox are: Emma Lou, wife of Earl Rutledge, of Peoria; Elizabeth, wife of John Babb, of Peoria; Miss Harriet, a student at Peoria; and Jerry C. and Maxine.

ALBERT E. STOLZE is an Edwardsville business man whose record is one that is abundant testimony to his remarkable initiative and enterprise. He took heavy responsibilities when almost a boy, and has built up one of the largest retail lumber organizations in Illinois, the Stolze Lumber Company.

He was born at Edwardsville, October 3, 1878, son of John and Louise (Grebel) Stolze. His father, a native of Germany, came to Illi-

E. W. Brace. Ella B. Brace.

nois when four years of age, while the mother was born at Edwardsville, of a pioneer family of German origin. Mr. Albert Stolze's mother is still living. His father died in 1921. The late John Stolze was at one time mayor of Edwardsville, and during his term in office the water works system was constructed. He was always a factor in civic affairs.

The lumber business now controlled by the Stolze family in Edwardsville was established in 1874 by John Stolze. Albert Stolze, the oldest of the six sons, and second child among ten children, was reared and educated in Edwardsville, and was only eighteen years of age when, in 1897, he took charge of the lumber business, showing an energy and careful judgment that would have been a credit to a much older man. He has since become president of this business, and has expanded it to five retail yards, the others outside of Edwardsville being at Staunton, Illinois, at Benld, at Wood River, and at Granite City. The company also owns the Edwardsville Wood Works, manufacturing interior trim and other building materials.

Mr. Stolze in later years has achieved a number of other business interests. He is one of the directors of the firm of the Stickle Lumber Corporation at Dallas, Texas, and is a director of the Bank of Edwardsville and the Peoples Loan Association of Edwardsville. He is a member of the Chamber of Commerce. Mr. Stolze for several years has been an operator in real estate, and has put on the market, developed and improved one of the fine residential additions to Edwardsville, building homes which are sold on time payment.

On January 25, 1905, he married Miss Hilda Weder, of St. Louis, Missouri. Their three children are: Irma, Paul and Evelyn. Mr. Stolze is affiliated with the Knights of Columbus, and he and his family belong to St. Boniface Catholic Church.

EDGAR E. BRASS, owner of the Petersburg Canning Works, is a business man of outstanding ability, recognized as one of the leaders in the industrial development of Menard County. He was born in Cuming County, Nebraska, July 25, 1870, a son of Albert S. Brass, a native of Dexter, Michigan, but of English descent. His father, an Englishman, upon his arrival in the United States settled in Michigan, and his life closed in Washtenaw County. The grandfather married a member of the Stevens family, also of English birth, and they had thirteen children who reached maturity, among them being Walter, Horace, William (who died while serving in the Union army), Albert S. and Mrs. Emma Davis. Horace Brass, of the above family, was also a Union soldier, and he, while he lived long enough to return home, died soon thereafter from disability incurred in the service.

Albert S. Brass moved to Nebraska soon after the close of the war between the states and homesteaded in Cuming County. Owing to the scarcity of building materials in that region the pioneers built their first homes partly of sod, and it was in one of these primitive shelters that Mr. Brass of this review was born. While this pioneer home was replaced by a better one as the years passed, Albert S. Brass continued on the farm until he retired, at which time he moved to Beemer, Nebraska, and there he died when he was fifty-seven years old. While his education was limited to what he acquired in the country schools, he was an intelligent and well-informed man, and always stood well with his neighbors. During the war between the states he enlisted in a Michigan regiment, and served until the close of the war. Although twice slightly wounded, he escaped being captured, and his service was rendered as a guard for the steamboats of the Union army along the lower part of the Mississippi River, a most dangerous work. Albert S. Brass married at West Point, Nebraska, Harriet A. Hall, a daughter of Daniel Hall, and she was born at Chippewa Falls, Wisconsin. She survives her husband and is now a resident of Stevenson, Washington. Mr. and Mrs. Brass had the following children born to their marriage: Edgar E., who was the first born; Alice, who died in infancy; Horace, who died in Omaha, Nebraska, in 1914, without issue, although he was married; Agnes, who married Ed Lindloff, of Portland, Oregon; and Clara, who is Mrs. Adolphus Kee, of Stevenson, Washington.

Growing up in his native county, Edgar E. Brass attended the country schools and remained on the farm until he was sixteen years old, at which time he went to Beemer and became a clerk in one of the stores of that village. When he began clerking he received his board, clothes and part time in school for his services, and when he completed his four years' connection with this store he was receiving his board and thirty dollars a month.

Too ambitious to be content with the progress he was making, Mr. Brass in 1891 became roustabout for a little cannery at Mount City, Missouri, and spent a season in that neighborhood, and in 1892, coming to Virginia, Illinois, in Cass County, he became foreman of the cannery he now owns, and the second year was made its superintendent. The third year he was with the company he was made its secretary, and the next year the duties of general manager were added to his other ones. In 1902 he moved the plant from Virginia, Illinois, to Petersburg, Illinois, and continued as secretary and general manager until 1918, when he purchased the entire stock and has since continued as its owner.

The capacity of the plant in output for 1925 was 38,000 cases of corn and 20,000 cases of pumpkin, two dozen cans per case. Additions have been made, as needed to the plant, beginning in 1902, and there are now half a dozen buildings, with a floor space of 30,000 feet. The buildings are steel and concrete and are modern and thoroughly sanitary. Employment is given to from thirty to eighty people, and this is one of the chief industrial plants of Petersburg.

In addition to his canning plant Mr. Brass is an active farmer and has other interests, is secretary of the Shale Products Company of Petersburg, of which he was one of the promoters, and he has aided in its continued life and activity during the last few years. For ten or twelve years Mr. Brass has been a member of the Petersburg Board of Education. He was a charter member of the Petersburg Rotary Club, and belongs to the Knights of Pythias. His first vote was cast for William McKinley for president, and he has since faithfully maintained his allegiance to the republican party and was nominated for Congress from the Twentieth District in 1912. This is, as is well known, a democratic stronghold, but he polled a surprising vote and when required to file his campaign expense account he humorously gave it as "one can of pumpkin." His family have always been republicans since the organization of the party in the early '50s.

In addition to all of the above-mentioned activities Mr. Brass constructed the first hard road built in Menard County. There were no bidders for the contract, and he was awarded it, and built his first section of it from the north limits of Petersburg to a point one-half mile in the country. Another contract he took was for a piece of road the same length running west from the town, and the third contract was for a similar piece east of Petersburg up Rose Hill. Taking the contracts at the state's estimate, he built the roads at a personal loss.

During the late war he operated his plant to full capacity and furnished canned food to the government to some extent. A son and a son-in-law were in the service, the latter going overseas and the former being stationed in the lumber camps of the State of Washington, where he was engaged in getting out airplane material from the virgin forests.

On February 23, 1890, Mr. Brass married in Beemer, Nebraska, Ella B. Potter, daughter of Edwin H. Potter, who died at Mound City, Missouri, in 1902. Mrs. Edwin H. Potter before her marriage was Lucy Snyder, and both she and her husband moved from South Bend, Indiana, in 1870 to South Dakota, where they resided for some time. Their children were: Frank, who died in 1904; Mrs. Brass; Kate, wife of Joseph Caldwell, of Chicago; Carrie, who died in 1912, wife of Charles Book, of Mound City, Missouri; and Edwin H., now of St. Louis, Missouri.

The following children have been born to Mr. and Mrs. Brass: Hazel A., who married Edward S. Mitchell, of Petersburg, Illinois; Lloyd L., who married Dorothy Barnes, and is the soldier of the family and is now located at San Diego, California; Glenna, a teacher in the public schools and residing in Petersburg, the widow of Lloyd T. Mitchell, who died from the effects of gas and exposure during the war, and has a son, Lloyd T., Jr.; Laverne, a school teacher of Petersburg; Jean, attending training school for nurses in Decatur, Illinois; Edgar E., Jr., a student in the graded schools of Petersburg; Mary Lou and Ward Randolph, the little ones of the family, also attending the graded schools of Petersburg.

DELMONT L. SCHAEFFER, cashier of the Farmers Bank of Trenton, has spent practically all his life in Clinton County, and is one of the favorably known financiers and citizens of that locality.

He was born at Trenton, September 12, 1889, son of William and Ida (Hohe) Schaeffer. William Schaeffer was born in Switzerland and on coming to America first worked in the coal mines, learned surveying and for many years was one of the prominent officials and business men of Clinton County. He was a veteran of the Civil war, enlisting June 25, 1861, and became bandmaster of the Twenty-second Illinois Regimental Band from Belleville. In after years he served as sheriff and tax collector of Clinton County and conducted a hotel at Trenton. He was a member of the Masonic fraternity as well as other lodges.

He was twice married, Mrs. Ida Hohe Schaeffer, still living, being his second wife. After that marriage there were two sons, Delmont L. and William. Adolph, of the first marriage, graduated from the United States Naval Academy at Annapolis in the same class as Admiral Hobson, but subsequently resigned from the navy and started for Alaska, since which time no word has ever been heard from him.

Delmont L. Schaeffer was reared in Clinton County. He was eleven years of age when his father died in 1900. His mother being a Catholic, Mr. Schaeffer received his early advantages in parochial schools, but after the age of twelve attended the public schools at Trenton and Carlyle, Illinois. He also spent one year in the University of Illinois. After completing his education he returned to Trenton and became bookkeeper in the Farmers Bank of that city. He was with this bank seven years, then removed to Albers in Clinton County as cashier of the Peoples Bank there, and also served as president of that institution. He was at Albers from 1916 to 1923 returning in the latter year to Trenton, where he has since served as cashier of the Farmers Bank.

Mr. Schaeffer during the World war was put in the fourth class and was unable to get into active service as a soldier. He is unmarried and adheres to the faith of his mother, being a member of the Catholic Church.

RAYMOND B. PEARCE. One of the names most important and conspicuous in the annals of the community of White Hall, Greene County, is that of Pearce. The old White Hall Republican became one of the leading newspapers in this section of the state as a result of the labors of the late Captain E. J. Pearce and his son, Raymond B. Pearce. The latter is now postmaster of White Hall.

The Pearce genealogy dates back to 1608. During the Revolutionary war William Pearce was a soldier in the cause of independence from Pennsylvania. According to a record in the war office under date of February 1, 1782, he was captain, ranking No. 10 in the Continental Line of the Pennsylvania Artillery. A son of this Revolutionary soldier was Elisha Pearce, and a son of Elisha was Joseph Pearce, a native of Pennsylvania, who followed the trade of hatter. Joseph Pearce married Sarah Ann Allen, and their children were: Ebenezer James; Mary, who died unmarried; John Mansfield and Ethan Allen, both of whom were soldiers in the Civil war; Emily Ann, who became the wife of Frank Dossett; and Francis Joseph, who died young.

Ebenezer James Pearce, the pioneer of the family at White Hall, Illinois, was born Octo-

PLANT OF PETERSBURG CANNING WORKS

Showing "Vineyard Hill," Home of the Brass Family, in the Background.

ber 6, 1839, in Evansburg, Pennsylvania, and was reared on a farm in the environment of one of the pioneer districts of Pennsylvania. He acquired a good education and during the late '50s came overland to Illinois. In Greene County he taught what is now known as the Gregory and Maples Grove schools near White Hall. Not long afterward, the war having opened, he joined the Union army as a member of Company G, Ninety-first Illinois Infantry. For a time he was second lieutenant, was promoted to captain, and during the siege of Vicksburg was assigned special duty as assistant provost marshal. His command was finally sent to Brownsville, Texas, and he was mustered out at Camp Butler, Illinois.

After the war Captain Pearce resumed teaching and for a time was a government gauger of the Peoria district. In 1877 he established the White Hall Republican, and devoted the rest of his active life to newspaper work. He was also in the insurance business. His activities, attainments and character made him a man of genuine distinction in his community. He was an able public speaker, and was a member of the Grand Army of the Republic and Independent Order of Odd Fellows. In religious matters he was liberal. He possessed culture due to the thorough reading of an unusual range of literature, his favorite works being the classics, history and biography, and he accumulated a fine private library. He was one of the early temperance workers, and his newspaper from the beginning advocated temperance and was the first outspoken temperance journal in this section of the state. Captain Pearce died April 30, 1907. He married Margaret Carr, who died a year before him. She was born at White Hall, daughter of William Carr. Their children were: Frederick V., of Mount Morris, Illinois; Edward Carr, of White Hall; Raymond Blair; Mrs. Laura Pritchett, of White Hall; and Mrs. Mabel Meisenbach, of St. Louis.

Raymond B. Pearce was born at White Hall, July 9, 1875. He has never married. He attended the grade schools of his native town and when about fourteen years of age became self-supporting, earning his first money around the Alton station in White Hall. He learned telegraphy under George W. Secor, and was a telegraph operator at the age of sixteen, working at different stations on the Burlington between Rock Island and St. Louis. Leaving that service, he returned to White Hall, went to work in the White Hall Republican office and was actively associated with his father in the newspaper business and eventually became editor of the Republican. He gave up his newspaper work in 1916, the year the Republican was merged with the White Hall Register. Mr. Pearce during the World war returned to the vocation of his boyhood and made good use of his knowledge of telegraphy by serving in an emergency capacity at Roodhouse for the Chicago & Alton Railway. He continued in that service until he was selected as postmaster to succeed Richard T. Clark, temporary postmaster, and has been in charge of this office since May 1, 1923.

While engaged in newspaper work Mr. Pearce became interested in historical research and the preservation of all historical records particularly related to this section of Illinois. He helped promote the Soldiers Monument at White Hall, and he has compiled a complete record of all the soldiers in the various wars, beginning with the Revolution and ending with the World war, who might properly be credited to Greene County, or who spent part of their lives in the county. At the beginning of 1926 a White Hall Historical Society was formed, and one of the plans of the society is the establishment of a museum. Another direction of his interests while in the newspaper business was weather bureau reporting, and he has continued his daily observations and his reports to the agriculture department, issuing the daily forecast for this locality. Mr. Pearce has handled the publicity work of the Men's Bible Class of the First Baptist Church at White Hall.

ROBERT ROY TINSLEY, president of the Grand Avenue Lumber & Supply Company, has been a lumber merchant at Waukegan since locating here. Most of his early life was spent in Chicago. He comes of a family which for two generations have been identified with railroading.

Mr. Tinsley was born at London, Ontario, Canada, February 13, 1891, son of Robert and Jennie A. (Petrie) Tinsley, and grandson of Edwin and Jessie (Chisholm) Tinsley, who were natives of England. Edwin Tinsley when about twenty-one years of age and after his marriage came to America, locating at Hamilton, Ontario. There he entered the service of the Grand Trunk Railroad Company and was with that company a period of forty-five years, being one of the oldest men in the service when he retired. After retirement he was appointed chief game warden and superintendent of fisheries in Ontario, and continued so until his death in 1918, when about eighty-five years of age. His wife died in 1916.

Robert Tinsley was born in Canada, as was his wife, attended public schools there, and also entered the employ of the Grand Trunk Railroad Company, being with that company many years. In 1893 he removed with his family to Chicago, and he and his wife still live in that city. In Chicago he was with the Pullman Car Company until he retired in 1910, being manager. After that he engaged in the railway supply business, and is now Chicago representative for the Oxford Varnish Company of Detroit. During the World war his business experience made him valuable to the Government and he was given the rank of major in the Thirty-fifth Engineers and was stationed at La Rochelle, France, in charge of car building. His wife is an active church worker.

Robert Roy Tinsley was a small child when brought to Chicago. He attended grammar and high school there, was a member of the class of 1910 in Lake Forest Academy, and then entered Cornell University with the intention of pursuing a law course. After a few months he left college and returning to Chicago, became associated with his father in the railroad supply business for about a year. For about four years he was in the general mercantile business at Chicago, up to

1916, and following that for a few months was with the Sherwin-Williams Company, paint manufacturers.

Mr. Tinsley in April, 1917, moved to Waukegan and engaged in the lumber business, he and his associates, Mr. Brannum, D. Q. Hart and James Brannum, purchasing the Waukegan Lumber Company. This business had steady growth under the new organization and handled business all over Lake County. Mr. Tinsley on account of the enlarged business outlook subsequently started a new lumber plant, known as the Grand Avenue Lumber & Supply Company, of which he is president, M. B. Tinsley, vice president, and G. C. Richardson, secretary. They have erected a large plant on Grand Avenue.

Mr. Tinsley is a member of the lumbermen's fraternity, the Hoo Hoos, belongs to the B. P. O. Elks, the Waukegan Chamber of Commerce, Phi Gamma Delta college fraternity, and is a charter member of the Kiwanis Club of Waukegan. He belongs to the Glen Flora Country Club, Bonnie Brook Golf Club, is a republican and a member of the Presbyterian Church. Mr. Tinsley moved to Waukegan about the time America entered the World war. Shortly after going into the lumber business he was accidentally injured in the lumber yard, and that injury incapacitated him for active army duty. He took part in all the war drives, including the sale of Liberty Bonds, and was active in the Red Cross and other organizations. He is a charter member of the Waukegan Building & Loan Association.

He married in Chicago, January 9, 1917, Miss Marjorie Brannum, who was educated in the grammar and high schools of that city and in Lewis Institute, and finished her education in Dana Hall Girls School. She is active in church and woman's club life. Her father, W. S. Brannum, has for many years been in the lumber business in Chicago, and he and his wife still live in that city. Mr. and Mrs. Tinsley have four children: Marjorie, Robert Roy, Jr., Thomas James and Nancy Brannum.

JOHN VARDAMAN DILLMAN, M. D., is an accomplished physician and surgeon whose work for a number of years has identified him with the city of Louisville in Clay County. He was a medical officer during the World war, and is also known in his home community as a banker.

Doctor Dillman was born on a farm in Clay County, July 31, 1869, son of Lewis and Harriet B. (Smith) Dillman, and a grandson of Vachel Dillman, who established his family in Clay County in 1854. Vachel Dillman after a brief residence in Illinois returned to his home state of Kentucky, where he died. Lewis Dillman was born in Henry County, Kentucky, in 1836, and for many years was a Clay County farmer, his interests also extending to banking. He died at the age of seventy-five and for several years prior to his death had been president of the Clay County State Bank. He was a democrat in politics. His widow survives him and is now eighty-six years of age. She was born in Hancock County, Tennessee. Of her eleven children nine grew to mature years and seven are still living.

John Vardaman Dillman was reared on a farm, and while a boy in the country attended rural schools. He continued his education in the Greenlaw School at Flora, the Union Christian College at Merom, Indiana, and for several winters taught school. In 1899 he graduated in medicine at Washington University at St. Louis, and for six years practiced at Bible Grove, Illinois, four years at Ingraham, and after a year on the Pacific Coast located at Louisville, where he has become one of the very busy men of his profession and has achieved a front rank as a physician and surgeon in this section of the state. He is a member of the Clay County, Illinois State and American Medical Associations, is the designated examiner in Clay County for the Veterans Bureau, and is also chairman of the Citizens Military Training Committee for the county.

Doctor Dillman in September, 1917, volunteered and was commissioned a first lieutenant in the Army Medical Corps. He was called to active duty at Camp Wadsworth, South Carolina, later performed special duty at the University of Pennsylvania, for a time had charge of a hospital at the Virginia Polyclinic Institute at Blackburg, and finally returned to Camp Wadsworth, where he acted as receiving officer until after the armistice, when he was discharged with the rank of captain. He is now a member of the American Legion. Doctor Dillman is a thirty-second degree Scottish Rite Mason, member of the Independent Order of Odd Fellows, the Christian Church and is a democrat in politics.

His father was the first president of the Clay County State Bank. The second president was W. H. Dillman, a brother of Doctor Dillman. Doctor Dillman succeeded this brother as the third president. During his absence in the army while the World war was in progress Doctor Dillman's place was filled by his brother-in-law, the late Dr. G. W. Steely. Now Doctor Dillman is again president of this institution. He is also owner of a large amount of farm and fruit growing land.

In 1918, while home on leave of absence from the army, Doctor Dillman married Miss Lula Goodnough. She died November 14, 1924, leaving two children, Jean Vardaman and Wilbur Lewis Dillman.

CHARLES W. MOORE was born and has spent his life in Carroll County, where he is prominently known as a farmer and banker and a citizen of marked public spirit.

He was born near Mount Carroll March 19, 1868. His grandparents were Charles and Jane (Ross) Moore, natives of Ireland, who brought their family to America about 1842 and settled near Hanover in Jo Daviess County, Illinois, where Charles Moore spent the rest of his life as a farmer and where he died and is buried. He was the father of a family of eight sons, William, Robert, Charles, Samuel, George, Thomas, James and Josiah. The only one now living is Thomas, of Galena, Illinois.

Yours very Truly
Rev. P. J. Eickmann

Robert Moore, father of Charles W., of Mount Carroll, was born in Ireland and was twelve years of age when he came to America. He grew up in Jo Daviess County, finishing his education in public schools there. In 1852, as a young man, he went over the plains to California, and for two years lived on the Pacific Coast engaged in mining and other business. After returning to Illinois he located on a farm, married, and subsequently bought a farm near Mount Carroll, where he lived, enjoying prosperity in proportion to his diligence and industry. In 1898 he retired and spent his last years at Mount Carroll, where he died in 1914. His wife was Anna Mackay, who died in 1923. They were the parents of four sons and four daughters: Jennie is the wife of Ed Rankin, of Los Angeles, California; Nettie, now deceased, was the wife of Harvey Graham, of Monmouth, Illinois, and her son, Harold Graham, died while in service during the World war at Dayton, Ohio; Robert lives at Los Angeles; Charles W.; Alice is a resident of Mount Carroll; Duncan lives at Los Angeles; Retta, who died January 6, 1925, was the wife of Dan Connell; and Josiah died in infancy.

Charles W. Moore was reared on a farm, attended public schools in Mount Carroll and Carthage College at Carthage, Illinois, also the Davenport Business College. After this liberal education he took up farming, and that has been his chief vocation. He is one of the progressive men in the agricultural affairs of Carroll County, and he still owns the old homestead near the county seat and another farm within the city limits of Mount Carroll. Mr. Moore is a director of the First State Bank of Mount Carroll and is president of the Farmers State Bank of Chadwick.

He has been a good business man without neglecting calls upon his service in the community and for many years has been a school director. He is a member of the Glengary Country Club, is a republican and a Methodist.

Mr. Moore married at Monmouth, Illinois, October 27, 1897, Miss Blanche Pogue, who attended public schools and Monmouth College and taught for a year in Henderson County, Illinois, prior to her marriage. Mrs. Moore takes an active part in Sunday School, teaching a class of girls at the Francis Shimer Academy, and is also a member of the Woman's Community Club of Mount Carroll. Her parents were Thomas and Emaline (Spears) Pogue, farmers near Monmouth. Her grandfather was one of the early settlers in that vicinity. Mr. and Mrs. Moore have four children, Helen, Gertrude, Charlotte and Marjorie. Helen attended public schools, graduated from the Francis Shimer Academy in 1918, from the University of Illinois in 1920, and is now in Chicago as secretary to the advertising manager of the Union Trust Company. Gertrude graduated from the Mount Carroll High School in 1921, from Francis Shimer Academy in 1923, and from the University of Illinois in 1926. The daughter Charlotte finished the work of the Mount Carroll High School in 1924 and graduated from Francis Shimer Academy in 1926. Marjorie is a member of the high school class of 1929.

Mr. and Mrs. Moore have been very generous in providing their children with complete educational advantages in some of the best institutions of the state.

REV. CHARLES J. ESCHMANN. At Waterloo, Monroe County, the Catholic priest is Rev. Charles J. Eschmann. The community, Catholic and non-Catholic, have come to appreciate the broad mindedness and sincere public spirit of this church man. Several other communities in southern Illinois have known him for much longer pastorates than that he has spent at Waterloo.

He is a native of southern Illinois. His father, John Eschmann, was born in 1828 at Deidesheim, Rhinish Palatinate, Bavaria, and in 1859 came from Germany to Illinois. Locating at Belleville, he worked in a flouring mill and eventually became wheat buyer for the company. He continued in the milling business until his death in 1901. He married, in 1860, Madaline Hasenstab, who was born at the village of Obernan, near Frankfort-on-the-Main in 1839, the oldest of seven children. In 1853 her father, Peter Hasenstab, brought the family to America. He was a blacksmith by trade and opened a shop at Belleville, Illinois, but died within the era of his coming to this country. Mrs. Madaline Eschmann lived to the age of eighty-three, passing away in 1922. Charles J. was the oldest of her ten children. The other sons still living are: Adam, a carpenter at Belleville, George at Cairo, Illinois, John, in the boiler and real estate business at St. Louis, Michael now a resident of the State of Washington, who served three years in the Phillipines in the United States Cavalry following the Spanish-American war.

Rev. Charles J. Eschmann was born at Belleville January 11, 1862. He grew up in that St. Clair County community, attending parochial schools and the Catholic High School. His education was continued in the Franciscan College at Teutopolis, Illinois, in the seminary at Milwaukee, and from there he went abroad to attend the famous university at Innsbruch, Austria, where he completed his classical and theological courses and was ordained April 6, 1889.

On returning to America Father Eschmann took charge of the parish at Mount Vernon, Illinois, with several missions in Jefferson, Hamilton and Washington counties. In 1891 he was transferred to St. Patrick's parish at Cairo. His service there covered a period of eleven years and gave him opportunity to prove his constructive ability. During his pastorate he erected the fine new St. Patrick's Church and also the St. Mary's Infirmary. His church superiors learned that in Father Eschmann was a minister capable not only of the routine service to a parish but the organizing zeal that makes a parish grow and the church and community prosper. Consequently in 1902 he was selected by the Bishop to take the St. Joseph's church and parish at Prairie Du Rocher in Randolph County. Here he remained through nine happy and prosperous years. From there he was assigned to the church at Duquoin in Perry County, and again he was permitted to remain a period of eleven years. From the Sacred Heart Church at Duquoin he was transferred in 1922 to Centralia. While there only two years he brought new vitality into the parish, and among other accomplishments brought about the building of an extensive addition to St. Mary's Hospital at Centralia. In August, 1924, his Bishop assigned him to Waterloo, Monroe County, where he has charge of Sts. Peter and Paul Church.

Father Eschmann has a splendid education. He has been much interested in matters of civic leadership in community, county and state. He is a deep student of local history, and for many years has been a member of the Illinois State Historical Society. He has done much to secure the preservation of historic sites in southern Illinois. He went to Springfield to help urge the Legislature to appropriate money for the restoration and protection of the famous old Fort Chartres Magazine and its surroundings.

JAMES E. FURLONG, owner of the leading furniture and undertaking establishment at Galena, is a native of Jo Daviess County, and among his property possessions is some of the land which was acquired by his grandfather in pioneer times in the county.

This grandfather was John Furlong, who was born and reared in County Wexford, Ireland. He married Mary Carroll. About 1820 they came to America, and subsequently settled in the northwestern corner of Illinois, where they took up land direct from the government. This land has been in the possession of the Furlong family for nearly a century, and the old homestead is now owned by James E. Furlong and his sister, Mary Furlong. Their father, John E. Furlong, was born at the old farm, in the Vinegar Hill locality of Jo Daviess County, and attended public schools and the Brothers College at Sinsinawa Mound, Wisconsin. After completing his education he returned to the farm and was engaged in agriculture and the growing of pure bred cattle and hogs until his death on February 18, 1913. John E. Furlong married Catherine Murray, who was born and reared at Sinsinawa, Wisconsin, attending public schools there. She was the first graduate of St. Clara College at Sinsinawa, and after graduating she taught in that college for a number of years, and among other subjects was a teacher of music. She was a daughter of John and Mary (Sheridan) Murray, of Sinsinawa. Mary Sheridan was a distant relative of Gen. Phil Sheridan. John Murray was a farmer and a miner, owning a lead mine on his farm.

James E. Furlong was born at the Furlong homestead at Vinegar Hills, near Galena. He attended the local schools, the high school at Hazen Green, Wisconsin, Palmer's Business College at Cedar Rapids, Iowa, and Coe College at Cedar Rapids. Leaving college in 1887 he spent the following six years as an employe of the American Express Company at Sioux City, Iowa. In 1893, while the World's Fair was in progress at Chicago, he went to that city and spent two years with the undertaking firm of Ralston & Company, after which he entered the service of the P. J. Hursen Company, an organization with which he was identified for eleven years. After this long experience in training Mr. Furlong in 1906 returned to Galena and formed a partnership with William A. Uhren, furniture and undertakers, establishing the firm of Uhren & Furlong, which name is still retained, though Mr. Uhren died January 15, 1924. Mr. Furlong subsequently acquired the Uhren interest from his estate, and is now sole owner. The business has grown until it occupies three stores, and in point of service and equipment the undertaking department is unsurpassed by any similar concern in northwestern Illinois.

Mr. Furlong is a very popular citizen and business man, and has proved his sincere public spirit on many occasions. He is affiliated with the B. P. O. Elks, Eagles and Moose, is a member of the Kiwanis Club, Galena Golf Club, is a democrat and a member of the Catholic Church.

ALEXANDER H. BELL, a former grand master of the Masonic Grand Lodge of Illinois, is a resident of Carlinville, where he has rounded out nearly half a century of practice as a lawyer.

He was born at Troy, Illinois, October 29, 1853, about two years after his parents, Thomas H. and Julia A. (Hubbard) Bell, settled in that community. His parents came from the eastern shore of Maryland. Alexander H. Bell acquired his early education in public schools and at Blackburn University at Carlinville, where he was graduated in June, 1875, with the Bachelor of Science degree. In later years Blackburn bestowed upon him the LL. D. degree. In June, 1897, he was admitted to the bar and first began practice at Carlinville. He served as city attorney in 1878, as state's attorney of Macoupin County from 1880 to 1884, was mayor of Carlinville about 1890, and for several terms was president of the local Board of Education and for six years held the office of master in chancery of Macoupin County.

Judge Bell is a democrat in politics. His position as grand master of the Grand Lodge of Illinois Masons was held two terms, from 1907 to 1909. He has been a member of the Masonic Order and a student of Masonry for forty-six years.

Judge Bell married at Carlinville, December 20, 1877, Flora G. Mounts, daughter of Leander W. Mounts. Her father's people were natives of Ohio, and her mother was of a Kentucky family. The two children of Judge and Mrs. Bell are Elizabeth and Robert H. Elizabeth is the wife of Francis Baldwin, an attorney in the employ of Swift & Company at Chicago. Robert H. Bell, now practicing medicine at Carlinville, married Miss Minnie Dilks, of Springfield.

ALBERT L. HALL is a member of the Waukegan bar, is city attorney and has built up a successful law practice there after getting his early training and experience as a lawyer in Chicago.

He was born at Worcester, Massachusetts, November 25, 1889, son of John E. and Augusta (Olson) Hall. The parents were born and reared in Sweden, and his father came

to America when about sixteen years of age, in 1879. He met and married his wife at Worcester, and in 1892 moved with the family to Waukegan, Illinois. John E. Hall for many years was an employe of the American Steel & Wire Company, and since 1919 has been superintendent of the rolling mills for the Interstate Iron & Steel Company of Chicago, and is a resident of that city.

Albert L. Hall grew up at Waukegan, attending grammar and high schools of that city. He graduated from the Waukegan High School in 1908, and in 1912 took his law degree from the University of Illinois. Mr. Hall was admitted to the Illinois bar in 1913 and soon afterward opened a law office and practiced in Chicago, and as a lawyer represented some important interests during the years he was engaged in that city.

Mr. Hall in July, 1918, joined the colors with the Officers Training School at Camp Taylor, Kentucky, where he was in training for the artillery until December, 1918, when he received his honorable discharge. He then resumed his law practice in Chicago, but in 1921 returned to Waukegan and has gained a large clientele in the city where he grew up and spent his youth. During 1921 he was an assistant state's attorney of Lake County and for the past three years has been city attorney. Mr. Hall is a member of the Masonic order, Knights of Pythias and B. P. O. Elks, and is a past commander of Homer Dahringer Post of the American Legion at Waukegan. He is a past president of the Waukegan Rotary Club, a member of the Glen Flora Country Club, Lake County Bar Association, Delta Tau Delta college fraternity, and is president of the Waukegan Y. M. C. A. Mr. Hall is a republican and a member of the Baptist Church.

He married at Chicago, August 25, 1915, Miss Orpah Starratt, of Honolulu, but formerly of Waukegan. She is a daughter of Samuel and Caroline Starratt, who lived in Waukegan for many years but are now residents of Honolulu, Hawaii. Mrs. Hall was reared and educated at Waukegan and taught school there for several years. Mr. and Mrs. Hall have three children, Katherine S., Elizabeth S. and Albert L., Jr.

AUGUST B. EGGLER. In both the yesterday and today of Dundee the jewelry establishment now operated by August B. Eggler has proved a substantial force among the rising institutions of the town. No branch of merchandising is slower in its growth or more conservative in its methods than the jewelry business. Non-fluctuating values largely are responsible for the condition, and, latterly, the same are intensified by the exactions of the associations to which most jewelers belong. It follows, therefore, that men engaged in the calling are of calm and non-speculative mind, reliable as to morals, definite in their purpose and not easily led from accustomed grooves. No exception to this conclusion has been found in the career of August B. Eggler, who came to Dundee in 1880 and in 1897 established the business which has weathered the storms and changes of more than a quarter of a century.

Mr. Eggler was born in Germany, September 12, 1865, and is a son of Benedict and Josephine (Miller) Eggler, natives of Germany, who passed their entire lives there. He was given a public school education in his native land, and was about fifteen years of age when he bid good-bye to his parents to sail for the land of promise, the United States. This was at the earnest entreaties of an uncle, who had preceded him to this country and, having established a successful business here, desired that his nephew be given the opportunity to gain independence and a competence. Accordingly, about 1880, the youth arrived from the Fatherland, and, making his way to Dundee, immediately began to learn the business under the preceptorship of his uncle, who was a skilled jeweler and expert watchmaker. Every branch of the trade was taught him in its entirety, and after seventeen years, or about the year 1897, when his uncle was ready for retirement from business, the nephew bought same, and has conducted it to this time. Mr. Eggler is the owner of the building in which the establishment is situated and of other property and real estate at Dundee and in Kane County. His career has been characterized by industry and economy, and by well directed interest in the affairs which have helped to build up the town. While not a politician, he has always voted the republican ticket. He holds membership in several clubs and fraternities, and all in all takes an energetic and helpful part in the various activities which make up the life of this thriving little Illinois and Kane County city.

On February 28, 1901, in Dundee, Mr. Eggler was united in marriage with Miss Ellen Lewis, who was born in Wassaic, New York, the daughter of Charles E. Lewis, former superintendent of the Gail Borden Condensed Milk Company. To this union there have been born three children: Aloysius A., Marrilla J. and Charles B.

CHARLES I. PIERCE, president of the Saline County Coal Corporation, with offices in the Bell Building at Chicago, has been identified with manufacturing and coal mining in Illinois for over thirty years. He represents a family of manufacturers and business men and pioneers in northern Illinois.

He was born in the city of Kewanee, Illinois, March 24, 1871, son of John Henry and Sarah (Ingals) Pierce. Through his mother his ancestry runs back to Edmund Ingals, who came to this country in 1628, first locating at Salem, Massachusetts, and afterwards at Lynn, Massachusetts. The paternal grandparents of Charles I. Pierce were Thomas and Ruth (Powell) Pierce, the former a native of northern Wales. Thomas Pierce came to Illinois overland, and was one of the earliest pioneers of Kane County in the Fox River Valley, settling there in 1836. He and his wife had three sons and one daughter, the youngest being John Henry Pierce, who was born in Kane County, January 11, 1843. John Henry Pierce was one of the pioneer builders of the manufacturing industry that has long distinguished the city of Kewanee. He was one of the organizers of the Haxtun Steam Heating

Company, later the Western Tube Company; was a banker and connected with a number of business and civic organizations and served one term in the Illinois Senate. He was a republican in politics. John Henry Pierce died July 22, 1908. His wife was born in Lee County, March 6, 1850, and is now seventy-five years of age. There are three children, two sons and one daughter.

Charles I. Pierce studied mechanical engineering in the University of Illinois and in 1891 became associated with his father in manufacturing and coal mining. Since 1904 he has been actively engaged in mining and is now president of the Saline County Coal Corporation. This is one of the largest coal producing companies in Illinois, obtaining its products chiefly from mines in Saline County. The executive offices of the company have been in Chicago for some years. Mr. Pierce is a director in the National Bank of the Republic of Chicago.

He is a director of the Illinois Manufacturers Association, is a republican, a member of the Chicago, Union League, and the University Clubs. In Masonry he is a member of the Kewanee Knights Templar and belongs to Oriental Consistory of the Scottish Rite and Medinah Temple of the Mystic Shrine at Chicago.

Mr. Pierce married, Feb. 20, 1896, Miss Louise Lyman, of Kewanee, who died June 17, 1901, the mother of two daughters, Katharine and Adelaide. On June 8, 1911, he married Miss Grace V. McCarthy, of Chicago. By this marriage there is one son, Charles I., Jr.

FRANK P. WORACK is owner of one of the largest insurance agencies in the Waukegan district. He is a leader in Waukegan business and civic affairs, and gained his early business experience with the Chicago Board of Trade.

He was born at Muskegon, Michigan, November 16, 1894, but his home since early infancy has been in Chicago or Waukegan. His parents were Anthony L. and Cecelia (Hortiz) Worack. His grandfather, Anthony Worack, was born and reared in Prague, Austria, and on coming to America settled with his family at St. Louis, Missouri. Anthony L. Worack was born and reared in St. Louis, attended public schools there and learned the trade of hardwood finisher and piano maker. When about forty years of age he moved to Chicago, later to Muskegon, Michigan, and in 1895 returned to Chicago and was with the Newman Brothers Piano Company. In 1896 he was elected president of the Piano Makers Union of Chicago and served in that capacity four years. He retired in 1923, and he and his wife still reside in Chicago. His wife was born in St. Louis, of French parentage, and was educated in a convent.

Frank P. Worack attended public schools in Chicago, including the Waller High School and the LaSalle University. He left school in 1909 and became an employe of the Chicago Board of Trade and was in the service of that institution in various capacities until June, 1918, when he joined the colors with the Ninth Regiment of Field Artillery. He was trained at Camp Jackson, Columbia, South Carolina, remaining there until January 2, 1919, and received his honorable discharge at Camp Grant January 11.

After leaving the army Mr. Worack resumed his work with the Chicago Board of Trade and was soon made a director in the Sawers Grain Company. In 1922 he transferred his business interests to Racine, Wisconsin, where he was connected with the machinery business. On April 1, 1924, he bought the insurance agency of his deceased brother, Charles A. Worack, who had died March 1, 1924. As owner of this agency he has done much to extend the scope of the business. His agency handles business for the Franklin Life Insurance Company, the Bureau Group Fire Insurance and the United States Fidelity & Guaranty Company in Lake and McHenry counties. Mr. Worack is in every sense a business hustler, makes a success of what he undertakes and has a host of friends in Waukegan and other parts of northern Illinois.

He is grand knight of the Knights of Columbus, is a past secretary of the Waukegan Lions Club, member of the Colemar Golf Club, the Germania Club of Chicago, Fort Dearborn Town Club of Chicago, American Legion and the Forty and Eight Military Society, Bobadil Caravan of the Order of the Alhambra, B. P. O. Elks. He is a republican and a Catholic.

Mr. Worack married at Chicago, September 10, 1919, Miss Dorothy Riedl, who was educated in parochial schools in that city and takes an active part in church and club life at Waukegan. She holds a card of honorable mention for the work done in the Red Cross drive during the World war. Her parents are Mr. and Mrs. Christopher Riedl, of Chicago. Her father for many years was a bicycle manufacturer. Mr. and Mrs. Worack have one son, Frank P., Jr.

LOUIS J. YAGER is the official head of the commission or mayor of the city of Waukegan. That city was his birthplace and for many years he was active in its commercial life and is a successful business man who has utilized his experience and training in handling the important responsibilities of the city government.

He was born near Waukegan July 21, 1871, son of John and Eliza (Brochon) Yager, and a grandson of Philip and Eleanor (MacMichael) Yager. His grandparents came from Erie, Pennsylvania, to northern Illinois about 1846 and were pioneers of Lake County, entering a tract of government land near Waukegan. Philip Yager in addition to developing a farm established a brick making plant and supplied brick for many of the early buildings in Waukegan and vicinity.

John Yager was born at Erie, Pennsylvania, and was about ten years of age when the family came to Lake County, Illinois. Two of his brothers, George and William Yager, were Union soldiers in the Civil war. John Yager spent his active life as a farmer and also learned the brick maker's trade and continued the brick kiln established by his father for many years. A few years before his death he sold his farm and moved to Waukegan, where he was associated with his brother Ezra in the ice business. He died in 1887, at the comparatively early age of fifty-six. He was the youngest of the thirteen children in the family of Philip Yager.

Louis J. Yager attended grammar and high schools at Waukegan and after school clerked in general stores for eight years, and in 1898 engaged in the mercantile business for himself, handling men's clothing and shoes. He built up a prosperous business and continued it for eighteen years, selling out in 1916. He then took up another line of business, promoting a chain of bakeries in six towns of northern Illinois, known as the Federal System of Bakeries. After giving effective direction to these bakeries he sold out in 1921. Mr. Yager was one of the founders and is a director of the Waukegan National Bank.

In 1923 he was elected a city commissioner, becoming commissioner of accounts and finances, and as such vice president of the council. He has given his full time to the duties of this office, and Waukegan as a city has been greatly benefited by his business wisdom and has appreciated the splendid service he has rendered. On the death of Mayor Theodore H. Durst in February, 1926, he became mayor or head of the commission. He is a member of the Glen Flora Country Club, a director of the Rotary Club, is a republican and a Baptist, and since early manhood has been active in church work. For twenty-eight years he has held the office of superintendent of the Sunday School.

Mr. Yager married at Waukegan, June 22, 1898, Miss Margaret Webb, who was educated in the grammar and high schools of Waukegan. She also takes an active part in church work with her husband and is a member of the Woman's Club of Waukegan. Her parents were Chase E. and Jeanette (Minto) Webb, representing an old family of Lake County. Her father was a farmer and stock buyer and at one time served as sheriff of the county. Mr. and Mrs. Yager have one son, Philip Yager, who graduated from the Waukegan High School in 1926 and is enrolled in Carleton College at Northfield, Minnesota.

CLAIRE C. EDWARDS, Circuit Court judge of the Seventeenth Circuit, is a resident of Waukegan, and has been a prominent representative of the bench and bar of Lake County for many years. His family has been identified with Lake County since the very beginning of white settlement there.

Judge Edwards is a descendant of Robert Edwards, who came from England about 1640 and located in Massachusetts Colony. He married Mary Churchill. From Massachusetts the Edwards family moved to Connecticut. Judge Edwards has in his possession a deed given to one of his ancestors in 1772 during the reign of King George III, conveying property in Middletown, Hartford County, Connecticut, to Churchill Edwards.

The grandfather of Judge Edwards and the pioneer of the family in Lake County was also named Churchill Edwards. Churchill Edwards married Louisa Wright, daughter of Capt. John Wright, who was a soldier in the Colonial army during the Revolution. Judge Edwards' sister, Mrs. Maud Coulson, is an active member of the Daughters of the American Revolution, in which she holds membership by virtue of her descent from Captain Wright. Churchill Edwards came to Illinois in 1833 and spent some time in Chicago. That was the year of the cholera epidemic and he helped bury many victims of the plague. For that reason he did not carry out his intention of filing a homestead in the present Chicago district. In 1835 he returned to Watertown, New York, where he married, and coming back to Illinois, settled in Avon Township, near what is now the City of Waukegan, where he acquired land from the Government and spent the rest of his days in improving his holdings. His first house was a log cabin and his neighbors were all Indians. Frequently on cold and stormy nights these Indians sought shelter in the Edwards cabin, and it was filled to overflowing. Churchill Edwards died in 1885. He and his wife had six children: Amanda, who is now the oldest living native white child in Lake County, wife of Daniel Whiteman, of Avon; Mrs. Mary L. Bard, deceased; Henry C.; Charles G.; Mrs. Alice Cribb, deceased; and William W.

Henry C. Edwards, father of Judge Edwards, is now in his eightieth year and resides at Grand Avenue and Jackson Street in Waukegan. He was born near that city in 1847, was educated in public schools and the Waukegan Academy, and has spent his active career in farming. He has held a number of public positions, including county assessor and supervisor and has also assisted in taking the census. Henry C. Edwards married Margaret Sherman, who was born and reared at Libertyville, Lake County, Illinois. She died in 1914. Her father, William Sherman, was born and reared in Pennsylvania, and settled in Lake County, Illinois, about 1850, after having gone to California in search of gold. He died about 1889. The Sherman family is one of numerous connections in Lake County, and every year a family reunion is held there.

Claire C. Edwards, son of Henry C. and Margaret (Sherman) Edwards, was born in Avon Township, near Waukegan, August 31, 1876. He attended the grammar and high schools of the county, spent one year in Northwestern University, taught a term of school in Lake County and followed that with two years in Wheaton College. He graduated from Valparaiso University in Indiana in 1896, and in 1899 took his law degree from the Chicago-Kent College of Law. Judge Edwards after graduating in law spent some time in farming, and in 1900 was admitted to the bar and opened his first office at Grays Lake. After about a year he removed to Waukegan, the county seat, and has lived there and practiced law for a quarter of a century. He soon established a reputation for great resourcefulness and skill in handling criminal cases, being regarded as one of the ablest criminal lawyers in Northeastern Illinois. Judge Edwards for one year served as a member of the Board of Review. In 1914 he was appointed by a democratic governor to succeed Charles Whitney as judge of the Seventeenth Circuit, and in June, 1915, was regularly elected and was reelected in 1921, so that his judicial service covers a period of twelve years. In that time Judge Edwards has presided over many important trials. Probably the two that attracted the greatest public attention were the governor conspiracy case, a trial lasting sixty-three days and ending with acquittal, and the Delavan Smith will contest, which consumed about six weeks for trial.

Judge Edwards is one of the directors of the First National Bank of Waukegan. His father still owns the old homestead on which Judge Edwards' grandfather settled in 1835. Judge Edwards is a Knight Templar Mason and Shriner, member of the B. P. O. Elks, Hamilton Club, Glen Flora Country Club, is a life member of the Illinois State Bar Association and member of the American Bar Association. During the World war he performed much important service as a member of the War Camp Community Service, which expended over $300,000 in Waukegan in providing recreation and entertainment for the boys in training at the Great Lakes Naval Training Station. For several months he also held court at Camp Grant in naturalizing citizens while the Eighty-sixth Division was in training there. He naturalized over a thousand applicants a week, and in one week the applicants represented twenty-six different nationalities. Judge Edwards was recommended by Colonel Kimball for a position on his staff as judge advocate. He enlisted in the Chemical Warfare Division, but on account of age was rejected.

Judge Edwards in 1916 was elected president of the Jane McAlister Hospital of Waukegan. This institution at that time had accommodations for only thirty patients and was entirely inadequate for a hospital in a growing commercial and industrial city like Waukegan. Judge Edwards at once called together a number of business men and financiers of the community, and after a visit of inspection in the hospital the movement was started for the construction of the Victory Memorial Hospital, a general hospital that now has equipment of a hundred beds and cost $350,000, including a memorial to the soldiers of the World war, of whom there were six thousand from Lake County, this memorial costing $40,000. Judge Edwards remained as president of the hospital association until the hospital was built and paid for, and then resigned in 1923. This was a piece of constructive citizenship that gives Judge Edwards as much satisfaction as any other one achievement of his career.

Judge Edwards is a member of the faculty of the John Marshall Law School and the Chicago Law School at Chicago. For many years he was a member of the Waukegan Rotary Club, and in politics is a republican.

He married at Waukegan, June 30, 1909, Miss Harriet G. Erskine, of Waukegan, who was educated in the grammar and high schools of that city and a business college at Kenosha. Mrs. Edwards' primary interests have been in her home. She is a daughter of Fred S. and Emily (Sunderlin) Erskine, her father a native of Lake County and her grandfather coming from Scotland, while her grandmother came from the West Indies and was of Spanish descent. Her maternal grandfather, Emsley Sunderlin came to Waukegan as a pioneer, and at one time owned all the land on which the city was founded and gave the site for the court house. Fred S. Erskine spent his active career in the insurance business at Waukegan, carrying on the insurance agency established by his father, D. M. Erskine, in 1863.

Judge and Mrs. Edwards became the parents of four children, one dying in infancy. The son Erskine Churchill Edwards is in high school and is planning to take up the law and follow in his father's professional footsteps. The two daughters are Avis Harriet and Eleanor Claire.

RUSSELL H. EDWARDS has been one of the most active men in recent years in Waukegan in real estate subdivisions and development work. He is a member of a family that has lived in Waukegan for many years, owns individually a large amount of property in Lake County, and most of his operations have been conducted with his own property. He is a brother of Judge Claire Edwards of Waukegan.

He was born on a farm near Waukegan, December 10, 1891, son of Henry C. and Margaret F. (Sherman) Edwards. His grandfather, Churchill C. Edwards, was born and reared in New York State and about 1830 came to Northern Illinois and settled at the community known as Little Fort, now Waukegan. He took up land from the Government, bought other lands and was one of the pioneer farmers and one of the leading landowners in the county. His daughter, Amanda E. Edwards, who became the wife of Daniel Wightman, of Lake County, was the first white child born in the county. Henry C. Edwards was born near Waukegan in 1846, was reared there and devoted most of his active life time to farming, and still owns the homestead which his father entered from the Government. For a number of years he served as assessor of Avon Township and was township supervisor twenty-five years. He is now eighty years of age and a resident of Waukegan, where he has lived retired since 1916. His wife, Margaret F. Sherman, was born and reared in Lake County, was a real home lover and home maker and greatly beloved by her children and all friends and acquaintances. She died March 14, 1912. There were seven children in the family: Judge Claire C.; Royal S., deceased; Maude, wife of Hervey C. Coulson, of Waukegan; Harry J.; John J.; Cosie, deceased; and Russell H.

Russell H. Edwards attended public schools at Lake County, finishing his high school work at Waukegan in 1910. After leaving school he spent some time at farming and in 1912 went to Waukegan for his future, opening his office at 222 Washington Street. Mr. Edwards in handling his property has specialized in subdivisions and has carried out an extensive home building program, totaling during 1925-26 over 150 houses. During the last three years he has subdivided seventeen different tracts, including such properties as the Glenwood Heights subdivision.

HESS MEMORIAL

Erected by George W. and C. Josephine Hess to the memory of the Boys of Union County who died in the World War. Anna, Ill.

Mr. Edwards is affiliated with the Knights of Pythias, the B. P. O. Elks, is a charter member of the Kiwanis Club of Waukegan, a republican and a Methodist.

He married near Waukegan, July 30, 1916, Miss Blanche M. Doolittle, who was reared in Lake County, attending public school there and the State Normal College at DeKalb. She was a teacher in Lake County until her marriage, and since then has been active in church and club life at Waukegan. Mr. and Mrs. Edwards have three children, Harold, Shirley and Roger.

JOHN M. ETCHISON, present county treasurer of Clay County, is a member of two old and prominent families of that section of Illinois. His own life has been largely spent in the county, where he has been identified with agriculture, the live stock business and many other matters, some of them direct public interests.

He was born on a farm in Blair Township, Clay County, November 16, 1866, son of John Coston Etchison and Nancy (Blair) Etchison. His grandfather, Silas Etchison, came from North Carolina and was a pioneer settler of Clay County, Illinois, spending the rest of his life in Louisville Township. John Coston Etchison was born in Rowan County, North Carolina, and was a small boy when the family settled in Clay County. He followed farming in Blair Township after his marriage until 1886, when he moved to a farm near Louisville, where he died in 1895. He was a republican and seventeen times was elected supervisor of Blair Township. He and his wife were Baptists. His wife, who died in 1901, was born in Indiana and was a small girl when her father, Josiah Blair, came to Clay County and settled in the township which was named for him.

John M. Etchison was the seventh in a large family of nine children. He was reared on a farm, attended country schools, and has had a long and active experience in farming and the live stock business. For a year after his marriage he continued to live in Blair Township, following which he spent five years in the great Platte River Valley of Nebraska, near North Bend. On returning to Illinois he settled in Bible Grove Township, Clay County, which was the scene of his activities for about twenty-two years, from 1896 to 1918. Since then his home has been at Louisville.

Mr. Etchison served one term as president of the town board of Louisville. In 1922 he was elected for a term of four years as county treasurer and ex-officio collector and supervisor of assessments. In this position he has enjoyed contact with his friends and fellow-citizens from all parts of the county and has given a most efficient administration. Mr. Etchison is a republican, belongs to the Masonic Lodge, Independent Order of Odd Fellows, Modern Woodmen of America and the Methodist Church.

He married, March 7, 1886, Miss Anna Cook. Four children were born to them: Archie C., Arkell L., Lindsey A., who died at the age of sixteen years and seven months, and Delbert E., who died at the age of nineteen. Archie C. was with the colors during the World war, but was not permitted to go over seas. He was commissioned a second lieutenant and is now a member of the American Legion. He is a veterinary surgeon at Assumption, Illinois. Arkell L. is also a veterinary surgeon and a live stock dealer at Louisville. Both sons are graduates of the Chicago Veterinary College. The sons, like the father, are republicans in politics, and active workers in the party, the older being clerk of the Christian County Republican Central Committee.

GEORGE W. HESS, one of the capitalists of Union County, now living retired at Anna, is one of the representative men of this region, and one who in former years was very active, especially in agricultural circles. His benefactions are many and one that commends itself to the people of the county is the purchase of a lot and the erecting on it a $1,500 monument to commemorate the services of the soldiers of Union County in the World war. In this beautiful tribute Mr. Hess was joined by his wife. He was born in Union County, Illinois, November 20, 1854, a son of Silas and Mary E. (Hileman) Hess, both born in Union County. Silas Hess was a son of Joseph and Mary (Hartline) Hess, natives of Rowan County, North Carolina, and his wife was a daughter of Christian and Nancy (Davis) Hileman, also natives of North Carolina. The Southern Illinois State Hospital stands on land once owned by Mr. Hileman. Silas Hess died December 31, 1899, and his wife died in 1909. Joseph Hess, the grandfather, was among the earliest settlers in the vicinity of Saint John's Church in Perry County, Illinois, and here he was engaged in farming. Silas Hess was also a farmer. The following children were born to Silas Hess and his wife: Henry Lafayette and L. Jasper, both of whom are deceased; Mary E., who married William T. Boswell, of Anna; George W., who was the fourth in order of birth; Silas Franklin, who is deceased; Nancy C., who married T. J. Stokes, of Mount Pleasant, Illinois; John W., who resides at Anna; and Frances I., who married D. F. Rendleman, of Union County.

After attending the district schools George W. Hess had one term at the Anna schools, and at the age of twenty-two years began teaching, and followed that calling for six terms. He then bought a farm and began growing fruit, his first farm being near Dongola, Illinois. Two years later he sold this farm and bought another one four miles northwest of Jonesboro, and for eight years carried on general farming and stock raising. Once more he sold his farm, and bought another one just east of Anna, and on it he farmed and raised and dealt in stock for thirteen years. At the end of that period he sold and moved to Creal Springs, Illinois, but a year later went to East Saint Louis, Illinois. A few months later he located at Anna, buying one and one-half acres, on which he built a residence and occupied it for a year or two. This residence not suiting him, he bought two lots on South Main Street, on which he had built an elegant eight-room modern residence, with all improvements, and here he is living retired.

On September 7, 1879, Mr. Hess married Josephine Wilson, born in Union County, Illinois, January 31, 1858, a daughter of Daniel and Mary E. (McCasland) Wilson, natives of middle Tennessee, who, in 1853, came to Union County. Mr. and Mrs. Hess have no children. They are Congregationalists. In political faith they are democrats. Mr. Hess belongs to Anna Lodge, I. O. O. F., and has been through all the chairs, and he and his wife belong to the Rebekahs. Mrs. Hess is a member of the Daughters of the American Revolution, and has four certificates. She organized the Anna Woman's Club and also a Household Science Club for her home community. Both she and Mr. Hess are very popular all over the county, and their many kind deeds and thoughtful acts have endeared them to those with whom they are associated.

CLAUDE V. PARSONS is superintendent of public schools for Pope County. He is one of the outstanding younger men in educational affairs in southern Illinois, and has identified himself with the cause of better schools and better educational facilities in general throughout his section of the state, especially in the field of moral education.

Mr. Parsons was born on a farm in Pope County, October 7, 1895, son of Charles M. and Tennessee (Reid) Parsons. His grandfather, William B. Parsons, was born in Breckenridge County, Kentucky, in 1828, and was an early settler in Pope County, Illinois. He married a daughter of Preston L. Reagan, who was born in Virginia in 1818, and when a boy went over the mountains into Tennessee, then to Kentucky, and during the '40s settled in Illinois. The father of Preston L. Reagan was a soldier in the War of 1812, and his grandfather was a Revolutionary soldier. Charles M. Parsons was born in Johnson County, Illinois, February 14, 1861, and spent his active career as a farmer in Pope County. He was a democrat and he and his wife, Baptists. He died in 1916. His widow now resides with her son Claude at Golconda. Charles M. Parsons married Tennessee Reid, who was born in Johnson County, December 25, 1865, daughter of William Liggett and Sarah Priscilla (Robinson) Reid. William L. Reid was born in Tennessee, in 1826, his father having been a native of Virginia. William L. Reid settled in Johnson County, Illinois, in the '40s, and he and his brother cast two of the four votes passed for Lincoln in 1860 in their township of Johnson County. Charles M. Parsons and wife had four sons: Ernest W., Elisha Young, Jewell T. and Claude V., all of whom grew up on a farm in Pope County.

Claude V. Parsons after graduating from common schools was granted a teacher's certificate when only fourteen years of age. At the age of nineteen he began teaching, but for five years was employed by a utility company at Paducah, Kentucky. In 1923 he graduated from the Southern Illinois State Normal at Carbondale. In 1922 he was elected county superintendent of schools for Pope County, being the first democrat elected to a public office in Pope County in a period of forty years. Mr. Parsons is a member of the Illinois State Teachers Association, president of the Southern Illinois Teachers Association and is vice president of the Illinois State County Superintendents Association. He attends the Methodist Episcopal Church and teaches a class in Sunday School. He is a member of the Masonic Lodge and Eastern Star, and was one of the founders of the Sigma Alpha Pi fraternity at Carbondale, the only men's fraternity in the Normal School there. He was also active in organizing the Agro Debating Club at the Normal. He is president of the Egytian Benefit Association, a fraternal protective organization of Pope County.

JOHN C. STIRES has been a resident of Ogle County seventy years or more, has been known in his community as a man of soundest integrity and business capability, and a citizen ever ready to participate in movements for the general upbuilding and welfare.

Mr. Stires was brought to northern Illinois when a child from his birthplace, Pattenburg, Hunterdon County, New Jersey, where he was born February 6, 1852. The Stires family came from England before the Revolutionary war. His grandfather, Tunis Stires, lived at Pattenburg, New Jersey. Thomas J. Stires, father of John C., was born and reared in New Jersey, attended public schools there, and in 1855 brought his family to Illinois and the following year bought a quarter section of land near Byron. This old homestead is now owned by his son Ira Stires. Thomas J. Stires followed farming in Illinois until his death in 1864. His wife, Jane Conover, was born and reared in Hunterdon County, New Jersey, and her family came to America about 1660. Thomas J. Stires and wife had a family of five sons and five daughters: Watson, who died when six years of age, Hiram, Ira, Garrett and John C.; Malinda, deceased, who married N. J. Hewitt; Margaret Swackhamer, of White House, New Jersey; Carrie M.; Hannah, who married Frank Noyes of Byron; and Mrs. Alice Court of Creston, Iowa.

John C. Stires acquired a district school education in Illinois, and as a boy he learned the principles of farming and was engaged in farm work until 1890. Mr. Stires for over a quarter of a century was in the live stock business with headquarters at Byron, buying and shipping stock to the Chicago market. He retired from business in 1916 and has since looked after his private affairs. He is a democrat in politics and attends the Congregational Church.

Mr. Stires married at Byron, December 28, 1875, Miss Hattie N. Wilbur, of Byron, daughter of Charles and Ann (Shaw) Wilbur, both of whom were born and reared in Oneida County, New York, and came to Illinois in 1845, being early settlers in the vicinity of Byron, where they located on a farm. Her father served thirty-eight years as justice of the peace in his community. Mr. and Mrs. Stires became the parents of four children: Mabel, who died in 1890; Elva J., who died in 1910, wife of A. R. Mize, formerly of Byron, now cashier of the Bank of Leaf River; Anna E., married in 1902 to L. T. Barrick, who is a member of the mercantile firm of Barrick & Hunter at Byron, and they

LIVING ROOM OF MR. AND MRS. GEORGE W. HESS, ANNA, ILLINOIS

have a daughter, Evlyn Barrick, now attending the University of Chicago; and Margaret Grace Stires, who attended the grammar and high schools of Byron and the University of Chicago, and for several years taught school, until her marriage to Mack Defouw, who is connected with the Hoover Realty Company of Chicago.

HUGO M. FRIEND. Successful in the practice of his profession, and now one of the judges of the Circuit Court of Cook County, Hugo M. Friend for a number of years has represented a type of high minded and earnest citizens, with a sincere devotion to a public welfare and the solution of its social problems.

Judge Friend was born in Prague, Bohemia, July 21, 1882, son of Marcus and Emilie (Straschnow) Friend. His parents were natives of Prague, and in 1884 they came to the United States and settled in Chicago, where his father was connected with the wholesale dry goods business until his death in 1911, at the age of sixty-six. Hugo M. Friend was the youngest of seven children, three of whom are still living. He was two years of age when brought to Chicago, and grew up in that city, attending the Doolittle Grammar School and the South Division High School. He graduated from high school in 1901, and then entered the University of Chicago, where he took his Bachelor of Philosophy degree in 1905, and in 1908 received the degree J. D. from the University Law School. For about ten years Judge Friend was in active practice, at first associated with the firm Felsenthal, Foreman and Beckwith, then with Foreman, Levin and Robertson, and after 1912 in individual practice and subsequently as a member of Rothschild & Schaffner, and Schaffner & Friend.

In July, 1916, he was appointed master in chancery of the Superior Court by Judge Albert C. Barnes, and from that position was appointed by Governor Frank O. Lowden judge of the Circuit Court to succeed Judge J. W. Pinckney, and in 1921 was regularly elected judge of said court.

Judge Friend is a member of the Chicago, Illinois and American Bar Associations, is a republican, has served as president of the Young Men's Associated Jewish Charities, is a member of the City Club, Social Service Club, Collegiate Club, and has been actively identified with a number of movements for good local government and patriotic purposes.

Judge Friend married, June 30, 1920, Miss Sadie Cohn, a native of Omaha. They have three children: Robert, Marion and Hugo, Jr.

DAVID A. WARFORD is a member of the law firm of Watson & Warford at Elizabethtown. Mr. Warford was born in Hardin County, is a member of a prominent family there, and before practicing law was in military service during the World war.

He was born at Elizabethtown, November 14, 1895, son of William P. and Maggie A. (Price) Warford. Both the Warford and Price families are of English ancestry. The Warfords settled a number of generations ago in Virginia. William N. Warford, grandfather of David A., was a pioneer physician in the northern part of Hardin County, Illinois. William P. Warford was born in Indiana, grew up in Hardin County, and for many years has been a prominent business man at Elizabethtown, first as a merchant and then as a private banker, and is now president of the First State Bank. He is a republican, a Master Mason and member of the Knights of Pythias and the Christian Church. William P. Warford married Maggie A. Price, who was born at Elizabethtown, daughter of Thomas Price, a farmer and blacksmith of Hardin County.

David A. Warford was the only son of his parents. There were two daughters. He grew up in Elizabethtown, attended the public schools, took his high school work in the Southern Illinois State Normal at Carbondale, and for two years was a student in the School of Commerce at the University of Illinois. Following that he attended the Law School of the university, graduating LL. B. in 1920 and admitted to the bar the same year. For a short time he was at Springfield engaged in drafting bills in the Legislative Reference Bureau. For one year he practiced at Aurora, and since then in his native town, becoming associated with one of the veteran attorneys of Hardin County, James A. Watson. Mr. Warford is a member of the Masonic fraternity and B. P. O. Elks, and in politics is a republican. He is unmarried.

On September 18, 1917, he went into training, going to Camp Dodge at Des Moines, Iowa. Subsequently he attended an officers' training school and was commissioned second lieutenant of infantry June 1, 1918. He was sent to Camp Pike, Little Rock, Arkansas, two weeks later to Camp McArthur, at Waco, Texas, with a replacement camp, and remained there until honorably discharged December 10, 1918. Mr. Warford is a member of the American Legion.

BERTHOLD L. BOGGS is president of the Boggs & Agey Funeral Home, Incorporated at Centralia.

Mr. Boggs was born near Walnut Hill in Marion County, Illinois, October 18, 1885. He represents a family that was established in this section of southern Illinois in pioneer times, when the land was open to entry and required the labor of an entire generation of pioneers to lay the foundations of settled conditions. His grandfather, Spruce M. Boggs, first came to Illinois in 1823. He soon returned to his home state of North Carolina, where he married, and in 1825 he brought his wife and family to Illinois and settled on a farm in Section 33, Township 1, Range 2 E. That constituted the pioneer Boggs homestead in Illinois. Hugh M. Boggs, father of B. L. Boggs, was born in Marion County and spent his active life as a farmer. He died August 16, 1906. His wife, Mary D. (Watson) Boggs, a native of Marion County, now lives at Centralia. Berthold L. Boggs was the second in a family of three sons. He was educated in local public schools, attended Valparaiso University in Indiana and took his professional course in embalming in the Barnes School of Anatomy and Science in Chicago, where he was graduated in 1911. Mr. Boggs in 1912 established his undertaking business at Centralia, subsequently admitting a partner. The firm was Boggs & Agey until 1925, when it was incorporated as the Boggs & Agey Funeral Home, Incorporated, of which he is president. Mr. Boggs has developed the most complete mortuary in southern Illinois, his well equipped establishment being at 134 South Elm Street. He is also secretary and treasurer of the Hillcrest Memorial Park Company, owning and operating a cemetery. Mr. Boggs is a member of the Illinois and National Funeral Directors Association, the American Institute of Funeral Directors, is a republican is a past noble grand of the Independent Order of Odd Fellows, member of Centralia Lodge No. 201 of the Masonic Order, the Tribe of Ben Hur, Rotary Club, Chamber of Commerce, and the Methodist Church.

He married at Irvington, Illinois, December 3, 1916, Miss Myrtle Armstrong, daughter of J. T. and Frances Armstrong. Mrs. Boggs is assistant mortician and has been immediately identified with and responsible for much of the success of the business. She is secretary of the corporation. She is a member of the Centralia Woman's Club, the Rebekahs, Royal Neighbors, Maccabees and W. R. C. They have one daughter, Thelma Alice Boggs.

LOUIS B. JOLLEY, M. D. A resident of North Chicago, Doctor Jolley for some years engaged in the general practice of medicine and surgery there, but in recent years has had his offices in Waukegan and his work is now confined to eye, ear, nose and throat, in which he is a specialist.

Doctor Jolley was born at Fontana, Kansas, February 16, 1878, son of James L. and Margaret (Bryan) Jolley. His great-great-grandfather, John Jolley, was a soldier in the Revolutionary war. His grandfather, Jerry Jolley was born in Union County, Ohio, was a tanner by trade and about 1858 moved out to Kansas and settled near Fontana, taking up land from the government. He died about 1899. James L. Jolley was born in Union County, Ohio, in 1853 and was a boy of five years when he went to Kansas. He was reared on the old homestead farm, and farming was the occupation which he followed with much industry and success until 1903, when he turned his experience to advantage as an employe on the farm of the Kansas State Agricultural College at Manhattan. He and his wife still reside at Manhattan, he being seventy-three years of age. His wife, Margaret Bryan, was born in 1856 and was reared in Iowa, being educated in public schools in that state. Her parents were Harvey Newton and Margaret Bryan. Harvey Newton Bryan became a soldier in the Union army and died at Ft. Scott, Kansas, where he is buried.

Doctor Jolley spent his early childhood in eastern Kansas. When he was eight years of age his parents moved out to western Kansas, built a sod house, and for a time he continued his education in a sod school house. Later he attended village schools at Kingman, and his education was continued in the Kansas State Agricultural College at Manhattan, from which he was graduated with the Bachelor of Science degree in 1901. While at college he paid his own expenses by work in the library, in a boarding house, and clerking in a store. Before he left Manhattan he married, and shortly afterward he and his wife went to Chicago, where he enrolled as a student in the Hahnemann Medical College. Having little money, he managed his studies so they would not conflict with his work as a wage earner. He was conductor on the elevated railway and also clerked in a store, and during vacations was employed as a practical nurse. He graduated M. D. in 1905 and was engaged in private practice at Gurnee, Illinois, until 1909, in which year he established his home and offices in North Chicago. He still retains his home at North Chicago, but in 1901 established his office in the Waukegan National Bank Building and has since specialized in the treatment of eye, ear, nose and throat. Doctor Jolley did post-graduate work in the Chicago Polyclinic in 1920-21, and also spent the summer of 1925 abroad, taking special work in his line at the University of Austria at Vienna. His time and energies are now fully occupied by the heavy demand placed upon him as a specialist.

Doctor Jolley is a director of the Lake County State Bank, having held that position since the bank was organized in North Chicago. He was mayor of North Chicago during 1915-16. He belongs to the Lake County, Illinois and American Medical Associations, the Waukegan Chamber of Commerce, Rotary Club, Glen Flora Country Club, is a thirty-second degree Scottish Rite Mason and member of Medinah Temple of the Shrine at Chicago, and also belongs to the Knights of Pythias. His favorite sport is fishing.

He married at Manhattan, Kansas, September 11, 1901, Miss Bertha E. Evans. who was educated in public schools in Iowa and Kansas, and was a student at the same time with him in the Agricultural College at Manhattan. Mrs. Jolley takes an active part in the Presbyterian Church at Waukegan and the Waukegan Woman's Club. Her parents were George W. and Luretta (Amons) Evans, who were born and reared in Pennsylvania and moved from there to Iowa and later to Mason City, Illinois, then back to Iowa and finally to Kansas. Mrs. Jolley is of Colonial-American ancestry and one of her ancestors was a soldier in the Revolution, by virtue of which she is a member of the Daughters of the American Revolution. Doctor and Mrs. Jolley had five children, and the four now living are Geraldine, Eleanor, Burton and Paul. Geraldine was educated in the high schools of North Chicago and Waukegan, spent one year in the University of Illinois and one year at the Chicago Conservatory of Music, and was teacher of music in North Chicago until her marriage to Rollo Western. They now reside at Rapid City, Michigan, where he is superintendent of the Bay Lake Fruit Farm. Mr. and Mrs. Western have a son, Robert. The second daughter, Eleanor, was educated at North Chicago and in the Waukegan High School, and is now the wife of Marshall Emmons, of Waukegan, an employe of the American Steel & Wire Company. Mr. and Mrs. Emmons have a son, John. Burton Jolley graduated from the Waukegan High School in 1926, and his plans for his continued education include the University of Illinois and the Boston Institute of Technology. The other son, Paul, is a member of the class of 1929 in the Waukegan High School.

HARRY WILLIAM SCHUMACHER, M. D. A physician and surgeon at Altamont in Effingham County, Doctor Schumacher was reared in that community, and brings to his profession the qualifications gained not only by training in the best medical schools but also the experience of a medical officer overseas during the World war.

He was born on a farm near Altamont, April 7, 1890, son of John F. and Bertha (Klitzing) Schumacher. His parents were born in Germany and were children when brought to the United States. His grandfather, Charles Schumacher, first settled at Blue Island, Illinois, later at Manhattan, Illinois, and about 1866 moved to Effingham County, settling on a farm in Mound Township. He lived there until his death, and his widow subsequently went to Nebraska, where she died and was buried. Doctor Schumacher's mother was a daughter of Carl F. and Wilhelmina Klitzing, early settlers of Effingham County. John F. Schumacher died in 1923 and his wife, in 1920. They were reared in the German Lutheran faith and later became Methodists. John F. Schumacher was a farmer throughout his active career and always voted the republican ticket. Of their nine children two are now deceased.

Harry William Schumacher spent his boyhood on the farm, graduated from the Altamont High School in 1911, following which for one year he was a student in Central Wesleyan College at Warrenton, Missouri, and for a similar period in the University of Illinois, where he took the pre-medical course. Doctor Schumacher in 1917 graduated with the medical degree from Washington University at St. Louis. He was an interne in the Children's Hospital of St. Louis from June, 1917, to May, 1918. In May, 1918, he was commissioned a first lieutenant in the Army Medical Corps and on May 22 was called to active duty, being sent to Camp Jackson at Columbia, South Carolina, and on the fifth of July was ordered to Camp Merritt, New Jersey. On July 14, 1918, he sailed for overseas, landing at Liverpool July 26, then going to Cherbourg, France. His company went over as casuals. He was sent to a replacement camp at Saint Aignon and later was on active duty in hospital work at Brest. He remained until the spring of 1919, and on May 2, 1919, was commissioned a captain. He was honorably discharged at Camp Grant at Rockford June 28, 1919.

After the war Doctor Schumacher engaged in private practice at Altamont until March 1, 1920. He then accepted appointment as a member of the Illinois State Department of Health, with headquarters at Springfield, but on October 1, 1921, resigned and resumed his private practice at Altamont. He is secretary of the Effingham County Medical Society and is a member of the Illinois State and American Medical Associations.

Doctor Schumacher is affiliated with the Masonic Order, Independent Order of Odd Fellows, is a republican and a Methodist. He married, January 10, 1922, Miss Helen Dollarhide, who was born and reared at Paris, Illinois. Her parents were Mr. and Mrs. Horace Dollarhide.

FRANKLIN B. PEARCE, M. D., is a physician and surgeon at Eldorado, where he has practiced his profession for the past ten years. He is a native of Saline County, and since boyhood has been known for his persevering industry and enterprise in making the most of limited advantages.

He was born on a farm in Saline County, July 10, 1874, son of Allen M. and Martha J. (Mason) Pearce. Both parents represented pioneer families of southeastern Illinois, his father's people having come to Saline County in early days, while the Masons were of a White County family. Allen M. Pearce was a farmer, a democrat and a member of the Primitive Baptist Church, and both he and his wife were good, respected people, but with the support of eight children they never achieved considerable wealth.

Franklin B. Pearce was sixth in this family of eight children, and as a boy he was left an orphan to fight the battles of life on his own account. After the country schools he earned his own higher education, working on farms and in other occupations. He attended the Saline County Normal School at Harrisburg and at the age of twenty-four volunteered during the Spanish-American war, becoming a private in the Ninth Illinois Volunteer Infantry. He was with this regiment in Cuba, and at the close of the war was a corporal. He then clerked in a store five years, and for five years was a merchant on his own account at Carriers Mills, Illinois.

Doctor Pearce prepared for his medical profession in Loyola University at Chicago, entering there when a married man and with limited means. He supplemented rigid economy by earning part of his living as a night clerk in the post office. He was graduated M. D. from the university in 1915, and for one year following held a state position in Illinois. When he began practice at Eldorado he had only twenty-five dollars in capital and had to meet the competition of other well established physicians. A successful operation for the removal of the appendix of a boy gave him his reputation as a surgeon, and he has been best known as a surgeon and now gives the greater part of his time to that work. He owns the Eldorado Hospital, which he established in 1923, and is a member of the surgical staff of St. Mary's Hospital of Evansville, Indiana. Doctor Pearce is a member of the Saline County, Illinois State and American Medical Associations.

During the World war he volunteered in the Army Medical Corps, was commissioned a first lieutenant, and for eight months was on duty at the base hospital at Camp Dodge, Iowa. Doctor Pearce is vice president of the Tiger Oil Company and is a director in the summer resort and hotel organization known as the Big Lake Company. Fraternally he is a thirty-second degree Scottish Rite Mason and Shriner, member of the Independent Order of Odd Fellows, Knights of Pythias, B. P.

O. Elks and Red Men. He votes as a republican and is a member of the Methodist Church.

Doctor Pearce married, in 1900, Miss Gertrude Brewner, who was born and reared in Saline County, daughter of James and Ella (Andrews) Brewner. They have two children, Eva and James Lee.

ALFRED HERMAN BEIMFOHR. The love of the soil is inherited, and those who have this instinct are certain to succeed in agriculture. No man makes much progress unless he is interested in his work, is able to put his soul into it, and take a pride in what he produces. Alfred Herman Beimfohr, one of the most progressive and extensive farmers of Peoria County, comes of a long line of farmers, and he was taught from early childhood to care for the land, and to look forward to ownership of a farm of his own. His training has been thorough, and he is a firm believer in farm land as the basis of all real wealth. In addition to his farm activities he has built up a large connection in the dairying branch, and for a quarter of a century he has been selling milk.

Alfred Herman Beimfohr was born in Pekin Township, Tazewell County, Illinois, August 26, 1873, a son of Casper Beimfohr, one of the outstanding characters in the earlier life of Pekin Township. A native of Hesse-Darmstadt, Germany, Casper Beimfohr was one of a family of three sons and four daughters born to his parents, namely: Bernard, Casper, Herman, Mrs. Anna Weichter, Mrs. Mary Vooth and two daughters who died young. After the death of his father Casper Beimfohr's mother was married to Herman Siefer, and they came to the United States, Casper Beimfohr being at that time sixteen years old. Mr. and Mrs. Siefer located in Tazewell County, and they died here and are buried in Lakeside Cemetery.

Casper Beimfohr, following the admirable custom of his native land, was taught a trade, and was made a wagonmaker, but he followed this calling for only a short time, as his heart was set on farming. As soon as he had managed to acquire a little money, through work in the wagon shop, and as a farm hand, he rented land. His mother and stepfather could give him no assistance, for they had been bitterly poor in Germany. Their leaving their native land and risking the long trip to a new land was the result of failure to wrest a living from the land that gave them birth. So many of the better class of Germans left Germany during the '40s for the same reason, and some of the best and most patriotic citizens this country has ever possessed, some of its most gallant officers during the war between the states, belonged to this same class of Germans driven forth because of economic or political conditions.

Notwithstanding the fact that he was forced to make his own way, Casper Beimfohr prospered almost from the first, for he knew how to work and save, and how to so invest his money as to make it produce an income. It was not long after he became a tenant farmer that he was able to make a payment on a farm of his own that secured him possession of it, and this property is now a unit in the magnificent Tazewell Farms plant owned by Adolph Neirstheimer and his wife, the latter of whom is a daughter of Casper Beimfohr. Experiments proved that the best results were secured from corn and cattle raising, and he became one of the leading agriculturists of this neighborhood, and when he retired, at the age of sixty years, he was a very wealthy man. While he did not serve in the war between the states, he took out his citizenship papers as soon as the law permitted, and he continued a loyal supporter of his adopted land until his death, which occurred January 9, 1923, when he was eighty-four years old. First a democrat, he later became an ardent advocate of the prohibition party. Early uniting with Grace Methodist Episcopal Church of Pekin, he remained with it the rest of his life, and long was one of its stewards. For thirty years he was a director of his school district, and in every way measured up to high standards.

Casper Beimfohr married Louise Frentrup, a daughter of Henry Frentrup, the latter also a native of Germany, and a man of great industry. Mrs. Beimfohr survives her husband, and is living at Pekin. Their children were as follows: Otto, Alfred H., Edward, Ida, Anna, now Mrs. Adolph Neirstheimer, Clara Beimfohr, and several who are deceased.

Growing up on his father's farm, Alfred Herman Beimfohr attended the Sand Hill school, and remained on the homestead until his marriage. Following that event, in 1900, he became a tenant farmer on the homestead, but in 1914 purchased the Jacob Herr farm at Mapleton, Peoria County, which contains nearly an entire section of land. The residence and one of the present barns were on the property when Mr. Beimfohr purchased it, but he has erected all of the other buildings, and made all of the other most substantial improvements, until he now has one of the finest farming properties in his neighborhood. His farming program has been diversified, with considerable activity in dairying. His returns from his dairy have formed the basis of his present prosperity.

His first presidential vote cast for William McKinley, he has continued in the ranks of the republican party ever since, but aside from serving as one of the directors of the Mapleton school district he refuses office because of the demands made upon his time by his engrossing interests. Both he and his wife belong to the First Methodist Episcopal Church of Pekin.

On March 8, 1900, Mr. Beimfohr married, at Springfield, Oregon, Olive Dougherty, a native of Lancaster, Pennsylvania. She is a daughter of Simon and Lizzie (Simon) Dougherty, and the oldest of a family of two sons and three daughters born to her parents. The sons are deceased, but the daughters, in addition to her are: Mrs. Grace Exley, of Portland, Oregon, and May, who is Mrs. Arthur Newman, of California. The Dougherty family, after some years spent in the vicinity of Pekin, moved to Springfield, Oregon, and Mrs. Beimfohr accompanied her parents on the westward migration. Mr. and Mrs. Beimfohr have had the following children born to their

marriage: Helen, who is a graduate of the Pekin High School, took two years at the Illinois State University, and is now a teacher in the public schools of Mapleton: and Lois, who is the wife of Carl Walker, of Mapleton, has one daughter, Bettie Virginia.

During the World war Mr. Beimfohr was engaged in producing foodstuffs. He was registered in the second draft, and had submitted his questionnaire, but the armistice was signed before he was called into the service. He is a Blue Lodge Mason, and served as worthy master for five years of Hollis Grange, No. 1778, and he also belongs to the local farmers' organization.

HOWARD L. HOLLAND, undertaker and embalmer at Waukegan, was born in Lake County, and represents some of the old families who settled in northeastern Illinois in pioneer times.

He was born on a farm near Waukegan, July 15, 1888, son of Warren P. and Mary (Skinner) Holland. His grandfather, John Holland, brought his family from New York state and settled on a farm in Lake County. When the Civil war broke out he enlisted with a son in an Illinois regiment of infantry and participated in many battles of the war, being wounded in one engagement. After the war he lived on his farm, near Waukegan until his death in 1898. Warren P. Holland was born and reared in New York state and was about eighteen years of age when he came to Illinois, subsequently acquiring a government homestead in Lake County. He was a farmer and died in 1915. His wife died in 1917, and both are buried in Oakwood Cemetery at Waukegan. She was a native of Ashtabula, Ohio, and was about four years old when her parents, Isaac L. and Mariah (Fickinger) Skinner, moved west and settled near Waukegan, where they homesteaded land from the government. Her mother died in 1902 and her father in 1904.

Howard L. Holland grew up on his father's farm, attended grammar and high schools at Waukegan and finished a business course in the Waukegan College in 1908. Mr. Holland after leaving college became secretary and stenographer to the Noel Construction Company, then handling the contract for erecting the buildings at the Great Lakes Naval Training Station. He was with the construction company about two years and in 1910 engaged in the undertaking business as a member of the firm White & Holland. Mr. Holland has been a Waukegan undertaker for fifteen years, and is now in business under the name Howard L. Holland, Undertaker and Embalmer, operating one of the best equipped establishments of its kind in Lake County, at 419 Washington Street in Waukegan.

Mr. Holland left his business in 1917 to join the colors, enlisting in Company G of the Three Hundred and Forty-second Infantry, Eighty-sixth Division. He was in training with this division at Camp Grant for about seven months, and accompanied it overseas to France, sailing from New York September 9, 1918, and landing at Liverpool September 21st. He walked part of the way across England to Southampton, crossed the Channel to Havre, France, and the division was then sent to a camp near Bordeaux, where it served as a replacement division. He remained in France after the armistice, returning home on the steamship Mount Vernon in April, 1919, and received his honorable discharge at Camp Grant May 8, 1919, with the rank of sergeant, Three Hundred and Fifth Infantry, Seventy-seventh Division. He then immediately resumed his business connections at Waukegan.

Mr. Holland is a member of the Masonic Order and Mystic Shrine, Independent Order of Odd Fellows, B. P. O. Elks, Knights of Pythias, Lions Club, is a republican and a Methodist and a charter member of Homer Dahringer Post of the American Legion.

Mr. Holland married at Peoria, Illinois, August 12, 1918, Miss Eveline Martha Cheney, who was reared and educated in Chicago, being an adopted daughter of Mr. and Mrs. Charles Melbourne, of Chicago. Her father was in the railroad service for many years, an assistant yard master of the Chicago Junction Belt Line. Mr. and Mrs. Melbourne now reside at Delavan, Wisconsin.

EDWARD JAMES FUCIK is a Chicago boy who early developed special technical genius and for many years has been prominent in engineering circles. The chief field of his experience has been as a river and harbor improvement engineer.

He was born at Chicago, January 26, 1880, son of Frank and Anna (Kakuska) Fucik. Both parents are of Bohemian ancestry and his mother, who was born in Chicago in 1854, represented one of the earliest of Bohemian families in that city. Frank Fucik, still a resident of Chicago, has been an honored citizen of his community and well known in political circles. He was born in Bohemia, now Czecho-Slovakia, of a family that for generations has been identified with teaching and the scholarly profession. Frank Fucik came to America and settled in Chicago in 1867, and for many years was active in public service. He was West Town clerk in 1881 and 1882. He served as special bailiff in Judge Tuthill's court at the time of the famous trial of Doctor Cronin. He was personally intrusted by Judge Tuthill with the task of raising a jury for this trial. Such was his known reputation for rectitude and sound judgment that he was selected for this duty, and the selection was approved by both the prosecution and the counsel for the defense. At all times he has enjoyed the confidence and esteem of all who have come in contact with him, and has discharged well and honorably every responsibility or duty. He and his wife gave college educations to their children.

Edward James Fucik while a boy in Chicago attending the grammar schools, English High School and the Manual Training School, now the Crane Technical High School. From high school he entered the University of Illinois and was graduated in 1901 with the degree Bachelor of Science in civil engineering. Mr. Fucik from 1901 to 1907 was a construction engineer on the Randolph and Dearborn Street bridges. In 1903 he wrote an article on the first use of steel sheeting on piling, an article published in the University of Illinois Technograph. This style of sheeting is still in general use. One of his outstanding achievements was designing and building the 700 foot concrete dry dock at South Chicago in 1915. During the World war Mr. Fucik was engaged in harbor and industrial construction in the Calumet steel district. From 1921 to 1926 he was vice president of the Great Lakes Dredge and Dry Dock Company, and at the present time is associated as vice president and general manager of the Fitzsimons & Connell Dredge & Dock Company of Chicago. This is an organization that has been in existence for many years and has handled an immense volume of the harbor and river improvements in the Chicago district.

Mr. Fucik is a member of the American Society of Civil Engineers and Western Society of Engineers. His business office is at 10 South LaSalle Street, and his home is at 3852 North Hamlin Avenue. He also has a summer home on Lake Superior in the Upper Peninsula of Michigan. He is a member of the University and Park Ridge Country Clubs, is a thirty-second degree Scottish Rite Mason and Shriner and a member of the Independent Order of Odd Fellows. His chief recreations are reading and golf.

Mr. Fucik married, September 3, 1912, Miss Agnes M. Montford, of Marquette, Michigan. The Montfords were a family of old Virginia and a Joseph Montford, of Halifax County, North Carolina, was an officer in the Continental line in the Revolutionary war. Mr. and Mrs. Fucik have two sons, Edward Montford and Frank Montford Fucik.

HAROLD J. HANSEN has practiced law since 1913, at first in Chicago and is now one of the well established attorneys at Waukegan in Lake County. The only interruption to his professional service came during the World war, when he went overseas with the American Expeditionary Forces.

Mr. Hansen was born in Oslo, Norway, February 18, 1887. In September of the same year, when he was about six months old, his parents, Sophus and Olia (Gundersen) Hansen, came to America, settling in Chicago. His father has been in the tailoring business in that city for forty years and is now one of the oldest men in that line still active.

Harold J. Hansen acquired his education in grammar and high schools of Chicago, attended the Chicago Seminary of Sciences and in 1913 graduated from the Chicago Law College. He was admitted to the bar and practiced law in the city until 1918. He joined the colors and was sent for training to Camp Wheeler at Macon, Georgia, where he was put in Company B of the One Hundred Seventeenth Machine Gun Battalion. After about four months in training camp his battalion was sent overseas, and shortly after arriving in France he was transferred as an instructor in machine gun practice and assisted in training machine gunners for the front until the armistice. Mr. Hansen received his honorable discharge with the rank of sergeant at Camp Grant, Illinois, February 12, 1919.

In March of the same year he resumed his professional work at Chicago, and in June, 1922, moved his law office to Waukegan. He has been identified with a growing and important general law practice. He is secretary and treasurer of the Community Chest of Waukegan and North Chicago, is a director of the Lions Club, member of the Fort Dearborn Town Club of Chicago, is a past master of Progressive Lodge of Masons No. 954 of Chicago and has attained the thirty-second degree of the Scottish Rite. He is also a past noble grand of Wicker Park Lodge, Independent Order of Odd Fellows, is a member of the B. P. O. Elks, Chamber of Commerce, Phi Alpha Delta college fraternity, American Legion and Lake County Bar Associations. He is a republican and a member of the Methodist Episcopal Church.

Mr. Hansen married at Waukegan, December 26, 1925, Miss Blanche Adams, of that city. Mrs. Hansen was educated in the public schools of Waukegan and has been much interested in church and social affairs in that city, being a member of the Woman's Auxiliary of the American Legion. She is a daughter of David and Lora Belle (Bristol) Adams. Her father for many years owned and directed valuable farming interests near Waukegan, but is now living retired in that city. Her mother died in February, 1926. The Adams family were among the pioneers of Lake County, Illinois. David Adams for many years served on the Board of Supervisors and assisted in laying out the first rural mail route out of Waukegan.

ERIC LOUIS KOHLER is a certified public accountant whose name and work have been made familiar outside his immediate clientage by reason of his connection with the Northwestern University School of Commerce and also as author of several books on accounting. Mr. Kohler is a resident of Chicago and is head of the firm of certified public accountants Kohler, Pettengill & Company, with offices in the Tribune Tower.

He was born at Owosso, Michigan, July 9, 1892, son of F. Edwin and Kate Evelyn (Bentley) Kohler. He spent some years of his youth and early manhood at Ann Arbor, Michigan, graduating from high school there in 1910. He took his A. B. degree at the University of Michigan in 1914, and soon afterward came to Chicago. He was graduated Master of Arts from Northwestern University in 1915, and received the degree Certified Public Accountant from the University of Illinois in 1916. Mr. Kohler during 1915-17 was a member of the staff of Arthur Anderson & Company, certified public accountants, and again during 1919-20 was associated with the same firm. The only important interruption to his profession and work as a public accountant came during the World war period. In 1917 he attended the First Officers' Training Camp at Fort Sheridan. Throughout the remainder of the war he held the rank of captain in the Quartermaster's Corps, stationed at Camp Grant and in Chicago.

Captain Kohler became an instructor of accountancy in the Northwestern University School of Commerce, later was made assistant professor and associate professor in that institution, and in 1922 was promoted to the

rank of full professor. This position he has held continuously since.

Mr. Kohler is a member of the Illinois Society of Certified Public Accountants, American Institute of Accountants, National Association of Cost Accountants, and is author of "Accounting Principles Underlying Federal Income Taxes," and co-author of "Principles of Auditing" and "Principles of Accounting." He has contributed a number of articles to magazines on Federal Income Taxes and related subjects.

Mr. Kohler is a member of the Michigan Society of Chicago, the college fraternities Phi Mu Alpha, Beta Gamma Sigma, Beta Alpha Psi, and of the last he was grand president in 1924-26, and belongs to the City Club, Chicago Town and Tennis Club. He is a republican. His home address is 5314 Glenwood Avenue.

HENRY STEIN, M. D., has been a resident of Altamont and a professional man of that community for over thirty years. His has been a career of important service to his fellow men. In attaining to the capacity to serve others he has overcome many difficulties, not only those involved in poverty but in ill health as well.

He was born at Sigourney, Keokuk County, Iowa, November 19, 1869, son of Joseph and Louisa (Sheets) Stein, natives of Germany, who came to America when children and were married in Iowa. Joseph Stein followed the occupation of farming and died in 1874, when his son Henry was five years of age. He was the father of three sons and one daughter, and his widow subsequently had a daughter by her second husband, Jacob Mertz. Mrs. Mertz is still living at Sigourney, Iowa.

Henry Stein on account of the early death of his father was deprived of many of the advantages that might have been normally his to enjoy. He attended the common schools of his native county and at the age of eighteen became a teacher. For several years he taught and attended school alternately. He was a student in the University of Iowa for two years and then entered the Medical School of Washington University at St. Louis, where he was graduated M. D. in 1894. Doctor Stein on account of ill health was unable to take up the active practice on graduating. As a youth he was afflicted with tuberculosis, and he spent much time in Colorado and Kansas in getting free from the disease. For many years examinations have shown no evidence of this scourge, though his entire life has been a battle against weakness and impaired vitality, and the service he has rendered stands out the more conspicuously on that account.

Doctor Stein located at Altamont, Illinois, in 1895, and has carried on a very successful general medical practice through all the subsequent years, being the loved and respected physician to many families of Effingham County. He is a member of the various medical organizations, and for several years has been president of the Altamont Board of Education. He is a republican voter.

Doctor Stein married at Mount Vernon, Illinois, in 1895, Miss Clara Williams. They have two children: Helen, wife of J. B. Austin, of Glendale, California; and Victor Stein, who is now connected with the United States army.

RAYMOND P. MYER, certified public accountant, is manager of the Waukegan office for Kohler, Pettingill & Company, certified public accountants. Mr. Myer is also secretary of the Rotary Club of Waukegan and has made himself a very popular and esteemed citizen of that community.

He was born at Kingston, Illinois, January 21, 1898. His father, John George Myer, was born in Germany in 1856, and was brought to America in 1860. He was reared near Kingston, Illinois, and as a young man bought a farm of his own in that vicinity and devoted the rest of his years to agriculture. He died January 31, 1925.

Raymond P. Myer spent his boyhood days on the farm near Kingston, attended public schools there, and prepared for college in the Northwestern Academy at Naperville, Illinois. He then entered Northwestern University at Evanston, Illinois, and was graduated with the Bachelor of Science degree in commerce in 1922. Mr. Myer during 1922-23 was in New Orleans as assistant registrar of Tulne University, and at the same time did postgraduate work in accounting. There he received the degree Certified Public Accountant on July 31, 1923. Mr. Myer since September, 1923, has been associated with Kohler, Pettingill & Company, certified public accountants at Chicago. He was sent to their office at St. Joseph, Missouri, where he remained until March, 1924, when he was transferred to Waukegan to open the office of the company in that city and act as manager of the business of this district.

Mr. Myer in addition to his position as secretary of the Rotary Club is a member of the Waukegan Chamber of Commerce, belongs to the Masonic Lodge, the Acacia College fraternity, B. P. O. Elks, Beta Alpha Psi accounting fraternity and the Beta Gamma Sigma honorary commerce fraternity. He is a republican and affiliated with the Methodist Church.

CHARLES G. SMITH, M. D. In the thirty years he has lived in the Red Bud community of Randolph County Doctor Smith has been a quiet, hard working physician, a professional man of most substantial attainments, and has well earned the esteem he enjoys.

He was born in Buffalo, New York, in 1869. His father was Rev. Franz Wilhelm Schmitt, a prominent minister of the Lutheran Church in New York State, who died in 1880. Charles G. Smith as a young man changed the spelling of his name to Smith. He was educated in grammar and high schools, attended Central University of Kentucky, and is a graduate of the medical department of St. Louis University. He also took post-graduate work in the Chicago Medical College. Doctor Smith in 1897 located at Red Bud in Randolph County, and the practice he enjoys is one of which any physician in a city of 200,000 people might be proud. Doctor Smith is a member of the various medical organizations. He has been much interested in local history and is well acquainted with all the historic sites of southern Illinois.

He married Altha Bockhoushe, of Wabash County, Illinois. They have two talented daughters. Irene Fern, graduate of the University of Illinois, is the wife of Dr. Julian F. Smith, a practicing physician at Akron, Ohio. The second daughter, Dr. Fanny Fern, is a graduate of Washington University at St. Louis and is now teacher of botany in the noted Lindenwood College at St. Charles, Missouri. The following is from a recently published article regarding Doctor Smith:

"The Missouri Botanical Garden has furnished one of the sources of laboratory research work of Dr. Fanny Fern Smith, who becomes the new professor of botany and bacteriology at Lindenwood College in September. She is now at the Marine Biological Laboratory at Woods Hole, Massachusetts.

"Doctor Smith is a graduate of Washington University, from which she has also received a graduate degree. She is a member of the Phi Beta Kappa, honorary fraternity, a member of Sigma Xi, and of Phi Sigma, an honorary biological society. Her home is in Red Bud, Illinois."

JOHN NUVEEN. The name Nuveen has been a familiar one in the commercial affairs of Chicago for over half a century. John Nuveen, named above, is founder and head of John Nuveen & Co., investment bankers, who are dealers in municipal, county and school bonds. This firm is one of the pioneer municipal bond houses in Chicago, established in 1898, with offices in the First National Bank Building.

John Nuveen represents the fifth consecutive John Nuveen in as many generations of the family. He was born at Altona, Schleswig-Holstein, Denmark (shortly afterwards Germany), of Dutch ancestry. His birth occurred there August 26, 1864. His parents were John and Margaret C. (Reimer) Nuveen. His father, John Nuveen, IV, was born in Amsterdam, Holland, and his grandfather, John Nuveen, III, was owner of five large ship building docks in Amsterdam, being in his time the largest ship builder in Holland. John Nuveen, IV, brought his family to the United States in 1866, locating in Chicago. One powerful incentive to come to this country was given him by reason of the many wars in which the European countries were then engaged. The choice of his location in Chicago was decided by the presence in that city of his brother-in-law, Rudolph Reimer, who had been a Union soldier in the Civil war. John Nuveen, IV, after locating in Chicago bought a stock of dry goods from the old firm of John V. Farwell and Company, and engaged in business as a merchant there for many years. He was well equipped for success in business and citizenship, having a fine education and speaking several languages, and all the qualities of a refined Christian gentleman. His achievements and character were unquestionably a real contribution to the citizenship of America. John Nuveen, IV, in 1875, retired from business and removed to Kalamazoo, Michigan, returning to Chicago three years later and again establishing a new dry goods business. He died August 21, 1892. He was a deacon in the Irving Park Baptist Church, and served as a trustee of the German Department of the Rochester German Baptist Theological Seminary, Rochester, New York.

John Nuveen, V, was less than two years of age when brought to Chicago. He completed the course at the Kalamazoo Grammar School and graduated with the first graduating class, in 1880, from the West Division High School of Chicago. In that class he was a schoolmate of Seymour Morris, Judge Mary Bartelme and George W. Perkins (partner of J. P. Morgan & Co.). After finishing his high school course and subsequently a course in commercial law, etc., in Souder's Business College, Mr. Nuveen entered his father's business and became identified with the wholesale dry goods trade. His purchasé in 1893 of an interest in the wholesale grocery house of Chapman and Smith Company gave him a new interest, and he was secretary of the company until 1898, when he sold out his holdings.

Mr. Nuveen established himself in the municipal bond business in the old First National Bank Building, and later became a tenant of the new building when it was completed at the corner of Monroe and Dearborn streets. He was one of the first investment bankers in Chicago to engage in the exclusive handling of municipal bonds, and owing to the small margin of profit on such bonds the outcome of his venture was at first problematical. It is properly a matter of pride for him that he has been the founder and directing head of one of the largest concerns of the kind in the country, a conservative yet progressive business and one in which not a single client has lost a dollar. Mr. Nuveen has had other connections with commercial activities, for the past thirteen years having been vice president of the Columbia Bank Note Company, although not taking an active part.

Mr. Nuveen is one of the prominent Baptist laymen of Chicago. He has been a member of that church since he was eleven years of age, baptized at Kalamazoo, Michigan, by Doctor Hodge. For over twenty years he has been superintendent of the Sunday School of the Immanuel Baptist Church, succeeding Mr. B. F. Jacobs. He was president of the Baptist Young People's Union of Illinois for two years, from 1893 to 1895, and was for many years chairman of the Board of Managers of the Baptist Young People's Union of America, has been treasurer of his church and member of the Board of Trustees for many years. He has served on the Board of the American Baptist Foreign Missionary Society, and is active on the finance committee of the Northern Baptist Convention, was president of the Cook County Sunday School Association for two years, and is a trustee of the Y. M. C. A. College (a position he has held for twelve years), is a trustee of the Chicago Y. M. C. A., and a director of the Sunday Evening Club.

On June 18, 1895, he married Miss Ida E. Strawbridge. She died January 23, 1910. In June, 1912, Mr. Nuveen married his first wife's sister, Anna Strawbridge. His first wife at the time of her death was president of the American Baptist Home Mission Society, and Mrs. Anna Nuveen likewise served that society as president and prior to that was treasurer. Mr. Nuveen by his first marriage has one son, John Nuveen, VI, who was born in 1896. During the World war he was in training as an aviator, and is an active associate of his father in the bond business.

Mr. Nuveen has many social connections in Chicago, being a member of the Union League Club, the Mid-Day Club, Hamilton Club, Quadrangle Club, Olympia Fields Country Club, Bankers Club (New York), White Lake Golf and Yacht Club (White Lake, Michigan), Knapp Island Gun Club and the Chicago Historical Society.

EDWARD D. ETNYRE is a manufacturer at Oregon, has been in business in that city for a great many years, and has made E. D. Etnyre & Company, of which he is president, one of the notable industrial organizations of the state, its manufactured products being distributed throughout the country and going to many foreign countries.

From a small local shop manufacturing tanks the E. D. Etnyre & Company has developed a very specialized business, manufacturing a line of equipment chiefly for the flushing of streets and also for distributing oil and other petroleum products as used in road building and maintenance. The Etnyre apparatus for these various purposes is regarded everywhere as the standard of efficiency and excellence. The business is now one involving a large amount of capital, a great plant with a large number of employes, and the business has been developed through long practical experience and the application of the best of modern engineering practice. The Etnyre machines are no longer mere tanks, but are pieces of complicated machinery, each one designed for the most perfect efficiency in its primary use.

Edward D. Etnyre was born at Oregon, Illinois, July 9, 1860, son of Daniel and Mary (Rice) Etnyre, his father a native of Pennsylvania and his mother of Hagerstown, Maryland. They were early settlers near Oregon, Illinois, where his father was a highly respected Ogle County farmer. Edward D. Etnyre was reared on a farm, was more or less actively identified with farming until 1898, and his early education in the public schools of Oregon was supplemented by attending Northwestern University at Chicago for three years. For one year he was in the west buying cattle and shipping them to the Chicago market.

Mr. Etnyre in 1895 began the manufacture of steel tanks at Oregon. For a number of years he manufactured the familiar types of gravity street sprinklers, but his business was a progressive one and rapidly outgrew its original scope. The company erected the present large factory in 1906. The Etnyre sprinkling apparatus has been designed for varied uses, and consists not only of gravity sprinkling but power flushing. This apparatus is used in many cities for streets, boulevards, parks, and special apparatus has also been built for use on golf courses, for road building and race tracks. Mr. Etnyre has been president of the company and the chief executive from the beginning.

He has taken a very active part in the civic welfare of his home community. He is a member of the Sigma Chi college fraternity and the B. P. O. Elks.

Mr. Etnyre in 1886 married at Sacramento, California, Miss Harriet Smith, who spent her early years in Illinois, attending public school at Oregon and the Rockford Seminary for Girls. After the death of her mother she went out to California with her father, and remained in that state until her marriage. Her parents were Mortimer and Sarah (Patrick) Smith, early settlers of Illinois. She is descended on one side from the Lee family of the Revolution. Mortimer Smith was a newspaper editor, conducted an abstract business, represented his district in the Illinois Senate, and in California engaged in farming, spending his last years in San Diego County.

Mr. and Mrs. Etnyre are the parents of six children, George Mortimer, Robert Daniel, Leland Edward, Horace Harding, Harriet Marie and Edwin Andrews. All the sons are actively identified with their father's growing business except Leland E., who is in the insurance and loan business at Dallas, Texas.

REV. JOHN WILLIAM ANTHONY FLEMING is organizer and priest of one of the newly established parishes of Lake County, St. Anastasia Church, one of the growing and prosperous religious communities in the industrial city of Waukegan.

Father Fleming, whose early work for the church was done in Chicago, was born in that city, January 29, 1888, son of Patrick and Johanna (Cronin) Fleming. His father was born in Ireland, and was nine years of age when his parents came to America, first living in New York City. He was educated in Ireland and in this country, and as a youth entered the service of the Rock Island Railroad Company, having moved to Chicago a year before the great fire of 1871. He was a locomotive fireman in the Rock Island Railroad service until his death in November, 1891. In Chicago he met and married in 1880 Johanna Cronin, who was born and reared in County Kerry, Ireland, and was fifteen years of age when she came to America, and her sister Catherine arrived in Chicago a year afterwards. She survives her husband and for many years has been active in her church and community in Chicago.

John William Anthony Fleming attended public and parochial schools in his native city, graduated in 1908 from the Carmelite College of Chicago and in 1912 completed his seminary course in Mount St. Marys of the West. After taking his orders as a priest he had charge of parochial work and spiritual ministrations in St. Jarlath's Parish and in the hospitals of Chicago for three and a half years. Father Fleming in 1916 was made assistant to Father Michael Sullivan of the Resurrection of Our Lord Church at Austin, Chicago, where he remained two years and nine months. In 1919 he was transferred as assistant pastor to St. Andrews Church on the North Side, and after the death of the pastor, Father Andrew Croke, he remained as acting pastor for a time.

Early in 1926 Father Fleming was given the important task of organizing and establishing a new parish at Waukegan, and formally took up the pastorate of St. Anastasia Church on April 29, 1926. The parish was organized April 3rd of that year, and the church property consisted of one block of ground at the corner of Glen Flora and Ash streets, while the boundaries of the parish extend north as far as the Wisconsin line. Already the parish contains over 200 families. Father Fleming has rapidly carried out the work of organization, and plans have been made for the erection of a beautiful school and auditorium of the English-Gothic style of architecture. The first mass in St. Anastasia parish was said May 9, 1926.

Father Fleming is a member of the Holy Name Society and was chaplain of that society at St. Andrews Church in Chicago, and was chaplain of the Chicago Council and the Hughes Council of the Knights of Columbus, and also a member of the Chicago Kiwanis Club. He is a member of the Alumni Association of Mount St. Mary's Seminary, and in politics is non-partisan.

FRANCIS M. BROCK is a resident of Fairfield, known for many activities and relationships, county official, merchant, lumber dealer, banker and former postmaster.

He was born on a farm in Wayne County, Illinois, January 15, 1852. His family was one of the first to settle in the Ohio River Valley. The founder of the family there was Jacob Brock, a native of Pennsylvania, of English ancestry. Isaac A. Brock, son of Jacob, was born April 26, 1790, in a block house that stood on the original site of the settlement at what is now Cincinnati, Ohio. Isaac Brock finally came to Illinois and spent his last years on a farm in Wayne County, where he died April 28, 1870. He had married Elizabeth Mugg, and they were the parents of Malinda Matilda, John W. M., Jacob C., Melissa and Isaac. Of these children John W. M. was a soldier in the Civil war.

Jacob C. Brock, the father of Francis M., was born near Stafford, Ohio, December 17, 1827. He married in Ohio Rebecca Flick, and in 1851 they accompanied the rest of the family to Wayne County, Illinois. Rebecca Flick was a native of Pennsylvania, of Pennsylvania-German ancestry. Jacob C. Brock followed farming in Wayne County, was a republican in politics, and he and his wife were members of the Christian Church. He died March 16, 1901, and his wife lived to the age of eighty-four. Their children were Allie, Francis M., Viola, Charles, Jennie and Irwin.

Francis M. Brock lived on a farm to the age of twenty, getting his education in the common schools, and his independent career started with no special advantages to mark him out and make his course easier than that of other young men of his age. On leaving home he spent two years in Missouri, following different lines of work, and for four years was a traveling salesman for a hardware house, with headquarters at Austin, Texas. Returning to Illinois, he married in 1878 Miss Ella Collins. She was born in Ohio and came with her parents to Wayne County, Illinois, in the late '50s. Mr. Brock after farming a year engaged in the grain and seed business at Cisna, and then for four or five years was a general merchant there. In 1886 he was elected county clerk on the republican ticket and in 1890 was reelected, holding this office eight years. For over thirty-five years since leaving this county office he has been financially interested and more or less active in the lumber business. Mr. Brock in 1904 became cashier of the First National Bank of Fairfield, serving seven years. In 1910 he was appointed postmaster, and filled that office a little over four years. Since 1911 he has been president of the Southern Illinois Lumber Company, which now operates nine yards in different towns in the southern part of the state. Since 1920 he has been president of the First National Bank of Fairfield. Mr. Brock through all the years has been active in local politics and for some time was chariman of the County Republican Committee. He is a member of the Christian Church, is a Royal Arch Mason and a member of the Independent Order of Odd Fellows.

His first wife died in 1919. She was the mother of the following children: Glenn, wife of S. T. Pendleton, of Fairfield; Edna A., wife of Robert A. Cox, of Phoenix, Arizona; Frank Leslie, of Fairfield, secretary and treasurer of the Southern Illinois Lumber Company, who married Mary Moran. Mr. Brock in 1921 married Mrs. Alice M. (Hill) Freshwater.

G. P. KOENEKE, of Waukegan, is a man of most interesting business experience. For a number of years he was interested in the house wrecking industry, supervising the dismantling of plants and equipment in many sections of the United States, including some of the great army cantonments. Mr. Koeneke on coming to Waukegan purchased an automobile sales, garage and service station on Sheridan Road, and is one of the successful and popular men of that North Shore community.

Gottlieb Koeneke was born in Chicago, February 4, 1890, son of Gottlieb and Madeline (Luncas) Koeneke. His father was a native of Bremen, Germany, educated in public and military schools there, and when a young man, just after the close of the Civil war, came to America and located at Chicago. He was a florist up to the time of the great Chicago fire, his plant being on ground now included in Lincoln Park. The old relic house, now used as a residence, contains glass which was a part of the glass from his old greenhouse. After the Chicago fire he conducted a cigar factory in Chicago until his death in 1909. He is buried in St. Luke's Cemetery of Chicago. His wife was also born and reared in Bremen, and came to America when a young woman and was married in Chicago. She is still a resident of that city. There were eight children: Anna, wife of Albert Gschwind, a manufacturer of woman's shirt waists at Dowagiac, Michigan; George, who died in Chicago at the age of thirty-four; Hattie, wife of Edmund Gschwind, office manager for Landers, Frary & Clark, in Chicago, and the mother of three children, named Edmond, John and Helen; Edward Koeneke, who died in Chicago in May, 1926, the result of an auto-

mobile accident, leaving a widow and one child, Raymond; Rosie, wife of Paul G. Krien, a manufacturer of women's garments in Chicago, and mother of two children, Harold and Jeanette; John, a Chicago insurance man, who is married and has one daughter; Augusta, who married Jay Clark, of Chicago, later of Nome, Alaska, where he died several years ago, and she and her two daughters, Ethel and Anna, reside in Chicago.

Gottlieb P. Koeneke, youngest of this family of children, attended public schools in Chicago, but left school at the age of eleven and satisfied a craving for travel and excitement, normal in any boy of those years, by going about the country with a carnival company, and that was his line of work and experience until he was about sixteen. Returning to Chicago, he spent a year and a half in the service of the Singer Wrecking Company, and in 1906 he built a yard and plant for the American House Wrecking Company, taking charge of the plant and managing it for about a year. He then became purchasing agent and superintendent of the Chicago House Wrecking Company, and filled that position until 1923. In 1924 he leased the Hotel Clayton Garage at Waukegan, and continues the business as the Hotel Clayton Garage, G. P. Koeneke, proprietor. He also handles the local sales agency for the Locomobile Company. He conducts a well equipped garage, service station and auto laundry at the Hotel Clayton, and in no small degree his success in business has been due to his close personal supervision and a courteous service rendered the large daily patronage that comes to his headquarters along the Sheridan Road.

Mr. Koeneke was called during the draft in the World war. At that time he was in the employ of the Harris Brothers Wrecking Company, an auxiliary of the Chicago House Wrecking Company, and was superintending the dismantling of the Alton, Jerseyville & Peoria Railroad. All this equipment had been requisitioned by the Government, the rails being shipped to the United States Shipping Board at Newcastle, Delaware. On account of the importance of his service in that capacity the shipping board ordered him to remain at his duty, and he continued the work until after the armistice. After the war he purchased and wrecked a number of army and navy cantonments, including the largest of these cantonments sold by the Government, Camp Merritt, New Jersey. He bought $1,500,000 worth of war supplies after the armistice, superintending the distribution of these supplies from France to the various public warehouses in America.

Mr. Koeneke is a member of the Kiwanis Club and in politics is an independent voter. He married in Chicago, June 14, 1909, Miss Susan Vitula Wittenburg, who grew up in Chicago, attending public schools there and the Lewis Institute. She is a daughter of Henry C. and Myrta E. (Whiteside) Wittenburg, both of whom spent all their lives in Chicago. Her father was a manufacturer of ladies dresses on Milwaukee Avenue for many years, and died in 1918. Her mother, still a resident of Chicago, is now the wife of William Schuh, an employe at the court house in Chicago. Mrs. Koeneke's mother was a cousin of Brigadier General Whiteside, a distinguished Union officer of the Civil war. Mr. and Mrs. Koeneke have one daughter, Charlotte K., member of the class of 1928 at Waukegan High School.

WILLIAM MICHAEL EDDLEMAN. The affection in which a physician is held by those to whom he has ministered is of a character that excites admiration and inspires respect. The medical man occupies a position that is unique, for in his hands lie the lives of those entrusted to his care and upon his knowledge, skill and poise in times of danger depends the future of the community. To the credit of the profession be it said that very few of the men who devote their lives to the healing art fail to live up to the highest standards of fine manhood and citizenship. They put self second, and give lavishly of their time and professional services often without thought as to recompense. They not only care for the ailing, but through their foresight and ability to provide for contingencies preserve the public health and enforce sanitary regulations which oftentimes revolutionize the general soundness of the people, and establish a salubrity in their communities not dreamed of until they came into the locality with their scientific knowledge. One of the men of Illinois who belonged to this distinguished class, and lived up to its highest ideals, was the late Dr. William Michael Eddleman, of Anna, whose faithful service is remembered by all with whom he was brought into contact both as a physician and as a man.

Doctor Eddleman was born near Dongola, Illinois, March 22, 1858, a son of Eli and Mary Ann (Halterman) Eddleman, and grandson of Joseph and Susan (Hess) Eddleman, natives of North Carolina, of which state the maternal grandfather, Noah Halterman, was also a native. Eli Eddleman was born in Union County, Illinois, but his wife was born in North Carolina. Growing up on his father's farm in Union County, Doctor Eddleman attended the local schools, and continued his educational training at the University of Valparaiso, Indiana, and University of Louisville, Kentucky, and took up the study of medicine at the Medical College of the University of Nashville, Tennessee, from which he was graduated in 1882, with the degree of Doctor of Medicine. Immediately following his graduation he began the practice of his profession at Anna, and continued in it until death summoned him, April 1, 1925. During the many years he was in continuous practice in Union County he became a well-known figure all over this section, and was recognized as one of the most highly skilled general practitioners in this part of Illinois. He belonged to the Union County Medical Society, the Illinois State Medical Society, the Southern Illinois Medical Society and American Medical Association. Believing the principles of the democratic party more nearly express the ideal of a true democracy, Doctor Eddleman supported them, and became one of his party's leaders. For two terms he was coroner of Union County, and for four terms served Anna as mayor, and few men have given a more loyal service in either office. While he occupied the office of chief executive of Anna he inaugurated many very important improvements, and established certain sanitary reforms that have played a very important part in the improvement of the health of the community. When this good man and skilled and beloved physician passed away the whole community mourned the loss of a personal friend, and his place will not easily be filled.

On March 22, 1887, Doctor Eddleman married Dora E. Sifford, who was born near Cobden, Union County, Illinois, March 23, 1862, a daughter of Daniel and Susan (Casper) Sifford, natives of Union County. The paternal grandparents of Mrs. Eddleman were Peter and Leah (Mull) Sifford, natives of North Carolina, who came to Union County, Illinois, in 1819; while her maternal grandparents were Henry and Eliza (Rich) Casper, natives of North Carolina and Tennessee. Doctor and Mrs. Eddleman became the parents of the following children: William Ralph, who was born in 1888, is a practicing physician and surgeon of South Dakota; Ruth Marie, who was born in November, 1891, died in January, 1894; Glenn C., who was born in September, 1894, is a resident of Union County; and Daniel S., who was born in March, 1897, died in infancy. Mrs. Eddleman still maintains her home at Anna, residing in the handsome brick house which Doctor Eddleman built several years ago. She is a graduate of the Southern Illinois Normal School, and is an educated lady, and very active in the work of the Anna Lutheran Church, of which she has long been a member.

RABBI RUDOLPH FARBER, rabbi of the Jewish Congregation Am Echod in Waukegan, is a native of old Hungary, now the new Republic of Czecho-Slovakia, where his people on both sides for generations have been rabbis of the church. He was reared and educated there, but more than thirty years of his service had been rendered in America. He is greatly beloved by his people in Waukegan, being a man of exalted ideals, of remarkable scholarship and of complete devotion to the welfare and interest of his community.

Rabbi Farber was born at Nitra, Hungary, in what is now Czecho-Slovakia, April 5, 1865, son of Rabbi Jacob and Rose (Gertreider) Farber. His father spent his life in Hungary as a rabbi, for many years conducting a rabbinical college at Nitra, where he died in 1909 and is buried. Both he and his wife were of families that have been rabbis to the faith for many generations. Rose Gertreider still lives at Nitra, Hungary, at the age of ninety. Her father was Rabbi Aaron Gertreider.

Rudolph Farber was educated at home, obtained a secular education from a Catholic priest, who prepared him for entrance into the gymnasium, and in 1878 he entered the Ober Gymnasium. After graduating he was sent to Prague, Bohemia, where he pursued his rabbinical studies, obtaining his rabbinical authorization from the seminary in 1884. His education was continued in the Kaiser Wilhelm's University at Strassburg, Alsace, where he specialized in oriental philology. He was graduated in 1887, and after submitting his dissertation he was granted the Doctor of Philosophy degree in 1888 by the Philosophical Faculty of that university. Doctor Farber then spent a year and a half traveling and studying in the Holy Land, visiting every place of Biblical or archaeological interest. On returning to Bohemia in 1890, he took charge of a district rabbinate in the District of Klattau, serving there until 1894.

He first came to America in 1893 to visit the World's Fair at Chicago, and in 1895 he accepted a call which had previously been urged upon him to a South Side Hebrew Congregation in Chicago. He acted as rabbi in that congregation only a short time and then accepted a call to the care of oriental languages and philosophy at Union College at Schenectady, New York. In this congenial post of duty he remained for five years. Doctor Farber for eight years, 1900-08, was rabbi of a congregation at Vancouver, British Columbia. was rabbi four years at Des Moines, Iowa, and in 1912 returned to his former work in British Columbia, remaining there seven years, until 1919. From 1919 to 1923 he was rabbi at Texarkana, Texas, and in the latter year came to Waukegan as rabbi of the Congregation Am Echod.

He is an honorary life member of Border Lodge No. 672 of the Masonic order of Texarkana, is a life member of Texarkana Lodge No. 60, Knights of Pythias, life member of the B. P. O. Elks, member of the I. O. B. B. and the Deutsch Morgenlaendische Gesellschaft of Leipzig and Halle. He has been a member of the Rotary Club, the Lions Club, Kiwanis Club in different cities, being now a Kiwanian at Waukegan. He is also serving as a member of the Waukegan Board of Education. In politics Doctor Farber is an independent.

He married in Chicago, March 10, 1896, Miss Etta Crocker, who was reared and educated in Chicago, attended grammar and high school there. She takes an active interest in church and woman's club activities in both Chicago and Waukegan. Her parents were Morris and Theresa (Summerfield) Crocker of Chicago, where her father spent his life as a merchant. He died in 1919 and her mother still resides in Chicago. Doctor and Mrs. Farber have three children. Leona is the wife of Ben Heilbron, a merchant in Texargana, Texas, and has two children, Jerome K. and Marion Celeste. Arnold S. Farber graduated from the Texarkana High School in 1917, took special work in finance and banking with the Columbia University Extension Department, for nine years was with the State Bank of Texarkana, and is now with his father in Waukegan. Nettie Farber, the youngest child, is the wife of Max L. Heyman, a merchant at Okmulgee, Oklahoma, and they have one child, Max L., Jr.

EDMUND HOWARD CHILDRESS is one of the outstanding business men and citizens of Wayne County. A teacher in early life, he turned to the newspaper profession as the work best suited to his talents, and as editor and manager of the Wayne County Press has had the satisfaction of building up one of the most prosperous papers in Southern Illinois.

Mr. Childress represents several lines of pioneer Illinois ancestry. He was born at

Bridgeport in Lawrence County, January 12, 1873, son of George L. and Alice (Leach) Childress. His great-grandfather, Isham Childress, was a soldier of the American Revolution. He was born in Virginia and was one of six brothers, all of whom at one time or another took part with the Continental forces in the struggle for independence. Isham Childress was a pioneer of Lawrence County, Illinois, settling there about 1818, when he came from Tennessee. He died and was buried in Lawrence County. A son of Isham Childress was William Childress, who married Prudence Howard, daughter of William Howard, another pioneer of Lawrence County. George L. Childress, son of William and Prudence (Howard) Childress, was born in Lawrence County May 17, 1839. He served forty-five months as a soldier of the Union in Company I of the Sixty-sixth Illinois Infantry. While a soldier he kept a complete diary of his experiences, and that diary was later deemed so valuable for its historical contents that it was published. George L. Childress was a man of sound talents, popular, a useful member of society, though never a money maker, and he struggled much of his life with circumstances verging on poverty. He followed farming, and in the early days he taught many "singing schools" and was a good violinist. His home was in Lawrence County until 1883, and after that he lived in Wayne County until his death at Golden Gate in 1905. He was an active member of the Disciples Church, and after the war was a republican in politics. George L. Childress married Alice Leach, who survived him until April, 1923. They reared a family of six children. Alice Leach was born in Edwards County, Illinois, January 20, 1849, the fourth daughter of Rev. Daniel Bassett Leach. Rev. Mr. Leach was a native of Chenango County, New York, and came in early times to Edwards County, Illinois. His father, David L. Leach, was a New Englander, born in 1779 and died in 1870. David L. Leach married Millenia de Grassee Pardie, whose father was one of the French officers who came over at the time of the Revolution to help the American colonists. Rev. Daniel Bassett Leach was a pioneer Methodist minister in Illinois and lived for many years at Bone Gap. His wife was Marie Lois Root, who was born in Virginia and whose father came in pioneer times to Illinois.

Edmund Howard Childress spent his boyhood days on a farm, and from an early age had borne in upon him a serious sense of responsibility, doing his utmost to assist the family in making a living under trying circumstances. All of this work and training became valuable to him in his later years. He attended the country schools, but beyond them he earned all his education except for a sum of eight dollars given him by his father. At the age of twenty-one he began teaching. He spent four years as a student of the Southern College Institute at Albion, Illinois, graduating in 1898, and for two years after that taught in Tennessee. While in Tennessee he met and married Miss Isadora Butler Snell, of a prominent Tennessee family.

After leaving Tennessee Mr. Childress returned to Illinois and went to work on the Albion Journal. In 1904 he became assistant editor of the Wayne County Press at Fairfield. In 1909 he and W. M. Knodell bought the Press, and that paper has enjoyed its period of best prosperity and growth under the firm of Childress & Knodell as publishers. Mr. Childress has the responsible duties of editor and manager. He is well known among Illinois journalists, and for the past four years has served as treasurer of the Illinois Press Association.

For many years he has been an active member of the Christian Church at Fairfield, serving twenty years or more as church treasurer. He was a member of the building committee which in 1924 completed the beautiful modern church edifice at a cost of $55,000. As a token of their special interest in the church and as a means of inspiration to the community, Mr. and Mrs. Childress were the donors of the $7,150 Wurlitzer pipe organ, which was a prominent feature of the church at its dedication in December, 1925.

Mr. Childress has accumulated many other interests in addition to his successful newspaper plant. He was one of the organizers of the Albion Shale Brick Company. He is a republican in politics, is a member of the Masonic order, Independent Order of Odd Fellows, Knights of Pythias, and belongs to the Rotary and Good Fellow Clubs at Fairfield. He has achieved more than ordinary success and business prominence, and has always kept in mind the struggles of his own youth and has used his means and opportunities to benefit and assist many younger men in realizing their aspirations.

ORVILLE G. ST. PETER has for a number of years been a well known business man along the North Shore district in Lake County, and is now proprietor of the Green Mill Cleaners establishment at Waukegan, operating probably the largest cleaning and dyeing concern in Northern Illinois.

He was born at Highland Park in Lake County, February 22, 1879, son of Alford J. and Mary Ann (Mowers) St. Peter. His family is one that has many historical associations with the Highland Park section of Lake County. His grandfather, Joseph St. Peter, was a French Canadian of Quebec, Canada, was born and reared there, became a stone cutter and about 1870 came to Chicago, where he followed his trade as stone cutter for a number of years. He finally moved to Highland Park with his son Alford J. and lived at his home until his death about 1892, at the age of eighty-five. Alford J. St. Peter was born in Quebec, Canada, in 1843, and grew up among the French Canadians, learning to speak the French language fluently. In 1865 he came to Illinois and settled at Highland Park. The rest of his life he was in the general contracting business under the name of A. J. St. Peter, contractor and builder, and figured in the building operations during the pioneer period in that locality. He died at Highland Park in 1919. His wife, Mary Ann Mowers, was born in New York State and was eight years of age when her parents, Peter and Mary Ann (Truex) Mowers, came to Illinois in 1848. They first located at Halfday in Lake County, where her uncle operated the pioneer hotel, which was the stopping place for the stage coach line between Chicago and Milwaukee. Her parents soon moved to the lake front and lived for a time on the site now occupied by Fort Sheridan, and then to Highland Park. Their old home is 227 North Green Bay Road in Highland Park. Her father was educated in New York and after coming to Illinois took up the study of medicine and for some time was the only physician in the Highland Park district of Lake County. He died about 1876. He owned the first brick plant north of Chicago, and much of the brick was hauled along the lake shore on a scow boat drawn by a team of horses to market until the construction of the North Western Railroad through his property. The location of this plant was formerly known as Port Clinton. Mrs. Mary Ann St. Peter died in 1921.

Orville G. St. Peter attended public schools at Highland Park and in 1892, at the age of thirteen, went to work for the Fort Sheridan laundry. That was the beginning of an experience that has qualified him in such exceptional manner for the business in which he is now engaged. His first employment at the Fort Sheridan Laundry lasted about two years. After that he went with the North Shore Laundry at Highland Park, and in 1898 with the Lake Forest Laundry as a helper in the wash and starch room, remaining there until January, 1899. He then returned to Highland Park and bought the North Shore Laundry, and eighteen months later erected a complete new plant, which served the purpose for about five years. About a year after returning to Highland Park he took in his brother, Solomon A. St. Peter, as a partner. In 1906 they built a new model plant, still known as the Reliable Laundry of Highland Park. Mr. St. Peter in 1924 sold out his interest in this business to his brother and to L. B. St. Clair, who still continue it. At that time he removed to Waukegan and bought the Sanitary Cleaners and Dyers, renaming it the Green Mill Cleaners. He has practically made over the business, installing equipment and machinery that make it one of the most modern cleaning establishments in the country. Besides having all the mechanical facilities, Mr. St. Peter has given the business a personal touch and the benefit of his broad experience, as a result of which the volume of business has doubled about twelve times in the brief time since he took over the management.

Mr. St. Peter has been interested in a number of other business undertakings. In 1921 he was one of the associates who started the Waukegan Foundry and is still a director. He was also a director for five years in a woodworking establishment at Tuscaloosa, Alabama, and for two years, until 1925, he was secretary of the Scomatal Company of America at Highland Park.

Mr. St. Peter is a member of the Lodge, Royal Arch Chapter, Council and Knight Templar Commandery of Masons, was the first chaplain of Highland Park Lodge of Elks, belongs to the Knights of Pythias, Modern Woodmen of America, Royal Arcanum, and while living in Highland Park he served four years on the East Park Board. He is a republican and his church affiliations are with the Episcopal denomination.

He married at Waukegan, November 22, 1902, Miss Bessie S. Rogers, of Waukegan, who was educated in grammar and high school there for a number of years took an active part in the work of the Methodist Episcopal Church. Her parents, Henry and Rhoda Ann (Houston) Rogers, were born and reared in the Volo section of Lake County, where her father for many years conducted a general store, but in 1898 moved to Waukegan, where he was in the dry goods business until he retired. He died in 1914, and her mother is still living at Waukegan. Mr. and Mrs. St. Peter have three children, Marion, Mildred and Ruth. Marion is the wife of Harry Clovey, in the nursery business at Deerfield Park, Illinois, and they have a daughter, Bessie Ruth. Mildred married George Rudolph, of Highland Park, an electrician with the Hoover Electric Company. Miss Ruth is attending school at Highland Park.

SHERBURN V. WIRICK is a native of Illinois, spent a number of years in the railroad service, and is now one of the leading members of the bar of Ogle County, practicing at Rochelle.

His grandparents were Jacob and Mary (McCoy) Wirick, the former of Pennsylvania Dutch and the latter of Irish parentage. Jacob Wirick was born in Pennsylvania, May 22, 1787, and his wife in the same state, December 12, 1795. A few years after their marriage they moved to Coshocton County, Ohio, and several years later to Richland County in the same state, living there from about 1811 for twenty-five years, in the meantime developing a farm from the woods. They were the parents of seven sons and five daughters, and five sons and all the daughters reached good old age. Jacob Wirick while living in Ohio became a convert of the Mormon faith and left Ohio to join the Mormon colony in Northwestern Missouri, locating in the vicinity of the Mormon capital at "Far West" in Caldwell County. He acquired 160 acres there. Not long afterward occurred the difficulties between the Mormon colonists and other settlers, and by order of the governor and under the force applied by the Missouri militia the Mormons were driven out, most of them coming East and settling in the vicinity of Nauvoo, Illinois. Jacob Wirick left his Missouri farm unsold and spent the first year in Illinois about twenty-five miles from Quincy, and then bought eighty acres four miles from Nauvoo, in Hancock County. Not long afterward he became convinced that the church of the Mormons rested upon human rather than divine doctrines, and selling his farm he left the Mormon community and moved to East Paw Paw in DeKalb County, Illinois, where he and his wife lived out their years. He died February 6, 1868, and his wife, January 31, 1872. Their children, with dates of birth, were: John, 1812; Harriet, February 25, 1815; Cornelia, October 3, 1816; William, May 13, 1818; George, 1820; Samuel, who died in infancy; James, 1823; Edmund, June 25, 1825; Rebecca, March 13, 1827;

Mary, April 23, 1829; Valentine, March 25, 1831; and Nancy, March 5, 1839.

Of this large family of children Valentine Wirick was the father of Sherburn V. Wirick. He was six years of age when the family left Ohio, and most of his boyhood was spent in DeKalb County, Illinois. In 1849, at the age of eighteen, he and his older brother, Edmund, started with others for the gold fields of California. At Council Bluffs Edmund turned back on account of the report of cholera and Indian hostilities on the plains. Valentine remained there for a time and then went on to Salt Lake and from there to California, where Edmund joined him in 1850. They engaged in mining on the south fork of the American River, and were getting good returns for their labors until the rainy season began and their dam across the river was destroyed. They then took a boat at San Francisco, crossed Nicaraugua, thence by boat to Havana, Cuba, and back to the States at New Orleans, reaching home at Paw Paw, Illinois, January 2, 1851. In the spring of 1852 Valentine and Edmund, together with their brothers William and James and their sister Mary, started again for California, crossing the plains by the Salt Lake route and finally reaching Sacramento. They spent two or three years in California, returning to Illinois about 1854. Valentine Wirick was a carpenter and wagon maker, and died July 12, 1903. He married Janet Coulthard, and their son, Sherburn V. Wirick, was born at Evanston, Illinois, September 19, 1872.

Sherburn V. Wirick attended schools at Rochelle, and at the age of sixteen began assisting his father in drilling wells. After two years he went to work for the Chicago and Northwestern Railway Company as telegraph operator, and continued as such until he was appointed station agent at Rochelle in 1900. During the year he was in charge of that station he suggested improvements in certain methods of handling freight traffic. These suggestions were adopted and the officials of the road soon afterward made him traveling freight agent, with headquarters at Cincinnati. He was traveling freight agent four years and in 1903 was transferred to the Galena Division of the Chicago & Northwestern Railway as freight traffic solicitor in Northern Illinois. For some years he had been studying law, having been persuaded to do so by Delos W. Baxter, an attorney who had recognized his particular capability in that line. In 1907 he was admitted to the Illinois bar, and has busied himself with a growing law practice. He was in partnership with Delos W. Baxter in the firm of Baxter & Wirick until January 1, 1919, when Mr. Baxter retired. He then formed a partnership with his brother, Fred A. Wirick, under the name of Wirick & Wirick, and that is still one of the leading law firms of Ogle County.

Mr. Wirick is a thirty-second degree Scottish Rite Mason, a member of the B. P. O. Elks and belongs to the Rochelle Chamber of Commerce. He married near Rochelle, October 8, 1901, Miss Laura Cobb, daughter of Henry B. and Helen (Beamer) Cobb. Her father was born in Tolland County, Connecticut, and came to Illinois in 1852. He was a farmer, and became known as one of the largest cattle feeders in Northern Illinois. At the time of his death he owned over 1,800 acres of superb Illinois farm lands. He died November 2, 1918. One of his ancestors was one of the early assemblymen of the State of Connecticut.

THOMAS DIVEN HUFF. Included in the roster of able corporation lawyers of the middle west is Thomas Diven Huff, who is recognized as an authority on corporate organization, management and financing, having specialized in this branch of the legal profession from the very beginning of his practice. He is frequently retained as associate counsel in that connection. He is one of the ablest trial lawyers in Chicago, and has been retained in many notable cases; has had largely to do with the judicial interpretation of the present revenue laws of Illinois, and has served as counsel on many bondholders and reorganization committees of large public utilities and industrial corporations. Mr. Huff is Illinois editor of the "Corporation Manual," published at New York City; western counsel of the United States Corporation Company of New York, which corporation has an office in every state of the Union, the provinces of Canada, the Latin American countries, and the principal countries of Europe, and is engaged in the business of organizing and representing corporations in all of the same, and therefore his business is more or less international. He is also a director, secretary and treasurer of The Stoneman Company, besides being a director and stockholder in numerous other corporations. He is associate counsel to Messrs. Johnson, Heymann, Galston & Holstein of New York, probably the leading Latin American lawyers of the United States. Mr. Huff has also served as assistant corporation counsel of Evanston.

Thomas Diven Huff was born at Eldora, Iowa, January 9, 1872, a son of Hon. Henry Lewis and Elizabeth (Diven) Huff. The former, born in Pennsylvania, had the misfortune to lose his father when he was eight years old, and his mother when he was twelve, and from the latter tender age he was self-supporting. While serving an apprenticeship with a tailor he studied law and prepared himself for the legal profession. Coming west, he located in Harding County, Iowa, and became one of the leading railroad attorneys of his time. For many years he was counsel for the Chicago & Northwestern Railroad, later holding the same position with reference to the Illinois Central Railroad, and still later with the Iowa Central Railroad. A man of strong character and unquestioned ability, he was very active in the republican party, served two terms in the Iowa State Assembly, and was a member of the National Republican Committee in 1880, the year that James A. Garfield was elected to the Presidency of the United States. Of the eight children born to him and his wife three sons and two daughters survive, and of them all Mr. Huff of this review was the fifth in order of birth.

Growing up at Eldora, Thomas D. Huff there attended the grammar and high schools, and later continued his studies in the academy and college at Grinnell, Iowa. During his vacations he worked in his father's office, his early grounding in his subsequent profession thus being acquired under the supervision of one who had already achieved considerable fame. In 1893 he took up his legal studies in the Northwestern University Law School, Chicago, and was graduated therefrom in 1895, with the degree of Bachelor of Laws. From 1895 until 1903 Mr. Huff was associated in practice with Thomas J. Diven, and was also a member of the firm of Huff & Cook, Horace Wright Cook being the junior member. This latter connection was maintained undisturbed until 1911, when Joseph Slottow was admitted to partnership, under the name of Huff, Cook & Slottow. The firm is now Huff & Cook, with offices at 29 South LaSalle Street.

When Mr. Huff began his practice American business was assuming such proportions that the formation of corporations was a necessity, and as Chicago was the center of much of this new form of commercial organization Mr. Huff saw the value of specializing in what he knew would become a very important branch of his calling. It was with this object in mind that he first made a careful study of corporation law and delved into the intricacies of that subject with the purpose of acquiring an intimate knowledge of its every detail. His present position and international reputation prove that he has succeeded in marked degree, and that his decision at the outset was a wise and logical one.

On August 18, 1903, Mr. Huff married Ethelyn K. Allen at Helena, Montana. They became the parents of three children: Emorie Cannon, Lewis Stevenson, deceased, and Curtis Allen Huff. Like his father, Mr. Huff is a stanch republican. He belongs to the American Bar Association, Chicago Bar Association, Illinois State Bar Association, and Chicago Law Institute. He also is a member of the Hamilton Club of Chicago and Rolling Green Country Club, as well as of numerous other clubs and societies, and he and his family reside at Evanston.

CHARLES MONTAGUE WRIGHT, M. D., has been a practicing physician and surgeon at Altamont in Effingham County for a quarter of a century. His professional work covers the same territory in which his father labored so many years. The two together have been identified with the medical fraternity in Effingham County for sixty years or more.

His father was the late Dr. Charles M. Wright, Sr., who was born in Knox County, Ohio, December 8, 1834. The Wright family came from England and settled in Massachusetts in the early Colonial period. Dr. Charles M. Wright, Sr., was reared in Ohio, acquired his literary education in local schools and graduated from the Jefferson Medical College of Philadelphia. About 1858 he came to Illinois and settled in Ewington, then the county seat of Effingham County. The county seat the following year was moved to Effingham and he then located at Freemanton in the same county and in 1871 at Altamont, where he made his home until his death. He was the leading doctor and also the leading citizen of that community in its early years, and he carried on his professional work at the expense of great physical hardships and disabilities, riding to remote sections on horseback and frequently walking. He continued in active practice until 1878 and in that year organized and established at Altamont the private banking firm of C. M. Wright & Company. In 1893 he retired, after having been president of the bank. He died in 1898, at the age of sixty-four. Dr. Charles M. Wright, Sr., married Mattie Belle Patterson, who was of Scotch ancestry, the Pattersons having moved from Virginia to Indiana, and her parents came to Illinois from Indiana. She was born in Columbus, Indiana, and died in March, 1925, at the age of eighty years. Doctor and Mrs. Wright had three children: Lottie, wife of G. C. Dial, of Altamont; Miss Mabel Maude; and Charles M.

Charles M. Wright, Jr., was born at Altamont April 13, 1879. He grew up there, supplementing his public school education in Austin College at Effingham, from which he was graduated in 1898. Doctor Wright in 1902 received his degree in medicine from Washington University at St. Louis, and since that year has made his professional services available to his home community of Altamont. He is a member of the Effingham County, Illinois State and American Medical Associations, and during the World war was on the local examining board, was chairman of the local Red Cross and was a Four Minute Speaker.

Doctor Wright is a republican and a member of the Presbyterian Church. He married, in 1907, Miss Ella May Hobbs, a native of Knox County, Illinois. They have one son. Charles Montague Wright III.

GEORGE W. JOHNS, veteran lawyer and banker of Fairfield, is one of the youngest survivors of the veterans of the Civil war. His career as a lawyer and business man began more than half a century ago and he is still active.

He was born at Albion, Illinois, March 7, 1849, son of George J. and Harriet (Smith) Johns. His father, a native of England, came to Illinois when a young man and at Albion became a blacksmith and carriage maker, being one of the early manufacturers of wagons, buggies and plows in that community. He married at Albion Harriet Smith, who was born there. Her father, Moses Smith, was also a native of England and for many years a leading merchant at Albion, buying and shipping pork and beef. George J. Johns and wife lived out their lives at Albion. George J. Johns in 1862 raised a company which became Company B of the Sixty-third Illinois Infantry, and went out as its captain. He died in 1874, and his wife passed away in 1852, when George W. Johns was only three years of age.

George W. Johns was the only child of his parents to grow up. He spent the first twelve years of his life at Albion. In 1864, when only fifteen years of age, he enlisted and was enrolled as a member of Company H of the One Hundred and Thirty-sixth Illinois Infantry. A record of his service is a certificate of honorable service, signed by A. Lincoln. At the age of seventeen, soon after the war, he enrolled as a student in the University of Indiana, graduating from the literary department in 1869, and from the Law School in 1870. He also read law privately at Fairfield and was admitted to the Illinois bar in 1870. Mr. Johns for two years practiced at Carmi, and since 1872, at Fairfield, where he became a member of the law firm of Robinson, Boggs & Johns, an association which continued until Judge Boggs' elevation to the bench and the firm was then Robinson & Johns until Mr. Robinson's death. The bar of Wayne County presented Mr. Johns in 1922 with a testimonial, signed by each of its sixteen members, saying: "The fiftieth anniversary of his entering the practice of the law in this county affords a fitting opportunity for us to testify our appreciation of his sterling character and high ideals, as well as his distinguished ability and clear legal mind." Mr. Johns has always taken a leading part in civic affairs and in republican politics, and he served with the rank of colonel on the staff of Governors Cullom, Hamilton and Oglesby, but was never an office seeker.

In 1893 was organized Pendleton, Johns & Company, bankers of Fairfield. In 1903 this private bank was succeeded by the Fairfield National Bank, and Colonel Johns has continued as vice president of this institution. He is a member of the Grand Army of the Republic, belongs to the Phi Kappa Psi college fraternity, the Independent Order of Odd Fellows and the Knights of Pythias.

In 1875 he married Miss Mary E. Barnhill. Of the children of their marriage two daughters died young, one at the age of five and the other, Nellie Johnson, after her marriage. The two surviving daughters are Mary E. Phillips, wife of an attorney at St. Louis, and Ann Shaeffer, wife of David H. Shaeffer, of Fairfield, Illinois.

JOHN R. FULTON, head of one of the most successful real estate, insurance and loan organizations in the Waukegan district, prior to entering that field had many years of experience in the banking institutions of Waukegan, and he brought to real estate, therefore, a wide knowledge of financial conditions and an extensive acquaintanceship with men and affairs along the North Shore.

He was born at Waukegan, April 30, 1871, son of William and Elizabeth (Jenkinson) Fulton. His father, a native of Scotland, was reared and educated there and learned the cabinet making trade. When he came to America as a young man he lived for a few years in New York State and in 1857 located at Waukegan, then a small manufacturing town. He followed his trade as a cabinet maker and carpenter contractor until he retired, and then spent his declining years with a son, Albert, at Spencer, Iowa, where he died in 1919. His wife was born in Queen's County, Ireland, and was a small girl when she accompanied her family to America. One of her sisters died during the voyage and was buried at sea. Her family moved from New York to Waukegan about 1857, and she married William Fulton about 1860. She was a member of the Episcopal Church, and after her home and children was deeply interested in church matters. Her death occurred in 1923. All of the nine children of William Fulton and wife are living, Matilda, Joseph, William T., Nellie E., Albert J., John R., Robert C., Ada E. and Frank H. Matilda is the wife of William B. Hayden, a hardware merchant at Cassopolis, Michigan, and mother of four children, named Joe, Belle, Stella and Bernice. Joseph, a Burlington Railway engineer at Kansas City, Missouri, and for a number of years secretary of the Brotherhood of Locomotive Engineers, married Jennie Porter of Racine, Wisconsin, now deceased, and their four children were Harry, William, Ada and Josephine. William T. Fulton, a resident of Chicago and connected with the Chamberlin Weather Strip Company of Chicago, married Barbara Robling, and their children are Howard, Robert, Geraldine and Gardner. Nellie E. Fulton married Fred Shober, in the mail delivery department of the Waukegan Post Office, and their children are Lois, Charles, Albert, Joseph, Ethel and Ruth. Albert Fulton, formerly of Spencer, Iowa, now a farmer and truck grower at Gurnee, Illinois, married Nannie Seibel, who died in 1903, leaving three children, Frank, Ada and Clara. Robert C. Fulton is a musician, a pipe organ player and proficient on other instruments, and for a number of years has been active in musical affairs at Pasadena, California, where he resides, having conducted the Fulton Orchestra. He married Grace Kines, and their children are Dorothy, Lloyd and Billie. Ada Fulton is the wife of August W. Groth, a farmer and breeder of pure bred Poll Angus cattle at Spencer, Iowa, and they have one daughter, June. Frank H. Fulton, a carpenter contractor at Waukegan, married Mabel Gilbert and has children named Hayden, Harold, Edward, Lillian and Anabel.

John R. Fulton grew up at Waukegan and attended grammar and high school, graduating from the latter in 1890. Soon after completing his education he became a messenger boy in the First National Bank of Waukegan and was in the service of that institution ten years, reaching the position of head bookkeeper. In 1900, upon the organization of the Peoples State Bank of Waukegan, he became cashier, and served in that capacity for eighteen years. He left banking to engage in real estate, conducting a brokerage business in city, suburban and rural property, also handling loans and insurance, and has operated to some extent on his own properties, putting on the market several subdivisions. His organization was one of the few in Lake County which during the past year recorded sales in excess of two million dollars.

Mr. Fulton has always been generous of his time and means to promote the civic welfare of his community. He is a Royal Arch Mason, member of the Eastern Star, was a charter member of the Kiwanis Club, belongs to the Royal Arcanum, is a republican and a member of the Episcopal Church, and since 1903 has been on the Board of Vestrymen and for three years has been junior warden of Christ Church, and for twenty years church treasurer.

Mr. Fulton married in Waukegan, October 15, 1895, Miss Addie B. Pollock, of Millburn, Illinois. She finished her education in the University of Illinois and taught in public schools in Lake County before her marriage.

She is a member of the Eastern Star and has given much time to church work. Her parents were James and Isabelle (Mason) Pollock, of Millburn. Her father for a number of years conducted a grain and wool warehouse and commission business at Wadsworth, and at one time was a representative in the Illinois General Assembly, being one of the 103 members of the Legislature who after a prolonged deadlock elected John A. Logan to the United States Senate. Mr. Pollock died in 1919 and his wife in 1920. Mrs. Fulton had a brother, Robert, now deceased, another brother, Henry, who is associated with Mr. Fulton in the realty business at Waukegan, and her sister Bertha became the wife of J. Campbell Carey, a distinguished cartoonist who died in 1925. Mr. and Mrs. Fulton have two sons, James W. and Donald L. James W. graduated from the Waukegan High School in 1918, and from the mechanical engineering course in Armour Institute of Technology in 1924. He married Bessie Hoak of Fort Atkinson, Wisconsin, formerly a teacher in the schools of Waukegan. Donald L. Fulton, the younger son, graduated from the Waukegan High School in 1924, receiving the Craftsmanship Shield, the highest award of the high school. He is now in the class of 1928 at Lake Forest University.

McKINLEY J. ANDERSON is a representative of the third generation of the Anderson family in Ogle County, long and prominently known for their connection with the agricultural, industrial and civic interests of that locality.

The founder of the family was John Anderson, who was born in Scotland in 1807, son of Joseph and Jane (Clark) Anderson, who spent all their lives in Scotland. John Anderson had a natural genius for mechanics, learned the trade of millwright, which was also his father's occupation, and he worked in his father's mill in Scotland. He was one of a family of eleven children. Coming to America in 1832, he landed in Nova Scotia, but soon settled in Delaware County, New York, where in connection with the operation of a mill, which he built, he also engaged in farming. He married in Delaware County, September 18, 1834, Miss Margaret Sim. She was born and reared in Scotland, daughter of Alexander Sim, who brought his family to America and settled in Delaware County, New York.

It was in 1845 that John Anderson brought his family to Illinois and settled in Ogle County, acquiring the nucleus of what has long since been known as the Anderson homestead farm, one of the best improved country places in the county. He entered eighty acres from the Government. On this land he erected a small home. At Eagle Point he put up a shop where he did wagon making and general repair work. Subsequently he removed the shop to his farm. His increasing prosperity was represented by repeated additions to his land holdings until he owned about three hundred acres, improved with one of the best residences in the township, and with stock and equipment that he took pride in making the best. John Anderson died while visiting in Rockford, March 21, 1886, two years after he and his wife had celebrated their golden wedding. His widow survived him until June 1, 1892. Both are now at rest in Fairmont Cemetery. John Anderson was a republican, and for a number of years was a justice of the peace in his township. He and his wife had seven children: Joseph A. and George, both of whom went out to Oregon, Jane A., who married G. J. Monroe, James D., John, who became a Chicago building contractor, Nettie A., who married W. W. Pierce, and Margaret C., who became the wife of George Gibbs.

James D. Anderson was born at Andes, Delaware County, New York, October 12, 1842, and was three years of age when the family came to Illinois. He was reared on the farm, attended the common schools, and in 1868 became the responsible manager of the farm. After the death of his father he bought the interests of the other heirs, and for many years was known as one of the most progressive representatives of agriculture in Ogle County. He increased the original farm to four hundred acres, and for years regularly returned a large part of the net profit of his farming to new improvements, building large barns and other facilities for handling his live stock. He was a raiser and feeder of stock for the market, and for years was one of the largest individual shippers from Polo.

James D. Anderson for twenty-five years was interested in the Eagle Point Mutual Fire Insurance Company and for a time was its president. He served eighteen years as commissioner of highways, as township treasurer for a similar length of time, was township collector, and was a delegate to the county and congressional conventions of the republican party. He was a past grand in Polo Lodge, Independent Order of Odd Fellows.

James D. Anderson in March, 1910, moved to Polo and occupied a beautiful home he purchased there until his death on September 26, 1911. He married in Brookville Township, Ogle County, April 2, 1885, Miss Addie L. Gibbs, who was a native of the county, daughter of Leonard Gibbs, an early settler. To their marriage were born two children, Grace B. and McKinley J. Anderson.

McKinley J. Anderson was born at the homestead near Polo, September 22, 1894, was educated in the grammar and high schools of Polo, and since his father's death has been the responsible manager of the farming, live stock and other Anderson interests in that locality. He and his sister still own the fine Anderson farm of 400 acres near Polo, and they occupy the old home in the City of Polo. McKinley Anderson is a member of the Masonic order, is a republican, a Lutheran, and belongs to the Edgewood Country and Golf Club.

He married at Polo, March 27, 1913, Miss Anna Beard, of Polo, daughter of Dr. L. A. and Frances (Strickler) Beard, and a granddaughter of Solomon and Sarah (Laudenslager) Beard, who came to Illinois from Maryland in pioneer times. Dr. L. A. Beard was born and reared at Polo, attended public schools there and graduated from Northwestern University School of Medicine at Chicago, and also took post-graduate work in Germany. He practiced medicine until 1905, and since

John L. Walker

then has lived retired. Mr. and Mrs. McKinley Anderson are the parents of four children, Anna Frances, James Robert, Helen Ruth and Mary Adelaide.

HOWARD CARLISLE HOAG, M. D. A Waukegan physician and surgeon, member of the staff of the Victory Memorial Hospital, Doctor Hoag has been a resident of that city since 1919. He is regarded as one of the most accomplished men in his profession in Lake County, and his experience has demonstrated the wisdom of his choice of a career.

He was born at Waterloo, Wisconsin, July 31, 1887, son of Porter E. and Emma S. (Lackey) Hoag, and grandson of W. L. and Caroline Hoag, the grandfather born and reared in New York State and was an early settler at Waterloo, Wisconsin. The Hoag family is of English ancestry and the line is traced back to the English nobility. Porter E. Hoag was born and reared at Waterloo, Wisconsin, was educated in public schools there and for many years was a general merchant of the town. He retired from business in 1924, and he and his wife still reside at Waterloo. They had a family of four children, the oldest, William, dying in infancy. The second is Howard C., and the two younger are Mrs. Hazel Hoag Wilcox and Robert Lee Hoag. Mrs. Hazel Wilcox is the wife of Raymond B. Wilcox, who is plant pathologist at the Agricultural Experiment Station at Wooster, Ohio. Mr. and Mrs. Wilcox have a daughter, Elizabeth. Robert Lee Hoag is a resident of Beloit, Wisconsin, and married Lyla White, of Waterloo.

Howard Carlisle Hoag attended public schools at Waterloo, graduating from high school in 1906, and during the next few years was employed as a bookkeeper by the Farmers & Merchants State Bank of Waterloo. In 1910 he entered the School of Osteopathy at Kirksville, Missouri, graduating in 1913. In his career as an osteopathic physician, Doctor Hoag practiced one year at Beloit, Wisconsin, and five years at Oak Park, Illinois. While practicing at Oak Park he pursued the regular course in medicine and surgery at Loyola University in Chicago and was graduated M. D. in 1918. Doctor Hoag after graduating spent a year as an interne in the West Side Hospital and also attended the Illinois Post-Graduate School of Medicine. In 1919 he located at Waukegan, opened an office and has built up a very extensive general practice and is now serving as vice president of the staff of the Victory Memorial Hospital. He is president of the Lake County Medical and a member of the Illinois State and American Medical Associations. His offices are in the Waukegan National Bank Building. In 1924 he was elected city health officer.

Doctor Hoag has taken a commendable interest in the affairs of his community and was president of the Kiwanis Club two years, 1920-21. He is a thirty-second degree Scottish Rite Mason, belongs to Medinah Temple of the Mystic Shrine at Chicago, Waukegan Lodge No. 702, B. P. O. Elks, Glen Flora Country Club, and is a Methodist.

He married at Beloit, Wisconsin, October 20, 1914, Miss Grace L. Curns. Mrs. Hoag was educated in the public schools of Fort Worth, Kansas, and in the Chicago Heights High School, and is an active member of the Methodist Episcopal Church and the Waukegan Woman's Club, the Eastern Star Chapter, and the P. E. O. Her parents were Robert L. and Sarah Curns, formerly of Beloit, Wisconsin, now of Springfield, Massachusetts. Her father is a retired contractor, and for many years was successfully identified with that business at Chicago Heights. Doctor and Mrs. Hoag had two children, Howard Porter, who died in infancy, and Robert Curns Hoag.

JOHN DANIEL WALKER. Among the officials of Will County who have demonstrated the possession of qualities eminently fitting them for the positions which they now hold, none have vindicated the confidence reposed in them in greater degree than has John Daniel Walker, the incumbent of the shrievalty. His official career in this and other offices has been a long and honorable one, and Sheriff Walker has the added distinction of being a self-made man in all that the word implies.

John Daniel Walker was born at Braidwood, Illinois, March 26, 1874, and is a son of John P. and Eliza (Steel) Walker, natives of Scotland. The father immigrated to the United States alone in 1866 and took up his residence first at Braidwood, where he was joined by his wife and elder children in 1867. A coal miner by trade, he found employment at that calling, but in 1875 moved to Joliet, where he found better employment in the rolling mill of a steel company. He was thrifty and enterprising, saved his wages, and in later life became a merchant and accumulated a modest property. He died in 1920, at the age of eighty-two years, and is survived by his widow, who is now eighty-one years of age. They were the parents of twelve children, of whom four are living: Anna, the wife of James McCulloch, of Joliet; John Daniel, of this review; Jessie, a merchant of Chicago Heights, Illinois, and the wife of Joseph Wattleworth; and Peter, who resides with his mother at Joliet.

The boyhood of John Daniel Walker up to the time he was twelve or thirteen years of age was passed in attending the public schools and in doing such odd jobs as came his way, but finally he secured steady employment with what was then the Joliet Steel Company, now a part of the Illinois Steel Company. This position was known as that of "pull-up boy," calling for twelve straight hours of hard manual work, for which he was remunerated to the extent of seventy cents per day. Gradually he worked his way to the position of charger, in which he received $2.25 per day when he started, and eight years later $3.39 per day, and then advanced to the post of heater. After eighteen years in this capacity Mr. Walker decided that there was no future for him, and he accordingly resigned to accept the post of keeper in the new penitentiary at Joliet, holding this position for six and one-half months. He then secured employment in the office of the secretary of state as an automobile investigator, and for two and one-half years covered the counties of Kankakee, Grundy, Kendall and Will, and April 11, 1922, was nominated for the office of sheriff of Will

County. Elected November 7, 1922, he took office December 4 of that year, and since that time has made an excellent record. He is a member of the Illinois State Sheriffs Association, and at Peoria, in 1923, was elected president thereof, an office which he held one year. He has also served as tax collector of Joliet Township two years, and as county oil inspector of Will County, by appointment, four years. One of the best-known and most influential republicans in his part of the state, Sheriff Walker is chairman of the County Central Committee, and was manager of the campaign of Governor Small and Oscar Carlstrom in his county. His religious faith is that of the Presbyterian Church. He has been a Mason since 1901 and in 1925 was elevated to the Scottish Rite, in addition to which he is a member of the Mystic Shrine, the Independent Order of Odd Fellows, the Benevolent and Protective Order of Elks, the Loyal Order of Moose and the Modern Woodmen of America. He likewise maintains membership in the Rivals Club, the Speed Boys Club and the Irwin Athletic Club.

On August 17, 1895, Sheriff Walker married Miss Mary Puhek, who was born at Joliet, a daughter of Mathew and Catherine Puhek, natives of Austria, and to this union there have been born the following children: Anna, the wife of Frank Smith, of Joliet; Elizabeth M., the wife of Alfred Jancovas, of Joliet, who has two sons, Alfred Hughes and John Daniel; Lillian K., who married John Turney, of Chicago, and has four children, Marie, Jack, Bernard and Bernice; John J. and Frank C., who live with their parents; Mathew, who died in infancy; and Alexander G., Eliza Steel and Grace Scott, twins, and James D., all at home.

ROBERT EDWARD BROWN. The qualities of adaptability, persistence, common sense and good judgment have prevailed in the energetic life of Robert Edward Brown, winning for him an enviable rank among the financial, business, political and social elements of the city of Anna. A resident of this thriving community since infancy, he has grown with its growth, developed with its development and prospered with its prosperity, and at present occupies the position of secretary and manager of the Anna Loan and Improvement Company. He also has numerous other interests, but has found the time to give of his services and ability to all worthy and beneficial movements.

Mr. Brown was born in Tarrant County, Texas, September 19, 1871, and is a son of Andrew C. and Emma (Elkins) Brown, natives of Union County, Illinois. His paternal grandfather was Tolbert Brown, a native of North Carolina, who in early days migrated to Tennessee, whence he came to Union County, Illinois. The maternal grandparents were Benjamin C. Elkins and Angeline (Williams) Elkins, natives of Virginia, who had accompanied Mr. and Mrs. Brown to Tennessee and then made their way in the same party to Union County. Benjamin C. Elkins served as a justice of the peace for many years, and both he and Mr. Brown were substantial citizens of their community. However, they were not satisfied, and in 1866 they answered the call of the West and with their families moved by wagons, driving thirty-six head of cattle, across the seemingly endless plains to Tarrant County, Texas. The trip took from April until September, and when they had arrived at the destination all of the cattle with which they had started the journey had died and they were forced to secure more before starting their agricultural activities. While living at Anna grandfather Brown had been a flour miller, while grandfather Elkins was a blacksmith, his shop still standing as one of the old landmarks. However, in Texas, both became farmers, entering land which they improved.

When the parents of Robert Edward Brown reached Texas they found a wild country, uninhabited save for much game. It was not long, however, before the country began to settle up and with the western flow of civilization came the usual lawless element, which made much work for that intrepid little organization which was to become world-famous as the Texas Rangers. Andrew C. Brown, who was a fearless man of somewhat adventurous spirit, joined this organization, and in April, 1872, while in the discharge of his duty, was killed by a desperado. Soon thereafter his sorrowing widow and her two small sons returned to Anna and settled on a farm just east of town. There Mrs. Brown married again, her husband being W. H. Thiell, who died in 1902, while Mrs. Thiell survived until 1916, dying while on a visit to her other son, Leonard U., at Ardmore, Oklahoma, he following her in death in 1917.

Robert Edward Brown attended district school, and for seven years taught in district schools during the winter months, while at the same time advancing his own education in the summer months at the Southern Illinois Normal School. He then took up his permanent residence at Anna, where he was elected secretary and manager of the Anna Loan and Improvement Company, a position which he still retains. In 1916 Mr. Brown was one of the main factors in the organization of the Anna State and Trust Bank, which opened its doors for business June 9, 1917, with C. D. Harris as cashier. In 1919 Mr. Brown was elected cashier and held that position for four and one-half years, when he resigned and was succeeded by C. R. Ford, the other officers being Rad Burnett, president; W. F. Bruchhauser, vice president; and Robert E. Brown, J. H. Ligon, E. P. Owen, A. W. Walter, Jr., and W. H. Crane, directors. Mr. Brown is also director of the Anna Products Corporation and the Ligon Lumber Company. He was the organizer of the East Side Apartment Building Corporation, which has just erected a three-story brick building with twelve complete apartments, with electric ranges and thoroughly modern, ten individual rooms with Murphy folding beds, and three store rooms on the first floor. Politically Mr. Brown is a republican. He is much interested in fraternalism, being a member of the Knights of Pythias and a former delegate to the Grand Lodge; the Independent Order of Odd Fellows, in which he has passed through the chairs and been a representative to the Grand Lodge and Grand Encampment; the Rebekahs, in which

he has been through the chairs; the Modern Woodmen of America, of which he is venerable counsel; and the Springfield Life Insurance Company; while in the old Court of Honor he was supreme delegate for twenty years. Mrs. Brown has passed through the chairs of the Rebekahs and several times has been a delegate to the Grand Lodge. She is a member of the Lutheran Church.

On February 23, 1902, Mr. Brown was united in marriage to Miss Mayme West, who was born in Union County, Illinois, a daughter of A. J. and Lucinda A. (Treece) West, the former born in Indiana and the latter in Union County, and a granddaughter of Benjamin and Mary West, of Indiana, and Maston and Sarah Treece of Union County. Mr. and Mrs. Brown are the parents of two children: Roy A., born February 21, 1905; and Robert W., born December 22, 1908.

CLARENCE W. BALKE, research chemist and expert in rare metals, has been director of the laboratory of the Fansteel Products Company at North Chicago for the past ten years. With the generous support and cooperation of the president of that company, James M. Troxel, he has carried out some remarkable investigations and experiments, and his success in producing on a commercial scale the rare metal, Tantalum, has made possible some of the most remarkable developments of the radio industry.

Doctor Balke was born at Auburn, Ohio, March 29, 1880, son of William F. and Clara (Class) Balke. His father was born in Germany, in 1850, came to America when about eighteen years of age, and as a tinsmith located at Chagrin Falls, Ohio, where he was employed as a journeyman at a wage of $75 for the first year. He succeeded in saving $50 from his wages and with that sum bought a set of tools and started a business of his own at Auburn. Later, in connection with his tin and sheet metal works, he conducted a hardware store there, and finally another hardware business at Chagrin Falls, and continued active in business, except for a brief respite in 1891, until 1900, when he retired. He died in 1908. His wife, Clara J. Class, was born and reared on a farm adjoining the Rockefeller estate in Northern Ohio. She now resides with her children, Doctor Balke, at Highland Park, and her daughter, Mrs. Walter H. Loomis, at Cleveland.

Clarence W. Balke attended public school at Auburn, was in the class of 1896 in the Chagrin Falls High School, was graduated with the A. B. degree at Oberlin College in 1902, and during 1902-03 pursued post-graduate work in chemistry at the University of Pennsylvania. During the summer of 1903 he was instructor in chemistry at Oberlin College, was acting professor of physics and chemistry at Kenyan College at Gambier, Ohio, in 1903-04, and then returned to the University of Pennsylvania as a fellow and post-graduate student. In 1905 he was awarded the Doctor of Philosophy degree. He remained another year at the University of Pennsylvania as an honorary research fellow in chemistry. While at the university he studied the compounds of the rare metals, Tantalum and Columbium, and determined the atomic weights of these two elements. His results in both cases were accepted and approved by the international committee of atomic weights. During 1906-07 Doctor Balke was instructor in chemistry at the University of Pennsylvania. From 1907 to 1916 he was in the chemistry department of the University of Illinois, first as associate in chemistry and later professor of inorganic chemistry and head of the division of inorganic chemistry. In June, 1916, he went to the Pfanstiehl Company of North Chicago, now the Fansteel Products Company, and has since been chemical director of this successful manufacturing concern. It was the result of several years of patient work carried on under many discouragements that he finally succeeded in producing at the laboratory chemically pure Tantalum. The secret of producing Tantalum on a commercial scale came at the phychological moment in conjunction with the development of radio. Tantalum is the essential element in what is known and appreciated by all radio experts and users as the Balkite system of charging batteries.

Doctor Balke is author of a number of articles which have been published in engineering and technical publications, including the story of the production and uses of Ductile Tantalum, which appeared in the Smithsonian report for 1923. Doctor Balke is a member of various technical societies, among which are Sigma Xi, the American Chemical Society and the honorary fraternities of Phi Lambda, Phi Eta and Epsilon Chi. Doctor Balke married, April 21, 1905, Miss Minnie Maud Coddington, of Sussex, New Jersey, whom he met in Oberlin College. She was a teacher before her marriage and is still active in educational affairs. Doctor and Mrs. Balke have five children, two sons, Claire Coddington, member of the class of 1927 in Deerfield-Shields High School, and Roger Redfield, member of the class of 1929, and three daughters, Barbara, Hildegarde and Abigail, who are in the Lincoln Grammar School of Highland Park.

ROBERT E. SMITH, a Franklin County attorney, has practiced law at Benton since 1913. Besides a large private practice his work has involved important service to both county and state legal departments and his reputation as a lawyer is by no means confined to his native locality.

His family has been in Franklin County for over ninety years. His grandparents, John A. and Nancy J. Smith, the latter a native of McNairy County, Tennessee, moved from Tennessee to Franklin County in 1834, settling five miles east of Benton, where they lived out the rest of their lives as farmers. Their son, Albert C. Smith, was born in Franklin County, devoted all his active years to agriculture, and died in 1911. He was a soldier during the Civil war in the Tenth Illinois Cavalry for three years and four months. Albert C. Smith married Judea Maddox, a native of Tennessee, who was brought by her parents to Illinois. She died in 1909.

Robert E. Smith was born on the home farm June 8, 1877, grew up there and attended country schools. He now owns the farm where he was born and in a measure has always kept in touch with agricultural interests. He finished his literary education in Ewing College and Dixon College, and in 1903 began the study of law at Benton under Judge W. S. Cantrell. While studying he made his living in the real estate business. Mr. Smith was admitted to the bar in 1913. He has been particularly successful as a jury lawyer. His law offices are in the Swofford Building at Benton.

Mr. Smith served as United States commissioner from 1914 to 1918. For eight years he was an assistant attorney general of Illinois under Attorney General Brundage. His special assignment of duties was in handling cases in the inheritance tax department. He also acted four years as city attorney and for four years was assistant state's attorney under W. P. Seeber. Thus he has been intrusted with a large volume of public business. Mr. Smith in 1920 became a member of the Board of Education of the consolidated school district. He has filled all the chairs in the local lodge of Knights of Pythias and is a member of the B. P. O. Elks and Modern Woodmen of America.

He married Miss Verna Thurmond, daughter of W. B. Thurmond of Spring Garden, Jefferson County, Illinois. Their one son, Goffrey, a graduate of the Missouri Military Academy, is now county surveyor of Franklin County.

JOHN WILLIAM BOSTICK, cashier of the First National Bank of Albion, has well earned all the successive stages of his promotion, including all his education above the fundamentals. The productive period of his career began about the time he came to Edwards County, Illinois, some fifteen years ago.

He was born on a farm in Boyd County, Kentucky, September 9, 1882, son of William N. and Mary (Elswick) Bostick, and grandson of Mortimer Bostick. William N. Bostick was born in Indiana and was a small boy when the family moved to Illinois, where he grew up in Adams County. The Civil war came on and at the age of seventeen he enlisted, serving one year. He was discharged in Tennessee, and returning north he married in Kentucky, his wife being a native of Virginia. After his marriage he settled in Boyd County, Kentucky, and when John W. was about seven years of age the family moved to Lawrence. William N. Bostick was a miner in early life and later a farmer, and he and his wife now live in Greenup County, Kentucky. Of their five children John W. is the oldest.

John William Bostick up to the age of seventeen had the privilege of attending public schools only about two months a year. His people were in rather limited circumstances and since the school year ran from July to December he was never able to enter the term until all the farm work was done late in the fall. Between the age of seventeen and nineteen he attended a normal school. Leaving home at the age of twenty-one, he went to Cincinnati and worked his way through a commercial college, paying his expenses by dish washing and waiting on table, and even so he was in debt when he completed his course. He showed such proficiency that he became an instructor in a business college, giving six years altogether to that work. He spent five years at Terre Haute, Indiana, and one year at Jacksonville, Illinois. A breakdown of health caused him to leave school work and spend several months recuperating in the mountains of Kentucky.

Mr. Bostick in 1909 married Amy Jennings, daughter of Ernest M. Jennings, of Grayville, Illinois. Mr. Bostick had located at Grayville after his sojourn in the Kentucky mountains. In 1911 he became bookkeeper and teller of the Farmers National Bank of Grayville, and subsequently was cashier of that institution. In 1916 he took over the West Salem Brick Plant, and in 1920 he became cashier of the First National Bank of Albion, and is also vice president of the Brown State Bank. Thus his interests have been accumulating rapidly within the past ten years.

Mr. Bostick is a Council degree Mason and is an active worker in the Christian Church. He and his wife have three children: T. Jennings, William E. and Harriet.

GEORGE H. ANDREW, former county treasurer of Ogle County, is one of the oldest living native sons of the county, and for many years was engaged in farming and in business, but is now enjoying a well earned retirement.

He was born in Pine Rock Township, near Oregon, July 16, 1855, son of Nicholas and Margaret (Eychaner) Andrew. His grandfather, John Andrew, lived in New York State and was of English ancestry. Nicholas Andrew was born in Herkimer County, New York, where he was reared and married. In 1842 he came west and in the new district of Ogle County, Illinois, acquired land from the government at $1.25 an acre. He subsequently bought other land and became a prosperous farmer, one of the leading stock and grain raisers there. He died in 1856, fourteen years after coming to Illinois. The wife of Nicholas Andrew, Margaret Eychaner, was a daughter of Conrad and Catherine (Boody) Eychaner, who came to Illinois in 1843 and were also early settlers in the vicinity of Oregon. Conrad Eychaner was born at Albany, New York, in 1792, and was an American soldier in the War of 1812. He died in 1866.

George H. Andrew grew up on a farm, attended public schools and Mount Morris College, and after completing his education engaged in farming, which he followed for many years. He has always kept in touch with agricultural interests, since he has been a large land owner. Mr. Andrew was sheriff of Ogle County from 1897 to 1905. In 1906 he was elected county treasurer, and administered that office with a high degree of efficiency until December 1, 1910. For three years he was also deputy county clerk. Mr. Andrew is a Royal Arch Mason, and was a member of the Knights of Pythias until its lodge was abandoned.

He married at Freeport, Illinois, September 19, 1878, Miss Ida M. Eddy, daughter of Horace and Jane (Woodward) Eddy, whose home was near Creston, Illinois. Her parents were born and reared in Rhode Island and came to Illinois about 1850, taking up land in DeKalb County. Mr. and Mrs. Andrew have two children, Eddy Glenn Andrew and Edith L. Andrew. Eddy Glenn was born January

21, 1881, was educated in public schools, in the University of Illinois, in a business college at Rockford, and from 1906 to 1922 was deputy county treasurer. In the latter year he became county treasurer and is the present incumbent of that important county office. He married Helen Kohler, of Oregon. Edith L. Andrew was born February 19, 1884, and is the wife of Francis Burchell, a practicing attorney at Oregon.

PETER CHARLES WALTERS, former judge of Edwards County, is a resident of Albion, has a successful law practice, and has been well known in that section of the state since early manhood as a teacher, lawyer and public official.

He was born in Dearborn County, in Southern Indiana, January 29, 1881, son of John and Catherine (Altherr) Walters, his father a native of Germany but reared in Indiana, while his mother was born in Indiana. A year after the birth of Peter Charles Walters the family moved to Illinois and settled in White County, close to the Edwards County line. Peter Charles Walters grew up on a farm, learning farm work as part of the normal routine of his boyhood. He attended local schools and in 1897 was graduated from the high school at Grayville. During the next seven years he alternately taught and attended school, being a student in the Southern Illinois Normal University at Carbondale. While teaching he took up the study of law, was admitted to the bar in 1908, and subsequently he completed his law course in the University of Illinois, graduating in 1912. After his admission to the bar he practiced two years at Graysville, and in 1910 was elected for his first term as county judge. After graduating from the University of Illinois he was again elected county judge, and held that office continuously until 1918. Since then he has given his time to an increasing general law practice. He also supervises some farming interests, and thus keeps in touch with the occupation of his youth.

Judge Walters is a republican and has been quite active in the party. He is a Royal Arch Mason and a member of the B. P. O. Elks. He married in 1909 Ethel Faarnsworth, who was born in Richland County, Illinois. They became the parents of two children, Richard F., who died in infancy, and Charles J.

HOWARD K. BAUERNFEIND, superintendent of city schools at Polo, is a native of Iowa, but finished his education in Illinois, and has been identified with the educational interests of Ogle County since 1922.

He was born at Council Bluffs, Iowa. His grandparents, Mathias and Amanda (Keller) Bauernfeind, were natives of Maryland and were pioneer settlers of the State of Minnesota. Rev. James H. Bauernfeind, father of the Polo school superintendent, was born near Faribault, Minnesota, and finished his education in Northwestern College at Naperville, Illinois. He has been a prominent minister of the Evangelical Church. He was in the ministry in Iowa until 1912, and since that year has been in charge of the Evangelical Hospital in Chicago. He married Matilda Koenig, who was born in Baltimore and was about nine years of age when she moved with her parents to LeMars, Iowa, and taught in the public schools in that state until her marriage. Her father, Henry Koenig, came from Maryland.

Howard K. Bauernfeind attended grammar and high schools at Waterloo, Iowa, and Chicago, Illinois, and in 1921 was graduated from Northwestern College at Naperville, Illinois. He has also had two summers of graduate study in the University of Chicago. In 1921 he became an instructor in the high school at Polo, and since March, 1922, has been superintendent of city schools. He is a young man of ambition and well qualified leadership in educational affairs, and has thoroughly identified himself with the best interests of Polo. He is treasurer of the Northwestern Division of the Illinois State Teachers' Association, is a Mason and a member of the American Legion. During the World war he was a member of the Student Officers Training Corps at Naperville. He is a republican, a Methodist, and is teacher of the Men's Class in the First Methodist Church.

He married at Kokomo, Indiana, August 9, 1922, Miss Lorraine Shrock, who was educated in the Kokomo High School and Northwestern College at Naperville, Illinois. Her parents were John N. and Etta May (Whittaker) Shrock, of Kokomo, her father born and reared in Indiana, and has given practically all his life to the real estate business, being a member of the Shrock Realty Company of Kokomo. Mr. and Mrs. Bauernfeind have one son, Robert Howard, born July 19, 1925.

J. DONALD WALKER. After a remarkable record of individual real estate salesmanship J. Donald Walker organized and became head of the J. Donald Walker Realty Company, a Chicago firm that is specializing in the high class properties of the North Shore district. Mr. Walker grew up in the Austin section of Chicago, and many who followed his career in school and after school have been vitally interested in his success and have backed him in his independent business undertakings.

Mr. Walker, who was reared and educated in Chicago, was born in Rochester, New York, March 13, 1901. The family came from Rochester to Chicago in 1913. J. Donald Walker completed his education in the Austin High School, and while there he won eleven letters in athletics.

When he was eighteen years old he took a job with the Butler Paper Company, shoving paper around on the floor for eighteen dollars a week. He was promoted to the city sales force of the Butler Paper Company and remained there a year and a half. Since then his work has been in the real estate field. For three years he was with Pray & Sons, Oak Park and Austin, handling mortgages and selling property. He then entered the subdivision field with the Frederick H. Bartlett Company, one of the oldest and largest real estate organizations in Chicago and one which has been famous for years for its successful subdivision and development undertakings. During the two years he was with the Bartlett Company Mr. Walker made a remarkable record as a salesman. He won virtually every sales contest conducted by this company during the last year, and in eight months he sold property to the amount of $261,000. Though one of the junior men in the sales department his record put him at the very top of Bartlett salesmen.

An acknowledged leader in salesmanship and with a broad knowledge of the real estate business in general, Mr. Walker in February, 1926, organized and established the J. Walker Realty Company, with offices in the State-Lake Building at the corner of State and Lake streets. The firm is specializing in property along the new extensions of the North Shore Electric Lines, its first subdivision being a tract of land on Belvidere Road near Green Bay Road. An important factor in Mr. Walker's success in business has been his honesty of purpose and his ability to make and hold friends.

Mr. Walker married Miss Edith Cummings, of Oak Park, daughter of Mr. and Mrs. William A. Cummings. The Cummings family were pioneers in Chicago. Mrs. Walker's grandfather was for many years owner of the old Tribune Building, now the Union Trust Company Building, at the corner of Madison and Dearborn streets.

CHARLES W. MCPHERSON, M. D. Since 1887, a period of forty years, Dr. Charles W. McPherson has been a physician and surgeon at Polo, a man of utmost devotion to the duties and responsibilities of his profession, and hundreds speak of his work in the community as an indispensable service.

Doctor McPherson was born at Eagle Point, in Ogle County, October 19, 1861. His grandparents, Charles W. and Anna (Hicks) McPherson, were natives respectively of Scotland and Philadelphia. Anna Hicks was a descendant of Elias Hicks, founder of the Hicksite branch of the Quaker Church. Charles W. McPherson moved West to Illinois in 1854. He became a Union soldier during the Civil war in Company I of the Sixty-third Infantry and participated in many battles. At the close of the war, after his honorable discharge and while on the way home, he died from chronic diarrhœa. Dr. M. C. McPherson, father of Charles W., was one of the early physicians of Ogle County who had a medical college diploma. He was born and reared in Philadelphia, attended grammar and high schools there and was graduated in 1854 from the medical department of the University of Pennsylvania at Philadelphia. Coming to Illinois, he settled at Eagle Point, and practiced medicine there continuously until his death in June, 1887. His wife Mary Schoemaker, was born and reared at Eagle Point and completed her education in the Frisby Academy, near what was then known as Buffalo Grove, now Polo. Her parents were Pearson and Elizabeth (Parker) Schoemaker. Her father was born and reared in Ohio, was of German ancestry, and came to Illinois in 1833, at the close of the Black Hawk Indian war entering land from the government and spending the rest of his life as a farmer. He and his wife reared eight children. His wife, Elizabeth Parker, was born in Grayson County, Virginia, daughter of Samuel Parker and granddaughter of General Parker, an officer in the English army at the time of the American Revolution, who was killed in one of the battles with the Continental forces. His family afterwards came to America and settled in Grayson County, Virginia.

Charles W. McPherson was reared in Ogle County, attended public schools, the St. Joseph Academy at Dubuque, Iowa, finished his course in Rush Medical College at Chicago in 1882, and in 1887 received another diploma at the University of New York. He practiced for a time at Eagle Point and Hazelhurst, and since 1887 his home has been at Polo, where he is still engaged in practice. Doctor McPherson is a Catholic in religious affiliations.

He married at Dixon, Illinois, Miss Lydia A. Zendt, of Sterling, Illinois. She died July 19, 1908. On October 18, 1910, Doctor McPherson married at Polo Miss Maud Allen. She was born in London, England, and when six years of age came to America with her parents, Fred and Emily (Hodge) Allen, who settled on a farm near Polo. Doctor and Mrs. McPherson have two sons: Fayette J. and Donald Francis, both attending school at Polo.

ALEXANDER Z. RICE. Educator, business man and banker, Alexander Z. Rice has for many years been prominently identified with the community of Warden in Southern Illinois. Though his primary interest since early youth has been school work, Mr. Rice has carried a number of important responsibilities in the local business world and also in public affairs.

He was born at Du Bois, Illinois, June 1, 1871, son of Alexander and Mary A. Rice. His ancestors came to this country from England about the time of the Revolutionary war first settling in Virginia, from there going to Tennessee and Kentucky and came to Illinois about 1828. His father, Rev. Alexander Rice, was born at Pinckneyville, Illinois, September 1, 1834, and died at Worden in December, 1914, at the age of eighty years. He became a minister of the Baptist Church and for a number of years was a missionary preacher of the Nine Mile Baptist Association. His wife, Mary A. Rice, was born in January, 1836, near Nashville, Illinois, and died at Du Bois in December, 1891.

Alexander Z. Rice began teaching at the age of eighteen and except for a few years has been either a teacher or a student in higher institutions of learning. He attended Ewing College, Valparaiso University in Indiana and is a graduate of the Southern Illinois Normal University at Carbondale. He has served as principal of schools at Richview, Du Bois, Okawville and Worden, Illinois, and has been almost continuously identified with the Worden schools for twenty years. He is now principal of the high school there, and for two years he was connected with the International Harvester Company. For a number of years he has been a secretary of the Worden Building & Loan Association, has maintained a mercantile insurance agency at Worden for fifteen years, is vice president of the First National Bank of Worden and president of the Worden Telephone Company.

From 1914 to 1922 Mr Rice was postmaster of Worden, being commissioned by former President Wilson. He has been a democrat in national politics. From 1908 to 1912 he served as a member of the Worden Village Board. During the Spanish-American war Mr Rice joined Pittinger's Provisional Regiment and was commissioned second lieutenant by Governor John R. Tanner. During the World war he acted as chairman of the local Council of Defense, as chairman of the Red Cross drive, treasurer of the Y. M. C. A. drive, and chief registrar of the Registration Board of Worden. At the same time Mrs. Rice organized Unit No. 9 of the Madison County American Red Cross, and has been chairman of that unit ever since. She has been recorder of the Camp of the Royal Neighbors of America for seventeen years, is a member of the Eastern Star, the Rebekahs and is affiliated with the Baptist Church. Mr. Rice is a member of the Masonic Lodge at Staunton, Illinois, the thirty-second degree Scottish Rite Consistory and Shrine at East St. Louis, belongs to the Independent Order of Odd Fellows and for a number of years has been active in the Knights of Pythias, being district deputy chancellor in 1906. He is a member of the Modern Woodmen of America.

Mr. Rice married at Richview, Illinois, July 5, 1900, Miss Ora V. Chapman, daughter of Samuel J. and Elizabeth P. Chapman. Her grandfather came from England and was a soldier in the Revolutionary war. Her father, Samuel J. Chapman, was born in 1815 and participated as a soldier in the Seminole Indian war. He came to Illinois from Tennessee and for a number of years owned a dry goods and grocery store and the hotel near what is now Richview and subsequently was proprietor of the flour mills at Richview, moving from there to Ashley, where he died in 1896. Mrs. Rice is a graduate of the Ashley High School, attended the Southern Illinois Normal University at Carbondale and was a teacher in the Richview and the Ashley public schools. Two daughters were born to the marriage of Mr. and Mrs. Rice. The younger, Allyne Virginia Rice, was born at Worden October 9, 1903 and died January 16, 1916. The living daughter, Lois Marie, born at Okawville, Illinois, July 12, 1902, graduated from the Worden grade schools in 1915, from the Edwardsville High School in 1919, attended the University of Illinois for three years, and then attended Iowa University at Iowa City, Iowa, getting her degree in 1925. During 1925 and 1926 she taught in high school at Modale, Iowa, and at the conclusion of her school she was married to Kenneth Hunt, a graduate of Illinois University. He is now connected with an insurance company with headquarters at Omaha, where they make their home.

CURTIS ARTHUR HUNSAKER, M. D. One of two elementals make the successful physician —marked talent or marked industry. Emerging from the former are the majority, who lend brilliancy and color and emphasis to a profession resting upon the hard rocks of science, while to the latter class is given the task of upholding the solid pillars of the calling. When both qualities are found in the same individual the combination produces the ideal man of medicine. Among the practitioners of Union County, Illinois, whose careers would seem to indicate that they have reached this desirable position is found Dr. Curtis Arthur Hunsaker, who has been engaged in practice at Anna since 1915, and who is not only a general practitioner of skill and experience, but also a specialist in the treatment and cure of diseases of the eye, ear, nose and throat.

Doctor Hunsaker was born September 10, 1887, in Union County, Illinois, and is a son of William Franklin and Hulda Catherine (Stout) Hunsaker, natives of Union County. Doctor Hunsaker's grandparents were Samuel and Elizabeth Hunsaker, early settlers, as were also his maternal grandparents, William and Catherine Stout, who came to Union County from Pennsylvania among the pioneers of this region. The parents of Doctor Hunsaker now reside on a small piece of land one mile north of Anna, Illinois, although Mr. Hunsaker also owns 420 acres of land in the vicinity of Cobden, Illinois. They are highly respected residents of their community, where they are the center of a circle of warm friends.

Curtis Arthur Hunsaker attended the public schools of Union County until reaching the age of fifteen years, and then assisted his father on the home farm and prepared himself for college until entering the St. Louis College of Physicians and Surgeons, where he spent two years. Later he attended the University of Illinois, from which he was graduated June 9, 1908, with the degree of Doctor of Medicine, and immediately commenced practice at Western Saratoga, Illinois, where he remained until July, 1910. At that time he accepted a position as physician in the United States service at Schurz, Nevada, where he ministered to the physical ills of the Piute Indians, government wards, but in the following year returned to his home, where he remained until April, 1912, then again entering the Indian service at Lame Deer, Montana, where he remained three months. In July, 1912, Doctor Hunsaker started private practice at LaPlace, Illinois, and in October, 1915, settled at Anna, which has since been the scene of his professional activities. Doctor Hunsaker has continued to be a student of his calling, and has had several post-graduate courses. In June, 1921, he went to Chicago, where he took a special course in diseases of the eye, ear, nose and throat, and in September of the same year took a similar course in the hospital of that name at West Frankfort, Illinois. Returning to Anna January 1, 1923, he has continued a general and special practice and has been in the enjoyment of a constantly growing professional business. He belongs to the Union County Medical Society and the Illinois State Medical Society, as well as to the American Medical Association, and keeps fully abreast of all the advancements being made in his calling. In his political affiliations he is a democrat, while as a fraternalist he is identified with B. P. O. Elks Lodge No. 1340 of West Frankfort, Illinois. Mr. Hunsaker's public service includes eight years as coroner, a position to which he was first elected in 1916 and reelected in 1920. During his career Doctor Hunsaker has lived close to high ideals, and his citizenship has imparted strength and substantiality to all undertakings in which his abilty and worth have been enlisted. During the World war he was commissioned First Lieutenant in the Medical Corps, May 19, 1917, serving until February 17, 1919, when he was commissioned captain and served until discharged, August 12, 1919. He served overseas from August 22, 1918, to July 19, 1919.

On September 30, 1908, Doctor Hunsaker was united in marriage with Miss Nora Belle Johnson, who was born in Union County, Illinois, a daughter of Samuel and Nancy Johnson, agricultural people of that county, and to that union there have been born six children: Franklin S., Clara Idel, Robert Lee, Hiawatha Catherine, Curtis Eugene and Kenneth Ray. Mrs. Hunsaker is a member of the Methodist Episcopal Church at Anna and is much interested in its work.

JOSEPH O'SULLIVAN. Pulaski County contains its full quota of capable and industrious attorneys, skilled in their profession and well grounded in its principles, so that the bar compares favorably with that of any of her sister counties of the same size in the state. Among these, one of the rising young legal lights is Joseph O'Sullivan, city attorney of Mound City, secretary of the Mound City Building and Loan Association, and a veteran of the World war, in which he saw active overseas service.

Mr. O'Sullivan was born November 1, 1895, at Mound City, Illinois, a son of Daniel and Julia (McNeil) O'Sullivan. Daniel O'Sullivan was born at Mound City, May 14, 1869, a son of Timothy and Katherine (Shay) O'Sullivan, natives of County Cork, Ireland. The grandparents immigrated to the United States in 1840 and first located in the state of Maine, where Timothy O'Sullivan was engaged in railroad building, and this kind of labor he followed at various places, being at Union City at the time of the outbreak of the Civil war. Being a Union man in sentiment, and doubtful of the state in which he was residing, he left Tennessee and came direct to Cairo, Illinois, soon changing his residence to Mound City, where he spent the rest of his life, passing away in 1883, while his wife died in 1888. They left a large family.

Daniel O'Sullivan attended the public schools until his father's death, when he, then a lad of fourteen years, went to work on "The Ways," in boat-building. There he served his apprenticeship to the carpenter's trade, and has been identified with this work to the present time. He rose through the various minor positions until given a foremanship in 1893, and remained in the same capacity until 1901, when he became superintendent of the plant. On January 22, 1925, the plant was sold to the Ayer & Lord Company, builders and repairers of boats, and Mr. O'Sullivan was retained in the capacity of general superintendent. A master of his craft, he is also possessed of much executive ability, and possesses the confidence of his superiors and the respect and friendship of his men. He is independent in his political views and has served his city for years as a member of the school board and as alderman. With his family he belongs to the Immaculate Conception Catholic Church, of which he is a trustee, and also holds membership in Cairo Council, Knights of Columbus. In 1892 Mr. O'Sullivan was united in marriage with Miss Julia McNeil, who was born at Washington Court House, Ohio, a daughter of Patrick and Bridget (O'Gara) McNeil, the former born in Ireland and the latter in Illinois. To Mr. and Mrs. O'Sullivan there have been born the following children: Joseph; Albert, a graduate of Notre Dame University, class of 1918, now an attorney of Chicago; Walter, a graduate of the United States Naval Academy, now an ensign on the U. S. Simpson, torpedo boat destroyer; Daniel, a graduate of Notre Dame, now employed by his father; and George, who is taking a medical course at the University of St. Louis. Prior to her marriage Mrs. O'Sullivan was for several years a high school teacher.

Joseph O'Sullivan graduated from the high school at Mound City, following which he pursued a course at Notre Dame University, from which he was duly graduated with the class of 1916, receiving the degree of Bachelor of Laws. He was admitted to the bar in December of the same year and commenced practice at Mound City, where he was making rapid progress until interrupted by the demands of the World war. In April, 1918, he enlisted in the United States Marines and was assigned to the Second Division, Sixth Regiment, which he accompanied to France. This regiment saw some of the hardest fighting of any of the American troops, taking part in the St. Mihiel offensive, fighting through the Champagne sector, and playing an important part in the Meuse-Argonne drive. The regiment was on the front line when the armistice was signed, following which it served with the Army of Occupation until April 1, 1919, and finally received its honorable discharge May 29, 1919.

Returning to Mound City, Mr. O'Sullivan at once resumed his law practice, which has assumed large and important proportions. Since January 1, 1920, he has been secretary of the Mound City Building and Loan Association. A republican in politics, he is the present city attorney of Mound City, and has discharged the duties of that office in an entirely capable and commendable manner. Mr. O'Sullivan belongs to Cairo Council, Knights of Columbus.

CHARLES OTTIS OTRICH. Trained faculties and an enlightened understanding in these modern days contribute materially to individual success, and more and more is the world at large asking for educated men not only for the accepted professions, but also for those along agricultural lines. The trained thinker is demanded for the deciding of public questions which, while they may be perplexing problems to the general public, must be clear to the law maker. In Charles Ottis Otrich Union County has a man of scholarly attainments, who has been one of the most energetic and constructive educators of this region for many years, and who now is serving as county superintendent of public schools.

Mr. Otrich was born at Dongola, Illinois, in 1878, a son of George W. and Martha A.

(Stokes) Otrich, natives of Union County. George W. Otrich, who was born in 1855 died in 1887, while Mrs. Otrich survived him for many years, dying October 6, 1925. Charles Ottis Otrich attended the district schools, and then spent two summer terms in a normal school, after which he went to the Creal Springs Baptist College eight months and Dixon Normal School for a like period. During the next six winters he taught in the rural schools, and in the summer months furthered his own studies by attendance at the Southern Illinois Normal School. In 1914 he was elected county superintendent of schools of Union County, a position which he has retained to the present time, and at the close of this term he will have held the office longer than any other county superintendent in the history of the county.

In 1904 Mr. Otrich was united in marriage with Miss Mabel E. Hileman, who was born at Anna, Illinois, a daughter of Hamilton and Catherine E. (Fuller) Hileman, of Union County, Illinois, and to this union there have been born two children: Charles Clyde and George H., both of whom reside with their parents.

Mr. Otrich is a Baptist and a teacher in the Sunday School, and was formerly superintendent of the Union Sunday School. Politically he is a democrat, while his fraternal connections are with the Masons, the Independent Order of Odd Fellows and the Modern Woodmen of America. Professionally he holds membership in the Union County Teachers' Association, the Southern Illinois Teachers' Association, the Illinois State Teachers' Association and the National Education Association, and was a delegate to the World's Congress in 1923 at San Francisco, and the National Education Association at Oakland in 1925. Always interested in all matters pertaining to the welfare of his city, he is now serving as treasurer of the Jonesboro Chamber of Commerce, in addition to which he is a member of the Chamber of Commerce of Anna, Illinois. During the World war he was a member of the National Defense organization, and in 1919 was assistant superintendent of the Boys State Fair School at Springfield.

Numerous honors have been bestowed upon Mr. Otrich as an educator, and in return he has rendered his profession most splendid service. He is a former member of the resolutions committee of the Illinois State and Southern Illinois Associations; at present is a member of the executive committee of the Southern Illinois Teachers' Association, of which he was formerly second vice president, now first vice president, also president of the rural division of the body and many times a delegate. He was also at one time president of the superintendents' division of the Teachers' Association of the Southern Division. Other services rendered by Mr. Otrich during the war period included the putting on of a drive for funds by the Young Men's Christian Association, of which he was chairman, and having charge of community organization for all war drives. Mr. Otrich has farmed while teaching and is still the owner of a forty-acre property, which he devotes to fruit and vegetables. He is a charter member of the Farm Bureau, and in 1918 was chairman of the Pig and Calf Club organization.

During the time that Mr. Otrich has been in office many things have been done for the betterment and advancement of the school system of Union County, among them being the following: Every schoolhouse in the county has been remodeled to meet the requirements of the sanitary laws; three high schools have been erected; all high schools have been placed on the recognition list by the State Association, and two placed on the list by universities, and sixty-nine rural schools have been made standard schools. In October, 1925, Mr. Otrich was one of the leading factors in the staging of a students contest at the Farmers Institute, and served as a member of the committee. This was a very interesting affair, the displays including grain, vegetables, canned fruit, fruit, bird houses, poultry houses, crocheting, weaving, hand sewing, machine sewing, woodworking, display of industrial work, etc. It stimulated interest in these subjects and brought out the ingenuity of the students, as only a contest can.

A friend of good roads, in November, 1924, Mr. Otrich worked energetically in the drive of that nature. He is chairman of the Union County Historical Society and a member of the committee to encourage the marking and purchasing of historical spots of Union County in order that they may be preserved for future generations. Likewise he has taken an active part in city improvement projects at Jonesboro, and has advocated plans for the bringing of industrial plants into Union County. In fact, anything that makes for the betterment of conditions, educational, moral, commercial or civic, finds him a willing and generous supporter, and no list of supporters of such movements is considered complete that does not include his name.

CLEVELAND MORSE has been a Chicago business man since 1914, and is president of the Standard Steel & Wire Company of that city. Outside of business and domestic interests his chief activities have been in military organizations.

Captain Morse was born at Clinton, Massachusetts, in 1886, of old Colonial New England ancestry, a son of G. W. and Lydia Ann (Bates) Morse. His mother was a descendant of Clement Bates, who came over at the time of the Mayflower. Captain Morse grew up at Clinton, attended public schools there, was a student in Worcester Academy from 1900 to 1903, and from 1903 to 1907 attended Harvard University, from which he was graduated with the A. B. degree. In university he was a Kappa Gamma Phi and is a member of the Harvard Alumni Association.

After his university career he spent several years in business in his native city of Clinton and took an active part in local politics, serving as chairman of the Board of Selectmen.

Captain Morse came to Chicago in 1914. The Standard Steel & Wire Company, of which he is president, are manufacturers of steel and wire products with plant located on Cortland Street near the North Branch of the Chicago River. This is one of the industries that contribute to the enormous volume of Chicago's commerce.

In both his native state and in Illinois Mr. Morse had a long military experience. In Massachusetts his first service, beginning in 1910, was as second lieutenant of K Company, Ninth Massachusetts Volunteer Infantry. For two years he was an aide on the staff of Gen. William E. Pew, a West Point man, commanding the Second Brigade of the Massachusetts Volunteer Militia. With this organization he was called for active duty in the great strike of the textile industries at Lawrence in 1912. On October 11, 1917, during the World war, he was commissioned first lieutenant of what was at first known as the Illinois Volunteer Training Corps, later the Illinois Reserve Militia. He was promoted to captain October 31, 1917, and was assigned to duty in the First Regiment, of which he was made regimental adjutant, and was under Colonel Pelouze and General Stewart. Mr. Morse is a member of the Illinois Commandery of Knight Templar Masons and of the Bunker Hill Country Club.

His home is at Glencoe. He married in Chicago Miss Effie Thurom Ladd. They have three children, Betty Jane, Patricia Bates and Helen Winifred.

WALTER W. WAITE. The prosperity and progress of a county may well be measured by the character of its officials, for if they be lacking in desirable qualities, or unwilling to exert themselves to bring about necessary changes, the county they represent is apt to fall behind the others better provided for in this respect. Judging by such standards Pulaski County has every reason to continue to advance, for the men holding its most important offices are beyond the ordinary, and stand deservedly high in popular esteem. One of them deserving of more than passing mention is Walter W. Waite, county clerk, a man of ability, sound judgment and unblemished character, and a public-spirited citizen well known all over the county.

Walter W. Waite was born in Pulaski County, Illinois, June 21, 1890, a son of John F. and Sophronia (O'Hara) Waite, he born in Cuyahoga County, Ohio, and she born near Nashville, Tennessee. Taking up the study of medicine, he was graduated from the Cleveland Medical College, and then was engaged in the practice of his profession in Ohio, New Jersey and Maine. When war was declared between the two sections of the country, Doctor Waite enlisted in the Union army from Ohio, but later was transferred to an Illinois regiment, and continued in the service from 1861 until peace was declared. Following his honorable discharge he was engaged in practice at Saint Louis, Missouri, and was also interested in the manufacture of drugs. Subsequently he went to Arkansas, and still later came to Pulaski County, and here he continued in an active practice until his death in 1902. The mother survives him and makes her home at Villa Ridge, Illinois.

Supplementing his public-school training with a business college course, Walter W. Waite taught school for a year, and then for two terms attended the Southern Illinois Normal University, following which he resumed teaching and for ten years was one of the most successful educators of Pulaski County, for two years of that period being principal of the schools of Olmstead, Illinois. In the meanwhile he had made his influence felt in the local republican party, and in 1918 was elected county clerk, and four years later was reelected to succeed himself in this office, in which he is giving such complete satisfaction.

In 1912 Mr. Waite married Emma P. Mangold, a daughter of Henry and Anna (Odle) Mangold, of Pulaski County. Mr. and Mrs. Waite have three children: Claude Whitman, Ruth Eleanor and Kenneth Milton. They are members of the Methodist Episcopal Church. Fraternally Mr. Waite belongs to the Independent Order of Odd Fellows and the Modern Woodmen of America. Both he and Mrs. Waite have many friends in this part of the state, and are prominent socially, their hospitable home oftentimes being the scene of pleasant gatherings.

MILLER S. MCCORD, the efficient and popular station agent of the Mobile & Ohio Railroad at Jonesboro, Union County, was born at Oraville, Jackson County, Illinois, in November, 1890, and is a son of William F. and Susan (Doty) McCord, both of whom were likewise born and reared in that county, where they now reside at Murphysboro, the county seat, the father there being yard foreman for the Jackson County Lumber Company.

In the public schools of his native county Miller S. McCord continued his studies until he was sixteen years of age, when he initiated his apprenticeship at the art and trade of telegraphist in a local office of the Mobile & Ohio Railroad. He has since continued his association with this railroad corporation, for which he has served as telegraph operator at various points, he having been advanced in 1908 from the position of night operator to that of day operator in the station at Elco, Alexander County, Illinois. In 1911 he was advanced to the dual position of station agent and telegraph operator at Pomona, Jackson County, where he remained seven years. He then, in 1917, was assigned to a position in the train dispatcher's office at Murphysboro, and in April of the following year he assumed his present office of station agent at Jonesboro. No further evidence of his unqualified popularity in his present home community is needed than the statement that in April, 1923, he was elected mayor of Jonesboro, and that in the spring of 1925 he was re-elected to this chief executive office of the municipal government, in which his vigorous and progressive administration has met with high approval.

Mr. McCord is found loyally aligned in the ranks of the republican party, he is an influential member of the Jonesboro Chamber of Commerce, and he is affiliated with the Masonic fraternity and the Independent Order of Odd Fellows, in the former of which he was master of the local lodge of Ancient Free and Accepted Masons in the year 1923. While a resident of Pomona he there served as a member of the Board of Education.

The year 1908 was marked by the marriage of Mr. McCord and Miss Bessie C. Isom, who was born at Ava, Jackson County, this state, and whose parents, Albert W. and Isabelle

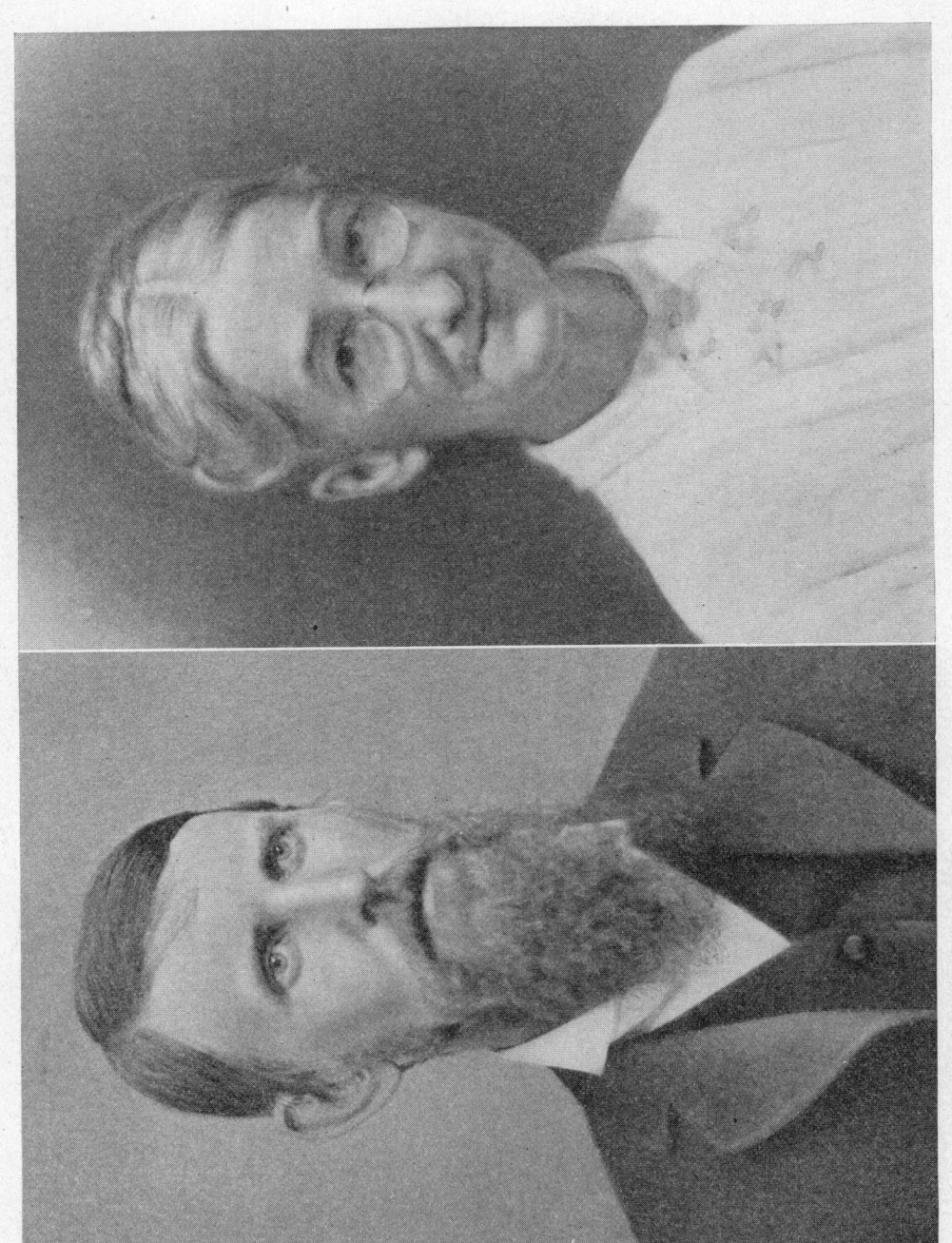

Arthur J. Moss Alice S Moss

(Clelland) Isom, likewise were born and reared in that county. Mr. and Mrs. McCord have four children: Albertine, William Claude, Elizabeth Jane and Jean.

CHRIS C. WENDT, postmaster of Dundee, and one of the most representative of its citizens is a native son of Dundee, where he was born July 9, 1871, a son of Chris C. and Carrie (Schuttz) Wendt, both of whom were born in Germany. In childhood they were brought to the United States, their parents locating at Dundee. Here they met and later were married. They located on a farm in Kane County, and for a number of years the father was one of the substantial farmers of this region, but he subsequently retired, and both he and the mother died at Dundee. Six children were born to them, namely: Henry, who is deceased; William, who is a resident of Huntley, Illinois; Chris C., who was the third in order of birth; John, who is a resident of Elgin; Charles A., who is a resident of Dundee; and Frank C., who is also a resident of Dundee.

Until he was seventeen years old Chris C. Wendt remained on his father's farm, and then he began learning the trade of a tinner with Wendt & Morse, of which his uncle was senior member. For fifteen years he continued with this house, in later years becoming a partner of Mr. Morse. This association was severed with his appointment, October 1, 1922, as postmaster of Dundee by President Harding. Since Mr. Wendt assumed the duties of his office its affairs have been put in excellent order and a very efficient service is being rendered for Postmaster Wendt is a good executive and knows how to get satisfactory results from the men under him.

On June 21, 1893, Mr. Wendt married Minnie Kamp, a native of Dundee. Two children were born to them, namely: Olive E. and Clarence D. Mr. Wendt belongs to the Lutheran Church of Dundee, and is generous in his support of it and the good work it is accomplishing. In political faith he is a republican, and during all of his mature years he has been a loyal party worker, and one who has never failed to respond to calls made upon him. In all respects he measures up to a high standard of American citizenship, and the people of Dundee are very well satisfied with his work as postmaster.

ROBERT T. COOK is called the dean of the bar of Herrin, having practiced in that Williamson County community for over twenty-five years. In knowledge of the law and all the resources that make the successful trial attorney Judge Cook has few equals in Southern Illinois, particularly in handling criminal cases.

He comes of a family that has long been well and favorably known in this section of Southern Illinois. His father was Dr. William Henry Cook, who was born near Lexington, Kentucky, and on coming to Illinois settled at Mulkeytown in Franklin County. He became known far and wide as an exceptionally skilful and able physician and surgeon. He died in Mulkeytown in 1872. His wife was Margaret C. Davis, and she died in 1891.

They had three sons. Rufus E. Cook earned an unusual distinction in having been the first republican elected to the office of sheriff in Franklin County. William D. Cook was long a prominent merchant at Mulkeytown, and died in 1902.

Robert T. Cook was born March 1, 1864, and was eight years of age when his father died. His early education was received in the grade schools, and for two and a half years he attended Duquoin College while that institution was conducted by Professor Stone, a very able educator. He studied law at home and in the office of W. F. Spiller at Benton, and in 1900 took the examinations in Chicago and was admitted to practice.

Judge Cook then established himself at Herrin, which was just coming into prominence as a coal center. In 1906 the firm of Neeley, Galimore, Potter & Cook was formed, and Judge Cook has handled the business of the Herrin office of this organization ever since. Mr. Potter retired from the firm in 1917 to become assistant United States attorney. The firm have offices in Marion.

From 1910 for eight years Judge Cook served as city judge of Herron and he was reelected to the Herrin bench in September, 1926, and is now incumbent of that office. While a large part of his practice has been criminal cases, he has also had much business in the Chancery and Civil Courts. In 1912 he became affiliated with the progressive wing of the republican party and was candidate for Congress on that ticket. He is a member of the Masonic lodge at Herrin.

Judge Cook married Miss Effie C. Kirkpatrick, daughter of John Kirkpatrick, of Franklin County. They have one daughter, Ethel Irene, who was the wife of Dr. Frank E. Stephens, of Indiana Harbor. Mrs. Stephens died in 1925, at the age of thirty-one. Judge and Mrs. Cook had three grandchildren: Frank, who died when eighteen months old, Richard and Sylvia.

ARTHUR H. MOSS. For many years one of the substantial business men of Anna, the late Arthur H. Moss won and held the confidence and respect of his fellow townspeople, and when he died his loss was felt by all with whom he has been associated. For a long period he had been connected with the pottery industry, not only in this region, but elsewhere, having owned potteries in Pulaski and Grand Junction, Tennessee. He was born in Lawrence County, Ohio, October 30, 1844, a son of Alfred and Sarah (Fisk) Moss, the former a native of New York. A potter by trade, he worked at his trade in Indiana, later at Mound City, Illinois, and finally at Anna.

Learning the potter's trade, Arthur H. Moss was engaged in this line of business all his life, and was a successful man. His death occurred April 10, 1908. On November 8, 1868, Arthur H. Moss married, at Anna, Alice Susanna Miller, born at Jonesboro, Illinois, September 2, 1847, a daughter of Henry and Catherine (Cover) Miller, he was born in Rowan County, North Carolina, and she at Hagerstown, Maryland. They were married in Union County, Illinois. A tanner by trade, he worked as a tanner all of his life, and conducted a tannery at Jonesboro and also at Caledonia, Illinois. Mr. and Mrs. Moss had the following children born to them: Charles H., who is deceased; Harry Arthur, who is a resident of Anna; Francis M., who is a druggist and lives at home; and William Clark, who is a carpenter of Anna.

Mr. Moss attended the Presbyterian Church, but his widow belongs to the German Reformed Church. He was a member of the Independent Order of Odd Fellows. Interested in local matters, Mr. Moss was always willing to do everything in his power to serve his community. In 1899 he erected a handsome residence at 120 West Chestnut Street, and here Mrs. Moss still maintains her home. She belongs to the local chapter of the Eastern Star, and she is a member of the Domestic Science Club. It is a source of pride to Mrs. Moss that her father was connected with a number of public enterprises at Anna, among which was the erection of the German Reformed Church, now the Evangelical Church. When he came to Anna he bought sixty-six acres of land in Union County, to which he kept adding until the property now comprises 160 acres, and Mrs. Moss owns an interest in it, and she is also a stockholder in the Anna Building & Loan Association. As the farm is now included in the city limits of Anna the heirs are enjoying a not inconsiderable income from the foresight of Mr. Miller. Mrs. Moss is held in the highest esteem, and has many warm personal friends at Anna and throughout Union County.

LAWSON FRANKLIN ROBINSON, whose death occurred in the fine little city of Anna, Union County, on the 16th of April, 1917, here maintained his home for half a century, and upon this community he left the impress of an unassuming life of sterling integrity and productive usefulness. He was a skilled workman at the carpenter's trade, and was long one of the successful contractors and builders of Union County. Mr. Robinson was an implacable adversary of the liquor traffic and became well known as a worker in behalf of the temperance cause. Though born in the South and reared in an atmosphere impregnated with the full flavor of democratic principles, he became in Illinois a stalwart supporter of the cause of the republican party. His life was guided and governed by high ideals and principles and he was an earnest member of the Methodist Episcopal Church.

Mr. Robinson was born near Statesville, North Carolina, in the year 1831, and his death occurred a short time prior to the eighty-sixth anniversary of his birth. He was a son of Henry and Nancy (Ward) Robinson, who were born in South Carolina and who moved from North Carolina to Arkansas in the year 1860, the remainder of their lives having been passed in the latter state.

Lawson F. Robinson was reared and educated in North Carolina, and there as a young man he married Miss Margaret Araminta Day, whose death there occurred August 16, 1864. The children of this union were five in number and the first born was Melmuth Harley, who is deceased; Ella Blanche is the widow of William Misenhimer and resides at Anna, Illinois; Dora Alice died in infancy; Jane died at the age of five years; and Robert Lawson Day Robinson resides at Perryville, Arkansas.

The subject of this memoir arrived at Anna, Illinois, October 26, 1866, and here his marriage with Miss Clarissa Isabella Spence was solemnized April 22, 1869, his widow being still a resident of this place, which is endeared to her by many gracious memories and associations. Mrs. Robinson was born at Mount Pleasant, this county, January 15, 1851, and is a daughter of the late Merideth Williams and Hazy Merida (Davidson) Spence, the former of whom was born September 1, 1814, and the latter on the 4th of October of that year, both having been natives of the state of Tennessee. Mr. Spence was a son of Daniel and Rebecca (Chapman) Spence, who made the long overland trip from their native Tennessee and settled at Jonesboro, judicial center of Union County, Illinois, in the year 1819. They were among the earliest pioneers of the county and did well their part in advancing the development of this section of the state. Daniel Spence was a man of strong mentality and of deep Christian faith, he having given service as a local preacher of the Methodist Episcopal Church in the pioneer period in this section of Illinois.

Lawson F. Robinson and his family established their home in a house on West Davie Street at Anna, and there he continued to reside forty-one years. He then sold the property and removed to the new house that he had erected on Dewey Street, this latter residence having been his place of abode at the time of his death. His widow and their daughter Cora M. now occupy a house of modern architecture and modern facilities at 412 North Main Street, where they established their home in November, 1923. Of the children of the second marriage of the late Lawson F. Robinson the following brief record is offered: Mrs. Flora Howell resides in Indianapolis, Indiana; Miss Cora M. is chief nurse at the Anna State Hospital at Anna, and of her individual mention is made in the sketch following; Idella died in infancy; Ellen is the wife of Robert Duncan and they reside at Anna; Adolphus likewise is a resident of this place; Claude died in infancy and Ada, at the age of three years; and Terrell Ambrose maintains his home in Indianapolis, Indiana.

CORA M. ROBINSON has the distinction of being chief nurse in the Anna State Hospital, located in her native city of Anna, Union County, and her professional skill is on a parity with her unqualified personal popularity in the community that knows her best. Miss Robinson was born at Anna on the 5th of September, 1872, and is a daughter of Lawson Franklin Robinson and Clarissa Isabella (Spence) Robinson, the former of whom was born in North Carolina and the latter near Mount Pleasant, Union County, Illinois. The first wife of Mr. Robinson was survived by three children, and by his marriage with Clarissa I. Spence he became the father of eight children. He was a carpenter and builder by vocation and his death occurred

April 16, 1917, his widow being still a resident of Anna, where she makes her home with her daughter Cora M., of this review. After profiting by the advantages of the public schools of Anna Miss Cora M. Robinson here continued her studies in Union Academy. Thereafter she taught one term of school and she then took a position as attendant in the Southern Illinois State Hospital. In 1908 she became a graduate nurse, after completing the prescribed course in the training school maintained in connection with this institution, with which she continued her service until 1911, when she was assigned to the position of supervising nurse at the Watertown State Hospital at Watertown, Illinois, where she was advanced, in 1918, to the position of chief nurse, an office that she retained until 1922, when she was transferred back to the hospital at Anna, where she has since continued her earnest and efficient professional service as chief nurse. Miss Robinson is an active and popular member of the Nurses Association of the Fifth District Association of Graduate Nurses, the headquarters of which are in the city of Moline, Illinois, and she is an instructor in the Training School for Nurses conducted in connection with the Anna State Hospital. In advancing herself in her chosen profession she has taken several post-graduate courses in the city of Chicago.

Miss Robinson has due appreciation of the privileges of woman suffrage, is well fortified in her political convictions, and gives her allegiance to the republican party. She and her mother are zealous members of the Methodist Episcopal Church in their home city and she is a member of its Official Board. In the preceding sketch of this publication is dedicated a memoir to Lawson F. Robinson, father of the subject of this review, and to that article reference may be made for further details concerning the family history.

CHARLES CARROLL CRAWFORD has won success and secure status as one of the able and representative members of the bar of Union County, where he is engaged in the general practice of his profession in the city of Jonesboro, judicial center of the county. In connection with his character and achievements there can be no application of the scriptural aphorism that a prophet is not without honor save in his own country, for he is a native son of Jonesboro and has here found ample opportunity for effective stewardship in his chosen profession.

Mr. Crawford was born at Jonesboro on the 13th of September, 1872, and is a son of Judge Monroe Carroll Crawford and Sarah Illinois (Wilbanks) Crawford, the former of whom was born on a farm near Benton, Franklin County, this state, and the latter at Mount Vernon, Jefferson County. The marriage of the parents was solemnized at Benton, and within a short time thereafter they established their home at Jonesboro, where Judge Crawford engaged in the practice of law and became one of the leading lawyers and jurists of this county, he having been called upon to serve as state's attorney and county judge and also on the bench of the Circuit Court of this circuit. Judge Crawford was a vital and influential advocate of the principles of the democratic party, and was one of the venerable and honored veteran members of the Union County bar at the time of his death, which occurred March 19, 1919, when he was eighty-four years of age.

Judge Monroe C. Crawford was a son of John and Elizabeth (Randolph) Crawford, the former of whom was born in Virginia and the latter at Murfreesboro, Tennessee, to which state her ancestors moved from Virginia. Both the Crawford and Randolph families were founded in the historic Old Dominion of Virginia in the Colonial period of American history. John Crawford became one of the early settlers of Illinois, whither he made his way in 1811. His marriage occurred in 1830, and he and his wife maintained their home in Franklin County, this state, during the remainder of their lives.

At the age of six years Judge Monroe C. Crawford was taken into the home of Col. Tilman B. Cantrell, of Franklin County, and that he made good use of the educational advantages afforded him is evident when it is stated that at the age of sixteen years he initiated his successful service as a teacher in the district schools of the period. With the money he earned he paid the expenses incidental to his attending McKendree College, and he had also fifteen months of effective preceptorship while a student in the law office of Judge William K. Parrish, of Franklin County. He thereafter passed the examination that made him eligible for the practice of law in his native state, and, as previously noted, he became one of the leading members of the bar of Union County. The Judge early began to take lively interest in public affairs, and in 1856, when he was but twenty years of age, he was elected circuit attorney. His marriage occurred in 1858, and thereafter he continued in the active practice of his profession until he subordinated that and all other personal interests to respond to the call of patriotism and go forth as a soldier of the Union in the Civil war. On September 11, 1863, Judge Crawford enlisted in the One Hundred and Tenth Illinois Volunteer Infantry, in which he was elected lieutenant colonel and with which he served as a gallant soldier and efficient officer until the close of the war. He became circuit attorney in 1860, and retained this office during the period of his military service in the Civil war. In 1867, upon his retirement from this office, he was elected to the bench of the Circuit Court of the First Judicial Circuit, and to the latter office he was reelected in 1873. In 1886 he was elected judge of the County Court of Union County, and of this office, by successive reelections, he continued the incumbent for the long period of thirty-two years. Judge Crawford gave two terms of characteristically loyal and efficient administration as mayor of Jonesboro, besides which he long held membership on the Board of Education. He was specially prominent in the Masonic fraternity and was for two terms grand master of the Illinois Grand Lodge of Ancient Free and Accepted Masons. It has already been noted that the death of Judge Crawford occurred in 1919, his wife having passed away in September, 1905. John, eldest of the children, is successfully established in the real estate and insurance business in Jonesboro; Charles C., of this review, was the next in order of birth; George W. resides at Anna, Union County; and Mary is teacher of Senior English in the Community High School of Jonesboro and Anna, in Union County, and resides at Jonesboro.

Charles C. Crawford is indebted to the public schools of Jonesboro and the Union Academy at Anna for his early educational discipline, and, beginning in 1889, he was for seven years engaged in teaming and contract work at Jonesboro and Anna. Thereafter he began the study of law under the able preceptorship of his father, and he has been successfully established in the practice of his profession at Jonesboro since his admission to the bar in 1900. He has given three years of service as state's attorney of his native county, and two terms as city attorney of Jonesboro. He has been influential in the advancing of educational interests in his home county, was one of the originators and promoters of the movement that resulted in the establishing of the Community High School at Jonesboro and Anna, of the Official Board of which he is now president, he having also served about ten years as president of the Jonesboro Board of Education. His political allegiance is given to the democratic party, he is an active member of the Commercial Clubs of Anna and Jonesboro, and is a charter member of the Anna-Jonesboro Rotary Club. Like his father before him, Mr. Crawford is prominently affiliated with the Masonic fraternity, in the Blue Lodge and Chapter of which he has passed the various official chairs, his maximum York Rite affiliation being with the Commandery of Knights Templars at Carbondale, and he being a Noble of the Temple of the Mystic Shrine in the city of East St. Louis.

On the 25th of September, 1904, Mr. Crawford was united in marriage with Miss Emma Lence, who likewise was born in Union County and who is a daughter of Alfred and Martha (Hardin) Lence, the former a native of this county and the latter of the state of Kentucky. After having completed her studies in the public schools Mrs. Crawford attended St. Vincent's Academy at Cape Girardeau, Missouri, and the Southern Illinois Normal University. Prior to her marriage she had been a popular kindergarten teacher and had given a number of years of service in the primary department of the Jonesboro public schools. Mr. and Mrs. Crawford have two children: Martha, who was a student in Lindenwood College at St. Charles, Missouri in 1925, graduated from the Southern Normal at Carbondale in 1926, and is now a teacher in the public schools in Jonesboro, and Mary is a student in the high school at Jonesboro.

ANDREW JACKSON MILLER passed his entire life in Union County, Illinois, was a representative of one of the sterling pioneer families of this county, and his active career was one of close association with mercantile enterprise, of which he was a prominent exponent in the village of Cobden at the time of his death, he having passed away April 29, 1899. Mr. Miller was a leading merchant and influential citizen of Cobden, here served as a member of the village board, was a republican in politics, and was affiliated with the Masonic fraternity. His religious faith was that of the Presbyterian Church, of which his widow, who still resides at Cobden, is likewise a zealous member.

Mr. Miller was born at Jonesboro, the judicial center of Union County, January 8, 1844, and was a son of Henry and Catherine (Cover) Miller, the former of whom was born in Roane County, South Carolina, on the 13th of August, 1814, and the latter of whom was born in Frederick County, Maryland, September 26, 1822. Henry Miller became a pioneer settler in Union County, Illinois, and here he and his wife continued to maintain their home until their deaths.

Andrew J. Miller was reared at Jonesboro and received the advantages of the common schools of the locality and period. He continued to reside at Jonesboro until he was nineteen years of age, when he took a position in the general store conducted at Cobden by the late Adam Buck, with whom he continued to be associated for the long period of fourteen years, at the expiration of which he here established the general merchandise business that he thereafter successfully conducted until the time of his death. He was thirty-three years of age at the time he engaged independently in the mercantile business, and during a period of nearly a quarter of a century he continued to figure as one of the representative citizens and business men of this community, where his was ever an inviolable place in popular confidence and esteem.

On the 19th of February, 1880, was solemnized the marriage of Mr. Miller and Miss Allie Phillips, who was born at Cobden on the 1st of February, 1858, and who is a daughter of the late Isaac N. and Nancy E. (Phillips) Phillips, both of whom were natives of Illinois and members of honored pioneer families of this state. Isaac N. Phillips was born at Belleville, St. Clair County, in 1830, and his wife was born at Centralia, Marion County, in 1835. Mr. Phillips was in the employ of the government in the Civil war period, became one of the large landholders and substantial farmers of Union County, and he served several years as postmaster at Cobden, besides having been otherwise prominent and influential in community affairs. In this connection it may be noted that the original name of the little village of Cobden was South Pass, and that the present name was given at the time when the railroad was built through this section and the name of its station at South Pass was made Cobden in honor of Lord Cobden of England, who, with his father and brother, had visited Union County in an early day and who here acquired a large tract of land. The village of Cobden was incorporated in 1869, and in a general way it has kept pace with the march of improvement and progress in the intervening years. Of the children of Mr. and Mrs. Miller the eldest is Henry P. who was born September 30, 1880, and who is now serving as postmaster at Cob-

Harold R. Heat
Co. E. 737st Inf.
33 D

den; Nettie A. died in 1886, at the age of four years; Charles Herbert, who was born August 26, 1884, resides at Benton, Franklin County, is a lawyer by profession and is now presiding on the bench of the Circuit Court; John A., who was born April 19, 1887, died June 14, 1922; Grace, who was born August 26, 1889, remains with her widowed mother and is a popular teacher in the public schools of Cobden; Paul, who was born October 11, 1890, is a successful farmer near Anna, on the farm formerly owned by his grandfather; Ruth, who was born August 1, 1894, is the wife of John W. Chidester, of Malvern, Arkansas; and Harriet, who was born August 15, 1895, died December 11, 1897.

Mrs. Miller is the owner of fifty acres of valuable land, the most of which is within the village limits of Cobden, and this tract has fine fruit orchards, besides which a portion of the land is devoted to gardening. In 1919 Mrs. Miller erected in Cobden the fine brick house that is now her place of residence and that is one of the most modern and attractive places in this part of Union County. As chatelaine of this beautiful home she makes it a center of gracious hospitality and delights to extend welcome to her many friends in the community that has represented her home from the time of her birth and that is endeared to her by many hallowed memories and associations. She has long been a popular figure in the social activities of her home village and is a loyal and zealous worker in the local Presbyterian Church.

OSCAR HOUSE, M. D. A physician and surgeon at Desoto in Jackson County, Doctor House has come to be regarded as an indispensable citizen of that locality, where he has been prompt and ready with his professional service for twenty years.

His grandfather, Eli House, came from Kentucky and established his home near Murphysboro in Jackson County many years ago. The family was originally from West Virginia. Arthur C. House, father of Doctor House, was born in Kentucky, and married Mary Ann Swaar, a native of Tennessee and of an old Tennessee family.

Oscar House was born at the old homestead in Jackson County, had a farm training, attended country schools and later the schools at Murphysboro. He was a student in the Southern Illinois Normal University at Carbondale during 1902-04, and in 1907 was graduated from the College of Physicians and Surgeons of St. Louis. He practiced five months near Centralia and then located at DeSoto, in Jackson County, where he has found his real work and the associations of life that may be considered permanent.

Doctor House married Ida Blanche Wayman, who died March 4, 1923. He has one daughter, Ida Gladys, now attending the Southern Illinois Normal University. Doctor House was in the World war, receiving a commission as a first lieutenant in the Medical Corps. On August 15, 1917, he was sent to the Medical Officers Training School at Ft. Riley, Kansas, and three months later was stationed at Camp Pike, Arkansas, where he was on duty until December 12, 1918, when honorably discharged. Doctor House's office and residence was badly damaged in the tornado of March, 1925.

JOHN EDWIN HEAP. That agriculture can be made one of the most agreeable and satisfying occupations of human life, that industry, good judgment and perseverance transform an individual's dreams into realities, and that honesty and fair-mindedness are among the most useful of human assets, are facts emphasized in the life of the late John Edwin Heap, whose life was passed in Kendall County, and who in passing away August 27, 1915, left behind him the splendid heritage of an honored name and a large property which had been gained fairly and without animosity.

Mr. Heap was born on a farm in Seward Township, Kendall County, Illinois, February 15, 1865, a son of Ralph and Eliza (Coop) Heap, natives of England, and a grandson of Edwin Heap and John and Nancy Coop. Both the Heap and Coop families originally settled in Big Grove Township, Kendall County, where they followed the pursuits of the soil. Following their marriage Ralph and Eliza Heap settled down in Seward Township and there passed peaceful lives, the only break in which was when Ralph Heap served his country as a soldier during the dark days of the Civil war.

John Edwin Heap grew up in an agricultural atmosphere and acquired his education in the district schools of his community. Upon his arrival at man's estate it was but natural that he should adopt farming as his means of livelihood, and he was thus engaged in Seward Township until the time of his marriage, when he changed his residence to the vicinity of White Willow, that community continuing to be his home until his death. He was an able and industrious farmer and made the most of his opportunities, using modern methods and directing his efforts with able management. He was reared in the faith of the Congregational Church and was a friend of all worthy movements. Politically a republican, he was called to serve in several township offices, but was not a politician in the generally accepted meaning of the word. He belonged to the Masonic fraternity at Minooka, Illinois. Mr. Heap's life was a full and useful one, and in his death his community lost a reliable and substantial citizen.

On December 17, 1890, Mr. Heap was united in marriage with Miss Elnora R. Widney, who was born at White Willow, Kendall County, a daughter of John and Emily (Van Duser) Widney, the former a native of Miami County, Ohio, and the latter of Will County, Illinois. Her paternal grandparents were John and Mary (Henderson) Widney, the former a native of Ohio and the latter of Pennsylvania, and her maternal grandparents were George and Elmira (Mellon) Van Duser, the former born in New York state and the latter in Vermont. To Mr. and Mrs. Heap there were born the following children: John Claude, engaged in operating the home farm in Kendall County, who married Erma Cunningham and has four children, George Edwin, Claude Harold, Wayne Donald and May Gertrude; Harold Ralph, who enlisted May 17, 1917, was attached to the 131st Infantry, Company E,

Thirty-third Division, arrived at Brest May 30, 1918, and was killed in action July 4, following, being buried in France; and Florine Emily, the wife of Maurice Garrett Stokum, a salesman for the Sinclair Oil Company.

Following the death of her husband Mrs. Heap moved to Joliet, where she owns a beautiful residence at No. 507 Union Street, and since her arrival has been prominent in various women's activities of the city. She is a Universalist in religion and active in religious work. She was a charter member of Lisbon Chapter, O. E. S., of which she was worthy matron two years, and now belongs to Joliet Chapter of that order. During the World war she was very active in Red Cross work, and was the first president of Joliet Chapter under charter of the American War Mothers, being at present a member of the auxiliary to Harwood Post No. 5, American Legion; and president of the Ladies of Company E. She belongs also to the Woman's Club, the Women's Christian Temperance Union and the Will County Historical Society, and is a woman of broad interests, wide outlook on life and much executive capacity.

EUGENE COHN, M. D., F. A. C. S., of Kankakee, Illinois, was born in 1875 in Germany, where he obtained his general education in the public and high schools of that country. Coming to America in 1891, he first settled in Michigan, where he continued high school and college work until 1895, when he entered the Detroit College of Medicine. After spending one year at this school he moved to St. Louis, Missouri, continuing his medical work there and graduating as an M. D. in 1898. He practiced his profession in Madison County, Illinois, until 1905, when he entered Northwestern University Medical School as a postgraduate, receiving the degree of M. D. from this school also, and becoming a life member of the Northwestern Alumni Association. Doctor Cohn also spent some time as a postgraduate student in New York and Europe. In 1917 he was made a fellow of the American College of Surgeons (F. A. C. S.). Since 1906 he has served the State of Illinois as medical officer in various charitable institutions, filling the positions for fifteen consecutive years as chief of staff of the Anna, Peoria, Kankakee and Chicago State Hospitals and from 1917 to 1921 as superintendent of the Kankakee State Hospital. He resigned in 1921 to devote himself to private work and now practices in Kankakee, Illinois, limiting himself to surgery and office consultations. He is a member of the Kankakee County and Illinois State Medical Societies, the American Medical Association and Association of Military Surgeons, having been a medical reserve officer in the U. S. Army for a number of years. In politics Doctor Cohn is a republican. He is a thirty-second degree Mason, Knight Templar, Shriner, Elk, Moose, etc., and is a member of the Kankakee Rotary Club and Chamber of Commerce.

He married Alexandra May Ross, of Grand Rapids, Michigan, in 1895. They have three children, Eugene Ross, of Milwaukee, Wisconsin, Ewald S., of Chicago, and Miss Dorathea, who lives at home.

JOHN J. BROWN, a member of the bar of Vandalia for over forty years, has enjoyed several distinctions outside his home locality. He was a member of the State Centennial Commission and has served as supreme chancellor of the Knights of Pythias of Illinois.

He was born in New York City, November 15, 1852, son of James and Mary Brown, who came to this country from Dublin, Ireland. John J. Brown was reared and educated in Illinois and graduated from the law department of Illinois Wesleyan University in 1882. He taught school for several years, and then engaged in practice at Vandalia, where he still carries on a large general practice. He served as city attorney and has been a director and attorney for the First National Bank of Vandalia.

Mr. Brown has filled positions by appointment from three Illinois governors, as a member of the commission of the Southern Illinois Penitentiary under Governor Fifer, on the World's Fair Commission under Governor Yates, and the Centennial Commission under Governor Lowden. He has always been a republican, and was once delegate from the Twenty-third Congressional District at the National Convention of the party, and at one time was a delegate at large. He was also a member of the Illinois State Legislature.

Besides his service as supreme chancellor of the Knights of Pythias he has been grand master of the Illinois Independent Order of Odd Fellows. Mr. Brown is a member of the Rotary Club, the Hamilton Club of Chicago, Vandalia Chamber of Commerce, is a member of the Masonic fraternity and the Methodist Church.

He married at Vandalia, May 29, 1883, Miss Nellie G. Blackwell, daughter of Col. Robert Blackwell. Mrs. Brown has been a member of the Vandalia School Board and Library Board, treasurer of the Missionary Society of the Southern Illinois Conference of the Methodist Episcopal Church and president of the Women's Federation of Clubs in the Twenty-third Congressional District. Mr. and Mrs. Brown have one daughter, Mary Lucille, wife of Don Buchanan, of Hillsdale, Michigan.

LAWRENCE A. GLENN, representing a pioneer family of Coles County, Illinois, is a lawyer by profession, and for some years he and his brother Otis have been associated in one of the leading law firms of southern Illinois at Murphysboro.

The founder of the family in Coles County was his great-grandfather, Thomas Glenn, who moved from the Carolinas to Hardin County, Kentucky, and from there to Illinois. The grandfather of Lawrence A. Glenn also bore the name of Thomas. The father was Joseph C. Glenn, who was born in Coles County in 1846, and became widely known over the state through his transactions as claim agent for the Illinois Central Railroad. He was a lawyer by profession. In 1880 he began buying land in Jackson County, Illinois, having been attracted by the great opportunities which he saw in the possibilities of reclaiming areas of land that had theretofore been completely waste. He was the first to reclaim the river bottom lands by a system of drainage

and dredging. He possessed legal knowledge, but even more important had a large fund of common sense and business ability. From Mattoon he moved his family to Champaign in 1896 for the purpose of educating his children at the State University. For many years he was a member of the State Board of Equalization. He died in 1904. Joseph C. Glenn married Mary C. Ferguson, daughter of Myron Ferguson, and member of a New York family. They had four children: Leslie L., an attorney at Champaign, Otis F., Eleanor and Lawrence A.

Otis F. Glenn was graduated from the University of Illinois in 1900, and in 1904 engaged in law practice at Murphysboro as an associate of the late Hon. James H. Martin. Otis Glenn came into particular prominence on account of his remarkable record in the prosecution of riot cases arising at Herrin and his record in the State Senate, where he served from 1920 to 1924. He served under a special appointment from the governor to represent the state and he handled the matters with a fearlessness that earned him the gratitude of the entire state. Since then his reputation as a lawyer has been state-wide, and in order better to care for his large law practice he opened offices in Chicago in 1925.

Lawrence A. Glenn was born at Mattoon, Illinois, in 1887, and was nine years old when the family moved to Champaign, where he attended public schools and graduated from the Law School of the university in 1911. For several years he practiced at Champaign and was city attorney from 1913 to 1917. In 1917 he removed to Murphysboro, where he joined his brother in the firm of Martin & Glenn, a firm title that had been retained after the death of Mr. Martin in 1915. Lawrence Glenn has been successful in handling the large business of this firm in southern Illinois.

He is a member of the Masonic fraternity. He married Mary Schneider, daughter of William C. Schneider, of Vermilion County, Illinois.

ZACHARIAH HUDSON, M. D. For half a century the name Hudson has been associated with the practice of medicine and surgery in Williamson County. Dr. Zachariah Hudson, of Marion, represents the third generation of the family in this profession and is a son of Dr. Theodore Hudson, one of the oldest medical men in the county.

The Hudson family is of Scotch-Irish ancestry. The grandfather of Dr. Zachariah Hudson was John Atchison Hudson, a native of Pennsylvania. From Pennsylvania he moved to Tennessee and later to Illinois, founding the family in Williamson County. Dr. Theodore Hudson was born in Pennsylvania, August 12, 1850, and was a child when his parents went to Tennessee. In the early '70s he came to Illinois and established his home six miles south of Marion. He went back to Tennessee to attend the Medical School of the University of Nashville, where he was graduated in 1876. He then located at Hudgens in Williamson County, and remained the medical and surgical advisor of that community until 1904, since which year his home has been in Marion. He looked after an extensive general practice until early in 1925, when his health failed, and he has since been practically retired from practice. He is a member of the Williamson County, Illinois State and American Medical Associations, is a charter member of Fountain Lodge of the Independent Order of Odd Fellows at Hudgens, is a charter and life member of the Elks Lodge at Marion, and also belongs to the Moose.

Dr. Theodore Hudson married Emma Hudgens, daughter of Zachariah Hudgens, the founder of the Hudgens community in Williamson County. There were four children: Nannie, who died in 1890, when eighteen years old; Dr. Zachariah; Clara, who died in childhood; and an infant who died with its mother in 1886. Dr. Theodore Hudson in 1888 married Ella Norris, of Williamson County. The two children of this marriage are: John Atchison Hudson, proprietor of a drug store in St. Louis; and Mattie Davis Hudson, who was married to E. A. Lainson, of Boone, Iowa.

Dr. Zachariah Hudson was born August 21, 1883, and acquired his early education in his native community of Hudgens, and after a preparatory course he entered St. Louis College of Physicians and Surgeons, where he was graduated in 1907. He served as an assistant to Dr. Otto Sutter in Jefferson Hospital at St. Louis for a few months and then returned to Marion and became associated with his father, taking more and more of the heavier responsibilities of his practice. Since 1917 he has specialized in industrial surgery.

Doctor Hudson is unmarried. He belongs to all the medical organizations, also to the B. P. O. Elks and Moose. In 1915 he became financially interested in the automobile business. This business has steadily grown and is now the largest agency in the county, handling the Hudson and Essex cars. The sales and service force comprise seven persons.

ARLIE O. BOSWELL, state's attorney of Williamson County, is a young man, member of one of the old settled families of southern Illinois, and has had experience as an educator, was with the colors during the World war, and is rapidly achieving a name for himself in the profession of law.

His great-grandfather, Thomas Boswell, came from Kentucky and was a pioneer in Union County, Illinois, where he developed a farm and occupied it until his death. He was in the Civil war as a Union soldier, returning with the rank of captain. William Thomas Boswell, grandfather of the state's attorney, was born at the old homestead in Union County, and after many years of farming is now living retired at Anna, Illinois. He married Elizabeth Stokes. She died two years after the birth of her son Thomas William Boswell, who was born on the Union County farm in August, 1877. He, too, has been a farmer, but in conjunction therewith he taught for twenty years in country schools in winter terms and for twenty years held the office of justice of the peace, and at one time was republican candidate for sheriff in a strongly democratic county. He married Minnie Idell Hill, daughter of James Hill, and their five children were: Arlie O.; Edith, wife of Roy

Williams, of Detroit; Fred; Thomas William; and Charles Calvin, who is now a student in the University of Michigan.

Arlie O. Boswell was born at Anna, February 11, 1897. He grew up on the farm, attended district schools, and at the age of sixteen entered the Southern Illinois Normal University at Carbondale, where he was graduated in 1917. At that time his plans were for school work, and in the fall of 1917, after graduating, he was engaged as principal of the schools at Sesser in Franklin County.

He resigned in order to join the colors, and in January, 1918, was sent to Jefferson Barracks at St. Louis and assigned to the Medical Corps. Next he was sent to Fort Oglethorpe, Georgia, being put with Field Hospital No. 42, and after three months was transferred with a detachment of men to the embarkation port at Newport News and was assigned duty in the Embarkation Hospital at Camp Stuart, remaining there until his discharge in June, 1919.

After he left the army he decided to study law, and attended the University of Chicago, Law Department, part of the time teaching to defray his expenses, but all the while keeping up a diligent study of law. He qualified for admission to the Illinois bar in December, 1921, and was graduated from law school in February, 1922. In April of the same year he located at Marion, and soon made his name well known among the active younger men of his profession. He was nominated and elected state's attorney in 1924, being chosen on the republican ticket.

Mr. Boswell is a past commander of the local post of the American Legion, having been honored with that office in 1923. He is a thirty-second degree Scottish Rite Mason and Shriner, member of the B. P. O. Elks, and holds a commission as first lieutenant in the Officers' Reserve Corps in the Judge Advocate's department. He is a member of the University of Chicago Acacia fraternity, membership in which is limited to Masons.

Mr. Boswell married Antoinette Joyner, daughter of Ernest Joyner, of Stonepoint, Illinois. They have one son, Arlie O., Junior.

JACKSON L. HAMMOND, owner of the Anna Weekly Democrat, published in Union County, has been prominent in politics in that section of the state for a number of years, and has served two terms in the Legislature.

He was born at Hagerstown, Maryland, in 1865 and was two years of age when his parents moved to Illinois. His father was a Lutheran minister in Illinois and Wisconsin. Jackson L. Hammond grew up and received his education in public schools in different localities, attending college at Carthage, Illinois, for two years. He learned the newspaper business at Murphysboro, Illinois, was for four years chief clerk at the Illinois Southern Hospital for the Insane at Anna, and then became editor and manager of the Anna Weekly Democrat. He has kept that paper in line with the most progressive weekly publications in the southern part of the state.

Mr. Hammond was for six consecutive terms city clerk of Anna. From 1913 to 1917 he was law clerk in the index department in the secretary of state's office at Springfield. In 1918 he was elected a representative to the General Assembly from his senatorial district and was reelected in 1920. He is a democrat, a member of the Court of Honor and was active in the organization and for two years was secretary of the Anna Commercial Club.

On September 11, 1894, he married Miss Martha Aden. They became the parents of two children: Mary Frances and Josiah.

GEORGE T. WEBER, M. D. One of the private hospitals of Illinois with more than a statewide reputation is the Olney Sanitarium. The founder of this institution more than twenty-five years ago was George T. Weber. Doctor Weber has given the hospital its distinctive service and value and has raised an organization remarkable in skill and facilities. Several of his brothers are associated with him on the staff, and his two sisters are in charge of the nursing department.

Doctor Weber was born on a farm in Jasper County, Illinois, December 10, 1868, son of Benedict and Regina (Schafer) Weber. His father, now ninety-three years of age, was born in Baden, Germany, and was a young man of twenty-four when he came to the United States. His wife, Regina Schafer, was born at Haubstadt, in Gibson County, Indiana, of German parentage. After their marriage they settled on a farm in Jasper County, Illinois, near the town of Ingraham, in Clay County. The mother lived there until her death in 1898. Their children were: Mrs. Barbara Nix, of Poseyville, Indiana; Dr. George T.; Anton, a farmer in Clay County, Illinois; Benedict, a farmer at the old homestead in Jasper County; Dr. Joseph Cornelius, who graduated in medicine from Washington University at St. Louis and is a specialist in eye, ear, nose and throat work, being a member of the staff of physicians and surgeons of the Olney Sanitarium; Dr. Frank J., also a graduate of Washington University, a skilled general surgeon, also a member of the staff of the Olney Sanitarium; Philomena and Katherine, both graduate nurses, connected with the Olney Sanitarium; Dr. James A., a graduate of Washington University and on the Olney Sanitarium staff.

George T. Weber was reared on a farm, attended country schools, and in qualifying himself for a medical career had to depend on his earnings to complete his literary as well as professional education. He attended the academy at Princeton, Indiana, under the noted educator Prof. John Runcie. For two years he taught school in his native county. He was graduated with the M. D. degree from Washington University at St. Louis in 1894, and for four years practiced at Ingraham, Clay County, near his old home.

Doctor Weber in 1898 located at Olney and purchased an old hotel building which he converted into a general hospital with sixteen beds. That was the beginning of the Olney Sanitarium, which has steadily grown and has facilities now equalled only by those of the hospitals of large cities. The original building was replaced in 1906 by a modern brick structure with a capacity of seventy-five beds. In 1912 a building was erected for clinical purposes. There are nine physicians and surgeons on the staff, and their aggregate skill and attainments have made the institution deservedly famous. The active head of the institution as manager is Dr. George T. Weber, whose specialty is diagnosis, in which he has few peers in Illinois. He and his assistants every year take post-graduate work and come in contact with the work of great physicians and surgeons all over the country. Doctor Weber is a man of highest standing in his profession, but personally is plain and unassuming, sympathetic and pleasant in manner, and is justly loved in the community where he has spent more than a quarter of a century in his chosen work.

He is a member of the Richland, County, Illinois State and American Medical Associations and the American College of Surgeons. He married, in 1894, Miss Elizabeth Hauser. They are the parents of a large family of fourteen living children. The oldest is Bernard Weber, who graduated in medicine from St. Louis University in 1926 and is now a junior member of the medical staff of Olney Sanitarium.

RAD BURNETT. In business circles of Anna, Illinois, a well-known figure is Rad Burnett, who is serving as general agent for the Illinois Central Railroad at that point. He commenced his career as a school teacher, but gradually drifted into the railroad business, which latter brought him into connection with other interests, so that today he finds himself at the head of a number of prominent enterprises. He has also been a leader in the public life of the community, where he wields a distinct and beneficial influence.

Mr. Burnett is a product of the agricultural districts of Williamson County, Illinois, having been born near Marion December 9, 1878, a son of Wesley F. and Samantha (Tanner) Burnett, natives of Williamson County. Wesley F. Burnett passed his life in agricultural operations in Williamson County, and he and his worthy wife are now deceased. Rad Burnett attended district school, this being supplemented by a course at the Crab Orchard Academy, from which he was graduated as a member of the class of 1898. At that time he entered upon his work as a teacher in the rural schools, but after three years decided there was no future in educational work for him, and therefore turned his attention to railroading, as a telegraph operator. In 1900 he became an operator for the Illinois Central Railroad, on the St. Louis Division, subsequently being transferred to the station at Freeburg, Illinois. In 1906 he came to Anna, where he is now general agent, with offices in the Illinois Central freight office.

Without neglecting his duties to the railroad company, Mr. Burnett has become prominently interested in a number of other enterprises. At this time he is president of the Anna State and Trust Bank, one of the strong financial institutions of Union County, president of the Anna Products Corporation, president of the East Side Apartment Corporation and a director in the Anna Loan and Improvement Company. All of these companies have profited by his business acumen and energy, and his associates have every confidence in his ability and judgment. Mr. Burnett has been prominent in the work of the local Presbyterian Church, in which he is elder and clerk of the sessions, and is likewise treasurer of the Home Mission of the Cairo Presbytery. A republican in his political affiliation, he has served his city twice in the capacity of mayor, and was city treasurer for a like period, giving his fellow-citizens excellent service in each case. As a fraternalist he is a past master of his Blue Lodge and a member of the Royal Arch Chapter in Masonry, and has been national delegate of the Modern Woodmen of America on three occasions. He likewise belongs to the Chamber of Commerce and the Rotary Club, and in the latter was chairman of the committee on boys' work for one year. In 1920 Mr. Burnett was a candidate for the Illinois Legislature, but met with defeat in the primaries.

On February 20, 1900, at Mount Vernon, Illinois, Mr. Burnett was united in marriage with Miss Lulu Nation, who was born at Mount Vernon, daughter of W. A. and Lydia (Adams) Nation, of Jefferson County, Illinois. Mr. Nation, a retired merchant, now resides on a farm.

CHARLES ROLAND CLOTHIER, a graduate pharmacist, is proprietor of the leading drug business at Polo.

He was born at Polo, October 10, 1882, son of William F. and Della (Hawes) Clothier. His father was born near Brockville, Ontario, Canada, and came to Illinois about 1880, settling at Polo. He was a buggy maker by trade and worked in the Brown & Company shops at Polo, for fourteen years was clerk for the Thomas Company, and for the past five years has assisted his son in the Clothier Drug Store. He married in 1881 Della Hawes, who was born and reared near Milledgeville, Illinois, and had a public school education. Her father was John Hawes, whose father was a native of Kentucky and among the pioneer settlers of Illinois. William F. Clothier and wife had four children: Charles Roland, Hazel, Belle and Ruth. Hazel is the wife of C. G. Franks, of Norfolk, Virginia. Miss Belle is a graduate of the Presbyterian Hospital of Chicago, was overseas with a hospital unit a year during the World war, and was a professional nurse employed by the Burlington Railway Company in Chicago. She is now the wife of Dr. William Sweeney, of Chicago. Ruth Clothier is the wife of John Smith, formerly of Polo, now a representative of the Shell Oil Company at Freeport.

Charles Roland Clothier attended grammar and high schools at Polo, and was graduated in 1904 from the Northwestern University School of Pharmacy at Chicago. Returning to Polo, he was employed a year and a half as a clerk in the C. E. Bamborough Drug Company. For another year and a half he was an assistant in the pharmaceutical laboratory of Northwestern University School of Pharmacy. In March, 1907, he bought the Bamborough drug business at Polo, and about 1919 acquired the C. A. Dingley Drug Store, absorbing the stock and business and closing out the store. In 1923 he moved to his present location on Mason Street, and has made his store conspicuous as one of the best establishments of its kind in this section of the state. Mr. Clothier has been interested in the general welfare of his community, and has given his aid and support at all times to worthy movements. He is a Mason and Shriner, member of the Independent Order of Odd Fellows, the Polo Merchants Club, the Noonday Lunch Club, and is a member of the public school board. He is a steward in the Methodist Church and treasurer of the church.

He married at Dixon, Illinois, October 13, 1917, Miss Cecile Cortright, who attended grammar and high schools at Dixon, was a member of the class of 1911 in the State Normal School at DeKalb, and then for four years was a teacher, spending two years in the public schools of Polo. She is a daughter of Nathan A. and Catherine (Burkett) Cortright. Her father was born and reared near Dixon, was a farmer and one of the influential citizens of that locality, having been a school director and road supervisor. After selling his farm he retired to Dixon, where his wife died in 1922, and he then lived at Polo with his daughter, Mrs. Clothier, until his death in 1923. His parents came from Pennsylvania and were early settlers near Dixon. Mr. and Mrs. Clothier have three children, Marion Cecile, born August 27, 1918, and Robert Roland, born April 4, 1920, both now attending public school, and Patricia Ann, born January 21, 1926.

COL. EDWARD A. WELLS, president of the City National Bank of Murphysboro, has in the course of a long and honorable career been one of the strong men of his community and has earned repeated distinctions over the state at large.

Colonel Wells represents a family that was established in southern Illinois at the close of the territorial period. A great many of the soldiers and officers of the Revolutionary war were attracted to the western country and pushed their settlements close upon the fields of the receding Indians. One of these veterans of the war for independence was Louis Wells, who in 1817 brought his family by wagon from North Carolina and acquired attractive government land in Perry County, Illinois. He cleared the land and developed a good farm, and remained on it until his death at the ripe old age of ninety-six. His son, also named Louis, had served in the War of 1812, and came to Illinois about the same time. He also acquired land and made a home out of the wilderness in the same community where his father had located. This land acquired by the younger Louis Wells is still in the possession of his heirs. No deed of conveyance has ever been recorded against it. It was on this farm that Ferdinand Wells was born. Ferdinand Wells in 1859 drove an ox team from the Mississippi River to Pike's Peak during the gold excitement in the Colorado country. Not long after his return he enlisted for service in the Civil war, being a sergeant in the Eighty-first Illinois Infantry. Thus members of three consecutive generations of the family proved their sturdy patriotism in time of war. Ferdinand Wells married Mary C. Rees. Her grandfather migrated from Kentucky in 1815 and settled in Perry County, Illinois, on a stream of water that ever since has been known as Rees Creek. Her father, Hon. Ephraim T. Rees, was one of Perry County's best known citizens, serving for twenty-one years as associate judge.

Edward A. Wells, who represents the fourth generation of the Wells family in southern Illinois, and is a son of Ferdinand and Mary C. (Rees) Wells, was born at the old homestead in Perry County, August 13, 1858. When he was a small child the family left the farm and located in the village of Duquoin, two and a half miles distance. Up to the age of fifteen Colonel Wells attended the village schools. The family then removed to Grand Tower in Jackson County. This was the beginning of Colonel Wells' residence in Jackson County, dating from 1873, a period of over half a century. He inherited the military spirit of his ancestors, and one of his boyhood ambitions was to become an officer in the regular army. His studies and efforts for a number of years were directed to that end. Finally he passed a successful examination and was admitted as a cadet in the West Point Military Academy in 1879, and was a tent made of Major General George W. Read. After pursuing his studies for two years and giving a good account of himself ill health compelled him to resign. He then returned to his father's home in Grand Tower. While preparing for entrance to the Military Academy he had taught school in Perry County three years. After recovering his health he was appointed deputy sheriff of Jackson County in 1882, and in 1886 was elected sheriff on the republican ticket. He served in that capacity four years. On leaving office he was in the real estate business until 1894, when he was again elected sheriff, his second term in that office closing in 1898. About the time he left the sheriff's office the country was engaged in the war with Spain, and looking upon this as an opportunity to follow the example of his father, grandfather and great-grandfather, he assisted in raising a volunteer regiment, and was commissioned its lieutenant colonel. This regiment, like many others, did not reach the scene of action.

Colonel Wells in 1891 was elected state commander of the Sons of Veterans. In 1901 he was appointed a member of the staff of Governor Yates, with the rank of colonel, and served four years.

Colonel Wells has been prominent in banking at Murphysboro for a great many years. In 1882 was established a small private bank known as the J. E. Walker & Company Bank. In 1892 this became the City National Bank, with Mr. Walker as its first president. The bank was started with a capital of $50,000 and total assets of $112,000. Other men associated with Mr. Walker at that time were C. O. Pellett, a merchant, George W. Smith, then a congressman, George E. Kirtchner, J. C. Clark, president of the Mobile and Ohio Railroad, A. B. Minton, James H. Martin, attorney, and James D. Kelley. In 1895 Mr. Walker retired, and was succeeded by Coram Norman as president, and he very shortly was succeeded by Joseph Van Clooster, who served as

GEORGE M. LeCRONE

president from 1895 to 1899. In 1899 John G. Hardy, who had been cashier, was elected president. It was Colonel Wells who took the place of Mr. Hardy as cashier of the City National Bank, and he served in that capacity until 1905, when he organized a land company, bought a patch of land in Missouri and built the town of Fornfelt, where he established a bank. Some years later, when Mr. Hardy's health was failing, Colonel Wells at his earnest solicitation again became an officer of the bank, vice president, and since 1922 has been president. The City National Bank is one of the strongest institutions in southern Illinois, with deposits around $1,300,000.

Colonel Wells in 1917 was made chairman of the Jackson County Exemption Board, and served until the close of the war. For six years he was president of the Township High School Board. He is affiliated with the Knights of Pythias, B. P. O. Elks, Sons of Veterans, and the First Methodist Episcopal Church.

Colonel Wells in 1886 married Susie Chiles, daughter of James J. Chiles, of Kansas City, Missouri. Her grandfather, James J. Chiles, was a colonel in the war with Mexico, and in 1857 was elected speaker of the Missouri House of Representatives. Colonel and Mrs. Wells were the parents of two sons and two daughters. Joseph V. Wells, the oldest son, spent one year at Camp Taylor, training as a soldier during the World war, and for the past eight years has been clerk of the Circuit Court of Jackson County. Edward A. Wells, Jr., was with the colors eighteen months during the World war, thirteen months overseas with the army. He is a graduate of the Bernaar McFadden Physical Culture School of Chicago, and was a physical director in that school until he entered the army, and is now connected with the Chicago post office. The daughter Lulu is the wife of C. E. Tudor, of Herrin, Illinois. The daughter Emma is the wife of Harry E. Strong, a resident of Duquoin and manager for the Hayes interests in southern Illinois.

GEORGE M. LECRONE, of Effingham, has had more than forty years of consecutive working experience in the newspaper business. He is still proprietor and editor of the Effingham Daily Record, but has turned over the active management of that very successful newspaper to his son.

While he has been a resident of Effingham County practically all his life, Mr. LeCrone is undoubtedly one of the best known citizens of southern Illinois, made so by his activities in the newspaper field and in public affairs. He was born at Ewington, the old county seat of Effingham County, December 23, 1853. His father, Dr. John LeCrone, was a beloved physician whose practice identified him with this section of Illinois for half a century or more. Dr. John LeCrone was born in Fayette County, Pennsylvania, December 12, 1816. With his parents, in 1832, he moved to Fairfield County, Ohio, living there for twelve years. He taught school, and continued his own education in Marietta College of Ohio. He studied medicine at Rushville, Ohio, and was licensed to practice in 1842, when twenty-six years of age. Doctor LeCrone in the fall of 1844 came to Illinois and located at Ewington. The county seat was changed from Ewington to Effingham in 1859, and Doctor LeCrone followed the general exodus of population to the new site in the spring of 1861. For three months in 1864 he was on duty with the Union army as a surgeon of the 155th Illinois Regiment. Doctor LeCrone practiced medicine for fifty-five years. All but two years of that time was spent in Effingham County. His abilities gained him recognition and he attended a large practice in surrounding counties. Doctor LeCrone died in 1897, when eighty-one years of age. He was always a busy doctor but found time for public duties, serving three terms as mayor of Effingham and two terms as county clerk. He was a life long democrat, was a Royal Arch Mason, member of the Independent Order of Odd Fellows and a Presbyterian, while his wife was a Methodist. Dr. John LeCrone in 1836 married Miss Elizabeth Allen in Ohio. In 1886, at Effingham, they celebrated their golden wedding anniversary, a notable event that attracted hosts of friends and admirers to visit this old couple on this anniversary. Their married life was continued six years longer, until broken by the death of Mrs. LeCrone in 1892.

George M. LeCrone was eight years old when his parents established their home in Effingham. As a boy he attended public schools there, and was graduated in 1873 from the Illinois State Normal University at Normal. Since then he has had fifty-three years in which to pursue his varied and purposeful activities, and nearly half a century of that time has been devoted to journalism. He taught for several years and for two years was deputy circuit clerk of Effingham County. In 1878 he acquired a half interest in the Effingham Democrat, a weekly newspaper. He sold this interest in 1881 and for several years was engaged in the real estate business. Then, in 1883, he rebought the Effingham Record, and has been its sole owner now for forty-three years. In 1898 the Effingham Daily Record was founded and it is now published by the LeCrone Press, with Mr. LeCrone as its proprietor and editor. In 1924 he turned over the business management to his son, Byron K. LeCrone. The home of this newspaper is the LeCrone Press Building, a modern and thoroughly equipped newspaper plant, which of itself testifies to the business efficiency with which the LeCrone newspaper interests have been handled.

Mr. George M. LeCrone in 1897 organized at Effingham the American Fraternal Order, a beneficiary insurance organization. As its secretary and general manager he developed an extensive membership and gave an admirable administration of its affairs through twenty years. In 1917, just as America entered the World war, this order was merged with the Standard Life Insurance Company of Decatur, Mr. LeCrone becoming a member of the Board of Directors of that company. The Standard Life Insurance Company subsequently was merged with the International Life Insurance Company of St. Louis, and Mr.

LeCrone is on the Board of Directors of that institution. He is also a director of the First National Bank of Effingham.

As a newspaper man Mr. LeCrone has had an unofficial but none the less active and influential part in the political and municipal record of Effingham and Effingham County for over forty years. He has served as councilman and for many years as a member of the Effingham City Board of Education, of which he was president five years. In 1894 he was elected a member of the Lower House of the State Legislature, serving one term and refusing to be a candidate for a second term. His friends in 1906 urged him to become a candidate for the democratic nomination for Congress, but his refusal to accept certain conditions kept the nomination from him. Mr. LeCrone is a Royal Arch Mason.

He married, in 1879, Miss Frances K. Nitcher, of Effingham. They became the parents of four sons: Byron K., now manager of the Effingham Daily Record; Hugh, deceased; George M., Jr., who is in the newspaper business at Colorado Springs, Colorado; and John H., who was a wireless operator with the United States navy during the World war and is now in the newspaper business at Vandalia, Illinois.

PETER W. GRIFFITH, of Murphysboro, at the age of four score looks back in his recollections for three quarters of a century in Jackson County. He is one of the oldest living natives in this section of the state and is one of the few men whose memories go direct to the original pioneers of this section.

In 1830, when Illinois had been a state only twelve years, his father, John J. Griffith, Jr., came to Jackson County, Illinois, from Chicago. The Griffiths were a Welsh family in Pennsylvania. John J. Griffith, Sr., had come from Wales and settled in Pennsylvania in 1793. He spent his last years in Jackson County, Illinois. John J. Griffith, Jr., left Pennsylvania and on coming to Illinois bought forty-five acres located in the present business district of the city of Chicago. He soon concluded that the land was too swampy for farming, and attracted by the favorable report concerning the beautiful country in the southwestern part of the state he came to Jackson County and in time acquired and developed 440 acres. He died in 1863, at the age of fifty-two. The Griffiths were from the vicinity of Somerset, Pennsylvania, and a number of other settlers from that region came to Jackson County, consequently Somerset Township was named for their former place of residence. Another Jackson County family that came from Somerset, Pennsylvania, were the Wills, and Harriett Wills became the wife of John J. Griffith, Jr. Harriett Wills within three months lost her father, one brother and three sisters by typhoid fever. John J. Griffith, Jr., had his home a few miles north of Murphysboro. On that farm Peter Will Griffith was born December 28, 1845.

In the fall of 1851, at the age of six, he walked away from his home for his first day in school, which was kept in a log building with seats of slabs and a long table where the children did their writing. Peter W. Griffith attended such a school two months in the year, helping in the work of the home and on the farm mornings and evenings, and throughout most of the year giving the benefit of his growing strength and willingness to the heavier burdens of the farm. He was sixteen years old when the Civil war broke out, and he desired to enter the Union army at once. However, he deferred to the wishes of his father for two years. Then, at the age of eighteen, he entered the Eighteenth Illinois Infantry and later was assigned duty with the Mississippi Marine Brigade, and continued in the service until the end of the war. He then returned to his home farm.

He remained on the farm just a year and then became associated with Dr. Frederick C. Bierer in the mercantile business, succeeding Robert Worthen as a partner. The location of this store was at Eleventh and Walnut streets, the present site of the Citizens State & Savings Bank. Mr. Griffith was identified with this business for ten years, at the same time retaining his interests in farming. He rented large acreage from coal companies, owners of great bodies of fine farm land with underlying coal veins. Mr. Griffith has always had the faculty of managing men and varied interests, and made a success of farm management beyond the ordinary. After selling his interests in the mercantile business he was induced by Doctor Bierer to take charge of his mill property in the flats. The mill had not been profitable, but Mr. Griffith with his usual energy put it on a paying basis and ran it for two years, at the end of which time the owner sold out at a profit of five thousand dollars. Mr. Griffith next took up logging, contracting with the Mount Carbon Company. He purchased sixteen yoke of steers and used them with a number of men in getting out logs. However, the logging business during the two years he followed it was not profitable. Mr. Griffith's chief success has come from farming. For some years he owned and operated over 700 acres of Jackson County's best farm lands. After retiring he sold all but 320 acres located near the Mississippi River. He induced his son, Frank P. Griffith, to take the management of this land. Frank Griffith, his only child, had been a locomotive engineer with the Mobile and Ohio Railroad for sixteen years, but he now lives on the farm. Frank P. Griffith married Ada Wilkinson.

Prior to the advent of the automobile Peter W. Griffith owned and operated a livery stable at Murphysboro for eight and a half years. With his usual success he soon had all the business of the town. He has been interested in a large number of other enterprises. He was instrumental in the building of the Reliance Mills, and was one of the founders of the Anchor Ice & Packing Company, in which he is still a stockholder. He is vice president and a large stockholder in the City National Bank. His home at Murphysboro was badly damaged by the tornado of 1925, and in another part of the city two houses he owned were totally destroyed.

Mr. Griffith has been a man of kindly, impulsive and helpful efforts through all the years of his life. He married Miss Leona

Sams, daughter of former Sheriff B. F. Sams. As noted, they had only one son. However, they adopted Frederick A. Pope at the age of eleven years, reared and educated him, and he is now a well known business man of Murphysboro and served several terms on the City Council. Mr. and Mrs. Griffith enjoy life today as is proper for those to enjoy it who have such an enviable record behind them. They take great pleasure in recalling the days of their youth, and particularly the old scenes and companions of a generation of whom they are now almost the only survivors. Both are members of the Lutheran Church.

GEORGE E. SHAW is assistant land appraiser for the Elgin, Joliet & Eastern Railroad, his home being at Joliet, in which city he was born and where the Shaws have lived since pioneer times.

The Shaw family came originally from England. One of the ancestors of Mr. Shaw was a soldier in the American Revolution. His grandparents were James and Mary (Hardy) Shaw, of Boston, Massachusetts. James Shaw was born in 1811, and in 1847 moved with his family to Joliet, Illinois. He arrived there in time to take up land from the Government, and soon afterward founded one of the pioneer brick plants in the Illinois River Valley, and thus started an industry with which the name and fortunes of the Shaw family were closely identified until a very recent date. He gave his personal supervision to the brick plant until his death in 1871. This brick plant was started about the time the old Illinois and Michigan Canal was completed, and such of the brick as was not used in the immediate locality was transported largely by canal boats. Many of the early buildings of Joliet were built from brick made in the Shaw plant. After the death of James Shaw the business was continued by his sons, Jesyrus and Silas, until about 1915, when they retired. There were several other sons of James Shaw. Among them were Nicholas Shaw, William Shaw and Isaac Shaw, all of whom were soldiers in the Union army during the Civil war. Nicholas Shaw was with Company K of the Forty-fifth Illinois Infantry and was killed in action at the battle of Lookout Mountain. William Shaw was in the One Hundredth Illinois Infantry, participated in many battles, and is still living, blind, at the Soldiers Home at Kansas City. Isaac Shaw was an engineer and served the Union cause by pulling troop trains in the movement of soldiers, and spent all his active life in railroading. He died in 1921.

Alexander Shaw, father of George E. Shaw, was born at Ogdensburg in Northern New York, April 7, 1843, and was four years of age when the family located at Joliet. After reaching his majority he entered the service of the Illinois Steel Mill and for many years was yard master of that plant in Joliet. In the course of his service he conceived the original idea of removing the slag from the cupolas by dynamite, perfecting a process which brought him an ample measure of income and which is still followed in many of the steel plants. In later years he was with the South Chicago Mills of the United States Steel Corporation, and was killed there September 30, 1905, by a falling brick from some reconstruction work. He married Katherine Kase, who was born in 1858 at Joliet and was reared and educated there in the public schools. She was a daughter of Frantz and Dorothy Kase, who came to America from Alsace-Lorraine, France, in 1850, first settling at Huntington, Indiana, and about 1856 establishing their home at Joliet, where Frantz Kase for many years engaged in business and the trade of cabinet manufacture. He finally retired, and died in 1886, and her mother died in 1900. The children of Alexander Shaw and wife besides George E. were: Frederick A., William R., Robert E. and Laura M. Frederick, who lives with his mother in Joliet, is a dye maker and engraver. William R., in the garage business at Joliet, married Margaret Hoffer, of Joliet, and has three children, William, Robert and June. Robert E. is an employe in the electrical department of the Elgin, Joliet & Eastern Railroad at Joliet. Laura married H. C. Hagedorn, of Cleveland, Ohio, where he carries on an extensive real estate business and is also superintendent of the Western Division of the Manufacturers Appraisal Company of Philadelphia. Mr. and Mrs. Hagedorn have one child, Jean.

George E. Shaw was born at Joliet, February 4, 1899, and graduated from high school in his native city in 1918. From high school he went to work for the Manufacturers Appraisal Company of Philadelphia, and remained in that service until 1923. Since 1923 he has been assistant land appraiser for the Elgin, Joliet & Eastern Railroad, a subsidiary of the United States Steel Corporation. During 1923, before joining the railroad company, in its valuation department, he did some appraisal work for the City of New London, Connecticut.

Mr. Shaw is affiliated with the B. P. O. Elks, is a democrat and a member of the Lutheran Church. He married at New London, Connecticut, March 22, 1922, Miss Judith Nelson, of Joliet, where she was reared and educated, graduating from high school in the same class with her husband. She also took a course in the Joliet Business College. Her parents, August and Sophie (Jacobson) Nelson, came from Sweden to America about 1880 and settled at Joliet, where her father for thirty-nine years was foreman of the blast furnaces of the Illinois Steel Company, continuing active until his death in 1923. Mrs. Shaw is one of five children, the others being Arthur, Grant, Lillian and Mabel.

URIAH C. DAVIS. When large and substantial business enterprises of Morris, Illinois, are mentioned, an important one that comes under consideration is the Davis Undertaking Company, with which the Davis name has been identified for almost forty-five years. It is an honorable old pioneer name in this section of Illinois, for the founder of the family came here when Grundy, Kendall and adjacent counties had comparatively few permanent settlers on their wide and fertile prairies.

Uriah C. Davis, who died January 15, 1926, after a sickness lasting six weeks, was for many years the head of the Davis furniture firm at Morris, but did not take an active part, being more interested in the undertaking end of this business. He was born on his father's pioneer farm in Kendall County, Illinois, November 15, 1851, second son of Phineas and Maria L. (Phipps) Davis. His father, Phineas Davis, was born in Livingston County, New York, January 24, 1827, and his mother, Maria L. Phipps, was born in New Jersey, in 1822 When twenty years of age Phineas Davis came to Illinois to look the country over and decide for himself as to permanent settlement, and finding prospects promising, he purchased a tract of wild land in Kendall County, set about its clearing and development, and twenty-seven years later, when he retired to a more easeful life at Morris, he owned one of the best cultivated and productive farms in the county.

Uriah C. Davis and his brother, James L., two years his senior, grew up on the farm, assisting their father, and through boyhood attended the country schools. Uriah C. was a studious youth and early decided to prepare for a wider field of interesting effort than that offered on the farm at that time, and through his own enterprise made possible an educational course in Fowler's Institute, in the Normal School at Morris, and later in the State Normal School. After teaching for some time in the country schools he became principal of the public schools at Mazon, in Grundy County, where he continued for two and a half years, although this necessitated a weekly walk of nine miles to his home at Morris.

Although by this time Mr. Davis had really accomplished a great deal through individual effort and was very satisfactory as a teacher, he was not quite satisfied as to the future, this commendable anxiety making him wide awake to substantial business propositions, and in 1881 he bought an interest in the furniture store of William R. Cody, 94-96 Liberty Street, Morris, and the new firm began to do business as Cody & Davis. In 1882 James L. Davis bought the Cody interest, and for the next ten years the brothers operated the business as partners. In the manwhile, as undertaking became a large feature in the business, special provisions were made, and Uriah C. Davis became a licensed embalmer, the first one in Grundy County, and the sixty-ninth registered in the state. A change in business ownership came about when failing health caused James L. Davis to retire and in 1892 Uriah C. Davis purchased his interest and thereafter conducted the business alone until his two sons became mature enough to assume responsibility and were admitted to partnership.

At Morris, Illinois, Mr. Davis married Miss Nellie Cody, daughter of William R. Cody, and they have three children: Edith, who was born September 12, 1881, and is now Mrs. Harry B. Brayton; and William C., born November 3, 1883, and Ralph C., born October 9, 1887, both of whom are substantial business men and representative citizens of Morris. William C. Davis was educated in the public schools and the Dixon Business College, Dixon, Illinois, and since 1923 has been a member of the Board of Education at Morris. He married Miss Edith Brayton, daughter of Frank W. and Ella (Burleigh) Brayton. Ralph C. Davis was educated in the public schools, the Aurora Business College, Aurora, Illinois, and the Barnes School of Embalming, Chicago. Both brothers are members of the Odd Fellows fraternity and belong also to the Knights of Pythias, W. C. Davis being one of this fraternity's charter members. The extensive furniture store of the firm is located on Washington Street and in 1923 was completed the new addition on the corner of Washington and Liberty which houses the modern undertaking establishment and chapel.

Uriah C. Davis was always active in civic affairs, and as one of the city's most reputable business men, was frequently elected to the City Council, where his public spirit was shown in such matters as giving hearty encouragement to the building of the present admirable water works system. From youth he belonged to the Methodist Episcopal Church. He was a Mason of advanced degree, wore the twenty-five-year jewel of the Order of Odd Fellows, and long had membership also in the Knights of Pythias order.

CAPT. RICHARD E. SMITH. Waukegan as a lake port for over eighty years has been the home of many men of interesting experience and achievement as mariners on the Great Lakes. One of them is Capt. Richard E. Smith, a veteran of the lake fishing industry and owner of the Smith Fishing Company, one of the largest and most complete establishments of its kind on Lake Michigan. It is a business that was founded by his father.

Richard E. Smith was born at St. Joseph, Michigan, October 1, 1856, son of William and Sophia Smith. His father was a native of Bavaria, but came to America in 1839 and located in Milwaukee when that was a small village. He lived in Milwaukee when a large part of the population of the country inland was made up of Indians. He was about sixteen years of age when he came to America, and the rest of his life was spent in the fishing industry. He established a fishing business at Milwaukee in 1848, in 1856 moved his headquarters to St. Joseph, Michigan, and in 1882, to Frankfort, Michigan, where he continued his business until 1888. In that year he established his home at Kenosha, Wisconsin, and in 1893 moved to Waukegan, where he continued active until his death in 1894. At the time of his death he owned a fleet of steam tugs, other fishing boats, and all the varied equipment and apparatus for handling fish, including smoking plants and warehouses. It was then the largest fishing industry in the State of Illinois, and under his son that reputation has not been diminished. Mrs. Sophia Smith, his wife, was a native of Hanover and was brought to America when seven years of age, about 1839, her parents also settling in Milwaukee, where her father was a gardener. Mrs. Sophia Smith died in 1900. She was the mother of a family of thirteen children, Capt. Richard being the oldest. Two died in infancy and eleven reached mature years. The children who grew up were: Capt. Richard E.;

Lena; Henry; William, deceased; Laura; Charlie; Clara; Alice; Robert, deceased; Frank; and Emma, deceased. Lena became the wife of Herman Rehmer, of St. Joseph, Michigan, for many years associated with Captain Smith in the fishing industry. He died in 1910, and his widow is still living with three children, Richard, Elmer and William. William Smith married Anna Snaknus, of Waukegan, and had seven children, the five living being Henry, Chester, Josephine, William and Bert. Laura Smith became the wife of Charles Shearer, who for a number of years was in the clothing business at Benton Harbor, Michigan, and since then has been a clothier at Rochester, New York, and they have two children, named Flossie and Warren. Charlie Smith is a dentist at Davenport, Iowa, and is married and has two children, named Laura Ruth and Mary Jane. Clara Smith resides at Waukegan. Frank is a salesman at Rochester, New York, and is married and has one child.

Capt. Richard E. Smith attended public schools at St. Joseph, Michigan, and was still a boy when he began making regular trips with his father in the fishing business. It has been a lifelong experience, and has involved remarkable adventures and vicissitudes. He has been a most capable business man, and still directs a large and complete organization embracing every facility for the smoking, storage and curing, and the distribution and sale of fish from the Great Lakes. Captain Smith has been a man noted for his generosity, a friend of his employes and a willing contributor to many public causes. He has been on the Great Lakes in many of the historic storms that have overtaken that body of water. He was out in the same storm when the Steamer Gilcher with all hands was lost between South Fox and North Manito. At another time he was out in the storm when the Steamer Chicora went down at St. Joseph, Michigan, with the loss of twenty-two. A Chicago newspaper of February 13, 1899, told a thrilling story of an ice bucking record when Captain Smith as captain of the tug Alice started from the harbor at Waukegan with the thermometer 22° below zero, and spent sixteen hours bucking the ice in an effort to reach some students from Lake Forest University reported to be stranded on an ice floe in the lake. The tug broke through the ice for a distance of thirty-five miles going and coming, and at the time it was claimed that this was the longest record of ice bucking in the annals of the Great Lakes.

Captain Smith is a Royal Arch Mason, a member of the Isaac Walton League, a republican and a liberal member of the Baptist Church.

He married at St. Joseph, Michigan, June 9, 1880, Miss Augusta Neimetz, who was reared and educated there and was not only a most capable home-maker but was interested in church and church activities. She died July 2, 1900. Captain Smith and wife had five children, all of whom are living. Belle is the wife of State's Attorney A. V. Smith, of Waukegan. Ailene, who finished her education in the high school at Waukegan, resides with her father. Lawrence W., married Edna Sabra, is manager for one of the Armour and Company branch plants at Erie, Pennsylvania, and has two children, Billie and Helen. Elsie, a graduate of the Waukegan High School, is cashier and secretary to the manager of the Elgin, Joliet & Eastern Railway. Nellie M. is the wife of Bruno Henderson, a jewelry merchant at Waukegan, and they have a daughter, Suzanne, whom Captain Smith claims is his sweetheart girl.

RAYMOND W. FAIRCHILD. There is no other calling which makes such heavy demands upon its followers as does that of school-teaching. Not only does a conscientious educator feel that he must carefully prepare himself, and develop his natural leaning toward his work, but he can never, if he hopes to reach satisfactory heights, relax his efforts, but continues a student to the close of his life. The rewards for this constant and heavy work are not all material ones, but those most appreciated are those whose value can only be discerned by the whole heartedness centered in the work, and their influence upon the plastic minds of their charges. Raymond W. Fairchild, superintendent of schools of the city of Elgin, is a man who belongs to this class of earnest, devoted educators, and his career is one that sets an example for others in his same line to follow if they, too, hope to produce the best results.

Raymond W. Fairchild was born at Bismarck, near Danville, Illinois, September 9, 1888, a son of Wilbur D. and Susan M. (Johnson) Fairchild, both natives of Illinois. The grandfather, Harrison Fairchild, was a veteran of the war between the states, and he, as the other members of his family, was well known in and about Danville. Wilbur D. Fairchild was a clergyman of the Methodist Episcopal Church. Two children were born to him and his wife, namely: Professor Fairchild and Donald H., the latter being a mining engineer located at Chicago.

The elementary schools of Greencastle, Indiana, and Murdock, Illinois, grounded Raymond W. Fairchild in his education, and he supplemented this early training with courses at Illinois Wesleyan Academy in Bloomington, with which his father was then connected, the University of Illinois and the University of Michigan, and took his degrees Bachelor of Arts and Master of Arts from the last-named institution. He assisted in biology at Wesleyan University, Bloomington, for two years, following which he became assistant principal of schools at Vandalia. After a year he went to Moline, Illinois, as assistant principal of its high school, and spent three and one-half years in that position, and for six and one-half years was a member of the faculty of the State Normal School at Stevens Point, Wisconsin, in the capacity of dean of men. For the following three and one-half years he was superintendent of schools at Fond du Lac, Wisconsin, and then, in 1923, was appointed superintendent of schools of Elgin.

An outstanding accomplishment of national importance has been the formation and development of a course in Character Education used in the Elgin schools and now a part of similar courses in cities of thirty-three states. This course was worked out by Mr. Fairchild and the assistant superintendent at Elgin.

On June 25, 1913, Professor Fairchild married Miss Nellie M. Bronson, and they have two children: Ralph B. and Robert E. Professor Fairchild is a republican He is a past-president of the Elgin Club, and is a Rotarian and an enthusiast with reference to what is being accomplished through the medium of this movement in the way of awakening the people to the responsibilities of good citizenship. Fraternally his affiliations are with the Knights of Pythias and the Benevolent and Protective Order of Elks, while in religion he is a member of the Methodist Episcopal Church.

FRANKLIN NATHANIEL HULL. The life history of the late Franklin Nathaniel Hull, of Morris, is an unusual one in that after years of confining work, during which he acquired ample means, he retired from the fields of activity in which he had been so successful at a time when his affairs were in a most flourishing condition. To be satisfied with a sufficiency of this world's wealth is unusual, but it is commendable, for it not only provides leisure for enjoyment of the fruits of honorable labor, but also leaves open opportunities for others to achieve similar prosperity.

The Hull family is an old and honored one in Grundy County and was established in this region by Birdsey Hull's father, Samuel Hull, who came to Morris by wagon from his home in Ohio, and in this little city Birdsey Hull found work at his trade as a painter. Two years later the Crumb family came to Grundy County from New York State, and among its members was Cynthia Crumb, then twelve years old. She grew to beautiful young womanhood in this county, and here she was married to Birdsey Hull, and the two subsequently became the parents of Franklin Nathaniel Hull.

Of their nine children, Franklin Nathaniel Hull was born in Morris, October 26, 1864. The public schools educated him to the age of sixteen years, but, an ambitious lad, he wanted to get an early start in business life, so left school at that age. With the good judgment which characterized him through life, he decided to master some one thing. Naturally fond of the printing business, he learned the trade, and with the exception of a few years spent in Michigan, resided in Morris all his life. At the age of twenty-five Mr. Hull formed a partnership with several fellow citizens under the firm name of Kutz, Hull & Murray, and they founded and began the publication of the Morris Daily Post.

It was not long before Mr. Hull purchased the interests of his partners, and from then on until 1909 he continued to issue this paper. In the latter year he sold it to the Morris Herald. At the time of the sale Mr. Hull retained the mechanical part of the plant and conducted a job printing business until 1916, when he retired.

During his long and successful career Mr. Hull was assisted in his work by the lady who subsequently became his wife. On the day the Post was founded Miss Helen Hitchcock became the bookkeeper for the firm, and in 1891 she and Mr. Hull were married, and to her able assistance he always contributed the larger portion of his success. Like the late Mrs. Warren G. Harding, Mrs. Hull continued to take an active part in her husband's newspaper work, and Mr. Hull, as did the late President Harding, always realized the debt he owed to her wise counsel, knowledge of affairs, and good business judgment. As they made money they invested it in local realty, including a half interest in the Hull Opera House.

In 1916 Mr. Hull suffered a stroke of paralysis, and July 2, 1920, he was stricken with the second one, which proved fatal. He had a wide circle of friends won by his wholesome generous nature and winning personality. A true friend, he was always ready and willing to aid those whom misfortune had overtaken. While he never cared for politics, he was always favorable to anything which promised to be for the community's good. In fraternal matters he affiliated with the Benevolent and Protective Order of Elks.

Mrs. Hull, who survives her husband, is the daughter of Hiram Dwight and Mary (Cutting) Hitchcock, who came to Morris from New York State in 1867. Mr. and Mrs. Hull had no children. Mrs. Hull is one of the most highly-esteemed ladies of the county seat, and one whose philanthropies are many, although a number of them never are made public. She is highly cultured, and her influence has always been exerted in behalf of the welfare of Morris and Grundy County.

CYRUS HILARY ANDERSON. Many of the most skilled physicians and surgeons of Illinois are devoting their talents and energies to special lines of work connected with their calling, in this way rendering a better service than they feel they could do if they confined themselves to a private practice. The work of the medical men is the highest form of service to humanity, and those who take their obligations seriously strive to produce the most lasting results for the greatest number. Dr. Cyrus Hilary Anderson, late superintendent of the Anna State Hospital for the Insane, and now associated with the Watertown State Hospital of East Moline, Illinois, is one of the members of the medical profession who has given much time and thought to the treatment of those whose minds are disordered, and his appointment to these institutions was felt to be a long step forward in the securing for them the best of care and treatment.

Doctor Anderson was born at McLeansboro, Illinois, September 15, 1869, a son of John T. and Martha E. (Patrick) Anderson. His paternal grandparents were Edmund and Nancy (Turrentine) Anderson, natives of Illinois, and his maternal grandparents were Hilary and Martha Patrick, natives of Tennessee. John T. Anderson was born in Hamilton County, Illinois, near McLeansboro, and his wife was born in Tennessee. They were married at McLeansboro, Illinois, and settled on a farm in its vicinity, where they continued to reside until his death in 1912. She survives her husband and makes her home at McLeansboro, where she is held in high esteem. Mr.

Anderson was one of the solid men of his community, and in his death a good citizen is lost.

Growing up within a strictly Christian environment, Doctor Anderson was taught habits of thrift and industry which he has never forgotten, and was sent to the local schools through the high school course. Early displaying scholarly instincts, he was encouraged by his watchful parents to develop his talents, and he entered the Southern Illinois College, where he secured the degrees of Bachelor of Science and Bachelor of Arts. Subsequently he took his medical training at the Missouri Medical College, and was graduated therefrom with the degree of Doctor of Medicine. In later years he took two post-graduate courses in New York City. In 1898 Doctor Anderson established himself in a general practice at McLeansboro, where he remained until 1907. In the meanwhile he had given considerable attention to diseases of the mind, and contributed papers upon this subject to different medical journals. Attention was attracted toward him because of his success in handling such cases, and in 1907 he was appointed managing officer of the Chester Illinois State Hospital, and immediately entered upon the discharge of his duties. His work in this institution is a splendid record of his skill and knowledge, as well as his sympathetic understanding of the people placed in his charge. Kindness, tempered with judicious firmness, without any harshness, has always characterized his relations with the mentally diseased, and his patients have always improved under his ministrations. In 1913 he resigned his position with the Chester institution, and, returning to McLeansboro, resumed his private practice. The need for men of his experience, however, was too great for him to remain out of the field for which his studies and experience so eminently fit him, and in 1917 he was induced to accept appointment at the Anna State Hospital. In this connection he duplicated his success at Chester, and added to the laurels already won. Recently Doctor Anderson was transferred from the Anna State Hospital, Anna, Illinois, to the Watertown State Hospital, East Moline, Illinois. The transfer was made May 15, 1926. Doctor Anderson is an accepted expert along the lines he has been following, and recently read a much-discussed paper before the meeting of the Psychological Society at its annual convention at Richmond, Virginia. He is oftentimes called as an expert alienist in criminal cases all over the country.

On August 16, 1893, Doctor Anderson married Mary E. Williams, who was born in Hamilton County, Illinois, a daughter of Rev. G. W. Williams, also a native of Hamilton County. Doctor and Mrs. Anderson have had the following children born to them: Ruth, who is at home; Winfield Scott, who died at the age of twenty-one years; and Anna, who is the wife of Dr. C. M. Rile, a dental surgeon of Chicago, Illinois. Doctor Anderson has always been very active in the republican party, and for years was chairman of the County Central Committee of Hamilton County, and was a member of the Board of Education of McLeansboro. He is a member of the Presbyterian Church. After going to Anna he associated himself with its Rotary Club, in which he took a forceful part. The Hamilton County Medical Society, the Illinois State Medical Society, the American Medical Society, the Southern Illinois Medical Society and the American Psychological Association all hold his membership. Very high in Masonry, he has been advanced in that order to the thirty-second degree.

JOHN WILLIAM BARWELL. Among the accumulating institutions that make Waukegan one of the important industrial cities of Northern Illinois, the plant and factory of the Blatchford Calf Meal Company, built there in 1900 by John William Barwell, president of the company, constitutes a business of no mean proportions and has served to identify with the city Mr. Barwell, a man of exceptionally high character both in business and citizenship, whose public spirit and generosity have been reflected in many ways.

Mr. Barwell was born in Leicester, England, November 2, 1854, son of Thomas and Elizabeth (Hannam) Barwell, and member of a family that has been identified with Leicestershire for many generations. They have been farmers and for over a century have been identified with a business of handling agricultural seeds, cakes and meals, as dealers and importers. Two uncles of John W. Barwell lost their lives in the foreign service of the British government, one in the Crimean war and the other in the Indian mutiny. Mr. Barwell's father, who gave most of his life to the business of handling agricultural seeds and the linseed and cotton seed cake, was also a member of the Town Council, a charter member of the Royal Agricultural Society of England, and a member of the Masonic fraternity. He died in 1896.

John William Barwell was educated in English schools, attending a private school in Leicester and Trent College, after which he passed the Oxford local senior examination. At the age of seventeen he began work in his father's office. Thus Mr. Barwell for over half a century has been in close contact with the fundamentals of the industry of which he is now the head. He worked in his father's seed and cake warehouse at Leicester, this being the business established by the Barwells as early as 1800. After two years he began an apprenticeship with a firm of general produce brokers at Liverpool, remaining there for years. When he had completed his term he returned to his father's business for two more years. His father at that time was importing large quantities of linseed and cotton seed oil and cake, and John W. Barwell was selected as a proper representative to look after the American interests of the business. Consequently in 1878 he came to America and settled at Chicago, where he was a buyer of cotton seed and linseed cake, also clover seed and other agricultural products, and was the local representative not only of his father's firm but of other similar firms in England. While in Chicago, in 1881, he became identified with E. W. Blatchford & Company in the manufacture of Blatchford's calf meal and other products utilizing linseed and cotton seed cake.

Blatchford's Calf Meal for several generations has been a familiar feed on dairy and live stock farms. It is based on an old English formula, and besides seed cakes other ingredients of the manufacture include locust beans, anise seed and fenugreek, products imported from the shores of the Mediterranean.

Mr. Barwell in 1896 bought from the E. W. Blatchford & Company the calf meal department, and in 1900 he built at Waukegan the Blatchford Calf Meal Factory, using Waukegan as his location primarily because it was his wife's old home. Since then he has been at the head of this large and profitable industry. In 1913 he was elected president of the Waukegan National Bank and is now chairman of its board of directors.

He is a director of the Waukegan Y. M. C. A., charter life member of the Glen Flora Country Club, member of the American Association for the Advancement of Science, the Chicago Historical Society, the Art Institute of Chicago, is a trustee of the Good Fellowship Settlement, member of the Illinois Manufacturers Association, Waukegan Chamber of Commerce, and in politics is a republican. He was elected an alderman of Waukegan in 1909, but declined to serve, and in 1910 was appointed president of the Civil Service Commission of the city and in that capacity he and his associates did some good work for the community. He has for many years been an official of Christ's Episcopal Church of Waukegan and was a director of the Lake County Tuberculosis Institute when first organized.

He married in Waukegan, October 27, 1887, Miss Harriet Frances Porter, daughter of Henry F. Porter, a pioneer Waukegan groceryman. Mrs. Barwell died January 15, 1915. She was deeply interested in charitable and general welfare work in her home city, and as a memorial to his wife Mr. Barwell founded the Hattie Barwell Goodfellowship Settlement House for working girls and boys and home improvement which through his generosity is a self supporting institution and is operated on the basis and policy of good fellowship settlement houses here and elsewhere.

LYMAN J. WILMOT. One of the oldest families of Lake County is that of Wilmot. The Wilmots took up land from the Government more than eighty years ago, and they have been identified with the agricultural, business and public interests of the county ever since. Lyman J. Wilmot, of this family, has spent practically all his years since leaving school in the court house at Waukegan, and in the service of one office, of which he is now chief, that of Circuit Court clerk.

He was born at Deerfield, Lake County, July 16, 1885. The Wilmots are of English ancestry. The great-grandparents of Lyman J. Wilmot were Jesse Wilmot and wife, of New York State. His grandfather and the pioneer in Lake County was Lyman Wilmot, who came to Northeastern Illinois from Greenwood, Steuben County, New York, about 1840 and took up Government land, a part of which is now included in the limits of the Village of Deerfield. Lyman Wilmot became one of the substantial farmers of the community. For a number of years he held the office of squire or justice, and during the Civil war he acted as a recruiting officer, two of his own sons, Virgil and Levi, being in the army. His son Levi was wounded in battle. Lyman Wilmot was a resident of Deerfield more than half a century and died there about 1897, when ninety-one years of age. He married Clarissa Dwight, who died shortly after her husband at the age of ninety.

Warren H. Wilmot, father of Lyman J., was born and reared at Deerfield, attended public schools in the county and the Naperville School in Illinois. His work for a number of years was divided between farming and teaching school. He taught both in Lake and in Iroquois counties. In 1890 he engaged in the real estate business in Chicago and Deerfield, and also did a great amount of auctioneering. In 1905 he was made deputy United States marshal for the Northern District of Illinois, which position he held until his death on January 1, 1912. He married Minnie Vining, who was born and reared in Iroquois County, Illinois, and was educated in public schools there and subsequently taught in that county until her marriage. She died in 1888. Her parents were Jefferson and Minnie Vining, of Iroquois County, farmers of that section of the state.

Lyman J. Wilmot received his early advantages in the public schools of Deerfield, graduated from the Waukegan High School in 1903, and in December of that year began the performance of clerical duties in the office of Circuit Court clerk. In 1908 he was made deputy clerk of the Circuit Court. In December, 1924, he was elected clerk of the Circuit Court. Hardly any one in Lake County is officially better known than Mr. Wilmot, and at all times he has shown a willingness to take up civic burdens and exemplify the general spirit of service. He is a director of the Waukegan Public Library and the Waukegan Y. M. C. A., is a member of the B. P. O. Elks, Modern Woodmen of America, has served as a director for a number of years and is now president of the Waukegan Rotary Club, and in politics is a republican. He is a member of the Congregational Church and for fifteen years was superintendent of the Sunday School. He is president of the Waukegan Independent Chautauqua.

Mr. Wilmot married at Waukegan, December 25, 1908, Miss Laura Brockway, who graduated from the Waukegan High School in 1900. She is active in church work, is a director and vice president of the Waukegan Y. W. C. A., is treasurer of the P. E. O. Sisterhood and a member of the Woman's Club. She is also president of the Parent-Teachers Association of the Glen Flora School. Mrs. Wilmot is a daughter of Lewis O. and Abi (Vant) Brockway, of Waukegan. Her father was born and reared at Lake Zurich in Lake County, attended public schools and was a teacher for a number of years at Deerfield. In 1890 he became a clerk in the Census Bureau at Washington, where he lived several years. On returning to Lake County he became deputy county clerk under A. L. Hendee, then county clerk. In November, 1900, Mr. Brockway was elected clerk of the Circuit Court, an office which then included the duties

Frederic E Legris

also of recorder of deeds. In 1924 this office was divided, one branch being handled by a recorder of deeds and the other by a Circuit Court clerk. Mr. and Mrs. Wilmot are the parents of four children: Helen E., Lyman J., Jr., Marshall B. and Robert M., all attending the public schools at Waukegan. Mr. Wilmot during the World war was active in the work of the United War Charities at Waukegan.

GUERDON LYNN BREWSTER has given the greater part of his business career and service to the Chicago Hardware & Foundry Company at North Chicago, of which he is assistant manager and director. Mr. Brewster is a member of a family that has been active in the commercial life of Waukegan for three generations.

He was born at Waukegan, February 11, 1883, son of Jay L. and Altie (Derrick) Brewster, grandson of Daniel and Anna (Montgomery) Brewster, and a descendant of the noted Elder Brewster, one of the most conspicuous figures in the early Colonial settlement of Massachusetts. Daniel Brewster was born and reared in New York State, acquired his education in public and private schools, and in 1840 came to Illinois and settled at Waukegan, then known as Little Fort. He was a saddle and harness maker, and set up a shop of that kind at Waukegan, eventually building up a large and prosperous industry which at one time employed about forty harness makers. He died in 1904, and after his death the business was continued by his son Jay L. Brewster. Jay L. Brewster was born and reared at Waukegan, attended grammar and high schools there and also the University of Michigan, and after finishing his education he entered his father's harness and saddlery shop, and devoted to that business the full energies of his career until he retired about 1920. Jay L. Brewster was one of the most prominent members of the Masonic order of Northern Illinois, attaining the thirty-third supreme honorary degree in Scottish Rite Masonry. He died in 1924, at the age of seventy-six, and his death, the result of heart failure, occurred while he was in uniform engaged in Masonic degree work in the Waukegan Masonic Temple. His wife, Altie (Derrick) Brewster, was born at Troy, New York, attended public schools and a girl's seminary there, and for many years has been an active worker in the Presbyterian Church. She now divides her time between her son, Guerdon L., and her daughter, Lucy, wife of H. S. Miller, a real estate man at Pasadena, California. Mr. and Mrs. Miller have three children, Altie, Helen and Seymour.

Guerdon Lynn Brewster grew up at Waukegan, graduated from high school in 1900, and during the next five years was engaged in railroad service, beginning as a clerk in the office of the Chicago & Northwestern. Subsequently he was with the Rock Island, Burlington, Wabash, Mexican Central and other lines. In 1905, returning to Waukegan, he became bookkeeper for the Chicago Hardware and Foundry Company, from bookkeeper was promoted to traffic manager, then to office and credit manager, and since 1924 has been assistant general manager and a director of the company at North Chicago, and also a director of the branch plant at Toronto, Canada.

Mr. Brewster is a director of the Waukegan-North Chicago Chamber of Commerce, is a past master of the Waukegan Lodge of Masons, a past commander of Waukegan Commandery, Knights Templar, belongs to the Modern Woodmen of America, Rotary Club, Glen Flora Country Club and Illinois Athletic Association. He is a republican and a member of the Presbyterian Church.

Mr. Brewster married at Waukegan, July 18, 1906, Miss Florence Pienkowsky, who was reared and educated at Waukegan, and after her high school course there attended the State Normal College at DeKalb. She taught in grade and high schools of Illinois until her marriage. Mrs. Brewster takes an active part in the work of the Presbyterian Church and the Waukegan Woman's Club. She is a direct descendant of Count Sobieski, the famous Polish patriot who rendered such signal service to the American colonists at the time of the War of the Revolution. Mrs. Brewster is a member of the Daughters of the American Revolution. They have two children: Elizabeth Norton and Derrick Lynn, the former a member of the class of 1927 in the Waukegan High School.

FREDERIC E. LEGRIS, whose home is in Kankakee, for many years has been prominent in business and public affairs at the town of Bourbonnais. He was born in that town, and has given the community the benefit of his mature judgment and experience as a business man, serving many years in the office of mayor.

He was born at Bourbonnais September 7, 1860, son of Joseph and Cleophe (Sylvester) Legris. Both his parents were born in Quebec, Canada, and the grandparents, also natives of Canada, were Moses J. Legris and Eusabe Sylvester. The families were early settlers in the farming districts of Kankakee County. Joseph Legris and wife after their marriage in 1857 settled at Bourbonnais. He had spent several years in California and invested the gains he had made in that state in Kankakee County land. He died in 1888, and his widow still occupies the old homestead.

Frederic E. Legris attended St. Viators College until 1878, after which he was on the farm with his father. After the death of his father he took over the latter's business, and subsequently with his brother Harvey J. and Mr. Frazer started the Legris Brothers & Frazer Bank. On January 1, 1921, the controlling interests of the bank were acquired by Harvey J. Legris, who died two months later. It is now the Legris Trust & Savings Bank, with Frederic Legris, president and C. M. Clay Bunlain, vice president. The bank has capital of $100,000.

Mr. Legris married, February 3, 1886, Miss Mary Joubert, a native of Kankakee, daughter of Joseph and Mary Rose Joubert, natives of Canada. The children born to Mr. and Mrs. Legris were: Mariette, a Catholic Sister who taught twelve years at Staten Island, New York, six years at Ottawa, Canada, and since September, 1925, at Bourbonnais; Joseph and Ralph, both of whom became priests in the Catholic Church, the former a resident of Quebec, Canada, while the latter died in October, 1918, at the age of twenty-four; Frederic E., of Bourbonnais, who married Arselie Sanasack, and their six children are Ambrose, Homer, Mariette, Ralph, Cecilia and Bernard; Maximillan, who died of the influenza while on his way overseas to France; Noel, of Chicago; Sylvester, who died at the age of two years; Gabriel; Sylvester, second of the name, who died in infancy; Gerasme, who at the age of eighteen has become a novitiate in the Jesuit Order at St. Louis.

Mr. Legris was for twenty years mayor of Bourbonnais. His administration corresponded with the period of greatest growth and development of the municipal improvements. Water works and sewerage were installed and many other improvements. Mr. Legris is a democrat and is a member of the Catholic Church.

GEORGE C. KENRY, division superintendent of the Chicago North Shore and Milwaukee Railroad at Waukegan, is one of the youngest railway executives in Northern Illinois, and he is one of the officials who has contributed to the remarkable prosperity of this system of electric transportation.

Mr. Kenry was born at Junction City, Kansas, August 16, 1891, son of George C. and Elizabeth A. (Purbaugh) Kenry. His father, a native of Germany, came to America when about eighteen years of age, lived for a time in Maryland and while there joined the First Maryland Volunteer Infantry at the outbreak of the Civil war. As a Union soldier he was in the war practically until its close. He was wounded in the battle of Antietam. After the war he remained in the regular army, participating in some of the Indian campaigns in the West and being stationed at many army posts over the country. He was still in the service when the Spanish-American war broke out and was a sergeant in Captain Grimes' battery. This battery shared in the brilliant record of the American forces at San Juan during the siege of Santiago. At this battle a shrapnel shell burst near him and he was hit by nine pieces of the shell. After recovering from the wounds he was honorably discharged, having a record of forty-three years in the service of Uncle Sam. He was retired with the rank of captain. Captain Kenry after leaving the army became chief of police at Highwood, holding that post for two years. He died March 5, 1917. His widow was born at Hyndman, Pennsylvania, was educated in public schools in that state and now resides at Highwood, Illinois. She has always been interested in church work.

George C. Kendry was a child when his parents located at Highwood, Illinois, and attended school there and the Deerfield Township High School at Highland Park. He left school in 1908, and for one year was in the service of the Chicago, Rock Island and Pacific. In 1910 he joined the staff of the Chicago & Milwaukee Electric, now the Chicago, North Shore and Milwaukee Railroad. He has been in its service throughout the period of development which has made this one of the most remarkably successful and efficient electric transportation lines in the Middle West. His hard work and loyalty brought him repeated promotions until in July, 1922, he was made division superintendent.

Mr. Kenry is affiliated with the B. P. O. Elks and has been very prominent in the work of the Kiwanis organization, being a director of the club at Waukegan and also affiliated with Kiwanis activities in Chicago. He is a member of the American Association of Railway Superintendents, the Western Railway Club, the Wisconsin Utilities Association, the Bonnie Brook Golf Club, and in politics is a republican.

ALFORD E. BUDDE, M. D. In the community chosen for his profession as a physician and surgeon, North Chicago, Doctor Budde is admired not only as a skilful physician but as a man of rare accomplishments and experience.

He was born near Madison, Wisconsin, March 19, 1885, son of William and Augusta (Kropf) Budde, and grandson of Charles and Amanda Budde, who were early settlers near Madison, Wisconsin. Charles and Amanda Budde had two children, Amelia and William. Amelia became the wife of Alexander Harfell, and they are living retired on their farm at Verona, Wisconsin. William Budde, father of Doctor Budde, was born and reared near Madison, attended public and district schools there and became a blacksmith, but is now living retired and since 1912 has had his home at North Chicago. His wife, Augusta Kropf, was also born at Madison, Wisconsin, and attended public schools there. Her parents were Robert and Mary (Reel) Kropf. Her father was a printer and for many years was an employe of the Wisconsin State Journal at Madison.

Doctor Budde when four years of age, in 1889, was taken by his parents to Illinois, near Harvard, and he first attended the Big Foot district school near Harvard, graduating from high school in 1902. In that year he went to Milwaukee and was in the office of the commercial agent of the Santa Fe Railway Company there for about two years. In 1904 he entered the medical department of Northwestern University at Chicago, graduating M. D. in 1908.

Doctor Budde served as an interne in the Milwaukee County Hospital and in 1909 became a contract physician and surgeon with the Penn Iron Mining Company at Norway, Michigan. He was engaged in industrial practice until 1911, and on December 26th of that year came to North Chicago and established his office. That community has had the benefit of his training and broad experience for fifteen years except for the two years he was with the colors during the World war.

Doctor Budde in 1916 was commissioned a first lieutenant in the Medical Corps and was awaiting duty during the Mexican border trouble. On March 17, 1917, he was re-assigned under a new ruling as first lieutenant of the Medical Reserve Corps, and on August 12th was ordered to report at Fort Sheridan. For two weeks he was in the hospital there, was next sent to Camp Grant at Rockford as recruiting officer for the Eighty-sixth Division, and at the same time was on the staff of the Base Hospital. In January, 1918, he was ordered to Chicago for intensive training in military and orthopedic surgery, and in April, 1918, was ordered to Camp Custer and assigned to duty with Base Hospital No. 14, which had been organized in Chicago as a Red Cross unit from St. Luke's and the Michael Reese Hospitals. In July, 1918, this unit was sent overseas to Mars Sur Allier, France, and he was orthopedic surgeon in charge of Ward 1 in Base Hospital Unit No. 14. The cases sent to his ward consisted of compound fractures of the long bones. He remained on duty at this hospital until January, 1919, after the armistice, and was then ordered for duty in Camp Hospital No. 1 at Gondrecourt, France. About March 1, 1919, he was sent to England for post-graduate work in medicine and surgery, having been awarded a fellowship.

Doctor Budde on April 16, 1919, at London, married Miss Madeleine DeColnet D'Huart of Brussels, Belgium. This was the culmination of a romance that had started a number of years before. She had been to America in 1914 as bridesmaid of a friend at Winnipeg, Canada, and while visiting in Chicago she and Doctor Budde began their acquaintance and became engaged to marry. Her parents were Louis and Frances (DeMiromont) DeColnet D'Huart of Luxemburg.

Not long after his marriage Doctor Budde returned home, was honorably discharged at Camp Grant August 6, 1919, and then reopened his office and has since been one of the busiest professional men of North Chicago. Doctor Budde is a member of the Masonic order, the Royal Arcanum, Mystic Workers of the World, the American Legion, in politics is a republican, and is a member of the Presbyterian Church.

JOSEPH KROOTH and ARTHUR S. KROOTH. There has always been a supposition that the members of a family should display absolute and undying loyalty to each other, and this condition no doubt prevails at least in the great majority of cases, and particularly in the business world where those related are associated in the same enterprise. Not so often, however, is it displayed in such a high and harmonious degree as in the case of Joseph Krooth and Arthur S. Krooth, brothers, and this although one is a professional man while the other is identified purely with business affairs. The deep-rooted affection that has ever existed between them prevailed even through war times, when they served with the same outfit in France, and they have been practically inseparable companions except as the exigencies of business and professional life have served temporarily to keep them apart.

The brothers, now in their early '30s, were born and reared on the South Side, Chicago, and are sons of Mr. and Mrs. Isaac M. Krooth. The father, who has now retired from active business life, has lived in Chicago for about forty-five years, and for many years was a prominent manufacturer of the city. Joseph Krooth graduated in 1909 from the Frances E. Willard High School. As a youth he engaged in business pursuits, but later, in 1916, entered the office of Foreman, Robertson & Bloomrosen, attorneys, as a law student and law clerk. The senior member of this firm was Col. (now Gen.) Milton J. Foreman, a distinguished member of the Chicago bar, who made a brilliant record during the World war at the head of the Illinois troops and is now commanding general of the Thirty-third Division. Both as a law student and later as a soldier Joseph Krooth had a genuine friend in General Foreman.

Joseph Krooth enlisted in the Signal Corps, United States army, as did his brother, Arthur S. Krooth, at Chicago, early in 1917. They went overseas together in April, 1918, on detached special service. Landing in Scotland, they saw service throughout the western front of the war, all the way to and including Italy. So far as known there is no record, at least among the Illinois troops, of two brothers serving continuously throughout the war, as these two did, continuously together in exactly the same service and in the same areas, from the beginning of their enlistment until the time of their discharge from the army in the spring of 1919. They have taken a very prominent part in the councils of the Veterans of Foreign Wars and are the leaders in making this organization a flourishing and permanent institution at Chicago and in the state of Illinois. Arthur S. is commander of Christopher J. Burke Post No. 177, V. F. W., of which Joseph is adjutant. The latter is also judge advocate for the Department of Illinois, V. F. W., and editor of the V. F. W. News, the official organ of this organization for Illinois.

Before the war Joseph Krooth had taken academic courses both at Chicago University and Northwestern University, and subsequent to the war took law courses in the Law School of the latter institution. He was admitted to the bar in 1922 and since that time has built up a prominent and lucrative practice, which is confined almost exclusively to constitutional and corporation law and legal matters related to finance. He occupies offices in the New Metropolitan Building at Randolph and LaSalle streets, and is a member of the Chicago Bar Association and the Illinois State Bar Association.

Arthur S. Krooth has remained in business life, in which he has shown such diligence and astuteness as to gain the highest regard and confidence of those with whom he has been associated, and a place of honor and esteem in the business world that is a permanent asset to him and an assurance of his continued and added success in the future. He has a splendid executive and advisory position with the well-known firm of Gross, Ray, Eberhart and Harris, one of the largest provision concerns operating on the Chicago Board of Trade. Starting in with this corporation as a clerk, he rose within three years to his present position of responsibility. He is also engaged in the insurance business.

The brothers, with their father, all belong to the same lodges in the Masonic, Odd Fellow and Knights of Pythias fraternities, and Joseph Krooth is a member of the Fort Dearborn Town Club. The genuine affinity existing between the brothers, which has lasted from childhood, not only has shown itself during the dark days of the war, but in every other relationship they have been equally inseparable as genuine pals and friends. Though not necessarily holding the same views on all questions that come up between them, there never has been the slightest discord on any subject. They not only have business interests in common, and a joint bank account, but in their social affairs as well, in their recreations and diversions, in their attendance at theatres, dances, or other entertainments, they are invariably found together.

ROBERT MURDOCK came to Oregon, Illinois, from the east, where he had gone through the early stages of his business training. At Oregon he has built up one of the largest mercantile establishments in Ogle County and ranks as one of the men of first importance in that community.

He was born at Hagerstown, Maryland, January 27, 1880, son of John W. and Elizabeth (Moser) Murdock. His paternal grandparents were natives of Ayrshire, Scotland, and moved from there to the north of Ireland, where they died of the cholera in 1830. John W. Murdock came to America in 1850. He was three years of age when his parents went to Ayrshire, Scotland, to Ireland, and in the latter country he acquired his education. He settled at Baltimore and later became a farmer. He retired from the farm at the age of sixty and died in 1904, when seventy-seven years of age. His wife, Elizabeth Moser, was born and reared in Pennsylvania, daughter of John and Mary Moser, of Franklin County, that state.

Robert Murdock attended public and private schools at Hagerstown, Maryland, finished a course in the Hagerstown Business College in 1899, and soon afterwards became clerk in the Byers Grocery Company at Hagerstown at three dollars a week. He had two years of working experience there and then going to Pittsburgh, became a salesman for the National Biscuit Company, and was a representative of that corporation, selling goods in Pittsburgh and surrounding territory, for a period of ten years.

It was in 1911 that Mr. Murdock came to Oregon, and in partnership with his brother, Edward E. Murdock, engaged in the retail grocery business. In fifteen years this has become the largest retail grocery establishment in Oregon and vicinity. The Murdock brothers are thorough going merchants, and are no less valued as citizens. Robert Murdock is a stockholder in the Ogle County State Bank and in several public utility companies. He is a member of the Masonic Order, B. P. O. Elks, Rock River Golf Club, and is a member of the Official Board of the First Methodist Episcopal Church at Oregon.

He married at Pittsburgh, March 20, 1908, Miss Rebecca Reno. They are the parents of three children, Robert Reno, born January 27, 1909, and Rebecca Elizabeth, born in October, 1910, both students in the Oregon High School, and David Reno Murdock, born in September, 1918.

Mrs. Robert Murdock is a member of one of America's most distinguished families of French ancestry. She is in the eighth generation of descents from Phillipe Renaud or Renault (pronounced Reno). Phillipe Renault was born in 1654, was a metallurgist and iron worker in France, and developed improved methods of refining iron. He died in 1744. His wife was Marie Jean Baillet, who died in 1727. The oldest of their sons, Phillippe Francois, was a central figure in a notable episode in French Colonial exploitation and finance. He was selected by a French company to come to the new world and carry on an extended exploration for minerals in the French possessions, which then extended from Canada to the Gulf west of the Alleghanies. His expedition, made in 1717, resulted in the discovery of the great lead deposits in Missouri and other regions of the Mississippi Valley. The French Company itself went on the rocks as a result of the feverish speculation, which is recorded in general history. Phillippe Francois was recompensed by extensive grants from the French government to lands in various localities of the Mississippi Valley, including the tract of land on which the city of Peoria, Illinois, was built.

The ancestor of the Renault family in America was Jean or John Renault, a brother of this Phillippe Francois. He came to America in 1719, landing at Charleston. He was born in 1685 and died in 1790, at the age of 105 years. His son John was born April 13, 1715, and died in 1800. John Reno married Susannah Thorne, who was born in 1716 and died August 29, 1773. They moved into western Pennsylvania in 1765, and after the death of his wife, John went into the Tennessee country, taking with him the family Bible, which is still in the possession of his descendants and which contains many of the family records. One of the sons of John and Susannah was Rev. Francis Reno, who was the first ordained Episcopal minister west of the Alleghany Mountains, serving churches and missions in the vicinity of Pittsburgh.

Benjamin Reno, of the fourth generation, and second son of John and Susannah, was born February 3, 1740. November 26, 1766, he married Jane Sevier, a daughter of John Sevier, one of the distinguished characters of the Revolution and later period of the Carolinas and the Tennessee country. John Sevier was the hero in the battle of King's Mountain in the Revolution, and afterwards became the first governor of the state of Tennessee. Benjamin was a land owner in Allegheny County, Pennsylvania. All of his sons were participants in the Whiskey Rebellion and all were engaged in the river traffic, so important in the early developments of the western country.

Zachariah Reno, son of Benjamin and Jane, was born December 7, 1776, and died April 29, 1861. He married Martha McMichaels, whose father, General McMichaels, was a commanding officer of the Revolutionary war. Zachariah Reno was a boat builder, having his boat yard in Pittsburgh, on the present site of the Exposition Building. One of his daughters, Amanda, became the wife of C. L. Magee, and the grandmother of William A. Magee, the present mayor of the city of Pittsburgh and one of the most prominent lawyers of that city.

Samuel Jackson Reno, son of Zachariah and Martha Reno, was born October 20, 1808. He

Judson E. Harriss

was a famous river man of his day, owning and commanding some of the finest packets along the Ohio and the Mississippi. He commanded the Buckeye State, said to be the fastest packet ever on western waters. He married Eliza Briceland Magee, a sister of Christopher L. Magee, previously mentioned.

One of their children was Samuel J. Reno, born September 23, 1843, and died February 26, 1905. He was also a captain and pilot of river boats between Pittsburgh and New Orleans, commanding some of the famous boats on these rivers in his time. He married, December 3, 1872, Rebecca Margaret Stephenson, daughter of Robert and Margaret Suter Stephenson. The youngest of the children of Samuel J. Reno was Rebecca Margaret, born April 6, 1887, now the wife of Mr. Robert Murdock, of Oregon, Illinois.

JUDSON EMORY HARRISS, serving his second term as state's attorney of Perry County, is a former member of the Legislature, and has been one of the very forceful men in the law and in public affairs in his section of Illinois for the past fifteen years.

Not far from Duquoin is located the old Harriss homestead, which was entered from the government nearly a hundred years ago by his grandfather and has never been transferred out of the family name. This grandfather was Jordan Harriss, who was born in Laurens district, South Carolina, in 1800, moved over the mountains to Tennessee, and in 1828 settled on his farm northwest of Duquoin. He lived there until his death in 1874. The five sons of his family were Johnson C., John H., Hiram M., Marion and J. Carroll, and two daughters who lived to old age in southern Illinois were Sarah Jane, who married Roberts Teague, a pioneer merchant and farmer; and Nancy, who married Edmund Dry. Rev. Marion Teague, long a leader in business and church affairs, is a grandson of Jordan Harriss.

J. Carroll Harriss, who died in 1919, at the age of seventy-nine, was a man of versatile gifts and is properly credited with a great amount of service to humanity. For many years he was a minister of the Missionary Baptist Church, and in the ministry was especially well known in "Egypt," but also was active as an evangelist in Kentucky, Missouri and other western states. He was born in Perry County, September 8, 1840, was educated in common schools and left Shurtleff College at Upper Alton to join the Union army in Company A of the Eighty-first Illinois Infantry. His regiment was engaged in many battles in the Mississippi Valley, including the siege of Vicksburg, Port Hudson and the battle of Guntown, Mississippi, where Mr. Harriss and many of his comrades were cut off from their troops, and after their ammunition was exhausted they were captured. For eleven months he was held a prisoner in the Andersonville prison and endured all the hardships and indignities of that notorious place.

In 1866 he was elected on the republican ticket sheriff of Perry County and after one term was selected and served four years as county clerk. He then became a grain merchant and farmer at Duquoin, and was one of the conspicuous men in the breeding of high grade live stock for many years. After gaining competency he left his farm and moved into Duquoin, where he resided until his death. In early manhood he was ordained in the Missionary Baptist Church and was one of its ministers for more than forty years.

His first wife was Valerie Thornton, whose father, William Thornton, came to Illinois from Kentucky and was a farmer and minister. Mrs. Viola H. King, of Ewing, and Hon. Clarence W. Harriss, of Mt. Vernon, were the children of this union. The second wife of J. Carroll Harriss was Eliza A. Strait, daughter of Judge H. H. Strait. The children of the second marriage were: Rev. Walter H., Herschel, who died at the age of seven years, Alva, who died in infancy, Grace, who became the wife of W. O. Kind, Wilfred C., who died when thirteen years old, Judson E. and Earle B.

Judson E. Harriss was born at the old homestead in Paradise Prairie in Perry County, November 5, 1884. He attended public schools in Duquoin, graduating from high school in 1904, spent the year 1904-5 as a student in the University of California, attended the business college at Quincy, Illinois, and for one year was an employe of Marshall Field & Company at Chicago. During the year 1907 Mr. Harriss was traveling in Europe, a year that he has always regarded as the most profitable of his life from the point of view of general education and inspiration. In 1910 he was graduated from the University of Illinois College of Law, was admitted to the bar in February, 1911, and at once opened his office in Duquoin and was elected city attorney. In 1912 he was elected on the republican ticket to represent the Forty-fourth District in the Forty-eighth General Assembly. He was a member of the Legislature one term and was author of the bill making the appropriations to preserve the old Fort Chartres and to establish a state park at that place on the Mississippi, and he introduced another bill to purchase the old home or Gen. John A. Logan at Benton Illinois. This bill was vetoed by Governor Dunne. Mr. Harriss was urged to be a candidate for the State Senate, but declined in order to give his time and energy to his growing law practice. After his term in the Legislature he was again made city attorney. In 1920 he was elected state's attorney and was re-elected for a second term in 1924. Although not called by the "draft" in the World war, Mr. Harriss voluntarily enlisted for service in 1918, and was ordered to report for duty at training camp at Claremont, California. The plans for this camp were delayed and the armistice caused its abandonment. Mr. Harriss' brother, Earle B. Harriss, now of Memphis, Tennessee, was an aviator with commission as lieutenant in the World war.

Mr. Harris is a member of the First Baptist Church of Duquoin and of the Masonic Order, Eastern Star, Independent Order of Odd Fellows, B. P. O. Elks, Modern Woodmen of America, Moose and Red Men; belongs to the Beta Theta Pi college fraternity and the

Phi Delta Phi legal fraternity. He is also a Rotarian.

He married Miss Claire Barton, of Fayette, Missouri. Her father, P. M. Barton, was a grandson of Levi Barton, a prominent man in the early life of the state of Missouri. His uncle, Senator David Barton, was author of the legislation creating the University of Missouri. He was a cousin of Clara Barton, long famous as head of the American Red Cross. The mother of Claire Barton Harriss was a member of the McCrary family of Howard County, Missouri, likewise well known in that state.

Judson E. Harriss has long been known as one of the best political leaders of southern Illinois, and his fame is widespread for his remarkable memory for names and faces of people whom he has met. Few young men of Illinois have more extensive acquaintance in this great commonwealth than has "Jud" Harriss of Duquoin.

He is the father of four fine children: Judson E., Jr., Vivien, John Carroll and Willard. The Harriss home in Duquoin is a favorite stopping-place for hosts of friends, and the circle of friends is ever widening.

JUDGE JOHN W. BROWNING is Circuit Court judge of the Third Judicial District, with residence at Harrisburg.

The Brownings have been a prominent family in the southern half of Illinois for several generations. His grandfather on coming to the state located near Quincy, but later moved to a farm near Stonefort in southern Illinois. Thompson Samuel Browning, father of Judge Browning, was born in Pope County, spent his active life as a farmer there, and served as a soldier in the Civil war.

John W. Browning was born in Pope County May 7, 1869. He was reared in the country, and early determined on the vocation of law. He continued his early education in the Southern Illinois Normal College at Carbondale, and then took up the study of law in a law school at Benton conducted by Judge Duff. In 1896 he was admitted to the bar and began practice at Golconda in Pope County. He served three terms as state's attorney and for a time was master in chancery. Judge Browning carried on an extensive general law practice until 1922, when he was elected to fill an unexpired term as judge of the Circuit Court in the Third Judicial District, and at that time moved to Harrisburg in Saline County, where he now resides. He is a member of the Masonic Order, the Methodist Church and is a republican. Judge Browning married Josephine Barker, daughter of George W. Barker, of Saline County.

J. Roy Browning, only son of Judge Browning, is a resident of Marion, Williamson County, and is also an attorney by profession. He was born at Golconda in Pope County, February 28, 1897. After attending the public schools of Golconda he spent two years as a student in the Illinois Normal University at Normal and then entered the law department of the University of Illinois.

In May, 1918, he joined the colors and was sent to the Great Lakes Naval Training Station. Three weeks later he was assigned duty on the receiving ship at Ellis Island, and after a week was sent by transport to Queenstown, Ireland, where he was assigned to the U. S. S. Texas as a yeoman and was with that ship, a unit of the Fifth Battle Squadron of the English Grant Fleet, until after the armistice. He received his honorable discharge in July, 1919, and then returned to the university, where he was graduated in law in 1920 and was admitted to practice the same year.

He engaged in practice with his father at Golconda, but three months later was selected by Chief Justice Duncan of the Illinois Supreme Court as his private secretary, and has filled that position for six years. He is a member of the Lodge and Royal Arch Chapter of Masons at Golconda, the Knights Templar Commandery at Metropolis, and has filled all the successive chairs except that of exalted ruler in the Elks Lodge at Marion.

J. Roy Browning married, October 2, 1921, Miss Bertha John Raum, daughter of John and Bertha Raum, of Pope County. They have one son, John, born May 20, 1923.

THOMAS P. HOUSTON is the founder and president of the Gold Medal Products Company at North Chicago, one of many thriving industries that have been attracted by the exceptional commercial facilities of the Waukegan-North Chicago district.

Mr. Houston, who is at once a thorough business executive and a man of wide experience in mechanical and manufacturing lines, was born at Ironton, Pennsylvania, February 20, 1865, son of Conrad and Mary (Bonner) Houston. His father was a native of County Cork was educated in public schools in Ireland, and coming to America when a young man, spent the rest of his life as a miner. For many years he was in the employ of the Colerain Mining Company at Ironton, Pennsylvania, where he died in 1867. His wife was also born and reared in Ireland and came to America when a young woman. They were married at Catasauqua, Pennsylvania. She died in 1915. She was the mother of a large family of children, only three of whom are now living. These children were John, Hannah, Ellen, Amandus, Francis, Michael, Thomas, Winnie, Hannah, Mary and Annie.

Thomas P. Houston was educated in the grade and high schools of Pennsylvania, and was only two years of age when his father died. As soon as his schooling was over he went to work with the Lehigh Zinc Company at Friedensville, Pennsylvania, spending about six years in the service of that company as a miner. In 1881 he transferred his employment to the Bethlehem Steel Corporation at Bethlehem, Pennsylvania, as a member of the rigging gang for four years. In 1885 he went with John D. Cutter & Company's silk mills at Bethlehem, for three years having charge of belting and machinery.

Mr. Houston came to Illinois in 1888. At Chicago for a time he was employed as a fireman in the court house and for six years was a fireman at the old Tremont Hotel. In 1894 he removed to Racine, Wisconsin, where he went with S. E. Johnson & Company, manufacturers of floor wax, and was with that well known Racine industry until July 10, 1907.

At that date he engaged in business for himself, organizing the Gold Medal Polish Company, with plant at Racine. It was in 1925 that Mr. Houston removed his factory to North Chicago. This business was started in a small way, but the quality of goods put out under the Gold Medal brand and the energy of Mr. Houston have accomplished the upbuilding of an extensive industry. Prior to the removal from Racine the plant facilities were contained in a building 28 by 100 feet. The present plant in North Chicago is in a large building 54 by 100 feet. The Houston's Gold Medal products comprise paste wax, liquid wax, powdered wax, water putty, pastewood filler, wax stain remover and metal polishes, and these products are familiar articles in daily use throughout the United States and extensively sold in foreign countries.

Mr. Houston acknowledges his chief hobby and recreation as fishing. He is a member of the Loyal Order of Moose, is independent in politics and his church affiliations are Catholic.

He married at Chicago, October 9, 1888, Miss Anna Foley, of that city. She was reared and educated there and was for many years active in church and social life at Racine. She died May 26, 1926. Her parents, Thomas and Catherine (Burke) Foley, came from Ireland, first settling in Canada and then in Chicago, where they located some time before the great Chicago fire. Her father for many years was in the service of the Illinois Central Railroad Company. Mr. and Mrs. Houston had no children of their own but reared two adopted children, Marie and William. Marie was educated in the public and parochial schools at Racine and is the wife of Joseph Houlb, who is with the Belle City Malleable Company at Racine. Mr. and Mrs. Houlb have three children, Thomas, Richard and Robert. The adopted son, William Houston, married Ellen Nelson, of Racine, and they have one child. He is connected with the Frank A. Luxem Company of Racine.

JAMES T. HAYES. One of the oldest manufacturing concerns in the Waukegan district is the Chicago Hardware Foundry Company of North Chicago. James T. Hayes has been identified with the business over forty years. He entered the service as a moulder, and for a number of years has been a stockholder and one of the officials, being now vice president. In no small measure the success of this business has been due to Mr. Hayes' thorough knowledge of every technical operation in the plant.

Mr. Hayes was born at Chicago, March 11, 1863, son of James S. and Mary (Lynch) Hayes. His father was born and reared in County Tipperary, Ireland, and in 1847, when about eighteen years of age, came to America in company with other young immigrants from that island. He became an employe of one of Chicago's pioneer packing houses, the Higgins Packing Company, being an engineer in the plant for about ten years. Later he moved to Omaha, Nebraska, and was lard engineer with the Omaha Packing Company. Ill health finally compelled him to retire and he spent the last few years of his life at Chicago, where he died in 1887. He married in Chicago, in 1857, Mary Lynch, a native of County Cavan, who had also come to America about 1847. She died in 1912 in North Chicago. Her parents were Edward and Rose Lynch, farmers of County Cavan. James S. Hayes and wife had five children, two dying in infancy. The survivors are Mary, James T. and John Edward. John Edward is the present water commissioner of North Chicago. James T. Hayes has never married, and he and his brother and sister all reside together. His sister married James Lester, of Medina, New York, where for many years he was in the service of the Adams Express Company. Mr. Lester died in Chicago in 1888, and his twin daughters, Marion and Elizabeth, are both teachers in the public schools of Lake County. John E. Hayes married Mary Canobay, of Beloit, Wisconsin, who died in 1902. The three children of that marriage are Frank L., Florence and John E., Jr., John being a reporter for the Waukegan Daily News.

James T. Hayes attended public schools in Chicago, including the old Kinzie School, and finished his work in the North Division High School. In 1878, on leaving school, he became an apprentice moulder with the Lake Shore Foundry Company. He served a thorough apprenticeship of five years, and in 1883 spent a year as a journeyman employed by various foundries in Illinois and Wisconsin.

It was in 1884 that Mr. Hayes went with the Chicago Hardware Foundry Company as a moulder. There has been no interruption to his service and he enjoyed many promotions, being made foreman, superintendent, and is now vice president, director and a stockholder. He is also a director and one of the founders of the Lake County State Bank and is a trustee of the North Shore Sanitary District, having served in that capacity since the organization of the district in 1914. For ten years he was a member of the North Chicago Park Board and for three years on the Library Board. In politics he is independent. He is a member of the Loyal Order of Moose, Knights of Columbus, and is a Catholic in his church affiliations.

FRANK M. OPEKA is one of the most popular young business men of Lake County, where he has lived practically all his life. He was a Marine during the World war, and since the war has had an interesting participation in the business life of his community. He has had experience in banking, is a qualified attorney, but devotes most of his time to a very prosperous real estate and insurance business at 1645 Sheridan Road in North Chicago.

He was born at Waukegan, October 13, 1898, son of Frank and Gertrude (Straziser) Opeka. His father was born near Laibach, Austria, in what is now Jugo Slavia, attended school in his native country and in 1890, on coming to America, located at Waukegan, where he was an employe of the American Steel & Wire Company for a number of years. Later he took up the mercantile business at North Chicago and is head of a prosperous clothing and dry goods business under the name of Frank Opeka. His wife, Gertrude Straziser, was born and reared in Jugo Slavia and came to

America about 1890, joining her father and brother, who had previously located in Waukegan. Shortly afterwards she met and married Mr. Frank Opeka. She and her husband had nine children, and the eight still living are Frank, Michael, John, Andrew, Anthony, Francis, Jennie and Mary, all except Frank, the oldest, being still members of the family circle.

Frank M. Opeka attended parochial school in Waukegan, was a student in the Waukegan Township High School and finished his education in St. Viator College with the class of 1918. In June, 1918, he enlisted in the United States Marines, was trained at Paris Island, South Carolina, and in July, 1918, went to Charleston and from there embarked with other Marines for duty in Haiti, West Indies. He was one of the force of Marines preserving order on that island until August, 1919, when he was sent to the Brooklyn Navy Yard and honorably discharged in October, 1919.

Mr. Opeka after his military service returned to Waukegan and was bookkeeper in the First National Bank until June, 1920, when he became assistant cashier of the Lake County State Bank at North Chicago, and subsequently was promoted to cashier. In March, 1923, he left the bank to engage in the real estate and insurance business on his own account, and incidentally also made the race for city treasurer. He was elected and served one term in that office, until May 1, 1925. His business now takes up his full time and energies. He has handled many important real estate transactions and also writes a large volume of insurance as representative of the Northwestern Mutual Life Insurance Company, Columbia Casualty Company, Ocean Accident & Guarantee Corporation, Commercial Union Assurance Corporation, Limited, Detroit Fire & Marine Insurance Company, Equitable Fire & Marine Insurance Company, Employers Fire Insurance Company and the Reliance Insurance Company.

For several years he pursued the study of law in the night classes of the Chicago Law College, and completed his course in 1926. He is secretary and treasurer and a director of the North Chicago Real Estate Improvement Corporation.

Mr. Opeka is a deputy grand knight of the Knights of Columbus, is a member of the B. P. O. Elks and Moose, the Phi Alpha Delta law fraternity, is a Catholic, belongs to the American Legion and the Forty and Eight Society, is secretary of the Association of Commerce of North Chicago, member of the Frontenac Athletic Club of Chicago, and in politics is a republican.

He married at Chicago, June 28, 1922, Miss Vera Carroll, of Des Plaines, Illinois. She attended grammar and high schools in Chicago, is now secretary of the North Chicago Library Board and has accepted many opportunities to render service to the community in a social, religious and charitable way. She is a member of the choir of the Holy Family Church of North Chicago. Mrs. Opeka was a student of music for a number of years. Her parents were James T. and Julia (Heumos) Carroll, of Chicago, where her father for a number of years was in the mercantile and restaurant business. Her parents now reside at Des Plaines, where her father is proprietor of a merchant police or detective bureau. Mr. and Mrs. Opeka have one child, Francis Carroll Opeka.

THOMAS H. McKINNEY has been a prominent figure in the business life of North Chicago for thirty-five years. He located there after a successful experience as a lumberman in the Northern Peninsula of Michigan, and was a retail lumber merchant along the North Shore for many years. He is now president of the McKinney Steel & Sales Company, a very successful organization furnishing structural steel to contractors all along the North Shore district.

Mr. McKinney was born in County Tyrone, Ireland, February 6, 1862, son of James and Sarah (Hamilton) McKinney. His parents spent all their lives in Ireland, where his father was a shoemaker and farmer. He died in 1905. Thomas H. McKinney acquired his public school education in County Tyrone. In the spring of 1882, when twenty years of age, he came to America, and for several years lived in Chicago, and from there went to Menominee, Michigan, where he became associated with his brother, George McKinney, in the lumber industry. Mr. McKinney on August 17, 1891, located at Waukegan, and soon afterward organized and established four lumber yards, one at Waukegan, one at Evanston, one at North Chicago and one at Wilmette. The Waukegan Lumber Company handled the business of the yards at North Chicago and Waukegan. The yard at Evanston was operated under the firm name of T. H. Lindsey and T. H. McKinney, and the other yard was conducted by the Wilmette Lumber Company. Mr. McKinney was active in this very successful business until about 1917, when he sold out his lumber interests. At that time, in association with his son, Harry J. McKinney, he established a hardware business in North Chicago, and this was his chief enterprise until 1924. On January 22, 1924, having sold the hardware business, they organized the McKinney Steel & Sales Company of North Chicago. They handle everything in steel from small rods to the largest of structural steel units, and are jobbers and distributors for this product to a large number of factories, building contractors and other customers in the Waukegan district.

Mr. McKinney has been president of the Sheridan Building and Loan Association since it was organized four years ago. For one term he was alderman of North Chicago, but has steadfastly refused the repeated efforts of his friends to get him to accept nomination for the office of mayor. He is a Chapter Mason, is senior warden of North Chicago Lodge No. 1095, A. F. and A. M., is a life honorary member of the Trowel Club of the North Shore Masonic Club, and Masonry has been his hobby. He is a republican and a member of the Presbyterian Church, he and his wife being the oldest living members of the North Chicago Presbyterian Church. He was chairman of its Board of Trustees when the church was built more than thirty years ago.

Mr. McKinney married at Piper City, Illinois, April 26, 1887. Miss Anna E. McKinney, who was reared and educated there. During her married life she has constantly associated herself with the work of her church and its Ladies Aid Society, and is also a member of the North Shore Woman's Club. Her parents, William and Rebecca (Thompson) McKinney, were well known citizens of Piper City, where her father was in the lumber and hardware business until his death in 1885. Her mother died in 1886. Mr. and Mrs. McKinney became the parents of two sons, one of whom died in infancy.

Harry James McKinney, the surviving son, was educated in public schools at North Chicago and the high school at Waukegan, and after leaving school in 1908 became associated with his father in business and is the active man in the McKinney Steel & Sales Company. He married in North Chicago Laura Mae Shoup, who was a teacher in the public schools of Lake County for a number of years prior to her marriage, and is active in church and social life. Her father was Clinton C. Shoup, for many years chief of police of North Chicago. Harry J. McKinney and wife had two children, one dying in infancy and the other being Emily Mae McKinney, now attending school.

CHARLES A. BONNIWELL,* who represents an historic American family, is assistant secretary of the nationally known investment banking house of S. W. Straus & Company of New York and Chicago.

The Bonniwells (Norman-French, de Bonneville, Bonevil, etc.), had their original seat at Rouen, Normandy, where the ruins of their castle may still be seen. The progenitor of the family in England and later in America went with William the Conqueror into England, taking part in the battle of Hastings in 1066, as attested by the famous Battle Abbey Roll.

That the family quickly adapted itself to their new home is evidenced by the numerous entries in English records of the eleventh to fifteenth centuries, the family reaching the zenith of its fortunes in England when King Henry VI summoned to Parliament Baron William de Bonville, Lord of Bonville and Chuton, honoring him with the Order of The Garter. Baron de Bonville espoused the cause of the House of York in the "War of the Roses" and was made prisoner at the second battle of St. Albans and later beheaded. He was subsequently declared innocent by Act of Parliament 1, Edward IV. The Heralds Visitations gave nineteen different shields of arms of the Bonniwell family.

The ancestors of the American branch came to America very early in the Colonial period, settling in Maryland, taking an active part in the development of the new colonies, owning five thousand acres of land and five hundred slaves. William Bonniwell, the great-grandfather of the subject of this sketch, came west with his wife and children and six brothers. They stopped in Chicago in 1829, but on getting a touch of malaria moved on to Wisconsin, building their homes about twelve miles north of the site of Milwaukee and known in the old historical atlases as "Bonniwell Settlement," nearly twenty years before the state was admitted to the Union. They erected the first schoolhouse in the state, where many of the teachers rose to considerable prominence in the educational history of the state.

Evander B. Bonniwell, father of Charles A., was born at "Bonniwell Settlement" May 12, 1847. The call to arms issued by President Lincoln stirred his martial blood to its depths, and failing to get his father's consent to enlist (being only fourteen years old at the time) he ran away to Milwaukee. There he was enrolled November 12, 1861, as a private in Company I, Second Wisconsin Cavalry, to serve three years. In January, 1863, he was appointed bugler, and on December 17, 1863, re-enlisted as a veteran volunteer and was mustered out at Austin, Texas, on November 15, 1865. One of his brothers was killed in action, and his uncle, William Capes, served as foreman for Erickson in the building of the "Yankee Cheese Box," the Monitor.

After a visit home he returned east, finally settling in Philadelphia, where on February 21, 1871, he married Elizabeth Ann O'Doherty, lineal descendant of O'Dochartach, Lord and Prince of Innishowen, County Donegal, Ireland, and cousin of his Eminence the late John Cardinal McCloskey, America's first cardinal, their union being blessed with seven children. In Pennsylvania the name Bonniwell acquired great political distinction through the renomination by the democratic party of Judge Eugene C. Bonniwell for governor of the state. He was nominated for this exalted position in 1918 and again in May of 1926. Judge Bonniwell, a prominent jurist of Philadelphia, is the oldest brother of Charles A. Another brother, Captain Thomas J. Bonniwell, now a resident of Florida, served in the Spanish-American war, the Philippine insurrection and the World war. A third brother, Reverend William Raymond Bonniwell, O. P., served in the World war as a chaplain with the rank of first lieutenant.

Charles A. Bonniwell, born in Philadelphia, was educated at the Broad Street Military Academy, Philadelphia, and after graduation became associated with his father. On account of defective hearing he was refused service in the Spanish-American war. The same slight physical defect again prevented his serving his country during the World war, as his ancestors had done for hundreds of years, service being refused even after he had appealed to President Wilson. In a final supreme effort, a remarkable document in the form of an eighteen page book was addressed to President Wilson, wherein he states in part, "—I will gladly waive all rights or claims to a pension that could possibly be based on this disability—defective hearing—if so doing will enable me to get into active service." This original "Application for Military Service" is now in the Congressional Library at Washington by the authority of the War Department.

Since the government would not utilize his services in a military capacity he had to confine his efforts to serve his country to non-com-

---

* Coat of Arms—Or On a Bend Sable, Three Mullets (6) Argent.

batant activities, serving as a member of the General Committee of National Security League; American Protection League; Liberty Loans and Red Cross drives, etc.; civilian recruiting for both marines and navy, also submitting valuable suggestions to both the War Department and secretary of the treasury.

Upon retirement from active business by his father, Mr. Bonniwell came to Chicago, subsequently becoming associated in increasing responsibilities with the great financial house of S. W. Straus & Company, of which he is now assistant secretary. He married, February 23, 1908, Zita M. Welch, daughter of Richard I. and Mary A. (Hogan) Welch, her father having been a soldier in the Union army from Missouri. The six children of Mr. and Mrs. Charles A. Bonniwell are Charles A., Jr., Donald R., Adrienne E., Eloise M., John R. and Mary E.

He is a contributing author to the LaSalle Extension University; National Salesman's Training Association; special feature writer for the Chicago Herald and Examiner, as well as the International News Service on psychology and character analysis. Many of his articles on advertising and selling, as well as short stories, have appeared in some of the current magazines.

Mr. Bonniwell's ancestors have served in every war of this nation from King Phillip's war in 1633 to date. Fourteen Bonniwells from Maryland and Virginia served in the Revolutionary war, five in the War of 1812, etc. He is secretary-treasurer of the Illinois Society of the War of 1812, former secretary of the Sons of Revolution; vice deputy commander, Order of Washington; vice commander, Order of White Crane; Sons of Veterans, etc., and a descendant of Thomas Rogers, sixteenth signer of the Mayflower compact.

CHARLES O. MOLZ, M. D. Most of the qualities considered essential in the character of an able physician are present in the personality of Dr. Charles O. Molz, including liberal medical education, broad mindedness, skill, proficiency and experience. Doctor Molz stands high in the profession in his section of the state. He is an ex-president of the Southern Illinois Medical Society, and for several years was president and secretary of the Jackson County Medical Society.

His father, Matthias Molz, came from Germany in 1860 and settled in Christian County, Illinois, where he followed the trade of blacksmith. He died there in 1876. Matthias Molz married Ellen Kempf, whose family came from the vicinity of Greensburg, Indiana, to Fayette County, Illinois.

Dr. Charles O. Molz was born in Christian County, Illinois, June 2, 1872. He came to manhood with the self reliance obtained by reason of having supported himself from an early age. He attended public schools, but at the age of fifteen went to work in a drug store in the town of Pana, in the southeastern part of his native county. He was a clerk in this store three years and at the age of eighteen went on the road as a traveling salesman for a wholesale drug house, continuing that work three years. Later he entered the Missouri Medical College, now a part of Washington University at St. Louis, and during his school term he was associated with Dr. A. V. L. Brokaw, who was professor of Anatomy and Surgery. He was graduated in 1898 with the highest honors of his class. He spent one year as an interne in the St. Louis City Hospital and first engaged in practice at Bedford, Indiana, where he remained two and a half years. For two years he practiced at Pana in Christian County, and since 1904 has been a leading representative of his profession at Murphysboro. He has a well equipped office on the ground floor of the building on Chestnut Street owned by him.

Doctor Molz married Miss Margaret Shea, daughter of Patrick and Mary Shea, of St. Louis, Missouri. They have a daughter Cleopha, wife of Richard Scholz, a resident of Quincy, Illinois, and attorney for the Travelers Insurance Company.

HAROLD CHARLES GILBERT is a Kankakee manufacturer, an electrical engineer by profession, and has a record of service in the World war.

He was born at Kankakee in 1896, son of Otto and Ella (Sauerman) Gilbert, his father a native of Sweden and his mother of Kankakee. His mother is deceased and the father is now associated with the son in business.

Harold C. Gilbert attended grammar and high schools, and continued his education in the University of Chicago and in the New York Electrical School, where he completed his course in 1921.

In the meantime, in March, 1917, he had enlisted and was one of the American volunteers in the French army. He went overseas, and six months later at Paris joined the First Pursuit, Aerial Squadron. He continued in the air service until March 4, 1919, when he was discharged with the rank of lieutenant at Mineola, Long Island.

Mr. Gilbert for some time did a general brokerage business in electrical supplies. In May, 1925, he established a mill for woodworking and the manufacture of toys, located at Wall Street and the New York Central Railroad. It is an industry that is increasing Kankakee's fame among Illinois cities. Mr. Gilbert is unmarried. His home is at 655 South Evergreen Avenue. He is independent in politics and a member of the First Methodist Episcopal Church.

CAPT. JOHN W. SINDING. From the Nordic stock has come much that is great and good, and this country has today no better citizens or higher-minded men and women than those who have been born in those northern countries of the Old World, or are descended from that sturdy people whose industry, thrift and Christianity are known the world over. One of Chicago's representative business men and public-spirited citizens who belongs to this class is Capt. John W. Sinding, vice president and manager of the Tompkins-Kiel Marble Company, and president of the Norwegian Club of Chicago, whose life was for many years spent as a deep-sea captain.

Captain Sinding was born in Oslo, Norway, in 1882, and when only fourteen years old he went to sea, and in different capacities with

the sea-faring industry, went to all parts of the world and rose to the position of master mariner and captain of a steamship. About 1909, however, he retired from the sea, and coming to Chicago, engaged in the marble business in this city. He began his connection with it as a salesman of his present company, a New York concern, and has risen to be its vice president and manager in charge of the Chicago office. The Tompkins-Kiel Marble Company is one of the leading concerns in the country furnishing marble for all purposes in building and construction work.

Ever since he located here Captain Sinding has taken an active part in civic and social affairs in Chicago, participating effectively in all movements for the advancement of his adopted city. He has for several years been a zealous member of the Norwegian Club of Chicago, and is now its president. He also belongs to the Adventurers Club, the Lake Shore Athletic Club, the Swedish Club, the Illinois Golf Club and Rotary Club of Chicago.

Captain Sinding married Miss Ingeborg Catherine Arnet, and they have three children: Thomas Arnet, John Renard and Marjorie Renard. The family residence is at 1513 Sherwin Avenue, and Captain Sinding maintains his office at 414 Wrigley Building, 400 North Michigan Avenue, Chicago. Both he and his wife are enthusiastic with reference to Chicago and its great possibilities.

MARTIN H. FINNERAN has rendered good account of himself as a representative member of the bar of Cook County and is engaged in the successful practice of his profession at Calumet City, where he is president of the Board of Education, his membership in which has covered a period of a decade, as he was first elected in 1915. He had previously served twelve years as village clerk of West Hammond, and he was for two years city treasurer of Calumet City. In 1924 Mr. Finneran was elected representative of the Seventh District in the Illinois Legislature, and in this office his service has proved of characteristically loyal and efficient order. He initiated his career as a legislator when the Fifty-fourth General Assembly of the Illinois Legislature convened in January, 1925, and he was assigned to the following committees of the House of Representatives: Judiciary, civil service, farm drainage, roads and bridges, and uniform laws. Mr. Finneran gave much time and effort to championing a bill for the benefit of the smaller towns and cities of Cook County, this bill making provision that each municipality should have the right to collect special assessments up to August 1st of each year, a privilege already accorded to the city of Chicago. This measure was passed by both Houses of the Legislature, but was vetoed by the governor. Mr. Finneran has been an active and resourceful worker in connection with the councils and campaign activities of the democratic party in Cook County, and he is now a member of the party's advisory committee for this county. In a fraternal way he is affiliated with the Benevolent and Protective Order of Elks and the Loyal Order of Moose.

Mr. Finneran was born at Valley Falls, a suburb of the city of Providence, Rhode Island, in the Centennial year 1876, and he was a child at the time of the family removal to Cambridge, Massachusetts, where he was reared to the age of eight years, the family having then come to Cook County, Illinois, where its members arrived on the 4th of July, 1883. The home was established at West Hammond, which is now Calumet City, and here the subject of this review has continued to reside during the intervening years, which have been marked by large and worthy achievement on his part. After his graduation from high school in the city of Hammond Mr. Finneran continued his studies in what is now Valparaiso University, at Valparaiso, Indiana, and thereafter he continued his association with business and industrial affairs until he realized his ambition by entering the Kent College of Law, Chicago, in which institution he was graduated in June, 1920, his reception of the degree of Bachelor of Laws having been forthwith attended by his admission to the Illinois bar. Mr. Finneran has proved a resourceful trial lawyer and well fortified counselor, and in the practice of his profession he maintains an office not only in Calumet City but also an office in the Burnham Building in Chicago.

Mr. Finneran is a director of the First Trust & Savings Bank of Calumet City and also of the Calumet City Trust & Savings Bank. He is a member of the Illinois State Bar Association and the Chicago Bar Association and of the Chicago Historical Society. In 1925 he was renominated for the legislature without opposition.

Mr. Finneran married Miss Blanche S. Stevens, of Blue Island, Cook County, and they have a fine son, Clarence H.

MAUDE FRAKER JERICHO has been a resident of Kankakee for a number of years. Since the death of her husband she has built up a business service based on her knowledge of and skill in the science of electrolysis.

She was born at Rose Hill, Iowa, in 1888, daughter of Dr. Joseph Wesley and Martha Jane (Broyle) Fraker, the former a native of Chattanooga, Tennessee, and the latter of Greenville, Tennessee. Her father was a Methodist minister and is now living at Mt. Pleasant, Iowa. Mrs. Jericho attended public schools in Iowa and the Iowa Wesleyan University at Mt. Pleasant. She was married January 28, 1908, to Warren B. Jericho, who was born at Mt. Pleasant, Iowa, in 1885. His parents were Gus and Belle (Davis) Jericho, the former a native of Chicago of German parentage, and the latter a native of Henry County, Iowa. Warren B. Jericho graduated in pharmacy from Northwestern University in Chicago and for one year was manager of a drug store at Colfax, Washington, another year at Grangeville, Idaho, then a year at Mt. Pleasant, Iowa, and for three years was proprietor of a drug business at LaHarpe, Illinois. On selling out he removed to Kankakee and continued his service as a pharmacist, but aside from this he and his wife established a Kankakee Photo Finishing Company, and handled a large volume of business for amateur photographers. He died February 18, 1923.

Mrs. Jericho was graduated in August, 1922, from the Hall School of Electrolysis, and has used this scientific knowledge successfully in the treatment of superfluous hair and skin blemishes. She has her studio in the Cobb Building at Kankakee and is a member of the National Cosmeticians. Her home is at 158 N. Schuyler Avenue. She has one son, Jack Fraker, born November 12, 1908. Mrs. Jericho is a Methodist and a republican, and her husband was a member of the Phi Chi fraternity and the B. P. O. Elks.

JOHN CUYLER BAKER, vice president of the Fansteel Products Company of North Chicago, has been identified with the growth and development of that industry since 1912. Mr. Baker had the training of a technical engineer and was a teacher in mathematics until he became associated with the Fansteel Products Company.

Mr. Baker is a member of a prominent family in the vicinity of Manhattan, Illinois, where he was born June 1, 1885, son of John Cuyler and Elizabeth (Hopson) Baker, and grandson of a pioneer settler and land owner in that section, Clark Baker. The Baker family has been in New England since Colonial times. Two members of the family, Benjamin Baker and his son, were soldiers in the Revolutionary war. Clark Baker, who married Lucinda Welch, was born in New York state before the close of Washington's term as president. He was a soldier in the War of 1812. In 1846 he came out to Illinois and settled at Manhattan, and later was joined by other members of his family. He acquired extensive land in that rich agricultural section, and some of those lands are still owned by his grandchildren. John Cuyler Baker, Sr., was born at Hoosac, New York, November 10, 1842, and spent his active life as a farmer and stock man at Manhattan, where at one time he owned over a thousand acres of land. He was a breeder of blooded stock. He died in 1919. His wife, Elizabeth Hopson, was born in New York State, and died at the age of thirty-five at Manhattan in 1888. She was the mother of three children, and the two living are: John Cuyler and Helen Mary, wife of Healy Alexander, a farmer at Lockport, Illinois. Mr. and Mrs. Alexander have eight children, named Mary, Elizabeth, James, John, Margaret, Caroline, Hayes and Ruth.

John Cuyler Baker attended a private school, graduated from the Joliet High School in 1903, from Beloit College of Wisconsin in 1907, and did post-graduate work in the Massachusetts Institute of Technology and the University of Chicago, and pursued a special engineering course in the Armour Institute of Technology at Chicago. In 1908 for a few months he was a teacher in the high school at Denison, Iowa, then became head of the mathematics department in the Oak Park and River Forest Township High School, where he remained until 1911, and for one year was head of the mathematics department of the high school at Pamona, California. Returning east in June, 1912, he became purchasing agent for the Pfanstiehl Electrical Laboratory, now the Fansteel Products Company. He is now in charge of the purchasing and production departments of this industry, and in the meantime has become vice president and a director of the company. He is also a director of the Potter Manufacturing Company of North Chicago, manufacturers of electrical condensers.

Since coming to Lake County Mr. Baker has had his home at Lake Bluff and for several years was a member of the Village Board. He is a member of the Beta Theta Pi college fraternity, the Glen Flora Country Club, the Episcopal Church and in politics is an independent voter.

He married, June 17, 1910, at Chicago, Miss Helen Cody, who was educated in grammar and high schools in Chicago and with the class of 1912 at the University of Chicago. Mrs. Baker is much interested in literary organizations and is a member of the Woman's Club of Lake Bluff and the Lake Bluff School Board and Library Board. Her parents are Arthur B. and Grace (Goodrich) Cody, of Chicago, her father being manager of the real estate department of the Chicago Trust Company and president of the Cody Trust Company. He is a member of the Cody Clan, and is a third cousin of the famous scout and frontiersman, the late Buffalo Bill Cody. Mr. and Mrs. Baker have two children, John Cuyler Baker III, and Philomela Baker, and one adopted son, Albert Grover Baker. John Cuyler Baker III, is a member of the class of 1929 in the Highland Park, Deerfield Shields High School, and Philomela is attending grammar school. Albert Grover Baker is a member of the high school class of 1927.

JOSEPH A. JADRICH is a resident of North Chicago, a man with many useful and important relationships with the community, being a newspaper editor and real estate operator. He has shown a most commendable attitude in assisting all worthy projects in his community.

Mr. Jadrich was born at Joliet, Illinois, August 15, 1892, son of Joseph and Catherine (Pacunka) Jadrich. His father was a native of Jugo Slavia, was reared and educated there, and in 1888, on coming to America, settled at Joliet, where he lived for some years, and in 1898 moved to Lake County, Illinois, where he was an employe of the American Steel & Wire Company. Later he became a farmer and teamster and is now living retired at North Chicago. He married at Joliet Catherine Pacunka, and they were the parents of the following children: Francis Spillman, who died in 1926; Joseph A.; Mrs. Mary Rogan, of Kenosha; Mrs. Anna Kupski, of North Chicago; Mrs. Catherine Flament, of Waukegan; Helen, Arthur and Elmer.

Joseph A. Jadrich was about six years old when the family moved to Lake County and he attended public schools there, including the Waukegan High School with the class of 1912. In 1919, after his army experience during the World war, Mr. Jadrich graduated from the Kent College of Law at Chicago, was admitted to the Illinois bar that year and in 1920 opened his law office in North Chicago. He devotes most of his time to newspaper and real estate work. His real estate business, comprising sales of his personal property and also a general brokerage business, has been markedly successful during the past year. Mr. Jadrich owns the North Chicago Journal, a weekly publication, and devotes part of his time to its editorial management. He acted as city attorney of North Chicago from 1921 to 1923, and was secretary of the zoning commission. He was one of the organizers of the Sharvin American Legion Post.

In June, 1918, he joined the colors with the Forty-sixth Regiment, one of the regular infantry regiments, and was in training at Camp Sheridan, Alabama, and later at Camp Taylor, Kentucky. When the armistice was signed he was a victim of influenza in the Base Hospital at Camp Taylor. He received his honorable discharge there December 6, 1918, and after returning to North Chicago completed his law course.

Mr. Jadrich is affiliated with the B. P. O. Elks, Loyal Order of Moose, Knights of Columbus, American Legion, Association of Commerce of North Chicago, the Waukegan-North Chicago Chamber of Commerce. He is a republican and a Catholic.

Mr. Jadrich married, November 3, 1920, Mrs. Josephine Stavorski of Chesterton, Indiana, where she was reared and educated. She has become well known socially in North Chicago and Waukegan, being a member of the Woman's Club and the American Legion Auxiliary. Mrs. Jadrich is a daughter of Joseph and Agnes Stachowiak, who came from Germany and settled near Chesterton, Indiana, in 1870, and are still living in that vicinity, substantial farmers of northern Indiana. Mrs. Jadrich's first husband was Paul Stavorski, of Joliet, a cousin of Mr. Jadrich. He died during the influenza epidemic in 1918, leaving one son, Raymond, who has been reared and educated by Mr. and Mrs. Jadrich. Mr. and Mrs. Jadrich have two children of their own, Sylvia and Clarence.

DONALD RANDALL RICHBERG, who has practiced law at Chicago since 1904, has become a prominent figure in the professional and literary life of the city. Much of his work has brought him in contact with some of the large national problems of business and politics.

He was born at Knoxville, Tennessee, July 10, 1881, son of John Carl and Eloise Olivia (Randall) Richberg. Eloise Olivia Richberg was born November 12, 1849, in Woodstock, Vermont. Her father was Dr. Nathaniel Randall and her mother, Dr. Mirenda Briggs Randall. Doctor Richberg's mother was reputed to be the third woman physician in the United States, having graduated with special honors from Penn College of Medicine, Philadelphia, in 1856, with the degree of M. D. Eloise O. Richberg graduated from Woodstock High School at the age of fourteen, being given her teacher's diploma on condition that she would not teach until seventeen years old. She taught in Vermont district schools after 1866 until she came to Chicago early in the '70s, and taught in the Chicago public schools, becoming eventually principal of the Clark School.

When Mrs. Richberg was fifty-five years old she was able to realize a life long intention of studying medicine and becoming a practicing physician, following in the footsteps of her mother and father. She entered Hering Medical College in 1904 and received the degree of M. D. in 1908 and subsequently lectured on dietetics and hygiene and became professor of embryology and physiology in the same institution. She also obtained the degree of Doctor of Orthopedic Surgery. She began and continued in active general practice, specializing in chronic diseases, for sixteen years, until her death October 7, 1924. She was the author of many books, including fiction, poetry and a brochure on diet entitled "Eat, Drink and Live Long." She also contributed extensively to medical and philosophical magazines. She was a member of the American Institute of Homœopathy, Illinois Homœopathic Medical Society of Chicago, and at the time of her death was vice-president of the International Hahnemannian Association. She was also a member of the Daughters of the American Revolution. She was a forceful and trained public speaker, having taught elocution for many years, and at various periods was quite prominent in activities in women's clubs in Chicago.

John Carl Richberg, lawyer, was born in Romrod, Germany, a son of Louis and Katharina (Mesz) Richberg. He was educated in Knox College, Galesburg, Illinois, and in the United States Naval Academy (LL. D. Knox College, 1909). He practiced law at Chicago many years, until retiring from practice three years before his death which occurred in 1918. He was a member of the Board of Education, Chicago, for three terms, president two terms, 1874-76 and 1879-81. His administration was notable for placing the salaries of women teachers on a par with those of men; and eliminating bible reading in the schools. He was president of the Illinois Commission on Uniform State Laws; member of the Board of Visitors to United States Naval Academy, 1896, member of Grand Army of the Republic, and commander of Farragut Naval Veterans' Association.

Donald R. Richberg attended the University of Chicago, graduating with the class of 1901 (with the degree of A. B. In 1904 he received the degree of LL. B. from Harvard Law School, and in the same year began the work of his profession at Chicago. Mr. Richberg has always been a scholar and thinker in his profession. He was active in the progressive party during its existence, and was chairman of the resolutions committee of the National Progressive Convention July 4, 1924. In 1922 he served as chief counsel for the Railway Unions in the government injunction suit; and drafted the Railway Labor Act which became federal law May 20, 1926. In 1923 he was appointed general counsel for the National Conference on valuation of railroads. Since 1915 has been special counsel for the city of Chicago in the gas litigation. In Michaelson vs. United States he sustained in the Supreme Court of the United States the right of trial by jury in contempt cases.

Mr. Richberg was special assistant state's attorney of Cook County from 1913 to 1915, republican nominee for Circuit Court in 1915 and master in chancery of the Circuit Court of Cook County from 1916 to 1919. He served as director of the National Legislative Reference Bureau, progressive party, and is a member of the Chicago, Illinois State and American Bar Associations, the Chicago Law Club, is a Phi Gamma Delta, and belongs to the Harvard Club of New York, the Cosmos and Racquet Clubs of Washington and the University, Olympia Fields, Quadrangle Clubs of Chicago.

Mr. Richberg has contributed a number of articles on current problems to magazines and reviews, and his published books are: "The Shadow Men," published in 1911; "In The Dark," 1912; "Who Wins in November, 1916;" and "A Man of Purpose," 1922. He married, December 24, 1924, Florence Weed, of Lansing, Michigan, a daughter of Herbert M. Weed, of that city. They are the parents of one daughter, Eloise, born August 25, 1926.

WILLIAM D. WHYTE, real estate and insurance, has been one of the prominent men in that business at Waukegan for a number of years. Waukegan has been his home practically all his life, and he is member of one of the notable families attracted here by the industrial opportunities. He is one of the eleven children of the late George and Isabelle Primrose Whyte.

The late George Whyte was born in Fifeshire, Scotland, May 3, 1844, in the same town as Andrew Carnegie, and Mr. George Whyte died at Waukegan August 12, 1919, just a day after the death of the great iron master and philanthropist. George Whyte became an engineer by trade. He married in Scotland Isabelle Primrose. In 1883 they brought their family to America and located in Chicago, where they had their home for about ten years. George Whyte at Chicago was an engineer with the Frazier Chalmers Company, now the Allis Chalmers Company. About 1891 he became chief engineer in the Washburn-Moon Steel and Wire Mills at Waukegan, now the plant of the American Steel & Wire Company. He remained at his duties in the power plant until he retired in 1908, and later was put on the pension roll of the steel company. He enjoyed the high respect and esteem of his community at Waukegan and it was well said that in the "business and professional world the sons of George Whyte have made their way. No family of boys in this community have earned a better place in the esteem of the public than those who called this man father." His widow, who survived him until 1922, was always very active in church work and a devoted home maker. She had the typical love of Scotch people for her early surroundings, and among many bits of verse which she composed, one is entitled Heathery Hill Road, of which the following lines are characteristic:

"I am faur frae Bonnie Scotland,
   The land I love sae well,
   Where the thistle and the Heather wave,
   Beside the sweet blue bell,
   But the dearest to my memory,
   In that land o' mist and rock,
   Is whaur I pu'd the rasps and brummels
   Doon Heathery Hill Road."

Eleven sons and daughters of George Whyte are still living, a brief record of them being as follows: George, head of the George Whyte Rope Manufacturing Company of Kenosha, Wisconsin, married Anna Jessel, of Chicago, and has a son, Jessel Stewart Whyte; Prof. James Whyte, member of the faculty of Bucknell College at Lewisburg, Pennsylvania, is married and has two children, Lucy Primrose and James; Mary is the widow of Robert Drysdale, who was Chicago representative of the MacWhyte Rope Company of Kenosha, and died in 1926, the two surviving children being George W. and Isabelle. Maude, another daughter, died in 1925; Ann married Charles Simpson, now with the Whyte Rope Company at Kenosha, and their children are Isabelle, Gladys, Eugene, Jessie, Harriet, Cecelia, Margaret and Mary; John, secretary of the O. C. Keckley Company of Chicago and a resident of Waukegan, married Minerva Thompson, of Waukegan, and has three children, Margaret, George and John Stewart; Charles, head of the Whyte Furniture Company of Waukegan, married Minnie Tompkins, their two children being Charles and Jessie; Isabelle is the wife of Oliver S. Thompson, superintendent of the high school at Compton, California, and they have four children, named Marjorie, Clare, Ruth and Virginia; Margaret married Lawrence Doolittle, present sheriff of Lake County, and has two children, Donald and Charlotte; William D. Whyte is next in age of this family; Robert is superintendent of the MacWhyte Rope Company of Kenosha, and he and his wife have five children, named Mary, Robert, Jean, Donald and George; Harry is with the Martin Teaming Company of Chicago and a resident of Waukegan, and he married Belle Pillifant.

William D. Whyte, the Waukegan real estate man, was born in Chicago, October 7, 1883, and began his education in the public schools of that city, continuing in the schools of Waukegan. After high school he completed a course in the Bryant and Stratton Business College in 1904, and left college to become timekeeper in the plant of the American Steel & Wire Company at Waukegan. He was with that company four years, then, in 1908, went with the Western Coal & Dock Company, and beginning in 1910 spent seven years with Cyclone Fence Company and the Dearborn Chemical Company of Chicago. Mr. Whyte in 1917 became manager of the Genesee Hotel of Waukegan, and conducted that popular hostelry five years. He has been in the real estate business since 1922, and his knowledge of conditions and energetic service have made him remarkably successful. He handles acreage and industrial property, also residential, and in the insurance business represents the Eagle Star Insurance Company and the British Dominion Insurance Company.

Mr. Whyte is a baseball fan and for several years was a semi-professional player with the Chicago Marquettes. He is a republican and a Methodist. He married at Waukegan, June 17, 1908, Miss Lydia Gertrude Dahringer. She grew up in Michigan, attending grammar and high schools at Ludington, and also at Sheboygan, Wisconsin, and Waukegan, Illinois. She is a member of the Methodist Church and is active in club and social life. Her parents were Henry W. and Anna M.

(Robison) Dahringer, who for a number of years lived at Lowellville, Ohio, later at Ludington, Michigan, where her father was superintendent of a salt company, and in 1905 the family moved to Waukegan, where her father has since been superintendent of the Ruggles & Rademacher Salt Company. Mrs. Whyte is a sister of Homer Dahringer, in whose honor was named the Homer Dahringer Post of the American Legion at Waukegan. Homer Dahringer was a graduate of the University of Illinois, a civil engineer by training and early profession, went into the Aviation Corps soon after America became involved in the World war, and as a first lieutenant was killed during the St. Mihiel drive, September 18, 1918. Mr. and Mrs. Whyte have had four children: Dorothy Marie, member of the class of 1927 in the Waukegan High School; Russell James, a high school freshman; and Harry Walston. Another boy, William Dahry, died in infancy during 1919.

JOHN CALVIN SCOTT was a resident of Illinois from his youth until the time of his death, was a member of one of the honored pioneer families of this state, became a prominent member of the Illinois bar, and his life was one of signal worthiness, every phase of his career having been marked by fine ideals and loyal personal stewardship. He gave twenty-eight years of effective service as attorney for the American Book Company in Illinois and Indiana, and he was one of the influential and highly honored citizens of Jonesboro, Union County, at the time of his death, which occurred February 22, 1902.

Mr. Scott was born in Pittsburgh, Pennsylvania, August 29, 1835, and was a son of Dr. R. K. and Matilda (McElhinny) Scott. Mrs. Mary A. Fish, a sister of the subject of this memoir, and a resident of San Francisco, California, has prepared a most interesting record concerning the family ancestral history, and it is gratifying to the publishers of this work to be able to reproduce, with but slight change in statement, this valuable record, which touches in a prominent way the earlier history of Illinois. The text of Mrs. Fish's article is substantially as follows:

"Dr. R. K. Scott was born in Butler County, Pennsylvania, in the year 1805, and was of Scotch and English parentage. His paternal grandfather was a Scotch highlander and became a successful ship carpenter and contractor. This sterling Scotch ancestor assumed a contract to build a ship for an English nobleman, and the young artisan and a daughter of the nobleman fell deeply in love with each other. The father of the young woman would not consent to her becoming the wife of any man except one of title, but love is ever a law unto itself, and the young folk contrived to make their way to the city of Belfast, where their marriage was solemnized and where their son, father of Dr. R. K. Scott, was born, this son having eventually become a pioneer settler in Pennsylvania. Matilda (McElhinny) Scott was born in Pittsburgh, Pennsylvania, in 1811, and her father was in training for service as a soldier in the War of 1812 when he contracted an illness that terminated in his death. His widow then took her three small children to the home of her parents, who resided on a well improved farm twelve miles distant from Pittsburgh and near the village of Library. Mrs. McIlhinny's father, Rev. David Phillips, was a Baptist clergyman, and he was much gratified to receive into his farmstead home his widowed daughter and her children. Mrs. McIlhinny assumed charge of the domestic economics of her father's home, and there reared her children. Mr. Phillips and his wife were growing old and all of their children were married and departed from the parental roof at the time when Mrs. McIlhinny returned, with her children, to the old home. The father of Rev. David Phillips had served as a patriot soldier in the War of the Revolution, in which he was a captain in the army of General George Washington, his home at the time having been near Philadelphia, Pennsylvania, and it is worthy of special mention that his two brothers were respectively first and second lieutenants in the company of which he was the captain, so that all of the commissioned officers of the company were the three brothers. Rev. David Phillips was the first Baptist clergyman to establish residence west of the Alleghany Mountains, and he bought a large tract of land at the low prices then asked by the government, so that he was able to provide most of his sons with farm homes in the same locality. He built a little church of log construction, later replaced this with a frame building, and finally a substantial brick edifice was erected. His earnest pastoral service was given in each of these three pioneer church buildings. Annual reunions are now held by representatives of this Phillips family, and the descendants number more than 5,000. John C. Scott's sister, Mrs. Mary A. Fish, of San Francisco, California, wrote to a Baptist minister in Pittsburgh relative to his relationship to Rev. David Phillips, and he promptly responded with the statement that Rev. David Phillips was his great-great-grandfather. In Wales the ancestral line of the Phillips family is traced back to the eleventh century, and the family line was the same as that of the ruling family of England. The present-day Baptist clergyman in Pittsburg gave the following statement in his letter to Mrs. Fish: 'None of the many descendants has ever been in prison or the poorhouse; they are a frugal and industrious people.'

"From Pennsylvania Dr. R. K. Scott moved to Ohio, and in the latter state he resided in the city of Cincinnati until 1854, when he came with his family to Illinois and established his residence in Champaign County, where he remained until 1859. In the Circuit Court of that district Abraham Lincoln was accustomed to appear and plead cases each spring and autumn term, and about 1857 suit was brought in this court against Doctor Scott in connection with some intricacies in land titles. Doctor Scott stated that he would retain Lincoln in the handling of his cause, as some other lawyers would not take the case, owing to their lack of understanding of its intricacies. On the first day of the court session Doctor Scott made an early appearance, in order to be sure of obtaining the services of Lincoln. Only a few were in the court room, but near the front Doctor Scott observed Lincoln sitting beside the man who had brought the suit against the Doctor. The two were in close conversation, and the Doctor took a seat back of them. After some time had passed, Lincoln straightened himself up and said: 'No, sir, I can not take your case. It is an unjust suit, and I can not plead an unjust suit.' The defendant could have either a jury or permit the judge to make the decision. Judge David Davis, of Danville, was presiding, and was a wise and just man, as the history of Illinois jurisprudence amply testified. In behalf of the cause of Doctor Scott, Lincoln did not speak more than twenty minutes, but so clear was his exposition that Doctor Scott felt assured of a favorable decision. Judge Davis promptly decided the case in favor of Doctor Scott, who later wrote an article concerning the same, this contribution having been published in St. Louis papers at the time of the presidential campaign of 1860, when Lincoln was the republican candidate for the presidency of the United States. In the meanwhile Doctor Scott had removed with his family to Salem, Marion County, and there he organized parades and was otherwise active and influential in the national campaign of that year.

"Doctor Scott's first son, John Calvin Scott, was at this time attending college at Jacksonville, and while in Springfield waiting for a train to Salem, he decided to make a call upon Abraham Lincoln. The two sat down together and had a mutually pleasing conversation and visit, Young Scott having thereafter given an effective stumping campaign in support of Lincoln. After his election to the presidency Lincoln appointed John C. Scott postmaster at Salem."

As intimated in the foregoing review, John C. Scott received the advantages of Illinois College at Jacksonville, and he became one of the successful and influential members of the Illinois bar, he having been for nearly thirty years, as previously noted, attorney for the great American Book Company. He served as county superintendent of the public schools of Richland County, and in the Civil war period he served as provost marshal under General Grant. He eventually aligned himself in the ranks of the democratic party, he was affiliated with the Masonic fraternity, and his religious faith was that of the Church of the New Jerusalem, of which his widow is a devoted member, she having been virtually an invalid since 1901.

On the 8th of December, 1894, was solemnized the marriage of Mr. Scott and Miss Mary A. Sowers, of Jonesboro, she having been born in the fine old homestead that is her present place of residence at Jonesboro, December 10, 1851, being a daughter of David and Mary (Cruse) Sowers. David Sowers was born in Davidson County, North Carolina, and his wife was born near Dongola, Union County, Illinois, the date of the former's birth having been October 11, 1820, and that of the latter April 1, 1829; their marriage was celebrated September 23, 1849. David Sowers came to Illinois in an early day, and as a young man he served as guide or pilot for a woman and her three daughters who, with three slaves, were making their way from North Carolina to Fort Smith, Arkansas. He made this trip successfully, and was equipped with a gun to protect his charges if it became necessary. In 1846 he returned with his horse to Jonesboro, Illinois, and in this county his marriage occurred about three years later. He purchased a farm adjacent to Jonesboro, and to the same he removed on the day that marked the assassination of President Lincoln. In a grove near his home he had the privilege of listening to one of the now historic series of debates by Lincoln and Douglas, at the time when these two great Illinois citizens were candidates respectively on the republican and democratic tickets for the presidency of the United States. Mr. Sowers brought his farm of eighty-nine acres under effective cultivation and on this fine old homestead he and his wife passed the remainder of their lives, he having been called to eternal rest November 15, 1910, and his widow having passed away November 13, 1912. Of their children the first son, Walter Willard, died in infancy; Mary A., widow of the subject of this memoir, was the next in order of birth, and she resides on the old homestead of her parents, a place endeared to her by gracious and hallowed memories of the past; Sarah Jane, the younger daughter, is the wife of John W. Grear, of West Frankfort, Franklin County, Illinois; and James C. remains with his widowed sister in the old homestead. Mr. and Mrs. Scott had no children.

John C. Scott was a man whose life was guided and governed by the highest principles of integrity and honor, and he well upheld the prestige of a family name that has been long and worthily associated with the annals of American history. Mrs. Scott, a woman of culture and most gracious personality, was graduated from the Southern Illinois Normal School as a member of the class of 1881, and she gave many years of effective service as a popular teacher in the public schools of Illinois, her pedagogic activities having continued from 1868 until her marriage, in 1894. It may be noted that the father of Mrs. Scott was one of the first carriage and wagon makers in this part of Illinois, and that a wagon made by him was used in completing the long overland trip from this state to California in the early '50s, the vehicle not having lost a bolt or required any repairing on the entire journey.

DAVID L. JASINSKY is an engineer by training and profession and since leaving technical college his experience has been with the Public Service Company of Northern Illinois, being now superintendent of the plant at Waukegan. He is one of the popular and esteemed citizens of Waukegan.

Mr. Jasinsky was born at Bellefontaine, Ohio, December 30, 1889. His people have been in that section of Western Ohio since earliest pioneer times. His great-grandfather, John Jasinsky, was a Philadelphian, and about the year 1800 moved to Ohio and homesteaded and acquired by purchase many hundreds of acres in and around the pleasant City of Bellefontaine. He developed and carried on a large farm, and eventually divided his extensive land holdings among his three sons, William, George and John.

The grandfather of David L. Jasinsky was William Jasinsky, a native of Philadelphia, and was a small child when taken to Ohio. He gave his life to farming, and lived out his life in the vicinity of Bellefontaine. He married Julia M. Rudey.

The father of David L. Jasinsky is Gideon Jasinsky, who married Effie Grabiel. Both were born and reared at Bellefontaine, completed their educations in high school there, and Gideon Jasinsky for many years was proprietor of a buggy, implement and blacksmith shop, and later operated a garage and conducted an automobile sales business at Bellefontaine. Since 1924 he has been retired. He and his wife had five children: David L.; Guy G., Fred, who now continues the Bellefontaine Automobile Company; Gail, a farmer; and Muriel, wife of Albert Zoz, proprietor of the Logan County Lumber Company at Bellefontaine. Mr. and Mrs. Zoz have two children, Elizabeth and Dorothy.

David L. Jasinsky attended the grade and high schools of Bellefontaine, completing his high school course in 1908. He spent four years in Ohio State University as a student of mechanical and electrical engineering, graduating in 1912. Shortly after leaving college Mr. Jasinsky came to Illinois and has been continuously in the employ of the Public Service Company of Northern Illinois. He was fuel engineer at the Blue Island station of this company from 1912 to 1916, was then assistant engineer in charge of the Blue Island station from 1916 to 1922, and in 1922 was promoted to superintendent of Station 1 and Station 6 at Waukegan. This is the largest station operated by the corporation and also is regarded as the most efficient station in the Chicago district.

Mr. Jasinsky is a member of the Masonic order, the Western Society of Engineers, the Masonic Engineers, the Sigma Pi college fraternity, is a republican and a Presbyterian.

He married at Blue Island, Illinois, March 22, 1913, Miss Emily Daniels, who graduated from the Blue Island High School in 1910. She is a daughter of Charles Daniels, who was born and reared in Chicago and is now superintendent of the two plants of the Illinois Brick Company at Blue Island.

HARMEDOIS A. LANGLOIS is a retired business man of Kankakee and most of his life has been spent in Kankakee County, where he grew up on a farm and where for many years he was identified with agriculture as a farmer or land owner.

Mr. Langlois was born in Manteno Township, Kankakee County, February 12, 1861, son of Napoleon and Zilia E. (Longtin) Langlois. His parents were both born in Ontario, Canada, and all his grandparents were likewise natives of Canada, of French ancestry. His grandparents were Antoine and Mary (Boudreau) Langlois, and Peter and Mary (Delude) Longtin. The Langlois family settled at Bourbonnais, Illinois, in 1846, and the Longtin family, in 1847, both becoming pioneer farmers and land owners in that section. Napoleon Langlois after his marriage lived for a time in Manteno, and was a successful farmer and served as highway commissioner. He died July 7, 1890, and his widow, in 1895.

One of ten children, Harmedois A. Langlois grew up on a farm, was educated in district schools, and followed farming. For two years he was in the saloon business at Manteno, and for one year operated a milk route in Chicago. On the death of his mother he was appointed executor of the estate, and married and lived in Manteno two years. After the estate was settled he took possession of his inheritance of 125 acres, and on this land he built a house and engaged in practical farming for six years. Leaving the farm, he returned to Chicago, where he was in the saloon business a year and a half, then at Bradley, in Kankakee County, one year, and two years at Kankakee. For fifteen years he handled the district agency for the Blatz Brewing Company, selling and distributing the product over a territory for a radius of fifty miles around Kankakee. Since giving up this business he has lived retired. He owns a residence in Bradley, and his home in Kankakee is a modern house at 309 North Greenwood Avenue. He still owns his farm, which is operated by a tenant.

Mr. Langlois married, February 5, 1890, Miss Lydia Dubois, a native of Kankakee, daughter of Louis and Zoa (Brouillette) Dubois, natives of Ontario, Canada, where they were married. Her parents with three children in 1868 came to Kankakee and subsequently bought land in Iroquois County, Illinois, and spent their last years at St. Ann, where her father died September 25, 1919, at the age of eighty-three. Her mother died in the fall of 1872, and her father's second wife was Selma Gagnon, a native of Quebec, Canada. Mr. Langlois' children were: Harvey Louis, born January 15, 1891, a well known physician at Kankakee, who married May Quinlan, of Pesotum, Illinois; and Elroy Nelson, born October 23, 1892, who was a musician with the Marine Corps, and died of influenza at Hampton Roads, Virginia, October 18, 1918, and was buried at Kankakee. Mr. Langlois and family are members of the St. Rose Catholic Church. He is a democrat and has served as judge of elections.

REV. EDWARD FRANCIS RICE, pastor of the parish of Our Lady of Peace, grew up in Chicago and has been laboring in the priesthood for twenty-five years. He was a chaplain with the Expeditionary Forces overseas.

He was born at Mitchellstown, County Cork, Ireland, November 25, 1875, son of Cornelius and Mary (Brown) Rice, both natives of County Cork. His parents were married in February, 1865, and they had a family of seven sons and two daughters, Edward F. being the sixth child. The latter was five years of age when his parents settled in Chicago. He attended St. Pius parochial school in that city, also St. Ignatius College and completed his seminary and classical education in Niagara University, New York. He was ordained at Chicago May 24, 1902, by Bishop Peter J. Muldoon.

His first service after ordination was as assistant pastor to Rev. E. A. Kelly, pastor of

St. Cecelia Church. Father Kelly with some of the prominent laymen of Chicago formed the Associated Catholic Charities, under the direction of Cardinal Mundelein. He was then transferred to the Church of the Nativity as assistant pastor, and in the fall of 1917 was appointed president and spiritual director of the St. Vincent De Paul Society for the state of Illinois.

Having previously served as chaplain for the Seventh Regiment of the Illinois National Guard, he volunteered soon after America entered the World war and was appointed a chaplain in the National army, being assigned duty as chaplain of the One Hundred and Twenty-second Field Artillery in the Thirty-third Division, under Col. Milton J. Foreman. He was with his command at Camp Logan in Texas and overseas during 1918, remaining until after the armistice. He returned in May, 1919, and in September of the same year was appointed pastor of the new parish of Our Lady of Peace on East Seventy-ninth Street in Chicago. He has carried out the organization plans and has a prosperous congregation with a new church and school erected in 1925. During the Eucharistic Congress he was south side chairman of the Entertainment and Reception Committee. He took care of the information bureaus at all the railway terminals and at the large hotels. He also had charge of the civic reception to the Apostolic Delegate at the Coliseum on Friday, June 18, 1926.

HAROLD J. TALLETT is one of the active young leaders in the commercial life of North Chicago, Lake County. He was overseas during the World war. He has had a long experience in the building industry, is now head of a prominent real estate firm and also holds office as a police court judge at North Chicago.

He was born in Chicago, Illinois, April 23, 1895. His father was named Corcoran, but Mr. Tallett took the name of his stepfather. His parents were James and Catherine (Donnevan) Corcoran. The Corcorans have been a prominent family in the east, and in honor of one of them is named the famous Corcoran Art Gallery at Washington. They were also related to the Carey family of Pennsylvania. James Corcoran was born in Shamokin, Pennsylvania, attended public schools in that state and about 1885 located in Chicago, where he was connected with one of the industrial plants, being sales manager at the time of his death in 1898. His wife, Catherine Donnevan, was born and reared at Grand Mound, Iowa, and is now a resident of North Chicago, being active in church work. Her parents, Mr. and Mrs. James Donnevan, were natives of Ireland and were early settlers at Grand Mound, Iowa, where her father followed farming until the Civil war. He joined the Union army, and was in many battles, including Vicksburg, where he was severely wounded and died as a result of the wounds two years after the war. Mrs. James Corcoran in 1900 was married at North Chicago to Mr. John Tallett, who was connected with the Chicago Hardware Foundry Company until his death on May 21, 1916.

Harold J. Tallett attended public school at North Chicago, graduating from the Waukegan High School in 1915. For six months he was a student in Lake Forest College, but abandoned his college course to take employment with the National Kellastone Company of Waukegan.

Mr. Tallett in 1918 enlisted in the Thirty-eighth Division, being a member of the supply train. On going overseas he was a passenger on the Adriatic, a troop ship that when ten hours out of Liverpool was torpedoed, but was able to continue the voyage unassisted to Liverpool. Mr. Tallett was with his command overseas until after the armistice and was honorably discharged at Camp Grant in June, 1919. He then resumed work with the Kellastone Company at Waukegan, and this brought him an extensive experience in building construction. In August, 1925, he resigned his position as superintendent to engage in the real estate business. He and W. E. Janson opened their real estate office in North Chicago February 22, 1926. The firm of Tallett & Janson is one of the most energetic sales organizations in the real estate field in Lake County, and the first year their business aggregated a value of over $500,000. Mr. Tallett has had several years of experience in real estate management and sales. For several years in connection with his other work he attended law classes in the Kent College of Law of Chicago and was graduated in 1926, so that he is now a qualified attorney. Mr. Tallett is a director and secretary of the Sheridan Road Building & Loan Association. He is justice of the peace of Shields Township, including Lake Bluff, Lake Forest and part of North Chicago, and holds court as a police judge in North Chicago. He is a republican in politics, is a member of the Knights of Columbus, B. P. O. Elks, American Legion, and is a Catholic.

He married in North Chicago, June 23, 1920, Miss Irma Ruth Dickson, who was born at Fort Wayne, Indiana, and attended school there and high school at Waukegan, being a member of the class of 1919. She is active in the American Legion Auxiliary and in social and club life. Her parents, John and Eva (Seymour) Dickson, lived in Fort Wayne for many years and later moved to North Chicago, where her father is superintendent of the Thomas E. Wilson estate. Mr. and Mrs. Tallett have one son, John Harold.

WALTER A. HOMRICH, assistant cashier of the First State & Savings Bank of Galena, was born in that city, and was one of the young men who left business to join the colors at the time of the World war and saw active service overseas in the culminating campaigns of the great war.

Lieutenant Homrich was born at Galena February 12, 1888, son of Louis and Della (Charter) Homrich. His grandparents, Anton and Dorothy Homrich, came from Germany to America about 1835 and were among the early settlers of Jo Daviess County. Louis Homrich was born in Galena, Illinois, and has been a substantial business man and citizen of Galena for many years. He was educated in public schools and the State Normal School, and soon after leaving school entered the monument business. He was connected with

that business at Galena until he retired in 1924. He served two different terms as sheriff of the county, was an alderman for one term, and in many other ways has enjoyed the confidence and trust of his fellow citizens. He is now chairman of the Jo Daviess County Democratic Central Committee. He is a charter member of the Lodge of Elks and is affiliated with the Knights of Pythias and Woodmen of the World. His wife, Della (Charter) Homrich, who died in 1910, was born and reared near Warren, Illinois, attending public schools there. Her father, Charles Charter, was a bridge carpenter and contractor, and lived in the vicinity of Warren, where among other work he erected many wind mills.

Walter A. Homrich was educated in the public schools of Galena, and after high school attended the Brown Business College at Rockford. In 1908 he began working for his father in the monument business, in what was then known as the Homrich Monument Works. Since his father retired this has been the Vincent Monument Works. In 1913 Mr. Homrich entered the service of the newly organized First State & Savings Bank as bookkeeper, and from bookkeeper was promoted to assistant cashier in 1916.

This office he resigned when America entered the World war, and on August 27, 1917, he began training in the Second Officers' Training School at Fort Sheridan, Illinois. He was commissioned a first lieutenant of infantry and from December 14, 1917, to April 15, 1918, was attached to Company L, Three Hundred and Thirty-third Infantry, Eighty-fourth Division; was assigned to Fourth Company, First Replacement Regiment at Camp Gordon, Georgia, April 15, 1918, to July, 1918; left Camp Gordon in command of Fourth Company with the July Automatic Replacement Draft and arrived at the American camp, St. Aignan, France, August 15, 1918, after passing through England. He helped train replacement troops until October 10, and was assigned to the Seventy-seventh Division, then fighting in the Argonne Forest, and was in command of Company B of the Three Hundred and Eighth Infantry. His company at that time had only a total strength of sixty, but received seventy replacement troops the next day. This company was one of the so-called "Whitley's Lost Battalion," which was surrounded by Huns for five days, October 5 to 9th, during which they received no food. None of the original officers were with the company at the time, a sergeant and corporal being the highest in rank. Lieutenant Homrich was at the battle front from the time he joined the Seventy-seventh Division until the signing of the armistice. He took part in the advance through and the capture of St. Juvan, Oaches, Stonne, Harricourt, Raucourt and clear up to the gates of Sedan.

Lieutenant Homrich was honorably discharged May 10, 1919, and soon afterward resumed his position as assistant cashier of the First State & Savings Bank. In 1921 he was elected city treasurer of Galena, serving until 1923, and since 1925 has again held that position. He is a Knight Templar Mason, and was exalted ruler of the local lodge of Elks when he entered the army. He also belongs to the Eagles, American Legion, Kiwanis Club, Galena Golf Club, is a democrat in politics, belongs to the First Presbyterian Church, and for over ten years has been treasurer of School Township 28, Range 1 West.

AMBROSE WYRICK, concert and operatic singer, president of the Wyrick Studios, Inc., School of Music and Drama, at Chicago, is a young man who has opened many doors into experience, the works and the delights of the world about him, and in reaching a position of solid fame and achievements in the musical world has not sacrificed the interests that comprise a well balanced career. Mr. Wyrick has enjoyed a many sided contact with his environment, and his many friends appreciate his interest in business, politics, sports and other matters, as well as his perfect artistry.

His musical talents were discovered early, while living in a rural community in Michigan. He was born at Greenville in that state, February 11, 1891, son of Michael and Elizabeth (Van Horn) Wyrick. After attending public schools he took up his advanced musical education at Chicago under Herman DeVries during 1907-09. From 1909 to 1911 he was under the great master David Bispham of New York City. He enjoyed great favor as a pupil of the eminent Jean de Reszke in Paris in 1913. In his earlier years he had attracted attention while a singer in churches at Grand Rapids, Michigan. After completing his European training he made a tour of the world, including South Africa, singing in concert in fifty-six countries. This tour extended from 1911 to 1914. The managers of his tour billed him as "the silver-toned tenor." He appeared at Albert Hall in London, Eng., (10,500 Seats), and at St. Andrews Hall, Glasgow, Scotland (4,500 seats). Mr. Wyrick has sung before a total of seven million paid admissions during his career. In 1913 the Lord Mayor of Glasgow and members of his cabinet gave this singer a token of their appreciation in a gold watch charm with the Scotch Thistle and his initials on one side. Engraved on the back was the tribute "To Ambrose Wyrick, from his Glasgow admirers, 1913-14." During the season of 1919-20 Mr. Wyrick was engaged by the Boston Opera Company.

His talent was given freely to patriotic services during the World war. For three months in 1917 he was a Y. M. C. A. secretary, and in 1918 he was with the colors as first sergeant in the Ninety-ninth Division. During 1917-19 he was a soloist touring with national speakers in four Liberty Loan drives.

Soon after the World war Mr. Wyrick established himself permanently in Chicago, where he has built up a large clientele. The Wyrick Studios on East Jackson Boulevard, under his direction, comprise a staff of distinguished teachers of music and drama. Mr. Wyrick is also a composer and publisher of music. He sings for the Gennett records, and has composed the words and music of several songs, including "Mother," "DansLa Nuit," and "Under the Western Sky."

Outside the environment of his studio he is known as an enthusiastic follower of such sports as fishing, hunting, tennis and golf. He has membership in the Chicago Association of Commerce, the Kiwanis Club, Co-Operative Club, the Executive Club. He is a member of the Masonic Order and Knights of Pythias, and is an honorary member of the Gyro Club of Davenport, Iowa. On December 17, 1921, Mr. Wyrick married Miss Helene Lelah Ann Turnage, a daughter of James and Della E. (Lance) Turnage, of Carterville, Illinois. Mrs. Wyrick before her marriage was a public accountant.

JOHN P. WYLLIE is proprietor of one of the most successful retail stores in Waukegan, his place of business being known and widely patronized as "Wyllie the shoe man." Mr. Wyllie has been identified with Waukegan both as a business man and citizen for the past ten years.

He was born at Andover, Massachusetts, February 11, 1888, and is of Scotch ancestry, both his parents having been born and reared in Scotland. He is a son of Alexander and Grace (Penny) Wyllie. His father was reared and educated in Scotland and at the age of eighteen came to America and spent a short time in New York City. He then went back to Scotland, remained about four years, and while there married Grace Penny, who had grown up in the same locality as her husband. They came to America and Alexander Wyllie located at Andover, Massachusetts. He was a flax dresser by trade and for about forty-five years was in the service of the Smith & Dove Manufacturing Company at Andover. He retired about 1919 and spent his last years with his son in Waukegan, where he died in July, 1921. He was buried beside his wife in the South Congregational Cemetery at Andover, Massachusetts. She passed away in June, 1918. Alexander Wyllie was a member of the famous Stewart Clan of Scotland.

John P. Wyllie grew up at Andover, Massachusetts, attended grammar and high school there and on finishing his education in 1904 he became clerk in a retail shoe store at Lawrence, Massachusetts. He was at Lawrence about seven years and in 1911 went with the R. H. White Company, shoe merchants at Boston, with whom he continued another five years. Mr. Wyllie in 1916 came west to Waukegan and for three years managed the store of Doolittle & White. In 1919 he bought out the business and has since conducted it under his own name and has developed the store to one of the largest and best patronized establishments of the kind along the North Shore.

Mr. Wyllie has shown a public spirited interest in civic and welfare movements in Waukegan. He is a past commander of Waukegan Commandery of the Knights Templar, is patron of the Eastern Star Chapter, is a past secretary of the Rotary Club, member of the Glen Flora Country Club and the Medinah Athletic Club. He is a republican and is treasurer of the First Congregational Church of Waukegan.

Mr. Wyllie married at Andover, Massachusetts, June 6, 1911, Miss Elizabeth Cunningham, of Andover. She attended grammar and high schools in her native city and also spent some time in Edinburgh, Scotland, where she continued her education in French, German, English and Latin. She is a past matron of Waukegan Chapter of the Eastern Star and is a worker in the church. Her parents, William and Janet (Wright) Cunningham, were natives of Edinburgh, Scotland, where her father for many years was in the hotel business. About 1893 the family came to America and located at Andover, Massachusetts, where her father was in the florist business at Lawrence. He died in June and his wife in October, 1919, and both are buried at Lawrence, Massachusetts. Mr. and Mrs. Wyllie have three children, Alexander Bennett, Janet A. and Robert John. Alexander B. is now in high school at Waukegan and Janet is in grade school.

EVERETT JENNINGS, master in chancery of the Superior Court of Cook County, has for a number of years been a well known member of the Chicago bar and has figured in many notable cases.

He is a Kentuckian, born at Providence, Kentucky, in 1876, and is of pioneer ancestry of the Blue Grass State. His forefathers came over the Blue Ridge Mountains from Virginia not many years after the beginning of the state under Daniel Boone and his associates. Mr. Jennings' people were Kentucky planters. He finished his literary education in a famous institution attended by many of Kentucky's best known sons, Center College at Danville. He was graduated in 1896, with the A. B. degree, and in the same year was admitted to the bar, soon afterward engaging in practice at Chicago, where he has been a lawyer now for twenty-five years. He was engaged in a general law practice until 1913, when he was appointed an assistant state's attorney. Subsequently, from 1914 to 1917, he was general consul for the State Public Utilities Commission, later an assistant attorney general of the state, and in December, 1925, was appointed by Judge McGoorty as master in chancery. He was a presidential elector from Kentucky on the democratic ticket in 1904.

Mr. Jennings has his offices at 10 South LaSalle Street and his home in Chicago. He has one daughter, Miss Maud Mason Jennings.

WALTER L. ATKINSON, the present mayor of North Chicago, grew up as a boy in that community, and has been associated with some of the leading industries of Lake County, for a number of years having held responsible positions in the plant of the Fansteel Company.

Mayor Atkinson was born on a farm near North Chicago, October 19, 1893, son of Joseph S. and Lucy (Meyers) Atkinson. His grandfather, John Atkinson, came from Texas to northern Illinois and was a pioneer of Lake County, taking up some land from the government and buying other lands, from which he improved a farm and home. There he and his wife lived out their lives. Joseph S. Atkinson was born in Texas and was about two years of age when the family settled in Lake County. After attending the public schools he took up farming as a vocation and lived on his farm until his death in 1910. His wife, Lucy Meyers, was born in Chicago, and was a small child at the time of the great Chicago

fire of 1871. It is supposed that her home and parents and other members of the family were destroyed in that great calamity. After the fire she was brought to Lake County and grew up in the home of a farmer named Kelly, near North Chicago. She was never able to trace her family in Chicago.

Walter L. Atkinson attended the grammar and high schools of Lake County at Waukegan, leaving high school in 1911. From that time until 1914 he was in the pattern department of the Chicago Hardware Foundry Company and for a year was shipping clerk with the North Chicago Foundry Company. Mr. Atkinson in 1915 entered the service of the Fansteel Products Company of North Chicago, starting in the production end of the business. He was with the company during the World war, when its facilities were devoted to government work. He is now foreman of the rare metals department of this notable industry.

Mr. Atkinson for some years has been deeply interested in civic affairs, and was city treasurer of North Chicago from 1921 to 1923. In 1925 he was elected mayor, being at that time thirty-two years of age and the youngest mayor of any city in northern Illinois. He is greatly admired for the splendid work he has done in this office and the spirit of service he has exemplified in all civic relations. Mr. Atkinson is a republican and is affiliated with the B. P. O. Elks.

He married at North Chicago, July 29, 1918, Miss Margaret McLearn, who attended public schools in North Chicago. Her parents were H. B. and Hattie (McKinney) McLearn. Her father for many years has been a blacksmith at North Chicago. Mr. and Mrs. Atkinson have one son, Walter, Jr.

KARL D. SANDERS, M. D. The sterling character and the professional ability and loyal stewardship of Doctor Sanders mark him as one of the representative physicians and surgeons of his native county, and he has been established in successful general practice at Jonesboro, judicial center of Union County, during a period of nearly a score of years. He was born in Williamson County, February 8, 1880, and is a son of Dr. David R. and Lydia E. (Ranch) Sanders, the former of whom was born in Tennessee and the latter in Ohio. Dr. David R. Sanders was long engaged in the successful practice of medicine at Jonesboro, and also served as a local preacher of the Baptist Church.

The earlier educational discipline of Dr. Karl D. Sanders was obtained in the public schools of Jonesboro, and when he chose as his life work the profession that had been dignified and honored by the services of his father, he entered Endsworth Medical College at St. Joseph, Missouri, where he completed the prescribed curriculum and was graduated as a member of the class of 1908. After thus receiving his degree of Doctor of Medicine he engaged in the general practice of his profession at Jonesboro in August, 1908, since which time he has here continued his able and earnest service as a well fortified physician and surgeon who keeps in close touch with the advance made in his profession. He has active affiliation with the Union County Medical Society, the Southern Illinois Medical Society, the Illinois State Medical Society, and the American Medical Association.

Doctor Sanders holds staunchly to the faith of the republican party, but has had no desire for political preferment. He is an active and valued member of the Jonesboro Chamber of Commerce, and is affiliated with the Masonic fraternity, as well as with both the lodge and encampment bodies of the Independent Order of Odd Fellows. He and his wife hold membership in the Baptist Church in their home community and are popular figures in the representative social activities of Jonesboro.

In the year 1909 Doctor Sanders wedded Miss Ella Pickles, who was born at Goreville, Johnson County, Illinois, a daughter of Moses M. and Martha (Hudgons) Pickles. Mrs. Sanders received the advantages of the Southern Illinois Normal University at Carbondale, and also those of the great University of Wisconsin. She has been continuously engaged in teaching in the public schools since 1903, and has been a successful and popular teacher in the Jonesboro High School from the time of its establishing. Doctor and Mrs. Sanders have no children.

JAMES EDGAR RHODES, manufacturer and banker, was born and reared at Altamont in Effingham County, where his business abilities and civic interests have been displayed in enlarging the commercial activities of the community and in improving its resources as one of the prosperous smaller cities of southern Illinois.

He was born at Altamont, June 20, 1878, son of John and Samantha Louisa (White) Rhodes. His grandfather, Joseph Rhodes, was of Pennsylvania Dutch ancestry and a native of Pennsylvania, coming from that state to Illinois and settling in Fayette County, where he lived out his life. John Rhodes, father of James E., was born in Fayette County, Illinois, and after his marriage engaged in farming in that county. He was one of the early settlers in the little town of Altamont, and followed various business lines there. During the '80s he started a small factory for the manufacture of egg cases and shipping boxes. He was more or less actively identified with this industry the remainder of his life. The business was incorporated as the Altamont Manufacturing Company in 1891. John Rhodes died in 1900. He married in Illinois Samantha Louisa White, who was born in Missouri, daughter of John White, also a native of that state. John White was a Union man at the time of the Civil war and lost his life at the hands of Confederate guerillas. His widow with her family moved to Illinois. John Rhodes and wife had the following children: Mary, deceased; J. M. Rhodes; J. E. Rhodes; Elsie, deceased; G. C. Rhodes; T. A. Rhodes; and J. A. Rhodes.

The Rhodes sons early became identified with the Altamont Manufacturing Company, and their business genius and enterprise have made it one of the largest box and container manufacturing plants in the state. The headquarters of the business remain at Altamont, but there is another factory at Cairo, Illinois.

James Edgar Rhodes was educated in the common schools of Altamont and completed a scientific and commercial course at Valparaiso University of Indiana. In 1900 he became president of the Altamont Manufacturing Company, and for over a quarter of a century has directed the business. He has also been president of the Altamont Lumber & Grain Company and is treasurer of the Johnson-Hicks Mill Company. Mr. Rhodes in 1910 assisted in organizing the First National Bank of Altamont and has since been its president.

He has filled several local offices and for seven years has been mayor of Altamont, his progressive ideas having been carried out in street paving and many other modern improvements. He has also served on the Board of Education. He is a democrat in politics, is a thirty-second degree Scottish Rite Mason and Shriner, member of the B. P. O. Elks and Knights of Pythias, and is active in the Chamber of Commerce and the Effingham Country and Vandalia Country Clubs. He is a generous supporter of the Presbyterian Church.

Mr. Rhodes married, January 1, 1920, Miss Elnora Schilling.

WALTER E. JANSON, member of the real estate firm of Tallett & Janson at North Chicago, is familiar with business conditions in that locality from the standpoint of a varied experience and participation in commercial affairs. In early life he was in the railroad service, went overseas as a transportation expert, was also in the lumber business for a time, and is a thoroughly practical man who has contributed much to the splendid success achieved by this firm of real estate operators.

He was born in Chicago, Illinois, January 6, 1896, son of Axel and Augusta (Gustafson) Janson. His parents were born and reared in Sweden. His father attended public schools near Stockholm and at the age of sixteen came to America. His wife came later and they met and were married in Chicago. Axel Janson was an iron moulder with the Allis-Chalmers Company until 1902, in which year he moved to North Chicago and was with the Chicago Hardware Foundry Company until he retired in 1921. He still resides at North Chicago. His wife, who died in 1907, had been a captain in the Salvation Army in Sweden before coming to America, and she always devoted much time to church and charitable enterprises.

Walter E. Janson attended school in North Chicago, graduated from the Waukegan High School in 1912, at the age of sixteen, and at once began his working experience. He was chief clerk in the Chicago & Northwestern freight office at North Chicago until the outbreak of the World war. He then enlisted in the Army Transportation Corps early in 1918, and after some training at Camp Grant went overseas to France about the first of May, 1918. He was with the Transportation Corps at Vierzon Cher, France, much of the time on detached duty as an interpreter. More than 350,000 troops were checked through his station. He remained on duty there until June, 1919, was then sent home and in July, 1919, received his honorable discharge at Camp Grant.

Then, after a civil service examination, Mr. Janson was appointed to take charge of transportation at the Great Lakes Naval Training Station, and held that position about three years. He resigned this work in 1922 to become office manager and general manager of the Goldstein Clothing Company of Waukegan. In October, 1924, he bought an interest in the Victor Gustafson Lumber Company in northern Wisconsin. This business he sold in 1925, and returning to North Chicago, entered the real estate business as a salesman for several realty companies. In January, 1926, he and Harold J. Tallett formed the partnership of Tallett & Janson, and due to the great energy of these two young men, both of whom have lived in Lake County most of their lives, they have done a business hardly surpassed by any firm in point of sales, their aggregate sales of property during 1926 having aggregated nearly a million dollars.

Mr. Janson is a member of the Masonic Order and Knights of Pythias, is a republican, and a Lutheran. He married at Waukegan, May 16, 1923, Miss Nellie Glosson. She was educated in grammar and high school at Lincoln, Nebraska, daughter of Peter Glosson and Anna (Beller) Glosson, who for many years were dairy farmers at Lincoln. Mr. and Mrs. Janson have one son, Walter E., Jr. Mr. Janson has two sisters, Edith, wife of Arthur Shumaker, of Scranton, Pennsylvania, now a resident of Detroit, where he is a draftsman and designer of automobile bodies with the Chevrolet Company; and Isabella, an art student in New York City.

JOHN FRANCIS HOOD. Few men render a service of more lasting value than does the one who insures his fellow citizens against loss of all kinds. The changes of a rapidly expanding civilization have so materially increased the risks of accident and sudden death, while those of fire, tornado and other calamities remain as dangerous as ever, and therefore no person ought to fail to take advantage of the opportunities offered him to provide against any and every contingency by having his life, person and property fully covered. On the face of it this would appear a self evident fact, and yet any insurance man will tell you that the educational work he is compelled to carry on is immense, and that the majority must be convinced, practically against their will, that there is a crying necessity for their providing such protection for themselves and their families. The insurance business, therefore, in all of its ramifications has grown into a very important feature, and requires the services of men of exceptional character, men who are willing to become educators in the working forces of public welfare, as well as super-salesmen. Anna has one of these aggressive and successful insurance men of high character in the person of John Francis Hood, who after a wide experience as an insurance agent has gone into business for himself, and is writing all kinds of insurance.

John Francis Hood was born at Lick Creek, Illinois, one of the small communities of

Union County, December 30, 1872, a son of Hiram Newton and Mary (Drake) Hood, natives of Tennessee and Illinois, respectively. They were married in Union County and settled on the farm he owned, and there they rounded out their useful lives, he dying in 1890 and she in 1909. The following children were born to them: Milanda Ann and William T., both of whom are deceased; Joseph, who resides at Anna, Illinois; Lucy, who is Mrs. Edwin Penninger, a widow of Anna; Martha, who died at the age of two years; Caroline, who is Mrs. William T. Brading, of Anna; John Francis, whose name heads this review; Edgar, who resides at Stephens, Minnesota; and Etta, who is Mrs. W. Elijah Gurley, of Union County.

Attending the district schools of Union County until 1893, John Francis Hood secured in them the fundamentals of an education, and entered the work of an educator in the country regions of Union County, Illinois, continuing in this calling for fourteen years, during the winter terms, and during the summer months he followed farming. In the meanwhile he also became interested in the mercantile business in partnership with his father-in-law, F. M. McGinnis, at Lick Creek. In 1918 this store was sold by the partners and Mr. Hood came to Anna, where for a short time he taught school. The epidemic of influenza caused the schools to be closed and Mr. Hood was one of those stricken down with the dread malady, but fortunately he recovered and as soon as he was able went on the road as a traveling representative for the Bump Confectionery Company, with whom he continued for eighteen months. Later he served in the same capacity for Proctor & Gamble, in these connections becoming thoroughly acquainted with the selling end of business. On October 1, 1920, he entered the insurance field as agent for the Roberts Insurance Company, and in August, 1924, he established a general insurance agency of his own at Anna, and has met with remarkable success.

On July 25, 1897, Mr. Hood married Levia Alvincia McGinnis, who was born in Union County, a daughter of Francis Marion and Sarah (Keller) McGinnis, natives of Illinois and Tennessee, respectively. Mr. McGinnis has long been a merchant at Lick Creek, Illinois, but his wife died in 1913. Mr. and Mrs. Hood became the parents of the following children: Lois Alvincia and Nina Pearl, both of whom died in infancy; and Oral Francis, who was born May 25, 1909.

The Cumberland Presbyterian Church holds the membership of Mr. Hood, and he has always been active in its good work, having served as clerk of the church sessions for twenty-four years. For many years he has been a teacher in the Sunday School, and his classes have been largely attended, for he is earnest and effective in his work. A democrat, he is one of the local leaders in his party, and has served as township trustee and school director. He is also a notary public. Since 1907 he has been a member of the Independent Order of Odd Fellows, having first belonged to Evergreen Lodge No. 581, from which he was transferred to Hiawatha Lodge No. 491. He also belongs to Anna Encampment No. 269 of the Odd Fellows, and to Anna Lodge of the Rebekahs No. 262. Through the Anna Chamber of Commerce he is working for the good of his home community. At present he owns eighty acres of land, section 3, township 12 in Union County, that he rents to a tenant. In the fall of 1924 he sold a forty-acre farm he had, section 35, township 11, Union County, to Clebe R. Bullock. He owns his comfortable residence, 409 North Main Street, Anna, and he maintains his office at 325 South Main Street.

CLAIR R. WOODRUFF, mayor of the city of Polo, is a business man of wide and varied experience in a number of localities. Polo has been the scene of his activities for some years and the esteem paid him as a business man has been reflected in the honor conferred upon him by his fellow citizens in election to the office of mayor.

Mr. Woodruff was born at Polo, December 28, 1884. His great-great-grandfather was a soldier in the American Revolution, and the Woodruff family is of English origin. His great-grandparents, Thomas and Silence Woodruff, came from Binghampton, Massachusetts, to Illinois in 1838, making the journey by wagon and team. Newton Woodruff, son of Thomas, was born and reared at Binghampton, Massachusetts, and accompanied his parents to Illinois in 1838. They entered land near Polo in Elkhorn Grove Township. A few years later a party of slaves that were on their way north stopped at the Newton Woodruff farm and they were given work, and in consequence Newton Woodruff became known as a black abolitionist. The descendants of this family of colored people are still living in Carroll County, and some of them still occupy the same house. Newton Woodruff owned 320 acres of some of the finest land in northern Illinois. He died about 1890. His wife, Maria Hacker, came from England with her parents about 1838, being about five weeks on the sailing vessel, which once was stopped by a band of pirates.

I. T. Woodruff, father of the Polo mayor, was born and reared near Polo, attended public schools, spent one year in Northwestern University at Evanston, and was actively engaged in farming until 1920, when he sold out and now lives retired at Polo. He married Della Fender, who was born and reared near Dixon, Illinois, daughter of Hiram and Mary (McConnell) Fender, who came from Indiana, where they were reared. They were settlers at Sugar Grove, near Dixon, Illinois, in pioneer times before the Indians had left that part of the country. Hiram Fender was a son of Absalom Fender, who on coming to northern Illinois in 1835 acquired 1400 acres of government land.

Clair R. Woodruff was educated in grammar and high schools, completed a course in the Sterling Business College in 1906, and then for a year and a half was employed by the W. M. Welch Manufacturing Company, acted as secretary to Warden Hunter of the Iowa State Penitentiary, and following that was a clerk in the transportation department of Armour & Company at Chicago for four years. In 1911 he returned home, spending a year in recuperating his health, and in 1913 he went to Alberta in western Canada and engaged in the mercantile business at Camrose until June, 1915. He remained another year in western Canada engaged in farming, and since 1916 has been a business man of Polo, handling tractors and automobiles. Among other interests he acts as jobber for the Westinghouse Electric Manufacturing Company in eight counties of western Illinois. He handles the Willys-Knight and Overland automobiles, and has built up a tremendous volume of business in this section of the state. In 1920 he built a fine sales room and garage, which was burned down December 16, 1924. It was rebuilt in the spring of 1925, and is acknowledged one of the best appointed automobile sales buildings in Ogle County.

Mr. Woodruff was elected mayor of Polo in April, 1925. He is a republican, and a Knight Templar Mason and Shriner. He married at Vermilion, South Dakota, June 29, 1910, Miss Ida Marie Iverson, who was educated in public schools in South Dakota and in the Girls Seminary at Red Wing, Minnesota. She is a graduate nurse of Wesley Hospital of Chicago. Her parents, Olie and Anna Iverson, came from Christiania, Norway, her father having been brought to America when a child. The family first located in Wisconsin and later homesteaded in South Dakota. Mr. and Mrs. Woodruff have two sons: Ralph Hiram, born March 12, 1917, now attending public school at Polo; and Lloyd Wilbur, born April 19, 1921.

THOMAS JEFFERSON HILLIARD, M. D., has practiced medicine in Wayne County thirty-five years, and while his usefulness to the community has been chiefly measured by his devotion to his profession, he has accumulated other interests, being a banker and business man as well.

Doctor Hilliard was born on a farm near the center of Wayne County, January 25, 1864, son of George H. and Amanda Elizabeth (Green) Hilliard. His grandfather, George Bell Hilliard, was born in Ireland, and lived in Ohio for some years, where he married a Miss Foraker, an aunt of the famous governor and United States Senator from Ohio. George Bell Hilliard in the late '30s moved his family to Illinois, locating seven miles west of Jeffersonville, where he died in 1885, at the advanced age of ninety-five years. He was the father of a family of eight children, most of whom lived and reared families in Wayne County. George Bell Hilliard was a soldier in the War of 1812 and was wounded in one battle. The Hilliard family for many years were Catholics and later became members of the Church of the Latter Day Saints.

George H. Hilliard, father of Doctor Hilliard, was born in Stark County, Ohio, in November, 1838. After coming to Wayne County he married Amanda Elizabeth Green, daughter of Dr. T. P. Green, who came to Illinois from Tennessee in 1838, and for over half a century practiced medicine in Wayne County, his home having been on a farm two miles north of Jeffersonville. Doctor Green died at the age of eighty-six. Amanda Elizabeth (Green) Hilliard died April 13, 1881, leaving a family of ten children, all of whom grew to mature years. Later George H. Hilliard married again, sold his farm in Illinois and moved to Missouri, and died at Independence in that state in 1913. He became prominent in later years in the Latter Day Saints organization, representing the organized church as a preacher and bishop. He was not only devoted to his religion, but in every sense of the word was a truly good and just man.

Thomas Jefferson Hilliard grew up on the home farm, attending the country schools with his brothers and sisters, and in 1887 graduated from Hayward College at Fairfield. He also attended the Central Normal College of Indiana at Danville, taught for four years in country schools in White County, Illinois, and began the study of medicine in the Kentucky School of Medicine at Louisville. On March 19, 1891, he was graduated from the Indiana Medical College of Indianapolis, and returning to Wayne County, settled down for practice at Jeffersonville. He remained in that community for fifteen years and since then has made his home at Fairfield, where he is still in active general practice. He has taken post-graduate work and is a member of the County, State and American Medical Associations.

Doctor Hilliard is a director and vice president of the First National Bank of Fairfield, is a director in five retail lumber companies and president of two of them. He is a director of the Bloomfield Brick Company, of which his son-in-law is general manager. In politics he is a republican, member of the Methodist Church, a Royal Arch Mason, belongs to the Independent Order of Odd Fellows, Modern Woodmen of America, Rotary Club and Chamber of Commerce.

He married, in 1892, Miss Stella M. Hunter, daughter of Dr. C. T. and Sarah Hunter, of Springerton, Illinois. They had two children, daughters, Wanda Lucile and Lyndal, the former educated in the Woman's College at Oxford, Ohio, and the latter in the University of Illinois. Wanda Lucile married Knight O. Holland, and died at the age of twenty-five. Lyndal, who took a course in the Southern Illinois Normal University at Carbondale, taught for a year in the schools of Fairfield, and is now the wife of D. T. Bunting, a resident of Bloomfield, Indiana.

EDWARD L. BENCINI is president of the Egyptian Iron Works at Murphysboro. The name of the company is comparatively modern, dating from 1917. The president and other men in active control were the organizers of the business nearly twenty-five years ago. However, the industry has a consecutive history running back fully half a century. It is an industry that long since has grown beyond a local enterprise. Mining districts all over the United States and Mexico are familiar with the chief output of the company in mine cars and shaker screens. The company also manufactures the Reid safety frog used in mine and street railways, and many other articles. It also does a general foundry business for the manufacture of castings and bronze plates and tablets.

In 1874 James and Walter Alexander, two Scotchmen, located at Murphysboro and start-

ed the Alexander Brothers Foundry and Machine Shop. They continued this very successful enterprise as a general machine and repair shop until 1897, when they sold out to John Lewis. Mr. Lewis continued it until his death in 1903.

In the meantime, early in 1902, four mechanics employed in the shops of the Mobile & Ohio Railroad at Murphysboro laid plans to start a business of their own. These men were E. L. Bencini, W. H. Michael, T. J. Burton and Wienand Schauerte. Mr. Burton's stock has been purchased by the stockholders, he having retired, and now Mr. Grover F. Blankenstock is a stockholder and fills the position of secretary and sales manager. The four men negotiated with Mr. Lewis for the purchase of his plant, but failing in that, they organized the Southern Illinois Foundry and Machine Company, with a capital of six thousand dollars, most of it borrowed capital, and two of these expert mechanics started the operation of their modest shop in the old cannery. About two years later they succeeded in acquiring the Lewis foundry, and through great self denial and by constant exercise of the skill each of them possessed in the mechanical industry they put the new company on its feet and built up the business to very successful proportions.

Edward L. Bencini, president of the company, bears a name indicating his Italian ancestry, but he is a member of a family that has been in America four generations. His great-grandfather, Lorenzo Bencini, on coming from Italy settled in Virginia, where he married a Southern girl. He acquired the ownership of an extensive plantation, using many slaves in the labor of the fields. He remained in that state the rest of his life, a highly honored citizen. His son, Lorenzo W. Bencini, moved from Virginia to North Carolina, locating at Charlotte, where he engaged in planting and also operated a hotel.

William B. Bencini, representing the third generation, was born at Charlotte, North Carolina, in 1853. Before he was ten years of age misfortune had overtaken the Bencini family, as it did practically all the other Southern families who were holders of property and business. From North Carolina Lorenzo W. Bencini removed to Kentucky, where he engaged in the hotel business at Ft. Jefferson. His son, William Bencini, as a boy began construction work on railroads. In 1889 he removed to Murphysboro, and spent many years in the service of the Mobile & Ohio Railroad Company, eventually becoming yard master. He died in 1912. He married Esther Bailey, of Pana, Illinois, who died in 1922.

Edward L. Bencini was born May 2, 1874, while his parents were still living at Ft. Jefferson, Kentucky. He was about fifteen years of age when the family located at Murphysboro. During his youth his father had moved about almost constantly engaged in railroad construction work, and the boy had little opportunity to attend school regularly. However, he managed to get the equivalent of a common school education. When he was fifteen years old he was working as water boy for a large construction gang on the Mobile & Ohio, and the following year entered the shops at Murphysboro as a machinist's apprentice. After finishing his apprenticeship he worked in shops in different parts of the country as a journeyman. In 1898 he married Marie Stewart, daughter of Peter Stewart, of Murphysboro.

Mr. Bencini was a machinist in the Mobile & Ohio shops at Murphysboro from the time of his marriage until 1913. After assisting in organizing the Southern Illinois Foundry & Machine Company he had wisely kept his position in the railroad machine shops, putting all his savings into the new business and in every way possible assisting the company through its early struggles. By 1913 he was justified in leaving the railroad and giving his entire time to the business, of which for many years he has been president. The original capital of the company was increased from six thousand to fifty thousand dollars, and now the company gives employment to fifty skilled workmen and does an annual business valued at over a quarter of a million dollars.

FRANK GEORGE NELSON. In every important center of commercial life may be found able business men who through devotion to their task and ability to perform it have won financial success together with the confidence and sincere respect of their fellow men. Such men are found in the great city of Chicago, and one who is deservedly honored is Frank George Nelson, vice president and member of the managing committee of the Illinois Merchants Trust Company.

Frank G. Nelson was born at Saginaw, Michigan, December 25, 1869, one of a family of four sons and two daughters born to Julius and Susan (O'Brien) Nelson. The father was born at Alborg, Denmark, and the mother in County Sligo, Ireland. Before coming to Saginaw, Michigan, in 1865 his life had been mainly spent on the sea, and his business at Saginaw was to become manager of the Blanchard line of vessels on the Great Lakes. He spent the rest of his life in these waters, being captain and owner of different vessels up to the time of his death, and was the builder at Bay City of the Goshawk and the Zachariah Chandler, two of the largest full rigged schooners on the lakes at that time. Captain Nelson was widely known and held in high regard.

Mr. Nelson attended the public schools and O'Donnell College at Saginaw until he was about fifteen years of age, then spent some time working in a plumbing shop, but really began his business career as a clerk with the Saginaw Valley Freight Transportation Company in 1885. Shortly afterward, however, he became a messenger in the Home National Bank at Saginaw, where he continued until 1891, in the meanwhile applying himself closely to his duties, gaining promotion, and acquiring a general knowledge of the banking business at that time as it came within his experience.

In 1891 Mr. Nelson came to Chicago and secured a clerkship in the Merchants Loan & Trust Company, one of a number of other ambitious young men, but the only one who received such rapid promotion that within ten years he had become assistant cashier in this great financial institution, and in 1910, a vice president. He continued to devote his time and energy to this bank until it merged with the Illinois Trust & Savings Bank and the Corn Exchange National Bank on April 1, 1923, the consolidation being effected under the name of the Illinois Merchants Trust Company, when Mr. Nelson became vice president of the new organization and a member of its managing committee. He has additional important business interests, being vice president of the John M. Smyth Company of Chicago, the largest furniture house in the United States; president of the Terrebonne Land Company, Louisiana, and the owner of an extensive plantation near Columbia, Louisiana, which he devotes to livestock and grain farming.

Mr. Nelson married at Lake Geneva, Wisconsin, October 17, 1908, Miss Mary Angela Smyth, daughter of the late John M. Smyth.

A busy man with such responsibilities as Mr. Nelson must to some extent limit his hours of leisure, but he is a member of a number of representative social and philanthropic organizations that claim some of his time, and he finds congenial friends on every side, in the Bankers, the Lake Shore Athletic and the Attic Clubs. In political life he is a republican, and he is a member of the Union League Club and a life member of the Art Institute and the Field Museum.

ALBERT J. KENT. From railroading, a career to which his energies were devoted from early boyhood, Albert J. Kent after many years as the agent representative of the Mobile & Ohio at Murphysboro, retired to engage in business for himself. He has built up one of the largest general insurance agencies in Jackson County.

Mr. Kent is the son of a railroad man, and he therefore had the constant example before him to stimulate his ambition for railroading as a career. His grandfather, William C. Kent, Sr., was a native of England and in 1845 came to America and settled near Vicksburg, Mississippi. He acquired and owned a large plantation, working it with slave labor, and became prosperous and influential. He died just before the outbreak of the Civil war, thus being spared the loss and devastation that followed in the wake of the armies that ruined his home and plantation. William C. Kent, Jr., was born on the plantation near Vicksburg, July 5, 1854. As a boy of nine years he was almost an eye witness of the great struggle going on for the capture of the Vicksburg stronghold. After the fall of that city and when the center of the fighting in the middle South was transferred to Atlanta, Mr. Kent was taken a prisoner, and probably was a willing captive under the spell of the fascination of army life. He was held in the Union army, working in the messes until Sherman's invaders arrived at Charleston. He was then put on the cars and sent back home. At the end of the war his widowed mother had lost practically all her property, and William C. Kent had to go to work. He learned telegraphy, and in 1870 came to Carbondale, Illinois, acting as railroad agent. When the old St. Louis Central built its line from Pinckneyville to Carbondale he was made agent at Murphysboro. This line later became the Cairo Short Line and still later was incorporated in the Illinois Central System. William C. Kent after leaving the railroad engaged in the general merchandise business at Murphysboro as a member of the firm Kent, Chapman & Thomas, with store on the present location of the Bert Davis Stores. In 1888 he retired from this firm and engaged in business alone, erecting a two-story frame building on Walnut Street, the first business block west of the Illinois Central tracks. In 1890, instead of a frame building, he put up a substantial brick structure, and in that building his son Albert J. now has his offices. William C. Kent, Jr., sold out his business interests at Murphysboro in 1897 and then returned to the old plantation near Vicksburg to take care of his aged sister, who declined to leave that old home. He remained there until his death in 1915. William C. Kent married Ada E. Kirkpatrick, daughter of Joseph K. Kirkpatrick, a prominent citizen and one time mayor of Belleville, St. Clair County, Illinois. She died and was buried at Murphysboro in 1891, and when her husband, over twenty years later, died the son brought his body back from Vicksburg and buried him, as he always wished, beside his wife.

Albert J. Kent was born at Murphysboro December 7, 1871. He attended public schools, but even while in school he worked in his father's store on Saturdays and also studied telegraphy as a means to entering the railroad service. He learned telegraphy in his father's office and was able to send and receive messages by the time he was eleven years old. At the age of twenty he was given his first permanent position in the railroad service, and in 1892, a year later, was employed in the office of H. W. Clark, superintendent, being shortly afterward sent to Sparta, Randolph County. His next promotion took him into the office of the superintendent of the St. Louis Division, Murphysboro district of the Mobile & Ohio, and in 1895 he became local agent for that company at Murphysboro. Mr. Kent was the agent representative of the Mobile & Ohio for a period of twenty-three years, and his business promptness and efficiency and personal popularity did much to popularize the railroad with Murphysboro business men and the public generally.

Mr. Kent on leaving the railroad organized the firm of Kent & Saurer, handling four well known makes of automobiles. This prosperous business was sold out to the Diamond Motor Sales Company in 1922. In the meantime, in 1917, Mr. Kent had become the local representative of an automobile insurance company, and when he gave up handling cars he branched out into the general insurance business. In 1925 he became the district manager of the Belt Auto Indemnity Association of Chicago, and in the same year was made general agent for the Providential Life & Accident Company, covering seven counties in Southern Illinois. In addition to his office at Murphysboro he has offices at Benton, Carbondale, Herrin, Grand Tower and Marion.

Mr. Kent is a member of the Murphysboro Chamber of Commerce, belongs to the Masons, Knights of Pythias, B. P. O. Elks and Country Club, and is a member of the Presbyterian Church. He married Miss Katherine Alexander. She is a daughter of James and Jessie Alexander, one of the old and prominent families of Murphysboro, where her father settled in 1870 and for many years was a prominent foundryman and manufacturer.

AUGUST G. WILLI. In the tornado of March, 1925, the Anchor Ice & Packing Company did not escape the almost general destruction meted out to the little City of Murphysboro. The manager of that company, Mr. August G. Willi, like other local business men, rose to the emergency and by the most strenuous efforts managed to fulfill his contract with his customers in spite of the fact that the machinery of the plant was out of commission for ten days after the storm. The Anchor Ice & Packing Company are ice manufacturers, have cold storage facilities and also deal in coal. The main plant is at 734 North Seventeenth Street, and a branch is maintained at 1110 Locust Street.

Mr. Willi represented a syndicate of men from Duquoin and in June, 1911, came to Murphysboro as manager of the local plant. He entered the ice and cold storage business at Duquoin in 1906 as bookkeeper there. He rapidly mastered the business in its various details and was assistant manager when he left in 1911. He and his Duquoin associates had purchased a controlling interest in the Murphysboro plant. However, the Anchor Ice & Packing Company at Murphysboro has always been a separately managed concern. The plant in 1911 had a capacity of forty tons of ice per day and the capacity is now seventy-five tons, with cold storage facilities of 3,500 tons, used chiefly in the storage of apples. The company manufactures and supplies ice not only for Murphysboro but neighboring towns and sells large contracts with the Mobile & Ohio Railroad.

Mr. Willi's father was Christian Willi, a native of Switzerland, who on coming to Illinois settled at Lebanon, where he for many years conducted a prosperous general store. August G. Willi was born at Lebanon in 1872. He attended grade and high schools there and at the age of seventeen began an apprenticeship at the machinist's and moulder's trade. After his apprenticeship he followed the trade as a journeyman for some years. When he was twenty-five years of age he left his trade to take up the life insurance business, becoming local agent for a company at Murphysboro, and six months later was promoted to district superintendent with headquarters at Alton, Illinois, and still later was sent to represent his company at Dallas, Texas. Mr. Willi was a successful insurance man and attributes most of his success in later years to the training he acquired during the seven years he spent in the insurance business.

He takes an active part in public affairs, though his time is fully employed by the Anchor Ice Company. His disposition is such that he never fails to respond to the calls of his fellow business men. He is president of the Commercial Club, is an alderman and chairman of the finance committee of the council, a position of great importance now on account of the condition of the city's finances following the reconstruction era after the great tornado. Mr. Willi is an active member of the Presbyterian Church, belongs to the B. P. O. Elks and is a director in the State Bank of Murphysboro.

He married Miss Katie Wildy, of Pinckneyville, Illinois. They are the parents of two daughters: Mildred, who taught for two years in the Pinckneyville High School and is now attending the University of Illinois; and Katheryne, a student in the Illinois Woman's College at Jacksonville.

WILLIAM H. MICHAEL, treasurer of the Egyptian Iron Works at Murphysboro, is an expert machinist and has had a long experience in the manufacture and repair of mining equipment and other machinery. He is one of the men who are promoting the modern industrial prosperity of Murphysboro.

His father, Frederick W. Michael, was born at Dissen, Germany, in 1840, and coming to America about 1860, lived for a short time with his older brother, Henry Michael, a farmer in Washington County, Illinois, and then went to St. Louis and followed his trade with the Lueking Wagon Factory. At St. Louis he met Johanna Noltkamper, who was born in Germany in 1839. After their marriage they removed to Wentzville, Missouri, where he established a wagon shop. About 1889 he sold his interest and engaged in a similar business at Huey, Illinois, and in 1905 removed to Murphysboro, where he was employed as a wood worker by the firm then known as the Southern Illinois Machine and Foundry Company. In 1908 his wife, while visiting a daughter at Ferren, Illinois, was accidentally injured and died several weeks later at the age of sixty-nine. Frederick W. Michael died at Murphysboro December 27, 1912.

William H. Michael, the oldest son of his parents, was born at Wentzville, Missouri, September 1, 1870. After a common school education he began his apprenticeship, at the age of fourteen, at the wagon maker's trade under his father. After two years he qualified as a journeyman, worked for a brief time at Wentzville, Missouri, then with the St. Charles Car Company at St. Charles, Missouri, in 1888 was following his trade at Winfield in Lincoln County, Missouri, and on December 28th of the same year began an apprenticeship at the machinist's trade with Fisher & Davis at Main and Carr streets in St. Louis. Unsteady employment caused him to seek more remunerative opportunities elsewhere and through a friend he secured employment with the Chicago & Texas Railroad Company at Murphysboro, beginning his work October 1, 1896, during the great Free Silver presidential campaign of that year. He left the railroad to take a better position with the Big Muddy Coal & Iron Company, and left that for something still better with the Mobile & Ohio Railroad Company in March, 1897, under Foreman James A. White and General Foreman B. A. Orland. On March 28, 1902, he retired from the railroad service and with four other men established the Southern Illinois Machine & Foundry Company, a corporation. Its title in 1917 was changed to the Egyptian Iron Works. For over twenty years this company has rendered a notable service throughout the mining territory adjoining Murphysboro in the manufacture and repair of mining equipment. Mr. Michael for some years was secretary-treasurer and manager of the company, and is now its treasurer and purchasing agent.

At St. Louis, Missouri, May 27, 1897, just a year after the devastating tornado which struck that city, Mr. Michael married Miss Pauline May, a daughter of Carl May, of St. Louis, Missouri Her people were German Lutheran pioneers who, seeking better opportunities for religious worship, came to this country and settled at Altenburg, Missouri. Mr. and Mrs. Michael became the parents of seven children, two of whom died in infancy. The oldest of those living is Eleanor, who was married May 6, 1920, to E. A. Kraft, a journeyman plumber, and they with their two infant daughters reside at Murphysboro. Lydia, the second child, was married November 12, 1925, to Frank Loy, a plumber at Murphysboro. Harry A., the third child and oldest son, spent three years at the University of Illinois, and is now storekeeper at the Egyptian Iron Works. He married, September 6, 1924, Frances Webb. W. Carl, the second son, is a senior and basketball star at the Murphysboro Township High School and is planning to continue his education in a general course in commerce at Valparaiso, Indiana. E. Albert, the youngest of the family, is a sophomore at the Murphysboro Township High School, and his present choice of a profession is that of cartoonist.

ERNEST KLEINE. The automobile industry in its various branches has of recent years opened up a new field of opportunity for energetic and ambitious young men, many of whom, now successful, had but a casual acquaintance therewith before identifying themselves with its activities. At least this has been the experience of Ernest Kleine, former sales manager for Ford and Lincoln cars and now connected with the Cadillac and Chevrolet agency at Rockford, an enterprising young business man and a veteran of the World war of overseas experience.

Mr. Kleine was born at Rockford, April 16, 1893, and is a son of Christ F. and Mattie Kleine. His father, a native of Germany, immigrated to the United States when he was still a child and was reared to an agricultural life. He followed farming until about 1890, when he came to Rockford and established himself in the grocery business, with which he has since been identified. Both he and Mrs. Kleine still reside at Rockford, where they are numbered among the city's highly respected residents. They have been the parents of four children: Roy, who is deceased; Minnie, the wife of Oscar Wick, of Rockford; Ernest, of this review; and Elsie, the wife of Elmer Anderson, of Rockford.

Ernest Kleine attended the public schools in his boyhood and added to the family exchequer by selling newspapers on the streets of the city of his birth. In order to qualify himself for a more ambitious position he managed to secure a commercial course in Brown's Business College, and upon his graduation therefrom obtained employment with the Rockford Gas Light and Coke Company. During the nine years that he was connected with that concern he rose from a humble position to that of salesman, which position he was occupying at the time the United States entered the World war. Mr. Kleine went overseas with Company K, One Hundred and Twenty-ninth Illinois Infantry, with which he saw two years of active service on the battlefields of France, participating in several important engagements, but receiving no serious injury. He won promotion worthily and when he received his honorable discharge it was with the rank of sergeant. On his return to the city of his nativity Mr. Kleine turned his attention to the automobile industry, securing a position in the Ford and Lincoln agency at Rockford, where he held the position of sales manager until July 1, 1926, and since then has been connected with the A. C. Price Company, Cadillac and Chevrolet dealers of Rockford. He has been instrumental in materially increasing the sales of his company and in making it one of the successful and important enterprises of a city which does not lack for substantial enterprises and industries.

On August 15, 1923, Mr. Kleine was united in marriage with Miss Beatrice Miller, of Rockford. Politically Mr. Kleine is a supporter of the principles of the republican party. As a fraternalist he holds membership in the Benevolent and Protective Order of Elks and the Loyal Order of Moose, and he is also identified as a member with the American Legion and the Young Men's Business Association of Rockford.

THOMAS H. BRACKEN has been in business as a merchant at Polo perhaps longer than any of his contemporaries. He was born in that town, and his entire life has been associated with the community, and always in a constructive and a public spirited manner.

He was born at Polo January 26, 1857, son of Robert and Ann (Conway) Bracken and were Robert and Julia (Conway) Bracken, life long residents of Ireland and farmers there, Robert being a native of Westmeath and his wife of Kilkenny. Robert Bracken, father of Thomas H., was born in Ireland, and came to America about 1852, on a sailing vessel which was eight weeks making the voyage. For two or three years he lived in Chicago. He was with the construction forces during the building of the Illinois Central Railroad. He served about fifteen years as pump man for that railroad, and after the installation of a pumping station operated by steam power he had charge of one of such stations until he was retired on a pension about 1905. His wife, Ann Conway, was born in County Kilkenny, Ireland, and came to America in 1853,

landing in New York and coming out to Illinois about 1854. Her parents were James and Julia Conway, farmers.

Thomas H. Bracken grew up at Polo, and after completing his high school education worked on a farm. In 1886 he became a clerk in the clothing store of Henry H. Nye. Two years later, in 1888, he went with the Strickler & Kreidler Company, dry goods and furniture, and was with that firm a period of twenty-one years, making his service indispensable to them. In 1909 he and his brother, Peter W. Bracken, became equal partners in the firm of Bracken Brothers, conducting a dry goods store and also an undertaking business. Peter W. Bracken died in 1915, and since then Mr. Bracken has been sole owner, his business being conducted under his individual name of T. H. Bracken Style Shop. From a small dry goods shop he has developed a business that is now a department store, occupying a large part of the Masonic Building. It is the largest department store in Polo, and carries a complete stock of dry goods and garments. Another branch of his business is undertaking, with quarters on Franklin Street.

Mr. Bracken has been wrapped up in the progress and prosperity of the City of Polo, and his public spirit has brought him general esteem in that community. He served twelve years as an alderman. He is a member of the Woodmen of the World, Knights of Columbus, Edgewood Golf and Country Club, is a republican, and is a member of the Catholic Church.

He married at Polo, in 1885, Miss Nora Denny, daughter of Dennis and Mary (Sullivan) Denny, who were born and reared in County Kerry, Ireland, coming to America about 1831 and settling near Polo. Her father was a stone mason, and there is an example of his craftsmanship still to be seen in Polo, a road bridge near the Burlington Railway station. He died about 1911, surviving his wife a short time. Mr. Bracken by his first marriage was the father of seven children, the oldest dying in infancy. The son Albert James, popularly known as Bert, attended grammar and high schools of Polo and is now associated with his father in business. The daughter Anna is the wife of John Kramer, a sign painter at Polo. Mr. and Mrs. Kramer have four children, Hanora, Dorothy, Jeanette and Barbara. Hanora Kramer is a graduate of the Polo High School and the Bush Conservatory of Music in Chicago, is now connected with the teaching staff of the Bush Conservatory and has frequently been heard as a performer in radio concerts. The other Kramer children are still in school at Polo. The third child, Julia Ann Bracken, is a graduate of the Polo High School and is at home. The second son, William Thomas Bracken, attended the Polo High School, a business college at Sterling, Illinois, and is now secretary and treasurer of the Illinois Public Service Company at Kewanee. William Thomas Bracken enlisted in the navy during the World war, was transferred to the paymaster's department at Puget Sound, and remained there until the armistice. His brother, Bert Bracken enlisted in 1917, was assigned duty in the quartermaster's corps at Camp Jackson, later went to France and was on duty at St. Nazaire and at Samur until the armistice. These brothers are members of the American Legion. The fifth child of the family is Robert V. Bracken, who finished his education in the Polo High School and is now connected with the Niman Grocery Company of Polo. George B. Bracken, the sixth child, attended Polo High School and is now member of the firm of Clark & Bracken, electrical supplies, at LaCrosse, Wisconsin.

Thomas H. Bracken on November 1, 1900, married at Polo Jennie Wood, who was reared and educated at Polo, daughter of Gaylord and Eller (Sherman) Wood. Her father was born and reared in Susquehanna County, Pennsylvania, served as a private soldier in Company L of the Second Regiment of Pennsylvania Heavy Artillery, participating in many battles and campaigns, including Missionary Ridge, Lookout Mountain, siege of Atlanta, and was with Sherman's army on the march to the sea. After the war he settled in Illinois and was a farmer and livery man until he retired and died in 1910.

HON. CHARLES H. WEBER. Numbered among the reliable realtors of Chicago, Hon. Charles H. Weber has in this connection won high standing among the worthwhile citizens of the metropolis of the west, but he is also an outstanding figure in state politics, and as a member of the Lower House of the Illinois General Assembly has made his name a household one all over the state. He is a native son of the city in which his life has been spent, and to whose prosperity and prestige he has made valuable contributions. He was born at Chicago in 1893, and his education was acquired in the parochial school of Saint Alphonsus parish. Of German parentage, his political support has largely come from those of German birth or descent, and the people of his district feel that in him they have one who understands them and their needs.

For some years he has been engaged very successfully in the real-estate business at 2922 Southport Avenue, and he was born just across the street from his office, and has lived within a block of his birthplace during his entire life. When this country entered the World war Mr. Weber attended the Officers Training Camp, Northwestern University, Evanston, from whence he was sent to Jacksonville, Florida, where he was commissioned a second lieutenant, and was sent overseas to France, where he served for thirteen months, with the Thirty-third Division.

In 1922 Mr. Weber was elected a representative from the Sixth Senatorial District of Illinois, and served in the Fifty-third Session, and was re-elected in 1924 to succeed himself as a member of this body, where he has acquitted himself most creditably and with the enthusiastic approval and endorsement of his constituents. In the ever-present "wet" and "dry" issue as relating to the Eighteenth Amendment Mr. Weber has in the Legislature been a consistent "wet" and the leader of those possessing the same ideas. In doing this he not only expresses his own preference, but reflects the sentiments of practically the entire body of his constituents. In the Fifty-fourth Session, 1925, Mr. Weber was a member of the important appropriations committee, as well as of other leading committees. He is head of the famous Charles H. Weber Bowling Team, champions of Illinois, and belongs to the Knights of Columbus, the Benevolent and Protective Order of Elks, National Union, Loyal Order of Moose, Catholic Order of Foresters, Independent Order of Foresters, and the German and Athletic Clubs.

Not only is Mr. Weber an astute business man and able legislator, he is a warm-hearted, generous person, who responds quickly to any demand made upon his sympathies. In December, 1924, learning of the shortage of Christmas trees, and the consequent exorbitant price for this essential of a child's enjoyment of the season, he went personally to his 1,000-acre farm in northern Wisconsin, near Mercer, and ordered his employes to chop down and send to Chicago a sufficient amount of Christmas trees, at least six feet in height. Through the co-operation of a local newspaper these trees were distributed to 1,823 children of Chicago who without the thought and liberality of Mr. Weber would have been deprived of this enjoyment. The munificent gift was very characteristic of this open-handed son of Chicago.

The same month that saw his energetic efforts to make happy the poor children of his native city brought to him an appreciation from his friends that was gratifying and stimulated him to renewed efforts. These friends tendered him a dinner at the Parkway Hotel in celebration of his re-election to the State Assembly, at which every democrat of note in Chicago and Cook County was present, and he was presented with a watch and fob valued at $1,000.

FLETCHER LEWIS, an ex-service man of the World war, is one of the rising young attorneys of the City of Murphysboro, Jackson County.

His father, John A. Lewis, a descendant of Francis Lewis, one of the signers of the Declaration of Independence, came from his home near Atlanta, Georgia, to Cairo, Illinois, in 1880. At Cairo he married Phoebe Potter, daughter of Fletcher Potter, a former officer in the Union army during the Civil war and for many years well known as a newspaper man at Cairo. John A. Lewis after a brief residence at Cairo moved to Murphysboro, which remained his home for forty years, until his death in 1923. All his active career was given to railroading. Soon after his marriage he became a fireman on the Mobile & Ohio Railroad, and remained in the service of that company nearly forty years, nearly all of the time as an engineer.

Fletcher Lewis was born December 8, 1892, at Murphysboro. He attended public schools there, continued his education in Valparaiso University of Indiana, and took his law course there and at the University of Illinois. In 1918, during the World war, he left college to enlist in the Field Artillery, and after a brief time spent at Kansas City, Missouri, was sent to the Artillery Training Camp at Camp Taylor, Kentucky. He was a corporal. He was scheduled for overseas duty when the armistice was signed. He was given his honorable discharge in December, 1918. He at once resumed his law studies and was admitted to the bar in 1919, and returning to Murphysboro, formed an association with W. F. Ellis. They were associated for two and a half years, and since then Mr. Lewis has been engaged in a growing individual practice. In 1921 he was made assistant state's attorney.

He took a prominent part in organizing Paul Stout Post of the American Legion at Murphysboro. This post was named in honor of the first Jackson County boy killed during the war. Mr. Lewis is a past commander of the post, and was one of those active in organizing the State Legion, being on the first executive committee.

Mr. Lewis married Miss Rose Mitchell, daughter of Mike Mitchell. Mrs. Lewis is a native of Murphysboro, and a very able business woman, being now assistant cashier of one of the leading banks of Murphysboro.

HENRY H. ROTH, M. D. One of the leading members of his profession in Jackson County, Doctor Roth is a native of the City of Chicago, and came to Southern Illinois after completing his general medical education. Doctor Roth is particularly well known as a specialist in eye, ear, nose and throat work.

His people on both sides came from Germany. His mother's family, the Bomhakes, came across the ocean in a sailing vessel in 1844, landing at New York, and from Pennsylvania going out to Chicago, where the head of the family became a tanner. The paternal ancestors of Doctor Roth on coming from Germany settled at Dubuque, Iowa, where his father, Nicholas Roth, was born. Nicholas Roth subsequently removed to Chicago, where he followed the trade of carriage painting. He married Mary Bomhake in that city.

Henry H. Roth was born in Chicago in 1875, attended public schools there, and took his degree in medicine at the Illinois Medical College. He subsequently did post-graduate work in the Chicago Polyclinic and the Chicago Eye, Ear and Throat Infirmary. On coming to Jackson County he engaged in general practice at Oraville, but in 1906 removed to Murphysboro, where he has had increasing opportunity for his special talents and training in eye and nose work. To increase his proficiency in that line he attended and received a degree at the New York Post-Graduate Medical School in 1914.

Doctor Roth married Sylva Reiman, daughter of Edwin Reiman, a Jackson County farmer. Doctor Roth is public spirited, a dignified and highly esteemed citizen, is devoted to his profession and without political aspirations, though his interest in good schools caused him to accept a place on the Murphysboro School Board.

REED GREEN, member of the Illinois bar since 1888, has achieved numerous distinctions in his home community of Cairo, as an attorney, banker and public official. He is president of the Cairo Public Library.

He was born at Mount Vernon, Illinois, son of William H. and Ann Letitia (Hughes)

Green, his father a native of Danville, Kentucky and his mother of Morganfield, Kentucky. William H. Green was an attorney and lived at Metropolis, Illinois, and later at Cairo. He was a man of prominence in the southern part of the state, serving as a state senator, circuit judge and president of the State Board of Education. He died at Cairo June 2, 1902.

Reed Green was only an infant when his mother died. He was given a liberal education and advantages, attending the Normal University and the Southern Illinois Normal and took his law course in the law department of Illinois Wesleyan University at Bloomington. He was admitted to the bar in June, 1888, and since that date has practiced in Cairo with a reputation extended out over many adjacent counties.

In December, 1912, he married Miss Lula Young, who was born at Wickliff, Kentucky, daughter of Newton and Ida A. Young. They have two children: Marion and Martha Reed.

Mr. Reed Green was for two terms a member of the Lower House of the Illinois Legislature and has been a member of the Illinois State Senate. He was elected as a democrat and has been active in the affairs of that party. Mr. Green has filled all the chairs of the Lodge of the Knights of Pythias; is a member of the Independent Order of Odd Fellows and B. P. O. Elks, belongs to the Kiwanis Club, Association of Commerce and the Cairo Country Club. Since 1921 he has been a member of the Board of Election Commissioners, is president of the Cairo Board of Education and also president of the Public Library Board. He is president of the First Bank & Trust Company of Cairo.

JAMES O'NEAL, Wayne County attorney, was born in that county and before practicing law was a teacher and business man. He was born on a farm five miles south of Fairfield, March 11, 1882, son of Patrick and Zipporah (Skinner) O'Neal. His father was born in Ireland and was about twelve years of age when he came to the United States from Canada, where his parents settled. His father died at Kingston, Canada, and his mother later came to the United States and settled in Lake County, Illinois. The mother of our subject was born at Stratford-on-Avon, England, and was also twelve years of age when her parents came to the United States, settling in Edwards County, Illinois. Patrick O'Neal and wife married in White County, Illinois, and shortly afterward moved to a farm in Wayne County. They had a family of nine children, the youngest being James.

James O'Neal lived the first eighteen years of his life on the home farm, getting his education in country schools and completing a high school course at Fairfield. Later he studied in Central Normal College at Danville, Indiana. Beginning at the age of eighteen, he was a teacher, and from teaching earned the money to get his advanced education and open up other opportunities in life. For five years he was in Washington as a bookkeeper and in the railway mail service. He was in the insurance business at Fairfield, where he carried on the study of law, and also studied in the Danville Law School. Mr. O'Neal was admitted to the bar in 1918, and since that year has been steadily making his way to the front as a capable lawyer, engaged in a general practice in Fairfield, Illinois.

Along with his law practice he has participated in local affairs, serving two terms on the county board, two terms as city attorney and one term as mayor. He has served several terms as secretary and chairman in the democratic party and is otherwise active in political organizations. Mr. O'Neal is a Master Mason, member of the Knights of Pythias and Independent Order of Odd Fellows. He married, in 1905, Miss Fannie Powell. They have three children, Carroll, Lillian and Kathleen.

WILLIAM C. SCHIELE, M. D., after graduating from medical college had several years of industrial practice in the Lake Superior iron mining district, then was with the colors at home and overseas during the World war, and since the war has been located at Galena, where he has earned the reputation of being a very thorough, capable and conscientious practitioner.

He was born at Joliet, Illinois, June 3, 1887, son of Rev. Richard A. and Elwine (Ruehmann) Schiele. Her father was born in Saxony, Germany, son of Adolph Schiele and wife. Richard A. Schiele entered the ministry of the Lutheran Church and in 1877 came to America as a missionary, located at the German Sailors' Home. Three years later, in 1880, he moved to Chicago and was pastor of the Ashland Boulevard Lutheran Church in that city until 1886. From Chicago he was transferred to Joliet and served as pastor of the First Lutheran Church of that city for thirty years, his ministry ending with his death in 1916. Rev. Richard Schiele was an uncle of Martin Schiele, a former minister in the Cabinet of President Von Hindenberg of Germany, and now a member of the German Reichstag. The mother of Doctor Schiele, Elwine Ruehmann, was born and reared in Mecklenburg Schwerin, Germany, and came to America with her mother and brothers in 1877, locating in Chicago. She was married to Rev. Mr. Schiele at Albany, New York, shortly after her arrival in this country. She had been exceptionally well educated in Germany and was teacher of French in a woman's college at Berlin for some years before coming to America. She was a devoted helper and assistant of her husband in his ministerial labors, taking part in all the auxiliary organizations of the church, in addition to performing the duties devolving on the mother of a large family of children. She now resides with her son at Galena.

William C. Schiele attended grammar and high schools in Joliet, graduating from high school in 1906. He took the Bachelor of Science degree at the University of Chicago in 1910, doing the first two years of his medical work there, and graduated M. D. from the University of Illinois in 1912. For a year and a half he was an interne on the staff of the Lying-In Hospital of Chicago and in 1913 went to Virginia, Minnesota, where he served as a surgeon for the United States Steel Corporation in the iron mines. He remained there five years, only leaving to join the colors for military service.

Doctor Schiele went overseas as a captain in the Medical Corps with the Forty-first or Sunset Division, the Companion National Guard Division of the Forty-second or Rainbow. Prior to going overseas he had attended the Medical Officers' Training School at Fort Riley, Kansas, two months. He was overseas eleven months, spending much of his time training medical troops in first aid work. He was also at the front in the Toul sector. Doctor Schiele was honorably discharged April 1, 1919, at Fort Sheridan, Illinois, and shortly afterward opened his office at Galena, where he has practiced medicine and surgery. He is rated as a very skillful surgeon. He still holds a commission as captain in the Medical Officers' Reserve Corps.

Doctor Schiele is a member of the American Legion and the Forty and Eight Society, belongs to the County and State Medical Associations, is a fellow of the American Medical Association and the Military Surgeons of the United States. He belongs to the Masonic Order, Independent Order of Odd Fellows, B. P. O. Elks, Knights of Pythias, Kiwanis Club and Galena Golf Club. In politics he is a republican and is a Lutheran in religion.

Doctor Schiele married at Hanover, Illinois, August 15, 1917, Miss Ann Reifsteck, of Hanover. For some years before her marriage she had been primary supervisor of schools in Virginia, Minnesota, where she and Doctor Schiele became acquainted. Her parents were Andrew and Anna (Millhouse) Reifsteck, well known citizens of Hanover, Illinois, where they still reside. Her father is a retired merchant. Mrs. Schiele died April 10, 1922, leaving one daughter, Elizabeth Jane, who now resides with her maternal grandparents and attends public school at Hanover.

WILLIAM H. TROBAUGH, a native of Jackson County, member of one of the pioneer families, is general manager of the Murphysboro Construction Company. This company was organized October 1, 1909, for the purpose of doing contract cement work in Murphysboro and vicinity. The first president and organizer was Walter C. Alexander, and his associates were Joseph Borgers, Sr., Edward Corley, A. J. Kent, John Borgers and A. L. Smith, who was the first manager. The business was started at 802 North Nineteenth Street, with a capitalization of ten thousand dollars. In 1911 the other stockholders acquired the interests of Mr. Smith, and L. B. Wright of St. Louis became manager. He was succeeded March 1, 1914, by J. J. Hagenlocher. On April 1, 1917, William H. Trobaugh became general manager as successor of Mr. Hagenlocher.

Mr. Trobaugh has been interested as an employe or in other executive capacities with the Murphysboro Construction Company since twenty-two days after its organization. When in 1911 the company acquired the interests of Mr. Smith the contracting end of the business was discontinued, and since then the company has devoted its resources exclusively to the retail lumber business and the manufacture of cement blocks. On the death of Joseph Borgers the interests of the Borgers estate were purchased by the remaining stockholders. Joseph Berra in 1913 became a stockholder and a director. The present officials of the concern are: W. C. Alexander, president; Edward Corley, secretary and treasurer; A. J. Kent and Joseph Berra, directors.

William H. Trobaugh was born in Jackson County, on his father's farm on the main road midway between Murphysboro and Carbondale. His grandfather, William M. Trobaugh, moved from Virginia to Tennessee, and from there to Jackson County, Illinois, where he established the old homestead. John W. Trobaugh, father of William H., was born in Jackson County, and was one of the substantial farmers of the county until his death. He married Mary Jane Hale, a native of Tennessee, who died March 14, 1926. Her family moved to Hamilton County, Indiana, and later to Owen County in that state.

William H. Trobaugh was educated in rural schools, attending school in a frame schoolhouse, whereas his father had gone to school in a log cabin. His schooling continued six months of the year while the rest of the season he labored in the fields. As soon as old enough he entered the Normal College at Carbondale, driving to Carbondale during the spring and fall, and after stabling his horse walking a mile to the college building. During the winter weather he usually remained in Carbondale, having a room and cooking his own meals to save expenses. After his normal course he taught in rural schools and was principal of the Ava School during 1887-89. He left teaching to engage in farming, and in 1902 was elected county treasurer on the republican ticket. He was in the office of county treasurer four years and for two years following that was in the county clerk's office. In 1908 he became connected with the Jackson County Lumber Company and from that went with the Murphysboro Construction Company and has had an important part in the management for the past sixteen years. The buildings of this company were badly damaged during the tornado of 1925, but no personal injuries resulted.

Mr. Trobaugh first married Jessie Palmer, a daughter of John R. Palmer. She died in 1904, leaving four children, Ernest, Ralph, Ethel and Helen. In 1906 Mr. Trobaugh married Emma M. Nettles, a daughter of John C. Nettles. Mrs. Trobaugh was a teacher before her marriage.

ORMAN H. GABEL has become one of the prominent exponents of the life insurance business in his native state of Illinois, and since 1915 he has been in charge of the Joliet agency of the Illinois Life Insurance Company of Chicago, his well appointed offices in the City of Joliet being in the Orpheum Theater Building. Prior to directing his attention to the insurance business Mr. Gabel had been identified with banking enterprise and had also made a successful record as promoter of an interurban electric railway.

Mr. Gabel was born on the homestead farm of his parents in Kendall County, Illinois, January 26, 1878, and on this old homestead his parents, Lewis J. and Grattee L. (Alford)

Gabel, still reside, the former being, in 1925, seventy-nine years of age and the latter, seventy-one years.

Lewis J. Gabel was born in the oft war-torn province of Nassau, Germany, a son of Henry and Anna Gabel, and he was four years of age when his parents came to the United States and settled on a pioneer farm near Somonauk, Dekalb County, Illinois, this old homestead being still in the possession of the family. Henry Gabel obtained this land from the government and from the raw prairie reclaimed a productive farm, he and his wife having been sterling and honored pioneer citizens of Illinois at the time of their deaths. Mrs. Lewis J. Gabel was born near Plattville, Kendall County, Illinois, and is a daughter of the late Frank and Lydia Alford, who came in an early day to that county, both having been born and reared in the State of Maine.

The boyhood and early youth of Orman H. Gabel were compassed by the influences and activities of the home farm, and in the meanwhile he profited by the advantages of the rural school of the home district. Later he completed a three years' course in the Dixon Business College, and he then passed a year on the old home farm. Upon severing his association with farm enterprise Mr. Gabel took a minor position in the old Second National Bank of Aurora, Illinois, and in this institution he worked his way forward to the position of assistant cashier, an executive office which he retained eleven years. He then effected the organization of the Aurora Trust & Savings Bank, and after three years of service as assistant cashier of this institution he went to Gary, Indiana, and devoted three years to the promotion and development of an electric interurban railroad. He next associated himself with the Illinois Life Insurance Company, and after serving eighteen months as an agent for this corporation he was made manager of its agency at Bloomington, Illinois, this being known as the Illinois Corn Belt Agency at that time and having since become the Illinois and Indiana Corn Belt general agency of the company. After leaving Bloomington Mr. Gabel was for four years representative of the company in the City of Aurora, and since 1915 he has been in charge of the important general agency at Joliet, besides which he has maintained since 1921 the supervision of the company's agency at South Bend, Indiana. He is known as a vigorous and resourceful representative of the insurance business, in which he has made a record of splendid success.

Mr. Gabel is found aligned in the ranks of the republican party, and his wife pays allegiance to the democratic party. His Masonic affiliations include membership in the Shrine, Medinah, at Chicago, and he is a member also of the Loyal Order of Moose, the Independent Order of Odd Fellows, the Joliet Association of Commerce, the Joliet Country Club, the $100,000 Insurance Club of Chicago and the $1,000,000 Agency Club of the Illinois Life Insurance Company.

January 26, 1924, was marked by the marriage of Mr. Gabel and Miss Jane C. Hamilton, who was born at Lancaster, Kentucky, a daughter of Isaac and Sarah Hamilton, both likewise natives of the fine old Bluegrass State. Mrs. Gabel is a representative of a family that was founded in America in the early Colonial period, and she is a direct descendant of John Alexander Hamilton, who served as a patriot soldier of the Continental Line in the War of the Revolution. In Joliet Mr. and Mrs. Gabel maintain their home at 111 Buell Avenue, and they are popular figures in representative social circles in this city.

WILLARD GILBERT WALL. In the profession of banking and finance the late Willard Gilbert Wall attained a place of conspicuous success in Southern Illinois. For twenty-five years he was identified with banking and business at Murphysboro.

His father was Judge George Willard Wall, a distinguished lawyer and jurist of Perry County, Illinois. Judge Wall came to Illinois from Chillicothe, Ohio, and began his professional career at Duquoin. He was one of the founders of the First National Bank of Murphysboro. He married Celeste Nettleton, who was of French ancestry.

Willard Gilbert Wall was born at Duquoin, attended public schools there and continued his education in Illinois College at Jacksonville and at Racine, Wisconsin. As a youth he chose banking as his vocation, and his higher education was pursued with a view to fitting him for that career. For several months for the sake of experience he was employed in the offices of the noted hotel at French Lick, Indiana. He then became cashier of a bank owned by W. K. Murphy and George W. Wall at Pinckneyville, Illinois, and while there gave evidence of his marked ability and sound judgment in matters of finance.

The First National Bank of Murphysboro was organized and began business May 13, 1889, taking over a private bank known as the Jackson County Bank. The three men most active in the founding of the First National were William K. Murphy, George W. Parker and George W. Wall. Mr. Murphy served as president until 1907. The first cashier of the bank was Willard Gilbert Wall, and to his ability, integrity and industry a large share of the success of the institution was due. In 1907 he became president of the bank and continued in that position until his death, July 13, 1915.

In addition to being president of the bank he was president of the Murphysboro Gas, Electric & Water Company, president of the Southern Illinois Milling Company, and his business interests were widely diversified. He was very popular and a generous and helpful worker in civic affairs. He was president of the Jackson Club, and was a member of the Masonic Order, Knights of Pythias and the B. P. O. Elks. He was a member of the Episcopal Church, but as there was no church of that denomination in Murphysboro at the time he became affiliated with the Presbyterian Church and at the time of his death was acting treasurer.

Mr. Wall in March, 1889, married Mary Alexander. Mrs. Wall, who resides at 724

Walnut Street, Murphysboro, is a daughter of James and Jessie Alexander, who came to America from Scotland in 1860, and after residence at Galesburg and St. Louis located in Murphysboro in 1870. Her father in 1874 became one of the founders of the old Alexander Brothers Foundry & Machine Shops, an industry that is still in existence under the name of the Egyptian Iron Works. Mrs. Wall is a sister of the well known capitalist Walter C. Alexander and John Alexander, president of the City National Bank of Herrin. Mrs. Wall was born in Galesburg, attended public school there and the Girls' Seminary at Duquoin and the Normal University at Carbondale. She also attended the Conservatory of Music at St. Louis, and her accomplishments in music are well known. To this union was born one daughter, Miss Jessie Celeste Wall, now the wife of Benjamin A. Daniel. They have one daughter, Jessie Marie Daniel. Mrs. Wall has also interested herself in various organizations, having served many years as president of the Murphysboro Woman's Club, was district president of the Woman's Club of the Twenty-fifth Congressional District, is second vice president of the Illinois Federation of Women's Clubs, is a member of the Chamber of Commerce and the Eastern Star, and was the first president of the League of Woman Voters in her district. She has also availed herself of exceptional opportunities for personal culture and study, and has several times made tours to Europe.

ADOLPH GEORGE ZELLE is a business man at Murphysboro, proprietor of a funeral home which in equipment and service is one of the best in the southern part of the state.

Mr. Zelle, whose early ambition was directed toward another line, has found both happiness and success in his present profession. He was born January 10, 1878, on his father's farm in Mason County, Illinois.

Frederick Zelle, his grandfather, came from Germany in 1858, bringing his wife, Henrietta (Oettermohen) Zelle, and their son, G. H. Carl Zelle, then only seven years old. One motive which prompted Frederick Zelle to leave Germany was the cruel treatment frequently accorded German soldiers. The family landed at New Orleans, came up the Mississippi and Illinois rivers and settled on land in Mason County. Frederick Zelle took out papers as a naturalized American citizen, and was a man of most substantial character. He acquired a farm of 240 acres, and lived on it until his death. His son, G. H. Carl Zelle, was born in Germany in 1851. Opportunities for schooling were very poor in Mason County during the early years of the Zelle family residence, and the father of Carl employed a private instructor in his home for the benefit of his children. Carl Zelle as a young man engaged in farming, and an industrious career made him one of Mason County's leading agriculturists. He and his wife are now living retired at Lincoln in Logan County, Illinois.

Adolph G. Zelle while a boy on the farm attended the country schools, which were much superior to those in his father's day. He also attended high school at Havana. His working experience was on his father's farm until the age of twenty-one. About that time he became a salesman for the International Harvester Company and represented that corporation several years. His ambition had been to become a machinist, since he manifested an evident genius in mechanical lines. In order to promote his opportunities in that direction he secured a position at Shelbyville. While there the influence of a friend diverted him from machinery to the embalming profession. He engaged his services to this friend, spending several months in apprenticeship in his establishment, and subsequently taking a course in an embalming school at Chicago. Following that he was employed by several funeral directors. In 1910 he entered the service of D. L. Boucher, then the leading funeral director of Jackson County, at Murphysboro. His salary was fifteen dollars a week. In the same year he married Kathryn Fryer, daughter of Samuel B. and Mary (Core) Fryer. Her father was a native of Ohio and spent most of his life at Lincoln in Logan County, Illinois. Mrs. Zelle attended school at Lincoln, also the Normal University at Normal, and for nine years taught at Mount Pulaski, Illinois.

Mr. and Mrs. Zelle have cooperated perfectly in their joint business undertakings. Mr. Zelle gave up his position working for others and in 1915 started a business of his own, practically all his capital being obtained from banks. Since then he and Mrs. Zelle have kept their business and service improving until it is now represented by a modern equipped funeral home. Mrs. Zelle in 1917 completed a course in the Chicago School of Embalming. She is a member of the Woman's Club, and both are popular members of many organizations in Murphysboro.

During 1924-25 Mr. Zelle was president of the Illinois Funeral Directors and Embalmers Association, and is on several committees of the National Association. For the past three years he has been chairman of the Egyptian Funeral Directors Association.

MAJOR FLOYD F. PUTMAN has been a member of the bar of his native County of Fulton for twenty years, a member of the law firm Taff and Putman at Canton. He earned a distinguished record as major of the One Hundred Twenty-fourth Machine Gun Battalion with the Thirty-third Division, Expeditionary Forces, during the World war.

Major Putman was born in Putman Township of Fulton County, October 8, 1880. This family was founded in South Carolina before the American Revolution. The spelling of the name until recent generations was Putnam. It has been Putman since the migration to Fulton County, Illinois. Major Putman is a descendant of Daniel Putnam, who served with South Carolina militia during the Revolutionary war. A son of this Revolutionary soldier was Hazael Putnam, who settled in Fulton County, Illinois, in 1820. The family has therefore been in the county for more than a century and has been represented by at least four generations. Harrison Putman, son of Hazael, was the grandfather of Major Putman.

Francis Putman, father of the Major, was born in Fulton County, October 27, 1837, and devoted his active life to farming. He served three years in the Civil war with the Seventh Illinois Cavalry, being for a time a messenger to General Grant. He participated in the Vicksburg campaign and in the Grierson raid. Two of his brothers were also soldiers. He was a member of the Grand Army of the Republic, and in politics was a democrat. He died at Canton March 20, 1908. His wife, Clarissa Saunders, daughter of Christopher and Aurillia (Putney) Saunders, died at Canton April 17, 1923.

Floyd F. Putman lived on a farm for the first fifteen years of his life, attended country schools, later graduated from the Canton High School, and for four years was a student in the University of Michigan, spending one year in the literary department and three years in the Law School, where he was graduated in 1904. He was admitted to the bar in Michigan and Illinois, and in 1905 engaged in practice at Canton. He was successful in winning his first case, a civil suit.

He was elected in 1908 and served two terms as city attorney of Canton. He was assistant state's attorney under W. S. Jewell from 1908 to 1912. In 1920 he was elected state's attorney and served until 1924, it falling to his official lot to handle prosecutions under the new national prohibition amendment. He collected in fines and fees for the county something like $21,000, and earned a very successful record.

Major Putman was in the National Guard before the World war, enlisting in Company M of the Fifth Illinois Infantry in 1899, serving two and one-half years. In 1908 he was made captain of his company, holding that rank until 1912, and from 1912 to 1917 was major of a battalion of the Fifth Infantry. He went out with the National Guard by proclamation of the President March 26, 1917, doing guard duty, and on October 13th commanded the battalion when it went into camp at Camp Logan at Houston, Texas, forming one of the units of the Thirty-third Division. He became commander of the One Hundred and Twenty-fourth Machine Gun Battalion, and was its major until discharged from the service June 19, 1919. Major Putman sailed from Hoboken, New Jersey, on the Mount Vernon May 16, 1918, landed at Brest May 26th, and saw his first service with the British Fourth Army along the Somme from May 31 to August 23, taking part in the defensive operations near Albert in conjunction with the Australian and British troops and was in the Somme offensive August 15 to 20. The division was then sent to the American sector near Verdun, where his battalion was in the defense of sector near Verdun September 10 to 25, was in the Meuse-Argonne offensive September 26 to October 20, was then in the Troyon sector and was on general duty until the armistice on November 11. After the armistice his battalion became part of the reserve to the Army of Occupation at Luxemburg from December 20, 1918, to April 26, 1919. On May 9, 1919, his battalion embarked at Brest, returned on the Mount Vernon, arriving at Hoboken May 17, just one day over a year after he sailed. Major Putman for exceptionally meritorious service was cited by his division commander and also by General Pershing. Since the war he has been a member of the American Legion.

He is a member of the Sigma Nu fraternity, is a thirty-second degree Scottish Rite Mason, a member of the Knights of Pythias, the Elks, Sons of Veterans, Canton Rotary Club and Chamber of Commerce. In politics he has been aligned with the republican party. He and his wife are members of the Congregational Church.

Major Putman married at Canton, June 16, 1909, Miss Clara Thompson, daughter of Lewis and Mary (Bailey) Thompson. She was born near Canton May 17, 1882, and finished her education in the Canton High School. Major Putman and wife have four children, Mary Elizabeth, Lewis T., Charles Francis and Helen Louise.

CHARLES A. WIGHTMAN, pioneer real estate man at Evanston, was one of the founders and is a past president of the Evanston Real Estate Board. Mr. Wightman has used much of the income from a successful business conducted through many years to pursue his hobby as an art collector, and in his knowledge of art work he has few peers in the middle west.

Mr. Wightman was born at Kenosha, Wisconsin, in 1861, son of Addison P. and Jane (Richards) Wightman. The Wightman's were Colonial settlers in America, locating in Connecticut. Addison P. Wightman was born in western New York and in the late '30s came west, first stopping in Chicago and then going to Kenosha, Wisconsin. He was a pioneer in wagon manufacture in that city, at first associated with the Mitchell wagon interests, and later as a manufacturer on his own account. He finally sold his industry to the Bain Wagon Company and in 1868 removed with his family to Evanston, Illinois, where he was associated with his brother in the hardware business under the firm name of Wightman & Brother. The Wightman Wagon was noted for its sturdiness and seemed to reflect the personal caharacter of its builder. Some of these old Wightman wagons were still in existence and use until comparatively recent years.

Charles A. Wightman was a boy when the family removed to Evanston, and after the public schools he attended Northwestern University, graduating Bachelor of Philosophy in the class of 1885. In 1925 the honorary degree Doctor of Laws was conferred upon him by Notre Dame University of Indiana. Mr. Wightman entered the real estate business at Evanston in 1889, and all of his contemporaries of that date have retired or died or moved to other locations. For many years he was in business under the name of Charles A. Wightman & Company. He now has charge of the loan department and acts in an advisory capacity to the Edmund J. Smith & Company, the active head of which is his son-in-law, Edmund J. Smith.

The Evanston Real Estate Board of which Mr. Wightman was the founder and is past president, was one of the first real estate boards in the United States to own its own building. Mr. Wightman took an active part in bringing about the construction of this building. He also erected the University Building at the corner of Davis Street and Chicago Avenue, and the Security Building on Sherman Avenue, where his business had its headquarters for a number of years and where he also conducted the Evanston Bond & Mortgage Company. He sold his interest in the latter institution in January, 1926, and at that time returned to his original location in the University Building. Mr. Wightman has not only been a constructive business man but a public spirited factor in the life of the Evanston community and for one year served as an alderman.

His long and patient study of art and collection of art objects have made Mr. Wightman deservedly known as one of America's foremost art collectors. He has acquired one of the largest and most valuable private collections of paintings, prints and rare engravings in the country. Mr. Wightman has given collections of art works to a number of institutions, the largest being the Wightman Memorial Gallery of Paintings given as a memorial to his wife to Notre Dame University of Indiana. This gallery contains about two hundred subjects, some of them outstanding examples of their class.

Mrs. Wightman, who died in January, 1925, before her marriage was Cecelia A. Daley, member of a pioneer family of Kenosha County, Wisconsin. Mr. and Mrs. Wightman had four children: Miss Catherine and Miss Margaret; Alice, wife of Edmund J. Smith; and Rosemary, wife of Doctor Westcott.

HON. HERBERT E. TORRANCE. A leading member of the Livingston County bar for many years and very prominent in the law and in civic affairs at Pontiac is Hon. Herbert E. Torrance, formerly master in chancery and ex-mayor of the City of Pontiac. He bears an old and honored Illinois name that has belonged to the state and been identified with her history for more than sixty years.

Herbert E. Torrance was born at Chatsworth, Livingston County, Illinois, April 4, 1870, son of George and Eliza M. (Fenn) Torrance, and grandson of David Torrance and Elim P. Fenn, the paternal grandfather coming to Illinois from near Lancaster, Ohio, in 1862, and the maternal grandfather from Connecticut, in 1856. Both were agricultural families and became well and favorably known in Bureau, Vermilion and Livingston counties.

George Torrance was born in Ohio, May 14, 1847, and he accompanied his parents to Vermilion County, Illinois, in 1862, and at Danville enlisted in the One Hundred Forty-ninth Illinois Volunteer Infantry, and as a member of this famous body of Illinois soldiers, continued until the close of the Civil war. In 1867, then only twenty years old, he came to Chatsworth, where he secured employment as a clerk in a general store, and it was while so employed that he fitted himself for the career in which he later became so eminent, was admitted to the bar and opened his first law office at Chatsworth. In 1881 he removed to Pontiac, where he continued in the practice of his profession until he retired, in 1897, having in the meanwhile served with honesty and usefulness, from 1881 to 1889, as a member of the State Legislature. After retiring from active practice George Torrance was appointed, in 1897, superintendent of the Illinois State Reformatory at Pontiac, a position he continued to fill with the utmost efficiency until his retirement in 1904, his death following in 1905. He married Miss Eliza M. Fenn, of New England ancestry and daughter of Elim P. Fenn, and they had two children.

Herbert E. Torrance received his early educational training in the public schools at Chatsworth, and after the family removal to Pontiac, continued in school there until his graduation from the Pontiac High School. For two years, 1888 and 1889, he attended Northwestern University, after which he studied law in his father's office, was admitted to the bar in 1894, and then formed the law partnership with his father which continued until 1897, when the latter retired from active practice.

Mr. Torrance continued the practice of the old firm at Pontiac, where it always has had many most important connections in almost every branch of the law, until 1903, when he accepted a call to Washington, D. C., and spent the following three years in the office of the assistant United States attorney for the Department of the Interior. In 1906 he returned to Pontiac and received the appointment of master in chancery, in which important public office he continued to serve until 1913, and on retiring from the same, resumed the general practice of the law, representing large interests all over the country.

Not only professionally does Mr. Torrance enjoy the respect and confidence of his fellow citizens at Pontiac, but personally as well, as an earnest co-worker for the welfare of the city, and as neighbor and friend, and his election to the mayoralty of the city in 1915 was a marked testimonial to the universal regard he has inspired. For the past eight years he has been a member of the Board of Education, and in 1920 he was a member of the Constitutional Convention. During the World war he was chairman of the Livingston County Board of Exemption, and he was the first chairman of the executive committee of the Red Cross.

Mr. Torrance married first Miss Cornelia M. Holtzman, who died in 1919. In 1924 he married Sara Pond Alle, who was born in Connecticut and traces her family to early Colonial settlement in New England.

JOSEPH TRIMBLE KAY. Among the old and honorable names representing for generations a family that has belonged to America for more than 200 years is that of Kay, which first became a possession of Illinois in 1859. In the entourage of William Penn when he came to this country from England in 1682, were John Kay and his wife, probably of the religious faith of the Quakers, and undoubtedly pious and thrifty people, for it was with such material that Penn succeeded in building up the great commonwealth of Pennsylvania.

To this first John Kay, sometimes spelled Key, and his wife a son, John, was born in December, 1682, the first American Kay, his birth taking place near the Delaware River, on ground subsequently taken into the first plat of the City of Philadelphia. He maintained his home there all his life and died there at the age of eighty-five years. He was survived by a son John, who was born at Philadelphia, September 12, 1728, and became a man of business importance, a manufacturer of fire-arms for the Colonies during the Revolutionary war. He died in his native city in 1793.

Isaac Kay, youngest son of the above John Kay, was born at Philadelphia, September 14, 1778, and was the first of the Kays to show an enterprising spirit that in young manhood led him to adventure so far as Mason County, Kentucky, but finding Indian and frontier troubles still interfering with peaceful settlement, removed to Brown County, Ohio, where he followed farm pursuits until the close of his life, his death occurring October 9, 1858. In Mason County he married a member of the Wiseman family, who was born May 2, 1781, and died March 18, 1858. They were the grandparents of one of Livingston County's best known and most highly respected citizens, Joseph Trimble Kay, now retired, but for many years a prominent political factor and substantial business man of Pontiac.

John Kay, eldest son of Isaac Kay's eight children and father of Joseph Trimble Kay, was born in Mason County, Kentucky, January 21, 1808, and grew to manhood in Brown County, Ohio, where in 1833 he married Miss Joanna Wiley, and of their family of thirteen children Joseph Trimble was the eighth in order of birth, the others being: Helen Ann, born November 14, 1834, married a Laycock; Margaret Bythena, born January 28, 1836, married John W. Smith! Augusta Katherine, born July 23, 1837; Amanda Eveline, born March 11, 1840, married L. Armstrong; Minerva Frances, born October 13, 1841, died at the age of twenty-three years; Viola Susana, born December 16, 1843; Jerusha Rebekah, born March 23, 1845, married Rev. P. Smith; Zacheus Lafayette, born August 1, 1849; Thomas Wiley, born August 21, 1852; Isaac Newton, born January 25, 1855, died one month later; Samuel Lee, born March 26, 1858; and John Fletcher, born February 24, 1860, died July 28, 1866.

In 1859 John Kay with his wife and eleven children set out from Ohio to find a home on the fertile prairies of Illinois, of necessity traveling by wagon, for those were yet pioneer days through many sections of the West. They found a pleasing prospect in Livingston County and John Kay bought a farm a short distance west of what was then the village of Pontiac. He was a man of industry, energy and enterprise, developed and improved his land and so prospered that when ready to retire from active labor he was able to build himself a comfortable home in Pontiac and there his last years were spent, his death taking place in 1886, universally respected.

Joseph Trimble Kay was born at Georgetown, Ohio, April 23, 1847, and was twelve years old when he accompanied his parents to Livingston County, Illinois. Through accident he had suffered injuries that rendered him physically unfit for the hard labor of the farm, and thus his education, to some extent, was directed along lines that would best prepare him for other lines of effort. Fortunately he possessed the quick mind and studious habit that brought quick and satisfactory results, both in the public schools at Pontiac and the Bryant & Stratton College at Peoria. After completing his college course he found employment in the office of the county clerk, where he worked for several years, in the meanwhile taking an active and intelligent interest in politics, and in 1869 entered the county treasurer's office os deputy county treasurer. Mr. Kay continued in the above position until 1874, when he was made deputy county clerk, and when he retired from this office it was to embark in business for himself along the lines of real estate and insurance.

In the first year that Pontiac emerged from a village status into that of a city Mr. Kay, as one of her most progressive and hard-working citizens, represented the Third Ward in the City Council, 1873-1874, and served again in 1887, 1888 and 1889, and finally in 1890, 1891 and 1892, and at times in other such offices as justice of the peace and city clerk. His public spirit as well as his good judgment have been very generally recognized in promoting the welfare of Pontiac.

In 1916 Mr. Kay relieved himself of former business responsibilities and took up his residence on one of his farms situated a short distance from Pontiac, and interested himself for five years in raising thoroughbred horses, but in 1921 he placed the farm in charge of a reliable tenant and returned to the city to again occupy his handsome residence on East Washington Street and perhaps to keep in little closer touch with passing events in which he was so important for so long a time, and to associate more frequently with the congenial friends of a lifetime, won through his own kind neighborliness and geniality.

Mr. Kay married, October 15, 1872, Miss Anna A. Gore, born in Illinois June 25, 1852, daughter of William Gore, who had come from Adams County, Ohio, in 1851. The death of this greatly beloved lady took place May 27, 1925. Two sons were born to them: Claude D., born December 10, 1873, died March 18, 1875; and Joseph Robert, born June 30, 1886, who is a prominent business man and sterling citizen of Pontiac. Joseph Robert married Miss Ruth Sparks, of Fordyce, Arkansas, on September 7, 1915, and they have two children, Joseph Robert, Jr., born November 4, 1916, and Joann Ruth, born June 11, 1920.

ARTHUR L. JOHNSON, postmaster of Rockford, and one of the aggressive business men of Winnebago County, is a man who is universally esteemed by all who know him. He was born at Rockford, June 14, 1885, a son of Gust and Anna C. (Olson) Johnson, both natives of Sweden, who came to the United States as children and located at Rockford. For sixteen years he was chief deputy sheriff of Winnebago County. His death occurred March 8, 1916, but he is survived by his widow, who maintains her home at Rockford. They had the following children, Postmaster Johnson being the youngest, the others being

Edna E., who died in infancy; and William G. and Ernest V., twins, who are residents of Rockford.

At the age of fifteen years Arthur L. Johnson was graduated from Brown's Business College, and for the subsequent four years was a bookkeeper, and then was placed in charge of the order and shipping department of the Union Overall Company of Rockford, and was also city salesman for this company. In the meanwhile, when still a boy, he had established a bicycle business, which grew to such an extent that he was finally forced to resign from his position with the Union Overall Company in order to look after his own interests. He branched out to include the handling of motorcycles, motors and automobiles and auto accessories, and did an excellent business. Two years later he began handling the White Motor truck, the highest-priced truck on the market, and for three years did a big business and was very successful, and then sold at an excellent figure. In October, 1921, he was appointed postmaster of Rockford, and still holds this office. For five years he served as a member of the election commission, having been appointed to it by Judge Reckhow and Judge Carpenter. He has been very active as a republican, serving as secretary of the First Voters Club, secretary and later president of the Young Men's Republican Club, and was secretary three terms of the Winnebago County Republican Committee, and he has also served it as treasurer, and for two terms was its chairman. He is a member of the Board of Directors of the Rockford Chamber of Commerce, Rockford Boy Scouts and Rockford Boys Club, and was president of the Kiwanis Club, 1926.

On September 19, 1907, Postmaster Johnson married Lillian M. Lundine, and they have two children: Marguerite and Arthur L., Junior. He has been advanced through the Scottish and York rites in Masonry, and was worthy patron of Forest City Chapter, Order of Eastern Star, 1923-1924, watchman of Shepherd's Oriental Shrine No. 5, W. S. J. F. for the year 1925, and chaplain of Winnebago Chapter No. 24, Royal Arch Masons. He also belongs to the Benevolent and Protective Order of Elks, and the Loyal Order of Moose. He is a member of Trinity Lutheran Church and is vice president of the Lutheran Trinity Church Brotherhood. Since he has taken charge of the postoffice he has greatly bettered the service, and is giving satisfaction to the people of the city and its vicinity, as well as to the employes under him. He is a man who can accomplish much because he is able to secure a hearty cooperation from others. He was president of the Illinois Association of Postmasters 1925-1926 and vice president of the National Association of Postmasters 1925-1926.

EDWARD OSGOOD BROWN was one of the oldest members of the Chicago bar when death came to him on December 18, 1923. He had come to Chicago soon after the great fire and did his first professional work in the city in the years of reconstruction. He enjoyed many of the best distinctions of his profession. For a number of years he was judge of the Circuit Court of Cook County, and practically all the time he was on the bench he was assigned to the Appellate Division.

Judge Brown was born at Salem, Massachusetts, August 5, 1847, and died at the age of seventy-six. His parents were Edward and Eliza (Dalton) Brown. He was liberally educated, graduating from Brown University at Providence with the A.B. degree in 1867. He studied law at Salem, his native town, in the Harvard Law School and in 1870 was admitted to the bar, and during 1870-71 acted as assistant clerk of the Supreme Court of Rhode Island. In 1872 he began the practice of law with the firm of Peckham & Brown at Chicago. Judge Brown was regarded as an invaluable counsel. From his private practice his attention was diverted to the duties of public office for many years. He served as counsel for the Lincoln Park Board of Commissioners from 1894 to 1897. He was elected judge of the Circuit Court of Cook County for the term 1903-09, and in 1904 was appointed a justice of the Appellate Court of the First District. On retiring from the bench after his first term he was associated as a member of the prominent law firm of Peckham, Brown, Packard & Walsh until 1910. In that year he was again elected judge of the Circuit Court, and on December 1 of the same year was again appointed justice of the Appellate Court of the First District. On resuming private practice in 1915 he became a member of the law firm Miller, Starr, Brown, Packard & Peckham.

Judge Brown was recognized for his thorough scholarship, not only in matters of his profession but on a wide range of economic topics. He was a pronounced single taxer, though in politics he was a thorough going democrat. He wrote a great deal on the subject of the single tax and other economic problems, also on political and historical subjects. His opinions as a judge are found in Volumes 117-192 of the Illinois Appellate Court reports. Several of his legal papers and pamphlets treat of the literal rights on Lake Michigan.

Judge Brown was a member of the Illinois, Chicago and American Bar Associations, the University Club, City Club, Chicago Literary Club, Law Club, Mid-day Club, Press Club and Iroquois Club. He married, June 25, 1884, Helen Gertrude Eagle, of Chicago. The children of their marriage were Edward Eagle, Helen Dalton, Walter Elliott, Robert Osgood and Mary Wolmarth.

IRA M. LISH, general superintendent of the Illinois State Reformatory at Pontiac, occupies a position of singular importance. At a time when crime is rampant and all influences are necessary to maintain law and order, it is decidedly desirable to have as the heads of our penal and corrective institutions men of sound intellect, practical and straightforward views and moral courage who can govern their charges with justness and kindness, without allowing to enter into their administration of either the corrosion of sentimentality or of pernicious influences. During the time that he has occupied his present position Mr. Lish has

demonstrated that he is possessed of the necessary qualifications, and his official record is an admirable one.

Mr. Lish was born July 16, 1855, on the Lish farm in Kankakee County, Illinois, and traces his family back to the original ancestor who came to America prior to the Revolutionary war and took up his residence in New Jersey. Henry Lish, the grandfather of Ira M., was born in that state, which he left in 1848, and after having spent a short time near Joliet, Illinois, took up his residence near Essex in Kankakee County. He was one of the hardworking and highly respected men of his time and community, and was engaged in agricultural pursuits until he met an accidental death by drowning in the Des Plaines River near Joliet. His son, John Lish, the father of Ira M. Lish, was one of the well-known farmers of his community, and, like his father, met an accidental death, dying from the effects of the kick of a vicious horse in 1883. He married Miss Susan Wood, who was born in New York State and accompanied her parents to Illinois, and they became the parents of seven children: Anna, who died in 1862; Ira M., of this review; Ada J., now Mrs. Thomas Rankin, of Lake Bluff, Illinois; Henry, of Wichita, Kansas; and Frank, Burt Elmer and Lulu, who died in 1877 during an epidemic of diphtheria and were laid to rest in a single grave.

As a lad Ira M. Lish attended the country school in the neighborhood of the home farm, and later had the advantage of attendance at the Channahan High School. Like other farmers' sons of his time he went to school during the winter terms and worked hard on the farm in the summer months, and at the age of seventeen years left the parental roof to work on the lands of neighboring farmers. Agricultural life, however, did not appeal to him. He was anxious to get into commercial enterprises and with that end in view was careful of his savings and thrifty in his habits. When he was twenty-three years of age he was united in marriage with Miss Caroline A. Spencer, of Minooka, Illinois, whose people were early Illinois settlers from Vermont, and not long after his marriage Mr. Lish obtained a position as clerk in a general merchandise store at Mazon, Illinois. Here he worked hard and faithfully until 1883, the year of his father's unfortunate death, when he went to Essex and formed a partnership with Mack White in the general merchandising business. This was continued for two years, when Mr. Lish disposed of his interest to his partner and removed to Saunemin, Livingston County, in which little community he embarked in the same line of business on his own account. While at Essex he had entered upon a political career, although it was much against his inclination, having been elected to the office of supervisor, from which he resigned when he moved to Livingston County in 1885. In 1898 he was elected a member of the Board of Supervisors of Livingston County, representing Saunemin Township. By 1906 his business had grown to such proportions that he found it advisable to take in a partner, P. H. Lannon, who was the owner of a private bank located at Saunemin, and at the same time became financially interested in the latter enterprise. In 1911 this was reorganized as the State Bank of Saunemin, of which Mr. Lish was elected president, a position which he still retains. Mr. Lish continued as a supervisor of the county from 1898 to 1904, during two years of which time he was chairman of the body. In 1902 he was elected to the State Legislature and in 1904 declined to run again as supervisor, but was nominated and elected to the State Senate, to which he was reelected in 1908, but went down to defeat in 1912, like many other members of the republican party, owing to the "Bull Moose" movement. In 1916 he was urged to make the race again, but declined the honor. Mr. Lish had never desired public preferment, but had accepted the offices to which he was elected as a matter of public duty, feeling that no business man should seek to evade the responsibilities of citizenship.

As a good business man and a good executive, doing well all that he undertakes, Mr. Lish attracted the attention of not only his party and constituents, but the general public as well, and in 1921 he was requested by Governor Len Small to accept the appointment as general superintendent of the Illinois State Reformatory at Pontiac. His record in that office is an open book and his service has been one in which he has worked conscientiously for the betterment of the institution and for the welfare of its unfortunate wards.

Mr. Lish suffered a severe loss in the death of his mother, which occurred on her ninety-third birthday in February, 1925, the shock being all the more severe because she had apparently been in the best of health.

GEORGE M. TEARNEY, a Chicago attorney, with offices in the downtown district, is best known in the community where he was born and reared, the southwest section of the city, the McKinley Park district, where for a number of years he has been engaged in real estate and in building and community promotion.

Mr. Tearney was born in Chicago in 1890, son of Thomas H. and Bridget E. (Larney) Tearney, both members of pioneer families of that city. His mother was born in Chicago. His father was born at Covington, Kentucky, February 12, 1861, and was five years of age when the family settled in Chicago in 1866. The Tearneys located in the vicinity of Archer Avenue, the historic "Archey Road," in what is now McKinley Park in the southwest section of the city. Thomas H. Tearney was for several years a civil engineer with the Sanitary District Canal and is now living retired.

George M. Tearney attended parochial schools, a Chicago high school, and since early manhood has engaged in the real estate business. In the meantime he studied law in the Chicago-Kent College of Law, and was graduated Bachelor of Laws in 1919 and Master of Laws in 1920. He conducts a general law practice.

His activities as a builder and financier have been responsible for many notable improvements in the McKinley Park section of the city. He was one of the men responsible for the construction of a great motion picture house at McKinley Park. A site for such a theater was secured and he and others interested capital which resulted in the building of the huge Mid-West Ascher's Theater at Archer Avenue and Hamilton Street, an institution that gives distinction to that section of the city. In March, 1926, he completed the organization of the M. T. & O. Company for the purpose of promoting, financing and operating moving picture houses in different sections of the city. The work of this company is an outgrowth of Mr. Tearney's broad conception of real estate development in general. He realizes that the bringing of a fine modern moving picture theater to a community is in reality an uplift and inspiration to such community, giving enjoyment, entertainment and a gratification of a desire for the beautiful to the masses of the people. The Asher Mid-West Theatre cost $600,000, seats 2,500 people, and the splendid building also contains rooms for eleven stores and twenty-four apartments.

Mr. Tearney served two years as president of the McKinley Park Business Men's Association, which has supported many laudable community projects, including the Mid-West Theatre. Mr. Tearney is a member of the Collegiate Club of Chicago and International Lions Club, the Fraternal Order of Eagles, the Mutual Protective League, Chicago Bar Association and Illinois Bar Association.

He married Miss Nellie Sanders, member of a well known Chicago family. They have one son, Thomas Woodrow Tearney.

LAWRENCE ARVIL BLACKBURN, produce merchant, has through his remarkable energy and faculties for handling a business made up of many details developed the largest independent produce commission business in Southern Illinois, with headquarters at Fairfield. It is said that Mr. Blackburn started his business career with only $20 in cash and a debt of $6.

He was born on a farm in Wayne County, Illinois, November 10, 1887, son of George W. and Ella (Paul) Blackburn. He is of Colonial and Revolutionary ancestry. His father, George W. Blackburn, was a son of Johnson Lourana (Wallace) Blackburn, a grandson of William Blackburn, who married a Miss Wolfe, great-grandson of Joseph and Mary May Blackburn, and Joseph was a son of John Blackburn, who was born in Pennsylvania in 1752 and died in Shelby County, Kentucky, in 1835. John Blackburn served as a soldier of the Revolution, enlisting from Little York, Pennsylvania. His first enlistment for one year began May 18, 1776, and on July 18, 1777, he enlisted for three years. The Blackburn family is English, Scotch and Irish.

George W. Blackburn was born in Indiana and moved to Illinois in 1861. He married in Wayne County Ella (Paul) Durell, a native of Ireland. He followed farming and in later years was engaged in business with his son. He died in 1919. By his first marriage there were four children, and later he married Sina Keen, by which union there were six children.

Lawrence A. Blackburn grew up on the farm, attended country schools and completed a commercial course at Indianapolis. He had two years of business experience and training as a bookkeeper at Indianapolis and in 1906 located at Fairfield, where with his father as senior member of the firm he established G. W. Blackburn & Company, produce dealers, handling poultry and eggs. This business has grown in keeping with the energy of Mr. Blackburn, reaching the great volume where its annual turnover is now approximately two million dollars. Branch houses are maintained in many towns of Southern Illinois, Mr. Blackburn's brother, L. C. Blackburn, having the management of the business at Olney. Mr. Blackburn is also a director in the First National Bank, and is interested in two garages at Fairfield and in the Fairfield Lumber Company, and is owner of some valuable farm land. In 1926 he completed perhaps the finest residence in Fairfield.

He has long been active in the Methodist Church as a trustee. He is a Royal Arch Mason, member of the Independent Order of Odd Fellows, Rotary Club and Chamber of Commerce. Mr. Blackburn in 1911 married Miss Winona Black, a native of White Hall, Illinois. They are the parents of four daughters, Helen, Marjorie, Grace and June.

GEORGE W. CROSSMAN, judge of the Probate Court of Madison County, has been an able member of the bar at Edwardsville for seventeen years. Edwardsville is his native town, and he is a member of a family that has been actively identified with professional and public affairs there for a great many years.

He was born at Edwardsville February 12, 1883, son of W. R. and Julia (Bicklehaupt) Crossman. His father was born in Hamilton County, Ohio, and his mother in Madison County, Illinois, and both are living at Edwardsville.

The oldest of three children, George W. Crossman graduated from high school at Edwardsville in 1901. Subsequently he entered the law department of Northwestern University at Chicago, graduated, and in 1907 was admitted to the bar. He soon engaged in private practice at Edwardsville, and in a few years he was enjoying a profitable private practice. From 1909 to 1911 Judge Crossman was city attorney of Edwardsville, and from 1913 to 1917 was corporation counsel for the city. In 1916 he was elected to the office of probate judge and for eight years has given considerate and discriminating attention to the many important matters for decision.

Judge Crossman before completing his law studies, from 1901 to 1904 was assistant postmaster of Edwardsville. He is unmarried, is a member of the college fraternity Delta Chi, and is a Knight Templar Mason and Shriner.

LOUIS R. WAYMAN, M. D., well known physician of Murphysboro, was first known in this portion of Southern Illinois in the capacity of teacher and educator.

He was born in Kenton County, Kentucky, in 1880. His father, S. Louis Wayman, died in 1904. His mother, Anna J. Arnold, was of an Ohio family and died in 1918. Four years after the birth of Louis R. Wayman his parents moved to Northern Indiana, and in 1899 came to Jackson County, Illinois, where his father spent the rest of his life as a farmer.

Louis R. Wayman was reared in Jasper County, Indiana. He attended school there, and made the best of his advantages with a view to qualifying as a teacher. In 1898 he came to Jackson County, Illinois, a year before his parents moved here. His uncle, John W. Wayman, was an old settler of Jackson County, having come from Kenton County, Kentucky. For many years John W. Wayman lived in the vicinity of Brownsville and later at Murphysboro.

Louis R. Wayman taught a country school in 1898-99. After that between school terms he continued his education in the State Normal at Carbondale and in 1902 graduated from Ewing College. He acted as principal of schools at Elkville and Mount Carbon. Through his association with Doctor Etherton of Murphysboro he became interested in the study of medicine, and by teaching paid his way through the St. Louis College of Physicians and Surgeons, where he was graduated M. D., in 1909. He had additional training as interne in the Jefferson Hospital and Clark Sanitarium. Doctor Wayman then established himself in private practice at Murphysboro, and has made an enviable record in his professional work. He is a member of the various medical societies, is a member of the Murphysboro School Board, is affiliated with Murphysboro Lodge of Masons, the Mystic Shrine at East St. Louis and the Independent Order of Odd Fellows.

Dr. Wayman married, in 1910, Levissa Etherton, daughter of H. H. Etherton, of Murphysboro. She died December 13, 1918. Doctor Wayman on April 17, 1924, married Mrs. Nell Brandon, of Murphysboro.

THOMAS N. SCOVILLE. Among the progressive and enterprising business men of the younger generation, who through natural ability, acquired experience and progressiveness are forging rapidly to the front, few have met with the prosperity that has attended the efforts of Thomas N. Scoville, president of the Resco Electric Supply Company of Rockford. From the time he left school in young manhood he has been energetically identified with various lines of business, in each of which he has displayed versatility.

Mr. Scoville was born August 7, 1900, at Fulton, New York, and is a son of Nesbit and Ita (Leitch) Scoville, the former a native of Michigan and the latter of Wisconsin. His father has been for many years identified with the theatrical business, has traveled extensively and has made his name well and popularly known in various large cities. He and Mrs. Scoville became the parents of two children: Carrie, the wife of Dan Deal, of Wauwatosa, Wisconsin, and Thomas.

Thomas N. Scoville received his education in the public schools of Wisconsin, and then accompanied his parents to Chicago, in which city he secured employment in the printing establishment of the Buckley-DeMent Company. This kind of work did not suit him, and after a short time he entered the service of Peter E. Powers, a furniture manufacturer's agent. His next experience was in the United States navy, during the World war, and in 1918, after one year, received his honorable discharge as a petty officer in the radio department. During the next five years he was engaged as a traveling salesman for various electrical concerns, including radio, but in 1924 located at Rockford, where he became the organizer of the Resco Electrical Supply Company, capitalized at $25,000, of which he is president, his associate officers being D. R. Peterson, vice president; and Kent A. Hemming, secretary and treasurer. The company has already built up a large and lucrative business under Mr. Scoville's energetic direction, and promises to become one of Rockford's successful and prominent enterprises within the course of a few years.

Mr. Scoville married Miss Iva Dell Cassidy, of Boone, Iowa, January 1, 1925. Fraternally he is affiliated with the Masons and the Elks, and also holds membership in the American Legion.

RALPH E. CHURCH, prominent Chicago attorney, member of the law firm of Church, Traxler and Kennedy at 10 South La Salle Street, has to his credit also a record of six consecutive terms in the Illinois Legislature as representative from the Sixth District.

Mr. Church was born on a farm near Catlin in Vermilion County, Illinois, May 5, 1883, son of Henry G. and Lola May (Douglas) Church, of that county. Ralph E. Church acquired a liberal education, but earned his way through his university and law school courses. He graduated from the Danville High School in 1903 and completed his academic education in the University of Michigan, where he was graduated A. B. in 1907. He is an alumnus of the Northwestern University School of Law, which awarded him the degrees Master of Arts and the LL. B. in 1909. In that year he was admitted to the bar and has had a very successful law practice in Chicago, being now senior member of a law firm that ranks among the leaders in general practice. He is a member of the Chicago, Illinois and American Bar Associations.

Mr. Church in the Legislature has earned the special commendations of such organizations as the Legislative Voters League, which said of him: "Highly recommended by prominent lawyers and citizens; an industrious, independent, conscientious member. He is finishing his fifth term, during which he gave the public faithful service as usual."

Mr. Church resides at 300 Church Street, Evanston, in one of the notable residence districts of that city. The Sixth Senatorial district comprises a large section in Chicago and suburbs, including Evanston, Rogers Park, Ravenswood and the north section of Chicago to the Chicago River. Mr. Church was elected a member of the House for the Fiftieth General Assembly in November, 1916, as a republican, and was reelected to the Fifty-first, Fifty-second, Fifty-third, Fifty-fourth and Fifty-fifth General Assemblies. Throughout his several terms he was a member of the judiciary committee. During his legislative service he has been a member of such committees as banks and banking, building and loan associations, judicial departments practice, civil service, charities and corrections, education, insurance, municipalities, revenue and has served as chairman of the committee on elections. He sponsored and had passed the Credit Union Bill, formulated under the Filene plan, under which industrial workers in specified groups are enabled to lend money among themselves.

Mr. Church performed some valuable service in the preparedness activities leading up to the World war. He attended the original Citizens' Training Camp at Fort Sheridan in the summer of 1915, two years before America entered the World war. This was the second training camp for citizens, the first one having been carried out at Plattsburg, New York, under General Leonard Wood. At that time Mr. Church took part in the organization of the Fort Sheridan Association, formed to carry out various helpful activities for the benefit of young men taking training and to have the federal government offer inducement to such in the way of financial remuneration. Mr. Church was one of a committee that went to Washington and brought about an arrangement whereby men offering for training for military service in these camps were to receive pay of one hundred dollars a month. He was a member of the executive committee of the Central Department Citizens Military Training Camp Association in 1916. In May, 1917, while serving his first legislative term, he volunteered for military duty and entered the First Officers' Training Camp at Fort Sheridan, commanded by Colonel W. J. Nicholson. He had nearly finished his term of training when he was taken with the mumps. This ailment was followed by more serious complications and finally, upon medical examination, he was disqualified for active service in the army. This prevented him from active participation in the further events of the World war. He is a member of the American Legion, Evanston Post, and is a member of Wayfarers Lodge No. 1001, A. F. and A. M. His other social connections are with the Lake Shore Athletic Club, of which he is a life member, the Hamilton Club, of which he is a life member; Union League Club of Chicago, the Executives Club of Chicago and the Kiwanis Club of Chicago. He is also a member of the First Methodist Church of Evanston, of the Phi Kappa Psi and Delta Chi fraternities, Loyal Order of Moose, Evanston University Club and the Evanston Country Club.

Mr. Church married, December 21, 1918, Marguerite Stitt, of New York City. They have two children: Ralph Edwin Jr., and William Stitt.

CAPT. LEON M. SHUGART. The average man is seldom brought face to face with the stern realities of life before he has reached years of near maturity. He is generally given the opportunity of making a choice of occupations, allowed to follow his inclinations in as far as circumstances do not prevent. Showing an early predilection for a certain vocation, he may be given his chance to develop his talents along his chosen line, and his success or failure rests upon the manner in which he exercises his inherent gifts. It is not, however, the average man who always reaches the highest goal. History and biography conclusively prove that many men who have reached high positions have had their start in obscurity and have had to fight their own way and make their own opportunities. Capt. Leon M. Shugart had no golden youth. He was but fourteen years of age when he joined the world's workers, and since then he has continued to be an energetic, forceful and industrious laborer in whatever field he has found himself. Today he occupies the position of sheriff of Livingston County and a place in the esteem and confidence of his fellow citizens at Pontiac.

Captain Shugart was born in McLean County, Illinois, in 1893, and is a son of John C. and Anne (Seddith) Shugart. His father came to that county from Virginia and followed his trade of harnessmaker there until his removal to Pontiac, where he resided for many years and was known as an industrious workman and a good citizen. The last three years of his life were spent at the home of Captain Shugart, where his death occurred September 18, 1925. He and his wife were the parents of three children: May Ione, the wife of Edward Schneckenburger, a prominent farmer of Pike Township, Livingston County; Robert Zachariah, a business man of Atlanta, Georgia; and Leon M., of this review.

Leon M. Shugart attended school only through the eighth grade and when fourteen years of age began to be partly self-supporting. His first employment was at stripping tobacco after school and during the evenings, but he soon found that his earnings were small and that the best way to forge ahead was to master a trade. Accordingly he learned the vocation of cigarmaking, but when he had completed his trade and had worked for a time as a journeyman he felt that he could better himself, and sought and obtained employment with P. D. Bagnall, a leading plumber of Pontiac. After learning the plumber's trade he remained with Mr. Bagnall for a period of fifteen years. While attending strictly to business, he found pleasure and benefit in military affairs and prior to the World war had been a member of the local company of the Illinois National Guard, in which he rose to the rank of sergeant. Before this country had become embroiled in the great struggle that raged overseas he had retired from the Guard, but the moment the call was issued for volunteers he enlisted as a private in Headquarters Company, 129th Infantry Regiment, 33rd Division, Illinois National Guard. On May 10, 1918, his regiment landed at Brest, France, and from that time forward he was constantly with his unit, participating in all the engagements and movements of that splendid body, as related elsewhere. After the armistice he was promoted to a lieutenancy in the regular army and assigned to Headquarters Company of the Fifty-second United States Infantry, in the Sixth Division, a part of the Army of Occupation. In the early part of June, 1919, the work of the army being completed, the Fifty-second was sent to Brest and June 12 sailed for the United States, and upon arrival was sent to Camp Grant. While Captain Shugart was an officer in the regular army, and with a fine record as a soldier, he did not want a permanent military life and upon his own request was retired as captain on August 23, 1919. He at once returned to Pontiac and to the employment of Mr. Bagnall. In February, 1922, the republicans nominated Captain Shugart for the office of sheriff of Livingston County, and, being elected in the fall, assumed the duties of that position December 4, 1922. His record is an excellent one and he has been highly successful in the maintenance of law and order and in discharging the other duties of his office. When the local post of the American Legion at Pontiac was organized Captain Shugart was elected its first adjutant. He is a Scottish Rite and Knight Templar Mason, and belongs to the Modern Woodmen, the Elks, the Loyal Order of Moose, and Independent Order of Odd Fellows.

At Pontiac Captain Shugart was united in marriage on August 1, 1920, with Miss Florence Gieseking, of Centralia, Illinois. Mrs. Shugart has been very active in the work of the American Legion Auxiliary and has served as president of that organization, and is also an active worker in the Eastern Star in Pontiac.

JOHN HILL MCFADDEN. While the residence of John Hill McFadden at Pontiac, which has now covered a period of eleven years, has been replete with engrossing professional employment which has placed him in the front rank of practicing lawyers, he has found time to devote to various branches of public service, which his liberal training fits him to execute and appreciate. His career has been one of useful and active participation in the affairs of his adopted community, and at present he is acting as attorney for the Board of Supervisors of Livingston County.

Mr. McFadden was born near Arcola, Douglas County, Illinois, in 1880, and is a son of John W. and Martha (Hill) McFadden. His father, a native of Tuscarawas, Ohio, came to Illinois in 1859 and settled on a farm near Arcola which he had purchased from the Illinois Central Railroad Company, and on which he passed the remainder of his life in the peaceful pursuits of agriculture. Mrs. McFadden, who is also deceased, was, like her husband, a native of Ohio.

John Hill McFadden grew up in an agricultural atmosphere, and, like most of the farmers' sons of his day, spent the summer months in assisting his father on the home farm, his primary educational training being acquired in the district school during the winter terms. In 1897 he graduated from the Arcola High School, and, ambitious and industrious and with a determination to follow a professional career, he attended Illinois Wesleyan College, where he took both the literary and law courses. He graduated from the latter with the class of 1905, receiving the degree of Bachelor of Law, and circumstances led him to Fairbury, Livingston County, where, having been admitted to the bar, he commenced the practice of his profession. During the decade that followed he built up an excellent clientele and acquired such prominence that he became the republican party's candidate for the office of state's attorney, to which office he was duly elected in 1916, at which time he took up his residence at Pontiac. By reelection he held this office until 1924 and made an enviable record for brilliant handling of the many cases that were entrusted to his care. Shortly after retiring from that office he was appointed attorney of the County Board of Supervisors by action of that body. While living at Fairbury Mr. McFadden served eight years in the capacity of city attorney.

Mr. McFadden has never married. A large and jovial man, he is very popular, particularly among his fellow members in the Kiwanis Club, the Elks, Odd Fellows and Masons, in the last-named of which he has passed through all the chairs in the Blue Lodge. He belongs to the Methodist Church. Mr. McFadden takes a keen and intelligent interest in all matters pertaining to the betterment of the community, and has been active in child welfare work and similar accompaniments of civilization.

WILLIAM OSBORN DAVIS. The Bloomington Daily Pantagraph has for many years enjoyed a rating as a successful newspaper. It has been successful not only as a business enterprise and in the measure of its circulation, but as a newspaper of character and standards such as have entitled it to the respect of discriminating critics. In its broader and better success The Daily Pantagraph reflected the personal character of the late William Osborn Davis, who was its responsible editor and publisher from 1868 until his death in May, 1911. Since his death The Daily Pantagraph has been published by a corporation, composed of members of his family.

William Osborn Davis was born and reared on a farm in eastern Pennsylvania, in the historic and cultured region around Philadelphia, and was of Quaker stock. His ancestors had come to the United States at the time of William Penn. The farm of his father, Hibbard Osborn Davis, and of his grandfather, William Osborn Davis, was included in the site of the battle of the Brandywine of the Revolution. While his parents were farmers, they enjoyed more of the comforts than the substantial farmers of the middle west at that time. Mr. Davis grew up in a substantial house, built of stone, and comfortably furnished according to the standards of that time. There were nine children, and they were given the advantages of boarding schools in addition to the facilities of the local institutions of learning. William Osborn Davis was afforded every possible opportunity to pursue his natural bent for knowledge, and something was also done to develop his talent for drawing and sketching.

Not far from the home of the Davis family in Chester County, Pennsylvania, was the home of the Fell family, one member of which, Jesse W. Fell, had come out to Illinois and was conspicuous as founder of the town of Normal, and prominent in public affairs. When William O. Davis as a young man came to Illinois he visited at the Fell homestead in McLean County, and on his return from a trip to Colorado he was induced to remain and teach a winter term of the district school in the then sparsely settled region of Normal.

About that time his father purchased land in central Illinois, and William Osborn Davis established himself as a farmer on this place about two miles north of Normal. When the Civil war broke out Mr. Davis went to Washington and served with the paymaster's department of the army. In 1863 he married Eliza Fell, daughter of his old friend Jesse W. Fell. For several years he was engaged in farming and teaching, and in 1868 first became interested in newspaper work, and Jesse W. Fell had something to do with the history of newspapers at Bloomington, being one of the proprietors of The Observer, the first paper published in that city, in 1837. Mr. Fell, Mr. Davis and James P. Taylor acquired the daily and weekly Pantagraph in 1868. Thereafter for forty years Mr. Davis gave his time, thought and wise management to the development of this newspaper. A job printing shop was formerly connected with the newspaper, but Mr. Davis disposed of that to a separate company, and gave his undivided attention to the newspaper. His breadth of view, his instinctive knowledge of what the reading public wanted, and his eminent fairness gave his paper a standing and prosperity seldom equalled by any newspaper published in a city of similar size.

In 1908, a few years before his death, the business was incorporated with Mr. Davis as president, his son Hibbard O. Davis as vice president, and C. C. Marquis, secretary.

One of the chief reasons assigned to Mr. Davis' success as a newspaper manager apart from his individual genius was his faculty for choosing competent people for the detailed work and then keeping them for long terms in my employ after his training had made them valuable assistants. The Pantagraph is noted for the number of men and women who have served it many years.

After the death of William O. Davis his son Hibbard O. Davis succeeded him as managing editor and continued the policies of his father. On account of ill health he retired from the active management in 1923, and died in 1924. His interests are now looked after by Davis Merwin, a grandson of the late William O. Davis.

Mrs. William O. Davis died nine years before her husband. The two surviving daughters of Mr. Davis are: Helen, wife of Lewis G. Stevenson, a son of Adlai Stevenson, former vice president; and Jessie, wife of Louis B. Merwin, of Bloomington.

ROY J. OSTRANDER. Three generations of the Ostrander family have lent strength and dignity to the institutions of Livingston County, where its members have continued to contribute materially to the welfare and development of various communities. A worthy representative of this family is found in Roy J. Ostrander, who since 1920 has conducted a modern funeral directing establishment, and who is one of Pontiac's reliable and public-spirited citizens.

Mr. Ostrander was born June 10, 1886, at McDowell, Livingston County, Illinois, and is a son of Joseph K. and Ophelia (Foster) Ostrander. His grandfather, Dr. C. B. Ostrander, was one of the earliest settlers and best known men of Livingston County. Having fitted himself for the practice of his profession in his native state of New York, he made his way as a young man to Illinois and settled on a farm about seven miles from the village of Pontiac, at a time when there were less than a dozen houses at that place and too few citizens to support a physician depending on his profession alone. For several years he operated his farm, but answered calls to all parts of the county made by the sick and injured, riding horseback as the brave and unselfish set of men of that day did, night or day, in all kinds of weather, gone for a week at a time, and with little hope of financial remuneration. After a time this kindly country doctor was able to purchase a buggy, in which he soon became a familiar figure, driving all over the countryside, and only using his saddle-horse when the roads and streams were so bad that they were impassable for vehicles. Incidentally that was the first buggy used in Livingston County. He became widely known and greatly beloved, doing much good among the poor and needy, and as the population increased he sold his farm and moved to Fairbury, where he lived to the ripe old age of ninety years, passing away in 1902. He and his worthy wife had no children of their own, but adopted two or three children whom they reared to honorable man and womanhood.

Among these children was Joseph K. Ostrander, the father of Roy J., who was born in 1846. Working on his adopted father's farm during the summer months, he acquired an education in the district school during winter terms, and was only a lad when he enlisted for service in the Civil war, during which he underwent hardships and injuries that affected his health during the remainder of his life. When he was twenty years of age he went to McDowell, in the same county, a village on the Wabash Railroad, and there entered the grain business. Two years later he bought a grocery store in that village and ran it in connection with his grain business, and at the same time discharged the duties of station agent of the Wabash Railroad at that point. For twenty years he conducted his store successfully, but in 1898 the building and stock were destroyed by fire, and at that time he retired from that line of business and devoted himself to his increasing duties as agent. In 1923 his health failed and he considered it advisable for him to resign his railroad position. His death occurred October 10, 1925. Mr. Ostrander was a man of integrity, who had the good will and confidence of the people of his community. He married Miss Ophelia Foster, daughter of Russell B. Foster, one of the early settlers of the county, Mrs. Ostrander having been six years of age when brought by her parents from her native state of Indiana. She died April 2, 1923, having been the beloved mother of eight children, of whom six still survive.

Roy J. Ostrander attended the public schools at McDowell and the high school at Pontiac, following which he taught school for three years in the rural districts. He then went to Chicago, where for the following ten years he was employed in various undertaking establishments, during which time he learned the business in every department. In 1920 he took up his residence at Pontiac, where he purchased the business of George Rice, who had

Fanny Posey Hacker

been engaged for years in the furniture and undertaking line. Mr. Ostrander immediately sold the furniture department, and has devoted his entire attention to the undertaking line, having built up a large patronage and unbounded confidence, and is conducting one of the most modern establishments of its kind, fully equipped for the reverent care of the dead. Mr. Ostrander has a number of civic and social connections, but takes only a good citizen's interest in public affairs.

Mr. Ostrander married Miss Eleanor Scheve, a daughter of Henry Scheve, of Cincinnati, Ohio, and they are the parents of two children, Dorothy Opelia and Robert Joseph, both born in Pontiac.

Mrs. Ostrander is a licensed embalmer and a trained registered nurse. Mr. Ostrander belongs to the B. P. O. E. No. 1019, of Pontiac, I. O. O. F. of Pontiac, No. 262, Vermilion Encampment No. 54, and Modern Woodmen of America.

JOHN E. CROSS had a notable career to his credit as an educator in Ogle County, where for over forty years he was identified in some capacity with the public schools at the time of his death, October 2, 1926, and was county superintendent of schools with headquarters in the courthouse at Oregon.

He was born in Ogle County, February 1, 1861, son of James L. and Mary A. (Rathbun) Cross, and grandson of John and Sophia (Hardesty) Cross. John Cross came from Coshocton County, Ohio, and settled on land taken up from the Government in Ogle County in 1842. When Sophia Hardesty was a child Indians were numerous in this section of Illinois, and during their yearly visit to the Hardesty neighborhood and while camping near Rochelle, Illinois, they sometimes called at the Hardesty home and named the child Sophia the White Papoose. James L. Cross was born in Coshocton County, Ohio, and was a child when brought to Illinois. He spent his life as a farmer in Ogle County and died in 1920. His wife, Mary A. Rathbun, was the first white child born in the eastern part of Ogle County. She died in 1886.

John E. Cross attended grammar and high schools in Ogle County, grew up on a farm, and it is doubtful if any other citizen of Ogle County knew more of the people more intimately and understood conditions better than he. He attended a training school for teachers and first began teaching in 1883. He taught in country schools, town and city schools, and after twenty-three years in the school room he, in 1906, was appointed assistant county superintendent of schools at Oregon. In 1910 he was elected county superintendent, and by reelection held that position over fifteen years. Since 1910 the public schools of the county have marked a great advance in equipment and general raising of standards. The teachers are better prepared and today there are eight community and consolidated high school districts in the county.

Mr. Cross was president and a director of the Restitution Publishing Company of Oregon. He was affiliated with the Independent Order of Odd Fellows, Woodmen of the World and the Church of God. He married at Chana, in Ogle County, November 2, 1887, Miss Nellie I. Booth, daughter of J. W. and Fanny (Collins) Booth. Her father was born and reared in Indiana and her mother, in England, and early in their married lives they settled in Illinois. Mr. and Mrs. Cross had four children, Leroy B. (deceased), Clarence S., Cecile N. and Maude F. Leroy married Clara Williams and they had two children, Verna and Margaret. Clarence married Ruth Chamberlain, of Oregon, who died in 1916, leaving a son, John Eugene, and in 1918 he married Lois Brandel, of Wisconsin, and by this marriage has four children, named Robert, Donald, Roland and Richard. Cecile Cross became the wife of Ward J. Scott, of Oregon, and their three children are John W., Margaret Jane and Marilyn C. Scott. Maude Cross is the wife of Rolland Stilson, of South Bend, Indiana, and they have a family of three children, named John E., Donald and Joy.

CAPT. JOHN STUART HACKER. One of the men who played an important part in the early history of Alexander County and the City of Cairo, has been Capt. John Stuart Hacker, who for years was one of the leading business operators of this section, and a most public-spirited citizen. He was born at Washington, District of Columbia, in 1854, a son of William H. and Angelina Hacker, also natives of Washington City. In 1856 the family moved to Jonesboro, Illinois, where William H. Hacker was engaged in the practice of law, and became one of the distinguished men of his profession. He served as a member of the Illinois State Legislature, and was instrumental in having the county seat of Alexander County moved from Thebes to Cairo.

Captain Hacker attended the public schools, and his first contact with business was gained when he was employed in painting wagons. Becoming interested in river traffic, he became in the course of time general manager of three ferry boats, the Kiwanis, Tri-State and Cary Bird.

In March, 1877, Captain Hacker married Fanny Posey, born at Henderson, Kentucky, a daughter of Washington and Hannah (Sublet) Posey. The paternal grandparents were Fayette and Louisa (Edwards) Posey, natives of Virginia and Tennessee. The great-grandfather, Gen. Thomas Posey, was a state senator in Kentucky, and a pioneer of Posey County, Indiana, which was named in his honor. Mrs. Hacker attended the primitive backwoods schools of Kentucky, later a preparatory school in Indiana, and finally a high school in Kentucky, and subsequently she took up post-graduate work in several educational institutions, becoming famed for her intellectual attainments. In 1910 she was elected county superintendent of schools for Alexander County, Illinois, and served the full term of four years. Captain and Mrs. Hacker became the parents of the following children: Loulow, who is Mrs. A. W. Danforth, of Cairo; Daisy, who is a resident of Halliday House, Cairo; Hannah, who is Mrs. Fowler, of Los Angeles, California; Nick, who died at the age of twenty-nine years; Alice, who is living with her parents at 415 Washington Avenue; and Dimple, who is a school teacher in the Philippine Islands, the wife of Shannon Richmond.

Mrs. Hacker is a member of the Woman's Club of Cairo, which she has served as secretary, also served as president of the Wickliff Woman's Club of Wickliff, Kentucky, of which she is a charter member, and she is now president of the Delphium Society. In religious faith she is an Episcopalian. She has always been deeply interested in public affairs, and has possessed the ability to participate in them, and to lead others of her sex in similar work. It has always been her contention that it is a woman's duty to work in behalf of civic movements, and that in so doing she does not need to neglect her home or family. Proper planning will enable her to do her duty as a citizen while looking after her domestic cares, and in her own operations she has proven the truth of this. A very ambitious girl, she carried on the studies begun in the backwoods of her native state until she was chosen to lead in educational matters in her county. Her influence in club affairs is unquestioned, and many look to her for proper guidance.

ISAAC FUNK was truly one of the founders of Illinois' greatness as a state. In the domain of agriculture his achievements were fully as impressive and important as those of Pullman and Armour in the field of industry and only less notable than those of Lincoln in statesmanship. It is possible to assert that the full significance of the phrase "The Illinois Corn Belt" would never have been realized without the leadership and the constructive and creative ability of Isaac Funk and his descendants.

In 1924 the Funk family of McLean County celebrated the one hundredth anniversary of its establishment in Illinois. Isaac Funk, the founder, was born in Clark County, Kentucky, November 17, 1797. He arrived in Illinois, coming from Ohio, in 1824, and at that time was burdened with a debt of some two thousand dollars. His place of settlement has long been known as "Funk's Grove." The only capital he possessed was industry, perseverance and integrity. In 1826 he married Cassandra Sharp, of Peoria, who had come from Maryland. He soon formed a partnership with his brother Absalom and engaged in the business of buying cattle and horses and selling them at various markets, chiefly Chicago. After 1841 Isaac Funk continued the business alone, and was one of the largest drovers of his time, sometimes driving as many as 1500 cattle and 1000 hogs to Chicago. From the profits of his dealings in live stock he invested in land on a large scale. Long before his death he was the foremost live stock raiser and dealer, and one of the largest land owners in Illinois. He never speculated in land, since he bought for use and not for sale. His purchases between 1829 and 1853 aggregated 25,000 acres, and most of that land is still comprised in the various Funk farms around Bloomington. Many larger areas of land have been held by a single family in the United States, but no land anywhere surpasses it in value for purely agricultural purposes.

Isaac Funk was a pioneer. He grew up on the frontier of the middle west, and had only the simplest literary advantages. His distinguishing virtues were his remarkable energy and industry, his rugged integrity and his exemplification of the simple fundamentals of private and public life. He was elected a member of the Legislature in 1840, and in 1862 was sent to the State Senate, serving during the Civil war. He made a speech in the Senate in February, 1863, that has been regarded as one of the most memorable of all war speeches. President Lincoln ordered the speech read before every Union regiment then in the field. The occasion of the speech was the critical time in the Illinois General Assembly, when the war and emancipation policy of President Lincoln was being bitterly arraigned. A few sentences from Senator Funk's speech are best quoted in Smith's "Student's History of Illinois:" "I can sit here no longer and not tell these traitors what I think of them; and while so telling them, I am responsible, myself, for what I say. I stand upon my own bottom, I am ready to meet any man on this floor in any manner, from a pin's point to the mouth of a cannon upon this charge against these traitors—I came to Illinois a poor boy; I have a little something for myself and family. I pay $3,000 a year in taxes. I am willing to pay $6,000 a year; aye! $12,000. Aye! I am willing to pay my whole fortune, and then give my life to save my country from these traitors that are seeking to destroy it. Yes, these traitors and villains in the Senate are killing my neighbor's boys, now fighting in the field. I dare to say this to these traitors right here, and I am responsible for what I say to any and all of them. Let them come on, right here. Mr. Speaker, I must beg the pardon of the gentlemen in this Senate who are not traitors, but true, loyal men, for what I have said I only intend it and mean it for secessionists at heart."

Isaac Funk and his good wife Cassandra both died on the same day, January 29, 1865. They were survived by eight sons and one daughter. The careers of these children might be regarded as the greatest glory and honor of Isaac and Cassandra Funk. Their names and a brief reference to their positions in business and public affairs are as follows:

George W. Funk (1827-1911) owned and operated a 2600 acre farm, was a director of the First National Bank of Bloomington, and served in the Legislature and on the Board of Supervisors.

Jacob Funk (1830-1919) owned and lived on a 2600 acre farm, was president for thirty years of the State National Bank of Bloomington, was a charter member of the Funk Brothers Seed Company, and had an international reputation as a breeder and feeder of Angus cattle.

Duncan M. Funk (1832-1910) in addition to the management of his 2700 acre farm served thirty-six years as president of the First National Bank of Bloomington. He was in the Legislature, served twenty-five years as a member of the Board of Supervisors, and for eighteen years was a trustee of the Soldiers Orphans Home.

LaFayette Funk (1834-1919) like his brothers owned a farm over 2,200 acres, was a breeder of Shorthorn cattle, a director of the Union Stock Yards of Chicago, and a charter member of Funk Brothers Seed Company. For twenty-nine years he was a member of the State Board of Agriculture, and served several terms in the Illinois General Assembly.

Francis M. Funk (1836-1899) owned a 2,200 acre farm. He was a generous benefactor of the Methodist Church and for over twenty years was president of the Board of Education of Bloomington.

Benjamin F. Funk (1838-1909) also owned a 2,200 acre farm and was a charter member of Funk Brothers Seed Company. He served a term in Congress, was for twelve years mayor of Bloomington, and was chairman of the Board of Trustees of the Illinois Wesleyan University.

Absalom Funk (1841-1915) lived on a large farm near Bloomington, served five years as president of the First National Bank, was a charter member of the Funk Brothers Seed Company, and was a very successful feeder and breeder of Shorthorn cattle. He served as a soldier in the Civil war.

Isaac Funk, Jr. (1844-1909) was also a soldier of the Civil war. He engaged in live stock and grain farming on his 2,200 acre place, was a charter member of Funk Brothers Seed Company and a director of the State National Bank of Bloomington.

The only daughter was Sarah Funk Kerrick (1846-1907), wife of Hon. L. H. Kerrick, who at one time was president of the Board of Trustees of the University of Illinois.

EUGENE DUNCAN FUNK, grandson of Isaac Funk, has been an outstanding figure in the third generation in carrying on the work for which the name Funk will longest be known in the history of Illinois.

Eugene D. Funk was born at Funk's Grove, McLean County, September 3, 1867, son of LaFayette and Elizabeth (Paullin) Funk. His mother is still living. LaFayette Funk, who died September 6, 1919, for many years owned and operated one of the extensive Funk farms, was a breeder of Shorthorn cattle and was several times winner on the best Shorthorn carload lot exhibited at the International Fat Stock Show in Chicago. He was a director of the Chicago Union Stock Yards, and he served in the Lower House of the Legislature in the Thirty-third General Assembly, and succeeded Governor Fifer in the State Senate in the Thirty-fourth and Thirty-fifth sessions. He was also a director of the State National Bank in Bloomington.

Eugene D. Funk was educated in country schools, attended Wyman's Institute at Upper Alton, Illinois, Phillips Andover Academy, Andover, Massachusetts, and spent three years in Yale University. Instead of continuing in college to graduation he spent a year abroad in practical contact with farmers and in the study of agriculture in England, Belgium, Holland, Germany, France, Switzerland and Italy.

Eugene D. Funk for over thirty years has specialized in the growing of pure bred seed, and since its organization in 1901 has been president of the Funk Brothers Seed Company of Bloomington. This company specializes in seed corn, grown and tested on the thousands of acres comprised in the Funk farms in McLean County.

During the World war Mr. Funk was one of the twelve men selected by President Wilson to fix the price of wheat in 1917, and subsequently was one of the twenty-four that acted in the food department under Herbert Hoover and the agricultural department under Secretary Houston. He was a dollar-a-year man. He was appointed by Governor Lowden as chairman of the seed planting crops for the state of Illinois, also was chairman of the National Committee for the same purpose, member of the agricultural advisory committee of the food administration, member of the agricultural committee of the Chamber of Commerce of the United States, and treasurer of the State Live Stock Association of Illinois. He has served as president of the National Corn Association of the United States since 1907. He is president of the American Seeds Trade Association of the United States, which handles seventy per cent of agricultural seeds sold in the United States and Canada. He is also president of the Poinsetta Pork Company of Winter Haven, Florida, and has served for about twenty-five years on advisory committees for the College of Agriculture, University of Illinois and at present a member of a committee. When the Department of Agriculture in 1918 undertook cooperative experimental work in the study of plant diseases affecting corn, Mr. Funk placed at the disposal of the federal and state scientific men his buildings, his farms, his crops, his men and even a great deal of his own time. Some branch of this great work has been carried on at his farms ever since.

Mr. Funk is a York and Scottish Rite Mason and Shriner, member of the Bloomington Country Club, is a charter member of the Rotary Club, member of the Bloomington Association of Commerce. He owns a winter home at Winter Haven, Florida.

Mr. Funk takes reasonable pride in the achievements of his grandfather and the members of the second generation of this family, derives no small measure of satisfaction from the activities that have been guided by his own hands, but still another source of gratification is the splendid family of boys and girls who have grown up in his own household and who constitute some of the men and women of the fourth generation of the Funk family who may be depended upon for the work and responsibilities in which they are already engaged or which are awaiting them. Mr. Funk married at Portland, Oregon, in 1894, Miss Mary Anderson, daughter of Mrs. A. B. Anderson, of Portland. Of their children the oldest is Gladys, wife of C. A. Rihtmeier, of Pittsburgh, Pennsylvania, and the mother of four children, Betty, Robert, Josephine and Calvin. LaFayette Funk, Jr., the oldest son, married Cleda Otto and has a son, LaFayette III, thus making the fifth generation now living on the Funk farm. Elizabeth Funk is the wife of Robert S. McCormick, of Gibson City, Illinois. Eugene Funk, Jr., now an associate with his father in business, married

Maeotta Divelbiss. The two younger sons, Paul Allen and Theodore, are both students in the University of Illinois. The daughter Ruth was an art student in the Carnegie Institute of Technology at Pittsburg, and was recently married to Waldo Roth, of Gibson City, Illinois. Mary, the youngest daughter, is at home, attending high school.

EDWARD A. PETERSEN is an electrical contractor, member of a firm with well established connections and extensive business over northern Cook and Lake counties. Mr. Petersen, with M. R. Kordick, conduct the business known as the Kordick Electric Company at Winnetka, Illinois.

Mr. Petersen was born at Mamaroneck, New York, November 16, 1893, son of William A. and Sophie C. (Lenz) Petersen. Both his parents were born and reared in Germany, were educated there, and in 1890 came to America and settled in Mamaroneck. From there in 1901 they removed to Chicago. William A. Petersen has been retired from business since 1925. His wife died in Chicago in 1924.

Edward A. Petersen was eight years old when the family moved to Chicago, and he attended public schools there, and subsequently in the intervals of his working experience continued his education in the night schools of the Y. M. C. A. at Lewis Institute, and later took a course in accountancy at Northwestern University. For some time he was an employe of the Continental Fire Insurance Company. After his work at Northwestern University he became estimator for the Chicago Mill & Lumber Company, serving about two years. In 1916 he went with the Commonwealth Edison Company of Chicago in the maintenance department, and was there about eight months before he was called to the colors.

In September, 1917, he enlisted in the Headquarters Company of the Thirty-third Division, and was in training at Camp Logan at Houston, Texas. In November, 1917, he was transferred to the One Hundred Eighth Field Signal Battalion. He went overseas to France in May, 1918, and was on duty on the front lines during the Somme offensive, the St. Mihiel offensive and the Meuse-Argonne campaign. During the Argonne campaign he was slightly wounded by shrapnel, but after first aid treatment continued with his outfit. The scar of those wounds are still on his body. He was with the Army of Occupation in Luxemburg until returning home, and he received his honorable discharge at Camp Grant June 7, 1919.

After the war Mr. Petersen became an electrician in the building trades of Chicago, a line of work he followed about two years. He then engaged in electrical contracting for himself, locating at Winnetka, where he formed a partnership with Joseph L. Kordick. In 1926 a third partner came into the firm, S. Harry Fish, and in April of that year the firm established the North Chicago branch of the Kordick Electric Company. As electrical contractors the firm handles a business that is constantly growing, including important contracts along the North Shore.

Mr. Petersen is a Knight Templar Mason, is a member of the Lutheran Church and in politics votes as an independent. He married at Chicago, in July, 1919, Miss Anna Dahlstrom. She was born and reared in Chicago, attending grammar and high schools there. They have two children, Edward A., Jr., and Dorothy Jean.

FRANK M. BULLOCK. Throughout his entire business career Frank M. Bullock has been a railroad man. He has held positions with several of the leading southern railroads, and came to Illinois as an official of the Mobile & Ohio. At the present time he is superintendent of the St. Louis Division, Murphysboro district, of that railroad, with headquarters in the Mobile and Ohio offices at Murphysboro.

He was born at Rockmart, Georgia, and grew up and received his early education there. His parents were John Grey and Sarah Rebecca (Randall) Bullock, both of Southern birth and parentage. His father likewise spent his life in railroad work and died in 1913.

Frank M. Bullock at the age of nineteen began his career as a railroad man in the transportation department of the Southern Railway and later with the Seaboard Air Line Railroad. His work centered at Atlanta. At the end of fifteen years he had reached the position of assistant chief train dispatcher, and subsequently became chief train dispatcher. These two positions he held for a total of six years.

On leaving Atlanta Mr. Bullock became trainmaster of the Southern Railway at Columbus, Mississippi, and a year later was advanced to a similar position at Jackson, Tennessee, with the Mobile & Ohio, where he likewise remained a year. In 1921 he came to Murphysboro as trainmaster, and on January 1, 1926, was promoted to superintendent of the Murphysboro district of the St. Louis Division. He is a vigorous yet popular railroad official, and in his promotions he has followed closely in the footsteps of Superintendent Blaney B. Tolson, another veteran employe of the Mobile & Ohio, who on January 1, 1926, was made assistant to the general manager, being succeeded by Mr. Bullock as superintendent of the district.

Mr. Bullock is a member of the Masonic Order and belongs to Yaarab Temple of the Mystic Shrine at Atlanta. He married Jane Newman, daughter of Benjamin Newman, of Selma, Alabama.

ARCHIBALD D. BRUBAKER has been identified with some phase of the grain business since early youth. He is now general manager of the Southern Illinois Milling Company at Murphysboro. This company was incorporated and began operations for the manufacture of a high quality of flour at Murphysboro in 1892. A large part of the output of the mills from the beginning was marketed in the South. The two principals in the organization were Theodore Ismert and Phillip H. Eisenmayer. Eisenmayer became the first president and general manager of the company. The mills and elevators are located directly east of the Illinois Central Railroad passenger station. Steam power is used. The equipment installed in 1892 has since been

Owen Meredith Fox.

replaced by the most modern type of flouring machinery.

The officers of the company today are: Edward R. Hincke, of Pinckneyville, who has been president since 1922; Dr. A. R. Carter, vice president; Walter C. Alexander, secretary and treasurer; and Archibald D. Brubaker, general manager. Mr. Brubaker has been general manager and assistant treasurer of the company since 1924.

He was born at Washington, in Tazewell County, Illinois, in 1872. His father, Peter Brubaker, now living at Eureka, Illinois, came to this state from Mansfield, Ohio, and for many years has been identified with the grain business. Peter Brubaker married Almeda Cress, a native of Illinois, her parents coming from Virginia. Peter and Almeda Brubaker celebrated their sixtieth wedding anniversary December 14, 1925.

Archibald D. Brubaker grew up at Washington, Illinois, attended public schools there, and by working for and with his father he acquired an extended experience of the grain business. It was in 1914 that he became identified with the Southern Illinois Milling Company in the capacity of traveling salesman, covering an extended territory in the South.

Some years ago while on the road as a flour salesman he moved his home and family to Carbondale as a city not only with excellent transportation facilities for his own convenience, but with splendid schools. He has been one of the respected and public spirited citizens of that educational community of Southern Illinois. Mr. Brubaker is a Mason, member of the Knight Templar Commandery at Carbondale, the Temple of the Mystic Shrine at Peoria, and belongs to the B. P. O. Elks and Modern Woodmen of America.

In 1900 he married Miss Catherine Thomas, daughter of Charles C. Thomas, of Southern Illinois. They have one daughter, Dora E., who graduated in 1924 from the Southern Illinois State Normal University at Carbondale, and is now an instructor in the high school at Cobden, Illinois.

ANDREW HOUSER SHUMAKER is a veteran newspaper man, publisher and editor, and has given all the years of his life since early manhood to that calling.

He was born at Farmer City, Illinois, December 26, 1869, son of Hardy and America Shumaker. His paternal grandparents came from the South, while his mother's people were New Englanders. Mr. Shumaker first attended public school at Farmer City, and his last days in school were in McLean County. In 1896 he became owner and publisher of the newspaper at Villa Grove in Douglas County, and has found his time and energies fully absorbed in the varied responsibilities of publishing and operating a high class country newspaper.

Mr. Shumaker is a democrat, is chancellor commander of the Knights of Pythias, member of the Masonic Lodge and the Methodist Episcopal Church.

He married at Farmer City, June 8, 1898, Miss Maude Rinehart, daughter of A. R. and Mary Rinehart, who came to Illinois from Pennsylvania in 1879. Mr. and Mrs. Shumaker have three daughters, Marguerite Y., Madge M. and Stella. Marguerite is the wife of Ira Beaman and is the mother of two children, named Gloria and Marna.

OWEN MEREDITH FOX. When in August, 1925, Owen Meredith Fox was appointed executive vice president of the Chicago Coal Merchants' Association, due recognition was given to the abilities and character of one of the best known men in the coal trade of the country, and one thoroughly informed as to conditions therein as well as in other lines of industry.

Mr. Fox was born in December, 1885, at Goddard, Kansas, and is a son of Thomas J. and Belle (Matlock) Fox. Thomas J. Fox was born near Indianapolis, Indiana, whence he went to Kansas and became a public school teacher in the little town of Goddard, where a land boom was then raging. Later he went to Wichita and then to Garden City, in the same state, and finally, when the boom burst, to Colorado, where he still makes his home at Colorado Springs and is now secretary of the Board of Education. Mrs. Fox, who is now deceased, was born in Rush County, Indiana, a member of a large and prominent family of that historic section of the state.

The public schools of Colorado, including the high school, furnished Owen Meredith Fox with his educational training, and during the years of his boyhood he resided at Leadville and Cripple Creek, two of the greatest gold mining camps of the time. This was during the time that the Western Federation of Miners, under the leadership of the notorious Moyer, Heywood and Pettibone, was striving for control of the quartz mining industry, and the youth received impressions of union misrule, as an eyewitness of the bloody riots at these two mining towns which became indelible. Later, as a member of the Colorado National Guard, he had a further contact with the then embryonic Industrial Workers of the World, the so-called "wobblies," at Telluride, Trinidad and Cripple Creek. Recognizing the handicap placed on earning power by the large number of tubercular refugees who were willing to work for a bare living, Mr. Fox went east in 1910, following several years of clerical work in a large wholesale grocery concern. He spent a year at Kansas City and a short time at Oklahoma City, and then took up his permanent home at Chicago. It was here that he first entered the office of the Western Electric Company, where he spent four years, next becoming assistant to the general plant superintendent of the Michigan State Telephone Company, an allied concern, at Detroit.

When he returned to Chicago one year later Mr. Fox became assistant to the secretary of the Western Society of Engineers, a position which brought him into wide contact with men of large affairs and which gave him opportunity to study economics, a subject in which he had always been greatly interested. In 1917 he became an employe of the McGraw Hill Company, publishers of trade journals, where for four years he wrote on business subjects for various papers, including the Engineering

News Record, Electrical World, American Machinist and Coal Age. His next connection and one that remained up to his selection as executive head of the retailers of Chicago, was with the Black Diamond, a leading publication of the coal industry, where, as associate editor, he became thoroughly acquainted with the problems with which the coal industry is faced. Thoroughly convinced that it is only through education of the coal man and of the public that prosperity may come to the coal industry, the new connection has given him the best possible opportunity for the working out of his views. The Chicago Coal Merchants' Association is the largest and strongest organization of its kind in the country. With the addition of Mr. Fox to its executive staff the association began increasing the scope of its activities, and in the rendering of substantial aid in the meeting of inroads of competitive fuels, in providing a modern advertising service for its members, in the establishment of a common meeting place for coal men where problems mutual to all may be freely discussed, in the establishment of connections with the daily press, and in various other ways its worth to its members will be greatly increased.

Mr. Fox married Miss Mary Elizabeth Sholty, who was born at Springfield, Illinois, but was reared and educated at Chicago, being a graduate of the Marquette School and the John Marshall High School. They have one daughter: Annabelle Lorayne. The pleasant family home is located at Oak Park, where Mr. Fox has many friends and is one of the valued members of Oak Park Lodge No. 1295, B. P. O. E.

JAMES A. WHITE, United States marshal for the eastern district of Illinois, is a resident of Murphysboro, and for many years has been one of the prominent republican leaders in that section of the state.

His grandfather, James White, moved from Iowa in 1868 and settled at East St. Louis. He was an Iowa pioneer, going there from the State of Ohio. He had also lived in Pennsylvania, where Henry White, father of James A., was born. Henry White married Hannah Parkinson in Iowa, and throughout his active life he was a farmer.

James A. White was born at Fairfield, in Jefferson County, Iowa, in September, 1868, and was only a few months old when the family moved to East St. Louis. He grew up there, attending public schools, and learned the machinist's trade. This was his occupation from 1885 to 1898.

In the meantime, in 1888, he established his home at Murphysboro. Mr. White in 1898 was appointed postmaster of Murphysboro by President McKinley. He was postmaster sixteen consecutive years. During that time many improvements and extensions were made in the postal service, including the establishment of rural delivery and other features, and the efficiency of the local office was kept at a high standard, and Mr. White was given equal credit with the congressmen from the district for the fine new Federal building.

Mr. White retired from the postoffice in 1913. In 1914 he was elected sheriff of Jackson County. This office he resigned after three and a half years to become warden of the State Penitentiary. He served as warden until September 1, 1920, and January 1, 1921, was appointed United States marshal for the eastern district of Illinois, with headquarters at Danville.

Mr. White was an alderman of Murphysboro from 1894 to 1896. He became a member of the Republican State Central Committee in 1900, and for many years was chairman of the Republican Central Committee of Jackson County. He is a member of the Masonic Order, Knights of Pythias, B. P. O. Elks and Modern Woodmen of America. His wife died in 1918.

E. MARIE JOHNSON, Doctor of Naprapathy, has practiced her profession at Kankakee for the past eight years. She is a graduate and registered nurse, and followed that profession prior to her study of naprapathy.

She was born at Peotone, in Will County, Illinois, in 1886, daughter of Peter and Catherine (McFarlin) Johnson. Her father was a native of Denmark and her mother was born at Manhattan, Illinois. Her father on locating in Will County, Illinois, took up horticulture as his chief business.

E. Marie Johnson was educated in public schools, and in 1915 graduated from the Illinois Masonic Hospital as a nurse. For one year she was connected with the Iowa University Hospital, and followed her profession in Will County and Chicago. Then, in 1919, she graduated from the Chicago College of Naprapathy, having previously become greatly impressed by the results she had observed in the treatment of chronic and acute cases of disease by the naprapathic methods. Doctor Johnson has her offices at Kankakee, in the City National Bank Building.

She is a Presbyterian, a member of several of the women's organizations at Kankakee and belongs to the Eastern Star Chapter, White Shrine of Jerusalem, Young Women's Christian Association. Her home is at 622 South Greenwood Avenue.

JUDGE S. N. HOOVER is an Illinois attorney who for thirty years has performed varied services of his profession in the City of Aurora. He is serving his third term as county judge of Kane County.

Judge Hoover was born in Claremont County, Ohio, December 27, 1867. His parents were P. H. and Anna (Prather) Hoover, both natives of Ohio and now deceased. The father was a farmer by occupation. There were five children: Orlando, deceased; Nettie, wife of W. P. Jones, of Bloomington, Illinois; Thomas H., deceased; William W., of Sioux Falls, South Dakota, and S. N. Hoover.

S. N. Hoover grew up on a farm, lived there to the age of twenty and attended local schools. He finished his literary education in Illinois Wesleyan University at Bloomington, and began the study of law in law offices. In 1888 he became principal of schools at Rankin, Illinois, and continued his law studies at night. Removing to Colorado, he was admitted to the bar at Denver on June 1, 1891, and for about three years practiced in that state. In

Fay F. Christian

September, 1893, he located at Aurora and has since engaged in a general civil and criminal practice. He was elected judge of the County Court in 1914, and since then has been twice reelected to that important office.

During the World war Judge Hoover was chairman of the Board of Registration and also chairman of the Legal Advisory Board of the same county. He is an active republican, is a Mason, Elk, Knight of Pythias and Moose, and is a member of the Peoples Church of Aurora. He married Miss Clara A. Luck on June 25, 1901.

ERNEST G. WILSON, M. D. While engaged in general practice, Doctor Wilson is best known over Kankakee County as a very skilled surgeon. His offices are in the Cobb Building at Kankakee, and he has practiced in that city for the past fifteen years.

He was born at St. Paul, Indiana, October 2, 1884, son of Dennis G. and Jessie C. (Allison) Wilson. His father was a railroad man and was born at Waldron, Indiana, and died in 1924. His mother was born at St. Paul, Indiana, and now resides at Kankakee.

Ernest G. Wilson received most of his early education at Indianapolis, graduating from the Manual Training School of that city in 1902. In 1906 he was graduated from the Indiana Medical College. Doctor Wilson had the benefit of post-graduate work and experience at Vienna, Austria, and London, England. For two years he practiced at Reddick, Illinois, and one year at Essex before moving to Kankakee in 1911, and in this city his skill as a surgeon has brought him a very heavy practice. He is a member of the various medical and surgical organizations.

Doctor Wilson married, in 1909, Ilah Patchett, a native of Reddick, Illinois, and daughter of Frank R. and Clara (Hulbert) Patchett, natives of Canada. They have two children, Donald P., born January 30, 1916, and Elizabeth June, born April 9, 1919. Doctor Wilson has served as a member of the Official Board of the Methodist Episcopal Church, is a Mason and a republican.

FAY F. CHRISTIAN, a prominent and popular business man of Mount Carroll, is a member of one of the oldest families in Carroll County. Some four or five generations of the family have lived in the county and in every successive epoch have carried their share of responsibilities in business and good citizenship.

One of the soldiers of the American Revolution who came out to northern Illinois and spent his last years in Carroll County was Daniel Christian, Sr., whose home was at Boonesboro, Maryland. He married Elizabeth Nikirk. He first enlisted from Reading, Pennsylvania, in September, 1776, serving two months under Captain George Wills. Again he enlisted, in December, 1778, serving two months under Captain Kit. Again, on June 1, 1780, he was with the Colonial forces seven months under Captain Spoon and Colonel Butler. References to official documents authenticating these services are found in Pennsylvania Archives, Volume 10, Page 592. His application for a pension, dated April 4, 1833, was allowed June 21, 1833, and payable at Baltimore, Maryland. At that time he was living in Washington County, Maryland. The record of this is found in Pension Office Book E, Volume 5, Page 102. Daniel Christian, Sr., came to Mount Carroll in 1839, being then seventy-seven years of age. He lived there until his death on December 26, 1847, and was buried at Mount Carroll.

His son, Daniel Christian, Jr., was born June 4, 1788, and was a soldier in the War of 1812. He married Christina Anspiger, who was born February 12, 1791. From Boonesboro, Maryland, they came out to Illinois and settled at Mount Carroll in the spring of 1837. Daniel Christian, Jr., on coming to this locality of Illinois, became associated with Nathaniel Swingly, Samuel L. Hitt and George Swaggert in a company which bought from Otis and Matthews a claim including a mill site and the land on which much of the present city of Mount Carroll now stands. They paid $1,400 for the claim. Daniel Christian, Jr., hewed the timbers and put up the frame for the sawmill on Carroll Creek and the mill was in operation by the fall of 1837. This company in 1840 sold the mill site to David Emmert and Nathaniel Halderman, and in 1842 they erected a large flouring mill of stone construction, and also built a stone dam. This dam stood until washed away in September, 1911. Daniel Christian, Jr., on coming to Mount Carroll moved his family into the house vacated by Matthews and subsequently erected additions to the house and occupied it until his death on January 14, 1848. He and his wife had eight children.

Their son, Joseph C. Christian, grandfather of Fay F. Christian, lived at this old homestead until his death on August 23, 1905. Joseph C. Christian was born at Boonesboro, Maryland, April 8, 1827, and was about ten years of age when brought to Mount Carroll. During his long and active life he was engaged in farming. He married Elizabeth Freed, who was born January 28, 1834.

Their son, Herbert J. Christian, was born and reared at Mount Carroll, was educated in public schools there, and then engaged in farming. He left his farm in 1908, and since 1911 has been in the mercantile business at Newell, South Dakota. Herbert J. Christian married Mary C. Tipton, and their son, Fay F. Christian, was born at Mount Carroll January 27, 1886. He attended public schools, graduated from high school in 1906, spent one year as a student in William Jewell College at Liberty, Missouri, and another year in the University of Illinois. He left the university in 1909 and during the following year was a clerk at Joliet in the office of the Elgin, Joliet and Eastern Railway. In 1910 he became associated with his father in the milling business and in the spring of 1911 went to South Dakota, but in the fall of the same year entered the Barnes School of Anatomy, Sanitary Science and Embalming at Chicago, where he completed the course and received his diploma in November, 1911. Mr. Christian then returned to Mount Carroll and engaged in the furniture and undertaking business. This business has grown until it is the largest enterprise of the kind in Mount Carroll. Mr. Christian is greatly esteemed and admired for his amiable disposition and spirit of helpfulness and service, which he has always manifested. He is a member of the Masonic Order, Independent Order of Odd Fellows and Knights of Pythias, and is also a member of the Illinois Chapter of the Sons of the American Revolution. He belongs to the Sequoia Club, and is a republican and a Baptist. He is now serving on the Mount Carroll School Board and holds a commission as notary public.

He married at Mount Carroll, September 12, 1911, Miss Laura E. Gillagly, whose home was near Savanna, Illinois. She was educated in public schools in Carroll County, attended the Francis Shimer Academy, and for four years was a public school teacher. She is a daughter of Robert F. and Celia Gillagly, whose home is near Savanna. Her people were early settlers and prominent farmers of Washington Township, Carroll County. Her father died October 23, 1920. Mr. and Mrs. Christian have one child, Herbert O., now attending public school at Mount Carroll.

THOMAS H. HODSON volunteered into the Union army as a recruit in Company E of the Fifteenth Illinois Veteran Volunteer Infantry in the great Civil war before he was seventeen years of age, and is one of the few survivors of that great host which saved the Union. For upward of forty-five years past he has practiced law at Galena, and was former state's attorney of Jo Daviess County for two successive terms, or from 1888 to 1896.

He was born at North Riding, near Arkandale, Yorkshire, England, on January 28, 1848, of English parents who brought him to America when he was but three years of age. They crossed the Atlantic on a sailing vessel to New Orleans, and then came up the Mississippi River by boat to Galena and settled at Council Hill in Jo Daviess County. He is the eldest son of Mark and Elizabeth (Coates) Hodgson, both of whom represented old and respected English families. The name "Hodson" was originally spelled "Hodgson" in England. The father, Mark Hodgson, died at Council Hill soon after coming to this country, and the mother, Elizabeth (Coates) Hodgson, afterward married John Atkinson, and as the Mark Hodgson children were growing up everybody in America spoke and wrote their name as "Hodson," which grew into a custom on account of the American manner of both speaking and writing the name.

On coming to America the father settled at Council Hill, Illinois, taking up government land. He was by occupation a miner, and during most of his years in this country worked in the lead mines in the vicinity of Galena. He also operated a farm. His death occurred in 1856, at Council Hill. There were five children, Sarah H. being the oldest and Thomas H., the second, and he is now the only survivor. The other children were John, William T., Nehimiah and Sarah. All married and left children except Nehimiah. Nehimiah for many years was engaged in teaching in the public schools of Illinois. William T. Hodson, who married Addie Rivenberg, of Apple River, became a successful lawyer at Galena, was a graduate of Ann Arbor College of Law or Law Department of the University of Michigan, and for a number of years served as county judge of Jo Daviess County. Judge W. T. Hodson grew to prominence in the state of Illinois in the Order of Knights of Pythias. He was also at one time selected from Galena as a delegate to the National Republican Convention. He passed to the great beyond at the age of seventy-one, at Galena, after a busy and useful life, on November 3, 1922, beloved and honored by all who knew him. The son John Hodson after his marriage moved to San Francisco, California, where he was a photographer and artist, and his family still live there. The daughter Sarah became the wife of John W. Langdon, of Galena, a merchant, and of their four children one, Charles, is an artist in San Francisco, and Bessie is the wife of Doctor Stephenson of Galena.

Thomas H. Hodson was educated in public schools in Jo Daviess County and in the intervals of his school work did farming. On April 10, 1864, after the Civil war had been in progress just three years, he enlisted as a volunteer and became a recruit of Company E of the Fifteenth Illinois Veteran Infantry. That regiment had seen hard service and its ranks were heavily depleted, and young Hodson was one of those who shared in the splendid record of the regiment during the last year of the war. His first duty was in the vicinity of Huntsville, Alabama. He was in the Atlanta campaign with General Sherman, participating in many of the skirmishes and battles between Chattanooga and Atlanta. In June, 1864, he assisted in building the forts and breastworks in the mountains for the defense of Altoona Pass, where Sherman had stored his supplies during the march against Atlanta. At this point were located three large government warehouses. After the fall of Atlanta, and about the first of October, 1864, the Confederate General Hood with sixty thousand men started on his memorable campaign back through Tennessee in the futile effort to divert Sherman from his march to the sea. One of the first objects of Hood's attack was the supply point at Altoona Pass. On the afternoon of October 3 the advance guard of the Confederate forces struck the Fifteenth Illinois Regiment, stationed about five miles south of Altoona Pass. This regiment was ordered to hold the Confederates until reinforcements could be concentrated. Mr. Hodson and his comrades were in a screen of woods, and the men were stationed about thirty feet apart, over a front extending two or three miles, and they made such determined resistance that they gave the impression of being a much larger force. From four o'clock in the afternoon until ten o'clock the next morning this one regiment held the Confederates at bay until Hood's cavalry got in behind them and between the regiment and Altoona Pass. The Fifteenth Illinois was thus surrounded and compelled to surrender, but in the meantime reinforcements had arrived from towns and army posts further north, filling the Pass with Union soldiers, including General Corse's cavalry from Rome, Georgia, so as to frustrate Hood's attack upon Altoona Pass. By this gallant resistance the Federal supplies were saved and Sherman was permitted to carry out his remarkable march to the sea. Mr. Hodson and his comrades, as prisoners of war, while being marched to the rear of Hood's army witnessed the famous signal sent from Kenesaw Mountain by General Sherman's Signal Corps for eighteen miles over the heads of the entire Confederate army, then in the valley, to Altoona Pass, "Hold the fort for I am coming," words that later inspired one of the most familiar of the old hymns. This signal was seen and enjoyed by the old Fifteenth Illinois boys while being marched through the valley by their captors between Kenesaw Mountain and Altoona Pass.

Mr. Hodson's next experience took him to the prison stockade of Andersonville, where he and many of his comrades of the Fifteenth Illinois were held for seven months. He went into that prison weighing 136 pounds, having had but one meal a day, of coarse corn bread, for seven months, and on his release and on reaching Jacksonville, Florida, he weighed only seventy-two pounds. On being released he and his comrades were taken to Baldwin Station, Georgia, then the end of the railroad, and there they were informed that the war was over and that Lincoln had been assassinated. They had to walk over the demolished railroad track, a distance of twenty miles, to Jacksonville, Florida, where they were met and welcomed and feasted by the citizens. After ten days at Jacksonville and after partial recuperation from the horrors of starvation Mr. Hodson and some of his comrades went on board the steamship Daniel Webster, were taken to Washington, and a few days later traveled to Springfield, Illinois, where he and about two hundred other survivors of the Fifteenth Illinois received their final discharge. Many of this famous regiment died in Andersonville. By volunteering as a recruit to help fill up the depleted ranks of the Fifteenth Illinois Infantry Mr. Hodson served at the front on the Atlanta campaign during the entire summer of 1864, and under General Sherman until captured while defending Altoona Pass, where valuable army stores were located, which supplies were absolutely essential to carry out the plans of General Sherman, and had the regiment retreated back to the Pass during the night of October 3, 1864, the army of General Hood would probably have taken all of said army stores, but during that night heavy reinforcements of Union soldiers arrived from the north and prevented the capture of the Pass, while the Fifteenth Illinois, and parts of other regiments fought in the woods all that night to keep the enemy from advancing, hence the famous signal from the top of Kenesaw Mountain by Sherman's advanced guard.

Mr. Hodson used his army pay and bounty money to educate himself after the war. He graduated in 1867 from the Rock River Seminary at Mount Morris, now Mount Morris College. For a few years he taught in public schools, also engaged in farming, and in 1879 he was graduated from the Union College of Law at Chicago and admitted to the Illinois bar the same year. He then joined his brother William T. in practice at Galena, and has been steadily at work through all the subsequent years, engaged in a general law practice and handling office routine.

Mr. Hodson served as state's attorney of Jo Daviess County for two terms, from 1888 to 1896. He is now president of the Jo Daviess County Bar Association and of the board of school trustees of his township. Mr. Hodson is the present commander of E. D. Kittoe Post No. 502, Grand Army of the Republic, Galena, and was one of the comrades who organized this post on April 9, 1885, and has been one of its most faithful and active members for over forty years. He is also affiliated with the Knights of Pythias.

Mr. Hodson married at Apple River, Illinois, in March, 1869, to Miss Julia Alice Wright, daughter of John Wright. Her people settled in the Apple River district from New England. Mr. and Mrs. Hodson became the parents of three children. The son Harry R. is a professor of music in Chicago. The daughter, Sadie B., is the wife of Dr. Philip F. Kittoe, a doctor of dental surgery at Galena. The youngest is Raymond Hodson, who is now working in the lumber business in Idaho. Julia Alice Wright Hodson, wife of Thomas H. Hodson, died in Galena, on March 18, 1920, aged seventy-two years, beloved and honored by all, as a worthy and noble wife and mother.

E. D. Kittoe Post No. 502, G. A. R., was named in honor of Edward D. Kittoe, surgeon of volunteers of the Forty-fifth Illinois Infantry, Civil war. The Philip F. Kittoe, named above as husband of Mr. Hodson's daughter, Sadie, is a grandson of said E. D. Kittoe, who was surgeon of volunteers.

EDWARD EVERETT PEVERLEY, JR. Material success is essential to the ideal business life, and the wise man never belittles it. Success in life is the inspiration of all ambition, and is acquired through different avenues and qualifications, among them being grip and grit, the bulldogs of business life; and character is another necessary element, and the foundation of character building is truth. Truthfulness is the best policy in business life, for it is its very web. Faithfulness and faith are others, and both are very necessary. The man who has faith in himself, and who practices faithfulness toward others, is not liable to go far wrong in his contact with the business world. That many of the leading citizens of Joliet have followed the rules above indicated is a well-known fact, and one of them deserving of special mention in this connection is Edward Everett Peverley, who is recognized as one of the leading sign painters of Will County, and a citizen of the highest standing.

Edward Everett Peverley was born in Chicago, November 22, 1902, a son of Edward Everett and Louise (Pillath) Peverley, he born in Hartford, Michigan, and she in Manitowoc, Wisconsin. The Peverley family is an old and honored one of this country and traces descent through different branches from George Washington, Israel Putnam, and the Adams family which gave two presidents to the country. The parents of Edward Everett Peverley of this review were married in Chicago, where the father was a sign painter, and where they continued to reside until 1904, when removal was made to Joliet. There he continued in business until July, 1925, where he turned his contracts over to his son, and, moving to Marseilles, Illinois, went into the restaurant business, which he is now conducting with satisfactory returns.

The younger Edward Everett Peverley is the only living child of his parents, and he was educated in the public schools and an electrical school, and he left the latter at the age of eighteen years. For a year thereafter he was in the employ of the Western Electric Company, and then, joining his father in Joliet, he learned the sign-painting trade, and is now continuing the business he received from his father. He does all kinds of sign painting, and not only understands the mechanical side of the work, but possesses the true artistic taste which is so essential an attribute of this business, and his contracts are increasing rapidly, as a result of the entire satisfaction he gives. In political faith he is a republican, although he is not active. He is a Universalist. As a member of the Advisory Committee of the North American Auto Club, he is rendering an excellent service to autoists, and he also belongs to the Masonic fraternity, and is active in the Boy Builders, the junior branch of that order, and in the Alumni Association of the Coyne Trade & Engineering School of Chicago.

On December 13, 1924, Mr. Peverley married Linda Marie Dieter, born in Lockport, Illinois, a daughter of Philip and Bertha Dieter, natives of Minnesota and Lockport, respectively.

ANDREW JOHN GOODWIN, M. D., physician and surgeon, well known in Kankakee County, has his offices in the Cobb Building at Kankakee, while his home is at Bradley, where he first engaged in general practice.

Doctor Goodwin was born at Flat Rock, Illinois, in 1879, son of James and Caroline (Maddox) Goodwin, his father a native of Ohio and his mother of Crawford County, Illinois. John Goodwin, his grandfather, was a native of England and an early settler in Crawford County, Illinois. The maternal grandparents were David and Mary (Cushman) Maddox, the former a native of Ireland. James Goodwin followed a career as a farmer and died in 1903, and is survived by his widow at Flat Rock.

Andrew John Goodwin was reared on a farm, attended district school in Montgomery Township, and through teaching paid most of the expenses of his professional education. In 1902 he graduated from the Central Normal College at Danville, Indiana. He taught school three years in Crawford County, Illinois. Doctor Goodwin spent one year as a student of pharmacy in Northwestern University at Chicago, and then for three years attended the Illinois Medical College, where he was graduated in 1907. During his senior year he was an interne in the Illinois Medical Hospital. He then took the state board examination and in 1908 located at Bradley, building up a general country practice in that vicinity. Since 1917 he has had offices in the Cobb Building at Kankakee. For six months in 1913 Doctor Goodwin held an internship in the Post-Graduate Hospital in Chicago.

He married, in 1907, Miss Leona York, a native of Robinson, Illinois, and daughter of Willis and Julia (English) York. They have one son, James Willis, born January 13, 1908. Doctor Goodwin is a republican, is a Royal Arch Mason, member of the Independent Order of Odd Fellows, B. P. O. Elks, Modern Woodmen of America, Woodmen of the World, and belongs to the Kankakee County and Illinois State Medical Associations.

DAVID B. PENNIMAN, M. D. Numbered among the skilled physicians and surgeons of Winnebago County, Dr. David B. Penniman holds the confidence and respect of his fellow citizens, and enjoys an extensive practice at Rockford and throughout the county. He was born at Woodburn, Macoupin County, Illinois, June 9, 1867, a son of Dr. Alexander Brown Penniman, born near Lake Champlain, in New York State, in April, 1824. He, too, was a physician, having graduated from Eclectic College of Cincinnati, Ohio, in 1859. For a few years he was engaged in the practice of his profession in Canada, but later went to Missouri. During the war between the North and the South he served for three years as regimental surgeon. At the close of the war he located in Macoupin County, where for thirty years he continued in practice. At the close of that period of faithful service to humanity he moved to Oberlin, Ohio, and there his useful life was terminated by death in 1887. In May, 1865, he was united in marriage with Sarah Barton, who died at Argyle, Illinois, in 1910. They had two children born to them, namely: Dr. David B. Penniman, of this review; and Ira B., who is a teacher of voice culture at Canton, Ohio.

Graduated from Oberlin College in 1889, with the degree of Bachelor of Arts, Dr. David B. Penniman took up the study of medicine in the medical department of Northwestern University, and was graduated therefrom in 1893, with the degree of Doctor of Medicine. Subsequently Oberlin College conferred upon him the degree of Master of Arts. Immediately following his graduation Doctor Penniman established himself in a general practice at Argyle, Illinois, and for nineteen years remained in that locality, ministering to the afflicted, and rendering an efficient service as well through his public-spirited efforts to secure better sanitary conditions and normal ways of living. In December, 1912, he came to Rockford, and since coming to this city he has continued to rise in public esteem until today he is rightly regarded as one of the leading representatives of his profession in this part of the state. He has always maintained membership with the different medical societies and associations for he believes in them and their value to the profession and the world at large.

On September 13, 1893, Doctor Penniman married, at Shelby, Iowa, Miss Corda Shively, who died in November, 1907, leaving two children: Lawrence W., who is a graduate of Northwestern University, is an expert on the prevention of forest fires, and during the World war he served for seventeen months in

the army. He is married and has a son, John. Alford, who is a resident of Memphis, Tennessee, is unmarried.

Doctor Penniman has always taken an intelligent interest in local affairs, co-operating with his vote and support to the advancement of the republican party and its candidates. He belongs to the Masonic fraternity, the Benevolent and Protective Order of Elks, the Modern Woodmen of America, and the Harlem Hills Golf Club. Both as a member and elder of the First Presbyterian Church of Rockford he is a potent factor in religious work, and few men stand as high as he in their home community.

T. BARNEY THOMPSON, former pastor of the First Congregational Church of Rockford, is a man of scholarly attainments and convincing sincerity, and his work here, as elsewhere, is marked by remarkable and constructive progress. He was born at Nashotah, Wisconsin, January 20, 1876, a son of O. B. and Rachel (Nohr) Thompson, natives of Lillehammer, Norway, who came to the United States following their marriage in 1870, and first located at Chicago. The father was superintendent of bridges and building on the old Wisconsin Railroad. His death occurred at Christiania, Norway, while he was there on a visit, in 1904, and he is buried in one of the cemeteries of that city. The mother survives, and lives in North Central Wisconsin, Clark County, where the family residence has been maintained since 1880. Ten children were born to the parents, of whom eight are living, T. Barney Thompson having been the fourth child. There were nine sons, one of whom died at Chicago in infancy, in 1871, and another in young manhood, November 2, 1918.

When only thirteen and one-half years old T. Barney Thompson was serving as telegrapher in Wisconsin for the Wisconsin Central Railroad, and at that tender age began taking a night shift, and continued to do so for two years, and then for three years he worked during the days. From childhood he had been ambitious, and, deciding to devote himself to his Master's work, he laid his plans accordingly, and conscientiously carried them out. Entering a divinity college at Chicago, he studied there for one year, and took a four-years' collegiate course at the Mount Hermon, Massachusetts, School, from which he was graduated in 1899, as valedictorian of his class, and he also took the prize for four years of excellence that was bestowed by Cambridge University. During the next four years he was a student of Beloit College, from which he was graduated in 1903, magna-cune-laude, with the degree of Bachelor of Arts. In the fall of that year he became pastor of the First Congregational Church of Watertown, Wisconsin, and remained there until January, 1906, when he became junior pastor of Plymouth Church, Milwaukee, Wisconsin, the church made famous in the annals of religious freedom by the thirty years' militant pastorate of the late Judson Titsworth, and continued to hold that charge until January 11, 1909, when he assumed the pastorate of the First Congregational Church of Rockford. Until New Year's Day, 1914, he continued his ministry, and then, feeling that journalism would afford him a broader field of labor, he became part owner, with Harry M. Johnson and four other associates, of the Rockford Republic, succeeding Charles L. Miller as editor. He is a strong republican.

On September 21, 1904, Mr. Thompson married, at Watertown, Wisconsin, Priscilla Teall, of Sparta, Wisconsin, a former classmate, and three children were born to them: Priscilla, Phoebe and Robert George, the last named living only two months. Mr. Thompson belongs to Rockford Lodge No. 102, A. F. and A. M.; the Benevolent and Protective Order of Elks; and the Izaak Walton League.

MARTHA PARK. A brief sketch of Martha Park is introduced because the subject is that of an unusually successful business career for a woman. Her life has been spent at the city of Murphysboro. Before her marriage she clerked for a time in a small grocery store. Later, a widow, she took employment again as clerk, and from that position has risen to the post of general manager of one of the largest and most prosperous retail dry goods stores in southern Illinois.

Her maiden name was Martha Stuart and she was born and educated in Murphysboro, being a daughter of William and Jane (Butcher) Stuart. She was eighteen years of age when her father died. Her mother, a native of Jackson County, died in 1909. Since that time her mother-in-law, Jane Ann Park, who was born in England, has lived with Martha Park.

At the age of eighteen Martha Stuart had taken a position in a small grocery store run by Alexander Hutton. At the time she was doubtful as to her ability as a clerk, since the range of experience had never been outside the home. Her pay was two dollars a week. At the end of three years she was married to William Park, in 1892, and she gave up her work in the store. William Park was a railroad man and was killed in an accident at Springfield on the Chicago, Peoria & St. Louis Railroad in 1895. Mrs. Park was then left with an infant son and a mother to care for. In this emergency she accepted a position in a store called The Fair and was one of the employes of that house for eight years.

In 1904 Oscar S. Young, a St. Louis merchant, opened a small dry goods store in Murphysboro on Walnut Street, opposite the Logan Building. He started with a staff of four clerks, securing two of them from The Fair, one of them Mrs. Park. At the end of four years Mr. Young decided to return to St. Louis in order to give his personal attention to his business in that city. This necessitated leaving the Murphysboro store under a competent manager, and from his various employes he selected Mrs. Park as the person best fitted for the post. Under Mrs. Park's management the Young Dry Goods Company grew rapidly, and in 1916 the store was moved to larger quarters in the Logan Building, and still further increases were made to facilities by the extension of the building. In the new store fifteen clerks were employed. In 1924 the Young Dry Goods Company bought the stock and equipment of the Herrin Supply Company, and remodeled the building into one of the most complete business houses in southern Illinois. This store has fifteen thousand square feet of floor space, woman's rest room, passenger elevators, sprinkling system for fire protection, and altogether it is a business establishment that much larger cities would be proud of. The house now employs about thirty persons. Mrs. Park disclaims much of the credit assigned her by others and is enthusiastic over the co-operation afforded her by her working associates. For a number of years she has been buyer as well as manager, and makes frequent trips for that purpose to New York, Chicago, Cleveland and St. Louis.

Mrs. Park is a director of the Murphysboro Chamber of Commerce. She is active in club work, is a member of the Eastern Star and White Shrine of Jerusalem, and the Centenary Methodist Church.

Her son, George Park, born January 27, 1894, was educated in the Murphysboro grade and high schools and for one year attended the University of Illinois. Returning to Murphysboro, he was given employment in the Young Dry Goods Company and has thoroughly mastered the business, being now office manager. During the World war he was sergeant of an ambulance company and spent one year overseas. George Park married Beulah McCord, daughter of Z. V. McCord, an official of the First National Bank of Murphysboro.

REV. KASPER SCHAUERTE was for thirty-seven years the beloved pastor of St. Andrews Catholic Church at Murphysboro, and that service is destined to make his name revered in that community throughout the memory of the present generation and the present generation's children.

He was born in Westphalia, Germany, March 7, 1862, son of William and Regina (Matzhauser) Schauerte, the oldest of four sons and three daughters. His brother Wienand Schauerte is a well known business man of Murphysboro.

Kasper Schauerte was educated in Germany, and in 1880, at the age of eighteen, came to America. He attended Teutopolis College in Effingham County, Illinois, and graduated from St. Francis Seminary at Milwaukee, being ordained to the priesthood June 24, 1887. A few weeks later he came to Murphysboro as substitute to Rev. F. Bergmann, then pastor of St. Andrews Church, and before the close of the year was made the regular pastor. This church enjoyed continued growth and prosperity under his administration. He erected the church, parish school, parish home and hospital and convent during his administration, and also erected churches at Carterville and Ava.

Father Schauerte for several years before his death suffered ill health. After vain resort to hospitals in several cities, including the Mayo Brothers at Rochester, Minnesota, he returned home and died December 22, 1924.

WIENAND SCHAUERTE is a practical machinist as well as a very capable business man, and was one of the founders and for many years has been identified with the growth and upbuilding of the Egyptian Iron Works at Murphysboro, an industry of which he is vice president.

Mr. Wienand Schauerte was born in Westphalia, Germany, April 28, 1873, son of William and Regina (Matzhauser) Schauerte. His parents spent all their lives in their native land. William Schauerte was a tailor by trade, though most of his time was devoted to farming.

Wienand Schauerte was given good educational advantages. At the age of seventeen, in 1890, he came to America and joined his older brother, Father Kasper Schauerte, at Murphysboro. Kasper Schauerte was for thirty-seven years the beloved pastor of St. Andrews Church at Murphysboro, and a sketch of his career precedes this. Wienand Schauerte became almost as well known in business as his brother was in church circles.

At Murphysboro Wienand Schauerte went to work in the shops of the Mobile & Ohio Railroad as a machinist's apprentice, at a wage of ten cents an hour. After his apprenticeship he removed to St. Louis and for seven years worked in the St. Louis rolling mills. While there he met and married Anna Able, a native of St. Louis, of German ancestry. Returning to Murphysboro, Mr. Schauerte again went into the Mobile & Ohio Railroad shops, this time as machinist under the master mechanic, A. B. Minton, who is still a prominent citizen of Murphysboro.

In 1902 Mr. Schauerte and three other machinists at the shop decided to start a business of their own. They tried to purchase the Lewis Foundry, but failing in their negotiations the four started a small shop in the old canning factory, Mr. Schauerte and one other handling practically all the work at the beginning. A year later they reached an agreement and purchased the Lewis Foundry at the present location, and thus came into existence the Egyptian Iron Works, which today represents an enlargement of the original factory and equipment and a general foundry and machine repair service for mining and other industries. The company was first incorporated with a capital of $10,000. The first president of the company was Martin Schauerte, and his brother Wienand, vice president. Martin soon sold his interest and left Murphysboro and was succeeded by Joseph Borger, and he in turn, in 1915, was succeeded by Edward Bencini. The treasurer and purchasing agent of the company is William H. Michael, the secretary is Grover Blankenship, while Howard Jacob is foundry foreman.

Mr. Wienand Schauerte's son Edward learned the machinist's trade in his father's establishment and is now finishing his technical education in a school in Kansas City.

GEORGE HUTHMACHER is proprietor of the Jackson County Lumber Company at Murphysboro. This has been his chief business interest for nearly thirty years. At the same time he has been interested in other lines of activity, and is one of the very influential figures in the citizenship of his home city and county.

His father, Charles F. Huthmacher, was born in Baden, Germany, in 1834, and on coming to this country settled at Central City,

Illinois, and afterwards at Sandoval, Illinois. From there he removed to Grand Tower in Jackson County, where he engaged in business until his death on September 25, 1875. He was a democrat in politics. Charles F. Huthmacher married Josephine Lienert, who was born at Zurich, Switzerland, and was brought to the United States when a child. She now resides at Murphysboro.

George Huthmacher was born on a farm at Sandoval, Illinois, February 1, 1869, and a few weeks after his birth his parents removed to Grand Tower, where he grew up and attended the public schools. Later he attended the Bryant and Stratton Business College in St. Louis. Mr. Huthmacher from 1890 to 1894 was deputy sheriff of Jackson County. For a time he was engaged in the furniture business at Joplin, Missouri, and in the fall of 1898 he and his brother, A. J. Huthmacher, bought the Jackson County Lumber Company. Since 1905 they have also handled hardware, and this is now the largest business of its kind in Murphysboro. The firm have acquired extensive tracts of timber land in Arkansas, and are lumber manufacturers as well as dealers and distributors. The headquarters of their business is at 101 North Thirteenth Street. In the tornado of 1925 the second story of their busines block was badly wrecked, and in the remodeling only one story was returned. For a number of years the Huthmacher brothers have been among the largest commercial growers of asparagus in this section of Southern Illinois. They have a farm of forty acres devoted to that crop, located two and a half miles northeast of Murphysboro. All the buildings on this farm were wrecked in the tornado. There are also thirty acres in peaches on this farm.

Mr. Huthmacher is a democrat in politics, has served as alderman of Murphysboro, is a member of the Elks and the lumbermen's social organization known as the Hoo Hoos.

BURTON WILLARD NORTON. One of the able attorneys practicing at the bar of Winnebago County, Burton Willard Norton, of Rockford, has won distinction in his chosen profession, and is ranked as one of the most representative men of this part of the state. He was born at Weybridge, Vermont, July 23, 1867, a son of Calvin and Charlotte (Hagar) Norton, natives of New York and Vermont, respectively. They had six children born to their marriage, namely: Henry C., who died at Addison, Vermont, in May, 1926; Burton Willard, whose name heads this review; Sarah, who is the wife of Ward B. Brown, of Milford, Connecticut; Laura E., who is deceased; Benjamin H., who is a resident of California; and Gideon R., who is a resident of Toledo, Ohio. For many years the father was engaged in farming, and both he and the mother died in Vermont.

Given excellent educational advantages, Burton Willard Norton first attended the local graded and high schools, and Middlebury, Vermont, College, and was graduated therefrom in 1890. For the subsequent year he was a schoolmaster in a local school, but was then made principal of the public schools of Oakland, Iowa. After a year in that city he came to Rockford and began the study of law with L. L. Morrison. In 1897 he was admitted to the bar of Illinois, and commenced at once a general practice, in which he continued steadily for eighteen years, during that period gaining a deeply-rooted reputation for his sagacity and knowledge of the law. In 1915 he was elected police magistrate of Rockford, and served very capably as such for three terms.

On June 14, 1899, Mr. Norton married Miss Flora E. Helnibolt, of Orfordville, Wisconsin. They have no children. Mr. Norton is a republican, and has always been interested in local politics. He belongs to the Masonic fraternity, the Benevolent and Protective Order of Elks and the Knights of Pythias. The Congregational Church holds his membership, and he is a deacon in the Rockford body of this denomination. A man of high principles and ideals, Mr. Norton has lived according to them and his record is one of which any man might well be proud.

WILLIAM L. DORMAND, who has spent most of his life in Illinois, is a lawyer by training, but in recent years has made his chief mark in the real estate business in the city of Evanston as head of the firm of W. L. Dormand & Company at 605 Davis Street. Mr. Dormand is a former president of the Evanston Real Estate Board.

He is a native of Missouri, but when only three weeks of age his parents settled at Spring Valley, Illinois. He spent some of his early years in that famous mining locality, but completed his education in Ohio Northern University at Ada. Ohio Northern University for many years has had a splendid reputation as an institution of learning, and particularly for the thoroughness of the instruction and the earnestness of the great majority of the student body. It has a long list of prominent alumni. Two of them are the present United States senators from Ohio, Willis and Fess. Mr. Dormand completed both his academic and law education at Ohio Northern. He was admitted to the Ohio bar and the Illinois bar.

During the World war he was with the air service of the United States army on detached duty at various places. Then, in 1919, he returned to Illinois, and locating at Evanston, engaged in the real estate business. His law practice is confined largely to interests connected with his real estate operations and matters relating to property. W. L. Dormand & Company occupies handsome quarters on the second floor of the W. L. Dormand Building on Davis Street, and in a few years the company has become one of the largest concerns of its kind operating in the great North Shore district.

Mr. Dormand was elected and served as president of the Evanston Real Estate Board for the year 1925. The Evanston Real Estate Board was the second organization of the kind in the United States to build and own the building which furnishes it its headquarters. The building at Evanston is one of the important additions to the commercial architecture of the city, and besides facilities for commercial uses it provides ample quarters for the Board and also contains a fine auditorium.

Mr. Dormand is one of the active leaders among the younger element in working for the general welfare of Evanston and continuing the prestige of the city as a great educational center and community of wealth and culture. He is a member of the Evanston Club, Evanston Rotary Club, is a Scottish Rite Mason and Shriner, member of the Medinah Country Club, Wilmette Golf Club and Medinah Athletic Club. He married Miss Velda Holman, of Wisconsin. Their two children are Jean Elaine and William L., Jr.

U. CLINTON HENDEE, who resides at Round Lake, in Lake County, is a contractor and builder, associated with his brothers in that business, and the firm for many years has handled important contracts in the building line all over this section of Illinois.

The Hendee family were pioneer settlers in the Grays Lake section of Lake County, where U. Clinton Hendee was born June 20, 1876, son of Eugene and Anna R. (Ingrish) Hendee, and grandson of Uz and Eunice (Rathburn) Hendee. His grandparents came from Genesee County, New York, where they were reared and married and about 1831 came to Lake County, settling near Grays Lake, where the grandfather took up Government land. He cleared and improved one of the first farms in that section. The family made the trip west by canal and boat around the Great Lakes. Uz Hendee spent his life as a farmer and died about 1898, and his wife, in 1906. The family came originally from England and has lived in America since prior to the Revolutionary war. Eugene Hendee was born and reared at Grays Lake, attended public school there and from early manhood occupied his energies with farming in his native community. In 1920 he sold his farm, having lived retired for four years before that, and he is now seventy-six and his wife, seventy-two, and they live at Grays Lake. His wife, Anna R. Ingrish, was born and reared in Austria and came to America at the age of eighteen. She lived in Chicago for some time, being there during the great fire of 1871, and was in the path of destruction wrought by the flames. She saved her trunk by dragging it along the street until her brother Joseph arrived with a wagon and took her and her possessions to safety. After the fire she joined her parents at Grays Lake and while there met and married Eugene Hendee. Her parents, Anthony and Anna Ingrish, came to America two or three years after their daughter, and he followed his trade as a tinner for a time at Chicago, and then bought a farm at Grays Lake, where he lived out his life, dying about 1901, and his wife, in 1904. Eugene Hendee and wife had four children: U. Clinton, Edward E., Louis F. and Leo, three of whom are partners in the contracting and building business. Edward, one of the firm of contractors, lives at Round Lake, and married Maud Etinger, of Volo, Illinois. Louis F. Hendee, who is with the S. L. Trip Lumber Company at Mundelein, Illinois, married Mayme Decker and had six children, five of whom are now living. Leo E. Hendee, also in the contracting business, married Elizabeth Kretchmer of Grays Lake, and has two children, Hildred and Leroy.

U. Clinton Hendee was educated in public school at Grays Lake and after school learned the carpenter's trade, a vocation he has followed and has made the basis of his successful contracting business. He has been a contractor since 1908, and in recent years has built a number of homes on his own property in the vicinity of Round Lake. In connection with contracting he owned and operated for a number of years a farm, but sold this land in 1921. He is a member of the Association of Contractors and Electricians of the Public Service, is affiliated with the Modern Woodmen of America and is a republican.

Mr. Hendee married at Waukegan, November 7, 1900, Miss Bertha E. Davis, of Grays Lake. She was educated at Fort Hill and at high school in McHenry County and has had much part in the social and church life of Grays Lake and Round Lake. Her parents, F. P. and Martha (Harman) Davis, were well to do farming people in the Fort Hill community near Fremont Center, but her father is now retired and lives at Grays Lake. Her mother died in 1920. Mr. and Mrs. Hendee have three children, Florence, Elmer I. and Harmon. Harmon died when five years old. Florence is the wife of Anthony Leonard, a carpenter at Lake Villa, and their only child, Eddie, died in infancy. Elmer is a member of the class of 1927 in the Libertyville High School.

FRED ARNOLD. Provided a man is endowed by nature with ordinary intelligence there is no reason why he cannot advance through industry and economy. The cause of so many failures is lack of ambition and unwillingness to work and save. Some of the most successful business men today are those who started out in life penniless. They had, from the start, to rely upon their own resourcefulness, and so early developed a strength of character that has carried them far. Such a man is Fred Arnold of Rockford, who owns the largest retail auto supply house in Illinois. His entry into the business arena was through the selling of newspapers while still a lad of tender years, and from that humble beginning he has gone steadily forward, never shirking work nor failing to save something no matter how small an amount he earned.

Fred Arnold was born at Rockford, April 10, 1894, a son of Gadlip and Anna (Meyers) Arnold, both natives of Germany. The father came to the United States in 1890, and the mother, in 1892, and they settled at Rockford in 1893. A stone mason, the father worked at his trade until his death. The mother survives him and is still residing at Rockford. The following children were born of their marriage: Fred, whose name heads this review; Theresa, who is the wife of William Anderson, of Rockford; Robert, who is a resident of Rockford; and Calvin, who is also a resident of Rockford.

There were not many advantages offered Fred Arnold, and his earnings were early required to help support the family. As a newsboy he proved alert and obliging, and later carried these same qualities with him when he began working in a garage. While maintaining this connection he was learning the requirements of the automobile users, and in 1916, with a capital of $1,000, the total of his savings, he established in a small way the business he now owns, handling those supplies and accessories his experience had taught him would meet with a ready sale. One of his strong selling points has been the service he renders, and his business has so advanced, as before stated, it leads all others of its kind in the state.

On April 10, 1918, his birthday, Mr. Arnold married Sarah Ann Ganley, who was born at Rockford, and they have two sons, Robert and Frederick. Mr. Arnold is a stanch republican, although not an office seeker, and gives his party loyal support. He is a thirty-second degree Mason. The American Business Men's Club and the Rockford Chamber of Cammerce afford him opportunities for civic betterment work. An enthusiastic sportsman, he belongs to the Izaak Walton League, the Rockford Athletic Association, and the Winnebago Outing Club, and in these connections he is able to obtain healthful recreation and enjoy association with congenial friends. Rockford has every reason to be proud of Mr. Arnold and what he has accomplished, and his example ought to stimulate others to renewed effort in different lines in which they may be interested.

OGDEN P. BOURLAND is one of the veteran and honored representatives of banking enterprise in Livingston County, at whose judicial center he is president of the Pontiac National Bank. In connection with financial affairs his experience covers a wide range, and he has effectively directed affairs through various periods of financial depression and panic, including that of 1873. He has proved reliable, resourceful and well poised as an exponent of banking, a line of enterprise through which are protected and conserved the varied interests of every community. Mr. Bourland is not only one of the honored and influential citizens of Pontiac but also has the distinction of being a native son of Illinois and a scion of one of the sterling pioneer families of this commonwealth.

Ogden P. Bourland was born at Peoria, Illinois, in the year 1850, and is a son of Benjamin L. T. and Julia (Preston) Bourland, the former of whom was born in Trigg County, Kentucky, in the year 1825, and the latter of whom was born in one of the counties of western New York.

Benjamin L. T. Bourland was reared and educated in the old Bluegrass State under the tutelage of his father, who was his schoolmaster. As a pupil he made a rare record of successful scholarship, besides having gained high reputation for his skilful penmanship, a prominent feature in education at that time. He was still a young man when he came to Illinois and established his residence at Vandalia, which was then the capital of the state. There his excellent penmanship had much influence in securing for him a position in the office of the auditor general of Illinois. While thus engaged he became well acquainted with Hon. Stephen A. Douglas, and the "Little Giant" became so much interested in young Bourland as to obtain for the latter a position in the Chicago offices of Ogden, Jones & Company, which was at that period the largest real estate and financial concern in the west. In 1845 this influential firm made Mr. Bourland its representative at Peoria, and while he was in charge of the branch establishment and business in that city he formed the acquaintanceship of Mr. Phelps, a man of sterling character and good business judgment, this acquaintanceship eventually leading to the formation of the firm of Phelps & Bourland, which there engaged in the real estate and loan business, Mr. Bourland having at this time severed his alliance with Ogden, Jones & Company. In 1867 Mr. Bourland accepted the position of district financial agent for the Aetna Life Insurance Company, and of this position he continued the incumbent until his final retirement from active business, he having been one of the venerable and revered pioneer citizens of Peoria at the time of his death, in 1915, and having long survived his wife.

At the time of the birth of Ogden Preston Bourland his native city of Peoria was a place of about 4,000 population, but it was already a vital and important business center in that section of Illinois. He duly profited by the advantages of the public schools of the locality and period, and he early manifested a perhaps inherited predilection for financial affairs, in connection with which his father had gained no minor prestige. Thus he initiated his business career by taking a position as messenger boy and ex-officio assistant janitor in the Merchants National Bank of Peoria. He applied himself diligently, and his receptiveness enabled him to profit greatly by the experience that he gained while allied with this institution.

At the age of twenty-one years Mr. Bourland came to Pontiac to assume the position of bookkeeper in the banking house of Joseph F. Culver & Brother, besides being assigned to the guardianship of his father's interests in the institution. Joseph F. Culver was a man of marked versatility, as is evident when it is noted that he was a lawyer, a preacher, a farmer, a philosopher and a would-be banker, his success as a financier having been of somewhat negative order, as his philanthropic expenditures continued as long as his own funds or money intrusted to him by others were available. Of his connection with banking enterprise it has consistently been said that he was "a good deposit-getter, but a poor caretaker." The Culver bank contrived to survive the panic of 1873, but soon afterward its affairs became so deeply involved that it was compelled to terminate its operations. Under these conditions Mr. Bourland returned to the parental home, but it seemed that the business men of Pontiac had been so favorably impressed with his resourcefulness in carrying the affairs of the Culver bank through the panic of 1873 that they looked to him for co-operation when was essayed the organizing of the Pontiac National Bank. He was called back to Pontiac for this purpose and was prominently concerned in the organizing, in May, 1874, of the substantial and influential institution of which he is now the executive head and the affairs and policies of which he has directed with consummate wisdom and discrimination, with the result that he is now one of the influential representatives of stable banking enterprise in this section of his native state, with an enviable place in the confidence and esteem of the community that has represented his home somewhat more than half a century.

HOWARD D. RYAN. Among the young and progressive element of Rockford's business life is found Howard D. Ryan, who has already written his name in strong and legible characters of the city's mercantile and manufacturing pages, although still in the prime of young manhood. During his short but vigorous career he has been identified with a number of business enterprises, all of which have benefited by his energy and progressiveness, and at present he is devoting his abilities to forwarding the interests of the Rockford Star Motor Company, of which concern he is general manager.

Mr. Ryan is a native of Rockford, born February 4, 1897, a son of Daniel W. and Alice (Sargent) Ryan, the former a native of New York and the latter of Pennsylvania. Daniel W. Ryan was but a boy when brought by his parents to Rockford, and here he grew to manhood, acquiring his education in the public schools. For many years he was employed by the Roper Corporation, and became one of that concern's most trusted employes, filling a number of important positions. His death, which occurred in October, 1923, removed from the city one of its highly respected citizens and a man who had always been a supporter of worthy and beneficial civic movements. His worthy and faithful wife had passed to the great beyond in 1905. Four children were born to Mr. and Mrs. Ryan: Mabel, the wife of Fay Jacobs, of Rockford; Gertrude, the widow of Richard Condon; Eva, who resides with her brother; and Howard D.

The public schools of Rockford furnished Howard D. Ryan with his educational training, and when he was seventeen years of age he felt ready to embark on a career of his own. Accordingly, in 1914, he became associated with Arthur L. Johnson in a number of different business operations, and continued with him until becoming manager of the Rockford Star Motor Company, a position which he still retains.

Mr. Ryan served in the World war six months, of which five months were spent in France. He was with the Fifth Anti-Aircraft Machine Battalion. Enlisting in August, 1918, he was first stationed at Camp Wadsworth, Spartanburg, South Carolina, later sailed from New York to France, in September, 1918. Returning to the United States in February, 1919, he received his discharge at Camp Grant in February, 1919, and returned to Rockford. He served as a private.

Mr. Ryan is a man of astuteness and progressive ideas, and has the full confidence of his business associates, as well as their friendship. He has been too actively occupied with his business interests to engage in politics, but he votes the republican ticket, and all worthy measures enlist his interest and intelligent co-operation. He holds membership in the local lodge of the Benevolent and Protective Order of Elks and is a prominent Mason and a member of the Mystic Shrine. Mr. Ryan is unmarried.

ROLAND H. SHUMWAY was one of the important contributors to Rockford's position as a commercial center with trade relations far beyond the boundaries of the state. More than half a century ago he started a seed business, at first supplying only a local market, but eventually making it primarily a mail order house that advertised nationally and did practically a nation wide business. It is a flourishing institution today, its active head being his son, M. Raymond Shumway.

Roland H. Shumway's life spanned the existence of Rockford from a pioneer community with Indians as close neighbors until it came to rank among the first of Illinois cities outside the metropolis. He lived there for more than eighty-three years. He died in Saint Anthony's Hospital at Rockford January 2, 1926, as the result of having been struck by an automobile a few days previously. He was laid to rest in Cedar Bluff Cemetery, Rev. John Gordon officiating, and with the impressive ceremonies of the Grand Army of the Republic conducted by G. L. Nevins Post No. 1. Mr. Shumway never really retired from business, continuing daily his routine of walking from his home to his offices, preferring the walk to riding. He was known all over the country among seed men as one of the oldest in the business.

He was born July 26, 1842, on the site of an old Indian camp in Winnebago County, a short distance south of Camp Grant, and the longest time he was ever away from his birthplace at Rockford was the years he spent in the service of the Union Army during the Civil war. His parents, David S. and Sally (Greeley) Shumway, were natives of Vermont, his father born at Jamaica, that state, March 27, 1803, and his mother at Andover, Vermont, February 8, 1806. She was a cousin of Horace Greeley, the famous editor. They were married at Andover, November 20, 1825, and in 1828 they started West with a yoke of oxen and two horses and a buggy, settling in Lorain County, Ohio. At Carlisle in that county David Shumway erected a sawmill. In 1836 he left Ohio and came out to Winnebago County, Illinois, preempting land from the Government near the junction of the Kishwaukee and Rock rivers. Their first home was a log cabin. David Shumway built a sawmill and he also operated a tavern and a stage coach between Rockford and Dixon. When Roland H. Shumway was five years of age his father was captured by the Driscoll bandits and was tied up in his mill, after which the structure was set on fire. Some Indians discovered the blaze and rescued David Shumway before he was harmed. The mill was rebuilt and subsequently the old tavern was remodeled as the "Old Shumway Homestead," the name it still bears. David Shumway died July 31, 1879, and his wife,

August 8, 1888. Their eight children were: Rosanna, born February 9, 1827, died September 3, 1839; Romanzo Greeley, born February 12, 1832, died March 30, 1908; Rolenzo Bartlett, born May 25, 1835, died December 31, 1911; Alvaro, born April 11, 1838, died at Tacoma, Washington,; Rosetta, born December 2, 1840, died September 3, 1841; Roland H.; Monroe B., born March 31, 1845, also deceased; and Rosalinda, born January 12, 1848, died August 20, 1852.

Roland H. Shumway grew up at the old homestead, attended country schools, worked on the farm and in the mill, and on June 2, 1862, before he was twenty years of age, enlisted in the Union army. While home after the expiration of his first enlistment he married, but soon reenlisted and received his honorable discharge after the close of the war, on July 26, 1865. While in the army he suffered an attack of bronchitis, affecting his hearing, and eventually he became totally deaf. After the war he settled on a farm near his birthplace. It was his ability to recognize an opportunity that brought him into the seed business. In the fall of 1870 he was asked by a neighbor if he had a surplus of a certain seed for sale. It was not long after that he and his brother-in-law, Ed Davis, began a business for supplying the local growers with seed, and after a year or so they located in Rockford in order to be nearer postal and other transportation facilities. The first home of the business in Rockford was on the site of the present Hess Brothers Dry Goods Store, next the upstairs in a building over the present East Side Smoke Shop, and during the early '80s Mr. Shumway bought property in the 100 block on South First Street, on which was erected a building properly equipped for the business. The business grew and prospered, supplying an ever widening range of customers, its trade extending throughout the United States and to the island possessions of America. While Roland Shumway never left the business altogether, since 1912, its active management has devolved on his son, Raymond. He was identified with the Congregational Church, a republican in politics, and long an active member of the Grand Army. He married at Lanark, January 16, 1864, Miss Emma Davis, of Clyde, New York, who died in 1899. They were the parents of six children: Leroy, born October 17, 1870, died May 26, 1924; Leora D., born December 14, 1871, died November 15, 1924; Myra May, born May 7, 1874, died January 7, 1885; Roland H., born December 28, 1880, died May 7, 1906; M. Raymond; and Greeley Davis, born January 29, 1893, now a resident of San Diego, California.

M. Raymond Shumway, whose home is at 1955 Harlem Boulevard, was born at Rockford, March 9, 1884, was well educated in local schools and from boyhood was associated with his father's business, becoming active manager in 1912. He is a member of the Rotary and Country Clubs and the B. P. O. Elks, a republican and a member of the Congregational Church. On May 29, 1906, he married Miss Alice Johnson, and they have two children, Mary V. and William David.

ALEXANDER W. HUTCHINGS. Standing as he does among the ablest men of his profession practicing at the bar of Washington County, Alexander W. Hutchings, of Nashville, is enjoying a very large practice, and the confidence of his fellow citizens. He was born in Perry County, July 26, 1861, his family being the first one to settle in that county. The first settlement in township 4, range 2 west, which includes Beaucoup precinct and the northwestern corner of Pinckneyville, Perry County, Illinois, was made by John Hutchings in 1816, and William Hutchings, his brother, two years before Illinois was admitted to statehood.

The Hutchings were natives of North Carolina, from whence with their wives they went to Tennessee, stopping there a short time, but, not being satisfied, they pushed forward to the territory of Illinois, their original stopping point being Missouri. In May, 1816, they camped on the banks of Beaucoup Creek, and were so pleased with their surroundings that there they made their permanent settlement. John Hutchings with his wife and four children had a colored man named London Parks, and his wife, Agis, and another colored woman named Dinah. William Hutchings had a wife and six children, and with them was a young lady, Delilah Jones, who subsequently became the wife of John R. Hutchings, his eldest son. Here on the banks of the little creek they found game in abundance, rich soil that they felt would be productive of a varied crop, and they were all so delighted that they abandoned their project of going on into Missouri. They did, however, go on as far as Ratcliffe, or Sawyer's Point, in Washington County, but this only confirmed their first choice, and they returned to their camp on Beaucoup Creek and began their preparations for permanent settlement, and all of this was done within sight of a large body of Kaskaskia Indians. John Hutchings built his first cabin on the northwest quarter of section 19, township 4, range 2 west, which he entered July 25, 1817. Later he built a two-story house near the cabin, which was known as the "Travelers Inn." This latter building was a landmark for over fifty years.

William Hutchings built first on the south side of Hutchings Prairie, in 1819, but moved later to Watson Place, where he continued to reside until his death, about 1829. William's second son, Eli J. Hutchings, the paternal grandfather of Alexander W. Hutchings of this review, was a well-known figure throughout the county, having been a country schoolmaster and Justice of the Peace. John R., the eldest son of William, aided in the organization of the county in 1827, was one of the commissioners to locate Pinckneyville as the county seat, and subsequently served as county judge.

Wesley W. Hutchings, son of William Hutchings, was born October 4, 1822. Mary Hutchings, a daughter of John Hutchings, the original settler, was five years old when brought by her father to Illinois, and she became the wife of Hiram Rice.

Martin Van Buren Hutchings, son of Eli J. Hutchings, grandson of William Hutchings, the original settler, and father of Attorney

Hutchings, died in November, 1865, from the effects of sickness contracted while serving in the Union army, dying in a hospital at Victoria, Texas. His wife had passed away in July of that year, and their only child, Alexander W. Hutchings, was left an orphan at the age of four years. His grandfather took him, but at his death the child was placed in the care of his great uncle, Wesley Hutchings of Washington County, where he owned a farm, and it was on this property that the orphaned boy grew to manhood.

The district schools gave him the beginnings of an education, and he further advanced himself at Ewing College, and in 1893 he began reading law in the office of Edward Merrick. In November, 1895, Mr. Hutchings was admitted to the bar, and began the practice of his profession at Nashville. Later he made an abstract of the county, and branched out into the real estate and farm loans business, and now specializes in real-estate law.

In April, 1888, Mr. Hutchings married, at Saint Louis, Missouri, Emma Isabelle Whelan, a daughter of Nicholas Longworth and Mary J. (Duggen) Whelan, the former from Cincinnati, Ohio, and the latter from Covington, Kentucky. Both are now deceased. Mr. and Mrs. Hutchings have two children: Norma and Alexander W., Junior, the latter now being a student of Washington University, Saint Louis, Missouri. Norma married Dr. G. F. Schroeder, who is now at the Edward Hines Hospital, Maywood, Illinois. Doctor Schroeder volunteered for service in the late war, and was overseas at Toul, France, with the rank of captain of dental surgery. He returned home in July, 1919.

J. H. HALLSTROM, mayor of Rockford, veteran of the World war, and a man of unusual abilities and good citizenship, is capably discharging the duties of his high office, and living up to the principles of the labor party which nominated him. He is a native of Sweden, having been born in that country November 18, 1888, a son of Karl and Mina Carlson, both of whom are deceased, having had six children, namely, Henrik, who lives in Sweden; Hulda, who is married and also lives in Sweden; Hialmar, who lives in Sweden; Hilda, who is the wife of B. Esgquist; J. H., whose name heads this review; and Hilding, who is deceased.

When only eleven years old J. H. Hallstrom began to take care of himself, and in February, 1908, having lost his father, he came to the United States. After arriving in this country he went direct to Rockford, and first worked as a building laborer. He then learned the trade of a bricklayer, and followed it until 1921, when he was elected mayor of his home city.

With the entry of this country into the World war he entered the service and was overseas with the Thirty-second and Forty-first Divisions. After eighteen months in the army he was honorably discharged as a corporal, and returned home and resumed work at his trade.

In September, 1922, Mayor Hallstrom married Ruth Hammerstrand, and they have two children: Ruth Irene and Roy Herman. Fraternally Mayor Hallstrom is an Odd Fellow. He and his wife belong to the Lutheran Church. A practical man, he is very progressive in his ideas, and anxious to make his administration one of constructive worth to his city. His election as a labor candidate was a triumph, not only for trade unionism, but for him personally, and what he has accomplished proves the good judgment of the voters in putting him in office and keeping him there. What every city needs at present is clean, honest government, and it can only be brought about by the election to office of men who will live up to their oath of office, and enforce the laws. Such a man is Mayor Hallstrom.

WILLIAM ZIOCK. One of the best known manufacturers of Rockford passed away March 21, 1905. He was born in Hattingen, Germany, April 2, 1830, and would have been seventy-five years of age had he lived a few days longer. He came to America when a lad of nineteen with no capital save his hands and brain. He remained in Philadelphia for some years, and then came to the West, settling in St. Louis, where he engaged in the wholesale business with success and laid the foundation for his fortune.

He secured an interest in a hosiery plant at Manchester, New Hampshire, and later in another at St. Charles, Missouri. In 1877 he gained an interest in the knitting machines of Burson & Nelson in this city and placed them in operation in his mills in New Hampshire and Missouri. In 1883 he removed to Rockford and took charge of the Rockford Mitten and Hosiery Company, organized two years before. He was induced to come by Ralph Emerson, who had an acquaintance with him and recognized his ability. The small industry he found here was soon enlarged and later additions were made until it became one of the largest plants in the city, with 500 machines and 650 employes, sending its goods all over the world.

In addition to this company, to which he devoted most of his effort, he was vice president of the Burson Knitting Company, a director in the Winnebago National Bank, and held other offices in various companies.

Another enterprise of Mr. Ziock was the rehabilitation of the old Horsman Block in North Town. This he took as an investment and converted it from almost waste space into a populous community with accommodations for thirty families. It was known as Ziock Terrace. This was an idea which he lived to see practically completed and which is carried on by his heirs.

Mr. Ziock married in St. Louis, Missouri, Miss Elizabeth Bollinger, May 26, 1855, and the wife died in Rockford, Illinois, March 12, 1900. There were six children born to this union, two sons and four daughters, of whom one son, William H., who has separate mention following, and one daughter, Miss Mathilde Ziock, of Rockford, are living.

The death of Mr. Ziock was received with sorrow by his business associates, his employes and his friends in general. He was a man of reserved habits and perhaps of forbidding exterior and inclined to the brusque on slight acquaintance. Beneath all this there

Jas. W. Gibson

Mrs. Jas. W. Gibson

beat a heart as tender as a woman's and once the first crust of reserve was passed he was as genial a man as could be found and a true friend. In his home life he was the patriarch, the father, in the Biblican sense, the head of the family. His home was the center, and although the children had homes of their own, his was the rallying place and about his board on Sabbaths and holidays all were gathered in frequent reunion. He lived for his family, and this stood first, even ahead of his most cherished business plans.

WILLIAM H. ZIOCK. One of the leading business men of Rockford, and one who occupies a commanding position in the industrial life of Winnebago County, is William H. Ziock, president and treasurer of the Rockford Mitten & Hosiery Company. Mr. Ziock was born in St. Louis, Missouri, November 26, 1863, a son of the late William and Elizabeth (Bollinger) Ziock, of whom a more extended mention appears in the preceding sketch.

After attending the public schools William H. Ziock took a two-years' course in a private school, and then, entering his father's mercantile establishment in St. Louis, was a clerk for a year. For another year he worked in a hosiery mill at Manchester, New Hampshire, following which he came to Rockford and was associated with his father in the Rockford Mitten & Hosiery Company until the latter's death, when he succeeded him in the business. In addition to his responsibilities in connection with this company Mr. Ziock is also president of the B-Z-B Knitting Company, of the Ziock Paper Box Company, and of the T. N. T. Printing Company; is vice president of the Nelson Knitting Company, and a director of the Rockford National Bank.

On April 24, 1889, Mr. Ziock married Lulu Mackwitz, of St. Louis, and four children have been born to them, namely: Juanita, who is at home; William H., Jr., Roy and Carl M. In political faith Mr. Ziock is a republican, and belongs to the Benevolent and Protective Order of Elks.

JOHN V. RILEY, editor of the Rockford Morning Star, has had many activities in the business life of the City of Rockford during the past thirty years.

He was born at Henry in Marshall County, Illinois, son of John and Mary Amanda (Clisbee) Riley. All his grandparents came from Ireland, the Clisbees being Methodists and the Rileys Presbyterians. John Riley was a contractor and builder at Henry, and erected many churches, factories, schools and residences in that portion of the state. His wife took a very leading part in church and social affairs.

John V. Riley finished his education in the Henry High School, and his first business was in retail dry goods. He left a retail store to become a traveling salesman, and in 1895 entered the newspaper business as a part owner of the Rockford Morning Star and has been the man chiefly responsible for making that one of the most influential newspapers in Northern Illinois. He is now half owner of the Rockford Star and is also secretary of the Rockford Apartment Corporation, is vice president of the Palm Theatres Company and the Rockford Theatres Company, is a stockholder in three Rockford banks, in the American Insurance Company and several of the large manufacturing establishments of Rockford.

Mr. Riley served one enlistment with the First Regiment of the Illinois National Guard and for a time was also with Company I of the Michigan State Troops, in what was known as the Custer Guard. He has served on the public library board of Rockford.

Mr. Riley married at Grand Rapids, Michigan, in June, 1891, Miss Lenore Hooker. They have one son, John Stewart Riley, who is a director of the Rockford Star Printing Company.

JAMES WATT GIBSON, of Murphysboro, who died February 27, 1926, had an unusual record of public service. For nearly a quarter of a century he had been in some office of direct importance to the people of Murphysboro or Jackson County. He served as sheriff of the county, and spent many years in the postal service, having been the postmaster of Murphysboro at the time of his death.

His father, James Watt Gibson, Sr., spent most of his life in railroading. Born in Scotland, in 1830, he came to America in 1848, at the age of eighteen, and in Jackson County, Illinois, found employment during the construction of the Illinois Central Railway. He drove a team delivering provisions to the construction force and money for the pay roll. It was about that time that the bridge was being built on the line between DeSoto and Carbondale. For many years after that he was a supervisor in the maintenance of way departments of railroads, chiefly in Texas. He died at the home of his son, James W., in 1902. His wife, Rachel Crews, was born in Somerset Township, Jackson County, in 1839, and died January 28, 1899.

James Watt Gibson, of this review, was born in Somerset Township, Jackson County, April 13, 1870. He acquired a public school education at Murphysboro, but like many other boys of the time he went into the coal mines as a worker and followed mining as an occupation for some years.

When in May, 1899, a free delivery service was established at the Murphysboro post office, Mr. Gibson was one of the three mail carriers appointed. He also had the duties of stamping clerk. Mr. Gibson carried mail eleven years, and for three years, beginning in 1910, was one of the regular clerks in the office. He finally resigned from the postal service to engage in the furniture business. However, there was no long interval between his public service record. When James A. White was sheriff Mr. Gibson was made deputy, serving three and a half years, and was then appointed sheriff to serve the unexpired term of Mr. White, and following that was regularly elected to the office. He had been sheriff three years and seven months when he resigned to accept appointment under the federal government as postmaster.

Mr. Gibson married Etta Hamilton, daughter of Alexander P. Hamilton, who came from Virginia and settled in Franklin County, Illinois. Mrs. Gibson was one of the victims of the fatal tornado of March, 1925. She and Mr. Gibson were at their home, which was totally destroyed, and Mr. Gibson himself was severely bruised. Mr. Gibson was the father of a fine family of five sons and one daughter: Raymond H., employed at a Murphysboro bank; Earl and James W., Jr., both clerks at the post office; Louise, Joseph F. and William Blake.

COL. TRYGGVE ALBERT SIQUELAND. During the entire history of this country some of its most distinguished men and ardent patriots have been those born in foreign lands, and who, coming here in search of a greater measure of liberty and better opportunities, gladly offer to the nation to whose government they have obligated themselves a service that is self-sacrificing and efficient beyond the ordinary. To such men all Americans must accord a support and respect that is only given for actual value in character and citizenship. One of the representative men and financiers of Chicago who is entitled to this distinction is Col. Tryggve Albert Siqueland, manager of the foreign department, State Bank of Chicago, who served in the World war with rank of colonel and who is now holding the same rank in the Reserve Corps of the United States Army.

Colonel Siqueland was born in Stavanger, Norway, June 16, 1888, a son of Capt. Ludvig Albert Siqueland, and his wife, Hanna (Aske) Siqueland. Educated in the Latin School in his home town, Colonel Siqueland was graduated therefrom in 1904, and in September of that same year, coming to the United States, he continued his studies in this country, taking a college course, and later a legal course at the Chicago Law School, from which he was graduated in 1909, with the degree of Bachelor of Laws "cum laude." That same year he was admitted to practice at the Illinois bar. However, he was not contented with the knowledge he had already gained, nor the position he held, and during 1910, 1911 and 1912 he studied political economy, finance and banking and accountancy, School of Commerce of Northwestern University. At the same time he was engaged in the practice of his profession, and he continued in practice until 1917. While he was carrying on a general practice, gradually he was becoming known as an expert in those matters of jurisprudence to which he had given so much thought and study, and he was connected with many corporations as president or secretary or treasurer.

When the United States entered the World war in April, 1917, he was a member of the law firm of Blum, Teed, McKinley & Siqueland. For nine years he had served in the cavalry branch of the Illinois National Guard, rising from the rank of private to that of an officer, and when he offered his services to the United States Government he was appointed captain of the regular army, and called into active service in July, 1917. His period of service continued until September, 1919, when he was put on the reserve list with the rank of lieutenant colonel. During the war he spent the greater part of his time as military attache in Copenhagen, Denmark, and had charge of the important work for the army at that post. He was decorated by the King of England with the Order of Honorary Commander of the Order of the British Empire; by the King of Denmark with the Knighthood of Danebrog and the Sleswig Medal; by the King of Norway with the Knighthood of Saint Olav first class, and received from the American Government the Victory medal with citations. At present he is a colonel in the reserves, United States Army, commanding the Three Hundred and Seventeenth Cavalry.

Upon his return to Chicago Colonel Siqueland associated himself with the State Bank of Chicago as manager of the foreign department, and still maintains this connection. He was one of the organizers and is a director of the Pioneer Trust and Savings Bank of Chicago and chairman of the Board of Directors of the Elmwood Park State Bank. He is a member of the Union League Club, Chicago Bankers Club, Adventurers Club of Chicago, of which he is treasurer and ex-president; he is an ex-president of the Norwegian Club of Chicago and the Douree Club; is a member of the White Paper Club, the Sojourners Club, the Advertisers Golf Club, and was treasurer of the Army and Navy Club.

In 1910 Colonel Siqueland married Lovey Thorp, and they have two children: Alice Victoria, who was born in 1912, and Margaret Ida, who was born in 1914. The family residence is at 2156 Caton Street, Chicago, and a summer home, "Wildaire," is also maintained at Bridgeman, Michigan.

WILLIAM H. MCDERMAID. In an important manufacturing city, where many interests meet and supremacy is maintained only through the exercise of unusual business ability, importance attaches to those whose foresight and good judgment, supplemented by experienced trade knowledge, enable them to safely guide their enterprises through the shoals when there are unsettled commercial conditions. By no means all of the business ventures entered into at Rockford some thirty years ago can be located at the present time, although many started with far better prospects than did William H. McDermaid, whose modest beginning was carefully nourished and substantially developed. Today Mr. McDermaid finds himself at the head of a prosperous coal and wood business, being also the oldest manufacturer of barrel churns in the United States.

Mr. McDermaid was born at Rockford, August 11, 1872, and is a son of John and Isabel (Ralston) McDermaid, natives of Scotland. The parents came to the United States in 1861 and shortly thereafter the father enlisted in the United States Navy for service during the Civil war, at the close of which he came to Rockford and here Mr. McDermaid followed the trade of cooper until 1875, when he invented the barrel churn and which he manufactured until his death in 1918. A man of much mechanical ability, he conceived the idea of a barrel churn, which he patented and manufactured for many years, gradually improving it. His widow still survives him and is one of the highly respected residents of Rockford. They were the parents of six children: Elizabeth, the wife of Matson Morrill, of Los Angeles, California; William H.; Daniel, of Rockford; Robert, deceased; May, the wife of Theodore Robinson, of Chicago; and D. Howard, of Rockford.

William H. McDermaid received a public school education in the community of his birth, and when he was fifteen years of age entered his father's shop and began to learn the trade of cooper. When the elder Mr. McDermaid died the son became the head of the churn manufacturing business, and the "Belle" and "Star" churns, both hand and power, have had a wonderful sale throughout the country, Mr. McDermaid having manufactured as many as 40,000 in a single year. This is now the oldest established firm of churn manufacturers in the United States. In the meantime Mr. McDermaid has built up a prosperous coal and wood business and occupies large and modern yards, employing a fleet of automobile trucks to deliver his product, insuring rapid and active service. In politics he is a republican and for some time was actively interested in public affairs, having filled the offices of supervisor and road commissioner of the township. His military service includes participation in the Spanish-American war, during which he rose to the rank of sergeant. Fraternally he is a Mason and Shriner and holds membership in the local lodge of Elks.

On April 26, 1899, Mr. McDermaid was united in marriage with Miss Lillian May Ward, a native of Rockford, and they have one son, Donald, born August 7, 1907.

J. EDWIN RACKAWAY is one of the principals in the publishing of the Mount Vernon Daily Register-News at Mount Vernon, and is editor of the well ordered and influential newspaper of Jefferson County. He was born at Mount Vernon, September 6, 1889, and has here found opportunity for successful achievement in the field of practical and constructive journalistic enterprise. In this city his parents, John H. and Martha (Welch) Rackaway, still maintain their home, and he is the elder of two children, the younger son, Walter, likewise being a resident of Mount Vernon. He married Miss Fern Burke, and they have one child, Elizabeth. John H. Rackaway was born in Washington, D. C., and was about twenty-five years of age when he established his residence in Mount Vernon, Illinois, in the early '70s. Here he was for several years engaged in the drug business, and he has here gained substantial success, with status as one of the prominent capitalists and liberal and progressive citizens of Jefferson County. He is a director of the Third National Bank of Mount Vernon and also of the Mount Vernon Car Manufacturing Company, besides being financially interested in other representative business concerns in his home city.

After completing his studies in the Mount Vernon High School J. Edwin Rackaway was for two years a student in the great University of Chicago, where his course was of general literary order. After leaving the university he initiated, at Denver, Colorado, his association with the newspaper business, he having there remained about five years, within which he was first allied with the Denver Republican and later with the Denver Times. In 1913 Mr. Rackaway returned to Mount Vernon, where he became editor of the Daily News, besides acquiring an interest in the business. In 1920 he effected a consolidation of the Daily News and the Daily Register, and the business was thereupon incorporated under the title of the Mount Vernon Register-News Company. He is secretary and treasurer of the company and is editor in chief of the paper, which under his vigorous and progressive editorial direction has greatly expanded the scope of its service and influence. In the World war period he was active in local patriotic service and in registration for active military duty he was assigned to the fourth class. He is a Knight Templar Mason and an Elk.

May 21, 1916, recorded the marriage of Mr. Rackaway and Miss Bernice Chapman, one of the six children born to the late William and Nevada (Holcomb) Chapman, who were residents of Mount Vernon at the time of their deaths, the father having passed away in 1904 and the mother in 1917. Mrs. Rackaway is the youngest of their six children; Charles is still a bachelor; Edith is the wife of Edward Garrison; Lena is the wife of J. H. Maxey; Nell is the wife of Clyde King, and they have two children, William and Martha; and Lynne is the wife of Frank Thompson. Mr. and Mrs. Rackaway have two children—John and Chapman.

The paternal grandfather of Mr. Rackaway was born in Germany and came to the United States about 1840. He established his residence at Washington, D. C., where he engaged in the tobacco business, and later he removed to St. Louis, Missouri, where he passed the remainder of his life. The maternal grandparents of the subject of this review were Edwin and Elizabeth (Boswell) Welch. The Welch family was founded in New England in the Colonial era and gave patriot soldiers to the Continental Line in the War of the Revolution. Representatives of the family later settled in Indiana, and it was at Princeton, that state, that the mother of the subject of this sketch was born, her father having been widely known as a specially skilled accountant. He died while serving in the Union army during the Civil war.

LAWRENCE J. BOYD, postmaster of Lewistown, and one of the most representative of its citizens, belongs to one of the old families of Fulton County. He is a native son of Lewistown, where his birth occurred August 21, 1871, but his father, the late Thomas Alexander Boyd, was born at Bedford, Pennsylvania, in 1830, and came from that city of the Keystone State to Lewistown not long before the breaking out of the war between the states. An attorney by profession, he had been liberally educated in the college of Pennsylvania, Mercersburg, and was admitted to the bar of his native state. His father died when he was a child, but he left an estate that was ample to educate his son.

When war was declared Thomas Alexander Boyd enlisted for service in the Union army, and was made a captain of one of the companies of the Seventeenth Illinois Volunteer

Infantry, and as such participated in some very heavy fighting during the earlier part of the war, but was honorably discharged for disability. Returning to Lewistown, he resumed his practice of law, and was connected with some of the most important litigation of his times and locality. Entering politics as one of the leaders of the local republican party, he was first sent to the Lower House of the Illinois State Assembly, and later to the Illinois State Senate, and finally was elected to the National Congress, to which body he was re-elected, his period of service covering the latter part of President Hayes' term and the beginning of that of President Garfield. Upon his return to Lewistown he resumed his law practice once more, but was not long left in private life, as he was elected county judge of Fulton County, and he was reelected to the same office. After serving two years of his second term he was stricken with paralysis, and resigned. His death occurred in 1887, thus removing from Fulton County one of its most distinguished and honorable representatives, and a man who held the warm friendship of its people, to whom he was known as Judge Boyd.

Judge Boyd married, in Washington, Miss Laura James, born in the capital city in 1833, a daughter of William and Mary James. She died at Lewistown June 4, 1897. The children born to Judge and Mrs. Boyd were as follows: Thomas A., who died in University Place, Nebraska, leaving a widow and three daughters; Mary, who married E. C. Miles, and resides at Lewistown; John W., who is a business man of Lewistown; Margaret, who died unmarried; Lawrence J., whose name heads this review; and Hobart S., who is an attorney of Lewistown, and a member of the strong legal firm of Boyd & Weber.

A product of the grammar and high schools of Lewistown, Lawrence J. Boyd is a credit to them and the careful rearing of his parents. His first connection with business life was as a member of the mercantile firm of Hamblin & Boyd, and his brother, John W. Boyd, was also a partner. After five years of this association Mr. Boyd retired from the mercantile field and entered upon the official duties of the office of circuit clerk of Fulton County, to which he was appointed. After leaving that office he was connected with the selling force of Groat & Strode, merchants of Lewistown, and when he left that firm he entered the Lewistown postoffice, under Postmaster F. M. Love, as a clerk. Rising in the government service, he became assistant postmaster, which office he held for ten years, and March 3, 1922, he was appointed postmaster by President Harding, to succeed J. B. Henry. Since taking charge of the Lewistown postoffice Mr. Boyd has greatly improved the service, and has placed the affairs of this office upon a sound basis that meets the approval of the Government and the people alike. His first presidential ballot cast for Benjamin Harrison, Mr. Boyd has continued in his allegiance to the republican party, and is proud of the fact that his vote went to swell the majorities given to William McKinley, Theodore Roosevelt, William H. Taft, Warren G. Harding and Calvin Coolidge.

On January 11, 1921, Mr. Boyd married in Nehawka, Nebraska, Myrtle Creamer, a native of that city, where she was reared and educated. She is a daughter of Lincoln and Ida (Thompson) Creamer. Mr. Creamer was formerly a farmer of McLean County, Illinois, but is now a farmer in the neighborhood of Nehawka. Mr. and Mrs. Creamer have had the following children born to their marriage: Lee, Blanche, Helen and Mrs. Boyd. Mr. and Mrs. Boyd have no children. Beyond the age for registration during the late war, Mr. Boyd's participation in it was confined to a zealous support of local war work, and he was particularly active in the sale of Liberty Bonds and War Savings Stamps. He is a Knight of Pythias. While he was reared an Episcopalian, he now belongs to the Presbyterian Church. Both he and his wife are very popular socially, and are recognized leaders in a congenial circle of Lewistown.

GUY C. STUTZMAN is superintendent of city schools at Hanover, Illinois. He is an ex-service man of the World war, and taught in Iowa before taking up his present duties in Jo Daviess County.

He was born at Buda, Illinois, November 12, 1894, son of Adam L. and Mary (Schur) Stutzman, of Buda. His father was born and reared near Harrisburg, Pennsylvania, acquired his education in public schools in his native state, and coming to Illinois about 1880, settled at Buda. He moved out to Kansas and homesteaded and taught school a few years in that state. Returning to Buda, he bought a farm and lived on it until his death in 1913. His wife, Mary J. Schur, was born near Tiffin, Ohio, and was educated in Kansas, her parents moving out to that state about the close of the Civil war and homesteading near Minneapolis, Kansas, where she was reared. Her father came to America from Germany at the age of twenty-one, first settling in Ohio. He served in the Union army under General Sherman in the quartermaster's department, being assigned duty making and repairing shoes and harness for the army. At the close of the war he married and moved out to Kansas.

Guy C. Stutzman acquired a public school education in Illinois, graduating from the Buda High School in 1912. In 1917 he was graduated from Knox College at Galesburg, and in the same year he enlisted for service in the Army Medical Corps, spending two weeks at Jefferson Barracks, St. Louis, and one month in training at the Medical Officers' Training School at Fort Riley, Kansas. In August, 1917, he was put on duty at Camp Dodge, Iowa, remaining there about a year. He was made a sergeant first class. In August, 1918 he went to England and from there to France, and was a participant in the concluding scenes of the great war, particularly in the Meuse-Argonne campaign. Mr. Stutzman in June, 1919, was honorably discharged at Camp Dodge, Iowa. During 1920-22 he taught in the public schools of Iowa, and in 1923 he was graduated Master of Arts from the University of Iowa. On graduating he accepted his present position as superintendent of schools at Hanover, Illinois. Mr. Stutzman is a Mason, member of the college frater-

A. H. ROBERTS
In 1862

nities Lambda Chi Alpha and Phi Delta Kappa, is a member of the Hanover Men's Community Club, is a democrat and is affiliated with the Church of God.

He married at Anamosa, Iowa, May 19, 1922, Miss Gertrude Crispin, who was educated in grammar and high schools of Anamosa and spent two years in Coe College at Cedar Rapids. She taught for two years in the public schools of Onslow, Iowa. Mrs. Stutzman is a daughter of Miller C. and Irene (Snyder) Crispin, of Anamosa. Her father was born and reared in Ohio and accompanied the family to Iowa. Mr. and Mrs. Stutzman have one daughter, Dora Jane.

ALEXANDER HAMILTON ROBERTS. The Roberts were unquestionably one of the oldest and most eminent families in Scotland, being of that royal house which occupied the throne and kingdom during the eleventh, twelfth and thirteenth centuries. They were descended from the ancient earls of Athol, which house sprang from Duncan, King of Scotland, eldest son of Malcolm III, surnamed Canmore. The ancient celtic earls of Athol were the ancestors of the Roberts of Strowan.

Crinan, Lord or Earl of Athol, Abbott of Dunkeld and Abthane of Dull, married Beatrice, daughter of King Malcolm II, so that they became the ancestors of all the Scottish kings from Duncan I to Alexander III in the male line except Macbeth, and to James VI, in the female line, and were therefore of the Roberts blood. The name Roberts, meaning the son of Robert, is Saxon in its derivation, but the race was a Gaelic one. They fought under Sir William Wallace, the great patriot warrior, also served with distinction under Robert Bruce at Bannockburn in 1314, when with thirty thousand Scots he routed King Edward II of England, with a hundred thousand English troops.

In 1437 Robert of Strowan, chief of the clan, arrested Graham, one of the murderers of King James I of Scotland, and as a reward for that service his lands were made a barony, and he was granted an honorable addition to his arms, consisting of a man lying in chains, a hand holding a royal crown and the motto "Virtutis Gloria Merces" meaning "Glory the reward of bravery." This was the first coat of arms possessed by the Robert family. Robert of Strowan married Lady Margaret Stewart and they had: Alexander, Robert and Patrick. From him is derived the surnames Roberts and Robertson, both meaning the son of Robert. Since then the names have been often used interchangeably. There were numerous founders of the family in America.

Alexander Hamilton Roberts has the distinction of being Murphysboro's oldest active business man. His direct associations with the city's commercial activities extend over a period of more than half a century. He is a senior member of the firm A. H. Roberts & Sons, hardware, furniture and undertaking.

Mr. Roberts was born at Jonesboro, Illinois, April 13, 1847, son of Joshua and Caroline (Cruse) Roberts. The father was commissioned a second lieutenant in 1846 in the War with Mexico by Gov. Thomas Ford, of Illinois. Joshua Roberts' father, of Scotch-Irish ancestry, was born near Zanesville, Ohio, was a carpenter by trade, and when a young man went down the Ohio and Mississippi rivers to New Orleans. At that distant place he learned of the plans to erect a new court house at Jonesboro, Illinois. Coming north to Jonesboro, he found work as a carpenter on the new construction. While thus engaged he boarded at the home of Peter Cruse, a blacksmith and native of North Carolina, and one of the earliest settlers of Jonesboro and Union County. He had come to Illinois as early as 1815, three years before the territory was admitted to the Union. Joshua Roberts loved and married Caroline Cruse, one of the seven daughters and thirteen children of Peter Cruse, and she herself became the mother of thirteen children, five of whom are still living. She was born in North Carolina and reached the advanced age of ninety-two. Joshua Roberts saw service as a soldier in the war with Mexico. Besides his work as a carpenter he taught school at Jonesboro, and was a man of unusual education. Finally he took up the manufacture of furniture and burial caskets, and a natural and almost necessary auxiliary of such a business at that time was performing the duties of undertaker. In this work he continued until his death in 1866.

In the log cabin where Alexander Hamilton Roberts was born he learned at the knee of his mother the principles that have guarded him through his career as a successful business man. He also attended the public schools, and learned his father's trade. He was fifteen years old when the Civil war broke out, and his desire to become a soldier immediately was thwarted because of his age. The following year, however, he enlisted in Company F, of the 109th Illinois Infantry. After the capture of General Morgan, the famous Confederate raider, Mr. Roberts' company was in charge of the prisoner. Through negligence Morgan was permitted to escape. Mr. Roberts witnessed the escape and gave the alarm to his lieutenant, who, however, did not take the proper step to effect his recapture. Several of the officers were cashiered, and Mr. Roberts was transferred to Company D of the Eleventh Illinois Infantry. He was in the army three years and three months, and was a participant in sixteen battles.

After being mustered out at Springfield, Illinois, Mr. Roberts returned home to Jonesboro and was associated with his father's business until the latter's death. As a step toward increasing his business opportunities Mr. Roberts moved to Murphysboro, Jackson County, in 1872. For nine months he was in partnership with C. C. Culey as a furniture dealer and undertaker, at the northeast corner of what is now Ninth and Chestnut streets. After the firm dissolved he continued the business alone, and in 1874 bought property on the southeast corner of the same street and erected the large business block still used by the firm. The corner store-room provides quarters for the hardware store, while the east room is the undertaking parlors. It is one of the oldest business establishments under one name in southern Illinois. In the '70s Mr. Roberts served one term as mayor of Murphysboro, and was also a supervisor.

Mr. Roberts gave his children good educational opportunities. His three sons are licensed embalmers. Two of them, Hamilton S. and Alexander Joshua Roberts, are now members of the firm A. H. Roberts & Sons. The youngest son, Homer E., is still in training.

Mr. Roberts married Miss Frances Sanders, daughter of Jacob Sanders. Mr. Roberts at the age of eighty is still active, attending to business every day. He has an interesting memory of events running back to Civil war times. In his younger years Mr. Roberts was frequently imposed upon by going security for friends. He always paid such debts, but long since has ceased to worry about such losses, and that attitude is a characteristic one and has perhaps been responsible for his long life. He is quartermaster of the Grand Army Post at Murphysboro. At one time this post had 225 members, while now the membership is only thirteen.

CAPT. EBENEZER JAMES PEARCE, of White Hall, Illinois, attained a place of prominence in his home county and state as an orator, editor, educator and patriot. Captain Pearce was a native of Pennsylvania, born October 6, 1839, at Evansburg, Crawford County, in that state. His schooling was very meagre, attending a few three-month terms, working on a farm in the summer and cutting cord wood in the winter. He attended an academy at New Lebanon, Pennsylvania, for a short time, but his education and vast store of general knowledge were obtained by unceasing home study, and a quick comprehension of facts as he found them.

He taught several terms of school in his native county, and then came to Illinois, reaching White Hall in 1860. He was engaged in teaching school until the call of Lincoln in 1862 caused him to resign school work and join the army. For a time he was engaged in recruiting soldiers, but enlisted in Company G, Ninety-first Illinois Infantry, being at once made sergeant, and in succession second lieutenant, first lieutenant and captain. In July, 1863, Gen. John A. Logan appointed him as assistant provost marshal. In March, 1865, he was made acting assistant general of the Second Brigade, Third Division, Thirteenth Army Corps, retaining this position all through the Mobile and New Orleans campaigns.

After the war he resumed teaching at White Hall, and in 1877 established the White Hall Republican, which he continued to publish until his death in 1907. He was widely quoted as an editorial writer, it being known that one of his editorials appeared in the London Times without credit. He advised the Republican National Committee on the issues of the national campaign of 1896, when McKinley made his first race for the presidency, advocating the tariff as the leading issue of that notable campaign. Captain Pearce's writings on the tariff issue and especially his arguments with T. C. Willson, tariff editor of the New York World, formed much of the campaign material of the republican party in that year.

His wife died July 30, 1904, leaving surviving five children, as follows: Frederick Vinton Pearce, Mount Morris, Illinois; Edward Carr Pearce, postmaster Raymond Blair Pearce and Mrs. Laura Pritchett, White Hall, Illinois; and Mabel, wife of Dr. A. E. Meisenbach, of St. Louis.

Mr. Pearce was founder and editor of the White Hall Republican for many years. After his death it was sold to the White Hall Register, the name of the two papers since that time being Register-Republican.

DON I. KIRKHAM, judge of the County Court of Alexander County, has been a prominent factor in development work, particularly the drainage of low lands in Southern Illinois.

He was born at Princeton in Kosciusko County, Indiana, November 17, 1886, son of Richard M. B. and Kate (Voke) Kirkham, his father born near Louisville, Kentucky, and his mother near Oblong, Illinois. His parents were married in Crawford County, Illinois. His father was in the lumber mill industry, and lived for many years in Edgar County, Illinois. He died November 24, 1922, and his wife, on January 19, 1922.

Don I. Kirkham was educated in grammar and high school, completed his education in Westfield College in 1907 and for ten years was engaged in teaching. In the meantime his father had bought a tract of timber land in Alexander County, Illinois, and Don Kirkham, moving to Olive Branch, organized the Richland Drainage District, draining part of the area and afterwards selling the land. He and his brother, Wendell B., organized the Olive Branch Bank, of which Don Kirkham became president. With his brother he then bought another farm and in association with Walter Withburn, organized the Olive Branch community high school district, purchasing the site for the school. This was the first school in Southern Illinois to operate motor busses for the transportation of the pupils. Pupils are now brought over four school routes. Mr. Kirkham with his brother organized another drainage district and he and his brother, with R. J. Hooks and C. A. Clark of St. Louis, built a cotton gin at Cairo, which during one season ginned over 900 bales of cotton raised in this section.

Mr. Kirkham married, July 10, 1909, Miss Alice Chandler, a native of Tuscola, Illinois, and daughter of Thomas and Jennie (Gurnea) Chandler. The children of their marriage are six in number: Ruth, Audrey, Shirley, Virginia, Alice and Don. Mr. Kirkham was reared in the faith of the Methodist Episcopal Church, is a republican and for twelve years held the office of justice of the peace and was elected judge of the County Court of Alexander County in November, 1924. His offices are in the courthouse at Cairo.

REV. P. J. HENNESSY, resident priest of Saint Mary's Catholic Church, Joliet, is one of the scholarly men and eminent divines of his calling, and one who has won the confidence of the people of the city, irrespective of their religious connections, because of his whole-souled work in behalf of public well being. While he is not native-born, he is a true American in the highest and best sense of the word, and to his advice and admoni-

tions are due many of the improvements which have been recently secured in this section of the state.

Rev. P. J. Hennessy was born in Limerick, Ireland, in 1876, a son of James and Margaret (Collins) Hennessy, both of whom came to the United States, and settled in Chicago, in 1898, and there they died and are buried. These excellent and devout parents sent their son to the public schools in his native land, and dedicated him to the service of the church. He was a student of Saint Francis College, Brooklyn, New York, and Saint Mary's Seminary, Baltimore, Maryland, and in 1902 he was ordained to the priesthood by the late Cardinal Gibbons. After six months in parish work in New York City, Rev. P. J. Hennessy was sent to Chicago, and a year later was stationed in Saint Mary's parish, Evanston, Illinois, where he remained for seven years. He was then sent to Braidwood, Illinois, where he spent ten years, after which he was at Elmhurst for three years. Then, in April, 1924, he assumed his present duties in connection with Saint Mary's Church, Joliet. His assistants are Revs. Ed. Sendek, L. J. Kiley and J. T. Farrell.

A man of broad vision, Rev. P. J. Hennessy believes in acting with various community organizations, and is a valued member of the Joliet Kiwanis Club and of the Public Health Council. He belongs to the Knights of Columbus, and is chaplain of the Joliet Council of that order, and he is an ex-grand knight of the Braidwood Council, Knights of Columbus, and Joliet A. O. H. Reverend Hennessy is interested in many philanthropies and reforms which indubitably add value and dignity to his name and calling and his identification with the higher life of this city is unquestioned, nor is his leadership in many things disputed.

WILLIAM THOMAS LAKIN, son of Alexander and Maria Lakin, was born near Carrollton, Illinois, July 2, 1845, his birth occurring on the old Lakin homestead. He assisted on the farm during the summer months, and during the winters applied himself to studies, by which means he acquired quite a liberal education. At sixteen years he became apprenticed to the trade of harness making with N. Williams, of White Hall, and at the end of two years became baggage master with the St. L., J. & C. Railroad at Carrollton, which later became the C. & A., and while in this capacity, on November 5, 1866, he fell in attempting to board a moving train, his injuries necessitating the amputation of part of one hand and his leg. While recovering from this accident he took up the study of telegraphy, and for nine years followed railroad telegraphing on various roads over the country. In 1875 he became a citizen of White Hall, where he established the Greene County Democrat. From this time forward Mr. Lakin was active as a country editor and news correspondent for various metropolitan papers as well as a typesetter. He died February 6, 1916, with the record of having launched more country newspapers than any other man in the country. He was survived by two children at the time of his death, these being Lena, wife of Harry Watt, Jerseyville, and George A., St. Louis. The remains were interred in White Hall Cemetery.

ARTHUR L. WHITMER. One of the notable examples of western perseverance and success gained through the well-directed application of modern methods in a field of ever-widening opportunity has been the career of Arthur L. Whitmer, chairman of the board of directors of the Chicago National Life Insurance Company, of which he was the founder and formerly was president. Mr. Whitmer had only ordinary advantages in his youth and in every sense has been the architect of his own fortunes. Starting in the insurance business only twelve years ago, he is now one of the best known and most highly connected men in this field, in addition to which he is associated with other lines of business endeavor.

Mr. Whitmer was born at Emporia, Pennsylvania, October 27, 1890, and is a son of William and Grace Whitmer. He was granted the advantages of a grammar school education and as a youth learned the trade of carriage painter, which he followed only for a short time. After traveling for a jewelry house as a salesman for two years, in 1912 he became identified with the Joslin Dry Goods Company of Denver, Colorado, and in 1914 received his introduction to the insurance business with the California State Life Insurance Company at Oakland, California. From 1915 until 1917 he was agent at San Francisco for the International Life Insurance Company of St. Louis, Missouri, and from 1917 until 1919 was agent for the Reserve Life Insurance Company of Indianapolis, Indiana, in the state of Pennsylvania and at Chicago, settling permanently at the latter in 1919. In 1922 Mr. Whitmer founded and organized the Chicago National Life Insurance Company, of which he was at first president and is now chairman of the Board of Directors. At the time of its organization it was the youngest of about 256 life insurance companies writing business in the United States, being the twenty-second going company organized in the State of Illinois. At that time it possessed a capital of $100,000, and surplus of $78,125. It occupied two rooms, whereas now it has the entire fifteenth floor of the Century Building. So rapid was its growth that in 1924 it had attained to third rank in the state in the amount of insurance, according to the reports of the Illinois State Insurance Department, being surpassed by only two companies, one of which had been doing business for thirty years and the other for seventeen years. The advancement, while seemingly spectacular, under Mr. Whitmer's wise direction has been healthy and consistent. The home office has been expanded from 300 feet of floor space to over 3,300 square feet, the agents have increased from thirty-five to about 160, the capital has grown from $100,000 to a capital and surplus including a reserve of over $900,000, and with over $20,000,000 of insurance in force, the territory had been extended to six states, Illinios, Indiana, Iowa, Missouri, Kentucky and Kansas, from a single policyholder to more than 7,000, and from a production during the first six months of an average of $100,000 a month to a production of nearly $1,000,000 a month for the first six months of 1926. In addition to his connection with this very successful enterprise Mr. Whitmer is president of the United States General Agency Company, exclusive general agency in the United States of the Chicago National Life, president of the Illinois National Underwriters Company, president of the Industrial Hotel Supply Company, president of the Premium Petroleum Company, and a member of the directorate of the First National Bank of Oak Park. Politically he is a republican, but his numerous business duties have precluded his taking an active part in politics or public matters, although always a constructive supporter of worthy civic movements. He is a thirty-second degree Mason and Shriner, and a member of the Medinah Athletic Club, the Medinah Country Club, the Mid West Athletic Club and the Hamilton Club.

On July 16, 1923, Mr. Whitmer was united in marriage with Miss Florence Heaney, of Chicago, and they are the parents of one son, Raymond Howard.

THOMAS JEFFERSON ALBERT was born in Carrollton, Greene County, Illinois, in 1842. On attaining his twentieth year his parents, John and Nancy D. Albert, moved to Milton, Pike County, and thence to Pearl Prairie. At the latter place the head of the family continued farming until his death in the spring of 1877, at the age of seventy-seven years. In 1868 Thomas Jefferson Albert purchased a farm in Missouri of 130 acres. He received his preliminary education in the district schools, later attending business college and a normal school, and on attaining his majority taught the village school of Pearl, Pike County, and later taught near Mexico, Missouri. His longest tenure as teacher was at Patterson, Greene County, for upwards of ten years, previous to which he conducted a store at Patterson. In 1876, in connection with John M. Ferris, he began the publication of the Greene County Democrat, whose columns always teemed with well-written articles. At the outbreak of the Civil war he enlisted in Company I, Ninety-ninth Illinois Infantry, at Milton, Pike County. He was then in his nineteenth year. His death occurred October 1, 1905, at Parsons, Kansas, where he had resided for a number of years. The remains were brought back and interred in White Hall Cemetery, where they occupy an honored and well-remembered soldier's grave.

Mr. Albert married Miss Etta Doyle, sister of Wilson L. Doyle, near White Hall, Illinois. Two children were born of this marriage, Arla and Aura. Both grew to young womanhood. Aura died in Kansas City, Missouri, and was buried beside her father in White Hall Cemetery at White Hall, Illinois. Arla became the wife of Creighton A. Henshaw, of Greene County, Illinois, and was killed in an automobile accident in the City of St. Louis soon after the death of her husband and is buried in the same cemetery.

Mr. Albert in the early eighties was elected and served as circuit clerk of Greene County for one term of four years.

GEORGE F. M. WARD, president of the Ham National Bank at Mount Vernon, judicial center of Jefferson County, was born at Harwinton, Connecticut, October 11, 1854, and has been a resident of Illinois since he was a child of about three years, his parents having established their residence at Carbondale, Jackson County, this state, in 1858. He is a son of Henry and Lucy Adeline (Todd) Ward, who were honored pioneer citizens of Illinois at the time of their deaths, the father having been venerable in years when he passed from the stage of life's mortal endeavors in 1906, and the mother's death having occurred about four years previously. Henry Ward was a farmer by vocation throughout his active life, was active and influential in community affairs, and ever commanded unqualified esteem. Both he and his wife were representatives of families that were founded in New England in the early Colonial era. The subject of this review is the only survivor of a family of six children, the others having been Elmina, Julius Henry, William Dwight, John Nelson, and Samuel Whitemore.

The youthful experiences of George F. M. Ward included a goodly share of service in connection with the work of the home farm and a due amount of application to study in the district school, besides which he was for three years employed as a clerk in the clothing store of M. Goldman at Carbondale. During the ensuing two and one-half years he was similarly engaged in the Joe Solomon clothing store at Duquoin, and he then was admitted to partnership in the clothing business established by Ward & Solomon at Mount Vernon. It was in 1879 that Mr. Ward thus became a resident of Mount Vernon, and three years later he purchased Mr. Solomon's interest in the business which had been conducted under the firm name of Ward & Solomon, his independent association with this enterprise having been actively continued until January 20, 1909, when, as a matter of commercial expediency in the handling of the large and greatly amplified business, he effected its incorporation under the title of the Mammoth Shoe, Clothing & Dry Goods Company. Of this representative business corporation he has since continued the president, and as such he now figures as one of the veteran merchants of the city that has represented his home for nearly half a century and in which he has at all times stood exponent of loyal and liberal citizenship. He has done much to advance the civic and material interests of Mount Vernon, where he is president of the Ham National Bank and of the Mount Vernon Lumber Company, besides being a director of the Mount Vernon Car Company and several other local business corporations. The Ham National Bank is the direct successor of the First National Bank, and C. D. Ham, its president and principal stockholder, eventually surrendered its charter, and after Mr. Ham had conducted a private banking business for a number of years the institution was reorganized and was chartered as the Ham National Bank, inasmuch as it was impossible to resume the former title of First National Bank. Mr. Ward's daughter,

Leota Pope, became the wife of Grant T. Ham, a son of C. D. Ham. Her husband is now deceased, and their daughter, Helene Elizabeth, is a gracious young woman of seventeen years (1925).

The political allegiance of Mr. Ward is given to the democratic party and he was several times mayor of Mount Vernon. He is affiliated with the Independent Order of Odd Fellows, the Knights of Pythias, the Modern Woodmen of America, the Improved Order of Red Men and the Elks. He and his wife hold membership in the Christian Church.

At Duquoin, this state, June 2, 1880, Mr. Ward was united in marriage with Miss Sarah Elizabeth Pope, daughter of the late Dr. B. W. and Emeline Pope. Of the other children of the Pope family it is to be recorded that Bryan is deceased; Judge B. W. Pope died in 1924; P. V. is engaged in the dry goods business at Duquoin. The late Dr. B. W. Pope was long one of the representative physicians and surgeons of Franklin and Perry County, with residence at Duquoin, and after retiring from the active practice of his profession he was there engaged in the lumber business. He was a leader in public affairs in his community and was called upon to serve in various offices of trust, including that of mayor of Duquoin. Mr. and Mrs. Ward became the parents of three children: Todd P. Ward, M. D., who is a representative physician and surgeon of Mount Vernon, married Miss Virginia Watkins, of Owensburg, Kentucky, and they have two children: Letitia and George F. M. (II), named in honor of his paternal grandfather; Henry Ben Pope, the second son, married Miss Aline Emmerson, whose father, Hon. L. L. Emmerson, is the present secretary of state for the State of Illinois, and the one child of this union is a son, Louis Emmerson, named for his illustrious grandfather. Leota Pope, only daughter of the subject of this review, became, as previously stated, the wife of Grant T. Ham, their one surviving child being Helene Elizabeth.

WILLIAM A. KIRCHNER, a representative of the Kankakee Food Clinic, is a native of Kankakee County and represents a family that has lived there through three generations.

His grandfather, Harman Kirchner, was a native of Germany, and coming to America in 1847 after a brief residence at Chicago settled in Salina Township of Kankakee County. His son, William Kirchner, was born in Germany, March 9, 1838, and was about nine years old when the family settled in Kankakee County, where he followed farming until he retired. He is now living at 740 North Rosewood Avenue in Kankakee. William Kirchner married Lydia Hertz, who was born in Pennsylvania, July 25, 1846, daughter of David and Mary (Trump) Hertz, who subsequently crossed the country in wagons and settled in Salina Township of Kankakee County. The children of William and Lydia Kirchner are: William A., of Kankakee; Samuel S., on the old home farm; Benjamin, of Salina Township; Mary A., wife of William Dazey, of New Castle, Indiana; Amelia C., wife of George L. Caldwell, of Kankakee; Emma E., Mrs. George Williams, of Bradley, Illinois; Minnie G., widow of Edward Foreman, of Kankakee.

William A. Kirchner was born in Salina Township September 25, 1866. Until the age of seventeen he lived at home and attended school. After that he worked as a farm hand by the month. When he was twenty years of age he became a mission worker in the Salvation Army, serving in some of the large cities in the states of Indiana, Illinois, Missouri and Minnesota for six years, then learning the trade of sheet metal worker at Joliet. He later returned to Kankakee, and for twenty-three years followed his trade, twenty-one years of the time as shop foreman. During this time he was also interested in raising pet stock, being a member of local, state and national pet stock associations, in which he held a number of official positions. Since then he has been a distributor in Kankakee, Bradley and Bourbonnais of whole grain wheat products made at Momence, distributed through the Kankakee Food Clinic, which is a member of the American Educational Food Council. His business headquarters are at 1235 East Chestnut Street. He also operates a small printing plant in connection with his work.

Mr. Kirchner married, in 1893, Fannie B. Morris, a native of Peoria, daughter of David and Cynthia Morris, her father an Ohioan and her mother a Pennsylvanian. The children of Mr. and Mrs. Kirchner are: William C., at home; Clarence S., of Bradley, who married Vera B. Potts and has a son, Harlan; Elmer L., at home; Herbert O., of Kankakee, who married Elizabeth Rogers; Nellie A., Mrs. Matthew Meents, and has a son, Willard Elmer; Loretta Pearl; Mrs. Howard Fitzpatrick, of Kankakee. Mr. Kirchner is a member of the Church of God and interested in Sunday School work and a member of the County Council of Religious Education.

JACOB W. RAUSCH, of Morris, is a native of Ohio. In 1848 his grandparents on both sides immigrated from Germany and settled in Tuscarawas County, Ohio. His parents were Philip G. Rausch and Philipina-Helter Rausch. The subject of this sketch was born November 1, 1870, on a farm near the historic village of Gradenhutten, Ohio. He was the seventh son of a family of ten children. In 1885 Jacob left his home in Ohio and came to Bradford, Illinois, where two of his older brothers, Philip and John, were located. Here Jacob worked for different farmers during the summer seasons, while he attended the Bradford High School during the school year. After two years of study he was granted a teacher's certificate by William R. Sandham, county superintendent of schools of Stark County, Illinois. Commencing in the fall of 1887, Jacob taught the Franklin School, near Modena, on the Spoon River, for two years. During the winter seasons he organized a literary and debating society which became famous and furnished entertainment and instruction for the entire community, people coming for many miles to attend these exercises.

In 1889 Jacob Rausch entered the Illinois State Normal University as a student. He graduated from this institution in 1894. While attending the university he taught school one year at Shirley and one year at Godfrey. At the university Jacob developed great ability as a ready debater and public speaker. After his graduation he was principal of the Mazon public schools for three years. While teaching he studied law and he was admitted to the bar by the Supreme Court in 1898. Since then he has been engaged in the active practice of his profession. His practice extends to the State and Federal Courts. He has been engaged in many important cases.

In 1901 Jacob W. Rausch was united in marriage with Colette Beatrice McCambridge. Mr. and Mrs. Rausch have one child, Mary Colette, who is now a student in the University of Southern California.

Mr. Rausch is an authority on governmental problems and constitutional law. He has always taken a keen interest in public affairs. He served the city of Morris as city attorney from 1899 to 1901, and again from 1907 to 1909. In 1912 he was a candidate for Congress, but was defeated at the election by a narrow margin. He was a member of the Fifty-third General Assembly and at once took rank as one of the ablest, best informed and most influential members of that body. At the end of his term he resumed the practice of the law.

Mr. Rausch's father served four years in the Civil war. During the World war Mr. and Mrs. Rausch devoted practically their entire time to war activities. Patriotism is his creed. He has always performed official duties in such an efficient manner that he has conferred more honor upon the office he held than the office has conferred upon him.

REV. NORMAN TAYLOR ALLEN, of Galesburg, has been in the ministry of the Methodist Episcopal Church for over half a century and has the distinction of being the oldest surviving native born citizen of Galesburg.

He was born in that city, which has been his home practically all his life, on August 15, 1844. His grandfather, Chester E. Allen, came from Connecticut and was an early settler in Illinois, living in this state until his death at the age of seventy-six. The father of Rev. Allen was Sheldon W. Allen, who was born in New York State, and in 1835 married Fidelia Leach. In 1837 they came west with a colony which settled on the site of Galesburg, and who founded Knox College, erecting log cabins and establishing what was known as "Log City." Three years later Sheldon W. Allen established his home on what is now Mulberry Street in Galesburg, and lived there until his death. Before the days of railroads and before the Michigan and Illinois Canal was constructed he hauled grain in wagons to Chicago, sleeping underneath the wagon at night. He died January 18, 1893, at the age of eighty-five and his wife passed away in 1855, when in middle life. Sheldon W. Allen was one of the original Abolitionists in north central Illinois, and was one of the conductors on the underground railway.

Norman Taylor Allen was one of a family of seven sons and one daughter. He grew up in Galesburg, attended college there and completed his theological education in the Garrett Biblical Institute at Evanston. In 1869 he entered the Central Illinois Conference, his first pastorate being French Creek circuit, afterward at Biggsville and later at Wataga, Roseville and other places. In 1881 the conference selected him to publish its minutes, he having for five years prior to that, been the assistant publisher, a work so ably done that he was retained for that service and in 1926 the last issue of the annual report of the conference was published by him. It was the forty-ninth such report under his editorial supervision. He is now with one exception the only survivor of his early colleagues in the conference.

On May 26, 1867, Rev. Allen married Amelia Kent, adopted daughter of Rev. L. B. Kent. She died March 14, 1921, fifty-four years after their marriage. Of their five children Willie R. died at the age of six months and Adah E. died at the age of sixteen years. The daughter Eva A. is the wife of A. N. Hughes, superintendent of animal industry at Peoria. Norman C. is superintendent of Wood Brothers Construction Company of Lincoln, Nebraska. The daughter Grace F. is the wife of Harry Dale Weaver, of Galesburg.

Rev. Allen has been prominent in the civic life of Galesburg, assuming many responsibilities outside of his regular routine as a minister. He once served as poormaster of the city. He is a man richly endowed with qualities of mind and heart that make the real spiritual leader.

AUSTIN JULIUS SMITH. The history of Grundy and adjoining counties of Illinois would be entirely incomplete without extended record of Austin Julius Smith, who for many years was a man of note in this section of the state, where the greater part of his useful and achieving life was spent. Of New England birth and ancestry, he possessed and illustrated in his life many of the admirable characteristics that have long been attributed to the hardy descendants of the Pilgrim argonauts.

Austin Julius Smith was born at Otter Creek, Vermont, November 14, 1849, son of William G. and Isabel M. (Bressee) Smith, who migrated to Illinois when he was five years old and settled on a farm in Kendall County, five miles south of Yorkville. In 1868 the family removed to a farm located near what is now known as Handford's Landing, in Will County, on which farm William G. Smith died in 1876.

Having no leaning toward an agricultural life, after the death of his father Austin J. Smith left the farm and went to Wilmington, Illinois, where he went into business for himself, purchasing a water right and operating a planing mill for the next two years. But he was a young man, with but little business experience, and in 1878 displayed native common sense in disposing of his Wilmington interests and accepting a railroad position with the Chicago and Alton Railroad Company. After a short season of work as a brakeman he was put in charge of the switching crew at Braidwood, where his services in a position of authority were found so valuable that no change was made in the next four years, or

until Mr. Smith's enterprise and progressive spirit led him in another direction.

About this time the coal interests of this section became very important, and Mr. Smith was tendered and accepted the position of superintendent of a coal mine at Tracy, a mining town situated two and a half miles east of what is now South Wilmington, and for a number of years afterward he was identified to some extent with positions and concerns largely dependent on this great industry, filling offices of business responsibility with such efficiency that he gained the respect, confidence and esteem of all with whom he came in contact. In 1884 he became manager of the general store of Ray and Felton at Coal City, and shortly afterward he was appointed postmaster at Coal City by President Harrison, which public office he held until 1893, when he retired in order to identify himself with the General Wilmington Coal Company, a new business organization, of which he became general shipping clerk, and continued with this company until 1901, when he embarked in the clothing business at Coal City and was conducting his own store at the time he was elected county clerk of Grundy County. Previously he had served one term as assessor at Braidwood and had been postmaster at Coal City, but the county clerkship was a public office of such importance that Mr. Smith felt much gratified over the evidence of public regard in which he was held by his fellow citizens. He served in the office of county clerk until 1910, retiring from the same only to enter upon another field of activity, satisfying an ambition he had more or less cherished from his youth. In 1911, although then sixty-two years of age, he was admitted to the bar of Illinois, and became a member of the law firm of Smith, Smith & Smith at Morris, a very prominent firm at the present time in Grundy County.

Mr. Smith married, November 14, 1872, Miss Lucy Vining, who was born January 8, 1853, on a farm in Kankakee County, Illinois, daughter of Samuel and Jane Vining, and to this union a son and daughter were born: Henman Bressee and Edith Maude.

Henman Bressee Smith, an able member of the Morris bar and senior member of the present law firm of Smith & Holderman, was born at Wilmington, Illinois, July 8, 1876. In 1902 he was graduated from Northwestern University, and in 1905 from the Law School of Harvard University, and in the same year was admitted to the bar and entered into practice at Morris, and it was in his office and under his supervision that his father and his talented sister also were prepared for their law examinations. Mr. Smith married Miss Margarette Livermore, a native of Kansas. Edith Maude Smith, now Mrs. A. G. Harrison, and formerly a junior member of the law firm of Smith & Smith at Morris, but now retired from practice, was graduated from Hedding College, Abington, Illinois, read law in her brother's office and was admitted to the bar in 1911. In 1917 she went to France as secretary of a Y. M. C. A. unit and remained on duty for more than a year.

Throughout life Austin J. Smith was an advocate of temperance, and even in his youth his strong and compelling personality made his influence widely felt. He was instrumental in organizing two Good Templar lodges in industrial centers, and for years was an active worker in the Band of Hope, a temperance organization in Coal City. From the age of twenty-one he was a member of the Masonic fraternity, becoming a member of the Blue Lodge and Chapter at Wilmington, and at the time of his death was a member of Blaney Commandery, Knights Templar, at Morris, by affiliation, being originally a member of Ivanhoe Commandery at Kankakee, and at the time of the fiftieth anniversary of Blaney Commandery, 1908, was eminent commander. He was a member of Medinah Temple, Scottish Rite Masons, Chicago, and had membership also in the Modern Woodmen order at Coal City.

For several years after entering upon the practice of law Mr. Smith seemingly greatly enjoyed the new interests coming into his life, taking pardonable pride in the professional victories of his talented children with whom he was associated, but always finding time to lend assistance to his beloved wife in her numerous charities. She was an active member of the Methodist Episcopal Church. With her illness and subsequent death on February 11, 1914, however, a change came, the savor of life for him seemed to depart, and his own death followed on November 14, 1915, The record of his sterling character, his upright, industrious life, his high aims and integrity in public office belongs to the state that claims no higher prestige than the true nobility of its citizens.

WILLIAM JOHN HENRY ARBEITER is one of the very popular and successful young business men of the city of Murphysboro. He knows the automobile industry both from the mechanical and business standpoint. He has been one of the most successful sales agents in this section of the state, and is proprietor of one of the best equipped sales, service and garage stations in Jackson County.

His father, Ernest William Arbeiter, was born in Baden, Germany, in 1847, and came to America at the age of seventeen, landing at New York, and from there coming out to Illinois to join his brother, Henry Arbeiter, who already had become well established as a prosperous farmer in Jackson County. Ernest W. Arbeiter was at the time unable to speak English. He worked on his brother's farm, and later acquired a good farm of his own four miles east of Murphysboro. That was his home the rest of his life. His death in 1918 resulted from a railroad train striking an automobile. He married Engle Bellman, a native of Germany, who still occupies the old homestead.

William John Henry Arbeiter was born while his parents were operating a farm in the Mississippi River bottoms, but he grew up on the old homestead near Murphysboro, attending the rural school at Fountain Bluff. At the age of twenty-one he left the farm and served an apprenticeship as a machinist. Mr. Arbeiter is a thorough machinist, and that has been fundamental in his success in the automobile business. He followed his trade until

1915, when, in order to get into business for himself, he took up contracting, but during the same year started an automobile repair shop. The following year he took the agency for the Patterson car, establishing his garage and repair shop in the old Sailor Building on Nineteenth Street at Murphysboro. In 1917 he became the local agent and distributor for the Hudson and Chevrolet cars, and in 1918 his business had grown so as to necessitate his removal to larger quarters at Sixteenth and Walnut. Since 1919 Mr. Arbeiter has handled the local sale and distribution of the Hudson and Essex cars. In 1920 he arranged for the construction of his present large and modern garage and sales room at the corner of Eighth and Walnut streets, where he has a one-story brick building 65 by 175 feet.

He married Miss Martha Gandlitz, of Effingham County, Illinois. Three children were born to their marriage, Viola, a student in high school; Eunice, who died when eleven years old; and Helen, attending grade school. Mr. Arbeiter is a member of the Rotary Club, is a member of the Park Board and is a very loyal citizen of Murphysboro, always ready to take his share of civic responsibilities.

HON. GEORGE BEDFORD. In the ancestry of Hon. George Bedford, prominent attorney of Morris, Illinois, and formerly judge of the County Court for a number of years, appear old pioneer names that have belonged to this section of the state for seventy-six years, and during this three-quarters of a century the old Bedford farm in Kendall County has remained in the possession of the Bedfords.

Judge Bedford was born on the old family homestead in Kendall County, Illinois, February 16, 1865, second son of William and Sarah Ann (Bowden) Bedford, and grandson of William and Sarah (Wood) Bedford. The grandparents were born, reared and married at Stockport, England, and from there, in 1849, came with their children to the United States, and journeying westward in search of a new home, found promising conditions in northern Illinois, and the grandfather soon purchased eighty acres of land in Kendall County, the present old Bedford homestead.

William Bedford, son of William and father of Judge Bedford, was born at Stockport, England, November 25, 1838, and was a sturdy youth of eleven years when the family came to Illinois, and did his part in assisting his father in developing the pioneer farm. In later years he acquired a farm of his own, located just across the road from the homestead, which he developed into a valuable property and resided there until his death in 1912, a man of sterling character and widely known. He married Miss Sarah Ann Bowden, a member of an English family which came also from Stockport to the United States, and in 1853, after a short period spent at Peoria, Illinois, came to Kendall County and settled permanently near their old neighbors, the Bedfords. An interesting and somewhat unusual fact in the lives of Judge Bedford's parents was that they were born in the same town in England, in the same year and on the same day of the month. She was survived two years by her husband, her death occurring February 26, 1910. They had nine children: William H., George, Frank, Fred J., Elizabeth M. O'Brien, Ida M., Arthur T., Charles and Irwin, the youngest two dying in infancy.

George Bedford grew up on the home farm but very early began to feel the urge for wider educational opportunities than those afforded by the country schools, and willingly went to some trouble to attend school at Minooka and Morris, and, as may be supposed, one so earnest and studious made rapid progress, but an education for the law, just then, seemed far away. Yet, with this cherished ambition as a goal, the young man accomplished wonders by himself. At that time valuable books in that section were luxuries and few of his friends or acquaintances owned law libraries, but by persistent seeking he was able to borrow a few volumes at a time, and devoted himself to absorbing their contents whenever he found leisure from his duties on the farm, as a country schoolteacher or other gainful occupations.

In February, 1903, Mr. Bedford successfully passed his examinations at Ottawa, and in April of that year was admitted to the bar, and in September following he came to Morris and opened a law office, establishing here his permanent home and becoming an active and useful member of the community by which he has long been held in high esteem.

Soon recognized as an able lawyer, in 1905 Mr. Bedford was elected city attorney of Morris and at the close of his term was elected justice of the peace. He retired from that office in order to accept the republican nomination for judge of the County Court, to which high office he was elected in 1910, and for twelve succeeding years, or until he declined reelection, Judge Bedford served with such faithfulness and ability that his record on the bench is unassailable, reflecting honor upon himself and Grundy County. Upon retirement from public life he resumed private practice and has many important legal connections.

Judge Bedford has long been an important factor in republican politics in the county and is a loyal supporter of the national administration. He is a Knight Templar Mason, a member of Blaney Commandery No. 5, Medinah Temple, Chicago, and belongs also to the Eastern Star and the Knights of Pythias at Morris. He is a familiar figure on the golf links, a scientific player and the winner of many high scores. Although he has never married, he maintains a hospitable bachelor home, in which may be seen a rare collection of relics of early days in Illinois, the search for these historical mementoes having contributed to his happy vacation jaunts for many years. Another pastime of which he has made a finished art is photography, in which he is a noted amateur.

CAPT. EDWARD WOOD HERSH, who gained his military title by commanding a company of Illinois troops during the Spanish-American war, is a resident of Newton, Jasper County. At one time he was a practicing lawyer there, but the activities which constitute his largest and most important service to the community have been through banking, and as a pioneer in raising the standards and conditions of agriculture, horticulture and live stock industry.

Captain Hersh was born at Mount Vernon, Ohio, January 10, 1866, son of Dr. John and Nancy J. (Dowd) Hersh, natives of the same state. His paternal grandfather was of Pennsylvania German ancestry, and from Pennsylvania moved to Lima, Ohio, and later to Mount Vernon, where he died and was buried. Captain Hersh's maternal grandfather was a native of Scotland, and coming to the United States when very young spent the rest of his life at Amity, Ohio. Dr. John Hersh served three years as a Union soldier in the Civil war, being a private in Company G of the Thirty-eighth Ohio Infantry. In 1875 he moved from Mount Vernon to Defiance and in that city practiced medicine until his children had completed their public school education. Then, in order to provide a better environment for his sons, he moved to a farm nearby, and he and his wife spent the rest of their days in that rural neighborhood. Their six children were Jennie, Hamilton, Lou, Edward W., Nell and William S.

Edward Wood Hersh was nine years old when his parents moved to Defiance, Ohio, grew up there and attended the local schools and later graduated from the Chautauqua literary and scientific course. On account of ill health he came to Illinois and spent one year canvassing over the state, selling family Bibles. He left that to become stenographer and typewriter in the law office of Gibson & Johnson at Newton, and in that way became identified with the community in which he has rendered such important service for so many years. While working for the law firm he studied law, was admitted to the Illinois bar in 1890, and a year or so later engaged in practice at Newton in connection with the real estate and farm loan business.

Captain Hersh in 1898, with A. F. Calvin, bought the Bank of Newton, a private institution, and for nearly thirty years has been one of the city's leading bankers. The bank was incorporated in March, 1901, under charter of the First National Bank of Newton, and since that date for a quarter of a century Captain Hersh has been its president, and its largest shareholder.

About the time he entered banking Captain Hersh responded to the call for military service at the outbreak of the Spanish-American war, and as captain of Company B of the Fourth Illinois Infantry National Guard was mustered into the United States Volunteer forces in April, 1898. From Springfield the regiment went to Jacksonville, Florida, where it remained during the summer, and on January 1, 1899, crossed over to Havana, Cuba, and was employed in police duty in that city until April, 1899. Captain Hersh is a member of the Spanish-American War Veterans, and so far as business has permitted has taken an active interest in the organization.

Immediately on his return from the army he gave his undivided attention to his bank, and has made it one of the largest and strongest institutions in this section. In 1914 Mr. Hersh acquired an interest in the private bank of Rose Hill, Illinois, which was afterward incorporated as a state bank, under the name of the State Bank of Rose Hill; and a few years later he organized the State Bank of West Liberty, Illinois, in both of which banks he is the largest stockholder and president.

Captain Hersh is a banker with a sense of responsibility to the community, and he has used his advantages to the betterment of Jasper County in general, and individually has probably contributed as much as any other man to raising and improving the standards of country life. On his farm he has grown pure bred Hereford cattle, and some years ago he came into possession of a twenty acre apple orchard, one of many orchards in the county that had suffered neglect and were commercially unproductive. Captain Hersh set into operation a rigid plan of pruning and spraying, showed a profit on his individual orchard and set a good example for other fruit growers. Later he bought another unproductive orchard of 125 acres, and that, too, became profitable. Jasper County in recent years has become one of the leading apple producing counties in Illinois. Captain Hersh for many years has been a believer in the commercial value of pure bred live stock, and has developed one of the finest herds of Hereford cattle in the state.

His home community of Newton has likewise been benefited by his enterprise and public spirit. Largely through his instrumentality the town was given an adequate water plant, affording filtered water to consumers, one of the best guarantees of community health. He was one of the organizers of the Rotary Club of Newton and its president in 1925, and has been active in church and school matters. He is a member of the Methodist Church, is a Knight Templar Mason and Shriner and member of the Knights of Pythias, and has always been a staunch republican. During the World war he was chairman of the local exemption board and personally acted as a leader and contributed much to the success of the Liberty Loan drives, taking the county over the top each time. He also applied for active service in the field, but was advised that he could do most at home.

Captain Hersh in 1891 married Miss Flora Shup, a native of Newton. Their only son died when seven years of age, and their daughter, Marjorette, died of the influenza at the age of twenty.

RUBEN H. WOOD, M. D. The record of Doctor Wood as a practicing physician and surgeon at Mount Carroll covers a period of nearly thirty years. He is one of the very able men of his profession in Carroll County, and has founded himself securely in popular regard and esteem there.

Doctor Wood was born at Stowe in Lamoille County, Vermont, April 19, 1859, but has spent most of his life in the middle west. His grandparents were Nathaniel and Emily (Gillette) Wood, of Stowe, Vermont. Nathaniel Wood was born and reared in that state, was a farmer, and in the War of 1812 served as a captain of infantry with the American forces, participating in the battle at Plattsburg, New York. He reached the remarkable age of ninety-eight years. The Wood family is of

English ancestry and was established in America before the Revolution. Hiram D. Wood, father of Dr. Ruben Wood, was born at Fairfax, Vermont, was educated in public schools there and in St. John's Academy, and after leaving school learned the tinner's trade at Montpelier, Vermont. In 1869 he moved with his family to Minneapolis, and became one of the pioneer merchants of that city. He was in the hardware business until 1891, when he sold out and retired. He is now ninety-three years of age and makes his home with his son Daniel Wood at Minneapolis. He is a member of the Masonic Order. Hiram D. Wood married Louise C. Slayton, who died in June, 1923, at the age of eighty-five. She was born and reared at Stowe, Vermont. Her brothers, Abial H. and Jerome Slayton, went to California around the Horn during the gold rush, and returned east across the plains. Abial H. Slayton at the time of the Civil war served as captain of Company I of the Seventeenth Vermont Infantry and was made a prisoner at Petersburg, and for six months endured the tortures of confinement at Andersonville. Hiram D. Wood and wife were the parents of eight children, Ruben H. being the oldest. The others were: Clara, who died in 1896, wife of Albert E. McMullen, a lumberman at Minneapolis; Erving E., who has one surviving child; Charles E., who died in September, 1922, survived by six children, who with their mother reside at Long Beach, California; Dr. H. D. Wood, Jr., a practicing physician at Minneapolis, who married Bessie Jennings and has a daughter, Esther Jennings Wood; Daniel B., who graduated in law from the University of Minnesota and is now northwestern manager for the Fidelity Deposit & Security Company of Baltimore at Minneapolis; and William B., who lives in northern Minnesota.

Ruben H. Wood was ten years of age when the family moved to Minneapolis. He had attended school in Vermont, and in Minneapolis continued his education through high school. In 1896 he graduated from the Hahnemann Medical College and Hospital of Chicago, and for a year after graduating was assistant to Dr. A. L. Blackwood of Chicago. In 1898 he located at Mount Carroll, and his professional career as a physician and surgeon has been continuous in that locality except for the years 1906-07, which he spent in Alaska. Part of the time he was located at Sitka and he also was in the back country engaged in fishing, hunting and prospecting. Doctor Wood has a very large general practice, and at all times has shown a very helpful spirit in carrying out community projects. He is a Royal Arch Mason, member of the Methodist Church, and a republican in politics.

He married at Minneapolis, May 17, 1883, Miss Nellie M. Nash, of that city. She was educated in high school there and in Bennett Seminary, and for many years has been a very active worker in the Methodist Church, teaching a class in the Sunday School. Her parents were Edgar A. and Virginia (Bartholmew) Nash, of Minneapolis. Her father was born at Penyan, New York, and when about twenty-one years of age settled at Minneapolis, where he was in the hardware business and continued active until his death in 1916. Mrs. Wood's maternal grandfather was Gen. Riley L. Bartholomew, an adjutant-general of Ohio militia, and later a member of the first Territorial Legislature and also the first State Legislature of Minnesota. The Bartholomew family is said to have been founded in America by the descendants of two brothers named Bartholmy, French Huguenots, who at the time of the religious persecution culminating in the massacre of St. Bartholomew made their escape from France in hogsheads to Holland.

FRANK D. CONDON. One of Grundy county's influential citizens and reliable public officials is Frank D. Condon, circuit clerk and recorder, a life long resident of Grundy County, for many years a leading business man of Morris, and long active in the political affairs of this city.

Frank D. Condon was born at Morris, Grundy County, Illinois, November 15, 1879, son of Cornelius and Evaline (Davidson) Condon. The late Cornelius Condon, well and favorably known for years at Morris, was born in County Limerick, Ireland, February 12, 1847. When three years old his parents, David and Margaret Condon, with their children, left Ireland for the United States with the port of New Orleans for their goal, and safely crossed the Atlantic in a sailing vessel. From New Orleans they proceeded up the Mississippi River to Hanesville, Kentucky, where Cornelius received his schooling and grew to manhood. In 1869, when twenty-two years old, he came to Illinois and located at Morris, where he operated a brickyard for a time before becoming a miner in the coal districts in this region. He continued in the mining business until he was forced to retire because of failing health. He served as city marshal under Mayor Palmer but never accepted any other public position. He was a man of sterling character, a faithful member of the Congregational Church, and one of the early members of Star Lodge, I. O. O. F., and before his death, on June 26, 1923, had the satisfaction of wearing the twenty-five-year membership jewels of that organization. On October 30, 1870, Cornelius Condon married Miss Evaline Davidson, of East Morris, Illinois, whose people had come to this state from New York. Eight children were born to them: Robert, Mrs. W. T. Williams, Fred, Hattie, Frank D., Walter, Irwin, and Mrs. W. B. King, all of whom, with one exception, survived to mature years.

Frank D. Condon has practically spent his entire life at Morris, receiving his education in her excellent public schools, and while still a youth completing his apprenticeship to the cigarmaker's trade, and showing a large measure of good judgment when, at the age of twenty-one, he purchased the business of T. B. Hinds, his employer. Mr. Condon continued in that line of business for twenty years, building up a substantial enterprise of his own and establishing a reputation for business sagacity and integrity that still prevails. In Grundy County there still is held the old-fashioned idea that an honest and industrious business man possesses qualities that are needed in

public officials, and therein, perhaps, lies the reason that the lamentable irregularities that have disturbed business and even penetrated into social life in some sections in the past few years have been unknown in Grundy County.

Mr. Condon has been an earnest worker in the republican party ever since becoming old enough to take an intelligent interest in politics, and in the course of years found himself highly valued by his party organization, and tendered offices of trust and responsibility. For four years he served as city clerk of Morris, and for two years was city treasurer, serving efficiently in these offices while still carrying on his private business, but in 1920, when elected circuit clerk and recorder, he sold his business and since then has devoted himself entirely to public duties, in 1924 being reelected circuit clerk and recorder.

Mr. Condon married Miss Martha H. Emerson, daughter of Elias Emerson, the family being well known in Grundy County. For many years Mr. Condon has been a member of the Masonic fraternity, and he is also a member of Star Lodge No. 75, I. O. O. F., with which his father was so long identified, and of Shabbona Encampment No. 155. He is also a charter member of the Fraternal Order of Eagles at Morris and has passed the local chairs in this organization.

JOHN C. FOLEY, M. D. Until death stayed his hand and stilled his voice on January 22, 1924, the wisdom and skill of Dr. John C. Foley had been an asset of immeasurable importance to the city and community of Waukegan, where he had practiced for thirty-four years.

Doctor Foley was born at Kenosha, Wisconsin, July 29, 1863, son of Captain James and Onnie (Farrell) Foley. His father, who was an early settler of southeastern Wisconsin, enlisted at the time of the Civil war in the Union army, rose to the rank of captain, and served until he met death leading his company on one of the fields of battle in the South. Onnie Farrell, mother of Doctor Foley, was born at Oswego, New York, and was a child when her parents, John and Catherine (Hopkins) Farrell, moved west about 1841 to Wisconsin, establishing their early home at Kenosha.

Dr. John C. Foley attended school for a time at Kenosha and for several years of his boyhood lived in Kansas, where he saw much of pioneer life. He attended school at Republican City, Kansas. Through his earnings by teaching and other work he continued his education in the University of Iowa, and paid his way through Rush Medical College of Chicago, graduating in 1890 with the M. D. degree. Doctor Foley immediately after graduating came to Waukegan, opened his office and continued in practice with few vacations and an ever increasing burden of responsibilities until about the year before his death, when his health compelled him to give over some of his activities, and he was in quest of strength at Miami, Florida, when his death occurred. He had taken post-graduate work in Johns Hopkins University.

His range of activities was a wide one. He was a director and promoter of the old Lake County Tuberculosis Sanitarium, was closely associated as a director and staff surgeon with the Victory Memorial Hospital at Waukegan, was one of the charter members of the Lake County and a member of the Illinois State and American Medical Associations, and his attainments as a surgeon were recognized by a fellowship in the American College of Surgeons. He was an organizer of the Lake County Clinic and a supporter of the Hattie Barwell Good Fellowship Club. He was also a charter member of the Waukegan and North Chicago Chamber of Commerce, a member of the American Legion, the Knights of Columbus, B. P. O. Elks, Kiwanis Club, and other organizations. He was one of the first physicians from Waukegan to enlist at the time of the World war, being commissioned a captain in the Medical Corps and was stationed on duty at Fort Sill, Oklahoma, and Fort Johnson at Jacksonville, Florida. Three organizations that formally participated in his funeral services represented many of the important activities of his life. There were the Homer Dahringer Post of the American Legion, the Lake County Medical Society and the staff of the Victory Memorial Hospital. Doctor Foley was a republican in politics and a member of the Catholic Church.

He married at Waukegan, November 10, 1898, Miss Frances Donnelly, who grew up at Waukegan, attending high school there and graduated from Saint Catherine's School for Girls at Racine, Wisconsin. She has been active in church work, in the Waukegan Woman's Club, and she still occupies the family home in Waukegan. Since 1912 she has served as a member of the Waukegan Board of Education. Her parents, John and Catherine Donnelly, came from the vicinity of Albany, New York, to northeastern Illinois. Doctor and Mrs. Foley had three sons, John D., Joseph C. and Francis E., and it was Doctor Foley's ambition that all his sons should follow in his professional steps. John D. graduated from the Waukegan Township High School in 1918, took his pre-medical course at the University of Chicago, and is a member of the class of 1927 in Loyola University School of Medicine. Joseph C., the second son, graduated from high school in 1920, and received his Bachelor of Science degree from Notre Dame University of Indiana in 1925. Francis E., the youngest, graduates from the Waukegan High School with the class of 1927.

In the career of a man like the late Doctor Foley the formal facts of biography are insufficient to constitute a just appreciation of what he was and what he did. One tribute that supplements the facts given above is found in an editorial in the Waukegan Daily Sun, which said: "Waukegan's health physician for many years, whose life terminated so unexpectedly at Florida where he had gone for his health, was one of Waukegan's most prominent citizens. He was one of the most loyal and honored and one of the most sincere citizens of the community. He was a man who was ever ready to lend his support to civic matters and he was keenly interested in the development of Waukegan morally, commercially, industrially and in a civic way. He was one of those fellows who always had a cordial greeting for those he knew and he was typical of those men who have helped to make Waukegan what it is. He was a man who had confidence in Waukegan, but his line of activity was more along the lines of health rather than commercially. To him to a large extent was due much of the progress that has been made in Waukegan health matters, and no doubt had he not been so active in his profession he could have achieved more for the community in general. He gave much of his valuable time to the city's official business despite the fact that his personal services were called for with such continued frequency that it was almost impossible for him to devote the necessary time to the work of health physician. Yet his insistent interest in that work caused him to neglect his own interests in his private practice many times to carry out the bigger work."

A more rounded tribute to this Waukegan surgeon is found in the editorial column of the Waukegan Daily News at the time of his death. Editorially the News said: "Doctor Foley was an exemplary citizen, giving ungrudgingly of his time and effort to public activities despite the constant demands upon him because of his professional skill and ability. His community interest was intense—he loved Waukegan and Waukegan loved him for just what he was, a great hearted, good man.

"This city can ill spare Doctor Foley. He was our leading surgeon, conscientious and untiring in his devotion to those whom he so capably served, and a friend of every man, woman and child in Waukegan who was privileged with his acquaintance.

"It avails little to list Doctor Foley's public activities by way of emphasizing his splendid devotion to his city, nor will the unostentatious help and generous aid he offered the less fortunate be known, but it earned him the esteem and love that is so universally expressed today, just as his surgical skill and valued friendship earned him the respect and allegiance of men in the profession he graced.

"Fine and typical expression is given the high regard and estimation in which Doctor Foley was held in Waukegan in an unsolicited communication to this paper by one of his admirers. We append it herewith:

"'When men die it is a custom, and a commendable one, to always speak well of them. But in many, many cases it is the language of courtesy, not conviction. How different from all this is the choking gasp with which this community greets the news of Dr. J. C. Foley's passing. Always appreciated, it is probable that it is now for the first time the immense value of the great life that is gone is fully realized. His death was not unexpected; it was a matter of common knowledge that the long years of intensive devotion rendered to the multitudes who had placed their lives into his hands had so sapped his vigor that he could not be saved from the fate from which his skill had rescued so many.

"'And so it was, that during these past months the homes of so many were made wretched by the sense of their futility in an hour when their friend lay stricken, and they could not lend a hand to save.

"'Of course, none could know better than this wise and experienced physician, what the tolling of his feeble heart forboded; but his cheerfulness was not abated, nor the bright smile nor the ready jest. It was his way. None of the trials of life had daunted this great patient, courageous man—and the last adventure of all could not. Those who knew Doctor Foley best, best knew that great as he might be as a surgeon, he was still greater as a man. Plain, simple—more than unassuming—laying claim to no special virtue, there never lived a man of higher principals or more unblemished life. It is no exaggeration to say that he wholeheartedly offered himself as the servant of his kind, and God and man both know how faithful a servant he was.

"'His once robust body has been worn out and his life has gone much before his years would justify; but in the three score years he lived he allayed the suffering of thousands, furnished an ideal of citizenship and made his chosen community infinitely better for his having lived. Such was the kind of success he coveted, such the success he achieved. Can there be a greater one?'"

M. O. WILLIAMSON, a former state treasurer of Illinois and a Galesburg banker, has spent practically all his life in Knox County, and in that community his business enterprise and faithfulness to private and public duty laid the foundation of the esteem which has made him one of the notable and representative men of Illinois.

Mr. Williamson was born July 14, 1850, on the Atlantic Ocean while his parents, William and Margaret Williamson, were coming to America. His parents were natives of Sweden. The family arrived in Victoria, Knox County, Illinois, in November, 1850, and after spending the winter there settled in the spring of 1851 on a farm in Sparta Township. Two years later, in 1853, the father died. The widowed mother was left with the care and responsibility of six children, and bravely and well she played her part in rearing them to manhood and womanhood. Her death occurred in 1886.

M. O. Williamson lived during the first thirteen years of his life on a farm, had only a few brief terms of school, and his chief discipline was manual labor. At the age of thirteen he began a three years apprenticeship at the harness-maker's trade, learning it in a shop at Wataga. In skill of workmanship he was qualified to engage in business for himself, but realizing the deficiencies of his early education he waited until he had attended the village schools of Wataga for a time, making the utmost of these advantages. He then set up a harness shop of his own at Wataga and was a substantial business man of that village for a quarter of a century. During part of that time he also operated a flouring mill.

His political advancement had begun while he was in business at Wataga. In 1886 he was elected county treasurer of Knox County for a term of four years. In 1890 he was elected county clerk, was reelected in 1894 and again in 1898. His service as county clerk continued ten years, at the end of which time he resigned to become state treasurer of Illinois. He was elected state treasurer in 1900 for a term of two years. His record was one of exceptional efficiency at Springfield. According to the law he was ineligible to succeed himself, and on returning to Knox County he organized, in 1903, the Peoples Trust and Savings Bank. He has been continuously president of this substantial institution for twenty-three years.

Mr. Williamson moved his home to Galesburg in 1890, and has been an honored resident of that city for thirty-five years. His success in life must be credited in part to an early sense of responsibility, the habit and power of doing work well, and a faithfulness in all the varied relations of life.

In politics he has ever been a staunch republican and one of the strong men in his party in the state. He is well known as a member of the Hamilton Club of Chicago, and was also active in the Swedish-American Republican League of the state of Illinois, now known as the John Ericson Republican League of Illinois. He was one of the organizers and served as president of the league in 1897. For two years he was a member of the Lincoln Monument Association of Illinois, and during that time the monument at Springfield was completed and received the mortal remains of the great president. Mr. Williamson is a Knight Templar Mason, a member of the Independent Order of Odd Fellows, B. P. O. Elks, and is affiliated with the Congregational Church.

He married in 1871 Miss Mary A. Driggs. Their marriage companionship endured for more than half a century, death finally parting them in March, 1925. To their marriage were born a son and two daughters, the son dying in infancy. One daughter, Adelaide F., is the wife of Edward Clyde Slocumb, a resident of Minneapolis, and who served with the rank of major in the World war. The other daughter, Nellie W., is Mrs. C. C. Davis, of Galesburg.

EDWARD SIMMONS STICKNEY, judge of the County Court of Knox County, has practiced law at Galesburg for ten years. He was born and grew up in the section of Illinois where his professional career has been centered.

Edward Simmons Stickney was born on a farm a few miles west of Woodhull, in Henry County, August 13, 1888, son of Alfred and Eugenia (Simmons) Stickney, and grandson of Henry and Mary Ann (Wood) Stickney, natives of Vermont and of English lineage, their ancestors having come from the vicinity of London. Henry Stickney was an Illinois pioneer, moving out in 1851, but subsequently returning to Vermont. The next year he brought his family to Henry County, settling on a farm, and lived there until he was killed by a runaway team of horses at the beginning of the Civil war. He left a family of three sons and one daughter. Alfred Stickney, who was born at Grafton, Vermont, July 3, 1840, was twelve years of age when his parents moved to Illinois. After his marriage he settled on a farm, and for many years was a substantial factor in the agricultural affairs of Henry County. He married Eugenia Simmons, who was born at Youngstown, Ohio, October 4, 1844, daughter of William H. and Mary (Griggs) Simmons, who moved to Illinois in 1856.

Edward Simmons Stickney after the country schools attended the Woodhull High School, graduated, and then went east to complete his education in Harvard University, where he received the A. B. degree in 1909, and took his law degree at the Harvard Law School in 1912. On graduating he was admitted to the Massachusetts bar and later to the Illinois bar. For two years Judge Stickney remained in Boston, where he gained valuable experience in law practice. In 1915 he located at Galesburg, and has steadily practiced law in that city to the present time. He was elected on the republican ticket to the office of county judge in 1922, for a term of four years.

Judge Stickney during the World war served on the exemption board. He is a Knight Templar Mason, a ruling elder of the First Presbyterian Church of Galesburg, and is a member of several clubs, including the Kiwanis Club, of which he was elected president in 1925.

Judge Stickney in 1916 married Miss Lyle Mackey, of Woodhull. They have two children, Edward Simmons, Jr., and Elizabeth Lyle Stickney.

HARRY LEROY HEER, of Galena, is judge of the Fifteenth Judicial Circuit and for many years has been an honored member of the bar, having practiced both in his native community of Galena and at Rockford. Judge Heer occupies one of the most responsible positions in the county, but is not the only official member of his household. Mrs. Heer has long been prominent as an educator and is the present city superintendent of schools at Galena.

Judge Heer was born near Galena January 22, 1873, son of David and Martha (Evans) Heer. His father came from Germany and his mother from Wales, and they were brought to this country when children, before the Civil war. David Heer was a farmer and a veterinarian, and during the Civil war enlisted in Company F of the Ninety-sixth Cavalry, seeing service in many battles. At the close of the war he returned to Galena and engaged in farming and the work of his profession until his death in February, 1907.

Harry Leroy Heer was reared on a farm, finished his high school course in Galena and also attended the Northern Illinois College at Dixon. After his college course he taught in the public schools of Jo Daviess County a number of years. While teaching he studied law, passed the Illinois bar examination in 1903, and in 1904 was elected clerk of the Circuit Court. He was Circuit Court clerk eight years. In 1912 he opened a law office at Galena, but in 1914 removed to Rockford, where he conducted a successful general practice three years. In 1917 he returned to Galena, partly to supervise his interests in the lead and zinc mines. He also resumed his law practice. In 1922 he was elected county judge and in 1924 was elected judge of the Fifteenth Circuit for a term of five years. Mr. Heer is a thirty-second degree Scottish Rite Mason and Shriner, member of the Independent Order of Odd Fellows, B. P. O. Elks, Moose, Kiwanis Club, Izaak Walton League, Galena Golf Club, is a member of the Jo Daviess County and Illinois State Bar Associations and the Chamber of Commerce. He is a trustee of the First Presbyterian Church.

At Warren, Illinois, April 18, 1914, Judge Heer married Miss Myrtle Renwick. Mrs. Heer graduated from the Warren High School in 1893, took the Bachelor of Arts degree from Monmouth College in 1899, and from the same institution was awarded the Masters degree in 1907. For two summers she took graduate work in Columbia University at New York City. Mrs. Heer after graduating from Monmouth College taught school at Clarinda and Creston, Iowa, being an instructor in the high schools in those towns. In 1906 she was appointed county superintendent of schools of Jo Daviess County, holding office under appointment nine months, and was then regularly elected for a term of four years. In 1911 she became superintendent of schools at Stockton, Illinois, serving two years, from 1911 to 1913. After their marriage Mr. and Mrs. Heer lived in Rockford three years. In 1921 Mrs. Heer was chosen superintendent of the city schools of Galena and has made a splendid record in that position. She is a daughter of Robert Bruce and Alzina (Cornelius) Renwick, whose home was near Stockton, Illinois. Her father was born and reared in Jo Daviess County, and at the time of the Civil war enlisted in Company F of the Seventeenth Illinois Cavalry. After the war he engaged in farming until 1897, when he retired. He spent his last years at Warren, where he died January 18, 1922. He was a son of George and Henrietta (Horton) Renwick. George Renwick was a native of Scotland and on coming to this country lived for a time in New York State before settling near Stockton, Illinois, where he followed farming until his death in 1870. Judge and Mrs. Heer have one son, Robert Renwick Heer, born February 8, 1915.

C. HAROLD HIPPLER, practicing lawyer in Fulton County since 1914, has earned much prominence through his official relations with the Kiwanis Clubs and as a leader in community affairs.

Mr. Hippler was born at Geneseo, Illinois, September 27, 1890. His grandfather, Charles Hippler, was a native of Heidelberg, Germany, and came to America soon after the German Revolution, first living at Rock Island and in 1860 settling in Geneseo, where he became a grocer. He married Theresa Banscher, and they became the parents of four children. Charles A. Hippler, father of the Canton attorney, was born at Rock Island, March 25, 1859, and spent his active career in the grocery business at Geneseo, where he died April 23, 1914. He married Minnie Bradley, who is still a resident of Geneseo. Her parents were James A. and Sarah (Hodges) Bradley.

C. Harold Hippler was educated in the Geneseo High School, and is an alumnus of the University of Michigan, where he was graduated A. B. in 1912, and received his law diploma in 1914. After being admitted to the bar he engaged in practice at Lewistown, in Fulton County, until January 1, 1917, and tried his first law suit there. Since that date he has conducted a general practice at Canton. He has been city attorney of Canton since 1918, except during a portion of the war period. For the past four years he has served as master in chancery of the City Court.

Mr. Hippler volunteered during the war and was in training at the Great Lakes Naval Station for the office of ensign until after the armistice. He was one of two delegates from his congressional district to the first meeting of the American Legion held at St. Louis, and was the first regular commander of the Canton Post. He is also a member of the "Forty and Eight" military society.

Mr. Hippler in the spring of 1925 was elected president of the new Chamber of Commerce of Canton. He was the first president of the Kiwanis Club, organized at Canton in 1920, and held that office until January, 1923. He is a former trustee of the Kiwanis, and for two years has been lieutenant governor of Division No. 3 of the Illinois-Eastern Iowa District, with sixteen clubs under this jurisdiction.

Mr. Hippler did the legal work connected with the organization of the Canton Park District and is attorney and secretary for the Board of Park Commissioners. Matters of wholesome recreation and sound sports have been causes in which he has been deeply interested for years. He was prominent in athletic circles at the University of Michigan, playing football, baseball and basketball, and was a member of the Michigan baseball team which won the inter-collegiate championship in 1914. For two years he was a catcher for George Sisler, who afterwards became famous in the major meet. For several years he played semi-pro baseball. Mr. Hippler is a democrat and cast his first presidential vote for Woodrow Wilson.

July 13, 1920, at Lewistown, he married Mary Lucille Lilly, daughter of Fayette L. and Grace G. (Boyd) Lilly, being the youngest of their six children. She is a graduate of the Lewistown High School and the Brown Business College of Peoria. Mr. and Mrs. Hippler have one son, Jack Bradley Hippler, born January 25, 1924.

GLENN RATCLIFF. Well known alike for his ability as an attorney and his enterprise as a good citizen, Glenn Ratcliff, of Lewistown, stands deservedly high in popular confidence. He was born near Casey, in Cumberland County, Illinois, July 7, 1889, a son of Thomas Ratcliff, and grandson of Moses Ratcliff, a native of Ohio, who came to Illinois about 1854 and settled in Cumberland County, which continued his home for some years.

Thomas Ratcliff was for a long period one of the leading farmers of Cumberland County, his homestead being near Greenup. During the '70s one of the movements of great interest to the farmers was that made in behalf of the Grange, and Thomas Ratcliff was not only a supporter of the Grange, but a leader of the movement. Politics also inter-

ested him, and while he now and then held some local office, he enjoyed participating in the different campaigns without particular thought of his own advancement. He married Sarah Reed, a native of Cumberland County, a daughter of John S. Reed, also a native of Ohio, and a farmer of Cumberland County. Mrs. Ratcliff died in 1917, having borne her husband the following children: Cloe, wife of F. S. Marrs, and resides at Sutton, North Dakota; Rev. Leo, who is a clergyman of the Methodist Episcopal Church, stationed at Page, North Dakota, at the time of his death, which occurred in December, 1925; Glenn, who was the third in order of birth; and Rev. John, who is a clergyman of the Universalist faith, stationed at Beverly, Massachusetts. Thomas Ratcliff died in 1900, many years before his wife.

Reared amid healthful rural surroundings, Glenn Ratcliff assisted with the work of the farm, and attended the local schools, being graduated from the high school course at Greenup when he was twenty years old. For the subsequent year he was engaged in school teaching, after which he entered the academic department of the University of Illinois, and after two years took up the study of law, which he completed, receiving his degree of LL. B. from the University of Illinois in 1915. Passing the state examinations, he was admitted to the bar, and began his practice at Toledo, Illinois. The state's attorney's office being vacant, Mr. Ratcliff was appointed to fill out the term, and made so favorable an impression upon the people of Cumberland County by the vigor with which he brought criminals to justice that he was elected to this office for the full term of four years. While serving as state's attorney he was noted for the number of cases he brought to trial, and the high percentage of convictions he secured.

His usefulness in office and his profession was interrupted by this country's entry into the World war, and he volunteered, went to the Officers Training Camp at Camp Gordon, Georgia, and was there when the armistice was signed. Honorably discharged from the army, he returned home in December, 1918, resumed the duties of his office, and completed his term in 1920. Coming then to Lewistown, Mr. Ratcliff formed a partnership with Harvey H. Atherton, under the style of Atherton & Ratcliff, which was maintained until December, 1924, when Mr. Atherton moved to San Diego, California, since which time Mr. Ratcliff has continued alone. His practice is a general one, and he has had his fair share of the important litigation of this part of the state. Before he entered the army Mr. Ratcliff was chairman of the Cumberland County Chapter, American Red Cross, and after his return he was chairman of the Victory Loan campaign, and he was also governmental appeal agent for the county. Politically Mr. Ratcliff has always been a democrat.

On June 10, 1915, Glenn Ratcliff married, in Cumberland County, Maude Hadley, a native of Brazil, Indiana, and a daughter of Lot Hadley, and his wife, Hattie (Mercer) Hadley. Mrs. Ratcliff was one of two children born to her parents, her brother being Roy L. Hadley, of Casey, Illinois. Mr. and Mrs. Ratcliff have one son, Gene Hadley Ratcliff, who was born August 12, 1920. Mr. Ratcliff is master of Lewistown Lodge, A. F. and A. M., and a member of the Scottish Rite Consistory of Peoria, Illinois. The American Legion holds his membership, he is vice president of the Lewistown Kiwanis Club, one of the directors of the City Improvement Association of Lewistown, and president of the Lewistown School Board. From the above list it is easy to see that Mr. Ratcliff is one of the public-spirited citizens of Lewistown, and his usefulness is not confined to these activities, but carries him into every movement which has for its object the betterment of existing conditions, or the advancement of the community with whose welfare he has so thoroughly identified himself.

ALSIE N. TOLLIVER, a life long resident of Clay County, grandson of a pioneer settler there, has given his active years to teaching and the law, and has enjoyed a station of success and influence in his community.

He was born on a farm in Hossier Township, Clay County, October 12, 1870. The Tollivers were of French-Huguenot stock and first settled in North Carolina, then becoming soldiers at the time of the American Revolution. The grandparents of the Louisville lawyer were Isom and Phoebe (Way) Tolliver, natives of North Carolina, who came to southern Illinois at an early day and settled in Hossier Township, Clay County. Isom Tolliver was a prosperous farmer and a man of substantial character, well known in his locality, and died in middle life. His son, John H. Tolliver, who was born in Lawrence County, Indiana, in 1844, grew up in Clay County and for several years was a druggist at Ingraham in that county, and during the last twenty years of his life engaged in farming and merchandising in the country. He had no natural tendency toward politics, and yielded with reluctance to the request of his friends to perform the duties of several local offices. He was a Union soldier in the Civil war, and afterwards a staunch republican in politics. John H. Tolliver married Margaret Lauchner, who was born in Tennessee, daughter of Daniel Lauchner, another early settler in Hoosier Township, Clay County. John H. Tolliver and wife were members of the Baptist church. Their children were: Alsie N.; Fred D., who lives on the old homestead; Dora S., a farmer in Hoosier Township; Minnie, wife of Sidney Odell, a farmer in the same locality; Myrtle, widow of James Barnett; Cora, wife of Lewis Erwin, and is now deceased; and Claudia, deceased.

Alsie N. Tolliver grew up on the farm, was educated in country schools, and after that accomplished an unusual degree of higher education as the result of private study, qualifying in that way for the duties of teacher and afterwards for the legal profession. For ten years he taught during winter sessions and engaged in farming in the summers. After the required examination he was admitted to practice by the Supreme Court of Illinois December 5, 1903. After two years as superintendent of schools at Louisville he established his law offices there and has enjoyed a successful law practice for over twenty years.

He has been interested in politics since early youth. While on the farm in Hoosier Township he held several local offices. On beginning law practice at Louisville he formed a partnership with Thomas S. Williams, now a member of Congress from Illinois. They were together until 1906, when Mr. Tolliver was elected county judge of Clay County, and in 1910 was re-elected for a second term of four years. Then for an interval of several years he was permitted to concentrate his entire time and energies on his growing law practice. In 1920 he was again called to public duties by the votes of his fellow citizens, being chosen state's attorney and served one term of four years. Judge Tolliver has done much for the cause of public education in his home county, and for eighteen consecutive years has served on the Louisville Board of Education. He has long been a member of the Republican Central Committee for Clay County, being now chairman of the committee, has been affiliated with the Masonic fraternity for over thirty years, is a member of the Mississippi Valley Consistory of the Scottish Rite at St. Louis, and is a Baptist.

Judge Tolliver married, in 1892, Miss Elizabeth Bryan, a native of Clay County, who died in 1910, leaving five children, Zola, Flossie, Lowell S., Bryan and Elizabeth. In 1914 Judge Tolliver married Miss Rachel Kincaid. By this marriage there are two children, Vincent and Charles E.

JAMES E. STEVENS is master mechanic of the Mobile & Ohio Railroad Shops at Murphysboro. Murphysboro's future was assured when in 1873 the old narrow gauge railroad, the St. Louis and Cairo, was built through that village. The St. Louis and Cairo subsequently became an important unit in the expanding Mobile & Ohio system. That railroad as originally chartered was established about 1851, building north from Mobile, Alabama. It was almost obliterated during the Civil war, but by 1873 had been completed north to the Ohio River at East Cairo. Traffic was ferried over the river to the Illinois side. About that time the St. Louis and Cairo narrow gauge was undertaken, construction being started at both ends. The northern terminal of the Mobile and Ohio remained at East Cairo until 1886. In that year the company acquired a lease on the St. Louis and Cairo, subsequently purchasing the road outright. This brought the northern terminal of the Mobile and Ohio to St. Louis. The first shops of the St. Louis and Cairo were located at East Carondolet. At that time Col. Charles Hamilton was superintendent and later was president of the road, while L. C. Mayes was master mechanic. A year later the shops were moved to East St. Louis. In 1888 the Mobile and Ohio shops were established at Murphysboro, and the subsequent growth and development of Murphysboro largely dates from that event. At first the shops were small, but they have kept pace with the increased facilities demanded by modern railroading. At the present time there are about 135 skilled mechanics employed there, the pay roll reaching nearly $100,000. Modern railroad shops are vastly different from those of fifty years ago, when the rolling stock of a railroad company, including the engines, were simple pieces of mechanism, compared to the cars and locomotives themselves and also the elaborate equipment such as electric lights, air brakes, steam heat. Today the demand for skilled labor is greater than the supply and in spite of the yearly output of graduates of universities, colleges and manual training schools the larger railroads do their utmost to educate and train men in their own ranks to the higher technical positions.

In the company's employ at Murphysboro are three typical self made railroaders, William B. B. Tolson, now assistant to the general manager, Mr. F. M. Bullock, division superintendent, and Mr. J. E. Stevens, master mechanic. All of them started at the bottom and rose to their present position by proficiency. Mr. Tolson was the first agent of the Mobile & Ohio at Enterprise, Mississippi, subsequently became brakeman, then yard master, and in 1913, superintendent at Murphysboro. His first work was piling wood and hauling water at a salary of $12.50 a month. He was then fifteen years old. On January 1, 1926, he became assistant to the general manager, and was succeeded by Mr. Bullock as superintendent.

James E. Stevens, the master mechanic, is one of many men whose career was affected directly or indirectly by the great Civil war. Before the war the Stevens family had been plantation and slave owners. The march of Sherman's army liberated three hundred slaves, and brought such ruin to the plantation itself that the property was practically abandoned by the family. The founder of the family was Henry M. Stevens, great-grandfather of James E. He had come from England in Colonial times. Mr. Stevens' grandfather had a summer home at Marietta, Georgia, and a winter home at Thomasville, Georgia, spending his last days at Thomasville. On the old home plantation there still remain broken pieces of field artillery and other evidence of battles fought there by the Northern and Southern armies. The mansion house itself was burned. James E. Stevens, Sr., father of the master mechanic, after the war became a planter in Mississippi. He married Josephine Chatten, a native of Camden, South Carolina. Her father, a native of Pennington, New Jersey, was an architect and furniture manufacturer in Camden, South Carolina. James E. Stevens, Sr., died when his son was eighteen months old.

James E. Stevens was born on his father's plantation in Mississippi, January 16, 1880. His uncle, Henry Porter Stevens, who had served in the army of Lee during the war and who was captured and spent two years in a northern military prison, subsequently married Mrs. James Stevens and reared her two sons, James E. and Henry Chatten Stevens. Both sons became railroaders and Henry is now master mechanic at Alamosa, Colorado, for the Denver & Rio Grande Railroad. Another uncle of these boys is John M. Stevens, a graduate of the Marietta Military Academy and a First Lieutenant in the Confederate Army, now residing in Thomasville, Georgia.

The sons were able to attend school only through the seventh grade. Both served their apprenticeship at the machinist's trade in the railroad shops of the old Plant System Railroad at Waycross, Georgia. James E. Stevens in 1906 went to work for the Mobile & Ohio at Tuscaloosa, Alabama, as a machinist. As a youth he recognized the handicap imposed by his lack of a technical education, and he applied himself with a thoroughness and persistence that has brought remarkable results. He mastered one correspondence course after the other, going through mechanical drawing, locomotive running and general shop practice, mechanical engineering and electrical engineering. Even yet his text books are his daily companions.

Mr. Stevens in 1908 was sent to Montgomery, Alabama, as terminal foreman, four years later became assistant general foreman at Meridian, Mississippi, and in 1915, three years later, was promoted to valuation engineer for the Mobile & Ohio system. In 1920 he became general foreman at Meridian and on January 1, 1922, came to Murphysboro as master mechanic of the shops there.

Mr. Stevens from his individual experience has been so impressed with the value of the work done by good correspondence schools that he aided the adoption of a plan by the railroad company whereby twenty per cent of the cost of correspondence courses is paid for by the company, and twelve hours full pay each month given to each student apprentice in the employ of the company as an inducement for them to qualify themselves for better positions. Besides the 138 skilled employes in the shops there are sixteen apprentices. The shops were totally destroyed by the tornado of 1925.

Mr. Stevens married Kathryn Darden, of Tuscaloosa, Alabama Their three children are James S., Henry P. and Kathryn D. Their home was badly injured in the tornado. Mr. Stevens' grandmother, Elizabeth Law, descendant of John Law, Scotch mariner, was representative of a Scotch family that settled at Midway, Georgia, a community in its original population made up almost entirely of Scotch people. Mr. Stevens has all the appearance of a typical railroad executive, and has the characteristic modesty of a successful railroad man. He is a Scottish Rite Mason and Shriner, having his membership at Meridian, Mississippi.

CARL P. MORGAN. After a record of brilliant success as a reporter on the staff of the Hearst papers in Chicago, Carl P. Morgan entered journalism as a publisher, and in what was regarded up to a few years ago as a field in which financial success was extremely hazardous, the publishing of newspapers in neighborhood communities of a large city. Mr. Morgan has reversed and upset the usual rules, and has become wealthy and influential through his enterprise. He is owner and editor of the Calumet Index and several other papers in the southern section of Chicago.

Mr. Morgan was born at Joplin, Missouri, in 1884, son of William Lawrence and Elvira (Moffitt) Morgan. His father was an educator and for several years was a professor in Kansas University. His mother was a sister of the late E. H. Moffitt, a famous mining king of Idaho.

Carl P. Morgan attended public schools, completing his education in college, and was seventeen years of age when he began reporting for the Chicago American. He was with the Chicago American about twelve years, and became one of the star members of its staff. He supplied many of the most important details in the investigation and story of a number of murder cases, both in Chicago and elsewhere.

On December 1, 1913, Mr. Morgan purchased the subscription list and good will of the Calumet Index, issued at Roseland. This weekly had been established in 1905 by Charles H. Gallion, and Mr. Morgan bought the paper from his widow, Mrs. Lucile B. Gallion. The Index at that time was printed by the Western Newspaper Union. Without capital, Mr. Morgan borrowed money for his venture, and since 1918 Mr. Floyd E. Haas has been associated with him. During the winter of 1914 occurred a slump in the business of the Pullman Company, the largest industry in the territory where the Index circulated. As a result a payroll of 13,500 men was cut down to about 2,000. Every business in the district suffered, and the Index experienced the full force of the reaction. However, Mr. Morgan persevered, and gradually developed his paper and printing plant until the Index came to command a tremendous circulation and represents a very prosperous business. In addition to the Calumet Index Mr. Morgan and his partner, Mr. Haas, are owners and publishers of three other papers, the Woodlawn Gazette, the South Shore News and the Chicago Telegram, published at Grand Crossing.

Recently Mr. Morgan was elected president of the Calumet Security Industrial Finance Company, organized by business and professional men of the Calumet region to aid worthy borrowers and defeat the aims of loan sharks. The company is incorporated for $125,000.

He owns a beautiful home in Beverly Hills. He is an enthusiastic motorist and a member of many of the prominent clubs and civic organizations. While never seeking office, he has been a power in city, county and state politics. He numbers among his personal friends such well-known Illinois leaders as former Governor Frank O. Lowden. Personally he is a democrat and a member of the Carter Harrison faction of the democratic party.

Mr. Morgan organized the Calumet Commercial Club, which has a membership of 150, and owns its own building. He is a member of the South Shore Country Club, the Pullman Club, the Woodlawn Temple Club, the Midway Athletic Club, the La Salle Club, various Masonic bodies, and the South End Chamber of Commerce. During the World war he was secretary of Draft Board No. 22 of Cook County.

Mr. Morgan in 1917 married Miss Lillian Evans, of Chicago. As a proper celebration of this event a thousand friends of Mr. Morgan in the Calumet steel district presented him and his bride with a rich and beautiful chest of silver. Mr. and Mrs. Morgan made an extended tour of Europe during the summer of 1925.

ANTON T. NADIG, M. D. Born and reared in Jo Daviess County, member of one of the pioneer families there, Doctor Nadig for many years has practiced medicine and surgery at Elizabeth. He stands high in his profession and his fellow townspeople also admire him for his loyalty and unselfishness and his willingness to act for the best interests of the community at all times.

He was born in Rush Township, Jo Daviess County, son of Jacob and Theresa (Schultz) Nadig. Jacob Nadig was born in Germany and at the age of eleven years was brought to America by his parents, who settled in Jo Daviess County in 1851. Jacob Nadig early in the Civil war enlisted in Company K of the Ninety-sixth Infantry. He was in many battles and was wounded at Missionary Ridge. He still carries in his body the bullet which made those wounds. After the war he engaged in farming until about 1911, and now resides on one of his farms in Rush Township at the age of eighty-six.

Anton T. Nadig grew up on a farm, attended country schools and the Galena High School, graduated from the Northern Illinois College at Dixon and took his medical degree from the University of Illinois School of Medicine in 1902. After practicing one year at Nora in Jo Daviess County, he located, in 1904, at Elizabeth and has been the tried and trusted physician and surgeon of that community ever since. He is a member of the County, Illinois State and American Associations, is a Scottish Rite Mason, member of the Independent Order of Odd Fellows, Knights of Pythias and Fraternal Order of Eagles. He is a director of the Elizabeth State Bank.

Doctor Nadig married at Stockton, Illinois, September 12, 1905, Miss Sarah J. Bartch. Mrs. Nadig died in December, 1919, leaving one son, Clyde. The son is now in his third year at Dubuque University, taking the premedical course.

CHARLES SIMONSON BRANTINGHAM, president of the Emerson-Brantingham Company of Rockford, is one of the responsible business men of Winnebago County, and one who plays an important part in the industrial life of this community. He was born at Rockford, Illinois, a son of Cornelius Corson and Katherine Elizabeth Brantingham. The Rockford public schools gave Charles Simonson Brantingham a practical education, and he has made good use of his training, adding to his store of knowledge by observation and contact with men.

The great industrial plant, occupying a site of 190 acres and employing 1,000 persons, was founded in 1852, for the purpose of manufacturing farm implements, which have attained to an international reputation. It is capitalized at $22,000,000. Associated with President Brantingham, who has held the office of chief executive since 1912, are the following officials: E. P. Lathrop, vice president; A. T. Jackson, vice president; H. H. Biggert, vice president; and C. F. Sanders, secretary and treasurer.

The Emerson-Brantingham Company manufactures a full line of plows, harrows, planters, cultivators, machinery and appliances for the planting and cultivation of cotton. The sales territory embraces the entire United States, the agricultural countries of Western Europe, South America and Australia. The great body of business, however, is done in the territory west of Chicago, and in the southwestern part of the Mississippi Valley, on the Pacific Coast, and in the western provinces of Canada, including Manitoba. These products are eagerly sought because they are so admirably fitted for the purposes for which they are designed, and the annual sales show a healthy increase.

On November 10, 1897, Mr. Brantingham married Sara McCulloch, a daughter of Henry D. McCulloch. They have three children, namely: Helen Louise, Charles Alan and Kathryn Elizabeth. Mr. Brantingham has always voted the republican ticket. His fraternal affiliations are those he maintains with the Benevolent and Protective Order of Elks of Rockford. He also belongs to the Rockford Country Club, the Rockford Rotary Club, the Union League Club of Chicago, and the Old Colony Club of New York City. The Second Congregational Church of Rockford holds his membership and receives his generous support. While he has not cared to come before the public for office, his time being fully occupied by his business responsibilities, he has always taken a deep interest in civic matters, and lends his assistance in bringing about various improvements.

COLEMAN MILES is the present mayor of Mount Carroll. He represents a family that has given several valuable citizens to this community. Mr. Miles is perhaps best known for his invaluable service in developing a musical organization and musical taste in Mount Carroll.

He was born in that Illinois town November 30, 1890, son of Joseph S. and Grace (Coleman) Miles, and grandson of Owen P. and Hannah (Shirk) Miles, who came from Pennsylvania to Mount Carroll in the early '50s. Owen Miles was a miller by trade, and followed that occupation at Mount Carroll. He became active in public affairs and for four years was county treasurer, and later entered the First National Bank of Mount Carroll and was cashier of that institution at the time of his death in 1896. He and his wife had eight children, six of whom are still living: Joseph S.; Charles K., of Savanna, Illinois; Jessie N., of Waynesboro, Pennsylvania; Jacob H., of Mount Carroll; A. Judson, of Mount Carroll; Mary D., of Mount Carroll; while one died in childhood, and the other deceased child was Susan M. Campbell.

Joseph S. Miles was born and reared at Mount Carroll, and after finishing his high school course entered the First National Bank as bookkeeper and has been identified with that institution ever since. He is now vice president and is one of the oldest bankers in northern Illinois, having been continuously

with one bank for over forty-five years. He is a Royal Arch Mason, member of the Eastern Star, a Baptist and a republican. His wife, Grace Coleman, was born and reared in Mount Carroll, being educated in the public schools there and the Frances Shimer School for Girls. Her parents were John and Mary (Dresbach) Coleman, who came from Pennsylvania to Mount Carroll about 1865. John Coleman engaged in the grain business and followed that line until his death in 1917. His wife died in 1907. Joseph S. Miles and wife had five children: Nathaniel, Coleman, Theodore, Owen P. and Elizabeth.

The son Nathaniel Miles was educated in the grammar and high schools of Mount Carroll, graduating from high school in 1906, and from Beloit College of Wisconsin in 1911. After his college career he was teller in the First National Bank of Mount Carroll until 1913, was then made assistant cashier, and in 1926 became cashier. He is also a director of the Mount Carroll Daily Mirror-Democrat and a director of the Frances Shimer School. He is a member of the Masonic Order, Sequoia Club, is a republican and is treasurer of the First Baptist Church. Nathaniel Miles married at Portage, Wisconsin, August 29, 1913, Miss Jane Johnson, of Portage, who graduated from the high school of that city in 1908, and from Beloit College in 1912. She is a daughter of Knute A. and Susanna (Whitlaw) Johnson, her father a native of Wisconsin and for some years a member of the Wisconsin Legislature. Nathaniel Miles and wife had four children, the three now living being Nathaniel, Jr., Suzanne and Theodore Robert.

Coleman Miles, who was born at Mount Carroll November 30, 1890, graduated from high school in 1908. He spent four years in the Warren Military Band School at Warren, Ohio, graduating in 1912. While there he had a thorough training that developed his natural talents as a musician, and has since been one of the most successful band leaders in the country. He spent one year with the Gilliland Band, one season with the Brooks Chautauqua Band, a year with the Park Prentiss Band at Venice, California, and for several seasons appeared on Chautauqua circuits. Mr. Miles in 1914 returned to Mount Carroll, and his attention has been primarily directed toward the development and training of the Mount Carroll Band. He also teaches music in the grammar and high schools. The Mount Carroll High School Band, of which he is a director, is a notable organization, and won first place in the state contest at Urbana in 1926 in high school bands of Class B. Through this organization and through his other activities Mr. Miles has done much to develop a sound taste for good music in Mount Carroll and vicinity.

Mr. Miles owns an attractive bungalow on the south side in Mount Carroll, together with several acres of land, where he pursues his hobby of poultry raising. In 1923 he was elected mayor of Mount Carroll. His administration of municipal affairs was so satisfactory to all concerned that he was reelected in 1925. He is a member of the Masonic Order, is a republican and a Methodist and has charge of the Sunday School orchestra in the First Methodist Episcopal Church.

He married at Los Angeles, California, February 16, 1914, Miss Mabel E. Rhodes, member of a well known family of Mount Carroll, where she was reared and educated, graduating from high school in 1912. She is a daughter of Thomas B. and Emma (Chambers) Rhodes, who were born and reared at Savanna, Illinois, her father moving to Mount Carroll about 1886. Here he engaged in the coal and lumber business and owns one of the leading establishments of the kind. Mr. and Mrs. Coleman Miles have one daughter, Mary Jean.

CHARLES W. HADLEY, lawyer and banker of Wheaton and assistant attorney general of the state of Illinois, is without question one of the ablest attorneys of the state. In the course of official duty or by special assignment he has participated in some of the most famous trials within recent years in Illinois.

Mr. Hadley is a member of one of the oldest families of DuPage County. He was born on a farm near West Chicago, five miles west of Wheaton, that county, and his parents, Philip L. and Mary (Roundy) Hadley, were also natives of DuPage County. His grandfather, Hiram H. Hadley, descended from the same family that settled Hadley, Massachusetts, came west from Vermont and settled in DuPage County about 1838. Mr. Hadley's maternal grandfather was Major Roundy, and the Roundys came to DuPage County several years earlier than the Hadleys. Major Roundy was an officer in the militia, and organized a troop of Home Guards later incorporated in the State Militia before the Civil war. He married a Miss Kimball, of English ancestry.

Charles W. Hadley was reared in the rural districts around Wheaton, graduated from the high school there and from Wheaton College in 1899, and in 1902 took his degree in law at Northwestern University in Chicago. Admitted to the bar in that year, he engaged in practice, with offices both at Wheaton and in Chicago. He kept his Chicago office until 1906, when he was elected state's attorney of DuPage County. In no small measure Mr. Hadley's reputation as a trial lawyer is based upon his splendid record while state's attorney of DuPage County. He was re-elected to that position and served continuously until 1920. As a prosecutor he was vigorous, resourceful and able. He prosecuted the case against Henry Spencer, known as "the man without a soul," and who finally was executed for his crime. In 1920 Mr. Hadley became a candidate for appointment to the office of United States district attorney for the Northern District of Illinois. However, Edward Olson was appointed to that office. Shortly afterward Mr. Hadley was appointed by Edward J. Brundage, attorney general of Illinois, to take charge of the criminal proceedings against the mayor and other officials and citizens of Rock Island, where vice conditions had reached a point where the entire machinery of city government had broken down. Mr. Hadley tried the case for conspiracy and secured the conviction and penitentiary sentence for the mayor and chief of police, and incident to the same general conditions four others were tried on murder charges and convicted and sent to the penitentiary. One of the men indicted in the conspiracy trial was John P. Looney, long known as the vice lord of Rock Island. His trial was delayed and only recently, in December, 1925, at Galesburg, he was found guilty of murder in the first degree.

In the fall of 1923 Mr. Brundage called Mr. Hadley to assist in the prosecution of perhaps the most famous case in Illinois judicial history in recent years, for the recovery of interest on public funds handled by Governor Len Small while state treasurer of Illinois. This is a case that has made history in Illinois, has attracted nation wide attention, and has involved not only the law, the ethics of public business, but also personal friendship and politics. Finally, on December 16, 1925, the Supreme Court of Illinois handed down its decision that Governor Small must return to the state the interest collected on state funds while he was state treasurer, amounting to approximately $1,000,000.

Mr. Hadley was attorney for the administrators of the estate of William P. Cowan, who at his death was president of the Standard Oil Company of Indiana. Cowan died intestate, and there followed a celebrated scramble for a division of his property, claimants from all parts of the county seeking a share on the basis of more or less remote cousinship to the oil magnate.

Mr. Hadley is counsel for and a director of the First National Bank of Wheaton, and the DuPage Trust Company of Glenn Ellyn, is president of the First Trust Bank of Lombard, is an attorney for the Chicago & Northwestern Railway and the Chicago, Milwaukee & St. Paul Railway. He has also been active in real estate developments in his home vicinity and was responsible for laying out one of the highest class resident subdivisions in the vicinity of Wheaton. Mr. Hadley is a Knight Templar Mason and a member of the First Methodist Episcopal Church of Wheaton.

In public office for a number of years and always concerned in public movements, Mr. Hadley puts into his addresses and into counsel a broad measure of experience and statesmanlike talent, and in consequence no one in his home county wields more influence in civic affairs and large undertakings involving the common welfare. Without doubt he is one of the most influential figures in northern Illinois today.

ALBERT EDGAR TAFF. Undoubtedly while some men achieve success along certain lines and in certain professions, there are those who are born to them, their natural leanings and marked talents pointing unmistakably to the career in which they subsequently reach distinction. With some the call of the church cannot be disobeyed; to others the science of healing appeals; the business mart or the political arena engage many, while there are still others who clearly see in their visions of the future their achieving in the law the summit of their ambition. To respond to this call, to bend every energy in this direction, to broaden and deepen every possible highway of knowledge, and finally to enter upon this chosen profession and find its rewards worth while, has been the happy experience of Albert Edgar Taff, one of the able attorneys of Canton.

Albert Edgar Taff was born at Bartonville, Arkansas, July 28, 1876, a son of George Taff, whose death occurred when his son was two years old, and he is buried in one of the national cemeteries in Arkansas, never having recovered from his service in the Union army during the war between the states, in which he enlisted from Indiana. He married Susan Downing, a daughter of A. G. Downing. She was born in Illinois, and she died near Canton, Illinois, two years after her husband, having returned to her own people when she was made a widow, and she is buried on the Downing homestead. Three children were born to her and her husband, namely: William M., who is chairman of the Fulton County Board of Supervisors, and a farmer in the Canton locality; Charles J., who is an attorney of McMinnville, Oregon; and Albert Edgar, whose name heads this review.

Left an orphan at the early age of four years, Albert Edgar Taff was taken by his maternal aunt, Mrs. M. V. Seaton, of Canton, and he was reared in Fulton County, where he alternated farm work with attendance at the district schools. Later he had the advantages afforded by the Canton public schools, and commenced his training for professional life by taking a course at the Western Normal School, Bushnell, Illinois. After he left normal school he taught school in the country districts of Fulton County for three years, and with the money thus earned he entered the law department of the University of Illinois, from which he was graduated in 1903, with the degree of Bachelor of Laws, and was admitted to the bar.

Mr. Taff immediately established himself in a general practice at Canton, and his ability soon received recognition. After he had acquitted himself satisfactorily as assistant state's attorney under W. S. Jewell. Judge H. C. Moran, in 1912, appointed him master in chancery, and he held that office until 1922. Mr. Taff was a member of the Constitutional Convention of the state held in 1920-1922. He was also appointed special master in chancery for the important case known as the "Thompson Lake" case. After hearing the testimony he rendered a decision to the effect that the State of Illinois could not enjoin the parties from draining Thompson Lake, as it was private property, and the owners had a right to use it as such. The case was appealed from his decision and taken to the Supreme Court of Illinois, where he was sustained. Early in his professional life he became a member of the Fulton County Bar Association, and was its president 1916-1917. During the World war he was a member of the legal advisory committee, and government appeal agent of the local draft board of Fulton County. Registered in the final draft, he submitted his questionnaire, and tried to get a release from his connection with the local board, but the adjutant general of Illinois refused to grant his request, as his services were more needed at home. He also served as chairman of the Home Service Section of the American Red Cross. Fraternally he belongs to the Benevolent and Protective Order of Elks, and has twice been exalted ruler of Canton Lodge No. 626 of that order, and was chairman of the committee that had in charge the erection of the Elks Building at Canton. After serving for four years as a member of the Board of Trustees of the Fulton County Tuberculosis Sanatarium, he declined re-appointment. From 1912 to 1914 he was city attorney, and he has never failed to respond to the call of his community upon his professional experience and knowledge. In addition to his professional interests, Mr. Taff is vice president of the First State Bank of Canton, which office he has held for the past decade; is a member of the Canton Chamber of Commerce, and is president of the Mutual Homestead & Loan Association.

Albert Edgar Taff married, at Galesburg, Illinois, in 1905, Miss Neta Michaels, a daughter of Wesley Michaels, now deceased, although the mother is living. The Michaels were farming people, and Mrs. Taff, born near Raritan, Illinois, was reared in a country home, and educated in the rural schools and the Western Normal School at Bushnell, Illinois. She is the younger of two children born to her parents, her brother being Fred Michaels, of Macomb, Illinois, where he is living retired from former agricultural activities. Wesley Michaels, their father, was a soldier in the Union army during the war between the states, having enlisted for service from Illinois. Three children have been born to Mr. and Mrs. Taff, namely: Clarice, who was graduated from the Canton High School, is a student of Vassar College, having won the Graham scholarship through a competitive examination in 1925, and is the first to win this scholarship, and she is regarded as a very brilliant scholar, and one who reflects great credit on Canton as well as on her parents; Maurine, who is a student of the Canton High School; and Albert W., who is also a high school student. Mr. and Mrs. Taff stand deservedly high in the confidence of the people of Fulton County, and they are very prominent socially, their culture and interest in the better things of life giving them a standing second to none in this community.

CHARLES F. HURBURGH, Galesburg business man, is widely known throughout central Illinois because of his activity in politics. He has been a county official and for a number of years was in the Legislature.

Mr. Hurburgh has spent practically all his life in Illinois. He was born in Sweden, January 10, 1873, son of Charles and Susanna Hurburgh. About a year later his mother started for America, the father remaining behind to complete other arrangements. Before he left Sweden he was taken ill and died there. Charles F. Hurburgh from early infancy was reared at Altona, in Knox County, Illinois, completing his high school work there. In 1892 he graduated from Abingdon Normal College of Illinois, taught school for a year, and through his own efforts paid his way through Knox College, where he was graduated in 1895. He is one of the honored alumni of that institution. For five years after graduating he taught at Maquon in Knox County.

Mr. Hurburgh for two years was deputy county sheriff and in 1902 was elected sheriff of Knox County, holding that office four years. In 1906 he was elected a member of the Illinois State Senate, and served in that body with distinction for two successive terms. Such was his personal popularity and influence in central Illinois that in response to the urging of his friends he was a candidate for the republican nomination for governor in 1914.

Mr. Hurburgh is a building and general cantractor who has handled many important projects, involving not only general building construction but such undertakings as drainage of farm land areas. His business requires an office in Chicago as well as in Galesburg.

Mr. Hurburgh is a Royal Arch and Council Degree Mason. He is a member of the Trinity Lutheran Church of Galesburg. In 1902 he married Miss Anna Scott, a native of Stark County, Illinois. They have one son, Richard Charles Hurburgh. Mr. Hurburgh has his business offices in the Mail Building at Galesburg.

MARK B. WHITE is secretary-treasurer and manager of the Hanover Woolen Manufacturing Company, an industry founded by his grandfather, and with which three generations of the White family have been associated. The business is the foundation of Hanover's prosperity and is one of the largest woolen cloth manufacturing establishments in the Mississippi Valley.

The founder of the business was J. W. White, who was born and reared in Hillsboro County, New Hampshire, and was educated in a private school at Lowell, Massachusetts. He married Almira Jenks, of Lowell, and in 1837 moved to Savanna, Illinois, where he conducted a mercantile establishment, and in 1845 purchased the water power and about 200 acres of ground at Hanover, where he established first a sawmill and later a flouring mill, which he operated until 1864.

In 1864 he built the Hanover Woolen Mills, which name was later changed to the Hanover Woolen Manufacturing Company, which has enjoyed an existence of over sixty years and in the year 1921 was more than doubled in size by the building of an entirely new building and the addition of new machinery to take the place of that so long in use. The finished wool cloth manufactured at Hanover is used entirely for men's suitings, and is sold directly to manufacturers of men's clothing through their own offices and sales agents located in New York City and Chicago.

J. W. White, the founder of the business, died in 1906. He was succeeded by his son, A. B. White, who was born and reared at Hanover, attended grammar and high schools there, and finished his education at Notre Dame University of Indiana. After completing his college work he returned to Hanover, entered the woolen mills, learned the industry in all its phases, and became secretary and treasurer of the company, and on his father's death became president of the company, which position he still holds. He is a member of the Masonic Order, various clubs, and is a Presbyterian. He married Martha Reynolds.

Mark B. White, son of A. B. and Martha (Reynolds) White, was born at Hanover, January 1, 1885. He graduated from the Hanover High School, and likewise attended Notre Dame University, where he was graduated in 1907. As his father had done, he returned from the university to go into the mills, and served in every department of the factory, gaining an experience that thoroughly qualified him for his duties as secretary-treasurer and manager of the company. He is a Knight Templar Mason and Shriner, member of various clubs, and a republican. He married at Savanna, Illinois, October 5, 1917, Miss Ruth M. Morrison, who was educated in the Savanna schools and in Downer College of Milwaukee. She is a daughter of G. R. and Flora (Eaton) Morrison, of Savanna, her father being an official of the Chicago, Milwaukee and St. Paul Railroad.

HAMPTON S. BURGESS, lawyer, legislator and prominent citizen of Fairfield, was born and reared on a farm in Wayne County, Illinois. He was born December 5, 1866, a son of John H. and Mary (Williams) Burgess. His father was born in the County of Wayne, in the State of Tennessee, in 1826, and at the age of twenty-two years came to Illinois, settling on a farm in Wayne County. When the Civil war came on he volunteered his services in defense of the Union, becoming a private in Company D, Fifth Illinois Cavalry, in which he served for two years. Afterwards he resumed the pursuit of farming in Wayne County, and continued that occupation until he departed this life in 1897, at the age of seventy-one.

In the country schools Hampton S. Burgess received his early education, which was supplemented by attending old Hayward College at Fairfield. He became a teacher in the public schools and for nine consecutive years continued to teach with gratifying success. Meanwhile Mr. Burgess took up the study of law, and in 1895 was admitted to the bar. Two years later he quit the school room as a teacher and gave all his time to his practice at Fairfield. He has long ranked among the leaders of the Wayne County bar. Since early manhood he has been active in public affairs and in the councils of the democratic party. He has held numerous offices, including township assessor for two terms, township supervisor two terms, serving one year as chairman of the county board of supervisors, and in 1900 was elected city attorney of Fairfield. Later Mr. Burgess served for two terms as mayor of his home city. His administrations as mayor were marked by efficiency and wisdom. In 1908 he was elected state's attorney of Wayne County, an office he filled two terms, giving a record as an able and vigorous prosecutor. In 1922 he was again called into official life by election to the Lower House of the General Assembly of Illinois. As representative he served with credit to himself and constituents, gaining the merited recognition of being nominated for state senator from the Forty-sixth District in 1924. He was elected, and in the State Senate his record has been such as to meet with the approval of all concerned. In his official and public career the service and conduct of Mr. Burgess have been such as to inspire wholesome respect for his character and abilities. He is plain and unostentatious in manner, direct in utterance, and is a citizen to be trusted.

In church faith Senator Burgess is a Methodist, and in fraternal relationship he is a member of the Independent Order of Odd Fellows. On December 27, 1893, he and Miss Lillie Harlan were united in marriage, and they have eight children, three girls and five boys. Mrs. Burgess is a daughter of Mr. and Mrs. William D. Harlan, of Wayne County, Illinois.

MIKE H. HUSSEY, of Waukegan, had his early experiences in the lumber camps and lumber mills of Wisconsin, where he grew up and has been more or less closely identified with the lumber industry ever since. He has been one of the men most vitally interested in the upbuilding of Waukegan as an important industrial and civic center of Northeastern Illinois. He was responsible for giving Waukegan its first modern public utility plant. He is still the head of the extensive Hussey lumber interests, though his sons have taken over many of the details of management.

Mr. Hussey was born in Manitowoc County, Wisconsin, April 9, 1856, son of Mike and Helen (Thornton) Hussey. Both parents were natives of County Clare, Ireland. They were brought when children by their parents to America about 1840. They grew up and met and married at Akron, Ohio, and subsequently became pioneer settlers in the great lumber woods of Manitowoc County, Wisconsin. Mike Hussey, Sr., cleared up a farm and spent the rest of his life on it. He died in 1911, at the age of eighty-four, and his wife, in 1922, at the advanced age of ninety-four.

Mike H. Hussey had a farm training, attended public schools in Manitowoc County, and after several years of farming routine he went into the logging and lumber camps, and his experience has made him familiar with every phase of the industry from the felling of the trees to the marketing of the finished product.

Mr. Hussey became a resident of Waukegan in 1890. Waukegan then was a country town of about 4,000 population, without paved streets, electric lights, telephones or other essentials of a modern community. He organized the Waukegan Electric Light Company, which built the first electric plant in Lake County. Mr. Hussey operated this public utility and in connection the company also built and operated a central heating plant for the downtown stores and courthouse. These public utilities were sold in 1900 to the Public Service Company of Northern Illinois and now constitute an important unit of that corporation's widely extended service. On retiring from the public utility field Mr. Hussey resumed the lumber business at Waukegan, operating a retail lumber and building material organization which has enjoyed steady growth. The company now owns the original yard of the M. H. Hussey Lumber Company, also operates a yard at Lake Forest, one at North Chicago, conducts a coal and building

material yard at North Chicago and operates the Waukegan Coal Yard, including the largest coal dock on the North Shore between Chicago and Milwaukee. About ten years ago the company also extended its business by establishing a large lumber yard in Detroit. The general manager of this branch of the business is J. E. Hussey, one of Mr. Hussey's sons. The company owns a manufacturing plant on the Pacific Coast at South Bellingham, Washington. This is the Puget Sound Saw Mill & Shingle Company. The son who has active charge of this business is John Earl Hussey.

Mr. Mike H. Hussey is a director of the Security Savings Bank of Waukegan, is a member of the Modern Woodmen of America and the Glen Flora Country Club, is a democrat and a Catholic.

He married in Manitowoc County, Wisconsin, February 8, 1882, Miss Margaret Earles, who was reared and educated in that section of Wisconsin. She takes an active part in church work at Waukegan and the Woman's Club. Her parents, Thomas and Catherine (McMahon) Earles, came from Ireland and were early settlers in Manitowoc County. Mr. and Mrs. Hussey have seven children: J. E. Hussey, general manager of yards, who was educated in the grammar and high schools of Waukegan and Notre Dame University of Indiana, and married Mabel Mackey, of Waukegan; Lillian, wife of R. J. Rich, formerly of Seattle, Washington, now in the simonizing business in Chicago, and they have four children, named Bill, Betty, Peggy and Jerry; Ruth Hussey, who from the high school at Waukegan attended a girls' seminary and is now traveling and studying abroad in Europe; Florence Hussey, who attended the public schools, the Sacred Heart College at Lake Forest, and is the wife of J. N. Heath, in the real estate business at Coral Gables, Miami, Florida; John E. Hussey, who after graduating from the Waukegan High School spent two years in Culver Military Academy in Indiana and Notre Dame University, and now has charge of the M. H. Hussey Pacific Coast lumber interests at Bellingham, Washington; Harold and Thomas, the two youngest sons, both educated in the Waukegan High School and Campion College at Prairie du Chien, Wisconsin, and are now associated with their father in the lumber business at Waukegan.

BENJAMIN FRANKLIN THOMAS, attorney at Fairfield, came to the bar thirty years ago, and the measure of his service and achievements can be found in the splendid record he made while state's attorney of Wayne County, the extensive general practice that has rewarded his abilities and efforts, and the frequent recognition of his leadership from outside his home community.

Mr. Thomas was born on a farm in Wayne County, four miles north of Fairfield, August 18, 1873, son of Jason H. and Rebecca (Puckett) Thomas. His father, who was born at Salem, Ohio, July 9, 1826, settled in Wayne County in 1854, and for many years was a respected farmer of the county. He died at the advanced age of eighty-seven. He was a soldier three years in the Civil war with Company D of the Eighty-seventh Illinois Infantry. He was a private, and participated with his regiment in its various campaigns. He was a member of the Grand Army of the Republic, a republican in politics, and was a Methodist. His wife, Rebecca Puckett, was born in Tennessee, daughter of Mr. and Mrs. Thomas Puckett, who while she was a girl settled on a farm south of Fairfield. Jason H. Thomas and wife had nine children, of whom six are living, four sons and two daughters.

Benjamin Franklin Thomas was next to the youngest in the family and was four years old when his mother died. He grew up on a farm, attended country schools and at the age of eighteen began teaching in country districts. He taught five winter terms and in the meantime attended Hayward College at Fairfield, where he was graduated in 1893. While at college he began the study of law in the law office of T. H. Creighton. Mr. Thomas was admitted to the bar in January, 1897, and in March of the same year formed a partnership with Mr. Creighton, and they have been associated in their law work and as close friends now for thirty years. They constitute one of the oldest law firms in southern Illinois. Mr. Thomas has practiced before all the state and federal courts. In June, 1924, he was appointed by the Illinois Supreme Court a member of the committee on the character and fitness of applicants for admission to the bar. In June, 1925, he was appointed one of the judges of the Court of Claims, being appointed by Governor Small. Mr. Thomas has extensive interests outside his professional work. He owns 560 acres of farming land and supervises the farm and his live stock. He also is interested in a chain of lumber yards in southern Illinois. He is vice president of the First National Bank of Fairfield, is a stockholder in several automobile companies, and also in wholesale produce houses at Olney and in Newton, Illinois.

Mr. Thomas in November, 1900, was given the distinction of being the first republican ever elected state's attorney of Wayne county. In 1904 he was re-elected, serving eight years. In the first election he was successful by a margin of seventy-three votes, while in 1904 his majority was 401 votes. His administration was a splendid justification of the faith shown in him by the people. He secured a larger number of convictions than was credited to the office in any like period in the county. He was also for one term of two years master in chancery for Wayne County. For over eighteen years Mr. Thomson was secretary of the Wayne County Central Republican Committee and is now republican chairman for the First Judicial District of the Supreme Court. He was a delegate to the National Republican Convention at Cleveland in 1924, being chosen as a Coolidge supporter. During the World war Mr. Thomas managed the Red Cross, Liberty Loan, and Y. M. C. A. campaigns in Wayne County. He served two years as chairman of the Fairfield Chamber of Commerce, is vice president of the Rotary Club, is president of the Board of Directors of the Fairfield Public Library, and in a similar way has been identified usefully and helpfully with many of the civic causes and local enterprises that have marked the progress of his home city and county. He is active in the Christian Church, is on the church board and was chairman of the building committee which in December, 1925, completed the beautiful $55,000 new church edifice at Fairfield. He is a thirty-second degree Scottish Rite Mason and Shriner.

Mr. Thomas married, January 1, 1901, Miss Minnie Farmer, of Noble, Illinois. She had taught in the schools of Richland County a number of years and at the time of her marriage was primary teacher at Fairfield. They have one daughter, Majorie, who graduated in 1924 from the University of Wisconsin and followed her university career with an extensive tour abroad, during which she visited eleven countries in Europe.

HON. HOBART SHEARMAN BOYD, one of the distinguished attorneys practicing at the bar of Lewistown, is senior member of the reliable legal firm of Boyd & Weber, and he is also an ex-judge of the County Court of Fulton, and a public-spirited man. Lewistown is proud of the fact that it is entitled to the honor of being his birthplace, for he came into the world in this city, October 17, 1876, and here his useful life has been spent, and here his deepest interest center, although, of course, his public duties have made him include a wider territory in his field of labor.

Judge Boyd is a son of Thomas A. Boyd, and he inherits his professional abilities, for the father also made a name for himself in the legal profession. Thomas A. Boyd was born in Franklin County, Pennsylvania, and he died at Lewistown in 1898, at the age of sixty-three years. Following his graduation from Mercersburg, Pennsylvania, College, he came to Illinois in 1860, and had barely established himself at Lewistown when the war cloud, so long hovering over the country, burst in all its fury, and he, with the other young men of his times, was drawn into the vortex, and commanded Company H, Seventeenth Illinois Volunteer Infantry. This unit saw the greater part of its service under General Grant, and although in the hardest of fighting, Mr. Boyd escaped without being wounded or captured. With the termination of war and his honorable discharge from the army Mr. Boyd returned to Lewistown and resumed his practice. It is interesting to note that he also served in the Illinois State Senate, holding the office for two terms, and he was also county judge of Fulton County, and represented the Ninth District in Congress, holding that office for two terms. He was a member of the House during the first free silver controversy, in 1873. A useful citizen, he not only held these high public offices already referred to, but was mayor of Lewistown, although he did not complete his term in office owing to ill health. While he opposed the open saloon, he believed that as long as the liquor traffic was permitted under the law those engaging in it should be treated fairly. He was not a member of any religious organization, nor was he identified with any fraternity.

Congressman Boyd married Laura James, born in Virginia, near Washington, District of Columbia, a daughter of William James. Mrs. Boyd was a graduate of the local high school, and she outlived her husband until 1908, when she passed away, aged sixty-two years. The following children were born to them. Thomas A., who died at Lincoln, Nebraska, where he was in the service of the United States government, leaving a widow and three children; Mary C., who married Edward C. Miles, of Lewistown; John W., who is a resident of Lewistown; Margaret L., who died unmarried; Lawrence J., who is postmaster of Lewistown; and Judge Boyd, whose name heads this review.

Graduating from the Lewistown High School when he was eighteen years old, Hobart Shearman Boyd began the study of law, but soon realizing his need for a training in the higher branches, he entered the University of Illinois, where he spent two years in the academic and art departments, following which he entered the law department, and was graduated from that institution in 1900, with the degree of Bachelor of Laws. Taking his bar examination at Springfield, he was licensed in the fall of that same year.

Returning to Lewistown Judge Boyd began the practice of his profession, and in 1905 was appointed master in chancery by Judge John A. Gray of the Circuit Court, and served for two years. He then resumed active practice, in which he continued until 1910, when he was elected county judge of Fulton County, succeeding Judge Breckenridge, the present incumbent. After twelve years in the office he retired to resume his law practice, and became a member of his present firm. A strong republican, Judge Boyd cast his first presidential vote for William McKinley, and since then has warmly and intelligently supported the tenets of his party, honestly believing them to be the best ones to secure its continued prosperity. In a community like as Lewistown where the paramount industry is farming, the population is not transitory, and the people become well acquainted with each other, and willingly follow the leadership of a man in whom they realize they can place implicit trust. Therefore Judge Boyd has always had the support of his fellow citizens, as did his father before him. Registering in the second draft, he filled out his own questionnaire and was classified. In addition to his professional interests Judge Boyd is president of the Lewistown National Bank, of which he was a stockholder and director prior to his elevation to his present office.

On February 5, 1907, Judge Boyd married at Cambridge, Illinois, Elizabeth Walker, who was born in Fulton County, a daughter of Robert K. and Mary (Harris) Walker, who had three daughters and three sons born to their marriage, of whom five are now living. Mrs. Boyd is a product of the public schools of Fulton County. Judge and Mrs. Boyd have three children, namely: Robert Walker, Hobart L. and Margaret Louise. These children are being carefully reared, and are taught to be proud of their family record. The brilliancy that Judge Boyd displays in his professional work and in politics may also be inherited from his mother as well as from his father, for she came of those people who have given this country some of its most distinguished statesmen and lawyers. Miss Laura James at the time of her marriage to Congressman Boyd, was a lady of great intellectual vigor, and strength of character. Not only was the name of Boyd represented during the war of the '60s in an Illinois regiment, but a brother of Congressman Boyd, Robert Boyd, carried it on the battlefield in a Pennsylvania regiment, and following the close of the war he returned to the Keystone State, where the remainder of his life was spent.

COL. BURNETT M. CHIPERFIELD, an attorney of great repute engaged in the practice of his profession at Canton, and ex-congressman representing his district in the Sixty-fourth National Assembly, is one of the most distinguished citizens of Illinois, and a man whose honorable life and public-spirited principles have centered upon him the attention not only of the people of Illinois but of the country as well. He is a native of Illinois, as he was born at Dover, Bureau County, June 17, 1870, a son of Rev. Thomas and Hannah M. (Reynolds) Chiperfield, the former of whom, a clergyman of the Methodist Episcopal Church, came to the United States from England in 1854, and held pastorates at different points, especially in Illinois, including those at Sandwich, Sterling, Marseilles, Seneca, Rock Falls, Kankakee, Chillicothe and Chicago, and for many years was recognized as an eminent divine.

After attending school in the different localities to which his father's ministerial duties took him, Colonel Chiperfield became a student of Hamline University at Saint Paul, Minnesota, which is an educational institution of the Methodist Episcopal Church. When he left the university he began that preparation for a successful professional career which included not only the tenets of the law, but business as well, and acquired practical ideas for the latter in a Chicago banking house. Not long afterwards, however, he joined a surveying party which went through the Northwest, in which expedition he secured an experience of outdoor life which was beneficial and instructive. Before entering upon the regular study of the law, he identified himself with educational work as a member of the faculty at a school of Green Prairie, Minnesota. Later he was assistant principal of schools at Cuba, Illinois. By this time he has passed his majority, and he re-entered, with customary vigor, on the active acquisition of the essentials in legal principles and practice for early admission to the bar of Illinois, and that same year successfully passed the required examinations. Immediately following his admission to the bar, he established himself in practice at Canton, and subsequently became a member of the firm of Chiperfield & Chiperfield, his partner being Judge C. E. Chiperfield. It was not long before this new firm won the confidence of litigants, and the public generally, for both were able attorneys and alert practitioners. Not only were the partners' aid sought in the local courts, but their clientele came to represent every phase of human activity. It was not long before the name of this firm was found on one side or other of almost all of the important lawsuits tried in the Circuit and the higher courts of the state. One of the cases of chief moment in the professional career of Colonel Chiperfield was that of the Bar Manufacturing Company and its employes, the latter of whom demanded a nine-hour day instead of a ten-hour day without a reduction in wages. Before the board of arbitration which was provided to settle the differences between the contending parties Chiperfield & Chiperfield represented the men, and Reeves & Boyes, of Streator, Illinois, represented the company. Colonel Chiperfield and his partner secured a verdict in favor of their clients, with the result that the men not only secured the reduction in the number of hours of work per day, without any loss of wages, but they received pay for the extra hour each day which they had agreed to work pending the settlement of the case. This great victory secured for labor by the firm added to the prestige of the partners, and the personal popularity of each man, and Colonel Chiperfield found he had gained many friends. Another important case with which Colonel Chiperfield has been connected was that when he appeared as the attorney for the Sanitary District of Chicago in the case of Congressman Graff and Judge Curran, who asked $55,000 damages from the district for the alleged overflow by the Drainage Canal of 700 acres of land. The case occupied eleven weeks in the trial court, and the jury brought in a verdict for the plaintiffs for $750.

In 1894 Colonel Chiperfield first came before the people of Canton for the office of city attorney, and he was elected to that office by an excellent majority. One of the results of his service in that office was the complete revision of the city ordinances and a thorough systematizing of the city legal department. He was the instigator of the practice of suspending fines for good behavior, and of suspending sentences when the convicted man agreed to seek work in other fields and begin life anew. In the disposition of some 500 criminal cases prosecuted by him the city won all but two or three, and there was more than $150,000 litigation in which the city was involved.

From the city attorney's office Colonel Chiperfield went to that of state's attorney for Fulton County, to which office he was elected as the first republican incumbent. In that office he soon showed himself so relentless a prosecutor that accused men followed the dictates of their guilty consciences and oftentimes pleaded guilty, rather than to fight the long battle for liberty, only to be convicted at its end and sent to prison. He held his oath of office sacred and conducted its business as he would that of his private practice, a line of conduct he has always followed. Like Martin Luther before the Diet of Worms, he has stood upon his convictions and could not do otherwise, for such is the character of the man. His record as state's attorney served to commend him for other political honors, even more important and distinguished, and these he also carried with dignified capability.

Elected as a member of the Forty-third General Assembly of Illinois from Fulton and Knox counties, Colonel Chiperfield declared he had accepted the office: "To favor such legislation as is desired by the United Mine Workers of this state; to advocate the passage of a bill prohibiting any employer from requiring his men to sign a contract permitting said employer to retain ten per cent of their wages without interest; to require manufacturers to furnish sanitary shops for employes and to take all necessary and proper precautions to prevent the escape of wood, emory and other dust and dirt into such places of employment, to the detriment of the health of those employed there; to advocate the passage of a bill to deduct from the assessed valuation of farm lands and other real estate, where mortgaged, the value of the mortgage, and to compel the holder of the mortgage and the owner of the farm or other real estate to pay the tax only on the remaining values."

Notwithstanding that this program of legislation represented much labor and seemed to many difficult of accomplishment in the face of strenuous opposition, Colonel Chiperfield achieved his object and succeeded in placing laws upon the statutes, with the aid of friends of labor, which covered these proposals and also rendered valuable aid in putting over beneficial legislation upon other subjects, financial and economic, which have served to mark his worth as a public servant, right at the fountain head. He was chairman of the committee on penal and reformatory institutions, and a member of the committees on corporations, fish and game, judiciary and judicial appropriations, military affairs, mines and mining, railroads, rules and the Republican Steering Committee of the House.

In 1914 Colonel Chiperfield was elected to the Sixty-fourth Congress, and while in that body was a member of the committee on rules, and a member of the investigating committee which handled the charges of Thomas W. Lawson regarding an alleged leak of the President's message. At the invitation of Congress he delivered the Lincoln oration in the House of Representatives in February, 1917.

Colonel Chiperfield has been connected with the Illinois National Guard for twenty-five years, being promoted by successive stages from lieutenant to colonel. He subsequently was commissioned a colonel in the United States service by President Wilson. He has had commissions from Governors Yates, Deneen, Lowden and Small, and is now judge advocate general of the National Guard of Illinois. During the World war he was made judge advocate general of the Army of Occupation in Germany, of the Third Army Corps. He entered the war early in 1917 as assistant to Gen. E. H. Crowder, provo marshal general. He had charge of the organization of the troops in Illinois and surrounding territory. Afterwards he was sent to the Thirty-third Division at Camp Logan, Houston, Texas, and was on the staff of Maj.-Gen. Geo. Bell, Jr. Early in 1918 he went to France with the division and participated in all the activities of the division until after the armistice. He was cited for exceptionally meritorious and conspicuous service by General Pershing, and for gallantry in action against the enemy by the commander of the Thirty-third Division; was recommended for the Distinguished Service Medal, and had other honors bestowed upon him.

Other distinctions have been bestowed upon him, for he was one of the trustees of the Illinois State Normal School from 1900 to 1903; was delegate to the Republican National Convention in 1920 and was chairman of the Canton Centennial Commission in 1925. He belongs to the American Bar Association, the Illinois State Bar Association, the American Association of Military Law, is ex-president of the States Attorneys Association of Illinois, is a member of the Phi Alpha Beta, the Order of the Coif, the Union League Club of Chicago, the Army and Navy Club of Washington, District of Columbia, the Lincoln Club of Denver, Colorado, and the Creve Coeur Club of Peoria.

As an advocate Colonel Chiperfield perhaps has few equals and no superiors in the courts, on the stump or in the halls of legislation. His personal magnetism, his attractive personality, his great storehouse of information, and his wonderful voice, all contribute to the success of his achievements in life, and have contributed to send him to the halls of our national Congress. He was nurtured in a republican home and the policies of this grand old party have been sacred to him through life. Sometimes differing from other leaders upon essential matters of public policy, he has not always yielded to the judgment of the majority, and has not always been proven mistaken when adverse judgments have been registered against him. He has carried his message to the people of Illinois in his several campaigns in recent years, and he has faced audiences upon political occasions in many of the states of the Union. Many of his addresses are notable in the annals of the locality where they were delivered, one of them being the one he gave the people of Quincy, Illinois, upon the anniversary of the birth of Abraham Lincoln. Another one of his notable addresses was the one he delivered before the Illinois Press Association, at which time he appeared to great advantage. He is ever in his element when addressing an audience of his fellow citizens, and it makes little difference what the occasion or subject may be, Burnett M. Chiperfield always brings inspiration to it, and leaves it with the feeling that it was good to be there.

On November 12, 1895, Colonel Chiperfield married, at Canton, Illinois, Miss Clara Louise Ross, a daughter of Dr. Pike C. Ross. Doctor Ross belongs to the oldest family of Fulton County, and he married Margaret Irwin, a daughter of Judge Irwin, of Fulton County. Mrs. Chiperfield was born in Canton, and was graduated from its high school. She was one of four children born to her parents. Colonel and Mrs. Chiperfield have the following children: Robert B., who was graduated from Harvard University, was admitted to the bar in 1925, and is now engaged in practice with his father's firm; Claud B., who is a junior in Syracuse University, New York; and Margaret Ross, who attended the Ward-Belmont School, of Nashville, Tennessee, and Wellesley College, the famous New England educational institution.

JAMES EDMUND COLEMAN, M. D. Genius may be the motive power of success, but many who take the trouble to study the lives and leading characteristics of the men of the country who have accomplished something are led to believe that experience and sound judgment must be combined with natural inclination to produce the best results. In the majority of cases where a man has risen above his fellows it will be found that his rise has come gradually through persistent fighting in spite of all opposition. There are many qualities which help to form character, such as self-reliance, conscientiousness, energy and honesty, and they all work together to produce the highest standing and most satisfactory rewards. The above is certainly true of the professional career of Dr. James Edmund Coleman, of Canton. In no other profession is the true character of a man brought out so prominently as that of medicine, and as he really is, so is he held by his professional associates. All who have the honor of Doctor Coleman's acquaintance admit that he is respected, honored and beloved, not only by his associates but by those to whom he is a ministering friend. He made an enviable record professionally in the World war, and he is equally useful in his home community as a good citizen and upright man.

Doctor Coleman was born in Fulton County, February 28, 1863, a son of Ezra Coleman. The Coleman family was founded in the American colonies by Noah Coleman, who settled in Massachusetts in 1630, ten years after the landing of the Pilgrims. Later he went to Deerfield, Connecticut, and was one of the survivors of the Deerfield massacre, in which so many of the settlers were killed by the Indians. The line of descent from him to Doctor Coleman is as follows: John, Noah, Benjamin, John and Ezra. Benjamin Coleman, great-grandfather of Doctor Coleman, was a soldier in the American Revolution, in which fifteen bearing the name were under arms in the Colonial army.

Ezra Coleman was born in New Jersey, in 1818, and came to Illinois in 1826, being brought here by his parents, who made the journey in the historical "covered wagon" of the period. John Coleman, the grandfather of Doctor Coleman, brought with him a stock of goods from New York City, and with it opened the first store at Canton. In addition to being a merchant he was a manufacturer of axes, operated a gristmill, later was a banker, and during all of the time he was developing into the leading business man of the settlement he was also engaged in farming. For many years he was connected with practically every local activity, and to him is due the credit for much of the early prosperity of Canton. His death occurred about 1843, and he is buried in the Canton Cemetery. His wife, Elizabeth, was a French lady, a member of the nobility, who, during the French Revolution, managed to escape, after horrifying experiences in which she saw her relatives murdered. She was spared the same fate through a happy chance which enabled her to get away dressed in the garments of a peasant boy. A servant, faithful to the family, hurried her away to Holland, and from there she went to England, there taking the name of Pool. She was reared by an English governess. Her escape from massacre was not more wonderful than that of her husband's ancestor, Noah Coleman, so many years previously. He happened to be away from home when the Indians descended upon the little Deerfield settlement. Two sons, Noah and John, a daughter, Anna, and an infant, together with their mother, were captured by the Indians. The infant was later murdered, the mother died of the shock, but the other children were ransomed by the father.

Ezra Coleman was a farmer throughout his life. Too many family responsibilities kept him from enlisting for service during the war between the states, and he was not active in politics. He married Sarah Beard, a daughter of Philip Beard, a soldier of the War of 1812, who was issued a land grant in Illinois as recompense for his service. His remains now lie in Canton Cemetery. Ezra Coleman and his wife had the following children born to their marriage: Oscar, Dora, Mrs. Alice Fidler, Mrs. Louella Meeker, Charles, Frank and Doctor Coleman, whose name heads this review. Mrs. Coleman died in 1864.

Doctor Coleman was reared at Canton, and after he had completed his studies in the grade and high schools of this city he entered Rush Medical College, and was graduated therefrom with an honorary degree, and that of Doctor of Medicine. His entire professional experience has been gained at Canton, where he is accepted as one of the most able medical practitioners in this part of the state. During the World war he was very active as a member of the draft board, examining soldiers, and he was also a member of the Reserves. Other than exerting his right of suffrage, he has not participated in politics, and in national matters he is a republican. He belongs to the Canton Rotary Club and the Canton Chamber of Commerce, is a park commissioner of Canton, and served on the Canton School Board for seven years, for five of these years having been its president. He is a thirty-second degree Mason, and belongs to the Independent Order of Odd Fellows, the Knights of Pythias, and the Benevolent and Protective Order of Elks, and is a delegate to the Grand Lodge of the Knights of Pythias, and holds offices in the other fraternities. Doctor Coleman has been city health officer and county physician of Fulton County, and belongs to the Fulton County Medical Society, the Illinois State Medical Society and the American Medical Association, and is a fellow of the American College of Surgeons. He is also a member of the Civil Legion. For the past thirty years he has been surgeon for the International Harvester Company of Canton and the P. and O. Works.

On September 27, 1887, Doctor Coleman married at Canton Miss Nettie Porter, a daughter of Lafayette Porter, and granddaughter of a Revolutionary hero, through whom she is a member of the local chapter of the Daughters of the American Revolution. This ancestor was in the battle of Bunker Hill, enlisting for service from Massachusetts. Mrs. Coleman was educated at Canton, where her father was a well-known figure as a painter. Doctor and Mrs. Coleman have one son, Dr. Everett Porter Coleman, a noted surgeon, who is engaged in practice with his father at Canton.

Dr. Everett Porter Coleman was born September 10, 1891, and was graduated from the Canton High School, and from the medical department of the University of Illinois, with the degree of Doctor of Medicine. Following his graduation from the university he took an internship at Cook County Hospital, Chicago, Illinois. With this country's entry into the World war he offered his services to the government, was commissioned a captain, and was sent to France, where he was stationed at Evacuation Hospital No. 4. During the latter part of the war he was on duty for twelve hours out of the twenty-four for three months, and during the greater part of each daily period of service was operating. Following the signing of the armistice he was returned home, and was honorably discharged. Returning to Canton, he entered upon an active practice with his father. He is a member of the staff of Graham Hospital, Canton, as is his father, and is a thirty-second degree Mason, an Odd Fellow, Knight of Pythias, a Modern Woodman and an Elk, and also belongs to the American Legion. He is also a fellow of the American College of Surgeons.

Dr. Everett Porter Coleman married Miss Gladys Hough, and they have two daughters, Eleanor and Louise.

PAUL KERZ, county judge of Jo Daviess County, has for many years successfully practiced law at Galena and is a member of two of the prominent pioneer families in the northwestern corner of Illinois.

Judge Kerz was born at Galena April 27, 1872, son of Paul and Barbara (Yunker) Kerz. His father was born near Mainz, Germany, and about 1854 came to America, and after stopping for a time at Buffalo, New York, came on to Galena in 1855. He settled near Galena at what was then known as the California Diggins. He soon entered the river service and with his brothers built a steamboat named the Charley Rogers, which was engaged in freight and passenger traffic between Bellevue, Iowa, and Galena, making daily trips. Afterwards the Kerz brothers owned the Sterling, and when this was sold to W. J. Young & Company, lumber dealers, Paul Kerz entered the service of the Young Company. This was about 1867, and he continued with that organization until his death on December 19, 1893. He was captain of boats and superintendent of the fleet of the Young Company and superintended the building of many of their boats, including the Douglas Bordman and W. J. Young, Jr. Barbara Yunker, mother of Judge Kerz, was born and reared near Manz, Germany, and was educated in that country. Her father, Philip Yunker, came to America about 1855, landing at New Orleans. His mother died on the boat from cholera on the voyage up the Mississippi to Galena. Philip Yunker acquired mineral lands in the California Diggins near Galena and spent the rest of his life as a lead ore operator.

Judge Paul Kerz attended parochial and public and high schools at Galena, graduating from high school in 1891. He studied law in the University of Wisconsin, taking his degree in 1894, and in July of that year he opened his law office at Galena. For over thirty years he has been one of the able representatives of his profession in that city. He formed a partnership with John J. Jones, which continued for sixteen years, until Mr. Jones, on account of ill health, retired in 1900. Since then Judge Kerz has practiced alone. He is a director in the Merchants National Bank of Galena and was a member of the Board of Education from 1896 to 1902. He was then elected city attorney, serving eight years, and after an interval of two years was again elected and held the office six years more. In April, 1925, he was elected to fill an unexpired term as county judge, and in 1926 was renominated. He is the first democrat to hold the office of county judge in Jo Daviess County. Judge Kerz during the World war was chairman of the Four Minute Speakers and a member of the Local Draft Board. To the utmost of his ability he has discharged his obligations as a citizen and as a public spirited member of his community. He is a Catholic, is affiliated with the Knights of Columbus, B. P. O. Elks, the Izaak Walton League, was the first president of the Kiwanis Club, and a member of the Jo Daviess, Illinois State and American Bar Associations.

Judge Kerz married at Dubuque, Iowa, October 3, 1899, Miss Eleanor Trout, who was reared and educated at Dubuque. Her parents were Paul and Louisa (Yager) Trout. Her father was one of the leading business men of Dubuque, and many of that city's foremost institutions reflect his wise management and participation. He was largely instrumental in securing the location at Dubuque of the enameling works. He was a director in several lumber mills, and had a prominent part in organizing and bringing harmony to the conflicting elements that first constituted the Dubuque Malting Company, which became one of the city's largest and most profitable enterprises. He was vice president and director of the company for several years. He was also manager of the Iowa Coffin Company and was cashier and president of the German Trust & Savings Bank. He held the office of county treasurer, and in that capacity won the admiration of the financial interests by the ability with which he disposed of Court House Bonds and paid off the floating indebtedness of the county. He was the father of the following children, Eleanor, Frank, Louisa, Matilda, Mamie, Edward, Erma and Adam H. Paul Trout died May 28, 1898. Judge Kerz lost his first wife by death January 31, 1908. Of the children of this marriage the oldest is Paul A., now associated with the Keller Electric Company at Dubuque. Marita was educated in the Galena High School, St. Clair Academy and the Gregg Business School, and

is now in office work in Chicago. Louise graduated from the Galena High School, is a graduate nurse from Mercy Hospital and is following her profession in Chicago. Eleanor M. graduated from St. Mary's College at Prairie du Chien, Wisconsin, and is now in a nurses' training class in the Michael Reese Hospital in Chicago. The son Arnold died on Decoration Day of 1925, being a member of the class of 1924 in the Galena High School. Judge Kerz on June 6, 1916, married, near Crown Point, Indiana, Miss Sylvia McKinney, who was a graduate nurse, daughter of William and Catherine McKinney, of Chicago. Her father was a mining man and for an umber of years was interested in mines in Cripple Creek, Colorado.

SAMUEL SCHWARTZ, of Waukegan, has enjoyed all the honors paid to a substantial business man, and to one who has mingled public spirit with all his activities so that his character to the public eye represents generosity as well as forcefulness in action and achievement.

Mr. Schwartz has been a resident of Waukegan since 1889. He was born in Jassy, Rumania, a town that figured prominently in World war annals, June 8, 1865, son of David and Elizabeth Schwartz. His father spent most of his life in Rumania and was a cattle shipper and for many years operated a stock yard in Jassy. In 1915 he came to America and lived several years near his son in Waukegan, and about a year before his death went to New York City, where he died in 1906.

Samuel Schwartz had a public school education in his native country, and had some experience in the retail meat business at Jassy. In 1883 he married, sold out his business and came to America. For a few months he was a retail meat merchant in New York City, but lost all his capital in that venture. From New York he went on to Chicago, and there found employment with the Anglo-American Provision Company at $1.25 a day. For four years he worked for wages, gradually getting experience and a modest capital, with which in 1888 he embarked in the meat business again in Chicago. This, too, was unprofitable, and in 1889 he arrived at Waukegan and for about four years was employed by the F. J. Deuse Brewing Company, and then became a wholesale distributor at Waukegan for the Pabst Brewing Company. He maintained his active connections with the Pabst Company for twenty-six years.

In the meantime Mr. Schwartz, in 1913, engaged in the furniture business, starting a small store which became the nucleus and foundation for what subsequently became the leading furniture business in northeastern Illinois outside of Chicago. After a few years he established a branch store at Kenosha, Wisconsin, and after a fire destroyed his Waukegan store in March, 1924, he rebuilt and re-established a store second to none in appointment, stock and service. Mr. Schwartz has shown a capacity for handling a great variety of business interests. He has been a regular investor in Waukegan real estate, owns a large amount of business property, and has built and remodeled over a score of buildings since he came to Waukegan. He gave the city its first legitimate theatre, and he was one of the founders of the Northern Illinois Industrial Association, which has provided publicity, finance and general cooperation for industries seeking favorable locations in this section of Illinois. At least half a dozen of the large factories now at Waukegan were influenced to locate there through the Northern Illinois Industrial Association. Mr. Schwartz served both as vice president and president of the association.

He was responsible for organizing the first Jewish Congregation in Lake County. This was in 1896. He and his friends organized and built the Church of the Congregation Am Echod at Waukegan. The splendid service he has rendered through all the years in behalf of the institution was gratefully and fitly memorialized in the annual meeting of the Congregation on September 14, 1926, when an official record of the society closed with the following words: Samuel Schwartz, the father of the Congregation, the leader of civic, social and religious affairs of the Jewish community of Waukegan, was honored with the office of honorary president for life, and he will be looked upon as a guiding light in the future development of the Congregation Am Echod. This honor was paid him after it had been recalled that Mr. Schwartz had started the Congregation with only thirty members, and the association had since grown to a membership of 125, and his election as honorary life president coincides with a movement now well under way for the building of a handsome Temple on Sheridan Road that will serve as the home of one of the most active organizations representing people of the Hebrew faith in northeastern Illinois.

Mr. Schwartz has been a member of the Elks Lodge since shortly after its organization, is a member of the Knights of Pythias, the B'nai B'rith, the Covenant Club of Chicago, and is a republican in politics.

Mr. Schwartz has found his greatest happiness in his home circle. He married at Jassy, Rumania, June 10, 1883, shortly before setting out for America, Mary Jacobson, who was reared and educated there and shared with her husband the various vicissitudes, good fortune and bad fortune, and contributed to the notable success he made as a business man in Waukegan. She died June 11, 1925. Her father, Harry Jacobson, was a metal work contractor in Rumania. Mr. and Mrs. Schwartz had seven children, the only daughter dying young. The six sons are Jacob, Emanuel, Dr. Benjamin, Abe, William and Harry, and all but the youngest of these were enlisted in the service of the government during the World war. Jacob, the oldest son, graduated from Lake Forest College and Harvard Law School, and is now in Chicago, an associate of the distinguished law firm of Mayer, Meyer, Austrian & Platt. He married Clarissa Claster, of Harrisburg, Pennsylvania, and has two children, Betty and Norman. The two sons Emanuel and William, were educated in the Waukegan High School, William being a graduate of the University of Wisconsin, and they are now together in the real estate business at Waukegan. Dr. Benjamin was educated in the Lake Forest College, graduated in medicine from Northwestern University in 1916, and was attached to the Wesley Hospital in Chicago until the World war, when he volunteered and was commissioned a lieutenant, remaining in the service until 1919, going overseas to France, where he was promoted to the rank of captain. He is now one of the leading physicians at Kenosha. The sons Abe and Harry finished their high school work at Waukegan. Harry attended the University of Wisconsin, and they are now associated with their father in the furniture business. Abe married Myrtle Zediker of Waukegan, and has two sons, Bobby and Dick. The family is one of the oldest and most distinguished in the city and very highly regarded by the entire community.

JONATHAN JONES, father of Walter Clyde Jones the Chicago attorney, was one of the earliest settlers on the Iowa side of the Mississippi River, locating in the southwestern corner of the present State of Iowa many years before there was sufficient population to qualify the country for statehood.

Jonathan Jones was born in Harrison County, Ohio, in 1815. His family was one of the many Quaker families to settle in that section of Southeastern Ohio. Jonathan Jones himself exemplified the manner and character of the Society of Friends all his life. In 1833 he started west, traveling down the Ohio River and up the Mississippi, leaving the river in the extreme southeastern corner of Iowa at Keokuk. Some miles west of the Mississippi he preempted Government land, and there laid out the townsite and founded the village of Pilot Grove, named for an Indian grove of beech, elm and oak trees. For his first home Jonathan Jones built a small log house. He lived close neighbors to the Indians, but like other Quakers had no trouble with them. As other white settlers came in he was chosen to act as their representative not only in settling disputes but in marketing their produce, which was at first hauled to Keokuk and later transported down the Mississippi to St. Louis. Soon after the close of the Civil war and about the time he retired from active farming he founded the village of Pilot Grove, where he erected one of the first brick houses of this western country. It was a commodious residence for those pioneer days. The brick was made at Keokuk and hauled overland. Jonathan Jones in 1873 removed to Keokuk in order to give his children better educational advantages. He had begun his political affiliations as a whig and became one of the first members of the republican party in Iowa.

Jonathan Jones died at Keokuk in 1883. He had two daughters and four sons, one of them being Walter Clyde Jones, of Chicago. Sarah Buffington, his wife, a native of Fayette County, Pennsylvania, died in 1914.

WALTER CLYDE JONES, a resident of Chicago since about 1889, first educated for the profession of mechanical and electrical engineering, has practiced law for thirty years, specializing in patent law, and has exhibited other marked gifts and talents by important service and attainments in the public life of his city and state. In the political history of Illinois his name is associated with several reform movements and measures. He was progressive republican candidate for governor in 1912.

He was born at Pilot Grove, Iowa, December 27, 1870, son of Jonathan and Sarah (Buffington) Jones. During his early childhood the family moved to Keokuk, where he was educated in the public schools. From there he entered Iowa State College at Ames, where he was graduated in 1891 with high honors in mechanical and electrical engineering. During vacation periods he had worked in the iron mining districts of Northern Michigan. While there he assisted in installing the first electric lights that were ever installed in mines, and even at that early date Mr. Jones learned that progressiveness is not always popular. When the lights were turned on the miners went out on strike, refusing to use the brilliance of electric lamps to illuminate the dangers of their work. On coming to Chicago in 1892, after graduation, Mr. Jones was employed in engineering and electrical work, chiefly with the Aeromotor Company and the Edison Company. In 1893 he was awarded a prize by the Electrical Engineering Magazine for an essay on "Electricity at the World's Fair." An article he wrote many years ago, first read before the Chicago Electrical Association and since published and republished, is regarded as a classic on the subject of the "Evolution of the Telephone." Mr. Jones was one of the founders of the Chicago Electrical Association and in 1896 was chosen its president.

In the meantime Mr. Jones was studying law in the evening sessions of the Chicago College of Law, then the law department of Lake Forest University. He graduated in 1895. His graduation thesis was entitled "Trusts and Trade Monopolies," and was published in a number of law journals. While a law student he frequently served as an expert witness in litigation involving electrical and mechanical questions. Thus his early experience prepared him for and inclined him to the practice of patent law. He began practice with an office in the Chicago Title & Trust Building in 1896, and three years later formed a partnership with Keene H. Addington under the name Jones & Addington. He is now senior member of the law firm Jones, Addington, Ames & Seibold, with offices both in Chicago and New York. Mr. Jones in the past thirty years has been identified with the general range of law practice, but chiefly in cases involving patent and corporation law. He has acted as counsel for a number of large corporations. One of his early cases involving matters of general popular interest at this time as well as then was his service in behalf of an automobile company in 1898 to contest the ordinance of the Board of South Park Commissioners at Chicago excluding automobiles from the boulevards and parks on account of danger from frightened horses. After a bitter fight in the courts the ordinance was declared void. It was perhaps the first important decision affecting the rights of automobiles on streets and highways.

Mr. Jones has been an important contributor to the literature of the law. He and his partner, the late Keene H. Addington, were joint authors and editors of Jones & Addington's Annotated Statutes of Illinois, published in six volumes; Illinois Notes or Cyclopedia of Illinois Law, published in fifteen volumes; and Appellate Court Reports of Illinois, in seventy volumes.

Mr. Jones was one of the organizers of the Benjamin Electric Manufacturing Company of Chicago, of which he is a director and vice president. He also helped organize and is a director of the Benjamin Electric, Limited, of London, and the Benjamin Electric Manufacturing Company, Limited, of Canada. The Benjamin Electric Manufacturing Company furnished a large part of the lighting equipment used on ships built by the Government during the World war.

Mr. Jones for a number of years lived in the Hyde Park district of Chicago and was one of several notable leaders in Illinois public life to come from there. He was elected from the Fifth District to the Illinois Senate in 1906 and served two terms, in the Forty-fifth, Forty-sixth, Forty-seventh and Forty-eighth General Assemblies. During his second term he was leader of the republican majority of the Senate. Senator Jones was author of the first direct primary law of Illinois, of the law limiting hours of labor of women to ten hours a day, and of the rules for reformed legislative procedure adopted by the Senate and later by the House, insuring majority control, and was a leader in the movements for civil service reform. Before going to the Senate he had helped organize and was influentially identified with the Legislative Voters League. and is now a member of the Executive Committee. He was a member of the Chicago Charter Convention which drafted the proposed charter for Chicago in 1906-07. His political principles and attitude toward political problems naturally allied him with and made him an admirer of Theodore Roosevelt and his political principles, and he was a leader in the organization of the progressive party in 1912. The following sentence is from a letter written by Roosevelt to him: "In this great fight for elementary justice and decency for fair play and industry no less than in the political world, and for honesty everywhere, there is a body of men to whom I feel peculiarly grateful, not only personally but for what they have done for the people as a whole—you come high among them."

During the World war Mr. Jones was a member of the War Industries Board. For thirty years he has regularly taken part as a speaker in municipal, state and national campaigns. His home in recent years has been in Evanston. He is a member of the Chicago, State and American Bar Associations, the Union League Club, University Club, Hamilton Club, City Club, Press Club and Literary Club of Chicago, Evanston University Club, Evanston Country Club and Evanston Golf Club, Lawyers' Club and Engineers' Club of New York and Cosmos Club of Washington. He also belongs to the Franklin Institute of Philadelphia and the American Society of Mechanical Engineers. His favorite recreations are horseback riding and golf. He assisted in organizing and was president of the Equestrian Association of Chicago and also in organizing the Evanston Saddle Club of which he was the first president.

Mr. Jones married, in 1896, Miss Emma Boyd of Paullina, Iowa. They have three children, Walter Clyde, Jr., a graduate of Yale; Helen Gwendolyn, a student at Smith College, and Clarence Boyd, a student at the Hill School. Mr. Jones has a summer and country residence, known as Clydellyn, on Gull Lake, near Battle Creek, Michigan.

EARL D. DEAN was superintendent of the Township High School at Rochelle. His experience as an educator has been in several states as well as in Illinois and he is the type of high minded and progressive school man.

He was born at Binghamton, New York, June 1, 1892. His grandfather, Ransom S. Dean, was a Pennsylvania farmer. Wallace H. Dean, father of Earl D. Dean, was born near New Milford, Pennsylvania, attended school there, took a business course, and has given his later years to active work in education. He has taught manual training in a number of schools, such as Olive Hill, Kentucky, and is now a teacher in the Meisenheimer School in North Carolina. He married Minnie Greene, who was born at Troy, New York, and was educated in public schools of that city, also attending the Girls Seminary. She has been interested in missionary work and teaching and is now associated with her husband in Meisenheimer School.

Earl D. Dean attended grammar and high schools at Binghamton, New York, graduating from high school in 1911. In 1916 he received the Ph. B. degree at Valparaiso University and a year later was awarded the A. B. degree at the same institution. He is a member of the Phi Delta Kappa honor fraternity. After completing his training at Valparaiso he was a teacher in the high school at Philip, South Dakota. On August 21, 1918, he went into training at Camp Custer, Michigan, held the rank of sergeant major and remained there until April 1, 1919, when he was discharged. During the remainder of the school year he was supervisor of English in the high school at Clinton, Indiana. He was for one year principal of the high school at Weiser, Idaho. Following this he was superintendent of schools at Edgemont, South Dakota, for a period of two years, and in June, 1922, came to Rochelle as superintendent of the Rochelle Township High School, completing four years in this position. In June, 1926, he was elected to the principalship of the James Whitcomb Riley Junior High School at South Bend, Indiana. The James Whitcomb Riley Junior High School is one of the outstanding junior high schools in the country, having a teaching staff of some fifty teachers and a student enrollment of 1,400. The building is complete in every respect and far surpasses many of the smaller colleges in the country today. The James Whitcomb Riley Junior High School is often referred to as the "Show Place" of South Bend, and rightly so. In the meantime, by work in summer vacations at Northwestern University, he was awarded the Master of Arts degree in 1926.

Mr. Dean is a member of the B. P. O. Elks, the American Legion, and is a member of the

Methodist Church. He married at Valparaiso, Indiana, August 20, 1917, Miss Mildred Florence Stoner. She graduated from the Valparaiso High School and took several summer courses at Purdue University. Until her marriage Miss Stoner taught for several years in the schools of Indiana. Her parents, George A. and Mae (Carpenter) Stoner, reside near Valparaiso, both having been born and reared in Indiana. Her father is the owner of several large farms near Valparaiso, one of them being the original homestead of his grandfather. Mr. and Mrs. Dean have one son, Jack Donald Dean.

CHARLES MANNING FISH. Among the more notable real estate men of Joliet who have established reputations for integrity and have achieved notable and well-merited success in their calling, none are more worthy of mention than Charles Manning Fish. A resident of the county seat for many years, he fully exemplifies the alert, energetic character for which the people of his city have been noted, and in addition to having played a prominent part in business affairs has fully discharged the duties of citizenship.

Mr. Fish was born at Joliet, August 1, 1859, and is a son of Henry and Mary V. (Manning) Fish, and traces his ancestry back on the paternal side to John Alden and on both sides to Colonial days in America. His direct ancestor, William Manning, came from England to America in 1634, taking up his residence at Cambridge, Massachusetts, and later being selected, with Deacon Cooper, to rebuild old Harvard College, in 1672. The paternal grandparents of Mr. Fish were Calvin Bacon and Clarissa (Sterling) Fish, the former born at Norwich, Connecticut, December 15, 1779, and the latter at Sterling City, Lime, Connecticut, February 18, 1870. They became farming people of Jefferson County, New York, and Calvin Bacon Fish died at Rutland, New York, in 1830. The maternal grandparents of Mr. Fish were Joel and Diza (Jenkins) Manning, the former born at Andover, Vermont, October 9, 1793, and the latter in Tennessee, October 15, 1806. She was a sister of Elizabeth who married Dr. John Logan, father of Gen. John A. Logan; and of Hon. Alexander M. Jenkins, who served as lieutenant governor of Illinois in 1834. Mr. and Mrs. Manning made their way by boat and Indian trails to St. Louis and finally located at Brownsville, Jackson County, Illinois, where Mr. Manning engaged in the practice of law for some years. He was appointed by the governor as secretary of the Board of Commissioners of the Illinois and Michigan Canal, and during the early days of Chicago resided on the present site of the Conway Building corner of Clark Street and Washington in that city. When the office of the commissioners was moved to Lockport, Illinois, he took up his residence there and continued to make his home in that city until 1861, when he and Mrs. Manning moved to Joliet. At that place Mrs. Manning died November 27, 1861. Mr. Manning died January 8, 1869.

Henry Fish was born at Watertown, New York, December 19, 1819, and married February 1, 1854, Mary V. Manning, who was born at Brownsville, Illinois. He came to Joliet in 1834, and Mr. Fish engaged in the real estate, lumber and grain business, with which he was identified during the remainder of his life. In 1873 he became the organizer of the Will County National Bank, of which he was the first president, and later organized a private bank, which he operated for many years. He died June 22, 1899, his widow surviving him until October 3, 1903. They were the parents of the following children: George Manning, born January 27, 1855, who died August 15, 1917; Jennie Clara, born March 31, 1857, who died September 3, 1858; Charles Manning, of this review; and Henry Manning, born February 12, 1862, who died December 11, 1915. After meeting with financial reverses with his brothers, in 1893 Henry Manning Fish took up the study of medicine and was graduated from Hahnemann Medical College, Chicago. He spent 18 months at the renowned hospital in Vienna where he specialized in the study of diseases of the eye. He returned to Chicago and became a noted eye specialist, and to him the present successful treatment of eye disease is largely indebted.

Henry Fish took a great interest in public affairs and was a delegate to the national convention of the republican party which nominated Abraham Lincoln for the presidency. Mrs. Fish was also a woman of attainments, and for many years served as a trustee of Northwestern University. As a small child she witnessed the parade past their home at Clark and Washington streets, Chicago, of the Indians who received payment in money for the site of Chicago, and often related to her children in later years the ludicrous appearance of the Indian princess who rode a horse astride, wearing proudly a man's silk hat. Mrs. Fish's sister, Mrs. Cornelia A. Miller, the widow of Edmund Miller, of Waterloo, Iowa, moved to Joliet in 1883. She was a world traveler and collector of rare curios and in 1886 made a trip to the Orient in company with Bishop and Mrs. Warren to inspect missions of the Methodist Episcopal Church bringing back with her many specimens of oriental art, including rare porcelains and lacquer work of great value. She was a generous contributor to the Methodist Episcopal Church and gave $30,000 to Garrett Biblical Institute of Northwestern University. In 1896 she became an invalid and so continued until her death April 14, 1906. During that time she was cared for by her nephew, Charles Manning Fish, in her beautiful Joliet stone residence at 205 Richards Street, at the corner of Lincoln, which was bequeathed to Mr. Fish at the time of his beloved aunt's death. Mr. Fish has since torn down this residence, considered the finest in Joliet, and erected a large apartment building, metropolitan in all respects, where he resides with his family.

Charles Manning Fish attended the public schools of Joliet and after his graduation from high school became a student at the Pennsylvania Military College, from which he was graduated as a member of the class of 1882, with the degree of Civil Engineer, and was one of the six honor students whose names were presented to the governor of Pennsylvania, and the leader of his class. At the time of his graduation he and his brothers embarked in the manufacture of all kinds of wire, and built the largest and best equipped

wire drawing plant in this part of the country. At the end of the year 1892 through the machinations of several designing business men their wire mill and other business properties were swept away. Soon after Mrs. Miller, the aunt of Mr. Fish, suffered a stroke of apoplexy and Mr. Fish devoted his time for the next ten years to the care of his invalid aunt and her business. Afterwards Mr. Fish became greatly interested in suburban real estate and opened an office at Joliet, where he has since been engaged in a constantly growing business. He has been identified with a number of large and important transactions. Mr. Fish has been for over fifty years a member of the Methodist Episcopal Church, is a republican in his political views, and has been a member of the Sons of Colonial Wars, Sons of the American Revolution, Mayflower Society of Illinois, Midlothian Country Club and Joliet Country Club for many years.

On February 1, 1887, Mr. Fish was united in marriage with Louise Steel, who was born at Joliet, September 23, 1866, and died February 8, 1892, daughter of William A. and Frances Louise (Sanger) Steel, and to this union there was born one daughter: Mary Louise, born June 5, 1889, at Joliet, who married Paul W. King, of Evanston, Illinois, June 4, 1910, and has one daughter Frances Louise, born April 30, 1911. Mr. Fish was again married, May 18, 1898, to Miss Helen E. Thompson, who was born April 8, 1872, at Joliet, daughter of Maj. J. M. and Mary J. (Davidson) Thompson, the former born at London, Canada, October 22, 1832, and the latter in Will County, Illinois, January 15, 1840. To this union there were born four children: Jennie, born February 20, 1899, who died March 30, 1908; Manning, born November 20, 1903; Charles M., Jr., born May 11, 1906, a student at the University of Illinois; and Allen Miller, born July 9, 1907.

WALTER C. ALEXANDER. In connection with the industrial, public utility and commercial affairs generally of southern Illinois no name has appeared more frequently in the last quarter of a century than that of Walter C. Alexander, of Murphysboro, whose career comprises an unusual range of business achievements.

He was born at Glasgow, Scotland, May 24, 1865, and three years later, in 1868, his parents, James and Jessie Alexander, came to America, living for a time at Philadelphia, later in St. Louis, and in 1870 establishing their home at Murphysboro, Illinois. James Alexander was an iron worker and followed his trade at these several points, and for a brief time was master mechanic for the Burlington Railway at Galesburg, Illinois. On locating at Murphysboro he became a general merchant, and in 1874 he and his brother, Walter Alexander, established the Alexander Brothers' Foundry & Machine Shop. They made this the leading establishment of its kind in Jackson County. The business was discontinued by the brothers in 1896. James Alexander died October 4, 1899, and his wife, on January 4, 1908. Mr. Walter C. Alexander had a sister, Janet M., who married Edward Morrison, for many years engaged in the office and school supply business at Boston, Massachusetts, where Mrs. Morrison died January 8, 1926.

Walter C. Alexander began his education in the public schools at Murphysboro. His youthful experience included an apprenticeship in his father's shop and foundry, work as a telegraph operator with a coal company, employment as a chainman and in other capacities in railroad surveying and for several years the general practice of civil and mining engineering at Duquoin, Illinois. On returning to Murphysboro he became manager and superintendent and a director of the Murphysboro Water Works, Electric, Gas and Light Company, serving five years. After that the scope of his enterprise was greatly enlarged. Mr. Alexander organized the Chicago and Herrin Coal Company at Herrin, becoming its president, was also president of the Carterville-Herrin Coal Company, but about ten years ago disposed of his interests as a coal operator in Williamson County. He organized and was president of the Chew Mercantile Company at Herrin, organized and became president of the Anchor Ice & Packing Company of Murphysboro, organized the Murphysboro Construction Company in 1910, became president of the Republican Era Printing Company, publishers of the leading daily newspaper at Murphysboro, and has been an executive official or directors in the Murphysboro Telephone Company, Ohio & Mississippi Valley Telephone Company, Murphysboro Electric Railway, Light, Heat & Power Company, Murphysboro and Southern Illinois Electric Railway Company, the City National Bank of Herrin. In 1917 he and associates constructed the interurban line from Murphysboro to Carbondale, and he is now manager of that line.

Mr. Alexander has been active in the Murphysboro Commercial Association, has been a trustee of the First Presbyterian Church of Murphysboro, for several terms was on the Murphysboro Board of Education, is a republican, member of the Masonic fraternity, Knights of Pythias and B. P. O. Elks.

He married, November 22, 1905, Miss Martha M. Forbes, daughter of Charles and Sophia B. (Trowbridge) Forbes. They have one son, Forbes, born January 4, 1907.

REV. WALTER HENRY SPEEMAN took the orders of priesthood in the Catholic Church twenty-one years ago, has given faithful service in various localities, both in Canada and the United States, and is now pastor of Mother of Dolors Church at Vandalia, Illinois.

He was born at Krefeld, Rhineland, Germany, January 25, 1881, son of Franz and Katharine (Terhoeven) Speeman, grew up at Krefeld, and from early youth his education was directed with a view to his entering the church. After grammar school and college at Krefeld, where he received the B. A. degree in 1899, he entered Holy Cross College at Uden, Holland, and took his philosophical course in Immensee at Lucerne, Switzerland, where he was graduated Bachelor of Science in 1902. From there he came to America and pursued his theology in the Grand Seminary (Lavalle University) at Montreal, Canada. He was graduated in 1906, and on June 29th of that year was ordained to the priesthood by Most Rev. Archbishop Ad. Longevin, D. D., Archbishop of St. Boniface, Manitoba, Canada. He was ordained for the Diocese of Alton, Illinois. His early service included two years as auxiliary professor at St. Joseph's College at St. Boniface, Manitoba, Pro Tempore Missionary in the Diocese of Fargo, North Dakota, and four years and six months as missionary in the Diocese of Springfield, Massachusetts. He was also assistant pastor of the Holy Family Church at Union Hill, New Jersey, in the Newark Diocese. Father Speeman's first pastoral work in Illinois was at St. Alphonsus Church at Brighton, where he remained three years. On October 15, 1925, he became pastor of the Mother of Dolors Catholic Church at Vandalia and is not only a very energetic priest, but a very popular citizen of that historic city of Illinois. Father Speeman is a fourth degree Knight of Columbus, member of the Vandalia Chamber of Commerce, Rotary Club and Country Club.

GUSTAVUS FRANKLIN SWIFT. The first slaughter house erected in Chicago was built by Archibald Clybourn in 1827, on the south bank of the north branch of the Chicago River, near what was known as the Bloomingdale Road, and the original aim of the proprietor was the killing of cattle to supply the needs and meet the requirements of the military garrison at Fort Dearborn. It was built of logs and was followed by a frame structure which remained standing for more than fifty years. That was the real start of the meat packing business in Chicago, which eventually was to grow to such stupendous proportions. The idea of the establishment of the Union Stock Yards took tangible form in 1865, when a prospectus was issued which resulted in subscriptions for stock to the extent of $1,000,000. To trace the history of the packing business, year by year, would prove a wearisome repetition of the same story, and it suffices to say that it is one of steady and almost unexampled growth. From year to year new firms embarked in the business, until today there are approximately fifty meat packing houses centered in the Yards, employing some 50,000 people. One of the greatest of these firms is that of Swift & Company, the founder of which was the late Gustavus Franklin Swift, who from the time of his arrival in Chicago in 1875 until his death in 1903 was one of the city's most forceful business men, sterling citizens and great philanthropists.

Mr. Swift was born at West Sandwich, sometimes called Scussett, now known as Sagamore, Massachusetts, in 1839, a few miles north of Buzzards Bay, and only a mile or two from the southeast boundary of Plymouth County, on what is called the shoulder of Cape Cod. The Massachusetts Swifts have made their home there since 1630, when the first of the family came from England and after a few years at Boston or its vicinity settled at Sandwich. Mr. Swift was in the seventh generation from William and Elizabeth Swyft (as the name was then spelled). The founders of the family doubtless were of Pilgrim sympathies, and formed a part of that first great migration in which about 300 of the "best Puritan families" of England came to the New World and founded the colony of Massachusetts Bay and the city of Boston. The Swifts were for the most part farmers and Gustavus Franklin Swift was in the direct line which had for more than 200 years clung to the soil where the family first settled.

The town of Sandwich was first occupied by white settlers in 1637, a grant of land having been made by Plymouth Colony to a company formed at Lynn. The original settlers were joined by others from Duxbury and Plymouth, and among these was William Swyft, who is believed to have been one of the earliest among them. He lived only until 1642 or 1643, but in the latter year his son William is recorded as one of the sixty-eight men between the ages of sixteen and sixty liable to bear arms. In 1655 this William Swift and three others were engaged to build the town mill, and the same year his name appeared on a subscription for the building of a new meeting-house. Of the forty subscribers only seven gave more than he. Soon thereafter he united with eighteen others in a request to a minister to supply them with preaching, giving him this assurance: "We will not be backward to recompense your labors of love." In 1672 William Swift was one of a committee of seven prominent men who were "requested" to go forward settling and confirming the township with the Indian chiefs and to prevent the town of Barnstable from encroaching on the domains of Sandwich. In 1730, among 136 heads of families, ten were Swifts, these being the recognized people "besides Friends and Quakers," but there were Swifts among the latter also, for Jane Swift had the doubtful honor of being fined ten shillings by this Pilgrim colony for attending Quaker meetings.

Like other families of this early period, the Swifts are to be found in every part of the United States, but many of them lingered long in the Cape Cod community and among these were the forebears of Gustavus F. Swift. His father, another William Swift, was a farmer, and his mother, Sally Sears (Crowell) Swift, was a descendant of Elder William Brewster, one of the best known of the Pilgrim Fathers, and was related, as her name indicates, to two of the leading families of the Cape. Perhaps the most illustrious of her relatives was Barnas Sears, president of Brown University and first secretary or agent of the Peabody Fund. Mr. Swift was born June 24, 1839, the ninth child and fifth son in a family of twelve children. Reared on the farm, he was given only the advantages of a common school education, and the school could not have been of a very high standard, while the months of a farmer's son were restricted as to attendance, and he was only fourteen years of age when he laid aside his few school books. However, it is not to be said that the boyhood and youth of young Swift and his brothers were intolerable, or at least that they ever noticed it, for in addition to the practical education and primitive pleasures of the farm these resourceful, self-reliant and industrious youths enjoyed the facilities for swimming, sailing and fishing in Buzzards Bay, only three miles from their home, as did Barnstable Bay, the woods were at hand for hunting and nutting, and in winter, sleighing, coasting and skating were easily to be found.

A story of the business acumen of the youth is told. He was but a lad when one day he entered the home of his maternal grandfather Crowell and stated: "Grandpa, I will give you forty cents for that old white hen," and when the deal had been accomplished he left the house with his purchase. His grandmother told the relator of the story that he bought a hen almost daily, and found a customer for it somewhere, always making enough to pay him for his trouble in the transaction. He was then only nine years of age, but inspired with business ambitions. When he was fourteen years of age he went to work for his brother, Noble, nine years his senior, and the village butcher. At first he was paid one dollar per week, but this was gradually increased to two dollars per week, and there is a tradition that before he left his brother's employment at the end of two or two and one-half years he was receiving three dollars. At sixteen years of age he exercised his qualities of initiative, ambition, self-reliance and an intuitive genius for business, and started out for himself, although he had little education, no money and no influential friends, and there were perhaps millions of boys in America in 1855 who had far more brilliant prospects. The business opportunities offered to a farmer's son on Cape Cod were next to nothing, save to about one boy in a million. He happened to be that boy, and at sixteen was already one of vision. While he possessed in full degree ambition and courage, his initial efforts were necessarily humble.

Like many youths of that day, and of later times, he turned his eyes longingly toward New York City. His father persuaded him, however, to remain at home by advancing him a capital of twenty dollars, the nucleus for the present stupendous business of Swift & Company. He invested this capital in a heifer, which he killed and dressed and disposed of among the surrounding neighbors, probably netting himself a capital of ten dollars. Thus encouraged, a short time later he secured a loan of $400 from his uncle Paul Crowell, the village storekeeper, went to the Brighton stockyards and bought pigs, and thus cleared up another excellent profit. The business of buying and selling pigs was confined for the most part to two or three months in the spring, when the people were buying shoats to fatten for their own use. During the rest of the year young Swift followed the business of butcher and meat seller at the stockyards at Brighton, and while his capital was small his ambition was large. His method of procedure may prove interesting: On Friday he would buy a fat steer in the Brighton market outside of Boston; Saturday he would slaughter it and hang up the quarters over Sunday; Monday he would load the meat into his old democrat wagon and start for Cape Cod, fifty miles away, and during the rest of the week he would peddle the meat from house to house. Friday he would return to Brighton to start repeating the process. Thus he continued until the winter of 1859-1860, when he opened a modest meat market at Eastham, taking with him his brother, Nathaniel, several years his senior, who had also learned the business under the still older brother Noble.

On January 3, 1861, at Eastham, Mr. Swift was united in marriage with Miss Annie Maria Higgins, a descendant of Richard Higgins, one of the seven original proprietors who settled at Eastham in 1643-44, and not long thereafter returned with his bride to Sagamore and entered the same business, having surrendered his Eastham enterprise to his brother. At Sagamore was born his eldest son, Louis F. Swift, for many years president of the firm of Swift & Company. After several years Mr. Swift moved from Sagamore to Barnstable, where he became the village butcher and extended his knowledge and reputation as an expert judge of cattle. This latter reputation soon caused him to make a further step in his consistent progress, as he began buying and selling cattle, and his butchering business became a side issue. He resided at Barnstable for about eight years, and there were born four more children: Edward Foster; Lincoln, who died there; Annie May and Helen Louise. In 1869 his increasing business called the family away from Barnstable, and they made their home first at Clinton and later at Lancaster, about forty miles west of Boston, in Worcester County. There the fourth son, Charles Henry, was born in 1872. While continuing his cattle buying operations, Mr. Swift also established a meat market at Clinton, a few miles south of Lancaster, where he put his brother Nathaniel in charge. From this point as a center he sent his meat in wagons about the towns of Bristol County, and a little later opened another market at Freetown, between Fall River and Taunton, which he put under the charge of a lieutenant, sending his wagons out among the towns of that community, and, in these undertakings, unconsciously commenced preparing himself for the future, then quite undreamed of, when the field of his operations should embrace the world. During this time, however, he began to get a vision of the possible development of the cattle-buying business in which he had been feeling his way, and looked longingly toward Albany and Buffalo, where great cattle yards had been established.

In 1872 Mr. Swift entered into partnership with James A. Hathaway, who was doing a large business in meat at Boston. Hathaway & Swift combined the dressed-meat business with buying and selling cattle for the Boston market, Mr. Hathaway taking care of the former and Mr. Swift of the latter. Mr. Swift in his capacity soon extended his operations to Albany and Buffalo, and eventually came to the conclusion in the '70s, that if he desired leadership in the cattle business eventually he would have to make his headquarters in Chicago. The firm of Hathaway & Swift was doing well, but Mr. Swift persuaded his partner to consent to the transfer of the cattle-buying department of the business to Chicago, and the year 1875 found him among the cattle-buyers of the Chicago Stock Yards. Mr. Swift soon discovered that the future belonged not to the buyer and seller of cattle, but to the packer, and he quickly decided to enter the meat-packing business. This business, in 1877, when his advent was made, was a totally different affair from what it has since become—different not only in size but in kind. The men engaged in business were essentially pork curers and packers, winter jobs only, and the distributing of the product followed during the succeeding warm weather, when killing and curing could not be done.

This was all to be changed however, for Mr. Swift entered the field of shipping dressed beef to the eastern markets instead of the live cattle. Naturally this innovation was fought with great obstinacy and bitterness. The railroads did not want it because of the reduction in their freight bills, and the eastern stockyards and butchers fought it tooth and nail because it threatened their business. In spite of all obstacles Mr. Swift began, in the winter of 1877, to make shipments. The success achieved was such that Mr. Swift became more and more determined that the eastern market be supplied the year around, and this was to be the work of the refrigerator car, upon which his mind had been fixed from the beginning, and the devising of which had dated back for more than ten years. Here again there were difficulties, but by this time difficulties had become to Mr. Swift only something to be overcome. The Grand Trunk Railway, to whom he went for cooperation, welcomed his proposal to give them new business, but could not visualize the idea of building refrigerator cars. Whereupon Mr. Swift made the proposal, which was accepted, that he would build the cars if they would run them. Ten cars were immediately built and put into use, and during the twenty-five years that followed these cars grew into the thousands. The dressed-beef industry was the fore-runner for dressed mutton and pork and finally for all kinds of meats, and the industry became fully established as one of the greatest in the world.

In 1877-78, when Mr. Swift decided that the future belonged not to the cattle buyers but to the beef packers, Mr. Hathaway withdrew from the concern. For a time, however, Mr. Swift continued buying cattle for his own use, and Louis F. Swift has been reported as saying: "I can remember when my father bought all the cattle we handled. He did not need any help. Then came the time when he had to go to the packing house and offices, and I took up the buying alone and did all of it. My five brothers followed me. I well remember when we were able to ship one whole car of beef in one day. It marked an epoch in our business." While he was training his sons for the business, Mr. Swift began to realize the need for a partner, and he decided upon his brother Edwin C. Swift, ten years his junior, who had last been heard from on the Pacific Coast. Failing to locate him, he sent his cousin to San Francisco with explicit instructions to bring him to Chicago. After two months the cousin located the brother with a railroad contractor's gang in the Rocky Mountains, and succeeded after some effort in persuading him to return to Chicago. After the brothers had met Gustavus F. Swift, then thirty-nine years old, made Edwin C., twenty-nine, his partner and sent him to Boston to take charge of the eastern end of the business under the style of Swift Brothers, although the name of the concern was G. F. Swift & Company.

Mr. Swift and his brother adopted a liberal policy toward the trade, and in the important centers either engaged the leading meat dealer as their agent or entered into partnership with him to his great advantage, forming in a few years more than a hundred of these partnerships and thus sharing their prosperity with the trade. Mr. Swift had no sympathy with the practice of some packers, whose first appearance in a town was as rivals to the butchers of the place whom they were powerful enough to drive out of business. Operations expanded, and in 1885 the business was incorporated as Swift & Company with a capital stock of $300,000, Mr. Swift becoming president and remaining in that capacity until his death. By 1887 the capital was increased to $3,000,000. After the refrigerator car came the refrigerator ship, and with that the extension of the business to England and the Continent. In this great undertaking it is stated that Mr. Swift made as many as twenty trips abroad. In 1880 the packing industry began the transformation of former waste into by-products, one of the first of which was oleomargarine, followed by glue, beef extract, pepsin, soap, oil, fertilizer and others. This not only meant more profit to the packer, but to the farmer for his live stock and to the public cheaper meat, and at the same time provided many things, some never known before, that contribute to the general welfare.

The first branch of Swift & Company was established in 1888 at Kansas City, in 1890 came the Omaha branch, in 1892 that at St. Louis, in 1896-97 St. Joseph, Missouri, St. Paul in 1897 and Fort Worth, Texas, in 1902. Meanwhile, in 1896, the capitalization of the company had increased to $15,000,000, and before 1903 had reached $25,000,000. It is not surprising that Mr. Swift did not live to an advanced age. It is said that he worked harder than any man in his employ. His mind was incessantly engaged on the new and perplexing problems of a business that developed and expanded in every direction with bewildering rapidity. To meet the demands for new capital to finance such a vast enterprise called aloud for more and more money, and while Mr. Swift was an extraordinary man, this work exhausted even his wonderful vitality and nervous energy. When he passed away March 29, 1903, there were in the various establishments controlled by his company above 7,000 employes, and the yearly business exceeded $160,000,000. Among the published maxims attributed to Mr. Swift, the following have been selected as characteristic: "The best a man ever did shouldn't be his standard for the rest of his life." "When a clerk tells you that he must leave the office because it is 5 o'clock, rest assured that you will never see his name over a front door." "The secret of all great undertakings is hard work and self-reliance. Given these two qualities and a residence in the United States of America, a young man has nothing else to ask for."

In writing of Mr. Swift in the University Record for April, 1921, Thomas W. Goodspeed said, in part: "The only time I ever saw G. F. Swift, the first week in April, 1890, he gave me a subscription of $1,000 toward the fund for the founding of the University of Chicago. I went to the Stock Yards rather expecting he would be too busy to see me. He was not in his office, and I found him outside apparently at leisure. His talk was that of any ordinary man of business. But his face took me wholly by surprise. It was not the face of a typical business man, but that of a scholar, or a poet, or an artist. It looked like the face of a man who might see visions and dream dreams. And his fundamental characteristic as a man of affairs was his business imagination. From his youth up he was always seeing possibilities that other men could not see. He was like an explorer in a new country. Every step in advance opened up new vistas. Every new achievement gave him a new vision of something bigger beyond. He was a man of business vision. . . . Behind all his plans was the driving-power of tremendous and tireless energy. . . . His success was no happy accident. He was no lucky child of fortune. He toiled as few men toil. He contended with difficulties such as few men meet, and he did it with surpassing courage, patience, perseverance, purpose and success. . . . It must be added to all this that he had an undoubted genius for business. Some men gain wealth because opportunities are thrust upon them. But opportunity never knocked at G. F. Swift's door. It was he that knocked at her door, or, rather, he beat the door down and forced an entrance."

Mr. Swift had few interests outside of his business. It left him scant time for general society. He was too busy for club life. He shrank from publicity and did not take that interest or that place in public affairs which a man of his abilities and wealth, perhaps, should have taken. But he had two great interests outside of his business. These were his family and the church. The six children born to Mr. and Mrs. Swift before they came to Chicago in 1875 have been mentioned. Five more came to them. Herbert L., George Hastings, Gustavus F., Jr., Ruth May and Harold Higgins. The oldest son, Louis F. Swift, succeeded to the presidency, and his younger brothers are united with him in the management. It is an unusual example of family solidarity. The children not only inherited great business ability from their father, but his spirit of liberality also descended to them.

Mr. Swift joined the Methodist Church of Sandwich in his youth and religion continued always to be one of the great interests of his life. On February 18, 1877, less than two years after they settled at Chicago, Mr. and Mrs. Swift became charter members of the nine persons who formed the congregation of the newly-organized Winter Street (now Union Avenue) Methodist Church, of which Mr. Swift became a trustee and a steward. For twenty years Mr. Swift continued to reside in a modest home on Emerald Avenue, among, or very near, his employes. In 1898 he moved two miles directly east and built a modern home on a spacious lot at 4848 Ellis Avenue. His attention was centered immediately upon a new religious enterprise, but he neither forgot nor neglected the little church near the Stock Yards, in which he continued his official relations and liberal interest. The new religious work was the founding of St. James Methodist Church, the first meeting for the organization of which was held in his home while he was still residing on Emerald Avenue. Associated with him was N. W. Harris, who shared all expenses with him. After his death, in token of their affectionate remembrance of him, the people made the north window of the church a memorial of Mr. Swift. Six years later his portrait was hung in one of the church rooms, and in 1914-1915 Mrs. Swift and her children presented to the church the great memorial organ. In 1907 the Union Avenue Parish House, consisting of a parsonage, gymnasium, baths, bowling alleys, library and reading room, and later, a playground, both connected with the Union Avenue Church, were given and endowed by Mrs. G. F. Swift and the other members of her family as a memorial to Mr. Swift, in the place where and among the people with whom he had lived for many years and raised his family. These institutions are now ministering in a very helpful way to many young people and are open to Protestant, Roman Catholic and Jew alike. Later, the pastor, Reverend Clancy, added to this statement that Mrs. G. F. Swift, the daughter, Mrs. Helen Swift Neilson, and the six sons, all maintained a fine, strong interest in the church and parish house, and contributed regularly and liberally to the support of the church. Louis F. Swift is one of the trustees of the church, and Edward F. Swift and G. F. Swift, Jr., are members of the parish house board of managers. His memory is also kept fresh by the beautiful G. F. Swift Memorial Church at Sagamore, the home of his boyhood and the place of his spiritual birth.

Mention has been made of Mr. Swift's initial contribution to the University of Chicago. In the thirty-six years that have passed since that first gift the family of Mr. Swift has contributed over $1,000,000 to the various needs of the University. Mrs. Swift has endowed the Gustavus F. Swift Fellowship in Chemistry as a memorial of her husband and has given large sums for the medical and other departments. Two sons, Charles H. and Harold H., and a daughter, Mrs. Neilson, also have made large contributions. With C. H. Swift's last gifts it amounts to more than $425,000. Mr. Swift had no taste for display, and none of the arrogance of wealth. He valued money for what he could do with it in his developing business and in helping others. He gave a large sum toward building the Annie May Swift Hall at Northwestern University, a memorial of a daughter Mr. and Mrs. Swift had lost in 1889, when she was twenty-two years old, and gave the initial $25,000 for the Hyde Park Young Men's Christian Association Building. These contributions only hint at the ceaseless flow of similar gifts to churches, colleges, universities, missions, hospitals and charities that has sent out increasing and widening streams to bless the world.

VICTOR C. CARLSON is head of the Victor C. Carlson Organization of Evanston, an organization that represents every phase of service connected with development, building, financing, ownership and operation of real estate holdings. It has played a notable part in Evanston's modern development and has also participated in other directions of Chicago's metropolitan development.

Victor C. Carlson was born at Evanston in 1888. He had a public school education and since boyhood has been associated with the building industry, learning it technically, practically, and at the same time studying architecture, real estate law and building construction. Mr. Carlson financed and built and owns some of Evanston's most notable buildings, including the beautiful Orrington Hotel, the Library-Plaza Hotel, and the Carlson Building. The most thoroughly modern office building in Evanston is the Carlson Building, which with its tower is an example of architecture that would be a credit to any city in the United States.

The most recent project of the Victor Carlson Organization is the development of a subdivision of 524 acres at Western Avenue and Sauk Trail, in the southwestern section of Chicago. This is known as Indian Wood, a name well justified by historic associations with one of the famous trails and grounds of a tribe of Indians at one time well known in the Great Lakes country. One other item of history attached to this locality is that in a field of grain there many years ago Cyrus McCormick made the first successful trial of his reaping machine. The complete scheme of development at Indian Wood, now in progress, will comprise a residential community of great charm and beauty, it being Mr. Carlson's purpose to make it one of the finest communities of homes in the country.

Mr. Carlson is a business man who enjoys his work and finds a pleasure and satisfaction in constructive enterprises quite apart from the financial reward. He is a popular and active member of Evanston's business and social community, and is a member of the Evanston Club and Masonic Club. He married Miss Charlotte Carlson, and they have four children, Virginia, Victor, Jr., Robert and Roberta.

JOSEPH D. HERB has his farm home seven miles northwest of Polo, in Ogle County. That community has been fortunate in having among its most progressive and enlightened citizens members of the Herb family for three generations.

The Herb family lived for many years in Pennsylvania. That was the home of Daniel Herb and wife, in Northumberland County. A son of Daniel Herb was Samuel Herb, who married Polly Zartman. Both were natives of Northumberland County, Pennsylvania, and in 1845 they removed to Illinois and bought the large tract of land known as the Chambers farm in Ogle County. Along with the land Samuel Herb acqquired a grist mill, sawmill and small store, and looked after these various interests until his death in 1873. The four children were Daniel, Isaac, Sarah and Eliza. Daniel and Isaac Herb were closely associated in their business interests in Brookville Township for many years.

Isaac Herb was born in Northumberland County, Pennsylvania, and was thirteen years old when the family came to Illinois. They made this journey by canal boat and river to St. Louis and thence up the Mississippi to Savanna, Illinois, from which river landing wagons conveyed them overland to Brookville. Isaac Herb assisted in developing the various interests of the family in that township. The store grew to be one of an important character, meeting the needs of the population of a large section. After the grist mill was burned in 1888 it was not rebuilt, and subsequently the store was moved to Brookville. Isaac Herb continued to give his attention to stock raising, milling and mercantile interests until his death on March 24, 1894. He married Sarah Messner, who was born in Pennsylvania and came to Illinois in 1848, her father, John Messner, settling near Brookville. The Messners were a family of farmers, and Sarah Messner was one of three daughters and two sons, Henry, John, Sarah, Elizabeth and Mary. Of these, Henry Messner, is now living retired at Naperville at the age of ninety, being the oldest minister of the Evangelical Church and a man of saintly character, who for a number of years was presiding elder in the Illinois conference.

Joseph D. Herb was born at Brookville in Ogle County November 6, 1870, attended public schools, and since early youth his interests have identified him with the rural community in which he was born and grew up, and he owns the farm where his grandfather settled eighty years ago. He has 360 acres of some of the best of Illinois land. In addition he is vice president of the Exchange National Bank of Polo and is school treasurer of the Brookville and Lima Township School. Mr. Herb has given an energetic direction to his business affairs and has been equally generous of his time and means to promote every movement for the general good of his community. No one has worked more wholeheartedly for the improvement of the roads, and he was an early advocate of hard permanent roads. He has been a stock feeder and shipper for many years. He is an active member of the Evangelical Church, and when the church in his community burned in 1920 he was put on the building board and with the loyal cooperation of his associates raised the funds and made it possible to erect a handsome new church, which was dedicated in 1921.

HENRY BORGSMILLER. The same indomitable spirit that has so frequently been attributed to Murphysboro as a community, after it raised itself out of the wreckage and ashes of a destructive tornado and fire, has long been a characteristic of one of the city's leading business men, Henry Borgsmiller, Sr., wholesale grocer.

Mr. Borgsmiller was born in Germany, in 1867 and was a boy when his father died. Subsequently his step-father came to America, in 1880, and found employment in the coal mines of Southern Illinois. The remainder of the family joined him at Duquoin in Perry County. Henry Borgsmiller was then thirteen

Amante Rongetti, M.D., C.M.

years of age and was without the command of a word of English when he arrived in this country. For a time he attended parochial schools, and at the age of sixteen went to work in the mines. Up to the age of eighteen he had only the prospects of a youth whose life had been one of manual labor and with very meager educational equipment.

Mr. Borgsmiller, in 1885, moved to Murphysboro in Jackson County. "That," he says, "was the next best thing I ever did in my life. The best thing I ever did was to meet and marry Elizabeth Borgers on November 15, 1887. To her I owe my success in life as well as my happiness."

After moving to Murphysboro he continued his labors in the coal mines nearby until 1890. After his marriage he acquired a little home on North Ninth (then known as Cherry) Street, and had a savings account of about four hundred dollars. Through a friend he became acquainted with a traveling salesman for a St. Louis, Missouri, wholesale grocery house. His capital of four hundred dollars was soon invested in a stock of groceries, which was put on display in the front room of his cottage. Trade developed gradually, and in the meantime Mrs. Borgsmiller looked after the store as well as her family, while he took outside work. Undoubtedly he had inherited from his father, an old German merchant, some exceptional business instincts, and of these he made the best possible advantage. After a few months, from the profits of the store and his earnings outside, Mr. Borgsmiller built a small frame store building on old Cherry Street, opposite the old Turners Park. In 1896 he bought the stock of W. C. Kent, together with the store building, and from that time had two retail stores in operation.

It was in 1902 that he advanced to the stage of wholesaling, with a warehouse on North Seventeenth Street. He was his own traveling salesman, covering the territory within a radius of forty miles from Murphysboro. Competition was strong, and it was no easy matter for Mr. Borgsmiller to demonstrate to the wholesalers of the large city that he could adequately serve the Murphysboro territory. In the meantime his retail business was discontinued and from the age of fourteen their son Henry was an industrious and intelligent factor in the business.

Mr. Borgsmiller in 1918 erected a large business structure on North Seventeenth Street. This structure was entirely destroyed by the tornado of March, 1925. Also in 1918 the business was incorporated as H. Borgsmiller & Sons. He became president, his son Henry, vice president, his son Herman, secretary and treasurer, while two other sons, Joseph and William, are directors. Borgsmiller Produce Company was started in 1919. Herman is manager of this company. The manager of H. Borgsmiller & Sons Wholesale Grocery is Henry Borgsmiller, Jr. The other wholesale business is handled under the name of Murphysboro Grocery Company, the manager being Joseph Borgsmiller, assisted by John and Theodore. Joseph Borgsmiller served in the navy during the World war.

The Borgsmiller family is almost unique in the loyalty among its members and the ability to do team work in promoting and managing the different branches of their great and prosperous business.

The solid character of Mr. Borgsmiller and his business met its severest test in the tornado of 1925. Twenty-eight buildings owned by him were either totally destroyed or badly injured. Mr. Borgsmiller himself was taken out of the wreckage senseless and badly injured, and required hospital care for many weeks. On the site of the wholesale warehouse and offices a large and handsome brick building, 100 by 62 feet, is now in course of construction, and will give adequate quarters for the business when completed. Mr. Borgsmiller's losses from the tornado amounted to over $65,000. The Red Cross offered financial assistance to enable him to ease the burden of his loss, but his reply was that he required no help and that instead help should be given to others who needed it more. His beautiful home in the western part of the city, erected in 1912, was also badly damaged by the storm. For more than a year since this catastrophe Mr. Borgsmiller, leaving the practical details of his business to his sons, has been rebuilding thereby giving employment to many and as a leading business man showing a faith in the future of his community which has been invaluable in the rehabilitation of that city.

AMANTE RONGETTI, M. D. A Chicago surgeon whose work has brought him more than ordinary fame and has enabled him to serve mankind not only through the scope of his individual abilities, but in extending the knowledge and the instruments of science over disease, Dr. Amante Rongetti has been a resident of Chicago for over twenty years and is chief surgeon of the Ashland Boulevard Hospital.

Doctor Rongetti was born in Sepino del Sannio, Italy. The following record of the Rongetti family history is quoted from the Instituto Araldico ed Artistico, Roma:

"Noble and ancient family of French origin of which they were first noticed in the XIII century. Came to Italy and took permanent residence in the Kingdom of Napoli under Carlo d' Angio, and here its members occupied in all epoch the highest and elevated office of Magistrature, always noted for public and private virtue.

"About the beginning of the XV century the secondary branch of this most distinct family transplanted in Sannio where they gave to this new country personage most expert in Army, Giuriconsulti and dotti Prelati."

Dr. Rongetti was first impressed with an appreciation of the power of the capable physician to help mankind and gained his ambition to study medicine about the time he completed his grammar school course and himself fell victim to a long and serious illness. He resisted the desire of his parents that he should study for the priesthood, and instead followed the studies that would prepare him for his chosen vocation.

After a year in a gymnasium or high school he came to America in 1900, and while working in New York continued his preparatory studies. From there he came to Chicago and entered St. Ignatius College, where he took his pre-medical course and graduated with honors in 1910. From there he entered the medical department of Loyola University, and in 1914 was graduated with the M. D. and C. M. degrees. Doctor Rongetti was an interne in Columbus Hospital and for several years was a member of the staff of the Jefferson Park and the West End Hospitals. He has long enjoyed an extensive private practice in the South Ashland Boulevard district, and in 1920 he organized the Ashland Boulevard Hospital, located at Ashland and Polk streets. As chief surgeons he has given this hospital much of its reputation for splendid and efficient service. In his private practice and through the facilities of the hospitals Doctor Rongetti has given much time and study to research in cancer, and he has become one of the foremost authorities in America on the cure or control of this malignant disease. He also enjoys a fine reputation for his gland research work.

Doctor Rongetti has been chief surgeon of the Elmwood Park Hospital, is surgeon of the Glaziers' Union and associate national medical director of the Society of Friends of America. Besides contributions to medical journals, he has written several books, two titles by him being "Modern Sanitary City" and "The Human Organism."

Doctor Rongetti is a member of the B. P. O. Elks, Golden Rule Lodge of Masons, and in the Independent Order of Odd Fellows is a member of the Oriental Order of Humility and Perfection.

His skill as a surgeon, his devotion to the science and profession of medicine, and his work for humanity gained him signal recognition in March, 1923, when Pope Pius conferred upon him the Papal blessing. Doctor Rongetti is the only Chicago physician except the late John B. Murphy to be so honored.

GEORGE HARRISON RIPPETOE. Success in any one calling is an indication of close application and industry, and therefore the world is made better for the life of every successful man. The men who have accomplished the most good in the world are not the ones who through exceptionally favorable opportunity have, in a comparatively short period of time, gained both wealth and prominence, but the men whose careers have shown a steady and gradual development. George Harrison Rippetoe, vice president and superintendent of the Anna Stone Company, is eminently one who has risen gradually through his own efforts, and demonstrated what can be accomplished through pluck and perseverance. He has not only achieved an honorable business success, but he has also won and holds the confidence of his associates, and has been the recipient of public honors in election to office.

George Harrison Rippetoe was born at Colchester, Illinois, August 22, 1886, a son of John and Caroline (Underhill) Rippetoe, native of McDonough County, Illinois, and Akron, Ohio, respectively. John Rippetoe was a son of Caleb and Anna Rippetoe, natives of Kentucky, who came to Illinois at an early day and settled in McDonough County, where Caleb Rippetoe was engaged in farming and coal mining. John Rippetoe was a mining engineer and mine operator, and was chief engineer of the Quincy Coal Company for thirty-four years. He bought two mines near Colchester, which later became the property of the Quincy Coal Company, and later he and his son sunk three mines and continued to operate them until they were stripped. Another enterprise in which father and son were interested was the operation of mines of potters' clay, and they also had some experience with stone quarries. In fact, as can be easily seen from the above, John Rippetoe was one of the leading men in the development of the natural resources of his part of Illinois during the time he was active, but increasing years have led to his retirement and he is now living at Colchester, removed from his former activities.

George Harrison Rippetoe went to school, taking both the grammar grades and the high school courses, and then took up the study of electrical engineering through the medium of the International Correspondence School, while at the same time he was associated with his father in his different mining enterprises. In 1913 Mr. Rippetoe left Colchester and went to Macomb to become superintendent of the Central Illinois Public Service Company, having already had some experience in this line of work at Colchester, and through it being thoroughly competent to take the position offered him at Macomb. Until 1922 he continued in the employ of the public service corporation, but in that year came to Anna to assume the duties of the Anna Stone Company, of which he is now also vice president. This company is one of the substantial ones of Union County, and its object is the crushing of limestone for building concrete products, including agricultural limestone. The main office of the company is at Chicago, but the plant is located at Anna. The territory of the company covers a wide area, and the annual volume of business shows a steady and healthy increase.

In 1907 Mr. Rippetoe married Leona Stevens, who was born at Monmouth, Illinois, a daughter of W. O. Stevens. Mr. and Mrs. Rippetoe have four children: Catherine, Isabelle, Virginia and Billie. A stanch republican, Mr. Rippetoe has always been active in local politics, and served for two terms as township clerk while a resident of Colchester. While not a member of any religious organization, Mr. Rippetoe attends the services of the Presbyterian Church. He belongs to Macomb Lodge No. 1009, B. P. O. E.; to Anna Chamber of Commerce, which he represented at the state meeting held at Chicago in 1924; to the Anna Rotary Club, and to the Hamilton Club of Chicago. In every way he measures up to the highest standards of honest business and good citizenship, and is rightly regarded as one of Anna's most representative men.

JAMES MORSELL GASSAWAY, M. D. For more than thirty-seven years engaged in the practice of medicine and surgery at Cairo, Dr. James Morsell Gassaway is at once one of the best known, most highly skilled and most greatly beloved members of his profession in Alexander County. His has been a full and busy life, crowded with interesting experiences and unselfish works, all of which have tended to mellow his nature and to make him a profound and accurate judge of human nature.

Doctor Gassaway was born at Georgetown, D. C., January 7, 1848, and is a son of Rev. Stephen Griffith and Isabella Virginia (Beache) Gassaway, the former born at Elk Ridge, Maryland, and the latter at the Navy Yard, Pensacola, Florida. He was an Episcopalian clergyman for many years, married Miss Beache at Gambier, Ohio, and died at St. Louis, Missouri, February 14, 1854, while she survived him some years, passing away at Washington, D. C., in 1881.

James Morsell Gassaway attended the public schools of Philadelphia, Pennsylvania, the Episcopal High School at Alexandria, Virginia, the Protestant Episcopal Academy of Philadelphia and Columbia College. On leaving school he became a telegrapher, and by 1872 was manager of the Franklin Telegraph Company and the Southern & Atlantic Telegraph Company at Washington, D. C. In the meantime he had been pursuing his medical studies, and in 1872 received his degree from the National Medical College at Washington. Some ten years later, in 1882, he was given his degree by Jefferson Medical College of Philadelphia. In 1872 he entered the Government service as correspondence clerk for the United States Lighthouse Board, and three years later was made scientific proofreader in chief of the Engineer's Office, United States Army. In 1876 he obtained a transfer to the United States Marine Hospital service, now known as the United States Public Health Service, with which he labored for a number of years, but from which he has since retired. On January 21, 1888, Doctor Gassaway came to Cairo, where he has since been in continuous practice. He stands high in his profession and in the esteem and confidence of the people. His record as physician, citizen and man is an open book. In addition to the various organizations of his calling, Doctor Gassaway belongs to the Masons, being a Knight Templar and having attained to the Scottish Rite; is a past exalted ruler of the B. P. O. Elks Lodge No. 30 of New Orleans, Louisiana; and grand commander of the Knights of Pythias. His religious faith is that of the Episcopal Church.

On April 30, 1873, Doctor Gassaway married Susan Elizabeth Ramsey, who was born at Georgetown, D. C., daughter of James Murphy and Mary Eleanor Addison (Tyler) Ramsey, and to this union there have been born the following children: James Ramsey, deceased; Stephen Griffith, of Oklahoma City, Oklahoma; Mary Eleanor, professor of French at Beloit (Wisconsin) College; Alexander S., chief engineer in Unted States Marines at Oakland, California; Crosby Mitchell, of Portsmouth, New Hampshire; and Frederick Garish, manager of the Chamber of Commere, Wilmington, Delaware. All of the sons saw service during the World war.

THOMAS P. FLYNN, a native Chicagoan, whose business activities have been chiefly in the field of crushed granite and construction materials, has been very popular and prominent in Irish organizations in Chicago, and is now president of the Irish Fellowship Club of that city.

Both his parents were born in Donegal, Ireland. Mr. Flynn was born in Chicago, February 22, 1868, son of Thomas and Bridget (Hassett) Flynn. After completing his education in St. Patrick's Academy at Chicago, he engaged in business, and for many years has had extensive interests and connection with the granite quarry industry and as a dealer in construction materials. He is president of the Waushara Granite Quarries Company, of the Badger Crushed Granite Company, and the Du Ro Asphalt Products Company. His business offices are at 133 West Washington Street.

The famous Irish Fellowship Club, of which Mr. Flynn has the honor of being president, was launched many years ago to promote concerted action and good feeling in all things relating to the welfare of Ireland. Its membership has included not only Irishmen, but friends of Ireland, among others including even non-Catholics and Jews. Its banquets and meetings have been frequently starting points for great and important discussions and movements, as well as scenes distinguished by the wit and wisdom of eloquent speakers. The greatest of these banquets was given since Mr. Flynn became president in honor of His Eminence Patrick Cardinal O'Donnell, Primate of All Ireland, at the Palmer House during the great Eucharistic Congress in June, 1926.

Mr. Flynn for a number of years has been prominent in the Knights of Columbus and other Catholic organizations, being former president of the American Federation of Catholic Societies, former vice supreme master of the Fourth Degree Knight of Columbus, former vice president of the National Council of Catholic Men. During the World war he was director of personal overseas secretaries of the Knights of Columbus. Mr. Flynn is a democrat, member of the B. P. O. Elks and Catholic Order of Foresters. He married, November 26, 1890, Miss Catherine Kenny, of Prince Edward Island, Canada. Their home is at 6544 Harvard Avenue.

IRA WILSON ELLIS, M. D. Thirty-five years of earnest and hard working service as a physician and surgeon have brought Doctor Ellis a well defined position in the citizenship of Murphysboro. However, his fellow citizens have not allowed him to serve them entirely in a professional capacity. Due to their repeated insistence and his sense of civic obligation Doctor Ellis has been mayor of Murphysboro for at least ten out of the past thirty years.

Doctor Ellis attributes his powers of physical endurance and his present physical good health to the inheritance of qualities from his father, John R. Ellis, who led a strenuous but successful life in the lumber and mill business. John R. Ellis was born in Ohio, and as a young man moved to Franklin, Indiana, where he established and operated the Indiana Lumber Mills. In Ohio he lived at Georgetown, where he married Susan Slack. In 1884 John Ellis moved his business to Murphysboro, Illinois, and continued it as the Indiana Lumber Mills. His trade covered several counties in the southern part of the state, and he was active in business until he retired at the age of seventy-four. He is now eighty-nine, vigorous and contented, and a resident of East St. Louis. His wife, Susan Slack, died at the age of fifty-two. Ira Wilson Ellis was born at Franklin, Indiana, November 23, 1858. He attended grade and high schools there. His father and mother urged him to take up the law as a profession. However, during his boyhood he had spent many hours reading medical works in the office of his cousin, Doctor Slack, at Franklin. This early reading interested him to the point of determining that medicine should be his permanent profession. After high school he took his literary course at Butler College, and in 1883 was graduated in medicine from the Butler Medical Department. His medical college work was supplemented by private study in the office of Dr. E. B. Willum, at that time a very prominent Indiana physician.

Doctor Ellis after graduating was located for six months at Stinesville, a village near Bloomington, Indiana, then practiced a short time in a suburb of Indianapolis, and from there went to Linton, Indiana, as surgeon for the Island City Coal Company.

Doctor Ellis in 1889 removed to Murphysboro. Thirty-five years ago Murphysboro was one of the typical inland towns of southern Illinois, almost isolated for several months in the year except by railroad, because of the condition of its highway. Over such roads, on horseback or in buggy, Doctor Ellis carried out the routine of an old time country doctor. He had that sense of duty, the willingness to serve, the defiance of obstacles and the joy in his work which have been described so frequently as a characteristic of the old time doctor. His professional career is a complete link between the conditions of that day and the present. He now has a modern uptown office in a modern building, with every facility at his hand for immediate service, including telephone and automobile, and no one appreciates the contrast between such facilities and the old time methods to a higher degree than Doctor Ellis. He has retained and preserved his physical health and strength, his spirit, and while a great deal of his service was never compensated he has managed to accumulate a sufficiency of this world's goods.

Doctor Ellis was mayor of Murphysboro for the years 1897 to 1900, 1903-04, 1907-08 and 1911-12, a total of ten years.

He married Miss Mary Acuff, a native of Owen County, Indiana. Doctor Ellis' partner and associate in practice now is his son Edward Kent Ellis. This son was born at Murphysboro in 1892, attended grade and high school in his home town, and in 1915 graduated from the St. Louis Medical College. For a year and a half he was interne in the St. Louis City Hospital. When America entered the World war he joined the Medical Corps, rose to the rank of captain, and was on duty fourteen months overseas. He still has a commission in the Medical Officers' Reserve Corps. Since returning from the war he has been associated with his father. He married Pauline Steinle, a daughter of Joseph Steinle, of Murphysboro.

MATTHEW M. MORALEE, general insurance and real estate dealer at Murphysboro, has the bearing of a man whose associations have always been with business leaders and men of affairs. To some extent he inherited that qualification, and it is also derived in part from his former relations with some of the leading financiers of New York and the east.

Mr. Moralee's grandfather, Michael Moralee, was a native of northern England. Matthew M. Moralee, Sr., was born at Springfield, Massachusetts, and was a California forty-niner, crossing the plains, and during his brief stay in California having moderate success in his quest for gold. After returning east he located in the lead mining district of southwestern Wisconsin, and subsequently moved to Hancock, Michigan, where he engaged in the lumber business and where he remained until his death in 1897. He married Mary Ann Ford, of Louisville, Kentucky.

Matthew M. Moralee, of Murphysboro, was born at Hancock, Michigan, July 14, 1870. He was reared there, attending public schools to the age of sixteen, and then entered Kenyon Military Academy at Gambier, Ohio, where he was graduated with high honors, being chosen captain of Cadets, a position given only to select students of highest scholarship and ability. His ambition in those days was for the law. After leaving the academy he entered the law offices of Chadbourne and Reese at Houghton, Michigan, pursuing his studies for a year and a half. His legal knowledge and training has been of the greatest value to him in his business career. The father's urgent desire was that the son should succeed him in the lumber industry. The son yielded to the wishes of his father and after spending one year in the Michigan College of Mines he joined his father in the lumber business in 1894. After the death of his father in 1897 he took up railroad construction, a business he followed until 1903. This work has brought him in contact with a number of big men in the financial and business world. In 1903 he was given preference over a number of other applicants by M. S. Daniels, noted financier and operator, as a business manager of Mr. Daniel's private properties. For the next two years he was engaged in laying out farms, planning and erecting buildings, and carrying out many similar plans. Then, in 1905, he was induced to enter the service of John W. Sterling, New York financier, a close associate of Rockefeller and James J. Hill, the railroad magnate. Mr. Moralee in this capacity located at Rye, New York, taking charge of the Sterling estate and of the Meriam Osborn Memorial Home Association, an institution maintained for aged gentlewomen, the home having been founded by Charles J. Osborn, the banker. The estate comprised five thousand acres. Mr. Moralee had under him seven superintendents and three hundred employes.

Mr. Moralee was business manager of the Sterling holdings for twelve years. During this time he took courses in landscaping and agriculture at Columbia University at New York. Then, in 1917, he came to Murphysboro and purchased the old established business of Robert A. Watson, general insurance. He soon added a real estate department, and

has had a very successful business in that line ever since.

Mr. Moralee married, in 1902, Miss Mabel Ashman, daughter of Andrew Ashman, of a prominent family of Jackson County, Illinois. Her father, Andrew Ashman, with Peter Jeffrey sank the first coal shaft in the county. Mrs. Moralee was born in England was brought to America at the age of four years.

Mr. Moralee is a Knight Templar Mason, member of the Shrine at East St. Louis, belongs to the Independent Order of Odd Fellows, B. P. O. Elks, the Murphysboro Chamber of Commerce, is a trustee of the Presbyterian Church, is president of the Jackson Club, the oldest social organization in southern Illinois, and is a member of the Jackson Country Club and charter member of the Rotary Club.

EDGAR B. JONES. The largest industrial establishment in Ogle County is the Schiller Piano Company at Oregon, manufacturers of the Schiller-Grand piano patented construction, the Schiller grand reproducing piano with the Welte-Mignon reproducing action, and the Schiller upright piano and Player piano.

The dominating factor in the success of this notable industry has been the personal energies and idealism of two generations of the Jones family. The man who built up the business was the late Frederick George Jones, and since his death his sons have maintained it at the same high ideals and have greatly increased the commercial prestige of the output of the factory.

The Jones family is of Welsh ancestry. John Henry Jones was born in Hertfordshire, England, May 24, 1819, and married Rachel Dean, who was born in Northumberland County, Canada West. John Henry Jones was a tailor by trade, who followed his business at Cobourg and Port Hope, Ontario, until his death on August 7, 1904. His wife died October 5, 1899.

Their son, Frederick George Jones, was born at Cobourg, Ontario, Canada, March 19, 1847, and up to the age of twelve years attended school in Port Hope. During the following two years he was employed in a book store. At the age of fourteen he was put in charge of a book store at Lindsay, in Canada West, and remained there until 1865, when, at the age of eighteen, he came to the United States, and on the eighth of May arrived at Oregon, Illinois. He was a farm hand during that summer, then for two years clerked in the store of John P. Wooley, and afterwards in the dry goods department of W. W. Woods & Company of Rockford, Illinois. Returning to Oregon, he engaged in merchandising with F. G. Petrie as silent partner. At the end of thirteen years Mr. Jones bought out the interest of his partner and continued it under his own name for fifteen years.

Mr. Jones in 1885 became financially interested in and took over the active management of a small factory on the banks of the Rock River where pianos were made. With characteristic progressiveness he completely reorganized the business, and soon began manufacturing Schiller pianos, choosing the name of the great German poet in response to an idealism which was always foremost in Mr. Jones' career as a manufacturer. In 1893 he became president of the Schiller Piano Company, and guided the business through its successive stages until his death in 1913. In the meantime he had made the Schiller piano an instrument recognized everywhere as possessing the qualities which are the first essentials in piano construction. He made a success of his business also by setting and maintaining certain business standards. He refused to follow the policy of conditional sales, the expenditure of large sums for advertising and the use of traveling salesmen. He made an instrument that could be recommended on its own intrinsic merits, and the business has grown through the cumulative process rather than by artificial stimulation. During his life time the capacity of the plant was increased from some three hundred to about three thousand pianos annually, and from 250 to 300 persons were employed in the plant. The Schiller Piano Works never had a shut-down, never missed a pay day, and the demand for the output has steadily grown throughout the United States and also in Canada, Mexico, Italy and the Hawaiian Islands.

While developing this large piano industry, Frederick G. Jones acquired and served for years as president of the Oregon Electric Light & Power Company, the Oregon Foundry and Machine Company, the Standard Player Piano Company, and at one time was the sole owner of the Oregon Water Power. The use of this water power has been a tremendous advantage to the Schiller Piano Company. Mr. Jones developed it primarily for use in the piano plant, but continued its development until it furnished light and power for nine cities. Finally it was sold to one of the large public utility companies, but in the contract the Schiller Piano Company for all time has guaranteed electricity sufficient to run all machinery in the plant. This free power alone enables the company to meet all competition, and give to the Schiller instruments increased qualities of power and tone at a lower general cost.

Frederick G. Jones was a republican in politics. In 1870 he was elected an alderman of Oregon on the no license ticket, and served continuously until 1886. From 1887 to 1897 he was a member of the Oregon Board of Education. He was an active member of the Methodist Episcopal Church.

He married at Oregon, November 19, 1872, Miss Chloe B. Brockway, a native of North Bangor, New York. The five children of their marriage were: Edith Blanche, born October 2, 1873; George Henry, born October 29, 1875; Edgar Brockway, born May 20, 1880; Mildred Gardner, born February 10, 1885; and Cyrus Frederick, born April 16, 1887.

The present executive officers of the Schiller Piano Company are Edgar B. Jones, president; F. M. Hood, vice president; C. F. Jones, treasurer; B. F. Shelley, secretary; and Roland B. Jones, assistant secretary.

Edgar B. Jones, the president, was liberally educated, attending public school at Oregon and receiving special musical advantages in the University of Leipzig, Germany, under Professor Mueller. On returning home in 1900, he went to work in the factory under his father, and filled a number of positions in order to acquaint himself with every practical detail of the business. In 1902 he was assigned duties in the office, serving as shipping clerk, bookkeeper, secretary, and in 1910 was made sales manager and also secretary and treasurer.

Mr. E. B. Jones is also a director in the Ogle County State Bank of Oregon. He is a member of the City Commission, a member of the National Piano Manufacturers Association, the Piano Club of Chicago, the Lions Club, is a Knight Templar Mason and Shriner and one of the endowment members of the Oregon Golf Club. He is on the Official Board of the Methodist Church and a church trustee.

He married at Shabbona, Illinois, October 30, 1901, Miss Carolyn Mohr, daughter of George and Mary (Nau) Mohr, of Shabbona. They have two children, Roland B. Jones and Rogene Gardiner Jones. Miss Rogene was born October 4, 1912, is a student in the Oregan High School and her talents are also being trained in music, particularly the violin and piano.

Roland B. Jones, the son, was born July 14, 1902, attended public schools, academies at Beaver Dam, Wisconsin, and Elgin, Illinois, and after working about two years in Chicago became an employe of the Schiller Piano Company, of which he is now assistant secretary. He married at Chicago, February 11, 1922, Miss Dorothy Bowermann, of Leaf River, Illinois, daughter of Dr. H. E. and Frances (Nally) Bowermann. They have a daughter, Patricia Ann, born December 13, 1923. R. B. Jones is also talented musically, plays the piano, and is a popular vocalist.

FLETCHER F. CLARK, of Manchester, Illinois, is the sole survivor of Company G, Ninety-first Illinois Infantry, and still resides at Manchester, where he was born December 17, 1835, being a very lively individual at the age of ninety-one years. He is president of the Farmers & Traders Bank. His birth occurred in a log house on the corner site in Manchester, where his daughter and son-in-law, Mr. and Mrs. L. C. Funk, now reside in a modern home. Another daughter is Mrs. M. T. Cuddy, of Roodhouse. A son, Ted Clark, resides in Oklahoma. Mr. Clark is remarkably active for his years, having taken some long auto trips during the past summer.

JESSE W. FELL. On the campus of the Illinois State Normal University was erected in 1918 a woman's dormitory known as Fell Hall, and so named to commemorate a zealous friend of the cause of industrial education and a pioneer in that direction in Illinois. Jesse W. Fell was the founder of the city of Normal and was a leader in the movement which resulted in the establishment there of the Normal University. Following are a few facts of his biography.

He was born in Chester County, Pennsylvania, about 1808. In 1828 he started west on foot, and after spending some years at Steubenville, Ohio, came to Delavan, Illinois, in 1832, and in 1833 located at Bloomington, being the first attorney in that new town. Subsequently he served as agent for school lands and the State Bank. In 1837, after the financial panic of that year, he resumed his law practice. For several years his home was at Payson, in Adams County. From there he returned to Bloomington, and was instrumental in securing the location of the Chicago & Alton Railway through that town. His name is associated with the founding of such Illinois towns and cities as Clinton, Pontiac, Lexington and El Paso. He was a pioneer exponent of the "City Beautiful" idea, and was instrumental in the planting of hundreds of shade trees at Bloomington and Normal, many which now are giants in size and are enjoyed by a generation few of whom know the identity of their benefactor.

Jesse W. Fell was an intimate friend of Abraham Lincoln. It was to him that Mr. Lincoln addressed his celebrated biography. In the spring of 1860 he served as secretary of the Republican State Central Committee. In 1862 President Lincoln appointed him paymaster of the regular army, and he served in that capacity two years. Jesse W. Fell died at Bloomington January 25, 1887.

EDWARD S. NICHOLS, of Roodhouse, Illinois, holds the distinction of being the oldest conductor in the service of the Chicago & Alton Railroad Company. He began his railroad career as a newsboy on his father's run between Joliet and Chicago in 1870, his father being Edwin O. Nichols, a veteran railroader, who served in Company D of the Nineteenth Massachusetts Infantry during the Civil war, and who died January 5, 1919, at Roodhouse.

E. S. Nichols again served as newsboy on the old North Missouri line between St. Louis and Ottumwa, Iowa, before entering the service of the C. & A. in 1874 as passenger brakeman. In 1879, with the opening of the western division between Roodhouse and Kansas City, he was given a run as baggageman between those points. In 1880 he served a few months as freight brakeman, when he was made freight conductor, serving until April, 1883, when he was given a regular run as passenger conductor between Roodhouse, Bloomington and St. Louis. He has followed a frugal and correct life, and his excellent physical condition, while still in the harness, is token of the reward of one who never undertook to cheat the laws of God or nature.

FRANK J. WISE. Since his admission to the bar of Illinois in 1904 Frank J. Wise has lent dignity and stability to professional affairs at Joliet, and thus has maintained a reputation for ability and resourcefulness. A broad-minded and progressive practitioner, a careful observer of the amenities and courtesies of his profession, and at all times seeking its most intelligent and praiseworthy compensations, he occupies a high place in the esteem of the general public and the profession, and as city attorney of Joliet is conserving and protecting the community's interests.

Mr. Wise was born at Joliet, November 22, 1880, and is a son of James and Katherine (Conklin) Wise. His father, a native of New York City, chose railroading as his life's vocation when a youth, and for many years was thus employed on various lines, for the most

part as a locomotive engineer. Of more recent years he has been employed by the city of Joliet in various capacities. He married Katherine Conklin at Joliet, she being a native of Beloit, Wisconsin, and they have two children: Anna, a graduate of the Junior High School at Joliet, who is now a teacher in the Chicago public schools; and Frank J., of this review.

Frank J. Wise attended the public and high schools of Joliet, and after some further preparation enrolled as a student at the Kent College of Law at Chicago, from which he was duly graduated with the degree of Bachelor of Law as a member of the class of 1904. He immediately returned to Joliet, where he has since been engaged in the general practice of his profession, having built up a large and remunerative clientele. He maintains offices in the Joliet National Bank Building, as well as his official offices in the City Hall. Mr. Wise has been identified with some of the most important litigation that has come before the courts in recent years, and his average of successful verdicts is high. He is well founded in the principles of his profession, of which he is a close and careful student, and his clients have his support from the lowest to the highest court of appeal. In 1913 Mr. Wise was first elected city attorney of Joliet, a position in which he served until 1915. In May, 1923, he again took this office, this time by appointment, and has occupied it to the present, with a splendid record. Mr. Wise subscribes to the principles of the democratic party, and in 1924 was chosen a delegate to the national convention of that party. He has several fraternal connections and is a communicant of St. Patrick's Catholic Church.

In 1908, at Joliet, Mr. Wise was united in marriage with Miss Mae McFadden, who was born at Joliet, and a daughter of John McFadden, a well-known resident of the city, and to this union there have been born three children: Donald F., Mary C. and Helen M.

Acc. B. MINTON, of Murphysboro, has for many years figured prominently in the business life of that section, particularly as a capitalist and promoter of urban and interurban transportation.

Mr. Minton was born in Virginia, in October, 1854, son of Edward and Mary (Ritchey) Minton. From Virginia the family moved to Tennessee, and were living there when the Civil war broke out. Edward Minton sympathized with the Union, and experiencing the hostile attitude of the people of Tennessee, he left that state and removed to Indiana, settling at Danville.

Acc. B. Minton grew up and received his education at Danville, Indiana. He came to Murphysboro, Illinois, at the age of twenty-one. For many years he was a railroad man, being in the service of the Mobile & Ohio Railroad and rising to the position of master mechanic, which he held for twenty-three years.

Since leaving the railroad service he has engaged in real estate and the wide scope of enterprises that reflect his executive ability and judgment. He has been unusually successful, and it has been his temperament never to waste energy or worry over mistakes and failures that, taking his career as a whole, have been very minor incidents.

Mr. Minton, in 1890, was associated with others in planning and carrying out the building of a street car line from East Murphysboro through Walnut Street to what is now Twenty-second Street. The rails used were thirty pound rails, narrow gauge, and the small cars were drawn by mules. In 1896 Mr. Walter Alexander became associated with Mr. Minton. Since then they have worked together in the handling of many important transactions. Largely due to the enterprise of these two men the street car line in 1910 was rebuilt and electrified. The Murphysboro Street Railway Company, organized at that time, had Mr. Minton as president, Thomas Logan, secretary and treasurer, and Mr. Walter Alexander, manager. The gauge was made standard and a heavier rail put in. These two men had as their active associate P. H. Eisenmeyer, then president of the Southern Illinois Milling Company, the late Willard P. Wall, then president of the First National Bank of Murphysboro, Joseph VanCluster and John L. Alexander, a brother of Walter. The line was extended on Twenty-second Street to the Iron Mountain depot. In 1917 the company built the interurban line from Murphysboro to Carbondale. Walter Alexander handled the preliminary survey for this line, after which R. C. Smith, of St. Louis, was employed as consulting engineer. This line, like all interurban lines over the country, has been affected by competition of "bus lines," but the company has met this by establishing a bus line of its own, using the most up to date motor busses.

Mr. Minton married Mary McNelly, daughter of Robert McNelly, who was editor and owner of the Cleveland Banner at Cleveland, Tennessee, where Mr. and Mrs. Minton were married. They have two sons, Robert, of East St. Louis, and Edward, of Murphysboro.

RONALD KINGSLEY, a veteran of the World war, who served with the Canadian Expeditionary Forces until disabled by wounds, is secretary of the Cairo Association of Commerce and has had a wide experience in commercial organization work.

He was born at Philadelphia, Pennsylvania, in November, 1890, son of Henry and Alice Elizabeth (Pratt) Kingsley. His parents were natives of England. His father served for a number of years with the rank of colonel in the English army, most of his service being in India. Ronald Kingsley attended public schools in Detroit, Michigan, and at the age of seventeen went abroad and lived for four years in England on the European continent. His early training took him toward the mining profession. After returning to America he went into the Hudson Bay district of Canada and was identified with the gold mines of the Porcupine district in northern Ontario until September, 1914.

Coming to the United States, he spent a brief time at Pittsburgh and then returning to Canada, enlisted in the Canadian infantry. With the Canadian contingent he went overseas and was in active service until wounded in the battle of the Somme, being injured in both legs and arms and in the right lung.

For fourteen months he was in a hospital and was then discharged on account of disability.

On returning to this country he was assigned duty with the United States Speakers' Bureau and did notable service in the Liberty Loan and other war drives, speaking in thirty-three states of the Union. In April, 1919, he became affiliated with the War Camp Community service.

After the war Mr. Kingsley was made secretary of the Chamber of Commerce at Scotts Bluff, Nebraska, and a year later organized the Chamber of Commerce of Falls City, Nebraska, serving as its secretary one year. He was then secretary of the Braddock Chamber of Commerce in Pennsylvania and in June, 1924, accepted the call to his present duties as secretary of the Association of Commerce at Cairo, handling the program of development work and other activities for Cairo and the southern Illinois district.

He married, August 8, 1920, Miss Wilhelmina Westfall, a native of Seward, Nebraska, and daughter of August H. Westfall. Mr. and Mrs. Kingsley are members of the Christian Science faith. He is a republican, is affiliated with the Masonic fraternity and belongs to the Egyptian Country Club at Cairo.

WILLIAM WILFORD KARRAKER is now living virtually retired at Dongola, Union County. In his years of activity he made a record of successful achievement as one of the prominent farmers in this county and also as an efficient and popular teacher in the public schools in rural districts.

Mr. Karraker was born in Pulaski County, Illinois, in the year 1851, but was reared from childhood in Union County. He is a son of the late Rev. Jacob and Mary (Peeler) Karraker, and is a representative of a sterling family that was founded in southern Illinois more than a century ago. Jacob Karraker was born in Union County, on the ancestral farmstead on which his son William W. was reared, and he was a son of Daniel and Rachel (Blackwelder) Karraker. Daniel Karraker was born in Cabarrus County, North Carolina, and was reared to manhood in that historic old commonwealth. In 1818 he made the overland journey, with team and wagon, to Illinois, and in what is now Union County he entered claim to a quarter section of timber land in Township Thirteen, Range One, East. He reclaimed this tract into a productive farm and here he remained, one of the highly esteemed pioneer citizens of the county, until his death in 1861. He was born in the year 1793, his wife having likewise been a native of North Carolina, where she was born in 1794. Surviving him by a score of years, she was eighty-seven years of age at her death, in 1881.

Mrs. Mary (Peeler) Karraker, mother of him whose name initiates this review, was a daughter of Christian and Rachel Peeler, who were born and reared in Tennessee and who thence made the overland journey to Illinois in the year 1817, they having been numbered among the earliest settlers in Union County, where their old homestead farm lay near the Johnson County line, on the main road between Dongola and Metropolis, and near Bethany Church, which was erected many years ago. The marriage of Jacob Karraker and Mary Peeler was solemnized in 1842, and they established their home on a farm in Pulaski County, where they remained several years and where their son William W., of this sketch, was born. After their return to Union County they settled on the farm near Dongola, and in that village they passed the closing years of their earnest and useful lives. Jacob Karraker was born in 1822 and died in 1910, his wife having been born in 1823 and having passed to the life eternal in 1900. Of their children the first two, Rachel and Malinda, are deceased; William Wilford, of this review, was the next in order of birth; David W. is deceased; Henry W. is a resident of Dongola; Julius and Calvin are deceased; Ella is the widow of Dr. George W. Ausbrooks and maintains her home at Dongola. The parents were devout members of the Baptist Church, in the faith of which they carefully reared their children.

William W. Karraker gained his rudimentary education by attending district schools, thereafter he was for two terms a student in the public schools at Anna, besides which he profited by the advantages of a select school at De Soto, Jackson County, and a school of normal order at Irvington, Washington County, the latter institution having closed when the Southern Illinois Normal University was established at Carbondale. At the age of twenty years Mr. Karraker began teaching in district schools during the winter terms and attending school during the summers.

After his marriage Mr. Karraker passed five years on the farm that he had acquired near Mount Olive Church, and in 1880 he purchased the old homestead farm that had been originally entered by his paternal grandfather. He continued to give his attention to farm enterprise and to teach school during winter terms during a total period of twenty-seven years, and to the old Karraker homestead he added until the place is now a fine farm of 190 acres. He now rents this farm to an approved tenant, and in the same section of the county he owns likewise another well improved farm of 100 acres and which is rented. In a general way Mr. Karraker still maintains an executive supervision of his farm estate, but when he retired from the farm he purchased a modern house, with five acres of land, at Dongola, where he and his wife now reside and where in June, 1925, their children and grandchildren helped them celebrate their fiftieth wedding anniversary.

Mr. Karraker has been progressive in his association with community affairs. He is township treasurer of schools for his home township and save for an interval of three years has held this office continuously since 1878. He has been interested in the work of the local Farm Bureau, and he and his wife are earnest members of the Baptist Church, in which he is a deacon.

In the year 1875 was solemnized the marriage of Mr. Karraker and Miss Sarah E. Richardson, who was born in 1853 in Williamson County, near Marion, and from the age of five years lived in or near Dongola, Union County. She is a daughter of the late Rev.

Francis Marion Richardson and Elizabeth J. (McCown) Richardson, the former of whom was born in the state of Georgia and the latter in Tennessee. Ira O., eldest of the children of Mr. and Mrs. Karraker, is president of the First National Bank of Jonesboro and is the subject of a personal sketch following this. Orville M. is president of the First National Bank of Harrisburg, Illinois. Carrie is the wife of Rev. Fred R. Johnson, of Atlanta, Illinois. Ray R. is cashier of the St. Louis National Bank of St. Louis, Missouri. Guy W. is associated with the United States Gypsum Company and lives in Chicago.

IRA OLIVER KARRAKER, president of the First National Bank of Jonesboro, the judicial center of Union County, is a native son of this county and a member of a family that was founded in southern Illinois in the early pioneer days—more than a century ago.

Mr. Karraker was born on the farm near Dongola, Union County, April 19, 1876, and is a son of William Wilford Karraker and Sarah Ellen (Richardson) Karraker. A personal sketch of his father precedes this, and in the article is given also a general review of the family history, so that it is unnecessary to repeat the data in this connection.

Reared on the home farm, Ira O. Karraker found in the district school his first medium of educational discipline, and later he was for two years a student in Union Academy at Anna, this county. He next completed a four years' course in the Southern Illinois Normal University, in which he was graduated as a member of the class of 1896. He taught school two years, one year as principal of the high school at Marion, Williamson County, and the ensuing year as superintendent of the public schools of that place. He then became bookkeeper in the Bank of Jonesboro, in which he was advanced to the position of assistant cashier and eventually to that of cashier. In 1913 the institution was incorporated as the State Bank of Jonesboro, and in 1923 it received its charter as the First National Bank of Jonesboro, Mr. Karraker having become president of the bank January 1st of that year and having since continued as its chief executive. Thomas Rixleben is vice president of the bank and Ed L. Karraker is its cashier. The bank has recently established headquarters in the modern building erected for its use, and this is recognized as one of the most attractive and best equipped bank buildings in this section of the state, with facilities that are usually to be found only in places of much larger population than that of Jonesboro.

Mr. Karraker is one of the public-spirited citizens of Jonesboro. He is president of the local Chamber of Commerce, and he has also served as a member of the Jonesboro Board of Education, of which he was the president four years. In the Masonic fraternity he is a past master of the local lodge of Ancient Free and Accepted Masons, his political alignment is with the democratic party, and he and his wife are members of the Baptist Church in their home community, he being the treasurer of the same.

February 5, 1913, recorded the marriage of Mr. Karraker and Miss Elsie Rendleman, who was born and reared at Jonesboro and who is a daughter of Drake H. and Nettie (Eddleman) Rendleman, both likewise natives of Union County. Mr. and Mrs. Karraker have two children: Ira Oliver, Jr., and Mary Elizabeth.

HARRY R. ROW. To Harry R. Row, growing up on a farm in southern Illinois, the work that made the strongest appeal to his ambition for a career was teaching, and in that profession he has achieved more than ordinary distinction. Mr. Row is now superintendent of city schools of Murphysboro. As a young man, he contrived most of his own opportunities. While his father was financially able to give him an education after the common schools, Mr. Row chose to earn his own way, and in carrying out this determination he tested his ability in a way that impressed all his subsequent efforts.

Mr. Row is Irish on his father's side and Holland-Dutch through his mother. He has the keen wit and pleasing personality of the educated Irishman and the thrift and tenacity of the Hollander.

His grandparents, Jacob and Mary Row, came from Ireland and settled in southeastern Missouri, where many of their descendants have made names in the professions, business and politics. However, politics never made an appeal to Adam Row, their son and the father of Harry R. Row. Adam Row, after reaching manhood, left Missouri and settled in Illinois. He married America Josephine Holland, whose ancestors came from Holland in Colonial times. Her parents lived near Jonesboro in Union County, Ohio. Her grandfather was a pioneer and a cousin of Daniel Boone and companion of that famous frontiersman in several of his trips over the mountains from Carolina to Kentucky.

Harry R. Row was born on his father's farm near Makanda, Illinois, in 1882. He attended country schools through the eighth grade, and in 1898 was graduated from high school at Cobden. Soon afterward he became a teacher, being employed in the schools of several villages and country communities. Teaching alternated with his own periods of work as a student while getting his higher education. At different times he attended the State Normal University at Carbondale, and in 1924 graduated from its Teachers College. Soon after graduating he became principal of the Washington School at Murphysboro. This school building was severely damaged by the tornado of March, 1925. Not long afterward, in the chaotic conditions that followed this disaster, Mr. Row was elected city superintendent, and has shown a wonderful degree of executive ability in restoring the school system to normality. In that work he has had the full and hearty cooperation of his principals and teachers.

Mr. Row married Miss Grace Brooks, daughter of A. H. Brooks, one of the prominent fruit growers of southern Illinois, living near Cobden in Union County. The two children of Mr. and Mrs. Row are Anna Mary, who graduated with the class of 1926 from the Normal University at Carbondale; and Harry, Jr., who graduated in 1926 from the Murphysboro High School.

FREDERICK G. BIERER. The name Bierer is one about which has gathered a peculiar measure of esteem in Jackson County throughout a period of over four score years. The representative of the family there today is Frederick G. Bierer, for a quarter of a century a leading member of the Murphysboro bar.

He was born at Murphysboro, June 1, 1875. His father was the late Dr. Frederick C. Bierer, an old time resident of Jackson County whose name and work will not soon be erased from the county's records. He attained distinction and real success in his profession and gave the best in him to further all enterprises for the general welfare.

Frederick C. Bierer was born in Pennsylvania, January 6, 1820. He was graduated from the Jefferson Medical College of Philadelphia in 1843. In 1844 he drove in a buggy from Pennsylvania to Effingham, Illinois. Shortly afterward he located at Murphysboro. He possessed unusual natural qualifications for his profession, and had the additional distinction of being one of the few doctors in that part of Illinois who at that time were graduates from a school of medicine of equal standing of old Jefferson Medical College. He practiced medicine with the best spirit of the old time country doctor, with utmost self abnegation. He traveled on horse back, went over almost impassable roads, and under conditions that tested alike his physical powers and his devotion to work. In 1861, at the outbreak of the Civil war, Doctor Bierer enlisted in Company H of the Twenty-seventh Illinois Infantry as a private. He was soon promoted to lieutenant, and after the regiment reached the front he was assigned duty as hospital surgeon. However, his health did not long stand up under the stress of his army duties. He had to resign his mission and return to Murphysboro, broken in health and unable to resume his private practice. Soon afterward he formed a partnership with Robert Worthen, and afterwards with P. W. Griffith, and for eighteen years was associated with one or the other in the mercantile business.

Doctor Bierer spent his last years at St. Louis, Missouri, where he died in January, 1893. It is only just to quote a happy tribute to him, previously published in a history of southern Illinois. "Doctor Bierer was a man of courtly person, marked vitality and most progressive ideas. . . . Served as mayor of Murphysboro in 1869 and thereafter was a member of the city board of aldermen for a considerable period. He was one of the originators of the Southern Medical Association and served several terms as president of the same. He was one of the founders of the First Lutheran Church of Murphysboro, and served as superintendent of its Sunday School for twenty-two years."

Doctor Bierer married in February, 1865, Sabina U. Griffith, daughter of John J. Griffith, a pioneer of southern Illinois. She made her home in Murphysboro until her death in 1916. Of her four children two died in infancy, and the two survivors are Frederick G. and Ella.

Frederick G. Bierer as a boy at Murphysboro attended the grade and high schools. He also had the training of work in his father's store. This experience showed him that a mercantile career was not the goal of his ambition. Therefore, he entered the law department of Washington University at St. Louis, and in 1900 was graduated LL. B., and in the fall of the same year was admitted to the Illinois bar. Mr. Bierer from that date has been engaged in a general practice at Murphysboro, and has made a wide reputation as a trial lawyer and counsellor. He served two terms as city attorney prior to 1911, and at this writing again holds that office. He has much of the public spirit and progressiveness that characterized his father, and his helpfulness was much in evidence after the appalling disaster of the tornado of March, 1925. He served as treasurer of the local relief organization and was one of the untiring workers in the rehabilitation of the stricken town.

Mr. Bierer is a director of the Citizens State & Savings Bank, which he was instrumental in organizing. He is attorney for the Southern Illinois Building & Loan Association and the Murphysboro Park District, is a director of the Jackson County Fair Association. Fraternally he is a past exalted ruler of the B. P. O. Elks, a member of the Knights of Pythias, Modern Woodmen of America, and is a republican.

He married, June 1, 1910, Miss Nellie S. Peirson, daughter of John J. and Anna K. Peirson, of Murphysboro. They have one son, Frederick Peirson Bierer. Mr. and Mrs. Beirer are active members of the First Presbyterian Church.

HERMAN GATEWOOD EASTERLY, prominent Jackson County farmer, known all over the state for his activities in betterment of farming conditions, was a pioneer in the organization of farm bureaus and other bodies that represent the modern cooperative spirit of agriculture. During 1903-04 he was president of the Illinois State Farmers Institute and was the first director of that association for his district.

Mr. Easterly spent both time and money in improving soil conditions in Jackson County, not only on his own farm but elsewhere. For some time he was one of the committee to locate soil stations. His own farming had been handicapped by poor soil conditions and in former years he frequently regretted that his father had not located in a part of Illinois now famed for its fine farms. The regret was overcome by his adoption of the methods recommended by the great experts in treating the soil by application of limestone, phosphate and other conditioners. Mr. Easterly carried out a program of this soil treatment on his own place in 1905, and was one of the first in his section of the state to prove its advantages.

Mr. Easterly's grandfather, Casper Easterly, was born in Germany and there were three brothers in the family who came to America, two settling in Virginia and one later moving over the mountains into Tennes-

see. Elbert Easterly, a son of Casper, in 1849 left Tennessee and came to Jackson County, Illinois, securing a tract of raw, unimproved land three miles west of Carbondale. He was then twenty-one years of age. On the land was a small log house. Its enlargement and improvements represented the successive stages of Elbert Easterly's prosperity. The old log part of the house is still standing, a part of the Easterly home, though the logs are now covered over with weather boarding. Casper Easterly subsequently joined his son and took up land adjoining, and two uncles did likewise, so that a considerable colony of Easterlys was established in that part of the county. On coming from the Tennessee the Easterlys traveled by the Tennessee River to Cairo, and thence up the Mississippi, and by boat as far as Murphysboro. Elbert Easterly died in 1874. He married Ellen Hinchcliff, whose father settled three miles southwest of Carbondale. She died in 1910.

Herman Gatewood Easterly was one of twelve children and was born at the old homestead in Jackson County September 2, 1858. As a boy he attended the country school located on his father's farm. His father had given half an acre of land as a site for the school and had also donated an acre as the ground for the Methodist Church. While not in school Mr. Easterly had the occupations and pastimes of other Illinois farm boys. Farming appealed to him rather than any other vocation. For a time he attended the Normal School at Carbondale, but at the age of sixteen, after his father's death, he had to take most of the responsibilities of the farm on his own shoulders. At the age of twenty-one he went out to California and for two years worked in the lumber camps in the midst of the giant forests of that state.

On returning to Illinois Mr. Easterly bought the interests of the other heirs of the old farm and has since made it his home. There he has spent a normal, happy, industrious and productive life. Some years ago he retired from the active labors of farming, which he turned over to his son Frank, who lives nearby. He has been a strong supporter of the Christian Church and his public spirit has been displayed on numerous occasions. During the World war he was engaged by the government as a buyer of corn, a work of great responsibility, also on the District War Board.

Mr. Easterly married Anna Arnold, of an old Connecticut family. She died in 1894, the mother of two sons, Frank and Charles. In 1898 Mr. Easterly married Mary Caldwell, daughter of Isaac H. Caldwell. She was born in Kentucky and her father came to Jackson County, Illinois, after the Civil war. Mrs. Easterly is, like her husband, generous, thoughtful of others and a leader in woman's work. She began teaching at the age of seventeen and at the time of her marriage was an instructor in the Normal University at Carbondale. For years she has been a member of the Illinois League of Women Voters and is now a director in that organization.

In conclusion some notes should be made of Frank and Charles Easterly, the two sons of Herman Gatewood. Frank was born October 25, 1888, and Charles, October 28, 1889. Frank Easterly married Pearl Williams, of White County, Illinois. Charles married Madge Davis, of Neligh, Nebraska. Both sons were educated in the public schools and Normal at Carbondale, and Frank attended the University of Illinois. Charles Easterly on July 27, 1917, entered the Second Officers Training School at Ft. Sheridan, Illinois, and on November 27 was commissioned a first lieutenant and ordered to Camp Lee, Virginia. On September 1, 1918, he was commissioned a captain, commanding the Provost Guard Battalion and served as assistant provost marshal at Camp Lee from December 1, 1918, to April 4, 1919, when he was given an honorable discharge. On returning to Carbondale he bought out the J. M. Johnson Lumber business, and has since operated that establishment.

VERY REV. JAMES F. GREEN, of the Augustinian Order of Priests, the oldest teaching order in the Catholic Church, came to Chicago on June 24, 1905, under appointment to organize St. Rita of Cascia Parish in a new and fastly developed section of the southwest side and also to erect a college for the education of boys. During twenty years the tide of population has spread far beyond the original limits of the parish, and St. Rita has become a mother church for other churches and institutions in that section of the city. Father Green laid the corner stone of the college at Sixty-third and Oakley on October 26, 1905, and in the college chapel first mass was celebrated in April, 1906. In 1915 the cornerstone of the present school building was laid at Sixty-second Street and Washtenaw Avenue and about seven years later preparations were begun for the erection of the new St. Rita Church, the cornerstone of which was laid in May, 1923. In 1926 was completed the largest convent in the city of Chicago, with accommodations for fifty nuns.

James Frank Green was born in Philadelphia, March 1, 1867, and as a boy he attended grammar and high schools there. At the age of seventeen he made definite choice of the priesthood as a career, and entered the Augustinian College at Villanova, Pennsylvania, and after three years was admitted to membership in the order of Friar Hermits of St. Augustine. He received his Holy orders from Archbishop Ryan of Philadelphia on June 11, 1892. In 1917 in St. Rita Church at Chicago was celebrated his silver jubilee. His first appointment was St. Mary's Church at Lawrence, Massachusetts, where for four years he rendered invaluable service as a priest in that textile center. In January, 1896, he went to the church at Hoosick Falls, New York, and in July, 1898, was appointed to labor with the Augustinian Missionary Band and as an assistant rector carried the word of God throughout the length and breadth of land. In January, 1901, he was appointed to his first independent care in the Parish of St. Joseph, Greenwich, New York, and during the four years he was there he completed the house and church and left the parish in a very prosperous condition.

Then, in June, 1905, he came to Chicago, where durnig the next twelve years he succeeded in laying the corner stones and completing the building of five combination churches and schools and a high school edifice within the limits of his original parish. Marking his constructive achievements, he was awarded the degrees Bachelor in Sacred Theology May 3, 1908. He served several terms as president of the college section of the Catholic Educational Association and has been a member of the general executive board.

During the Eucharistic Congress in Chicago he was chairman of the committee on health and sanitation.

Many tributes were paid him at the time of the celebration of his silver jubilee in 1917. To conclude this brief biography, one of those tributes may properly be quoted: "He has builded well, the priest who now celebrates his twenty-fifth anniversary of ordination to the priesthood. His labors have brought a suspicious thinness to his once luxurious hair, they have streaked the lines of gray among the black, worry grooves appear upon his brow. It may be that his time of rest has not yet arrived, but when it does he can point with pardonable pride to the result achieved in Chicago. All honor to Father Green, builder of churches; may he live long years of further usefulness in the priesthood that he honors."

JOHN G. HARDY. This is a name that has been significant in Murphysboro and Jackson County for a great many years. The late John G. Hardy, Sr., was a well known banker, and was in the banking business thirty years. His son, John G. Hardy, Jr., is manager at Murphysboro of the Illinois Southern Telephone Company.

The late John G. Hardy was born at Vienna, in Johnson County, Illinois, April 16, 1859, son of William B. and Malinda (Willis) Hardy. His parents were natives of Kentucky and were pioneer farmers of Johnson County, Illinois. John G. Hardy, Sr., was reared on a farm, finished his education in the Southern Illinois Normal University at Carbondale, and for four years taught in rural schools. In 1884, he was appointed deputy county clerk of Jackson County and was a member of the staff at the courthouse until 1892.

He participated in the organization of the City National Bank of Murphysboro in 1892, this succeeding the older bank of Murphysboro. He became cashier of the new institution, and on May 1, 1899, was elected president. He guided the destiny of this bank until failing health compelled him to retire, when he was succeeded by Col. E. A. Wells. John G. Hardy, Sr., died in 1923. He had also been treasurer of the Murphysboro Telephone Company and the Ohio and Mississippi Valley Telephone Company, was secretary and treasurer of the Murphysboro Electric Railway, Heat, Light & Power Company, and a director of the Jackson County Building & Loan Association.

John G. Hardy, Sr., was a democrat and for many years was a member and at one time president of the Murphysboro Board of Education. He and his wife were Methodists, and he was affiliated with the Royal Arch Chapter of Masonry, Independent Order of Odd Fellows, Knights of Pythias, and the Eastern Star and Daughters of Rebekah.

John G. Hardy, Sr., married, January 6, 1886, a daughter of Henry B. Neal, of Murphysboro. The children of their marriage were Ruth, Nell, John G., Jr., Carl N., Robert H., Mary E. and Esther.

John G. Hardy, Jr., possesses many of the attributes of character and business ability that distinguished his late father. He was born at Murphysboro in 1892. After finishing his education in the grade and high schools he went to work, at the age of eighteen, for the local telephone company, then known as the Murphysboro Telephone Company. It was his intention to master every technical and business detail of the telephone industry. Accordingly he started work as a lineman helper. He was promoted to lineman, later to wire chief, in 1915 to plant chief, and in 1916 became manager of the Murphysboro Telephone Company. In 1923 this became the Illinois Southern Telephone Company, with Mr. Hardy as manager.

During the World war he had a service record of two years and eleven days as an electrician in the United States navy. He has taken a keen interest in civic, educational and commercial organizations in southern Illinois.

Mr. Hardy married Ruth Redd, daughter of James Redd, of DeSoto.

NATHAN HENRY DOWDELL. At Carbondale, in Jackson County, is located the largest tie treating plant in the world, owned by the Ayer & Lord Tie Company. Edward E. Ayer, one of Chicago's most distinguished citizens, eminent as an archeologist and long actively identified with the Field Museum, was reared in northeastern Illinois, and in 1881 engaged in the cedar tie and pole business, delivering same to Chicago via boat, and afterwards developed the tie and lumber business in the southwest, supplying ties and timbers for railroads. He established the Ayer Lumber Company in 1882, and from the southwest the business was extended to Chicago, where an immense yard was established for the storage of ties, telegraph poles and other railroad material. Mr. Ayer in 1893 became associated with John B. Lord in the Ayer & Lord Tie Company. Mr. Lord was born in Massachusetts, but as a young man located at Paris, Illinois.

In the early years of the Ayer & Lord Tie Company the chief material for ties was white oak timber, which was very plentiful. As this material became scarcer and as other lumber substitutes did not stand up so well, various methods of treatment were introduced to prolong the service. In 1902 the company built a plant at Carbondale, adopting what was called the zinc treatment. This was subsequently discarded for the creosote method of treatment. Great quantities of creosote were shipped from Germany before the war, the German creosote being the best in the world. Creosote manufacturers of England mastered the secret of the manufacture of the best creosote, which is a coal tar product. The company now obtains the greater part of this material from England.

Nathan Henry Dowdell became associated with the tie and railroad material business founded by Mr. Ayer in 1888. He began as buyer of material, and when a plant was established at Carbondale he was put in charge of general superintendent and purchasing agent. At that time he removed with his family to Carbondale and for many years has been one of the city's valued residents. While now retired from active business, he is a director and stockholder in the Ayer & Lord Tie Company and is also a director of the First National Bank.

His father, Henry Dowdell, was a farmer and later a carpenter and builder. Nathan Henry Dowdell was born in Fountain County, Indiana, in 1858. He had only a few terms of schooling and otherwise helped his father on the farm and worked as a carpenter. For a few years he was employed in bridge building on the Clover Leaf Railroad between Toledo and St. Louis. At that time he realized the opportunities in the railroad material business. As he could save or raise the money he bought small tracts of timber, employed men to hew the ties, and he himself did the arduous work of hewing ties in the woods. He began supplying small quantities of such material, and his energetic ways attracted the attention of the Ayer & Lord Company and he was brought into their service.

Mr. Dowdell married Miss Julia Lucas, of Pike County, Indiana. She died in 1922, the mother of seven children. Two of the sons made records as soldiers in the World war. Dick Derwood Dowdell while in France was severely wounded in battle and reported as dead, and six weeks passed before his father and mother learned otherwise. He never fully recovered from his wounds. The other soldier son, Frank Edward Dowdell, was in the Air Corps stationed at Berkeley, California, and since the war has continued in the service, now with the rank of lieutenant.

HOMER D. LEE. One of the best known men in the city of Carbondale is Homer D. Lee. He is not only well known, but respected and popular, though a man of quiet and modest demeanor, never prone to advertise himself.

Mr. Lee was born February 4, 1872, at Pomona, Jackson County, Illinois, son of Arthur M. Lee and grandson of Arthur Lee. His father, Arthur M. Lee, was born on the old homestead near Campbell Hill in Jackson County, and served four years in the Union army with the rank of captain. He was wounded in battle, a bullet passing through his chest and lodging in the muscles of his back. That wound was the eventual cause of his death, though he lived many years after the war. He was a student of medicine in Rush Medical College when the great fire occurred in that city in 1871. Rush Medical College being destroyed, he continued his professional education in Nashville, Tennessee. He practiced at Pomona in Jackson County, and afterwards at Carbondale, where his professional work continued until his death in 1907. He was on the first board of pension examiners, served as a member of the Legislature and for several years was chief surgeon to the Southern Illinois Penitentiary. He married Sarah Jane Heiple, of De Sota, Illinois, who died in 1917. They were the parents of six children.

Homer D. Lee spent his early years at Pomona in Jackson County and was sixteen years old when his parents moved to Carbondale on account of the better school facilities there. He was graduated from the Normal University in 1895 and continued his studies in Ewing college. Mr. Lee for three years taught in the Carbondale schools. For twelve years he was connected with the Carbondale post office, beginning as money order clerk and subsequently was assistant postmaster. His servive in the post office was not continuous. For four years of that time he was county treasurer, being elected in 1910. On retiring from the office in 1914 he went back to the post office and was assistant postmaster when America entered the World war.

Mr. Lee endeavored to get into the army, but postal officials declared that he was greatly needed in the post office. Finally he resigned and from August 1, 1918, to July 5, 1919, was with the Y. M. C. A. in its overseas work, and part of the time was in the very front line trenches. After the war Mr. Lee returned to Carbondale and has since been active in merchandising in that city.

He married, in 1896, Miss Rosa Williams, daughter of C. W. Williams, of Carbondale. Their son, George D. Lee, enlisted soon after America entered the war, was trained at Jefferson Barracks, then at Kelley Field, Texas, with the Flying Corps, and spent eighteen months in France. He went in as a private, and was promoted to second lieutenant. George D. Lee is now field superintendent for the Hamilton Construction Company of Carbondale.

CORAL T. HEYDECKER was educated both as a mining engineer and as a lawyer, and was identified with the mining industry of the West for a time. Since returning to his native City of Waukegan he has practiced law and carried on a real estate business.

Mr. Heydecker is a son of the veteran Waukegan attorney, Christian T. Heydecker. Christian T. Heydecker among other labors of a busy and useful life compiled and published the geneaology of the Heydecker family, a valuable account, both historical and reminiscent and genealogical of this family in Europe and America, running back to about the year 1000 A. D., with a consecutive record of his particular branch of the family to 1643. The home of this branch of the Heydecker family for many generations has been at Kempten, in Bavaria, Germany, where is still standing the attractive old home built some time before 1750. The first ancestor in consecutive line was Joachim Heydecker, whose first marriage occurred in 1643. His son, Joachim II, was born August 12, 1657, and died February 1, 1722. His son, Markus, was born April 19, 1697. Joachim III, son of Markus, was born February 26, 1731. He was the father of Joachim Heydecker IV, who was born February 2, 1774, and died November 26, 1839. He was twice married and was the father of twenty-four children. His second wife was Euphrosina Abrell, who was born October 28, 1785, and died March 20, 1847.

Charles Frederick Heydecker, the pioneer of the family in Lake County, Illinois, was born at Kempten, Bavaria, July 27, 1814, and came to America in 1838, at the age of twenty-four. In the old country he had been given a fine training as a gardner. In 1844 he settled in Lake County, Illinois, buying land from the government, and eventually improving his farm of 200 acres. He lived in Lake County until his death on April 16, 1896. The first six years after he came to America he lived in the vicinity of Richmond, Virginia, and there came to entertain a strong dislike for slavery, and after coming to Northern Illinois was a staunch abolitionist. He joined the republican party at its organization.

Charles F. Heydecker married, May 1, 1845, Mary Ann Townsend, who was born in New York State, February 15, 1821, daughter of John and Hannah Townsend. The Townsend family came to America in 1630, settling near Boston, but being Quakers they suffered persecution and subsequently settled at Oyster Bay, Long Island. Mary Ann Townsend was a daughter of Lawrence Townsend, who during the Revolution was captain of a company of New York militia. Through this ancestor Coral T. Heydecker is eligible to membership in the Sons of the American Revolution. Mary Ann Heydecker died January 24, 1884. She came to Lake County alone in 1844, and was married the following year. She was survived by seven children.

The oldest of these is Christian Townsend Heydecker, of Waukegan, who was born September 4, 1846, in Lake County, Illinois, and died at San Diego, California, February 25, 1926. He was reared on a farm, attended a log schoolhouse, and at the age of twenty-one began study in a law office at Waukegan and was admitted to the bar by the Supreme Court of Illinois in 1870. He was engrossing clerk of the Illinois Legislature in 1871, was speaker's clerk in 1875 and 1885 was appointed public administrator of Lake County in 1872, serving over twenty years, and in 1890 was elected, running on an independent ticket, as state's attorney of Lake County. He was re-elected in 1892 and again in 1896. One of his notable services was in presenting a plan for the reorganization of the Modern Woodmen of America in 1890, at a time when that organization was practically bankrupt. He was chosen a member of the board of five directors and for many years devoted much of his time to putting the business affairs of the order on a sound basis. He has been a member of many other fraternal organizations. He cast his first vote for General Grant in 1868 and carried a torch in a rally at Waukegan when Abraham Lincoln delivered a campaign speech in 1860. He was a long and faithful member of the Baptist Church and for many years taught a class in the Sunday School.

Christian T. Haydecker married, May 22, 1872, Lorina Townsend, who died November 14, 1873. On April 18, 1875, he married Carolina Alice Gourley, who was born January 25, 1851, daughter of James and Lucy Ann (Poe) Gourley. They became the parents of four children: Coral T.; Nina Louis, who died in infancy; Bessie Irene, who married James Fred Berry; and Alice Emma, wife of Edward Dethloff, formerly of the United States Navy.

Coral T. Heydecker was born at Waukegan and was educated in grammar and high schools there, graduating from high school in 1901. In 1904 he completed the course of the Chicago-Kent College of Law and subsequently took a special mining course in the Missouri School of Mines at Rolla. He was admitted to the Illinois bar in 1904. In 1909 he removed to Idaho and spent four years in mining, and in the practice of law. On his return to Waukegan he resumed the general practice of law with his father under the firm name of Heydecker & Heydecker, and is also engaged in real estate operations, handling largely his own property. During his residence in the West he served as city clerk of Hailey, Idaho, two years. For two years he was probation officer of Lake County. Mr. Heydecker is a past high priest of Waukegan Chapter, Royal Arch Masons, is a Knight Templar Mason, member of the Eastern Star, Knights of Pythias, Elks, Modern Woodmen of America and Tribe of Ben Hur, belongs to the Kiwanis Club, the Pi Kappa Alpha fraternity, the Glen Flora Country Club and is a republican.

He married at Waukegan, June 8, 1910, Miss Edith Dunakin, daughter of Edson A. and Effie (Wiswell) Dunakin. Her parents came to Lake County from Ohio, and her father was a broom maker and carpenter. Mr. and Mrs. Dunakin now reside with their daughter, Mrs. Heydecker. Effie Wiswell had four brothers, Henry, Oliver, Wilson and Edmond, who all enlisted in an Ohio regiment for service in the Civil war and all of whom survived their military experience, the first to pass away being Edmond, who died in 1924. Mr. and Mrs. Coral T. Heydecker have three children: Robert Coral, Edwin Murray, and Marjorie Edith, all born in Waukegan.

COL. THOMAS B. F. SMITH. A resident of Carbondale since early manhood, Colonel Smith has long enjoyed a successful practice and standing as a lawyer, and among other experiences and attainments has an interesting record as an American officer in the World war.

He was born in Lyon County, Kentucky, May 12, 1877, and in 1889, when he was twelve years of age, his parents, William F. and Sarah (Nickell) Smith, moved to Southern Illinois and located on a farm in Williamson County. Colonel Smith had a farm training, attended country schools and in 1897 moved to Carbondale, where in the intervals of teaching he attended the Southern Illinois Normal University, where he was graduated in 1901. He had five years of experience as a teacher. For two years he was superintendent of schools at Jonesboro, in Union County. He studied law at the University of Illinois, was graduated in 1905 and admitted to the bar in February of the same year, and at once engaged in general practice at Carbondale. He was elected city attorney in 1905, and has held this office for sixteen years and was also elected to the Board of Equalization in 1916. Colonel Smith is a well trained lawyer and has long enjoyed prestige as a trial attorney and as a very popular public speaker, and has been one of the able campaigners of the republican party in his section of the state. He was republican candidate for state's at-

torney in 1912, and for the State Senate in 1924. Colonel Smith is a Rotarian, has been a deacon in the Presbyterian Church, and is now a trustee, is a Royal Arch Mason, member of the B. P. O. Elks, Knights of Pythias, Independent Order of Odd Fellows and Modern Woodmen of America. He married September 9, 1903, Miss Bessie Johnson, daughter of James M. and Sarah A. (Harvey) Johnson. The father served as local commander of the G. A. R. Mrs. Smith is a member of the D. A. R., a descendant of Sir William Harvey. Colonel and Mrs. Smith had a son, now deceased.

Colonel Smith was a volunteer in the World war, being above the age included in the age period of the first draft law. On August 27, 1917, he entered the Second Officers Training Camp at Fort Sheridan, and on November 27th was commissioned a captain of infantry. He was given secret orders to sail for France, and sailing at once arrived in France on January 7th. For three months he had special training in trench warfare in a special school for offices under French and English instructors. He was then assigned to the Eighty-second Division, spending several weeks behind the front lines as instructor. He was next sent to the Fourth Division as instructor in trench warfare, and was then assigned to the Three Hundred and Eleventh Infantry Regiment, Seventy-eighth Division, as company commander of Company F, Second Battalion. He participated in the splendid record of that fighting unit during the second Somme offensive, the Oise-Aisne offensive and in the Somme defensive was cited for bravery and decorated by the French government with the Croix de Guerre. Though broken in health and suffering from partial shell shock he made no complaint and asked for no rest. However, in September, 1918, he was ordered to report to general headquarters and was assigned duty with the adjutant general of the American forces. In February, 1919, he was ordered to Beaune, Cote d'Or, the location of a proposed university which soldiers of the United States and France could attend. There he was put in charge of the buildings and grounds and continued in service and on duty, being promoted to major, until on July 9, 1919, when on account of his health he was relieved and returned to America. He now has the rank of lieutenant colonel in the Officers Reserve Corps.

HOSEA E. SKINNER. At the beginning of the nineteenth century the Skinner family was living at Wilmington, Delaware. In that city was born in 1801 a boy named John Skinner. Later in the same year his parents started west, with a view to prospecting for a new home on the prairies of the Mississippi Valley. They traveled in a prairie schooner drawn by six horses, but most of their personal possessions were left behind at Wilmington until they were established. While passing through Indiana the six-horse team ran away. The father of John was killed and his mother injured, while the infant son escaped death through the presence of mind of his mother in throwing him from the speeding wagon well wrapped in a blanket. A year later the mother of John married again and the family established their home near Springfield, Illinois. John Skinner grew up in this frontier community, and attended such schools as were maintained by subscription in the community. At the age of seventeen, the same year that Illinois became a state, he engaged in farming on his own account, locating six miles south of Carterville in Williamson County. This was the beginning of the Skinner homestead farm, one of the farms that has been in uninterrupted ownership by one family for more than a century. John Skinner lived in that home until his death in 1889.

His son, Nelson Skinner, was born at the homestead in 1838. Nelson Skinner was a citizen of Williamson County who commanded more than ordinary respect and esteem. He looked after his own affairs and business as a farmer, directing them to substantial success. He was also strong minded and possessed both physical and moral courage. He believed that every one should obey the law no matter what this law was, and he put this principle into practice during the sixteen years he was constable and also as deputy sheriff under Sheriff Hartwell Duncan. For many years he was a trustee of his local schools and was a pronounced democrat in a strong republican community, but was elected by large majorities when prevailed upon to become a candidate for office. Nelson Skinner lived to the same age as his father, passing away May 1st, 1926, aged eighty-eight. He married the daughter of a Baptist minister, George W. Ellis. Mary Elizabeth (Ellis) Skinner is now seventy-five years of age and still makes her home at the Skinner farm. There were four children: Miss Tranquil; Hosea E.; Leroy, now connected with the Missouri Pacific Railroad Company at Jefferson City Missouri; and Miss Jessie Delaware.

Hosea E. Skinner, who is successfully established in law practice at Marion, was born November 16, 1876. He lived at the Skinner homestead, and completed his eighth grade education in the country schools. At the age of fifteen, in 1891, he entered the Southern Illinois Normal University at Carbondale and spent two summers there. The intervening winters, in spite of his youth, he taught school. Later he entered Valparaiso University in Indiana, was graduated Bachelor of Science in 1904, and following that for a year was superintendent of schools at Watseka, Illinois. As a further means of broadening his education and business experience he took a position with the International Harvester Company and traveled over the states of Wisconsin, Michigan and the Dakotas. Mr. Skinner in 1908 accepted appointment as a clerk in the War Department at Washington, and while thus employed he attended George Washington University, from which he obtained the B. A. degree in 1910. following that with a law course in the Georgetown University School of Law, from which he received the LL. B. degree in 1913 and the Master of Laws degree in 1914. Mr. Skinner was admitted to the bar of the District of Columbia in 1914, and in the same year returned to Illinois and was admitted to practice in the courts of this state. Mr. Skinner in 1916 again resumed employment with the International Harvester Company, this time as field secretary. For three years his duties required a great deal of travel through western Canada. In 1918 the company decided to send him on a special mission to South America. On the way he stopped at his old home in Williamson County, and while there the company decided that on account of war conditions the trip to South America should be postponed. His father being in poor health at the time, Mr. Skinner in order to remain at home accepted some commissions as an attorney, being employed by the city of Cartersville to revise its ordinances, and he was also employed as counsel for the objectors to the organization of the community high school. Much other business came to him practically without solicitation on his part, and this demand for his professional services in the end caused him to locate permanently in his native county. In 1921 he moved to Marion and shared the office of Judge Hartwell, and two years later secured separate offices in the Marion State & Savings Bank Building, where he now directs a large and important practice.

Mr. Skinner, who has never married, took his first degrees in Masonry at the age of twenty-one in the Lodge of Cartersville. He became a Royal Arch Mason at Washington, D. C., and has membership in other bodies, including the Shrine at East St. Louis. He also belongs to the Elks. He was one of the leaders among the progressive younger business and professional element of Marion in instituting the Marion Golf Club, which now has a fine course.

LEWIS M. CROW, whose home is at Grand Tower, is one of the best known citizens of this section of the Mississippi Valley. For many years he was on the Mississippi as a steamboat man, and is one of the comparatively few old river men still found whose recollections go back to the time when the river was one of the greatest arteries of traffic in the United States.

Mr. Crow's father, James Crow, was born in 1824, and settled in Jackson County at a time when Brownsville was its only post office. James Crow married Melissa Logan, of the noted Logan family of southern Illinois. She was a native of Holly Springs, Mississippi.

Lewis M. Crow was born at Carbondale, Illinois, October 11, 1858. He first attended a school on the west side of Carbondale, his teacher being Lucretia Brush. He was eight years old when the family moved to Grand Tower, a beautiful village located on the banks of the Mississippi. Her father was an employe of the Illinois Central Railroad Company, having charge of the handling of freight between the railroad and the river boats at that point and was freight agent of the Grand Tower Mining & Manufacturing Transportation Company on wharf boats.

Thus the river and its traffic exercised an early fascination upon Lewis M. Crow. As soon as old enough he began making trips on the river boats and in time had worked up to and qualified as chief engineer, a position of great responsibility, requiring nerve and brain. He was engineer on some of the noted boats along the river in that day and saw some of the famous races that made steamboat travel so exciting.

Mr. Crow left the river when he became postmaster of Grand Tower on April 1, 1899. He was appointed by President McKinley, succeeding Tiffin Jenkins. Mr. Crow has held the office of postmaster a period of twenty-seven years, his being one of the longest continuous services in an office of that kind in this part of the state. While postmaster he also served as cashier of the Bank of Grand Tower from 1905 to 1917, entering that bank soon after it was organized by Charles C. Huthmacher. Since 1917 he has given all his time to his duties as postmaster.

Mr. Crow for many years was a member of the local school board and is a veteran member of the Masonic Order. He married Dora A. East, daughter of James A. East, of Jackson County. His son, Lewis M. Crow, Jr., was in the railroad artillery service in France during the World war as a duty sergeant. He is now a trusted employe of the National City Bank of New York City in its Chicago branch.

IDA GEORGIANNA VANDERWATER, of 654 East Chestnut Street, Kankakee, represents a family that has been identified with this county for a great many years.

She was born at Belleville in Hastings County, Ontario. Her parents were Elias and Amanda H. (Yates) Vanderwater, also of Hastings County, Ontario. The Vanderwater family first settled in New York colonies and were of pure Holland Dutch descent. Elias Vanderwater brought his family to Kankakee in 1864. During the first winter he husked corn and did other farm labor, but in the spring rented a farm near Pilot Grove. He then bought a place three miles west of Manteno, remaining on it for seventeen years. When he retired he located in Kankakee, where he died in September, 1898. His wife passed away in January, 1898.

Of eleven children, Ida G. is one of two survivors. Her brother, Walter Singleton, is head of the Vanderwater Clothing Company of Kankakee.

Miss Vanderwater was educated in public schools, attended college at Valparaiso, Indiana, and for a number of years has been a Christian Science practitioner. She owns a 120-acre farm at Manteno, and also owns the comfortable residence in which she resides in Kankakee.

PHIL CLINE is proprietor of the Phil Cline Drug Store at Eleventh and Walnut streets in Murphysboro. He learned the business under his father, a veteran druggist of Williamson County, and is one of the very popular and progressive younger business men of Murphysboro.

He was born at Marion, in Williamson County, son of John M. Cline and grandson of Jefferson Cline, who came from Pennsylvania, first locating in Kentucky, where John M. Cline was born. John M. Cline on moving to Marion, Illinois, opened a drug business and continued its active operation forty-two years, until his death in 1922. He married Mary A.

Vick, of Marion, whose family came from Virginia. She was a daughter of Samuel S. Vick.

Phil Cline attended public schools in Marion, worked in his father's drug store, and in 1916 graduated from the School of Pharmacy of Northwestern University at Chicago. He then returned to his father's business at Marion and from there came to Murphysboro, working in the old Post Drug Store on the site now occupied by Louis Hoffman's clothing store at Tenth and Walnut. After the death of Mr. Post his son operated the store until it was sold to a brother and cousin of Phil Cline, L. V. Cline and S. S. Vick. They continued it as the Cline-Vick Drug Company. In 1923 Phil Cline engaged in business for himself at 1603 Walnut Street, and remained in that location until his store was wrecked by the tornado of March, 1925, and totally destroyed by the fire which followed. After the fire Mr. Cline bought the interests of the Cline-Vick Drug Company and has built up a splendid business.

Mr. Cline married Mabel Carter, daughter of Albert R. Carter, one of the leading physicians and surgeons of Jackson County. Mr. Cline is a Knight Templar Mason and Shriner.

HARRY W. RENDLEMAN. One of the greatest horticultural regions in the United States is a rugged section of southern Illinois, in Egypt, one of the men who has exploited the great fruit producing possibilities of the section and given it fame is Harry W. Rendleman, a resident of Carbondale, but whose home during the fruit growing season is on one of the picturesque hills of Union County at Alto Pass.

His father, Joseph Rendleman, was born in Union County, Illinois, and is now living retired at West Frankfort. The Rendlemans came from North Carolina. Joseph Rendleman married Catherine Landreth, a native of Tennessee. Their son, Harry Rendleman, was born at Cobden, Union County, June 17, 1873. He attended school at Cobden, but after the age of eight years at Alto Pass in the same county. Beginning while a boy, during school vacations he engaged in the fruit brokerage business. At the age of nineteen he was traveling out of Chicago as a fruit broker.

His knowledge of the fruit business was gained while in the brokerage work, and he had very little to start with on his account except this experience and a credit which enabled him to start his orchard planting. In 1901 he acquired his present farm at Alto Pass. As a producer he grows apples and peaches. His apples are the Transparent, Duchess and Winesap, planted in blocks that gives him an opportunity to sell in three seasons. His peaches are the Albertas. From the top of the great pyramid Bald Knob in Little Egypt the view in all directions is one of the most beautiful in the world, particularly in the fall when the leaves are colored by nature, and again in the spring when the orchards are in bloom.

Mr. Rendleman built his modern home on the farm in 1910. During the winters he has his residence in Carbondale. He married, in 1893, Miss Cora Abernathy. They are very congenial people, popular, hospitable, and while the fruit business requires their close attention and a great deal of hard work, they have also found pleasure in the esthetic side of the industry and delight in showing visitors about the orchards.

Mr. Rendleman owns 220 acres in his farm at Alto Pass. Within a radius of four miles of his orchards the fruit produced commercially totals an annual average of five hundred carloads of apples and peaches. This fruit is sold "on the track" at Alto Pass. Mr. Rendleman employs six men all the year round and during the summer months employs from seventy-five to eighty additional men and women.

ALFRED CLINTON HOY, member of the Chicago bar, a specialist in real estate law, is a member of one of the most notable pioneer families of Du Page County.

Mr. Hoy was born at Warrenville, in Du Page County, Illinois, January 26, 1882, son of Clinton H. and Mary A. (Manning) Hoy. His grandfather, Reuben Hoy, was a native of Pennsylvania, and settled in Du Page County among the first pioneers. He developed a large farm there, and exerted a valuable influence in the progressive development of the community. While holding the office of roadmaster he built the first steel bridge over the Du Page River. He was also a school director, and in politics a whig until the formation of the republican party. He and his wife had seven children.

Theodore Marshall Manning, maternal grandfather of A. C. Hoy, came to northern Illinois from New York state with his parents, who made the journey overland and settled at Warrenville, in Du Page County. He attended schools in New York and also in Du Page County, was one of the early graduates of the old Union College of Law of Chicago, and earned a place of distinction in the early bar of that city. He was a personal friend of Abraham Lincoln.

Clinton H. Hoy was born in Pennsylvania, attended school at Warrenville, Illinois, Northwestern College at Naperville, and lived in Du Page County from the age of about twelve years. For several years he was traveling collector for the Johnson Harvester Company, and subsequently was with the Deering Harvester Company. From 1894 to 1898 he was sheriff of Du Page County, was a school director and trustee for over a quarter of a century, and for a number of years has been a member of the County Republican Central Committee. He is now living retired on the old Manning homestead, which at one time was owned by his wife's grandfather, Rockwell Manning. His wife was born at Warrenville, in Du Page County, and they were married there. They had six children: Mabelle A., wife of John Thorso; Alfred C.; Bertha M.; Elsie L.; Ralph M., who married Alice S. Saylor; and Truman J.

Alfred C. Hoy attended the schools of Wheaton, graduating from high school there in 1900, as president of his class. After spending about three years on the old homestead farm he taught school five years, four years of that time being principal of the Bloomingdale School. He then entered Northwestern University School of Law at Chicago, was graduated in 1911, and since then has had a steadily growing practice in Chicago and in his native county, largely in real estate law. He is also head of a successful real estate organization, and in 1926 was elected president of the Du Page County Real Estate Board.

Mr. Hoy was for ten years president of the Warrenville School Board, and served as public administrator of Du Page County under Governor Lowden and two years under Governor Small. He is in the tenth year of his service as a republican precinct committeeman. He is a member of Wheaton Lodge No. 268, A. F. and A. M., Wheaton Chapter, R. A. M., Oak Park Lodge No. 1290, B. P. O. Elks, the Hamilton Club of Chicago, Realty Club of Chicago, and Antlers Country Club. Mr. Hoy married, December 27, 1917, Miss Martha Carrol, of Chicago. They have two children, Louise Carrol and Alfred Clinton, Jr.

JAMES A. PATTERSON is one of Carbondale's leading merchants, has been in business there for a quarter of a century, and has earned his prosperity on his own merits and energy. He inherits many of the qualities of his respected and esteemed father, one of the best known of the old time citizens of Jackson County.

His father was the late Gabriel William Patterson. He was born in Ireland, in 1842, of a well-to-do family of that country. He was still a child when his father, John Patterson, died. According to the laws of the country the homestead was inherited by the oldest son. The other members of the family at different times sought homes in the new world. Two sailing vessels, each of which carried a Patterson as one of its passengers, were lost at sea. Gabriel Patterson at the age of eleven, in 1853, accompanied his mother, Ellen Patterson, who first settled in Ohio and later in the same year moved to southern Illinois, near Makanda in Jackson County. Here Gabriel William Patterson grew to manhood. He worked on farms, and while he had little opportunity to attend school, his taste for good reading brought him advantages superior to many college bred men of his time.' His thrifty and energetic habits enabled him while still a young man to buy a farm at the edge of the village of Makanda. He engaged in farming and cattle raising there, and in 1867 opened a small general store in the village. His energy was remarkable, enabling him not only to operate his farm but look after his store, and he also engaged in buying and selling grain, and was prompt and ready with his volunteer services at every call made by the community for his church. He was a leading prohibitionist in his time and helped drive the saloons from his village. During 1884-88 he was postmaster of Makanda, also served on the school board, and was an active Methodist.

Gabriel W. Patterson died in 1901. He married, October 28, 1871, Susan Catherine Zimmerman, a bright, lovely woman who now resides at Carbondale. Her father was Samuel Zimmerman, a merchant of southern Illinois, and her grandfather, Jacob Zimmerman, moved from Pennsylvania to Kentucky and thence to Illinois, where he served in the State Legislature. The children of Gabriel Patterson and wife were: George, a building contractor; James A.; Mary Estelle, wife of Dr. Fred Lingle; Edward E., who now operates the old homestead farm; Dr. Herbert W., a dentist at Carbondale; Mabel, wife of L. R. Harrington, of the Hamilton Construction Company of Carbondale; and Samuel, a Carbondale merchant.

James A. Patterson was born at Makanda in Jackson County, January 15, 1878. His advantages in the village schools were supplemented by a course in McKendree College. At that time he intended to become a lawyer. The death of his father interrupted his plans, since he felt an obligation to get into business for himself. Returning home, he worked in the store and post office, and after a time moved to Carbondale, in 1903, and began taking orders for made-to-order clothing. His genial personality and honest endeavor to please won him a large custom. At the same time he clerked in the Leader Shoe Store. After five years of hard work and saving he was able to open a men's furnishing store in the room adjoining the Frank Hewitt Drug Store. He remained there one year, and in 1909 he organized and incorporated the James A. Patterson & Company, with himself as president and L. R. Harrington as secretary and treasurer. The firm then moved to its present quarters, where the business has had a constant growth and increasing prosperity. J. A. Patterson now owns the building. He also served four years as City Commissioner. When Mr. Harrington retired to become connected with the Hamilton Construction Company his place was taken by W. J. Brown, who is now secretary and treasurer of the company.

Mr. Patterson is a member of the Methodist Church. He married, in 1903, Miss Florence Brown, daughter of William J. Brown, the present city clerk of Carbondale. They have three children: Vernon R., a graduate of high school and the Normal University and now attending Washington University at St. Louis; Alice, aged sixteen, who is a talented pianist; and Florence, a pupil in the public schools.

ALBERT R. CARTER, M. D. A physician and surgeon and horticulturist, Doctor Carter has lived most of his life in Jackson County, and in notable measure has satisfied the chief ambitions of his nature for accomplishment and service to his fellow men.

Doctor Carter's grandfather, William Carter, came to Illinois from Missouri when a young man and settled on a farm near Campbell Hill, where he lived all his life. Doctor Carter's father, John Allen Carter, the eldest son of William Carter, was born near Campbell Hill, Illinois, where he became a well-known farmer. After retiring in 1913 he lived eight years at Campbell Hill, and in 1921 removed to the town of Ava, where he died in February, 1923. His wife was Susan T. Phoenix, a native of Williamson County, Illinois, and daughter of Frederick Phoenix, who at one time was a merchant in partnership with Peter Keefer at DeSoto, Illinois. He spent his last years on a farm in Bradley Township, Jackson County, Illinois.

Albert R. Carter was born September 17, 1867, in Bradley Township, Jackson County. His birthplace was what was known as the old Abe Koen farm. His father at that time operated the farm under lease. He later bought a farm in Bradley Township, where he lived until 1913, when he retired, moving to Campbell Hill. The old Carter home is now owned by the youngest brother of Doctor Carter, William Frederick Carter. Albert R. Carter while a boy on the farm shared in its work, and secured his early advantages in a country school. The first school he attended was the Barrow School, two and a half miles from the Carter home and near the old Bradley station. This station was subsequently moved down the line of the St. Louis and Cairo narrow gauge railroad and became Campbell Hill Station. A better school was then conducted at Campbell Hill, taught by John W. Jeffery, and Doctor Carter attended this school, though it was farther from home. Doctor Carter also attended the Southern Illinois Normal at Carbondale. He had an ambition to teach in higher schools, having had some experience as a teacher in rural districts at Sugar Hill, the old Jones School, and elsewhere in Jackson County.

Doctor Carter in 1890 married Augusta Schlegle, daughter of Julius Schlegle, who came from Germany and settled in St. Clair County, Illinois. Julius Schlegle was highly educated, a master of several languages, and was a railroad man and farmer. Doctor Carter graduated in 1895 in the medical course from Washington University at St. Louis. For three years he practiced at Campbell Hill, and ten years at Cora City, where he built up a large general town and country practice. In 1908 he sought a still larger field and established his home and professional offices at Murphysboro, opening his office in the Herbert Block. He continued in private practice there until 1917. Doctor Carter volunteered and was commissioned a first lieutenant in the Army Medical Corps and was stationed at Camp Wadsworth, South Carolina, while the Twenty-seventh Division was in training there. On account of disabilities incurred in the line of duty he received his honorable discharge in May, 1918, and then returned to Murphysboro, where he opened his offices at his present location.

Doctor Carter has a fine farm of 165 acres in Jackson County. Sixty-five acres of this land is devoted to apples and peaches. His chief commercial apple crops are the Yellow Transparent and Winesap, together with several blocks of Red and Yellow Delicious. His peaches are the Elberta, J. H. Hale and Cap Eads.

Doctor Carter is an ardent fisherman, is also fond of golf, and one of his pleasures is taking charge of the Boy Scouts on their camping trips. He was the first president of the Jackson Country Club. He has long been a student of pre-historic relics and his personal discoveries have brought him a collection regarded as one of the best privately owned in the state. Doctor Carter is a member of the Masonic Order, the Mystic Shrine, the B. P. O. Elks, Modern Woodmen of American and Rotary Club and president of the Jackson County Medical Society and chairman of the local chapter of the American Red Cross.

During the tornado aftermath in 1925 Doctor Carter had charge of medical men sent to give relief to the district. He was a member of the advisory board of working out the adjustment of losses in connection with the Red Cross. His entire family were in the midst of the storm, but none was injured. Doctor Carter himself was attending a patient, and the house was almost totally destroyed. His wife was at home, and the Carter house was all but torn to pieces, but she was in that portion left standing. Their son, Albert R., Jr., was in high school where many were killed. Doctor Carter's daughter, Mabel Florence, is the wife of Phil Cline, formerly of Marion, Illinois, now a druggist at Murphysboro. The Cline home was also destroyed in the tornado, but none of the inmates injured. The first three children of Doctor and Mrs. Carter died in infancy.

MARSHALL E. KEIG. The career of Marshall E. Keig, executive vice president of the Consumers Company of Chicago, has been a varied and interesting one. Largely self-educated, he has worked his own way to prominence at an age when many men are only entering upon their real careers.

Mr. Keig was born February 7, 1887, in DuPage County, Illinois, and is a son of John J. and Margaret (McHugh) Keig. John J. Keig was born on the Isle of Man of Scandio-Celtic origin, and received his education in his native land. He came to the United States when twenty years of age. He worked in the dry goods business, and later he became a pioneer merchant of Lace, a little community in DuPage County, hauling his goods from Chicago. Money was scarce at the time, and Mr. Keig took in exchange for his merchandise hides, eggs and farm products, which he was forced to haul to Chicago for disposal over rough and at times almost impassable roads. While he was industrious and painstaking, his business cares were too great a strain and in 1893 he sold his store and entered the traffic department of the Santa Fe Railroad, with which he was identified for a number of years prior to his retirement. He was independent in his political views and served in a number of township and county offices, having the full confidence and respect of his fellow citizens. His wife was born in Ireland and is widely known for her industry and charitable disposition. She has devoted her life to her family and her neighbors. There were five children, of which Marshall was the second, all brought up on the old-fashioned theory of having chores to do and studies to master.

Marshall Keig attended public school, meanwhile earning money at odd jobs available in the neighborhood, and graduated from Lockport Township High School in 1906 as valedictorian of his class. He then secured employment in the construction department of the Santa Fe Railroad, and successively worked in the telegraph and interlocking departments. For one year he taught school, following which he came to Chicago and entered the purchasing department of the Santa Fe Railroad in the general offices. Subsequently he was engaged in the railroad supply business, becoming vice president of the Charles R. Long, Jr., Company, manufacturers of paint, of Louisville, Kentucky. His next position was that of secretary and treasurer of Harry Vissering & Company, in the foundry and machine shop business at Chicago, and later secretary and treasurer of the Okadee Company, railroad supplies. During the World war period he served for a time in the Signal Corps, U. S. army, and in 1919 became assistant to Fred Upham, who was then president of the Consumers Company. He consistently won promotions and is now the executive vice president of Consumers Company, the largest ice, coal and building material concern in the world.

Mr. Keig took correspondence courses and attended night schools for many years in an effort to broaden his experience and acquire knowledge.

He is favorably known as one of Chicago's substantial business citizens and has a number of important interests and connections.

Mr. Keig has held important offices in the trade associations, local and national. He is chairman of the Highways Committee of the Chicago Regional Planning Association. He also holds memberships in the Mechanical Engineers Club, Union League Club, Racquet Club, Bob-o-Link Golf Club, Commonwealth Club, Swedish Club of Chicago, Chicago Yacht Club and the Joliet Country Club. His political belief makes him a republican. On January 10, 1925, Mr. Keig was united in marriage with Miss Gertrude Woodruff, of Joliet.

REV. HOWARD E. GANSTER, Rector of Christ Episcopal Church at Waukegan since 1913, has not only performed congenial and useful duties in this large and wealthy church, but has made himself a citizen of force and influence in the entire city.

Rev. Father Ganster was born at Phoenixville, Chester County, Pennsylvania, April 30, 1879, son of William Allaman and Mary Alice (High) Ganster, and grandson of Joseph and Sophia Allaman Ganster, who for some years lived at Saarbruecken, Germany, and brought their family to America in 1848, at the close of the Revolutionary troubles. He located at Reading, Pennsylvania. William Ganster was born in Saarbruecken in 1842 and was six years of age when brought to America. He attended public schools in Pennsylvania, became an iron worker, and left his trade when the Civil war broke out to enlist, at the age of nineteen, in the Union army. He joined Durrell's Battery of Pennsylvania Light Artillery, and was in some of the heaviest fighting of the war in the Virginia district with the Army of the Potomac. In the last year of the war, during the siege of Richmond, Virginia, he had a leg shot off at Petersburg, Virginia, by a bursting shell, and was in a hospital at Washington for many months, until honorably discharged some time after the war closed. On returning home he learned telegraphy, and was a telegraph operator with the Philadelphia and Reading Railroad for twenty-six years, until his death on January 28, 1895. His wife, Mary A. High, was born in Oley Township, Berks County, Pennsylvania, January 1, 1844, was reared and educated there, and now resides with her son, Calvin B. Ganster, at Philadelphia, at the age of eighty-two. She has throughout her life been a devout church member. Her parents, Jerimiah and Henrietta High, were born and reared at Reading, Pennsylvania.

Rev. Howard E. Ganster received his early education in the public schools of Phoenixville in Chester County, Pennsylvania, not far from Philadelphia. Later he attended high school at Dayton, Ohio, graduating in 1900, and in 1904 received the degree of Bachelor of Arts from Northwestern University. In 1907 he was graduated from the Western Theological Seminary. Father Ganster during 1902-03 was pastor of the church at Glen View, Illinois, and in 1904-05, at Franklin Park, Illinois. In 1906 he was made curate of St. Luke's Episcopal Church at Evanston, and from 1907 to 1913 was rector of St. John's Church in Chicago. Then, in 1913, he came to Christ Episcopal Church at Waukegan. Father Ganster is a man of high character, and is greatly beloved both in his church and among all classes of people in Waukegan.

He is president of the Victory Memorial Hospital Association, is a member of the Waukegan Park District Commission, is on the Council of the Boy Scouts of America, and is affiliated with the Ancient Free and Accepted Masons, Royal Arch Masons, Knights of Pythias, Loyal Order of Moose, Elks, Rotary Club, and in politics is a republican.

Father Ganster married at Chicago, Illinois, February 2, 1906, Miss Lilliam Catherine Gordon, of Dayton, Ohio. She is a graduate of the Steel High School, Dayton, Ohio, of the Deaconess Training School, Chicago, and of the Nurses Training School of the California Hospital of Los Angeles. She takes an active part in the church and civic work of the city. Mrs. Ganster is a daughter of Harry and Della (Reid) Gordon, of Dayton, Ohio. Her father for a number of years was superintendent of the Dayton and Union Railroad Company and later was president of the Gordon Manufacturing Company of Dayton. He died in 1925, and her mother, in 1897. Rev. Father and Mrs. Ganster had two children, William Allaman and Gordon Elwood, the latter of whom died in infancy. William A. Ganster graduated from the Waukegan High School with the class of 1926, being an honor man in his class, and is now a student of architecture at the University of Illinois.

EDWIN AHLSTROM. As sheriff of Lake County Edwin Ahlstrom has had many responsible contacts with affairs in the North Shore district between Chicago and the Wisconsin line. He was born and reared at Waukegan, and before going into politics was an electrical engineer and contractor. He is an ex-service man of the World war.

Sheriff Ahlstrom was born at Waukegan May 10, 1893, son of Charles A. and Maria (Eckerman) Ahlstrom. His parents were born near Stockholm, Sweden, and came to America about 1890. Charles A. Ahlstrom first located at Worcester, Massachusetts, where he

became an employe of the old Washburn-Moen Steel Company, subsequently made a subsidiary of the United States Corporation. From Worcester he was transferred to the steel works at Waukegan, and is now master mechanic of the Waukegan plant of the United States Steel Corporation and has been continuously in the service of that institution for over thirty years. He is a member of the Modern Woodmen of America. His wife died December 25, 1906.

Edwin Ahlstrom attended grammar and high schools at Waukegan, spent one year in the Christian Brothers College at St. Louis, and on leaving college in 1914 went to work in the electrical engineering department of the Public Service Company of Northern Illinois. He was with that public utility until 1917, gaining a wide and practical experience in electrical engineering. In 1917 he became construction engineer for the Cyclone Fence Company of Waukegan.

In May, 1918, he enlisted in the United States Marine Corps, but was later given special training in the Lewis Institute at Chicago and was transferred to the Officers Training Camp at Camp Gordon, Georgia, where he received a commission as second lieutenant of infantry October 15, 1918. He was put on unassigned duty at Camp McClellan at Anniston, Alabama, and received his honorable discharge December 10, 1918.

Mr. Ahlstrom then returned to Waukegan and became associated with Russell W. Ames in the electrical contracting business, establishing the firm of A. & A. Electric Company. He gave his full time and energies to developing this prosperous business until 1921.

Mr. Ahlstrom in 1922 was elected sheriff of Lake County and has served a term of four years, during which he has set a standard of official conduct that has merited the phrase bestowed upon it by the best citizens of that rich and populous county. Sheriff Ahlstrom's military experience and training, his familiarity with situations growing out of the massing of large bodies of people, and his natural executive gifts stood him in good stead when for the Twenty-eighth International Eucharistic Congress held at Mundelein in June, 1926, he was appointed chairman of the police committee for Lake County. This brought an unparalleled gathering of people, congesting and taxing every facility of transportation, but with such excellent discipline were the traffic regulations carried out that the vast crowds were handled with a minimum of accidents and with notable absence of confusion. His associates gave Sheriff Ahlstrom a notable measure of the credit for this orderly celebration, and Cardinal Mundelein personally extended him congratulations for his splendid work as chairman of the county police organization.

Mr. Ahlstrom is a Royal Arch Mason, member of the B. P. O. Elks, Knights of Pythias, American Legion and the Sojourners, an organization composed of former officers of the Army, Navy and Marine Corps of the World war and other war services. While in business at Waukegan he was a member of the Rotary Club. He also belongs to the Waukegan Chamber of Commerce. He is a republican in politics and was elected on that ticket to the office of sheriff. His church affiliations are Methodist.

Sheriff Ahlstrom married at Danville, Illinois, June 2, 1917, Miss Hazel A. Cole, of Waukegan, who was educated in the grammar and high schools of that city and prior to her marriage was employed in stenographic and secretarial work at Waukegan. She is a member of the Christian Church and active in its various departments, also belongs to the Eastern Star and Ladies Auxiliary of the American Legion. Her parents are John C. and Grace A. (Levagood) Cole, of Waukegan. Her father for many years was a merchant in that city, but is now living retired at Clear Water, Florida. Mr. and Mrs. Ahlstrom have two daughters, Phyllis Jeanne and Barbara Ann.

COL. GEORGE F. NIXON, of Chicago, was recently the central figure in a story illustrating some of the remarkable turns in the fortunes and destiny of an individual. It was recalled that as a boy on the streets of Chicago he had carried and sold the daily editions of the Chicago News. Then, not so many years later as an individual career is measured, following the death of the late Victor F. Lawson, owner and publisher of the Daily News, the same George F. Nixon was one of the principal financial figures in the organization of the corporation which purchased and took over this great newspaper publication.

In a business way Colonel Nixon has been most familiar to the Chicago public through his extensive real estate operations. He is president of the George F. Nixon Company. Colonel Nixon was born in Chicago, January 29, 1892, son of George Adam and Julia (Heintz) Nixon. His education ended with graduation from grammar school. He was an errand boy, then a newsboy, and his connection with newspapers brought him eventually into the advertising department of the old Record-Herald, then owned by the late Victor F. Lawson. He left the newspaper business to take up real estate. That was in 1913, at the age of twenty-one. In thirteen years Colonel Nixon has accomplished probably a greater success in the real estate business than can be credited to any other individual operator.

The George F. Nixon Company which he founded and of which he is president has from the first done business on a large scale, handling large acreage, subdivisions and development. It has selected its properties with remarkable foresight along lines of rapid transportation. Its first big undertaking was in Ravenswood. Then, during a lull in the extension of transportation lines in Chicago, Colonel Nixon concentrated his attention on the building of business blocks on prominent transfer corners in various sections of Chicago. His organization then went out north in advance of the construction of the rapid transit lines to Niles Center, and handled a tremendous business in that section, following that up with further development of properties on the recently completed Skokie Valley line of the Chicago North Shore & Milwaukee Railroad. The George F. Nixon Company has been one of the largest operators in the Libertyville-Mundelein area.

The culminating undertaking of the George F. Nixon Company is the model suburban community of Westchester, started early in 1926 along the proposed extension of the rapid transit lines south and west of Maywood at Roosevelt Road. He organized and is now carrying out the building of a model and entirely modern suburb, with every possible utility and convenience both for business and for residence, including a zoning plan approved by the Chicago Regional Planning Commission. Westchester is one of the most ambitious suburban community developments undertaken in recent years around Chicago.

Colonel Nixon has also been a prominent leader in real estate and other activities in the Wilson Avenue district. In 1926 this company acquired the old Fort Dearborn National Bank Building at the southwest corner of Clark and Monroe streets, and this is now known as the Nixon Building, the general offices of the Nixon Company being on the second and third floors. As noted above, he is one of the principal stockholders in the corporation which took over the Daily News in the spring of 1926.

Colonel Nixon has for several years been an important member of the Chicago Real Estate Board and chairman of the State Association Committee of the Board. He is former president of the Uptown Chamber of Commerce, a member of the Chicago Association of Commerce, is a Knight Templar and Scottish Rite Mason and Shriner, member of the Edgewater North Shore and Evanston Golf Clubs, and president of the North Shore Polo Club. Colonel Nixon in May, 1926, was honored by being made a colonel on the staff of the governor of Illinois, and holds that rank in the National Guard of Illinois. He has been a particular friend to the famous 202d Coast Artillery of Chicago, having donated valuable property to that organization. The 202d Regiment is designated by the war department as one of the best equipped and best officered National Guard units in the United States.

Colonel Nixon owns a magnificent estate, "Glen Ayre," at Glenview. He married Miss Elsa Witte. Their two children are Robert and Consuelo.

BENJAMIN FRANKLIN URAN, M. D., is dean of the medical profession of Kankakee. He has given his efforts to his vocation in that community fifty-four years, and with a degree of skill and unselfishness that has made him a greatly beloved figure in the community.

Doctor Uran was born January 26, 1848, in Bourbonnais Township, in what was then Will, now Kankakee, County, Illinois, son of Jonathan and Lucinda (Legg) Uran. His paternal ancestors were French. They came to America in the early part of the eighteenth century, one branch settling in Vermont and the other in Massachusetts, near Boston, where many of their descendants are still found. Jonathan Uran was born at Pawlett, Vermont, May 10, 1810, and in 1838 settled in Bourbonnais Township, Will County, Illinois. He died at Kankakee March 16, 1885, at the age of seventy-five. Lucinda Legg was born at Greencastle, Indiana, June 1, 1826. Her father, George Legg, moved his family in the spring of 1829 to Fort Dearborn, Illinois. In 1837 he established his home at Bourbonnais in Will County, locating on the Kankakee River in the spring of that year, at the village of Bourbonnais, in the log cabin that had been erected in 1832 by Noel Le Vasseur. This was the first cabin erected on the Kankakee River in what is now Kankakee County. In 1839 the Legg family moved into another log cabin that had been built in 1834 by Francois Bourbonnais on the site of the present county court house. This was the home of the Legg family for some years, and George Legg died there in 1844. Thus the mother of Doctor Uran had some very intimate associations with the first homes constructed in the wilderness of what was then Kankakee County. She and Jonathan Uran were married October 15, 1846. She lived to an advanced age and died December 3, 1902.

Benjamin F. Uran attended public schools in his home neighborhood, also the high school at Kankakee and St. Paul's Academy there. For two years he studied medicine in the medical department of the University of Michigan, and then in the Bellevue Hospital Medical College in New York, where he was graduated in 1872. While a student of medicine he taught school, in that way paying part of his expenses. Since graduating in 1872 he has given all his efforts to his profession, and has satisfied his ambition in that calling rather than in outside business undertakings or in politics. Doctor Uran after beginning practice took special work in Rush Medical College at Chicago. During the World war he devoted much of his time to the examination of men and fitting them for service, being president of the Medical Advisory Board, District No. 12. With several friends he organized the company that constructed the North Kankakee Street Railway in the early '90s, and served as president of the company thirteen years. He has always been a republican in politics, was for many years a member of the Royal Arcanum and acted as local examiner, and has been president of the Kankakee Historical Society. He is a member of the Kankakee City and Kankakee County Medical Societies, the Illinois State and American Medical Associations.

Doctor Uran married, September 10, 1874, at Kankakee, Susan W. Troup, daughter of Dr. Joseph Alfred and Margaret Weaver (McQueen) Troup. Her father practiced medicine and surgery for a number of years at Emmitsburg, Maryland, and on removing to Illinois was with the wholesale and retail drug firm of Fisher & Troup at Peoria, and from that city, in the early '60s, moved with his family to Kankakee, where he was a member of the firm Troup & McCullough, operating a woolen mill for the manufacture of all kinds of woolen goods. Doctor and Mrs. Uran had three sons and one daughter. The oldest son, Howard Hale, married Marie Dee Rankin, and after her death, Miss Olga De Marre, of New Orleans, and they now reside at Kansas City, Missouri. The second son, Dr. Joseph A. Uran, married Imogene Morgan, has four children and resides at Riceville, Iowa. The third son, Benjamin Franklin Uran, Jr., married Florence French, of Mattoon, Illinois, and has two children. The daughter, Bertha Margaret, is the wife of Frank Thornton Bowles, of Richmond, Virginia.

FRED E. STERLING, lieutenant governor of Illinois, is one of the distinguished men of Rockford and the state, whose long public service, solid characteristics and honorable record entitle him to the confidence of his constituents. He was born at Dixon, Lee County, Illinois, June 29, 1869, and he is a product of the public schools which he attended, first at Dixon, and later in Huron, South Dakota, to which city his parents moved in 1880. His early training was received amid rural surroundings, and like so many of the great men of the country, he was reared to farm work. However, he did not choose agriculture as his life work, but entered the newspaper field, and for thirty years worked in it at Rockford, and was one of the publishers and editor of the Rockford Daily Gazette.

Entering politics in young manhood, he soon became one of the leading figures in the local republican party. For ten years he served as a member of the Rockford City Council, and for twelve years was either secretary or chairman of the Winnebago County Republican Committee. In 1914 he was elected to membership on the state committee of his party from the Twelfth Congressional District, and was reelected to that committee, and made its chairman in 1916, and in that office directed very successfully both the national and state campaigns for Illinois. In 1912 he was a Roosevelt delegate to the Republican National Convention held at Chicago, but continued a regular republican after the nomination of Mr. Taft. In 1920 he was also a delegate to the National Convention held at Chicago. From 1904 to 1912 he was a member of the Board of Managers of the Illinois State Reformatory and from 1912 to 1913 was secretary of the Illinois State Board of Arbitration. On July 1, 1917, Governor Lowden appointed him a member of the Public Utilities Commission, in which position he continued to serve until January 1, 1919, when he resigned to take up his duties as state treasurer, to which office he was elected in November, 1918, by a plurality of nearly 150,000. In 1920 he was the republican primary nominee for lieutenant governor, and in November of that year was elected for a term of four years by a plurality of 715,473, and reelected to the same office in 1924.

Mr. Sterling is married and has a son and daughter. He belongs to the Masonic order, in which he has been advanced through the Scottish and York Rite to the Consistory and Commandery, and he is a member of the Benevolent and Protective Order of Elks, the Knights of Pythias, Loyal Legion, Modern Woodmen of America, Loyal Order of Moose, American Brotherhood, the Kiwanis Club, and the Hamilton Club of Chicago. While of late years much of his time has, of necessity, been spent at Springfield, Mr. Sterling continues to maintain his residence at Rockford, and his interests are centered in the further growth and prosperity of the city in which he lived and worked for so many constructive years. Outside of his prominence in politics his name has long been a household one throughout Winnebago County and Western Illinois because of his editorial connections, and no man is more popular with his fellow citizens than he.

ADOLPH MUELLER is president and treasurer of the Mueller Company of Decatur. In the line of water, gas and plumbing brass goods this company has for many years represented the largest industry in America. It is a business closely associated with the industrial growth and prosperity of Decatur. The company celebrated its fiftieth anniversary in 1907. At that time it was estimated that the persons on the payroll of the company equaled the entire population living in Decatur in 1857. The honored founder of the business was Hieronymus Mueller, one of the most noted inventors and experts in mechanical technique who ever lived in Illinois. He developed the business to successful proportions, and it was his good fortune that he had six stalwart sons to become associated with him as they reached manhood and were well qualified to take control of the business in the intense competition of the present century, and carry the Mueller standard to new heights of success.

Hieronymus Mueller was born in the village of Wertheim, Germany, July 16, 1832, son of John M. and Ursula Elizabeth (Kast) Mueller. His father was born in Wertheim in 1794 and his mother, in 1795. Hieronymus Mueller was educated in the schools of his native village and early manifested a mechanical bent of mind. He acquired the machinist's trade by a thorough apprenticeship in the City of Manheim and in 1850, at the age of eighteen, came to America, following his two brothers, Adolph and Henry. For several years he lived in Chicago and Freeport, Illinois, and in 1857 came to Decatur. His mother subsequently joined him in this country, and lived in Decatur until her death at the age of ninety-two.

H. Mueller came to Decatur a short time after his marriage, and his first undertaking was the establishment of a small shop and business as a gunsmith. He gave this up, yielding to the excitement of the mining discoveries around Pike's Peak, but after eight months returned to Chicago, where he joined his wife and in 1858 they returned to Decatur, where he resumed business, occupying several shops in different locations in the city. The gunsmithing shop was maintained until 1872, when the growth of his business justified the erection of a three-story building at Main and State streets. It was in 1872 that he invented the water taping machine, this being the first important piece of machinery manufactured by the Muellers in a line of supplies long considered indispensable to the plumbing, water and gas industries. H. Mueller was a genius in mechanics, possessing an understanding of the basic principles that made their application to any line a simple matter, resulting in his gradual entry into new fields. In 1882 he invented and patented the water pressure regulator.

In following years there came about a rapid expansion of the business. In 1885 a gun store was established as a separate institution, and in the same year the firm began the manufacture of a line of brass goods. In 1886 his sons Henry, Philip, Fred, Robert and in 1890 Adolph were admitted to partnership. Owing to an increasing demand for the Mueller brass goods, the plumbing business was made a separate department in 1887, and in 1891 the Decatur Plumbing & Heating Company was organized.

It was in 1893 that the Mueller Manufacturing Company was organized with a capital stock of $68,000.00. In 1895 construction was begun of a complete new factory building to provide facilities for the tremendous demand for Mueller goods. At that time the principal product of the company was corporation stops and then orders from one company for 10,000 such stops annually was an important reason for the expansion of the manufacturing facilities. This increasing demand for the company's products made the original department, the plumbing and gun business, secondary features, and in 1896-7 the plumbing business and the gun store were sold. This permitted the sons of Hieronymus Mueller to return to the manufacturing end of the business.

On March 1, 1900, occurred the death of the founder of the business, and in the reorganization that followed his son Henry Mueller became president; Oscar B., vice president; Adolph, secretary and treasurer; Robert, assistant secretary and treasurer; Philip, superintendent; and F. B. Mueller, field manager of the salesmen.

Heironymus Mueller had an interesting and pioneer part in the introduction of the automobile. He recognized the possibilities of the horseless carriage when such a vehicle was still in the domain of theory or shop experiment. In 1895 he imported from Germany the Benz motor wagon, one of the very first types of motor propelled vehicles. This Benz wagon was by no means perfect, its defects being manifested in sudden refusals to start and inability to readily ascend grades. Mr. Mueller applied himself to a correction of these defects and in the course of a year there was little to distinguish the wagon except its name Benz. He merely improved on the fundamental rule of power and its transmission without infringing in any way on the Benz patent. Mr. Mueller's wagon was entered in the first automobile race, held under the auspices of the old Chicago Times Herald in November, 1895, and the Mueller wagon was declared the winner. In a second race a few weeks later Mr. Mueller's wagon was second. At the time of his death Hieronymus Mueller had under construction the working parts of three distinct automobiles and had already secured a number of patents on his ideas. After his death the parts of the machines were disposed of, the company deciding not to follow the father's plans, but to confine their attentions strictly to manufacturing brass goods.

Originally Mr. Mueller was a republican, continuing to support that party until the Greeley movement of 1872. Afterwards he was a democrat, and was especially pronounced in his support of Cleveland. He refused steadfastly any political honors, declining to become a candidate for mayor only a few years before his death. Until his business reached the proportions of a great factory Hieronymus Mueller regularly entered the shop and, picking up his tools, took his place beside the other workmen. Necessity did not force this upon him. The pure love of shaping with his hands the inventions of his brain prompted him to daily labor. He loved to toil. It was a part of his nature, and his daily efforts brought him the recompense of peace and contentment. Labor with him was honorable and uplifting.

In moments of relaxation and leisure the social side of Mr. Mueller's nature shone out brightly, revealing a man whose heart grew light while his hair grew gray. To those who did not know him thoroughly, his manner smacked of brusqueness, but his real nature was one of gentleness and kindness. He was a man of pronounced convictions, but his beliefs were not given freely and never forced on others. His thoughts found expression in few words that carried his meaning directly and plainly. He was tenacious in his opinions when convinced he was right but there was no bigotry in his makeup and he conceded to all men the same liberty of conscience that he claimed as his inalienable right, and which he stoutly contended for. The absence of fraud and deception in his own composition made him a hater of dissembling in others, and his contempt for this class was so pronounced that he did not seek to conceal it.

At Freeport, Illinois, May 26, 1856, Hieronymus Mueller married Miss Fredericka Bernhardt. She was born in Minden, Prussia, in 1839, daughter of Christian and Annie Mary Bernhardt. She came to America when a young girl, and in Freeport she met and married H. Mueller. Her life for half a century was one of continued domestic activity, her household duties and her children demanding her care for many years, and she showed that rare ability to retain the interest of her children in their home and make the home a magnet for all its members after the work of the day was done. She was the mother of nine children, seven of whom grew to mature years: Henry, who succeeded his father as president of the H. Mueller Manufacturing Company, but is now deceased; Philip; Fred B.; Robert; Adolph, and Oscar B., all now active in the company. The only daughter is Mrs. Leda Cruikshank.

Adolph Mueller, president and treasurer of the company, was born at Decatur, May 8, 1866. He was educated in high school and in the University of Illinois, specializing in the study of mechanical engineering. For a number of years he was associated with various mechanical departments of the business, including the gunsmithing and plumbing departments, and also became familiar with the bookkeeping and clerical sides of the business.

Mr. Mueller married, June 14, 1893, Miss Minnie Bachman. Three children were born to their marriage: William Everett, Charlotte A. and Charles Philip. Charles P. died when three years old. Mr. Mueller is a member of

the Christian Science Church, is a Mason, belongs to the Decatur and Country Clubs, a member of the University Club, and has shown a very deep interest in the educational, material and moral welfare of his community.

EZRA JOSEPH WARNER. The house of Sprague, Warner and Company has been a conspicuous name in the wholesale business of Chicago for many years, and in fact this house was one of the pioneers in making Chicago a distributing agency for the supplies of the Middle West. The two names Sprague and Warner have been closely associated in the history of the firm practically from its founding in the early part of the Civil war. Ezra Joseph Sprague, Sr., came into Chicago and joined A. A. Sprague and Mr. Stetson, soon afterwards established themselves in business. The late Ezra Joseph Warner was actively identified with the business for nearly forty years, until his death, and his son, Ezra Joseph Warner, Jr., is now president of the company.

The Warner family is of old New England stock, first established in Connecticut, and there was a succession of Joseph Warner through six generations or more. Joseph Warner of the sixth generation was born in Vermont in 1803, succeeded his father as a merchant and the latter part of his life, up to his death in 1865, was spent as the cashier of the Bank of Middlebury, Vermont. He married Jane Meech, of Colonial ancestry.

Ezra Joseph Warner, Sr., son of Joseph and Jane (Meech) Warner, was born at Middlebury, Vermont, March 8, 1841. He graduated from Kimball Union Academy in New Hampshire in 1857, and was graduated valedictorian of his class at Middlebury College in 1861. Forty years after his graduation he completed Joseph Warner Science Hall on the campus of Middlebury College as a memorial to his father, and throughout his life he was deeply interested in the college and his native town. After leaving college he studied law for a brief time in Wisconsin, but in the summer of 1862 moved to Chicago and early the following year became associated with Albert A. Sprague in what became known as Sprague, Warner and Company. Mr. Sprague and Mr. Warner each borrowed from his father $3,000, this $6,000 constituting the original capital of the wholesale grocery business. In 1871 their business was wiped out by the great Chicago fire, all they had left being a wagon load of dried blackberries and some worthless insurance policies. They quickly reestablished the business and in 1893 it was incorporated, Ezra Joseph Warner serving as vice president, and after the death of J. A. Sprague became president, an office he held until his death on September 10, 1910. He was for fifteen years chairman of the Board of Directors of the western branch of the Liverpool, Lumbermen Globe Insurance Company. He was a republican, a Presbyterian, and a prominent pioneer resident of Lake Forest and was a trustee of Lake Forest College. He married, in 1861, Miss Jane Remsen, daughter of William H. and Sarah Remsen, of Middlebury, Vermont. She died January 7, 1911. Of the seven children born to their marriage two died in infancy, and the fifth in order of birth was Ezra Joseph Warner, Jr.

Ezra Joseph Warner, Jr., was born at Lake Forest, Illinois, March 10, 1877. At the age of twelve years he was taken to Europe, spending two years in a private school at Dresden, and in 1895 graduated from Lake Forest Academy, and took his B. A. degree at Yale University in 1899. Since his university career he has been identified with the wholesale grocery house of Sprague, Warner and Company, a business he learned by working through many of the departments. In 1902 he was made secretary and director, subsequently was elected chairman of the board and is now president. He is also a director of the Northern Trust Company.

Mr. Warner is a Zeta Psi, a member of the Chicago University and City Clubs of Chicago, the Onwentsia, Shore Acres Clubs of Lake Forest, and the Yale Club of New York. He married, November 26, 1902, Miss Marion Aline Hall, of Lake Forest. They have three children, Marion, Jane and Ezra Joseph III.

W. I. BACCUS. Among the men of Pulaski County who are entitled to bear the title of self-made, none deserves it in greater degree than W. I. Baccus, superintendent of the Mound City plant of the Inman Company, manufacturers of furniture materials. Entering on his independent career when he was but fourteen years of age, he worked his way upward to a prominent position in his chosen field of endeavor, only to see his efforts and means of a livelihood swept away by fire. Nothing daunted, he again started the arduous climb and has succeeded in attaining a leading place and the respect that is given to all who overcome obstacles and discouragements.

Mr. Baccus was born at Metropolis, Illinois, in 1873, a son of William Sardin and Sarah (Garrett) Baccus, tne former born in Massac County, Illinois, and the latter in Pope County, this state. The father, who was an agriculturist in early life, later became the owner of spoke mills, which he conducted until his death in 1917. W. I. Baccus was given only meagre educational advantages, as he did not attend school after he was seven years of age, and when he was fourteen years old he found conditions so little to his liking that he ran away from home and secured work in a sawmill, a course of action which shaped his entire life. For many years he worked in mills at various places, learning the business from the bottom upward, but, finding his education inadequate to meet the requisites of the higher positions, he took a course in steam and electrical engineering from the Scranton Correspondence School. With the knowledge thus gained he secured employment with the West Constance Chair Company, Mound City branch, and at first worked as a log scaler, from which position he rose to be master mechanic of the plant. Later he was made assistant engineer, subsequently engineer, and finally superintendent of the mechanical department, a position which he was filling six years later when the plant was destroyed by fire. On January 1, 1911, Mr. Baccus joined the Mound City plant of the Inman Company, manufacturers of furniture material, as engineer and saw filer, his initial wages being three dollars per day. In 1913 he was made assistant manager and superintendent of the plant, and his present salary is $6,000 per year, in addition to which he is the owner of stock in the plant, which he purchased in 1917. Mr. Baccus is a thorough master of his craft and possesses good executive ability which assists him in the handling of the men in his charge. A republican in politics, while residing at Olmstead, Illinois, he served several terms as alderman. He belongs to the Independent Order of Odd Fellows and the Modern Woodmen of America, in both of which he is popular, and his religious faith is that of the Congregational Church.

In November, 1894, Mr. Baccus married Mertie Shelton, who was born in Pulaski County and educated in the public schools, daughter of James and Louise (Kraatz) Shelton, natives of Germany. Mrs. Baccus died September 10, 1910, leaving two children: Myrtle, who died March 23, 1913, at the age of seventeen years; and William Paul, of Mound City, born October 8, 1904. Mr. Baccus's second marriage occurred February 28, 1914, when he was united with Hazel Born, who was born at Mound City, February 1, 1893, a daughter of John and Mary (Deahl) Born, natives of Illinois. They became the parents of the following children: Hazel Loretta and Myrtle Juniata (died about 1917), twins, born January 28, 1915; William Ashton, born November 27, 1917; and Harry Edward, born March 20, 1919, who was killed by an automobile August 20, 1920. In 1925 Mr. Baccus purchased eighty-two acres within two miles of Mound City, a fine country home, where he intends to reside when he retires.

THOMAS WILLIAMSON in the thirty years he has practiced law in Madison County has performed services of a master of his profession, is an eloquent speaker and has lent the power of his mind and logic and his wise influence to the settlement of many important questions both within the strict limits of the law and in public affairs. Mr. Williamson was United States attorney from 1922 to 1926.

He has come to dignified and successful position through the power within himself to rise above circumstances. His father was a native of Ireland, and in 1860 came from Philadelphia and acquired a place of forty acres in Macoupin County, Illinois, clearing away the timber for a field and using some of the logs to construct the little house in which his son Thomas Williamson was born May 19, 1867. The son was reared in the home of his uncle and aunt, John and Mary Williamson, who when he was nine years old moved to Madison County. He made a record of promptness and studious attention while attending public school and at the age of seventeen was given a license to teach. For several following years he taught the country schools, worked for railroad contractors, and combined both mental and physical labor in his program of getting ahead. With two borrowed volumes of Blackstone he began the study of law in 1890, and after completing a course in the St. Louis Law School he was licensed to practice by the Illinois Supreme Court in May, 1891. For eight years he practiced at Mount Olive and in September, 1899, moved to Edwardsville, and has been one of the members of the bar of that city for a quarter of a century. He is a member of the well known firm of Warnock, Williamson & Burroughs.

Mr. Williamson has been a power in the republican party in Southern Illinois for a number of years. He delivered his first public speech in the campaign of 1892, and has long held the record of being a polished orator, used his eloquence in many worthy causes. He has been reading clerk in the Legislature, chairman of county conventions, has served as president of the school board of Mount Olive and Edwardsville, and is a member of the Madison County and Illinois State Bar Associations. He is a trustee of the Presbyterian Church. Mr. Williamson was attorney representing the United Mine Workers during the strike of 1898. He has been an official in the Modern Woodmen of America, the Knights of Pythias, is a member of the American Federation of Musicians, and is a Knight Templar and thirty-third degree Scottish Rite Mason and Shriner.

On October 14, 1891, he married Miss Mattie L. Binney, daughter of Walter P. Binney, of Madison County. The children born to their marriage were Bessie E., Jessie C., Thomas Binney and Robert W.

FRANK O. LOWDEN has been conspicuously one of the foremost Illinoisans of his generation. Fully a score of years before he was elected governor of the state he was an increasing influence in the republican party. Illinois was fortunate in having him governor during the critical period of the World war. In reorganizing the state government he performed one of the biggest tasks of constructive statesmanship in the present century. Since leaving the governor's chair his influence has been growing rather than declining. He has been unofficially, though none the less genuinely, a leader of the Mississippi Valley, a recognized spokesman of the dominant part of progressive agriculture in the Middle West, and altogether is one of the able men of the country whose ability and integrity inspire confidence among all classes.

Frank Orren Lowden was born at Sunrise City, Minnesota, January 26, 1861, son of Lorenzo O. and Nancy Elizabeth (Greg) Lowden. His parents were among the territorial pioneers of Minnesota, having gone to the northern frontier about 1858 from Pennsylvania. His father was a blacksmith and farmer. When Frank O. Lowden was seven years old the family moved to Hardin County, Iowa. Here, with few opportunities to study and attend school in the intervals of his work on the farm, he made the best of them and at the age of fifteen had qualified as a teacher. He taught five years. The subsequent story of Governor Lowden's rise in the world desires to be told in the language used in an article published about the close of his term as governor.

A fine education was his goal. His salary as a teacher was so small that he undertook the cleaning up of his own school room to earn a few extra dollars. Saving and studying, he managed to save money to enter the University of Iowa when twenty years old. His money ran out and he was compelled to get another school. He succeeded in keeping up his studies so he was able to return to the university, from which he was graduated at the head of his class.

The first goal attained, his eyes turned to another—a legal degree. By teaching in Burlington, Iowa, and working as a law clerk at $8 a week in Chicago, to which he came in 1886, he made his way through the Union College of Law, now Northwestern. He was graduated in 1887, having completed the work of the two-year course in one year. Here again he was valedictorian of his class, receiving the first prize for his oration and the first prize for scholarship.

In the same year he was examined for admission to the bar by the committee of the Appellate Court for the First District of Illinois and outranked all who at that time took the examination. Admitted to the practice of law, the next eight years were filled with work—hard and trying as the previous years. Success, however, was assured by his early training. The boy of the prairie was more than able to hold his own among the brilliant minds practicing law in Chicago.

Along with those qualities indispensable to the lawyer—and a keen, rapid, logical mind, plus the business sense, and a ready capacity for hard work—he brought to the starting point of his legal career rarer gifts—eloquence of language and a strong personality. An excellent presence, an earnest, dignified manner, marked strength of character, a thorough grasp of the law, and the ability accurately to apply its principles were factors in Colonel Lowden's effectiveness as an advocate.

In 1896 he married Miss Florence Pullman, daughter of one of America's greatest business men, the late George M. Pullman of the Pullman Company. One son and three daughters were born to them.

A new period of life now opens. Popular, brilliant and untiring, he turned his attention to politics. He entered the presidential campaign and devoted his great speaking ability to electing William McKinley President of the United States. After election President McKinley offered him a high office in Washington, but Colonel Lowden was not ready to abandon his profession. In 1903 friends urged him to seek the nomination for governor of Illinois. After a terrific campaign and a convention lasting twenty-one days he was defeated by Charles S. Deneen. In the campaign following the convention Colonel Lowden devoted his time to the election of Mr. Deneen for the governorship.

The call of the soil from which he came as a western pioneer always had sounded sweet in his ears. In 1900 he purchased a farm in Ogle County, in the beautiful Rock River Valley, near the town of Oregon. To it he moved his family, with a view to making it his permanent home.

But his neighbors were not content to let him rest in peace. They drafted him in 1906 and sent him to Congress to represent the Thirteenth District in the national House of Representatives. He served them two terms, retiring voluntarily to regain his health and devote his energies to the development of the great agricultural resources of his farm, which he named Sinnissippi Farm.

Colonel Lowden was a hard worker in Congress, as he always had been in everything. He voted for the bill limiting the hours of labor of train crews, the employers' liability act, the act regulating child labor in the District of Columbia, the measure establishing a Bureau of Mines and the bill creating the postal savings bank system. He supported a constitutional amendment providing for an income tax. He delivered a notable speech advocating publicity in connection with the big industries of the country.

Though Colonel Lowden retired from politics after two terms, his party required his services, and in 1908 he was elected national committeeman for Illinois, serving in that capacity for eight years.

All this while his unflagging interest in agriculture was manifest. He increased his farm acreage. He was also raising cotton in Arkansas and Texas, attending to his big business interests. Between overseeing the development of his lands, the breeding of fine stock, dairying, road building and planting 500,000 pines on Sinnissippi Farm he was a very busy man.

Colonel Lowden was not so engrossed, however, that he could not devote some of his great energies to aiding his fellow men. He gave liberally to deserving causes. He aided in the development of a vocational or training school for youth at Pullman—a mangnificent useful institution. He served as trustee of numerous small colleges that needed his ability in their development. The young man struggling for an education found a sympathetic and wise counselor in him because he remembered his own hardships.

In his work he has a strong supporter in Mrs. Lowden, whose unostentatious charities have endeared her not only to the countryside but to the poor of Chicago. She built and furnished two cottages which she called Hilltop on the farm overlooking the beautiful Rock River. To this haven crippled and orphaned boys and girls were taken from Chicago hospitals and tenements, and kept until they regained their health before being sent back to the crowded districts of the city.

The people of Illinois, a majority of them, at least, were not willing that Colonel Lowden should remain on his farm, where he finds so much happiness. They wanted him for their governor. After a year of insistence he became a candidate for the republican nomination. On September 13th the primaries were held. He was nominated by a plurality of 120,214, or a majority of 34,711. On November 7 he was swept into office by a tremendous vote—a majority of 149,842.

Upon assuming the duties of his office, January 8, 1917, Governor Lowden immediately turned his attention to the great things in the program he had promised the people. Foremost among them was the consolidation of 125 commissions, boards and bureaus into nine major departments with a director at the head of each who would be required to live in

Springfield and give his entire time to the state. Before he had been in office sixty days this consolidation act had passed both houses of the General Assembly and become a law.

In addition to abolishing many useless agencies and improving the efficiency of existing divisions, the new law, called the Civil Administrative Code, provided for making a budget in the Department of Finance and its presentation to the Legislature by the Governor. Upon this appointment, July 1, 1917, the Director of Finance and his assistants began the study of the finances of the state. Their work was so well done that when the taxing body, consisting of the governor, the state treasurer, and the auditor of public accounts, met in December, 1918, they were able to present such an accurate report of the finances that—notwithstanding the United States had been at war twenty-two months and war prices had prevailed—the tax rate was reduced from 90 to 75 cents on the $100 taxable valuation. This meant a saving of $4,000,000 to the taxpayers of the state. Efficiency in the nine departments, more accurate knowledge of the state's needs and constant watchfulness over expenditures contributed toward that saving.

Illinois needed a new constitution, the present constitution having been adopted in 1870. The Governor recommended that a resolution be passed by the Legislature submitting to the people the question of whether or not they wanted a new constitution. The Legislature concurred in the recommendation and the people voted in November, 1918, by 74,239 majority, to call a constitutional convention.

For fifteen years Illinois had been trying to get out of the mud. Governor Lowden recommended a $60,000,000 bond issue to build 4,800 miles of roads. The Legislature approved the suggestion and it was submitted to the people. At the November, 1918, election by a constitutional majority of 212,404 they said they wanted good roads. Governor Lowden recommended state supervision for all private banks, and notwithstanding the opposition of a powerful lobby the bill was passed. Upon submission to the people at the November election it was approved by a large vote.

When war was declared by President Wilson February 3, 1917, Governor Lowden issued a statement to the people of Illinois in which he declared, "It is the solemn duty of all Americans to rally to his support." Three days later he went before the Legislature in joint session and said to its members, "We may have many sympathies; we can have but one allegiance and that allegiance is to the United States."

Illinois was regarded by the Washington authorities as dangerous territory, perhaps the most critical of any state in the Union. Governor Lowden appointed a State Council of Defense, representing all parties and elements. That council made a remarkable record. With only $50,000 appropriated by the state it did work that in some states cost $5,000,000 and achieved efficiency that placed it in the van. It raised and equipped 15,000 Home Guards besides sending thousands of fairly well trained young men into the service where they obtained immediate recognition as non-commissioned officers.

Governor Lowden visited the Illinois troops in camps and spoke to them. He bade them good-bye at the seaboard, sending them on their mission with cheering and inspiring words. One of the regiments, the old First Illinois National Guard, subsequently the One Hundred Thirty-first Infantry, was the regiment of which he was lieutenant colonel for three years. In the Prairie Division to which the One Hundred Thirty-first as assigned, was his own son, Pullman.

When the Fifty-first General Assembly met January 8, 1919, the House of Representatives was organized the first day. Within a week both bodies had ratified the dry amendment to the federal constitution—Illinois being the twenty-first state to enter the Union. In his message to the 1919 General Assembly the Governor recommended a waterway from Chicago to St. Louis; a general revision of the revenue laws; a reduction in the cost of primaries and elections; an adequate law for corporation; larger powers for courts, and an eight hour day for women. He suggested a state housing code; greater development of agriculture with a land tenure act; the planting of trees and the reorganization of all state and municipal pension systems.

ROBERT E. L. BROOKS has been identified with the real estate business in Chicago for thirty-eight years. He is president of the Robert E. L. Brooks, Incorporated, real estate and first mortgage loans. He is a former president of the Cook County Real Estate Board, and the real estate and financial interest of the city and county recognize especially the important nature of his service and long and persistent fight in behalf of the introduction of the Torrens system for registration of real estate titles in Chicago and Cook County. He is former president of the Torrens Land Title Registration League.

He came to Chicago in 1887 and has been a business man of that city since, 1892. The headquarters of Robert E. L. Brooks, Incorporated, of which he is president, are in South Chicago, at 10101 Ewing Avenue in the East Side Trust & Savings Bank Building. He is a director of the Calumet National Bank, director of the Suburban Trust & Savings Bank of Oak Park, chairman of the Board of Directors of the East Side Trust & Savings Bank, director of George H. Taylor Real Estate Mortgage Company, director of the South Chicago Masonic Association and president of the South Chicago Community Hospital.

The Torrens system for transferring and guaranteeing real estate titles was adopted in Illinois in 1897 and has been in force in Cook County since that date, and notwithstanding the opposition of large interests the system has made great progress in the county, but memorably so since the Cook County Real Estate Board in 1911 adopted what is known as the Brooks Resolution for active support of the system. This board, together with the Torrens Land Title Registration League, are the only organization whose members have given their time and money without stint in

promoting land registration, and for fifteen years they have conducted an intensive campaign to bring about the general adoption of the system throughout the state.

Mr. Brooks was chairman of Local Draft Board No. 20 at Chicago during the World war. He is a past master of Harbor Lodge No. 731, A. F. and A. M., a past high priest of Sinai Chapter No. 185, Royal Arch Masons, past master of Calumet Council No. 76, R. and S. M., past commander of Calumet Commandery No. 62, Knights Templar, and past patron of Lady Garfield Chapter No. 91, Order of the Eastern Star.

Mr. Brooks married Miss Josephine Johnson. They have two children, Mrs. Juanita L. O'Brien and Robert E. L. Brooks, Jr.

JAMES E. MITCHELL, vice president and cashier of the First National Bank of Carbondale, comes of a family of bankers and men long prominent in the affairs of southern Illinois.

His grandfather, William N. Mitchell, was born in McNairy County, Tennessee, in 1814, and came to Illinois in 1832. At Old Frankfort he taught subscription schools, studied surveying and used his knowledge in running the lines which separated Williamson from Franklin County. He was also a farmer. In spite of his advanced years he volunteered as a soldier in the Civil war, becoming captain of Company E, Sixtieth Illinois Infantry, and was wounded during his service. In 1865 he was elected county clerk, and served as postmaster of Marion during the administrations of Grant and Hayes. He died at Marion December 30, 1879. The wife of William N. Mitchell was Rachel Roberts, daughter of John Roberts. She died August 30, 1866.

One of their sons was Edward Mitchell, a former state treasurer of Illinois. The other son, James Cafield Mitchell, is now president of the First National Bank of Marion. He was born in Williamson County, October 30, 1852, was educated in common schools, worked as a drug clerk at Marion, was elected county clerk and in 1890 was reelected for another four year term. At the close of his second term he became a cashier of the First National Bank of Marion and is now president of the highly prosperous institution.

James Cafield Mitchell married, October 21, 1872, Miss Lillie White. Her father, Col. John H. White, assisted in raising the Thirty-first Illinois Infantry, Col. John Logan's old regiment, and himself became colonel of the regiment. He was the first Union officer killed in the siege of Ft. Donelson on February 14, 1862. Mrs. Lillie Mitchell died November 22, 1901. James C. Mitchell on December 7, 1901, married Julia Dunaway.

James E. Mitchell, son of James C. and Lillie (White) Mitchell, was born at Marion, Illinois, and attended public schools there, graduating from high school in 1901. For a quarter of a century his time and energies have been fully absorbed in banking. He became a clerk in the old National Bank of Carbondale in 1903. This was before the institution had absorbed the trust company. He has filled various positions in the bank and since 1911 has been its vice president and cashier. Mr. Mitchell is a member of the Masonic Order, Knights of Pythias and B. P. O. Elks. He married, in 1908, Mollie Vancil, a native of Joplin, Missouri.

FRANK EDWARD ROBISON is president and general manager of the Murphysboro Paving Brick Company. The Murphysboro Paving Brick Company utilizes strictly home resources, the shales and clays found only a few feet beneath the surface, the coal for fuel mined in the locality, and manufactures a paving brick not surpassed anywhere. This paving brick has probably done more to make the name of Murphysboro familiar in distant towns and regions than any other one thing. The company has an almost international business.

The coal mining operations in the vicinity of Murphysboro revealed many years ago the presence of clays and shales of supreme quality for brick making. However, at that time the coal was the only commercial product taken from beneath the earth's surface. It was with the general advent of automobiles and the nation-wide demand for good roads that the manufacture of paving brick became an industry to attract capital. The Murphysboro locality is fortunate in having the clays and shales near enough to the surface so that they can be uncovered by stripping operations with shovels.

It was in 1908 that William H. Hill, at that time a prominent business man of East St. Louis, a dealer in building materials, was attracted by the possibilities offered for the manufacture of brick at the shale deposits in Jackson County. He and Henry Jenkins, a Murphysboro plumber, organized and on March 9, 1909, incorporated the Murphysboro Paving Brick Company with a capital stock of one hundred thousand dollars. Frame buildings were erected and the first experiment produced a brick of such superb quality that the business was on a firm footing practically from the beginning. Mr. Hill became the first president of the company and Mr. Jenkins, secretary and treasurer, and from the beginning S. D. Sexton has been vice president. In the course of time the frame buildings were replaced by solid brick structures and the capital increased to $160,000. Modern machinery and modern methods were adopted and the capacity of the plant enormously increased. At the beginning there were forty employes, now there are 140. The capacity of the six kilns at the beginning was 20,000 paving bricks daily, and this capacity has since been increased to around 100,000 paving brick. The company also manufactures a special line of brick used for packing house floors, and some of the facilities of the plant are devoted to the manufacture of face building brick, though only to meet an unsolicited demand. The United States government used five million paving bricks manufactured at the Murphysboro plant in the canal zone cities of Balboa and the Colon. Murphysboro paving blocks were used to pave the wide roadway on the top of the dam at Muscle Shoals, Alabama. Carloads of brick from Murphysboro have been shipped to Canada and to nearly every state in the Union. During the

World war the plant was kept in operation on a restricted basis and at a loss to the company, but the facilities and organization were preserved so that little time was lost in returning to normalcy after the war.

Frank Edward Robison, the president of the company, was born at Lafayette, Indiana, November 19, 1884. His father, Dell Robison, was a native of White County, Indiana, and as a youth entered the service of the Monon Railroad Company. In 1890 he moved to East St. Louis, and for many years was a conductor on the Baltimore & Ohio fast express trains between that city and Cincinnati. He died in 1911. His wife was Ann W. Sills, of Smithland, Kentucky.

Frank E. Robison during his boyhood lived with a sister at North Vernon, Indiana, attended public schools there, graduating from high school. His boyhood ambition was to become a mechanical engineer. However, he never had the money to attend a technical college, and after passing a civil service examination he became a clerk in the post office at North Vernon, remaining there three years. Going to East St. Louis, he went to work in the local plant of the Armour Packing Company, a clerk in the wholesale market department at $12.50 a week. For eleven years he remained with the Armour Company, his ability and forcefulness securing his promotion from time to time until he became assistant to the general manager.

Having almost reached the position which had been his objective when he entered the business, he then sought a still broader field. It was about that time that he accepted the proposition of William H. Hill to become identified with the paving brick industry. Therefore, in 1917, he bought the interest of Mr. Jenkins in the Murphysboro Paving Brick Company and became secretary and treasurer of the plant. His associates give Mr. Robison great credit for the remarkable increase in the business during the past ten years. Recently he has become president of the company. On October 1, 1925, Mr. Robison sold 36,000,000 paving brick to the city of Orlando, Florida, which was the largest paving contract ever awarded in one contract of any material. This represented a sale of approximately two million dollars. Mr. Robison is also secretary and treasurer of the Hill Brick Company of East St. Louis.

Mr. Robison married, in 1917, Miss Gertrude E. Hill, daughter of William H. Hill.

Henry O. Clausen, now proprietor of the New Hundley Hotel, which he has made one of the best managed hotels in southern Illinois, has the abundant energy and enterprise that qualifies him for success in everything he undertakes. He has been engaged in the hotel business only a few years. He is perhaps best known on account of his long and important service as an educator.

Mr. Clausen is a son of Henry and Catherine (Peterson) Clausen. His parents had a remarkable similarity of circumstances in their life history. Both were born in the same community, Alse, in the Province of North Schleswig, Germany, and both on the same day, January 16, 1840. They were baptized and confirmed at the same time and in the same church and they came to America on the same ship, locating at Shelbyville, in Shelby County, Illinois. However, it was after they came to America that their acquaintance ripened into marriage. They were married in 1870. Catherine Peterson was a daughter of John and Christina Maria Peterson. Henry Clausen was a citizen of Denmark, highly educated, master of several languages, and became an officer of the Danish army. In 1865-66, when Germany wrested the Province of Schleswig from Denmark, he was one of the formal officers of the Danish army who refused to take the oath of allegiance to Germany, and to escape the consequences of that act he immigrated to America in 1868, and during the rest of his life was a farmer in Rose Township, Shelby County, where he died December 24, 1881. His widow survived until January 5, 1895. There were five children, Mary, Peter J., Henry O., Christina C. and John P.

Henry O. Clausen was born in Rose Township, Shelby County, February 21, 1876. He was five years old when his father died. As a boy he showed a studious disposition, inherited his father's love of learning, and made the best of his rather limited school advantages. After the death of his mother he left school and became a teacher in the school at Sylvan, in Holland Township. Following that he taught a year at Henton and the next year at Sandyhill. In 1898 he became principal of the school at Fancher, and was with that one school community continuously until 1917, except for two terms. Thus for practically twenty years he was director of the educational interests of one community. There were other opportunities outside of teaching which he accepted and made use of. He conducted a farm, for a time was interested in a livery stable at Shelbyville, and for four years, a merchant there. In 1899 he and J. E. Gallagher and the late W. B. Lantz organized the Holland Township Telephone Company, building the line, which started with only three telephones. This is now one of the prosperous exchanges and Mr. Clausen still owns an interest.

Mr. Clausen in 1920 was induced to come to Carbondale to take charge of the New Hundley Hotel, which was owned and operated by his cousin, John Mart Brown. Mr. Brown was in ill health and for that reason persuaded Mr. Clausen to take charge. The latter, in 1925, bought the building, which has the best location in the city, also the furnishings, and has shown splendid ability in directing the establishment.

As a young man he was an Evangelical Lutheran and subsequently joined the United Brethren Church. He married, December 24, 1902, Miss Bertha Terwilliger, daughter of John and Mary (Fortner) Terwilliger, of Holland Township. They have three children: Mary Fay, who is the wife of Floyd Blain, an electrician at Cartersville, and the mother of one son, John D. Blain; George C., a civil engineer in the service of the Illinois Central Railway Company, and who married Mary Rodd; and William Orville, a student in high school at Carbondale.

EARL H. HOSTETTLER has been three times elected to the office of county superintendent of schools of Richland County. This is impressive testimony to the ability and faithfulness with which he has conducted his office. His administration has been one synonymous with marked advancement in all phases of popular education in this county.

He was born on a farm in Richland County, March 11, 1887, son of Cornelius F. and Emma (Persoon) Hostettler. His grandfather, Frederick Hostettler, was a native of Berne, Switzerland, and on coming to America first settled in Ohio and later in Illinois, locating in Richland County about 1870. He was a farmer. Cornelius F. Hostettler, one of two sons and six daughters, was born in Ohio and was a child when brought to Richland County, where his active career has identified him with farming. His wife was born in Richland County, daughter of Frederick Persoon, a native of Germany, who came to this country about 1860 and settled in Richland County, where he likewise was a farmer.

Earl H. Hostettler, one of two sons and three daughters, grew up on the farm, attended country schools and continued his education and his professional preparation in the Southern Illinois State Normal University at Carbondale and also in the Illinois State Normal University at Normal.

He has given about twenty years to teaching and school administration, beginning at the age of nineteen, in 1906, when he taught a term of country school. For a number of years he taught in winter and attended school in summer. Mr. Hostettler in 1918 was elected for his first term as county superintendent of schools, was reelected in 1922, and in 1926 had no opposition as a candidate either in the primaries or the general election.

Mr. Hostettler is a democrat, a member of the Independent Order of Odd Fellows and Woodmen of the World, and is a Methodist. He married, in 1912, Miss Nettie Lewis, a native of Richland County and daughter of Thornton and Florence (Stiff) Lewis. She taught several terms of school before her marriage. The children of Mr. and Mrs. Hostettler are Aleene, Georgia, Roy, Marjorie, Eugene and Robert.

JOHN J. NICHOLSON. One of the well-known figures of Joliet and Will County is Judge John J. Nicholson, police magistrate, a man whose sound judgment and strong sense of justice make him one of the best men for the office he holds that could be found, and so wise are his decisions that only a few of them are ever reversed by the higher courts. He was born at Bloomington, Illinois, November 25, 1865, a son of Daniel and Ellen (O'Neil) Nicholson, both of whom were born in Ireland. They were married at Boston, Massachusetts. A stone mason by trade, he worked at his calling in Boston, and at Bloomington, after he came to Illinois about 1856. His death occurred in 1879, and she died in 1917.

Judge Nicholson attended the public schools until he was thirteen years old, at which tender age he began working, and was employed in a nursery at Bloomington until 1880, when he came to Joliet, and for ten years was in the rolling mills. After leaving these mills he entered the clothing business as a clerk, and maintained that connection for twenty years. Appointed superintendent of the broom shop in the Illinois penitentiary, he held that position for eighteen months, and then resigned to accept his present office, to which he was elected in 1917, and which he has held continuously ever since.

In March, 1890, Judge Nicholson married Cecelia Cummings, born at Niagara Falls, New York, a daughter of Lawrence and Margaret (Callinan) Cummings, natives of Ireland. Judge and Mrs. Nicholson have had the following children born to them: Hazel, who is at home; Edward, Raymond and Lawrence, all of whom are residents of Joliet. Judge Nicholson belongs to Saint Mary's Catholic Church. He is a democrat in politics and served for four terms as alderman from the First Ward, and for two years was city treasurer. His fraternal affiliations are many, and he belongs to the Fraternal Order of Eagles, of which he has been president several times, the Benevolent and Protective Order of Elks, the Knights of Columbus and the Loyal Order of Moose.

WILL G. SHAW. For over half a century the Shaw family has been prominent in the business and civic affairs of Jackson County. During most of this time there has been a Shaw Drug Store at Murphysboro. The late Miles W. Shaw was in the drug business many years, and his son, Will G., has followed in the same line.

Miles W. Shaw prior to 1871 was a resident of Pennsylvania, a school teacher near the City of Altoona. Then and afterwards he was known as a man of exemplary habits, conscientious, acting always in the light of his ideas of right and wrong. On coming to Illinois in 1871 he located at Murphysboro, in Jackson County. He had also studied law and civil engineering. After coming to Jackson County he taught school, and among his pupils was the well known banker, the late John Hardy. In addition to his local interest as a druggist he went on the road as traveling representative of a wholesale house, and during the early '80s moved his home to Lebanon, Missouri, as a more central location in his territory. Subsequently he was made sales manager for his company. Some years later he moved out to California and in 1907 was killed by an accidental explosion of gasoline.

Miles W. Shaw in 1875, while serving as deputy clerk of the Circuit Court, became associated with Mr. Bond in the purchase of a drug business owned by G. E. Zimmerman. This is now the Werner Drug Store. The business of Shaw and Bond soon became prosperous. Mr. Shaw bought out the interest of his partner and continued in business many years. He was at one time supervisor from Somerset Township, and while serving in that capacity has been given credit by those familiar with the tax question of saving the county thousands of dollars.

Miles W. Shaw married Siddie E. Griffith, daughter of Peter Griffith, who came from

Pennsylvania and settled in Somerset Township, Jackson County, giving the name to that township. Mrs. Miles W. Shaw was a prominent woman of Murphysboro and was killed in the tornado of March 17, 1925, while in the home of a neighbor, which was totally destroyed.

Will Griffith Shaw was born at Lebanon, Missouri, September 23, 1885. He has four brothers: Howard M., an employe of a light and power company at Chicago; Ray C., an oil operator at Oklahoma City; Earl J., general Company of California: and Frank C., a dealer in real estate in Florida.

Will G. Shaw attended public schools in Missouri to the age of nine years. When the family returned to Murphysboro he continued his education there, spending two years in high school. With his father as an ideal of a man, he studied hard to fit himself for business, and worked in his father's store, where he acquired a practical knowledge of business. He also attended night school, taking courses in commerce, telegraphy, shorthand and bookkeeping. For several years he was clerk in the Murphysboro postoffice. Feeling that his opportunities were limited in that line of work, he determined to engage in the business so successfully carried on by his father. His father's store had first been sold to W. C. Rambow, and in 1915 to Wallace Werner. Mr. Shaw established his business at 1328 Walnut Street, known as the Shaw Drug Store. He followed his father's example in square dealing. However, his father by reason of his too generous nature never accumulated a substantial competency, and his son, though thoroughly public spirited and generous, has sought to guard his own interests and has done so, still holding the respect and esteem of his townspeople.

Mr. Shaw married Miss Nellie Decker, daughter of Clint Decker, an early family of Jackson County who came from New York State. Mr. Shaw's life has been saddened by numerous tragedies. His father was killed in an accident, his mother and brother-in-law lost their lives in the tornado, and in 1924 his three year old son, Robert B. Shaw, was killed by an interurban car in Murphysboro.

During the World war Will G. Shaw was secretary of the Jackson County Finance Committee for the raising of funds for the Government by the sale of bonds. This committee made a splendid record. In numerous counties of the United States the war organizations felt compelled to adopt vigorous and sometimes strong methods in raising their quotas. The Jackson County Committee on the other hand went over the top on every drive and yet, in a manner that was not offensive. Mr. Shaw spent night and day with his war organization, almost wholly neglecting his own business.

BENJAMIN F. KILGORE, M. D., is a physician and surgeon, member of the firm Doctors Pautler & Kilgore, physicians and surgeons at Waterloo, and is a young professional man of high standing and thorough training and qualifications.

He was born at Des Moines, Iowa, August 31, 1899, son of Warren B. and Elizabeth (Salter) Kilgore. His mother was born in Vermilion County, Illinois, and his father, in Indiana. The parents reside at Des Moines, where his father is a druggist. There are two children, Sally Louise and Benjamin F.

Benjamin F. Kilgore received his early education in the schools of Des Moines, graduated in 1922 from the University of Iowa, and in 1924 completed his medical course and received the M. D. degree at the University of Illinois School of Medicine. Doctor Kilgore spent one year as an interne in the St. Louis City Hospital, and since then has been practicing at Waterloo in Monroe County.

Doctor Kilgore is a member of the Phi Rho Sigma college fraternity, belongs to the Monroe County and Illinois State Medical Associations, and to the American Medical Association. In politics he is a republican.

MARION C. COOK, a lawyer by profession with an extensive practice, is a resident of Duquoin, Perry County, and has enjoyed many official honors in that community.

He was born at St. John, Illinois, March 7, 1877. His grandfather, Moses Cook, came to Illinois from Kentucky and was a farmer. Benjamin O. Cook, father of Marion C., was born in Franklin County, Illinois, June 16, 1849, became a cooper, and in 1874 located in Perry County and for many years conducted a barrel making industry. He married Nancy J. Phillips. Her father, Jesse Phillips, came to Illinois from Alabama, but when the Civil war came on he joined the Union army and was killed on the second day of the battle of Shiloh. Mrs. Benjamin Cook died March 26, 1911.

Marion C. Cook had a common school education. He and all his brothers learned the cooper's trade under their father. Later he engaged in mining, and was a coal miner when he was injured in the machinery of a coal plant, January 18, 1902. As a result of the injury he lost his right arm, and it was this accident that caused him to study and prepare for the profession of the law. He studied in the office of Isaac R. Spillman of Duquoin, and was admitted to the bar October 7, 1908. He has done a large business as a lawyer, though much of his time has been taken up with the duties of public office. Before his admission to the bar he was made city attorney of Duquoin, and held that office eight years, being in charge of the legal details of all such public improvements as sewer and water systems and electric lighting plant. He was elected on the democratic ticket county judge in a county normally republican, and defeated the republican incumbent of the office by a majority of 186, and four years later, in 1910, was reelected by a majority of 394. In 1913 he was appointed postmaster of Duquoin by President Wilson, and held that office until March 17, 1923. Judge Cook was postmaster throughout the World war period, and a large amount of unusual business was crowded in on his official routine. Outside of his official position no one in Perry County worked harder for the success of the various campaigns during the war than Judge Cook. He was chairman of the County War Work Committee, was chairman of the committee managing the drives for the United War Work campaign, was chairman of the committee in charge of the War Savings Stamp drive. He spoke at every mine in Perry County in behalf of the Liberty Loans and frequently was called to Chicago headquarters in an advisory capacity during the Liberty Bond campaigns. When the bodies of Perry County soldiers were brought back from France he was placed in charge of the local ceremonies, being ably assisted by the Presbyterian minister, Rev. Mr. Maxton.

Judge Cook has long been prominent in the Improved Order of Red Men, is a past sachem of the Duquoin tribe No. 168, became great sachem of the Red Men of Illinois in 1919, and is now head of the Junior Guards of the United States, while on October 25, 1925, Mrs. L. M. Cook, his wife, was made head of the Degree of Pocahontas of Illinois. He is also affiliated with the Independent Order of Odd Fellows, Modern Woodmen of America, and is a member of the First Missionary Baptist Church. He married at Freeburg, Illinois, February 12, 1902, Lula M. Parker, daughter of Ira G. Parker, of Perry County. Judge and Mrs. Cook reared an adopted daughter and a niece of Judge Cook, Celeste Newell Cook, now Mrs. Elvain.

NICHOLAS SAUER. The history of Evansville in Randolph County runs back into the territorial era of Illinois, and involves many names and events. Since the close of the Civil war, however, probably no one family has meant so much to the constructive advantage of the community as that of Sauer. Fully three generations of the family have impressed their activities and spirit on the growth and development of the locality. The most conspicuous member of the family was the late Nicholas Sauer. Both his father and his brother were identified with Evansville, and the men of the present generation of the family are still carrying on the work there.

The founder of the family in Illinois was Philip Sauer, a native of Germany, who when a young man came to America, landing at New Orleans, coming up the Mississippi to St. Louis, and making his first permanent home in Monroe County, Illinois, where he developed a farm. After the war he was for a time associated with his son Nicholas at Evansville, but then returned to the farm and died in 1891, at the age of eighty-six. His wife died in 1878, aged fifty-six. The three sons, all of whom were residents of Randolph County, were Nicholas, William and Philip.

Nicholas Sauer was born at the farm near Redbud, in Monroe County, March 21, 1841, and was educated in the common schools of the locality and in St. Louis. He taught two terms of country school and in 1865 became a general merchant at Mascoutah, in St. Clair County. In 1866 he and his father bought a flour mill at Evansville. This industry had been established before the war by John Wehrheim and was one of the old time mills. Under the new firm of N. & P. Sauer it was continued until 1868, when William Sauer succeeded his father, Philip, and the firm became N. & W. Sauer. Later, in 1899, the Sauer Milling Company was incorporated, and the business is now conducted by the third generation. This milling company has been one of the central factors in giving permanent vitality to the commercial life of Evansville. The firm greatly improved the mill, introducing modern machinery, and it was one of the first mills in southern Illinois to adopt the roller process. The old plant was destroyed by fire in 1904, but a new mill was constructed. Since the death of Nicholas Sauer his son, Philip E., has been president of the company. The mill has a capacity of seven hundred barrels of flour daily.

From Illinois Nicholas Sauer and his sons extended their milling connections to the great wheat belt of Kansas and purchased a mill at Cherryvale in that state, known as the N. Sauer Milling Company, of which Philip E. Sauer is now president and his brother George, vice president.

For many years the prosperity of Evansville depended upon its river transportation. A railroad was vital to its continued place among the commercial centers of Randolph County. Nicholas Sauer was perhaps the man chiefly responsible for effecting the building of the Illinois Southern Railroad to Evansville. He contributed liberally to the cash bonus and helped secure the right-of-way, and after many discouragements and the lapse of fifteen years of effort saw the railroad built. Nicholas Sauer in 1894 organized the Bank of Evansville, and was president of this bank until his death. George Sauer, his son, is now president and Philip E. Sauer, vice president.

Nicholas Sauer was not less active and influential in bringing to Evansville the institutions that expressed the ideals of a people in respect to educational and religious facilities. He was for twenty-one years a member of the Board of Education. He was a devout member and liberal supporter of the German Evangelical Church and was an active member of the Masonic Order. In politics he was a republican. Socially Nicholas Sauer was an interesting man, with a democratic and genial personality. He possessed a mind well matured by reading and broad experience and contact with the world. He loved his home and family, but at all times was public spirited and generous in doing for others.

Nicholas Sauer died October 21, 1908, at the age of sixty-seven, his death being the result of an accident, so that the community felt the greater grief because of his taking away in the prime of his matured powers and character. He married, July 22, 1866, Miss Elizabeth Gerlach. She was born in Virginia, but was reared in Monroe County, Illinois. Her parents were also natives of the same section of Germany from which the parents of Nicholas Sauer came. The children of Mr. and Mrs. Sauer were: John, who was educated as a mining engineer and later became manager of the milling business of the Sauer Company at Cherryvale, Kansas; Magdalena E.; Philip E.; Dr. William E., who after a liberal education in this country and abroad became a specialist in ear, nose and throat at St. Louis; George N., who is president of the Bank of Evansville, and secretary of the Sauer Milling Company.

Philip E. Sauer was born at Evansville January 11, 1873, was educated in public schools, the Southern Illinois Normal University and Shurtleff College, and since early youth has been associated with the milling business of his father. He and his brother George have been closely associated in carrying on the many varied interests started by their father. He and his brother were responsible for the laying out and development of the beautiful cemetery on the hill at the edge of Evansville, named the Nicholas Sauer Cemetery. Philip Sauer is president of the Evansville School Board. He married, September 18, 1907, Miss Alice Harmon, of Chester, Illinois, and they have one daughter, Elizabeth C., attending Lindenwood College of St. Charles, Missouri. His brother, George Sauer, was born February 10, 1879, was also educated at Shurtleff College, and after leaving college went to work in the flour mill.

CAROLINE MARGARET MCILVAINE, librarian of the Chicago Historical Society, has always regarded her position as an opportunity and has utilized it as an important source of service and a great contribution to the educational and cultural activities of a great city.

Miss McIlvaine was born and reared on the Chicago North Side, and is a daughter of John Slaymaker and Laura Jane (Hinds) McIlvaine. Her parents were of Scotch, English and German ancestry. Her earliest American forebears were identified with the New England and Pennsylvania colonies. Her father's grandfather, Andrew McIlvaine, came to America from the North of Ireland in 1719 and settled at Lewes, Delaware. Her mother was a descendant of William Hinds, who came to this country from England about 1630 and settled in Salem, Massachusetts.

Miss Caroline McIlvaine was educated in Chicago public schools and under private tutors. At the time of her graduation from the grades, business matters required the family to live temporarily in Minneapolis, and thus her first two years of high school were spent in that city. One of her classmates was Louise Beatty, subsequently known to operatic fame as Madame Homer. Miss McIlvaine continued the study of languages and other subjects after graduating from high school and pursued several courses at the University of Chicago.

Miss Caroline and her sister, Miss Mabel McIlvaine, were early attracted to the library service in the Newberry Library, and eventually Dr. William Frederick Poole, head of the library, consented to give them a chance for an apprenticeship in library science. The instruction they received under the notable group of scholars and other library workers assembled by Doctor Poole—Miss McIlvaine has always regarded as a very broad foundation for administrative work in the museum or library field.

At the Newberry Library she worked in every department, and at the end of five years was head cataloguer and director of the index of genealogy. From this office she was called in 1901 by the Chicago Historical Society to take charge of its Library and Museum of American History at Dearborn and West Ontario streets. In that work she has rounded out a quarter of a century of important service to her native city. Beyond the routine activities of efficient administration Miss McIlvaine has aimed at, and in the judgment of all who know something of the Historical Society has been abundantly successful in achieving, two general objects: One, the cultivation of good citizenship and patriotism through the study of American institutions and ideals, and the other to adapt the work of the historical society to the young by means of visual education.

Miss McIlvaine is well known in the official organizations of library workers and has membership in such organizations as the American Association of Museums, Chicago Academy of Science, Chicago Library Club, Prairie Club, Friends of Our Native Landscape and Wild Flower Preservation Society.

ALLAN PINKERTON, the most celebrated man who ever lived in Dundee, Illinois, was born in Glasgow, Scotland, in 1819. His father, William Pinkerton, had been a sergeant of police and in the Glasgow riots received injuries which left him an invalid. He died when his boy was fourteen, but even before that Allan had begun to make his own way and at twelve had been apprenticed to the trade of cooper. For years the family knew pinching poverty, and he and his brother Robert were the main support of the widowed mother.

The one outstanding characteristic of Pinkerton was his dauntless courage. With shams or half way measures he had no patience. Injustice was to him intolerable and this disposition to plunge in and straighten out the crooked at whatever cost led him at the age of nineteen to join the Chartist movement.

To the average American the Chartist demands (the abolition of a property qualification for a seat in parliament, equal representation, payment of members and universal suffrage) appear almost as inalienable rights but the government of that day did not so regard them, and when young Pinkerton, who belonged to the branch known as "the physical force men," showed a prompt willingness to fight for his faith the united kingdom speedily became too hot for him.

In 1842 he sailed for Canada, but on the day before embarking he married Joan Carfrae, a young woman born in Edinborough. Their honeymoon was as adventurous as a novel. Off the coast of Sable Island a storm descended upon them and they were wrecked. The passengers, however, escaped and the Pinkertons managed, with difficulty, to reach Montreal, and thence worked their way westward by way of the Great Lakes to Detroit. There they invested practically all they had in a horse and wagon and drove overland to Chicago, where Pinkerton found work at his trade.

In 1843, influenced probably by the number of his countrymen living in the vicinity, Pinkerton moved to Dundee. A cooper shop was established and grew until in time it employed eight or nine men. Among these were often a few negroes, for the same intolerance of oppression which made Pinkerton a

Chartist made him also an anti-slavery man. Indeed his aloofness from the organized church (profound as was his friendship with many deeply religious men) is probably to be attributed to the temporizing attitude of many church members toward slavery.

The beginning of a new career came in odd fashion. While foraging for his cooper's supplies, hickory hoops cut on an island in the Fox River, Pinkerton stumbled upon a cache of counterfeit money. With a canniness characteristic of his race he told no one of his find excepting the sheriff, who appointed him a special deputy, with instructions to keep watch for any one who might come to dig up the hoard. No one now living can tell exactly what happened, but Pinkerton watched, there was a chase, a fight, and the ultimate capture of the counterfeiters—a formidable gang of men and women, interested in diversified criminality, including horse-stealing and murder.

After this Pinkerton, like John Burns of Gettysburg, went back if not to his bees and his cows, then to his casks and barrels. He had not the vaguest idea of having found a new calling: He had simply been one of a posse to round up a bunch of bad men. But he had made a beginning and it was not long ere greater responsibilities were thrust upon him.

One hot July day in 1847 Cooper Pinkerton was busy in his shop, arrayed in hickory shirt, overalls and nothing more when a hurry up call came from a prominent merchant and not bothering even to slip on his boots he answered it. What was offered him was virtually a job in the detective line and the future terror of crooks and criminals laughed it to scorn. What did he know about detective work! But two prominent citizens were insistent and he reluctantly submitted; only insisting that for this special piece of work, the capture of a counterfeiter, he was especially unfitted. "Why, I never saw a ten dollar bill in my life." And he later declared that this statement was strictly true.

The task for which he had been summoned was to "get" a man at that moment across the street and thither Pinkerton went, playing the village loafer to such good purpose that the stranger decided he had found a man to give circulation to his wares and in the woods on the other side of the Fox River explained his terms to Pinkerton and showed his product. It would be needless to give the story in detail, for Pinkerton himself wrote it in one of the books which during his life time had such a wide circulation; and it is available to such as would seek it. Suffice it to say that Pinkerton, with money furnished by his Dundee backers, bought $500 worth of bogus money and thereafter arrested the man who had sold it to him. His anger may be imagined when one adds that after being safely lodged in jail the criminal finally slipped through the hands of the law, evidently by corrupting the sheriff.

Pinkerton's work, however, had been widely discussed and it had two far-reaching effects. It made the Fox River valley unhealthy for counterfeiters, their Golden Age was over; and it launched the fame of the man who had protested that his business was coopering and not chasing criminals. Calls came that gave him work county wide, state wide and then nation wide. He was the first detective employed by the Chicago police department; in 1850, under a guarantee of $10,000 a year from several railroads, he established the Pinkerton Detective Agency; and in 1860 he went to Washington and organized the government Secret Service.

His larger work brought him not only fame and fortune, it brought him also great friendships. John Brown was one of his friends; Abraham Lincoln was another and probably the proudest achievement of his life was to be able, just on the eve of the inauguration, to save the great emancipator from assassination.

OSCAR B. ORMSBY, M. D. No name has been more honored in the medical profession in Jackson County than that of Ormsby. Two members of the family, father and son, have practiced there covering a period of sixty years or more.

The first was the late Dr. Orange B. Ormsby, who was born on a farm near Greenville, Bond County, Illinois, in 1836. His father was one of the pioneers of Bond County. Orange B. Ormsby was a graduate of Rush Medical College of Chicago. For two years he practiced in his old home community of Greenville. Then the Civil war began and he went into the army as a private. After ninety days it was discovered that he was a physician and he was appointed assistant surgeon in the Eighteenth Illinois Infantry. Later he was made surgeon with the rank of major and transferred to the Twenty-second Illinois Infantry. The hardships of the strenuous campaigns in Georgia and around Atlanta undermined his health, and when Sherman reorganized his army for his famous march to the sea Major Ormsby was told by his superior that if he attempted to march he could not possibly survive, and recommended him to accept an honorable discharge. Convinced that this was the only course open to him, Major Ormsby resigned his commission and, returning to Illinois, located at Murphysboro, where he engaged in his long and successful career as a physician and surgeon. For a few years he lived in a log cabin located on fields at one time devoted to the cultivation of cotton. Few modern citizens of Jackson County even know that cotton was ever grown here. In his practice he walked, rode horseback and in a cart over the surrounding country, frequently being gone two or three days at a time and returning physically exhausted. He went through the hardships and rendered great service so frequently credited to those famous old time country doctors. Dr. Orange Ormsby married Susan Butler at Rockford, Illinois. After some years of arduous practice in Jackson County, on account of his health, he went out to California, locating at Bakersfield. After three years in California he returned to Murphysboro and remained there the rest of his life, which came to its close June 13, 1899.

Dr. Oscar B. Ormsby, the present representative of the family in the profession of medicine, has spent nearly all his life in southern Illinois, but is a native of California.

He was born at Bakersfield during the residence of his parents there, on October 24, 1876. He was educated in the grade schools in Murphysboro and attended the Normal University at Carbondale. His father had always said that he would permit no boy of his to enter the medical profession. However, Oscar Ormsby had a natural inclination for that work, also an admiration of the splendid qualities of his father, and he finally overcame the old doctor's objections and entered the St. Louis College of Physicians and Surgeons. He was graduated in 1897, and practiced with his father during the last two years of the latter's life. He has carried on a general practice and made a splendid success of his career.

Doctor Ormsby married Grace Holden, of Carbondale, daughter of William Holden. They have one daughter, Julia Elizabeth, who is a graduate of Northwestern University of Chicago, and is a talented musician, being now a teacher of music.

DAVID McWILLIAMS. Well may this history pay a tribute of honor and appreciation to the McWilliams family, which has played a prominent part in Illinois development and progress from the early pioneer period to the present time. The richest heritage that shall ever remain in the keeping of the generations to come is the simple story of the struggles, the sacrifices and the triumphs of the men and women who planted in the wilderness the home, the school, the church and the state. We shall never know that story in its fullness, for the noble men and women who thus opened the way for civilization in all this western country have long since passed away, leaving but meager records of the vicissitudes through which they passed. Time has, in many instances, obliterated even the names of those who thus planted where others have reaped and garnered, and whose lonely, self-sacrificing but resourceful lives entitle them to a place in the breviary of civilization. In this day of swift communication, of manifold advantages for the transacting of business and for the indulgence in pleasures, it is difficult to realize adequately the hardships and reverses experienced by those who figured as the early pioneers. Following the nationalization of the colonies there was a great national unrest. There were frontiers in those days, and something beyond the horizon. The man of Ohio who had come into that country as a pioneer and there developed his farm into a paying proposition would hear of better lands further on, including those of Illinois, where the corn grew so tall that one could for days be lost in its mazes. Whereupon he assembled his family, locked the door of his cabin and set forth for the new fields of conquest. There continually came the challenge and thrill of a new country—something always a little bit better a bit farther on, and thus came the natural urge to benefit thereby. Those were the days of the poor man's chance.

Influenced by this feeling of unrest and by the reports concerning the beauty and attractiveness of the Illinois country James McWilliams, in company with his family, left the home in Ohio in the year 1838 and in a primitive boat drifted down the Ohio River to the Mississippi, and then proceeded northward to the mouth of the Illinois River. Up the Illinois River Mr. McWilliams continued his way until he reached Pike County. The natural hardships of that long and tiresome journey were augmented by illness among members of the family. Reaching a point on the river east of the site of the present town of Griggsville, Pike County, Mr. McWilliams made a landing for the night. To the settler in a new country, with neighbors few and far removed and with conditions that will barely serve in time of health, family illness came in a darker garb and presented a more disheartening aspect. Seeking better shelter than the usual night camp afforded, in order better to care for his sick child, Mr. McWilliams pushed on four or five miles back from the river, and there found and purchased a hut owned by a squatter. The life of the child could not be saved, however, and sadly was the little form laid to rest by the devoted father and mother. An excessive spring flood had covered the bottom lands till the middle of summer and then dried off with extreme hot weather in August, thus causing much sickness and many deaths along the rivers that season, the while fears were expressed that the locality would always be unhealthful.

James McWilliams was not to be daunted by any misfortune, for he recognized the possibilities offered by the new country—a virgin soil, clean and rich, inviting the plow; boundless meadows waiting the scythe; the summer paradise of the flocks and herds that were to occupy them; a teaming richness of oil whose golden harvests should one day glut the markets of the world—all this could but excite the imagination and constructive resourcefulness of a man like James McWilliams, who thus became imbued with the liveliest hope, the most ardent anticipation and ambition. The day's experience was but a miniature picture of the hopes and sufferings of pioneer life.

James McWilliams became one of Pike County's leading men, and there he engaged eventually in the lumber business at Griggsville, where he became also the president of the First National Bank. He was one of the honored and influential pioneer citizens of that county at the time of his death, in 1886.

David McWilliams, son of this sterling Illinois pioneer, was born in Belmont County, Ohio, and was an infant in arms at the time of the momentous journey from the old Buckeye state to the new home in Illinois. He received somewhat better educational advantages than the average youth of the locality and period, and he seemed to have inherited from his father the faculty of discerning the future possibilities of the county in which he had been reared. In the '50s, before railroads had entered the present city of Dwight, Livingston County, James McWilliams had made a tour of inspection in both Livingston and La Salle counties, and had purchased large tracts of land. In 1855 David McWilliams established his residence in Dwight, which was then a mere village, and here opened a small general store, in which he conducted also the banking business of the community. Through the years of hardship incidental to the development of that section of Illinois, and through discouraging periods of industrial and general financial depression, David McWilliams was at all times ready to encourage and aid to the best of his resources and powers. In this connection may be noted an incident that affords high light upon his character and his communal attitude. A settler came to his store to secure a plow. "When can you pay?" asked Mr. McWilliams. "When my corn is gathered next fall," was the response. "What if your crop fails?" "I'll pay you the next year," was the rejoinder. "What if your second crop fails?" "I'll pay you with the next crop," replied the prospective buyer. "All right, take the plow," said Mr. McWilliams, and it is to be recorded that the plow was paid for with the fourth-year crop of the purchaser. In fact, at that period there were so many crop failures and so many years of low prices for farm products that many Illinois farmers sold their farms far below value and sought land in Kansas and Iowa. Here may be related another incident relative to Mr. McWilliams' business methods. One farmer had been running an account at the McWilliams store until the same had raised his credit score to $500. Discouraged by repeated poor crops, this farmer, feeling that he had exhausted his credit, offered his farm to Mr. McWilliams in payment of the debt. While the farm was worth much more than the amount of the debt, Mr. McWilliams refused to take the property, extended further credit to the farmer and encouraged the latter to try again, the result being that the man eventually became one of the most substantial farmers of the community. In manifold services of this order David McWilliams contributed far more than his normal share to the development and progress of this now prosperous and favored section of Illinois, and here his name and memory are held in enduring honor.

In 1896, Charles D. McWilliams, his youngest son, just graduated from Northwestern University, entered his father's banking house, where he has remained until the present day in various capacities. In 1906 David McWilliams and Charles D. McWilliams organized the Bank of Dwight, which had run as a private institution since the year 1855, into a state bank, known as the Bank of Dwight, to succeed the former private bank. David McWilliams continued to be its president until the time of his death, which occurred in 1909.

David McWilliams married Louise Weagley, who was born in the state of Maryland, and who is now deceased. Upon the death of Mr. McWilliams his son Edward succeeded to the presidency of the Bank of Dwight, an executive office that he still retains, while another son, Charles, is vice president of the institution. Mr. McWilliams gave excellent educational advantages to each of his three sons, Edward, John P. and Charles, and all are well upholding the prestige of the family name. John McWilliams, a brother of David, was captain of a company in an Illinois regiment in the Civil war, and thereafter he became a successful banker and leading business man at Odell, Livingston County. Both of these brothers were known as loyal, liberal and progressive citizens and both commanded inviolable place in popular confidence and esteem.

SHURTLEFF COLLEGE is the oldest college in Illinois and one of the oldest west of the Alleghanies. It was founded less than ten years after Illinois was admitted to the Union and ten years before Chicago was incorporated as a city.

The founder of Shurtleff College was John M. Peck, who was born at Litchfield, Connecticut, in 1789. He was sent by the Baptists of the East in 1817 to establish a so-called "domestic mission" in the frontier mission territory. No sooner had he received his appointment than he began to dream of a school in this great territory, and he wrote: "It had been our plan at first, even before we left Philadelphia for this region, to establish a seminary for the common and higher branches of education, and especially for the training of school teachers and aiding of preachers, now in offices or who may hereafter be brought forth in our schools. The education of the ministry is of primary importance in all new countries."

On January 1, 1818 Peck opened a Baptist school in St. Louis, but conditions in that city were not favorable for a permanent location for the school, and in January, 1927, the Rock Spring Theological and High School was opened at Rock Spring, Illinois. This is regarded as the real founding of Shurtleff College. In 1832 the school was removed to Upper Alton and was called Alton Seminary. Rev. Hubbell Loomis was its first principal. The first building erected, in 1832-33, bears his name, and is still used as the Chemical Laboratory. In 1835 "Alton College of Illinois" was duly granted a charter from the Legislature.

In 1835, too, the college received from Benjamin Shurtleff, M. D., of Boston, a gift of $10,000, one-half of which was to be used for buildings, and one-half for founding a professorship of oratory. This amount was a munificent gift for the times, and in honor of it the name of the school was changed to Shurtleff College, and the charter was amended to accord with this action.

The first president of Shurtleff College was Rev. Adiel Sherwood, who served from November, 1841, until 1845. Succeeding him, after a period of five years without a president, was Dr. Norman Wood, 1850-1855, during whose administration Elijah Gove, of Quincy, Illinois, contributed nearly $60,000 to the college, the largest amount ever given by any individual; Daniel Read served from 1856 to 1870, a period including the dark days of the Civil war, when the attendance was naturally greatly decreased and the finances of the school were so depleted that the very life of the college was threatened; Dr. A. A. Kendrick was next, from 1872 to 1894, whose administration was longest of all, and who increased the endowment funds to nearly $100,000 besides building the chapel, a dormitory for girls and a gymnasium; from 1895 to 1900 Dr. Austin K. deBlois was president, and continued to increase the prosperity of the school; Dr. Stanley A. McKay followed from 1900-1905; and then Dr. J. D. S. Riggs, who completed an endowment campaign for $50,000 and succeeded in securing a Carnegie Library building.

After the resignation of Doctor Riggs in 1910 a period of depression followed. The student body decreased in number, many of the investments were bringing little income, and a feeling was prevalent that Shurtleff's day was done. In 1912 the trustees called to the presidency George Milton Potter, who began his administration on August first of that year. He undertook what was regarded as an almost hopeless task, many of the trustees themselves being doubtful as to the advisability of opening for another year. There was no interest in the school on the part of local citizens and very little among the Baptists of the state. But the work of reconstruction began and the new president gradually removed the incubus of the indebtedness, slowly won the confidence of the constituency in the state and awakened a new spirit of appreciation in Alton. A plan of expansion was formulated and almost at once new property contiguous to the small campus of eight acres began to be acquired, until at present the college owns about thirty-five acres, which includes a large athletic field. The productive endowment funds which in 1912 amounted to only about $85,000 have been increased by two campaigns. In 1919, $320,000 were added, of which Alton citizens contributed about $102,000. In 1923 the Centennial campaign was begun to meet a conditional pledge of the General Education Board of New York. This board offered to pay one-third of the whole amount if $400,000 could be added to the endowment. This campaign was completed in June, 1926, and when all the funds are paid in in 1928 the endowment will be $725,000.

Part of the increased acreage provides a campus for women, on which a beautiful stone dormitory has already been erected. A new gymnasium has also been built. The student body has grown from seventy-two to over two hundred in the college proper, while the establishment of a Conservatory of Music, with courses leading to a degree, a summer school and a night school, makes the total enrollment considerably larger. The faculty has been increased from ten to eighteen. The library has 18,608 volumes and is in charge of a trained librarian. The academy has been discontinued and the college has been made fully accredited, being a member of the North Central Association of Colleges and Secondary Schools.

In June, 1927, Shurtleff College will celebrate its Centennial, and will start on a new century with all things pointing to a bright future.

JOHN S. MURPHY made his life expressive of the best attributes and influence of a strong and noble nature, his course was guided and governed by high principles, and his ability enabled him to achieve through his own efforts a large measure of temporal success. He was long numbered among the representative business men and loyal and public spirited citizens of Pontiac, and material property gave him the means to indulge his earnest desire to be helpful to others. He merited and received the unqualified popular respect and esteem expressed in the following memorial tribute written by Rev. John H. Ryan, D. D., at the time of the death of Mr. Murphy, which occurred in the home of his son Rupert in Miami, Florida, February 27, 1924:

"The announcement of the death of this very unusual man will be received with real sorrow by a wide circle of friends and associates who have sustained intimate relations with him in all the business, educational and philanthropic activities that have distinguished our city of Pontiac for the past thirty-five years."

John S. Murphy was born at Campbellsford, Province of Ontario, Canada, August 18, 1855, and was thus about five years of age when the family came to Illinois and established a home in Pontiac. He was a son of Peter and Anna Murphy, who continued to reside in Illinois during the remainder of their lives, the other children of the family having seen Susan, James, Peter, Jr., Patrick, Mary, William and Joseph, and only three of the number survive at the time of this writing—Peter, Mary and Joseph.

Quoting further from the tribute of his pastor, Doctor Ryan:

"The education of John S. Murphy was received in the common schools of Pontiac, supplemented by wide reading, extended travel, and association with alert business and professional men, whereby his keen and active mind was equipped for the responsibilities that he so efficiently carried through the best years of his life. The problem of carving out his own destiny confronted him in early years. As a boy he did willingly and well what his hands found to do, and at the age when most boys were living the child life, care free, he was at work in the woolen mills and at such other forms of employment as the town afforded at that time. In 1868 he entered the drug store of Caldwell & McGregor, where he immediately gave evidence of the business acumen that assured his success in later years. Mr. McGregor stated, near the close of his life, that of all the young men who had been trained for business in his store John S. Murphy was one of two outstanding examples of efficiency.

"It was due largely to his natural and acquired gifts, joined with his integrity, devotion and purpose, that Mr. Murphy was given by C. W. Sterry an opportunity commensurate with his talents, and Mr. Sterry was easily induced to furnish Mr. Murphy the means for independent activity in the establishing of the John S. Murphy drug and stationery store. Mr. Sterry took no part in managing the business, but his judgment and confidence were rewarded by returns which proved to be one of his most profitable business adventures. This business enterprise was launched in 1885, and the firm relation was sustained till 1898, when Mr. Sterry's interests were purchased by Mr. Murphy, who continued the business as its sole owner until 1911, when he retired, as he supposed, but his counsel and cooperation had proved too valuable not to be actively enlisted up to with-

in recent months, when his health made imperative a change of program.

"Mr. Murphy was largely responsible in inducing Mr. Sterry to finance the first shoe manufacturing enterprise in Pontiac. C. E. Legg, at the time, had received a flattering offer to begin the manufacture of shoes at Kankakee. However, when Mr. Sterry assured his support the citizens gave cooperation. Later, when the A. M. Legg Shoe Company was organized, Mr. Murphy became identified with the company as stockholder and director. He had been from the beginning financially interested also in the Pontiac Shoe Company, of which he became the vice president.

"Mr. Murphy was one of the organizers of the Pontiac Chautauqua, and was a director through all the years of its history. He was associated with others in establishing the Pontiac State Bank, and was one of its directors until recent months. With the LaCrosse Land Company he sustained a like relation, and with his associates he pioneered in the development of the Kankakee Valley. He was a member and director of the original Allen Candy Company of Pontiac; was superintendent of the Pontiac Light & Water Company for most of the period between the death of Mr. Carothers and the transfer of the plant to the Public Service Company; as postmaster of Pontiac he first filled the unexpired term of D. C. Eylar, and thereafter he succeeded to a full term, he having served eight years as postmaster, under the administration of President Wilson, and having retired from this office August 29, 1923. He was a member of the City Council, from the First Ward, in 1900-01. No activity that promised a larger and a better Pontiac was without the support of his talents and means.

"Within the pastorate of Rev. E. Wasmuth, of the Methodist Episcopal Church in Pontiac, Mr. Murphy, together with Mr. A. M. Legg, was given the difficult task of working out a financial program that would meet not only the demands of the church's activities but also the confidence and approval of men of affairs, and as a result the society took rank with the leading churches of the Conference, and has sustained a position of unquestioned leadership during a period of more than thirty years. While Mr. Murphy actively supported the Y. M. C. A. and was one of its original organizers in Pontiac, his sympathy was especially enlisted in hospital service, and those agencies, wherever they ministered, found him a generous and constant friend. Mr. Murphy had been identified with the local Methodist Episcopal Church since his early manhood, was treasurer of the church more than twenty-five years, and he was the oldest trustee in time of service at the date of his death."

On the 30th of January, 1878, was solemnized the marriage of Mr. Murphy and Miss Ella M. Moody, who died in Miami, Florida, December 29, 1925. Mrs. Murphy had long been a gracious and popular figure in the representative social, cultural and church circles of Pontiac. She was eligible for affiliation with the Daughters of the American Revolution through service by both paternal and maternal ancestors as patriot soldiers in the great war for national independence. Her paternal ancestor who accorded such service was Captain Moody, and her maternal ancestor of similar service, Private Rawlins, or Rollins, as the name is sometimes spelled. Mr. and Mrs. Murphy became the parents of five children, the first of whom died in infancy; Emily Marie died at the age of twenty-three; John Ray and Erroll Rupert are now residents of Miami, Florida; and Kenneth is secretary of the A. M. Legg Shoe Company of Pontiac.

KENNETH M. MURPHY, secretary of the A. M. Legg Shoe Company of Pontiac, is a son of the late John S. Murphy and at the present time the only remaining representative of that well known family in Pontiac.

He was born in that city March 19, 1892. After completing his course in the public schools he attended during 1912-13 the Kansas Agricultural College, returning from college to take up work with the Pontiac Shoe Company. Upon the incorporation of the A. M. Legg Shoe Company he was made secretary and handled the executive responsibilities of that position ever since.

Mr. Murphy is an alert and capable business man and well known for his public spirit and usefulness in his community. He is a member of the City Council of Pontiac and has been on the council for five years, in 1926 becoming a candidate for reelection. He is a member of all the Masonic bodies at Pontiac, including the York and Scottish Rite, belonging to the Scottish Rite Consistory at Bloomington and the Mystic Shrine Temple at Springfield. He is a past commander of Pontiac Commandery No. 85, Knights Templar. Mr. Murphy is also a member of the Loyal Order of Moose and the Modern Woodmen.

He married Miss Amy Berry, daughter of John A. Berry, of Pontiac.

FRANCIS MARION HEWITT is one of Carbondale's business men who has been active in the affairs of that city for more than a quarter of a century. The experiences and activities of Mr. Hewitt have been those of a more than ordinarily successful man.

In his early life, however, he had to struggle and make his own way, since he was left an orphan at a very early age. He was born in Johnson County, Illinois, May 3, 1870, son of John L. and Mary Ann (Casey) Hewitt, farming people. Two and a half years after his birth his father died, and a few years later his mother passed away. He had a few brief terms of schooling in Johnson and Williamson counties, but all the time was engaged in whatever work he could find to do. He made the best of his opportunities and at the age of nineteen was teaching a school near Marion in Williamson County. Going to Chicago, he studied pharmacy in Northwestern University, paying his own expenses while there. He was graduated in 1893, and a few months later located at Carbondale, where he was a pharmacist three years. From 1896 to 1899 he was employed by the Yeiser Drug Company at Paducah, Kentucky, and another year at Clarksville, Tennessee. Mr. Hewitt in 1900 started a drug store at Carbondale, and has been continuously in business, and is owner of one of the city's best known mercantile establishments. Mr. Hewitt was one of the founders and became a director and vice president of the Carbondale National Bank. He is also a member of the Carbondale Building & Loan Association and is a director in that institution.

Mr. Hewitt in 1911, on the adoption of the commission form of government, was chosen commissioner of health and public safety, and did much to insure the early popularity of the commission form of government. Subsequently he was elected a member of the Illinois State Senate, serving in that office from 1916 to 1920. He was a member of the Senate during the World war and participated in the important legislative program of that period. Mr. Hewitt is affiliated with the Masonic Lodge at Carbondale, the Independent Order of Odd Fellows, has been chancellor commander of the Knights of Pythias, and joined the Order of Elks at Paducah, Kentucky.

He married, January 24, 1907, Miss Winifred Harker. Her father was the distinguished lawyer and judge, Oliver A. Harker, of Carbondale. Mr. and Mrs. Hewitt have three children, Francis Marion, Jr., Winifred Harker and Mary Ann Hewitt.

FRANCIS NEWTON SMITH has long been one of the representative business men and loyal and honored citizens of Pontiac. Though now living virtually retired, he is still the senior member of the firm of F. N. Smith & Son, conducting a large and prosperous general lumber business. He was founder of this business. The advancement of Mr. Smith to the status of leading representative of the lumber business in the city of Pontiac runs its course from the time when he left the parental homestead farm in the state of New York and determined to carve out for himself a successful career in connection with business affairs. He has been in the fullest sense the architect of his own fortunes, and his substantial success has been worthily won.

Mr. Smith was born in Orange County, New York, and he early gained a full share of experience in connection with the work of the home farm, his educational advantages in the meanwhile having been those involved in his attending the district school during the winter terms, when his service was not in such great demand in connection with the farm work. His ambition to identify himself with business found expression in 1881, when, at the age of seventeen years, he came to Illinois and in Chicago found employment in a grocery store. In Chicago he had befriended another youth who was out of work and without money. For a term of weeks Mr. Smith permitted this youth to sleep in his room, besides which he paid for the meals of his supposed friend. He had accumulated a reserve fund of about forty dollars, which he intended to use in making his way further to the west, in search of more profitable employment. One day both his companion and his money disappeared, and he was more hurt by the ingratitude than he was by the loss of his savings. This was not the last time advantage has been taken of his sympathetic and generous nature. Mr. Smith refused to be disheartened or discouraged, and he soon made his way to Pontiac, where, a few days later, he found employment in the lumber yards of the Chicago Coal & Lumber Company, the headquarters of which were in Chicago, the yards in Pontiac being situated near the passenger station of the Wabash Railroad. He applied himself diligently and loyally, and at the age of twenty-one years he was made manager of the company's Pontiac branch and business. At the end of his first year of service in this executive position Mr. Smith was confronted with the problem of finding a new location, as the owner of the land demanded a virtually prohibitive rental in connection with renewal of the lease. The company having authorized him to use his own judgment, he purchased for the company a piece of land in block No. 2 of the Ladd & McDowell Addition to Pontiac. Within a comparatively short time after the requisite buildings had been erected on this new site and the lumber yards here established fire destroyed both buildings and stock of lumber, but new structures were promptly built and the yards replenished with stock. At that period a competing concern purchased lumber yards that had been established in the west end of Pontiac, on the line of the Chicago & Alton Railroad. In the vigorous competition that continued with the opposing concern in the ensuing period of two or three years victory was finally won by Mr. Smith, whose aggressive leadership gained for his company this precedence, the Chicago Coal & Lumber Company having purchased and absorbed the business of the opposing concern.

In 1896 Mr. Smith decided that he was entitled individually to the full benefits of his industry and experience, and he therefore severed his alliance with the Chicago company and engaged independently in the lumber business at Pontiac, where he initiated operations on the site of his present large and well equipped yards, his original buildings having been a small office structure and sheds of limited capacity. With no capital save his own reputation for integrity and his proved ability as an executive in this line of industrial enterprise, Mr. Smith encountered no little difficulty in obtaining his first stock of lumber. When the first two carloads of lumber for his new yards arrived in Pontiac the company from which the stock had been purchased demanded payment before unloading, in spite of a previous agreement to give Mr. Smith sixty days in which to meet the bill. It was then that the reputation of Mr. Smith stood him well, for a local banker, upon being informed of conditions, advanced him $5,000 on his personal note and thus enabled Mr. Smith to release his first stock of lumber. Fair and honorable dealings and effective service gained to the new enterprise a constantly expanding trade, and with the passing years Mr. Smith gained precedence as one of the leading exponents of the lumber business in this part of the state. In 1915 he established a branch lumber yard at Saunemin, this county, with C. C. Ridinger as a partner in the latter place.

In May, 1923, the well established business that Mr. Smith had built up in Pontiac was taken over by the newly organized firm of F. N. Smith & Son, the junior member of the firm being his older son, Francis L.

Francis N. Smith is one of the loyal and public spirited citizens of Pontiac, and has long been one of its influential business men. His political allegiance is given to the democratic party, he has given a long period of service as a member of the city Board of Aldermen, and he has served also as a member of the Board of Supervisors of Livingston County. He has passed the various official chairs in the local lodge of the Independent Order of Odd Fellows, is affiliated also with the Benevolent and Protective Order of Elks, the Loyal Order of Moose and the Modern Woodmen of America. He and his wife are members of the Methodist Episcopal Church.

Mr. Smith married Mrs. Clara A. (Moreland) Lambert, whose one child by her previous marriage is a daughter, Edith. Mr. and Mrs. Smith have four children: Ida Corwin, Gladys Moreland, Francis Lynden and Donald Ezra.

FRANCIS LYNDEN SMITH, junior member of the firm of F. N. Smith & Son, lumber dealers at Pontiac, was born in that city February 18, 1896. His early education was acquired in the public schools of his native city, including high school. In 1917 he was graduated in both the literary and law departments of Illinois Wesleyan College, from which he received the degrees Bachelor of Arts and Bachelor of Laws, his law course having been as an incidental preparation for his association with business affairs. Prior to his graduation in the college he had, in May, 1917, volunteered for service in the United States army, less than a month after the nation entered the World war. He completed his college courses after this enlistment and in July, 1917, he was assigned to the machine-gun company of the One Hundred and Twenty-ninth Illinois Infantry. In the following September he accompanied his command to Texas, and November 1st he was there transferred to the headquarters company at Camp Logan and assigned to the Intelligence section, with the rank of sergeant. In May, 1918, he was sent to Long Island, New York, and on the 3rd of the following month he landed at Brest, France. He was assigned to duty with the Australian troops, as a member of the Intelligence section. In September, 1918, Mr. Smith was ordered back to the United States and to report for duty as an instructor at Camp Dodge, with the rank of second lieutenant. In the following month the armistice brought the war to a close, and Mr. Smith received his honorable discharge in January, 1919. Later he was commissioned captain in the reorganized Illinois National Guard, and still holds this rank.

At the close of his World war service Captain Smith returned to Pontiac and became associated with his father's lumber business. He was admitted to the partnership of F. N. Smith & Son in May, 1923. His father had largely retired from active association with the business, and the enterprise is now virtually maintained under the active supervision of the junior member of the firm, who is well upholding the honors of the family name both as a vital young business man and as a loyal and progressive citizen of his native city. His parents have a winter home in Florida where they spend the greater part of each successive winter season.

Captain Smith was the democratic nominee for mayor of Pontiac in 1922, and while he had no expectation of being elected, owing to the great republican preponderance in the city and county, he had the satisfaction of greatly reducing the republican majority, as he was defeated by only sixty-six votes. The result gave evidence of his unqualified popularity in his native city. Captain Smith has passed the official chairs in the Pontiac Lodge of Elks, his Masonic affiliations include membership in the Mystic Shrine, and he is affiliated also with the American Legion and the Loyal Order of Moose. He married, November 17, 1919, Miss Marion Eleanor Williams, daughter of William Williams, a resident of the state of Washington. Captain and Mrs. Smith have one son, Francis Newton, II, named in honor of his paternal grandfather.

CAPT. EDWARD A. EVERS, captain of the Ninth Naval District, United States Naval Reserves, who has given nearly thirty years to active or reserved duty with the navy, is a Chicago business man, and for a number of years was in business as a machinery manufacturer.

Captain Evers was born in New York in 1878, but Chicago has been his home since 1893. After attending public schools he qualified for the work of mechanical and electrical engineer through shop practice. Until the time of the World war he was in the manufacturing industry as president of the Evers-Sauvage Company, manufacturers of special machinery. He still has financial interests in that corporation.

Captain Evers first volunteered for naval duty in 1897, and was called to active duty during the Spanish-American war in 1898. He was on the U. S. S. Indiana, one of the capital battleships of that period. He was on that ship at the battle of Santiago, and was one of the boat crew that rescued Admiral Cervera of the Spanish navy from his sinking flag ship. Following the war he continued with the Naval Reserves as seaman, and in 1900 was advanced to the rank of ensign. Other promotions followed until in October, 1911, he was commissioned captain and put in charge as commanding officer of the Naval Reserve of Illinois, with headquarters in Chicago. That position he has filled now for nearly fifteen years.

Captain Evers took an active part in preparing the Naval Reserve in his district for the event of America's participation in the World war. Immediately after the declaration of war, in April, 1917, he sent 600 trained men to the Naval Station at Philadelphia. These men, all Illinoisians, were assigned individually into every branch of the naval service, including duty on ships in the European battle area. Captain Evers had these men ready for entraining within forty-eight hours after the telegram came from Washington to mobilize.

In January, 1922, Captain Evers began the reorganization of the Naval Reserve forces in the Ninth Naval District. Now he has

1,400 men under his command, all of whom are given training on regular cruises of the U. S. S. Wilmette, the training ship. Each member of the Naval Reserve during training must take a fifteen day cruise. The Ninth Naval District has more men in the reserve than any other naval district in the United States, including New York. The authorities at Washington have pronounced it one of the most efficiently organized and trained naval districts in the country, a fact largely due to the personal leadership and experience of Captain Evers. On account of his long service Captain Evers is now the senior ranking officer of Naval Reserve in the United States, qualified for duty on a combatant ship.

He is an ex-president of the Army and Navy Club of Chicago, served five years as president, and is now vice president of the Naval Reserve Officers Association. Captain Evers married Miss Florence King, of Chicago. Their three children are Jean, Virginia and Marjorie. His home is in Wilmette and his official headquarters are at the U. S. S. S. Commodore.

JOHN A. LYNCH. For thirty-two years as president of the National Bank of the Republic John A. Lynch has been one of Chicago's leading financiers. He was one of the organizers of this bank, and its solidity and continued prosperity have been absorbing interests in his busy life. In directing its public policy he had ever shown the careful conservatism of a wise, clear-headed business man, and in private administration had been watchful and generous as is a father to his favorite son.

John A. Lynch was born at Chicago, Illinois, June 11, 1853, son of Thomas and Ann (Flanagan) Lynch. His father, a native of Barntick, County Clare, Ireland, came to the United States in 1845 and soon afterward had made a home for his family in the growing town of Chicago, Illinois, on the shore of Lake Michigan, and here, in the course of time, through industry and business ability, he became a man of importance. At first, as a laborer, he became connected with the Crosby Distillery, later acquired an interest in the business, still later became the head of this pioneer industry and operated at first under the name of Thomas Lynch & Co., and still later as H. H. Shufelt & Co., under which name it was sold to the late Lyman J. Gage in 1891, Thomas Lynch retiring at that time.

John A. Lynch attended the parochial and public schools of his native city, and in 1869 was graduated from Dyenforth College. A six months' course at Bryant and Stratton Business College followed, and the day after receiving his diploma he entered the firm of Thomas Lynch & Co., distillers, which shortly afterward became H. H. Shufelt & Co. When the business was sold in 1891 Mr. Lynch, consulting his own taste, made plans for a period of travel, a taste that still prevails and is Mr. Lynch's chief source of recreation today.

In the meanwhile, however, Mr. Lynch had assisted in the organization of the National Bank of the Republic, an unusually important financial venture at that time. The Board of Directors of the bank heard of Mr. Lynch's plans with regret, for they had hoped he would consent to assist in the bank's management, realizing the helpfulness of his honorable name and the value of his sound judgment and business sagacity. Their arguments prevailed with Mr. Lynch, and in January, 1892, he accepted the presidency of this institution, and held this office continuously until January 8, 1924, when he was elected chairman of the Board of Directors.

The National Bank of the Republic opened for business August 3, 1891, and in January, 1892, when Mr. Lynch became its president, its capital was $1,000,000, no surplus, undivided profits, $17,342.35, deposits, $1,156,801.55. On July 1, 1902, the bank's capital was increased to $2,000,000, and on that date the surplus was $700,000, undivided profits, $55,269.34, deposits, $14,600,466. On November 20, 1918, the capital was $2,000,000, surplus $1,000,000, undivided profits, $348,316.53, deposits, $32,039,115.88. On October 10, 1924, the capital was $2,000,000, surplus $1,000,000, undivided profits and reserve for taxes, interest and contingencies $1,311,250.39, deposits, $47,152,938.83. During Mr. Lynch's presidency the bank paid in dividends to its stockholders $3,685,000.

During his many years of wise and profitable administration of the affairs of this institution Mr. Lynch's fidelity and devotion to its interests, particularly during the anxious periods of business depression and financial stress over the entire country, manifested to his close associates, but unselfishly kept to himself as closely as possible, bore fruit, the National Bank of the Republic being one of the impregnable financial institutions of the country. Grateful acknowledgment of Mr. Lynch's faithful stewardship was voiced by William F. Fenton, vice president of this bank, in an address at the fifteenth annual meeting of the Board of Directors, which address was spread upon the minutes and made a part of the official records of the bank. After referring feelingly to his warm personal esteem for Mr. Lynch, Mr. Fenton said: "President Lynch has been the bank's most faithful friend. During the perilous days of 1893, 1894, 1895 and 1896 he placed his entire fortune at my disposal, in case it should be necessary to use it for the protection of the bank. Time and again he sold securities at a sacrifice and turned the money into the vaults of this bank for its protection. Once during the financial panic of 1893 he got up from a sick bed and came to me one morning at the bank to tell me that he had money enough to pay every dollar that was due to the bank's depositors and that he would do it if necessary. I cannot begin to enumerate the instances of substantial support he has given to the bank in times when disaster seemed to threaten its career." During the panic of 1907 the National Bank of the Republic, at considerable expense, imported $1,000,000 in gold to meet the possible currency requirements of its customers and correspondents and increased its own circulation an additional million, thus obviating the necessity for calling a single loan or distressing a single customer during the entire period of disturbance. For three years Mr. Lynch was president of

the Chicago Clearing House Association, and a member of the Clearing House Committee.

Mr. Lynch married, January 21, 1896, Miss Clara, daughter of John Schmahl, of Chicago. He has long been helpfully interested in civic improvement and social welfare, and has been notably generous in the field of benevolence. He is treasurer of the Catholic Church Extension Society and the Catholic Home Finding Association; past president (1904-17) of the Board of Trustees of St. Mary's Training School; a governing member of the Chicago Art Institute, and a member of the Chicago Athletic, Bankers, Mid-Day and Edgewater Golf Clubs.

WALLACE C. PURDY, assistant postmaster of Murphysboro, is a veteran of the postal service, and has been continuously identified with the post office at Murphysboro for a quarter of a century.

The Purdy family has been in Jackson County since pioneer times. As a family they have had their best distinctions perhaps not in the material success of business careers but in the fine influence they have exerted in upholding religion, morals and educational ideals.

Isham Purdy, grandfather of Wallace, came from Vermont, and in 1832 settled near Vergennes, in Jackson County, Illinois, a locality that was named for an old Vermont town. His son, Charles W. Purdy, was born at Vergennes in 1840. He lived all his life in the northern part of Jackson County, and no one there was held in finer esteem. Both he and his father were church workers, and the first sermon preached in the Vergennes locality was in the home of Isham Purdy. Charles W. Purdy was one of the interested Sunday School workers for many years. He died February 2, 1912. Charles W. Purdy married Rachel Outman, whose family came from New York State in 1848 by way of the Erie Canal, Great Lakes and Illinois River. She died July 4, 1912, about five months after her husband.

Wallace C. Purdy was born at the Purdy homestead, Jackson County, February 2, 1869. As a boy he worked on the farm and attended country schools. In carrying out his early plans to become an educator he entered the Normal College at Carbondale in 1889 and attended nine terms there. His first teaching was done at Finney in Jackson County. Later he was principal of schools at Pomona and Vergennes.

In 1900 the first civil service examination was held for positions in the Murphysboro post office. He took this examination and on September 1, 1901, began work which has proved consecutive and permanent. He started as substitute clerk and substitute carrier, in 1903 was promoted to clerk, and on May 1, 1906, became assistant postmaster, a position he has now filled for twenty years under various postmasters. On the death of Postmaster Gibson he was made acting postmaster, February 10, 1926. Mr. Purdy has the characteristics of the family, quiet, industrious, unselfish and faithful to duty. He is a member of the Masonic Order, Knights of Pythias, Woodmen of the World, and belongs to the Methodist Episcopal Church.

He married, in 1896, Ellen Whisler, daughter of Christian W. Whisler, a farmer near Ava. To this marriage were born six children, Anna, Lois, Lela, Geraldine, Pauline and Margarette. The daughter Pauline was considered hopelessly injured in the great tornado of 1925, but after spending four months in a hospital recovered. Mr. Purdy after the death of his first wife married Henrietta Strohm, of St. Louis.

ALVIN JOINER, lumber manufacturer, farmer and business man, is a native of Ogle County and for many years has been one of the most influential citizens of Polo.

He was born at Buffalo Grove, Ogle County, November 13, 1848. His parents, Charles W. and Harriet M. (Waterbury) Joiner, settled in Illinois in June, 1837. Alvin Joiner attended school in Illinois for several years. In 1857, when he was nine years of age, his parents moved to Sanilac County, Michigan. He attended school there, and continued his education in an academy at Royalton, Vermont, and the Hillsdale Business College in Michigan. At the age of twenty-one he was admitted to a partnership in his father's lumber manufacturing business. The Joiners owned and operated several sawmills and owned extensive tracts of pine lands in eastern Michigan. The headquarters of their manufacturing enterprise were in Huron County. During 1870 they bought some large tracts of pine timber in Lake County. In 1871, the year of the great fire of Chicago, there were unprecedented forest fires in Michigan, which destroyed a large part of the timber holdings of the Joiners in the eastern section of the State. Consequently, the Joiner family centered their operations on their new holdings in Lake County, where they erected mills and laid out the town of Chase on the Pere Marquette Railroad. Mr. Alvin Joiner was actively associated with his father in the firm of C. W. Joiner & Son, Michigan lumbermen, for a period of twenty-seven years. A strange freak of fate in connection with their lumber interests is that their saw and shingle mills were destroyed by fire six times.

In May, 1884, Mr. Joiner resumed his residence in Ogle County, Illinois, and has had many business interests there as well as elsewhere. He has been financially interested in real estate properties in Illinois, Michigan, Wisconsin, South Dakota and Florida. Mr. Joiner still owns the Joiner homestead where he was born. He is also owner of telephone lines connecting three counties in Wisconsin. One of his very active interests, constituting a hobby, is a 300-acre farm in Carroll County, Illinois. This model farm is operated by his two sons, to whom he deeded the place. They operate this farm under the firm name of Joiner Brothers.

Mr. Joiner served as mayor of Polo, and under his administration the city's water system was installed. He is a trustee of the Carnegie Library and was on the board when the library building was erected, and has served as president of the board since that time. While a practical man of business, he is inclined to literary pursuits, and is one of the best read men in Ogle County. In the publication known as the Illinois Libraries, issued by the library extension division, in volume 6, No. 2, of April, 1924, is an article under the title of "Great Books," written by Mr. Joiner.

Mr. Joiner married in Wood County, Ohio, June 14, 1873, Miss Ida P. Wood. Her father, Henry L. Wood, assisted in the building of the second railway in the United States. He was a member of the Ohio Legislature and was a quartermaster in the Union army during the Civil war. Mr. and Mrs. Joiner became the parents of three daughters and two sons. The daughter, Jennie H., was formerly a teacher of music in Blair Hall, New Jersey, and at Danbury, Connecticut, and became the wife of John M. Siddall, who was a graduate of Oberlin College of Ohio, subsequently attended Harvard University, and became one of the editors of the American Magazine. Mr. Siddall died in 1923, and his widow now spends her summers in New York and her winters at her sister's home in Florida.

Alice Joiner, the second daughter, graduated from a private school in Wisconsin, and spent three years in Leland Stanford University in California. She is the wife of Ralph C. Bryant, of Princeton, Illinois, and a nephew of the poet, William Cullen Bryant. Ralph C. Bryant was the first person in the United States to receive a diploma in forestry, graduating from the forestry department of Cornell University. He is now connected with the forestry department of Yale University. He went to the Philippines as assistant to the chief forester under the United States government, taking his bride to those islands immediately after their marriage. Mr. Bryant is a well known authority on forestry, is author of two books on the subject, and one of them is used as a state text in China. The two children of Mr. and Mrs. Bryant are Betenia, a daughter, and Ralph, Jr.

Charles H. Joiner, the older of the two sons of Mr. and Mrs. Alvin Joiner, spent two years at Leland Stanford University in California, took a special course in agriculture at the University of Illinois, and is now engaged in the practical phases of agriculture of his father's farm above mentioned. He married Florence Hostetter, and has a son, named Richard Vaniah Joiner, and a daughter, named Jean Adell Joiner. His younger brother, Alvin Joiner, Jr., also attended Leland Stanford University, and is especially interested in the animal husbandry side of farming. He married Zella G. Mackay, of Carroll County, and their two children are Alvin III and Joan.

Flora Isabel Joiner, the youngest of the family, attended Barnard College at New York, did special work in domestic science at the University of Illinois, and was married to Vaniah Hostetter, of Rockford, Illinois. Mr. and Mrs. Hostetter have a son, Carl.

EDWARD TURNER JEFFERY, a well known American Railway official, was born at Liverpool, England, April 6, 1843, son of William S. and Jane (McMillan) Jeffery. His father, born at Greenock on the Clyde (Scotland), entered merchant marine engineering service in the early days of steam navigation and later became a chief engineer in the British navy. He died in Woolwich in 1849. In 1851 the mother brought her family to America and settled in Wheeling, Virginia (now West Virginia), where she had relatives and where Edward Turner Jeffery attended school.

In 1856 the family moved to Chicago, then a city of 68,000 people, and in October, 1856, when about thirteen years old, Edward Jeffery entered the employ of the Illinois Central Railroad Company as office boy to the superintendent of machinery, Samuel J. Hayes. At the end of five months he commenced as an apprentice in the tin and coppersmith shop; soon transferred to the machine shop to learn the trade of machinist; served about half of his apprenticeship as machinist and was retransferred (July, 1858) by Mr. Hayes to the office of superintendent of machinery as office boy and apprentice to mechanical drawing and engineering, with instructions never to be idle; either to keep at work or at study. He studied mechanical engineering and manifested deep interest in that special branch of railroading, and also in all its other branches. He was an indefatigable student for ten years and overcame the deficiencies in his general education due to commencing work, of necessity, at an early age. At the age of twenty he became a regular draughtsman; at twenty-two he was placed in full charge of the department of mechanical drawing and became also private secretary to the superintendent of machinery. In February, 1872, he accepted from Major General George B. McClellan (retired) the position of general manager of the United States Rolling Stock Company in New York, of which company General McClellan was president. General McClellan had been vice president and chief engineer of the Illinois Central before the Civil war. The arrangement was mutually cancelled at the request of Mr. John Newell, president of the Illinois Central, and Edward T. Jeffery was appointed assistant superintendent of machinery, and he served in that capacity for the ensuing five years under Mr. Samuel J. Hayes, the superintendent of the department.

His zeal and business activity attracted the attention of the management of the company. In 1877 he was appointed general superintendent and acting chief engineer of the Illinois Central System under the presidency of Mr. William K. Ackerman, and on January 1, 1885, was elected, by the Board of Directors, general manager of all departments of the railroad. In September, 1889, he resigned for the purpose of obtaining needed rest, after thirty-three years in the service of the company.

In 1885 he was the representative of the Illinois Central and two other companies at the first International Railway Congress, which convened in Brussels under the auspices of King Leopold of Belgium, and was the only American delegate present.

His personal influence with working men was generally recognized, as he had grown up amongst them and retained their confidence and friendly cooperation. In his early years his warmest friends and associates were working men, and it was their interest in him, their intelligence, and their sound advice to him as to right habits of life and the upbuilding of character that stimulated his efforts. For three years in those early days he was librarian of the Illinois Central Workingmen's Library in Chicago, and he formed friendships there with workers of all classes which left a lasting impress for good upon his life and character. To working men he has always felt and acknowledged his indebtedness for their helpfulness and support.

On resigning the general managership of the Illinois Central Railroad Company, Mr. Jeffery was elected by the mayor and other leading citizens of Chicago interested in projecting the Columbian Exposition to visit and report on the International Exposition in Paris, and at the same time to promote in every way practicable the claims and desirability of Chicago as a site for the Columbian International Exposition of 1893. In this mission he was entirely successful. He declined compensation for this and other services in connection with the Exposition. Chicago is indebted to his influence that the enterprise was located there. In January, 1890, he made an able argument before the U. S. Senate which was largely influential in achieving the desired result. Upon the organization of the directory he was chosen a member of the board and was strongly urged to accept the position of director general, but refused this honor, as well as a candidateship for the presidency of the Board of Directors to succeed Lyman J. Gage, resigned. He was chairman of the committee on grounds and buildings for a year and a half, however, and in recognition of his many services to the Exposition was presented with a memorial by the Board of Directors calling him "The Father of the World Columbian Exposition."

For several years he was a member of the Young Men's Literary Society of Chicago; of the Chicago, Iroquois and Calumet Clubs; Masonic Fraternity; and the American Railroads Master Mechanics Association.

On October 1, 1891, he accepted the position of president and general manager of the Denver and Rio Grande Railroad Company. He continued his service as general manager until 1900, and as president until January, 1912, when he was elected chairman of its Board of Directors. He retired from official connection with the company in January, 1917.

In 1905, when the Western Pacific Railway Company was organized to build a low grade line of railroad from Salt Lake City to San Francisco in the interest of the Denver and Rio Grande Company, he was made president and devoted some of his time to the construction of this important enterprise, about one thousand miles long. He retired as president in 1913, but remained two years longer as chairman.

Mr. Jeffery has been for a number of years a director in the First National Bank and the First Trust & Savings Bank of Chicago; and of the Equitable Trust Company of New York, and the Manhattan Railway Company of New York.

His clubs are the Chicago Club (Chicago); Denver Club (Denver) and Metropolitan, Lawyers and Railroad Clubs (New York).

He married, in 1877, Virginia Osborn Clarke. Their son, James Clarke Jeffery, was a well known Chicago attorney. His sketch follows this. Their daughter is Mrs. E. J. Doering, Jr., of Chicago.

JAMES C. JEFFERY was a member of the Chicago bar for about twenty-two years, in the course of which he made a large circle of friends and formed a wide acquaintance in various parts of the country. His natural abilities and genial temperament brought him a degree of leadership in his profession that enabled him to manifest much influence as a citizen in his home city of Chicago and also, at times, in national affairs when his professional duties permitted. He was born in Chicago on January 1, 1879, and was the son of Edward T. and Virginia O. Jeffery. His father was connected with the Illinois Central Railroad Company for about thirty-three years and retired as general manager in the latter part of 1889. He is one of the well known American railway presidents and a sketch of his career immediately precedes this.

James C. Jeffery was educated in private schools, principally the University School of Chicago. He graduated from Yale University in 1899 and followed a law course at Harvard University, graduating in 1903 with the degree of LL. B. and the following year entered upon the practice of law in his native city. He made a specialty of interstate commerce law, to which he devoted much of his time for a number of years, although engaged in the general practice of law. He acted as attorney for several railroad companies and for other business corporations and was also one of the attorneys for the Chicago Board of Trade. He was a member of the law firm of Jeffery, Campbell and Clark from 1917 to 1924, when it merged with another Chicago firm under the name of Jeffery, Townley, Wild, Campbell and Clark, and he continued with it until his death, December 5, 1924, in Chicago.

Mr. Jeffery was a well known member of the Chicago Bar Association; was one of its Board of Governors in 1921-1923; and a member of the finance and entertainment committees, and he took an active interest in the affairs of the association. He was also a member of the Illinois and American Bar Associations.

In politics he was a democrat. He was at one time president of the Iroquois Club, Chicago; president of the Forty-second Ward Democratic Club, and for a couple of years president of the Yale Club of Chicago, in the welfare of which he felt much interest.

When Mr. Jeffery was candidate for judicial office the Chicago Bar Association Committee summed up his qualifications concisely as follows:

"His genial disposition attracts many friends. He possesses requisite education and experience. His integrity is of the highest. He is well qualified for the office of Judge of the Superior Court."

During the World war period Mr. Jeffery was one of the original organizers of the "Four Minute Men" movement throughout the United States, acting as vice chairman of the

Four Minute Men for the state of Illinois, and chairman of the same organization for the city of Chicago, and during this time devoted considerable time to making speeches and attending to other details of these organizations.

Mr. Jeffery was a member of the Chicago Club, the University Club, Racquet Club, Legal Club, the Law Club, Chicago Literary Club, the Riverside Golf Club, and he belonged to the Chicago, Illinois State and American Bar Associations.

He married at Chicago, April 21, 1906, Clara Louise Whedon, daughter of James P. and Clara W. Whedon. Mrs. James C. Jeffery died November 18, 1918. One daughter, Frances Clarke Jeffery, survives both parents.

THE ELGIN DAILY NEWS, of which Richard Lowrie was editor and Lyman F. Black publisher, the two operating under the name of Lowrie & Black Company, is one of the leading newspapers of this part of the state, and the mouthpiece for the best element of Elgin and Kane County. It was established by S. A. Taylor in 1872, and in 1883 it was purchased by Adam H. Lowrie, father of Richard Lowrie, then owner of the Daily and Weekly Advocate. For several years he continued issuing both papers, but subsequently discontinued the Advocate, and in 1890 associated with him in the publication of the News, Willis L. Black, father of Lyman F. Black.

Adam H. Lowrie was born in Berwickshire, Scotland, October 29, 1836, but was brought to the United States when he was six years old by his parents, who settled at Cleveland, Ohio, and it was in that city that he was reared, his education being obtained in its public schools during the preliminary stages. Subsequently he attended the University of Michigan, and his final year was spent at Adrian, Michigan, College. For the following two years he held a tutorship, and then became superintendent of schools of Marion, Ohio. After two years in this position he left to become superintendent of a Cleveland city school, and two years later was made head of the school system of Bellefontaine, Ohio. Resigning the latter position, he took the chair of English literature and political economy at Adrian College, and for the following fifteen years held it, during two years of this time being acting president of the college.

Resigning from the educational field Mr. Lowrie then entered that of journalism as proprietor of the Adrian Times and Expositor, and in 1882 came to Elgin to purchase first the Advocate and later the News. During his editorial career Mr. Lowrie was one of the founders and an honorary member of the Inland Daily Press Association; for several years he was treasurer of the National Editorial Association, and took great pleasure in the annual excursions of this body of newspaper men to all parts of the country. In 1892 and 1893 he was United States consul to Freiburg, Germany, under the administration of President Harrison, and was always prominent as a republican. He was present at the birth of the republican party in 1854, and took a more or less active part in a great many of the campaigns from that date until his death, and for more than a quarter of a century he was one of the most prominent republicans of Kane County.

Mr. Lowrie was always a forceful figure at Elgin, and for more than thirty years was a member of the Board of Directors of the reliable financial concern, the Elgin City Banking Company, an institution in whose growth and progress he took great pride and interest. He was always active in church work at Elgin, and preached from many of the city pulpits, and was particularly zealous in behalf of the building of the First Congregational Church structure. During his lifetime many honors were bestowed upon him, including several college degrees from the University of Michigan, the University of Florida, and others in the South where he had lectured on political and economic subjects. He was, at all times, deeply interested in the public schools of Elgin, and at one time was president of the school board, and the A. H. Lowrie School on Oak Street was named in his honor.

On September 11, 1858, Mr. Lowrie married Miss Mattie B. Pease, of Jackson, Michigan, who was at the time of her marriage instructor in French at Adrian College. Mrs. Lowrie survived her husband, as did their two sons: Will L. Lowrie, who was United States consul general at Athens, Greece, for four years and in 1925 was transferred to Wellington, New Zealand, where he now holds a similar position, he having been in the diplomatic and consular service for over twenty years, and Richard Lowrie, who served as editor of the Elgin Daily News after his father's death until his retirement.

WILLIS L. BLACK was a commanding figure in the newspaper world of Elgin, the partner of Adam H. Lowrie, and his associate in many public-spirited movements. Mr. Black was born at Elgin, on the present site of the First Baptist Church, April 18, 1855, a son of Lyman Black, and he died in the same city February 9, 1916. The public schools of Elgin gave Mr. Black his beginnings of a fine education, and he supplemented this training with attendance at the Elgin Academy and the University of Chicago, entering the latter in 1874, and being graduated from it in 1878. After some years with the office force of the Daily News and Advocate Mr. Black, in 1886, purchased an interest in the papers, the two having by this time been consolidated, and he and Mr. Lowrie entered upon their long association, a partnership inherited by their sons. Mr. Black was also active in business life and was president of the First National Bank, vice president of the Elgin City Banking Company, and the principal stockholder in both banking houses. He was a member of the Board of Directors of the Elgin Wind, Power and Pump Company, and was widely connected with many other commercial and industrial concerns of the city, for his business acumen was widely recognized, and his association desired. The social side of his nature was not neglected and he was a welcome addition to the Country, Elk and Century Clubs, the National Editorial Association, the Press Club of Chicago and the Inland Press Association.

For years he found much enjoyment and relaxation in traveling, and about 1910 he and his wife and family made a trip around the world.

On September 4, 1884, Mr. Black married Miss Etta D. Roe, of Chicago, and they became the parents of two children: Lyman F. and Mareta V.

Under the second generation the Elgin Daily News continued to sustain its high reputation. The office was constructed in 1893, but has been remodeled until it is now one of the most modern newspaper offices in Illinois. The News is republican and exerts a powerful influence in the community in behalf of the public schools. Within the past two years the entire plant has been reequipped with new machinery, including linotype machines and presses, and it compares favorably with any in the country. The new tubular press has a capacity of twenty-four pages ready to double whenever occasion warrants. The plant and offices, together with three stores, are located in a building, owned by the firm, which is one of the most prominently situated in the business part of the city. The circulation of the News is nearly 9,000. The officers of the Lowrie & Black Company were: Richard Lowrie, president and editor; Mrs. Willis L. Black, vice president; Lyman F. Black, secretary and treasurer.

On January 1, 1926, the News was consolidated with the Elgin Daily Courier under the name of the Elgin Courier-News, with circulation of over 17,000 daily.

NICK A. MASTERS is one of the very prosperous young business men of Carbondale. He went from Carbondale for soldier service in the great war, and in that and in many other ways has shown an admirable spirit of patriotism and citizenship.

He was born in Greece August 15, 1892, but came to St. Louis, Missouri in 1907. He is a son of Arthur and Helen Masters. The mother died while Nick was away in France. Arthur Masters was born in Greece, and for many years lived at St. Louis, but finally returned to his native land, where he is still living.

Nick A. Masters attended public schools for a few years, but at the age of twelve was employed as a helper in a machine shop at sixty-five cents a day. After that he continued his education in night school. By the time he was fourteen he had advanced so far in proficiency that he commanded a wage of three dollars a day. He worked five years, saving his money, and in September, 1916, came to Carbondale, where he invested his entire capital in the purchase of the Carbondale Candy Kitchen. It was a small beginning, but his hard work and close attention to details brought him a large and profitable business.

Soon after America entered the World war he turned over his business to his young brother, Chris, and on September 17, 1917, was enrolled in the training camp at Camp Taylor, Kentucky. On June 4, 1918, he was on his way to France and spent ten and a half months overseas. After the armistice and his honorable discharge he returned to Carbondale and resumed his business, taking the financial loss incurred during his absence as only a necessary part of patriotism. The business subsequently grew and in January, 1924, he bought a cafe which for many years had been conducted by L. T. Barnes. He modernized and enlarged this, doubling its capacity, and has a thoroughly up-to-date restaurant.

Mr. Masters married, January 20, 1924, Pearl Ebbs, of Carbondale, and they have one daughter, Helen Elizabeth. He has been much interested in the American Legion and has given generous response to many calls upon his generosity as a soldier and as a citizen.

HAROLD C. LEWIS as president of the Coyne Electrical School has made a distinctive contribution to the city of Chicago as both a great industrial and educational center. Mr. Lewis is a dynamic character, forceful and resourceful, a skilled and successful administrator and organizer, and is equally gifted with the inspiring, human and kindly qualities that has gained him the trust and admiration of his students.

Mr. Lewis was born at Des Moines, Iowa, was reared in Council Bluffs of the same state, and the advantages of the public schools were supplemented by the practical education derived from the necessity of earning his own living. Thus his personal experience has made him completely sympathetic of the situation in which many of the pupils who attend his school are placed.

He came to Chicago in 1909, and for several years was connected with the great mercantile house of Carson, Pirie, Scott & Company. He began as stock boy in one of the departments of the wholesale concern, and his ability won him advancement to the position of assistant to the buyer of a department.

In 1919 he assumed the management of the Coyne Electrical School, of which he is president. This school was founded in 1899, and for some years was conducted as a general trade school, teaching many different trades. Mr. Lewis from the first recognized the value of specialization, and has made the Coyne School exclusively a school for teaching the various branches of the electrical profession. The Coyne School fully bears out the reputation it enjoys of being America's oldest practical school of electricity. The emphasis is on the practical training. The student is always in the atmosphere of close contact and the real work connected with the various branches of the electrical industry. There are no class rooms, text books, lectures or formal recitations. It is a vocational school with its methods of instruction rigidly conforming to the necessities of training men for immediate and vital contact with the electrical trade. It is shop practice and shop training, and the school is operated six days in the week and every week of the year without any arbitrary date for beginning or end of sessions nor graduation time, a student being promoted or getting a diploma of proficiency only when he has done the required work.

The Coyne School occupies spacious quarters in the seven-story building at the northwest corner of Harrison and Throop streets, but its large facilities are so taxed that in 1927 the school removed to a modern building erected especially for its use, at Congress and Paulina streets, at an expenditure of approximately $300,000. Thousands of young men have received their training in this institution, and their characters and practical services in the electrical field demonstrate the thoroughness of their training and in every sense the best advertising for the school itself. While there are opportunities offered to students for prolonged training in some special line, the regular course of instruction for a student runs through a circuit of related departments, beginning with the elementary department, then going through the circuit department, the construction department, illumination department, sign department, armature department, direct current and alternating current departments, following which the complexities of automotive engineering so far as it involves electrical work are taken up, and also there are battery departments, drafting departments, and finally the radio department. As a practical asset to the radio department the Coyne School owns and operates radio station WGES, with studio in the Guyon Paradise Ball Room at 121 North Crawford Avenue. This is one of the very popular broadcasting stations of the central west, and the students of the Coyne School have an opportunity to learn every phase of radio engineering. Mr. Lewis extends a cordial invitation to all those interested in vocational training, as well as those interested in electricity and the electrical industry, to visit the school at any time. He would be especially interested in a visit from those interested in or connected with vocational training in the high schools and he would be pleased to offer any suggestions or aid in organizing this work in the public schools of any state.

Mr. Lewis in 1915 married Georgia C. Chapp, daughter of Joseph Chapp, of Chicago. They have one son, William C. Mr. Lewis is affiliated with Chicago Lodge No. 4, B. P. O. Elks, Illinois Chamber of Commerce, Chicago Chamber of Commerce, West Town Chamber of Commerce, and is a member of the Midwest Athletic Club, American Institute of Electrical Engineers and the Hamilton Club. He is independent in politics and a member of the Episcopal Church.

REV. TILGHMAN HOLTON, a retired resident of Bloomington, has lived a long life, many years filled with intense labors, a remarkable career of devotion to humanity and the cause of religion.

His grandfather, William Holton, moved from Fauquier County, Virginia, to Mason County, Kentucky. He was a soldier under Harrison at the battle of Tippecanoe and subsequently served through the War of 1812. He took part as a member of the first legislative body of Kentucky, and was a contemporary and associate of the great Kentuckians Felix Grundy and Henry Clay. William B. Holton, father of Rev. Mr. Holton, was born at Minerva, Mason County, Kentucky. As a young man he was sent by his father to look after some land on Stone River, Tennessee, and while there he met Miss Sallie Price Tilghman. She was born in Albemarle County, Virginia, and as a girl was among the young people entertained at Monticello, the home of Thomas Jefferson near Charlottesville. She accompanied her father, John Tilghman, to Wilson County, Tennessee, the family settling near Hermitage, fourteen miles from Nashville, and there they became friends and acquaintances of President Jackson. After the marriage of William B. Holton and Miss Sallie Tilghman they lived in Wilson County, near Hermitage, Tennessee, and six children were born to them there. William Holton, Sr., subsequently bought a patch of land in Brown County, Ohio, near Aberdeen, fronting on the Ohio River and just across the river from Maysville, Kentucky. His two sons, Dr. E. G. Holton and William B. Holton, joined him in the purchase and removed to that locality.

Rev. Thomas Tilghman Holton was born after his parents moved to southern Ohio, on November 17, 1839. He was the ninth in a family of thirteen children. He attended local schools, the Hill Seminary at Aberdeen, Ohio, and at the close of his fifteenth year entered what was then known as the Southwestern Normal School, subsequently the National Normal University at Lebanon, Ohio. The head of that school was then Prof. Alfred Holbrook, one of the greatest educators of his time. Mr. Holton received a certificate with grades of a hundred per cent, and at the age of seventeen became principal of a school near Lebanon. The following year he was again in the Normal and in October, 1858, he entered Bethany College in what subsequently became the state of West Virginia. He was a student there four years. The president of the college was the celebrated Alexander Campbell, founder of the Church of the Disciples or Christian Church. Mr. Holton graduated valedictorian of his class and soon afterward was called to a professorship in Jefferson College at Jeffersontown, twelve miles from Louisville, Kentucky. Early in 1864 he established an academy in Selma, Kentucky. In connection with teaching he had been filling pulpits in many churches. In 1866 he formally entered the Christian ministry, his first regular pastorate being at Vincennes, Indiana. In 1868 he came to Illinois, was a pastor at Springfield and while there at different times acted as chaplain in the Legislature. He was pastor and the principal of schools at Berlin, Illinois, and for many years was in charge of the Christian Church at Lincoln, Illinois. He has enjoyed an extensive acquaintance and service in many communities of central Illinois, including Pekin, Atlanta, Broadwell, Emden, Bethel, Delavin, Old Union, Hallville and Waynesville. His friends have frequently admired his versatile talents and remarkable industry. For many years he has performed the labor of two men. In connection with the ministry and teaching he filled positions in commercial establishments and for eight years was clerk of the circuit court of Logan County. In the early '90s he moved to Tallula, Illinois, and served the church there four years, was also pastor at DeLand four years. In 1907 he bought his home at Bloomington, and while nominally retired has answered many calls to temporary positions in the ministry.

Rev. Mr. Holton married Miss Ellen Margaret Campbell, daughter of Archibald and

Ann (Carr) Campbell. Her parents came from Newry, County Down, Ireland, when Mrs. Holton was a child. Mr. and Mrs. Holton were married in the old Bethany Church in West Virginia, November 18, 1862, the ceremony being performed by Alexander Campbell, president of Bethany College. Rev. and Mrs. Holton enjoyed a married life of nearly sixty years. She passed away April 8, 1922. Rev. Mr. Holton is the father of six children: Helen King, born at Falmouth, Kentucky, now Mrs. Lucas, and living with her father in Bloomington; Campbell, born at Vincennes, Indiana, president of the Campbell Holton Company, wholesale grocers at Bloomington; Pauline, born at Springfield, Illinois, widow of D. G. Evans and a resident of Rocky Ford, Colorado; Mary, who was born at Berlin, Illinois, the widow of R. B. Rush and lives at Tallula, Illinois; Annie, also born at Berlin, the wife of Frank McConnell, living near Lincoln, Illinois; and Bettie, who was born at Lincoln and died in 1905, wife of W. H. Armstrong, of Mechanicsburg, Illinois.

CAMPBELL HOLTON is president of the Campbell Holton Company, wholesale grocers at Bloomington. Mr. Holton has had over forty-five years of consecutive mercantile experience, and has developed one of the organizations which contribute to the prestige of Bloomington as a wholesale center.

He is a son of Rev. Tilghman Holton, whose career is sketched preceding this. He was born at Vincennes, Indiana, August 11, 1866, was educated in public schools, graduating from the high school at Lincoln, Illinois, in 1882. Then, at the age of sixteen, he went to work in the grocery store of C. E. Ross at Lincoln. After six years he formed a partnership with Mr. Reynolds in the firm of Holton & Reynolds, and in 1895 removed to Bloomington. Mr. Holton for a number of years was associated with the J. F. Humphreys Company. In 1907 he established the Campbell Holton Company, and that business has enjoyed a prosperous growth for twenty years.

He married Miss Adelaide May Blake, daughter of J. H. and Susan (Ford) Blake, of Clinton, Illinois. They have two children, Campbell Blake Holton and Ellen Margaret. The son is now associated with his father in business. Mr. Holton is a Scottish Rite Mason, being a member of the Consistory at Bloomington and the Shrine at Peoria. He was active in the Red Cross and other war causes during the World war.

JAMES T. CALLAHAN, one of the veteran newspaper men of southern Illinois, is a native of Alton, and has spent most of his life in that city. He is still active in newspaper work, but most of his time is devoted to his duties as clerk of the City Court.

He was born there July 25, 1856, son of Thomas and Mary (Cronin) Callahan, natives of Ireland, where they were married. During the forties they crossed the ocean, accompanied by two children, and at once settled at Alton, Illinois. James T. Callahan was the eighth among ten children and he and a younger brother are the only ones now living.

Reared in Alton, where he attended the public schools, he completed his literary education in St. Joseph College in Effingham County and in Sacred Heart College in Randolph County, Illinois. Mr. Callahan studied law, and has been admitted to the bars of Illinois, Missouri and California.

In 1874, fifty years ago, and when a youth of eighteen, Mr. Callahan acquired his first experience in newspaper business, working on the old Alton Democrat. He has been reporter, editor and special writer for newspapers and magazines with little interruption since then and at the present time is a staff member of the Alton Daily Telegraph, contributing a column of paragraph to that paper under the title of "Stray Scraps." Under this heading he has become one of the noted newspaper paragraphers in the middle west, and several years ago a volume of collected specimens of "Stray Scraps" was published under the title, and is one of the most fun provoking books ever published by a member of the newspaper fraternity.

Soon after Grover Cleveland was elected president of the United States he appointed Mr. Callahan, in 1885, a special agent of the Interior Department for duty in the territories of New Mexico and Arizona, and he spent about three years in the southwestern Country. He then returned to Alton, and subsequently for about a year was on the staff of the Decatur Review and he also worked on a paper in Chicago, and for about six years was affiliated with the publishing interests of Mr. Charles Boeschenstein of Edwardsville.

Mr. Callahan in 1919 was elected clerk of the City Court of Alton, and reelected for a four year term in 1921. In 1908 he was elected a member of the Illinois Legislature, but in a contest he was finally beat out of his seat. He has for many years been active in the interest of the democratic party in southern Illinois.

On June 27, 1893, Mr. Callahan married Miss Margaret McGinnis, of Alton, where she was born, reared and educated. They have three sons and one daughter, James, Jr., William P., Joseph M. and Margaret M. The daughter is now deputy clerk under her father. All three sons were in the World war, William spending two years in the army during that period. The family are members of the Catholic Church and the sons belong to the Knights of Columbus.

ELMAR LOUIS SCHIERHOLZ is a sheet metal, roofing and furnace contractor, learned his business at Kankakee with one of the old firms of that city, and has a growing and prospering business of his own.

He was born in Chicago, in 1896, son of Henry and Bertha (Dierking) Schierholz, his father a native of Hanover, Germany, and his mother of Kankakee. His parents now reside at 397 South Myrtle Street in Kankakee. Elmar Louis Schierholz was educated in public schools up to the age of fifteen. He had one year of experience as a farm worker and then became an employe of Reuter Brothers, sheet metal workers and roofers. He remained with that firm eight years, then for two and a half years was employed in stove works, and at the end of that time returned to Reuter Brothers for another two years. He then bought out a shop and has since been making a prosperous business of his own, handling roofing and sheet metal and furnace installation. His plant is at 1154 East River Street, where he has a new shop building, 30 by 46 feet. His home is at 607 South Elm Street.

Mr. Schierholz married, in April, 1923, Elma Leuth, a native of Kankakee, daughter of George and Anna Leuth, her father a native of Kankakee and her mother of St. Louis, Missouri. Mr. and Mrs. Schierholz have two children, John Howard, born in April, 1924, and Juanita Jean, born in July, 1925. The family are members of the Lutheran Church, and he is an independent republican in politics.

WILLIAM DAVID HIGDON, editor and publisher of the Monticello Bulletin, is a veteran educator and newspaper man.

He was born in Missouri, in 1869, son of John Brantley and Hester Ann Higdon. Ancestors on both sides were soldiers in the Revolution. He is a descendant of the King family of Georgia and the Fishburne family of Virginia. Mr. Higdon was reared in Jasper County, Missouri, attended country schools there, and his higher education was the result of subsequent periods of study in De Pauw University in Indiana, the University of Missouri and the University of Illinois. Mr. Higdon was a farmer for some years, but then entered educational work and gave twenty-three years of his life to teaching. He has been in printing and journalism for eleven years, and has made the Monticello Bulletin the leading newspaper of Piatt County.

Mr. Higdon is independent in politics and is a member of the Methodist Episcopal Church. He married at Decatur, Illinois, December 26, 1900, Miss Lena Biehl, daughter of George Biehl. They have one daughter, Gertrude Brantley Higdon.

FRED WESLEY SARGENT is president of the Chicago and Northwestern Railway and Chicago, St. Paul, Minneapolis and Omaha Railway Companies. He is an executive of broad and practical ability, thorough, determined, alert, versatile and resourceful.

Mr. Sargent was born at Akron, Iowa, May 26, 1876, and is a son of Edgar Wesley and Abbie E. (Haskell) Sargent. His father, a native of Ludlow, Vermont, was born in 1840, and received his education in the public schools of his native state. When eighteen years of age he decided to try his fortunes in the fast-growing west, and accordingly made his way to Marshalltown, Iowa, whence he made his way by horseback to Sioux City, Iowa, that being the only means of transportation available. Sioux City at that time was only a small trading post where a desultory business was carried on with the Indians. For a time Mr. Sargent remained at Sioux City, and then commenced the erection of a line of flour mills, operated by water power, along the Big Sioux River, an enterprise in which he was a pioneer, as he was also, later, in the construction of a line of grain elevators along the same stream. He became the founder of the village of Partland, and later of the city of Akron, and was one of the largest landholders in his section. In 1899 Mr. Sargent retired from business activities and disposed of all his holdings and interests with the exception of his land. His death occurred in 1916, in the faith of the Unitarian Church, Boston, of which he had been a lifelong member. First a whig and later a republican, he took a good citizen's interest in politics, but never cared for public office. Mr. Sargent married, in Iowa, Miss Abbie E. Haskell, who was born in 1848, in New York State, and who died in 1925. In addition to their son Fred Wesley, who was their first-born, they were the parents of three daughters.

Fred Wesley Sargent attended the public schools of Akron, Iowa, and then entered Iowa State University, from which he was graduated with the class of 1901, receiving the degree of Bachelor of Laws. He first took up his residence at Sioux City, where he engaged in the general practice of law, and in the meantime became attorney for the Chicago and Northwestern Railway. In 1906 he was elected city attorney of Sioux City, an office to which he was reelected in 1908. In 1912 he removed to Des Moines, Iowa, and engaged in private law practice and also with the legal department of the Chicago, Rock Island & Pacific Railroad for the state of Iowa. He continued as a resident of Des Moines until 1920, when he was appointed general solicitor for the Chicago and Northwestern Railway, with office at Chicago. This post he held until December, 1923, when he was elected vice president and general counsel of the Chicago & Northwestern and Chicago, St. Paul, Minneapolis & Omaha Railway Companies. On June 23, 1925, he was elected president of both companies. Since coming to Chicago he has allied himself with a number of progressive civic movements and has evidenced a desire to take part in the enterprises that are holding the interest of men of public spirit and enlightened views. He is a member of the Masonic fraternity and of Sioux City Lodge No. 412, B. P. O. Elks, and also holds membership in the Union League Club, and Evanston, Glen View and Old Elm Clubs, Chicago. His political allegiance is given to the republican party.

On January 9, 1902, Mr. Sargent was united in marriage with Miss Mary Minier, who was born in Minnesota, and to this union there have been born two sons and one daughter: Minier, Haskell and Fredericka.

CLYDE JAMES CHAMNESS, M. D. After graduating from the Chicago College of Medicine and Surgery in 1910, Doctor Chamness in the fall of the same year located at Elkville, in Jackson County, and for fifteen years has handled a large volume of general practice with considerable industrial surgery.

He is a member of an old and well known family in Jackson County. His great-grandfather, Joseph Chamness, was of Danish descent, and lived in Virginia, later in Tennessee. His son, James P. Chamness, came with his parents to Illinois from Tennessee when very young, and during his active life time was a farmer in Williamson County. His son, William Harbert Chamness, was born in

Williamson County in 1866, and likewise followed farming as an occupation. William H. Chamness married Cora Kimmel, daughter of Joseph Kimmel and member of another old family of Williamson County.

Their son, Clyde James Chamness, was born December 24, 1887, on the home farm in Williamson County. He attended country schools, spent one term in the State Normal at Carbondale, also attended the Crab Orchard Academy near Marion, and took his pre-medical course in Valparaiso University of Indiana. His service as an interne was rendered in several large Chicago hospitals, and he came to his work in Jackson County with a splendid equipment and has made an enviable reputation as a successful doctor.

On December 14, 1917, he enlisted for service in the World war, being commissioned a first lieutenant, and after training at Fort Riley, Kansas, was commissioned captain on June 1, 1918. He went overseas August 30, 1918, with Hospital Train No. 38, and later was appointed to command that train. He was stationed at Brest until June 10, 1919, and arrived in New York on June 19th and was discharged at Fort Sheridan September 4. He immediately returned to his practice at Elkville. Doctor Chamness is vice president of the State Bank of Elkville.

He married Miss Beulah Lipe, daughter of Elsworth Lipe of Elkville. They have two daughters, Darlie and Glennabelle.

JAMES EDWARD GORMAN was born in Chicago, December 3, 1863. He commenced railroad service in August, 1877, with the C. B. & Q. Railroad, and has been president of the Chicago, Rock Island & Pacific Railway Company since July, 1917.

LOYD M. BRADLEY, judge of the City Court of Carbondale, is a prominent young attorney of that city, has practiced law for ten years, and was with the Aviation Corps during the World war.

The Bradleys came from old Virginia, where one of the family was Governor Bradley. The Illinois branch of the family on coming west were attacked by Indians near the Ohio River and the father of the family at the time, with his youngest child, was killed by arrows. The mother bravely pushed out into the river on a boat and saved herself and other children. She found refuge in a fort, which was besieged by the bloodthirsty savages for the entire night.

The Bradleys on coming to Illinois settled at Sugar Hill near Ava. James Bradley, grandfather of Judge Bradley, became a soldier in the Civil war. He was seriously wounded in one battle, and after partial recovery served in the commissary department. He had a family of seven sons and seven daughters. One of these was Lewis Marion Bradley, who died in 1917 and is well remembered as one of the prominent lawyers of this section of the state. He practiced law at Mound City for a number of years and after 1905 at Carbondale. He married Mary Ellen Williamson, who now resides at Berkeley, California, with her daughter, Lucille Bradley, who is a practicing attorney at Berkeley.

Loyd M. Bradley was born at Mound City, May 3, 1895. He attended public school there, the Normal University at Carbondale, and was graduated from the University of Illinois School of Law in 1917. Returning to Carbondale, he engaged in private practice and was associated with C. E. Hamilton until elected judge of the City Court in 1920. On February 20, 1918, he was ordered to the Massachusetts Institute of Technology at Boston in training with the Naval Air Service, and after completing the course was sent to the flying field at Akron, Ohio, in the Balloon Corps, with the Goodyear Flying School. He received rank as ensign in the navy, and was finally at the Naval Air School at Rockaway, Long Island, where he was honorably discharged February 3, 1919. Judge Bradley married Mary E. Fraley, a daughter of William Henry Fraley.

DELIA CALDWELL, M. D., of Carbondale, is one of the comparatively new women graduates in medicine who prepared for and began a career in that profession prior to the present century. Doctor Caldwell for many years enjoyed an enviable and useful place in general practice, but for several years has used her professional experience and abilities in the Southern Illinois Normal University, where she is instructor in the department of biology.

Doctor Caldwell was born at Hopkinsville, Kentucky, in 1860, and is a member of the historic Caldwell family of America, of Scotch-Irish ancestry. John Caldwell came from Ireland and settled at New Castle, Delaware, in 1727, later moving to Lancaster County, Pennsylvania, and in 1742 settling in Charlotte County, Virginia, where he was joined by other Caldwells, forming what was known as the Caldwell settlement. John Caldwell was the first justice of the peace and his son the first militia officer commissioned by King George, II, for that region. The third son of John Caldwell was David Caldwell, while the seventh son, James, was one of the founders of Princeton College. Martha Caldwell, a granddaughter of John Caldwell, became the mother of John Caldwell Calhoun, the great American statesman from South Carolina. One of the sons of David Caldwell was named for his grandfather, John. This John was a soldier in the Revolution and married Dicey Mann, and among their many descendants one is Dr. Delia Caldwell. Beverly Caldwell, grandfather of Doctor Caldwell, was born in Green County, Kentucky, and that was also the birthplace of Isaac Caldwell, father of the Doctor. Isaac Caldwell was a prosperous lawyer, banker and tobacco dealer until his fortunes were ruined by the Civil war. In 1868 he removed with his family to Carbondale, Illinois, and was well known as a lawyer throughout the southern part of the state. He died in 1901. His wife was Evaline Sharp Stites, representing two of Kentucky's well known families. She was born in Christian County, Kentucky, and died in 1900.

Delia Caldwell was eight years of age when her father moved to Carbondale. She had her first advantages under a tutor hired by her father. She also attended a pay school taught by Clark Brayden at Carbondale and later entered the public schools. She was one of the first students enrolled at the opening of the Normal School and graduated in 1878 with the third graduating class. After graduating Doctor Caldwell taught in Illinois, Missouri and Idaho. She then carried out her ambition of long standing to prepare for the profession of physician. She attended the Northwestern University Medical College for Women, at that time a separate department or institution. She was graduated M. D. in 1896, and had interne experience in New England Hospital for Women and Children, Boston, Massachusetts. Doctor Caldwell's career as a physician is best known in Paducah, Kentucky, where she had a large practice for twenty years. While there she served six years as a member and two years as president of the school board.

About the time America entered the World war, Doctor Caldwell decided to return to her old home in Carbondale, doing so in 1918. For a year and a half she continued the practice of medicine, and then became school physician to the Normal University, also medical inspector and advisor, and instructor in the department of biology.

CHARLES HAROLD LOGAN, SR., a native of Illinois, a country boy, has for many years been an active factor in the business life of the city of Decatur, where he is president of the Decatur Coffin Company.

He was born in the country near Edinburg, Illinois, March 6, 1877, and spent his early childhood and youth in that community. He attended the grade and high schools of Edinburg. When he was about eighteen years of age, in 1895, he became an employee of the Decatur Coffin Company, and has been with that business and industry for thirty-one years. The company was founded in 1873, and is now a business employing sixty men and forty women. The company has a model factory, manufacturing caskets and burial dry goods.

In May, 1900, Mr. Logan married Mabel E. Tomlinson of Springfield, Illinois. They have four sons. The oldest, Charles Harold, Jr., was born at Decatur, May 14, 1902, graduated from the Decatur High School and the University of Illinois, and is now the accountant with the Decatur Coffin Company. The second son, Robert T. Logan, born at Decatur, February 19, 1904, is an employee of the Wabash Railway Company at Decatur. Edward A., born December 22, 1906, is employed in New York City and Frederick W., born October 7, 1910, is a student in the Decatur High School.

Mr. Logan is vice president of the National Casket Manufacturers Association and the Decatur Club, president of the Country Club, a member of the Rotary and City Clubs, and a member of the Association of Commerce. He is a thirty-second degree, Scottish Rite Mason. A sister, Mrs. E. A. Vigal, resides in Edinburg, Illinois.

ROLAND WHEELOCK GRIFFITH is one of the leading younger members of the Granite City bar and represents a pioneer family of Madison County. However, he was born in St. Louis, Missouri, May 1, 1888, son of William Edwin and Mary Elizabeth (Wheelock) Griffith. His father was born near Collinsville in Madison County, Illinois, son of one of the pioneer settlers.

R. W. Griffith is one of a family of three sons and three daughters. Most of his boyhood was spent in Granite City, where he attended grammar and high schools. He graduated A. B. from the University of Illinois, which he attended from 1906 to 1910, and in 1910 entered the law department of Washington University at St. Louis, where he was graduated LL. B. in 1912. He was admitted to the bar October 2, 1912, and in the same year engaged in practice at Granite City. He served as assistant state's attorney of Madison County from 1912 to 1916, and from 1912 to 1914 was master in chancery of the city courts. In 1917 he became city attorney of Granite City, resigning in June, 1918, when he enlisted for service in the World war joining the naval reserves. He was at the Great Lakes Training Station until honorably discharged January 5, 1919. For about a year previous to his war service he was also corporation counsel of Venice.

After the war Mr. Griffith removed to Okmulgee, Oklahoma, and engaged in the practice of law and in the oil business. In 1921 he returned to St. Louis, was engaged in professional work there until 1922, and then resumed his law practice at Granite City. He is serving as corporation counsel of Granite City, and is an active leader in the democratic party. He is a thirty-second degree Scottish Rite Mason and Shriner and a member of the Elks.

He married Miss Florence Caroline McElroy of Arenzville, Cass County, Illinois, in 1921. They have one son, Roland W., Jr.

A. R. BOONE is superintendent of the Community High School of Carbondale. This is one of the numerous high school institutions that in recent years has been organized as community schools and which serves to enhance the splendid reputation Carbondale has long enjoyed as a school center.

The Community High School was organized at Carbondale in 1920. It has an enrollment of over five hundred pupils. The building, completed in 1923, is one of the best structures erected for high school purposes in southern Illinois in recent years. In many respects the high school and the building reflects the energy and idealism of Mr. Boone, who took charge of school work at Carbondale in 1918. Throughout he has had the cooperation of a splendid Board of Education. The president of the school board is John D. Dill, and another valuable member is G. Riley Huffman.

Mr. Boone is a native of Kentucky. He has had a long educational experience, having taught in a rural academy in Fulton County of his native state. For three years he was in charge of a Methodist school and for eight years was superintendent of schools at Charleston, Missouri. Following that for three years he was in charge of the high school at Hickman, Kentucky, and from there came to Carbondale. At Carbondale he is successfully solving the problem of negro education by providing the negro schools with well educated college instructors. Mr. Boone has all the personal qualities of a successful educator, being a man of fine address, education and executive power. He is a member of the Masonic fraternity.

FRED A. MIER, present county clerk of Bond County, grew up in the Pocahontas community of that county, and became well and favorably known to the citizens of this section during his many years of trading and dealing in live stock.

He was born at Pocahontas December 12, 1877, son of Frank and Nettie R. (Gilmore) Mier. His father was born in Germany and was eight years of age when brought to the United States by his mother about 1850. He grew up in the old Swiss and German settlement at Highland, Illinois, and on September 14, 1880, was naturalized as an American citizen. At the age of seventeen he had moved to Bond County, and from that time was engaged in the live stock business. He bought his first hogs from a man named Charles Plant, borrowing the money from Mrs. Whirli to complete the deal. Mrs. Whirli had defended him when others were not inclined to trust him on account of his youth. He showed his remarkable business ability and continued in the live stock business until his death on September 13, 1917. It is reported that he sold the first carload of cattle sold at the National Stock Yards in East St. Louis. His widow is still a resident of Pocahontas. There were two sons, Frank E., who died in 1910, and Fred A.

Fred A. Mier supplemented his early advantages in the public schools of Pocahontas by attending Greenville College, from which he was graduated in 1896. He then became associated with his father in the live stock business in the firm of Mier & Son, and contributed much to the wide spread and successful operations of that firm.

Mr. Mier was appointed county clerk to fill the vacancy occasioned by the resignation of W. H. Koonce on December 12, 1921. On November 4, 1922, he was elected for a regular four year term in the office and in 1926 was renominated by the republicans. In his home community of Pocahontas he served as school director for several years. During the World war he assisted in the work of the registration board.

Mr. Mier is affiliated with Pocahontas Lodge No. 473, Ancient Free and Accepted Masons, belongs to Greenville Lodge No. 3, Independent Order of Odd Fellows, Robert K. Dewey Encampment No. 21, is also a member of the Greenville Chapter of the Eastern Star, the Maccabees, the Chamber of Commerce and attends the Methodist Church.

He married at St. Louis, April 30, 1902, Miss Minnie R. Senn, daughter of Frank and Minnie (Idler) Senn. This is an old family in the vicinity of Pocahontas and her grandfather for many years was in the hotel business there and later a farmer. Mrs. Mier takes an active part in church work. They have one son, Gerald O., a graduate of high school.

DR. WILLIAM E. WALSH, M. D., was born at Ormstown, near Montreal, Canada, in September, 1867, a son of George and Janet (Bryson) Walsh, of Irish and Scotch descent, respectively. His father was a farmer who died when William E. was about eight years old. His mother still resides at Ormstown, Quebec, and was ninety-six years old in 1926 and in good health.

The early training of Doctor Walsh was secured in the Canadian common schools and Huntington Academy. When fourteen years of age he helped to take charge of a general store and sawmill, where he worked for three years. After this he attended McGill University in Montreal, from which he graduated in 1892, when he came to Morris and entered into a general practice, since then becoming one of the leading physicians in Grundy County.

In 1894, Doctor Walsh married Mrs. Edith (Cryder) Wilson. After her death, Doctor Walsh married, June 1, 1898, Emeline Nelson, daughter of John and Mary (Campbell) Nelson, natives of Ohio. They have three children: Marjorie, who graduated from Wellesley College 1922, Anita, from the University of Chicago, 1926, and Edmund. In his church connection the Doctor is a Presbyterian; in politics he is independent; and he belongs to the Knights Templar. In 1913 Doctor Walsh was elected mayor of the city of Morris on the citizen's ticket, with the law and order platform. He is deeply interested in all public movements and is one of the closest scientific students in Morris. He made a careful study of the disease known as "Milk Sick" or White Snake Root Poisoning, and his invaluable discovery of acidosis as the cause of death in this mysterious disease and its treatment and cure has given him national recognition. His most valuable work has been in collecting the remains of the Red Man's culture as found in Grundy County and vicinity. He founded the Grundy County Historical Society in 1923, and donated to it one of the best Indian collections in the state. He is interested in farming and has farm lands in Indiana, which he is trying to make as near one hundred per cent perfect as possible.

CLARENCE E. HOILES, a native of Bond County, where the Hoiles family have resided for eighty-six years, is a lawyer by profession, but his time and energies have been fully absorbed by his extensive banking connections. He is president of the State Bank of Hoiles & Sons, an institution which was founded by his grandfather more than a half a century ago and has continued with unimpaired credit and strengthening resources through all the years.

His grandfather was Charles Hoiles, who was born at Burlington, New Jersey, March 28, 1819, son of Charles Hoiles. Charles Hoiles in 1837, leaving New Jersey, moved to Salem, Ohio, where he learned the tailor's trade. In 1840 he located at Greenville in Bond County, Illinois. For two years he followed the work of his trade and then engaged in merchandising, building up a large and successful business with a trade over a wide surrounding country in those early days. His integrity and sound business judgment were important assets when in 1869 he founded the bank known as Hoiles & Son. Charles Hoiles continued the active head of this private banking institution until 1881.

This bank, for many years known under the style of Hoiles & Son, has continued the business with only a slight change in name, and is now known as the State Bank of Hoiles & Sons, but the name Hoiles, like its capital, has remained an essential part of the institution. Charles Hoiles, the pioneer banker, was one of the strong men of his time and one who helped shape history in southern Illinois. He was a member of the State Assembly on the democratic ticket, and assisted in the vote in the election of his friend Stephen A. Douglas as United States senator.

Charles Hoiles died May 14, 1884. Death came to him suddenly while he was with his wife in the Union Passenger Station at St. Louis. He married, November 24, 1842, Elizabeth Morse, who was born in Lowell, Massachusetts, in 1812, daughter of Stephen and Susan (Parker) Morse, natives of New Hampshire. Stephen Morse died in Massachusetts and his widow, Susan, subsequently moved to Illinois with her sons and daughters, and died at Greenville in 1852. Charles Hoiles and wife had a family of five children, three of whom died in infancy. The two to grow up were Charles Douglas and Stephen Morse Hoiles, both of whom became associated with their father in banking.

Stephen Morse Hoiles was born in Bond County, Illinois, April 18, 1852, and from early manhood until his death in January, 1901, was associated with the banking firm of Hoiles & Sons. He married Wilma C. Stoutzenberg, a native of Madison County, Illinois.

Their son, Clarence Eugene Hoiles, was born at Greenville August 17, 1875, and has lived his entire life in that community. He was graduated from the Greenville High School in May, 1891, and subsequently completed a business course in Greenville College. In 1896 he was admitted to the bar, and practiced law for twenty-three years. After his admission he became a member of the copartnership of Northcott, Fritz & Hoiles. The senior member of this firm was his uncle, Mr. Northcott, who subsequently became lieutenant governor of Illinois, serving in that office from January, 1897, to January, 1905. For several years the law firm was Fritz & Hoiles, and after the death of Mr. Fritz, Mr. Hoiles practiced alone until 1919.

In that year he became president of the State Bank of Hoiles & Sons, which had been founded by his grandfather in 1869. His interests and responsibilities as a banker have greatly increased. Since 1923 he has been principle owner and president of the Bond County State Bank at Pocahontas. He is also a director in the State Bank of Keyesport and is secretary-treasurer of the Bond County Abstract & Title Company of Greenville. In 1922 he organized the Central Illinois Joint Stock Land Bank at Greenville, with capital of $250,000, later increased to $600,000. This bank operated under government charter in Illinois and Indiana until the fall of 1925, growing to a ten million dollar institution. In 1925 it was sold to the St. Louis Joint Stock Land Bank of St. Louis. Mr. Hoiles also owns extensive real estate interests in Illinois, Missouri and Indiana.

During the World war he acted as secretary of the Military Exemption Board and was chairman for the county in two of the Liberty Loan drives. He is a democrat, but has never held any public office, though his business and professional connections have always been vested with more or less of public service. He is a thirty-second degree Scottish Rite Mason, member of the Knights of Pythias and Modern Woodmen of America, belongs to the Greenville Country Club, and the Episcopal Church of Greenville. His favorite recreation is camping and hunting in Canadian wilds.

He married, October 20, 1897, in Bond County, Miss Lena Ethel Moss, daughter of James Howell Moss, who was a pioneer of that county. Mrs. Hoiles is a member of the Greenville Library Board, belongs to the Pierian Club, Presbyterian Church and the Daughters of the American Revolution. They have two children, James Moss, born in 1911, and Clarence Eugene, Jr., born in 1913.

THEODORE C. KELLER began his career as a railroad clerk in Chicago. For many years he has been a prominent figure in coal operations in Indiana and Illinois, being president of the Indiana and Illinois Coal Corporation and interested in a number of other business enterprises. His business offices are in the Old Colony Building on Van Buren Street.

He was born at Boston, Massachusetts, January 7, 1864, son of Christian and Henrietta (Burkhert) Keller. His parents were natives of Germany. He was the youngest of two sons and three daughters. Theodore C. Keller acquired a grammar and high school education, attended the Bryant and Stratton Business College at Chicago and his first work was as office boy with J. B. Brown, president, and Andrew Crawford, vice president of the Chicago & Western Indiana Railway Company. Later he worked in the auditor's office, was a clerk in the treasury department, bookkeeper and car accountant in various departments of the Chicago & Western Indiana Company. He was head bookkeeper for the Great Creek Coal Company, this constituting his first active connection with the coal industry.

Mr. Keller in 1889 was appointed general manager and superintendent of the Great Creek Coal Company. On June 9, 1891, he acquired a quarter interest in the City Coal Yards of the company and later bought the entire business, organizing the T. C. Keller Coal Company and has been president of the company for many years. Later he acquired 640 acres of coal land in Indiana, developed it and as an operator has figured in a number of coal mining districts in Indiana and Illinois. He organized the Northwestern Powder Company at Newport, Indiana, for the manufacture and sale of blasting powder and was president of the company three years, until the business was sold to the Laflon Dupont Powder Company. One of his transactions was the purchase of seventeen hundred acres of land in Sullivan County, Indiana, and the coal op-

erations there were developed under the name of T. C. Keller & Company. This property Mr. Keller sold to the Chicago, Rock Island & Pacific Railway Company, consisting of 3,000 acres of coal land in Franklin County, Illinois, in 1905. This is the Sesser Coal Company and until he sold out in 1918 he was president of the Sesser Coal & Land Company. Mr. Keller was executive and trustee with Mr. Alexander Crawford and daughter in settling the Crawford estate, doing this work without bond. He has been a director of the Graham & Morton Steamship Company. Some years ago he acquired a large block of property at Twenty-third Street, adjoining the Chicago & Western Indiana tracks in Chicago, using it as a site for coal yards, but subsequently sold the land to the Chicago & Western Indiana Railway. He sold the Keller Coal Company's business at Clinton, Indiana, to the Oak Hill Coal Company. He formerly owned a piece of property on West Fifteenth Street, at Canal and Union streets in Chicago, which he sold to the Chicago Terminal Transfer Railway Company. In 1916 he was appointed receiver for the coal lands of the Chicago & Eastern Illinois Railway Company, and after paying all the debts he reorganized the property as the Indiana & Illinois Coal Corporation. Since the reorganization he has been president and treasurer. In 1918 he became a director of the Pittsburg Railway & Coal Company.

Mr. Keller is a successful business man who has been an interested participant in many movements and undertakings for the general welfare of his home city. During 1893-94 he had a contract for filling and raising the grade of the city streets in South Chicago. He is a trustee of Beloit College at Beloit, Wisconsin, is a member of the Westchester Club and the Country Club of New York, the Union League Club of Chicago, the Evanston Country Club and Glenview Golf Club. For many years he was a director of the National City Bank, until it was consolidated with the National Bank of the Republic, of which he is a director. Mr. Keller in politics is a republican.

He married, June 13, 1889, Miss Jessie Price Smith, a native of Chicago. They have five children: Theodore Price, Jessie Ruth, Marion Virginia, Paul Joseph and Jeanette. The son, Theodore Keller, since completing his education at the University of Michigan has been associated with his father in the coal industry.

JOHN J. MOYNIHAN, who claims to be the only pure-blooded Irishman in White Hall, was eighty-three years of age July 12, 1926. Mr. Moynihan resides with his daughter, Miss Mae, in the family homestead on Franklin Street. His whole life has been dependent on his daily toil, and he has wrought a wonderful life. He followed the other members of his father's family from Millstreet, County Cork, Ireland, when a boy, traveling alone, and was located at New York for a short time after his arrival. He then spent three or four years in Massachusetts before coming to White Hall, where he has since resided continuously, a period of more than sixty-three years.

He reared a large family of the most upright men and women, but surviving him are only the daughter at home and two sons, Leo, master mechanic with the Santa Fe Railroad at Newton, Kansas, and Hon. C. J. Moynihan, of Montrose, Colorado. Lawrence, John and William are dead. The latter was a veteran in the Spanish-American war, serving in Company K, Fourth Illinois.

Mr. Moynihan is a beloved old citizen.

JAMES S. BROOKS, a resident of White Hall for sixty-six years, was a native of Tennessee, and resided in Pike County for a time after coming to Illinois. His residence in White Hall dated from 1856 until his death in 1922, at the age of ninety-one years and seven months. His wife died in 1914, she being the daughter of Aaron Reno, who came to White Hall in 1828 and was a long-time merchant, serving as postmaster in 1859. In 1846 Mr. Reno had in his employ as clerk one John G. Nicolay, who afterwards became noted as Lincoln's private secretary during the Civil war and an authentic biographer of the great emancipator.

James S. Brooks was an early stage driver, and in later years conducted a transfer business in White Hall. He was the father of twelve children, nine of whom survive, as follows: F. A. Brooks, J. O. Brooks, White Hall; J. Albert Brooks, Greenview, Illinois; Emma, wife of Dr. J. S. Graves, Inman, Kansas; Mary, wife of C. J. Chapman, Corona, California; Lucy, wife of J. V. Nevius, White Hall; A. D. Brooks, Auburn; A. H. Brooks, St. Louis; Katie, wife of Bert Moore, Hutchinson, Kansas.

SAMUEL W. ANDREWS is a Greenville citizen whose energies and enterprise have been a responsible factor in some of that community's most important undertakings. His friends and associates in commenting on his success emphasized the fact of his persistence in gaining an education as a preparation for life. He spent several years in earning his way through college and the higher schools.

He was born near Greenville, in Bond County, October 11, 1878. The Andrews family still owns land that was taken up as a homestead by his grandfather, John Andrews, in pioneer times. He is a son of Samuel W. and Catherine (Hawley) Andrews, both natives of Illinois. His father, who died in 1921, spent his life as a farmer and for twenty years was a school director and held other local offices. The widowed mother still lives in Greenville, and of her family of nine sons and three daughters Samuel W. was the fourth.

Samuel W. Andrews while a boy on the farm and one of a large family of children had only the advantages of the rural schools. For two years he hired out as a farm worker in Christian County and for a time attended high school at Taylorville. For five years he was a teacher in business colleges, one year in Frederickstown, Missouri, three years in South Dakota, and for one year he worked in a bank in South Dakota and also was employed for sometime in a bank in St. Louis. In 1911 he graduated Bachelor of Science from the Greenville College, Greenville, Illinois. A part of his college work was done at the University of Illinois. Two years before completing his course at Greenville College he took the position of bookkeeper during vacations for the Model Glove Company. Then, in 1911, he bought an interest in this local enterprise and subsequently reorganized and became its president. He still carries on that successful Greenville industry. He is also president of Andrews Brothers Company, hardware and implements, at Greenville, and is president of the Hygienic Ice Company of that city. His holdings and interests have increased rapidly since he started on the basis of a thorough education. He is owner of some 700 acres of farm land in south central Illinois.

Mr. Andrews is now secretary and a member of the Board of Trustees of Greenville College and takes a deep interest in educational affairs. For eight years he was a member of the City Council and in 1918 was elected mayor of Greenville. During the great war he was a Four Minute Speaker and active in the Liberty Loan and Red Cross campaigns. He is a past president of the Chamber of Commerce, member of the Greenville Country Club, is a republican, and on the Official Board of the Free Methodist Church. His favorite sports are hunting and other forms of outdoor life.

He married at Greenville in September, 1903, Miss Ola Bost, daughter of Joshua and Margaret Bost. Their children are Dorothea, Kathryn, Isabel, Joyce Kilmer and Dorris Christine.

JONATHAN YOUNG SCAMMON. Some historians declare that Chicago was destined to become one of the leading cities of the country because of its geographical positions, but the more astute recognize the fact that it has been dveloped from a frontier settlement surrounding little Fort Dearborn to the second city in the country because of that fact that it was particularly fortunate in its pioneers. The men who came to the mouth of the little stream emptying into Lake Michigan were of such forceful character, possessed so broad a vision and thorough appreciation of the natural resources and possibilities of this locality that expansion was but the logical outcome of their continued residence in the village they created. Many of the names now famous because of their connection with the early history of the city and county are borne today by worthy descendants, or their blood still flows in the veins of others who trace proudly back to them on the maternal side. One of these notable pioneers was the late Jonathan Young Scammon, still represented in the city of his pride by his daughter's son, Clark Scammon Reed, one of the eminent attorneys practicing at the Chicago bar.

The year 1835 was a very important one for Chicago, as it saw the settlement here of men of the caliber of Jonathan Young Scammon, who was born at Whitfield, Lincoln County, Maine, July 27, 1812, a son of Eliakim and Johnna (Young) Scammon, the latter a daughter of David Young, a soldier of the American Revolution, and a member of the ill-fated expedition against Quebec. Subsequently he became a very prominent man and represented Pittston in the General Court of Massachusetts before Massachusetts and Maine were separated. Eliakim Scammon was one of the pioneers of Kennebac County, Maine, which lies just west of Lincoln, and as he grew older the confidence he inspired in his fellow citizens resulted in his election to the Lower and later the Upper House of the State Assembly.

Trifles so often determine careers, and in the case of Jonathan Young Scammon this was certainly the case. Reared on his father's farm, he was planning an agricultural life when an accident, while he was still a youth, deprived him of two fingers of his left hand, and thus rendered him unfit for efficient work on a farm. Realizing that their manly, intelligent son deserved the best life could give him, his parents decided that Jonathan should receive a better education than fell to the lot of the average farmer's son of those days. He was therefore sent to the Maine Wesleyan Seminary at Readfield, and later the Lincoln Academy at New Castle, both in Maine. In the autumn of 1830, when eighteen years of age, he entered Waterville College, now Colby University, and while he only remained there a year, he gained an augmented love of knowledge which enabled him to pursue by himself his studies to such an extent that he came to be recognized as an exceptionally well-educated man, and in 1862 the old University of Chicago conferred on him the degree of Doctor of Laws, and this same honor was accorded him by Waterville College in 1869.

Having decided to enter the legal profession, Mr. Scammon, about 1832, entered the office of Hon. John Otis, of Hallowell, a small village of Kennebec County, and after close study, alternated with school teaching in order to secure his living expenses, he was admitted to the bar in 1835. The ambitious young man had no intention to be limited by the narrow confines of a country village in the conservative East. His eager eyes turned to the West, but it was of some of the flourishing cities along the Mississippi River that he thought when he started out on his long journey. This was made by way of the Erie Canal from Albany to Buffalo; thence he traveled round the Great Lakes to Chicago on the steamboat Pennsylvania, and the voyage was so tempestuous that when he reached Chicago he was glad to seek a haven until the storms had abated. Thus it was that he secured temporary accommodations in the log cabin of Mark Beaubeen, corner of Market and Lake streets, intending to further pursue his travels in a few days.

Fortunately for Chicago the embryo attorney made the acquaintance of Alonzo H. Moore, deputy clerk of the Cook County Circuit Court, and through him of Colonel Hamilton, judge of the Probate Court, clerk of the county commissioners, school commissioner, recorder of deeds, notary public, bank commissioner and county treasurer. Colonel Hamilton and Mr. Moore recognized the ability of the young New Englander, and induced him to become the former's deputy in the Circuit Court. This Mr. Scammon consented to do, and for the succeeding fifty-five years Chicago continued his home. In December, 1835, Mr. Scammon took the state examinations and was admitted to the bar, and began his legal practice in the office of the clerk.

Mr. Scammon arrived at Chicago when the future metropolis had a population of 1,500, but before the close of the year 1835 so large had been the influx this had been increased to 3,265. Having won the confidence of Colonel Hamilton and others in the rapidly growing village, Mr. Scammon soon found himself a very busy man, his occupations covering many lines outside of his professional claims and his political duties. By the end of 1836 his practice had so increased that he formed a partnership with Morris S. Buckner, under the firm name of Buckner & Scammon, but it was terminated by the former's election to the office of mayor to succeed William B. Ogden.

It was during this first partnership in 1837, that Mr. Scammon was made attorney for the Chicago State Bank, and his experience in this connection drew his attention to the abuses which existed in the conduct of banks, for this was during a deplorable period in Illinois finances, and led him to a study of banking that determined his future. It is believed that he did more than almost any other man to secure better banking laws for Illinois. After he had secured some improvement, in 1851, he established the Marine Bank, the first under the new law, and was its president. Under his wise direction this institution became the head of the moneyed institutions of the entire Northwest. Subsequently, owing to his absence, and the dishonesty of others, the bank's assets were diminished, and with the opening of the war their value was destroyed, and the bank suspended. Mr. Scammon, however, extricated it from its difficulties and reestablished its former prosperity.

A private bank he had established in 1861 became, under the national banking law, the Mechanics National Bank, and he also served it as president. In spite of all he had secured in behalf of sound currency, state bank bills continued to be used. Chicago was flooded with a depreciated currency. In 1864 Mr. Scammon, with others of the Chicago Board of Trade, took the matter up, and at the April meeting the following resolution, offered by Mr. Scammon was adopted:

"Resolved, That each member of the Board of Trade pledge himself to make no business transactions except on the basis of legal tender treasury notes or their equivalent, and that he will keep no account with any banker, broker or banking house except in legal tender treasury notes or their equivalent, and that he will not pay out nor circulate at par any money or bank notes which are not equivalent to legal tender treasury notes." With the going into effect of this resolution, May 16, 1864, the City of Chicago, for the first time in its history, conducted its business on the basis of a national currency.

Prior to his entry into banking Mr. Scammon had become interested in business enterprises. He revived a charter that had been granted, some years before, to the Chicago Marine and Fire Insurance Company, and developed it into a very successful concern. Chicago's first railroad, the Galena and Chicago Union Railroad, owed much of its prosperity to him, for in 1846-7 he joined with William B. Ogden and other Chicago men in buying the land, improvements and charter of the old company chartered in 1836 so as to form a new corporation. It was through the financial strength of Mr. Scammon that sufficient funds for the extension of the work were raised, and he continued with the directorate until 1850. He and Mr. Ogden were instrumental in bringing the Michigan Central Railroad into Chicago in 1852, and he never lost his interest in increasing the transportation facilities of the city.

It was Mr. Scammon who made possible the creation of its public school system. He wrote the ordinances on the public schools, secured their passage by the city council, and served as a member and secretary of the school board which they created for many years. From 1845 to 1848 he was president of the board. In appreciation of his services one of the schools of the city bears his name.

While acting as reporter for the Supreme Court of the state, from 1839 on, he published four volumes of reports which bear his name and are still recognized as models of perspicuity and brevity, and are admitted to be the first books published in Chicago.

The firm of Buckner and Scammon being dissolved in 1838, Mr. Scammon took as his second partner Norman B. Judd, under the name of Scammon & Judd, and this association continued until 1847. In 1849 the firm of Scammon & McCagg came into existence, the junior member being E. B. McCagg, and these partners were joined several years later by Samuel Fuller, the firm then becoming Scammon, McCagg & Fuller, but in 1872 Mr. Scammon retired from it, and thereafter gave his attention to his private affairs.

During his early life Mr. Scammon was an ardent admirer of Henry Clay, and consequently a whig in his political views. When Henry Clay entered the race for the presidency in 1844 Mr. Scammon, with others, bought the Express and founded the Chicago Evening Journal and conducted as a strong whig organ supporting Clay. With the latter's defeat the stockholders sold their interests to Richard L. Wilson, who, with others, placed the paper on a solid basis that stands today. In 1865 he again entered the newspaper field, and, with others, founded the Chicago Republican, whose career was terminated by the great fire of 1871. The only asset of this journal remaining after the fire was its Associated Press franchise. This Mr. Scammon bought, and he continued issuing the paper for a short time, and then, March 25, 1872, he issued the first number of the Inter Ocean. The disastrous panics of 1873 and 1874, however, compelled him to sell it in 1875.

Mr. Scammon consented to become a nominee for the office of alderman in order that he might carry out his public school plans, and was elected by a gratifyingly large majority in 1840. At that time there was but one decent schoolhouse in the city, corner of Madison and Dearborn streets, known as the Dearborn School. As soon as he took his place in the council Mr. Scammon was made chairman of the committee on schools, and soon secured the erection of a brick schoolhouse on the

North Side, and a little later one on West Madison Street, east of Halstead.

In so brief an article as this it is impossible to do full justice to as ideally a good citizen as Mr. Scammon, only the leading enterprises with which he was connected can be touched upon. In 1847 he, with others, issued a call for the Great River and Harbor Convention which met on the Fourth of July of that year, at which 10,000 delegates represented eighteen states. He was one of the organizers of the Old Settlers Society, in 1855, and he was its first treasurer. In 1856 he was one of the organizers of the Chicago Historical Society, and served it first as vice president and later as president. One of the leaders of the movement which resulted in the incorporation of the Chicago Academy of Sciences, in the early '60s, he served it as its president until 1883. One of the first to introduce homeopathy in Chicago, in 1859, he was instrumental in organizing the Hahnemann Medical College, donated the land on which Hahnemann Hospital was built, and for many years served as a trustee of both the hospital and college. In 1861 the Old Ladies' Home was begun, and four years later he was one of the men who incorporated it. Always a friend of the University of Chicago, he was early made a regent of the first institution, and also served it as a trustee, and from 1862 to 1879, was its vice president. His son Charles was one of its first graduates. In 1862-3 he, with others, organized the Chicago Astronomical Society, and furnished the $30,000 required for the construction of an observatory on the campus of the University of Chicago. It was known as Dearborn Observatory, so named in honor of Mrs. Scammon. Mr. Scammon served this society as president until 1882. When the university closed its doors he managed to save the great telescope to the society, and it is now in use at the observatory of Northwestern University. In 1872 Mr. Scammon was one of a committee of citizens who prepared a bill for the creation of the Chicago Public Library. He was one of the early members of the Union League Club that was organized in 1879. When the Sons of Maine was organized, in 1880, he was made vice president and a member of the Board of Directors of that body. When he was in his seventy-third year, in 1885, he delivered the speech of welcome at the Grand Pacific Hotel to the New York delegation who carried to the National Republican Convention the name of President Chester A. Arthur for renomination. In commemoration of the interest he had always shown to the old University of Chicago Mr. Scammon's daughter created the Scammon Scholarship to be used for the benefit of a Chicago pupil, at the present University of Chicago. Mrs. Scammon as a lasting memorial to the university of her celebrated husband conveyed, in 1901, to the university the site of the School of Education, and this property is known as Scammon Court. At the time of the conveyance this property was valued at $61,050. As he was, perhaps, the most liberal supporter of the old university, it is but just and very appropriate that his name should be perpetuated in association with its successor.

In 1837 Mr. Scammon married Miss Mary Ann H. Dearborn, of Bath, Maine, and the two, after establishing themselves at Chicago, were instrumental in organizing a church of the Swedenborgian faith, to which he continued loyal the remainder of his life. For ten years he was vice president of the New Jerusalem Church of the United States. Mr. and Mrs. Scammon had three children: Charles Trufant, Florence and Ariana, the elder of the daughters being the mother of Clark Scammon Reed, following this. While the family were abroad for the purpose of giving their children every advantage Mrs. Scammon died, in 1858, and was buried in Germany. On December 5, 1867, Mr. Scammon married Mrs. Maria Sheldon Wright, who survived him.

CLARK SCAMMON REED. Numbered among the able and resourceful attorneys practicing at the Chicago bar is Clark Scammon Reed. He was born on Ladies Island, near Beaufort, South Carolina, February 14, 1878, a son of Joseph Sampson and Florence Ann Dearborn (Scammon) Reed. Joseph Sampson Reed was born at Boston, Massachusetts, December 13, 1841, and passed away in January, 1898; his wife was born at Chicago, November 12, 1844, and still survives and makes her home at Chicago. Of the two sons and three daughters born to this couple four survive, and Mr. Reed was the youngest.

Joseph Sampson Reed was graduated from Harvard University with the class of 1860, and as a young man went to Ladies Island, South Carolina, where he bought a plantation and engaged in raising cotton. Later he came to Chicago, and was in the employ of the Marine Bank, which was organized by Jonathan Young Scammon. At that time this bank led among the monied institutions of the entire northwest. After some time at Chicago he returned to his plantation, and continued his cotton operations until his retirement. His last years were spent at Beaufort, Beaufort County, South Carolina, where his death occurred. For several terms he was treasurer of Beaufort County, and he was always active in the democratic party. He was a Swedenborgian in religious belief.

Clark Scammon Reed attended the public schools of Columbia, South Carolina, and during 1894 and 1895 was a student of South Carolina College. Matriculating at the University of Chicago, he was graduated therefrom in 1900, with the degree of Bachelor of Philosophy. His legal studies were taken in the law department of Northwestern University, and he was graduated from that institution in 1902, with the degree of Bachelor of Laws. Admitted to the bar, he for a short time was associated with Holt, Wheeler & Sidley and then entered upon an independent practice, and immediately received the recognition to which his talents entitled him. Between 1910 and 1912 he served as assistant attorney of the Sanitary District. At present he is a member of the Board of Managers of the Chicago Law Institute, having been its president 1925-1926, is a member of Chi Psi fraternity, the Chicago Bar Association, the Illinois Bar Association, the American Bar Association, life member of the Chicago Art

Margaret Imhoff

Institute, the Hamilton Club, the University Club, the Skokee Golf Club, and the Chicago Literary Club. He belongs to the Masonic fraternity. In addition to maintaining his residence at Glencoe, Illinois, Mr. Reed has a summer home, Arvilla Cottage, on the Kalamazoo River in Michigan. His offices are in the Union Trust Building on South Dearborn Street, Chicago. Like his grandfather, he believes in the principles enunciated by the republican party, and gives them his support. The Church of Christ, Scientist, holds his membership.

On June 21, 1905, Mr. Reed married Miss Mabel Arvilla Lewis, who was born at Chicago, a daughter of Charles W. and Mary (Calahan) Lewis, both of whom were born at Cleveland, Ohio. Mr. Lewis is still living, but his wife passed away in 1923. Mrs. Reed is the youngest of the four children born to her parents. Mr. and Mrs. Reed have had two children: Charles, who passed away in infancy; and Clark Lewis.

During the late war Mr. Reed was assistant director of the Investigating Department of the United States Food Administration of Illinois, and was otherwise active in local war work. Through his paternal great-grandfather, Rev. John Reed, first chaplain of the Colonial navy, and his maternal great-grandfather, David Young, Mr. Reed is a member of the Chicago Chapter, Sons of the American Revolution, and is proud of the fact that he is descended from one of the men who developed this city along so many and varied lines that it is almost impossible to mention an advancement of any kind during the period between 1835 and 1875 with which his maternal grandfather, Jonathan Young Scammon, was not connected as organizer, or potent adherent. It was Mr. Scammon who established the public school system; organized the first state bank, and the first national bank of the city; with William B. Ogden brought the first railroad to Chicago, and a little later the Michigan Central Railroad; placed the finances of the city and state upon a stable basis; assisted in establishing the old Chicago University, to which he was a most liberal contributor, his donations including a $30,000 telescope, which is now in the possession of the Dearborn Observatory at Northwestern University, and in founding the Old Settlers Association, the Chicago Public Library, and many other similar organizations. He was instrumental in founding the Chicago Evening Journal, the Chicago Republican and the Chicago Inter Ocean. Many sound business projects were inaugurated by him and carried on very successfully. For several years he was a member of the City Council, and he was one of the organizers of the republican party, after a long adherence to the principles of Henry Clay and the whig party. The Swedenborgian faith had in him a zealous supporter, and he and his first wife, the grandmother of Mr. Reed, together with one other person, were the charter members of the first church of that belief in Chicago. During the greater portion of the fifty-five years he was a resident of Chicago, Mr. Scammon was actively engaged in the practice of law, and was associated in it with some of the leading legalists of the state. Did his reputation rest alone upon his capabilities as a lawyer he would still be numbered among the most prominent men of his day and city.

MARY MARGARET IMHOFF. An educator well known and deservedly so in Jackson County and other sections of southern Illinois is Mary Margaret Imhoff, at present assistant county superintendent of schools of Jackson County. Her work and career as a teacher and educator has brought her a wonderful degree of esteem in this section of the state.

Her father, John M. Schroeder, was long a highly esteemed citizen of Jackson County. He was born in Prussia, February 2, 1833, son of John Henry and Elizabeth Schroeder. Elizabeth Schroeder died in the old country in 1841. In 1844 the remaining members of the family immigrated to America, making the voyage on a sailing vessel, which was forty days on the sea before they landed at New Orleans. Coming up the Mississippi River, they stopped for a time at St. Louis, and from that city John Henry Schroeder prospected for land, eventually buying a tract of public land near Belleville, in St. Clair County, Illinois. He had hardly begun the task of clearing and developing a home there when death overtook him in 1845.

John Martin Schroeder was only twelve years of age when his father died, and after that was thrown more or less on his own resources. With all the necessity of work he found means to satisfy some of the thirst for an education. It was a remarkable contrast between the schoolhouse built of logs, with slab and plank benches, heated by a smoky fireplace, which he attended, and the splendid brick and stone school houses in Jackson County where his daughter has taught. John Schroeder, in 1853, left Illinois and went out to California by way of New Orleans, and spent three years seeking his fortune there. Returning to Belleville, he remained a resident of that city until 1887, and then moved to Somerset Township, Jackson County. In 1891 he bought the farm which remained his home until his death in 1914.

John Martin Schroeder married Amanda Levina Wilderman, daughter of Joseph Henry Wilderman. He was a soldier with a Pennsylvania regiment in the Revolutionary war, and was a pioneer of Illinois. He donated the land for the first school in his neighborhood.

Mary Margaret Schroeder received her early advantages in the schools of Belleville. Later she completed a course in the State Normal School at Carbondale. In attending the normal school she had to depend upon her own earnings, and after one year of teaching she had sufficient to maintain herself at Carbondale the following year. Altogether she remained there as a student three years. In 1889 she first became connected with the schools of Murphysboro, in which she taught for six years. Then followed seven years of teaching at Belleville, another four years at Murphysboro, and from 1911 to 1913 she taught in the city schools of Carbondale. Since 1913 her work has been at Murphysboro. After ten years in the city schools she became assistant county superintendent in 1923. She takes an active part in public affairs, has been president of the Murphysboro Woman's Club, a club affiliated with the State Federation of Women's Clubs, the League of Women Voters and during the World war was in charge of the sale of savings stamps. She is a member of the First Methodist Episcopal Church. She has always been very active in her church work, taking part with all the organizations and especially the missionary work, being a descendant from the late Bishop Homer D. Stuntz. Mrs. Imhoff has recently completed her lineage record, making her eligible for membership in the Daughters of the Revolution.

McKENDREE COLLEGE, at Lebanon, claims to be the oldest Methodist college west of the Alleghany Mountains. In a little log church that stood on the present college campus Rev. William, afterwards Bishop, McKendree addressed the Ogle class of nineteen members in 1807. Rev. Peter Cartwright, attending the Methodist Conference at Mount Carmel in September, 1827, presented a memorial from Greene County, asking the conference to take steps to establish a conference seminary. In February, 1828, the people of Lebanon, then a town of two hundred, drew up articles of association "for the erection of an edifice for a seminary of learning." The school was opened in the fall of 1828, one year after the opening of the famous Rock Springs Seminary by Rev. John M. Peck. The first year, the school was housed in two buildings belonging to the public and used for subscription schools. Mr. E. R. Ames, afterwards bishop in the Methodist Episcopal Church, was the first principal. His assistant was a Miss McMurphy. The college building was completed by the fall of 1829. It burned in 1856. In 1830 the Methodist Conference accepted the offer of the Board of Trustees and the school was taken under the fostering care of the Methodist Church. At this time it was known as the Lebanon Seminary. About 1831 Bishop McKendree made a gift to the school of 480 acres of land. In 1835 the Illinois Legislature created four college corporations, one being "The Trustees of the McKendreean College," but in 1839, through the co-operation of Abraham Lincoln, then a member of the General Assembly, the name was changed to McKendree College.

McKendree College has lived long and has had an honorable career. In its earlier years it was obliged to accept the student whose preparation was necessarily of a very limited character. In more recent years all lines of work not purely collegiate have been eliminated, making it a standard classical and scientific college. The first president under the charter was Peter Acers. The first class was graduated in 1841, seven in all, and all classical students. In 1848 a paper was started known as the Illinois Advocate and Lebanon Journal. It was a religious paper and was eventually moved to St. Louis and called the Central Christian Advocate. Its editor while it was in Lebanon was Dr. Erastus Wentworth.

For a number of years the school has been greatly benefited by the interest taken in it by former Governor Charles S. Deneen, who has been a member of the Board of Trustees. Governor Deneen's father was a teacher in the school for many years and the governor himself was a student there.

The president of McKendree College since 1923 has been Dr. Cameron Harmon. His uncle, John Francis Harmon, was president of the college from 1908 to 1915, going from there to the presidency of Kansas Wesleyan University, and subsequently into the efficiency work for the Methodist Conference. His home is now at Louisville, Illinois.

The grandfather of Dr. Cameron Harmon was John Harmon, a native of Indiana, who married Charity Bullard, a native of Ohio. The Harmons came to the United States in 1735, and there were sixty-one Harmons in the War of the Revolution.

William A. Harmon, father of Dr. Cameron Harmon, has for many years been a prominent citizen of Clay County, Illinois; a farmer and banker, serving four years as county treasurer, and organized and was president of the Clay County State Bank. William A. Harmon married Sarah C. McKnight, who died November 29, 1920. Her parents were Cameron and Sarah (Field) McKnight. William A. Harmon was the father of a large family of children: Vestilla J., who is the mother of six children by her marriage to John B. Carmichael; Belle, wife of John W. Wattles and mother of thirteen children; Charity, who married Ezra Gould and has six children; Cameron; Ruth, who married Charles Gibson and has three children; Lydia, who married George Smith, and is the mother of three children; Alfred Roscoe, father of two children by his marriage to May Foster; Grover C., who married Lola Wood and has six children; Nell, who married Fred Vapp and has three children; William A., Jr., deceased; Mollie, deceased; John F., who married Esther Kettlekamp.

Cameron Harmon was born at Louisville, Illinois, April 7, 1876, and during his youth had the wholesome environment of a farm in Clay County. He attended district schools, did his preparatory work at Lebanon in McKendree College, and took the classical course in the college, graduating with the A. B. degree in 1903. In 1916 Lebanon conferred upon him the Doctor of Divinity degree. He was ordained to the Methodist ministry in 1900 and was pastor of the Washington Street Church in Alton from 1900 to 1902; the First Church at Granite City, Illinois, in 1902-03; was pastor at Grayville from 1903 to 1906; at McLeansboro from 1906 to 1910; at Murphysboro from 1910 to 1914, and at East St. Louis in the First Methodist Church of that city from 1914 to 1917. In 1917 Doctor Harmon accepted a call to the presidency of Missouri Wesleyan College at Cameron, Missouri, and was with that institution during a period of much growth and development, and during the extraordinary circumstances of the World war. He left there in 1923 to become president of McKendree College.

Dr. Cameron Harmon enlisted as a private in Company L of the Fourth Illinois Volunteer Infantry in May, 1898, during the Spanish-American war, and was appointed wagon-master of his regiment in March, 1899. He was honorably discharged after eighteen months of service. Doctor Harmon is a forceful speaker, and has delivered many addresses, on patriotic, educational and fraternal occasions; was a delegate from the Third Congressional District of Missouri to the Democratic National Convention at San Francisco in 1920. He was elected leader of the Ministerial Delegation of the Southern Illinois Methodist Episcopal Conference to the General Conference at Springfield, Massachusetts, in May, 1924. Doctor Harmon is affiliated with the Masons, the Independent Order of Odd Fellows and the Knights of Pythias.

In December, 1903, he married Miss Nina May Large, daughter of James and Mary (Lingerfelter) Large. She died in October, 1908, the mother of two children, Dorothy and Nina May. On October 18, 1910, Doctor Harmon married Miss Ruby Wilson, of McLeansboro, Illinois, daughter of Judge A. M. and Sallie J. (Morgan) Wilson. The father died in 1916. Doctor and Mrs. Harmon have one child, Marion.

EDWIN PERCY BAKER, dean of McKendree College at Lebanon, is a veteran and greatly beloved teacher who has been with that institution as a member of the faculty and in administrative responsibilities for thirty years.

He was born at Mechanicsville, Ohio, October 23, 1868, son of Edwin S. and Marie Ann (Norton) Baker. His grandfather, Frederick Augustine Baker, was a native of Vermont, and as a young man moved to Ohio, marrying Julia Hagley, a native of Pennsylvania and of German ancestry. The maternal grandfather, Andrew Norton, was born in Belfast, Ireland, and when about twenty-five years of age came to this country with his wife, whose maiden name was Mary Anne Wilson, a native of Manchester, England. Edwin S. Baker, father of Edwin P., was a minister of the Methodist Church with the East Ohio Conference, serving twenty-seven years in various pastorates, and was active in the ministry until about two years before his death, which occurred in 1904.

Edwin Percy Baker attended public schools in various communities of Ohio, and took his preparatory work in a splendid old institution of the Western Reserve, the Grand River Institute at Austenburg, Ohio, where he spent two years. For three years he attended Northeastern Ohio Normal College at Canfield, and subsequently entered Ohio Wesleyan University at Delaware, where he graduated with his A. B. degree in 1893. After graduating he came to McKendree College as professor of Latin and German. The summer of 1896 he spent in Amherst College in the school of languages, and in 1897 was abroad in study and travel in Berlin and other European centers. After his return from abroad he held the chair of German in McKendree College. In 1917 he was made acting president of the college, serving three years, until Rev. George E. McCameron became president. With the resignation of Doctor McCameron Mr. Baker was again called to the president's chair, serving until Cameron Harmon was elected president in 1923. Since 1919 Mr. Baker has been dean of the college.

He married at Canfield, Ohio, December 29, 1897, Miss Mary Spaeth King, daughter of Martin Van Buren King, who was a Union soldier in the Civil war, and was wounded at the battle of Chickamauga, being left on the field for dead. After two days he was picked up and did not fully recover from the wound through the lung for a number of years. He was a druggist at Canfield. Mr. and Mrs. Baker have one son, Lee Robert. He is a member of the Official Board of the Methodist Episcopal Church, has been a member of the City Council at Lebanon, is a republican, and has identified himself with many of the community affairs of the town.

RANSOM S. MARTIN, of Eldorado, had good natural endowments of ancestry and inheritance, but he was reared in a country community, a poor boy, and his very successful career has represented an achievement of personal character and industry that is very unusual.

He was born on a farm in Rector Township, Saline County, December 14. 1874, son of George W. and Eliza (Baldwin) Martin, his mother a native of Saline County. His father was born on a farm not far from Nashville, Tennessee, and was brought as a child by his parents to Illinois. At the time of his marriage he located on a farm and spent his life there. He and his wife reared five of their six children, three of whom are still living.

The Martin family for some years lived in a log cabin home, and they lived on a plane of utmost simplicity, the children having no advantages outside of the rural schools. The parents were active members of the Primitive Baptist Church. After the children had grown up and left home the parents removed to Eldorado, where for several years George W. Martin engaged in the harness business. He died in 1920 and his wife, in 1914.

Ransom S. Martin shared in the work of the farm almost from his earliest recollection. When he went to school he wore patched clothing, often went barefooted, and on several occasions his mother wrapped his feet in rags to protect them from the snow. He ate his lunch of corn bread and molasses alone, so that his schoolmates would not know the simple quality of his fare. However, he was one of the best of the students and made such good use of his opportunities that before he was eighteen years of age he had qualified for a teacher's license, and the county superintendent of schools, knowing his earnestness and capability, stretched the law slightly to give him his license before the time required by the law. In the fall of 1892 he began teaching his first term of country school. He taught school, also attended school, being a pupil in the Normal at Carbondale, Illinois, and in the college at Merom, Indiana. For three years he was principal of the high school at Eldorado, for one year was superintendent of schools at Galatia, Illinois, was superintendent at Eldorado two years, and for several summers he was employed in teaching select or normal schools. He had become one of the well known educators in this section of Illinois and had been identified with school work thirteen years when impaired health caused him to give up the vocation of educator. For four years Mr. Martin was in the vehicle and implement business at Eldorado, but since 1905 has been an undertaker and has the only establishment of its kind in Eldorado. He prepared for the work of funeral director at Cincinnati under Prof. W. H. Clark, founder of the science of embalming. His ability as a teacher was recognized by Professor Clark, who made him instructor while he was a student of embalming. Mr. Martin has a complete establishment, with all the equipment and facilities for his work. Altogether he has prospered remarkably in his business career, owns one of the finest homes in the town and other real estate, besides several tracts of good farming land. He is a director of the First National Bank of Eldorado.

Mr. Martin has allied himself with all movements for the advancement and improvement of his home locality. He is a member of the Merchants Association, in 1926 was president of the Rotary Club, is a thirty-second degree Scottish Rite Mason and Shriner, member of the Knights of Pythias, Independent Order of Odd Fellows and B. P. O. Elks. He and his family are active workers of the Christian Church, and he has served as city clerk of Eldorado, and has been clerk of the Board of Trustees since the organization of the Eldorado Township High School. He is a republican in politics.

Mr. Martin married, in 1899, Miss Elizabeth Westbrook, a native of Saline County, where her people were among the respected pioneer families. The children of Mr. and Mrs. Martin are: Nina A., wife of Earl L. Pillers, manager of the New Mexico Utilities Company at Clovis, New Mexico; Cecil L., who graduated from the University of Illinois and is now a student of medicine in the University of Chicago; Margaret E., a student in Hardin College at Mexico, Missouri; and George R., attending the Eldorado Township High School, from which the three older children are all graduates.

OSRO SHIRK. Under modern conditions and organization the office of sheriff of an important community like Massac County is one of the most important in the service, and its management requires abilities of an executive nature, good diplomatic powers, the bravery of a soldier and the judgment of an able general. All of these traits are possessed in an eminent degree by Osro Shirk, who is serving his second term as sheriff of Massac County and has established an excellent record in the discharge of his duties.

Sheriff Shirk was born at Joppa, Massac County, Illinois, in 1881, and is a son of Joseph J. and Sarah Alice (Carsons) Shirk, the former a native of Metropolis, this state, and the latter of Joppa, and a grandson of James Shirk, a native of Pennsylvania, and of Andrew Carsons. In his younger days Joseph J. Shirk was engaged in blacksmithing, but subsequently turned his attention to agricultural pursuits, and at this time is living in comfortable retirement at Belknap, Illinois. Mrs. Shirk died in 1905.

Osro Shirk attended the common schools until he reached the age of eighteen years, following which he associated himself with his father in his farming activities and continued to be so engaged until he reached the age of twenty-two years. He and his father then embarked upon a mercantile venture at Joppa, in which they continued for about five years, and at the end of that time Osro Shirk was appointed a deputy sheriff and was the incumbent of that position for one year. Returning to Joppa, he was again engaged in business with his father for one year, and then purchased twenty acres of land at the city limits of that place, on which he engaged in truck gardening. Later he was a rural mail carrier for two years, and in 1914 was first elected sheriff of Massac County, having continued in that position for four years. During the four years that followed he farmed and engaged in the timber business, and in 1922 was again elected sheriff of Massac County, for a four-year term. He has discharged the duties of his office conscientiously and is accounted one of Massac County's able officials.

On December 5, 1906, Mr. Shirk was united in marriage with Miss Ophia Mae Wilcox, who was born in Massac County, in May, 1891, a daughter of Lee and Martha Elizabeth (Hendrix) Wilcox, natives of the same county. The Wilcox grandparents were from Virginia, grandfather Wilcox and three of his brothers being the earliest settlers and original founders of the town of Metropolis. The Wilcox family contributed the land upon which the courthouse now stands. Dr. Delbert Hendrix, the maternal grandfather of Mrs. Shirk, was one of the early physicians of Massac County. To Mr. and Mrs. Shirk there have been born the following children: Richard T., born March 12, 1908; Austin F., born October 12, 1910; and Joe D., born April 7, 1912. Mrs. Shirk attended the public school and is a member of the Christian Church, to which her husband also belongs. In politics he is a republican, while his fraternal affiliations are with the Benevolent and Protective Order of Elks and the Independent Order of Odd Fellows, in the latter of which he has filled some of the chairs.

During his career Mr. Shirk has had a number of interesting experiences, one of which occurred in his boyhood, when as a small lad he accompanied his father and mother and two sisters, Sina and Libby, and an uncle, Richard Shirk, to Comanche County, Kansas, where his father homesteaded a tract of 160 acres. There the family's home consisted of a dugout. The subsequent life of the father was somewhat of a roving one, for after improving his Kansas property and residing thereon for two years he disposed of it by sale and moved to Evansville, Kentucky, where he resumed the trade of blacksmithing. After two years he again turned his face to the West, this time going to El Reno, Oklahoma, where he set up the portable house and blacksmith shop which he had formerly used in Kansas. After eight years he finally returned to Massac County.

M. W. Baysinger, M.D,
and family.

HON. GUY R. WILLIAMS, judge of the Eighth Judicial Circuit of Illinois, is one of the leading citizens of Havana, and a man of high standing and unblemished reputation. He won distinction as a member of the legal profession before he was elevated to the bench, and his record is one that reflects credit alike upon himself and his honored calling. He was born at New Vienna, Ohio, March 8, 1872, the only child born to the late Richard and Adelia (Rulon) Williams.

Richard Williams was born at New Vienna, Ohio, as was his wife, the latter being a daughter of Joseph and Adelia (Crawford) Rulon. Richard Williams died at Havana, Illinois, where he had long been engaged in business as a druggist, in 1908, but his widow survives him and continues to reside at Havana. He was a graduate pharmacist, and was a man who held the respect and confidence of all who knew him.

Reared in a comfortable home by watchful parents, Judge Williams was given educational advantages and encouraged to prepare himself for a professional career. Entering the University of Ohio, he took four years of literary work, after which he studied law in the legal department of the same institution, and was graduated therefrom in 1895. He took his bar examinations the same year and was admitted to practice. While in university he became a member of Sigma Chi and Phi Delta Phi, the latter the legal Greek letter college fraternity.

In 1895 Judge Williams came to Havanna, entered the office of H. R. Northrup, and a year thereafter was admitted to the bar of Illinois, according to the provisions of the law governing such matters. He remained in Mr. Northrup's office until January 1, 1897, at which time he formed a partnership with Lyman Lacey, Jr., a son of the late Judge Lacey, and they formed the firm of Lacey & Williams, which association was maintained until January 1, 1901, when Judge Williams withdrew to enter upon the duties of the office of state's attorney, to which he had been elected in November, 1900. Later he formed the firm of Northrup & Williams, with H. R. Northrup, and this connection continued until 1906, when Judge Williams was chosen to fill the unexpired term of Judge Mehan, judge of the Eighth Judicial Circuit. In June, 1909, Judge Williams was elected for a term of ten years, and has twice been re-elected to the same office, being now in his third full term on the bench. As state's attorney he succeeded S. A. Murdock, and his courage and fearlessness in handling some important local cases brought him before the public as the logical candidate for the bench. As a judge he has presided with dignified capability, and his decisions have been recognized as masterpieces of legal astuteness and impartial judgment. Very few of them have been reversed by the higher courts.

During the long period he has resided at Havana Judge Williams has participated in all of the activities of the Havana community, has united with the Riverside Club, the local Commercial Club and the Knights of Pythias, and in his political affiliations has given support to the democratic party. During the World war he was chairman of the Havana and Mason County board, which prepared the returns for his district for the United States Government.

On November 23, 1898, Judge Williams married, at Havana, Miss Elizabeth Rhodes, born at Havana, a daughter of John W. and Cyrene (Hancock) Rhodes. They had two children, Walter H. Rhodes being the elder of Mrs. Williams. She was educated at Rockford College, Rockford, Illinois. Judge and Mrs. Williams have three surviving children: Kathrena, who resides at Lynn, Massachusetts, the wife of Paul F. Bauer; Margaret Elizabeth, who is a graduate of the Havana High School, and now a student of the University of Illinois; and Guy Rhodes, who is a high school student. The eldest child, Richard Rhodes Williams, died at the age of five years.

MILLARD WINFIELD BAYSINGER, M. D., is one of the veteran physicians of southern Illinois. His professional career covers a period of over forty years. His home and the scene of his practice has been at Grand Tower, and up and down the Mississippi River Valley for many miles his name and good deeds are well known and fondly recalled.

Doctor Baysinger was born in Breckenridge County, Kentucky, August 15, 1857, son of Daniel Harding and Elizabeth (Claycomb) Baysinger. On November 20, 1870, when he was thirteen years of age, the family located at Grand Tower, Illinois. That community has been his home ever since, except during the years 1875 to 1879, when he lived in Murphysboro.

Doctor Baysinger was educated in public schools and graduated from the Missouri Medical College at St. Louis in 1883. In youth and through the years of maturity he has kept an ardent spirit for new knowledge and attainments, and intellectually he is regarded as one of the brightest men in his profession in spite of his seventy years. During 1890-91 he completed a course in the medical department of the University of the City of New York, from which he graduated in 1891. Doctor Baysinger worked as a physician in the years when there were few telephones and no good roads in the modern sense of that term. He is still active, answering calls and going about in all kinds of weather.

Dr. Baysinger is a member of the Jackson County Medical Association, the American Medical Association, the Southern Illinois Medical Association, American Association of Railroad Surgeons. He is local surgeon for the St. Louis Division of the Illinois Central Railroad, and is medical examiner for a number of life insurance companies. He has been engaged by the Employees Compensation Commission to attend the sick and the injured employees of the various industries in his locality. Doctor Baysinger is affiliated with the Independent Order of Odd Fellows and Modern Woodmen of America.

On December 30, 1887, he married Martha Ella Congleton. Mrs. Baysinger is one of the remarkable women of southern Illinois. She has been totally blind since the age of eight years, but that misfortune did not prevent her from becoming a splendid wife, mother and citizen. She has taken an active part in community and social affairs, is an interesting talker and has frequently addressed public gatherings and Sunday School organizations. Her Sunday School work is well known not only in Jackson County, but all over southern Illinois. Mrs. Baysinger graduated at Jacksonville in 1883, and taught music up to the time of her marriage. Doctor and Mrs. Baysinger had a family of five children: Helen, who died when three and a half years old of diphtheria; Millard Winfield, Jr., a resident of Carbondale; Ralph Waldo, of Centralia, Illinois; Ruth, wife of Ralph Pirtle, of St. Louis; and Maude, wife of Dr. Eugene F. Naylor, of Springfield, Illinois.

CLYDE HAGER has made for himself a place of prominence and influence in connection with the radio art and industry, even as he had previously gained no minor fame as a versatile vaudeville artist and as a writer and interpreter of songs that have scored large in popular favor. Mr. Hager is now the efficient and popular director of Station WMBB, which is one of the most important of the radio broadcasting stations in Chicago and which is established at the famous Trianon Building at Cottage Grove Avenue and Sixty-second Street.

Mr. Hager was born at Mitchell, South Dakota, December 2, 1886, and is a son of Arthur W. and Mary T. (Phillips) Hager, who removed from Iowa and became early settlers at Mitchell, South Dakota. The parents of Mr. Hager were both graduated from the University of Iowa and the father became one of the prominent pioneer members of the South Dakota bar, though he came to Chicago and here established the family home in 1888, his ability having here made him successful in the practice of his profession. Mrs. Mary T. (Phillips) Hager was born at Oelwein, Iowa, and for several years she was a successful teacher in the public schools, she having been, as previously noted, a graduate of the University of Iowa. She was prominent in social and cultural circles, and held various positions of official order in civic and social organizations, including that of president of the Woman's Relief Corps, auxiliary of the Grand Army of the Republic.

Clyde Hager was a child of two years at the time of the family removal to Chicago, and here he received the advantages of the public schools, including those of high school. From a recently published newspaper tribute to Clyde Albert Hager are taken the following statements relative to his early career:

"It wasn't long until Clyde got a blow. He found he would have to work for a living. He recovered from the shock and started out to be a business man. Stenography was the gate by which he decided to enter the business world. He had read of stenographers who had become head clerks, and, as his parents would not let him join a circus or become a fireman, he determined to work up, eventually, to be a head clerk—which to his youthful eyes was about as high as the chimes on the great Straus Building in Chicago. For some time he was amanuensis to some of Chicago's best known business men. He was well on his way to the head-clerk job, which by now was to be just a springboard to railroad president or bank board chairman. Then someone in the office declared he was 'funny as a clown.' That sowed a seed. He did make life merry for the office force and for his boss, who was always sending somebody to 'find Hager,' generally engaged in entertaining somewhere instead of figuring out the funny marks in his notebook so as to put them in English. It was not long until he had developed into such a 'funny guy' that he got a job as a vaudeville artist. Good-by business work; good-by railroad presidency or anything else to do with such sordid business. It was easy for Clyde to make crowds laugh and chuckle, and he loved his work.

"Yes, it took some schooling to get to be a stenographer, and while he was at it Clyde got a good education. Moreover, he was strong for athletics, and strong at all games. He spent a large part of his time out of school in wrestling bouts and practicing football. He was halfback on a team with Alderman George M. Maypole and 'Tubby' Graham, later famous Michigan guard. He also chased the pigskin with Waterson R. Rothacker, president of the Rothacker Film Company. Hager's athletic ability brought him no small amount of attention during his school days in Chicago, and to take a look at him today you would know that he is a trained athlete.

"In his kit bag Clyde has ten different song characterizations and also a 'Ballyhoo' number that is a dandy."

In continuing its estimate of the talent and work of Clyde Hager the same Chicago newspaper article speaks as follows: "'Git away, boys, you botham me.' And from that introduction all those who have listened in on the radio set to amount to anything know that this story is about Clyde Hager, director of Station WMBB, located on the roof of the Trianon Ballroom. Also those who follow radio to any extent know how the rise of Mr. Hager in the radio world was meteoric. He was heard one night, from WQJ, giving his song characterizations and 'Street Faker' selection, and most radio folks said: 'Here is a friend; come right into the family and have a chair.' He came in, and he has been made welcome ever since. Clyde Hager was a find by Jerry Sullivan of WQJ, and Jerry was safe in offering Mr. Hager to his listeners, because Jerry knew Mr. Hager had been a hit in vaudeville for years. * * * For fifteen years Mr. Hager played most every vaudeville circuit in the country, and has entertained thousands in almost every city in the country. And another thing about Mr. Hager. Millions have sung one of his songs, and it is well known throughout the nation. He wrote 'That Wonderful Mother of Mine,' which about ten years ago was the rage in mother songs. He dedicated that number to his own mother, Mrs. Mary T. Hager, who for years was a resident of Chicago. When the WMBB management was looking for a director and announcer for its new station, it was a popular man who was being sought. Though he had been heard in Chicago on the air for a short time only, Clyde Hager attracted attention and got the job. When he opened the station it jumped into immediate popularity. * * * The station is well run, and all who listen feel a friendly attitude coming right out of the receiving set. In turn, the fans are friendly."

In conclusion of this review may be made a brief reference to the domestic chapter in the life history of Mr. Hager. He married Miss Alice Garland, and they have three children: Kenneth Clyde, Genevieve Alice and Mary T.

COL. LAWRENCE V. REGAN. The reverberations of the great World war, the most stupendous catastrophe of all times, are gradually dying out as those who wore their country's uniform have taken up the duties of peace, but the services rendered by the men who during the dark period when the integrity of the world had to be preserved on battlefields will never be forgotten. These soldiers of a great cause developed into fearless men who have since rendered valuable service to their communities during the years of peace in which the clash of competing ambitions has been contributory to civic advancement as well as personal aggrandizement. One of the men who has proved his worth as a private citizen and business man quite as effectively as he did as a soldier is Col. Lawrence V. Regan, of Chicago, secretary-treasurer of the Pearsons-Taft Land Credit Company.

Colonel Regan was born at Omaha, Nebraska, in 1891, and was but a lad when brought to Chicago by his parents. He attended the public schools of the metropolis and was then sent for further preparation to St. Mary's College, Oakland, California. On his graduation from that institution he started his business career in finance in the offices of the Harris Trust and Savings Bank, Chicago, where he remained for four years. Subsequently he became associated with the Pearsons-Taft Land Credit Company of Chicago and San Francisco, and has since risen to the post of secretary and treasurer of this organization. It is one of the largest and most successful concerns of its kind in the country and for a long number of years has maintained a place of the highest standing in financial circles. In his identification with this enterprise Colonel Regan has contributed materially to its continued advancement and success, and has the full confidence of his associates as a man of the highest ability and character. In addition to his Chicago interests he is a member of the directorates of the Maverick Mills, the Congress Rubber Company and the Steadman Products Company, all of Boston, Massachusetts.

Colonel Regan's military career began in 1913, in which year he enlisted as a private in the old First Illinois Cavalry, Illinois National Guard. He continued as a private until this organization went to the Mexican border in the summer of 1916, when he was advanced to the rank of sergeant. Successively he was advanced to sergeant-major, second lieutenant, first lieutenant and captain, and after the close of the World war was promoted to his present rank, that of lieutenant colonel. He served under Col. (now Maj.-Gen.) Milton J. Foreman in the One Hundred and Twenty-second Field Artillery, Thirty-third Division, in France, establishing a splendid record. Colonel Regan is now assistant chief of staff of the Thirty-third Division, in charge of personnel and also is a member of the Officers Reserve Corps, United States Army, with the rank of lieutenant colonel. He belongs to the Army and Navy Club of Chicago and the Bankers Club of New York City, and has a number of civic and fraternal connections. His name is always found on the lists of the backers of progressive civic movements.

Colonel Regan was united in marriage in 1921 with Miss Marguerite J. Dahlquist, of Chicago, and they make their home at 7637 Greenview Avenue.

CARL A. STEINHOUSER, JR., is proving admirably fortified for the responsible executive duties that devolve upon him as manager of the Illinois Power & Light Company, and he is one of the representative business men of the younger generation in the City of Mount Vernon, Jefferson County. Mr. Steinhouser was born at Craig, Missouri, June 14, 1889, and his parents, Carl A. and Leona (Carlton) Steinhouser, now reside at Nashville, Washington County, Illinois, the subject of this review being the eldest in a family of two sons and three daughters. Carl A. Steinhouser was born and reared in Germany, and was a lad of twelve years when he accompanied one of his older brothers to the United States. He soon proved his independence and resourcefulness by finding practical employment that provided for his needs. He was associated with farm work in different states of the Union and finally he learned the trade of flour miller, in which connection he has erected and operated a number of large mills, including one at Craig, Missouri. In 1904 he built a modern mill at Nashville, Illinois, and in connection therewith installed an electric light plant to furnish general service to the community. In 1908 he sold his mill to local citizens and the electric plant to the Southern Illinois Lighting Company, of which he became the local manager at Nashville. In 1916 the Southern Illinois Lighting Company became a part of the Illinois Power & Light Company, and Mr. Steinhouser has since been retained as manager of its local plant and business at Nashville. He was doubly orphaned when he was but a boy, and it was under these conditions that he was brought by his older brother to the United States, where he has made substantial and worthy achievement and stands exponent of loyal and appreciative American citizenship. The parents of his wife were John and Leona Carlton, both of whom were born and reared in Illinois.

After completing his studies in the high school at Nashville Carl A. Steinhouser, Jr., became actively associated with the operation of the electric lighting plant that his father had there established, he having been there employed even before he left school, at the age of seventeen years. He eventually acquired an interest in the business, and later, after the transfer of the property by his father, he became superintendent of construction for the Illinois Power & Light Company. While in this service he met with an accident that necessitated the amputation of his left arm. Later he was made assistant commercial manager for this company at St. Louis, Missouri, and in August, 1920, the company made him manager of its plant and business at Mount Vernon. This Mount Vernon plant was originally constructed by local capitalists as a municipal system, later it was sold to the Trowbridge-Niver Company of Chicago, and thereafter it was owned by Henry M. Daugherty, of New York, who, after an interval of about five years, sold to the Southern Illinois Lighting Company, which transferred the plant, about two years later, to the Illinois Power & Light Company.

In the World war period Mr. Steinhouser was able to "do his bit" in an effective way, especially in the construction of electric lines for Government use, including the one to Scott Field. Mr. Steinhouser is a man of sterling personality, a citizen of loyalty and progressive spirit, and his is an impregnable place in popular esteem. He is president of the Mount Vernon Chamber of Commerce and is a leader in movements that make for the civic and material progress and prosperity of his home city. He is affiliated with the Independent Order of Odd Fellows and the Knights of Pythias, and he and his wife hold membership in the Methodist Episcopal Church.

On the 21st of October, 1910, Mr. Steinhouser was united in marriage with Miss Lillian Hasemier, daughter of Louis and Emma Hasemier, who are well known residents of Nashville, Illinois, where her father was formerly engaged in the grocery business, and where he and his wife still reside, he being now a traveling commercial salesman. Mrs. Hasemier is a daughter of the late Doctor and Emma Bahrenburg, the former of whom was a representative physician who served as a surgeon in the Civil war and who was a leader in his community, where he has long engaged in the practice of his profession and where also he held the office of justice of the peace. Mr. and Mrs. Steinhouser have two children: Jack Malcolm, born in 1912, and Carl Louis, born in 1915.

HENRY HARRISON PELHANK is a banker, and his career has been identified with the detail work and management of banks in Southern Illinois since early manhood. He is president of the First National Bank of Eldorado.

Mr. Pelhank was reared in Illinois from early boyhood, but was born at Portsmouth, Ohio, September 19, 1870, son of Henry and Harriet (Massey) Pelhank, and a grandson of Frederick Pelhank. Henry Pelhank was born at Dresden, Germany, and was two years of age when the family came to America. Frederick Pelhank for many years was a clothing merchant at Cincinnati. Henry Pelhank was reared in Cincinnati and after the discovery of gold in California went across the plains to that state. After his return to Ohio he married Harriet Massey, a native of Ross County. About 1875 they removed to Illinois and settled on a farm in Saline County, where Henry Pelhank died and where his widow still resides. They reared a family of five sons and two daughters.

Henry Harrison Pelhank grew up on the old homestead in Saline County, was educated in country schools and normal schools, and as a youth he spent four years as deputy county treasurer under D. B. Chase. His first work in a bank was as bookkeeper in the First National Bank of Harrisburg, where he remained about six months. For three years he kept books for J. M. Potter, owner of a grain elevator at Harrisburg.

Mr. Pelhank in 1903 became associated with David Weideman and Charles W. Weideman in opening the Hardin County Bank at Cave in Rock. Mr. Pelhank was the active officer of this institution until 1911. He was cashier of the First National Bank at Equality from 1911 to 1917, and after selling his stock in that institution became cashier of the First National Bank of Eldorado. Since 1923 he has been president, and the bank during his connection with it has steadily grown and prospered. Mr. Pelhank has other business interests and has identified himself with the progressive welfare of the community, though he has never sought nor shared political honors. He votes as a republican and is a prominent Methodist layman, being chairman of the Board of Trustees of the church at Eldorado and a member of the Board of Hospitals of the Southern Illinois Methodist Conference.

He married, in 1896, Sarah B. McCormick, a native of Saline County, daughter of John W. and Isabel (Galespie) McCormick. Mr. and Mrs. Pelhank have three children. Mabel married Elza C. Brown, and they reside at St. Petersburg, Florida, where she is a kindergarten teacher. Hobart D. Pelhank, a student in the University of Illinois, and a member of the Student Officers Training Corps during the World war, is now in the real estate business at Tampa, Florida, and married Mamie Schrieffer. The youngest child is Kenneth Judson Pelhank.

MARTIN J. ISAACS has been a hard working Chicago attorney for more than thirty years, and is perhaps best known to members of the bar rather than to the general public, though for many years he has been master in chancery of the Superior Court of Cook County.

He was born at Memphis, Tennessee, January 13, 1870, son of Joel D. and Amelia (Josephi) Isaacs. His father was born at Liverpool, England, and his mother at Washington, D. C. Joel D. Isaacs during his early manhood was in the British army service, and was on duty in Australia and New Zealand and became an expert interpreter because of his knowledge of the various dialects and languages of native tribes. He finally came to America, and he died at the age of eighty-two. Of his five children Martin J. is the second, and four are living.

Martin J. Isaacs spent his youth in Chicago, graduating in 1892 from the Chicago College of Law, the law department of Lake Forest University. He had been admitted to the bar of Illinois October 13, 1891. For three years he engaged in practice at Plano, Illinois, and since then in Chicago. He is a member of the law firm McGoorty, Silber, Isaacs & Woley. Since 1910 he has been master in chancery of the Superior Court. He has been mentioned prominently as a candidate for the

Omer N. Custer

bench and the Chicago Bar Association's committee on candidates recently reported: "He is well qualified for the office of judge of the Superior Court."

Mr. Isaacs is a life member of the Chicago Bar Association, and for three years was a member of its Board of Managers. He also belongs to the Illinois State and American Bar Associations. During the World war he was an active member of the war committee of the bar association, this committee having charge of the legal relief for soldiers and sailors and their families. He was also a member of the Legal Advisory Board of Division No. 7. Mr. Isaacs is a member of the Idlewild Country Club, the Iroquois Club, the B. P. O. Elks, and is a democrat. Mr. Isaacs married, October 25, 1895, Miss Hetty Reinhard. She was born at Niles, Michigan. Their home is at 425 East Forty-eighth Street, Chicago. The three children of their marriage are Robert, Edward and Richard.

WILLIAM G. GOLDMAN is one of the prominent younger men in the real estate business at Chicago, organizer and active head of the North Side Realty Company, with offices in the Chicago Temple Building.

He was born in Roumania, May 24, 1902, son of Lazarus and Rebecca (Bernstein) Goldman, natives of the same country. His parents came to America and settled in the northwest of Canada and are now living at Vancouver, British Columbia, where his father is in the hotel business. He is also a large land owner.

William G. Goldman was the ninth in a family of ten children. He acquired his early education in the schools of Alberta, Canada, and in 1918, as a youth of sixteen, came to Chicago, and his experience has since been continuous in the real estate business. In 1921 he organized the North Side Realty Company, subdividers and home builders, and has made this one of the very prosperous realty firms in the city. He is a member of the Chicago Real Estate Board and the National Real Estate Exchange.

GEORGE FRANCIS HOGAN has been a Chicago manufacturer and business man who has developed a small industry into one of notable proportions and has kept the distinctive name of his company and its products constantly before the public. He is president and owner of the Heco Envelope Company, which is probably the largest individual envelope manufacturing plant in the country.

Mr. Hogan, who is better known as Frank Hogan than by his full name, was born in Chicago in 1873. As a boy he was familiar with the city, particularly the North Side, during the '70s and '80s. His manufacturing plant is at 361 East Ohio Street, and not far from that site he hunted ducks on the lake shore during his youth. In addition to the public schools he attended Racine College in Wisconsin.

Mr. Hogan in 1900 engaged in his present business starting the Hogan Envelope Company, manufacturers of envelopes. This business he later sold but continued as a manufacturer under the new name of Heco Envelope Company, of which he is president and principal owner. A quarter of a century ago he started out to make his business prosperous and successful, and through unusual advertising methods brought knowledge and appreciation of his product before the public. Mr. Hogan recently contributed to the pamphlet of "Illinois Facts," issued by the Illinois Chamber of Commerce, an article on envelope manufacturers, recounting that Illinois has thirty envelope factories, and that in the aggregate they constitute a large and important industry, whose output is indispensable to modern business.

Mr. Hogan finds his diversion from business at his farm in Waukesha County, Wisconsin. He has made his farm a breeding ground for pheasants, prairie chickens, partridges and other bird and animal life. Mr. Hogan married Miss Virginia Pickrell, member of a pioneer Illinois family whose home for many years was at Mechanicsburg in Sangamon County. She is a daughter of Arthur A. and Theodosia (Bone) Pickrell and a granddaughter of William Pickrell. The only child of Mr. and Mrs. Hogan is George Francis Hogan, Jr.

HON. OMER N. CUSTER, state treasurer of Illinois, and secretary and treasurer of the Galesburg Printing and Publishing Company, was born in Fayette County, Pennsylvania, December 25, 1873, a son of Herman K. and Dorcas A. (Nixon) Custer, natives of the Keystone state, the father a carpenter by trade. The son worked with the elder man in his youth, and in the meantime attended the public schools and gained an elementary education that has been supplemented in the school of experience.

Very early in his career Mr. Custer began the battle of life for himself. After going west and spending three years in Colorado and then returning to Pennsylvania for one year, in 1894 he located at Galesburg, Illinois, which city has since been his place of residence. His first employment was in a grocery store, but shortly thereafter he began his real career in the newspaper business, first as a solicitor for the Galesburg Republican-Register. Through constant promotions he gradually rose to higher and higher positions until he was finally elected secretary and treasurer of the Galesburg Printing and Publishing Company, owners and publishers of the above-named newspaper, and this position Mr. Custer has continued to hold.

Not long after entering the newspaper business Mr. Custer became active in the councils of the republican party, and in 1906 won election as treasurer of Knox County. In this office he served with credit until February, 1909, when he resigned to become postmaster of Galesburg, to which office he was appointed by President Roosevelt that same month, and acted in that capacity for four years. During the World war Mr. Custer served as a member of the Illinois State Industrial Commission, under appointment by Governor Lowden. In 1924 he won the nomination as the republican candidate for state treasurer of Illinois, and was successful of election at the polls in the fall of that year. He is the present incumbent of the office, with a splendid record to his credit.

Mr. Custer has always manifested faith in the future of Galesburg and has been one of its ardent supporters and active in promoting the city's interests and development. He and his associates are holders of extensive real estate at Galesburg and are the builders and owners of Hotel Custer, named in his honor.

In 1896 Mr. Custer and Miss Olive F. Temple were united in marriage, and they are the parents of two children: Ethel M., the wife of Lester Pritchard; and Howard T., who married Miss Josephine Wood.

HUMBERT A. BERRA. A family that has been prominent with the best citizenship of Southern Illinois has been that of Berra, represented for many years both at Murphysboro and at Herrin. The Berras are of Italian ancestry, and Joseph Berra, now a retired business man of Murphysboro, is a native of Italy.

Joseph Berra was born in the town of Cuggiono, Province of Milano, Italy, August 31, 1866, son of Antonio and Maria (Gallina) Berra, who spent all their lives on a farm in that section of Italy. His education was continued in a school in his native community until he had completed the equivalent of fourth grade studies. After that he worked on a farm. At the age of sixteen he came to America, and from New York City came West to St. Louis. At that time he had a cousin, John Berra, living at Murphysboro. John Berra was killed in the tornado of March, 1925. From St. Louis Joseph Berra went to Pilot Knob, where he worked eight months for a coal and iron company, then three months in stone quarries at Merrimac, Missouri, until the quarries shut down, and after that nine months in a coal mine at Troy, Illinois. Joseph Berra first came to Murphysboro in 1885. Here he also found employment in a coal mine. All this time he was steadily striving to perfect his knowledge in the English language and acquaint himself with American customs as a basis for citizenship. Before he was twenty years of age he met with a serious accident in a mine, one leg being broken and his back badly injured. He spent six months in the Mullanphy Hospital at St. Louis, and on returning to Murphysboro resumed work in the mines. About that time he had a letter from his mother in Italy urging him to return and serve in the Italian army as required by law. He was quite desirous himself to return for a visit, but supposed that on account of the injuries he had sustained he would be rejected for duty in the army. However, when he went back he was accepted and served thirty-three months with the military establishment of Italy. At the close of his army service he returned to America, and at Detroit spent six months learning the iron moulder's trade. He abandoned his apprenticeship, and returning to Murphysboro, again worked about a year in the mines. His first opportunity to engage in business for himself was a partnership with Dominic Cesare in the purchase of a saloon at the corner of Ninth and Walnut streets. He had only four or five hundred dollars in savings, but his reputation as a steady young man of good ability and habits enabled him to procure a loan from a local business man for the rest of the capital. After six months Cesare sold his interest to Enrico Taveggia, and he and Berra were in partnership two years. Taveggia's interests were then sold to Louis Dell'Era. This was the beginning of a very successful and notable partnership between Joseph Berra and Louis Dell'Era. Both of them had been soldiers together in Italy and were friends in everything, not merely in business. In 1898 these partners established another retail store at Herrin, with Mr. Berra in charge.

A year later Joseph Berra married Emilia Merlo, who was born at Castelletto, of Cuggiono, Province of Milano. After this marriage the two partners exchanged places of residence, Dell'Era going to Herrin, while Joseph Berra located at Murphysboro as a more desirable place to rear a family. The partners also engaged in the real estate business, buying land and platting it as the Berra and Dell'Era addition to Herrin. Prosperity seemed to smile on everything they undertook. In 1904 they built at Herrin the first real opera house in that town. This structure was burned January 13, 1917. They also built the European Hotel at Herrin.

Louis Dell'Era, one of the conspicuous citizens of Southern Illinois, died October 2, 1914. In 1919 Joseph Berra sold his interest in the Herrin property to the Dell'Era estate. Joseph Berra has lived retired during the past six years. He was formerly a director in the City National Bank of Herrin. He and his wife had two children, a daughter, Maria, dying at the age of eight years.

The only son and surviving child is Humbert A. Berra, a prominent and popular young business man of Sesser, Illinois. He was born at Murphysboro, January 19, 1900, and was given very liberal educational opportunities, attending the parochial schools in Murphysboro and graduating from Notre Dame University at South Bend, Indiana. In school he specialized in journalism and did newspaper work for a time at Indianapolis and at Alliance, Ohio. On returning to Murphysboro to live with his father and mother he accepted employment in the Phil Cline drug store and later with his father purchased a drug store in Sesser, Illinois. He is unmarried.

THOMAS FLINT, one of the proprietors of Flint's Sanitary Dairy, at 406 Collins Street, Joliet, came to that Illinois city when a boy, grew up there, and has been closely identified with the dairy business for about thirty years.

He was born at Skane, in the south of Sweden, in 1869. His mother died there and in 1881 the father brought his family to the United States and first located at Lamont, Illinois, and about 1889 removed to Joliet, where he died in 1913. He was a quarryman by trade. The children of the family were: Nels, of Sweden; August and Axel, of Joliet; Johanna, wife of Peter Munson, of Joliet; Thomas; Oliver, of Joliet; Anna P., Mrs. M. C. Linburg, of Rock Island, Illinois; Wilhelmina, wife of Ernest Anderson, of Joliet.

Thomas Flint acquired a common school education in Sweden and attended school in Joliet for several years. In 1888 his brother Axel started a dairy business, handling milk, both wholesale and retail, and in 1890 Thomas Flint became associated with the business, so that his continuous record of activity therein covers a period of thirty-five years. In 1891 another brother, Oliver, joined in the firm. Axel, in 1923, sold his interest and since then Thomas and Oliver have continued the business of the Sanitary Dairy, of which Thomas Flint is president. Since 1900 the business has been located at 406 Collins Street. It is now wholesale, and handles a large volume of business between the producers and the retailers in milk, cream, ice cream and butter.

Mr. Thomas Flint married, in 1895, Miss Anna Marie Anderson, a native of Sweden, who came alone to the United States at the age of sixteen and lived in Joliet until her marriage. The children of Mr. and Mrs. Flint are: Clara, Mrs. Edwin Johnson, of Joliet; Theodore and Gertrude, both at home. Mr. Flint is a trustee of the Lutheran Church, is a republican and is an active member of the Association of Commerce.

CLAUDE RAY YOUNG after some youthful experience in other lines of work took up railroading, and that is a career and profession that has brought him deserved advancement until he is now superintendent of transportation of the Illinois Central Railroad System at Chicago.

Mr. Young, who is known among his friends and associates as Cy Young, represents old Kentucky families and was born at Oakland, Kentucky, May 25, 1885, son of Samuel Murrell and Isabel Elizabeth (Ray) Young, the former a native of Marion County and the latter of Warren. During the early childhood of Claude R. the family moved to Bowling Green, where he attended public schools. He had a college course at Ogden College. At that time his choice among the professions was that of medicine. With that in view he became a drug clerk. Leaving that, he tried journalism, working for newspapers at Louisville. He gave that up to take a commercial course in the Bowling Green Business College, and with qualifications as a stenographer took up railroading. Mr. Young has always been grateful for these three successive experiences. His college course gave him a good fundamental education. Journalism was a school of training that no other business or vocation offers. His industrious application and efficiency has carried him far along the road of accomplishment in the railroad service.

In 1905, at the age of twenty, he became stenographer to the chief train dispatcher of the Illinois Central Railroad at Fulton, Kentucky. From this position he was promoted to that of car distributor. In July, 1906, he was made clerk and timekeeper in the trainmaster's office at Princeton, Kentucky. June 1, 1908, he was transferred to the office force of the general superintendent at Memphis. In 1910 A. E. Clift, then general superintendent, moved his headquarters from Memphis to New Orleans, Mr. Young going along. For a number of years his home was in New Orleans. In May, 1911, he was promoted to chief clerk to the superintendent at Fulton, Kentucky, and served in that capacity until 1917, when he was appointed yardmaster at Fulton; in 1918 he was made trainmaster, and two years later made superintendent of the Tennessee division, with headquarters at Fulton. In 1924 he was appointed superintendent of the St. Louis division, with headquarters at Carbondale, Illinois, and in July, 1926, was promoted to superintendent of transportation of the Illinois Central Railroad System, moving to Chicago with his family.

He married Mary Louise Ellis, of Bowling Green, Kentucky. Her people came out of Virginia and were early settlers at Hopkinsville, Christian County, Kentucky.

JOSEPH J. THOMPSON, LL. D., an able lawyer practicing at the Chicago bar, now assistant corporation counsel of the City of Chicago, was born on the Military Tract in Warren County, Illinois, January 14, 1868. His parents, John W. and Hannah (Crofton) Thompson, were both natives of Ireland, but came separately to the United States when young and were married in New York. In the '30s they came to Illinois, and participated in the scenes and incidents of pioneer life. Joseph J. Thompson was the youngest of twelve children. He was principally educated in the country schools, Mercer County High School at Aledo, and the Northern Illinois Normal School, Dixon, Illinois. He took his legal training in Wesleyan University, Bloomington, Illinois, from which he received his degree of Bachelor of Laws.

For seventeen years following his admission to the bar Mr. Thompson was engaged in the general practice of law at Bloomington, and during that period taught law in Wesleyan University. Coming then to Chicago, he became a member of the faculty of Lincoln Law School of Loyola University, and at the same time was engaged in the practice of his profession. Subsequently he received the honorary degree of Doctor of Laws.

To inaugurate and develop the Legislative Reference Bureau at Springfield, he resigned his connection with Lincoln Law School. The purpose of this organization was to prepare the bills for the Legislature, advise as to their constitutionality and supervise their enactment. Mr. Thompson served under the administrations of Governors Dunne and Lowden, and during this period had under consideration some 2,000 bills. In 1909 a law in Illinois was enacted to provide for the appointment of five commissioners to act with other commissioners from other states to bring about the uniformity of state legislation. Mr. Thompson has ever since served on that commission, and except for the first year has been, and now is, secretary of the commission. He has, at the instance of the Illinois State Bar Association, formulated all the laws to which all the territory now known as Illinois was ever subject up to the constitutional convention of 1818. His work in this connection familiarized him with many historical subjects, particularly with those embracing legal matters. In connection with this work his researches led to his intimate knowledge of the early exploration in Illinois of the Catholic missionaries, and in the early French and Irish settlements. Mr. Thompson's contributions on the history of laws in the Illinois Law Journal have attracted much attention, and he has also contributed to the press much valuable data on various historical subjects.

Mr. Thompson married, when twenty-one years old, Miss Julia McNamara, the daughter of a neighbor, and she bore him four daughters, all but one of whom are married. Mrs. Thompson died in 1918. In 1922 he married Mary Josephine Riley.

THOMAS D. SHIPTON, retired merchant, lives at Hanover, in Jo Daviess County. He belongs to the pioneer element of citizenship in Northwestern Illinois. He has been successful in business and is also well known for his attainments in scientific lines, particularly as a mineralogist, archaeologist and paleontologist.

His father was Joseph Shipton, who was born in Alabama in 1812, and in 1827, with his mother and three brothers and one sister, came from the Muscle Shoals district of Alabama to Galena, Illinois, by way of the Mississippi River. Joseph Shipton was a blacksmith by trade and operated a shop at Galena until 1840, when he moved to Derinda Township, where he engaged in farming. In 1850 he went out to California, spending about a year and a half as a mining prospector in the Far West. He returned to Galena by way of the Isthmus of Panama, and then around Cape Horn to the United States. The receipt given him for his sailboat fare from San Francisco to Panama is now preserved by Thomas D. Shipton, as well as a number of letters written during his perilous journey across the plains. The Shipton family were living in Jo Daviess County at the time of the Black Hawk Indian war and active in defense of Galena.

Joseph Shipton in 1838 married Mary McGrath, who had come with her parents from the vicinity of Pittsburgh, Pennsylvania, to Galena in 1836. Her father, Rev. Samuel McGrath, was a widely celebrated Methodist circuit rider and was instrumental in organizing with two other men the first Methodist Church at Hanover. He was noted for the tirelessness with which he prosecuted his duties as a minister. He was hardly less famous as a pedestrian. Frequently he walked instead of riding horseback in his ministry. It is told of him that on one Sunday he walked from his home in Derinda to Savanna, a distance of twelve miles, preached there in the forenoon, then walked ten miles to Mount Carrol, where he held afternoon services, and after a four mile walk to Cherry Grove, where he preached at night, he walked all the way back home to Derinda, eighteen miles away, thus in twenty-four hours having covered about forty-four miles on foot and having preached three sermons.

Thomas D. Shipton was born and reared in Derinda Township. Since 1896 his home has been at Hanover. In the spring of 1879, before his marriage, he went to Montana, traveling up the Missouri River on a steamboat that was forty days in reaching the head of navigation, Fort Benton. He engaged in mining and also at times was interested in stage coach operation. He spent altogether about six years in Montana, Utah, Wyoming and the Black Hills district of South Dakota. On one of his trips back home he married. In 1896, for the sake of his health, he spent the summer in Montana, Idaho and Utah, and in 1897 made an extended trip over the Black Hills country of South Dakota. Thomas D. Shipton in 1904 was appointed postmaster at Hanover, succeeding Charles A. Como, and also acquired the store which has been conducted by Mr. Como. He served as postmaster from March 1, 1904, to March 1, 1916. As a merchant, handling men's clothing and furnishing goods, he continued active until 1922, when he retired. Since his retirement he has found congenial and constant occupation and study in his chief hobbies, mineralogy, archaeology and paleontology, along which lines he has been an investigator and student for a great many years. He became strongly interested in mineralogy while prospecting over the West. His knowledge of geology is thoroughly practical. He has gathered together one of the finest collections of geological and archaeological specimens found anywhere outside of a museum.

He is a member of the National Geographic Society, the Mississippi Valley Historical Society, Illinois State Historical Society, American Mineralogical Society, Wisconsin Archaeological Society and the Archaeological Institute of America. He has been affiliated with Masonry for thirty years, is a past master of his lodge, member of the Eastern Star and a past patron, and a Royal Arch Mason. He is well read in history and the general sciences, and has also derived great pleasure from poetry. His favorite verses, by an unknown author, are:

MY WISH

A thickety path that clambers high
From a winding road where the world goes by.
A bit of hut on a wooded hill,
Where wind and weather may have their will;
A bit of a door that has no key,
That calls to the traveler "Open Me."
A bit of a hearth with a shelf above
Just enough to hold the books I love,
A bit of a nook in the fire's red glow
To dream of my love of long ago.
A pipe to smoke when the crickets cry,
Far away from the road where the world goes by."

Thomas D. Shipton married Hattie A. Campbell, who was born and reared in Derinda Township, daughter of William and Mary (McDonald) Campbell, and granddaughter of Robert Campbell. Robert Campbell was a Scotchman, came to America and entered the service of the Hudson Bay Fur Company, and spent a number of years in western Canada and other British possessions of the north. William Campbell, father of Mrs. Shipton, was born in 1830 on the Red River of the north and was a small boy when his parents, in 1836, settled in Hanover, Illinois. The Campbells took up the first claim of land in Derinda Township. Mrs. (Mary McDonald) Campbell, wife of William Campbell and mother of Mrs. Thomas D. Shipton, was a daughter of John McDonald, who came to Jo Daviess County and settled at Elizabeth, near the Apple River Fort, and he and his wife were in the Fort

when it was attacked by Indians in 1832. Some of the relatives are yet in possession of a wardrobe which plainly shows the marks of the tomahawk. The Indians having broken into the house and after having taken such articles as they desired, smashed the furniture, leaving a wreck behind them. Mr. and Mrs. Thomas Shipton are spending their last years in a very comfortable home and have the sincere esteem and interest of a large circle of friends. They became the parents of four children: Charles C., born November 27, 1886; Mary, who was born November 23, 1890, and died May 8, 1903; Washburn D., born January 19, 1893; and William J., the oldest, born July 15, 1885. The son Charles is now connected with the income tax department of the Internal Revenue Bureau at Washington. He married Florence Davy, of Elizabeth, Illinois. Charles was a graduate of Hanover High School and also of Coe College, Cedar Rapids, Iowa. The son Washburn D. graduated from Hanover High School, from Coe College at Cedar Rapids, Iowa, and from the University of Iowa, and in December, 1917, enlisted in the service of his country as a flying cadet and subsequently was commissioned a second lieutenant in the Signal Officers' Reserve Corps. He was discharged in November, 1918. He spent some time in the training camp at Berkeley, California, and also at Kelley Field at San Antonio, Texas. He has the strong bent of his father for scientific work, and is now connected with the Washington University at St. Louis as associate geologist.

William J. Shipton, present county treasurer and former sheriff of Jo Daviess County, was born in Derinda Township, July 15, 1885, was educated in the grade and high schools at Hanover, and had considerable practical experience in farming and also in his father's store, and was clerk in the postoffice when his father was postmaster. In 1913 he went with the Hanover Lumber Company. Mr. Shipton in November, 1918, was elected sheriff of Jo Daviess County, serving until 1922. In that year he was elected county treasurer, the office he now fills.

He is a thirty-second degree Scottish Rite Mason and Shriner, being a past master of Hanover Lodge No. 905, A. F. and A. M., member of Savanna Chapter No. 200, Royal Arch Masons, Ely S. Parker Council No. 60, R. and S. M., is a past commander of Galena Commandery No. 40, Knights Templar, and a member of the Consistory at Freeport and Tabela Temple of the Mystic Shrine at Rockford. He is a past exalted ruler of Galena Lodge No. 882, B. P. O. Elks, is a member of the Galena Gold Club and belongs to the Presbyterian Church.

ROY W. HARRELL, M. D., executive medical officer of the Christopher Hospital, had his training in medical college and as a hospital interne, supplemented by a year of service in the Army Medical Corps during the World war, and is one of the exceptionally well equipped surgeons in Franklin County.

His father was a prominent doctor in Southern Illinois, Jerome L. Harrell, who was born in Gallatin County, this state. The father of Jerome Harrell came to Illinois from North Carolina. Jerome L. Harrell graduated from the Eclectic Medical College of Cincinnati, then practiced at Gossett and Ridgeway, Illinois, and in 1890 located at Norris City, White County, where he continued his work as a physician and surgeon for many years. He married Mary Cook, also of Gallatin County.

One of two children, Roy W. Harrell, was born at Norris City, White County, September 16, 1891, and received his early school advantages there. He was graduated in 1912 from the School of Pharmacy of the University of Illinois and in 1913 entered the medical department of Loyola University at Chicago. He took his M. D. degree in 1917, and had eighteen months of hospital experience as an interne in St. Bernard's Hospital of Chicago.

Doctor Harrell in the spring of 1918 was commissioned a lieutenant in the United States Army Medical Corps and was assigned duty with the General Hospital at New Haven, Connecticut, and a month later was sent to Camp Funston, Kansas, and put on the medical examining board, where he remained a year. His final service was at Fort D. A. Russell, Wyoming.

After returning to Illinois, Doctor Harrell practiced a year at Galatia and since then has been at Christopher, in charge of the Christopher Hospital. This hospital, established by Dr. Albert Willis, is limited in its accommodations, but has splendid equipment and personnel for handling its cases.

Doctor Harrell married Miss Florence Curran, a daughter of P. L. Curran, of Buckner, Illinois.

DR. HENRY A. WEBER, optometrist at Murphysboro, is a native of southern Illinois, grew up on a farm, and while educating himself for his profession worked in various commercial lines at St. Louis.

His grandfather, John Weber, on coming from Germany, settled near Waterloo, in Monroe County, Illinois, and established a farm there. On this farm his son Matthew Weber was born in March, 1863. Matthew Weber since 1901 has lived near Somerset in Jackson County. He married Katherine Welsch, who was born and reared in Monroe County, her parents also coming from Germany.

Henry A. Weber was born on the farm then occupied by his father near Waterloo, in November, 1889. His first opportunities were given him by the country schools and he had his full share in the heavy work of the farm while growing to manhood. For two years he attended the State Normal University at Carbondale. While ambitious for a higher education, he was unwilling to burden his father with the expense of acquiring it. Therefore, at the age of twenty he removed to St. Louis, and for three years worked in a clothing factory, and then for eighteen months in a shoe factory. While working during the day he attended night school, and finally from his earnings was able to devote all his time to study. He attended the Missouri College of Optometry and was graduated in May, 1915. Doctor Weber in the fall of 1915 established his office at Murphysboro and has gained an extensive business all over this part of the state.

He married Theresa Paul, daughter of Mr. and Mrs. H. G. Paul, of Murphysboro, October 22, 1918. They have two children, H. Paul Weber and Margaret Ann Weber.

Doctor Weber is a member of the Murphysboro Rotary Club, Chamber of Commerce, B. P. O. Elks and K. of C. Also the Illinois State and National Society of Optometrists, and Beta Sigma Kappa, an international honorary fraternity.

JUDSON D. NICHOLS is one of the survivors of the real pioneer era of Kankakee County, and for many years was active in business, but is now retired, with home at 323 North Indiana Avenue in Kankakee.

He was born in Wayne County, New York, April 8, 1828, son of Roswell C. and Mary (Durfee) Nichols. His father was born in Connecticut, in 1795, and his mother, in Rhode Island. Her parents drove across the country in a very early day and were pioneer settlers at Palmyra, New York. Subsequently the Erie Canal was constructed through part of the Durfee farm. Roswell Nichols after his marriage engaged in the tanning industry. After selling his business he bought the farm where Joseph Smith, the Mormon leader, was reared, and where subsequently the famous plates were found for the Book of Mormon. In 1841 Roswell Nichols sold his farm, and, coming to Kankakee County, Illinois, purchased seven hundred acres along the banks of the Kankakee River. He moved from New York, bringing his household goods, traveling by canal to Buffalo, and on a side wheel steamer to Chicago, being nine days on the voyage. At Chicago the family remained in a tavern two days while he was buying supplies and securing the services of seven teams to haul his family and goods to his farm in Kankakee County.

Judson D. Nichols was about thirteen years old when the family came west. Prior to that he had attended public schools at Palmyra, New York. He shared in the heavy work of converting the virgin land of Kankakee County into a farm, and on April 8, 1849, at the age of twenty-one, he married Ludelia Arnold. She was born at Tonawanda, New York, daughter of Orin Arnold, who brought his family to Kankakee County with wagons and teams. Mr. Nichols after his marriage moved to land which his father had given him and where he built a stone house that is still standing. After a short time he left the farm and went to Joliet, where for two years he was a tie contractor for railroads. With his brother-in-law, Jefferson Edmonds, he went to Missouri, and together they did the grading and laid the ties on the first miles of the Hannibal & St. Joseph Railroad. He was in Missouri three years.

In the fall of 1857 his first wife died, leaving two children, Eugene, now of Montreal, Canada, and Orin, of Kankakee. On December 31, 1859, Mr. Nichols married Mary Isabel Denny, a native of Terre Haute, Indiana, and daughter of David and Emily (Nichols) Denny. By this marriage he has the following children: Hattie Ann, at home; Claribel, wife of Judge John Small, of Kankakee; Helen Emily, widow of J. Frank Gibbs, of Bellingham, Washington; David D., of Kankakee.

In the fall of 1877 Mr. Nichols moved from his 280 acre farm into Kankakee, putting on an addition to a house he owned there. His brother, Argailus B., was a noted auctioneer, and the two brothers became associated in the ownership and management of a general store. They were partners ten years, after which Mr. Judson Nichols started a general furniture business on Court Street. This was the first exclusive furniture store in Kankakee. It is a business house with a long and honorable record, and is now managed by the sons of Mr. Nichols and is located at 141 N. Schuyler Avenue.

Mr. Nichols has served as constable and his father was a justice of the peace and postmaster during the early days in Kankakee County. He is a republican, has served as township treasurer and county supervisor, and since 1863 has been a member of the Masonic Order.

ELIZABETH MARGARET THURSTON MANN, juvenile probation officer of Kankakee County, was born at Manteno, in Kankakee County, in 1882, daughter of Fred and Georgiana (Grant) Thurston, her father a native of England, while her mother was born at Manteno, Illinois. Her grandparents, John and Ann (Cox) Thurston, came from Utica, New York, in 1857, and soon afterward settled in Sumner Township of Kankakee County. Her maternal grandparents were Daniel and Margaret (LaBounty) Grant, the former a native of New York State and the latter of Montreal, Canada. Fred Thurston and wife after their marriage settled at Manteno, where for many years he was in business as a hardware merchant, and later for seven years was an employe of the Illinois Central Railroad Company, until his death on March 26, 1925. The widowed mother still lives at Manteno.

Mrs. Mann graduated from high school in 1899 and in the same year was married to William Alexander Mann. Mr. Mann was born in Rockville Township, Kankakee County, in 1872, son of Samuel James and Mary Ann (McIntosh) Mann. Mr. Mann attended grammar and high school at Manteno and was engaged in farming until 1913. In that year he moved to Kankakee and established his home at 429 East Locust Street. He served as car inspector for the New York Central lines until 1919, and since that year has been practically an invalid.

Mrs. Mann after the organization of the American Legion became president of Kankakee Unit No. 85, and two years later was made district committee woman, and the following year elected senior vice president of the Department of Illinois, and the next year was reelected, serving until the fall of 1925. She has been state finance chairman for the year 1924-25-26. She is a member of the Gold Star mothers and a member of the American Legion Auxiliary. Mrs. Mann in May, 1924, was made juvenile probation officer and is also superintendent of charities and county truant officer.

Her only son, Russell Gilbert Mann, born January 8, 1901, graduated from Our Ladies Academy at Manteno and the Kankakee High School, and in July, 1918, before he was eighteen years old, entered Medical Supply Depot No. 3 and sailed for France with that unit on November 11, Armistice Day. He died at Gievres, France, March 3, 1919, and his body was subsequently brought home and laid to rest in Kankakee Cemetery. Mrs. Mann is a republican, is a member of the Woman's Club and the Pythian Sisters.

HENRY POLK LOWENSTEIN, of the prominent Lowenstein family of White Hall, Greene County, gained his early experience as an attorney in Illinois, but for forty years has been a resident of Kansas City, Missouri.

Mr. Lowenstein was born March 14, 1859, in Monroe County, Tennessee, fourteen miles south of Tellico Plains. As recounted in the sketch of his parents, published elsewhere, he lived in Georgia until 1869, then in northwest Arkansas, and in southern Missouri until 1873, when the family settled in Greene County, Illinois, at Wilmington, now Patterson, and after 1877 at White Hall. Mr. Lowenstein lived on farms in Georgia, Arkansas and Missouri, attended subscription schools a few months each year, but his chief advantages were acquired in the common school at Patterson and high school at White Hall. He studied law in an office at White Hall, was admitted to the bar by the Supreme Court in 1881, and first located at Roodhouse, but soon afterward returned to White Hall. In 1884 he went out to Ottawa, Kansas, for a brief time, returning again to White Hall and in 1886 began his career at Kansas City, which has been his home except for a few months in 1892 when he lived in Memphis, Tennessee. He has made real estate and law a specialty and is regarded as an authority in that branch of the law.

Mr. Lowenstein has always had a strong inclination for literature, is familiar with a wide range of writings, ancient and modern, and as inspiration has moved him he has written much verse, but none for publication until after the beginning of the World war. Since then he has published many short poems, usually in rondeau form, which have received wide newspaper and magazine publication. One poem that measured up to the highest standards of patriotic verse and is justly included in the notable poetry of war times was his answer to the famous "In Flanders Fields" by Lieutenant Colonel John McCrea. (See below.)

Mr. Lowenstein is a York and Scottish Rite Mason and Shriner, and holds a life membership in various bodies of the order. His first wife was Rebecca C. Dempsey, of Danville, Indiana. She died July 7, 1900. On June 25, 1907, he married Mrs. Belle Van Natta Dom, of Kansas City. Mrs. Lowenstein is an accomplished artist. Mr. Lowenstein has one son, Henry Polk Lowenstein, Jr., who served as a lieutenant, junior grade, in the navy during the World war and is still in the Naval Reserve, with rank of full lieutenant, and is now engaged in law practice with his father in Kansas City.

Mr. Lowenstein is at this time preparing a history of Josiah Lamborn, attorney general of Illinois 1840-43, who was closely associated with Abraham Lincoln and many other prominent lawyers of his day.

H. P. Lowenstein, Jr., was married April 24, 1919, to Rowena Belden of Belden, California. Two children have been born to them, Henry Polk Lowenstein III, five years of age, and Helen Edna Lowenstein, three years of age.

O LET ME SLEEP IN FLANDERS FIELDS.

In Flanders Fields, O let me sleep,
And wake me not and never weep
  For me. I rest in perfect peace;
  And till all earthly strife shall cease.
I shall in silence slumber deep.

You do me wrong to stir and sweep
Away my fondest hopes and keep
  Me from my rest and just release,
    In Flanders Fields.

Disturb me not, but let me sleep
Right where I am and never weep
  Again, for I shall never cease
  To live and make my light increase,
As Time rolls on in silence deep,
  In Flanders Fields.
      —Henry Polk Lowenstein.

EDWARD BAKER LEIGH, president of the Chicago Railway Equipment Company, was born in Townsend, Massachusetts, April 13, 1853. In 1855 his parents, Dr. Edwin and Susan Scollay Leigh, moved to St. Louis, Missouri, where they established their home, and where Edward Baker Leigh received his education at the City University, and Washington University. Compelled by ill health to relinquish scholastic study at the age of fifteen, a year later he entered business life as a clerk in the St. Louis office of the Pennsylvania Railroad. In 1875 Mr. Leigh left the employ of that company to become the assistant secretary of the St. Louis Grain Elevator Company, and, shortly thereafter, took up the added duties of secretary of the East St. Louis Grain Elevator Company, an affiliated interest. However, with an acquired taste for railroad and collateral activities, Mr. Leigh reentered the railroad field in 1882, as manager of the American Brake Company. Under his direction that company was brought to a high degree of success, and was absorbed by the Westinghouse Air Brake Company.

In 1887 Mr. Leigh's attention was directed to the invention of a trussed, metal brake beam with a hollow compression member. Quickly recognizing not only the intrinsic merits of this new device, but its accompanying opportunity, which he promptly seized, a company was organized under the name of the National Hollow Brake Beam Company, with Mr. Leigh as its vice president and general manager, for its production, introduction and sale. Six years later, in 1893, to broaden the field of activity of this rapidly growing industry, Mr. Leigh organized the Chicago Railway Equipment Company, which took over the business of the National Hollow Brake Beam Company, and in addition acquired, in 1899, the businesses of the American Brake Beam Company and the Kewanee Manufacturing Company, followed, in 1902, by the acquisition of the Monarch Brake Beam Company and the brake beam business of the Sterlingworth Railway Supply Company.

The Chicago Railway Equipment Company, under Mr. Leigh's presidency and active management, has made an enviable record in its gradually broadened sphere, having acquired the Grand Rapids Malleable Works, Grand Rapids, Michigan; the Marion Malleable Iron Works, Marion, Indiana; and the Franklin Steel Works, Franklin, Pennsylvania, all owned and controlled by the parent company, and operating both as contributors of their products to it, and as producers and sellers of their varied products in their respective fields generally.

With watchful care in its days of small things, and clearly visualizing the widening scope of its possibilities, Mr. Leigh from the inception of the industry has been the leading and most constructive force in its development. The company today is not only the pioneer and the largest in its field, but commands the highest esteem in both industrial and financial circles.

Mr. Leigh is a descendant, on the paternal side, of Thomas Leigh of Dunster, Somerset, England.

Capt. Thomas (2) Leigh, his first American paternal ancestor, born in England in 1735, came to this country in 1770, and settled in Portsmouth, New Hampshire, where he died in 1815.

Major Thomas (3) Leigh, son of Capt. Thomas (2) Leigh, was born April 13, 1775.

Dr. Edwin Leigh, son of Major Thomas (3) Leigh, and father of Edward Baker Leigh, was born in South Berwick, Maine, September 10, 1815, and died at the age of seventy-five years, April 9, 1890, at Stoneleigh Ranch, Kerr County, Texas, while visiting a son. Doctor Leigh was a man of rare mental endowment, of prophetic vision, and with an inherent love of study and research. A deep thinker and a clear analyst, his contributions to the thought and to the literature of his day, while too numerous to record, won for him a distinguished place in his chosen fields of activity.

Apart from his immediate business interests, but springing from them, Edward Baker Leigh has devoted much time and thought to the many problems and to the complex conditions surrounding and affecting industry in general, and especially to such as bear upon the great railway system of this country. From close observation over a period of many years Mr. Leigh evolved and demonstrated the accuracy of the theory that "Railway Buying Measures General Business Prosperity." This doctrine has been presented from time to time in the forms of printed pamphlets, addresses before national trade bodies, and to congressional committees charged with the consideration of pending legislation. These and other contributions of a similar character, together with his standing as an industrial leader of high aim and fine purpose, have brought Mr. Leigh authoritative recognition as one of the soundest of advisers on the industrial and commercial problems of the day.

Among his affiliations are: Membership on the executive committee of the Railway Business Association; director and vice president of the National Association of Manufacturers; member of the National Industrial Conference Board—all organizations of national scope and character, whose common purpose is that of constructive thought and action for the betterment of national industrial and commercial conditions. Mr. Leigh's club memberships are: Chicago Athletic, Illinois Athletic, Press and Union League, Chicago; St. Louis Club, Detroit Club, City Club of New York City. He also has been a member of St. Louis Lodge, Benevolent and Protective Order of Elks, since 1882.

Mr. Leigh married, November 15, 1876, Clara Norton Furness, daughter of Edwin Leigh Furness, Esq., Furnessville, Indiana. His only surviving son is Edwin F. Leigh, now general manager of the Marion Malleable Iron Works.

THOMAS McCLELLAND was one of the lofty men in the recent educational history of Illinois. For a quarter of a century his work and the influence of his character enriched the scholastic atmosphere of Knox College, of which he was president and president emeritus. He died at his home in Galesburg January 29, 1926, when in his eightieth year.

He was born at Quilly, in County Derry, Ireland, May 1, 1846, son of William and Margaret (Smiley) McClelland. His father during his life in Ireland followed farming and school teaching, and in 1849 brought his family to America, setting at Catasauqua, Pennsylvania, where he had contracts for moving ore for the steel mills. Ten years later, in 1859, he moved to a farm near Mendon in Adams County, Illinois.

Thomas McClelland was about thirteen years of age when the family came to Illinois. He was the youngest of thirteen children. After the common schools his education was dependent upon his own efforts. He attended the academy at Denmark, Iowa. In 1875 he was graduated with the A. B. degree from Oberlin College. which in 1883 made him Master of Arts. In the meantime he attended Oberlin Theological Seminary, Union Theological Seminary, and in 1880 was graduated from the Andover Theological Seminary. In the ministry of the Congregational Church and as a teacher he spent half a century. From 1880 to 1891 he was professor of philosophy in Tabor College, Iowa. At the conclusion of his service there in 1891 Tabor gave him the honorary degree Doctor of Divinity. From 1891 to 1900 he was president of Pacific University at Forest Grove, Oregon. Doctor McClelland was called to the presidency of Knox College at Galesburg in 1900. He served actively in that position until 1917, and for the last ten years of his life was president emeritus. So far as his strength and health permitted he kept in close touch with the affairs of the college until the end.

The University of Illinois in 1905 gave him the honorary degree Doctor of Laws, and he was similarly honored by Grinnell College of Iowa in 1915. He acted as trustee of the Carnegie Foundation for the Advancement of Teaching from its foundation in 1905 until 1917. He was a corporate member of the American Board for Foreign Missions from 1891 to 1915. He was a republican in politics, a member of the honorary scholastic fraternity Phi Beta Kappa, the University Club of Chicago and the Galesburg Club.

Doctor McClelland married at Denmark, Iowa, August 19, 1880, Miss Harriet Caroline Day, daughter of Kellogg and Mary (Ingals) Day. Her father was a teacher and missionary, and was teaching in the old Dwight Mission in Indian Territory when Mrs. McClelland was born. Doctor and Mrs. McClelland had three children: Kellogg Day, who married Jean N. Campbell; Cochran Bruce, who married Helen Moir; and Miss Ruth Marjorie McClelland.

CHARLES HEFTER is a Kankakee merchant. His early business career was spent in Chicago, but for many years he has been one of the proprietors of a store patronized by all of Kankakee County. In a different realm Mr. Hefter has something perhaps more than a national fame. His name is known wherever the game of checkers is played. For a number of years he was Illinois state checker champion.

Mr. Hefter was born at Mobile, Alabama, November 28, 1860, son of Louis and Ricca (Goldstein) Hefter. His father was born at Neustadt, in eastern Germany, and came to the United States about 1840, landing at New York City. He was a tailor, and established a clothing and tailoring business at Mobile, Alabama. He left there during the Civil war and moved to Chicago, his wife and family following him a year later. He and a brother conducted a clothing business in Chicago. Their establishment was burned in the great fire of 1871, but after that he continued as a retail and wholesale merchant for many years. He died in 1897 and his wife, in 1893.

Charles Hefter was a small child when his parents moved to Chicago, where he attended grammar and high schools to the age of seventeen. He then became office boy in a wholesale clothing store, also kept books, and in 1893 he and his brother and cousin formed a company to engage in the wholesale clothing business. Mr. Hefter on February 1, 1907, engaged in business at Kankakee, and since then has been one of the proprietors of the Chicago Store, a general department store. He is treasurer of the company, while Fred Hefter is president, E. Mock is vice president and B. E. Gast, secretary. The company in 1916 erected a three-story brick building, a part of it being 125 by 95 feet in dimensions, and another portion, 145 feet. It is located on Schuyler Avenue and Merchant Street.

Mr. Hefter married, January 24, 1884, Miss Emma Herzog, a native of Chicago and daughter of Ignatz Herzog. Her father was a native of Hungary and was one of the pioneer furriers of Chicago. Mr. and Mrs. Hefter have three children: Mattie, widow of Samuel Spielberger; Fred C.; and Edna, wife of Harry Spielberger, all residing in Kankakee.

Mr. Hefter has been a director of the Kankakee Chamber of Commerce. He is a republican, a Rotarian, a member of the B. P. O. Elks, Kankakee Country Club, Covenant Club of Chicago, Chicago Chess and Whist Club, and honorary member of the Chicago Checker Club. He was state champion checker player of Illinois for a quarter of a century. His home is at 1334 East Court Street. Mrs. Hefter is active in various social clubs of the city.

HOMER HARRISON DAVIS, Doctor of Chiropractic, at Kankakee, is a native of Illinois, born at Bloomington in 1893.

His parents were Harry H. and Margaret (Gambon) Davis, his father a native of Mahomet, Illinois, and his mother of Bloomington. His father was in the undertaking business and died in 1921. The widowed mother now resides at Kankakee, at 310 East Court Street.

Doctor Davis lived at Kankakee from the age of five years, attended public schools there, and after high school continued his literary education in the Grand Prairie Seminary at Onarga. Doctor Davis in June, 1922, graduated from the National College of Chiropractic at Chicago. For eighteen months he followed his profession at Battle Creek, Michigan, and while there completed a course in the Battle Creek Sanitarium. Since then he has been a busy member of his profession in Kankakee.

He married, in 1917, Lucille Gardner, a native of Battle Creek, Michigan. Doctor Davis is a member of the Masonic fraternity, B. P. O. Elks, Mystic Workers of the World, and is a republican and a Presbyterian.

REV. JOHN SHERIDAN MORRIS, pastor of St. Felicitas Church on Eighty-first Place in Chicago, is a native of Illinois and during a quarter of a century of earnest labor in the Chicago diocese has become widely known in several Catholic communities.

Father Morris was born at Beardstown, Illinois, July 13, 1871, son of John and Catherine (Sheridan) Morris. His parents were natives of County Cork, Ireland, his father born December 26, 1835, and his mother in 1842. They were married October 5, 1864, and were the parents of seven children, two of whom died in infancy while four grew to adult age. John Morris was well educated, became a surveyor and civil engineer and in 1865 came to the United States landing at New York City. Subsequently he was in Chicago and Shreveport, Illinois, as a railroad man and for a number of years acted as railroad agent at Beardstown, Illinois. He died March 9, 1912, and his wife on July 29, 1884.

John Sheridan Morris attended public schools between the ages of six and nine and from 1880 to 1884 was a pupil in the Holy Family parochial schools. Subsequently through seminary and college he completed his classical and theological courses and on June 9, 1900, was ordained a priest. From June, 1900, to March, 1901, he served as assistant pastor of the Holy Angel Church in Chicago. He was pastor of St. Catherine's Church from 1901 to 1909, and was pastor of other churches, including St. Albilba Mission at 8061 Stony Island Avenue in Chicago. On July 1, 1920, he was assigned to St. Felicitas Church at Eighty-first Place and Blackstone Avenue and has since built a handsome church, school and convent, the buildings being dedicated on Sunday, April 27, 1924. In his parish at the beginning he only had fifty families, while at this writing about 230 families are communicants of St. Felicitas.

JOSEPH S. WALDMAN, M. D. While he has earned wide recognition through his success as a general practitioner of medicine and surgery in Williamson County during the ten years he has been located at Herrin, Doctor Waldman has been particularly successful in treatment of the eye, ear, nose and throat, and as a specialist his name promises achievements of the very highest order, since he is still a very young man.

He comes of a family and ancestry noted for earnestness and thoroughness in everything they do and undertake. His father, Samuel Waldman, was born in the historic city of Cracow, then in Austrian Poland, now Poland, in 1856. He lived there and attended school until the age of fourteen. Then his father, Leo Waldman, who was a man of the better class and hoped for better conditions for his children in America, came to this country, landing at New Orleans and coming up the Mississippi and crossing overland to Kansas. Leo Waldman subsequently settled in Jefferson County, Missouri, and was a prosperous farmer and business man there. He lived out the last years of his life at St. Louis, where he died at the age of seventy-three. Samuel Waldman after coming to this country had private instructors and was rewarded with success in his effort to master the English language. He remained a student of literature, politics and affairs to the time of his death and was constantly seeking to improve his own talents. For forty years he was a traveling salesman out of St. Louis, covering the entire south and middle west, at first as representative of optical goods houses and later was in business for himself with headquarters at St. Louis. His sincerity and upright manner brought him a large business, which he carried on until his death in August, 1923, at St. Louis. Samuel Waldman married Caroline Hertz, who was born on the Rhine at Mayenz, Germany, and was sixteen years of age when she accompanied a married sister to America, her sister's family first locating at Indianapolis, Indiana, and afterwards in St. Louis. Samuel Waldman and wife had two sons and two daughters: Joseph S.; Albert; Rose, wife of John Goldsteni of St. Louis; and Anna, wife of Edward Lustig of St. Louis. All these children were born in the city of St. Louis.

Dr. Joseph S. Waldman was born April 11, 1885. He was educated in grade schools, graduated from the Central High School of St. Louis, and followed that with a business course in Jones and Henderson's Business College in that city. During the winter of 1906-07 he studied in the St. Louis Dental College. During these years of school attendance he worked on the side, showing his native thrift and enterprise. In 1910 he entered the medical department of St. Louis University. His energy and mental abilities attracted the attention of F. C. Pauley of St. Louis, well known for his interest in bright young men and who had founded a medical scholarship, and this scholarship was awarded to young Waldman. He continued his studies of medicine in St. Louis University from 1910 until graduated in 1914. He was an interne at the St. Louis City Hospital from July, 1914, to January, 1915, and then received an appointment in the Out-patient Department of the Skin and Cancer Clinics of Washington University, a position he held six months. Doctor Waldman first located for private practice in Jefferson County, Nebraska, but remained only until the spring of 1917, when he yielded to the wishes of his own family and his wife's family to locate in the vicinity of St. Louis. In August, 1917, he accordingly established his home and office at Herrin in Williamson County, Illinois.

Almost from the first Doctor Waldman has shown unusual proficiency in handling cases involving the eye and the ear, and so far as practical he has specialized in those lines and concentrated his advanced studies. In April, 1922, he received the appointment, after taking the civil service examination, as resident surgeon at the Illinois Charitable Eye and Ear Infirmary in Chicago, and remained with that institution until September, 1923. He then returned to Herrin and established his present offices and laboratories in the New Herrin Building. Doctor Waldman is a member of the County and State Medical Associations.

He married in June, 1916, Miss Eva Shapiro, a St. Louis girl, daughter of Elias and Leah Shapiro. They have three children, Joneva Sylvia, June and Shyrle.

JOHN T. JOYCE, of the firm McCauley & Joyce, real estate and insurance at Chicago, has proved a vigorous young leader in political affairs in his native city and is now a member of the Illinois State Senate.

He was born in Chicago in 1894. His parents, Thomas J. and Anna (Carlin) Joyce, were born in Ireland, were married after coming to America, and have made their home in Chicago for nearly half a century. Senator Joyce still lives with his parents and practically all his life has been spent in one community in Chicago. His home is at 227 Oak Street, in what was the old Twenty-first ward, now the Forty-second Ward.

After attending the parochial and public schools and the Lane Technical High School, John T. Joyce engaged in business until the World war. On December 8, 1917, he enlisted for service in the United States navy, and was on duty at the Great Lakes Naval Training Station until honorably discharged in December, 1918. Since then he has made himself a factor in business and is a member of one of the leading real estate and insurance firms, with offices in the Wrigley Building.

Mr. Joyce, in 1920, was elected to represent the Twenty-ninth Senatorial District in the General Assembly, serving one term, and in 1922 was elected a member of the State Senate from the same district. He was the youngest

J. S. Waldman, M. D.

state senator in the Fifty-fourth General Assembly. During the session of 1923 he was chairman of the committee on parks, boulevards and playgrounds. In that capacity he introduced the bill providing for expanded parks and driveways on the North Shore in Chicago. He was also identified with other legislations, particularly such as affected the city of Chicago. Mr. Joyce is a member of the American Legion, and is affiliated with the B. P. O. Elks, Knights of Columbus and the Owls.

JOEL CHURCHILL FITCH is a descendant of ancient and noble English families both paternally and maternally. The Fitch family and the Richardson family in the early part of the seventeenth century sent their most fearless and intrepid sons and daughters to brave the perils and hardships of the then little known America and to take an active part in the progress and advancement of what was destined to become the United States of America. This the scions of both families did to the fullest degree and today the records of their achievements form an integral of the early history of this great country.

The Arms of the Fitch family are:
Arms—Vert, a chevron between three leopards' heads, or
Crest—a leopard's head caboshed, or in the mouth, a sword proper, hilt gules.
Motto—*Nulla dies sine linea.* (No day without lines.)

The Rev. James Fitch and his brother, Thomas Fitch, were the immigrant ancestors of the Fitch family in America. A great grandson of Thomas Fitch was colonial governor of Connecticut from 1754 to 1766.

I. Rev. James Fitch, son of Thomas and Anna (Pew) Fitch, of England, who came to America in 1638, was ordained minister at Saybrook and later removed with his congregation to Norwich. He was one of the most prominent clergymen of the colony. He married (first) Abagail Whitefield and (second) Precilla Mason, a descendant of Capt. John Mason. To this union were born several children, including James, of whom further.

II. Major James Fitch, son of Rev. James and Abagail (Whitefield) Fitch, was the founder of Canterbury, Connecticut and for many years was one of the most influential men of the colony. He married (first) a sister of his father's second wife, and (second) Mrs. Alice (Bradford) Adams, widow of the Reverend Adams of Dedham, Massachusetts, and a granddaughter of Governor Bradford of Plymouth Colony. He gave the glass and nails for the first building of Yale College and later, in 1701, rescued that institution from financial embarrassment by a grant of seven hundred and thirty-six acres of land. He was one of the leaders in the movement that deposed Governor Andras and restored the "Charter Government" of the colony. An extended and interesting account of Major Fitch and his public services to the colony is contained in Larned's "Historical Gleanings." Of the latter marriage were born several children, including Daniel, of whom further.

III. Daniel Fitch, son of Major James and Alice (Bradford-Adams) Fitch, married Anna Cook, of a notable family of Windham County and a descendant of Stephen Hopkins, a signer of the Mayflower Pact. Among the children of Daniel and Anna (Cook) Fitch was William Fitch, of whom further.

IV. William Fitch, son of Daniel and Anna (Cook) Fitch, was born at Canterbury in 1720. He married Mary Paine, a daughter of the Rev. Elisha Paine, of Canterbury, a descendant of Stephen Hopkins and prior to entering the ministry was one of the prominent lawyers of Connecticut. Mr. Paine became the leader of the "Separate Movement" in the Congregational Church and was thrice imprisoned for his advocacy of doctrines and principles which are now accepted as fundamental in that denomination. To them were born several children, among whom was Elisha, of whom further.

V. Elisha Fitch, a son of William and Mary (Paine) Fitch, was born at Canterbury, Connecticut, May 6, 1749. He settled at Pawlet, Vermont, where he enlisted in the Revolutionary war and served throughout the campaign against General Burgoyne. He was one of the organizers of the Congregational Church at Pawlet, and a selectman of the town. In 1793 he removed to Scipio, Cayuga County, New York, and was prominent in the public affairs of the county during the next twenty years. Elisha Fitch married Rachel Kellum, and to them were born nine children, one of them being Chester, of whom further.

VI. Chester Fitch, son of Elisha and Rachel (Kellum) Fitch, was born at Pawlet, Vermont, in 1786. He married in Cayuga County, New York, October 6, 1811, Elizabeth Richardson, a daughter of Judge John Richardson, of Pennsylvania and New York. (See Richardson V, infra.) They removed to Crawford County, Illinois, in 1816 and founded the village of York, now in Clark County. This marriage united the two old English families of Fitch and Richardson. Of this union there were several children, including George Richardson, of whom further.

VII. George Richardson Fitch, son of Chester and Elizabeth (Richardson) Fitch, was born in York, Clark County, Illinois, October 29, 1834. He attended Wabash College and Hanover College in Indiana, graduated from the Law School at Cincinnati, Ohio, and removed to Vandalia, Illinois, where he died in 1866. He was an effective public speaker and acquired a high standing as one of the younger members of the southern Illinois bar. He married Emily Churchill, a daughter of Joel and Eliza Churchill, of Albion, Edwards County, Illinois, who were among the earliest of the English settlers of that county. Emily Churchill was born at Albion December 16, 1839, educated at Kalorama, Bishop Smith's School for young ladies, near Louisville, Kentucky, and at Dr. Beatty's Seminary at Steubenville, Ohio, and died in Chicago, Illinois, August 24, 1918. To this union were born (1) Edward Churchill Fitch, (2) Joel Churchill Fitch, of whom further, and (3) George Richardson Fitch, who died in infancy. Edward Churchill Fitch has attained high rank in his profession as a lawyer. He was educated in the public schools of Albion, Illinois, and Evansville, Indiana, and graduated from the University of Indiana in 1885 and received the degree of Master of Arts from the same institution in 1891. He was admitted to the bar of Illinois in 1888; was county superintendent of schools of Edwards County, Illinois, from 1886 to 1890; was assistant city attorney of Chicago from 1904 to 1913, having charge of the Appellate and Supreme Court Division of that office; was a member of the House of Representatives of the Forty-fifth General Assembly of Illinois from the Thirteenth Senatorial District from 1907 to 1909; was appointed assistant attorney general of Illinois in 1917, and from thence hitherto has held and now (1926) holds that office. He is a republican and an effective public speaker, and has frequently been called to stump the middle west in behalf of that party. He is a member of the Phi Kappa Psi college fraternity, a Mason, a Knights Templar, a Shriner, an Elk, a member of the Sons of the American Revolution and of the Society of Mayflower Descendants. He married Alice S. Soringer October 4, 1887. Of this union one child, a daughter, Helen Churchill Fitch, was born July 1, 1888. She was married to Clark Webster Gould October 24, 1912, and they have two children, Clark Webster Gould and Janet Churchill Gould.

VIII. Joel Churchill Fitch, son of George Richardson and Emily (Churchill) Fitch and a representative of the eighth generation of the American branch of the Fitch family and a lineal descendant of three ancient families long seated in England, was born at Vandalia, Illinois, November 29, 1863. His early education was obtained in the public schools of Albion, Edwards County, Illinois, following which he entered the preparatory department of the University of Indiana, from which he graduated in 1882 and then entered the University of Indiana, from which institution he graduated with the class of 1886 with the degree of Bachelor of Philosophy. After his graduation he returned to Albion, Illinois, and studied law in the law office of Judge J. M. Campbell and was admitted to the bar of Illinois in August, 1888. After his admission to the bar he practiced his profession at Albion. He served as city attorney of that city until his election as state's attorney. In 1896 he was elected state's attorney of Edwards County and was reelected in 1900 and in 1904 he voluntarily retired from that office and resumed the general practice of law. In 1906 he was appointed assistant attorney general of Illinois, and held that office until 1913. He then resumed the general practice of law and frequently represented the insurance department of Illinois in legal matters connected with that department. He was elected judge of Edwards County in 1918, reelected in 1922 and was again elected to that office November 2, 1926. He is frequently called by the chief justice to serve as judge of the Municipal Court of Chicago and has spent a large part of his time serving in that capacity. By reason of his broad experience and ability in handling intricate and important legal matters he has attained high rank in his profession. He is a member of Hermitage Lodge No. 356, Ancient Free and Accepted Masons, Albion Illinois; of Albion Chapter No. 237, Royal Arch Masons; of Mt. Carmel Commandery No. 82, Knights Templars, Mt. Carmel, Illinois; a thirty-second degree Mason of the Springfield (Illinois) Consistory and a Shriner, being a member of Ansar Temple, Springfield, Illinois. He is a member of the Phi Kappa Psi college fraternity, a member of the Sons of the American Revolution and of the Society of the Mayflower Descendants and of the Episcopal Church. He is a republican and takes an active part in political and civic affairs. He is a bachelor and resides in the old homestead acquired by his maternal grandfather in 1823 and maintains it now as it has been maintained for more than a hundred years, as the traditional gathering place of the Churchill kin.

The Richardson Line:

I. Samuel Richardson, the progenitor of the American branch of the Richardson family, was a stalwart and dominant Quaker, born and reared in old England. He came to America while a young man and settled at Philadelphia, Pennsylvania. Two theories exist concerning him: One is that he went directly to Jamaica and because of an earthquake removed to Pennsylvania; the other, that he was first a settler with William Penn and then went to Jamaica and later returned to join Penn's Colony. He became a well known judge, legislator and councillor for the early settlement and was a member of the Colonial Assembly of Pennsylvania at various times for most of a period of thirty years. At one time his seat in the Governor's Council was declared vacant because he disapproved of some of the policies of the deputy governor. He immediately became a candidate to succeed himself and was vindicated by reelection. He is the subject of an interesting sketch entitled "Samuel Richardson, Councillor, Judge and Legislator of the Olden Time," by Governor Samuel W. Pennypacker, in a volume entitled "Historical Biographical Sketches." Samuel Richardson died June 10, 1719, leaving three daughters and one son, Joseph, of whom further.

II. Joseph Richardson, son of Samuel and Eleanor Richardson, became a prominent land owner. He married, in 1696, Elizabeth Bevan, a daughter of John Bevan, a noted Quaker preacher and his wife, Barbara Aubrey, and had seven children, one of whom was Edward, of whom further.

III. Edward Richardson, son of Joseph and Elizabeth (Bevan) Richardson, was born at or near Philadelphia, Pennsylvania. His religion was Quaker, that of his ancestors, and for years he sat at the head of the Providence meeting. He married Ann Jones. They had five sons and two daughters, one of the sons being William, of whom further.

IV. William Richardson, son of Edward and Ann (Jones) Richardson, was born near Philadelphia, Pennsylvania, and after middle age settled at Levanna, New York, where he died February 20, 1823, aged ninety-two years. He was married three times; by his first and second wives he had ten children and five by his third wife, who was Elizabeth (Beck) Richardson. This line descends through John Richardson, a child of the first marriage.

V. John Richardson, son of William Richardson, became equally as well known and prominent in public affairs as his pioneer great-great-grandfather. He became a judge of the Court of Common Pleas of Onondago County, New York, and was a representative and also a senator of the State Legislature of New York. Through his eloquence and indefatigable work the bill passed which made the Erie Canal an actuality, and he dug the first spade full of earth in the construction of the first canal of that system. In the year 1816 he moved to Crawford County, Illinois, and founded the town of York, now in Clark County which was for many years a thriving and bustling community but which has declined until now it is little more than a deserted village. In the year 1829 he published a book entitled "A New Theory of the Causes of the Motion of the Planetary Bodies belonging to the Solar System" printed at Vincennes, Indiana. While his theory was not in accord with the scientific men of that day and the book is now obsolete, it indicates at least a glimmering of some of the discoveries of the last ten or twelve years. Judge John Richardson is buried at York, Illinois. He married Hannah Fisher a daughter of George Fisher, who founded the town of Middletown, Pennsylvania, and whose great-grandfather, John Fisher, came from England in the ship "Welcome" with the illustrious William Penn. George Fisher married Hannah Chamberlain, a daughter of Jonas Chamberlain, of Salisbury Township, Lancaster County, Pennsylvania. The children of John and Hannah (Fisher) Richardson are as follows: Elizabeth, born December 14, 1789, died at York September 25, 1869; married Chester Fitch (see Fitch VI, supra); John, George, Nancy, Charlotte, Clarinda, Roxetta, Mary, Sarah Julia and William.

Elizabeth Richardson, wife of Chester Fitch, was the great-great-granddaughter of John Bevan and his wife, Barbara Aubrey. In a book entitled "Thomas Family as Descended from David and Anna Noble Thomas," published in 1907, a copy of which is in the Congressional Library at Washington, William Thomas Lyle has traced the pedigree of John Bevan back to Edward III of England and that of Barbara Aubrey back to Alfred the Great, Charlemagne and William The Conqueror. Mr. Lyle cites a number of ancient records and reputable genealogical works as authority for these pedigrees.

AXEL FLINT, president of the Joliet Calendar Company, manufacturers of art calendars and other commercial printing, has been a resident of that city for many years, and was formerly in the dairy business.

Mr. Flint was born at Lands Krona, Sweden, in 1864, son of Nels and Gertrude (Nelson) Flint. His mother died in Sweden, and in 1881 the father came to America. He was a stone quarry worker and lived at Lemont, Illinois, for a time, but in the fall of 1883 removed to Edmondson County, Kentucky, where he bought land and farmed. Later returning to Illinois, he was again at Lemont, but about 1889 settled in Joliet, where he died in 1913.

Axel Flint attended common schools in Sweden and also in Illinois, and from the early age of nine years had a working experience as a farm boy in his native country. In 1883 he accompanied his father to Kentucky, but in 1884 returned to Illinois and for a year and a half worked in the mills at Lockport, Will County. For one year he was with C. M. Sprague in Du Page County, thus acquiring his first knowledge of the dairy business. Later he drove a delivery wagon at Joliet for Mr. Sprague, and subsequently, in association with his brothers, engaged in the wholesale and retail milk business as distributors. This became the Flint Sanitary Milk Company. Mr. Axel Flint sold his interest in 1916 and has since been president of the Joliet Calendar Company, with a complete general printing establishment, specializing in the manufacture of art calendars. Mr. C. H. Peterson is secretary of the company, while Mr. Flint is its president and treasurer.

Mr. Flint, who has never married, is a member of the Lutheran Church, belongs to the Joliet Chamber of Commerce, the Knights of the Maccabees, and in politics is an independent voter.

HENRY PINKNEY BIGGS, whose son, John D. Biggs, is the present judge of the County Court of Bond County, was for many years one of the large land owners and substantial farmers and citizens of that county.

He was born in Callaway County, Kentucky, June 15, 1847, son of David and Mary Elizabeth (Green) Biggs. Both parents were natives of Tennessee and were married in 1829, after which they moved to Kentucky, where David Biggs engaged in farming and stock raising. His first wife died when her son Henry Pinkney was only three months old. Later, in 1850, he married Mary Elizabeth Phillips. In 1855 the family left Kentucky and traveled by ox team and wagon to St. Clair County, Missouri, where David Biggs entered 320 acres of government land. He lived there until 1863, when, during the Civil war, he moved to Macoupin County, Illinois, and later in the same year to Bond County. David Biggs died in that county in 1865 and is buried in McKendree Chapel at Tamalco. After his death his widow returned to the old homestead in St. Clair County, Missouri, and lived there until her death.

Henry Pinkney Biggs was eight years old when the family located in St. Clair County, Missouri. As a boy there for several years he attended school conducted in a log cabin. After the family moved to Illinois he had no opportunity to attend school until 1864, when he became a student in the Tamalco Township School. In spite of lack of early advantages and the necessity of making his own way in the world he achieved more than ordinary success, proving a good business man and capable and honorable in all his relationships. He owned and operated about 1500 acres of farming land in Bond County. He retired from business in 1909 and thereafter lived in Greenville until his death in 1922.

Henry Pinkney Biggs was nineteen years old when, on September 6, 1866, he married Miss Delphia Holsberry. Her father, John Holsberry, was born in Indiana and was an early settler in Bond County. Mrs. Biggs died in 1900. They were the parents of four children: Alice Eveline, deceased; Lillie F., now Mrs. Iva Whitford; Elizabeth Pauline, who is Mrs. W. E. Taylor, of Pensacola, Florida; and Judge John David, of Greenville.

JOHN DAVID BIGGS, judge of the County Court of Bond County, was born and reared in that county and he has been practicing law at Greenville since 1911.

He was born near Tamalco, Bond County, February 23, 1888, son of Henry P. and Delphia M. (Holsberry) Biggs. Some of the details of the family history are given in a sketch of his father preceding this. Judge Biggs grew up on the home farm in Tamalco Township, where his father was one of the leading farmers and land owners. He attended public school there, and during 1904-05 attended Greenville College, and in 1907 graduated from Whipple Academy at Jacksonville, Illinois. He then entered the law department of the University of Illinois, in 1907, and was graduated with the LL. B. degree in 1911. While attending university he took the examinations for the bar at Chicago in 1910 and passed and was admitted to the bar, but returned to complete his law course and graduate at the university.

He at once engaged in practice at Greenville, and in 1912 won the democratic nomination and was elected state's attorney. He was state's attorney until 1916. On retiring from office he bought the law library and practice of Clarence E. Hoiles, the well known Greenville banker, and has been intrusted with the management of many important interests. In 1922 he was elected county judge, and in 1926 received the honor of having his name placed on both the democratic and republican tickets for election to that office, and will be elected county judge without opposition for 1926 to 1930. Judge Biggs in 1921 was democratic nominee for the office of circuit judge, being the youngest man ever nominated for that position in this circuit. He served as city attorney of Greenville from 1918 to 1920.

During the World war Judge Biggs was county food administrator and member of the Legal Advisory Board. In addition to his routine of duties in Bond County he is frequently called to Chicago to act as a special judge in the Cook County courts. He is president of the Bond County Bar Association, member of the Illinois State Bar Association, member of the Masonic Lodge and Eastern Star, Greenville Lodge No. 245, Independent Order of Odd Fellows and the Encampment, and the Greenville Country Club. His chief recreation is golf.

Judge Biggs married at Greenville, October 4, 1913, Miss Mabel Grace Davis, daughter of John H. and Paulina Davis, of an old family of Bond County. Mrs. Biggs is a member of the Delphian Society, the Eastern Star and the Methodist Church. They have one child, Delphia Pauline, born in 1914.

WILLIAM FRANKLIN LODGE, general contractor, was born and has spent most of his life at Monticello, and for many years has been actively identified with nearly every important material as well as cultural organization in that locality.

He was born at Monticello, November 12, 1868. His father, William E. Lodge, was born at Mount Hope, Ohio, December 8, 1834, was admitted to the Illinois bar in 1858, and for over forty years practiced law. He died at Monticello September 24, 1901. His parents were Benjamin F. and Julia A. (Brooks) Lodge. William E. Lodge married, January 30, 1868, Frances Ann Piatt, a daughter of William A. Piatt, and a granddaughter of James A. Piatt, the Illinois pioneer for whom this country is named. Frances Ann Piatt was born May 10, 1843, and died September 16, 1895.

William F. Lodge was liberally educated himself and has always been interested in educational movements and causes. He attended the University of Illinois during 1889-90, and in 1893 graduated from the law department of Northwestern University at Evanston. His experience as a practicing attorney covered only one year at Monticello. As a young man he was interested in brick manufacture. His chief business experience has been general contracting, including the building of hard roads, and he has constructed many miles of Illinois hard roads during the present century. For four years he was president of the Illinois Association of Highway and Municipal Contractors. Mr. Lodge built the first electric light plant in Monticello. He built and still owns the first telephone exchange of Piatt County, and he also owns a large amount of farming land near Monticello.

Mr. Lodge served two terms as a school director, has been president of the Community Club and Cemetery Association at Monticello and has been a member of the various social organizations in his community. In 1924-25 he was president of the University of Illinois Dads Association. He is a member of the Illinois State Historical Society and the State Horticultural Society. In politics he acts as an independent, believing that a certain number of citizens have a duty to perform in casting their ballot independently to preserve the regular parties from atrophy.

Mr. Lodge married at Monticello, January 19, 1904, Miss Sarah Elizabeth Tinder, daughter of Lineas B. and Elizabeth (Babcock) Tinder. They have one son, William Tinder Lodge, born July 4, 1905.

REBECCA HARLAN BRICE KAUFFMAN, whose home for many years has been at Oregon, was born and brought up near the Susquehanna River in Pennsylvania, and married Horace Greeley Kauffman, whose home was at Greencastle in the Cumberland Valley of the same state. They had been classmates in school and their wedding journey brought them to the middle west. The first year they taught school at Mount Morris in Ogle County, living on a salary of sixty dollars a month, and afterwards they taught at Batavia in Kane County, spending their vacations in Chicago studying, reading law and taking business courses. While living at the edge of Mount Morris their son Harlan Brice Kauffman was born. Later the call of the river drew them to Rock River at Oregon, where they built the house on the block of ground just south of the Fair Grounds, where they lived thirteen happy

John D. Biggs

years. While there Mrs. Kauffman, urged by her husband, became president in 1901 of the Oregon Woman's Council, which was being organized by some of the progressive women of that city. Through this council she effected some valuable work in saving the "White Pine Forest of Ogle County." Mrs. Kauffman has been a keen student of nature since girlhood, having been trained an alert observer by her mother and her step-father at their home in Sunbury, Pennsylvania. Mr. Kauffman shared with her an enthusiastic love of the out-or-doors. A similar interest has been a strong characteristic of their son, who in his term in the Illinois Legislature of 1921, representing Ogle County, presented and worked assiduously for two bills to establish state parks for Illinois. The son at the beginning of his Junior year transferred his studies from Lake Forest College to Stanford University on the Pacific Coast, and the parents also went to California in 1910, remaining until the son graduated from Stanford. In 1912 they again took up their residence at Oregon.

To the Kauffmans as to many others the World war was an unsettling period. The son went to the Second Officers' Training Camp at Fort Sheridan August 27, 1917. His father had preceded him by two days to take the place of the dean of the Pullman Free School of Manual Training at Pullman, Chicago, the dean having also entered the Officers' Training Camp. The son received his commission as first lieutenant and was assigned, December 10, 1917, to Camp Lee, and on September 1, 1918, sailed for overseas, being in France, Germany and England before he returned. He was in the army altogether two years.

Early in the war Mrs. Kauffman, as chairman of the Committee of National Defense, organized Ogle County until at the time of the armistice she had under her twenty-five township chairmen and fifteen county department chairmen. She also rented the law office at Oregon and worked with her husband in Chicago. It was overwork under the heavy strain of war responsibilities that sapped the strength of Mr. Kauffman and resulted in his death January 8, 1920. He is buried in Riverview Cemetery, Oregon. After his return from the war the son began the practice of law, having been admitted to the bar in the winter of 1917, while teaching Latin at Mount Morris College. The son is now postmaster of Oregon.

After the death of her husband Mrs. Kauffman returned to Chicago and took a position in the English department of the Pullman Free School of Manual Training, and has continued that work ever since. She is a member of the Republican Woman's Club of Chicago, has been a member of the Prairie Club of that city, is a member of the English Club of Greater Chicago, a charter member of the Illinois Forestry Association, member of the State Art Extension Committee, and member of the Illinois Audubon Society. She and her son keep their home at Oregon, not far from Rock River. Her love for the country has never abated, and next to being a lawyer her preference would be for farming. She and Mr. Kauffman wrote the historical part of the Ogle County history published in 1909, and for years they carried on a joint study of local and state history. Mrs. Kauffman has written for a number of years and supplied pictures for the State Arbor Bird Day and Memorial Day annual publications. The Illinois State Historical Society has printed in one of its annual numbers a paper by her on all that she could learn about Governor Ford in Ogle County, and the Illinois State Horticultural Society has in one of its annual volumes a paper on "Wild Flowers and Their Preservation," read by Mrs. Kauffman at the society's meeting at Princeton, Illinois.

ALBERT H. SEVERINGHAUS. The work of the successful business men of the big cities is necessarily steady and progressive. In many cases the intelligence and energies of an individual have been centered in a certain line of endeavor, and this has been the case with Albert H. Severinghaus, president of the G. A. R. Laundry of Chicago, who has been a consistent and persevering worker since boyhood, and who since 1893 has been identified with his present line of work. Likewise he has found the time to devote to numerous public movements which have established him firmly in the confidence of his fellow-citizens.

Mr. Severinghaus was born at Batesville, Ripley County, Indiana, in 1870, a son of Judge J. H. and Louise (Newkirk) Severinghaus. His father, who was prominent in his locality as judge of one of the township courts in Ripley County for about twenty years, died when Albert H. was still a boy, and in order to assist the family income he started to work when he was but fourteen years of age, leaving his widowed mother to go to Dayton, Kentucky, where he secured employment on a dairy farm. This vocation was not to his liking, however, and as soon as he could make arrangements he went to Indianapolis, where he learned the trade of machinist in the plant of the Dean Brothers Steam Pump Works. At the age of eighteen years, in 1888, he came to Chicago, which city has been his home ever since and the scene of his success. During the five years that followed his arrival he worked at his trade as a machinist, but being ambitious to be the proprietor of a business of his own, at the age of twenty-three years, in 1893, took the venture of establishing a laundry, the G. A. R., located at 3122 Armitage Avenue. His initial venture was necessarily a modest one, as his capital was small, but he has since developed this into one of the best and most successful enterprises of its kind in the city. Mr. Severinghaus has become widely known in the trade, is an ex-president of the Illinois State Laundrymen's Association and a member of the National Association of Laundrymen. He bears the well-merited reputation of being a man of the soundest ability and sterling integrity, and has the full confidence of his associates and the respect and good will of his employes.

Mr. Severinghaus has been favored with honors in public life. He served for four years as a member of the Chicago Board of Education, establishing an honorable reputation as a member of this important body. Prominent in the councils of the republican party at Chicago and in Illinois, he was a delegate to the National Republican Conventions of 1916 and 1920, and in the national election of 1924 was presidential elector of the republican party from Illinois, representing the Seventh Congressional District. Mr. Severinghaus is the owner of a beautiful summer home and estate at Piskakee Bay, McHenry County, in the Fox River Valley of Illinois.

Mr. Severinghaus married Miss Ernestine Nieland, and they are the parents of two children: Minerva and Gladys.

JOSEPH S. REED. The life story of Joseph S. Reed, the present county clerk of Livingston County, is illustrative of the lives of most of the men of the state who have risen not only in a business way but in the estimation of their fellow-citizens and friends. Mr. Reed had little opportunity to gain a reputation by attending school, and like most of the boys of his generation was compelled, although glad to do so, to work hard during the summer months and to gain what education he could in the winter terms of public school.

Mr. Reed's parents, Henry B. and Esther (Beck) Reed, the latter a daughter of George Beck, were born and reared in Pennsylvania. They were married there, and soon after their union, in 1854, removed to the new west, settling at Bloomington, McLean County, Illinois. Henry Reed became an apprentice to the boot and shoemaking trade, and at the end of his apprenticeship embarked in business on his own account and conducted an establishment for a number of years. While proprietor of this enterprise he had as an apprentice at one time a lad who was to become one of the leading citizens of the state and its lieutenant-governor. During 1860, because of business matters, Mr. Reed was compelled to return to Pennsylvania, taking with him his family, but at the outbreak of the Civil war came back to Bloomington and enlisted in the Twentieth Regiment, Illinois Volunteer Infantry. During his year in the service with this regiment he rose to the rank of lieutenant, and on being mustered out of the service returned to Bloomington and moved his family to Pontiac, where immediately he began to busy himself in raising an infantry company. When this company, which was G of the One Hundred and Twenty-ninth Illinois Volunteer Infantry, was organized he was elected captain and with his company was sent at once to the front. They took part in the March to the Sea with General Sherman and then pursued their way north, taking part in the Grand Review at Washington, D. C.

Returning to Pontiac after receiving his honorable discharge, Mr. Reed opened a boot and shoe shop which he continued to conduct until poor health compelled him to retire from active affairs. He lived at Pontiac until his death in 1900, and was honored and respected by all who knew him.

Joseph S. Reed, who was one of a family of nine children, was born at Pontiac, August 25, 1864, and spent part of his boyhood in attending public school. At the tender age of ten years, desiring to be of some help to his family, he secured employment on a farm several miles from town, and worked in planting when the corn seed was dropped by hand, and in the harvesting season at five dollars per month and "keep." The following spring he secured his same job at the same price, but in the next year transferred his services to another farmer and was paid ten dollars per month. In the following year, being then a strong and willing boy of thirteen years, he obtained employment at a local brick yard in the capacity of an "off-bearer," where the required amount of work was 5,000 bricks per day, in addition to which the bricks much be "edged." If it chanced to rain the bricks had to be covered, and many nights, at all hours, the lad would be awakened to hurry to the brick yard, three-quarters of a mile from home, to assist in the covering of the newly-moulded bricks. Destruction of the product meant loss of pay to the ambitious youth, which would have been a great calamity.

During the three years he worked at the brick yard Mr. Reed attended school as much as possible, for it seemed that he was possessed of enough wisdom even then to know that an education is one of life's most valuable assets. When he was sixteen years of age he obtained a position as clerk in the grocery store of J. W. Babcock, where he remained four years. He was now twenty years of age, had always saved his money, was industrious and quiet, and always attended strictly to the business at hand, although he was of a happy and sociable disposition and when possible took part in all the worth-while activities of the young people of his day. He especially enjoyed church work, and was very active in the interests of the Methodist Church. It was but natural that he should attract the attention of the business men of the community, especially of W. H. Bruner, at that time one of Pontiac's leading merchants. Although the youth was but twenty years old, Mr. Bruner offered him sixty dollars per month to clerk in his store, a sum which was a large salary for a clerk at that time. The offer was accepted, but at the end of the year another proposition confronted the young man. Philip Arman, a man of experience and means, proposed that he and young Reed start a store as partners, offering to supply all needed capital. By that time Joseph had saved about $200, above what he had spent in aiding his father's family. The new store was started on Mill Street, under the name of Arman & Reed, and the venture was a success from the start.

At the age of twenty-three years Mr. Reed married Ezzie Ross, a daughter of Richard Ross, of Pontiac, and in the following year Mr. Reed bought the interest of Mr. Arman in the store, and conducted it under his own name for a number of years, then selling a one-half interest to Thomas W. Kay. After several years under the new firm name Mr. Reed, desiring to retire from such active business life, sold to his partner. However, he did not care to live wholly in inactivity and accordingly entered the real estate and insurance business, in which he continued until elected county clerk in 1918. Previous to this he had served twelve years as county assessor. Mr. Reed was reelected in 1922 and at the

R. C. Woolsey

present time has no opposition for the nomination in 1926.

Mr. Reed is an active republican. Fraternally he is a thirty-second degree Mason, an Odd Fellow and a charter member of the local camp of the Modern Woodmen. Following his marriage he joined the Episcopal Church, of which Mrs. Reed is a member.

FLOYD J. TILTON, descended from one of the pioneer families of northern Illinois, has for many years practiced law at Rochelle, and while a professional man he still keeps in touch with the landed interests which have always distinguished his family.

Mr. Tilton was born near Chana, in Ogle County, May 24, 1875. The Tilton family came from England about 1769, and one of them became an officer in the Continental army during the war for independence. Richard Tilton, a native of New Jersey, when a young man went to southwestern Pennsylvania, subsequently to Ohio, and in 1849 came to northern Illinois and settled near Chana, where he entered land from the government. Chana was then known as Washington Grove. This Richard Tilton was a substantial farmer and one of the very able citizens of his time and locality. His son, Elijah Tilton, was born in Pennsylvania, not far from Wheeling, West Virginia, and lived in Knox County, Ohio, until about 1850, when he brought his family to Rochelle, Illinois. He lived there for a number of years and then bought a farm near Chana, on which he spent the rest of his life engaged in farming and stock raising. He died in 1871. His wife was Elizabeth Stout. They were the parents of William W. Tilton, who was born near Danville, in Knox County, Ohio, and was eight years of age when the family came to Illinois. He attended public school at Rochelle and after that engaged in farming and stock raising. At the time of his death, in 1913, he owned the same farm which his father had bought when he first moved to Illinois from Ohio. William W. Tilton married Alice Carnavan, who was born in Ireland and was four years of age when brought to America. She lived for some years in Knox County, Ohio, graduating from the Mount Vernon High School of that state. She also completed a teacher's training course in Illinois and was a teacher in this state for a number of years, until her marriage, her husband being a member of the school board in the district where she was employed as teacher. Her parents were John and Catherine Carnavan, of County Monoghan, Ireland, and her mother died in that country.

Floyd J. Tilton was reared on the farm, attended public schols, graduated from the high school at Rochelle in 1895, and during the Spanish-American war in 1898 he served as a non-commissioned officer in the Third Illinois Volunteers. He was under the command of General Brooks in the Porto Rican campaign. Mr. Tilton attended law school in Northwestern University, Evanston, was graduated in 1900 and admitted to the bar in June of the same year. For one year he was a collector for the Steel Hardware & Implement Company in Kansas, and first engaged in practice as an attorney at Kewanee, Illinois. In the fall of 1907 he returned to Rochelle, and has handled a large general law business there. He still owns the farm near Chana which his grandfather entered, and thus has some of the finest agricultural lands anywhere in the world. Mr. Tilton is president of the Rochelle Township School Board and for over seven years has held the office of city attorney of Rochelle. He is also secretary of the Chamber of Commerce. During the World war he was secretary of the local draft board of Ogle County. Mr. Tilton is a democrat, is a Knight Templar Mason and member of the B. P. O. Elks.

He married at Kewanee, Illinois, June 11, 1909, Miss Martha C. Bailey, daughter of Norval D. Bailey and wife. Her father for many years was superintendent of the Western Tube Company at Kewanee. Mr. and Mrs. Tilton are the parents of five children, Mary N., John W., Norval B., Catherine L. and Charles F., all of whom are in grammar or high school at Rochelle.

ROBERT CUSHMAN WOOLSEY, prominent Galesburg attorney, is a native of Knox County and came to the work of his career with a very liberal education. He represents several of the old and prominent pioneer families of north central Illinois.

He was born on a farm near Victoria, in Knox County, on December 3, 1881, son of Thomas Nelson and Mary (Fifield) Woolsey, grandson of Deo Woolsey, whose wife was an Olmstead, and a great-grandson of John Woolsey, who was one of the early pioneers to locate at Sycamore, Illinois. John Woolsey also lived for a time at Victoria, in Knox County, but went back to Sycamore, where Deo Woolsey grew to manhood. Deo Woolsey was a native of Ohio. He married at Victoria, and finally returned to Sycamore and settled on a farm there. He died quite young, leaving to the care of his widow the rearing of the following children: John, Russell, McKendree, Thomas Nelson and Hannah.

Thomas Nelson Woolsey was born at Sycamore, DeKalb County, Illinois. In 1864, at the age of seventeen, he enlisted in a regiment of Illinois infantry and served until the close of the Civil war. In after years he was an active member of the Grand Army of the Republic.

Farming was his occupation during his long and industrious life. He died in 1921, at the age of seventy-four. He was always a staunch republican in politics, and a member of the Congregational Church. His wife, Mary Fifield, who died at Galesburg, in August, 1926, was born near Victoria, daughter of Dr. Langdon and Laura (Cushman) Fifield. Doctor Fifield and wife were born, reared and married in New Hampshire. He graduated from Dartmouth Medical College, and, shortly after his marriage, came up to Illinois in 1836, living for some years at the town of Rochester and in 1848 moving to a farm just east of Victoria, in Knox County. This was the home of Doctor Fifield and wife for the rest of their years. He did his part as a pioneer physician, and was a man of real distinction in his profession. His daughter, Mrs. Woolsey, was a pioneer of Knox County. Several years ago she wrote a history of Victoria Township, where she was born and reared, one of the valuable documents in local Illinois History. Both Thomas and Mary Woolsey were always faithful members of the Congregational Church. Their children were four in number and are: Ralph B., Ross A., Laura E., who is now deceased, and Robert Cushman.

Robert Cushman Woolsey, whose middle name is in honor of his maternal grandmother, was educated in the grade schools at Victoria, spent two years at Hedding College at Abingdon, and for five years had experience as a teacher at Wataga and Williamsfield in Knox County. His literary education was finished in Knox College at Galesburg, where, after three years, he was graduated with the A. B. degree in 1909. The following year he and Claude H. Gamble, now an editor of the Peoria Star, spent in a European tour, including the British Isles, Norway and Sweden and the continent. After his return Mr. Woolsey, who in a competitive examination had been awarded a scholarship from the Harvard Club of Chicago, spent a year in post-graduate study at Harvard, from which he received the Master of Arts degree in 1910. Mr. Woolsey is a graduate from the University of Chicago Law School, taking the degree Juris Doctor in 1913. He was at once admitted to the Illinois bar and set up in general practice at Galesburg, where he has enjoyed a splendid success. His first partner was Walter C. Frank, until the latter became Circuit Judge in January, 1922. He is now a member of the law firm of Woolsey & Lucas, with Ralph D. Lucas as his partner.

He has given his time and energy to the law and its practice. However, he has served two terms as a member of the Galesburg Board of Education. He is a republican, a Master Mason, a Rotarian and a member of the Congregational Church.

Mr. Woolsey, in 1915, married Inez Oberholtzer, of Williamsfield. They are the parents of four children: John Langdon, Mary Allerton and Donald Cushman (twins), and Esther Carolyn.

GEORGE W. BOLLING. With the extensive and important harbor development and other improvements that are being carried forward in the Calumet Lake district of Cook County the civic and industrial precedence of that section of the county is being rapidly advanced, and growth and progress are in the very air. As editor and publisher of the Daily Calumet at South Chicago Mr. Bolling finds wide scope to exert influence in the promotion of the development and general interests of the Calumet district, and he has reason for taking pride in being the editor and executive head of the daily newspaper that can claim pioneer priority in this district, the Daily Calumet having been founded nearly half a century ago and its influence having been large and benignant in connection with the development and progress of the great industrial district that it represents.

Mr. Bolling is a native of the historic old state of Virginia, where the Bolling family has been for many generations one of prominence and influence, the widow of the late President Woodrow Wilson likewise being a member of this historic family of the Old Dominion. Mr. Bolling received in his youth excellent educational advantages and was reared in a home of patrician influences. Many years ago he came to Chicago, and he soon associated himself with the Daily Calumet at South Chicago, he being now editor and publisher of this successful and influential paper, which he makes a most effective exponent of the varied interests of the great industrial district of which South Chicago is the center—one of the greatest in the United States, especially in connection with the manufacturing of steel. Through his paper Mr. Bolling has been one of the most vigorous leaders in promoting the continued progress of this celebrated district and in expanding the scope of its industrial activities. He was able to make the Daily Calumet an important medium for gaining the cooperation of the United States government in the dredging of Lake Calumet and the Calumet River for the purpose of making Chicago a deep-water port, and the Daily Calumet has likewise had leadership in all matters of local improvement, including streets and highways, extension of water and sewer facilities, providing of modern street lighting, and the furtherance of other municipal enterprises making for civic and material betterment. Mr. Bolling is duly valued as one of the most loyal, liberal and progressive citizens of the city of South Chicago and the great Calumet industrial district.

ACHALIS M. LEGG, who is treasurer of the A. M. Legg Shoe Company, one of the important and well ordered manufacturing concerns that lend industrial and commercial precedence to the city of Pontiac, Livingston County, has been a resident of this county since his boyhood and here he has achieved advancement and success through his own ability and well ordered efforts. Mr. Legg has depended upon no extraneous aid or influence in making his way forward to the goal of business success, and thus it is of the greater significance that he is now one of the prominent figures in the industrial and civic life of his home city and county.

Mr. Legg was born in the state of Virginia, of Colonial ancestry in the historic Old Dominion, and he was but a child when his parents came to Illinois and established their home on a pioneer farm seven miles west of Pontiac. The father, the late Jesse Legg, became one of the substantial exponents of farm industry in Livingston County, where he and his wife passed the remainder of their lives, secure in the respect of the community in which they long lived and labored to goodly ends.

The boyhood and early youth of Achalis M. Legg were marked by a plethora of arduous work on the home farm, and the limited education that he gained by attending the district schools during the winter terms has been supplemented by the valuable lessons gained under the preceptorship of that wisest of all head-masters, experience. As a lad of thirteen years Mr. Legg found employment in the Pontiac drug store of the firm of Caldwell & McGregor, and within a short time thereafter he transferred his services to the Lyon Shoe Store, he having there remained for a long period and having learned with thoroughness all details of the business. Mr. Lyon eventually admitted Mr. Legg to partnership, and this alliance continued until Mr. Legg retired from the firm to become a traveling salesman for the Pontiac Shoe Company, with which he eventually became interested in a financial way. He continued his association with this corporation until he became one of the organizers of the shoe-manufacturing concern that bears his name, the A. M. Legg Shoe Company having been incorporated in 1917, and its business being now one of substantial order —contributing in large measure to the precedence of Pontiac as a manufacturing and distributing center. Mr. Legg is treasurer of this company, his son, Clark L., being its president, his younger son, Howard, being the vice president, and Kenneth M. Murphy being the secretary. Of Mr. Murphy specific mention is made on other pages of this publication, in the memoir dedicated to his honored father, the late John S. Murphy.

Achalis M. Legg has gained standing and high reputation as a reliable, resourceful and progressive business man, and is also a loyal and public-spirited citizen of the county that has represented his home from his boyhood to the present. Clark L. Legg, president of the A. M. Legg Shoe Company, was born at Eureka, Woodford County, Illinois, in 1885, his father having at that time conducted a shoe store in that place. Mr. Legg received not only the advantages of the public schools but also those of the University of Illinois, and from 1906 until the organization of the A. M. Legg Shoe Company, in 1917, he was connected with the Pontiac Shoe Company. As president of the A. M. Legg Shoe Company from the time of its organization he has brought to bear careful and progressive policies that have worked greatly to the cumulative success of the business, and his brother, Howard, the vice president, has proved a valued coadjutor, as has also Mr. Murphy, who is the secretary. All of these executives are native sons of Illinois and all are honoring the state by their characters and worthy achievements.

IRA W. SIMS since 1916 has been proprietor of the I. W. Sims College at Murphysboro, one of the best of the educational facilities of that city. It affords high grade instruction to those preparing for a business career in bookkeeping, shorthand, typewriting, penmanship, spelling, letter writing, commercial law, commercial arithmetic, rapid calculation and other subjects. Mr. Sims in February, 1916, purchased the Southwestern Business College at Murphysboro, which had been established by C. L. Padgett. At the time of the purchase he changed the name to its present title and has had remarkable success in developing the school and realizing his ambition for a business school of the first rank. The prosperity of the school has been attended by several removals to larger quarters. The present home of the school is a new business block erected and completed in the fall of 1925, and already its facilities have been outgrown.

While occupying the third floor of the Crane Building it was realized that the location was not well adapted to the purposes of the college, and Mr. Sims obtained temporary quarters by the purchase of the South Methodist Church property, using the church for his school and the parsonage for his residence.

The college building was severely damaged by the tornado of March, 1925, and work of instruction could not be resumed until the new building had been completed. This resulted in great loss of patronage, but within a few months that handicap had been practically overcome. The enrollment is largely drawn from the eight surrounding counties, but several pupils are registered from Indiana and Missouri.

Ira W. Sims was born in Franklin County, Illinois, August 22, 1885, on his father's farm, at the present site of the town of Zeigler. His grandfather, Andrew Jackson Sims, came to Franklin County from Tennessee. He was a Union man and went into the Union army during the Civil war, giving up his life for the cause at the battle of Nashville, and was buried there in his native state. His son, Andrew Jackson, Jr., was born in Franklin County, Illinois, but since 1895 has been a resident of Malden, Missouri, where he carries on a prosperous mercantile business. He married Elizabeth Browning, a native of Franklin County.

Ira W. Sims was ten years of age when his parents moved to Malden, Missouri, where he attended grade and high schools. He graduated from the Fort Berry Military Academy, and subsequently attended the Gem City Business College at Quincy, Illinois, graduating in 1915. He followed that with a normal course in the Brown Business College at Marion, and in the same year established a school of his own, naming it the Simerian Business College. Shortly afterward he was attracted by the opportunity to purchase the Southwestern Business College at Murphysboro.

Mr. Sims married Ethel M. Chamberlain, a daughter of Joseph P. Chamberlain, of Murphysboro. They have three sons, named Ira W., Jr., born in 1920, Joseph Andrew, born in 1923, and Milford Lee, born in 1924.

H. S. PETTIS, formerly a practicing attorney in Chicago, now of Wheaton, is both a lawyer and engineer, and his professional experience has brought him contact with interests, many of which are entirely outside the general run of the professional routine of either the lawyer or engineer.

Mr. Pettis was born at Newport, Kentucky, but grew up at Chattanooga, Tennessee. His early education was under the direction of private tutors and in private schools. He attended Benedict College in Georgia, and his early training fitted him for engineering. In 1899, following the Spanish-American war, he went to Cuba in the government service as a sanitary engineer. In that capacity he was identified with the great work instituted and carried out by the army and government engineers of cleaning up the city of Havana. It was in the early stages of this colonial enterprise on the part of America that the scientific cause of yellow fever was practically demonstrated, and means contrived for stamping out that tropical scourge. Still later Mr. Pettis was associated with the great staff of sanitary engineers under the direction of General Gorgas in the Isthmian Canal zone during the preliminary measures leading up to the construction of the canal. Mr. Pettis spent several years in Washington associated at different times with governmental departments, including the Bureau of Corporations and Bureau of Standards. While there he took up the study of law in Georgetown University and was graduated with the degree Bachelor of Laws. He was also employed by the government as an investigator of labor conditions and other phases of the shipbuilding industry, and in various iron and steel industries.

Mr. Pettis located at Chicago in 1911, and at that time engaged in the private practice of law. However, his activities for several years brought him association with the iron and steel industries of the city and vicinity, particularly in the adjustment of legal difficulties requiring skilled technical engineering knowledge such as Mr. Pettis had acquired.

On retiring from his professional work in Chicago in 1913 Mr. Pettis established his permanent residence at Wheaton, the rich and rapidly growing county seat of DuPage County. There he purchased a beautiful home, besides other property, and has become assistant to the city attorney, in charge of the legal department and also of the various public works for the city of Wheaton. In recent years Wheaton, like other cities and villages in the west suburban district, has more than doubled its population and has undertaken and carried out notable projects involving the expenditure of millions of dollars in improved streets, park development, sanitary provisions and the modifications required by zoning plans. As a skilled engineer as well as lawyer, Mr. Pettis is an invaluable assistant to Wheaton in supervising various phases of this work. He has been the engineer in charge of the construction of the sewage disposal plant, one of the finest in the country and which places Wheaton in the front rank of cities that have sanitation as nearly perfect as modern science and engineers can make it. This enterprise is carried out by the Wheaton Sanitary District.

Mr. Pettis is a member of the college fraternity Phi Alpha Delta, is a Knight Templar Mason, and at Wheaton belongs to the Lions Club and Business Men's Association.

HON. WILLIAM R. JOHNSON, congressman from the Thirteenth Illinois District, is a Freeport manufacturer, active in an industry that has been conducted by the Johnson family at Freeport for many years. Mr. Johnson had spent many years in Washington as a government employe prior to going to that city as representative of the Thirteenth District. His record during his first term in Congress earned him the republican nomination by an overwhelming majority in April, 1926.

Mr. Johnson is a native of Illinois, born at Rock Island May 15, 1875. His parents, Richard and Jane (Horner) Johnson, were born and reared and married in England, growing up in the country near Leeds. Just at the close of the American Civil war they came to this country, first settling at Kingston, Canada, two years later coming to Rock Island, Illinois, and about a year later going to what was then the far west, Cheyenne, Wyoming, where they remained about two years. Richard Johnson was an employe of the Union Pacific Railroad Company. Cheyenne was then the terminus of this road. Returning to Rock Island, he remained in that city about a year, and during this time his son William R. was born. In 1876 the family located at Dixon, Illinois, where Richard Johnson was superintendent of the Grand Detour Plow Works. In 1878 the family moved to Freeport, and in 1882 acquired the property where Congressman Johnson now resides. Richard Johnson for many years was connected with the Barnes Manufacturing Company, later was foreman of the Illinois Central Railway Shops, and in 1895 engaged in business for himself, manufacturing the patented Johnson self feeder as an equipment for thrashing machines. He also manufactured an automatic cylinder wrench and an automatic coupler. These inventions of his own genius were the foundation for a successful manufacturing industry which he built up and continued until his death on November 24, 1917. He and his wife had eight children: Henrietta, Anna, Mary Elizabeth, Laura, William R., J. H., Richard and B. F. Johnson. All are living except Henrietta.

William R. Johnson was educated in the grammar and high schools of Freeport, and attended the Freeport College of Commerce in night classes. As a youth he served an apprenticeship at the blacksmith's trade, and early became identified in a practical working capacity with the Johnson Manufacturing Industry. Since his father's death he has been active manager of that business, which is one of the important industrial enterprises of the city of Freeport.

Mr. Johnson in 1901 was given a position at Washington by the late congressman Robert R. Hitt. He was in Washington throughout the sessions of Congress and spent his summer vacations in his father's plant. At Washington he finally became superintendent of the folding department in charge of all government documents assigned to members of Congress. In this position he had under his supervision a chief clerk, four bookkeepers, a foreman and sixty other employes, and he had the responsibility of looking after the distribution of all the documents. Frequently as high as a million parcels were mailed out in a single month. Mr. Johnson was daily on the floor of the House and had an opportunity to familiarize himself with the workings of Congress and parliamentary procedure, an experience that in itself was a remarkable training for the duties of congressman.

In 1924 Congressman John C. McKenzie voluntarily resigned and Mr. Johnson entered the primary as a republican candidate, defeating four rivals. In November, 1924, he was elected by the largest vote ever given a congressman in the Thirteenth Illinois District, getting over forty-nine thousand votes out of a

total of sixty-three thousand. His opponents, a democrat, a socialist and an independent republican had between them only a little more than thirteen thousand votes. For a first term member Mr. Johnson had a remarkable record of achievement during the Sixty-ninth Congress, closing March 3; 1927. He received assignment to four House committees, accounts, census, claims and merchant marine and fisheries. The census committee has jurisdiction over all statistical matters of the government and country, while the claims committee considers all claims against the United States government. The merchant marine and fisheries committee has long been an important committee of Congress, having jurisdiction over matters pertaining to the merchant marine and other matters of navigation, and also jurisdiction of the radio. Mr. Johnson introduced and assisted in securing the passage of a large number of bills, including many private pension bills for veterans of the Civil, Spanish-American and World wars. He secured an appropriation of $220,000 for the enlargement of the Freeport Government Building, and also secured an appropriation for the construction of a sea wall along the Mississippi River in Carroll County to protect parks and play grounds. He was active in supporting the general Revenue Bill, which passed the House December 22, 1925, and which saved the taxpayers of the nation over $382,000,000 annually, eliminating from the income tax rolls more than two million persons who formerly were compelled to file schedules and pay taxes on limited incomes. Mr. Johnson has recently been pushing a bill for the straightening of the Galena River to prevent floods in the city of Galena.

On April 13, 1926, Mr. Johnson was again nominated as the republican candidate, being given an overwhelming majority in that primary. He carried every county in the district, including the one in which his principal opponent resided and carried his own county by a vote of seven to one.

Mr. Johnson's home in Freeport is on the site where the noted Lincoln-Douglas debate occurred. Just in front of his home rests a boulder erected by the Freeport Woman's Club and dedicated by President Roosevelt in 1903. Mr. Johnson is affiliated with the B. P. O. Elks and is a member of the Methodist Church. He is unmarried. At the time he took his seat in Congress in March, 1925, he took his mother with him to Washington to witness the inauguration of President Coolidge. However, this happy occasion was turned into sadness, since his mother took suddenly ill on March 3rd and died on the following day, the day of the inauguration. Her body was brought back to Freeport and laid to rest beside her husband, Richard Johnson.

DAVID HILL. With a record behind him of over half a century of successful effort in horticulture at Dundee, David Hill is recognized as one of the leaders in his line in his part of Illinois, and the evergreens, in which he specializes, are sought by customers from all over a wide territory. He was born in England, January 17, 1849, a son of Henry and Martha (Graves) Hill, both of whom died in England, never having left their native land. Of the eight children born to their marriage, David Hill is the eldest.

In 1872 David Hill came to the United States, and after a short stop in Connecticut, located at Dundee, where for a time he was in the employ of a Mr. Hill, a Scotchman, who, although he bore the same surname as Mr. Hill, was no relation to him. When David Hill married he began, with the five acres of land owned by his wife, to make a specialty of growing evergreens. His business prospered to such an extent that he now has 400 acres of land and fifteen greenhouses, the latter being used to propagate fine and new varieties of evergreens. These greenhouses are 70 x 200 feet.

Mrs. Hill was Maggie Grant before her marriage, and she is a niece of her husband's former employer. He brought her to the United States from Scotland, of which land she is a native, together with his father, the latter living to be over ninety years of age. Mr. and Mrs. David Hill had seven children born to them, namely: George W., who is associated with his father in the nursery business; Arthur H., who is now manager and treasurer of the nursery business; Maud, who is the wife of George Shurtleff, of Peoria, Illinois; Mabel N., who is a resident of Washington, District of Columbia; Vernon D., who is associated in business with his father; Florence, who is the wife of Isaac C. Pratt, of Warren County, Illinois; and a daughter who died in infancy. Mr. Hill is a republican, but he is not active in politics. The Masonic fraternity holds his membership. In religious faith he is a Baptist. A quiet, steadfast man, working hard, and planning wisely, he has succeeded in a wonderful manner, and has become one of the representative men of his city and county.

ROBERT E. WRIGHT was admitted to the bar soon after the close of his service in the navy during the World war period, and is engaged in a successful practice at Greenville in Bond County.

He is one of the four sons of Judge William B. Wright, present judge of the Fourth Judicial Circuit and a resident of Effingham. Robert E. Wright was born at Effingham February 13, 1895. His father was born at Ewington, Illinois, and his mother, Dora (West) Wright, was a native of Mattoon.

Robert E. Wright attended public schools in Effingham and Illinois Wesleyan University at Bloomington. He was a student in law school when America entered the war, and he then enlisted in the navy and spent twenty-six months in the service. He was at the Great Lakes Naval Training Station and later was supply and dispersing officer on the U. S. S. Essex. He received his honorable discharge in August, 1919, with the rank of lieutenant, junior grade. He took the bar examinations in the summer of 1919, and after being admitted engaged in practice two years at Centralia in partnership with Judge Wilson in the firm of Wilson & Wright. Mr. Wright since October, 1921, has conducted an individual law practice at Greenville.

He is a member of the Illinois State and American Bar Associations, belongs to the

American Legion, is a republican, a member of the Masonic Order and the Eastern Star, the B. P. O. Elks and the Greenville Country Club.

He married at Effingham, June 26, 1917, Miss Adeline Schafer, daughter of Charles Shafer. They have one son, Robert, Jr.

JOHN LYNCH for forty years has practiced law at Olney and has found duties and responsibilities that satisfy a man of normal ambitions to be useful to his community and state.

His father, the late Colonel John Lynch, was one of the most distinguished soldiers from Richland County during the Civil war. Colonel John Lynch was born in Richland County, November 8, 1831, and took up civil engineering as a profession. He did a great deal of surveying of land boundaries and he also ran the original survey for the Illinois Central Railroad through Richland County. When the Civil war came on he raised in Richland County Company D of the Eighth Illinois Infantry and was elected its captain. In that capacity he presented the company, the first in the state outside of Springfield, to Governor Yates in answer to President Lincoln's first call for troops. It was a three months' company, and after this period had expired Captain Lynch returned home. He then raised Company E of the Sixth Illinois Cavalry, was elected first lieutenant and was with that regiment throughout the period of the war, rising to the rank of colonel. For many years after the war he was a prominent member of the Grand Army of the Republic and the Loyal Legion. Colonel Lynch after the war settled down to farming, superintending the operations of his farm from his home in the city of Olney. He was active in this business until his death, which occurred August 24, 1906. He took much interest in public and civic affairs, though was never a candidate for office. He was a republican.

Colonel John Lynch married Margaret Nelson, who was born in Richland County, November 20, 1843, and died November 24, 1895. They were the parents of three children: John; Frank, who became a lawyer and in 1890 moved to Chicago, where he gained success as a corporation lawyer, but died at the early age of thirty-eight; and Tinnie, wife of Joseph Morrow, living in Kansas.

John Lynch was born at Olney, January 13, 1865, only a short time before the close of the Civil war. He grew up in his native town, worked on his father's farm two miles distant, and after completing a high school course began the study of law in the office of Wilson & Hutchinson. His entire professional career has been associated with the office in which he studied, anl for many years he has owned that law office. He was admitted to the bar in May, 1886, and has enjoyed a large clientage, involving a general practice, and has appeared in many important cases in the courts of the county and district. He has been very successful as a corporation attorney. The only public office he has held was that of city attorney for Olney.

He has been a leader in the republican party in Richland County. Through his efforts in securing a redistricting of judicial circuits, efforts that failed of their object because of opposition, his republican friends insisted that in 1903 he become the party candidate for circuit judge. The district was overwhelmingly democratic, but he made a most creditable race, being defeated by only about two hundred votes. Since then he has been popularly known as Judge Lynch. He owns and operates the old homestead farm of his father. During the World war he gave much of his time to patriotic causes, serving on the advisory council and as a member of the food administration. Judge Lynch married, May 1, 1890, Miss Edith Bunch, a native of Illinois.

REV. JOHN F. RYAN is pastor of St. Bernard's Parish, one of the large Catholic Churches on the South Side of Chicago. His labors as a priest cover a period of a quarter of a century, nearly all the time in Chicago.

Father Ryan was born in County Tipperary, Ireland, January 17, 1871, son of Stephen and Margaret (Lanigan) Ryan, also natives of County Tipperary. He was next to the youngest in a family of eight children, two of whom still are living.

Father Ryan was educated at Thurlow in County Tipperary, attended St. Patrick's College and Seminary, and in 1899 was ordained a priest. Coming to Chicago, his first assignment of duty was with St. Melo Church, where he remained seventeen years as first assistant. For one year, during 1916, he was pastor of St. Patrick's Church at Kankakee, Illinois, and in 1917 was installed as pastor of St. Bernards on West Sixty-sixth Street. Father Ryan has made himself very popular with his parishioners, exercises a strong influence over young people and has given an energetic and forceful administration of the large school and church. The school has an enrollment of six hundred, with a hundred in the high school department.

FRANK H. JUST as editor and proprietor of the Waukegan Daily News is one of Illinois very successful newspaper men. He served an apprenticeship when a boy in a newspaper printing plant, and since then has had working contact with and experience in every phase of the printing and newspaper business, his career for many years having made him well known in Lake County.

He was born at Rockford, Illinois, September 2, 1871, son of Christian and Alice (LaBarre) Just. His grandfather, Adam Just, and family, coming from Hesse-Darmstadt, Germany, located at Barton in Washington County, Wisconsin, in April, 1847. Christian Just was born in August, 1847, in a log cabin, which his father a short time previously had built in the virgin forest. Christian Just at the age of nineteen became an apprentice harnessmaker at Berlin, Wisconsin, and on completing his trade married Alice LaBarre. Removing to Rockford, Illinois, he was employed as a carriage trimmer and harnessmaker with Hall & Bartlett, carriage manufacturers. In 1875 he removed with his family to Waukegan, forming a partnership with A. O. Ferguson, harness makers and carriage trimmers. Later he established a business of his own and continued his chosen work until obliged to retire owing to failing health. His death occurred, after a lingering illness, in 1922 at Libertyville. His widow is still living at Waukegan, where she has long been active in church and community affairs. For fifty years she has been a member of the Congregational Church, for three years was recording secretary of the State W. C. T. U., has been a delegate to many state and national conventions and has held the office of president of the district, county and local W. C. T. U., and of the Federation of Women's Clubs of Waukegan. Although she has passed the three score and ten mark, she still holds office in the W. C. T. U., the First Congregational Church and Lake County Sunday School Association, and takes a keen interest in community affairs in general as well as her domestic duties as home keeper. She was born at Lowrytown, Pennsylvania, daughter of Hampton and Matilda (Hughes) LaBarre, whose earlier home was in Corbin County, Pennsylvania, where their daughter Alice was born in 1852. In 1855 they came west and settled at Berlin, Wisconsin, where Hampton LaBarre was active in business, at one time conducting the hotel now known as the Berlin Hotel. While in Pennsylvania he owned and operated a canal boat, carrying coal from the mines near Wilkes Barre to Philadelphia.

Frank H. Just was four years of age when the family moved to Waukegan, where he attended public schools. In 1887, at the age of sixteen, he left school and began his apprenticeship in the printing plant of the Waukegan Gazette. During the next four years he acquired a high degree of skill as a compositor and experience in all branches of printing and the details of a country newspaper office. Leaving Waukegan, he had several years of experience in Chicago, working as a printer, and eventually he bought the Harvey Headlight, a weekly paper, the name of which he changed to the Harvey Tribune. He conducted this as a daily during the World's Fair of 1893, and sold out in 1894. At that time Mr. Just removed to Lake County, which has been his home and center of his business activities now for over thirty years. His first location was at Libertyville, where he bought the Lake County Independent. In 1898 he acquired the Waukegan Daily Sun, and conducted both papers until 1911, when he sold them to their present owners. In 1916 he established the Lake County Register, a semi-weekly paper, and still owns it. It is one of the few prosperous semi-weeklies in northern Illinois. In 1902 Mr. Just established the Waukegan Daily News. This is a republican paper and has the largest circulation of any paper published in Lake County. Both through his newspaper and as an individual Mr. Just exerts himself public spiritedly and loyally wherever and whenever the welfare of the community is at stake. He is a member of the Chamber of Commerce, belongs to the B. P. O. Elks, is a republican, and his family are Methodists.

He married at Libertyville, in 1897, Miss Mary Evelyn Davis, of that town, a graduate of high school and active in music and other social organizations there. Her parents were William E. and Margaret (Murphy) Davis.

Her father for a number of years was principal of schools at Libertyville, also owned farms near there, and after he retired from school work he engaged in the mercantile business at Libertyville for a number of years. He died in 1919 and his wife, in 1898. Mr. and Mrs. Just had four children, William LaBarre, Margaret E. (deceased), Franklin Ward and Mary E. William L. was educated in Culver Military Academy of Indiana, served with the Marines at Quantico, Virginia, during the World war, and is now a resident of Evanston, connected with the Triangle Motors Company. The second son, Franklin W., was educated in grammar and high schools at Libertyville, and is now a reporter on the staff of the Waukegan Daily News. The daughter, Mary, is a member of the class of 1928 at the Libertyville High School.

FREDERICK T. HASKELL. Among the prominent business men of Chicago, Frederick T. Haskell has long been a representative of financial strength, and as vice president of the Illinois Merchants Trust Company ably fills a position of immense responsibility, and his wisdom as a banker is equaled by his uprightness as a citizen.

Frederick T. Haskell comes of old New England ancestry and of Revolutionary stock. He was born at Ogdensburg, New York, January 11, 1854, a son of Ralzaman and Annette (Ray) Haskell, both of whom were born in Connecticut, where their forefathers settled in Colonial days. The mother of Mr. Haskell died when he was but six months old, and death claimed his father six months later, following which the child was taken into the family of his uncle and reared there. This uncle, Frederick Haskell, was the founder of the Haskell & Barker Car Company at Michigan City, Indiana.

From the public schools of Michigan City Mr. Haskell entered Lake Forest Seminary, Chicago, and when nineteen years old became a messenger in the employ of the Merchants National Bank of this city, and since that time has been more or less continuously identified with the banking business. He had become teller of the Merchants National before he transferred to the Illinois Trust & Savings Bank, where he became third vice president, then second vice president and in 1910 was elected first vice president of that institution. Mr. Haskell continued to devote himself in this capacity to the affairs of the Illinois Trust & Savings Bank until the merger, on April 1, 1923, consolidated the Merchants Loan & Trust Company with the Illinois Trust & Savings Bank, under the name of the Illinois Merchants Trust Company, when he became vice president of this vast aggregation of capital and interests. Other old and solid corporations with which he is officially connected include the Bankers Trust Company of New York City and Paris, France, of which he is a director; is a director in the Elgin National Watch Company; and is president and a director of the Illinois Trust & Safety Deposit Company.

Mr. Haskell married, December 31, 1881, Miss Mary I. Magone, of Ogdensburg, New York, who died December 30, 1911. His second marriage, December 19, 1919, was with Mrs. Lila (Ross) Holtz, daughter of Dr. Joseph Ross, of Chicago. They are members of Trinity Episcopal Church, in which Mr. Haskell has served as vestryman and warden for twenty-three years. He stands foremost among the city's philanthropists, for years having been a quiet, unostentatious contributor to charity through the avenues of his church and otherwise, supporting many benevolent causes.

In political conviction Mr. Haskell is a republican, entirely so in national affairs, but in matters purely local often exercising his own judgment as a voter. He has been an extensive traveler both in the United States and in Europe, and in this and other countries has a wide social as well as business acquaintance. He is a valued member of many representative clubs, including the following: Lake Geneva Country Club, the Onwentsia, the Saddle & Cycle, the University, the Mid-Day and the Attic Clubs; the South Shore Country Club; the Union League Club of Chicago; the Maganassife Club of Ottawa, Canada, and others equally famous in New York City and Paris, France. Mr. Haskell belongs also to the Sons of the American Revolution, to the Sons of Colonial Wars and to the Mayflower Division Knights.

JOHN F. GILCHRIST, vice-president of the Commonwealth Edison Company, entered the service of the old Chicago Edison Company as an office boy in 1887. He is a native of Chicago, had only the ordinary advantages of a comparatively poor boy growing up in the city, and from his industry and fidelity and his faith in himself has become an executive in some of the most powerful public utility organizations in the middle west.

John Foster Gilchrist was born in Chicago March 14, 1868, son of James M. and Mary (Foster) Gilchrist. After completing his high school course he went to work for the Chicago Edison Company at the age of nineteen, and subsequently he pursued a law course in Lake Forest University. For thirty years he had some important executive responsibilities in what since 1907 has been the Commonwealth Edison Company. He was assistant to the manager of the Electrical Sales Department from 1894 to 1896; contract agent from 1896 to 1906; assistant to the president from 1906 to 1914; and since February, 1914, has been vice-president in charge of purchasing stores, transportation and statistical department.

Mr. Gilchrist has also since its organization in 1912 been identified with the Middle West Utilities Company, the holding company owning and controlling twenty-two operating companies furnishing electric light and power and public service to hundreds of communities distributed over fifteen states. Mr. Gilchrist has also been an official in the Public Service Company of northern Illinois, one of the units owned by the Middle West Public Utilities Company. He is treasurer of the Federal Sign System (Electric). Mr. Gilchrist is a member of the Industrial Club of Chicago, the Engineers Club of Chicago and Engineers Club of New York, and belongs to the Chicago Stock Exchange, Union League, Chicago Athletic, Chicago Yacht, Flossmoor Country and South Shore Country Clubs. He is a democrat and a Presbyterian. On November 19, 1896, he married Emma Lockboard. They have three children, John M., Marion B. and Dorothy F.

CHARLES WHAM is an attorney with a successful law practice at Centralia, Illinois, where he and his brother Fred are associated in the law firm of Wham and Wham. His grandparents were among the early settlers of Southern Illinois in Marion County. He was born near Cartter, in Marion County, Illinois, August 1, 1887, and is the son of Henderson B. and Nancy (Stonecipher) Wham, both of whom were born in Illinois. Henderson B. Wham was a successful farmer and school teacher, and held several local township offices. He died August 26, 1923. His widow is still living, and a brief record of their children is as follows: George D., a member of the faculty of the Southern Illinois State University at Carbondale; Eunice, wife of T. E. Maulding of Centralia; Phoebe, wife of E. P. Gaston of Champaign, Illinois; Edgar B., merchant at Cartter; Fred L. and Charles, Lawyers at Centralia; Florence, employed in the U. S. treasury department at Chicago; and Benjamin, an attorney at Chicago.

Charles Wham attended the public school at Panhandle, near Cartter, Illinois; high school at Olney, Illinois, and the Southern Illinois State Normal at Carbondale. He graduted from the College of Law of the University of Illinois in 1912 with the degree of LL. B. During the past fourteen years he has earned an enviable record of success as a practicing lawyer. He is a member of the Marion County and Illinois State Bar Associations.

While at the university he was active in athletics and earned his letter in football. He was a member of the University debating team and was a member of Sigma Chi, Delta Sigma Rho, and the Order of the Coif, Mauanda, etc.

When the United States entered the World war Mr. Wham raised and served as captain of Company I, of the Ninth Regiment, Illinois National Guard. Later he entered the U. S. Field Artillery Officers Training School at Camp Taylor, Louisville, Kentucky, where he was commissioned a second lieutenant. At the close of the war he was discharged into the Reserves. He is a republican, a Royal Arch and Knight Templar Mason, also thirty-second degree Mason, member of the Independent Order of Odd Fellows, Elks, Modern Woodmen of America and American Legion. He belongs to the Meadow Woods Country Club, golf being his favorite sport. He is a member of the Chamber of Commerce and Rotary Club.

Mr. Wham married Miss Pauline Bundy, daughter of the late William F. Bundy, at Centralia, on October 27, 1915. Mr. Wham was associated in the practice of law with Mr. Bundy until his death in 1916. Mrs. Wham attended the University of Chicago and Northwestern University; is a member of the

Kappa Kappa Gamma sorority and is a member of several social clubs at Centralia. They have two children, James B., born in 1918, and William B., born in 1922.

EDMUND H. HAEGER. Ordinarily heredity has no rights which the biographers of successful men, especially those of the middle west, feel bound to respect. However, it counts for much in shaping the course of some men, and emphatically must be noted when the tendency born in a man is fostered by an ever-present influence along the same lines, crowding other avenues of thought, and compelling minute attention to the demands of one's surroundings. Supplementing environment and training, heredity has counted in the case of Edmund H. Haeger, president of The Haeger Potteries, Inc., of Dundee, which has been in existence since 1919. Mr. Haeger has been grounded in the brick and tile business ever since childhood, and there are few men in the country similarly employed who have a more comprehensive grasp of this important industry.

Mr. Haeger was born at Dundee, Kane County, Illinois, May 20, 1886, and is a son of David H. and Mary (Weltziem) Haeger, natives of Germany. His father, born in 1839, was a lad of fourteen years when he came to the United States, and first located at Barrington, Illinois. There he met and married Mary Weltziem, who had come to the United States in 1857, and in 1871 they moved to Dundee, where David H. Haeger purchased the interest of a Mr. Hibbard in a brick yard. He then began the manufacture of brick and subsequently bought out another partner. His operations rapidly extending their scope, in 1883 he started a brick yard at Elgin, Illinois, and two years later was the builder of the first drain tile factory in this part of the state. Later he became interested in farm lands, and at the time of his death, in 1900, was the owner of 2,300 acres of valuable property, which land was divided into dairy farms. Mr. Haeger was at all times interested in matters pertaining to the welfare of his adopted community, and as a friend of the schools was for some years president of the Board of Education. He and Mrs. Haeger, who survives him as a resident of Dundee, became the parents of the following children: Emma, the wife of F. W. Estergren, of Algonquin, Illinois; Thusnelda, the wife of Dr. G. T. McCullum, of Oak Park, Illinois; Edna, the wife of H. W. Walker, of Dundee, Illinois; David C., of Aurora, Illinois; Mary, who resides at Elgin; Edmund H., of this notice; and Elsa, of Oak Park, Illinois.

At the time of the death of the father, in 1900, the business came under the management of an estate, and was thus conducted until 1908, at which time it was incorporated under the name of the Haeger Brick & Tile Company, the corporation operating the farm lands and the plants at Elgin and Dundee, with David C. Haeger, president, and Edmund H. Haeger, secretary and treasurer. In 1919, however, Edmund H. Haeger purchased the Dundee plant and formed a separate corporation known as The Haeger Potteries, Incoporated, of which Mr. Haeger has since been president and W. F. Rowe, secretary. This concern has grown and prospered and is now accounted one of the substantial and important industries of Dundee. The Haeger Potteries, Inc., do a nation-wide business, and have sales offices in New York and Los Angeles. Mr. Haeger is a business man of acknowledged ability and marked energy and one who has the thorough confidence of his associates. With his years of experience, his excellent business foresight and his managerial ability, it is needless to add that he accomplishes the best possible results with his manufacturing plant. It is his habit to employ good workmen and pay them good wages, a common sense view which saves him thousands of dollars yearly. In politics he is a republican. Like his honored father, he is interested in public affairs, as are all good citizens, and like the elder man also, he has been president of the Board of Education, a position in which he served capably from 1918 until 1925. He is a Mason, a member of the Sigma Chi college fraternity and the Hamilton Club of Chicago, director of Dundee State Bank, and with his family belongs to the Congregational Church.

On October 7, 1913, Mr. Haeger was united in marriage with Miss Vera Mills, of Jefferson, Iowa, and to this union there have been born two children: Barbara Mills and Marcy Mills. Mr. Haeger is a man of leading characteristics, public spirited, popular, honorable in all his dealings, and, through his upbuilding of one of the town's most worthy industries, a commercial factor of widespread influence.

WALTER HOWARD ROSS, district manager of the Peoria Life Insurance Company at Danville, has made a distinctive success of insurance as a profession and business and is one of the leading producers among men of his age in eastern Illinois.

He was born at Eugene, Indiana, September 12, 1894. Ross is an English-Irish name. His grandfather was Peter Ross, a Baptist minister, who spent his last years in Illinois. His father, Homer Ross, was born in Virginia, July 25, 1831, and in August, a few days after his birth, his parents moved to Westfield, Illinois, where he spent some of his boyhood. He also lived a few years in Missouri, after which he returned to Illinois. Receiving a teacher's license, he also studied medicine three years, but never practiced. He taught school for several years in Indiana and was married at Yeddo, that state, where he lived a year. The business he followed was that of painting, and he was a painting contractor for a number of years. He followed that business at Eugene, Indiana, until 1900, when he located on a farm southwest of Eugene, giving most of his time to the management of the farm until 1907. He then operated for a year a restaurant at Cayuga, and at Quaker, Indiana, was engaged in the painting and decorating business until 1911. On retiring he moved to Humrick, Illinois, in 1911, and that was his home until his death, though he died in a hospital at Danville in April 1924. He was a republican and a member of the Masonic fraternity. Homer Ross married Clara Grace Bonebrake, who was born at Yeddo, Indiana, in 1868 and died at Quaker in 1909. They had a family of seven children: Lena, wife of Claude Banta, a carpenter at Ridge Farm, Illinois; John Homer, a railroad worker at Quaker; Walter Howard; Frank Harrison, a farmer at Newport, Indiana; Dorothy Leah, wife of James Loop, a steam shovel worker and strip miner at Humrick, Illinois; Grace Merle and Blanche Pearle, twins, both attending the Vermilion Academy at Vermilion Grove, Illinois.

Walter Howard Ross acquired his education in the public schools of Eugene, Indiana, the Flats school house southwest of Cayuga, and the public schools at Quaker. He left school when only fifteen years of age, and until reaching his majority worked for his father in the painting trade. He then became a clerk and for six years was employed in the grocery store of H. L. Brown at Humrick, Illinois.

Mr. Ross took up the insurance business in 1922 and for eighteen months wrote life insurance with headquarters at Chrisman, Illinois. In June, 1924, he was promoted to the responsibilities of district manager for the Peoria Life Insurance Company at Danville. His district comprises the counties of Vermilion, Edgar, Coles, Clark, Cumberland and Douglas. His offices are in the Baum Building.

Mr. Ross was inducted into the United States service June 26, 1918, being sent to Camp Jackson, South Carolina, where for a time he was in the personnel company, a branch of the adjutant general's department, and later was transferred in the same service to Camp Sevier, South Carolina. He received his honorable discharge, with the rank of sergeant, March 11, 1919. He is a member of Fletcher Post of the American Legion at Ridge Farm. Mr. Ross married, September 8, 1916, at Danville, Miss Grace Patten, a native of Ridge Farm, Illinois.

ANNA STONE COMPANY. A brief sketch of this industry is interesting not only as the story of an individual undertaking but also as reflecting the distinct modern trend of developments in southern Illinois in the building of hard roads and soil conservation.

Southern Illinois in general is deficient in limestone rock, but at Anna is a deposit of limestone several hundred feet in thickness, containing the highest grade of calcareous rock. The quarry site owned by the Anna Stone Company covers fifty-four acres. The operation of the quarry was started in 1900 for the purpose of manufacturing lime. A small kiln was erected and steam power was used. Later a small crushing mill was installed to reduce the stone for ballast and road making purposes. The industry went through many vicissitudes and finally, in 1921, the property was acquired by the present Anna Stone Company. Under the active personal management of G. H. Rippetoe, vice president of the company, a new era dawned for the industry. Steam power was abandoned, and Mr. Rippetoe's previous experience in electrical and mining practice enabled him to re-equip the industry with modern electric equipment, the total cost of the development reaching the figure of $250,000. As now constituted the plant has a daily capacity of two thousand tons when operated on a single ten-hour shift. The output in 1925 was over 240,000 tons. The finished product now include agricultural limestone, crushed stone for ballast and concrete uses, fine stone for coal mine dusting and stone for use as asphalt filler, these products being distributed through southern Illinois, western Kentucky and Tennessee. Machinery, operated by electric power, has enabled the plant to greatly increase its output at a lower cost per ton of the finished product, one electric shovel now doing the work which formerly required sixty men. The reorganization of the industry came at just the opportune time, when enormous quantities of limestone were required for the hard road building program of Illinois. The educational campaign conducted for so many years to restore soil conditions by the addition of lime also contributed to the prosperity of the business. The continued prosperity of this industry probably depends largely on the growing demand by farmers for agricultural limestone. Illinois farms in 1925 used more than 800,000 tons of limestone, and the area in which the application of lime is most important is in southern Illinois. In supplying this essential element to the soil building program the industry at Anna has unrivalled facilities in the matter of situation.

The vice president and superintendent of the Anna Stone Company is George Harrison Rippetoe, who was born at Colchester, Illinois, August 22, 1886, son of John and Caroline (Underhill) Rippetoe, and grandson of Caleb and Anna Rippetoe. His grandparents were born in Kentucky, and were early settlers in McDonough County, Illinois, where Caleb Rippetoe was a farmer and coal miner. John Rippetoe, a native of McDonough County, became a mining engineer and mine operator, for thirty-four years was chief engineer of the Quincy Coal Company, and later bought two mines near Colchester, which became the property of the Quincy Coal Company. Later he and his son sunk three mines and continued to operate them until they were worked out. John Rippetoe and his son, George H., were also interested in mining potters clay and in stone quarrying. John Rippetoe is now retired, a resident of Colchester. His wife was born at Akron, Ohio.

George Harrison Rippetoe finished a high school course, and in connection with his practical work with his father in coal mining and quarrying pursued technical courses in electrical engineering at the International Correspondence Schools. In 1913, leaving Colchester, he became superintendent of the Illinois Public Service Company at Macomb, having previously had some experience in this kind of work at Colchester. He was with the public Service Company at McComb until 1922, when he took the active management of the Anna Stone Company.

Mr. Rippetoe in 1907 married Leona Stevens, a native of Monmouth, Illinois, daughter of W. O. Stevens. They have four children, Catherine, Isabelle, Virginia and Billie. Mr. Rippetoe was for two terms township clerk at Colchester, is a republican, attends the Presbyterian Church and is affiliated with Macomb

Lodge No. 1009, B. P. O. Elks. He represented the Anna Chamber of Commerce in the state meeting at Chicago in 1924. He belongs to the Anna Rotary Club and the Hamilton Club of Chicago.

HENRY G. MILLER. In the general practice of law, as well as in the special fields of commercial and corporation procedure, Henry G. Miller has come rapidly to the forefront during recent years at East St. Louis, where he is a member of the firm of Keefe, Baxter & Miller. While his career has not been as extended as some of the other biographies appearing in this work, his experience has been extensive and of a nature calculated to advance him in his calling.

Mr. Miller was born May 25, 1889, at Kansas City, Missouri, and is a son of Charles A. and Emma (Schimpff) Miller. His paternal grandfather was William Miller, a native of Germany, who came to the United States because of his political connection with the German revolution of that time and settled at Peoria, Illinois, where he met and married a native of that state. Charles A. Miller was a musician during his early years, and as such did quite a bit of traveling, although when his son Henry G. was a child he settled down at East St. Louis, where he now occupies the position of truant officer. Mrs. Miller also survives. They have been the parents of seven children: G. A., president of the Union Trust Company of East St. Louis, who married Mayme Kelly and has three children; Charles A., Jr., who married Jennie Weiss and has two children; Frank M., who married Jeannette Studer and has one child; Hon. Edward E., former state senator and now congressman of the Twenty-second Congressional District, who married Mabel Brown and has three children; Loretta, who married Robert Jost and has two children; Henry G., of this review; and R. W., who married and has one child.

Henry G. Miller attended the public schools of East St. Louis, and in 1908 was commissioned by President Roosevelt a midshipman in the United States navy, in which he served one year and three months. When he left the navy he became private secretary to Congressman W. A. Rosenberg, of the Twenty-second Illinois Congressional District, a position which he held for ten years, being also for five years clerk of the Flood Commission of the House of Representatives. In the meantime he entered the National University at Washington, D. C., where he pursued a course in law, and was graduated as a member of the class of 1913. This was supplemented by a course at Cumberland University, Lebanon, Tennessee, by which institution he was also granted his Bachelor of Laws degree, graduating in 1914, and in 1915 started practice at St. Louis, Missouri. After one year he came to East St. Louis, where he now belongs as junior member to the firm of Keefe, Baxter & Miller, doing a general practice, but interested chiefly in corporation law as counsel for several railroads and large corporations. Mr. Miller belongs to the St. Clair County Bar Association, the Illinois Bar Association, the Missouri Bar Association and the Tennessee Bar Association and has been admitted to practice in the Supreme Court of the United States. He belongs to Tennessee Lambda Chapter of the Sigma Alpha Epsilon. He has taken an interest in all matters pertaining to the welfare of his adopted place, and at present is a member of the City Board of Education. His religious connection is with the Presbyterian Church.

On February 11, 1918, Mr. Miller married at Lebanon, Tennessee, Miss Lilla Mace, daughter of B. M. and Ella (Cook) Mace, both of whom survive. Mr. Mace, a retired attorney, taught school during his earlier years, but later acquired a high position in the profession of law and was at one time a member of the State Legislature of Tennessee. To Mr. and Mrs. Miller there has been born one daughter: Anne Nicholson.

LUTHER A. FULWIDER for over twenty years has been principal of the high school at Freeport and has been closely identified with the civic as well as the educational life of that city. Mr. Fulwider is author of a history of Stepenson County, published in 1910.

He was born at Acton, Indiana, August 19, 1870, son of Jacob S. and Nancy B. (Moore) Fulwider, and grandson of Moses Fulwider, who came to Indiana from Virginia, was a pioneer and followed the occupation of stone mason and farmer. The maternal grandparents of Luther A. Fulwider were Thomas E. and Lucy Moore, who settled in Indiana from Kentucky. Jacob S. Fulwider was born and reared on a farm near Acton, Indiana, had a public school education and was a farmer and grain raiser. His home for many years was on a farm in Boone County, Indiana, where he died in 1919. He was a soldier of the Union, enlisting in Company B of the Tenth Indiana Infantry and participated in many battles, including Perryville, Kentucky, Murfreesboro, Missionary Ridge and Lookout Mountain. His wife, Nancy Moore, was born and reared in Indiana and taught for several years prior to her marriage.

Luther A. Fulwider has been an educator since early manhood. He attended grammar and high school in Indiana, and in the intervals of his higher education taught two years in schools in Boone County. He attended Butler College at Indianapolis and in 1895 was graduated A. B. from Indiana University. Later he took graduate work in the University of Chicago, and in 1905 received the Master of Arts degree from Indiana University. After graduating in 1895 he taught three years in the Lebanon High School of Indiana, and also found time for editorial work on the Lebanon Daily Reporter. For four years he was principal of the high school at Petersburg, Indiana, and in 1902 came to Illinois and for two years was high school principal at Jacksonville. In 1904 he entered upon his duties as principal of the Freeport High School, and has been the administrative head of that school ever since. He has been responsible for many improvements that have kept the Freeport High School apace with the best secondary educational units in Illinois. At the same time he has cooperated with his fellow citizens in every movement for the general welfare of the community, and for a number of years served as a director of the Freeport Chamber of Commerce. He is a member of the Freeport Public Library Board, is a thirty-second degree Scottish Rite Mason, a director and vice president of the Illinois Athletic Association, is a past president and former director of the Freeport Rotary Club, a past president of the Illinois Teachers Association, member of the Freeport Country Club and in the Presbyterian Church has for the past eight years taught the Men's Bible Class.

He married at Lebanon, Indiana, in January, 1892, Miss Augusta F. Simmons, who was born and reared at Lebanon and was educated in the grammar and high schools there. Her parents were James and Harriet (Higgins) Simmons, who settled at Lebanon, Indiana, from Kentucky. Her father was a farmer and stock raiser. Mrs. Fulwider is descended from two Revolutionary soldiers, James Higgins and Joab Simmons. Mr. and Mrs. Fulwider have three children, Byron S., James H. and Marjory Frances. Byron S. was educated in the grammar and high school at Freeport, the University of Illinois, and as a member of the Illinois Naval Reserves went into active training at the Great Lakes Naval Training Station at Chicago, and later was transferred to the station on Long Island, where he remained until the armistice. He is now manager of the S. S. Kresge Store at Clinton, Iowa. He is a member of the American Legion and is a Knight Templar Mason and Shriner. The second son, James H., after his high school course at Freeport attended the University of Illinois, was in training as an aviator there, and subsequently was in the flying service at Love Field and Ellington Field near Dallas, Texas, and was preparing for overseas duty when the armistice was signed. He held the rank of second lieutenant in the Aviation Corps. He is now owner, president and manager of the Franklin Radio Company of Chicago. The daughter, Marjory Fulwider, is still attending school at Freeport.

FRANCIS WAYLAND SHEPARDSON, former director of the department of registration and education in the government of Illinois, was one of the original faculty at the founding of the University of Chicago and has been identified with educational work in Chicago and Illinois for over thirty years.

He was born at Cheviat, Ohio, October 15, 1862, son of Daniel and Eliza (Smart) Shepardson. He is a descendant of Daniel Shepardson, who settled at Sale, Massachusetts, in 1628. The ancestral line, beginning with this Daniel, included: Daniel, Daniel, Jonathan, Nathaniel, Jonathan, Daniel, Daniel and Francis Wayland. Daniel Shepardson, D.D., father of Francis W., was one of the founders of Shepard College at Granville, Ohio. His wife, Eliza Smart, descended from a family that settled at Hingham, Massachusetts, in 1631.

Francis W. Shepardson received his collegiate education at Denison University, Granville, Ohio, graduating B. A. in 1882. He received a similar degree from Brown University in 1883, was awarded the Master of Arts degree by Denison in 1886, and in 1906 Denison bestowed upon him the honorary LL. D. degree. Doctor Shepardson for several years taught in the Young Ladies' Institute at Granville. During 1887-1890 he was a printer and editor. He was engaged in graduate study from 1890 to 1892, and in the latter year was awarded the Doctor of Philosophy degree by Yale University. Doctor Shepardson came to Chicago as a member of the University of Chicago faculty in 1892, the year the university was founded. He was engaged in teaching and administrative work at the university a quarter of a century, until 1917.

After the reorganization of the state government of Illinois by Governor Lowden in 1917, Doctor Shepardson was called to the new department of registration and education as its first director, and served until the close of Governor Lowden's term in 1921. Since 1921 he has been director of the Julius Rosenwald Fund.

Doctor Shepardson was an editorial writer for the Chicago Tribune from 1906 to 1910. Of the Beta Theta Pi college fraternity he was general secretary from 1907 to 1917, and since 1917 has been president and editor. He was grand president from 1910 to 1914 of the Acacia fraternity and its grand editor during 1918-19. He was president from 1908 to 1913, and from 1915 to 1918, of the Illinois Society of the Sons of the Revolution. Since 1913 he has been senator, and since 1919, vice president, of the Phi Beta Kappa honorary scholarship fraternity. He is a member of the Royal Arch Chapter, Council, Knight Templar Commandery, Consistory and Shrine in Masonry, the Knights of Pythias, and is a republican and a Baptist.

He married at Clinton, Indiana, September 3, 1894, Cora Lenore Whitcomb, daughter of John and Margaret (Whitcomb) Whitcomb. The Whitcomb family ancestry dates back in Massachusetts to 1631. Doctor and Mrs. Shepardson have one son, John Whitcomb Shepardson.

HON. JAMES HENRY FERRISS, long one of Will County's most representative citizens, and who passed away March 17th, 1926 in West Park, Joliet, held valuable interests in several of Joliet's important business enterprises, and from 1922 was park commissioner of the public parks of Joliet. He was born in Kendall County, Illinois, November 18, 1849, a son of William Howard and Eliza (Brown) Ferriss, natives of New York and Pennsylvania, respectively. The paternal grandparents were Nathan Reed and Lydia (Ricketson) Ferriss, he born in Vermont and she in New York. They came to Illinois in 1833, coming by way of the Erie Canal and Lake Champlain to Detroit, Michigan, from whence the remainder of the journey was made with teams to Kendall County. The maternal grandparents were Stephen W. and Adeline (Sloan) Brown, natives of Pennsylvania, who were also early settlers of Kendall County, to which they came by way of the Great Lakes as far as Chicago, and completed the journey with teams. Nathan Reed Ferriss was a carpenter and Stephen W. Brown was a millwright and tanner, and both of these pioneers secured farms. After their marriage the parents of Mr. Ferriss of this review settled on a farm in Kendall County, and the father alternated his farm work with carpentering. His death occurred in 1915, but his wife survives, although now ninety-five years of age, and resides in Aurora.

His education completed as far as his attendance at the public schools was concerned, James Henry Ferriss in 1870 went into the newspaper field and for nine months conducted the Yorkville News. In 1871 he began his long connection with Joliet, when he, Robert W. Nelson and Horace E. Baldwin bought the Joliet Daily News, now the Herald-News, and for thirty-eight years Mr. Ferriss and Mr. Baldwin conducted this old and reliable journal, but at the expiration of that period they sold to the present company.

Mr. Ferriss was always a prominent figure in city affairs, and displayed his faith in Joliet by investing in local undertakings. His home, which is a landmark, was erected in 1892, and is one of the finest residences in West Park. For eight years Mr. Ferriss was prominently before the public as national chairman of the populist party, and he was up to the time of his death very much interested in current events. The First Presbyterian Church of Joliet held his membership, and he was a member of the Rotary Club and the Association of Commerce. Mr. Ferriss was always deeply interested in the public parks of his home city, and did much to beautify them, among other things traveling through both the eastern and western mountain regions to collect hardy shrubs and flowers for these beauty spots of Joliet.

In 1880 Mr. Ferriss married Olive Hunt, who was born in Litchfield County, Connecticut, a daughter of Chauncy L. and Rutheda (Peck) Hunt, natives of Canaan, Connecticut, who settled in Kendall County about 1859. Mr. and Mrs. Ferriss had no children, and therefore were more than usually interested in many philanthropies and reforms, all of which gave indubitable value and dignity to their name.

WILLIAM P. STRUNK. In 1920, rounding out forty years of service as engineman on the Chicago & Alton Railroad at Roodhouse, William P. Strunk resigned from active service, although his name was continued on the roster of engineers. This decision was revealed in letters from W. G. Bierd, president, and A. P. Titus, general manager, both of whom wrote very cordial communications to the veteran engineer, inviting him to meet them at any time it might be convenient for Mr. Strunk to do so. In a note concerning some soldier matters, Mr. Strunk remarked: "I will now surprise you by letting you know that I have resigned my position with the Chicago & Alton Railroad, after forty years of service with them. I have passed the eightieth milestone in life's journey, and expect to enjoy a rest the remaining days I may be spared." Roodhouse has thus the distinction of having the oldest engineer on the Chicago & Alton Tonica line as its citizen, but White Hall has the distinction of having as a citizen the man who laid the first railroad track through Roodhouse and White Hall, Lyman C. Wright, who celebrated his eighty-fourth birthday anniversary last month.

Mr. Strunk's railroad career embraces almost every department of railroad operation. He was born at Reading, Pennsylvania, April 24, 1840, and at the age of eighteen years became machinist helper in the Pennsylvania Railroad shops at Altoona, Pennsylvania, where at that time the late Andrew Carnegie was a train dispatcher for the same road. Mr. Strunk became fireman on a construction train and then engineer. His description of the engines of those days is in marked contrast to the powerful and speedy locomotives of the present day. In 1862 Mr. Strunk came west and engaged in farming in Will County, Illinois, but within two months Lincoln's call came, and he enlisted in the 100th Illinois Infantry at Joliet. He was in all the engagements and marches of that regiment when not laid up with wounds or illness. He was on the seventy-two day march to Atlanta, and after that battle encamped until Sherman marched to the sea, when they followed Hood to Nashville, being discharged at Camp Douglas, Chicago, July 1, 1865.

He then returned to his old home at Reading, Pennsylvania, and entered the service of the East Pennsylvania Railroad, performing the various duties of yardmaster, conductor, dispatcher, baggageman, fireman, brakeman, engineer, engine inspector and wrecking boss. His fixed salary was $75 per month, receiving extra compensation when serving as conductor or engineer. In 1868 he came to the Wabash at Lafayette, Indiana, as fireman, and two years later had a collision that resulted in his going to the Mobile & Ohio at Macon, Mississippi, as conductor, but was almost immediately pressed into service as an engineer. He was with other roads with varied experiences until coming to the Chicago & Alton in January, 1880, where he has remained continuously in active service until the present time. He is allied with religious, fraternal, patriotic and labor organizations on the principles of improving the condition and character of his fellow men. He is one of the best known men along the Chicago & Alton Railroad, and one of the grand characters of Greene County.

HORACE H. SHEETS, M. D. Among the original settlers and pioneers of Ogle County in the vicinity of Oregon were members of the Sheets family. They have been sterling and industrious citizens of that locality ever since. The present generation is represented by one of the very capable and thorough physicians and surgeons of Oregon, Dr. Horace H. Sheets, who has practiced medicine there for over twenty years.

His grandfather, David Sheets, came from Pennsylvania and made his first location in the country west of Aurora, Illinois. From there he moved to Oregon and bought a farm, part of which is now included in the city. He spent the rest of his life engaged in farming in that locality. He had come to Illinois overland in prairie schooners, and the family endured many of the privations of life on the frontier in that day.

Benjamin F. Sheets, father of Doctor Sheets, was born in Pennsylvania, and was about ten years of age when brought to Illinois. He was for over forty years a leading hardware merchant at Oregon, continuing active in that business until 1905. Benjamin F. Sheets was a lieutenant colonel of the Ninety-second Illinois Infantry in the Civil war. His regiment was one of the first to occupy Chattanooga after the battles of Missionary Ridge and Lookout Mountain. He was in many of the hard fought campaigns of the war and was a staunch friend of the old soldiers. He was active in the Methodist Episcopal Church at Oregon and for over thirty years superintendent of the Sunday School. For two terms he represented the counties of Ogle and Winnebago in the State Senate, serving up to 1892. While in the Senate he secured the passage of the law changing the Illinois State Reform School to a reformatory, and he acted as first superintendent of that institution, during 1891-93. Benjamin F. Sheets married Catherine Hornell, daughter of Lewis C. and Nancy (Grann) Hornell. Her father was a native of Germany and came to America about 1840, living for several years at Dayton, Ohio. While there he joined the volunteers for service in the Mexican war and became a captain in the army of General Scott. After that war he located at Oregon, Illinois.

Horace H. Sheets was born in Oregon November 24, 1877. He attended grammar and high schools in his native town, continued his higher education in Northwestern University at Chicago and was graduated from Rush Medical College of that city in 1902. For about a year he practiced at Byron, Illinois, and since 1903 has been active in his profession in his native community. Doctor Sheets enjoyed the possession of one of the honored family names in Oregon, but his professional success has followed in consequence of individual abilities of high order and a constant devotion to the best ideals of his calling. Doctor Sheets is a member of the Masonic fraternity and B. P. O. Elks, belongs to the Ogle County, Illinois State and American Medical Associations, is a member of the Dixon Country Club at Dixon, the Edgewood Golf Club at Polo, the Rock River Golf Club, the Lions Club of Oregon and the Methodist Church.

He married at Oregon, September 4, 1902, Miss Gussie J. Wilson, daughter of Lyman and Rhoda (Rogers) Wilson, of Oregon. Her father was born and reared near Oregon and attended public and private schools at Grandetour. For the greater part of his life he was a farmer and after retiring located in Oregon. The father of Mrs. Sheets twice ran away from home to join the Union army and was finally accepted as a member of the 140th Illinois Infantry, under General Rosecrans, and participated in the battles of Lookout Mountain, Missionary Ridge, Chickamauga, and was in the rear guard of Sherman's army on the march from Atlanta to the sea.

Doctor Sheets was one of Illinois' physicians who offered their services to the country during the World war. He was a captain in the Medical Corps from October 3, 1918, until June 18, 1919. From October to December he was stationed at Fort Oglethorpe, Georgia, helping train and drill hospital outfits. In December he was sent to Fort Riley, Kansas, where he assisted in the discharge of disabled overseas soldiers until May, 1919. During the last month of his service he was at Camp Grant, Rockford, Illinois, engaged in general hospital work. Doctor Sheets since 1909 has held the office of county physician of Ogle County.

SILAS HARDY STRAWN, a director of the First National Bank of Chicago, has been an active representative of the legal profession in the metropolis for the past third of a century, and since the 1st of January, 1918, has practiced as a member of the firm of Winston, Strawn & Shaw. He was born in the vicinity of Ottawa, Illinois, on the 15th of December, 1866, his parents being Abner and Eliza (Hardy) Strawn. He graduated from the Ottawa High School in June, 1885, and then engaged in teaching for two years, after which he read law in the office of Bull & Strawn of that city. Silas H. Strawn passed his examination for admission to the bar on May 22, 1889, and practiced in LaSalle County during the succeeding two years. He became a resident of Chicago in September, 1891, and until the following April was in the employ of the law firm of Weigley, Bulkley & Gray. He was a clerk for Winston & Meagher from April, 1892, until September 1, 1894, when he was admitted to partnership. This association continued until January 1, 1902, when Mr. Meagher retired from the firm, and its style became Winston, Babcock, Strawn & Shaw, which, by the admission of Judge John Barton Payne on the 1st of October, 1903, became Winston, Payne, Strawn & Shaw. This firm style was maintained until January 1, 1918, since which time practice has been carried on under the name of Winston, Strawn & Shaw. Although the business of the firm is general, it is largely corporation practice and conducted in the higher courts. Messrs. Winston, Strawn & Shaw act in the capacity of counsel for the receivers of the Chicago & Alton Railroad, as general counsel of the Chicago Great Western Railroad Company, as general counsel for the Union Stock Yards & Transit Company and as solicitors for the Michigan Central Railroad Company.

Mr. Strawn has argued many important cases in the Illinois courts of last resort and the Supreme Court of the United States. His high standing in professional circles is indicated in the fact that he was chosen president of the Illinois State Bar Association for the years 1921 and 1922 and has also been honored with the presidency of the Chicago Bar Association. He is likewise an active member of the American Bar Association. Aside from his professional activity he is serving as a director of the First National Bank of Chicago, as chairman of the Board of Directors of Montgomery Ward & Company, director of the Hurley Machine Company, and of other corporations. His successful achievements in professional, financial and business lines have gained him an enviable and well merited reputation in his adopted city.

Mr. Strawn was selected by President Coolidge as one of the two delegates representing the United States at the conference respecting

Chinese Customs Tariff, and as sole commissioner of the United States on the commission investigating extraterritorial jurisdiction in China, both of which bodies sat in Peking in 1925-1926. Mr. Strawn was chairman of the Extraterritorial Commission.

On the 22d of June, 1897, Mr. Strawn married Miss Margaret Stewart, of Binghamton, New York. They are the parents of two children, Margaret Stewart, now Mrs. James A. Cathcart, and Katherine Stewart, and make their home at 229 Lake Shore Drive, Chicago. Mr. Strawn has various club connections, belonging to the Chicago Law Club, the Commercial Club, the Chicago Club, the Mid-Day Club, the Old Elm Club and the Industrial Club of Chicago and being an ex-president of the last named. He is also an honorary member of the Chicago Athletic Club and he has membership connections as well with the Chicago Club and the University Club of Chicago, the Metropolitan Club of New York, the Chevy Chase Club of Maryland, the Burning Tree Club of Washington, the Medwick Country Club of Los Angeles, California, the National Golf Links of America and the United States Golf Association, of which he formerly served as president.

CLIFFORD EARL BEACH. For thirty years Mr. Beach has been engaged in a law practice that makes him one of the outstanding members of the bar of eastern Illinois. The full experience of his lifetime has brought him in contact with business and public affairs as well as his profession.

Mr. Beach, now a resident of Gilman, was born at Onarga, Illinois, May 16, 1866, son of Freedus Poe and Nancy (Lewis) Beach, and a direct descendant of Gresham Beach, who served as Colonial Governor of the Town of Wallingford, Connecticut, in 1647. There were also ancestors in the Revolutionary war. Mr. Beach's great-grandfather, Samuel Beach, was a pioneer settler of central Ohio, his name appearing in the early records at Worthington and Columbus. The Beach family is of direct Welsh ancestry.

Clifford E. Beach was liberally educated, attending the Grand Prairie Seminary at Onarga, and completing his law course in the Illinois Wesleyan University at Bloomington. For several years he was associated with his father in the general store, grain and stock business at Delrey, Illinois. On July 16, 1894, he engaged in law practice at Paxton, and on August 1, 1919, moved his home and offices to Gilman. Mr. Beach has a reputation in several counties of eastern Illinois as a trial lawyer, and has appeared in many notable criminal cases. During 1899-1900 Mr. Beach was city attorney of Paxton and was mayor of that city during 1907-08.

He has normally been a democrat in politics, though in 1908 he was candidate for lieutenant governor of Illinois on the independent party ticket. He had three years of military training, from 1893 to 1896, while a member of the Third Regiment, Illinois National Guard Band. In the Knights of Pythias he has filled all the chairs in the subordinate lodge, has been a member of the Grand Lodge, is a Mason, and belongs to several literary, chess and skat clubs. Out of his experience as an attorney he has prepared several articles published in law journals and his liberal views on philosophy and religion have also been expressed in articles written by him. He edited and copyrighted the book "Eternity of Matter" by Lockhart Brooks Farrar.

Mr. Beach has been twice married. On March 10, 1921, he married Mary Essie Wells, daughter of Gideon W. and Mary E. Wells, representing an old family of West Virginians. Her great-great-grandparents figured in the records of the Revolutionary war. Mr. Beach's two children are by his first marriage: Nita, wife of Frank Weber, and Leola, who married Paul Boomer.

GUSTAF J. JOHNSON, who has served three terms in the Illinois General Assembly from Ford County, has for thirty years been one of the constructive business men and citizens of Paxton.

Mr. Johnson was born at Skenninge, Sweden, September 8, 1872, son of Carl J. and Augusta Johnson. His early education was the product of the public schools of Sweden up to the age of fourteen. Soon afterward he came to America, and for two years lived in Kansas, where he attended public school at Clay Center. From Kansas he removed to Chicago, became clerk in a clothing store, and in 1889 attended the North Side Business College, that city. He learned the business of watchmaker, and was watchmaker and clerk in a jewelry store in Chicago until October, 1894. At that date Mr. Johnson became a citizen of Paxton, and from that time to the present his business energy has been a factor in the life of that community and has also brought him responsibilities outside his home community. He was engaged in the jewelry business in King & Helmer's Drug Store for a time, but later established the Johnson Jewelry Company, which he conducted until 1912, when he sold out. At that time Mr. Johnson engaged in the real estate business. He is president of the Paxton Building Loan & Savings Association. One of his important business undertakings was the reorganization and rehabilitation of the Central Telephone & Telegraph Company of Paxton, and he is now president of that public utility.

Mr. Johnson was one of the organizers of the Ford County Chautauqua Association, served as a member of the Illinois Educational Commission in 1923-24, was a member and secretary of the Illinois Legislative Relief Committee for the cyclone sufferers in Southern Illinois in 1925-26, and is also a member of the Illinois Great Lakes-St. Lawrence Deep Waterway Commission. During the World war he was chairman of the Ford County Fuel Administration. In his home city he was alderman from 1907 to 1909, and from 1909 to 1915 held the office of mayor. Mr. Johnson was elected a member of the Illinois General Assembly in 1920, serving in the session of 1921, and was reelected in 1922 and 1924 and again in November, 1926, for a fourth term. He has been one of the very influential members of the Legislature. Mr. Johnson was a delegate to the Republican National Convention in the historic year of 1912.

For eight years he was chairman of the Ford County Republican Central Committee and in the spring of 1926 was elected as a member of the Republican State Central Committee representing the Seventeenth Congressional District. Although a new member was unanimously elected chairman of that committee.

He has filled all the chairs in the subordinate lodge of the Independent Order of Odd Fellows. Has held position as grand marshal of the Grand Lodge and Grand Encampment. For sixteen years was local clerk of the Modern Woodmen of America and is a Mason, belonging to the Royal Arch Chapter and the Bloomington Consistory of the Scottish Rite. Mr. Johnson is a member of the Hamilton Club of Chicago, the Kiwanis Club of Paxton and the First Lutheran Church of Paxton.

He married August 17, 1898, Miss Jennie Frederickson, daughter of Gustaf and Anna Frederickson. Her father was a farmer and stock raiser and director of the First National Bank of Paxton and frequently honored with positions of public trust. The five children of Mr. and Mrs. Johnson are Lester, Noble, Raymond, Emily and Virginia.

CHARLES CALEB ROBERTS made a valuable contribution to the industrial and commercial interests of Metropolis, Illinois, when he and his brother John N. here established a fruit-box factory, the enterprise having grown to one of broad scope and importance and Mr. Roberts having continued his active association with the business until his impaired health necessitated his retirement, when a sale of the property and business was made to Liggett Brothers, the present owners. Mr. Roberts was a man of sterling character and of marked business ability, and he was one of the honored and venerable citizens of Metropolis at the time of his death, November 3, 1916, his widow being still a resident of this fine little city, which is the judicial center of Massac County.

Mr. Roberts was born in the State of Ohio, in 1840, and was there reared and educated. He early proved his capacity for successful business achievement, and his association with civic and business affairs in the old Buckeye State continued until his removal to Illinois, where, as already noted, he became associated with his brother in founding the fruit-box manufacturing industry at Metropolis. He was a man of strong convictions, was liberal, loyal and progressive as a citizen, and while he manifested no desire for political office, he was a staunch supporter of the cause of the republican party, his religious faith having been that of the Methodist Episcopal Church and he having been identified with various fraternal and social organizations.

The first marriage of Mr. Roberts occurred in Ohio, and the death of Mrs. Roberts occurred in 1909, the one surviving child of this union being Percy, who now resides at Venice, California.

On the 14th of September, 1911, was solemnized the marriage of Mr. Roberts to Mrs. Millie (Green) Jackson, widow of Capt. J. S. Jackson and daughter of the late Dr. D. K. and Irrelda (Winans) Green, she having been born at Jamestown, Ohio, July 13, 1850, and her parents likewise having been born in Ohio. Dr. Green was born at Bainbridge, Ohio, and his education included thorough preparation for his chosen profession, he having been long and successfully engaged in practice as a physician and surgeon and both he and his wife having been residents of Illinois, at the time of their death. In the Civil war period Doctor Green served as a member of the Illinois State Board of Medical Examiners.

Capt. J. S. Jackson, the first husband of Mrs. Roberts, was born and reared in Ohio and there their marriage occurred May 13, 1869. Captain Jackson gave gallant service as a soldier and officer in the Civil war, in which he was captain of Company G. Twenty-second Illinois Volunteer Infantry. He became the owner of a well improved farm near Iuka, Marion County, this state, and was one of the prominent members of the bar of that county, besides having been a citizen of prominence and influence in that section of the state. He served as county clerk and also as state's attorney of Marion County, and represented that county as a member of the Illinois Legislature. He was a cripple during the last twenty-three years of his life, and was a resident of Springfield, Illinois, at the time of his death. While he was a member of the Legislature Captain Jackson's wife there became postmaster of the House of Representatives, an office that she retained during the legislative session during the long period of twenty-three years, at the expiration of which she resigned. In this connection Mrs. Roberts became well acquainted with many of the leading men of Illinois, besides having been in close touch with public affairs in the state. Her daughter, Ella M. Jackson, was the only girl who has ever served as a page of the Illinois Legislature, and she is now the wife of Thomas S. Marshall, of Jackson, Mississippi. Cordelia, the other child of the first marriage of Mrs. Roberts, died at the age of fifteen months. In the early '90s Mr. Roberts erected in Metropolis the attractive residence that is still the home of his widow, at 200 East Third Street, and Mrs. Roberts is not only the gracious chatelaine of this home, but is also a popular figure in the representative social and cultural circles of the community. Mrs. Roberts is a stockholder in the box-manufacturing concern that was here founded by her husband, and is a stockholder also in the First National Bank and the City National Bank of Metropolis.

WILLIAM HENRY HART, former county judge of Franklin County, has to his credit thirty-five years of law practice and a variety of business and civic activities.

He was born in Williamson County, Illinois, August 31, 1862, son of William Jasper and Sarah Ann (Murphy) Hart, his father a native of Kentucky and his mother of Indiana. William J. Hart was an early settler in Illinois and spent the active part of his life as a farmer. He was a democrat and his wife a member of the Missionary Baptist Church.

William Henry Hart after a public school education became a teacher and taught for ten years in Franklin, Jackson, Randolph and

Monroe counties. He studied law under Daniel M. Browning, who subsequently became commissioner of Indian affairs during Cleveland's administration. He was admitted to the bar in February, 1889, and for a time practiced with Judge Browning, subsequently was a partner of W. S. Spiller, and in 1898 was elected and served one term as county judge of Franklin County. In 1906 he became a partner of W. W. Williams and now has his sons as his law associates, with offices in the Hart and Williams Building at Benton. He has also been interested in the coal industry, and was secretary and treasurer of the Hart-Williams Coal Company.

Judge Hart has always been allied with the democratic party and from 1900 to 1902 was a member of the State Democratic Committee. He is a Royal Arch Mason and he and his family belong to the Christian Church.

He married in 1890, Miss Mary W. East, who was educated in the Southern Illinois Normal University at Carbondale and taught school before her marriage. They have four children, William W., Marion M., Mary M. and Mebel E.

William W. Hart was born at Benton, Illinois, in 1894, attended grammar and high school there, graduated from the law department of the University of Illinois in 1916, and was admitted to the bar October 4, 1916. With a very brief experience in the practice of law he volunteered in the fall of 1917 and went into training with the Ninetieth Division at Camp Travis, Texas, being assigned duties in the judge advocate general's department. He served with his division in France one year and was recommended for a commission as captain, but was never commissioned on account of the early signing of the armistice. He had formed a partnership with his father in the firm of Hart & Hart before entering the army, and since the war has earned a substantial position in the bar of Southern Illinois. Since 1922 he has served as United States commissioner for the Eastern District of Illinois.

William W. Hart married Alberta Andrews, whose father, William E. Andrews, became well known in Southern Illinois as an educator. They have one child, William Ward, Jr.

Marion Murphy Hart, second son of Judge Hart, was born at Benton, and while a student in the University of Illinois joined the colors in May, 1917, and was assigned duty with the One Hundred Third Ammunition Train in the Twenty-eighth Division at Allentown, Pennsylvania. He continued his training at Camp Hancock and going overseas spent seventeen months in France. In March, 1919, he was one of about a thousand American soldiers selected from the Expeditionary Forces to attend different universities and colleges in France and England. He entered the University of Edinburgh, where he studied law and attended other lectures until August of that year. After the return of his division to the United States he reentered the University of Illinois, and was graduated from the law school in 1920, having been admitted to the bar in the same year before graduating. Since 1922 he has been associated with his father in practice. He married Constance Skinner, daughter of F. L. Skinner of Benton.

Mary Miller Hart, older daughter of Judge Hart, is a graduate of the National Park Seminary of Washington and the University of Illinois, and is teacher of English in the Benton Township High School. The second daughter, Mabel C. Hart, graduated from the National Park Seminary, spent two years in the University of Illinois, and is now the wife of Elles W. Krieckhaus of Dania, Florida.

The wife of Judge Hart has been a prominent leader in woman's club activities in Illinois and in recent years has been honored with the office of president of the Federated Women's Clubs of the state, serving two years.

EDMUND JANES JAMES, president of the University of Illinois from 1904 to 1920, shared with his predecessor, Andrew S. Draper, the distinction of guiding the university through the most important era of its expansion and development.

Doctor James was born at Jacksonville, Illinois, May 21, 1855, son of Rev. Colin Dew and Amanda K. (Casad) James. For many years before taking up his duties at the university he was one of the foremost scholars in the country on political science and economy. He was educated in the Illinois State Normal, in Northwestern and Harvard Universities, took his Doctor of Philosophy degree at the University of Halle in 1877, and a number of institutions conferred upon him the honorary degree Doctor of Laws. For one year he was principal of the high school at Evanston, and from 1883 to 1895 was professor of public finance and administration in the Wharton School of Finance and Economy of the University of Pennsylvania, and during this time was also professor of political and social science at the University of Pennsylvania. In 1896 he was called to the University of Chicago as professor of public administration and director of the extension division, holding that position until 1901. From February 1, 1902, until September 1, 1904, he was president of Northwestern University. He was head of the University of Illinois sixteen years, retiring with the rank of president emeritus.

The following list of his affiliations, proof of his scholarship and other activities, is taken from Who's Who: Editor of Publications, University of Pennsylvania, Political Economy and Public Law Series, 1886-95, member board of trustees, Illinois State Historical Library, 1897-1907; National Municipal League since 1896; president Illinois State Highway Commission, 1904-09; secretary Illinois State Geological Commission since 1906; member Board of Natural Resources and Conservation; president Economic Association; founder and president of the American Academy of Political and Social Science, 1889-1901 (editor of its "Annals," 1890-95; associate editor, 1895-98); American Society for Extension of University Teaching, 1891-95; International Arbitration Society, Chicago, 1903; Illinois Association for Prevention of Tuberculosis, 1905; fellow Royal Statistical Society, Dublin; member Societe d'Economie Politique, Paris; Phi Kappa Psi, Phi Beta Kappa. Clubs: City (New York); Cosmos, University (Washington); Press, Quadrangle, University, Union League

(Chicago); Evanston (Evanston, Illinois); Champaign (Champaign); University (Urbana). Author: "Relation of the Modern Municipality to the Gas Supply," 1886; "The Legal Tender Decisions," 1887; "The Canal and the Railway," 1890; "Federal Constitution of Germany," 1890; "Federal Constitution of Switzerland," 1890; "Education of Business Men in Europe," 1899; "Charters of City of Chicago," 1900; "Growth of Great Cities in Area and Population," 1900; "Government of a Typical German City—Halle," 1900; "The Land Grant Act of 1862," 1910; "A National Economic Program," 1916; "Military Training in Our Land Grant Colleges," 1916; "A Naval Program," 1916.

CARL F. MEYER. The late Carl F. Meyer is numbered among the men to whose energy, business foresight and good judgment much of the present prosperity of Mound City is due, for without the sound foundation laid by these earlier settlers the superstructure of today could not have been reared. Mr. Meyer was born at Mound City, Illinois, December 23, 1862, a son of G. F. and Lena Meyer.

G. F. Meyer, his father, was for thirty years closely identified with the business affairs of Mound City. He was born in Bielefield, Germany, October 26, 1835, son of G. F. and Caroline Meyer. He graduated at the age of eighteen from Bielefield College, for several years had charge of his father's estate, and in 1858 came to America, reaching Mound City on the 15th of April. While he had no knowledge of the English language, he immediately became a partner in a grocery business, and after 1867 continued the business alone under his own name. His store transacted an immense volume of business during the Civil war period. He mastered the English language both spoken and in reading and writing, and kept in close touch with all the vital interests of the community. In addition to his grocery business he became a dealer in lumber and staves, buying up the products of the mills and shipping them to outside markets. As a dealer in cooperage stock his business was almost nation-wide, and he even exported some materials. In 1877 he built a large factory at Mound City for dressing staves. Both his store and factory were destroyed by fire in 1879, but he soon resumed business on a larger scale than ever. He was also instrumental in establishing at Mound City a furniture factory.

G. F. Meyer died April 29, 1888. Something of his character and standing as a citizen of Mound City are conveyed in the following quotation from an editorial in Pulaski Patriot: "Mr. Meyer was a friend to Mound City in the truest meaning of the word; a person could not quicker arouse his displeasure than to talk against it. He always stood by the little city of his adoption; in adversity as in prosperity and when others seem to doubt the future, then was the time he was always starting new enterprises to give confidence to the people. But his life is ended. The loved and loving husband, father, friend, died where manhod's morning touches noon. While yet enraptured with the world he passed to silence and pathetic dust. This brave and tender man in every storm of life was oak and rock, but in the sunshine he was vine and flower. He was a far-seeing financier, and when the money market was flush he launched out in business transactions, and when a financial crisis was about to affect the business of the country he had the faculty of seeing it and preparing for it."

G. F. Meyer married at Bielefield, Germany, in October, 1859, Miss Lena Meyer, who was born in 1835. They became the parents of eight children, who all died at an early age except one, Carl F.

Carl F. Meyer attended the public schools of Mound City, and when, in 1888, his father died, he and his mother took charge of the stave factory and general mercantile business, and Mr. Meyer inherited the property at the death of his mother, and continued to conduct them for a number of years, but subsequently sold his store. On April 29, 1909, the factory was destroyed by fire, removing one of the landmarks of Mound City. From then until his death, October 11, 1911, Mr. Meyer continued to live retired in his beautiful home at Mound City.

On October 26, 1909, Mr. Meyer married Agnes E. Westermann, born at Mound City January 10, 1887, a daughter of William and Agnes (Schulte) Westermann. He was born at Germantown, Illinois, October 27, 1853, and she in Hanover, Germany, April 21, 1857, a daughter of Bernard and Agnes (Luehermann) Schulte, who came to Saint Louis, Missouri, in 1864. Mr. Westermann was bookkeeper and manager of the Meyer Stave Company. His death occurred January 21, 1921, and since his death Mrs. Westermann has lived with her widowed daughter, Mrs. Meyer. Mr. and Mrs. Meyer had one son, Carl F., who was born May 18, 1911, who is now a student at Clayton, Missouri. In religious faith Mr. Meyer was Lutheran, but his widow is a Catholic, and he was a democrat in his political belief. He was not one who mingled to any great extent in public affairs, but he continued to maintain his interest in his home city to the day of his death, and contributed generously toward its advancement in every way he thought best. When he died Mound City lost one of its best citizens, and his family a kind and loving husband and father.

JOHN J. FAULKNER, former postmaster of East St. Louis, for many years prominent in public life and business in that city, was born in Richardson County, Nebraska, November 5, 1861, son of George and Luemma (Songer) Faulkner.

His grandparents were Virginians, the Faulkners having been prominent in Botetourt and Montgomery counties of that state. His grandfather, Stephen Faulkner, served in the Quartermaster's Department of the army during the war with Mexico. The maternal grandparents were Joseph and Amanda Songer, also Virginians.

George Faulkner, who was eight years old when his father died, was a pioneer of Nebraska Territory, settling in Richardson County, where he became a farmer and stock raiser. For ten years he was sheriff of Richardson County. He took an active part in

securing the admission of Nebraska to the Union and served as a member of the Territorial Legislature when the capital was at Omaha. From Nebraska he removed to Hodgeman County, Kansas, and served as county commissioner for a number of years. He died in 1893, and his wife in 1905. Their children were: Mary, who married Randolph R. Hanna, and they reared eleven children; John J.; Charles W., who married and had three children; Susan, widow of Samuel Grundy, who died in 1923, and has six surviving children; Mrs. Alice Pitts, a widow with two children; and Mrs. Olive Smith, mother of four children.

John J. Faulkner spent his early life in Southeastern Nebraska. He graduated from the Falls City High School in 1876. For a number of years his work was chiefly in the field of education. He taught in Richardson County, served as county superintendent of schools, and for several years was also editor and manager of the Falls City Journal of Nebraska. As a commercial salesman he represented a wholesale general merchandise supply house, and from 1898 to 1911 was a representative of the American Book Company, part of the time as field manager for that educational publishing house. While on the road he established his home at East St. Louis, and on leaving the book company he engaged in general construction and paving supply business. At East St. Louis he became active in municipal affairs, and on June 21, 1921, was appointed acting postmaster and was commissioned postmaster on the 8th of November of the same year. He was postmaster until November 23, 1925.

He married August 15, 1883, Miss Agnes Abbey, daughter of Wallace W. and Alzina (Worthe) Abbey. Her father died in 1914 and her mother in 1894. Her father entered the Union army as a captain, became colonel of his regiment, and at one time was provost marshal of Louisville, Kentucky. One of his brothers served on the staff of General Grant. Mrs. Faulkner is connected with the Scofield and Simmons families of Illinois, prominent tobacco dealers and growers, and also with the Pepoon and Boone families. Wallace W. Abbey became a prominent citizen of Nebraska. He was a farmer and stock man, also conducted a nursery, and in later years was engaged in the furniture and undertaking business. Active in state politics, he served on the prison board, was chairman of the Nebraska State Fair Executive Board, and one of the Nebraska Live Stock Commission under Governor Thayer. Mrs. Faulkner's brothers and sisters were: Charles S.; Mamie, who married Edward S. Steele; Myrta, who became the wife of Charles F. Reavis, member of Congress, and later assistant attorney general of the United States; Nell, who married August E. Hagensick.

Mr. and Mrs. Faulkner have one son, Worthe Wallace. He graduated from the East St. Louis High School, spent two years in Washington University at St. Louis, studied art and music in the Cincinnati College of Music, and has gained considerable distinction in his profession and art, having played a leading role in "Maytime" at New York City.

Mrs. Faulkner is member of the Christian Science Church. Mr. Faulkner was the first exalted ruler of the local lodge of Elks, and has been one of its active members for twenty-five years. He was grand trustee of the United States Grand Lodge for five years. For forty-three years he has been a member of the Knights of Pythias.

John Crerar, Chicago merchant and philanthropist, was born in New York in 1827 and died October 19, 1889. In New York he earned a partnership in a large mercantile house, and while in that city was president of the Mercantile Library Association. He moved to Chicago in 1862, as representative of his firm, a railway supply house, and subsequently became head of Crerar, Adams & Company and engaged in the same line of business. Under his direction this became one of the largest concerns of its kind in the Middle West. He also assisted in the development of such institutions as the Pullman Palace Car Company, the Chicago & Alton Railway, the Illinois & Joliet Railroad, the Illinois Trust and Savings Bank, and the Liverpool, London and Globe Insurance Company.

During his lifetime he gave generously to many causes and at his death, being without wife or children, he bequeathed a million and a half dollars to various institutions of a religious, historical and literary character, also the great sum of four million for a free public library. The Crerar Library has become one of the great libraries of the Middle West and for some years past has been housed in the splendid Crerar building, opposite the Chicago Public Library.

Rev. P. J. Hennessy, resident priest of Saint Mary's Catholic Church, Joliet, is one of the scholarly men and eminent divines of his calling, and one who has won the confidence of the people of the city, irrespective of their religious connections, because of his whole-souled work in behalf of public well being. While he is not native-born, he is a true American in the highest and best sense of the word, and to his advice and admonitions are due many of the improvements which have been recently secured in this section of the state.

Rev. P. J. Hennessy was born in Limerick, Ireland, in 1876, a son of James and Margaret (Collins) Hennessy, both of whom came to the United States, and settled in Chicago, in 1898, and there they died and are buried. These excellent and devout parents sent their son to the public schools in his native land, and dedicated him to the service of the church. He was a student of Saint Francis College, Brooklyn, New York, and Saint Mary's Seminary, Baltimore, Maryland, and in 1902 he was ordained to the priesthood by the late Cardinal Gibbons. After six months in parish work in New York City, Rev. P. J. Hennessy was sent to Chicago, and a year later was stationed in Saint Mary's parish, Evanston, Illinois, where he remained for seven years. He was then sent to Braidwood, Illinois, where he spent ten years, after which he was at Elmhurst for three years. Then, in April, 1924, he assumed his present duties in connection with Saint Mary's Church, Joliet. His assistants are Revs. Ed. Sendek, L. J. Kiley and J. T. Farrell.

A man of broad vision, Rev. P. J. Hennessy believes in acting with various community organizations, and is a valued member of the Joliet Kiwanis Club and of the Public Health Council. He belongs to the Knights of Columbus, and is chaplain of the Joliet Council of that order, and he is an ex-grand knight of the Braidwood Council, Knights of Columbus, and Joliet A. O. H. Reverend Hennessy is interested in many philanthropies and reforms which indubitably add value and dignity to his name and calling and his identification with the higher life of this city is unquestioned, nor is his leadership in many things disputed.

JAMES JACOB HOFFER, M. D., who is also Doctor of Dental Surgery, is one of the highly qualified men in the modern field of oral surgery and dentistry in Illinois. He enjoys a large practice at East St. Louis.

He was born at Mansfield, Ohio, April 28, 1878, son of Isaac Bell and Katherine (Leiter) Hoffer. For some years he was sheriff of Cumberland County, Pennsylvania. The maternal grandfather of Dr. Hoffer was Jacob Leiter, who moved from Pennsylvania to Ohio in about 1823, and settled near Mansfield, where he was a blacksmith. Some years later there visited him a nephew, L. Z. Leiter, on his way west to Chicago. L. Z. Leiter later was a partner of Marshall Field, and one of the founders of the great Marshall Field establishment in Chicago. Isaac Bell Hoffer was a butcher and retail meat merchant. One of his customers in Mansfield, Ohio, was the late distinguished Ohio statesman, John Sherman, and Dr. Hoffer as a boy frequently delivered meat to the Sherman Home. Isaac B. Hoffer was an enthusiastic republican in politics. From Ohio he moved out to Tacoma, Washington, where he continued in the same line of business. He was deputy sheriff at one time. He died in 1898 and his wife in 1912. They were the parents of seven children: James, who is married and has one child; Frances, wife of Alexander Doutrick; Grace, wife of Hugh King and the mother of one child; Brainard, who married Minnie Morris and has two children; Brink, who died unmarried; Katherine, who is the wife of C. H. Knapp and has one child, and Doctor James Jacob Hoffer.

James Jacob Hoffer received his early education in the public schools of Mansfield, Ohio, and in 1896 graduated from the high school at Tacoma, Washington. Returning to the middle west, he entered the dental department of Northwestern University at Chicago; graduated Doctor of Dental Surgery in 1901. For three years he practiced at Peoria, and then took a regular medical course in the National College of Medicine at Chicago, receiving his M. D. degree in 1907. He had specialized in oral surgery and diseases of the mouth. For some years Dr. Hoffer was in practice at Chicago and for one year in Omaha, Nebraska, and in 1921 located at St. Louis, where he is a specialist in dental surgery, and diseases of the mouth, his reputation attracting cases to him from all southern Illinois. Doctor Hoffer tried to get into the navy during the World war, but was put in class four. He is a member of the College Dental Society Psi Omega, thirty-second degree Scottish Rite Mason, and a member of several professional organizations.

Doctor Hoffer married at Oak Park, Chicago, in December, 1910, Miss Elsie Nye Gibbs, daughter of Joseph and Katherine (Jarvis) Gibbs. Her father died in 1884 and her mother in 1919. Her father was a soldier with an Illinois regiment in the Civil war, and after the war drew a pension and was a member of the Grand Army of the Republic. Mrs. Hoffer is related to the Swift family, the Calvin Brice family of Ohio, and Senator Cullom family of Illinois. She has one brother William J. Gibbs in the shoe department of Marshall Field & Company, Chicago. He married Maud Brothers, and has a son William. Mr. and Mrs. Hoffer have a son James J. Jr., born in 1912.

Dr. Hoffer finds his recreation largely in literature and is himself well known in the literary field. He writes in a humorous vain, but with keen observation and discrimination. His nom de plume is "Jerry." One article which attracted much notice was a burlesque on the Bok Prize, and also some articles on the political situation of 1924.

EDWARD RECTOR, of the Chicago Bar, who died August 1, 1925, began the study of law and had his first experience and practice with a firm that handled a considerable amount of patent cases. He became fascinated with this branch of the law, and gave it a degree of study and investigation that for a number of years made him a well known authority among the patent attorneys of Chicago, where he practiced in that branch of the law for thirty years.

Mr. Rector represented an old American family of Revolutionary stock and was himself born in southern Indiana in Lawrence County, July 6, 1863. His grandfather, Jesse Rector, was a native of Virginia, served with the Virginia Continental line in the Revolution under General Washington, participating in the siege of Yorktown at the close of the war. He then engaged in farming in Virginia, but in 1821 yielded to the call of the West, and with wife and children crossed the Alleghany mountains, and by laborious stages reached a new home in Lawrence County, Indiana, where frontier conditions still prevailed to a large extent.

Isaac Rector, father of the Chicago attorney, was fifteen years of age when his parents went to Indiana. He was reared on a farm, and became a very successful banker in Bedford, Indiana. In 1881 through the influence of a distinguished Indianan, his brother-in-law, Colonel Richard (Dick) Thompson, who was then secretary of the navy, he was induced to remove to Washington and accept a special appointment in the Navy Department. He died at Washington in advanced years in 1899.

Isaac Rector married Juliet B. Gardiner, Her father, James B. Gardiner, was a man of prominence in Ohio the early half of the last century. His home was at Marietta, the site of the first permanent settlement in the northwest territory. Subsequently he removed to Franklintown in Franklin County, where for a time he published a newspaper and later was engaged in the newspaper business at Columbus. He was a man of more than ordinary mentality and influence.

Edward Rector, son of Isaac and Juliet B. (Gardiner) Rector, was reared in Lawrence County, Indiana, where he attended the common schools. In 1882 at the age of nineteen, he began the study of law at Cincinnati in the office of Stem & Peck, and also attended the University of Cincinnati Law School, where he graduated with the LL. B. degree in 1885. For six years following, he engaged in practice at Cincinnati as junior member of the firm of Peck & Rector. During that time Mr. Rector sought every opportunity for experience in litigation relating to patents for invention, personally handled an increasing practice in that line, and his success justified him in making it his specialty. In order to have a more central location, for a practice that is never altogether local in nature, Mr. Rector in 1892 removed from Cincinnati to Chicago. In thirty years he enjoyed rank as a leader in his specialty, and one of the men of genuine prominence in a city that has been famous for the high standards set by the legal profession.

The success Mr. Rector achieved in his profession was turned to the benefit of many others besides himself. He was always mindful of his own early struggles for an education, and used some of his means to afford readier opportunities to other youths. He established a number of years ago, the Rector Scholarship Foundation at De Pauw University at Greencastle, Indiana, and altogether afforded opportunity for more than seven hundred students at that institution of learning to have the normal burden of college expenses lightened. He was a trustee of De Pauw University. Mr. Rector never sought or desired political office, being content to exercise the right of franchise and exert such influence as he might toward clean government and wholesome conditions. He was a member of the American, Illinois State and Chicago Bar Associations, and the Chicago Association of Patent Lawyers. The wife of Mr. Rector, to whom he was married in 1893, was formerly Miss Lucy Rowland, of Cincinnati.

August W. Thode, veteran Galena business man, and former mayor of that city, was born at Galena December 5, 1868, son of August N. and Sophie (Seamann) Thode. His father was born and reared in Hanover, Germany, and came to America about 1850. For two years he lived in New York City, and moving from there to Galena met and married Sophie Seamann. He was a cabinet maker, but after a few years entered the grocery business and was active as a local merchant until his death in 1901. His wife died in 1897, and both are buried in the city cemetery. They had five children: Ernestine, who married Alfred M. Brickler; Edward J., of Fort Dodge, Iowa; Johanna, who married W. F. Claussan; Herman, of Fort Dodge, and August W.

August W. Thode was educated in public schools in his native city and finished in the German-English College. From early boyhood he had working experience in his father's store, and practically grew up in the grocery business. In 1891 he sold out his interest in his father's store and then built an independent establishment at the corner of Ridge and West streets. This has been the familiar store which has supplied food for the people of Galena and vicinity for over thirty years, and has become famous for the advertising which has made the store noted far and wide. Mr. Thode's store slogan and sign is "Thode on the Hill."

Mr. Thode through all the years of his active business career has identified himself with every project for the general welfare and upbuilding of the community. He has been a director in a number of business enterprises and he owns over a thousand acres of bottom land along the Mississippi River. He plans to make this into an extensive park, to be known as Thode's Park. It has wonderful natural resources and attractions. For many years it has been a favorite picnic ground. Mr. Thode is also proprietor of the Galena Land & Pickle Company, which ships many carloads of pickles to all parts of the United States.

Mr. Thode for a number of years was assistant fire marshal and fire marshal of Galena, served as an alderman and president of the Galena Fire Association, was the first president of the Southern Wisconsin and Northern Illinois Firemen's Association, holding that office from 1910 to 1911, and was president of the Illinois State Firemen's Association in 1903-04. He held the office of mayor for a number of years. In 1912 he was president of the National Rock Club of America and Canada, and has been president of the Jo Daviess County Poultry and Pet Stock Association. He belongs to a number of fraternities, including the Independent Order of Odd Fellows and Elks, Rebekahs, Knights of Pythias, Eagles, Owls, Woodmen of the World. He is a member of the Illinois Farm Bureau and the Jo Daviess County Horticultural Association, Galena Chamber of Commerce, Kiwanis Club, and is president of the Izaak Walton League at Galena. Mr. Thode is a republican in politics and a member of the Lutheran Church.

He married at Galena, August 27, 1892, Miss Emma J. Meller, who was reared and educated at Galena, completing her studies in St. Mary's College at Galena. For twelve years she was a student of music, and comes of a family distinguished for its artistic attainments. Mrs. Thode is a member of the Eastern Star, Rebekahs, Pythian Sisters, the Needle Work Guild of America, and has been active in clubs and church work. She is one of the large family of Joseph A. and Theresa (Haser) Meller. Her father was born and reared in Cologne, Germany, and came to America at the age of fifteen, and shortly afterwards settled with his father at Galena. The Meller family is a large and prominent one in Northwestern Illinois, Mrs. Thode being one of fourteen children, eight of whom are still living. Mr. and Mrs. Thode have no children of their own, but two nieces of Mr. and Mrs. Thode, Miss Marguerite and Miss Irene C. Meller, have made their home with Mr. and Mrs. Thode, since the death of their mother, Mrs.

Cory Meller, who died May 10th, 1926, their father dying in 1924.

Miss Marguerite is an accomplished pianist of Galena and Miss Irene C. Meller is office manager for the Galena Water Works and Electric Light and Power Company of Galena, Illinois. A sister, Madeline Meller, married Edward Johnson, a road contractor and builder, now of Hampton, Iowa. They have one child, Major Meller Johnson.

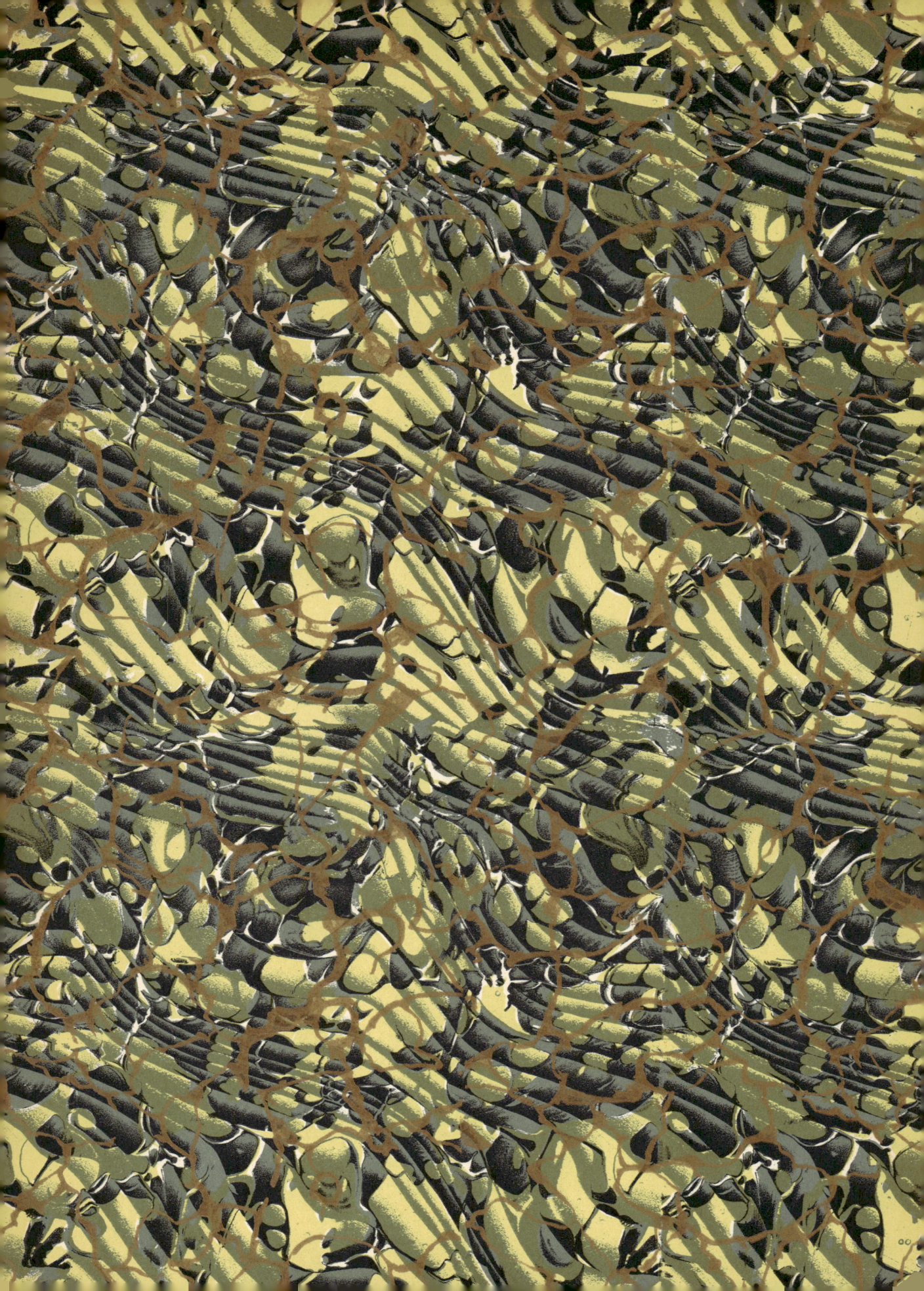

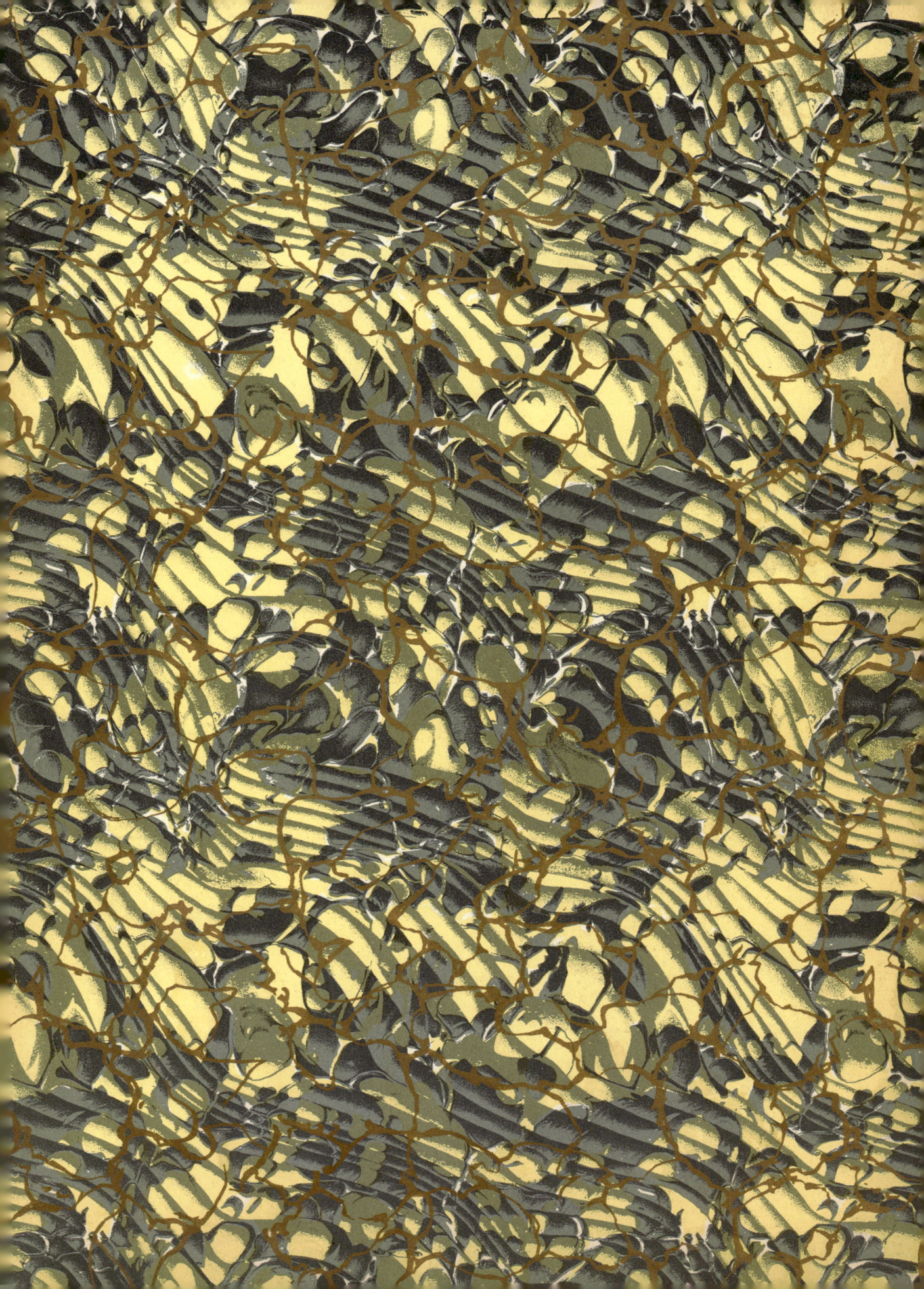

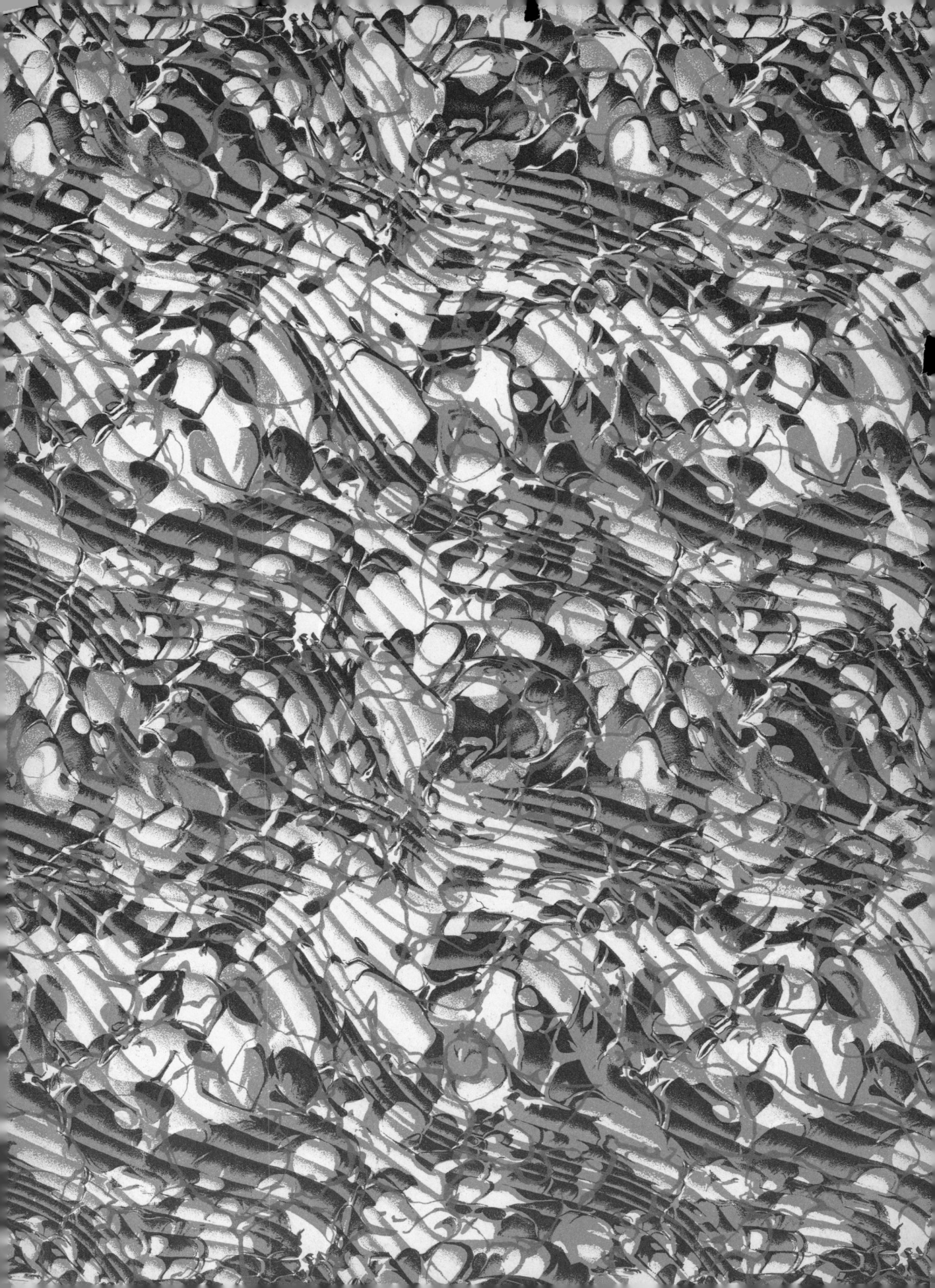

HISTORY

OF

ILLINOIS

AND

HER PEOPLE

BY

PROFESSOR GEORGE W. SMITH, M. A.

*Head, Department of History, State Teachers College, Carbondale, Illinois;
Author of a Student's History of Illinois; Member Board
of Directors, State Historical Society*

Assisted by an Advisory Board

IN SIX VOLUMES

ILLUSTRATED

VOLUME VI

PUBLISHERS
THE AMERICAN HISTORICAL SOCIETY, INC.
CHICAGO AND NEW YORK
1927

COPYRIGHT 1927
THE AMERICAN HISTORICAL SOCIETY, INC.

History of Illinois

JOHN B. LORD. The Ayer and Lord Tie Company of Chicago is the oldest and largest organization of its kind in the country, manufacturers and dealers in railroad ties and other heavy timbers. The operations of this company are nation wide, and the mills, timberlands and distributing facilities comprise an imposing industry.

One of the founders of the business and continuously active therein for nearly half a century is Mr. John B. Lord, a Chicagoan who deserves mention among the constructive citizens of Illinois.

He was born at Newton, Massachusetts, June 5, 1848, son of Brackett and Clarissa (Winslow) Lord. On both sides he is of Colonial ancestry. Reared in Massachusetts, attending public schools at Newton, and finishing his education in Wilbraham Academy, he then assisted his father in the hay and grain business at Newton. About the time he reached his majority he had made a resolve based on Horace Greeley's injunction that young men should go West, and accordingly he came to Illinois. At Paris in Edgar County he engaged in the grain business.

While there he met C. W. Powell, whose influence had a marked bearing on his subsequent career. Later for a time he continued in the grain business at Toledo, Ohio. On one of his buying trips in Illinois he learned that the Wabash Railroad Company was preparing to let a large tie contract. This information he imparted to his friend Mr. Powell, who had been a tie contractor for a number of years and was then about to retire from business. In consequence of this information the two formed a partnership, secured the Wabash contract, and fulfilled its conditions by delivering 300,000 ties. In that way was laid the basis of the present Ayer and Lord Tie Company of Chicago. The firm of Powell and Lord extended its interests and activities and for a number of years maintained its headquarters in Chicago. Upon the dissolution of the partnership in 1892 the Ayer and Lord Tie Company was organized, Mr. E. E. Ayer becoming senior member of that corporation. This company has continued now for over thirty years, and Mr. Lord never has owned less than a half interest in the business. The first year of its existence the concern produced 1,750,000 ties. The largest production of any year for the company was 12,650,000 ties. Besides the ties the company deals in telegraph poles, bridge and other heavy timbers. The company started with a capitalization of $100,000, the present capital being $1,650,000 in common and $750,000 in preferred stock.

By 1903 the tie business was confronted with a radical change, owing to the scarcity of white oak timber. To meet the increased demands various other woods were made available by chemical treatment. The Ayer and Lord Tie Company built its first treating plant at Carbondale, Illinois, in 1903, and since then has established plants at Grenada, Mississippi, North Little Rock, Arkansas, Louisville, Kentucky, and Montgomery, Alabama. The plant at Louisville is the most complete plant of its kind in the world. The Ayer & Lord Company is the largest user of creosote in the United States. The corporation found the greater part of its timber in the states of Kentucky, Tennessee, Mississippi and Arkansas, and it has been expedient for the company to buy the land outright on which the timber grows. As the material is largely along water courses, the company also built and owns its own fleet of steamers and barges, and at Paducah, Kentucky, maintains marine ways to repair its boats and furnish a general marine service.

In the upbuilding of this gigantic industry John B. Lord has been a dominant factor. In Chicago, likewise, as a citizen he has been esteemed for nearly half a century. He is a Presbyterian, a republican and a member of the Chicago, the Midday and Onwentsia Clubs and the Midwick Country Club of California.

Mr. Lord is a director of the Harris Trust Company, is one of the Board of Managers of the Y. M. C. A. and a member of the Board of Directors of the Presbyterian Hospital.

In 1876 he married Miss Anna E. Steele, her parents being natives of Staunton, Virginia, and she having been born in Illinois. Her parents moved to Edgar County, Illinois, in pioneer days. Mr. and Mrs. Lord had four children: Clara, wife of William E. Pratt; Mary T., wife of Robert E. Ross; Margaret, wife of J. H. King; and Russell. Russell Lord, now president and business manager of the Ayer & Lord Tie Company, earned a meritorious distinction in the World war, where he obtained the rank of captain and regimental adjutant in the One Hundred and Twenty-fourth Field Artillery of the Thirty-third Division. For about four weeks he was a continuous participant in the Argonne offenses.

CHAUNCEY B. BLAIR. During an extended and somewhat varied business career Chauncey B. Blair has been identified with several lines of endeavor, holding high positions in enterprises of Chicago which have been benefited by his ability and industry. At present he is representative at Chicago for the Bankers Lien Corporation, and his connection with this and other important activities gives him a substantial standing among the city's men of worth.

Mr. Blair was born at Lake Forest, Illinois, August 18, 1886, and is a son of Chauncey J. and Mary A. I. (Mitchell) Blair. His father was born at Michigan City, Indiana, in 1845, and received good educational advantages, completing his study at the University of Indiana. Following his graduation from that institution he embarked in the hardware business with his uncle, William Blair, at Chicago, but later transferred his services to the Merchants National Bank of Chicago, where his abilities gained him rapid promotion and he rose to the position of president, in which capacity he was active at the time of his death, May 10, 1916. Mr. Blair was widely known in financial circles and for a number of years took a prominent part in civic affairs.

Chauncey B. Blair attended the Chicago public schools, The Hill School in Pennsylvania and Yale University, from the last-named of which he was graduated with the class of 1909. At that time he became the secretary and treasurer of the Kennicott Company, acting in those capacities until 1916. During 1917 and 1918 he was cashier and a member of the Board of Directors of the famous Chicago Morris Plan Bank of Chicago, and in the latter year entered the United States service as a member of the Naval Reserve Force at the Great Lakes Training School In 1919 he received his honorable discharge, and in the same year returned to civilian life as treasurer of the Dearborn Trust Company. In 1924 he became president of the Manufacturers and Dealers Finance Corporation, but at present is applying himself to his duties as Chicago representative of the Bankers Lien Corporation, maintaining offices at 166 West Jackson Boulevard, Room 535. He is also president-treasurer of Blair and Hailand, Inc., insurance brokers and agents. Mr. Blair is a member of the University Club, the Harvard, Yale, Princeton Club, the Onwentsia Club, the Saddle and Cycle Club and The Casino Club. In his political adherence he affiliates with the republican party, but has had no active part in political matters save as a public-spirited citizen.

On January 3, 1913, at Chicago, Mr. Blair was united in marriage with Miss Mildred Marshall, who was born at Chicago, and to this union there has been born one son: Chauncey B., Jr. The family home is at 515 Blair Place, Chicago.

WILBUR C. HADLEY had the distinction of having served continuously for a third of a century as president of the State Bank of Collinsville, having been the first president of that institution, one of the strong and prosperous banks of Madison County. As a business man and citizen he was active at Collinsville for over sixty years. His death occurred December 9, 1925.

Mr. Hadley was of old Colonial ancestry and Revolutionary stock and a member of the family that has been in Southern Illinois for over a century. His grandfather, John Hadley, was a soldier in the War of 1812, and came from Kentucky to Collinsville Township in 1817, developing a farm from the wilderness north of Collinsville. Of his three sons two became ministers of the Gospel.

William Hadley, his son, was widely known for his early work in the Methodist ministry and his splendid Christian character at all times. He was born in Kentucky in 1806, and was eleven years of age when the family came to Illinois. Growing up in pioneer surroundings he taught himself the alphabet and had only six weeks of attendance at any school. He was ordained to the ministry in 1833, and was distinguished for his broad culture and solid learning, having been a deep student not only of the Bible but of other literature. For five years he followed the trade of carpenter, and in 1831 began farming. He developed one of the finest farms in Madison County, and gave his active supervision to the farm until 1863, when, following the death of his first wife, he turned his attention to fruit growing in Jackson County. He made his home at Collinsville after 1883, and died November 4, 1896. His home was just across the street from the polling place, and his death occurred only a few hours after he cast his vote in the general election of 1896, when William McKinley was chosen President. The election judges conferred upon him an unusual but well deserved honor, carrying a ballot across the street to his home and then receiving his vote and depositing it in the ballot box. He had been a republican since the organization of the party.

Rev. William Hadley married in 1830 Diadema McKinney. She was born in 1809, daughter of John and Katherine (Eaves) McKinney. John McKinney, a native of South Carolina, was a soldier of the Revolution, serving with Morgan's Rifles and later as a corporal and scout in the Continental Line. He was one of the followers of the famous Revolutionary leaders, Morgan and General Marion, and for particularly meritorious service was presented with a pair of silver spurs by General Marion. He was then only sixteen years of age. Diadema McKinney died in 1863.

Wilbur Clay Hadley was the last surviving child of three sons and two daughters. He was born on his father's farm in Collinsville Township, August 28, 1842, and had the advantage of a later generation than his father, but even so he first attended the subscription school taught in a log cabin. Later he attended school at Collinsville, spent a portion of two years in McKendree College at Lebanon, and completed a course in the Jones Commercial College at St. Louis. In his early life he was a farmer, a school teacher and for a short time conducted a hotel in St. Louis. He then managed his father's farming property, and engaged in merchandising at Collinsville, where he conducted a store from 1871 to 1880, and again from 1884 to 1891. He had been a permanent resident of Collinsville since 1869.

When the State Bank of Collinsville was organized in 1891 the directors conferred upon Mr. Hadley the honor of electing him first president, and he was the executive head of that bank continuously for a third of a century and wisely guided its prosperity and made it an instrument of great service to the community.

Wilbur C. Hadley was one of the prominent Masons of Illinois. He was a life member of Oriental Consistory of the Scottish Rite in Chicago, and was Grand High Priest of the Royal Arch Masons of Illinois, and for many years acted as master of his home lodge and as high priest of his chapter. His affiliations were with Collinsville Lodge No. 712; Unity Chapter No. 182, R. A. M.; Belleville Council, R. and S. M.; Tancred Commandery No. 50, K. T.; and Ainad Temple of the Mystic Shrine of East St. Louis. He was the responsible leader in giving the Masonic bodies at Collinsville an appropriate home and was master of the lodge when the Collinsville Masonic Temple was constructed.

Mr. Hadley served as a member of the State Central Committee of the republican party for the Twenty-second Congressional District, and for one term he was a member of the Madison County Board of Supervisors and was county treasurer in 1889. He was a member of the Society of Sons of the American Revolution. Wilbur C. Hadley was a brother of the late W. F. L. Hadley, who was a lawyer, banker and congressman, and one of the most distinguished citizens of Edwardsville.

Wilbur Clay Hadley married, in 1866, Miss Mary S. Smith. She was born in 1847, at what is now Granite City, Illinois, daughter of Sydney and Sina (Davidson) Smith. She finished her education in Monticello Seminary at Godfrey. Mr. and Mrs. Hadley became the parents of six children: Alice, who married R. S. Louden; Bertha M., who married Alonzo Coombs; Josephine, who became the wife of J. A. Yates; William E. Hadley, a prominent Illinois lawyer and jurist, whose career is given in the following sketch; Mary, deceased, wife of Edward A. Langan; and Mattie Strong, who died in infancy.

WILLIAM EDWIN HADLEY was admitted to the Illinois bar in 1894, and for nearly thirty years was engaged in a practice of growing importance at Collinsville and East St. Louis. He was honored with election and gave distinguished service as judge of the Circuit Court for six years. Recently he gave up his law practice to become vice president of the State Bank of Collinsville, and upon the death of his father, succeeded him as President of the bank.

He is a son of Wilbur C. Hadley, for over thirty years president of the State Bank of Collinsville, a prominent citizen of southern Illinois and member of a pioneer family of the state. A more complete account of Wilbur C. Hadley and the Hadley family is published in the preceding sketch.

Judge William Edwin Hadley was born at Collinsville, January 16, 1873, only son of his parents. He graduated from high school in 1890, entered the law department of McKendree College at Lebanon, where he received his law degree, and was admitted to the bar on his twenty-first birthday. He began practice at Collinsville, and subsequently opened another office at East St. Louis, and was one of the busy attorneys in these two cities for fifteen years. In June, 1909, he was elected judge of the Third Judicial Circuit, and proved a most capable and well qualified judge in that circuit for his six year term. After retiring from the bench he resumed his extensive law practice at East St. Louis, but in 1922 retired from his professional work to become active vice president of the State Bank of Collinsville. Judge Hadley for a number of years handled a law practice largely commercial and corporation in character. He is interested in a number of banks and mining and other enterprises.

In October, 1899, Judge Hadley married Miss Kate L. Powell, of Collinsville, daughter of Dr. A. M. Powell, who for many years was a successful physician in that community. Mrs. Hadley died in April, 1923, the mother of two children: Louise H., who is the wife of C. H. Helm, of East St. Louis; and Wilbur Powell, who finished his education in the University of Illinois, graduating in June, 1925.

Judge Hadley has always been actively affiliated with the republican party except while on the bench. During the World war he was a Four Minute Speaker and otherwise identified with patriotic causes. He is a Knight Templar and Scottish Rite Mason and Shriner, and is a member of the Elks Lodge at East St. Louis, the Moose and the Episcopal Church.

HON. WALTER C. LINDLEY, since September 29, 1922, judge of the United States District Court for the eastern district of Illinois, is a native of this state, graduating with honors from the Colleges of Liberal Arts and Law at the university, and in a career of twenty years as a member of the bar has fully justified the expectations entertained of him while a university man.

Judge Lindley was born on a farm in Big Spring Township, Shelby County, Illinois, July 12, 1880. His paternal ancestors came from England and settled in New Jersey in Colonial times. Subsequently a branch of the family moved to North Carolina. There they became affiliated with the Quaker Church, and Judge Lindley's grandfather on coming north first lived in the noted Quaker community of Wayne County, Indiana. This grandfather was Osmond Lindley, who was born at Guilford Court House, North Carolina, in 1837. As a young man he moved to Wayne County, Indiana; married there, and became a pork packer and farmer. In about 1866 he moved with his family to Shelby County, Illinois, and was a school teacher and farmer there until his death in 1879. His wife was Achsah Wilson, who was born at Guilford Court House, North Carolina, in 1839, and died at Fairmount, Indiana, in 1919.

Alfred W. Lindley, father of Judge Lindley, was born at Dublin in Wayne County, Indiana, September 7, 1856, and was about ten years of age when his parents moved to Shelby County, Illinois, where he was reared and finished his education. The greater part of his active life has been spent as a farmer. He has been an important and successful figure in the agricultural life of Shelby and Cumberland counties, and still owns a large amount of farm lands in those counties. He also engaged in banking and was president of the First National Bank of Chrisman and of the Neoga National Bank and is still a director of those institutions. His home was in Shelby

County until 1895, when he removed to Neoga. Alfred W. Lindley is a republican, has served on the Board of Supervisors in Shelby County, and is an active worker in the Presbyterian Church, though reared a Quaker. He married Irena Carey, who was born in Grant County, Indiana, September 7, 1858. Walter C. is the oldest of their children. Miss Jennie A., at home with her parents, is a teacher of music. The two other children were Virgil, who died at the age of two years, and Vernon, who died when ten years old.

Walter C. Lindley during his youth lived on a farm and in the town home of his parents at Neoga; was educated in common schools in Shelby County; graduated from the Neoga High School in 1897, and from 1897 to 1901 was a student in the College of Liberal Arts at the University of Illinois, taking his A. B. degree in 1901. From 1901 to 1904 he attended the College of Law, graduating LL. B. in 1904. In 1910 the College of Law awarded him the degree Doctor of Jurisprudence. From 1901 to 1905 he was instructor of rhetoric in the Academy of the University. At the University he was a member of the Phi Gamma Delta social fraternity; was elected to the honorary scholarship fraternity Phi Beta Kappa; was a member of the Phi Delta Phi legal fraternity; and the Theta Kappa Nu honorary legal fraternity. Judge Lindley while at the University was managing editor of the Daily Illini; was president of the Students' Republican Club; associate editor of the Illinois Magazine; chairman of the Senior Ball Committee, and the Cap and Gown Committee. He graduated at the head of his class from the law school, and stood second in the entire graduating class of the University, a class numbering two hundred and forty-five.

Admitted to the bar June 30, 1904, Mr. Lindley began practice at Danville, and until 1922 was a member of the firm Lindley, Penwell & Lindley, handling a large general practice in all the courts of eastern Illinois. From 1912 to 1918 he served as master in chancery of the United States Court, and from 1916 to 1920 was a member of the Board of County Commissioners of Vermilion County. The late President Harding appointed him judge of the United States District Court on September 29, 1922. His eastern district comprises forty-five counties, extending from Kankakee County on the north to Alexander County, including the City of Cairo on the south and St. Clair County on the west.

Judge Lindley is a member of the Presbyterian Church, Olive Branch Lodge No. 38, A. F. and A. M., Danville Consistory of the Scottish Rite; Medinah Temple of the Mystic Shrine at Chicago; Danville Lodge No. 332, B. P. O. Elks; White Oaks Lodge No. 469, Knights of Pythias. He is a director of the Danville Chamber of Commerce; is former president and director of the Danville Country Club; former president of the Vermilion County Bar Association; served on important committees of the Illinois State Bar Association; is a member of the American Bar Association; was for two years president and is still a member of the College Club of Danville; is a member of the Kiwanis Club; is president of the Alumni Association of the College of Law; has served on the Advisory Committee of the Board of Trustees in the College of Law, and for a number of years was a member of the Executive Committee of the Alumni Association of the University of Illinois.

Judge Lindley is a director of the Second National Bank at Danville. During the World war as a Four Minute Speaker he made more than two hundred speeches in counties of eastern Illinois in behalf of the Liberty Loan and Red Cross drives; and was a member of the Legal Advisory Board of Vermilion County. Judge Lindley for three years was on the Board of Education in Danville, and during this time the new million dollar high school was built. His home is at 1212 Logan Avenue, Danville, and he is interested in farming lands in Vermilion County and in the state of Nebraska.

Judge Lindley married, April 30, 1913, at North Egremont, Massachusetts, Miss Louise Dewey Brown, daughter of Charles F. and Carrie (Dewey) Brown, both now deceased. Her father was a prominent bridge contractor, for many years having his headquarters in Chicago. He helped build the bridge across the Mississippi at Memphis, the bridge at Thebes, Illinois, and many others over the United States. The three children of Judge and Mrs. Lindley are: Mary Aletta, Louise Dewey and Walter C., Jr.

MACLAY HOYNE. In the public life of Illinois during the past several decades there has been no more spectacular figure than Maclay Hoyne, of Chicago. A true representative of western progress and spirit, during a number of years he was before the people as their protector in the office of state's attorney, as well as in other important capacities, and it can be stated with truth and without fear of contradiction that no citizen of our day has brought into the conduct of the affairs of his office a stronger personality, greater courage or deeper conscientiousness as to the discharge of his responsibilities.

Mr. Hoyne was born at Chicago, October 12, 1872, and is a son of Thomas Maclay and Jeanie Thomas (Maclay) Hoyne. One of his great-grandfathers, Patrick Hoyne, fled the tyranny of British government in Ireland and in 1815 landed at New York, penniless and with a wife, to begin life afresh. Another great-grandfather was Rev. Archibald Maclay, a Baptist minister then stationed at New York, and a third was Dr. John Temple of Virginia. Great-grandfather Hoyne and his wife died within a year of one another and left an eight-year-old son, Thomas Hoyne, who had up to that time been attending a parish school. The law appointed as his guardian the Protestant Doctor Maclay, and while the lad was growing up in the Maclay home, in 1833, Doctor Temple moved from Virginia to Chicago, bringing his daughter, Leonora. Doctor Temple became one of the widely-known men of his day, being one of the thirteen original incorporators of Chicago, the founder of the first stage-coach line which connected Chicago with the settlements on the Illinois, and built the house of worship occupied jointly by the original congregations of the First Baptist and First Presbyterian churches. His daughter was one of the first women baptized in Chicago, being immersed in the waters of Lake Michigan.

Thomas Hoyne had been born at New York, February 11, 1817, and when still quite young was apprenticed to a manufacturer, and not only performed his work faithfully but joined the Literary Association, which included in its membership such men as Horace Greeley, George Manierre and Charles P. Daly. As an apprentice he also attended two night schools, in one of which he made a study of English grammar and elocution, and in the other gave particular attention to Greek and Latin. When he was eighteen years of age he became clerk in a large jobbing house in order to obtain money to continue his education, and in 1836 began the study of law in the office of Hon. John Brinkerhoff. The reports of his fellow debater and old friend, George Manierre, who had been a resident of Chicago for two years, were of such an encouraging nature that Mr. Hoyne decided to join him in the raw young city of the sloughs and plains, and later in the year 1837 he started for the west, at Detroit boarding the brig "John H. Kinzie" for Chicago. Two weeks later he reached Chicago, where Mr. Manierre, who was clerk of the Circuit Court, found a way to have Mr. Hoyne assist him at a salary of $10 per week. In the autumn of 1838 he took charge of a public school on the West Side, subsequently entering the law office of J. Young Scammon as a student. In the fall of 1839 he was admitted to the bar, and from that time until his death, with the exception of two years spent at Galena, practiced his profession at Chicago, making a brilliant record at the Cook County bar and also appearing before the Supreme Court of Illinois and the United States Supreme Court. He early associated himself with Benjamin F. Ayer, and in January, 1864, Oliver H. Horton entered the partnership, of which Thomas M. Hoyne, the son, became a member in 1867, the style of the firm being thus changed to Hoyne, Horton and Hoyne, which remained unchanged until the death of its senior member.

On September 17, 1840, Thomas Hoyne was united in marriage with Leonora M. Temple, and soon thereafter, because of the stringency of the times at Chicago, the couple went to Galena, Illinois, where business in the lead mines was still flourishing. After two years the family returned to Chicago and there made their permanent home. At Chicago Mr. Hoyne was elected probate justice of the peace, and held that office until it was abolished in 1848 and succeeded by the county judgeship. Although a firm democrat, he became a "free soiler." In 1848 he was presidential elector, and stumped the northern half of Illinois in support of Van Buren and Adams. In 1853 he received from President Pierce the appointment of United States district attorney for Illinois. In 1859 he entered upon his duties as United States marshal, and in 1860 superintended the census for the northern district of his state. No man in the west was more patriotic and broadly useful during the Civil war. He was a very active member of the Union Defense Committee, and with tongue and pen, to the utmost limit of his powers, assisted in the preservation of the cause. He was nominated by acclamation for Congress in the Chicago district in 1870, but declined to run. Two years later he was a presidential elector on the ticket which had put forth Horace Greeley, the friend of his youth, to lead the liberal democracy. During the early '70s he commenced a vigorous agitation to further the purificaton of local politics and in the spring of 1876 led the reform movement for mayor on the Citizens ticket. He was elected by a majority of 33,000, the largest at that time ever given a municipal chief magistrate in the city. Mayor Colvin contested the election and the Circuit Court sustained the regular democratic candidate. Although it was believed that he might have appealed with success to the Supreme Court Mr. Hoyne considered the outcome so unjust that he never after would consent to be considered a candidate for office. As a private citizen, however, he was Chicago's devoted friend, and his support was always proffered for any measure which he believed to be for her advancement. He gave his strength, mind, heart and soul to the upbuilding of the city from the period of his early manhood until he was so suddenly snatched away in a vigorous old age. He was one of the fathers of the city who assisted in laying its material foundation broad and deep, and at the same time gave his best efforts toward the establishment of an honest public administration. His nature was both practical and ideal, and founded upon a fine enthusiasm based upon common sense. It was such men as he that Chicago needed in the early times, and to them, more than to all else, must be credited the remarkable impetus which the city acquired even in the pioneer period, and fortunately has never lost.

Mr. Hoyne assisted to found a chair of international and constitutional law in the University of Chicago in 1859, and this institution, of which he was for years the friend and adviser, conferred upon him the degree of Doctor of Laws in 1862. He also secured the great Lalande telescope and was the chief promoter and first secretary of the Chicago Astronomical Society. He was a life member of the Mechanics' Institute, the Academy of Sciences and the Chicago Historical Society, and by contributions and other active work furthered their best interests. In June, 1873, when the University of Chicago and the Northwestern University founded the Union College of Law, Mr. Hoyne was chairman of the Board of Trustees in behalf of the Chicago University for 1873-74 and in 1877 was chosen president of the joint board of management, holding that position at the time of his demise. Mr. Hoyne was also one of the most active in founding and fostering the free Public Library, of which he wrote a most interesting historical sketch in 1877. Of his other writings, of particular interest to pioneers of Chicago, may be mentioned "The Lawyer as a Pioneer," covering the period of the Illinois and Chicago bar from 1837 to 1840, which were the years of his introduction to the community in which he afterwards became so commanding a figure.

Still a vigorous man at the age of sixty-six years, in the summer of 1883 Mr. Hoyne decided to take an eastern tour of rest and recreation, planning to descend the St. Lawrence and pass on to the refreshing beauties of the White Mountains. But on the evening of July 27, three days after he left Chicago, he was killed in a railway collision at Charlton, Orleans County, New York, and his body was brought back for burial to the mourning city of his adoption.

Thomas Maclay Hoyne, father of Maclay Hoyne, continued the substantial work begun by his father, after whose death the firm became Horton and Hoyne, and so continued until 1887, when Oliver H. Horton was elevated to the bench. The firm of Hoyne, Follansbee and O'Connor then came into existence, and in 1899 Thomas M. Hoyne, Maclay Hoyne, John O'Connor and Harry D. Irwin organized the co-partnership of Hoyne, O'Connor and Hoyne, which continued until July 1, 1903, when Maclay Hoyne withdrew, the style then becoming Hoyne, O'Connor and Irwin. Thomas Maclay Hoyne was born at Galena, Illinois, July 17, 1843, and attended the public schools of Chicago and a German school on the North Side, being nineten years of age when he graduated from the old Chicago High School. He made his first practical start in life as a draughtsman for a New York concern engaged in the manufacture of engines and machinery, at a salary of $2.50 per week, but within a year returned to Chicago and in 1866 graduated from the Law School of the old University of Chicago. In 1867 he commenced his long legal career in Chicago, and for forty years had his office at 88 LaSalle Street, removing in 1907 to the Stock Exchange Building.

Under the act of 1901 Mr. Hoyne became a candidate for one of the three additional Circuit judges of Cook County, but although he received a large plurality vote, the Supreme Court declared the law unconstitutional. In 1904 he was again nominated for judge of the Superior Court, but was defeated. These were Mr. Hoyne's sole movements toward public preferment, but while never prominent in politics he always took the interest of a typical American in public affairs. He was one of the founders of the old Chicago Democratic Club, which in 1881 was succeeded by the Iroquois Club, of which he was president in 1897. He was long an honored member of the Illinois State and Chicago Bar Associations, the Chicago Law Institute and the Law Club and served as president of the last-named organization, and the Chicago Bar Association. He also was twice president of the Northwestern Law School Alumni Association, and outside of his success as a practitioner was recognized as a large figure in the fraternal and educational circles of his profession.

In 1871 Mr. Hoyne married Miss Jeanie T. Maclay, daughter of Moses B. Maclay, a well-known New York lawyer. Maclay Hoyne of this review is the eldest of their six children. Thomas Temple Hoyne, Archibald Lawrence Hoyne, Mrs. Susan Hoyne Ingraham, Eugene Hoyne and Mary Hoyne.

Maclay Hoyne attended the Chicago public schools, Williams (Massachusetts) College, from which he was graduated with the degree of Bachelor of Arts in 1895, and the Northwestern University School of Law, from which he was graduated in 1897 with the degree of Bachelor of Laws. At college he played halfback on the varsity teams of both schools, at Williams was a member of the track team and for some time held the college bicycle record for one mile, and also added to his prestige on the baseball diamond. He was always active and interested in athletic sports, being gifted alike with a sound mind and a sound body, and both on the athletic field and in the courts of law has been an aggressive and fair fighter and one hard to defeat. Admitted to the bar in 1897, he joined his father, as heretofore noted, and soon began his long record of public service. From 1903 to 1905 he was assistant corporation counsel under Mayor Harrison the younger, from 1905 to 1907 held the position of first assistant corporation counsel under Mayor Dunne, and later was special counsel for the city of Chicago and for the city council committee on gas, oil, electric light and telephone matters under Mayor Busse. From 1911 until December, 1912, when he became state's attorney, he was first assistant corporation counsel under Mayor Harrison. In 1906 he drafted the Chicago Telephone Company ordinance, which reserved to the city the right to regulate telephone rates every five years. It was he who devised and conducted the litigation resulting in the reduction of telephone rates and of the payment by the telephone company to the city of Chicago a large sum, with a proportionately large benefit to the subscribers. Mr. Hoyne is also the author of the 70-cent gas ordinance and conducted the litigation for the city of Chicago. While first assistant counsel under Mayor Harrison, as counsel for the Chicago Harbor and Subway Commission he became the author of the ordinance creating several harbor districts.

Mr. Hoyne was secretary of the conference of the Chicago Bar Association and State Bar Association for the reform of pleadings and procedure, and has twice served as a member of grievance committees and once on the committee on admissions of the Chicago Bar Association, of which body he was a member of the Board of Managers from 1923 to 1925. The high opinion in which he is held by the legal fraternity is shown by the fact that, while a democratic candidate, he has on two different occasions been decisively endorsed by the Chicago Bar Association, which is conceded to be composed of not less than a three-fourths republican membership. In 1916 he was a delegate to the Democratic National Convention.

Mr. Hoyne was first elected state's attorney in 1912 and received the re-election to that office in 1916, serving until 1920, since which time he has been engaged in the general practice of law at 10 South LaSalle Street. As to his work in the state's attorney's office, a contemporary states: "When it comes to his work as state's attorney I feel that I can justly say that never before in the history of this office in Cook County have the sterling traits of honesty, fearlessness and efficiency been so strikingly exhibited. He has elevated the state's attorneyship to a dignity and importance never before attained, and has made it truly the bulwark of the people's rights and liberties. He possesses in high degree the attributes of moral courage, so desirable but so

Charles S. Thornton.

often lacking in public prosecutors. He has demonstrated in scores of prosecutions that he is fearless in the pursuit of big criminals and the unearthing of organized crime, and he has been relentless in the prosecution of its perpetrators, its protectors and its more remote beneficiaries. The Hoyne record, on the other hand, is not one of drastic, harsh and relentless prosecutions. No public official or private citizen, minister, priest or rabbi ever asked leniency or mercy for the young, ignorant, poor or misguided first offender in vain. It was to the habitual criminal and betrayers of public trusts alone that a deaf ear was turned. That the vast power placed in his hands was wielded impartially and fearlessly by Mr. Hoyne is known to be universally admitted by those who have access to the facts. That it has been efficiently and wisely exercised is proved by the number and character of convictions secured by him as compared with others who have held the office." While Mr. Hoyne possesses a mind essentially legal, it has not that machine-like coldness which is a defect of many brilliant intellects in the professions. He is capable of a very warm sympathy, which he showed very conclusively in July, 1915, when the strike on the surface and elevated railway lines had paralyzed business and threatened to become an endurance test between the car men and the companies. Arbitration was proposed, and the strikers, in acknowledgment of the fact that Mr. Hoyne had always proven himself a sincere and effective friend of labor and honest unionism, asked him to act as their representative on the arbitration committee. This responsibility he accepted, though his friends advised him that the chances of a favorable award were so slight that he must almost surely hurt himself politically through an appearance of indifference and inefficiency. The result of the arbitration, however, was the best award that labor ever received in Chicago. His entire record in office showed that he could neither be cajoled, coerced or intimidated by improper influences, political or otherwise. Mr. Hoyne belongs to the Chicago Bar Association and the Chicago Law Institute; the University, South Shore Country, Law, Legal and Lake Shore Athletic Clubs, and the Delta Upsilon and Phi Delta Phi fraternities.

On June 14, 1897, Mr. Hoyne was united in marriage with Miss Marie Jacobs, daughter of the late Benjamin F. Jacobs, who had been superintendent of Immanuel Baptist Sunday School, which Mr. Hoyne attended in his youth. They are the parents of two sons: Thomas Maclay II and Francis J.

CHARLES SOLON THORNTON came to Chicago to practice law in 1873, two years after the great fire. In the colorful and changing panorama of developments out of which has evolved one of the great cities of the world, Mr. Thornton's career as a lawyer and citizen has been one of rich and significant usefulness, touching the life and affairs of the community at many points. Future students of the law and its application and interpretation in noted cases, students of municipal history in Chicago and of educational reform will meet again and again the name, Charles S. Thornton in connections that redound to his secure reputation and honor.

He was born in Boston, Massachusetts, April 12, 1851, son of Solon and Cordelia A. (Tilden) Thornton, the former a native of Lempster, New Hampshire, and the latter of Marshfield, Massachusetts. His mother was a descendant of Peregrine White of Mayflower fame, and both parents represented old New England families of Colonial stock. He was reared and educated at Boston, attending the famous Boston Latin School six years, and was graduated with the degree of A. B. from Harvard University in 1872. While in university he had resolved upon the law as his vocation, and among other studies had pursued courses in the Roman law and in the history and principles of the English law. One of his teachers was the late Henry Adams. He continued his studies in the Boston Law School until March, 1873, when he moved to Chicago, and in September of that year passed the examinations for admission to the Illinois bar before the Supreme Court. He was subsequently admitted to practice in the Federal Courts of Illinois, Michigan, Ohio and New York, and the United States Supreme Court. One of the oldest law firms in Chicago is that of Thornton and Chancellor, which except for two years has been an active partnership between Charles S. Thornton and Justus Chancellor since 1886. In real estate law Mr. Thornton has been one of the acknowledged authorities of the Chicago bar since the early years of his practice. The firm has also handled much corporation business, and on several occasions Mr. Thornton was a leading counsel in important criminal cases. One trial of general interest to the public and of great importance to the banking interests of the United States was the case of The People vs. Charles R. Williams, indicted for the embezzlement of several million dollars and for the forgery of a large amount of commercial paper. The case was on trial before Judge Burke for six weeks, and Mr. Thornton, representing the defendant, occupied two days in the delivery of his final speech to the jury, winning the case and at the same time establishing a reputation as a jury advocate that has remained with him through all the years.

While the high point of his public service was reached in the two years he was corporation counsel for the city of Chicago, he had previously laid the foundation for that service by his earnestness and skill in handling the duties of corporation counsel for the town of Lake. He was elected to this office in 1888, prior to the annexation of Lake to Chicago and at a time when the town contained a population of 100,000. He served as president of the Auburn Park Board of Education before the annexation of that suburb to Chicago, and soon after the annexation of Lake he was elected, in 1893, a member of the Chicago Board of Education for three years. He also served three years as a member of the Cook County Board of Education, declining re-election in 1894. In January, 1895, he was appointed by Governor Altgeld a member of the State Board of Education. He was appointed by his associates to make an investigation of the condition of the Cook County Normal

School, and his published report received wide circulation and became the basis of important reforms in the normal and secondary schools of the city and county. He also originated the plan of the college preparatory schools, the system of truant schools, and advocated military drill for the pupils of the high schools of Chicago. Mr. Thornton in 1895 framed and personally presented to the Illinois Legislature the Teachers Pension Bill for all teachers and employes of the public schools. This bill, probably the earliest enactment of this kind in the country, was passed by a large majority in both Houses and approved by the governor.

Mr. Thornton was corporation counsel of Chicago from April 15, 1897, to May 1, 1899. Those familiar with Chicago municipal history will readily understand the importance of his administration when it is recalled that his official routine involved such cases as the Lake Front case against the Illinois Central Railway, the intercepting sewer cases, and his personal intervention in obtaining a decision from the Supreme Court awarding to the city the right to operate street railways and purchase their franchises. He refused to accept for himself and his assistants passes issued and presented by the railroad companies. He reorganized the special assessment department and rigidly enforced a rule permitting no reduction whatever for political or personal favorites in the amount of any special assessments excepting as ordered by the court after a hearing upon the merits. As corporation counsel he rejected claims against the city aggregating over fifteen million dollars, and in several instances exercised his personal influence against the combinations of many powerful political, business and other interests in defeating what he considered unjust claims. One case in which he won a favorable decision from the Supreme Court was that confirming the city ordinance fixing a fee of a hundred dollars for a license to vend cigarettes, a measure designed to prevent the sale of cigarettes by school stores to school children.

As an indication of the scope of his work as corporation counsel Mr. Thornton rendered over 2,500 opinions to heads of departments and others of which only three were ever successfully attacked. Of 3,500 special assessment cases, less than one per centum were lost. Out of fifty-seven special assessment cases in the Supreme Court only three were lost, and in nisi prius courts out of 2,010 contested cases the city won 1,938.

A more thoroughly merited official endorsement of service was never given than in the words of the mayor of Chicago when Mr. Thornton retired as corporation counsel: "In accepting your resignation I desire to congratulate you upon the splendid service that you have given to the city in the past two years. I think it is generally understood among lawyers that the work of the department has never been in as good shape or so thoroughly cleaned up as it is at the present time, and this condition is unquestionably due to the discipline you have installed in the department as well as your own personal ability and industry."

When he retired from office in 1899 he resumed his active place in the partnership with Mr. Chancellor. During the next ten years he gave almost his entire time to the litigation of the Booth Company, winning all of its cases, some fifteen in number, six of which were of the very first magnitude. One of these in the United States District Court of Detroit, and another in the United States Circuit Court of Cleveland, involved among other questions the violation of anti-trust laws in many parts of the United States. In each of these cases more than 1,600 witnesses were subpoenaed and heard. The Detroit case went to the United States Court of Appeals at Cincinnati and thence to the Supreme Court of the United States, in each of which a decision favorable to Mr. Thornton's client was rendered.

During the Spanish-American war Mr. Thornton was secretary of the Naval Reserve Association of Illinois and later became president of the Association. This organization received the commendation of the United States government for its action in sending about eight hundred naval reserves fully trained, equipped and able to at once take their places upon the government warships ready for service.

Mr. Thornton has been a stalwart democrat in politics. His name appeared on the ticket as an Illinois presidential elector in 1916, the year President Wilson was re-elected, and again in 1920, when James M. Cox was candidate, and in 1924, when the democratic candidate for president was John W. Davis. Mr. Thornton has been identified with many civic organizations in Chicago and Illinois. He is a Knight Templar and thirty-second degree Scottish Rite Mason, is an Odd Fellow and he prepared the Illinois Odd Fellows' code of 1896.

Mr. Thornton for many years has resided in the Englewood district, at 7600 Stewart Avenue. He married in September, 1883, Miss Jessie F. Benton, of Chicago, daughter of Francis and Esther (Kimball) Benton. They have four children: Mabel J., wife of John T. Walbridge, a Chicago civil and electrical engineer; Pearl E., wife of Carl H. Knoettge, a civil engineer of Chicago; Hattie M., wife of Dr. Frank G. Douglass, a prominent physician and surgeon of Chicago; and Chancellor B. Thornton, in the building construction business.

JUSTUS CHANCELLOR. For many years Justus Chancellor, of Chicago, has been one of the leaders of the Illinois bar, and has been a resident of this city since he came to it, a youth of nineteen years from his father's Indiana farm. During the ensuing years he has gained a knowledge and mastery of the law, and since rising to his present enviable position in public confidence, has steadily maintained his leadership in the very front ranks of an able and accomplished bar. At an early period of his professional career he was fortunate in securing the confidence and esteem of those engaged in large affairs, and these men have grown to appreciate him so that no interests are so important that those concerned with their management hesitate to commit them to him, when the occasion arises, either for counsel or the assertion or defense of their rights in the

Justus Chancellor

courts. In fact his entire life is so dominated by a stern integrity, an integral trait of his character, that confidence follows as a matter of fact. His attention is almost wholly occupied by corporation, municipal and real-estate law.

Mr. Chancellor is proud of the fact that he is a product of the rural regions, and looks back with pleasurable emotion to his birthplace, the homestead adjoining the town of Oxford, Indiana, where he was born October 12, 1863. He is a son of John Cooper and Elizabeth Jennie (Justus) Chancellor. The Chancellor family has been an American one for over three centuries. Richard Chancellor, the American founder, came to Westmoreland County, Virginia, from London, England, in 1682, and like many others of that period came to the American colonies because of religious persecution. He had been a captain in the Royal army under Charles II, but because he resisted the encroachments of that monarch upon the Established Church he, with others of similar opinions, was indicted for conspiracy. Fortunately he escaped, with the consent of the monarch, to America, and therefore was never apprehended or prosecuted. On the broad acres of the plantation he subsequently developed he found peace and plenty, and brought up his family in the fear of God and love of freedom. His descendants are numbered among the substantial and solid men and women not only of Virginia, but other states to which those bearing the name, during the intervening period, migrated, and among them was William Cooper Chancellor, the paternal grandfather of Justus Chancellor. On his mother's side Justus Chancellor traces back to another honored family, his maternal grandfather having been Basil Justus.

Justus Chancellor attended the public schools of Vincennes from 1873 to 1882, the latter year marking his graduation from high school. His father was a man who believed in solid educational advantages, and he encouraged the ambitious youth in his aspirations to train himself for a professional career. Therefore with a body made strong by his healthy rural surroundings and a mind kept clean through watchful parental care and supervision, Justus Chancellor at the age of nineteen years came to Chicago and entered the Union College of Law, from which three years later, in 1886, he was graduated with the degree of Bachelor of Laws. The Chicago Law School conferred upon him the degree of Master of Laws in 1923.

In 1884, in order to secure an income while he was pursuing his studies, Mr. Chancellor had entered the employ of Charles S. Thornton as a clerk, and he continued to hold that position until after his admission to the bar. In 1888 he and Mr. Thornton formed the firm of Thornton & Chancellor, a partnership which is still maintained. This is admittedly one of the strongest legal combinations in the city, and has been connected with some of the most important jurisprudence in the state.

For years Mr. Chancellor has taken a prominent part in various professional organizations, and for three successive terms he has been president of the Lawyers Association of Illinois. He is a member of the executiv committee of the American Branch of the International Law Association, and belongs to the International Law Association, the American Bar Association (in which he represented Illinois as local counsel), the Illinois State Bar Association, the Chicago Bar Association, the Chicago Law Institute (where he is a member of the board of managers), and the Chicago and Cook County Real Estate Boards. A man of social proclivities, he is a member of the Southern Club, the High Noon Club, the Press Club of Chicago, the Missouri Athletic Association, the North Woods Hunting Club, the Pistaqua Heights Country Club, the Illinois Chamber of Commerce, Northwestern University Club, life member of the Field Museum and also the Art Institute, Grand Council Fire of American Indians, Chicago Historical Society (Governing Annual Membership), Chicago Motor Club, and Chicago Association of Commerce and the Cook County Real Estate Board. Fraternally he belongs to the Masonic Order, in which he has been advanced through all of the bodies of both the Scottish and York Rites, and is a Knight Templar and thirty-second degree Mason, and a member of Medinah Temple, A. A. O. N. M. S., and he is a member of the Knights of Pythias.

On May 2, 1889, Mr. Chancellor married, at Vincennes, Indiana, Miss Hattie Theodocia Lincoln Harper, a daughter of Rev. William W. Harper, of Hartford City, West Virginia. Three children were born of this marriage, namely: William Chancellor, who died in infancy; Leola Chancellor Gates; and Justus Chancellor, Junior, the latter being associated with his father and Mr. Thornton in the practice of law.

HENRY S. BAKER. Now not less than at any time in the past century the name Baker has been associated with some of the most outstanding abilities in the legal profession of Southern Illinois. Henry S. Baker has been a member of the Alton bar forty years, and in his younger career was associated with his father, Henry S. Baker, Sr., a great lawyer and Illinois statesman, which the first generation of the Illinois family was headed by David J. Baker, a conspicuous figure in the political life of early Illinois.

This branch of the Baker family was established in New England, about 1670. Both the grandfathers of David J. Baker were soldiers in the Revolutionary war. David Jewett Baker was born at East Haddam, Connecticut, September 7, 1792, and in 1800 his parents Bayze and Johanna Baker, moved to New York State. He was reared on a farm, prepared himself for College, graduated in 1816, from Hamilton College, and subsequently was admitted to the bar. In 1818 he came West, traveling by flat boat down the Ohio, and arrived at Kaskaskia when that old town was still the Illinois capital.

He was one of the early probate judges of Randolph County, and in 1830 was appointed by Governor Edwards, United States Senator, to fill a brief vacancy. President Jackson in 1833, appointed him United States attorney for Illinois, and he was reappointed by President Van Buren in 1837. In 1844 he removed to

Alton, and for ten years had an extensive practice as a lawyer there. In 1848 he was the unsuccessful candidate against another Alton citizen, Lyman Trumbull, for judge of the Supreme Court. He had a personal encounter with Governor Reynolds on the streets of Kaskaskia, due to his staunch opposition to slavery in Illinois. In 1854 he assisted in the organization of the republican party. At the time of his death Chief Justice Sidney Breese, one of his close friends said: "He was a ripe scholar, a genial gentleman, a faithful friend, a true patriot, and a Christian, and well worthy of the honors this day done to his memory."

David J. Baker who died at Alton, August 6, 1869, at the age of seventy-seven, married Sarah T. Fairchild, who died in 1859, and his second wife was Elizabeth Swanwick. Among his sons by the first marriage were David J., Jr., who became Chief Justice of the Supreme Court of Illinois; E. L. Baker, who was in the United States Diplomatic Service; and Henry Southard Baker, Sr.

Henry Southard Baker, Sr., who was born at Kaskaskia, Illinois, November 10, 1824, was educated in Shurtleff College, in Brown University, studied law under his father, and began practice at Alton in 1849. He had a successful law practice, and by election he held the office of judge of the City Court of Alton from 1865 until 1880. He retired from his law practice in 1888, and died March 5, 1897.

He came upon the stage of public affairs when the issues were being closely drawn over slavery and freedom. He was of the same temper as his father as regards slavery, and in 1855, he was elected a member of the State Legislature, as an anti-Nebraska democrat. It was his vote that practically decided the election of Lyman Trumbull of Alton to the United States Senate. In 1860 he served as secretary of the National Republican Convention, and was a republican elector in 1864.

Judge Henry S. Baker, Sr., married Emily Blair Bailey who died in 1862, and his second wife was Mary F. Adams. The three children of his first marriage were Henry S., Jr., Sidney Blair and Jennie B.

Henry S. Baker, Jr., was born at Alton, June 7, 1859, and is a graduate of the Alton High School and of Shurtleff College and was admitted to the bar in 1883. From 1884 to 1890 he served as city attorney of Alton, was corporation counsel from 1894 to 1900, and for many years has had a practice in corporation law, including many clients among the public utilities and leading industries of that city, and is general attorney for the Illinois Terminal Railway. He is a member of the Madison County and Illinois State and American Bar Association, and is a member of numerous clubs and fraternal organizations, being a charter member of the Alton Lodge of Elks. In 1912 he married Miss Florence H. Lang, of Alton.

THE BURNHAM FAMILY. No record concerning the history of Champaign County, and especially the city of Champaign, can exercise consistent functions if there be failure to give appreciative tribute to the honored and influential representatives of the Burnham family, who have marked their course with high integrity, surpassing civic loyalty, and large and worthy achievement. Two of the noblest and most objectively benignant public institutions in the city of Champaign stand as enduring monuments to and specifically perpetuate the name of Burnham, these being the Burnham Athenaeum, known as the Champaign Library, and the Julia F. Burnham Hospital.

Albert C. Burnham was born at Deerfield, Lenawee County, Michigan, February 20, 1839, and that his parents had pioneer precedence in Michigan is indicated by the date of his birth, which occurred within less than two years after Michigan Territory had been admitted to statehood. The life span of Albert Calvin Burnham counted in large and noble works on his part, and he was one of the most honored and influential citizens of Champaign, Illinois, at the time of his death, September 13, 1897. He was reared to the sturdy discipline of a pioneer farm in Michigan, and that he made good use of the advantages afforded in the schools of the locality and period became manifest when he proved himself eligible for successful service as a teacher in the public schools. He finally came from Michigan to Illinois, and it is a matter of record that he was a successful teacher in the schools of Iroquois County in the years 1860 and 1861, he having taught during the winter terms. In the spring of 1862 this ambitious young representative of the pedagogic profession came to Champaign and in an unassuming way initiated his preparation for another of the learned professions. Here he entered the law office of the late J. B. McKinley, under whose preceptorship he continued his studies until he gained admission to the Illinois bar, after proving himself well fortified in the principles and minutiae of the involved science of jurisprudence. In the light of later events Champaign may well be considered fortunate in having become the stage of the life activities and service of this ambitious young lawyer, who here became the junior member of the law firm of McKinley & Burnham, as coadjutor of his former and honored preceptor. Concerning this period in his career a record of special interest is that here reproduced: "From the first this firm had influential financial connections. Through its instrumentality a large amount of eastern capital was brought west to invest in farm securities in and around Champaign. The Middle West was not then overflowing with wealth, as it is today, and the money brought in by this firm was not only greatly needed but was also wisely expended in the improving and upbuilding of many farm properties —a basic medium for the advancing general civic and material prosperity."

Mr. Burnham soon gained reputation as an able and successful lawyer and as a man of exceptional business acumen. He continued an active member of his original law firm, one of large business and important interests, until 1876, when he found it expedient to retire virtually from the practice of his profession and to give his attention to business enterprise, more specifically that of the banking house of Burnham, McKinley & Company, Mr. McKinley having retired from the banking firm in that year, 1876, and J. R. Trevett and R. R. Mattis having become members. Of the old, substantial and influential banking house of Burnham, Trevett & Mattis Mr. Burnham thereafter continued the executive head until his death, and as such has been continued by the two remaining partners and incorporated under the name of the Trevett Mattis Banking Company. Worthy of perpetuation in this review are the following extracts from a previously published memoir to Mr. Burnham:

"It was Mr. Burnham's privilege and good fortune to witness a marvelous development in Champaign County in the course of his active career. That development was primarily based upon the increasing agricultural resources. While not a tiller of the soil and not otherwise concerned in a direct way with farm industry, Mr. Burnham was able wisely to employ the constructive forces of capital in the furtherance of agricultural development and his banking house was always, and justly, considered an integral part of the business and industrial structure of his home city and county. He was liberal and public spirited in the fullest degree and took a deep interest in all that tended to advance civic morality and educational interests."

Ever appreciative of, and an exemplar of the highest of human ideals and ethics, broad in his intellectual ken, and trained and efficient in the practical affairs of life, Mr. Burnham long cherished his plan for making some definite and enduring contribution to the cultural advantages of his home city. In consonance with this fine civic ambition two years prior to his death he gave to Champaign a princely benefaction. He provided a splendid site, that of his former home near the business center of the city, and accompanied this by the gift of $50,000 to be expended for the erection and maintenance of a public library building. The concrete realization of his dream and loyal ambition is shown in the fine Burnham Anthenaeum, which is a library of metropolitan proportions and service and which constitutes a real civic center. As has been said, "It is a monument to the memory of this sturdy banker and noble citizen. Thousands have benefited from the service it affords and future generations shall continue here to find a source of inspiration and incentive." For the maintenance of the Burnham Athenaeum and its work Mr. Burnham's son, the late Robert D. Burnham, left an additional endowment of $10,000.

In the winter of 1893 and 1894 Mr. and Mrs. Burnham, after considerable contemplation, began active planning for a hospital in Champaign and 1895 saw the results of their efforts consummated in the opening of the Julia F. Burnham Hospital which immediately became a real memorial, due to the death in October, 1894, of Julia F. Burnham, wife of A. C. Burnham. The hospital proved of inestimable value to the people of the city and county during the long intervening period of thirty years, a noble memorial to a noble woman. Mrs. Burnham was an earnest and devoted member of the Presbyterian Church and was instant in its support and service.

In the year 1866 was solemnized the marriage of Mr. Burnham and Miss Julia F. Davison, who was born in New York City, April 16, 1839, and who was again in her native city at the time of her sudden death, October 25, 1894. She was reared and educated in the City of Newark, New Jersey, and remained in the east until she came to Champaign as the bride of Mr. Burnham. Concerning her the following appreciative words have been written: "Mrs. Burnham, while ever devoted to her home, had many other interests through which she expressed her gracious personality and distinctive culture. She was zealous in the service of her church, was earnest in the support of charitable and benevolent agencies, and was ever ready to aid those in affliction and distress and was long prominent in the representative social and cultural circles of her home city. Mrs. Burnham gave many years of efficient and loyal service as secretary of the Illinois State Board of Charities; was one of the first women members of the Champaign Board of Education and was an active member of the Champaign Art Club. Mr. and Mrs. Burnham were survived by one son, Robert D., a memorial tribute to whom is given in the paragraphs that here follow. A daughter Mary Bruce, an equally wonderful daughter of a remarkable mother, and who is mentioned at length in another portion of this work under the record of the Harris family, was born June 29, 1873. She was married, November 17, 1897, to Newton Harris at Champaign and died January 10, 1921.

Robert Davison Burnham was born at Champaign on the 19th of February, 1872, and here his death occurred March 31, 1920. In all of the relations of life he well upheld the prestige of the honored family name. He was the eldest in a family of five children, three of whom died in infancy.

After having profited by the advantages of the public schools of Champaign Robert D. Burnham attended the old and well known collegiate preparatory school at Lawrenceville, New Jersey. Later he was a student in the University of Illinois, though he did not complete a full course. After leaving the university he was associated with the business of his father's bank, that of the Burnham, Trevett & Mattis Banking Company until he formed a partnership with his brother-in-law, Newton M. Harris, and engaged in the farm loan and investment business in Champaign County, his association with the business having continued until his death. Mr. Burnham, like his father, was generous, tolerant and kindly of nature; was liberal and public spirited as a citizen and gained vantage ground as one of the substantial and influential business men of Champaign County. In a preceding paragraph mention is made of the gift of the father, A. C. Burnham, to the Burnham Athenaeum, and at the time of his death he was president of the Board of Trustees of this institution. He was a republican in politics and while never a seeker of public office he gave loyal service as a member of the park commission of his native city. He was a member of the Sigma Chi fraternity of the University of Illinois and a thirty-second degree Scottish Rite Mason, a Knight Templar and a member of the Mystic Shrine. He was an earnest communicant of the Protestant Episcopal Church, as is also his widow, who still maintains her home in Champaign and who is a popular factor in the leading social and cultural life of the city.

December 4, 1895, recorded the marriage of Mr. Burnham and Miss Mae Wilcox at Magnolia, Illinois, who was born and reared in Champaign. Mrs. Burnham is a daughter of the late Dr. Levi S. Wilcox, who is represented in a memorial tribute in this publication. Mr. and Mrs. Burnham became the parents of three children: Robert D., Jr., Sidney Wilcox and Albert C. II. Robert Davison Burnham, Jr., was born September 14, 1896, and in 1914 was graduated from the Lawrenceville preparatory school, in which his father likewise had been a student at Lawrenceville, New Jersey. Thereafter he was for three years a student in Yale University, in which he was a member of the class of 1918. He remains with his widowed mother in the beautiful family home at Champaign. Sidney Wilcox Burnham was born August 23, 1898, attended the Champaign schools and the Hotchkiss Preparatory School, Lakeville, Connecticut, from which he graduated in 1918, and for three years was a member of the class of 1921 in Yale University, from which he withdrew at the time of his father's death. He was a member of the Yale Battery of field artillery two years, having volunteered for service with it in the World war, in which connection he gained a commission as a second lieutenant. He is a member of the Zeta Psi of Yale Chapter, and a thirty-second degree Mason of the Ancient Accepted Scottish Rite at Dayton, Ohio. He is now president of the National Recording Pump Company at Dayton, Ohio. On September 1, 1921, he married Miss Arlene Weis, of Quincy, Illinois, and they have three children: Joan, and twin sons, Sidney Wilcox II and William Dennis. Albert C. Burnham II, youngest of the three sons, was born October 1, 1900, and his death occurred May 4, 1923. He likewise attended the Hotchkiss Preparatory School for two years and entered the Sheffield Scientific School of Yale University in the fall of 1919, remaining three years, after which he proceeded into business in the automotive field, where he gave through his executive ability in controlling men an indication of the talent of his forefathers. He was steadily promoted from one position to another. He was a member of the Berzellius and the Colony at Yale.

HALE HOLDEN. No one outside of those who have direct dealings with the railroad companies upon an extensive scale have any comprehension of the magnificent part they have played in the opening up and development of the country, nor how dependent all business is upon their proper operation and maintenance. The problems confronting the officials of these roads are stupendous and wide-reaching, and only a man of executive ability and great force of character can hope to cope with them in a satisfactory manner. One of these astute men of broad vision and efficient capability is Hale Holden, president of the Chicago, Burlington and Quincy Railroad Company, with headquarters at Chicago. He is a man carefully trained for a learned profession, who found in the intricacies of railroading a broader scope for his abilities than had been offered him in the practice of the law, and his remarkable success in his present work proves the wisdom of his final choice of an occupation.

Hale Holden was born at Kansas City, Missouri, August 11, 1869, a son of Howard M. and Mary F. Holden, and of their two sons and one daughter he was the second in order of birth. Howard M. Holden was born at Malden, Massachusetts, August 26, 1837, and his wife was born at Hanover, Pennsylvania, in 1841. He died at Kansas City in 1912 and she died in 1922.

After attending Harvard University, when only nineteen years old, Howard M. Holden came West, and after a short time spent at Chicago, went to Muscatine, Iowa. There he was in the employ of the banking house of Greene & Stone, first as bookkeeper and later as cashier, and while in Iowa became so prominent in politics as a republican that he was sent to the Iowa State Assembly for several terms. Going to Kansas City, Missouri, in 1867, he organized the old First National Bank, with which the present institution of that name has no connection. This bank he served as cashier and president for a number of years. He was a man of strong character and had a deep and abiding faith in the future of Kansas City and the Southwest. It was through his influence and personal efforts that the Kansas City Board of Trade was organized and placed on a solid basis, and he served it as its first president. For years he was an active member of the Kansas City Livestock Exchange. While he was developing his other interests he had acquired very substantial land holdings, at one time owning 6,000 acres of land and large herds of cattle. Realizing the possibilities of Kansas City as one of the great centers of the cattle industry, he exerted himself to awaken an interest in this important branch of business, and, in order to stimulate it, and enable men of moderate means to enter it, he loaned many who later became extensive stockraisers the money for their initial venture. It is, without doubt, largely due to him that Kansas City is now numbered among the large and important centers of the country, for, in addition to what has been enumerated, he was during his active years ever zealous in behalf of his community. The Presbyterian Church long had in him one of its most highly prized members. He was always a strong republican.

Hale Holden attended the common and high schools of Kansas City, Williams College, Massachusetts, and Harvard University, in which he took up the study of law. Leaving the last-named institution in 1892, without being graduated, he entered the law office of Warner, Dean & Hagerman, of Kansas City, and in 1895 became a member of the firm of Warner, Davis, McLeod & Holden, which association was maintained until 1907. The combination

was a strong one, and Mr. Holden soon gained notice for his work as a corporation lawyer, and attracted the attention of the Chicago, Burlington & Quincy Railroad Company, and in 1910 was offered the position of general attorney of the road, with offices at Chicago, and, accepting, entered upon a new phase of his career. In 1910 he was made assistant to the president and in 1912 he became a director and vice president, and in 1914 he was elected president of the road, and that same year was also elected president of the Colorado and Southern Railroad Company.

Many honors have been accorded Mr. Holden, and he has never failed to live up to their multiple responsibilities. He was a trustee of Williams College for five years, where once he was a student, and in 1926 was given the degree of LL. D. by that institution. He is a director of the Illinois Merchants Trust Company, of the Union Trust Company, of the First National Bank of Saint Paul, Minnesota, was for two years chairman of the Association of Railroad Executives; is vice president and a director of the American Railroad Association, and is connected with numerous other organizations. A man of social proclivities, he holds membership in the Chicago Club, the Onwentsia Club, the University Club, the Mid-Day Club, the Shore Acres Club, the Saddle and Cycle Club, the Casino Club, and the Old Elm Club, all of Chicago; of the University Club of New York City and the Denver Club of Denver, Colorado. Like his father, he is a zealous republican.

Mr. Holden married, September 18, 1895, Ellen M. Weston, who was born at Dalton, Massachusetts, a daughter of Byron and Julia (Mitchell) Weston, both of whom were born in Massachusetts. Mr. Weston was a prominent manufacturer of paper, and in the political life of Massachusetts, and he served the commonwealth for two terms as lieutenant governor. He and his wife had eleven children, of whom Mrs. Holden was the second in order of birth. Mr. and Mrs. Holden have three children: Eleanor W., Hale, Junior, and Philip D.

CHARLES HULL EWING. In the history of real estate operations in Chicago the name of Charles Hull Ewing has been prominent for over thirty years. Mr. Ewing is individually a large property owner both in Illinois and in Florida. His career is interesting because of his family connections. He was a relative of the late Charles J. Hull, whose name is commemorated in the famous social center, Hull House. Mr. Ewing is a nephew of the late Helen Culver, one of the most distinguished pioneer women citizens of Chicago.

Mr. Ewing was born at Randolph in Cattaraugus County, New York, July 11, 1868, son of Robert Finley and Aurelia (Culver) Ewing. The name Ewing has been in America since early Colonial times. In the paternal ancestry were various members of the Finley family, including Samuel Finley, a great-uncle of Charles Hull Ewing, who at one time was president of Princeton University. This same branch of the family included Samuel Finley B. Morse. Aurelia Culver was a sister of the late Miss Helen Culver.

Helen Culver, who died at her home in Lake Forest in August, 1925, was a Chicago school teacher before the Civil war, and in the year following the war was one of the first women to take up a practical business career. For many years she was busy with the care of her manifold interests, and the direction of her extended philanthropies. She was born in New York State in 1832, and after the death of her father in 1851 she came to Illinois, and in DeKalb County started a select school. In 1854 she removed to Chicago and became principal of the primary department of one of the six public schools of the city at that time. Later she taught in the new high school on Madison Street. Her cousin, Charles J. Hull, lived in a spacious residence on Halsted Street, and after the death of Mr. Hull's wife, Miss Culver took over the care of the Hull home, which was then in a fashionable residence district. This home was abandoned by the family in 1868, and more than twenty years later Miss Culver consented to its use by Jane Addams for a social center. On the death of Mr. Hull in 1889 he left all his property to Miss Helen Culver. In his memory she subsequently devoted a large part of her fortune to the public welfare. Thus for many years she was best known for the uses to which she put her extended fortune. She did much to finance Hull House, and in the course of her lifetime and after her death bequeathed more than one and one-half million dollars to the University of Chicago, furnishing the funds for the building and endowment of the Hull Court biological group on the campus.

For thirty years Miss Culver's chief assistant in the management of her business interests was her nephew, Charles Hull Ewing. Mr. Ewing is a graduate of Yale University, taking his A. B. degree in 1893, and during the following year attended the Northwestern University Law School. For one year he was manager of a stave manufacturing company in Mississippi, and from 1896 to 1908 was manager of the Helen Culver Fund of the University of Chicago. He has been in the general real estate and investment business since 1903, with valuable property in Illinois and also in the Southern states, particularly in Florida. His interests in Florida are at Bradenton and Sarasota and vicinity. For many years past he has maintained a home at Sarasota. He has a summer residence at Lake Forest, Illinois.

Mr. Ewing is a life member and has served for two terms as president of the Geographic Society of Chicago, and established its endowment fund during his administration. He organized the Oberlin Men's Club of Chicago. He is a life member of the Art Institute, the Field Museum of Natural History, and of the Press Club of Chicago; is a trustee of Hull House Association and a member of the Elihu Club,, Phi Beta Kappa and Phi Delta Phi college fraternities, and of the City, University, and Yale Clubs, and the Historical Society of Chicago; also of the Onwentsia, Knollwood and Winter Clubs of Lake Forest, and of the Bradenton Golf and Country, Palma Sola Country, and Longboat Key Golf and Country Clubs in Florida. On October 8, 1906, he married Miss Mary Sleight Everts, who was at that time Dean of Women of the State University of Iowa. They have two daughters, Katherine Everts, a graduate of Ferry Hall, Lake Forest, and a student at Vassar, and Helen Culver, a student at Ferry Hall, Lake Forest.

JAMES H. CARTWRIGHT. In the history of Illinois jurisprudence the name of Judge Cartwright must ever stand forth as that of one of the really great jurists and constitutional lawyers of the state, and as that of a man whose character and services gave him distinction as one of the strongest and sanest of the fine group of representative legists who have served as chief justice of the Illinois Supreme Court. The service of Judge Cartwright on the bench of the Supreme Court of Illinois covered more than a quarter of a century, and there have been comparatively few others whose records on this bench can connote equal duration. The final term of Judge Cartwright as a justice of the Illinois Supreme Court terminated in 1924, the twenty-fifth anniversary of his assuming this judicial office having been celebrated December 17, 1920. His name and work are written large upon the history of Illinois jurisprudence. His death occurred May 18, 1924, and this publication consistently enters a tribute to his memory and to his achievement.

Judge Cartwright was a scion of the stanchest of English ancestry and of the purest of American stock, the Cartwright family having been founded in New England in the Colonial period of our national history. In a pioneer log cabin that stood at the forks of the Maquoketa River in the territory of Iowa James H. Cartwright was born December 1, 1842, and his native heath is now the site of the vital city of Maquoketa. In a family of six children he was the eldest of the three sons. He was a son of Rev. Burton Hall Cartwright and Jane Chloe (Benedict) Cartwright, and his father was one of the pioneer clergymen of the Methodist Episcopal Church in Iowa Territory. He later became a circuit rider of his church in the northern part of Illinois, the family having removed to this state in the year following the birth of the future chief justice of its Supreme Court.

Judge Cartwright was reared under the conditions and influences that marked what may be termed the middle-pioneer period of Illinois history, and he had the advantages of a home of culture and refinement. He attended the schools of the period, including those at Mount Morris, where he finally entered Rock River Seminary. In this institution he continued his studied at intervals, and in the meanwhile he gave his attention to assisting in the work of the small farm that his father has acquired in that locality. He had also his quota of experience in teaching school, and he was nineteen years of age at the inception of the Civil war. He subordinated all personal interests to the call of patriotism, and as soon as possible, in April, 1862, he enlisted for service in defense of the Union. He became a member of the Sixty-ninth Illinois Volunteer Infantry, with which in the summer of 1862 he assisted in guarding Confederate prisoners at Camp Douglas, Chicago. Later he was assigned to duty in connection with the exchanging of prisoners at Vicksburg, Mississippi, which city at that time was held by Confederate forces. At the expiration of his three months' term of enlistment he found it incumbent upon him to return home and aid in the care of his mother and the younger children, his father having in the meanwhile entered service as chaplain in the army commanded by General Sherman. In June, 1864, Judge Cartwright again enlisted, he having at this time become a member of the One Hundred and Fortieth Illinois Infantry, in which he was elected captain of his company. Captain Cartwright's company thereafter passed three months in guarding railroad lines in the vicinity of Memphis, Tennessee, next was assigned to guard duty in Memphis, and finally was ordered to Camp Fry, Chicago, where it was mustered out October 29, 1864.

In the autumn of 1865 Judge Cartwright entered the law department of the University of Michigan, and from the same he received his degree of Bachelor of Laws in the spring of 1867, he having soon afterward been admitted to the Illinois bar and having engaged in the practice of law at Oregon, judicial center of Ogle County. In 1868 he was selected as general attorney and solicitor of a company that projected the building of the Chicago & Iowa Railroad, now a part of the Chicago, Burlington & Quincy Railroad. Of his interposition in this connection the following statement has been written: "Out of this employment came a vast amount of experience in condemnation work which today makes Justice Cartwright so particularly well qualified in the law of eminent domain."

The young lawyer was retained as general attorney for this railroad company until it went into the hands of a receiver, and even after this he continued service in connection with the general affairs of the railroad. It is interesting to record that during a part of the time in this early period of his professional career Judge Cartwright maintained a Chicago office in a small frame house that stood on Dearborn Street, just to north of the present Great Northern Hotel, and that after his retirement from the Supreme Bench he established his Chicago headquarters in the building of the First National Bank—a great metropolitan structure in marked contradistinction to that in which he had his office in the early days.

In 1876 Judge Cartwright resumed the practice of law at Oregon, and from that year until 1888 he served as master in chancery of the Circuit Court for Ogle County. In 1888 he was elected judge of the Circuit Court, and after his re-election in 1891 he was assigned to Appellate Court duty in the Second District, at Ottawa. In 1895 he was elected to the bench of the Illinois Supreme Court, to fill the vacancy caused by the death of Judge Bailey, and thus was initiated his long and able service as a justice of the Illinois court of last resort, which has been dignified by his character and his achievement.

In an editorial that appeared in the Illinois Law Review of November, 1920, reference is made to the statement of Justice Orrin N. Carter to the effect that in the previous

twenty-five years of his service on the bench of the Supreme Court Justice Cartwright had written an average of seventy-five opinions each year, and the editorial estimate then continues as follows: "In substantiation of that statement we have turned to the Supreme Court reports of this state for the period immediately following Justice Cartwright's first election—a period in which we should expect him to make his smallest contribution—and in 1896, the first year after his election, we find that he wrote sixty-six opinions; the following year he had increased this number to ninety-six; that he delivered seventy-nine opinions in 1898, fifty-seven in 1899, and seventy-seven in 1900. When we consider how short a time each year can be spent by the Supreme Court justices in writing opinions, Justice Cartwright's record seems almost unbelievable. In order to perform such a vast amount of labor and to withstand the attendant physical strain one must of course possess a remarkable physique, together with extraordinary good health and powers of endurance. And Justice Cartwright is fortunate in possessing all three. The rugged life he was obliged to lead while a boy not only helped him to overcome the frailties of his youth but seems also to have given him a constitution which no strain of later life has been able to impair. His health is remarkable. In the past twenty years he has not once been confined to his bed with sickness, but on the other hand has been in constant attendance at the terms of the Supreme Court, and in the twenty-five years of his service has not been absent more than three or four days, all told. We are told that he always has a fixed time for everything, and that everything is done precisely at the appointed time. As for his relaxation Justice Cartwright has adopted an interesting plan. Just outside of the town of Oregon he owns a large farm, a part of which is covered with heavy timber. In this timber area he has built a small, restful cottage, and to this place he repairs when the strain of his work becomes too heavy. A few days spent in the quietness of these surroundings revives in Mr. Cartwright his original vigor and enables him to return to his work and attack it with his customary energy.

"It might be thought that because of the great rapidity with which Justice Cartwright works, that his opinions would lack the close consideration which would result from a greater deliberation. Such, however, seems not to be the case. Justice Cartwright's mind is distinctly and emphatically judicial. His thinking is clear-cut, analytical, direct. He has the faculty of going at once straight to the heart of a case. Consequently he is able to arrive at a decision in a minimum of time, and the opinion, moreover, is logical and concise.

"Stopping merely to catalogue certain other of Justice Cartwright's characteristics—his extreme positiveness on all questions, and especially public questions; his brusque manner, particularly on the bench, which is nothing more than a mask for the genial nature that lies behind it—we come to an interesting sidelight on the man, in his choice of an avocation, namely the breeding and training of fast trotting horses. Barring his interest in his chosen profession, no other interest so absorbs his time and attention. So extensive has been his study of the theoretical perfection of the trotting horse that he can be classed as an authority on the subject. His theories have been carefully put into practice on the large farm which he maintains near Oregon, with the result that from his stables have come some of the fastest horses on the Grand Circuit.

"Justice Cartwright's other hobby is the study of Illinois political history. Here again he is accorded the rank of authority. It is said, indeed, that few men in the state * * * can claim such an intimate knowledge of the history and workings of our political institutions."

To review in detail the career of Justice Cartwright on the bench of the Illinois Supreme Court must be left to more specifically technical publications, as such indulgence is impossible in a sketch so necessarily circumscribed as this memoir. It is well, however, to incorporate here the final paragraph written by Judge Orrin N. Carter in giving an appreciative estimate of the services of his distinguished confrere on the Supreme Bench, and that paragraph is as follows:

"I am confident that more and more, as the years pass by, the leaders of the bench and bar of this state will rank the opinions of Judge Cartwright along with those of Scholfield, Breese, Lawrence and our other great judges, and that judges and lawyers the country over will frequently consult and quote from his opinions, particularly on constitutional questions, as among the most profound, the clearest and sanest written."

The opinions handed down by Justice Cartwright cover a wide range, as touching human motives and actions, and have to do with matters of the greatest importance to the State of Illinois and its people. His have been the highest of civic, social and professional ideals, and he wrought mightily and well. Of his attitude in regard to the service of the Supreme Court of which he was so long a member, an idea is conveyed in the following extract from one of his public addresses:

"This court has been required to keep pace with the rapid growth of the state. Beginning with the simple questions arising between the settlers concerning their rights, it has sought to apply the same principles of right and justice to the many questions arising from more complex conditions and the restless energy of a great people, as well as from new legislation. While the principles upon which justice is administered have always been the same, no two sets of circumstances are precisely alike, and the growing complexity of social conditions often renders their application difficult, but the court has sought to select and apply such rules as would accomplish justice in each case. The work has not been perfect, as no work of human hand or brain is perfect, but it has never been questioned that the motives have been pure and that there has been a conscientious effort to fulfill the high mission of establishing and maintaining justice. So far as there are imperfections, they fade away with maturer judgment and consideration, and that which is in accordance with the eternal principles of right endures."

Loyal and public-spirited as a citizen, and characteristically well fortified in his convictions concerning matters of political and economic import, Judge Cartwright was ever a stanch advocate of the principles of the republican party. Until his death he continued to maintain the idyllic semi-rural home at Oregon.

On the 26th of November, 1873, was solemnized the marriage of James Henry Cartwright and Miss Hattie L. Holmes, of Oregon, Ogle County, and their devoted companionship of more than half a century was severed only by the death of the honored subject of this memoir. Mrs. Cartwright still maintains the beautiful home at Oregon, and two sons and three daughters likewise survive the distinguished father: James Henry, Jr., the elder son, is a member of the representative Chicago law firm of Winston, Strawn & Shaw, and in the World war he was in overseas service during a period of four months, as a member of the Three Hundred and Thirty-first Field Artillery of the American Expeditionary Forces. Horace A., the younger son, likewise volunteered for service in the World war, and he was still attending an officers training camp at the time when the armistice brought the war to a close. He is now a resident of Fremont, Ohio. Of the daughters it is to be recorded that Miss Ada M. resides in the city of Chicago; Grace C. is the wife of Charles W. Townley; and Genevieve C. is the wife of Robert Salmon.

HON. WILLIAM BROWN MCKINLEY,* senior United States senator from Illinois, has been in Congress continuously except for two years since 1905, at first as representative of the Nineteenth Illinois District. For much longer time he has been a real and vital force in Illinois business and politics. His home since early boyhood has been at Champaign, and the university and the community as a whole have shared in his personal success.

Senator McKinley was born at Petersburg, Illinois, September 5, 1856, son of George and Hannah (Finley) McKinley. His grandfather, Thomas McKinley, was a native of County Donegal, Ireland, but of Scotch ancestry. Coming to the United States when a young man in 1801, he lived for a time in Southern Pennsylvania, where he married Alice Barclay, also a native of Ireland. Later they moved to Ross County, Ohio, and were farmers in that section. The father of Senator McKinley was a Presbyterian minister. When William B. McKinley was a small child his parents moved to Champaign, and George McKinley was a well loved minister in that city. The McKinley Memorial Presbyterian Church at Champaign was erected in honor of his memory by Senator McKinley.

William B. McKinley is a product of the old school of self-reliance and industry. He lived with his parents on a small farm and had his share in the routine duties before and after school. He was a good student and at the age of thirteen entered the University of Illinois, where he spent two years. At the age of fifteen he began clerking in drug stores. In 1875, when nineteen, he went to work as a clerk in the brokerage and banking house of his uncle, James B. McKinley, at Champaign. It was his ability that permitted him to enter a partnership in 1877, and he has been a partner in the old establishment firm of J. B. and W. R. McKinley, banking and mortgage loans, since that year. This was a pioneer concern in representing eastern capital for loans on Illinois farming land.

In Central Illinois W. B. McKinley is better known for his constructive work in developing an electric traction system than in politics. He has had a part in the public utility field since 1885, in which year he built the Champaign and Urbana water works, an electric lighting system. In 1890 he undertook the construction of the Champaign and Urbana Electric Railway. During the next twenty years he took an increasing part in electric interurban traction until he became head of a great system known as the McKinley Lines. Officially this is the Illinois Traction Company, one of the largest systems of its kind in the United States. He has been president of this company for a number of years. It will be recalled that in 1910, when his company was forbidden the use of the railroad bridge over the Mississippi into St. Louis, his company built an independent bridge at a cost of five million dollars.

From 1902 to 1905 Mr. McKinley served as a trustee of the University of Illinois. That brief service, however, does not measure his real interest in the cause of education. From his personal fortune it is estimated that he has given more than one million dollars to worthy causes, largely of an educational nature, the greater part going to the University of Illinois, the Y. M. C. A., Y. W. C. A., the McKinley Memorial Hospital and also to the McKinley Foundation for Presbyterian Students. He was responsible for the donation of a $55,000 loan fund to be loaned to worthy students with no other security than their personal notes at five per cent. The plan among other things has demonstrated to his satisfaction the innate honesty of ambitious students, since the losses have been negligible and the repayment of the loan has proved the value of helping others to help themselves.

Mr. McKinley has been a forceful and interesting figure in Congress. He has been there as a representative from Illinois more than a partisan or representative of any faction. He has given the counsel of a very successful business man and executive and his service has been of a quality that deserved repeated endorsement at the hands of his constituent. He was first elected to represent the Nineteenth District in 1904, taking his seat in the Fifty-ninth Congress in 1905. He served continuously until 1913, being defeated in the historic year 1912. In 1914 he was again sent back from the same district, serving throughout the war period until 1921. In 1920 he was elected United States senator, his term being for the years 1921-27. Senator McKinley is a member of the Union League and Hamilton Clubs of Chicago, the Cosmos Club of Washington and the Country Club of Champaign. His favorite pursuits are business and

Anthony P. Hunt

politics. He married, in February, 1881, Miss Kate Frisbee, of Chicago.

The qualities that have earned him success have undoubtedly been persistency and fairness. It has never occurred to him to quit in any undertaking he thought worth while. In his public addresses he has emphasised as elements of achieving success such qualities as industry, good judgment, honesty with self as well as with every one else and a pleasing personality. His friends claim he has exhibited all these in abundance in his own career. When he was a poor clerk working for twenty dollars a month and board he saved something and demonstrated ability to handle his own affairs long before he sought any offices of trust or responsibility from others.

* Died December, 7, 1926.

CLARENCE S. DARROW. In preparing a biographical sketch of such a man as Clarence S. Darrow, whose brilliant professional achievements are based on an intimate knowledge of the intricate subjects of law, human failings and human emotions, the historian feels the limitation of his knowledge as well as like limitations that attach to the ordinary reader. In truth, any just biography of such a man should be prepared by one having some adequate professional knowledge, and might better be presented in the pages of legal journals whose readers are en rapport with the subjects which have engaged his thoughts, and can follow the line of original investigation and action which it has been his fortune to take while advancing to an undisputed position among the leaders of the bar of the country.

Clarence S. Darrow, lawyer of Chicago, was born at Kinsman, Ohio, April 18, 1857, and received his education in the public schools of his native state, following which he took up the study of law and was admitted to the bar in 1875. Not long thereafter, seeking a broader field for his activities, he took up his residence at Chicago and for some years was a member of the law firm of Altgeld, Darrow & Thompson, later of Darrow, Masters & Wilson, being now the senior partner of Darrow, Smith, Cronson & Smith, with offices at 77 West Washington Street. After coming to Chicago his rise in his profession was rapid and he was eventually retained as attorney for the Northwestern Railway. He developed great ability and reputation as a trial lawyer and soon was identified with important litigation in cases against monopolies, including the gas trust of Chicago. He was chief counsel for the anthracite miners in the anthracite coal strike arbitration at Scranton and Philadelphia, Pennsylvania, in 1903, on the commission appointed by President Roosevelt. He was counsel in the Debs strike case and a large number of labor injunction and labor conspiracy cases, always on the side of labor. In 1911 Mr. Darrow was counsel for the McNamara brothers in the Los Angeles Times dynamite case; and was also attorney for the defendants Moyer, Haywood and Pettibone, who were charged with the murder of ex-Governor Steunenburg of Idaho. The recent Franks murder case, in which he was counsel for the defendants, Leopold and Loeb, is of such recent date as to need no mention; as is also the famous trial at Dayton, Tennessee, where Mr. Darrow, on the side of Evolution, was pitted against the late William Jennings Bryan. Mr. Darrow's splendid powers of oratory have been used to good advantage on the lecture platform, where his services are constantly in demand, as they are at public meetings and as an after-dinner speaker. While he has been active in politics as an independent democrat, his only important public office was that of member of the State Legislature in 1902. He is a member of the Illinois State Bar Association, the Chicago Bar Association and the Illinois Lawyers' Association, and belongs to the Chicago Athletic, South Shore Country and Press Clubs. While his legal abilities have been such as to overshadow his activities in other fields of endeavor, Mr. Darrow is possessed of marked literary ability, and is the author of a volume of essays, "Persian Pearl"; a novel, "Farmington"; "Resist Not Evil"; "An Eye for an Eye"; "Crime, Its Cause and Treatment," and various pamphlets on social and economic questions. He has been twice married and resides at 1537 East Sixtieth Street.

ANTHONY A. HUNT. Not only is Anthony A. Hunt, of East St. Louis, well known as a brilliant and successful practitioner of law, but almost equally well in the world of letters, where he has gained considerable reputation as a writer on commercial subjects and man of affairs. For forty years he has mingled with the people of East St. Louis, and during this time has been a leading factor in many of the progressive movements inaugurated, although he has consistently and steadfastly refused to consider the acceptance of public office.

Mr. Hunt was born January 19, 1869, at Bellville, St. Clair County, Illinois, and is a son of Bernard M. and Anna Marie (Kaelch) Hunt, the former a native of Germany and the latter of France. His grandparents on both sides of the family were born in the old country, and except for a short visit by his mother's people, spent their entire lives there. Bernard M. Hunt was given a good education in his native land, but at the age of seventeen years came to America in order to escape military service. The Baden youth soon established himself in business at Louisville, Kentucky, as the proprietor of a book store, and also dealing in art objects and doing bookbinding. In the latter for the wonderful artcraft displayed in the binding of books he gained a reputation all over the country by men engaged in the business. A man of broad views and comprehensive mind, at the time of the election of President Lincoln his was one of the two votes cast at Louisville for the Great Emancipator. At that time he was the owner of two large book and art stores at Louisville, and it was no uncommon thing for him each week to sell two wagonloads of the Saturday Evening Post without taking them into the stores. His courageous action in voting as he did caused public sentiment to run high against him, and after he had been visited by more than 1,000 citizens of Louisville he decided to adopt tactics of discretion and accordingly he left the city for a time. Later, however, he returned and when war was declared between the South and the North he secured a commission from President Lincoln as a captain in the Sixth Regiment, Kentucky Volunteer Infantry. He raised a company which served throughout the struggle and participated in many of the great engagements, including Shiloh, where Captain Hunt lost ninety percent of his men and was slightly wounded himself. At the close of the war he moved to Belleville, Illinois, where Anthony A. Hunt was born, all the other children before him having been born in Kentucky. Bernard M. Hunt gave up his former business and went in for the construction of large buildings and railroads, a vocation in which he was remarkably successful. His work carried him to various cities all over the country, as he gained a reputation for being capable in the handling of large projects. His death occurred in 1914, when he was eighty-three years of age. He and his worthy wife, who is also deceased, were the parents of the following children: William B., who is married and has two sons; August C., who is married and has two children: Anna J., who married Louis Huber; Matilda O., who married Charles C. Johnson and has four children; Helen C., who married August C. Friess and has two children: Florens J., who married Marie Hemmer and had two children who are now deceased; Anthony A., of this review; Rose, who married Henry Rentchler and has two children; and Benjamin M., deceased, who married Dora Dorlark and had one child.

The early education of Anthony A. Hunt was acquired in the public schools of Belleville, he having graduated from the high school as a member of the class of 1884, following which he pursued a course at the Jones Business College, St. Louis, Missouri. Next he began the study of his calling at McKendry College, Lebanon, Illinois, from which he was graduated in 1893, and in 1894 was admitted to the bar and commenced practice in June at East St. Louis, where he has built up a large and influential clientele. As before noted, he has refused all offers of public office with the exception of one term as city attorney early in his career. During the World war he was chairman of the Instruction Board. Mr. Hunt is general counsel for the St. Louis National Life Insurance Company and has represented numerous other large companies. As a writer on commercial subjects and prominent men his name has appeared frequently in leading periodicals. A man of interesting personality, he occupies a place high in the esteem of the people.

In 1897 Mr. Hunt married Miss Maud Virginia Little, whose brothers and sisters were: A. Platte, who married Minie Dill and has one child; Samuel, who married Annie Bauchens and had one child; Carrie E., who married Charles Smiley and has three children; and May, who married William Hauss and has two children. By his first wife Mr. Hunt has one daughter: Helen Virginia, who married Lewellyn Mills. On June 29, 1907, Mr. Hunt married Miss Nellie Brockman, and they are the parents of one daughter: Lorraine Josephine, who resides with her parents and is attending school. Mrs. Hunt's brothers and sisters are: Arthur, who married Minnie Peel; Annie, who married Arnold Zerwick and has two children; Col. Phil Henry, who married Anna Skippe; and Dorothy, who married Frank Galloup. Mr. and Mrs. Hunt are members of the Presbyterian Church. He is one of the oldest Masons in St. Clair County, and also holds membership in the Illinois State Bar Association, the St. Clair County Bar Association and the East St. Louis Bar Association.

NATHAN WILLIAM MACCHESNEY began the practice of law at Chicago in 1902. For many years he has been almost daily in the courts, and for a successful corporation lawyer has given an unusually close and personal attention to the diverse interests he represents. He is senior member of MacChesney, Weaver, Evans & Robinson, a firm that is a continuation of Carter & Becker, established nearly seventy years ago. This firm enjoys a high standing in real estate, banking, railroad and corporation legal matters. It may be of interest to recall the fact that among the cases in which he has been engaged have been the preparation of the briefs of arguments in the Supreme Court of the United States in such matters of vital importance as power of federal government to control the organization and discipline of state troops. The constitutionality of Selective Service Act, Child Labor Legislation, constitutionality of Real Estate License Law, in which case he sustained for the first time the right of a state to regulate the personnel of a business as distinguished from the business itself, and he has participated in numerous other litigated matters of local and national importance.

The attainments thus briefly suggested would be worthy of almost a lifelong devotion of the best energies of a normally ambitious lawyer. They measure, however, only a fraction of the activities and interests of one of the most intensive individuals of the present generation who, says one who knows him well, has become almost an "institution" of the city in which he lives. It has been a constant cause for marvel on the part of his admirers that he could expend himself so effectively on so many diverse avocations and keep the resources of his mind fresh and unimpaired for the heavy routine of his working day. One writer has enumerated among his exertions "lecturing on legal ethics in law schools, directing the affairs of a bank or social mission, taking part in the management of a large university, improving penal conditions, helping in the editorial direction of law journals, investigating a high-pressure fire system and municipal art, striving for uniformity in legislation and for labor and industrial laws, taking an active part in military affairs, writing law articles, and laboring in one way and another in a considerable variety of other organized undertakings; to say nothing of what is required of the time and energies of a lawyer actively and successfully practicing his profession and participating in a normal way in the affairs of family, church and social life." Even this census, having been taken about ten years ago, makes no account of his distinguished service to the American cause during the

World war nor of the intense zeal he has given to patriotism and patriotic education since the war.

General MacChesney during his earlier years was actively interested in athletics, and while in college took an active part in them, but more recently his time along this line has been absorbed by his military activities, in connection with which he has kept up his interests in horses. He has a farm in Lake County, Illinois, which he is interested in developing and where he raises pure blooded horses and cattle.

General MacChesney is only forty-eight, and new directions and purposes are being given to his many-sided activities every year. In many senses he is a true progressive, but for that very reason his career does not submit to still-life representation. The above is a more or less temporary estimate of the range of his activities, and beyond indicating the orbit and force of his career any estimate will be premature.

However, as one of the distinguished Illinoians of the present age the formal facts and interests of his life should be set down, letting these facts speak for themselves and pointing the significance to the brief interpretation attempted above.

The MacChesneys came from Scotland, but more remotely were of Norman-French stock. They were Scotch Presbyterian transplanted to Northern Ireland, and from there John MacChesney, of County Antrim, was "expelled for adhering to the Presbyterian faith," coming to America and landing in New Jersey, July 19, 1689. From New Jersey the family settled in Rockbridge County, Virginia. The great-grandfather of the Chicago attorney was a Virginia soldier in the War of the Revolution. The grandfather, Nathan MacChesney, served in the War of 1812 as a second lieutenant. He was paid in land script, and to make use of it he came to the Military Tract of Illinois and settled in Mercer and Knox counties. He was a pioneer, and is remembered among other things more especially for helping found Knox College at Galesburg.

Alfred Brunson MacChesney, father of Nathan William, was reared in Knox County and like his brothers attended Knox College, continuing his education in the University of Michigan, University of Pennsylvania, Jefferson Medical College at Philadelphia, and Bellevue Hospital at New York. For a time he was professor of surgery in the Jefferson Medical College of Philadelphia. He practiced medicine in Quincy and Alton, Illinois, and during the Civil war became a surgeon in the Union Army and attained the rank of lieutenant-colonel during his army service, which continued for some years after the war.

The mother of Nathan William MacChesney was Henrietta Milsom, of London, England. Her father was a professor of Greek at Oxford and an abolitionist in sympathy. Two of his sons came to America to fight for the cause of the Union during the Civil war. One of them was wounded in the battle of Atlanta, and his sister, Henrietta, having come to this country went South to nurse him, and in that way met Mr. MacChesney. After the war she studied medicine and was with Dr. Emily Blackwell and Dr. Mary Thompson in charge of the first "out-work" among the poor on the east side of New York. Later she married Dr. MacChesney. Her life was devoted to the service of other people, and she and her husband provided home or school advantages for a large number of young people.

Nathan William MacChesney was born at Chicago, June 2, 1878, acquiring part of his education in the public schools of that city. He was a student at Stanford University in California in 1896-97, graduated A. B. at the University of the Pacific in 1898 and was a student and instructor in the University of Arizona in 1899 and attended Northwestern University Law School at Chicago in 1899-1900. He graduated LL. B. in 1902 from the Law School of the University of Michigan. Twenty years later Northwestern conferred upon him the honorary degree Master of Laws.

General MacChesney in 1911-12 was special assistant attorney general of the United States; 1913-1923, served as special assistant attorney general of Illinois; and special counsel for the City of Chicago, 1924. He is general counsel of the National Association of Real Estate Boards; is a member and was president from 1912 to 1917 of the Illinois Commission on Uniform State Laws; was a state delegate to the International Prison Congress at Washington in 1910; since 1922 has been president of the National Conference of Commissioners on Uniform State Laws; is a member of the commission on Uniform Industrial and Insurance Legislation of the Chicago Plan Commission, the Chicago City Council Crime Commission and was appointed by the city council a member of the Air Board of Chicago. He was appointed by Secretary of Commerce Hoover chairman of National Conference Committee on Street and Highway Safety; of counsel for United States Senate in investigation of United States War Veterans Bureau; of council for United States Senate for Rent Control legislation in the District of Columbia; of council for war department in United States Supreme Court, 1914-17; National Council on Religion in Higher Education; trustee of the Institute for Research in Land Economics and Public Utilities. He was law member of the State Board of Examiners in Accountancy, 1914-17; is president of the Northwestern University Press; has been a director of the United Charities, Emerson House and South End Settlements; is a trustee of Northwestern University, trustee of Olivet Institute, trustee of the Public Health Institute; a member of the Advisory Board of the Salvation Army, of the National Convocation of Universities and Colleges on International Relations; and he is consul-general for the Kingdom of Siam and has recently been decorated by the King for his services.

He served with the National Guard during his youth in Arizona and California, and with the Illinois National Guard from 1893 to 1895, and during the Spanish-American war did garrison duty on the Pacific Coast. From 1911 to 1917 he was Judge Advocate General of the Illinois National Guard and in 1916 was one of the first six officers to be commissioned in the new Judge Advocate General Reserve Corps of the United States Army.

During the World war he served with Major Generals Crowder, Berry, Carter and Wood at Camps Grant and Custer and in the Central Department, was also on special duty in the office of the Secretary of the War and on February 13, 1918, was commissioned lieutenant colonel of the United States Army. He was a judge advocate at the General Headquarters of the American Expeditionary Forces in France, and also served with the Thirty-third Division, in connection with which he was an inspector and reported upon disciplinary conditions in occupied territory, and was recommended for the Distinguished Service Medal, General Pershing awarding him a citation for "exceptionally meritorious and conspicuous service." He was recommended for the Distinguished Service Medal by the Judge Advocate General for the American Forces in France and Germany as follows: "For exceptionally meritorious and conspicuous service. As chief of the section of Dishonorable Discharge Cases Branch Office of the Judge Advocate General in France his breadth of view and executive ability contributed greatly to the carrying out of the policies established by the Secretary of War for the maintenance of discipline and proper legal procedure in our Army." He was also recommended for the French Legion of Honor at G. H. Q., A. E. F., France, 1919, and for the British Order of St. George and St. Michael and by Belgium and Italy for recognition of his services. He was promoted to the grade of Brigadier General, August 4, 1917 "For long and distinguished service," and in September, 1919, placed on the retired list of the Illinois National Guard.

He was also officially thanked by the Illinois State Council of Defense and presented with the Commemorated Sabre "in recognition of his fine spirit and efficient, invaluable and distinguished services."

General MacChesney is vice president of the American Bar Association, is a member and director of the American Judicature Society, a member of the American Society of International Law, of the American Prison Association, is on the National Council of the National Economic League, is a member of the American Political Science Association, American Institute of Criminal Law and Criminology, of which he was president in 1910-11, the American Society of Military Law, of which he was president in 1913-14, a member of the National Commission on Prisons and Prison Labor, the National Civic Federation, Illinois State Bar Association, which honored him with the office of president in 1915 to 1916, and is an honorary member of the Tennessee, Iowa and Pennsylvania State Bar Associations. He is chairman of the Conference of Bar Association Delegates, succeeding Hon. Charles Evans Hughes in that position. He is also, of course, an active member of the Chicago Bar Association, Chicago Law Club and other professional associations of Chicago, in which he has had an active part, and is a member of the Association of the Bar of the City of New York. He is a member of the Sons of the American Revolution, was president 1912-14 of the Society of the War of 1812, is a past commander of the Sons of Veterans, a member of the Advisory Council of the American Legion, of which he was a charter member, as he was also of the Military Order of the World war, was national president in 1910-13 of the Order of the Coif, of which he was one of the co-founders. His college fraternities are Phi Kappa Psi, Phi Beta Kappa and Phi Delta Phi. He was president 1922-24 of the Northwestern University General Alumni Association. General MacChesney is an honorary life member of the Chicago Historical Society, is a Presbyterian, a member of the National Council of the Schools of Religion. He has served on the executive committee of the Republican National Convention. He is a Mason and belongs to the Army and Navy Club of New York, the University, Chicago, Racquet, Union League, City, Chicago Literary, Exmoor Country, Knollwood, Chicago Yacht clubs, Northwestern University Club of Chicago, of which he was president 1920-21, and Michigan Union at Ann Arbor.

General MacChesney was a lecturer at the University of Illinois from 1908 to 1916. He was a managing editor of the Illinois Law Review, of which he was one of the founders sixteen years ago, and an associate editor of the Journal of Criminal Law and Criminology. His writings in the field of property and corporation law and management with respect to labor and child labor legislation, military law and other subjects are numerous. His work as an author is identified by the following: "Abraham Lincoln, the Tribute of a Century," published in 1910; "The Significance of the War of 1812"; "The Prototype of American Citizenship"; "Uniform State Laws"; "French Contribution to American Life"; "Challenge to American Ideals"; "Military Policy of the United States"; "Race Development"; Principles of Military Law"; "MacChesney on Real Estate Law (1924)."

General MacChesney married December 1, 1904, Miss Lena Frost, daughter of William E. Frost, of Riverside, Illinois. She is of Old New England stock and her people were pioneers in the State of Wisconsin. Her father was one of the leading lumbermen, millmen and builders of his generation in Chicago. Mrs. MacChesney is an A. B. graduate of the University of Michigan in the class of 1901, and subsequently studied in the University of Berlin and the University of Chicago. She is much interested in and devoted much time to civic and welfare work in addition to her home duties as mother of two sons, Alfred Brunson MacChesney III, and Gordon MacChesney.

General MacChesney's city home is at 568 Hawthorne Place, while his summer home, known as Riverhill Farm is at Belvidere Road and Desplaines River, northwest of Lake Forest, in Lake County, Illinois. His office is at 30 North LaSalle Street, Chicago.

His brother, Captain Chester M. MacChesney, who also was educated at the University of Michigan, served with the Eighty-sixth Division in France and was a member of the American Commission to Italy which made the valuations for the Peace Conference on the devastated regions there.—Luther B. Hill.

Benedict K. Goodman

HON. FRED J. KERN. In the person of Hon. Fred J. Kern, Belleville, Illinois, possesses a citizen who has not only assisted the city in its progress and advancement, but who through his writings as editor-in-chief and owner of the News-Democrat has gained a reputation that extends far beyond the limits of his city and state. During a long, active and successful career he has been the incumbent of a number of official offices, in which he has displayed courage, fidelity and industry.

Mr. Kern was born September 2, 1864, on a farm near Millstadt, St. Clair County, Illinois, and is a son of Henry L. and Katherine (Engler) Kern. His father, a native of Germany, was six years of age when he accompanied his parents to the United States and settled in St. Clair County, where he passed the remainder of his life in agricultural pursuits. He was prominent in various local activties, being particularly interested in public, welfare, and served as a member of the school board and as road supervisor. He belonged to the Evangelical Church, in the faith of which he died in 1914. His wife came to the United States with her parents, who were driven out of Germany because of their political tendencies during the revolution of 1848. Her death occurred in 1909. She was the mother of six children.

Fred J. Kern received good educational advantages in his youth, attending first the district schools and later the Illinois State Normal School at Normal, and while he did not graduate from the latter he secured a teacher's certificate and for five years taught school at various points. When he left the classrooms he entered the newspaper field and worked his way to the editorship of the East St. Louis Gazette. In 1890 he purchased the News-Democrat of Belleville, of which he has since been the editor and owner. While favoring the democratic candidates and principles, Mr. Kern is independent of all parties and stands for what is right in a very fearless way. Without a doubt he is an outstanding American citizen from every viewpoint. A fearless writer, he gives the best that is in him to the common good, and his editorials have attracted widespread attention, particularly one of recent date regarding an international wedding, which one of the contracting parties tried to suppress, but of which tens of thousands of copies have been mailed to those requesting same, not only in this country but others, notably England.

In 1892 Mr. Kern was elected chief enrolling and engrossing clerk of the State Senate during the administration of Governor Altgeld, and held that position for one term. In 1900 he was elected to Congress from the Twenty-second Congressional District, but after serving one term was gerrymandered out of the body. Following this he was elected and served five consecutive terms as mayor of Belleville, and during that time there were built seventy-five miles of sewers and sixty miles of paved streets. In 1912 he was made president of the State Board of Administration, a body which has charge of all the state institutions, and held that post until 1916, four years under Governor Dunne and six months under Governor Lowden, while the board was in session during the World war. During that titanic struggle Mr. Kern devoted his paper to America first and the citizen's duty to their country, made speeches all over the state and was active in all loan and other drives. In 1908 he was a delegate to the Democratic National Convention, and again at St. Louis and Baltimore, when President Wilson was nominated and was made the standard-bearer of his party. Mr. Kern has various important club, business and civic connections, and takes an active part in every phase of the city's life.

In August, 1898, Mr. Kern was united in marriage with Miss Alma Eidmann, of Mascoutah, Illinois, daughter of Louis F. and Katherine Eidmann, the latter of whom died in 1918, while the former is a retired agriculturist. Three sons have been born to this union: Alfred E., who died February 4, 1926; Robert L. and Peter Richard, who are associated with their father. Alfred, editor of the News-Democrat, was the very first to enlist from St. Clair County in the World war, entering the navy, where he left a splendid record for efficient, self-sacrificing and distinguished service.

BENEDICT K. GOODMAN. In a city where great undertakings are a commonplace Benedict K. Goodman has achieved a rare distinction by reason of the fact that at the age of thirty-four, with only a few years between him and the poverty in which he grew up he has been the central figure in perhaps the greatest single improvement in the modern constructive era of the city.

Mr. Goodman was born in one of the crowded sections of the West Side of Chicago, in 1891, son of David and Feige (Goldberg) Goodman. His parents represented old families in the city. Mr. Goodman never knew luxury or wealth during his boyhood. His environment was that of self respecting poverty. As a boy he attended the Garfield public school, graduating in 1905, graduated in 1909 from the Crane Technical High School, and subsequently paid his way through the University of Chicago, where he was graduated in 1913.

Mr. Goodman's first employment was as clerk in the Fort Dearborn Trust and Savings Bank. By 1916 he had been advanced to manager of the real estate loan department. He then resigned from the Fort Dearborn Institution to establish his present mortgage, banking and investment business under the firm name of B. K. Goodman & Company, located at 111 West Washington Street. This business was concerned almost exclusively with finance until Mr. Goodman's achievement of building the Chicago Produce Market, since which time he has combined building construction with financial transactions.

The building of Chicago's great produce market, beginning in January, 1925, and completed in seven months, at a cost of seventeen million dollars, is easily one of the greatest single construction achivements in history. The enterprise was originated and carried out by a comparatively young man, who in less than a dozen years has reached the plane of a financier of the first rank in one of the greatest cities of the world.

The new produce market of Chicago in its new location is the result of the condemning of South Water Street and the construction of the new Wacker Drive along the river front where the old market stood. The new location is Fourteenth Place, South Racine and South Morgan. One hundred and sixty-five buildings were constructed in a six months period over an area of almost six acres. The site for the present market was once the habitat of Chicago's worst West Side gangsters and bad men. Through the enterprise of B. K. Goodman and Hugh McLennan hundreds of dilapidated shacks were torn down and a place of filth and crime was cleaned up to make way for the structures that now house the greatest and best known market place in the world. In the immediate district are twenty-five railway terminals and the market has a bank of its own, known as the Commerce Trust and Savings Bank.

This new market was formally opened August 22, 1925, in the presence of such officials as Secretary of Commerce Herbert Hoover, United States Senator Deneen and Mayor Dever. Mayor Dever in the course of his address said: "This is one of the greatest days in the history of Chicago," and went on to point out that this market, providing a wholesome and sanitary center for the handling of the big food supplies of Chicago and the Middle West, was in reality an enterprise conducive to the public wealth and welfare of not only a city but a nation. The business of the produce merchants, whose headquarters are in the market, amounts to half a million dollars daily.

Mr. Goodman is a member and director of the North Moor Country Club, member of the Standard Club, Chicago Mortgage Bankers Club, Press Club, Association of Commerce and the Chicago Real Estate Board. On August 21, 1916, Mr. Goodman married Irene E. Kesner. They are the parents of two daughters, Joan and Nancy, and a son, Bruce Kay. The Goodman home is in Highland Park.

HON. HARVEY MARION TRIMBLE. An Illinois lawyer and jurist and soldier of the Civil war, the career of the late Hon. Harvey Marion Trimble was chiefly identified with his home community at Princeton, but he likewise came into national prominence as commander-in-chief of the Grand Army of the Republic.

Illinois was the home state of Judge Trimble from his infancy, but he was born near Wilmington, Clinton County, Ohio, January 27, 1842, a son of Mathew and Lydia (Thatcher) Trimble. The founder of the Trimble family in America was his great-grandfather, James Trimble, who came from the north of Ireland and settled in New York state in 1792. About eighteen months after the birth of Harvey M. Trimble the parents started from Ohio and arrived at a farm near Princeton, Bureau County, Illinois, October 25, 1843. The Trimbles had a home on this farm until 1867, when the parents moved to Princeton and spent the rest of their lives in that town.

Harvey Marion Trimble was reared on a farm, acquired a good elementary education and grew up in a community whose strong, able and earnest citizens did much to influence the forming of his character. After attending the common schools he entered Eureka College, Eureka, Illinois, but left college to enter the Union army during the Civil war. He enlisted in Company K, Ninety-third Regiment, Illinois Volunteer Infantry, August 21, 1862, and upon the organization of the regiment was elected sergeant-major, September 8, 1862. He was promoted to first lieutenant and adjutant of the regiment April 13, 1864, and served as assistant adjutant-general of two brigades during the closing months of the war. He was mustered out June 23, 1865, having been with his regiment on every march except a distance of fourteen miles, and in every battle, although on January 13, 1863, while on scouting duty in the execution of commands from his superior officer, he was captured by the enemy near Ridgeway, Tennessee, and held as a prisoner of war fourteen days. The date of his release coincided with his twenty-first birthday. His service record included the siege of Vicksburg, the battles of Jackson, Champion Hill, Missionary Ridge and Altoona and the celebrated march to the sea. He participated in the Grand Review of Sherman's forces at Washington, D. C., May 25, 1865, and was mustered out at Louisville, Kentucky, and honorably discharged at Chicago. For half a century after the war Judge Trimble was prominent among his old comrades and enjoyed the highest honors within their power. He served as commander of Ferris Post, G. A. R., at Princeton in 1897-98, was elected and served as commander of the Department of Illinois during 1902-03, and August 25, 1911, received the culminating honor of election at Rochester, New York, as commander-in-chief of the National Grand Army of the Republic.

Shortly after he returned from the war to civic life Judge Trimble was appointed deputy clerk of the Circuit Court at Princeton, December 4, 1865, and held that position until November 20, 1867. In the meantime he had studied law, and, being admitted to the bar on the latter date, engaged in practice and quickly arose to distinction and success. During a half a century he was a member of law firms that stood at the front of the bar in Bureau County. He was associated in practice with another honored soldier who spent twenty years in Congress, Gen. Thomas J. Henderson. He was a member successively of the firms of Paddock & Trimble, Henderson & Trimble, Henderson, Trimble & Butler, and finally with his son in the firm of H. M. and Cairo A. Trimble.

Judge Trimble was master in chancery of the Circuit Court of Bureau County from 1868 until 1877. He was county judge from 1877 until 1890, and from 1894 until 1897. His service on the Circuit bench of the Thirteenth Judicial District was from 1897 until 1903. He had a deep interest in educational and community affairs, serving as a member of the Board of Education of graded schools from 1878 until 1897, and being a member of the Princeton Township High School Board from 1881 until 1886. He was one of the organizers and a member of the first Board of Directors of the Princeton Public Library, serving from 1886 until 1888, was president of the Bureau County Soldiers' Association, an ardent republican in politics, and a member of the Christian Church. He was a thirty-second degree Scottish Rite Mason. Judge Trimble was the author of "The History of the Ninety-third Regiment, Illinois Volunteer Infantry," published in 1898. He passed to his final rest January 10, 1918.

On October 9, 1866, shortly after the close of the Civil war, Judge Trimble had married Margaret S. Dakin, and October 9, 1916, they celebrated their Golden Wedding Anniversary. The children of that marriage were: Winfred K., an attorney who died at the age of fifty-two years; Cairo A., a leading member of the Princeton bar, who was for years associated with his father in practice; Robert C., a resident of Florida; Harvey, who died at Indianapolis, Indiana, at the age of thirty-four years; and Perry D., also a prominent Princeton lawyer.

Mrs. Margaret (Dakin) Trimble, who was for many years an outstanding figure in the educational and civic life of her community, and founder of the Princeton Woman's Club, died April 10, 1925. Mrs. Trimble was born January 2, 1842, at Wilmington, Ohio, a daughter of Perry Dakin. She was but a child when she accompanied her parents to Bureau County, and prior to her marriage to Judge Trimble taught in the Arispie school and later in the old Lincoln school on Euclid Avenue, Princeton. Mrs. Trimble for sixteen years was president of the Woman's Club of Princeton and after her retirement from that office in 1907 was elected president emeritus, an honor which she held at the time of her demise. She was a member of the Matson Public Library Board for thirty years, and had been prominently identified from 1880 with the Friends in Council, a well-known literary society. She was also a member of the Woman's Relief Corps and the Missionary Society of the First Christian Church. Mrs. Trimble's varied activities, extending over many years, revealed a mind exceptionally active, strong and resourceful. She became a charter member of the missionary organization of her church and served faithfully for many years as one of those who carried on the work of the Master. Only a week prior to her death she had attended a meeting of the society. There could not have been found in the community a more capable and discerning person to serve on the book selecting board of the Public Library. She was chosen for this work in 1896, and served faithfully until her death, and those who served with her on that board trusted her judgment, being aware that her eager mind was always seeking for the best to put into the hands of the reading public. In 1880, when there was organized at Princeton a literary group known as the Friends in Council, she became a charter member and whenever possible attended the meetings of this organization, the work of which has always been of a high order. Always an attentive and appreciative listener, when her turn came she was a valuable leader. The very fact that she remained a member of a literary club for forty years is itself a compliment to her ability and interest in things of a high literary order. On April 13, 1891, in response to a call in the city newspapers, about fifty women met in the reception room of Apollo Hall, Princeton, to consider what they believed to be a practical temperance work. Mrs. Trimble was selected chairman of this meeting, and after committees had been appointed on constitution and nomination of officers, she was elected its first president and served until 1901. She was again chosen president in 1907, serving this time until 1913.

The following tribute paid to Mrs. Trimble came from the pen of one of her close friends of many years standing, Darlene Stevens Reeve: "In the cherished picture of old Princeton which hangs on memory's wall and which time can not dull, nor distance dim, no figure stands forth in more vivid colors than that of Margaret Dakin Trimble. We loved her when, as a child, we went to school to sweet Maggie Dakin; and our love grew into admiration when the passing of the years witnessed her assumption of the duties of wife and mother, and cares multiplied fast and ever faster, and to the succession of little sons was added the responsibility of an invalid brother and of two old people to whom she gave a daughter's devoted attention in her own overflowing little home. To love and admiration was added reverence for the high serenity and courage with which she met her problems and the cheerful spirit with which she pursued her daily round, radiating sunshine and warmth upon each and any who were so fortunate as to come within her orbit. She was greatly blessed by the possession of an equable and serene temper whose roots were grounded and nourished in a sane and controlled mind. She possessed to a marked degree the calm reasonableness of the philosophic temperament. For years she was the presiding officer of the Woman's Club of Princeton, which she had founded. Time and again she served as president of the Friends in Council and of other organizations of which she was a member, and never in all the years of active service did any one see her at a loss in handling a situation however awkward or untoward. With her acute, scholarly mind, she possessed the critical attitude toward books, measures and things, but toward her fellow-creatures her judgment was as large as charity itself. She spoke no evil, she thought no evil of any one. Hers was a soul without rancor, nor was there one harsh note in its gamut. She was an insatiable reader, and how, with all her manifold duties, she found time to read all she did and be so conversant with past history and present events was ever a mystery to her friends. It may have been because knowing the value of time she never wasted it, but used every minute to the uttermost in seeking only the true and the genuine in literature. The cheap and the spurious were not for her, and the nucleus of a good reading in the Matson Library, which has since expanded into such admirable proportion, was due largely to her insistent effort that something more than current novels should be found upon its shelves. She loved her country and was concerned for its welfare. She loved the town of Princeton, in which her life was spent in ever blazing the trail to highest civic effort in all things educational and cultural. She knew life to the full. None of its experiences of joy or sorrow were withheld from her brimming cup. With a deep-seated faith in the goodness and wisdom of God the Father, she submitted without a murmur to the enforce inactivity of her later years, to the loss of sight, and to the death of her loved ones. She often expressed herself as blest above women in the devotion of her children and the number of her friends. Thus serene, confident and unafraid, she passed out from mortal sight, through the sunset bars and twilight stars of that portal which opens into Resurrection Morning."

For two years prior to her death Mrs. Trimble had been in declining health. Early in April, 1925, she caught a slight cold, which was followed by more serious complications, and Tuesday night, April 7, she had a sinking spell that alarmed her relatives and resulted in a hurried call for Cairo A. Trimble, her son, who with his wife and son, Cairo Dakin Trimble, was on a vacation trip to Sea View, New Jersey. Perry D. Trimble, another son, who had recently returned from California, was in constant attendance at his mother's bedside. Upon receipt of the urgent message that his mother was dying, Cairo Trimble hurried to New York and there engaged an airplane to speed his journey home, so as to reach his mother before she died. He was about to take off from Curtiss Field, Lond Island, Wednesday afternoon, when a long distance message from Princeton announced that Mrs. Trimble was unconscious and sinking fast, and his friends in New York persuaded him to give up the hazardous flight, which would have required nine hours in the air and a perilous landing at Princeton at 11 o'clock at night. Mr. Trimble made the trip to Chicago on the fastest train running out of New York, and arrived at Princeton April 9. After his arrival Mrs. Trimble rallied long enough to recognize him before she died. Services were held from the family residence, 425 South Church Street, and interment was in the family lot at Oakland Cemetery.

CAIRO A. TRIMBLE for over thirty years has ranked as one of the ablest lawyers and most influential citizens of Princeton, and his name is also well known throughout the state as a leader in the republican party and a former trustee of the University of Illinois. He is a son of the late Judge Harvey M. Trimble, lawyer and former commander-in-chief of the Grand Army of the Republic. A brief sketch of his honored father precedes this.

Cairo A. Trimble was born at Princeton in Bureau County, March 15, 1869. He received his public school education at Princeton, graduating from the Princeton Township High School in 1889. He then attended business college and studied law in his father's office, and in June, 1892, was admitted to the Illinois bar. For many years he was associated in a law firm with his father.

His practice has been principally civil and corporation work, and in volume and importance has far exceeded that usually attained outside of the very large cities. He served several years in his early career as official reporter of the Circuit Court of Bureau County. In 1898 he was elected a member of the Board of Education of the Princeton Township High School, and served in that capacity thirteen years, part of that time as president of the board. In 1919 Governor Lowden appointed Mr. Trimble a member of the Board of Trustees of the University of Illinois, to fill a vacancy, for two years, and in 1919 he was elected on the republican state ticket to serve a full term for six years on that board, his term ending in March, 1925.

Mr. Trimble has been a delegate to many local and state republican conventions, was one of the republican electors from Illinois voting for President Taft, and from early manhood was actively interested in the success of party campaigns. He is a member of the Illinois State and American Bar Associations, a Knight Templar and Shriner, and member of the Methodist Church, in which for many years he addressed a large men's class on Sunday mornings.

He married in 1895 Alice M. McKey. She died in 1916, leaving two children, Margaret Victoria and Cairo Dakin. Mr. Trimble in 1919 married Miss Nancy Creswell Kyle, of Princeton.

PERRY DAKIN TRIMBLE is the youngest of a notable family of Bureau County attorneys. He is a son of the late Judge Harvey M. Trimble, and is a brother of Cairo A. Trimble, who is now and has been for thirty years a leading member of the Princeton bar, and with whom he is associated with in practice.

Perry D. Trimble was born in Princeton, November 3, 1888. He was educated in the Princeton grade schools, was graduated from the Princeton Township High School and then entered the University of Chicago, where he was graduated with the Ph. B. degree in 1910, and with the J. D. degree from the University Law School in 1912. In the same year he was admitted to the Illinois bar. During the World war, in December, 1917, he volunteered and was commissioned as second lieutenant of Air Service Aeronautics, spending most of his time on Long Island. He is a member of Delta Tau Delta and Phi Delta Phi fraternities, the American Legion, the Masonic fraternity, the B. P. O. Elks, being the first exalted ruler of the Princeton Lodge, the Princeton Rotary Club and the Methodist Church, and is secretary of the Board of Education of the Princeton city schools. In politics he follows the traditions of his family as a republican. He married, in 1921, Carolyn F. Lawton.

D. L. MUSSELMAN, president of the Gem City Business College of Quincy, is the oldest son of the founder of that institution. The college celebrated its semi-centennial a few years ago and it has long ranked as one of the largest and best-known commercial schools of America.

D. Lafayette Musselman, Sr., founder of the school, was born in Fulton County, Illinois, April 21, 1842, and died June 18, 1910. In 1862 he entered the Union army with the Eighty-fifth Illinois Infantry and subsequently became second lieutenant, participating in many battles, including Perryville in the fall of the year of his enlistment and continuing through the Chickamauga and Atlanta campaigns. He had been a farmer's son, learned the carpenter's trade and after the war attended college and subsequently was a student in the Eastman Business College. He first taught penmanship in the Eastman College, then bookkeeping and penmanship for the Bryant & Stratton schools and for several years was head of the commercial department of the old English and German College of Quincy. In 1870 he established the Gem City Business College at Quincy, with three students, the enrollment being increased to thirty-three by the end of the year. For over thirty years he was the vital factor and directing influence in the school's development. Through his college he made Quincy known to the outside world, contributed to its material prosperity and was always deeply concerned with its welfare. He was a republican and a member of the Methodist Church; was active in the Park and Boulevard Association and in the Chamber of Commerce. D. L. Musselman, Sr., married Mary McDavitt, a native of McDonough County, Illinois. Their four children are all living: Hattie V., D. Lafayette, Virgil George and Thomas Edgar, all the sons being executives in the Gem City Business College. D. Lafayette Musselman, Jr., was born at Macomb, McDonough County, Illinois, March 31, 1879, but has spent practically all of his life at Quincy, where he was educated in the high school, attended the Shattuck School at Faribault, Minnesota, the Gem City Business College, and also studied law. In 1898 he commenced teaching and in 1900 he was elected secretary and treasurer of the Gem City Business College. Since the death of his father in 1910 he has been president of that institution.

Mr. Musselman has always been alert to his opportunities and responsibilities as an educator, and has been keenly interested in civic and public affairs generally. For over twenty years he has been a member of the National Commercial Teachers' Association, serving as president of the association in 1907, and is a member of the National Association of Accredited Schools. In about 1910 he was elected a director of the Quincy National Bank, and when this bank was consolidated in 1922 with the Ricker National Bank he continued as a director of the larger institution. He was a member of the school board of Quincy from 1916 to 1924. He was one of the charter members of the Adams County Chapter of the Red Cross in 1917, serving as first chairman of the chapter and continuing in that office throughout the war. He is a director of the Park and Boulevard Association; is a trustee and treasurer of the Woodland Home for Orphans and Friendless; for several years was a director and vice president of the Chamber of Commerce; is a member of the Rotary Club and during 1919 was chairman of publicity and education for the old Twelfth District of International Rotary. Mr. Musselman is vice president of the Chaddock Boys' School at Quincy, a trustee of the Illinois Wesleyan University at Bloomington, and a member of the Board of Education of the Illinois Conference of the Methodist Episcopal Church, and is president of the Laymen's Association of the Methodist Church, Illinois Conference. He served as a member of the General Conferences of the Methodist Church at Des Moines in 1920 and at Springfield, Massachusetts, in 1924. He is secretary of the Chicago Area World Service Council of the Methodist Church and is a trustee of the Vermont Street Church in Quincy. Mr. Musselman is a Knights Templar and thirty-second degree Scottish Rite Mason and a member of Medinah Temple of the Mystic Shrine at Chicago.

His brother, V. G. Musselman, vice president of the Gem City Business College, was educated in the Quincy High School and the University of Illinois. He is secretary of the Board of Trustees of Blessing Hospital at Quincy; for fourteen years was secretary of the Board of Directors of the Y. M. C. A.; is trustee of the Woodland Cemetery Association; and has served as director and vice president of the Chamber of Commerce. During the World war he participated in the different drives, several times acting as captain of a district. He is a director of the Quincy Park & Boulevard Association, is a member of the Quincy Rotary Club and of the Sigma Chi college fraternity, and is a Knights Templar Mason.

The youngest of the brothers, T. E. Musselman, secretary of the college, has national distinction as an ornithologist. He was graduated from the University of Illinois with the degrees of Bachelor of Arts and Master of Arts. Under the direction of the United States Biological Survey he has done a great deal of research work for the government on bird migration in all parts of the country. He is undoubtedly one of the outstanding authorities on birds and wrote the history of the birds of Illinois and bird migration for the State Historical Society, and bird articles for the newspapers, and also many articles published in the bulletins that go out from the Department of Education of the State of Illinois. He delivers many lectures before schools, colleges and service clubs on bird life and nature subjects.

T. E. Musselman is well known in amateur sports, particularly tennis. He was captain of the tennis team at the University of Illinois for several years, and has won a number of tennis championships since he graduated from the university. He was in the semi-finals in the western tennis championship several years ago. T. E. Musselman is a member of the Masonic Order; is scribe for the Kiwanis Club; member of the Phi Gamma Delta college fraternity, and of the Kappa Delta Pi, the honorary society in education; secretary of the Quincy Country Club; trustee of the Anna Brown Home for the Aged; secretary of the Inland Bird Banding Association; and has been prominent in the Boy Scout Organization.

That three sons should train themselves and devote most of their active lives to making a success of the institution founded by their father is in itself an unusual distinction. The Gem City Business College is an institution that honors not only its founder, but his successors. For some years past the annual attendance at the school has been between twelve hundred and fifteen hundred students. The founder of the business erected a splendid building at a cost of $100,000 some thirty years ago. The students at the Gem City Business College come from thirty states in the Union and from many foreign countries, and during the fifty-six years since it was founded the college has educated over fifty thousand students. Some of the most prominent business and professional men of America received their commercial training at the Gem City Business College.

Bernard De Bear, managing director of the De Bear Schools in London, in his report before the annual conference of the De Bear Schools at Liverpool in 1920, said, "Then I went to a little place called Quincy and visited the Gem City Business College, one of the most wonderful schools I have seen. It is certainly one of the most beautiful, well equipped, well organized and efficient commercial schools in the world." During Mr. De Bear's trip to the United States he visited over twenty of the leading business colleges of America, and the only one he honored by special mention in his report was the Gem City Business College.

Mr. D. L. Musselman on October 7, 1908, married Miss Harriet Evans Wells, daughter of Mr. George Wells, of Quincy, and member of one of the most distinguished of the pioneer families of that city. The Wells family is of English ancestry and represents old New England stock. Her grandfather was a conspicuous figure in the pioneer life of early Quincy. Mrs. Musselman attended Quincy schools and later graduated from Miss Hazen's School at Pelman Manor, New York. During the World war she was chairman of the knitting department of the Adams County Chapter of the Red Cross and has interested herself in a variety of causes. She is treasurer of the Ladies Executive Board of the Woodland Home for Orphans and Friendless, treasurer of the Quincy district of the Woman's Foreign Missionary Society of the Methodist Church; and has been active in several of the literary clubs in Quincy.

HARRY E. BELL is proprietor and editor of the White Hall Register-Republican, one of the veteran institutions of journalism of Greene County. Mr. Bell has played a useful part in the affairs of Greene County during his life, having formerly been identified with educational work. His family is one of the oldest in this section of Illinois, its residence in Greene County dating from the year that Illinois was admitted to the Union.

His pioneer Illinois ancestor was Francis J. Bell, who came from Kentucky about 1818. For a time he lived on Apple Creek prairie, but the absence of timber there caused him to change his location to a more wooded section. He was a mill man rather than a farmer, and was the founder of the pioneer mill in the community named in his honor, Belltown. He placed a dam across Apple Creek, and his mill was used not only for grinding grain but carding wool. His successors at the mill were his sons, John J. and Francis M., who kept up its operations for the grinding of grain, carding wool and sawing lumber. Francis J. Bell, the pioneer, is buried in the family plot at the old town named in his honor. He reared the following children: Daniel, William, John J., Francis M., Mrs. Mary (Polly) Allen, and Margaret, who married John Howard.

The son, John J. Bell, was a Union soldier during the Civil war, serving in the Ninety-first Illinois Volunteer Infantry. After the war he resumed his activities at the mill, also conducted a farm, and died January 1, 1875. He was a democrat, which has been the political complexion of all members of the family from the time of Jefferson and Madison. John J. Bell never held a public office, but his brother Francis was once sheriff of Greene County. John J. Bell was a staunch Presbyterian and was one of the pioneer advocates of temperance in his locality. He married Emeline Morrow, born December 9, 1818, and died September 23, 1860. Their children were: Allen, Harvey, Finis E., John, Sarah, who became the wife of Delaney Hutchens, and Miss Delilah.

John J. Bell had a great admiration for one of the pioneer missionary preachers of this region, Rev. Finis Ewing, who held meetings in Greene County. In consequence John J. Bell named one of his sons Finis E. This son was born June 14, 1849. He attended one of the pioneer schools of the day, with its slab bench seats. He had the mechanical genius of the family, operated a sawmill and threshing outfit, and his death on July 7, 1897, was the result of being crushed by a traction engine. He was a huge man physically, weighing almost 300 pounds. He was one of the most industrious and thrifty members of the Bell family. His first wife was Mary McFarland, who died August 13, 1879, leaving one son, Harry E. His second wife was her sister Elizabeth. His third wife was Albinah Teaney, who was the mother of three children: Charles, who died in infancy; Paul, a World war soldier who died at White Hall in February, 1925; and Blanche, wife of H. S. Ford, of White Hall. Finis E. Bell was devoted to the church of his ancestors, and was a member of the Masonic fraternity.

Harry Eugene Bell, representing the fourth generation of this family in Greene County, was born February 12, 1873, and was reared on the banks of Apple Creek in the village of Belltown. He worked on the farm, attended the common schools of the country and is a graduate of White Hall High School. He was a student in the high school there under the instruction of Professor George W. Smith. After leaving high school he engaged in teaching in the rural districts, and for two years was an instructor in the White Hall High School. In 1898 he was elected county superintendent of schools of Greene County, serving a term of four years. While county superintendent Mr. Bell inaugurated a unique campaign for better school buildings. The county then had a large number of the old type of country school house, a building that at one time had perhaps been in keeping with the homes of the community, but which had been preserved unchanged while the prosperity of the country district was reflected in better residences and better barns for live stock. Mr. Bell took his camera and went about over the various townships making pictures of the school houses. These pictures he mounted on a wall map, and inserted among them some of the fine and expensive barns found in the neighborhood of some of the worst types of school buildings. The pictures were a direct challenge to the civic pride of the people of the county. However, it introduced controversy, raising the fear of additional taxes, and the result was that Mr. Bell was defeated for nomination for a second term. Nevertheless, his campaign of education had its effect, and during the term of his successor many of the antiquated school buildings were removed and definite progress made toward better school houses over the county.

In June, 1902, shortly after retiring from the office of county superintendent, Mr. Bell bought the White Hall Register. This paper had been founded by the firm of Davis and Johnson in August, 1869. In 1917 Mr. Bell acquired the White Hall Republican and by consolidation has made the Register-Republican. This newspaper is primarily devoted to publishing the news and promoting the welfare of the home county, and incidentally is democratic in politics. It is published every Friday.

Mr. Bell has been a busy man in conducting his newspaper business for the past quarter of a century. He has served as a central committeeman of the democratic party and has frequently attended state and national conventions. For twenty-one years he represented the Knights of Pythias Lodge in the Grand Lodge, and is a member of the Masonic fraternity. He adheres to the same church as his ancestors, the Presbyterian.

He married, October 23, 1895, Miss Stella Chapin. Their wedding was celebrated on the anniversary of Mr. Bell's parents' wedding. The same minister officiated at the marriage of both parents and son. Mrs. Bell was born at White Hall, January 14, 1874, one of the three children and the only survivor of Wesley C. and Lucy (Adams) Chapin. Mrs. Bell graduated from the same class in high school as her husband, and four other couples from that class also linked their lives in matrimony. Mr. and Mrs. Bell have a son, Richard Chapin Bell, born in April, 1909. This son is a senior in the White Hall High School and is editor-in-chief of the school paper, The Weekly Echo.

HENRY W. SHIRLEY is secretary of the White Sewer Pipe & Stoneware Company of White Hall, and has been a factor in the business affairs of Greene County since early manhood.

He was born at White Hall, September 7, 1885. His grandfather, George Y. Shirley, was a native of Kentucky, and disagreed with other members of his family on the question of slavery. In consequence he moved north of the Ohio River to a free state, settling in Morgan County, Illinois. He was a medical college graduate and practiced medicine in Illinois until his death. His wife was Emily Brown, a native of Ohio.

One of their six children was Dr. Edwin K. Shirley, who was born at Jacksonville, Illinois, in 1855, and died at White Hall in January, 1913, at the age of fifty-eight. He finished his education in the Missouri Homeopathic College at St. Louis, remained there a year and spent the rest of his life in his profession at White Hall. He was a member of the Independent Order of Odd Fellows and Knights of Pythias and was a Methodist. Doctor Shirley married at White Hall, Miss Annie L. White, who died March 22, 1926, at Calgary, Canada. She was a daughter of Alfred and Elizabeth (Hubbard) White, her father a native of Ohio. Henry W. is the oldest of their children. Lina is the wife of Roy Beavers, of Calgary, Alberta, Canada. Anna married Elmer Hoagland, also of Calgary. Albert Edwin, the youngest, lives at Spokane, Washington.

Henry White Shirley acquired a public school education, completing the high school course at the age of seventeen. For a year he taught country schools and then went to Arkansas and spent a year in the office of the Frank Kendall Lumber Company near Pine Bluff. In 1905, having returned to White Hall, he began work for the sewer pipe company, and since October, 1923, has been secretary and director of this important local industry.

Mr. Shirley for eleven years was a member and secretary of the local board of education. During that time the high school was erected. For eight years he was on the local Board of Management of the Chautauqua. He has served as secretary and is now president of the Men's Brotherhood. Mr. Shirley was registered and classified during the World war. He is a republican, casting his first vote for William H. Taft. He has filled chairs in the Knights of Pythias Lodge, is a Mason, and was reared a Methodist, but is now a Presbyterian.

He married at White Hall in November, 1909, Miss Lucy North, daughter of Marcus North and member of the prominent family of that name in Greene County, as recorded more at length elsewhere. Mrs. Shirley was born in Greene County, May 25, 1887. They have two sons, Richard Henry, born November 29, 1911, and Donald North Shirley, born November 17, 1913.

EDWARD N. BAUER, of Decatur, who for over a quarter of a century has been in the soft drink and bottling industry, represents one of the old established families of Macon County.

He was born there July 29, 1869, son of Henry and Maria (Revelley) Bauer, his father a native of Germany and his mother of Maryland. Henry Bauer was brought to this country when four years of age, and as a youth located in Macon County, Illinois, where for many years he was engaged in the grocery business. He and his wife had eight children, Edward N. being the oldest. Phillip is deceased, also Phiabena and three others who died in infancy; Henry lives at Decatur; and Minnie is the wife of Frank Welton, of Urbana, Illinois.

Edward N. Bauer was reared and educated in Macon County, leaving school at the age of fifteen to take his place as a clerk in his father's grocery store. When he was twenty-one years of age he entered the service of the America Express Company, and was with that corporation altogether eight years. Since 1898 he has been associated with George

W. Kraft in the bottling and soft drink business, and is now active manager of the Whistle Manufacturing Company at Decatur, a business owned by Mr. Kraft, who is its president.

Mr. Bauer married, May 5, 1891, Miss Rosa Karlowski. They are the parents of four children: Helen, wife of Otis Perkiser, of Tegunja, California; Gertrude, deceased; Emma, wife of Irvin Knapp, of Chicago Heights; and George E., of Decatur. Mr. Bauer is a republican. He is affiliated with the Masonic fraternity and Loyal Order of Moose, and is a member of the Grace Methodist Church.

HOWARD T. WHARFF, M. D., who died May 26, 1924, was the oldest practicing physician and surgeon in Madison County. His home for many years was at Edwardsville, and in addition to his private practice he served as a railway surgeon and in the public health movement.

Doctor Wharff was born in Washington County, Maine, September 20, 1844, the only son of the three children of Thomas E. and Mary Ann Wharff. His father was a native of Massachusetts, of English ancestry, and was a tailor by trade and for many years was in business in that line at Robinson, Maine, where he died at the age of forty-seven.

Dr. Howard T. Wharff was reared in Maine, and as a youth enlisted in Company A of the Ninth Maine Infantry, and was in active service through three years and three months of the Civil war. Most of the time he was a hospital steward. After the war he took up the study of medicine, and was a graduate of the Bellevue Hospital Medical College at New York City. After graduating he came to Madison County, and was in continuous practice until his death, most of the time at Edwardsville. For fifteen years he held the position of surgeon for the Clover Leaf Railroad, and at his death was county physician of Madison County. He was a member of the County Medical Society and other organizations.

In 1873 Doctor Wharff married Miss Mary J. Carney, who was born in Ireland. She died in 1922, a short time before they would have celebrated their fiftieth or Golden Wedding Anniversary. Doctor Wharff and wife had three children: Emma, Edith and Dr. Howard E., a prominent specialist in eye, ear, nose and throat diseases at Edwardsville.

Doctor Wharff at the time of his death was commander of Post No. 461 of the Grand Army of the Republic at Edwardsville. He was always a staunch republican, and was affiliated with the B. P. O. Elks, the Independent Order of Odd Fellows and the Knights of Pythias.

CLARENCE E. POTTS has devoted all his active life to farming interests, having been a practical farmer himself, and is now manager of the Farmers Elevator at White Hall. He is a member of a family that has been in Greene County since early pioneer times.

His grandfather, William Potts, was a native of England, was brought to America when nine years old, was reared in Greene County, and the farm he owned had been taken up as government land. That land has never been out of the possession of the Potts family since the government deed was given to it. Its present owner is Mr. Clarence E. Potts of White Hall. The children of William Potts were Elam A., John H., Anthony, Samuel and Mrs. John Grimes, all of whom reared families.

Elam A. Potts was born in Greene County, attended pioneer country schools, and gave his life to his farm, where he died in July, 1888, at the age of seventy-six. He married Naomi Zollinger Hackney, who was born in Indiana, a daughter of Joseph Zollinger, and was reared in the home of the Hackney family. She died August 18, 1900, at the age of sixty-two. Her two children were Clarence E. and Maude E., the latter dying in 1889, at the age of thirteen. By a former marriage Elam A. Potts had a son, Marshall L., who died at Grand Rapids, Michigan, in December, 1922.

Clarence E. Potts was born on a farm just west of White Hall, February 9, 1874. He attended the common schools and the White Hall High School, where he was a pupil under Professor Andrews, and during his junior year under George W. Smith. After leaving high school he devoted his energies to farming in his home locality until 1919. In that year he moved his residence to White Hall, took an active part in the organizing of the Farmers Elevator Company and was elected president, and has since served in that capacity and as manager of the business.

Mr. Potts has made himself a useful citizen in his community without special participation or interest in politics. He was registered under the second draft act during the World war, but was not called to duty. His son was also registered and was ready to leave for the front when the armistice was signed.

Mr. Potts married in Greene County, February 8, 1895, Miss Ada Danforth. She was born in the same neighborhood as her husband, March 12, 1873, daughter of George B. and Kate (Worcester) Danforth, the latter a daughter of Mark Worcester, who was a pioneer of Greene County. Her father was born in Southern Illinois, was a traveling salesman for a time and later a merchant at White Hall, where his widow survives him. Mrs. Potts has a sister, Mrs. Grace Chapin, at Jacksonville, Illinois. The two sons of Mr. and Mrs. Potts are Danforth E., born November 12, 1897, and Franklin Potts, born June 12, 1909. The son Danforth attended high school at White Hall and since his school days has engaged in farming. He married Hilda Davis, daughter of William W. Davis, and they have a daughter named Peggy.

WILLIAM C. BAKER, now living retired at White Hall, has had a career that merits him the high respect and esteem of his fellow citizens. He was a youthful soldier in the Civil war, going in when a boy shortly after his father, who had also been a soldier, died, and after the war he was engaged in farming in Greene County until his retirement.

He was born August 18, 1848, in Scott County, Illinois, five miles northwest of Winchester, in what is now called the Smithson locality. His grandfather, John Baker, was born March 22, 1753, and on September 17, 1797, married Mary Combs. John Baker died at Winchester, Kentucky, April 3, 1803, and in the following year his widow became the wife of Peter Evans. He was the father of two sons, the only one growing up being Cuthbert B. Baker.

Cuthbert B. Baker on April 13, 1820, married Sallie McCarty, who died August 12, 1832, and there were eight children of this marriage. On September 8, 1835, he married Elizabeth Ecton, and of the two sons and four daughters born to this union, the three survivors are William C. Baker, of White Hall, Nancy J., also of White Hall, widow of David Henderson, and J. S. Baker, of White Hall. Cuthbert B. Baker after his second marriage came to Illinois, driving overland from Kentucky, and established a home in Scott County. When the Civil war came on he joined the Second Illinois Battery in General Grant's army, was in some of the heavy campaigning around the Mississippi River Valley, participated in the battle of Shiloh, and soon afterward was sent home incapacitated and died at Roodhouse, Illinois, in June, 1863, at the age of sixty-one.

Shortly after the birth of William C. Baker the family removed to Tazewell County, near Pekin, where his mother died in 1853, being buried in the cemetery in the Spring Lake locality of the county. After her death the family moved to Greene County, locating at Roodhouse. William C. Baker lived for a time with his half-sister, Mrs. Isaac Tunison, and afterwards with his own sister, Mrs. Griswold. Before he was sixteen years of age he left the home of his sister, Mrs. Griswold, to enlist in February, 1864. At Jacksonville he enlisted, was assigned to Company I of the Ninety-first Illinois Infantry, and joined this regiment on Mobile Bay participating in the siege and capture of Fort Spanish and Blakeley on the bay, and also participating in the last skirmish of the war, when his command was attacked at Whistler, some miles from Mobile, by Confederate forces after General Lee's army had surrendered. He fell ill and was in a hospital in Mobile until September, 1865, and was then transferred to Company I of the Twenty-eighth Illinois Infantry, which he joined at Brownsville, Texas, and remained there until mustered out.

He returned home in February, 1866. Realizing his early lack of educational opportunities, he attended school for some time after the war and also worked as clerk in a mercantile store until 1870. After his marriage he took up farming, and located two and a half miles southwest of White Hall, where for many years he grew grain and live stock, achieved prosperity and took an active part in the public affairs of the community until he left the farm to live in retirement at White Hall. Mr. Baker has always been a strenuous republican. In 1872 he cast his first vote for General Grant for president, and has never missed a national election since then. He is a member of the Grand Army of the Republic, but otherwise has never joined an order or church.

He married at St. Louis, Missouri, October 6, 1870, Miss Alice Griswold, daughter of Damon and Luthera (Swallow) Griswold. Her father came to Illinois from Vergennes, Vermont, and was a farmer in Greene County.

Mrs. Baker was born in White Hall Township, Greene County, August 6, 1849, youngest of three children and the only one to grow up and marry. She graduated from Monticello Seminary at Godfrey, Illinois, had also been a student in Boston, Massachusetts, and was a woman of intellectual culture and beautiful character. She was actively identified with the Baptist Church. Mrs. Baker died August 14, 1913. She was the mother of five children: Mabel, wife of A. G. Fehr, of Belleville, Illinois; Fred E., of Kansas City, Missouri; Edgar D., of Louisiana; Nellie, wife of Joseph Wiesner, of Greenfield, Illinois; and Miss Laura, of White Hall.

JOSEPH M. PAGE, of Jerseyville, has been an important man of that community for over half a century, and his activities as a newspaper publisher, public official and political leader has made him well known not only over the state but in other states as well.

He was born at Stoughton, now a suburb of Boston, Massachusetts, May 20, 1845, son of Elisha and Almira (Wightman) Page. His great-grandfather was one of the Massachusetts patriots called out by Paul Revere for service in the Lexington alarm. Other members of the family participated in the War of 1812. Elisha Page and wife had five children, and the three to grow up were: Miss Elizabeth, who spent her active life as a teacher at Boston; Elisha, who died at Rochester, Minnesota; and Joseph M.

The father of Joseph M. Page was a shoe manufacturer and promoted several shoe stores over the State of Massachusetts when that was the only shoe manufacturing state in the Union. Joseph M. Page completed the equivalent of a grammar school education at Stoughton. He was only sixteen when the Civil war broke out. Health and physique caused his rejection when he enlisted for service in the Twelfth Massachusetts and later in the Thirty-fifth Massachusetts Regiment. The commander of the Thirty-fifth was Col. Fletcher Webster, a son of Daniel Webster. About that time Mr. Page came west to St. Louis, clerked in a store and then enlisted and was accepted, becoming a member of Company F of the Fortieth Missouri Infantry, under Captain Green and Col. Samuel Holmes. Not until he had participated in one or two engagements did he inform his mother of his enlistment. His first battle was at Pulaski, Tennessee, and he was in the skirmish at Columbia, later at Spring Hill and Duck River, and in the bloody and important battles of Franklin and Nashville, where Hood's army was destroyed. Subsequently he participated with the land forces in the reduction of the force guarding Mobile Bay, and remained in the army until August, 1865, his record including ten battles and skirmishes. He then visited his mother in Stoughton, Massachusetts, and returning to Illinois stopped at Jerseyville, where he arrived penniless. He bound himself out to William Embley, a carpenter, for three years at $2 a week and board, but at the end of six months had acquired such a knowledge of his trade that Embley hired him out for $2.50 a day, working a ten-hour day. Nevertheless, he completed his three-year contract and for nine years after that was a journeyman carpenter.

During a great strike centering at Pittsburgh, in 1877, but extending out over the country, Mr. Page was selected as chief of police of Jerseyville, largely because he was known as a man who did not drink and was not afraid to do his duty. The first day he counted a thousand and fourteen tramps in Jerseyville. There were thirty saloons in the place. He established a rock pile and soon collected a large number of vagrants and set them to work. He announced that he was going to dinner and would be back, and when he returned all the forced workers had disappeared. He also recaptured a freight train which tramp laborers and railroad men to the number of 250 had captured. For this act the Chicago & Alton railroad officials gave him and his wife a life pass over all their roads. Another episode was his arrest of the mayor whom he found in a saloon after closing hours playing cards and drinking beer with his friends. He continued to serve as the chief of police for several years, and by his fearlessness and impartiality made many friends and never injured a man in the discharge of duty.

Mr. Page in 1880 bought the Jersey County Democrat from J. I. McGreedy. He had previously acquired some experience as an editorial writer. He had to borrow the capital of $4,500 to pay for the plant. The shop contained an old Washington hand press, two job presses, seven columns of advertising and 700 subscribers. Mr. Page for over forty-five years has been the business head of the Democrat, and has kept the paper growing in influence and facilities apace with the community until it is now a modern printing plant, with linotype machines, power presses, and the paper has 2,000 subscribers and twenty-six columns of advertising.

Mr. Page in 1885 was appointed master in chancery of the Circuit Court by Judge Herdman, and has served continuously, constituting a record of continuous service in that office. The annals of Jerseyville will always give him a prominent place on account of his constructive service as mayor. After he had served on the council he was first elected mayor in 1887. This town of 2,500 people at that time had neither paving nor waterworks, the old brick yard water tank furnishing the water supply for street sprinkling. During his term the city voted $30,000 for water works, and an artesian well was sunk 1,600 feet to the St. Peters sandstone, the water head driving within sixty feet of the surface. A tower was built for pressure, mains laid, and for nearly forty years Jerseyville has had a water supply. In 1914 Mr. Page was again elected to the office of mayor, this time against the opposition of both the W. C. T. U. and the saloonkeepers. He was elected two to one, and distinguished his term by a period of progressive municipal improvements, including the building of $100,000 worth of brick pavement, extension of water mains two miles and sewers one mile, overhauling of the water plant and increasing the flow from 70,000 gallons daily to 200,000 gallons in eight hours. He declined a second term. Many of the enemies he made while carrying out his paving programs have since become enthusiastic over the improvement.

Mr. Page is a democrat, and he had an uncle who was the first democratic mayor of the City of Boston. He has been active in politics since 1873. He was a member of the National Editorial Association when the meeting was held in Boston, and for a number of years was corresponding secretary of the association, and for fifteen years handled many conventions, during which the association traveled through every state and territory of the Union and twice through Canada and once through old Mexico on free trains. Mr. Page is a member of the Grand Army of the Republic.

He married at Jerseyville, March 29, 1879, Miss Sarah Remer, a native of New Jersey, and brought to Jerseyville at the age of two years by her parents, Abram and Deborah (Nutt) Remer. Her father was a wagon maker. Mr. and Mrs. Page for four years after their marriage rented and lived in two rooms. They have one son, Dr. Theodore H. Page, now of Peoria, who was a medical officer during the World war. Dr. Theodore Page married Matilda Heidrich, member of the well known Peoria family owning a big cordage company there. The two children of Doctor and Mrs. Page are Frances and Theodore, Jr.

PAUL M. HAMILTON is a Jerseyville attorney, member of the second generation of the family to practice law there, and his individual career has been part and parcel of the continuous history of the Hamilton family in Southern Illinois since Illinois became a state.

His great-grandfather, Thomas McClure Hamilton, was born at Tinmouth, Vermont. From New England he came West, living for a time at Athens, Ohio. He left there in 1818, traveling by flat-boat which he built on the Muskingum River, and came down the Ohio and up the Mississippi, landing at the old capital of Kaskaskia. He first settled at New Design, and in 1830 came to Jersey County, where he continued his vocation of farming in Otter Creek Township until his death in 1835. He married Apphia Brown, and both are buried side by side in Jersey County. Their children were: Nathaniel, Benjamin B., Joseph O. and Adeline the latter of whom became the wife of John M. Hull.

Nathaniel Hamilton, member of the second generation in Jersey County, was born in the vicinity of Athens, Ohio, in 1809. He was nine years of age when brought to Illinois, and his educational opportunities were altogether those of the primitive subscription schools. He became a carpenter as well as a farmer, and he died at Jerseyville. His first wife was Mary Dougherty, who was the mother of Oscar B. and Thomas Hamilton. His second wife was Nancy Spaulding, and the children of that marriage were Henry H., Mrs. Grace Robinson and Mrs. Frank Hartman.

Oscar B. Hamilton of the third generation of the family, was for many years one of the ablest lawyers of Jersey County. He was born in the county January 31, 1839, and died April 10, 1919, at the age of eighty. He grew up near Otterville, attended school there and taught for several years. He was in business

Fred Ranke

as a merchant at Grafton and Otterville, studied law privately and in the St. Louis Law School, and was admitted to the bar in 1869. In 1874 he located for practice at Jerseyville, and became associated with Orville A. Snedeker, one of the leaders of the bar at that time. Their firm was Snedeker and Hamilton. He was partner in the firm of Hamilton and Slaten, his partner being Allen M. Slaten. In 1886 he moved out to Meade, Kansas, where he practiced law and engaged in banking with the Farmers & Stock Growers Bank. Governor L. U. Humphrey appointed him a temporary judge of the District Court of Kansas. In 1890 he returned to Illinois, resuming law practice with Otis D. Leach in the firm of Hamilton & Leach, and two years later formed a partnership with his son-in-law, L. E. Brown, as Hamilton and Brown. In 1895, after his son Paul was admitted to the bar, they practiced together as Hamilton & Hamilton until the death of Judge Hamilton twenty-five years later. Oscar B. Hamilton was president of the Jersey County Historical Society for many years, and in 1918 edited a history of Jersey County. He was president of the Jersey County Bar Association when he died. He was a very influential republican, attended many state conventions and was an Illinois delegate to the National Convention of 1880, and one of the 306 delegates who supported General Grant until the bitter end. He was an official of the Methodist Church and a Royal Arch Mason.

Oscar B. Hamilton married in Jersey County October 25, 1860, Miss Eliza M. Brown, who was born in Jersey County July 31, 1842, daughter of Chauncey Brown, who came from Ohio and was an Illinois farmer. Chauncey Brown and wife had two sons and five daughters: Wat, who served as a soldier in the Union army and died soon afterward; Thomas, who lived to old age; Mrs. Elizabeth Whitcomb; Mrs. Delia P. Lurton, the only survivor, now living at Jerseyville at the age of ninety-five; Mrs. Sarah H. Squier; Mrs. Lucretia Ruckstuhl; and Mrs. Eliza Hamilton, who died September 23, 1925. The children of O. B. Hamilton and wife were Miss Clara, who died in 1919; Bertha, wife of George M. Cockrell of Omaha, Nebraska; Rose, wife of L. E. Brown, of Victor, Iowa; Silas E., of Hayes, Kansas; Paul M.; John J., of Grand Junction, Colorado; Dr. Fred W. of Robinson, Illinois; Dr. Ray A., of White Hall; Miss Margaret, of Jerseyville; and Ethel, wife of Leslie Noble, of Alton.

Paul M. Hamilton was born in Jersey County, December 18, 1872. He attended school at Jerseyville, high school at Meade, Kansas, took up the study of law with his father at the age of nineteen, spent one year in the St. Louis Law School, and in 1895 was admitted to the bar after examination before three lawyers selected by the Appellate Court. He then joined his father in the firm of Hamilton and Hamilton, and since 1921 has been senior member of the firm Hamilton and Cross. His partner, Hugh W. Cross, a son of Edward Cross, is a graduate of the law department of the University of Illinois. Mr. Hamilton for thirty years has been engaged in a general law practice frequently involving some of the most important cases on the dockets of the local courts. He served a term as city attorney and in 1916 had the distinction of being the first republican elected to the office of state's attorney in Jersey County. He succeeded Walter J. Chapman in that office. In 1920 he was reelected, and his eight years of service included the World war period and its aftermath, with duties and responsibilities such as none of his predecessors had to meet in their official routine. He retired from office in December, 1924. Mr. Hamilton during the World war was also a member of the Legal Advisory Board of the county. He was elected the first president of the Township High School, helped organize it and was on the board until after the high school building was erected and the school started. Later he served still another time, retiring in 1925. He has been a director of the Chamber of Commerce, is a Royal Arch Mason and a past master of Jerseyville Lodge No. 394, A. F. and A. M., and is a member of the Presbyterian Church. By appointment of Governor Lowden to carry out a provision of the Legislature, Mr. Hamilton was appointed a member of the commission which used a fund of $10,000 for the erection of an appropriate monument to Governor T. J. Carlin in the public square at Carrollton, Illinois.

Mr. Hamilton married, September 3, 1896, at Jerseyville, Miss Alma W. Carlin. Her father, Major Walter E. Carlin, was a nephew of Governor Carlin. Major Carlin was an officer in the Union army. Mrs. Hamilton and Mrs. Eugenia Vandenberg, of Peoria, are the only two daughters of her father's first marriage, and there were also two daughters by a second marriage: Clara, deceased, who was the wife of E. L. Alexander; and Julia B., wife of Harold Curdie, of Springfield. Mr. and Mrs. Hamilton had three daughters: Helen Eugenia, Pauline Cross and Mary E. Mary died in infancy. Helen is the wife of Donald D. Mills, of Chicago, and Pauline is the wife of John G. Farnsworth, of Albany, New York.

FREDERICK ADOLPH RANKE, president and manager of the F. Ranke Fur Company of Chicago, is a veteran in experience in his line of business, which he learned in Europe. He has been identified with the furrier business in Chicago for over forty years, and has built up one of the largest concerns of its kind in the middle west.

He was born in Hassel, Germany, March 24, 1857, son of Christ and Sophia Ranke. His people were well educated and substantial citizens of eastern Germany, where his parents spent all their lives. His father was a German farmer and died at the age of eighty-seven, his wife passing away at the age of eighty-six. Frederick Adolph was the third in a family of four sons and one daughter.

He grew up in a rural district in Germany, attended common schools and after the age of fourteen learned the trade and art of a furrier. Coming to Chicago June 28, 1881, he was employed at his trade by Charles Glanz, and remained in the service of others for twenty-four years. In 1906 he engaged in the furrier business for himself, and is now sole owner of the F. Ranke Fur Company, which has its quarters on the third floor of the Capitol Building, the old Masonic Temple. He is a manufacturer of fur garments and does an extensive general business in the handling of furs of all kinds. This is one of the old and honored concerns of its kind in Chicago.

Mr. Ranke is affiliated with the I. O. O. F., having been a member of Atlas Lodge No. 261 since 1886. Since 1882 he has been a member of the Mutual Benefit and Aid Society, and since 1886 has been treasurer of this organization and a member of the Board of Directors. In politics he is a republican. Mr. Ranke married, June 13, 1886, Miss Minnie Scharlau, a native of Chicago. Both the children born to their marriage are now deceased.

LOUIS A. SCHLAFLY became identified with the Citizens National Bank of Alton when it was organized twenty-seven years ago, and has been in the service as an executive officer for many years, being now vice president and a director. The Citizens National Bank of Alton is one of the stronger banking institutions of southern Illinois, with total assets of over five million dollars and with capital, surplus, undivided profits and reserves of $700,000.

Mr. Schlafly was born at Carlyle, in Clinton County, Illinois, February 4, 1877. His father, August Schlafly, one of the organizers of the Citizens National Bank of Alton, was born in Switzerland and was four years of age when he came with his father, John Schlafly, to America. The family established a home in the Swiss colony at Highland, Illinois, and later moved to Carlyle. August Schlafly, after organizing the Citizens National Bank at Alton in 1899, served as its president for about two years. He and his wife now live at St. Louis.

The second child and oldest son in a family of six, Louis A. Schlafly was educated in parochial schools at Carlyle, attended the Christian Brothers College at St. Louis, and his first regular employment was with the Carlyle Mill & Grain Company. He acquired his early training in banking at a private bank in Carlyle, and in 1899 became assistant cashier of the Citizens National Bank at Alton. For some years past he has been vice president of that institution. He is treasurer of the Illinois Terminal Railway Company.

Mr. Schlafly is affiliated with the Knights of Columbus and the B. P. O. Elks. In 1918 he married Jean Van Gent, of Minneapolis, Minnesota. They have one daughter, Jean Louise.

GILBERT K. HUTCHENS, present county judge of Greene County, is a native of that section of Illinois, and hard work and determined effort have brought him to a successful position in professional and public life there.

He was born in Woodville Township, Greene County, January 21, 1888. His grandfather, Brazwell Hutchens, was born in the same section of Illinois, followed farming, and died when forty years of age. He married Caroline Landon, of Jerseyville, Illinois, and who before her marriage had taught school in Greene County. Brazwell Hutchens himself was a pupil of Caroline Landon at Mount Gilead. They had a family of twelve children, the survivors being: Horace, Elkanah, Lucius, Julius, Jasper, Augustus, Gilbert, Julia, wife of Harry Glassner, Marie, wife of Lewis Resinger, Ellen, wife of Fred Martin, and Mary, wife of Horace Smith.

Jasper Hutchens, father of Judge Hutchens, was born in Greene County, in 1862, has devoted his active life to farming and is now living retired at Carrollton. He married Fannie Kaffer, daughter of Frank and Catherine (Goede) Kaffer, who came from Alsace-Lorraine. The children of Jasper Hutchens and wife are: Judge Gilbert K., Norbert L., of Denver, Colorado;; Oma, wife of Joseph Cordes, of Carrollton; Paul V., of Tipton, Iowa; Jasper J., of Denver; and Martin L., of Carrollton.

Gilbert K. Hutchens was reared in the vicinity of the villages of Woody and Kane, attended rural schools, but had to pay his way through high school. For two years he worked for Capt. William Fry, taking care of stock, in order to have the privilege of attending the high school at Carrollton. After the death of Captain Fry he made arrangements with his father to repay such money as was required to complete his high school course. He also arranged with Samuel Thomas to break a mule to ride and to work, and he rode that animal two years, until he had finished his high school course in 1907. He was president of the graduating class and has been president of the Carrollton High School Alumni. Several times he was chosen president of the Greene County Teachers Association. He spent a year in Illinois Normal University, and while there he won first place on the Triangular Debate Team. Judge Hutchens taught in rural districts in Greene County three years, at Green Summit and Woody, and in 1910 organized a high school at Hillview in the same county. While teaching there he was appointed, in April, 1913, county superintendent of schools to fill out the unexpired term of George B. McClelland. He was not yet twenty-five when appointed, and thus became the youngest county superintendent in the state. After finishing out the unexpired term he declined a nomination for that office and resumed his work at the Hillview High School, where he continued until the spring of 1918. Judge Hutchens for five years was superintendent of city schools at Roodhouse. During his administration the Roodhouse High School was changed to a community high school. While there he studied law with Attorney A. B. Johnson of Roodhouse, and subsequently took the course of the American Extension University of Los Angeles. He was admitted to the Illinois bar on examination before the Supreme Court in April, 1923, and on June 1st of the same year formed a partnership with Judge Thomas Henshaw at Carrollton. Judge Henshaw was one of the veteran lawyers of this section of Illinois.

Judge Hutchens tried as his maiden case an issue involving prominent parties. He appeared for the defense of a former sheriff who had been charged with defaulting to the amount of some $4,000 of public money. The sheriff had disappeared and had been gone for several years. On being returned he declined to plead guilty and take a modified sentence with a chance for freedom in about a year. He was without funds to fight his case, but Judge Hutchens offered to appear in his behalf without remuneration. In spite of able counsel arrayed on the side of the prosecution and in a trial involving a great deal of publicity in this section of the state, Judge Hutchens won a victory. Later he was one of the attorneys for the defense in a prominent murder trial at Carrollton, and the jury acquitted the defendant in ten minutes.

Judge Hutchens on June 2, 1924, was elected county judge as successor of the late Judge Mark Meyerstein. In this campaign he opposed his old preceptor, Mr. Johnson, who was the republican candidate. Judge Hutchens comes of a democratic family and cast his first presidential vote for Woodrow Wilson. His people were North Carolina democrats and his ancestors when they came West brought their slaves as far as Kentucky, where they freed them before moving into Illinois. Judge Hutchens registered during the World war and was active in Red Cross and other drives. He is a Thirty-second degree Scottish Rite Mason in the Consistory at Springfield, and is a director of the Carrollton Chamber of Commerce.

Judge Hutchens married at Normal, Illinois, April 22, 1915, Miss Grace Schutz, who was born at Hillview in 1895, daughter of Charles and Jane (Martin) Schutz. Mrs. Hutchens was for three years a student in the Hillview High School while Judge Hutchens was principal. She and Judge Hutchens have one daughter, Bettylee.

ELMER LINCOLN WENDELL, a resident of White Hall, has spent many years in the ministry, is also a lawyer, and is now giving most of his time to his duties as justice of the peace. He is a member of a pioneer family of Illinois.

John D. Wendell, one of his ancestors, served with the rank of captain in Washington's army during the Revolution. David H. Wendell, a son of John D., was also a Revolutionary veteran. In the attack on the Judge Chew mansion at the battle of Germantown he had his arm shot off. David H. Wendell married Cornelia Finch, who was one of the few who escaped from the massacre in the Wyoming Valley of Pennsylvania during the Revolution. She was the mother of Daniel Finch Wendell, the pioneer of the family in Illinois.

Daniel Finch Wendell was born at East Orange, New York, in 1801, and from the age of ten years lived at Ogden, in Monroe County, that state. He became a carpenter by trade. In 1833 he came to Illinois, located at Alton and followed his trade there the rest of his life. He died in 1869. He was a justice of the peace for many years and a deacon of the Upper Alton Baptist Church. Daniel F. Wendell married Harriet Ollcott, who was born at East Haddam, Connecticut, in 1803, and died in 1867, daughter of Oliver Ollcott. She was a direct descendant of Thomas Ollcott, who came from Northamtonshire, England, to America in 1636.

Capt. William H. Wendell, youngest child of Daniel F. Wendell and wife, was born at Upper Alton, Illinois, November 11, 1836. He was educated in Shurtleff College at Upper Alton, attended a business school in St. Louis, from which he graduated in 1856, and for several years was clerk in the store of his uncle, Alvin Ollcott. He also learned the trade of carpenter. On May 7, 1861, he enlisted in Company B of the Twenty-second Illinois Infantry, was mustered in June 20, and participated at Fort Donelson, Shiloh, Corinth and LaGrange, Mississippi, and in the blockade of Nashville in 1862, being at that time with the pioneer corps of the Army of the Cumberland. He was in the battle of Murphreesboro and the Chattanooga campaign, where he was detailed to the quartermaster's department and became quartermaster sergeant until mustered out July 11, 1864. On July 30 of the same year he was commissioned a lieutenant of volunteers by President Lincoln, and during the rest of the war served as assistant quartermaster of the Third Division of the Seventh Army Corps, being promoted to captain quartermaster in September, 1864. In May, 1865, at the close of the war, he acted as post quartermaster at Fort Gibson, Indian Territory, boarding with the famous Cherokee Chief Ross, and following that was on duty at Fort Scott, Kansas, and Fort Leavenworth, Kansas, and finally took command of the military prison at Alton as quartermaster in charge of government stores. The stores were sold October 1, 1865, and he was mustered out and honorably discharged November 20, 1865. His older brother, David, in the early part of the war was an overseer on his sister's plantation in Mississippi County, Missouri, and became a Southern sympathizer. He was captured and was put in the military prison at Cairo, where Captan Wendell visited him several times, and he finally took the oath of allegiance and served as civilian clerk under his brother.

After the war Captain Wendell followed the trade of carpenter until 1877, and then located on a farm in the east portion of Madison County, near Worden. From 1882 to October, 1892, he lived on a farm in Livingston County, Missouri. On returning to Illinois he established his home at White Hall, where he died in February, 1913. He was a Royal Arch Mason, a Baptist and a republican. Captain Wendell married Sarah Emily Pritchett, daughter of David and Lydia W. (Peas) Pritchett. Her father was born in Montgomery County, Kentucky, in 1816, and died in Jersey County, Illinois, in October, 1892.

Elmer Lincoln Wendell, oldest of the children of Captain Wendell and wife, was born at Upper Alton, Illinois, December 26, 1866. He attended public schools there and in Madison County, also in Livingston County, Missouri, and took a preparatory course in William Jewell College at Liberty, Missouri, was a student of theology three years, and his knowledge of the law was gained by study at White Hall. He was admitted to the Illinois Methodist Conference on probation in 1897, and became a full member in 1899. For several years he preached in North Dakota and South Dakota. Returning to Illinois in July, 1903, he was pastor of several churches. In July, 1907, he went to Oklahoma and was pastor of the Baptist Church of Okemah, and two years later became district missionary in

Eastern Oklahoma. He had united with the Baptist Church while in North Dakota in 1901. His ministerial service took him to a number of localities in Oklahoma, Missouri, Kansas and finally again in Illinois. For four years he was employed by the Burlington Railway at Beardstown, Illinois. He was elected justice of the peace at White Hall in April, 1922.

Mr. Wendell is president of the White Hall Historical Society, with Raymond B. Pierce, its secretary and treasurer. He is also a member of the Chamber of Commerce and is a republican. He has one son, Elmer L., Jr., who is a sergeant in the Aviation Corps, stationed at Chanute Field, Rantoul, Illinois.

HON. MALBERN MONROE STEPHENS. For many reasons one of the most interesting personalities and foremost citizens of St. Clair County is Hon. Malbern Monroe Stephens, mayor of East St. Louis and, in a manner of speaking, he may be called the father of this prosperous southern Illinois city. From early boyhood entirely dependent upon his own efforts, he has risen through sheer ability to influence and high position among his fellow citizens, and to none of them is more credit due for the material upbuilding of the most important enterprises of East St. Louis during many years of civic development.

Mayor Stephens was born February 7, 1847, in Luzerne County, Pennsylvania, son of Ziba and Mary (Travis) Stephens, and grandson of William Stephens, all of whom were born in Pennsylvania. His father served in a Pennsylvania regiment in the Civil war, afterward for a time was in the hotel business but later became a contractor in railroad construction. Of his family of five children, Malbern Monroe was the eldest, the other being: Charles E., who was unmarried and died; Mary Frances, who died when fifteen years old; William Henry, who married and has one child; and Ziba, who died when one year old.

The only actual schooling Mr. Stephens ever received was in the district school near his home in Luzerne County, this being interrupted when he went to work when eleven years old. One year later he left home, facing the world alone with the feeble strength and childish experience of twelve years. That he possessed even then a personality that attracted attention and inspired confidence may be assumed, for at the age of about fifteen he is found acting as a brakeman on the Delaware, Lackawanna & Western Railroad. On leaving that work he entered the employment of the Delaware and Hudson Coal & Railroad Company, part of the time firing and in railroad shops learned the trade of machinist, and after that worked in the machinery department of said Delaware & Hudson Coal and Railroad Company.

In 1866 Mr. Stephens came to the Big Muddy coal fields of Jackson County, Illinois, as a mechanic, and for three years was employed in erecting engines and machinery in the coal plants and running a locomotive. In 1869 he came to East St. Louis, Illinois, as an engineer, and ran a locomotive between East St. Louis, Illinois, and Vincennes, Indiana, on the old Ohio and Mississippi Railroad, now the Baltimore & Ohio, and from that time until the present, has been a resident of this city, of which he has nine times been elected mayor, and if he serves this term out, to April, 1927, he will have served the city twenty-two years as mayor.

It was in 1878 that Mr. Stephens first came into public notice as a political factor, being elected alderman of the Fourth Ward of East St. Louis for a term of two years and subsequently re-elected for a second term. In April, 1887, he was first elected mayor of the city, in which office he continued until 1895, and it was during this interval of eight years that his fellow citizens learned to know, and in a manner to appreciate, his courage and public spirit in behalf of civic improvement. Viewing the beautiful, prosperous city of East St. Louis of today, with its healthful environments, it is difficult to remember its unsightliness in a low-lying swamp, as was its condition forty years ago. Upon becoming mayor of the city the energetic young engineer, who through courage and determination had overcome so many obstacles in his personal career upward, began to plan many changes and reforms, although he fully realized that he had strong private interests to contend with. Always practical, he called in the city engineer to supply him with necessary data, and, as a beginning, in a secret session of the City Council submitted plans for raising the grade of Broadway about twelve feet, at this time simply asking the City Council to think it over for two weeks. At the end of that time he found the council unanimously in favor of the ordinance, which was approved and passed, then the work was immediately begun, by building retaining walls, sewering, filling, grading and paving of Broadway, which necessitated the raising of all connecting streets, and thus East St. Louis entered upon a new era, and the firm foundation was laid for its present expansion and prosperity. As sometimes happens, a people or community for a time are blind to their best interests and revile instead of praising their benefactor. At first there was bitter feeling against Mayor Stephens by property owners, although before the great work was finished property values had increased 200 per cent and more.

Mr. Stephens retired from the mayor's office in 1895, when he was appointed postmaster of East St. Louis by President Cleveland, and served as such until 1897, when he was again elected mayor and continued again at the head of municipal affairs until 1903, retiring then only to be recalled in 1919 and in 1923 was re-elected for another term of four years.

Mayor Stephens married first, in 1872, Miss Mary Elizabeth Beam, of East St. Louis, Illinois, who died in 1895, the mother of three children, two sons, one son who died in infancy, and one died at seven years of age, and a daughter, Leonora Frances. His second marriage took place in 1896, to Miss Sarah J. Bolte, and they have one daughter, Malberna Jane.

An active democrat all his public life, Mayor Stephens was chairman of the Illinois Waterways Commission under Governor Dunn, and has been tendered other high political positions outside his own city but has never been will-

ing to accept them. During the World war he was patriotically active along every line of effort, and specially had charge of all building material in this section for the U. S. government. He is a Knight Templar Mason and Shriner, and belongs also to the Elks, the Moose and the Knights of Pythias. He has been prominently identified with the Brotherhood of Locomotive Engineers for many years and has served in all the offices of the local lodge, and is now and long has been secretary and treasurer of the insurance department. For many years he has been preserving data published by local newspapers concerning the marvelous growth of East St. Louis, and when a faithful and accurate historian compiles and publishes it, one of the most informing chapters of the book may give some idea of the storm and stress through which the ship has been safely guided for so many years by the sturdy captain who is still at the helm.

HARLIN MELVILLE STEELY, for forty-five years has been a practicing lawyer in Vermilion County, one of the attorneys of widest and most successful experience at Danville. He is a native of Vermilion County, and his people were among the earliest pioneers of Western Indiana, in what is now Fountain and Warren counties.

He was born in Vermilion County November 25, 1856. The Steely family has been in America since Colonial days, coming from Scotland and settling in the Carolinas. Gabriel Steely, a great-grandfather of the Danville attorney, was born in one of the Carolinas, and served as a private in Captain Jehiel Gregory's company of Ohio in the War of 1812. Altogether there were fifteen members of the Steely family in the war for American independence. This Gabriel Steely, born August 19, 1763, died May 2, 1830. He moved West in 1805 from Pennsylvania, and spent his last years in Pickaway County, Ohio. His son, George Steely, grandfather of Harlin M., was born in Pennsylvania, May 20, 1788, and in 1805 went to Pickaway County, Ohio. He enlisted with the volunteers under General William Henry Harrison, and fought at the Battle of Tippecanoe November 7, 1811. In the War of 1812 he served as a private in Captain Jacob Catterline's Company and as a lieutenant in Captain George Wolfe's Company in the Second Ohio Regiment during that war. At its close he moved still further West and settled in what is now Fountain County, Indiana, entering land there in 1823. He built up a large estate and at his death left eighteen hundred acres to his heirs. His wife whom he married November 24, 1811, was Elizabeth Emerson, born November 16, 1791, a native of Maryland, who died February 10, 1853, in Fountain County. Her father, Captain Thomas Emerson, was commissioned captain of the Sloop Lethe April 5, 1782, a private in the War of the Revolution; also served on the American sloop Franklin, and was captured by the British, being taken to England and committed to the Old Mill prison. Later he was exchanged under an agreement made by Benjamin Franklin and returning home, was commissioned captain of the sloop Lethe, which carried twelve guns and a crew of fifty-six men. This Captain Emerson moved from Hampshire County, Virginia, to Pickaway County, Ohio, in 1806, and was a farmer. He married Mary Downey on November 12, 1779, a native of Maryland.

George Steely, Jr., father of Harlin Melville Steely, was born in Fountain County, Indiana, September 6, 1830. He was reared there, finished his education in old Asbury University, now De Pauw University, at Greencastle, Indiana, and after leaving college became an extensive farmer in Vermilion County, Illinois, locating here in 1854. He was a well known and substantial citizen of this section and died at his home near Hoopeston August 15, 1907. He held various town offices, was a soldier in the Mexican war, a member of the Masonic fraternity and a republican in politics. George Steely, Jr., married Hannah Hiser October 22, 1854, who was born in Warren County, Indiana, February 16, 1836, and died in Vermilion County, Illinois, September 11, 1892. She was a great-granddaughter of Lieutenant-Colonel Alexander Lawson Smith, who was commissioned a captain in the War of the Revolution July 13, 1776. He also served as major, and in October, 1780, resigned his commission as captain to become lieutenant-colonel of what was known as the Regiment Extraordinary, being with that command until the end of the war. George Steely, Jr., and wife had a family of ten children, five of whom died young. Harlin Melville is the oldest of those who grew to manhood; William Wallace is in the loan business at Bloomington, Illinois; Mrs. Clara I. Stone died at Gibson City, Illinois, in 1902, wife of a banker at Gibson City; Zaidee is the wife of Abraham L. Phillips, a lawyer at Gibson City and former member of the Illinois House of Representatives, and former state's attorney of Ford County. The son Mark A. has been in the West for a great many years.

Harlin Melville Steely was reared on his father's farm in Vermilion County, attended public schools, graduating from the Hoopeston High School, and when not in school gave most of his time to farm work until he was twenty-two years of age. During his seventeenth and eighteenth years he taught a country school in Vermilion County, and in 1878-79, at Potomac, Illinois, was principal of the high school. In the meantime he was pursuing the study of law, and on September 17, 1880, was admitted to the bar. He practiced law from an office in Hoopeston, but since March, 1892, has had an active membership in the Danville bar, carrying on a general law practice. His offices are in the First National Bank Building. He has a large clientage of corporation interests, being attorney for the Chicago & Eastern Illinois Railway and also for the Lake Erie & Western, and Toledo, St. Louis & Western Railways, both lines comprising branches of the Nickel Plate System. He is also attorney for the Illinois Power & Light Corporation of Danville, which owns the street railway system. Mr. Steely also has accumulated a number of real estate investments, including his home at 920 North Vermilion Street, two farms in Vermilion County, and two farms in Warren County, Indiana.

He is a republican in politics. For six years he was master of Star Lodge No. 709, A. F. and A. M., at Hoopeston; is a past high priest of Hoopeston Chapter No. 181, Royal Arch Masons, and a member of Olivet Commandery No. 38, Knights Templar, at Paxton. He performed his share of patriotic duties with the various committees during the great war.

Mr. Steely married in Vermilion County, August 25, 1878, Miss Mariam M. Marquess, daughter of James and Sarah E. (McLean) Marquess, now deceased. Her father had a long career as a farmer and school teacher in Indiana and in Vermilion County, Illinois, and was county superintendent of schools in Hodgeman County, Kansas. Leaving Kansas, he moved to Fountain County, Indiana, and lived there until his death. Mr. and Mrs. Steely had three sons. The oldest, George Steely, graduated Bachelor of Science from the University of Chicago; took his degree in medicine from the College of Physicians and Surgeons at Boston, Massachusetts, and for a year was on duty with the Army Medical Corps, with the rank of captain in the Receiving Hospital at New York City. He is now engaged in practice as a phyisician at Danville. The second son, Robert W., ran away from college to enlist in the Spanish-American war, and subsequently entered the University of Illinois and was a student of that institution when he was killed in a railroad accident on August 29, 1903. The youngest son, Harlin Melville, Jr., graduated with the PH. B. degree from Yale University, and studied law in the University of Illinois and in his father's office, now being junior partner in the law firm of Steely & Steely at Danville. He was accepted for service during the World war, but the armistice was declared before he was inducted into duty.

JACK C. SPENCER is president and manager of the Illinois Condensed Milk Company of White Hall, and has been an active figure in the milk industry for many years.

He was born near Rolla, Phelps County, Missouri, September 30, 1879. His father, James A. Spencer, was born at Belleville, Illinois, was reared there and in Madison County, and in about 1858 moved to Phelps County, Missouri. He served with an Illinois regiment in the Union army during the Civil war, being in General Sherman's army on the march to the sea and back through the Carolinas to Washington. He has been active in school and church in his home locality. In Phelps County he married Sarah J. Turner; whose parents came from South Carolina to Missouri in an ox wagon. She died in 1912, at the age of sixty-five, and of her three sons and three daughters those now living are Jack C., James A., of Texas County, Missouri, and Ellen, wife of Frank Morris, of Phelps County, Missouri.

Jack C. Spencer was first engaged in the milk business at Smithboro, where he had charge of the local plant of the St. Louis Dairy Company four years. While there he served as town clerk. In 1906 he located at White Hall and assisted in organizing the Illinois Condensed Milk Company, supervising the building of the plant. This plant has a capacity of 20,000 pounds, or ten tons of milk daily. The plant is in operation 365 days of the year and the market for the product is in Illinois towns as well as in St. Louis.

Mr. Spencer became interested in the Peoples First National Bank upon the consolidation of the two older institutions, and is now a director. He was for twelve years a director of the Board of Education of White Hall, being chairman of the building and grounds committee during the entire time of the erection of the modern high school. He also served two terms as an alderman, is a director of the Chamber of Commerce, is a member of the Masonic fraternity, Knights of Pythias and Independent Order of Odd Fellows, and is a Presbyterian. During the World war he was a member of the County Fuel Administration and was registered under the second draft.

He married in Macoupin County, Illinois, Miss Bertha Baker, a native of that county and daughter of John and Sarah Baker.

BAE STEWART, sheriff of Iroquois County, has earned the complete confidence and esteem of his fellow citizens in his official capacity. He is an honored veteran of the World war, having been in service in France with the Thirty-third Division.

He was born at Wellington, Iroquois County, son of Daniel and Almira (O'Connor) Stewart, and grandson of John and Elizabeth Stewart. Sheriff Stewart was reared on a farm, attended school at Wellington, and his experience up to the beginning of the World war was all derived from the farm.

On July 8, 1917, at the age of twenty-eight, he enlisted in Company B of the Third Illinois Infantry. He was with that command when it was mustered into the Federal service on August 5, 1917, becoming the One Hundred and Twenty-ninth Infantry, Sixty-fifth Brigade, Thirty-third Division of the United States army. September 13, 1917, he entrained for Camp Logan at Houston, Texas, remaining there for about eight months in training. On May 2, 1918, he left Camp Logan, arrived at Camp Upton, New York, and on May 6th, and on May 10th sailed on the U. S. S. Covington, formerly the Hamburg-American Liner Cincinnati. Arrival was made at Brest on May 24th, and on June 18 his outfit entrained for the front, arriving at Oisemont at 12:40 a. m., and detraining at 3:30 a. m., making the march to Menesles, 35 kilometers, (twenty-two miles) where the First Battalion assembled and where they received horses, rolling kitchens, and drew their equipment of British Enfield Rifles and gas masks, all this taking place between 4:30 p. m. and 12 o'clock midnight. From that time until November 11 Mr. Stewart's outfit was on or near the battle lines, sharing in the glorious record of his regiment, brigade and division. The full history of the Thirty-third Division has been published in the volumes of Illinois in the World War. Mr. Stewart was mustered out June 6, 1919, nearly two years after his first enlistment.

Mr. Stewart is a republican, and was nominated by that party and elected November 4, 1922, sheriff of Iroquois County. He began his official duties December 4, 1922. He is a popular member of a number of organizations, social and civic. He became a member of Wellington Lodge No. 785, Independent Order of Odd Fellows, on January 10, 1912, was elected noble grand in 1916, was a delegate to the State Grand Lodge at Springfield in 1922, and is a member of the Encampment at Watseka and Prairie Rebekah Lodge No. 622 at Hoopeston. In 1908 he became a member of Hoopeston Lodge No. 1227, Loyal Order of Moose, also a member of Star Camp No. 1003, Modern Woodmen of America, at Wellington. He was raised in Watseka Lodge No. 446, A. F. and A. M., June 30, 1925. Sheriff Stewart is a member of American Legion Post No. 23, and of its 40 et 8 Society, and is a member of the Iroquois Club at Watseka. He holds membership in the Methodist Episcopal Church at Wellington.

Mr. Stewart married at Danville, Illinois, November 12, 1919, Miss Amy Hazel Harris, daughter of Edward V. and Amy L. Harris, and a granddaughter of Hezekiah Harris, who served as a Union soldier in Company G of the Sixty-second Michigan Infantry during the Civil war. Her grandfather, Jesse B. Thompson, was related to former president Rutherford B. Hayes. Her great-great-grandfather, Joseph Parrot, was a captain in the Revolutionary war. Mrs. Stewart is a member of the American Legion Auxiliary Post No. 23.

BENJAMIN JORDAN. In the modern road building program of Illinois during the present century, one man who has contributed a notable share in technical and actual construction work in his home county, Iroquois, is Benjamin Jordan, for thirteen years county superintendent of highways. Mr. Jordan is a veteran road builder, and his early experience in that line antedated the modern construction of the functions of a highway system.

Mr. Jordan was born on a farm near Corydon, Indiana, February 27, 1874. He represents an old American ancestry. His great-grandfather Jordan was a Hessian soldier during the Revolutionary war, and after the war remained in America, settling in the Shenandoah Valley in Virginia. Mr. Jordan's grandfather, Benjamin Jordan, came from Virginia and settled about three miles south of Corydon between 1818 and 1820, being one of the pioneers in that section of Indiana. Mr. Jordan had another ancestor, a great-grandfather, Patrick Hunter, who was with Captain Lochry in his attempt to join Gen. George Rogers Clark's expedition to the Northwest Territory. He and his companions were captured by the Indians on Blennerhassett's Island in the Ohio River, were taken to Detroit, and there made to run the gauntlet. It is a tradition that Patrick Hunter was such a fast runner that none of the Indians could hit him. He survived the ordeal and subsequently settled at Rehoboth in Harrison County, Indiana, where he died.

Mr. Jordan's father, David Mitchell Jordan, was born January 15, 1836, and died in Harrison County, Indiana, December 27, 1916. His life was spent as a carpenter and farmer. In the Civil war he enlisted in 1861, became captain of Company C of the Sixty-sixth Indiana Infantry, and at the battle of Richmond, Kentucky, he and nineteen men of his company escaped while all the other Union forces were captured. He also participated in the battle at Winchester, Virginia; Corinth, Mississippi; Colliersville, Tennessee; several battles around Atlanta, and was with Sherman on his march to the sea and north to Washington. He was finally mustered out in 1865. David Mitchell Jordan married Sarah Catherine Sieg, whose parents came from Westmoreland County, Pennsylvania and settled in Harrison County, Indiana.

Benjamin Jordan grew up on his father's farm in Harrison County, Indiana, attending grade school No. 6 there, and subsequently graduating from the high school at Corydon. While reared on a farm, he also worked as a carpenter, and from 1898 to 1904 was employed as road engineer of Harrison County, Indiana.

His training as an engineer was amplified by his work as a transit man on the location of the Chicago Southern (the old Walsh Road) and as resident engineer on construction at Donovan, Illinois. During the years 1906 to 1913 he was engaged in general engineering work, chiefly drainage surveying in Iroquois County. Then, in 1913, he was made county superintendent of highways, and has filled that office continuously, giving the utmost of his training and experience to the county in the transformation of its highways, which make the county a distinctive unit among Illinois counties. He has charge of construction of many miles of concrete and gravel roads and bridges, including the large grade and bridge over Sugar Creek, west of Milford.

Mr. Jordan is a republican, and attends the Methodist Church. At Corydon, Indiana, December 25, 1904, he married Miss Christine Jane Mathes, daughter of Eli and Elmira Mathes, and granddaughter of John Mathes, who served as a member of the Second Constitutional Convention of Indiana. Mr. and Mrs. Jordan have two children, Juanita and Wayne Jordan.

JAMES MCNABB. Few men have a wider diversity of work, service and honor than James McNabb, of Carrollton.

Mr. McNabb was born at Clarksville, Pike County, Missouri, November 14, 1857. His father, Hugh McNabb, was a native of County Tyrone, Ireland, and after coming to the United States was a farmer and merchant in Calhoun County. He married in Ireland Rosa McQuade. He died in 1861, at the age of forty-five, and his wife, in 1889. Their children were: Patrick, who was killed while a soldier in the Union army at the battle of Corinth; John, a farmer, who died in Calhoun County; Frank, a Calhoun County farmer; and James, twin brother of Frank.

James McNabb was an infant when his parents settled in Calhoun County, Illinois. He grew up on a farm, attended country schools, and in the intervals of his teaching he continued his higher education, spending two years, beginning in 1888, as a student in the College of Physicians and Surgeons at St. Louis. He took special training in elocution and literature under John R. Scott at Washington University in St. Louis, and completed a course in law with the New York Correspondence School of Law. He was in school work twelve years, ten years of that time as county superintendent in Calhoun County. He was given a certificate to teach in March, 1874, at the age of seventeen, and on March 17, 1877, was appointed county superintendent, and was twice elected to that office. Mr. McNabb has been in newspaper work forty years. On March 19, 1881, he purchased the Calhoun Herald, and in addition to other duties edited it for six years. In 1886 he bought a half interest in the Carrollton Gazette, and has been the responsible editor in charge since July 19 of that year. On January 14, 1895, he was admitted to the Illinois bar, and on January 5, 1897, was admitted to practice in the United States District Court. Governor John P. Altgeld appointed him a member of the State Board of Charities on May 1, 1893, and he served four years. His chief service in the legal profession has been rendered as master in chancery for the Circuit Court of Greene County. He was first appointed March 10, 1895, by George W. Herdman, was reappointed March 10, 1899, by Judge O. P. Thompson, and subsequent appointments came from Judge R. B. Shirley, Judge Frank W. Burton and Judge Norman L. Jones. He was elected mayor of Carrollton April 17, 1917, and for the past six years has been a member of the City Board of Health.

Since October 15, 1910, he has been a member of the Democratic State Central Committee from the Twentieth Congressional District, and on the death of the chairman was automatically made acting chairman. He has been a director of the Greene County National Bank since January 14, 1908. He cast his first presidential ballot for General Hancock, and has regarded voting as an essential privilege and duty of every citizen. He is a member of the local Chamber of Commerce.

Mr. McNabb married, June 26, 1880, Louise M. Pierson, at Carrollton, where she was born, daughter of Ornan and Maria (Stryker) Pierson. She was educated at Carrollton and in the Illinois Woman's College of Jacksonville. Mr. and Mrs. McNabb have one son, James P., who graduated from the Carrollton High School and the University of Colorado, and is now in the real estate business at Hollywood, California. During the World war this son was in the auditing department of the American Expeditionary Forces, located at Paris, France.

WILLIAM C. DICKSON is one of the oldest residents of Pittsfield, has personal recollections of the community during the '40s and '50s, is a survivor veteran of the Civil war, and his active career for upwards of half a century was devoted to business, especially merchandising. The name Dickson has figured in the commercial life of Pittsfield from almost the founding of the town.

His father was Thomas Dickson, who located at Pittsfield in 1838. Thomas Dickson was born on the Orkney Islands of Scotland in 1815, the year of the battle of Waterloo. At the age of eighteen he came to America, locating first in New York City. He had been trained to the tailoring trade, and at New York he was employed as a "bushelman" in a tailoring establishment. While in New York he married Isabella Foster, a native of New York. Leaving the east, he moved out to Ohio, and from there in 1838 came to Illinois, having traded his furniture and other goods for a one-horse covered wagon in which the family, consisting of himself, his wife and one child, drove overland to western Illinois. He passed through Griggsville, then an important village, and was urged to stop there. He arrived in Pittsfield in August, 1838. It was his good fortune to fall in with the genial and popular citizen of Pittsfield, Doctor Worthington, who had come to the town from Tennessee. Doctor Worthington was so accommodating as to make room in his own family so that Thomas Dickson had two rooms in which to live for a time. He soon bought a lot on the town square. This lot is now included in the property of his son William. On this he erected a frame house and also a shop, and there engaged in the tailoring business. In 1850, with three companions, he went to California over the plains, but after a year returned with little more wealth than he took away. Thomas Dickson then clerked for a dry goods firm at Pittsfield and after two years engaged in business for himself, at first in the firm of Watson, Abbott & Dickson, then Gay, Abbott & Dickson. In the summer of 1861 he took his share of a third of the goods and fitted up his old home on the square as a store. He became a merchant, and continued active in business until his death in 1885. His wife passed away in 1906.

Thomas Dickson was a man of public spirit and an earnest worker for improvements in his community. He sponsored the movement for setting out the trees on the public square, which when he came to Pittsfield was just part of the open prairie. He and a companion brought in a wagon load of trees and each one was turned over to an individual citizen who planted it and made himself responsible for its care. As a result of this bit of enterprise the square at Pittsfield has a small grove of towering trees. Thomas Dickson was also one of the charter members of the First Congregational Church. After the formation of the party he became a republican, but his only public service was on the town board. He was a member of the Order of Good Templars. He and his wife are buried in Oakwood Cemetery at Pittsfield. Their children were: Elizabeth married J. W. Nesmith, and both died in Denver, Colorado, leaving two daughters; Isabella married John T. Lynch, and they went to Salt Lake City, where Mr. Lynch was postmaster, and at their death they were survived by two daughters; Julia married Watson Goodrich, and both died at Pittsfield; the next in age is William Carter, who was named in honor of Rev. William Carter, a beloved minister of the Gospel at Pittsfield for thirty-eight years; James has always lived at Pittsfield; Thomas became a leading lawyer at Leadville, Colorado, and died leaving two sons and two daughters.

William C. Dickson was born at Pittsfield, October 10, 1843. As a boy he attended private schools. He was a pupil in the school conducted by Mr. and Mrs. John D. Thompson, a school that was justly famous because of the fine character and scholarly abilities of

Lotte E. Jones

Mr. and Mrs. Thompson. Mr. Thompson was an educated Irishman, a classical scholar, and had formerly been a bookkeeper in the Bank of London. His wife was an Irish lady and well versed in French. William C. Dickson later attended a school conducted by John Shatid and also one conducted by Mr. Sanders.

He was not yet eighteen years of age when the Civil war broke out. In August, 1862, he enlisted as a private in Company A of the Ninety-ninth Illinois Infantry, and was on duty with the regiment in Missouri several months, then at Memphis, and as part of Grant's army was at Milligan's Bend, participated in the battles of Magnolia Hill, Port Gibson, Raymond, Mississippi, Edwards Station, Jackson, Champion Hill, Big Black, and for forty-seven days was in the siege of Vicksburg, from May 19, 1863, until the surrender on July 4th. He witnessed the preliminaries of the surrender, seeing General Pemberton come out of the city and meet General Grant, and he also saw the Confederate forces march out of the city and stack their arms. From Vicksburg the Ninety-ninth Regiment went to Jackson, Mississippi, and fought with General Johnston's army, thence went to New Orleans by boat, over to Algiers and Brazier City, was in the Tesch country of Louisiana and by gulf went to Mobile Bay and participated in the reduction of Spanish Ft. Blakely, took possession of Mobile, was at Spring Hill, and subsequently returned to Louisiana and was in camp at Carrollton, near New Orleans, for a time. From there the regiment went to Shreveport and after a few weeks was ordered to Baton Rouge, where it was mustered out July 31, 1865. Mr. Dickson was discharged at Springfield and returned to Pittsfield August 19, 1865. He had been in the service three years and was never wounded. After the war he joined the Grand Army of the Republic as a charter member of his post, and has attended numerous national reunions and has served on the staff of the Illinois State Commander.

Following the war Mr. Dickson resumed work for his father in the store. Subsequently he and James Rhea from Missouri built up a good business as manufacturers of plug tobacco at Pittsfield. Mr. Dickson handled the sales end of this business. He continued in the tobacco business until 1872. At that time Thomas Dickson had erected the Dickson brick building on the site of the old home on the square, and the son then accepted his invitation to join him in merchandising. After the death of Thomas Dickson, William C. bought the business and continued it six years longer, his own son becoming a clerk in the store. After selling the store at Pittsfield Mr. Dickson became a commercial salesman, representing a rubber paint company of Chicago. He next accepted a flattering offer to handle mining machinery for the Colorado Iron Works. After a few years he resigned and since 1905 has been altogether retired from the active responsibilities of business.

Mr. Dickson married at Pittsfield, October 10, 1866, Miss Josephine Topliff, who was born in Vermont and came to Illinois at the age of thirteen, growing up at Pittsfield. Her parents were Madison and Sarah (Carpenter) Topliff. Mrs. Dickson died October 17, 1903. There were two sons, William H. and Joseph Dickson. Joseph died at the age of thirteen. William H. since leaving Illinois has been a prominent lawyer at Denver, Colorado, is former attorney-general of Colorado and former speaker of the House of the Colorado Legislature. He married Winona Holeman, of Chicago, and they became the parents of three children, the daughter Lucia being deceased. Winona is the wife of William Kirby, and Wellington N. lives in Florida.

MISS LOTTE E. JONES, author and lecturer, is a resident of Danville and an Illinois woman widely known for her interest and education and in the preservation of Illinois history. She was born close to the Illinois line on the banks of the Wabash River at Covington, Indiana. Miss Jones is in the ninth generation of two of the early Colonial New England families, being a descendant of Rev. John Jones of Fairfield, Connecticut, and also of George Wheeler of Concord, Massachusetts, both of whom came to America before 1638. Rev. John Jones (Joanes) was a dissenter from the Church of England who with his family came to America on the ship Defense in 1635 and was one of the founders of Concord, Massachusetts, a minister of the Congregational Church. His son, grandson and great-grandson all bore the name of John and were all likewise ministers of the same denomination. The great-great-grandfather of Miss Jones, also John Jones, went west to the Hudson River and the John Jones of the following generation went further west, to the Genesee Country, where he lived as a farmer, and died in Spencer, New York. Miss Jones grandfather, James Mandeville Jones, was born at Peeksville, New York, and died at Spencer of the same state, spending his life largely as a farmer. His wife, Elizabeth Sproson, was a native of New York City. Her father, John Sproson, was one of the founders of the John Street Methodist Church.

Miss Lotte Jones is a daughter of the American Revolution, belongs to the Sons and Daughters of the Pilgrims, Daughters of the Revolution, and the Daughters of Colonial Wars and other patriotic organizations requiring direct ancestry for eligibility. Miss Jones is a member of the Lincoln Circuit Marking Association.

The father of Miss Jones was Doctor John Sproson Jones, who was born at Peekesville, New York, and was reared there; was educated in Vermont for the medical profession and practiced in New York State for ten years. In 1849 he moved to Covington, Indiana, and in the early seventies removed to Danville, Illinois, where during his final years he practiced his profession. Doctor Jones was a whig and later a republican in politics. He was a member of the New School Presbyterian Church. Doctor Jones married Charlotte Wheeler, a native of Bath, New York. Her father, George Wheeler, was a farmer and for many years postmaster at Kanona, New York. His home, yet standing, has been in constant use for generations by the Wheeler family, from the time it was built in 1814. Doctor Jones and wife were parents to the following children: George Wheeler Jones, a physician and surgeon in the Civil war with the Sixty-third Indiana Infantry, was a thirty-second degree Mason and died at Bermuda in 1900. James, the second son, was also a soldier in the Civil war, in the quartermaster's department of the Sixty-third Indiana Infantry, a druggist by profession, a member of the Masonic fraternity, and died at Danville. Lydia, Mary and Lotte, the daughters who lived beyond infancy, are in Indiana and Illinois.

Lotte E. Jones was educated in the public schools of Danville, having graduated from the Danville High School. She completed her education in the Northwestern University at Evanston. She was a primary school teacher in Danville for nearly twenty years, and a great many people remember her chiefly for her kindly and effective work in starting them on the road to education. In later years she lectured extensively on historical and educational themes. Miss Jones is the author of a work on Illinois history called "Decisive Dates of Illinois History," and also is the author of the historical work entitled "The Heart of the Nation," beside other books and pamphlets. Miss Jones has been conspicuous in her efforts to mark the old Lincoln Circuit. This historic highway passes through seventeen counties of central Illinois, through which Abraham Lincoln traveled twice each year in the practice of his profession of law from 1849 to 1860, when he was elected President of the United States. These counties are Sangamon, Tazewell, Woodford, McLean, Logan, DeWitt, Piatt, Champaign, Vermilion, Edgar, Shelby, Coles, Moultrie, Macon, Christian and Mason. A marker is placed at each county seat and one at the county limits along the way, with an extra one in Vermilion and in Logan County. These markers at the county seats were designed by Henry Bacon, the artist of the great Lincoln Memorial at Washington, D. C. This work of marking the Lincoln Circuit was done primarily by the Daughters of the American Revolution of Illinois, financed by the people through the County Boards of Supervisors along the circuit. The permanent care of the marking is vested in an incorporated organization called the Lincoln Circuit Marking Association, under the auspices of the Daughters of the American Revolution of Illinois. Miss Jones has been a never failing supporter of the Circuit Marking and it is conceded that to her efforts and those of her associates the success of the undertaking is due.

EMIT W. JOESTING is a native son of Alton, and has spent the greater part of his mature career with the Citizens National Bank of Alton. He is the present cashier of that institution.

He was born at Alton January 19, 1884. His grandfather, Frederick C. Joesting, was born in Hanover, Germany, in 1807, and spent his life in educational work. Several of his children came to Alton, one of them being the late Gustav A. Joesting. He came to this country when sixteen years of age, about 1863, and to the end of his life, more than half a century later, was actively identified with the city's financial affairs. For a number of years he was cashier for the Alton Savings Bank and later became cashier for the Citizens National Bank of Alton. He had started his banking experience as a clerk in the old First National Bank. He was cashier of the Citizens National Bank until his death in 1918, when seventy years of age. He married Fannie E. Volz, who survives him. She was born at Alton, daughter of Christian Volz, a native of Germany.

Emit W. Joesting was the fourth in a family of eight children, five of whom are still living. He was educated in the public schools of Alton, including high school, and after the completion of his education he became a clerk in railroad offices. In 1905, as a young man of twenty-one, he went to work in the Citizens National Bank on the books, and has successively mastered many other responsibilities in the banking service, so that he was eminently well qualified to succeed his father as cashier upon the latter's death in 1918.

On June 14, 1910, Mr. Joesting married Miss Irene C. Threda, of Alton. They have on daughter, Jane J. Mr. Joesting is affiliated with the Masonic fraternity and the B. P. O. Elks, and is interested in all the constructive movements for the city's growth and welfare.

LYNN CLARENCE SMITH, a member of the firm Lowenstein and Sons, merchants at White Hall, represents one of the old and prominent families of Greene County.

He was born at White Hall, November 24, 1889. His father, Edward B. Smith, was born ten miles east of White Hall, was reared on a farm, was sergeant in a company with an Illinois regiment in the Civil war, and after the war was employed for some time at White Hall in the Culbertson and Smith Pottery, in which his brother, Tom Smith, was a partner. He also followed the trade of stationary engineer. At one time he traveled with the noted Duncan Sisters, singers. He was very active in the republican party, served as county supervisor, was sergeant at arms in the National Republican Convention at Philadelphia, and for a time held an appointive position at Springfield under Andrew Russell. He died at White Hall. His wife was Caroline Lowenstein, a daughter of Isaac Lowenstein and a sister of the Lowenstein brothers of White Hall. Their only child is Lynn Clarence Smith. The late Edward Smith was a brother of Prof. George W. Smith, head of the history department of the Southern Illinois Normal University of Carbondale. Professor Smith himself spent his early life in Greene County and for several years was superintendent of schools at White Hall.

Lynn Clarence Smith graduated from the White Hall High School in 1909. He also took the agricultural course in the University of Illinois a year and a half. Mr. Smith for one year was employed by the street car company at Springfield as a conductor. Since returning to White Hall he has been active in the firm of Lowenstein & Sons, and is one of the partners and active principals in that large and successful business.

He served as the last tax collector under the old township system for two years. He is a member of the White Hall School Board and Chamber of Commerce, belongs to the Masonic Lodge, and in politics is a republican,

having cast his first presidential vote for William H. Taft.

He enlisted June 27, 1918, at Norfolk, Virginia, and was on board the Pamlico, a training ship for officers' material school. He received his honorable discharge in December of the same year. He is one of the charter members and has been a commander of White Hall Post of the American Legion.

WALTER E. HOWDEN, superintendent of highways for Madison County, is an engineer by training, and has had many years of actual contact with the great modern road building program of the state of Illinois.

Mr. Howden was born in northwestern Missouri, December 1, 1886, son of Andrew F. and Nora (Wright) Howden. His father was born at Camp Point, Illinois, while his mother was born at Marysville, Missouri. His parents now reside at Kansas City, Missouri.

Second of three sons, Walter E. Howden was reared and educated in northwestern Missouri, and was about twenty years of age when he came to Illinois in 1905. For two years he was with an engineering party locating railroad lines, and on September 26, 1907, he became an employe of the Illinois Highway Commission. His active experience has covered every phase and department of highway construction, and he has spent many years in the field during actual road building. Among other places where he has been located in the service for more or less longer time were Mount Sterling, Effingham, Collinsville, White Hall, Salem, McLean and Joliet.

On January 1, 1914, Mr. Howden was appointed superintendent of highways for Madison County, and thus for ten years has been the technical man in charge of the program of highway building in this rich and prosperous southern Illinois county. Mr. Howden married, September 26, 1910, Miss Ruth C. True, of Canton, Illinois. In politics he is a republican.

THE BURNHAM ATHENEUM of Champaign, is one of the older public libraries of Central Illinois and in its history reflects entirely the generosity and public spirit of the community. The library now contains 76,745 volumes and thirty-five percent of the city's population are borrowers from the library. The city provides annually about $12,000 for the maintenance of the institution.

The Atheneum had its inception in a meeting held April 28, 1868, when the Champaign Library Association was organized. A reading room was opened and maintained for a short time. Later the movement was revived in 1871 and in September, 1876, the association conveyed its property to this city on condition that the city appropriate $1,000 annually to support the library. This was the beginning of the Champaign Public Library reading room. The library was maintained in rented quarters for some years and in 1889 was moved to a room in the city hall.

In December, 1894, A. C. Burnham announced a generous gift of $40,000 for a library building and $10,000 as an endowment fund. A residence, the former Burnham homestead, on West Church Street, was conveyed as a site for the Burnham Atheneum and Julia F. Burnham endowment fund of $10,000 was provided for the purchase of books and in 1920 an additional sum of $50,000 was given by the will of Robert D. Burnham for the further purchase of books to be known as the Robert D. Burnham Endowment Fund. The permanent home of the Burnham Atheneum was opened December 17, 1896. It was designed by a leading Boston architect with the idea of combining beauty in simplicity in a type of architecture that would be correct and enduring. The building is of light gray brick, with a beautiful Colonial front and the library has occupied this structure since June 1, 1896.

The librarian of the Burnham Atheneum since 1915 has been Miss Ethel G. Kratz.

HUGH E. BOUTON soon after finishing his high school course entered the navy for service in the great war, and after that experience took his law course and is now one of the prominent and influential young attorneys of the Danville bar.

He was born at Sparland in Marshall County, Illinois, October 20, 1899. His family has been in this country for a number of generations, their first place of settlement being in Massachusetts. They came here from France, but more remotely the name was English and spelled Boughton. The grandfather of the Danville attorney was Nathaniel D. Bouton, a native of New York State, and a minister of the Methodist Church. He was killed in a railway accident in New York. Jesse Roe Bouton, father of Hugh E., was for many years well known as a school man in the different communities of Illinois. He was born in Wenona, this state, October 6, 1869; spent some of his boyhood in the Town of Magnolia, and graduated from Highland Park College at Des Moines, Iowa, with the Bachelor of Science degree and the degree Master of Didactics. He was a teacher in the rural schools of Marshall County, Illinois, until 1895, following which for fourteen years he was principal of the Sparland High School in the same county. Then, in 1909, for a year he was principal of the high school at Wapello, Illinois; for two years was principal of the high school at Pawnee, and during 1911-12 was high school principal at Herin in Southern Illinois. From 1912 to the fall of 1918 he was principal of the high school at Vermont, Illinois, and then for three years was high school principal at Greenfield, and since 1920 has been principal of the high school at Sidell. He is an independent in politics; a member of the Methodist Church and the Masonic fraternity.

Jesse R. Bouton married Marie M. Barton, who was born at Wenona, Illinois, December 25, 1863, and died at Sidell July 13, 1923. Their oldest child was Jesse Roe, Jr., who studied medicine in the medical department of the Northwestern and Loyola Universities at Chicago, also in the St. Louis University, and during the World war was a pharmacist mate in the United States Navy, stationed at the Great Lakes Naval Training Station, having been in the service one year and four months. He died at Chicago April 8, 1921. Hugh E.

Bouton is the second child. The youngest is Mildred E., a student in Knox College at Galesburg.

Hugh E. Bouton received his early training in the public schools of Sparland, Pawnee, Herin and Vermont, Illinois, graduating from the Vermont High School with the class of 1917. On April 16, 1917, ten days after America declared war on Germany, he volunteered, though at that time he was not yet eighteen. He entered the navy and after some training was assigned to duty on a transport and was overseas four times. He received his honorable discharge at the Great Lakes Naval Station in Illinois August 2, 1919.

He then entered the law department of the Illinois Wesleyan University at Bloomington, and was graduated with the LL. B. degree in the class of 1922. He was a member of the Phi Alpha Delta legal fraternity. Mr. Bouton in 1922 engaged in practice at Danville, and has already acquired a profitable civil and criminal practice in the local courts. He is a republican and a member of the Methodist Church. His offices are in the First National Bank Building in Danville.

Mr. Bouton married Harriet M. Terry, daughter of Harvey G. Terry, a prominent farmer who has a large farm of over eight hundred acres situated near Sidell. H. G. Terry's father migrated from New York into Illinois early in 1840, settling in Vermilion County, in what was known as the Vermilion swamp. This land was drained in the sixties and now is considered the finest tillable agricultural land in the State of Illinois.

GEORGE FRANCIS BATTY, postmaster of Greenfield, was born and reared and has spent all of his life in Greene County, has been a farmer and stock man, and prominently identified with politics and public affairs for many years.

He was born on a farm near Wrights, in Greene County, August 18, 1875. On the same farm was born his father, James F. Batty, who gave his active years to its cultivation and management, though for some time he was postmaster of Wrights. He was a republican in politics. In Macoupin County James F. Batty married Miss Martha Ann Witt, daughter of Elijah and Elizabeth (Johnson) Witt. Mrs. James F. Batty died in 1892, and he passed away in 1901. Their children were: George F.; Agnes, wife of Arthur Blaney, of Alton, Illinois; Olive, wife of H. W. Sonneborn, of Webster, North Dakota; Florence, of Hettick, Illinois, widow of Milton Braden; William E. of Greenfield; and James E., of Hettick.

George F. Batty was reared on the farm, and obtained his educational advantages in the Batty school near Wrights. He then went to farming, beginning as a renter, achieving the ownership of a farm, and was one of the capable farmers and stock men in the locality until 1914, when he removed to the town of Greenfield. Mr. Batty was clerk in a mercantile establishment until the beginning of the World war. During the war he was a member of the local exemption board and was himself registered and classified. With a partner he erected the Batty and Gustine garage at Greenfield, and was identified with its management for three years. After selling out he devoted his attention chiefly to his duties as township supervisor until October 1, 1923, when he became postmaster of Greenfield as successor of William M. Cannedy.

For twenty years or more Mr. Batty has been more or less continuously occupied with some official duty. He was tax collector of Rubicon Township, was deputy assessor of Rockbridge Township, then became deputy collector under County Treasurer C. R. Angle, and was elected and for five years was supervisor of Rockbridge Township, resigning to become postmaster. He was a member of the finance committee of the Board of Supervisors. A republican, he cast his first presidential vote for Major McKinley in 1896, and has never missed an election in thirty years. He is affiliated with the Modern Woodmen of America and is a member of the Methodist Church.

He married October 11, 1899, Miss Maggie Short, who was born in Greene County, January 20, 1875, daughter of Joshua M. and Maria (Ferguson) Short, a well known family of farmers in this section. Mrs. Batty was one of a family of four sons and four daughters, seven of whom are living. Her brothers are George L., Frank M., Barney and Lewis H., all residents of Springfield, Illinois. The other two surviving daughters are Mrs. Delia Wright of Wrights, Illinois, and Mrs. J. Frank Doyle, of Greenfield.

ALONZO FRANKLIN GOODYEAR, vice president of the First National Bank of Watseka, president of the Board of Trustees of the Iroquois Hospital, is also one of the leading attorneys practicing at the bar of Watseka, and a man whose name is known very favorably all over his part of Illinois. He was born at Morton, Tazewell County, Illinois, August 30, 1860, a son of Alonzo P. and Mary (Humphrey) Goodyear, and a lineal descendant of Stephen Goodyear, one of the founders and deputy governor for thirty years of the New Haven Colony, Connecticut.

Grounded in the fundamentals of an education in common and high schools, Alonzo Franklin Goodyear took his professional training at Union College of Law, Chicago, and has long been connected with important litigation in Iroquois County. In order to earn the money to secure his legal training Mr. Goodyear taught school for several years, being as thorough in the schoolroom as he has since been in other avenues of activity, and had he cared to remain an educator could have risen far in that calling. He has never lost his interest in the public schools, and served for one term as assistant county superintendent of schools, and as a member of the local school board. His public service, however, has not been limited to educational matters, for he has served Watseka as an alderman for several terms, has long been master-in-chancery, and in 1920 he was a member of the Constitutional Convention of Illinois. Since he cast his first vote Mr. Goodyear has been a staunch supporter of the republican party, and has become one of its leaders in his city and county. High in Masonry, he belongs to Watseka Commandery, K. T., and Medinah Temple, A. A. O.

N. M. S., Chicago, and is zealous with reference to his fraternity. Through his membership in the Commercial Club he keeps in close touch with the affairs of business in Watseka, while the Methodist Episcopal Church of the same city is his religious home, and he is one of its most steadfast members.

On January 8, 1889, Mr. Goodyear married, in Donovan, Illinois, Stella M. Myres, a daughter of Matthew D. Myres, and they have the following children: Robert F. and Lawrence M. Goodyear. Robert F. Goodyear was born August 26, 1893, and is unmarried. He is an attorney, secretary of the Republican County Central Committee, and inheritance tax attorney for Iroquois, Grundy and Kankakee counties. Lawrence M. Goodyear was born September 5, 1897, and he is assistant cashier of the First National Bank of Watseka. He married Grace Davis. Both of these young men are held in high esteem, and have succeeded in establishing themselves in public confidence. They, with their father, are regarded as leading exponents of the best element in Watseka and Iroquois County, and can be depended upon to forward all movements looking toward the maintenance of the public welfare.

ADOLPH B. HAMMEL. As a business man and also in the public spirited activities of the citizen the outstanding member of the community of Trenton in Clinton County is Mr. Adolph B. Hammel, president of the Farmers State Bank and of the Trenton Milling Company.

His people are of the old Swiss-German stock, so prominently identified with a number of communities in southern Illinois. Mr. Hammel was born at Trenton, in August, 1874. His parents, Sebastian and Elizabeth (Mautchinbock) Hammel, are residents of Trenton, and an occasion of much interest to that community was the celebration of their fifty-eighth wedding anniversary on December 13, 1924. Sebastian Hammel is now eighty-four years of age and his wife, seventy-nine. They had only two sons, Adolph and Rudolph. The latter married Estelle Schuerer. Sebastian Hammel came to America when seventeen years of age. His parents remained in the old country. He soon located at Trenton and for a number of years followed the mechanical trade. He conducted an implement shop in Trenton, and in 1895, with others, organized the Trenton Milling Company, in which he has ever since been one of the large stockholders. In 1905 he organized the Farmers State Bank, serving as its vice president. He has been a successful business man and has given generously of his time and means to the advancement of the community, being interested in education and serving on the school board for a number of years. He has also been a member of the City Council.

Adolph B. Hammel grew up in Trenton, attending grammar and high school there, and finished a commercial course in the Jones Business College at St. Louis in 1892. For about two years he worked in his father's implement shop, but in 1895, upon the organization of the Trenton Milling Company, he became identified with that industry. For thirty years his experience has covered every phase of flour milling, from the mechanical processes of the mill itself to the problems of distribution and organized marketing. He worked in every department of the mill, and in 1899 was promoted to the post of general manager, and still holds that office. The Trenton Milling Company, Inc., is practically owned by Mr. Hammel and his father. Mr. Adolph Hammel is president of the company. He has also become president of the Farmers State Bank of Trenton, one of the leading financial institutions of Clinton County.

Mr. Hammel is a member of the Southern Illinois Millers Association, of the American Corn Millers Association, the Millers National Federation and the St. Louis Millers Association. As a miller he rendered some special service, drawing upon his business experience in behalf of the government, during the World war. For nine years he served as a member of the city school board and has served as a member of the City Council. He has since been elected mayor of the city of Trenton. He and his wife attend the Methodist Episcopal Church. He is a Knight Templar, Scottish Rite Mason and Shriner, and is a charter member of Trenton Lodge, Knights of Pythias.

Mr. Hammel married in February, 1909, in Highland, Illinois, Edna K. Kinne, member of one of the prominent families of that historic community founded by Swiss people in Madison County. Her parents were Louis and Carrie (Thorp) Kinne, and she was the youngest of their four children, the others being Orville, now deceased, Miss Helen, and Irene, wife of Rev. D. Z. Davis. Louis E. Kinne, who died in 1916, was a prominent merchant and banker of Highland, also a leader in politics in that section of the state. He served with the rank of colonel on Governor Yates' staff, and held some of the local offices in Highland. Mr. and Mrs. Hammel have two children: Richard Kinne, born in 1910, and Jerome Kinne, born in 1912.

JOSEPH E. BARNES has been a member of the Illinois bar for a quarter of a century, and during most of that time has practiced law at Havana. His work as a lawyer has particularly identified him with land and drainage district litigation.

He was born at Forest City, Mason County, April 11, 1862. His father, George E. Barnes, was born in Greenville, New Hampshire, came west in September, 1851, over the Erie Canal, around the Great Lakes and by the Illinois and Michigan Canal, and settled twenty miles east of Alton, Illinois, where he followed farming. In April, 1857, he settled near Forest City, in Mason County, and lived there the rest of his life, passing away July 13, 1916, when almost eighty-four years of age. He held several local offices, was always a republican and a member of the Baptist Church.

His wife, Clarissa H. Hovey, was born at Charlton, a suburb of Boston, in October, 1835, daughter of Perez G. and Hannah (Packard) Hovey. Her father's grandmother was a sister of John Adams, the second president of the United States. Her grandfather was connected with the Cranes, one of the very prominent Massachusetts families. One of the Crane daughters married a Mr. Hovey.

The Hovey family sent soldiers to every war in America. A great-great-grandfather of Mr. Barnes on his mother's side was a lieutenant in Captain Towne's Company, was a minute man of Lexington and helped remove the stores from that town before the arrival of the British. His son was a Colonial soldier of the Revolution. Perez G. Hovey, father of Clarissa H., was in the militia during the War of 1812. Clarissa H. Hovey was reared in Madison and Macoupin counties, Illinois, coming to this state when four years old, in September, 1839. She died August 16, 1914.

Joseph E. Barnes was reared on a farm to the age of twenty-one, attended local schools and the Mason City High School, walking fifteen miles twice a week to reach that school. In 1884 he entered Westfield College at Westfield, Illinois, and graduated Master of Arts in 1888. This school produced a number of noted men, and among his schoolmates were B. A. Sweet of Colorado, L. S. Cornell, superintendent of schools in that state, T. J. Hines, an Illinois legislator, and others. Mr. Barnes was in educational work for ten years or more, most of the time in Illinois, but two years in Bourbon County, Kansas. He studied law in the office of A. T. DePue at Havana, was admitted to the bar April 5, 1900, and after his last term of school work, in 1903, engaged in practice and has handled an important array of criminal and civil cases since then. He was associated with I. R. Brown from January 1, 1908, until the death of Mr. Brown October 26, 1920. For one term he served as county surveyor, and previously for six years was deputy surveyor. In this connection he handled a number of contested cases growing out of boundaries. He served on four different commission surveys, and in these cases his notes and decisions were never reversed or set aside. Mr. Barnes is a commissioner of the Garden Special and of the Mason County drainage districts, of the Langelier Drainage and Levee District of Macoupin County, and the West Matanzas Drainage and Levee District of Fulton County.

He has been prominent in republican politics and was a candidate in one convention for nomination to the Legislature, this contest going to four hundred ballots before he finally failed of the nomination.

Mr. Barnes married at Westfield, Illinois, September 4, 1889, Miss Nellie Allen, daughter of Samuel B. and Elizabeth (Smith) Allen. Her father for fourteen years was president of Westfield College, and for seven years was an instructor and two years acting president of Otterbein University in Ohio. Mrs. Barnes graduated from Westfield College and for several years taught music.

Maurice E. Barnes, son of Joseph E. Barnes and wife, was born in Mason County, June 3, 1890, graduated from the Havana High School and took his law degree at the Illinois Wesleyan University at Bloomington in 1915. As a youth he learned telegraphy, becoming an expert operator. When America entered the World war he became a wireless operator with Company A of the One Hundred and Fifth Field Signal Battalion, in the Thirtieth Division, serving on the Ypres front with the British forces. He was at the battle of Bellecourt, where the first breach was made in the Hindenberg line. In April, 1919, he returned home, was discharged at Camp Grant, and since the war has engaged in practice. In the fall of 1920 he was elected on the republican ticket as clerk of the Circuit Court and recorder, and in 1924 was re-elected by three times his first majority. He is a charter member of Havana Post of the American Legion. Maurice Barnes married Margaret Egan, whose father was a Union soldier in the Civil war.

HON. WILLIAM PERRY HOLADAY, who had the distinction of succeeding Joseph G. Cannon when the latter retired in 1923 after nearly half a century in Congress, has been a practicing lawyer in "Uncle Joe's" home town of Danville for twenty years, and has been almost continuously in some public service, having a record of seven terms in the Illinois Legislature.

Mr. Holaday was born at Ridge Farm in Vermilion County, Illinois, December 14, 1882. The Holaday family came from Ireland and settled in North Carolina in Colonial times. They have been Quakers or Friends in religion for many generations. The grandfather, William Holaday, was a native of Ohio, and in 1837 moved to Vermilion County, Illinois, being one of the pioneer settlers, and owned and operated a large farm. He died at Vermilion Grove in 1880. His wife was Elizabeth Hayworth. George M. Holaday, father of the congressman, was born in Vermilion County in 1848; was reared there, finished his education in Purdue University in Indiana, and during his active career has been identified with farming and live stock raising, and is now living practically retired at Georgetown in Vermilion County. He is a republican and has been a staunch Friend in religion. His wife, Martha S. Smith, was born in Vermilion County in 1849. They had a family of three children: Ola, who lives on a farm near Georgetown in Vermilion County, the widow of William H. Hopkins; Anna, who died in 1900, wife of Jesse Hester, a farmer at Earlham, Iowa; and William P.

William P. Holaday was reared on a farm, attended public schools, graduated in 1901 from Vermilion Academy at Vermilion Grove, following which he spent a year in the Penn College at Oskaloosa, Iowa; for one year was a student in the law department of the University of Missouri, and completed his professional preparation with two years in the Law School of the University of Illinois. He is a member of the Phi Alpha Delta college fraternity. Admitted to the bar in October, 1905, he established himself for practice at Danville, and has had a growing connection with the important litigation with the courts of that district for twenty years. He is member of the law firm Hall & Holaday, with offices in the Daniel Building at Danville.

Mr. Holaday was for two years an assistant state's attorney of Vermilion County. He was elected to the House of Representatives of the Illinois Legislature in 1908 and re-elected for a consecutive two year term, his last election being in 1920. He was one of the representatives of the Twenty-second Sen-

atorial District, being a member of the House fourteen years. For six years he was chairman of the judiciary committee, acting in that capacity during the forty-seventh, forty-ninth and fifty-first General Assemblies. In the fiftieth Assembly he was chairman of the committee on efficiency and economy that prepared the civil administrative code of the state. In the fifty-second Assembly he was the republican floor leader. Mr. Holaday in November, 1922, was elected to Congress to succeed Joseph G. Cannon, who had voluntarily retired. In the sixty-eighth congress he was active in framing and passing the restrictive immigration law. He was reelected in 1924 and is the author of the Holaday Alien Criminal Deportation Bill.

Mr. Holaday is a member of the Georgetown Friends Church, Russell Lodge No. 154, A. F. and A. M., at Georgetown; is a thirty-second degree Scottish Rite Mason; and during the World war, was government appeal agent for Vermilion County.

He married in September, 1906, at Indianola, Illinois, Miss Blanche Gorman, daughter of John and Eva (Hill) Gorman, her father and mother deceased. Mr. and Mrs. Holaday have two children: Helen, a student in Ward-Belmont School, Nashville, Tennessee, and William, Jr., attending grade schools at Georgetown.

MARK CARLEY was, in one sense, the father of the town of Champaign, having erected the first residence on the town site just before the first trains were run over the Illinois Central Railway from Chicago, and likewise he was responsible for much of the early business enterprise attracted to that center. While thus identified with Champaign County, his character and experiences made him bulk large as an American pioneer whose life was connected with the development of the great work throughout the middle decades of the last century.

He was born at Hancock, Hillsboro County, New Hampshire, August 24, 1799, his native home being near the birthplace of Horace Greeley, whom he knew in his boyhood. His father was Elijah Carley, and his mother, who represented an old New Hampshire family, was Agnes Graham. His paternal grandparents were Joseph and Sarah (Washington) Carley, his grandmother being a member of the distinguished family of Washburns. The New England Carleys were of Scotch-Irish ancestry, of ancient lineage, their coat of arms having been handed down to the present generation of the family. A family document, still carefully preserved, is the discharge from the Continental Army, signed by George Washington, of Jonathan Carley, an uncle of Mark Carley. The Carleys were related by blood and marriage with many other distinguished families of New England, New York, Kentucky, Ohio and Illinois, including the Stevensons of Vermont, the Harrimans, Fisks, Lawsons and Kendalls of New York, the Carley Chess family of Kentucky, and the Goulds and Boutons of Chicago. A sister of Mark Carley, Louise, was an artist and became the wife of L. M. Lawson, dean of the Medical College of Ohio and of the Medical College of Lexington, Kentucky.

Mark Carley from the age of eleven years lived with his parents in Vermont, had the limited educational advantages of that day, learned the trade of carpenter and millwright, and at the age of twenty started out to see the world, first going to New Brunswick, from there sailing to New Orleans. His vessel was shipwrecked and finally landed at Savannah, Georgia. From there he went to Havana, Cuba, and on April 24, 1820, reached New Orleans. He became a builder of mills and cotton gins in La Fourche Parish, Louisiana, spending his winters in New Orleans. He continued his building business in Feliciana Parish until 1837, in the meantime making occasional visits to the North. During one of these visits, in 1830, he married Abigail Weatherbee Stevens, daughter of Silsby Stevens, of Springfield, Vermont.

Mark Carley, in 1837, established his home in Clermont County, Ohio, acquired large farming interests and also engaged in boating down the Ohio River. In 1850 he sailed from New York for the Pacific Coast, and for a time was a conspicuous figure in the California mining district, being chosen a judge of the Miners' Court. After a year he returned to Ohio, and in 1853 he located at Urbana, in Champaign County. Early the following year he built the first dwelling house at Champaign, also erected the first grain warehouse, and introduced the first steam engine, using it to operate his elevator and corn sheller. He built the agricultural warehouse on the Illinois Central Railway at the Main Street crossing, and at the northeast corner of Church and Randolph streets he erected the substantial homestead which was owned until recently by his granddaughter, Mrs. Mattie K. Weston, who sold it in 1916. The property is now owned by the Knights of Pythias Order in Champaign.

Mark Carley also built the first grain warehouse at Tolono, in Champaign County, built the railway siding and made other improvements there. He acquired a large acreage in this portion of the Illinois corn belt, and left a large amount of real estate to his family. A man of tremendous energy, keen in business, kindly in his relationship with his fellowmen, he enjoyed an exceptionally long and useful life and was nearly eighty-nine when he died, February 3, 1888. In politics he was a whig, and his family preserved the snuff-box given him by Henry Clay, a statesman whom he particularly admired. Later he became a republican, being identified with the founders of that party in Illinois. Abraham Lincoln and other distinguished men were visitors at his Champaign home. Mrs. Mattie K. Weston still has a letter written to Mark Carley by A. Lincoln, dated February 25, 1858. Mark Carley was a liberal in religious matters, and was one of the early students of such great scientific thinkers as Huxley, Tyndall, John Stuart Mill and others.

His wife died November 12, 1871. Of their three children the only survivor is Mrs. Isota Carley Mahan, of Los Angeles. A son, Graham Carley, died in Chicago in 1893.

The oldest child, Mary A. Carley, who was born in Clermont County, Ohio, and was married in 1851 to Dr. Samuel W. Kincaid.

The original member of the Carley family in this country, Mary Chilton, came over on the Mayflower, and was the first white woman to set foot on Plymouth Rock in Massachusetts.

Mrs. Mattie K. Weston has in her possession the Kincaid coat of arms, bearing the name Kincaid, which has been handed down from the eleventh or twelfth century, and also a silver dollar of 1799, the year of Mr. Mark Carley's birth.

SAMUEL W. KINCAID, a physician and surgeon, one of the pioneers of his profession in Champaign County, was born at West Union in Adams County, Ohio, July 15, 1823, son of Judge John Kincaid, an Ohio jurist and a brother of Hon. W. P. Kincaid, who for several years represented a certain Ohio district in Congress. The family is descended from the "Lairds of Kincaid," of Sterlingshire, Scotland, whose history began back of the twelfth century. Probably the first Kincaid in America settled in Virginia in 1707, being Capt. John Kincaid, who was a native of the North of Ireland. Captain Kincaid married Margaret Lockhart, a native of Scotland. Their son, Captain James Kincaid, was a soldier of the Revolution, and married a niece of James Wilson, a signer of the Declaration of Independence.

Dr. Samuel W. Kincaid received his academic education in the schools of Cincinnati, studied in the Medical College of Ohio, at Cincinnati, where he was graduated in 1853, and soon afterward he located at Tolono, Illinois, and in 1855 established his home in Champaign. Then followed a long and eminently creditable career as a physician and surgeon, a kindly advisor of the community, a public spirited citizen and a genial gentleman of the old school. When he retired from medical practice he returned to Adams County, Ohio, and lived quietly near the scenes of his boyhood until his death. He was an early member of the American Medical Association and of the Illinois State Medical Society, and one of the founders of the Champaign County Medical Society. He was a charter member of the First Lodge of Odd Fellows organized in Champaign.

Doctor Kincaid married in Ohio, in August, 1851, Miss Mary A. Carley, daughter of the Champaign County pioneer, Mark Carley. Mrs. Kincaid was born in Clermont County, Ohio, in the same neighborhood as Gen. U. S. Grant, and attended the same school as did the Grant children. Most of her life was spent at Champaign, where she died February 3, 1907. After the death of her husband she traveled extensively in the United States and Europe, accompanied by her daughter, Mrs. Mattie Kincaid Weston. Her home was a center of the cultivated thought and society of her generation. The greatest harmony in intellectual pursuit existed between her and her daughter Mrs. Weston. Mrs. Kincaid's tastes from early childhood were highly artistic, and as a young woman she executed some rare designs in wood carving, one of these being a facsimile of a famous piece of wood carving in Hampton Court Palace, London. Mrs. Kincaid graduated from the Chautauqua Circle at Lake Chautauqua when President Garfield and other distinguished personages were in attendance there. She and her daughter were collectors of curios and historical relics for many years. Mrs. Weston still preserves many quaint and interesting and beautiful things gathered in travel. Mrs. Kincaid was during her lifetime, and Mrs. Weston continues to be, members of the Daughters of the American Revolution and the Society of Colonial Dames, and both were eligible to membership in the Society of the Mayflower Descendants. Mrs. Weston has carried out researches in her family history to England, using the Winslow coat-of-arms as used by Governor Winslow of Massachusetts. This coat-of-arms has been reproduced in Heraldic colors upon canvas, surrounded by an ebony frame of a special antique pattern much used for coats-of-arms up to about 200 years ago.

Martha Kincaid was liberally educated in music one of her vocal teachers having been the great operatic instructor, De Campi, at one time head of the National Conservatory of Music of New York. Martha Kincaid married Charles Weston, who was president of the class of 1876 at the University of Illinois, and subsequently was elected auditor of the State of Nebraska. His death occurred a number of years ago.

Mrs. Mattie K. Weston has now in her possession the first piano that was ever brought to Champaign County. This instrument has twice crossed the Atlantic.

HERMAN R. DE LONG is an insurance man, a business with which he has been identified since early manhood, and his abilities and success have gained him honors and recognition in Illinois insurance circles. He has developed a very large general insurance agency at Danville.

He was born near Indianapolis, Indiana, July 25, 1884. His father, Isaac Nelson De Long, was born in the state of Maine, in July, 1850, and from early manhood lived the life of a farmer at Pittsboro, near Indianapolis, where he died November 14, 1902. He was a Civil war veteran, serving the last three years of the war with the Tenth Indiana Regiment. He always voted as a republican and was a leading layman of the Methodist Episcopal Church. His wife, Merinda Susan Dickerson, was born near Indianapolis, in 1854, and died there in June, 1904. They had a family of five children: Oris, a farmer at Pittsboro, Indiana; Homer O., a foreman with the Standard Oil Company at Indianapolis; James A., an Indianapolis merchant; Herman R.; and Effie Ivy, wife of Edward Culbertson, a carpenter living in Indianapolis.

Herman R. De Long was reared on an Indiana farm, attended public schools in Hendricks County and the Pittsboro High School, and at the age of seventeen began making his own way. For two years he was employed as stockkeeper for the H. Lauter Furniture Company at Indianapolis. For two years he was a coffee and tea salesman in that city,

KINCAID ARMS

WINSLOW ARMS

Mattie Kincaid Weston

leaving that to get his initial experience and training in the insurance business. For five and a half years he was with the Indianapolis agency of the Prudential Insurance Company, following which he was with the Empire Accident Insurance Company at Indianapolis, at first as agent and then as field auditor four years, and left Indianapolis to go to Chicago as a superintendent for the Washington Life and Accident Insurance Company in that city. Mr. De Long has been a resident of Danville since 1916. Since February, 1920, he has been in the general insurance business, developing a thorough service, handling all branches of insurance in Vermilion County. He is a member of the Danville Fire Insurance Board, the Illinois State Association of Insurance Agents; the National Association of Insurance Agents; is former president of the Illinois-Ohio Farmers Agents' Association. In his business at Danville Mr. De Long has as his associate partner Mr. Fred Myers, present city comptroller of Danville. Their offices are in the Baum Building.

Mr. De Long is a republican; member of the First Baptist Church at Danville; is a past prelate of White Oak Lodge No. 469, Knights of Pythias; is a member of Danville Camp No. 63, Woodmen of the World; belongs to the United States Chamber of Commerce at Washington.

He married at Indianapolis, June 25, 1913, Miss Jennie Estelle Johnston, daughter of Clayborn and Sarah Johnston. Her parents are now deceased, her father having been a farmer at Greencastle, Indiana.

HON. FRANK PERRIN, deceased, judge of Probate for twenty-two years, was before the public as an official of Saint Clair County for thirty-four years, and was one of the most representative men of Belleville. A man of scholarly attainments, and unusual intellectual capabilities, he long gave considerable attention to historical matters, and at the time of his death was county historian. He was a native son of the county, having been born in Mascoutah Township September 10, 1858, a son of Frank and Katherine (Pfeifer) Perrin, and grandson of George Perrin and Sebastian Pfeifer.

George Perrin, the paternal grandfather, was born in Lorraine, France, but came to the United States in 1833 and settled in Saint Clair County. His wife, Susan Adams, was also a native of Lorraine, France, and she came to this country about the same time as Mr. Perrin. They were married in Illinois. The maternal grandfather of Judge Perrin, Sebastian Pfiefer, was also born in Lorrain, France, and he married a lady whose first name was Katherine, and she, too, was a native of Lorraine. The Pfiefers also came to the United States in the early '30s.

Frank Perrin, father of Judge Perrin, died in 1904, the mother having passed away in 1872. They had five children, as follows: Nicholas, who died in 1919, married Amelia Fuess, and they had children, George, Ada (deceased), and Teressa; Mary Teressa married Mr. Moll, and they had three children, Frank, Albert and Emma; Rosa died unmarried; and Judge Perrin was the youngest of the family.

The father was a farmer, and was always interested in matters of public moment, and for over thirty years he served as a member of the local school board. In religious faith he was a Catholic.

After he had attended the district schools of his native county Judge Perrin took the academic course at the Saint Louis University, Saint Louis, Missouri, and was graduated therefrom in 1878. His legal training was obtained in the law department of McKendry College, Lebanon, Illinois, from which institution he was graduated in 1890. Returning then to Mascotah, he remained in that locality for a few months, after which he came to Belleville, and became city attorney, which position he held for about ten years. For the subsequent two years he was assistant state's attorney, and then for eight years served as chairman of the county board. From 1898 to 1902 he was county judge of Saint Clair County, and in 1902 was elected judge of probate, which office he continued to hold, with dignified capability, until his death. He was also judge of the Juvenile Court. A man of the highest character, learned and able, he brought to the bench a matured judgment and profound knowledge, not only of the law, but of human nature and the motives which govern men and their actions. Few men in the state were held in higher esteem than he, and he was in no sense a politician, his long public life having been the result of the office seeking the man, and not that of a man striving for honors at the hands of his fellow citizens. A man of letters, he turned his attention to historical writing, and was the accepted authority on historical matters, especially those pertaining to the affairs of Saint Clair County and the state of Illinois.

Judge Perrin was twice married, first in 1884, to Amelia Letherbury, who died in 1898. There were three children born of this marriage: Benjamin, who is unmarried; Winona Rosa, who married George Fiedler, and they have two children, Alice and Lois; and Albert Emmett, who married a Miss Green. Judge Perrin married June 21, 1900, Ida Ludwig, and they had one child, LeRoy Frank.

CAPT. CORYDON B. HOPKINS is a native Chicagoan, bearing a family name that for many years has been an honorable one in that city. Captain Hopkins, who outside of business is best known for his activities in promoting Americanism, and as a captain in the Officers Reserve Corps, was born in Chicago in 1874, son of Benjamin Lansing and Louisa Emily (Turner) Hopkins. His father and mother represented pioneer families in Chicago. Both parents were born in New York State, but lived in Chicago from the '50s.

Captain Hopkins married Laura E. Whipple in 1901. They have two daughters, Charlotte and Ruth, a son having died in infancy.

Captain Hopkins was an early volunteer when America entered the World war in 1917. He was captain of a company in the American Protective League operating in Chicago and vicinity. His immediate staff comprised about 150 men, all particularly well qualified for carrying out a program of immediate assistance to the Department of Justice. No group did more to break down organized disloyalty during the World war and bring to prosecution many of the prominent individuals and organizations who were fostering opposition to the war. After the armistice the American Protective League was disbanded, but Captain Hopkins was one of its members who has continued to exert the full strength of his influence in patriotic activities.

At the close of the war he was assigned for duty as a special representative of the Department of Justice working among radicals and later as an agent for the Army Intelligence Bureau.

Captain Hopkins was one of the charter members and first president of the Military Intelligence Association of the Sixth Corps Area of Chicago. Its principal objects are to advance military intelligence, foster patriotism and promote national defense and the upbuilding and maintaining of American ideals. Its membership is composed of reserve officers of the United States Army, practically all of whom saw service in the World war. As a member and official of this organization Captain Hopkins has delivered a large number of addresses and lectures on the wisdom and duty of supporting the government in all matters of national defense, emphasizing that such support is not for the purpose of making or causing war, but for preventing war.

When in January, 1925, Captain Hopkins retired from the presidency of this association he received special commendation for intelligence and faithful performance of duty, exhibition of a peculiar type of leadership so necessary in work with the organized reserves, and for his efforts as a speaker and otherwise in behalf of the program of national defense. In addition to his speeches Captain Hopkins has written a great deal for the press as a means of educating the public on the principles and ideals of the national defense program and also calling attention to the insidious character of many of the so called "peace organizations." He is the author of "Radicalism in Churches, Colleges and Schools" that appeared in the Iron Trade Review and has been extensively circulated. As a captain in the Officers Reserve Corps Captain Hopkins is assigned to military intelligence and attached to the Headquarters Staff of the Sixth Corps Area in Chicago. He is a Royal Arch Mason, a director in the Chicago Kiwanis Club, a member of the Fraternity Club and a communicant of the Methodist Episcopal church.

MAJ. JAMES E. WHITE, president and manager of the White Audit System, Chef de Gare of the 40 et 8 Society, and a veteran of the World war, is one of the representative professional men of Chicago, and one who stands deservedly high in public esteem. He was born at Nebraska City, Nebraska, in 1874 a son of Henry and Sarah (Jones) White, of Iowa. During the war between the states Henry White served in the Twentieth Iowa Volunteer Infantry, and he was one of the pioneers of Nebraska City, in which locality his family had settled.

Growing up amid rural conditions, and experiencing the necessary hardships of life incident to pioneer days in Iowa and Nebraska, James E. White worked as a farm hand and on railroad construction, and at intervals attended the public schools, and also studied by himself, in this way acquiring an excellent educational training. Many years ago he came to Chicago as an employe and later as an officer of the Chicago & Northwestern Railway Company. In 1913 he established his present business, the White Audit System, which does special auditing for railroad companies, with offices at 1240 Transportation Building. Since its inception Mr. White has been president and manager.

When war was declared with Spain in 1898 James E. White volunteered for service and was a member of the Fifty-first United States Volunteer Regiment, and he was in the Philippines following the close of the Spanish-American war. In 1917, when this country entered the World war, Mr. White was one of the first to offer his services, as he volunteered in April of that year, and was commissioned a captain of infantry at Fort Sheridan, Illinois, in August, 1917, and was assigned to the Three Hundred Forty-third Infantry, Eighty-sixth Division. For a year he served with this unit as captain, and then, in August, 1918, was raised to the rank of major, went overseas with the Eight Hundred and Third Regiment of Infantry, and served in the Second Army at Metz. Following the armistice he served in the German Occupation, and was returned home and honorably discharged in July, 1919. He is now a reserve officer of the United States army with the rank of major.

In June, 1925, Major White was elected Chef du Gare of the Cook County Organization of the 40 et 8 Society, and he has been prominent in this organization since it was founded. He is also a member of the National Committee of the 40 et 8 Society on child welfare. The Cook County organization is known as Voiture No. 220. He is also a member of the American Legion, the Army and Navy Club, the Hamilton Club, and the Lake Shore Athletic Club. He is a thirty-second degree Mason and a Shriner, belonging to Medinah Temple.

Major White married Miss Madge McMillan, now deceased. They had one son, John M. White, an engineer now with the Illinois State Highway Department at Springfield, Illinois.

KELLY A. CARDIFF, postmaster of Hoopeston, is a member of an old family of Vermilion County, and his individual activities have made him a man of mark and leadership in his home community.

Mr. Cardiff was born at Rankin in Piatt County, Illinois, April 6, 1875. The name Cardiff is of Scotch ancestry. His great-grandfather came from Scotland to America. His grandfather, David Cardiff, was a native of Ohio, and when a comparatively young man moved to Vermilion County, Illinois, and acquired extensive farming interests. He died at what was then called Higginsville, near Jamesburg, in Vermilion County. John W. Cardiff, father of the Hoopeston postmaster, was born in Ohio, September 25, 1844, and as a young man settled near Pilot, Illinois, where he married. Shortly after his marriage he

John Ruf, Jr.

moved to a farm near Rankin, in 1880 settled at Danville, and in 1881 moved to the vicinity of Jamesburg in Vermilion County. He was a farmer and at different periods engaged in the building contracting business. In August, 1893, he removed to Hoopeston, where he died in December, 1893. He was a democrat and was a local preacher of the Methodist denomination. John W. Cardiff married Ella Johnson, who was born in Vermilion County, July 3, 1852, and resides at Hoopeston. They had five children, Kelly A. being the oldest. Ralph died when two years of age; John Robert and Edwin Franklin are twins, the former a retired business man of Hoopeston, while the latter is superintendent of a tin factory at Simcoe, Ontario, Canada; and Mark W., a window trimmer and card writer at Hastings, Nebraska, is a World war veteran, having been trained at Camp Taylor.

Kelly A. Cardiff was educated in public schools in Vermilion County, attending high school at Hoopeston. On leaving school at the age of seventeen he spent five years clerking in a grocery store of J. S. Dunscome at Hoopeston and then followed various occupations. During McKinley's term he was assistant postmaster of Hoopeston. He spent eleven years with the Burton & Norris Furniture Store at Hoopeston, resigning in 1922 to accept appointment as postmaster on August 12th of that year. During 1917-18 he also served as tax collector of Grant Township, Vermilion County.

Mr. Cardiff is a republican, a member of the Methodist Episcopal Church of Hoopeston, Star Lodge No. 709, A. F. and A. M., at Hoopeston, Danville Consistory of the Scottish Rite, Hoopeston Lodge No. 498, I. O. O. F., Hoopeston Lodge No. 1227, Loyal Order of Moose, and is a director of the Hoopeston Chamber of Commerce and the Hoopeston Commercial Club. He has considerable real estate in Hoopeston, including his residence at 1015 West Main Street. During the World war he was active in committee work in behalf of the various drives.

Mr. Cardiff married, June 25, 1899, Miss Mabel Claire Sherrill, daughter of James W. and Mollie (Van Cleve) Sherrill, the latter now deceased. Her father is a retired resident at Danville, where he had been engaged for some years in the transfer business. Mr. and Mrs. Cardiff are the parents of six children: Esther Lucile, wife of Harold McVicker, a farmer at Stockland, Illinois; Marguerite Irene, who spent two years in the University of Illinois and is a teacher in a public school in Iroquois County; Harold Edwin, who graduated from the Hoopeston High School in 1923, and is employed in the cost department of the Sprague Sells Corporation; Edith Claire and Robert Burle, both students in the Hoopeston High School; and Kelly, Jr., a primary school pupil.

JOHN LAWRENCE HAYES RUF, JR. Clinton County not only enjoys the reputation of being the home and birthplace of many of the representative and substantial citizens of Illinois, but in the hearty support given to its schools and local newspapers, proves its high degree of intelligence. Taking precedence in the matter of age the Union Banner, published at Carlyle and owned by John Lawrence Hayes Ruf, Jr., is probably the best known journal in the county, for it has been a welcome weekly visitor to homes and business houses for the past sixty-one years. It is the leading organ of the republican party in the county, and during its long term of existence has had but three active editors and proprietors.

John Lawrence Hayes Ruf, Jr., was born at Carlyle, Illinois, January 12, 1879, second son of John and Josephine (Hubert) Ruf, and grandson of John Ruf and Jacob and Catherine (Souter) Hubert. The paternal grandfather, John Ruf, was a native of Germany, where he lived until 1840 and was a man of consequence, being burgomaster of his village. Because of what he considered oppression in the military laws, he left Germany in the above year and came with his family to the United States and settled at Waterloo in Monroe County, Illinois. Many years later he returned for a visit in his native land and died while there.

John Ruf, son of John and honored father of John L. H. Ruf, is widely known in Illinois journalism. He learned the printer's trade in youth and has been identified with newspapers all his life, and still, although retired from active control, occasionally wields his ready pen in an editorial that shows the weight of eighty-three years has not dimmed his active brain. He founded several papers before he became identified with the Union Banner, the first one being a German newspaper, the Clinton County Pioneer. In 1874 he started the Sued Illinois Zeitung, but later became interested in the Union Banner at Carlyle. The Union Banner was founded in 1863 by James W. Peterson, who died in 1884, at which time Mr. Ruf bought a half interest in the property and conducted the paper for Mrs. Peterson until 1890, when he bought her interest. In 1894 he discontinued publishing the Sued Illinois Zeitung. For many years afterward he conducted the Union Banner in association with his son, the present owner, and then retired in the assurance that the high standards he had set up in newspaperdom would be still maintained.

John Ruf, Sr., married Miss Josephine Hubert. Her people came to the United States about 1840, her father and mother both being born in Alsace-Lorraine. Of the eleven children born to his parents John L. H. was the third in order of birth, the others being: Jacob Edward, who died January 10, 1896; Josephine, who lives with her parents; Harry, who died in 1904; Elsie, who is the wife of John Dieterich; Martha, who is the wife of William P. Hinkel and they have five children, Margaret, Martha, William, Mary Jane and Bettie; Leo, who lives at home; Ernest, who was a soldier in the World war and lost his life in France September 26, 1918; and Bruno and Paul, twins, born June 13, 1891, and died in infancy.

John L. H. Ruf attended the public schools of Carlyle until fourteen years of age and then settled down to learn the printer's trade in the Union Banner office, although long before this, in fact when only nine years old, he had learned many details, for the work attracted him from the beginning. Mr. Ruf is a practical printer, having devoted his energies to this line from the age of sixteen years without change, gradually assuming duties and responsibilities to assist his father, who, in 1900 gave him a one-fourth interest in the Union Banner. Later he acquired a one-half interest and in 1914, when his father retired from the active management, he took over the latter's interest. Mr. Ruf has a wide journalistic acquaintance, and as a man of public spirit and sterling character enjoys the confidence and friendship of many of the distinguished men of his own political party and of his fellow citizens generally.

Mr. Ruf married at Waukegan, Illinois, June 10, 1912, Miss Eda Buhler, and they have one daughter, Hazel Virginia. Mrs. Ruf is a daughter of John Emil and Bertha (Luescher) Buhler, of German ancestry. She is the youngest of their family of six children, losing her mother when only about one and one-half years old. Her father, whose death occurred November 29, 1925, formerly owned and operated a fruit and truck farm near Centralia. Mrs. Ruf's brothers and sisters were: August, who married Elizabeth Banks and they have one son, Ralph; John Emil, who married Lena Merten, and they have had two children, Harry and Elvera; Ernest, who died in 1899; Herman, who married Hilda Selle, and they have two children, Vera and Marvin; and Bertha, wife of William Edwards, and they have three children, William, Harold and Florence Betty. Mr. Ruf belongs to the Mutual Protective League, to various newspaper and political organizations, and is a Mason, belonging to the Blue Lodge, A. F. and A. M., Scott Lodge No. 79, at Carlyle.

ALEXANDER HAMILTON REVELL for many years has been one of the great merchants of Chicago. However, it is an unusual distinction that many times he has represented Chicago in more or less semi-official ways, not as a great business man or political leader but as a citizen whose character and interests have been most completely expressive of one of the largest centers of population in America.

Mr. Revell is in every sense a real Chicagoan. He was born in that city January 6, 1858, son of David James and Margaret (Dorgan) Revell. He was educated in public schools, and since the age of twenty-one has been identified with furniture manufacturing and the retail furniture business. As president of Alexander H. Revell & Company he built up a business which for over forty years has been a mercantile establishment as familiar as almost any institution in the city. For many years he was president and is now chairman of the board of this great business. He is also a director of the Central Trust Company of Illinois and at different times has been an officer in various other banks and business corporations.

Mr. Revell was a member of the executive committee of the World's Columbian Exposition of 1893. He has repeatedly held positions that present great opportunities for unselfish devotion and service to the community without corresponding material rewards. He has been a member of the Chicago Board of Education, is a trustee of Northwestern University, and a leader in many reform movements. He was made a member of the Legion of Honor of France in 1908. He is a republican, member of the Hamilton Club, Chicago Club, former president of the Chicago Athletic Association, member of the Commercial Club, Onwentsia Club, Old Elm Club, Arts Club, Congressional Country Club of Washington, National Golf Links Club of Long Island and Everglades Club of Palm Beach. He is a member of the Fourth Presbyterian Church of Chicago.

Mr. Revell married Miss Maude Richardson. He is the father of three children: Margaret (Mrs. Loring R. Hoover); Alexander H., Jr., who married Isabel Joan Watkins; and Richardson Revell.

REV. CHARLES A. O'REILLY has been distinguished by a service of thirty-two consecutive years as pastor of Mt. Mary's Catholic Church of Edwardsville. His pastorate has been in service both within and out of the parish, a contribution to the general welfare of the community as well as to the success of his church and his people.

Father O'Reilly was born at Amboy in Lee County, Illinois, May 29, 1867, one of the twelve children of Patrick and Ann (Lee) O'Reilly. His parents were natives of Ireland and came to the United States when young and were married in New York. Patrick O'Reilly, who was born May 29, 1812, and came to America in 1832, was a merchant and contractor, and for many years was identified with railroad construction in the middle west. After a brief residence in Illinois he established his family at Fort Dodge, Iowa, and lived in that city until his death in very advanced years.

Charles A. O'Reilly was educated at Fort Dodge, Iowa, spent three years at St. Joseph's College at Dubuque, and in 1883 graduated from St. Ambrose College in Davenport. His philosophical and theological studies were pursued in the Catholic University at Niagara Falls. He was ordained a priest June 11, 1892, and was immediately assigned to duty in Madison County, Illinois, being a curate under Bishop Ryan at Alton a year and three months. In October, 1893, he removed to Edwardsville as pastor of St. Mary's Catholic Church. The first church of this parish, a frame building, was erected in 1847, and just four years before Father O'Reilly came to Edwardsville a predecessor had completed a new brick church, and one of the tasks accomplished by Father O'Reilly was freeing the parish from the heavy debt incurred by this construction. He has added other material improvements as well, and has greatly increased the membership of his church.

CHARLES BRADSHAW is editor and proprietor of the Carrollton Patriot, one of the oldest republican newspapers in southern Illinois. S. P. Ohr founded the old Carrollton Press, but left it to go into the Union army as a soldier in the Civil war. The plant was taken over by D. Pearson & Company, and the first issue of the Patriot appeared May 14, 1864, with Elder E. E. L. Craig as editor. The

Pearsons sold out to William B. Fairchild, who was succeeded by Edward Miner as editor, and in 1875 Clement L. Clapp became editor and continued until Mr. Charles Bradshaw took charge.

Mr. Bradshaw was born at Sheffield, in Bureau County, Illinois, December 30, 1856, son of James F. and Mary M. (Smith) Bradshaw, his mother being a daughter of John Smith. James Bradshaw was a native of Kentucky, came to Illinois at the age of seventeen, and for several years followed his trade as a cabinet maker at Canton, Illinois, and was married in Fulton County. He engaged in farming, later in business at Kirkwood, and lived out his last years at Carrollton, where he died in 1896, at the age of sixty-five, and his wife, in 1917, aged eighty.

Charles Bradshaw, only son of his parents, was reared in town and county communities, had some training as a farmer, attended school at Kirkwood, and was qualified to teach. Instead, he went into the office of the Kirkwood News at two dollars a week, remaining only a short time. He was associated with his father in merchandising, and after several years bought the Kirkwood Leader and was its publisher six years. On selling out his interest in the Kirkwood newspaper he acquired the Patriot at Carrollton. This paper is republican in politics, but under Mr. Bradshaw it has expressed the progressive tendencies of the community and is first and last a home paper. Mr. Bradshaw was honored with election as president of the Illinois Press Association in 1903.

He has served on the Board of Education, is a member of the Baptist Church and the Chamber of Commerce.

He married at Pasadena, June 17, 1915, Miss Emma Smith, a native of Stark County, Illinois. She is very active in club work, being a member of the Delphian Chapter and the West End Reading Circle, and during the World war was in charge of local Red Cross work.

JAMES WILSON KERN has been a member of the bar of Iroquois County thirty-five years, and has become one of the outstanding citizens of Watseka.

Mr. Kern was born at Bedford, Indiana, September 24, 1865, son of Alvin Green and Elizabeth (Boyd) Kern. His father grew up in the district west of Bedford, Indiana, was a farmer, and served as a Union soldier in the Civil war. James W. Kern had the early environment of a farm boy, and his education beyond the common schools which he attended in Lawrence County, Indiana, was continued in Eureka College at Eureka, Illinois, where he was graduated with the A. B. degree in June, 1887. After his Eureka College course the remainder of his education was acquired largely through his own efforts. In 1890, on account of advanced work done, this college conferred upon him the Master of Arts degree. Mr. Kern also, in 1890, graduated from the law department of the University of Michigan with the LL. B. degree. Since November, 1890, he has practiced law with accumulating success and prestige. In the early period of his practice he served one term as city attorney of Watseka, and for four terms was state's attorney of Iroquois County. Since holding these offices his time and energies have been quite fully taken up with his general law practice.

Among other interests Mr. Kern is president of the Watseka Building & Loan Association. He is a director in the Life & Casualty Insurance Company of Chicago. During the World war he was chairman of the Iroquois County Chapter of the American Red Cross, and for several years was a member of the Watseka Board of Education. He has been active in the republican party, is affiliated with the Masonic bodies at Watseka, the Knights of Pythias at Sheldon, Modern Woodmen of America at Watseka, and Improved Order of Red Men at Watseka. He also belongs to the Iroquois Club of Watseka and the Shewami Country Club.

Mr. Kern married at Eureka, Illinois, in June, 1887, Miss Caddie A. Davidson, daughter of Calvin and Eliza (Kinnear) Davidson. Her people were pioneers of Woodford County, Illinois. Mr. and Mrs. Kern are the parents of two sons, M. A. Kern and L. D. Kern, both now residents of Chicago.

HON. CHARLES V. BARRETT, a leading member of the Chicago bar, president of the Board of Review and an active and prominent republican leader of the State of Illinois, is a true son of the city and state, having been born at Chicago, March 19, 1882, and being a product of its educational institutions. His career has been one in which he has earned prominence and position through the exercise of native talent and industry, and within the span of comparatively a few short years he has gained a standing and reputation that most men would consider sufficient if attained after a lifetime of arduous struggle.

The parents of Mr. Barrett were both of Irish extraction and were early residents of Chicago, whence the father enlisted for service in the Union army during the Civil war. The lad acquired his early education in the public schools of the city of his birth, following which he entered the law department of the University of Illinois, from which he was duly graduated with the degree of Bachelor of Laws as a member of the class of 1903. Admitted to the bar during the same year, he engaged in practice and has become recognized as one of the most capable members of the great galaxy of legal talent practicing at the Chicago bar. He is now associated with his brother, ex-Judge George F. Barrett, with offices at 140 North Dearborn Street, the brothers having been formerly associated with ex-Judge Robert E. Crowe, who is now serving as state's attorney for Illinois. Both of the Barrett brothers are members of the honorary legal fraternity known as the Order of the Coif, and to various other organizations of their calling.

From the outset of his career Charles V. Barrett has been interested in politics, in public matters and in civic affairs. Through a real genius for leadership he has gradually risen to a position of much power in the ranks of the republican party, where he is now an accepted leader. In 1918 he was elected a member of the Cook County Board of Review, of which important body he is now chairman. He is a popular member of the Hamilton Club, the Chicago Athletic Club, the Mid-Day Club and the Evanston Golf Club, and also has a number of connections with fraternal bodies.

Mr. Barrett married Miss Helen V. Colohan, of Chicago, and they are the parents of a happy and interesting family of four daughters and two sons: Helen V., Marion, Gertrude, Ruth, Charles V., Jr. and Edward J. The family home is at 541 Hawthorne Place, Chicago.

JESSE MORTIMER SMITH, interested in a job printing business at Watseka, is a native of Iroquois County, and member of a well known family there.

He was born at Watseka, in 1877, son of Lorenzo Nye and Marian Wallace (Burlew) Smith. Mr. Smith was reared and educated in Watseka, attending high school, and soon afterward began his apprenticeship as a practical printer. He has been in that business for many years, and since 1914 has developed a successful business of his own, handling all classes of job and commercial printing.

Mr. Smith is a democrat, a member of the Masonic fraternity and the Presbyterian Church. He married at Watseka, in 1902, Miss Clara Mae Schaeffer, daughter of Jacob Schaeffer. They have one son, Frank Smith, born in 1919.

GEORGE GARVIN is a native son of Shelby County, a representative of one of the old and honored families of this section of Illinois, and since the year 1885 he has been successfully engaged in the hardware and farm-implement business in Windsor, one of the progressive little cities of his native county. He was born at Shelbyville, judicial center of Shelby County, March 9, 1854, and is a son of Shem and Katherine Garvin, the former of whom was born in the state of Maryland, and the latter of whom was born in Ohio.

Shem Garvin became one of the pioneers in the milling business in Shelby County, and for a number of years operated the old water-power flour mill at Shelbyville, he having removed from the county seat to Windsor in 1866, and both he and his wife having here passed the remainder of their lives. They were members of and attended the Methodist Church. Mr. Garvin was a staunch republican in his political alignment.

The public schools of Shelbyville and Windsor afforded George Garvin his youthful education, and he early became associated with his father's milling business, his alliance with this line of enterprise at Windsor having continued from 1872 until 1885, in which latter year he established his present hardware and implement business, the substantial success of which during the long intervening years has been based on fair and honorable dealings and effective service.

Mr. Garvin is not only one of the veteran and honored business men of his community but is also a loyal and liberal citizen whose influence has been potent in advancing the general welfare of the community. He is a stalwart in the local ranks of the republican party, and his was the distinction of having been the first republican candidate to be elected supervisor of Windsor Township. He is a director of the Windsor Telephone Exchange and of the Windsor Building & Loan Association. He and his wife are zealous members of the Christian Church, and he is affiliated with the Masonic fraternity and the Modern Woodmen of America.

In the year 1876, at Windsor, was solemnized the marriage of Mr. Garvin and Miss Bell Bruce, a daughter of the late John D. and Eleanor Bruce, who were long residents of Shelby County. Mrs. Garvin is a popular figure in the social activities of her home community, as well as in the affairs of her church and those of the local chapter of the Order of the Eastern Star, she having filled the office of Worthy Matron and Mr. Garvin later holding the office of Patron. Mr. and Mrs. Garvin have four children; Leota Alice, Katherine Eleanor, Grace Maude and Bruce.

GEORGE A. RAY is a resident of Rossville, Vermilion County, and has lived in that community all his life, for a quarter of a century being the leading lawyer there and a man naturally looked to for leadership in all public matters.

He was born in Ross Township, Vermilion County, January 12, 1869. His grandfather, John Ray, was a native of Pennsylvania, and was a pioneer settler of Vermilion County, Illinois, locating in Ross Township in 1829. He was a man of great industry, developed a farm from the wilderness and eventually became owner of several sections of rich land in that locality. He was a soldier in the Mexican war, and died at his homestead in Ross Township. George T. Ray, father of the Rossville attorney, was born in Pickaway County, Ohio, in 1827, and was an infant when his parents moved to Ross Township. He received his education in Georgetown Seminary at Georgetown, Illinois, and gave his active life to farming. He died at his homestead in Ross Township, in January, 1914. He was a democrat and a member of the I. O. O. F. His wife, Mary E. Hickman, was born at Georgetown, Vermilion County, in 1840, and died at the home farm in 1902. They had a family of five children: Dr. Daniel V., physician and surgeon at Rossville; George A.; Frank H., secretary and treasurer of the South Water Street Teamster's Union; Charles, owner and operator of a grain elevator at Koutz, Indiana, and Benjamin, who now owns the old homestead.

George A. Ray spent the first twenty-three years of his life on the home farm, assisting in its cultivation when not in school. He attended public schools, graduated from the Indiana Normal College at Covington, Indiana, in 1890, and after leaving the farm spent a year as clerk in the shoe and grocery store of W. T. Cunningham at Rossville, three years as clerk in the hardware and implement store of Adam Hoover, also at Rossville, and for two years was assistant postmaster of Rossville. Having taken up the study of law, he spent the year 1897 in Chicago attending lectures at the Northwestern University School of Law and the Kent College of Law. He was

admitted to the bar in November, 1897, and since that date has handled a general law practice at Rossville. For six years he was a member of the Village Council of Rossville, and he was elected to represent the Twenty-second District in the Forty-ninth General Assembly of Illinois. Mr. Ray is a democrat, is a member of Rossville Lodge No. 527, A. F. and A. M., Danville Lodge No. 332, B. P. O. Elks, and a member of the Vermilion County Bar Association. For eighteen years he has acted as attorney for the Rossville Building & Loan Association. Mr. Ray owns a very modern and attractive seven room brick home on West Attica Street, and also owns his brick office building and an adjoining building, besides other real estate in Rossville and some property in Arkansas. During the World war he devoted most of his time to the work of committees and other organizations handling the Liberty Loan, Red Cross and other drives, and was also a member of the local draft board.

Mr. Ray married at Marshall, Illinois, March 25, 1907, Miss Josephine Colvin, daughter of Lewis L. and Emma Colvin. Mrs. Emma Colvin resides with Mr. and Mrs. Ray. Her father was a locomotive engineer and died at Joliet, Illinois. Mrs. Ray is a sister of W. C. Colvin, present superintendent of pardons and paroles of Illinois.

HARRY FAULKNER. Within three years after his admission to the bar Harry Faulkner had achieved a place of definite trust and success as an attorney at Granite City. He brought to his profession unusual qualifications and further training, and is regarded as one of the most resourceful lawyers and public men in Madison County.

He was born in Staffordshire, England, October 15, 1885. In 1886 his parents, Steven and Maria (Edwards) Faulkner, came to America, first locating in Jefferson County, Missouri, and subsequently living in Indiana and in another state. His parents are still living, and his father for many years has been a glass worker. At one time he was a sailor, and he served his time in the English army. In the family were two sons and two daughters. The Illinois attorney is the second child.

Harry Faulkner acquired his early education in the schools of Kokomo and Elwood, Indiana, and after the family moved to St. Louis he attended St. Louis University one year, graduated in 1906 from the Normal Academy at Columbia, Missouri, and took his law course in Washington University at St. Louis, where he was graduated in 1909. At Washington University he won his letter as a member of the athletic team, was active in the College Debating Society and the fraternity Phi Delta Phi.

Admitted to the Illinois bar in 1909, Mr. Faulkner chose Granite City as the scene of his professional work and has been practicing law there for seventeen years. He was associated with O. H. Jones in the firm of Faulkner and Jones, handling a general practice in law and also in the real estate business. Mr. Faulkner was elected city attorney of Granite City in April, 1911, and he also served as master in chancery of the City Court and as corporation counsel. For three terms he was a member of the Board of Review. Mr. Faulkner has been actively identified with the republican party organization in his county and state, and has been a delegate to several congressional and state conventions. He is a Royal Arch and Knight Templar Mason, a member of the Elks and Moose, belongs to the Madison County and Illinois State Bar Associations and the Granite City Commercial Club. He and his family are Episcopalians.

He married in 1912 Miss Kate Voight, of Granite City and a native of Illinois. They have four daughters: Margaret Maria, Catherine Louise, Clara Virginia and Florence Ruth.

WILLIAM C. TIMM, sheriff of Vermilion County, is a veteran of the World war, and for some years was in the railway service, resigning as a conductor on the Chicago & Eastern Illinois to take up his duties as sheriff.

Sheriff Timm was born December 26, 1887, son of William Timm, who was born April 14, 1865. Both of them were born in a house on a farm near Danville. His grandfather, Philip Timm, a native of Germany, was one of the pioneer settlers in Vermilion County, Illinois, locating there during the decade of the '20s, nearly a century ago. He was a farmer, and before coming to this country had training as a German soldier. He married Elizabeth Hagaman, also from Germany. William Timm devoted the active years of his life to farming, and was one of the prosperous representatives of the agricultural industry in Vermilion County. Since 1922 he has lived retired at Danville. He is a republican and an active supporter of the Lutheran Church. William Timm married Miss Anna Schonbeck, who was born at Danville, May 30, 1870. They have three children, William C. being the oldest child and only son. The daughter Esther married Edward A. Prettyman, who is a conductor with the New York Central Lines, living at Danville. Anna married Eric Klein, who is in the automobile business, agent at Danville for the Hudson and Essex cars.

William C. Timm had all the variations of experience and work on the home farm to the age of twenty-one. In the meantime he attended public schools, including the Danville High School. He left school at the age of sixteen, and after he left the farm he entered the service of the Chicago & Eastern Illinois Railway Company, rising to the rank of conductor in the train service. Mr. Timm was quite young when he began taking an active interest in military affairs. He was one of the chief figures in the organization of Company I of the Fifth Illinois Infantry in 1905, and in 1907 was made a second lieutenant of the company, and in 1909 promoted to first lieutenant. When this organization was mustered into the national army in 1917 he went into training with it and subsequently was with the American Expeditionary Forces overseas. He had experience of two years and eight months as a soldier in the World war. Mr. Timm participated in the Somme offensive, where he was wounded; also in the St. Mihiel campaign and the Meuse-Argonne campaign, and was also in the Toulon sector. In

August, 1918, he was promoted to the rank of captain. Captain Timm received his honorable discharge at Camp Lewis, Washington, December 14, 1920. He is a member of the American Legion.

Soon after his release from military service he resumed his position in the train service with the Chicago & Eastern Illinois Railway, but in November, 1922, was elected sheriff of Vermilion County, and on the first Monday of December of the same year entered upon the duties of that office for a term of four years. Sheriff Timm is a republican, and is a member of the Immanuel Lutheran Church of Danville, and also belongs to the Masonic fraternity, Knights of Pythias, Knights of Khorassan, Moose, Woodmen of the World and Veterans of Foreign Wars. He has acquired some property interests at Danville, including his home on Robinson Street, a residence built in 1924.

He married at Terre Haute, Indiana, May 18, 1912, Miss Julia E. Newell, daughter of Eugene E. and Julia Newell. Her father was a merchant at Aurora, Illinois, and her widowed mother now lives at San Diego, California. Mrs. Timm is a graduate of the high school at Bloomington, Illinois.

CHARLES EDWIN SHAW. There has been five generations of the Shaw family represented in the citizenship of Paris and Edgar County. The history of Paris as a settled community begins with the grandfather of Charles Edwin Shaw, whose life covered a period of over seventy years, the greater part of which was devoted to business.

His grandfather was Smith Shaw, who was born in Guilford County, North Carolina, June 20, 1783, and married Elizabeth McMinn. born July 20, 1788. They were married in Wilson County, Tennessee, February 12, 1805. In 1821 Smith Shaw and his son James Dyer Shaw came into the wilderness country represented by the present Edgar County and selected the site for a new home. He and his son got out and prepared the logs for a house. In the spring of 1822 Smith Shaw returned with his family and erected a double log cabin at the southeast corner of the intersection of East Washington and Monterey streets. This was the first permanent dwelling within the limits of the present city of Paris. In 1825 he built a house on the hill on East Crawford Street, being attracted to the new location by several springs. It is on these premises that Charles Edwin Shaw resides today. Smith Shaw and wife had ten children when they came to Illinois and five more were born here.

The sixth child was Elvis Perry Shaw, who was born in 1816, and lived to a ripe old age at Paris. At the age of sixteen he began carrying the mail on horseback from Paris to Springfield, making the trip twice a week. In this way he came to know Abraham Lincoln, and Lincoln usually inquired of him as to the welfare of people he knew in Paris. Elvis Perry Shaw served as a soldier in the Civil war, reaching the rank of major. At the Vicksburg battlefield a monument marks the situation of his regiment and a marker shows where Major Shaw stood. Elvis Perry Shaw married Emily Street, and they had one child, Charles Edwin Shaw, born in Edgar County November 24, 1853, and died on the 21st of December, 1925.

Charles E. Shaw was educated in the country schools, and graduated from the Philadelphia School of Pharmacy and the Commercial Business College at Terre Haute, Indiana. In 1872 he entered the drug business, but after 1880 he gave his attention to manufacturing enterprises, a bottling business, the operation of a grain elevator and other interests. Mr. Shaw lived retired from business from 1907. He was a republican in politics, and in Masonry was affiliated with Prairie Lodge No. 77, A. F. and A. M., Royal Arch Chapter No. 32, and Knight Templar Commandery No. 27.

He married at Paris, December 12, 1878, Miss Lilla Jane Sheppard, daughter of Isaac Newton and Sarah (Shrewsbury) Sheppard. The Sheppards came from Kentucky to Illinois and settled in Edgar County in 1865. Isaac Newton Sheppard was a manufacturer of farm implements, but about the close of the Civil war he established a business at Paris that is still conducted as the Jones Dry Goods Company. Mr. Charles E. Shaw and wife had five children: Elvis Perry, born September 30, 1879; Isaac Newton, born April 2, 1881; Charles Edwin, born August 26, 1883; McMinn Buchanan, born September 16, 1885; and Nell Eugene, born September 26, 1887. The son Isaac Newton married Elinor Virginia Dyas on October 27, 1905. She died October 6, 1918, leaving two sons; Joseph Edward, born January 17, 1907, and Charles Edwin III, born February 5, 1911. These represent the fifth generation of the family and there are others of the same generation here. Charles Edwin Shaw, Jr., married, November 27, 1912, Alta Elva Gaumer and the three daughters of their marriage are Lilla Jane, born December 5, 1913, Elinor Virginia, born May 14, 1916, and Phoebe Ann, born June 21, 1919. Mr. C. E. Shaw's sons Isaac and McMinn are engaged in the banking business at Paris. His son Elvis Perry served two years in the Spanish-American war in the Philippines. Charles Edwin, Jr., is in the contracting business, associated with the Cunningham Construction Company of Indianapolis, Indiana.

ROBERT E. HIERONYMUS, an active educational worker in Illinois for forty years, since 1914 has been community adviser with the University of Illinois. His addresses before and participation in meetings for the discussion of various problems affecting community life have brought him in contact with practically every locality in the state.

Robert Enoch Hieronymus was born near Atlanta, Logan County, Illinois, December 8, 1862. The Hieronymus family had its original seat in the vicinity of Frankfort, Germany. One branch of the family left there in 1755 and immigrated to Virginia, later going across the mountains into Kentucky. In 1828 the family moved out of Boone County, Kentucky, to what is now Tazewell County, Illinois. Their place of settlement, ten miles north of Atlanta, became known as Hieronymus Grove. The parents of Robert E. Hieronymus were Benjamin R. and Susan Mary (Mountjoy) Hieronymus. His father served as a lieutenant in the One Hundred and Seventeenth Illinois Infantry during the Civil war. His early life was spent as a farmer, but for more than forty years he was a banker. He organized the Illinois National Bank of Springfield and for many years was its president. He was always deeply interested in educational and religious work.

Robert E. Hieronymus graduated from the Illinois State Normal University in 1886, took his A. B. degree at Eureka College in 1889, and two years later the Master of Arts degree. In 1914 Eureka College bestowed upon him the honorary Doctor of Laws. He was a student in the University of Michigan during 1887-88. In the meantime he had taught in rural schools in Tazewell County, and during 1886-87 was principal of the high school at Carrollton. From 1890 to 1897 he was professor of the department of English language and literature in Eureka College, and during the last two years of that period was vice president of the college. During 1897-98 he was teacher of English and history in the State Normal School at Los Angeles, California, and served as superintendent of university extension work in Southern California in 1898-99. He then resumed the chair of English in Eureka College and in 1900 became president, serving until 1909.

In 1907 Mr. Hieronymus was made a member of the Educational Commission of the State of Illinois, and in 1910 was elected its secretary, serving in that capacity until 1913. Since 1914 he has been community adviser in charge of an important department or service of the University of Illinois. Doctor Hieronymus was vice president for two years and president of the Federation of Illinois Colleges from 1906 to 1911, president of the Illinois School Masters Club in 1907-08, and president of the Illinois Chautauqua Alliance in 1911-13.

He has always taken an active part in civic affairs, though maintaining a non-partisan or independent attitude in politics. He is a member of the Civic Club of Chicago and belongs to the Church of the Disciples of Christ.

He married, June 26, 1890, Miss Minnie Frantz, daughter of Henry J. Frantz and sister of Frank Frantz, who was the last territorial governor of Oklahoma. Mr. Hieronymus and Miss Frantz were married at Enid, Oklahoma. The Frantz family came from Illinois. Mrs. Hieronymus died October 27, 1898. On August 30, 1900, he married Lois Campbell, of LaHarpe, Illinois, daughter of C. S. Campbell. Doctor Hieronymus is the father of five children: Faith Helene; Frantz Mountjoy; Rex Eugene, who married Wilma Graham; Grace Maurine, deceased; and Robert Crawford.

WILLIAM SABIN DEWEY is now in the twenty-fifth year of his career as an attorney at the Cairo bar, and is one of the best known citizens of extreme Southern Illinois.

He was born at Irvington, Washington County, Illinois, August 25, 1869, and is of New England ancestry. His father, Edmund S. Dewey, was a son of Oliver and Eliza (Sabin) Dewey and was born at Lenox, Massachusetts, November 10, 1836. He spent the greater part of his life in Southern Illinois and died at Cairo November 28, 1906. Edmund S. Dewey married Jane French, who was born at West Swanzey, New Hampshire, July 12, 1847, and died at Cairo January 29, 1889. She was a daughter of Rev. David P. and Mahitable (Foster) French. Edmund S. Dewey and Marie Jane French were married at Irvington, Illinois, June 16, 1868.

William S. Dewey was reared at Cairo, where he attended public schools. In June, 1889, he graduated from the Sioux Falls College of Sioux Falls, South Dakota, and soon afterwards, returning to Cairo, he served as deputy circuit clerk of Alexander County from January 1, 1890, until December 1, 1894. In the meantime he studied law and on June 20, 1892, was admitted to the bar by the Illinois Supreme Court. Since that date he has practiced law, and since September, 1919, has been senior member of the firm Dewey & Cummins, his partner being W. E. Cummins. On December 1, 1894, Mr. Dewey became county judge of Alexander County, and held that office for a consecutive period of twenty years, until December 1, 1914. Since May 1, 1915, he has been corporation counsel for the City of Cairo. Thus his public service record has been practically uninterrupted for over thirty-five years. He is also attorney for the Cairo National Bank and is a director of the Cairo Association of Commerce.

Judge Dewey is a republican. He is a past president of the Cairo Rotary Club, is a member of Cairo Lodge No. 237, A. F. and A. M., Cairo Chapter No. 71, Royal Arch Masons, Cairo Commandery No. 13, Knights Templar, Ainad Temple, A. A. O. N. M. S., of East St. Louis, and Southern Lodge No. 741, Knights of Pythias. He is a member, trustee and elder of the First Presbyterian Church of Cairo.

Judge Dewey married at Cairo, June 14, 1904, Miss Katherine Kleir, daughter of Francis and Phoebe Kleir. She was born at Cairo, March 3, 1880. They have one daughter, Mary Katherine Dewey, born at Cairo March 9, 1914.

WARREN R. HICKOX, in the abstract and title business at Kankakee, is a lawyer by training, but has successfully carried on a business established by his father prior to the Civil war.

He was born at Kankakee, June 26, 1877, son of Warren R. and Georga A. (Griffith) Hickox. His father was born at Baldwinsville, New York, and his mother at Pollock, Vermont. His father established an abstract business at Kankakee in 1859 and continued it until his death.

Warren R. Hickox, Jr., was educated in grammar and high schools, attended the Shattuck Military Academy at Faribault, Minnesota, and in June, 1897, took charge of the abstract business established by his father. In 1900 he graduated from the law department of Lake Forest University at Chicago. For a number of years he has been an active executive in the abstract business founded by his father, and which is now known as the Kankakee County Title & Trust Company.

January 11, 1900, he married Miss Laura M. LaParle, a native of Kankakee, daughter of Alphonse B. and Mary LaParle. Her father was born in Canada. They have two children, Junior and Edith Ann. Mr. Hickox is a member of the vestry of the Episcopal Church. For three terms he was an alderman from the Second Ward, and for a number of years on the police pension board. He is a republican, a Royal Arch, Knight Templar and Scottish Rite Consistory Mason and Shriner, a charter member of the B. P. O. Elks, a past president of the Kiwanis Club, and now lieutenant governor of Eastern Iowa and Illinois District of the Kiwanis International, president of the Mound Grove Cemetery Association; vice president of the Salvation Army Local Council, member of the Board of Directors of the Y. M. C. A., secretary of the Masonic Temple Association, and secretary and director of the Kankakee Country Club.

JOSEPH CHAMBERS DODDS, M. D. Now in the prime of a successful career, Doctor Dodds is an honored resident of Champaign County. He practiced medicine for over a quarter century, but now gives his time chiefly to business, connected with the Twin City Ice & Cold Storage Company at Champaign.

Doctor Dodds was born at Dover, Long Island, July 15, 1864, and came to Champaign, Illinois, at the age of ten, being reared in the home of his maternal uncle, Dr. J. G. Chambers. He acquired a liberal education, graduating from the Urbana High School and in 1886 completing the regular course in literature and arts at the University of Illinois. He studied medicine first in the University of Michigan and then in Northwestern University at Chicago, where he took his M. D. degree in 1889. Doctor Dodds was an interne in the Marine Hospital at Chicago and later served on the staff of the Eastern Illinois Hospital for the Insane at Kankakee.

Doctor Dodds practiced medicine in 1901 at Denver, Colorado, returning to Tolono, Illinois, in 1902, where he was engaged in the general practice of medicine for nine years and during which time he was active in the civic affairs of that place. He was a district surgeon for the Illinois Central Railway between Gilman and Effingham, and in 1908 was appointed state medical director of the Modern Woodmen of America, acting six years in this capacity.

Doctor Dodds discontinued the general practice of medicine in order to devote his time to business affairs. He was superintendent and secretary-treasurer of the Twin City Ice & Cold Storage Company. He is a man of public spirit and has always been generous of his time and resources to help others. He is president of the Burnham Public Library Board at Champaign and held that position for about ten years. He is also one of the trustees of the Urbana-Champaign Sanitary District and for twelve years has been vice president of the Citizens State Bank. Fraternally he is affiliated with the B. P. O. Elks, the Modern Woodmen of America, has held membership in the County and State Medical Societies and is a Knight Templar Mason and a member of the Country Club.

On January 1, 1891, he married Miss Minna Brown, of Newport, Indiana. Three children were born to their marriage. Eva, a graduate of the University of Illinois, is the wife of B. H. Crowder, residing at Seattle, Washington. They have two children, a son, Richard, aged seven, and a daughter, Janice, aged five. Miss Josephine graduated A. B. from the University of Illinois in 1917; in 1921 completed the course in landscape gardening at the University and is now practicing the profession of landscape gardener in association with Irving L. Peterson at Champaign. The only son, Donald C. Dodds, graduated from the Champaign High School and at the end of three years left the University of Illinois as a volunteer in Battery F, with which he went to Texas and was one of the National Guardsmen, becoming a corporal in Battery F of the One Hundred Forty-ninth Field Artillery in Texas. During the World war this organization was held intact and he was a member of the One Hundred Forty-ninth Field Artillery, Forty-second (Rainbow) Division in France. After his service overseas he resumed his course in the College of Commerce at the University of Illinois and is now president of the Twin City Ice & Cold Storage Company at Champaign. Donald Dodds married, in the fall of 1924, Miss Harriet Amsbery, daughter of F. G. Amsbery, of Champaign. They have one child, Helen Chambers Dodd, born February 27, 1926.

JOHN WESLEY MARTIN. For over twenty years Dr. John Wesley Martin has been one of the prominent medical men of Edgar County. He is the present county coroner, and had a medical service as a medical officer in the World war, having been on duty overseas.

He was born March 15, 1882, in Jacksonville, Illinois, son of John B. and Caroline (Weisenberger) Martin. His mother was born in Germany and came to this country at the age of eighteen, locating in Illinois, where she was married. John B. Martin came from Vermont, where the Martin family had settled on coming from England in 1810. John B. Martin located at Mineral Point, Wisconsin, and three years later moved to Springfield, Illinois. He followed the railroad business, and at Jacksonville in 1882 entered the ministry of the Methodist Church and gave more than thirty-five years of his ablest efforts to the cause. He died in June, 1919.

John Wesley Martin was educated in public schools in various localities in Illinois, graduating from the high school at Pawnee, and took his medical course in the Barnes Medical College at St. Louis, this being at that time the medical department of the University of Missouri. He was graduated M. D. in June, 1907, and during his senior year he was appointed and served as an interne at St. John's Hospital at St. Louis. He began the practice of medicine at Henton, Illinois, having passed both the Illinois and Missouri State Boards of Examiners at the time of his graduation. In 1908 he moved to Oliver, Edgar County, and carried on a successful country practice in that community until he entered the army and after that until January, 1921, when he re-

moved to Paris to perform his duties as coroner of Edgar County, an office to which he was elected in the preceding fall. He was elected in 1921 and reelected in 1922 president of the Edgar County Medical Society.

In February, 1917, before America entered the World war, Doctor Martin volunteered for the Medical Corps. He was commissioned lieutenant in the Medical Reserve Corps in June, 1917, and in February, 1918, was called to active duty. He went overseas in July of that year as a battalion surgeon, and was abroad during the last months of the great struggle. He received his honorable discharge at Camp Grant April 2, 1919. Doctor Martin is a republican in politics, is a Methodist, is a member of the American Legion and the Forty and Eight Society, is affiliated with the Elks Lodge at Paris, Independent Order of Odd Fellows there, Lodge No. 268 of the Masonic fraternity and the Scottish Rite Consistory at Danville.

In 1921 Doctor Martin had the distinction of tracing and proving the transmission of bovine tuberculosis to the human family. This discovery was proven in the famous Kelly family case that attracted the attention of the entire medical world, as it established beyond any question of doubt the actual transmission of the disease. In this work he was assisted by the United States Health Department and the National Live Stock Breeders Association. These organizations cooperated with Doctor Martin. including Commissioner of Health Dr. John Dill Robertson and Professor Smith of the National Live Stock Breeders Association. All the live stock papers of the country gave accounts of this splendid effort. Due to this discovery and subsequent testing and destruction of infected cattle Edgar County stock brings ten per cent higher premiums above the market price at the Chicago Stock Yards. Some idea of the value of Doctor Martin's work can be estimated by this effort if one will pause a moment and compute this sum in dollars.

Doctor Martin married on December 7, 1910, his wife being a daughter of Charles A. and Mary Catherine Rahel. They have three children: Carrie Pauline, born July 18, 1913; John Wesley, born February 11, 1916; and Paul, born September 22, 1922.

CHARLES HELMUTH SEYBT was a resident of Highland for over half a century, and one of the citizens who did most in a constructive way in making it one of the leading industrial centers of Southern Illinois and a community long noted for its civic enterprise and character.

Mr. Seybt, who for many years was president of the Highland Milling Company and known throughout the Middle West as a leader in milling organizations, was born March 16, 1840, at Bautzen, Saxony, Germany, son of David and Julia (Burmeister) Seybt, his father being a minister of the Lutheran Church.

Charles H. Seybt was well educated in his native land, but left there at the age of sixteen to come to America. He landed in this country with very little money, one of his fellow passengers having borrowed most of the sum with which he set out. He was further handicapped by the lack of knowledge of the English language, but while working on a farm in Wisconsin he accepted every opportunity to master the new tongue, and in a short time spoke it well. In the fall of 1857 he came South to St. Louis, and for a time followed the trade of lithographer, having special talents in that line. At that time photography had reached only the stage of making portraits, and all representations of buildings or outdoor scenery required the services of a lithographic artist. In January, 1861, his employers sent him to Highland to make a picture of the town and its principal residences. That was the beginning of his long and useful residence in the city.

On November 23, 1861, he married Frances A. Suppiger. Her father was Joseph Suppiger, one of the founders of Highland, and also one of the founders in 1837 of the milling business now known as the Highland Milling Company. Her mother's maiden name was Mary M. Thorp.

In the early days of the Civil war Mr. Seybt founded the Highland Union as an aggressive paper for the Union cause. He managed it one year, and then turned his attention to varied business and commercial interests. He was one of the leaders in that section in raising funds to induce the Vandalia Railroad to build through Highland. He became a director of the Vandalia Railroad Company, and served in that capacity until late in life and after it was absorbed by the Pennsylvania System. In 1867 Mr. Seybt formed the company for the erection of a brick flouring mill at Highland. In 1875, feeling the need of reasonable insurance for flour mills, he drove to the leading millers in Southern Illinois with the object of forming a mutual fire insurance company. In May, 1876, the first policy was issued, and this modest beginning developed into the Millers National Insurance Company of Chicago. Mr. Seybt served as president of that company from its inception until the end. Later he helped organize the Illinois Millers Mutual Fire Insurance Association of Alton, and served on its board of directors until his death. He was instrumental in opening the first coal mines along the Vandalia Railroad and later organized the Coal Operators Mutual Fire Insurance Company at Springfield, Illinois, being made its president. When a few years before his death the Illinois Legislature passed laws holding employers responsible for injuries sustained by employes, he organized the Millers Mutual Casualty Company, which enjoyed a wonderful success from the start. He was president of this company until his death.

Mr. Seybt in 1875 became one of the early exporters of flour from Southern Illinois. He successfully applied his idea of direct trading between the mill and the importers of the British Isles. He handled the export for a number of leading mills in the Central Western States.

In the spring of 1917 Mr. Seybt underwent an operation for the eye, and while it was successful he was much weakened physically, and he was one of the victims of the influenza-pneumonia epidemic of 1918, dying December

13, 1918. Mr. Seybt was greatly respected at home and abroad. He was well known both in St. Louis and Chicago, where he maintained his business offices. He was a man of strong character, and many institutions benefited by his wise guidance and influence.

His wife died April 25, 1915. They had two children: Alice Josephine Spindler, who died December 30, 1904; and Irma Adele, who passed away June 9, 1905. Mr. Seybt was survived by eight grandchildren: Miss Martha Spindler, Julius J. Spindler, Mrs. Solomon Suppiger, Alexander Spindler, Mrs. Birdie Volz, Miss Bessie Spindler, Curtis and John Louis Spindler.

MARTIN HUBER is secretary, treasurer and manager of the Highland Milling Company, one of the leading flour manufacturing concerns of Southern Illinois. The company conducts one of the oldest flour mills in Illinois under continuous operation, it having been established in 1837, more than eighty-five years ago.

Mr. Huber, who has been a leader in other lines of business and in civic activities at Highland, was born on a farm near Grant Fork in Madison County, January 23, 1877. He is the oldest of a large family of children born to Adam and Margaret (Kopp) Huber. His father, who died April 14, 1897, was born and reared in Baden, Germany, came to the United States about 1873, and spent his active career as a farmer. His wife was a native of Illinois.

Martin Huber was three years of age when his parents moved to Highland. He attended parochial schools, and as a youth went to work in a flour mill. He has had a thorough experience in both the grain and flour manufacturing business. For eleven years he was with the well known flour exporter, C. H. Seybt, and for two years was with the Meek Milling Company at Marissa, Illinois. Mr. Huber in 1903 became a mill manager for the Wisconsin Power Company, at first in the mill at Rice Lake, Wisconsin, and then at Menominee, where this company had one of its largest mills. Returning to Highland in 1906, Mr. Huber became sales manager for the Highland Milling Company, subsequently was made one of the directors, and is now the chief executive officer of that prosperous industry.

Since January 1, 1920, Mr. Huber has been president of the Farmers and Merchants Bank of Highland. He is also director of the Highland Brick and Tile Company, and was a member of the advisory board of St. Paul's Catholic Church. He served for nine years as grand knight of the Knights of Columbus of Highland, and is one of the prominent men of his church in Madison County. During the World war he was active in the various loan drives and also in the drive for the Knights of Columbus.

Mr. Huber is a member of the St. Louis Millers Club, of the Country Club of Highland, is second vice president of the Business Men's League, is a life member of the Red Cross Chapter and is a republican voter. He has never been a candidate for public office.

He married, November 8, 1910, Miss Ida R. Burke. She was born at Du Bois, Pennsylvania, was educated in parochial schools at Altoona, Pennsylvania, and is a graduate of King's School of Oratory at Pittsburgh, and of the Chicago Conservatory of Dramatic Art. For a time she was a teacher of elocution at Pittsburgh. Mr. and Mrs. Huber have three daughters and three sons: Irma C., Mary Frances, Thomas M., Edmund Burke, Robert C. and Idagene.

TREVETT-MATTIS BANKING COMPANY, one of the oldest farm loan organizations in Illinois, established more than half a century ago at Champaign, was broadened into a general banking service, now known as the Trevett-Mattis Banking Company. The two men who give the name to this corporation are still active in the business and have been associated together for over half a century.

The business itself was first started by A. C. Burnham, about 1861, as a farm loan agency. On March 1, 1876, the firm of Burnham, Trevett & Mattis came into existence, the two new members being J. R. Trevett and Ross R. Mattis. About 1890 a general banking business was added, though farm loans continued to be the essential feature. After the death of A. C. Burnham, in 1897, the firm became Trevett & Mattis, remaining a private company until 1903, when the Trevett-Mattis Banking Company was incorporated under the laws of Illinois. The Trevett-Mattis Banking Company occupies a modern banking structure, erected in 1910 especially for this company and the business. It is a substantial two-story building of Indiana limestone, with large Colonial columns of stone from the base to the top of the second story. Inside the banking rooms are finished in marble and mahogany. With possibly one exception this is the oldest farm loan business in Illinois. The scope of its business is state wide. The company has capital and surplus of $200,000.

The present officers of the company are: Ross R. Mattis, president; John R. Trevett and John H. Trevett, vice presidents; W. P. Spalding, cashier.

Ross R. Mattis, president of the company, was born in Philadelphia, Pennsylvania, in February, 1849, and has been a resident of Champaign since May, 1865. For a time he was employed in the hardware store of his uncle, Joseph McCorkle, and in 1875 entered the farm loan business conducted by A. C. Burnham. In 1876 he and Mr. Trevett came into the business as partners, and Mr. Mattis has been vitally identified with the growth and development of the company through succeeding years.

Mr. Mattis married, May 4, 1875, Miss Mary E. McKinley, sister of United States Senator William B. McKinley, of Champaign. In the spring of 1925 they celebrated their golden wedding anniversary. There were four children: George M. Mattis, until recently vice president of the Illinois Traction Company; Miss Julia R., of Champaign; Ida M., wife of Allan Macdonald, of Danville, Illinois; and Mary, wife of Major T. J. Camp, of the United States Army.

John R. Trevett, vice president of the Trevett-Mattis Banking Company, is a native of Chicago, and came to Champaign about 1858

with his parents, Oliver Trevett and wife. His father conducted a baking business at Champaign, and died when his son John was a child. John R. Trevett about 1870 went into the office of A. C. Burnham, learned the farm loan business there, and in 1876 had qualified as one of the two partners of Mr. Burnham. Mr. Trevett served one or two terms as city treasurer of Champaign, and for some years was a trustee of the University of Illinois.

In May, 1875, he married Miss Helen M. Lenington. Like his business partner and wife, he and Mrs. Trevett in May, 1925, celebrated their golden wedding anniversary. To their marriage were born four children, two sons and two daughters: Ross L., who died in 1913; John H., vice president of the banking company, who married Flo T. Flower, of Chicago; Helen M., wife of Dr. James H. Finch, of Champaign; and Bessie H., wife of Lawrence T. Allen, of Danville.

LEVI SPENCER WILCOX, long and successfully engaged in the practice of his profession at Champaign, was one of the representative physicians and surgeons of Champaign County. His professional stewardship, able and faithful, was maintained on a high plane, and the same spirit of fidelity marked his course in all other relations of life. He was a veritable guide, counselor and friend to the community in which he long lived and in which he consecrated himself to helpful service. The Doctor was a native of Illinois, his birth having occurred at Lacon, Marshall County, August 7, 1847, and his death having taken place in Los Angeles, California, on the 5th of August, 1910.

Doctor Wilcox was a son of Levi and Nancy (Rogers) Wilcox, the former a native of Hadden, Connecticut, and the latter of Columbiana County, Ohio, and both parents died in Illinois. Doctor Wilcox was but four years of age at the time of his father's death, and he early began to depend largely on his own resources. He found employment at farm work, and he gained in the rural schools of the period his early education. His ambition to gain a liberal academic education and also to prepare himself for the medical profession was not to be thwarted by any adverse circumstance of time or place, and induced him to use his entire patrimony and his own earnings for that purpose. Thus he was graduated from Northwestern University, Evanston, Illinois, as a member of the class of 1871 and with the degree of Bachelor of Arts. There he formed the acquaintance of Miss Alice Yaple, who was graduated in the same year from Northwestern Female College, which later became an integral part of the university. The marriage of the two young students was solemnized July 2, 1873, the year marked also by the graduation of Doctor Wilcox from Long Island Medical College, Brooklyn, New York. Mrs. Wilcox was born and reared at Mendon, St. Joseph County, Michigan, a representative of one of the old and influential pioneer families of that section of the Wolverine State and a sister of the late Hon. George L. Yaple, who served with distinction in the United States Congress in the late '80s and upon the bench of the Circuit Court in Michigan. Prior to entering Northwestern Female College Mrs. Wilcox had been a student in Albion College, Albion, Michigan.

To fortify himeslf still more fully for his exacting profession, Doctor Wilcox later completed an effective postgraduate course in his alma mater, Long Island Medical College. After receiving his degree of Doctor of Medicine and taking unto himself a gracious and talented young wife, in 1873, Doctor Wilcox first engaged in the practice of his profession at Magnolia, Putnam County, Illinois, and it was there that his daughter Mae was born, who is now the widow of Robert D. Burnham, her husband being specifically mentioned on other pages of this publication, in the memorial dedicated to the distinguished Burnham family of Champaign County. Mrs. Burnham was an infant at the time of the family removal to Champaign, in which city she still maintains her home. In her youth she attended the University of Illinois one year and Northwestern University two years. Doctor Wilcox built up a substantial and representative practice at Champaign, where he established his residence in 1875, and he was a leader not only in his profession but also in the ordering of civic affairs in the community. He was an active worker in the ranks of the republican party, served several terms as township supervisor, and gave three terms of signally resourceful and progressive administration as mayor of Champaign. In the late '80s his impaired health caused him virtually to retire from the active work of the profession that he had dignified alike by his character and his able services, and he soon afterward accepted the position of United States collector of internal revenue in his district, a position that he retained four years. Doctor Wilcox was an unswerving lifelong republican, whose untiring zeal and unflagging efforts were felt in county, state and national politics. In 1897 distinction came to him when he was appointed United States consul to China, where he continued eight years in this diplomatic service, he having in the meanwhile been there advanced to the status of consul general. He was there in discharge of official duties at the time of the great Boxer uprising in 1900, and in appreciative recognition of his zealous and effective service in getting all of his countrymen safely out of the danger zone at the time of this menacing insurrection, the Chinese government, on the 1st of September, 1903, awarded to Doctor Wilcox a distinguished decoration of honor, that of the Eight Pointed Star, the highest tribute awarded by that government to foreigners.

In 1905 Doctor Wilcox returned from the Orient to his native land and to his home in Champaign. His first wife died March 19, 1888, and on the 28th of January, 1891, he was united in marriage with Miss Nina Dickenson, of Jacksonville, Illinois, who still maintains her home in Champaign, no children having been born of the second marriage, and the daughter Mae, widow of Robert D. Burnham, being the only child of the first marriage.

After his return from China Doctor Wilcox traveled somewhat extensively through Europe and the United States, and he was sojourning in Los Angeles, California, at the time of his death. His was a life of signal honor and usefulness, and his character was the positive expression of an intrinsically strong and noble nature, so that his name and memory are honored in the city and county that long represented his home and the center of his interests.

CAPTAIN EDWARD BAILEY, long one of the honored and influential citizens of the City of Champaign, passed away October 5, 1925. He was living virtually retired from active business, though he was still the president of the Champaign National Bank, with status as the only survivor of those who figured as the organizers of this old and staunch financial institution, which was founded nearly half a century ago and which has always stood exponent of honorable and conservative banking policies.

Captain Bailey was born at Bloomfield, Edgar County, Illinois, September 8, 1843, a son of David and Hannah (Finely) Bailey, who established their residence in Champaign, this state, in the spring of 1856, and he was one of the early merchants here. David Bailey was one of the organizers of the First National Bank of Champaign, in 1865, and later he became one of the organizers of the Champaign National Bank. He was one of the liberal, enterprising and highly honored citizens of Champaign, and after leaving this place he resided for a time at St. Joseph, Missouri, where occurred the death of his first wife. He passed the closing years of his life mainly in his native state of New Hampshire, but he had erected in Champaign, Illinois, in 1897, a fine new house on the site of that which had here been his former home. He had just taken up his abode in this new residence when his death here occurred December 17, 1897. David Bailey was born at Salem, Rockingham County, New Hampshire, August 2, 1814, and thus he was eighty-three years of age at the time of his death. His character was as staunch as the hills of his native Granite State, and he lived a life of honor and usefulness, of human kindliness and human helpfulness, so that his name and memory merit enduring veneration.

Capt. Edward Bailey attended the common schools of Illinois in his boyhood and early youth, later was a student in an academy at Atkinson, New Hampshire, and in the fall of 1860 he entered Douglas University, the nucleus of the present great University of Chicago. At this school he joined an independent military company that was formed at the inception of the Civil war, and this company had the place of honor at the funeral of Hon. Stephen A. Douglas. In 1862 Captain Bailey enlisted in Company K, Sixty-seventh Illinois Volunteer Infantry, and was elected first lieutenant of his company. At the expiration of his original term of enlistment he received his honorable discharge and returned home. In 1864 he reenlisted and was made captain of Company B, One Hundred and Thirty-fifth Illinois Volunteer Infantry, with which command he served until the close of the war. After the close of his military service Captain Bailey had experience as clerk in mercantile establishments, and finally acquired an interest in the Champaign firm of Richards & Brother. In the fall of 1879 he became associated with W. S. Maxwell and James C. Miller in the organizing of a private banking business, the same being conducted under the firm name of Bailey, Maxwell & Miller. In 1882 these principals, with six other stockholders, organized and incorporated the Champaign National Bank, the operations of which were based on a capital stock of $50,000. Of the new institution Captain Bailey was elected the first president, and of this office he continued the incumbent during the long intervening period of more than forty years, and up to his death, a record probably unequaled by that of any other Illinois bank president of the present time. Of the Champaign National Bank brief specific record is given elsewhere in this publication.

In 1868 was recorded the marriage of Captain Bailey and Miss Josephine S. Richards, who was born in the State of Maine and who had accompanied her parents on their removal to Champaign, Illinois. Captain and Mrs. Bailey had three children: Fred S., who is now president of the Champaign National Bank and who is individually mentioned on other pages of this volume; Josephine Belle, who is at home; and Angeline, who is also at home. Captain Bailey was a stalwart veteran in the ranks of the republican party, and he was long and actively affiliated with the Grand Army of the Republic. He was a citizen who did much for Champaign, and this community accorded to him the fullest measure of confidence and esteem.

FRED S. BAILEY. In his native city of Champaign, where he is president and major active executive of the Champaign National Bank, is well upholding the prestige of a family name that has been one of prominence and large influence in connection with civic and business affairs in this city and county. Of his venerable father, Capt. Edward Bailey, who died October 5, 1925, one of the organizers and the president of the Champaign National Bank up to his death, individual mention is made in the preceding sketch, so that further review of the family history is not here demanded.

Fred S. Bailey was born in Champaign on the 19th of April, 1871, and in the public schools of this city he continued his studies until his graduation from high school as a member of the class of 1889. Thereafter he here continued his studies in the University of Illinois, where he followed literary and scientific courses until his impaired health compelled him to leave the university. By passing a year in Colorado he recuperated his physical well-being, and in the early '90s he assumed a clerical position in the Champaign National Bank, with which he has since been continuously connected and in which he has won advancement through the various grades of executive responsibility until he now has the active supervising management of this old and staunch financial institution, of which he is now president, succeeding Capt. Edward Bailey, his father. Mr. Bailey gave effective service as cashier of the bank prior to his election to the office of vice president and later president of which positions he has been

the incumbent since 1909 and in which he has ably directed the policies and general administration of the institution. A record concerning the bank may be found in the following sketch.

Mr. Bailey takes loyal interest in all that concerns the welfare and progress of his native city and county, is a liberal and public-spirited citizen, is a republican in political allegiance, and is affiliated with the Champaign Lodge of the Benevolent and Protective Order of Elks.

On the 12th of August, 1901, was solemnized the marriage of Mr. Bailey and Miss Mabel Bennett, who was born at Pontiac, this state, and whose parents are now deceased. Her father, the late Havilla S. Bennett, resided for a time in Kansas, thereafter the family home was maintained at Cairo, Illinois, and finally, in 1892, removal was made to Champaign, where he served as station agent for the Illinois Central Railroad and where he and his wife maintained their home until their deaths, he having in later years been concerned in the land business in the State of Mississippi. Mr. and Mrs. Bailey have no children.

THE CHAMPAIGN NATIONAL BANK has gained secure place as one of the substantial and well ordered financial institutions of Illinois, and its history has been one of careful and honorable methods and policies, of consecutive advancement in the scope and importance of operations, and of inviolable place in the confidence of the people of the community that it has long and faithfully served. In the city of Champaign the private banking house of Bailey, Maxwell & Miller was established in 1879, and in 1882 the same was succeeded by the Champaign National Bank, which was incorporated with a capital stock of $50,000. The new bank was incorporated October 20, 1882, and those who were concerned in this incorporation were James B. McKinley, Francis T. Walker, George F. Beardsley, Isaac S. Raymond, David Bailey, Barnard Kelley, James C. Miller, William S. Maxwell and Capt. Edward Bailey. Captain Bailey up to his death was the only surviving member of this company of corporators, he had been president of the bank during the entire period of its existence up to his death, October 5, 1925, and of him individual mention is made elsewhere in this publication. The other officers of the bank at the time of this writing, in 1926, are as here noted: Fred S. Bailey, president; J. W. Stipes, vice president; P. L. McPheeters. cashier; and John H. Snider, assistant cashier. The resources of the Champaign National Bank now total more than $1,000,000, the capital stock is still retained at the original figure of $50,000;; the surplus and undivided profits aggregate over $183,000, and the deposits as indicated in the last official statement are $788,558.22.

HERMAN C. HORNEMAN, an expert in dairy products, has been the guiding genius in the development of one of the largest manufacturing and distributing concerns in the United States handling dairy products, particularly butter. This is the Sugar Creek Creamery Company, Inc., of which he is president. The main offices of the company are at Danville, where Mr. Horneman has resided for several years.

He was born at Harlan, Kansas, May 13, 1884. His father, Charles Horneman, was born at Pottsdam, Germany, in 1838, was reared and educated there and learned the machinist's trade, and at the age of nineteen ran away from home, coming to the United States. For several years he followed his trade as a machinist and blacksmith in De Kalb County, Illinois, and in 1879 moved to Harlan, Kansas, where he was a blacksmith until he retired, removing to Los Angeles to spend his declining years. He died in that city in August, 1916. He was a republican in politics, and an active worker in the German Lutheran Church. Charles Horneman married Caroline Leifheit, who was born in Schleswig-Holstein, Germany, and was a young child when her parents came to the United States. Her father, Henry Leifheit, settled in De Kalb County, Illinois, and became an extensive and prosperous farmer there. Mrs. Charles Horneman is now living at Long Beach, California. Her children were: C. Frank, an employe of the Sugar Creek Creamery Company at Danville; Albert, a machinist who died at Des Moines, Iowa. when twenty-eight years old; Christina, wife of Harry C. Jones, a dentist at Los Angeles; Walter A., manager of the Sugar Creek Creamery Company's plant at Louisville, Kentucky; and Herman C.

Herman C. Horneman attended public schools at Harlan, Kansas, at Norfolk, Nebraska, and Des Moines, Iowa, spending three years in the West Des Moines High School. He graduated from Iowa State College at Ames, Iowa, with the class of 1908 and the degree Bachelor of Science in agriculture. In 1920 Iowa State College, in recognition of his services and technical proficiency, awarded the honorary degree Master of Agriculture. After graduating in 1908 he remained for a year and a half in the dairy extension department of Iowa State College. For nearly a year following that he was with the Blue Valley Creamery Company of Chicago as head of the creamery department, supervising all the plants of this company.

Mr. Horneman at Watseka. Illinois, engaged in the creamery business for himself, establishing the first plant of the business now known as the Sugar Creek Creamery Company. He developed the enterprise rapidly, extending and building new plants, incorporated the company in 1914 and has since been its president. The main offices are at 123 Washington Avenue, in Danville. This company now operates plants at Danville, Watseka and Pana, Illinois, St. Louis and Marshfield. Missouri, Indianapolis and Evansville, Indiana, and Louisville, Kentucky, and maintains branch sales offices at Jacksonville, Florida, and Pittsburgh, Pennsylvania.

Mr. Horneman since coming to Danville has been an interested and public spirited citizen, and since April, 1924, has been president of the Danville Board of Education. He is a republican, was baptized and confirmed in the German Lutheran Church. is a member of Watseka Lodge, Watseka Chapter and Mary

Commandery of the Knights Templar, all at Watseka, Illinois, Danville Consistory of the Scottish Rite Masons, and Ansar Temple of the Mystic Shrine at Springfield. He belongs to the Sigma Alpha Epsilon social fraternity and the honorary agricultural fraternity Delta Theta Sigma; is a member of Danville Lodge No. 332, B. P. O. Elks, Danville Chamber of Commerce, and the Danville Country Club. He owns a home at 1119 Sherman Boulevard in Danville, resident property at Long Beach, California, and has a seventy-acre farm east of Danville.

During the World war Mr. Horneman devoted much of his time to his duties as a member of a committee on perishable food, including butter, a committee of the Food Administration under George Haskell, who was head of the Dairy Products Bureau of the food administration.

Mr. Horneman married at Wheaton, Illinois, December 2, 1909, Miss Florence Coe, daughter of Seymour R. and Caroline (Peterson) Coe, residents of Ames, Iowa, where her father is a retired farmer. Mr. and Mrs. Horneman have one son, Kenneth Herman.

JAMES EDWIN FILSON, popularly known as Edwin Filson, president of the Illinois Trust and Savings Bank of Champaign, is one of the men of this region who is making banking history, and one whose uprightness and high personal character have won him the appreciation and esteem of his fellow citizens. He was born on a farm in Caldwell County, Missouri, October 28, 1883, a son of Thomas and S. Zelma (Adams) Filson.

With the exception of a few years spent in Kansas Mr. Filson resided in Missouri until 1903, and in 1901 was graduated from the high school at Hamilton, Missouri, and following that event worked in his father's law and abstract offices, supplementing former work done while attending school, so that in all he had about four and one-half years' training, and gained an excellent knowledge of business and exactness in carrying on transactions of any nature. In 1903 he came to Champaign to join a boyhood friend. When he arrived in the city he had $1.65 as his capital. Two days later he secured employment with the Champaign County Abstract Company, first located at Urbana, but later at Champaign. In the fall of 1904 he entered the College of Law of the University of Illinois for a three years' course, but at the same time continued his work in the abstract office. In time he was made manager of the Champaign office of the company, and at the same time was graduated with the degree of Bachelor of Laws. Subsequently Mr. Filson was placed on a profit-sharing basis, in 1920 became a partner, and in 1923 he bought the business and is now sole owner of it. In 1921 he was elected cashier of the Illinois Trust and Savings Bank of Champaign, later became vice president and in 1926 was made president. He rendered a public service as a member of the city council from 1911 to 1915, elected to that office on the republican ticket. During 1922 and 1923 he was president of the Champaign Chamber of Commerce, and he is still a member of that body, and he has been very active in the Rotary Club, serving it for four years as secretary. For six years he was secretary of the Illinois Abstractors Association, and he was its vice president for a year, and for one year was its president. He was also vice president of the American Association of Title Men.

On December 26, 1906, Mr. Filson married Lena Will of Hamilton, Missouri, whom he has known since childhood. They have four children: Kathleen, James, Beth and Jean. Mr. and Mrs. Filson belong to the Presbyterian Church, which he is serving as clerk of the session and clerk of the congregation, and was chairman of the Budget and Finance Committee of the Synod of Illinois, and now holds the same office with the Bloomington Presbytery. Fond of golf, which he regards as a healthful recreation, Mr. Filson believes in enjoying the good things of life, to which his hard work and good management entitle him. A social favorite, he maintains membership with the Champaign Country Club. His fraternal connections are with the Masonic fraternity, to which he had been advanced in the York Rite to the Commandery, and the Knights of Pythias and the Independent Order of Odd Fellows.

THE ILLINOIS TRUST & SAVINGS BANK of Champaign specializes in city and farm loans, and does a city loan business that is probably larger than that of any of the other banks in Champaign. It was incorporated in 1912, and has a capitalization of $150,000. This institution succeeded to the business of the Illinois Title & Trust Company, which had been incorporated in 1902, with a capital stock of $100,000, with the following officers: F. B. Vennum, president; V. W. Johnston, vice president; Shields A. Blaine, cashier; and G. R. Shawhan, manager of the savings department.

The present officers of the bank are: Edwin Filson, president; H. E. McNevin, vice president and cashier; S. A. Wright and L. F. Lawhead, assistant cashiers; and H. C. Augustus, manager of the savings department.

The structure occupied by the bank was erected by it in 1912, solely for banking purposes, and is a beautiful building of Bedford stone, with a tall, arched entrance on either side flanked by large stone columns. Inside is a very large counting room, in height about three stories, the light coming through a ceiling of stained art glass, this ceiling being arched with heavy beams. In the interior decorating, as well as the architectural design, a highly artistic effect has been secured that compares favorably with any banking house in the state. The people of Champaign are naturally very proud of this monument to the enterprise and artistic taste of their fellow citizens, and point to it as illustrative of what can be accomplished outside of the great centers of the country.

CHRISTIAN GOTTLOB HIRSCHI is a native of Illinois and for thirty-five years has been a competent member of the bar, engaged in an extensive general practice at Watseka.

He was born in Saline Township, Madison County, Illinois, October 18, 1861, son of Christian and Elizabeth (Plocher) Hirschi. His

father was born in Switzerland, son of Christian Barbara Hirschi. Madison County was settled by a great many colonists from Switzerland. Elizabeth Plocher was born in Wurttemberg, where her parents were also born.

Christian G. Hirschi after the common schools entered Eureka College of Illinois, and on completing his literary education attended the University of Michigan Law School, where he was graduated LL. B. June 25, 1891. Soon afterward he was admitted to the Illinois bar, and most of his practice has been in Iroquois County. He served as city attorney of Watseka from May 1, 1895, to May 1, 1897. Later he was appointed master-in-chancery of the Circuit Court, and served one year in this capacity.

Mr. Hirschi is a republican and a member of the Iroquois Club of Watseka. He married, September 20, 1893, Miss Capitola H. Davidson.

THOMAS O'DONNELL, general foreman of the Nickel Plate Railway at Rankin, is a veteran in the railroad service, and comes of a family of railroad men.

He was born at Lima, Ohio, June 28, 1893. His father, Thomas O'Donnell, was born at Fremont, Ohio, in 1857, grew up there and as a youth took up railroading, reaching the position of passenger conductor for the Lake Shore & Michigan Southern, now part of the New York Central Lines. From Fremont he removed to Cleveland and in 1890 to Lima, where he became a freight conductor for the Lake Erie & Western Railway. He was in the service until injured in February, 1908, and died March 3 of that year at Lima. He was a democrat, a Catholic and a member of the Order of Railway Conductors. Thomas O'Donnell, Sr., married Mary Casey, who resides at Lima, in which city she was born May 28, 1856. A brief record of their children is as follows: Bernard, assistant shop superintendent for the Nickel Plate Railway at Lima; Thomas; John Daniel, a pipefitter for the Nickel Plate Railway at Lima; and Miss Anna Mary.

Thomas O'Donnell was reared in Lima, and attended the public and parochial schools of that city, graduating from high school in 1908. During the next four years he served as a machinist apprentice at the Nickel Plate shops in Lima. As a machinist he followed his trade with the Nickel Plate, the Wheeling & Lake Erie, the Big Four and Baltimore & Ohio railways at different points until 1917. In that year he was foreman of the roundhouse of the Nickel Plate Railway at Muncie, Indiana, and was a resident of that city four years. Then, in February, 1921, he was transferred to Rankin, Illinois, as general foreman of the roundhouse. The roundhouse and offices of the Nickel Plate are situated a mile east of Rankin proper. Mr. O'Donnell has forty-four employes under his supervision. He is a thorough master of the mechanics of railroading and a very capable and popular executive. His particular service during the World war was in his position as a railroad man.

He votes independently, is a member of the Catholic Church and is affiliated with Muncie Council No. 560, Knights of Columbus, Lima Council No. 1331, Catholic Order of Foresters, Muncie Lodge No. 245, B. P. O. Elks, and is a member of the New York Central Insurance Organization.

Mr. O'Donnell married at Loda, Illinois, December 29, 1922, Miss Elsie Sours, daughter of John and Mary (Miller) Sours, residents of Geneva, Indiana. Her father is a farmer.

NORMAN SMITH STARR, M. D. A physician and surgeon at Charleston, Doctor Starr has practiced medicine for over ten years, and was in service as a medical officer during the World war.

He was born September 28, 1888, son of Dr. Nathan and Ida Green Starr. His father is a physician who has practiced for thirty-five years in Charleston, Illinois, and is still actively engaged in practice at this place. Norman Smith Starr graduated in medicine in 1915 from the University of Michigan, and has practiced in Illinois, at Moweaqua and Charleston, being at present associated with his father, practicing under the name of Drs. Starr & Starr. His military service began in August, 1917. He was commissioned a first lieutenant in the Army Medical Corps and was overseas from June 1, 1918, until February, 1919, receiving his honorable discharge in the latter year.

Doctor Starr is a past commander of the Raymon Harlan Post of the American Legion at Moweaqua and is vice commander of the Andrew Dunn Post at Charleston. He is a republican, and a member of the Masonic Lodge, Knights of Pythias and Lodge No. 623, B. P. O. E. He is a Methodist.

On June 24, 1916, at Hoopeston, Illinois, Doctor Starr married Miss Ferne Baxter, daughter of William Baxter, of Hoopeston. They have three children, Norman Baxter, born April 27, 1918, and Susan and Robert, twins, born July 28, 1921.

MOSES ELMER NEWELL, a prominent Edwardsville lawyer, has had a busy career divided between education and the legal profession, and all his attainments have been due to a persistence of purpose and well directed energy, beginning when as a young man without capital he had to work to secure his advanced education.

Mr. Newell was born near Farmersville in Montgomery County, Illinois, October 23, 1878, son of Moses A. and Samantha (Green) Newell. His mother was born in Fairfield County, Ohio, in 1850. His father was born in Greene County, Illinois, in 1847, and now resides at Girard, this state. The Newells are of English ancestry and have been in the United States for a number of generations. Moses Elmer Newell was fourth in a family of six children, the others being: Jesse W., Cora Lillian (who died in infancy), Agnes L., Ralph G. and Jeduthun E.

Moses E. Newell passed his boyhood days on the farm, attended the old Lake District School in his home community, and in preparation for his work as a teacher he spent one year in the Illinois Normal College at Normal. For a year he was employed as a clerk in the freight office of the Terminal Railway Association at St. Louis. Mr. Newell subsequently graduated from Greer College at Hoopeston, Illinois, with the Bachelor of Pedagogy degree. He was president of his graduating class in 1902. For ten years after graduating he consecutively taught school, the first year in Grant County of Oklahoma Territory. After his return to Illinois he was principal of the schools at Moro in Madison County two years, then for two years was principal of the Bethalto School and his final five years' work as a teacher was done as principal of the Brighton School in Macoupin County.

In the fall of 1912 Mr. Newell entered the law department of the University of Illinois at Urbana, and was graduated LL. B. in 1915 and admitted to the Illinois bar the same year. He, with the assistance of his wife, earned the money necessary to defray the expense of his law education operating a photograph studio in the university district. He forthwith entered practice at Edwardsville, and has been known as an industrious attorney, giving an adequate service in every case in which he is engaged. He was alone in his law work until January 26, 1917, when he and Jesse R. Brown formed the partnership of Newell & Brown. On September 19, 1917, Mr. Brown answered the call to the colors, leaving the practice of the firm in the hands of Mr. Newell. On August 31, 1917, Edwardsville's postmaster, Frank Stillwell, died, and on the twentieth of October Mr. Newell was appointed his successor, and capably administered the affairs of the local office until July 15, 1920. In the meantime Mr. Brown had returned from the army and the active partnership relations were resumed. On June 21, 1921, Mr. Perry H. Hiles became the senior member of the firm of Hiles, Newell & Brown. This firm today is one of the most successful in Southern Illinois. Since Mr. Hiles became a member the firm has maintained an office at Alton as well as at Edwardsville.

On August 17, 1904, Mr. Newell married Miss Frances S. Carriker, also a native of Montgomery County, Illinois, and of a pioneer family there. Mr. Newell is a Royal Arch and thirty-second degree Scottish Rite Mason and a Shriner, and a member of the Eastern Star. He has interested himself in public affairs, but in politics has largely worked for the other fellow. He is a member of the Methodist Episcopal Church.

DAVID ANDREW PHILLIPPE passed his entire life in Champaign County, Illinois, and was a representative of a family that was here founded more than a century ago—a family whose name has been worthily associated with the civic and industrial annals of the county from the very early pioneer era to the present day. David A. Phillippe long followed the ancestral vocation of farm industry, and was one of its substantial and progressive exponents in Champaign County. His memory compassed much of the development and progress of this favored section of Illinois, he did well his part as a loyal citizen and substantial man of affairs, and he ever commanded high place in popular confidence and goodwill.

David A. Phillippe was born in Hensley Township, Champaign County, August 29, 1843, and thus he was seventy-eight years of age at the time of his death, March 18, 1922, he having passed the closing years of his earnest and worthy life in the beautiful home in which his widow still resides in the city of Champaign. Mr. Phillippe was the only child of Hezekiah and Elizabeth (Howell) Phillippe, the former of whom was born in Loudoun County, Virginia, and the latter near Louisville, Kentucky. Hezekiah Phillippe was a son of John Phillippe, and about the year 1818 he accompanied his parents on their immigration to Illinois, which state was then on the western frontier. John Phillippe came with his family to Champaign County and here took up a tract of government land in Henley Township, about ten miles northwest of the present city of Champaign. Old parchment deeds to this homestead and other government land here secured by the Philippe family are preserved as valuable and historical heirlooms and are now in the keeping of the children of the honored subject of this memoir, whose widow passed them on to her children after the death of the devoted husband and father. John Phillippe reclaimed and developed one of the productive pioneer farms of Hensley Township, and on the old homestead he and his wife passed the remainder of their lives. His sons Hezekiah and John, Jr., succeeded him in the vigorous carrying forward of farm industry in the old home township, and by their practice of securing an additional forty acres of land each successive year during an appreciable period they accumulated one of the large and valuable landed estates of the county in which they were substantial and highly respected pioneer citizens at the time of their death.

David A. Phillippe was reared to the sturdy discipline of the pioneer farm, and his rudimentary education was acquired in a primitive log schoolhouse not far distant from his home. Thereafter he attended the Urbana schools a few terms, and later, in intervals of his farm work, he attended Wesleyan College at Bloomington. His entire active career was one of close and successful association with the great basic industries of agriculture and stock-growing, and, as the only child, he inherited the valuable farm estate of his father. For more than a half century Mr. Phillippe was actively engaged in progressive farm enterprise, and it was given him to witness and take part in the development of the county from the pioneer conditions to its present status of opulent prosperity. He made the best of improvements on his farm property and continued to reside on the old homstead until 1910, when he and his wife removed to the city of Champaign, where he passed the gracious evening of his life in well earned retirement and under the most grateful of conditions and influences. Though he never had any desire for political activity or public office, Mr. Phillippe was loyal and liberal as a citizen and was aligned in the ranks of the republican party. He was an earnest member of the Methodist Episcopal Church, as is also his widow. He long maintained affiliation with the Masonic fraternity.

In the year 1874 was solemnized the marriage of Mr. Phillippe and Miss Rachel J. R. Harris, who was born and reared in Champaign County and who is the only surviving child of the late Benjamin F. and Mary (Heath) Harris. The father of Mrs. Phillippe was one of the influential and distinguished pioneer citizens of Champaign County, and a tribute to his memory is entered on other pages of this work. Mr. and Mrs. Phillippe became the parents of five children: G. Prank, who resides on and has active management of the fine old homestead farm of his father, married Miss Edna Pippenger, of Lincoln, this state, and they have three children, Margaret, Frances and Elise. Harris, the second son, died in infancy. Ida is the wife of Milton W. Gatch, of Baltimore, Maryland, and their two children are Phillippe and Rachel. Olive is the wife of Charles H. Strawbridge, of River Forest, a suburb of Chicago, and their children are Richard and Elizabeth. Edith, youngest of the children of the subject of this memoir, is the wife of John W. Armstrong, and they reside with her widowed mother in the beautiful home at Champaign. This home, one of the show places of the city, is one of the most attractive and artistic in Champaign. The substantial and spacious house is set in the midst of beautiful grounds that constitute an entire city block, and the home is known as a center of gracious and refined hospitality, with Mrs. Phillippe as its popular chatelaine.

CAPT. EARL HUNTER, who was an American officer in the Mexican border troubles of 1916 and was on duty overseas for many months, is one of the popular and successful business men of Paris, Illinois. Captain Hunter was born at Paris, March 5, 1889, son of Robert and Margaret (Gorman) Hunter. His grandfather Hunter came to this country from Ireland in 1854, settling in Edgar County. He made a return trip to Ireland and brought back his son Robert and subsequently made other trips for the remainder of his family, there being fourteen children altogether. Robert Hunter, father of Captain Hunter, was educated in country schools, and was identified with farming until 1888, when he moved to Paris to engage in business. Captain Hunter's maternal ancestors, the Gormans, came to this country about the same time as the Hunters and also settled in Edgar County. Both families were represented by soldiers in the Civil war.

Earl Hunter was educated in public schools at Paris, including St. Mary's Parochial High School. As a boy he engaged in the furniture and undertaking business, and from that took service with the American Express Company, beginning as clerk and was later promoted to traveling auditor and finally was made agent of the company at Paris.

While in high school Captain Hunter was an enthusiastic member of the Cadet Corps. Subsequently he enlisted as a private in Company D of the Fourth Illinois Infantry, National Guard, and was a captain when called to duty on the Mexican border in 1916. The Fourth Illinois Infantry at the time of the World war was designated as the One Hundred Thirtieth Regiment of Infantry, and Captain Hunter was mustered into the National Army with the rank of captain and went overseas in May, 1918. He saw duty on the British, French and American fronts with the Thirty-third Division, and he has a citation for splendid performance of duty and gallantry in action on October 10, 1918. He returned to this country in May, 1919, and was mustered out June 23, 1919.

Captain Hunter organized Paris Post No. 211 of the American Legion, was elected its first post commander and he also organized and was the first president of the Forty and Eight Society, a social branch of the American Legion. He is independent in politics, is a Catholic and has held all the offices in Paris Council No. 860 of the Knights of Columbus.

Captain Hunter married, November 28, 1917, at Houston, Texas, Miss Nell Timmons, daughter of John and Mary Timmons. They have four children: Mary Margaret, born January 15, 1919; Virginia Ann, born September 23, 1920; Jean and Joan, twins, born September 26, 1923.

ALBERT THOMPSON SCOVILL, educator and lecturer, is proprietor and manager of Brown's Business College at Sterling and Freeport. He has made a notable success of commercial education, and for many years has been one of the outstanding men in the community of Sterling.

He was born at Cleveland, Ohio, March 7, 1875. His grandfather, Stephen Thompson Scovill, was a native of Connecticut and during the '40s of the last century went West and settled in Lee County, Illinois. Homer W. Scovill, father of Albert T., was born in Oneida County, New York, and was three or four years old when the family moved to Northern Illinois. He grew up there, was educated for the ministry and was attracted to the oil fields of Pennsylvania in the early days. This industry brought him considerable financial success. Later he moved to Colorado, where he embarked his capital in the lumber business. Forest fires wiped out his business and his capital. At Chicago he had married Miss Mary Louise Fisk. She died in Colorado soon after the family had moved to that state, in about 1880. Homer W. Scovill after the loss of his wife and his lumber business never retrieved his former business energy and ambition. For several years he lived at Denver in a home presided over by his daughter. In later years he drifted from place to place, was in California for a time and finally returned to Sterling and lived with his son Albert T., until he died recently.

Albert Thompson Scovill spent his early years in Colorado. When he was about thirteen his aunt, Mrs. Thomas Leake, visited the family in Colorado and took him back to her home at Amboy, Lee County, Illinois. In the meantime he had been without school advantages and while at Denver earned part of his own living by selling newspapers and blacking boots. In the home of Mr. and Mrs. Leake at Amboy, Illinois, he attended public schools and at the age of seventeen graduated from the county graded schools. He continued his education in Steinman's Institute at Dixon, and had post-graduate training at Cedar Rapids, Iowa.

Mr. Scovill had three years of practical business experience as a stenographer and bookkeeper in Chicago. He then became head of the commercial department of the Northern Illinois College, and while there pursued work in the collegiate department, graduating in the scientific course. At that time he was offered a position by G. W. Brown, then proprietor of sixteen business colleges, the base college being at Jacksonville, Illinois. Mr. Scoville for three years was an instructor in the college at Galesburg and for two years at Lancaster, Pennsylvania. Following that he became principal of Brown's Business College at Sterling and in 1915 bought this institution, while in 1917 he acquired the Brown School at Freeport. These colleges he has brought to the first rank as institutions of business education.

Mr. Scovill in addition to his responsibilities in administering two successful schools, is a public accountant and handles business for an extensive clientele in that line. As a lecturer his platform subjects are of a philosophical nature and he has entertained many audiences with his lectures under titles of "Tin Cans," "Bumps," "Making Faces" and "Fifteen Steps in the Stairway to Success." For many years he was an active anti-saloon league worker. As a candidate on the dry ticket he was defeated by a very narrow margin for mayor of Sterling. In national politics he is a republican, is a member of the Methodist Church, a Master Mason and Elk and is a member of several fraternal insurance orders, including the Mystic Workers of the World. Mr. Scovill in his home community has been honored with the office of president of the Sterling Chamber of Commerce.

He married in 1901 Miss Josephine Waters, of Dixon. They have five children: Harold H., Myron M., Wilford W., Lois E. and Evaline L.

DAVID O. THOMPSON, president of Homestead Films, Incorporated, former executive secretary of the Illinois Agricultural Association, is a man to whose broad vision and tireless energy is due much of the improvement among the agriculturists of Illinois, if not of the country, for the improvements he has been able to effect in this state are being adopted by others in different localities, and in his new undertaking he is but carrying on, in a different way, the work he began when he aided in building up and financing his former association. He was born at East Troy, Wisconsin, in 1881, a son of Orrin D. and Carrie (Funk) Thompson, both of New England ancestry.

Going to the University of Wisconsin, Mr. Thompson specialized in agricultural science, and was graduated therefrom in 1905. Following his graduation he spent two or three years, under state auspices, in the cut-over timber regions of Wisconsin, instructing farmers in the use and development of the cut-over lands. Taking up as a specialized study animal husbandry at Purdue University, Indiana, he spent two years at that institution, and then, in 1915, came to Illinois as farm advisor for the McLean County Farm Bureau at Bloomington, which position he retained until 1919.

It was while there that Mr. Thompson became embued with the idea of a state association of agriculturists, and a meeting was held in 1917 to take initial steps looking toward such an organization. However, it was not until 1918 that this association was perfected, and it now is a highly organized concern, which handles the various problems of production, marketing, transportation, taxation, legislation and similar phases of agricultural life. The success of this association today is largely due to the energy and skilful management of Mr. Thompson, who particularly emphasized to the farmers of Illinois the essential necessity of having plenty of money to carry on the work of the association, and he succeeded in so financiering its affairs that it was placed on a solid moneyed foundation with present resources of nearly $500,000.

When Mr. Thompson had completed the initial work of organization and financiering of the Illinois Agricultural Association his active mind turned in another direction, and he resigned from the office of executive secretary to become president of Homestead Films, Incorporated, which he brought into existence. This corporation produces educational films on agricultural and industrial subjects, much of the product being distributed to and exhibited by farm bureaus, so that in this work he is but continuing his campaign of education begun in his former organization work, now one of the powerful factors in the agricultural industry of the state.

Mr. Thompson married Cellah Waterhouse, a native of Chicago, and they have three children: Kathleen, Dorothy and David. The family home is at Wheaton, DuPage County, Illinois.

DONALD FRASER MCPHERSON has practiced law at Chicago since 1909. Occupying a strong position in his profession, he has attended to many patriotic and civic interests outside, particularly in his home community of Winnetka, where he is a member of the Village Council.

He was born at Buffalo, New York, August 26, 1884, son of Donald Fraser and Mary Adelaide (Gowens) McPherson. Several years of his boyhood were spent at Lausanne, Switzerland, where he attended a private school. He was a student in the Lawrenceville Preparatory School in New Jersey, graduated A. B. from Princeton University in 1906 and received his Master of Arts degree from the same institution in 1909. He attended the Harvard Law School and in 1908 entered the law firm of Holt, Wheeler & Sidley at Chicago as a clerk, at the same time carrying on his studies in the Northwestern University Law School, from which he was graduated LL. B. in 1909, being admitted to the Illinois bar the same year. Mr. McPherson since 1913 has been a member of the well known Chicago law firm of Cutting, Moore & Sidley at 11 South LaSalle Street.

During the World war his chief service was rendered as purchasing agent on the staff of General Dawes. He went to France on this duty in December, 1917, remaining in Europe until February, 1919. While overseas he acted as purchasing agent for Switzerland and also for England.

Mr. McPherson is a member of the Chicago Bar Associaton, is a republican and a Presbyterian and a member of the following clubs:

Chicago, Attic, Law, Caxton, University, Princeton, Harvard, Indian Hill Country. His recreations are golf, riding and fishing.

His home is in Pine Lane at Winnetka. For several years he has been a member of the Council Organization, and is chairman of its committee on judiciary. He has been closely identified with the organized activities and undertakings that have made this suburban community one of the most distinctive in the country in the accumulation of institutions and facilities that most thoroughly express the ideals of a model community. The completion early in 1926 of the new Village Hall, one of the finest anywhere, called further attention to the enterprise and public spirit of the citizens of Winnetka.

Mr. McPherson married Miss Frances Ogden West, of Chicago, on January 15, 1913. They have one daughter, Frances Ogden.

ALEX CARLTON JOHNSON. A railroad man since early youth, Alex Carlton Johnson first entered the service of the Chicago and Northwestern Railway Company forty years ago. For thirty years his official connection with that great system of transportation has been continuous. He is regarded as a master mind in traffic organization and administration. Mr. Johnson has had a steady promotion to increased responsibilities, and for several years has been vice-president in charge of traffic for the Chicago and Northwestern Railway Company, and is also vice-president of the Chicago, St. Paul, Minneapolis and Omaha Railway.

He was born in Crawford County in western Pennsylvania, May 20, 1861, son of Abraham Carlton and Clara (Sigler) Johnson. His parents were natives of Pennsylvania and his father died at the age of eighty-eight and his mother, at fifty.

Alex Carlton Johnson, the oldest of three children, was educated in public schools and Meadville College, and was a young man of twenty-three when, in 1884, he began his service with the Chicago and Northwestern Railway. After that followed an interval with other lines and service, but in 1894 he returned to the Chicago and Northwestern as special agent, and since then has had a steady promotion. In 1899 he was made general agent for South Dakota; in 1900, general agent for Minnesota and South Dakota, in 1905, general freight and passenger agent of the P. R. C. and N. W. Railway; in 1910 was promoted to passenger traffic manager and in 1916 to general traffic manager for the Chicago and Northwestern Railway Company. When the railways were taken over by the United States Railroad administration, in 1918, Mr. Johnson was assigned duty as chairman of the Western Freight Traffic Committee, acting as such until 1920, and during the same period was assistant traffic manager and traffic manager for the Chicago and Northwestern Lines. On April 1, 1920, he resumed his former post as general traffic manager, and on January 1, 1921, was given the office of vice-president in charge of traffic. Since June 16, 1924, he has been vice-president in charge of traffic for the Chicago, St. Paul, Minneapolis and Omaha Railway.

Mr. Johnson is well known in Chicago fraternal and social circles, being a member of the Union League Club, Traffic Club, Rotary Club and is a Knights Templar and thirty-second degree Scottish Rite Mason and Shriner and Elk.

He married in 1888 Miss Ida R. Devare, who is likewise a native of Crawford County, Pennsylvania. Their three children are: Eveline, wife of J. G. McFarland and the mother of two sons; Alda, wife of C. H. McNie, and they have two children; and Carlton D., who married Marion Finarud.

GRANT HOLMES is president of Robert Holmes & Brothers, one of the old established business concerns of the City of Danville, in existence fully forty years. The company handles hardware, operates foundry and machine shops, and the executives of the business from the beginning have been practical machinists and foundrymen.

Grant Holmes was born at Galion, Ohio, December 26, 1865. His father, William Henry Holmes, was born at Lawrence, Massachusetts, in 1837, was reared in that state and in New Jersey, and was married at Mount Vernon, Ohio. A machinist, he was employed at Mount Vernon by the C. & G. Cooper Company, but soon after his marriage removed to Sandusky, where he followed his trade. In 1864 he located at Galion, where he established an iron works, foundry and machine shop. This plant subsequently he removed to Marion, Ohio, and developed an extensive business. These works founded by William Henry Holmes are now owned by the Huber Manufacturing Company, which has an international reputation for its machinery products. William Henry Holmes was a republican in politics. He died at Marion in 1872. His wife, Rebecca Thomas, was born at Carnarvon, Wales, and died at Marion. They had a family of nine children: Robert, founder and former president of Robert Holmes & Brothers at Danville, where he died May 18, 1918; Mary Ellen, wife of Dr. William Snavely, a physician and surgeon at Tampa, Florida; Mattie, who died at Thonotassassa, Florida, in 1921, wife of John A. Johnson, an orange grower in that section of Florida; William H., a machinist who died in Colorado; Laura, who died when nineteen years old; Mrs. Hattie Bradley, of Los Angeles, Mr. Bradley being a carpenter; Sherman, who is vice president of Robert Holmes & Brothers at Danville; while the ninth and youngest child, a son, died in infancy.

Grant Holmes was about seven years of age when his father died. He grew up at Marion, and his education in public schools there terminated at the age of thirteen. He went to work in the Huber Shops, serving his apprenticeship as a machinist, and subsequently was with the Marion Steam Shovel Company, in which service he was promoted from machinist to assistant superintendent of the plant.

Mr. Holmes in 1893 removed to Danville, where he joined the firm of Robert Holmes & Brothers, a business that had been founded by his brother Robert about 1885. Robert Holmes & Brothers own and conduct a flourishing hardware business at 26-28 North Hazel Street, and they also operate a foundry and machine shop at 520 Junction Avenue, owning all the land and building and plant facilities at both locations. The firm formerly operated the Holmes Garage Company, but sold that business in 1909.

Mr. Grant Holmes succeeded to the presidency of the firm in 1918 after the death of his brother. He is vice president of the Vermilion County Building & Loan Association and has interests in coal operations in Ohio. He is a republican, a member of the Episcopal Church at Danville, Olive Branch Lodge No. 38, A. F. and A. M., and Danville Consistory of the Scottish Rite. He also belongs to Danville Lodge No. 332, B. P. O. Elks, and is a director of the Chamber of Commerce. He did his full part as a citizen in promoting the success of the various drives during the World war.

His home is at 215 West North Street in Danville. Mr. Holmes married at Marion, Ohio, September 20, 1893, Miss Jessie Henrietta Porter, daughter of Mr. and Mrs. Henry Porter, now deceased. Her father was a dyer by trade. The only child of Mr. and Mrs. Holmes is John K., now connected with the engineering department of the Marion Steam Shovel Company at Marion, Ohio. He is a veteran of the World war, having been in the service two years. For a little more than a year he was stationed at Camp Custer at Battle Creek, Michigan, and in July, 1918, went overseas to France with the Three Hundred and Tenth Signal Corps. He was all through the St. Mihiel campaign, went into Germany with the Army of Occupation and while there attended a special school for about three months at Mayence. He received his honorable discharge in May, 1919.

EDWARD J. HUGHES. In the effort toward solving Chicago's modern traction and transportation problems probably no one has supplied more practical data and rendered greater intelligent support through the Legislature than State Senator Edward J. Hughes of Chicago. Mr. Hughes is a native of Chicago, was trained for the law, but for a number of years has been well known as an engineer and contractor specializing in underground construction, and is associated with Nash Brothers.

He was born in Chicago in 1888. Both his parents were natives of Ireland, and they came to Chicago from New York in 1871. Edward J. Hughes was educated in public schools, attended the Lincoln College of Law, but turned away from the law as a profession to take up construction work. His experience has brought him an exceptional reputation as an authority on underground construction for municipalities and public service corporations. Nash Brothers, contractors and engineers at Chicago, with whom he is connected, has handled the technical problems of many difficult contracts and projects in Chicago and all over the middle west.

Mr. Hughes was elected a member of the Illinois State Senate in 1914, representing the Twenty-first Senatorial District. He was born and reared and has resided in that district all his life. He has continued to represent the district in the Senate successively now for a dozen years. He is a democrat in politics. Important committees of the Senate of which he is a member include canal and waterways, corporations and industrial affairs, harbors, highway transportation, boulevards, public utilities, mines and mining, highways and bridges, state university and normal schools, education, criminal procedure, judiciary, judicial department and practice.

Throughout his legislative record he has specialized in all problems in traffic and transportation brought to the Legislature largely from their point of origin in Chicago. During the 1925 session of the General Assembly he was appointed a member of the Commission, composed of members of both Senate and House of Representatives, including the Lieutenant Governor, to investigate the workability of the terminal permit scheme as relating to the operation of public utilities in Illinois. Mr. Hughes was one of five members of this Commission, including Lieutenant Governor Sterling, who in the summer of 1925, at their own expense, made a tour of British and Continental Europe cities for the purpose of studying the operation of public utilities. This journey, though partly for pleasure, resulted in the gathering of a mass of data of real and tangible value to Chicago and Illinois in the solution of some of the most critical problems now before the public.

Senator Hughes married Miss Winifred Ronayne, of Chicago. They have one daughter, Mary Elizabeth.

JOSEPH GRANT KILGORE, M. D. The Kilgore family has been identified with Edgar County for nearly a century. Joseph Kilgore has long sustained a reputation as an able medical practitioner in Vermilion, and he has a son following the same calling there.

Joseph Grant Kilgore was born in Edgar County, January 26, 1866, son of Joseph and Mary (Meadows) Kilgore. His father came from Kentucky in 1831 and his mother in 1832, and they spent the rest of their lives in Edgar County.

Dr. Joseph G. Kilgore was educated in common schools, and pursued a course in the Literary Department of DePauw University and in the Kentucky School of Medicine at Louisville, where he completed his course and was graduated M. D. in 1888. For over thirty-five years now he has performed all the duties of a general country physician and surgeon, with home at Vermilion.

Besides the work of his profession he served two terms as township supervisor, as mayor of Vermilion, was on the Edgar County Pension Examining Board from 1896 to 1912, and is affiliated with the republican party. He belongs to the Independent Order of Odd Fellows and the Modern Woodmen of America.

Doctor Kilgore married at Vermilion, April 4, 1889, Lulu McCloud, daughter of Dr. W. H. H. and Helen McCloud, of Vermilion. Dr. Floyd Vernon Kilgore, only child of Doctor Kilgore and wife, was born January 27, 1890. He was educated in DePauw University, where he graduated in 1912, and attended Rush Medical College and Northwestern Medical College at Chicago, where he graduated in 1916. He

then completed a course in the Army Medical School in Washington, D. C., in February, 1918, and received a commission in the regular army as first lieutenant. He still remains in the service as captain in the Medical Corps of the United States Army. For three years he was engaged in a base hospital at Honolulu and is now located in Walter Reed Hospital, Washington, D. C. He enlisted in the Medical Reserve Corps in 1917, serving at Camp Taylor and at other base hospitals during the World war period.

COLONEL NATHANIEL LAMSON HOWARD in his forty-second year, and eighteen years after he had begun railroading, was made president of the Chicago Great Western Railroad. It was claimed at the time that he was the youngest president of a Class 1 railroad in the United States.

Colonel Howard, who gained his military title by distinguished service with the Railway Engineers in France, was born at Fairfield, Iowa, March 9, 1884, son of Elmer Addison and Mary (Lamson) Howard. His father was also a prominent railroad official. Both parents were natives of Fairfield, Iowa, the father born in 1858 and the mother in 1861. Elmer Addison Howard, who died in 1921, had been for several years a vice president of the Chicago, Burlington & Quincy Railway. The widowed mother is still living and there are three children, Nathaniel L., Hubert Elmer and Eugene Addison.

Nathaniel L. Howard was thoroughly educated, being graduated from the United States Military Academy at West Point in 1907. Instead of remaining in the army he at once became a civil engineer with the Chicago, Burlington & Quincy Railroad, and spent eighteen years with that system. He was successively trainmaster, assistant superintendent and division superintendent. From May, 1917, to May, 1919, he was in the army. He returned to civil life as assistant to the Federal manager of the Chicago, Burlington & Quincy, and in November, 1919, was made general superintendent of the Missouri district at St. Louis. In July, 1923, he became superintendent of transportation, with headquarters at Chicago. In June, 1924, he was appointed general manager of the Chicago Union Station Company, and resigned that position in 1925 to succeed Mr. Felton as president of the Chicago Great Western Railroad.

On account of his training at West Point and his qualifications as a railroad man Colonel Howard was in a position to render important service to the American government at the very outset of the World war. In May, 1917, he was commissioned lieutenant colonel and assisted in organizing the Thirteenth Regiment of Railway Engineers, which was the first regiment to go overseas from Illinois. This outfit went overseas in July, 1917, and from August, 1917, until the spring of 1918 Colonel Howard was on duty with the Director General of Transportation in France. Later he took personal command of the Thirteenth Railway Engineers, and in July, 1918, was promoted to the rank of colonel. For his military service he was awarded the Croix de Guerre and the French Legion of Honor.

Colonel Howard married in June, 1915, Miss Marie Blaul. He is a member of the Masonic fraternity, Knights Templar and A. A. O. N. M. S., also of the Chicago Athletic Club, Indian Hill and Sunset Country Clubs.

HARRY BOYD HURD, Chicago attorney, at 231 South LaSalle Street, has practiced law thirty years, and the line of work most congenial to his talents and in which he has achieved special success has been in the law affecting corporations and public utilities.

Mr. Hurd was born in Livingston County, Missouri, January 8, 1875, son of Inscoe E. and Harriet Jane (Andrew) Hurd. He was only two years of age when his father died in 1877. His mother, who was a native of Ohio, lived until 1911. Harry Boyd was the oldest of three children. He has a brother, H. Clark, and a sister, Lena, the wife of C. Theodore Boroughs.

Harry Boyd Hurd graduated from the high school at Muscatine, Iowa, at the age of sixteen and soon afterward came to Chicago. He learned stenography and typewriting, and while employed in clerical work attended night classes of the Chicago College of Law. He was graduated in 1895, at the age of twenty, and in January, 1897, was admitted to the Illinois bar. He has been continuously engaged in practice since that date. He is a member of the Chicago, Illinois State and American Bar Associations, belongs to the Chicago Athletic Club, Mid-Day Club, Evanston Golf Club, Bobolink Golf Club, and is a republican in politics.

He married, December 25, 1902, Miss Margaret Julia Frank, a native of Sterling, Illinois. They have three children, Harriet Margaret, Anna Catherine and Harry Boyd, Jr.

HILMAR C. LINDAUER. A man of personal worth and of professional prominence in St. Clair County is Hilmar C. Lindauer, of Belleville, state's attorney, who has many notable achievements to his credit since assuming the duties of this responsibile office. Mr. Lindauer is a native of this county and comes of old pioneer stock that settled in Illinois some seventy-five years ago.

Hilmar C. Lindauer was born at New Athens, St. Clair County, Illinois, March 15, 1888, son of Charles and Minnie (Horn) Lindauer, the latter of whom died March 17, 1917. Her father, Christian Horn, was a native of Germany and came to the United States about 1850, established his home in St. Clair County, Illinois, where he became a substantial farmer and respected citizen. The mother of Mr. Lindauer was born in St. Clair County. Charles Lindauer was born in Germany and was four years old when his parents brought him to the United States and settled as farming people in St. Clair County, Illinois. He has always followed agricultural pursuits and still lives on his farm near New Athens. To his marriage with Minine Horn six children were born: Eleanor, who is the wife of John Mooles, and they have one child, Minora; Edmund, who married Miss Wilberger, and they have one child, Wilbur; Richard, who married Barbara Hohm, and died in 1914; Hilmar C.; Walter, who married Elsie Wolf, and they have one child, Ethel; and Curt, who married Louise Brinkman, and is an assistant in the state's attorney's office.

Hilmar C. Lindauer spent his boyhood on the home farm and attended the public schools. Later he became a student in the Central Wesleyan College at Warrenton, Missouri, and subsequently taught school in St. Clair County for three years. Having early decided upon the law as a career, as soon as the time seemed propitious he entered the University of St. Louis, Missouri, where he completed his law course with credit and was graduated in 1913. In the fall of that year he entered into a general practice of law at Belleville, where he soon found recognition and by 1916 had built up a very satisfactory practice. In December of that year he was appointed assistant state's attorney under State's Attorney Hubert Shaumleffel, where he continued until the death of his chief in March, 1922. In April, 1922, Mr. Lindauer was elected to fill the vacancy, which he did with such complete efficiency that in November, 1924, he was re-elected state's attorney of St. Clair County, the second largest county in Illinois. Under Mr. Lindauer the work of his office has benefited St. Clair County greatly, and his honest, fearless administration has but added to the respect and confidence that he has long enjoyed from his fellow citizens generally.

Mr. Lindauer married, July 2, 1917, at Ruma, Randolph County, Illinois, Miss Mae Boul, daughter of Arthur and Elizabeth (Kurtz) Boul. Her father, a retired farmer, died in 1914. Mrs. Lindauer's brothers and sisters were: Jerome, now deceased, survived by widow and six children; Adolph; Forene, who is the wife of Frank Fleshren, and they have four children; Estelle, who is the wife of Herman Bartel, and they have four children; Luella, who is the wife of Albert Eisenhaver, and they have one child; and Lillian, who is an accomplished young lady and the competent stenographer of the state's attorney. Mr. and Mrs. Lindauer have one son, Richard, now six years old, and one daughter, Jean, now six months old. The state's attorney finds little leisure time at his disposal so that his recreations are somewhat limited, but in the Knights of Pythias, Elks and Moose lodges he finds congenial companionship and is a past chancellor of the order of Knights of Pythias. He is a valued member also of the Illinois State and the St. Clair County Bar Associations.

CHARLES E. HAMILTON is president of the Hamilton-Hoffman Construction Company of Carbondale. He organized this company in July, 1924. He is president of the company, with Mr. Hoffman, vice president, and his son, Ralph E. Hamilton, secretary and treasurer.

The company has the capital and the equipment for handling the largest class of contracts in general construction. Their operations have extended over Missouri, Illinois, Kentucky and Tennessee. The company has handled the $374,000 contract for the building of the new water works system of Carbondale. During the year 1924 this company built twenty-five miles of concrete road in Illinois and Missouri.

The personnel of the company comprises several men of exceptional qualifications for engineering and construction service. Mr. Hoffman has had extended experience, having for several years been connected with the Illinois Traction Company, and also superintendent of the Terminal at Springfield. Ralph Hamilton attended public schools in Carbondale and the Normal University, and has had actual experience in construction work. Another member of the staff is Charles H. Gibbs, a graduate engineer from the University of Illinois. George Lee, superintendent of field work for the company, is a practical civil engineer of several years' experience.

Charles E. Hamilton, the president of the company, was born in Jefferson County, Illinois, March 6, 1873, son of William J. and Catherine (Garner) Hamilton, farmers. He was reared on a farm, and attended public schools and the Southern Illinois Normal University at Carbondale. For three years he studied law in private offices, attended the Illinois College of Law, and in 1901 was admitted to the bar. Mr. Hamilton practiced for several years at Carbondale, but during the past twenty years his time and talents have been quite fully taken up with his varied enterprises in the public utility field. In 1908 he helped organize the Citizens Water, Light & Power Company of Carbondale, becoming its vice president and general manager. He also established the Hamilton Utility Company at Benton, supplying water, light and ice to Benton and Franklin counties.

Mr. Hamilton is a democrat. He has served as president of the Carbondale School Board, is a member of the Independent Order of Odd Fellows, Modern Woodmen of America, and the Methodist Church. He married, July 28, 1894, Miss Dora Hayes, daughter of Richard L. Hayes. The five children born to their marriage were Ralph E., Lola, Catherine Jewell, Charles Morrison and Helen.

MAURITZ P. NORDELL. The career of Mauritz P. Nordell, one of the successful younger element in Rockford's thriving manufacturing circles, has been characterized by steady and energetic adherence to the development of his abilities, so that at the age of thirty-three years he finds himself in the responsible position of superintendent of the Rockford Drop Forge Company, a concern doing a business of $1,000,000 annually. His success has been all the more remarkable in that it has been self-gained, for he began to be at least partly self supporting when still a lad of tender years, and has earned his advancement by hard and conscientious work.

Mr. Nordell was born at Rockford, July 19, 1892, and is a son of Frank A. and Ellen (Carlson) Nordell, natives of Sweden. His father, who had learned the trade of tailor in his native land, immigrated to the United States in young manhood, eventually taking up his residence at Rockford, where for many years he has conducted a tailoring establishment. He is one of the highly respected citizens of his adopted community and a man of public spirit and reliability. Mr. and Mrs. Nordell are the parents of five children: Mauritz P., of this review; Ruth, who is deceased; Ethel, Alvin and Eleanor, all of Rockford.

The parents are faithful members of the Swedish Mission Church of Rockford.

During the boyhood of Mauritz P. Nordell the family finances were not excessive and accordingly the lad before and after school hours conducted a regular daily newspaper route. This he continued until he was fifteen years old, when he was seized with a desire to learn the trade of machinist, although for two years he continued his education in high school. He learned his trade with the Rockford Drilling Machine Company, but left Rockford to accept employment in a large automobile plant at Detroit. This position did not suit him, however, and within a short time he was back in Rockford, where he entered the service of the National Lock Company, where he remained five years and had charge of the tool department. In 1915 he transferred his services to the Rockford Drop Forge Company, and after spending one and one-half years at the bench was made assistant foreman of the die room. Further advancement marked recognition of his fidelity and ability when, in 1919, he was put in charge of the die room, and in 1924 he was honored by his promotion to the position of superintendent of the entire works. This is a nationally known concern, its product being distributed throughout the United States, with an annual business of $1,000,000. The superintendency of such a plant is a position of decided responsibility, but Mr. Nordell has been capable of handling affairs in every emergency and bears the unqualified confidence of his superiors and the respect and good will of the men under his charge.

On June 14, 1918, Mr. Nordell was united in marriage with Miss Ruth Cedarleaf, a native of Chicago, and to this union there has been born one daughter: Muriel Edith. Mr. and Mrs. Nordell are members of the Swedish Mission Church. In his political sentiment he is a republican.

RAYMOND WALTER BEACH and his brother, Elmer Ellsworth Beach, have been associated in the law firm of Beach & Beach at Chicago for thirty-seven years. Of the hundreds of law firms in Chicago it is doubtful if any has continued without change in title or in essential membership through so many years.

Raymond Walter Beach was born at Percival, Iowa, November 29, 1863, son of Henry Walter and Eva (Canfield) Beach. His father was a native of New York state and his mother, of Vermont, and the father died at the age of seventy-five and the mother at seventy-six. There were five children, four sons and one daughter. Three sons are still living. Besides the two lawyers the other surviving brother is the distinguished author Rex Beach, one of the supreme masters of story writing in America, author of a large number of "best sellers," including some that have been dramatized and most of them have been put on the screen.

The grandfather of these brothers was Artemus Beach, a miller, furniture manufacturer and farmer in New York State. He had a family of eleven children, the oldest son being Henry W. Beach, who after growing up and receiving his education in New York State, went west to Wisconsin and thence overland by wagon to the territory of Nebraska. He took up a homestead of 160 acres near Lincoln, put up a house and dug a well, but soon afterward was driven out by the Indians. He sold his homestead rights for an Indian pony and saddle and then moved into southwestern Iowa. His son, Elmer E., was born in Fremont County in that state, while Raymond W. was born two years later in the locality called Percival. The father was a pioneer in the saw milling industry there. He was also a staunch abolitionist, and largely through his agency Percival became one of the stations on the underground railroad. On account of the troubled conditions of that locality during the Civil war period he moved to Atwood on the mouth of Grand Traverse Bay in Michigan, where he engaged in farming and lumbering. Later he removed to Tampa, Florida, and his death occurred in Chicago. His wife, Eva Canfield, was a great-granddaughter of one of the Green Mountain boys who followed Ethan Allen in the capture of Fort Ticonderoga in the Revolutionary war.

Raymond Walter Beach acquired most of his early education at Grand Rapids, Michigan, graduating from high school in 1882. In 1886 he received the Bachelor of Science degree in civil engineering at the University of Michigan, and for several years worked as a railroad engineer, being with the engineering department of the Chicago, Milwaukee & St. Paul Railroad in the Dakotas, later with the Atchison, Topeka & Santa Fe Railway Company. He returned to the University of Michigan and took his law degree in 1889. In 1910 the Chicago Law School awarded him the degree J. D. Since 1889 Mr. Beach has been associated with his brother Elmer in practice at Chicago. His brother had located in Chicago a year before Raymond W. The principle field of work for this firm has been corporation and commercial law. Raymond W. Beach has been vice president of the Manufacturers Equipment Company and vice president and director of the Howard Avenue Trust & Savings Bank. He is a member of the Chicago, Illinois State and American Bar Associations and is a dean in the Chicago Law School.

Mr. Beach is a member of the Delta Upsilon law fraternity, the Phi Alpha Delta, the Masonic fraternity, Hamilton Club, is a past vice president of the Edgewater Golf Club, and a member of the Edgewater Athletic Club. His chief recreation is golf. He married, October 4, 1892, Miss Jennie C. Healy. They have one daughter, Ethel Corinne, wife of C. B. Beebe.

HERBERT J. CAMPBELL is a Chicago lawyer, member of one of the leading general law firms of that city. His father practiced law in Chicago with distinguished success up to the time of his death, and through his mother Mr. Campbell represents one of the pioneer families of northern Illinois.

He was born at Chicago, Illinois, December 9, 1880, son of William J. and Rebecca (McEldowney) Campbell. Both the Campbells and McEldowneys were Scotch, but they lived in the north of Ireland before coming to

America. The maternal grandfather, John McEldowney, came from the north of Ireland to the United States in 1833 and located in what is today Chicago Heights, being a pioneer farmer in that section. He and his wife were the first couple married in Will County, of which Joliet is the county seat. William J. Campbell, son of John and Mary Campbell, was born in Philadelphia, December 12, 1850, and was about one year old when his parents came to Illinois and settled at what is now Chicago Heights. He attended public schools and later the University of Pennsylvania, in the class of 1871, and graduated from the Union College of Law at Chicago in 1873. As an attorney he was associated in practice with W. C. Goudy, later was with Jacob R. Custer in the firm of Campbell & Custer, and for a time former governor Hamilton was associated with this firm. William J. Campbell for a number of years prior to his death was general counsel for Armour & Company, also a trustee of and one of the men most active in founding the Armour Institute of Technology. He served several terms in the Illinois State Senate and for a year was president of that body. For a long time he was the member for Illinois of the National Republican Committee. He belonged to the Chicago Club, the Union League Club, the Chicago Athletic Club, Lawyers Club of New York, and the Chicago, Illinois and American Bar Associations. He was a Presbyterian. William J. Campbell, who died March 4, 1896, married Rebecca McEldowney, who was born in Cook County, Illinois, October 8, 1851, and is still living. There were four sons and one daughter, Herbert J. being the third in age.

Herbert J. Campbell received a public school education at Riverside, Illinois; then entered Armour Institute of Technology, graduating in 1897, and in 1901 graduated from the literary department of the University of Michigan. He took his law course in the Northwestern University Law School at Chicago, was graduated in 1904, and since then for a period of twenty years has been one of the busy attorneys of the Chicago bar. He was associated with the law firm of Eddy, Haley & Wetten; later with Jeffery, Ott & Campbell, succeeded by Jeffery & Campbell, and then followed the firms of Jeffery, Campbell & Clark, and the present Townley Wild, Campbell & Clark. Their offices are at 105 South La Salle Street.

Mr. Campbell is a member of the Chicago, Illinois State and American Bar Associations, the University Club, the Chicago Literary Club; the Riverside Golf Club; the Racquet Club, the University Club of Washington; and is a member of the college fraternities Phi Kappa Psi and the Phi Delta Phi. He is a republican in politics. Mr. Campbell married Nancy P. Lambertson on October 6, 1921. She was born at Lincoln, Nebraska.

THURLOW G. ESSINGTON was born in and until recently was a resident of Streator, where he built up a large general law practice and where he enjoyed a number of public honors. Mr. Essington became one of the best known and most discussed citizens of Illinois in the gubernatorial campaign of 1924, when he was put forward by a group of independent republicans as candidate for the nomination for governor. Mr. Essington is now a resident of Chicago and is practising law in that city.

He was born at Streator, May 19, 1886, son of John and Mary (Gault) Essington. His father was born in DuPage County, Illinois, December 10, 1855, and his mother, on Staten Island, New York, March 27, 1857. They were married at Odell, Illinois, July 2, 1885. John Essington was a farmer, teacher, then became a lawyer and for a time was editor of a paper at Pontiac. He practiced law at Streator from 1881 until 1892, and after that was engaged in the real estate business until his death on September 29, 1912.

Thurlow Gault Essington attended the city schools and the township high school at Streator, graduated A. B. from the University of Illinois in 1906, and completed his law course at the University of Chicago, where he was graduated J. D. Cum Laude in 1908. Mr. Essington established his reputation as a very able attorney and built up a large law practice at Streator before his name was known beyond his local community in politics. He continued to practice in that city until March, 1926, when he removed to Chicago and formed the partnership of Essington & McKibbin, his associate being George B. McKibbin, formerly of the firm of Good, Childs, Bobb & Wescott. They have their law offices at 231 South La-Salle Street.

Mr. Essington served as city attorney of Streator from 1915 to 1917, and was mayor of the city from 1917 to 1919, during the period of the World war. In 1918 he was elected a member of the State Senate and was re-elected in 1922. Mr. Essington by his scholarship earned membership in the Phi Beta Kappa and was also a member of the social fraternity Delta Kappa Epsilon and the law fraternity Phi Delta Phi. He is a member of the University Club, Hamilton Club and Union League Club of Chicago, is a Royal Arch and Knight Templar Mason at Streator, member of the Bloomington Consistory of the Scottish Rite, Mohammed Temple of the Mystic Shrine, and held membership in various clubs and civic organizations at Streator. He married, February 16, 1913, Miss Davie Hendricks, at Madisonville, Kentucky. They have one daughter, Elizabeth. Mr. and Mrs. Essington reside on East Fifty-Sixth Street in Chicago.

HENRY RUSSELL PLATT, who came to Chicago in 1891, is a member of one of the largest law firms in the middle west, that of Mayer, Meyer, Austrian & Platt, the head of which for many years was the late Levy Mayer.

Mr. Platt was born at Plattsburg, New York, March 4, 1866, son of Theodorus and Marietta S. (Nichols) Platt. His father was born at Plattsburg, New York, in 1811, and died in 1887, while his mother was born at Vergennes, Vermont, in 1818, and died in 1895. Henry R. was the youngest of a large family of three daughters and eight sons, only two of whom are now living. His father was a farmer and business man, was a whig in politics and later a democrat.

FLETCHER LADD McCORDIC

Henry Russell Platt graduated from high school in 1883, and in 1887 took his A. B. degree at Williams College. He studied law with Judge George E. Lawrence at Rutland, Vermont, was admitted to the bar there, and about a year later came to Chicago and was admitted to the Illinois bar in 1891. For about three years he practiced with Judge Isham, then a member of the firm Stein & Platt for ten years, was alone in practice for three years, then practiced with the firm of Musgrave, Platt & Lee, and from that joined the organization of Mayer, Meyer, Austrian & Platt. Individually or through his firm he has been connected with many large interests. He is counsel for the Leiter estate. He also acted as counsel in the merger of the Armour and Morris packing interests in 1923. He is a director of Albert Pick & Company and several other corporations. Mr. Platt is a member of the Chicago, Illinois State and American Bar Associations, the Chicgo Bar Institute, and is a member of the Union League, University and Glenview Country Clubs, the Mid-day Club and Law Club.

He married, August 27, 1895, Miss Helen Sherwood Kyle, a native of Vergennes, Vermont. They have three children, Theodora, Henry Russell, Jr., and Sherwood Kellog.

FLETCHER LADD MCCORDIC, first lieutenant, Eighty-eighth Aero Squadron, American Expeditionary Forces, was an Illinois boy, a resident of Winnetka, son of a Chicago attorney. When a mere boy he saw as in a vision the possibility of the control of the air and the great uses to which this control might be put. He saw the vision in the workshop and the camp; he followed it upon the field of battle; it dominated all his thoughts. He loved it with a boyish love, pure, single and serene. He never had the pain as a man of seeing this vision "fade into the light of common day." But on the contrary he saw it prevail in a great cause and gave his meed of effort that it might prevail. He died in its hour of triumph, realizing that his belief in it had been justified. This was his reward.

He was born December 1, 1891, son of Alfred E. and Jane Augusta (Ladd) McCordic, his father of Scotch and his mother of Colonial English ancestry. His father was born in Canada, graduated from the Harvard Law School, and directly after his marriage engaged in practice at Duluth, Minnesota, where his son Fletcher was born. In 1896 the family established their home at Winnetka, and since then Alfred E. McCordic has been practicing law in Chicago. Fletcher Ladd McCordic attended the public schools of Winnetka, the College School of Kenilworth and the Chicago Latin School. He early developed mechanical taste and had a home shop where he reveled in electrical and mechanical contrivances. He also had a great love of sport and outdoor life, but especially enjoyed those sports involving the exercise of mechanical skill. He was physically well made and especially strong in his back and arms, and was fond of rowing, camping and motoring. When very young he had interested himself in making "gliders" and toy planes. A serious trouble of the eyes interrupted his plans to enter college, but he devoted his leisure to mechanical pursuits. As his eyesight improved he attended Lewis Institute at Chicago for a number of terms, and had a rather extensive apprenticeship, working in a freight car factory, with the General Electric Company in Massachusetts and in an automobile school at Detroit. He finally bore down his parents' opposition to take up aviation, and in the fall of 1916 entered the Wright Flying School at Hempstead, Long Island, where he was graduated and received a pilot's license from the Aero Club of America. On the establishment of the Aviation Officers' Reserve Corps camps in January, 1917, he enlisted, being given the rank of sergeant. He was in the training camp at Memphis until June, then was assigned to Chicago, and in July to Chanute Field. Early in September he was sent to Kelly Field in San Antonio, Texas, and after two weeks was ordered to Minneola, Long Island. He sailed for overseas October 27, 1917, and on November 20 reached Issoudun, the first great training field in France for the American air forces. Here he went through that rigorous and intensive training required of air pilots. While he was distinguished by a remarkable concentration on the technical branches of his work, he also steadily won the respect and esteem of his associates. In the words of his biographer: "He combined a peculiar reserve of manner and reticence of speech with a gravity of countenance that seldom betrayed his thoughts. His willingness to accept responsibility and in turn his resolve to exact obedience recall his bob-sled days. He claimed as pilot entire direction of the machine. He accepted from his observer no suggestions and listened to no complaints. On the other hand, while always willing to assist, Fletcher left the observer's special task entirely to him. It was only as time went on that his comrades discovered the boyish good-nature that went with these deeper traits. While leader of a training squad at Issoudun because of his grave demeanor he was nicknamed "General" (usually abbreviated to "Gen.") which clung to him throughout the war."

After nearly three months of training and service at Issoudun, McCordic was assigned to the Eighty-eighth Aero Squadron, Maj. H. B. Anderson commanding. The Eighty-eighth Squadron was what is now known as a "Corps Observation Squadron." It belonged to that part of the air service that has given to the service as a whole the name "Eyes of the Army." The Squadron was the fifth American aero squadron to go to the front, the first having preceded it by only a short time. It was engaged in each of the great offensives in which the American troops shared; it took part in the capture of the St. Mihiel salient which was virtually the achievement of the Americans alone; and was one of the seventeen squadrons serving at the front when the fighting ceased. It accompanied the American Army of Occupation into Germany.

Except for two weeks' sick leave, in August, 1918, Fletcher was with the squadron during the entire period of activity. During this time he suffered no serious mishap and was not interrupted even for a day in the discharge of his duties. Writing shortly after the armistice, Fletcher says: "I was in all the big drives—first at Chateau-Thierry, then at the Vesle, then when we moved to Souilly for the St. Mihiel drive and then at the Meuse." He remained with the Army of Occupation for several months and until his death.

Writing after his death his commanding officers said: "During the war there was no one more willing and capable to undertake any mission. No matter how hazardous the undertaking a smile would always come to his face when he was detailed on the patrol. He had next to high man in the squadron in flying time over the lines."

This brief sketch can do little justice to the detailed work and service rendered by Lieutenant McCordic. This work and service earned two citations. The third is as follows: "France, December 31, 1918. The Air Service Commander, First Army, cites for exceptional devotion to duty: First Lieutenant Fletcher L. McCordic, A. S. U. S. A., pilot, 88th Aero Squadron served with never failing loyalty and spirit since February, 1918. By his ability and initiative, he contributed greatly to the success of the squadron. By Order of Colonel Milling."

The second was based on one day's duty. October 23, 1918, he was serving as "protection," helping to guard another plane engaged in taking photographs over the lines. In the battle that followed he brought down two of the hostile planes. The citation giving recognition to this day's work was not awarded for more than a month after McCordic's death.

"First Lieutenant Fletcher L. McCordic, A. S. Pilot, 88th Aero Sqdn. for Distinguished and Exceptional Gallantry at Aincreville, France, on 23 Oct. 1918, in the operations of the American Expeditionary Forces. In testimony thereof, and as an expression of appreciation of his valor, I award him this Citation

JOHN J. PERSHING,
Commander-in-Chief."

Awarded on 27 March 1919.

Fletcher McCordic was so engrossed in his work and so loved the wonderful art of flying that he was careless of honors except as they were real opportunities for better service. He declined the post of commanding officer of another squadron. In January, 1919, he was made flight commander of the Eighty-eighth, and was serving as such when he died.

An official account of the last scene in the career of this brilliant Illinois airman is contained in a special report made by Maj. Howard C. Davidson, A. S., U. S. A.: "Lieut. Fletcher L. McCordic took off from the airdrome at Treves, Germany, at 13:40 H. on March 1, 1919, flying a Fokker D VII with two hours fuel. He stunted over the field for about fifteen minutes, showing perfect control of the plane, and then flew north over Treves, disappearing in the direction of Coblenz. The motor seemed to be turning up regularly. At 14:15 he was seen flying low over a forest just east of Waldweiler. His motor was turning up very irregularly and he was evidently trying to glide to an open space north of the woods. Seeing that he did not have enough altitude for that he banked up to turn to a little clearing of stumps on the left. It is impossible to tell from the account of a German that saw it whether it side-slipped and fell on this turn or went into a spin, at any rate he was just above the woods when he banked. He fell very near to where he made the turn and investigation shows that his fall was almost vertical. The left lower wing was torn off on a tree. As the motor hit the ground the fuselage swung around and hit a large tree, Lieut. McCordic's head being caught between the tree and the machine guns as the cockpit crumpled. His skull was fractured and face very badly bruised. A German got there in a few minutes and Lieut. McCordic was unconscious but still alive. He died in a few minutes. He was buried from Base Hospital No. 19 on March 3rd, 1919, in the American section of the Trier cemetery.

"Lieut. McCordic was assigned to the 88th Squadron on February 22, 1918, at Amanty, France, being one of the fifteen original pilots to go with the Squadron. He went to the front on May 28, 1918, Station Ourches (Toul Sector); from there he moved with the Squadron to the Chateau-Thierry sector, Stations at Francheville, France, Ferme de Greves, Goussaincourt, from July 6 to September 12. He took part in the St. Mihiel and the entire Meuse-Argonne offensives with stations at Souilly and Bethelainville from Sept. 12 to Nov. 11th. On December 5th he moved with the Squadron to the Army of Occupation.

"Lieut. McCordic was, without question, one of our best and most daring pilots. He has had over a hundred hours over the enemy lines, has been engaged in several air battles and has always shown the greatest skill and liking for the work.

"The above is a very complete record of the accident of Lieut. McCordic. He was one of the best flyers in the Squadron, and no one can tell just what happened to him to make him fall."

After resting more than a year on the banks of the Moselle his body was brought home and on November 6, 1920, in the presence of the Winnetka Post of the American Legion, was laid to rest in Graceland Cemetery at Chicago.

In conclusion should be quoted a few sentences from a letter written by Maj. K. P. Littauer, who was one of the commanding officers of the Eighty-eighth: "I want to add my own tribute to the memory of the best beloved officer of the Eighty-eighth. In my three years of service with the French and American flying corps I never met a man who was at once so gallant and so modest as your son. The grandstand meant no more to him, apparently, than his exploits did which—when they were heard from other lips—excited its applause. I believe it never crossed his mind that anything in his consistent record for skill, devotion and gallantry, was worth mentioning. He seemed as oblivious of recognition as he was of danger. Had he, single-handed, put the entire German Army to rout, I am perfectly certain that he would have returned to the airdrome and written in the squadron log, 'Nothing to report.'

"I think none of us can look back on 'The General' without a feeling of reverence and awe. Brave to the point of fearlessness, loyal, devoted to the utmost limit, he was the Bayard of the Eighty-eighth, 'sans peur et sans reproche.'"

WILBUR J. CARMICHAEL, a graduate of the School of Agriculture of the University of Illinois and an expert in animal husbandry, has since 1922 been secretary and traffic manager for the St. Louis Live Stock Exchange, an organization designed generally to promote the welfare of the live stock market at the National Stock Yards at East St. Louis.

Mr. Carmichael has been familiar with the live stock industry since early youth. He grew up on his father's blooded stock farm in northern Illinois, and is regarded as one of the best informed men on the technical and marketing problems of the business. He was born in Ogle County, Illinois, June 15, 1888, son of James and Alma (Knight) Carmichael. His maternal grandparents were Joshua Adams and Achsa James (Davis) Knight, the former a native of Herkimer County, New York. James Carmichael was born in County Donegal, Ireland, and was seven weeks old when his parents, with their three children, sailed for America, the other two children being John and Eliza. They were nine weeks in crossing the ocean, landing in Philadelphia. They immigrated from Ireland on account of the historic potato famine of the year 1849. About 1851 the family settled in Ogle County, Illinois. James Carmichael for forty-five years has been a breeder of blooded stock in that county, and is one of its most prominent citizens, esteemed for his integrity of character as well as for his success in business. For over twenty-one years he has served on local school boards, and has been identified with a number of organizations in that rich and prosperous county. He and his wife had six children: Robert married Jessie Downs, and their four children are Alma Josephine, George James, Edna and Robert. Burton married Nell Holmes, and their two children are Elizabeth and James Holmes. Miss Edith J. is unmarried. Elwood is unmarried. Leonard D. married Mabel Somers, their two children being Leonard D. and Virginia May.

Wilbur J. Carmichael, youngest of the family, was educated in the district schools of Lynnville Township, Ogle County, attended the Rochelle High School and in 1909 entered the School of Agriculture of the University of Illinois, receiving his Bachelor of Science degree in 1913, and the Master of Science degree in 1916. From 1912 to 1915 he was an assistant in the department of animal husbandry, and in 1915 was made inspector of animal husbandry, remaining at the university until the spring of 1918. His special assignment was in swine work. From the university he was called to Washington, D. C., and for one year was in charge of field work for the Department of Agriculture and from 1919 to 1922, inclusive, was secretary of the National Swine Growers Association. He then accepted his present responsibilities as secretary and traffic manager of the St. Louis Live Stock Exchange.

Mr. Carmichael is a Mason, and is a member of the social and agricultural college fraternities of Delta Phi, Sigma Xi, Alpha Zeta and Gamma Alpha. He belongs to the Methodist Church.

He married at Middlebury, Indiana, November 23, 1916, Miss Florence Varns, daughter of Ellsworth and Jennie (Thompson) Varns. Her father is in the hardware and agricultural implement business in Indiana and has served on the school board more than twenty years. Mrs. Carmichael has a brother, Reginald C., who married Adda Prouch, and their two children are Abbie Jane and William Ellsworth. The second wife of her father was Clara Hoover, and by that union three children were born, Clarence, Catherine and William, the two latter deceased. Clarence Varns married Wilura Swartz and has a daughter, Geraldine. The two children of Mr. and Mrs. Carmichael are Ellsworth Varns and William Jerome.

FRED CLARK MYERS was city comptroller of Danville, is an ex-service man of the World war, and a popular leader among the younger group of men in his native city.

He was born at Danville, February 1, 1895. This branch of the Myers family came from England, three brothers of the name settling in western Virginia, near the present city of Wheeling, West Virginia. His grandfather, James A. Myers, was one of the early day merchants of Danville. His father, Frank P. Myers, was born at Danville, March 3, 1855, and spent all his life in that city. He was the first mail carrier of Danville after free delivery of mail was started. He filled the position nine years, and while thus engaged he conceived the idea and put into effect the plans for distributing hand bills of sales for the department stores by the house to house method. He rapidly developed this into a systematic business and gradually added a bill posting and sign board service, so that he was the real pioneer in the advertising business at Danville. He continued his advertising business very successfully for twenty-two years, until his death on September 24, 1907. He was a democrat in politics and was affiliated with Olive Branch Lodge No. 38, Free and Accepted Masons, Danville Camp, Modern Woodmen of America, and Danville Lodge No. 332, Benevolent and Protective Order of Elks. Frank P. Myers married Mary Ellen Hannah, who was born at Danville, August 14, 1861, and still lives in that city. They had three children: Hubert, who died at the age of eighteen months, Wilber Ernest and Fred Clark. Wilber Ernest, now manager of the Hassler Shock Absorber Company at St. Louis, Missouri, during the World war tried to get accepted into the infantry service but was rejected for disability, though subsequently mustered in and during the rest of the war period was clerk at the St. Louis arsenal.

Fred Clark Myers was educated in public schools at Danville, attending high school into the senior year. He left school in 1915, and during the next four and a half years, except for the war period, was a salesman of Cadillac cars employed by the Home Garage Company at Danville. During 1920-21, he was with the Chevrolet Motor Company at Danville as salesman, and for one year wrote life insurance, with offices at Danville, for the Mutual Trust Company of Chicago. Following that Mr. Myers took up the general insurance business with H. R. DeLong of Danville, but resigned on May 1, 1923, to accept appointment from Mayor T. F. Shouse as city comptroller. He has since held that position and is the youngest city comptroller in the United States, as was proven at the National Convention of the Comptrollers and Accountants, held in the City of Milwaukee in 1923.

Mr. Myers is a republican, is a member of the Second Presbyterian Church of Danville, Olive Branch Lodge No. 38, A. F. and A. M., and the Lodge of Perfection with the fourteenth degree of Scottish Rites Masons. He is unmarried.

He enlisted May 20, 1918, being sent for training with the Engineers' Corps to Camp Meade, Maryland. On June 2, 1918, he was transferred to the American University Camp at the extreme northwestern edge of the City of Washington, and on July 10, 1918, was transfered to Fort Myer, Virginia, just opposite the Arlington National cemetery. There he was in charge of the engineers' automotive transportation service until November 15, 1918, when all the engineers were discharged except the transportation service men, who were assigned duty with the Motor Transport Service and as such he remained at Fort Myer until his discharge on January 20, 1919.

EDWARD ROSS. One of the most progressive spirits in the agricultural community around White Hall, Greene County, is Edward Ross, who has lived all his life in the rural district just southeast of White Hall.

He represents a pioneer family. His father was the late Simeon Ross, who was born at Rahway, New Jersey. When a young man he clerked in a store in New York City, and had some property in the east. After his marriage he exchanged this property for what was reputed to be improved land in central Illinois. In 1844 he brought his wife and one child to White Hall. The land he had bought comprised twenty acres. It had been represented that two good houses stood on the land, but on inspection they were found to be two log cabins. The Ross family moved into one of these cabins and unpacked a few goods, thinking that they would remain temporarily and after selling out return to the east. In a year or so Simeon Ross found his engagements and responsibilities such that he could not carry out the plan, and so became a permanent resident. After farming a time he formed a partnership with Judge Worcester to engage in the general store and grocery business at White Hall, which was then a very small village. He prospered, and the business grew and brought substantial prosperity to Simeon Ross. For a number of years he made the daily trip to and from the store on foot. He invested his surplus capital in land, and at the time of his death owned over 1,200 acres.

Simeon Ross, who died February 6, 1893, was a generous and public spirited citizen of Greene County. He aided in the erection of schools and churches, in the building of Union Hall, and while a republican voter he took little interest in politics. The only office he ever held was that of school director. Simeon Ross married Eveline Brant, who died January 4, 1888. Her children were: Francis A., who died at Bloomington, Illinois; Simeon, Jr., of Perry, Missouri; Milan, who died at White Hall; Annie, who married Frank Armstrong and died at Ogden, Utah; Hettie, who died unmarried; Daniel, deceased; Emily, who died unmarried; Elliott, a farmer near White Hall; Adelaide, who married Doctor Foreman; and Edward.

Edward Ross was born on the family homestead near White Hall, April 27, 1860, and grew up just across the road from his present home. He attended schools in White Hall, and for over forty years has been a farmer, chiefly a grain grower. In recent years he and his son Arnold have been growers of seed corn, and is one of the leading men in his community specializing in the breeding of Chester White hogs. He has been a feeder and shipper of fat stock for a number of years. In addition to his farming he was at one time connected with the Sewer Pipe Company at White Hall and the Illinois Milk Condensery. He is a director of the Peoples First National Bank. Mr. Ross is a member of the Methodist Church, is a republican, casting his first vote for Blaine and Logan in 1884, and has served as a member of the school board.

He married in the White Hall community, October 29, 1884, Miss Ellen A. Tankersley, who was born January 6, 1863, daughter of William A. Tankersley, a farmer in Greene County. The three children of Mr. and Mrs. Ross were: Bernice, wife of Ernest Boggess, of White Hall, and their children are Isaac, Marjorie, Mary E., and Henry E; Clemma, deceased, who married George North, and their children are Isaac and Marion A.; and Arnold Ross, a farmer associated with his father. Arnold Ross married Grace Piper, and they have two children, named Eugene and Gerald.

CHESTER A. ALDRICH, publisher of the Chronicle-Herald of Hoopeston, went to work in a newspaper and printing plant when a boy, and his experience has made him one of the ablest newspaper publishers in Illinois.

Mr. Aldrich was born at Wapella, Illinois, October 5, 1874. His grandfather, David Aldrich, was of English ancestry, the Aldrich family having been established in Rhode Island in the latter part of the seventeenth century. David Aldrich was a native of Pennsylvania, and spent most of his life in northern Ohio and northern Indiana. He died at Mishawaka, Indiana. His son, David Aldrich, father of Chester A., was born at Mishawaka, Indiana, in 1844, became a farmer at Wapella, Illinois, where he married, and served as a soldier in the Union army. From Wapella he removed to Du Quoin, Illinois, where he was a prosperous farmer for thirty-five years. He is now living retired at Cobden, this state. He is a republican, a Baptist and a member of the Grand Army of the Republic. David Aldrich married Ann Eliza Burroughs, who was born at New Paris, Indiana, and died at Wapella, Illinois, in 1877. Her father, Chester S. Burroughs, was a native of Northampton, Massachusetts, went to Indiana at an

early day, served as a soldier in the Mexican war, and followed the occupation of carpenter and builder. He married Permelia Mills, a native of Ohio, who died at Niles, Michigan. The Mills family came from England and were among the early colonists of Virginia, being related to the Custis family, of which Martha Custis Washington was a member. Chester S. Burroughs was a cousin of the Chicago merchant, Marshall Field.

Chester A. Aldrich was the youngest of three children, the oldest, Nathaniel, dying in infancy. His sister, Amy Permelia, is the wife of Fred Jansen, a cigar manufacturer at Denver, Colorado. Chester A. Aldrich was only three years old when his mother died, and he grew up in the home of his grand parents at Niles, Michigan, attending public schools there to the age of sixteen. He then served a nine-month apprenticeship in the office of the Niles, Michigan, Democrat, and for eleven months was a reporter for the Niles Daily Star. He had three months experience as a reporter for the Detroit Evening News, and then returned to Niles, where for one year he was city editor of the Niles Daily Star, following which he became associated with Major L. A. Duncan as editor of the Niles Daily Sun and Niles Republican. After four years he went to Poplar Bluffs, Missouri, and established the Poplar Bluffs Sentinel, which he published two years, selling that paper in 1900.

Then for another year he was city editor of the Niles Daily Sun, and for a year was city editor of the Mattoon, Illinois, Morning Star. He then became managing editor and publisher of this Mattoon paper and remained in that city until 1911.

Mr. Aldrich in 1911 acquired the Hoopeston Evening Herald. On April 15, 1921, he bought the Republican Daily and Weekly Chronicle, the consolidation of the two papers resulting in the Chronicle-Herald, which has both daily and weekly issues. The Chronicle is the oldest newspaper of Hoopeston, having been established in 1872 by Mr. Dale Wallace, still a resident of that city. The Chronicle-Herald is independent in politics. The paper is now owned and published by the Aldrich Printing and Publishing Company, Inc., which Mr. Aldrich incorporated in 1921 with a capital of forty thousand dollars. He is president and managing editor and general business manager of the corporation . The plant and offices are at 201 East Main Street. This is a very successful newspaper, and few cities of the size of Hoopeston anywhere can claim a newspaper so well edited and possessing more of the qualities of a really good newspaper.

Mr. Aldrich is a member of the Illinois Press Association, belongs to the Hoopeston Chamber of Commerce, to the Commercial Club and to the Hubbard Trail Country Club. During the World war he put his newspaper and all its facilities completely at the disposal of the government in giving publicity to war measures. He is independent in his political views, is a member of the First Methodist Episcopal Church, and of Mattoon Lodge No. 495 B. P. O. Elks. Mr. Aldrich owns an attractive home at 626 Washington Street, and has other real estate in Hoopeston.

He married at South Bend, Indiana, July 16, 1897, Miss Hattie Hudson. She was born at Rockton, Illinois, in 1878, and died in a Chicago hospital in 1904. By this marriage there were four children: Rita Amy, wife of Clarence W. Murray, of the A. W. Murray Plumbing Company of Hoopeston; Erma Anna, wife of J. Franklin Murray, who is a pressman in the Chronicle-Herald plant; David R., linotype operator for his father; and Lucretia E., wife of Marvin G. Probst, a resident of River Forest, Illinois, Mr. Probst being a member of Graham, Andersen, Probst & White, Chicago architects, who have designed and built some of the finest business and public structures in Chicago and the middle west.

Mr. Aldrich on October 1, 1906, at Clayton, Missouri, married Miss Georgia Jane Gibler, a native of Mattoon, Illinois. By this marriage there are two children: Helen Czarine, in the second year of high school at Hoopeston; and Richard Wayne, a freshman in the high school.

FRANK C. RATHJE. Perhaps in no other city in the world can be found a greater number of able professional men than in Chicago, a fact attested by remarkable achievements along every line. To this prestige the Chicago bar has contributed largely, and a representative member of this important body is Frank C. Rathje, specialist in banking law, who is at the head of the prominent law firm of Rathje, Wesemann, Hinckley & Barnard, with offices at 29 South La Salle Street, Chicago.

Frank C. Rathje was born at Bloomingdale, Dupage County, Illinois, son of William and Louise (Ehlers) Rathje, and grandson of Frederick Rathje, all natives of Hanover, Germany. The grandfather was born in that province in 1802. Early in the fifties he came to America and settled in Illinois, buying 210 acres of land in Dupage County, securing it for $10 an acre, and resided there until his death in 1886.

William Rathje, who was born October 30, 1832, came alone to the United States when only thirteen years of age, showing a spirit of courage and resourcefulness that characterized him throughout subsequent life, making him a successful business man and useful and respected citizen. He crossed the Atlantic ocean in a sailing ship that took six weeks to complete the voyage but finally landed its passengers safely, and shortly afterward William Rathje found himself where he wanted to be, in the midst of a great agricultural section, and began life in new surroundings as a farm hand in Dupage County, Illinois, and already had made some headway and many friends when his father, Frederick Rathje, joined him. The latter had brought capital to invest and soon father and son were hard at work converting the 210 acres of wild prairie into a fertile farm. William Rathje remained on this farm, and acquired additional land in the meanwhile, until 1888, when he gave up farming, having already established himself in the fire insurance business and as an auctioneer at Bloomingdale. In 1897 he bought 400 acres of land near Roselle, in Dupage County, but in 1901 retired from business and moved to Chicago, where his death took place November 30, 1907. He was active in republican politics in Dupage County, for a long time was a justice of the peace and for twenty-eight years was supervisor of his township, where he was also a member and liberal supporter of the German Lutheran Church.

In Dupage County, March 7, 1863, William Rathje and Louise Ehlers were married. She was born in Hanover, Germany, February 13, 1842, and died in Illinois January 30, 1920. Of their family of ten children, four sons and six daughters, eight are living, Frank being the tenth in order of birth.

Mr. Rathje attended public schools in Dupage County and afterward St. John's Military School at Delafield, Wisconsin, then became a student in Armour Institute, Chicago, and in 1907 completed his course in the law department of Northwestern University, Chicago, and in July of that year was admitted to the Illinois bar. He entered upon the practice of law May 1, 1908, and in 1910 organized the firm of Rathje and Wesemann. In 1919 the firm name was changed to Rathje, Wesemann, Hinckley & Barnard, one that has an honorable record in court proceedings over the state for over a decade.

Mr. Rathje married, October 16, 1915, Miss Josephine Logan, a native of Chicago, and they have three children: Theron Logan, Josephine and Franklyn C.

In political life Mr. Rathje is a republican, a quiet and influential worker for his party's supremacy because he believes in its principles, but too devoted to his profession to seek political office. He is president of the Chicago City Bank & Trust Company and president of the Mutual National Bank. He is a member of the Chicago Bar Association and the Illinois State Bar Association, and is a Knight Templar Mason and a Shriner.

CHARLES WILLIAM MOREY is president and founder of the Chicago Technical College, which is one of the oldest and largest schools of specialized engineering in the country. It was founded in 1904. The school was the outgrowth of a practical experience on the part of several engineers, including Mr. Morey, who had great difficulty in finding competent men educated in the fundamentals of engineering to assist in the organization of which Mr. Morey was then a part. The school has had a steady growth and offers courses in architecture, civil, mechanical, electrical and structural engineering. Since the first year Mr. Morey has been president of the school. For a number of years the school had its quarters in the Athenaeum Building, but since 1923 has occupied a large and well equipped building of its own at Twenty-sixth Street and Indiana Avenue.

Mr. Morey was born at Quincy, in Branch County, Michigan, March 26, 1875, son of John R. and Amanda E. (Bickford) Morey. Mr. Morey graduated with the degree Bachelor of Science in electrical engineering from Purdue University in 1897. For one year he was chief draftsman for the Austin Manufacturing Company, and from 1900 to 1904 was an engineer for the American Bridge Company. One of his associates in this work was Carl T. Newgard, and both of them were associated in the founding of the Chicago Technical College, Mr. Newgard being vice president of the school corporation. In addition to the management of the college, Mr. Morey was for some years engaged in engineering and construction enterprises in Chicago, being a member of the firm Morey, Newgard & Company. This firm designed a number of important buildings in Chicago.

Mr. Morey is a member of the Western Society of Engineers, the American Association of Engineers, the Engineers Club of Chicago, the Society for the Promotion of Engineering Education, and is a member of the City Club and Collegiate Club. He married Dollie N. Cosper, of Coldwater, Michigan, September 20, 1899. They are the parents of three children: Leslie G., Elinore G. and Francis C.

WALTER C. SHOUPE. No name in Clinton County, Illinois, is better known in newspaper circles than that of Shoupe, its connection with the Constitution, at Carlyle, covering a period of forty-five years, and for thirty-six years it has been owned by a Shoupe. Its present owner and publisher, Walter C. Shoupe, is an able journalist known all over the state, and one of Carlyle's leading citizens.

Walter C. Shoupe was born at New Athens, St. Clair County, Illinois, March 25, 1874, second son of Theodore D. and Louisa G. (Moore) Shoupe. His paternal grandparents were Abraham and Catherine (Tannehill) Shoupe, the former of whom was born in Westmoreland County, Pennsylvania. In company with his three brothers he came to Illinois in 1830 and to Belleville in 1831. He was a carpenter and builder. At Belleville he married Catherine Tannehill, whose people came from Kentucky, and at that time were conducting a hotel at Belleville, the same hostelry in which Charles Dickens was once a guest. The maternal grandparents of Mr. Shoupe were Risdon and Louisa (Mitchell) Moore, the former of whom was a native of Georgia.

For many years the late Theodore D. Shoupe was a prominent and influential man in Illinois. He was born at Belleville, November 24, 1837, and died at Carlyle January 9, 1920, at that time being the oldest newspaper man in the state and considered one of the ablest. In his youth he attended school at Belleville and then learned the carpenter trade with his father's approval, and the printer's trade to suit himself, worked in both lines up to 1861, when he made a definite stand by going to work in the printing office of the Daily Eagle, the first newspaper in St. Clair County, and during the rest of his active life was identified with journalism. From Belleville he went to Tamaroa, in Perry County, where he published The True American until 1871, when he sold that paper and moved to New Athens, in St. Clair County, where for three years he published the New Athens Era and served also as postmaster of New Athens. He then moved his family back to Belleville and for a time was a compositor on the Missouri Republican at St. Louis. On July 4, 1881, in partnership with Risdon Moore, he purchased the Constitution, a newspaper published at Carlyle, in Clinton County. After four years Mr. Moore sold out to R. H. Norfolk, and upon the death of Mr. Norfolk Mr. Shoupe purchased his interest. Mr Shoupe was active in politics, and among the distinguished men of the state with whom he was intimately acquainted were Abraham Lincoln and Stephen A Douglas.

In 1858 Theodore D. Shoupe married Louisa G. Moore, who died in 1917. The children born to them were: Ella, who died in infancy; Lillie, who is unmarried; Fannie, who is the wife of Henry Gross and they have two children, Theodore and Dorothy; Risdon Moore, deceased, who married Mary Rogan, now deceased, and they had three daughters; Alethea, who married Ralph Williams, and they have two children, Margaret Louisa and Robinson; Mary Louisa, who married Gerald Gray, and they have one child, James Risdon; Margaret, who married Ellwyn Alvorson, of Washington, D. C., and they have one child, Joan; the four other members of the family of Theodore D. Shoupe are: Jessie, who is unmarried; Walter C., whose interests for over thirty years have been centered at Carlyle; Mabel, now deceased, who was the wife of Archibald Bean, and they have one child, Eleanor; and Nellie, who is a government clerk in the Agricultural Department at Washington, D. C.

Walter C. Shoupe was educated in the public schools of Carlyle and immediately after graduating from high school, in 1890, became associated with his father in the newspaper business, subsequently succeeding to its ownership and entire management. The Constitution is an old democratic landmark in the state, an organ of great influence politically, while as a welcome visitor in the majority of the homes in Clinton County it fulfills every demand made of the modern newspaper. Mr. Shoupe has been chairman of the Democratic County Committee and has been secretary of this body for eighteen years. In 1907 he was appointed master in chancery and served four years, and under appointment by the late President Wilson served eight years as postmaster of Carlyle.

Mr. Shoupe married, October 25, 1919, at Carlyle, Miss Mabel H. Robinson, third member of a family of six children born to John W. and Lydia (Hall) Robinson. Her mother passed away many years ago, but her father survives and is in the lumber business, with sawmill and yards at Carlyle. The brother and sisters of Mrs. Shoupe are: Charles, who married Lillian Gross, and has four children, Claude, Harold, Lillian and Lucille; Edith, who is the wife of John Luepke, and they have three children, Joseph, John Paul and Jane; Ruth, who is the wife of Maurice Johnston, and they have one child, William Jerome; and Emma, who is unmarried.

Mr. and Mrs. Shoupe have three children, two little daughters and an infant son: Lydia Robinson and Louisa Moore, twins, and Walter C., Jr. Mrs. Shoupe is a member of the Episcopal Church and interested in many charities. Mr. Shoupe was reared in the Baptist faith and is liberal in his support of both church organizations, and through his newspaper and otherwise continually shows his sincere concern as to the welfare of Carlyle. He is a thirty-second degree Mason and a Shriner and is a past master of the Blue Lodge at Carlyle, and belongs also to the Modern Woodmen, the Odd Fellows and in Knights of Pythias, being chancellor commander of the latter order.

ALBERT GOTTLIEB GUMM. In the twenty-three years he has represented his profession in Paris, Doctor Gumm has become noted as a surgeon, one of the most skillful operatives in this part of the state. He came to Paris with most liberal educational advantages and learning under the greatest man of his profession.

Doctor Gumm was born at Paris, May 24, 1876, son of Frederick J. and Anna (Graf) Gumm. His mother came from Zurich, Switzerland, to the United States in 1851, being a girl of fourteen at the time. Frederick J. Gumm, in company with his mother, two brothers and three sisters, came to the United States from the village of Horn, Prussia, in 1848, first settling in Sheboygan, Wisconsin, later coming to Illinois. For many years he was engaged in farming. Before the first railroads were built through this section of Illinois he delivered his surplus produce in Chicago by wagon. His record was one of unusual industry and of perfect integrity of character, so that his word was considered as good as his bond.

Albert Gottlieb Gumm was educated in the public schools at Paris, and took his literary and general science course in Valparaiso University, receiving his degree Master of Science in 1901. He is the only physician at Paris who possesses the M. S. degree. In 1901 he also graduated M. D. from the Northwestern University Medical School at Chicago, and after graduating remained for some time as an instructor in the University Medical Department, giving instruction in surgery under the late Dr. John B. Murphy, professor of surgery in that institution. On leaving Chicago Doctor Gumm practiced a short time at Oakland, Illinois, and in 1903 returned to Paris, where with few interruptions has been engaged in practice for twenty years.

Doctor Gumm was commissioned a captain in the Medical Corps of the United States army on September 4, 1918, and was held for active duty until November 30, 1920. He served several terms as member of the Board of Health, and since 1922 has been police surgeon at Paris. He is an independent in politics.

Doctor Gumm is a member of the Aesculapian Medical Society of the Wabash Valley, the Edgar County, Illinois State and American Medical Associations, belongs to the American Legion and the Forty and Eight Society and fraternally is affiliated with Lodge No. 268 of the Masonic fraternity, Lodge No. 91 of the Independent Order of Odd Fellows, Lodge No. 768, B. P. O. Elks, the Modern Woodmen of America and the Royal Neighbors. He has been an elder in the Presbyterian Church since 1904.

Doctor Gumm married at Paris, June 27, 1900, Miss Anna B. Morris, daughter of O'Neil and Susannah Morris. The Morris family were among the early settlers of eastern Illinois, coming by wagon from Ohio. Her father became one of the extensive land owners in Edgar County. Mrs. Gumm was born October 28, 1874, and died July 11, 1917. The only child of Doctor Gumm is Miss Anna Louise Gumm, who was born March 30, 1903. Since childhood she has been distinguished by her capable gift and talent in music, and was thoroughly educated in both instrumental and vocal music and esthetic dancing and now devotes her entire time to her art. She was with the Chicago Civic Opera Company, the past season, 1925-1926, as a member of the Pavley-Oukrainsky Ballet. She is in Chicago studying voice and expression, and will be with the Chicago Opera Company during the coming season.

Doctor Gumm was united in marriage, June 12, 1926, with Miss Margaret (Blau). The present Mrs. Gumm was born in Chicago, June 17, 1891, where she resided until recently.

WILLIAM G. BIERD, president of the Chicago & Alton Railway, is a railway official whose career has consisted of something more than a steady advancement in his responsibilities. His life has been of more than ordinary interest considered from that standpoint alone, since his is the typical story of the poor boy who educated himself and earned his early promotions when he had the competition of hundreds on the same scale as himself. Mr. Bierd has enjoyed the additional distinction of always helping others as he has come up the ladder of success.

He was born at Baltimore, Maryland, May 24, 1864, son of Obediah and Mary (Morgan) Bierd. Beyond the advantage of the common schools his opportunities were limited to such time as could be applied after the work required for earning a living. For five years he attended night schools, and for many years after that kept up his studies as a supplement to his advancement. At the age of seventeen he was working as a bridge gang laborer for the Chicago & Northwestern Railway. After five years he left that branch of the service, and his subsequent promotions during the next fifteen or sixteen years were as follows: Overseer of construction for the Chicago, Burlington & Quincy Railroad; yard master for the Union Pacific Railroad at Cheyenne, Wyoming; trainmaster for the Norfolk & Western Railroad at Roanoke, Virginia, and also for the Lehigh Valley Railroad at Buffalo, New York. From 1902 to 1904 he was trainmaster and division superintendent, and in 1904-05 assistant to the general manager of the Chicago, Rock Island & Pacific Railway. An interesting variation from his steady railroad service came during the years 1905-07, when he was general superintendent and general manager of the Panama Railway & Steamship Company at Colon, Panama. From 1907 to 1910 Mr. Bierd was general superintendent of the N. Y. N. H. & H. Railroad, and from 1910 to 1914 was vice president and general manager of the Minneapolis and St Louis Railroad. Mr. Bierd became president of the Chicago & Alton Railroad in 1914. In the general offices of the company at 340 West Harrison Street it is said that Mr. Bierd knows practically all the several hundred employees, so that he addresses them by name. His recognition does not stop there, since a great many cases have come to general notice of individuals whom he has helped out of trouble, has sent to hospitals and has enabled to seek change of climate and other advantages for health and improvement.

Mr. Bierd advocates and practices the gospel of self help. One of the institutions which has been notable in Illinois for many years as a source of inspiration and training for boys and girls without the means to take the course of a regular college or university is Blackburn College at Carlinville, Illinois. He is one of the trustees of that institution and not long ago erected a new building on the campus. He is also chairman of the finance committee of one of the best and most exclusive schools for girls in the middle west, Monticello Seminary at Godfrey, Illinois. Mr. Bierd is a member of the Chicago Club and Chicago Golf Club. His home is at 2258 Lincoln Park, West.

He married, February 25, 1891, Miss Maude Chapman, daughter of Mr. and Mrs. Edward Chapman, of Fulton, Illinois.

LLOYD A. BARTLETT, former proprietor of the Lebanon Advertiser, was born at Marshall, Clark County, Illinois, November 26, 1895, a son of Frederick J. and Mary E. (Wooster) Bartlett, and grandson of Archer Bartlett, the first settler of Clark County, to which he came from New York State. He married Martha Quick, a member of the old New York State family of that name. Lloyd A. Bartlett had four ancestors in the American Revolution, and his family record is an interesting page in the history of this country.

Frederick J. Bartlett, whose death occurred in 1911, was for years a prominent attorney of Marshall, and a law partner of B. M. Davison, former head of the Illinois State Board of Agriculture. Mr. Bartlett also served as city attorney of Marshall, was a master-in-chancery, and took an active part in public affairs. In religious faith he was a Congregationalist. His wife died in 1909, leaving four children, namely: Lloyd Archer, who is the eldest; Sidney Ganong, who married Ruth Sweet, of Marshall; Ralph Quick, who is unmarried; and Martha Wooster, who is also unmarried.

Following the death of his father at Marshall, Lloyd A. Bartlett went to work in a printing office at Tuscola, Douglass County, Illinois, but after a few months went to Saint Louis, Missouri, where, in the plant of one of the largest printing companies of the city, he learned the printing business.

On March 26, 1918, his unit of the National Guard, later known as Company L, One Hundred and Thirty-eighth U. S. Regiment of Infantry, in which he had enlisted the previous month, was ordered into the service and sent to Fort Sill, Oklahoma, where they were in training for a short time. From Fort Sill they were sent to Camp Mills, New York, and

then over seas, landing at Liverpool, England. After a brief stop at Winchester they went across the English Channel to La Havre, France, and thence to near the Somme Sector for training under the British army. His unit was twice in the trenches of the Voges Mountains in western Alsace, and were participants in the major offensives being in action at Saint Mihiel, where they were held in reserve, and in the Muese-Argonne, where they were at the time of the signing of the armistice. For sixteen weeks thereafter Mr. Bartlett was an instructor on the 37 millimeter gun, and at the termination of that period he attended the American E. F. University at Baune, Cote d' Or, for instruction in journalism, and remained there for four months. He then sailed from Marseilles, France, for the United States, landing at Hoboken, New York, from whence he was transferred to Camp Merrit, and later to Camp Taylor, Kentucky, where he was honorably discharged.

Upon his return to Missouri Mr. Bartlett entered the printing establishment of George D. Barnard, with whom he remained until May 23, 1921, when he came to Lebanon and purchased the Advertiser, which he conducted as an independent newspaper until October, 1925, when he sold his business to S. E. Williams, of Lebanon, Indiana.

On November 24, 1920, Mr. Bartlett married, at Webster Groves, Missouri, Dorothy I. Field, a daughter of Alexander M. and Maud O. (Rathel) Field, and they have two children, Lloyd A., Junior, and Jayne. Mr. and Mrs. Field, both of whom are living, have five children: Eugene R., who married Madge McLaughlin, and has two children, Elaine Louise and Eugene R., Junior; Mrs. Bartlett, who was second in order of birth; Alexander, Junior, who married Dorothy Pearson, of Webster Groves, Missouri; Alice and Robert.

Mr. and Mrs. Bartlett are members of the Baptist Church. They both belong to the Eastern Star, and he is a Blue Lodge and Chapter Mason, and belongs to the Independent Order of Odd Fellows and the American Legion.

WILLIAM GRANVILLE COCHRAN. One of the distinguished members of the bench and bar of Central Illinois is Judge William Granville Cochran, of Sullivan, Moultrie County. Judge Cochran was born in Ross County, Ohio, November 13, 1844, son of Andrew and Jane Cochran, both of whom were natives of Ohio. His paternal grandparents moved to Ohio from Pennsylvania in 1801. His maternal grandparents came from Ireland. William G. Cochran as a youth had the opportunity to attend district schools only about three winters. He was reared on a farm, and in July, 1862, when in his eighteenth year, he enlisted in the Union army. He was in the army until the close of the war. He then resumed farming, also took up the study of law, and was admitted to the bar. Judge Cochran has been successful as a lawyer, has won high honors on the bench, and has been a leader in the republican party in this section of the state. He has been a campaign speaker for the republican ticket in every campaign through forty years. He served three terms in the Illinois Legislature and was twice elected speaker of the House. Judge Cochran was on the Circuit Court bench a period of eighteen years, three terms. He is former department commander of the Department of Illinois Grand Army of the Republic and is a Knight Templar Mason and Odd Fellow. He has been identified with the Methodist Church fifty-nine years.

In token of the high esteem in which Judge Cochran is held the Moultrie County Bar Association directed the painting of a lifesized portrait, and this portrait was hung on the walls of the Circuit Court room at Sullivan and publicly dedicated November 13, 1924, on the eightieth birthday of Judge Cochran. An interesting ceremony and program attended the dedication. The presiding judge of the court during the program was Judge George A. Sentel, and from his sketch and estimate of Judge Cochran as published in the proceedings of the dedication ceremony, the following is taken as perhaps best expressing the life and services of this honored Illinois jurist: "A real man of the common people; his foundation and support were his great memory, honesty and activity; his service was his success.

"Judge William G. Cochran of Sullivan, Illinois, was born of poor parentage; he served his masters with faithfulness; he had the love of God in his heart; he overcame almost unsurmountable difficulties; formed a character that is held in the highest esteem by all who know him; and now has almost ended a useful, honorable and exemplary life.

"Judge William G. Cochran was born November 13, 1844, in Ross County, Ohio, moving to Moultrie County, Illinois, when almost five years of age. He attended the district school about three months each year until he was seventeen years of age, and left home at the age of seventeen. He worked on the farm, herded and fed cattle on the prairies of Illinois and when seventeen years of age enlisted in the Federal army, on July 31, 1862, a private in Company A, One Hundred Twentysixth Illinois Infantry. There were fortynine men who joined the Union army on July 31, 1862, just west of Lovington, Illinois, on that day, all of whom except Judge Cochran have passed to the Great Beyond.

"Judge Cochran served three years in the Union army, being at the siege of Vicksburg and was mustered out of the service on August 2, 1865, at the close of the Civil war.

"Upon his return from the army he resumed farming and was married to Miss Charlotte A. Keyes on September 13, 1866, by Rev. William Rhodes, minister of the Christian Church.

"For several years he engaged in farming; during the lonely nights his good wife taught him the rudiments of a higher and better education which was to be the foundation of an active and successful life. Giving up farming, he engaged in the restaurant business for two years, then acted as a clerk in a general store for several years. One Saturday night he told his employers, Foster & Gregory, that 'that was the last package of coffee I'll ever tie up.'

"Judge Cochran was twice elected constable and twice elected assessor of his township.

He did a collection business, wrote fire insurance and made farm loans for loaning companies. In 1876 he began the study of law, while doing his other work, and was admitted to the bar on May 23, 1879, practicing with H. M. Minor, now of Colorado, and Judge M. R. Davidson, now county judge of Piatt County, since which time the law has been his life.

"Judge Cochran united with the Methodist Episcopal Church in October, 1866, and in 1872 became a local preacher and has remained such to the present time. He has often filled many pulpits in the Methodist Church to the pleasure of the congregation. He once filled the local circuit at Bethany for six months, for which he received the munificent sum of $22.50. In speaking of this incident he smilingly surmised, 'I guess they thought that was more than the services were worth.' But he had the satisfaction, on his return home from the services, of seeing his good wife waiting for him with a piece of hot mince pie and a glass of cold milk to satiate the physical inner man.

"He has lived a good Christian life; his friends are those whom he meets, his peace of mind is his; he lives imbued with the faith and hope that when his life's journey is ended he will safely rest in the arms of his Maker.

"Judge Cochran has, from early manhood, been a representative of his local church in Lay Conferences and was the first president of Lay Conferences of the Methodist Episcopal Church of Illinois and succeeding himself to said presidency. He was elected as a delegate to two General Conferences of his church when they were held in Chicago in 1900 and in Baltimore in 1904.

"In June, 1883, Judge Cochran with his family moved to Hebron, Nebraska, taking with him his team, surrey, household goods and dog, landing there on July 2nd. He made a patriotic speech in a grove on the Fourth of July, the second day after his arrival. He organized the first Sunday School in Hebron. He came back to Moultrie County, however, within thirty days because of his dislike of the prairie country with its windstorms and cyclones.

"Judge Cochran early entered into public life and was elected to the State Legislature in November, 1888, and was made speaker of the House of a special session of that body in 1890. He received the nomination for state senator in 1890, but as the district was strongly democratic, he being a republican, there was no chance of his election. In 1894 he was again elected to the Thirty-ninth General Assembly and at a July special session in 1895 he was again chosen speaker of the House. He was again elected in 1896 as a member of the General Assembly; while serving as a representative he was prominently mentioned over the state as republican candidate for governor, but he never entered the field for that honor. While a member of the Legislature in 1897, he was chairman of the judicial apportionate committee and chairman of the subcommittee. He wrote and fostered the bill which created the present judicial circuits of the State of Illinois. He was instrumental in having passed by the Legislature, bills, among which were the location of the site of the World's Fair in Chicago, the amendment of the law of chattel mortgages, which amendment required that chattels taken under chattel mortgages be sold in the county where the same were located after giving due notice to the mortgagor and requiring mortgagees to render a statement in full to the owner of the property; a bill creating a jury commission for Cook County; a bill to erect a monument to soldiers at the battle grounds of Shiloh; a bill transferring title of Lincoln monument from Lincoln Monument Association to the State of Illinois, and where a fee of twenty-five cents was therefore charged, but this bill was abolished and each visitor was given, free of charge, a leaflet outlining a description of the monument and a brief history of the life of Lincoln.

"Judge William G. Cochran was a successful practitioner of the law, and because of his natural flow of langue and eloquence, was considered a power in his pleas before a jury. He moved from Lovington to Sullivan, the county seat, in 1891, and formed a partnership with Hon. F. M. Harbaugh for the practice of law.

"Judge Cochran was elected to the circuit bench of the Sixth Judicial Circuit of the State of Illinois in June, 1897, and held this position as judge of the Circuit Court for three successive terms of six years each until his health failed and he was compelled to retire from the bench in 1915, refusing to be a candidate for reelection.

"As a jurist he was conscientious, honest and frank; he used his good common sense along with his great knowledge of the law and was always a gentleman on the bench. He believed in the young man, the young lawyer and rendered much assistance to them. His great memory—that great storehouse of knowledge—was his means of success. He never forgot, hence his education and knowledge of the law was rapid and firm. No one ever questioned his honesty and uprightness, and because of his training in religion he 'judged with mercy.'

"While a jurist he tried many important cases, among which were the Warner will case, the Bondurant will case, the Snell will case, the Magill murder case, the Appleton murder case, the Adkins will case and many more which involved millions of dollars and life itself to some defendants in the court. Judge Cochran has known every circuit judge who held court in this part of the state from Judge Treat down to the present time.

"When Judge Cochran had his nervous breakdown, during the period of his recovery he wrote a pamphlet of the early history and progress of Lovington Township, which was first published in a newspaper and afterward 250 copies were delivered to friends in many states of the Union who were interested.

"Judge Cochran has been a member of the Grand Army of the Republic since its organization and has held about every office in said organization, including department commander of the State of Illinois and judge advocate general of the Grand Army of the Republic. While he was department commander he reduced the time of their encampments from four to three days, since which time the encampment has been held only three days. He has attended most of the Grand Army Encampments of the United States in the last fifty years. These encampments form a large part of the pleasure in Judge Cochran's life. He attends all that his health will permit and always has a prominent part in the programs and policies. He is known in Grand Army circles from one end of the country to the other as a first-class and entertaining speaker and good story teller and is much in demand. There is always fun and pleasure and a good time experienced when Judge Cochran is among them.

"In politics Judge Cochran has been a consistant republican and has made political speeches all over the state in many campaigns. He has been with the National Republican Campaign Speakers' Committee in several campaigns and made speeches in Kansas and Michigan for President McKinley during his campaigns. He has attended about every Republican National Convention since 1888.

"Judge Cochran has always been the friend of the poor man—sympathy could control him but money would fail. In fact, the judge has always served his clients for a moderate fee and is now far from being a rich man. However, he is still a practicing lawyer, always prompt in his business and in court and still flashes the fires of former days when he feels his clients rights are being jeopardized. He is the senior member of the firm of lawyers of Cochran, Foster & Cochran of Sullivan, who enjoy a lucrative practice, his oldest son, Judge Oscar F. Cochran, being the third member of the firm.

"Judge Cochran was the father of five children who grew to maturity, three boys and two girls: Judge Oscar F. Cochran, Mrs. Grace Richardson, Archibald B. Cochran, of Springfield, Illinois; Arthur G. Cochran, an attorney of Tulsa, Oklahoma; and Laura O., the wife of Frank J. Thompson, now deceased. He has several grandchildren, who believe in their grandfather's wisdom and religion."

J. FRANK WILSON, M. D. A native of southern Illinois, Dr. J. Frank Wilson has been engaged in practice as a physician and surgeon for over a quarter of a century in Brown County. His home is at Versailles.

He was born at Perry, Illinois, October 23, 1876, and comes of a family of physicians and professional men. His grandfather was Dr. Benjamin Wilson. His father, Dr. S. J. Wilson, was born near Portsmouth, Ohio, in 1852, and was a child when his parents moved to Illinois He grew up in the home of a country physician, and he graduated from the College of Physicians and Surgeons of Keokuk, Iowa, just twelve years before his son J. Frank. He practiced at Versailles, Illinois, but for the last twenty years has given up the work of his profession and is now in business at Versailles as a druggist and optician. Dr. S. J. Wilson married at Chambersburg Miss Emma Metz, daughter of Joseph Metz, of an old Illinois family. They had three children: Dr. J. Frank; Elsie, wife of John M. McCoy, of Springfield; and Della, wife of Sherman Thomas, a farmer in Brown County.

J. Frank Wilson was six years of age when the family moved to Versailles, where he attended public schools. He was a member of the first graduating class at the high school, being then seventeen years of age. Before taking up the study of medicine he spent one year in Illinois College at Jacksonville. For one year he attended Keokuk Medical College and spent two years at Barnes Medical College, St. Louis, now part of the medical department of the University of Missouri. He was graduated in 1899, winning a gold medal for excellence in surgery and honors for excellence in other subjects. Immediately after graduating Doctor Wilson engaged in practice at Versailles, spending two years with his father. From 1901 to 1903 he practiced at Bluffs, and then returned to Versailles and bought his father's practice and has been one of the leaders of his profession in Brown County since that date. He is a member of the various professional societies, including the Illinois State and American Medical Associations. He has served as examiner for a number of the leading insurance companies and is a member of the Brown County Board of Pension Examiners. The severest test upon his professional and physical powers came during the influenza epidemic of 1918 and 1919.

Doctor Wilson is treasurer of the Versailles Commercial Club, is vice president and a director of the Versailles State Bank, which he helped organize, has been a director of the local school board and a member of the town board. He owns farming interests and is vitally identified with all matters affecting his community. He is a member of the Christian Church, is a past master of Versailles Lodge of Masons, member of the Meredosia Royal Arch Chapter and the Quincy Consistory of the Scottish Rite. In politics he is a republican.

Doctor Wilson married at Quincy, Illinois, September 30, 1900, Miss Della Vandeventer, daughter of William H. and Jane (Walker) Vandeventer. Her father was one of the pioneer settlers of Brown County. Doctor and Mrs. Wilson have two sons, Howard and Roy, both graduates of the Versailles High School. Howard subsequently graduated with the A. B. degree from the University of Chicago, specializing in history, and is now a teacher there in the department of history, doing work towards his Masters degree.

ALVIN C. KOCH, president of the Breese Grain Company at Breese in Clinton County, also financial secretary of the Clinton County Agricultural Fair Association, in May, 1926, was elected president of the Illinois Grain Dealers' Association at the convention held in Peoria, Illinois. He is an active young business man of the community, and is continuing a line of business which was established by his grandfather and which has been continued by members of the family for a period of fifty years or more.

Alvin C. Koch was born at Breese, October 17, 1886, son of Fred and Katherine (Hoffsommer) Koch. His grandparents were John and Frederica Koch, both natives of Germany. John Koch was an early pioneer in southern Illinois, founder of the grain business at Breese and a man of prominence in other affairs as well. The maternal grandfather, Castar Hoffsommer, was born in Germany and settled in Clinton County about 1840. Katherine Hoffsommer Koch is still living. Fred Koch, who died in 1901, was a general merchant at Breese and an active man in that community, but not a participant in politics. He was a member of the Evangelical Church. Alvin C. Koch is the oldest of four children. Walter died December 25, 1925, in Denver, Colorado, from a tonsil operation, and his twin sisters are Hulda and Alma, Hulda being the wife of John Reeves.

Alvin C. Koch attended public schools in Breese and the Carlyle High School, and for two years was a student in the University of Illinois at Urbana. He left the university before graduating in order to become associated with his two uncles and mother, who organized and opened coal mines, Alvin becoming secretary of the Mining Company in charge of the office. Then, in 1918, he took an interest with his uncle in the grain business. These uncles, J. O. and Henry, had been in the grain business for many years, and on their death Alvin C. Koch took over the active management and has continued it in connection with his brother Walter.

Alvin Koch married at Breese in September, 1909, Miss Ada Dorries. Her father, Carl Dorries, who died in 1921, was a soft drink manufacturer at Breese. The children in the Dorries family were Emelia, Riecke, Martha Koch, Nellie Schroeder, Selma Hildebrand, Gust and Carl, Jr. Mr. and Mrs. Koch are the parents of three children: Bernice, Carl and Ada. They are members of the Evangelical Church.

SAMUEL EDGAR CULBERTSON has lived at White Hall most of his life, has been well known as a teacher and business man, and is a member of a fairly numerous family which came to this section of Illinois many years ago.

The history of the early generations of the family is largely traditional. According to that four brothers came from Scotland to America before the Revolution, three of them locating in the South and one in Pennsylvania. From the Pennsylvania branch the family moved into Ohio. John Culbertson lived in Ohio and died leaving his widow with a large number of children. She reached the age of more than ninety years and died and is buried at White Hall. Some of her children were bound out, as was the custom at that time, and thus grew up practically among strangers. Among her children were: Mrs. Anna Cornhaus, who after moving to Kansas married a Mr. Miller; Henry, Aaron and William, none of whom ever lived in Illinois; and Samuel, David, John and Levi, who all settled in Greene County, Illinois, David and John coming first.

Samuel Culbertson was one of the children who grew up among strangers. He was born in Richland County, Ohio, April 21, 1842, and followed his brothers to Illinois. He had a limited education in country schools, was a farmer, and at White Hall became identified with the clay working industry with his brother David, who conducted a tile factory, in which his brother Samuel became foreman. Later this was changed to pottery works, and was conducted as the D. Culbertson & Son and later as the Western Pottery Company. Samuel Culbertson earned a competency from his long service in the pottery industry and retired at the age of sixty-eight. He died August 25, 1921.

He was a Union soldier in the Civil war, enlisting at White Hall in Company D of the Fourteenth Illinois Infantry. His first battle was at Shiloh. He was with Sherman's army in the Atlantic campaign and the march to the sea, also the march through the Carolinas, terminating in the Grand Review at Washington. While a soldier he was injured in a railroad collision, being knocked off a car and sustaining injury to his head and breast. After the war he received a pension. He was an active worker and comrade in the Grand Army of the Republic and frequently attended state encampments. He was a staunch republican and for many years identified with the Christian Church, his only fraternity being the Modern Woodmen of America.

Samuel Culbertson married Louisa Jones near Virden, Illinois, daughter of William Jones. She died in February, 1907, at the age of seventy-three. Her children were: Anna, who died in childhood; Samuel Edgar; John Frank, who died when comparatively a young man, leaving children by his marriage with Sarah Evelyn Baker; Edith B. Bishop, of Alton, Illinois; Ethel May and Harold Culbertson, both of White Hall.

Samuel Edgar Culbertson was born April 19, 1868, while his parents were living on a farm at White Oak, Illinois. He attended school at White Hall after 1877, graduated from high school, and was employed for a time in a pottery and later in a chair factory. For twenty years he was an educator, teaching in a number of country districts. His last work was done in the schools of Belltown, Greene County. Since leaving school work he has been connected with the White Hall Lumber Company.

Mr. Culbertson, who has never married, is a charter member of White Hall Lodge of the Knights of Pythias. He cast his first presidential vote for Benjamin Harrison in 1892, and has steadily supported the republican platform and candidates since that date.

JOHN A. HEATON, Doctor of Dental Surgery, has been the leading representative of his profession at Hoopeston for over a quarter of a century, and he has held the office of mayor of Hoopeston for six years.

Doctor Heaton was born in Grant Township, Vermillion County, Illinois, August 12, 1872. His grandfather, Isaac Heaton, was born in Ireland, in 1791, came to the United States when a young man, first living in Coshocton, Ohio, and during the seventies moved to Grant Township, Vermilion County, Illinois, where he followed farming until his death in 1883. His son, Hugh Heaton, was born in Coshocton, Ohio, December 9, 1822, was reared there, was married in northern Indiana, but before his marriage located in Grant Township of Vermilion County. He was one of the substantial and energetic farm-

ers of that locality and was widely known as a man of splendid integrity. He died December 9, 1885. He was a republican and a member of the Methodist Church. Hugh Heaton married Mary R. Reece, who was born at North Liberty, Indiana, July 27, 1839, and died at the old homestead in Grant Township in December, 1923. They had a family of eight children: Edmond M., a teacher who died at Boswell, Indiana, at the age of forty-eight; Joseph W., member of the firm Heaton & Evans, clothiers, who died at Hoopeston in 1911, aged fifty; Lincoln L., a fruit grower at Harlingen, Texas; Nannie, wife of Lynn H. Griffith, present county auditor of Vermilion County; Sarah Alice, of Hoopestown; John A.; Orrie, a clerk in the post office at Hoopeston; and Reece, in the real estate business at Los Angeles.

Dr. John A. Heaton spent his early years on his father's farm in Grant Township, attended rural schools and the Hoopeston High School and subsequently prepared for a professional career in the Chicago College of Dental Surgery. He was graduated in 1898 with the degree D. D. S., and is a member of the Delta Sigma Delta fraternity. Doctor Heaton has continuously practiced at Hoopeston and has enjoyed a reputation for exceptional skill and success in his professional work. His offices are in the First National Bank Building. He has prospered in a business way, owning in addition to his residence at the corner of Fifth and Washington streets some five other dwelling houses in the city. He is associate director of the Chicago National Life Insurance Company.

Doctor Heaton from 1909 to 1918 was a member of the Hoopeston School Board. It was in 1919 that he was elected mayor of Hoopeston, and his fellow citizens have given him a repeated vote of their confidence every two years since then. He is a republican, a trustee of the First Methodist Episcopal Church, a member of Star Lodge No. 709, A. F. and A. M., and the Hoopeston Chamber of Commerce.

He married at Kankakee, Illinois, September 5, 1900, Miss Bessie A. Cowles, daughter of Herbert and Fannie (Hawkins) Cowles, now deceased. Her father was a farmer at Kankakee. Mrs. Heaton is a graduate of the Illinois State Normal School and for two years before her marriage, taught at Hoopeston. They have had four children: Bernice A., who graduated with the A. B. degree from De Pauw University and is connected with the Chronicle-Herald of Hoopeston; Kingsley, who died at the age of thirteen; and John Richard and Herbert Francis, both attending grammar school at Hoopeston.

CHARLES R. HALL. Among other things for which Chicago is famous is its magnificent Coliseum, the home of conventions, in which have been held some of the largest and most remarkable gatherings of the country. The project of erecting, within convenient distance of the loop district, a convention hall large enough to accommodate the vast crowds which attend such great events evolved from the fertile brain of that eminent and public-spirited citizen, John Gibson, who not only brought the matter before the city, but financed the undertaking, and served as treasurer of the Coliseum Building Corporation until his retirement January 4, 1926. During all of the initiatory work he was associated with the late Stewart Spalding, the latter being secretary of this great undertaking. One of the men now carrying on the work so ably begun is Charles R. Hall, president of the corporation, and one of Chicago's foremost business men. He was born in Afton, Iowa, in 1866, and came to Chicago as a youth. Learning mechanical and electrical engineering, he began his practical career as an employe of the Coliseum Building Corporation as an assistant mechanical and electrical engineer during the process of its construction, and has continued with this corporation, steadily rising, until in 1920 he was made its president, which office he has held since. He is a Mason and has been advanced through the different bodies of both the York and Scottish Rites, and he also belongs to Medinah Temple, A. A. O. N. M. S., and to the Royal Order of Jesters, a Shrine organization. For many years he has been closely connected with civic affairs.

The charter for the Coliseum Building Corporation was issued December 22, 1898, and construction began soon thereafter. On account of some unavoidable delays the building was not completed until some two years later. Five republican national conventions have been held within its walls, which alone would make the building famous, but there have been many other important events held there, including the following: National Automobile Show, American Road Builders Exposition, National Shoe Retailers Convention, National Railways Appliance Show, Six-Day Bike Races, Chicago Merchandise Fair, Travel and Outdoor Life Exposition, Own Your Home Exposition, Sells-Floto Circus and Menagerie, Ringling Brother Circus and Menagerie, Barnum and Bailey's Circus, National Business Show, Food and Household Exposition, Enclosed Automobile Show, Used Car Automobile Show, Automotive Accessory Show, Chicago Radio Show, Poultry Show, Graphic Arts Exposition, Window Display Men's Exposition, American Mining Congress, Restaurant Show, Hotel Men's Show, Chemical Show, Health Show, Brewery Show, National Confectionery Show, Music Show, Motorcycle and Bicycle Show, Athletic Entertainments, Saengerfest, Skate Tournament, Allied Bazaar, large banquets and balls, National Beverage Show, Electrical Show, Moving Picture Show, Vocational Show, Specialty Salesmen's Exposition, Horse Show, Tribune Land Show, and 101 Ranch Wild West Show.

The Coliseum is located from 1439 to 1513 South Wabash Avenue, and it is this great hall that has given Chicago the name of the Convention City. Some idea of the accommodations afforded here may be had from the following figures. The Coliseum itself has a seating capacity of 14,000; its floor space is 52,000 square feet, in a hall 303x172 feet. The North Hall has a seating capacity of 4,500, and a floor space of 18,000 square feet, the hall being 105x172; while the South Hall, with three floors, each 70x172, contains the ballroom which seats 1,200 people.

Associated with Mr. Hall in the management of the Coliseum Building Corporation are George Bogart, vice president; R. T. Badger, treasurer and vice president of the Equitable Trust Company of Chicago; and Charles R. Francis, secretary, ex-commissioner of public works, City of Chicago; all well-known figures in Chicago's commercial and financial circles.

Mr. Hall married in September, 1889, Miss Rosella Prickett, of Kirkville, Missouri. They are the parents of one child, Hazel, living with her parents at 111 Linden Avenue, Wilmette, Illinois. Mr. Hall is a director of the Chicago Motor Club, treasurer of the Exhibitors Service Company, secretary of the Coliseum Athletic Club, secretary of the Chicago Merchandise Fair, member and vice president of the Auditorium Managers Association of North America, and also belongs to Chicago Lodge No. 4, B. P. O. Elks, and is a life member of the Loyal Order of Moose.

EDWARD THOMAS GUTHRIE. The prosperous banker and business man illustrates in his experience the ups and downs of financial and commercial affairs, their fascinating promises of fortune, as well as their equally abundant opportunities for failure. Most energetic men have their full share of both, and it is the persevering men of native talent who eventually gain success. Edward Thomas Guthrie, president of the First State Bank of Mattoon, and a leading citizen of Coles County, while he has made money and attained prominence as a banker, has not been content to rest upon the honors thus gained, but has ever reached out to grasp other opportunities, developing them not alone for his own benefit but for the betterment of the community.

Mr. Guthrie was born on a farm in Coles County, Illinois, November 3, 1873, and is a son of William J. and Martha E. (Threlkeld) Guthrie, the latter being a daughter of Mathew P. Threlkeld, one of the early settlers of Coles County. The country school in the vicinity of his home furnished Mr. Guthrie with his early educational training, following which he pursued a course at Lee's Academy, which was located at Loxa, Coles County. This training was supplemented by a business course at the Terre Haute Commercial College, from which he was graduated in the spring of 1892. In the fall of the same year he became a clerk in the First National Bank of Mattoon, of which institution he became assistant cashier in 1896. He was cashier of the Mattoon National Bank in 1902 for about a year and then turned his attention to the general insurance and real estate business, in which he achieved marked success, and was an independent adjuster of fire losses for leading fire insurance companies for eighteen years. In January, 1924, Mr. Guthrie became the organizer of the First State Bank of Mattoon, of which he has been president since its inception and which is accounted one of the substantial and reliable institutions of this part of the state and which has grown and developed rapidly under Mr. Guthrie's able administration of its affairs. He is the largest stockholder of this bank and a member of the Board of Directors, and has several other connections of a business character at Mattoon, being a director in the National Building and Loan Association, vice president and a director of the Mattoon Crystal Ice Company, and a director in the Association of Commerce, of which body he was president in 1924. Politically a republican, and always voting the regular ticket, he was a member of the county Board of Supervisors for two terms, from 1907 to 1911, and resigned from that body in the spring of 1911, when elected mayor of Mattoon, an office in which he served one term, from 1911 to 1913. For twenty-two years Mr. Guthrie has been a member of the Knights of Pythias, is a past chancellor of Palestine Lodge No. 46, was grand chancellor of the order in the state from September, 1919, to September, 1920, and at present is one of the five supreme representatives from Illinois in the Supreme Lodge. He also belongs to the Improved Order of Red Men. He belongs to the Mattoon Country Club. His religious connection is with the Central Church of Mattoon, an independent church of the Protestant faith which is formed of a combination of Congregationalists, some Presbyterians and others.

On June 3, 1896, at the home of the bride about five miles east of Mattoon, in Coles County, Mr. Guthrie was united in marriage with Miss Jennie E. Herman, daughter of John and Amanda Herman, old residents of Coles County, and to this union there have been born two children: Helen, the wife of George M. Montgomery, a resident of Wichita, Kansas; and Lawrence, now a student of the University of Illinois.

CHARLES B. CAUDLE is one of the veteran business men at the National Stockyards of East St. Louis. He began his career there as a cattle salesman and now for a number of years has been head of one of the best known and most successful live stock commission firms.

He was born in Harrisonville, Missouri, October 25, 1869, son of Patrick D. and Dora R. (Crow) Caudle, and grandson of Patrick Caudle and Joshua Crow, both natives of North Carolina. Joshua Crow was ninety years of age when he died. Patrick D. Caudle was born and married in North Carolina, and three children were born in that state. After the war he moved to Missouri, in 1868, and during the rest of his active life was a farmer and dairyman and much interested in public affairs in his home community. He died in 1894. His widow is now eighty-seven years of age. They had six children: Arthur B., who married Grace Price and they have two children; Luella, who married C. P. Gibson and left two children; Anna B., wife of William H. Simonson, mother of two children; Charles B.; Fannie, wife of William Hoelscher and mother of one child; and Mayme, wife of Albert Garrison, and they have one child.

Charles B. Caudle was five years of age when his parents moved to Iowa and he grew up and attended school at Centerville. Much of his early experience was gained in farm work and around live stock. He was on his father's farm to the age of eighteen. He then learned and followed the barber trade for four years, and following that came to the

National Stockyards at East St. Louis. He began his service there for the White & Williams Company, serving them for four years and then became cattle salesman for the C. M. Keys Live Stock Commission Company. Since then he has been in business for himself. For four years he was a member of the partnership Dimmett, Caudle & Smith, but in 1917 established the Caudle Live Stock Commission Company, and has made this one of the best known firms of the stock yards. His son is now associated with him in business.

Mr. Caudle married at Bentonville, Arkansas, Miss Matha G. Williams, daughter of Washington and Rilla (Lattimer) Williams. Her mother died in 1904. Washington Williams, who died in 1914, was one of the prominent men at the National Stockyards, for many years having been a commission dealer there and was member of the firm White & Williams, the first employers of Mr. Caudle. In the Williams family were three children: Arden, deceased; Dwight L., manager for the Dawson Fuel & Coal Company at Dallas, Texas; and Mrs. Caudle. Mr. Caudle has one son, Arden A., and a grandson, Charles Joseph Caudle. Mr. Caudle is prominent in church work, being a member of the Official Board of the Methodist Episcopal Church, a trustee and chairman of the Finance Committee and member of the Evangelical Association of the Methodist Episcopal Church at St. Louis and secretary of the Sunday School. He is also a trustee of Trinity Methodist Episcopal and Wesley churches of St. Louis.

Esco N. Bowen has been practicing law at Herrin since 1918. He is the present judge of the City Court and enjoys high standing both professionally and as a citizen.

His great-grandfather, James Bowen, was a pioneer settler of Lawrence County, Illinois, coming from Virginia. He was an officer in the Black Hawk war and he also saw service as a soldier in the War of 1812. He was a farmer, and after settling in Lawrence County lived there until his death. His son, also named James, was a boy when brought from Virginia to Illinois, and was likewise a farmer in Lawrence County. He married Marion Perkins, who was born near Lexington, Kentucky. She attained to the advanced age of ninety-three years, and her death occurred only recently, in 1925, at Sumner, Illinois.

George Bowen, father of Judge Bowen, was born on the old homestead in Lawrence County. He lives at the edge of Lawrenceville, not far from his birthplace, and for many years has enjoyed unusual prosperity and success as a farmer, owning several farms in Lawrence County. He married Julia Loos, a daughter of Daniel and Mary Elizabeth (Tilton) Loos, her father of Pennsylvania ancestry while her mother represented a well known Ohio family.

Esco N. Bowen was the only child of his parents and was born at Chauncey, Illinois, May 27, 1893. He attended the grade schools of his home locality, spent three years in the Lawrence High School and graduated from Sumner High School. His work in public schools was supplemented by three years in the Illinois Normal University at Normal, following which he taught a term of school in Lawrence County.

In 1915 he was graduated from the Blomington Law School, was admitted to the bar the same year and opened his first law office at Bridgeport, Illinois, where he remained three years. He acted as city attorney of Bridgeport for three years and for one year was assistant state's attorney under R. M. Shaw. Judge Bowen gave up his law practice at Bridgeport on account of failing health, and spent a winter recuperating in Southwest Texas. He returned to Illinois in 1918, and in the same year married Beulah Schraeder, daughter of Joseph H. Schraeder, of Eldorado, Saline County. She was born and reared at Murphysboro, Illinois. After his marriage Mr. Bowen opened his law office at Herrin and has gained a large clientele there. He was elected judge of the City Court in 1922 on the Independent ticket. Judge Bowen is a member of the Masonic Lodge at Sumner, having taken his first degrees at the age of twenty-one. He is affiliated with the B. P. O. Elks, Eagles and Knights of Pythias at Herrin, the Independent Order of Odd Fellows at Chauncey, and the Improved Order of Red Men at Bridgeport. Judge and Mrs. Bowen have two children, Anna Marie and Betty Jule.

JOHNSTON CITY STATE BANK. This is an institution that reflects not only the commercial growth and prosperity of the community where it is located, but also some of the activities of a very prominent family of this section of Williamson County, that represented by the president of the bank, Mr. Peter Wastier, who is now eighty-five years of age and has long since turned over the details and executive duties of banking to the younger men, his grandsons being the active officials of the institution. However, Peter Wastier still appears at the bank daily and his appearance lends confidence to those who for so many years have looked upon him as one of the chief bulwarks of the business prosperity of the village.

The Johnston City State Bank was organized December 31, 1904, the active men in the organization being Peter Wastier, Ed. Duncan, Lon Peterson, A. C. Stiritz and one or two other citizens of what was then a comparatively new town. Peter Wastier was elected president and has served continuously from the beginning. He and A. C. Stiritz, now vice president, are the only two members of the original board still active as directors. The first cashier was Mr. Lorenzo Felts, and there were several cashiers during the early years. W. S. Hardesty was cashier for a number of years, until succeeded on November 15, 1924, by Mr. William O. Huck, who is a grandson of Peter Wastier. Two other grandsons of the venerable banker, Albert Becker, bookkeeper, and Leo Becker, are both assistant cashiers. This bank was started with a capitalization of $25,000. This was increased in 1907 to $50,000. The first home of the bank was a building on the south side of West Main Street. In 1912 the present modern bank building, 48 by 148 feet, two stories and basement, was completed and occupied. The cost of this substantial banking structure at pre-war prices was

$27,000. The Johnston City State Bank today has total resources of over a million dollars, the deposits amounting to approximately $982,000. The bank has a surplus of $50,000. The directors besides Mr. Wastier and Mr. Stiritz are Ira M. Leigh, vice president, H. J. H. Becker, J. F. Becker, A. A. Becker and Ed M. Stotlar.

Peter Wastier was born December 16, 1841, in southern Illinois, son of Peter Wastier, Sr., a native of Alsace-Lorraine, who came to the United States when a young man and located in that section of Illinois east of St. Louis. He married Mary Wesser, who died in 1846. He died in 1861, at the age of seventy. Their son, Peter Wastier, as his long life shows, has always been possessed of wonderful physique and vitality. He began life in humble circumstances, with little education, and after the death of his mother he lived with an uncle, whom he accompanied to Williamson County in 1859. He grew up on a farm three miles north of the site of Johnston City, and he lived in that locality, engaged in farming, for forty years. He had a natural aptitude for business, and his vision of opportunities led him to anticipate the development of several communities in southern Illinois. With the building of a railroad and the establishment of a station at Frankfort he bought land there and platted nine additions to the town. He also became president of the Frankfort State Bank. He likewise anticipated the development of an important town at Johnston City, bought farm land and divided it into lots and has been a resident of the locality since 1902. He is a member of the Masonic fraternity and is a republican in politics.

He married, May 30, 1864, Miss Barbara Rigel. She died in February, 1906. Of this marriage there were two daughters who reached mature years: Caroline, who became the wife of Henry Becker; and Mary Lucy, who became the wife of John Huck, Jr. John Huck, Jr., is now practically retired but lives on his farm near Johnston City. His father was John Huck, Sr. John Huck, Jr., and wife became the parents of seven children, and four are now living, three daughters and one son.

The one son of Mr. and Mrs. Huck is William O. Huck, cashier of the Johnston City State Bank. He was born on the Peter Wastier homestead three and a half miles northeast of Johnston City, January 15, 1894. Mr. Huck was educated in rural schools, and also attended the Southern Illinois State Normal University at Carbondale. He has been connected with the Johnston City State Bank since 1915, beginning as bookkeeper and in 1924 was elected cashier. He is unmarried.

HOWARD E. BARBER has done some big things in transportation work in Illinois. He received his training in steam railroading, and has had a long experience in every phase of railroad work, but his outstanding achievement has been in providing an adequate system of motor bus transportation for southern Illinois. Mr. Barber is president and general manager of the Egyptian Transportation System and is also president and general manager of the Marion and Eastern Railroad. His home headquarters are at Marion.

In 1917, as representative of some eastern capitalists, he was sent to southern Illinois to view and investigate conditions preliminary to the building of electric interurban lines. He was favorably impressed with many conditions, particularly population and need for better transportation facilities. At the same time he was more impressed with the idea that the facilities of such transportation should be on the basis of hard roads and by motor driven busses, rather than trolley cars. His report favoring this was ridiculed, but eventually he won over his financial backers, and brought about the formation and incorporation of the Egyptian Transportation System. In 1918 that system started operation with one bus between Harrisburg and Marion. The officers of the company were: Howard E. Barber, president and general manager; E. G. Bolger, vice president; A. W. Haggerty, secretary, treasurer and accountant; and D. E. Burnett, superintendent.

In recent years the system has developed rapidly. In 1922 the line was put in operation between Marion and Carbondale. The greatest expansion came in 1924, with the installation of service between Carbondale and Centralia, Duquoin and Benton, Marion and Mount Vernon, Mount Vernon and Centralia, Carbondale to Johnston City by way of Herrin. In 1925 a through service was installed at all points in southern Illinois to and from St. Louis. At the present time plans are being made to extend the service as far north and east as Danville, Illinois. This system has some of the best equipment found anywhere in America, including thirty-two modern motor busses.

In achieving these results Howard E. Barber has gone at the task with an indomitable will and energy that have been characteristic of his entire career. He was born at Dixonville, Pennsylvania, October 3, 1885, and was reared on the farm of his parents, Robert S. and Martha Barber. Up to the age of fifteen he attended country schools, then worked in a sawmill and later in logging camps. When he was seventeen he went to work for the Pennsylvania Railroad System as a lineman. By paying close attention and through the power of intense interest he learned to read messages as they were being received by the operators. However, while he could understand the message perfectly he could not at the same time write it word for word as it came over the wire. His mind had not yet been trained to do two things at once. With the perseverance characteristic of him he soon overcame this fault, and was assigned duty as an operator at Bradley Junction, Pennsylvania, being the first new operator put to work without having gone through the regular apprenticeship in an office. In 1903, desiring to learn actual railroading, he entered the train service as a brakeman and the following year was made conductor, being then only nineteen years old. Six months later he decided to broaden his knowledge of railroading by experience in the motive department. Hence he was given a job as fireman, and six months later was an engineer and for eighteen months had a regular run on the Pennsylvania system lines east of Pittsburgh. In 1906 he returned to the telegraphic department and in 1907 was made

Robert L. McKinlay

train dispatcher at Cresson, Pennsylvania, and eighteen months later was promoted to assistant train master at the same point.

Mr. Barber in 1909, leaving the Pennsylvania System, went with the New York Central Lines as train dispatcher, and soon was made general yard master at Albany. From that he was promoted to assistant train master at Clearfield, Pennsylvania.

He resigned this position to go out to East St. Louis and take charge of the East St. Louis & Suburban and the Alton, Granite & St. Louis Traction Lines, thus coming directly into contact with electric interurban transportation. In 1916 he went to Texas, and for a time was president and general manager of the Sugarland Railroad, one of the short lines of Texas. This position he resigned in 1917, and soon afterward accepted the commission from eastern capitalists to investigate transportation conditions in southern Illinois, with results that have already been described.

On coming to Marion he was called upon to undertake the management of the Marion & Eastern Railroad, which had been built to reach eleven coal mines, but which both as a physical property and growing business concern was in a bad way. As president and general manager he undertook the complete rehabilitation of the road, including the making over of the physical property by the laying of new ties and ninety pound rails.

Mr. Barber is a member of the Marion Golf Club, is affiliated with the Lodge of Masons at Pennsylvania, belongs to the Scottish Rite Consistory and Shrine of East St. Louis, is a member of the Marion Lodge of Elks, the Knights of Pythias at Cherrytree, Pennsylvania, and the Independent Order of Odd Fellows. When America entered the World war he enlisted, and went into training with the railway engineers at Camp Humphries, Virginia, but was soon taken out by Secretary McAdoo as a man whose highest usefulness to the government consisted in what he could do for the railroads at home.

Mr. Barber married, in 1918, Miss Estelle Pironi, of St. Louis.

ROBERT LANG MCKINLAY. A resident of Illinois almost half a century, the late Robert Lang McKinlay was distinguished as an attorney, practicing law at Paris from 1868 to 1917, had a reputation throughout his part of the state as an orator and debator of great eloquence, served in the Legislature and obtained some of the highest honors and positions in the Masonic fraternity in Illinois.

He was born at Cincinnati, July 14, 1839. His father, James McKinlay, a native of Campbelltown, Scotland, was a mechanical draftsman. He came to this country from Scotland in 1829 with three Campbelltown friends, one of whom was George Armour, the prominent grain merchant who settled in Chicago. James McKinlay died in 1893, and at that time two of the pumping engines (the Harkness and the Powell), of the Cincinnati Water Works system, for which he had drafted the patterns, were toiling smoothly on as they had been for fifty years.

Robert L. McKinlay became interested in his fathers work and at the age of fourteen drafted the patterns, made the castings and finished a miniature steam engine with the usual slide valve, pitman, crank and fly wheel, for which he received a special premium of $50 at the fourteenth annual exhibition of the Ohio Mechanics Institute held in Cincinnati in 1855, this being the prize offered for the best invention or work of a minor mechanic of the Valley of the Mississippi. From childhood, he was a careful student and, after attending Hughes High School, entered the Naval Academy at Annapolis. He received his appointment as acting midshipman U. S. N., in February, 1857, through his own efforts; at first applying to the congressman of his district, who wrote him that there was no vacancy and to apply for the one from the nation at large but not to be discouraged if he did not receive this appointment "that the same indomitable spirit which you manifest in reference to this matter would, if persisted in, secure your success in any profession or calling you might select." Many of his classmates were prominent during the war with Spain. Rear Admiral W. F. Sampson, Rear Admiral F. J. Higginson and Commodore John W. Phillip. Rear Admiral George Dewey had entered in 1854 and Commodore W. S. Schley in 1856. After making a cruise in the U. S. Steamship Preble, visiting France, Spain and the Madeira islands, the service became distasteful to him and he resigned. On his return to Cincinnati he began the study of law in the office of R. A. Johnson, and was graduated from the Law School of the Cincinnati College April 16, 1860, being admitted to the Ohio bar the same day and later engaged in practice at Cincinnati.

At the outbreak of the Civil war he enlisted in Company I of the Twenty-second Ohio Regiment, being elected first lieutenant and at the organization of the regiment was made adjutant. His commission was dated April 21, 1861, ten days after the firing upon the flag at Fort Sumter. In August of that year his regiment was mustered out, having completed more than the term of service for which the members had enlisted. Returning home, he was very active in recruiting the glorious old Fifty-ninth Ohio Volunteer Infantry, becoming captain of Company A, commission dated September 12, 1861. He saw hard service in West Virginia and Tennessee, but on account of ill health was compelled to resign May 26, 1862.

Mr. McKinlay later resumed the work of his profession in Cincinnati. In the fall of 1868 he moved to Paris, Illinois, and was admitted to the Illinois bar at Ottawa. He early established a large practice as a successful lawyer. He was corporation attorney for the Big Four Railroad for a period of approximately twenty-five years. During his association with this corporation, there was much local litigation against the R. R. Co.; the value of his services in local and state courts in behalf of his clients is attested to by his long and honorable service with the Big Four Railroad Company. During his long life in his adopted city he was closely identified with affairs of state and was a prominent character in the democratic party. Although a strong partisan, he in a great measure enjoyed the respect of his political opponents and held their confidence. Another tribute to Senator McKinlay is quoted from J. B. Watson's Biograpical Sketches, "Either as an orator or a debater—there is wide distinction—Mr. McKinlay may have an equal in the assembly, but he certainly has no superior. Listening to some special argument in support of or against some measure before the Senate or to reflections cast upon his party by the opposition, according to the mood he is in, he either bursts forth like a torrent, unable to give sufficient rapidity of expression to his thoughts, or, in his usual calm and deliberate manner, pulls his adversary's argument to pieces and places it in just the kind of light he wishes it to appear; the stranger, listening to him today, while speaking, would be amazed on the morrow to hear him when hurling his arguments and defiance across the Senate. Yet Mr. McKinlay can speak in another vein; when the lawyer pleading his case, or the statesman speaking in support of a party measure is put aside and the man only is speaking—speaking from the heart and not from the lips—then Mr. McKinlay is heard at his best. In making a eulogistic speech before the House of Representatives on Judge John Scofield, shortly after that gentleman's death, his great heart swelled when speaking of the friend whom he had known so many years and only found relief in the utterance of the sweetest thoughts and the kindest sentiments, in tribute to his departed friend and brother, in one of the most beautiful, chaste and eloquent orations ever uttered within the walls of the Capitol." Having unusual ability he was recognized as a man of power and was held in the highest esteem.

He was elected and served four terms as city attorney of Paris in the years 1876-1878-1882-1892-1894, he was elected a member of the Illinois State Legislature, the first four terms to the House of Representatives and in 1894 to the Senate. In the thirty-eighth General Assembly he was recognized as the leader, was chairman of the appropriation committee, chairman of the steering committee and the orator of his party. Quoting from the "Illinois State Messenger" of December 25, 1897, "Honorable R. L. McKinlay is the pride of his constituents. His hard and honest efforts, in behalf of the common people, have won for him a place in the heart of every man, woman and child in the Forty-third Senatorial District. His uncompromising disposition when convinced that he is right has brought for him the title of leader for the Democratic side of the Senate. He is firm and decisive in his convictions. The high honor in which he is held by the frequenters of the Senate chamber is certainly surprising and we feel safe in saying that Paris, Edgar County, has furnished a people's savior if they will only continue him in office."

In 1880, when General Hancock was a candidate for the presidency, Mr. McKinlay was a presidential elector from the old Fifteenth Congressional District. In 1884, when Carter Harrison was a candidate for governor, Mr. McKinlay was a candidate on the same ticket for attorney general, and during this state campaign he received the title of "Honest Bob."

In fraternal orders he was a member of the Independent Order of Odd Fellows for more than fifty years, receiving the veterans jewel. In 1892, when that order was in its prime, he was elected and served two years as grand master of the Ancient Order of United Workmen of this state. To the Ancient Free and Accepted Masons of Illinois he gave every possible allegiance serving as worshipful master of Prairie Lodge a number of terms, high priest of Edgar Chapter, Royal Arch Masons, eminent commander of Palentine Commandery. On December 10, 1869, he was created a Knight Templar, a year later was elected eminent commander, being elected for three consecutive years, and first represented his Commandery in the Grand Commandery at Chicago in October, 1871. At the opening of the conclave in 1872 he was appointed to fill a vacancy as grand senior warden pro tem and the same day was duly elected grand warden. Within six years he was elected grand commander of Illinois. He attended the Grand Commandery forty-two years in succession, always taking an active part and being chairman of one of the most important committees for many years. For several years before his final illness he presided at the annual Past Grand Commanders' dinner. Also the Grand Royal Arch Chapter elected him to the position of grand master of the First Veil at its annual convocation in Chicago in 1894. He was regularly promoted and in 1903 was installed as Grand High Priest of the Grand Royal Arch Chapter of Illinois. He became a member of the Oriental Consistory of the Valley of Chicago in April, 1904, being chosen orator of the class and for about thirty years was a member of Medinah Temple of the Mystic Shrine at Chicago. He served as grand master of the Grand Lodge, A. F. and A. M. He also belonged to the Grand Army of the Republic.

Mr. McKinlay's first law partner was Judge A. Y. Trogden and afterwards he became a partner of Attorney Robert N. Bishop, who died in 1881. At that time John H. Anthony, who had been a student in their office, became Mr. McKinlay's law partner, continuing until Mr. Anthony accepted a government position at Washington during Cleveland's first administration. Mr. McKinlay then engaged in the practice of law alone until his son George M. McKinlay was admitted to the bar in January, 1892, when they formed a partnership.

Mr. McKinlay was a devoted member of St. Andrew's Episcopal Church and for many years was senior warden. He had been reared by Scotch Presbyterian parents, but became attracted to the Episcopal form of worship while attending the Naval Academy. The late Mr. McKinlay married Miss Margaret McMurchy, of New Richmond, Ohio. She passed away in 1897. To their marriage were born one son and two daughters: George M., who passed away in 1916, before his father; Helen Mar, who died in 1884; and Marie, the only surviving member of the family.

While Robert L. McKinlay was a power as a lawyer and a statesman he was one of the kindest most refined and considerate of men.

That he was surely beloved, one among many evidences is a letter written him by a prominent friend in Chicago: "Of all men whose friendship I esteem and whose affection I wish for, you are first among them." A number of years ago when he was on the program to make an address before a large audience at the Fair Grounds, and when there were also speakers from a distance, a republican friend who was acting as master of ceremonies announced: "Last but not least is our Bob, our Mack, the silver tongued orator of Edgar County." At another time, at a Masonic Home Coming, on his going to the platform to make an address the chairman said, "This is our brother whom we all love." So after living the greater part of his life in this community. where he had served its interest faithfully and well, he came to the end of this life esteemed by his fellow men, loved and trusted by all who knew him, old and young alike. Mr. McKinlay loved his friends and no one could be more appreciative of them. He passed away at his residence in Paris January 23, 1917.

LA FAYETTE PARRISH, who engaged in the house-furnishings and undertaking business in the city of Metropolis, Massac County, maintains his large and well equipped business establishment at the corner of Sixth and Metropolis streets. He was born at Stonefort, Saline County, Illinois, August 1, 1878, and he was a small child at the time of the death of his parents, Frank and Dora (Smith) Parrish, his father having been born in South Carolina. The orphaned boy was taken into the home of his maternal grandmother, Mrs. Sarah J. (Williamson) Smith, whose home was in Pope County and who was the mother of seven children, she having been of venerable age at the time of her death, May 30, 1916.

While residing in the farm home of his grandmother Mr. Parrish attended the neighboring district school until he was twelve years of age, when, in September, 1890, he became a student in the public schools of Metropolis. He here continued to attend school and to be employed during vacations and other leisure periods in the Toles flour mill until 1893, when he found employment on a farm near this city. In 1897 he returned to Metropolis, and after here being employed one year in a woolen mill he took a position in the undertaking establishment of J. M. Elliott on the 9th of January, 1899. In this connection he gained knowledge and experience in all details of the business, his association with Mr. Elliott having continued until October 2, 1911, when he engaged in the undertaking business in an independent way. In July, 1913, Mr. Parrish purchased a store that has been devoted to the sale of second-hand household furnishings, etc., and this he converted into one of the largest and finest retail furniture stores in Southern Illinois. Here he now carries a comprehensive and select stock of furniture and general house furnishings, and in the establishment is maintained also the modern undertaking department, with facilities that insure the highest grade of service. Mr. Parrish has made a record as one of the enterprising and progressive business men of Metropolis and is a citizen who takes loyal interest in all that concerns the communal welfare. He is a member of the directorate of the First National Bank of Metropolis and is the owner of several residence properties in the city, including his own modern and attractive home place.

Mr. Parrish is a staunch supporter of the cause of the republican party, though he has had no desire to enter the arena of practical politics. He has membership in the Illinois and Kentucky Undertaking Association, and is affiliated with the Independent Order of Odd Fellows, the Knights of Pythias and the Benevolent and Protective Order of Elks.

June 22, 1909, recorded the marriage of Mr. Parrish and Miss Virginia L. Greene, who was born at Portsmouth, Ohio, and who is a daughter of E. B. and Virginia (Moore) Greene, both likewise natives of the old Buckeye State. Prior to her marriage Mrs. Parrish had been a successful and popular teacher in the public schools, and after her marriage she continued her pedagogic service as a substitute or cadet teacher until 1920, since which year she has been the efficient science teacher in the community high school of Metropolis. Mr. Parrish is a deacon in the Christian Church, and his wife is a member of the Presbyterian Church. He has been liberal and public-spirited as a citizen and served one term as city treasurer of Metropolis. Of the two children of Mr. and Mrs. Parrish the elder, LaFayette, Jr., is living, his birth having occurred July 30, 1911, and he being now associated with his father's business. The younger of the children was Virginia Moore, who was born December 10, 1913, and whose death occurred February 25, 1919.

WILLIAM HARVEY WARD, M. D., is practicing medicine and surgery at Sesser in Franklin County, where his father was a pioneer doctor and one of the first citizens of that mining and agricultural community.

The Ward family originated in England. William Ward, a native of Virginia, came to Illinois at an early date and settled at old Duquoin. In 1849 he left the county and with ox teams and wagons traveled across the plains to California, where he enjoyed moderate success in his quest for gold. Returning to Illinois, he bought land and lived a long and honored life in Perry County.

He was the father of the late Dr. Emza E. Ward, who was born at the old homestead in Perry County in 1866. He had the advantages of the common schools of the country, and from youth was distinguished by his alert intelligence and ambition. For three years he taught school, then attended Ewing College, and in 1889 graduated in medicine from the old University of Missouri. He opened his office and practice at Winfield and in 1900 moved to Sesser, Franklin County, where his family was the third to locate in the new town. He established the first drug store and conducted it for several years. He continued his valuable work there as a physician and surgeon until his death in 1921. He was a thirty-second degree Scottish Rite Mason. At Winfield Dr. Emza Ward married, in 1889, Miss Alice Cleveland, daughter of James Cleveland, who was a first cousin of President Grover Cleveland. Mrs. Ward still lives at Sesser.

Her son, William Harvey Ward, was born at Winfield May 29, 1890. He attended grade schools there and at Sesser, was graduated in 1910 from Ewing College, and for a time attended the Barnes Medical College at St. Louis, and in 1914 graduated from the National University of Arts and Science. He at once returned to Sesser and was associated in practice with his father until the latter's death.

In May, 1917, he enlisted in the Medical Corps, spent six weeks in training at Camp Gordon, Georgia, and from Boston went to England and three weeks later to France with the Fifth Regiment, a regiment of replacement troops. He was assigned duty at a base hospital in France and continued in the service there fourteen months. Doctor Ward is a man of progressive ideals and enjoys a large practice. He is a member of the medical societies, the Masonic order, and the M. W. of A. He married, August 10, 1921, Miss Irene Cox, daughter of William Cox, of Ina, Illinois. To this union was born one girl, Neva June Ward, January 31, 1924.

THURLOW G. LEWIS. Admitted to the bar and beginning practice in 1915, Thurlow G. Lewis has since become one of Franklin County's most prominent attorneys. He is a member of a leading law firm of Benton, Williams & Lewis, his partner being Hon. Walter Williams.

Mr. Lewis represents a family that has been in Franklin County for over ninety years. His great-grandfather, Andrew Jackson Lewis, came from Tennessee in 1834 and settled in Franklin County. Two or three years after coming to the county he was drowned in Middle Fork Creek. His son, Andrew Jackson Lewis, Jr., was born in Tennessee, was a boy when brought to Franklin County, and spent his mature years as a farmer in the Mount Pleasant settlement. He was the father of Adam Franklin Lewis, who was born at the old homestead in May, 1859. He has lived on that one farm all his life, and has been identified with the substantial interests of the farm and community, where he is well known and esteemed. He married Louisiana Isabelle Galloway, whose family also came from Tennessee.

Thurlow G. Lewis, one of the nine children of Adam Franklin Lewis, was born on a farm in Franklin County October 6, 1886. He had the usual life and environment of a country boy. Beyond the public schools his education depended upon his own initiative and resourcefulness. For a time he was a student in Ewing College. He early decided upon the law as his future vocation, but having to make his own way it was some years before he was able to attend law school and qualify himself. In 1915 he graduated with his law degree from the University of Illinois, was admitted to the bar the same year and at once engaged in practice at Benton. Some valuable professional training came to him as assistant state's attorney under W. F. Spiller. For a year and a half he was a law partner of James T. Mooneyham. Since July, 1918, he has been in partnership with Walter Williams in the firm of Williams & Lewis, and they have a very large and profitable practice.

Mr. Lewis while still teaching and attending school married, at the age of twenty-one, Miss Edna R. Moore, daughter of George B. Moore, of Franklin County. They have five children, Loren Elmer, Frieda, Wayne, Lilla and June. Mr. Lewis is a member of the Masonic fraternity and the Baptist Church.

OSCAR HARRISON KIMMEL is the executive head and controlling stockholder of the Mount Vernon Printing Company, and is editor of the Daily Herald, which is published by this company. He has representatives standing in the field of newspaper enterprises in southern Illinois, and is a liberal and progressive citizen who takes vital interest in all that concerns the civic and material welfare and advancement of his home city and county.

Mr. Kimmel was born at Auburn, Sangamon County, Illinois, May 17, 1877, and is a son of John M. and Hannah (Garber) Kimmel, the former of whom died in 1896 and the latter in 1907. Concerning the other children of the family the following data are available: Missouri is the wife of Charles Ecker and they have four children; Jesse A. married Edith Kenney and they became the parents of seven children; Jennie is the wife of Thomas E. Bawden and they have two children; J. Lewis married Jeneva Crozier and they became the parents of five children; Grace M., next younger than he whose name initiates this review, is the wife of H. J. Cusker and they have five children; and Ruth N., wife of Walter M. Atkinson, has two children.

John M. Kimmel was born on a pioneer farm about one mile distant from Dayton, Ohio, his father having there settled about 1807, upon removal from his native Virginia. In the old Buckeye State John M. Kimmel was reared and educated, and there he continued to reside until 1866, when he came to Illinois and engaged in farming enterprise in Sangamon County. In 1891 he sold his old homestead farm in that county and removed with his family to Mount Vernon Township, Jefferson County, where he purchased a small farm, not far distant from Mount Vernon, and where he lived virtually retired until his death. The Kimmel family was founded in Virginia in the early Colonial period of our national history and about 1807, as already noted, the name became associated with pioneer activities in Ohio. The paternal grandmother of the subject of this sketch was a McMurray, the prefix of the name having eventually been dropped, so that the form Murray was held as the patronymic, Judge Murray, of Springfield, Ohio, having been a representative of this family. Allen Garber, the maternal grandfather, moved from Virginia to Ohio about the same time as did the Kimmels, and thus Os-

Albert H. Veeder

car H. Kimmel is a scion of Ohio pioneer ancestry on both the paternal and maternal sides.

The preliminary education of Oscar H. Kimmel was acquired in the district schools of his native county, and he was about fourteen years old at the time of the family removal to Jefferson County, where he completed a high-school course by attending the Mount Vernon Collegiate Institute. Thereafter he was for one year a student in the Illinois State Normal School at Normal, and in 1901 he was graduated from Ewing College, from which he received the degree of Bachelor of Science. He taught five years in the district schools of Jefferson County and two years in the graded schools of Mount Vernon. He next became principal of a school at East St. Louis, Illinois, where he was later advanced to the position of superintendent of the public schools of the city. This executive and pedagogic office he resigned in 1914, when he became vice president of the National American Insurance Society, a fraternal organization with headquarters in Kansas City, Missouri. He retained this office for some years, and in November, 1921, he resigned and returned from Kansas City to Mount Vernon, where he became editor and part owner of the Daily Herald, in the publishing of which he is now the president of the Mount Vernon Printing Company. He has brought the Herald up to high standard and has made the business successful through his careful and progressive policies. In the World war period he was registered for service and was assigned to the fourth class. He was active in local patriotic movements and service, and both he and his wife were specially influential in furthering the work of the Red Cross.

Mr. Kimmel is a stalwart advocate of the principles of the republican party, and he and his wife are zealous members of the Methodist Episcopal Church. He is affiliated with the Masonic fraternity, the Modern Woodmen of America, the Security Benefit Association, the American Insurance Union, and the Illinois State Newspaper Association, besides which he is a loyal and influential member of the Rotary Club in his home city.

In August, 1905, Mr. Kimmel wedded Miss Anna Aulbach, of Woodlawn, a part of the City of Chicago, where her widowed mother, Mrs. Augusta Aulbach, still maintains her home, the other children being Otto P., who married Helen Marquett and who has two children, Walter and Helen; and Agnes, who is the wife of Frederick H. Lacey, their children being two in number. Lizzie, eldest of the Aulbach children, is deceased, and Mrs. Kimmel was the next in order of birth. The father gave the greater part of his active life to farm enterprise. Mr. and Mrs. Kimmel have one child, Clelamae Lois.

ALBERT HENRY VEEDER, who died at Chicago July 13, 1914, had been a member of the Chicago bar forty years and in that time had achieved a notable place not only in his profession but in the business world also.

His first American ancestor was Simon Volkertse Veeder, who visited this country in 1644 and in 1652 permanently settled at New Amsterdam or New York. The late A. H. Veeder was in the seventh generation from this pioneer. His great-grandfather, Lieut.-Col. Abraham Veeder, was an officer in the American army during the Revolution.

Albert Henry Veeder, son of Henry and Rachel (Lansing) Veeder, was born at Fonda, New York, April 1, 1844, and was prepared for college in the elementary and high schools at Fort Plain in his native state. He graduated with the A. B. and M. A. degrees from Union College at Schenectady at the age of twenty-two and coming west, was superintendent of schools at Galva, Illinois, and while there read law in the office of John I. Bennett. He was admitted to the bar in 1868, and practiced several years in Galva before removing to Chicago in 1874. For a time he was attorney for the Town of Lake, the only position he ever held that brought him in any way in touch with politics.

His longest service as a lawyer was rendered as general counsel for Swift & Company, an office he held from 1885 until the close of his career. In this capacity he directed the preparation and frequently handled the entire course of litigations in which not only Swift & Company but the other packing interests were involved during the last thirty years of his life. The more notable of these cases are on record in the United States court, including the litigation growing out of the efforts of certain states to discriminate against products and industries of other states in favor of themselves by means of inspection and similar laws, the Oleo Margarine litigation in the State and Federal courts and the litigation against the so-called beef trusts beginning in 1902. Mr. Veeder was a director in Swift & Company, the St. Louis National Stock Yards, the San Francisco Land & Improvement Company, Libby, McNeil & Libby, the Chicago Junction Railway and Union Stock Yards Company and the St. Joseph Stock Yards Company.

He found time for active work in a number of civic organizations for the promoting of the best interests of Chicago and its people, and socially was a member of the Chicago Club, the Chicago Athletic Association, the University Club, the Mid-day Club, and was a Knight Templar and thirty-second degree Mason and Shriner.

A more intimate picture of his fine and signal character is afforded in the following words: "Mr. Veeder was a man of sound judgment, strong and cultivated intellect, vigorous character and conversant with and interested in all the great questions of the day. He maintained a reputation for zeal, self-sacrifice and devotion to duty, showing at all times masterful leadership by respect for the rights and opinions of others. As characterized by an intimate acquaintance, he was renowned for purity of character and an intense love for usefulness; independent though earnest in the support of what he thought right, rather than what was expedient; never an aspirant for office, and valuing only that popularity which follows a good man; practicing warm hearted charity in thought, word and deed, and always evincing an ability more than adequate for all he undertook."

Albert Henry Veeder married, August 15, 1866, Miss Helen L. Duryee, daughter of Rev. Isaac G. Duryee, of Schenectady, New York. Four children were born to their marriage: Henry, Albert H., Jessie and Paul L.

HENRY VEEDER is a son of the late Albert Henry Veeder, whose career as one of the conspicuous Illinois attorneys of his generation has been sketched above. Henry Veeder succeeded his father as general counsel for Swift & Company and has also had an extensive general practice for many years.

He was born at Galva, Illinois, May 13, 1867, son of Albert Henry and Helen L. (Duryee) Veeder. His home has been in Chicago since he was seven years of age. He attended schools at Englewood until 1880, was in preparatory school in the old Chicago University from 1880 to 1886, and in 1890 graduated with the B. A. degree from Yale University and in 1892 received his law degree at the Northwestern University Law School in Chicago. In the same year he engaged in practice with his father, and for a number of years past has been a member of the law firm Albert H. & Henry Veeder. He was made general counsel of Swift & Company in 1902, and has served in a similar capacity in a number of other business corporations.

He is a member of the Chicago, Illinois State and American Bar Associations, belongs to the Chicago Club, the Chicago University Club, the Chicago Athletic Association, the South Shore Country Club and Yale Club of New York. He married at Chicago, December 29, 1892, Miss Darlene Gibons, daughter of George Gilbert Gibons, who was a well-known Chicago attorney. The children of their marriage are Albert Henry and Helen Frances Veeder. The son Albert Henry is now assistant corporation counsel of the City of Chicago.

JOHN M. REID is a native of Williamson County, grew up there, and is now successfully established in the practice of law at Marion. From the time he left home as a young man until ten years ago he was away from his native county, attending school, teaching and practicing law, his experience taking him to many communities in many states.

As an introduction to the individual career of this Marion attorney some interesting facts should be stated regarding his ancestry. He is of a staunch old American family, and in one line his forefathers have been in this country for two centuries. From researches in genealogy conducted by Alice O'Rear MacFarlene of the Supreme Court of Missouri, the following data is compiled concerning his ancestry in the Woods line. Michael Woods, born in County Meath, Ireland, in 1684, came to America in 1726, bringing his two sons, William and John. They first settled in Lancaster County, Pennsylvania, and in 1734 moved to Virginia, Michael Woods being an early settler of Albemarle County. John Woods, second son of Michael, was born February 19, 1713, and died in Albemarle County, October 14, 1797. A large part of his life was spent in military service. He was with the Virginia Militia defending the frontier against the Indian attacks, and held a commission of major and lieutenant-colonel from the Virginia government. John Woods married Susanna Anderson and had six children. Their second son, James Woods, born January 21, 1748, married Mary Garland, February 25, 1779. John Woods was likewise a man of military experience and was colonel of a regiment of Virginia infantry. During the Revolution he was commissioned an officer of the Continental troops, November 12, 1776. His regiment was known successively as the Fourth, Eighth and Twelfth Virginia. Colonel James Woods, in 1790, with his family moved to Kentucky and settled in Gerrard County, where he died September 11, 1822.

The eleventh of the thirteen children of Col. James and Mary (Garland) Woods was Elizabeth Garland Woods. She became the wife of Garland Reid. John Reid, father of Garland Reid, and the earliest known ancestor of John M. Reid in the Reid line, lived in Kentucky and in 1836 removed with his family to Missouri. Garland Reid was born in Kentucky February 5, 1791, and he grew up in the home of well-to-do parents, was well educated for that time, became a teacher and was an able instructor of music, conducting singing school. After going to Missouri and settling in Randolph County he served as captain of the Missouri State Militia, and later was commissioned a colonel. Garland Reid and his wife, Elizabeth Garland Woods, had a family of eleven children, the ninth of these children being William M. Reid.

William M. Reid was for many years a resident of Williamson County, Illinois. He was born in Kentucky, went to Missouri in early manhood, was a Union soldier in the Civil war, and when a young man moved to Illinois and had his home for many years two and a half miles north of Marion. He was a substantial and respected farmer in that community until his death on May 4, 1917. He married at Marion, Bethany Jane Spiller, daughter of Elijah Spiller, who in his day was considered a wealthy man, owning a large tract of land underlaid with coal. William M. Reid's land was at the place called Spillertown, and along with farming he engaged in the production of coal. Mrs. Bethany Jane Reid died August 9, 1921. She and her husband had ten children: Zula R., who married Judge W. F. Slater of Marion; Dr. W. Edward, a graduate of the American School of Osteopathy at Kirksville and the Marquette Medical College of Milwaukee, who married Anna Goodall Borton, of Marion; Carrie E., widow of Dr. Chester I. Pease, and a resident of Chicago, four children; Dr. Charles C. Reid, of Denver, Colorado, whose record is given elsewhere; James Franklin, an osteopathic physician and surgeon at Warren, Ohio, who has a family of three children; John M. Reid, the Marion attorney; George W. Reid, osteopathic physician and surgeon at Worcester, Massachusetts, who married Dr. Eva Green, and had two children; Gertie M. Reid, who died in infancy; Ella, who married Dr. Edgar Austin, and lives at Huntington, West Virginia, the mother of two children; and Nellie Reid, who married Bert Stotlar, and both died, leaving one child.

Of this immediate family and ancestry, John M. Reid was born October 7, 1877, on the home farm, and during his boyhood in

the country he determined to become a lawyer. After the common schools he entered the Southern Illinois Normal University at Carbondale in the spring of 1896, and was graduated from the Marion High School at Marion in 1898, after which he taught a year in country districts and two years in the Marion High School. During one summer he attended the Kirksville Normal School in Missouri, and then spent two years in Hiram College of Ohio, the school of which President Garfield was at one time the head. Leaving the Ohio college, he went west and entered the University of Denver, from which he graduated in 1906 with the degree B. A. and LL. B., and at the same time passed the bar examination and was admitted to practice in the courts of Colorado. In 1907, after a period of residence and study, he received his Masters degree at Columbia University in New York. For three years he practiced law at Denver and for two years was in partnership with Frank H. Mason, now of New York.

Mr. Reid had for a long time carried the plan of completing his education by a trip around the world, but this necessitated earning the funds as he went. In 1913 he left Denver and spent a year as principal of schools at Montpelier, Idaho. From there he went to Spokane, Washington, then to Marshall in the same state, where he was principal of the high school, and in 1914 he had accumulated enough to start him on his world pilgrimage. Then the World war broke out and the project had to be abandoned. Instead he went to Alaska and practiced law at Anchorage until the death of his father in 1917 called him home, and while looking after his widowed mother he opened a law office, forming a partnership with R. R. Fowler. They were associated five years, and since 1924 he has carried on an individual practice in Marion.

Mr. Reid in 1918 was made assistant state's attorney and served eighteen months, handling many important cases during that time. He is a member of the Lions Club, B. P. O. Elks, Loyal Order of Moose, Independent Order of Odd Fellows and Rebekahs and the Knights of Pythias. He married, in 1919, Miss Anna Hearn, daughter of Ebenezer W. Hearn, of Marion, Williamson County.

CHARLES DURFEE, of Golconda, has been an educator, business man, banker and lawyer in southern Illinois through a busy career of forty years or more.

He was born in Saline County, Illinois, November 21, 1863, son of William Fielding and Lucretia (Moore) Durfee. His grandfather, Ebenezer Durfee, was of French ancestry, the original spelling of the name having been d'Arfe. William Fielding Durfee was born at Zanesville, Ohio, July 4, 1818, and died in Massac County, Illinois, in March, 1876. He came to Illinois from Covington, Kentucky, in 1856, settling at Stone Fork in Saline County. He was a man of versatile talents and training, was a civil engineer, owned a farm, became a merchant, but for the greater part of his active life practiced medicine. In politics he was a democrat. His first wife, whom he married in Ohio, was Mary Morrell. She died leaving children named Michael, Margaret, Samuel S. and William Fielding. Doctor Durfee married Lucretia Moore in Kentucky. She was born at Rising Sun, Indiana, of Irish parentage, and she died May 4, 1865. Her children were Alice, Andrew J., Lewis, Laura, Charles and Frank. The third wife of Dr. William F. Durfee was Mrs. Jane Barnett, and by this union there was one child, Joseph Alonzo.

Charles Durfee was only two years old when his mother died. He had limited opportunities during his boyhood, and from the age of nine was largely dependent on his own resources. He was thirteen years old when his father died. Mr. Durfee for about seven years did farm labor as a wage worker. He attended common schools, made the best of his advantages and secured a teacher's license, and gave twelve years to teaching as a profession. In the meantime he studied law, and for four years was county surveyor of Saline County. He was admitted to the bar in 1893, since which time he has practiced law at Golconda. Mr. Durfee served two terms in the Illinois General Assembly, elected first in 1906 and again in 1908, and subsequently served one term as mayor of Golconda. Besides his law practice he is president of the Pope County State Bank. In 1926 he was elected judge of the county court of Pope County, without opposition, and also was elected a Republican State Central Committeeman from the Twenty-fourth Congressional District. He was a delegate to the Republican National Convention in 1920. He attends the Methodist Church, is a Knight Templar Mason, and a member of the Independent Order of Odd Fellows.

Mr. Durfee married Mary Catherine Murphy on January 1, 1885. She died in 1893, the mother of two children: Dr. Claude Durfee, of Rosiclare, Illinois; and Mrs. Mary Steyer, deceased. In 1895 Judge Durfee married Lucy Berry. They have one daughter, now Mrs. Veneva Durfee Chandler.

CHARLES M. SEXTON is owner and editor of the Freeburg Tribune, one of the successful newspapers published in St. Clair County. He began learning the printing trade at the age of thirteen, and except for the service he gave during the World war, has been continuously at work in some phase of the newspaper publishing business ever since.

He was born at Sturgeon, Missouri, October 20, 1891, son of Middleton and Ida L. (Matthews) Sexton. His grandfather, John Sexton, a native of Missouri, who died in 1923, at the age of ninety-two, married Margaret Dustin, of the famous Massachusetts family of that name, one of whose members was Hannah Dustin, whose exploit in making her escape after capture by the Indians has been read by every American school boy and girl. The maternal grandfather of Mr. Sexton was David Matthews, who came from Kentucky. Middleton Sexton was a farmer, member of the Christian Church and died in 1891, before the birth of his son Charles. The widowed mother is still living at the age of sixty. The two other sons were: John Sexton, who married Myrtle Miller and has two daughters, Catherine and Louise, and William, who married Catherine Kimberland and has a son, Winton K.

Charles M. Sexton completed his high school course at Sturgeon, Missouri. In the meantime, at the age of thirteen, he began using the hours after school and Saturdays and holidays in the employ of D. Gray, who had the reputation of publishing the best newspaper in Missouri outside of St. Louis and Kansas City. In the Gray office he learned printing and much of the general business of publishing a newspaper. When he was eighteen he gave up his school work and gave all his time to his new profession, and at the age of nineteen came to Illinois and at Sesser in Franklin County bought the Herald. He was publisher of this paper three and one-half years, selling out and coming to Freeburg and purchasing the Tribune in 1916.

Mr. Sexton leased his paper during the World war period, making provision that the lease would terminate as soon as he returned from the service. In April, 1918, he enlisted, and was put in training in the Ray Automobile School at Kansas City, taking a six months' course in training to handle army trucks. In October, 1918, he sailed from Hoboken and landed at Brest with the Three Hundred and Second Water Transport Trucks for front line work. He went to the headquarters at Commercy, France, his special work being to supply the fighting lines with water. Owing to eye trouble he was in a hospital in France for two months, and in May, 1919, returned and landed at Cape May, New Jersey, and in June, 1919, was discharged. Since then he has given his time and best energies to making the Tribune one of the live organs of publicity in St. Clair County.

He married at Edwardsville, Illinois, December 22, 1916, Miss Myrtle Carter, daughter of George and Susie Carter. Her father is a coal mine operator. The other children of her parents are: Ethel, wife of Clarence Hertel; Bess, wife of Dr. R. J. Joseph, of New Athens, Illinois, and mother of two daughters, Harriet Jean and Doris May; Elmer G., who married Esther Bucksciedel; and Harry Carter. Mr. Sexton is a member of the Christian Church, while his wife is a Methodist. He belongs to the Printers Union and is affiliated with the Masonic Lodge and Knights of Pythias. He and his wife have two children: William Carter and Bettie Jane.

LEWIS C. MORGAN, M. D., who is president of the Jefferson State Bank at Mount Vernon, and who has been engaged in the practice of his profession during a period of nearly forty years, was born near Dahgren, Hamilton County, Illinois, January 18, 1861. The Doctor is a son of Philip W. and Harriet J. (Daymon) Morgan, the former of whom died in the year 1881 and the latter of whom is still living in 1925. Concerning the other children of the family the following brief data are available: Mary became the wife of W. I. Riddle, and they have two sons and three daughters; Annie became the wife of Augustus Irwin and is now deceased, their children being two sons and four daughters; Dr. Lewis C., of this review, was the next in order of birth; Nora, deceased wife of John R. Graves, became the mother of three sons and three daughters; William G. married Sallie Karns and they became the parents of one child; O. A. is the father of three sons and one daughter, the family name of his wife having been Grigg; Emma became the wife of Willis Shipley and is now deceased; and the next child died in infancy. The late Philip W. Morgan gave the greater part of his active life to productive farm industry and was one of the influential and highly respected citizens of Hamilton County, he having served in various local offices of public trust, including that of county commissioner, of which he was the incumbent three terms, his political allegiance having been given to the republican party. He was born in Kentucky, in 1839, and was a boy at the time of the family removal to Illinois, where he was reared and educated under the conditions of pioneer days. He went forth as a member of an Illinois regiment in the Civil war, and one of his brothers met his death on the battle line in that great conflict. The father of Philip W. Morgan was born in Virginia, of Colonial ancestry in the Old Dominion, and thence he removed to Kentucky, from which state he came with his family to Illinois about the year 1845. Here he passed the remainder of his life as a farmer and here also occurred the death of his wife, whose maiden name was Fannie Thompson and who was born and reared in Kentucky.

Mrs. Harriet J. (Daymon) Morgan was born in the State of Massachusetts, and is a daughter of Owen and Jerusha (Williamson) Daymon, her father having been born in Vermont and having been a representative of a staunch Colonial New England family that gave patriot soldiers in the War of the Revolution, on which score the sons and daughters of the subject of this sketch all have active affiliation respectively with the Sons of the American Revolution and the Daughters of the American Revolution.

Doctor Morgan passed his boyhood days on the home farm, and after having profited by the advantages of the district schools he continued his studies by attending Ewing College, in which he was graduated with the degree of Bachelor of Arts. Thereafter he completed a course in the Evansville Medical College at Evansville, Indiana, in which institution he was graduated in 1886. After thus receiving his degree of Doctor of Medicine he further fortified himself by the valuable clinical experience he gained in one year of service as an interne in a leading hospital in Nashville, Tennessee. He then initiated the practice of his profession at Dahlgren, in his native county, where he built up a large and representative general practice and where he continued to reside until 1905, since which year he has been engaged in successful practice at Mount Vernon, judicial center of Jefferson County. In the period of the nation's participation in the World war, Doctor Morgan served as medical examiner for the draft board of Jefferson County, and within his tenure of this position he made examination of more than 1,500 young men who had been called into service. The Doctor has proved one of the most loyal and public-spirited citizens of Mount Vernon, and was mayor of the city in the period of 1909-11. In 1905 he here effected the organization of the Jefferson State

Bank and became a member of its original directorate. He has had much to do with the shaping and ordering of the policies that have made this one of the substantial and important financial institutions of this part of Illinois, and he has been president of the bank since 1915. He is likewise a director of the First National Bank of Dahlgren, he having been the leader in its organization, in 1889, and having served as its president prior to his removal to Mount Vernon.

Doctor Morgan is found loyally arrayed in the ranks of the republican party, he and his wife hold membership in the Baptist Church, he has membership in the Jefferson County Medical Society and the Illinois State Medical Society, and in the Masonic fraternity his maximum York Rite affiliation is with the Mount Vernon Commandery of Knights Templars, the while he has received the thirty-second degree of the Scottish Rite and is also a Noble of the Mystic Shrine, besides having membership in the Independent Order of Odd Fellows, the Benevolent and Protective Order of Elks, and the Modern Woodmen of America.

At Dahlgren, in the year 1882, Doctor Morgan wedded Miss Jennie Brumbaugh, daughter of Dr. Andrew Brumbaugh and Sadie (Blake) Brumbaugh, the former of whom died in 1910 and the latter in 1918, the other two children being Carma, who is the wife of Rev. Theodore Gates, a clergyman of the Methodist Episcopal Church, and Della, who is the wife of Lewis Kuykendall, of Portland, Oregon. The children of Doctor and Mrs. Morgan are: Della, the wife of W. P. Wood, who is engaged in the insurance business at Mount Vernon, and they have three children, Vermadell, John L. and William (Billie); and Chloe, the wife of Irving Levhart, of Mount Vernon, and their one child is a daughter, Janice.

MYRON D. KING. The record of Pittsfield and surrounding district in matters of business, industry and public improvements has numerous occasions to make reference to the name of M. D. King, the veteran miller, a resident of Pittsfield for over half a century, and a man who at all times has exemplified the progressive spirit.

Mr. King was born near Monson, in Hampden County, Massachusetts, December 11, 1849, and represents the eighth generation of the King family in New England. Thomas King settled at Scituate, Massachusetts, in 1835, being the first of this generation. The ancestors of Myron D. King were soldiers in all the early wars and many of them in the War of the Revolution. His father, Dwight King, born January 29, 1810, was a Massachusetts farmer, and while he had few educational advantages himself he saw that his children were well provided for. He died July 28, 1888. He married Martha Vinton, born February 14, 1813, of another Massachusetts family. She died at the age of eighty-six, in 1899. They had three sons and one daughter, the daughter, Mrs. Waterman, dying at San Diego, California. The sons were: Frank M., who died at Monson, Massachusetts; Myron Dwight; and Judge Henry A., a distinguished lawyer of Springfield, Massachusetts.

Myron Dwight King attended the common schools and Monson Academy in his native town, was reared on a farm, but at the age of sixteen began an apprenticeship to learn the trade of straw hatter. He worked in one shop seven years. Then, in April, 1873, he started for the West. He spent a couple of weeks at Cameron, Missouri, where his sister then lived, was also in Kansas City, and then went to St. Louis, where a friend was engaged in the commission business and was incidentally interested in a flour mill at Pittsfield, Illinois. In that way Myron D. King arrived at Pittsfield June 1, 1873, and was given employment in the mill of C. P. Chapman & Company. Chapman had come from the vicinity of Hartford, Connecticut, in 1847, and was prominently connected with the grain milling industry of Pittsfield for many years. While in Massachusetts Mr. King had been earning wages of $90 a month. In Illinois he was paid $7.50 a week and performed work ranging from that of roustabout to loading cars, buying wheat and grain. He found increasing responsibilities in the Chapman Grain Mill and continued with the firm until the death of Mr. Chapman in February, 1899, when he acquired the interest of Mr. Chapman and organized the new firm of Dow & King.

Mr. King's personal experience affords an interesting view of changing conditions in the milling industry in this section of Illinois. When he came to Pittsfield there were seventeen mills in Pike County, and fully half a million bushels of grain annually was delivered by local farmers to the town of Pittsfield. At the present time the King Mill is the last survivor of the flour mills of the county except a midget mill at Kinderhook. Farmers immediately tributary to the mill deliver not to exceed 50,000 bushels of wheat annually. In the early days there were no elevators for the storage of grain, but now there are elevators at various points in the county, the King Milling Company being interested in more than half a dozen of them tributary to Pittsfield. Fifty years ago the local mills depended entirely upon wheat and other grains produced by the local farmers. Today a large part of the wheat ground at Pittsfield is raised in Kansas and Missouri. The mill of Dow & King was burned in 1899. It was rebuilt and the present plant was opened in April, 1900. In 1909, with the death of Mr. Dow, the business became incorporated under the name of the M. D. King Milling Company, with Mr. King and his two sons the active managers and owners. The mill has a capacity of 500 barrels of flour daily, and a large part of the product is sold outside of Illinois in Southern markets. Mr. King in 1911 organized the Barry Mill & Grain Company, of which he is president, and in 1918 the King Milling Company acquired three elevators in Pike County from the firm of Anderson & Garner. Mr. King while with the Dow & King firm built an elevator at Fall Creek, in Adams County.

Various other business interests has engaged the attention of Mr. King. Since 1898 he has been a director of the First National Bank of Pittsfield. He has served fifteen years as a director of the Millers Mutual Fire Insurance Company, and for ten years has been president of the Louisiana & Pike County Railway Company, which connects Pittsfield by rail with the Wabash Road.

One thing which should be especially remembered in his constructive citizenship was his leadership in promoting the hard road movement. He was a member of the Board of Supervisors when the proposition for building the first stretch of hard road in Pike County came up, and was the only one of the twenty-four supervisors to vote yes on the proposition. He personally advanced more than $8,000 for its construction and was given permission by the board to locate the new road, selecting a stretch extending east from the limits of Pittsfield on East Washington Street. The first construction involved only a mile and a half of road, and it was used to demonstrate the value of such construction and furnish the object lesson in a general campaign for the education of the public. Mr. King is chairman of the Pike County Hard Road Committee. He has been an alderman at Pittsfield, for many years treasurer of Newburn Township, and in politics has always been a republican, casting his first presidential vote for General Grant in 1872. He was a delegate to the Republican National Convention at Cleveland in 1924. He was an original Frank Lowden supporter for governor. Mr. King was made a Mason while living at Monson, Massachusetts. He is a member of the Hamilton Club of Chicago, the Missouri Athletic Club and Merchants Exchange of St. Louis.

Mr. King married at Pittsfield in November, 1876, Miss Rosabelle Chapman, daughter of C. P. and Amelia (Shaw) Chapman, who came from Wilbraham, Massachusetts, and were early settlers of Pike County, locating here in 1847. Her father was born in Tolland County, Connecticut. Mrs. King died in 1911, the mother of two sons, Lyndle C. and Vinton S. Lyndle C. was born in August, 1886, at Pittsfield and is now actively associated with his father in the milling business. He married Bertha Hesley, and has a son, Clark C., who is the third generation of the family interested in the milling business. The son Vinton S. King died January 28, 1922. He was educated in the local high school, the Western Military Academy at Alton and the Ferris Institute at Grand Rapids, Michigan. Vinton King married Lucile Hough and is survived by four children, Vinton S., Helen Rosebelle, Myron D. and Frank M.

Mr. Myron D. King married for his second wife, in Pittsfield, in January, 1913, Fannie (Webster) McCann.

BENJAMIN FRANKLIN ANDERSON. The duties and responsibilities of public office have claimed the greater part of the energies and time of Benjamin Franklin Anderson since he qualified for practice as an attorney. He had served three terms as county judge of Pope County. Judge Anderson has won professional success on merit, and thoroughly deserves the confidence and esteem which have so richly rewarded him.

He was born on a farm in Pope County, October 2, 1883, son of John G. and Elizabeth (Gilbert) Anderson, also natives of Pope County. His grandfather, William Anderson, a native of Pennsylvania and of Pennsylvania-German lineage and Quaker faith, came to Golconda in early life. He built the first stone house at Golconda. He died while the Civil war was in progress, when about sixty years of age. William Anderson married a Miss Gallimore, and they reared a large family of children. John G. Anderson was a farmer and country merchant in Pope County. He and three of his brothers were Union soldiers in the Civil war. He was in Company E of the One Hundred and Twentieth Illinois Infantry, and after the war was active with the Grand Army of the Republic. He always voted as a republican, and was a Methodist. He died at his home in Golconda in 1910, and his wife passed away in 1918. They were the parents of a large family of fourteen children. Elizabeth Gilbert, the mother of these children, was a daughter of James Gilbert, who was of English ancestry and a native of North Carolina. James Gilbert for his service as a soldier in the War of 1812 received a grant of land in the Rock Island district of Illinois, but subsequently moved to the southern part of the state and settled in Pope County. He married a member of the Rose family, one of the earliest in Southern Illinois, and they had a large family of children.

Benjamin Franklin Anderson spent the first eighteen years of his life on his fathers' farm. While there he attended common schools and for two terms taught in rural districts. Judge Anderson for several years lived in St. Louis, where he was employed, and in the intervals of employment attended Washington University as a law student. He paid all the expenses of his professional education. Later, on October 26, 1911, he received his law degree from the University of Michigan, and a year later was admitted to the bar in Illinois. Judge Anderson for a time was deputy county clerk and for two years master in chancery in Pope County. In 1914 he was elected county judge and was re-elected in 1918 and 1922, giving a continuous service of twelve years in that important office. He is a Knight Templar Mason.

Judge Anderson married, in 1913, Miss Chrystia Baker, a native of Golconda, daughter of the late John C. Baker, who was a lieutenant in an Illinois regiment during the Civil war and afterwards for many years a merchant in Golconda, and was postmaster when he died. Mr. and Mrs. Anderson have two children, Beverly Baker and Ben Franklin Anderson.

HENRY CUMMINGS ADDERLY, M. D., is one of the old time physicians of southern Illinois. His home for half a century has been at Chester. The good work he has done all over that section of the country has derived not only from his skill and ability as a physician but from his essential kindliness and constant desire to be of use to his fellow men.

His grandfather, William Adderly, came to America in 1834 and lived the rest of his life at Pittsburgh, Pennsylvania, where he became a prosperous merchant. Joseph Adderly, father of Doctor Adderly, was seventeen years of age when the family came from England. He finished his education in Pittsburgh and entered the ministry of the Episcopal Church. While in charge of a parish at Newcastle, Pennsylvania, he married Hannah Peters, whose family came from Plymouth, England, in 1836, and also settled in Pennsylvania. From Newcastle, Pennsylvania, Rev. Joseph Adderly moved to Stevens Point, Wisconsin, where he preached for a few years. He had a church at Hannibal, Missouri, when his son Henry Cummings was born, June 24, 1854. At that time the Episcopal Rectory stood four doors from the home of Mark Twain. Henry Cummings Adderly attended for a very brief time school at Hannibal, and the family then removed to Jefferson City, Missouri, where his father in addition to a regular pastorate was made chaplain of the State Penitentiary by Governor Price. Jefferson City remained the home of the family six years. The next call to duty took them to Mishawaka, Indiana. Doctor Adderly, a boy of eleven years, has a vivid recollection of the scene attending the passage of the train through Chicago bearing Abraham Lincoln through Mishawaka to Washington, D. C., to become President. From the Indiana town Rev. Joseph Adderly was next transferred to a church at Carlyle, Illinois, and in 1876 to Chester, where he was pastor of the Episcopal Church about a year. He died there in 1877, being survived by his wife until 1898.

Henry Cummings Adderly as a boy planned a career as a doctor. After completing his high school work he entered the St. Louis Medical College, where he was graduated M. D. in 1875. He first established his practice at Kemper in Jersey County, Illinois, but the following year removed to Chester in order to be near his father in his declining years. Thus Chester became his permanent home. Doctor Adderly practiced for many years when the work of the medical profession was exceedingly arduous, when there were no telephones or good roads, and when a doctor endured every conceivable inconvenience and hardship in all kinds of weather. He still maintains an office, though he has been quite willing that the younger generations of doctors should assume the burdens he carried so faithfully and well.

Dr. Adderly in 1904 was elected mayor of Chester and while he was never a willing candidate he was kept in that office for ten years. For several years he acted as prison physician at Chester, under appointment from Governor Deneen. Doctor Adderly for twenty years was a member of the Republican County Central Committee, and was for several years its chairman. He served twelve years as secretary of the pension board, and as county physician eight years.

He married Miss Della Wassell, daughter of Charles Wassell, of Chester. Mrs. Adderly died in 1921. Doctor Adderly takes justifiable pride in his four children. The oldest, Joseph C., is a graduate of McKendree College, and is now president of the Integrity Casualty Insurance Company of Chicago, where he resides. The second child, Lola D., is the wife of Frank Albright, of Chester. The younger son, William H., is vice president of the Integrity Casualty Insurance Company and has charge of the New York City business. The second daughter is Elizabeth, wife of Henry Lemerman, of Chester.

EARL C. FRANKLIN, superintendent of schools at Carlyle, Clinton County, is one of the leading educators of this part of the state, and a man whose scholarship is combined, most admirably, with executive ability of a high class. For over a score of years he has been giving the best of himself to educational work, and is, today, one of the best-known men of his profession in the State of Illinois.

Professor Franklin was born at Spencer, Owen County, Indiana, July 26, 1880, a son of R. B. and Susan (Wakefield) Franklin, grandson of John and Susan (Moore) Franklin, natives of North Carolina and Indiana, respectively, and grandson, on the maternal side, of S. H. and Emaline (Young) Wakefield, natives of Kentucky. The Franklin family descends in a direct line from Benjamin Franklin.

R. B. Franklin was in young manhood a blacksmith, and for years was superintendent of schools. The Methodist Episcopal Church has in him a zealous member. He belongs to the Improved Order of Red Men. Children were born to him and his wife as follows: Earl C., Nora, Irvin, Jesse, Leota, Herman, Fern, Wallace, Fred and Freda, deceased, and Fred.

Growing up in Owen County, Earl C. Franklin attended the local schools, and later the Indiana State Normal School at Terre Haute, from which he was graduated in 1915, and in 1922 he was graduated from the University of Illinois at Urbana. During the years between 1903 and the present writing he has been engaged in teaching, first in the district schools, then in the graded schools, rising to be principal of the school at Coal City, Indiana, in 1906, and there he remained until 1912. For the following year he was principal of the school at Long View, Illinois. While thus engaged Professor Franklin has continued his own studies, and is well abreast with the advancement in his calling. In the latter part of December, 1925, and early part of 1926, he completed his reading for his Masters degree. In September, 1922, he came to Carlyle as superintendent of its schools, and has since then been discharging his manifold responsibilities with dignified capability.

Professor Franklin married, in 1902, at Freedom, Indiana, Bell Dyer, a daughter of K. S. and Elizabeth Dyer, the former of who is living, but the latter is deceased. He is a farmer, and he and his wife had thirteen children, of whom Mrs. Franklin is the tenth in order of birth. One child, a son, was born to Professor and Mrs. Franklin, namely: Burns Maurice, who was graduated from the University of Illinois at Urbana in 1923, with the degree of Bachelor of Science. He is now director of physical education in Southwestern College, at Winfield, Kansas. In religious faith Professor Franklin is a Methodist. He is a Blue-Lodge Mason, and belongs to the college fraternities Kappa Delta Pi and Phi Delta Kappa, and to the Illinois Teachers' Association. Both he and Mrs. Franklin are prominent socially, they being the center of a congenial group at Carlyle, and he stands deservedly high in public esteem, for he is a man of unusual attainments, and a citizen whose sense of civic responsibility is keen.

HERMAN P. FRIZZELL, who is giving a most able and loyal administration as United States Commissioner for the Southern District of Illinois, with residence and executive headquarters in the city of East St. Louis, St. Clair County, is a native son of Illinois and a representative of one of the honored families of this state, his paternal grandfather, whose family was early established in Kentucky, having come from that historic old state to Illinois in the pioneer days, and the same condition having been true of the maternal grandfather, S. D. Poor, the original representatives of the Poor family in Kentucky having come from one of the eastern states.

Mr. Frizzell was born at Metropolis, Massac County, January 27, 1892, and his early education was obtained in the public schools of Johnson County, where his parents established their residence when he was a child. There he was graduated from the high school at Vienna, and in 1916 he was graduated in the law at Bloomington, and after thus receiving his degree of Bachelor of Laws and being admitted to the bar of his native state he was engaged in the practice of his profession at Vienna, judicial center of Johnson County, until, within a short time after thus initiating his professional work, he subordinated the same to the call of patriotism when the nation became involved in the World war. Early in 1917 Mr. Frizzell, as a volunteer, enlisted in the United States army, and was assigned to Jefferson Barracks, St. Louis, for preliminary training. Later he served five months as sergeant at the headquarters of the medical department at Fort Riley, Kansas, and he then crossed the Atlantic, and, as hospital sergeant was stationed in London, England, until after the historic armistice brought the great conflict to a close. In February, 1919, he returned to the United States, and at Camp Grant, Illinois, he received his honorable discharge on the 10th of the following month. He returned to Vienna with the purpose of resuming his law practice, but he was soon afterward appointed deputy clerk of the United States District Court at Danville. Later he was transferred to similar service at East St. Louis, and here he continued his service as deputy clerk until December 1, 1922, when he was appointed to his present office of United States commissioner. In addition to holding this office he is engaged also in the general practice of law in this city, and success is attending his work in both of these connections. Mr. Frizzell is aligned in the ranks of the republican party, he and his wife hold membership in the Methodist Episcopal Church, and he is affiliated with the Masonic fraternity and the Phi Delta Phi college fraternity.

At Vienna, Johnson County, on the 10th of June, 1921, was solemnized the marriage of Mr. Frizzell and Miss Mary V. Hooker, daughter of the late Doctor and Margaret (Simmons) Hooker, both of whom died when she was a small child, her father having been a prominent physician and surgeon at Vienna and the other surviving child, Grace, being the wife of J. Ladd Mozley and the mother of one child, Margaret. Mr. and Mrs. Frizzell have a fine little son, Lewis H., named in honor of his paternal grandfather.

Herman P. Frizzell is a son of Lewis H. and Sidney I. (Poor) Frizzell, both of whom passed their entire lives in Illinois, the father having died September 25, 1910, and the mother on the 15th of November, 1918. Of the children the eldest is Lewis H., Jr., who is still a bachelor; Rista is the widow of Ernest Moore and has two children, Lynn W. and Ernest, Jr.; the second daughter is the wife of Thomas D. Johnson, and they have one child, Thomas D., Jr.; and Herman P., of this review, is the youngest of the four.

At the time of his death Lewis H. Frizzell, Sr., was general agent for the Franklin Insurance Company, and he had previously given twelve years of service as sheriff of Johnson County, besides which he had represented that county in the Lower House of the State Legislature. He was a stalwart democrat and his personal popularity was shown in his being elected to office in a county that gives a large republican majority normally. In earlier life he had been engaged in the dry goods and clothing business. He was one of the honored and influential citizens of Johnson County and its county seat, Vienna, at the time of his death.

JAMES C. MITCHELL has played a part of large and varied usefulness in the affairs of Williamson County. For over thirty years he has been identified with the First National Bank of Marion, and as cashier has been the man who has chiefly represented the bank to the public and undoubtedly has been the principal influence in building the institution up to rank with the strongest banks in Southern Illinois.

The Mitchell family has been identified with this section of Illinois for nearly a century. His father, William N. Mitchell, who was born in Tennessee, in 1814, came to Illinois in 1832, and first lived at Old Frankfort, where he taught several terms of subscription schools. He became a surveyor, and was one of the surveyors who ran the lines separating the new Williamson from the old Franklin County, his residence being in the new county, and he became its county surveyor. He also developed a farm in what is now Northern Township of Williamson County. William N. Mitchell during the Civil war became captain of Company E of the Sixtieth Illinois Infantry, but after being wounded in battle resigned his commission. In 1865 he was elected county clerk and subsequently was postmaster of Marion during the administration of Grant and a part of that of Hayes. He was one of the staunch republicans of the county. He died at Marion December 30, 1879. William N. Mitchell married Rachael Roberts, daughter of John Roberts. She died August 30, 1866. Besides their son James C., another son was Edward Mitchell, whose name is familiar in Illinois history as state treasurer from 1911 to 1913.

James C. Mitchell was born on his father's farm in Williamson County, October 30, 1852,

and has been a resident of Marion since 1867. His early training was on the farm, where he attended country schools. He was a drug clerk in Marion and for several years was in the drug business, until in 1886 he was elected county clerk and reelected in 1890. During his eight years as county clerk Mr. Mitchell had much to do with refunding and paying off the bonded debt of Williamson County incurred in the early days in behalf of railroad subsidies. Before the expiration of his second term Mr. Mitchell was elected cashier of the First National Bank, and he left the courthouse to go immediately to his duties in the bank. He has continued as cashier to the present time, with the added honor and dignity of vice president. Thirty years ago the First National Bank had capital of $50,000, but deposits of only $30,000. A recent statement in the spring of 1926 showed the First National Bank of Marion possessed of total resources of approximately $2,240,000. It has capital stock and surplus of $200,000, and the deposits have reached the impressive figure of well upwards of $2,000,000.

Mr. Mitchell married, October 21, 1872, Miss Lillie White, who was born at Marion and died in that city November 22, 1900. Her father, Colonel John H. White, helped raise the Thirty-first Illinois Infantry, the first commander of which was Colonel, afterwards General, Logan. He attained the command of this regiment and was killed as its colonel at Fort Donelson February 14, 1862. Mr. James C. Mitchell married, December 7, 1901, Miss Julia Dunaway, daughter of Thomas Dunaway, of Marion. The children, all by his first marriage, are: John; Frank, James; Rose, wife of Fred Taylor; Verna, who married Samuel Parker; Dessie; and Edward Everett.

The youngest son, Edward Everett, is a contractor and member of the Mitchell Construction Company, a well known organization in Southern Illinois, which is now building ten miles of concrete road on Route No. 1 from Metropolis to Vienna in Johnson County. Edward Everett Mitchell was born in Marion January 14, 1888, and finished his schooling with two years in the University of Illinois. He married Helen Hartman, daughter of Charles Hartman, of Los Angeles. They have two children, Charles and J. C.

NATHANIEL SEDGWICK MONROE is an Illinois inventor and manufacturer, maker of machinery that has helped to lighten the labor of the world, and improve the conditions under which men work and live. He is still active head of the business of N. S. Monroe & Sons at Arthur, in Douglas County.

Mr. Monroe was born January 8, 1851, in Shelby County, Indiana, where were born also his parents, Andrew Jackson and Julia Ann Monroe. In the paternal line he is Scotch-Irish, while through his mother he has a mingling of German and English blood. He attended common schools in Shelby County, but many years ago came to Illinois and engaged in farming in Douglas County. His home was six miles southeast of Arthur. Like all other farmers of Central Illinois at that time, he contended daily with the handicap of poor roads, a heavy tax upon all phases of agricultural production as well as upon wagons and horse power. Mr. Monroe possessed the practical and mechanical mind, and in 1894, while still living on his farm, he perfected his first road making machine, a leveler, the first of the famous line of "Jumbo" levelers and road making machines that have been the typical product of the Monroe establishment for over thirty years. His first leveler was built entirely of wood in a shop on the farm. In operation it proved a remarkable success over all existing types of machines for leveling dirt roads in that part of Illinois. Within two years a new machine was built, adding more steel, and eventually twelve machines of that type were put together on the farm shop. In 1896 the business was moved to Arthur, where a small factory was erected. In that year Mr. Monroe demonstrated the practical value of his machines over roads in other districts and counties, and there has been a steady progression in the business as to facilities and output of the plant, as well as new improvements and entirely new machines made and invented by Mr. Monroe's organization. In 1913 a large factory and warehouse were erected on the site of the original factory at Arthur. Since then the road making machinery has been of all steel construction. At the present time the Monroe road machines of the "Jumbo" type are used in every part of the country from the Atlantic to the Pacific. The output of the factory now comprises a complete line of equipment for every purpose in the grading, leveling and perfecting of roads and highways.

For many years Mr. Monroe has had associated with him his sons, A. Johnson and George W. Monroe. A. Johnson Monroe was especially interested in the mechanical side of the industry and was given every encouragement by his father to perfect his talent. He worked out and improved many of the inventive ideas of his father. When, in 1913, the firm of N. S. Monroe & Sons was established and a new factory built, A. Johnson Monroe took charge of the plant and the production end of the business. His brother, George W. Monroe, also had a thorough apprenticeship in the shop and factory, but his chief service has been in the administrative and sales departments, and under him the sales of the Monroe road machines have been extended far and wide.

Mr. N. S. Monroe has been a sturdy and successful business man and always a public spirited and substantial citizen of his community. He served twenty years as a school official, for twenty years has been associated with a loan association, has served as highway superintendent, and is a staunch republican, having cast his first presidential vote for U. S. Grant. He has been a member of the Masonic Order for forty years and identified with the Methodist Episcopal Church sixty years of his life.

On February 23, 1876, at the home of Irvin Johnson in the north end of Coles County, Illinois, Mr. Monroe and Miss Martha Alma Leggitt were married. Two of her brothers were soldiers in the Civil war. The children of Mr. and Mrs. Monroe are: Charles Walter, who is married and has one child and three grandchildren; Andrew Johnson Monroe, who married Dora Corbett; Margaret May, wife of J. F. Smith, of Decatur, Illinois; Julia Eveline, wife of E. W. Boyd; George Washington, who married Drew Harrison; Ora Bell, wife of Jesse H. Dickson; and Alice Josephine, wife of Wilson P. Boyd, of Kenny, Illinois.

ALEX P. HENSLEY is a member of one of the prominent firms of livestock commission merchants at the National Stock Yards of East St. Louis. His experience since boyhood has been with live stock, both on the farm and as a buyer and shipper, and his enterprise has been a contributing factor in making the national stockyards one of the important livestock centers in the country.

He was born on a farm in Montgomery County, Missouri, March 10, 1885, son of A. B. and and Mattie (Palmer) Hensley. His mother died in 1920. A. B. Hensley has for many years been one of the most extensive farmers and stock growers and stock dealers in central Missouri, having a six hundred acre farm and ranch in Montgomery County He has been a sheep and cattle grower and one of the leading stock dealers in his section of the state. A. B. Hensley and wife have three sons and three daughters: Maggie, who was married and has two children; Alex P.; F. L., who is married and has one son; Mary, who has four children; Burton, who has two children; and Miss Catherine. A. B. Hensley is a son of Pittman and Dorcas Hensley, natives of old Virginia. Mrs. Mattie (Palmer) Hensley was a daughter of George Palmer, who also came from old Virginia.

Alex P. Hensley attended public schools in Montgomery County, and after his schooling he engaged in the elevator and milling business in his native county. This he followed for five years, after which, in 1908, he located at East St. Louis and engaged in the live stock commission business in the partnership firm of Hensley, Gant & Carter, live stock commission company. They have a large clientele, representing farmers and stock raisers all over the middle west.

Mr. Hensley married in June, 1907, in Montgomery County, Mina Agnes Dunham, of Prices Branch. They grew up on neighboring farms and her father was one of the prosperous farmers and stock men of that section of Missouri. She is a daughter of William L. and Sarah (Dyke) Dunham, her mother still living. Her father died in 1918. Mrs. Hensley has a sister, Mrs. Lessie Northcutt, who has two children, and a brother, Fred, who is also married. The three children of Mr. and Mrs. Hensley are: Leroy, Louise, and Mary Agnes. The family are all members of the Christian Church. Mr. Hensley is affiliated with the Masonic Lodge and the Modern Woodmen of America.

JAMES ANTHONY WATSON, attorney at Elizabethtown, has the distinction of being the first republican elected to the office of state's attorney in that county. He has served as state's attorney and also as a member of the Legislature.

Mr. Watson was born at Elizabethtown, July 31, 1874, son of Thomas S. and Sebary (Casad) Watson. His father was born in Livingston County, Kentucky, December 28, 1847, and died at Elizabethtown, Illinois, in July, 1901. He was a son of Thomas Watson, a native of Tennessee, while his grandfather was born in Virginia, and the family is of English ancestry. Sebary Casad was born at Elizabethtown, Illinois, daughter of Thomas Casad, a native of Ohio, a pioneer of Hardin County, Illinois, and a Union soldier in the Civil war. Thomas S. Watson followed farming, was also a timber dealer, was always a republican in politics, and he and his wife were Baptists in church faith. They reared a family of ten children, and nine are still living.

James Anthony Watson was reared at Elizabethtown and on a nearby farm, attended common schools and became a school teacher. He pursued the study of law under Judge John J. Ledbetter at Elizabethtown, and in 1896 was admitted to practice, so that he has rounded out three decades of work as a lawyer in his native county. Mr. Watson filled the office of state's attorney of Hardin County from 1900 to 1908. From 1910 to 1922 he was a member of the General Assembly and one of the most capable legislators this district has ever had. He was chairman of the election and labor committees, and during his last term was chairman of the judiciary committee. Mr. Watson is a Master Mason and a member of the Baptist Church. He has had a successful law practice, and has turned some of his surplus capital into farming land, on which he has developed a peach orchard, producing a fine quality of fruit.

He married in 1901 Cora Flanary, a native of Kentucky. They have three children, Deneen A., Mildred and Imogene.

FRED L. WHAM, attorney, is a member of the law firm of Wham and Wham at Centralia, his professional associate being his brother Charles.

Fred L. Wham was born near Carter, Marion County, June 15, 1884, son of Henderson B. and Nancy (Stonecipher) Wham. His father was a farmer and school teacher, and died in August, 1923. Fred L. Wham was one of several brothers who were prominent in university circles at Champaign for several years. The oldest, George D., is now dean of the faculty in the Southern Illinois Teachers College at Carbondale. Charles, Benjamin and Fred L. were all students in the College of Law at the University of Illinois after having received their early training in the Southern Illinois Normal University at Carbondale. Fred L. Wham attended the University of Illinois from 1904 to 1906, and from 1907 to 1909, and graduated from the College of Law with the degree of LL. B. in the latter year. He earned his letter I three different seasons with the football team, and was selected as one of the members of the All Western team during his senior year. He was a member of the Phi Alpha Delta fraternity and also the honorary scholastic fraternity of the College of law known as Theta Kappa Nu.

After completing his law course Mr. Wham engaged in practice for two years at Fort

Smith, Arkansas. Four years following that he was established at Fayetteville, Arkansas, in the legal department of the St. Louis and San Francisco Railroad Company, and then went to Washington, D. C., as an attorney for the Department of Agriculture. In 1917 he came to Centralia, Illinois, and entered into a partnership with his brother Charles in the practice of law under the firm name of Wham & Wham.

Fred L. Wham during the war was a member of the Legal Advisory Board and a four minute speaker. He is a republican and was for five years president of the local Board of Education. He is now one of the trustees of the University of Illinois, a director of the Chamber of Commerce, a member of the Meadow Woods Country Club, where he plays golf, the Rotary Club, is a Royal Arch and Knight Templar Mason, also belongs to the Scottish Rite bodies and Shrine, and is a member of the Independent Order of Odd Fellows and B. P. O. Elks. He is on the Board of Sessions of the Presbyterian Church and superintendent of the Sunday School.

Mr. Wham married, June 16, 1909, Miss Carrie Hitch. She died in Washington, D. C., in 1917, leaving one son, Fred L., Jr. In August, 1918, Mr. Wham married Miss Nina Shanklin, daughter of Phil and Belle Shanklin, members of old families of Sandoval and Centralia, Illinois. Mrs. Wham is a member of the Woman's Club, the Eastern Star and White Shrine of Jerusalem. They have two children, Donald and Robert.

ANTHONY V. KANEY, president of the Kaney Ice Cream Company of Centralia, was born and reared in Marion County, and from a mine laborer has made himself one of the most progressive business men and citizens of Centralia.

He was born July 15, 1882, son of John and Margaret (Merkel) Kaney. His parents were natives of Indiana and settled in Centralia in 1880, still living there. His father has spent most of his life as a miner and for several years held the office of state mine inspector. Anthony V. Kaney is the second in a family of four sons and five daughters.

Like his brothers and sisters, he was educated in parochial schools of Centralia and at the age of fifteen left school and became a worker in the mines. Mr. Kaney gained his early commercial training working for eight months in a recreation parlor, one year in a retail confectionery store, was then in the confectionery business for himself twenty-six months, and after selling out he returned to the Schultz Candy Kitchen for four years. Mr. Kaney in 1912 engaged in business as a manufacturer and wholesaler of ice cream and dairy products, and has enjoyed a steadily increasing and prospering business, supplying the chief service of the kind not only to Centralia but many outlying towns. The Kaney Ice Cream Company was incorporated in 1919, with Mr. Kaney as president and manager. He is also vice president of the Centralia Clothing Manufacturing Company.

Mr. Kaney is an independent democrat, is affiliated with the Knights of Columbus, B. P. O. Elks, Catholic Church, Meadow Woods Country Club, Chamber of Commerce, Rotary Club, United Commercial Travelers, and Illinois Ice Cream Manufacturers Association. His favorite sports are fishing, hunting and golf.

Mr. Kaney married at Centralia, October 2, 1907, Miss Magdaline Egger, daughter of Jacob J. Egger, of an old family of Marion County, originally from Germany. Mr. and Mrs. Kaney have two children, Anthony Vernon, Jr., and Roland John.

WALKER BUTLER. In the few years since his admission to the bar Walker Butler has performed some services and achieved distinction that gives promise of a career of large and important usefulness in his native City of Chicago.

He was born in Chicago in 1896, son of Michael J. and Margaret F. (McKevitt) Butler. Michael J. Butler was for many years a well known labor leader and man of affairs in Chicago and throughout the Middle West. He was born in Carbondale, Pennsylvania, coming to Chicago in early manhood, in 1873. For over forty years he was active in the councils of the democratic party. He was born in the same neighborhood in Pennsylvania that was the birthplace of Terrence V. Powderly, famous as the national leader of the Knights of Labor, and between these two there existed a life long association and friendship. Michael Butler served as state president of the Knights of Labor for Illinois and was one of the forceful men who directed the organization of labor in Illinois and over the nation. His home was in the Fourth Senatorial District and twice he was honored with election to the Legislature, serving as a member of the House of Representatives from 1896 to 1900, and as a member of the State Senate from 1900 to 1904. Michael Butler died in 1917, at the age of sixty-three.

Walker Butler was liberally educated, attending Loyola Academy, Campion College at Prairie du Chien, Wisconsin, and was graduated A. B. from Loyola University in 1916. He took his law course at Loyola University, graduating LL. B. in 1920. Since that year he has been engaged in private practice and public duties, and now has his law offices in the Conway Building at 111 West Washington Street. In addition to his private law practice he is an assistant state's attorney of Cook County, and has handled many violations of the Eighteenth Amendment.

During the World war he made several applications for enlistment, but was rejected on account of an affection of the eyes. Two of his brothers, Frank and Joe, upheld the patriotic record of the family by service with the American forces in France. Joe Butler was a member of the Illinois, or Thirty-third, Division. Frank Butler, who was a lieutenant of engineers in the Thirty-fifth Division, made the supreme sacrifice, being killed in action at the battle of the Argonne.

Walker Butler lives on the South Side and is a member of the South Shore Association of Commerce, the South Shore Congress, and for several years has been prominent in Knights of Columbus circles, being grand knight of Calumet Council, and as chairman of its building committee he inaugurated the program for the erection of the splendid home of Calumet Council at Stony Island Avenue and Marquette Road. He is a member of the Chicago and Illinois Bar Associations.

MARTIN LAFAYETTE RITTENHOUSE, member of an old time family of Edgar County, and active in business at Paris, the county seat, is the present mayor of Paris.

He was born in that city, February 29, 1884, son of Marquis Lafayette and Amanda (Lane) Rittenhouse. The Rittenhouse family in Edgar County is descended from one of seven Rittenhouse brothers who came to America from Holland in Colonial days and settled in Pennsylvania. Amanda Lane was born in Edgar County, Illinois, her parents coming from Pennsylvania in 1818. The Lane family is of early Puritan stock. Marquis Lafayette Rittenhouse came to Illinois from Ohio when about ten years of age, settling in Edgar County. He was a farmer there, and subsequently engaged in the nursery and florist business at Edgar.

Martin Lafayette Rittenhouse was educated in the public schools of Paris, and as a boy and young man became associated with his father in the nursery and floral business and for a number of years has been manager of that very successful enterprise, the largest in Edgar County.

Mr. Rittenhouse has also been deeply interested in public and civic work at Paris. He was appointed an alderman in 1908 and filled that office until 1912. In 1923 he was elected on the republican ticket mayor, and has given Paris a very businesslike administration. He is affiliated with Prairie Lodge No. 77, A. F. and A. M., Edgar Lodge No. 91, Independent Order of Odd Fellows, and is a member of the Methodist Episcopal Church.

On April 28, 1909, he married at Paris Miss Lena Rivers Preston, daughter of Samuel Hamilton and Laura (Lycan) Preston. The Prestons settled in Edgar County among the pioneers in 1831. Mr. and Mrs. Rittenhouse have one son, Martin Preston, born in 1911.

PHIL A. CRAIG is editor and proprietor of the Golconda Enterprise. Forty-five years of continuous experience in the printing and newspaper business makes him one of the oldest members of the profession in southern Illinois.

He was born on a farm about a mile from Golconda, March 19, 1867, son of Joshua and Aly (Campbell) Craig, the former a native of Tennessee and the latter of Illinois. Joshua Craig was a carpenter and contractor, and about 1870 located at Golconda, where he lived until his death in 1880. He was a republican in politics. He and his wife had ten children, eight of whom grew up, and Phil A. Craig and six sisters still survive.

Phil A. Craig was three years old when his parents moved to Golconda, and he grew up there, attending public schools. At the age of thirteen he went into the printing office of the Pope County Democrat, learning the trade, and has never been long absent from the printing office or newspaper business through the forty-five years since he began his apprenticeship. All of his experience has been in Golconda. In 1887 he and Sim V. Clanahan established the Enterprise.. About two years later the Enterprise was merged with the Herald, under the name of Herald-Enterprise. They were associated in the ownership and publication of this well known southern Illinois republican newspaper until 1924, when Mr. Craig became sole owner and publisher. It is a weekly paper and circulates throughout Pope and adjoining counties.

Mr. Craig in 1888 married Hester Clanahan, a sister of his business partner. She has been closely associated with her husband in newspaper work for many years, and is a very talented editor and writer. The two children born to their marriage are deceased. Mr. Craig while active in the republican cause has never sought the honors of office. He and his wife are Presbyterians, and he has been a ruling elder in the church for twenty-five years.

NICHOLAS B. PAUTLER, M. D. Both in Randolph and Monroe counties the name of Dr. Nicholas Pautler stands for broad usefulness and efficiency in the medical arts and surgery, and also for professional success and business prosperity. Doctor Pautler is one of the leading citizens of Waterloo.

His grandfather, Joseph Pautler, came to America from Alsace-Lorraine, settling on a farm in Randolph County, near Evansville, where he spent the rest of his life. His son, also named Joseph, was a child when brought to America, grew up on a farm and gave his active life to farming. Dr. Nicholas B. Pautler was born on the farm near Evansville June 19, 1872. He attended what was known as the Pautler district schools, located on his father's farm. Afterwards he attended school in Evansville, and in 1893 was graduated from the Missouri Medical College.

Doctor Pautler for ten years practiced medicine at Evansville and since then at Waterloo. He owns a fine home and office, and his reputation as a physician and surgeon extends for miles around Waterloo. On moving to that city he formed a partnership with the late Doctor Meyer. After the death of Doctor Meyer he practiced alone until the fall of 1925, when to relieve him of some of his professional burdens he took into partnership Dr. Benjamin F. Kilgore.

Doctor Pautler has numerous business interests. He helped organize in 1912 and is vice president of the First National Bank of Waterloo. He is president of the St. Louis Seed Company and president of the Crescent Steel Company of St. Louis.

He married Elizabeth Thummel, of Evansville, who died in 1903. Four sons were born of this marriage. His second wife was Mrs. Mamie Payne, who died June 22, 1922. Subsequently he married Felicia Copp, of Waterloo, who for twenty-one years was a teacher in that town. Doctor Pautler is a member of the Sts. Peter and Paul Catholic Church of Waterloo. During the World war he was a member of the County Exemption Board. Stephen, his oldest son, is interested in racing stock. Sylvester I., the second son, is manager of the St. Louis Seed Company. Raymond W. is manager of the Crescent Steel Company. Erwin

graduated in 1926 from the St. Louis University, becoming associated with his father in practice. Roy, the youngest son, is attending college at Chaminade, St. Louis. Doctor Pautler also adopted the two children of his second wife, Mrs. Payne. Her daughter, Arlon, is now a nun in a convent at San Diego, California. The son, Jefferson Payne, is a prominent leader in politics in Monroe County, and was nominated for county clerk on the republican ticket.

HOWARD HORACE HITCHCOCK is one of the veterans of Chicago's banking fraternity. His service, counting his clerical apprenticeship, has covered a period of more than half a century.

A native of Illinois, Mr. Hitchcock was born at Lee Center in Lee County, December 10, 1858, son of Charles I. and Mary (Bodine) Hitchcock. During his childhood his parents moved to Chicago, where he attended public schools. On January 18, 1875, at the age of sixteen, he went to work in the office of Preston, Kean & Company, bankers. This banking firm was succeeded May 12, 1884, by the Metropolitan National Bank, at which time Mr. Hitchcock was made assistant cashier. In 1894 he was promoted to cashier. With the consolidation of the Metropolitan National Bank with the First National Bank on May 31, 1902, Mr. Hitchcock became a vice president of the First National, and continued one of the executive officers of that great institution for a number of years. He is now associated with Hitchcock and Company, investment securities, at 39 South LaSalle Street.

Mr. Hitchcock is a republican in politics, is a member of the Union League, Mid-Day and Exmoor Country Clubs in Chicago and belongs to the Los Angeles Country Club in California. His home is at Highland Park. He married in Chicago, October 24, 1883. Nellie Watters. They have a son, Fremont Bodine, and a daughter, Agnes Jean, now Mrs. Theodore C. Butz.

WILLIAM GILHAM WILSON, county judge of Marion County, has practiced law twenty years and has earned a successful professional career in the same county where he was born and reared.

He was born in Marion County, August 26, 1872, son of John C. and Eliza Ellen (Gilham) Wilson. His father was born in Ohio and came to Illinois in the early '50s and engaged in farming until his death in 1900. Eliza Ellen Gilham, who died in 1917, was born at Edwardsville, Illinois, and was a member of one of Madison County's most prominent families.

The youngest child of his parents, Judge Wilson grew up on a farm, attended rural schools, and after that his education came as the product of his own efforts. He taught school for ten years, using the means thus earned to advance him toward his goal as a lawyer. He studied law with Schafer & Rhodes at Champaign and lated with Earl C. Higgins at Kinmundy. He was admitted to the bar in 1908, and for a number of years carried on his practice with law offices at Salem, but since 1919 has been a resident of Centralia.

When his sons came to the bar they joined their father in practice, and the law firm is now Wilson & Wilson, with offices in Centralia and Salem. Mr. Wilson is also a partner in the Wilson-Millure Insurance Agency.

During the World war he was chairman of the educational committee of the county, a Four Minute Speaker, government appeal agent, and member of the Legal Advisory Board. Judge Wilson is a republican and he was elected judge of the County Court of Marion County in 1914. He is now serving his third term in that office. He is affiliated with Salem Lodge of Masons, the Independent Order of Odd Fellows of Centralia, belongs to the Meadow Woods Country Club and the Marion County and Illinois State Bar Associations.

Judge Wilson married at Alma, Illinois, April 7, 1907, Miss Mollie J. Poole, daughter of Abraham and Martha Poole. There were four children: William Basil Wilson, attorney, who looks after the business of the firm at Salem; Russell Wilson, an attorney at Centralia; Ruth, wife of R. N. Millure; and Byron Vincent, who died in 1914. Another member of Judge Wilsons' household is his granddaughter, Ruby, a daughter of his son William Basil Wilson. William B. Wilson during the World war was in the Second Division of the United States Marines, while Russell saw service with the American Third Division, being a corporal.

WERNER W. SCHROEDER. Keen, logical and astute, Werner W. Schroeder is regarded as one of the outstanding figures in the legal profession in Illinois, and a man whose ability will carry him far in his profession and political life. He was born in Kankakee, Illinois, December 20, 1892, a son of Frederick and Sophia (Steinmeyer) Schroeder. After a thorough grounding in the public schools of the city of his nativity Werner W. Schroeder matriculated in the University of Michigan, from which he was graduated in 1914 with the degree of Bachelor of Arts, and in 1916 with the degree of Juris Doctor. During the latter part of his life at the university he was instructor of political economy.

Returning to Kankakee, Mr. Schroeder became a member of the strong legal firm of Small, Bratton & Schroeder, maintaining this connection for several years, and winning the confidence of the people by his masterly handling of the cases placed in his hands. In 1921 he most successfully defended Governor Len Small, governor of Illinois, in the suits instituted against him, and in this connection became a state-wide figure. In 1921 Mr. Schroeder was appointed secretary of the Legislative Reference Bureau, and in this very important office he drew up 1,000 bills for the members of the Fifty-second General Assembly, many of which are now on the statutes of Illinois. The masterly manner in which these bills were drawn not only demonstrates the thorough knowledge of the law with relation to each bill that is possessed by him, but also the necessity for so drawing them that they might present the intent of the Legislature in passing them in a clear and lucid manner, easily understood by the masses. Mr. Schroeder's abilities are not confined to the mere practice of his profession, for he is the author of several tomes that are accepted as being in the highest degree authoritative. Since February 14, 1925, Mr. Schroeder has been attorney for the public administrator of Cook County. He belongs to the Illinois Bar Association and the Chicago Bar Association and to the Hamilton Club. Politically he is an active republican.

On September 22, 1920, Mr. Schroeder married Elizabeth More, of Milwaukee, Wisconsin. Mr. Schroeder's public duties keep him in his office at 33 South Clark Street, Chicago, during the greater portion of the time.

H. KAUL has no minor measure of personal popularity and influence in his home city of Forest Park, Cook County, one of the attractive and progressive suburbs of Chicago, and evidence of this is given when it is stated at the time of this writing, in the autumn of 1925, he is serving as mayor of his home city and is also editor and publisher of the well conducted German paper known as Nachrichten aus Schleswig-Holstein.

Mayor Kaul was born in the fine old province of Schleswig-Holstein, in the year 1861, that province having then been a part of Denmark but having been carried over to the governmental control of Germany in the year 1864. In his native land the early educational advantages of Mr. Kaul included those of what was called "A First Class Citizen School," which corresponds to the high school of the United States, and his higher academic education was obtained in a college in the City of Hamburg, Germany. Mr. Kaul was about twenty-one years of age when he came to the United States, in 1883, and he passed the first eight years in Iowa—at Muscatine and Boone. In 1892 he came to Chicago and two years later established his residence in the western suburb of Forest Park, where he has since maintained his home and where he has wielded no little influence in advancing the civic and material upbuilding of the city. Prior to coming to this country Mr. Kaul had served as a newspaper reporter in his native land, and he has continuously been associated with journalistic and newspaper work during the entire period of his residence in the United States. Thirty-eight years ago he founded at Boone, Iowa, the Nachrichten aus Schleswig-Holstein, a fortnightly paper devoted to the interests of the American citizens who were born in or are descended from natives of the fine old province of Schleswig-Holstein, and the paper is maintained at a high standard as a vehicle for literary information and general news, its columns giving to readers full information concerning affairs in Schleswig-Holstein and of the sons and daughters of the province who are now American citizens. The paper is published in the "high" and "low German" language. Low German is the common speech of the province mentioned, and its circulation has been extended far outside of mere local boundaries. Through the medium of this influential newspaper was recently collected about $50,000 for the relief of children left destitute in Schleswig-Holstein as an aftermath of the World war, and Mr. Kaul sent these funds to his native land, he having there provided for the distribution of the money through proper channels. In the World war period, both in an individual way and through the columns of his paper, Mr. Kaul gave loyal service in upholding the United States Government and in advancing the various patriotic measures and enterprises, he having delivered speeches in support of the Government war loans, Red Cross work, etc., besides which one of his sons, Armin, volunteered and served in the United States Navy, in which he was in active service in the war zone and in which he won his service stripes. In politics Mr. Kaul gives his allegiance to the democratic party, and he and his wife are zealous communicants of St. John's Evangelical Lutheran Church in their home city.

Forest Park has the commission system of municipal government, and under this system Mr. Kaul has served for the past nine years in the office of mayor. Years before he had served as a member of the Forest Park Board of Education. He has never entered the arena of practical politics, but his civic loyalty led him to consent to become a candidate for the office of mayor in order to protect the interests of the citizens and home-owners of Forest Park. The old Harlem race track brought to Forest Park saloons, gambling and other evil influences, and for home protection the city government put forth its best efforts for the elimination of such influences as work against the general well-being of the community.

Mr. Kaul was united in marriage with Miss Elizabeth Steuber, who was born in the City of St. Louis, Missouri, of German ancestry, her parents, however, having been born in the United States. Mr. and Mrs. Kaul have four children: Henry, Armin, Gerhardt, and Irma.

JAY AUSTIN COLVIN. One of the most successful automobile sales organizations in the City of Chicago has been the Triangle Motors, Incorporated. This is the organization with which Jay Austin Colvin has been most closely identified in recent years. He has been handling automobiles for over ten years, but has made his distinctive success in the Triangle Motors, handling the Lincoln cars.

Mr. Colvin was born in Chicago, in 1890, son of Edwin Meric and Clara (Fuller) Colvin. His father, who died in Chicago, May 16, 1926, was one of the outstanding leaders in the printing industry. For nearly forty years he was associated with the W. F. Hall Printing Company, one of the largest commercial printing concerns in America. For many years prior to his death he was vice president and general manager of the company, and was regarded as an authority on printing and its allied arts. Mr. Colvin through his mother, Clara (Fuller) Colvin, is a direct descendant of John and Priscilla Alden. His maternal grandfather was the late Jerome Fuller. The Fuller genealogy reveals names of prominence and distinction in American history from the earliest Colonial times, including the late Chief Justice Fuller from Illinois.

Jay Austin Colvin attended public schools in Chicago and was graduated with the A. B. degree from the University of Illinois in 1913. He has been in the automobile business since 1916, beginning as distributor for the Scripps-Booth car, and following that successively he

had the sales rights for the Stephens car and the Haynes car. Several years ago he became Chicago distributor for the Lincoln car, and in that connection he founded and became president of his own company, Triangle Motors, Incorporated. The headquarters of this organization are at 2229 South Michigan Avenue, but branches are also maintained at Park Avenue and St. John Street in Rogers Park, and at 1824 Ridge Avenue in Evanston.

Mr. Colvin is a member and director of the Chicago Automobile Dealers Association. He is a member of the Chicago Yacht Club, Edgewater Athletic Club, American Athletic Club, Hamilton Club, Westmoreland Country Club, and for a time was a lieutenant of the Supply Company in the Illinois National Guard. He is a republican, a member of the Methodist Church, and is affiliated with the Theta Delta Chi college fraternity, Edgewater Lodge No. 901, A. F. and A. M., Liberty Chapter No. 251, R. A. M., and the Medinah Temple of the Mystic Shrine.

Mr. Colvin resides at 5900 Sheridan Road. He married, September 26, 1914, Agnes Porteus McDowell. Their two children are Janet Agnes and Priscilla Alden.

WILLIAM H. SCHUWERK, of Chester, state's attorney of Randolph County, is the oldest son of Judge William M. Schuwerk, of Evansville in the same county. He has distinguished himself by his all around ability as a lawyer since his admission to the bar fourteen years ago.

He was born at Evansville, February 10, 1890. The career of his honored father is sketched elsewhere. William H. Schuwerk was educated in public schools and McKendree College, studied law under his father and was admitted to the bar in 1912, at the age of twenty-two. For several years he practiced with his father and in 1915 moved his office to Chester. He was chosen city attorney in 1916. In the spring of 1918 he joined the colors, attending training camp at Hattiesburg, Mississippi, was assigned duty in a machine gun company and later in the One Hundred and Forty-fourth Infantry. He went overseas, spending thirteen months in France. Since the war he has been one of the leading members of the bar of Chester, and in November, 1925, was elected state's attorney, and has earned distinction in that office by his vigorous efforts at law enforcement. He has filled chairs in the Masonic Lodge at Evansville. He married in November, 1917, Dorothy Crisler, daughter of Arthur E. Crisler, a prominent attorney. They have one son, William A.

FRANK ADAMS MITCHELL is a Chicago manufacturer, his chief business in recent years being the Ceresit Waterproofing Corporation, manufacturers of a line of waterproofing materials. Mr. Mitchell is a successful business man and is one of the influential members of the Chicago Association of Commerce.

He is a son of Rev. Thomas and Martha (Adams) Mitchell. At the time of his birth his parents were living at Fountain, Colorado, for the benefit of the health of his mother, who subsequently died in that state. Frank Adams Mitchell was born at Fountain, Colorado, April 17, 1879. Subsequently his father returned to his home state of Pennsylvania, where he was active in the ministry of the Baptist Church for over sixty years.

Frank Adams Mitchell was reared and received his early education in the town of Troy, Pennsylvania. He finished his literary and technical training in Bucknell University at Lewisburg, Pennsylvania. After leaving college he spent several years employed in manufacturing concerns at New York City, and in 1906 removed to Chicago, where for twenty years he has had an increasing part in the city's industrial life. Mr. Mitchell is president of the Ceresit Waterproofing Corporation and is also president and treasurer of the American Builders Corporation.

For two years, 1924 and 1925, he was chairman of the important ways and means committee of the Chicago Association of Commerce. In 1926 he was honored by being elected general secretary of the association. He is a member of the Illinois Athletic Club, and is a Baptist. Mr. Mitchell is a man of literary taste and inclination and is author of a volume of verse entitled "War Rhymes and Peace Poems," written and published during the World war period.

His home is at LaGrange, Illinois. He married, May 29, 1909, Miss Helen Judson Dye, of Brooklyn, New York. They have one son, Thomas Kent, born April 20, 1910.

SARAH A. JARMAN HOSPITAL is located at Tuscola, and was opened to the public April 1, 1919. It bears the name of the wife of William F. Jarman, for many years a well-known citizen of Douglas County. He was born in Kentucky in 1843, came to Douglas County when a youth, and though he had few school advantages and was without means and earned his living as a farm laborer, his industry brought him the rewards of success. He was a farmer and merchant and became rated as one of the men of substantial means in the county. His wife was Sarah A. Porter, and they reared only one child, Nellie B. Mr. Jarman was an invalid the last twenty-five years of his life, and for many years was lovingly cared for by his wife and daughter. His wife died in 1910 and his daughter in 1913. Alone in the world, he determined to devote some share of his wealth to the benefit of the poor and afflicted. He first offered 160 acres of his land for the purpose of founding a public hospital, provided the citizens of Douglas County raised $40,000 to meet his gift. Sufficient interest could not be aroused to raise the sum. Then came the summer of 1916, with a memorable typhoid fever epidemic at Tuscola, where more than one hundred persons were stricken with the disease, and many of them died. Mr. Jarman then renewed his offer, but reduced the demand for subscriptions to $10,000, and the conditions of his gift were met by the active efforts of J. H. Chadwick, a leading attorney of Tuscola, who himself went to the public and through his own personal efforts raised the money. Mr. Jarman conveyed the land on August 30, 1916. He died March 1, 1917, not living to witness the completion of the building. Since the hospital has been opened it has cared for between

1,000 and 2,000 patients. By the provisions of the charter the hospital is non-political and non-sectarian control, and its facilities so far as possible are available to the poor and distressed without pay. The president of the Board of Trustees of the hospital is L. R. McNeill, who for many years has been in the drug business at Tuscola.

EDWARD H. WEIHE was born and reared in Chicago, is one of the younger group of active business men of that city, and has to his credit a conspicuous service with the Twenty-first Engineers during the World war and continued activity in the Illinois and Federal military organizations since the war.

He was born in Chicago, in 1894, son of Henry W. and Sadie (Hoffman) Weihe. Both his father and mother are of pioneer Chicago families. His grandfather, John C. Weihe, came to Chicago in the early '50s and for many years was active in business, being proprietor of a wholesale crockery house, at one time the largest in Chicago, located on the site of the present Marshall Field store on State Street. His establishment was burned out in the Chicago fire of 1871. Sadie Hoffman's father was Louis Joseph Hoffman, who at one time was secretary to the great Chicago merchant, Marshall Field. Henry W. Weihe was born in Chicago in 1866, and in 1917 established a manufacturing furrier business at 127 North Dearborn Street. This has become a very prosperous and widely known establishment. It is conducted under the title of Henry W. and Edward H. Weihe. Edward H. Weihe has been associated with his father in business since completing his education in the public schools, except during the two years of his army service.

Mr. Weihe volunteered before America entered the war, joining Company I of the Eleventh Infantry, Illinois National Guard, on December 1, 1916. With that organization he remained until November, 1917, being called out for duty during the Springfield riot and at other points in Illinois. On November 15, 1917, he enlisted with the Twenty-first Engineers at Camp Grant. The Twenty-first Engineers was purely a volunteer regiment made up almost altogether of Illinois men. It made a wonderful record in the war zone in France, and was known as the "orphan" regiment on account of its being assigned to detached and unusual duties. Mr. Weihe sailed with the organization for France on December 26, 1917, and for several months was engaged in railway construction for supplies and equipment transportation in various combat sectors, including St. Mihiel, Argonne, Toul, Xivray, Seicheprey, Belleville and Baccarat. After the armistice Mr. Weihe accompanied the Twenty-first in the Army of Occupation and was stationed in Luxemburg. In 1919 Mr. Weihe as drum major of the Twenty-first Engineer Band accompanied the organization on its notable journey to the French-Spanish border, it being the first American band to cross the international bridge between the two countries.

Returning home, Mr. Weihe was honorably discharged June 18, 1919. However, he has maintained an almost continuous connection with some branch of the military service since then. On November 1, 1919, he enlisted in the Thirty-third Division, Illinois National Guard, being assigned to duty in the tank battalion. He began as first sergeant, was commissioned second-lieutenant March 2, 1920, first lieutenant July 21, 1920. April 6, 1922, he joined the Officers Reserve Corps, United States Army, and on May 6, 1923, was commissioned second lieutenant in the Officers Reserve Corps, Military Intelligence Section, and in April, 1926, was assigned to duty in the General Staff section of the Corps Area Headquarters, Chicago, on duty in the Communications Division, Military Intelligence.

Mr. Weihe is a member of Theodore Roosevelt Post No. 627, American Legion, the Forty and Eight Society, and became a member of the American Sea and Field Lodge No. 3 of the Masonic fraternity at Le Mans, France. He is a thirty-second degree Scottish Rite Mason and Shriner, member of the Riviera Masonic Club at Nice, France, is a director of the Associated Fur Industries of Chicago, member of the Hamilton Club, Army and Navy Club, Isaac Walton League, Lincoln Park Boat Club and the Chicago Association of Commerce.

HARRY J. FAWCETT since early manhood has been identified with the hotel business and has been a resident of Chicago since 1915. The outstanding and culminating achievement of his career was the building of the Shoreland, of which he is managing director as well as president of the Shoreland Hotel Company, owners of this magnificent residential hotel, the latest creation of America's genius for creating beauty and convenience in living environment.

Mr. Fawcett was born at Hewlett, New York, August 6, 1890, son of Henry A. and Frances (Pension) Fawcett. He acquired his early education in the grammar and high schools at Lawrence, New York, attended St. John's College at Brooklyn, and in 1911, at the age of twenty-one, began his hotel experience as steward for the Long Island Railroad Company at Brooklyn. The success which made him favorably known in hotel circles in the East was his management for three years of the Cedarhurst Country Club in New York. He was also connected for a time with the Grand Trunk Railway, and at San Francisco was identified with the management of the Grenada and Plaza Hotels, and for a time was manager of Kansas City's exclusive residential hotel, the St. Regis. Coming to Chicago in 1915, Mr. Fawcett was manager of the Chicago Automobile Club, the Lake Shore Club at Glencoe and the Down Town Club in Chicago.

Early in 1925 he organized the Shoreland Hotel Company, his wide and successful experience in hotel management enabling him to perfect an organization with ample financial backing for building a hotel unsurpassed in equipment and furnishings, designed to provide the privacy of an individual home, and in a wonderful setting of park, lake and boulevard. The Shoreland, which opened its doors in May, 1926, is located on South Shore Drive immediately north of Fifty-fifth Street. Some of the features of the Shoreland are thus noted in an article in a hotel publication:

"Unlike any existing Chicago residential hotel, each apartment has separate entrances for servants and guests, full sized kitchens laid out along the lines detailed by eminent authorities on domestic science to eliminate labor, electric ranges controlled by time clock switches permitting the housewife to shop while the dinner previously prepared and placed in this most wonderful range automatically starts to cook at the desired time, electric ice boxes, irons, toasters, percolators, in fact every labor-saving device possible. No breakfast nooks or in-a-door beds in this hotel-home, but full size dining and bed rooms—each with its private bath. A beautifully proportioned living room makes up the unit of four rooms, and to this unit any number of bed room can be added to suit the requirements of any family.

"The furnishings do not follow the hotel trend but were executed by the manufacturer of America's finest furniture and are of pure period design, the pieces and coverings varying so that a wide range is offered the prospective tenants. In every detail the commonplace practice in hotel furnishings was disregarded so that from the lowest to the highest priced suite has the finished atmosphere of the well appointed home."

The Shoreland has approximately a thousand rooms. Adjoining and connected and under the same management are the Jackson Shore Apartments, one of the highest type of apartment buildings in the United States, eleven stories high but containing only twenty-apartments.

Mr. Fawcett is a member of the Hotel Men's Mutual Benefit Association, International Stewards Association, Club Managers Association, American Caterers Association. He also belongs to the Chicago Motor Club and the Masonic fraternity, and while a resident of New York he served an enlistment in the National Guard. In 1918 he married Bonnie Lockwood Paul, of Caney, Kansas. They have one daughter, Helen Marie.

EDWARD EVERETT GORE, a former president of the Chicago Association of Commerce, and member of the firm of Smart, Gore & Company, public accountants, has during his residence there of thirty years been one of Chicago's most useful and public spirited citizens.

Mr. Gore was born in Macoupin County, Illinois, and he came to Chicago after some years of experience in the state auditor's department at Springfield. His father, the late David Gore, was a conspicuous figure in Illinois agriculture and politics. The first Gore ancestor came to America from England in 1630. One branch of the family went South, and the direct ancestors of Mr. Gore were in Virginia before the Revolution. His great-grandfather, Eleazer Gore, was a native of Virginia, but served in the Revolution with South Carolina troops. Michael Gore, the grandfather, was born in South Carolina and moved over the mountains to Kentucky. David Gore, of Illinois, was a native of Kentucky, but was a small child when in 1835 the family came to Illinois and settled in Madison County, and later in the vicinity of Carlinville, Macoupin County. David Gore when a boy volunteered and served with the American troops in the war with Mexico. In after years, while again and again a leader in politics and a representative of progressive movements, his chief energies were devoted to farming. He became one of the best farmers in the state, and from early manhood was a successful experimenter in agriculture science. He applied the principles of soil renewal and enrichment by legumes thirty-five years before that practice was generally advocated and applied. He was a democrat in politics, but during the early '70s he became identified with the farmers' movement for political action to restrain corporate interests. In 1873 the anti-monopoly party was organized, and it later became the greenback party. In 1874 this party nominated a state ticket, including David Gore for state treasurer. In 1884 David Gore was elected a member of the Illinois Senate from the Thirty-eighth District and served in the Thirty-fourth and Thirty-fifth General Assemblies, 1885-87. He was a member of the State Board of Agriculture for twenty years, beginning about 1878, and was president of the State Board in 1892. In that year he was elected state auditor of public accounts, and served from January 10, 1893, to January, 1897. In 1893 he was a vice president of the Illinois World's Fair Commission.

David Gore married Cinderella Davis Keller, and their son, Edward Everett Gore, was born at Carlinville, December 4, 1866. He was educated in Blackburn College at Carlinville, in a business college at Jacksonville, and in the University of Illinois. For four years he pursued the study of law in private law offices, and while his legal training has been invaluable to him he has never practiced law as a profession. From 1889 to 1893 he was a justice of the peace at Carlinville. He went with his father to Springfield and from 1893 to 1897 was chief of the building and loan department in the state auditor's office, and from 1895 to 1897 was chief of the state banking department of the same office.

Mr. Gore came to Chicago in 1897 and engaged in the practice of the profession of public accountant. He was one of the pioneers in that comparatively new business vocation. Until 1908 he carried on an individual practice. He was vice president of the Assets Realization Company from 1908 to 1910; member of the firm Barrow, Wade, Guthrie & Company, public accountants, from 1908 to 1922; and in 1922 became one of the founders of the present firm of Smart, Gore & Company, public accountants, at 111 West Monroe Street. He is a member and had the distinctive honor of being president from 1922 to 1924 of the American Institute of Accountants. He is a fellow of the Illinois Society Certified Public Accountants, of which he served as president in 1907.

His service as president of the Chicago Association of Commerce during the year 1922 was a tribute to his business position and his qualifications for leadership. He has been president of the All Chicago Council since its organization. In 1925 he was elected president of the Chicago Crime Commission, a position offering remarkable opportunities for constructive public service. He is a member of the Sons of the American Revolution, is affiliated with the republican party, and belongs to the Union League Club. He is a member of the Masonic fraternity and of the Knights of Pythias. Mr. Gore married Amanda Jeannette Burgdorff, daughter of William F. Burgdorff, of Carlinville. They were married October 6, 1892, and their four children are Florelle Jeannette, Mary Amanda (Mrs. Frank W. Hawley), Virginia Cinderella (Mrs. Edward Dyers Wilcox), and Alexander Burgdorff. Mr. Gore's residence since 1904 has been at Lagrange, a suburb of Chicago.

MAJ. WENDELL SYDNEY MERICK is an engineer of broad and important experience and service, and in recent years has been prominently identified with Chicago's constructive progress, particularly on the South Side. He is president of the Merick Construction Company.

Major Merick was born at Fenton, Michigan, June 14, 1879, son of Sydney Gideon and Alice Anne (Wills) Merick. He received his early education in the grammar and high schools of Flint, Michigan, attended normal school at Fenton, and graduated from Michigan State College at Lansing with the Bachelor of Science degree in mechanical engineering in 1904. After graduating he was assistant manager and engineer of the Michigan Manufacturing Company at Kalamazoo from 1904 to 1906, was assistant sales manager of the Ball Engine Company of Erie, Pennsylvania, in 1906-07, and was with the Loew Manufacturing Company of Cleveland from 1907 to 1910. Major Merick's business interests extended to Chicago in 1906, and since 1910 he has been a resident of that city.

He was works manager and vice president of the Chicago-Riverdale Steel Company from 1910 to 1912, and for the following five years, until America entered the World war, engaged in a consulting engineering practice. While in college he had received military training and was promoted to captain of cadets. After America entered the World war he joined the Three Hundred and Ninth Engineers, a combat engineer regiment and a unit of the Eighty-fourth Division. He was overseas in France, serving with the rank of captain. Since the war he has remained in the service and is now major of engineers in the Officers Reserve Corps, United States Army, attached to the Three Hundred Eighty-first Engineer Regiment, Sixth Corps Area.

The company of which Major Merick is now president and general manager started operations in 1914 under the name of the Merick Construction Company, and in 1923 the Merick Construction Company was incorporated, of which he is president and general manager. Major Merick built the East End Park Hotel and is president of the East End Park Building Corporation, owners of this exceptionally fine apartment hotel in the heart of the Hyde Park hotel district. Through the Merick Construction Company he has been carrying out notable developments along the South Shore, outstanding examples of which are Flossmoor Park and South Shore Park. These are subdivisions which have been equipped with every possible public utility, streets, sewers, pavements, water supply, sewage disposal, electric lights and gas, and they rank among the finest residence subdivisions in the entire metropolitan area of Chicago. Similar developments under the auspices of the Merick Construction Company are being carried out in Palos Park.

Besides the Merick Construction Company, Major Merick is treasurer of John A. Carroll & Company, one of the oldest and largest real estate organizations in Chicago. He is a director of the Hyde Park Investment Company, and is president of the Jackson Park Hotel Association. He is a very popular citizen and belongs to a number of civic and community enterprises, particularly those connected in some way with the South Shore and the South Side. He took the lead in the movement to commemorate in fitting manner the completion of the electrification of the Illinois Central suburban lines in 1926, this being in reality an historic achievement, not only in the annals of the Illinois Central Railroad, but of Chicago and the State of Illinois. Major Merick is a member of the American Society of Mechanical Engineers, Western Society of Engineers, American Military Engineers, American Legion, belongs to the Adventurers Club and the Olympia Fields Country Club. He is a Catholic and a republican.

In 1908 Major Merick married Ethel Carroll, of Chicago. She died in 1915. In February, 1926, Major Merick married Miss Catherine Shaughnessy, of Chicago. Her father, now deceased, was a vice president of the Soo Line Railroad. She is a niece of Sir Thomas Shaughnessy, one of the greatest railroad men in America, president of the Canadian Pacific Railroad.

JOY MORTON has been a Chicagoan since 1879. His interests and activities rank him among the nation's leaders in business and industry. Throughout his very successful business career he has been dominated by the statesmanlike and constructive principles which a previous generation admired in his father, the late J. Sterling Morton. Joy Morton is one of the wealthy men of Chicago who has more than a temporary interest in the broader phases of its development and growth.

His father, J. Sterling Morton, was for many years a national figure and was a descendant of Richard Morton, who is of record at Plymouth, Massachusetts, as early as 1625. J. Sterling Morton was a Nebraska pioneer, going to that territory soon after the passage of the Kansas-Nebraska Bill in 1854. He became territorial governor under appointment from the President, and had a long career in the public affairs of the state. He was called by President Cleveland to the office of secretary of agriculture in 1893. His home was at Nebraska City, and he gave it the name "Arbor Lodge." Governor Morton died in 1902. In 1923 Joy Morton donated the old homestead to the State of Nebraska; it is now a state park of remarkable beauty and fitly commemorates the man who instituted "Arbor Day," which, for over fifty years, has been observed by schools and other organizations throughout the land. J. Sterling Morton married Caroline Joy, of Detroit, a descendant of Thomas Joy, who built the first town house of Boston, in 1650. A replica of this

town house is now owned by the Morton Salt Company on Pier No. 1, near the mouth of the Chicago River.

Joy Morton was born at Detroit, Michigan, September 27, 1855, during a visit of his mother back to her old home. He spent his boyhood at Nebraska City, finishing his education at Talbot Hall there. He moved to Chicago in 1879, and since 1885 has been senior member of the firm Joy Morton & Company, financiers. He is doubtless best known in a business way as president of the Morton Salt Company, which celebrated its seventy-fifth anniversary in 1923. The Morton Salt Company is the largest organization in America manufacturing and distributing salt, and has numerous plants in Michigan, Kansas, California, Texas, and other states. Mr. Morton is also a director of the Chicago & Alton Railroad; director of the Western Cold Storage Company of Chicago; director of the Equitable Life Assurance Society of the United States, of which his brother, the late Paul Morton, was president; and has been identified with many banks and other organizations. Mr. Morton built and is president of the company which owns the Railway Exchange Building in Chicago, one of the largest of the great office buildings in the early years of the present century. In 1926 Mr. Morton built and owns the twenty-three-story Morton Building at Wells and Washington streets, one of the largest and finest of the office buildings of the era since the close of the World war.

During the World war Mr. Morton was appointed a member of the Inland Waterway Transportation Committee of the Council of National Defense. He has membership in many clubs and other organizations, including the Chicago Historical Society, Caxton Club of Chicago, Lawyers Club of New York. His home is one of the magnificent country estates in the territory west of Chicago in Du Page County. On 400 acres of this land he is carrying out the great tradition of his father, having established the foundation of what is regarded as one of the finest benefactions in the Chicago metropolitan district, *The Morton Arboretum*. It is a great experimental laboratory for the cultivation and propagation of trees, shrubs and plants, established primarily to encourage practical forestry as a means of serving and increasing the timber resources of the Middle West. Already some 4,000 different species and varieties of wooded plants are growing there, comprising an estimated total of more than 250,000 trees and shrubs. A formal statement of its purposes and aims is contained in the following quotation from the declaration of trust establishing it: "Creating a foundation to be known as the Morton Arboretum, for practical, scientific research work in horticulture and agriculture, particularly in the growth and culture of trees, shrubs and vines, by means of a great outdoor museum arranged for convenient study of every species, variety, and hybrid of the woody plants of the world able to support the climate of Illinois, such museum to be equipped with an herbarium, a reference library, and laboratories for the study of trees and other plants, with reference to their characters, relationships, economic value, geographical distribution and their improvement by selection and hybridization; and for the publication of the results obtained in these laboratories by the officials and students of the arboretum, in order to increase the general knowledge and love of trees and shrubs, and bring about an increase and improvement in their growth and culture."

Mr. Morton has been married twice. In 1880 he married Carrie Lake, daughter of Judge George B. Lake, of Omaha, who is the mother of his two children. She died in 1915. Mr. Morton married, in 1917, Margaret Gray, daughter of James Gray, Esq., of Newburg, Indiana. Mr. Morton's oldest child, Jean, married Joseph M. Cudahy in 1904. They have no children. His son, Sterling, married Preston Owsley in 1910. They have two daughters, Suzette and Millicent. Sterling Morton is an officer of the Morton Salt Company and also president of the Morkrum-Kleinschmidt Corporation, manufacturers of telegraphic machines.

ROBERT BLACK, a well known Chicago building contractor, has been a resident of that city since 1909. The Robert Black Company, contractors and builders, comprise an organization that does a business by no means of local character, and the company has its headquarters and executive offices at 122 South Michigan Avenue.

Mr. Black, who is a prominent figure among Scotchmen and Scotch organizations in Chicago, was born at Bladnoch, Wigtonshire, Scotland, in 1881, and was reared and educated there. Leaving home as a young man, he spent a short time in Liverpool, England, lived for three years in South Africa, and in 1906 arrived on the western coast of the United States. He spent some time in California, and in 1909 established himself in Chicago. Here he has built up and developed the Robert Black Company, which represents not only his skill as a builder, but as a capable executive who has assembled both the personnel and the facilities for handling practically every class of building work in a large city like Chicago. His work is exemplified in commercial structures, industrial plants, and particularly in residences of the finer type. His building work includes some of the most beautiful and attractive homes of wealthy residents in Lake Forest and other suburban communities.

An ardent Scotchman, devoted to the memories and traditions of his native heath, Mr. Black has for years been a leader in Scotch organizations and in social and benevolent enterprises among Chicagoans of Scotch birth or ancestry. He appreciates as a genuine honor and a high distinction his election and present incumbency of the office of president of the Illinois St. Andrews Society. The St. Andrews Society of Illinois is the oldest incorporated benevolent institution in the state, having been instituted in 1846 and incorporated in 1853. The particular care and object of the activities of this society is the Scottish

Old People's Home at Riverside. The home, built and maintained by the society, is an ideal institution of its kind. The old people who live there are actually guests and not "inmates," and are men and women of Scottish birth and ancestry who in their closing years have found themselves without relatives or friends to care for them. The home is a modern structure set in the midst of a beautiful landscape, with five acres of ground, and the furnishings, equipment and conveniences are fully in keeping with the atmosphere of happiness that pervades the institution.

Mr. Black is always a prominent figure in celebrations by Scotch people, has been closely associated with the Scottish Choir of Chicago, and was for six years president of the Dumfries and Galloway Association of America. He is vice president of the Braid Hills Country Club, member of the Mid-West Athletic Club, High Noon Club, and is a past chief of the Order of Scottish Clans.

Mr. Black's home is at 112 N. Kenilworth Avenue, Oak Park. He married Miss Effie Barr, and their two children are Robert Barr and Agnes Barr Black.

ERNEST X. LE SEURE. Among the men of affairs at Danville, Ernest X. Le Seure, president of the Second National Bank of Danville, was recognized as one of the most astute, sagacious business men of this section of the state. During the greater part of a busy life he was identified with banking, and frequently his financial wisdom was of great assistance in furthering worthy local enterprises.

Ernest X. Le Seure was born at Danville, Illinois, March 24, 1864, and died at Danville April 3, 1926, son of Prosper and grandson of Pierre Le Seure. The older generations of the Le Seure family belonged to Nancy, France, where Pierre Le Seure was born and married, and came from there to the United States with his family in the boyhood of his son Prosper. He settled first in the southern part of Indiana, but later came to Danville, to which city Prosper Le Seure had come in early manhood, and both died here. Prosper Le Seure was a leading merchant and banker of this city for many years, was an active citizen and gave his political support to the republican party. He married Miss Harriet G. Crane, who was born in Vermont and died at Danville. They were members of the Presbyterian Church.

Mr. Le Seure attended the public schools at Danville, completing his high school course and later studied in Stuttgart, Germany, and Paris before turning his attention to business. When about twenty-one years old he became a bookkeeper in the State Bank of Danville, where his industry, proficiency and integrity soon won promotion and he became cashier of that institution. Subsequently he became assistant cashier of the Second National Bank of Danville, but a year later accepted the responsible position of general manager of the Danville Street Railway & Light Company, and continued to be so identified for the six succeeding years. Upon retiring from this connection Mr. Le Seure organized the Danville National Bank, becoming its president, and when, later, this bank was consolidated with the Second National Bank, he was made president of the financial consolidation, one of the strongest and soundest in this part of the state.

Mr. Le Seure married at Danville, Illinois, June 9, 1891, Miss Mabel Cannon, daughter of Hon. Joseph G. Cannon of this city. A sketch of this distinguished statesman appears in this work. Mr. and Mrs. Le Seure had two daughters: Virginia, who is the wife of William Houghteling, of San Francisco, California; and Helen, the wife of Dorsey L. Richards, who holds an office in the State Department, Washington, D. C. Mr. Le Seure was a vigorous member of the Danville Chamber of Commerce. In political sentiment he was a republican, a consistent party man but has never accepted political office. He was prior to his death a member of the First Presbyterian Church at Danville, of which his wife is still a member.

In commemoration of Mr. Le Seure's death Mrs. Le Seure purchased a set of beautiful chimes that toll in a clock installed in the Presbyterian Church at Danville as a loving tribute to his memory.

ANDREW CUSTER METZGER, as a plumbing and heating contractor and engineer, has had a business experience in Chicago of thirty-five years. The firm of Walsh & Metzger, which he helped establish, has had a long and enviable record in this line of business. Mr. Metzger for many years has also been a local leader in the republican party.

His father is Mr. William Metzger, a notable Chicagoan, who is now eighty years of age. At the age of fourteen he enlisted at Chicago as a drummer boy in the famous Board of Trade Regiment, Seventy-second Illinois Volunteers, and after that regiment was mustered out he joined the regular United States Army for continued service in the Civil war. He was commissioned lieutenant of a company composed of colored troops commanded by white officers. For many years after the war William Metzger was associated in the wholesale glass business at Chicago with the firm of Tyler & Hippich, an organization that is the leader in handling and installing plate glass in the Chicago district. William Metzger at the age of eighty has sixty-four living descendants, children, grandchildren, great and great-great-grandchildren. He married Annie Gabrielson.

Their son Andrew Custer Metzger was born in Chicago, October 18, 1873. He was educated in public schools, and at the age of seventeen, in 1890, took up the plumbing trade and has had a remarkably diversified as well as successful business as a plumbing and heating contractor and engineer. He and Mr. David Walsh in 1895 established the firm of Walsh & Metzger, whose main plant and offices are at 6828 South Chicago Avenue. This business was incorporated in 1923. He is senior partner in the firm of Davis-Metzger Company, power plant engineers. Either individually or with his associates he has installed a large number of important plumbing

and heating contracts in Chicago. His contracts include the plumbing and other equipment for the Lincoln Park Aquarium, Southmoor and Wedgewood hotels, Tilden Technical and Crane high schools, Trianon Ball Room, and for the state institution, the Colony for the Feeble-Minded, at Dixon, Illinois.

Mr. Metzger has the executive offices of his business at 30 North LaSalle Street. His home is at 7444 Blackstone Avenue. As a resident of the Eighth Ward he has filled precinct and various committee chairmanships of the republican organization, was on the staff of the sheriff of Cook County from 1906 to 1910, was secretary of the Republican Central Committee of the county and committeeman for the Seventh Senatorial District in 1920, and a member of the Republican State Central Committee in 1924. In the primaries of April, 1926, he was nominated by the republican party as candidate for the Cook County Board.

Mr. Metzger was for fifteen years secretary of Aaron Lodge, A. F. and A. M., is a Knight Templar Mason and Shriner, member of the Independent Order of Odd Fellows, Knights of Pythias, Royal Arcanum, Modern Woodmen of America, and belongs to the Press, Midway Athletic and Swedish clubs, and to the Fort Dearborn Town Club.

CAPT. ALBERT SELLNER GARDNER, president of the Metcalf Stationery Company, stationers and engravers at Chicago, is a member of a prominent St. Louis family, but business interests have identified him with Chicago since the close of the World war, in which he served actively until wounded in the closing weeks of the great struggle.

The Gardners are in direct descent from Sir Joshua Gardner, who was a Lord Admiral in the British navy. The ancestral record of this family is traced back definitely in England to the year 1006. William Henry Gardner, grandfather of Captain Gardner, was of Virginia parentage and lived and died in Tennessee. During the Civil war he fought on the side of the Confederacy. He married Mary Ella Dozier, who introduced a number of other distinguished names into this ancestral record of Captain Gardner. The mother of Mary Ella Dozier was Lavinia Green Russell, who in her turn was a daughter of John Coates Russell. His father, William Russell, was one of the authors of the resolutions which were later redrafted into the Declaration of Independence. He was a colonel in Washington's army and distinguished himself as an officer. He witnessed the surrender of Cornwallis at Yorktown. William Russell, a brother of John Coates Russell, was the grandfather of Carter Harrison, Sr., of Chicago. John Coates Russell married Anne, a sister of Henry Clay. The Russells were of French origin, being the founders of the Norman House of Du Rozel, Vicomtes de La Manche. On emigrating to England they took the name of de Russell and formed the Ducal House of Bedford. The first of the family to settle in Virginia, in 1710, was sent to America by the King as an emissary of peace. Besides the Russell and Clay families and the Harrisons, another family connected with the paternal line were the Whiteheads, of Richmond, Virginia.

William Alfred Gardner, father of Captain Gardner, was the first of the family to settle in St. Louis, where he went as a young man and where later he was joined by his brothers, Frederick Dozier Gardner and Russell E. Gardner, also natives of Kentucky. Frederick Dozier Gardner was governor of Missouri from 1917 to 1921, including the period of the World war, and gave a most notable administration of the affairs of that state. William Alfred Gardner is a prominent financier, a member of the New York Stock Exchange, and for years has been a figure of power and influence in the affairs of St. Louis. He was a member of the Board of Directors of the World's Fair in that city in 1903-04, and in many other ways has been a leader in causes of civic advancement.

William Alfred Gardner married Julia Sellner. Her father, Alfred Christian Sellner, was born in Germany. His grandfather was forester to Frederick the Great, a position in the Imperial Council of Germany corresponding to the secretary of agriculture in the Cabinet of the President of the United States. Alfred Christian Sellner renounced his rights to succession of title and position of his grandfather, came to America in the midst of the Civil war and immediately volunteered his services in the cause of the Union and fought as a soldier until the end of the war. He first settled in Fort Wayne, Indiana, and later removed to St. Louis, where he died in 1924.

Capt. Albert Sellner Gardner, of Chicago, is a son of William Alfred and Julia (Sellner) Gardner. The ancestral record, briefly outlined, justifies the pride of this family in the fact that their people in each generation from early Colonial days to the present have when occasion required given freely of their services and talents to the public good and to the defense of the country, leaving an honorable record that is a written heritage to their descendants.

Albert Sellner Gardner was born at St. Louis, June 7, 1895, and was educated in Culver Military Academy of Indiana, and in the Lawrenceville Preparatory School at Lawrenceville, New Jersey, where he graduated in 1914. Captain Gardner first came to Chicago in 1915, but after America entered the World war he returned to St. Louis and on May 15, 1917, entered the First Officers' Training Camp at Fort Riley, Kansas. Later he was commissioned lieutenant of infantry and in April, 1918, went overseas with the Thirty-fifth Division. In August, 1918, he was promoted to captain of infantry in the One Hundred and Fortieth Regiment of the Thirty-fifth Division. He was severely wounded in action during the Argonne offensive on September 29, 1918. From the base hospital he was brought home and was treated in the hospital at Fort Sheridan, Illinois, until October 1, 1919, when he was granted his honorable discharge. Captain Gardner is now a member of the Officers' Reserve Corps, with the rank of captain, and is attached to the Three Hundred and Forty-second Infantry.

Recovering sufficiently to reengage in business, Captain Gardner from 1920 to 1922 was assistant to the general manager of the Calumet Baking Powder Company of Chicago. During 1924-25 he was vice president of the Ster-Electron Corporation, manufacturers and distributors of devices for deodorizing and sterilizing. Since September 9, 1925, he has been president of the Metcalf Stationery Company, located at 605 South Clark Street.

Captain Gardner takes an active part in the republican party, being a member of the Young Men's Republican Club of the Twenty-first Ward, and in 1920 was a member of the Ways and Means Committee of the national republican organization. He is a member of the Episcopal Church, Covenant Lodge No. 526, A. F. and A. M., and his chief recreations are tennis, swimming and sailing.

Captain Gardner married, June 10, 1922, Miss Caroline de Windt, of Winnetka, daughter of Heyliger Adams and Bertha (Mandell) de Windt. In the paternal line she is a great-great-great-granddaughter of John Adams and a descendant of John Quincy Adams, who were second and sixth presidents of the United States. Mr. and Mrs. Gardner, who reside at 456 Surf Street, have two children, a daughter, Carol, and a son, William Alfred, II.

JOHN H. CLAYTON, former city judge of Johnston City, has practiced law in that community of Williamson County since 1910. He is a member of a family that has been identified with this section of the county since pioneer times, and Judge Clayton's birth occurred on the site of Johnston City when the land was all woods and fields.

He is a son of Walter E. Clayton, a retired business man of Johnston City, who was born in Robertson County, Tennessee, January 18, 1856. The father of Walter E. Clayton was Lambert S. Clayton, who was born in Tennessee, June 23, 1822, and married Mary Ann Dorris, daughter of Simpson Dorris. They came to Williamson County, Illinois, in 1858, and Lambert S. Clayton died at Johnston City in May, 1909, and his wife in 1907.

Walter E. Clayton was reared at the old Clayton homestead, three miles north of Johnston City, was educated in district schools, became a buyer and shipper of live stock and for a number of years was a familiar figure on the markets of Chicago and St. Louis. He spent several years as a railroad contractor, assisting in grading and other phases of construction work for the Chicago & Eastern Illinois, the Illinois Central, and later went to Oklahoma during the territorial period and built portions of the Frisco Railroad at Choctaw, Oklahoma and Gulf, through districts then owned and largely occupied by the Creek Indians and some of the semi-civilized tribes. On returning to Illinois he engaged in business as a merchant at Johnston City, and was one of the organizers of the Pioneer Building and Loan Association in 1913. He also assisted in founding and became a director of the Johnston City State Bank. He has served as superintendent of the Missionary Baptist Church at Johnston City.

Walter E. Clayton married, September 14, 1876, Miss Cora E. Harper, daughter of John Harper. She was born in North Carolina. Their children were Leonard L., Mary A., John H., Della, Gracie, Eula and Ruby.

Judge John H. Clayton was born on the site of Johnston City, March 25, 1885. His early advantages were supplied by rural schools, and later he attended Ewing College, and in 1903 completed a course in the Gem City Business College at Quincy. After some business experience he entered the law department of the University of Illinois, remaining a student there three years and graduating in 1910. He was admitted to the Illinois bar the same year and at once opened an office at Johnston City. He served as city attorney from 1911 to 1915, and as city judge for eight years, from 1915 to 1923. Since retiring from the bench he has given all his time to his large and important general law practice. Judge Clayton became the first secretary of the Pioneer Building and Loan Association when it was organized in 1913. Two years later, in 1915, he was succeeded by his brother, Leonard L., who is still the secretary. Judge Clayton's sister Ruby is also connected with that organization.

Judge Clayton is a member of the Baptist Church, the Masonic order and the Lions Club. He married, in 1913, Miss Winnie Black, daughter of J. Edward Black, of Lawrence County, Illinois. They have three children, John H. Jr., Eleanor and Marjory.

HARRY W. BRACY, of Marion, is one of the young business men of Southern Illinois typifying the modern spirit of commerce with its ability to realize visions of undertakings that an earlier generation would have been content to achieve after many years of slow but steady growth. Mr. Bracy is the founder and proprietor of H. W. Bracy & Company, wholesale grocery company.

This business has a history of less than ten years. It was started on a very modest scale as the Bracy Fruit and Produce Company at Herrin, in Williamson County, in 1917. At that time Mr. Bracy's territory was confined to Williamson County. He had only three or four men employed. He was the salesman who covered the territory. The growth of the business was represented in 1919 by the establishment of another branch at Johnston City, this employing three men. At Herrin a building was erected with 16,000 feet of floor space. In order to facilitate the service of the company through its rapidly growing territory a modern cold storage plant was constructed, with basement for storage of bananas and other fruit. In 1922 the headquarters of the business were removed to Marion, and at that time H. W. Bracy & Company was established as successor to the Bracy Fruit and Produce Company. At Marion the company leased a large building with 14,000 square feet of

space, formerly occupied by the Goddard Grocery Company, a St. Louis firm. In 1921 the fourth chapter in the progress of the business was written with the opening of the West Frankfort branch. To accommodate the business at that point a building said to be one of the most complete in Southern Illinois for its purpose was erected. In the meantime the business in its various branches had grown so that it afforded employment to from forty to fifty persons, including ten salesmen covering a large part of the territory in Southern Illinois.

Mr. Bracy, proprietor of this business, represents an old family of Southern Illinois. His grandfather, John Bracy, was reared in Tennessee, lived in Kentucky for some years, and on coming to Illinois settled in St. Clair County, and soon afterward in Williamson County. He was a farmer and lived on and owned the farm known as the Brooks Farm, three miles west of Marion, a property he purchased in 1861. This farm contained a brick residence, which is still standing, and which has sheltered several generations of the Bracy family. John Bracy lived there until his death in 1893. He married a Miss Felz, and they had four sons, Thomas, William H., Benjamin D. and Abner.

Abner E. Bracy was born in Kentucky, in 1858, and was three years of age when the family came to Illinois. He was reared on a farm, but his inclinations have been entirely commercial, and since early youth he has been identified with the grocery or dry goods business. He went into business at the age of nineteen at Carterville, and subsequently at Marion was employed at wages of a dollar a day by A. L. Cline, remaining with the Cline establishment five or six years. He then started in the retail grocery business for himself with a store on the Public Square. On account of poor health he sold this business and since 1905 has been a traveling salesman on the road, representing a dry goods house. Abner E. Bracy married Florence Craine, daughter of Lorenzo Craine. Lorenzo Craine was an early settler of Williamson County, was a farmer, and lived in the Craineville community, where for many years he served as justice of the peace. Abner and Florence Bracy are the parents of five children: Charles E., Harry W., Reba, wife of Fred O. Lough; Leon and Ralph.

Harry W. Bracy was born at Marion, September 17, 1887. Up to the age of eighteen he lived at home and attended the city schools. At that time his brother Charles was selling fruit and produce for a St. Louis house, and enjoyed a prosperous clientele. However, desiring to go into business for himself, he turned over his road connections to his brother Harry. Harry Bracy was on the road selling fruit, produce and groceries from 1905 to 1917. He then utilized his experience and his connections to start in business for himself, and by calling upon every ounce of his energy and resources for several years he laid the foundation of a business that is one of the most successful of its kind in Southern Illinois.

Mr. Bracy is a member of the Marion Country Club and the Elks Club. He married Maud May Duncan, daughter of George Duncan, of Johnston City. They have one daughter, Virginia Duncan Bracy.

JAMES HENRY ELLIOTT, president of the Elliott Lumber Company, Inc., of Danville, has been in the lumber business since 1904, and during his earlier career was a school man in Vermilion County.

He was born in Jamaica Township, Vermilion County, June 2, 1876. His grandfather, William Elliott, was a native of North Carolina, and when a young man moved to Indiana, being a pioneer blacksmith in Washington County, and later followed the same occupation in Vigo County of the same state. James Henry Elliott's grandmother, Nancy Byerly, was a native of South Carolina. Richard M. J. Elliott, father of James H., was born in Washington County, Indiana, December 25, 1841, was reared in that county and in Vigo County, was married at Terre Haute and engaged in farming near that Indiana city until 1864. In that year he moved to Vermilion County, Illinois, and continued farming the rest of his life. He died in 1916 and is buried at the Wood Lawn Cemetery, near Indianola in the same county. He was a staunch democrat, and a member of the Church of Christ. During the Civil war he was a soldier with the Eighty-fifth Indiana Infantry. Richard Elliott was the fifteenth of a family of sixteen children, all of whom lived to maturity. He married Jane E. Jackson, who was born in Fleming County, Kentucky, January 12, 1837, and died in 1911. She was the daughter of Dr. Harrison Jackson. Her mother's maiden name was Elay. Doctor Jackson practiced medicine in Vermilion County for about thirty years. They had a family of seven children: William Harvey, a farmer near Sidell; Harrison Grant, a retired farmer at Danville, Illinois; Nancy Ann, wife of Oliver Sullivan, a retired farmer at Urbana, Illinois; Emma Frances, wife of Arch Carrington, a farmer at Georgetown, Illinois; James Henry; Josephus Allen, who died on the home farm at Sidell in 1888; and Charles Clarence, a farmer at Sidell.

James Henry Elliott attended common schools in Vermilion County and in 1895 completed the scientific course at the Northern Illinois Normal School at Dixon, graduating with the degree Bachelor of Science. For some ten years or more most of his time was given to school work in Vermilion County, and his last four years in teaching were spent as principal of the Oakwood school. In 1904 he entered the employ of Trent Brothers, lumber dealers at Danville, and later became secretary and treasurer of the corporation. He resigned his position in December, 1921, and in January, 1922, established the Elliott Lumber Company, Inc., of which he since has been president. This company has its offices, yards and planing mill at 640 East Fairchild Street in Danville, and is one of the leading enterprises of its kind in Vermilion County.

Mr. Elliott in 1910 was supervisor of Oakwood Township in Vermilion County. Since

1918 he has been chairman of the Democratic County Central Committee and was a member of the Democratic State Central Committee for two years. He is a member of Further Light Lodge No. 1130, A. F. and A. M., Danville, Danville Consistory of the Scottish Rite, and Ansar Temple of the Mystic Shrine at Springfield, Danville Lodge No. 332, B. P. O. Elks, and Damascus Lodge No. 84, Knights of Pythias.

His home is at 1126 North Vermilion Street in Danville. Besides this property he has eighty acres of farm land in Jamaica Township. He married at Danville, March 22, 1900, Miss Verna O. Villars, daughter of George H. and Martha (Brewer) Villars. The only child of Mr. and Mrs. Elliott, Paul Villars, died in infancy.

BENJAMIN F. TAYLOR was born at Lowville, New York, July 18, 1819, and died February 24, 1887. He graduated from Madison University at Hamilton, New York, in 1838, and in 1845 came to Chicago and was on the staff of the Chicago Evening Journal until 1865, during the greater part of that time as literary editor. He was also a war correspondent and wrote probably the most famous descriptions of "The Battle Among the Clouds" and the "Storming of Mission Ridge." After leaving daily journalism at Chicago he spent much of his time in travel, and his death occurred at Cleveland, Ohio. He was a contributor of prose and poetry to the Atlantic, Harpers, and Scribners, and attained high rank as a poet. His most popular poems were: "The Isle of Long Ago," "Rhymes of the River," and "The Old Village Choir."

EARL GEORGE GUBBINS is senior member of the firm Gubbins & McDonnell, real estate operators, which has chosen for its special field of real estate construction and financing the Rogers Park district of Chicago. Mr. Gubbins is one of the most successful younger men in real estate operations in Chicago today.

He was born in that city, January 27, 1896, and both his parents are also natives of Chicago. His father is Joseph John Gubbins, who was born in Chicago in 1861.

Earl George Gubbins after a public school education was for several years a clerk in the Chicago postoffice. In the spring of 1917 he volunteered for service in the World war and was assigned duty at the Great Lakes Naval Training Station, where he remained more than a year. One of his brothers, John Joseph Gubbins, who had been in the old Illinois National Guard before the war, enlisted in the One Hundred Thirty-second Infantry at Chicago, one of the regiments of the Thirty-third Division. With this he went overseas, and received eighteen wounds in the front lines at Chateau-Thierry. There are living only three men of the company of the One Hundred Thirty-second, of which this young man was a member. A younger brother is William W. Gubbins, now a cadet at the United States Naval Academy at Annapolis. He was formerly a student at the University of Illinois, where he made a notable record in mathematics and subjects relating to architecture and engineering. Among the group of young men who were applicants for the appointment to Annapolis he made by far the highest record in competitive examinations.

Earl George Gubbins since the war has made remarkable progress in the real estate field. The firm of Gubbins & McDonnell was established in 1919. For the year ending in the summer of 1926 the firm built thirty fine houses and apartments and completed general construction work totaling $3,000,000, all located in Rogers Park. They were one of the first firms to take up the new trend of coöperative apartment buildings, and they have financed and built a number of such structures, all of them notable for beauty of architecture and arrangement. The firm also deal in first mortgages and have the facilities for a complete service in every phase of home and apartment building and ownership. The firm are members of the Chicago Real Estate Board, the Cook County Real Estate Board, Illinois State Association of Real Estate Boards, and National Association of Real Estate Boards.

Mr. Gubbins has scarcely any diversions in the way of club life recreations which in some way are not immediately connected with the business and profession represented in the firm of Gubbins & McDonnell. Through this organization he has participated in various projects of civic betterment in Rogers Park, such as zoning plans, parking, good roads, state, city and county paving, sanitation, better housing and living conditions, and all of this constitutes his hobby as well as his primary occupation.

JOHN W. CLAYTON, M. D. Since 1904 one of the able physicians of Johnston City in Williamson County, Dr. John W. Clayton is a member of a well known family of Williamson County and Southern Illinois.

Doctor Clayton's grandfather, Lorenzo Dow Clayton, came from Kentucky and settled in Franklin County, Illinois, during the '50s. He was a prosperous farmer and when he retired he lived at Old Frankfort until his death at the age of eighty. Granville M. Clayton, son of Lorenzo D. and Johanna Clayton, was born at the Clayton homestead, and likewise followed the activities of agriculture until he retired with a competency. He then moved to Johnston City and died there in 1920. His wife was Ellen Dorris, whose family came from Tennessee.

Dr. John W. Clayton was one of nine children and was born on his father's farm in Williamson County January 8, 1875. He made the best of rather limited opportunities when a boy, most of his time being taken up with farm duties. He had the privilege of attending country schools only about 2½ months each winter. When he was eighteen years of age the family moved to Ewing, Franklin County, where he spent three years as a student in Ewing College. He taught school three years in Franklin County, and while teaching decided to qualify for a career as a

Rev. J. J. Klaes.

physician. In 1904 he was graduated from the medical department of St. Louis University, and on July 7th of the same year established himself at Johnston City and engaged in general practice. His time and energies have been fully occupied by his professional duties, and for a number of years he was one of the hardest working doctors in Southern Illinois. He did his work for the love of it and humanity, and a great deal of his professional service was never recompensed. In recent years he has influenced the natural increase of his profession toward younger doctors, and has afforded himself a well earned leisure. Doctor Clayton is a member of the various medical societies. He is on the Township High School Board and is a member of the Masonic order and the Franklin Country Club. He married, in 1904, the same year he located at Johnston City, Miss Anna Cox, daughter of Thomas A. Cox. She died in 1914, leaving four children, Ward, Lester, Vernie and Alva. In 1915 Doctor Clayton married Agnes Doty, daughter of Henry Doty, of Marion. They have one son, John William.

EARL B. JACKSON, cashier and vice president of the Marion State and Savings Bank, has been the official in closest touch with the public and the patrons of that bank since it was established under its present title and charter, and the remarkable strength and success of the institution reflect his individual service and ability as a banker.

The predecessor of the Marion State and Savings Bank was a private banking house started in 1890 by the father of Congressman E. E. Denison and the father of John Searing, the present state's attorney of Jackson County, Illinois. The home of this bank was at the northeast corner of the Square. After six months John Burnett purchased a one-third interest and at the end of two years John H. Searing sold out to Denison & Burnett. It was maintained as a private bank for twelve years. On July 23, 1902, a reorganization was effected, the Marion State and Savings Bank being chartered with capital of $60,000. The first president was Mr. C. H. Denison. At that time Earl B. Jackson, who had for several years been a bookkeeper in the Bank of Marion, was called to the new institution as its cashier. This position he has held now for nearly a quarter of a century and in addition is also vice president of the bank. The president is J. H. Burnett, and the directors comprise some of the best known citizens of Williamson County. The Marion Savings Bank has its home in one of the best bank and office buildings in Southern Illinois, a five-story modern structure with elevator service, built at a cost of $140,000 in 1914. In 1907, the bank having a surplus of $40,000, a stock dividend was declared and the capital increased to $100,000, its present figure. The bank now has a surplus of $90,000, deposits of over $1,750,000, and total resources of nearly $2,000,000. For several years the bank has regularly paid its stockholders 10 per cent dividends.

The father of Earl B. Jackson was James C. Jackson, who came from Gallatin, Tennessee, to Williamson County, Illinois, in 1861, at the age of nineteen. He came to Illinois to escape forced allegiance to the cause of disunion at the time of the Civil war. He was a democrat in politics. In early manhood he was a carpenter and for thirty years was a furniture merchant on West Main Street in Marion. He still lives in that city at the age of eighty-four. For one term he served as county clerk and for three terms was mayor of Marion. James C. Jackson married Elizabeth Calvert, a native of Williamson County and still living at Marion.

All the three children were born in Marion, including Earl B. Jackson, whose birth occurred October 9, 1874. He was educated in public schools, attended the Southern Illinois Normal University at Carbondale two years, and for a year and a half was assistant postmaster under John Goodall. Since then for about thirty years his experience has been in the field of banking. For eighteen months he was an employe of the Bank of Norris City, and in 1898 became a bookkeeper in the Bank of Marion, a position he held until he was appointed cashier of the Marion State and Savings Bank. He is also treasurer of the Marion Building and Loan Association. Mr. Jackson was mayor of Marion during 1917-19, during the period of the World war, when the office involved many unusual duties and responsibilities. Mr. Jackson is a member of the Marion Golf Club, and fraternally is affiliated with the Masonic fraternity, Knights of Pythias and B. P. O. Elks.

He married Miss Carra Barnes, daughter of Charles E. Barnes, of Norris City. They have a daughter, Pauline, now the wife of Charles B. Cochran, of Marion.

REV. JOHN JOSEPH KLAES, pastor of St. Jerome's Catholic Church at Troy, Illinois, was born in Weidenbach, Rhine Province, Germany, on December 15, 1887, the son of John Joseph and Anna Mary (Simons) Klaes.

He received his elementary education in the schools of Weidenbach, and at the age of sixteen came to the United States in company with two older brothers. In 1910 he received the degree of Bachelor of Arts and in 1911 the degree of Master of Arts from St. Francis College, now Quincy College, where he studied classical subjects and philosophy. The same year he received his American citizenship papers, in the Circuit Court at Quincy, Illinois.

For three years thereafter he studied theology in the American College of Louvain, leaving in 1914, when the World war forced the college to be discontinued. His studies were resumed at Canisianum Seminary, a Jesuit school in Innsbruck, Austria.

On June 30, 1915, he was ordained by Dr. Sigismund Waitz, Bishop of Feldkirch, at Holy Trinity Church, Innsbruck, and he celebrated his first mass on July 4, 1915, in the parish church at Kesseling.

Returning to the United States, Father Klaes was appointed assistant at St. Mary's Church, Quincy, Illinois, on October 15, 1915. He was named to have charge of the hospital at Highland, Illinois, on April 25, 1919, and directed the missions at Pocahontas and St. Jacobs. On July 1, 1920, he was appointed pastor of St. Jerome's Church, Troy, Illinois, with a mission at Black Jack.

LLOYD C. CAMPBELL is vice president of the First National Bank of Marion. He is a veteran banker, and few men in the state have exceeded his record of continuous service with one institution. He started in with the First National Bank at the age of eighteen and has given it almost thirty-five years of uninterrupted work, good will and loyalty. In that time the First National Bank has developed from a small country bank, with limited resources, until now its resources reach the impressive total of approximately $2,240,000. The bank has capital and surplus of $200,000, and deposits averaging over $1,800,000.

The Campbell family has been in Williamson County since the close of the Civil war period. His grandfather, Samuel C. Campbell, was born in South Carolina, lived for many years in the vicinity of Princeton, Kentucky, and in 1865 came to Illinois and settled on a farm three miles east of Marion, in Williamson County. He lived there until his death in 1879. His wife, Louisa Howard, was a native of Kentucky, and they were married in that state.

James M. Campbell, father of the Marion banker, was born in Kentucky, October 24, 1849, and was sixteen years of age when the family came to Williamson County. In Kentucky and also after coming to Illinois his routine was attending rural school in winter and working on the farm in summer. On reaching his majority he left the farm to become clerk in the old Goodall & Campbell store, a general merchandise establishment at Marion. He was connected with this enterprise for a number of years, later was deputy county clerk under County Clerk W. H. Eubanks, and after leaving that office spent some time in Carbondale as an employe of the North-Campbell store, located on the present site of the Roberts Hotel. In the spring of 1885, on returning to Marion, James M. Campbell became associated with his brother, William H. Campbell, and James W. Pillow in the purchase of a general merchandise store located where the Whitington & Wallace Drug Store now is. In 1895 he sold his interest to Mr. Pillow, and he then became associated with L. E. Dennison & Company, who were in business where the First National Bank Building now stands. After several years with this firm he rejoined his brother, William H., in a partnership engaging in the general merchandise business in the room now occupied by the Economy Store. William H. Campbell died November 11, 1918, armistice day. James M. Campbell then retired from business, and his own death occurred almost exactly five years later than his brother, on November 15, 1923. His death followed a week later after an injury when he was struck by an automobile in crossing a street. James M. Campbell married Mary L. Eubanks, daghter of William Eubanks, of Williamson County. There were four children: Lloyd C., Gertrude, who died in infancy; William Harris and Hortense.

Lloyd C. Campbell was born at Marion, October 6, 1874, and his education was supplied by the grade and high schools of his native town. Soon after leaving high school he became a clerk in the Burkhart & Binkley store. In September, 1892, at the age of eighteen, he took the opportunity to enter the First National Bank as clerk and bookkeeper. The bank was then, as noted above, a comparatively small organization, and the clerk and bookkeeper had many other duties than those familiar to the title of his position, including sweeping out the banking room. At the age of twenty-one he was made assistant cashier under Mr. J. C. Mitchell, who was then and is now cashier of the bank. Subsequently Mr. Campbell was promoted to active vice president, and has had a prominent part in making the bank what it is today.

Mr. Campbell was for two years an alderman of Marion and served four years as city treasurer, and he helped organize and is treasurer of the Rose Hill Cemetery, and was one of the organizers of the Coal Belt Building and Loan Association in 1921 and has since been its secretary. He became an active member of the Methodist Episcopal Church at the age of eighteen, has been church treasurer since 1893, and was superintendent of the Sunday school from 1897 to 1913. Mr. Campbell is a charter member of the Lions Club and its treasurer, and belongs to the Marion Golf Club. He married Miss Nettie House, daughter of Columbus H. House, of Washington County.

LOUIS HECKMAN. A man whose example and conversation are a constant inspiration to his associates, Louis Heckman, one of the successful merchants of Manito, operating under the caption of Louis Heckman, is a real optimist, at peace with everybody and the world, and a firm believer in the desirability of Illinois as the Garden Spot of America. His wholesome outlook on life, his sound business principles and his pleasure in his home community, state and country all play an important part in his own good health and happiness and the encouragement of others less fortunate than he. His wealth, which is considerable, has been acquired through legitimate channels of business activity and from his agricultural pursuits, and he is turning a fair proportion of it back into the section from which his money has been drawn by investing in local enterprises, and assisting worthy movements. Such men as he are a very valuable asset to their fellow citizens wherever they are found.

Louis Heckman was born in Mason County, Illinois, February 19, 1869, a son of George Heckman, the latter a German by birth, who came to the United States in boyhood from the vicinity of Heidelberg and settled at Pekin, Illinois. Here he earned his first American money working to learn the blacksmith trade, and he continued a blacksmith throughout his life, although he retired several years prior to his death, which occurred when he was sixty-four years old. He married, at Pekin, Mary Weber, a daughter of J. Weber, a German. Mrs. Heckman was born in Hergetstown, Germany, and was brought to the United States when a girl of nine years. She lived to be seventy-eight years old, and died at Pekin, where she and her husband are buried. Their children were as follows: George, who lives in Pekin, a cabinetmaker for years; Philip, who was formerly the partner of his brother Louis, and is now a resident of Muskogee, Oklahoma; Arthur, who died in Mason City, Illinois; Anna, who is the widow of the late John B. Hacker, of Pekin; Louis, whose name heads this review; Dr. Lydia Holmes, who resides at Bloomington, Illinois; Mrs. Ida Seidens, who resides at Pekin; Frank, who died in young manhood at Pekin; and Edna, who is the wife of John Smith, of Pekin.

The public schools of Manito gave Louis Heckman his schooling, and he started to learn blacksmithing from his father, but the latter soon saw that his son had no real aptitude for the trade and so he advised him to seek some other calling. Finding that his inclinations were for a mercantile life, the young man entered the employ of L. Burchett of New Holland, Illinois, and remained with him as a clerk for nine years. Leaving that community, Mr. Heckman went to Mason City, Illinois, and worked for Mr. Cargill as a clerk for a year. With the experience he had thus gained he and his brother Philip went into a general mercantile business at Manito, under the name of Heckman Brothers. After many years together Louis Heckman bought his brother's interest, and has since continued alone. A few years ago he restricted his stock to furniture and carpets. In addition to his store at Manito he owns a hardware, implement and furniture store at Delavan, and this was formerly the McKinstry store, one of the leaders of its kind in Tazewell County. Mr. Heckman has also long been engaged in farming, and owns a fine farm in Mason County.

Other interests have claimed Mr. Heckman at different periods of his career, and he was one of the founders of the Manito State Bank, and served as one of its directors at that time. As a community man he has always taken a hand in local affairs, but has studiously refrained from politics, although he votes the straight republican ticket, and is proud of the fact. When the matter of rehabilitation of the Chicago, Peoria & St. Louis Railroad came before the people of Mason County it was Mr. Heckman who was one of the real leaders in that great work, which resulted in saving for Manito its railroad connection with the rest of the state. Long a consistent member of the Methodist Episcopal Church, he is identified with the church board, and is one of the most energetic workers in behalf of the church. During the late war Mr. Heckman was active in the Mason County Chapter of the American Red Cross, was one of the three fuel administrators, and was otherwise zealous in behalf of local war work.

While his life has been a strenuous one, Louis Heckman has found time for some recreation, and he is now able to so arrange his business affairs that he and his wife can travel. They have covered the Western states, principally with their car, and have toured in the North and South as well. In 1925 they covered 7,600 miles between August 6 and October 18. The East has not either been neglected, and there are few places of interest in any part of the country that Mr. and Mrs. Heckman have not visited. The more places they visit the more firmly is Mr. Heckman impressed with his good fortune in belonging to the most wonderful country in the world, and he has never found a single section, however advantageous the surroundings might have been, that he would exchange for his own home community.

On April 22, 1895, Mr. Heckman married, at Manito, Louise Pollard, a daughter of Maj. Andrew Pollard, one of the conspicuous merchants of Manito, and a veteran of the Union army. Mrs. Heckman was born at Manito, in 1875, being one in a family of nine children, and one of the younger members of the family. She was educated at Manito, and here her life has been happily spent. While she is not a leader, she is deeply interested in the progress made by her sex, and glad to assist in every way she can in forwarding the good work. However, it is as the homemaker that she finds her most congenial work, and is noted for her ability in this direction. Mr. and Mrs. Heckman have no children. It can be safely said that no one ever comes to these excellent people for help in vain. Not only are they generous in their donations of money, but they are equally lavish in their kindly sympathy and encouragement, and they have warm personal friends wherever their travels have led them, in addition to the host they possess in Mason County.

WILLIAM CLINTON JOHNSON, who is chairman of the examining committee for real estate brokers in Illinois, has been a business man in Danville for over forty years, and one of the citizens most active in the industrial upbuilding and functions of that city.

He represents distinguished ancestry on both sides and is a member of the Sons of the American Revolution. His father, the late Richard H. Johnson, was one of the most successful newspaper men in the Middle West, and founded several papers that have been in existence for half a century or more. He was born at Covington, Indiana, July 15, 1826, son of one of the first pioneers in that section of Indiana. He grew up there, finished his education in DePauw University at Greencastle, Indiana, and as a youth learned the printer's trade. One of his early achievements was founding a newspaper at Bloomington, Illinois, which is now the Bloomington Pantagraph, one of the best papers in the state. After publishing this a year he sold out and going to Des Moines, Iowa, started another paper, now the Des Moines Register, without doubt one of the outstanding newspapers in the Middle West. From Des Moines he removed to Richmond, Kentucky, founding the Richmond Messenger, which he published until 1865. In that year President Andrew Johnson appointed him collector of internal revenue at Richmond.

On December 10, 1866, Richard H. Johnson became a resident of Danville, Illinois. Here he was connected with the Danville Commercial, and in 1872, with the late W. R. Jewell, founded the Danville News. He acted as city editor of the News until 1876, when, selling out, he acquired an interest in the Danville Commercial, and was with that newspaper until he retired in 1904. He was therefore identified with both the papers now consolidated as the Commercial-News. For four years after retiring from the newspaper business he held the office of county coroner of Vermilion County. His death occurred at Danville, in May, 1911. He had begun voting as a whig and later was a republican, was an elder in the Christian Church and a member of the Masonic fraternity. Richard H. Johnson married Susan Goodloe, a daughter of Judge William C. Goodloe, who lived at Richmond, Kentucky, and for thirty-six years was on the bench as judge of the Circuit Court. Her maternal grandfather was Governor William Owsley, of Kentucky. Her paternal grandfather was also one of the eminent jurists of Kentucky. Susan Goodloe was born in Richmond, Kentucky, in December, 1826, and died at Danville in 1910. She was the mother of four sons and three daughters: Almira, of Danville, widow of John W. Osborne, who was a farmer; William C.; Milbrey J., wife of John T. Campbell, of Bismarck, Illinois; Curran S., owner of the C. S. Johnson printing establishment at Danville; Richard Harvey, whose home is at Danville and who for thirty-five years has been a flour salesman for the Page Milling Company at Topeka, Kansas; Elizabeth J., wife of Edward S. Moore, a building contractor at Danville; and Archibald G., a real estate broker at Danville.

William Clinton Johnson was born at Richmond, Kentucky, December 28, 1858, and was about eight years of age when his parents came to Danville. He grew up here, attended the public schools and at the age of thirteen entered the printing office of the Danville News. He learned the printer's trade and many of the details of the newspaper business in general. At the age of twenty-one he became assistant postmaster at Danville, serving from 1880 to 1885, following which for four years he was in the grocery business, and from 1889 to 1891 was again assistant postmaster. Mr. Johnson was in the life insurance business for six years, and since 1897 has devoted his attention to the real estate business, having developed in that time a complete organization and real estate service for Danville and Vermilion County. His offices are on Main Street.

Mr. Johnson served as assessor and collector of Danville Township from 1899 to 1904. He is a republican. During the World war he was food and fuel administrator of Vermilion County, and for eighteen months of that period put in eighteen hours a day, expending his energies and resources without stint to the cause. Fraternally he is affiliated with Olive Branch Lodge No. 38, A. F. and A. M.; Vermilion Chapter No. 82, R. A. M.; Athelstan Commandery No. 45, K. T.; Danville Consistory of the Scottish Rite; is a past exalted ruler of Danville Lodge No. 332, B. P. O. Elks. From 1920 to 1924 he was president of the Danville Chamber of Commerce.

Mr. Johnson married at Danville, October 12, 1882, Miss Ida M. Meyers, daughter of Leonard and Susan Meyers, now deceased. Mrs. Johnson died February 7, 1899. There were four children: Meta J., the oldest, is the wife of Frank H. Lewis, general manager, secretary and treasurer of the Feldkamp Candy Company at Danville. Helen married Alden F. Barker, president of a financing company at Danville. The son Clinton G. was with the Students' Army Training Corps while a student at the University of Illinois, remaining in the university nearly through his senior year and is now connected with the Onarga Nursery Company at Onarga, Illinois. The younger son, Philip L., was also in the Students' Army Training Corps at the university, where he completed his sophomore year and is now a traveling salesman with home at Indianapolis.

Mr. Johnson is individually a large real estate owner in Danville, having an attractive home at 1622 North Vermilion Street, and he owns several extensive farms on the Wabash River in Indiana. As a real estate man he has laid out and sold several additions to the city. He was associated with Col. George Buckingham in donating seventy-four acres of ground to the Chicago & Eastern Illinois Railways as sites for the $3,000,000 shops located there, these constituting perhaps the largest single industrial resource of the city. Mr. Johnson lent effective aid in securing several other large factories for the city. The building of Danville has been a matter of pride and enthusiasm with him as well as business. He served several years as president of the Danville Real Estate Board. He assisted in forming the Real Estate Association of Illinois in 1916, being its first president, and holding that office three years. It was through the Real Estate Association of Illinois that the law was placed on the statute books requiring that real estate brokers be licensed as a measure of protecting the public from the dishonest practice of men posing as real estate brokers. This law was confirmed and took effect January 1, 1922, and Governor Small appointed Mr. Johnson as one of the three commissioners to enforce the law and he is now chairman of the commission.

JOHN MINTON MITCHELL has been identified with the business life of Mt. Carmel over forty years, at first as a merchant and later as a banker. He is president of the American National Bank of Mt. Carmel. He has also been long and prominently identified as a layman with the Methodist Episcopal Church. Three generations of the Mitchell family have

lived in southern Illinois, the residence of the family having been continuous since the year of Illinois' admission to the Union.

His grandfather, Sion F. Mitchell, was of Scotch-Irish ancestry, and his forefathers on coming from England first settled in Connecticut, later went to North Carolina and finally to Tennessee. Sion F. Mitchell left Tennessee in 1818 and came to Illinois, settling in Franklin County. He was accompanied on that migration by Braxton Parrish. Each of them had a wife and baby, and the wives rode horseback while the husbands walked. Both were local Methodist preachers and had an active part in upbuilding the Methodist Church in southern Illinois.

Jesse G. Mitchell, father of John M., was born in Franklin County, in 1835, and spent his entire life there. At his marriage he gave the minister who performed the ceremony the only dollar he possessed. He was a school teacher before that time, later a farmer, and subsequently conducted a general store at Locust Grove, where he was a dealer in grain and tobacco, and for many years postmaster of the community. He proved his native ability by achieving a successful business career, and was likewise a natural leader of men. He was optimistic, generous, good natured, was a local preacher in the Methodist Church and at all times exercised an influence for good. Selling his farm and other business interests in 1880, he removed to Benton, where he died at the age of fifty-nine. Jesse G. Mitchell married Asenath E. Marvel, who was born in Posey County, Indiana, in 1837, daughter of George R. Marvel, who served with the rank of colonel of the Forty-eighth Illinois Cavalry during the Civil war.

John Minton Mitchell, one of five children, was born on a farm in Franklin County, July 16, 1862. After completing a high school education he attended the Southern Normal University at Carbondale, and in 1882 graduated from the Central Normal College at Danville, Indiana. His experience outside of school had been acquired on his father's farm and in the store at Locust Grove and at Burton, Illinois. Mr. Mitchell engaged in business for himself at Mt. Carmel in 1883, at first as a clothing merchant and subsequently adding dry goods. His mercantile business was sold in 1894, and since then he has been a banker, guiding the destiny of three institutions successfully for thirty years. He first became president of the Wabash Savings Bank of Mt. Carmel. He continued as president of its successor, the American State Bank, and this in 1901 became the American National Bank, of which he has been the head for a quarter of a century. Other business enterprises have naturally attracted a portion of his time and attention and he has been the source of much constructive work in Mt. Carmel and vicinity. He is a republican, is a Knight Templar Mason and Shriner, member of the Independent Order of Odd Fellows, B. P. O. Elks, the Moose and Woodmen. Mrs. Mitchell and their daughters are also active Methodists.

His record in the Methodist Church calls for more than passing mention. Mr. Mitchell for thirty years has been superintendent of the Sunday school of his home church. For five consecutive terms he was selected as a delegate to the General Conference; has served for eight years as a member of the Sunday School Board of the World; has been on the Board of Control of the Epworth League; for eight years on the Board of Foreign Missions; for twenty-five years on the Board of Trustees of McKendree College at Lebanon, and eight years of that time as president of the board, and is treasurer of the College Endowment Fund. Mr. Mitchell also served as president of the Conference Claimant Society, which provides for aged and incapacitated ministers.

On June 1, 1886, he married at Mt. Carmel Miss Della Russell, daughter of Charles R. and Frances Russell. Her grandfather, Abraham Russell, was a pioneer of Mt. Carmel, where he settled in 1817. Mrs. Mitchell was born at Mt. Carmel March 28, 1868. The three daughters of Mr. and Mrs. Mitchell are: Grace, an instructor in the Christian College at Columbia; Frances, wife of E. E. Fearheiley, of Mt. Vernon, Illinois, and Elinor, wife of Loren C. Hill, of Mt. Carmel.

WILLIAM PATTERSON MACCRACKEN, JR. At its annual convention in Detroit in September, 1925, the American Bar Association chose as its secretary for the following year a well known Chicago attorney, William Patterson MacCracken, Jr. This is one of numerous distinctions that have come to this Chicago lawyer since he began practice fifteen years ago.

He was born in Chicago, September 17, 1888, son of Dr. William P. and Mary Elizabeth (Avery) MacCracken. His early education was acquired in Chicago except for one year at Hillside, Wisconsin, and one year at Montclair, New Jersey. He attended the South Side Academy, graduated from the University High School in 1905, took his Bachelor of Philosophy degree at the University of Chicago in 1909, and was graduated J. D. from the University of Chicago Law School in 1911. He was admitted to the Illinois bar in October of the same year. He served as legislative secretary to Hon. Morton D. Hull in 1911. From the date of his admission until February 1, 1916, he was employed by the law firms of Steere, Williams & Steere, Steere & Steere, George S. Steere, and Montgomery, Hart, Smith & Steere. In 1916 he became a member of the firm Montgomery, Hart Smith & Steere, and is now a parnter in the firm of Montgomery, Hart & Smith. During 1923 he served as special assistant to the attorney general of Illinois in connection with the City Hall graft investigation, and as assistant state's attorney of Cook County was especially assigned to try cases growing out of this investigation.

Mr. MacCracken enlisted in July, 1917, was on duty at the Rock Island Arsenal until August of that year, and during August and September attended the Fort Sheridan Training Camp, Sixth Battery. He was in the School of Military Aeronautics at the University of Illinois in October and November, and was at Rich Field, Waco, Texas, from December, 1917, to September, 1918, as cadet. After being commissioned second lieutenant there he served as flying instructor until transferred to Ellington Field, Olcott, Texas, in September, 1918, and was discharged January 7, 1919. Mr. MacCracken was a member of the committee on the law of aviation in the American Bar Association in 1920-21, and was chairman of the committee on the law of aeronautics from 1921 to 1925. He was commander of Aviation Post of the American Legion in 1925. As a member of the National Aeronautics Association he has been governor at large since 1923, and chairman of the legislative committee also since 1923. He is a member of the Aero Commission of the City of Chicago, appointed by Mayor Dever, and participated in the organization of the National Air Transport, Inc., and is general counsel of this organization.

Mr. MacCracken has been an active member of the Illinois State and Chicago Bar Associations, and served as member of admissions and rules of court committees, and as chairman of the committee on rules of court, 1925-26. He is a past president of the Chicago University Law School Alumni Association, member of the Commercial Law League of America, member of the Hamilton Club, Kenwood Evangelical Church, superintendent of the Sunday School of Christ Church at Winnetka, member of the Sunset Ridge Country Club, is a past regent of Garden City Council of the Royal Arcanum, and a republican in politics.

Mr. MacCracken married, September 14, 1918, at Waco, Texas, Miss Sally Lucile Lewis. They have one son, William Lewis MacCracken, born August 24, 1923.

WHITSON WILFORD DAILY, state's attorney of Hamilton County, served two terms as county superintendent of schools of that county and for the past ten years has enjoyed an extensive and successful practice as a lawyer.

He was born on a farm in Stone County, Missouri, January 14, 1880, but represents some pioneer families of Hamilton County, Illinois. John Daily, a native of Kentucky and of Virginia ancestry, came to Hamilton County fully a century ago and helped develop the country from a wilderness condition. His son, Lewis J. Daily, was born in Hamilton County, but subsequently moved to Missouri, where he spent the rest of his life. His wife was Celia Maulding, a native of Hamilton County, and who finally returned to that county and died there at the age of ninety-two. Her father was William Maulding, and her grandfather, Ambrose Maulding, was a soldier of the Revolutionary war and one of the early settlers of Hamilton County, Illinois, where he died. His descendants recently erected a monument at his grave at Ten Miles to commemorate his services as a Revolutionary patriot. Wilford C. Daily, son of Lewis J. and Celia (Maulding) Daily, was about fifteen years old when his parents moved to Missouri, and he was reared there and engaged in farming. He married Martha J. Kirk, and in 1892 he returned with his family to Hamilton County, Illinois, and he is now seventy-four, and his wife sixty-nine. Both are members of the Missionary Baptist Church. They reared a family of five sons: Robert Z., James H., Whitson W., William H. and Lewis A.

Whitson W. Daily was twelve years old when brought to Illinois. He grew up on a farm, was educated in rural schools, and at the age of nineteen began teaching. He did a great deal of private study at home and he also attended Ewing College, from which he was graduated in 1902. For eleven years he attended and taught school alternately, during which time he was principal of schools at Broughton, and in 1910 was elected county superintendent of Hamilton County, and reelected in 1914. On account of a change in the law regulating the term of office he served eight years and eight months as county superintendent.

In the meantime Mr. Daily, in 1915, graduated from the American College of Law at Chicago and was admitted to the Illinois bar in 1916. On retiring from his office as county superintendent he engaged in practice at McLeansboro, and in 1920 was elected on the democratic ticket state's attorney of Hamilton County. He was reelected in 1924, and has set a high standard of efficiency in law enforcement in Hamilton County.

Mr. Daily is a deacon in the Missionary Baptist Church. He is a member of the Masonic Order and Independent Order of Odd Fellows. He married, in 1902, Miss Nora E. Davis. She was born and reared at Broughton, Illinois, and was a teacher before her marriage. They have two sons, Joe Whit Daily and John Davis Daily.

GEORGE W. HOGAN was admitted to the Illinois bar forty-six years ago, and while one of the oldest active men in the profession in Hamilton County, he is also well known for his participation in other activities, particularly as a banker. He is president of the Peoples National Bank of McLeansboro, and also of the Walpole State Bank at Walpole, Illinois.

He was born on a farm in Hamilton County, April 9, 1858. His grandfather Hogan was a native of Georgia, and on coming to Illinois settled in Franklin County, where he died some years later after a surgical operation. His son, John H. Hogan, was born in Franklin County, Illinois, was reared in Franklin County and in 1854 went out to California as a gold digger. He had a moderate success in the quest of gold and on returning to Illinois located in Hamilton County. When the Civil war broke out he enlisted as a private in a company organized in Franklin County, a part of the Fifteenth Illinois Cavalry which afterwards was attached to the Thirty-first Illinois Volunteer Infantry, commanded by Gen. John A. Logan. He was commissioned a second lieutenant and then a first lieutenant. John H. Hogan was in service until the close of the war and in after years was generally called Captain. His father-in-law, Capt. James Wallace Flannigan, was a soldier in both the Mexican and Civil wars. John H. Hogan married Constance Flannigan. While he was in the army he sent part of his salary home to his wife, who used it to buy half a section of land in Hamilton County. After the war he located on this land, but three years later returned to Franklin County. His last years were spent at McLeansboro, where he died May 2, 1913, at the age of eighty-two. He was a democrat until he went into the Union army, but came back from the war a republican and ever after supported that party. He and his wife had a family of ten children, and seven are now living.

George W. Hogan spent most of his youth on a farm, attended country schools, continued his education in Ewing College and read law at Benton and McLeansboro. He was admitted to the bar in 1880, and for ten years was associated in practice with John C. Hall. In later years his law work has been largely confined to chancery and probate practice.

Mr. Hogan in 1903 organized the First State Bank at Elizabethtown, Illinois, and was its president five years, until selling his interest. He organized the Peoples National Bank at McLeansboro in 1909, and he has been its president from the beginning. In 1924 this bank and the First National Bank of McLeansboro took over the Cloud State Bank of that city, and since then the Peoples National Bank has occupied the former building of the Cloud institution. Mr. Hogan is regarded as one of the leading financiers of Hamilton County, and is in close touch with a wide variety of business interests.

He has given a generous share of his time and abilities to the public service. He served a term as mayor of McLeansboro, and after an interval served two other terms. During the second period of service he led the movement for the building and installation of water works and street improvements, carrying the issue against strong opposition. He was a delegate to the last state constitutional convention of Illinois. Mr. Hogan has always been a staunch republican, is a thirty-second degree Scottish Rite Mason and Shriner, member of the Knights of Pythias and the Methodist Church.

He married, September 14, 1888, Miss Pearl Thompson, daughter of Richard Thompson, of Thompsonville, Illinois. They have two children, Lila Thompson and George W., Jr. His son was a soldier in the World war and is now practicing law at McLeansboro.

PETER J. KOLB. The most forceful and youthful of the pioneers of Wabash County are represented in the family and ancestry of Peter J. Kolb, prominent attorney of Mt. Carmel, who for his own part has displayed exceptional ability and integrity in the course of his life work in that locality.

Mr. Kolb was born on a farm three miles west of Mt. Carmel, August 5, 1874, son of Adam and Anna (Kohlhaas) Kolb. His paternal grandparents were Suitbert and Elizabeth (Dunkel) Kolb. In 1840 they immigrated to the United States and bought a small tract of land a few miles west of Mt. Carmel, in Wabash County. A large part of it was covered with heavy woods. Suitbert Kolb built for his family a log cabin, began the work of clearing the timber, and as evidence of his prosperous career as a farmer he increased his holdings to 160 acres. He died in 1885. About ten years later his widow moved to Mt. Carmel, where she died in 1906, at the age of eighty-nine. Of their nine children six reached mature years, named Adam, Lawrence, John, Joseph, Mary and Margaret.

Adam Kolb, father of the Mt. Carmel attorney, was born at Thulba, Bavaria, Germany, February 22, 1835, and was five years of age when brought to America. He grew up on the farm in the midst of pioneer conditions, learned to work from an early age, and had only the advantages of the neighboring schools. In 1860 he married Josephine Melcher, who was born at Louisville, Kentucky. The two children born to this marriage died in infancy, and the wife passed away in 1863. After her death Adam Kolb sold the farm which he had purchased near Rochester, in Wabash County, and in 1867 he married Anna Kohlhaas. She was born in Wabash County, daughter of John and Mary Ann (Leipold) Kohlhaas, the former a native of Prussia and the latter of Hesse-Darmstadt, Germany. John Kohlhaas arrived at Baltimore, Maryland, in 1836, went from there to Natchez, Mississippi, then to Louisville, Kentucky, and there he married. His wife had come to America with her parents, who located at Louisville. John Kohlhaas for several years after his marriage lived in Louisiana, and then moved to Salem, Illinois, and five years later located on a farm near Friendsville in Wabash County. His wife died in 1856, and afterward John Kohlhaas lived with Mr. and Mrs. Adam Kolb until his death in 1875, at the age of eighty-one.

Adam Kolb after his second marriage located on a farm about three miles west of Mt. Carmel and remained there until 1901. Then selling the old homestead, he moved to Mt. Carmel and was retired until his death on May 2, 1917. He was a democrat in politics, took an active interest in local affairs, and he and his wife were Catholics, and lived industrious and well ordered lives. Mrs. Kolb died May 28, 1925. They reared three sons and two daughters: Charles, George, Peter J., Mary and Laura.

Peter J. Kolb was reared on a farm, attended rural schools, and at the age of nineteen began teaching. His work as a rural school teacher continued four years, and for a year and a half he was an instructor in the high school at Mt. Carmel. In the meantime he was using the intervals of teaching to advance his own education. The winter of 1892-93 he spent in the Illinois Normal University at Carbondale, attended the Indiana Normal College at Danville in the summer of 1895, and the summer of 1896, in Austin College at Effingham, Illinois. In the fall of 1896 he began the study of law in the office of Leeds and Ramsey, Mt. Carmel attorneys. During the summer of 1897 he was a student in the Illinois Wesleyan University Law School at Bloomington. Mr. Kolb in December, 1898, became deputy county clerk, holding that position for two years. In the meantime, in December, 1899, he was admitted to the bar after examination at Mt. Vernon, Illinois. In September, 1900, he formed a law partnership with Judge S. Z. Landes, and they practiced together until Mr. Landes retired upon election to the office of county judge. He was states attorney of Wabash County from 1904 to 1908, and served as master in chancery of that county for two years. In the course of a quarter of a century Mr. Kolb has achieved a position of fine distinction among the lawyers of southern Illinois. He has handled a large volume of varied and important practice in all the courts in the southern part of the state. Since 1911 he has been district attorney for the Cleveland, Cincinnati, Chicago & St. Louis Railway. He is a director of the First National Bank of Mt. Carmel, and during 1906-08 was associated with A. E. Smith in the ownership of the Mt. Carmel Register.

He is a democrat in politics, and he and his family are members of the Catholic Church. He has been active in the Rotary Club, serving as governor of the Forty-fifth District. Mr. Kolb organized the Knights of Columbus at Mt. Carmel and for several years was grand knight, and is a past exalted ruler of the Mt. Carmel Lodge of B. P. O. Elks.

He married, October 15, 1902, Miss Helen Fridrich, a native of Mt. Carmel, daughter of Nicholas and Margaret (Peters) Fridrich. Nicholas Fridrich, who was born at Mt. Carmel October 10, 1839, and died there February 29, 1908, was a son of George and Mary (Wirth) Fridrich, natives of Germany, who settled in Wabash County in 1838. Nicholas Fridrich was a carpenter contractor, later a furniture dealer and undertaker, and one of the highly esteemed citizens of Mt. Carmel. He was a Union soldier in the Civil war. Mr. and Mrs. Kolb have two children, Margaret and Walter. The daughter is a graduate of the University of Illinois and is a teacher. The son is in his second year as a student at Notre Dame University.

JAMES R. WINN is president of the Winn Lumber Company, one of the leading concerns of its kind in Jefferson County, where it maintains large and well equipped yards both at Mount Vernon, the county seat, and in the village of Waltonville. Mr. Winn has achieved substantial success through his own ability and efforts and has high standing in the business and social circles of his home city of Mount Vernon. On a farm near the village of Hillsboro, Arkansas, and at a point more than fifty miles distant from a railroad, James R. Winn was born in the year 1873, a scion of sterling American ancestry on both the paternal and maternal sides. He is a son of Powhatan and Ada L. (Oakes) Winn, both representatives of families that were founded in the southeastern part of the United States in the pioneer days, Mrs. Winn having been descended from a Colonial New England family that early sent representatives into Ohio and that has figured also in the development and progress of other states of the middle west and southwest. Powhatan Winn likewise was a native of Arkansas, was a plain, industrious and law-abiding citizen, and belonged to that large and eminently respectable class of yeomenry that in an unassuming way has ever added stability to the body politic and aided in advancing human progress and prosperity, his active career having been marked by close alliance with productive farm industry. His was the distinction of having been a loyal and valiant soldier of the Union in the Civil war, he having been a member of the One Hundred and Seventy-seventh Ohio Volunteer Infantry and his military career having covered virtually the entire period of the war. At the close of the great conflict through which the integrity of the nation was perpetuated he received his honorable discharge, and in later years his continued interest in his old comrades was shown in his appreciative affiliation with the Grand Army of the Republic. His death occurred in 1898, his wife having passed away in 1890, both having been held in unqualified esteem in the community where they had lived and wrought to goodly ends and where they had stood as representatives of the staunchest type of sterling American citizenship, sincere and earnest and living useful lives "far from the maddening crowd's ignoble strife." This worthy couple became the parents of a large family of children, seven of whom attained to maturity: James R., of this review, is the eldest of the surviving children. Frank E. was a member of an Arkansas regiment in the Spanish-American war, and is engaged in saw-mill operations. Richard P. is now a resident of Cleveland, Ohio, to which state he removed from Pine Bluff, Arkansas. Owen O., who resides in California, married Bonnie Lamont, who is deceased and who is survived by three children, Everett E., Earl and Ada May. Clyde M. married Jessie Hopper, who is deceased and whose surviving children are Marion and Rosella. Flora is the wife of John E. Graves and they reside in Nevada. Lois M., the third child, and Everett, the youngest of the number, are the two who are deceased. The Winn family has been worthily concerned with civic and industrial development in various parts of Ohio, Illinois, Arkansas and Mississippi and with other states of the southwest.

James R. Winn, of this sketch, was named in honor of his paternal grandfather, the late James R. Winn, who was born in Mississippi, and who was a successful planter and influential citizen of his home county, where he served as sheriff, besides holding other local offices, and where he did well his part in the development of the agricultural and other resources of the district. He was a pioneer in Arkansas, where he settled prior to the admission of the state to the Union, and he was one of the first settlers and exponents of plantation industry in what is now Union County, that state. Concerning him the following record has been written: "He made the journey to the new country under many difficulties and hardships, he having found it necessary to cut his way for many miles through dense forests, into the depths of certain parts of which no white man had previously penetrated, besides which he had to traverse many swamps and make difficult crossings of swift-rushing streams—all this implying much labor and not a few perils. He became a leader in his pioneer community,

there rose to a position of prominence, became widely known, largely through his influential participation in the councils and campaigns of the democratic party, and at one time he was earnestly importuned by party leaders to become a candidate for governor of Arkansas, an office for which he was well qualified but for which he refused to consider nomination by his party. This honored and public-spirited citizen died in the year 1884, secure in the high regard of all who knew him."

There was little of the unusual and the dramatic in the youthful life of James R. Winn of this sketch. He was a child at the time of the family removal from Arkansas to Ohio, where he was reared on the home farm and received the advantages of the district school. After a few years the family returned to Arkansas, and there Mr. Winn became associated with the timber industry, as a buyer and later as a saw-mill manager for a St. Louis lumber company. Still later he engaged independently in the manufacturing of lumber, and after two years had passed he organized the Winn Lumber Company, of Mount Vernon, Illinois, Incorporated, of which he is now the president and general manager. The business, which was incorporated in 1905, has steadily grown in magnitude and now covers a broad range, the enterprise including not only the handling of lumber products of all kinds but also the manufacture of brick and concrete building blocks and other concrete products. The business is one of major importance in Jefferson County, and the branch at Waltonville has greatly facilitated the operations of the company in the district from which that village is a distributing center. In the management of this large and constantly expanding business Mr. Winn has shown exceptional initiative and administrative ability. Methodical and intensely practical, he keeps in close touch with every detail of the business, and he formulates plans with discrimination and with a clear apprehension of future demands, his mature judgment causing his policies and plans to make for cumulative success. He has worthily gained rank among the successful and representative business men of Jefferson County and has done much to promote the material advancement of his home city and county and to make Mount Vernon one of the important business centers of southern Illinois, the while he stands exponent of loyal, appreciative and progressive citizenship and takes deep and constructive interest in all that concerns the communal welfare. His success has been in consonance with his energetic application and honorable and enterprising business policies, and he commands unequivocal popular confidence and esteem. He has refused to hold as any significant handicap the physical infirmity that is his through having met with an accident that necessitated the amputation of his left arm. Mr. Winn is well fortified in his convictions concerning economic and governmental policies, his patriotic loyalty is of the staunchest type, and while he has had no desire for political preferment or public office, he is a stalwart advocate of the principles of the democratic party, in the faith of which he was reared.

He is affiliated with several fraternal organizations and is popular in both the business and social circles of his home city and county, where his friends are in number as his acquaintances. His advancement has been won entirely through his own ability and efforts, and he well merits that proudest of American titles, "self-made man." He is in the very prime of strong and resourceful manhood and his continued advancement in business success and influence is normally assured. The name of Mr. Winn is still permitted to be enrolled on the list of popular and eligible bachelors in Jefferson County.

PROF. RUFUS MARTIN UTTERBACK. In the development of a career which has been characterized by marked industry and energy and the achievement of merited success the younger generation should take interest, for in this way lessons of incalculable value may be learned. Such a career has been that of Rufus Martin Utterback, president of Utterback's Business College at Mattoon, who, commencing his independent life with little to aid him save faith in himself and a good education, with some experience as a teacher and a large amount of native ability, has steadily advanced in the field of commercial education until now he has three branch schools in addition to the parent school at Mattoon and is accounted one of the leaders in his field of effort in the state.

Professor Utterback was born May 21, 1878, at Dundas, Richland County, Illinois, and is a son of Martin and Eliza (Burgess) Utterback. Martin Utterback was born near Elizabethtown, Hardin County, Kentucky, his birthplace being near that of Abraham Lincoln, and was three years of age when he was brought to Illinois by his parents, the remainder of his life being passed in Richland County, where he helped to haul logs for the first court house of the county. He was of German descent from both ancestral parents, but the family has been long in this country and his grandfather Snyder was present at the signing of the Declaration of Independence, clad in homespun linen uniform, as sergeant-at-arms. At Claremont, Illinois, in 1857, Martin Utterback married Eliza Burgess, of Scotch descent, a daughter of James Burgess, a veteran of the War of 1812 and one of the early pioneers of Ohio.

Rufus Martin Utterback acquired his early education at Dundas, Illinois, where he attended the rural school, and followed this by a course at Valparaiso University. Later he took a course at the Southwestern Business College. He commenced his career as a teacher in the public school and was so engaged from 1896 to 1904. He then spent one and one-half years as a stenographer, and in 1905 turned his attention to business college work, with which he has been identified to the present, although it was not until 1909 that he purchased and started operation of what has since been known as Utterback's Business College, of which he has been president since its inception. In 1919 Mr. Utterback organized the branch school at Paris, Illinois, in 1921 the second branch school, located at Olney, Illinois, and in 1925 the third branch school, at Danville, Illinois. These have all proved decidedly successful under his careful and capable management, and there are already found a number of successful men and women in the business world who received their training at the Utterback schools. Mr. Utterback has given his chief attention to the management and direction of these establishments, but has not overlooked the duties of citizenship, and from 1915 to 1917 served as a member of the City Council of Mattoon. He is a republican in politics, as a fraternalist is a member of the Danville Consistory and is a thirty-second degree Mason, an Odd Fellow and a Modern Woodman of America, and belongs also to the Rotary Club and the United Association of Accredited Private Business Schools. Until 1922, from 1896, he was a member of the Baptist Church, but now belongs to the Methodist Episcopal faith.

On July 19, 1905, at Calhoun, Illinois, Professor Utterback was united in marriage with Miss Leona A. Bartley, a daughter of Edward T. and Elvira Jane Bartley. Edward T. Bartley, who died in May, 1925, was a descendant of Governor Bartley of Ohio, a Union soldier during the Civil war, and a great-nephew of William Hooper, one of the signers of the Declaration of Independence. William Hooper was born at Boston, Massachusetts, June 17, 1742, and was graduated from Harvard College in 1760, following which he practiced law in North Carolina and early became interested in the Colonial struggle with Great Britain. Elected to the Continental Congress in 1774, he became a signer of the famous document of July 4, 1776. He died at Hillsboro, North Carolina, in October, 1790. Mrs. Bartley, who still survives her husband, is a descendant of the old Scotch Covenanters. To Mr. and Mrs. Utterback there have been born two children: Ethel Elvira, who was born December 27, 1913, and died six hours later; and Mary Elizabeth, born March 3, 1917, who is attending the public schools of Danville.

JAMES ROMULUS CAMPBELL, who attained the rank of brigadier-general of volunteers during the Spanish-American and Philippine wars, was one of Southern Illinois' most distinguished citizens, long prominent in civil affairs as a lawyer and banker. His home was at McLeansboro, where he died August 20, 1924.

He was born on a farm in Crook Township, Hamilton County, May 4, 1853, son of John and Mary (Coker) Campbell. John Campbell was a native of Ireland, and settled in Hamilton County in early manhood, where he met and married Mary Coker. Her father, Rev. Charles Coker, was well known throughout Southern Illinois in the early days as a Methodist minister. John Campbell was a farmer and stock man, and as a stock buyer his business took him all over Southern Illinois. He resided on and paid taxes on the same farm for fifty years. He was a democrat in politics and was reared a Catholic, but his wife was a Methodist.

James R. Campbell was reared on his father's farm, attended common schools, and subsequently Notre Dame University at South Bend, Indiana. He showed his unusual business enterprise at an early age. Before reaching his majority he obtained a sub-contract for the construction of several miles of the Big Four Railroad. He studied law at McLeansboro and was admitted to the bar in 1877. From 1879 to 1899 he published the McLeansboro Times. While practicing law and publishing the newspaper he exercised an influential leadership in the democratic party. He was a member of the Illinois House of Representatives from 1884 to 1888, and of the Senate from 1888 to 1896. In 1896 he was elected a member of the Fifty-fifth Congress and resigned his seat in Congress in 1898 to serve as a soldier in the Spanish-American war. He was colonel of the Ninth Illinois Volunteer Infantry, was mustered into service June 28, 1898, and was with his regiment in Cuba. He was mustered out May 20, 1899, and on July 5, 1899, was commissioned lieutenant-colonel of the Thirtieth United States Volunteer Infantry, with which he went to the Philippines. He saw active service during the Philippine insurrection and was promoted to the rank of brigadier-general of volunteers January 3, 1901. He received an honorable discharge March 25, 1901. He was the highest ranking officer from Illinois during the Cuban and Philippine wars.

General Campbell after his military service devoted most of his time to banking, though he remained prominent in the democratic party until his death. In 1902 he organized the First National Bank of McLeansboro and was president of that institution until his death. He was also president of the Campbell Milling Company at Carmi, Illinois. General Campbell was a man forceful in action and in thought, and though a leader in the democratic party he never hesitated to condemn a measure which his convictions and judgment would not approve. He was one of the four delegates at large from Illinois to organize the progressive party in 1912.

General Campbell married, December 18, 1879, Miss Kittie Benson, who survives him. The only son and child is Valentine B. Campbell, who is a well known figure in many of the same lines distinguished by his father. He was born at McLeansboro, October 1, 1880, and was educated in public schools and West Point Military Academy. Since his father's death he has been president of the First National Bank of McLeansboro, in which he was a former cashier. He is the most extensive breeder of thoroughbred running horses in Illinois. A democrat in politics, he was for eight years treasurer of the State Democratic Central Committee, and has been a committeeman from his senatorial district. He married Madeline Flannigan.

JOHN C. HALL. Admitted to the bar in 1871, John C. Hall has outlived all his early contemporaries at the bar of McLeansboro. He has been a lawyer and citizen of high standing in that community for over half a century. Along with the practice of law he has handled an extensive business in real estate.

He was born on a farm in Hamilton County, August 1, 1849. His grandfather, John Hall, was a native of Kentucky and one of the early settlers of Hamilton County, Illinois, where he followed farming and the trade of blacksmith. He reared a large family of children by his marriage to Nancy Shirley. Her father Moses Shirley, came from Kentucky to Illinois in an early day.

Hiram Wesley Hall, father of John C., was born in Hamilton County, Illinois, and lived a long and conspicuously useful life. He was a farmer, and served as a soldier with the American forces in the war with Mexico. When the Civil war came on he organized two companies for the Fortieth Illinois Infantry and was captain of Company A of that regiment. After the battle of Kenesaw Mountain he was promoted to lieutenant-colonel and commanded his regiment in Sherman's army on the march to the sea, and was in the Grand Review at Washington. Colonel Hall after the war returned to his farm, but was a man of such character as to exercise wide influence in his community. He was a thinker in advance of his times in many lines of thought, served as justice of the peace and for one term was a member of the Legislature. He was on the commission which located and built the State Asylum at Anna. He had taught school for a number of years. He was a member of the Missionary Baptist Church and superintendent of the Sunday School. He cast a vote for Lincoln in 1860, and ever afterward was a republican in politics. Hiram Wesley Hall lived to be nearly ninety-nine years of age. His wife, Julia Ann McLean, was born in Franklin County, Illinois, daughter of James A. McLean, who came to Illinois from Indiana, and the family at a still earlier date lived in South Carolina. She died at the age of eighty-six.

A brief record of the children of Hiram W. Hall and wife is: John Carroll Hall; Wilford F., deceased, a physician at McLeansboro; Columbus McLean, deceased, a farmer in Hamilton County; Casander, deceased, who married R. Medly Knight; Nancy M., deceased, who was the wife of James Hall; James P., a farmer who died unmarried; Dr. William W., a prominent physician of McLeansboro; Dr. Andy Hall, of Mount Vernon, Illinois, who was a soldier in Cuba during the Spanish-American war, also went to the Philippines, attained the rank of major in the medical department, and also rendered service during the World war; and Lydia, wife of John Norris, a farmer at McLeansboro.

John Carroll Hall was educated in the common schools and in DePauw University at Greencastle, Indiana, and took his law course at Northwestern University in Chicago. He had taught school as a means of furthering his education. He was admitted to the bar in 1871, and his professional career has been identified with McLeansboro as his place of residence. Mr. Hall is a republican in politics, but has seldom been a candidate for office. He is a member of the Missionary Baptist Church and is affiliated with the Masonic order and Independent Order of Odd Fellows.

He married, in 1877, Lila Isabel Hogan, daughter of John H. Hogan. They are the parents of four children: Dr. Charles W., of Mount Vernon, Illinois; Dr. J. Carl, of Centralia, Illinois; Vinita H.; and Julia C., wife of Nelson Layman, of Duquoin, Illinois. Both sons were volunteers in the Medical Corps during the World war and attained the rank of major. Dr. Charles went to France and the other son was with the American forces on duty at Arch Angel, Russia.

CAPT. JOHN H. STELLE, who won his military rank as an officer in the World war, represents a prominent family of Hamilton County and has been actively identified with the professional and business interests of McLeansboro since early manhood. He is a lawyer and manufacturer.

Captain Stelle was born at McLeansboro, August 10, 1891. His great-grandfather Stelle was an early settler of Hamilton County, coming from North Carolina. His grandfather, Jacob Stelle, was born in Hamilton County, was a Union soldier in the Civil war, and followed farming as his occupation. Thompson B. Stelle, father of Captain Stelle, was born and reared in Hamilton County, acquired a common school education and taught school for a time. He graduated in law from McKendree College and was engaged in practice at McLeansboro until his death in 1907, at the age of sixty years. Thompson B. Stelle had unusual gifts not only in his profession but in business, and successfully conducted a number of interests. He became one of the largest land owners in Hamilton County, accumulating an estate of about 2,000 acres. He also operated a general department store at McLeansboro. As a lawyer he enjoyed exceptional skill in the criminal branch of practice. He served one term as judge of Hamilton County and was a democrat in politics. Thompson B. Stelle married Laura Blades, a native of Hamilton County, who died in 1919. Their children were: Eleanor, wife of Z. W. Graff, of McLeansboro; Edith, who married C. C. Wright; William H., who practiced law at McLeansboro until his death in 1908; Cyrus B.; Raleigh B.; Elsie, wife of Dr. W. H. Weirick, of Jacksonville; and John H.

John H. Stelle finished his high school course at McLeansboro, attended Western Military Academy, and was graduated in law at Washington University of St. Louis. From 1908 to 1913 he played professional baseball with several leagues. He was admitted to the bar in 1916 and was engaged in practice at McLeansboro when America entered the World war.

He volunteered in 1917, attended the First Officers Training School at Fort Sheridan, and was commissioned a first lieutenant. In January, 1918, he went overseas with the Seventy-seventh Division, and subsequently was detailed for service with the Twenty-eighth and Thirtieth Divisions, and finally with Company B of the One Hundred Fifteenth Machine Gun Battalion. He was in much of the fighting in France during the year 1918, and in December of that year was promoted to the rank of captain. Captain Stelle received his honorable discharge May 19, 1919. He attended the first meeting of the American Legion in this country and is a past commander of the post at McLeansboro.

Captain Stelle has given much of his time since the war to business and industrial interests. Since 1920 he has been owner of the

McLeansboro Creamery, a successful industry manufacturing ice, ice cream and butter. He is president of the McLeansboro Shale Products Company, manufacturers of brick, drain tile and building blocks. He was president in 1923 of the Hamilton County Fair Association, of which he was an organizer, and was elected president for 1926 of the McLeansboro Chamber of Commerce. Captain Stelle is a Royal Arch Mason, member of the Independent Order of Odd Fellows, Knights of Pythias and B. P. O. Elks. He is a democrat and a Methodist. He married, in 1913, Wilma Wiesehardt, of Shawneetown, Illinois. They have two children, John Albert and Russell Thompson Stelle.

JOHNSON HILL LANE. As an educator, lawyer and public official, Johnson Hill Lane has been prominently identified with the County of Hamilton for over forty years. The best elements of success have been combined in his career. He has been dependent on his own exertions since boyhood, and has lived a clean, vigorous and useful life.

He was born on a farm in Crook Township, Hamilton County, December 13, 1858, son of John W. and Teresa (Mitchell) Lane, and grandson of Lewis Lane, who came from Tennessee and was one of the pioneers of Hamilton County, Illinois. Lewis Lane was elected and served as the first sheriff of the county, and was a farmer by occupation. He died in 1876, when about eighty-five years of age. He and his wife reared two sons, Joel P. and John W., and one daughter, Eliza. John W. Lane was born in Tennessee and was young when brought to Illinois. He followed the vocation of farming and died about 1866, aged fifty-seven years. He was a Methodist and reared his family in that faith. He was twice married. His first wife was a Miss Shirley, by whom he had several children. His second wife, Teresa Mitchell, was born in Hamilton County, daughter of Ichabod and Mary (Lane) Mitchell. Her father came from Tennessee, was a Hamilton County farmer, and died when about eighty-five years of age at the homestead where he first settled.

Johnson Hill Lane was one of a family of five children. He was about eight years old when his father died, and three years later his mother passed away, and from that age he has been in an important sense the master of his own destiny. He grew up on a farm, attended country schools, and at the age of seventeen had qualified for work as a teacher. He taught in rural districts for four years, and by teaching was enabled to attend Hamilton College at McLeansboro. He studied law under the late Judge T. B. Stelle of McLeansboro, and was admitted to the bar before the Illinois Supreme Court in 1881. In 1882 he graduated from the law department of the University of Michigan. On returning to McLeansboro he resumed teaching, and was connected with the schools of that city four years, for three years of that time being superintendent. In 1886 he was elected county superintendent of schools of Hamilton County and served efficiently for eight years.

Mr. Lane then gave his full time to the practice of law in partnership with the late Judge Isaac H. Webb. He was elected state's attorney in 1904, and held that office three consecutive terms, a total of twelve years. His record in this office was that of a vigorous prosecutor, and he won the reputation of being one of the most forceful state's attorneys of Illinois. Mr. Lane has been a stockholder in the First National Bank of McLeansboro since its organization, and is now vice president of that institution.

For many years he has been a prominent figure in the democratic party in his section of the state. He was a delegate to the national conventions of 1908, 1912, 1916 and 1924. He is a member of the order of Knights of Pythias, and the Methodist Episcopal Church.

Mr. Lane married, in 1885, Miss Carrie Harvey, a native of McLeansboro, and daughter of Felix A. and Lurina C. (Inman) Harvey. Her people came from the South and were early settlers in Gallatin County, Illinois. Mr. and Mrs. Lane have one daughter, Hazel, wife of Dr. Douglas A. Lehman, who is a prominent and successful physician and surgeon of Harrisburg, Illinois, specializing in the treatment of the eye, ear, nose and throat.

In addition to his faithful attention to the practice of his profession, his loyalty to his clients and his devotion to his constituents when a public officer, Mr. Lane has not neglected the home duties. He idolizes his daughter and granddaughter, Jane, and they are a source of great pleasure to him.

JOHN L. GUINGRICH, a prominent real estate and insurance man of Hoopestown, Illinois, is a business man of varied experiences and during his active career has been identified with a number of Illinois committees. He was born near East Lynn in Iroquois County, Illinois, January 4, 1877. His early school days were spent in the Carey school district in Iroquois County. Until nineteen years of age he and his brothers had the responsibility of their mother's farm, their mother having been left a widow when the children were mere boys. At the age of nineteen he went to Claytonville, where he worked as an apprentice in the profession of pharmacy for four years. He then attended Greer College in Hoopeston and completed his pharmacy course. The following year he worked as a pharmacist in Elliott Brothers' drug store at Hoopeston and in the spring of 1900 he moved to Peoria, where for three years he was employed as pharmacist in the drug house of William P. Oberhauser. He was employed by John Kneer in 1904. Leaving Peoria, he went to Ottawa, Illinois, where he was employed as pharmacist at T. E. Gapen and Sons. In 1906 he was called to Alton, Illinois, to work in the large drug firm of Sam Wyss, where he stayed for three years. Mr. Guingrich then bought a drug business of his own, which he conducted for four years, until the ill health of his mother called him to Cissna Park, Illinois. In the spring of 1910 he purchased a farm at Warsaw, Hancock County, Illinois. On March 27, 1910, he was united in marriage with R. Lena Herman, daughter of Mr. and Mrs.

John Herman, of Cissna Park, Illinois. Mrs. Guingrich was a prominent and successful teacher of Iroquois County. They lived on their farm for two years, improving it with new buildings. Mr. Guingrich became interested as a real estate broker while in the profession of pharmacy, and in the year of 1912 became an active real estate broker at Cissna Park, Illinois. In the spring of 1920 he returned to Hoopeston, where he has done a thriving real estate, insurance and loan business at his offices at 207½ East Main Street.

Mr. Guingrich served a year as city treasurer of Cissna Park and in the capacity of justice of the peace for twelve years. He is an independent voter in politics; is affiliated with the Christian Science Church of Hoopeston; is a member of Cissna Park Lodge No. 205, Knights of Pythias, Tribe of Ben Hur, Alton Fraternal Order of Eagles, Junior Order United American Mechanics and is a member of Ku Klux Klan. He belongs to the Hoopeston Chamber of Commerce and is president of the Hoopeston Real Estate Board, which he was instrumental in organizing. Besides several properties in Hoopeston Mr. Guingrich owns eighty acres of valuable farm land in Hancock County, Illinois, and 160 acres of Wisconsin land.

Mr. Guingrich's father, John Guingrich, was born near Hamilton, Butler County, Ohio, August 24, 1832. He was educated in the public schools of Ohio. In 1849, at the age of sixteen, he accompanied his father to California. He became a successful gold digger and remained on the Pacific Coast for eight years. He then returned to the east and settled in Tazwell County, Illinois, where he cleared land for farming. In 1870 he settled on a farm two and a quarter miles northeast of East Lynn, Illinois, where he lived until his death in September, 1882. He began voting as a whig, but later became a republican. He was a member of the Masonic fraternity.

On May 7, 1867, he was united in marriage to Susan Bahr, who was born near Bavaria, Germany, in 1844. To them were born ten children: Anna, wife of Henry C. Ziegenhorn, of Independence, Missouri; Joseph P., a grain buyer of Gridley, Illinois; Samuel, who died on the old homestead farm at the age of twenty-eight; Benjamin F., who is connected with a sweet corn factory at Garrison, Iowa; Sadie, wife of August F. Ziegenhorn, a druggist and veterinarian of Claytonville, Illinois; Adena, who died at the age of two; John L.; Ada, wife of Frederick D. Frank, a farmer near Claytonville, Illinois; Emanuel, a farmer who died at Latty, Ohio, in 1918; and William, a farmer of Francisville, Indiana.

It is interesting to know that to this John Guingrich belongs the credit for laying the first drain tile in that section of Illinois and proving the success of sub-drainage. In 1876, while laying tile through a swamp on his farm, Mr. Guingrich came across some mammoth bones which caused considerable comment over that section of the country. On investigation by a well known professor of zoology from Yale University the bones were discovered to be the skeleton of a Mastodon. It was at that time one of the first to be found.

Mr. Guingrich's grandfather, Joseph Guingrich, was born in Alsace-Lorraine, France. He served in the regular French army during his youth, and on coming to the United States he cleared land for a farm in southwestern Ohio near Hamilton, Butler County. There he married a Miss Gerber, also of Alsace-Lorraine, France, who died in 1840. To this union was born one son, John, and four daughters, Anna, Lydia, Barbara and Kate.

Joseph Guingrich was a "Forty-niner" who helped blaze the trail to California during the gold rush. He left for the west early in the spring of 1849, taking with him his son, a boy of sixteen, who became the father of John L. Guingrich. They made the journey in a covered wagon, driving oxen and enduring all the hardships of that first emigrant procession which started westward for the California gold fields in the spring of 1849. He remained there for a period of four years, during which time he accumulated a fair amount of gold. He left his son there and returned to his home in Ohio for a time. In the spring of 1854 the gold fever again seized him and he returned to California to be with his son. Both father and son returned to Illinois in 1857 and settled on a farm in Tazewell County. In 1860 he was united to Mrs. Summers, nee Verkler, a native of New York State. He remained on his farm at Danvers, Tazewell County, until his death. Joseph Guingrich was the grandfather of John L. Guingrich, the subject of this biography.

W. E. SULLIVAN, founder and president of the Eli Bridge Company at Jacksonville, is a mechanical genius and inventor, and through the work he has done in perfecting the all steel portable Ferris wheels, and thereby contributing to the innocent pleasure of the world's children, has been a real benefactor of mankind.

Mr. Sullivan was born near the present site of Roodhouse, Illinois, July 3, 1861. His grandfather, John Sullivan, was for many years a steamboat man on the Mississippi River. The sinking of his boat caused him to settle at Carrollton, Illinois. William A. Sullivan, father of W. E., was a teacher and farmer, and died in 1875. His wife, Elizabeth Heaton, was the daughter of parents who were pioneers in Illinois, and she was descended from the Deem family that furnished several heroes to the War of the Revolution.

W. E. Sullivan grew up on a farm to the age of eighteen. His uncle, Mark Heaton, persuaded his mother to allow him to learn a trade, having decided that he would never make a farmer. For some years he worked as a carpenter and then became a machinist, for which he had special inclinations. He is naturally of an inventive turn of mind.

Many years ago Mr. Sullivan saw the original Ferris wheel at Chicago, one of the features of the World's Fair in that city. He then conceived the idea of adopting a smaller type of such wheel to popular amusement and set himself to construct one that would be safe, portable and readily installed and taken down. He built his first Big Eli wheel in the winter of 1899-1900, and started to operate it the following season. He built others, putting into one improvements that he had worked out as a result of his previous experience, and from 1900 to 1905, through six summer seasons, he operated his wheels until he had finally achieved his ambition of perfecting an absolutely interchangeable wheel and one that he could with confidence manufacture and sell to a public that was already waiting for it. He first operated as a copartnership, and in the fall of 1905 incorporated the Eli Bridge Company, starting with a small capital and using a shop thirty by sixty feet at Roodhouse. He has given the manufacturing end his close personal supervision, and has introduced innumerable improvements. The business has steadily grown on merit and in 1919 a large modern plant was built and equipped, a one-story structure, 150 by 225 feet and a two-story office, 20 by 50 feet. There are near fifty employes. Lee A., son of the president, is secretary, treasurer and superintendent, while Ben O. Roodhouse is sales manager and advertising manager. For some years the company used as its chief advertising medium the Billboard Magazine, but in 1916 the company established a periodical publication of its own known as the Optimist, now the Big Eli News. The Big Eli Ferris wheels are now in operation in twenty countries, and they are a feature of every fair and amusement park.

Mr. Sullivan married Miss Julia L. Crayne on July 3, 1881, at Athensville, Illinois. They have three children. Lee A., born July 3, 1889, married Nell M. Griffiths and they have three children, Katherine L., William E. and Lee A., Jr. Olive M., born March 28, 1892, married I. V. Page and lives at Roodhouse, Illinois. Leta L., born March 12, 1894, is at home.

Ross Carlos Hall. A member of the Illinois bar since 1889, and in practice in Chicago since 1893, Ross Carlos Hall has gained his chief distinction in the field of municipal law. He is a native of Illinois, and his forefathers were pioneer characters in the west central part of the state.

Mr. Hall was born at Rushville, Schuyler County, October 29, 1866. His birthplace was a house erected by his grandfather. It was also the scene of the birth of his own father. His grandfather, the builder of the home in Schuyler County, was Robert C. Hall, a native of Ireland who was born near Belfast in 1798. On coming to America he first settled in Baltimore, and in 1834 moved to Schuyler County, Illinois, where he was one of the early settlers. He married Elizabeth Graflin, and they were the parents of six children. Their son, Thomas M. Hall, was born at Rushville in 1840, and died in 1897. He married Harriet Ross, who was born at Canton, in Fulton County, Illinois, in 1844, and died in January, 1926. She was a daughter of Harvey Lee and Jane R. Ross, and a granddaughter of Ossian M. Ross, who served with the rank of major in the War of 1812. Major Ross came to Illinois in 1819 and was one of the first settlers on the military tract in the western part of the state. He founded Lewiston and Havana, Illinois. Harvey Lee Ross, who was born at Seneca Falls, New York, and came to Illinois with the rest of the family in 1819, was a mail carrier and carried mail on horseback to Salem and other towns while Abraham Lincoln was postmaster of Salem. Thomas M. Hall and Harriet Ross were the parents of three children: Ross C.; Louise, who died in 1922; and Elizabeth, wife of Warren R. Willard, of New York.

Ross Carlos Hall was graduated in 1885 from the Macomb High School, and then entered Georgetown College at Washington, D. C., where he took the literary course two years and graduated from the law department in 1888, and was admitted to the bar in the District of Columbia the same year. In 1889 he was admitted to practice in Illinois, and for several years followed his profession at Macomb and Rushville. In 1893 he removed to Chicago and has been a member of several well known law firms in that city, handling a large volume of practice involving municipal law.

Mr. Hall was honored with election as president of the Iroquois Club on February 15, 1926. He has been active in the democratic party and was a delegate to the National Convention of 1904 and the Baltimore Convention of 1912. For a time he was first assistant attorney of the Sanitary District of Chicago. Mr. Hall was a member of the Fortieth Illinois General Assembly in 1897-98, and has been attorney for the town of Cicero. He is a member of the Chicago, Illinois and American Bar Associations and the Oak Park, Iroquois and Crystal Lake Country Clubs.

Mr. Hall married, August 19, 1890, Miss Catherine Twyman, a native of Macomb, Illinois. They have three children, Carlos, George R. and Charles M.

Beauchamp A. Harvey. One of the oldest families in Wabash County is represented by Beauchamp A. Harvey, lawyer and abstractor at Mt. Carmel, who has himself been well and favorably known in that county for a great many years.

His grandfather, Beauchamp Harvey, arrived on the Illinois side of the Wabash River, in what is now Wabash County, in 1819. He was born at Baltimore, Maryland, December 5, 1789, and was of English ancestry, the family having come to America in Colonial days and was represented by soldiers in the War of the Revolution. Beauchamp Harvey's parents were John and Teane (Beauchamp) Harvey. Beauchamp Harvey was a Friend in religion, but the next generation of the family became Methodists. He was reared and educated in Baltimore, and on going west first located at Piqua, Ohio, where in 1816 he married Hester Saylor. She was a daughter of Jacob and Elizabeth Saylor. Then, in 1819, he and his wife arrived at Mt. Carmel, Illinois, and he was connected with mercantile interests for many years. He died in 1859. Beauchamp Harvey had the following children: Jane, who married Silas Kneippe; Sally, who never married; James; Mary; David Saylor Harvey; Judith; and William P.

Dr. James Harvey, father of Beauchamp A., was born at Mt. Carmel, April 6, 1821. In early life he adopted the profession of medicine, and after qualifying engaged in practice at Mt. Carmel and was an honored physician of that city until his death on April 12, 1896. He was a democrat in early life and finally joined the prohibition party. Dr. James Harvey married Elinor Tougas, descended from some of the French stock that settled in the Wabash Valley around Vincennes. She was born in Wabash County, Illinois, but was reared at Vincennes, and was a daughter of Augustus Tougas, and her grandfather, also Augustus Tougas, was the first settler in Wabash County, founding the trading post at Rochester, but finally moving to Mt. Carmel. Dr. James Harvey and wife had the following children: Beauchamp Augustus; Mary Alice, who married J. Fred Steine; Julia, who became the wife of Robert T. Wilkinson; James W., who died in California; Ellen M., who married John S. White, of Chicago; Miss Laura E., principal of the Longfellow School at Mt. Carmel; and Orien Ross, deceased.

Beauchamp Augustus Harvey was born at Rochester, in Wabash County, October 4, 1850. He grew up at Mt. Carmel, acquired his education there, and after pursuing a course of law studies was admitted to the bar in 1878. For nearly half a century he has upheld the dignity of the law as a practitioner at Mt. Carmel, is now president of the local bar, for many years has been engaged in the abstract business and is recognized as an authority on questions of land titles throughout the county. Mr. Harvey is a democrat, but has not been active in politics. He is unmarried. For many years he has been affiliated with the Independent Order of Odd Fellows, and is a member of the Illinois State Historical Society. He has cultivated the subject of history as a hobby, and through articles written for the press and other periodicals has been instrumental in preserving the important early history of this section of Illinois.

VOL E. RICHARDSON, the efficient and popular cashier of the Jefferson Bank in the city of Mount Vernon, Jefferson County, was born near McLeansboro, Hamilton County, Illinois, December 5, 1884, and is a son of Austin H. and Martha (Compton) Richardson, the former of whom died April 24, 1908, and the latter of whom still maintains her home at Mount Vernon, to which city the family removed about 1890. The subject of this review is the younger of the two children. The elder son, John H., is a resident of Mount Vernon, he having married Miss Nellie Patterson and their one child being a son, John Russell. Austin H. Richardson was a skilled artisan at the carpenter trade and after coming to Mount Vernon he was employed at his trade in the shops of the Mount Vernon Car Works.

After he had completed his studies in the Mount Vernon High School Vol E. Richardson eventually made his way to Dublin, Texas, where he was employed one year in a furniture store. He then returned to Mount Vernon and took a position as salesman in the clothing and shoe departments of the Boston Store, with which he continued his service two and one-half years. In 1907 he assumed the position of bookkeeper in the Jefferson Bank, which had organized in 1905, and his efficiency led to his advancement to the position of assistant cashier and finally to the office of cashier, of which he has been the incumbent since 1916 and in which he has given an executive administration that has greatly forwarded the success of the business. In the World war period he was active and influential in local patriotic movements, was manager of the drives in support of the government war loans, and in his registration for active military service he was assigned to the fourth class and thus was not called to active duty. Mr. Richardson is loyal and progressive in his civic attitude, is a republican in politics, and has given effective service as city treasurer of Mount Vernon, an office to which he was elected in 1921. He is affiliated with the local Blue Lodge, Chapter and Council of York Rite Masons, as well as with the Odd Fellows and Knights of Pythias, and he and his wife hold membership in the Methodist Episcopal Church.

May 2, 1908, recorded the marriage of Mr. Richardson and Miss Helen Hartnagel, the only child of John T. and Lora (Ridgeway) Hartnagel, who are well known citizens of Mount Vernon, where the father was chairman of the city park commission, he being a traveling commercial salesman by occupation. Mr. and Mrs. Richardson have one child, a winsome daughter who bears the name of Eleanor.

Aaron Richardson, grandfather of the subject of this review, was born and reared in Ohio and from that state he came to Illinois prior to the Civil war. He enlisted for service soon after the inception of the Civil war, and became a member of the Fortieth Illinois Volunteer Infantry, commanded by Col. H. W. Hall. After the expiration of his original term of enlistment he re-enlisted, and he was with his command in the state of Mississippi when he contracted typhoid fever and died as a result of this disease. His wife, whose family name was McClure, died at the birth of her son Austin H., father of him whose name initiates this sketch. John and Elizabeth Compton, maternal grandparents of Vol E. Richardson, were born in Tennessee and came from that state to Illinois in the pioneer days. Both the Compton and McClure families gave patriot soldiers to the war of the Revolution, and by similar ancestral prestige Mrs. Vol E. Richardson is eligible for and affiliated with the Daughters of the American Revolution.

OLIVER BATY CUNNINGHAM, the only child of Frank Simpson and Lucy (Baty) Cunningham, was an Evanston boy who met his death in the great World war while accomplishing dangerous reconnaissance work on the firing line near Thiaucourt, France.

All questions as to the adequacy of service were answered in this youth's sacrifice. For Captain Cunningham "one crowded hour of glorious life was worth an age without a name." His parents, wishing to perpetuate their son's service, have in various modest ways sought to give continuity to the idealism and influence of character which were his. Their first gift for this purpose was the erection of a Parish House adjacent to St. Mark's Episcopal Church of Evanston, of which he was a communicant. This building is known as the Oliver Baty Cunningham Memorial House, and is used for all manner of activities connected with the church.

Through Captain Cunningham's Alma Mater his parents found another channel of service, and in 1920 they established at Yale University what is known as the Oliver Baty Cunningham Publication Fund, the income from which is used for the publishing of books of unusual merit.

Perpetuity of altruism was further fostered by Mr. and Mrs. Cunningham when, in September, 1920, they established the Oliver Baty Cunningham Memorial Prize, which is awarded the male member of the Senior Class of the Evanston High School who is adjudged to rank first among the members of his class in all around manly qualities, including intellectual ability, high character, capacity for leadership and spirit of patriotism.

Not only have the parents of Captain Cunningham sought ways to fittingly commemorate his life and death, but the citizens of Thiaucourt themselves, when erecting a monument in tribute to their honored dead and as material evidence of the friendship between France and America, chose the likeness of this courageous Evanston boy to represent America. A life-size bronze portrait statue of Captain Cunningham clasping the hand of a French poilu, symbolizing the undying affection which is the war's bequest to the two nations, stands in the Thiaucourt City Square fronting the church. This monument was unveiled November 8, 1925, and the dedicatory address was made by Myron T. Herrick, United States Ambassador to France.

Inhabitants of Thiaucourt had previously felt the beneficent influence of this young soldier's immolation when in 1923 Mr. Cunningham's business associates on the Board of Directors of Butler Brothers, the nationally known wholesale concern of which he is president, caused to have hung in the village church a set of chimes in memory of Oliver Baty Cunningham to replace the original bells which had been confiscated by the Germans and melted into ammunition.

The story of such a life, however brief, should be told in words of friendship, and the following paragraphs are abbreviated excerpts from an appreciation written shortly after Captain Cunningham's death.

To die bravely requires instant courage, to live rightly requires enduring courage, to do both is to achieve life's complete success, and on the 17th day of September, 1918, on his twenty-fourth birthday, Capt. Oliver Baty Cunningham was killed in action and completed his life's success. He was born in Chicago on September 17, 1894. Until his eleventh year he went to school in Riverside. The family then moved to Evanston where for several years Oliver attended the Lincoln School. He spent one year at Howe Military Academy at Howe, Indiana, and four years at The Hill School at Pottstown, Pennsylvania.

Though Oliver was at all times a fine, clean, bright lad, he gave, in his early years, no promise of exceptional achievement. At about fifteen he seemed to wake up to the fact that he was not making the best of himself. Realizing that he must be his own keenest critic, the change in the boy was soon apparent. And in his bright, buoyant way he now showed such a determination to develop his brain, as well as his body, and was so honest at all times with himself that his companions and his teachers began to recognize in him the coming man.

In 1913 he went to Yale. Though a hard and consistent student at college, Oliver found plenty of opportunities to mix with his fellows. He soon became a member of the Yale Daily News, and in the years following was elected to the Psi U Fraternity, the Elizabethan Club, and Skull and Bones. Because of his excellent scholarship he was made a member of the Phi Beta Kappa. The Francis Gordon Brown Memorial Prize, given to that member of each Junior Class at Yale "who most closely approached the standards of intellectual ability, high manhood, capacity for leadership, and service to the University" was awarded to Oliver near the close of his Junior year.

During the summer before Oliver's Sophomore year the Great war clouds suddenly appeared on the European horizon, and their shadows began to creep slowly toward the western hemisphere. Oliver's keen insight and his fine sense of honor made him quickly realize that the issue of the war might involve his country, and he began to prepare for his country's call. An artillery corps, affiliated with the Connecticut State, was formed at Yale, and Oliver at once became a member of it. When the Mexican crisis arose in 1916 the organization was given active training at Tobyhanna, Pennsylvania.

The war clouds had now settled heavily over America, and when in April, 1917, we declared war on Germany, Oliver withdrew from college and joined the First Officers' Training Camp at Fort Sheridan. During his absence from college, and by a unanimous vote of the faculty, he was graduated from Yale with honors. Believing that service under Regular Army officers would give him better training and enable him to get into fighting earlier than remaining in the Reserve Corps, he made application for and secured a second lieutenancy in the Regular Army. He made this choice, although he had every reason to believe that otherwise he would have received a higher rank in the Reserve Corps at the close of the training period.

Lieutenant Cunningham was stationed first at Sparta, Wisconsin, then at Plattsburg, and finally at Watertown, New York. On December 12, with the Fifteenth Field Artillery, he sailed for Europe and arrived in France on New Year's day. For a few months he was in training at the French Artillery Camp at Valdahon. During April and May, in a quiet sector near Verdun, he was regimental adjutant and operations officer. Though these positions are usually held by two officers, yet when his regiment came into action Oliver's work was so thorough and efficient that his colonel found it advisable to keep him at the two jobs.

In May the Fifteenth Field Artillery was transferred to the more active fighting front as a part of the Second Division. With that division Oliver took part in the second battle of the Marne and in the engagements of Chateau Thierry, Vaux and Belleau Woods. In the first offensive action in which the American army fought as a unit Oliver was with

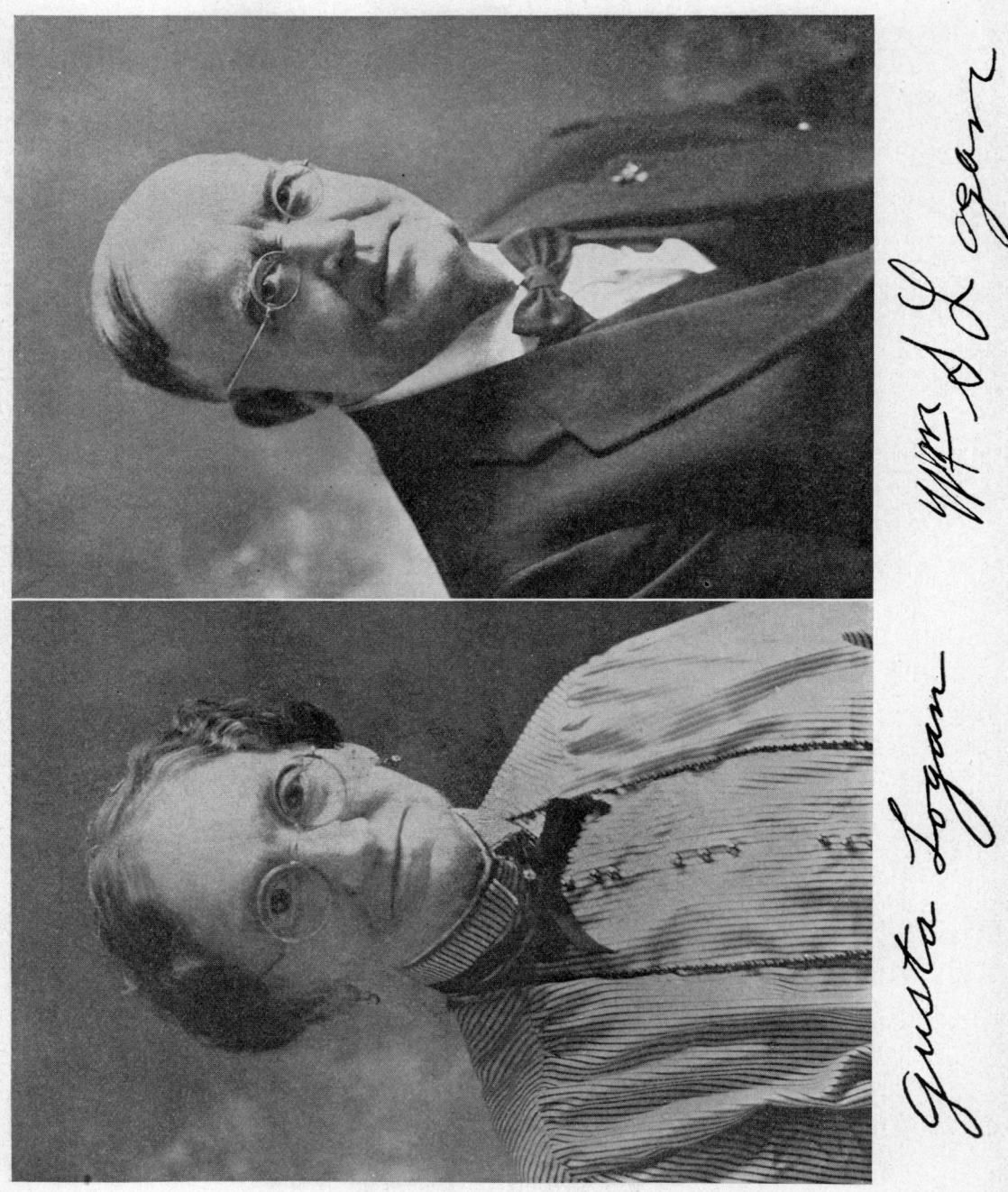

Gusta Logan   Wm A Logan

his regiment in the engagements around Soissons and the forest of Villers-Cotterets.

Oliver was then doing staff duty. Strongly desiring to experience fighting service with a battery, Lieutenant Cunningham had repeatedly urged his colonel to assign him to that work, and on September 2 this change was reluctantly made.

On September 12 began the first All-American offensive, directed at St. Mihiel. Lieutenant Cunningham had volunteered for an especially dangerous duty. On September 17, while doing reconnaissance work in the extreme front line trenches, near the town of Jaulney, which is not far from Thiaucourt, death came to him instantly on the tide of a victorious advance. At the time of his death Oliver wore the silver bar of a first lieutenant. On the next day a captain's commission, dated September 11, arrived for him. While German airplanes were hovering overhead, and enemy shells bursting near, Captain Cunningham was laid at rest by his comrades-in-arms on a spot half way up a gentle hillside in French Lorraine. "Greater love hath no man than to give his life for his friends."

DELWIN MORTON CAMPBELL, who for a number of years has been one of the most widely known veterinarians in America, is a resident of Chicago. Retiring several years ago from the routine practice of his profession, he is now interested mainly in editorial and publishing work. He is editor of "Veterinary Medicine" the leading veterinary magazine in the country. He has found an interesting diversion and supplement to his business duties in the publication of a magazine for his hobby of golf. He is interested actively in the publication of Golfers Magazine.

Doctor Campbell is a native of Topeka, Kansas, where he was born January 19, 1880, son of Newton Josephus and Mary Jean (Mitchell) Campbell. He is of Scotch ancestry, but the Campbells have been in America since Colonial times, first settling in Virginia. Doctor Campbell's paternal grandfather moved with his family to Kansas territory in 1857, and had a part in the tragic events along the Missouri-Kansas border, involving the historic stages in the establishment of free soil on the territory of Kansas. Doctor Campbell's father was nine years old when taken to Kansas.

Delwin Morton Campbell attended the Kansas State Normal in 1897-98; the Kansas State Agricultural College, 1903-05; and in 1907 was graduated from the Kansas City Veterinary College with the degree Doctor of Veterinary Medicine. Doctor Campbell in 1907 located at Shawnee, Oklahoma, and for about a year remained in veterinary practice in the then territory of Oklahoma. Returning to Topeka, he was city milk and dairy inspector there from 1908 to 1910. In the meantime, in 1908, he had established the American Journal of Veterinary Medicine at Topeka. In 1910 he accepted an offer to come to Chicago as head of the veterinary department of the Abbott Laboratories. He held this position until 1914, and in 1916 gave up active practice. In a period of twenty years he has practiced in three states, Oklahoma, Kansas and Illinois; served in the Federal Bureau of Animal Industry, as an army veterinarian, as a municipal food inspector, in commercial veterinary work and to a considerable extent in literary pursuits.

Doctor Campbell is president and manager of the Veterinary Magazine Corporation and editor of the Veterinary Medicine, published at 4753 Grand Boulevard. He is vice president of the Golfers Magazine Company, and acts as circulation manager for the Golfers Magazine. One feature of his work in connection with the Golfers Magazine has been conducting a number of personally conducted tours or pilgrimages of golfers. One of the most notable was the Dixie Golf Pilgrimage in February-March, 1926, comprising 257 persons and requiring two special Pullman trains. The itinerary embraced Hot Springs, New Orleans, Gulfport, Biloxi, Pensacola, Daytona, Sarasota, Coral Gables, Hollywood, Palm Beach, Orlando, Augusta, Pinehurst, White Sulphur Springs, French Lick Springs and back to Chicago. The most notable tour of all, in July and August, 1926, was named "A Pilgrimage to St. Andrews." It started from Montreal, including a journey through France, England and Scotland, culminating at St. Andrews, the shrine of the ancient game of golf. The idea of this pilgrimage was suggested by Mr. Opie Read of Chicago, author and enthusiastic golfer.

Doctor Campbell is a major in the Veterinary Reserve Corps of the United States Army and is division veterinarian of the Sixty-fifth Cavalry Division, U. S. A. He is the author of a number of recognized works on veterinary science and is a member of the American Veterinary Medical and other veterinary associations, the Art Institute of Chicago, the Field Museum, the B. P. O. Elks, the Modern Woodmen, and in politics is a democrat.

WILLIAM SNYDER LOGAN is the oldest director of the Edgar County Bank at Paris. Mr. Logan is a native of that community and has been active in its business affairs since early manhood.

He was born at Paris, March 8, 1852, son of John J. and Martha (Birtch) Logan. His mother was born in England and was brought to America when a child. The Logan family were pioneers of Indiana. William S. Logan attended the public schools there and as a youth had eight years of experience in the flour business. He was also in the grocery business for a time, and in 1874-1875 was a grain dealer. Since 1875 he has been steadily, for half a century, engaged in the lumber business at Paris. He has also been a dealer in live stock, and many years ago became identified with the Edgar County Bank as a director.

Mr. Logan is a republican and has been quite active in the republican party in his section of the state. He is a member of the Elks Order, of the Paris Country Club, Chamber of Commerce and is affiliated with the Christian Church, of which both his parents were charter members.

He married at Paris, September 11, 1873, Gusta Everance. Her father was buried at sea and her mother died in Germany. As an infant she was adopted by the Parish family.

The oldest of the children of Mr. and Mrs. Logan was Robert Parish Logan, born January 18, 1875, and died December 4, 1907. He married Hattie Beard, and she survives with three children: Dorothea, Marion and William. The second child, Charles Shaw Logan, born in 1877, married Carrie Rittenhouse, and has one child, Harry. Harriet Parish Logan, born in 1879, is the wife of C. L. Sawyer, and has four children. Exia Pinelle was married to Arthur Reese and has children: George Hughes, deceased; Martha Marie, who was married in June, 1922, to Dr. R. M. Quigley, a veterinary doctor at Tyrone, Pennsylvania. Benjamin Harrison Logan was born August 25, 1888, married, November 3, 1913, Miss Bertha Russell. Beulah Partlow, born June 28, 1891, was married December 18, 1922, to Alfred Gilbert and died leaving one daughter, Mary Martha Gilbert.

FRANCIS JOHN FESSANT, president of the First National Bank of Vermilion, has been actively identified with the business and civic interests of Edgar County for over thirty years.

He was born in Edgar County, December 31, 1875, son of Richard Henry and Mary (Smith) Fessant. The Fessant family came from England in May, 1843, and settled in Canada, later coming to Illinois, and were among the earliest pioneers of Edgar County, Illinois.

Francis John Fessant was educated in country district schools, and first engaged in farming, and through all the years has kept in touch with agriculture, having considerable investments in farming land today. On leaving the farm he became a dealer in agricultural implements, and was also in the undertaking business for several years. In 1911 he was called to succeed his father as president of the Farmers & Merchants Bank of Vermilion. In 1915 the bank was reorganized as the First National Bank and Mr. Fessant has continued to serve it as president and as a director. In 1926 he was elected president of The Paris State Bank of Paris.

For twelve years Mr. Fessant has been president of the school board. He is a republican, is affiliated with the Masonic and Odd Fellows Lodges of Vermilion, the Paris Country Club, the Methodist Episcopal Church. He married at Terre Haute, Indiana, October 1, 1902, Miss Minnie L. List, daughter of Samuel V. and Ellen List. They have one daughter, Dorothy List, born December 3, 1905.

HENRY AUGUSTUS BRIDGMAN has been a business man of the City of Paris, in Edgar County, for over thirty-five years, being founder and proprietor of the Bridgman Cigar Factory there.

He was born at Farmington, Iowa, November 27, 1866, son of Albert Henry and Josephine (Hartness) Bridgman. His parents came from Massachusetts and the Bridgmans are an old Colonial family of Massachusetts of English ancestry.

Henry Augustus Bridgman was reared at Paxton, Illinois, was educated in the public schools there and during his early life was identified with the work of a farm. In 1888 he established a drayage business at Paris, and he continued that enterprise for nine and one-half years. In November, 1898, he organized the Bridgman Cigar Factory. This factory has been in existence for over a quarter of a century, and has become noted for the uniformly high quality of its product. The factory manufactures large quantities of cigars, kept under private brand, but its special output is three brands and grades of cigars known as the Bridgman Hand-Made, the Don Elmo, and the G. A. B.

Mr. Bridgman is a republican in politics. He is affiliated with Lodge No. 664 of the Independent Order of Odd Fellows at Paris, is a charter member of Paris Council of the United Commercial Travelers, belongs to the Chamber of Commerce, the Methodist Church, and is superintendent of the adult department of the Sunday school.

He married at Paxton, Illinois, September 19, 1887, Miss Ella Hall, daughter of George A. and Martha C. Hall, of Paxton. They have two children: George Albert, born February 12, 1890, was educated in the Paris High School and Paris Business College, and after graduating entered business with his father and has also served as secretary of the Chamber of Commerce. He married, June 19, 1910, Miss Lena Step, of Paris, and they have one child: Harold Austin, born June 3, 1918. The second child of Mr. and Mrs. Bridgman is Margaret Frank, born November 17, 1893. She married Bruce Bass, of Paris, and their two children are: Philip Henry, born July 7, 1916, and Robert Bruce, born May 7, 1919.

ASHER LINCOLN RICHMOND has been a well known figure in the Illinois journalism for a number of years. He is editor and publisher of the Mt. Carmel Republican-Register.

He was born at Brighton, Ontario, Canada, May 18, 1872, son of Ichabod and Mary (McGuire) Richmond, and grandson of Sylvester and Dorothy (Strievel) Richmond. Sylvester Richmond was a native of Brookline, Massachusetts, and subsequently established his home at Brighton, Ontario, where he was a lumberman and farmer. Ichabod Richmond was born at Brighton, Ontario.

Asher Lincoln Richmond acquired a high school education at Brighton, and at the age of seventeen went to Rochester, New York. He acquired his early training and experience in the newspaper business in that city, remaining there for twelve years. For about four years he was a student in the University of Chicago, specializing in subjects connected with journalism. As an Illinois publisher Mr. Richmond was first known as proprietor of the Daily Standard at Sterling, Illinois. He published and edited that paper until 1916, when he sold it. Mr. Richmond in 1919 acquired the Mt. Carmel Register. He and the late D. E. Keen subsequently bought the Mt. Carmel Republican, consolidating the two papers as the Mount Carmel Republican-Register. Since the death of Mr. Keen in 1923 Mr. Richmond has been sole publisher and editor, and continued to make this one of the livest and most influential newspapers in southeastern Illinois.

Mr. Richmond is an independent republican in politics, is a Methodist, was commander of Mt. Carmel Commandery No. 82, Knights Templar, in 1924, and is a Shriner. He was the organizer and first president of the Mt. Carmel Kiwanis Club. He belongs to the B. P. O. Elks. Mr. Richmond married at Rochester, New York, in 1902, Miss Margaret Powers, a native of that city. They have two children, Mabel, born in 1911, and Asher M., born in 1912.

G. CARROLL FANNING for thirty years has been a familiar figure in the mercantile life of White Hall. He is a partner in the well-known mercantile firm of Sykes & Fanning of that city.

He was born at White Hall, October 2, 1879. His father, George Richard Fanning, was born near Murrayville, Scott County, Illinois, August 10, 1858, was reared on a farm, learned the carpenter's trade, was a carpenter in White Hall for many years, and finally engaged in the restaurant and hotel business until his death on July 23, 1901. He was a staunch democrat. He married in 1877, Maggie L. Harper, who was born in Kentucky, June 16, 1860, daughter of William B. and Mary K. (Cogdell) Harper. Her parents came to Illinois from Kentucky. Her father served as a soldier in the Mexican war and for many years drew a pension for that service. The children in the Harper family were: Mrs. Jennie Cotter, of Wichita, Kansas; Mrs. Alice Johnson, who died at White Hall, leaving a daughter, who is now Mrs. George B. Morrow; Sallie Ann, who died in early womanhood; and Mrs. George R. Fanning. The two sons of George Richard Fanning and wife are G. Carroll and William C. The latter is a linoleum contractor in Chicago, and married Carrie Caldwell.

G. Carroll Fanning was reared at White Hall, graduated from high school in 1897, and for a time was employed in delivering goods for a local feed store. His real insight into mercantile business was acquired as clerk for C. H. Black & Brother, dry goods, groceries and hardware. He was with this firm five years, next became associated with M. S. Kawin in his dry goods and clothing store, and in 1908 engaged in business for himself, purchasing the interest of Francis Fowler in the firm of Fowler and Sykes. This was the beginning of the firm of Sykes and Fanning, dry goods and clothing, a business partnership that existed and prospered through a period of eighteen years.

Mr. Fanning served one term as township tax collector. He helped organize the local Chamber of Commerce, served as a director and is now president of the Chamber. He is a member of the Knights of Pythias, is a trustee of the Presbyterian Church and a member of the Church Brotherhood of White Hall. He is a democrat, but is largely independent in local elections. He was registered during the World war and did a great deal of work as a member of local committees. He married at Jacksonville, Illinois, October 20, 1920, Miss Elizabeth Baker, daughter of Mr. and Mrs. J. R. Baker. She was born near Roodhouse, Illinois, and is a high school graduate. Her sisters are Mrs. Rebecca Greenwalt, Mrs. Ola Travis, Mrs. Anna Wintler, Mrs. Roe Lee, Edith, deceased, and she has a brother, Dwight Baker, a farmer near Roodhouse. Mrs. Fanning is a member of the Presbyterian Church and is active in woman's club work at White Hall.

JUDGE DAVID DAVIS was one of the most eminent jurists and statesmen of Illinois, one of the most distinguished in that group of men who were contemporaries and associates of the life and times of Abraham Lincoln.

David Davis was born at the Rounds, Sassafras Neck, Cecil County, Maryland, March 9, 1815, son of David Davis, a physician of Cecil County, and grandson of Naylor Davis, of Prince George County.

He attended the schools of his native county and Kenyon College, from which he graduated in 1832. He then studied law with Judge Henry W. Bishop at Lenox, Massachusetts, and at the Law School at New Haven, Connecticut, under Judges Daggett and Hitchcock, and was admitted to practice in 1835. He located in Pekin, Illinois, but due to the unhealthy climate of this district removed in 1836 to Bloomington, Illinois. In 1844 he was elected to the Legislature of Illinois as a Henry Clay whig, and in 1847 was a delegate to the State Constitutional Convention. Upon the adoption of the new constitution in 1848 he was elected judge of the Eighth Judicial District of Illinois, without opposition, and at a time when the circuit was strongly democratic; and was reelected in 1855. He gained the friendship of Abraham Lincoln, and for years they together rode the circuit, which extended over fourteen counties. He supported Mr. Lincoln in his canvass against Judge Douglas for United States senator in 1858, and in 1860 was sent by the Republican State Convention to Chicago as a delegate-at-large to the National Convention, where his leadership brought about the nomination of Abraham Lincoln. After the election Judge Davis was chief councillor of the President, and accompanied him to Washington in February, 1861. After the inauguration he returned to his duties on the circuit, and used his efforts toward a peaceful adjustment of the questions at issue between the states. He was reelected a second time judge of the Eighth Circuit in 1861. President Lincoln appointed him, with Hugh Campbell of St. Louis, and Joseph Holt, former secretary of war in Buchanan's cabinet, as a committee to adjust the war claims against the Department of Missouri, and to investigate the conduct of General Fremont in the administration of the affairs of the department. In 1862 Abraham Lincoln appointed Judge Davis a visitor to the United States Military Academy, and the same year to the seat on the bench of the United States Supreme Court made vacant by the death of Mr. Justice McLean. He became a firm friend of Chief Justice Taney, and this friendship was maintained up to the time of the death of the latter. He administered the estate of Abraham Lincoln in 1865. In 1870 he signed the minority report of the Supreme Court, giving as his opinion that the Act of Congress making government notes a legal tender for the payment of debts was unconstitutional. At this time the ex parte Mulligan case, one of the most important cases of the period and one exciting wide public interest, was assigned to him. It involved the question of individual liberty and the power of the government in the times of war. The leading thoughts of Justice Davis's decision are: "The Constitution of the United States is a law for rulers and people in war and in peace, and covers with the shield of its protection all classes of men, at all times and under all circumstances. The government, within the constitution, has all the powers granted to it which are necessary to preserve its existence, as has been happily proved by the result of the great effort to overthrow it." In 1872 he accepted the nomination of the Labor Reform party as its candidate for President, and his name was also presented at the Liberal Republican National Convention at Cincinnati, where he received ninety-two and a half votes on the first ballot. On the nomination of Mr. Greeley, however, he withdrew from the field as the candidate of the Labor Reform party. It was in first accepting the nomination that Justice Davis made use of the oft-quoted expression: "The chief magistracy of the republic should neither be sought nor declined by any American citizen." In 1876 the independents of the Illinois Legislature united with the democrats and elected Justice Davis to the United States Senate. He resigned his seat on the bench of the United States Supreme Court and took his seat in the Senate March 4, 1877. He served on the committee of the judiciary, and in 1881, on the reorganization of the Senate, under the administration of President Garfield, he declined the chairmanship of the judiciary committee. Upon the accession of Vice President Arthur to the presidency Senator Davis was elected president of the Senate at the convening of the Forty-seventh Congress, December 5, 1881, and accepted the position with the frank statement that "if the last party obligation had been made a condition directly or indirectly I would have declined the compliment." He resigned from the Senate in 1883 and retired to his farm near Bloomington, Illinois.

Judge Davis died at Bloomington, June 26, 1886. He married, October 30, 1838, Sarah W. Walker, daughter of Judge William Perrin Walker, of Lenox, Massachusetts. Mrs. Davis died November 9, 1879. In 1883 Judge Davis married Adeline E. Burr. By the first marriage there were two children, George Perrin and Mrs. Sarah D. Swayne. George Perrin Davis graduated from the University of Michigan Law School in 1867 and became a lawyer at Bloomington. A grandson and namesake of Judge Davis is a resident of Bloomington.

JOHN A. KOONS, present mayor of the city of Mount Vernon in Jefferson County, has been a merchant and business man there for thirty-five years and is a native of southern Illinois.

He was born in Franklin County, Illinois, December 27, 1861, son of Nathan W. and Anna Rebecca (Bates) Koons. His paternal grandfather, Jonathan Koons, was a native of Germany and was very liberally educated, a man of scientific training, well versed in philosophy, astronomy and history and wrote a great deal on those subjects. He came to Illinois in 1859. In Germany he had been a shipbuilder and he followed that occupation in this country for a time at Philadelphia and Erie, Pennsylvania. He died in Illinois at the age of ninety-eight. Nathan W. Koons was a farmer, merchant and nurseryman in Franklin County, lived for some years at Piedmont, Missouri, where he conducted a sawmill and general store, and he served as a Union soldier with the Fourth Illinois Regiment. He and several of his brothers were in the war. He was always active in the Grand Army of the Republic, held local offices and was a republican in politics. He died in 1923. His wife, Anna Rebecca Bates, who died October 30, 1899, was a daughter of Samuel Bates, a tanner in New York City, and he and his wife, Margaret (Turnbull) Bates, are of old American families of Revolutionary stock. Nathan W. Koons and wife reared the following of their seven children: George, who married Paulina Jones and had five children: John A.; Robert, who married Della Pierson and has one child; Leota, now Mrs. E. B. Moss, of Mount Vernon; Samuel Allen, who married Miss Elly; J. B., who married Ora Englett and had six children.

John A. Koons acquired his early education in public schools in Franklin County and Piedmont, Missouri, where he finished his education when about nineteen years of age. As a youth and young man he was associated with his father in work at the store, the farm, and the sawmill. Later he engaged in farming and sawmilling on his own account and also operated a threshing outfit and was a grain raiser and wheat dealer. Returning to Franklin County, he conducted a farm and in 1886 removed to Mount Vernon, where for thirty-five years he has been a leading furniture and hardware merchant. In the course of his business experience he has also handled a number of contracts for road building and street paving.

Mr. Koons has been a man of prominence in local affairs and politics, has been township supervisor, highway commissioner and served several terms on the City Council of Mount Vernon and in 1923 was elected for a two year term as mayor. He was nominated for re-election without opposition on the republican ticket.

Mr. Koons married, in 1884, Miss Eldorado Robinson, who died in 1908. The only child of their marriage was Leo, who died October 19, 1897. In 1911 he married Mrs. Delia Kerr, of Jonesboro, Arkansas. He met her while engaged in paving the streets of that city. Her parents, Mr. and Mrs. James H. Williams, are now deceased. By his second marriage Mr. Koons has one son: John A., Jr., born October 18, 1912.

SHELDON CLARK is a native son of Chicago, and his prominence in his native city is twofold, based on business leadership and close association with organizations designed to make the most of Chicago's position as a civic and commercial center.

Mr. Clark was born at Chicago August 29, 1878, son of Sheldon Adelbert and Nannie A. Clark. His father, a native of Michigan, served with the Sixth Michigan Cavalry in the Civil war and soon afterward moved to Chicago, first locating on the West Side and afterwards in what was then the choice residential section around Calumet Avenue and Thirty-second street. In that community Sheldon Clark spent his boyhood, attending grammar and high schools, and finished his education in the University of Colorado. Mr. Clark's main business activities have been identified with the commercial side of the oil industry. His prominence in the oil business is sufficiently described when it is stated that he is vice president of the Sinclair Refining Comuany and the Sinclair Navigation Company. He is first vice president of the National Petroleum Association, a director of the American Petroleum Institute, and a director in the American Oil Men's Association. He is also a director of the Lake Shore Trust & Savings Bank.

Some of the avenues taken by his civic energy are denoted by his membership in the Chicago Plan Commission, former membership and vice presidency of the Lincoln Park Board, member of the Executive Committee of the Chicago Association of Commerce. He was presidential elector on the republican ticket for Illinois in 1916 and served as secretary of the Chicago National Republican Convention Committees in 1916 and 1920.

A large section of the public knows the name of Sheldon Clark largely through its frequent association with sports and athletics. He is a former commodore of the Chicago Yacht Club, the oldest and premier yacht club of the Great Lakes. He was interested in boating and sailing from his early youth, and his schooner, the Rainbow, has won many honors in the aquatic events of the Great Lakes. Mr. Clark is chairman of the athletic committee of the Chicago Athletic Association, and through that organization and individually has done much to promote the prestige of the Chicago district in American sports. He is also a member of the University Club, Saddle and Cycle Club, Onwentsia Club, Racquet Club, Forty Club, Bobolink Golf Club, New York Yacht Club, Royal Automobile Club of London, and his college fraternities were Delta Tau Delta and Delta Chi.

Mr. Clark is married and at present resides at 1367 North State Street, Chicago, with his family, consisting of three sons and one daughter, Sheldon A., Harry, Carrington and Bonnie-Jean.

G. THOMSEN VON COLDITZ, M. D., has been active in his profession at Chicago since 1907, is widely known as a surgeon and specialist in eye, ear, nose and throat, and has devoted much time and attention during and since the World war to military affairs, holding the rank of major in the United States army.

He was born at Chicago, October 21, 1877, son of Julius and Ida L. (Schloesser) Thomsen von Colditz. His early education was acquired for the most part abroad in Germany, attending a gymnasium at Dresden. He attended Rush Medical College of Chicago and the Illinois Medical College, Loyola University, graduating in 1902, and subsequently did work in the New York Post-Graduate Medical School and spent two years at the University of Heidelberg, Germany, as assistant to Professor Leber in the eye department. Later he attended clinics at Vienna, Strassburg and Zurich. He practiced at Mt. Clemens, Michigan, for several years before returning to Chicago. Doctor von Colditz has had a very successful experience in the special field he has chosen. He is attending otologist and rhino-laryngologist to Grant Hospital and the Chicago Home for Young Girls, attending ophthalmologist and oto-laryngologist to Olivet Dispensary, and is a trustee of Olivet Institute. For a number of years he taught at the Chicago Policlinic, Illinois University and Loyola University. He is a fellow of the American Academy of Ophthalmology and Oto-Laryngology, and the German Ophthalmologische Gesellschaft, Germany, besides being a member of the Chicago Ophthalmological Society and the Chicago Medical, Tri-State, Illinois State and American Medical Associations.

At the time of the World war he volunteered and was assigned to examine candidates for aviation in the army. He has served at several military posts throughout the country, and holds the rank of major in the Officer's Reserve Corps. He has been appointed chairman for Evanston of the Citizens Military Training Camp. Major von Colditz organized the North Shore Cook County Reserve Officer's Association, of which he was elected first president. He graduated as flight surgeon in 1925 from the Aviation School of Medicine, United States Army, at Mitchell Field, Long Island, New York, and is assigned as flight surgeon for the Three Hundred and Ninth Attack Guard, Air Service, United States army. He is a member of the Military Intelligence Association of the Sixth Corps Area, Reserve Officer's Association of the United States and the Association of Military Surgeons of the United States. He is also a member of the Chicago Athletic Club, Evanston Golf Club, Army and Navy Club, Physician's Club and is a Knight Templar and Scottish Rite Mason and Shriner, and a Sojourner, also a life member of the Art Institute of Chicago.

He is the author of articles on: Surgical Technique of Tonsillectomy; Unusual Reactions Following Atropine in the Eye; Treatment of Otitis Media with Tuberculin, etc.

Dr. von Colditz married, December 3, 1912, Miss Ruth Ware, daughter of J. H. Ware, late of New York. They are the parents of three children, Elizabeth Louise, Herbert and Paul. Doctor von Colditz has his office at 25 East Washington Street, Chicago, and 708 Church Street, Evanston. His residence is at 1621 Judson Avenue, Evanston, and he has his summer home at Martha's Vineyard, Massachusetts.

PEARL SMITH, chairman of the Board of Supervisors of Madison County, has been active in politics there for twenty years, and has been a resident of the town of Madison and one of those most active officially and in a private capacity in promoting its growth and prosperity.

Pearl Smith was born at Bowling Green in Pike County, Missouri, July 31, 1877, son of J. T. and Frances Smith. His father and also his grandfather, John S. Smith, were natives of Kentucky and of German ancestry. J. T.

Smith was born in Harrison County, Kentucky, in 1852, was a small child when the family moved to Bowling Green, Missouri, and he held the office of justice of the peace there for thirty-five years. He died at the age of sixty-two. His wife was born and reared in Missouri, her people being pioneers of that state. She died when about thirty-two years of age, the mother of three daughters and two sons, Pearl being the oldest.

Pearl Smith grew up at Bowling Green, attended high school there, and at the age of twenty-one came to Madison County, Illinois. His home has been in the town of Madison for twenty-five years. He learned the undertaking business, securing a diploma in Chicago in 1901, and followed his profession at Madison until 1904, since which time his energies have been mainly taken up with politics and public affairs. In 1904 he was elected supervisor of Venice Township, and has held that position continuously. For eighteen years of that time he was clerk of the Board of Review, and has been chairman of the Board of Supervisors in 1922-23-24-25. In his home town he has been superintendent of the streets and inspector of sewers and plumbing for eight years, and also president of the Illinois State Fireman's Association. As a leader in the democratic party he is senatorial committee man for the Forty-seventh Senatorial District, comprising Madison and Bond counties and is the nominee for sheriff on the democrat ticket for November 2, 1926. During the World war he had charge of the local Red Cross and was chairman of the Advisory Board. He is on the Advisory Board of St. Elizabeth Hospital of Granite City. Mr. Smith is an active member of the Madison County Country Club, is affiliated with the Elks, Eagles and the Lodge and Encampment of the Independent Order of Odd Fellows.

He married in 1903 Miss Maud Laird, of Carryville. They have twin daughters, Nadene and Irene, now nineteen years of age. Mr. Smith is affiliated with the Presbyterian Church.

HUBERT HENRY FLETCHER, M. D., had for many years practiced medicine at Winchester and in Scott County. His friends have been much impressed with his remarkable ability not only in his profession but in business and affairs and the energy that has enabled him to keep in contact with a wide range of active interests.

Doctor Fletcher was born at Milmine, in Piatt County, Illinois, July 27, 1872. His grandfather, Thomas Fletcher, was a planter and slave holder of old Kentucky, but died comparatively young. He was the father of five sons. They divided their allegiance almost equally between the North and the South at the time of the Civil war. Two of them, Woodson and Larkin, were enrolled as soldiers of the Confederacy. James, Robert G. and Columbus were on the Union side, James and Columbus serving as soldiers.

Robert G. Fletcher was the father of Doctor Fletcher. He was born at Bowling Green, Kentucky, was reared there and about the time of the Civil war came to Illinois. On account of an injury he was never mustered into the army. He spent a life of usefulness as a farmer in Scott County, near Winchester, and died in 1913, at the age of eighty-nine. He was a republican and a Baptist. He married in Scott County Mary Elizabeth Schnell, who was born in Pennsylvania in 1824 and died in May, 1921. Her father, James Schnell, was a native of Scotland and married Betsy Hickernell. There were four sons and five daughters in the Schnell family. The children of Robert G. Fletcher and wife were: James S., of Fredonia, Kansas; Charles C., of Hebron, Nebraska; Woodson T., who died in childhood; Ulysses S., who died in Winchester in 1920; Jennie, wife of J. M. Stowe, of St. Francis, Illinois; and Dr. Hubert H.

Hubert Henry Fletcher at the age of nine years removed with his parents to White Hall and four years later, in 1885, to the vicinity of Winchester, where he grew up on the farm, and shared in its labors to the age of eighteen. He attended school under Prof. George W. Smith at White Hall, was in high school at Winchester and at the age of nineteen began teaching, a vocation he followed over a period of seven years, including eleven terms. His last school work was done in the Claywell School in Scott County. While teaching he studied medicine. For four terms he attended Valparaiso University in Indiana, and in 1899 was graduated in medicine from the Barnes Medical College of St. Louis. After a brief experience of practice he returned for another year of medical work and received another diploma in 1901. Doctor Fletcher has also had the advantages of residence and study abroad, spending over a year, from July, 1905, to October, 1906, in Europe, chiefly in the clinics and hospitals of Vienna and London, taking work in pathology, medicine and surgery. He then resumed his active practice at Winchester.

Doctor Fletcher rendered special duty in the Army Medical Corps following the World war, being stationed at Camp Greenleaf, Georgia, from August, 1919; until November 24th, and was then made puss surgeon at Camp Logan, Houston, Texas Base Hospital, remaining until the hospital closed. He left there in May, 1920, and then resumed practice in Winchester. He is one of the consulting surgeons of the Baptist Hospital of St. Louis. He was elected president of the Mercer County Illinois Medical Society in 1903, president of the Tri-State Medical Society in 1912, secretary of the Scott County Medical Society from 1907 to 1925, inclusive, and is a member of the Illinois State and American Medical Associations and the American Association of Railway Surgeons.

Doctor Fletcher is a member of the American Legion. He took his first degrees in Masonry at Winchester and is a member of the Scottish Rite Consistory at Quincy, the Mystic Shrine at East St. Louis, and is a patron of the Eastern Star. He is a charter member of the Winchester Kiwanis Club.

Doctor Fletcher cast his first presidential vote for Major McKinley in 1896, and has frequently been a delegate to Republican State Conventions and served on the advisory board of the Twentieth Congressional District. He is a director of the First State Bank of Winchester, is secretary of the Board of Commissioners of the Big Swan Drainage District and

Thomas Kennedy.

is one of the directors of the Association of Drainage and Levee Districts of the State. For fifteen years he was president of the Winchester Board of Education and president of the library board three years, and served two terms as mayor. While he was mayor the water system was installed.

Doctor Fletcher married at Winchester, November 8, 1899, Miss Mary Isabel Murray, a native of Scott County. She was educated in the schools at Winchester. She is a daughter of Rev. George W. and Lucinda (Taylor) Murray. Her father was born in Greene County, Illinois, and was a descendant of Henry Murray, who fought with a Pennsylvania regiment in the American Revolution, while his son, Arthur Murray, was a soldier in the War of 1812, and fought in the battle of that war at New Orleans. Mrs. Fletcher has a sister, Millie A., wife of S. M. Smithson, a sister Grace, wife of Normal B. Getty, and a brother, Melvie B., of Winchester.

The only child of Doctor and Mrs. Fletcher is Charles Wayne, who was born in 1901, finished his high school work at Winchester, and at Washington University in St. Louis, took four years of law and had one year of medicine in St. Louis University. While splendidly qualified for a professional career, he had developed while in college remarkable ability as a banjo player and showed pronounced talent and versatility in music, and since leaving college he has been a composer of music for the banjo and is widely known both as a player and composer. He is spending the summer of 1926 in Europe as banjo player and tenor soloist, and has engagements to play for the President of France and King Albert of Belgium and other eminently well known people in Europe. He contracted to take his orchestra, The Washington University orchestra, with the Cunard S. S. line.

THOMAS KENNEDY was admitted to the Illinois bar in 1886. For over thirty years he was one of the leading attorneys of Woodford County, and was honored with some of the important offices connected with his profession. He now practices in the City of Bloomington, one of his sons being his law partner.

Judge Kennedy was born on a farm in Minonk Township, Woodford County, December 6, 1858. His father, Thomas Kennedy, was born at Lismore, County Waterford, Province of Munster, Ireland. The Kennedys have been a family whose name has appeared in the history of Munster as far back as the ninth century (Ency. Britt., Vol. IV, Eleventh Ed. 515; Historians' History of the World, Vol. XXI, 350). Members of the family are still living in Munster. Thomas Kennedy, Sr., at the age of eighteen left his native place, and after living about four years on the Isle of Jersey came to Boston, Massachusetts, where he married Catherine Flynn. After their marriage they came out to Illinois and lived at Lacon until 1856, when they moved to a farm in Minonk Township, Woodford County. Thomas Kennedy, Sr., died there in 1878. His wife, Catherine Flynn, was born in New Hampshire, moved to Boston, and was living in the family of Leonard Stone at Roxbury at the time of her marriage. She died at Minonk in 1863.

Thomas Kennedy, the attorney, was four years old when his mother died. He grew up on his father's farm and worked for his father until he was nineteen years of age. After the death of his father he worked with his brother on a farm for two years and for about one year was a hired farm hand. In the meantime he was getting his education through opportunities provided by his own industry and economy. He attended country schools, the city school at Minonk, and for about three years taught in country school districts, and for one year in the city schools at Minonk. He had studied at every opportunity while working on the farm, and in this way was able to pass an examination for a teacher's certificate. He studied law in the office of Martin L. Newell at Minonk in 1884-86, and, as noted above, was admitted to the bar in June, 1886. After practicing a year at Minonk he moved to Metamora and opened an office a few doors west of the old court house, which is now the Lincoln Memorial Building. About the time he was admitted to the bar he became city attorney of Minonk, in 1886. During 1887-88 he served as master in chancery of Woodford County. In 1888 he was elected state's attorney of Woodford County, and then returned to Minonk and formed a partnership with Martin L. Newell under the firm name of Newell & Kennedy. This partnership was dissolved in 1893, when Mr. Newell removed to Springfield to take up his duties as assistant attorney general of the state. Mr. Kennedy served two consecutive terms as state's attorney, retiring from the office in 1896. In 1912 he was again elected state's attorney, serving until 1916. From 1898 to 1906 he had served as county judge of Woodford County. In connection with the duties of these offices he carried on a general law practice in Woodford and adjoining counties until the winter of 1918, when he moved his home to Normal and opened his law office in the Greisheim Building at the northeast corner of the court house square in Bloomington. That office is the headquarters of the law firm of Kennedy & Kennedy, his junior associate being his son Kaywin Kennedy.

Judge Kennedy owns farms in Woodford, LaSalle, Tazewell and McLean counties. During the World war he was a member of the advisory board and on the council of defense of the county. He is a democrat in politics, and is affiliated with Lodge No. 377, Independent Order of Odd Fellows, at Minonk, and is a charter member and was first consul of Camp No. 952, Modern Woodmen of America, at Minonk. He is a member of the College Alumni Club of Bloomington, the Bloomington Country Club and the Maplewood Country Club at Normal. Members of his family belong to and attend the Second Presbyterian Church of Bloomington.

Judge Kennedy married at Bloomington, July 12, 1894, Miss Clara Hart, member of a prominent family of Woodford County, daughter of Allen and Martha A. (Baldridge) Hart. She was born in Palestine Township, Woodford County, and lived on the Hart homestead there, removing with her widowed mother to Bloomington. Allen Hart, who was a member of the Hart family of White Plains and New York City, New York, came to Illinois as a pioneer in 1836 and for a short time conducted a store at Hudson, and then moved to the Hart homestead in Woodford County. He was on the first petit jury in Woodford County after its organization as a county, and was one of the twelve who brought in a verdict of guilty in the case of People vs. Gardiner, the first case tried in the county. Allen Hart made a visit to New York City in 1853. On his trip home he rode from LaSalle to Bloomington on the first train over the Illinois Central Railway to enter Bloomington. Martha A. Baldridge, the mother of Mrs. Kennedy, came from Ohio with relatives in a prairie schooner. All the experiences and changes in this section of the state from frontier days to modern times were unfolded before her eyes, as she survived to the advanced age of ninety-one, passing away February 8, 1925.

Judge and Mrs. Kennedy have two sons. Kaywin Kennedy, born December 24, 1895, married Bernice Phillips and has two children, Kathryn and Martha Jean. Thomas Hart Kennedy, born April 4, 1901, married Marion Carter, daughter of Wilbur M. and Leila Van Loo Carter, of Bloomington. Both sons are veterans of the World war, both having been honorably discharged from the service with the rank of second lieutenant. Kaywin Kennedy was attached to the United States Signal Corps, saw service overseas and after the armistice was in the Army of Occupation in Germany. He was admitted to the bar of the State of Illinois in the latter part of 1920, and since then has been associated with his father in practice. Thomas Hart Kennedy was interested in aviation during the war. In 1923 he traveled in Europe, mostly by airline, and after his return wrote a book entitled "An Introduction to the Economics of Air Transportation." He was a student in the Northwestern University School of Law at Chicago, and is now pursuing his law studies in the University of Southern California at Los Angeles.

GEORGE NORTH is one of the younger representatives of one of the oldest families of Greene County. His career has identified him with farming, land ownership and business. He is chairman of the board of the Peoples First National Bank of White Hall.

Mr. North was born in White Hall Township, March 2, 1886, son of John and Lora (Twitchell) North, and grandson of Marcus North, and great-grandson of Asahel North. His American ancestor was John North, who sailed from England in 1635. His descendants have since scattered to practically all sections of the United States.

Asahel North, founder of the Illinois branch of the family, was born at Farmington, Connecticut, September 3, 1782. On August 26, 1819, he married Prudence Swallow, who was born at Windsor, Vermont, September 10, 1799. Their wedding tour was a trip to the west. They left a few days after their marriage and after a long journey overland in wagon arrived in Illinois, and in the spring of 1821 settled on Apple Creek Prairie in Greene County. They bought the primitive home of a squatter until the public land came into the market. Then Asahel North entered over 800 acres at $1.25 an acre. The rest of his life was spent in that community and in the development of his land. The town site of White Hall includes a portion of the original farm holdings of Asahel North. He died at his home near White Hall March 19, 1846, and both he and his wife were buried on the old North farm. There were twelve children, and those to grow up were: Lucy, who became Mrs. Edward Griswold; Marcus; Sylvia, who married Isaac McCollister; John; and Mrs. Mary Stewart.

Marcus North, Sr., father of the present Marcus North of White Hall, was born in Greene County, December 6, 1824. He was a farmer during his brief career of thirty years. He died November 28, 1854, and is buried in the White Hall Cemetery. He married Elizabeth Wales, who was born at Ferrisburg, Vermont, and was a girl when brought to Illinois. She was a daughter of Charles Wales and a direct descendant of William Brewster of the Mayflower Colony. Mrs. Marcus North lived a widow after her husband's death for fifty-six years. She was the mother of the following children: Edward, for many years a banker at White Hall, who subsequently went to Houston, Texas, and later to Memphis, Tennessee, where he died in 1923; Lucy, who died at White Hall, wife of Charles I. McCollister; and Marcus.

John North, father of George North, was born March 6, 1835, was reared and educated in Greene County, was a farmer and land owner and became one of the founders of the old Peoples Bank of White Hall. For a number of years he was engaged in the cattle business. He died in 1897, at the age of sixty-two. Lora Twitchell, his second wife, was born near Greenfield, Illinois, in Rubicon Township, Illinois. Her father was an Illinois pioneer and in erecting his pioneer residence he had to haul the lumber a great distance from the nearest saw mill, hauling it with wagon and ox team. Lora Twitchell's brothers and sisters were: Maria, who married Milton Wilder; Ada, who married George Melvin, of Greenfield; Grant; and Ralph Twitchell, the only surviver, a resident of Baldwin, Kansas.

George North soon after his birth was taken by his parents to Nebraska, and he lived for five years in the vicinity of Kearney. His mother died at Kansas City, Missouri, and was brought back for burial in the White Hall Cemetery. George North was the only child of his parents. He was reared by relatives in White Hall and after the age of seven lived with Mrs. F. E. Turneaure, near Madison, Wisconsin. He finished his early education in the Hillside Home School at Spring Green, Wisconsin. Then returning to Illinois he took a course in Brown's Business College, later a short course in agriculture at the University of Wisconsin, and for eight years was successfully engaged in the business of farming in White Hall Township. Mr. North disposed of his farm land in that township in 1918 and removed to White Hall. Since then he has invested heavily in lands in Walkerville and Patterson townships, and gives much of his time to their supervision. He is also one of the partners in a syndicate engaged in clearing up a section of land in the Illinois River bottoms.

Mr. North while on the farm became a stockholder in the Peoples Bank of White Hall, and when that bank was consolidated with the First National, becoming the Peoples First National Bank, he continued his financial interests and is now chairman of the Board of Directors.

Mr. North is a York and Scottish Rite Mason, having taken his first degree in White Hall Lodge No. 80. He is a member of the Springfield Consistory and Ansar Temple of the Mystic Shrine. He is a trustee of the Presbyterian Church, is a member of the White Hall Chamber of Commerce, and during the World war was active in the various drives. He was registered for service but never classified.

He married at White Hall, December 3, 1908, Miss Clemma E. Ross, who was born April 19, 1888, daughter of Edward and Ella (Tankersley) Ross. Her parents were born in Greene County and were farmers and stock raisers there. Mrs. Clemma North had a sister, Bernice, who married H. E. Boggess, and a brother, Arnold Ross, a farmer of Greene County. She was educated in the White Hall High School and was a talented pianist. Mrs. North died November 26, 1918, leaving a daughter, Marian Ada, now a student in the Monticello Seminary at Godfrey. Mr. North's second wife was Grace Elizabeth Tankersley, a native of Scott County, Illinois, and daughter of W. A. and Margaret E. (Coltas) Tankersley. She was one of the eleven children, seven daughters and three sons to reach mature years. Her brothers and sisters were Mrs. Edward Ross, Mrs. Addie Lorton, Mrs. Arthur McMahan, Mrs. George Hill, Mrs. Clarence Tunison, Mrs. Nora Davis, William O., Kirby and Bert C. Tankersley.

COL. PAUL HENDERSON. One of the most memorable achievements in modern history, the inauguration of the Transcontinental Air Mail Service, was projected and put into successful operation under the official authority and direction of Col. Paul Henderson, a Chicago man, and one of the prominent figures in modern commercial aviation.

Colonel Henderson was born at Lyndon, Kansas, in 1884, but when a small boy was brought to Chicago by his parents. He was reared and educated in that city, and prior to the World war he was engaged in the road building and road building material business. He became president of the Western Stone Company, one of the large organizations handling raw material for street and road building. Later he was an executive in the Brownell Improvement Company, the largest producers of crushed stone in the world.

During the World war Colonel Henderson volunteered, was commissioned captain and was assigned duty as ordinance officer of base section No. 1 at St. Nazaire, France, where he had charge of the transportation and storage of ammunition, high explosives and other materials. While in France he was promoted to lieutenant colonel, and now holds that rank as reserve officer, Air Service Corps, United States army.

Colonel Henderson in April, 1921, was appointed assistant postmaster general in charge of postal transportation; this includes railway, steamship, motor and air services. He was appointed during the Harding administration and was continued in the Coolidge administration until the fall of 1925, when he resigned. As assistant postmater general he perfected and closely supervised the working details of the air mail service, and personally organized the night air mail. Colonel Henderson returned to Chicago in 1926, and has since been general manager of the National Air Transport, Incorporated, which was organized and incorporated under the laws of Delaware May 21, 1925. The stockholders of this corporation include many men of wealth—bankers, manufacturers and others all over the country. The primary purpose of the corporation is to carry mails and express by air. The first operations of the corporation were inaugurated in the spring of 1926. An article from the Chicago Commerce of February 27, 1926, affords a prevision of what may be expected of this development in commercial aviation: "Within a short time there will be in operation out of Chicago the most extensive system of air lines anywhere in the world. One of the most important "airways" that will connect Chicago with other parts of the United States is the one promised by the National Air Transport, Inc., which plans to operate a fleet of planes from the southwest to New York City by way of Chicago. Plans for this latter highly important service are maturing rapidly. Chicago, and in fact every considerable manufacturing city in Illinois, by the combination of the National Air Transport, Inc., Air Mail and Express Lines, from Chicago to the southwest, and by its express lines from Chicago to New York, will be placed in the most advantageous position with regard to the extension of executive control from headquarters throughout the undeveloped sales and distribution market of the southwest."

Colonel Henderson has his offices in the Straus Building on Michigan Avenue, and his home is at Hinsdale. He is a member of the Hinsdale Club, Hamilton and Union League Clubs of Chicago and the Engineers Club of New York.

THE MILITARY TRAINING CAMPS ASSOCIATION OF THE UNITED STATES has its national headquarters in Chicago, its president being Mr. Charles B. Pike, and a brief account of the association is more properly included in a history of Illinois than in that of any other state.

The association was formed in 1916 by the graduates of Plattsburg and other pre-war camps throughout the country. During 1917-18 the association assisted in the selection of nearly 100,000 men, who were trained and added to the commissioned personnel of the national army. The purpose of the association is to support a sane and adequate policy of national defense, represented by the army of the United States, including the Regular Establishment, the National Guard and the Organized Reserves. It is especially devoted to the principle of voluntary training through the plan known as the Citizens' Military Training Camps, and for these it acts in large measure as an enrollment agency cooperating with the War Department and with the commanding generals of the different corps areas. The organization has been perfected through the appointment of corps area and state civilian aides and of county representatives, until every section of the country has easy access to this first aid to national defense.

Since the close of the great war the work of the association has been primarily to carry out the program laid down in the National Defense Act of 1920. The Citizens' Military Training Camps were first established in 1921, and through appropriations from Congress the accommodations and facilities have been steadily increased, Congress in 1924 providing for the training of almost 35,000 men in fifty camps throughout the country. President Coolidge has called the camps "Schools of Citizenship," such camps, in his opinion, "are an essential in the plan of national security. They promote obedience to law and respect for the institutions of a well-ordered society. Young men are helped to physical health, mental vigor and moral excellence. Social understanding and democratic feeling are developed; love and reverence for the flag are the natural outcome of the training. I hope that each year an increasing number of young men may take advantage of the opportunity which is afforded them."

Perhaps the most valuable commentary on the work of this association is contained in a letter from the late John W. Weeks, secretary of war, to the president of the association. In his letter the honored secretary of war makes the following statements:

"Since their establishment in 1921 the Citizens' Military Training Camps have had a steady growth. They have shown in a very decided manner the intelligence and energy which you and your associates have devoted to this matter. By giving them indispensable aid you have been instrumental in informing thousands on thousands of American youths of the three fundamental elements which the country will need in time of emergency. The Citizens' Camps have developed the hygienic and physical fitness of young America. They have imparted the basic facts underlying coordinated action. They have created and spread a clearer conception of loyal patriotism and responsible citizenship. Of course these camps do not bind those who attend them to any obligations and make no attempts to enroll anyone for future service. Yet, their extraordinary success and the unprecedented enthusiasm they have brought out this year serve as indications of what the Republic may well expect her young men to offer in an hour of danger. I feel certain that if peril should again threaten the Government of the United States the young men who have attended the summer camps and there learned the spirit of national service will freely offer their support.

"For the work which you have done towards creating this very favorable condition I desire to reiterate the thanks which I have already expressed on several occasions in the past. You will have the satisfaction of knowing that you have contributed something towards the betterment of the people of the Nation and towards a more definite assurance of its welfare."

The Military Training Camps Association is the recognized civilian agency of the War Department in helping to enroll through its county representatives young men for the Citizens' Camps. In addition, through the Civilian Aides, who are appointed from its membership and on its recommendation by the secretary of war and through its local committees which are organized in every part of the country it seeks to promote the comfort and the pleasure of the candidates at the various training centers. It offers the much-prized medals "for excellence;" it helps to secure in neighboring communities prizes for the military and athletic events at each camp; excursions, admission to ball games and theaters, as well as other forms of entertainment are frequently provided by civic committees at its suggestion; each year a series of CMTC Annuals is published by the association on the request of corps area and camp commanders; the young men who have attended the summer camps are united in local and state organizations with the cooperation of representatives of the association; visiting committees are appointed for each training center. In these and in many other ways the Military Training Camps Association supports the National Defense Act and serves as the civilian link between the war department and the people of the United States in a plan of voluntary training, which is attracting each year greater numbers of young men of the nation.

In the history of Illinois, Chicago deserves a special mention for its hearty support of the Military Training Camps Association. Its advisory and executive committees number such representative men as Frank O. Lowden, Cyrus H. McCormick, Stanley Field, James Simpson, R. T. Crane, Dr. Frank Billings, Marshall Field III, George M. Reynolds, Robert Gardner, Julius Rosenwald, Joseph T. Ryerson, John A. Holabird, Noble Brandon Judah and Charles G. Dawes. The national officers include Henry S. Drinker, honorary president; Charles B. Pike, president; Charles S. Dewey, treasurer; Tom R. Wyles, secretary, and Dr. George F. James, executive secretary. The national offices of the association are at 6 North Michigan Avenue, Chicago, Illinois.

HORACE GREELEY RUSSELL. Although a member of the Illinois bar and present judge of the City Court at Beardstown, the chief distinction of Horace Greeley Russell was the long and capable service he gave to the cause of education, chiefly in Illinois.

Judge Russell was born in 1860, and was sixteen years of age when his parents, in 1876, came from Hendricks County, Indiana, to a farm near Newman in Edgar County, Illinois. His father, Silas Russell, was born near Danville, Kentucky, in 1830, and through practically all his life was identified with agriculture. He was in the grain and elevator business at Chrisman, Illinois, for several years, until his death in 1905. He was a republican and a member of the Christian Church. He married Nancy Jane Moreland, whose father

was a farmer in that vicinity and had come from Kentucky. Mrs. Silas Russell died in 1904, at the age of seventy-three. They were the parents of nine children, and those to grow up were: George W., of Indianapolis; Horace G.; Mrs. Fannie Pounds, of Newman, Illinois; Mrs. John H. Chadwick, of Tuscola, Illinois; Clark A., a government grain inspector at Indianapolis; and Miss Dorothy, of Indianapolis.

Horace Greeley Russell continued his education after coming to Illinois, attending the Newman High School, and in intervals of teaching and other work attended and paid his way as a student at Illinois Wesleyan University at Bloomington. He taught two years in rural schools, four years in the villages of Scotland and Dudley in Edgar County, was for three years superintendent of schools at Hartley, Iowa, and for thirteen years was superintendent of schools at Greenfield, Illinois. From Greenfield he removed to Beardstown in 1910 and for twelve years held the office of superintendent of city schools. When he retired from the schoolroom in 1922 it was after thirty-four years of earnest and high-minded labors in the field of education. During these years he was an honored member of the State Teachers Association, the National Education Association, was for two years secretary of the City Superintendents Association of Illinois, and became especially well known as a lecturer before county institutes and other organizations on various phases of the boy problem. Early in his teaching he showed a singular faculty in handling boys and directing their activities and characters into useful lines. For twenty-five years he taught in county institutes and also lectured before farmers' institutes on practical phases of education. He was a member of the faculty of the Grout Farm School for Boys, founded by a group of successful farmers of Scott County, Iilnois. This school did a splendid work in the practical training of farm boys and girls in the state, and the work is still continued under the auspices of the Illinois State Fair. As is the case of all real educators, it is impossible to estimate the tremendous good acomplished by his precept and example.

Judge Russell during his early career as a teacher studied law, chiefly for the training and culture it would give him, and in 1887 he passed a successful examination for the bar at Springfield. Since leaving school work he has utilized his learning as a lawyer, and after some months spent in recuperating his health in California he was elected, in 1923, judge of the City Court of Beardstown. For many years he was chairman of the board of the Christian Church of Beardstown, is a director of the Chamber of Commerce, an honorary member of the Rotary Club, and has been identified with numerous public undertakings. He took his Masonic degrees at Hartley, Iowa, and in politics has always been a republican nationally, casting his first presidential vote for James G. Blaine in 1884, and while in Illinois Wesleyan University was president of the Blaine and Logan Club. During the World war he was a member of the local Council of Defense and Four-Minute Speakers, and for two years chairman of the local Red Cross.

Judge Russell married at Paris, Illinois, April 11, 1888, Miss Nellie Denton, born at Paris, daughter of John W. and Nannie E. (Dorsey) Denton, who came from Kentucky. Mrs. Russell was educated in Paris, and had been a teacher before her marriage and continued educational work for many years, for most of the time being principal of schools where her husband was superintendent. Mrs. Russell has a sister, Mrs. Harriet Graham, living at San Diego, California; another sister, Miss Minnie Denton, also at San Diego, and a brother, John, at St. Louis. The only child of Judge and Mrs. Russell was a daughter, Helen, who died when five years old.

JOHN CHARLES WESTERVELT, M. D., now has secure standing as one of the veteran and honored physicians and surgeons in the city of Shelbyville, judicial center of Shelby County, where he has been engaged in the practice of his profession nearly half a century and where he is a citizen of distinctive prominence and influence aside from his faithful and efficient professional stewardship. The Doctor has given four terms of service as mayor of Shelbyville, and this fact offers significant testimony to his high place in communal confidence and esteem, besides attesting the efficiency of the service that he thus gave as head of the municipal government. Doctor Westervelt is vice president of the First National Bank of Shelbyville and also of the Shelbyville Loan & Trust Company, and he is president of the Shelbyville County Fair Association and the Citizens Savings & Loan Association, besides which he is treasurer of the Kaskaskia Life Insurance Company.

The history of the Westervelt family in Holland is traced back to 1500, and the family was founded in America in the Colonial period of our national history. Doctor Westervelt was born in Westerville, Ohio, June 7, 1855, and is a son of the late James L. and Mary A. (Connelly) Westervelt, who came to Illinois when their son John C., of this review, was a boy and who established their home in Livingston County, the remainder of their lives having been passed in this state. The public schools of Livingston County afforded Doctor Westervelt his earlier educational discipline, which included that of the high school at Fairbury, and as a youth he formulated definite plans for his future career. In consonance with these plans he finally entered the Bennett Medical College in Chicago, in which institution he was graduated as a member of the class of 1877 and with the degree of Doctor of Medicine. In the following year he there received a supplemental degree of Doctor of Medicine from the fine old Hahnemann Medical College. During the long intervening years Doctor Westervelt has not failed to keep in touch with the advances made in medical and surgical science, and he has long been one of the leading physicians and surgeons of Shelby County, as well as a citizen of unbounded loyalty and public spirit.

The republican party has ever received the unqualified allegiance of Doctor Westervelt, he and his wife are zealous members of the Methodist Episcopal Church, and he is affiliated with the Modern Woodmen of America and is an active member of the Rotary Club in his home city. He has long retained membership in the Shelby County Medical Society, the Illinois State Medical Society and the American Medical Association.

On the 28th of July, 1880, was solemnized the marriage of Doctor Westervelt and Miss Mary L. Webster, daughter of Simon H. and Lucy Webster, of Shelbyville, Mr. Webster having long been one of the representative business men of this city and having also served as postmaster of Shelbyville during a long term of years. Doctor and Mrs. Westervelt have three children: Grace L. is the wife of Edward H. Christman, of Shelbyville; Leverett C. was married to Donald Fought, of Altannet; and Floyd C. married Miss Mayme Rowling, their home being in New York City.

JAMES N. MCMINN is a veteran figure in Chicago real estate. In one particular section of the city he is not only the oldest operator but probably the outstanding authority on everything connected with value and the other factors that enter into and affect the real estate market. That section is the famous World's Fair district, bounded by the great artery of traffic leading up to the Fair entrance, Sixty-third Street.

Mr. McMinn was born at Potters Mills, Center County, Pennsylvania, and in 1878 came to Illinois. The following year his widowed mother joined him, and it has always been one of the satisfactions of his life that he abundantly and tenderly cared for her throughout the many years she lived in Illinois. He first located at Rock City in Stephenson County, learned the jeweler's trade and followed it for a time at Freeport, and in 1879 came to Chicago. He had studied telegraphy and in Chicago was employed as train dispatcher for the Chicago and Alton Railroad, from 1879 to 1890. He then entered the service of the Illinois Central Railroad Company, and just prior to the opening of the World's Fair was given charge of the station at Sixty-third Street, one of the stations practically at the gate of the Fair grounds. However, he resigned to take advantage of the business opportunities offered by the Fair, and at what is now 1407 Sixty-third Street he opened a lunch room, having one of the first permanent establishments of the kind on that street. From the restaurant business he engaged in the jewelry business, and on account of the confining nature of retail work he took up real estate. He did some building and real estate work in LaGrange, and for twenty years he had his offices at 8 South Dearborn Street. Through all these years he was interested in South Side development, particularly the district along Sixty-third Street from Cottage Grove east, in what is known as Woodlawn.

Finally, in the spring of 1925, Mr. McMinn determined to transfer his headquarters to the Woodlawn section, and in the fall of that year he moved into a building which he especially erected for his purpose at Sixty-third Street and Evans Avenue. This is a two-story building, with his own offices and two stores on the first floor, and offices on the second floor. Sixty-third Street is the dominating commercial and financial center of the South Side, and has grown into a great shopping area, the home of prosperous banks, hotels, business establishments of great variety, magnificent moving picture houses. In 1920, in a period of depression, there were twenty-three vacant stores east of Cottage Grove Avenue. Mr. McMinn was resuming his real estate activities about that time, and within four years he was personally responsible for tenanting all but one or two of these buildings, and also brought about the erection of a number of new places, also making many ninety-nine year leases, securing the S. S. Kresge Company a prominent location and many others.

Mr. McMinn for many years was a well known figure for civic betterment. For four years he was secretary of the Chicago Dry Federation and was a potent factor in the movement, consummated many years ago, for making Hyde Park and the Woodlawn sections of the city dry territory. In later years he continued vigilance in fighting gambling and vice elements in that section of the city. Mr. McMinn is a life member of the Midway Athletic Club, and is a member of Blaney Lodge of Masons.

He married Miss Cora Hartman, of Freeport, Illinois, and they have one daughter, Ida May, wife of Dr. James Gregory. Mr. McMinn and family are members of the Christian Science Church, Chicago, and occupy their own flat building at 7006 Oglesby Avenue, Chicago.

JAMES M. BANDY for a quarter of a century was a figure of more than ordinary prominence in the law and in the public life of Madison County. His home community, which especially esteemed him, was Granite City. Some years before his death his son, Harold J., took up the practice of law there and continued to add honors to the name in the legal profession.

James M. Bandy, who died February 25, 1923, was born in Greene County, Illinois, in 1867, son of Walter and Mary (Courcy) Bandy and grandson of Elijah Bandy and great-grandson of Hugh Bandy. Hugh Bandy died in Greeen County when ninety-eight years of age. The maternal grandfather of James M. Bandy was John Courcy, a Kentucky land and slave owner who about the time of the Civil war moved to Illinois and settled in Greene County.

James M. Bandy was reared on a farm, attended country school and the Roodhouse High School and also a high school at Garden City in western Kansas. For several years he taught country school in Illinois and in 1890 became an employe of the Chicago & Alton Railway Company. For six years he was yardmaster at Roodhouse, and in the meantime applied himself with such diligence to the study of law as to bring about a breakdown in health. In 1897 he was admitted to the Illinois bar, and for one year engaged in practice at Greenfield, following which he located at Granite City. Besides a large general practice he served two years as city attorney, was elected in March, 1910, the first judge of the City Court of Granite City, and in 1912 was the successful democratic candidate for the office of state's attorney. He was also a member of the Board of Education at Granite City, was a member of the Council of Venice, and was vice president of the Madison County Bar Association. He was a democrat and popular in several fraternities, including the Elks.

Judge Bandy married, in 1889, Mae Sullivan, who was born in Greene County, Illinois, in 1869, daughter of Timothy and Mary (Mahoney) Sullivan. Her parents were born in Ireland. Mrs. J. M. Bandy was educated at Carrollton, Illinois, and was a teacher before her marriage. She was the mother of three children: Harold J., Gertrude and Zella. Gertrude graduated valedictorian and youngest member of the class of 1910 of McKinley High School at Granite City, continued her education in music in St. Louis and is the wife of Hubert Ratliff of Dallas, Texas. The other daughter, Miss Zella, is a teacher in the Granite City public schools.

Harold J. Bandy was born at Roodhouse, Illinois, May 24, 1891, and has lived at Granite City since he was ten years of age. He is a graduate of the McKinley High School there, spent three years in the University of Illinois, and graduated in 1912 from the law department of Washington University at St. Louis. While in the university he was a member of the debating team. He was admitted to the bar in 1913, and has since been engaged in practice. He served one year as corporation counsel of Granite City, and is a member of the Tri-City Bar Association. He is an Elk and is active in the democratic party.

He married, in 1916, Edna Pinson, of St. Louis. They have two children: Helen, born in 1917, and James, born in 1919.

CLEMENT STUDEBAKER, JR., whose business activities for some years have made him a resident of Chicago, represents the third generation of one of the most notable families in American industrial history. He is a grandson of the John Studebaker who many years ago at the village of South Bend was proprietor of a country blacksmith shop. That was the acorn from which grew the spreading oak of one of the largest industrial organizations in the country, the Studebaker Corporation. John Studebaker had five sons, best known to fame as the Studebaker Brothers. They had the mechanical genius of their father and also an unrivaled ability as organizers, executives and salesmen, and their genius laid the foundation for the great Studebaker Brothers Manufacturing Company, whose output and service are now practically world wide.

One of these five Studebaker brothers was the late Clement Studebaker of South Bend, Indiana, who died November 27, 1901. He married Ann Milburn, daughter of George Milburn, and member of another distinguished family of South Bend. The ancestors of the Studebaker family were of Dutch origin.

A son of Clement Studebaker, Sr., Clement, Jr., was born at South Bend, August 11, 1871. After the public schools he attended Northwestern University at Evanston, Illinois. In 1891, at the age of twenty, he went to work in the offices of the Studebaker Company in the humble position of bill clerk. From that he was advanced to cashier, and subsequently was elected treasurer of the Studebaker Manufacturing Company. He held that office until the merger and the incorporation of the present company, March 7, 1911, under the title of Studebaker Corporation. He became treasurer and second vice president of the corporation, and on December 9, 1911, was elected first vice president and chairman of the committee of control.

Up to 1914 Mr. Studebaker gave all his energies to the industry founded by the Studebaker Brothers. Since then his interests and activities have taken him into a comparatively new field. He is one of the notable figures in the public utilities of the middle west. On April 16, 1915, he was elected president of the North American Light & Power Company, and became chairman of its Board of Directors July 23, 1920. On May 28, 1923, he was elected president of the Illinois Power & Light Corporation, and on March 19, 1925, became chairman of its finance committee. He was elected chairman of the board of the Illinois Traction Company September 5, 1923, and on May 28, 1924, was elected chairman of the Board, and on November 12, 1924, was made president of the Illinois Traction, Incorporated. He became president of the Missouri Power & Light Company October 18, 1923, and since March 19, 1925, has been chairman of the finance committee of that company. During the years 1901-08 Mr. Studebaker was treasurer of the South Bend Fuel & Gas Company, which company was practically owned by his father's estate.

April 27, 1893, he married Alice Rhawn, of Philadelphia. Her father, the late William H. Rhawn, was former president of the Bankers Association. Mr. and Mrs. Studebaker's two children are Clement Studebaker III, and Esther Studebaker.

WILLIAM C. BLAIR, whose death occurred on the 7th of March, 1926, was a member of the bar of Jefferson County for a period of somewhat more than thirty years, was called upon to serve in various offices of public trust, and long held prestige as one of the strongest and most resourceful criminal lawyers of Illinois. He was a native son of this state and honored it by his character and his large and worthy achievement. He was born at Nashville, Washington County, Illinois, May 24, 1861, a member of a fine family of eleven children born to William and Mary (Crain) Blair, both natives of the State of Missouri, where the former was born at Cape Girardeau, his father, Francis Blair, having been a native of Georgia and a scion of sterling Irish ancestry. Francis Blair removed from Georgia to Missouri and eventually came with his family to Illinois and established his residence in Washington County, where he and his wife passed the remainder of their lives, their old home farm having there been located south of Nashville. William Blair, whose death occurred about 1900, passed the greater part of his life in Illinois, was a skilled stone and brick mason, and as such was for a number of years engaged in the contracting business. In 1872 he removed with his family to Jefferson County, where he reared his children and where he and his wife maintained their home until their deaths, Mrs. Blair having passed away about 1904, and both having been consistent members of the Methodist Episcopal Church. It is possible at this juncture to give a brief record concerning the children: Nancy became the wife of Benjamin Parker and both are deceased; Caroline married James R. Pearcy and both are now deceased; James R., who married Maria Graham, was at one time president of the Chicago, Rock Island & Pacific Railroad, and retired from his office by reason of his impaired health, he having been a man of distinctive initiative and executive ability and one of the prominent railroad men of the country; Sallie Love died when about sixty-eight years of age; William C., of this review, was the next in order of birth; Francis G. and his wife reside in the City of Springfield, where he is serving as Illinois state superintendent of public instruction; Minnie was the wife of Rev. C. R. Phillips, a clergyman of the Methodist Episcopal Church; Thomas L. and George W. died young; and two children died in infancy.

William C. Blair gained his early education in the public schools, and was but eleven years of age when he decided to become a lawyer. In following the course of this ambitious purpose he was compelled to overcome many obstacles. He finally directed his close attention to the study of law, and after passing a year in a law office in Mount Vernon, where he received effective preceptorship, he passed a successful examination and was admitted to the bar of his native state in 1889. He forthwith began the practice of law at Mount Vernon, and it was assured that a young man who had by his own efforts made himself eligible for practice had the courage and ambition that were certain to make for success in the vocation for which he had thus equipped himself. He soon made a record that gave him reputation as a resourceful trial lawyer, and in 1892 he was elected police magistrate, which office he retained four years. He next gave four years of service as state's attorney of Jefferson County, and it was in this connection that he first gained fame as a vigorous and versatile criminal lawyer. He held for eight years the office of master in chancery, and in the meanwhile he gained leadership in the councils and campaign activities of the democratic party in this section of the state. He served on the county committee of his party and also as a member of its state central committee, the while he gained high reputation as a vigorous and convincing campaign orator. In 1906 Mr. Blair was elected to the Illinois Legislature as representative from the Forty-sixth District, and in 1908 he was re-elected by a greatly increased majority, he having become the leader of the democratic contingent in the House of Representatives and having wielded much influence in the promotion of wise and constructive legislation. After his retirement from the Legislature Mr. Blair served as city attorney of Mount Vernon, and in 1924 he was again elected police magistrate, of which judicial office he was the incumbent at the time of his death. As a criminal lawyer of distinctive ability Mr. Blair appeared in many important cases in most of the counties of Illinois, and at all times honesty and fearlessness marked his professional stewardship.

Mr. Blair was affiliated with the Independent Order of Odd Fellows, the Knights of Pythias, the Fraternal Order of Eagles, the Court of Honor, and the Modern Woodmen of America. He was an active member of the Methodist Episcopal Church, as is also his wife.

December 24, 1883, marked the marriage of Mr. Blair and Miss Laura E. Johnson, daughter of the late Leander C. and Martha (Piper) Johnson, the former of whom was born in Indiana, a son of John T. and Rachel (Prather) Johnson, Leander C. Johnson having been a pioneer minister in Illinois, and his wife's father having been the first sheriff of Jefferson County, this state. Mrs. Blair is a member of a family of six children, all daughters; Ida May, eldest of the number, became the wife of Angus Moss, and the mother of seven children, she being now deceased; Mrs. Blair was the next in order of birth; Eva married C. K. Etta; Mary became the wife of John H. Burns, and their only child is Clyde Burns; Ruth Menzer is the widow of Frank Menzer; Pet is the widow of Arthur Bateman, and she and her one child reside in Springfield, Illinois. In conclusion is entered record concerning the children of Mr. and Mrs. Blair: Ethel May was the wife of George H. Stein, who was engaged in the practice of law in the City of St. Louis, Missouri, and they had two children, Margaret M. and Mary K. Mary John is the wife of Russell R. Clark and their one child is a son Francis Blair. Mr. Clark is with the State Board for Vocational Education. Katherine L. is the wife of Thomas Kelley, who formerly served as athletic instructor and football coach at various colleges in Missouri, Alabama, Kentucky, Pennsylvania and other states, and who is now with the Johnson-Endicott Shoe Company. Mr. and Mrs. Kelley reside at Henderson, Kentucky, and their two children are Caroline and Katherine. William Lee married Sylvia Morse, and their one child is William Lee, Jr. Albert Watson, the next younger son, married Kathryn Marvin, whose father was president of a bank at Urbana, Ohio, and they have one child, Katherine Ann. Albert W. Blair, a lawyer by profession, volunteered for World war service in May, 1917, shortly after the nation entered the great conflict. He entered the Training Camp at Fort Benjamin Harrison, Indianapolis, Indiana, where he was commissioned captain. He now resides at Fort Wayne, Indiana, where he is connected with the law firm of Yaples & Teeters.

HON. JOSEPH SABATH was appointed to the Superior Court bench of Cook County in 1916. Previous to that time he had for six years been judge of the Municipal Court. For fifteen years it has been his business to discern the actions and purposes of men, and it is generally recognized by practitioners and litigants that no one on the local bench is better

informed on criminal procedure or inspires greater confidence in the prompt and impartial administration of justice than he.

Judge Sabath was born at Zabon, Bohemia, March 2, 1870, and is a son of Joachim and Barbara (Eisenchimel) Sabath, natives of Bohemia, who spent their last years in Chicago. The father, born in 1815, died in 1893, while the mother, born in 1835, survived her husband until 1918. They were the parents of twelve children of whom Joseph was the fourth in order of birth. He acquired his early education in the public schools of his native land, including the high school at Pilsen, and following this was brought to the United States and settled at Chicago. Having decided upon a career in the law, after some preparation he entered the Chicago College of Law, Lake Forest University, and was graduated therefrom June 1, 1897, receiving the degree of Bachelor of Laws. He was admitted to the bar in the same year and immediately engaged in the practice of his profession. By industry, ability and fidelity to the interests of his clients he soon built up a gratifyingly large practice, to which he devoted himself unsparingly during the following years. The success which he gained as a practitioner soon came to the attention of the public, who recognized in him good judicial timber, and in 1910 he ascended the bench as a judge of the Municipal Court. In that capacity he served until July, 1916, when he was appointed to complete an unexpired term as a judge of the Superior Court of Cook County by Governor Edward F. Dunne, and elected to the full term in November, 1916. In June, 1922, the people placed the seal of approval on his service by reelecting him. With all of his years of experience with the delinquent element of society, while it has sharpened his insight of the faults and guile of mankind, Judge Sabath has preserved and constantly manifests a fairness in dealing with litigants that makes him one of the most esteemed judges in Cook County. His unfailing common sense saves him from the pedantry of law, and having been a close and careful student, under the impetus of his own determination he has become fully and practically equipped to meet any emergency within the scope of his judicial duties.

Judge Sabath has always tried in his court to reconcile parties applying for divorces where he figured that the causes leading to such applications were not vital and that by a spirit of mutual concession a divorce would not be necessary. In this effort he has been greatly successful and has won the gratitude of a large number of claimants. He is the author of a play, "Trial Divorce," which will shortly be produced.

Judge Sabath is a member of the Lawyers Association of Illinois, the Illinois Bar Association, the American Bar Association, the Law Institute, the Royal Legion of America, the Covent Club, the Press Club, the Idlewild Country Club and the B'nai B'rith; a member of all Masonic orders up to the thirty-second degree and of the Order of the Eastern Star; a life member of Chicago Lodge No. 4, B. P. O. Elks, and a member and an ex-president of the Mystic Golf Association. He is now serving his seventh term as president of the American Theatrical Hospital Association. In politics he is a democrat.

Judge Sabath was united in marriage with Miss Regina Mayer, who was born in Heidelburg, Germany, and to this union there have been born three children: Albert, who married Olive Oberndorf and has two children; Stella, who married Harry S. Grollman and has two children; and Milton, who married Dorothy Johnson and has one child.

ABNER W. FOREMAN, M. D. Of the old-time characters perhaps none has been more justly celebrated than the country doctor. An unusually fine example of the old country doctor, a man of education, friend to all, confidant of every family, respected and honored by his years of usefulness, was the late Dr. A. W. Foreman of White Hall. Doctor Foreman when he died, December 31, 1925, had reached the great age of eighty-five years, nine months, six days. He had been retired from the practice of medicine fifteen years, but had given half a century or more to the work of his profession.

He was born in Warren County, Indiana, March 25, 1840, son of David and Elizabeth (Purcell) Foreman. Each of his parents had been married before, and Doctor Foreman was the last survivor of the nineteen children of his parents. It is said that fourteen of them lived to be seventy years old or more. David Foreman was descended from a Saxon ancestor who came over with the Baltimore colony. His wife, Elizabeth Purcell Watson, had seven children by her first marriage, and she and David Foreman had also seven children.

In the fall of the year after Abner W. Foreman was born his parents removed to Pike County, Illinois, and settled in Newberg Township, where he was reared and where he attended an old time subscription school. His father built the schoolhouse which he attended. Later he himself taught in that school. He began the study of medicine with Dr. George C. Pitzer, a local doctor, and continued it until February 18, 1865, when he enlisted in Company D of the Seventh Illinois Infantry under Captain Hubbard and Major E. S. Johnson. He was detailed for duty as captain's clerk and received his honorable discharge at Louisville July 9, 1865. In after years he became a prominent worker in the Grand Army of the Republic, serving as commander of Culver Post at White Hall, and attended many state and national encampments.

While reading medical books Doctor Foreman had the advantage of experience with a busy country doctor, riding about with him and also compounding his medicine. In this way he acquired a knowledge of the practical duties of a medical man and also of a pharmacist. He read medicine at Detroit in Pike County, and succeeded his preceptor as village doctor there. Subsequently he attended the Eclectic School of Medicine of Cincinnati, Ohio. Doctor Foreman after several years work at Detroit moved to White Hall on July 5, 1869, and that date began his notable career of service as a physician in town and country. For years and years he went about attending calls regardless of weather, bad roads and other conditions, and in spite of his strenuous service he seemed to bear a charmed life, being practically immune to the various epidemics that from time to time visited the locality. Even after he retired he was frequently called upon for consultation. He owned one of the largest private libraries in Greene County and was probably one of the best read men on scientific subjects at White Hall. He was also interested in the affairs of the community, serving on the City Council at the time the water system was installed, on the Board of Education, and was one of the founders of the old White Hall Library Association. He was a republican and a member of the Modern Woodmen of America.

Doctor Foreman married in Pike County, April 5, 1859, Elizabeth Rebecca Hayden. Of the eleven children born to their marriage four died in infancy, and the son Dr. Claude Barnard died November 27, 1916. The children who survived their father were: Dora, wife of Dr. H. W. Hand, of San Diego, California; Grant Foreman, an attorney at Muskogee, Oklahoma; Dr. Ernest J., of Trinidad, Colorado; Lois, wife of C. E. Ellis, of California; Bertha, wife of Dr. W. L. Ellis, of San Diego, California; and Herbert S., an attorney at Los Angeles. The mother of these children died November 21, 1896. On January 11, 1898, Doctor Foreman married Miss Adelaide Ross, who survives him. Their only daughter, Adelaide, is the wife of Charles G. Purl, of Carrollton. Mrs. Foreman was born at White Hall and is a daughter of Simeon Ross. Simeon Ross was one of the prominent characters of Greene County for many years. He came from the East, traveling from Pittsburgh by the Ohio and up the Mississippi and Illinois rivers to Bedford. He located on a farm near White Hall, but soon entered business and devoted many years to merchandising, investing in land and becoming one of the largest land owners in Greene County. The Ross family had the first spring wagon in the vicinity of White Hall, and though it was put to almost constant use by members of the Ross family and neighbors, it lasted long and well. Simeon Ross was a man of ordinary height and build, and through all the years of his active career was seldom absent from his accustomed place of business. Doctor Foreman when not engaged in practice was always busy at home with his family and flowers.

JOHN ALLEN MCGEE, M. D. Known all over Cass County as a skilled and able physician and surgeon, Dr. John Allen McGee is enjoying a large practice in his neighborhood, and is recognized as one of the leading citizens of Virginia. He was born near Chrisman, Edgar County, Illinois, April 26, 1873, a son of John Wesley McGee, and grandson of William and Susan (Dawson) McGee, both of whom were born and reared near Londonderry, Ireland. Some time after their marriage the grandparents immigrated to the United States and settled near Roanoke, Virginia. From that locality they subsequently migrated to Ohio, where William McGee continued his lumbering, and where he was killed in an accident, a tree he was felling falling on him. At the time of his death he was forty-five years old. He and his wife had the following children: John, Elisha, Thomas, Samuel, Sarah and another daughter. All the children married, and the daughters lived and died in Wabash County, Indiana.

John Wesley McGee was born near Roanoke, Virginia, October 19, 1827, and when he was two years old his parents moved to the vicinity of Sandusky, Ohio, where he was reared and educated. Coming to Illinois in young manhood, he entered land from the government near Chrisman, Edgar County, and there he died May 21, 1897, having been a farmer all his life, and a successful man of affairs He was an important part of the community life, represented his locality in county matters as supervisor of his township, and he was a justice of the peace for many years. Long identified through membership with the Methodist Episcopal Church, in religious work he was a leader in it and Sunday School activities, and served the local church as steward. During the war between the states he served in an Edgar County company for a short time, but was discharged on account of disability incurred in service along the Mississippi River.

John Wesley McGee married Nancy A. Byram, a daughter of William and Mary (Clark) Byram, the latter of whom was a direct descendant of James Clark of Virginia, of whom Gen. George Rogers Clark was also a descendant. Mrs. McGee was born in Ross County, Ohio, October 26, 1836, and died August 6, 1924, long outliving her husband. Their children were as follows: Doctor McGee, whose name heads this review; Florence, who died in childhood; Henry Arthur, who resides at Terre Haute, Indiana; and Odis Wesley, who is a resident of Dana, Indiana.

Growing to manhood amid the rural surroundings of his father's farm, Doctor McGee first attended the district schools, and later the Chrisman High School, entering the latter at the age of sixteen years. Still later he was a student of the Vermilion Grove Academy, after which he entered Hahnemann Medical College, Chicago, and was graduated therefrom in 1896, with the degree of Doctor of Medicine.

Following his graduation Doctor McGee established himself in a general practice at Virginia, where he has since remained. While he is not interested in politics save as a voter of the republican ballot he has served on the local school board, and for some years was city physician of Virginia. Made a Mason in Virginia Lodge No. 544, A. F. and A. M., in 1899, he is a past master of it, and he belongs to Beardstown Chapter, R. A. M. Doctor McGee is also a member of the local lodge of the Knights of Pythias, of which he is a past chancellor commander, and he belongs to the Cass County Medical Society, the Illinois State Medical Society, the American Medical Association, the Illinois State Historical Society, and he served the local medical society as secretary for some time. He is a past commander of Walter Reed Post No. 258, American Legion, is county commander of the Legion, and annually is sent to the state conventions of the Legion. For the past twenty-five years Doctor McGee has been connected with Saint John's Hospital, Springfield, and during the period he has been in practice has taken up considerable post-graduate work along special lines at different times.

In June, 1917, Doctor McGee was commissioned a lieutenant of the Medical Corps of the United States Army, in which he had enlisted, and was first sent to Camp Fort Oglethorpe, Georgia, General Hospital No. 14. While there he was transferred by special order to Chattanooga, Tennessee, during the influenza epidemic, but subsequently was returned to Fort Oglethorpe, where he was stationed at the time of his honorable discharge following the signing of the armistice. Returning to Virginia, he resumed his practice. Doctor McGee was appointed field officer in the United States Public Health Service, continuing in it and with the United States Veterans Bureau, with which it was merged. On July 24, 1924, he was commissioned captain in the Officers Reserve Corps and is still holding that rank.

Doctor McGee married Alice E. Constans at Ridge Farm, Illinois. She was born at Paris, Illinois, and was a daughter of Fred and Mary (Cook) Constans, the former of whom was of French origin, while the latter came of Dutch stock, and both were born in Pennsylvania. By trade a cabinet-maker, Fred Constans spent the last years of his life at Ridge Farm, and there he is buried. He and his wife had three daughters and two sons, all of whom are living except Mrs. McGee, who died July 21, 1924. She was reared and educated in Illinois, attending the public schools of Paris and Farm Ridge, and was a lovely Christian lady of many virtues, a consistent member of the Presbyterian Church. During the late war she was very active in knitting for the soldiers, and she also took a deep interest in her work in connection with the Virginia Woman's Club. Doctor and Mrs. McGee had four children born to their marriage. A. Donovan McGee was graduated from the Virginia High School, and then volunteered for service during the World war. In 1917 he was commissioned a first lieutenant, Fort Benjamin Harrison, and went overseas as adjutant of the Three Hundred and Thirty-fifth Infantry, Eighty-ninth Division, and was promoted to the rank of captain. Returning to the United States after the close of the war, he was honorably discharged, located in Columbus, Ohio, and is now a wholesale furniture buyer with the Carlyle Company. He married Miss Lillian Flanagan, and they have two children, Robert Allen and Eiline Alice. Florence, the second child of Doctor and Mrs. McGee, is a graduate of the Virginia High School and of Blackburn University, Carlinville, Illinois. Lela Irene, the third of the family, is also a graduate of the local high school and Blackburn University, and she is the wife of Charles Montgomery, of Petersburg. Lillian, who is the youngest, went through the Virginia public schools, married Harry C. Chittick, of Springfield, and they have a daughter, Marjorie Ellen.

PAUL WILLIAM ZERWEKH. Admitted to the bar in 1916 and locating at Alton, Mr. Zerwekh was with the Aviation Corps for about a year of the World war, and has since achieved a reputation as a sound and able lawyer and man diligent and efficient in public affairs.

He was born at Pekin, Illinois, November 26, 1892, son of William G. and Wilhelmina (Zerweck) Zerwekh. His parents were also born in Illinois, his father at Peoria and his mother at Lebanon, and she is still living, while the father is deceased. Paul was the only son. His sister is Elizabeth.

When a child Paul W. Zerwekh was brought to Alton by his parents, was reared in that city and educated in the public schools. For six months he continued his higher education in the University of Missouri at Columbia, and then took the full four year course in the law department of the University of Michigan at Ann Arbor, where he was graduated with the LL. B. degree. On December 13, 1916, he was admitted to the bar, and set out at once to make his professional name known in his home city. In the spring of the following year, 1917, he was elected city attorney, and he was subsequently reelected and filled the office four years, being the last city attorney chosen by popular vote, that office now being an appointive one.

In the meantime, in December, 1917, he enlisted, was trained in the air service, and in July, 1918, was commissioned a second lieutenant. He received his honorable discharge in January, 1919. While in the army he was located at various flying fields in Texas, and had completed all the training and was thoroughly qualified for duty as an air pilot when the armistice was signed. After his discharge he was returned home and resumed his special duties and his private practice, and in 1921 became assistant state's attorney of Madison County. In June of 1926 he moved to Springfield to continue at that place in the general practice of law. Mr. Zerwekh is a member of the American Legion and the 40 Hommes et 8 Chevaux, and during 1924-25 was State Treasurer of the 40 and 8. He is an active worker in the republican party. On November 14, 1922, he married Miss Helen Holl, of Alton.

DE WITT W. BUCHANAN, a mechanical engineer by training and profession, has for many years been identified with coal mining operations and is one of the leading coal operators of Illinois, being president of the Old Ben Coal Corporation and an official in a number of other industries.

Mr. Buchanan is a native of Chicago, where he was born May 16, 1876, son of Milford De Witt and Sophia (Wheeler) Buchanan. His father was born at Fairfield in Herkimer County, New York, April 10, 1835, and died December 2, 1905. His mother was born at Niles, Michigan, December 27, 1839, and is still living. His parents were married October 10, 1861, and their five children were: Gordon, Mary C., Margaret and Genevieve, twins, and De Witt W.

Milford D. Buchanan was for many years a well known figure in banking and other lines of business in Chicago and Illinois. He was educated in public and private schools and an academy at Utica, New York; clerked for a time in the office of General Wilkersons at Utica, and at the age of sixteen was appointed agent for the Rome, Watertown and Ogdensburg Railway at Rome, New York. Subsequently he became teller of the Oneida County National Bank at Rome. In 1857 he went West to Iowa and engaged in locating soldier's land warrants, with headquarters at Fort Dodge and later at Des Moines, where he operated a general mercantile business. For several years he was in Chicago associated with Chapin & Wheeler, private bankers, and at Lincoln, Nebraska, he organized a state bank for private parties and acted as its cashier. After again returning to Chicago, he became cashier of the Commercial National Bank and was one of the organizers of that institution. He was also interested in and cashier of the Manufacturers National Bank and subsequently helped organize the Commercial Loan Bank, of which he became vice president. He was also interested in coal mining in Grundy County, Illinois.

De Witt W. Buchanan was liberally educated, attending the Harvard and University schools at Chicago, and completed his technical education at Purdue University, Lafayette, Indiana, graduating in 1898 with the degree Mechanical Engineer. Following his graduation he was with the engineering department of the Illinois Central Railway at the Burnside shops during 1898-99 and for a time was in the general offices as draftsman. He resigned his position with the railroad to enter the coal mining business with the Wilmington Star Mining Company, becoming its secretary and treasurer. He was associated with his father in organizing the Bituminous Coal Washing Company and became secretary and treasurer. He was secretary and treasurer and one of the organizers of the Old Ben Coal Corporation and since 1917 has been president of the corporation, with mines in Franklin County. It is one of the largest of the Southern Illinois mining companies.

Mr. Buchanan is a member of the Union League Club and the Chicago Athletic Club, the South Shore Country Club, the Flossmoor Country Club, Knowlwood Country Club and belongs to the Oconomowoc Lake Club and Oconomowoc Country Club in Wisconsin, where he maintains his summer home. He is a director of the National Bank of the Republic of Chicago and in the line of his profession is a member of the Western Association of Engineers, the American Society of Mining and Metallurgical Engineers and is a republican in politics. His recreations are yachting and hunting.

Mr. Buchanan married, April 12. 1905, Miss Grace G. Follansbee, who died July 19, 1906. On November 16, 1915, he married Helen S. Stoppenbach, of Jeffersons, Wisconsin. There are two children: De Witt, Jr., and Barbara Anna.

ALEXANDER D. CULLINANE. Belonging as he does to one of the old and honored families of Mason County, Alexander D. Cullinane, of Havana, is sustaining its prestige and is rendering a most efficient service to his community in the office of master-in-chancery, as well as representative for a dozen or more reliable insurance companies. He was born at Havana, December 3, 1871, a son of Daniel Cullinane.

Daniel Cullinane was born at Scarte Glenn, Ireland, from whence he came to the United States in company with some of his neighbors, but following his parents who had already immigrated to this country and settled in Knox County, Illinois. Later removal was made to Pekin, Illinois. While still a young man he located at Havana, and his brother Dennis also became a resident of this locality, the two commencing their connection with this community in 1865. With but an ordinary education Daniel Cullinane began work at Havana as a teamster, but, possessing shrewdness and good judgment above the ordinary, it was not long before he began trading in stocks, and later he operated extensively in real estate, both city and rural. His success in these lines brought him wealth, and when he died he was one of the rich men of Mason County. Politics never attracted him, although he gave the democratic party his support at elections.

In 1869 Daniel Cullinane married at Havana, Jennie Stuart, a daughter of Alexander Stuart, who also came to this country from Ireland, and settled at Havana, where Mrs. Cullinane was born July 4, 1850, he coming here as a mate on a boat running on the Illinois River. He and his brother quarried the stone to lay the foundation of his home at Stuart's Landing, Havana, Illinois, where he continued to live until 1887, when he moved to 125 North Broadway, Havana, where he died at the age of eighty-two years. For many years he was actively engaged in merchandising. His wife belonged to the Gardner family, pioneers of Fulton County, and she is buried in the Gardner Cemetery in her native county. Mrs. Cullinane died March 1, 1922, having survived her husband but a few months, as he passed away December 27, 1921. The children born to them who reached maturity were: Alexander D., whose name heads this review; Margaret, who lives with him at Havana; Wilson, who died unmarried August 6, 1923; and Stuart, who died in young manhood, August 6, 1899.

Alexander D. Cullinane was reared at Havana, where his life has been spent, and he is naturally attached to it and interested in its progress. Its schools gave him his education, and he taught in the rural regions of Mason County for some year, preparing for his calling by a course in Illinois College, Jacksonville. The Quiver school was the last one in which he taught, for he left the schoolroom to engage in the insurance business, in which he has been very successful. His insurance business is confined to fire risks. For some years he has acceptably filled the office of mastery-in-chancery, and he has held some of the local offices, including that of alderman for eight years, and while a member of the City Council he served on the important finance committee of that body as its chairman. Casting his first presidential ballot for William Jennings Bryan, Mr. Cullinane has continued his support of democratic candidates in the national campaigns ever since, and has been chairman of the Mason County Central Committee of his party for several terms. Oftentimes sent to the Democratic State Conventions, he was a delegate to the one which

Adam Meisinger

nominated Judge Dunne for governor, and was active in his campaign. Upon several occasions he has been the alternate delegate to national conventions of his party, including the historic one at Baltimore, Maryland, in 1912, which nominated Woodrow Wilson, but has never attended any of them. In addition to his other interests he has been vice president of the Havana National Bank for many years, and prior to his election to that office he was on its board of directors. During the World war he was assistant food administrator for Mason County, was active in the work of raising war funds, helping in organizing the county for that purpose, and in carrying on the various drives, particularly the ones in behalf of the Red Cross. While he belongs to the Knights of Pythias, he is not active in that fraternity. Mr. Cullinane is unmarried. In everything he has undertaken he has proved his worth as a man and good citizen, and has fairly earned his present high standing in his community.

GEORGE A. FOX, executive secretary of the Illinois Agricultural Association, is one of the solid citizens of DeKalb County whose work in behalf of the agriculturists of Illinois is of a most constructive character, and productive of much improvement in methods of farming and advancement in the value of farm lands. He was born in Miami County, Ohio, on his father's farm, and he was reared on a farm, and has always been connected with the agricultural industry.

When he was thirteen years old his parents moved to Barry County, Michigan, where George A. Fox attended the public schools and later the University of Michigan at Ann Arbor, from which he was graduated in 1905. Coming then to Chicago, Mr. Fox entered the Law School of Northwestern University, and was graduated therefrom in 1907, with the degree of Bachelor of Laws, but did not take up the practice of law. Instead he went to Sycamore, DeKalb County, Illinois, where he began farming, and there he has continued to maintain his residence, although his business location is Chicago. Since 1918 he has been connected officially with the Illinois Agricultural Association, first as treasurer, and since 1922 as executive secretary.

The Illinois Agricultural Association is a highly organized and thoroughly efficient business concern carried on to advance the interests of all the farmers of Illinois. It has a trained, efficient staff of experts for each branch of its activities, which includes the problems of marketing, transportation, taxation, legislation and innumerable other phases that directly affect the welfare and prosperity of the farmer. It is said to be the best organized and most efficient state organization of farmers in the country, and is officered and directed by the best brains among the agricultural interests of the state.

In 1912 the first county farm bureaus were organized in Illinois, and within a comparatively short period most of the counties were thus organized. In 1916 representatives of the various county farm bureaus met for the purpose of setting up a state organization. An effective organization, however, was not achieved until 1917, when a representative body of farmers from all over the state met at Peoria and organized the present Illinois Agricultural Association, adopting its present constitution and bylaws, providing for cooperation between the farm bureaus and the state organization. It also provided a substantial method for financing both the farm bureaus and the state organization.

ADAM MEISINGER. A man can have no more valuable heritage than that of a good name or the privilege of tracing back through a line of honorable ancestors. The Meisinger family, of which Adam Meisinger, of Sand Prairie Township, is a worthy and esteemed representative, has been located in Tazewell County for more than three-quarters of a century, during which time it has contributed many men of more than local note to agricultural pursuits, banking, business, the professions and the public and political arena. Mr. Meisinger in a long and useful career has fully lived up to the family traditions for steadfastness of purpose, fidelity to duty and integrity in business affairs, as well as in good citizenship.

Mr. Meisinger was born on a farm in Sand Prairie Township, Tazewell County, on the farm where he now lives, January 11, 1870, and is a son of J. George and Mary (Orth) Meisinger. His paternal grandfather was Balz Meisinger, who was born in Hesse-Darmstadt, Germany, and was there reared, educated and married. When he came to the United States he brought with him his wife and six children, and his first settlement, about 1848, was near Belleville, Illinois. There, however, he remained only a week or two, subsequently moving to Tazewell County, where he took up his residence on a farm located about one and one-half miles east of the present residence of his grandson, Adam Meisinger. A man of sturdy worth and sound integrity, Balz Meisinger soon made himself felt as a force in his community, where he was not only successful as an agriculturist, but won and held the respect and esteem of his fellow-citizens. He lived beyond the Psalmist's "three-score-and-ten" years and is buried in the old Sand Prairie Cemetery. His widow survived him for some years, being an octogenarian at the time of her demise and was laid to rest at his side. They were the parents of the following children: J. George, the father of Adam; Maggie, who died as the wife of Leonard Orth and left a daughter, who died as Mrs. Landes. Elizabeth, who married George Weyrich and died in the Sand Prairie locality: Catherine, who married Adam Weyrich and lived out her life in Tazewell County; Lizzie, who married Jacob Hoerr and resides at Pekin, Illinois; Eva, who married George Meisinger and resides in Nebraska; and Anna, who married another George Meisinger and resides in the same Nebraska town.

J. George Meisinger was born in Germany and was a child of six years when he was brought to the United States. He received only a limited education in the primitive schools of his day in Tazewell County, but was a man of intelligence who added to his education in later years through study, reading and observation. He spent his entire life in the pursuits of the soil, and possessing industry and native ability made a success of his operations so that he became one of the substantial men of his community. Mr. Meisinger located where his son now lives when he was a youth and there rounded out an honorable and useful career, meriting and winning the respect and confidence of those among whom he lived and labored. His death occurred March 10, 1924. During his life Mr. Meisinger took an interested and helpful part in public affairs, and served his township as road commissioner and his district as director of the school board. As a Lutheran he was one of the church officers late in life, and in politics he was always a democrat. He was almost a straight grain farmer, raising only such stock as the farm needed. In Tazewell County Mr. Meisinger was united in marriage with Miss Mary Orth, a daughter of Peter Orth, who was born in Hesse-Darmstadt, whence he immigrated to Canada and there spent the rest of his life. Mrs. Meisinger, who came to the United States with an uncle, was the only one of the family to remain here. She died in May, 1891, when she was forty-six years of age. She and her husband were the parents of the following children: Eva, who died as Mrs. Leonard Vetter and left four children: Adam, of this review; Leonard, a farmer of Sand Prairie Township, located near his brother, Adam; and Mary, who married Leonard Vetter and lives in Sand Prairie Township.

Adam Meisinger was reared in the community in which he now lives and received a limited education in the rural schools. The home in which he was born now forms a part of the residence which now shelters his own family, and he has spent his life, with the exception of two years, right at this location. His own program as a farmer has been the same as was that of his father, and in the growing of grain on his well-cultivated 180 acres, and the raising of live stock, he has met with the kind of success that results from good management and a thorough knowledge of farming conditions and methods. Mr. Meisinger has discharged fully and well the duties of citizenship, and for a quarter of a century has been a member of the board of school directors of the same school which he attended in boyhood. In politics a democrat, he takes an interest in public affairs, while his religious relationship is with Sand Prairie Lutheran Church, of which he is a member of the Board of Trustees.

On March 21, 1895, in Sand Prairie Township, Mr. Meisinger married Miss Mathilda Proehl, a daughter of Louis Proehl, a review of whose career will be found in the sketch of the latter's son, John A. Proehl, elsewhere in this work. Mrs. Meisinger was born at Pekin, Illinois, December 26, 1871, and she and her husband became the parents of the following children: Ida, the wife of Harry Weyrich, of Pierce County, Nebraska, who has two children, Harold and Alvin; Louis, an agriculturist of Cincinnati Township, Tazewell County, who married Emma Ripper and has two children, Melvin and Elaine; Dora, who married George Timke, of Spring Lake Township, Tazewell County, and has a daughter, Lorena; and Louisa Pauline, Mary and Gertrude, who reside with their parents. Theodore and Lorene are deceased.

RICHARD J. LYONS grew up in the very heart of the great city of Chicago, was born on the old West Side in the vicinity of Blue Island Avenue and West Eleventh Street, and was a typical boy of the loop, at the age of ten beginning work as a messenger for the Postal Telegraph Company. His education was acquired in public schools in intervals after and between the work that earned him a living. It was an environment calculated to result in the survival of the fittest, and gave him at an early age a resourcefulness and ability to solve problems arising from constant contact with men and situations such as no college education could confer.

From messenger boy he became a telegraph operator for the Postal, and later was promoted to branch manager of one of the company's Chicago offices. From this position he went as salesman for The Johns-Manville Corporation, manufacturers of asbestos roofing products. At the age of twenty-one he had reached the position of sales manager for the territory comprising the North Shore district of Illinois.

From the city he moved, in 1918, to what was then a rural village some forty miles from the center of Chicago. The name of this village was Area, located in Lake County. There he started a grocery business, his personal capital being only thirty dollars. Not long afterwards the site of Area and much of the surrounding country was acquired by the Catholic Church and dedicated as the site of a great Arch Diocese center, and subsequently the name was changed to Mundelein in honor of the Catholic Cardinal. Mr. Lyons rapidly built up a business until its annual volume represented $90,000 a year. From this he retired in 1925 to engage in the real estate business with John H. Rouse at Mundelein, under the firm name of Lyons & Rouse. Through his foresight and acumen Mr. Lyons has taken full advantage of the marvelous increases in land values in the Mundelein section. The firm has sold about $3,000,000 worth of property in the Mundelein district in about eleven months. This has been the scene of perhaps the most remarkable development in real estate in the Chicago metropolitan district. To a large extent this has been due to the activities of the Catholic Church in building up some of its important institutions at Mundelein and to Mr. Samuel Insull's great development plans. In 1926 occurred the Eucharistic Congress, the greatest event of its kind in the history of the Middle West. Attending this Congress were the highest church dignitaries from all over the world, together with hundreds of thousands of devout Catholics.

Mr. Lyons at the age of thirty, when most men are just getting started in their careers, is reputed to possess a comfortable fortune. He was born in 1895, son of Thomas J. and Mary Ellen (Welch) Lyons. His father is deceased and his mother now resides at Hollywood, California. Richard J. Lyons has been prominent in all civic enterprises and philanthropic movements in the Mundelein-Liberty-

Mathilda A. Meisinger

ville region. In April, 1926, he was elected a member of the Mundelein Village Board. He served on two prominent committees in connection with the Eucharistic Congress, the Parking Committee and the General Activities Committee. He is vice president of the Lake County Real Estate Board. He is a precinct committeeman in the Lake County organization of the republican party, is a member of the Hamilton Club of Chicago, the B. P. O. Elks and the A. F. and A. M., Lodge No. 492, Libertyville, Illinois.

Mr. Lyons married Miss Blanch Mitchell, of Lake County. They have two children, Lucile Mae and Richard.

CHARLES HENRY REYNOLDS, president of the North Shore Bond and Mortgage Company of Evanston, is a son of the late Bryson James Reynolds, and both father and son were intimately identified for a number of years with the early development of one of the most remarkable commercial organizations of the age, the United Cigar Stores Company.

In the late '80s the Reynolds family moved from Chicago to Grand Rapids, Michigan, where Bryson James Reynolds became a tobacco dealer. Some time later George Whalen, proprietor of a small cigar stand in a hotel at Syracuse, New York, conceived the idea of establishing a chain of cigar stores. The chain idea in merchandising was then novel and had very few successful examples. George Whalen in investigating the possibilities and seeking backing and cooperation visited Grand Rapids, and with Bryson James Reynolds further elaborated his plan. Together they made many of the plans entering into the very foundation of what since became the nation-wide chain of United Cigar Stores.

Charles Henry Reynolds was born at Chicago in 1881, and was a boy when his parents moved to Grand Rapids. His mother, Katherine Reynolds, is still living. Charles Henry Reynolds first attended public school in Grand Rapids and then attended the University of Michigan and was graduated in 1900 with the degree of Ph. B. and LL. B. and admitted to the practice of law in Michigan the same year. He then went into partnership with his father and for several years acted as a salesman and sales manager in and out of Chicago for the United Cigar Stores Company. His father held the position of executive vice president and director in this company for the territory embracing most of the Mississippi Valley. In 1902 the Reynolds family returned to Chicago from Grand Rapids.

Charles Henry Reynolds since 1904 has been a resident of Evanston, and after retiring from the tobacco business he founded, in January, 1925, at Evanston, the North Shore Bond & Mortgage Company, of which he is president. This is a successful and expanding house dealing largely in mortgages. As a financier Mr. Reynolds is repeating the success he made in the cigar business. He is also vice president of the Commercial Trust & Savings Bank of Evanston and is an active and public-spirited participant in the civic and social affairs of that city. He is a member of the Evanston Rotary Club, Evanston Chamber of Commerce, Evanston Club and a vestryman of St. Luke's Episcopal Church. He is a member of Delta Upsilon fraternity and DeWitt Clinton Consistory of the Masonic order, DeMolay Commandery, K. T., Grand Rapids, Michigan, and Saladin Temple, A. A. O. N. M. S., also Evanston Lodge, B. P. O. E.

Mr. Reynolds married Miss Louise Freeman, of Grand Rapids, Michigan. Their family of five children are named Bryson James II, Katherine, Richard Freeman, William Graham and Robert David. They reside at 1426 Hinman Avenue.

LAFAYETTE E. TALBOTT. New eras of improvement have been inaugurated through the mental alertness, energy and determination of the business men of today whose standing is conspicuously high, for, with competition so strenuous, none but the efficient and capable can aspire to success. These men have risen to their present positions along no royal road to fortune, but rather because of constructive thinking and aggressive action, which is gaining for Illinois an extraordinary amount of the country's business. One of the men of the present stirring generation whose interests are heavy and whose territory is wide is Lafayette E. Talbott, manager of the Grangers Elevator Company at Manito, a real estate dealer of some years of experience, and an agriculturist who is operating 1,000 acres of valuable land in Mason County.

Mr. Talbott was born October 11, 1883, at Manito, Illinois, and is a son of O. L. and Clara E. (Willard) Talbott. The family traces its ancestry back for a number of generations in this country, its early residents being members of the community of Talbott County, Maryland, which was doubtless named for some branch of the same family which spelled the name in that manner. The great-grandfather of Mr. Talbott was born in that county, but in young manhood went to Kentucky and later to Indiana, where he established a home and engaged in agricultural pursuits, clearing a farm from the wilderness and developing a productive property, on which he passed the remainder of a long and useful life. His son, John B. Talbott, the grandfather of Lafayette E. Talbott, was born in Indiana, where as a young man he learned the trade of steam mill engineer, a vocation to which he devoted practically his entire life. He came to Illinois in 1862, during the Civil war, and soon thereafter enlisted in Company G, Eighty-fifth Regiment, Illinois Volunteer Infantry, with which he served until the close of the great struggle between the North and the South, establishing a splendid record for bravery and fidelity to duty. At the close of hostilities he returned to his Illinois home and resumed his calling, in which he continued to be engaged until his death at Manito during the '90s. He was a man of real worth and had the confidence of his associates and the esteem of a wide circle of friends. John B. Talbott married Catherine McIntosh, who preceded him in death in the '80s, and they became the parents of the following children: Coleman B., who became a successful agriculturist of the Manito locality; James M., also a cultivator of the soil in the vicinity of Manito; Othnial L., the father of Lafayette E.; Rose, the widow of William Sterrett, of Manito;

Olive, the widow of Erastus Stufflebean, of Easton, Illinois; and Jeanette, the wife of Philip Fox, a ranchman of Clayton, New Mexico.

Othnial L. Talbott was born at Terre Haute, Indiana, September 9, 1859, and was three years of age when brought by his parents to Manito, Illinois. Here he grew to manhood, acquiring a public school education, and on entering upon his independent career chose the vocation of farming as his life work, an occupation in which he found success and contentment and in which he was active until his recent retirement, since which he has resided quietly at Manito. Mr. Talbott is an unostentatious man who has never cared for the honors of public life, nor has been active in fraternal bodies or church work. He married at Manito Miss Clara E. Willard, a native of the same community, and a daughter of Samuel E. and Sibyl H. (Ebbe) Willard, and a member of one of the old and honored families of Macon County, members of which have been prominent in merchandising, politics and the professions. She was born at Carlyle, Pennsylvania, where her father carried on a mercantile business for some time, and is one of a family of two sons and four daughters, the surviving members of the family being: Eugene F.; Anna, the wife of John Skinner, of Norborne, Missouri; Nellie, the wife of John Schantz, of Bogard, Missouri; Clara E., who is now Mrs. Talbott; and Catherine, the widow of Wellington Herrman, of Parkland, Tazewell County, Illinois. The other son, George W., a farmer near Manito, died unmarried. Four children were born to Mr. and Mrs. Talbott: Lafayette E., of this review; Gail, a farmer of Manito, who married Maud Hunt; Ray, likewise an agriculturist of Mason County, who married Myrtle Eidman, and Glenn, a farmer who married Nida Withers.

Lafayette E. Talbott grew up at Manito, where he attended the graded and high schools and after his graduation from the latter, at the age of eighteen years, started to farm and continued farming up to the age of twenty-six, then started as traveling representative for the International Harvester Company. Later he held a like position with the Hayes Pump and Planter Company and finished his work on the road with the Rock Island Plow Company, his entire career in this vocation covering a period of ten years. This gave him much valuable experience and a wide acquaintance, both of which have been useful to him in his subsequent activities. Leaving the road in 1919, Mr. Talbott turned his attention to the real estate business, having gained rather definite ideas and information regarding land values during his travels through the state, and still devotes a large part of his time to buying and selling land. Also, in 1923, he took over the management of the Grangers Elevator Company at Manito, of which he is still the directing head, and has made this one of the sound and profitable enterprises of the county, doing a large business. In addition to these lines Mr. Talbott has important agricultural holdings and at the present time is operating 1,000 acres of land, carrying on all departments of agricultural work. He uses the latest approved methods and the most modern machinery and his property includes commodious and attractive buildings and the most up-to-date improvements. As an active community man, Mr. Talbott has displayed a most commendable interest in the cause of education, and for the past five years has been president of the Board of Trustees of the grade schools. During the period of his incumbency of this office a splendid modern school building has been erected and the landscaping of the campus has been given due and proper attention. During the World war Mr. Talbott was registered and classified, and while he was not called for service to camp or field, discharged his full duties as a civilian in behalf of the raising of funds and in other directions. He has several fraternal connections and has not been indifferent to appeals from civic and religious enterprises and movements.

At Manito, April 11, 1907, Mr. Talbott was united in marriage with Miss Pearl Gay, a daughter of John F. and Jennie (Cogdal) Gay, the latter being a daughter of Eli Cogdal, a carpenter by vocation and a representative of one of the old-time families of Mason County. Mrs. Talbott has two sisters: Hazel, who is a resident of Manito; and Opal, who is the wife of Ernest W. Seelye, assistant cashier of the State Bank of San Jose, Illinois. Six children have been born to Mr. and Mrs. Talbott: Jennie, Richard, Florence, Ruth, John and Betty. Mr. and Mrs. Talbott occupy a pleasant home at Manito, where they have numerous friends.

ROBERT EMMET SHAW is owner of the White Hall Lumber Company, and has been one of the very progressive and enterprising business men of Greene County for the past twenty years.

Mr. Shaw's parents were living in Natchez, Mississippi, before he was born, but they went back to their native county, Longford, Ireland, on a visit and while there Robert Emmet Shaw was born in 1867. William Shaw and Maria (Kerr) Shaw, his wife, parents of Robert Emmet Shaw, on returning from Ireland settled in White Hall, Illinois, in 1867 with their family of four children. Here Robert Emmet Shaw was reared, attending the public schools, and after leaving school became clerk in a general store, where he learned the fundamentals of commercial life. He was connected with that business for ten years, under several different owners. Later for six years he was with the White Hall Fire Clay Works. Leaving Illinois in 1902, Mr. Shaw, accompanied by his family, went to Kansas to enjoy the experience of a comparatively new country, and at Hutchinson became connected with a large wholesale grocery and continued that work three years.

Returning to Illinois in 1905, Mr. Shaw engaged in the lumber business as successor in the ownership of a plant established by the E. R. Darlington Lumber Company. He has been the active head of this business ever since. Mr. Shaw is a sterling citizen and has served four terms as alderman, and was a member of the City Council when the water works and storage systems were installed. He has been a life-long loyal member and supporter of the Presbyterian Church

On September 19, 1893, Mr. Shaw married Miss Catharine Augusta Staats, a charming and highly esteemed instructor in the public schools. Mrs. Shaw was born at White Hall, Illinois, the daughter of James Voorhees and Mary (Wyatt) Staats. Her father, a highly respected citizen of the White Hall community and a charter member of the First Presbyterian Church of that place, came from New Brunswick, New Jersey, a son of Peter P. Staats, a prominent educator of New York City. Her mother was a native of White Hall.

Mr. and Mrs. Shaw have one son, Robert Voorhees, one of the talented and popular young men of the White Hall community. He finished high school at White Hall, and during the World war served nearly two years with the A. E. F. in France. After returning home he graduated from Illinois College, receiving the A. B. degree, and is now associated with his father in business. He is well known in musical circles, possessing a splendid tenor voice, and before joining his father in business had a wide and successful experience as teacher of voice. He is active in musical work in the Presbyterian Church at White Hall and is a member of the Masonic fraternity.

JOHN D. PROEHL. From the earliest times the possession of land has given an individual standing among men. Long before the gathering together of people in settled communities there were standards, just as there are today, by which a man's importance was judged, and chief among them all was the number of acres he could lay claim to. Down through the ages that standard has remained practically unchanged, for primarily from the soil man draws his sustenance and from it must come wealth and position. It is taken for granted that the man who has the ability to acquire large landed interests is one who also possesses the characteristics that go to make for good citizenship, as in the case of John D. Proehl, who possesses 345 acres of splendidly productive soil in the Mackinaw river bottoms of Spring Lake Township, and who is one of the constructive and reliable citizens of the Manito community.

Mr. Proehl was born December 25, 1873, in Spring Lake Township, Tazewell County, and is a son of Louis and Augusta (Bodtke) Proehl. His father was born in Seleska, Germany, and was a young man when he arrived in the United States, coming directly to Pekin, Illinois, where he arrived in 1871. He made his appearance here in July of that year and in the folowing December married Miss Augusta Bodtke, whom he had accompanied to this country together with Mrs. Proehl's sister, Ida Bodtke, and another young woman. In the Fatherland, in his youth, Louis Proehl had been fond of hunting and had acquired quite a reputation as a marksman. On coming to the United States to seek his fortune he brought with him his favorite fowling piece, and during his few leisure hours was often to be seen in search of game. However, he had little time during his early years for sport. He was busily occupied in learning the English language so that he could get along with his new neighbors, and his services were almost constantly in demand as a brick and stone mason, a trade which he had learned in his youth and which he followed with success at Pekin for two or three years. Not only did he know this trade but he was likewise an all-around mechanic, and when he went from Pekin to Sand Prairie he contributed much to the comfort of the early settlers and to the tenability of their primitive homes by digging the first cellars, building the first chimneys and whitewashing the rooms. After spending a year there he moved south of the Mackinaw River and engaged in agricultural pursuits. He spent his first eight years in the bottoms near where he finally settled permanently, and in 1884 moved to the farm where he finished his life. This property lay right against the timber, and when he commenced life in this community his home was a story and one-half frame house, which is still standing, and which sheltered him for ten or twelve years. Later he built the commodious home which now shelters his children, and in which he resided until his death, May 13, 1925, burial being made at Manito. Mr. Proehl's program as an agriculturist was the growing of corn, wheat and oats, and the raising of cattle and hogs, and he acquired title to 345 acres of good farming land before retiring from his active labors. He was a man of progressive ideas and modern methods, and his high principles invited the confidence of the people of his community. He early became a citizen of his adopted country and lived up to its laws, and took a good citizen's interest in public affairs. Politically he was a democrat, while his religious faith was that of the Lutheran Church. At Pekin Mr. Proehl married Augusta Bodtke, who still survives him at the age of seventy-four years, her sister also living as a resident of near Pekin. They became the parents of four children:: Matilda, who is the wife of Adam Meisinger, a farmer of Sand Prairie Township, Tazewell County; John D., of this review; William A., a farmer near Forest City, Illinois; and Augusta, who married Otto Garlisch and resides near Manito.

John D. Proehl has passed his entire life in an agricultural atmosphere. He never left his parents, caring for them in the evening of their lives, and always showing filial affection and respect. Mr. Proehl is now the owner of 345 acres of the Mackinaw bottoms of Spring Lake Township and his farming process has been the same as that of his father. He has added improvements for the shelter of his hogs and cattle, as well as to the tenant accommodations of the farm, and carries on his operations in a highly modern manner, being a close student of his vocation and fully alive to all its discoveries and advancements. Mr. Proehl is a stockholder of the Peoples State Bank of Manito and has other interests. One of the stanchest friends of education in his community, for some twenty years he has served as a member of the Board of Directors of the Parkland School. He shows his good citizenship by always voting at elections, and cast his first presidential ballot for the late William Jennings Bryan, whom he supported on two other occasions for the presidency. As a religious man Mr. Proehl is identified with St. John's Lutheran Church. During the World war he was registered for service, and while he never received his questionnaire he did his full part as a civilian, contributing generously of his time, means and ability in the cause of the success of American arms.

In Sand Prairie Township, Tazewell County, October 13, 1899, Mr. Proehl was united in marriage with Miss Emma E. Ripper, a daughter of P. E. and Elizabeth (Schaefer) Ripper. Mrs. Proehl died about two years later, leaving a daughter, Charlotte, who is now the wife of Henry Fischer, a farmer of Tazewell County, and has three sons, John Louis, Henry William and Melvin Frederick. For his second wife Mr. Proehl married Anna E. Getz, who was born June 7, 1874, in Carroll County, Illinois, one of the nine living children of George and Elizabeth (Wademan) Getz, agricultural people of that community. Four children have been born to Mr. and Mrs. Proehl: Martha A., Louis G., Walter William and Mabel Louise. Mr. Proehl is interested in the work and movements of St. John's Lutheran Church.

PAUL DEMOS is a Chicago lawyer, with office at 160 North LaSalle Street, and is particularly well known through his leadership in Greek-American organizations engaged in civic, benevolent and patriotic programs.

Mr. Demos was born and received his academic education in Greece, and coming to America, located in Chicago in 1912. He studied law in the Chicago Law School, from which he was graduated with the degree Master of Laws in 1916. While his ability and industry has won him a profitable practice in his profession, much of his time has been taken up with other interests and movements. He is president of the Greek-American Republican Club of Cook County, one of the strongest organizations of its kind. During the World war he had charge of a section of the Foreign Language Bureau in the sale of Liberty Bonds. Among other civic and benevolent organizations with which he is identified is the Greek Relief Committee, whose benevolent activities extend not only through Chicago but frequently in response to outside calls for aid. The American Association of the Greek Community of Chicago, of which Mr. Demos is president, is similarly engaged in a large program of benevolent work. Mr. Demos is a past district president of the Ahepa Society in Chicago. This is a national organization engaged in educational work among Greeks in America, particularly in behalf of Americanization work.

ALBERT E. PIKE is a Southern Illinois business man who has shown capacity for accomplishing broad and successful results in the handling of enterprises from public utilities to banks. He is president of the Christopher State Bank in Franklin County, and a brief history of that bank is a practical illustration of his forcefulness as an executive.

This bank was chartered in April, 1912, with a capital of $35,000, T. P. Harrison being the first president and H. M. Rea the first cashier. The bank opened for business in a frame building on the north side of Market Street. While the bank was in those quarters the present handsome bank building was in course of construction on the south side of the street. Mr. Albert Pike was financially interested but was not a member of the official personnel of the bank in the beginning.

On June 18, 1915, Mr. Harrison having resigned as president, Mr. Pike was elected his successor. At that time the bank had deposits of about $92,000. In the spring of 1926 the deposits had reached the impressive total of $996,460, while the total resources of the institution were over a million dollars. The bank has capital, surplus and undivided profits of over $82,000.

Of the charter directors of the bank the two still serving are T. P. Harrison and F. G. Rea. Mr. Pike's brother, Charles L. Pike, was bookkeeper of the bank for several years and is now cashier.

Mr. Pike's grandfather came from Tennessee and settled near Campbell Hill in Illinois. He was a land owner and business man, and is especially well remembered because of his passion for education. He donated land for a school which became known as the best in Jackson County, the Shiloh Hill School. One of the early pupils of this institution of learning was John A. Logan, afterwards known to fame as General Logan.

The parents of Albert Pike were William B. and Eliza (Tudor) Pike. His father was a prosperous farmer and died June 4, 1894. The mother passed away July 5, 1912. Her ancestors, the Tudors, first settled near Grand Tower and from there moved to the Campbell Hill neighborhood.

Albert E. Pike was born July 27, 1865, at Degognia in Jackson County. His early environment was the country and he attended country schools until he entered the Southern Illinois Normal University at Carbondale. He had four years of experience as a country school teacher, worked three months in a general store at Ava, and had seven years of commercial training and experience at St. Louis. On returning to Campbell Hill he operated a hardware and grocery store two years and then engaged in the milling business at Ava. After two years he took charge of the Ava Light & Power Plant, and here he demonstrated his unusual capacity for handling business in building up a public patronage. He was with the light and power plant at Ava for nine years, during which time his work attracted attention among public utility men. In 1910 he removed to Christopher and assisted in organizing the Christopher Electric Light Company, with H. M. Rea as president and Mr. Pike as secretary and treasurer. He was an officer of that company four years and laid the foundation for its permanent success. In 1914 he was called to Pinckneyville to take charge of an ice plant, but soon afterward returned to Christopher as representative of the city in the capacity of inspector of the dam. While thus engaged he was elected president of the Christopher State Bank as successor of Mr. Harrison.

Mr. Pike has left a record of public spirit in the several localities where he has made his home in Southern Illinois. He served as a member of the Board of Trustees of Campbell Hill and was mayor while living at Ava. In politics he has always been a staunch re-

publican, but is usually non-partisan in local affairs. He has filled all the chairs in the Lodge of Odd Fellows and is a member of the B. P. O. Elks.

Mr. Pike married Miss Hattie M. Redfield, daughter of John Redfield, of Campbell Hill, Jackson County. They have a daughter, Mary E., now attending the university at Urbana.

Mr. Pike's brother, Charles L., entered the Ava State Bank at the age of eighteen, was an employe there several years, spent three years with the Dean Milling Company and clerked for a mining company at Christopher. He went with the Christopher State Bank when it opened as bookkeeper and for a number of years now has been its cashier. He married Eva Ruth Allais, daughter of Victor Allais. She is of French ancestry.

HOWARD E. KIMMEL for twenty years has been a practicing lawyer in his native town of Duquoin, Perry County, and State of Illinois, and represents a number of the earliest families coming to the United States from foreign countries, and among those who were pioneer families of Egypt. Mr. Kimmel has been interested in the family history of a number of families in his community aside from the Kimmel line, and is preparing data for a history of the Kimmel family.

Jost Kimmel, born in 1592, is the earliest ancestor he has been able to locate and obtain any information about. He was the great-grandfather of Michael Kimmel. Michael Kimmel, who was born near Gimbscheim, near Hessen, Germany, was the father of three sons, Jacob, Valentine and Phillip, who eventually came to America. Jacob Kimmel and Henry Lohman brought their followers to Ephrata in Lancaster County, Pennsylvania, where they established a religious sect, living on a common property basis, known as the "Church of God" and later developed into a sort of Dunkard religion. Jacob Kimmel was accompanied by Valentine, his brother, who settled in York County.

Jacob and Valentine Kimmel came to Philadelphia in 1751, the other brother, Phillip, landing with five of his sons at what is now known as Alexandria, Virginia, in 1755, the sixth son being sent to America previously to locate Jacob and Valentine.

When Phillip landed in 1755 Braddock and Washington were preparing their ill-fated expedition to Fort Pitt. Phillip and his sons went with them as far as Frederickstown, Maryland, where they dropped out and went from there into York County and purchased the farm of Valentine Kimmel, where they lived until his death. Of Phillip's six sons, Jacob, Michael and George served in the Revolutionary army, the other three being Nicholas, Phillip and Anthony.

The subject of this sketch is a descendant of Phillip (2nd). It was Phillip, son of Phillip (2nd) and Abraham Kimmel, his son who settled in Somerset County, Pennsylvania. Abraham's son Henry moved to Richland County, Ohio, and in 1840 to Jackson County, Illinois. The subject of this sketch is also a descendant of George, the son of Phillip Kimmel (1st) through Catherine Kimmel, a daughter of George Kimmel, having married Jacob Schwartz, a Revolutionary soldier in 1799 and settled in Somerset County, Pennsylvania. Jacob Schwartz in 1817, in ill health, stayed with his daughter Josephine Dively, while the mother and eight children same on a flat boat down the Ohio to Kaskaskia and from there to Brownsville, then to Southern Illinois, where she joined her brother Peter and where she lived until her death.

Catherine Kimmel Schwartz was the ancestor of the Schwartz family so prominent in the history of Jackson and Union counties. Edward Schwartz, a son of Catherine, married Sarah Pyle in 1824, and they settled a mile and a half west of Elkville on a farm that was in the family until about 1924. Isabella Schwartz, a daughter of Edward Schwartz, married Joseph Kimmel, a son of Henry Kimmel, heretofore referred to, there being only one surviving child, Edward Kimmel, the father of the subject of this sketch. The wife of Edward Kimmel was Alifair Onstott, a daughter of Elihu Onstott, of Washington County, Indiana, who was a descendant of John Onstott, a subject of Bavaria, Germany, who came to Virginia in 1749 and later to Indiana.

Edward Kimmel, son of Joseph Kimmel, was for a number of years engaged in the mercantile business at Elkville, Illinois, and in 1875 came to Duquoin, where he engaged in the hardware business with his brother-in-law Don Onstott. Later he operated the Duquoin Milling Company Mill, and later, in 1899, engaged in the hardware business with John Yeihling.

The children of Edward and Alifair Kimmel were: The subject of this sketch, Howard E. Kimmel; Maurice E.; William A., engaged in the hardware business at the stand opened up by Elihu Onstott about 1860 in Duquoin, Illinois; Ruth I. Kimmell; and Dr. Fred J. Kimmel, now a resident of Billings, Montana.

Howard E. Kimmel was born November 23, 1879, in Duquoin, and was educated in the public schools. He later took the literary and law courses at Illinois University, from which institution he graduated in 1906. He opened a law office in Duquoin in 1906, and has enjoyed a very large practice since that time. He married Gertrude Humphrey, the daughter of John F. Humphrey, in 1915, from which marriage there were two children, Patricia Ann and Gloria Gertrude. John F. Humphrey the father of Gertrude, was for over forty-five years a merchant of Duquoin, Illinois. He was a descendant of the old Humphrey family that came from Maryland to Kentucky and then to Illinois in 1865.

The early history of Perry County is incomplete without some information in connection with the Pyle and Wells families that settled in the vicinity of Duquoin, Illinois.

John Pyle, a doctor and a colonel in the British Army during the Revolutionary war, was appointed commissioner of peace for Chatham County, North Carolina, by the Newburn, North Carolina, Court in 1768. John Pyle was highly praised in the Historical Record of North Carolina for his activity in the

Revolutionary war, in behalf of the British. He also had a son who was a doctor and soldier with the British.

This son John left North Carolina after the Revolution and settled in Greenville District, South Carolina, where two of his sons, John Jr., and Abner Pyle, married Mary and Sarah Wells, daughters of Lewis Wells, a soldier of the Revolution, and from South Carolina the families of Lewis Wells and John Pyle, Sr., moved to the present site of Hopkinsville, Kentucky, in 1806. In 1817 they came to Illinois.

John Pyle, Jr., settled at the present site of Duquoin, and together with his sons, Octavius, Cortez, Hiram and Ulysses, owned most of the land on which Duquoin is now situated. When the Illinois Central Railroad Company came through this territory, they sold out their holdings, and moved to Worth County, Missouri, where their descendants now live.

Hiram Pyle after going to Worth County, returned to Duquoin, and settled about three-miles southwest on the site of the original homestead entered by his grandfather, John Pyle. Hiram Pyle was a doctor and was prominent in politics until the time of his death in the '70s.

Nicholas Pyle, a son of the original Doctor and Col. John Pyle, settled in Perry County in 1820, but later moved with his family to Sangamon County in 1829. The Pyle family now in Sangamon County are the descendants of this Nicholas Pyle.

The Wells family heretofore referred to settled southwest of Duquoin about three miles, and through their marriages became closely allied to the various families of the counties of Jackson, Franklin, Perry and Washington, and have held numerous county and city offices from the beginning of the respective counties down to the present date.

ROSCOE TYGETT is an attorney who has practiced at Christopher since 1913. He is former postmaster of that city in Franklin County and is one of the county's best known citizens.

His great-grandfather Tygett came from Ireland and founded the family in Kentucky. The grandfather, John Patrick Tygett, came from Kentucky and was a pioneer of Williamson County, Illinois, where he founded what was long known as the Tygett settlement. He lived in that county as a farmer. William F. Tygett, who was born in Williamson County in 1862, after reaching manhood bought a farm not far from his birthplace, and was one of the substantial agriculturists of that vicinity until 1898, when he sold out and moved to Carbondale. At Carbondale he engaged in the livery business until the business became unprofitable through the advent of the automobile. He died at Carbondale in 1911. William F. Tygett married Alma Fox, daughter of Enoch Fox, a farmer in the Zion Church settlement of Jackson County. They had two children: Roscoe and Lloyd J. Tygett. Lloyd is now in the drug business at Valier in Franklin County.

Roscoe Tygett was born July 28, 1886, on the farm of his father in Williamson County, was a farm boy through his youth, attending country schools, and in 1898 he continued his education in the normal at Carbondale, graduating in 1906. In 1909 he graduated from the law department of the University of Illinois and was admitted to the bar in October of the same year. Mr. Tygett in 1910 removed to Oklahoma City and opened a law office in the new state of Oklahoma, practicing there until May, 1911. On returning to Illinois he was associated with A. S. Caldwell, and in 1913 located at Christopher. Mr. Tygett was appointed acting postmaster of Christopher January 1, 1919, by President Wilson, and soon afterward was regularly commissioned postmaster and handled the business of the postoffice for five years. In addition to his general law practice he acted as first assistant state's attorney of Franklin County under W. F. Spiller in 1913-14, and in 1924 he was democratic candidate for state's attorney in this strongly republican county. He served as city attorney of Christopher in 1914-15, and again in 1925-26.

Mr. Tygett married Miss Iva Tweedy, daughter of Willis Tweedy, of Union County. They have three children, James Roscoe, Katherine and William Tweedy Tygett. Mr. Tygett is affiliated with the Modern Woodmen of America.

WILLIAM EDMOND CARRINGTON is not only a successful business man but has shown such ability in municipal administration that he has been again and again elected mayor of his home City of Onarga.

Mr. Carrington was born at Howard City, Kansas, February 20, 1877, son of Edmond Hamilton and Sarah Elizabeth Carrington. When he was a child he was brought to Illinois, attended common schools at Woodland and had two years of academic training in the Grand Prairie Seminary at Onarga.

Mr. Carrington in a business way is prominently known for his connections with the canning industry. He is the executive official of one of the largest canning companies in Eastern Illinois, the Iroquois Canning Corporation, of which he is director, secretary and treasurer and general manager.

Mr. Carrington for six years represented the Second Ward in the City Council of Paxton. He was mayor of Onarga from May 1, 1919, to May 1, 1925, and on December 15, 1925, was again called to the office of mayor. He is a republican, is a past grand of the Independent Order of Odd Fellows and a member of the Masonic Lodge and the Presbyterian Church.

He married at Onarga, July 19, 1899, Mary Essie Leef. They have one daughter, Edith Anna.

GEORGE LANGER SCHEIN at the beginning of his law practice identified himself with some of the investigations and prosecutions of more than ordinary current interests in Chicago at the time, and the vigor and ability he applied to his early work brought him favorable attention and what has proved to be a growing reputation in the law and in business.

He was born in Chicago, July 4, 1889, son of Louis and Frances (Langer) Schein. His parents were natives of Germany, and George L. was fourth in their family of eight children.

After completing his high school course in Chicago he attended Lake Forest University and had two years in the law department of

John P. Burry

Northwestern University, graduating with the class of 1910. In the same year he was admitted to the Illinois bar and in 1919 was admitted to practice in the United States Supreme Court. He was one of the young lawyers attracted to the staff and leadership of the late John E. W. Wayman, then state's attorney of Cook County. In 1914 he engaged in an individual practice, and as a young lawyer of twenty-three he had an active part in the Chicago Tribune's Anti-Loan Shark campaign. His professional career has been chiefly identified with corporation laws. He is counsel for a number of large firms in Chicago, being a director and counsel for Oscar Mayer & Company, the Victor Mayer Company, general counsel for the Great Lakes Boat Building Company, counsel for Blair & Company, investment bankers. Since 1921 he has been a law partner of Judge Beckwith, former corporation counsel for the City of Chicago.

Mr. Schein is a member of the Chicago, Illinois and American Bar Associations, the Chicago Legal Club, Chicago Yacht Club, a life member of the Press Club, Lake Shore Athletic Club, a member of the City Club, the Lincoln Club, Association of Commerce, Standard Lodge No. 873, A. F. and A. M., and Chicago Lodge B. P. O. Elks. In politics he is a republican.

Mr. Schein married, August 23, 1918, Louise Mayer, a native of Chicago. They have three children: George L., Jr., Louise and Elizabeth.

LEWIS WINE BREMERMAN, M. D. A distinguished Chicago surgeon, Doctor Bremerman has for a number of years probably ranked first as an authority on urology in the Middle West. Among specialists his name is one of the best known in the Middle West.

Doctor Bremerman was born at Washington, D. C., August 12, 1877, a son of Laban Trout and Helen Kate (Rhinehart) Bremerman. He was educated in grammar and high schools at Washington, took his A. B. degree at the Central High School at Philadelphia in 1897 and in 1905 that school awarded him further with the A. M. degree. In the meantime, in 1900, he graduated M. D. from the Jefferson Medical College at Philadelphia. He served as an interne in the Pennsylvania Hospital for Injured Persons at Fountain Springs during 1900 and at the W. W. Beckus Hospital at Norwick, Connecticut, in 1901.

Doctor Bremerman was engaged in the general practice of surgery in New York from 1903 to 1907 and in the latter year located in Chicago, where he practiced as a specialist in diseases of the kidney and bladder. In addition to his private practice he was for several years surgeon on the staff of the Oak Park Hospital, was consulting urologist of the Illinois Central Railway and a director of the Bremerman Urological Hospital. For two years he was a surgeon with the rank of lieutenant colonel in the United States Army. During 1904-05 Doctor Bremerman was associate professor of urology and was professor during 1905-07 in the New York School of Clinical Medicine. In 1910 he was professor of urology in the Bennett and Practitioners' Medical Colleges at Chicago and during 1914-15 served as professor of genito-urinary surgery at the University of Iowa.

Doctor Bremerman has written over one hundred periodicals for medical journals. The profession has been waiting for several years the appearance of a text book on surgical subjects which Doctor Bremerman has in preparation. He is a member of the Chicago Medical Society, the Mississippi Valley Medical Association, has served as president of the Ohio Valley Medical Association, the Chicago Urological Society and the American Urological Association. He is a member of the Illinois Athletic and Olympia Field Country clubs.

Doctor Bremerman's offices are at 104 South Michigan Avenue and his home in the Surf Hotel. He married, September 26, 1905, Miss Helen Tope, of Oak Park, Illinois. She died September 13, 1906. In 1912 he married Mrs. Margaret E. (Thomas) Alexander.

ST. MARY'S CATHOLIC CHURCH OF CHAMPAIGN, established about 1858, was the first church of this denomination in the entire county, and the entire county was the original parish, from which have since been carved fourteen parishes, while there are now four churches in the twin cities of Champaign and Urbana.

The founder of the parish was Rev. P. Toner, a splendid type of the pioneer minister and missionary. He was a man of rugged constitution and well able to stand the hardships of winter night drives of twenty or thirty miles to visit the sick or dying. The original church building started by him on the site of the present St. Mary's was a small, strange structure, at first without lath or plaster. Improvements were added from time to time, a school being started in 1877, and in September, 1879, a brick building of eight rooms was provided for the school. In 1915 a modern schoolhouse was erected, including a fine auditorium with stage, and also a well equipped gymnasium. The school provides both elementary and high school instruction, the graduates being qualified to enter the State University.

In connection with St. Mary's Church and School Mercy Hospital was opened in September, 1923. During the first year it took care of more than one thousand patients. The hospital, rectory, church and school occupy about one and one-half blocks of land in the City of Champaign, located on East Park Street.

The present pastor of St. Mary's Church is Rev. John P. Barry, who has had many years of experience as a Catholic priest in this section of Illinois.

He is a native of Champaign County, born in Urbana Township, September 28, 1863, son of Bartholomew and Ellen (Lane) Barry. His parents came from County Cork, Ireland, were married at Joliet, Illinois, January 11, 1861, and at once settled on land previously purchased near Urbana. Bartholomew Barry engaged in farming there until advanced years, and about 1899 located at Philo, where his son was then priest of the parish. In 1914 he bought a home in Champaign, opposite St. Mary's Church, and at that home passed away September 4, 1924, aged ninety-one years and nineteen days. His widow is now in her ninety-third year and still occupies the old homestead. The late Bartholomew Barry was a man of splendid habits and character, temperate, kindly, and enjoyed the complete confidence of his friends and neighbors.

Rev. John P. Barry was reared on the home farm near Champaign to the age of fourteen. He has seen the twin cities during most of their important progress and development. His early education was acquired in St. Mary's School, supplemented by attendance at St. Viator's College, near Kankakee, where he graduated in 1885, and in 1888 he graduated from St. Mary's Seminary at Baltimore, and was ordained a priest October 20, 1888.

Father Barry has given more than thirty-five years of service to the church. He was assistant at Ivesdale two years, one year at Holy Trinity Church at Bloomington, and then took charge of the parish at Gibson City, where very little work had been done, so that his tasks and responsibilities were those of the pioneer. He had charge of twenty-two towns and stations in a territory twenty by sixty miles. At the end of six months he was able to report to the Bishop that he had removed the church from its former location in the negro section of the city to a better neighborhood, had remodeled the building and had a class ready for confirmation. His next charge was at Piper City, with an outmission at Forest, Illinois. Here he repeated the good work done at Gibson City. After two years and nine months he was sent to Philo, near his boyhood home in Champaign County. In this charge he succeeded in harmonizing the discordant interests, built Memorial Chapel, a rectory and school, and two new church buildings, one at Philo and one at the out station. In these congenial labors he was engaged for a period of seventeen years, leaving there in 1914 to accept transfer to Odell, Illinois. At Odell he continued his prosperous work until July, 1924, and there built up the parish, erected a new high school and paid off the debt on the new church building. While at Odell he was responsible for the erection of a fine modern convent, a building that has since been duplicated at six other places.

In July, 1924, he came to St. Mary's Parish at Champaign.

JAMES W. HAMILTON, M. D., is established in the successful practice of his profession at Mount Vernon, judicial center of Jefferson County, and he has gained secure vantageground as one of the leading surgeons in this section of the state. As a specialist in the surgical branch of his profession the Doctor is fortified alike through broad and varied experience and through availing himself of the advantages of many of the leading surgical clinics of the United States. He has to his credit innumerable surgical operations of most important order, both major and minor.

Doctor Hamilton was born on the old homestead farm of his father in Blissville Township, Jefferson County, April 24, 1871, and he is a scion, in the third generation, of a family that was founded in this county nearly a century ago. His paternal grandfather, Orange Hamilton, was born and reared in the State of New York and upon coming to the West he first settled in Ohio, from which state he came to Jefferson County, Illinois, about the year 1830, he having here passed the remainder of his life, as did also his wife, whose family name was Ashley. They were sterling pioneers of Illinois and did well their part in civic and industrial progress in their home community.

Josiah A. Hamilton, father of him whose name introduces this review, was born in Ohio and was a child at the time of the family removal to Illinois, where he was reared and educated under the conditions of the pioneer days and where he followed farm industry during virtually his entire independent career, besides which he represented Jefferson County as one of the valiant young soldiers of the Union in the Civil war, he having been a member of Company K, Thirty-second Illinois Volunteer Infantry and having served during nearly the entire period of the war. He was long numbered among the substantial citizens and progressive farmers of Jefferson County, and here his death occurred in the late '90s, his widow, whose maiden name was Anna E. Boswell, having survived him about eighteen years and having attained to the venerable age of eighty-six years. Her father, Samuel Boswell, was a pioneer in Illinois, to which state he came from Tennessee. Orange, eldest of the children of Josiah A. and Hanna E. (Boswell) Hamilton, first married Mary Blackwell, who was survived by one child, Emza, the second wife of Orange Hamilton having died without issue. Lucretia is the widow of Leslie Mannen, their eight children being: Cora, Lydia, James, Ira, Earl, Roy, Ethel and Grace. Elenora is the wife of Daniel Webb, and they have two children, Raymond and Ruby. Vincent married Martha Hartley, and to them were born six children: Hugh, Walter, Lawrence, Blanche, Hazel and Helen. Charles, who married Ollie Barrett, is deceased, and is survived by his widow and their one child, Harry. Dr. James W., of this sketch, was the next in order of birth, and is the youngest of the six children.

The childhood and early youth of Doctor Hamilton were compassed by the influences of the home farm, and his first educational advantages were those of the district schools. He eventually completed a high-school course, and in preparation for his chosen profession he entered the Barnes Medical College in the city of St. Louis. In this institution he was graduated as a member of the class of 1895, and after thus receiving his degree of Doctor of Medicine he was for two years engaged in practice in the village of Ina, Jefferson County. He then removed to Mount Vernon, the county seat, which has since continued the central stage of his earnest and successful professional activities, save for the interim of his World war service. In advancing himself in the surgical department of his profession Doctor Hamilton has taken post-graduate work in many of the leading medical schools of the United States—in New York City, Boston, Philadelphia, in the medical school of the great Johns Hopkins University at Baltimore, and in the world-famous Mayo Brothers Clinic at Rochester, Minnesota, besides which he has attended surgical clinics in the city of St. Louis. As a specialist in the practice of surgery Doctor Hamilton now has as his able coadjutor his son Dr. Clarence Hamilton, of whom more specific mention will be made in a later paragraph. Doctor Hamilton established, in 1909, the first hospital in the city of Mount Vernon, and to this he gave the title of the Egyptian Hospital, by reason of its field of service being in that part of Illinois that is commonly designated as Egypt. In 1921 Doctor Hamilton sold this hospital to Dr. S. A. Thompson, who now maintains the same as a general hospital in which Doctor Hamilton is retained for all surgical work. In the World war period Doctor Hamilton served as physician and surgeon for the exemption examining board for the thirty-three counties of Southern Illinois, besides which he was government surgeon for the railway administration. He is now local surgeon for the Louisville & Nashville, the Chicago & Eastern Illinois, and the Wabash, Chester & Western Railroads. He has active membership in the Jefferson County Medical Society, the Illinois State Medical Society, and the American Medical Association. The Doctor is affiliated with the Masonic fraternity, the Independent Order of Odd Fellows and the Knights of Pythias.

April 26, 1892, recorded the marriage of Doctor Hamilton and Miss Cora A. Webb, daughter of the late Daniel R. and Martha Webb, of Jefferson County, the children of the Webb family being three sons and three daughters: William is a resident of California; Otto resides in Jefferson County; Mary is the wife of Charles Spangler; Walter is still a resident of Illinois; Mrs. Hamilton was the next in order of birth; and Addie is married and living in California. Dr. and Mrs. Hamilton have two children, Dr. Clarence O., who is associated with his father in practice, and Opal, who remains at the parental home.

Dr. Clarence O. Hamilton was graduated from the Mount Vernon High School, and he then completed a course in the medical department of the National University of Arts and Sciences in the city of St. Louis. In this institution he was graduated as a member of the class of 1916, and he has since been actively associated with his father in the practice of his profession, in which both specialize in surgery. When the nation entered the World war Dr. Clarence O. Hamilton promptly volunteered for service in the Medical Corps of the United States army, in which he was commissioned a first lieutenant August 22, 1917. He soon went to England, where he was assigned to the First Battalion, One Hundred and Thirty-sixth Field Ambulance, Fortieth Division, and was stationed at Chiseldon Hospital. On January 31, 1918, he accompanied the Fortieth Division to France, and on the 17th of the following March he was assigned to duty with the Twenty-sixth Middlesex Battalion, One Hundred and Thirty-sixth Ambulance Corps. His next assignment was to the One Hundred and First Field Ambulance Corps of the Thirty-second Division, and he was thereafter with the Eighteenth Middlesex Battalion and with the Highlanders Light Infantry until the armistice brought the war to a close. He remained at Marseilles, France, until he sailed for the home land, and he received his honorable discharge May 16, 1919, at Camp Dix, New Jersey. The Doctor served with the British forces during the entire period of his stay overseas, though he had enlisted in the Medical Corps of the United States army, by which he was virtually "loaned" to the British service. The Doctor is a member of the Jefferson County Medical Society and the Illinois State Medical Society, and is affiliated with the American Legion, the Elks and the Knights of Pythias. On March 31, 1924, the Doctor wedded Miss Hilda Carr, who was born and reared in Jefferson County and whose father died when she was an infant, her widowed mother being now a resident of Jefferson County, and the other children being Wayne, Lorenzo and Dorothy.

GEORGE W. WARD had natural gifts and inclinations for business and has enjoyed every successive step in his business career, taking pleasure in the work itself as well as the promotions and rewards. Mr. Ward started in the ranks, and for a number of years has been connected with the First National Bank of Christopher in Franklin County, an institution that stands as one of the strong financial organizations in the southern part of the state. Mr. Ward is now president of this bank. The First National Bank of Christopher was established in 1906 by the late Nelson Browning, beginning with a capital of $25,000. The bank now has capital of $60,000, surplus and profits of similar amount, and its total resources are approximately $1,400,000, the deposits being one and a quarter millions.

George W. Ward was born at Greenfield, Tennessee, October 21, 1880, son of Isaac H. and Laura Ward. A few years after his birth his parents moved from Tennessee to Dunklin County, Missouri, where the son attended grade schools at Kennett. Later he attended a business college at Paducah, Kentucky, and for four years was employed as bookkeeper and clerk in a store at Caruthersville, Missouri. After ten months of further business training in the Gem City Business College at Quincy, Illinois, Mr. Ward came to Royalton, Illinois, and for eighteen months was an employee of a coal company.

In 1907 his parents moved to Royalton from Missouri and built a home there, but in 1915 moved to Flint, Michigan, where his father died in 1924, and where his mother still has her home.

George W. Ward for several years made changes in his employment, but each change was either a promotion or a larger opportunity. From the coal company at Royalton he spent six months as stenographer with the Benton Coal Company, and left that in 1908 to become bookkeeper for the First National Bank of Christopher. He joined the bank while it was still a modest financial institution. Not long afterward he was promoted to cashier, became a director, and served in that position until after the death of Nelson Browning, which occurred December 9, 1925. Mr. Ward was elected Mr. Browning's successor. Thus this bank has had only two presidents.

Mr. Ward married, in 1907, Mrs. Ada Campbell, daughter of Sydney Harrison, a prominent farmer living near Christopher. Mrs. Ward is a member of the Daughters of the American Revolution, being eligible through her Harrison ancestors. They have two children, Walter W. Ward, attending high school, and Helen Irene, also a student in high school. Mrs. Ward finished her education in the Southern Illinois Normal University at Carbondale and taught school in Franklin County before her marriage. Mr. Ward is a member of the Modern Woodmen of America and the Christian Church.

JOHN A. MARSHALL, a retired merchant at Manito, in Mason County, has been a resident of Illinois for more than three-quarters of a century.

He was born at Pleasant Valley, Ohio, September 23, 1846, and was two years of age when his parents came to Illinois and settled in Kankakee County. He is a great-grandson of John Marshall, a Virginian and not distantly related to the famous Chief Justice John Marshall. Joshua Marshall, a grandfather of John A. Marshall, was born in Loudoun County, Virginia, was a soldier in the War of 1812 and became a farmer in Franklin County, Ohio. He married Sarah Hagues. Of their sons Joshua Marshall Jr., was the father of John A. Marshall. He too was a native of Virginia, and while in Ohio followed the milling business, was in the hotel business for a time in the '50s at Kankakee, but otherwise spent his life as a farmer. In 1861 he moved to Mason County and also lived in Tazewell County. His death occurred in July, 1880, at the age of sixty-five. He was a director of the local schools and a republican. Joshua Marshall married Drusilla Rakestraw, daughter of Allen and Nancy (Harris) Rakestraw. She was born January 1, 1821, and died in 1882.

John A. Marshall was reared on a farm in Illinois, and engaged in farming as his vocation at Spring Lake near Manito until 1881. In the meantime, in 1878, he had engaged in merchandising at Manito, and continued in business there until having lost his store by fire. He retired in 1914. Mr. Marshall has always taken a keen interest in church, serving more than thirty years as a trustee of the Methodist Episcopal Church. He is a republican, having cast his first vote for General Grant.

Mr. Marshall married at Pekin, Illinois, October 23, 1873, Miss Mary E. Docker, who died October 1, 1882. Of her three children one died in infancy, and the son, Clarence E., lives at Chicago, and married Dorothy Smith, and the other son, Horace A., lives at Peoria and married Margaret Cosgrove. On December 10, 1884, at Peoria, Mr. Marshall married Sarah A. Strickler, a native of Philadelphia, Pennsylvania, daughter of Samuel and Mary E. (Smith) Stickler. Her father established the first book store at Peoria. Mr. and Mrs. Marshall have one son, Samuel J., who graduated from the Manito High School, from the Brown Business College at Peoria, and is now assistant cashier of the Peru State Bank, and is also in the life insurance business. He is secretary and treasurer of the LaSalle County Bankers' Federation, is secretary of the Peru Rotary Club and chairman of the Board of Directors of the Congregational Church. Samuel J. Marshall married Emma Patzer, and they have a daughter, Marion.

WALTER B. CRAWFORD, vice president of the West Frankfort Bank & Trust Company, has been more than a successful business man in his community. His character, personality and qualifications have led men naturally to select him for leadership and other responsibilities in connection with any project requiring united action. He has been engaged in community work not only in times of good fortune but in ill, notably following the great tornado of 1925, when he headed the local committee acting in cooperation with the American Red Cross in relief of distress in the devastated area.

Mr. Crawford was born at Frankfort Heights, Illinois, September 2, 1882. His father, Thomas Jefferson Crawford, came to Old Frankfort in the early '60s, and until his death in 1903 was a leading merchant of that community. His wife was Margarette Kirkpatrick, of a well known southern Illinois family.

Walter B. Crawford after finishing his education engaged in merchandising and for twelve years was a merchant at Frankfort Heights. After selling out he entered the West Frankfort Bank & Trust Company in 1916 as a clerk, and before the end of the first year was made cashier, and since then has been practically the active and responsible manager of the bank. The West Frankfort Bank & Trust Company was organized under a state charter in 1913. It has retained its original capitalization of $50,000, and now has surplus and undivided profits of almost equal amount. The first president was Mr. Harry Stotlar, who still continues in that office, though he is a resident of Benton and has many other outside business interests to occupy him, leaving to Mr. Crawford the direct management of the bank. The first cashier was W. A. Kelly, who was succeeded in 1916 by Mr. Crawford. In 1921 Mr. Crawford was promoted to the vice presidency, with the duties of cashier going to Lloyd F. Cox, who in turn, in 1923, was succeeded by Mr. L. B. Heard, the present cashier. The West Frankfort Bank & Trust Company now has total resources of over a million dollars, and these resources and the reputation of the bank for service and strength have been developed under Mr. Crawford's direct part in the management and are in no small degree due to his efficiency as a banker.

Mr. Crawford has been active in the Illinois Bankers Association since 1916, when he attended his first convention with the bankers of Group Ten, and in the following year was elected secretary of that group and since then has been vice chairman and chairman of the Group Organization, a member of the Executive Council. He was elected president of the State Bankers Association in 1926, and during 1924-25 was chairman of the Protective Committee. It was during these years that the state association adopted the Iowa plan of combating the bank bandit with his own methods, employing R. C. Saunders as active director of the entire anti-bank robber campaign, a policy that has resulted in a remarkable reduction in bank losses and attempted bank burglaries.

Mr. Crawford organized and is president of the West Frankfort Finance Company, is sec-

retary-treasurer of the Pyramid Coal Corporation, owning and operating mines at Marion and Pinckneyville, is president of the West Frankfort Mercantile Company, and is vice president of the West Frankfort Building & Loan Association, one of the largest and strongest loan institutions in southern Illinois.

Mr. Crawford was largely instrumental in securing the incorporation of Frankfort Heights as a municipality, serving as the first mayor, and was twice elected to succeed himself. Still later he led the movement for the annexation of Frankfort Heights as part of the largest city of West Frankfort. Following the tornado of March 18, 1925, he assisted in organizing and was elected chairman of the Franklin County Relief Association, through which body the American Red Cross expended more than a million dollars in rehabilitation and relief work. Mr. Crawford organized, in 1922, and was elected first president of the West Frankfort Rotary Club and was also instrumental in organizing and establishing the Franklin County Country Club. He was named a member of a citizens finance committee to work out a solution to the financial situation and restore West Frankfort to its proper credit among Illinois municipalities. Within less than a year the committee had reduced the municipal debt by one hundred thousand dollars, and had greatly relieved the financial strain on the city administration. During the World war Mr. Crawford was associated with all the organizations for raising money by sale of bond and stamps and participated in the Red Cross and other auxiliary war causes. He is a Knight Templar Mason and Shriner, a past noble grand of the Independent Order of Odd Fellows, and is a deacon in the First Christian Church. Mr. Crawford takes special pride in his position as president of the Men's Bible Class in the Sunday School, where for several years he has devoted himself to building the "big men's class," with the result that it is one of the largest men's Sunday School organizations in "Little Egypt."

Mr. Crawford married Miss Nell McIntyre, daughter of Dr. A. J. and Mamie (Poindexter) McIntyre, both of well known families in Southern Illinois. Mr. and Mrs. Crawford have two children. The daughter, Mary, born in 1907, is a graduate of St. Mary's College of Garden City, Long Island, and is an accomplished pianist. The son, Carl, born in 1912, is attending high school at West Frankfort.

LOUIS LOWENSTEIN, president of the Peoples First National Bank of White Hall, has been identified with Greene County over half a century, and his life record reflects an intensity of purpose, possibility of achievement and close contact with all the vital interests of his community, making him one of the outstanding Illinoians of his generation.

He was born in Sullivan County, Tennessee, June 2, 1855. His father, Isaac Lowenstein, was a native of Gimsheim, near the city of Wurms in Hesse Darmstadt. He left his native land at the age of eighteen, coming to America in 1852, first locating in Philadelphia, and soon became a peddler or traveling merchant. In Monroe County, Tennessee, he married Elizabeth A. Ghormley, daughter of Pleasant M. and Ann Ghormley. In 1857, when Louis Lowenstein was about eighteen months old, his parents moved to Murray County, Georgia. His father had a mail contract at the opening of the Civil war, carrying mail between Louden, Tennessee, and Dalton, Georgia. In 1862 he joined the Confederate army in General Joseph Wheeler's cavalry. In 1864 he was taken prisoner and was held at Rock Island, Illinois, until the close of the war. During his service he was wounded, once in the right knee and again in the left collar bone. After the war he tried farming, but in 1869 moved with his family to Washington County, Arkansas, along the border line of the Cherokee nation of old Indian Territory. In October, 1872, he removed to Pierce City, Missouri, and in 1873 brought his family by railroad to White Hall, Illinois, and located in the village of Patterson, where he conducted a small store for three and a half years. After that he lived at White Hall until his death in 1895, at the age of sixty-two. His wife died in 1909. Their children were: Louis; William P., who died at White Hall, December 31, 1916; Henry Polk, a lawyer of Kansas City, Missouri; Mary Caroline, who died at White Hall, wife of Edward B. Smith; Laura Ann, who died August 5, 1889, wife of George Gardner; Louise, wife of D. M. Fishback, of Carrollton, Illinois; Mark, of White Hall; Lena, wife of A. L. Eberhart, and she died at Austin, Minnesota; and Claud, of White Hall.

Louis Lowenstein lived in Tennessee, Georgia, Arkansas and Missouri during his boyhood, and was a youth of eighteen when he arrived at White Hall in 1873, the year of the great panic. His cash capital on arrival consisted of only two dollars. He had attended school only fifteen months, and realizing the handicap of lack of education set out to remedy that defect as soon as possible. He was given employment in a store, and was so well satisfied of being assured a place to sleep and something to eat that he did not inquire as to his salary. He made arrangement with a teacher who permitted him to take such subjects as would be suitable to him for a business career, and he attended school six months. A pupil with such earnestness as he had can accomplish a great deal in that time. Mr. Lowenstein has always been very grateful to the teacher whose grade he attended, and she is now a resident of Jacksonville and he visits her on every opportunity. He was employed in the store of Oswald and Mytinger. At the end of three months, desiring to attend an entertainment, he asked Mr. Oswald the loan of a quarter to buy some collars. Oswald referred him to the bookkeeper, and to his astonishment he found that all his bills had been paid, his washing and board attended to, and that he firm owed him a total of $105. One hundred dollars of this sum he loaned to the firm at ten per cent per annum, taking the firm's note. He was with the store three and a half years. Six months before leaving he arranged a partnership with a friend who had some surplus capital. Oswald and Mytinger tried to dissuade him from the move, offering him $125 a month for a period of five years. He was already getting $100 a month, being

10V6

one of the two young men in White Hall with that princely salary. However, he decided to go into business for himself, and that was the beginning of the firm of Lowenstein & Company. His associate was George M. Dallas, a marble cutter. They began handling hardware and groceries. In a short time he acquired the interest of his partner. At the end of six months an inventory showed him that he had not made a profit of $125 a month, but that did not deter him from proceeding with business independently. His father soon came into the business, the firm of Lowenstein & Son being formed in January, 1877, and with the addition of another son the following year the firm became Lowenstein & Sons. Louis Lowenstein sold his interest in this business in 1894, but the firm name still continues and is one of the oldest and largest mercantile concerns of Greene County.

Mr. Lowenstein set some precedents while he was a merchant at White Hall. His first decided departure from the custom of the times was his refusal to sell whiskey, long regarded as an indispensable part of a stock of groceries. Another custom was the marking of goods in characters instead of plain price figures, and in spite of predictions his business grew and prospered. For the first sixteen years he did a credit business, as did all the other merchants. He then installed a cash system, and again his initiative was rewarded. He also showed such ability in collecting old accounts that his losses over a long period of years averaged only fifteen cents on each hundred dollars sold.

About the time he retired from merchandising Mr. Lowenstein purchased the lands of the Seeley estate, some nine hundred acres. Seven hundred acres were covered with virgin timber. He worked this up, selling ties, wood and lumber, disposing of 35,000 cords of wood to the Alton Railroad Company. When the timber was cut off the land quickly grew up in blue grass, and he fenced it and engaged in the stock business. In this venture he was in partnership with his brother, William P. He proposed to his brother the possibility of reclaiming the river bottom lands of the now Hillview Drainage and Levee District, and when the brother did not regard this feasible Louis Lowenstein bought the partnership interests. He moved out to the farm and proceeded to organize the Hillview Drainage and Levee District of Greene and Scott Counties, Illinois. His improvements were located on a portion of the site of the present village of Hillview. A side track was already in, and he concluded it was a good place for a town. He platted twenty-six acres, naming the town Hillview. In one year he had sold that, and the sales totalled four hundred dollars more than he had paid for the entire nine hundred acres. Mr. Lowenstein then proceeded to carry out a grand purpose of reclaiming 12,000 acres of swamp lands adjacent to and a part of his present farm. He organized the Hillview Drainage and Levee District, securing the necessary signers after two years of trial. The original bonds were sold at par, the necessary engineering work was done, contracts for dredging let, and after eight years and the expenditure of $700,000 the entire 12,000 acres were brought under cultivation. From the point of view of public benefit this was the largest single undertaking of Mr. Lowenstein's career. On the reclaimed tract pumping plants to remove the excess rain fall were erected. In the plan to remove the flood waters twenty-seven miles of canals were made with a levee fourteen miles long. The expense to the district was sixty dollars an acre, which does not include tiling on each individual farm.

Mr. Lowenstein, regardful of his own educational limitations, was from the first a vigorous promotor of school facilities for his home community. He went on the school board soon after his marriage, and assisted in giving the district additional school buildings. Some years later he was on the board when other improvements were made, and more recently he was president of the school board when the new high school was erected. He also served as a member of the City Council and was mayor of White Hall when the water works were installed.

Mr. Lowenstein for many years has been interested in banking. He took stock in the White Hall National Bank, and later was a member of the syndicate that bought out the Peoples Bank, now the Peoples First National Bank, of which he is president. He still owns large holdings in farm lands. He has always been a republican, though his father was a democrat. He cast his first presidential vote for Rutherford B. Hayes. He is a thirty-second degree Scottish Rite Mason, member of the Consistory at Springfield, and also Ansar Temple of the Mystic Shrine. During the World war he had charge of the local Red Cross work.

Mr. Lowenstein married at White Hall, August 7, 1878, Ada V. Higbee, who was born at Havana, Illinois, October 10, 1860, and was brought to White Hall at the age of four years. She is a daughter of John E. and Abigail (Clement) Higbee, her father from Kentucky and her mother from Vermont. There were six daughters in the Higbee family: Miss Emma, Mrs. Belle Roberts, Mrs. Lowenstein, Fannie H., wife of William F. Dillman, a farmer in Greene County, Miss Lula May, and Jessie who died unmarried. Mr. and Mrs. Lowenstein have two sons, Carl and Guy. Carl, who is a farmer, married Ada L. White. Guy, cashier of the Peoples First National Bank, married Mabel Adams, and has one son, Louis.

CHARLES O. LANE, M. D. A native of Southern Illinois, member of pioneer families of this section of the state, Doctor Lane made the resolution when a youth to become a physician, and in attaining to the qualifications for such a career he made many sacrifices and labored earnestly, supporting a family before he had graduated. For some years he has been one of the very busy men in his profession at West Frankfort, Franklin County.

He was born on his father's farm in the Eastern part of Hamilton County, Illinois, June 26, 1876. His grandfather, John Lane, came from Tennessee and took up a tract of government land in Hamilton County, making a farm and occupying it until his death. George

Washington Lane, father of Doctor Lane, was born at that old homestead in Hamilton County in 1846. He was a farmer, but was also widely known over the county as a teacher, having taught for many years in different districts. He died in 1893. George W. Lane married Sarah E. Echols, daughter of Lofton Echols, who came to Illinois from Tennessee, and was a pioneer of Hamilton County.

Charles O. Lane had the working discipline of a farm during his boyhood. He attended country schools to the age of seventeen, and after that in order to carry out his plans he taught school in winter and worked on the farm during the summer until 1902, in which year he entered the St. Louis College of Physicians and Surgeons.

In the meantime, in 1901, he had married Miss Nora Weston, of Benton, Franklin County. His work in medical college was not continuous, as he had to leave school for one year and work in order to secure funds. However, he graduated with honors in 1907 and at once engaged in practice at Belle Prairie in Hamilton County. From there in 1914 he removed to West Frankfort, where he has a large business and a general practice. He is a member of the Franklin County, Southern Illinois, Illinois State and American Medical Associations.

Doctor Lane is affiliated with the Masonic order, having taken several of the degrees and orders, and is a member of the Mystic Shrine. He belongs to the B. P. O. Elks, Modern Woodmen of America and Rotary Club, the Franklin County Country Club and the Missionary Baptist Church. He and Mrs. Lane have an adopted daughter, Margarette.

DANN A. WOOD is a prominent young business man, supplying some of the energy which has helped create an extensive business in several towns of Southern Illinois in which the Wood family has played a prominent part. Dann A. Wood is general manager of the three West Frankfort "Woodway Stores," these being part of the system of stores established and operated by his father, Dann L. Wood, a prominent wholesale and chain store merchant. The home of Dann L. Wood is at Benton in Franklin County. There are two of the Woodway stores at Benton, one at Zeigler, one at Christopher, one at Johnston City, and three at West Frankfort.

Dann A. Wood, son of Dann L. and Eliza (May) Wood, was born at Enfield, White County, Illinois, February 22, 1890. He spent most of his boyhood and early youth at Eldorado, Illinois, where he attended public schools. For a time he was a student in the Meridian Male College of Mississippi. After returning to Eldorado he joined his father's establishment, the McClure-Wood Company, wholesale grocers, and his business training and education has been derived directly from his father.

Dann A. Wood left business in the spring of 1918 to join the colors, being assigned to the One Hundred and Fifty-ninth Depot Brigade. Later he was chosen for the officers' training course at Camp Gordon, Georgia, and was commissioned a second lieutenant, but the armistice was signed before he went overseas. After leaving the army Mr. Wood returned to Eldorado and continued with the wholesale house until 1921, when the company opened and established the stores at West Frankfort, of which he was appointed manager.

He married, in 1920, Ruth Shafer, daughter of Edwin and Elizabeth (Yost) Shafer, of Eldorado and Chester, Illinois.

WILLIAM S. RAINS, a Doctor of Dental Surgery, completed his dental course while serving in the army during the World war. He has a well established practice at West Frankfort.

Three generations of the Rains family have lived in the vicinity of and have been identified with what is now the thriving industrial City of West Frankfort. Altogether there have been four generations of the family in Southern Illinois.

The first was represented by Doctor Rains' great-grandfather, Rollo Rains, who moved from South Carolina to Tennessee in the early part of the nineteenth century and from Tennessee came to Southern Illinois, locating near Creal Springs in Williamson County. He followed farming in Williamson County until his death.

His son, Leroy Kendall Rains, was born in Illinois, and during the Civil war was with an Illinois regiment in the Union army. He spent his last years at Franklin Heights, now a part of the City of West Frankfort, and died there.

Elijah M. Rains, father of Doctor Rains, was born near Fitz Hill in 1869, but during most of his life lived in the Franklin Heights community. For several years he was police magistrate. He died in 1924. His wife, Hettie Bennett, was a daughter of Riley Bennett, of Franklin County, the Bennett family having come from Posey County, Indiana. Mrs. Hettie Rains still resides at Franklin Heights. She was the mother of five children, four of whom are living: Dr. William S.; Rollo Lee, chief billing clerk of the Old Ben Mining Company; Pearl, wife of Lum Kern; and Lena K., wife of Arnim K. Montgomery.

William S. Rains was born near West Frankfort, September 6, 1891. As a boy he attended country schools and later the Southern Illinois Normal University at Carbondale. He began teaching at the age of eighteen. In 1917 he joined the colors, and at Camp Taylor, Louisville, Kentucky, was assigned duty in the Medical Corps and was selected to complete a course in the Louisville Dental College, where he was graduated in 1918, and was then commissioned a first lieutenant in the Dental Corps. He was sent to Camp Greenleaf, Georgia, and remained there until shortly after the armistice, when he was discharged.

Doctor Rains on March 21, 1919, opened an office in West Frankfort, and enjoys a very large practice in his profession.

He is a thirty-second degree Scottish Rite Mason, being a member of the lodge at West Frankfort and the Consistory and Shrine at East St. Louis. He married, November 24, 1921, Miss Ethel Dorothy Sides, of Elgin, Illinois. Mrs. Rains before her marriage was supervisor of music in the West Frankfort public schools. They have one daughter, Dorothy May, born March 22, 1923.

ROBERT R. WARD, president of the Benton State Bank, is a member of a family of pioneers in southern Illinois not only in point of settlement but also frequently in matters of enterprise and achievement.

The family was founded by Abel and Polly Ann Ward. Both were born in the year 1800 in South Carolina and were married in 1819. Coming to Illinois, they settled in St. Clair County, and afterwards moved to Franklin County. Abel Ward died in 1886 and his wife in 1883. Their son, John Ward, was born in St. Clair County, Illinois, but spent all except the first six years of his life in Franklin County, where he died in 1902, at the age of seventy-eight. He had the distinction of installing the first roller process in a flour mill in the county. He was also a merchant.

William R. Ward, son of John Ward, was credited at one time with being the wealthiest man in Franklin County, and he made most of his wealth by the able management of diversified lines of business. He was born in Franklin County, August 12, 1848, and from the age of four years lived in Benton. He was educated in public schools there, attended Indiana University at Bloomington two years, and as a youth became associated with the general mercantile firm of John Ward & Company. Later he became a partner of Captain C. Moore in the firm of Ward & Moore. In 1871 they established the first bank in Franklin County, known as the Exchange Bank of Ward & Moore. In 1898 it was succeeded by the Benton State Bank, and William R. Ward served as its president until his death in March, 1905. Besides banking and merchandising he was heavily interested in the grain and milling business and was a director of the St. Louis, Alton and Terre Haute Railroad until it was absorbed by the Illinois Central. He was a democrat and Governor Altgeld appointed him a trustee of the Southern Illinois Normal School at Carbondale. He was a member of the Masonic Order and the Christian Church. William R. Ward married Imogene Snyder, daughter of Solomon and Mary (Russell) Snyder, and a granddaughter of Samuel T. Russell, who was one of the first settlers of Williamson County.

Robert R. Ward is a son of the late William R. Ward. He was born in Benton, August 9, 1879, graduated from the local high school, and in 1903 took the A. B. and LL. B. degrees from the University of Illinois. He was admitted to the bar in 1904, but has used his legal education in the management of his banking and other business interests. He was closely associated with his father in the latter's declining years, and in 1904 was elected vice president of the Benton State Bank, and now for a number of years has been president of that institution. His prominence as a banker led to his election as president of the Illinois State Bankers Association in 1918. He could also be classed as one of Illinois' largest and most progressive farmers. A mile and a half east of Benton he has a 700 acre dairy farm, with a herd of a hundred pure bred Holstein cows. He has derived a great deal of satisfaction as well as recreation from the management of this property.

Mr. Ward was a trustee of the University of Illinois at Champaign-Urbana from 1916 to 1921, elected on the democratic ticket. During Governor Lowden's administration he became a member of the State Fair Board, and is still serving on that board. During the World war he was vice chairman of the Eighth Federal Reserve District in handling the Liberty Loan campaigns. Most of his time was spent away from home and business at the district headquarters in St. Louis, and like many other prominent men at the time he worked without thought of physical limitations. Mr. Ward has a beautiful town home in Benton. He is a past high priest of the W. R. Ward Chapter of Royal Arch Masons, a chapter named in honor of his father. He is also a member of the Knights Templar Commandery, Scottish Rite Consistory and Shrine.

Robert R. Ward married, in 1905, Miss Terzie Kirkpatrick. Her father, R. D. Kirkpatrick, was one of the outstanding citizens and business men of Franklin County for many years. Mr. and Mrs. Ward are the parents of six children, the first three born being sons and the three youngest daughters. The sons are: William R., born in 1906, a student in the University of Illinois; Russell D., born in 1907, attending a preparatory school at Asheville, North Carolina; Leroy Albert, born in 1910, a student in the Benton High School. The three daughters are named Martha Imogene, Susan Esther and Mary Isabelle.

The brother of Robert R. Ward, George Snyder Ward, has gained a high place in the legal profession. He graduated from the University of Illinois in 1910, and from Columbia University in 1912. During the World war he was connected with the Alien Property Custodian's office, and he is now a legal specialist practicing in Washington, handling for the most part cases that come before the tax and shipping boards of the Federal government.

HOSEA AUGUST VISE, M. D., was graduated in medicine in 1905, and since 1908 has conducted a large general practice at Benton. He is one of the outstanding professional men of Franklin County, and is a member of a family that has lived prominent and useful lives in this section of Illinois for a great many years.

Originally the Vise family were Welsh. They came to America in Colonial times. One of the ancestors of Doctor Vise was a soldier under Washington in the Braddock campaign and later fought in the Revolutionary war as captain of a Virginia company, participating in the battles of Eutaw Springs and Guilford Court House. He is said to have reached the remarkable age of 103 years, while his wife died at the age of 107. They had a son named Nathaniel Vise, who married Dorcas Meadows, who was of English ancestry and a descendant of Pocahontas. Nathaniel Vise was the father of Hosea Vise, founder of the family in Illinois. He was born in the Spartanburg district of South Carolina in 1811. He married Lettie Moore, daughter of Ellsworth Moore. She was born in South Carolina in 1814. Their wedding is said to have been the first "temperance wedding" in South Carolina,

Anatol Gollos

marked by the absence of whiskey, a break in the common social custom which made Hosea Vise unpopular and was the main or one of the main reasons why he came west. In 1835 he settled in Posey County, Indiana, and a short time later came to Hamilton County, Illinois. He settled on a farm, but became widely known all over southern Illinois as a minister of the Missionary Baptist Church. He preached forty-eight years, and during that time filled all of his appointments but four, and for thirty-eight years was moderator of his district and missed only two meetings. He organized more churches of his denomination than any other man in southern Illinois, and he delivered the first temperance lecture in the counties of Hamilton and Franklin. In 1864 he established a general store at Macedonia. The Vise family have been merchants at Macedonia continuously since them. He was for twelve years postmaster of Macedonia and ten years pension agent. In 1861 he entered the Union army as captain of an Illinois regiment, serving twenty months. He gave his first vote to Andrew Jackson, but espoused the republican cause when Lincoln was nominated. Hosea Vise died February 11, 1897, and his wife in 1886.

Their son, Eliphas Vise, was born in the Spartanburg district, South Carolina, October 11, 1835, and died May 25, 1888. He was a farmer and merchant. His wife was Esther Choiser, whose father, William Choiser, lived to the age of eighty-six and had a military record of service in the Blackhawk Indian, Mexican and Civil wars.

Harvey C. Vise, son of Eliphas H. Vise, was born in Hamilton County, Illinois, October 17, 1856, finished his education in Ewing College and was admitted to the bar, though he has never practiced. In 1872, at the age of sixteen, he became interested in the store founded by his grandfather at Macedonia, and has made that business his principal concern ever since. He is president of the Farmers Exchange Bank of Akin and of the Bank of Macedonia since its organization in 1897. He also owns farming land in Franklin County. He is a republican, a Royal Arch Mason and Odd Fellow. Harvey C. Vise married Sarilda Plaster, daughter of John Plaster. She died in 1886, and of her three children the youngest is Dr. Hosea A.

Hosea August Vise was born on his father's farm at Macedonia, August 10, 1881. Prior to beginning his professional career he had a very thorough and liberal education. He attended village school at Macedonia, spent three years in Ewing College and two years in Washington University at St. Louis, and in 1905 was graduated from the St. Louis College of Physicians and Surgeons. Doctor Vise first practiced at Thompsonville, but in 1908 removed to the larger center of Benton, and has been busy in the performance of his professional duties both in that city and the surrounding country. He is a member of the various medical organizations and is affiliated with the Lodge and Royal Arch Chapter of the Masonic Order at Benton.

Doctor Vise married Miss Grace Mitchell, daughter of George O. Mitchell, of Marion, Williamson County. They have one daughter, Margaret, now attending the Southern Illinois Normal University at Carbondale and fitting herself for teaching.

MAJOR ANATOL GOLLOS, whose home has been in Chicago for about twenty years, is an electrical engineer whose achievements are well known to members of that profession. Major Gollos has participated in some of the triumphs of electrical engineering in America, and in some cases the general public have been aware of the importance of the work without knowledge of the identity of the man responsible for it.

Major Gollos, who is now serving as supervising electrical engineer for the Chicago Board of Education, was born at Berdansk on the Sea of Azov, Russia, in 1877. He grew up there, and in addition to the ordinary education received training in electrical engineering. This early training was supplemented by four years of practical experience as an electrical engineer in Germany. One of his achievements was the installation of the electrical plant for the Second Regiment Armory at Langfuhr near Danzig. Major Gollos came to America in 1903, while the work of construction was under way for the Louisiana Purchase Exposition at St. Louis. At St. Louis he first met Col. E. B. Ellicott, then electrical engineer for the Exposition and now president of the Chicago Board of Education. Major Gollos was employed under Colonel Ellicott at St. Louis. Later he was in the City of Mexico in charge of the underground electrical system for the Mexican Power & Light Company. In 1905 he established his home at Chicago, where he devoted his time chiefly to the practice of electrical engineering. He invented and perfected an automatic train control which has been approved by the Interstate Commerce Commission. In January, 1926, he was appointed supervising electrical engineer for the Chicago Board of Education, and thus again has come under the direct authority of Colonel Ellicott. Recently Major Gollos presented a plan for a type of electrical "feeder" installation in public school buildings that reduces the cost in this one item of many thousands of dollars in each building, and will amount to an imposing total in the course of a year's aggregate construction. The system which Major Gollos has carried out with the approval of Colonel Ellicott he had previously introduced in similar work which he designed and installed in the new Union Passenger Station of Chicago. For four and one-half years he was electrical engineer of the Union Passenger Station of Chicago.

Major Gollos rendered some notable service during the World war period. He was called upon as a civilian for duty in 1918 at Edgewood Arsenal, Maryland, the main plant of the Chemical Warfare Division of the United States army. Colonel Ellicott was an officer at the Edgewood Arsenal. After a short time Major Gollos was taken into the United States army and assigned to duty in the Construction Division of the Quartermaster's Department with the rank of captain. His duties were performed so efficiently and thoroughly as to draw from Colonel Ellicott a letter of the highest praise when Major Gollos took his discharge in March, 1919. He now has the rank of major in the Officers Reserve Corps. Major Gollos is a member of the Military Order of the World War, National Sojourners Association, Castle Post of the American Legion, the Quartermasters Association and the Society of American Military Engineers.

In 1905, soon after coming to Chicago, he married Miss Florence Hammersley. They have two children, Norman H. and Hortense Gollos, both native Chicagoans. The son was educated in the Senn High School and at the age of fifteen joined the National Guard of Illinois, becoming a private in the Two Hundred Second Anti-Aircraft Artillery, commanded by Col. C. J. Kraft, this being one of the crack units of the nation's military forces in the Chicago area.

REV. MICHAEL S. GILMARTIN has been a priest of the Catholic Church in Chicago and Illinois for over thirty years. His labors have been abundantly blessed and he is now head of one of the flourishing churches on the South Side of Chicago.

He was born in County Sligo, Ireland, on April 13, 1868, next to the youngest of the eight children of Dominick and Bridget (McGetrick) Gilmartin. Of the six sons and two daughters three are now living. Rev. Michael Gilmartin was educated in public schools in Ireland, and on coming to America attended St. Charles Seminary at Ellicott City and then St. Mary's Seminary at Baltimore. He was ordained to the priesthood June 19, 1892, and coming to Chicago, was assistant pastor of the Holy Angels Church for twelve years, serving under Father Tighe and Bishop McGavick. The late Archbishop Quigley appointed him in April, 1905, as pastor of St. Mary's Church at Woodstock, Illinois. He held that pastorate four years and in that time built a church and rectory and had both of them paid for when he left in 1909.

Father Gilmartin in that year was called upon to organize a new parish at the corner of Sixty-first Street and Michigan Boulevard. Acquiring two acres of land, he built a schoolhouse, rectory and convent, and at the present time about 500 children attend this school. A beautiful new church has been recently erected, which is one of the most artistic in the archdiocese, built at a cost of $300,000, and accommodates 1,500 worshipers.

JAMES C. SWOFFORD. One of the largest commercial establishment in West Frankfort is the J. C. Swofford Hardware Company. This business represents many years of close attention to a developing enterprise on the part of James C. Swofford. James C. Swofford has been fortunate in recent years in being able to turn over most of the details of active management to his son, Rassie A. Swofford.

James C. Swofford was born a few miles northeast of Benton, the county seat of Franklin County, August 16, 1868, son of Hezekiah Swofford. His father was a farmer and later for many years a merchant at Benton. James C. Swofford was reared and educated in the vicinity of Benton, and as a young man began his business career at West Frankfort as a dealer in lumber. Later he was associated with J. L. Smith in business at Royalton.

In 1907 he bought the hardware business of B. F. Murphy, then located in a small frame building where the Masonic Temple now stands. Mr. Swofford has kept his business growing apace with the rapid development of West Frankfort, which since 1905 has become one of the largest industrial towns of southern Illinois. Shortly after purchasing the Murphy store Mr. Swofford moved to the site of the State Bank. By 1916 his trade had reached such proportions that he required a larger and better store building. In consequence he erected the present splendid brick building, with a frontage of 63 feet and depth of 100 feet. The appearance of this building and store would do credit to a town of 100,000 population.

James C. Swofford married Miss Effie Deason. Their son, Rassie A. Swofford, was born January 16, 1889, two miles west of West Frankfort. Up to the age of thirteen his education was acquired in country schools. Since that time he has been identified with his father's business, serving an apprenticeship which was equivalent to a commercial education. He has a business type of mind, and has been successfully carrying the responsibilities of management of the hardware company.

He is a member of the Masonic fraternity and the Sunset Social Club. He married Beulah Adelsberger, daughter of Michael Adelsberger, of Franklin County. Their three children are Severne, Bernice and Jane Dean.

JOHN C. BLACK, M. D. A native of southern Illinois, representative of a pioneer family in that section of the state, Dr. James C. Black was reared and educated and spent the first years of his professional career in Arkansas. About ten years ago he returned to southern Illinois, and has built up an enviable reputation as a specialist of the eye, ear and nose, with home and offices at West Frankfort, Franklin County.

The pioneers of the Black family in southern Illinois were James and William Black, who came north from their former home in Mississippi, and taking up government land made themselves new homes out of the wild country of what then composed Williamson County. James Black was the father of John William Black, who was born at the farm in Williamson County in 1856. He grew up in the country, but farming did not appeal to him as a permanent career, and instead he became a merchant at Carrier Mills in Saline County. In 1894 he removed from Illinois and established himself in the lumber business in Arkansas, in which state he still lives. He married Mary Gold, daughter of John Gold, a Baptist minister, who at the time was living near Ewing in Franklin County. John W. Black and wife had a family of three sons and three daughters.

One of them is Dr. John C. Black, who was born at Carrier Mills in Saline County, April 29, 1887. He was seven years of age when the family removed to Clay County, Arkansas. He grew up at Corning, that county, and graduated from the high school there. In the mean-

H. Lucy Evans

time he had definitely decided to become a physician. In 1911 he was graduated from the medical department of the University of Arkansas, and had one year of additional training as an interne in St. Vincent's Infirmary at Little Rock. With this preparation Doctor Black engaged in general practice in his home town at Corning.

In 1916 he returned to southern Illinois and for five years carried on a general practice at Herrin in Williamson County. In 1920 he pursued a post-graduate course at Chicago in eye, ear and nose, and since 1921 has largely confined his practice to this special field, with home at West Frankfort. For three years and a half he was surgeon at the West Frankfort Hospital. He is a member of the various medical and surgical organizations, is a Knight Templar Mason and Shriner, member of the Franklin County Country Club and the Sunset Social Club.

Doctor Black married Miss Maude Oliver, daughter of G. B. Oliver, of Corning, Arkansas. They have four daughters, named Mary Oliver, Barbara, Julia and Joan.

ERNEST H. SMILEY was born and reared in St. Clair County, Illinois, and for thirty years has been one of the leading business men and public spirited citizens of O'Fallon. He is president of the First National Bank of that city.

He was born near O'Fallon, May 24, 1865, son of Samuel C. and Jennie I. (Simmons) Smiley. There were three brothers of the Smiley family who came from Ireland and settled at Philadelphia, where at one time they owned a large amount of land now included in the city. The grandfather of the O'Fallon banker was Matthew Smiley, a native of Illinois, who married Mary Christy. The maternal grandparents of Ernest H. Smiley were William and Lois (Peach) Simmons, the former from Vermont and the latter from Massachusetts.

Samuel C. Smiley, who died in November, 1916, was a farmer and stock raiser. During the Civil war he was with the One Hundred and Seventeenth Illinois Infantry, and while not wounded, was badly crippled from inflammatory rheumatism. He was an active leader in local politics, serving one term in the State Legislature and for many years as member of the school board and as township trustee. His wife died July 15, 1879. Of their four children Ernest H. is the oldest. He has never married. His brother, Charles T., who has suffered much ill health, has been a business partner of Ernest, and by his marriage with Carrie Little had four children. The daughter Josephine Smiley married George Remick and became the mother of three children. Jennie Smiley's first husband was Joseph Umbarger and she is now the wife of Thomas Lee and has two children.

Ernest H. Smiley attended district schools, the Smith Academy, St. Louis, and in 1894 graduated from the St. Louis College of Pharmacy at St. Louis. Mr. Smiley was in the drug business at O'Fallon actively for fourteen years. In the meantime, in 1903, he organized the First National Bank, and has continuously served as president and director, and since selling his drug business has devoted most of his time to his executive duties in the bank. He and his brother Charles organized the O'Fallon Telephone Company and built what is known as the Smiley Brothers Telephone Exchange. They still own this property, Ernest Smiley being its active manager, while his brother Charles is a director in the bank and telephone company.

Mr. Ernest Smiley has been township treasurer for twenty-five years, and also treasurer and one of the organizers and directors of the O'Fallon Building & Loan Association. He has been a leader in the republican party, serving more than twenty-three years on the County Central Committee, its vice-chairman twenty years and the present chairman. He was a delegate to the National Republican Convention at Cleveland in 1924, and has been an alternate delegate several other times. He has never consented to become a candidate for a political office. Mr. Smiley is a member of the Methodist Episcopal Church and is a Knight Templar and thirty-second degree Scottish Rite Mason and Shriner, and also belongs to the Independent Order of Odd Fellows.

H. LEROY EVANS is president of H. Leroy Evans & Company, a prominent real estate firm operating in the North Side and in north suburban properties of Chicago. Mr. Evans is regarded in Chicago real estate circles as a conspicuous authority on acreage values.

He was born in Kansas City, in 1894, and was reared and educated there. He had a thorough training and successful experience in the real estate business in his native city, and in the early part of 1923 came to Chicago and joined the organization of George F. Nixon & Company as vice president and general manager. He was with that company three years, and during that time did most of the buying of acreage for the company. Then, in April, 1926, he engaged in business for himself, founding the H. Leroy Evans & Company, with general offices in the McJunkin Building at Wilson Avenue and Broadway. The firm has a complete general real estate service, but also specializes in acreage and subdivisions, being one of the prominent firms operating in the new Niles Center, Mundelien and Highland Park sections in the north suburban district.

Mr. Evans is an active member of the Chicago Real Estate Board, and also a member of the Subdividers Division of the Chicago Real Estate Board. He belongs to the Illinois Athletic Club, the Edgewater Country Club and North Shore Polo Club. He is a member of Lawton Lodge No. 183, A. F. and A. M.

Mr. Evans enlisted with the Ambulance Company (unattached), with headquarters at Fort McIntosh at Laredo, Texas, when General Pershing invaded Mexico after Villa, and served there about one year and then received his discharge and returned to Kansas City. In the World war he again enlisted and was attached to the Thirty-fifth Division and sailed for France in November, 1916, and was in the St. Mihiel draft and through the Argonne and on the Verdun front. He received his discharge in June, 1919, and returned immediately to the United States and to Kansas

City. When the armistice was signed he was top sergeant of his company and with fourteen men was on his way to Metz. There were over 100 planes circling above him dropping shells, but he escaped uninjured.

Mr. Evans married Sophia Helen Reed, a native of Illinois. They have three children, Robert Leroy, William Reed and Martha Lee. Mr. Evans has his home in Oak Park.

FRITZ L. HASKELL. Few citizens of Scott County are better known than Fritz L. Haskell, former county treasurer, sheriff and present deputy sheriff. He has spent all of his life in the county, and probably no other family represented by descendants of the present generation settled earlier in this section of Illinois.

His grandfather and pioneer of the name in Western Illinois was Benjamin Haskell, born in Maine in 1798. He was of English ancestry. In childhood he moved with his parents to Massachusetts, and at the age of fourteen, to the neighborhood of Batavia, Ohio. He grew up and finished his scanty schooling there, and early showed a taste for adventure and changing scenes. He was a farmer, a carpenter and also a river man, a great disciple of Nimrod, being a real frontiersman in woodcraft. His favorite gun, "Long Tom," now much over 100 years old, is a curio in the courthouse.

Benjamin came to Illinois in 1826, and the following year entered his first eighty acres of land, near Exeter, building a log house with his own hands, which is still well preserved and is the property of his grandchildren. He is said to have been a volunteer in the Black Hawk war and in April, 1839, was united in marriage with Sally (Coonrod) Mills, this being the second marriage celebrated in Scott County after being set off from Morgan County the previous February. He departed this life in 1852.

Mrs. Mills was the widow of James Mills, a former pioneer, and the six children of her first marriage were James M., Sarah Snowden, George W., Julia Leeply, Eliza and Henry, the latter two dying in early youth. The children born to her marriage with Benjamin Haskell were Daniel W., Elizabeth Morris (of Nebraska), Beda, one child who died in infancy, and John H., late of California.

Mrs. Haskell came to Illinois from Virginia, her ancestors being of Scotch-Irish and of German descent. This trip was made entirely by water, previous to the advent of the steamboat, and she arrived near Naples in 1823, but a few years after the state was admitted to the Union, and even a less length of time after the greater portion of Central Illinois had been ceded to the government by the Indians. She began life here in a one-room log cabin, with no annex, no lean-to and no loft; in it the sparkling log fire played the lights and shadows over the pole rafters beneath the clapboard roof, upon which the sun beat down with all its intensity in the summer and through which the snow sifted from the blizzards of winter. She departed this life in March, 1883.

Daniel W., father of Sheriff Haskell, was born near Exeter, January 3, 1840. He served for three years in the Union army, a member of Company K, Fourteenth Illinois Volunteers. The morning of the battle of Shiloh he was severely burned, requiring several months to recover. Rejoining his company, he was made regimental color sergeant, a position he retained to the end of his three-year enlistment, participating in the battle of Hatchie, in the campaign against Vicksburg, and on Sherman's famous Meridian raid. After being mustered out in June, 1864, he soon returned to Nashville, Tennessee, where he was a civilian employe of the government until the close of the war.

Daniel was well known for his versatile gifts and ability. He had read deeply and extensively with a superior mind, and was particularly delighted with scientific and historical subjects. He was an extreme lover of nature and possessed an inventive turn of mind. He made a particular study of plant life and was familiar with a wide range of plant and animal life. To him all elements of nature had their place and a purpose and were entitled to respect. He was a splendid blacksmith, a carpenter, and loved to study mechanics. In reading matter he especially delighted in the political and evolutionary adventures of the race.

His death in November, 1912, was the result of an accident in which he was fatally burned. Thus in passing the whole of life seemed to have been an interesting study to him, and even in dying he appeared to be noting the sensations as the sparks of life ebbed away.

He was united in marriage with Sarah Eda Mills in 1869, she being the fifth child of a family of eight children of Alfred and Beda (Lowe) Mills. Mr. Mills came to Illinois in 1822 from Massachusetts, being one of the earliest settlers to enter land in this community. At least four previous generations of the Mills family had lived in New England. Mr. Mills died in 1885, at the age of eighty-five. Mrs. Mills was native of Tennessee, subsequently removing to Missouri, and her father, Aquilla Lowe, had served in the 1812 war under the leadership of the illustrious Jackson, and for a time had been a British prisoner at New Orleans; later he and a companion staked off and named what is now the City of Jacksonville.

Mrs. Sarah Haskell, the mother of our subject, was born March 19, 1843, and after reaching maturity she taught school for five years during and following the Civil war. Mrs. Haskell was particularly a home maker of a poetic turn of mind, a lover of flowers and cultivated them in great profusion. She had the widest range of accomplishments, and to her all worth while things were of equal importance, and every moment "jeweled with a joy." She departed life in April, 1912, seven months previous to that of her husband. The children of this union were: Maude, who died at the age of ten years; Fritz L.; and Dovie, now a resident of Winchester.

Fritz was born July 4, 1874, and lived the first forty years of his life on the home farm. After attending the rural school until grown he spent one winter at Dixon Normal College and the following winter took the agricultural course at the University of Illinois.

In 1914 he was elected county treasurer on the republican ticket. In this capacity he served four years and in 1918 was elected sheriff and collector. During the former term he introduced many reforms in the administration of affairs, especially in the care and improvement of county property, doing a great deal of landscape work and transforming the surroundings into scenes of beauty. The inside of the courthouse was also made attractive with pictures, curios and decoration. Many alterations came about by his diligent energies in their behalf.

During this term also came the World war, at which time Mr. Haskell was elected chairman of the County Red Cross Chapter, a position he still holds. This humane organization raised and expended more than $25,000. He was also secretary for the Exemption Board, precinct registrar, chairman of the "Four Minute Men," member of the State Council of Defense, member of the Eighth Federal Reserve Board during the Liberty and Victory bond sale drives and was chairman or secretary of nearly every drive put on in the county during the war, besides making out hundreds of questionnaires after registration.

During his term as sheriff came the flood of 1922, when much of the Illinois bottom was under water, including Naples. At that time much supervision was required in looking after the unfortunates and distributing the thousands of dollars in money and supplies contributed.

Following this came the railroad strike on the Wabash, when it was deemed necessary to have many deputies at Bluffs, which for a time required a good deal of supervision. During this term a number of improvements were made in the sanitary condition of the county jail.

At the conclusion of his term as sheriff he was appointed as deputy sheriff by his successor, Mr. Thomas, and is still serving in that capacity. During these twelve years of public service he has found much time for the collection of data and historical matter, a great deal of which has been published in local newspapers or in pamphlets. Recently the State Historical Society published a Civil War Diary by Col. William Camm, which was compiled by Mr. Haskell. He has made a detailed account of Scott County's participation in the World war.

Officially he has always believed a public servant owed the best there was in him to his constituency, that taxpayers were entitled to know what was going on, and he has taken no little pride in publishing such facts in both newspapers and pamphlets. Characteristic with his paternal ancestors, he is not given much to games and sports but as a hobby delights in plying mechanical tools and in creating useful appliances.

He is serving his seventh year as secretary of the Winchester Public Library, has been secretary of the Scott County Historical Society since its organization, is officially connected with the County Tuberculosis Society, a member of the Sanatorium Board, of the Winchester Mining Company, treasurer of the City Volunteer Fire Department, a member of the M. W. A., of the I. O. O. F. and the A. H. T. A.

He was united in marriage with Anna M. English, daughter of Rev. Nathan and Emma (Mills) English, at Arnold, Nebraska, on June 30, 1920. When a young man Nathan English, oldest son of George W. and Sarah (Bryant) English, of New Salem, Illinois, emigrated to Nebraska, where, after teaching school a few years, he married Emma, only daughter of William and Lucinda Mills, of near Lincoln. He entered the ministry of the Methodist Episcopal Church and became one of the leading pioneer preachers of that western country, devoting a total of thirty-five years to the church.

Anna (Mrs. Haskell) was born in a sod house near Arnold, Nebraska, and grew up in various parsonage homes. The family moved to Illinois when Reverend English entered the Illinois Conference. She taught school for a number of years, and during this time carried on her college work during the summers, receiving her diploma from the State Teacher's College at Kearney, Nebraska, in 1918 and her A. B. degree from the Illinois Woman's College in 1920. Rev. and Mrs. English had five other children, Lulu Downing, Herbert V., George William, and Florence Grim, all of Nebraska, while Raymond died at the age of eight years at Jacksonville, Illinois.

Mr. and Mrs. Haskell were the parents of one son, a beautiful, lovable child, born August 2, 1924. Daniel Mills, as he was named, lived but twenty-one months and twenty-one days, but in that brief span of time he became the seat and center of all family interest, budded, blossomed and bloomed—bubbled with mirth, tingled with attraction and glowed with affection, then sickened, faded and disappeared, leaving his parents submerged in the greatest sorrow they have ever known.

CARL CHOISSER joined the colors shortly after his admission to the bar, and since the war has practiced in Franklin County and is one of the able and successful lawyers of Benton. He is also a member of the Illinois Legislature.

Mr. Choisser is a descendant of Voltaire Choisser, who came from Montreal, Canada, with his family of eleven sons and one daughter and settled in southern Illinois, near Cairo, more than a century ago. This is one of the oldest and most influential families of southern Illinois. The name Voltaire has been handed down from one generation to another. The grandfather of the Benton attorney also bore the name Voltaire and owned and operated a large farm at Raleigh in Saline County. On this farm was born Ewing Choisser in 1875. Ewing Choisser has been a resident of Benton since 1896, and is now connected with the state government in carrying out the hard road building program. He married Emma Parrish, member of a prominent family of that name in Johnson County.

Carl Choisser was born at Ozark in Johnson County, July 10, 1895. He was reared at Benton, graduated from high school there in 1913, and in 1917 took his law degree at the University of Illinois. In the fall of that year he was admitted to the bar and in December, 1917, joined the colors, having enlisted in the air service. He had his ground training at Champaign and a few months later was transferred to Chanute Field, and from there was one of the men selected to attend the flying school of Cornell University in New York. He remained there until after the armistice, receiving his honorable discharge November 25, 1918.

Mr. Choisser then located at Benton and opened his law office. He has a general practice, much of it corporation work, and is also city attorney for Zeigler and North City. He was elected a member of the Legislature in 1922, was reelected in 1924 and also in 1926.

Mr. Choisser, who is unmarried, is a thirty-second degree Scottish Rite Mason, member of the Mystic Shrine at St. Louis, the Knights of Pythias, B. P. O. Elks, American Legion and belongs to the Baptist Church.

ONA M. KIRK. The Kirk family was established in southern Illinois a century ago, and four generations of the name have been noted as capable citizens, good farmers and business men. A representative of the fourth generation is Ona M. Kirk, present county treasurer of Franklin County.

The founder of the family in this state was his great-grandfather, a Scotch-Irishman who came from England and on locating in Illinois settled near Spring Garden in Jefferson County. He took up government land, and in time became one of the largest land owners in that locality, his land embracing several tracts in the southern part of Jefferson County, up to the line of Franklin County. Robert Kirk, grandfather of Ona M. Kirk, was born in Jefferson County, and the young man moved a few miles from the old homestead into Franklin County. His son, Matthew Kirk, born in Franklin County in 1839, is now eighty-seven years of age and is one of the oldest living native sons of the county. As a young man he drove ox teams from Franklin County to Virginia City and Helena, Montana, and spent three years prospecting in the mining regions there. In spite of sickness he was more successful than most miners, and on returning to Illinois had enough capital to buy sufficient land for a good farm in Franklin County. For many years he engaged in farming in Eastern Township, but is now retired and a resident of Benton. He married Ethelind Phillips, daughter of Peter Phillips. Peter Phillips came from North Carolina, and soon afterwards to Illinois, settling in Franklin County. He was a soldier in the Civil war, and after farming for some years engaged in merchandising at Benton. Mrs. Ethelind Kirk died in May, 1912. She was the mother of ten children: Mrs. Chloe Dollins, Alva, Mrs. Bertha Thredkeld, Victor, Mrs. Joyce Smith, Ona M., Harvey, Mrs. Lula Rogers, Mrs. Libby Frailey and Mrs. Katie Payne.

Ona M. Kirk was born on the old homestead farm, December 19, 1883. While a youth he attended country school in the winter, spent the rest of the year working on the farm, and at the age of twenty-one bought a small place of his own and engaged in farming as an independent vocation. By the time he was thirty years of age he had reached that degree of independence represented in the ownership of a farm of 120 acres, well cultivated and improved. This farm lies eight miles northeast of Benton. Mr. Kirk in 1906 left southern Illinois under the spell of the western fever, and moved out to Washington, where he tried the life of a cowboy and rancher. After one year he was satisfied to return to an Illinois farm.

Mr. Kirk in 1911 married Miss Maude, daughter of John King. In 1914 they left the farm and moved to Benton, where Mr. Kirk for eight years was an employe of the United States Fuel Company. In 1922 he was elected county treasurer, being elected on the democratic ticket in a republican county. Mrs. Kirk is his deputy treasurer, and together they have administered this office in a way to insure satisfaction to all concerned.

Mrs. Kirk's father, John W. King, was born on land now included in the city of Indianapolis, Indiana, and was a child when his parents settled in Franklin County. For many years he followed farming, but is now living retired near Ewing. Mrs. Kirk's mother was Eliza Morris, whose family came from Kentucky to Franklin County. Mrs. Kirk finished her education in Ewing College. They have one daughter, Virginia Kirk, born October 11, 1917. Mr. Kirk is a member of the Masonic fraternity, the Lions Club and the Christian Church.

ELMER RICH. In business affairs of great importance, as well as in civic movements which have contributed to the development of the city of his adoption, Elmer Rich has become well and favorably known to the present generation of Chicagoans. While a resident of this city only since 1912, his activities have been of such scope as to bring him prominently to the forefront, and at the present time he is president of the Simoniz Company and of the South Central Association.

Mr. Rich was born December 28, 1882, at Detroit, Michigan, and was about seven years of age when taken by his parents to Seattle, Washington, where he attended public school. He grew up in the period of Seattle's history that marked its emergence from a pioneer western town to a city that by its continued subsequent expansion has become one of the country's important metropolitan centers. In early youth Mr. Rich entered the office, first as a clerk, of Judge Thomas Burke, general western counsel for the Great Northern Railroad, and in time rose to a position of responsibility and importance as personal representative of Judge Burke and the executive department of the Great Northern in the management of large development enterprises in the state of Washington. These enterprises included the building of the extensive irrigation works at Wenatchee, Washington, that has made this one of the richest horticultural and agricultural sections of the country, the building of the first traffic bridge across the Columbia River in Washington, and various other projects of a similar nature in the northwest. Mr. Rich subsequently became associated in a similar capacity with the late Darius Miller, then president of the Chicago, Burlington & Quincy Railroad, which had come under the control of the James J. Hill interests. It was in this way that he located at Chicago in 1912, and this city has since been his home. After the death of Mr. Miller, Mr. Rich engaged in business on his own account at Chicago, and founded and is the president

of the Simoniz Company, the Chicago plant of which is located at 2114-20 Indiana Avenue, the other plants of the concern being at Seventieth Street and West End Avenue, New York City, and in London, England, and Paris, France.

Almost from the time of his advent at Chicago Mr. Rich has taken an active part in civic movements, his most important activity in this respect being as president of the South Central Association, composed of representatives of that rich commercial and industrial section of the city bounded by Van Buren Street on the north, Thirty-ninth Street on the south, and extending from the Lake to the south branch of the Chicago River. It was under the auspices of the South Central Association that the great celebration of the opening of the new outer drive along the South Shore was held July 15, 1925, in which the mayor and officials of the South Park Board officiated. This event marked the completion of the Twenty-third Street viaduct connecting the outer drive with South Park Boulevard, thus relieving the congestion of traffic from the South Side to the downtown section and solving the problem of southward expansion to relieve the central district, which has outgrown its facilities for serving a greater Chicago. This opening formed a part of the Chicago Plan that has been developing for several years, and is considered one of the most important steps Chicago has taken in its history. It was truly a notable event.

In addition to being president of the South Central Association Mr. Rich is a director in the Equitable Trust Company and a member of a number of clubs and organizations, including the American Athletic Club, the Lake Shore Athletic Club, the Exmoor Country Club, the Bobolink Country Club, the Arctic Club of Seattle, New York Athletic Club, the Chicago Association of Commerce, the Chicago Motor Club and the Chicago Auto Trade Association. Mrs. Rich was formerly Miss Josephine Sullivan.

MRS. MARY Y. RUNNELS is circuit court clerk of Franklin County. This is an office with a large volume of administrative and detailed responsibilities, but for many years no one more competent has filled the position than Mrs. Runnels.

She is a daughter of the late George Young, who came from Tennessee to Franklin County during the '70s, settling near Ewing. He was connected with the woolen mills of that vicinity until his death, which occurred January 2, 1926. George Young married Martha Seargeant. Her father, John L. Seargeant, came from Virginia and settled at Ashley, Illinois, soon after the Civil war.

Mrs. Runnels, one of a large family of ten children, was born in 1880 and was educated in public schools at Ewing, and for three terms was a student in Ewing College. After finishing her education she taught for several years in Franklin and Jefferson counties, and on December 23, 1906, became the wife of William E. Runnels, who was born September 1, 1880. Mr. Runnels was an assistant electrician in the mines. He died December 3, 1918, during the influenza epidemic.

Mrs. Runnels was left with a family of five children to provide for. These children are Robert E., born December 4, 1907; Margaret, born July 1, 1909; Doris, born October 30, 1910; George, born February 11, 1912, and Evelyn, born April 13, 1914. For two years prior to her marriage, Mrs. Runnels had been deputy clerk, and being a woman of thorough education, of experience in office routine, and well known to the voters of the county, she accepted nomination on the democratic ticket, and in a republican county was elected in 1924 to the office of circuit clerk by more than 1,000 majority.

GEORGE JUSTUS PEAK. Breeders of fine horses and cattle everywhere are familiar with some of the products of the Peak Stock Farm near Winchester in Scott County. Thus the business, profession and industry of one individual has brought some measure of substantial fame to one of the prominent rural communities of Illinois and has served to increase the reputation of this great state as a center of agriculture.

The founder of the Peak family in Scott County was Bird Peak, who in 1833 brought his family to Illinois from Tennessee, making the journey in an old fashioned covered wagon. The land he entered in Scott County is now owned by one of his great-grandsons, Keith Peak. Bird Peak achieved a full measure of success as a pioneer farmer. Among other accomplishments he was one of the most skilful of the old time penmen. He died in 1888, when well past the age of eighty years. He married a Miss Williams, and their children were: Reuben, James, Jacob, George, Samuel, Justus, Vallotta McLaughlin, Permelia, who married Jasper Claywell, Harriet, who became the wife of Jim Young, Sarah, who married Al Edmundson, and Lucy, who married John Waters.

Jacob Peak was born near Nashville in 1828. While making the journey by wagon to Illinois he fell out, and one of the wheels passed over his arm, breaking it and leaving it crooked the rest of his life. He had a limited education in a log cabin school near the old home. He worked hard, was a good manager, a splendid judge of live stock, and acquired a large body of farming land, though he had started life comparatively poor. He was interested in the breeding and feeding of cattle, and frequently exhibited his stock at local fairs, his example having inspired his son George J. for the work which has been the chief basis of his reputation in Central Illinois. Jacob Peak died in 1917. He married Mary Young, who died in 1921. Her father, Major James Young, came to Illinois from Kentucky, was a farmer and served as an officer in the Union army. The children of Jacob Peak and wife were: Howard, who died in 1904, leaving two children; Albert, who died at Winchester in 1921, leaving seven children; James, of Winchester; Alice, wife of Wesley Hamilton, of Winchester; George J.; Stella, wife of Edgar Hamilton, of Winchester; and Kate, wife of George Stewart, of St. Louis.

George Justus Peak was born December 5, 1860, on the farm in Scott County now owned by David Moss. Eight years later his parents moved to what is now known as the Peak homestead, and on that farm George J. Peak lived forty years. He had the opportunities of the country schools, and he remained at the home farm for ten years after his marriage. At the age of eighteen he began exhibiting live stock at county fairs. His first exhibit was a team of road horses, shown at Pittsfield. These horses were awarded second prize. With this as a beginning he has made his life work the breeding of blooded stock, chiefly standard bred horses and Shorthorn cattle. His horses have been chiefly of the Peter the Great strain. He developed Kentucky Peak, which was the grand champion at the St. Louis World's Fair of 1904. His Tommy Doyle was a well known champion, and at Kansas City, Missouri, won the highest prize ever offered for any show horse, and about six years ago Tommy Doyle and Tommy Piper won the championship in Kansas City in competition with Lula Long's famous exhibits. Peter Handsome was another of the roadster class bred at the Peak Farm and has been at the head of his class during the last four years. Another, St. Mesron, won the silver trophy at Los Angeles in 1926. Lillian Seidels is a mare which brought away the champion prize at the Chicago show in 1925, and is pronounced by many judges as the handsomest mare ever shown. The Peak Farm at this writing has about twelve show horses, including Jack London, the largest winner in any one show, having won prizes to the value of a thousand dollars during one week of exhibition at Los Angeles. The Peak Shorthorn cattle herd has been of growing note for a quarter of a century, and some have been in the champion class in the Chicago shows. King Foluto, winner of the championship over eighty-six entries, weighed a thousand pounds before he was a yearling.

Mr. Peak's life interests have been concentrated on this work as a horseman and cattle man, and through this industry he has contributed something worth while to his community. He took a prominent part in the local activities during the World war and secured the first load of hogs representing a donation from the county for food for the soldiers. He is a republican, having cast his first presidential vote for James G. Blaine, and for the past four years has been chairman of the Republican Central Committee of Scott County. He is a Baptist and is affiliated with the Independent Order of Odd Fellows.

Mr. Peak married at Winchester, November 24, 1897, Miss Nora B. Bush, a native of Scott County and daughter of Charles Bush. Her brother, Arthur Bush, lives at Winchester. Mr. and Mrs. Peak have two sons, Mark Charles and Ralph Peak. Mark is a stock man and farmer at the old homestead, and by his marriage to Roena Martin has two children, Alice Lenora and Thomas Martin.

MARTIN KENT NORTHAM, member of the Illinois Deep Waterway Commission, is a man of solid worth and astute business ability, which find expression in his present undertaking, the handling of railroad equipment, with offices in the New York Life Insurance Building, 39 South LaSalle Street, Chicago. The Northam family is an old one in America, of English origin, its founders in this country coming here from Northamptonshire, England, and becoming pioneers of the historic town of Williamstown, Massachusetts. Representatives of the family served in the Colonial army during the American Revolution, and others from that day on have been associated with the constructive development of this country, and the preservation of the institutions their forebears fought to establish.

The paternal grandfather of Martin Kent Northam, A. M. Northam by name, came from Williamstown, Massachusetts, at an early day and settled in LaPorte County, Indiana, arriving there during the early '30s, at a time when all that part of Indiana was undeveloped and inhabited mostly by Indians. He had the distinction of owning the first horse in the county. Martin Kent Northam was born at LaPorte, Indiana, in 1863, a son of D. K. and Lavina (Parsons) Northam, the former a native of Williamstown, and the latter of Virginia, but were only children when brought to Laporte County by their parents.

Although he spent a brief period at Chicago during the '80s, Martin Kent Northam began his actual business experience at Palatka in railroad construction work with the old Florida Southern Railroad, now a part of the Atlantic Coast Line. Subsequently he went into the traffic department of this road, and still later, not long after it was built by Henry Flagler, with the Florida East Coast Railroad. Continuing in railroad work, in 1895 Mr. Northam came back to Chicago as general agent for the Queen and Crescent Route. and held that position for three years.

In the meanwhile he, with others, had been working to perfect the modern refrigerator car, and when, about 1898, after many preliminary tests, it was decided that it could be used in a practical and satisfactory manner, cars were put into service for the shipment of fruit from California. This was the beginning of the great refrigerator-car transportation industry of the United States in the transportation of perishable freight, which has now assumed commanding proportions. The development of this car was the making of the California fruit industry, and through its almost universal use the people in all parts of the country are able to have fresh fruit and vegetables every month in the year. One of the early achievements of Mr. Northam and his associates was the shipment of refrigerated fruit direct from California to London. For many years past Mr. Northam has been engaged in the railway equipment business at Chicago, as above stated.

Mr. Northam maintains his residence at Evanston, and he is very active in the life of that suburb. He constructed the Evanston Golf Club, which was completed in 1919, serving on the board of directors line, and he belongs to the Evanston Country Club and the Indiana Society of Chicago. A member of the First Presbyterian Church of Evanston, he was for three years a member of its Board of Trustees. By appointment of Governor Small Mr. Northam is a member of the Illinois Deep Waterway Commission.

Mr. Northam married Miss Estelle MacChesney, a daughter of the late Dr. A. C. MacChesney, and a cousin of Gen. Nathan William

MacChesney, a prominent attorney of Chicago, a sketch of whom appears elsewhere in this work. Mrs. Northam was born in Wisconsin, but was reared in Chicago, and she has been thoroughly educated in both this country and abroad. She went from high school in Chicago to Lasell College, Massachusetts, and from there to the Mary Willard School for Girls at Berlin, Germany. Among her journeys from this school, with her teachers and classmates, was a notable one to the home of Count Tolstoy in Russia, and another to the home of Lady Somerset in England. Mrs. Northam has been for many years prominent in social, civic and woman's club affairs in Evanston, Chicago, and the state of Illinois. She was recording secretary of the North End Woman's Club, was later president of the Tenth District of the Illinois Federation of Women's Clubs. Still later she became recording secretary of the state organization, and for a time was president of the North End Woman's Club. In the national campaign of 1920 she was chairman of the Speakers Bureau of the woman's section of the Republican State Central Committee for Illinois, and is now member of the Normal School Board of the State Department of Education, to which she was appointed by Governor Small. A Presbyterian in religious faith, she is now president of the Woman's Division of the First Presbyterian Church of Evanston.

HON. SAM W. LATHAM, M. D. A physician and surgeon and a specialist for a quarter of a century, twice elected mayor of his home town of Eldorado, and a former member of the Illinois State Senate, Doctor Latham has a record reflecting his tremendous vitality and power of achievement.

He was born at Eldorado, April 12, 1878, son of Dr. John F. and Sarah (Westbrook) Latham. His father was born in Virginia, came to Illinois when a young man, and was a laborer while studying in preparation for a medical career. He graduated from the College of Physicians and Surgeons of Keokuk, Iowa, and then engaged in practice at Eldorado. He possessed great versatility and energy, and in the early years of his medical practice he studied law, was admitted to the bar, and for a time gave up medicine altogether and practiced law. He was elected and served four years as state's attorney. Later he resumed his medical practice and continued it until his death at Eldorado in 1884. He was a leader in republican politics and was a Protestant in religion, leaning to the Methodist Church. Sarah Westbrook, his wife, was a daughter of Samuel V. Westbrook, and was born in Saline County, Illinois, and reached the age of eighty years. Her father, Samuel V. Westbrook, was a Scotchman and bore a strong personal resemblance to Andrew Carnegie. He served as a soldier in the Mexican war, was an early settler of Saline County, Illinois, a farmer and a licensed exhorter of the Methodist Episcopal Church. He had a prominent part in building the Wesley Chapel in his community. When he died, about 1910, he had reached the remarkable age of ninety-nine years. Dr. John F. Latham and wife had three children, Belle, Oscar and Sam, all now living.

Sam W. Latham was about six years old when his father died. After that he grew up in the home of his maternal grandfather and lived there on a farm until the age of fifteen, having the advantages of a good country home and the guidance of a splendid Christian gentleman in his grandfather. From the age of fifteen, however, he has made his own way in the world, depending on his own exertions for his higher education and all his attainments. Doctor Latham has done nearly every variety of physical labor, including work as a section hand on the railroad. He was employed for a time in the flouring mill at Eldorado. After the public schools he spent two years in the Central Normal College at Danville, Indiana, and leaving there in the spring of 1897, in the fall of the same year he entered the St. Louis College of Physicians and Surgeons, in which he was graduated in 1901 with the highest honors, being valedictorian of his class. For six months he was an interne in the Jefferson Hospital of St. Louis, and then returned to his native city of Eldorado, where he soon acquired a good general practice. Subsequently he had three post-graduate courses of training in physio-therapy and X-Ray therapy both in Chicago and New York. For several years he has given practically all his time to this phase of the medical profession. He has a splendidly equipped office and laboratory, and it is said that his equipment for X-Ray and other apparatus cost more than $30,000. He is a member of the Saline County, Illinois State and American Medical Associations and the Radiological Society of America.

As a successful businessman he is treasurer of the Tiger Oil Company of Eldorado, of the Big Lake Company, an amusement corporation owning a summer resort and hotel in Gallatin County, Illinois, is a director of the Lions Park Company and the Lions Amusement Company at Eldorado, and a director of the Eldorado Building & Loan Association.

Doctor Latham was a volunteer for service during the World war, but was rejected from army duty on account of hernia. He has served as medical officer of the United States Compensation Committee and is now chief medical director of the Illinois Industrial Commission.

Doctor Latham was for six years secretary of the Eldorado School Board, at a time when the town was putting its school system on a modern basis, involving the erection of several handsome school buildings. In 1910 he was elected mayor of Eldorado and reelected in 1912, and his administration was responsible for a series of improvements that brought Eldorado into class with the progressive communities of southern Illinois in the matter of street paving and other improvements. In 1914 Doctor Latham was elected a member of the Illinois State Senate and served four years, being a member of the General Assembly during the World war period. Doctor Latham in 1924 was again elected mayor of Eldorado. At the outset of his administration he proposed a platform of administration and material improvements in line with his own progressive attitude as a citizen. A large group of taxpayers made strenuous objections to his proposed policy, and finally a special recal election resulted in a vote that deposed him from office.

Doctor Latham has always been a leader in the republican party in his home county. He is a thirty-second degree Scottish Rite Mason and Shriner, member of the Independent Order of Odd Fellows, Knights of Pythias, B. P. O. Elks, Red Men, Moose, and also belongs to the Lions Club. He is a Methodist. Doctor Latham married, in 1901, Miss Lura B. Osburne, daughter of Causey E. and Cynthia Osburne, her father a native of Kentucky and her mother of Illinois.

WILLIAM C. KANE, head of the law firm Kane & Scott at Harrisburg, is known throughout that section of Illinois as a very able lawyer, a man who has made a success of his professional work in all its varied relationships. He has filled public offices with credit and distinction, and his career has well deserved the esteem so abundantly paid him.

He was born on a farm in Saline County, Illinois, September 19, 1873, and his grandparents on both sides were among the earliest settlers of the county. His parents, Robert C. and Mary E. (Mingo) Kane, were born in Saline County. His grandfather, Hugh Kane, was a native of Allegheny County, Pennsylvania, and during the '30s came to Illinois, first settling at Shawneetown. Among the pioneers of that day he was a man of unusual education, having been trained both as a civil engineer and as a physician. He assisted in surveying portions of Saline County and made his permanent settlement on a farm in the northern part of the county. He lived there the rest of his life, and in the early years he taught school, did surveying and practiced medicine. He reared a family of four daughters and three sons.

James Mingo, maternal grandfather of William C. Kane, was born in North Carolina. Coming to Illinois between 1830 and 1835, he settled in Saline County. He went from this county some ten years later as a volunteer in the Mexican war. In the army he was a comrade and close friend of Gen. John A. Logan. He followed farming and reared a family of five sons and five daughters. The Kane and Mingo families are Baptists, and the Kanes were democrats in politics, while the Mingos were republicans.

Robert C. Kane spent his life of industry as a farmer in Saline County, and he also operated a pioneer grist mill, and was a genius in mechanical lines. He died at the age of fifty-six and his widow survived him until 1923.

William C. Kane grew up on a farm, and is one of many successful professional men who confess a heavy debt to the influence of country life and the training of the farm. He attended country schools, became a school teacher, and by teaching earned his higher education. He graduated in 1897 from the Central Normal College at Danville, Indiana. Mr. Kane taught eight terms of winter school and two summer terms. He was for a time teacher in the Harrisburg High School, and while there began the study of law with the firm of Choisser, Whitley and Choisser, then the leading attorneys of Harrisburg. He was admitted to the bar in 1898. He continued teaching for a time after that and then engaged in building up a law practice. When he was about thirty years of age Mr. Kane united with the Primitive Baptist Church and was soon afterward licensed to preach, and for several years was a pastor in Saline County. He gave up the ministry in order to devote his whole time to his increasing law practice. Except for one year at Poplar Bluff, Missouri, his professional career has been spent at Harrisburg. He has been associated with some of the eminent members of the Saline County bar. For thirteen years he was a partner of the late William V. Choisser. Other partners included the present circuit court judge, A. E. Sommers, S. D. Wise, W. W. Wheatley, and his present law partner is Miss Mabel Scott, a daughter of the late Winfield F. Scott, the firm name being Kane & Scott.

Mr. Kane was state's attorney of Saline County from 1908 to 1912. He was elected to that office as a democrat at a time when the county was giving large republican majorities. In 1912 he was again elected to office, being chosen a member of the Legislature from the Fifty-first Senatorial District. In 1914 he was reelected to the Legislature, and served two terms.

Mr. Kane in 1896 married Miss Mary Adda Berry. She died in 1917, leaving three children, John R., Byford C. and Mary Elizabeth. Mr. Kane in 1919 married Mrs. Ethel (Grace) Belt. The one son of this marriage is William B. Kane. The older sons, John R. and Byford C., are veterans of the World war. Both volunteered in 1917 at the outbreak of the war, John at the age of nineteen and Byford when only seventeen. Both enlisted in the Marines, and served in the Thirteenth Regiment of the Marine Corps. They were overseas, participating in the splendid record made by that organization. Byford C. was sent home and given an honorable discharge in June, 1919, and John did not return and get his honorable discharge until August the same year. Both sons are active members of the American Legion. John is now clerk in a Chicago law office and studying law in that city. Byford is a student of osteopathy. The daughter, Mary Elizabeth, is attending the University of Illinois.

WINFIELD F. SCOTT. A notable figure in the citizenship of Saline County was the late Winfield F. Scott. He was one of the younger veterans of the Union army in the Civil war. For many years he held a high position among Southern Illinois educators. After beginning the practice of law he achieved success out of the ordinary in that profession. Altogether his life was such as to deserve the distinction of long memory.

He was born in Hamilton County, Illinois, February 22, 1851. His grandfather, John Scott, was of Scotch nativity, a tailor by trade, and in 1815 brought his family to America, first settling in Gallia County and afterwards in Switzerland County, Indiana. Francis Scott, father of Winfield F., was born at Manchester, England, in 1811, and was four years of age when brought to America. In 1838 he settled in Hamilton County, Illinois,

Geo. W. Ziebold

and lived on a farm there until his death in 1865. He married Sarah Boster, who was of English, Scotch and Irish lineage. She was very energetic, possessed a keen intellect, and devoted her life entirely to her family and children.

Winfield F. Scott was twelve years of age when his mother died. His older brother, Philip, was then in the Union army. Winfield Scott for over a year worked in the Wabash bottoms for his uncle, George Boster, a man of strong Union sympathies, who had several sons in the army. Winfield Scott was unusually large for his age, and in March, 1865, soon after his fourteenth birthday, he sought out his brother in the Union army and enlisted as a private in Company A of the Eighty-seventh Infantry. In June, 1865, he was transferred to Company H of the Eighteenth Illinois Infantry. For seven months he served as dispatch orderly for General McCook, and was in the army until January 9, 1866, when honorably discharged.

Leaving the army about the time he was sixteen, he returned home, impressed with his need of a better education. He made the best of his advantages in schools, and at the age of nineteen qualified as a teacher. While teaching he continued his higher education. His education was the product of work in the common schools, Enfield College and the Northern Indiana Normal School at Valparaiso, where he was graduated Bachelor of Science. He was a teacher for thirteen years, his work in Illinois including two years in Jeffersonville, four years as principal at Xenia, two years at Fairfield, two terms at Enfield College and one year at Carmi. For five years he conducted the Wayne County Teachers Institute at Fairfield. In 1877 he was granted a life teacher's certificate by the state. During his practice as a lawyer he retained a keen interest in every matter of local and general educational progress.

While at Fairfield, in 1880, he took up the study of law under Judge Beecher. He was admitted to the bar in 1883, and the following year removed to Harrisburg, where he formed a law partnership with R. S. Marsh, his boyhood friend and schoolmate. The firm became Marsh and Scott. Their friendship remained unbroken throughout their lives. Mr. Scott brought to his profession sound scholarship, great perseverance, intellectual talents of a high order, and in time he stood among the leaders at the Saline County bar.

He was one of the organizers of the First National Bank of Harrisburg and for several years its president. He was a staunch republican, though he found his satisfaction in his law practice rather than in public office. He served one term as mayor of Harrisburg, for several years was a member of the school board, and was one of the prominent advocates of prohibition and during his last illness frequently expressed pleasure at having lived to see national prohibition as expressed in the Eighteenth Amendment. Shortly after his return from the Civil war he was converted at a Baptist meeting held in the Middle Creek schoolhouse in Hamilton County. Ever afterwards he was a faithful member of that church and for forty years a teacher in the Sunday School.

While a student in Enfield College he met Miss Julia Hunsinger, daughter of Ezekiel Hunsinger, of White County, Illinois. They were married September 7, 1877, while he was teaching at Xenia. That was the beginning of a happy married companionship that endured for forty-three years, until broken by his death on August 20, 1920. Mrs. Scott continues to reside at Harrisburg. There were five children, the only son dying in infancy. The four daughters are Mrs. Winifred Denning of LaGrange, Illinois, Mrs. Gertrude Barnes, Miss Mabel and Miss Edith.

Miss Mabel Scott has had the distinction of being the first woman admitted to the bar in Southern Illinois. She graduated from the Harrisburg High School, attended business college, and for several years was a stenographer in her father's law office, and while there studied law. She also attended the law department of the Northern Indiana Normal College at Valparaiso, and in 1911 was admitted to the bar. She has enjoyed a successful practice in Harrisburg and is now a member of the law firm Kane & Scott.

GEORGE W. ZIEBOLD. At one period, half a century or more ago, Illinois grew as much wheat as any other state in the Union. This supremacy has long been passed, but Illinois still remains a great flour milling state when the many mills are considered in the aggregate. One of the veteran millers of the state whose experience goes back to a time when practically all the mills ground home grown wheat is George W. Ziebold, proprietor of the Waterloo Milling Company at Waterloo in Monroe County.

Mr. Ziebold, whose experience in flour milling runs back considerably more than half a century, was born at California, Missouri, in 1860, and was seven years of age when his father bought a water mill at Monroe City, Illinois. He had in the meantime attended country schools a few months each year, but after the age of fourteen his education so far as schooling was concerned ended altogether. He was endowed with a gift for mechanics and a strong inclination for everything mechanical, and it was more a matter of pleasure than drudgery for him to work in his father's mill. After he left school he was a regular employe, serving an apprenticeship to learn every phase of flour milling, and some of the time driving the teams which in the early days hauled the flour from the mills to the river landing. When he was nineteen years of age his father bought a mill at Red Bud in Randolph County and installed the "roller process." It was one of the first of the then comparatively few roller mills in this part of the state. George W. Ziebold was put in charge of this plant. Four years later he returned to the mill at Monroe City and in 1886 he removed to Waterloo and organized the Waterloo Milling Company. This milling establishment is thoroughly modern, having been made so from time to time, all the machinery having been installed under the personal supervision of George W. Ziebold. Mr. Ziebold is also president of the G. Ziebold Milling Company at Red Bud. The capacity of the mills is 600 barrels per day. He is a former president of the Southern Illinois Millers Association and a member of the Millers National Federation.

During the World war he was chairman of the local board of Monroe County and also food administrator. He is president of the Harrison Bell Telephone System, a director of the Liberty Central Trust Company of St. Louis, director of the Commercial State Bank of Waterloo. He served ten years as mayor of Waterloo, and that administration included nearly all the progressive steps in the improvement of the municipality. The waterworks and electric light systems were built while he was mayor. Mr. Ziebold is a member of the Missouri Athletic Association of St. Louis, being a charter member of that organization, and his favorite sport is motoring.

He married in the fall of 1883 Miss Minnie E. Hoffmeister, of St. Louis.

A son, George C. Ziebold, who has followed in the footsteps of his father as a miller, was born at Monroe City, attended the parochial schools there and at Waterloo. He continued his education in St. Francis College at Quincy, Illinois, and at Notre Dame University at South Bend, Indiana, completed his junior year in law. He studied law not so much with a view to practicing it as a profession as to use it for the benefit of his personal business career. After completing his education he entered the Waterloo Milling Company, and is now business manager of that enterprise. He is chairman of the Waterloo Chamber of Commerce. He married Miss Viola E. Pinkel, daughter of Armin B. Pinkel, a Waterloo merchant. Their four children are Paul, Mary, Esther and an infant.

Max G. Ziebold, a younger son, is assistant manager of the Waterloo Milling Company. He was also educated at Notre Dame University. He is a public spirited young man and has been active in furthering matters pertaining to civic and social improvement, also a keen sportsman and secretary of the Mid-West Beagle Club. He married Edythe M. Brickey, daughter of Mr. and Mrs. F. M. Brickey, of Prairie du Rocher. They have one boy, Frank.

WILLIAM VOLTAIRE CHOISSER. For more than half a century the name Choisser has been distinguished in the legal profession of Southern Illinois, especially at Harrisburg. Harrisburg was the home of the late William Voltaire Choisser, who practiced law there until his death. Before his death his son, Robert E., was admitted to the bar, and he continued the name with honor and distinction in this profession.

William Voltaire Choisser was born on a farm near Mount Vernon in Jefferson County, Illinois, August 28, 1848. The Choisser family is of French origin. They were among the early settlers of Southern Illinois. Edmund Choisser, father of William V., was born in Illinois, and the claim is made that his father was one of the first native sons of the state. Edmund Choisser became a physician. He practiced in Jefferson County and afterwards in Saline County, near Eldorado. During the Civil war he served as a surgeon in the Union army.

William V. Choisser was a volunteer for service in the Union cause, and was perhaps the youngest regularly enlisted soldier from Illinois in the Union army. He was only thirteen and not old enough nor strong enough to perform the regular duties of a soldier, and was therefore made a drummer boy. After the war he attended Southern Illinois State Normal University at Carbondale, also continued his studies in Ewing College and McKendree College, and studied law privately. On being admitted to the bar he located at Harrisburg, and achieved a notable fame in the legal profession in that city. Mr. Choisser was known as a speaker of exceptional gift and eloquence. He was a leader in the democratic party for many years and took an active part in many campaigns. For one term he was state's attorney of Saline County and represented the county in the Lower House of the Legislature. He was a commissioner of the Southern Illinois State Penitentiary, and subsequently was appointed warden of the prison, and was holding that office at the time of his death, on May 18, 1917.

William V. Choisser was a Knight Templar and thirty-second degree Scottish Rite Mason and Shriner and an Elk. He was not a member of any church, but favored the Presbyterian denomination. He married, in 1880, Miss Kate Pearce, a native of Saline County. They became the parents of four children: Robert Edmund, Mary, Nellie and Roger M. Mary is the wife of E. F. Hayes, of Springfield, Ohio. Nellie married C. H. Reid, of Wichita Falls, Texas. Roger M. Choisser graduated from Rush Medical College at Chicago and in 1915 became a surgeon in the United States Navy and served with distinction during the World war at the Great Lakes Training Station, and is still with the navy, his home and headquarters being at Washington. Robert Edmund Choisser was born at Harrisburg, June 5, 1882. He graduated from the Harrisburg High School, in 1906 from McKendree College, and studied law under his father. He was admitted to the bar in 1909, and engaged in practice with William V. Choisser. He served six years as city attorney and is now in his second term as city judge. He also has an extensive private practice.

Judge Choisser is a democrat in politics, is a Scottish Rite Mason and Shriner, member of the B. P. O. Elks and the Presbyterian Church. He married, in 1915, Miss Elizabeth Grace. They have one daughter, Alice Choisser.

CHARLES HENRY THOMPSON, former state's attorney, has practiced law in Saline County since 1919, and is recognized as one of the most influential men in that section of the state.

He was born at Mt. Vernon, Posey County, Indiana, December 11, 1884, son of Lewis and Emma (Monroe) Thompson, also natives of Posey County. His grandfather Matthew Thompson, was born in the United States, but his great-grandfather, James Thompson, was a native of Ireland, and on coming to America landed at New York and soon went west to Ohio and from there to Indiana, locating near Mount Vernon in Posey County. The mother of Charles H. Thompson was a daughter of Edwin S. Monroe, an early settler at Mount Vernon, Indiana, and for many years a riverman engaged in flatboating down the Ohio and Mississippi. Subsequently he lived on a farm. Lewis Thompson was a farmer in early life, then became an employe of a coal mining company, was a foreman, and in 1886 removed to a farm near Eldorado, Illinois. Some seven years later the family moved to Harrisburg, where Lewis Thompson and wife have since had their home, and after years of employment he is now retired. There were two children, Charles H. and Elsie, the latter the wife of Thomas D. Gregg, a druggist at Harrisburg.

Charles H. Thompson was about one year old when brought to Illinois. He attended school while on the farm, completed his high school course at Harrisburg, and studied stenography, bookkeeping and accounting at the Massie Business College in Louisville, Kentucky. Mr. Thompson had valuable business training to supplement his legal education. For five years he was stenographer to the train master of the Big Four Railroad, and for about four years lived in Chicago, part of the time employed in the legal or valuation department of the Rock Island Railroad. While in Chicago he was a student in the Chicago Kent College of Law, graduating in 1918 and was admitted to the bar the following year. For one year he was clerk in a Chicago law office, and then, returning to Harrisburg, engaged in private practice. In 1920 he was nominated by the republicans and elected state's attorney. He gave a very capable administration of that office for a four year term and declined reelection. In 1926 he was a successful candidate for the republican nomination for the State Senate. Mr. Thompson is a member of the Masonic Order and B. P. O. Elks, was president of the Harrisburg Kiwanis Club in 1926, is a member of the Harrisburg Country Club and the Methodist Episcopal Church. He married, in 1916, Miss Ethel K. Knight of Saline County.

LUCIUS A. HINE, who for many years was a Chicago manufacturer, is a resident of Highland Park, and is a member of the firm Hine & Hine, real estate and investments. The record of his career has many points of interest. He was well past the age for military duty during the World war, but having had military training in former years he took an active part in the Illinois Reserve Militia and rose to the rank of lieutenant colonel.

Colonel Hine was born at Berlin Heights, Erie County, Ohio, in 1862, son of Daniel N. and Marinda (Brooks) Hine. Both parents were of Colonial ancestry. In the paternal line he is descended from Thomas Hine, who came from Yorkshire, England, and settled at Old Milford, Connecticut, on Long Island Sound, in 1636. Among the descendants of this pioneer were some of the founders of the Western Reserve in Ohio. In the maternal line Colonel Hine is a great-grandson of Capt. John Brooks, who was an officer under Washington in the Revolution. Both the Brooks and Hine families have participated in every war in America since Colonial times.

Lucius A. Hine was graduated an engineer from Ohio State University at Columbus in 1888. While in the university he had regular training for five years in the Cadet Corps under United States Army officers, and during that time his training experience brought him practical knowledge of the duties of private, sergeant, second lieutenant of artillery, second lieutenant of infantry, first lieutenant of infantry, acting battalion adjutant, captain of infantry, acting major of infantry.

After his university career Colonel Hine was employed as chemist and assistant superintendent for the Northwestern Iron Company at Mayville, Wisconsin, then as engineer in charge of surveys for the Sandusky and Columbus Short Line Railroad, and for three years he was principal of the high school of Sandusky. Later he was professor of civil and mining engineering in the State School of Mines of South Dakota at Rapid City.

After becoming a resident of Chicago, Colonel Hine for over twenty years was engaged in the manufacturing and jobbing business in that city. He retired in 1921 and has since given his attention to real estate and investments at Highland Park.

From April, 1917, when America entered the World war, until January, 1920, when he was honorably discharged, Colonel Hine was in continuous military duty during the World war period. He organized in April, 1917, the Highland Park Volunteer Patrol. Shortly afterward he was made captain of the Illinois Volunteer Training Corps Unit No. 309, and was promoter to major in that organization. On October 31, 1917, this Volunteer Training Corps became the Illinois Reserve Militia, and he was commissioned a major in that organization and assigned to the First Regiment of Infantry in command of the First Battalion. In March, 1919, Lieutenant Colonel Lorenzen was put in charge of the depot organization, consisting of fifty-four separate rifle companies, and at the same time Major Hine was assigned to the duty of acting adjutant general of the depot organizations. Later on Colonel Pelouze, commanding the First Regiment, was placed on the retired list and Lieutenant Colonel Lorenzen was promoted to the command of the First Regiment, at which time Major Hine was promoted to lieutenant colonel and placed in command of the depot organizations. Lieutenant Colonel Hine organized these troops into separate provisional battalions of four companies each and procured through Governor Lowden complete equipment from the United States Government, so that each soldier was prepared to take the field, and in the meantime the state government furnished these troops with light, heat and quarters at the state's expense.

After locating in Chicago Colonel Hine married Miss Winifred Otis, daughter of the late Frederick R. Otis, long one of the distinguished citizens of Chicago. Colonel and Mrs. Hine have two sons. The older, Frederick Otis Hine, now associated with his father in business, enlisted at the age of nineteen during the

World war and served as a lieutenant in the United States Army. The younger son, Lucius A. Hine, Jr., is a graduate of Cornell University and now associated with the well known Chicago firm of Joseph T. Ryerson & Son.

WILLIAM J. HOOD. This enterprising and successful merchant of Sparta, Randolph County, represents a pioneer family of southern Illinois, and a family which through the different generations has exemplified some very forceful and admirable traits of character.

The grandfather was John Alexander Hood. He was born in Ireland, and belonged to a family of fishermen. As a boy he accompanied his father and others on a fishing trip off the coast of Ireland. A great storm came up, and John Alexander Hood saw his father and brothers drown before his eyes. He was an expert swimmer and possessed great strength and endurance, and his life was saved because he was able to survive while clinging to a rock for three days until the storm subsided and permitted his rescue. Not long after that experience John Alexander Hood immigrated to America, first settling in South Carolina. At Charleston in that state was born his son, Samuel Bateman Hood, whose record as an educator forms the subject of another paragraph.

When Samuel B. Hood was eight years of age John A. Hood started with his family for Illinois, locating on a farm five miles west of Sparta, in a community known as Pleasant Ridge. John A. Hood developed a good farm and lived a life that commanded general respect and esteem. He was always known as a man strong in his convictions as to what was right and wrong. When he left the Carolinas to come to Illinois his wagon was one of a considerable caravan participating in the migration. On the arrival of the first Sunday the leaders of the party decided to keep on going. John A. Hood determined to observe the Sabbath and he stayed in camp and rested. He observed the same rule each succeeding Sunday, and he had some measure of satisfaction and reward when he discovered that he was the first of the party to arrive at their final destination in Randolph County. John Alexander Hood was a charter member of the American Sons of Temperance and one of the pioneer workers in the cause of temperance.

Samuel Bateman Hood from the age of eight was reared on the home farm in Randolph County. He was early distinguished by studious traits and had an ambition to secure a better education than could be obtained in the local schools. He finally attended the University of Michigan, where in addition to his literary studies he took a law course. After returning from the university he taught school at Eden. About that time the Civil war broke out and he enlisted as a private in Company I, Twenty-second Illinois Infantry. He was all through the war, and came out with the rank of captain in evidence of his soldierly conduct and ability as a leader. When he returned to Sparta after the war he resumed teaching. Subsequently he became a merchant at Sparta. His kindly spirit and easy ways with those who owed him soon demonstrated that he was not well qualified for merchandising. Consequently he resumed teaching, and that for forty years was his profession, and through it he realized the best distinctions of a worthy and useful career. For eight years he held the office of county superintendent. At one time he was a candidate for state superintendent of schools, but had none of the gifts of a politician to make his candidacy successful. Few men in the county have received such genuine respect and esteem as Samuel Bateman Hood, who died in February, 1914. He married Margaret Jane Frazier, of an old Virginia family. Of their nine children two died in infancy, and those now living are: Mrs. J. G. Klane, Willam J., John A., Samuel Bateman, Jr., George A., Robert D. and Allen C. The late Samuel Bateman Hood was an antiquarian and for years was a collector of relics, particularly those with some historical value showing the stages of settlement and history in Illinois. At his death he left to his son William J. one of the best private collections of the kind in the state.

William J. Hood was born at Sparta, Illinois, and was educated in the schools of that town. It was his boyhood ambition to become a merchant, and his career has shown that he possesses the proper qualifications for such a vocation. For several years he was employed as a clerk by the firm of Botton & Brown, and in 1902 he decided that there was proper opportunity for establishing a modern progressive mercantile store at Sparta. Having accumulated a small capital, he became associated with his brother George in forming the William J. Hood Dry Goods Company. This business has steadily grown and prospered during the past twenty years or more and is now one of the leading business establishments of its kind in southern Illinois, with a working force of twelve or fifteen clerks.

William J. Hood was born December 23, 1870. He married Bertha B. Bratney, daughter of James C. Bratney. Her father was a former merchant in Randolph County.

WILLIAM WALTER WHEATLEY had been in practice only a short time at Harrisburg when America entered the World war. He was in service until after the armistice, and since then has achieved a creditable record in his profession and in the civic life of his home community.

He was born at Tell City, Perry County, Indiana, September 6, 1887. His father, grandfather and great-grandfather were all named John T. Wheatley. The second John Thomas Wheatley was born in Indiana and died while a Union soldier in the Civil war. John T. Wheatley, III, was born at Tell City, September 15, 1862, and after the death of his soldier father was reared in the home of his grandfather, John T. Wheatley. He acquired a common school education, was a natural student and qualified as a teacher, a profession he followed seventeen years. On removing to Saline County, Illinois, he bought a tract of land in the black land or swamp belt of the county. He was very influential in bringing about the development of this district, becoming a director of the Black Land

Drainage District. These lands are now among the richest agricultural districts of Southern Illinois. John T. Wheatley gave his personal supervision to his farming interests until 1913, and since that year has been in the real estate and insurance business at Harrisburg. He was one of the first commissioners of Harrisburg after the commission charter was adopted. He is a democrat. John T. Wheatley married Augustine Fyie and they have three children, William Walter; Mary, wife of Dr. H. N. Jarvis, of Harrisburg; and Myrtle, wife of C. A. E. Hauptmann, a merchant at Harrisburg.

William Walter Wheatley was four years old when his father settled in Saline County. He lived on the farm to the age of seventeen, attending common schools and graduating from the Harrisburg Township High School. He then entered the University of Michigan, where he was graduated A. B. in 1913, and received his law degree in 1915. He then engaged in practice at Harrisburg, and has his law offices in the First Trust and Savings Bank, Rooms 504-505.

When the selective service act was put into effect in Saline County, Mr. Wheatley stood seventeenth on the roll of eligible men, and in September he went into training, first at Camp Zachary Taylor and then at Camp Sherman, Ohio, with the Eighty-fourth Division. He was assigned to the Fourth Officers Training School and on August 26, 1918, was commissioned a second lieutenant. He was scheduled for duty as an instructor in the Central Officers Training Camp at Camp Fremont, California, but the signing of the armistice caused his discharge before he went West, and he left the army at Camp Sherman December 7, 1918. Mr. Wheatley since the war has twice served as commander of George Hart Post of the American Legion, is the present adjutant of that post, and is a member of the military fraternity "40 and 8."

He is a democrat in politics, is a Catholic, a member of the Knights of Columbus, B. P. O. Elks, the Kiwanis Club and Country Club. Mr. Wheatley married, in 1917, Miss Nell Stanton, of Pana, Illinois. They have three children, John Walter, Dorothy Nell and Irene Patricia.

CLAYTON MARK. In manufacturing circles of Chicago and the middle west the name of Clayton Mark is one that stands for executive ability, organizing power, efficient management and admirable business ethics. A resident of Chicago since 1872, he has been identified continuously since 1876 with the manufacture of iron and steel products, and at present is president of Clayton Mark & Company, manufacturers of and dealers in steel pipe and water well supplies. It is not alone as a business man, however, that he is prominent, for the cause of education in his adopted city owes much to his enthusiasm and efforts, and he has likewise been active in other movements which have enlisted the support of farsighted and public-spirited citizens.

Mr. Mark is the product of a farming community near Fredericksburg, Lebanon County, Pennsylvania, where he was born June 30, 1858, a son of Cyrus and Rebecca (Strohm) Mark, and a direct descendant in the paternal line from William Killian Mark, who settled in that county and state in 1735. After acquiring a public school education in the states of Pennsylvania and Illinois, in 1872 he took up his residence at Chicago and four years later secured employment as a clerk with the Chicago Malleable Iron Company. Industry and fidelity had their reward and in 1880 he was made secretary of the company, and when its successor, the National Malleable Castings Company, was organized Mr. Mark was made director of its Chicago Works, subsequently becoming vice president of the company and a member of its directorate. In 1923 the National company was reorganized under the name of National Malleable and Steel Castings Company, and Mr. Mark is a member of its Board of Directors.

In 1888, while still secretary of the Chicago Malleable Iron Company, Mr. Mark founded at Chicago the Mark Manufacturing Company, an independent co-partnership for the manufacture and sale of water well supplies. This business was afterward enlarged to include the manufacture of steel pipe, whereupon pipe mills were built at Evanston, Illinois, and others bought at Zanesville, Ohio, and Mr. Mark became one of the pioneer steel pipe makers in this country. In 1908 he founded the Vinegar Hill Zinc Company for the mining of zinc ores, operating in the zinc fields of Illinois, Wisconsin, Oklahoma and Kansas. The National Zinc Separating Company was formed by him in 1914, to roast zinc ores. In 1906 the jobbing houses of the Mark-Lally Company in California were established, and in 1908 the Atlas Supply Company at Muskogee, Oklahoma, was incorporated, with a system of jobbing houses in Oklahoma, Kansas and Texas, these two organizations being primarily for the marketing of Mark Manufacturing Company products.

The Mark Manufacturing Company was incorporated in 1916, and began the erection, at Indiana Harbor, Indiana, of a self-contained steel plant to supply its requirements of steel, Mr. Mark being president of this company. Subsequently the Mark Company was merged with the Iroquois Iron Company, the Northwestern Iron Company and the Newport Mining Company to form the Steel and Tube Company of America, and Mr. Mark became chairman of its Board of Directors. In 1923 this company sold its business and properties to the Youngstown Sheet and Tube Company of Youngstown, Ohio.

Not being content with retirement from active participation in the world's work, Mr. Mark in 1924 organized and incorporated Clayton Mark & Company, and becames its president. This company manufactures and sells steel pipe and water well supplies, and has an office in the Conway Building, 111 West Washington Street, and a manufacturing plant at Seventy-fourth and Robey streets, Chicago.

Mr. Mark has been keenly interested in all matters of civic welfare, but his personal activities in this line have been chiefly with public education. For nine years, from 1896 until 1905, he was a member of the Board of Education of Chicago, and president of the board from 1902-3 to 1905. During his terms of service, due largely to his energetic advocacy of these matters, the superintendent of schools was freed from political interference, and the initiative in educational matters again placed in his hands; appointment and promotion of teachers were put upon a merit basis; vacation schools were recognized as entitled to support from public school funds, and school playgrounds were provided. In 1910 and 1911, while Mr. Mark was chairman of its educational committee, the Commercial Club of Chicago sent a commissioner to Europe to study its systems and methods of vocational education. The published report of this study, "Vocational Education in Europe," by Cooley, has had wide circulation in the United States; also in Europe and Canada. Later students of vocational education problems owe much to these investigations, which were due chiefly to Mr. Mark's personal inspiration and enthusiasm.

From 1907 to 1909 Mr. Mark was president of the Civic Federation of Chicago, and is president of this organization at the present time, also chairman of its executive committee. He is a member of the Board of Trustees of Lake Forest University, and holds memberships in the following societies and clubs: Chicago Historical Society, life member; Field Columbian Museum, life member; Art Institute of Chicago, governing life member; Arts Club of Chicago; Chicago Zoological Society, governing member; Commercial Club of Chicago, Chicago Club, Union League Club of Chicago, Union Club of Cleveland, Ohio, and the Old Elm, Onwentsia and Shore Acres Golf Clubs.

On September 27, 1880, Mr. Mark was united in marriage with Miss Anna L. Griffith, of Greeley, Iowa, who died in 1915. They were the parents of the following children: Clarence; Alice, the wife of Doctor McMicken Hanchett, of Council Bluffs, Iowa; Clayton, Jr.; Lydia, widow of John K. Saville; Phyllis, the wife of Everett L. Wyman; Cyrus; Scytha; Griffith; and Anna, the wife of Avery Rockefeller, all living. The family residence is at Lake Forest, Illinois.

JUDGE GEORGE W. DOWELL, a former judge of the Illinois Court of Claims, and a practicing attorney at Duquoin since 1909, has written many chapters in the book of experience, service, achievement and character, constituting the best record of a life well lived according to its opportunities and circumstances.

A native of Southern Illinois, he was born in Williamson County, August 18, 1879, son of William J. Dowell, a native of Tennessee, and grandson of David Dowell, who took his family from Tennessee to Arkansas. David Dowell was a merchant and race horse man, and died in Arkansas. William J. Dowell before the Civil war came to Southern Illinois. Not long afterward he enlisted as a Union soldier, joining on August 26, 1861, Company E of the Thirty-first Illinois Infantry. This was General Logan's old regiment. He was chosen regimental color bearer and served one enlistment of three years and then reenlisted so that altogether he gave five years of his life to military duty. He was a participant with his regiment at the battle of Shiloh, and while there he fought in the cemetery where his own mother was buried. At Vicksburg the flag in his hand was almost shot to pieces, there being counted after the battle 244 holes made by bullets. There were also fourteen bullet holes in his clothing and hat, and two in his body, but in spite of wounds and danger he held the flag. This flag which he so bravely carried is now a cherished possession of his son, Judge Dowell. William J. Dowell after the war followed farming, mining and the butcher's trade, and died January 5, 1923. His widow resides at Centralia, Illinois. Her maiden name was Mary E. Robinson. Her father, John Robinson, moved from Virginia to Kentucky and from that state to Illinois.

George W. Dowell was one of a large family of children and his father was never able to provide for them more than the simplest comforts and necessities. George W. Dowell spent his boyhood and youth at Marion, Carterville and Elkville, had experience in farm work, and for several years was employed in the coal mines. While he had only the advantages of a few terms of district school, his ambition was firmly set upon a career as a lawyer, but he remained in the mines, married and had children before he achieved that ambition. Some one well acquainted with the facts of his career told the story of his struggle in preparing himself for the bar so well that it deserves quotation at this point: "Since he could not enter high school because he was too old, he decided to attempt a high school course of his own. Therefore every night he would come home from the mines, weary from the physical labor, and after his often meagre supper, for it took so much money to buy books, would sit down close to the lamp and there in the company of his young wife would labor over knotty problems in algebra and geometry, and try to understand what Chaucer was talking about, or why 'Equal volumes of gas at the same temperature and pressure contain equal numbers of molecules.' Think of the struggles we ourselves had with the best of teachers and the most modern apparatus, studying at a time when our brains were most receptive and when facts found an easy lodgment therein, and compare our comparatively easy time with what this man had to contend with. With no scientific apparatus, no teacher to straighten out tangles, and with a brain that had passed the stage when it resembles a sponge, yet he determined that he would conquer, and he did. He completed all the work required in the curriculum of the high school and passed the examination given to him by the superintendent of schools. He had now taken the first and longest step. While he had been toiling over his school books he had also been poring over the massive tomes of legal knowledge that lay near by on his table. So he was ready to begin at once on his professional work. His first work was done by correspondence, in the Sprague Correspondence School of Detroit, Michigan, and later he entered the offices of Harker-Harker and Lightfoot in the City of Carbondale, Illinois. From Carbondale he moved to Herrin, and in 1907 took the bar examination in Northwestern University in Chicago, Illinois. He was one of fifty-two successful ones among more than two hundred applicants. He was admitted on the 23rd of June and was the first man to hand in his final paper to the examining commission, of which Judge George W. Wall, of Duquoin, was president."

Judge Dowell for a year or so had charge of the Herrin law office of Harker-Harker and Lightfoot, but on October 5, 1909, engaged in practice for himself at Duquoin. His abilities, his knowledge of men, his all around experience, have brought him steadily to the front as one of the leading members of the bar of Perry County.

Governor Dunne appointed him in 1913 one of the judges of the Court of Claims at Springfield to fill the unexpired term of Judge McMurdy. In 1912 he was a member of the State Central Committee of the progressive party and took an active part in the campaign of that year. In 1914 he was progressive candidate for Congress from the Twenty-fifth district. Otherwise his political affiliation has been republican. Judge Dowell was admitted to practice in the United States Supreme Court in 1921. In 1912 he was appointed special state's attorney to break up the activities of the Black Hand in Perry County, and succeeded in performing his duty, though exposing his life to grave risks many times. Judge Dowell during the World war period had charge of war work in Perry County as chairman of the County Executive Committee, and was tireless in prosecuting all measures recommended by the Government. He instituted the feature of closing the stores in order that the business men might go out and help the farmers cultivate and harvest their crops. Judge Dowell in 1917 laid out the town of Dowell in Jackson County. On account of the Katheline Mine operated by the Union Colliery Company this town has had a large and prosperous growth. Judge Dowell is a member of the Missionary Baptist Church and many years ago was licensed as a preacher. He is affiliated with the Independent Order of Odd Fellows, Modern Woodmen of America and the Elks.

Judge Dowell married, December 16, 1899, Miss Anna Midyett, daughter of John H. and Rebecca S. (Malory) Midyett. Her father, who died March 4, 1899, was a carpenter and architect in Franklin County. Judge and Mrs. Dowell have seven children, Noble Yates, Clara V., Reola Harker, George W., Jr., Anna Lee, Marion Richard and Theo. The son Noble was born October 26, 1900, at Elkville in Jackson County, graduated from the high school at Duquoin, and was not yet seventeen years of age when America entered the World war. Judge Dowell desired that he have military training in order to be in readiness if the country needed him, and he therefore attended and graduated at the age of eighteen from the Columbia Military Academy in Tennessee with the rank of lieutenant of cadets. Subsequently he attended the law department of Georgetown University at Washington, D. C., a year, and is now continuing his law studies in the University of Illinois, preparatory to practicing with his father.

ORVILLE MARION KARRAKER, president of the First National Bank of Harrisburg, first became identified with that community in the capacity of teacher and educator. He has been engaged in the banking business for a quarter of a century.

He was born on a farm east of Dongola, in Union County, Illinois, July 19, 1878. His grandfather, Rev. Jacob Karraker, was of Holland-Dutch ancestry and a native of North Carolina, but came in pioneer times to southern Illinois and covered an extensive territory as a missionary Baptist minister. Wilford W. Karraker, father of the Harrisburg banker, was born in Union County, Illinois, and married Sarah Richardson, a native of the same county, and daughter of Rev. Marion Richardson, who was also a Baptist minister in southern Illinois. The wife of Rev. Jacob Karraker was Mary Peeler, a native of Tennessee. Wilford W. Karraker was also a teacher in his early life, but for many years has followed farming, and he and his wife now live retired at Dongola. They are the parents of four sons and one daughter.

Orville Marion Karraker while a boy on the farm attended rural schools. He was graduated in 1899 from the Southern Illinois State Normal University at Carbondale. During the administration of Governor Dunne he was appointed a trustee of the Normal University at Carbondale and held that position while Mr. Dunne was governor. After graduating he came to Harrisburg as teacher of Latin and literature at the high school, and served in that capacity two years.

Mr. Karraker in 1901 entered the First National Bank as a clerk. For five years he was cashier of the bank, and since 1915 has been its efficient and popular president.

He has been active in public affairs, serving fifteen years as president of the Harrisburg Board of Education, and in 1913 was elected and served two years as mayor. He is a member of the Baptist Church, is a Master Mason and a member of the Rotary Club. Mr. Karraker married, in 1905, Miss Etta Joyner. She died in December, 1925, leaving one son, James Wilford Karraker.

ISADORE L. BUCHHALTER, Chicago musician, a resident of that city for nearly twenty years, is dean of the Chicago Philharmonic Conservatory.

Mr. Buchhalter was born in Russia, was brought in infancy by his parents to America and was reared at New Haven, Connecticut. His brother has adopted a somewhat different spelling of the family name from his father, who was A. Buchhalter and now signs it Bucharoff. His father was distinguished as an educator in Europe. He died in Chicago, as did also the mother. A brother of Mr. Buchhalter has won his place as a composer of operas, and one of the men high in the musical art at New York City.

Isadore L. Buchhalter was liberally educated in the high school at New Haven, attended Yale University there, and from early boyhood was a student of the piano. With the musical tradition of his family and his own enthusiasm he has achieved substantial renown in the musical art. For several years he has devoted himself to the pedagogy of the piano. As a teacher he has brought to life a number of pianists who under his skillful professional direction have likewise reached the goal of highest excellence.

Mr. Buchhalter's training was received under many noted masters, including Consolo, Von Schiller, Parker, Weidig and his brother Bucharoff. Mr. Buchhalter came to Chicago in 1907. The Chicago Philharmonic Conservatory, of which he is dean, is one of the noted musical institutions of the city, located in the Kimball Building.

A very interesting diversion from his musical career came to Mr. Buchhalter in the political campaign of 1924 when he was chosen one of the republican presidential electors from Illinois. Thus he had the privilege of passing one of the votes from his state for Calvin Coolidge. Mr. Buchhalter married Miss Elizabeth Hoffman, who was born and reared in Chicago and is one of the well known attorneys of Chicago. They have one daughter, Clarice.

WILLIAM ALDEN WILTBERGER is chief of police of the City of Evanston. His appointment to that office and confirmation by the City Council in June, 1925, attracted much attention as an unusual recognition of scientific training and efficiency rather than a mere service record as the chief qualification. Mr. Wiltberger is one of the few police chiefs in the country who has the scholastic degree of Master of Arts.

He was born at DeKalb, Illinois, October 17, 1897, son of William F. and Helen B. (Duffy) Wiltberger, also natives of DeKalb. He was reared in that city, and after two years of college training in Beloit College at Beloit, Wisconsin, he entered the army for service in the World war, enlisting in the Motor Transport Corps at Chicago early in 1918. He was on duty at Jefferson Barracks, Missouri, Camp Meigs at Washington, at Charleston, South Carolina, and finally at Fort Sheridan, Illinois as a sergeant, first class (sergeant-major) in the personnel office of the Motor Transport Corps.

On receiving his honorable discharge in January, 1919, he returned to Beloit College to complete some courses he had begun before the war. From Beloit he went to Berkeley, California, and received special training in the Berkeley Police School under Chief of Police Vollmer, nationally known as a "scientific chief." He was trained in all branches of the police profession, and in addition to this practical experience he took courses in criminology, police technique and related subjects at the University of California. His university training gave him a fundamental knowledge of such important subjects as social economics, education, psychology, psychiatry, economics, anthropology and related subjects. He remained at Berkeley three years, graduating with the degree Bachelor of Arts from the University of California. He was the first man in the University of California to be allowed academic recognition for professional training in police work, by being allowed to "minor" in criminology. This was on account of his special training in police work under the guidance of leaders in criminology and the police field.

On returning to Illinois Mr. Wiltberger on December 1, 1923, became an aid in the office of Dr. H. M. Adler, state criminologist, at Chicago, specializing in the work of the Institute of Juvenile Research, and the Illinois State Penitentiary. In 1924 he entered the School of Social Service Administration at the University of Chicago, taking further work in the field of criminology and public welfare administration. This led to the degree of Master of Arts.

Mr. Wiltberger took the position of chief of police of Evanston on July 1, 1925. He is a member of the Evanston Kiwanis Club, of several Masonic bodies, of the Phi Kappa Alpha fraternity, member of the American Legion and Congregational Church. He also belongs to such scientific organizations as the American Institute of Criminal Law and Criminology, International Association of Chiefs of Police, and at its meeting in Chicago in 1926 was made a member of its Executive Board and a member of the International Association of Identification and Illinois Police Association.

Mr. Wiltberger married in 1922, Miss Louise Walters, a native of Texas.

THOMAS B. STEPHENSON. One of the strongest forces in the progress and upbuilding of the little city of Sparta in Randolph County has been the Sparta Building & Loan Association, which was promoted in March, 1886, by James Bottom, with an authorized capitalization of $1,000,000. James Bottom was the first president, and the Board of Commissioners included James Bottom, H. R. Guthrie, G. W. McGuire, John Frohard, A. A. Brown, P. H. Murphy and J. A. Holdoway. Mr. W. J. Burnett was the first secretary. He resigned and the unexpired term was filled out by T. B. Stephenson. A. A. Brown was the next secretary, and in 1888 Thomas B. Stephenson became secretary and for nearly forty years has been the chief administrative official of this splendid organization. The first president was James Bottom, the second was J. C. Simpson, the third was W. J. Brown, who was followed by J. T. Clendennin, and later by J. C. Brown, who is now the president. In 1923 the authorized capital was increased to $3,000,000. The association now has assets of $1,150,000, and from the beginning the institution has used its resources in conformity with the essential principles of the charter, to promote home building and home ownership.

Thomas B. Stephenson has lived nearly all his life at Sparta, and while he has been abundantly prosperous he has given likewise of his talents for the larger welfare of the community. He was born in Lancashire, England, November 20, 1855, son of Edward and Elizabeth (Preston) Stephenson. In 1858 the family came to America and established a home near Toronto, Canada. Edward Stephenson died soon afterward, at the age of thirty-two. His widow subsequently married John D. Stephenson, brother of her first husband, and in 1860 they came to Illinois and settled at Sparta. John D. Stephenson was a carpenter and farmer, and died in 1907. The

mother of Thomas B. Stephenson died in 1923, when more than ninety years of age.

Thomas B. Stephenson was five years old when brought to Illinois. He attended public schools in Sparta, the Southern Illinois Normal University at Carbondale, and taught several terms of school in and near Sparta. In addition to his long connection with the Sparta Building & Loan Association he has had numerous other business interests. For a number of years, beginning in 1892, he was in the mercantile business, under the firm name of Stephenson & Beattie. He also helped establish the first modern creamery in Randolph County, the Sparta Creamery Company, and served as its treasurer. He was for a time bookkeeper and assistant cashier of the Merchants Exchange Bank. He was also one of the organizers and general manager of the Sparta Pressed Brick Company and secretary and manager of the Wilson Brothers Coal Company, operating one of the largest coal mines in Randolph County. Mr. Stephenson is a republican, and has taken a prominent part in Sunday School work, having been president of the County Sunday School Association and frequently a delegate to Sunday School conventions.

He married at Sparta, October 8, 1879, Miss Mary J. Beattie, daughter of Jacob Beattie. The Beattie family was established in Randolph County as early as 1812. Her father died in April, 1899, at the age of eighty years.

Edward B. Stephenson, oldest child of Mr. and Mrs. Thomas B. Stephenson, has made a brilliant record as a scientist and scholar. He graduated from the Sparta High School, then entered Knox College and was graduated Bachelor of Science in 1903. During 1906 he was a teacher in the high school at Geneva, Illinois. In 1907 he returned to Knox College as an instructor, having obtained the Master of Science degree at the University of Illinois in that year. Three years later, in 1910, he was awarded the Doctor of Philosophy degree by the University of Illinois. During the summer vacation of 1907 he was employed as a draftsman and rodman by the Chicago, Burlington & Quincy Railroad Company, and for several years he taught and worked alternately. While studying for his Doctor's degree he was a fellow in physics at the University of Illinois. In 1909 he became instructor in physics at the University of North Dakota, and from 1913 to 1917 was assistant professor in that institution. During the summer of 1911 he worked for the Western Electric Company at Chicago to increase his practical experience. In the summer of 1912 he worked for the Underwriters Laboratories, Incorporated, of Chicago, and each summer following until 1917 did research work in wireless telegraphy and wrote a number of technical articles. He is a Phi Beta Kappa, member of the social fraternity Sigma Gamma Alpha, the American Physics Society and the American Association for the Advancement of Science. When the United States entered the World war he resigned his position with the University of North Dakota, attended the Officers Training Camp at Fort Snelling, was commissioned a captain in the Engineer Corps and was on duty at Fort Leavenworth and Camp Humphrey. His ability and scholarship caused him to be retained in this country as an instructor, much to his disappointment, since he desired the experience of active service at the front. After the war the department requested that he remain in the regular army, but for the larger opportunities he secured transfer to the navy. Eventually he tired of the restrictions imposed by that department and resigned his commission, but was persuaded to remain as a civilian, and he has his headquarters at Washington, engaged in research and experimental work in behalf of the navy. He is regarded as one of the most promising of the younger scientists in the country today. Edward Stephenson married Adeline Alexander, of Geneva, Illinois.

The second son of Mr. and Mrs. Stephenson is Carl C., who graduated from Knox College Bachelor of Science, graduated in law from St. Louis Law School and is now legal advisor in the offices of the Sparta Building & Loan Association. He married Lena Dean, of Traverse City, Michigan. The only daughter, Bertha Elizabeth, is a graduate of Knox College, taught Latin two years in the Sparta High School, and in 1910 was married to Hugh K. Wilson, who is in business with the Witte Hardware Company of St. Louis.

ISAAC A. FOSTER, M. D., is a prominent physician at Ziegler, and has had a busy career in his profession covering a period of thirty-five years.

He is a member of one of the oldest families of southern Illinois. His great-grandfather, Asa Foster, came to Illinois when it was a territory, in the early years of the nineteenth century. He acquired his land direct from the government, and opened up one of the first farms in what is now Hardin, then Pope, County.

In this pioneer home of Asa Foster was born a son January 8, 1811, named Horace Foster. Horace Foster married Phoebe Davis. He died in 1847. He and his wife had four children, named Asa, Horace, Lyman, and Mary Jane.

Horace Foster, Jr., representing the third generation of this family in Southern Illinois, was born near Elizabethtown November 18, 1829. He married December 9, 1849, Elizabeth Ann Hobbs, a native of Missouri. Twelve children were born to their union, and those now living are: Thomas Jefferson, a resident of Franklin County, Illinois; John William, of New Haven, Illinois; Isaac A.; Mrs. M. L. Tyer, Mrs. John Blagg and Mrs. W. R. Patton.

Dr. Isaac A. Foster was born at the old homestead in Hardin County October 4, 1862. He had the normal experiences of a country boy, attended country schools, and eight years of his early manhood were divided between teaching and reading and study at home. He made himself proficient in civil engineering and in 1888 was elected surveyor of Hardin County. In 1891 he was graduated with the M. D. degree from the College of Physicians and Surgeons of St. Louis, and began his practice in the Rock Creek community, where he remained two years. For nearly a quarter of a century Doctor Foster was located at New

Haven, Illinois, and in 1917 removed to the mining community of Ziegler in Franklin County, where he has carried on a large general practice. He is a member of the Franklin County, Illinois State, Southern Illinois and American Medical Associations.

Doctor Foster is one of the prominent Masons of the state, being now the twelfth oldest grand lecturer of the order in the United States. He served several years as district deputy grand master, Forty-seventh Masonic District. He and his wife are active workers in the Eastern Star and he belongs to the Modern Woodmen of America and the Christian Church.

Doctor Foster married, in 1898, Miss Belle Chastain, of White County, Illinois. She had been a teacher before her marriage. Of their children the son Edward H. died September 19, 1908. The son John Paul is a graduate of the Southern Illinois Normal University at Carbondale and took his Bachelor of Science degree at the University of Illinois in 1925. The daughter, Alice Belle, is now a teacher in the State Normal at Carbondale. The son Isaac O., born June 1, 1895, from a former marriage, was educated in the Harrisburg High School, the Normal at Carbondale, graduated Bachelor of Science from the University of Illinois in 1923, and took his Masters degree at Illinois in 1924 and his Doctor of Philosophy degree in 1925. Since the fall of 1925 he has been a member of the faculty of the college at Battle Creek, Michigan.

DON B. STEWART, M. D., is a surgeon of brilliant qualifications, now in charge of the Ziegler Hospital and ranks among the best in his field in Franklin County.

His father, Dr. James C. Stewart, has for many years been an honored physician and surgeon in Southern Illinois, and lives at Anna. Dr. James C. Stewart was born in Johnson County, Illinois, in 1866, son of Thomas B. and Sarah J. (Lovelace) Stewart, who were Illinois farmers. He grew up on a farm, attended country schools and the Southern Illinois Normal University at Carbondale. He taught four years in the intervals of his medical studies. In 1891 he was graduated from the College of Physicians and Surgeons at St. Louis and for seven years carried on a successful general practice in Johnson County. He then removed to Anna, where for many years he has given special attention to diseases of the eye. He ranks as one of the able oculists in Southern Illinois. He completed post-graduate work in his specialty in the Illinois Post-Graduate Medical School of Chicago in 1900. He has been a member of the Joint Association of Surgeons of the Illinois Central, Yazoo and Mississippi Valley and Indiana Southern Railway Companies, belongs to the Union County, Illinois and Southern Illinois Medical Associations and the American Medical Association.

Dr. James C. Stewart married, in 1892, Miss Ada P. May, of Marion. Of the four children born to their marriage three died young. Don B. Stewart, the only living child of Doctor and Mrs. James C. Stewart, was born at Anna, Illinois, October 25, 1895. After attending grammar schools he was a student in the Union Academy at Anna, and in 1916 graduated with the Bachelor of Science degree from Northwestern University of Chicago and completed his medical studies at Northwestern University School of Medicine in 1919.

Doctor Stewart has accepted the opportunities that bring proficiency, though as the result of some years of hard work with comparatively little reward. For twenty-six months, beginning in 1921, he served as an interne in the Illinois Central Railway Hospital at Chicago. Since then he has been located at Ziegler, and is the surgeon in charge of the Ziegler Hospital, a modern institution with equipment of thirty-five beds and with a staff of three nurses. Doctor Stewart did post-graduate work in Tulane University at New Orleans in 1924. He is married, is a member of the Masonic fraternity, B. P. O. Elks, and Loyal Order of Moose.

H. EDWARD MORGAN has practiced law since 1913, and has achieved a place of secure prominence in his profession at Christopher, Franklin County.

He is a native of southern Illinois and is a son of the late Charles E. Morgan, who followed railroading in early life and was a constable in Perry County for about twenty-five years prior to his death. His home for many years was at Duquoin, Perry County, where he died in January, 1925. Charles E. Morgan married Ida Thimmig, a native of Perry County and daughter of Charles Thimmig. Charles Thimmig came to America from Baden, Germany, when an infant, his parents settling near Douglas in St. Clair County, Illinois. The Thimmig family has long been prominent in St. Clair and Perry Counties as farmers and dairymen, and they operated several creameries. H. Edward Morgan was born at Duquoin June 21, 1891, and was educated in public schools there, finishing his high school course. He then entered the University of Illinois, taking the law course and graduating in 1913. On being admitted to the bar he opened his office in Christopher, and has built up a large general practice as a lawyer. He served two terms as city attorney and one term as assistant state attorney.

Mr. Morgan is a member of the Rotary Club and the B. P. O. Elks. He married Miss L. Martin, daughter of Joseph F. Martin. They have one son, Robert E.

THEODORE MCGONAGIL, manager of the Zeigler Stores Company at Zeigler in Franklin County, has since early youth been engaged in commercial life and has filled a number of executive responsibilities in business establishments in southern Illinois.

The large mercantile institution of which he is now manager was established under the ownership of the Levi Leiter estate in 1904. Subsequently it was operated by the Zeigler Coal & Coke Company, and it is now one of the properties owned and controlled by Mr. Joseph Leiter of Chicago.

Theodore McGonagil was born at Carterville, Williamson County, Illinois, February 15, 1885. His father, John McGonagil, a native of Scotland, has spent his active life as a miner and mine superintendent. On coming to

America he located in Williamson County, being then a young man, and for many years served as superintendent of mines for the Hafer Wash Coal Company. After his health failed he retired and is now living in California. John McGonagil married Mary McEwan.

When Theodore McGonagil was a small child the family moved to Murphysboro, Jackson County, where he attended public schools. When he was eighteen years old the family returned to Carterville, and subsequently he completed a commercial course in the Gem City Business College at Quincy. On returning to Carterville he spent two years employed in a general store. For eighteen months he was payroll clerk for the Watson Coal Company in their offices at Herrin. The following four years were spent with Treece & Company at Herrin. He then joined the W. P. Wren Coal Company, which later became the Old Ben Coal & Coke Company. Mr. McGonagil had ten years of association with these corporations with various responsibilities in their general stores and offices. Then, in March, 1925, he was called to his present duties as manager of the Zeigler Stores Company.

Mr. McGonagil married Miss Ruth Perrine, daughter of George H. Perrine, of Herrin. He is a member of the Rotary Club and is affiliated with the Masonic fraternity and B. P. O. Elks.

JOHN FRANKLIN SMULSKI. For a quarter of a century no name has stood for a higher degree of integrity and ideals of public service and more complete business and personal integrity in Chicago than that of John Franklin Smulski, former state treasurer of Illinois, and both a lawyer and a banker.

His father William Smulski immigrated to the United States in 1869 and settled in Chicago, going into the printing and publishing business. Two years before, John Franklin Smulski was born in Posen, Poland, February 4, 1867, son of William and Euphemia (Balcer) Smulski. During five years of his early manhood Mr. Smulski was associated with his father in the newspaper and publishing business. He acquired a liberal education, attending a government military high school in Germany five years, spent two years in St. Jerome College in Canada, and took his law course in Northwestern University of Chicago. He was admitted to the bar in 1890, and for fifteen years was a member of the law firm of David, Smulski and McGaffey. In 1906 he organized and became president of the Northwestern Trust and Savings Bank of Chicago.

Early in his career Mr. Smulski identified himself with the republican party. He was elected and served as an alderman of Chicago from 1898 to 1903, and was city attorney from 1903 to 1907. The office of state treasurer of Illinois he held from 1907 to 1909 and in 1907 he was a candidate for the republican nomination for mayor. From 1907 to 1913 he was a member of the Board of West Park Commissioners of Chicago, and in 1917-18 was president of that board. He served as treasurer of the Chicago Association of Commerce in 1911. Mr. Smulski devoted practically all his time during the World war to patriotic engagements, not only those affecting the allied cause in general, but particularly all designed to promote the independence of Poland and the welfare of Polish volunteers from America. In December, 1921, he was decorated by the French government a Chevalier Legion d'Honneur and the order of Palonia Restotuta by the Polish Government. Mr. Smulski is a member of the Chicago Athletic and Union League Clubs and the Chicago Riding Club. He married Harriet Mikitynski, of Chicago, on June 7, 1899. They have two children, John J. and Harriet M.

COLONEL OSCAR C. SMITH, an Illinois man with a notable military record, in both the Spanish-American and World war periods, is a lawyer by profession, but for several years his discharged with a high degree of credit and efficiency his duties as managing officer of the Illinois School for the Deaf at Jacksonville.

Colonel Smith was born in Sullivan County, Indiana, January 1, 1876. His grandfather had come from Pennsylvania and became a settler near Bloomfield, Indiana. When Colonel Smith was a child his parents moved to Clark County, Illinois, where his father operated lumber mills. Colonel Smith had opportunities in the common schools of his locality, and beyond that had to employ his own efforts and resources in acquiring a higher education. He taught school and also worked as a coal miner, and without any assistance carried the high school subjects and also read law. In 1901 he was admitted to the Illinois bar in Franklin County, and for a number of years enjoyed a highly successful practice at Benton.

Prior to that, when the Spanish-American war broke out, he helped organize Company F of the Ninth Illinois, and subsequently enlisted and served as a private in the Fifth Illinois Regiment. About a year later he recruited forty-seven men for service in the Philippines during the insurrection, and he participated in the southern expedition in Luzon. Later he became captain of a company of the Fourth Regiment in the Illinois National Guard, and was with that unit on the Mexican border in 1916. The following year, when America entered the World war, his company was called into the Federal service, and he was promoted to the Judge Advocate General's Department. He had the distinction of heading the court which tried the famous forty-five conscientious objectors at Camp Travis. Colonel Smith crossed the ocean with the Ninetieth Division and at his personal request was assigned duty with the infantry as major in command of a battalion. While leading in a battle in the St. Mihiel campaign he was gassed and disabled from active duty, being in a hospital for six weeks. With his battalion he captured Stenay, headquarters of the Crown Prince, only a few minutes before the armistice was declared. On the same day he received his promotion to lieutenant colonel and subsequently was with the Army of Occupation. He was put in charge of civil affairs in a jurisdiction covering three kreises, including the important cities of Berncastle and Trier. Railroads, telegraphs, schools, courts, banks and other departments of business and civilian affairs were under his supervision. He had 170 army officers assisting, but so far as possible retained the German civil officers. In February, 1919, Colonel Smith returned and was granted an honorable discharge July 11, 1919. It is his distinction to have been the only American judge advocate that was awarded a wound chevron, a token of his disablement by gas during the St. Mihiel campaign.

During the years he practiced in Franklin County he won many successes, being assistant state's attorney, corporation counsel, and city attorney. Soon after his return from abroad he was elected city judge of Benton. As the court was well cared for, he responded to a request to serve as a judge in the Chicago courts, and held a court there for about a year.

In October, 1921, Governor Small offered him the position of managing officer of the Illinois School for the Deaf, paying him the honor of appointment largely in consideration of work done and a long and deep interest in child welfare and orphan home associations as county probation officer. He brought to this institution well digested ideas, the value of which have been duly demonstrated. He has made important innovations in teaching the deaf, and some of these changes have attracted attention generally and are now being adopted elsewhere. The Illinois School for the Deaf at Jacksonville was founded more than eighty-five years ago, and there are about 425 pupils with some fifty-five teachers and 100 employees. Besides the buildings there are over 150 acres of land, used for farming and truck growing. Much progress has been made in the teaching of backward children, and this school has introduced a normal training department to train teachers of the deaf.

Colonel Smith is affiliated with the Independent Order of Odd Fellows, Knights of Pythias and B. P. O. Elks, but his chief interest in such organizations is centered in the American Legion, and his efforts to secure for his comrades that consideration their services warrant. He was department commander of the Spanish-American War Veterans in 1923-24. Colonel Smith married Cora A. Crisp, of Franklin County, Illinois. They have three children: Irene J., Margaret Ellen and Allen Naylor.

CHARLES MARK BROOKINGS, M. D. For seventy years the name Brookings has stood for the highest attainments and skill in the profession of medicine and surgery at Duquoin. Dr. Charles M. Brookings has practiced medicine there a quarter of a century. His career supplements that of his father and also that of his uncle, Dr. Charles H. Brookings, a pioneer doctor of Perry County whose memory is still held in high esteem there.

The Brookings family were originally French Huguenots. The French spelling of the name was Broquin. Jean Broquin on leaving France found a home in Wales. His two sons, Charles and Richard Brookings, as the name was spelled after the family went to Wales, came to America in 1778 and settled in Cecil County, Maryland. Richard Brookings subsequently located at Connellsville, Pennsylvania, and became a mine owner and merchant. He was a man of distinction in the community and was impressive among other things for his great physical stature, being six feet, four inches tall.

A descendant of this pioneer of western Pennsylvania was the late Allan Clark Brookings, who was born at Connellsville, Pennsylvania, in 1840. He came west and graduated from Rush Medical College of Chicago. He had located at Duquoin in 1857, where his brother Charles had established his home. Dr. Charles Brookings practiced medicine and conducted a drug store at Duquoin until the outbreak of the Civil war, when he joined the Twelfth Illinois Infantry and later was made captain in the Eleventh Missouri Regiment, and was killed while leading his company in an assault in the siege of Vicksburg.

Allan Clark Brookings engaged in the drug business at Duquoin, soon became owner of a store and was the leading druggist of the community until his death on January 6, 1901. He was for many years a trustee of the First Baptist Church of Duquoin, also trustee of the Southern Illinois Normal University of Carbondale, Illinois. He organized the first company south of the O. & M. Railroad in Illinois which was the nucleus of the Twelfth Illinois Infantry, of which he was commissioned captain. He served with this regiment until the period of his enlistment expired. At that time the Illinois quota was full, so a large number of the boys of this regiment went to Missouri and enlisted in the Eleventh Missouri Regiment, in fact this regiment was composed almost exclusively of Illinois boys.

Allan Clark Brookings married, on June 25, 1867, Jane Amanda Winters, member of a very notable family of Perry County. Her father, Christopher Winters, moved to this section of Illinois in 1859. He had previously been a farmer in Putnam County, Illinois, owning several thousand acres of land there. Unfortunately he went security on the notes of some of his friends and their failure wiped out his entire fortune. When he came to Perry County he still owed $75,000, though he had never personally benefited a penny from this large amount. He started life over again, and set out an extensive peach orchard, now included in part of the town site of Duquoin. After his death his children continued paying off the debt, for which they could not be legally or morally held liable, until the entire sum was liquidated. The Winters family was largely responsible for establishing the First Baptist Church at Duquoin.

Dr. Charles Mark Brookings was born at Duquoin, May 27, 1868. He attended public schools, graduated from high school, was a student in the old Chicago University and spent two years in Northwestern University at Evanston. In 1889 he was graduated from the Northwestern University School of Pharmacy, and then became associated with his father's drug business at Duquoin. In 1898 he was graduated from the medical department of Washington University at St. Louis and for two years practiced at Rockford, Illinois. In 1901, on the death of his father, he returned to Duquoin and took charge of the drug business and engaged in general medical practice. As soon as the opportunity came he disposed of the drug business to its present owner, Mr. Angel. Doctor Brookings in experience and ability is one of the foremost physicians and surgeons of Perry County. He has a modern office in the Brookings Block on Main Street. Dr. Brookings is a trustee of the First Baptist Church and is president of the Duquoin High School Board.

In 1901 he married Miss Jessie Pope, daughter of Pleasant N. Pope, and member of an old family of Perry County. They have two children, Robert Lyle and Louise Brookings. The son graduated from West Point Military Academy in 1924, standing fourteenth in a class of 446. He has the rank of lieutenant and is now a registered graduate pilot in the flying corps. While in the Military Academy he ranked especially high in mathematics. The daughter, Louise, graduated from high school in 1925 and is now attending the University of Illinois.

JOHN FORESTER. Three generations of the Forester family have been identified with the mining industry in southern Illinois around Duquoin. The Foresters as a family have been distinguished by their ability as engineers. The first John Forester lived most of his life in England. However, he was employed in erecting the first bridge across the St. Lawrence River. This bridge was made in England, set up there, and after being dismantled was shipped to America and put across the St. Lawrence at Montreal.

The second John Forester lived for a time at Montreal, and was identified with the opening of the cannel coal fields of Ohio around Carrollton. In 1856 he moved to Duquoin, Illinois, where he lived until his death in 1874. He developed coal fields in southern Illinois. His wife was Elizabeth Thompson, who died in 1903.

John Forester, representing the third generation, was born in Northumberland, England, August 7, 1852, and was an infant when brought to America. He grew up at Duquoin, made the best possible use of his advantages in the public schools, and worked around the mines from boyhood. In 1873 he became clerk in the store of W. P. Halliday at St. John, and for over forty years was closely identified with Halliday interests. He became assistant superintendent and then superintendent of the Halliday Store. He was also employed in erecting the Halliday Coal & Coke Company's plant at Hallidayboro. In 1899 he built the Halliday Salt Works at St. John and managed the plant until it was abandoned. For a number of years he managed the Halliday estate. John Forester in 1903 organized the Forester Coal & Coke Company and erected its plant at Duquoin. He served as president of the company, and several of his friends became associated with him in that business. The company became one of the largest in Perry County, employing several hundred men in the mines and other departments of the plant. John Forester was also president of the Duquoin Planing Mill Company, was a member of the firm of merchants, Forester & Company, and a director of the First Bank & Trust Company. For many years he was regarded as one of the ablest men in business and community affairs at Duquoin. He was a member of the high school board from the time of its organization, and in politics was a democrat.

John Forester married at Duquoin, July 20, 1880, Miss Kate W. Jackson, who was born at Columbus, Ohio, daughter of J. B. Jackson. Their children were J. Howard, Robert J., Walter J., cashier of the First National Bank at Duquoin, and Frederick L. The three older sons all became actively associated with the Forester Coal & Coke Company.

Frederick L. Forester, the youngest son, was born at Duquoin, April 4, 1888, was educated in public schools and graduated with the first class at the Township High School in 1907. During 1908-09 he was a student in the dental department of Vanderbilt University at Nashville, Tennessee, and in 1910 graduated from Northwestern University College of Dentistry at Chicago. He practiced for a time at Farina, in Fayette County, and since then at Duquoin. Doctor Forester married Emily Pope, daughter of Pleasant N. Pope, a Duquoin banker.

NORMAN ALLYN JAY is postmaster of Steelville in Randolph County. The distinctive feature of his official position is the continuous service he has rendered, almost a quarter of a century, under democratic as well as republican control.

Mr. Jay, who devoted a number of years of his life to educational work, is a son of Rev. Charles F. Jay, who made himself widely known and beloved in the ministry of the Gospel in southern Illinois. He was born in Pennsylvania, in 1820, and coming to Illinois in 1837, settled in Richland County and later at Randolph. Entering the ministry of the Methodist Episcopal Church, he labored earnestly for many years, not only as a pastor but with missionary zeal in carrying the Gospel to isolated communities and building up all churches. Under his leadership the Methodist Church was established and built at Steeleville. He often preached there as well as at Chester. His primary interest was in agriculture, and when he retired from the ministry in 1856 he devoted the rest of his life to farming. He died in 1878. Rev. Charles F. Jay married Sarah Bryan. She was born January 8, 1821, and came to Illinois the same year as her husband's family. This remarkable woman reached the age of a century, passing away in 1921, newspapers all over the state taking note of her death at the century mark. She was the mother of eight children.

The youngest of these was Norman Allyn Jay, who was born October 11, 1864, on his father's farm two miles west of Steeleville. He attended country schools and three years in the village schools at Steeleville. As a boy he had an ambition to become an educator and was determined to complete the course of study in the Normal University at Carbondale. Like many of the young men of those days who eventually made a success, he had little or no money to spend on an education beyond what he earned himself. He taught school a year and the following year attended the Normal, and after ten years he was able to achieve his object and was graduated with high honors from the Normal School in 1894. After that he gave all his time to his chosen profession until 1902. In that year he was appointed postmaster of Steeleville. He has always been influential in politics and even more so as a recognized community leader. His administration of the post office was such as to gain him the support of all classes. During Wilson's administration an effort was made to turn the post office over to a representative of the democratic party, but the citizens, appreciating his efficiency and personality, prevented the change. As a result he has been in the office continuously for twenty-four years.

Mr. Jay married Clara M. Hyndman, daughter of Samuel Fleming and Sarah E. (Nimock) Hyndman. To their marriage were born six children, one of whom died in infancy. Helen is the wife of Rev. Charles L. Phifer, of Gonconda, Illinois. Herbert J., who was with the colors two years during the World war, spending eleven months in France with the Thirteenth Marines, is a member of the class of 1926 in the University of Illinois and is preparing for educational work. Ronald is an employe of the Wabash, Chester & Western Railroad Company. Norma married Everett R. Mathias, in the service of the Illinois Central Railroad; John J., the youngest, is attending high school.

WILLIAM M. SCHUWERK. An Illinois lawyer since 1882, Judge Schuwerk in his professional work has found many opportunities for loyal service to his community and state. No member of his profession is held in higher esteem in Randolph County.

Judge Schuwerk was born at Cleveland, Ohio, April 12, 1856, and was a child when brought to Randolph County, Illinois, by his parents, Paul and Elizabeth (Moser) Schuwerk. His father was born in Wurttemberg, Germany, in 1814, and came to America in 1844. He married at Cleveland and, moving to Illinois, he engaged in farming in Randolph County until his death in 1869. His wife was born in 1828, in Switzerland, and died in 1891.

William M. Schuwerk was thirteen years old when his father died. He had the training of a farm boy, and his first schooling was in a parochial school in Evansville, where his instruction was in the German language. Later he attended public schools, and in 1882 graduated Master of Science from McKendree College at Lebanon, an institution which all his children have attended. He also completed his law course there, and while getting his higher education he taught school for several years. He was principal of the Evansville school for a time after his admission to the bar. In 1885 he engaged in practice, and was a member of the firm Hood & Schuwerk, with offices at Evansville and Chester for several years. He has handled a general practice, appearing as lawyer for the defense in a number of criminal trials, and has also done a large amount of legal business for corporations. He assisted in organizing the Evansville Building & Loan Association, the Evansville Telephone Company and the N. & W. Sauer Milling Company, and helped raise the cash bonus and secure part of the right-of-way for the Illinois Southern Railroad, which was an important factor in the permanent prosperity of Evansville. Judge Schuwerk for many years has been a land owner and has been interested more or less actively in farming.

In politics he is a democrat. In 1889 he was elected a member of the Illinois General Assembly. For six years he was master in chancery in Randolph County, and in 1910 was elected county judge, an office he filled until 1918. He has distinction of being chosen master of Kaskaskia Lodge No. 86, the first Masonic lodge in Illinois. He is a member of the Royal Arch Masons, Tancred Commandery No. 50, Knights Templar, and has also held chairs in the Independent Order of Odd Fellows, is a member of the Knights of Pythias and Benevolent and Protective Order of Elks.

Judge Schuwerk married, June 7, 1883, Miss Mary M. Hoffman, who was born in Macon County, Illinois, June 25, 1862, daughter of Michael and Josephine Hoffman. Her father was a native of St. Clair County, Illinois, and her mother was born in Switzerland.

William H. Schuwerk, the oldest son of Judge Schuwerk, was born at Evansville, February 10, 1890, was educated in public schools and McKendree College, studied law under his father and was admitted to the bar in 1912, at the age of twenty-two. For several years he practiced with his father and in 1915 moved his office to Chester. He was chosen city attorney in 1916. In the spring of 1918 he joined the colors, attending training camp at Hattiesburg, Mississippi, was assigned duty in a machine gun company and later in the One Hundred Forty-fourth Infantry. He went overseas, spending thirteen months in France. Since the war he has been one of the leading members of the bar of Chester, and in November, 1924, was elected state's attorney, and has earned distinction in that office by his vigorous efforts at law enforcement. He has filled the chairs in the Masonic Lodge at Evansville. He married, in 1917, Dorothy Crisler, daughter of Arthur E. Crisler, a prominent attorney.

The second son of Judge Schuwerk is Walter J., who graduated from the Illinois Wesleyan University Law School at Bloomington and is now junior partner of his father. The son enlisted in the navy, in the medical department, in April, 1918, and was in service nineteen months. He married Treva Webster, of Steelville. The youngest son is Paul Edward, who graduated from McKendree College in June, 1926. The only daughter, Myrtle M., is the wife of Henry Sauer, a fruit grower of Jackson County, Illinois.

JOHN M. CREBS. This has been a distinguished name in White County for over seventy years. The present John M. Crebs for many years has been engaged in banking and is former president of the Illinois State Board of Agriculture. His father, Col. John M. Crebs, was an eminent lawyer, soldier and congressman.

Col. John Montgomery Crebs was born in Loudoun County, Virginia, April 9, 1830. He died at the age of sixty years at Carmi, on June 9, 1890. His parents were Berry and

Dr. C. F. Hampton.

Lucy (Wilson) Crebs, his father a native of Frederick County, Virginia, and his mother of Loudoun County. In 1836, when their son was six years of age, the family moved to White County, Illinois, settling on a farm about eight miles southwest of Carmi. Here John Montgomery Crebs grew to manhood, attending the common schools, and by dint of great industry and natural qualifications prepared himself for a career as a lawyer by private study at home. In 1852, at the age of twenty-two, he was admitted to the bar and at once engaged in practice at Carmi. He had reached a credible position as a young lawyer when the Civil war came on.

When the Eighty-seventh Illinois Volunteer Infantry was organized at Shawneetown August 12, 1862, John Montgomery Crebs was elected its lieutenant colonel. John W. Whiting was colonel, but on account of illness was unable to accompany the regiment to the front. Therefore Mr. Crebs was the commanding officer of the regiment and served as colonel through its various campaigns until July 5, 1865, when the regiment was mustered out. Having completed an honorable record as a soldier, Colonel Crebs resumed his law practice, and in subsequent years made himself one of the best known attorneys in Southeastern Illinois. In politics he was always an ardent democrat. In 1866 he was nominated, but was defeated in election for the office of superintendent of public instruction. In 1868 he was elected a member of Congress from the Thirteenth District, and was re-elected in 1870. Perhaps the most noteworthy incident connected with his congressional service was his refusal to accept the salary increase voted to members of Congress while he was in that body. It was the first case on record of a member of Congress declining such an increase. He declined on the ground that his election constituted a contract between himself and his constituents so far as the salary was concerned.

Colonel Crebs at the age of fifty-five retired from the practice of law and thereafter gave his attention to his farming and other business interests. He was one of the founders of the First Presbyterian Church at Carmi and for many years a deacon, and at the time of his death, treasurer. He was affiliated with the Independent Order of Odd Fellows. Colonel Crebs married, October 13, 1857, Annie Stewart, a native of White County and a daughter of Josiah Stewart. She survived her husband about ten years. They had the following children: Edwin E., Lucy, Berry S., John M., Annie, Stewart L. and Josiah. The son Josiah was drowned at the age of fourteen.

The present John M. Crebs was born at Carmi, January 24, 1869. His education was acquired in the public schools of his native town and in Wabash College at Crawfordsville, Indiana. Taking up a business career at Carmi, he engaged in banking. He was president of the Farmers and Merchants Bank when it was succeeded by the National Bank of Carmi, and he served as president of that institution until 1923, when he resigned. Since that date he has been chairman of the Board of Directors. He is also engaged in the real estate and loan business and for many years has supervised extensive farming interests. He has always been a democrat, but the only position he has held which might be regarded in any way as a political one was as a member of the Illinois State Board of Agriculture. He was first elected in 1896 and served continuously sixteen years, for the last four years being president. He was elected to this office by the district supervisors. Mr. Crebs is a member of the Presbyterian Church.

He married, in 1890, Elizabeth Powell, a native of Carmi and daughter of John G. Powell, for many years a merchant and at one time sheriff of White County. Mr. and Mrs. Crebs are the parents of four children. The daughter, Lorene, is the wife of Major W. M. Robertson, an officer in the United States Army. John Powell Crebs, a graduate of the University of Illinois, is now a member of the Board of Trade and Stock Exchange of Chicago. Elizabeth L. is the wife of C. W. Evans, a wholesale dry goods merchant at Los Angeles, California. John M. Crebs, the youngest son, graduated from the University of Illinois and the University of Wisconsin, and engaged in the bond brokerage business at Los Angeles, where he died in 1923.

SAMUEL FRANKLIN HAMPTON was one of the early merchants in the history of West Frankfort, beginning business there when the mining village was just beginning development toward the proportions of a city. His business career is a tribute to the power of thrift and industry and close attention to his work. Mr. Hampton is now living retired at West Frankfort.

He was born on a farm in Williamson County, Illinois, December 20, 1855. His father, William Hampton, came from Tennessee in the early '50s and located in Williamson County, where he followed farming. Samuel F. Hampton grew up on the farm, had the advantages of the country schools, and determined upon a career as a merchant rather than that of a farmer. When a young man he removed to Benton, where he had several years of valuable training and experience employed in a general merchandise store. While there he married Miss Laura Hays, daughter of Henry and Sarah Jane (Fidds) Hays. Both the Hays and Fidds families were among the early settlers of Franklin County.

Both Mr. and Mrs. Hampton were actuated by motives of getting ahead in the world, and after some years of close economy they decided in 1905 to go into business for themselves. With a limited capital they opened a grocery store in West Frankfort, their first location being marked by the present Strand Theatre. They kept an attractive store, followed good business methods, and after two years moved to better quarters on the site of the present American Store, and still later to the location of the Walker Store. Mr. Hampton in 1913, having taken a well advised measure of the future growth of West Frankfort, bought a building site west of the Chicago and Eastern Illinois passenger depot, and there erected the brick store building now occupied by the Hampton-Kelly Grocery Company. On the corner he put up a large brick building, now occupied by the Hampton Drug Company.

These buildings and the business conducted in them are a practical monument to the success of Mr. Hampton as a West Frankfort merchant.

He and his wife had six children, the five now living being Lucy, Henry, Bernard, Troy and Cecil. The sons, with the exception of Cecil, accepted the lead of their father and have achieved definite success in commercial careers. Henry is now head of the company operating two fine drug stores in West Franklin. The son Troy is head of another drug business at Christopher. Bernard is the manager of the Hampton-Kelly Grocery Company, under which title is continued the business founded by his father.

Cecil Franklin Hampton, the other son, is a professional man. He was born at Benton in 1902, but was reared at West Frankfort. He graduated from high school in 1919, and in 1923 received the degree Doctor of Dental Surgery from Washington University of St. Louis. The following year he engaged in practice at West Frankfort, and has well equipped offices in the Masonic Temple Building, and is one of the ablest representatives of his profession in Franklin County. He is a member of the Illinois State Dental Society, is affiliated with the Masons and Elks and is a member of the Franklin County Country Club.

GEORGE MATTHEW MILEY, senior member of the law firm of Miley & Combe at Harrisburg, was reared in that section of Illinois, began the practice of law there more than thirty-five years ago, and has won real eminence in his profession.

Mr. Miley was born at St. Louis, Missouri, July 22, 1865. His grandfather, Matthew Miley, was a native of Kentucky. His father, also named Matthew, was born at Paducah, Kentucky, and learned the cooper's trade. He came to Illinois, and when the Civil war broke out enlisted in Company B of the Eighteenth Illinois Infantry. He gave three and a half years of his life to the service of the Union. After the war he settled at Mount Vernon, Indiana, where he followed his trade and where he married Sarah Dunn, who was born at Mount Vernon, daughter of George Dunn. After their marriage they moved to St. Louis, Missouri, and about 1872 settled at Harrisburg, Illinois.

George M. Miley was reared at Harrisburg from the age of seven years, attended the public schools and as a youth learned the cooper's trade. As one of a family of seven children he had to depend upon his own exertions from early youth. At the age of nineteen he went to work in the circuit clerk's office. He studied law in law offices, and at the age of twenty-one was appointed master in chancery, a position which enabled him to live while studying law. He was admitted to the bar in 1890 and at once engaged in practice at Harrisburg. Some years later, on account of failing health, Mr. Miley removed to Thayer in the Ozark region of Missouri and practiced law there fifteen years. After regaining his health he returned to Harrisburg in 1913, and has since been busied with a very extensive practice, involving much corporation work for railroads, insurance companies, coal mining organizations, and public utilities.

Mr. Miley has taken an active part in the republican party since early manhood. Since 1920 he has been a member of the Illinois State Republican Committee. However, he has never sought any public honors or offices for himself. He is a Royal Arch Mason, and a member of the Knights of Pythias and B. P. O. Elks.

Mr. Miley married, in 1889, Miss Kate Anderson. They are the parents of six sons, Harker, Walter, Wayne, Robert, Clark and Delmas. Harker Miley is the present postmaster of Harrisburg. Walter Miley was in the United States navy, in the transport service, during the World war, received an honorable discharge and is now a sailor in the Merchant Marines. Wayne Miley enlisted at St. Louis, was trained in the field artillery and went overseas with the Thirty-fifth Division. He is now in business at Tulsa, Oklahoma.

ELROY W. HEOB, now superintendent of the city schools at Chester, Randolph County, was born in Southern Illinois, and is one of the popular young leaders in educational affairs in the state.

He was born at Ellis Grove, Randolph County, January 29, 1889, son of Joseph F. and Mary (Beare) Heob, and a grandson of Frederick Heob. His father has spent many years as a merchant in the Ellis Grove community. Elroy W. Heob attended school there, but his higher education was the result largely of earnings and efforts put forth by himself. He spent three years in the Southern Illinois Normal University at Carbondale. He taught in various schools, and eventually, in 1917, graduated A. B. from Valparaiso University of Indiana.

When the United States entered the World war he was superintendent of schools at Ava, Illinois. He enlisted, and was in service with the Field Signal Corps, Tenth Division, being stationed at Camp Funston, Camp McArthur and Camp Alfred Vail, serving as a non-commissioned officer, with the rank of sergeant, and at the close of the war was in line for a commission. After the war Mr. Heob was superintendent of schools at Stewardson in 1919-20, and since the fall of 1921 has been superintendent of the city schools at Chester. He married Miss Alice Staton, of Oklahoma.

ARTHUR W. DAGGETT, M. D., has practiced medicine and surgery at Duquoin since 1913. The Daggetts are of Welsh ancestry and on coming to America first settled in New York. Several representatives of the name were soldiers in the Continental army during the American Revolution.

Oran Daggett, grandfather of Doctor Daggett, came from New York State and settled in Marion County, Illinois, where he became a farmer and blacksmith. He died in 1885, when sixty-three years of age. He married a Miss Meyer, member of an Illinois pioneer family.

Their son, William R. Daggett, was born in Marion County, Illinois, in 1846, was a farmer by occupation and died in 1882, when only thirty-six years old. His wife was Isabell Creekmur, daughter of Richard and Nancy Creekmur, of Kentucky stock. Mrs. Isabell

Arthur W. St. Clair & Wife

Daggett now resides in Jefferson County, Illinois.

Arthur W. Daggett, the physician and surgeon, was born on his father's farm in Marion County, February 26, 1879. His first advantages while on the farm were supplied by the country schools. He lived at home to the age of twenty-two. His early literary advantages were supplemented by attending the college at Dixon and also at Charleston, Illinois, and later entered St. Louis University, where he was graduated A. B. and in 1908 received the degree Doctor of Medicine. For nearly a year he was an interne in St. Joseph's Hospital at St. Joseph, Missouri, and in 1909 he opened his office at Belle Rive, Jefferson County. He remained there eighteen months and then practiced in Franklin County until his removal to Duquoin in 1913.

Doctor Daggett married Miss Pearl Gilbert, of Belle Rive, daughter of Rev. B. R. Gilbert. Doctor Daggett is a member of the Knight Templar Commandery of Masons at Carbondale, the Mystic Shrine at St. Louis, and has filled many chairs in that organization, having been elected grand lecturer in July, 1925. He is also affiliated with the Independent Order of Odd Fellows and B. P. O. Elks.

WILLIAM H. BURKHARDT is cashier of the Red Bud Trust Company, the largest financial organization in Randolph County. It has a history of over thirty years. It was organized in 1895 as a co-partnership by Theodore Saxemeyer and others. In 1921 it was reorganized under a state charter as the Red Bud Trust Company, with August Eggerding, president, A. J. Ratz, vice president, and W. H. Burkhardt, cashier. With capital of $50,000, the company has deposits of over half a million, and its total resources are approximately $700,000.

William H. Burkhardt is a son of John M. Burkhardt, one of the best known citizens of Monroe County, who has served three terms as sheriff. The father of John M. Burkhardt was Conrad Burkhardt, who married Mary Fauerbach. Both were natives of Germany. They came to the United States in 1842, settling on a farm in Monroe County. John M. Burkhardt was born near Reneault in Monroe County, November 14, 1861, was reared and educated in that community and all his life has been more or less interested in farming. He built up an extensive business as a well drilling contractor, operating several outfits over Monroe and adjoining counties. His home is at Waterloo. He has been active in republican politics in Monroe County. In 1906 he was elected sheriff of the county, serving a four year term. In 1914 he was again elected to that office and was sheriff during the World war period. In 1922 he was elected for a third time sheriff. John M. Burkhardt married Louisa Wool, of Monroe County. The four children of their marriage were William, Olga, Sophia and Armin.

William H. Burkhardt was born at Reneault. Monroe County, June 26, 1888. He attended country schools and the village schools of Waterloo, finishing with a business college course in St. Louis. He was employed by the Commonwealth Trust Company of St. Louis and the St. Louis Union Trust Company, and after returning to Waterloo was appointed in 1917 a state bank examiner for southern Illinois. He also served as deputy sheriff under his father. Mr. Burkhardt in 1922 left the office of bank examiners to become cashier of the Red Bud Trust Company.

He married, in October, 1915, Miss Louise Burckhardt, daughter of Jacob Burckhardt, of Waterloo. They have one daughter, Dorothy W.

ARTHUR W. ST. CLAIR has the distinction of being the first mayor of the City of Nason, Jefferson County, a community that has consistently been designated as "the new town with the big future." This vital little industrial city is unique in the community of Illinois towns and cities, and its development and upbuilding are proving a marvel in modern urban progress.

Mr. St. Clair, the vital and progressive mayor of Nason, was born at Sullivan, Indiana, January 27, 1883, and is a son of Edon and Cecelia (Grizzle) St. Clair, who now reside on their fine homestead farm in Southeastern Missouri, near Charleston. The St. Clair family has pioneer distinction in the fine old Hoosier state. Thomas and Mary Ann St. Clair, grandparents of the subject of this review, passed their entire lives in Indiana, and Thomas St. Clair represented his native state as a valiant soldier of the Union in the Civil war. He participated in many engagements and in one of these he was rather severely wounded. His interest in his old comrades was shown during later years by his active affiliation with the Grand Army of the Republic. Andrew and Daura Grizzle, maternal grandparents of the mayor of Nason, Illinois, likewise were born in Indiana, and Mr. Grizzle thence went forth as a loyal soldier in the Civil war, as a result of which service he was eligible for and became an active member of the Grand Army of the Republic. Arthur W. St. Clair is a member of a family of eight children, four of whom died in early childhood and one of whom, Perry, met his death at the age of twenty-one years, when he was killed in an accident. Dora is the wife of Ulysses Cottenham, and they became the parents of eight children; Arthur W., of this sketch, is the next younger; and Elsie is the wife of Baxter Murphy, their children being seven in number.

In the public schools of his native state and county Arthur W. St. Clair continued his studies until he was seventeen years of age, and his discipline included that of the high school at Sullivan. There he learned the barber's trade, and after there following this trade two and one-half years he owned and conducted for two years a barber shop at Mosnee, Wisconsin. After selling this business he had a shop at Cairo, Illinois, and after selling this he had a shop in the City of St. Louis during a period of eighteen months. Thereafter he conducted shops at Collinsville and O'Fallon, Illinois, and in December, 1923, he became a pioneer settler in the new town of Nason, where he erected a house to be a home for his family and also built a barber shop for the conducting of his business. November 2, 1924, he was elected the first mayor of this vital young city, and in this office he is giving a most vigorous and effective administration that is justifying the popular choice that placed him in service as the executive head of the municipal government.

Nason is situated about eleven miles southwest of Mount Vernon, the county seat, and here in 1922 was opened the largest body of coal in the State of Illinois, under the control of the Illinois Coal Corporation. It was the initiation of the coal-mining industry here that led to the founding of Nason in 1923, and the place now has a population of 1,500. It is assured that by the close of 1925 Nason will have fully 2,500 inhabitants. The town is not one of mushroom growth, for its buildings are of substantial and modern order, including several fine brick blocks for business purposes, a modern bank building, and one unit of the public schools that are destined to rank with the best in the state. Nason has gained its city charter and is a community of industrial importance and modern facilities and improvements. The mayor and members of the council are liberal and progressive citizens, the City Council having as its members Albert Richardson, S. E. Martin, Carlow Geraldine, John Budislick, Alfred Mochnie, and Matthew Atkins. Robert Lance is police magistrate, Stanley Watson is city attorney, Mr. McIntyre is city treasurer, and Miss Ruth Martin is the efficient and popular city clerk.

The mayor of Nason is a republican in politics and he and his wife hold membership in the Methodist Episcopal Church. He was registered for service in the World war period, was assigned to the fourth class and was not called to active military duty, though he was able to make loyal contributions to the varied patriotic activities of the community in which he was then living.

August 3, 1908, recorded the marriage of Mr. St. Clair and Miss Mary Rossbach, eldest of the four children of Charles and Mary Rossbach, who are residents of Collinsville, Illinois. Emma, the next younger of the Rossbach children, is the wife of Edward Helmach, and they have two children; Kallie is the wife of Albert Gabower, and they have three children; and Charles is also married. Mr. and Mrs. St. Clair have two children: Cecelia and Eugene.

JAMES GLENN BEATTIE, M. D., represents the fourth generation of a family that has lived in Randolph County since territorial days in Illinois. His forefathers were all identified with the agricultural industry, but he has won success and distinction in the medical profession. His home is at Evansville, Randolph County.

He is of Scotch-Irish descent. His father, grandfather and great-grandfather all had the given name of John and all of them were farmers. His great-grandfather, John Beattie, came from South Carolina and settled near Preston, Randolph County, in the year 1809. Doctor Beattie's father married Agnes Faris, whose people had also come out of South Carolina and constituted a well known family in the vicinity of Sparta, Illinois.

James Glenn Beattie was born on the home farm between Sparta and Evansville, July 8, 1865. He was reared in the country, attended country schools and the high school at Sparta, and had several terms of instruction in the State Normal at Carbondale. He taught winter terms in country schools, and in that way defrayed the expenses of his higher education. After teaching for some time he entered the Barnes Medical College at St. Louis, from which he was graduated M. D. April 13, 1898. It is probable that his ambition to enter the medical profession was chiefly aroused by the example of his uncle, Dr. Andrew Bowers Beattie, who attained more than ordinary success in the profession and was for thirty-five years identified with one of the Illinois State Asylums. Doctor Beattie after graduating in medicine practiced at Preston for fifteen years, and since May 4, 1915, has been the leading representative of his profession at Evansville. He does a general practice, and looks after the health and well being of a large clientele for many miles around his home village.

Doctor Beattie married Miss Lillie Hogue, daughter of Archibald Hogue, of Randolph County. They have three daughters, Mary A., who is teaching in the Alton, Illinois, public schools, is a graduate of the Sparta High School and Charleston College. Flora I. is a graduate of the Sparta High School, was married to Philip Peters and lives in Detroit, Michigan. Lillian E. is a graduate of the Sparta High School and is at home. Mr. Beattie has a brother, John L., who is a graduate of the McCormick Theological Seminary at Chicago, and is located at Abingdon, Virginia. He married Elizabeth Roberts and they have one son, John.

PERCY E. STADLER. The International Shoe Company is one of the largest shoe manufacturing organizations in the world. Its headquarters and main plant are at St. Louis, Missouri. The company maintains forty-six subsidiary and branch plants over the country. With the subdivision and extension of the business through branch organizations the offices of the company in 1917 decided to locate a branch factory at Chester, Illinois. The first unit of the plant at Chester was built that year, and operations were begun with ten employes. Since then additions have been made so that about 500,000 square feet of floor space are now utilized. The equipment, needless to say, is of the most up-to-date and modern, representing the last word in new manufacturing facilities. The business at Chester now employs 625 persons. Since then as subsidiary to the Chester plant, auxiliary fitting plants have been established at Evansville and Steelville, both in Randolph County. These two smaller industries employ about 100 persons.

At the head of the business at Chester as general manager is Percy E. Stadler, a man who learned the shoe business in boyhood and has for many years enjoyed important executive positions. He came to Chester with his family in 1920 from Jefferson City, Missouri, where he had been in charge of a department of the International Shoe Company. His career has been an example of a steady climb to larger responsibilities with the help of his individual talents and industry. Mr. Stadler was born at Jefferson City, Missouri. His grandfather, Charles Stadler, was a native of Germany, but lived in Switzerland before coming to the United States. He settled in Pennsylvania and in 1849 started for the Pacific Coast during the gold discovery. He liked the Mississippi Valley and settled in Iowa, but soon afterward moved to Jefferson City, Missouri. Percy Stadler's father, Albert Stadler, was born at Jefferson City, and married Emeline Stone, of a prominent family of Kentucky.

Percy E. Stadler has the thrifty qualities of his ancestors. While attending public schools he carried newspapers, and as a boy became interested in shoe manufacturing. At that time the shoe plant at Jefferson City was largely manned by convicts, and there was very little chance for a free man to learn the business. During evenings after school and after he had finished his paper route Mr. Stadler studied shoe pattern making under a friend of the family. Becoming proficient, while still very young he found employment with the old Gieseke D'Oench Company cutting patterns by hand at three dollars a week. Later at St. Louis he found work in the pattern department of the Robert Johnson and Rand Company, and at the age of eighteen had been made manager or superintendent of the department. The Robert Johnson & Rand Company subsequently became the International Company and Mr. Stadler remained at St. Louis in its service until the period of the World war. During that time he was sent to Jefferson City as manager of the local plant there. This plant had been much beset by labor troubles, and Mr. Stadler had the responsibility of adjusting these disputes and bringing order and efficiency out of a very complicated situation. He understands not only every phase of the technical process of shoe manufacturing but is a thoroughly capable business executive as well.

Mr. Stadler though a resident of Chester only half a dozen years had become very popular as a citizen. He is president of the local school board and a member of the Masonic Lodge. He married Miss Ethel Crump, of Jefferson City. They have two daughters, Marcella, born December 16, 1916, and Fern, born April 28, 1918.

ULYS PYLE, former county judge of White County, represents some of the honored pioneer families of Southern Illinois, and during the greater part of his active career has practiced law at Carmi.

He was born on a farm in White County, April 10, 1880, son of John and Eliza (Stokes) Pyle, and a grandson of Nicholas Pyle, who came from Pennsylvania and was an early settler in White County. John Pyle was born in White County, but his wife, Eliza Stokes, was a native of Virginia. Her father, William H. Stokes, was born in New York State, and removing to Virginia, married Mary Margaret Cheek, member of an old family of that state. From Virginia they removed to Tennessee, and on coming to Illinois traveled by boat to Shawneetown, and thence by family coach to Carmi. William H. Stokes bought and settled on a farm ten miles southwest of the county seat, living there many years, but spending his declining days at Carmi, where he died in 1908 at the age of eighty-seven. Still another generation of the Stokes family was represented in White County during his later years. This representative was Rev. Thomas Stokes, a Baptist minister and father of William H. Stokes.

John Pyle and wife were married in White County in 1860. In 1861 he left his home to enlist in the Fortieth Illinois Volunteer Infantry, his wife's father, William H. Stokes, serving in the Eighty-seventh Illinois Cavalry. Both were soldiers throughout the entire war. Eliza (Stokes) Pyle was also in the war as a nurse, and she is one of the few women of Illinois who draw a pension for personal service in that struggle. She is now eighty-two years of age, lives at the old homestead in White County, but for more than thirty years has been afflicted with blindness. John Pyle died over a quarter of a century ago. He was a democrat in politics.

Ulys Pyle grew up on the home farm, attended country schools, and was the youngest of his parents' children. His brother, William H., has achieved distinction as an educator in the field of psychology and is the author of several books on that subject. He is now connected with the public school system of Detroit, Michigan. Another brother, John O., is a teacher in the public schools of Chicago.

Ulys Pyle graduated from the literary course at Highland Park College, Des Moines, Iowa, in 1902. He also studied law there, subsequently was admitted to the bar in Missouri, and for three years practiced in Dexter, that state. Mr. Pyle for five years was a practicing attorney at Stigler, Oklahoma. On returning to Illinois he established his law office at Carmi, and is one of the successful representatives of his profession there. He was elected on the republican ticket as county judge of White County in 1918, and served four years.

Judge Pyle married, in 1906, in Kansas, Clare Byerley. She is a native of Carroll County, Indiana. The three children of Judge and Mrs. Pyle are Mertice, Mabel and John.

FRANK C. SIBLEY, M. D. The name Sibley has enjoyed an honored prestige in the medical profession of Southern Illinois for half a century. Dr. Frank C. Sibley, of Carmi, is a son of the late Dr. Charles W. Sibley, for many years a physician at Fairfield, and the careers of the two men, father and son, cover exactly half a century.

Charles W. Sibley was a native of Trumbull County, Ohio, and son of Charles Sibley, a native of Connecticut and of English ancestry. Charles Sibley settled in the Western Reserve of Ohio after coming West, from thence moved to Southern Ohio, and in 1852 located at Fairfield, Illinois, where during the Civil war he held the office of postmaster. He lived at Fairfield until his death. Dr. Charles W. Sibley married in Ohio Mary LaLance, a native of Meigs County, Ohio, and of French ancestry. Her father died in Ohio. Charles W. Sibley and wife were married in 1868. He had made a gallant record as a soldier in the Civil war with the Thirty-fourth Illinois Infantry, and was wounded at the battle of Shiloh. He was sent to St. Louis for a surgical operation in which a part of his foot was amputated. Subsequently, when recovered, he engaged in recruiting and was detailed to drill negro troops in Kentucky. In after years he was a member of the Grand Army of the Republic and always a republican in politics. In 1870 he graduated in medicine from Ohio Medical College at Cincinnati, and in 1876 also took his medical degree at the Belleview Hospital Medical College of New York. For many years he was a physician of distinction in Fairfield, and continued his professional work there until his death in 1904. His widow survives him at the age of eighty-two and resides at Fairfield, where all of their six children were born and reared.

Dr. Frank C. Sibley was born at Fairfield, in Wayne County, April 30, 1875. After a common school education he graduated from Hayward College, and studied medicine in St. Louis University, where he took his M. D. degree in 1903. After an internship in a St. Louis hospital he located at Carmi, and has had a general practice as a physician and surgeon. In order to serve and practice the better and provide needed facilities at Carmi, he and Dr. John T. Legier, together with Miss Wilmina K. Pfeifer, in January, 1926, established the Carmi Hospital. Doctor Sibley is a member of the White County, Illinois State and American Medical Associations.

During the World war he served on the local exemption board until December, 1917, when having volunteered and having been commissioned a captain in the Army Medical Corps, he was called to active duty. He spent nine months at Camp Wadsworth in South Carolina, and in October, 1918, went overseas and was at the Base Hospital at Bordeaux. While overseas he was commissioned a major in the Army Medical Corps, and is now an active member of the American Legion. Doctor Sibley is a republican, a Presbyterian and a thirty-second degree Scottish Rite Mason and Shriner.

The citizens of Carmi hold his name in the highest esteem because of the three terms of capable service he gave as mayor of the city. He was elected to that office in 1915, 1917, and again in 1920.

Doctor Sibley married, in 1905, Mrs. Effie (Beck) Wilson. Their two children are: Dorothy Wilson Andress, of Tryon, North Carolina; and Hal K. Wilson, who graduated from the United States Naval Academy, and since leaving the navy has been an electrical engineer with the Bethlehem Steel Company at Johnstown, Pennsylvania. The chief intellectual hobby of Doctor Sibley is the collection of Indian relics. He is credited with having the finest and largest of such collections in Illinois.

JOHN A. SHORT is president of the First State Bank of Chester and is one of the youngest bank presidents in the state. In fact, Mr. Short is two years younger than the bank of which he is the active head.

This has long been one of the strong and prosperous financial institutions of Randolph County. It was founded as the Commercial Bank of Chester and opened for business October 24, 1888. The men active in its organization were William R. McKenzie, Isaac Meredith, T. G. Shadwick, who became its first president, Harvey Nevill, Theodore Saxenmeyer, Kate Gillette, and J. D. Gerlach, who was the first cashier. The bank started with a capital of $10,000. Later it was reorganized as the First National Bank of Chester, the two men most active in the institution at that time being C. B. Cole and M. C. Crissey. On January 12, 1897, the national charter was surrendered and it became the First State Bank. Its original capital was $25,000, later increased to $35,000, and finally to $50,000. The first president of the First State Bank was William R. McKenzie, who had been one of the original stockholders. Mr. McKenzie was succeeded by Isaac Meredith, and he in turn by Maurice A. Mudd. John A. Short first became active in the management of the bank in 1924 and was soon made president. In July, 1923, Mr. C. R. Torrence, the present cashier, entered the bank as assistant cashier and has held the first office since January, 1924. The vice presidents are David H. Holman and J. S. Morrison, with E. C. Richter assistant cashier. A report of the bank in April, 1926, showed total resources of over $600,000, with surplus of $25,000, undivided profits of $10,000, and deposits of over $500,000.

The grandfather of John A. Short was Richard J. Short, a pioneer settler of Southern Illinois, who located near the present site of the town of Percy in Randolph County, on a prairie afterwards called Short's Prairie. He lived out his life in that community. On the old farm there his son Allen A. Short was born April 5, 1856. Allen A. Short was a farmer and school teacher and remained in the home neighborhood until 1893, when he moved to Chester to take up his duties as county treasurer. After four years of service in that office he entered the grocery business with Isaac Meredith in Chester. The grocery business was consolidated with the mercantile business of Bernard Cohen, and the united enterprise became the Chester Supply Company. Allen Short sold his interest in this very successful business in 1917. He had for some years been financially interested in the First State Bank and was vice president of the institution when he died February 19, 1922. Allen Short married Ida Ella Monteith, of Scotch parentage. Her parents lived in North Carolina for some years before coming to Illinois. Mrs. Ida Short died in December, 1918.

John A. Short was born at Percy in Randolph County February 5, 1890, and his home has been at Chester since he was seven years of age. He graduated from high school there in 1908, spent two years in the Gem City Business College at Quincy and in 1911 became bookkeeper and treasurer of the Chester Knitting Mills. He was with that business two years, resigning to look after his father's mercantile interests during the failing health of his father.

As soon as America entered the World war he volunteered and had nineteen months of service in the navy prior to his honorable discharge. On his return to Chester he held

a position in the office of the International Shoe Company, one of the city's largest industries, until September, 1924, when he became president of the First State Bank. Mr. Short married Miss Lillian Etherton, of a well known family of Murphysboro, Jackson County, Illinois. They have one son, John A., Jr.

EDWARD J. BRUNDAGE began the practice of law at Chicago in 1893. He early became interested in politics, especially politics as a means to efficiency in the business of government. For twenty years he has been one of the leaders of real power and responsibility in the republican party of Illinois.

Edward Jackson Brundage was born at Campbell, New York, May 13, 1869, son of Victor and Maria L. (Armstrong) Brundage. He received his primary school advantages there. In 1880, when he was eleven years of age, his parents moved to Detroit, Michigan, where he continued his public education three years longer. Since the age of fourteen he has been self supporting. He worked in a railroad office in Detroit, and when the general office was removed to Chicago two years later he followed, and in 1888 had reached the position of chief clerk. While working he studied law, and was qualified and admitted to the Illinois bar in 1892. In 1893 he received the law degree from the Chicago College of Law. Except as his time has been required in public affairs Mr. Brundage has handled a large general law practice at Chicago for over thirty years.

In his early, as well as later affiliations with the republican party, he was distinguished by ability and integrity and fidelity to principle, and he has sacrificed none of those positions and qualities for the sake of advancement. In 1898 he was elected one of the representatives from the Sixth District in the Forty-first General Assembly, and in 1902 was again elected from the same district. In 1901 he served on the Board of Commissioners as vice president from Illinois to the Pan-American Exposition at Buffalo. In 1904 he was elected president of the Cook County Board and was re-elected in 1906. Under his administration for the first time the Board of County Commissioners earned a reputation for business-like methods in the management of county affairs. A great many citizens of Chicago first began to attach some special significance to the name of Edward J. Brundage because of the official part he had in the erection of the new county building during his administration. In the words of the Chicago Tribune of April, 1907: "Edward J. Brundage has made a remarkable record as president of the County Board. He will make an equally good one as chief of the city's law department."

Mr. Brundage resigned as president of the Board of County Commissioners April 16, 1907, to become corporation counsel of Chicago. He served in that position until the beginning of Mayor Dunne's administration in 1911. In his administration of the Chicago Law Department he made an unequalled record for the number of cases disposed of, advantageous settlements and judgments favorable to the city's interests. The work of the city law department was systematized and extended by him to adequately meet the requirements of the city government. The Chicago Evening Post said: "Mr. Brundage is regarded as the best corporation counsel Chicago ever had. His ability as an executive became recognized when the big municipal policies, now being worked out, were formulated during his tenure of this office. The Michigan Boulevard link improvement, the Twelfth Street widening, harbor development and parks consolidation, which came up in the form of new charter propositions were all subjects born in the Busse administration."

In 1911 Mr. Brundage resumed the private practice of law. During 1915-17 he served as judge of the Court of Claims of Illinois. In 1916 he was nominated by the republicans and elected attorney general of Illinois at the same time that Frank O. Lowden was chosen governor. His first term as attorney general coincided with the notable period of Lowden's administration. In 1920 he was renominated and re-elected and held the office of attorney general eight consecutive years, until 1925. Since retiring from office he has given most of his time to his law practice in Chicago.

Some of the outstanding features of his first term as attorney general were his successful defense of the two-cent passenger fare law, his vigorous prosecution of the riot cases in East St. Louis, his upholding of the constitutionality of the hard road act under which Illinois has since carried out its road building program, and in general his faithful efforts and impartial and thorough enforcement of the laws. His record was the subject of repeated comment and discussion in the Illinois Press, and probably one of the best opinions, one reflecting the general judgment of the people of the state and one of interest because coming from the old Edwardsville Intelligencer in southern Illinois, is the following: "It is a fact that from the moment he took office Brundage has been the servant of the public. It made no difference in what capacity his services were invoked, or if not invoked in what direction they were needed, he promptly met the need, and in such way that all efforts were directed toward the general good. He has not been a figure head in an important position, but a thoughtful, earnest and highly endowed public servant. Through his efforts in the enforcement of laws the state treasury has been enriched to the extent of many millions of dollars in funds which might otherwise never have reached there, and by this means the general burden of taxation was made this much lighter. Furthermore, in the enforcement of laws tending toward the betterment of public morals he has been prompt and efficient. Many people have come to know Edward J. Brundage well since he assumed the grave and important duties of attorney general of this great state, and this intimate knowledge has engendered in them a feeling of profound respect for his abilities and admiration and for his personal qualities."

In his second term General Brundage was presented with evidence of irregularities in the handling of state moneys in the treasurer's office. It was necessary in the performance of his duty for the attorney general to present this evidence to the state's attorney of Sangamon County, who in turn presented it to a grand jury which returned true bills against Governor Small, Lieutenant Governor Sterling and State Senator Edward C. Curtis, the two former being ex-state treasurers and the latter charged with being their associate in the misuse of public moneys. In addition to criminal charges civil suits were instituted. These cases were, perhaps, the most notable in the history of the Union. Governor Small was tried on the criminal charges and acquitted, but in the civil suit the Circuit Court at Springfield held him liable for an accounting and the Supreme Court affirmed its findings.

Mr. Brundage is a member of Chicago, Illinois and American Bar Associations, the Chicago Lawyers Association, is a Knight Templar and Supreme Honorary thirty-third degree Scottish Rite Mason, member of the Knights of Pythias, belongs to the Chicago Athletic, University, Industrial and Knollwood Clubs of Chicago, the Illini Country Club of Springfield. He married, December 7, 1913, Miss Germaine Vernier, of Caen, France. They have a family of two sons and two daughters.

ARTHUR WALTER CHARLES, of Carmi, has long been one of the influential leaders in the democratic party of the State of Illinois. In his home locality he has also been known as a veteran newspaper man and is now president of the National Bank of Carmi.

Mr. Charles was born on a farm in White County, February 14, 1866. His grandfather, Solomon Charles, was born in the same county, of Kentucky parentage and of an ancestry dating back to Colonial times. Daniel Charles, father of the Carmi banker, was born in White County and married Maria A. Clark. They were born and reared within a mile of each other, and after their marriage settled on a farm between the old Charles homestead and the Clark home. Maria A. Clark's father, George A. Clark, was a native of Vermont and of New England ancestry. Daniel Charles and wife finally left their farm and moved to Grayville, Illinois, where he died at the age of sixty-two and his widow died at the age of eighty, twenty-four years later. Daniel Charles was likewise a democrat with the influence of a leader in his community. He was a graduate of the University of Indiana, and a man held in high esteem for his culture and integrity. He and his wife reared nine of their ten children, and eight are still living. One son, Vane, died several years ago, and the survivors are: Arthur W., Belle, Nellie, Kate, Alice, Leda, Violet and Loren.

Arthur W. Charles while a boy on the farm attended country schools. At the age of eighteen he began the study of law at Carmi. He also taught two winter terms of school, and then for two years was a railway postal clerk, running between Cincinnati and St. Louis. He left this work at the beginning of the Harrison administration. During the following three years he was in Texas representing a wholesale farm implement house. From Texas he returned to Grayville, Illinois, and in 1896 engaged in the newspaper business as editor of the Grayville News. This paper was discontinued in 1897, and Mr. Charles then established the White County Democrat, and after two years as its owner and editor he consolidated it with the Carmi Courier, Mr. Charles P. Berry then becoming his partner. Mr. Charles gave most of his time to this publication until 1920, when he sold out.

Mr. Charles has been a director of the National Bank of Carmi since 1923, and in October, 1924, was elected its president. He took the active management of this bank after many years of service in political positions.

Mr. Charles soon after attaining his majority made himself an effective unit in the democratic party in his home county. For twenty-five years he was a member of the White County Democratic Central Committee, and in 1902 became a member of the Illinois State Central Committee, serving as its chairman three terms, from 1912 to 1918. He has attended some of the national conventions. Mr. Charles for twelve years was master in chancery of White County. Governor Deneen appointed him the minority member of the Board of Managers of the Pontiac Reformatory, and later to a like position as a member of the Rivers and Lakes Commission of Illinois. From this commission he resigned in 1912, but two years later was appointed chairman of the commission and served four years. Mr. Charles in 1918 became clerk of the United States Court at East St. Louis, and had served in that capacity five years when he resigned to become president of the National Bank of Carmi.

Mr. Charles married, in 1895, Annie G. Endicott. She was born in Posey County, Indiana, but was reared in White County, Illinois, and they were schoolmates at Phillipstown.

DAVID M. KINSALL is one of the old and honored residents of Shawneetown. For nearly half a century he practiced law and during many years was a public official. The community has honored him for his public spirit and the constant exercise of an influence for good.

The Kinsall family is one of the oldest in Illinois. John, Benjamin and William Kinsall, three brothers, natives of North Carolina and of English and Irish ancestry, came to Illinois about 1810 or 1812, settling in Gallatin County. Not long afterwards John Kinsall volunteered and was enrolled in the American forces during the War of 1812. He married a Miss Hancock, a native of Virginia. In 1827 he settled on a farm about a half mile east of the town of Omaha, in Gallatin County. He was one of the industrious farmers in that community, a man respected for his general works. He voted as a democrat, and was one of the organizers of the Omaha Cumberland Presbyterian Church. He died at his farm in 1853. He and his wife reared children named Hiram, William, Benjamin, Thomas, David, Moses and Jane.

Their son Thomas Kinsall was born in Gallatin County, likewise became a farmer, and his home was about a half mile southwest of Omaha. For many years he was a ruling elder in the Cumberland Presbyterian Church, and at election times always voted the democratic ticket. He died when sixty years of age and his wife was forty-seven when she died. Her maiden name was Malinda Harrell, a daughter of Cader Harrell, who was a native of North Carolina and a pioneer settler in White County, Illinois. The children of Thomas Kinsall and wife were: Judge David M., of Shawneetown, Alvin H., John H., Samuel M. and Virginia.

David M. Kinsall was born on a farm in Gallatin County, May 6, 1851, about forty years after his grandfather settled in the county. While growing up on the farm he attended public schools, also a select school at Fairfield, and spent about five years of his early manhood teaching. While teaching he began the study of law under Judge E. D. Youngblood at Shawneetown. For one year he was a student at the Bloomington (Indiana) Law School, and for another year studied in the office of R. W. Townshend, a member of Congress, at Shawneetown. He was admitted to the bar in June, 1877, and from that date continued the work of a practicing attorney until 1923, when he retired on account of failing health. Judge Kinsall was state's attorney of Gallatin County from 1880 to 1888. From 1890 to 1898 he served as county judge. He was for fifteen years president of the Board of Education at Shawneetown. Mention should also be made of another important public service he rendered the county. In the period of early railroad building Gallatin County was one of those that voted heavy bonds to railroad companies. Judge Kinsall volunteered his services as an attorney with slight remuneration to perfect a satisfactory liquidation of these old bonds, and he handled the matter very successfully for all concerned. During the World war he was chairman of the local Advisory Board. Judge Kinsall was one of the victims of the influenza epidemic during war times, and the results of that illness forced him to retire from active law practice a few years later.

Judge Kinsall has been identified with the democratic party, as was his father and grandfather before him. He is a member of the Cumberland Presbyterian Church and is a demitted member of the Masonic fraternity. He has farm interests in Gallatin County.

He married, in 1883, Miss Edith Lowe, who was born and reared at Shawneetown, daughters of Alexander K. and Casandra J. Lowe. Her father, a native of Maryland, was for many years a successful merchant at Shawneetown. Judge and Mrs. Kinsall have one daughter, Miss Edna.

WILLIAM C. SMITH, grain merchant, well known lay leader in the Presbyterian Church, and prominent citizen of White County, was born in that section of Illinois, and achieved success after a youth of considerable struggle and lack of advantages.

He was born on a farm in White County, March 31, 1856, son of William and Catherine E. (Barth) Smith. The parents were natives of Germany but were married after coming to White County, Illinois, where William Smith located on a farm. He was a blacksmith and wagon maker by trade, and made many of the heavy wagons or prairie schooners with which the California forty-niners crossed the plains. He also cleared away the timber and developed a farm in White County, and in this labor his son William C. Smith had a share in proportion to his strength and years. William Smith finally removed to Carmi, where he built a mill, and operated it for many years. His wife died at the age of seventy, and he was eighty-seven and a half when he passed away.

William C. Smith was one of a family of thirteen children. He was sixteen years old when the home was removed to Carmi. His school advantages were limited, but he had industrious habits and an inclination to make the best of his circumstances. For some time he was employed in a railroad office at Carmi. In 1882 he became an employe of North Storm in the grain business. In a year he had been granted an interest in the business, and subsequently he and Mr. Storm's brother Hail bought the business. Finally Mr. Smith became sole proprietor, and for years has handled a large share of the grain and other products sent to market at Carmi. His business position in later years is the more creditable because of the fact that he started life with less than $100.

Mr. Smith has successfully combined business and religion. For many years it has been the cardinal rule of his life to give at least a tenth of his earnings to church or charity. In early manhood he became a member of the First Presbyterian Church of Carmi and for many years has been ruling elder. He twice served as moderator of his presbytery, is a member of three committees of the general council of the Synod of Illinois, chairman of one committee of the synod, and is chairman of the National Missions Committee of his presbytery. Mr. Smith has always practiced a life of temperance, never having used tobacco or intoxicating liquors in any form. In politics he is a democrat, is a member of the Masonic fraternity and Eastern Star and the Kiwanis Club.

He married, December 27, 1882, Miss Emma R. *Cross, a native of White County and daughter of Thomas Cross, for whom the village of Crossville was named. They have two daughters: Lillian P., wife of Chester F. Rich, of Wellesley Hills, Massachusetts, and Emma E., wife of W. G. Boyer, of Carmi.

JEROME L. HARRELL, M. D. The Harrell family was established in southern Illinois the same year that Illinois came into the Union as a state. Three generations of the name have been honored, respected and useful citizens. Doctor Harrell for over forty years has practiced medicine. His home is at Norris City in White County. He is at the present time a member of the Illinois Legislature.

He was born in Gallatin County, Illinois, July 7, 1859, son of Benton R. and Dollie Emily (Abney) Harrell, both natives of this state, his father of White County and his mother of Gallatin County. The paternal grandparents were Cader and Polly (Garrison) Harrell. Cader Harrell came from his native state of North Carolina when a young man and settled in White County in 1818.

He married there and then located on a farm two and a half miles south of the present site of Norris City, where he devoted his long and exemplary life to agriculture. He died at the age of eighty-four. For many years he was a ruling elder in the Village Cumberland Presbyterian Church, one of the first churches organized in this section of Illinois. The maternal grandfather of Doctor Harrell was also a pioneer. He was James Abney, a Tennessean, who settled in Gallatin County in 1820. He was also a member of the Cumberland Presbyterian Church. Doctor Harrell's parents were life long members of that church and they reared their children in the same faith.

Jerome L. Harrell was one of ten children and grew up on a farm, his environment being rural and his early activities being connected with the farm until he was twenty-three. He attended country schools, the high school at Omaha in Gallatin County, taught school for several terms, and took one course of medical lectures in the Medical College at Evansville, Indiana, and on February 28, 1884, was graduated from the American Medical College of St. Louis. Doctor Harrell for five years practiced at Gossett, in White County, for two years at Ridgway in Gallatin County, and in 1891 began what has been a consecutive service of thirty-five years as a capable physician and surgeon at Norris City. By appointment he served two years, 1915-17, as superintendent of the State Hospital for the Criminal Insane at Chester. He is a member of the White County Medical Society, of which he is former president, and of the Illinois State and American Medical Associations.

Doctor Harrell has always been a staunch democrat. He was elected a member of the Legislature in 1924, being one of the three joint representatives from the Forty-eighth Senatorial District. In the Legislature he has maintained a consistent record for economy, voting against salary and other unnecessary increases, and at the same time favoring liberal appropriations for the state's charitable, penal and educational institutions. Like his parents and grandparents, he has always been a member of the Cumberland Presbyterian Church. He is a member of the Masonic fraternity.

Doctor Harrell married, in 1882, Mary A. Cook, of Omaha, Illinois. Three children were born, one dying in infancy. The son Roy W. was a first lieutenant in the army during the World war, but did not get overseas. He is now practicing medicine at Christopher, Illinois. The daughter Eva P., is the wife of L. L. Crow, and they reside at Fortuna, California.

IRWIN FROST COULTAS. In Scott County and vicinity one of the names most frequently encountered is that of Coultas. It is a family that was established here in pioneer times and has furnished many capable men and women to citizenship, agriculture, business and the professions.

The family lived in England for many generations. James Coultas was an Englishman, but in 1830 he brought his family to the United States. He left Scarborough and after six weeks on a sailing vessel embarked on a steamboat on the Mississippi and came up the Illinois River to Naples. He entered a small tract of forty acres about six miles east of Winchester. This land is now included in the Thomas P. Coultas estate. This was his home until 1853, when he moved to a place nearer Winchester and lived there until his death on February 2, 1859, at the age of sixty-one. James Coultas married Mary Foster. She was born in the same locality of England as her husband. She died April 18, 1872, when past seventy-six years of age. Her children were: James; Foster, born September 20, 1832; and Elizabeth, born December 30, 1834, and died in March, 1838.

James Coultas, second of the name, was born March 4, 1830, the same year that his parents came to the United States. He grew up in the log cabin days of Scott County. In 1861 he erected the brick home where he lived out his own life and where his son Irwin F. now resides. On that farm he spent his active career, and was regarded as one of the substantial men of the county. He served two terms as a county commissioner and had some official connection with the building of the present court house. He was a republican and a Methodist. James Coultas, II, died July 13, 1906. He married in Scott County Margaret Ann Frost, who was born in Sheffield, England, May 13, 1833. Her father, William Frost, was a portrait painter in England. In 1840 he came to America and settled in Scott County, just east of Winchester, but he soon succumbed to the hardships of life in the new world and was laid to rest in the old cemetery at Winchester. His wife was Elizabeth Peach, and she subsequently married Peter Barker and died when nearly eighty years of age. William Frost was the father of three daughters, Margaret Ann, Mrs. Georgiana North and Mrs. Elizabeth P. Hurd. Mrs. Hurd is the only survivor and a resident of Jacksonville. Margaret Ann Coultas died January 30, 1911. Her children were: Warren E., born January 25, 1854, a resident of Winchester; Irwin Frost, born October 27, 1855; Alber James, born September 29, 1857; Mary Ella, born February 12, 1860, wife of J. B. Campbell, of La Harpe, Illinois; Elizabeth Isabella, born March 25, 1862, died unmarried July 7, 1924; Lincoln Grant, born September 13, 1864, married Mayme Hawk, and died July 28, 1925; and Margaret Georgianna, born July 15, 1870, wife of Joseph Roark, of Winchester.

Irwin Frost Coultas represents the third generation of this family in Scott County. He acquired an education in the schools of the county, learned farming under his father, and after his marriage established his first home a mile west of the old place. He lived there fifteen years and after the death of his father he returned to the old homestead and has been managing its interests ever since. He has been a general farmer and stock raiser. For some years he raised and fed hogs, and has also been a cattle feeder, being one of the first to build a silo in Scott County and proved its value in cattle feeding.

Mr. Coultas has long been rated as one of the most prosperous farmers and land owners

in Scott County, and has stood equally high as a public spirited and generous citizen. He served as a member of the county Board of Commissioners from 1899 to 1905. In 1914 he was elected sheriff as successor of John E. Coultas. His term as sheriff was one of quiet routine administration. Only once was he required to make a trip to the penitentiary with a prisoner and once to the reform school at Jacksonville. He was elected sheriff on the republican ticket by a majority of 468 in a democratic county. The official business which has longest interested him in his community has been in his home school district. When his present term expires he will have served as a director twenty-seven years. A new school house was erected largely through his initiative. So well had he prepared the way that when the proposition was undertaken, including a site and voting of bonds, not a dissenting vote was cast at the election.

Mr. Coultas married at Winchester in April, 1885, Miss Eliza Townsend. She brought another English element into this strongly English family. She was born in Yorkshire, England, daughter of John Townsend, who brought his family to the United States when she was about five years of age. She grew up at Winchester, being one of a family of two sons and three daughters. Mr. and Mrs. Coultas have a family of talented children. Their daughter Mary, born October 30, 1888, graduated from the Winchester High School and has been a teacher in the schools of the county. The second daughter, Lois, born January 17, 1892, is a woman of exceptional attainments and experience. She graduated from the Winchester High School, graduated A. B. at the Woman's College at Jacksonville, and took a Masters degree in the University of Illinois. As a teacher she was a member of the faculty of the Woman's College at Jacksonville, taught English in the Community High School at Winchester, and then on invitation went to Japan and spent a year teaching in the mission schools in Tokio, rendering not only an important service but gaining at the same time a knowledge of the orient which has provided her interesting material for many public addresses since her return. She is now a teacher and dean of girls in a high school at Woodstock, Illinois. The third daughter, Margaret, born May 13, 1895, graduated from the Winchester High School and in the classical course at the Woman's College at Jacksonville, and is now the wife of R. M. Overton, a resident of Pittsburgh, Pennsylvania. The only son, James Irwin Coultas, was born February 16, 1901, attended the Winchester High School and is now engaged in the practical routine of farming in his home community. He married, December 24, 1925, Miss Beulah Green.

COL. ANTON F. LORENZEN. Many men of remarkable force and ability, men who have been assigned niches of fame as builders of Chicago, were at some time or other in their lives newsboys. One of the thousands of Chicago newsboys in the decade of the '80s was Anton F. Lorenzen. His business career has been somewhat a development of that first employment and interest. Colonel Lorenzen is president of Lorenzen & Thompson, Incorporated, newspaper representatives, one of the largest organizations of its kind in the country.

Colonel Lorenzen was born in Denmark, in 1876, and was five years of age when his parents, in 1881, settled in Chicago. He grew up in that city, and his early education was acquired in private schools and public schools. He was nine years of age when upon the death of his father he began earning his living as a newsboy on the streets of Chicago. In subsequent years he made his abilities known in different jobs and occupations, but for the most part has kept close to the publishing and advertising business. Lorenzen & Thompson, Incorporated, newspapers representatives, of which he is president, is a firm of nation-wide connections with newspaper publishers and handles advertising for many of the leading metropolitan dailies. The firm in addition to its headquarters in Chicago has branch offices in New York, Detroit, Los Angeles, San Francisco and Seattle.

While establishing himself in a successful business career Colonel Lorenzen has been also earning a distinguished military record. Only a brief outline of this record can be given. He enlisted in Company L, Second Infantry, Illinois National Guard, June 6, 1892; became corporal December 5, 1894; sergeant August 30, 1897; first lieutenant June 14, 1900; and captain June 26, 1902. During the Spanish-American war he was in Cuba with the Illinois troops, and as a lieutenant commanded the fortress which controlled the water supply of Havana. As a company commander he had the honor of leading the state of Illinois in rifle practice, and was the first man in his regiment to win the expert rifleman decoration when it was founded.

When America entered the World war Captain Lorenzen was given a position of unusual responsibility in the United States Secret Service. Later he was returned to active military duty with the First Infantry, Illinois Reserve Militia, of which he was commissioned major October 31, 1917, and advanced to lieutenant colonel March 7, 1918. Immediately upon his assignment to the First Infantry he undertook the task of recruiting and organizing troops at Chicago for service in the World war. The history of the First Infantry, I. R. M., and its distinguished services in training officers and men for the battle front has never adequately been recorded. Hundreds of the finest young men of Chicago and vicinity, many of them representatives of prominent and wealthy families, were trained and equipped for service by this organization and many of them made brilliant records for bravery. Numbers of these men remained permanently as officers in the United States army.

Following the World war Mr. Lorenzen was advanced to the rank of colonel. He was commanding the First Infantry, Illinois Reserve Militia, at the time of the great race riots in Chicago in 1919. At that time he rose to an extraordinary height of military efficiency. He had his regiment perfectly trained and all the men united in utmost loyalty and competence in him as a leader, and as a result his regiment rendered service during that tense and critical time in Chicago which won attention throughout the nation and brought from Governor Lowden and others many unusual tributes to Colonel Lorenzen's soldierly ability. One brief tribute to Colonel Lorenzen as commander during this riot may be appropriately noted in this brief sketch. It was written by Capt. La Mar Miller, a West Point graduate:

"I had been commissioned in the regiment for one hour when we were called out for riot duty. The promptness with which the men assembled and the evidence of cooperation and discipline surprised me, but I had little time to give the matter much thought until we had started down Michigan Avenue toward the Black Belt.

"It was then that I realized the magnitude of the undertaking—a regiment of business men gathered from all parts of Chicago and Evanston in two hours, armed and equipped, moving down the boulevard in one long line of a hundred and thirty yellow cabs to the scene of disorder. The whole result spelled complete cooperation and that evidence of response which is only shown in the presence of a real leader. And when the regiment detrained and moved into black territory in riot formation, stretching from house to house across the street with fixed bayonets, the colonel still leading by a hundred yards—a gray-haired boy—and I followed behind him, amazed at the irregularity of such an act on the scene of constant sniping, while enjoying its human side."

Colonel Lorenzen, whose home is at the Congress Hotel and whose business offices are at 122 South Michigan Avenue, is a Knight Templar Mason and Shriner, member of the Calumet Country Club, Lake Shore Athletic Club, the Detroit Athletic Club, Army and Navy Club and the Chicago Association of Commerce.

JUDGE JOSEPH B. DAVID has been a judge of the Superior Court of Cook County since June, 1916. His judicial services have won him the confidence and respect of the public of Cook County.

Judge David was born at Louisville, Kentucky, October 22, 1863, the son of Theobald and Adelaide David. His father was an expert accountant and also a teacher in Louisville. He was educated in the public schools at Louisville, and in 1881, at the age of eighteen, came to Chicago. He served his apprenticeship at law in the office of Judge Philip Stein and was admitted to the Chicago bar in 1885 and practiced continuously in Chicago until he was elected judge of the Superior Court. He was for some years a member of the law firm of David, Smulski & McGaffey, his partners being John S. Smulski, former city attorney of Chicago and treasurer of the State of Illinois, and Ernest McGaffey, at one time secretary of Mayor Carter H. Harrison II. Before he was elected to the bench Judge David had a high reputation as a successful trial lawyer, both in civil and criminal cases. Among the successful cases in which he was counsel were the famous "lottery cases" in which the Supreme Court of the United States ultimately decided that a lottery ticket was an article of commerce, and the prosecution growing out of the Burlington strike. While he was a practicing attorney he served at different times as special assistant states' attorney and special assistant city attorney.

Judge David was first elected to the Superior Court bench in June, 1916, to fill a vacancy, and was re-elected in November, 1917, and again in November, 1923, which term he is now serving. During his services as judge he has sat mainly in the civil branch, but has also presided in divorce cases and at various times has been one of the judges of the Criminal Court. He has twice served as chief justice of the Superior Court. Many cases involving unique, peculiar and important questions have been decided by him during his term of office, including the trials of Carl Wanderer and Mrs. Nitti for murder and the trial of Russell Scott for insanity after Scott had been sentenced to be hanged. Judge David's long and varied experience as a lawyer has made him unusually competent to meet the problems that have confronted him as a judge. With both the legal profession and the public he has gained a reputation for integrity, knowledge of the law, and absolute fearlessness.

Judge David married, on August 16, 1888, Miss Emma Siesel, the daughter of Salomon Siesel, of Chicago, who died June 27, 1924. The children of their marriage are Sigmund Walker, who is a practicing attorney in Chicago and a member of the law firm of Stein, Mayer & David, Louise, Adelaide and Cecil.

Judge David has always been a democrat in politics. He is a member of the Chicago, Illinois and American Bar Associations, the Iroquois Club, the Covenant Club of Chicago and the Irish Fellowship Club. He is at present serving as president of Adolph Kraus Lodge of B'nai B'rith, takes a deep interest in the Zionist movement and is affiliated with several Zionists organizations.

LEO VINCENT GATES, M. D. A graduate in medicine from the University of Illinois, Doctor Gates was a medical officer during the World war, and since the war has practiced in southern Illinois, being one of the highly qualified surgeons located at Duquoin in Perry County.

His father, Lawrence Gates, was of English ancestry and member of a family established in New York before the Revolution. Lawrence Gates was born in Minnesota, near Alma City, and became a merchant there. He died in 1889. His wife was a daughter of William Lawrence, of another New York State family. Branches of the Lawrence family settled in Indiana, Wisconsin, Illinois, Iowa, Montana, Wyoming and Colorado, and one branch in Honolulu. The Lawrences were all identified with merchandising.

Leo Vincent Gates was born at Alma City, Minnesota, May 29, 1888, at the home of his grandparents. At that time his father lived at Elgin City. Doctor Gates attended public schools at Elgin City, continued his education in Carleton College at Northfield, Minnesota, and in 1916 was graduated from the University of Illinois College of Medicine with the Bachelor of Science and Doctor of Medicine degrees. He had training as an interne in

St. Luke's Hospital in Chicago and also in Milwaukee, and for a few months was engaged in hospital duty at Zeigler in Franklin County, Illinois.

With a commission as lieutenant he was called to active duty in December, 1917, and assigned to the Three Hundred and Thirty-ninth Field Hospital, Eighty-fifth Division. He served with that division during its stay in France and returned home in April, 1919. He then took charge of the hospital at Zeigler, and remained until December, 1921, when he located at Duquoin to engage in private practice. He handles a general practice but his main work is industrial surgery, for which he has unusual qualifications. He is a member of the various medical organizations.

Doctor Gates assisted in organizing the Lodge of Masons at Zeigler. He is a member of the Mystic Shrine and the Elks. Doctor Gates married Emily Holt, of the Wisconsin branch of the Holt family.

J. C. McMILLAN, M. D. A native of Sangamon County, where his people have lived more than eighty years, Doctor McMillan has for over a quarter of a century practiced medicine and surgery in the community of New Berlin, and that locality has a high degree of esteem for him, both as a citizen and as a professional man.

He was born in Sangamon County, August 30, 1873, son of John A. and Cynthia Ann (Taylor) McMillan, his father a native of Sangamon County and his mother of Ohio. Both parents were born in the year 1844, his father on January 28 and his mother on January 4. They had a family of eight children, two of whom died in infancy, the others being: William H., of Arizona; J. C.; Kitty C., widow of Warren Wilcox, of Sangamon County; Hattie, Lucy and Leland, of California.

Doctor J. C. McMillan acquired his early education in the home locality, attended the Whipple Academy at Jacksonville, Illinois, and for one year taught school. He then entered the Missouri Medical College at St. Louis, was graduated M. D. in 1898, and for one year practiced in old Berlin, and since then at New Berlin.

Doctor McMillan married, October 11, 1900, Miss Maude E. Carpenter, daughter of Charles and Mary C. (Gibson) Carpenter, her father a native of Ohio and her mother of Sangamon County. Doctor and Mrs. McMillan have four children: J. Charles, Mary C., Lee Gibson and Ella Maude. Doctor McMillan is a democrat and a Baptist, is affiliated with the I. O. O. F., and belongs to the Sangamon County and Illinois State Medical societies.

ALFRED E. SCHUETTE is one of the conservative and successful members of the banking fraternity of Randolph County, and for over twenty years has been identified with the Bank of Evansville.

The Bank of Evansville was organized as a private institution in August, 1895, with William R. Borders as president, P. M. Holm as cashier, and Nicholas Sauer, vice president. The other stockholders included C. D. Pantler, V. Wehrheim, William Wolf, Henry Beare and J. H. Despain. Of these men constituting the original members Mr. Wolf is the only surviving director and has been continuously identified with the institution for over thirty years. Mr. Borders' interests were purchased by the late Nicholas Sauer, who had from the first been one of the most energetic factors in starting the bank. Nicholas Sauer was president until his death in 1908. and since then his son, George Sauer, has been president. This is one of the prosperous banks of Randolph County, with capital of $25,000 and surplus of $25,000.

Mr. Schuette, who became cashier of the bank in March, 1905, was born at Redbud, Illinois, November 10, 1881. His father, Louis Schuette, came to Randolph County, Illinois, from Germany in 1867 and spent the rest of his life as a blacksmith at Redbud. He married Caroline Eggerding, a native of Randolph County.

Alfred E. Schuette was educated at Redbud, and was sixteen years of age when he went to work for the Redbud Trust Company. He has spent practically all his mature years in the banking business. After six years with the trust company he came to Evansville, and has given his best talents to the institution of which he is cashier. He has always kept out of politics, but is an active member of the Evangelical Lutheran Church and is clerk of the Evansville School Board. He married Miss Emma Arras, a native of Randolph County.

ROY WINCHESTER is vice president and manager of the Community Lumber Company of Christopher. Practically his entire business experience has identified him with the lumber industry and it is doubtful if any lumber dealer in Southern Illinois has a better understanding of conditions affecting the trade than this live and enterprising young man, who is a native of Franklin County.

He was born on his father's farm in Franklin County, son of Joseph E. Winchester. His father was born in North Carolina and on coming to Illinois settled in Jackson County and then Franklin County, and after a career of well earned prosperity retired and now lives in Williamson County. Joseph Winchester married Julia Hiller, a native of Jackson County.

Roy Winchester was reared on a farm, attended country schools, and at the age of twenty-two became an employe of the Stotlar Lumber Company at Marion in Williamson County. He was with that concern four years. Then, in 1917, he and his brother Lloyd bought the lumber business at Sesser, operating it as the Winchester Lumber Company. In 1921 the Sesser business was sold to the newly organized and incorporated Winchester Lumber Company, of which Lloyd Winchester was president and Roy Winchester vice president and manager. The new corporation had also acquired lumber yards at Christopher and Valier. In 1923 the Park Lumber Company of Herrin was bought, and in 1924 Roy Winchester withdrew from the Winchester Lumber Company, his brother Lloyd having moved to Herrin in 1923 while Roy remained at Christopher. With the Christopher yard as a nucleus Roy Winchester organized the Community Lumber Company on August 4, 1924, J. M. Miller becoming president and L. T. Putnam treasurer, while Roy Winchester has the active management as vice president. The company operates two yards, one at Christopher and one at Sesser. The Sesser yard was destroyed by fire in 1926.

Mr. Roy Winchester while living at Herrin, on September 15, 1909, married Bessie Miller, born September 11, 1891, a daughter of Monroe Miller. He has one daughter, Violet, born May 27, 1912.

MARK CLANCY KELLER, states attorney of Lee County, has been a member of the bar of that county for a quarter of a century and has given creditable performance both in private practice and in public office.

He was born on a farm in Lee County, February 24, 1873, son of John and Amy (Brett) Keller. His grandfather Keller was a native of Ireland and going to Canada, located at Toronto, where subsequently he was appointed clerk of the Division Court, a position he held until his death. One of his sons became sheriff. John Keller, who was born and reared at Toronto, spent some of his boyhood as a driver of fast horses and drove in many races. He served as chief deputy sheriff under his brother. He married in Canada, Amy Brett, who was born in Liverpool, England, and went to Canada when a girl. Three children were born to John and Amy Keller while they lived in Canada: Lydia, Frank B. and Rebecca. This family on coming to the United States first settled in Whiteside County, Illinois. In that county children were added to the family circle named John, Ada, Charles and William. After the parents settled in Lee County six children were born: George, Mark C., Ralph, Densig, Lillian and Glenn. Glenn and Rebecca are now deceased. John Keller was an Illinois farmer, and was killed when his team of horses ran away, he being then sixty-two years of age. His widow reached the age of seventy-two.

Mark C. Keller in his youth and early manhood worked on the farm, learning the lessons of industry and perseverance which have contributed to his success in life. His parents were very worthy and industrious people, but means were limited to the income of the farm and they had a large family of children to share this income. Beyond the advantages of the country schools the children had to get their higher education and contrive their own opportunities in the world. Therefore, Mark Clancy Keller, while receiving encouragement and cooperation from his parents, had to earn his own education after leaving the country schools. He subsequently graduated from a business college at Chicago, and for several years taught in rural schools and also taught in Dixon College while attending that institution in the law department. He graduated with the degree Master of Laws in 1900, was admitted to the Illinois bar the same year, and since then has practiced in Dixon except for one year while he was connected with a law firm in Chicago. He has handled an important volume of general practice in all the courts of his district.

At the same time since early manhood he has been active in the councils of the republican party, serving as secretary of the County Central Committee. He was for six years justice of the peace, nine years city attorney for Dixon, master in chancery six years, and in 1920 was elected state's attorney, and in 1924, reelected. He has given an exceptionally able and forceful administration of this office.

Mr. Keller is a past master of his Masonic Lodge, a past high priest of the Royal Arch Chapter, a past commander of the Knights Templar Commandery, has served as district deputy grand master of the Grand Lodge of Illinois, and is a thirty-second degree Scottish Rite Mason and Shriner. He also belongs to the B. P. O. Elks, and is a member of the Country Club, Golf Club and Kiwanis Club at Dixon.

He married in 1904 Miss Mae Richardson, who was born at Lee Center, Illinois, daughter of George L. and Milla (De Wolf) Richardson. They have three children: Mildred Amy, Mark C., Jr., and John Richardson Keller.

COL. CHARLES RIDGELY VINCENT. Even the most ardent devotees of peace are compelled to acknowledge that warfare and its grim exactions develop character in a way accomplished by no other single medium. The appeal to the love of one's native land, the pride of birth and the determination to defend the honor of the country's flag bring out new traits and strengthen others so that it would almost appear that a new birth had taken place. No man who has passed through the ordeals attendant upon a war can be quite the same afterward. After he has faced the enemy of his country on the battlefield, risking life and limb as well as liberty, he is better able to meet the difficulties of everyday life during times of peace with fortitude and patience. The hardships of camp and the dangers of actual conflict tend to make the ills of civilian life of little weight, and he can, from such experience, look into the future with a clearer insight and with a much broader viewpoint than one to whom these great things of life are but words.

The World war was a terrible calamity, but it gave to the survivors a victory in the conquering of self, as many of them have proved in their subsequent service as reliable, successful and upright citizens, in which category is found Col. Charles Ridgely Vincent, of Chicago, a leading dealer in investment securities. Colonel Vincent was born at Springfield, Illinois, in 1888. His parents were both members of prominent and historic families of Illinois. His paternal grandfather, an intimate friend of Abraham Lincoln, at one time served as mayor of Springfield. Hon. William A. Vincent, his father, was born and reared at Springfield, and in early life achieved prominence and distinction as a lawyer. He was but twenty-six years of age when he was appointed by President Grover Cleveland as United States district judge for New Mexico, and after returning from that new state settled at Chicago, where he became one of the organizers of and counsel for the International Harvester Company, a connection which immediately put him in the front ranks of his profession and the business world. He also enjoyed a large general practice, and among other noted cases defended Luetgert, the sausage-maker, in his notorious murder trial of several decades ago. He was interested in numerous civic movements and was a member of the Board of Directors of the World's Fair at Chicago, and later, with Colonel Ferris, built the Ferris Wheel, which in its day was the wonder amusement device of the country. Judge Vincent married Miss Ridgely, a daughter of Charles Ridgely, and a granddaughter of Nicholas Henry Ridgely, a noted banker of Springfield and the founder of the first bank in Illinois, located at Springfield. A brother of Mrs. Vincent, the late William Barrett Ridgely, was comptroller of the currency during the administration of President Roosevelt.

Charles Ridgely Vincent attended Yale University, from which he was graduated in 1910 and for a time thereafter was a national bank examiner in New York state. Later he was assistant cashier of the National Bank of Commerce of Kansas City, but in 1913 returned to his native state of Illinois and took up his residence at Chicago. He got his start in military life in 1914 when he organized the Second Battalion of the First Illinois Field Artillery, which became a part of the Illinois National Guard, one of the batteries being located at the University of Illinois and two others organized at Chicago. He went to the Mexican border in the summer of 1916 as major of the Second Battalion, First Field Artillery of Illinois, and when the United States became actively engaged in the World war, in April, 1917, he was called to the First Officers' Training Camp at Fort Sheridan to assist in the training of officers. There he was recommended for the rank of lieutenant-colonel of artillery, and in the summer of the same year, 1917, was called to Springfield by Gov. Frank O. Lowden, who requested him to organize an additional regiment of infantry for the Illinois contingent. Colonel Vincent accordingly organized the Eleventh Infantry for World war service, accomplishing the remarkable feat of organizing a regiment of 1,183 men in ten days, fully equipped and ready for service. Then the Governor called on his abilities again, this time to assist the State Council of Defense in procuring recruits for the United States Marines. For this service Colonel Vincent raised 4,200 men in two and one-half months. As a merited reward for this extraordinary service the State Council of Defense, with the approval of the Adjutant General of the state, recommended Colonel Vincent for promotion to the rank of colonel, which was accordingly done, and with this rank he was assigned to duty as adjutant of the Twelfth Division, with which he went overseas in the summer of 1918. At that time he was the youngest colonel in the United States army. In his capacity of adjutant of his division he had charge of the flying service, and it was through his experience thus gained and his subsequent studies in aviation that Colonel Vincent has become known as an authority on the subject of flying. Following his honorable discharge from the service he located at Chicago, where he is now engaged in the investment securities business, with offices located at Room 907, 11 South LaSalle Street, being successfully connected with large banking and business interests. He has a number of civic connections and is a popular member of the Chicago Club.

Colonel Vincent married Miss Margaret Irving Tiffany, of Jacksonville, Illinois, granddaughter of Judge Berdan, one of the founders of Illinois College at Jacksonville. Mrs. Vincent, a graduate of Vassar College, died leaving two children: Charles Ridgely, Jr., and Tiffany. The pleasant Ridgely home is located at Winnetka, Illinois.

JAMES M. BURKHART, who died in 1922 at Marion had been a resident of Williamson County sixty years. In business he was successful as a merchant and banker, and he also revealed a stalwart character as an earnest and high minded citizen of his community.

The record of the Burkhart family in several generations passes from Germany to Virginia, thence to Tennessee, and from Tennessee to southern Illinois. George Burkhart, a native of Germany, came to Virginia about the time of or just at the close of the Revolutionary war, living for a time in Maryland, then in Virginia, and at Abingdon in the extreme southwestern corner of Virginia he conducted a tavern or inn. His son, Peter Buarkhart, was born at Hagerstown, Maryland, in 1785, and was seventeen years of age when the family moved to Abingdon, Virginia. He was reared there, getting a subscription school education. He had a military record of service in General Jackson's army in the Creek Indian war, participating in the famous battle of Horseshoe Bend. From Abingdon, Virginia, he moved down the great valley to Knox County, Tennessee, acquired a farm there and also followed the trade of carpenter. He was living there at the time of the Civil war, and like many others of eastern Tennessee, was a staunch Union man and espoused the republican party. He was a member of the Lutheran Church. He died in Tennessee in 1868. His second wife was Anna Gillian, who survived him until 1890, passing away at the age of eighty-nine. Of her three children the second was the late James M. Burkhart of Marion, Illinois.

James M. Burkhart was born in the vicinity of Knoxville, Tennessee, June 8, 1841. He grew up on a farm in eastern Tennessee, attended subscription schools, and about the time he reached his majority came to Illinois, settling in Williamson County. He taught school for a time and also followed the trade of carpenter in Marion and vicinity for ten years. He left his trade to become a clerk in the Goodall & Campbell store at Marion, and later formed a partnership with Hardin Goodall to engage in the general merchandise business. After eleven years he purchased the interest of Mr. Goodall, becoming sole proprietor, but subsequently took in A. J. Binkley, making the firm Burkhart & Binkley, and finally made his sons partners in the business of J. M. Burkhart & Sons. He was one of the organizers in 1891 of the First National Bank of Marion and served for a time as cashier. He was also one of the original stockholders of the Marion State & Savings Bank and became its vice president. He was one of the organizers of the Marion Electric Light & Power Company.

He cast a vote for Abraham Lincoln in 1864, and altogether voted in fifteen presidential elections and always as a republican. In public matters his chief interest was in education, and he served on the Marion school board and for a number of years was a trustee of the Southern Illinois Normal University at Carbondale. He became a member of the Masonic Order in 1865, was a past master of his lodge, past high priest of the Royal Arch Chapter and also served as district deputy grand master.

James M. Burkhart married, May 5, 1872, Miss Ellen Spiller, member of an old and prominent family of Williamson County. She was born in that county in 1850, daughter of Elijah Spiller. The children born to their marriage were: Annie and Lena, both of whom died in childhood; Carl; William S.; Jean; Kate; Ethel, who married Len Colp; Ralph; and Ruby, who married Paul Johnson.

Carl Burkhart has spent practically all his active life with the Benton State Bank in Franklin County. He was born at Marion August 11, 1876, attended public schools in his native town and graduated in 1897 from the Southern Illinois Normal University at Carbondale. The year following his graduation he went to work as a clerk in the Benton State Bank, and for a number of years past has been cashier of that institution.

Mr. Burkhart is a member of the Masonic Order, Knights of Pythias and B. P. O. Elks and the Benton Country Club. He married Miss Kate Hickman, daughter of Dr. Zachary Hickman. Her father at the time of his death in 1924 was the oldest practicing physician in Benton. Mrs. Burkhart died in 1920, leaving five children: Marjorie, who graduated in 1923 from the University of Chicago, did postgraduate work in Columbia University and is now a teacher in the Benton High School; Ellen, a Junior in the University of Wisconsin; George H., a student in the Benton High School; Gene M. and Kate, both attending public school.

COLUMBUS BROWN, M. D., a leading physician and surgeon of Herrin in Williamson County, has practiced for over a quarter of a century. He is a member of a pioneer family of Southern Illinois and one properly distinguished by the high character and the individual services of its members.

His grandfather was Rev. Jeremiah Brown, one of three brothers who came from Holland to North Carolina, thence removed to Tennessee, and about 1845 came to Illinois and settled in the hills of Union County. He was a Baptist minister.

Among his children was Capt. John Brown, who served in both the Mexican and Civil wars. He was born in Union County in 1826, a date which indicates that the Browns have been in Illinois for over a century. Capt. John Brown served in a regiment made up from Williamson and Union counties which marched to the relief of General Taylor at Buena Vista, arriving in time to witness the surrender of the Mexican troops. The regiment endured many hardships and sufferings in their southern campaign. After returning to Illinois Capt. John Brown settled on a farm near Jonesboro. While there he married Miss Martha J. Wilkins. They soon became members of the Baptist Church at Jonesboro, and then and throughout their lives were exemplary Christians. The two daughters born to them while they lived at Jonesboro were Fatima, who became the wife of Ephraim Herrin, the founder of the city of Herrin; and Josephine, now Mrs. John Herrin, of Marion. The children of these parents comprise a notable group of prominent names in the history and affairs of Williamson and adjoining counties. From the farm near Jonesboro they moved to Bainbridge, then the chief town of Williamson County. Here another daughter and a son were born. Captain Brown conducted a prosperous business there, but after Marion became the county seat and business centered around that point the family moved to the farm near Centerville known as the Brown farm. Here were born five daughters and one son, making a family of ten children in all. Captain Brown and wife helped promote good schools, though most of the children received their early advantages in log cabin schools. Hurricane Church was the scene of the religious activities of the family. The sons became honored physicians, the daughters, teachers, home workers and church workers. One daughter died at the age of sixteen. Capt. John Brown died at the age of seventy-three, in 1899, and his wife survived until June, 1910, passing away at the age of eighty-three. The son, Doctor Curtis, died at the age of seventy after a life of hard work for suffering humanity. The surviving son is Doctor Columbus, and the daughters are busy women, all devoted to their children and other activities. Besides those mentioned the daughters are: Gertrude, who is the widow of C. H. Murrah, and they were founders of Creal Springs College, and she has been the active head of that institution from its beginning, over forty years ago; Cornelia, who married Isaac Hammer; Florence, who became the wife of Thomas Stotlar, another well known name in the Herrin district; Orion J., who married A. K. Elles; and Cora, who married E. T. Steele.

In 1861 Capt. John Brown became captain of Company D of the One Hundred and Twenty-eighth Illinois Infantry. When he went away to war he left his wife with seven children and the care of a large farm. involving much work in looking after the stock and gathering in the crops. Three of the children, including Mrs. Murrah, were old enough to help her. She went through this period of her life a true heroine, wasting nothing, allowing nothing to suffer from neglect, and after the harvests were completed the children received more than half a term of school. When the war was over Captain Brown returned home and then followed many years of successful work in farming and merchandising and devotion to his family and to the best interests of his community.

Dr. Columbus Brown was born in Williamson County, on the home farm two and a half

miles west of Herrin, November 2, 1868. His opportunities in the country schools were supplemented by attendance at Creal Springs College under his sister. From there he entered Missouri Medical College, now the medical department of Washington University at St. Louis, and was graduated March 29, 1898. Doctor Brown returned to his old home at Creal Springs and practiced medicine for about eight years, and since 1906 his home has been in Herrin. In that city and over a large surrounding district his name is synonymous with the highest degree of skill and ability in medicine and surgery.

Since 1912 Doctor Brown has had as his professional associate his nephew, son of his sister, the president of Creal Springs College. In February, 1925, Doctors Brown and Murrah became the owners of the splendid Herrin Hospital. This is one of the best equiped private hospitals in Southern Illinois, having accommodations for forty patients and a fine building. The nurses staff comprise gradute and eight student nurses. Doctor Brown is a member of the Williamson County, Illinois State, Southern Illinois and American Medical Associations. He belongs to the Herrin Country Club and the B. P. O. Elks. He has served as a member of the Board of Education at Herrin and is a democrat in politics.

He married at Independence, Missouri, August 12, 1902, Miss Lula Slack, daughter of Anthony and Maria (Moore) Slack. Doctor and Mrs. Brown had four children. Martha is the wife of Cecil Dawson, of the Dawson Furniture Company of Zeigler, Illinois, and has a son, Richard Allen. John C. Brown graduated from the School of Commerce of the University of Illinois after special work in commercial law, insurance and accounting, with the class of 1926, and is now connected with the Metropolitan Life Insurance Company at Champaign, Illinois. He married Ruth Pace, daughter of A. T. Pace, of Herrin, and has a son, John Columbus, Jr. Anthony T. Brown, a graduate of the St. Louis School of Pharmacy, is now connected with the R. A. Carr Drug Company, of St. Louis. Curtis, the youngest, is attending the Herrin High School.

WILLIAM CALVIN FAIRWEATHER, publisher of the McLeansboro Times, is a native of Hamilton County, and is best known in that and other counties of southern Illinois on account of his prominence as an educator. For many years he was engaged in school work, and since retiring from that vocation has engaged in newspaper work.

He was born on a farm four miles south of McLeansboro, October 11, 1871, son of William and Rachel (Manning) Fairweather. His grandfather, Samuel Francis Fairweather, was a native of Lincolnshire, England, and brought his family to America, homesteading 160 acres in Hamilton County, Illinois. William Fairweather was a small boy when the family came to America, and he spent his life as an industrious farmer and influential citizen of Hamilton County, where he died in 1914, at the age of eighty years. His wife, Rachel Manning, was a native of Illinois, her people coming from Tennessee. She had four brothers who were soldiers in the Union army. William Fairweather and wife were members of the Missionary Baptist Church and he was a democrat in politics. Their children were: Sarah Elizabeth, deceased, who married John Brannon; Mary S., deceased, who married James Dudley; William Calvin; and Charles Arthur, who married Clara Brandt.

William Calvin Fairweather grew up on the home farm, and after the advantages of the common schools his advanced education was acquired as a result of his own effort, largely alternating with school teaching. He attended the State Normals at Carbondale and Normal, the Valparaiso University in Indiana, and had one year in the University of Illinois. Mr. Fairweather was engaged in school work for thirty years and is now on the teachers' pension roll. He taught a number of terms in country districts. For three years he was a teacher at McLeansboro, four years at Murphysboro, in 1902 was elected superintendent of city schools at McLeansboro and held that position ten years. For six years he was superintendent of schools at Nashville, Illinois, for two years superintendent of the grade school and township high school at Neoga, and held a similar position at Farmer City for one year.

Mr. Fairweather in 1923 bought the McLeansboro Times. This is a weekly newspaper, and has a large circulation and influence in Hamilton County. It is democratic in politics. Mr. Fairweather is himself a democrat, and is a member of the Fifty-first Senatorial District Committee. He is president of the McLeansboro Merchants Co-operative Association. He is a member of the Missionary Baptist Church and is affiliated with the Independent Order of Odd Fellows and Knights of Pythias. He married, September 8, 1900, Miss Excie O'Neal, who was born and reared in McLeansboro.

W. A. HASKELL, M. D. One of the able surgeons of his time, and active in his profession for thirty years at Alton, Doctor Haskell after retiring, though not losing an interest in professional progress, devoted most of his time to travel, books and literary associations.

He represented the fourth generation of the Haskell family in the medical profession of America. His great-grandfather, Abraham Haskell, practiced medicine in New England before the War of the Revolution. The grandfather, also named Abraham, was a physician and married Hannah Cotton, a descendant of Rev. John Cotton, and Rev. Cotton Mather.

Dr. Abraham S. Haskell, of the third generation, was a pioneer physician in southern Illinois. He was born in Massachusetts, March 19, 1817, studied medicine with his father, graduated from the medical department of Dartmouth College in 1839, and in 1843 settled in Montgomery County, Illinois. After 1864 he practiced at Alton, his home being in the section of the city known as Middletown, where he died. He married in 1844 Helen E. Parkhurst, daughter of Dr. William Parkhurst, of Worcester County, Massachusetts.

The late Dr. W. A. Haskell, only son of Dr. Abraham S. Haskell, was born at Hillsboro, Illinois, June 22, 1845. His death occurred just a hundred years after the birth of his great-grandfather. He attended the Hillsboro Academy, the Franklin Military School in Boston, and graduated in the classical course at Harvard University in 1866, and in 1869 received his medical degree at the Harvard School of Medicine. For thirty years he practiced medicine and surgery in Alton, and in 1872 was appointed surgeon in charge of St. Joseph's Hospital. His attainments as a surgeon were of the first rank. He was also a contributor to the literature of his profession, and in 1881 was appointed a member of the Illinois State Board of Health, being reappointed in 1888 and was president of the board from 1887 to 1892, when he resigned. He was the first president of the Alton Medical Society, and a member of the Madison County, Illinois State and American Medical Associations.

Doctor Haskell enjoyed literature, both classic and modern, the world's art and history, and his travels took him to nearly every part of the globe. He spent much of his time abroad, and when at home enjoyed best the associations of his beautiful residence, filled with books and objects he had collected from all the world.

On July 17, 1876, he married in Alton Miss Florence Ellen Hayner, only child and daughter of John E. Hayner, of Alton. Mrs. Haskell survives him. There were three children, but two are dead, Lucy J. and Florence H. The only one to grow up was John A. Haskell, born November 28, 1878. He married Ruth Hanna, and they have two children, Norman A. and Lucy.

JOHN E. HAYNER located at Alton in early manhood, and depending on his own resources and without friends or influence, made himself a power in the commercial world and a financier respected throughout the state. He possessed the highest integrity in business and in his personal relations, and was one of the generous benefactors of his home city of Alton.

He was born at Charlestown, New York, March 29, 1827, son of Alexander J. and Lydia (Gove) Hayner, and grandson of John Hayner, who, coming from Germany, joined the American colonists in their struggle for independence and served seven years and seven months.

John E. Hayner was reared on a farm near Yates, New York, attending country schools, and from the age of eighteen spent three years clerking in a dry goods store. In December, 1848, he arrived at Alton, then a town depending entirely on its river traffic. He continued clerking for a time, then engaged in the hardware business in the firm of Nelson & Hayner. He operated a saw mill and box factory, and J. E. Hayner & Company acted as the western representative of the Walter A. Wood Self-Binder Company. His connections in mercantile lines led to association with banks and a varied number of business enterprises not only in Alton but in Chicago and elsewhere. For many years he was president of the Alton Savings Bank and vice-president of the Alton National Bank.

By his marriage with Laura E. Scott, of Craftsburg, Vermont, he had one child, now Mrs. W. A. Haskell, of Alton. His second wife was Jane C. Drury, also of Vermont, and his third wife, Mary Caroline Keith, was also born in the Green Mountain State.

John E. Hayner died at Alton March 19, 1903, at the age of seventy-six. One who knew him intimately from the standpoint of long friendship and admiration for his business and civic work wrote an estimate of his character from which the following sentences will convey in concise manner the dominant elements in his personality:

"His interest and sympathy for young men was unbounded. Doubtless the memory of his own early struggles was ever present with him. Many now prominent men could be named who owe their station in life to the kindly advice, the helping hand and the material aid of John E. Hayner. His own success, instead of inspiring pride and arrogance, developed in him the desire to help others along the same road to high achievement, and he did this throughout his life. His material charity was abounding and perennial. He sought out and relieved the poor and needy. He comforted the sorrowing. His benevolence was unfailing. No good cause ever appealing to him found him unresponsive. The churches had in him a liberal and appreciative supporter. Ministers of the Gospel found in him a generous, sympathetic friend, who appreciated the work to which their lives were dedicated. His personality was engaging. He had a pleasant smile and a genial greeting for all he met. Rich and poor received from him the same unfailing courtesy. He was always and everywhere the polished, unassuming gentleman.

"As a citizen he loved the old Bluff City, and was interested in every project for its advancement. His many great enterprises did much for its upbuilding and the maintenance of its financial prosperity. He had been a friend and helper of the public library from early manhood. Even amid the later cares and exactions of his busy career he was interested in this means of advancing culture among the people. It came about normally, then, that when the time came that he could look back upon a life of satisfying achievement the desire should come to him to share his prosperity with others; and in no way could this be better done than by providing for the literary advancement of his own and future generations. In fulfillment of this desire he built and presented to the Library Association, for the use of the citizens of Alton, the splendid Hayner Memorial Library, which is one of the ornaments of the city.

"Mr. Hayner was himself a constant reader of the best literature, and his attainments were broadened by extended travels in this and foreign lands. He was thoroughly posted on political and economic topics, and while pronounced in his own views he was tolerant of others. During the war for the Union he was most liberal in his contributions in aid of the soldiers in the field and the sick and wounded in hospitals. He was the friend of every man who wore the blue. He was an ardent anti-slavery man, and was interested for many years in the project of building a monument in memory of Elijah P. Lovejoy, and those who were connected with him in forwarding

that undertaking can testify that his generous aid at its inception and the impulse he gave the Association were the mainsprings which resulted in the beautiful and stately memorial to the first anti-slavery martyr which now adorns the city cemetery. And within its shadow he lies at rest."

LOUIS B. GOETZMAN is a native of Gallatin County, and has been one of the active young business men of the city of Shawneetown, where he is well known as a banker.

He was born at Shawneetown, August 8, 1887, and is a son of Joseph L. and Ida M. (Bowers) Goetzman. His grandparents, Robert and Catherine (Frey) Goetzman, were natives of Baden, Germany, but were married after coming to the United States. Joseph L. Goetzman was born at Uniontown, Kentucky. He and his brothers, Louis W. and John R. Goetzman, have long been prominent as merchants in the city of Shawneetown, the firm of Goetzman Brothers having been established more than forty years ago.

Louis B. Goetzman was educated in public schools. For a time he was employed in the circuit clerk's office, and since leaving there all his time has been given to the National Bank of Shawneetown. He was first a bookkeeper and then assistant cashier, and since 1922 has been cashier of the bank. He is a democrat in politics and a member of the Catholic Church.

He married, in 1914, Miss Jessie McDaniel, a native of Louisville, Kentucky. They have two daughters, Katherine Taylor and Mary Jane Goetzman.

LOUIS W. GOETZMAN. No name is held in more deserved esteem at Shawneetown than that of Goetzman. It has been a name identified with business honor and integrity, success in private affairs, good citizenship at all times.

Louis W. Goetzman, one of the men who have contributed to the prestige of the name in that section of southern Illinois, is a merchant and former bank president. He was born at Uniontown, Kentucky, son of Robert and Catherine (Frey) Goetzman. His parents were born and reared in Baden, Germany, and were married after coming to the United States. Robert Goetzman was a participant in the German Revolution of 1848. Like many others, including Carl Shurz, he had to leave Germany after the collapse of the Revolution, and coming to the United States, set up in business as a merchant at Uniontown, Kentucky. He favored the Union cause during the Civil war and during that period moved his family for greater safety to Shawneetown, Illinois. After the war he returned to Uniontown and remained in that city until his death in 1869, his wife surviving him two years.

The three sons of Robert and Catherine Goetzman, Louis W., Joseph L. and John R. Goetzman, have spent most of their lives in Shawneetown. After their mother's death in 1871 they moved to that Illinois city and grew up in the home of an uncle, Lambert Elsasser. This is a remarkable example of fraternal companionship and work. The three brothers have maintained a remarkable unity of purpose and activity as well as affection. They had to earn their own living at an early age, and took up different lines of work, Louis W. and John R. becoming clerks in stores, and Joseph L. a barber. The brothers pooled their earnings and after a time were able to set up Joseph L. in business as a barber for himself. With subsequent accumulation of capital they entered the grocery business, and since 1883 they have constituted one of the leading mercantile firms of Shawneetown. Their lives have been plain and quiet, efficient in business, but at all times deserving the confidence of their fellow men. They are members of the Catholic Church and democrats in politics.

Louis W. Goetzman helped organize the National Bank of Shawneetown in 1905 and became its first president. He filled that office twenty years, until January, 1925, when he resigned. At two different times he was honored with the office of mayor of Shawneetown. For four years he was a member of the Illinois Board of Equalization. In 1916 the democratic party nominated him as a candidate for Congress. He gained the nomination without having expended a cent of his funds n the campaign and he made a most creditable race, though unable to overcome the republican majority in his district.

All three brothers have married and reared families. Joseph L. Goetzman married Ida M. Bowers and has seven children: Louis B., Carroll J., Josephine K., Marie, Dorris Ann, Fred P. and Elizabeth B. John R. Goetzman married Carrie Scheerer and had six children: Lawrence J., Margurete, Edward K., Helen K., Frances V. and Ralph A. Louis W. Goetzman married Fannie Cadle and they became the parents of one daughter, Louise, and a son, John Robert. John Robert Goetzman was a graduate of the Christian Brothers College at St. Louis. He became a civil engineer, and was employed in that capacity during the construction of Camp Knox for the World war. While there he contracted the influenza and died at Louisville. This son married Catherine McDaniels, and by the marriage left two children, Robert R. and Fannie L. Mrs. Louis W. Goetzman was born and reared in Gallatin County, a daughter of Joseph Cadle, of New Haven.

HENRY F. HECKERT, county clerk of Washington County, is one of the leading men of Nashville and the county, and a citizen whose public service is of constructive value. He was born in Washington County. Illinois. in December, 1861, a son of Rudolph and Mary (Luebke) Heckert. His paternal grandfather, Bardser Heckert, was a native of Germany, and came to the United States about 1844. His wife. Eliza, was also born in Germany. as were their two sons and four daughters. The maternal grandfather, Rudolph Luebke, was also a native of Germany, and he was there married. About 1844 he and his wife came to the United States and settled in Washington County, where, with the Heckerts, they became pioneers of this section of the state.

About fourteen years old when his parents brought him to the United States, Rudolph Heckert grew to manhood in Washington County, and in the course of time became a farmer. He was very active in public affairs, and during the war between the North and the South served as a recruiting officer. While oftentimes solicited to permit the use of his name on his party ticket, he could not be induced to accept nomination for any office. His death occurred in 1900. His wife died many years before him, passing away in 1868. Of the children born to them Henry F. Heckert was the sixth in order of birth.

The district and graded schools gave Henry F. Heckert his preliminary educational training, and he supplemented this instruction with a course at Jones Business College at Saint Louis, Missouri, where he acquired a thorough commercial training. In the meanwhile he had been doing some farming, and after he returned home from Saint Louis he spent two years with his father on the farm, and then began farming for himself, and for twenty-four years was numbered among the leading agriculturists of the county. During this period he served for twenty-two years as school director, six years as supervisor, and then, in 1906, was elected county clerk. So ably did he discharge the duties of this office that he has been reelected to this office at every subsequent county election, and is still in office. During the late war he was appointed food administrator, but, owing to his other duties, was forced to resign. As county clerk he had so much to do with the draft board and other war work that it was impossible for him to take upon himself other responsibilities.

In November, 1883, Mr. Heckert married Mary Strob, a daughter of Henry Strob, who died in 1901, and his wife, Mary (Holland) Strob, who died in 1883. Of the four children born to Mr. and Mrs. Strob all died in childhood with the exception of Mrs. Heckert. Three children were born to Mr. and Mrs. Heckert: Laura, who married John Yerel, and has one daughter, Helen, and Ida and Ella, both of whom are unmarried. The first Mrs. Heckert died, and Mr. Heckert married, December 9, 1921, Mrs. Katherine (Wueke) Finke, a daughter of Henry Wueke, now deceased. Mrs. Heckert lost her mother when she was seventeen years old. In addition to Mrs. Heckert there were six children in the Wueke family: John, William, Fred, Henry and Herman, all of whom are married except William, and Minnie, who married a Mr. Friderking, is now deceased. Mr. Heckert is a member of the Evangelical Church. He belongs to the Modern Woodmen of America.

Mr. Heckert is greatly interested in the history of Washington County, and with his deputy has published several very interesting and valuable booklets on this subject, one in 1916, another in 1918, and a third in 1919. At one time Washington County, as did the remainder of Illinois, belonged to Virginia; from 1812 to 1817 it was a part of Saint Clair County, but in the latter year an act was passed forming the county of Washington, which included what is now Clinton County. At that time the capital of the territory of Illinois was Kaskaskia, the state of Illinois not being created until a year later, so that Washington County as a separate unit is a year older than Illinois as a state. The first settlement in what later became Washington County was made in either 1810 or 1811 by two brothers-in-law, John Lively and David Huggins, and the latter has many descendants yet living in Washington County. The first court of the newly created county was held March 9, 1818; the first board of commissioners was elected in 1819; William H. Bradsby was the first clerk of the Circuit Court, was appointed in 1818 and continued to serve until 1839; Daniel S. Swearington was appointed in 1818 as first sheriff; Rufus Recker was appointed first assessor and treasurer in 1819; William H. Bradsby was appointed first county clerk in 1818, and continued to serve until 1832, and he was also the first probate judge, serving as such from 1821 to 1837; Thomas F. White served from 1849 through several terms as first county judge; John Crain was appointed first school commissioner in 1835 and continued to serve until 1842; William H. Clayton was elected in 1865 the first county superintendent of schools, and served until 1866; the first senator from this district was J. Maddox, who was elected in 1818, 1819 and 1820; Daniel S. Swearington was the first representative, being elected in 1818 and 1819. In 1827 Clinton County was formed from the original Washington County. These booklets from the pen of Mr. Heckert and his assistant contain many other facts worthy of preservation, and they are the result of thorough investigation into the records of the county, and careful compilation on the part of the authors. In work of this kind the utmost care must be exercised to separate hearsay from authentic facts, and that these gentlemen have accomplished this adds to the value of their work, and the debt owed them by their fellow citizens.

EUGENE S. CODDINGTON is now one of the veterans and influential figures at the National Stock Yards in East St. Louis, St. Clair County, where his activities have covered a period of more than half a century and where he is now the executive head of the Coddington-Leiner Live Stock Commission Company.

Mr. Coddington was born at Woodbridge, New Jersey, July 31, 1854, and is a scion of families that were founded in America in the Colonial period of our national history. On the maternal side, her parents were Crowell Martin and he married Sarah Burwell who died about three weeks after subject's mother was born. The grandparents on the paternal side being Isaac Coddington who married Catherine (Kittie) Clarkson. They had four daughters: Anne, Elizabeth, Charlotte and Mary Jane. Two brothers, Isaac and Samuel. He is a son of Randolph and Caroline (Martin) Coddington, and was an infant when, in 1855, his parents came to Illinois and established their residence in Hancock County, whence they later removed to Lewis County, Missouri, where they passed the remainder of their lives, the death of the father having occurred about the year 1904 and that of the mother about 1916. Randolph Coddington was actively associated with farm industry during virtually his entire active career, was a broad-minded and progressive citizen and was a stalwart advocate of the principles of the republican party, in the affairs of which he was an active worker, though he never consented to become a candidate for political office. Of the

C. J. Estes M.D.

family of eight children, Eugene S., of this review, is the third born, there having been five sons and three daughters, and the other two survivors are George M. and Carrie E. George M. Coddington married Fannie Bumbarger, whose death occurred August 14, 1924. Carrie E. is the widow of Robert Caldwell, and has two children, Spencer R. and Hazel, the former of whom married Miss Vivian Nelson.

Eugene S. Coddington was two years of age at the time of the family removal to Lewis County, Missouri, where he was reared to manhood and where he early gained full fellowship with the work of the home farm. In that county he attended the district schools during the winter terms until he had attained to the age of eighteen years, and he then came to East St. Louis and initiated his association with the industrial activities of the National Stock Yards. He entered the employ of the Cassidy Brothers Live Stock Commission Company, and with this old and important concern he continued his alliance twenty-nine years, he having eventually acquired an interest in the business and having been vice president of the company at the time when he severed his connection therewith. Soon after taking this action Mr. Coddington became associated with Frederick Leiner in the organizing of the Coddington-Leiner Live Stock Commission Company, and his long experience has been a potent force in the development of the large and substantial business controlled by this representative concern. Mr. Coddington is a charter member of the St. Louis National Live Stock Exchange, and has been for twelve years a valued member of its Board of Directors.

Mr. Coddington has long been a stalwart in the ranks of the republican party and has wielded much influence in its local councils and campaign activities. He was for four years chairman of the Republican City Committee of East St. Louis, and he simultaneously served as a member of the Board of Election Commissioners of St. Clair County, besides having been for two years chairman of the City Board of Police and Fire Commissioners. Under the administration of President Taft he held the office of postmaster at the National Stock Yards post office. Mr. Coddington has been long and prominently affiliated with the Knights of Pythias, he having been created a Knight October 28, 1881, in Eureka Lodge No. 81, in which he still maintains membership and in which he has passed all of the official chairs. He was for nine consecutive years master of the exchequer for this lodge, and for twenty consecutive years represented the lodge in the Illinois Grand Lodge of the Order, each newly elected grand chancellor having reappointed him a member of the finance committee of the Grand Lodge during all these years, and he being now grand trustee, in which he is serving, in 1924, his second term. In 1907 he was elected exalted ruler of East St. Louis Lodge of Elks, No. 664, East St. Louis, Illinois.

Mr. Coddington has been an earnest supporter of church work and, with a fine baritone voice, he was for eighteen years a member of church choirs, his wife being a zealous member of the First Methodist Episcopal Church of East St. Louis.

At Belleville, St. Clair County, Illinois, on the 22d of June, 1882, was solemnized the marriage of Mr. Coddington and Miss Lillie Louise Tompkins, and the one child of this union is Marie, who is the wife of Edmond J. Burgard, of Lebanon, Illinois.

A few interesting data concerning the paternal ancestry of Mr. Coddington are available. His grandmother, Catherine (Kittie) Clarkson, was a daughter of David and Peggy (Burrell) Martin, and the maiden name of the latter's mother was Mary Cobb. Mary Cobb was a member of one of the old and aristocratic families of Philadelphia and was a birthright member of the Society of Friends. In her marriage to Mr. Burrell, who was not of the Quaker faith and who did not meet the approval of her parents, she was estranged from her family and was disinherited. David Martin, who married Peggy Burrell, was a gallant soldier of the Continental Line in the War of the Revolution, his first enlistment having occurred January 25, 1777, and he having reenlisted September 16, 1780, after the expiration of his original term. He held the office of corporal at the time of his discharge, and was but forty-eight years of age at the time of his death, in 1803. His daughter Caroline became the wife of Randolph Coddington March 16, 1831, and these two were the paternal grandparents of Eugene S. Coddington of this review.

CLINTON J. ESTES, M. D., is a physician and surgeon now established in a successful practice at West Frankfort. His professional career covers a period of ten years, much of this in industrial practice.

He represents one of the old and honored families of Southern Illinois. His great-grandfather, John Estes, came out of Maryland and settled in what was then a part of Saline County, now Gallatin County, during the early '30s. On a tract of government land near what is now Equality he made a farm and spent the rest of his years. He was killed in a "hold-up" for the purpose of robbing him as he returned home from town. His slayers were never apprehended. His son, James G. Estes, was born at the old homestead and when the Civil war broke out enlisted in the Union army and was killed at the capture of Fort Donelson. Joseph H. Estes, father of Dr. C. J. Estes, was a son of this Civil war soldier, being the only boy in a family of five children. He was born at the home farm in Saline County March 15, 1856. His years and energies were occupied by farming, and he came to enjoy the general esteem and respect of his entire community. He died December 1, 1919. His wife, Margaret J. Travelstead, was of German ancestry, her people constituting a well known family of Saline County.

Clinton J. Estes, one of nine children, was born on the farm of his parents October 30, 1885. As a youth he determined to become a doctor, but had many difficulties to overcome before he was able to qualify for a professional career. He was educated in country schools and in 1904 entered the Southern Illinois Normal University at Carbondale, remaining there five terms. School teaching gave him part of the money necessary for his medical education. Finally, in 1915, he graduated from the Medical School of Valparaiso University at Chicago, and then engaged in general practice at Galatia, Illinois, a year and from there moved to Mason City. In 1922 he accepted the opportunity for experience as a surgeon for the Chicago & Northwestern Railroad, with headquarters at Kaukauna, Wisconsin. While there he was also employed as industrial surgeon for a number of the large paper mills in that locality. Doctor Estes had eighteen months of arduous service and experience in Wisconsin, and in July, 1924, returned to Southern Illinois and located at West Frankfort. He was associated in partnership with Dr. C. E. Koons until Doctor Koons retired in 1925, and since then he has carried on a large private practice alone. He is a member of the various medical organizations and is also affiliated with the Independent Order of Odd Fellows, Knights of Pythias, Modern Woodmen of America, and is a member of the Baptist Church.

He married, November 19, 1907, Miss Sarah Wallace, daughter of Aaron Wallace, of Saline County. They have three children: Esco Ellis Estes, who has finished his high school course and is now directing his education with a view to a medical career; Nina Marie, attending high school; and Joseph Aaron, a student in grade school.

JOE P. BENSON, who is descended from one of Williamson County's most prominent pioneer families, is the popular cashier of the City National Bank of Herrin. This institution has had a vigorous and substantial growth and service since it was organized in 1907, with capital of $50,000, its founders including such men as John Alexander, W. C. Alexander, W. H. Ford, J. D. Peters, Charles H. Pope, Frank Chew, John Rollo, Louis Dell'Era and R. A. Karr. John Alexander became the first and has been the only president. The first cashier was P. D. Herrin. The first quarters of the bank were in the Pope Hardware Building. Preparations were made for the erection of a modern bank building at 200 North Park Avenue, and that has been the home of the bank since 1909. P. D. Herrin was succeeded as cashier in 1914 by Frank Chew. Joe P. Benson has been cashier since 1917. This is one of the very strong financial institutions of Williamson County, having total assets of one and one-quarter million dollars.

The great-grandfather of Joe P. Benson was William Benson, who owned a farm including the present public square of Marion, the county seat. Williamson County was named in honor of this early pioneer. At first the name Benson was suggested, but since that would have invited a conflict of names, the entire name of William Benson was taken and shortened to Williamson.

Several other Bensons of the early day were prominent in the county. One of them, of whom the Herrin banker is a namesake, built the first brick house at Skohara Prairie, and he was one of the prosperous farmers in that vicinity and raised fine horses. Arch Benson, grandfather of Joe P. Benson, of Herrin, was a leading citizen and served with the rank of chaplain during the Civil war. The father of Joe P. Benson was William L. Benson, but better known throughout the county as "Lum" Benson. He was born at the old homestead and for many years engaged in merchandising, conducting stores at Marion and Creal Springs. He died at Marion in 1900. His wife was Mary Pope, daughter of William Pope. She died in 1892. They had a family of four children: Lois, wife of Dr. Frank C. Murrah, of Herrin; Celeste, wife of W. L. Smith, of Princeton, Indiana; Joe P.; and Gladys.

Joe P. Benson was born at Marion, December 14, 1889. He was three years old when his mother died and was taken into the home of his grandmother, Louisa M. Pope. While a boy there he attended rural schools and later entered the University of Illinois, where he was graduated with the A. B. degree in 1911. Mr. Benson for a year after graduating was in California, and on returning to Herrin became bookkeeper in the City National Bank, and five years later was promoted to the post of cashier.

He married Miss Marie Margrave, daughter of Rev. W. D. Margrave, and they have one child, Lou Ann, born September 5, 1924. Mr. Benson is a Royal Arch Mason, having filled the chairs in the local lodge, is affiliated with the Independent Order of Odd Fellows, Knights of Pythias, B. P. O. Elks, Lions Club, Franklin Country Club, Herrin Country Club. He is president of the Township High School Board. For three years he has served as district deputy grand master of the Ninety-fifth Masonic District of the A. F. and A. M. of Illinois. During the late World war Mr. Benson served for a time with the rank of sergeant, in one of the military training camps.

WILLIAM ELIAS BURNETT, M. D., has been a physician and surgeon over forty years, and for the greater part of that time has practiced at Norris City in White County.

Doctor Burnett was born on a farm in Hamilton County, Illinois, January 28, 1852. His father, William Green Burnett, was of English ancestry and a native of Rutherford County, Tennessee, where his parents had settled on coming from Virginia. William G. Burnett was reared in Tennessee and enlisted in the American army for service in the Mexican war. He was wounded in the hip by a gun shot at the battle of Buena Vista, and remained a cripple the rest of his life, though he conducted a farm with considerable success. After his military service he removed to Illinois and married Cordelia Davis. She was born near the old town of Roland, in White County. Her father, Rev. Robert Davis, was a pioneer minister of the Presbyterian Church in Illinois. She had a brother, also Rev. Robert Davis likewise a Presbyterian minister. William G. Burnett and wife were active members of the Presbyterian Church and he was a democrat in politics. He died at the age of seventy-two and his wife, at eighty-one. Of their eleven children nine are now deceased.

Dr. William E. Burnett was reared on a farm, attended country schools and first qualified himself for the vocation of teacher. He taught in rural school districts four years, using that occupation as a stepping stone to the medical profession. He first studied medicine under Dr. C. A. Smith at Galatia in Saline County. In 1884 he graduated from the medical college at Evansville, Indiana, and subsequently pursued work in the Post-Graduate School of Medicine at Chicago, and in 1898 in the medical department of Washington University of St. Louis. Doctor Burnett is a member of the White County and Southern Illinois Medical Societies.

He first engaged in private practice at Roland in White County. In 1893 he was appointed physician and surgeon among the White Mountain Apache Indians in the Southwest, and was in that branch of the government service for two years. Returning to Illinois, he has been one of the capable members of his profession, located at Norris City since 1896. Doctor Burnett is a democrat, and a member of the Presbyterian Church and Independent Order of Odd Fellows.

He married, in 1886, Belle Raney, a native of White County, Illinois, and daughter of James and Sallie Raney. She died November 3, 1923. Doctor and Mrs. Burnett had two sons. Walter J., a graduate in pharmacy, operated a drug store at Norris City, but sold out his business in preparation for joining the military service during the World war. However, the armistice came before he was inducted. He is now a traveling salesman living in Missouri. The second son, Ambrosia W., was overseas with the Marine Corps during the World war. He is also a pharmacist by profession.

ABRAM MIDDLESWORTH. With his noble head touched by the snows of eighty-eight winters and his strong face and capable hands bronzed by the sun which beat upon as many harvesting seasons, the late Abram Middlesworth, of Shelby County, passed to his final rest January 11, 1910. He was the personification of a life well lived, of energies well directed, of a mind attuned to the harmony of his surroundings and of a heart which lost nothing of its warmth and sympathy in its journey from the log cabin of the '40s to the affluence of the twentieth century. This vigorous personality, outlined against the background of events from 1840 in Shelby County, commanded the confidence and respect of as large a following as any who have helped to redeem the wilderness in this part of the state. He built up character as well as fortune and supported the substantial and fundamental processes of civilization.

Abram Middlesworth was born November 10, 1821, in Fairfield County, Ohio, of English and Pennsylvania Dutch descent, a son of Abraham and Barbara (Leathers) Middlesworth, the former a native of Beaver County, Pennsylvania, who brought his family to Illinois in 1840. The education of Abraham Middlesworth was of a very limited character in his boyhood and youth, but in later years he made the most of his opportunities and became a well-informed man. He was nineteen years of age when he accompanied his parents to Illinois, whence he volunteered for service during the Mexican war. He resided on the home farm until 1869, in the meanwhile becoming engaged extensively in the live stock business, and packed pork at St. Louis during the '60s and '70s, when that industry was in its infancy, and when it was all carried on during winters, when thousands of Illinois swine were driven across the Mississippi River on the ice. From young manhood Mr. Middlesworth had supreme faith in the value of Illinois farm land, and at one time probably owned more of the good black soil of Shelby County than any other individual. Likewise he probably had more to do with the development of Shelby County than any other man. He had a beautiful home at Shelbyville, reflecting his thoroughgoing character and regard for detail and method, and also evidencing his love of nature and the joy he experienced in collaborating with it. From 1876 until 1904 he was president of the First National Bank of Shelbyville. He was a faithful member of the Presbyterian Church, and was very much interested in the Illinois Children's Home and Aid Society, to which organization he gave his old homestead at Shelbyville, which was used for many years as a home for children. Mr. Middlesworth became a republican when the party was first organized and at a time when the prevailing political sentiment of Shelby County was such as to qualify the county for a location south of Mason and Dixon's line. He was a good capable man, one with a broad democratic view, of great generosity and wisdom of heart, and one who was greatly beloved for what he became as well as what he accomplished.

Mr. Middlesworth married Miss Elizabeth Goodwin, daughter of James Goodwin, who came from Virginia to Illinois and was one of the very earliest settlers of Shelby County. To this union there were born thirteen children, of whom three survive: Mrs. Isabel Scarborough, of Denver, Colorado; John W., of Hot Springs, Arkansas; and W. S., of Shelbyville.

FRANK FORREST SCATTERDAY, county superintendent of schools of Ford County, is a veteran educator whose name has been familiar as a school man in that section of Illinois, including several counties, for thirty years or more.

Mr. Scatterday was born April 22, 1872, on a farm southeast of Bellflower, in McLean County, Illinois. He is of Scotch-Irish, English, Welsh and German ancestry. The different branches of the families included in his ancestry were Scatterday, Pond, Ewers and Hays. The Scatterdays and Ponds were in this country prior to the Revolution, and these families were represented by soldiers in the war for independence. The colonies in which these families first found homes were New Jersey, Pennsylvania and Virginia. The Scatterdays settled near Leesburg, Virginia,, before the Revolution and records of the family at the court house there dates back to 1760. A later generation moved to Ohio, settling in Belmont County, not far from Wheeling, while others of the family found homes near Cincinnati. The great-grandfather of Frank F. Scatterday, John Scatterday, served for some years as a representative in the Ohio Legislature in the early statehood of Ohio. In politics the Scatterdays were whigs until the formation of the republican party, and their church affiliations for the most part were Presbyterian. In occupation they have followed chiefly farming. John L. Scatterday, father of Frank F., was a native of Belmont County, Ohio, and as a young man went west to Illinois and accomplished his ambition in making a farm from the virgin prairie of what is now the Illinois corn belt. His wife, Jane Ann Wilson, was a native of Virginia, was left an orphan in childhood and was reared among strangers, chiefly by the Lindsey family, with whom she came west from Ohio to Illinois. John L. Scatterday and wife were married at Champaign, Illinois, March 17, 1870, and first settled near Blue Ridge, in Piatt County.

When Frank F. Scatterday was fourteen years of age, in 1886, his parents moved to a farm near Paxton, in Ford County. His home has been at Paxton since 1889. As a boy he attended country schools in McLean, Piatt and Ford counties, later the grade and high schools at Paxton, and his advanced education was acquired in the Rice Collegiate Institute at Paxton and in Greer College at Hoopeston, Illinois. Mr. Scatterday gained due familiarity with the working discipline of a farm until early manhood. At the age of nineteen he began teaching. For ten years he was a teacher in rural schools in Ford and adjoining counties. For fifteen years he was principal and superintendent of grade and high schools. In vacation intervals of teaching and school administration he sometimes followed newspaper work. Mr. Scatterday has been county superintendent of schools of Ford County since August, 1923.

He is a republican in politics, is a member of Paxton Lodge No. 416, A. F. and A. M., Ford Chapter No. 113, R. A. M., Mt. Olivet Commandery No. 38, K. T., and Paxton Camp No. 259, Modern Woodmen of America. He is a member of the Paxton Methodist Episcopal Church.

Mr. Scatterday married at Watseka, Illinois, December 24, 1910, Miss Eudora Mertice Clause, daughter of Mr. and Mrs. Emanuel Clause, whose home was near Wellington, in Iroquois County. Mrs. Scatterday is of Pennsylvania German and Irish ancestry, though her parents were born in Indiana. The two children of Mr. and Mrs. Scatterday are Albert Leroy and Margaret Eleanor.

J. MAURICE STICE is one of the representative younger members of the bar of Shelby County, where he is established in the successful general practice of his profession in the city of Shelbyville, the judicial center of the county. He is attorney for the Effingham County Telephone Company at Altamont, and of the Fayette Home Telephone Company, St. Elmo, Fayette County, besides which he is vice president of each of these important corporations.

James Maurice Stice was born at Waverly, Morgan County, Illinois, August 4, 1900, and is a scion of a family that was founded in this state in 1816, about three years prior to the admission of Illinois as one of the sovereign states of the Union. Mr. Stice is a son of James A. and Hattie M. (Keplinger) Stice, both likewise natives of Illinois, the former having been born near Waverly, Morgan County, in 1866, and the latter of whom was born in 1870, a daughter of the late Benjamin F. and Rachel (Holliday) Keplinger, who likewise were residents of the Waverly district of Morgan County at the time of the birth of their daughter Hattie M.

James A. Stice was born October 8, 1866, and after profiting by the advantages of the Waverly public schools he attended Illinois College at Jacksonville. He thereafter made a record of effective service as a teacher in the public schools, and for a number of years he was successfully engaged in the mercantile business at Waverly, where as a lad he had served as the first newsboy of the village. About the year 1899 Mr. Stice became interested in independent telephone enterprise and service. He became connected with the Waverly Telephone Company, and after severing his association with the same he established, in 1903, the first telephone exchanges at Gillespie and Benld, both in Macoupin County. He has since given his attention to the developing and operating of independent telephone exchanges and he maintains his residence at Shelbyville, judicial center of the Illinois county of that name. In the year 1891 was solemnized the marriage of James A. Stice to Miss Hattie M. Keplinger, who was born near Waverly, June 26, 1870, and whose death occurred at Effingham December 14, 1924, she having been a devoted member of the Methodist Episcopal Church, as is also her husband, and having been loved by all who came within the sphere of her gentle and gracious influence. Mrs. Stice received her early education in the public schools of Morgan County, and thereafter took a course of higher study by attending the Illinois Wesleyan University. Mrs. Stice is survived by two sons, Earl F. and J. Maurice, the latter of whom is the immediate subject of this review.

J. Maurice Stice is of the sixth generation in direct descent from Andrew and Katron (Collins) Stice, who were born and reared in Germany, where their marriage was solemnized and whence they came to America and became the founders of the family in this country. They settled in Rowan County, North Carolina, fully a decade before the initiation of the War of the Revolution, as shown in the fact that in that county their son Andrew, great-grandfather of the subject of this sketch, was born in the year 1766, his death having occurred in 1818. In 1789 this Andrew Stice of the second generation in America married Nancy Green Wilson, who was born in 1771 and died in 1852, she having been a daughter of William Wilson, who was wounded in the Revolutionary battle of Bunker Hill, and having been a niece of James Wilson, who was one of the signers of the Declaration of Independence, a member of the convention that drafted the constitution of the United States and who served also as a member of the originally constituted Supreme Court of the United States.

Andrew Stice, Jr., son of Andrew and Nancy Green (Wilson) Stice, was born in 1803, as was also his wife, whose maiden name was

Rufus Putnam

Nancy Armstrong, he having died in 1855 and his wife having survived about five years, as her death occurred in 1860. About the year 1800 Andrew Stice II, in company with his immediate family and about twenty-five of his relatives and other friends, migrated from Rowan County, North Carolina, and made settlement in the vicinity of what is now the flourishing little city of Bowling Green, Kentucky. There Andrew Stice II reared his family of twelve children, including Andrew III, who, as previously noted, was born in 1803 and died in 1855, and who was thus about thirteen years old when he accompanied his parents and other members of the family to Illinois, as pioneers of the year 1816, when the family made settlement in what is now Madison County, this state.

Andrew Stice III married Nancy Armstrong, a daughter of Joshua and Sarah (Morris) Armstrong, and a granddaughter of Gen. John Armstrong, who was an officer of the Continental Line in the Revolution and who served as secretary of war under the administration of President James Madison.

James Pleasant Stice, son of Andrew and Nancy (Armstrong) Stice, was born near Jacksonville, Illinois, in 1826, and in 1848 he married Mary Margaret Conlee, daughter of the late Elder Isaac Conlee, who figured prominently in the spiritual development of Morgan County and also Macoupin County, this state. The death of James Pleasant Stice occurred in 1899, and his widow passed to the life eternal in the year 1919, she having been born in 1833. James P. and Margaret (Conlee) Stice became the parents of four children: Andrew J., Sarah Elizabeth (Mrs. Spires), Isaac Douglas and James A., the last named being the father of him whose name initiates this review. Mrs. James A. Stice, whose death occurred in 1924, as previously noted in this contest, was a daughter of Benjamin F. and Rachel (Holliday) Keplinger, the former of whom was born in 1844 and died in 1920, and the latter of whom is still living at the time of this writing, in 1925, her birth having occurred in 1848. Benjamin F. Keplinger was a son of John E. and Loretta (Harris) Keplinger, the former of whom was born in 1818 and died in 1890, and the latter of whom was born in 1823 and died in 1880. John E. Keplinger was a son of John and Elizabeth (Rubel) Keplinger, the former of whom died in 1858 and the latter in 1829, the Keplinger family likewise having been founded in America in the Colonial era.

The public-school advantages of J. Maurice Stice included those of the high school at Altamont, Effingham County, and at the age of sixteen years he endured an attack of poliomylitis, which thereafter incapacitated him for physical labor, and which, incidentally, was destined to prevent his entering the nation's military service in the great World war, he having, however, found other avenues through which to express his loyalty and patriotism after the nation became involved in this conflict. In preparation for his chosen profession Mr. Stice entered the law department of the University of Illinois, in which he was graduated as a member of the class of 1924, his admission to the Illinois bar having been virtually coincident with his reception of the degree of Bachelor of Laws, and he having forthwith established himself in the practice of law at Shelbyville, where excellent success is attending his professional stewardship. Mr. Stice is a staunch advocate of the principles of the democratic party, is affiliated with the Society of the Sons of the American Revolution and the Phi Delta Phi law college fraternity. He has active membership in the Rotary Club in his home city, and his religious faith is that of the Methodist Episcopal Church. His name still remains on the roster of eligible young bachelors in Shelby County.

MAJOR RUFUS W. PUTNAM, as officer of the United States Army was for five years assigned duty at Chicago as the army engineer in charge of the Chicago River and Harbor. He is a national authority on many phases of water resources and has been the responsible representative of the government in many negotiations of vital importance to Chicago and vicinity.

On July 1, 1926, Major Putnam left the service of the United States Government to become chief engineer in immediate charge of the Harbor Plan of Chicago. This position involves the preparation of a comprehensive plan for the harbor at Chicago. The work is under the direction of and financed by the Commercial Club and the results are to be available to the city free of cost. The work involves a study of prevailing practice abroad and in this country and consequently an extended tour of inspection of the principal parts of the world.

Major Putnam was born at LaCrosse, Wisconsin, June 30, 1891, and has a distinguished American ancestry. His father, William Rice Putnam, was born in Ohio, one of the family of Putnams that was established in 1788 at Marietta, the first permanent white settlement in the Northwest Territory. William Rice Putnam married Jane Willard, a native of Bloomington, Illinois. Her father, Samuel Willard, was an early teacher in the public schools of Chicago and left his mark on the early educational history of that city.

Rufus W. Putnam finished his high school course at Rushford, Minnesota, in 1908. In 1913 he was an honor graduate of the United States Military Academy of West Point and in 1916 he graduated from the United States Engineering School at Washington. In the routine army service he was promoted through the various grades to that of major on August 5, 1917. He was overseas in France during the World war, and while in France was commissioned lieutenant colonel August 23, 1918. On July 1, 1920, he resumed the rank of major in the regular army. He was on duty for a time at Fort Humphreys, Virginia, and in 1921 was assigned to Chicago as United States district engineer in charge of river and harbor improvements in the Chicago district. Major Putnam has been called upon to make reports and initial decisions on many intricate and technical problems connected with the water levels of the Great Lakes and their effect on lake commerce, diversion of water from Lake Michigan for the Chicago Sanitary District, and also on problems affecting the international interests of Canada in the Great Lakes and St. Lawrence River. His position as an army engineer has therefore been of much more than routine administration. Out of his experiences he prepared a brochure entitled "Diversion of Water from Lake Michigan," published in 1924. He also received the Arthur M. Wellington award of the American Society of Civil Engineers for the best paper on transportation, published in the proceedings of the society for 1924. He has contributed a number of articles to magazines and technical journals on port and terminal planning.

Major Putnam during his years of residence at Chicago became intimately identified with various civic, club and social activities. He is a director of the Chicago Regional Planning Association, Chicago Athletic Association, Traffic Club, University Club, Hamilton Club, Chicago Yacht Club, Riverside Golf Club, is a member of the American Society of Civil Engineers and is vice president of the Western Society of Engineers. His recreations are markmanship, golf, tennis and horseback riding. Major Putnam is a member of the Episcopal Church and is a republican in politics.

He married, September 4, 1914, Caroline Frances Hough, of Rochester, New York. They have three children, Persis, Rufus Willard, Jr., and Benjamin Olney.

CHARLES P. WITTERS, president of the First National Bank of Norris City, is a business man and citizen worthy of trust and respect, and trusted accordingly. His career reflects that ability to rise above circumstances and disadvantages which is one of the best elements of character as well as material success.

He was born on a farm in Lawrence County, Illinois, April 5, 1864. His father, William Witters, a native of Pennsylvania and of German ancestry, came to Illinois at the age of twenty-one. In Illinois he married Lavina (Barham) Sumner, widow of Samuel Sumner. Her people had come to Illinois from the Carolinas. In 1876 William Witters moved to Hamilton County, Illinois, where he died in 1896, at the age of seventy-six. His wife passed away in 1903, aged seventy-four. William Witters was a farmer and carpenter, a republican in politics and a member of the United Brethren Church. They reared a family of four sons and four daughters.

Charles P. Witters was member of a household that grew up in self respecting poverty. He had the discipline of hard work rather than the opportunity to attend country school, having attended not more than a few months a year. The most of his education has been gained in the school of experience. His early lack of advantages made an impression on him so that in his mature years and with increasing material success he has done his utmost to assist a younger generation to better opportunities than he had. For twenty years he has been a faithful worker for the cause of popular education, serving as president of the school board of Norris City. After reaching manhood he engaged in farming on his own account, but without capital. He continued farming until 1898, when he removed to Norris City. His ambition from early boyhood was for a career as a miller and grain merchant. On leaving the farm he began dealing in grain, and for twenty-five years was a leader in that line of business.

Mr. Witters upon the organization of the First National Bank of Norris City in 1905 became its vice president, and since 1914 has served as president. He is a republican, is affiliated with the Independent Order of Odd Fellows, attends the Methodist Church, and has always been generous in support of churches.

He married, in 1890, Miss Ada Mellon, a native of Hamilton County, Illinois. Two children were born to their marriage, namely, Ross E., who died aged eighteen years, and Merrell E., who died aged twenty-two years. They reared an adopted daughter, Ruth, now the wife of Donald Ogden, assistant cashier of the First National Bank.

RUFUS HENRY MAIN, M. D., of Barry, is a member of a family that has lived in Pike County, Illinois, for more than a century. He is himself, however, a native of Missouri, born in that state during the temporary residence of his parents there. The career of Doctor Main as a physician and surgeon has identified him with the Barry community for over thirty years.

Ezekiel Main, a native of England, settled at Stonington, Connecticut, in 1663, and was a founder of the branch of the family in America from which those in Pike County are derived. A later descendant was Philip Main, who was born in Gloucester County, New Jersey, in 1747. He was a soldier in the Twelfth Virginia Line in the Revolution. He was the father of Solomon Main, the pioneer of Illinois. Solomon Main was born in Beaver County, Pennsylvania, February 27, 1794, and as a young man he came west, down the Ohio River to Shawneetown, Illinois, from which point he crossed overland to what is now Pike County. He built his first cabin on land granted in the military tract for his service in the War of 1812. This old homestead now belongs to the Barber estate of Pittsfield. Solomon Main spent the rest of his life as a farmer, and he and his wife were buried in Highland Cemetery. He was the father of fifteen children, and many of them reared families.

One of these children was Andrew Main, who devoted his life to farming and lived near the Highland Cemetery, where he is buried. He was a soldier in the Mexican war, sergeant of a company in the First Illinois Regiment in General Taylor's army. He was a democrat in politics and an elder in the Christian Church. Andrew Main married Lutilla Johnson, and they were the parents of ten sons and three daughters.

The third of these children was Alvin Nye Main, who represents the third generation of the family in Illinois. He was born at the old Main homestead January 17, 1844, and has passed the age of four score. He attended local schools, gave his active years to farming, and is now a resident of Pittsfield. His grandfather was a soldier of the War of 1812, his own father a Mexican war veteran, and he himself continued the patriotic record by service in the Union army during the Civil war. He joined Company B of the Twenty-eighth Illinois Infantry, was at Shiloh and Corinth, and also in the Vicksburg campaign. He was a soldier three years, and since the war has been identified with the Grand Army of the Republic, has attended a number of national reunions and has frequently revisited the old Vicksburg battlefield. He is a member of the Christian Church and a democrat in politics. Alvin Nye Main married Lydia Foote, who also survives. She was born at Pittsfield, June 18, 1846, daughter of George Dorr and Abigail (St. John) Foote, and granddaughter of Josiah Foote, who was a direct descendant of Nathaniel Foote who settled at Wethersfield, Connecticut, as early as 1634. George Dorr Foote was born at Albany, New York, and as a young man came to Illinois in 1830, and two years later settled in Pike County. He was a carpenter contractor, and erected the first court house of the county at Pittsfield. He was also called upon to erect the first building on the campus of the University of Missouri at Columbia. Most of his life was spent on a farm near Pittsfield. Alvin Nye Main and wife had the following children: Miss Clara, librarian of the Carnegie Library at Lewistown, Montana; Dr. Rufus Henry; Josiah, of Hemet, California; Mrs. Blanche Gay, of Quincy, Illinois; Mrs. Rose Warden, of Lewistown, Montana; Dr. Roscoe C., of Monterey, California; and Frank A., of Pittsfield.

Rufus Henry Main was born near Troy, in Lincoln County, Missouri, September 5, 1868. When he was two years of age his parents returned to Pike County, and he grew up on the farm near Pittsfield. He attended the grade school at Time, and at the age of eighteen became a teacher. He followed teaching while getting the money necessary to complete his medical education. Doctor Main began the study of medicine at the age of twenty-one with Dr. J. H. Ledlie of Pittsfield. In 1894 he was graduated from the old Missouri Medical College, now the medical department of Washington University at St. Louis. Soon after graduating he located at Barry, and has been engaged in general practice, performing his service through a great variety of conditions, beginning in the era before good roads were known, almost before the introduction of telephones, and when the doctor who practiced in rural districts required not only a professional training and ability but the utmost physical consecration to his calling. The only two important epidemics that have visited the community were those of influenza. Doctor Main helped organize the County Medical Society and was its secretary many years, and is also a member of the Illinois State and American Medical Associations.

Through all the years he has taken an interest in the welfare of the local schools and has served on the Board of Education during most of his work as a physician. He has been master of Barry Lodge of Masons, is a Royal Arch Mason, a member of the Christian Church and in politics an independent. During the World war he was a member of the State Council of Defense and chairman of the local Red Cross.

Doctor Main married at Barry, October 9, 1895, Miss Helen Chrysup. She was born at Barry, April 7, 1872, daughter of George W. and Kate (Harvey) Chrysup, and granddaughter of Benjamin Barney Chrysup. Her father was captain of Company B of the Twenty-eighth Illinois Infantry, the same company Doctor Main's father was in. He was crippled by his war service. Mrs. Main is a graduate of Lindenwood School for Girls at St. Charles, Missouri, and taught in that school for several years. She has one living sister, Jane, wife of H. C. McCarrel of Nebo, Illinois. The children born to Doctor and Mrs. Main are: George Chrysup; Alvin Nye, who died when seven years old; Ruth, now a senior in the Barry High School; and Josephine and Philip Main. George Chrysup Main left his studies at the University of Illinois during the World war and was assigned duty in the pathological laboratory of the Debarkation Hospital at Ellis Island, New York. Subsequently he graduated from the medical department of St. Louis University and is now an officer in the Naval Medical Corps. He married Margaret Kubisch.

HENRY J. HARRIS has been identified with printing and the newspaper business since boyhood. He is founder and publisher of the Hoopeston Evening Times at Hoopeston and has published papers in Indiana, Ohio and other states.

He was born at Ellettsville, Indiana, May 12, 1883. The Harris family is of Scotch ancestry. His grandfather, Samuel B. Harris, was born in Kentucky in 1821, and as a young man moved to Ellettsville in Monroe County, Indiana, where he spent his active business career as a merchant and real estate man. He died in 1904. His wife, Endemile Chambers, was born near Spencer, Indiana, in 1821 and died at Ellettsville in 1905.

William B. Harris, father of Henry J., is a veteran Indiana newspaper publisher. He was born at Ellettsville, March 6, 1856, and that Indiana town has been his home all his life. He finished his education in De Pauw University and since early manhood has been publishing newspapers. He is now publisher of the Ellettsville Farm and Farm Magazine. Letters in his possession received from Washington, D. C., prove that he has entered as second class mail more newspapers than any other individual. For fifteen years he published fifteen newspapers each week. He founded many local papers in Indiana, Ohio, Illinois, Michigan and Kentucky. As a republican he was elected in November, 1924, to represent Monroe County to the Lower House of the Legislature, receiving a majority of about four hundred votes. He is a member of the Methodist Episcopal Church and active in all causes and belongs to the Masonic fraternity. He married Allie B. Braxton. who was born at Paoli, Indiana, December 29, 1858. They had a family of seven children: Carl B., who was publisher of the Cambridge City News in Indiana, and died at Ellettsville in 1900; Edmund B.; Henry J.; Miss Nellie. a registered nurse; Mary, wife of John W. Troth, carpenter and builder at Bloomington, Indiana; Frank B., a printer, who died at Chicago in 1914; William B., Jr., associated with his father in the newspaper business at Ellettsville and is a veteran of the World war. He joined the Rainbow Division during the World war and participated in the Chateau Thierry, Meuse Argonne and all the major offensives with the American forces, being overseas altogether eighteen months.

Henry J. Harris attended public schools in Ellettsville, including high school, graduating at the age of sixteen, meanwhile having worked for his father in the printing business. He continued his association with his father until 1905. He then started the Farmersville News at Farmersville, Ohio, and continued the publication of that newspaper until 1913. Going to Denmark, Wisconsin, he established the Denmark Press, but sold out a few months later, then spent a year with a newspaper at Camden, Ohio, and he established the News at Morrow, Ohio, which he published until 1917. In the spring of 1918 he established The Press at Otterbein, Indiana, and still owns that newspaper. Mr. Harris in August, 1924, established the Hoopeston Times, and has already brought this paper to a prosperous condition, with a circulation of seventeen hundred subscribers. The plant and offices are at 308 Main Street. The Times is independent in politics.

Mr. Harris himself is a republican. While at Farmersville, Ohio, he served as city clerk two terms, and was township clerk at Camden. He is a member of the Lutheran Church. He is affiliated with Otterbein Lodge No. 561, A. F. and A. M., Morrow Chapter No. 141, Royal Arch Masons, Otterbein Lodge No. 605, I. O. O. F., and is a past grand of the Odd Fellows Lodge at Farmersville.

He married at Farmersville, September 28, 1905, Miss Orpah S. Gilbert, daughter of Frank H. and Sabina (Recher) Gilbert, her mother now deceased. Her father is a blacksmith at Farmersville, Ohio. Mrs. Harris is a graduate of the Farmersville High School. They had two children: Beulah, attending the public schools, and Dorothy, who died when five years old.

THOMAS M. EDMONDS, for over twenty years has been identified with banking at Norris City, where he is cashier of the Norris City State Bank.

He was born on a farm in Gallatin County, Illinois, February 4, 1867, son of John I. and Mollie (Pearce) Edmonds. John I. Edmonds, of Scotch-Irish ancestry, was born near Clarksville, Tennessee, came to Illinois when a young man, about 1860, settling in Gallatin County, where he married. His wife, Mollie Pearce, was a daughter of Mack Pearce, while her mother was a member of the Harrell family, pioneers of Gallatin County. John I. Edmonds was a farmer in Gallatin County for ten years and then removed to a farm just west of Norris City, in White County, where he died at the age of seventy-eight. He was a democrat in politics and a member of the Cumberland Presbyterian Church. His first wife, Mollie Pearce, died in 1868, leaving three children, James M., Thomas M. and Ida M. The second wife of John I. Edmonds was Sarah Johnson, of an old White County family. By this marriage there were four children, Laura A., Hattie B., and two who died in infancy.

Thomas M. Edmonds was reared on a farm. He attended the common schools and the high school at Norris City, and for three years was engaged in the mercantile business at Norris City. In 1903 he took an active part in the organization of the Norris City State Bank. He became its cashier, and has served consecutively in that office ever since, and a great many patrons of the bank think of its service in terms of his personality. The late T. S. Barnes was the first president of the bank.

Mr. Edmonds has been active in the republican party. He is a member of the Independent Order of Odd Fellows, and attends the Presbyterian Church, of which his wife is a member.

He married, in 1887, Anna B. Kenedy, a native of Gallatin County. Five children were born to their marriage, two dying in infancy. The living children are: Miss Lena; Daisy, wife of Rev. J. W. Jenkins, a minister of the Missionary Baptist Church; and Lloyd L., who married Ruby Taylor and is now chief clerk of a coal mining company at Norris City. The son at the age of eighteen registered under the selective service act, but was not called into active service, owing to the close of the World war.

THOMAS ROBERTSON, M. D. Through a practice of nearly forty years Dr. Thomas Robertson has become one of the best known physicians and surgeons of Randolph County. His home throughout this long time has been at Steeleville, where he is now senior partner of Doctors Robertson & Wnorowski.

Doctor Robertson came to Chester, Illinois, in 1878, when a youth of nineteen, being attracted to this locality by the presence of his uncle, Dr. William R. McKenzie, who had located here many years before and was widely known as a physician in this section of the state. There were two other uncles, John and Daniel McKenzie, who had also settled in Randolph County prior to the Civil war. Both John and Daniel entered the Union army, John being killed at the capture of Fort Donelson, while Daniel went through the entire war uninjured.

Dr. Thomas Robertson was born at Churchville, Pictou County, Nova Scotia, March 8, 1859, son of John and Nellie (McKenzie) Robertson. His parents were farmers of Pictou County, Nova Scotia. The son was educated in public schools in his native country and also attended school for a time after coming to Chester. He was employed in the drug store of E. E. Holbrook and Alexander McKenzie at Chester until 1884. In that year he entered the St. Louis Medical College, now the medical department of Washington University, where he was awarded the M. D. degree in 1887. He at once returned to Chester, well qualified by education and training for practice, but being without money he worked for several months in a drug store. In the fall of the same year he located in the Steeleville community, and has been a faithful citizen as well as an able doctor in that locality ever since. He served twelve years as a member of the local school board.

Doctor Robertson in 1890 returned to his native town in Nova Scotia and married Minnie H. Cameron, daughter of Archibald Cameron. They have two children, Miss Marjorie Cameron Robertson and Donald Roderick Robertson. The latter is a graduate of the dental department of Washington University and is now well established in his profession at Belleville, Illinois. Doctor Robertson is a member of the Masonic fraternity and the Independent Order of Odd Fellows.

JOHN E. WALL has long enjoyed a position of acknowledged success as a lawyer and leadership as a citizen in his native community of Quincy, where as he grew up he earned his living as a newsboy and printer, but for thirty years has been busily engaged in the practice of law.

He was born at Quincy February 21, 1864, son of Edmund and Katherine (Gaffney) Wall, his father a native of Frostburg, Maryland, and his mother of Quincy, Illinois. Her father, John Gaffney, and his wife were from County Kilkenny, Ireland, coming to this country in the early '30s, and from New Orleans coming up the Mississippi Valley to Quincy, where John Gaffney died of cholera in 1849. His widow survived him and died at Quincy in 1892, at the age of ninety-two. The Wall family came from County Limerick, Ireland, David Wall came to this country between 1820 and 1830, being a pioneer on the border line between Maryland and West Virginia. He died leaving his widow, Mary Wall, and four children: Johanna, John, David and Edmund, the latter being then three years of age. The mother and her four children, being without means, moved west to Quincy, where she found such employment as was available to support and educate her family. Of her children John Wall studied medicine with Doctor Stahl, but died before beginning practice, while David Wall died very young. Edmund and Johanna Wall grew up, Johanna becoming the wife of Doctor Dowler of Beardstown, Illinois, and is now ninety-five years of age. The mother of these children reached the age of eighty-seven and died at Quincy in the early nineties.

Edmund Wall as a boy had to work to assist in supporting his mother, and many years of his life were accompanied by hardship and adversity. At the age of thirteen he began working away from home, and subsequently served an apprenticship to Mr. Slack to learn the blacksmith's trade, an occupation he followed for many years. At that time a blacksmith made his own as well as other people's tools, making plow shares, horseshoe nails and other implements. He was thoroughly self-made, and while working at his trade studied assiduously at night, familiarizing himself with Shakespeare, so that it is doubtful if any man in his community understood that author more thoroughly and comprehensively than Edmund Wall. He could quote long passages from memory up to within a few years of his death. After his marriage he took a course in the Bryant and Stratton Business College, one of the best commercial colleges in the country, and during that time he was working as a pressman for the Quincy Herald, then under the management of John P. Cadogan, former sheriff of Adams County. Later he was bookkeeper on the Quincy Herald until 1872, when he and Albert Demaree left Quincy for a venture which proved unsuccessful. During the Civil war he was in the service of the Union army. After his return to Quincy Edmund Wall followed the vocation of accountant, finally being bookkeeper for the Eagle Tobacco Company until two or three years before his death, which occurred in November, 1920. He served as alderman in his own ward for a number of years and on two or three occasions was first sergeant of police.

Edmund Wall married at Quincy, in 1862, Miss Katherine Gaffney, and of their eight children those now living are: John Edmund, Lenore, Thomas H. and Katherine Wells, the latter the wife of Neff Wells. George Albert died at Hollywood, California, in March, 1925.

John Edmund Wall was educated in the public schools at Quincy, and at the age of eleven began helping distribute the Quincy Herald, a morning paper. The carriers got up at two o'clock in the morning, folded their own papers, and distributed them to the subscribers. After this work he attended school. Later he was messenger for the Western Union Telegraph Company and became district messenger for the American Telegraph Company after it installed a system at Quincy during the '80s. Through this system the watchmen at a number of factories on the river front had to report to the central office every hour, and on failure to do so Mr. Wall had to ascertain the cause. The Quincy streets were not lighted by electricity then, a few gas lights being along the levee and no lights at all around the factories. Hence it was a matter of some courage to go into the factory district on that night, and in many ways the work had its unpleasant features. Mr. Wall subsequently worked as bookkeeper for the Cadogan-Gardner Company, and realizing the uncertainty of such clerical employment started to learn the trade of printer, serving his apprenticeship in the printing office of the Cadogan-Gardner Company. While thus employed he attended the night law school at Chaddock College. There were twelve students in the law class, including his own brother, Joseph William Wall, since deceased. At the end of the first year John E. Wall had the highest percentage in his studies of any member of the class, though the other students attended college in the day time and had other advantages as well. His brother, Joseph W., stood next in the class, the difference in their average being three-quarters of one per cent, while other students varied from five to twelve per cent. The second year the other students determined to outdo the Wall boys, but at the end of the year Joseph W. Wall's average was the highest, a difference of three-quarters of one per cent separating him from his brother John E. John E. was also awarded the medal for the best written thesis, his brother, Joseph W., coming next in honor.

After being admitted to the bar Mr. Wall went out to Salt Lake City to practice law, being admitted to the bar there in 1894. On account of the passage of the Sherman Act the previous year business in the West was so demoralized that Mr. Wall was compelled to turn to his trade and for about a month and a half worked as a job printer in the printing house at Leadville, Colorado. Returning to Quincy, he formed a partnership with Frank Penick, with offices in the Rogers Building, at the southeast corner of Fifth and Hampshire. Subsequently he moved to the Stern Building, at the northwest corner of Fifth and Hampshire, and in 1896 became associated with George H. Wilson, who was elected state's attorney on the republican ticket. Mr. Wall was assistant state's attorney during the following four years, and he and Mr. Wilson were partners until 1914, since which year Mr. Wall has practiced alone.

Mr. Wall has been attorney in some notable cases, including Converse versus Gardner Governor Company, and he assisted the state in the prosecution of Mr. Ray Pfanschmidt, charged with the murder of his parents, his sister and a visiting school teacher. This trial resulted in conviction with the death penalty, but on appeal to the Supreme Court the case was reversed and Mr. Wall did not participate in the second trial at Macomb. He was engaged to assist the prosecution in the third trial at Princeton, but was debarred by the presiding judge. Pfanschmidt was finally acquitted.

At the beginning of the World war Mr. Wall was appointed chairman of the Adams County Savings Stamp Committee. In a short time he found that the personnel of his committee was more ornamental than useful and he selected a committee of his own, which set to work and was the second in the state to secure its allotted quota. Mr. Wall was chairman of the Adams County Council of Defense, and participated in all the civilian activities of the war, making many speeches throughout the county and helping fill out questionnaires.

In politics Mr. Wall was a democrat until the nomination of William J. Bryan, during which campaign he became a republican, and continued to vote that ticket until 1912. He then voted for Woodrow Wilson and has since been affiliated as a democrat, though in the 1924 campaign he refused to vote for the Wall Street candidate, supporting the Lafollette-Wheeler ticket. In the McKinley campaign he made a number of speeches throughout the state and in the latter days of the campaign in Chicago. His speaking services were in great demand during the Woodrow Wilson campaign, and he delivered from fifty to seventy-five speeches in Illinois and Missouri. Mr. Wall is Catholic by faith but is not now a communicant. He is affiliated with the Bodley Lodge of Masons, the Masonic Grotto, the B. P. O. Elks and Eagles. At one time he was president of the Printer's Union, representing that union at the Trades and Labor Assembly, the forerunner of the Federation of Labor.

On October 10, 1899, he married Miss Belle Conley. Mrs. Wall has been an invaluable worker and executive in the institutional activities of the Young Women's Christian Association at Quincy, a cause to which she has devoted much of her time for the past fifteen years. She was instrumental in securing the Y. W. C. A. Home, is a member of the Board of Directors of the association, its treasurer, and in numerous campaigns has proved herself competent, capable and sincere, promoting the welfare of this institution. She was chairman of the second section of the Guild of the Congregational Church, and is prominent in that church as a member.

LEONARD T. STEARNS, clerk of the Circuit Court of Williamson County, is a member of a family that has lived in the county since pioneer times, and he has proved a very popular and efficient member of the court house family at Marion.

His grandfather, Thomas Stearns, came from Ohio to establish a new home in southern Illinois, and settled in Williamson County, two miles northwest of where Herrin later grew up as an industrial city. His work of improving and cultivating his farm was interrupted when the Civil war broke out, and he joined an Illinois regiment and fought for the Union until the end. After the war he resumed farming, and finally retired and lived at Herrin until his death.

Samuel T. Stearns, father of Leonard T., has long been one of the prominent citizens of the county. He was born on a farm northwest of Herrin, and is a farmer and land and property owner, and also a director of the Marion State & Savings Bank. He served two terms as chairman of the board of county supervisors and since 1918 has been a member of the Township High School Board. Samuel T. Stearns married Martha Benton, a native of Kentucky, who was brought to Williamson County when a child.

Leonard T. Stearns is one of four children, two sons and two daughters, and was born December 19, 1900, on his father's farm north of Carterville. On that farm has since been established the village of Colp. As a boy there he attended country schools, and in 1919 graduated from the Marion High School. During the following year, 1919-20, he was a student in the University of Illinois. Mr. Stearns gave up his university career to accept appointment as deputy circuit clerk of Williamson County. He served as deputy four years, and thus was thoroughly well qualified for the duties of chief of that office, to which he was elected on the republican ticket in 1924.

Mr. Stearns married, in 1923, Miss Thelma Fowler. Her father, Hiram Fowler, has been a well known contractor in Williamson County, and Mrs. Stearns was born at Herrin.

LEO E. WATSON is a member of a prominent pioneer family of Williamson County, and his own career has identified him with banking. He is assistant cashier of the Carterville State & Savings Bank of Carterville in that county.

His great-grandfather, William J. Watson, Sr., was a native of Virginia, served with the rank of sergeant in the War of 1812, and for some years lived in Tennessee, and later during the administration of President Franklin Pierce, moved his family to Williamson County, Illinois, obtaining a tract of government land, the title to which was signed by President Pierce. Both he and his son, William J. Watson, Jr., became well known farmers in the county where they lived out their lives. W. J. Watson, Jr., was born in Virginia, October 25, 1816, and died September 11, 1879. He married Martha J. Adams, who was born February 17, 1824, and died March 1, 1908. Elvis B. Watson, a son of William J., Jr., was born and reared in Williamson County, followed farming in early life, and after coal became the important resource of the county he took up the industry and had the distinction of stripping the first coal worked in the Carterville district. He has spent many years in the coal business, but is now practically retired and living in Florida. Elvis B. Watson married Unity C. Sizemore, who died at Carterville in 1902, daughter of William E. and Sarah Sizemort, and granddaughter of William Sizemore, a native of Virginia, whose father came from England. William E. Sizemore was born in Tennessee, in 1824, and on coming to Illinois lived for a time in Franklin County and then settled near Carterville in Williamson County.

Leo E. Watson, son of Elvis B. Watson, was born at Carterville, April 7, 1889. He attended public schools there, took a course in the Gem City Business College at Quincy, and in 1908, at the age of nineteen, entered the Carterville State & Savings Bank as clerk and bookkeeper. He has been assistant cashier since 1910, and since 1921 has been vice president of the Carterville Building & Loan Association.

Mr. Watson has also taken an active interest in local affairs in his home community. He was city treasurer, served seven years on the school board, and at times has been president and clerk of that body. He is a member of the Masonic order. His wife, whom he married October 24, 1910, was Maybel Youngblood, a daughter of Riley Youngblood. They have three children, Richard, Herbert and Robert Lee.

ORVAL NEWTON HURDLE, Doctor of Dental Surgery at Mt. Sterling, is an ex-service man of the World war, and since the war has engaged in a very successful practice at Mt. Sterling.

He was born at the Village of Clayton, in Adams County, Illinois, June 5, 1893. His grandfather, Newton Hurdle, was one of the early settlers in the LaHarpe community of Hancock County, Illinois, was a farmer and a Union soldier in the Civil war. He spent his last days in the Soldiers Home at Quincy. Newton Hurdle had three sons, Roy, Charles and Clinton, and one daughter, Mrs. Jetta McManus.

Dr. Roy V. Hurdle, father of the dental surgeon at Mt. Sterling, is also a well known member of the dental profession and resides at Danville, Illinois. He was born at LaHarpe, in Hancock County, graduated from the Chicago College of Dentistry, now the dental department of Northwestern University, and for many years engaged in practice at Mt. Sterling, but since 1921 has been located at Danville. While at Mt. Sterling he served on the City Council. He is a republican in politics. Dr. Roy V. Hurdle married Emma Jane Shutwell, who was born at Disco, Illinois, daughter of John Shutwell, and died at Mt. Sterling, April 8, 1917. She was the mother of three sons: Orval N.; Ennis C., who was in the World war service and is now a Y. M. C. A. worker at Toledo, Ohio; and Glen F., a graduate of the Illinois School of Pharmacy and a druggist at Chicago.

Orval Newton Hurdle lived in Adams County the first five years of his life and grew up at Mt. Sterling. He attended public schools, including high school, and studied dentistry at Washington University in St. Louis. He was graduated with his degree Doctor of Dental Surgery in 1916. With this preparation he returned to Mt. Sterling and engaged in private practice. Mr. Hurdle in 1917 was commissioned a first lieutenant in the Dental Corps, but was not called to active duty until September, 1918, when he was assigned to Camp Shelby at Hattiesburg, Mississippi. He remained there until his honorable discharge in May, 1919. Doctor Hurdle then resumed his practice at Mt. Sterling, and has not only advanced in his profession but has found opportunities for usefulness in the work of the community. He is a charter member of the American Legion Post at Mt. Sterling and its present adjutant, and is also a charter member of the Forty and Eight Society. In Masonry he is a member of the Scottish Rite Consistory and Mystic Shrine at Meridian, Mississippi.

Doctor Hurdle has been a member of the Board of Education of Mt. Sterling. He is a republican and a member of the Methodist Church. At Quincy, Illinois, August 5, 1917, he married Miss Letha E. During, a native of Chandlerville, Illinois, daughter of Joseph and Anna (Kischner) During. She grew up and finished her high school education at Mt. Sterling. Doctor and Mrs. Hurdle have two daughters, Elizabeth Ann and Dorothy Louise.

EDWIN C. O'BRIEN, postmaster of Barry, is the type of citizen who deserves well of his country and community. As a youth he was engaged in educational work. He volunteered and rendered service during the World war. After the war he resumed teaching, but was soon appointed postmaster and has made a splendid record in charge of the Barry post office during the past six years.

He was born at Barry, September 17, 1895. His grandfather O'Brien came from Ireland, joined a regiment in the Union army and lost his life during the siege of Vicksburg. His body lies in the National Cemetery at Vicksburg. His only child was Thomas O'Brien, who since early youth has lived at Barry and is one of the honest citizens of that locality. He finished his education at Griggsville, learned the tinner's trade, and after working at his trade engaged in the hardware and plumbing business, and for many years has been the leading representative of that line of business in Barry. Thomas O'Brien married Stella Churchill, daughter of Edwin F. Churchill, a brick layer by trade. The Churchills were among the earliest settlers of Barry in Pike County. Thomas O'Brien and wife had only one child, Edwin Churchill.

Edwin Churchill O'Brien was educated in grammar and high schools at Barry, and in 1917 graduated from the Western Illinois State Teachers' College at Macomb. Prior to that time he had taught in the rural schools, and after leaving the college at Macomb was elected principal of schools at Hull, Illinois.

When the World war came on he enlisted before the draft for service in the navy and was sent for training to the Radio School in Harvard University and then to the Radio Telephony School at New London, Connecticut. He was kept in service on this side of the water and honorably discharged February 20, 1919.

Mr. O'Brien after leaving the army resumed educational work as teacher of manual training in the public schools of Rock Island. He was there a year and in July, 1920, was appointed postmaster of Barry under the administration of Woodrow Wilson. Four years later he was reappointed by President Coolidge. He went into office in 1920 as successor of Mrs. Lucy Ware. Since he became postmaster the receipts of the Barry office have doubled, as also the volume of incoming and outgoing mail, and the office has been advanced to the highest grade of a first class post office.

Mr. O'Brien married Miss Mabel E. Hane, daughter of Mr. and Mrs. S. M. Hane, on June 3, 1926. He takes an active part as a citizen in the Barry Chamber of Commerce, and he is a member of the various Masonic bodies, being a past high priest of Barry Chapter, Royal Arch Masons, a member of the Scottish Rite Consistory at Quincy and the Mystic Shrine at Springfield. He was reared a Baptist, and also comes of a republican family, having cast his first presidential vote for Charles E. Hughes in 1916. He helped organize Barry Post No. 122 of the American Legion and is now its commander. He represented the post as a delegate to the Chicago Convention of the Legion in 1922.

ALBERT RICE. An early Colonial family of Pennsylvania that later became substantially established in Kentucky and still later in Illinois bore the name of Rice, a sturdy branch of an old clan of the Highlands of Scotland. A worthy descendant of this old family is found in Hon. Albert Rice, mayor of Potomac, Illinois, and president of the Potomac National Bank, with which financial institution he has been continuously connected for almost two decades.

Albert Rice was born on his father's farm near Potomac, Vermilion County, Illinois, August 20, 1877, son of William H. and Caroline (Sperry) Rice, and grandson of Enos and Elizabeth (Culp) Rice. Both grandparents were born in Kentucky. In 1860 they removed to Indiana and located near Battle Ground in Tippecanoe County, where Enos Rice died shortly afterward, his widow removing in the same year to a farm in Vermilion County, Illinois.

William H. Rice was born on a plantation south of Lexington, Kentucky, February 26, 1856, and was four years old when he lost his father and was brought to Vermilion County, Illinois by his widowed mother. He grew up on the home farm near Potomac, which, under his administration became a very valuable property, and for many years he was one of the leading farmers and stockraisers of this part of the county. In political life he was a republican and as a good citizen took a deep and intelligent interest in public affairs. His death occurred at Potomac on May 21, 1922. He married Miss Caroline Sperry, who was born near Potomac, Illinois, December 9, 1858, and died on the home farm July 18, 1898. Mr. Rice married for his second wife, Miss Mabel Ingersoll, who survives and is a resident of Champaign, Illinois. The children of the first marriage, five in number, were: Albert, who is mayor of Potomac; Bart, who is cashier of the First National Bank at Rantoul, Illinois; Fred, who is a farmer near Potomac; Clate, who died at Denver, Colorado, where he was in the clothing business; and Janet, who is cashier of the Potomac National Bank, and is the wife of Palmer C. Smith, who is assistant cashier. Two daughters were born to the second marriage: Mary, who is the wife of Victor Anderson, of Danville, Illinois; and Laverna, a senior in the University of Illinois, and the wife of O. D. Arnold, attorney-at-law at Rushville.

Albert Rice attended the public schools and was graduated from the Potomac High School in the class of 1900, after which he attended the Illinois State Normal Cchool at Normal, Illinois. In 1901 Mr. Rice became a teacher in the public schools at Potomac, and continued in that profession until 1905, when he became identified with the Potomac National Bank as a bookkeeper, later becoming assistant cashier, then cashier, and in 1923 was elected president. This old and trustworthy institution was founded as a private bank and opened for business in July, 1882, and was nationalized in 1903. It has always preserved the confidence of the public and has prospered exceedingly. Its present officers are: Albert Rice, president; George W. Judy, vice president; Janet Smith, cashier; Palmer C. Smith, assistant cashier. Its latest statement shows: Capital stock, $30,000; surplus and profits, $7,000; deposits, $125,000. Mr. Rice, additionally, has large farm interests in Vermilion County, and among other responsibilities at Potomac is president of the Potomac Building and Loan Association.

Although important business affairs have claimed much of his attention for many years, they have not excluded active and exceedingly valuable participation in public affairs both in county and city. He has long been an influential factor in republican political circles. In earlier years he served as tax collecter in Middlefork Township, Vermilion County, and from 1907 to 1909 was a member of the Board of Aldermen of Potomac. In 1909, in recognition of his sterling character and business sagacity, his fellow citizens elected him mayor of Potomac, and have reelected him regularly every two years since, with the exception of one term. To recount the reforms and public improvements that he has brought about would be to specify the most of the important evidences of civic progress the city has made in more than the last decade. Potomac is now a modern city with paved streets, cement sidewalks, water and sewerage systems well under way, and a finely equipped and efficient fire department.

Mayor Rice married, October 13, 1909, at Bloomington, Illinois, Miss Cora Goodwine, daughter of the late John and Alice (Lane) Goodwine, formerly of Potomac, where Mr.

Goodwine was a banker and interested also in farming. Mrs. Rice was cashier of the Goodwine State Bank for seventeen years prior to her marriage. Mayor Rice owns considerable valuable real-estate at Potomac, including a comfortable residence on State Street. He and his wife are members of the United Brethren Church. He is a thirty-second degree Mason and a Pythian; a member of Potomac Lodge No. 782, A. F. and A. M., Danville Consistory, S. P. R. S.; and also of Monte Christo Lodge No. 470, Knights of Pythias. He enjoys automobiling as a recreation and is a member of the Vermilion County Automobile Club.

WILLIAM AUSTIN COPE, an Illinois educator, is at this writing superintendent of the high school at Freeburg in St. Clair County.

He was born at Jerseyville, Illinois, June 24, 1890, son of William Jacob and Adelaide (Patterson) Cope. His grandfather, Andrew Cope, came from North Carolina to Illinois in 1840, and his wife, Susan Johnson, was born in Illinois, her mother being a daughter of Thomas Jefferson Hank. The Pattersons were a family originally from Virginia, but transplanted in Illinois from Lexington, Kentucky. They were of Scotch-Irish ancestry. William J. Cope has devoted his life to farming and stockraising, and has been active in local affairs, serving as school director. He is a member of the Methodist Church and the Modern Woodmen of America. His wife, Adelaide, is also a Methodist. They had four children: Bertha A., deceased; Orville Andrew, who married Clara Hester, and has two children, named Dwight William and Kenneth Andrew; Ollie M., who married John Sloffel, and William A.

William Austin Cope attended public schools at Jerseyville, and graduated from high school in 1909. Soon afterwards he began teaching, and after teaching about two years, entered the Macomb State Normal School, and continued his higher education during the summers while teaching the rest of the year. He also attended the State Normal at Carbondale, and the University of Chicago, and finished a special course in salesmanship from the Knox College of Business Efficiency at Cleveland. Mr. Cope in 1921 took charge of the highschool at Freeburg as principal. He has done much to improve the business department of the school. For several summer vacations he has been demonstrating his own ability in salesmanship. During the two months vacation of 1924 he represented a house and sold a volume of business amounting to over $50,000. He is a member of the Methodist Episcopal Church and the Masonic Lodge.

He married at Troy, Missouri, December 4, 1916, Miss Alice Naomi Sanders, daughter of Charles and Fannie (Harlan) Sanders. Her father was killed in April, 1922, while making some adjustments at one of the pumping stations of the Chicago & St. Louis Railway, being superintendent of the pumping station on that road. He was affiliated with the I. O. O. F. and Modern Woodmen of America. Mrs. Cope is next to the youngest in a family of five children. Her sister Hilda is the wife of Daniel W. Wastler and has a son Harlan; Floyd Sanders married Mary Naylor and has two children; Nita, who is the wife of David Rigsby, has two children; and Emma, the wife of D. Wilbur, has a child, Marion. Mr. and Mrs. Cope are the parents of two children: Orville Aaron and Norma Alice.

JOHN HENRY SEARING. The dignities, important responsibilities and honors of the legal profession have come rapidly to John Henry Searing of Carbondale. He is now serving his second term as state's attorney of Jackson County. He has a record as a soldier in the World war.

He was born at Carbondale, October 2, 1890, and is of Pennsylvania ancestry, his father being Harry R. Searing and his mother Nellie Sprague of old Vermont stock. His grandfather, John H. Searing, was a banker and dealer in timber land. Harry R. Searing came to Carbondale in 1885, and for many years was secretary of the Building & Loan Association. He died in 1912, and his widow now resides in Chicago.

John Henry Searing attended public schools at Carbondale, graduated from the Southern Illinois University in 1911, and for two years was a student in the University of Illinois. In 1915, he graduated from the Northwestern University School of Law at Chicago, and was admitted to the bar and at once opened an office at Carbondale. He had practiced only a short time when the World war came on.

On October 16, 1917, he joined the Colors at Camp Taylor, being assigned to Company B, of the Three Hundred Twenty-third Machine Gun Battalion, which became a part of the Eighty-fourth Division. He went overseas to France in September, 1918, and returned home and was honorably discharged July 8, 1919. He enlisted as a private, became a private of the first class, corporal, sergeant and finally regimental sergeant major.

After leaving the army, Mr. Searing was associated in practice with Judge W. A. Schwartz until 1920, when he was first elected to the office of state's attorney. In 1924 he was reelected. Mr. Searing received a distinctive honor when in December, 1925, at the annual session of the Illinois State's Attorneys Association at Chicago. He was elected president of the organization. He had previously served as secretary and vice president. Mr. Searing is a Royal Arch Mason, member of the B. P. O. Elks, the American Legion and the Sons of the American Revolution. He married in 1915, Miss Gale Shanoh of Washington, D. C.

BIRCHARD E. BAUM, municipal judge of Danville, had long been prominent in politics and business affairs in Vermilion County. Before removing to Danville, his home was at Ridge Farm and he was in the telephone business in that locality for many years.

Judge Baum was born at Point Isabel, Ohio, March 7, 1869. The Baum family is of German extraction, and settled in Pennsylvania at the time of William Penn. His grandfather, Joseph Baum, was a native of Reading, Pennsylvania, was a gunsmith by trade, and when in middle years removed to Point Isabel in Southern Ohio, where he lived until his death.

He died in 1876 at the remarkable age of 105 years. John C. Baum, father of Judge Baum, was born at Point Isabel in Clermont County, Ohio, March 19, 1846; was reared and married there and learned and followed during his active career the trade of blacksmith. In 1872 he removed to Palermo, Illinois, in 1876 to Georgetown this state and after 1877 his home was at Ridge Farm in Vermilion County. He died in Danville, January 1, 1914, and was buried at Ridge Farm. As a democrat he held several local offices, was an active worker in the Methodist Episcopal Church, and from early manhood was affiliated with the Masonic order. John C. Baum married Margaret J. Salt, who was born at Point Isabel, Ohio, June 7, 1848, and died at Ridge Farm, May 10, 1898.

Birchard E. Baum was three years of age when brought to Illinois, grew up at Ridge Farm, attended public schools there, completing his high school course in 1887. He had five years of experience clerking in a store and was postmaster of Ridge Farm during the Cleveland administration from 1893 to 1897. Mr. Baum for twenty-two years was superintendent of the Vermilion County Telephone Company and during that time he carried out a very effective organization and expansion of telephone facilities over the county, perfecting a service that was little more than nominal when he went into the business.

Mr. Baum removed from Ridge Farm to Danville in 1904. In 1918, after an attack of the influenza, he spent some months recuperating his health in Florida and Cuba, returning to Danville in 1919. He was elected municipal judge in May, 1924, with office in the Danville City Hall. Though formerly a democrat, Mr. Baum for some years was a republican. He was affiliated with the Methodist Episcopal Church and fraternally a member of Olive Branch Lodge No. 38, F. and A. M., Vermilion Chapter No. 82, Royal Arch Masons, Athelstan Commandery No. 45, Knights Templar, Danville Consistory of the Scottish Rite, Ansar Circle of the Mystic Shrine at Springfield, and Past Chancellor of Damascus Lodge No. 84, Knights of Pythias, at Danville, and a member of Danville Lodge No. 332, B. P. O. Elks.

Birchard E. Baum died October 10, 1925. He was married to Wilhelmine Keller, his nurse, daughter of John and Johanah Keller of Danville, Illinois. He is survived by his widow and two brothers, Perle M. Baum and George H. Baum.

JOHN T. LEGIER, M. D. Through half of a normal lifetime Doctor Legier has devoted himself faithfully to the practice of medicine and surgery in Southern Illinois, where he is highly esteemed. For more than a quarter of a century his home has been at Carmi.

Doctor Legier was born at Rochester Mills, in Wabash County, Illinois, October 19, 1867. His parents, George M. and Julia A. (Tugaw) Legier, were also natives of Wabash County and of French ancestry. George M. Legier was a general merchant, grain dealer and pork packer at Rochester Mills, but the later years of his life were given to farming. He died at the home of his son, Doctor Legier, at Carmi, in 1918, at the age of eighty-two, his wife having passed away aged sixty-five. Their children were: John T.; Frederick, now deceased; Mrs. Laura Stansfield; and Miss Naomi B.

John T. Legier was reared on a farm, and at the age of thirteen went to Keensburg, Illinois, where after completing his common school education he began the study of medicine under Dr. P. G. Manley. From there he went East to New York and in 1891 was graduated from Bellevue Hospital Medical College, one of the best medical schools in the country. Doctor Legier first engaged in private practice in the town where he had grown up, Keensburg, but on October 3, 1899, removed to Carmi, and where he still continues to look after and serve the many families and individuals who regard him as the leader of his profession in that community. In January, 1926, he and Dr. F. C. Sibley and Miss Wilmina K. Pfeifer founded the Carmi Hospital, of which they are proprietors.

Doctor Legier in the course of his practice took postgraduate work in the Chicago Post-Graduate School of Medicine and also at Tulane University at New Orleans. He is a member of the White County, Illinois State and American Medical Associations, and is a Methodist. For many years he voted the prohibition ticket, and in later years has usually supported the republican party. Doctor Legier married, in 1890, Margaret R. Rigg, a native of Wabash County, Illinois. They have three children: Paul Manley, who is married and is in the automobile business at Carmi; Mary Pauline, wife of E. E. Wilhoit, of Champaign, Illinois; and John A., who is married and is now preparing himself for the medical profession.

JAMES J. ELLIS, M. D. With a high standing as a physician and surgeon, Doctor Ellis is well known professionally in several communities of southern Illinois, but for the past twelve years his home has been at West Frankfort.

His father, Hiram Stanford Ellis, came from Tennessee and settled in Hamilton County, Illinois, where he followed farming until his death in 1889. He married Elizabeth Pulliam, of another Tennessee family that came to Illinois in early times. She died in 1888.

James J. Ellis was one of five children and was born on the home farm in Hamilton County April 17, 1882. He grew up in that rural community, attended district schools and afterwards Ewing College. Doctor Ellis on May 7, 1909, was graduated from the St. Louis College of Physicians and Surgeons and had one year of training as an interne in the St. Louis City Hospital. For five years he practiced at Walpole in Hamilton County, and in 1914 removed to West Frankfort, where his abilities have been taxed by a large practice in medicine and surgery. He is a member of the Franklin County, Illinois State and American Medical Associations and is a Scottish Rite Mason and Shriner, being a member of the Consistory and Temple at East St. Louis. He also belongs to the Lions Club.

Doctor Ellis married Helen D. Wilderman, daughter of John Wilderman. Doctor Ellis has

two sons. James Conrad Ellis graduated in 1926 from Rush Medical College of Chicago, having taken his A. B. degree at the University of Chicago in 1923, and is now serving as an interne in the General Hospital at Los Angeles, California. The younger son (Lester) Neal, is completing his college education in DePauw University in Indiana.

JUDGE CHARLES H. MILLER, judge of the Circuit Court of the Second Circuit, was thirty years of age when first elected to the bench, being one of the youngest circuit judges in the state. He is completing his second term, and has gained the general esteem of the bar and public for the splendid efficiency with which he has attended to the great volume of business in his court.

Judge Miller was born at Cobden, Illinois, August 6, 1884. He graduated from the public schools of his native village in 1899, and in 1906 completed his literary education at McKendree College. Judge Miller spent three years in the Harvard Law School, was admitted to the Illinois bar in 1909, and in the same year established his home and office at Benton. In 1910 he formed a partnership with W. F. Spiller, and they were associated in practice until 1915, when Judge Miller was elected for his first term on the circuit bench. He was commissioned June 21, 1915, and after the first term of six years was reelected for a second term in June, 1921. Prior to going on the bench he had been United States court commissioner for the eastern district of Illinois.

Judge Miller is a York and Scottish Rite Mason, and member of the Mystic Shrine at East St. Louis. He married, in 1915, Lillian R. Snyder, daughter of Solomon O. Snyder. They have two children, Mary Virginia and Joan.

MIKE FERRELL, whose family has been in Williamson County for three generations, is one of the county's substantial bankers and business men, being cashier and director of the First National Bank of Carterville.

The First National Bank of Carterville was organized in 1905, with A. K. Ellis president and A. J. Guerrataez the first cashier. The bank has operated on its original capital of $50,000, and now has surplus of $25,000, and total resources of nearly three quarters of a million dollars. The deposits according to a recent statement approximated nearly $600,000. Since 1923 Dr. F. M. Hiller has been president, and the executive responsibilities of cashier have reposed in the capable hands of Mike Ferrell since 1915.

Mr. Ferrell's grandfather, George Ferrell, was born in Tennessee, and on coming to Illinois settled in Williamson County, where he was a farmer and merchant, and where he died in 1856. Hosea Vice Ferrell, father of Mike Ferrell, was born in Williamson County in 1844, and at the age of seventeen enlisted for service in the Union army during the Civil war. He was with an Illinois regiment, was wounded in battle, and after the war came home and completed his education. He became a teacher in country schools, and was one of the able citizens of the county. He married Mildred Cassander Davis, who was born in Williamson County, Illinois, in 1848, her family likewise having come from Tennessee.

Mike Ferrell, one of eleven children, was born in Carterville June 4, 1878. As a boy there he attended the village schools, and after reaching years of maturity he engaged in farming and dairying, and later took up mining. Since 1915 he has been the official most frequently met with at the First National Bank. He is also secretary of the Egypt Building & Loan Association, which was organized in 1918 with an authorized capital of $1,000,000. This association is now one of the prosperous organizations of its kind in southern Illinois, having assets of over $500,000.

Mr. Ferrell for 1926 served as president of the Williamson County Bankers Association. At one time he was a member of the Board of County Commissioners, is a Knight Templar Mason and Shriner, member of the Independent Order of Odd Fellows, Knights of Pythias and Modern Woodmen of America.

He married Miss Daisy Phillips, of Williamson County, who died September 14, 1925. There are three children: Beulah, wife of Glenn Alcorn, of Carterville; George and Nora May, who are attending school.

J. W. MCCORMACK is founder and president of one of the successful firms of real estate operators and builders in the city of Chicago, the J. W. McCormack Company, Incorporated. This company has its headquarters in the downtown district at 111 West Washington Street, but the field in which Mr. McCormack's genius as a subdivider has been most conspicuously displayed is the southwestern section of the city, where recently his company has put on the market the Boulevard Manor Additions.

Mr. McCormack was born in Jefferson County, Missouri, in 1890, grew up on a farm, was educated in the schools at Festus, Missouri, and had his early training and experience in the real estate business at St. Louis. His father, George W. McCormack, who died at the age of eighty-four, was a pioneer of Jefferson County, Missouri, where he carried on farming operations all his life.

Since 1916 Mr. McCormack's home has been at Chicago, and he has had an increasingly prominent and successful part in the real estate business in that city. For several years he was connected with the William H. Britigan Realty Association. This is one of the old and prominent real estate organizations, and among other distinctions it has turned out a number of highly successful real estate men. Mr. McCormack in 1924 founded the J. W. McCormack Company, Incorporated. This company has already carried out several development projects, culminating in the present Boulevard Manor Additions, highly improved and residential section in Cicero, with Pershing Road as its southern boundary, and extending from Fifty-sixth Avenue on the east to the Berwyn-Cicero limits on the west, and to the Illinois Central right of way on the north. The property is only eight miles from the Loop district, and has as its main facilities for transportation the Burlington and Illinois Central Railways. The enterprise of Mr. Mc-

Cormack is developing this property attracted special attention through his independent undertaking of building a street car line from the existing terminus into and through his subdivision, paying the cost of construction and then turning it over to one of the railway companies for the operation of cars.

Mr. McCormack is a member of the Chicago Real Estate Board and the Chicago Association of Commerce. He married Miss Ida C. Kleinschmidt, of Missouri.

CITIZENS STATE BANK. The Citizens State Bank of Champaign was incorporated in 1908, at which time it was the smallest banking house in Champaign County. At the time of incorporation the officers were: A. M. Burke, president; E. I. Burke, vice president; and C. L. Maxwell, cashier. This bank under the wise and conservative management of President Burke has so expanded that it now does the largest banking business of any financial concern in the county, and is recognized to be without any peer in its solidity and resources.

According to the statement made at the close of the fiscal year June 30, 1925, this bank has total resources of $3,987,341.36. Its capital is $100,000; its surplus, $100,000, and its undivided profits, $19,573.71. It has deposits amounting to $3,761,103.16. Its banking house and fixtures are valued at $44,468,86, and its other real estate at $54,056.23. A general banking business is carried on in all commercial and savings lines, there are safety deposit vaults in the bank building, and special facilities are afforded for foreign exchange and the making of city and farm real-estate loans. Through the trust department the bank acts as executor, administrator and trustee for estates.

The present officers are: A. M. Burke, president; J. C. Dodds, vice president; E. I. Burke, vice president and cashier; F. L. Hutchins, S. A. Blaine and H. B. Wilson, assistant cashiers; and John A. Burke, auditor. The Board of Directors is composed of the following, all men of substance and high standing in the community: A. M. Burke, O. L. Percival, J. C. Dodds, E. I. Burke, A. L. Monroe, F. L. Hutchins, Jr., and D. B. Wright.

ARTHUR M. BURKE, president of the Citizens State Bank of Champaign, and treasurer of the University of Illinois, is one of the leading financiers and solid citizens of Champaign County. He was born in Condit Township, this county, November 6, 1870, a son of P. E. and Isabella Burke. P. E. Burke, a native of Davis County, Kentucky, came to Illinois about 1860 and purchased land in Logan County, on which he was engaged in farming until 1867. In the meanwhile he served for three years in the war between the states in Company F, Thirty-eighth Illinois Volunteer Infantry, participating in the battles of Stone River, Lookout Mountain, Chickamauga, and other major engagements.

In 1867 P. E. Burke moved to Condit Township, Champaign County, bought land, and was engaged in farming it until 1877, when he moved to Rantoul and embarked in a grocery and meat business. Later he was engaged in handling grain and coal. A man of great personal courage, he served first as deputy sheriff, and later as sheriff of Champaign County. The death of this widely and favorably known citizen occurred February 14, 1896, and in his passing his community lost one of its strong influences for good.

Arthur M. Burke completed his education in the Urbana High School, and then was employed for eighteen months by a wholesale commission house of Denver, Colorado. Returning then to Champaign, Mr. Burke served for a year as deputy sheriff, and for another year was reporter and collector for the Urbana Herald. From that time until 1897 he was a clerk in a local department store, but in February of that year formed a partnership with J. W. Lawder in a tailoring business, which they carried on until January 1, 1899, at which time Mr. Burke entered the Citizens Bank in a clerical capacity. The following August he and J. W. Orr bought the interest of John Armstrong in that institution, and it was continued as a private banking house until 1908, when it was incorporated under the name of the Citizens State Bank, with A. M. Burke as president; E. I. Burke, vice president, and C. L. Maxwell as cashier. At that time the bank was the smallest in Champaign County, but it now has more deposits and does a larger amount of banking business than any other in the county. Mr. Burke still continues as president, and devotes all of his time to the bank aside from overseeing his farming operations in Champaign County. While an active worker in the republican party, he has no personal ambitions for political prestige, and has more than once refused appointment to high-salaried positions. In April, 1921, he was made treasurer of the University of Illinois, which office he still holds with efficient capability.

On September 5, 1892, Mr. Burke married Miss Stella Innes, of Urbana, and they have two sons, John A. and Robert, the latter of whom, a lad of sixteen years, is attending high school. John A. Burke was graduated in mechanical engineering from the University of Illinois in 1920. During the World war he was commissioned a second lieutenant while in training at Fort Sheridan. Since January 1, 1924, he has been auditor of the Citizens State Bank. He married Miss Clyde Keene, of Kentucky, and they have two children, Arthur and James. Aside from his membership in the Knights of Pythias, President Burke has no fraternal connections, as his business cares absorb his time and attention. Not only does he take a deep pride in his home city and county, but he is willing and anxious to advance them in any way that lies in his power, but, being a conservative man, he will not support any movement that has not a sound and legitimate foundation.

PRESLEY GOLDONA BRADBURY was admitted to the bar and began practice in Crawford County in 1876. He is one of the few Illinois attorneys who have rounded out a career of half a century of continuous work in the legal profession. He has enjoyed success in his vocation, and his career has brought him a marked measure of community esteem and honor.

He was born on a farm in Hutsonville Township, Crawford County, October 6, 1847, son of John S. and Jemima (Buckner) Bradbury, and grandson of John and Mary (Hines) Bradbury. John Bradbury, his grandfather, was born in North Carolina, his wife being a native of Maryland. Their children were: Anna, who married Cornelius Martin; Peter; Martha, who became the wife of Bryant Cox; James; Morland; and John S. John S. Bradbury was born in North Carolina, August 17, 1822, and was six years of age when, in 1828, the family rigged up two two-wheeled carts and started on their westward migration, spending a brief time en route in Orange County, Indiana, but before the end of the year settling in Crawford County, Illinois. John Bradbury died the year following his Illinois settlement. His wife passed away in 1847. John S. Bradbury because of the early death of his father assumed responsibilities beyond his years and strength. He grew up and became a farmer and lived an industrious and exemplary life within a mile of where his father first settled in Crawford County. He cast his first presidential vote for James K. Polk and voted as a democrat all his years. He married, February 12, 1844, Jemima Buckner, whose parents, Henry and Martha (Evans) Buckner, settled in Crawford County about 1818. John S. and Jemima Bradbury had three children, James, Presley G. and Catherine. Their mother died in 1851 and subsequently Nancy Huckaby became the wife of John S. Bradbury, and by this marriage there were children named Andrew, John, Rosa, George, Alice, Albert, Willis and Nancy.

Presley G. Bradbury was one of the large household of children that grew up on his father's farm and up to the age of twenty-one he put his strength to test in farm work and in doing his share of the labors required for the support of the family. He attended the village school at York, a school at that time of high standing and one which provided unusual culture for its students. At the age of twenty-one Mr. Bradbury left home. His father's parting words, "Son, I am too poor to give you anything as a start in life, but if you ever need help let me know," contained both encouragement and incentive to the young man and deepened his determination to succeed. He secured a school, became a district school teacher, and for seven years following alternated between teaching and attending school himself. He continued his own education in the normal school at Normal, Illinois, and at Carbondale. His last school work was done at Palestine. In 1873 he was elected county superintendent of schools of Crawford County, and rounded out his educational career with three years of highly satisfactory work in that position, and resigned to become state's attorney.

While teaching he had diligently pursued the study of law and was admitted to the bar on July 4, 1876, the hundredth anniversary of the Declaration of Independence. Later in the same year he was elected state's attorney of Crawford County, and filled that office two terms, eight years. After retiring from the office he gained a large practice, and became distinguished over Crawford and adjoining counties for his skill and resourcefulness as a criminal lawyer, ranking as one of the ablest in that branch of the profession in the state. Mr. Bradbury has always voted for and acted with the democratic party. He has for over thirty years been a director of the First National Bank of Robinson. Mr. Bradbury is a member of the Presbyterian Church and is a Master Mason and Knight of Pythias. He united with the Presbyterian Church at Robinson in 1892, and soon afterward was made a ruling elder, regularly re-elected thereafter and recently electd ruling elder for life.

He married, December 31, 1877, Miss Jennie Kelley, a native of Sullivan County, Indiana. Her father was a pioneer settler there, a farmer and business man. To the marriage of Mr. and Mrs. Bradbury were born four sons and one daughter: John L., who died in 1908; Frances C., wife of Alonzo J. Goff, of Robinson; Palmer G., William E. and James Stanley. The son William E. graduated from the law department of Notre Dame University in Indiana, was admitted to the bar in 1916, and was with the colors during the World war in 1917-18. He is now practicing law with his father. James Stanley Bradbury is also a law graduate from Notre Dame and is practicing law in Chicago.

ENOCH E. NEWLIN has been a member of the Illinois bar and an attorney at Robinson forty-five years. Of that time he gave eighteen years to service on the bench as a judge of the Second Judicial Circuit. Judge Newlin was a farm boy in Crawford County, and all the opportunities for education beyond the country schools were supplied by his own initiative and effort. As a professional man and as a citizen he has been justly admired for the qualities that have raised him above the commonplace, for his rugged integrity and for the fine spirit that has characterized all his relations with the community.

In his individual record and in his ancestry no one could be more thoroughly an American. The history of the Newlin family has been traced back to Newland Hall, Essex, England, to about the year 1150. In England the name was spelled sometimes Newland and sometimes Newlin. At a later date appeared the ancestor of Nicholas Newlin, who was born at Canterbury, England, in 1580. His son Nicholas was born in Ireland. This Nicholas was the father of Nathaniel Newlin, who left his native country of Ireland and settled in Chester County, Pennsylvania, acquiring a land grant in that province as early as 1683. John Newlin, son of Nathaniel, moved to North Carolina. His children and grandchildren comprise a large group, accounting for many of the Newlins who lived in different parts of the country during the last century. The children and grandchildren were: John, father of Malinda, William, Rachael, Deina, Sargent, Sarah, Charles and Jacob; Jacob, father of Elias, John, Elihu, Sarah, Lidda and Zilla; James, father of John, Andrew, Hiram, Alfred, Abraham, Oliver, Nathan and Cyrus; Nathan, father of Hannah, Sarah, Elder, J. Nelson, Holiday P., Nancy, Fidelia, Elizabeth and Martha; Thomas, father of Matthew, Eli, Ahi, John D. and Rebecca; William, father of Jonathan, Richard, Mary, Elias, Andrew and Elizabeth; Sarah, who married John Mitchell and became the mother of James, Mary and John Mitchell; Mary, who never married and left no descendants; Jonathan, father of William, Ruth, James, Calvin, Clark, Eliza, Joshua, Charles, Lindsay, Alexander and Emily.

Eli Newlin, son of John and grandson of Nathaniel, and thus representing the third generation of the family in America, was one of the pioneer settlers of Crawford County, Illinois. He became the father of a large family of children, named: Jonathan, Mahala, Sarah, Enoch, Thomas, Frederick, John Kelley and Mary.

Of these Thomas Newlin was the father of Judge Newlin. Thomas Newlin was born after his parents settled in Crawford County. In 1861 he enlisted in Company I of the Seventy-ninth Illinois Infantry. His brother, John Kelley Newlin, was a soldier in the same regiment, and both died before the war was over. Thomas Newlin died in the hospital at Murfreesboro, Tennessee, in 1862. He married Mary Ruckle, a native of Licking County, Ohio. She was left a widow, and under difficult circumstances reared her children on the farm. She was always a devout Methodist and lived to be about sixty years of age. Her children were Martha, James M., George, Enoch E., LeRoy and Thomas J.

Enoch E. Newlin was four years old when his father died and in the years of his childhood and early youth he experienced some of the simple poverty that attended his mother's household. He was educated in the country schools, and at the age of sixteen qualified as a teacher. For seven years he taught in country districts, doing farm work in the intervals. While teaching he centered his ambition upon a career as a lawyer. He studied in the law office of Callahan and Jones at Robinson, and in 1882, at the age of twenty-four, was admitted to the bar. He at once engaged in practice at Robinson, which has been his home and the center of his professional activities ever since. Soon after beginning practice he was made city attorney of Robinson. In 1884 he was elected state's attorney of Crawford County, and by re-election he served eight years. Then followed a period when he was allowed to give his full time to his growing law practice. In June, 1897, he was elected judge of the Second Judicial Circuit. Six years later, in June, 1903, he was re-elected, and enjoyed the satisfaction of seeing his administration of justice approved a third time by popular vote in June, 1909. He rounded out the full three terms, a total of eighteen years, on the bench, and then voluntarily retired with a reputation as a jurist that will always make his name noteworthy in the annals of the bench. Since retiring from office he has been engaged in the quiet routine of a general law practice at Robinson.

Judge Newlin is a democrat in politics. He is a Knight Templar Mason, and he and his wife are active Methodists. For over thirty years he has been chairman of the Board of Trustees of his church.

He married, in 1885, Miss Clara A. Coulter, who was born in Crawford County, daughter of Melville and Mary Coulter. They have three children: Mary Fay, wife of E. C. Landgrebe of Huntingburg, Indiana; Frank E., who graduated from the law department of the University of Illinois, practiced for a time with his father at Robinson, but is now located in Florida; and Marian O., wife of F. W. Kessler, of Tulsa, Oklahoma.

JOHN C. EAGLETON is in his second term as judge of the Second Judicial Circuit. His home is at Robinson, and in that city he read law and began practice after his admission to the bar. Judge Eagleton has proved himself worthy of the honors bestowed upon him in the judicial office, and his career is also interesting because he has achieved success over difficulties.

Judge Eagleton was born on a farm, of poor but highly respected parents, members of pioneer families in Southern Illinois. His birth occurred in Crawford County April 10, 1866. His grandparents were James and Margaret or "Peggy" (Montgomery) Eagleton. They were one of the first couples to receive a marriage license in Crawford County, the date of their marriage being 1818, the same year that Illinois came into the Union. James Eagleton, of Scotch ancestry and Virginia stock, was born in Blount County, Tennessee. He came to Illinois to escape the institution of slavery. His location was a farm south of Palestine in Crawford County, in which county he died. His wife was a member of one of the very earliest families to come to Crawford County, and Montgomery Township in the county was named in honor of this family. Among the sons of James Eagleton, four served as soldiers in the Civil war. He and his wife were charter members of the first Presbyterian Church organized in Crawford County, and he was a ruling elder of the church.

James M. Eagleton, father of Judge Eagleton, was born in Crawford County, February 8, 1832, and lived there all his life, passing away in 1911. He was a farmer in early life, but for many years resided in Robinson. He offered his services in defense of the Union at the outbreak of the Civil war, along with his brothers, but was rejected for physical reasons. He cast his first presidential vote for John C. Fremont, the first standard bearer of the republican party, and he voted for the other successive candidates of that party for President as long as he lived. He and his wife were Presbyterians. James M. Eagleton married Nancy A. Baugess. She was a native of North Carolina and came to Crawford County, Illinois, alone. She was living in the home of James Eagleton when she and the latter's son, James M., were married. They had several children, but the only two to reach mature years were George Davis and John C., both residents of Robinson.

John C. Eagleton when a small child moved with his parents to Robinson, where he grew up, graduating from high school. He then learned the stone cutter's trade, and at one time worked as a section hand on the railroad. In these ways he supplied the capital for a

higher education, and his earnestness and industry commended him to the favorable attention of his fellow citizens even as a youth. While working at his trade as a stone cutter he studied law in Robinson under Judge Enoch E. Newlin, and was admitted to the bar in May, 1889. Judge Eagleton still has in his library the first law book he purchased. He earned the money for the purchase of these books by cutting stone for the schoolhouse at Palestine. In September, 1891, he engaged in law practice, and in a short time had a clientage that ranked him among the leading members of the local bar.

In the thirty-five years since he began the practice of law Judge Eagleton has received many honors at the hands of his fellow citizens. He has been city clerk, city attorney, mayor of Robinson, county judge, and by appointment of the Supreme Court served as one of the justices of the Appellate Court. He also served eighteen years on the school board of Robinson. For many years he served as a member and also as chairman and as secretary of the Republican County Central Committee. In June, 1915, he was elected judge of the Circuit Court in the Second Judicial Circuit, and succeeded on the bench his honored preceptor, Judge Enoch E. Newlin, who had served three terms and who was a democrat in politics. In 1921 Judge Eagleton was reelected, his present term expiring in 1927. His opinions and rulings have given evidence of a profound knowledge of the law and his entire administration on the bench has been approved by both the bar and the public. Judge Eagleton is a member of the Masonic order, Knights of Pythias and Woodmen of the World, and belongs to the Church of the Disciples or Christian Church.

He married April 6, 1892, Miss Lola M. Ritchie, daughter of Crawford B. and Caroline Amanda (Lemmon) Ritchie. She was born in Lawence County, Illinois, but was living in Crawford County at the time of and for many years before her marriage. Judge and Mrs. Eagleton are the parents of four children: Frank R., Mary Neal, Robley Neal and Richard H. Robley Neal is a dentist practicing at Decatur, Illinois. The son Frank R. during the World war was in the Field Signal Service, spent ten and a half months overseas and is an active member of the American Legion. He is a graduate of the Robinson High School and of the Illinois Wesleyan University School of Law, and is now an assistant attorney general at Springfield. Mary Neal is a graduate of the Northwestern University School of Oratory; and Robley Neal is a graduate of the Indiana State Dental School.

LEROY B. HOUSE is well established in the profession of dentistry at Herrin in Williamson County. He is a native of this section of Southern Illinois, and three generations of the family have lived there.

His grandfather, Henry Hill House, came from North Carolina, living in Tennessee for some years and later moving to Illinois, where he settled two and a half miles north of Benton, the county seat of Franklin County. In that community he lived out his life. James R. House, father of Doctor House, was born in North Carolina in 1849, but spent his active career as a farmer near Benton in Franklin County. He married Nancy A. Morris, a native of Illinois, where she was born in 1859. One of their thirteen children was Leroy B. House, who was born at the old homestead near Benton October 9, 1888.

Doctor House supplemented his rural school advantages by a period of study in the excellent normal school then maintained at Benton. In February, 1918, he enlisted in the Medical Reserve Corps and was stationed for duty at St. Louis, but continued his studies there without being called to active service. He received an honorable discharge from the Medical Reserve Corps in December, 1919.

Doctor House graduated in 1921 from the dental department of St. Louis University, and in December of the same year opened his office at Herrin. He is a member of the B. P. O. Elks. Doctor House married Lena Pool, daughter of Morgan Pool, of Hopkinsville, Kentucky. They have one child, Helen Virginia House.

JAMES L. MCDOWELL. The resourcefulness and the tenacity of purpose that signally marked the course of Mr. McDowell in advancing his education along both academic and professional lines have proved likewise potent in gaining to him success and prestige as one of the younger generation of lawyers in the great metropolis of Chicago. Objective recognition of his sterling character and his professional ability is betokened in the fact that at the time of this writing, in the autumn of 1925, Mr. McDowell is in active service as assistant United States district attorney for the Northern District of Illinois.

James L. McDowell was born at Fennimore, Wisconsin, April 16, 1884, and is a son of C. Lucien and Zoa Marie (Sellick) McDowell. His rudimentary education was received in the public schools of the Badger State, and he was a lad of nine years at the time of the family removal to Oregon, Ogle County, Illinois. There he continued his studies in the public schools until he had partially completed the work of his sophomore year in the high school, when he withdrew and found employment of humble order, so that at that early stage in his career he became in large measure dependent upon his own resources. For several years Mr. McDowell was employed by the Schiller Piano Company and as clerk in a cigar store at Oregon, and he had in the meantime gained the friendship and helpful interest of the late Judge James H. Cartwright of Oregon, who eventually became chief justice of the Illinois Supreme Court and who urged the young cigar clerk to resume his school work and gain a more advanced education as a proper fortification for a career of greater usefulness. Thus it was that Mr. McDowell took an unusual action, in that he resumed his high school studies when he was twenty-four years of age. In the Oregon High School, which he had previously attended, he was graduated as a member of the class of 1910, and he then followed again the kindly and earnest advice of Judge Cartwright by initiating preparation for the legal profession. He completed the three years' course in the law department of the great University of Michigan, in which he was graduated as a member of the class of 1913 and from which he received his well earned degree of Bachelor of Laws. He went to college without independent means and worked his way through the law department, by applying himself to service as a table waiter and by doing such other remunerative work as he could find.

In the year of his graduation from the law school Mr. McDowell was admitted to the Illinois bar and engaged in the practice of law in his home town of Oregon. In 1915 he was elected city attorney of Oregon, and of this office he continued the incumbent about three years or until the city adopted the commission form of government. In 1920 he was elected state's attorney of Ogle County, and in this position he gave a vigorous and successful administration of four years, at the expiration of which there came further recognition of his ability in that he was appointed an assistant United States district attorney for the Northern District of Illinois, under District Attorney Edwin A. Olson. At this time he removed to Chicago, the seat of this Federal jurisdiction, and he was assigned large responsibilities—those involved in the prosecution of all cases pertaining to the violaton of the Federal prohibition laws and the Harrison anti-narcotic Federal laws. It can readily be understood that in this connection have been effectively tested and proved the powers of this vigorous and fearless Federal law official, and his splendid work in unearthing and prosecuting infractions of the Federal prohibition and narcotic laws has become a part of the history of such important and difficult governmental service in the great city of Chicago, the while the professional reputation of Mr. McDowell has been signally advanced through the success of his work along these lines.

On January 27, 1916, Mr. McDowell married Frances M. Weatherby, of Chicago. He is a member of the various bodies of the Masonic and other fraternal organizations, including the Independent Order of Odd Fellows, Elks and Loyal Order of Moose. He is also a member of Tebala Temple, Ancient Arabic Order Nobles of the Mystic Shrine and a member of the Hamilton Club and Fort Dearborn Town Club.

JOHN CALVIN OXFORD has practiced law in Hardin County for over thirty years. He is the present state's attorney of that county and is a resident of Elizabethtown.

He was born in Hardin County, January 28, 1858. The Oxford family settled in that section of Illinois in 1837, the founder of the family being his grandfather, James Oxford, a native of North Carolina, who spent his last years in Hardin County. The state's attorney is a son of Samuel Calvin and Martha (Hodges) Oxford. His father was born in Tennessee, in 1827, and was ten years of age when the family came to Illinois. Martha Hodges, for many years affectionately known in her community as "Aunt Patsie," was born in Kentucky, a daughter of William Hodges. She had a twin sister, Tabitha, and both of them lived to be eighty-three years of age and died within forty-eight hours of each other. Samuel C. Oxford and wife were married in Hardin County and spent all their lives there. He died in 1884, having devoted his active years to farming. He and his wife were Baptists, and he was a Democrat. They had a family of nine children, five growing up, but John C. is now the only survivor.

John C. Oxford was reared on a farm, attended common schools and three terms of select school, and when twenty-three years of age became a teacher, an occupation he followed three years. He has been well known over the county since 1884, when he was elected circuit court clerk. He was reelected in 1888. He filled that office eight years, and during part of the time pursued the study of law under Judge Ledbetter. He was admitted to the bar in 1891, and on retiring from office in 1893 engaged in private practice. Mr. Oxford was elected state's attorney of Hardin County in 1924. He is a democrat. While engaged in the practice of law he has acquired farm lands and mining interests in Hardin County.

He married, in 1886, Martha Jane Wolrab, a native of Hardin County and daughter of John C. Wolrab. Mrs. Oxford passed away in death March 16, 1926. Three sons were born to their marriage, Grover C., born in 1888, and Paul, born in 1890, both of whom died in 1919; and Owen Scott Oxford, born in 1892. Grover C. Oxford left one son, Charles Grover Oxford, who resides at Murphysboro, Illinois. Paul Oxford died leaving a daughter, Hilda J., who also resides at Murphysboro.

GEORGE H. WILDEMAN, executive head of the firm of George H. Wildeman & Company, investment bonds, and president of the Greater Chicago Community Association, is accepted by a wide circle of clients as a skillful financier and an authority on conservative investments.

Born at Madison, Wisconsin, in 1892, George H. Wildeman remained in the city of his nativity until 1917, when he came to Chicago. He is a son of J. Wildeman and Barbara (Deneau) Wildeman, natives of Germany and France, respectively. Mrs. Wildeman's maternal grandfather Thierry belonged to the old and honorable French family for which Chateau Thierry was named, and, a man of great wealth, he helped to finance the Napoleanic regime.

Educated in part by his mother, a teacher and a highly-cultured woman, George H. Wildeman also attended the public schools and the University of Wisconsin, and was graduated from the latter institution in 1914. His initial experience in business finance was secured in connection with the commercial life of Madison, and since he has been located at Chicago he has devoted himself to finance and investments, on which subjects he has become an expert. His present bond house was founded by him soon after his arrival in the city.

In July, 1925, Mr. Wildeman was honored by election to the presidency of the newly-organized Greater Chicago Community Association, numbering among its founders many of the most substantial citizens of the city interested in its welfare. The principal object of this organization is to coordinate the work and activities of the large number of community civic associations throughout Chicago, each one of which hitherto has worked for its own neighborhood community. This association proposes bringing these different organizations together in such a way as to make their activities result in great good for the city as a whole. Mr. Wildeman is a young man of broad vision, and understanding mind, and a forceful personality that is productive of effective work. He not only can accomplish much himself, but is also able to inspire others with the spirit of his own enthusiasm, and remarkable changes are expected from the association of which he is the capable head.

AUSBY L. LOWE, a native of Crawford County, has been closely associated with the official and legal activities at Robinson for nearly half a century, attaining the qualifications of a lawyer in 1888, and has enjoyed unusual success and prominence in his work.

He was born at Hutsonville, Crawford County, November 18, 1857. His grandfather, William Lowe, was born in Virginia and was an early settler in Southern Illinois. Isaac N. Lowe, father of Ausby L., was born in Lawrence County, Illinois, and spent most of his life as a merchant at Hutsonville. He died May 6, 1882. Isaac N. Lowe married Amanda O. Hurst, who was born in Crawford County, daughter of John Randolph and Nancy O. (Barlow) Hurst, the former a native of North Carolina, where he was born August 7, 1811, and departed this life October 7, 1886, and was buried at Hutsonville. Nancy O. Barlow was born in Crawford County, May 5, 1818, her parents, John W. and Elizabeth (Gordon) Barlow, having come from Kentucky and settled just south of Hutsonville in territorial days. This good lady departed this life at Hutsonville July 23, 1900. The mother of Ausby L. Lowe died March 13, 1860, and he was reared in the home of his maternal grandparents.

After the common schools he entered Earlham College, a splendid Quaker institution at Richmond, Indiana, where he completed his literary education. On December 3, 1877, at the age of twenty, he became deputy clerk of the Circuit Court at Robinson. He filled that position seven years. On December 20, 1884, he entered the office of Callahan and Jones, distinguished attorneys, and under them prepared for the law. He was admitted to the bar in June, 1888, and was at once taken into partnership with his preceptors, when the firm became Callahan, Jones & Lowe. Mr. Lowe has maintained practically the same associations throughout his professional career. Since the death of Judge Callahan in 1918, the law firm has been Jones & Lowe, with offices on the east side of the square at Robinson.

Judge Lowe in June, 1893, was elected to fill an unexpired term as county judge, and in 1894 was defeated for this office, but was elected to the same office in 1898, and in 1902 he was elected his own successor. In 1915, by a margin of only two votes, he was deprived of the honor of being the democratic candidate for the office of Circuit Court judge.

In his successful professional career Judge Lowe has had the good fortune of association with very able legal minds. He has also owed much to two women, one his maternal grandmother and the other his good wife. He married, November 20, 1879, Miss Alice C. Hodge. Mrs. Lowe was born September 19, 1859, and died August 28, 1905. Judge Lowe has three sons and one daughter: Ausby Lyman Lowe, a physician and surgeon, and one of the two proprietors of the Robinson Hospital; Clarence H. Lowe, a dentist; Ethelbert Coke Lowe, a banker; and Florence, wife of Edward M. Pratt, and the mother of two children, and resides at New Rochelle, New York.

FREDERICK EDSON CLERK. School men and the public generally have long been accustomed to look upon the New Trier Township High School at Winnetka as one of the most distinctive educational units in Illinois. It is a large school, situated in a community of wealth and culture, but especially has developed standards and facilities with a personnel of instruction and a student body that have made it an object of admiration and study on the part of educators everywhere.

The present superintendent of this high school is Frederick Edson Clerk, widely known as an educator, lecturer and author, regarded as one of the most progressive leaders in secondary education in the country today. He was born at Newark, New Jersey, in 1880. He attended grammar and high schools in Newark, graduated in 1903 with the Bachelor of Philosophy degree from Yale University, and subsequently took his law degree from Lincoln-Jefferson College. He holds the Master of Arts degree from Northwestern University. On graduating from Yale in 1903 Mr. Clerk went to China as an attache of the Imperial Customs Department of the Chinese government at Pekin under the famous Sir Robert Hart, English statesman, diplomat and oriental authority. Following this interesting experience Mr. Clerk took up educational work, to which he has since devoted all his time. He was a teacher in Newark Academy, under the able educator Wilson Farrand. For two years he was head master of the Powder Point School at Duxbury, Massachusetts, next was a teacher in the high school at Brockton, Massachusetts, later he became principal of the high school and then superintendent of schools at Clinton, Massachusetts. While there he pursued postgraduate work in Clark University and the Harvard School of Education at Harvard University. For a time he was principal of the Arlington High School in Arlington, Massachusetts. From the East Mr. Clerk accepted a call to the far Northwest, and for a year was principal of the Lincoln High School at Seattle, Washington. This experience was followed by two years as assistant superintendent of schools at Cleveland, Ohio. During the World war he was a representative of the Federal Department of Justice.

From Cleveland Mr. Clerk went to Winchester, Virginia, on the request of the Board of Education and the Handley Foundation

Trustees of that historic city. He was intrusted with the responsibility of building a school system from the ground up, including not only the reorganization of the teaching staff and the curriculum, but the building and equipping of the physical property as well. Mr. Clerk spent four years at Winchester. He gave the city a model school system, one which is not only a source of pride to the people of Winchester, but is exercising a profound influence on educational standards throughout the famous Shenadoah Valley.

Mr. Clerk came to the superintendency of the New Trier Township High School in June, 1923. Here he has continued his work with the broader opportunities afforded by a great school in one of the richest communities surrounding Chicago. Mr. Clerk in the vacation periods has been a lecturer and teacher in various institutions of learning, including Harvard, the University of Virginia and the University of California. While at Winchester he organzed and was the first president of the Winchester Rotary Club, of which he is an honorary life member. He also became charter president of the Winnetka Rotary Club. He is a life member of the National Education Association, member of the Army and Navy Club of Washington, D. C., the University Club of Chicago, the Schoolmasters Club, the Colonnade Club of Charlottesville, Virginia, and is a member of the Officers Reserve Corps, United States Army, with the rank of major in the Military Intelligence Section. He belongs to the college fraternities Delta Kappa Epsilon and Phi Delta Kappa, and is a Knight Templar Mason. Mr. Clerk resides in the village of Winnetka. He married Miss Edith Louise Packard, of Springfield, Massachusetts, in 1907. They have two children, Edith and Frederick, Jr.

BION J. ARNOLD. If one were to make Colonel Arnold a direct inquiry as to the nature of his profession or business, it is certain that his equally direct and incisive reply would be: "Electrical engineer." But this modest statement falls far short of indicating the versatility and distinguished achievement of Colonel Arnold, who is consistently to be termed a scientist, an inventor and a veritable captain of industry, as well as an electrical engineer. A splendid co-ordination of constructive thought and research with direct and concrete translation into practical and productive action has significantly marked the career of this representative Chicago citizen who has attained to international fame in his chosen field of endeavor.

Bion Joseph Arnold was born in the village of Casnovia, Muskegon County, Michigan, on August 14, 1861, and is a son of Joseph and Geraldine (Reynolds) Arnold. Joseph Arnold later became a pioneer settler and representative member of the bar of Nebraska Territory, where he served as a member of the Territorial Legislature during 1865-66. The Arnold family was founded in Rhode Island prior to the opening of the eighteenth century and, at Smithfield, Rhode Island, the birth of Jeremiah Arnold occurred in the year 1700, and from him the line of descent to Col. Bion J. Arnold traces through his son Jeremiah (II), who married Elizabeth Knight; their son Ichabod having become the father of Jeremiah Arnold (III), who married Percy Rounds; one of the children of this union having been Joseph Arnold, father of him whose name initiates this review. Bion's maternal ancestor, Edward Rawson, was secretary of the Massachusetts Bay Colony for thirty-six years (1850-86); his maternal grandmother, Louisa Hale, was a member of the Hale family of Massachusetts. Edmund Rawson, grandson of Edward Rawson, and grandfather of Rhoda Rawson Taft, ex-President Taft's great-grandmother, and Susanna Rawson, grandmother of Constance Reynolds, grandmother of Geraldine Reynolds, mother of Bion J. Arnold, were brother and sister.

Bion J. Arnold gave in his boyhood days a distinct foreshadowing of his exceptional genius along mechanical lines. When he was six years of age he began to busy himself in making small boats, as well as sleds and models of farm implements. At the age of fifteen he made a small steam engine, in connection with which he devised and used the common piston valve, before he had seen it elsewhere and, in his seventeenth year, without previously having seen a vehicle of the kind, he constructed a bicycle, utilizing as his model a small advertising cut or illustration that had appeared in the *Youth's Companion*. In the construction of this machine he used the suspension type of wheel that is now common in bicycle construction, and originated it so far as he was concerned, but later learned that it had been previously invented. A year later, while a student at the University of Nebraska, he produced, at his home in Ashland and at Lincoln, a complete locomotive (one-sixteenth full size), operated by steam, and this miniature engine, which now stands in his Chicago office, attracted much attention at the time and has since been much in demand for exhibition purposes.

In the period of 1870-79, young Arnold was a student in the public schools at Ashland, Nebraska; in 1879-80 he attended the University of Nebraska; and in 1884 he was graduated from Hillsdale College, at Hillsdale, Michigan, with the degree of Bachelor of Science. In 1888-89 he took a post-graduate course in electrical engineering at Cornell University, Ithaca, New York. In 1887 he received from Hillsdale College the supplemental degree of Master of Science and, in 1889, this institution conferred upon him the degree of Master of Philosophy; besides which, in 1903, his alma mater gave a further evidence of appreciation by awarding him an honorary diploma for "distinguished achievement in invention and engineering." From the University of Nebraska he received in 1897 the degree of Electrical Engineer and, in 1911, the honorary degree of Doctor of Engineering. In 1907 Armour Institute, Chicago, awarded him the honorary degree of Doctor of Science. In recognition of his achievements in the domain of science and invention Mr. Arnold has received also medals from the Franklin Institute, Philadelphia; the Trans-Mississippi

Exposition, Omaha; the Pan-American Exposition, Buffalo; and the Universal Exposition, St. Louis.

After his graduation from Hillside College in 1884, Mr. Arnold became general agent and expert for the Advance Thresher Company and the Upton Manufacturing Company. Thereafter he served, in turn, as draftsman for the Edward P. Allis Company, Milwaukee, Wisconsin; chief designer for the Iowa Iron Works, Dubuque, Iowa; and mechanical engineer for the Chicago, St. Paul and Kansas City Railroad (now the Chicago Great Western).

During the years immediately following his graduation Mr. Arnold directed his work and policies to the securing of a broad and firm foundation for future and more important activities. Thus he resigned three good-paying positions, all of which he could have retained, and went to work for less than half of his former pay in order to obtain experience in different lines of engineering. After about five years of such experience he became convinced that electric railroading, which was then in its infancy, offered him the best future in his chosen profession. He thus decided to adopt electrical engineering as a specialty, and it was to fortify himself for this work that he passed the winter of 1888-89 in post-graduate engineering study at Cornell University, where he received his first technical instruction through the specific medium of an educational institution. Upon leaving Cornell, in the spring of 1889, he entered the employ of the Thomson-Houston Electric Company, and was placed in charge of its office at St. Louis, Missouri. The following year he was appointed consulting engineer of this company, after it had been consolidated with the Edison General Company to form the General Electric Company. In this capacity he designed and built the Intramural Railroad at the World's Columbian Exposition, Chicago, this representing the first commercial installation of the third-rail system on a large scale and proving the forerunner of the present day elevated electric railroads.

In October, 1893, Mr. Arnold resigned his position with the General Electric Company to open offices in Chicago and engage independently in the work of his profession as a consulting engineer. In this capacity and as head of the Arnold Engineering Company (which company he organized in 1895, to look after the details of his work), he has designed and constructed many properties throughout the United States and other countries, and perfected many inventions and improvements that have added materially to his reputation.

Early impressed with the value of storage batteries in connection with electric plants, Mr. Arnold set himself to perfecting plans for their use. He conducted experiments, largely in a laboratory which he fitted up in the basement of his home, and finally invested his entire available resources in their production. This business, after a long and desperate struggle, so common to the storage battery business of that period, survived the panic of 1893. In 1895, through the sale of the company and its rights, he realized a comfortable fortune and, thus reinforced in a financial way, he was in a position to advance more effectually his own ideas relative to electric traction and other problems.

Mr. Arnold has made valuable contributions to the problem of compact and efficient power plants for large buildings, his plan being to use steam generating units in conjunction with storage batteries, and to operate all machinery, including the elevators, by electric motors. This plan has been widely adopted, and was first used by him while he was acting as consulting engineer for the Board of Trade of the City of Chicago in 1895.

One of his earliest successes in the electric railway field was the equipment (1897-98) of the Chicago & Milwaukee Electric Railroad (now the Chicago, North Shore & Milwaukee), using high tension alternating current for power transmission, in combination with rotary converter storage-battery substations, by means of which the first cost and expense of operation of electric railroads have been largely reduced. In connection with this work the opposition to his ideas, owing to the road's having changed ownership during construction, was so great that Mr. Arnold was forced to take the contract for the completion of the road, thereby assuming the financial risk, under a bonus and forfeiture agreement, for its successful operation—in order to demonstrate the feasibility of the plan which he had laid down as consulting engineer on the work. This plan proved a success, rapidly becoming standard, despite the opposition encountered upon the start, and has since been almost universally followed in the construction of electric roads, the highest type of its development being represented in the equipment of the electric zone of the New York Central and Illinois Central Railroad companies, hereinafter described.

In 1901 Mr. Arnold was commissioned by the New York Central to study and report upon the feasibility of electrically operating its trains in and out of New York City, and he was a member of the Electric Traction Commission which carried out the work recommended by him, and involving the equipment of somewhat over 300 miles of track, which improvement, with the terminal thus created, required an expenditure of more than $65,000,000. By this system all passenger trains on the road within thirty miles of New York are propelled by electricity.

As further evidence of Mr. Arnold's pioneer spirit may be cited the fact that from 1900 to 1905, at his own expense, he carried on exhaustive experiments in Lansing, Michigan, in connection with the installation of the Lansing, St. Johns & St. Louis Railway, and demonstrated the practicability of operating electric trains with alternating current motors from a high potential, single phase alternating current. The use of single phase alternating current for the propulsion of trains has since been developed by different manufacturing companies, and is best exemplified in the conversion from steam to electrical operation of the St. Clair tunnel of the Grand Trunk Railway between Port Huron, Michigan, and Sarnia, Ontario, where Mr. Arnold (1907) as consulting engineer devised and installed the first single-phase high tension system for heavy electric railway work, using the Westinghouse system, a later development; and in the use of the same system by the New York, New Haven & Hartford and the Pennsylvania and the Virginia Railroad companies. He was also a member of the Electric Traction Commission for the Erie Railroad (1906-7). His more recent work along this line has been in his connection, as a member, with the Electrification Commission of the Illinois Central Railroad Company, which commission was formed in 1920 to consider and report, with recommendations, upon methods and processes advisable and necessary on the part of the railroad company in carrying out the obligations it had assumed in its acceptance of an ordinance, passed by the City Council of Chicago, July 21, 1919, for the electrification of the Chicago terminals. The commission's report was accepted by the railroad company September 20, 1922 and the system was formally placed in operation on August 7, 1926.

In the spring of 1923 Colonel Arnold was selected by President Truesdale, of the Delaware, Lackawanna & Western Railroad Company, to act as one of a committee of three prominent engineers to study and report upon the feasibility of electrically equipping the Scranton division of that system. This work involved the inspection of virtually all of the electrified steam lines in the United States, and also the analysis of a vast amount of data. To Colonel Arnold was assigned the work of preparing a special report on all matters pertaining to maintenance expenses and the relative merits of the different electrical systems, and the report which he thus presented is probably the most complete of its kind ever compiled up to the present time.

In 1902 Mr. Arnold was engaged by the City of Chicago to make an exhaustive study and report upon the entire traction system within its limits. The result was a report so complete and conclusive that his recommendations were in a large part adopted in the settlement between the city and the several traction companies, a settlement effected by the passage of the 1907 ordinances. These ordinances, which were submitted to popular vote on the part of the citizens of Chicago, named Mr. Arnold as chief engineer of the work and as chairman of the Board of Supervising Engineers, Chicago Traction, which board was created to see that the terms of the ordinances were carried out. Under the supervision of this board the companies have thus far expended about $110,000,000 in reconstructing and extending a system whose present value (1926) is in excess of $165,000,-000. The Colonel still retains his place as chairman of the board, with the respect of all sides, after nineteen years of service in a very difficult position.

In 1910 the Local Transportation Committee of the Chicago City Council commissioned Mr. Arnold to make a study of and prepare plans for a subway system for Chicago and in January, 1911, he presented complete plans for a most comprehensive subway system. In January, 1916, the Chicago City Council appointed him a member of the Chicago Traction and Subway Commission, which was formed to value and co-ordinate all of the present surface street and elevated railways of the city with a subway system, and to formulate a method of constructing, operating and financing such a system. The report was presented about the close of the same year. Largely due to political reasons, Chicago is still without semblance of a subway system. Mr. Arnold has acted also as chairman of the various valuation commissions that have valued all of the street railway properties of Chicago in the period of 1906-16. In 1913 he was chosen by the Citizens Terminal Plan Committee of Chicago to revise plans submitted by the Pennsylvania Railroad Company and others for terminals, and to recommend a comprehensive system of railroad terminals for Chicago. His complete report was produced and delivered in less than ninety days. In order to coordinate the work of the Citizens Terminal Plan Committee the Chicago Plan Commission and that of the City Council, in connection with steam railroad matters, the Chicago Railway Terminal Commission was created by authority of the City Council, and Mr. Arnold was appointed a member of the commission. With this commission he spent a part of the summer of 1914 in a study of railway terminals and harbors of Great Britain and the European continent, the survey being greatly shortened by the outbreak of the World war. He continued his services for seven years on this commission.

In 1908 Mr. Arnold was retained as consulting engineer for the Public Service Commission, First District, State of New York, to solve certain problems connected with the operation of the Interborough Rapid Transit Company's Subway System and the planning of the new subway systems of the City of New York. In this capacity he issued a series of very valuable reports. Many of his ideas were adopted and applied to the Interborough Rapid Transit System, thereby largely increasing its capacity, and also in the design of the new subways later constructed. He acted also as director of appraisals for that commission in the valuation of the surface line properties of the City of New York, and those of the Brooklyn Elevated Railway System.

Acting as consulting engineer, Mr. Arnold made exhaustive studies of and reports upon traction matters for the cities of Pittsburgh, 1910; Providence, Los Angeles and San Francisco, 1911; and Toronto and Cincinnati, 1912. In 1911 he was selected by the Public Service Commission, Second District, State of New York, to appraise for the company the properties of the International Traction Company at Buffalo, and afterwards he prepared for the commission data in connection with the reorganization of the company. He appraised also the properties of the Seattle Electric Company, Puget Sound Electric Railway Company, the Southern California Edison Company (Los Angeles), Metropolitan Street Railway System (Kansas City), and the Toronto Street Railway, in 1913, as well as many other properties. He has also been engaged by municipalities or by civic and commercial bodies to advise regarding steam and electric railway terminal and other matters in the cities of Des Moines, Omaha, Winnipeg, Sacramento, New Orleans, Detroit, Harrisburg, Rochester, Syracuse, and Flint (Michigan). Early in 1916 he was retained by the Public Service Commission, Commonwealth of Massachusetts, to review certain valuations and operating costs of the electric lines surrounding Boston. The report made by him, pointing out economies (aggregating $750,000) which could be effected, led to his being retained also by the Bay State Railway Company, at the request of the commission, to assist the company in producing the economies thus suggested. He has appraised the properties of the Chicago Telephone Company, the Lincoln Telephone & Telegraph Company, and the Mountain States Telephone & Telegraph Company (Denver), as well as the properties of the Brooklyn Rapid Transit Company, besides which he has acted on important engineering matters for the Hydro-Electric Power Commission of Ontario, Canada, and for many others too numerous to detail here.

Of late Colonel Arnold has devoted much time to an electric railway extending between Elgin and Belvidere, Illinois, a distance of about forty miles, and forming the connecting link between two other large electric railway systems for through traffic between Rockford and Chicago. As he owns this railway, he uses it as a sort of laboratory, and it was upon this road that the recently perfected automatic substation was developed and first utilized; the first concrete bridge built without false-work; and the one-man car, now so rapidly being adopted, was given one of its first practical tests, about seventeen years ago.

Colonel Arnold has written many valuable reports on engineering problems for virtually all the large cities of the United States and the Dominion of Canada. His "Report on the Chicago Transportation Problem," published in 1902, as well as his "Report on the Rearrangement and Development of the Steam Railroad Terminals of the City of Chicago," presented in 1913, have become authoritative text-books on electric traction and steam railroad transportation matters. He is the inventor of traction engine devices; method of connecting electric motors to electric railway trucks; magnetic clutches; electro-pneumatic and fluid variable speed gears; power station systems and single-phase alternating current railway system; was the first to recognize the advantage of and to put into practical use the recently developed automatically controlled substation for electric railroads.

In his home city of Chicago Colonel Arnold has membership in the following named organizations: The Chicago Club, the Union League Club, the Industrial Club (charter member), the Mid-Day Club, the City Club (charter member), Chicago Engineers, Electric Club, Press Club (life member), Army and Navy, The Aero Club of Illinois (president in 1913); South Shore Country Club (charter member; director 1912-15). His affiliations with patriotic, technical and civic organizations of varied order are here briefly designated: Naval Consulting Board of the United States; Military Order of the World War; American Legion of Illinois, in the organization of which he was especially active and in which he served as delegate to its first convention, district chairman and chairman of the finance committee, treasurer of organization committee, etc.; Army and Navy Association (Air), Washington, D. C., American Defense Society; Chicago Council, United States Junior Naval Reserve; National Bureau for the Advancement of Patriotism; Chicago Historical Society; Air Board of Chicago (of which he is president) besides being a member of the advance committee on organization of the National Aeronautic Association of the United States; American Institute of Electrical Engineers (president 1903-04); American Society of Civil Engineers; American Society of Mechanical Engineers; American Institute of Consulting Engineers; Western Society of Engineers (president 1906-07); Society of Automotive Engineers; New York Electrical Society; American Association for the Advancement of Science (vice-president 1916); American Society for Promotion of Engineering Education; honorary member Federated Service Council of Chicago; Michigan Society of Chicago; Hillsdale College Chicago Alumni, of which he is a past president, as he is also of the Chicago-Cornell Association and the University of Nebraska Alumni Association; member of Board of Trustees, Hillsdale College, Michigan, and Lewis Institute, Chicago; life member of the Chicago Art Institute. He is a member of the Delta Tau Delta and the Sigma Tau College fraternities, and an honorary member of the Tau Beta Pi fraternity.

It is possible here to give only the briefest of summaries of the really distinguished military and governmental connections of Colonel Arnold, but incidentally will be shadowed forth his admirable service of patriotism in connection with the World war.

Without formal marks of quotation is here incorporated a digest drawn from an article prepared by the United States army historian in September, 1919, slight changes being made in this reproduction:

In 1915 Col. Bion J. Arnold represented the American Institute of Electrical Engineers on a committee consisting of representatives of the four other main national engineering societies selected to confer with the military authorities at Washington, with a view to making the service of civilian engineers available in time of war. This committee's work resulted in the formulation of the Engineers' Reserve Corps Bill which, before it was finally passed, grew into the Officers' Reserve Corps Act. In recognition of his services in this connection President Wilson commissioned him major in the Engineer Officers Reserve Corps, January 23, 1917, his being the fifth commission issued under this act. He did not, however, enter active service until late in 1917, on account of his civilian duties and his services as a member of the Naval Consulting Board of the United States, to which he had been appointed by Secretary of the Navy Daniels, September 19, 1916, and of whose committee on transportation he was chairman until December 14, 1917, when he was commissioned a lieutenant colonel, Signal Corps (Aviation Section) Regular Army, and entered active service. He entered this service with the understanding that it was for overseas duty, and his order stipulated that he should be ready to go across within ten days, but the aircraft situation was acute, and he was assigned to the Equipment Division, to get acquainted with conditions. His previous experience in civil work and his work on the Naval Consulting Board made his services much in demand, and resulted in his being kept in this country and being called upon to act in an advisory capacity in connection with both the army and navy throughout his entire army service. In March, 1918, at the request of the Navy Department, he was detailed to work with Rear Admiral David W. Taylor, chief of construction in the United States Navy, on engineering work in connection with aircraft production for the navy. During this time he made extensive surveys of plants and personnel working on navy production and subsequently made a similar survey for the army. Being anxious to get across to the stage of conflict, he arranged, after the work was finished, to go overseas as lieutenant colonel with the Thirty-seventh Engineers, then being organized at Fort Meyer, but upon meeting the assistant secretary of war, that official stated that he had more important work for him to do on this side; work that, in his opinion, would be of greater value to his country. Thus again Colonel Arnold lost his chance to go into active service overseas. He was immediately assigned to work with the Snowden-Marshall Investigating Committee, which had just been appointed by President Wilson to go thoroughly into the aircraft production situation. He assisted in the selection of members of a technical committee, consisting of works managers of five leading manufacturers of the country; this committee was to obtain the exact situation at each aeroplane factory and to give the commission expert judgment as to future production. Colonel Arnold conducted the technical committee around the country, placed at its disposal his previously acquired knowledge of plant conditions, and brought it back to Washington, thus having made three complete surveys of conditions pertaining to aircraft production. Early in 1918 it became evident that there might be a shortage of aluminum for war purposes. At the request of the assistant secretary of war, Colonel Arnold made a thorough study of the aluminum situation and on July 31, 1918, submitted a report on the subject of aluminum and aluminum castings—a report that virtually became a Bible for the war department and aluminum producers, insofar as production and use of aluminum was concerned during the war period. So complete was this report that it will stand as a guide to the government in any future emergency. Colonel Arnold was then, upon the request of the secretary of the navy, temporarily detailed by the secretary of war to assist Maj.-Gen. William L. Kenly, director of military aeronautics, on important development work. For five months prior to the signing of the armistice he had complete control over the development, testing and arrangements for the production of Aerial Torpedoes, camouflaged for the purpose of secrecy, in war parlance, as "Automatic Carriers" and also sometimes referred to as Flying Bombs. This device originated with the Naval Consulting Board and after the navy type reached a certain stage of development the army, at the suggestion of General Squier, undertook the development of a type for its special use. Colonel Arnold assisted in coordinating the aerial torpedo work of the army and navy, and supervised the development of the Dayton type, the most successful torpedo for army service. January 31, 1919, he made a comprehensive report to the secretary of war on this subject, through the director of military aeronautics. The development work, of course, was all conducted very secretly, but the device had practically reached the stage of quantity production at the time of the signing of the armistice, and would probably have been in use, with all its powerful destructive force, by the thousands, on the western front, had the war lasted a few months longer. During this period Colonel Arnold made numerous trips in the air, aggregating something over 2,000 miles, using airplanes and seaplanes, as the occasion required, and seeking suitable sites for the testing of the torpedo. He flew a part of the distance from San Diego, California, to Palm Beach, Florida; thence to Key West and back to Miami, crossing the arid regions near the Pacific coast and the Everglades of Florida. After the completion of this report and the signing of the armistice Colonel Arnold was anxious to get back to civilian life and his professional duties, but was prevailed upon by the director of military aeronautics to make a survey of and report on the advisability of completing and retaining or abandoning Langley Field, Virginia, upon which the government had already spent some $7,000,000. The question was whether to abandon this investment or spend several millions more in completing the field and retain it as headquarters for the scientific development of the aeronautical department of the army. His recommendations were to retain the field and utilize the temporary buildings so far as possible, and gradually replace them with better structures, thus extending the future expenditures over a long period of years, and the policy thus outlined has since prevailed.

As he had already remained in service more than two months after the signing of the armistice, and as his business needed his personal attention, he again sought a release. On February 6, 1919, with a recommendation from his commanding general for a full colonelcy in the Reserve Corps, as soon as the laws were so modified as to permit this rank, he obtained his honorable discharge from the United States Army. He was commissioned major, aviation section, Officers' Reserve Corps, March 28, 1919, this being the highest rank that could then be given under the law. On September 13, 1919, after the law had been modified, he was raised to the rank of colonel, Air Service, Reserve Corps, and on August 14, 1926, having reached the age of retirement, he was commissioned a colonel in the Auxiliary Reserve of the United States Army.

The personality of Colonel Arnold rides with a stiff rein on the steed of action, and it needs

not to be said that each successive year of his life in counting in large and worthy achievements of things worth while.

January 14, 1886, recorded his marriage to Miss Carrie Estelle Berry, of Reading, Michigan. She died in Colorado Springs, February 1, 1907, and was survived by two sons, Stanley Berry and Robert Melville Arnold, and a daughter, Maude Lucille (later Mrs. Hartley Leroy Moss). Mrs. Moss, as the result of an accident, passed away on June 16, 1920, at Camp Grant, Illinois, where Captain Moss, her husband, was stationed. On December 22, 1909, Colonel Arnold married Mrs. Margaret Latimer Fonda, of New York City, and she is the popular chatelaine of their Chicago home.

GILBERT A. BARNES, M. D. V. One of the solid citizens of Mason County, who stands high in public confidence both as a farmer and as a veterinarian, is Dr. Gilbert A. Barnes of Topeka. He was born in Forest City Township, March 16, 1877, a son of John B. Barnes, the latter of whom was born at Greenfield, New Hampshire, in 1846. His parents left New Hampshire when he was five years old, and, traveling by way of the Erie Canal and the Great Lakes, reached Chicago. From what was then but a little village on Lake Michigan they came on the Illinois River and Hennepin Canal to Alton. The remainder of their trip was overland by team and wagon to Bunker Hill, Illinois. There the grandfather of Doctor Barnes passed away, and he was buried in the little Bunker Hill Cemetery. He was a typical Yankee and came of good, old New England stock, dating back to Colonial days. His wife was a member of the fine old family of Evans, and the following children were born to their marriage: Sarah, who married into the Blood family; Lydia, who married into the Chamberlain family; Rebecca, who married into the Hovey family; and Nathan, George, Reuben, Asaph, Almon, Joseph and John, of whom Asaph, Almon and Joseph were Union soldiers during the war between the states. They all survived and were honorably discharged from the service at the close of the war. John Barnes was also in the South during the war, and on account of his youth was not accepted for service, but was made a postal clerk, so that he saw a good deal of actual warfare, was at Savannah, Georgia, when General Sherman's army captured the city, and left it with the victorious troops, going north to New Berne, North Carolina, where he was honorably discharged and returned home.

John B. Barnes was reared at Bunker Hill, Illinois, and following the close of the war settled in Forest City Township, where he worked as a farm hand for a few years. When he married he established his home near the farm where he finally settled and later died. Absorbed in farming and stock feeding, he made a record in the latter. He was one of the promoters of the Garden Special Drainage District, was one of its first commissioners, and continued to hold that office for thirty years. For a long period he was a school director of the Brown school, and he long served as a trustee of the Union Christian and Baptist Churches of Pleasant Plains, and later served in the same capacity in connection with the Trinity Evangelical Church. During his younger years he was a republican, but later on in life became more independent, supporting the man more than the party.

John B. Barnes married June 9, 1869, after the close of the war, in Whiteside County, Miss Mary Smith, a daughter of Francis and Marcia (Blair) Smith. Mrs. Barnes was born in Illinois, and as her father was a preacher of the Wesleyan faith, his duties kept him moving about in various parts of Illinois and Iowa, and she secured her education as she could. Mr. Barnes died March 23, 1922, but Mrs. Barnes survives him, and still lives on the homestead. The following children were born to them: Ida M., who is the wife of James B. Whitaker, of Forest City Township; Harry W., deceased; Dr. Gilbert A., who was the third in order of birth; Alta R., who is the widow of Harmon D. Schierbeck and resides on the homestead, and has a son, Virgil. Mrs. Whitaker has four children: Floyd, Leslie, Mrs. Nelda Meeker and Mrs. Edith Meeker.

Growing up on the Barnes homestead, Doctor Barnes attended the local schools and the Gem City Business College, Quincy, Illinois, and when he was twenty-five years old he interrupted his farming activities to begin the study of medicine, entering in 1903 McKillip's Veterinary College, Chicago, from which he was graduated in 1906. Among his classmates in college was George McKillip, a son of the founder and president, who made a name for himself overseas in the World war, and several others who have turned their knowledge of their profession to use as meat inspectors at different packing plants.

After he had received his degree Doctor Barnes returned home and here entered upon a general practice of veterinary science. With the exception of several trips throughout the northwest, looking after some land investments, he has continued in the locality in which he was born, and has built up a wide professional connection, being accepted as one of the most skilled veterinary surgeons in this part of the state. During the cholera epidemics he has been particularly successful and the people here have come to depend upon him. He is living on the Barnes homestead which his father established, and this is regarded as one of the very valuable properties of Mason County.

On November 7, 1901, Doctor Barnes married, in Quiver Township, Mason County, Miss Hattie R. Schroen, a daughter of Justus and Catherine (Himmel) Schroen, the latter being a daughter of Adam Himmel, one of the Himmel brothers who founded this fine old family of German birth in Mason County. Justus Schroen was born in Niederula, Hesse Cassel, Germany, and came to the United States a youth of nineteen years, and he spent the remainder of his life in Mason County, where he was engaged in farming. When war broke out between the North and the South he served in the Union army, as a private of the Ninth Illinois Cavalry, was both wounded and captured, and confined in a Confederate prison at Cahaba, Alabama, until the close of the war. His wound was in his left leg, and was so severe that he was in a hospital at Florence, Alabama, for two weeks before he was taken to prison. Returning from the army he resumed farming and owned a valuable farm in Quinver Township, but he died at the home of his daughter, Mrs. Barnes, October 1, 1924, at the age of eighty-seven years. His wife died May 15, 1908. The following children were born to them: Sarah, who became the wife of John Grocenbach and resides near Washington, Illinois; Adam Schroen, who died near Washington, Illinois; Kate, who married Henry Kopp, and resides near Washington, Illinois; Lydia, who married William J. Heinhorst, of Pennsylvania Township, Mason County; Mrs. Barnes, who was born February 7, 1878; William E., who resides at Omaha, Nebraska; Fannie, who is the wife of Fred Worner, of Green Valley; Charles, who is a resident of Peoria, Illinois; and John W., who resides at Washington, Illinois.

Doctor and Mrs. Barnes have had five children born to them, namely: Mildred B., who is a graduate of the Forest City community high school, took normal-school work, and is now a teacher in the schools of Mason County; John J., who is attending the Brown grade schools; and Alfred S., LeRoy E. and Evelyn L., who are all in the Brown grade school.

During the World war Doctor Barnes was one of the men who devoted themselves to producing the heaviest possible crops of grain. He registered for service in the Veterinary Corps, submitted his questionnaire, and was expecting to be called, but the signing of the armistice made it unnecessary to further augment the army so he saw no service. Doctor and Mrs. Barnes are identified with the Union Church of their neighborhood, which is not confined to any one denomination, but is served by different ministers of varying faiths. He is superintendent of the Sunday school of Pleasant Plains, and in this capacity is accomplishing much along the lines of uplift work, in which he is greatly interested. He is also commissioner of the Garden Special Drainage District, having been chosen to that office soon after his father's death. He is now serving his fourth term as director of the Brown grade school board.

PETER FITZGERALD is a native of Alton, and his important distinction in that city has been gained through his service as chief of police. For a number of years he was connected with the glass industry, and has given a favorable account of himself in every public and private relationship.

He was born at Alton, August 8, 1870, son of Thomas and Mary (Shea) Fitzgerald, who were born in Ireland. Coming to America in 1840, they settled in Alton about 1852. They had a family of thirteen children, Peter being the ninth in age.

Reared and educated in Alton, where he attended the parochial schools, Peter Fitzgerald at the age of fifteen, in 1885, became an employe in the plant of the Illinois Glass Company. He was connected with the glass industry for over twenty years, being an expert glass blower. In 1911 he was appointed deputy sheriff of Madison County, serving until 1914, and from 1914 to 1916, was special agent for the Illinois Terminal Railway. He was first called to the executive head of the Alton police force on May 1, 1917, and served until May 1, 1921. During the next two years he was again associated with the Illinois Terminal Railway Company, and on May 1, 1923, Mayor Elble appointed him chief of police.

Chief Fitzgerald married, in 1895, Catherine Shelle, of Alton. They have seven children: Leo, who is in the coal business; Gertrude, with the Capital Life Insurance Company; Richard, of St. Louis; Florence, assistant to the city clerk of Alton; Virginia, with the Western Cartridge Company; Paul attending St. Vincent's College; and Kathaline. Chief Fitzgerald has been affiliated with the Knights of Columbus since 1901, is a democrat in politics, and he and his family are members of St. Patrick's Catholic Church.

REV. ALBERT HOMER JORDAN. Shelby County possesses in the person of Rev. Albert Homer Jordan, pastor-evangelist of the Christian Church at Shelbyville, one of the most human and wholesome of philosophers and most courageous and effective ethical teachers that the county has known. The extent of his insight and services, the encouragement to be found in his business success, the fragrance of his faith and the force and power of his public utterances in the maintenance of truth unite in the making of a career of more than ordinary scope, purpose and usefulness.

A. Homer Jordan was born April 28, 1883, at Point Pleasant, West Virginia, and is a son of John W. and Elizabeth Jordan. After attending the public schools of Huntington, in his native state, he pursued courses at Marshall College and the West Virginia State Normal School, and received the degrees of Bachelor of Arts and Master of Arts from Bethany College. Deciding upon a career in the ministry, he attended Oberlin Theological Seminary, and since then has held various pastorates in Ohio, Indiana, Kansas and Illinois, being at present pastor of the Christian Church at Shelbyville. His life has swept by with settings of increased prosperity and enlarging opportunities for usefulness, and his name is enrolled among those who are deepening and broadening the channels of human brotherhood. His civic services have been marked by the same public spiritedness which has characterized his other activities, and emphasize his nearness to the common needs of the people and his hearty sympathy with their ideals and aspirations. Doctor Jordan is a Knight Templar Mason, an Odd Fellow and a Pythian and an active member of the local Rotary Club.

At Pittsburgh, Pennsylvania, December 25, 1907, Doctor Jordan was united in marriage with Miss Elsie Gregg Watkins, and to this union there has been born one son: A. Homer, Jr.

JAMES WALLACE DUNNAN after his college career returned to Paxton and for over a quarter of a century has been known in that community as the influential editor and publisher of the Eastern Illinois Register.

He was born at Mt. Jackson, in Lawrence County, Pennsylvania, son of Hugh and Eliza Jennings (Wallace) Dunnan. His paternal grandparents were John and Ann (Smiley)

Hattie R. Barnes

Dunnan. John Dunnan came from Ireland and settled in Lawrence County, Pennsylvania. Ann Smiley was of Scotch-Irish ancestry. The maternal grandparents of Mr. Dunnan were James and Jane (Johnston) Wallace. The former was born in Mahoning County, Ohio, of Scotch-Irish parents, while the latter came from Belfast, Ireland, when only four years old. Hugh Dunnan was a Union soldier in the Civil war.

James Wallace Dunnan was reared from early childhood in Illinois, living with his parents on a farm in Dix Township, Ford County, until 1892, when the family moved to Paxton. He was graduated from the Paxton High School in 1896 and then entered Monmouth College at Monmouth, Illinois, where he took the degree Bachelor of Literature in 1899.

Mr. Dunnan since July 1, 1900, has been publisher of the Eastern Illinois Register at Paxton, and has kept that paper at a very high standard throughout all these years.

Some mention should be made of his interests and activities outside of his business and profession. While a student in Monmouth College he volunteered for service with a company organized at the college during the Spanish-American war. Beginning, in 1918, during the World war, and continuing until 1922, he was a first lieutenant in Company F of the Tenth Infantry, Illinois National Guard. Mr. Dunnan was an alderman of the city of Paxton from 1902 to 1904, and is now a director of the Paxton Carnegie Library. In politics he is an independent. He is a member of the Court of Honor, Modern Woodmen of America, Paxton Kiwanis Club, the United Presbyterian Church.

On July 16, 1903, at Paxton, he married Miss Mabel White, daughter of Mr. and Mrs. Weaver White, of Paxton. Her father for many years was circuit clerk of Ford County, Illinois. They have five children, Kathryn Jane, Martha Belle, Mabel Elizabeth, James Wallace, Jr., and Weaver White Dunnan.

CARL ROEDEL, a retired resident of Shawneetown, was admitted to the bar and began practice in the early '70s, and he continued the work of his profession for half a century. Roedel is a very honored name, and justly so, in Gallatin County.

Carl Roedel was born in Van Wert County, Ohio, September 30, 1842. His parents, Jacob and Barbara Roedel, were born, reared and educated in Germany. Barbara Roedel was a widow when she married Jacob Roedel. This marriage occurred after they came to the United States. She was the mother of Carrie, Carl, Mary and Edward Roedel.

Carl Roedel was a boy when his parents moved to Decatur, Adams County, Indiana, where he grew to manhood. His common school education was supplemented by a course in Vermilion Institute at Hayesville, Ohio. For three years he taught in the public schools of Indiana, for three years was principal of schools at Mount Carmel, Illinois, and in 1868 he became principal of schools at Shawneetown. Meanwhile, so far as his opportunities permitted, he had studied law. In order to have more time for this study he accepted the principalship of the schools at Grayville, Illinois, where the school term was shorter. He was there one year, and in 1871 was admitted to the bar. Mr. Roedel immediately engaged in practice at Shawneetown, and his abilities won him recognition so that for many years he was associated with many of the most important civil law cases in Gallatin County. In politics he became a republican, and for two terms he was mayor of Shawneetown. For over fifty years he has been a ruling elder in the Presbyterian Church, and for a quarter of a century was superintendent of the Sunday School.

Carl Roedel in 1868 married Sarah Frances Koser. They were married at Mount Carmel, Illinois, where she was born and reared. Her parents, William and Sarah Matilda (Goodyear) Koser, were natives of Pennsylvania and of German and French ancestry. The children born to their marriage were Mae, Rose, Sarah, Emma, Charles K., Lillie and Jacob K.

The active representative of the Roedel family at the Gallatin County bar today is Charles K. Roedel, who was born in Shawneetown, July 18, 1879. He graduated from high school, attended the Southern Illinois Institute at Albion, spent one year in Illinois College at Jacksonville, and studied law in the Illinois Wesleyan University at Bloomington. He was graduated LL. B. in 1904, and in July of the same year was admitted to the bar. Mr. Roedel then became a member of the law firm of Roedel & Roedel, practicing with his father at Shawneetown until the latter's retirement. In addition to his law practice he is vice president of the National Bank of Shawneetown. Mr. Charles Roedel has been city attorney, and a member of the City Board of Education. He is a republican, a thirty-second degree Scottish Rite Mason and a Presbyterian.

Charles K. Roedel married, December 31, 1910, Miss Laura Louise Peeples, daughter of William A. and Ada W. (Woods) Peeples. Her father, now a resident of Evansville, Indiana, was for many years a banker at Shawneetown. The third generation of the Roedel family in Shawneetown comprise Charles Koser Roedel, Jr., and John Peeples Roedel.

MRS. CLARA E. (BOHLS) HOLLY has been a contributor to the artistic and dramatic interests of the city of Peoria, having been by profession a teacher of dancing for a number of years and is proprietor of the Holly School of Dancing in that city.

She was born in Van Wert, Ohio. Her grandfather, Henry Bohls, was a native of Hanover, Germany, where he was reared and educated and served an apprenticeship at the carriage making trade. Coming to the United States, he lived for a time in New York City, then moved to Three Rivers, Michigan, where he established a carriage factory and continued its successful operation until his death. William Bohls, father of Mrs. Holly, was born in New York City, and learned his trade in his father's factory. Soon after his marriage he went to Van Wert, Ohio, where he established a carriage factory, but after a few years returned to Three Rivers, becoming associated with his father and after the latter's death moved to Indiana and established his home on the Indiana side of the state line but not far from the village of Hicksville, Ohio, where he subsequently bought and operated a carriage factory. He is now living retired. William Bohls married Miss Jennie Dean, who was born in New York City, daughter of Walker and Rebecca (Thornburg) Dean. Walker Dean was also a carriage manufacturer at Newville, Indiana. Miss Jennie Dean was a school teacher. William Bohls and wife reared eight children: Berdie, Clara E., Charles Roy, Pearl Edith, Harvey Clayton, Walter Highland, Calvin Ross and Karl Cecil. Mr. Bohls is a member of the Baptist Church and his wife is affiliated with the Christian denomination.

Mrs. Holly was educated in public schools and early manifested special gifts for music and dramatic art, and at the age of sixteen began regular instruction in dancing. At the age of twenty-one she became the wife of George Kinney Holly. They settled in Bloomington, Illinois, and in 1903 removed to Peoria. Subsequently they established the Holly School of Dancing.

Mrs. Holly's only daughter, Violette, learned to walk and dance at about the same time. After graduating from the Manual High School she continued her studies in dancing under Pavley and Owkransky and Muriel Abbot in Chicago, also under other masters of the art, and continued her training in New York City under the great Ivan Tarasoff. Violette Holly is a gifted and talented teacher of the advanced art of dancing at Holly School. This school has ample quarters, occupying quarters in the 100 block on South Adams Street, convenient to the entire shopping district of the city. The family are all members of the Episcopal Church.

HENRY C. SCHOTT during his active life time was closely identified with the community of Alton, a farmer by occupation, and he acquired and developed valuable property still owned by his family in that city.

He was born at St. Louis, Missouri, in May, 1861, and died at Alton March 25, 1903. After being educated in the common schools he took up farming, and made a success of that vocation. The present home occupied by his widow, Mrs. Schott, in Alton is on part of one of his farms, a forty acre tract, much of which has since been sold out in town lots. Henry C. Schott was brought to Alton when a small boy by his father, George Schott. Mr. Schott was a member of the Modern Woodmen of America.

He married at Alton, March 15, 1888, Emma Ducomum, who died leaving three children: Alice, Albert and Emma. On February 8, 1892, Mr. Schott married Emma Evans, who was born at Moro, Illinois, October 18, 1866, daughter of William and Mary (Phillips) Evans. Her father was born in Wales, March 12, 1824, and her mother, in Staffordshire, England, April 12, 1823. They came to Illinois many years ago and were substantial farmers in the vicinity of Moro, where they lived out their lives. Mrs. Schott is one of a large family of children.

Mrs. Schott became the mother of three sons, two of whom are now deceased. The living son, Henry C., was born September 22, 1900, and is a successful contractor, member of the firm of Schott Brothers. This firm laid out the Schott addition to Alton and has done much development work in that vicinity, having erected a group of six cottages on the property. The two deceased sons of Mr. Schott were: Augustus, born November 29, 1893, and died July 22, 1919; and Theodore, born November 10, 1901, and died November 25, 1901.

CHARLES F. GLORE. Prominent among the younger investment banking concerns of Chicago, one which has made rapid strides since its inception a few years ago and now has a large and prominent clientele is that of Marshall Field, Glore, Ward & Company. Much of the influence of this concern lies in the important connections of its members, among whom is Charles F. Glore, vice president, who is also interested in a number of other enterprises.

Mr. Glore was born at Eureka Springs, Arkansas, November 16, 1888, and is a son of Charles B. and Laura (McAdams) Glore. His father is now deceased, but his mother still survives. The only child of his parents, Charles F. Glore attended the public schools of his native community and was then sent to Lewis Institute, Chicago. This training was supplemented by a course at the University of Chicago, and therefrom he received his initiation into the banking business at Chicago with the firm of A. B. Leach & Company, bankers. In 1920 he became one of the organizers of the bond firm of Marshall Field, Glore, Ward & Company, at 120 West Adams Street, of which concern he has since been vice president. He has a wide acquaintance at Chicago, as well as at New York, where the firm also maintains an office, and has a reputation for foresight and shrewdness and a thorough knowledge of conditions pertaining to the marketing and handling of bonds and securities. Mr. Glore is also a director of the National Bank of the Republic, the Illinois Power and Light Corporation, the North American Power and Light Corporation, the Bucyrus Company and the American Multigraph Company. He is vice president of the United Charities of Chicago, having been chairman of the finance committee for three years, and has always taken an active interest in this worthy organization. He is also greatly interested in the Boy Scouts and is a member of the National Executive Board of the Boy Scouts of America. He is popular in club circles as a member of the Chicago Club, the Attic Club, University Club of Chicago, Saddle and Cycle Club, Racquet Club, Glenview Golf Club and Shore Acres. In political sentiments he is a republican. Mr. Glore saw active service abroad during the World war, serving as major of infantry attached to the general staff of the First American Army, A. E. F.

On April 11, 1914, Mr. Glore married Miss Ellen Hixon, who was born at LaCrosse, Wisconsin, a daughter of Frank Hixon, one of the prominent citizens of that community. To this union there have come three children: Frances H., Charles F., Jr., and Robert Hixon.

THE HENRY SCHOTT FAMILY AND HOMESTEAD ON MILTON ROAD, EAST ALTON

WILLIAM TELL HOLLENBECK. Five generations of the Hollenbeck family have been represented in the citizenship of Clark County, beginning in territorial times. Of this old family William Tell Hollenbeck has for thirty-five years been a practicing attorney at Marshall and has enjoyed high honors in the state at large.

He was born on a farm in Clark County, October 18, 1861. The Hollenbeck family is of Holland-Dutch ancestry and was established in New York in Colonial times. A native of New York was the Illinois pioneer, Lawrence Hollenbeck, who arrived within the borders of Illinois territory in 1815 and settled in Clark County, then practically a wilderness. He was the father of thirteen children. Lawrence Hollenbeck finally, about 1860, went to Texas, and acquired land, part of which is now within the limits of the City of Dallas. He died and was buried in Texas. His son, John Hollenbeck, married Isabell Houts. John Hollenbeck died a few years after his marriage, and his son, John Milton Hollenbeck, was reared in the home of his grandfather Lawrence. John Milton Hollenbeck was born in Clark County, and when the Civil war came on he enlisted in the Twenty-first Illinois Infantry, serving for a time as a Home Guard. He returned home after this service, but after the birth of his son William Tell Hollenbeck he reenlisted, this time in Company G of the Tenth Illinois Infantry, and was a gallant soldier of that regiment until the close of the war. He then resumed his life on a farm in Clark County and in later years became a merchant. He reached the ripe old age of eighty, passing away in 1918. John Milton Hollenbeck married Margaret Rebecca Neal, who was born in Clark County, daughter of Washington and Rebecca (Stephens) Neal, who came from Kentucky to Illinois about 1834. John Milton and Margaret Rebecca (Neal) Hollenbeck had seven children, four of whom are still living, namely: Elsie, who married George Holwick; William Tell, Charles G. and Washington. The mother died in 1876, and the father subsequently married Mrs. Susannah Winsett, who bore him a son, Homer, who is a resident of Missouri. For a third wife John Milton Hollenbeck married Sarah De Vee, and to that marriage five children were born, one that died in infancy and four living, namely: Effie, who married Otto Alabaugh, John Milton, Lawrence and Jenette. Thus John Milton Hollenbeck was the father of thirteen children, the same as his grandfather when he came to Illinois.

William Tell Hollenbeck was fifteen years old when his mother died. He spent his early life on a farm, attended a log cabin school house, and for several years of his early manhood alternated between teaching school and attending school as a student. His career has really been of his own making. During 1880-81 he was a student in the Southern Normal at Carbondale and he also attended the Indiana Normal School at Terre Haute and had a business college course in that city. Mr. Hollenbeck in 1889 expended some of the careful savings from his work as a teacher to take a trip abroad, in the course of which he visited the British Isles and traveled through Europe. After his return he diligently pursued the study of law, was graduated with the degree of LL. B. from the University of Michigan in 1892, and at once engaged in practice at Marshall. He was elected in 1894 and served one term as county judge. In 1906 he was elected a member of the Illinois Legislature and served with credit in the Forty-fifth, Forty-sixth, Forty-seventh and Forty-eighth General Assemblies, being a member of the Legislature from 1906 to 1914. Mr. Hollenbeck was elected in 1916 and served to 1918 as a member of the State Board of Equalization. He cooperated with Governor Lowden in getting the State Board of Equalization reorganized as the State Tax Commission, which in 1920 became a part of the State Finance Department. In 1920 he was elected a member of the Illinois Constitutional Convention, serving until 1922. Mr. Hollenbeck for over forty years has been one of the outstanding republicans in his section of the state.

During the World war he was advisor to the local examining boards and active in various campaigns, serving as chairman of the loan drives. His two sons, Neal and John, were both in training for soldiers. Mr. Hollenbeck is a Royal Arch Mason and a member of the Presbyterian Church.

He married, in 1898, Miss Louise Rackerby. Their three sons are Neal Augustus, John Milton and William Wayne.

GEORGE W. LACKEY in his career as an educator, lawyer and public spirited citizen has exemplified many of the sterling qualities of mind and character that are familiarly associated with Americans of pioneer stock. Mr. Lackey's ancestors were among the first settlers of Lawrence County, Illinois, and at least two of his forefathers fought for the independence of the colonies in the American Revolution.

His birth occurred on a farm in the northeastern part of Lawrence County, November 5, 1863. It was in the northeastern section of the county that the Lackey and Pinkstaff families settled in the early years of the last century and have remained numerously represented there ever since. Most of them have been farmers and in religion they have adhered to the Baptist faith. Mr. Lackey's maternal ancestors were the Seitzinger family, who at a later date came to Lawrence County from Pennsylvania. They likewise have been identified with agriculture, and their religious affiliation has been that of the United Brethren Church.

Adam Lackey, Sr., was a Virginian by birth. He was with the Virginia forces in the War of the Revolution. It was about 1810 or 1811 that he came west and settled in Lawrence County, and he is one of the Revolutionary soldiers buried in that county. Adam Lackey, Sr., was the father of John Lackey, who was born in Virginia and was about two years of age when the family settled in Lawrence County. John Lackey married Nancy Pinkstaff. Her father, John Pinkstaff, was a son of Andrew Pinkstaff, a native of Virginia and likewise a Revolutionary veteran. Andrew Pinkstaff on going west located in Kentucky, and from there came to Lawrence County, Illinois, where he died and is buried. John and Nancy (Pinkstaff) Lackey were the parents of James Lackey, who was born and reared in Lawrence County. He married Susanna Seitzinger, who was born near Harrisburg, Pennsylvania, and was about ten years of age when her father, Leonard Seitzinger, brought his family to Illinois and settled in Lawrence County. James and Susanna (Seitzinger) Lackey were the parents of three children. Susanna Lackey died in 1872, when about thirty-three years of age, and subsequently James Lackey married Eliza Highsmith. By his second marriage there were six children. James Lackey lived a quiet and respected life as a farmer and was an uncompromising democrat in politics. He died in 1914, at the age of seventy-five.

George W. Lackey was about nine years old when his mother died. As a boy on the farm he had the sturdy discipline of work in the fields, attended country schools a few months a year, and after a term of study in the Central Normal College at Danville, Indiana, he engaged in teaching. After that he followed the practice of teaching a term and then attending school, and in 1890 was graduated from the Central Normal College. While in college he took up the study of law. In 1890 he was elected county superintendent of schools of Lawrence County and served in that position four years. Meanwhile he continued his law studies under Judge Frank C. Messerve, of Lawrenceville, and in 1897 was admitted to the bar after examination before the Illinois Supreme Court. He at once engaged in practice at Lawrenceville, and from the first he has maintained a high standing at the bar. His law offices are in the First National Bank Building. He is a democrat in politics, and has had some unusual honors from his party. In 1900 he was nominated and was elected state's attorney, serving four years. In 1915 he was nominated for circuit judge. It was the first time a democrat from Lawrence County had been selected as the standard bearer of the party in the judicial or congressional district.

Having been a teacher in early life, Mr. Lackey has kept in close touch with educational affairs through his legal career. He was an earnest advocate of the township high school plan, and since the Lawrence Township High School was established in 1909 has served on its Board of Trustees a period of seventeen years. He has also been much interested in the work of the Christian Church, serving several years as superintendent of the Sunday School, and is still teaching a class. For more than thirty years he has been an active member of the Independent Order of Odd Fellows, and is also a Knight Templar and thirty-second degree Scottish Rite Mason and Shriner, member of the Knights of Pythias and Modern Woodmen of America.

Mr. Lackey on April 1, 1891, married Miss Theresa Whitenack. She was born in Hendricks County, Indiana, and is a graduate of the Central Normal College of Danville, Indiana, being a classmate of Mr. Lackey there. She taught school for several years. Mr. and Mrs. Lackey have given their children the best of educational opportunities. The daughter Ruth is a graduate of Transylvania University at Lexington, Kentucky. Miss Kate graduated from the University of Illinois. Miss Alice has had three years' work in the University of Illinois, and George A., the only son, is a member of the class of 1927 at the university.

PRINCE ALBERT PEARCE. One of the oldest and most prominent families of White County is that of Pearce. One of its talented members was the late Judge Prince Albert Pearce, able lawyer, and known all over this section of Illinois for his services on the bench. Two sons of Judge Pearce carry on the honored association of the family name with the profession of law in White County.

The pioneer of the family in Illinois was Hosea Pearce, who came from Tennessee and settled in White County in 1817. He was born in North Carolina, April 16, 1798, son of James and Betsey (Gomar) Pearce, the former a native of North Carolina and the latter of Maryland. The grandparents of Hosea Pearce were James and Jemima Pearce. Hosea Pearce was not only a very early settler but a founder and builder in White County. He was one of the founders of Herald's Prairie Church of the Old School Baptist denomination. This church erected the first religious edifice in White County, though it was only a log cabin. Hosea Pearce in 1830 was elected sheriff of the county, and filled that office six years. While sheriff he had the unpleasant duty of executing the death sentence pronounced by Judge Wilson on W. D. Ledbetter, the first of the two men ever hanged in White County. Hosea Pearce served as a colonel during the Black Hawk Indian War and with his regiment participated in the Battle of Bad Axe. The life of this splendid pioneer came to a close July 5, 1875. Hosea Pearce in 1818 married Nancy O'Neal, daughter of Hezekiah and Silvia (Moore) O'Neal, who also came from North Carolina.

Prince Albert Pearce, grandson of Hosea Pearce, the pioneer, was born on a farm in Herald's Prairie Township, November 22, 1850. His father, Russian B. Pearce, was born in White County, February 11, 1827. Prince Albert Pearce was reared on a farm, attended country schools, and continued his education in the Southern Illinois College at Enfield. He studied law in the office of Crebs & Conger at Carmi, was admitted to the bar in June, 1873, and at once engaged in practice at Carmi. His professional career covered nearly half a century. He always had a large private practice, and many times was chosen to positions of trust and responsibility. In 1876 he was elected state's attorney and was twice reelected, filling the office twelve years. In 1892 he was one of the four democratic presidential electors at large for the State of Illinois. In June, 1897, he was elected judge of the Second Judicial Circuit, and after his first term of six years was reelected in 1903. Judge Pearce was on the bench twelve years. His last public service was as a delegate to

the Illinois Constitutional Convention. He was the unanimous choice of both democrats and republicans of the Forty-eighth Senatorial District for that position. After retiring from the Circuit Bench he was not active in the practice of law, devoting most of his time to his farm and other business interests. Judge Pearce died October 29, 1922.

He married, September 25, 1873, Harriet Ellen Craw. She was born in White County and continues to reside at Carmi. They had three sons, Marcus A. dying at the age of two years. The surviving sons, both able lawyers at Carmi, are Roy E. and Joe A. Pearce.

Roy E. Pearce was born at Carmi, July 28, 1874. He was educated in public schools, in the Illinois Normal University, continued his education in DePauw University in Indiana, and in 1896 graduated in law at the Bloomington Law School. He was admitted to the bar in that year, and for three decades has been one of the leading representatives of his profession in the Second Judicial Circuit.

Roy E. Pearce married, in 1905, Annie Stewart Crebs, daughter of the late Col. John M. Crebs, of Carmi. They have one son, Stewart A. Pearce.

Joe A. Pearce in his professional career has emulated the honorable example of his father and in a measure has supplemented the splendid record set by Judge Pearce as a lawyer.

Joe A. Pearce was born at Carmi, September 8, 1881. After graduating from the Carmi High School in 1898 he entered the University of Illinois, taking a literary course, and studied law with the firm of Parker & Pearce at Carmi. After examination he was admitted to the bar in December, 1904, and since that year has been engaged in practice. In 1913 he was elected state's attorney to fill out the unexpired term of William L. Martin, deceased. In 1916 he was given the democratic nomination for reelection to that office, was elected, and in 1924, after an interval of one term, he was again chosen state's attorney. He has now filled that office almost as long as his father did before him. Reference has been made to the fact that his great-grandfather, Hosea Pearce, while sheriff of White County officiated in the first hanging in the county. As state's attorney, Joe A. Pearce handled the prosecutions and convictions of the second man who paid the death penalty for his crime. This was Frank Lowhone, who after his first conviction had the case appealed to a higher court, which ordered a retrial. On the second trial Mr. Pearce secured a second conviction, which was sustained upon appeal to the Supreme Court.

Joe A. Pearce is a thirty-second degree Scottish Rite Mason and Shriner, member of the B. P. O. Elks, the Loyal Order of Moose, belongs to the Missouri Athletic Association of St. Louis, is a past president of the Carmi Kiwanis Club, and a member of the Methodist Church.

By his first marriage he has one son, Kenneth Eldon Pearce, now associated with his father in the practice of law. Mr. Pearce's second wife was Mrs. Nellie (Boyer) Winner. By her first marriage she has a son, Roy P. Winner, now seventeen years of age.

HARVEY ELMER DUNCAN, a business man of Paxton and former mayor of that city, represents some of the pioneer families of southeastern Illinois, particularly Wabash County.

He was born in Wabash County, August 14, 1873, son of William and Mary Jane (Turner) Duncan. His grandfather Duncan came from Glasgow, Scotland, and was a weaver by trade. His grandfather Turner, whose ancestors were among the first settlers of New York, was a soldier in the Mexican war and afterwards settled in Wabash County, Illinois. He married Mary Smith, of old Virginia stock.

Mr. Duncan's father, William Duncan, was born at Shiloh, in Richland County, Illinois, July 8, 1849. His wife, Mary Jane Turner, was born in Wabash County, January 21, 1851. Harvey Elmer Duncan attended common schools in Edwards and Richland counties, and for many years has been in the restaurant and bakery business. He is a veteran of the Spanish-American war, having served during the years 1898-99. Mr. Duncan was elected mayor of Rantoul and served in 1913-14, and in 1925 was elected mayor of Paxton, and has given that city a most efficient administration of its municipal affairs. He is a democrat in politics and is affiliated with the Masonic fraternity, Independent Order of Odd Fellows and Modern Woodmen of America.

He married at West Salem, in Edwards County, Illinois, June 6, 1900, Elva Marx, daughter of John F. Marx. Of the five children born to their marriage two sons and one daughter are deceased. Miss Thelma A. is a student in the University of Illinois. Bernice J. was married in 1921 to Harry V. Leonard, and they have one child, Bonetta J. Leonard.

CHARLES N. SMITH has been an active citizen and business man of Madison, Illinois, since 1906. He is a native Illini, a prosperous merchant, banker and postmaster of Madison.

He was born at Hopedale, Illinois, November 26, 1867, son of Rev. Thomas A. and Miriam (Harlan) Smith. His grandfather, John Smith, was a native of Kentucky and an early settler in Illinois, entering lands from the government in Tazewell County. Rev. Thomas A. Smith, a native of Illinois, spent his active life in the Free Methodist ministry and died July 9, 1923, at the age of eighty-four. His wife, Miriam Harlan, was born at Dudleyville, in Bond County, Illinois, daughter of Captain William Harlan. Her father was a soldier and officer in the Civil war, was a native of Tennessee, and one of a number of Tennesseans who became pioneers in Bond County, Illinois. The Harlans were of Scotch ancestry.

Charles N. Smith is the only living child of his parents, there having been another son and a daughter. He was reared and educated at Hopedale, attending the common schools, and when sixteen years of age started to learn the trade of jeweler and watchmaker. After completing his apprenticeship as a watchmaker at Hopedale he removed to Kansas, locating at Moran, where he engaged in business for himself. At Moran on November 30, 1889, he married Miss Olive Cole, a native of Iowa.

After four years in Kansas Mr. Smith returned to Illinois, and was in business at

Tremont, and in February, 1906, removed to Madison, where he resumed his business career as a jeweler. He is also vice-president of the Tri-City State Bank.

Mr. Smith in 1912 was appointed postmaster by President Taft, serving the full four year term to a day. Then, on July 16, 1922, he was again appointed to this office. He served four years as a member of the Board of Education, and is a notary public. In politics he has been a faithful republican for many years, is a thirty-second degree Scottish Rite Mason and Shriner, and has filled all the chairs in the branches of Odd Fellowship up to Patriarch Militant. He belongs to a number of other social organizations and clubs. His hobby for years has been stamp collecting, and he has an unusually varied assortment and collection of stamps of American and foreign countries.

Mr. and Mrs. Smith have four children: Mrs. J. E. Neff, of Granite City; Mrs. J. E. Shone, of Madison; Mrs. J. A. Paterson, of Madison; and Marion Cole, who is attending the University of Illinois. The son has earned distinction as a Boy Scout and now has fifty-seven merit badges, more than any other boy in the state, and he was awarded second prize for making fire by friction at a contest held at Quincy, Illinois.

ORVILLE W. LYERLA since April, 1918, has been cashier of the Herrin State Savings Bank. This bank, located at Herrin, has capital and surplus of $85,000. The president is Mr. E. M. Stotlar, long prominently identified with business affairs in Williamson and adjoining counties.

Orville W. Lyerla prior to becoming actively identified with this bank was in the wholesale flour business at Herrin, and during 1912-15 had been principal of the city schools there. He is president of the organization composed of the building and loan associations of southern counties in Southern Illinois. He was also a member of the Herrin School Board and since 1923 has been township treasurer, and is vice chairman of the Herrin Library Board. In February, 1917, he married Miss Maybelle Jones, of Herrin.

JOHN GARVIN passed his entire life in Shelby County, Illinois, was a representative of one of the sterling families founded in this county in the pioneer days, and he became one of the substantial exponents of progressive farm industry in his native county, where he accumulated a large and valuable landed estate.

Mr. Garvin was born on the pioneer farm of his parents in Shelby County in the year 1849, the Garvin family having been founded in the United States many generations ago, and the original American representatives having come from Ireland. Mr. Garvin gained his education in the schools of Shelby County and in Avalon College at Avalon, Missouri, and Brown's Business College, Decatur, Illinois, and in the meanwhile had close fellowship with the work of the home farm, so that he was well fortified when he initiated his independent activities as an agriculturist and stock-grower. In 1872 was solemnized his marriage with Miss Adaline Green, who was born in Ohio, in 1846, and the young couple forthwith established their home on a farm ten miles north of Shelbyville, Mr. Garvin having made this place the stage of successful agricultural and live-stock enterprise and he and his wife having passed the remainder of their lives on this old homestead, both having been zealous members of the Christian, or Disciples, Church, active in the various departments of its work, especially that of the Sunday School. Mr. Garvin was a staunch advocate and supporter of the cause of the democratic party, and was influential in community affairs of public order in his township. The parents of his wife likewise became early settlers in Shelby County, whither they came from their old home in Ohio, and Mrs. Garvin was reared and educated in this county. Mr. and Mrs. Garvin became the parents of six children: Ida May, Charles B., James E., Jennie, Vivian and Ada.

Charles B. Garvin, eldest of the sons of the subject of this memoir, was born and reared on the old home farm and is indebted to the public schools of Shelby County for his early educational discipline. After severing his association with farm enterprise he was for twenty years a tobacco salesman, and since 1923 he has owned and successfully conducted the Garvin Cafe in the city of Shelbyville. The maiden name of his wife was Olka M. Mathews, and they have two sons, Charles B., Jr., and Edward D.

ROY CLIPPINGER, editor and manager of the Carmi Tribune-Times, grew up in the atmosphere of a printing office, and has known no other profession. He comes of a family of printers and newspaper men in southern Illinois.

Mr. Clippinger was born at Fairfield, Wayne County, Illinois, January 13, 1886, son of Anthony C. and Eliza B. (Donahey) Clippinger, and grandson of David Clippinger, a native of Pennsylvania, and of Samuel Donahey. Anthony C. Clippinger was born in Lawrence County, Illinois, and his wife, in Lawrence County, Indiana. After their marriage they lived a few years in Lawrence County, Illinois. Anthony Clippinger was a practical printer and for a time published the Sumner Press at Sumner. In 1893 he and E. M. Young established the Enfield Express, but selling his interests in this paper in 1895, he removel to Norris City, Illinois, where he lived until his death in 1919, at the age of sixty-one. At Norris City he was associated with Benjamin Miller in the establishment of the Norris City Record. Mrs. Anthony Clippinger still lives at Norris City. Their three sons, Ralph W., Roy and Cecil E., all learned the printer's trade under their father.

Roy Clippinger may be said to have started his practical apprenticeship as a printer when only ten years of age. He has been thoroughly experienced in every detail of printing and newspaper work. In the meantime he acquired a common school education. Mr. Clippinger became a resident of Carmi at the age of twenty-five. In 1909 he and Laurence M. Ross established the White County Tribune. In 1911 this was consolidated with the Carmi Times, and since that date Mr. Clippinger has

been editor and manager of the Carmi Tribune-Times, which is owned and published by the Carmi Tribune-Times Publishing Company. This is the only republican paper in White County and has the largest circulation of any paper published in Southern Illinois.

Mr. Clippinger is himself a republican, and has identified himself with a number of organizations for the promotion of the best interests of White County. He took the lead in bringing to Carmi the Carmi Manufacturing Company garment makers. He is secretary of the Commercial Association of Carmi, is vice president of the Kiwanis Club, is a steward and treasurer of the Methodist Church, and is a thirty-second degree Scottish Rite Mason and Shriner. Mr. Clippinger married, in 1911, Mary Land. By this marriage he has a son, John L. In 1917, Verna B. Essery became his wife. They have one son, Earl E.

GEORGE F. ILIFF. One of the most successful real estate operators of Chicago, who is also organizer and secretary of the South Central Association, George F. Iliff has always concentrated his best abilities and energies in those movements which his experience and trained knowledge have led him to believe are beneficial to the city and its institutions. His career has been one of consistent achievement, merited advancement and useful participation in civic affairs.

Mr. Iliff is a Chicagoan by birth, training and education. He was born in 1886, a son of John W. and Etta (Cram) Iliff, the former of whom is a business man of many years' standing at Chicago, while Mrs. Iliff is a daughter of George F. Cram, who for a half century has been head of the famous map-publishing concern of that name. The early education of George F. Iliff was acquired in the public schools of Chicago, and after graduation from high school he enrolled as a student at the Kent College of Law. While he graduated from that institution with the degree of Bachelor of Laws, with the class of 1913, and was admitted to the bar, he never practiced that profession, circumstances and his inclinations leading him into real estate, in which he has made a phenomenal success, now being one of the largest operators in the city. Prior to entering the real estate field Mr. Iliff had been identified for fourteen years with the State Bank of Chicago. At the present time Mr. Iliff is an official of the Bowes Realty Company, whose main offices are in the London Guarantee Building, while Mr. Iliff is in charge of the company's branch offices at 2446 South Park Avenue. He specializes in business property in the South Central District. In 1921 Mr. Iliff organized the South Central Association, of which he is secretary. This is an association of business men and property owners in the rich and very rapidly developing business section lying between Lake Michigan and the south branch of the Chicago River, and extending southward from Polk Street to Thirty-first Street. The president of this Association is Elmer Rich, in whose sketch, on another page of this work, a description of the association will be found. Mr. Iliff is not unknown to public life, having served in the Chicago City Council as alderman of the Third Ward for two years, from 1917 to 1919.

Mr. Iliff married Miss Ernestine Meehan, and they are the parents of one son: John W. The pleasant family home is situated at Wilmette.

THOMAS RUSSELL GOWENLOCK, who served with no minor distinction as an officer with the American Expeditionary Forces overseas in the great World war and who at the present time holds the rank of lieutenant colonel of infantry in the Officers Reserve Corps of the United States army, has proved alike his ability and resourcefulness in connection with the "victories that peace hath in store, no less renowned than war." In the city of Chicago he has achieved success and prestige as an advertising and selling counselor, his having been broad and varied experience in the advertising business, in which he is now vice president and general manager of Kling Gibson Company, one of the leading concerns in the advertising promotive field in the great western metropolis.

Colonel Gowenlock was born at Clay Center, Clay County, Kansas, February 14, 1887, but is a scion of a family that has a goodly measure of pioneer precedence in Illinois, his paternal grandfather having founded, at Mount Vernon, Jefferson County, this state, the car works from which has been developed the important industrial enterprise there conducted by the Mount Vernon Car Manufacturing Company of the present day.

Colonel Gowenlock is a son of Thomas and Emma Mabel (Allen) Gowenlock, whose marriage was solemnized in Jefferson County, Illinois, where the home of the bride was not far distant from Mount Vernon, and who eventually removed to Clay Center, Kansas. Colonel Gowenlock gained his early education by attending the public schools of his native town in the Sunflower State, including the high school, and thereafter he completed a course in the law department of the University of Kansas, in which he was duly graduated with the degree of Bachelor of Laws as a member of the class of 1909. The Colonel has maintained his home in Chicago since the year 1911.

When the nation became involved in the World war the subject of this review promptly volunteered for service in the United States army. In the Officers Training Camp at Fort Sheridan, near Chicago, he was duly graduated and was given the rank of captain of infantry. He was assigned to the Eighty-ninth Division at Camp Funston, Kansas, and there given command of Company K, Three Hundred and Fifty-third Infantry. Later he became assistant chief of staff of the Eighty-ninth Division, under General Leonard Wood. He accompanied his command to France, where he was transferred to and became assistant chief of staff G-2 of the First Division of the American Expeditionary Forces. After participating in the St. Mihiel drive he was promoted to the rank of major of infantry and made a general staff officer, he having later been advanced to the grade of lieutenant colonel of infantry and having eventually been made assistant chief of staff of the First Army Corps.

Colonel Gowenlock participated in the St. Mihiel, Argonne, Meuse and Sedan operations, and in operations in several defensive sectors, besides which, after the signing of the now historic armistice, he was with the allied Army of Occupation in Germany. He was wounded while at the front, and he received a number of citations, besides being given the following named decorations: Distinguished Service Medal, the Croix de Guerre, with Palm (France); and recommended for the Legion of Honor. Colonel Gowenlock had the further distinction of being the first American army officer with troops to cross the armistice line. He was one of the organizers of the American Legion both in France and the United States. As previously stated, he is now a lieutenant colonel of infantry in the Officers Reserve Corps of the United States Army, and he is vice-president and a director of the First Division Society of the United States, a trustee of the Illinois Veterans Trust, and a director of the Fort Sheridan Association. In addition to his affiliation with these organizations the Colonel is a member also of the Military Intelligence Association of the Sixth Army Corps, and of the advisory board of the Service Men's League of Illinois.

Colonel Gowenlock is a life member of the Chicago Art Institute and the Chicago Historical Society, and is vice-president and a trustee of the Chicago Public Health Institute. His exceptional promotive ability has been shown in his service as chairman of the organization committee of each the Lake Shore Athletic Club and the Illinois Woman's Athletic Club, both of Chicago. He has membership in the Racquet Club, of Chicago, the Chicago Athletic Association, the Chicago Golf Club, the Saddle and Cycle Club, the Lake Shore Athletic Club, and the Beta Theta Phi Club.

Prior to and since the close of the World war Colonel Gowenlock has been active and influential in the advancing of various civic and philanthropic enterprises, and it is to be recorded that he was specially active in the formulating and placing in service remedial measures for the aid of veterans of the World war. He had charge of one of the Salvation Army drives for funds, and in every way he is a worker in behalf of those things that make for civic betterment and human helpfulness.

Colonel Gowenlock was formerly associated with old Long-Critchfield Advertising Company and the Gundlach Advertising Company. Thereafter he was for ten years allied with H. W. Kastor & Sons Advertising Company, and Collins Kirk, Inc., since which time in his professional activities as an advertising and selling counselor and executive he has been associated with Kling Gibson Company, of which he is vice president and general manager.

Colonel Gowenlock married Miss Marjorie Gird of Pierre, South Dakota, and they are popular figures in representative social circles in their home city of Chicago.

JOHN WILLIAM BOWLING, M. D., is one of the older members of the medical profession in Gallatin County. His service in that profession covers a period of forty years. He began practice in the era before the general use and introduction of telephones, hard roads and automobiles.

Doctor Bowling was born near Catlettsburg, in eastern Kentucky, January 21, 1862. His parents, Jasper and Pauline (Crow) Bowling, were also natives of Kentucky, and in the fall of 1879 they came to Illinois and settled at Shawneetown. Jasper Bowling taught school a year in Gallatin County, then moved to Saline County, but after two years settled on a farm in Gallatin County.

Doctor Bowling spent most of his youth on a farm. His education in country schools was supplemented by terms at Ewing College and the Normal School at Carmi, Illinois. He taught for three terms, beginning at the age of nineteen. In the meantime he was privately pursuing the study of medicine and in 1887 he graduated from the Physicians and Surgeons College at Keokuk, Iowa. Doctor Bowling for fourteen years practiced his profession at Omaha in Gallatin County, and those were the strenuous years of his professional service, most of his practice being in a rural district. Since 1902 he has practiced at Shawneetown. For seven consecutive years he was honored with the office of president of the Gallatin County Medical Society. He is local surgeon for the Louisville & Nashville and the Baltimore & Ohio Railroads, and has held those offices for many years. During the World war he was chairman of the Registration Board, member of the local draft board of Gallatin County, and in many ways assisted in promoting the cause of the government. Since then he has been examiner for the Veterans' Bureau, and pension examiner for Civil war and other soldiers of the nation, holding this position since he came to Shawneetown. Doctor Bowling is a member of the Illinois State, American Medical, Ohio Valley, Southern Illinois and other medical organizations.

In politics he has been identified with the republican party. He is a Royal Arch Mason and a member of the Modern Woodmen of America. On April 30, 1885, he married Eliza Davis. They are the parents of three children: Albert Leslie, manager of the East St. Louis Journal; Emory Emmons, a merchant at Indianapolis; and Gail, widow of S. L. Miller, and a resident of Jacksonville, Illinois.

SEIBERT DAY WISE is one of the junior members of the Saline County bar, a highly qualified and educated young attorney, who also has a service record as a soldier of the World war.

His grandfather, Abram Wise, was born in Pennsylvania, of Pennsylvania-German ancestors. He was reared in Indiana, married in that state, and on coming to Illinois settled on a farm near Raleigh in Saline County. One of the landmarks of that community for many years was the Wise schoolhouse, which expressed his interest in educational affairs, and he was a leader in other community interests and a staunch Union man at the time of the Civil war. Abram Wise's children were Lewis F., Alice, George and Harrison D.

Lewis F. Wise has been a well known school teacher, farmer, stock raiser, dairyman and banker in Saline County. He was born in Washington County, Indiana, August 3, 1851, and was educated in public schools, in Ewing College and in a business college at Evansville, Indiana. While at Evansville he arranged to teach school at St. Phillips, Indiana. He taught three years, boarding with a German family named Seibert, and felt so kindly toward that family that he gave their name to his second son. Returning to Illinois, Lewis F. Wise married and settled on a farm near Raleigh. However, he continued teaching during winter terms. He engaged in stock raising and dairying, was one of the organizers of the First State Bank of Eldorado, served several years as its president and is still vice president. His has been a career exemplary and successful in the community, and a great many people have learned to respect his advice. It is a mark of genuine affection that the many people know him as "Uncle." Lewis F. Wise married Edith Jane Carnahan, a native of Saline County, where her father, Ellis Carnahan, was also born, and her grandfather, Thomas Carnahan, was a native of Ireland and a pioneer in Saline County. The Carnahans are of Primitive Baptist faith while the Wise family has long been identified with the Christian denomination. Mrs. Lewis F. Wise died at the age of fifty-two, the mother of two sons, John E., who died when nineteen years old, and Seibert Day.

Seibert Day Wise was born on a farm in Saline County, March 29, 1891. As a country boy he attended rural schools, graduated from the Eldorado High School, for one year attended the University of Illinois, and completed the three year law course at the University of Michigan in 1914. graduating LL. B. On returning home he engaged in practice at Harrisburg with W. C. Kane.

In January, 1918, he was appointed by Governor Lowden to fill an unexpired term as county judge of Saline County. He resigned this office in August, 1918, to enter the Central Officers Training School at Camp Gordon, Georgia, and on November 16, 1918, was commissioned second lieutenant of infantry. On account of the armistice he was discharged November 30, but retained the same rank in the Officers Reserve Corps. Mr. Wise in January, 1919, formed a law partnership with Charles D. Stilwell at Harrisburg. Mr. Stilwell died in October, 1923, and since then Mr. Wise has engaged in a successful individual practice.

He married, in 1922, Miss Virginia Eleanor Whitley, daughter of S. A. Whitley, of Eldorado.

PHILIP W. BARNES has a long record as a practicing attorney of Lawrence County, and was one of the first republicans elected to office in that county. In his profession he is widely known all over Southern Illinois.

Judge Barnes was born near Springfield, Ohio, July 17, 1858, and is descended, according to family tradition, from a Barnes who came from England and settled in Massachusetts. There were two brothers who came at the same time, one settling in New York and the other in Virginia. Judge Barnes' grandfather was Jonathan Barnes, who lived in New York and in Pennsylvania, dying in the latter state. Abram Barnes, father of Judge Barnes, was born in New York State, grew up near Erie, Pennsylvania, and was well educated. In company with Giles James and Whitelaw Reid he went to Ohio, all three stopping in the vicinity of Springfield, where they became school teachers. In that locality Abram Barnes met and married Amanda Woliston. They were married in 1856. She was born at Allentown, Pennsylvania, and was a small girl when her parents moved to Ohio. On account of failing health Abram Barnes left Ohio, and in 1863 located on a farm in Lawrence County, Illinois. There he lived out the rest of his life and also taught school for a time after coming to Illinois. He died December 17, 1904, at the age of seventy-three. His first wife died in 1875, leaving three children, Philip W., J. Judd and Otto H. Subsequently Abram Barnes married a second wife, but had no children by that union.

Philip W. Barnes was five years of age when the family moved to Lawrence County, and he grew up on the farm and shared in the routine work of a farm boy. After the country schools he attended high school at Olney, graduating there, and took his law course in the Illinois Wesleyan University at Bloomington. He was graduated LL. B. June 10, 1881, was admitted to the Illinois bar and at once located in Lawrenceville. Mr. Barnes began his professional career without money, but his abilities soon won favorable recognition and a growing clientele and many valuable interests and important cases have been intrusted to his care. For some years he was also interested in banking. In 1887 he and John W. McCleave organized a private bank known as the Lawrenceville Bank. They conducted it successfully ten years when it was succeeded by the First National Bank of Lawrenceville. Judge Barnes is a large owner of real estate in Lawrenceville and has in many ways identified himself with the progress of that community. He has never married. He is a member of the Independent Order of Odd Fellows and Knights of Pythias.

Judge Barnes soon after beginning law practice also undertook the task of organizing the republican party in Lawrence County. It had been normally democratic for many years, but under his energetic leadership a party spirit and organization were developed, and in 1882 he was nominated for county judge. He made his canvass from farm house to farm house mostly on foot, and he did his work so thoroughly that in the fall election he was chosen county judge and was subsequently reelected, serving in office for eight years. In 1900 he was elected one of the representatives of his district in the Legislature. Judge Barnes for over forty years has been one of the trusted leaders of his party in the county.

GEORGE M. LIVESAY, D. D. S. Although, as a rule, average Americans of the present day do not boast unduly of an ancient overseas ancestry that might once have been accounted royal, they have a high-reaching pride and loyal devotion to America and her ideals and institutions that make them cherish dearly an authoritative family claim that proves early colonial settlement. In the Livesay family, a prominent member of which is found in Dr. George M. Livesay, dental surgeon at Ashley, Illinois, this claim is a valid one, the Livesays being among the earliest English colonists of substantial character to settle in Virginia, and furthemore, three of the Livesays were Revolutionary soldiers under General Washington at Valley Forge. Doctor Livesay belongs to the Illinois branch of this family, established in this state by his great-grandfather.

George M. Livesay was born at Richfield, Illinois, December 9, 1887, youngest of a family of seven children born to William Jackson and Mary Ann (Patty) Livesay. William Jackson Livesay was a son of Thomas Livesay and both were lifelong residents of Illinois. The father died on his farm in Irvington Township, November 16, 1917. He was a man of sterling character, belonged to the Masonic fraternity, and was a member of the Methodist Episcopal Church. The mother of Doctor Livesay survives. She was born on the Isle of Man and accompanied her people to the United States in 1864. The brothers and sisters of Doctor Livesay are: Elizabeth, who is the wife of Joseph Randall, and they have three sons and four daughters; Flora, who is the wife of August Schmidt, and they have one son and two daughters; William T., who married Ida Goodman, and they have one child; Louis F., who married Dora Haun, and they have seven children; David Edward, who married Harriet Craig, and they have four children; and Ellen M., who resides with her mother.

George M. Livesay received his early educational training at the White District School in Irvington Township, after which he attended the Carbondale Normal School, and while there gave special attention to such branches of study as would best fit him for entering St. Louis University, St. Louis, Missouri, in which institution he became a student after one year at Carbondale, and was graduated from the University School of Dental Surgery in 1913, with his degree of D. D. S.

Doctor Livesay entered into the practice of his profession at Carbondale, where, among his other patients, he numbered the family of Prof. George W. Smith of the Normal School, and continued in active practice there until July 7, 1917, when he offered his services to the Government. They were accepted and he was commissioned lieutenant and sent to Camp Shelby, Mississippi, as chief dental surgeon, member of Dental Unit No. 1. Shortly afterward, through an accident, he broke his arm, which incapacitated him for some time, but after he left the hospital he remained at Camp Shelby until his honorable discharge on July 9, 1919. Shortly afterward he came to Ashley and has built up a substantial practice here, his skill being very generally recognized. While competent in every line of dental work, making use of the X-ray when necessary and other scientific modern inventions, he makes a specialty of plate work and has many well satisfied patrons.

Doctor Livesay married at Duquoin, Illinois, in June, 1921, Miss Jennie Marie Smith, daughter of William Henry and Frances Smith, the latter of whom passed away in 1917. The father of Mrs. Livesay is a physician in the State Health Department at Benton, Franklin County, Illinois. She is the third in a family of four daughters, her sisters being: Elizabeth, who is the wife of Adlai Munday, and they have four children; Elsie, who resides with her father; and Lola, who is the wife of Arthur Payton.

Doctor and Mrs. Livesay have two children, Francis Patty and Elizabeth Ann. Mrs. Livesay was reared in the faith of the Baptist Church, but the Livesays from far back have always been identified with the Methodist Episcopal Church. Doctor Livesay is a chapter Mason, and is a member of the County, State and National Dental Associations.

RAYMOND RYAN DENISON is editor and business manager of the Lawrenceville Publishing Company, publishers of the Daily Record and the Lawrenceville Republican, two papers, one a weekly and the other a daily, which are the chief medium of publicity in the county and carry the largest influence in politics and civic affairs.

Mr. Denison has been a successful newspaper man and prior to that was a capable educator, spending several years in his native county in school work. He represents some of the very oldest families of Lawrence County. He was born on a farm there April 29, 1885. His paternal ancestry in America begins with William Denison, who served as a patriot soldier in the Revolutionary war. After the war he moved to Kentucky, where he married, and in 1818 came with his family to Illinois, settling in Lawrence County. Denison Township of that county is named in his honor. He bought 160 acres of government land at $1.25 an acre, and developed a farm and lived there until his death. He is one of several Revolutionary war soldiers buried in Lawrence County. His religion was that of the Presbyterian Church and in politics he was aligned with the whig party. The children of William Denison were: Robert, Daniel, John, Alexander D., Madison, Elizabeth, Polly and Catherine.

Alexander D. Denison was born in Kentucky, August 16, 1807, and was about eleven years of age when brought to Illinois. He was reared in Lawrence County and the occupation of his mature years was farming in Lukin Township of the same county. He was a man of most substantial character, in business as well as in citizenship. He was a Presbyterian, and died at the age of sixty-three. Alexander D. Denison married Mary Ann Crane, who was born in Ohio, December 3, 1811, and was a small girl when her father, William Crane, settled in Wabash County, Illinois. The children of Alexander D. Denison and wife were: John, William D., Howard, Martha, Margaret, Sarah, Elizabeth, Catherine, Mary Ann and Alice.

William D. Denison, of the third generation of the family in Lawrence County, was born on a farm in Lukin Township, Lawrence County, March 20, 1850. He was educated in country schools, and on November 6, 1874, he married Miss Sallie Ryan, who was born

J. T. Wilson
Mrs. J. T. Wilson

and reared in Denison Township, Lawrence County. He has been recognized as a leader in agriculture and citizenship in his section of the county, has always been a staunch republican in politics, and he and his wife have been devout Methodists.

Mrs. Sallie (Ryan) Denison has an equally notable ancestry. Her grandfather was James Ryan, a native of old Virginia and of Irish ancestry. James Ryan married Sallie French, a native of Pennsylvania and of German stock. James Ryan on coming to Illinois in 1818 settled in Lawrence County. In his home the first Methodist Church was organized in the county. A son of James Ryan was Alexander B. Ryan, who was born at Wheeling in what is now West Virginia, November 15, 1815, and was only three years of age when brought to Illinois. He followed farming as his occupation, and was a republican in politics, both he and his wife being active Methodists, and both died when seventy-nine years of age. Alexander B. Ryan married, in 1843, Hannah Grant. She was born in England and was six years of age when her father, John Grant, brought his family to America, first locating at Philadelphia, and when she was twelve years of age settling in Richland County, Illinois. The children of Alexander B. Ryan were: Elizabeth Jane, Rachel Frances, Mary Ellen, Hannah, John G., Sallie, George L., William, James, Lydia and Zane.

William D. and Sallie (Ryan) Denison were the parents of the following children: William, Charles, Raymond R., Edgar, Albert, Roy, Walter, Carrie and Grace. Raymond R. Denison, as this account shows, has the advantage of a mixed ancestry, Irish in the Denison and Ryan lines, English in the Crane and Grant families, and German through the French contribution.

Raymond R. Denison grew up on the farm of his parents, attended the rural schools and in 1906 was graduated after a literary and agricultural course from the Winona Agricultural Institute. After teaching two terms he entered DePauw University at Greencastle, Indiana, and was graduated A. B. in 1910. For eleven years after graduating from DePauw he devoted practically his entire time to educational work. He taught a year in Lawrenceville, two years at Coleraine, Minnesota, for five years was principal of the high school at Brainard, Minnesota, and on returning to his native county served three years as superintendent of the Lawrence Township High School.

Mr. Denison in 1921 bought the Lawrenceville Republican, a weekly newspaper. In 1922 he established the Lawrenceville Daily Record, the first daily newspaper of Lawrenceville. At that time he organized the Lawrenceville Publishing Company as the majority stockholder, and this company owns and has the business management of both newspapers. The Record is a non-partisan paper in politics.

Mr. Denison himself is a republican, is a Methodist, a Master Mason, member of the Independent Order of Odd Fellows, and in 1926 was exalted ruler of the B. P. O. Elks Lodge at Lawrenceville.

He married, in 1911, Miss Barbara Crow, of Springfield, Illinois, member of an old family of this state and directly descended from the William Henry Harrison family. Her grandfather and greatuncle were soldiers with Abraham Lincoln in the Blackhawk Indian war. The three children of Mr. and Mrs. Denison are Ada, Raymond Robert and Barbara Jean.

JAMES T. WILSON, president of Neat Condit & Grout, Bankers, of Winchester, has been a remarkably successful man in the agricultural industry of Scott County. He began his career as a tenant farmer, and the thrift and energy with which he conducted his business brought him to the position of the largest land owner and tax payer in the county, and an interested factor and participant in various enterprises in that section of the state.

He was born in the south end of Scott County, November 14, 1864. His grandparents, James and Hettie (Rowe) Wilson, came to Illinois from the Blue Grass region of Kentucky, locating near Glasgow in Scott County, where they lived out their lives. James Wilson died before the Civil war, and his wife, when past eighty years of age. A record of their children is as follows: Jane married Joseph Gray and lives near Glasgow; Thomas and William, twin brothers, both reached a good old age and died in the Glasgow community; Eliza, who was married first to Clark Smith and later to August Miller; Narcissus became the wife of John L. Brown and died in Scott County; Monk was a soldier in the Union army and died at Manchester, leaving two children; Rowe spent most of his life in Scott County and was also the father of two children; Hettie became the wife of John Haney and was survived by a large family; Sarah became the wife of Benjamin Haney, leaving a son, Harrison; John H., the only survivor of this large family, is a farmer near Glasgow, and has two children.

Thomas K. Wilson, father of our subject, was born near Lexington, Kentucky, in 1834. He was self educated, a man of industry, and the efforts of his many years were directed largely in providing for his family. He died in 1914. His wife was Deborah Smith, daughter of William Smith, who came to Illinois from Henry County, Virginia. Their children were: James T.; William, of Glasgow; Mary, wife of Charles Schafer; Sophia, who married William Sherwin; Florence, who died while the wife of Fred Moore; Emilis, a farmer near Glasgow; and John A., also of Glasgow.

James T. Wilson, our subject, was reared on a small farm, with only such educational opportunities as the local school provided, and his practical experience and training on the farm were the only preparations he had for his successful career. He began as a tenant farmer near Glasgow, working three or four years, managing thriftily until he was justified in bargaining for eighty acres of land on the partial payment plan.

For twenty-one years Mr. Wilson was a tenant of the Grout property, known formally as the Carpenter property, and he laid the foundation of his prosperity by farming land owned by others. While a tenant on the

Grout farm he acquired several hundred acres of his own. Among other farms he then purchased were the old Brown farm, the William McKeevers farm, and the John Davis farm, living on the former for a number of years. At the end of twenty-one years as a tenant he was able to buy the Grout farm of 534½ acres and draw a check in full payment of it.

Mr. Wilson carried on a large business as stock raiser, feeder and shipper until 1920, when he sold off his stock and equipment, and is now the largest land owner in Scott County.

As a Winchester business man Mr. Wilson has been interested in the lumber business. He consolidated a yard he owned with another yard in Winchester and is still a stockholder in that company. In 1914 he became identified with the Private Bank of Neat, Condit & Grout, and when it was incorporated as a State Bank under the name of Neat, Condit & Grout, Bankers, he was elected its president, a position he has held ever since. This bank has a capital stock of $110,000.00 and a surplus of $55,000.00. The other executive officers are: George W. Woodall, vice-president, J. C. Neat, cashier, S. G. Smith and Paul E. Markillie, assistant cashiers.

Mr. Wilson was one of the founders of the Winchester Farmer's Elevator and Mercantile Company, and was its first president. For many years he was particularly active with the Scott County Farmer's Institute, much of the time as its president.

He was largely associated with experimental problems at the State University at Urbana, particularly the short course in agriculture, being for a number of years its president.

Politically Mr. Wilson is rather independent in local elections, but in national affairs has rather a straight republican record since casting his first vote for President Harrison. He is a member of the Masonic fraternity and a member of the Baptist Church.

A large proportion of Mr. Wilson's real estate lies in the Big Swan drainage and levee district, and he has spent much time and mental energy in the development of this drainage district, which is today one of the most perfect in central Illinois.

While still a very young man Mr. Wilson was united in marriage with Miss Ella Mundy, the only child of James L. and Lucinda Mundy. Mr. Mundy was a member of Company H, 129th Volunteer Infantry, and died during the war, giving his life for his country. His wife, Lucinda (Rowlin) Mundy, also died while her husband was in the war, leaving Ella in her infancy, without father, mother, brother or sister, and she was taken by her Grandmother Mundy and raised near Glasgow.

The children and grandchildren of Mr. and Mrs. James T. Wilson are as follows: Leila married W. C. Simmons and their children are Stanley and Eda; Charles R., a farmer near Winchester, first married Cassie Campbell, by whom he had one daughter, Opal, and his second wife was Hattie Campbell; Pearl is the wife of Roy Hoots, and their children are Bernita, Freda, James, Leroy, Maria, Ileene, Wilson and Murrel; Edward Wilson married Tillie Boes, and they have one daughter, Lucille; Bertha, the youngest of the family, is the wife of Rudolph Boes, and their children are Lula, Minnie, John, James, Gerald and Eugene. It is to be noted with interest that all of Mr. Wilson's children are farmers and reside in Scott County.

This completes the summary of one of Scott County's pioneer farmers, a self-made man who, beginning with nothing but the asset of a determination to accomplish what he set out to do, has through the application of thrift and perseverance achieved success financially, and through his efforts in drainage district work has materially benefited not only the farmers whose land is in the drainage and levee districts of Scott County, but the county itself, because owing to the increased revenue accruing as the direct result of this project the entire county has felt the indirect influence.

GEORGE F. WOMBACHER. A leading member of the St. Clair County bar, who has been engaged in practice at Mascoutah for nearly thirty years, George F. Wombacher occupies a firmly established place in the confidence of a large and representative clientele. At various times he has been called upon by his fellow-citizens to discharge the duties of political office, and in these incumbencies he has displayed the possession of characteristics which make him well equipped for public service.

Mr. Wombacher was born November 3, 1869, at Mascoutah, and is a son of Peter and Elizabeth (Wetzer) Wombacher, and a grandson of Peter and Mary (Michel) Wombacher, natives of Bavaria. On the maternal side his grandparents were Jacob and Mary Anna (Piefer) Wetzer, natives of Lorraine. Jacob Wetzer served as one of Napoleon's body-guards and later came to America with LaFayette, was wounded in battle, and died. Peter Wombacher, the father of George F., was born in Bavaria and was six years of age when he came to the United States with his parents. The family settled first in Pennsylvania, subsequently moving to St. Louis, Missouri, whence they came to St. Clair County. Here Peter Wombacher rounded out his life as an agriculturist and veterinary surgeon, and died in 1916. His widow, who was born in Lorraine, still survives him. They were the parents of eight children Charles D., who married Anna Loui and has six children; Nicholas, who married Maria Pond and has one child; Dominick, who married Katie Loui has three children; Margaret, who is single; Martin, who married Mary Meyer and has four children; George F.; Lizzie, who married Anton Myer; and Louis, who married Lizzie Rose.

George F. Wombacher acquired his early education in the grade and high schools of Mascoutah, following which he took up the study of his chosen calling at the Sprague Law School, Detroit, Michigan. He was graduated from that institution in 1896, and, being admitted to the bar in the same year, immediately took up the practice of law at Mascoutah, where he has since remained. He has a large and important clientele, practices in all the courts and stands high in his profession, where he is acknowledged to be a thorough, reliable and conscientious attorney. Mr. Wombacher, after serving in various local offices,

in 1900 was elected to the State Legislature, serving as a member of the Forty-second General Assembly and establishing an excellent record. He is a candidate for the office of probate judge in the election of 1926. He is a member of the Catholic Church and fraternizes with the Knights of Columbus.

On November 21, 1897, Mr. Wombacher was united in marriage with Miss Annie Glatz, daughter of Joseph and Mary (Wangler) Glatz, both deceased. Mr. Glatz, who was a baker by occupation, died many years ago. He and his wife were the parents of three children August, who married Annie Smith and has four children; Joseph, who married Mary Kroeger and has two children; and Annie, who is Mrs. Wombacher. To Mr. and Mrs. Wombacher there have been born three children: Alma Frances, residing with her parents; Laura, who married Edward L. Schmidt and has two children, George Edward and Anita Mary; and Leona T., who is single.

JAMES ORMEROD HEYWORTH is a native of of Chicago, has been prominent in its business and civic life, but enjoys a national reputation among contractors and engineers. In nearly all portions of the United States he has built railroads, industrial plants and is particularly well known in hydro-electric development.

He was born at Chicago, June 12, 1866, son of James Ormerod and Julia (Dimon) Heyworth. He is a descendant of the Lancashire family of Heyworths, the family name being variously spelled in the English records as Hayworth, Hyworth, Haworth and Heyworth. Many notable members of this connection are found in English history running back to the time of King Henry II, in the twelfth century. The grandfather of the Chicago contractor, Lawrence Heyworth, was born at West Darby, Lancashire, England, about 1800. He sat in Parliament for twenty-one years, was a man of great prominence in political and business life, and was a signer of the anti-corn league. He made millions of pounds in the South African trade, and lost several millions in the "South Sea Bubble." He became a large stockholder in the Illinois Central Railroad, and that was an important influence in one branch of his family locating in Chicago. One of his daughters married a president of the Grand Trunk Railway.

James Ormerod Heyworth, Sr., a son of Lawrence Heyworth, of England, was born in West Darby, Lancashire, in 1827. He was a graduate of Cambridge University, and coming to America, located in Chicago. He had large investments in the Illinois Central Railroad and his life was that of an English gentleman, free from commercial pursuits. His death on December 14, 1873, was the result of accidental injuries. He married Julia Frances Dimon, of Milan, Ohio, who survived him half a century. They had two sons, James Ormerod and Lawrence, and one daughter, all living in 1926. Lawrence Heyworth, also a native of Chicago, has been prominent in the real estate business there since 1900.

James Ormerod Heyworth, Jr., was liberally educated, graduating with the A. B. degree from Yale University in 1888. After preliminary experience with other firms he established a general engineering, contracting and building business on his own account in 1903. In 1894 he built the old Coliseum at Chicago, the building in which William J. Bryan was first nominated for the presidency. He was president of the company that owned the Coliseum until 1896. From 1897 to 1903 he was a member of the contracting firm of Christie, Lowe & Heyworth.

Much of his attention has been given to government contracts. He was the builder of the jetties at Port Arthur, Texas, and Fernandina, Florida, and of the locks and dams on the great Warrior River project in Alabama. He did railroad work for the Baltimore & Ohio, the Panhandle, the Chicago Junction and the South Side Elevated Railroads in Chicago and the Illinois Central Railway and Grand Trunk Railways. He has executed a number of contracts for the Steel and Tube Company of America, including the open-hearth furnace foundations, blast furnace, etc., and has executed large contracts for the Commonwealth Edison Company. He has carried out many difficult contracts in water power development in all parts of the country and under all climatic conditions. He had the contract for the Wisconsin River hydro-electric development, was builder of the Jefferson Street bridge at South Bend, Indiana, did important work for the Oliver hydro-electric plant at South Bend, and was a contractor in the hydro-electric development at Sault Ste. Marie, Ontario, and in the Calumet-Sag Channel Sanitary District of Chicago. He was a contracting engineer in connection with the restoration of the dam of the Elwha River in the State of Washington.

In July, 1917, Mr. Heyworth was given the contract by the bureau of yards and docks of the United States Navy to build the cantonments of Decatur, Farragut and Ross and also the Emergency Hospital at the Great Lakes Naval Training Station, finishing this work on scheduled time, November 30, 1917. In October, 1917, he was called to Washington by E. N. Hurley, and put in charge of all wood ship construction by the Emergency Fleet Corporation of the United States Shipping Board. He served in that capacity until after the war. His capability and efficiency were continually manifest in the thoroughness and rapidity with which he executed these government contracts, thus contributing in large measure to the welfare of the military forces of the country. When the war emergency had passed Mr. Heyworth returned to his private interests at Chicago, in May, 1919. He is a member of the American Society of Civil Engineers, of the Western Society of Engineers, the Chicago Historical Society, is a member of the Yale and Engineers Clubs of New York, the Chicago, University, Chicago Yacht and Engineers Clubs of Chicago, serving as president of the Engineers Clubs from 1910 to 1913. He also belongs to the Onwentsia, Old Elm, Shore Acres, Tolleston and Sanganois Clubs. His home is in Lake Forest.

On January 15, 1902, Mr. Heyworth married Martica G. Waterman, of Southport, Connecticut. She is a daughter of Edwin F. and Martica (Gookin) Waterman, granddaughter of Rev. Thomas Tileston Waterman, and represents the ninth generation in descent from Robert Waterman who came to America in 1636. The Waterman family has furnished many distinguished members to the professions, particularly the ministry. One of her ancestors, Capt. Nehemiah Waterman, commanded a company of militia during the campaign of 1779 in the Revolutionary war. Her grandfather, Rev. Thomas T. Waterman, was one of the ablest ministers of his time, and one of the pastorates he held in the Presbyterian Church was at Galena, Illinois. Two children have been born to Mr. and Mrs. Heyworth, a daughter, Frances Dimon Heyworth, on August 24, 1903, and James Ormerod Heyworth, Jr., on May 27, 1909.

WILLIAM A. MCCARTY, county judge of Crawford County, was admitted to the bar and immediately took a government position during the World war period. He has been engaged in a successful general practice at Robinson since the war, being member of the firm McCarty & Arnold.

He was born on a farm in Martin Township, Crawford County, July 27, 1892. His grandparents were Alexander and Harriet (Good) McCarty, the former a native of County Derry, Ireland, and the latter of Ohio. They were early settlers in Illinois. Their son, George D. McCarty, was born in Vermilion County, Illinois, May 31, 1867, grew up on a farm, and after the common schools attended the Normal University at Normal, Illinois, and the Central Normal at Danville, Indiana, and finally the Union Christian College at Merom, on the banks of the Wabash in Indiana. He was engaged in farming and school teaching, for two years being principal of the schools at Oblong, Illinois. While teaching he studied law, and in May, 1895, established his home at Robinson, and on August 25th of that year was admitted to the bar upon examination at Mount Vernon, Illinois. He became a member of the law firm Jones, McCarty & Arnold at Robinson, and finally of the firm McCarty & Arnold, and engaged in practice until his death on January 31, 1921. He was a republican, a Knight Templar Mason and Shriner, and a member of the United Brethren Church. George D. McCarty married Miss Laura Haskin, daughter of Robert E. Haskin, an early settler in Crawford County. She survives her husband and is the mother of the following children: Inez A., who married Carl Kibler, and died February 9, 1921; William A.; Prentice E., an electrician at Robinson; Palmer G.; Miss Gertrude; Harry Edward and Herbert Frederick, twins; and George H. The son Palmer G. was born at Robinson, August 19, 1896, and on August 31, 1918, entered as a volunteer the Officers Training School at Camp Gordon, Georgia, remaining there until honorably discharged November 30, 1918. He is a member of the American Legion. In June, 1919, he graduated with his law degree from Illinois Wesleyan University at Bloomington, was admitted to the bar in April, 1920, and is now practicing with the law firm of McCarty & Arnold. He is a republican, a thirty-second degree Scottish Rite Mason and Shriner and member of the Phi Gamma Delta college fraternity.

William A. McCarty, the oldest son of the late George D. McCarty, was reared in Robinson, graduated from the high school of that city in 1910, and spent several years clerking in a clothing store. He took a special course in mathematics at the University of Illinois in 1913 and then entered Illinois Wesleyan University at Bloomington, where he took his law degree in 1917. In October of that year he was admitted to the bar, and thereafter until February, 1919, was employed as an auditor in the Internal Revenue Bureau of the United States Government. He then became associated with his father's law firm, McCarty & Arnold, and continues practice with that firm, in which his brother Palmer is also associated.

He was elected county judge of Crawford County in 1922 on the democratic ticket, and was renominated as the candidate of his party in 1926. He is a thirty-second degree Scottish Rite Mason and Shriner and member of the Phi Gamma Delta fraternity. Judge McCarty married, August 2, 1917, Miss Elsie Allen. Their two children are Maxine and Margaret Alice.

GEORGE MORRIS. Steady application to one line of business endeavor is almost certain to bring about satisfying results if the individual so concerned possesses the native ability and industry which are necessary to success in any field of action. This was the case with George E. Morris, to whose skill and artistic taste many of the finest homes and buildings at Metropolis owe their attractiveness. Mr. Morris, whose death occurred August 5, 1925, was a paperhanger and plaster contractor during the greater part of a long and active career, and his fidelity and good workmanship contributed to his prosperity and gained for him public confidence and good will.

Mr. Morris was born on a farm in Williamson County, Illinois, August 3, 1856, a son of Overton Burrel Morris, a native of Virginia. He acquired a public school education in his youth and after leaving school adopted for a time the vocation of educator, subsequently teaching classes in various rural districts, including Hardin County, where he first met his future wife, who was one of his students. Following his marriage Mr. Morris became a clerk for a time and also received an appointment as sergeant-at-arms in the capitol at Springfield, a position in which he served for two terms. Not being satisfied with the advancement he was making he decided upon a steady trade and finally applied himself to the mastery of plastering, paperhanging and general decorating. For a time after coming to Metropolis, in 1892, he worked as a journeyman, but finally embarked in business on his own account as a contractor, and became one of the firmly established business men of Metropolis, where he built up a reputation for integrity and straightforward business dealing. Mr. Morris applied himself strictly to his business and never sought the honors of public life, although he took a good citizen's interest in affairs that affected the welfare of

Edmund D. Adcock.

his community. In his political allegiance he supported the principles and candidates of the republican party. His pleasant family home is situated at 615 Catherine Street.

In 1885 Mr. Morris was united in marriage with Miss Anna Hetherington, who was born in Hardin County, Illinois, a daughter of Richard Paxton and Jean (Little) Hetherington, natives of Scotland, who immigrated to the United States as a young married couple, landed at New York and then made their way to Hardin County. Mr. Hetherington was a skilled mechanic and a blacksmith of the old school, who followed his trade throughout his life. To Mr. and Mrs. Morris there were born the following children: Laura Jean, the wife of W. H. Smith, of Metropolis; Overton Paxton, who met a soldier's death in France during the World war; George H., of Metropolis; William S., who resides at home; and James H., who died at the age of two years. Mrs. Morris, who received a public school education, is active in the work of the Methodist Episcopal Church, its Sunday School and its various societies.

JOSEPH K. P. HAWKS, M. D., who has achieved special success and distinction in the field of surgery, has spent his entire professional career in his native city of Bloomington.

Doctor Hawks was born there in 1873, only son and child of Samuel and Emeline (Preston) Hawks. His father, a native of Scotland, came to Bloomington in 1854 and was one of the pioneer railroad men living in that city. He was a locomotive engineer. After air brakes were invented and were introduced on railroad cars he was appointed as superintendent of installation of such apparatus in the shop of the Chicago & Northern Railway. He died January 2, 1905. By his first marriage he had two children. Emeline Preston, his second wife, was born in Massachusetts and came to Bloomington in 1872. She died December 15, 1916.

Joseph K. P. Hawks was educated in public schools at Bloomington, graduated in 1896 from Illinois Wesleyan University, and took his Doctor of Medcine degree at Northwestern University School of Medicine in Chicago in 1900. In the same year he returned to Bloomington, and has always been known as one of the progressive men in his profession. For thirteen years he was associated in practice with the late Dr. W. E. Guthrie. He is now a member of the firm Hart & Hawks, physicians and surgeons, with offices in the Greisheim Building. Doctor Hawks for ten years was physician in charge of the Illinois Soldiers' Orphans' Home at Normal. He is a member of the staff of the Brokaw Hospital. During the World war he held a commission as captain in the Medical Corps and was assigned duty at Evacuation Hospital No. 46 at Fort Oglethorpe, Georgia. He is a member of the County, State and American Medical Associations.

Doctor Hawks is a republican, is a member of the Maplewood Country Club, Association of Commerce, Phi Gamma Delta fraternity and the First Presbyterian Church. His favorite sports are golf and fishing.

He married at Bloomington, February 3, 1912, Miss Esther Hart, daughter of Allen Hart, who was a pioneer settler of Woodford County, Illinois. She is a sister of Dr. Edson B. Hart, of Bloomington. Mrs. Hawks is a member of the Kappa Kappa Gamma sorority and is active in various social and civic clubs. They have two children, Esther and Allen Hart Hawks.

EDMUND D. ADCOCK, who has practiced law in Chicago since 1902, and for a number of years was general counsel for the Chicago Sanitary District, was born in the western part of the state and is a member of pioneer families of Warren and Knox counties.

The Adcocks have lived in Warren County a hundred years, Edmund Adcock having settled there in 1826, just two years after the first settlement was planted in that section of the state. The Adcocks were originally from Buckingham County, Virginia, moving from there to Kentucky, and spending two years in Crawford County, Indiana, while en route from Kentucky to Warren County, Illinois. Edmund Adcock, the pioneer, was the father of Joseph W. Adcock, who graduated from Knox College at Galesburg in 1848. Joseph W. Adcock was the father of the late William Adcock, who was born in Kelly Township, Warren County, July 3, 1850, and died in a hospital at Galesburg July 3, 1926, on his seventy-sixth birthday. He spent his active career as a farmer in Warren County, and was closely identified with public affairs in that section of the state. At the time of his death he was representative from the Thirty-second District in the Lower House of the Illinois General Assembly, having been elected on the democratic ticket in 1924. He was author of a resolution requesting Congress to pass legislation embodying a scientific plan or program by which reasonable export bounties could be paid on exports of American grains, live stock and their by-products. William Adcock graduated from old Abingdon College in 1871. He was elected supervisor in 1884, and for many years was on the board, being supervisor at the time the courthouse was built in 1894, and largely through his efforts as chairman of the board the county in 1890 was freed from its railroad debt of $200,000. He was also officially concerned with the provisions for the construction of the first hard road in Warren County. He became one of the charter members of the Farm Bureau, was a delegate to the Democratic National Convention of 1916, and during the World war was a member of the State Council of Defense.

The mother of the late William Adcock was Mary E. McMurtry. The McMurtrys, like the Adcocks, were a Southern family and were pioneers in Illinois, coming from Kentucky and settling in Knox County, adjoining Warren County, in 1828. Both the Adcocks and McMurtry families have had from their earliest generations in America a background of broad culture and education, and many of their name have achieved genuine prominence in academic and professional careers. The father of Mary E. (McMurtry) Adcock was William H. McMurtry, a prominent resident of Knox County, who served as lieutenant governor of Illinois from 1849 to 1853.

The late William Adcock married Mary Jane Henderson, who still resides in Warren County. They were the parents of three children: Edmund D.; Joseph, who was a midshipman on the battleship Missouri in 1918, during the World war; and Mrs. Bullman, of Galesburg.

Edmund D. Adcock was born in Kelly Township, Warren County, April 29, 1877. After the public schools he entered Knox College at Galesburg, was graduated with the A. B. degree in 1898, and in 1902 received his law degree at Northwestern University of Evanston, Illinois. After being admitted to the bar Mr. Adcock was associated with a well known Chicago law firm of which the head was Colin C. H. Fyffe. In December, 1912, he was made general counsel for the Sanitary District of Chicago, holding that position until January, 1919, and since then has frequently represented the Sanitary District in important legal matters, particularly the larger questions involved in the diversion of lake waters for this district, the source of many novel and important problems of both national and international interest. Mr. Adcock is now a member of the law firm of Haight, Adcock, Haight & Harris, with offices at 209 South LaSalle Street. He is a member of the Chicago Bar Association, Illinois and American Bar Associations and the Chicago Law Club. He also belongs to the Chicago Athletic Association, City Club, South Shore Country Club, and Midlothian Country Club. On August 31, 1905, Mr. Adcock married May Rex, of Creston, Iowa. She died June 15, 1918, leaving one child, Edmund Rex, born in Chicago, August 28, 1911. Mr. Adcock married, December 12, 1925, Miss Evelyn Ringland.

REV. GEORGE W. LOHMAN is pastor of St. Mary's Catholic Church at Centralia in Marion County. He is a native of Southern Illinois, and his duties since taking orders as a priest in 1913 have returned him to the congenial associations of his early life in this state.

He was born at St. Libory, St. Clair County, Illinois, July 25, 1887, son of Henry and Teresa (Lager) Lohman, both natives of Illinois, and a grandson of Herman H. and Mary (Bertke) Lohman, and Theodore and Gesina (Bergkoetter) Lager. His grandparents were among the early settlers of German nativity in Southern Illinois. His father, Henry Lohman, followed the occupation of farmer, and died in 1924, while the mother passed away in 1898.

George W. Lohman was educated in the parochial schools at St. Libory, graduating in 1901. In September of the same year he entered Josephinum College at Columbus, Ohio, and spent twelve years in his classical, philosophical and theological studies, ending with his ordination as a priest on June 7, 1913.

Father Lohman's first assignment was as assistant to Monsignor Charles Gilmartin in the Sacred Heart Church in East St. Louis. He was there three years, for four years was assistant at the Cathedral at Belleville, Illinois, and secretary to Rt. Rev. Bishop Althoff. For two and a half years he was pastor of St. Stephen's Church at Flora, Illinois, then returned to Belleville for two and a half years as secretary to the Bishop and chaplain at St. Elizabeth's Hospital. On August 4, 1924, he came to his present duties as pastor of St. Mary's Church at Centralia, and is now directing one of the most prosperous churches of his faith in the southern part of the state. He is a fourth degree Knight of Columbus.

MARY MOWERY GALLAGHER. Emerson says: "Every institution is but the lengthened shadow of a man." But, in the light of recent developments in business and in professions, that old saying will have to be amended. One of the most striking proofs of this epigram is found in the story of The Gallagher School of Kankakee, Illinois. In analyzing the causes which have led this big school to its present position as a leader in the business training world, it becomes more and more apparent that the school is but the lengthened shadow of its president, Mary Mowery Gallagher.

Miss Gallagher has not been content to follow the beaten path. By this we do not mean that she has shown an inclination to experiment with fads and fancies, but rather that with her school there is—and always has been—a restless ambition to delve deeper, to reach out farther, to do more and do it better. In other words, she has distinguished "The Gallagher School" from the hundreds of other so-called business training schools by making it progressively different. And in that difference lies in the secret of the splendid success of her graduates have achieved. It would be hard to find a finer executive at the head of any business training institution than she has proved herself to be.

From the beginning Mary M. Gallagher has been a leader. A keen student of the ways of business, she knows what busness men and women expect of their helpers. Her courses of study are not experiments, nor are they taught from the theoretical standpoint. This is why students desiring to train for business cheerfully travel many miles farther to attend her school in Kankakee. She has probably done as much to prepare young people for business and civil service, and to supply business with trained helpers, as any woman in America. She is not only training young people for success, she is building character.

Miss Gallagher was born in Cuba, Illinois, and is a daughter of Patrick William and Judith Caroline (Mowery) Gallagher, her father a native of Liverpool, England, and her mother of Cuba, Illinois. Patrick W. Gallagher for many years has been an Illinois attorney, having been located in Canton for over fifty years. The mother of Miss Gallagher died July 23, 1915.

Miss Gallagher's office is located at 153 South Indiana Avenue, in her new building, which was especially designed and built for school purposes. She resides at 740 South Greenwood Avenue.

Miss Gallagher is a member of the Woman's Club of Kankakee, the National Association of Business and Professional Women's Clubs, and of the Illinois Woman's Athletic Club of Chicago.

FRED BAGLEY, member of a family that has been in southern Illinois for three generations, is county clerk of Franklin County, an office in which he has demonstrated such fitness that the republican party gives him a nomination without any contest.

Mr. Bagley was born in Lola, Kentucky, July 15, 1886. His grandfather, Walter Bagley, came from Kentucky, and for the remainder of his years followed farming in Pope County. James Bagley, father of the county clerk, was born in Pope County, engaged in farming there, and also operated one of the first saw mills in the county. He was killed in his saw mill December 10, 1888, when a comparatively young man. His wife was Jeffie Bridges Bagley, a native of Illinois, now residing at Christopher in Franklin County.

Fred Bagley was two years old when his father was killed in the saw mill. He was born on a farm, was educated in country schools and from early years shared in the working responsibilities of the farm. When he left the farm he entered the service of the Chicago & Eastern Illinois Railroad Company, rose to the position of conductor, but after four years of service he was severely injured in a railroad wreck, losing his right leg. His home at that time was in West Frankfort, Franklin County. On recovering he removed to Benton and turned to an occupation where his physical handicap would not put him at a disadvantage. Mr. Bagley for several years was in the real estate business in the firm of Dial and Bagley, and helped build up a fine reputation and business for that firm.

Mr. Bagley during 1916-17 held the office of tax collector for Benton Township. In 1918 he was elected for his first term as county clerk and was reelected in 1922, and in 1926 received the renomination for a third term without opposition on the republican ticket.

Mr. Bagley is a member of the Masonic Lodge at West Frankfort. He married Miss Fannie Hunter on January 16, 1914. She was born December 25, 1887, daughter of Jasper Newton Hunter, of Union County. Two children have been born to them, Fred, Jr., August 1, 1918, and Marian F., September 9, 1920.

JESSE A. BEADLES. The business interests of Cairo are many and varied, and afford ample opportunities for development on the part of the men of this locality who are engaged in meeting the demands of the people, and among them none stands any higher in public confidence than does Jesse A. Beadles, vice president and treasurer of the McFarland Lumber Company, wholesale hardwood lumber dealers, one of the most substantial concerns in Southern Illinois.

Jesse A. Beadles was born at Moscow, Kentucky, April 7, 1878, a son of J. A. and Jennie (Long) Beadles, natives of Kentucky and Mississippi, respectively. He died in Kentucky in 1918, but she survives him and now makes her home at Kenton, Tennessee. Growing up in Kentucky until he was sixteen years old, Jesse A. Beadles attended its public schools, and after that completed his education in the schools of Obion, Tennessee. In 1902 he began his long connection with the lumber industry, when he entered the employ of J. H. Murry & Company, of Indianapolis, Indiana, at Kenton, Tennessee, continuing with this concern until 1907, when he came to Cairo and became a commercial traveler for the Thomas McFarland Lumber Company. For four years he continued with this company as an employe, and then took charge of the Cairo yards, became a stockholder in the company, and remained in that position for ten years. At the death of Mr. McFarland he bought more stock in the business and has since been vice president, treasurer and general manager. His associates in the business are: A. F. McFarland, president and John B. Rumsey, secretary.

On February 7, 1907, Mr. Beadles married at Kenton, Tennessee, Zada Wade, of that city, a daughter of W. H. Wade. Mr. and Mrs. Beadles have had the following children born to them: Louise, Thomas and Robert. Mr. Beadles belongs to the Presbyterian Church, and is chairman of the Board of Trustees of the Cairo body of this denomination. High in Masonry, he belongs to the Commandery and Shrine of that order, and he is a life member of the Benevolent and Protective Order of Elks. He belongs to the Association of Commerce, the Cairo, Illinois, Hoo Hoo Lumbermen's Club, which he has served as president, the Tri-State Bridge and Highway Association, the Egyptian Country Club, the International Rotary Club, and is a director of the Cairo Public Swimming Pool. A man of many interests, he is aggressive in behalf of his home city, and willing to exert himself to the utmost to advance its interests and promote its welfare.

WILLIAM CASWELL JONES. As lawyer, jurist, author and citizen, probably no resident of Crawford County lived a life richer in attainments, service and high purpose than the late William Caswell Jones. So far as possible the brief sketch of his career which follows is made up of the sincere tributes and estimates of his associates who best knew and understood him.

He was born at Hutsonville, Crawford County, Illinois, July 15, 1848, son of Caswell and Mary (Barlow) Jones. His father was a merchant at Hutsonville, and died there in 1853. In 1855 the widowed mother was married to Ethelbert Callahan, for many years a prominent attorney of the Crawford County bar. In 1861 the Callahan family removed to Robinson. From an interesting character sketch prepared by Ethelbert Callahan are taken the following sentences:

"He was but six years old when his mother became my wife and he became a member of our family. I assumed towards him the place, the duties, obligation and the responsibilities of a father. This relation was voluntarily assumed and harmoniously continued during his entire life. His mother and myself recognized in the boy elements of character that gave promise of an able and honorable manhood. We gave him opportunities for a liberal education to qualify him for the proper discharge of his public duties as a citizen and to enter upon industrial, commercial or professional life. The opportunities so given him were diligently improved by him. In his boyhood he was studious and industrious. He discarded idleness and sought employment. One summer he spent with my father on the farm and participated in the labors of the farm. His education began in the common schools of the county. Later he went to the Ohio Wesleyan University, where he continued until he determined to become a lawyer.

"In choosing his life work he hesitated for a time between law and business. When he finally decided upon the law he went to the Law School of the University of Michigan and took a course of legal study. He was admitted to the bar in June, 1868, and our partnership was immediately formed and continued for ten years. It was terminated by his election to the office of county judge. Durng this partnership he was elected and served as a member of the Twenty-seventh General Assembly of the State of Illinois, was the boy member of the House and was much favored by members who were veterans in the field of legislation. He was one of the young men who set at naught the caucus rule of their political party and voted for the Harper High License Bill. Two years afterward he was elected judge of the Circuit Court. In 1885 he was reelected. When this last term expired his eyesight had begun to fail. The clouds that shadowed his vision were very slight, but intensely ominous. He resumed practice as a lawyer and labored very industriously in the field of literature. In 1899 he was appointed by Governor John R. Tanner judge of the Court of Claims, which position he held for four years. As the years went by the shadows that came over his vision became deeper and darker until the curtain of almost total blindness closed around him never to rise again during his mortal life.

"On October 10, 1914, these shadows, that blinded him here, lifted and cleared his vision, in which the living cannot behold the beauty and splendor of the ever green mountains of eternal life.

"As a legislator he was conscientious and independent. As a judge he was impartial and administered the law as he understood it. Right and justice were the polar stars that guided him. Very few of his judgments or decrees were reversed by the Supreme Court. Success attended him and his future was full of promise until his failing eyesight obstructed his way and closed his career as a public man. His death brought to me a sense of loss that other members of the bar cannot feel. In his youth and young manhood he was a member of my family. Caring as I did with his devoted mother the responsibility of his education and moral training, he was greatly influenced by my advice in many things, particularly in the selection of his life work. For ten years he was my partner in the practice of law; for fourteen years he was a judge in whose court I practiced law, and for more than half a century we recognized the relation of father and son. I have a personal pride in all the successes of his life, in the honorable, upright and useful life that he lived, and in the untarnished reputation that he left as a legacy to his family and friends. From his childhood he was inclined to be religious. He held broadly the cardinal principles of Christianity. He was a Christian man of liberal views and not a sectarian in any offensive sense of the word. In the faith of a Christian he lived and died."

Judge Jones was a member of the Presbyterian Church, was a Knight Templar Mason, and politically was always a democrat. He exercised a determining influence on the side of high ideals in both business and civic affairs, and willingly put his means at the disposal of many causes that would benefit and beautify his city and county. In all things personal he was frugal, and not given to lavish expenditures of money. He was thrifty and accumulated wealth and used it unselfishly. One of his outstanding characteristics was his disposition to speak kindly of all whom he knew.

He possessed literary gifts and he used them to interpret his unusual experience and views of life. He was author of "Science of English Versification," "Birch Rod Days and Other Poems," and many minor contributions on current topics and legal themes. He and Judge Cunningham were joint authors of "Practice in County Courts."

Judge Jones married, November 25, 1869, Miss Mary H. Steel. Mrs. Jones since the death of her husband twelve years ago has continued to occupy the old homestead in Robinson at 306 West Locust Street. She is the mother of three living children, Caswell S., Dorothy and William C. Two, James H., and Emily H., are deceased, dying in infancy.

ETHELBERT CALLAHAN was a resident of Robinson sixty years, and at the time of his death was one of the oldest members of the Crawford County bar. He was born in Licking County, Ohio, December 17, 1829. His Irish ancestors had come to America in Colonial times. His paternal grandfather, Rev. George Callahan, was a soldier in the Revolutionary war and afterwards became a pioneer Methodist minister in Ohio.

Ethelbert Callahan at the age of twenty located in Crawford County, Illinois, where he taught school, edited a newspaper, studied law, and after his admission to the bar opened a law office in Robinson and was one of the busy men of his profession until late in life. He died at the ripe old age on June 20, 1918. He inherited sound abilities from an excellent ancestry, and his youth was passed among modest conditions that have produced the finest types of American citizenship. He was reared under Christian influences and taught the lessons of industry and frugality, love of knowledge and devotion to country. He became one of the founders of the republican party in Illinois and was one of its local leaders. He was an eminent lawyer, and in his offices he trained several young men who rose to distinction in the same profession. He married, in 1855, Mrs. Mary (Barlow) Jones, mother of the late Judge William C. Jones.

JAMES H. STEEL was a very able lawyer, a citizen of the finest integrity, whose personal history belongs in the annals of Crawford County. He was born of Quaker parentage in the City of Philadelphia, June 23, 1823. He

attended a Quaker school in his native city and coming West with his father, he lived for a time in Terre Haute, Indiana, and about 1846 settled in Crawford County, Illinois. Here he taught school, was elected and served about nine years as county clerk, and while in that office studied law. He was admitted to the bar in 1857, and acquired a strong position at the bar and continued in active practice until his early death on December 2, 1872, when in the fiftieth year of his life.

He was one of the founders of the republican party in Illinois and supported Abraham Lincoln, standing by the Government and the Union during the Civil war, physical disability keeping him out of the ranks as a soldier. He was well educated, possessed a high degree of intelligence, was an attractive personality and a noble character.

James H. Steel married, February 4, 1847, Emily J. Otey, daughter of James S. Otey, who was a pioneer settler at Palestine, Illinois. Mrs. Emily Steel was born at Palestine. She was the mother of four children: Mary H., who became the wife of Judge William C. Jones, of Robinson; James O.; Charles H.; and Frank O. Steel.

RALPH MARTIN SHAW since 1892 has practiced law in Chicago, and for a number of years has been a member of one of the most prominent firms of the city, Winston, Strawn and Shaw.

Mr. Shaw was born at Paris, Kentucky, February 18, 1869, son of Hiram and Harriet (Martin) Shaw. His father was a merchant in Lexington, Kentucky. Mr. Shaw is of Colonial ancestry. His ancestor, John Shaw, immigrated in 1645 from England and settled in Marlboro, Massachusetts. Members of the family and its collateral branches have served in all the wars of the nation. His maternal ancestor, Lieutenant Samuel Martin, immigrated from England and settled at Westbury, Connecticut, in 1640.

Ralph M. Shaw was liberally educated. He was graduated from Kentucky University in 1888; was graduated A. B. from Yale University in 1890, and acquired part of his legal education in the University of Michigan. He was admitted to the Illinois bar in July, 1892, and his first association with law practice in Chicago was with the firm of Aldrich, Payne and Washburn. Later he became an associate with the firm Winston and Meagher, after which he was admitted to membership and has been a partner in it and its successors during various changes to the present time. Mr. Shaw is a director of the Union Stock Yards and Transit Company of Chicago, the Joliet and Northern Indiana, and Chicago and Indiana Railroads, the American and Federal Creosoting Company, American Tar Products Company, the Los Angeles Corporation, the Los Angeles Union Stock Yards Company, and a number of brewing corporations and other business enterprises.

Mr. Shaw is a republican, a member of the Episcopal Church and belongs to the Chicago, Saddle and Cycle, Onwentsia, Yale, Mid-Day Law, Old Elm, Shore Acres and Racquet Clubs in Chicago, the Yale Club of New York, the Chevy-Chase Club in Maryland and Hyamnisport Golf Club of Massachusetts. He is also a member of the Chicago Bar Association, the Illinois State Bar Association, the American Bar Association, the Law Club and the Bar Association of the City of New York.

He is not particularly interested in politics or fraternal organizations. His great ambition, which he has realized in generous measure, has been to be a good lawyer in all that the term implies, to render valuable service to his clients in a satisfactory manner, and to command the respect of his fellow men. His own abilities have added something to the prestige of a law firm that for many years has been rated as one of the most successful at the Chicago bar. Mr. Shaw married at Geneva Switzerland, August 29, 1896, Mary Stevens. At her death she left one son, Ralph Martin, Jr. On September 29, 1914, Mr. Shaw married Louise Sheppard Tyler.

ISAAC LOWENSTEIN was a resident of White Hall from 1877 until his death on September 30, 1895. A biographer writing of him several years ago laid appropriate emphasis on the remarkable fact that his name a quarter of a century after his death was more deeply cherished than on the day of his funeral. Isaac Lowenstein was a man of character, a character that was exemplified in every day of his life and in every transaction of his business. He was the father of a large family. Some of his sons still remain at White Hall and carry on and continue the business which he founded. His children's lives have in a notable degree been a measure of the highest praise of his own lofty ideals and character.

Isaac Lowenstein was born at Gimsheim, a suburb of Worms, Germany, December 19, 1833. To escape the militarism of his native country he came to America in 1852, landing from a sailing vessel at Philadelphia after fifty-two days on the ocean. He was then a rather delicate youth, and is remembered by his old friends of White Hall as a man small in stature, about 125 or 130 pounds in weight, and never given to pretense or bluster physically or otherwise. After a year or so in Philadelphia he went into East Tennessee and about 1854 married Elizabeth Ann Ghormley, daughter of Pleasant Miller and Ann Ghormley, of Monroe County, Tennessee.

At the breaking out of the Civil war he had the contract for carrying the mail between Louden, Tennessee, and Dalton, Georgia. When Georgia seceded he went with his state and, enlisting in the Confederate cavalry, remained in the service until the close of the war. He was captured twice and slightly wounded twice. Following his first capture he was exchanged and reentered the army. He was again captured and sent to the military prison at Rock Island, Illinois, where he spent the last thirteen months of the war as a military prisoner. He never expressed regret at his captures nor complained of his treatment, but rather enjoyed his "sojourn" among the Union forces. His relations with the G. A. R. veterans in after years were always the most cordial. After the war he rejoined his family in Murray County, Georgia, about fifteen miles east of a little north of Dalton. In the fall of 1869 they moved overland to Washington County, Arkansas, settling near Evansville, on the border of what was then Indian Territory. In 1872 he moved temporarily to a place called St. Martha of Marthasville, about a mile and a quarter south of Pierce City, Missouri, and on July 24, 1873, located at what was then called Wilmington, now Patterson, Greene County, Illinois. He became a grocery merchant at Patterson and in 1874 erected a large store building. In 1877 he removed to White Hall and founded and conducted the business which since his death has been continued under the original firm name of Lowenstein & Sons.

Mrs. Isaac Lowenstein survived him fourteen years. She was a woman of glorious motherly character. There were eleven children. Two sons, Davis and Herman, died in infancy in Georgia. Two of the daughters, well remembered in White Hall, were the late Mrs. Edward B. Smith and Mrs. Laura Lowenstein Gardiner, the latter a teacher in the public schools. Two other daughters are Mrs. David M. Fishback and Mrs. A. L. Eberhart. Several of the sons were at some time identified with their father's business, but the two who have continued it until recent years are Mark and Claude Lowenstein. William P. Lowenstein, new deceased, was a member of the Lowenstein firm for a number of years and for twelve years he and his brother Louis were associated in the farm and live stock business. Louis Lowenstein, the oldest of the family, is a resident of White Hall and his conspicuous achievements have been in reclamation work in the Illinois Valley. Some account of his activities is given on other pages. One son, Henry Polk Lowenstein, has for forty years been a resident of Kansas City, Missouri, where he is a member of the law firm Lowenstein & Lowenstein, the firm consisting of father and son. His son, Henry Polk Lowenstein, Jr., who lived as a child at White Hall, Illinois, for seven years after his mother died in 1900, was a lieutenant in the navy during the World war and is still a lieutenant in the Naval Reserve. Henry Polk Lowenstein is also well known as a Middle West author, being president of the Kansas City Quill Club, and has published a volume entitled "Memorial Poems." Both he and his brother Louis are scholars and thinkers, and for many years have accepted the essential theories propounded by the late Henry George, though realizing the difficulty of practical application of those theories to the modern system of economics and business.

The lives of these sons and these daughters constitute one measure of the importance of the life of the late Isaac Lowenstein.

One of his friends said: "Isaac Lowenstein was the most industrious man I ever saw. I have heard him say many times that if he had a lazy bone in his body he would take a knife and cut it out. He never took advantage of the misfortunes of others. He always kept his word. He never swore or used profane language." He was a lover of children, and one of his chief interests in community affairs was proper provision for schools. It was one of his habits of merchandising never to allow a child to go out of his store without a stick of candy. Children knew him and valued his friendship. Isaac Lowenstein was an inveterate smoker, but advised his own sons aganst the custom, and not one of his five boys acquired the habit. He loved animals, especially horses. He was always prompt with his appointments and was scrupulously fair and honest in his dealings with others. He never signed a mortgage in his life. He sometimes borrowed money at the bank, but always on his note. At the time of his death he was serving as noble grand of Benevolent Lodge No. 227, Independent Order of Odd Fellows, and had been active in the affairs of Odd Fellowship since his initiation on December 26, 1887.

FRANK B. HILLER, M. D., of Pinckneyville, has the reputation of being one of the very best surgeons in Southern Illinois. That repuation is in part due to his wide experience, his constant application as a student, and also to unusual personal gifts and characteristics.

His grandfather, Peter Hiller, was well known over a number of counties in Southern Illinois for his religious activities. He established the "Hillerite" churches in Union County. His son, Walter Hiller, was born in Union County, east of Makanda, and now occupies a farm near Pinckneyville. Walter Hiller married Alethia Brooks, daughter of Larken Brooks.

Their son, Frank B. Hiller, was born February 7, 1881, near Progress, Union County, in what was known as the Hiller neighborhood. Up to the age of nine years his advantages were those of country schools. In 1890 the family moved to Carbondale, where he continued his education in the schools of that city. From early boyhood he was exceedingly fond of his uncle, Dr. Robert B. Hiller, a well known physician at Thebes, Illinois. Out of this admiration grew his determination to follow a career as a physician. His uncle did much to encourage and aid hm. Doctor Hiller worked and paid for all his educational opportunities after he left the common schools. He attended the Carbondale High School, the Normal University, and in 1910 graduated from the College of Physicians and Surgeons at St. Louis. For two and a half years after graduating he practiced at Vergennes in Jackson County, and then, in 1913, removed to Pinckneyville in Perry County.

Doctor Hiller, after America entered the World war, volunteered and spent two months in the Medical Officers Training School at Fort Riley, Kansas, and on July 5, 1918, was assigned duty at Camp Lewis, Washington and received his honorable discharge March 5, 1919. Doctor Hiller was somewhat dispirited on returning to Pinckneyville, feeling that his practice had disappeared during his military service. Through the encouragement of his wife, who has been his staunch comrade at all times, he resumed work and soon found that his practice was larger than before the war. He had previously recognized the great need of hospital facilities at Pinckneyville. In 1917 he erected a two-story buiding on a lot adjoining his residence. The facilities of this hospital soon became outgrown and in 1923 he put up a large building, comprising a mod-

ern twenty-bed hospital, equipped with everything found in the larger hospitals of the big cities. The old hospital is now used as a nurses' cottage.

Doctor Hiller, while possessing natural skill that makes him an unusual surgeon, has always sought to improve himself and has done post-graduate work in Chicago, took a course in X-ray at St. Louis, and he spent several weeks on three different occasions in the Mayo Brothers Hospital at Rochester, Minnesota. He is kindly, thoughtful and public spirited, and has a large general practice outside of his hospital work. Doctor Hiller married Margaret Rule, daughter of Samuel Rule of Perry County. Their three children are Lucile, Kenneth and Samuel Hiller.

Since 1925 he has had as his associate in surgical practice and the hospital Dr. Robert Clark Haynes. Doctor Haynes graduated A. B. from the University of Missouri in 1920, took his medical degree at the Medical University of Louisville in 1922, and was an interne in the Missouri Baptist Sanitarium during 1922-23. Following that he was a member of the staff of the Frisco Hospital at Springfield, Missouri, until he joined Doctor Hiller at Pinckneyville.

HON. FRANCIS SERVICE WILSON. A member of a family that has presented the bench and bar with many brilliant and distinguished men, Hon. Francis Service Wilson, judge of the Circuit Court of Cook County, has displayed the possession of talents which have made him a worthy representative of the name. A resident of Chicago for nearly thirty years, for a long period he occupied a leading position at the bar, having as associates some of the most eminent attorneys of his time, and since his elevation to the bench has evidenced a truly judicial mind, bearing with dignity the high honors of his office.

Judge Wilson was born at Youngstown, Ohio, February 7, 1872, and is a son of Hon. David M. and Griselda E. (Campbell) Wilson. David M. Wilson was born in 1823, in Medina County, Ohio, and was educated in the schools of his native county, where he studied law and was admitted to the bar in 1844. He continued to reside and practice law at Medina until 1862, when he removed to Canfield, the county seat of Mahoning County, and afterwards to Youngstown when the county seat was removed there. At Youngstown he established himself in the practice of law and from the start, aided by his ability, experience and success elsewhere, took a conspicuous place among the leaders of his profession. During the last five years of his life he was associated in practice with his nephew, James P. Wilson, of Youngstown. Northeastern Ohio has produced some of the most profound students and most eloquent exponents of the law that are to be found in the history of the state, and it is among these that Hon. David M. Wilson belonged and won his place at the bar. He was strong as a man and as a lawyer, holding high rank with very able contemporaries. He was a brilliant advocate, deep thinker, and was gifted with a clear, judicial mind, a penetrative and incisive wit and an intelligent grasp that has rarely been excelled. He was a forcible, vigorous and convincing speaker, and whether the subject was a case on trial or the principles of a political party, his hearers were equally impressed with his complete knowledge of the subject and his evident sincerity of expression. He was deeply earnest in all that he undertook. His manner was winning and cordial and made for him hosts of friends. A strong democrat, residing in an overwhelmingly republican district, he was nominated by his party for attorney general of the state in 1863 and in 1874 as candidate for representative in Congress, and by his personal popularity effected a change of more than 3,500 votes. He was one of the most active and prominent members of the Constitutional Convention of 1873, where he gave valuable aid to every suggestion that he believed to be for the best interest of the state. President McKinley at one time studied law in the office of Mr. Wilson, and the acquaintance thus formed ripened into esteem and friendship that was only terminated by his death. President Garfield was another intimate friend, and so close were their relations that a law partnership was at one time under serious contemplation by them. Some of the personal letters of Mr. Garfield still in existence evidence very clearly the confidence and the intimacy existing between the two friends. In one of them, dated January 27, 1874, the writer, doubtless for the first time, expressed the beautiful sentiment given to the public, with a variation of language, six years later in his speech accepting the high office of United States senator as the successor of Judge Thurman: "On the vines that grow over the walls of party politics are found the sweetest flowers that bloom in the garden of friendship." Mr. Wilson died February 11, 1882. He married in 1871 Miss Griselda E. Campbell, daughter of Thomas Campbell, of Old Town, Trumbull County, Ohio, and she survives him as a resident of Youngstown, where she is an earnest, devout member of the Presbyterian Church, to which she has always given her faithful support and adherence. They had but one child: Francis Service.

Francis Service Wilson attended a preparatory school at Hudson, Ohio, the Western Reserve University and the Western Reserve Law School, from which he was graduated with the degree of Bachelor of Laws. He began practice at Youngstown, and in 1896, when only twenty-four years of age, received the nomination of the democratic party for the office of judge of the Probate Court of Mahoning County. The republican party was in command, however, and he met with defeat. Not long thereafter he came to Chicago, where he became associated with ex-Gov. John P. Altgeld in the practice of his profession, and later had as an associate Clarence Darrow in the firm of Darrow, Masters & Wilson. In 1911 he was appointed county attorney of Cook County, a position which he retained during that and the following year, and from 1912 until 1918 was engaged in the practice of his profession. In 1918 he was appointed captain, J. A. G. Department, and stationed at Camp Sherman, Ohio, where he served until mustered out, February 1, 1919, at which time he was commissioned a major in the Officers Reserve Corps. In 1920 he was elected judge of the Circuit Court of Cook County to fill an unexpired term, and in June, 1921, was elected for a full term, acting as chief justice during 1922 and 1923. Judge Wilson since 1921 has been Chancellor of the Circuit Court. He is president of the judicial section of the Illinois Bar Association, and a member of the Chicago Bar Association and the Ohio Association of Chicago. He belongs to the University of Chicago Club, the Flossmoor Country Club, the Chickaming Club of Michigan, the Commonwealth Club of Chicago, the Delta Kappa Epsilon college fraternity and the Sons of the American Revolution.

At Youngstown, Ohio, November 18, 1903, Judge Wilson was united in marriage with Miss Caroline S. Siegfried, of Youngstown, and to this union there have been born two children: David M. and Francis Service, Jr.

ARTHUR DUNAS is founder and active head of Arthur Dunas & Company, subdividers and home builders in Chicago, with offices in the Chicago Temple. Mr. Dunas and his firm have achieved a memorable record in handling subdivisions on the north and northwest sides of Chicago along the North Shore, many of the finest localities for residence purposes having been improved and put on the market by this organization.

Mr. Dunas was born in Chicago, October 5, 1893, son of Cassel and Tillie (Kurtzon) Dunas. Oldest of four children, Arthur Dunas was educated in the public schools of Chicago, in the Lewis Institute of the city, and since 1919 has been a figure in Chicago realty circles as head of the firm Arthur Dunas & Company. Mr. Dunas has handled upwards of 100 developments in and around Chicago, and his attention is now devoted to the building of a town at Pinewald near Lakewood, New Jersey, and the development and colonization of a large tract in Florida. He is also financing homes for people of moderate means and is president of the People's Mortgage Company.

Mr. Dunas is a member of the Chicago Association of Commerce, the Chicago Real Estate Board and the Chicago Press Club. He married, August 25, 1919, Miss Flora Freedman. They have one daughter, Caryll, and one son, Edwin.

ALEXANDER WILLIAM NEFF. After years of successful operation in different lines Alexander William Neff is now living retired, his time being occupied with the care of his personal affairs, for he has large interests at Cairo and elsewhere in this vicinity. He was born at Cairo, Illinois, in 1854, a son of Peter and Elizabeth (Cruse) Neff, the former of whom was born in Germany, but came to the United States in young manhood, and was married in Union County, Illinois, where he resided for a time before settling permanently at Cairo, and establishing himself in the merchant-tailoring business, in which he continued until his death.

Following the completion of his studies in the public schools of Cairo Alexander William Neff attended the University of Saint Louis, and when he reached his majority he was appointed deputy clerk in the office of the internal revenue collector's office for thirty-six counties in Southern Illinois, comprising the Thirteenth Internal Revenue District, and he continued to hold this position for eight years. Business interests then claimed him, and he operated in hides and skins, and also handled clothing, and finally real estate, in the latter being associated with his brother Cal V. Neff. Mr. Neff's residence is 2611 Elm Street, Cairo, and his brother resides at 2009 Walnut Street in the same city.

On March 5, 1889, Mr. Neff married Amelia Osterloh, born at Cairo, Illinois, a daughter of Christopher M. and Catherine Osterloh, and the following children have been born to them: Alexander William, Jr., who resides at Cairo, is agent for a popular make of automobile, was in the World war, serving first in the Sixty-third Infantry, and in the aero squad in France; Herbert M., who is in partnership with his older brother, resides at Cairo, was also in the service in France as a member of the aero squad; Edwin P., who resides at Cairo, was at the Great Lakes Training Station, Chicago, Illinois, during the World war; Clarence Calvin, who is with his brothers in the automobile business, served on the battleship Connecticut during the World war; and Walter A. and Francis Charles are both mechanics working for their brothers at Cairo. Mr. Neff and his sons are all republicans, and fine citizens, who are held in high esteem by all who know them.

ISAAC NEWTON GRAVES, M. D. Usefulness in the form of active service to humanity has been the distinguishing fact in the career of Isaac Newton Graves, of Goreville, Johnson County. For many years he went wherever duty called him, when the lot of a physician was one of arduous labor and exposure. He is still in practice, but in recent years has been satisfied largely with an office practice and consultation and special work.

His grandfather, Frederick Graves, was one of the early settlers of Johnson County. His father died soon afterward and Frederick came to Illinois with a married sister. He grew up in Johnson County, and shared many of the vicissitudes of pioneer life there. He finally went to Texas to live with one of his children, and died in that state in 1878, at the advanced age of ninety-four.

His son, Joshua Graves, was born in Johnson County, grew up on a farm with few advantages at home or in school, and married Catherine Stewart, daughter of Thomas Stewart, who moved with his family from Western Tennessee to Johnson County. Joshua Graves was accidentally killed by a falling tree in 1858. He and a neighbor were on their way to work on a bridge and in crossing through the woods they stopped where a coon had been treed, and the young men felled the tree, which struck Joshua, resulting in his death. His wife died June 20, 1865. They had a family of five children, two sons and three daughters, and the only one now living is Dr. Isaac Newton Graves.

Doctor Graves was born on his father's farm in Johnson County, May 23, 1854. He

was four years old when his father died and only eleven at his mother's death. The rural schools he attended were maintained for only a few months each year and the teachers had very ordinary qualifications. At the age of twelve, after his mother's death, he went to live with a sister in Southern Indiana and attended school there for a time. He was fifteen when he returned to Johnson County. Doctor Graves as a boy showed a studious disposition and his desire to study medicine was encouraged by a local physician, Doctor Huggins, whom Doctor Graves greatly admired. He accompanied the old doctor on his professional rounds through the country and thus trained himself according to the best practice of former years, studying up on cases as he observed them. Soon after reaching his majority he was able to pass a successful examination and was licensed to practice, and found himself engaged in meeting the obligations of an increasing demand upon his professional abilities. At the same time he was studying for his individual improvement, and finally he entered the St. Louis College of Physicians and Surgeons, from which he was graduated with honors in 1890. Doctor Graves aside from fifteen months practice in Massac County, near Old Hilleuman has given his professional service in Johnson County, at first in the southern part of the county and since 1904 at Goreville. Soon after coming to Goreville he was appointed surgeon for the Chicago & Eastern Illinois Railway and is still performing the duties of that position. In recent years he has confined his work largely to eye, ear, nose and throat work.

Doctor Graves married Amanda Richardson, of Southern Illinois, daughter of Marion Richardson, of Union County. To their marriage were born seven children: Rolla A.; Cora, wife of Charles Stanley, of Johnston City; Daisy, who died in childhood; Izoria, who married Ray Bardley; James, who is agent for the Chicago & Eastern Illinois Railway at Marion; Mabel, wife of Frank Stevens; and Gladys, a public school teacher and also a student in the Southern Illinois Normal University at Carbondale.

WILBUR B. THISTLEWOOD is a civil engineer by training and profession, for a number of years was city engineer of Cairo, but is now head of a machine and repair and automobile business.

He was born at Cairo, August 30, 1877, son of P. J. and Harriet (Barney) Thistlewood, his father a native of Delaware and his mother was born in Edwards County, Illinois. P. J. Thistlewood was a well known and successful business man of Cairo for many years. He first engaged in business as a merchant at Mason, Illinois, but after his marriage moved to Cairo in 1871 and founded and conducted a grain business, and that business is still continued by two of his sons, being one of the factors in Cairo's importance as a grain marketing and handling center. P. J. Thistlewood died in 1903 and his wife, in 1919.

Wilbur B. Thistlewood was liberally educated, having attended the Pennsylvania Military College at Chester, Pennsylvania, and finished his course in civil engineering there in 1897. As a civil engineer he practiced for some fifteen years, and from 1903 to 1911 held the office of city engineer at Cairo. During that time he was the engineer in charge of all the technical work connected with the extensive street paving and sewerage program under Mayor George Parson. Mr. Thistlewood in 1911 bought the Vulcan Iron Works, including a general machine shop and iron foundry with special facilities for steamboat repairs. He has conducted this as a prosperous business and in addition is also local representative for the Chrysler automobile in Cairo and vicinity.

Mr. Thistlewood married in 1900 Miss Geraldine Lancaster, a native of Cairo and daughter of Charles and Sarah (Hodge) Lancaster. They have one daughter, Miss Geraldine. Mr. Thistlewood is a member of the Christian Church, is a republican, for eight years was a member of the Board of Election Commissioners and is a Knights Templar Mason, belongs to the thirty-second degree Scottish Rite Consistory, the Mystic Shrine and is a past commander of the Knights templar. He also belongs to Lodge No. 650, B. P. O. Elks, the Rotary Club, the Association of Commerce, and is a member of the Cairo Library Board. He is a director of the Alexander County Bank.

CAPTAIN ROYAL N. ALLEN for a quarter of a century has been a man of growing prominence in the city of Chicago, well known as a public speaker, active in behalf of many organizations and at the present time a department manager of the Chicago Motor Club.

He was born at Cedar Rapids, Iowa. His father was a native of Madison, Wisconsin. His grandfather, Cornelius L. Allen, came from Oneida County, New York, of English ancestry, related to the family of Ethan Allen of Vermont. Captain Allen's father was descended through his mother from Lieutenant Ranney, who served on the staff of General George Washington in the Revolution.

Royal N. Allen was reared and educated in Iowa, attending Coe College at Cedar Rapids and Cedar Rapids Business College. On coming to Chicago in 1901 he acted as secretary to Mr. George M. Reynolds, who has since become one of the most conspicuous financiers in the country, being president of the Continental & Commercial Bank. Captain Allen for some time was the local representative of the passenger department of the Baltimore & Ohio Railroad at Chicago, his duties being largely of a diplomatic nature. He has held several positions with other corporations, including that of secretary of the Insurance Federation of Illinois. He resigned this office in the latter part of 1925, and on January 1, 1926, became connected with the Chicago Motor Club.

During the World war period Captain Allen came into prominence as a special agent for the United States Department of Justice. The duties of this position took him all over the country, more particularly in centers where seditious and red activities were revealed. He was given the rank of captain in the United States army, and at the end of five years' service was awarded a certificate of the highest commendation for his skill and astuteness in apprehending seditious movements and traitorous characters.

Captain Allen for a number of years has been well known as a public speaker and organizer. He is a member of the Military Intelligence Association of Chicago, is a member, with the rank of captain, of the Reserve Officers Association, belongs to the Hamilton Club, Casa del Mar and Chicago Motor Club, to various Masonic bodies, to the Sojourners' Club, American Sentinels, Sons of the American Revolution, Sons of Veterans, Affiliated Clubs of Chicago and Cook County, Hawkeye Club, Association of Arts and Industries, English Speaking Union, American Road Builders Association and the Greater South Side Chamber of Commerce. Captain Allen married Miss May Coleman.

JOHN C. DEWITT. The manufacturing interests of Union County have grown to be of importance in the commercial and industrial world, and not the least among the various branches of manufacture is that pertaining to the making of boxes. In this line one of the well-known figures is John C. DeWitt, of Anna, whose plant of three large buildings on the Illinois Central Railroad right-of-way is conducted under the name of the Union Fruit Packers Company. Mr. DeWitt is a strictly self-made man who has won his own way and who is deserving of credit for what he has accomplished not only for himself but for the community of his adoption.

John C. DeWitt was born in Union County, Illinois, December 26, 1855, and is a son of Bennett M. and Elizabeth (Cruse) DeWitt. His father, who was born in Hopkins County, Kentucky, came to Union County, Illinois, settling in the Anna community in 1848. Here he met and married Elizabeth Cruse, who was born in Union County, a daughter of Jacob W. and Elizabeth (Hileman) Cruse, natives of North Carolina, who traveled overland in 1825 and settled as pioneers three and one-half miles south of Jonesboro. There they owned and improved a farm of 250 acres, on which both passed away. The parents of John C. DeWitt, following their marriage, settled down to farming, in which Mr. DeWitt continued until 1862, when he enlisted in the Union army for service during the Civil war, in which he lost his life. Mrs. DeWitt then returned to her father, and passed away in 1863.

John C. DeWitt, thus orphaned, lived with his grandparents and an uncle until he was fifteen years of age, in the meantime securing a somewhat limited education in the district schools. On entering upon an independent career he found employment in the timber business, at which he worked in a number of localities and capacities for eight years. Going then to Belknap, Johnson County, Illinois, he invested his small savings in a mercantile business, and spent six years therein. At the end of that period he moved his stock to Anna, and continued in the same line until 1901, when he was elected assessor and treasurer of Union County, in which capacities he served for a term of four years. When he left office, in 1905, he took charge of the Union Fruit Package Company, a farmers' co-operative concern. Starting with a capital of $5,000, this concern, under Mr. DeWitt's able management has grown and developed until it is now a $25,000 company, with three large buildings on the Illinois Central Railroad right-of-way. Mr. DeWitt's title in this enterprise is that of general superintendent.

On September 8, 1878, Mr. DeWitt was united in marriage with Miss Ludella Shadrick, who was born in Mercer County, Illinois, a daughter of John W. and Julia A. (Peeler) Shadrick, also natives of that county. To this union there have been born four children: Callie, the wife of C. H. Hunsaker, of St. Louis, Missouri, who has one daughter, Juanita DeWitt. Mr. and Mrs. DeWitt's other three children are deceased: Minnie J., who died in 1898, aged nineteen years; Elsie E., who died in 1902, aged eighteen years; and Stella, who died in infancy. Mr. and Mrs. DeWitt are members of the Methodist Episcopal Church, in which Mr. DeWitt has been custodian and a member of the Board of Trustees for a period of twenty-five years. A democrat in his political affiliation, he has served capably as city treasurer and alderman. In 1895 he was president of the Southern Illinois Fair Association, and belongs to the Chamber of Commerce, and is a director in the First National Bank and the Union County Lumber Company, and a stockholder in the Union Fruit Package Company. As a fraternalist, Mr. DeWitt is a thirty-second degree Mason and a member of the Independent Order of Odd Fellows and the Knights of Pythias.

HENRY EVANS HALLIDAY. In the development of the City of Cairo and its adjacent territory and commercial facilities no family has been more prominent than that of Halliday. The name appears again and again in the history of things done in improving the river transportation, in broadening the commercial outlook and trade of the city and in promoting its institutions in general.

A prominent member of this family is Henry Evans Halliday, who was born at Cairo, August 8, 1872. His parents were Henry Lang and Laura Evans Halliday, his father a native of Pomeroy, Ohio, and his mother of Batavia, Ohio. His paternal grandparents were William Wyatt and Louisa (Parker) Halliday, while his maternal grandparents were Joseph and Louisa (Parker) Evans, who came from the vicinity of Cincinnati, Ohio. William W. Halliday was a native of Edinburgh, Scotland, graduated from Edinburgh University and for several years after coming to this country was a teacher at Athens, Ohio. He married a native of Gallipolis, Ohio, and then settled on a farm near Pomeroy, where he lived out his life. Joseph Evans was a commission merchant and died of the cholera at St. Louis, Missouri, at the age of thirty-six.

About 1860 Henry Lang Halliday and five of his brothers located at Cairo, Illinois. He was in the hotel and the grain and elevator business, interested in public utilities and was identified with all the leading local industries of his day. His brother Thomas served several terms as mayor and is a member of the Illinois Legislature. Henry L. Halliday died in September, 1895, and his widow, in March, 1897. Their children were: Lila, wife of George H. Capen, of St. Louis; Laura, wife of Preston Kelson, of New York City; Henry E., and Douglas, who died at San Diego, California, in 1907.

Henry E. Halliday after finishing his schooling at Racine, Wisconsin, returned to Cairo, and was associated with his father's business until the death of the latter. He then became president of the H. L. Halliday Milling Company, and in 1898 organized the Halliday Elevator Company and has been president of this institution ever since, one of the largest of the grain milling concerns located at Cairo. He is also a director in the First Bank & Trust Company and was vice-president and part owner of the Cairo Bulletin Company until January, 1925.

Mr. Halliday married in April, 1896, Miss Nellie G. Galigher, a native of Zanesville, Ohio, and daughter of John and Eleanor Galigher. Four children were born to their marriage: Henry E., who died in February, 1924; Eleanor; Russell, a young man working in his father's office; and Jean, who died March 10, 1920, at the age of thirteen years.

Mr. Halliday was for twenty-five years vestryman in the Episcopal Church and is now rector's warden. He has been president of the Board of Trade and the Association of Commerce, is a republican in politics, a member of the B. P. O. Elks, the Egyptian Country Club, the Glen View Club of Chicago, Chicago Athletic Club, the Bell Reeve Golf Club of St. Louis, the Merchants Exchange of St. Louis, and the National Chamber of Commerce.

During the World war he had charge of purchases in the grain department of the Federal Control.

GEORGE FRENCH DEWEY, of Cairo, is an engineer of many years experience and practice, and his technical work has covered a broad field, including highway and railway construction, municipal engineering and general surveying.

He was born at Irvington in Washington County, Illinois, November 19, 1870, son of Edmund S. and Maria Jane (French) Dewey and a grandson of Oliver and Eliza (Sabin) Dewey, natives of Massachusetts. His grandparents came West and settled on a farm near Aurora, Illinois, in 1853. That farm is now in the heart of the City of Aurora. The maternal grandparents of Mr. Dewey were David and Mahitable (Foster) French, the former born at Bedford, New Hampshire, February 1, 1817, and the latter at Sullivan, New Hampshire, May 2, 1813. David French was a Baptist minister and in 1853 located at Jerseyville, Illinois, where he preached eight years, was at Greenville, Illinois, from 1861 to 1864, and from 1866 to 1871 preached at Irvington. In 1871 he became a Baptist minister for the General Association of Southern Illinois and died at Nashville, this state, in April, 1886.

Edmund S. Dewey was born at Lenox, Massachusetts, November 10, 1836, and his wife was born at Goffstown, New Hampshire, July 12, 1847. They were married at Greenville, Illinois. Edmund S. Dewey was a Union soldier in the 130th Illinois Infantry, was an adjutant and was discharged with the rank of captain. He was very proficient in mathematics and other branches and after the war became widely known as an educator, teaching mathematics, bookkeeping and military tactics. His wife was a graduate of the Boston Conservatory of Music and taught music privately and in various schools. Edmund Dewey served as deputy circuit clerk of Bond County, Illinois, and in the fall of 1872 removed to Cairo. In 1887 he was appointed circuit clerk and later was elected to that position. He was an elder in the Presbyterian Church. His death occurred in 1906 and his wife passed away January 29, 1889. Their children were: William Sabin, born August 25, 1869; George French, born November 19, 1870; Charles B., born November 27, 1872, a resident of Chicago; Jennie Elizabeth, born December 22, 1874, a teacher in the public schools of Cairo; John Myron, born November 2, 1877; Mira Josephine, born November 2, 1877, and died in 1923; Robert Edmund, born November 25, 1879, and died in infancy.

George French Dewey up to the age of seventeen lived at home and attended grade and high schools. For two years he was employed under his father in the circuit clerk's office. After that he attended the University of Illinois, from 1889 to 1894, taking the civil engineering course. During the spring of 1895 he was employed on levee construction in Missouri, then became acting county surveyor of Mississippi County, Missouri, serving two years, and in 1898 engaged in private practice and also farmed at Charleston, Missouri. Mr. Dewey on July 1, 1900, became resident engineer on construction of the St. Louis & Memphis Railway, now part of the Frisco System, and in January, 1901, was assigned work at Harrison, Arkansas, with the St. Louis & Northern Arkansas Railroad. Some months later he was with the St. Louis, Memphis & Southeastern Railway and in 1903 worked for the Mobile & Ohio Railroad on maintenance of way work, with headquarters at Cairo, Illinois, under John L. Lancaster. During 1904 he was engaged in private practice and from 1905 to 1910 was in charge of construction on the Cairo & Thebes Railroad during the building of that line and the making of connections between the Cairo and Thebes Bridges. Since 1910 Mr. Dewey has had a general private and consulting practice and has served as city engineer of Cairo.

On December 4, 1895, he married Margaret Sonora Clarkson, a native of Charleston, Missouri, and daughter of James S. and Fannie (Rouse) Clarkson, her father a native of Virginia and her mother of Kentucky. Mr. and Mrs. Dewey became the parents of three children: Frances Janette, born October 6, 1896, and died August 16, 1898; Edmund Dee, born May 16, 1900, at Cairo; and George William, born June 29, 1904, and died April 4, 1908. Mr. Dewey is a member of the Presbyterian Church, is a republican, for several years served as deputy collector and deputy circuit clerk, is a member of the Association of Commerce and belongs to the American Society of Engineers and the Illinois Society of Engineers, and the Institute of Portland Cement.

JOHN H. SPANN. The train of circumstances which lead to quickened activity the efforts of any one man, giving him an agreeable occupation and affording him an opportunity to invest his means and time in some profitable line of business, are not always known in entirety, but the ultimate results stand forth and demonstrate the fundamental gauge of the individual. The late John H. Spann, of Anna, was one who could always be counted upon to put his shoulder to the wheel of progress, and bring to bear upon every project with which he was connected that love of business that was in his blood. His day is past, his work on earth is completed, but the results live on, and stimulate others to like honorable achievements.

John H. Spann was born at New Orleans, Louisiana, February 5, 1847, a son of Silas H. Spann, who was born in North Carolina. When John H. Spann was a small boy his father moved to Jonesboro, Illinois, and was there engaged in merchandising and carpentering, but later in life conducted a general store at Alto Pass, Illinois. His education acquired in the common schools, John H. Spann learned the trade of cooper, and for a time worked at it for Captain Stinson. During the early '60s he was engaged in merchandising in Illinois, but subsequently moved to St. Louis, Missouri, and with a partnership carried on a boot and wholesale shoe business. After five years he returned to Illinois, and, locating at Anna, was engaged in the manufacture and sale of saddlery goods and harness. However, for some years prior to his death, in 1894, he was retired from all business activity.

On May 21, 1874, Mr. Spann married Harriet M. Naill, born at Jonesboro, April 17, 1850, a daughter of John E. and Anna (White) Naill, natives of Hagerstown, Maryland, and Livingston County, New York, respectively. They were married at Jonesboro, where Mr. Naill was a merchant for some years. He was a well-educated man, a graduate of Penna College, Gettysburg, Pennsylvania, class of 1838, and had studied law, although he did not practice, and naturally he became a leader of men and affairs. Not long after the close of the war between the states he retired from business. Mr. and Mrs. Spann became the parents of the following children: John Naill, who is deceased; M. Beatrice, who married John Bacon, a furniture dealer of Anna; Helen, who married R. H. Alden, of Anna; and Carita S., who married Everett H. Alden, and resides with her mother in her beautiful home, 611 South Main Street, Anna. Mrs. Spann is a lady who enjoys the respect of her neighbors and friends, for she has a kindly nature, and a character that reflects her many virtues. Left with ample means by her husband, she is ever generous in her donations, striving to carry out his wishes in disposing of her money. Many of her benefactions are never known to the public for she gives quietly, not desiring that her good deeds be known of men, but those who receive her help know the kindly spirit in which it has been given and remember her accordingly.

WALTER MCCAWLEY passed his entire life in Massac County and was one of the prominent business men and representative citizens of Metropolis, the county seat, at the time of his death, which occurred on June 7, 1907. He was a man of marked ability along business lines, upright and earnest in all of the relations of life, and was a citizen who commanded unqualified popular confidence and esteem.

Mr. McCawley was born at Brookport, Massac County, July 27, 1860, and thus was in the very prime of life at the time of his death. He was a son of William and Emma McCawley, his father having been born at Birmingham, Kentucky, where his parents established their home in the pioneer days, and he having become a successful hotel man at Metropolis, in which city he maintained his home until he moved to St. Louis, Missouri, where he died.

Walter McCawley attended the public schools until he had attained to the age of seventeen years, principally those of Metropolis, where he was reared to adult age. He was seventeen years old when he initiated a practical apprenticeship in connection with the milling business, and eventually he engaged in this line of enterprise in an independent way, he having conducted a well equipped flour mill in Metropolis for a term of years prior to his death. He was a staunch advocate and supporter of the cause of the republican party, and he was a zealous member of the Congregational Church, in which he held official position and of which his widow is a devoted member.

On October 22, 1888, was solemnized the marriage of Mr. McCawley and Miss Addie Quante, who was born and reared in her present home city of Metropolis, to the public schools of which she is indebted for her youthful education and in the social circles of which she has long been a popular figure. Mrs. McCawley is a daughter of August and Hannah (Foreman) Quante. August Quante was born in Germany and in 1850 he accompanied his parents, Frederick and Wilhemine Quante, on their immigration to the United States, he having soon established his residence at Metropolis, where he long continued to be engaged in the milling business and where he became a citizen of much prominence and influence. He served several terms as mayor of Metropolis and was president of the First National Bank of this city at the time of his death, in July, 1922, his wife having passed away in 1905 and having been a daughter of Henry Foreman, who was a native of Germany and who became a pioneer truck gardener at Metropolis, Illinois. August Quante did much to advance the civic and material progress of Metropolis and his name and memory are held in lasting honor in Massac County, where he lived and wrought to goodly ends. He was born in the year 1843 and thus was a lad of about seven years at the time when the family came to the United States, he having been reared and educated in Illi-

nois and having represented this state as a gallant young soldier of the Union throughout the course of the Civil war, in which he was a member of the Fifteenth United States Cavalry. Of the three children of the Quante family Mrs. McCawley is the only one living. Millie became the wife of William Sielbeck and both are deceased. Hiram, the only son, was about thirty-eight years of age at the time of his death. He had one son, August B. Mr. and Mrs. McCawley had no children. Mrs. McCawley is an active member of the Congregational Church in her native city, is prominently identified with the local chapter of the Order of the Eastern Star and with the Woman's Club of Metropolis, of which latter she served twelve years as treasurer. In the city and county that have ever represented her home her circle of friends is limited only by that of her acquaintances.

BENJAMIN CARPENTER is a member of a family that has made history in the city of Chicago, a family identified with commercial affairs for three-quarters of a century and hardly less prominent in the civic, philanthropic and artistic side of the city's activities.

Benjamin Carpenter, who was born at Chicago, September 16, 1865, is the oldest son of George B. and Elizabeth C. (Greene) Carpenter and a grandson of Benjamin Carpenter. Benjamin Carpenter, the elder, brought his family to Chicago in 1850, and he served as alderman of the old Ninth Ward of Chicago and was the first president, in 1861, of the Board of Public Works of the city. George B. Carpenter, whose name is retained in one of the oldest and best known commercial houses in Illinois, Geo. B. Carpenter & Co., was born at Conneaut, Ohio, in 1833, and was about seventeen years of age when he came to Chicago. He graduated at St. Mary's Academy by the Lake, and in 1857 became a partner in the firm of Gilbert Hubbard & Company, ship chandlers. On the death of Mr. Hubbard in 1881 he succeeded to the business, changing its name to Geo. B. Carpenter & Co. Later he took in his sons, Benjamin, Hubbard and John Alden as they successively graduated from Harvard College. George B. Carpenter long before his death had the satisfaction of seeing his business expand and become a notable organization, the largest of its kind in the middle west. His wife, Elizabeth C. Greene, possessed great musical ability and was one of the prominent women of Chicago in musical affairs during her generation. She was born at Pittsfield, New Hampshire, in 1840, and died at Chicago in 1905.

Mr. Benjamin Carpenter attended the University School of Chicago and graduated from Harvard University S. B. Cum Laude in 1888. For over thirty-five years he has given the best of his efforts to the upbuilding of Geo. B. Carpenter & Co., Inc. For some years he has been president of this company. This firm are jobbers, manufacturers and mill agents of cordage, twine, cotton duct, rubber goods, mill and railroad supplies, tents, awnings, flags and marine equipment; the business having broadened out over this extensive field from an original firm engaged in ship chandlery in 1840. Mr. Carpenter is also a director of the Elks Rapids Iron Company and the Elk Electric Company in Michigan. He is director and vice-president of the Anniston Cordage Company at Anniston, Alabama; a director of the Commonwealth Edison Company at Chicago and has served as a trustee of the estates of Helen P. Hubbard and N. K. Fairbank. He is a former director of the Corn Exchange National Bank, now a director of the Illinois Merchants Trust Company.

Mr. Carpenter in 1916 was commissioned a captain quartermaster, Officer's Reserve Corps, and was on active duty in the quartermaster general's office at Washington and New York during 1917-19, being promoted to the rank of major quartermaster in 1918 and lieutenant colonel in 1919. He is former president of the Associated Harvard Clubs and former Governor Deneen appointed him a director of the St. Charles School for Boys and subsequently he was elected president of the board. He is an independent republican, and while a member of no secret society, belongs to such permanent social organizations as the Chicago Club, University Club of Chicago, the Harvard Clubs of Chicago, New York and Boston, Saddle & Cycle Club, Onwentsia Club, Cliff Dwellers Club, the Chicago Yacht Club, Commercial Club; and is a life member of the Chicago Art Institute, the Chicago Field Museum and the Chicago Historical Society. He is a member of the Congregational Church.

Mr. Carpenter married at Chicago, September 18, 1893, Miss Helen G. Fairbank, daughter of N. K. Fairbank, who died in 1903 after a career that identified him in a notable measure with some of Chicago's leading manufacturing and civic affairs. Mrs. Carpenter has been active in charities, such as the Infant Welfare Association and the Henry Booth House, the Illinois Birth Control League, and for four years during the great war was vice-chairman of the Fund for French Wounded. She is active in the Girls' Club of America and the Chicago Women's Clubs. Mr. and Mrs. Carpenter are the parents of four children: Benjamin Carpenter, Jr., who graduated from Harvard A. B. in 1916 and now is with Geo. B. Carpenter & Co.; Fairbank Carpenter, who attended Harvard University in 1923-24 and is now associated with his father's business; Cordelia Fairbank Carpenter, who was married to Dr. N. S. Davis, third to bear a distinguished name in Chicago professional life, and they have two sons, N. S. Davis IV, and Graham Davis; and Elizabeth Webster Carpenter, who was married in 1925 to Thomas L. Marshall.

George Albert Carpenter, the younger brother of Benjamin Carpenter, was born in Chicago in 1867 and has made a notable career as a lawyer and jurist. He is a graduate of Harvard University, class of '88, and of the Harvard Law School, and after being admitted to the bar practiced as a member of the firm Pence & Carpenter. He was elected a judge of the Circuit Court of Cook County and served until 1909 and in 1910 was appointed by President Taft as United States district judge, and has served on the bench for sixteen years.

The two youngest brothers of Benjamin Carpenter, Hubbard and John Alden Carpenter, both of whom graduated from Harvard University with the class of 1897, are both identified with Geo. B. Carpenter & Co., the former as treasurer and the latter as vice president. John Alden Carpenter is well known in the world of arts and music. He inherited his mother's musical talent, and is one of America's foremost musical composers. He was decorated with the cross of the Legion of Honor by the French government in 1921, and a further mention of his musical work was recognized by Harvard University in 1922 in awarding him the honorary degree of Master of Arts.

NATHANIEL K. FAIRBANK. The present generation of Chicagoans has repeated occasion to admire the generous idealism and sound tastes as well as the constructive energies of those very practical and hard-headed men who dominated the commercial life of the city in the years following the great fire. One of the most important figures of that age and epoch of the city was Nathaniel K. Fairbank. The success he made of business was only one of many causes that relate his name and influence closely with some of the most permanent institutions of Chicago.

He came to Chicago when very young and was active in its business affairs for over forty years. He was born at Sodus, Wayne County, New York, in 1829, and had only a common school education. At the age of fifteen he began an apprenticeship as a brick layer at Rochester, later for several years was bookkeeper in a flouring mill, and in 1855, at the age of twenty-six, became western representative at Chicago for David Dows & Company, grain merchants. Mr. Fairbank was for many years an active member of the Chicago Board of Trade.

About the close of the Civil war he provided the capital for the construction of a lard and oil refinery on Eighteenth Street, west of the river. The first factory was burned, and a larger one was erected at Eighteenth and Blackwell streets. After a few years the business took the name of N. K. Fairbank & Company. During the first twenty years the primary output was lard and lard oil, and the lard manufactured under the company's brands had a world wide use and distribution. Later the facilities of the business were adapted for the manufacture of soaps, and it is with a line of high grade laundry and toilet soaps that the name has most familiar associations for the modern generations of Americans. About ten years after the business was established at Chicago a branch house was built at St. Louis, later another at Omaha, and long before N. K. Fairbank retired from active control of the business it had attained a national scope and importance.

Chicagoans of the present century will understand the broad sympathies and generous interests of N. K. Fairbank through mention of some of the institutions of which he was the benefactor. He donated the land and he and his wife were among the most liberal supporters of St. Luke's Hospital after that institution was transferred to its present site. Of the older Chicagoans none could surpass him in love of music, and he was president of some of the May Festival organizations in the early '80s, and throughout the rest of his life a generous supporter of the musical activities which came to a climax in the establishment of the Symphony Orchestra under Theodore Thomas. While his friend, George B. Carpenter, conceived the plan of constructing a hall particularly adapted for music, it was N. K. Fairbank who conducted the campaign and aroused the generous financial support needed for the construction of Central Music Hall, which served an entire generation of Chicagoans as the home of music and other arts. He was one of the most devoted members of the church presided over by Prof. David Swing, and he followed Professor Swing in the establishment of the Independent Church, which held its services in Central Music Hall. Mr. Fairbank also helped finance and put on a permanent financial basis the Chicago Newsboys Home. He took the initiative and assumed for a time the entire financial responsibility of building the home of the Chicago Club, which, prior to the great building era of the present century, stood on Monroe Street opposite the old Palmer House. These were some of the more familiar institutions that exemplified Mr. Fairbank's eminent public spirit, but there was no time in his life as a Chicagoan when he failed of either personal initiative or generous response in any movement characterizing the best ideals of the community.

Mr. Fairbank married, in 1866, Miss Helen L. Graham, of New York, and they were the parents of four sons and three daughters. The eldest daughter, Helen Graham Fairbank, married Benjamin Carpenter, a son of George B. Carpenter and president of the Geo. B. Carpenter Co., one of Chicago's oldest and most substantial commercial organizations. A son, Kellogg Fairbank, has for over thirty years practiced law in Chicago, and he married Janet A. Ayer, daughter of Benjamin F. Ayer. A son, Wallace Fairbank, married Josephine Nelson, daughter of Murry Nelson, and his youngest daughter married Laird Bell, a well known attorney and a member of the firm of Fisher, Boyden, Kales & Bell.

REV. PETER B. DUFAULT, pastor of one of the largest Catholic parishes in Illinois, at Kankakee, is a native of that city, and has been in the service of his church since early manhood.

He was born at Kankakee August 30, 1878, son of Peter and Mathilda (Charron) Dufault, his father a native of New York State and his mother of Canada. The paternal grandparents, Nelson and Lucy (Roy) Dufault, were natives respectively of Canada and New York, and settled in Kankakee about 1860, where Nelson Dufault followed his trade as a plasterer and mason. The maternal grandparents, Theophilus and Corinne (Chartier) Charron, came to Kankakee about 1850. Theophilus Charron was a blacksmith. Peter Dufault followed the trade of plasterer and died October 6, 1919. His widow resides at Kankakee.

Peter B. Dufault was educated in parochial schools, attended St. Viators College, and completed his theological course at Montreal, Canada. He was ordained a priest December 17, 1906, and for ten years was an assistant priest in St. Joseph's Church in Chicago. In 1916 he was appointed pastor of St. James Church at Irwin, Illinois, and on August 10, 1924, was transferred to St. Rose of Lima Church of Kankakee. This parish has a membership of about twelve hundred families and in membership is the largest parish in northern Illinois outside of Chicago.

The church was founded in 1855. The first pastor looked after the spiritual need of a number of parishes in that section of Illinois. Since 1857 the records of the church and parish have been maintained without a break. The second pastor was Father Mailloux, who was Le Grand Vicaire to the bishop of Quebec. He took charge of St. Rose Church at the age of sixty. Father Mailloux had come to Kankakee County in order to counteract the evil influence of Chiniquy among the French Canadians.

In 1852 St. Ann's Church, St. Anne, Illinois, was founded as a church for French Canadian families. Its pastor Chiniquy was excommunicated and formed a schism, a large number of his parishioners following him out of the church, but his attempt to found a new religion was unsuccessful. Rev. Mailloux was succeeded, in September, 1862, by James Cote, and after two years Joseph M. Langlois became pastor. Rev. Marschal was pastor from 1866 until May, 1871. Father P. Paradis became pastor September 13, 1871, and in the same year work was started on the stone structure of the present church, which was dedicated June 27, 1877, by Bishop Foley of Chicago. Rev. Ambrose D. Granger became priest March 28, 1898. In 1907 the church was enlarged, making the total length of the edifice 150 feet.

Father Dufault has two assistants, Joseph Tarean and John Justi. The St. Rose School for Boys and St. Joseph's Seminary for Girls provide complete educational facilities from the grammar through the high school grades for about 540 students. The church also established St. Mary's Hospital, a hundred bed hospital, conducted by the Sister Servants of the Holy Heart of Mary.

ROBERT LEROY DULANEY lived at Marshall in Clark County. He came here when a boy, grew up an orphan, and while he was liberally educated he never inherited wealth, yet he became one of the wealthy men of his generation in southern Illinois and enjoyed a commanding position and influence as a lawyer and financier.

He was born in Loudoun County, Virginia, September 12, 1818, and was a member of a family that had been in America for generations. He was a descendant of Thomas Dulaney, a native of Ireland, who with five sons came to America about 1700. The parents of Robert Leroy Dulaney were Zachary and Mary (Braden) Dulaney.

Left an orphan, at the age of twelve years he came to Illinois with a Doctor Allison, behind whom he rode on a horse. He was taken into the home of his uncle, Woodford Dulaney, who had settled at York in Clark County. While living in the home of his uncle he attended the village schools, and his literary education was rounded out at Indiana University at Bloomington. At Marshall he studied law under Judge Constable, completing his law course in Transylvania University at Lexington, Kentucky. He was admitted to the Illinois bar in 1843. For over thirty-five years he enjoyed an enviable position as a practicing attorney at Marshall. He retired from the law in 1879. He had practiced with Judge Constable for a time and for many years was the legal associate of Thomas J. Golden.

Perhaps of greater importance than his professional career was the active interests he held as a railroad man and banker. He was closely associated in banking and railroading with Riley McKeen of Terre Haute, Indiana. For years they were together on the Board of Directors of the Vandalia Railroad, of which Mr. McKeen was president. In 1880, after his retirement from law practice, Mr. Dulaney founded R. L. Dulaney & Company, a firm of private bankers at Marshall. In 1892 this firm was succeeded by the present Dulaney National Bank. Robert L. Dulaney served as president of that bank until his death on May 5, 1903.

Politically he began voting as a whig and later as a republican, but never sought any political honors. During the term of Governor Beveridge he served as a member of the commission that located the Illinois State Institution for the Feeble Minded. Prior to that Governor Oglesby had made him a trustee of the State Penitentiary, and he filled that office during a portion of Governor Cullom's administration.

Mr. Dulaney married, December 24, 1850, Elizabeth E. Bartlett, daughter of John and Jane Bartlett. She was born September 3, 1833, and died May 1, 1882. They were the parents of the following children: Charles W., who died in 1885 and married Mollie Clay Rice; Harry B., who married Edith Prevo in 1901; Eleanor, who married J. P. Barclay; Hector B., who never married; Eliza, who became the wife of W. C. Berry; Robert W., who never married; and Cecile, who became the wife of Dr. J. R. Burnett.

HON. GEORGE F. SEHRING. A lifelong resident of the city of Joliet, Hon. George F. Sehring is well known to its citizens as a man of integrity and ability who has been identified with a number of leading enterprises and whose business talents have been enlisted in the cause of public service much to the betterment of the community. In the capacity of mayor, an office in which he has served since the spring of 1923, he has established a splendid record for his businesslike methods of handling conditions which have come under his jurisdiction.

Mayor Sehring was born at Joliet, February 21, 1872, and is a son of Frederick and Eloise (Bez) Sehring, natives of Germany, the father of the province of Hesse-Darmstadt. The parents were married in their native land and not long thereafter immigrated to the United States, taking up their residence at Mokena, Illinois. Mr. Sehring became prominent in his community and served for a time as county recorder of Will County, and after moving to Joliet, was once a candidate for state senator. Having learned the art of brewing in his native land, he followed that calling on coming to the United States, and finally purchased the Columbia Brewery, which he conducted successfully until his death in 1892, his widow surviving him until 1911. They were the parents of the following children: Susan, of San Francisco, California; Louis J., of Joliet; Margaret, the wife of Henry F. Prepiepenbenk, of Joliet; Henry, of Joliet; Herman, who is deceased; Anna, the wife of Doctor Poehner, of San Francisco; and George F., of this notice.

George F. Sehring attended the public schools of Joliet, and after graduating from the high school as a member of the class of 1891 took a business course at the Metropolitan Business College of Chicago. He secured his first employment as collector for the Will County National Bank, where he rose to receiving teller and then to paying teller, but in 1904 resigned his position to become cashier and collector of the Fred Sehring Brewing Company. In 1922, because of national prohibition, the brewing company ceased business, and since then Mr. Sehring has centered his energies in looking after his large interests of a business and financial character and in attending to his official duties. In 1905 he was elected city treasurer, a position in which he served in that and the following year, and in the spring of 1923 was elected mayor of Joliet, an office which he retains, as above noted. Mr. Sehring is a Lutheran in religious faith and has a number of fraternal and civic connections.

On November 4, 1896, Mr. Sehring was united in marriage with Miss Louisa Kramer, who was born at Joliet, Illinois, a daughter of Frank and Mary (Weber) Kramer, of Germany. Mrs. Sehring, a member of the Catholic Church, died July 25, 1925, having been the mother of the following children: Margaret, who died as the wife of Joseph Smith; Gertrude, the wife of Joseph F. Lennon, of Joliet; Fred, who is employed in the Will County National Bank; George H., who is a medical student at the University of Michigan, Ann Arbor; and Louise, who formerly acted as secretary to her father on the Board of Local Improvements, and was married, June 14, 1926, to Mr. John J. Cassidy, who is located in Joliet, being associated with his father, Mr. Charles Cassidy, in conducting the J. O. Gorman Company, one of the pioneer wholesale and retail fruit dealers in Joliet.

JOSEPH L. ABELL is a veteran figure in river and transportation circles at Cairo, having been identified both with water and railroad traffic. He is wharf master at Cairo, and is a deservedly popular figure in that community.

He was born at Cincinnati, Ohio, October 9, 1863, son of Joseph I. and Cordelia E. (Goodwin) Abell, his father a native of Philadelphia, Pennsylvania, and his mother of Cincinnati, Ohio. Joseph I. Abell was a river boatman and merchant, and on January 2, 1864, after service as a Union soldier in the Civil war, he located at Cairo, Illinois, where for a number of years he was a steamboat agent and in the lumber business. Both parents are now deceased. Their children were: Alexander G., of Kansas City, Missouri; Joseph L.; Charles E., of Los Angeles, California; Lucy, who died at the age of ten years; Edward I. and Samuel J., both of Cairo.

Joseph L. Abell had a public school education to the age of seventeen. He grew up from early infancy in Cairo and has been an observer of the tide of traffic and boats and personalities on the river for a period of fifty years. His first service was as clerk on a transfer boat on the Ohio and Mississippi. July 1, 1887, he was appointed a city letter carrier of Cairo, being one of the first appointed after the free delivery system was introduced. Twenty-five months later, however, he resigned to go back to the river and was on the steamboat W. G. Duncan some years. In 1898 he became a clerk in the Mobile & Ohio Railway freight house, and was in the service of that road for seventeen years. In 1920 he was made wharf master at Cairo, and since the same year has also been steamboat agent for packets on the Ohio and Mississippi rivers.

Mr. Abell has never married. He is a democrat in his political affiliations and has been prominent in the Knights of Pythias order, serving in all the chairs of the lodge, is a member of the Pythian Sisters and belongs to the Knights of the Mystic Crew of Comas, a social order organized in 1867.

ROSS A. HARLE. From the time he was six years old Ross A. Harle, owner of the Breese Journal, has been interested in the printing business, and in his present work he is following his inclinations and giving his abilities their proper field of operation. He was born in Bible Grove, Missouri, July 13, 1899, a son of William Albert and Emily Harle, the former of whom died September 26, 1920, but the latter survives. He was a mine operator, having been connected with three mines, and he also operated in oil, owned several general stores and a drug store, the greater part of his property being in Adair County, Missouri. He also traded in live stock and farms, and was one of the leading men in his county, his ability as a business man and financier being unquestioned. He and his wife had five children, namely: William Boyd, who married Ethel Pritchard, has two children, Adah and Aline; Nellie, who married C. W. Wicher, had one child, Trecil; Iva, who married Harry Wilches, has five children, Norman, Harry, Nellie, Herbert and Margaret; Ethel, who married A. D. Jones; and Ross A., who was the youngest child.

After having been graduated from the high school of Kirkville, Missouri, in 1917, Ross A. Harle tried to enlist in the late war thirteen times, and even went to Calgary, Canada, but was each time rejected on account of defective eyesight. He has always, as before stated, been deeply interested in the printing business, and when only six years old used to work around printing offices, and was similarly engaged during his vacation periods as he grew older. When he was sixteen years old he went into the office of the Kirkville Daily News, and was with that concern for two years. After his repeated failures to get into either the army or navy he returned to the Kirkville Daily News, and spent two more years with this paper. Coming then to Breese, he bought one-half interest in the Journal, a weekly publication, and in September, 1923, became sole

owner through purchase of the other half interest. He conducts his paper as an independent organ, and has a wide circulation, and good patronage in advertising from the local business men.

On November 26, 1921, Mr. Harle married Miss Lillie Dodson, of Kirkville, Missouri, and their only child died in infancy. Mrs. Harle is a daughter of Theodore and Cora Dodson, the former of whom is living, but the latter died in June, 1923. Mr. and Mrs. Dodson had the following children: Thomas; Theodore; Myrtle, who married a Mr. Reynolds, and has five children; Nora, who married David Moore; Ruth, who married a Mr. Scarbrough, and has one child; Mrs. Harle, who was the next in order of birth; and Ophal and Mary Lee, both of whom are unmarried. Mr. Dodson is a resident of Kirkville at present, and is engaged in the teaming business, but for many years was a prosperous farmer.

CREAL SPRINGS COLLEGE supplies educational facilities of a high order to a community in Williamson County which otherwise has been noted as a quiet and orderly agricultural community and one which annually ships large quantities of its horticultural produce to outside markets.

Creal Springs College was founded by Mr. and Mrs. Henry Clay Murrah, of Frankfort, Illinois, and was opened September 22, 1884, as a seminary or junior college, including a department of music. Henry Clay Murrah at that time was a merchant at Frankfort. He bought five acres of ground at Creal Springs and erected the middle portion of what was to be a large three-story building. A charter was obtained from the state for "Creal Springs Seminary and Conservatory of Music." The seminary gave four years of academic and two years of college work. Courses were later added in normal, elocution and business training.

It was the intention of the founders to build a school for girls only, but the numerous applications from boys induced them to change their plans, and the school became co-educational. The following ten years were prosperous ones under the private ownership of the founders. In the meantime a substantial bequest was received and in 1894 the Baptists induced the founders to turn over the management to that organization. The change was consequently effected that year. Carrying out the request of the donor, all departments of the Seminary were preserved and the other two years of college work added under the new charter for "Creal Springs College and Conservatory of Music." Under the auspices of the Baptist Church the wings to the original building were added.

The president of the seminary and college since its founding has been Mrs. G. B. Murrah. The college grew rapidly to a Class A college with a faculty of ten and about two hundred students, the maximum for which provision could be made under the facilities. During the World war period the college met heavy financial losses and was closed.

Mrs. Murrah served as president continuously from 1884 to 1917. On the death of her husband, Mr. Murrah, in 1920, she began making plans for reopening the college, and the Board of Trustees retained their organization intact. In September, 1926, these plans were finally realized with the opening of the college in all departments.

HOWARD ERNEST CAMPBELL is one of the foremost radio engineers in the country, and is one of the few men in his profession who can claim fifteen years of consecutive experience in this giant but infant industry. Mr. Campbell has had experience as a radio expert, at first with the navy and later in commercial radio operation all over the country, and is now the chief radio engineer for the WLS Station, built, owned and operated by Sears, Roebuck and Company of Chicago.

Mr. Campbell is a native of Illinois, born at Greenup, May 25, 1886, son of Alven W. and Julia M. (Kirkendall) Campbell. His parents were born in Ohio, and his father and mother graduated from Ohio University at Athens in 1883. They moved to Illinois and settled at Greenup in 1885, and his father is now retired.

Howard Ernest Campbell after finishing his grammar school education in 1900 took up the study of the Morse system of telegraphy, graduating from Valentines School of Telegraphy in 1901. He then resumed his regular public school work, finishing high school in 1905, followed with four years at the University of Indiana, where he majored in physics and mathematics. In 1910 he graduated from the United States Naval Electrical School at Brooklyn. During 1911-12 he was radio electrician in the United States Navy, during 1912 acting as senior radio operator on the staff of Admiral Schroeder, the commander-in-chief of the Atlantic Fleet. Beginning in 1913 and continuing until America's entrance into the World war, he was identified with the commercial side of radio, with the Marconi Wireless Telegraph Company. With this company he was operating and installing radio engineer during 1913, for the first six months of 1914 was chief radio inspector of the port of New York City for the company, and during the last six months was assistant engineer in charge of the company's 300 kilo-watt Trans-Atlantic Radio Telegraph at New Brunswick, New Jersey, and was appointed engineer-in-charge of the station during 1915. In 1916 the Marconi Company made him associate engineer-in-charge of special research at the 300 kilowatt Trans-Pacific Radio Telegraph Station at Bolinas, California.

When this station was taken over by the government, April 7, 1917, he was continued there as officer-in-charge under the United States Navy. During 1918 he served as chief radio gunner, United States Navy, in charge of the United States Naval Radio Training School at Marshall, California. Following that, until September, 1919, he was radio communication officer on the staff of the Pacific Coast communication superintendent of the United States Navy.

On leaving the naval service in September, 1919, Mr. Campbell went with the Western Electric Company as radio designing engineer until May, 1922. During that time he designed the first 500-watt radiophone transmitter built by the company. From May, 1922, to January, 1924, he was radio engineer-in-charge of the Detroit News Broadcasting Station WWJ, and in January, 1924, became manager and chief radio engineer of the broadcasting division, Jewett Radio and Phonograph Company, erecting, installing and operating the company's 5000-watt broadcasting station WJR. In April, 1926, he took up his present work in Chicago as chief radio engineer for WLS Station. The physical plant of this station, one of the largest and finest equipped in the world, is located at Crete, Illinois, some thirty-five miles from Chicago. WLS is a radio station of outstanding achievement in the radio world. It has offered a program of great variety both in high class entertainments and in educational features, its educational service to farmers being unexcelled.

Mr. Campbell has successfully solved many of the intricate problems involved in broadcasting special programs, one of which was arranging for the broadcasting of the main features of the Eucharistic Congress at Chicago during June, 1926. Mr. Campbell has held a license as a first class commercial operator from the United States Department of Commerce since 1912. He has been a member of the Institute of Radio Engineers since 1914, and is author of various articles published in radio and trade magazines, and has also been a lecturer on technical problems of radio engineering.

JOHN MYRON DEWEY, clerk of the Circuit Court of Alexander County, is a native of Cairo and has been well and favorably known in business and public affairs there for a number of years.

He was born at Cairo, November 2, 1877, son of Edmund S. and M. Jennie (French) Dewey, his father a native of Lenox, Massachusetts, and his mother of Keene, New Hampshire. They were married at Irvington, Illinois, where his father was teacher of mathematics in Southern Illinois Agricultural College, his mother teaching in the music department of the same school.

John Myron Dewey graduated from high school at Cairo in 1897, following which he worked on farms in Northern Illinois for one and a half years, spent four years doing clerical work for the Wood & Bennett Company of Cairo and for several years had charge of the shipping department of one of Cairo's flour mills. Mr. Dewey since 1907 has been engaged in the abstract business, has a full set of the abstract records of Alexander County and performs most of the service in that line. His business is conducted as E. S. Dewey & Company, with offices in the courthouse.

He married, October 16, 1906, Miss Josephine P. Kaha, a native of Cairo and daughter of Louis H. and Josephine (Laurent) Kaha. Her parents were born in Germany, her father in the City of Hamburg and the mother on the Rhine. Mr. Dewey is a member of the Presbyterian Church and one of the deacons of the church at Cairo. He is a Mason, a member of the Eastern Star, belongs to the Kiwanis Club and Association of Commerce and is a republican.

From 1908 to 1912 he served as deputy circuit clerk and for a year and a half, in 1913-14, was deputy county clerk and at the same time deputy assessor. In 1916 he was elected to the office of Circuit Court clerk, and at the present time is serving his third successive term in that office.

DANIEL M. KELLY, a native of Cairo, has been identified throughout his business career with that city. He is an architect by training and profession, but his chief business activities have been identified with lumber manufacturing.

He was born at Cairo April 10, 1867, son of Daniel E. and Helen Kelly, both natives of Ireland. His father was born in County Cork in 1835 and died in 1917, while his mother was born in 1845 and died in 1905.

Daniel M. Kelly grew up at Cairo, attending parochial and public schools and as part of his training for the architectural profession, was a student in the Chicago Art Institute. From 1889 to 1900 he was associated with his brother in the contracting and building business, doing the work of an architect. However, since 1896 his time and energies have been chiefly given to the lumber milling business. He is a member of the Kelly Brothers Lumber Company, and his other business interests included the Mounds Lumber Company, the Wickliff Lumber Company, the Egyptian Box Company and the Ferguson Brick Company.

Mr. Kelly as a successful business man has been free of his time and means in behalf of community affairs. In 1912 he was elected an alderman of the city and since 1913 has served continuously as a member of the City Commission, his special duties being as commissioner of streets and public improvements. He was for many years a trustee of the B. P. O. Elks Lodge and is a member of the Association of Commerce.

He married, September 5, 1893, Miss Tensa Walsh, of Cairo. She died May 10, 1909, and surviving her are four children, a son, Lawrence Kelly, and three daughters, Helen, Mary and Ruth.

WILLIAM GEORGE, president of the old Second National Bank of Aurora, is a lawyer by education and profession and has been a conspicuous leader in the banking business, stock raising and other interests of northern Illinois for many years.

He was born at Sugar Grove in Kane County, Illinois, September 23, 1861, son of Alonzo and Lydia (May) George. His paternal grandfather, Ebenezer George, was a native of Keene, New Hampshire, the son of Benjamin George, a Revolutionary soldier, and Sarah Coolidge. His father, Alonzo George, for many years a resident of Aurora, was a native of Strafford, Vermont, and his wife, Lydia May, was a daughter of Col. Elisha May, of Fairlee, Vermont, who was directly connected with Capt. John May of Boston, who led the party, dressed as Indians which threw the tea overboard and which caused the Revolution.

Mr. George attended public schools at West Aurora, graduated from the West Aurora High School in 1879 and was a student in the University of Iowa at Iowa City with the class of 1884. He took his law degree at the Union College of Law in Chicago, now Northwestern College of Law, in 1885, and on being admitted to the bar engaged in practice at Aurora, where for about three years he was associated with former United States Senator Albert J. Hopkins, and with his partners, N. J. Aldrich and Frank H. Thatcher. Later he practiced alone and as a member of the firm of Aldrich, Winslow & George.

In the meantime Mr. George, in 1891, had taken an active part in the management of the old Second National Bank in the capacity of vice president. His father, Alonzo George, was at that time president. On the death of his father, in 1895, he succeeded to the office of president, and has been head of that financial institution for over thirty years. Mr. George is also a director in the Aurora Cotton Mills and many other manufacturing and business institutions.

He has long been conspicuously connected with the pure bred live stock interests of Illinois and is owner of the George stock farms near Aurora. He is former president of the Illinois Cattle Breeders Association, former vice president of the American Genetic Association, an ex-president of the American Hereford Cattle Breeders Association, a member of the Advisory Board of the National Soil Fertility League and a director of the Kane County Farm Improvement Association.

During 1903-04 Mr. George was president of the Illinois Bankers Association; was vice president for Illinois of the American Bankers Association and member of the executive council from 1905 to 1908 and again from 1909 to 1912. He has been president of the Kane County Bankers' Association. Mr. George is a republican, is a member of the Phi Delta Theta college fraternity and Phi Delta Phi law fraternity. During the World war was active in the Aurora Patriot's Committee; was chairman of the Kane County Y. M. C. A. war work; chairman of the Kane County United War Work; a member of the Kane County Council of Defense and treasurer of the Jewish Relief for Kane County. He is a member of the Union League, Hamilton, Saddle & Sirloin Clubs of Chicago, and the Union League Club of Aurora.

On October 11, 1887, he married Miss Alice Maude Lounsbury, of Dayton, Ohio, daughter of Rev. E. W. Lounsbury, D. D. They have two children: Alice May (Mrs. Eliot Winthrop Morrell) and Elizabeth Marcia.

LUCY BEATRICE TWENTE has the distinction of being the youngest county superintendent of schools in the state of Illinois, her position identifying her with the schools of Alexander County, of which Cairo is the county seat.

Miss Twente was born at Thebes, Illinois, in October, 1898, daughter of Asa D. and Mary A. (Miller) Twente. Her parents were both born near Olive Branch, Illinois. Her father spent his active career in educational work, as teacher and principal of public schools for a period of twenty-seven years, and for three years held the office of county superintendent of schools of Alexander County, dying in that office in 1922. His widow still lives at Cairo.

Lucy Beatrice Twente was educated in district schools to the age of thirteen, then attended the Thebes High School and in 1917 graduated from the Southern Illinois Normal School at Carbondale. She did her first work as a teacher in the Twente primary school in her old home community. She taught there a year, three years in the Thebes High School and then in the Community High School of Kaneville. For several summer sessions she was a student in the University of Illinois. She taught in the high school at Mound City and had completed one year of consecutive work at the University of Illinois when through the death of her father she left the university to accept appointment to fill out his term as county superintendent of schools and subsequently she was regularly elected to that office. Under her supervision are the many public schools in Alexander County, including seven for white and six for colored pupils in Cairo and outside of that city thirty-four school buildings for white scholars and twelve buildings for colored students. The total enrollment of scholars is 6,500. Miss Twente is a republican, is a member of the Methodist Episcopal Church and secretary of the Alexander County Sunday School Association.

WILLIAM M. LANGSTON has been a successful and influential figure in the life of his community in Mason County since early manhood. His principal tasks and duties have identified him with agriculture, and he has been a citizen willing at all times to cooperate and work for the general welfare.

He was born in a log house that stood on his father's farm near Manito, in Mason County, February 16, 1854. His father was a prominent pioneer figure known as Judge Matthew Langston, who settled in the Manito neighborhood prior to the Civil war. When the war came on he joined the Union army as captain of Company A of the Eighty-fifth Illinois Infantry, but in the course of the war he was obliged to resign on account of disability and return home. He had some years earlier given service to his country as a soldier in the Mexican war under General Taylor. Judge Langston for a number of years was a merchant at Manito. Later, attracted by the idea of securing land at a reasonable figure, he went to Kansas, remaining there until driven out by the scourge of grasshoppers. He then returned to Illinois and devoted his later years to farming in the vicinity of Manito, where he died in 1894. He had served as a member of the Illinois Legislature in 1872, was elected county judge in the early '60s as a war democrat and is a justice of the peace acquired the name and title of Judge Langston. He was of Colonial American stock. His grandfather, William Langston, served with North Carolina troops in the War of the Revolution, as shown by R. File No. 6149, in the Pension Office at Washington.

Judge Langston married Miss Sarah Havens. She was born in Scott County, Illinois, and died in 1915. Both are buried in the

Langston Cemetery in Manito Township. These parents had the following children: Daniel, who died in infancy; William M.; Elizabeth, who married Vernon C. Crosby and resides in Forest City, Mason County, Illinois; Rebecca, wife of W. W. White, of Forest City; Ella, deceased; Edward, who helped organize and was cashier of the Forest City State Bank, and he died in that city; and there were two other children who died in infancy.

William M. Langston was reared on the home farm, attended the common schools, and worked in his father's mercantile establishment and also on the farm. He has made a substantial record as a prosperous farmer in the community where he grew up and has carried his share of responsibilities in behalf of institutions and education and religion. He has always been a prohibitionist. He has filled offices as road commissioner and supervisor.

William M. Langston married Miss Hannah Kennedy, daughter of James B. and Mary (Watkins) Kennedy. The Kennedy family have been Illinois farmers for many years. James B. Kennedy on leaving the farm located at Forest City and engaged in the meat business and also as a stock dealer and shipper. Mrs. William M. Langston was born November 3, 1865. She and her husband have the following children: Vernon C., manager and secretary of the Farmers Elevator Company at Forest City; Lillie, wife of Floyd Whitaker, of Forest City; Lee M., who lives at home; Miss Gladys, at home; James, who married Carrie Leinweber and resides near Delavan, Illinois, while the three younger children, all at home, are Mabel, Ruby and Juanita.

VERNON C. LANGSTON. The Langston family is one of the old ones of Mason County, and those bearing the name have been connected with business and public life in this part of Illinois for many years. One of the younger members of the family, deserving of more than passing mention, is Vernon C. Langston, manager and secretary of the Farmers Elevator Company at Forest City. He was born at Forest City, April 11, 1896, a son of William M. Langston, and grandson of Judge Matthew Langston.

Judge Langston, judge of Mason County for a long period, was one of the well-known figures of this neighborhood. He came to the Manito neighborhood of the county prior to the outbreak of war between the North and the South, and served in the Union army as captain of company A, 85th Illinois Infantry. He also served in the Mexican war under General Taylor. Disability caused his honorable discharge before the close of the Civil war and he returned to Mason County. For some years he was engaged in the mercantile business at Manito, and then, attracted by the idea of securing land at a reasonable figure, he went to Kansas. He secured the land, but unfortunately, the plague of grasshoppers destroyed his crops, and he felt forced to return to his old home. For the remainder of his life he was engaged in farming in the vicinity of Manito, and he died there in 1894. He served in Legislature in Illinois in 1872. He married Miss Sarah Havens, born in Scott County, Illinois, and she survived him until 1915, when she passed away, and they are buried in the Langston Cemetery in Manito Township. Their children were as follows: Daniel, who died in infancy; William M., who is mentioned at length below; Elizabeth, who married Vernon C. Crosby and resides in Tazewell County, Illinois; Rebecca, who married W. W. White, of Forest City; Ella, deceased; Edward, who died at Forest City, cashier of the Forest City State Bank, which he helped to organize; and two, who died in infancy.

William M. Langston was born near Manito, in one of the old log cabins of the period, February 16, 1854. He remained with his parents until his father's death, when he began farming on his own account, and has continued to devote himself to agricultural pursuits. In politics he has always been a prohibitionist, and he has served as road commissioner and supervisor. He married Hannah Kennedy, a daughter of James B. and Mary (Watkins) Kennedy. Mr. Kennedy founded his family in Illinois, and after being a farmer for many years he settled at Forest City, engaged in the meat business and was also a stock dealer and shipper. Mrs. William M. Langston was born November 3, 1865. The following children have been born to Mr. and Mrs. William M. Langston: Vernon C., whose name heads this review; Lillie, who is the wife of Floyd Whitaker, of Forest City; Lee M., who is a resident of the Forest City locality; Gladys, at home; James, who married Carrie Leinweber and resides near Delavan, Illinois; and Mabel, Ruby and Juanita, at home.

Growing up on his father's farm near Forest City, Vernon C. Langston attended the local schools, and subsequently took a commercial course at Brown's Business College, Peoria. Mr. Langston was inducted into the United States army under the draft at Havanna, Illinois, and was sent to Camp Wheeler, Macon, Georgia, where he was assigned to Company E, One Hundred and Twenty-second Infantry, General Lyons Division, where he was still stationed when the armistice was signed, and he was there honorably discharged in December, 1918, and at once returned to Forest City.

From 1918 to 1922 Mr. Langston was engaged in farming, but in the latter year entered the Forest City Co-operative Grain Company as manager and secretary, and still holds these positions. He is a member of the Forest City Board, of the High School Board, and is superintendent of the Sunday School of the Baptist Church. He is a Blue Lodge Mason. One of the charter members of Havanna Post, American Legion, he is active in that organization. His first presidential ballot was cast for Warren G. Harding. He is a democrat.

On February 3, 1920, Mr. Langston married, at Greenview, Illinois, Miss Claudia Fricke, a daughter of Garrett Fricke, and his wife, Mary (Aben) Fricke. Mrs. Langston was born at Petersburg, Illinois, November 11, 1895, and was educated in her native city. Mr. and Mrs. Langston have one son, Ray Albert. Mr. Langston is recognized as one of the live young business men of Forest City,

and he and his wife are social favorites among the young married set of their beautiful little city.

GEORGE K. FARRIS, M. D., physician and surgeon at Vienna in Johnson County, has been an active representative of his profession for twenty years. His family is one that has been in this section of Southern Illinois for three quarters of a century.

Doctor Farris' father, Thomas G. Farris, was born in 1831 and came to Illinois from Tennessee in 1852. He settled three miles east of Vienna, made a good farm there, and was widely known as a stock raiser and stock dealer. He died in 1894. Thomas G. Farris married Mary Amanda Gillespie, also a native of Tennessee. She reached the age of eighty-four, passing away August 2, 1925.

Dr. George K. Farris was one of a large family of twelve children. He was born at the old homestead November 16, 1879, and spent the boyhood years of his life in the country. His advantages in the country schools were supplemented in the Vienna High School, and in 1906 he graduated from the medical department of St. Louis University. Doctor Farris in October of the same year engaged in practice at Vienna, and his professional work there was interrupted during the years 1913-15 while he was superintendent of the Chester State Hospital. After that official connection he returned to Vienna and is engaged in a very successful general practice.

For a number of years he was chairman of the City Board of Health, and is a member of the various medical organizations. He belongs to the Masonic Lodge at Vienna, the Temple of the Mystic Shrine at St. Louis, and is a member of the Knights of Pythias. Doctor Farris married Miss Edith Burnette, daughter of Frank Burnette, of Vienna.

W. P. SHERMAN, M. D. A professional service marked by many important responsibilities has comprised the career of Dr. W. P. Sherman for nearly thirty years as a physician and surgeon in the city of Aurora.

Doctor Sherman was born in Newark, Wisconsin, July 22, 1863, son of James B. and Katherine (Chase) Sherman, his father a native of Oswego, New York and his mother a native of the same state. His father was a farmer. They had a family of four children: Frederick G. and Nellie M., both deceased; Dr. W. P.; and Elizabeth, wife of E. J. Taylor, of Quincy, Illinois.

When Dr. W. P. Sherman was a small child his parents returned to Oswego, New York, and in 1871 they came west again, settling at Plano, Illinois, where Doctor Sherman acquired his public school education. In Chicago he attended Rush Medical College, graduating M. D. in 1889. Doctor Sherman for four and a half years practiced medicine at Leland, Illinois, and another four and a half years in Chicago. At the time of the Spanish-American war he located at Aurora and for many years has enjoyed a reputation second to none among the professional men of that city. He is one of the surgeons on the staff of St. Joseph's Hospital.

In 1882 he married Miss Belle B. Meisner, who died in 1892, the mother of three children: Rodger D., of Plainfield, New Jersey; Gertrude L. and Howard, both deceased. In 1899 Doctor Sherman married Addie B. Soffisburg.

Doctor Sherman is a republican, is affiliated with Aurora Lodge No. 254 of the Masonic Order, was formerly a member of St. Bernard's Commandery, Knights Templar, at Chicago, and the Aurora Commandery. He is a member of the Union League and Hamilton Clubs of Chicago, the Aurora Medical Society, the Kane County, Illinois State and American Medical Associations. His skill in surgery has brought him recognition as a fellow of the American College of Surgeons. He is a charter member of the American Society of Roentgenology. For a time Doctor Sherman was medical examiner for the Chicago Health Department.

LUCIEN GREATHOUSE was one of Illinois' conspicuous heroes of the Civil war. His name is held in particular veneration in Vandalia and vicinity.

He was born at Carlinsville, Illinois, June 7, 1842. He graduated from the Illinois Wesleyan University at Bloomington, studied law, but was only eighteen when the Civil war broke out, and he left his studies to volunteer as a private. After passing through every intermediate grade he was commissioned colonel of the Forty-eighth Illinois Infantry. His regiment bore a conspicuous part in the movements of the Army of the Tennessee, and he was present on the fields of battle at Fort Henry, Fort Donelson, Shiloh, Corinth, Stone River, Jackson, Black River, Vicksburg, Chattanooga, Lookout Mountain, Missionary Ridge, Altoona Pass, Kenesaw Mountain and all other engagements in Sherman's advance from Chattanooga to Atlanta.

He paid the supreme sacrifice during the battle of Atlanta, July 22, 1864, when he fell, with the flag of his nation in his hand, standing on the breastworks of the enemy.

General Sherman said: "His example was worth a thousand men." Gen. John A. Logan called him "the bravest man in the Army of the Tennessee."

CHARLES S. VALENTINE for many years has been a salesman, sales manager and organizer of business enterprises in New York and Chicago, and is now the active executive in the capacity of assistant to the president of the Orange Crush Holding Company. His business offices are at 225 North Michigan Avenue.

He was born at Litchfield, Hillsdale County, Michigan, in 1874. He grew up on a farm in Southern Michigan, and finished his education in Albion College at Albion in that state. He was graduated in 1895, and since then has had thirty years of varied business experience constituting a very successful business career not only on the sales but the executive side. He first located in Chicago in 1912. From 1918 to 1924 his business headquarters were in New York. In 1924 he returned to Chicago. Mr. Valentine was one of the organizers of the Orange Crush Holding Company, which controls the ownership and operation of the hundreds of plants throughout the United States engaged in the manufacture and sale of Orange-Crush, one of the most widely distributed soft drinks. As assistant to the president Mr. Valentine directs the general business of the company, since the president himself is not active.

Mr. Valentine takes an active part in civic affairs in his home city. He was one of the charter members and is still a member of the Chicago Kiwanis Club, which was organized late in 1915, and received its charter in January, 1916. He has been a member of the Union League Club since 1917, retaining his membership during his residence in New York. He is also a member of the Olympia Field Country Club.

Mr. Valentine married Margaret Edwards, of Kalamazoo, Michigan. They have a daughter, Allaseba B., wife of Dwight Harrison, Jr., of Birmingham, Alabama. The home of Mr. and Mrs. Valentine is at 5525 Hyde Park Boulevard.

CHARLES D. HENRY for many years has been a leading builder and architect at Kankakee, and is member of an old family of that county.

He was born in Kankakee County, September 26, 1859, a son of Andrew B. and Elizabeth D. (Dufford) Henry, natives of New Jersey, a grandson of Daniel and Catherine (Eversole) Henry, natives of New Jersey, and of Philip and Clarissa (Dickinson) Dufford, natives of the same state, and great-grandson of David and Catherine (Lutz) Henry, of New Jersey, and of Phillip Dufford, who was born in Germany and came to America, landing at Philadelphia September 11, 1738. Mr. Henry's parents were married in New Jersey and in 1852 came to Illinois, first settling at Aurora. His father was a mason by trade and subsequently bought a farm in Kankakee County, in Essex Township, but in 1861 moved to another farm in Salina Township, where he lived until his death on February 13, 1914. The mother died April 1, 1913. Their children were: Luther P., born December 6, 1852, a resident of Salina Township; George O., born March 3, 1854, of Manhatten, Illinois; Mary Emma, born December 16, 1855, widow of Gilbert V. D. Seward, of Chicago; Sarah E., born November 13, 1857, wife of Aaron D. Yates, of Salina Township; Charles D.; Edwin D., born September 24, 1861, and died in 1918; William A., born April 24, 1866, of Kankakee; and Alvah M., born March 18, 1868, of Salina Township.

Charles D. Henry had a public school education, and after leaving high school was a teacher for two years. He then took up building and architectural lines, and has followed that trade and occupation ever since. Mr. Henry has had his office in the Arcade Building since March 8, 1893, a period of over thirty-three years. He is a republican, a member of the Masonic fraternity, belongs to the Uniform Rank of the Knights of Pythias, Modern Woodmen of America and Sons and Daughters of the Pilgrims.

He married, September 4, 1889, Miss Viola E. Linton, who was born in Will County, Illinois, March 5, 1868, daughter of William and Mary Linton, her father a native of Indiana and her mother of Illinois. The children of Mr. and Mrs. Henry are: Charles D., born July 9, 1890, now a practicing attorney at Kankakee, who married Helen M. Oglesby; and Madeline E. Henry, born November 1, 1891, an employe of the department of purchase and construction of the state of Illinois.

LOMAN T. KING, secretary of the Chamber of Commerce of Kankakee, is thoroughly well qualified to cooperate with and carry out the plans of this organization for the broadening of Kankakee's commercial activities. He has been engaged in educational work, and is a graduate of the Illinois University School of Commerce.

He was born at Mount Vernon, Illinois, September 11, 1891, son of William Addison and Mary L. (Fry) King. His parents were born in Jefferson County, Illinois, and his father was a farmer there. Loman T. King after graduating from high school spent three years as a teacher in the rural schools, and for three terms attended the Illinois Normal University. At the same time he was principal of schools at Broadlands, Illinois. Mr. King for three years was superintendent of public schools at Cerro Gordo, Illinois, and then entered the University of Illinois, where he was graduated with the A. B. degree in June, 1923. He remained at the university as full time teacher in the College of Commerce and Business Administrations and at the same time pursued post-graduate work. For this he was given the degree Master of Arts in February, 1925. While at the university he carried on special research work on topics connected with Illinois education under the direction of C. M. Thompson, dean of the College of Commerce.

Mr. King on May 1, 1924, was chosen secretary and manager of the Kankakee Chamber of Commerce. He is also secretary of the state division of the Harding-Highway Association, and a secretary of the Kankakee River Development Association. Mr. King is a graduate of the School of Salesmanship of the International Correspondence School of Scranton, Pennsylvania.

He married, August 9, 1916, Ella I. Astell, a native of Broadlands, Illinois, and daughter of William and Lottie J. (Camerer) Astell, her father a native of Jacksonville, Illinois, and her mother of Indiana. Mr. and Mrs. King have two children, Merrill H., born September 11, 1918, and William Loman, born December 13, 1925. Mr. King is a member of the Official Board of the Methodist Episcopal Church. He is a Mason, a Phi Delta Kappa, a member of the Rotary Club. His home is at 876 West Jeffery Street.

HENRY REUTER has been a business man at Kankakee over forty-five years, and has one of the largest roofing and sheet metal works in Eastern Illinois.

He was born in Luxemburg, Germany, in 1856, son of John and Margaret Reuter, who spent all their lives in Germany. Henry Reuter was educated in the common schools and at the age of fourteen began his apprenticeship in sheet metal and roofing work. For seven years he was employed in France, being in Paris during 1878-79. Leaving there, he

came to America with his brother Nickolas, at first to Chicago, and in 1881 they came to Kankakee, where they handled all the roofing work for the State Hospital. In 1882 the Reuter Brothers established a shop of their own, and they made it a business known far and wide for perfect service. This firm handles some of the largest contracts in the state, and seventy-five per cent of the business still comes from sections outside of Kankakee. Nickolas Reuter, one of the original firm, was killed in an accident on the Big Four Railroad about 1914. The sheet metal works occupy a two-story brick building, 50 by 145 feet, at 151-153 South West Avenue.

Mr. Reuter married, in 1882, Catherine Glesner, also a native of Luxemburg. They became the parents of five children: Margaret, at home; Harry, who married Florence Barns; Frank, who married Evelyn Scott; Hazel, wife of Fred Seller; and Evelyn, Mrs. John S. Burton of Chicago. The family are members of St. Patrick's Catholic Church. Mr. Reuter was for twenty years an alderman either from the Sixth or Second Wards, and was assistant supervisor four years, and for two years mayor of the City of Kankakee. In politics he is a republican. He has filled all the chairs in the Independent Order of Odd Fellows, is a member of the B. P. O. Elks, Modern Woodmen of America, Kiwanis Club, and the Chamber of Commerce. His home is at 260 South Schuyler Avenue.

EDWARD HOENNICKE. The status of Kankakee among the industrial cities of Illinois is the result of a group of manufacturing establishments, several of which are among the largest of their class anywhere in the Middle West. One of these is the Bear Brand Hosiery Company, a plant with a tremendous output of manufactured goods that go practically to all parts of the world, and with an operating force that is one of the chief assets of Kankakee as a home city.

The secretary of this company is Edward Hoennicke, a native of Kankakee County, who has been well known in business there since boyhood. He was born in Salina Township of Kankakee County in 1875, son of Albert and Lena (Burghardt) Hoennicke, his father a native of Berlin, Germany, and his mother of Alsace-Lorraine. His paternal grandparents, Albert and Mary Hoennicke, were residents of Berlin, Germany, where they resided until their deaths. The maternal grandparents, John and Magdaline Burghardt, were old time hotel keepers in Kankakee, but later moved to a farm. Albert Hoennicke was a farmer in Salina Township, but for about eight years conducted a bakery business at Bradley. He died in September, 1917, and his wife, in October, 1921.

Edward Hoennicke was educated in grammar and high schools and when sixteen years old became an employe of the R. J. Hannah Bakery in Kankakee. Six years later he joined his father's baking establishment and took over the business when his father retired. He continued it about three years and then, returning to Kankakee, operated the South Side Dry Goods Store for thirteen years. After selling out his interest in that business he became office manager and secretary of the Bear Brand Hosiery Company.

Mr. Hoennicke married, April 23, 1902, Miss Mattie Wiechers, a native of Kankakee, daughter of Theodore and Lena (Smith) Wiechers, her father a native of Germany and her mother of Kankakee. Mr. and Mrs. Hoennicke have one son, Albert J., born August 2, 1904. Mr. Hoennicke is a trustee of the Emanuel Baptist Church, served one term as treasurer of Kankakee, is member and clerk of the Kankakee High School Board and has been town clerk. He is a republican, member of the Knights of Pythias, has held chairs in the Independent Order of Odd Fellows, belongs to the Modern Woodmen of America and the Chamber of Commerce. His home is at 1057 South Washington Avenue.

WILLIAM J. BAXTER, whose death occurred September 5, 1925, and who lies buried in Sunset Hill Cemetery, was a well known attorney in Madison County, practicing law both at Venice and at Granite City, and was one of the leaders of the republican party in the Forty-seventh District.

Mr. Baxter was born on a farm near Troy, Woodford County, Kentucky, June 13, 1879, son of Dr. and Mrs. James H. Baxter. His father was a graduate in medicine at Cincinnati, and had a successful career as a physician and surgeon. William J. Baxter attended public schools in Kentucky. In 1894, after his father's death, the family moved to Junction, Gallatin County, Illinois, where Mr. Baxter, though only fifteen years of age, contributed by his work most of the means of support for a family of four. He managed to continue his education, finishing his school work at Junction in 1901.

In April, 1902, he established his home at Venice in Madison County, and became a yard clerk. In the intervals of his employment he began the study of law in 1911, and in 1913 entered the City College of Law and Finance at St. Louis. He attended school at night, supporting his family by work during the day. In June, 1914, he graduated from the academy of the City College of Law and Finance and in June, 1915, received his law degree there. He was admitted to the Illinois bar October 13, 1915, and in the meantime had continued post-graduate work in the City College of Law, being awarded the degree Master of Laws in June, 1916. At the time of his death he was president of the Tri City Bar Association, and vice president of the Municipal League of Illinois.

Mr. Baxter, as these facts indicate, since early youth was dependent upon his own resources and his efforts, and made a noble use of his opportunities. In April, 1913, he was elected city attorney of Venice. Since he was not then a licensed attorney the city refused to pay him a salary, and he fought the case through the Supreme Court, which settled a disputed question. In April, 1915, he was reelected city attorney and also in April, 1916, continuing to serve as city attorney from 1913 until his death, with the exception of one year. In June, 1918, Mr. Baxter established his law offices in Granite City, and had an extensive private practice there.

Mr. Baxter served the republican party in nearly every position of responsibility in his home district. He was a member of the Central Committee and the Executive Committee of Madison County. He was a member of the Tri-City Edwardsville Boy Scouts of America, being official examiner and member of several sub-committees and also scout master of Troop No. 1 at Venice. He was president of the Venice School Board in 1921-22. In Masonry he was a member of the thirty-second degree Scottish Rite and the Mystic Shrine, was a Rebekah, a member of the legislative committee of the Grand Lodge of Odd Fellows of Illinois, at time of his death was secretary of the Twenty-ninth District, I. O. O. F., a past consul of the Modern Woodmen of America, for four years was president of the Venice City Council, and was president of the Tri-City Bar Association. During the World war, while not eligible for registration until the second draft act, he entered enthusiastically upon the entire program of war activities, being a member of the District Exemption Board and a Four Minute Speaker. His wife was chairman of the Venice Red Cross and very active in the organization. Mr. Baxter was a member of the Baptist Church, and his wife and children belong to the Presbyterian Church of Granite City.

On February 5, 1903, he married Miss Phena McDole, of DeKalb, Illinois. They are the parents of three children, one daughter and two sons. The daughter, Nona, graduated from the Illinois State Normal School at DeKalb in June, 1922, and became a teacher in the Venice public school. She married Elmer Holm, and lives in DeKalb, Illinois. They have one son, Warren. LaRue G. is an Eagle Scout and now is scoutmaster of Troop 18 and teacher in the Washington School in Granite City. He is now attending the City College of Law and Finance and is also a graduate of the Northern Illinois State Teachers College. He is also a member of the Red Cross. The youngest child, Thaddeus, is also an Eagle Scout and is a member of the Red Cross. He is a sophomore in the Venice High School.

MINOR E. WHITE, M. D., is a specialist of the eye, ear, nose and throat, being one of the very capable representatives of his profession at the City of Kankakee.

A native of Illinois, he was born in Fayette County, November 18, 1889, son of Elisha G. and Emma (Onins) White, his father a native of Middletown, Kentucky, and his mother of Maryland. Elisha White for some years followed the business of pilot on Mississippi River packets, but later engaged in farming, and died November 1, 1905.

Dr. Minor E. White was reared on a farm, attended public schools and through four winter terms taught in Fayette County. His higher education was acquired in the State Normal School at Charleston, also in Valparaiso University in Indiana, and he studied medicine in Loyola University School of Medicine at Chicago. He was graduated in 1918. For one year he was an interne in the Ohio Valley Hospital at Wheeling, West Virginia, and subsequently became first assistant surgeon under Dr. W. S. Fulton. For four and a half years he was engaged in a general practice in Martinton, Iroquois County, Illinois. Doctor White spent fourteen months in the Illinois Eye and Ear Infirmary, and with that special preparation located at Kankakee, where he has confined his attention to eye, ear, nose and throat work.

He is a member of the Kankakee County, Illinois State and American Medical Associations. He has served as treasurer of the Lodge of Independent Order of Odd Fellows and is a republican. He married in March, 1917, Jessie E. Roney, a native of Ontario, Canada. They have three children, Marion, Barbara and Minor Paul.

JAMES L. DIGGS, in the automobile business at Cairo, grew up from early boyhood in that Southern Illinois city and is one of the representative younger business men.

He was born at Bardwell, Kentucky, February 16, 1898, son of C. E. and M. L. Diggs, his father a native of Kentucky and his mother of Tennessee. C. E. Diggs moved to Cairo in 1912 and has been in the piano business for a number of years.

James L. Diggs after coming to Cairo attended grammar and high schools, and his schooling continued until 1916. In June of that year he enlisted in Company K of the 16th Illinois Infantry and was mustered in for service on the Mexican border. He remained in the federal service until discharged March 1, 1917. Then returning to Cairo, he was employed as an automobile mechanic by the Interstate Motor Company, remaining there fourteen months and continued with other automobile concerns for several years. In 1922 he established a vulcanizing and tire repairing shop, known as the Diggs Vulcanizing Company. He also has a sales agency for the Michelin tires.

Mr. Diggs, who is unmarried, is a member of the Episcopal Church, is an independent voter and is a Royal Arch Mason, having been master and junior overseer in the Chapter.

DANIEL JOSEPH O'LOUGHLIN, M. D. For a number of years Daniel J. O'Loughlin has had his home at Kankakee, where in addition to his private practice he is a member of the staff of the Illinois State Eye and Ear Hospital, and is also on the staff of St. Mary's Hospital.

Doctor O'Loughlin was born at Ackley, Iowa, January 16, 1881, son of James and Mary (Cooney) O'Loughlin. His parents were born in Ireland, but came to this country when young, and they spent most of their active lives on a farm in Iowa.

Daniel Joseph O'Loughlin after the common schools attended the University of Iowa, and studied medicine in Northwestern University at Chicago. He was graduated M. D. in 1904, and for one year was in the Illinois State Eye and Ear Hospital. For two years he practiced at Mattoon, Illinois, and since 1907 has been located at Kankakee. Doctor O'Loughlin is a member of the Kankakee County, Illinois State and American Medical Associations.

He married, in 1915, Miss Bertha B. Roberts, who was born at Champlain, New York,

in 1892, daughter of Gilbert Roberts. They have two children, Marie and Daniel. Doctor O'Loughlin is a member of St. Patrick's Catholic Church, is a democrat and is affiliated with the B. P. O. Elks and Knights of Columbus.

JOHN P. HICKEY is a native of Illinois, and for a number of years has been one of the very popular business men of Kankakee. He is a funeral director and has many other interests, both financial and civic. in his home locality.

He was born at Chebanse, Illinois, in 1880, son of Thomas and Beeze (Conley) Hickey. His father was a native of Ireland, son of Michael and Johanna Hickey, who settled at Chebanse, Illinois, in 1850. Thomas Hickey was a farm owner, merchant and banker, and died in 1915. His widow, a native of Ford County, Illinois, resides in Chicago, being a daughter of John and Mary (Gibbons) Conley, the latter still living.

John P. Hickey was educated in grammar and high schools, attended St. Ignatius College, St. Viators College at Bourbonnais, Illinois, the Athenaeum Business College, and for two years studied medicine. In 1903 he was graduated from the Chicago School of Embalming, and remained in that city for about two years. In October, 1905, he opened an undertaking establishment at Kankakee, and in 1922 established a Funeral Home, which is one of the most elaborate and complete in equipment and service outside the city of Chicago.

In 1910 Mr. Hickey married Miss Louise Trudeau, a native of Goshen, Indiana, and daughter of Peter Trudeau. They have two children: John Donald and Yolande. The family are members of the Catholic Church and Mr. Hickey is a democrat. He has fraternal affiliations with the Woodmen of the World, Ben Hur Tribe, B. P. O. Elks, Fraternal Order of Eagles, Loyal Order of Moose, Knights of Columbus and served four terms as grand knight of the Knights of Columbus. He is a member of the Kankakee Country Club. For fifteen years he was director of the Hickey Band and Orchestra, and is a member of the American Federation of Musicians, also of the Fish Fans Club of Chicago. His home is at 233 South Indiana Avenue. Mr. Hickey is a director of the Lake View State Bank of Chicago and owns a large amount of valuable real estate in the City and County of Kankakee, also in Chicago, Arkansas and Florida.

ALBERT HENRY HENNEBERGER is the sales representative of the Dodge automobiles at Kankakee. He is one of the alert younger men who have taken up the automobile business and has made a splendid success of it.

He was born at Fowler, Indiana, February 17, 1893, son of Charles and Mary (Seibert) Henneberger, his mother a native of Evansville, Indiana. His father was born in Germany and in order to escape the compulsory military service of that country came to America at the age of twenty and first located at Princeton, Indiana, where he followed his trade as a baker. Later he was in Evansville, Indiana, for two years conducted a bakery at Poseyville, Indiana, and afterwards a similar establishment at Fowler, Indiana, where he is now living retired. His wife died in 1911.

Albert Henry Henneberger attended the Sacred Heart Parish School at Fowler, and spent two years in St. Joseph College at Rensselaer, Indiana, taking the high school course for two years. He was employed as clerk in a grocery store at Fowler, and subsequently paid his way through four terms in the School of Commerce at Valparaiso University in Indiana. In 1913 he removed to Evansville, Indiana, doing office work in a wholesale china, queensware and grocery establishment, and for four years had charge of the accounting department of Graham Brothers. In 1921 he joined the sales department of the Dodge Brothers Company at Joliet, and in September, 1923, opened his salesroom for handling Dodge automobiles and Graham trucks at Kankakee. He also conducts a garage and has a well equipped building, two-story brick, 50 by 145 feet, at 344 South Schuyler Avenue.

Mr. Henneberger married, September 12, 1922, Mary Muller, a native of Indiana and daughter of Bernard and Catherine (Roth) Muller, her father a native of Germany and her mother born near Streator, Illinois. Her father at the age of eighteen came to Illinois, and died in 1909. Her mother now resides at Fowler, Indiana. Mr. Henneberger is a member of St. Patrick's Catholic Church. He belongs to the Knights of Columbus, Kankakee Country Club, Lions Club, Chamber of Commerce. His home is at 314 South Evergreen Avenue.

PERCY WILSON, president of the Percy Wilson Company, real estate, at 109 North Dearborn Street, has probably had as diversified and successful an experience in the real estate field as any of his contemporaries. Mr. Wilson served his novitiate with one of Chicago's oldest and best known real estate organizations, the Frederick H. Bartlett Realty Company, and is still a director of that company.

He is a native of Chicago, born October 31, 1890, but spent his boyhood years largely in one of the last remnants of the American frontier. When he was nine years of age, after he had been a pupil in the schools of Ravenswood for several years, his parents moved out to a homestead in northwestern Oklahoma, in what was then described in the geographies as "No Man's Land," the strip of land lying on the top of the Texas Panhandle. He lived there, doing ranch work and coming in contact with the varied types of civilization, until he was about sixteen years of age, when he returned to Chicago.

Mr. Wilson has made his own way in the world. After returning to Chicago he spent two years attending evening classes in the Chicago Business Law School. As an employe of Frederick H. Bartlett Company it is said that his first wage was six dollars a week, but he had rapid promotions, being made a subdivision manager at the age of eighteen. In 1916 he was made assistant general sales manager of this great organization, and on January 2, 1923, became a member of the company and subsequently was general sales manager and treasurer. During the nineteen years he was active in the Bartlett Company he assisted in distributing over two hundred subdivisions and thousands of acres of land besides scores of individual transactions in houses, flats, stores and vacant property. Among others he handled the Bartlett colonization project on 20,000 acres of land in Arkansas. He also spent much time on the road for the Bartlett firm, selling miscellaneous business properties.

In March, 1926, he established the Percy Wilson Company to handle real estate, mortgage loans and subdivisions, its first important undertaking being a million dollar development on Irving Park Boulevard in DuPage County. From the beginning of his business career Mr. Wilson has been noted for his remarkable ability as a salesman and his executive forcefulness. These qualities, combined with his exacting probity and straightforwardness, have accounted for his unusual success.

Mr. Wilson is a member of the Mid-Day Club, Hamilton Club, Bonnie Brook Golf Club and Olympia Fields Country Club. He married Miss Barbara Heggie, and they reside at 4919 Dorchester Avenue, Chicago, during the winter and in Lake Forest in the summer. Their three children are Patricia, Theodore and Robert.

GEORGE A. BISSEL. In the person of George A. Bissel, of Joliet, Will County possesses a citizen whose executive abilities have been used to good advantage in discharging the duties of important public office. The position of county treasurer is by no means a sinecure, the proper handling of its multifarious responsibilities calling for the possession of more than the average ability. That such ability is possessed by Mr. Bissel is shown by his past record and also by his present high standing in the confidence of his fellow-citizens.

Mr. Bissel was born at Bloomington, Illinois, October 19, 1862, and is a son of John and Mary (Yack) Bissel. His father, a native of Wurttemberg, Germany, came to the United States when still a youth, in 1850. He settled at Bloomington in 1858, where he was variously employed at honorable labor. Like many of his countrymen, he belonged to the German society known as the Turnverein. The local organization, seeing that war between the North and the South was inevitable, began training as early as 1858, and thus presented a trained and well-disciplined set of men. In June, 1861, Mr. Bissel enlisted in Colonel Hecker's Twenty-fourth Regiment, Illinois Volunteer Infantry, with which he fought bravely until incapacitated for further service when he received a gunshot wound and was honorably discharged in 1864. At the close of the war he moved to Joliet with his family, and was there engaged in merchandising until his death August 12, 1873, his widow surviving until 1917, when she passed away at the age of seventy-eight years. She was born at Chicago, a daughter of Michael and Teresa (Lehman) Yack, natives of Alsace-Lorraine, France. Mr. Yack came to the United States alone in 1838, but in the following year returned to the old country and was married, and then again came to this country and first settled at Chicago. He was a teamster by vocation, and for some years was employed in the construction of the Illinois and Michigan canal.

George A. Bissel attended the public schools until he was about fourteen years of age, at which time it was found necessary that he should become at least partly self-supporting, and accordingly he set about learning the barber's trade. This once mastered, he worked at the trade as a journeyman for ten years and finally opened an establishment of his own on Jefferson Street. This he conducted until 1891, when he changed his location to a larger and better-equipped place on Ottawa Street, where he now commands one of the best patronages in the city. He has hosts of friends and well-wishers and is known as a man of the soundest integrity. A republican in his political views, he has long been interested in public affairs. For two years he was tax collector of Joliet Township, and in 1922 was elected county treasurer of Will County, a position which he retains as noted above. Mr. Bissel is a Universalist in religion. Fraternally he is affiliated with Madison Lodge, A. F. and A. M., of which he is a grand lecturer; Joliet Chapter No. 47, R. A. M.; Joliet Council No. 87, R. and S. M.; Joliet Commandery No. 4, K. T.; and Oriental Consistory, and of Medinah Temple of the Mystic Shrine. He also belongs to the Loyal Order of Moose, the B. P. O. Elks and the Modern Woodmen of America, and other connections are with the Association of Commerce and the Sha-Bo-Na Club.

On April 15, 1886, Mr. Bissel was united in marriage with Miss Rosa Reinhard, of Joliet, a daughter of John and Mary (Kellar) Reinhard, born in Germany, and to this union there have been born two children: Edward, who died in infancy; and Marie, a graduate of Lake Forest Academy, who is a teacher in the high school at Dwight, Illinois.

ROY F. DUSENBURY, a veteran of the World war, is the present postmaster of Kankakee and has earned a most creditable record in both military and civil service.

He was born at Kankakee, November 28, 1889, son of Edward B. and Eugenia (Duga) Dusenbury, his father a native of Kankakee and his mother of Ford County, Illinois. His grandparents, William B. and Helen M. (Barnes) Dusenbury, were early settlers at Kankakee, where the grandfather was a painter and paper hanger. William B. Dusenbury was born in New York State and his wife in Vermont. Mrs. Eugenia Dusenbury died March 4, 1901, and her husband now resides at Chicago.

Roy F. Dusenbury was educated in public schools to the age of sixteen. He then enlisted in the United States Navy, and had the fortune to be with the North Atlantic Fleet when it made the memorable voyage around the world, starting in the winter of 1907-08. He was in the navy until honorably discharged November 27, 1910.

Mr. Dusenbury after leaving the navy was in the railway train service for the Illinois

Central Railroad. He resigned and on August 25, 1917, became first lieutenant of Company L in the One Hundred and Twenty-ninth Infantry, which was one of the units in the Illinois Thirty-third Division with the American Expeditionary Forces. He sailed for overseas May 13, 1918, being transferred August 23, 1918, and assigned to Company K, Fifty-eighth Infantry, Fourth Division, a regular army unit. He was with his command in the St. Mihiel campaign, the Meuse Argonne offensive, and also on the Albert sector, in addition to his experience in several defensive sectors. On October 4, 1918, at the climax of the Meuse-Argonne campaign, he was wounded by a machine gun bullet. This required the amputation of his left leg above the knee, and on December 24, 1918, he returned to the United States and for exactly one year was in hospitals, getting his honorable discharge December 24, 1919. After a course in vocational training he returned to his native city and was a manufacturer of furniture.

Mr. Dusenbury on August 15, 1922, was appointed postmaster of Kankakee, and has shown great ability in administering the work of the office. He has been prominent in the American Legion, having served as commander of the Kankakee Post, also as service officer and member of the Board of Directors. He is a republican and a member of the Presbyterian Church.

Mr. Dusenbury married, November 28, 1917, Miss Verlie E. Walker, who was born at Golconda, Illinois, daughter of Roy and Viola Walker. Mr. and Mrs. Dusenbury are the parents of three children, Roy E., Carolyn M. and Rex S.

C. M. CLAY BUNTAIN. One of the able members of the Kankakee bar for nearly a quarter of a century, the career of C. M. Clay Buntain is a realization of talent and industrious application that can be followed through well marked and definite details in the progressive development of his mind and character. These unusual details of biography are set down in the following paragraphs for their essential interest.

Mr. Buntain was born at Momence, Kankakee County, October 15, 1876, son of Thomas Jefferson and Anna (Van Kirk) Buntain. He was reared in Momence, attended public schools there, and on September 7, 1891, entered the Momence High School, where he graduated as class orator and valedictorian May 23, 1894. On September 12, 1894, he entered the Northwestern University Academy at Evanston, was graduated June 8, 1895; and on June 15, 1899, graduated with the A. B. degree from Northwestern University. On September 21, 1899, he was enrolled in the Law School of Northwestern University, and received his law degree June 19, 1902, at the same date receiving the Master of Arts degree from the same university.

Mr. Buntain's school record contains a number of other tokens of his scholarship and all around popularity. During his high school course he received many prizes and medals for scholarship and declamation. While in Northwestern University Academy he won second place in the Columbian Oratorical Contest on May 25, 1895. In the academy he was awarded in 1895-96, a state scholarship in Northwestern University for four years. In 1895-96 he was chosen Trig Cremation Orator. In 1896-97 he was a member of the Rogers Debating Club, and nominated by the class committee as editor of the Syllabus; in 1897-98 was chairman of the Pan Hellenic Association; leader of the Junior Promenade, February 18, 1898; member of the Junior Play Committee and Cast; elected a member of the Rogers Debating Club team for 1898-99; elected delegate to the province convention of the Phi Delta Theta fraternity at Lincoln, Nebraska, May 19, 1898; represented the same fraternity at its semi-centennial convention at Columbus, Ohio, November 21-25, 1898. On September 29, 1904, at St. Louis, he was elected vice president of the General Council of the Phi Delta Phi fraternity, and served as national president of this legal fraternity from 1903 to 1909 and since 1909 as chief justice of its Court of Appeals. He joined the Phi Delta Theta fraternity December 7, 1895; became a member of Theta Nu Epsilon fraternity May 13, 1898; was initiated in the Senior fraternity, Deru, on May 27, 1898; and on his scholarship record was elected a member of Phi Beta Kappa. During his summer vacation of 1898 he was a clerk in the adjutant general's office of the War Department at Washington. On October 28 of the same year he was a member of the winning team in the first semi-final debate of the Inter Society Debating League, and on January 13, 1899, was a Cleveland declamation contestant and a Lyman J. Gage debate contestant on April 14, 1899. He was initiated in the legal fraternity Phi Delta Phi on May 11, 1900. He was elected president of the class of 1902 for the senior year in Law School, May 24, 1901. He was elected a member of the Order of the Coif for excellence in scholarship in Law School.

Passing the state bar examination at Springfield in October, 1902, he was admitted to practice October 17, 1902, and from February 2 to May 6, 1903, was clerk in the law firm of Dupee, Judah, Willard & Wolf at Chicago. From May 14th to October 29th, 1903, he was assistant attorney for Farson, Leach & Company of Chicago.

Mr. Buntain on April 4, 1904, opened his law office in the Arcade Building at Kankakee, and has been steadily engaged in a general practice in that city ever since.

He was associate editor of the Illinois Law Review from 1906 to 1909. In 1921 he was appointed a member of the Illinois Deep Waterway Committee. In 1924 he was a member of the Local Council for Illinois for the American Bar Association. He is a member of the Kankakee County and Illinois State Bar and American Bar Associations, being president of the Illinois State Bar Association in 1924-25; he is also a non-resident member of the Chicago Bar Association. He was elected a life member of the American Law Institute; is also a member of the American Judicature Society; since 1925 a commissioner from Illinois of the National Conference of Commissioners of Uniform State Laws. Mr. Buntain is first vice president and chairman of the Board of Directors and attorney for the Legris Trust and Savings Bank of Kankakee, and a director and vice president of the Kankakee County Title and Trust Company.

He is a member of the First Presbyterian Church of Kankakee and fraternally is affiliated with Grove City Council No. 832, Royal Arcanum, B. P. O. Elks, Kankakee Lodge No. 627; Kankakee Lodge No. 389, A. F. and A. M; Kankakee Chapter No. 78, Royal Arch Masons; Ivanhoe Commandery No. 33, Knights Templar, Kankakee; Owisco Council No. 108, Kankakee; Bloomington Consistory of the Scottish Rite and Ansar Temple of the Mystic Shrine at Springfield, being a past commander of Ivanhoe Commandery of the Knights Templar. He is a member of and the founder of the Rotary Club of Kankakee.

Mr. Buntain married Alice G. Bellinger, of Momence. They have one son, Willard J. Buntain, now a sophomore in Northwestern University.

JOHN JOSEPH CLEARY. In the official machinery of any city as important as Joliet, one of the most responsible is that pertaining to its public utilities. Particularly is this true in a muncipality in which the manufactories are numerous and where much deepnds upon a proper regulation of the water supply. It is, therefore, fortunate that Joliet has as city commissioner of the water department, or the department of public property, such a capable and energetic individual as John Joseph Cleary, who has occupied this post since 1923 and has established an excellent record.

Mr. Cleary was born at Joliet, August 15, 1889, and is a son of Peter and Mary Catherine (Farget) Cleary. His father was a native of County Sligo, Ireland, where he was given a common school education and had some experience as an employe in steel mills, but found that he could make no progress in his native land and at the age of nineteen years immigrated to the United States and first located at LaSalle, Illinois. There he resided for one year and came to Joliet for the Illinois Steel Company, where he was employed twenty-four years. He was married in Joliet and here he has since made his home.

John Joseph Cleary attended the public schools and St. Mary's parochial school until reaching the age of seventeen years, when he began the battle of life as a crew caller for the Elgin, Joliet & Eastern Railroad. Being bright and energetic, he soon attracted the attention of his superiors, with the result that he started an upward climb that finally landed him in the position of chief timekeeper in the mechanical department of that railroad. He remained with the road until February 3, 1923, at which time he resigned his position to accept that of city commissioner in the water department, or department of public property, and commenced the discharge of his duties May 7 following. As previously noted, he has established a record that is a credit to his ability and to the department, and which has proven that his fellow-citizens' faith was not misplaced.

On May 30, 1922, Mr. Cleary was united in marriage at Joliet with Miss Mary Otto, who was born at St. Louis, Missouri, September 21, 1892, a daughter of Adolphus and Elizabeth Otto, the former a native of Germany and the latter of Pennsylvania. Mr. and Mrs. Cleary are the parents of one daughter: Ruth, who was born April 14, 1923. Mr. and Mrs. Cleary are consistent members of St. Mary's Catholic Church. In politics he maintains a non-partisan stand, subscribing to the principles of the candidate rather than of the party. Fraternally he is affiliated with Joliet Lodge of Elks No. 298, the Fraternal Order of Eagles, the Loyal Order of Moose, Joliet Council No. 385, K. of C.; the Ancient Order of Hibernians, Division No. 2, and the North East Athletic Club in all of which organizations Mr. Cleary is greatly popular.

JOHN BARNARD FITHIAN became one of the representative members of the bar of Will County, served four terms as judge of the Probate Court of this county, and was one of the honored and influential citizens of Joliet, the county seat, at the time of his death, which occurred March 8, 1917. This history of Illinois properly enters a tribute to the memory of Judge Fithian, who accounted well for himself and to the world in all of the relations of his busy and useful life.

Judge Fithian was born at Dansville, Livingston County, New York, October 26, 1849, and was a son of William and Eliza Jane (Clark) Fithian, his father having become a pioneer Presbyterian clergyman in Illinois, where he was for several years pastor of the church at Bunker Hill, Macoupin County. Thence he eventually removed with his family to Quincy, Adams County, where he was residing at the time when the Civil war was precipitated on the nation. He enlisted for service as chaplain of an Illinois regiment, and his death occurred within a few years after the close of the war, his wife having preceded him to the life eternal and having been comparatively a young woman at the time of her death.

John B. Fithian was but a boy at the time of his father's death, and at the age of thirteen years he found employment, working at whatever occupation he could obtain in order to provide for the maintenance of himself and his sister, their mother being deceased and their father having been at the time in service in the Civil war.

Mr. Fithian profited by the advantages of the schools of Quincy, which he attended until he was thirteen years of age, and his broader education, along both academic and professional lines, was gained through self-discipline and through dependence upon his own resources. He carried forward his study of law until he proved himself eligible for and secured admission to the Illinois bar in 1876, and was afterward engaged in the practice of law in the city of Joliet, he having thereafter continued as one of the honored and representative members of the Will County bar until the close of his life, and he having had the distinction of being chosen the first judge of the Probate Court of the county, an office in which he served, with characteristic loyalty and efficiency, during a period of four successive terms.

Judge Fithian was a well fortified advocate of the principles of the republican party, was a zealous member of the Ottawa Street Methodist Episcopal Church in his home city, as are also his widow and their only daughter, and he was a valued member of the Joliet Commercial Club. In the time-honored Masonic fraternity Judge Fithian received the thirty-second degree of the Ancient Accepted Scottish Rite, and he was affiliated also with the Modern Woodmen of America. At the time of his death he was on the Board of Directors of the Joliet Public Library. The Judge made judicious investment in Joliet real estate, including the home place of his widow and their only child, Miss Lillian Clare, at 370 Western Avenue. Mrs. Fithian and her daughter are popular factors in the social and cultural circles of Joliet, and Mrs. Fithian is here an active member of the Woman's Study Club.

At Carlinville, Macoupin County, on the 22d of January, 1878, was solemnized the marriage of Judge Fithian and Miss Edna Caroline Whitaker, who was born at that place and who is a daughter of the late Isaac and Virginia (Bement) Whitaker, the latter a native of the State of New York, where she was born at Canandaigua, Mr. Whitaker having been born at Bridgeton, Cumberland County, New Jersey, and having come to Illinois as a pioneer of the year 1831, he having been one of the early surveyors of this state and having profited through his well ordered real estate operations.

CHARLES D. HARBAUGH. Much is said in these days of the necessity of either personal or monetary backing in order that a man may win success along any line of endeavor. It is claimed by some that unless a man has wealth or influence he can not hope to climb far up the ladder of fortune. In spite of the statements of these pessimists there are many who have gained the topmost rung even though from youth they have been forced to grapple with life's problems unaided, mounting through sheer tenacity of purpose and native ability. To such men as these, commonly known among their fellows as self-made men, much credit is due, for beginning at the bottom each was but one in a throng crowding for a foothold. Of course those who have reached the upper rungs were of necessity men of more than the average ability, possessing the willingness to work and learn. Early discovering their bent in life, they developed themselves to meet emergencies and when the right opportunity presented itself proved their fitness and readiness. Among the men of this calibre in Tazewell County is found Charles D. Harbaugh, a prosperous and energetic grain and stock farmer of Spring Lake Township.

Mr. Harbaugh was born in the township in which he now resides, December 27, 1875, and is a son of Lewis F. and Mary J. (Van Orstrand) Harbaugh. The Harbaugh family is of Swiss origin and family tradition has it that the family was established in America in 1735 by a father and three sons who settled in what later became known as Harbaugh Valley, Frederick County, Maryland. There was born John Harbaugh, the paternal grandfather of Charles D. Harbaugh, who passed his life as an industrious agriculturist. Among his children were: Henry, Alexis, who fought as a soldier of the Union army during the Civil war; Lewis F., Margaret, Catherine and Susan.

Lewis F. Harbaugh was born September 22, 1837, in Frederick County, Maryland, and secured his education in the country schools of the Harbaugh Valley. He was still in his twenties and unmarried when he came to Illinois to seek his fortune, and while his capital was small his determination and ambition were great, and with these he laid the foundation for a career of signal usefulness and success. In order to get a start he accepted employment as a farm hand and gradually advanced to the status of a tenant farmer, from which his next step was to the ownership of a small property of his own. He became the proprietor of a quarter section of land which was known as the Harbaugh property, and this he made the old homestead, where he and his worthy wife passed the remaining years of their lives. Mr. Harbaugh was not one to court public preferment, but had the confidence of his fellow-citizens and represented Spring Lake Township as a member of the Board of Supervisors of Tazewell County, was road commissioner of the same township and for twenty-seven years continuously was a member of the board of school directors. He was reared in the faith of the Reformed Church, and his political allegiance was given to the democratic party. In the spring of 1873, at Pekin, Illinois, Mr. Harbaugh married Miss Mary J. Van Orstrand, natives of New Jersey. The Van Orstrand family is of Holland origin, the immigrants from that country having settled in New Jersey at an early day. John Van Orstrand came to Illinois and became a pioneer settler of Tazewell County, where he followed farming and blacksmithing, his home being the present farm of Carl Myers. Mrs. Harbaugh was one of four children: Charles G., who died at Pekin, Illinois; John Oliver, who died at Fairdale, Washington; and Elizabeth, who married Joshua G. Clayton and died in Caldwell County, Missouri. Lewis F. Harbaugh died in the Manito community August 31, 1914, and Mrs. Harbaugh followed him to the grave May 2, 1924, when she was almost seventy-three years of age. They were the parents of three children: Frank Leslie, who is carrying on large agricultural operations as a stock and grain farmer in Manito Township, Tazewell County; Charles Dana, who is engaged in farming near Manito; and Robert Huxley, a farmer in the same community.

Charles Dana Harbaugh has passed his life in the community in which he was born. His education was acquired in the community educational institution known as the County Line School, and at the age of eighteen years he laid aside his books and studies to apply himself to the work of farming, although he remained under the parental roof until long after he had attained his majority, being identified with grain and stock raising interests. At the time of his marriage he moved to the farm which he now owns in Spring Lake Township, a fractional quarter section originally, to which through good business management and industry he has since added considerably, now having 218 acres under cultivation, all producing abundantly. Mr. Harbaugh has limited himself to grain and stock farming and has found his choice a profitable and satisfying one. He is accounted one of the substantial men of his community, and all the improvements, save the residence and barn, have been added by him. A great believer in modern progress, he uses the most highly approved methods and up-to-date machinery in his work. He is a stockholder and member of the Board of Directors of the Grangers Elevator Company of Manito. For many years, as a friend of education, he has served as one of the directors of the County Line School. Politically Mr. Harbaugh has been connected with elections locally and nationally as a democrat, having cast his first presidential vote for William Jennings Bryan. While his parents were of the Reformed faith, he is not identified with any church, although a religious man. During the World war he was associated with the sale of war securities in his district and was in every drive for funds made. He registered in September, 1918, but did not find it necessary to return his questionnaire.

In Tazewell County, February 21, 1912, Charles D. Harbaugh was united in marriage with Miss May French, daughter of John and Anna (Hole) French, who came from Cass County, Virginia, to Illinois, and still resides at Pekin. They have two children: Mrs. Harbaugh, who was born December 2, 1890; and Keith, a public school teacher of near Pekin. Mr. and Mrs. Harbaugh have two sons: John Lewis, born November 15, 1912, and George Robert, born October 21, 1913.

WILLIAM A. HENNESSY, city commissioner of Joliet, in charge of the public health and safety of the people of his city, is a practical man, and one who has risen from patrolman to chief of police, and then to his present high office through his own efforts and integrity. He was born at Joliet, May 1, 1866, a son of David and Ellen (Fitzgerald) Hennessy, natives of Ireland, who were married after they came to the United States. They located at Joliet, where both died.

Commissioner Hennessy attended the parochial schools of Saint Patrick's parish, and also the public schools, until he was seventeen years old, and at that time began working on the farms of Will County. After three years in the rural regions he returned to Joliet and began railroading as brakesman on the Chicago, Rock Island & Pacific Railroad. After two years he left the railroad, and was a teamster until 1891, in which year he entered the fire department. In 1893 he returned to teaming, and followed that line of work until 1899, when he became a patrolman of the Joliet police department, and rose through different grades to be a plain-clothesman and in 1915 was appointed chief of police. This office he held until 1921, when he resigned it to accept the appointment as city commissioner to fill a vacancy. At the expiration of that term he was elected to the same office, and has continued to hold it ever since, having been reelected in March, 1923. He is an independent voter. Saint Patrick's Catholic Church is his religious home. He belongs to the Modern Woodmen of America, the Knights of Columbus, Western Catholic Association, and the Ancient Order of Hibernians.

On June 21, 1893, Commissioner Hennessy married Miss Anna Jenkins, born at Joliet, a daughter of James and Mary Jenkins, natives of Illinois, and the following children have been born to them: William J., who is in the employ of the Joliet Trust & Savings Bank as teller; Marguerite, who is the wife of George J. Puhentz, of Joliet; Regina, who is the wife of William R. Anson, of Joliet; Veronica, who is the wife of John J. Maloney, of Joliet; James P., who is a resident of Joliet; Helen, Robert and Raymond, all of whom are at home. A man of high character, strong in his convictions and willing to back them at any risk, with a thorough knowledge of the people and their needs, Commissioner Hennessy is well fitted for his office and is managing its affairs in a manner to win continued commendation from all classes.

HARRY P. REHR, Kankakee business man, is one of the live and energetic citizens of that community, where he has spent practically all his life.

Mr. Rehr was born at Kankakee in March, 1887, son of Peter H. and Caroline (Schlemme) Rehr, his father a native of Germany and his mother of Illinois. Peter Rehr came to Illinois when a young man and for many years was engaged in the shoe business.

Harry P. Rehr was educated in grammar and high school, and subsequently attended the Barnes School of Anatomy and Sanitary Science at Chicago, and the Cincinnati College of Embalming. At the age of twenty-one he became embalmer for Spicer Brothers and three years later bought out the Spicer undertaking business, and has had one of the leading establishments of its kind in Kankakee County. His business is located at 390 South East Avenue.

In 1914 he married Miss Phebe Ryden, a native of Paxton, Illinois. They have one daughter, Carolyn Ann. Mr. Rehr is now serving his third term as an alderman from the Second Ward. He is a republican, is a Royal Arch and Knight Templar Mason, member of the Knights of Pythias, Independent Order of Odd Fellows and Rebekahs, B. P. O. Elks, and belongs to the Kankakee Country Club and Chamber of Commerce.

OCTAVE J. CARTIER is a merchant and business man at Kankakee, where he has lived all his life and where his business, social and civic relations have made him well known and prominent.

Mr. Cartier was born at Kankakee September 9, 1873, son of Antoine and Rosalee (Brosseau) Cartier. His father, a native of Canada, went at the age of thirteen to Cambridge, Massachusetts, where he worked in a brick yard, and subsequently lived at St. Louis, and at the age of twenty-four moved to Bourbonnais, Illinois. He had learned the trade of broom maker and established a business of that kind in Kankakee, and was active in the management thereof until his death in 1910. He was one of a family of twenty children,

while his wife was one of seventeen sons and daughters. She survives him and resides at Kankakee.

Octave J. Cartier attended public schools and the St. Rose Parochial School, and at the age of fifteen began work as an apprentice at the tailor's trade. Subsequently he became exchange clerk in the First National Bank, which later became the Eastern Illinois Trust & Savings Bank, and is now the First Trust & Savings Bank. He was with that institution ten years, and gave up banking to engage in the grocery and meat business at 448 West Station Street. His residence is now located at 243 West Merchant Street.

Along with business Mr. Cartier has taken an active part in local politics. He served one term as city treasurer, one term as town clerk, two terms as town collector, and is the present coroner of Kankakee County.

Mr. Cartier married, in 1897, Miss Elizabeth Betourne, who was born at Clifton, Illinois, daughter of Louis and Adeline (Prarie) Betourne, natives of Kankakee County. The children of Mr. and Mrs. Cartier are: Frank P., of Kankakee; Charles, cashier for the Standard Oil Company at Kankakee; Armand, of Kankakee; Robert, of Kankakee; Louise; Louis; Vivian; Pearl; Gertrude; Joseph; Patricia and George, who died at the age of two years. The family are members of St. Rose Catholic Church. Mr. Cartier is a past dictator of the Loyal Order of Moose and has membership in the Loyal American Life Association.

WALTER B. WARD, engaged in the creamery business and an ice cream manufacturer at Kankakee, has spent the greater part of his active life in the dairy business, and his enterprise has been responsible for developing one of the leading concerns of its kind in Eastern Illinois.

Mr. Ward was born at Momence, Illinois, May 16, 1885, son of Charles F. and Alice (Hess) Ward, his father a native of Canada and his mother of Kankakee. Walter B. Ward was educated in district schools, and attended preparatory school at Winona Lake, Indiana. At the age of thirteen he had his first working experience in a creamery and in the ice cream business at Grant Park, Illinois. He was connected with a creamery and ice cream factory at Manteno, and after two years came to Kankakee, where he was employed by the Anderson-Wright Dairy Company. In 1909 he purchased the Kankakee Ice Cream Company, and this is the business which he directs today, though with many improvements and additions. The first part of the present modern plant was erected in 1910, and other building and equipment were added in 1919. There is now a two-story structure, 105 by 145 feet, with facilities for a large wholesale and jobbing business in ice cream, dairy products and other soda fountain supplies. Mr. Ward is president and manager of the business, with F. W. Holmes, secretary and treasurer, and J. W. Kisner, vice president.

Mr. Ward married, in 1906, Miss Matie V. Brown, a native of Decatur, Alabama, and daughter of William A. and Matie (Collins) Brown. They have two children, Elizabeth and William. Mr. Ward is a deacon in the Presbyterian Church, is a director of the Kankakee Chamber of Commerce, is president of the local Rotary Club and is a thirty-second degree Scottish Rite Mason and Shriner, a member of the Lodge and Encampment of the Independent Order of Odd Fellows, the Rebekahs, the Eastern Star, Sons of Veterans, B. P. O. Elks and the Kankakee Country Club. Mrs. Ward is a member of the Woman's Club and has affiliations with the Rebekahs and the Eastern Star.

WILLIAM O. WARREN, M. D. Recognized as one of the leading physicians and surgeons of Clinton County, Dr. William O. Warren, of Carlyle, is enjoying a large practice, and rendering a very constructive service both professionally and as a private citizen. He was born in Wayne County, Illinois, August 9, 1890, a son of John R. and Mary Ann (Burkett) Warren, and grandson of William and Vina Warren, natives of Illinois. The Warrens came, about 1830, from South Carolina to Illinois. William Burkett, the maternal grandfather, was a native of Illinois, to which state his father came from Louisiana about 1830. Members of both families served in the war between the North and the South, a paternal uncle, Adam Warren, having been killed in action, and a Burkett served in the American Revolution.

John R. Warren is a retired farmer, a Methodist in religious faith, and a member of the Masonic fraternity and the Independent Order of Odd Fellows. He and his wife had the following children born to them: Adam, who married Hassa Ellis, has a daughter; Halleck, who married Lola Kuehne, has two sons, Fred and William W., who is unmarried; Doctor Warren, who was next in order of birth; and Effie and Lou, both of whom are unmarried.

Following his leaving the district school Doctor Warren entered the Carbondale, Illinois, State Normal School and took the regular course, following which he entered the medical department of the University of Saint Louis and was graduated therefrom in 1915, with the degree of Doctor of Medicine. For the subsequent year he was interne at Saint Mary's Hospital, Saint Louis, Missouri, and then entered upon the practice of his profession at Carlyle, where he has since remained with the exception of the time he was in the service of his country. Each year he does post-graduate work at the Chicago Polyclinic or the University of Saint Louis.

During the late war he entered the Medical Reserve Corps and was commissioned a first lieutenant, and was called to the colors April 3, 1918. He was sent to Fort Riley, Kansas, with the First Army Ambulance Corps, and remained there for about three months. Ordered overseas, he sailed from Hoboken, New York, and landed at Brest, France. Sent to the front at once, he was at Chateau Thierry for two weeks as first aid, and served in a similar position for two weeks at Saint Mihiel. From there he was transferred to the Argonne front, and while thus serving the armistice was signed. So heavy had been his duties that he was then sent to a rest camp near Chateau Long, was later at St. Lazare, and thence back home, reaching Hoboken in March, 1919. For two days he was detained at Camp Mills, but was then sent on to Camp Grant, and was honorably discharged March 25, 1919, and returned at once to Carlyle and his practice.

In October, 1912, Doctor Warren married Flora Ellis, a daughter of Joseph and Grace (Harris) Ellis, both of whom are living, he being a retired farmer, and a Baptist in religious faith. Mr. and Mrs. Ellis have four children: Cora, who married Fred Hickey and has two children; Mrs. Warren, who was the second child; Lou, who married Ad Hickey, and they have two children; Elsie, who married Fred Kease, and they have one child. Doctor and Mrs. Warren have no children. He is a member of the Methodist Episcopal Church. The County, State and National Medical societies hold his membership, and he belongs to the Independent Order of Odd Fellows. Doctor Warren is a very interesting young man of exceptional ability professionally, and keeps abreast of the advancement in his calling. His standing in his home community is unquestioned.

JOSEPH MONTY lived during most of his long life in Kankakee County. He was a Union soldier in the Civil war, and in all relations commanded the respect and admiration of his fellow citizens.

He was born at Chambly, Quebec, Canada, June 17, 1836, son of Joseph and Isabelle (McQuaid) Monty. His father was a native of Canada, of French ancestry, while his mother was Scotch. In 1854, at the age of eighteen, Joseph Monty came to Kankakee County, Illinois, with his mother. He engaged in farming, and on August 1, 1862, enlisted in the Sixty-fourth Illinois Infantry. He was in the service until honorably discharged at Quincy, Illinois, in May, 1865, coming out as a corporal. He received a gunshot wound in one of the battles around Atlanta, and that wound troubled him more or less all the rest of his life. He followed farming in Kankakee County, also in Benton County, Indiana, and died at Goodland, Indiana, January 17, 1916.

In 1874 Joseph Monty married Hilda Bloom, who now resides at 169 South Wildwood Avenue in Kankakee. Mrs. Monty was born in Rockville Township, Kankakee County, in April, 1849, daughter of Henry Sterling and Elizabeth Ann (Kerns) Bloom. Her father was born in Bradford County, Pennsylvania, August 5, 1820, and her mother, in Montgomery County, New York, April 10, 1827. Elizabeth Kerns was a daughter of John and Margaret (Vrooman) Kerns, the former a native of Ireland and the latter of New York. They were married in 1825, and in 1837 settled in Will County, Illinois. David and Polly Ann (Rutty) Bloom, the paternal grandparents of Mrs. Monty, were also pioneers of Will County, Illinois, where they settled in 1834. He was born in Bradford County, Pennsylvania, in 1800, and his wife was born in 1799, in Pennsylvania. They were married in 1819. David Bloom was a millwright by trade and after coming to Illinois built one of the first sawmills in his section of the state, and also helped build the mill and dam at Bourbonnais. In March, 1837, he removed to Rockville Township, Kankakee County, where he secured a homestead. In 1849 he went out to California as a gold prospector and while at Marysville helped operate one of the first sawmills and also built one of the first hotels. Mrs. Monty's mother died in 1911. Her father who spent his active career on a farm in Rock Creek Township, died February 3, 1899. He had been a justice of the peace, was postmaster of Bloom Post Office at Rockville, and was on the Board of County Commissioners. Mrs. Monty is one of thirteen children, eight still living: Guy, of Joliet; Edith, of Kankakee; Mrs. Hilda Monty; Inez, of Kankakee; Linda, wife of Ernest Loring, of Yuma, Colorado; David, of San Francisco, California; Miss Bessie O., who lives with her sisters in Kankakee; and Margaret, wife of Fred H. Walkley, of Sacramento, California. Mrs. Monty is a worshiper at the Presbyterian Church.

EARL C. CASEY, who is a successful promoter of oil development industry and who is serving in the office of justice of the peace, maintains his office at 504 Morris Building in the city of Joliet.

Mr. Casey is a scion of the third generation of the family in Illinois, where his paternal grandfather, Zadok Casey, established residence in an early day. Mr. Casey was born on the homestead farm near Mount Vernon, Jefferson County, Illinois, in the year 1884, and is a son of Thomas Jefferson Casey and Jennie (Marteeny) Casey, the former of whom was born near Mount Vernon, this state, and the latter at Danville, Illinois. Thomas J. Casey was long engaged in business as a successful breeder and grower of high-grade horses and mules.

Earl C. Casey attended the public schools until he was sixteen years of age, when he initiated an apprenticeship in the milling and smelting of ores at Florence, Colorado. Five years later he associated himself with the oil-refining business at Boulder, that state, he having there been allied with his father-in-law in establishing one of the first refineries in Colorado, and having later become a pioneer in connection with oil production in the Spring Valley district of Wyoming. He there became one of the principals in establishing a refinery, and after serving as superintendent of the same three years he disposed of his interest in the property, which at that time was sold to the Utah Oil & Refining Company of Salt Lake City. Under the new ownership Mr. Casey was retained as superintendent of the Spring Valley refinery during the ensuing three years, and he then returned to Illinois and became assistant superintendent of the Lockport works of the Texas Oil Company. He was soon advanced to the position of superintendent of the plant, and after continuing his residence at Lockport four years he returned to Wyoming and associated himself with the Interior Oil & Development Company, in the Salt Creek fields and with headquarters at Casper. There he remained two and one-half years, at the expiration of which he established his residence in Joliet, Illinois, where he has since been engaged successfully in the oil-jobbing business and has also been associated with development work in the oil fields, he being now the president of the Northern Oil Development Company of Joliet, which has large interests in the vicinity of Minooka, Grundy County, this state, where wells are being driven and other development work carried forward at the time of this writing, in the autumn of 1925. Within the period of his association with the oil industry Mr. Casey has made a close study of geology, especially in its connection with oil development.

The republican party receives the loyal allegiance of Mr. Casey, and while he has not been a seeker of public office, he has held that of justice of the peace since May 4, 1925. He is affiliated with the four bodies of the York Rite of the Masonic fraternity, in which his main alliance is with the Commandery of Knights Templars in his home city, and he is likewise a Noble of the Mystic Shrine and a member of Joliet Lodge of the Benevolent and Protective Order of Elks. He is a member of the Speed Boy Club and the N. E. A. Club, and he and his wife hold membership in the Methodist Church.

In 1904 Mr. Casey was united in marriage with Miss Mabel L. Clark, who was born at Neodesha, Kansas, and whose death occurred in 1913, she being survived by one child, Clark Thomas, who was born April 19, 1911. In the year 1921 was solemnized the marriage of Mr. Casey and Miss Elizabeth Kirkham, who was born and reared in Joliet and who is a daughter of Thomas and Agnes (Cooper) Kirkham, the former a native of England and the latter of Scotland. Mr. and Mrs. Casey have a winsome little daughter, Virginia Agnes, who was born November 8, 1924.

THOMAS KILLMER SPRAGUE, auditor of Will County, is one of the substantial citizens and honored men of Joliet, of which city he is a native son, having been born here May 15, 1893. His parents, Charles Norman and Alice (Killmer) Sprague, were born at Du Page, Will County. The paternal grandfather, Thomas Jefferson Sprague, and the maternal grandparents, Reuben and Hannah Killmer, were New Yorkers who became early settlers of Will County, and there engaged in farming. Charles Norman Sprague in addition to his farming interests successfully engaged in the quarry industry in Will County. Later in life he became a dairyman, but he is now retired.

Growing up in his native city, Thomas Killmer Sprague attended its schools, and was graduated from high school in 1914. He succeeded his father in the dairy business, and continued to conduct it until in January, 1918, when he sold it to enter the World war. On April 29, 1918, he enlisted, and was assigned to the One Hundred and Twenty-fourth Machine Gun Corps, Thirty-third Division, of the United States army, and was in western Texas for about a month. Sailing overseas, he participated in the Meuse-Argonne offensive, the Saint Mihiel offensive, and others of the major engagements. Seven times he went over the top, and for his capture of fourteen Germans he received a citation for bravery September 26, 1918. After the armistice he was stationed in Luxemburg, and while there attended the university. He returned to the United States from Brest, France, with his regiment, and was honorably discharged May 30. 1919.

Upon his return to Joliet he was in the general insurance business until April, 1920, when he was elected a member of the Board of Supervisors of Will County, and served for two terms. Governor Small appointed him an examiner in the department of trade and commerce for insurance, and he continued to serve as such until December, 1924, when he was elected auditor of Will County.

On May 16, 1922, Mr. Sprague married Martha J. Streitz, born at Joliet, a daughter of Rudolph and Hermine Streitz, natives of Germany. Mr. and Mrs. Sprague have one son, Thomas Killmer, who was born March 24, 1923. Mr. Sprague is a member of the Presbyterian Church. In politics he is a republican. His fraternal connections are those which he maintains with the Masonic Order, in which he has been advanced through the Chapter, Commandery and Shrine; with the Benevolent and Protective Order of Elks, in which he has held all of the offices except that of exalted ruler; with the Loyal Order of Moose, and the Modern Woodmen of America. He also belongs to the Isaac Walton League, the Musicians Union and the Rivals Club, and is one of the most popular men of Joliet.

Charles Norman Sprague, father of Auditor Sprague, was born in Du Page Township, Will County, June 19, 1846. His parents were natives of Hamburg, New York, now Orchard Park, and there the father was born November 10, 1810. Coming to Will County, he drove overland, in company with a neighbor, Amos Paxton, and Thomas J. Sprague, the grandfather of Auditor Sprague, and father of Charles Norman, bought 160 acres of land in Du Page Township. Pioneer conditions prevailed, and this early settler, who had but little experience as a farmer, having been a merchant in his old home, found his greatest difficulty in getting his first forty acres cleared and fenced. After that his experience guided him. In farming he really found his life work, and became more than ordinarily successful, accumulating over 500 acres of land. His greatest success was achieved in raising stock, which he was able to let run on the unentered land, then called commons. After he retired he moved to Joliet, and here he died October 22, 1898. He was a staunch democrat, and belonged to Joliet Lodge No. 538, A. F. and A. M.

On January 9, 1845, Thomas J. Sprague married Mrs. Lydia (Swift) Godfrey, a daughter of Schubel and Eunice (Olmstead) Swift, natives of New York State, and widow of Charles Godfrey, a native of New York State, to whom she bore three children: Eunice E., who is deceased; Joseph, who lived at Plainfield, Illinois, where he died in 1925; and Julia M., who lives at Joliet. Thomas J. Sprague and his wife had the following children: Charles Norman, who was the firstborn; Elizabeth, who married Jonathan Mather and resides at the corner of Nicholson and Western, Joliet; and Harriet, who is the widow of Albert Phelps, of Du Page Township, Will County.

Charles Norman Sprague attended the district schools and those of Naperville, Illinois, for one winter, and remained on his father's farm until his marriage in 1869, after which he rented one of his father's farms, and spent three years on it. Returning to the homestead, he helped his father in the dairy business, which was so developed as to include the making of butter and cheese, and assumed such proportions that it was moved to Joliet October 1, 1886. Charles Norman Sprague retailed milk and produced high-grade butter and cheese for many years. After he left that business he and his brother bought 537 acres of land in one piece in Lockport Township, Will County, and on it conducted a dairy, selling rights to the railroad and other concerns. They also dealt in stone, which they quarried and sold, and continued in the stone business for about ten years, when they disposed of it, but kept on with the dairy, which was finally disposed of to the Flint Sanitary Milk Company. Since then Mr. Sprague has lived retired in his comfortable home at 805 Van Buren Street, Joliet.

On November 25, 1869, Charles Norman Sprague married Alice C. Killmer, born in Du Page Township, a daughter of Reuben W. Killmer, born at Essex, New York. Mr. and Mrs. Sprague became the parents of the following children: Harriet M., who is the wife of Robert Matheson, of Joliet; Mabel S., who is the wife of Oscar Kase and lives on Van Buren Street; and Thomas Killmer, whose name heads this review. Hannah, the oldest child died at the age of eighteen months.

Charles Norman Sprague belongs to the Central Presbyterian Church, but he attends services at the Universalist Church. In political faith he is a republican, and he served as assessor of Du Page Township. He is a Mason and belongs to the Joliet Chamber of Commerce.

RAYMOND J. FENTON is associated with his brother, James P. Fenton, in the conducting of a general insurance business in his native City of Joliet, and has won standing as one of the successful younger representatives of this line of enterprise in Will County. Mr. Fenton was born in the City of Joliet in the year 1904, and is a son of John J. and Maria (McCraney) Fenton, both likewise natives of the State of Illinois, where the former was born in Bureau County and the latter in Will County. The parents are sterling citizens of Joliet, where they have long maintained their home, John J. Fenton having been a foreman in the employ of the Chicago, Rock Island & Pacific Railroad Company, for the past forty-eight years. The subject of this review is the youngest in a family of five children, and his brother, James P., with whom he is associated in the insurance business, is the eldest of the number; Esther M. remains at the parental home; Marguerite died at the age of twenty years; and John J., Jr., died in infancy. The religious faith of the family is that of the Catholic Church.

Raymond J. Fenton gained his preliminary education by attending the parochial school of the Church of the Sacred Heart, thereafter continued his studies in De La Salle High School and effectively supplemented his earlier training, his brother, James P. being a graduate of the Joliet Township High School.

At the age of eighteen years Raymond J. Fenton took a position as salesman in a furniture store in his native city, and after he had been thus employed during a period of eighteen months he became associated with his brother, James P., in establishing the general insurance agency that they have since conducted with marked success, the excellence of service given having gained to the firm a substantial and representative support, and the well appointed offices of the firm being established at 405 D'Arcy Building. Mr. Fenton and the other children of the family remain at the parental home, 215 North Hickory Street, and the members of the family are all communicants of St. Mary's Catholic Church. James P. Fenton is affiliated with the Knights of Columbus and is a veteran of the World war, in which he was in active service overseas, he having been for eighteen months with the allied forces in Siberia.

HARRY A. HAMLIN has developed in the city of Joliet a substantial and prosperous direct advertising business, which is conducted under the title of the Harry A. Hamlin Company and which has the best of modern facilities for the turning out of high-grade printing and multigraphing work. Of this business Mr. Hamlin is the sole owner, and his well equipped headquarters are maintained in the Ottawa Building, 305 Van Buren Street. His home is on Campbell Street.

Mr. Hamlin was born at Morris, judicial center of Grundy County, Illinois, December 11, 1885, and is a son of Orrin R. and Imogene (Redfield) Hamlin, both natives of the state of New York, where the former was born at Ariskony Falls and the latter in Jefferson County. Oliver Hamlin, grandfather of the subject of this review, likewise was born and reared in the old Empire State, where the family was established in an early day. In New York State were likewise born Nathaniel and Sallie Redfield, maternal grandparents of him whose name introduces this sketch. The marriage of Orrin R. Hamlin and Imogene Redfield was solemnized at Lisbon, Illinois, and Mr. Hamlin gave the greater part of his active life to service as a skilled millwright. He located in Joliet in 1886, where he resided until his death in 1904. He was one of the founders of the Volunteer Fire Department. His widow is now a resident of Joliet. The other surviving son is Clarence Nathaniel, who resides in the city of Chicago and who is a train messenger for the American Railway Express Company.

Harry A. Hamlin continued his studies in the public schools until he had attained to the age of sixteen years, when he initiated his apprenticeship to the printer's trade in a job printing office in the city of Joliet, where he was thus engaged two and one-half years. He next passed a year in the job printing department of the Joliet Herald, and thereafter he was employed as pressman in the office of the Joliet Republican during a period of two and

one-half years. He was associated the following year with the Joliet Daily News, and thereafter he was again in the service of the Herald for some time. He next served three years as pressman in the local printing establishment of Garlach & Barklow, and he then became assistant circulation manager with the Joliet Daily and Sunday Herald, his work in this connection being at night and he having at the same time attended a local business college one year. After severing his association with the printing business Mr. Hamlin established and conducted the first motor parcel delivery business in Joliet, and after operating this successfully during a period of three years he sold the equipment and business and became associated with Earl C Hasey in the advertising service business, he having assumed sole control of the enterprise two years later and having since continued the same most successfully, under the title of the Harry A. Hamlin Company.

In national and state politics Mr. Hamlin pays loyal allegiance to the republican party, but in local affairs he supports men and measures meeting the approval of his judgment, regardless of strict partisan lines. He is affiliated with the Modern Woodmen of America, and of the local organization of the Loyal Order of Moose he served sixteen years as treasurer. He is an active member and supporter of the Joliet Chamber of Commerce, and is one of the progressive business men and citizens of his home city.

January 28, 1920, recorded the marriage of Mr. Hamlin and Miss Florence Elizabeth Barringer, who was born and reared in Joliet and whose youthful education was here received in the public schools, including the high school. Mrs. Hamlin is a daughter of Conrad and Florence (Wiser) Barringer, the former of whom was born at Troy, New York, and the latter at Joliet, Illinois. The paternal grandparents of Mrs. Hamlin were Andrew and Catherine (Sharp) Barringer, both natives of the state of New York, and her maternal grandparents were Samuel Henry and Elizabeth (Jones) Wiser, the former of whom was born at Elmira, New York, and the latter at Providence, New Brunswick, Canada. Mr. and Mrs. Hamlin have a fine son, Richard Earl, who was born July 29, 1922. Mr. and Mrs. Hamlin have membership in the Methodist Episcopal Church, and Mrs. Hamlin is active in the work of the Sunday School and the Ladies Aid Society.

BERNARD H. HERTENSTEIN. His modern department store that would be a credit to any community, standing as a monument to his sound business judgment and industry, Bernard H. Hertenstein, stands out as the leading merchant of New Baden, if not of Clinton County, and is a man who holds the full confidence of his fellow citizens. He was born in his present home city, January 3, 1889, a son of Rudolph and Ida (Monken) Hertenstein, and grandson of John and Christina (Leoffel) Hertenstein, natives of Germany, who came to the United States and settled at New Baden. On the maternal side of the family Bernard H. Hertenstein is a grandson of John and Mary (Gundlach) Monken, also natives of Germany. About 1880 they came to the United States and located at Belleville, Illinois.

Rudolph Hertenstein was born in Germany, October 1, 1850, as were his two brothers and two sisters. Accompanying the other members of the family to this country in 1854, he settled at New Baden, and advanced with the village until he stands today among its leading citizens. In 1872 he began his merchandising as a peddler, driving over the road between New Baden and Saint Louis, Missouri, and continuing this work until 1890, making money and saving enough to be able to open, in 1896, a store at New Baden. His education was confined, outside of what he had received in Germany, to a three-weeks session in a district school while he was working on a farm after he came to this country, and before he started on the road as a peddler. In 1896 his business was entirely wiped out by the tornado which visited this part of the state, but with characteristic persistency he began all over again, and at the time of his retirement he had a fine, substantial store, and handled dry goods, ready-to-wear clothing for both men and women, and groceries, all of his stocks being of excellent quality, while prices and services were eminently satisfactory. Under the present management the same policies are maintained, and the business shows a gratifying increase with each year.

Mrs. Hertenstein, mother of Bernard H. Hertenstein, died in 1914, having borne her husband the following children: John, who died in childhood; J. R., who first married Louisa Singler, by whom he had six children, of whom those living are Roland, George and Barbara, and after the death of his first wife, he was again married and had a son, Melvin, who is with his father; Emma, who married Frank Hess, and has one child, Murray; Otto, who was unmarried; and Herman, both of whom died with influenza in 1918, the latter having married Blanche Mitzel and they had six children, Olga, Daniel, Marybell, Clifford, Harold and Dorothy; George, who died in 1898; Bernard H., whose name heads this review; and Olga, who is unmarried.

After attending the graded schools of New Baden and Carlyle High School Bernard H. Hertenstein entered Central Wesleyan College, Warrenton, Missouri, from which he was graduated in 1910, with the degree of Bachelor of Science. For the subsequent three years he was engaged in teaching school in Missouri, then, returning to New Baden, he was assistant cashier of the New Baden Bank. After holding that position for six years he moved to Jackson, Mississippi, and became auditor of the Aviston Flour Company, but in 1918, upon the death of his brothers, then in charge of the New Baden store, he returned, and since then has been its manager, his sister Olga being in the store with him. Mr. Hertenstein is president of the school board of New Baden, was at one time village treasurer, and is one of the most representative of its citizens.

On September 18, 1913, Mr. Hertenstein married Miss Jennie Combs, of Memphis, Missouri, a daughter of W. T. and Mary (Hudson) Combs, both of whom are living. Mr. and Mrs. Combs have had the following children born to them: Victor R., who married Harriet Rebeccah Mahon, who died in 1924, having borne her husband six children, Harriet, Mary, William, Victor, Jackson and Georgia Ann; and Mrs. Hertenstein. One child has been born to Mr. and Mrs. Hertenstein, a daughter named Mary Louise. They are members of the Methodist Episcopal Church. He is a Knight Templar and Shriner, and also belongs to the Knights of Pythias. It is a source of great pride to Mr. Hertenstein that he can trace his family back in his home community through three generations, and for several more abroad. Honoring his father as he has always done, he appreciates what he owes to him, not only in a material way, but also for careful training and religious instruction, and it has always been his aim to live up to his father's principles and his expectations of him. For these and other equally cogent reasons Mr. Hertenstein is very prosperous, and his influence is a strong and uplifting one throughout a wide region.

W. A. YATES is a native of Eastern Illinois, but his home since early manhood has been at Kankakee. For a number of years he was connected with the State Hospital, and is now in the undertaking business.

He was born at Watseka, Illinois, in 1880, son of William and Elizabeth (Binning) Yates, his father a native of Illinois and his mother of New York. William Yates followed farming as an occupation and died in 1920, his widow residing at Watseka.

W. A. Yates grew up on a farm and shared in its work and activities to the age of twenty. Up to the age of eighteen he attended public schools in his home community. Mr. Yates was connected with the Illinois State Hospital a period of fifteen years. In the meantime, in 1909, he became a licensed embalmer, and in 1918 he engaged in the undertaking business with James Coen. In 1921 he became sole proprietor of the business, which is now located at 242 South East Avenue. Mr. Yates is a republican, a member of the Methodist Episcopal Church, and is affiliated with the B. P. O. Elks and Modern Woodmen of America. He has served as alderman from the Fourth Ward.

In 1902 he married Zilphy Stump, a native of Watseka and daughter of Henry and Alice Stump. Mrs. Yates died January 6, 1925.

JOSEPH ZALÁR, supreme secretary of the Slovenian Catholic Union, is one of the effective workers in behalf of the people of Slovenian birth in the United States, and one of the substantial citizens of Joliet. He was born in Slovenia, Jugoslavia, October 11, 1879. After attending the common schools in his native land he also secured a collegiate training there, and on July 8, 1899, came to the United States and joined his parents and brothers and sisters who had settled in Forest City, Pennsylvania. His first work in his new home was done in the anthracite coal mines.

On April 2, 1894, certain broad-minded persons had organized in Joliet, Illinois, the Slovenian Catholic Union, which was incorporated in the state of Illinois January 12, 1898, as a fraternity for Slovenian people now citizens of the United States, and Mr. Zalar became interested in this organization, and, being made supreme secretary of it in 1908, he came to Joliet in December of that year, and here he has since maintained his residence. The object of the society, in addition to taking care of its people, is to insure men, women and children. The national membership is over 30,000; the assets are $1,600,000, and the home office is at 1004 North Chicago Street, Joliet, Illinois.

Mr. Zalar married, June 25, 1902, Mary Dutchman, who was born in the same country as her husband, and they had the following children born to them: Marion, who is employed with Mr. Zalar; Vida, who is employed in the Joliet National Bank of Joliet; Joseph, who is a student of the University of Illinois College of Medicine; Doloras, who is a senior in Saint Francis Academy; Hubert, who is a student in the Joliet Township High School; and Richard, who is the little one at home. Mrs. Zalar died June 20, 1925. The family residence is at 819 North Nicholson Street. A Catholic, Mr. Zalar is a member of Saint Joseph parish, Joliet. He is a republican, and for two years served as city oil inspector in Joliet, Illinois. In addition to his connection with his insurance organization Mr. Zaler belongs to Saint Joseph's Society, Saint Peter's Society, Saint Babara's Society, the Loyal Order of Moose, the Modern Woodmen of America, and the Joliet Rivals Club, and is active in all of them. He stands very well with the general public, as well as with his fellow countrymen, and is an able officer of the union he is serving so faithfully.

FRED C. DAMES. There has been no era in recorded history when the care of the dead has not been a feature of even savage life and the ceremonies have been of a character marked by the measure of civilization. Study habits and customs of every nation and it will be found that a reverence has been paid to the deceased oftentimes such as was not given to the living. There never has been, however, a time when the proper, dignified, sanitary conduct of funeral obsequies and disposal of the remains of those whose life work has ended, has been so complete as at present. Funeral directors and morticians of this country are no longer merely mechanics, but, on the other hand, are carefully trained in their profession and are called upon to undergo a strict examination before allowed a license. One who is thoroughly and comprehensively prepared in his calling and who has always lived up to its highest ethics is Fred C. Dames, who is engaged in practice at Joliet.

Mr. Dames was born at Chicago, Illinois, October 14, 1897, and is a son of Joseph and Margaret (Cramer) Dames, the former a native of Joliet, and the latter of Chicago, where she still makes her home. Joseph Dames, who was engaged in merchandising at Chicago for a number of years, died there December 3, 1916. Fred C. Dames received his education in the public schools of Chicago, and after leaving high school at the age of seventeen years commenced to learn the undertaking

Charles A. Jackson

business with a Chicago concern. He remained in his native city until November, 1915, when he took up his residence at Joliet and continued to work at the same vocation until 1922. At that time he opened his present establishment at 111 North Joliet Street. He has a business that is up-to-date in every respect, is a licensed embalmer, and through his dignified manner of carrying on his business has won confidence and patronage. Mr. Dames is a member of the Fraternal Order of Eagles and the Loyal Order of Moose.

On June 29, 1920, Mr. Dames was united in marriage with Miss Louise Wilhelmi, who was born at Joliet, daughter of John P. and Louise (Bose) Wilhelmi, and to this union there have been born two children: Joan Louise and Marilyn O.

WILLIAM W. SMITH. The tiresome sameness that frequently ensue from the continuous following of a single line of endeavor has never been a feature of the career of William W. Smith. Gifted with mechanical ingenuity beyond the average, this well-known citizen of Joliet has, at different times, followed railroad construction, bridge building, carpentry and pattern making, and in the meantime has found the opportunity to serve his community well in various offices of public trust. At present he occupies the office of recorder of deeds of Will County, a position which he has held since 1908 and in which he has given the greatest satisfaction.

Mr. Smith is a product of the South, born in Madison County, Georgia, January 16, 1863, a son of William R. and Polly (Whitworth) Smith, natives of the same state, where they passed their entire lives in the peaceful pursuits of agriculture. William W. Smith was given only a log schoolhouse education and was brought up as the son of a farmer, but at the age of twenty-three years, in 1886, left the parental roof and went to Alabama, where he found employment in railroad construction work. He was thus employed at various points until 1891, when he formed a connection with the Schiffler Bridge Company of Pittsburgh, Pennsylvania, in the construction of bridges, and in 1893 located at Joliet, where he established himself in business as a carpenter and patternmaker for the Phoenix Horseshoe Works. In the meantime, as a republican, he had become interested in politics and public affairs, and in 1901 was elected a member of the Board of County Supervisors, a capacity in which he served until 1904. In 1905 he was elected tax collector of the township of Joliet, and in the fall of 1908 was elected county recorder of deeds, a position in which he has been retained by successive elections ever since. During his seventeen years of service in this office Mr. Smith has given his fellow-citizens the benefit of industrious and conscientious work, and the machinery of his office has worked in an expeditious manner.

Mr. Smith is a member of the Blue Lodge, Chapter, Council, Consistory and Commandery of Masonry at Joliet, and is a thirty-second degree Mason and a Noble of Ansar Temple of the Mystic Shrine of Springfield. He likewise holds membership in the Knights of Pythias, the Loyal Order of Moose and the Modern Woodmen of America. Interested in all things pertaining to the welfare of his adopted city, he is a working and constructive member of the Joliet Chamber of Commerce.

CHARLES ALBERT JACKSON is president of the A. D. Jackson Saddlery Company of Benton. This is a prosperous business, its products carrying the name of Benton to many remote localities in the United States. It is a business that has been in existence for over seventy years, always in the same family, and the great developments and changes in modern life have modified but not materially affected the success of the enterprise.

Charles Albert Jackson, whose father established the business, is a thorough going optimist in commercial matters and in his views of life in general. He recalls the fact that when his father began manufacturing saddles and harness predictions were made that the rapid growth of railroads would eliminate the horse and consequently the harness and saddlery business, but Mr. Jackson believes that the horse is a fixture as long as the human race endures. Mr. Jackson has maintained his business at a prosperous standard throughout a depression that has affected the industry as a whole on account of the general use of the automobile.

The founder of this industry at Benton was the late A. D. Jackson. His father, David Jackson, came from Ireland in 1828 and followed farming in the State of Pennsylvania until his death in 1880, at the age of eighty-four. A. D. Jackson was born in Chester County, Pennsylvania, February 9, 1829. In his youth he learned the saddler's trade in Philadelphia, and then traveled over the country as a journeyman. In the year 1855 he came to Illinois and first settled at Shawneetown, where he conducted a shop for a few months. In August of that year he moved to the then small village of Benton, where he opened the first harness shop. That was the beginning of the present A. D. Jackson Saddlery Company. A. D. Jackson was an expert in his trade, and his son Charles A. has thoroughly learned the technique of the business, and has been a master in resource at the commercial end. Consequently the business has always been on a sound footing. The heaviest misfortune it has suffered was a fire which destroyed the store in 1897, entailing a heavy loss. In that year the company was incorporated, the plant rebuilt and the output of harness, collars and saddles still goes in undiminished volume to a normal trade covering several states.

A. D. Jackson, the founder of the business, died May 11, 1906. He voted for Lincoln in 1860 and 1864, being one of the few men in the then strongly democratic county of Franklin to cast their votes in that way. He married Jennie R., the daughter of Charles Dudley, a native of Virginia. Mrs. Jackson, who was born in Kentucky July 20, 1834, died at Benton February 5, 1904.

Charles Albert Jackson was born at Benton, June 12, 1866. He attended the grammar and high schools of his native city, and supplemented this with a course at Bryant and

Stratton's Business College in St. Louis. For over forty years he has been closely identified with the A. D. Jackson Saddlery Company. He was its traveling salesman for fifteen years, and has been its president and treasurer since his father's death.

Mr. Jackson is a member of the executive committee of the National Wholesale Saddlery Association. He is a republican, a Royal Arch Mason, a member of the Consistory and of the Shrine. His wife and children are members of the Baptist Church.

He married, in 1893, Miss Daisy Webster, who died in 1894. Her father, Byron E. Webster, a pioneer druggist of Benton, was a Union soldier. Mr. Jackson in 1901 married Miss Carrie Layman, the daughter of Thomas J. and Elizabeth (Lemen) Layman. Mr. Layman, who died in 1892, was a veteran of the Civil war, and practiced law in Benton for many years. Mr. and Mrs. Jackson are the parents of two children, a daughter, Elizabeth Virginia, who is a graduate of Frances Shimer School of Mount Carroll, Illinois, and of the University of Chicago, and a son, Charles Abram, who is a student at Northwestern University, Evanston, Illinois, and is a member of the class of 1927. After his graduation he will be associated with the A. D. Jackson Saddlery Company, and will represent the third successive generation to engage in this business.

JOHN WALLACE SPEARS. While all honest business effort is commendable, the average person is apt to neglect the cultural part of life and forget that without it real progress can not be made. The arts are of paramount importance, and their cultivation is just as much of a national necessity as the manufacture of boots and shoes or the marketing of any commodity. One of the substantial citizens of Joliet who has long recognized these facts and used his talents and ability to afford the people of his vicinity an opportunity to develop whatever musical gifts have been bestowed upon them is John Wallace Spears, director of the Joliet Conservatory of Music.

John Wallace Spears is a native product, having been born in Joliet May 17, 1867, a son of William and Mary Ellen (White) Spears, natives of Scotland and Ireland, respectively. Both came to the United States when young, and subsequently, after some time spent in New York City, came to Joliet, and here they met each other and were married. The father was a carpenter by trade, and he developed into one of the important contractors and builders of Joliet, a number of the solid bridges, culverts, as well as handsome business blocks and residences in this vicinity being specimens of his skill and honesty. His death occurred in 1916, when he was seventy-one years old, but she survived him until 1918.

First attending the common schools of Joliet, John Wallace Spears had one year in high school and two years in Northwestern University. Early displaying musical talents of an unusual order, he began to study music under the best of teachers, including Emil Liebling, after which he went abroad and studied in Berlin, Germany, for two years and three months under Edouard Schriner, and altogether over one year in Paris under Martinus Sieverking. Upon his return to Joliet he began teaching music, and January 1, 1906, he opened his present conservatory of music, 205-7 North Chicago Street, Joliet.

On October 26, 1920, Mr. Spears married Mary Barry, born in the north of Ireland, foreign buyer for Marshall Field & Company. They maintain their residence at 500 South Ottawa Street, Joliet. Mr. Spears is a member of the Joliet Baptist Church, which he has served as organist for many years. His wife is an active worker of the Methodist Episcopal Church. In politics they are republicans. Mr. Spears is not only a musician of rare ability, but he is a practical man of affairs, and a public-spirited citizen, and has the distinction of being one of the first members of the Joliet Chamber of Commerce.

JOHN WILLIAM LEWIS owns and conducts a successful general insurance agency in the city of Joliet, with well equipped offices in the Will County Bank Building, and his suburban home is situated at Plainfield, Illinois, within easy access of the city.

Mr. Lewis was born in the city of Cleveland, Ohio, August 6, 1887, and is a son of William W. and Harriet (Rowland) Lewis, both natives of Wales, where the former was born at Dowlais and the latter at Swansea, both having been young folk when they came to the United States and their marriage having been solemnized in the state of Ohio. In 1896 William W. Lewis came with his family to Joliet, where he and his wife still maintain their home and where he was employed as an expert roller in the plant of the Illinois Steel Company, being now retired.

John W. Lewis was a lad of nine years at the time when the family home was established in Joliet, and he had previously attended the public schools of Akron, Ohio. He studied in Joliet schools and graduated in 1906 from the high school. In the same year he entered the employ of the Illinois Steel Company. After remaining thus engaged one year he completed an effective seven months' course in a local business college, and he thereafter was employed a few months in the maintenance-of-way department of the Elgin, Joliet & Eastern Railroad. During the ensuing three years Mr. Lewis held the position of chief clerk in the office of the Joliet Manufacturing Company, and thereafter he served about three years as cashier in the Joliet district office of the Prudential Life Insurance Company of Newark, New Jersey. During the next twelve years he held the responsible office of employment supervisor with the local plant of the American Steel & Wire Company, and since January 1, 1921, he has been engaged in the general insurance business as local representative of an excellent list of leading insurance corporations in the various lines, and with a substantial supporting patronage that indicates alike the effective service given by his agency and also his secure place in popular esteem in the community that has represented his home since his boyhood.

The political alignment of Mr. Lewis is with the republican party, in the time-honored Masonic fraternity he has received the thirty-second degree of the Scottish Rite, besides being a Noble of the Mystic Shrine, and he is affiliated also with the local organizations of the Benevolent and Protective Order of Elks and the Loyal Order of Moose. He is an active member of the Joliet Association of Commerce, and a popular member of the Shabbona Club, besides being manager of the male chorus of this club. He and his wife hold membership in the Congregational Church.

The year 1912 recorded the marriage of Mr. Lewis and Miss Ethel E. Anderberg, who was born at Walnut, Bureau County, Illinois, a daughter of Nelson and Freda Anderberg, who were born in Sweden. Mr. and Mrs. Lewis have three children, whose names and respective dates of birth are here recorded, as follows: John William, Jr., May 7, 1913; Ardath Harriet, February 1, 1916; and Judith Elaine, December 19, 1919.

WILLIAM H. ENGBRING. Residents of Effingham for over sixty years, the Engbring family has contributed a number of influential citizens and thoroughly capable business men to the community, including William H. Engbring, who for thirty years has been president of the Effingham State Bank.

He was born at Cincinnati, Ohio, March 24, 1860, and was four years of age when the family moved to Effingham. His parents, Gerhard H. and Katherine (Boedker) Engbring, were natives of Prussia, Germany, grew up there as school children together, but were not married until after they came to America. Their marriage was celebrated at Cincinnati in 1856. Gerhard H. Engbring at Cincinnati was in the grocery business. On moving to Effingham in 1864 he continued merchandising, conducting a general store until about 1883. Gerhard H. Engbring was associated at that time with Dr. Henry Eversman, Benson Wood and Virgil Wood as co-partners in a private banking firm known as Eversham, Wood & Engbring. He remained active in this banking institution until his death in 1903, at the age of seventy-eight. He was a democrat in politics, but never sought any public office, though several times he was given minor positions of trust and responsibility at Effingham. He was an honored, upright, progressive and very earnest citizen and business man, worshiped in the Catholic faith, and in that faith reared his family of three sons and two daughters. His wife died in 1901. Of their children Henry Engbring entered the Catholic priesthood and was one of the first American born Catholic missionaries to China, going to that country in 1888 under the auspices of the Franciscan Order, and after nine years of fruitful labor died there. Another son, John H. Engbring, is also deceased, leaving one daughter. Of the two daughters of Gerhard H. Engbring one, Mary Engbring, is now a Sister of the Notre Dame Order, and Annie Engbring is the widow of T. M. Lynch and lives at Mattoon, Illinois.

William H. Engbring grew up in Effingham, was educated in parochial schools there and spent one year in St. Joseph's College at Teutopolis, Effingham County. His practical business training, under the direction of his father in the store, began when he was only twelve years old. For one year he was employed as a teacher in a country public school. In 1879 he was given a position in the private bank of F. A. Von Gassy, at Effingham, and in 1881 entered the banking firm of Eversham, Wood & Engbring, and in 1885 attained to a partnership in this private bank. When out of this organization came the Effingham State Bank Mr. Engbring was chosen its first cashier. After ten years as cashier he was elected president, and no small degree of the strength and prosperity of this banking institution reflect the capable direction and character of Mr. Engbring himself.

He has been alderman of Effingham and for at least a quarter of a century has held the office of school treasurer. He is a democrat, a Catholic, member of the Catholic Knights of Illinois and also the Catholic Knights of America. He married, in 1887, Miss Louisa C. Eversman, daughter of Dr. Henry Eversman. Their family has consisted of the following children: Clara, wife of Joseph A. Feldhake, assisstant cashier in the Effingham State Bank; Mary, wife of Harry Underriner, a druggist at Effingham; Henry G., assistant cashier in the Effingham State Bank; Gertrude, a student in Loyola University at Chicago; Hilda, wife of Paul Feldhake, who is connected with the Effingham Republican; and Louise, an employe of the Effingham State Bank.

FRANK L. SHUP, veteran newspaper editor and publisher, has given nearly forty-five years of his life to the work of editing and publishing the Newton Press. He is also a lawyer by profession.

Mr. Shup was born on a farm in Jasper County, Illinois, about a mile and a half from Newton, July 4, 1854, the second son of William and Emily (Coffin) Shup. His grandparents were Jacob and Elizabeth (McNett) Shup, originally spelled Schuppe, natives of Pennsylvania, the former of Holland Dutch and the latter of Irish ancestry. Jacob Shup with his family moved from Pennsylvania to Ohio and settled in Highland County. William Shup, who was born in Greene County, Pennsylvania, served with an Ohio regiment in the war with Mexico under Col. George W. Morgan and General Taylor. Soon after that war he moved to Hancock County, Indiana, where he married, in 1851, Emily Coffin. She was born at Guilford Court House, North Carolina, of Revolutionary ancestry, being a descendant of Tristram Coffin, an Englishman who settled on the Island of Nantucket and was the founder of the Coffin family in America, representatives of which have been prominent in many sections. One branch of the family moved to North Carolina. Emily Coffin with her parents removed to Indiana. A year or so after their marriage Mr. and Mrs. William Shup came to Illinois and settled on a farm in Jasper County, where they reared their family and spent the rest of their lives.

Frank L. Shup acquired a common school education and for several terms taught in country schools. He studied law and was admitted to the bar in 1880 after an examination before the Supreme Court at Springfield. Mr. Shup had a pioneer's experience in Western Kansas. After being admitted to the bar he went out to Kansas and settled at Kingman where he practiced law, dealt in real estate, was assistant county superintendent of schools, and in March, 1881, became associate editor of the Citizen. He remained there until May, 1882, when he returned to Illinois and on June 2, 1882, began his long service as editor of the Newton Press. Since 1893 he has been sole owner of that newspaper, which in point of circulation and influence is one of the most successful newspapers in Southern Illinois.

Mr. Shup has always been active in the democratic party, and has labored for the political success of his party and his friends, most of the offices in which he has served being those honorary in character and without remuneration. He was the first village clerk of Newton. For three terms he was master in chancery for Jasper County. In 1905 he was selected as an Illinois commissioner to the exposition at Portland, Oregon, serving without pay. He served one term as vice president of the Illinois Press Association and during 1914-15 was manager of the publicity department of the Illinois State Fair Association, performing these duties without salary at Springfield. He served as commissioner of assay at Philadelphia in 1915, and in 1920 was district supervisor of the United States census. He is affiliated with the B. P. O. Elks and was formerly a member of the Independent Order of Odd Fellows and Knights of Pythias. He attends the Presbyterian Church, of which his son is a member.

He married, May 3, 1887, Miss Annie Richardson. Her parents were Lieut. Frank D. and Esther A. (Weer) Richardson.

Laurence Edgar Shup, the only son and child of Mr. and Mrs. Frank L. Shup, was born at Newton, Illinois, July 2, 1896. He graduated from the Newton High School, and in 1918 received the A. B. degree from the University of Illinois, where he had specialized in the school of journalism. While at the university he was in training for a soldier and remained with the colors until after the armistice. Since the war he has been actively associated with his father in the newspaper business and is now manager of the Newton Press. He is a member of the American Legion and of the Masonic fraternity.

Ties Velde. To those who have never had the opportunity of visiting a modern Illinois farm, the mention of farming may bring to mind a team of hot, tired horses, a hand plow, and a horny-handed, dusty son of the soil, toiling endlessly from sunup to sunset. Those who have such ideas would be considerably surprised if they visited the magnificent farm of Ties Velde northeast of Manito, where they would find powerful machinery taking the place of horse-driven appliances of former years, and comfort and recreation for all connected with this rural property. The very productive acres of this valuable farm have not always borne the abundant crops of today. When Dietrich Velde came to this region from Lincoln, Illinois, and bought a vast tract of swamp, people with less vision and practical knowledge than he laughed at his folly, and looked to see him bankrupted within a short time. Dietrich Velde, however, belonged to a sturdy race, and one accustomed to contend with difficulties. He was born in Ost Friesland, Germany, October 1, 1856, and was a son of Ties Velde, who in 1866 brought his family to the United States, and after a stay in Logan County, Illinois, settled in the vicinity of Lincoln. The German lad transplanted from German surroundings to the broader atmosphere of Illinois farm life was eager to create his own opportunities, and as soon as his meager savings gave him a little capital he looked about him for a suitable investment. By that time all of the desirable land had been acquired by the earlier settlers, but there were many acres of low land, lying during the greater part of the year under water, that could be secured for a small amount. Dietrich Velde saw his opportunity, and seized upon it. In the face of advice and considerable opposition he invested his little capital in a vast expanse of swamp grass and mud holes, and lived to become one of the wealthiest men of his section, and left behind him a large estate for his children. Experiments soon proved that this land, enriched by the ages of decayed vegetation was surpassingly fertile once it was properly drained, and not only was his tract in this condition, but many other acres of low land. Once he had proved this fact Dietrich Velde secured the interest and cooperation of other farmers, and the Hickory Grove Drainage District came into being, of which he was a commissioner from the beginning. He continued to hold this office from 1886 until his death, which occurred July 25, 1918, when he was sixty-three years old. For some years prior to that event he had been living retired at Peoria, Illinois, but he continued as president of the Peoples State Bank of Manito, and was a heavy stockholder of the Avery Manufacturing Company of Peoria, as well as owner of a large amount of valuable land.

The wife of Dietrich Velde was Rena Bruns, and she was a daughter of Henry Bruns, a native of Germany, who for many years was one of the substantial farmers of Logan County. The death of Mrs. Velde occurred on the homestead December 8, 1907. The children born to Dietrich Velde and his wife were as follows: Ties, whose name heads this review; Henry J., who resides at Manito; Dietrich W., who resides on a farm at Parkland; Tillie, who married John G. Golden, of Elmwood, Illinois; Lydia, who married William H. Traeger, of Peoria, Illinois; and Grace, who is the wife of Clarence Spreng, of Denver, Colorado.

Ties Velde was born in Spring Lake Township, Tazewell County, Illinois, December 21, 1879, and the local schools grounded him in the fundamentals of an education. Subsequently he took two years in the Bradley Polytechnic Institute of Peoria, and after he had completed this training he went into the Avery Manufacturing Company of Peoria, where he applied the technical knowledge of engineering he had acquired in the institute. However, this work did not suit him, and after a few months he abandoned it and re-

turned to the home farm. Still later he went to Manito, where he was engaged in the grain business as buyer for Smith-Hippin & Company, but six months of that connection satisfied him that farming was the vocation for which he was best suited, and once more he returned to the family farm. From 1905 to the present Mr. Velde has been engaged in operating this magnificent property, which is a portion of his father's original purchase. On it he raises grain and stock, and for many years he has been engaged in the threshing business with his brother Henry J. Velde. Mr. Velde is probably the oldest farmer in point of connection with the locality now operating in the township, and he is proud of what he is accomplishing, and his family's connection with the prosperity here.

Casting his first presidential vote for William McKinley, he has continued a republican ever since, and is quite active in local politics. Since the organization of the Community High School Board of Manito he has been one of its members, and he is now secretary of it. Long connected with the Hickory Grove Drainage District, he is one of its commissioners, his two associates being E. E. Ethel and Walter Meeker. At one time he was central committeeman for this locality, and he always places his party's success among the worthwhile things of life, and he never misses a national election. He was one of the many in the county during the World war to be engaged in promoting war activities, and he was very liberal in his purchases and donations. Fraternally he maintains membership with the Independent Order of Odd Fellows, is a past noble grand of the Manito Lodge, and has been a delegate to the Illinois State Grand Lodge.

On March 1, 1905, Mr. Velde married, at Parkland, Illinois, Miss Laura Starrett, who was born in Mason County, Illinois, a daughter of William L. and Roziltha (Talbott) Starrett, the latter a daughter of John Talbott. There were four children in the Starrett family, Mrs. Velde's three brothers being: William E. Starrett, who resides at Peoria; J. E. Starrett, who resides at Manito; and H. H. Starrett, who resides at Parkland, Tazewell County. Mrs. Velde was reared at Parkland and there she went to school. Mr. and Mrs. Velde are the parents of two children: Russell L., who is a graduate of the Manito High School, and is now a student of the Illinois State University; and Eleanor L.

COLONEL FREDERICK ALBERTIS LIND, a resident of Chicago fifteen years, earned his military title by service in the great war, and in his profession is widely known on account of his position as secretary of the Commercial Law League of America.

Colonel Lind was born on a farm near Greentop, Missouri, July 22, 1884. He is a son of Augustus M. and Caroline (Roberts) Lind, the father born in Pennsylvania and the mother in Indiana. The father was a contractor and farmer, and both are deceased. From an early age Colonel Lind has worked and paid his own way. He attended rural schools, graduated from the high school at Queen City, Missouri, attended the Athenæum Business College in Chicago, and for a time was employed as stenographer and cashier in the offices of the Rock Island Railroad Company. He took academic work in the University of Chicago, and studied law at the University of Missouri and Valparaiso University of Indiana, where he was graduated in June, 1909. In November, 1911, he removed to Chicago and the following year was admitted to the Illinois bar and became manager of the commercial law department of the law firm of Eastman, White & Hawzhurst, holding that position until America entered the World war.

He enlisted May 10, 1917, four days later was sent to the First Officers Training Camp at Ft. Sheridan, in August was commissioned a captain of infantry, and during the remainder of the war was at Camp Grant, commanding Replacement Battalion, training troops for overseas duty, serving as recorder and law member of the board that made settlements and adjustments with land owners concerning the rental and purchase of land at Camp Grant, and serving as trial judge advocate in three important trials. He was senior counsel for the defense in the famous military trial of the United States vs. Ray Smith, et al., wherein a number of negro soldiers were tried a second time for an alleged assault upon a white girl. The trial was famous not only because of the heinousness of the crime but because the detail of officers for the court martial was personally made by President Wilson, and because of the constitutional and other important points of law involved. It was one of the most unusual and extensive cases in the annals of American army court martial. Since the completion of the case a new manual for court martial has been issued by the war department, covering most of the irregularities brought out in the trial of this case. The result of the trial was the acquittal of eight and conviction of five, three sentenced to life imprisonment and two to hang. Twelve of these thirteen defendants had been previously convicted and sentenced to hang. The President later commuted the death sentences of the two to life.

Colonel Lind was commissioned a major of infantry August 24, 1918, but the commission was vacated September 14, 1920, since he was twenty-one days too young to hold the commission. At the same time he was commissioned captain of infantry in the regular army. This commission he resigned March 26, 1922, to become secretary of the Commercial Law League of America, an office he has held since April 1, 1922. Just prior to his decision to withdraw from the army he had received orders to report to the Forty-second Infantry in the Canal Zone. On April 27, 1922, he was commissioned a major and on December 1, 1923, was commissioned lieutenant colonel of infantry in the Army of the United States, and assigned to the 341st Infantry.

He became a member of the Commercial Law League in July, 1914. On January 1, 1926, Colonel Lind resigned as secretary of the Commercial Law League and became a member of the law firm of Eastman, White,

Hawzhurst and Lind, with offices in the Home Insurance Building.

Colonel Lind is a member of the University of Missouri Chapter of the Alpha Tau Omega, is a thirty-second degree Scottish Rite Mason and Shriner, member of the Elks, the Christian Church, the City Club of Chicago and the Chicago, Illinois and American Bar Associations. He is president of the Knights of the Chicago Round Table and a member of the Chicago Historical Society and president of the Eighty-sixth Division Infantry Association.

He married, July 1, 1909, Miss Minifredi Eastman, of Kingsville, Ohio. They have three children, Frederick A., born in 1911; Albert E., born in 1914; and Helen Minifredi, born in 1921.

WILLIAM W. HUCKINS. A resident of Kankakee County all his life, William W. Huckins has had many connections and contacts with business and public affairs there. He has been a farmer, public official and merchant, and his interests are all of a most substantial character.

Mr. Huckins was born in Otto Township, Kankakee County, November 25, 1860, son of George and Isabell (Christie) Huckins, his father a native of Vermont and his mother of Londonderry, Ireland. His parents were married at Elgin, Illinois, where his father for a time was in the shoe business. George Huckins lived in Illinois from boyhood, and at the age of fourteen he traveled over the site of the present city of Watseka and worked for a farmer there at eight dollars a month, breaking land now covered by some of the buildings at Watseka. As a youth he also hauled wheat to Chicago over the old trail that is now the Dixie Highway. In 1852 he moved to Kankakee County and paid a dollar and a quarter an acre for land in Otto Township. He was on the farm until 1872, when he removed to Kankakee, being elected sheriff of the county. He served two consecutive terms in that office, and later was again elected as an independent republican. George Huckins died in 1914 and his wife, in 1912.

William W. Huckins was liberally educated, attending the grammar and high schools and then the University of Illinois. He had two years of experience in a dry goods store at Kankakee and another two years was employed by Carson Pirie Company of Chicago. After returning from Chicago Mr. Huckins managed the old homestead farm of 320 acres. In the meantime he also engaged in the retail coal business at Kankakee, and for many years has conducted one of the leading fuel establishments in the city, his yards and offices being at Court Street and East Avenue. As an adjunct to his coal business he established, in 1923, a Sinclair gas station.

Mr. Huckins sold the old homestead farm, but still owns a place of 320 acres three miles east on Court Street. He is a director of the Kankakee Tile & Brick Company, of the Kankakee Title & Trust Company and the Majestic Theatre.

Mr. Huckins married in May, 1900, Miss Agnes Sinclair. She was born in Scotland, daughter of Donald Sinclair. Her father was a contractor with the Illinois Central Railway Company. The four children of Mr. and Mrs. Huckins are Donald, George, Warren and Margaret. The family are members of the Episcopal Church. Mr. Huckins was for two terms representative of the Second Ward in the City Council, and for four years he was circuit clerk and recorder of Kankakee County. He has been active in republican politics, is a thirty-second degree Scottish Rite Mason and Shriner, member of the B. P. O. Elks, Chamber of Commerce and the Kankakee Country Club.

WILLIAM ELDRIDGE ISLEY is a native and member of a well known family of Jasper County, Illinois, and for the past fourteen years has been engaged in a general law practice at Newton. He is a former state's attorney of the county.

He was born on a farm March 25, 1880. His parents, Emanuel and Vandalana (Apple) Isley, were both born in Indiana, of Pennsylvania Dutch ancestry, and were married in that state. His father was born June 18, 1839, son of Solomon and Margaret Isley. Emanuel Isley came to Illinois and settled on a farm in Jasper County in 1867, this farm being about eight miles northeast of Newton. He has acquired a large farm by industry and labor, 120 acres of which he has cleared from the brush and improved, and has been actively engaged in agriculture there for nearly sixty years. He and his wife are still living, and all of their eight children, there never having been a death in this immediate family. Emanuel Isley and wife are members of the Christian Church. He has always been a democrat, though never a seeker for public honors of any kind. Besides farming he taught school for some years after coming to Illinois. He has been a real friend of schools and has encouraged education in his locality not only for the sake of his own children but for others as well. The names of the eight children are Emma L., Albert E., Lydia, Augusta, William E., Myrtle, Leona and Phronia.

William E. Isley attended country schools in Jasper County and as a young man he taught in the country schools for two years. After that he alternated between teaching and attending school. He attended the Normal at Normal and Charleston, and in 1905 graduated from the law department of Valparaiso University, Indiana, being admitted to the Indiana bar the same year. On account of ill health he did not engage in active practice until 1912, when he located at Newton, Illinois. Mr. Isley was elected state's attorney in 1916, and was reelected in 1920, holding the office throughout the World war period and retiring after eight years of capable administration, at the beginning of 1925. He is now engaged in a successful general law practice. He and his family reside on a small farm just outside the city limits of Newton. He has other farm interests and has always retained his interest in agriculture.

Mr. Isley is a democrat. When sixteen years of age he made speeches in support of the first candidacy of William Jennings Bryan for president and has since been active in almost every campaign. Mr. Isley married, in

1906, Miss Naomi Stretcher. They are the parents of four children: Wayne E., Leonard C., Wendell H. and Eloise.

WILLIAM BENTON WRIGHT since June 21, 1915, has been judge of the Fourth Circuit, one of the three judges of the circuit comprising the counties of Effingham, Jasper, Fayette, Clinton, Marion, Clay, Shelby, Christian and Montgomery.

Judge Wright, who has had a long and honorable career as a lawyer and public official, was born at Ewington, the old county seat of Effingham County, June 7, 1860, son of William C. and Jemima (Rinehart) Wright. His grandfather, Jonathan Wright, was a native of New Jersey, of English ancestry, descended from a family of Wrights that settled in Massachusetts in Colonial times. Jonathan Wright and his brother David were pioneer settlers of Wayne County, Illinois. David Wright subsequently went to Iowa, while Jonathan Wright settled in Effingham County. He was a carpenter and brick mason. While employed in the construction of the old state capitol at Vandalia he was killed by a fall. Jonathan Wright married a Miss Hutchinson. Their son, William C. Wright, was born near Fairfield in Wayne County, Illinois, June 14, 1831, and died at Effingham December 25, 1892. He was reared at Ewington, married there, and engaged in farming and the real estate business, but in 1865 moved his home to Effingham, which had become the county seat. His wife, Jemima Rinehart, was born in Ohio and was a small girl when her parents, Daniel and Barbara (Kagay) Rinehart, came to Illinois and settled at Ewington. Her father was a merchant at Ewington and afterwards was elected county clerk and filled that office in the new county seat at Effingham.

Judge William B. Wright is the oldest in a family of seven children, the others being: Allen, who lost his life through an accident when a young man; David L., a leading attorney of Effingham; Dr. John R., of Louisville, Kentucky; George E., of Daytona, Florida; Mrs. Theo May Frye; and Benson, a lawyer living in California.

William B. Wright was five years of age when his parents moved to Effingham, where he grew up, attending public schools. In 1882 he graduated from the law department of Valparaiso University in Indiana, and was admitted to the bar the same year in Indiana and Illinois. Returning to Effingham, he engaged in practice, and in a short time had won prestige as a thoroughly trained and competent attorney. Judge Wright has filled many important offices in his home county. For thirteen years he was a member of the Board of Education of Effingham, served seven years as justice of the peace, for four years was county judge, and for eighteen years a member of the State Board of Law Examiners. He is the only living member of the original board first appointed under the existing law. Judge Wright was elected and was commissioned June 21, 1915, as circuit judge of the Fourth Circuit and was reelected in 1921 for a term expiring in June, 1927. His work on the bench has earned him a high measure of that esteem paid to the ablest judges of any generation.

Judge Wright is a member of the Illinois State and American Bar Associations. He is a democrat, a Baptist, and has the distinction of being a former grand master of the Grand Lodge of Masons of the state of Illinois. He held that position from 1903 to 1905. He is also a member of the Eastern Star.

Judge Wright married, in 1889, Miss Dora West, a native of Mattoon, Illinois. At the time of her marriage she was living at Effingham. Judge and Mrs. Wright have four sons, all of whom have earned success in their chosen careers and professions. The oldest is Dr. William B. Wright, an eye, ear, nose and throat specialist at Long Beach, California. David Lester Wright, now practicing law at Effingham, was an overseas soldier during the World war. Robert E. Wright is a lawyer practicing at Greenville, Illinois, and during the World war served with the rank of junior lieutenant in the United States navy. Branson Wright, the youngest son, the city attorney at Lincoln, Illinois, also had a service record in the navy during the World war.

JAMES P. JACK. The life of varied activities, many of them vested with public interest, continued over a period of forty years or more, has made James P. Jack one of the best known citizens of Jasper County. He is a lawyer, has held a number of public offices, and at all times has exemplified an admirable degree of public spirit.

He was born on a farm in Jasper County January 9, 1859, son of Jeremiah and Emeline (Thompson) Jack. His father was a native of Virginia, son of Samuel Jack, and of English ancestry. Samuel Jack from Virginia moved to Ohio, and then to Coles County, Illinois. Emeline Thompson was born in Kentucky, daughter of Frederick G. Thompson, who came to Illinois and settled in Coles County and afterwards in Jasper County. Jeremiah Jack and wife about 1853 settled on a farm in Jasper County and spent the rest of their lives there. He followed school teaching as well as farming, was a republican, and died at the age of fifty-two. Their family of children consisted of Samuel, Frederick G., Charles P., Elizabeth, John E., James P., Abigail, Thomas B., Laura, Lothario and Anselmo, twins, and the three now living are James P., Thomas B. and Anselmo.

James P. Jack was reared on a farm, was educated in country schools and for a time taught in country districts, his occupation paying the expenses of his higher education. He graduated from Lee's Academy in Coles County. His teaching experience covered a period of seven years in all, his last work being done in the city schools of Newton. Mr. Jack in 1884 was admitted to the bar, and since then has conducted a general practice at Newton. His home has been at Newton since 1882. Mr. Jack has been the outstanding leader and man of influence in the republican party in Jasper County for many years. For four years he was deputy treasurer of the county, having full charge of the office. In 1887 he was elected county judge, at a time when the county was almost overwhelmingly democratic. In that office he served four years. For eighteen years he was secretary of the Newton Building & Loan Association and developed that into a strong financial institution rendering valuable service for thrift and home building. He resigned as secretary to accept the office as postmaster, to which he was appointed by President Roosevelt. Mr. Jack was postmaster of Newton for ten and a half years. He has been president of the Newton City Board of Education and for five years was city attorney. In 1920 he was elected a delegate to the Illinois State Constitutional Convention. Mr. Jack is next to the oldest member of the Independent Order of Odd Fellows in Jasper County and is also affiliated with the Knights of Pythias, Modern Woodmen of America and Improved Order of Red Men.

He married, in 1882, Miss Laura Smith, who died in 1905, the mother of two children, Roscoe, now deceased, and Lester E., who is a hay merchant at Terre Haute, Indiana. Mr. Jack in 1906 married Della Waggy, who died in 1914. By this marriage there were three children, Vera May, James P., Jr., and Lawrence N. Mr. Jack in 1916 married Mrs. Winifred A. (Yelton) Robb. She graduated in 1901 from the College of Physicians and Surgeons of Chicago, now the medical department of the University of Illinois, and has to her credit a quarter of a century of very capable work as physician and surgeon and has achieved notable rank among the women physicians of Illinois.

WILLIAM I. LYON, real estate operator, is a native son of Waukegan, and is a grandson of one of the earliest merchants of the pioneer lake port known as Little Fort, Illinois, a town that was changed to the name of Waukegon in 1849.

His grandfather's name was Isaac Reed Lyon, whose early home was at Sutton, a suburb of Boston, Massachusetts. He was a descendant of old Colonial families of Massachusetts, his original ancestor, William Lyon, having come from England to Massachusetts as early as 1635. One ancestor was a general in the Continental army in the Revolution. This branch of the family was also connected with the Roxbury Lyons of Massachusetts, and the family have been in America for ten generations. Isaac Reed Lyon came to northern Illinois in 1842, and took up land from the government in Lake County and subsequently bought other tracts of land. On November 25, 1843, he established a general merchandise store at Little Fort, founding a business that was continued by him, his sons and grandsons for over seventy years. He started the business when much of his trade was with Indians in Illinois and Wisconsin. In the course of time his business developed as a department store. He was also one of the largest real estate owners in and around Waukegan. Isaac R. Lyon died about 1884. He married Lorinda Carpenter.

Their son, George R. Lyon, was born in Waukegon, was educated in public schools there and in Northwestern University, and he left college at the outbreak of the Civil war to join Yates' sharpshooters and later was transferred to the Sixty-fourth Illinois Infantry. He was in many of the important campaigns of the war, holding the rank of sergeant. He was at Lookout Mountain and Missionary Ridge, Chickamauga, was with Sherman's army in the Atlantic campaign and the march to the sea. After the war he became associated with his father in the mercantile business and continued active in its management until his death. He represented Lake County in the Illinois General Assembly four terms, a period of eight years, and he was a member of the committee which was largely responsible for the enactment of the Illinois pure food laws. He died August 7, 1914. George R. Lyon married Philippa Yeoman, who was born and reared at Boston, Massachusetts, and in 1848 came with her parents, James and Elizabeth (Pentecost) Yeoman, from Boston to Wisconsin. She attended school at Waukegon and Kenosha, and is now seventy-seven years of age, a resident of Waukegon. She has always been active in the work of the Presbyterian Church. Her father was born and reared in England, married there, and after coming west lived at Kenosha a few years and then in Waukegan, where her father was a pioneer merchant.

William I. Lyon was born at Waukegan, August 19, 1874. He attended public schools there, graduated from the Military Academy at Poughkeepsie, New York, in 1894, and in later years has taken a number of courses, not only in practical phases of business including real estate work, but also a number of scientific courses. He has always had a strong bent for scientific investigation, particularly in natural history. On leaving the academy in 1894 he returned to Waukegan and became associated with his father in the mercantile business. He and his brother, Charles R. Lyon, continued the old house as a modern department store until 1915, when in order to give their attention to the real estate interests owned by the family they disposed of the store to the Rubins Brothers, who still continue it. Thus the Rubins Department Store is the logical successor of a business established more than three quarters of a century ago. Mr. Lyon has been occupied with many important business interests, and involved in the handling of a large amount of valuable Waukegan real estate. He has been a figure in the improvement and marketing of several subdivisions and has used much capital in building homes. He is a director of the Surety Savings Bank, of which his father was a stockholder and president.

Mr. Lyon is a thirty-second degree Scottish Rite Mason and Shriner, member of the B. P. O. Elks, the Waukegan Rotary Club, Glen Flora Country Club, is a republican and a trustee of the First Presbyterian Church of Waukegan. For fifteen years he has been deeply interested in the Boy Scout movement, particularly the council of that organization at Waukegan. During the World war he held the rank of captain in the civil and army intelligence work of the northern district of Lake County. He is also a volunteer working in cooperation with the biological survey in collecting data regarding bird life and migrations, and is president of the Inland Bird Banding Association. He is former treasurer and vice president of the Wilson Ornithologi-

cal Club and a life member of the American Ornithologist Union.

Mr. Lyon married at Poughkeepsie, New York, Miss Mary Cantine, of Poughkeepsie, who was educated in Linden Hall of that city. She is a worker in church, civic and club organizations at Waukegan. Her parents were John J. and Laura (Van DerBilt) Cantine, her father of French ancestry, who was a captain of infantry in the Union army during the Civil war. Her mother's people, the Van DerBilts, were of Dutch ancestry of old New York Knickerbocker stock, and remotely connected with that branch of the family that has spelled its name Vanderbilt. Mr. and Mrs. Lyon are the parents of two children, George R. and Mary E. Lyon. George R. graduated from Dartmouth College in 1925 and is now in the class of 1928 at the University School of Law. The daughter, Mary, graduated from the Monticello and Bradford Academies and is a member of the class of 1927 in Northwestern University.

Charles R. Lyon, a brother of William I., was educated at Harvard University and after leaving that institution was associated with his father and brother in the mercantile business at Waukegan until 1915, and since then he and his brother have been together in the real estate business. He is a thirty-third degree Mason, member of the Mystic Shrine and Elks, a charter member of the Waukegan Rotary Club, member of the Glen Flora Country Club and is a republican and Presbyterian. He married, in Chicago, Miss Katherine Nash.

SAMUEL McELWEE WYLIE, M. D., of Paxton, whose death occurred July 18, 1926, for many years enjoyed a standing among the leading surgeons of America. From 1918 he was a fellow of the American College of Surgeons, which was organized in 1917. From 1913 he was a member of the American Association of Military Surgeons. He was a member of the County, Illinois State and American Medical Associations, and the American Veterans of the World War. In 1902, in company with the late Dr. Nicholas Senn, of Rush Medical College, Chicago, an international authority on civil and military surgery, he attended the seventh Red Cross Military Conference at St. Petersburg, Russia, and incidentally traveled 25,000 miles over three continents, visiting over 300 hospitals en route. Doctor Wylie was a delegate in 1906 to the International Medical Congress at Lisbon, Portugal, and in 1910 was a delegate from the American Medical Association to the seventy-eighth annual meeting of the British Medical Association at London. In May, 1902, he was granted a fellowship in the Deutches Gesellshaft for Chirurgerie of the German Empire, for orginal research on "The Traction Injuries of Arteries." He resigned from this society in 1914, after the German invasion of Belgium. Only ten surgeons in America had been granted a fellowship in this organization prior to 1914.

Doctor Wylie was born at Oakland, Coles County, Illinois, July 15, 1854. His Wylie ancestors came to this country from Scotland about 1717, settling in South Carolina. His paternal grandparents were Samuel and Elizabeth (Dixon) Wylie. Samuel Wylie was a slaveholder, but manumitting his slaves moved with his family to Bloomington, Indiana, about 1830, to be near the Indiana State University and the Scotch Covenanter (later the United Presbyterian) Church. Jonathan Wylie, father of Doctor Wylie of Paxton, was born in York district, South Carolina, February 8, 1825, and died at Paxton March 5, 1876. He attended the Indiana State University from 1840 to 1842, then entered Ohio Medical College at Cincinnati, from which he graduated in 1845. He moved to Illinois to practice and in February, 1867, located at Paxton. He was assistant surgeon with the Thirty-fifth Illinois Volunteer Infantry from December, 1862, until mustered out September 24, 1864, having in the meantime been present at the battles of Stone River, Chickamauga, Missionary Ridge and in all the battles of Sherman's army in the Atlanta campaign, including Resaca, Dallas and Kenesaw. Dr. Jonathan D. Wylie married at Cincinnati, April 3, 1845, Agnes Anderson Crawford, who was born near Beaver Falls, Beaver County, Pennsylvania, April 14, 1827, daughter of Samuel and Agnes (Anderson) Crawford. Both her parents were of Scottish ancestry and of pre-Revolutionary stock that settled in Pennsylvania in the Colonial period, about 1716 to 1720. Her ancestors participated in the Indian wars and the Revolution. The three sons of Dr. Jonathan D. Wylie and wife were: Samuel M.; Allen Dixon, born November 15, 1856; and Oscar Howard Wylie, born July 14, 1865. The Wylie family in South Carolina were tories in the early part of the Revolutionary war until the barbarities permitted by the forces under Cornwallis, Clinton and Tarleton drove them into the Revolutionary army for self-protection, and at King's Mountain and Cowpens they fought against the British.

Samuel McElwee Wylie was educated in the public schools of Paxton, attended the Indianapolis High School in 1871-72, was a student in Monmouth College in 1873-74, and in 1875 entered Chicago Medical College, now the medical department of Northwestern University. He graduated with honors as valedictorian March 8, 1878, and in the same month located at Paxton. He gave nearly half a century to the practice of medicine and surgery. Every year from 1881 to 1889 he pursued post-graduate instruction in the New York polyclinics and hospitals six weeks of each year. He made his first trip abroad in 1890, attending the Tenth International Medical Congress at Berlin, and also spent eight months in the clinics and hospitals of London, Paris, Berlin, Vienna and Munich. He served with the rank of captain in the Medical Corps of the Tenth Regiment of the Illinois National Guard, and was retired as major, and during the World war was medical member of the Ford County Exemption Board, serving without compensation. He was a member of the Army and Navy Club of Chicago and belonged to all the Masonic bodies at Paxton, having taken the thirty-second degree in Scottish Rite Masonry. He voted as a republican from his majority and was a member of the Federated

Church of Paxton, a church representing a union of the Congregational and United Presbyterian bodies.

Doctor Wylie on June 19, 1879, married Emily J. Bushnell, who was born at Lisbon, Kendall County, Illinois, March 4, 1853, daughter of Sherrill P. and Adeline (McEwen) Bushnell. The Bushnell and McEwen families were among the early pioneers of Kendall County, and both were descended from pre-Revolutionary families in Connecticut and New York. The Bushnell family included an ancestor who was a member of the Boston Tea Party. Both families were of the Congregational faith, and the Bushnells and McEwens produced a number of noted divines and educators.

HARLAN M. STONE has been known as a banker at Kankakee for over thirty years. He is president of the City National Bank and is one of the respected financial leaders of eastern Illinois.

He was born at Strongsville, in Cuyahoga County, Ohio, January 19, 1860, son of Montraville and Mary A. (Smith) Stone, his father a native of Vermont and his mother of Ohio. His father was a farmer, but in later years was president of the bank at Oberlin, Ohio.

Harlan M. Stone grew up in the region around the city of Cleveland, attended grammar and high schools and took special courses of instruction. When he was twenty-three years of age he went to work in a bank at Oberlin, and remained there five years as teller. On coming to Kankakee he was associated with R. G. Risser in the operation of a private bank for two years. The resources of this bank were then merged into those of the City National Bank, and Mr. Stone accepted the position of cashier of the larger institution. He was cashier about fifteen years and since then has been president of the bank. He is also president of the City Trust & Savings Bank, which was organized in 1893 and has been operated in affiliation with the City National Bank. Mr. Stone is a member of the Illinois State and American Bankers' Associations.

He married, in 1884, Miss Minnie C. French, a native of Cleveland, Ohio. They have one daughter, Miss Mary C. Mr. Stone is an elder in the First Presbyterian Church, is a republican, is affiliated with the Modern Woodmen of America, Round Table Club, Kankakee Country Club, Kiwanis Club and Chamber of Commerce. His home is at 1211 East Court Street.

JAMES F. HALEY. In Joliet, the judicial center and metropolis of Will County, the well appointed undertaking establishment of James F. Haley is to be found at 526-8 South Chicago Street, where the modern brick building, owned by Mr. Haley, has the best of modern equipment and gives effective service in all departments, the owner being recognized as one of the representative morticians of the city that he can claim as the place of his nativity.

Mr. Haley was born in Joliet on the 4th of September, 1890, and is a son of James J. and Elizabeth (O'Brien) Haley, the former of whom was born at Joliet, this state, and the latter at La Salle. James J. Haley was employed as a switchman on the line of the Chicago, Rock Island & Pacific Railroad during a period of twenty-five years, and thereafter he was long engaged in the livery business in Joliet, where his death occurred in August, 1922, and where his widow still maintains her home, at 707 Ottawa Street, she being a devout communicant of the Catholic Church, as was also her husband.

James F. Haley gained his early education by attending the parochial school of the Church of the Sacred Heart, and it is pleasing to note that he and his wife are zealous communicants of this same parish. After leaving school Mr. Haley was associated with his father's livery business until November 7, 1918, when he established his present undertaking business, which he has since conducted with marked discrimination, consideration and success, he having previously fortified himself by taking a course in the Worsham Training School for Funeral Directors and Embalmers in the City of Chicago.

Mr. Haley takes loyal interest in all that concerns the civic and material advancement and prosperity of his native city, is a republican in his political adherency, and is affiliated with the Knights of Columbus and the Ancient Order of Hibernians.

On the 24th of June, 1914, was solemnized the marriage of Mr. Haley and Miss Mary Holloway, who was born at Forrest, Livingston County, Illinois, a daughter of William and Mary (Wagner) Holloway, the former of whom was born at Roodhouse, Greene County, this state. Mr. and Mrs. Haley have one child, James F., Jr., born December 7, 1915.

ORSON BAILEY SPENCER, M. D., is in point of continuous service probably the oldest medical man in Kankakee County, where his name has been associated with some of the best of skill in his profession for over half a century.

Doctor Spencer comes of a family of physicians. Two of his great-grandfathers were colonels in the Revolutionary army. He was born at Winfield, in Herkimer County, New York, June 2, 1845, son of Nathan and Sophronia (Bailey) Spencer. Nathan Spencer was born in 1809 at Sangerfield, in Oneida County, New York. On account of ill health he went South and for three years managed a hospital at Key West, Florida. After that he returned to Winfield, New York, and remained there until his death on December 17, 1874. Sophronia Bailey, mother of Doctor Spencer, of Kankakee, was born at Brookfield, Madison County, New York, March 13, 1812.

Orson Bailey Spencer studied medicine with his father, and in 1868 graduated from the Homeopathic Medical College of Cleveland, Ohio. For several years he practiced in his home town of Winfield, and in 1872 located at Kankakee, where he has been engaged in practice fifty-four years. He is a member of the City, County, State and American Medical Associations, and is on the staff of St. Mary's Hospital. Fraternally he is affiliated with the Masonic fraternity and B. P. O. Elks, and is a republican.

Judge R. R. Fowler

Doctor Spencer married in the fall of 1868, Miss Mary S. Butler, who died in 1870, at the age of twenty-seven. She was a native of New York State and was a member of the Congregational Church. On October 16, 1878, Doctor Spencer married Miss Ida Peebles Wilcox, daughter of Judge C. C. and Alma (Chellis) Wilcox. Doctor Spencer had one son, Harry Stillman Wilcox, who was born in October, 1879, and graduated from the University of Chicago and from Rush Medical College of Chicago. He practiced in Kankakee for five years, until his death by accidental drowning July 17, 1913. He was a member of the various medical societies and was affiliated with the B. P. O. Elks.

Mrs. Spencer is an accomplished musician and was one of the organizers of the Kankakee Woman's Club, serving two terms as secretary and then as president. She has been actively identified with the Kankakee Public Library.

JOHN G. PAULISSEN is president of the Paulissen Manufacturing Company in Kankakee. This is a complete woodworking plant, manufacturing all kinds of interior finish and special dimension lumber for building purposes.

Mr. Paulissen was born in Kankakee, in July, 1862, and both his business and personal career has made him a citizen deserving of particular esteem in his native community. His parents were John G. and Anna (Mitchel) Paulissen, who were born at Duesseldorf, Germany, were married there, and in 1855 came to the United States and after a brief stay in Chicago moved to Kankakee about the time that city was founded. The father was a carpenter and contractor, and was active in business from the early days until his death in 1903. His wife died in 1890. Their children were: Isabelle, of Kankakee, widow of John W. Schneider; Mary, deceased, who was a Sister of Notre Dame; Theodore, deceased; John G.; Anna, of Wheaton, Illinois; and Frank, deceased.

John G. Paulissen attended the public and parochial schools in Kankakee until fourteen years of age. Following that he served a practical apprenticeship in the building trade under his father up to the age of twenty-two and after that was a journeyman carpenter until he was about thirty years of age. He then bought out the old Kankakee Planing Mill Company owned by the firm of Mateer and Scoville at 487 South Washington Avenue. He has since continued this business and in February, 1914, formed a stock company with himself as president, Andrew Paulissen as vice president, and Thomas Haggerty as secretary. This company has a model plant, 250 by 145 feet, with complete equipment of machinery for the manufacture of millwork and interior trim and other materials that enter into the construction of buildings. About twenty experienced men are employed.

Mr. Paulissen married, in 1886, Mary Verfurth, a native of Wisconsin, daughter of John and Mary Verfurth, who were also born in that state. The children of Mr. and Mrs. Paulissen were: Leo John, who was drowned in the Kankakee River when twenty-five years of age; Andrew, of Kankakee; Frances, at home; Loretta, wife of Donald A. Gallagher, of Missouri; and Rosella, at home. The family are members of St. Mary's Catholic Church. Mr. Paulissen was for three successive terms and alderman from the Third Ward. He is a democrat, for many years was a trustee of the Knights of Columbus, has filled chairs in the Catholic Order of Foresters and is a member of the Chamber of Commerce. His home is at 219 South Third Avenue.

RICHMOND R. FOWLER, judge of the City Court of Marion, was for three terms state's attorney of Williamson County, and has been known as a very capable lawyer, and courageous and energetic public official in that vicinity for over thirty years.

Judge Fowler's grandfather, James M. Fowler, came to Williamson County from Tennessee in 1825, more than a century ago. Buying a section of government land, he improved it as a farm and home and lived a respected citizen of the community the rest of his life. He married Sarah McHanna, the McHanna family coming originally from Virginia, but reaching Illinois after a sojourn in Tennessee. Joseph W. Fowler, father of Judge Fowler, was the second son of James and Sarah Fowler, and was born in Williamson County, where he spent an industrious career engaged in agriculture. He married Elizabeth Jane Davis, whose father was David Davis, and who represented a Virginia family that came to Southern Illinois in pioneer times.

One of five children, Richmond R. Fowler was born on the old homestead November 28, 1862. As a boy he attended rural schools, spent two years in Ewing College, and when a normal school was started at Marion, expecting to teach, he attended that. His experience as a teacher in Williamson County covered two years. In 1886 he was appointed and served for two years as deputy circuit clerk under Hartwell Hendrickson. Another experience that has contributed something to his knowledge of men and affairs was eighteen months as clerk in the Thomas Dunaway dry goods store at Marion. Following that he began in earnest his law studies under Judge Duncan, but at the same time he worked on the abstract books. This was a period when he did a great deal of hard work, spending eight hours a day as an abstractor, earning his living from that source, while another period of five hours was devoted to his law books. In 1890 he was elected justice of the peace, and that office brought him still closer to the law. All the time he was studying as opportunity offered and in 1892 passed the examination and was admitted to the bar. Judge Fowler began practice in 1893, forming a partnership with Ed. M. Spiller, which continued until 1895. His first term as state's attorney began in 1897. He was elected on the republican ticket in the great campaign of 1896. He served until 1900. In 1904, the year that Governor Deneen was first elected, he was again chosen state's attorney of Williamson County, serving until 1908. For his third term he was elected in 1916, serving until 1920, and was state's attorney of Williamson County throughout the World war period. Judge Fowler was elected city judge of Marion in 1923, and still holds that office. He was city attorney from 1908 to 1910.

Judge Fowler for a short time was associated in partnership with John L. Fowler, and in 1917 he and Mr. Reid formed a partnership, this continuing until Mr. Fowler went on the bench.

He married, November 23, 1893, Miss Lena Bundy, youngest daughter of Dr. S. H. Bundy. They have three children: Ailene M., born December 18, 1894; Frances C., born December 11, 1897; and Richmond Roe, Jr., born June 24, 1906. The son Richmond is now a student in the University of Illinois. Judge Fowler has been prominent in the Knights of Pythias Order, serving in the chairs of the local lodge and four terms as grand representative. He also belongs to the Moose and the B. P. O. Elks.

HENRY ERNEST KAMMANN was born in Kankakee and for a number of years has been in business in his native city.

He was born in 1885. His parents, Richard and Henrietta (Dahling) Kammann, were natives of Germany and were young people when in company with brothers and sisters they came to Kankakee, where they married. Richard Kammann was a coal dealer and subsequently organized the Kankakee Bottling Works. He died in June, 1888, and the business was continued by his widow until her death on December 6, 1925, and since then the active management has been under the direction of her son Louis Kammann.

Henry E. Kammann attended public schools at Kankakee, also took a business college course and in Chicago he learned the trade of electrician. He worked there about seven years, and in October, 1907, returning to Kankakee, established an electric repair shop at 138 South Schuyler Avenue. Mr. Kammann does an extensive business as an electrical contractor and handles a complete line of electrical appliances.

He married, in 1908, Lucy Klaiber, a native of Oak Park, Illinois, her parents, Carl and Eda Klaiber, having come from Germany. Mr. and Mrs. Kammann have four children, Henrietta, Lillian, Lois and Dorothy. Mr. Kammann is a Presbyterian, a thirty-second degree Scottish Rite Mason, member of the Knights of Pythias and the Modern Woodmen of America.

LOUIS J. BRAIS is one of the active younger men in Kankakee business circles. He was formerly in real estate and insurance, and is now in the coal business. He is an ex-service man of the World war.

He was born at Bourbonnais, Illinois, April 7, 1897, son of Eusebe and Denise (Betourne) Brais, who were born in the same Illinois locality. His grandparents were French Canadians and came from Canada as pioneers to Kankakee County. His maternal grandfather was Moses Betourne and his paternal grandparents were Michael and Aurillia (Contois) Brais. Michael Brais was a foreman during the construction of the Illinois Central Railway. Eusebe Brais followed the business of farming and died in October, 1916. The widowed mother still occupies the old homestead.

Louis J. Brais was educated in district schools, supplemented by six years in St. Viators College at Bourbonnais. For two years he was a student in Northwestern University at Chicago, and in 1919 he went to work in the offices of the Chicago Title & Trust Company as a title examiner. He had some valuable experience there for two and a half years, and then became associated with J. L. LeClaire in the real estate and insurance business at Kankakee. Two years later he became manager of the A. & B. Coal Company, and that is his business connection today. This is one of the largest retail fuel companies of Kankakee, located at Wildwood Avenue and the Big Four Railway.

Mr. Brais enlisted July 10, 1918, and was sent to the Great Lakes Training Station, but after two months was assigned duty in the Puget Sound Navy Yard. When he was discharged December 10, 1918, it was with the rank of chief storekeeper. Mr. Brais married in April, 1921, Miss Bernice Rivard, a native of Kankakee and daughter of George and Georgianna (Boudreau) Rivard. Mr. and Mrs. Brais have four children, Joseph Louis, Lorraine Marie, Donald Arthur and Constance May. The family are members of the St. Rose Catholic Church. Mr. Brais is an independent voter, is a member of the B. P. O. Elks, Knights of Columbus, Brotherhood of American Yeoman, the Catholic Order of Foresters, the American Legion, Chamber of Commerce and the Credit Men's Association.

ARTHUR H. PLANT is superintendent of the Mound Park Cemetery at Kankakee. He succeeded his father in that office, and together their service covers a period of over forty-four years.

Mr. Plant was born in Iroquois County, Illinois, January 20, 1869, son of Abraham and Odille (Morin) Plant. His parents were born at St. John, Canada, were married at Rouse Point, New York, and about 1854 settled in Kankakee County, Illinois. Abraham Plant was a farmer for a number of years, but in 1881 removed to Kankakee, at which time he became sexton of the Mound Grove Cemetery, and later was superintendent, serving in that capacity eighteen years. He finally retired and died in December, 1917. The widowed mother still resides at Kankakee.

Arthur H. Plant was educated in the public schools, attended the Metropolitan Business College of Chicago, and remained in that city as bookkeeper for a hardware concern six years. Following that he became a Pullman car conductor, with headquarters at New York, and was in that traveling service for six years. Mr. Plant in 1899 returned to Kankakee and succeeded his father as superintendent of the cemetery. This cemetery comprises fifty-five acres. Mr. Plant is also a city park commissioner and for six years held the office of superintendent of city parks.

He married in September, 1898, Edwidge Matthews, a native of Fort Wayne, Indiana. Her father, Stephen Matthews, was born in New York State, and her mother, Miss LaFountain, was a native of Montreal, Canada.

ELIZABETH J. TEMPLETON
DR. J. S. TEMPLETON
ANNA J. TEMPLETON

Mr. and Mrs. Plant have four children: Isabell, wife of George Law, of Kankakee; Florence, art supervisor in the schools of Princeton, Illinois; Ruth, wife of Harry Wilson, of Kankakee; and Mildred, at home. Mr. Plant is a trustee of the Presbyterian Church. Since 1918 he has been an alderman representing the Seventh Ward in the City Council. He is a republican, a member of the Kiwanis Club, Lions Club, B. P. O. Elks, and in the Independent Order of Odd Fellows is treasurer of the Encampment and the Canton, and a member of the Rebekahs.

HANNAH EINBECK. One of the popular photograph studios of Kankakee for a number of years has been the Einbeck Studio at 143 North Schuyler Avenue. Its artistic proprietor today is Mrs. Hannah Einbeck, widow of the founder of the business.

Mrs. Einbeck was born near Seattle, Washington, November 30, 1882, daughter of George and Johannah Harbitz. Her parents were natives of Norway, were married there, and on coming to the United States settled on a farm in Minnesota. In 1881 they removed to the State of Washington and remained there a vear and a half. During the infancy of Mrs. Einbeck they returned to their farm in Minnesota, where her father died in 1914. Her widowed mother and a brother still live on the old farm.

Mrs. Einbeck was educated in grammar and high schools, graduating at the age of sixteen. She remained on the farm until she was eighteen, and then took up dressmaking. She was married in Aurora, Illinois, in 1908, to Max E. Einbeck.

Mr. Einbeck was born in Monroe, Wisconsin, in 1876, son of Edward and Kathinka Einbeck, natives of Germany. He was educated in public schools in Wisconsin, and at the age of fifteen took up photography, an art and profession he followed the rest of his life. In 1909 he located at Kankakee and was connected with the Powell Studio until 1914, when he engaged in business for himself. Mr. Einbeck died December 15, 1923, and Mrs. Einbeck has continued the studio since that date. She is a member of the Lutheran Church.

HERMAN R. SCHERBARTH is editor of the Effingham Republican and president of the Effingham County Printing Company. His home has been at Effingham for over a quarter of a century.

He was born at Hanover, Germany, December 8, 1869, son of Robert T. and Wilhelmina (Bretschneider) Scherbarth, who spent all their lives in Germany.

Second in a family of four children, Herman R. Scherbarth was reared and educated in Hanover, attending the public schools there and serving an apprenticeship at the printer's trade. He also worked as a journeyman, and in 1900 came to America. He at once located at Effingham, where he found employment in the office of the German weekly paper known as the Effingham Volksblatt. In 1914 Mr. Scherbarth became the majority stockholder in the Effingham County Printing Company and was elected its president. This company bought the Effingham Republican, a weekly newspaper established in 1872, and the only republican paper in Effingham County. Mr. Scherbarth has given capable direction to this newspaper, not only editorially but as business manager.

He is a republican in politics and has been secretary-treasurer of the Effingham County Republican Central Committee and also its chairman. He is a Lutheran, affiliated with the Benevolent and Protective Order of Elks, and a member of the Rotary Club. Mr. Scherbarth is unmarried.

JAMES S. TEMPLETON, M. D., of Pinckneyville, Perry County, is a physician of nearly thirty years' experience, and has enjoyed more than an ordinary share of the service, responsibilities and honors of his profession in southern Illinois.

He was born in Perry County, March 23, 1871. His father, William H. Templeton, had a distinguished career as a Presbyterian minister and missionary among the Indians. William H. Templeton was born in Chester County, Pennsylvania, October 13, 1824, and after graduating from college went out to Indian Territory and spent seven years as a missionary among the Choctaws, Chickasaws and Seminoles. As a student at Washington and Jefferson College in southwestern Pennsylvania he was a classmate of James G. Blaine. After his missionary work in Indian Territory he settled in Perry County, Illinois, and continued active in his vocation until his death on March 27, 1910, at Pinckneyville. He married Margaret Eliza Craig, daughter of John M. Craig, and Dr. James S. Templeton is one of their eight children.

James S. Templeton was educated in public schools, attended the Southern Illinois Normal University, and for four years was a country school teacher. He left school work to prepare himself for a medical career, and graduated in 1898 from the College of Physicians and Surgeons of St. Louis. Doctor Templeton practiced five years at Cutler, Illinois, and for one year was physician to the Illinois Penitentiary at Chester. He then spent a year in post-graduate study in Rush Medical College of Chicago and in hospital work in that city, and in 1905 located at Pinckneyville, where he has enjoyed remarkable success in his professional work. For a number of years he has been county physician and during the World war he served as a member of the Board of Appeals. He is also an advisory member of the State Board of Health, is a member of the County, Illinois State, Southern Illinois and Americal Medical Associations. He is a member of the Masonic Order, Knights of Pythias, Independent Order of Odd Fellows, Modern Woodmen of America, belongs to the Rotary Club and the Presbyterian Church, and at times has taken a rather active part in republican politics, serving as a delegate to conventions. At the time of this writing he is a member of the republican state central committee, Twenty-ninth Congressional District, serving his second term, having been elected at the last primary without opposition. He is also a member of the Illinois State Medical Society Council, representing the Tenth District. He has been a director of the Pinkneyville Telephone Company and has a number of other business and investment interests in that community.

Doctor Templeton married, November 30, 1899, Miss Anna Galloway, and to their marriage was born one daughter, Elizabeth Jane. Elizabeth or Bessie, as she was familiarly known, graduated from the Pinckneyville High School, attended Lindenwood College and the Southern Illinois Normal, graduating from the latter institution. She taught school in Duquoin, Illinois, for a short time, was taken sick during the summer of 1922, and died in November of that year. Mrs. Templeton was the only child of John R. Galloway.

John R. Galloway was born September 8, 1836, in Ayrshire, Scotland, son of William and Jane (Robinson) Galloway, the former a tile maker. The Galloways and Robinsons had lived in Ayrshire for many generations. John R. Galloway at the age of eighteen sailed from Glasgow, bound for New Orleans, being on the voyage seventy-two days. From New Orleans he went up to St. Louis, and soon afterward to Randolph County, Illinois, where he became a farmer and carpenter. When the Civil war broke out he enlisted in Company I of the Twenty-second Illinois Infantry and participated in some of the early campaigns of the war, including Grant's operations at Belmont, Missouri, and later in Mississippi and Tennessee. In 1863 John R. Galloway was put on detached duty as a mechanic in the Engineering Corps, and was thus employed during the campaign against Chattanooga, and helped survey a military road over Lookout Mountain. In July, 1864, he was discharged at Springfield after three years as a soldier. He located at Sparta, Illinois, and for many years was a mechanic and farmer. In 1876 he settled in Perry County, and in 1906 retired from the farm and moved to Pinckneyville to live with his daughter, Mrs. Templeton. He had voted for Lincoln in 1860 and was an enthusiastic republican all the rest of his life. His wife, Jane Robinson, was of Irish parentage. They were married March 15, 1866.

JOSEPH H. SPEICHER, president of the Kankakee Pure Milk Company, has been a resident and business man of that city many years. His has been a long life of varied experience, beginning as a boy in the heart of the Pennsylvania anthracite coal district, where as a boy laborer he saw much of the conflict usually described as the "Mollie McGuire" disturbances of that period.

Mr. Speicher was born in Germany, in 1855. In 1864 his parents, George and Anna Maria (Bocken) Speicher, came to America and settled in Pennsylvania, where his father engaged in merchandising. Joseph H. Speicher finished his education in a public school at Scranton. When only eleven years of age he was working as a mule driver or slate picker in the anthracite mines at Archbald, Pennsylvania. He was also employed some five years of his youth in a hotel at Scranton and also at Wilkinsburg.

Mr. Speicher in 1876 came to Illinois, and at Kankakee worked three years as a carpenter. For two years he was in the hotel business at Herscher, in Kankakee County. Then followed a few years in the building contracting business at Kankakee, and from 1888 to 1908 he conducted a furniture and undertaking establishment. He sold this business to organize the Kankakee Pure Milk Company, with Robert Danforth, president, Mr. Speicher, vice president, Henry Backman, treasurer, and Grant Grinell, secretary. The company at first engaged in the distributing of milk over the city. Since 1909 Mr. Speicher has been president of the company, with G. W. Boyd, vice president and John Langham, manager. The company now uses its facilities for the evaporation of milk, which is distributed through wholesale houses in Chicago. The company has a model plant, a two-story brick building 150 by 145 feet, at 396 South Schuyler Avenue.

Mr. Speicher married, in 1881, Barbara Schubert, a native of Kankakee and daughter of John and Mary Jane (Free) Schubert, who came from Germany. The two children of Mr. and Mrs. Speicher are William and Clarence, both of Kankakee. Mrs. Speicher died in 1902. Mr. Speicher married Esther Whitehouse in 1904. No children have been born to this union. Mr. Speicher is a vestryman in the Episcopal Church at Kankakee. In politics he votes as a republican, is a member of the Chamber of Commerce and the B. P. O. Elks. His home is at 215 Sibley Avenue.

WILLIAM A. MCGREW is a Kankakee business man who has made a success of a local industry, a grist and feed mill, which was established by his father and which the son has operated, located at 495 North Fifth Avenue.

William A. McGrew was born in Iowa, in 1882. His parents were James and Ida (Stewart) McGrew, the former a native of Ohio and the latter of Iowa. James McGrew in early life followed the trade of piano tuner, his vocation taking him to many different localities. Finally he settled at Kankakee, where he took up the milling trade and established the grist and feed mill in 1900, which he continued for many years. He died March 2, 1924, and his widow is still a resident of Kankakee.

William A. McGrew was educated in grammar and high schools, and at the age of sixteen began working for his father. He is a veteran of the milling industry, and when he was twenty-two years of age he bought the business from his father and has continued it on successful lines ever since.

He married, in 1913, Opal McBroom, a native of Indiana. They have two children: Robert, born January 3, 1914, and Virginia, born March 3, 1919. Mr. McGrew is a member of the Methodist Church, is a republican, and is an official in the Royal Arcanum.

CLYDE J. WORTH has been a resident of Kankakee since boyhood. In business he has been chiefly engaged in real estate, and is also treasurer of the Kankakee Nursery Company. He is an ex-service man, active in the American Legion, and resides at 1006 Maple Street.

He was born at Buckingham, Illinois, May 16, 1888, son of Philip W. and Mary F. (Marsh) Worth, his father a native of Pennsylvania and his mother of Indiana. His grandfather, P. W. Worth, was born in England, lived in Pennsylvania for a time and then settled at Minooka, Illinois. Philip Worth and wife were married at Paxton, Illinois. He was a hardware merchant at Melvin and later at Buckingham, and in 1902 removed to Kankakee, where he was engaged in business until his death on January 25, 1920.

Clyde J. Worth attended grammar and high school and had two years of special training in the Y. M. C. A. College at Chicago. He acted as physical director of the Y. M. C. A. at Revelstoke, British Columbia, also at Jacksonville, Illinois. and two years at Mobile, Alabama. Returning to Kankakee, he was associated with his father under the name of P. W. Worth & Son in the real estate business, and he still continues work in that line, chiefly handling farm lands. Most of his time is devoted to the Kankakee Nursery Company, of which he is both secretary and treasurer.

In December, 1916, he enlisted in the navy and was sent to the Great Lakes Naval Training Station as instructor in the radio school and was discharged February 28, 1919, as radio electrician, second class. He is a member of the American Legion, the Masonic order, the Chamber of Commerce, is a republican and a member of the Methodist Episcopal Church. He married, September 25, 1924, Elinor M. Burrell, a native of Streator, Illinois, and daughter of Daniel W. and Cicely (Fairbairn) Burrell.

JOHN S. COLLIER. One of the first farm bureaus established in Illinois, though not under that name, was the outgrowth of a plan formulated in the mind of John S. Collier, an agricultural expert, who still continues as the executive officer and secretary of that body, which has the title of the Kankakee County Soil & Crop Improvement Company.

Mr. Collier was born in Tipton County, Indiana, in 1876, son of Abraham and Mary Elizabeth (Durham) Collier, his father a native of Johnson County, Indiana, and his mother of Shelby County in the same state. His paternal grandparents, Samuel and Elizabeth (Bills) Collier, were born in Edinburgh, Scotland, and on moving to Indiana as pioneers in that territory established in 1811 a town known as Edinburg. The maternal grandparents of John S. Collier were John and Elizabeth Durham, who were born near Heidelberg, Germany. Abraham Collier and wife were married in Indiana. He was a farmer and minister of the Methodist Church, and died in 1913, while his widow lives near Sheridan, Indana.

John S. Collier was thoroughly educated, attending DePauw University in Indiana, the University of Chicago, and was a graduate student in the School of Agriculture at the University of Illinois. He became an assistant in the School of Agriculture, and prior to that had been engaged in special service under the United States Department of Agriculture. It was in 1912 that he organized the Kankakee County Soil & Crop Improvement Company. This performed the general functions that have since been a familiar part of the program of the farm bureaus, though it antedated such organizations anywhere in the United States.

Mr. Collier is a republican in politics, a member of the Masonic Order and the Methodist Church. His home is at 832 South Wildwood Avenue in Kankakee. He married, in 1905, Lena Elizabeth Drayer, a native of Momence, Illinois, and daughter of Calvin and Carrie (Vining) Drayer, her father a native of Ohio and her mother of Kankakee. They have two daughters, Elizabeth Cameron and Agnes.

EDWARD ALLEN GRISWOLD was one of the very capable citizens of Greene County, was born there, and devoted most of his active years to civil engineering and the insurance business.

He was born on Apple Creek Prairie in Greene County, June 26, 1866. The Griswolds were among the pioneers of that region. His father, Edgar Griswold, came to Illinois when a young man and engaged in farming on Apple Creek Prairie, and spent the last years of his life in the home where his son Edward Allen Griswold lived. Edgar Griswold married Lucy North, daughter of Asahel and Prudence (Swallow) North, of another prominent pioneer family of Greene County. Edgar Griswold died July 18, 1892, and his wife, March 14, 1901. Their children were: Perry D., who died leaving a family at San Diego, California; Seth N., who died in White Hall; Chester S., who died in infancy; Mary Ellen, who died at Greenfield, Illinois, wife of Edward Boulton; Sylvia J., who died at White Hall, wife of George Whitaker; Martha A., who died in childhood; Damon A., a resident of Blue Mound, Illinois; Lydia, who died in childhood; Caroline, wife of Thomas Meek, of Rockbridge, Illinois; George A., who died in infancy; and Edward Allen, the youngest of the family.

Edward Allen Griswold was reared on the home farm, attended rural schools and the Jacksonville Business College, and studied engineering by correspondence. He was one of the assistant engineers under his cousin, Clinton Stewart, in carrying out the Hillview drainage district project. For three years he was city engineer of White Hall, having charge of the grading of the walks and the establishment of the grades for other purposes. He was very successful in the life insurance field, employed first by the New York Life Company and later by the Equitable Life of Iowa. Mr. Griswold also owned farming interests in Wrightsville Township. He was a republican in politics.

On April 30, 1891, at Virden, Illinois, Edward A. Griswold and Fannie E. Lorton were married by Rev. Mr. Coldwell. Mrs. Griswold, who survives her husband and lives in White Hall, is a daughter of James N. and Amy Ann (Baldwin) Lorton, and member of a prominent Revolutionary family. She is a descendant of Robert Lorton, who was born in 1767, and became a sergeant in John Morton's Company of the Fourth Regiment of General Foot, under Col. Thomas Elliott, in the war for independence. He married in Charlotte County, Virginia, Tabitha Ganway and they moved to Cumberland County, Kentucky, and in 1819 came to Bond County, Illinois, and two years later to Greene County, where this Revolutionary soldier died at White Hall May 16, 1833, and is buried in the cemetery there. His children were John, Robert, Thomas, William, Joseph, Mary Nance, Henry, Sarah Chipman, Mordecai and Susanna.

Thomas Lorton, son of the Revolutionary soldier and grandfather of Mrs. Griswold, was born in Virginia, December 29, 1784, and was one of the early pioneers of Greene County, Illinois. He married Francis Nance. Their children were: Betsy, whose first husband was Thomas Bell and second, Thomas Wiesner; Mrs. Sarah Campbell; Mrs. Nancy Grant, who afterwards married James Tallman; Robert; James Nance; Harvey Newton, who was a Union soldier; Mrs. Susan Bradshaw; Mrs. Lucinda Bradshaw, who afterwards married Thomas Johnson; Clarinda, twin sister of Lucinda, who married Luke Chapman; Julia, wife of William Benear; John; and Martha, who was married to a Mr. Stubblefield.

James Nance Lorton, father of Mrs. Griswold, was born on Lorton's Prairie, near White Hall, February 24, 1824, was reared in that locality when it was practically on the frontier, attended a country school and followed farming until his death on February 4, 1895. He married Amy Ann Baldwin, who was born in Indiana, February 7, 1830 daughter of Thomas and Anna (Stonebraker) Baldwin. She died April 26, 1918, and she and her husband are buried at Virden, Illinois. Their children were: Oliver C., of Virden; Thomas, who died in infancy; William H., of Springfield; John, who died in infancy; Fannie Ellen Griswold; and James H., of Virden.

Mrs. Griswold is the mother of one daughter, Lorene Ada. Mrs. Griswold finished her education in the high school at Virden. She is a republican, having cast her first presidential vote for Warren G. Harding. She is a member of the Methodist Church and the Royal Neighbors. She owns 240 acres in Wrightsville Township, Greene County, also a store building and ten acres and a nice home in White Hall. Mr. Griswold helped many young men in obtaining their education and to start in business, and was well thought of in this community.

PAUL TAYLOR is serving his second term as state's attorney of Effingham County. He is a comparatively young man in the profession of law, but has proved his abilities not only in the office he now holds but in general practice.

Mr. Taylor was born at Effingham, Illinois, March 9, 1890. The Taylors were among the early settlers, his forefathers having come to America prior to the Revolutionary war and settled in what is now Hampshire County, West Virginia. His great-great-grandfather Taylor was a soldier in the company forming Washington's bodyguard during the Revolution, and was severely wounded and crippled in battle. His grandfather, John Taylor, was killed in the Mexican war. His great-grandfather, who was then past the age of sixty years, volunteered at the opening of the Civil war, and incurred illness in service which caused his death shortly afterward. His father, John Wesley Taylor, at the age of fourteen, also entered the Union Army during the Civil war, and served throughout, and is still a resident of Effingham, being now in his eightieth year.

Paul Taylor's mother is Barbara Buehler Taylor, daughter of John G. Buehler, one of the early German immigrants who settled in Effingham County south of Dieterich, Illinois. She was born near Maysville, Kentucky, during her parents' journey to Illinois, and her home has been in Effingham County ever since they arrived here, she now being in her seventieth year.

Paul Taylor, only child of the second marriage to reach mature years, was reared in Effingham, where he graduated from high school in 1907. After a commercial course, including stenography, he entered the law office of the late Judge R. C. Harrah of Effingham. He performed clerical duties and studied law, and was admitted to the bar in 1911. Mr. Taylor was associated with Judge Harrah in law practice until the death of the judge. He also served as city attorney of Effingham until 1920, when he was elected state's attorney, and in 1924 was reelected. Mr. Taylor has depended on his own efforts and his abilities to advance him in life, and has had a very interesting career.

He is a democrat in politics. He is a Royal Arch Mason and member of the Eastern Star, having filled chairs in the Masonic Lodge, and has also filled all the chairs in the local Lodge of Elks. He is a member of the Presbyterian Church. Mr. Taylor married, in 1912, Miss Ruby Adams. They have two children, Shirley Bernice and Betty Jean Taylor. Mrs. Taylor is a native of Effingham, daughter of George W. and Mahulda Adams.

HESAKIAH K. POWELL in November, 1873, was elected county clerk of Jasper County. He had previously served as deputy county clerk. Election and reelection has followed as naturally as the regular recurrence of the seasons in Jasper County, and there was no interruption to his continued service in that position until at the close of 1926 he voluntarily retired, having been in office fifty-three years, which probably constitutes a record in Illinois and perhaps in many other states for continuous incumbency in one county office.

Hesakiah K. Powell was born November 12, 1847, and was in his seventy-ninth year when he closed his last term in the county clerk's office. His birth occurred on a farm in the northern part of Jasper County, Illinois, and he was two years old when his parents moved to Newton. His parents were John and Frances Arminta (McComas) Powell, the former a native of Ohio and the latter of Virginia. The McComas family was established in Jasper County in early days. John Powell died when his son Hesakiah was only nine years of age. Soon afterward he was thrown on his own resources and has had to make the best of his way through life, earning his living when most boys of his age were in school. He had a few terms in the public schools, and in the spring of 1864, at the age of sixteen, he enlisted in

Fannie E. Griswold

Company I of the One Hundred and Forty-third Illinois Infantry. He served until his honorable discharge at the close of the war, and is one of the youngest of the veterans of the great Civil war and one of the few survivors who are under four score years of age. He has been a member of the Grand Army of the Republic since its early years. Not long after the war Mr. Powell received appointment as a deputy in the county clerk's office, and that department of the county government has been the scene of his faithful labors and through which he has enjoyed the confidence of his fellow citizens and their general esteem. He has always been a staunch democrat in politics.

Mr. Powell married, January 11, 1870, Miss Dollie Ann Thompson. They were married at Olney, Illinois. Her parents were natives of Virginia, and came to Jasper County after the Civil war. Mrs. Powell was born in Missouri and spent part of her girlhood in Tennessee. Through the marriage of Mr. and Mrs. Powell were born four sons and two daughters, one son dying at the age of twenty-one. The daughter Julia C. is Mrs. Evans. The daughter Hattie has for many years been deputy county clerk under her father, and in 1926 received the democratic nomination and was elected county clerk to succeed her father. The three living sons are: Robert L., who has a record of service in the Spanish-American war and became deputy county clerk under his father; Thomas W., a resident of Chicago; and Boyce E., a resident of Tampa, Florida. The sons Thomas and Boyce were with the colors during the World war, so that the family has an unusual record of military service.

DR. EDD HOAGLAND. During a long and active career, Dr. Edd Hoagland, for many years a highly respected resident of Metropolis, has had a number of interesting experiences, perhaps the greatest of which came to him when, as a lad of twelve years, he enlisted in the Union army as a drummer boy and later became a full-fledged soldier. Since that time Doctor Hoagland, who is now the youngest Civil war soldier in the state of Illinois, has been principally engaged as the owner of livery and sales stables and as a veterinary surgeon, and it is in the latter capacity that he is probably best known to the people of Metropolis, who have relied on his skill and learning in the treatment of their ailing live stock.

Doctor Hoagland was born in Owen County, Indiana, in 1851, a son of John M. and Ruth (Grimes) Hoagland. His father, who was a native of Ohio, moved in young manhood to Indiana, and finally settled at Waynesville, Illinois, where for many years he conducted a mercantile establishment. Doctor Hoagland was a lad of ten years when the Civil war came on, and continued to attend school for two years more, when his youthful patriotism and love of adventure caused him to leave home and enlist, July 23, 1863, in the One Hundred and Fifteenth Regiment, Indiana Volunteer Infantry, as a drummer boy. Six months later he reenlisted in the First Indiana Heavy Artillery, became Gen. Gordon B. Granger's orderly, and with that regiment saw service in Tennessee, and also participated in the siege of Mobile, the battle of Fort Hudson and a number of hot skirmishes. Honorably discharged from the service January 10, 1866, he returned to Indiana, where he secured a position as clerk in a grocery store, a position which he held for one year. He went then to Terre Haute, Indiana, where he became foreman of a livery stable, having gained some experience with horses during his army service, and while thus engaged also bought horses and engaged in kindred activities. He left this position after two years and for a time his wanderlust carried him from place to place until 1872, when he located at New Columbia, Massac County, and there found employment on a farm, working by the month. Two years of this sufficed him, and he next purchased a livery stable at Vienna, Johnson County, Illinois, in the conduct of which he was engaged three years. Disposing of this enterprise, he first came to Metropolis and bought a similar establishment, but three years later sold out and applied himself to the study of veterinary surgery at Indianapolis, Indiana. He then returned to Metropolis, where he has since enjoyed a large and lucrative practice in his profession. Doctor Hoagland is a member of the Christian Church, and in politics is a democrat. He is an interested member of the Grand Army of the Republic and never fails to attend a reunion.

On November 7, 1878, Doctor Hoagland was united in marriage with Roberta Alice Kindred, who died December 5, 1924, having been the mother of the following children: Anna, the wife of Fred Kindred, of Indianapolis, Indiana; Bert, also a resident of the Hoosier capital; John, who died at the age of thirty years; Mamie, Mrs. A. J. Fritz, who lives with her father at 414 East Fifth Street; Dimple, who married Alfred T. Fugitt and also resides with her father; and Mabel, Mrs. John Mason, of Tampa, Florida.

FRED E. EVANS. Both individually, and through the medium of The Advocate, the leading newspaper of St. Clair County, Fred E. Evans is playing an important part in the life of Belleville and the county, and is making his journal one of the strong newspapers in the state. He is a native of Illinois, having been born at Greenville, Bond County, June 28, 1877, a son of Daniel B. and Eleanor D. (Johnson) Evans, and grandson of William M. and Mary Evans, of Indiana, and R. A. and Mary Johnson, natives of Hull, England. The maternal grandmother belonged to the old Revolutionary family of Weyman, descendants of the Dalrymple family of Scotland.

Daniel B. Evans was born in Indiana, and was seven years old when he was brought to Illinois by his parents when they settled in Hennepin County, they later locating in Bond County. He held several public offices, and was circuit clerk and recorder and an abstractor of Bond County for many years. Subsequently he was connected with the private state bank of Hoiles & Sons of Greenville. His death occurred in 1895, but the mother survived him for many years, passing away in 1919. They had two children: Fred E., whose name heads this review; and Woodford W., who married Ida Baurichter, and they have two children: Charlotte and Daniel Henry.

Following his graduation from the Greenville High School in 1894, Fred E. Evans took the academic course at Greenville College, although he is not a graduate of that institution. For a few years after he finished his collegiate course he was engaged in work as a bookkeeper for different mercantile establishments at Greenville, and then came to Belleville as a reporter on The Advocate. In 1908 he was made city editor of this thriving daily, and, acquiring an interest in the company, was made its secretary. In 1913 he, his brother and Walter D. Schmitt purchased all the other stock and became the owners of the paper, with Mr. Evans as president and editor, W. W. Evans as business manager, and Walter Schmitt, city editor. This paper is republican in policy, and through the energy and good management of the new company it has been placed at the front among the worthwhile newspapers in this part of Illinois. During the World war the paper and its owners played a very important part in forwarding all local war work.

Mr. Evans married, December 31, 1911, at Mount Carmel, Illinois, Miss Ida Fehr, a daughter of Adam Fehr, who died in 1917. He was a native of Germany, and a patternmaker during his active years. At the time of his death he was eighty-eight years of age. He and his wife, who died many years ago, had five children: William, who is unmarried; Adolph and August, both of whom are married; Alma, who is unmarried; and Mrs. Evans. Mr. and Mrs. Evans have no children. In religious belief Mr. Evans is a Methodist. He belongs to the Belleville Chamber of Commerce, to the Belleville lodge of Elks and to the Belleville Rotary Club. Outside of these organizations he has no affiliations, as his time is largely occupied with his newspaper, which is demanding more of his attention every year. He is a man who believes in developing a strong local pride, and giving to each home undertaking a proper support, and it is safe to say that there are very few movements of any real value that are inaugurated in this locality that do not receive a hearty cooperation from him and The Advocate, just as both are against lawbreakers in all ranks of life, and others who seek to lower the high standard of living so characteristic of the communities of St. Clair County.

NORMAN L. JONES, judge of the Circuit Court, who since 1921 has served as judge of the Appellate Court, Second District, has enjoyed many honors in the course of his public and professional career.

Judge Jones was born September 19, 1869, son of John and Minerva (Patterson) Jones. His parents now reside at Roodhouse, Illinois. His father was born in 1839 and his mother in 1844. Norman L. Jones was educated in public schools and attended the Northern Indiana State Normal. He entered politics and public affairs before his admission to the bar, having served as representative from Greene County in the Thirty-eighth and Thirty-ninth Illinois General Assemblies, from 1892 to 1896. He was admitted to the bar in May, 1896, and soon won secure prestige as a lawyer at Carrollton. He was city attorney from 1902 to 1912, and from 1912 to 1914 state's attorney of Greene County.

In 1914 he was elected to fill a vacancy as circuit judge of the Seventh Judicial Circuit, comprising the counties of Sangamon, Morgan, Scott, Greene, Jersey and Macoupin. In 1915 he was elected for the regular term of six years and was reelected in 1921. In June, 1921, he was selected by the Supreme Court to serve as one of the judges of the Second Appellate Court District at Ottawa, and he has since been fully occupied with the duties of that court.

Judge Jones is doubtless best known over the state of Illinois for his remarkable candidacy as democratic nominee for governor in 1924. In that election he ran more than five hundred thousand votes ahead of the democratic candidate for president in Illinois. Judge Jones married at Carrollton, June 28, 1906, Miss Meda Pegram, daughter of Mr. and Mrs. Alvin Pegram, of Carrollton. They have one son, Norman Pegram Jones, born February 7, 1912.

WALTER W. L. MEYER, Chicago attorney, master in chancery of the Circuit Court, was born in that city and has won a successful position in his profession and a place of influence in public affairs.

Mr. Meyer was born in Chicago June 23, 1892, only son of the three children of John J. and Maria (Gareiss) Meyer. His parents were also natives of Chicago. He is a graduate of the Lutheran parochial schools, the public schools and of the Armour Scientific Academy with the class of 1908. After a literary course in the University of Illinois he graduated from the Northwestern University Law School with the degree LL. B. in 1915.

Soon after being admitted to the bar he was appointed an assistant state's attorney under Maclay Hoyne, serving four years, 1915-18. He then engaged in private law practice and is a member of the firm of Rentner & Meyer, with offices at 160 North LaSalle Street. He was first elected master in chancery in 1922 by the judges of the circuit court and re-elected in 1924 and again in 1926.

Mr. Meyer is a member of the Illinois and Chicago Bar Associations, and is a member of the law faculty of Northwestern University and is professor of law at Loyola University, both in the under-graduate and post-graduate schools. He was appointed by President Coolidge captain of the Military Intelligence Reserve, and is a life honorary member of the Illinois Police Association.

His home is in Oak Park. One of the Kiwanis Clubs which he founded (The Forest Park Kiwanis Club) took the unprecedented action of suspending its by-laws and electing him a life honorary member, and also presented him with a solid gold card.

He is vice dictator of Greater Chicago Lodge No. 3 of the Loyal Order of Moose and chairman of the House Committee of the Moose Country Club House. He is a member of the

Board of Directors of the Chamber of Commerce of Forest Park, is deputy commissioner of Boy Scouts, life member of the Illinois Good Roads Association, a member of the Delta Theta Phi law fraternity, the Alumni Association of Northwestern Universty and the German Club of Chicago. He is vice president of the Pistaqua Heights Country Club and an honorary member of the Chicago Motor Club. In politics Mr. Meyer is a democrat.

He married, June 27, 1917, Miss Louise Wilkins, a native of Chicago. They have one son, John J.

GEORGE WILLIAM BOYD is vice president of the Kankakee Pure Milk Company, and through his own efforts and industry has reached a successful business position. At the same time he has interested himself in a number of organizations that reflect and express the progressive tendencies of his community, and he has allied himself actively with a number of these.

Mr. Boyd was born at Mount Sterling, Kentucky, May 5, 1882, son of Samuel J. and Julia E. (Rayborn) Boyd. His parents were born at Owingsville in Bath County, Kentucky, and his father was a farmer and tobacco raiser The father died in 1917 and the mother, in 1892.

George William Boyd attended public schools in Kentucky. At the age of sixteen he engaged in farm work, and two years later, in 1900, came to Kankakee, Illinois. After one year of farming he found work as a milk wagon driver in Kankakee. In 1910, when the Anderson milk business, with which he had been employed, was sold to the Kankakee Pure Milk Company, he was transferred to the factory of the plant, and two years later acquired stock in the business. Since 1920 he has been vice president of this company.

Mr. Boyd in 1908 married Dora M. Ortman, a native of Askum, Illinois, and daughter of Albert and Esther Ortman, natives of Germany. Mr. Boyd is a deacon in the Presbyterian Church. For two years he was city treasurer and is now a member of the City Park Commission, the first park commission organized in Kankakee. His political affiliation has always been with the republican party. In Masonry he is a member of the Royal Arch Chapter, Knight Templar Commandery, Council, Mystic Shrine and Eastern Star. He also belongs to the Knights of Pythias, B. P. O. Elks, Modern Woodmen of America and the Kiwanis Club. He is vice president of the Kankakee Chamber of Commerce, is vice president of the Y. M. C. A., is president of the Salvation Army, is a director in the Boy Scouts and is vice president and a director of the Red Cross Chapter.

JOAB GOODALL is a broad minded and successful business man of Carbondale, likewise a very generous and public spirited citizen, and is a member of one of the pioneer families in this section of the state.

His grandfather, Joab Goodall, settled in Williamson County, three miles southeast of Marion, and was one of the large landowners in that vicinity. John Goodall, father of Joab of Carbondale, was reared on the old homestead in Williamson County and for many years was a leading merchant at Marion, where he died in 1897. He married Sarah Scates, of an old Virginia family, who died the same year as her husband.

Mr. Joab Goodall was born at Marion, in Williamson County, in 1858. He attended public schools, subsequently attended the Normal University at Carbondale, and then engaged in farming at the old homestead. Along with farming he became interested in the horse and mule business and industry, beginning largely as a specialist in raising horses and mules on his own farm. He became a buyer and shipper on the market, and for a number of years past has practically eliminated farming in order to devote his entire time to the handling of a growing business. He formerly shipped his horses and mules to some of the leading markets, but in late years his reputation has enabled him to establish a market of his own at Marion. This is one of the leading supply points for horses and mules to southern buyers, and buyers from all over the South come regularly to his sales.

Mr. Goodall in 1914 removed his place of residence to Carbondale in order to give his children the advantages of the Normal University. He has one of the finest homes in that city. Mr. Goodall is a democrat, is a member of the Knights of Pythias and B. P. O. Elks and the Christian Church. He married Mamie Cobb, of Dixon, Kentucky. They have three children, the son John having taken the course in law at the University of Illinois and is now in Yale. Of the two younger children, Charles is in the University of Illinois, and Mary attended school at Carbondale and is now at a Young Ladies School at Denver, Colorado.

DR. H. A. BRENNECKE. Some cities are fortunate in having men with vision, ability and industry who found institutions which last long after the founders have passed on. Such a city is Aurora, Illinois, and such a man is Dr. H. A. Brennecke. The Brennecke Clinic is more than the personal property of one professional man. It is more than a clinic of specialists gathered together in the interesting and humanitarian work of caring for the sick. The Brennecke Clinic is a community institution! It is the dream of a dreamer come true. The work of a dreamer who has been strong enough and capable enough to make his dream materialize into the institution, which today is one of the things that Aurora people take pride in pointing out to visitors.

Doctor Brennecke was born at Watertown, Wisconsin, October 11, 1871; graduated from the Watertown High School at the age of fifteen; entered the famous old Rush Medical College at Chicago, and received his degree in 1896. His hospital experience included service in Augustana Hospital and the Cook County Hospital, and in December, 1897, he began private practice in Aurora.

In 1903 he went abroad and spent a year at Vienna, Austria, then the greatest center in the world for the mastery of medicine and surgery.

Also Doctor Brennecke always has kept in

touch with every progressive movement in his profession through clinics and conventions in this country.

Doctor Brennecke married Miss Bertha E. Fry on November 15, 1898. They have two children, John and Margaret. The Doctor is a republican, a member of the Masonic order, the Elks, the Union League and University Clubs of Chicago, and is affiliated with the County, Illinois State and the American Medical Associations.

CLARENCE C. THOMAS, Doctor of Dental Surgery, is one of the veterans of his profession in the city of Aurora, where he has practiced steadily for over a quarter of a century.

He was born near Eau Claire, Wisconsin, February 13, 1874, son of Frank and Mary (Cox) Thomas, his father a native of Ohio and his mother of Pennsylvania. Both parents are now deceased. His father was in the real estate and insurance business. Clarence is the only survivor of three children, his two brothers having been Halbert and Charles.

Clarence C. Thomas was educated in public schools and attended the Northern Illinois Normal at Dixon, where he graduated in 1892 and subsequently entered Northwestern University School of Dentistry, taking his degree in 1898. Since the year of his graduation he has practiced at Aurora and has been one of the most successful men in his vocation in that city. He now has charge of the dental department of the Brennecke Clinic of Aurora.

He married, June 25, 1901, Miss Pearl Larson, and they have two children: Marjorie and Halbert. Doctor Thomas is a member of the Fox River Dental Society, the Illinois State and National Dental Associations and is affiliated with the B. P. O. Elks and is a member of the County Club and Union League Club.

N. CURTIS CALHOUN, M. D., is a native of Effingham County, and has gained the appreciation and esteem of the community where he grew up by his services as a teacher, physician and surgeon.

He was born on a farm in Effingham County, January 9, 1881, son of Jeptha C. and Mary E. (Neal) Calhoun. His father was a descendant of the same family as that of John C. Calhoun of South Carolina. Doctor Calhoun's parents were born, reared and married in Ohio, and from that state moved to Illinois, settling in Effingham County. His father engaged in farming for a number of years, but during the last twenty years of his life operated a hotel in Effingham. He died in that city in 1925, at the age of seventy-six, and his wife passed away in 1908. They were the parents of four sons and four daughters.

N. Curtis Calhoun lived during his boyhood years on a farm, and his country school education was supplemented by courses in Austin College at Effingham. For eight years he taught school, this work being preliminary to his taking up the medical profession. In 1905 he began studying medicine and was graduated in 1909, after completing a four-year's course in the St. Louis College of Physicians and Surgeons. Doctor Calhoun practiced for ten years at Watson in Effingham County. He then left Illinois and spent five years in professional work at Cape Girardeau, Missouri. Since returning to his native county he has located at Effingham, and has a good general practice in the city and surrounding territory. He is at present county physician, and is a member of the County and Illinois Medical Associations and the American Medical Association. During the World war he volunteered for service in the Army Medical Corps, and was commissioned a captain, but was not called to active duty.

Doctor Calhoun is a member of the Masonic order, Benevolent and Protective Order of Elks, Modern Woodmen of America, is a democrat in politics, and while living at Watson was elected township supervisor. He married, in 1900, Miss Louise E. Klinger. They have one son, Cecil C. Calhoun.

HARRY S. PARKER of Effingham, has practiced law for thirty years, and his success in handling a large and important practice has given him the satisfaction that many other lawyers derive from participation in politics and public affairs.

Mr. Parker was born at Parkersburg in Richland County, Illinois, January 3, 1871, son of Thomas and Emma E. (Moore) Parker. His attainments in later years are the more noteworthy because he started the battle of life for himself when only twelve years old. He had to work his way, and for several years he was in the service of the Vandalia Railroad Company. He attended night school while working during the day. In 1896 he was admitted to the bar, having attended Austin College and the Kent College of Law a year, and he finished his law studies in the office of Wood Brothers at Effingham. Mr. Parker had practiced law about two years when the Spanish-American war broke out. He was in the service from the date of his enlistment, April 26, 1898, a few days after war was declared, until his honorable discharge on May 2, 1899. He became adjutant of the Fourth Illinois Regiment, and was detailed as assistant adjutant general, Second Brigade of the Second Division and of the Second Brigade of the Third Division, Seventh Army Corps. During his enlistment he spent three months in Cuba. After that war Mr. Parker was commissioned a lieutenant colonel in the Illinois National Guard.

Since then his time and energies have been fully taken up with a growing practice in the law. He is senior member of the firm Parker & Bauer, which is one of the successful law firms of Effingham County. They act as attorneys for five railroads and several other corporations.

Mr. Parker is a republican, but has never sought any honors from a political party. He is a Master Mason and has been a ruling elder in the Presbyterian Church since he was twenty-one years of age. He is also a member of the Effingham Chamber of Commerce. Mr. Parker is a prominent Rotarian. He was president of the Effingham Rotary Club, and in 1926 was elected governor of the Forty-fifth District Rotary, International. By virtue of

being district governor he is to be a delegate to the International Rotary Convention to be held in Ostend, Belgium, in 1927.

He married, in 1896, Miss Mary Stuart Rice. She was born at Altamont, Illinois, daughter of Doctor and Mrs. S. S. Rice. Mr. and Mrs. Parker have a daughter, Maurice, and a son, Howard S. Parker, the latter a railroad employe at Baton Rouge, Louisiana. The daughter is the wife of Leonard A. Steis, of Effingham, and they have a son, Parker Steis.

JOHN NIESS, M. D., has been a careful and reliable physician and surgeon of Carmi and White county, being now in the twentieth year of his practice in that community.

He is a native of Illinois and was born on a farm near Mascoutah, in St. Clair County, March 20, 1880. His parents, John George and Maria (Zolg) Niess, were born in Germany, where they were reared and married. They came to the United States soon after the Civil war, settled on a farm in St. Clair County, and were among the very capable and industrious people of their community. Both were active in the Evangelical Lutheran Church, and they did their utmost to give their children the benefits of superior educational advantages. All of their nine children are still living. John George Niess died in 1916, at the age of seventy-one. His widow died March 23, 1926, age of seventy-seven.

Dr. John Niess was reared on the farm, attended public schools, and after two years in Illinois Normal University at Normal he became a teacher in his native county. He taught for two years and then took up the study of medicine in St. Louis University, where he was graduated M. D. in 1907. Doctor Niess soon after graduating removed to Carmi, White County, and has been steadily engaged in his professional work there ever since. His success is measured by his active participation in professional affairs and also in local business. For several years he was secretary of the White County Medical Society. He is a member of the Illinois State and American Medical Associations, the Southern Illinois Medical Association, Ohio Valley Medical Society, and the New York Central Railway Surgeons Association. He is local surgeon for the Big Four Railway. Doctor Niess has prepared and read several papers before medical societies. For several years he was president of the local board of health, and was unremitting in his efforts to secure a pure water supply for Carmi until the filtering plant was installed at the water works.

During the World war he was commissioned a captain in the Medical Corps, but was never called to active duty. In home work he served as a member of the White County Exemption Board, and was its secretary and examining physician, and was also one of the organizers and chairman of the Red Cross Chapter of White County. Doctor Niess is president of the Carmi Building & Loan Association and assistant in organizing that institution. He has been president of the Board of Stewards of the Methodist Episcopal Church, is a democrat, a thirty-second degree Scottish Rite Mason and Shriner, and a member of Carmi Kiwanis Club. Doctor Niess married, November 9, 1909, Miss Louise Muehlhauser, of Mascoutah, Illinois.

EGBERT T. HUDGENS. The individual record of this well known Marion business man involves some of the earliest pioneer families of Williamson County. He and his brothers and sisters were all born at the Hudgens homestead, one of the few farms in the county which have not changed ownership during the past half century.

His grandfather, John Hudgens, traveled by wagon from Tennessee to Williamson County in the fall of 1816, two years before Illinois was admitted to the Union. He located in the southern part of the county, and started what afterwards became known far and wide as the Hudgens settlement. Later the town of Hudgens was established. John Hudgens was a real pioneer, a man of courage, industry and faith in the future, and he lived to see many of his hopes and expectations realized.

His son, Zachariah Hudgens, was born on the old homestead in Tennessee, April 3, 1833. He lived on the farm a number of years and later became a merchant at Marion, being associated with the firm of Campbell, Goodall & Company, which operated several general merchandise stores, commission houses and warehouses. One of the chief articles handled by the firm was tobacco. With the decline of tobacco growing in this section of southern Illinois Zachariah Hudgens withdrew from the firm and engaged in business for himself. He was a merchant and stock raiser, and continued active until his death in 1903. He was struck by an Illinois Central train and died from the injuries about a week later. In 1874 he was elected sheriff of Williamson County and held that office four years.

Zachariah Hudgens married Mary Jane Cooksey, daughter of Ephraim Cooksey, who was also one of the first settlers in Williamson County. He was born in Smith County, middle Tennessee, in 1821, and came to Williamson County in 1848, acquiring land from the government. The Cooksey farm later came into the possession of Zachariah Hudgens, and has since been known as the Hudgens homestead. Ephraim Cooksey died in 1886. His wife was Elizabeth Phillips, a native of Virginia, where her father, Thomas Phillips, died, his family shortly afterward moving to Tennessee. Zachariah and Mary Jane (Cooksey) Hudgens reared a family of fourteen children, all of whom were born at the Hudgens homestead and all of whom lived to mature years. They are now married and their homes are widely scattered, but all of them combine in pride in keeping up the old homestead which was the scene of their early years. The mother of this family, Mary Jane Hudgens, died in 1888. Zachariah Hudgens' second wife was Sarah E. Todd Allen, daughter of Peter Todd.

Egbert T. Hudgens, of Marion, was born at the Hudgens homestead June 27, 1878. He grew up there, attended rural schools and also had advantages in the schools at Creal Springs, to which place his father removed for the special purpose of educating his younger children. Mr. Hudgens as a youth was ambitious to become a physician, but on account of health and other reasons was never able to educate himself for that profession. In 1917 he graduated from Worshams Embalming School at Chicago, and obtaining his license, engaged in the undertaking business at Marion at 215 North Market Street. In 1926 his establishment was moved to 311 West Main Street, where he has one of the best equipped undertaking parlors in the county. When he first engaged in business in 1917 it was in partnership with G. J. Fricke. In 1920 the partnership of Hudgens & Scobey was formed, but since 1923 Mr. Hudgens has been sole proprietor of the business. He was elected city treasurer May 8, 1905, and served until May, 1907.

Mr. Hudgens has a brother, Lee R. Hudgens, who is also a well known business man of Marion and since 1923 has served as a city commissioner. Egbert T. Hudgens is a member of the Baptist Church, Knights of Pythias, Independent Order of Odd Fellows, the B. P. O. Elks, and was president for one year of the Lions Club.

He married Miss Bessie F. Wright, daughter of Francis M. Wright, of Creal Springs. They have one daughter, Muriel B., now the wife of Percy L. Garrison, connected with the Peabody Coal Company.

JAMES SHAW, librarian of the public library at Aurora, is a veteran of the Civil war, is an old time printer and for many years was in the printing and newspaper business.

He is a native of England and was born in County Lancashire, at Ashton-Underlyne, July 9, 1840. His father was also named James Shaw and in 1848 brought his family to America, locating at Portsmouth, New Hampshire. James Shaw from the age of eight grew up at Portsmouth, attended public schools there and served his apprenticeship at the printing trade. During the Civil war he enlisted in the Sixteenth New Hampshire Infantry, and saw active service with that regiment for nine months. He then returned to Portsmouth and in 1865 came west to Chicago, where he worked as a printer in the office of the old Republican, of which Charles A. Dana was at one time editor. He went from Chicago to Mobile, Alabama, being compositor on the Mobile Nationalist in 1866, and remained in Alabama altogether seven years.

Returning north, Mr. Shaw located at Aurora, and for seven years was one of the partners in the ownership and publication of the Aurora Herald. About that time he was appointed clerk of the City Court and in 1884, in addition to his clerkship, was made custodian of the public library. He also, in 1905, became secretary and a member of the Board of Education of West Aurora. He was clerk of the City Court sixteen years. In 1923 he resigned as a member of the Board of Education and now gives his entire time to his duties as librarian. In 1888 he was appointed official reporter of the Circuit Court of Kane County, and remained in that position until 1922.

Mr. Shaw is a republican, a member of the Union League Club, the Illinois State Library Association and Aurora Post No. 20, G. A. R. He married June 29, 1885, Ella D. Lowd, descended from one of the earliest Colonial families. They have one daughter, Alice, the wife of W. C. Shepherd, of Aurora.

ADAM E. DILLER, M. D. An accomplished physician and surgeon of Aurora, his attainments in surgery having brought him a fellowship in the American College of Surgeons, Doctor Diller has practiced at Aurora since 1909.

He was born in Otter Creek Township, La Salle County, Illinois, March 29, 1879, son of Adam and Carolina (Albrecht) Diller. The parents were natives of Germany, and on coming to America settled at Streator, Illinois, where they engaged in farming. The mother is still living, now a resident of Florida. There were three children: Doctor Diller; Charles E., of Princeton, Illinois; and Ada Christine, who is married and lives at Youngstown, Ohio.

Adam E. Diller was educated in district schools, grew up on a farm at Streator and near Sandwich in La Salle County, and in 1897 entered Northwestern College at Naperville. He completed the four years course there, and received his degree in June, 1903. In the fall of the same year he entered Northwestern University School of Medicine in Chicago, and was graduated in June, 1907. While in college he spent fourteen months as an interne at the Evangelical Deaconess Hospital in Chicago, and in September, 1908, became a member of the staff of the Chicago Lying-In-Hospital, serving six months. Since completing this training he has been engaged in practice at Aurora, handling a general practice as a physician and surgeon.

He married, April 27, 1907, Miss Leah Battermann. Three children were born to their marriage: John Adam, who died when five and a half years old; Dorothy Caroline and Robert Henry. Doctor Diller is a republican in politics. He is a member of the Aurora Medical Society, the Kane County and American Medical Associations and is a fellow in the American College of Surgeons. In religion he belongs to the Evangelical Association.

ROY L. SERIGHT since the age of sixteen has been identified with the printing and publishing business. His outstanding achievements in the journalistic field is the Daily Register of Harrisburg, of which he is managng editor.

He was born in Bethany, Illinois, March 3, 1885, son of David G. and Alice (Morris) Seright, the former a native of Illinois and the latter of Pennsylvania. David Seright's father was A. S. Seright, a native of Indiana and an early settler in Moultrie County, Illinois. David G. Seright and wife had three children, Roy L., May, a resident of Sullivan, Illinois, and Harry M. Harry M. Seright entered the army at the time of the World war, went overseas for service in France, and was one of "the unreturning brave."

When Roy L. Seright was six years of age his mother died and after that he was reared by his paternal grandparents at Sullivan, Illinois. He attended public school there and at the age of sixteen began his apprenticeship in a newspaper office, learning the printing trade. He worked on the Daily Review at De-

catur, Illinois, then bought the Herald, a weekly paper at Rockton, Illinois, which he edited and published three years. Following that he became manager of the Progress at Sullivan for a year, and at the end of that time removed to Louisville, Illinois, where he bought the Republican. He was editor and publisher of the Republican six years, and during that time served a term as mayor of Louisville. Mr. Seright in 1917 acquired the controlling interest in the Harrisburg Daily Register and has since been its managing editor. He has brought the Daily Register to a position where it ranks among the most influential and prosperous dailies published in any of the small towns of southern Illinois. It has a printing plant equipped with all the modern facilities and mechanical improvements.

Mr. Seright is a member of the Press Congress of the World, the National Editors' Association, the Inland Daily Press Association and the Southern Illinois Press Association. He is a republican in politics, is a Presbyterian, is a thirty-second degree Scottish Rite Mason and Shriner, member of the Elks, and is a charter member of the Harrisburg Rotary Club.

He married, in 1908, Miss Daisy Booze, a native of Illinois. They have one son, Morris Edwin Seright.

HENRY TAPHORN, M. D., has been a qualified physician and surgeon practicing in southern Illinois for nearly thirty years, the scene of his labors during most of this time being at Effingham. He has a large practice, is a man of recognized ability, and has identified himself with other affairs of the community in addition to his profession.

He was born on a farm in Clinton County, Illinois, August 1, 1871, son of John G. and Elizabeth (Werner) Taphorn. His father was born in Oldenburgh, Germany, grew up there and received his common school education, and left Germany at the age of eighteen to escape the compulsory military service. After coming to America he married Elizabeth Werner, who had been born in Hanover, Germany, and was brought to America when eight years of age. She died at the age of thirty-two, and John G. Taphorn subsequently married Elizabeth Pfiester, a native of the United States and of German parentage. By the first marriage there were seven children and ten by the second marriage. John G. Taphorn followed farming as a vocation, and his industry and honesty enabled him to provide sufficiently for his large family of children.

Henry Taphorn grew up on the home farm, living there until he was twenty-three years of age. Up to fourteen he had attended country schools, and finished his literary education in Shurtleff College at Upper Alton. In 1898 he was graduated in medicine from Washington University at St. Louis and for nearly a year he practiced his profession at Alton and four years at East St. Louis, where for three and a half years he was first assistant physician and surgeon at St. Mary's Hospital. Then followed another two years of practice at Alton, and in 1905 he came to Effingham, which has become his permanent home. He has a large private practice and is also local surgeon for the Illinois Central Railroad and is a member of the County, State and American Medical Associations.

Doctor Taphorn is a Catholic, is a member of the Knights of Columbus and Knights of America, and in politics, a democrat. He is now one of the city commissioners of Effingham.

He married, in 1901, Miss Genevieve Morrissey, of Alton, Illinois, who died five years later, leaving a daughter, Genevieve. Doctor Taphorn in 1908 married Elizabeth Eversman, daughter of the late Dr. Henry Eversman, of Effingham, the Eversman family having long been prominent in and closely identified with the banking and other interests of Effingham. Doctor and Mrs. Taphorn have four children, Mary, Pauline, Margaret and Frances.

GEORGE H. THOMPSON, who began teaching at the age of eighteen, is principal of the Marissa Township High School in St. Clair County. He came to Illinois from the adjoining state of Indiana, where for over twenty years he was superintendent of schools at Hobart in the northwest corner of that state.

Mr. Thompson was born at Fairplay in Cedar County, Missouri, March 6, 1869, son of George James and Mary N. (McNinch) Thompson. His maternal grandmother was Susan (Reed) McNinch. The grandfather, James Thompson, was born in Virginia, and was a slave owner in that state. Both the parents of George H. Thompson were natives of Tennessee, and in 1850 moved to Missouri. George J. Thompson was a Union soldier during the Civil war, at first with the Sixth Missouri Cavalry and then with the Fifteenth Missouri Cavalry. He participated in many battles and campaigns. After the war he was a farmer and for a number of years conducted a general store at Fairplay and was postmaster there. In 1877 the family moved to Independence, Kansas. George J. Thompson was born in 1827 and died in December, 1903, and his wife died in 1916. They had a large family of children: Donald, Robert, William, George H., Cynthia Ann, Quilla, Mary and Martha.

George H. Thompson attended public schools at Miami, Missouri, and was eight years of age when the family moved to Kansas. In that state he continued his education in the district schools, in high school and normal school, and at the age of eighteen, taught his first term in a school about six miles north of Coffeyville. He remained there four years, and in 1891 came to Indiana, entering Valparaiso University. He alternated between teaching and studying at the university for four years, and in 1895 took the principalship of the high school at Hobart in Lake County, Indiana. He remained at Hobart for twenty-three years, serving as principal from 1895 to 1905 and as superintendent from 1905 to 1918. This was a notable service. Mr. Thompson was an advocate and leader in educational progress, and while he was at Hobart all the schools of that township were consolidated in one, every one-room country school being abandoned. He left the Hobart Township school system one of the best in the state.

Then, in 1918, he came to Marissa, Illinois, as principal of the high school and in six years succeeded in establishing an enviable record for these schools, securing new buildings and greatly improving the general standards of construction. Mr. Thompson received the Bachelor of Science degree from Valparaiso University in 1907, and in 1913 was given the degree Bachelor of Pedagogy. He has also done post-graduate work in Washington University at St. Louis. Mr. Thompson is member of the Methodist Church, is a republican and is affiliated with the Masonic Order, I. O. O. F. and belongs to the National Education Association; the Illinois State Teachers' Association and the High School Principals' Association of Illinois.

He married at Hobart, Indiana, January 1, 1895, Miss Bertha Stilwell, daughter of Samuel S. and Jane (Gordon) Stilwell. Her father died in 1921, and her mother, in 1904. Her father served as a Union soldier with an Indiana regiment, was a native of New York State, and a carpenter and builder by trade, although the latter part of his life was spent on a farm. Mrs. Thompson is the youngest of four daughters. Her sister Ilda married Ernest Spencer; her sister Nora married Joseph Ditlow and has six children; and Lillie married William Weddle, who has six children. Of the children of Mr. and Mrs. Thompson the oldest, Ruth, is the wife of William Taylor Douglas, and both are teachers in the high school at Mobile, Alabama, and have two children, named William T., Jr., and Jean G. Mary Thompson, formerly a teacher in the Valparaiso High School and now teaching in a business college at Gary, Indiana, is the wife of Franklin Jones, of Gary. Wynne earned a fine record as a soldier in the World war, being two years in the service, enlisting April 5, 1917, in the coast artillery and is rated as a first class gunner; was overseas and also in the Philippines and in home posts. The son Milton McNinch is pursuing a civil engineering course in McKendree College. The younger children are Ella, a teacher, Maurice, in the U. S. Navy, and Kenneth, in school.

JORGEN P. RISING is president of the Rising Decorating Company at 527 South Peoria Street, Chicago. This is one of the leading firms of contracting painters and decorators in the city. Mr. Rising's approach to his important business position was through the long apprenticeship and service of a journeyman painter, and in no small measure his success has been due to his understanding of the conditions and problems of every employe under his jurisdiction.

Mr. Rising was born in Denmark, in 1878, but came to the United States in 1892. His home has been in Chicago since the World's Fair year. He had begun learning the painter's trade in Denmark and finished his apprenticeship in Chicago. He worked as a journeyman for several years before he started on a modest scale as a contracting painter and decorator. He has guided the business successfully and has always had the ability of securing cooperation and efficient service among his many employes. The Rising Decorating Company represents a large body of practical workmen, skilled men in their trades, and the business is a very solid one financially.

Mr. Rising for a number of years has been a prominent figure in the official organizations representing the painting and decorating trades. He served five years as president of the local association and in 1924 was elected president of the Illinois State Association of Master Painters and Decorators. In February, 1926, he was granted one of the rare honors bestowed upon the business men in America by his election as president of the International Association of Master Painters and Decorators of the United States and Canada. This was a fitting tribute to one who has zealously and willingly given so much of his time and energy to the cause of the organization, among not only contractors organized in his own trade but to contractors of organizations in all branches of the guilding industry. He has been a persistent and consistent worker in organized effort since he has been in business, and has always been ready to help in any way to promote the best interests of all concerned. Mr. Rising has been distinguished by a special courage of convictions, so that his loyalty to a cause has had a concrete meaning. He gave his earnest support to the citizens committee to enforce the Landis award in Chicago at the beginning, and is chairman of the painters and decorators committee for that purpose. He has thus contributed to the success of the Landis award committee as a whole in stabilizing the labor situation, preventing costly strikes and accelerating construction work generally, so that Chicago has been practically first among the large cities of the country for several years in the volume of its construction program.

Mr. Rising is also a member of the executive board of the Building Construction Employers Association of Chicago. He is a member of the Architects Club of Chicago, is chairman of the building committee of the Illinois Athletic Club, member of the High Noon Club, is a thirty-second degree Scottish Rite Mason and Shriner and member of the Medinah Country Club, and belongs to a number of other fraternal organizations. His Chicago home is at 2601 Morse Avenue, and he also has a beautiful home and estate near Lake Forest, where he and his family enjoy the summer months. This summer home gives him opportunity to pursue his chief hobby and recreation, the cultivation of flowers and vegetables.

J. NORMAN PIERCE is a Chicago electrical engineer and contractor whose ability and skill have developed the Pierce Electric Company into one of the most adequate organizations of its kind in the country. This company has handled many involved and difficult features of electrical engineering construction. Most notable was the electrical work in connection with the enormous project recently completed of the electrification of the Chicago terminal of the Illinois Central Railroad.

Mr. Pierce is a native of Missouri, born in Lockwood, that state, June 12, 1882, son of Howard and Mary (Mossman) Pierce. He was educated in district and grade schools and since early youth has followed a manifest bent and genius for electrical engineering, in which his training has been rigidly practical as well as theoretical.

Mr. Pierce in 1905 organized the Pierce Electric Company of Chicago, of which he is senior partner. This company has its executive offices and headquarters at 215 West Randolph Street. In the past twenty years the company has carried out a large number of electrical engineering and construction projects in Chicago and vicinity. Mr. Pierce has made it an organization representing not so much the power of capital and material facilities as the brains and skill of personnel. Consequently he and his staff have usually been engaged on special projects requiring unusual skill and knowledge. The operation of the first regular passenger train on the Illinois Central Railroad suburban service under electric power, on Wednesday, July 22, 1926, was properly regarded as a red letter day in the history of the city as well as in its transportation annals. The installation of the electrical equipment on these suburban lines, a work carried out without material interruption to the steam service, a work that has been repeatedly described in technical engineering papers as well as articles in the general press, was the great task on which Mr. Pierce's organization, including the services of about five hundred men, were engaged continuously for eighteen months. Another unusual piece of work by his organization was the construction of the gigantic switchboard built for the Aragon, one of Chicago's famous dance halls.

As an employer of skilled craftsmen Mr. Pierce for many years has been unusually successful as an arbitrator in preventing labor disputes, strikes and other troubles in the electrical industry in Chicago. As a member of the Arbitration Board he has rendered genuine service not only to the electrical industry but the public at large. He drew up the articles of agreement between the Electrical Contractors Association and the local union of International Brotherhood of Electrical Workers, articles approved and adopted for operation under the Landis award. Judge Landis in commenting on these articles said: "The parties to this agreement are to be highly commended for the brevity and the spirit of fairness and high regard for public interest indicated in this Section 12 as compared to the same section in former agreements."

Mr. Pierce is a director of the Pierce Wrapping Machine Company. He is a member of the Western Society of Engineers, the Chicago Electrical Contractors Association, of which he is former chairman and director, and the Chicago Association of Commerce. He is president of the Electric Club, is a life member of the Chicago Art Institute and Field Museum, is a progressive republican in politics, member of the Masonic Order, Sons of the American Revolution, Illinois Athletic Club, Prosperity Club, Hinsdale Golf Club, and Western Springs Men's Club. Most of his pastimes are outdoors, his favorite sports being golf and tennis.

Mr. Pierce is a resident of Western Springs, and that progressive village honored him and secured the services of one of the most competent engineers in the middle west when in 1925 he was elected president of the village board. Mr. Pierce married at Chicago, May 29, 1909, Miss Bertha Cappels. Their three sons are named Norman, Jack and Robert.

WILLIAM JESSE SUTHERLAND is a veteran Chicago business man, president of the Mooney-Boland-Sutherland Corporation. While this is the largest organization of its kind in the world, Mr. Sutherland has also gained distinction through his home and his hobby, the famous Polo Farm at Wheaton, of which he is owner and which is one of the beautiful country homes of that city.

Mr. Sutherland was born at Logansport, Indiana, November 3, 1863, son of George C. and Esther A. (Gerhart) Sutherland. He was educated in the public schools of Logansport, and at the age of fifteen went to work in the grocery store of A. H. McDonald in his native city. That was his preliminary business training. Mr. Sutherland came to Chicago in 1880. He has been continuously identified in varying capacities with what is now the Mooney-Boland-Sutherland Corporation. At first he was a clerk in the general office of the Mooney & Boland Agency, subsequently was general manager, vice president, partner, and in 1918 became president and sole owner of the Mooney-Boland-Sutherland Corporation. This is the largest organization of its kind in the country, handling confidential matters for the largest corporations and many prominent individuals. The corporation has offices also in New York, Detroit, and other large cities and maintain corresponding and official connections with similar organizations throughout the world. Mr. Sutherland is also vice president and general manager of the Employers' Protective and Bonding Association.

During his many years of residence in and around Chicago Mr. Sutherland has enjoyed a very extensive acquaintance both commercially and in social spheres, and is a member of many representative organizations, including the Chicago Association of Commerce, Apollo Commandery of the Knights Templar and the thirty-second degree Consistory and Shrine of the Masonic order, being a member of Medinah Temple. He belongs to the B. P. O. Elks, is a member of the Chicago Athletic, Hamilton, Press, Chicago Yacht, Chicago Riding and Driving, South Shore Country, and Business Men's Prosperity Club, is a Methodist and a republican. His favorite sports and recreations are motoring, yachting and horseback riding.

Mr. Sutherland had used his financial means to afford him opportunities for indulging his versatile tastes and activities. His purchase of the famous Polo Farm adjoining the City of Wheaton in DuPage County in 1921 was prompted by a desire to indulge his hobbies in country life, as well as to acquire a notable country home and estate. The farm, comprising about 100 acres, was originally owned by James Langford Stack, a polo player of international renown, who inaugurated polo at the Chicago Golf Club. He was a breeder of polo ponies, and had about fifty or seventy-five head when he established the farm. Mr. Sutherland retained the name Polo Farm, and has continued the breeding of polo ponies, but has greatly diversified the interests of the farm. He is well known as a breeder of Kentucky saddle horses, being owner of the champion stallion, Radiant King, a five-gaited Kentucky saddle horse, and of Missouri Chief, a five-gaited Missouri bred saddle stallion. He has other fine horses for sale and breeding purposes, and many fine colts are raised on the farm. It is also a general stock farm, departments being devoted to Duroc pigs, Leghorn chickens, White Pekin ducks, China geese, African geese, Egyptian geese, and, most interesting of all, the somewhat mysterious muscovy duck, an exceedingly attractive fowl in its black and white plummage. He also has kennels for the breeding of Dalmatian and Chow dogs. Polo Farm would be enviable property for any man of wealth, and it has brought Mr. Sutherland no end of satisfaction, not less because of the opportunities it affords for generous hospitality to his many friends. Mr. Sutherland married, May 30, 1888, Ella M. McMinnick, of Chicago.

FRANK L. BURNS, county superintendent of schools of Jo Daviess County, has given thirty years or more to educational work and is well known as a school man not only in northwestern Illinois but in southwestern Wisconsin, where he was born and reared.

He was born at Jamestown, Wisconsin, July 11, 1872, son of Edward and Mary (Tupper) Burns. His paternal grandparents came from Perthshire, Scotland, and settled in Canada. Edward Burns was born at Ottawa, Ontario, and when about fourteen years of age moved to northern New York, living a few years at Watertown, where he followed the trade of ship carpenter, building steamboats for navigation on the St. Lawrence River. Coming west, he lived in Chicago about four years. In Illinois he entered the service of the Illinois Central Railroad Company as a carpenter, and was transferred to various headquarters, including Bloomington, Amboy, Mendota, and in 1854 moved to Dunleith now East Dubuque, Illinois. After four years there he engaged in operating a lumber yard and in 1859 moved to Jamestown, Wisconsin, and bought some land, engaging in farming until he retired in 1905. He spent his last years at Platteville, Wisconsin, and at East Dubuque, Illinois, where he died in 1914.

His wife, Mary Burns, was born and reared at Rockton, Illinois, was educated in the Beloit Seminary at Beloit, Wisconsin, and taught some years in the public schools of Wisconsin prior to her marriage. She died in 1913. She was a daughter of J. B. and Rhoda (Bates) Tupper, and she had a great-grandfather who was a soldier in the Colonial army in the Revolution. J. B. Tupper was born and reared on a farm along the Erie Canal in Genesee County, New York. At the time of the Civil war he enlisted in a regiment of Wisconsin infantry, served under General Butler, and he was on duty at Fortress Monroe, Virginia, from which point he witnessed the memorable battle between the Monitor and the Merrimac. Later he sailed around to the Gulf Coast and was with General Butler's troops in the occupation of New Orleans, remaining there until the close of the war. He was wounded in one battle. After the war he engaged in farming and mining, and died in 1898.

Frank L. Burns is one of the two children of his parents, and his brother, C. C. Burns, is now county farm advisor of Champaign County, Illinois.

Frank L. Burns attended public schools in Wisconsin, including the high school at Platteville and the State Normal School there. He also was a student in the University of Wisconsin. He did his first teaching in 1893 and 1894, and after another interval of attending school he resumed his educational work in 1897. In 1908 he came to Illinois, and was superintendent of schools of East Dubuque from 1908 to 1922. In November, 1922, he was elected county superintendent of schools of Jo Daviess County, but continued as superintendent at East Dubuque until the end of the school year, when he removed to Galena and began his administration as county superintendent. Mr. Burns is a Royal Arch Mason, is a republican and a member of the Presbyterian Church.

Mr. Burns married at Chicago, Illinois, December 25, 1906, Miss Helen Seeney. Mrs. Burns is one of the very talented women of Illinois, an inventor, and for many years an educator. She was educated in grammar and high schools at Marinette, Wisconsin, studied journalism for a time and prior to her marriage taught in public schools in Wisconsin. Since 1921 she has taken out four patents on clothing and furniture and is now planning to place on the market and manufacture what is known as a "Teddie Toddler," a combination of dress and romper, which can be almost immediately converted from one to the other. The four patents, three of which were granted November 14, 1922, and the fourth on October 13, 1923, are: No. 1435147, combined dress and romper; No. 1435148, combined bassinette and swing; No. 1435146, a patent on children's apparel; and Patent No. 1472323, a nursery chair. Mrs. Burns is chief assistant to Mr. Burns in his work as county superintendent and is also serving as county truant officer.

Mrs. Burns is a daughter of Charles and Alice (Graves) Seeney. Her father was born and reared at Madison, Wisconsin, and spent most of his life in railroading, being in the service of the Santa Fe Railroad Company as an engineer for some time and later with the Chicago & Northwestern Railroad. His parents came from England. He died about 1910. Mrs. Burn's mother was a teacher for some time and had charge of a kindergarten and was librarian at Marinette for a number of years. She now resides at Milwaukee. Her parents were Morris and Abigail (Bingham) Graves. Morris Graves, a cooper by trade, was born and reared in New York state. His grandfather wrote a wonderful autobiography which is to be published.

Mr. and Mrs. Burns had six children, Helen dying at the age of five years, and those liv-

ing are Frank, Jr., Marion, Robert, Doris and Edward, all students in the schools of Galena, Frank being a member of the class of 1927 in high school.

JOHN P. VINCENT was born and reared in Jo Daviess County and is one of the veteran business men of Galena. On February 11, 1926, he celebrated his sixty-ninth birthday, and at the same time the forty-second anniversary of his active experience in the monument business, the firm now being known as J. P. Vincent & Sons.

Mr. Vincent was born at Weston in Elizabeth Township, Jo Daviess County, February 11, 1857, son of James and Grace (Pierce) Vincent. The Vincent family settled in northwestern Illinois on coming from Cornwall, England. The Vincents in southwestern England were miners, and the presence of the lead mines in northwestern Illinois decided their point of settlement. John P. Vincent's grandparents were Henry and Sarah (Mitchell) Vincent, who came to America in 1837 and settled near Galena. They took up 360 acres of government land in Galena, and some of that land is still owned by their grandchildren. Henry Vincent followed mining here, but chiefly engaged in farming and was known as "Farmer Vincent." He died about 1849. His son, James Vincent, was born in Cornwall, in 1828, and was eight years old when brought to this country. He attended public schools in Illinois, and for a time was associated with his father in the mines. He engaged in farming all through the Civil war. He was ineligible for military service for physical reasons, and he carried on the work of the farm and looked after the family while his four brothers were serving the flag of the Union. These brothers were William, Joseph, Charles and John. William was captain of Company A of the Ninety-sixth Illinois Infantry, and served in many hard fought campaigns, being wounded at the battle of Chickamauga, but rejoined his regiment before the end of the war. John Vincent was a member of the same company of which his brother was captain, and was wounded in the battle of Lookout Mountain. Joseph Vincent, in the Forty-fifth Illinois Infantry, was one of the first young men of Galena to enlist, and he was in Sherman's campaign through Georgia, and though exposed to the fire of the enemy many times in the course of his four years' service was never wounded. The youngest of the four brothers, Charles, joined as a recruit in the last year of the war, but saw some severe fighting before the end.

James Vincent became one of the very progressive farmers of Jo Daviess County and carried on agriculture on diversified lines. He died in 1912. His wife, Grace Pierce, born in 1819, was reared at St. Kevern, Cornwall, England, and was about twenty years of age when she came to America. She was well educated and had taught school in England.

John P. Vincent was educated in public schools in Jo Daviess County, and after school engaged in farming until the age of twenty-seven. On February 11, 1884, he acquired a half interest in the monument business of G. W. Ivey. and for thirteen years they continued the partnership of Ivey & Vincent. Mr. Vincent in 1897 bought out his partner and then became the sole owner, subsequently taking into partnership his two sons. The J. P. Vincent & Sons firm does an extensive business handling and placing monuments all over northern Illinois, portions of Wisconsin and Iowa. Mr. Vincent has an enormous acquaintance and friendship extending over the country many miles in a radius around Galena. On January 2, 1924, he bought the business of the Louis Hamrich monument dealers, and consolidated this with his own. He is still active in the firm and has been a very popular and efficient citizen as well as a capable business man.

Mr. Vincent has been affiliated with the Independent Order of Odd Fellows since 1882. For thirty-two years he has been a member of the Rebekahs and is one of the four original charter members still surviving. He is also a member of the Knights of Pythias, B. P. O. Elks and Modern Woodmen of America. He and his family are Methodists.

Mr. Vincent married at Galena, January 1, 1880, Miss Ella Morris, who was educated in the public schools of Illinois and was a daughter of Barzilla and Mary A. (Lawrence) Morris. Her father was born and reared in Jo Daviess County, and left his farm at the outbreak of the Civil war to enlist in the Union army. He was in many engagements and continued until the close of the struggle. Following the war he engaged in farming. His parents were among the pioneers of Jo Daviess County. Mrs. John P. Vincent died September 2, 1922, after a married life of forty-two years. She was survived by three children. The daughter, Ada M., is the wife of Frank C. Bray, who is superintendent of the Fort Atkinson city schools in Wisconsin. Mr. and Mrs. Bray have a daughter, Helen, now a student in the University of Wisconsin. The two sons of Mr. Vincent are Frank R. and Roy Grant, both associated with their father in the monument business. Frank R. married Helen Barlow, of Galena, and their two children are Frank, Jr., and Jean. Roy Grant married Priscilla Richards, of Galena, and they also have two children, John P., Jr., and Richard J.

J. R. HISTED is vice president and general manager of the Hudson Motor Company of Illinois, one of the largest organizations on "Automobile Row," at 2220 Michigan Avenue, Chicago.

Joseph Roland Histed was born at St. Louis, Missouri, January 3, 1877, son of Perry Gresham and Mary (DeVoy) Histed. He was educated in grammar and high schools at St. Louis and also attended Washington University there. His successful career has involved since early boyhood efforts at self advancement. He was an office boy in the offices of the Moffett-West Drug Company at St. Louis, and later became traveling representative of the Parke-Davis Company of Detroit, manufacturing pharmacists. He was on the road for this company from 1900 to 1908. Mr. Histed is one of the veteran automobile salesmen of the country, having entered that business in Kansas City in 1908, when the automobile was still in its experimental stage. From 1908 to 1911 he was an automobile salesman and from 1911 to 1915 he represented the J. I. Case Company of Racine, Wisconsin, and in 1915 was made manager of the New York office of the company. His business career has made him favorably known in various cities of the middle west, including St. Paul and Minneapolis. From 1915 to 1919 he was vice president and general manager of the Twin City Motor Car Company at Minneapolis, and is still a director in that company. Since 1919 he has been vice president and general manager of the Hudson Motor Company of Illinois. He is also a director of the Chicago Acceptance Corporation.

During the World war Mr. Histed was a major in the Minnesota National Guard, resigning in February, 1919, when he came to Chicago. He is a member and director of the Chicago Automobile Trade Association, of the Illinois Automobile Dealers Association, and is vice president of the South Central Association, an organization of property owners in the south central business district. Motor cars are his hobby as well as his business, and other recreations are golf, base ball and hand ball. He is a member of the Racquet Club, Exmoor Country Club, Minneapolis Club, Minnekahda Club and Lafayette Club. Mr. Histed is a republican, a thirty-second degree Scottish Rite Mason and a member of the Episcopal Church.

His home is at 1120 Lake Shore Drive. He married Julia Celeste Kelley, of Kansas City, December 25, 1901. Two daughters were born to their marriage: Mrs. Mauran Smith, of Chicago, and Margaret Sharpe, who is deceased.

GAIL BORDEN PUBLIC LIBRARY. As the village of Elgin increased in population and importance the people whose interest centered in books and intellectual pursuits naturally gathered together and eventually effected an organization. During the long winter evenings this organization promoted debates and similar diversions along the lines of the New England Lyceum movement. Here in the Middle West, as on the rock-bound shores of the Atlantic, this movement resulted in the creation of a little library for the use of its members, and this constitutes the beginning of a library in Elgin. The records of the winter of 1846 make mention of a small circulating library kept in the law office of Paul R. Wright. Later this library found a home in the office of Edward Gifford on Chicago Street, and he supervised the distribution of its small store of books. The Lyceum Club had now become a library association.

About 1851 or 1852 The Young Men's Association was organized, and to it was given the custody of the library and the responsibility for its growth. The inception of a public library at Elgin, or indeed in the state, is the direct result of the Chicago fire of 1871. At that time, learning of the terrible conflagration, the people of England, naturally supposing that the city's library had been totally destroyed, gathered a collection of books and sent them to Chicago. These generous people acted under a misapprehension. At the time of the fire Chicago had no library, nor had it any provision for one. In fact there was none upon the statute books of Illinois. The presence in Chicago of a library donated to the public gave impetus to a movement to secure necessary legislation to provide proper care for these books, and public purchase of additional books for the use of the public. On March 7, 1872, the Illinois Legislature passed a bill providing for this purpose, and almost immediately the city of Elgin voted for a public library to be created under this act. The following composed the first library board: I. C. Bosworth, Z. Eastman, J. A. Spillard, E. C. Lovell, J. W. Ranstead and H. H. Hintz.

The first home of the Elgin Public Library was in the Home Bank Building, and L. H. Yarwood was the first librarian. In 1880 the library was moved to larger quarters in the McOsker & Fletcher Building. In 1882 Mr. Yarwood resigned and Miss Cecil C. Harvey was appointed librarian. About this time Alfred B. and Samuel Church purchased the Scofield property on Spring Street for $12,000, and this property they gave to Elgin for a library upon the one condition that it should be called the Gail Borden Public Library. On February 22, 1894, the new library building, the first public buildings for library purposes in Elgin, was opened with a public reception. This building is much as it appears today. On June 7, 1903, Miss Harvey died, and Miss Katherine L. Abbott was chosen by the board as her successor.

Since its opening to the public there have been numerous improvements and enlargements, and the library is now thoroughly modernized. This library is now recognized as belonging to the first rank among libraries of Illinois. The present board is comprised of the following members: George W. Glos, A. L. Metzel, P. E. True, D. O. Richardson, W. W. McNeil and John C. Barclay. There are 65,500 volumes in the library, and about 600 volumes are taken out each day. Much of the efficiency and high standard of this library are undoubtedly due to the untiring efforts of Miss Abbott, whose love for her work and her capability and courtesy are unquestioned, and the patrons of it hold her in grateful appreciation.

ELAM L. CLARKE is a native of Waukegan and Lake County, and for over thirty years his name has been prominently connected with the law practice, public and business affairs in that city and county.

He was born at Waukegan October 7, 1861, son of Isaac L. and Lemira M. (Dean) Clarke. His grandparents were Elam and Cynthia (Lewis) Clarke, of Williamstown, Vermont, New England farmers, Elam having served as a member of the Vermont militia. Mr. Clarke of Waukegan has in his possession the commissions of his grandfather as corporal, sergeant and ensign in the Vermont militia. Isaac L. Clarke, father of Elam L., was born at Williamstown, Vermont, February 29, 1824, attended public schools in his native state and graduated in 1848 from Dartmouth College. In the same year that he graduated he came West to Waukegan, where for several years he was principal of the Waukegan Academy.

He also studied law, was admitted to the bar and practiced for some time at Waukegan. In 1862 he raised a company and became lieutenant colonel in the Ninety-sixth Illinois Infantry. With this regiment he went into service, and at the battle of Chickamauga, in September, 1863, was killed in action. Colonel Clarke married Lemira M. Dean, who was born at Grafton, Vermont, January 1, 1829, and was reared and educated in the public schools of that state. She survived her husband more than half a century, passing away at Waukegan in 1920, at the age of ninety-one. Lemira M. Dean was a daughter of Peter W. and Philinda W. (Willey) Dean, the former a native of Manchester, Vermont, and a son of Job and Mercy Dean, of Manchester. Job Dean prior to the Revolutionary war lived at Taunton, Massachusetts. In Volume 16, page 67, of the Revolutionary War Archives, is a muster roll of the James Williams, Jr., Company of minute men who marched from Taunton to Roxbury at the Lexington Alarm, each one from his respective home on the 20th day of April, 1775, and on that roll appears the name "Job Dean, Private, Discharged April 29; Miles Traveled, Eighty." Other references to his Revolutionary services are found in other volumes of the official records of the war. After the winning of independence Job Dean moved to Manchester, Vermont, where he engaged in farming. Peter W. Dean, grandfather of Elam L. Clarke, learned the woolen mill business in the Manchester Mills and later for many years was a manufacturer at Grafton, Vermont. He retired several years before his death, selling out his mills at Grafton, and died in 1879. In the maternal line Elam L. Clarke is also a descendant in the eighth generation of John Willey, who was a soldier in King Philip's Indian war.

Elam L. Clarke after the death of his father returned to Vermont, where he attended public schools, spent two years in Dartmouth College, and in 1885 was graduated from Brown University at Providence, Rhode Island. He then came to Waukegan, where he studied law with his uncle, Francis Clarke, then county judge of Lake County. He also studied law in Chicago and was admitted to the bar in 1888. Mr. Clarke practiced in Chicago for some years, until 1896, when he returned to Waukegan and formed a partnership with his uncle, Francis E. Clarke, a partnership that was continued until the death of his uncle in 1899. Since then, for over a quarter of a century, he has carried on an extensive general law practice under his own name. From 1903 to 1910 he served as master in chancery of the Lake County Circuit Court.

Many positions involving important public service without special remuneration have been held by Mr. Clarke and have contributed to the esteem in which he is held as a leading citizen of Lake County. He was president of the Waukegan Library Board from 1898 to 1910, and has been on the Board of Education of the Waukegan city schools and the Waukegan Township High School, and was president of the Waukegan Chamber of Commerce in 1917, and during the World war was chairman of the Lake County Finance Committee of the State Council of Defense. He is vice president of the First National Bank of Waukegan. He was a member of the Constitutional Convention of 1920. Mr. Clarke is affiliated with the B. P. O. Elks, Glen Flora Country Club, University Club of Chicago, Hamilton Club of Chicago, Sons of Veterans, Loyal Legion, the County, State and American Bar Associations, in politics is a republican and is a member of the Episcopal Church.

He married at Waukegan, June 24, 1903, Miss Georgia S. Douglas, of Waukegan. She received her education in the grammar and high schools of that city and at Kemper Hall at Kenosha, Wisconsin. Mrs. Clarke has an unusual range of interests both at home and in Waukegan's social and civic affairs, being active in church and in the Waukegan Woman's Club. She is a daughter of Robert J. and Margaret Ella (Steele) Douglas, and a granddaughter of Robert Douglas, a pioneer nursery man at Waukegan who gained a national reputation through his achievement in raising evergreens from seed, being the first nurseryman to make a practical application of this. Mrs. Clarke's father was for many years a Waukegan manufacturer, but is now in the real estate business. Of the three children born to Mr. and Mrs. Clarke one, Douglas, died in infancy. Lewis D. Clarke, the son, graduated from the Waukegan High School in 1925 and is now in his second year at Dartmouth College. The daughter, Sylvia Clarke, graduated from the Waukegan High School in 1926.

SYLVESTER F. HENRY, M. D., is one of the busy physicians and surgeons of Effingham County, where he has practiced fifteen years, with home in the city of Effingham.

His professional career has been in the same locality where he was born and reared. His birth occurred on a farm in Effingham County, December 12, 1881. His father, Martin Thomas Henry, was born near Orleans, Indiana, son of Sandford Henry and of the same Virginia stock to which Patrick Henry belonged. Martin T. Henry came to Effingham County, Illinois, when twelve years of age, and in 1863, at the age of sixteen, enlisted in the Union army, seeing service during the last two years of the Civil war. He was the youngest of the boys who went out from Effingham County for service as soldiers in that war. After the war he married and settled on a farm, and spent his active life in agriculture. His wife, Laura Lilly, was born in Effingham County, where the Lilly family have lived for a great many years.

Doctor Henry was one of a family of four sons, one of whom is now deceased. He acquired his early education in the country districts while living on the farm and assisting his father in the work of the fields. At eighteen he became a teacher, and during the next eight years he divided his time between teaching and attending school. He attended Austin College at Effingham and the Normal College at Charleston, and in 1911 was graduated in medicine from St. Louis University. For one year he was an interne in a St. Louis hospital and then returned to Effingham County and took up the work of his profes-

18V6

sion. He has been engaged in a general practice, and in late years has done a great deal of work in eye, ear, nose and throat. Doctor Henry has taken post-graduate courses in Chicago and with the Mayo Brothers at Rochester, Minnesota, and is a member of the Effingham County, Illinois State and American Medical Associations.

So far as his professional duties have permitted he has given time and effort to public causes and has served on the City Board of Education and twice was elected president of the board. In July, 1918, Doctor Henry volunteered his services to the Medical Corps of the United States army, and was commissioned captain and ordered to Camp Grant, thence to Camp Custer, serving most of the time with Field Hospital No. 256, Fourteenth Division. He received an honorable discharge in February, 1919. He is now a member of the American Legion. He is a republican, is a member of the Methodist Episcopal Church and a thirty-second degree Scottish Rite Mason and Shriner. Doctor Henry married, in 1901, Miss Minnie Davis, a native of Illinois. Her father, Lewis T. Davis, came from Tennessee. The two children of Doctor and Mrs. Henry are Ada Dayle and James Henry.

COL. CHARLES H. GREENE, mayor of Aurora, is a manufacturer and business man upon whom many unusual responsibilities have been laid by his fellow citizens. He has a distinguished record of service in the Illinois National Guard and as a soldier of the Spanish-American and World wars.

Colonel Greene was born at Syracuse, New York, August 19, 1869, son of Clarence W. and Henrietta (Collins) Greene, has father a native of Syracuse and his mother of Rome, New York. His grandfather, Capt. James K. Greene, had the honor of selling the first ticket out of Syracuse for transportation on Erie Canal boats. The father of Colonel Greene was likewise identified with transportation, being a conductor on the New York Central Railway. Both parents are now deceased. Colonel Greene was the oldest of four children. His sister Hattie B. is deceased; his sister Etta is the wife of Bernard Compton, of Aurora, and Ethel is deceased.

Charles H. Greene acquired a good practical education and then served a machinist's apprenticeship and has had a long and capable experience in all branches of tool manufacture. For a number of years he was superintendent and manager of the Independent Pneumatic Tool Company of Aurora and Chicago.

Mr. Greene in 1892 enlisted for service in the National Guard of Illinois, entering as a private, was promoted to lieutenant in 1893, to captain in 1896, to major in 1899, to lieutenant colonel in 1906 and on February 10, 1910, was commissioned a colonel. In 1921 he retired with the rank of brigadier general after thirty years of service with the National Guard. He was a captain in the Illinois Volunteer Infantry during the Spanish-American war, participating in the Porto Rican campaign. During the World war he was colonel of the One Hundred and Twenty-ninth Infantry from July 25, 1917, to July 9, 1919. He was in France sixteen months with the Thirty-third Division, being at base section No. 2, under Gen. W. D. Conners at Bordeaux. After returning to Aurora in July, 1919, he resumed the management of his successful manufacturing business.

Colonel Greene in 1921 was elected mayor of the city of Aurora and by reelection in 1923 continues the executive head of the municipal administration, which has been one of unusual efficiency and constructive progress. Colonel Greene is a republican, a Knight Templar Mason and Shriner, a member of the B. P. O. Elks, the Loyal Order of Moose and Modern Woodmen of America. He is a member of the Kiwanis Club and the Methodist Church. On July 2, 1894, Colonel Greene married Miss Jessie E. Luck. To their marriage were born four children: Charles E., Florence E., Harold B. and a daughter, Dorothy, who died in infancy.

BENJAMIN W. LANDBORG, postmaster of Elgin, and one of the most representative men of Kane County, was born at Geneva, Illinois, November 10, 1878, a son of Gust P. and Emma (Eck) Landborg, both natives of Sweden, who came to the United States in 1866 and settled at Geneva, where he was in business as a blacksmith for many years. He died in Elgin in 1914. The mother survives and makes her home in Elgin. They had five children: William E., who died February 18, 1925; Edward A., who is a resident of Elgin; Harry O., who is deceased; Benjamin W., who was the fourth in order of birth; and Florence B.

Following his graduation from the local high school Benjamin W. Landborg attended a business college, and then read law for a year. He then became bookkeeper and cashier for the Kerber Packing Company of Elgin, and held that position for eighteen months, leaving it to take charge of the office of the Selz-Schwab Shoe Company. He entered the Elgin postoffice as a clerk in 1902 and was appointed acting postmaster in June, 1923. He was appointed postmaster of Elgin March 1, 1924. Mr. Landborg was also associated with the Landborg & Collins Shoe Company, and served it as secretary and treasurer.

Mr. Landborg is a veteran of the World war, having served in it as a captain of infantry, and was assigned to duty on the United States Transport Pretoria as transport officer. Following the signing of the armistice he was honorably discharged and returned to Elgin.

On June 29, 1904, Mr. Landborg married Miss Marian Fairchild, and they have three children: Lesley, William F. and Benjamin W., Junior. Mr. Landborg is a republican, and has been active in local politics. He is a Shriner Mason and belongs to the Loyal Order of Moose and the Benevolent and Protective Order of Elks. He is a Rotarian, also a scout commissioner of Elgin Council, a member of the Weldwood Country Club and is president at this writing of the Braid Hills Country Club. The Universalist Church holds his membership and receives his support. Since he has assumed charge of the Elgin postoffice there has been a great improvement

in the service, and his administration of the affairs is giving widespread satisfaction, his former business experience being of great assistance to him in the management of the various problems which constantly confront him.

PROF. HENRY DONHAM SPARKS. In the life and career of Henry Donham Sparks, president of the Sparks College at Shelbyville, Illinois, is illustrated what can be accomplished by a man of strong convictions on subjects of public interest, although inclined to be liberal toward others who may have opposite opinions. He is at all times courteous and affable in social and business relations and is quick to make friends. These friends he holds because of his genial and wholesome disposition. He is always regarded as sincere, always helpful, and his word is always accepted as good as his bond. He is at all times very active in behalf of any movement that is calculated to make better and more wholesome the community in which he lives. He is a strong churchman and was very active in the building of a splendid church edifice at Shelbyville, and as chairman of the building committee exerted a powerful influence. He holds an uncompromising attitude in his opposition to any movement that in his opinion will work against the best interests of his community and particularly the church and the education of youth. He spends much time in working for the church and Bible school of which he is a member. He is opposed at all times to the liquor traffic and all other movements which destroy the efficiency of the youth or the citizen. Professor Sparks is the founder of Sparks College, an institution specializing in high grade commercial courses, music and elocution, and one which has taken front rank among similar institutions in the state.

Professor Sparks was born on a farm near Toledo, Cumberland County, Illinois, August 4, 1878, being a son of Bateman Ross and Mary Jane (Shupe) Sparks, and of Pennsylvania Dutch and English descent. His father was born at Terre Haute, Indiana, April 10, 1841, a son of a Missionary Baptist minister, while Mrs. Mary Jane Sparks was born in Parke County, Indiana, February 22, 1848, a daughter of a minister of the United Brethren Church. The paternal grandparents of Professor Sparks were natives of Kentucky and lived near Louisville until 1825, when removal was made to Indiana, and in 1854 they came to Illinois and settled on a farm near Toledo. The parents of Professor Sparks were agricultural people of Cumberland County, and were prominent in church and civic affairs. Bateman Ross Sparks fought as a soldier of the Union army during the Civil war, as did all four of Mrs. Sparks' brothers. Four sons were born to Bateman R. Sparks through a former marriage: Isaac, who died in infancy; John E., of Shelbyville; George A., of Brunswick, Georgia; and Ernest M., of Urbana, Illinois. To Bateman R. and Mary Jane (Shupe) Sparks there were born two children: Henry Donham, of this review; and Mrs. Mary Catherine Bruster of Shelbyville, Illinois.

Professor Sparks was brought up on the farm of his father and from earliest boyhood was a student, eagerly taking advantage of every opportunity to increase his store of knowledge. At first his thoughts turned toward a legal career, but later he abandoned this idea to become an instructor in special branches. He was graduated from the Toledo High School, the Northern Illinois Normal School, Dixon College, Northern Illinois College of Oratory, Rochester (Indiana) Normal University and Westfield (Illinois) College, and did special work in Iowa Christian College, Ewing College and Chicago University, holding the degrees of Bachelor of Science, Bachelor of Oratory, Master of Accounts and Master of Arts. While attending college he had some training as a cadet in a college military organization.

In order to secure sufficient funds to carry on his studies Professor Sparks solicited during one year for Highland Park College and Northern Illinois Normal School. He also taught country school, worked on the farm and did various other things, with the high aim in view of improving himself and fitting himself for his chosen work. After his marriage he moved to Rochester, Indiana, where he taught English and Elocution at Rochester University, building up an enviable reputation during this period. Following this he went to Madison, Indiana, as a commercial teacher in the high school, of which he was soon promoted to the principalship. He resigned this position, with promotion in sight, to take up commercial work, coming directly to Shelbyville. For many years he has made a close study of commercial conditions, so that when he established his college at Shelbyville he was enabled to make it a success from the beginning.

On June 28, 1905, Professor Sparks married in Rock Island County, Illinois, Lillian Bowes, a daughter of Mr. and Mrs. James Bowes. Professor and Mrs. Sparks have two children: Roger Ross, born June 21, 1908; and Madge, born November 16, 1909.

Professor Sparks belongs to the Knights of Pythias, Odd Fellows, Pythian Sisters, Rebekahs, Modern Woodmen of America and the Rotary Club, and is a thirty-second degree Mason and member of Ansar Temple, Springfield, Illinois, A. A. O. N. M. S. He has been active in the work of the Modern Woodmen of America, having been clerk for fifteen years; is a past chancellor of the Knights of Pythias; a member of the Anti-Horse Thief Association; is active vice president of the Rotary Club, of which he was secretary for several years; and has been prominent in the Chamber of Commerce, of which he was president three years, secretary three years and has been a member of the Board of Directors for a long period. He also holds membership in a number of civic and educational organizations. While acquiring his education he took an active part in the social life of his colleges. At one time during his senior year he was president of the Y. M. C. A. and of the Oratorial Club and Literary Society. He is a member of the Christian Church (Disciples of Christ) and has been heard to say in public addresses many times: "I believe the church of Jesus Christ is the biggest and greatest thing in the world." He has been chairman of the

Official Board of the church of his choice for many years and has served several years as superintendent of the Sunday School, and in fact is active in all movements of the church. While living at Madison he was an elder and holds the same office at Shelbyville.

Politically Professor Sparks is a republican, but is tolerant with those who disagree with him politically, always displaying a spirit of fair play. He was honored by the republican party in being elected to the Fifty-fourth General Assembly, in a field of four candidates, and in 1926 was again reelected to the Legislature, again leading in a field of four candidates. The Fortieth District, which he represents, is comprised of Cumberland, Fayette, Christian and Shelby counties. In the legislative halls Mr. Sparks has always stood for the same high-minded and broad-minded principles that have characterized his life in other activities. Competent critics say that he has made a good representative. Owing to his press of work, he has not been able to do any extensive traveling, but is a well-read man upon all subjects and countries and a most entertaining talker. He has something more than a local reputation as a public speaker, and is frequently called upon to address Sunday School conventions, religious meetings, school commencements and dinners and meetings of civic bodies.

All through his life Professor Sparks has been a constructive leader of the forces for clean living, civic righteousness and Christian ideals. He is one of those busy men who is always ready to give of his time and means to promote worthy causes. His school work occupies much of his attention, for he is not satisfied unless he attains to a high ideal, which comes near to being perfection. No student is allowed to pass through his institution without being impressed with the fact that nothing but the best will suffice. And to this may be attributed not only his own success, but that of so many of his graduates.

J. BRUCE AMELL, assistant state's attorney of Kane County, is a native of Illinois and for over fifteen years has given his time and talent to a growing general practice as a lawyer at Aurora.

He was born at Forrest in Livingston County, Illinois, July 7, 1884, son of Henry C. and Anna (Tapsfield) Amell, his father a native of Aurora, while his mother was born in London, England. Henry C. Amell, now deceased, was for a number of years well known in railway circles in northern Illinois, being superintendent of the Elgin, Joliet & Eastern Railway. The widowed mother is still living at Aurora. There were four children: Daisy, J. Bruce, Ada, wife of Paul Healey, of Aurora, and Bessie, wife of Albert Bean, of Chicago.

J. Bruce Amell was graduated from the Aurora high school in 1904. While getting his higher education he was employed at selling tickets in the Union station at Chicago. Mr. Amell attended the law department of the University of Illinois, was graduated in 1908 and was admitted to the Illinois bar the same year. He located at Aurora, and has had a promising private practice in connection with his public duties. In 1913 he was elected city attorney and was appointed assistant state's attorney in 1916.

Mr. Amell married, June 25, 1913, Miss Lillian Rackmyer. They have one daughter, Mary Ann. He is a republican, is affiliated with the B. P. O. Elks, the Loyal Order of Moose the Knights of Pythias, the Independent Order of Odd Fellows and is a Rotarian.

ALBERT M. SNOOK, president and manager of the Beacon Publishing Company, publishers of the Aurora-Beacon News, has been in the newspaper business in Aurora in some capacity for over thirty-five years.

He was born at Oswego, Illinois, December 4, 1869, son of Albert and Cornelia (Lawrence) Snook. His parents were natives of New York State and moved to Illinois in 1866. His father was an attorney by profession. Of their eight children six grew to mature years: Mattie, widow of Daniel Chaffee; Cornelia, widow of John W. Patterson, of Aurora; Marion, wife of William H. Henn, of Joliet; Albert M.; Fritz, of Plainfield, Illinois; and Otto, deceased.

Albert M. Snook since early boyhood has lived at Aurora, was educated in the public schools of that city and after graduating from high school with the class of 1888, went to work in the plant and offices of the Aurora Daily News. His experience has brought him in working contact with all the mechanical as well as the business details of the plant. In 1907 he left the News to become associated with Ira C. Copley, congressman from that district, in the Aurora-Beacon Publishing Company, assuming the offices of president, treasurer and general manager. In 1913 the Beacon absorbed the Daily News and the present Aurora-Beacon News inherits the honorable history of both papers. This is a newspaper that stands among the best in the cities of Illinois and as a business it has greatly prospered. The gross income of the Beacon in 1907 was $25,000 a year, while in 1924 the income amounted to over half a million. The newspaper is published in a modern fire-proof establishment and has a circulation of 20,000 copies.

Mr. Snook married, April 23, 1907, Miss Jane H. Kelley. Their four children are: John K., Janet, Albert M., Jr., and Eleanor. Mr. Snook is a republican, a member of the Masonic fraternity, Knights of Pythias and Elks and the Universalist Church.

D. LEWIS LEE has developed one of the most successful and interesting newspaper enterprises in southern Illinois. He has erected a modern, new building at Marissa, Illinois, and installed a new Hoe press that prints 15,000 twelve page newspapers per hour, this press, together with his other modern stereotype and linotype equipment, gives him a newspaper plant equal to that of the larger dailies. From this plant he prints a chain of weekly newspapers known as the 50th State Newspapers, covering six counties.

He is a son of Mr. and Mrs. J. K. Lee and a direct descendant of the famous Lee family of Virginia. His grandfather, Edward Lee, was killed in the Confederate army. His maternal grandparents, Mr. and Mrs. Louis Wilson, were farmers in South Carolina.

His entire family connection on both his father's and mother's side have passed away,

Judge D. D. Harris

leaving only one brother, T. A. Lee, in North Carolina and one sister, Mrs. Earl, in South Carolina, and one brother, John R. Lee, in Miami, Florida.

D. Lewis Lee received his education in the public schools of North Carolina, the prep school in Nashville, Tennessee, and finished in the Peabody Normal College, Nashville. For two years he taught school in the South.

He married in Tennessee, September 22, 1903, Miss Rebecca Stewart Swarbrick, daughter of Thomas Swarbrick. Mrs. Lee has a sister, Mrs. Gray, residing in Illinois, and a sister, Mrs. Spees, residing in St. Louis.

After spending a number of years in the printing and newspaper business in Texas Mr. Lee purchased the Marissa Messenger at Marissa, Illinois, in 1914, and through the assistance of his three sons, Thomas, Robert and Lewis, Jr., he has built up a wonderful printing and newspaper business extending over six counties, with the central plant at Marissa. His oldest son, Thomas Lee, is foreman of the Marissa plant and is taking advanced work in journalism at the University of Illinois.

Mr. Lee is affiliated with the Masonic Lodge and also the I. O. O. F. lodge, and he and his family are members of the United Presbyterian Church.

RAYMOND KENNETH KNAPP is a native of Illinois, and since early manhood except for his war service has been identified with the Bear Brand Hosiery Company, one of the largest hosiery manufacturing concerns in America. He is now superintendent at the company's plant at Kankakee.

He was born in Chester, Illinois, July 13, 1889, son of William and Elizabeth (Schoen) Knapp, both of whom were born near Chester, and grandson of Philip and Mary Knapp, natives of Germany and early settlers in Randolph County, Illinois, and of Philip and Elizabeth Schoen, natives of St. Louis, Missouri. William Knapp was a printer by trade and was the founder and publisher for many years of the Chester Tribune. He died in 1905 and his widow now resides at Hartford, Wisconsin.

Raymond Kenneth Knapp attended grammar and high schools, and at the age of sixteen learned telegraphy. He was employed as a telegraph operator three years, and in October, 1909, enlisted in the United States Marine Corps. He was in service four years with that famous organization, stationed mainly at Panama and in South America. After getting his discharge in 1913 he went to work for the Bear Brand Hosiery Company at Waupun, Wisconsin, becoming foreman in the plant there. He left the business in May, 1917, to enter the First Officers Training Camp at Ft. Sheridan, Illinois, was graduated August 1 with the rank of lieutenant of infantry and was assigned to the Eighty-fifth Division at Camp Custer. In December, 1917, he was promoted to first lieutenant of infantry, and in July, 1918, sailed for France and was with the Eighty-fifth Division until January, 1919, when he was transferred to the Second Division in the Army of Occupation in Germany. In May, 1919, he was again transferred, this time to the Seventy-eighth Division, with which he returned home and received his honorable discharge at Camp Dix, June 4, 1919. Mr. Knapp at once resumed his service with the Bear Brand Hosiery Company, becoming foreman of the plant at Beaver Dam, Wisconsin. On June 4, 1920, he was transferred to Kankakee, Illinois, as general superintendent of the industry in that city.

He married, July 7, 1917, Miss Vina Durae, a native of Beaver Dam, Wisconsin, and daughter of Alexander and Frances Durae. They have two children, Raymond Alexander, born August 22, 1918, and Bettie Frances, born June 6, 1920. Mr. Knapp is a republican, a member of the American Legion and the Rotary Club, and his home is at 553 East Bourbonnais Street.

JUDGE LOUIS P. HARRISS, attorney and judge of the city court of Duquoin, has a knowledge of men as well as the law, and has rendered a distinctive service during the few years he has been on the bench.

Judge Harriss is a self made man who has toiled upward from poverty. He was born on a farm in the Paradise Prairie community of Perry County, February 5, 1880. His people were highly respected, but in comparatively humble circumstances, and Judge Harriss had to work for all his advantages. His great-great-grandfather, Eward Harriss, better known as "Ned" Harriss, came from North Carolina and was a pioneer settler in Perry County. He was the father of John Johnson Harriss and grandfather of John Harriss. John Harriss, father of Judge Harriss, was born in 1850, in the Paradise Prairie community. He died in 1917. He married Emily Provart. Her grandfather, Phillip C. C. Provart, came from Lancashire, England, in the early part of the last century and settled in Perry County, where he distinguished himself by his qualities of natural leadership and character. He served as a member of the State Legislature.

Louis P. Harriss was reared as a country boy, went barefoot during a large part of the year, and worked in the fields except for a few weeks each year when in country schools. He was one of a large family of children. He kept up his studies at home and he also continued to study while mining coal, an occupation he followed for several years. As a coal miner he earned the money for maintaining a home of his own. Later he and his wife moved to Springfield, where he entered Lincoln College of Law and graduated as valedictorian of his class in June, 1918. On returning to Perry County he formed a partnership with Judge M. C. Cook. They were associated five years. In 1923 he was elected city judge. In his office he has concurrent jurisdiction with the Circuit Court in trials where the defendant is a resident of Duquoin or where the cause of action arose within the corporate limits of the city. Judge Harriss has shown such qualifications on the bench that he has been called to serve as a judge of the Superior and Municipal Courts in the city of Chicago at the request of judges of those courts, and has given nearly half of his time to the service. Judge Harriss is a member of the Independent

Order of Odd Fellows and various other fraternal orders. He married at the age of twenty, Miss Nora Bell Sronce, daughter of Peter Sronce.

ANDREW DAHLE, electrical contractor and dealer in electrical supplies at Galena, learned his trade in Norway, but has been a resident and business man of Galena for nearly twenty years.

He was born at Lyster, in Sogn, Norway, September 26, 1880, son of Johannes K. and Christiane (Hugen) Dahle. His father is still living in Norway, a merchant tailor at Sogn. Andrew Dahle attended the common and high schools at Lyster, and as a youth had experience working on a farm and later was an employe of the Norwegian Telephone Company, learning the trade of electrician. He was a young man of twenty-one years when he came to America in 1901. His first two years in this country were spent at Stoughton, Wisconsin, where he did farm work in summers and worked in town during the winter. In 1903 he went out to the Dakotas, but after a few months returned to Madison, Wisconsin, where he was employed about two years by an electrical contractor named E. E. Satter. On account of failing health he left this work and again followed farming for about two years near Madison.

Mr. Dahle came to Galena in the fall of 1908, and has since been in the electrical business, having a partnership with B. B. Boorman for about six months, and since then has been sole owner of a growing and prospering business. Mr. Dahle is the leading electrical contractor in this vicinity, and also does an extensive business in electrical supplies, and in recent years has been a dealer in radios.

He is a thirty-second degree Scottish Rite Mason and Shriner, member of the Knights of Pythias, B. P. O. Elks, Eagles and Kiwanis Club. He is not only popular socially but is a citizen willing to lend his hand in support of any worthy cause. In politics he votes as a republican.

HON. EARLE R. KELLEY. No man is elevated to the position of chief executive of a city without having accomplished something out of the ordinary, for an honor of this character is not bestowed until it has been earned. In the case of Mayor Earle R. Kelley, of Elgin, the people elected him because they recognized the high character of the man, his business strength and his unflinching integrity, and since he has assumed the responsibilities pertaining to his high office he has justified his constituents' choice of him. The progress of improvements and the growth in material prosperity has been steady, not spectacular, and his administration of affairs will not be soon forgotten.

Mayor Kelley was born at Huntley, Illinois, November 15, 1871, a son of Michael James and Sarah A. (White) Kelley, natives of Belfast, Ireland, and New York State, respectively. They came to Illinois in 1848, locating near Marengo, where the father was in the mercantile business for years, but has been deceased for some time. They had three children born to them: Mary Ellen, who is the wife of Lyman Forrey, of Skidmore, Missouri; Ernest E., who died in 1923; and Mayor Kelley, who was the third in order of birth.

Six years in the public schools of Huntley, two years of night work in the Elgin Academy, and four years under private tutors in public speaking prepared Mayor Kelley for contact with the world. For nine years he was an employe of the Elgin Watch factory, and then for twelve years he was a member of the advertising department of the headquarters office of the Union Southern Pacific Railroad at Omaha, Nebraska. Severing this latter connection, Mr. Kelley returned to Elgin and took over the management of the Todd homestead farm in the vicinity of Elgin, and for five years this work occupied his time. He was then, without any solicitation on his part, nominated and elected mayor of his home city in May, 1923, which office he still holds. He has always been independent in his political views. He has been advanced to the Chapter in Masonry, and is a past master of the Blue Lodge and a past high priest of the Chapter. The Congregational Church holds his membership.

On June 26, 1908, Mr. Kelley married Alice C. Todd, of Elgin, and they have one son, James Todd Kelley.

THEODORE F. EICHLER, M. D. Among the men prominently identified with the medical profession of Kane County who, by character and achievement, have attained notable distinction, the record of Dr. Theodore F. Eichler is found to be one that compels more than passing attention. Although numbered among the younger physicians of Dundee, where he is engaged in practice, he stands well to the head of his profession, and few men have attained a higher reputation both for ability and faithfulness. Not only, however, is he a well-known figure in his profession, but he has won appreciation as a man and good citizen, and is now serving Dundee as its mayor.

Doctor Eichler was born at Gary, Minnesota, January 14, 1892, a son of August and Sabina (Breitenbach) Eichler, both natives of Germany, who came to the United States about 1871. They landed in Louisiana, from whence they went north to Minnesota, there they bought land and became farmers. The mother died in 1901, having borne her husband nine children, of whom Doctor Eichler is the youngest. August Eichler was married a second time, and he and his wife are now residing at Dundee.

Growing up in his native state, Doctor Eichler was graduated from the Ada, Minnesota, High School in 1912, and he then entered the Chicago College of Medicine and Surgery, and was graduated therefrom in 1916, with the degree of Doctor of Medicine. Following his graduation he established himself in a general practice at Dundee, where he has since remained, building up a fine connection and winning the confidence of the people of his home community. Almost immediately he began to make his influence felt in civic affairs, and has served on the school board for the past two years and in the spring of 1925 was elected mayor of the city. He has been president of the City Club, is a member of the

Board of Directors of the Commercial Club, of the Braid Hills Country Club, is a director of the Elgin Radium Association, and a member of the Elgin Physicians Club and the American Medical Association. Fraternally he belongs to the Modern Woodmen of America and the Fraternal Order of Eagles. In political faith he is independent.

On December 25, 1916, Doctor Eichler married Miss Alice Thibodeau, and they have three children: Theodore F., Junior, Merlyn and Bruce.

OSSIAN COLE SIMONDS. One of the distinguished men in the profession of landscape architecture is Ossian Cole Simonds, of Chicago, whose work has contributed to the adornment and beautification of that city for over forty years.

Mr. Simonds was born at Grand Rapids, Michigan, November 11, 1855, a son of Joel A. and Harriet (Newell) Simonds. He finished his education at the University of Michigan in 1878, graduating with the degree of Civil Engineer. Shortly after, coming to Chicago, he was a member of the firm Holabird, Simonds & Roche, architects, from 1880 to 1883. The name Holabird & Roche have figured conspicuously in the architectural profession of the middle west. Mr. Simonds found his first important opportunities for service as a landscape architect in the position of superintendent of Graceland Cemetery, an office he held from 1881 to 1898. Since 1898 he has been a member of the Board of Managers and landscape architect for this beautiful cemetery.

He is also a member of the firm O. C. Simonds & Company, landscape designers, and has his office at 1101 Buena Avenue. Mr. Simonds designed the original plan for Fort Sheridan, also the Lincoln Park extension in Chicago. He has been consulting or active landscape gardener for public or municipal parks in Quincy, Springfield, Hannibal and many other cities throughout the middle west. His services have also been secured by numerous individuals in designing and developing private homes and estates and subdivisions.

Mr. Simonds is author of a book on landscape gardening. He has lectured on the subject at the University of Michigan. He is a member of the Western Society of Engineers, the American Society of Landscape Architects the Association of American Cemetery Superintendents. He belongs to the Delta Upsilon college fraternity and is a member of the University, City and Cliff Dwellers Clubs at Chicago. His home is 929 Montrose Avenue. On May 12, 1881, he married Miss Martha E. Rumsey, of Grand Rapids. They are the parents of five children: Gertrude, wife of W. E. Walker, of Chicago; Herbert, of Boston, Massachusetts, who is married and has three children, Robert, John and Eleanor; Marshall, of Green Bay, Wisconsin, who is married and has two children, Margaret and Barbara; Donald, of Boston, Massachusetts, who is married and has one child, Donald, Jr.; and Robert, of York Harbor, Maine, married but has no children.

JUDGE FRANK WILEY SHEPHERD. Officially connected with some of the most substantial of the financial and commercial houses of Elgin, Judge Frank Wiley Shepherd is recognized as a man of unusual business ability and astuteness, and his association with a concern is regarded as evidence of its solidity, for it is a well-known fact that he will not countenance anything that is unfair or speculative in character. Judge Shepherd is a product of Illinois, as he was born at Dundee, February 28, 1876, a son of Franklin L. and Helen (Kenyon) Shepherd, natives of New York and Vermont, respectively. They came to Illinois in 1855, and here passed the remainder of their useful lives, and here they died. For several years prior to his death the father had been living retired, but for a number of years he had been active as a farmer. Three children were born to him and his wife, namely: Carrie, who is the wife of Rev. Enos Holt of Coleta, Illinois; Jennie, who is the wife of John B. Newman, of Elgin; and Frank Wiley, who was the youngest born.

Frank Wiley Shepherd attended the Elgin High School, Leland-Stanford University, and the University of Michigan, and was graduated from the latter in 1899. He entered at once upon the practice of law, and achieved distinction in his profession, and since 1922, has been judge of the Probte Court of Kane County. In political faith he is a republican. As above stated, Judge Shepherd is connected with a number of important concerns, being vice president of the Home National Bank, treasurer and director of the Elgin Loan and Homestead Association, and a director of the Home Trust & Savings Bank. He belongs to the Methodist Episcopal Church. Fraternally he maintains membership with the Masons and Elks.

On February 14, 1923, Judge Shepherd married Ina Roberts Granke, a native of Wisconsin. By a former marriage Judge Shepherd has two children: Nan Jean and Caroline. Since he has assumed the responsibilities of his present office Judge Shepherd has demonstrated his fitness for his duties, and his administration of the affairs within his jurisdiction is giving universal satisfaction.

ARTHUR WILLIAM WEBSTER. The name Webster has been identified with the nursery business at Centralia since the decade of the '60s. A nursery and florist business conducted by Arthur William Webster at Fifth and South Locust streets is the oldest establishment of its kind in this section of Illinois. The third generation of the family is now active in the management, represented by Wendell W. Webster, a son of Arthur W. Webster.

Arthur William Webster was born December 17, 1865, at Sutton, Isle of Ely, England, son of William and Mary (Wybrow) Webster. The mother died in England in 1867. Soon afterward the father and sons came to America and settled at Sandoval, Illinois, where William Webster was in the nursery business until his death in 1872. Arthur William Webster, then seven years of age, came to Centralia to live with his uncle, Jabez Webster. Jabez Webster was the founder of the Webster nursery business near Centralia, and Arthur W. received ample training in the establishment during his youth. At the same time he attended public schools. He was actively associated with his uncle until August 1, 1896, when he withdrew to establish the business of his own at the corner of Fifth and South Locust streets, which has been the headquarters of the firm for thirty years. Mr. Webster in addition maintains a farm of three hundred acres, part of which is devoted to the cultivation of dahlia, gladiola and narcissus bulbs, trees and shrubs. Another department of the farm is a herd of Jersey cattle and dairy for the production of pure milk.

Arthur W. Webster is a democrat in politics. He is a past vice president of the Illinois State Florists Association and a member of the National Florists Association.

He married at Centralia, in 1895, Miss Mary Reichmann, daughter of William and Mary Reichmann, of a family that came from Germany. Wendell W. Webster, only son and child, was born August 10, 1896, was educated in public schools at Centralia, and since early youth has been associated with his father's business and is now manager of the retail store. He married Miss Fae Maxwell, daughter of George and Martha Maxwell. During the World war Wendell Webster was with the colors in training at Camp Bradley at Peoria.

HARRIET DOLBEE since 1912 has been librarian of the Hayner Memorial Library of Alton, succeeding in that office her sister, Miss Florence Dolbee, who was chosen librarian in 1879, when this library was first opened, and directed its work through a period of thirty-three years. She died in 1913. Miss Florence Dolbee succeeded her sister, Blanche, who was librarian from 1875 to 1878.

These noble women, so closely associated with the cultural life of Alton, were daughters of Shadrach Rodney Dolbee, a pioneer of Alton. He had lived in Columbus, Ohio, where he was an employe of Judge Baillache, Ohio state printer. After the latter moved to Alton Mr. Dolbee remained to close up the business and arrived in Alton six months before the Lovejoy tragedy. He was associated with Judge Baillache in the Alton Telegraph from May, 1838, to January, 1850. Mr. Dolbee was a skilful old time printer, a successful publisher, and after leaving the Telegraph he was called back to take charge of a difficult job of composition. In his later years he was in the real estate and insurance business. He died January 17, 1869. He was an active member of St. Paul's Episcopal Church, serving many years as senior warden. He was a whig and later a republican in politics.

S. R. Dolbee married, September 8, 1850, Hannah Elizabeth Pettingell. She died at Alton March 26, 1899. She was a direct descendant of Richard Pettingell, who was born in England in 1620, and was a resident of Salem, Massachusetts, before 1641. His descendant in the fifth generation was Edward Pettingell, a native of Maine and a large property owner in the City of Bath. He was a soldier in the Revolution. The Pettingells bought property at Bath, Maine, in 1661. Hannah Elizabeth Dolbee was born at Bath in 1820.

S. R. Dolbee by his marriage to Hannah Elizabeth Pettingell had six children: Blanche Owen, who married H. C. Cole and died October 19, 1910; Alfred Somers, who died in infancy; Cora, Mrs. Charles B. Rohland, a distinguished musician and musical director; Miss Florence, who died in 1913; William A., of Alton, who died in 1926; and Miss Harriet Cooper Dolbee.

HARRY MITCHENER SNYDER, well known in insurance and financial circles in Chicago, was born at McArthur, Ohio, July 2, 1882, son of Sanford B. and Jennie (Rigg) Snyder. His father was born at McArthur, March 3, 1848, and died October 13, 1918. His mother was born at Albany, Ohio, April 17, 1848, and died November 11, 1920. Sanford B. Snyder followed lumber manufacture for a number of years. He was the first man in the United States to manufacture ready made houses, a business he carried on under the name of Athens Lumber Company, of which he was general manager. He was also interested in railway building and contracting, and he handled wholesale building programs for coal companies, erecting entire towns in industrial centers. He was a staunch republican and a member of the Presbyterian Church. He and his wife had five children, one of whom died in infancy. The others were: William S., Hattie, Parker and Harry M.

Harry M. Snyder graduated from high school in 1899. During summer vacations he had worked in coal mines in Southern Ohio. He had also acquired some experience as a collection agent for merchants. For a time he sold books for the P. F. Collier Company, and spent some time in Missouri, Kansas, Oklahoma and Texas, working as a ranch hand and as an insurance adjuster. In 1903 he located at St. Louis, where he and his brother, W. S. Snyder, engaged in business as collecting agents. Later they entered contracting, remodeling various properties in hotels. He continued in the hotel business and contracting there until 1909. Following that he spent about three years at Independence, Kansas, in the insurance business, and he sold lands for farming purposes in Texas and New Mexico until the beginning of the Mexican border troubles. He engaged in the life insurance business, and in 1916 became vice president of a life insurance company. On April 1, 1919, he organized a Corporation Service Company at St. Louis, and on July 1, 1920, became president of the company.

Mr. Snyder is a thirty-second degree Scottish Rite Mason, a member of the Illinois Athletic Club and Hamilton Club of Chicago, the Adventurers Club of Chicago and the Missouri Athletic Club of St. Louis. His favorite recreation is hunting big game and he has spent a number of vacations in the big woods from Mexico to Alaska. He married, June 6, 1911, Miss Ida N. Shearer. They have two daughters, Dorothy Jane and Melba Elizabeth.

CHARLES EDWARD GILLESPIE is an earnest and high minded educator, a school man with a number of years of successful experience and is now county superintendent of schools in Clay County.

He was born on a farm in that county March 15, 1893, son of John and Maria (Rinehart) Gillespie, his father a native of Jasper

County, Illinois, and of Irish parentage, while his mother was born in Clay County, daughter of Jacob Rinehart. John and Maria Gillespie after their marriage lived in Clay County, then in Jasper County, and from there moved to the State of Arkansas, where John Gillespie died soon afterward. The widowed mother then returned to Illinois and reared her five children on a farm in Clay County.

Charles Edward Gillespie from boyhood felt the weight of unusual responsibility upon him and has done more than pull his own weight in the world. He acquired his early education in country schools, and at the age of eighteen qualified for teaching and took charge of his home school. Since then he has continued teaching and for several years attending school in the intervals of his instruction work. He took courses in normal schools and spent two years in Valparaiso University of Indiana.

His record as an educator aside from several terms of country school teaching comprise two years as principal of a ward school at Effingham, one year at Montrose, one year at Gifford, two years at Bible Grove. In 1922 he was elected superintendent of schools for Clay County. His offices are in Louisville.

Mr. Gillespie is a democrat, a member of the Masonic order and the Christian Church. He married, in 1915, Mary Chesnut, a native of Jasper County, Illinois. They have two children, Dale and Tempe.

D. A. McKENZIE. Having devoted his whole life to the newspaper business, D. A. McKenzie, president, business manager and editor of the Elgin Courier-News, is one of the best known men in journalistic circles Illinois possesses today, and his trenchant pen and wide-gauged policies have made the Courier-News a powerful organ throughout a wide territory. Mr. McKenzie's experience has been a varied one, and he understands the requirements of the public and how to meet them. He is a native of Dubuque, Iowa, where he was born December 18, 1871, and its public schools grounded him in the fundamentals of an education.

Mr. McKenzie's connection with the newspaper world began with his entry, in September, 1887, into the circulation department of the Dubuque Telegraph, and he remained with that journal, working in the circulation and advertising departments, until March, 1892. Leaving Dubuque, he went to Akron, Ohio, as secretary of the Journal Publishing Company, afterwards the Beacon Publishing Company, and he continued to hold that position until March, 1898. For five years Mr. McKenzie was associated with W. T. Clark, under the firm name of McKenzie & Clark, as traveling newspaper representatives of the Standard Fashion Company of New York City. They covered thirty states and made an excellent reputation for themselves as enterprising newspaper men.

Coming then to Elgin, Mr. McKenzie first had charge of the circulation department of the Elgin Daily News and the Weekly Advocate, and also paid special attention to increasing the advertising of these publications. His energy, astuteness and aggressive policies brought him recognition there, as elsewhere. During his last three years with the News he was vice president and one of the business managers.

On April 12, 1920, Mr. McKenzie became business manager of the Elgin Daily Courier, and a year later was also made its editor, and in 1922 was made president of the company, now the Elgin Courier-News Publishing Company, which three positions he is now holding with capable efficiency. He maintains membership with the Benevolent and Protective Order of Elks and the Loyal Order of Moose; he is a past president of the Elgin Rotary Club, is a member of the Weldwood Country Club.

On April 17, 1901, Mr. McKenzie married Miss Mary Edna Ellis, a native of Seneca, Illinois, and they have two children: Clark Ellis and Dorothy Lorraine. The McKenzie home is at 1028 Spring Street, Elgin.

HIRAM NYE JOHNSON was for many years a prominent Chicago business man, and a resident of Aurora, where he married a daughter of one of the founders of that city. Mrs. Johnson resides at Aurora.

Hiram Nye Johnson was born in Massachusetts, July 16, 1854, son of Gardner Nye and Eliza (French) Johnson. There were three sons in the family, Leland, Joseph French and Hiram N., all now deceased. Joseph French Johnson, who died January 22, 1925, was a distinguished figure in American scholarship and finance. He spent his early life at Aurora, Illinois, was in journalism and at one time financial editor of the Chicago Tribune, but was best known as professor of political economy and dean of the School of Commerce, Accounts and Finance at New York University. He is the author of many books and articles on financial and business problems, was the founder and president of the Alexander Hamilton Institute.

Hiram Nye Johnson spent his early life in Illinois, and after completing his education engaged in business as a merchant at Maroa for several years and later in Chicago. In 1907 he became president of the Chicago Rubber Company, and continued that business until his death on January 30, 1908. He was a republican, a Mason and an attendant of the Methodist Church.

On October 12, 1880, Mr. Johnson married Eva Dent McCarty, daughter of Samuel and Emily Ann (Swayzee) McCarty. Her father, Samuel McCarty, came to Illinois to join his brother Joseph, who in April, 1834, had located a promising site for a milling industry. Samuel McCarty arrived in November, 1833. The brothers, both millwrights by trade, erected and established on the bank of Fox River the mill which for several years was known as McCarty's Mill. This naturally became the center of increasing population of settlers who were locating in northern Illinois at that time. In 1835 a large colony arrived and settled around McCarty's mill. One of the new arrivals, Elias E. Terry, suggested that the name of the place be Aurora, a name unanimously agreed upon and thus substituting for the original McCarty's Mill. Mrs. Johnson is the mother of three children: Helen, wife of Robert McGregor Roy, of Aurora; Edwin Nye, of Aurora; and Lucy Gladys, wife of Ward J. Downs, of Brooklyn, New York.

GEORGE E. THOMPSON, superintendent of the Saint Charles Community High School, is one of the scholarly men of Kane County and one who is living up to the highest ideals of his learned profession. Trained faculties and an enlightened understanding in these modern days contribute materially to individual success, and more and more is the world at large asking for educated men not only for the accepted professions, but also for those along agricultural lines, and in the field of politics. The trained thinker is demanded for the deciding of public questions, which while they may be perplexing to the general public, must be clear to the lawmaker. Therefore, because of this almost universal demand for a more comprehensive and exhaustive training of the children of the country so that they may be adequately fitted for whatever demands are made upon them in after life, has come more exacting requirements of the educator. No longer is the half-baked lad, struggling each night to keep a day ahead of other pupils, or the girl filling in the time between her own escape from the schoolroom and her marriage, accepted as the school teacher. The training for this profession is long and arduous, and does not cease as long as its follower remains in the ranks. Professor Thompson has not only thoroughly prepared himself for his work, developing his natural abilities and keen love for his work, but he keeps well abreast of the advance in his calling, and is a recognized leader in educational matters in his part of the state.

Professor Thompson was born near Defiance, Ohio, May 1, 1894, a son of Charles H. and Gertrude (Dick) Thompson, both long residents of Ohio, where the mother still resides, but the father died in October, 1923. The following children were born to them: Bert, who is a resident of Toledo, Ohio; Clyde, who is deceased; Professor Thompson, who was the third in order of birth; Ray, who is a resident of Continental, Ohio; Glenn, who is deceased; Dale, who is a resident of Adrian, Michigan; Marvel, who is the wife of Edward Shafer, of Continental, Ohio; Jane, who is a resident of Saint Charles, Illinois; Robert, who is deceased; and Helen, who lives with her mother.

Following his graduation from high school in 1911, Professor Thompson entered Defiance, Ohio, College, and was graduated therefrom in 1915, with the degree of Bachelor of Arts. For the subsequent two years he was instructor in mathematics and director of athletics at his alma mater. For the following years he was principal of the Saint Charles High School.

In the meanwhile this country had entered the World war, and Professor Thompson, like other young men of his age, enlisted for service, entering the United States Navy destroyer branch. He was assigned to the Adriatic and Mediterranean Seas, where he remained for one year as an ensign. Following the signing of the armistice he was honorably discharged and returned to the United States. In September, 1919, he came back to the Saint Charles High School, and was made superintendent of the grade and high schools of this city. Professor Thompson has qualified at the Graduate School of Education, University of Chicago, and has nearly completed sufficient work for the Master degree, which degree he expects will be conferred upon him in the following year.

Professor Thompson married, March 3, 1919, Miss Mary Caldwell, a native of Ohio, and a teacher of music. Two children have been born to Professor and Mrs. Thompson: Robert C. and Mary Jean. He is independent in his political fealty, but not active in public matters, his time being fully taken up by his professional duties. He belongs to the Masonic fraternity, the Loyal Order of Moose, the American Legion and the Kiwanis Club, and is active in all these organizations.

HARRY A. BASTIAN is president and manager of the Millhouse Brothers Company, one of the largest general mercantile concerns in northwestern Illinois, located at Galena. Mr. Bastian has had a consecutive experience in business at Galena since early youth.

He was born in that city February 15, 1886, son of John and Eliza (Adams) Bastian. His grandfather, John Bastian, came from England and settled near Galena, taking up land from the government and spending the rest of his life on a farm. John Bastian, father of Harry A., was born in Cornwall, England, and was a child when brought to this country. He grew up near Galena, attended public schools there and for a number of years was engaged in farming. At the time of the Civil war he enlisted in the Ninety-sixth Illinois Infantry and saw hard service in many battles and campaigns, including Shiloh, Vicksburg, Chickamauga, Lookout Mountain. After the war he returned to Galena, resumed farming and was for some years in the hotel business. He died about 1890. His wife, Eliza Adams, was born six miles east of Galena, in the community known as Council Hill, and was educated in public schools. Her people were farmers and her father was an Englishman, but was acting as superintendent of a mine in Ireland when he died. Her mother and the children then came to America, settling near Galena.

Harry A. Bastian attended public schools in Galena until 1900, when, at the age of fourteen, he began working in the foundry of the John W. Westwick Company, spending about two years there. For another two years he followed the wood working trade with the Hubbard Furniture Company. Mr. Bastian in 1904 became an employe of Millhouse Brothers & Company, retail and wholesale hardware, as shipping clerk. He was given various promotions during the ten years of his service with that concern, finally being head clerk. In 1920 he took a prominent part in the organization of the Millhouse Brothers Company, now the largest mercantile establishment in Jo Daviess County. His associates in the business are: A. A. Genz, vice president and assistant manager; H. J. Toepel, secretary and treasurer; Mrs. William P. Swing and F. Menzemer. Mr. Bastian is also a partner in the Althauser Hardware & Variety Store at Dubuque, his associates in that business being George T. Millhouse and A. A. Genz.

Mr. Bastian is a member of the Galena Chamber of Commerce and the United States Chamber of Commerce, the Illinois Retail Hardware Dealers' Association, is a member of the B. P. O. Elks, The C. K. of A., the Catholic Church, and in politics is a republican.

He married at Galena, June 12, 1907, Miss Mary E. Bergman, of Galena, who was born and reared and educated in that city. Her parents were Henry and Mary (Leddy) Bergman, of Galena, her father a carpenter and contractor and for a number of years a furniture merchant at Galena, where he died in 1916. Her mother still resides at Galena. Mr. and Mrs. Bastian are the parents of six children, five of whom are living. The daughter Mary Elizabeth graduated from the Galena High School in 1925 and is a member of the class of 1926 in St. Mary's College at Prairie du Chien, Wisconsin; the son Harry David is a member of the class of 1927 in the Galena High School; Marco and Adelaide are pupils in the parochial schools; and the youngest of the family is Leddy James.

LEO E. ALLEN, clerk of the Circuit Court of Jo Daviess County, is a veteran of the World war, having served in the Illinois Division, the famous Thirty-third.

He was born at Elizabeth, Illinois, October 5, 1898, son of A. A. and Sarah (Steinberger) Allen. His parents were born and reared at Elizabeth, and were educated in the public schools of that locality. In 1914 the family moved to Galena, where the parents now reside. A. A. Allen is a son of John and Elizabeth A. (Clark) Allen. John Allen was born in Derbyshire, England, March 25, 1811, and coming to America, settled at Springfield, Illinois, in 1840, and in 1842 settled near Elizabeth in Jo Daviess County, Illinois. In 1851 he married Elizabeth A. Clark, who was born in Jo Daviess County in 1830. They were the parents of nine children, Mrs. Sarah Ann Gosney, William, John, Charles, Alphonso, Samuel, Robert, Joseph and Wilbur. John Allen owned 330 acres of land and was one of the men interested in the mining project known as the Wishorn Diggings. For many years his farm was carried on by his sons while he lived retired in Elizabeth.

Sarah Steinberger Allen is the daughter of John and Fredericka Steinberger. Both Mr. and Mrs. Steinberger were born in Germany, coming to this country in their early years. They are the parents of ten children: Mrs. Mary Leibert, Mrs. Barbara Groezinger, Mrs. Jennie Williams, Mrs. Christina Hill, Mrs. Sarah Allen, Mrs. Hannah Daniels, Miss Emma Steinberger, John, William and Michael (who died when a young man). Leo E. Allen has one brother and three sisters, Mrs. Clara Lawton, of Rockford, Mrs. Freda Willette, of Rockford, Miss Blanche Allen and Wilbur W. Allen, of Galena.

Leo E. Allen first attended public school at Elizabeth, also attended a school at Apple River, and then in Galena. He was a member of the class of 1917 in the Galena High School and was granted his diploma after he had joined the colors. On March 26, 1917, at the age of nineteen, he enlisted in the Sixth Illinois Infantry. When America entered the World war and the state troops were mustered into the National Army this became the One Hundred and Twenty-third Field Artillery. For a time he was in training at Camp Lowden, Springfield, and in August, 1917, entered Camp Logan at Houston, Texas, where he remained until May, 1918. He then went to Hoboken, New Jersey, embarked for Liverpool on May 15, landing at Liverpool two weeks later, and was soon with his regiment at a French artillery range. In August, 1918, the regiment went into the front line in the Verdun sector, participated in the St. Mihiel offensive, the Verdun defensive and the Argonne-Meuse offensive. His regiment received three citations for valor. After the armistice Mr. Allen was with his regiment in the Army of Occupation from January 1 to April 1, 1919. He arrived in the United States May 31, 1919, and was honorably discharged at Camp Grant, Illinois.

Following the war Mr. Allen spent four years in the University of Michigan Law School. After that he was for two years a teacher in the Galena High School. On November 4, 1924, he was elected clerk of the Circuit Court and began his four year term on December 1 of the same year. Mr. Allen is a member of the Masonic Lodge, is noble grand of Lodge No. 15, Independent Order of Odd Fellows, a member of the B. P. O. Elks and Eagles, the American Legion, the Galena Golf Club, and is a Presbyterian.

He married at Chicago, May 31, 1924, Miss Gladys Dahl, daughter of B. F. Dahl and wife of Chicago. Her father is a painter and decorator. Mr. and Mrs. Allen have one daughter, Dawn Elizabeth Allen.

MILTON VINCENT, sheriff of Jo Daviess County, was born and reared near Galena, and his people were among the very first settlers in this noted old mining district of Illinois.

His grandparents were Henry and Sarah (Mitchell) Vincent, who came from Cornwall, England, to America in 1837 and settled near Galena, where Henry Vincent took up land from the government. That land is still in the possession of his descendants, having remained without transfer since it was taken over from the government nearly ninety years ago. Henry Vincent was a farmer. His son, Capt. William Vincent, was born in Cornwall, England, and was fourteen years of age when his parents immigrated to America. He became a farmer, but also followed mining for many years. In July, 1862, he enlisted in Company A of the Ninety-sixth Illinois Infantry, and was in service with the regiment through the battles of Chickamauga, Atlanta, Franklin and Nashville. He was wounded in the second day's fighting at Chickamauga, September 20, 1863, and was returned home on a furlough until he recuperated. He went into the army as a first lieutenant and rose to the rank of captain, commanding his company after the battle of Chickamauga. At the close of the war he returned to his home near Galena and engaged in farming and mine operations until his death on October 13, 1921, at the ripe old age of ninety-eight. Three of his brothers were also soldiers in the Union army. One of them, Joseph Vincent, was in the Forty-fifth Illinois Infantry. John Vincent served with the Ninety-sixth Infantry, and in the battle of Lookout Mountain in December, 1863, was shot through the head, the ball ranging from a point just below the eye to the left ear. In spite of that serious wound he is still alive at the age of eighty-five and resides at Hampton in Franklin County, Iowa. The third brother, Charles, was a member of the One Hundred Fortieth Infantry. Capt. William Vincent in 1851 made the trip overland by ox wagon to California, spending about a year and a half in the gold fields. He returned east by way of Panama and up the Mississippi River to Galena, arriving in 1852. Capt. William Vincent married Eliza Bray, who was born in Cornwall, England, and at the age of ten years, in 1836, came with her parents to America. The Bray family settled near Cuba City, Wisconsin.

Milton Vincent was born near Galena, December 20, 1857, and was educated at Galena, attending high school there and subsequently took a business college course at Dixon, Illinois. After leaving school he engaged in farming, and farming was his occupation to the age of thirty. On leaving the farm he removed to Galena and engaged in the implement business until December 1, 1902. At that time he was appointed deputy in the sheriff's office at Galena, serving four years. In 1906 he opened a wagon repair shop, and gave it his personal management for eight years. In October, 1914, he was appointed deputy county clerk, serving fourteen months. On November 4, 1916, he was elected sheriff of Jo Daviess County to fill the vacancy caused by the death of John Bardell. He served out the two years term. In December, 1918, he resumed his wagon repair business. Mr. Vincent in November, 1922, was again called to the responsibilities of the office of sheriff, being elected on the republican ticket, and his present term expires at the end of 1926. Mr. Vincent is a Methodist.

He married at Galena, March 27, 1889, Miss Martha Jane Beck, of Galena. She attended public schools at Benton, Wisconsin, and prior to her marriage was employed in a dry goods store at Galena. Her parents were Thomas and Margaret (Alton) Beck. Her father was a merchant at Benton, Wisconsin, and later in business at Galena, and finally moved out to Aspen, Colorado, where he died in 1916. Mrs. Vincent's mother died May 30, 1900. Sheriff and Mrs. Vincent had twelve children, two of whom died in infancy. All the others are living, Augusta, Fred, Eliza, Margaret, William, Thomas, J. C., Dorothy, Dale and Ruth. The daughter Augusta is the wife of Charles R. Kuster, who is superintendent of the Vinegar Hill Mining Company at Benton, Wisconsin, and they have a son, named Bill. Fred Vincent during the World war was in training camp at Newport News, and also at Camp Sevier, South Carolina, and is now caretaker of the Government Building at Galena. He married Nellie Herbsleb, of Galena, and has a son, Harold. Eliza Vincent is the wife of Mr. Show, in the restaurant business at Quantico, Virginia. Margaret Vincent is business manager of the Galena Gazette, the oldest newspaper in northwestern Illinois. William R. Vincent, who served with the supply company of the One Hundred Twenty-third Heavy Artillery in the Thirty-third Division during the World war over seas, is now a government mail carrier, and by his marriage with Anna Cromer, of Galena, had two children, William and Charles. Thomas Vincent, rate clerk in the Illinois Central freight office at Waterloo, Iowa, married Mildred O'Connor and has a daughter, Beverly. J. C. Vincent is bookkeeper in the First National Bank of Galena. Miss Dorothy assists her father in the sheriff's office. Dale is in the United States Marine Corps, now located at Paris Island, South Carolina. Miss Ruth, the youngest, is a member of the class of 1928 in the Galena High School.

JOHN W. WESTWICK. An industry that has been functioning for over seventy years is a noteworthy institution in any community. More than seventy years ago at Galena was established a foundry and machine shop, now known as John Westwick & Sons, Inc., a business in which three generations of the Westwick family have been represented as owners and managers.

The founder of the business was the late John Westwick, who was born, reared and educated in England and married Mary Emerson, who was born and reared at Manchester, England. They were living at Manchester when their son John W. Westwick, present owner of the Westwick Foundry, was born December 20, 1851. A few months later, in 1852, the family started for America and settled at Galena. There in 1854 the father established a machine shop, which has had a consecutive record of growth and prosperity through seventy-two years. John Westwick, the elder, continued active in the business until 1885, when he sold out to his son J. W. Westbrook. He was an active member of the Baptist Church and superintendent of the Sunday School at Galena for many years. He passed away in 1902. He and his wife had seven children, John W., Charles, Thomas, Eunice, Mayme, Emma and Sarah.

John W. Westwick received his first school advantages at Galena, and in 1869, at the age of eighteen, went to work in his father's shop. He has given fifty-seven years of service in that one line of business, and is still active in the management. He has been manager of the plant since 1885, and after his father's death became its owner. In 1921 the business was incorporated, a closed corporation, with Mr. Westwick as president. In earlier years the plant did a general machine shop and foundry business, but in later years has somewhat specialized, manufacturing the Westwick warm air furnace and a variety of house heating appliances, products that are shipped to all parts of the United States. Most of the output is sold to jobbers.

Mr. Westwick has rendered his best service in building up and maintaining this business. However, for one term he was mayor of Ga-

lena. He is a member of the B. P. O. Elks, the Illinois Manufacturers Association, American Foundryman's Association, belongs to the Galena Golf Club and for many years took an active part in the Baptist Church.

He married at Galena in September, 1885, Miss Sarah Belle Evans, who was reared in Galena, and after graduating from high school taught school for several years, until her marriage. Her parents, W. P. and Mary Ann (Thomas) Evans, came from Devonshire, England, and settled in Galena, where her father was a merchant tailor until his death in 1896. Mr. and Mrs. Westwick had six children: Mary, Bella, Anna, John W., Jr., Dorothy S. and Martha. The daughter Mary is a graduate of the Galena High School and is now assistant librarian of the Galena Public Library. Miss Bella graduated from high school and Northwestern University and is a teacher at Watseka, Illinois. Anna graduated from the Galena High School and is the wife of E. B. Herron, local editor of the Galena Gazette, and is the mother of a daughter, Elizabeth Ann. The son, John W. Westwick, Jr., after finishing his high school course went to work in his father's plant, learned the foundry business from the bottom up, and remained there until America entered the World war. He joined the colors, went into training with the Eighty-sixth or Blackhawk Division, spending some time at Evanston, Illinois, and later at Camp Grant, and finally went overseas to Bordeaux, France, where the period of training had not expired when the armistice was signed. After returning to America he resumed work in his father's business and is now plant superintendent. The daughter Dorothy after finishing high school spent a year in Northwestern University, and when the war broke out returned to Galena and took charge of the bookkeeping and accounting in her father's business and still performs this responsible duty in the family corporation. The youngest child, Martha, attended high school and the University of Chicago, where she graduated, and is now a teacher in the Junior High School at Savanna, Illinois.

WILLIAM R. MCKERNON through a period of forty years has practiced law at Shawneetown. His professional abilities and his personal character have brought him a position of unusual esteem in that community, particularly among those who appreciate the early struggles of his orphaned boyhood.

Mr. McKernon was born on a farm in Gallatin County, Illinois, May 27, 1856. The earlier generations of the McKernon family lived in County Cavan, Ireland. An older form of spelling the name was McKiernan. Reuben McKernon was born in Ireland and also two brothers, Peter and Charles. When they were young their parents came to America, settling in what is now West Virginia. From West Virginia Reuben, Peter and Charles McKernon came out to Illinois and all were pioneers of Gallatin County. Reuben McKernon spent the rest of his life as a farmer in that county. He married a Miss Addison.

Henry McKernon, a son of Reuben the pioneer, was born in Gallatin County in 1829. On November 28, 1852, he married Lydia Spivey, daughter of Thomas S. Spivey, another early settler of the county. They became the parents of four children: Maria, now deceased, who was the wife of John McIntyre; William R.; Mollie; and Charles Henry, deceased.

Henry McKernon died in 1865, when his son William R. was nine years old. The mother of the family passed away six years later, in 1871. At the father's death the mother and children were left with a home on a little farm. William R., the boy of nine years, with his older sister, Maria, had to assume most of the responsibilities of the work on the farm and the care of their younger brother and sister. Occasionally William R. McKernon worked for neighbors, who paid him in provisions. His sister emulated the example of some of the earlier pioneer women, even to the extent of weaving and making clothing for the family. Mr. McKernon pays a high tribute to the devotion and character of that sister. In his youth William R. McKernon became familiarly known as "Bud" McKernon, and a great many of his admiring friends still know him by that title. With all the duties he had at home he was able to attend district schools only six months. Most of his education came from study at night, usually assisted by his older sister. When he was twenty years of age he qualified for teaching, and for several years taught winter terms of school. He also managed to attend academies at Enfield and Ewing. Up to 1888 he spent part of each year teaching the Waltonborough schools. In the meantime he studied law under the direction of Judge E. D. Youngblood of Shawneetown. Mr. McKernon was admitted to the bar in 1887. The following year he was elected state's attorney of Gallatin County and was re-elected in 1892, holding that office eight years. He has also been master in chancery and has held other minor positions, though on the whole he has preferred the routine of his general law practice to politics. He has always been active in the democratic party.

Mr. McKernon's parents and ancestors were Catholics in religion. In early manhood he united with the Cumberland Presbyterian Church and has continued that allegiance. He is a member of the Masonic Order, Independent Order of Odd Fellows and Knights of Pythias. Mr. McKernon married, in 1892, Miss Margaret Smith, of Indianapolis, Indiana. She died in 1893. In 1901 he married Grace Phile, daughter of William D. Phile, a pioneer of Shawneetown, and cashier of the First National Bank of that city for fifty-two years. He was a native of Germany, who came to the United States at the age of sixteen. At that time he could not speak a word of English, but became a good speaker of English, and was all his life a student and became a well-informed man. His character was above reproach, and he was esteemed and respected by all who knew him. He came to this county a poor youth; and by close attention to his endeavors he achieved gratifying financial success. He was a conscientious Christian gentleman, and for years a member of the Presbyterian Church. Such were the characters of Mrs. McKernon's father and her mother, whose maiden name was Nannie Martin. She possessed sterling qualities of heart and mind, and was a Presbyterian in church faith.

CHRISTIAN X. HEILIGENSTEIN. An interesting example of how one man or one family can influence, initiate and direct most of the movements and commercial undertakings that are fundamental in the life and prosperity of an entire community is provided in the career of Mr. Christian X. Heiligenstein, president of the Freeburg Milling Company and the outstanding man of affairs in the town of Freeburg, St. Clair County.

He was born at Freeburg August 8, 1861. His parents were natives of the border country between France and Germany. They were Xavier and Anna Marie Heiligenstein, the former, coming to America in 1853, and the latter in about 1855 with her sister. Xavier Heiligenstein married in St. Clair County, Illinois, was a farmer there, and died in April, 1861. His widow survived him until March 6, 1894. Their other children were: Frank X., Marie, Lena and Catherine.

Christian X. Heiligenstein attended the public schools at Freeburg, and then served a three years' apprenticeship, and for three years was a journeyman carpenter. He also learned the milling business with a local plant at Freeburg. For eighteen years Mr. Heiligenstein was in business as a soft drink manufacturer. He and his brother Frank in 1906 organized the Freeburg Milling Company, starting with a small plant and building up one of the largest flouring mills in the southern part of the state. His plant has a capacity now of three hundred and fifty barrels per day. Mr. Christian X. Heiligenstein is president of the company and his son is manager of the mill.

During the past forty years Mr. Heiligenstein has appeared again and again as the leading factor in the affairs of his locality. He has held a great many offices, including village and township tax collector, postmaster, president of the Board of Education for eighteen years, and he organized and is president of the Home Insurance Company of Freeburg, a notable example of economic efficiency in providing insurance against fire, its rates being based on actual cost. The president draws no salary. He also organized, in 1886, the Standard Coal Mining Company, and opened up some coal properties in the vicinity of Freeburg. He established a dairy, and started a lumber yard so that the people living in and around Freeburg might get lumber at reasonable prices. He was also founder and for many years President of a local singing society.

Mr. Heiligenstein married Miss Emma Heitzman, daughter of Engelberth and Maggine Heitzman. The oldest of their children is Xavier H., manager of his father's mill, who married Anna B. Hall and has three children: Evelyn, Christian Carl and Clinton. The son, Dr. R. C., married Edna Sefert and their one child is deceased. Martha M. married A. F. Klein, and their three children are: Isabelle, Wilson and Norman. The son Walter C. married Eina Burdo and has a daughter, Euphraine Emma. Christian, Jr., is a member of the class of 1925 in the University of Illinois, specializing in the banking and commerce course. Emma L. married Jacob Heid, and they have a silver fox farm in St. Clair County.

Mr. Heiligenstein is a thirty-second degree Mason and Shriner. His nephew, Frank X. Heiligenstein, now actively interested in the milling business, was born at Freeburg, September 3, 1884, son of Frank and Mary Heiligenstein. Frank X. was educated in the public schools of Freeburg, the State Normal at Normal, where he graduated in 1902, and for three years was a teacher. In 1906 he entered the milling business with his uncle and father.

He married, November 24, 1909, Miss Ida Sintzel, daughter of John and Mary Sintzel, and one of their seven children. Her father was a cigar manufacturer, and well known in Freeburg as the township and village clerk. Mr. and Mrs. Frank X. Heiligenstein have six children: Marie, Frank, John, Joseph, Gertrude and Madeline. Mr. Heiligenstein was active in Red Cross work during the World war, and was a member of the Exemption Board. He was president of the Red Cross Society for years.

EDWARD GRIMM is editor and owner of the Galena Gazette, the oldest newspaper in Illinois. Practically all his active working career has been identified with that newspaper plant at Galena. He served his apprenticeship there and has a thorough knowledge of all phases of the printing industry as well as a long and successful experience in business management of the newspaper.

Mr. Grimm was born at Galena, June 9, 1862. His parents, John F. and Henrietta (Goetze) Grimm, were born and reared in Germany. They came to America about 1850 and settled at Galena, where the father followed the trade of wagon maker the rest of his life. He died in 1876 and his wife, in 1906.

Edward Grimm acquired his education in the grammar and high schools of Galena. He was about thirteen years old when his father died in 1876, and in that year he began his association with the Galena Gazette as "printer's devil." In 1881, at the age of nineteen, he was promoted to pressman. In 1885 was made foreman of the Gazette office, and served in that capacity without interruption until 1906. Mr. Grimm in 1906 was appointed postmaster of Galena and filled that office for over two terms, nearly nine years. In 1916 he bought the plant of the Galena Gazette, and has since directed it as owner and editor. The Gazette from the beginning has been republican in policy, and under Mr. Grimm's control it has entered fearlessly into every fight for the best interests of the people.

Mr. Grimm is a past high priest of Jo Daviess Chapter, Royal Arch Masons, a past thrice illustrious master of Ely S. Parker Council, Royal and Select Masters, past commander of Galena Commandery of Knights Templar. He is a member of the Kiwanis Club and a Presbyterian.

He married at Galena, June 14, 1883, Miss

Catherine Ryan, who was educated in the grammar and high schools of Galena. Her parents, Thomas and Catherine Ryan, were born and reared in Ireland. Her father was a shoemaker by trade and for many years followed that occupation at Galena, where he died about 1905. Mr. and Mrs. Grimm are the parents of nine children, John Henry, James Edward, William F., Heiko B., Henrietta, Harriett J., Bertha L., Harry L. and Raymond. All received the advantages of the grammar and high schools of Galena. John Henry Grimm, the oldest, is now secretary of the Galena Gazette. By his marriage with Gertrude Hartzell, of Galena, he has one daughter, Alice Janette. James Edward Grimm, the second son, a farmer near Wascott, Wisconsin, married Elsie Goggin, of Emmettsburg, Iowa, and has a daughter, Marie. William F. Grimm a traveling salesman for the Barrett Wholesale Grocery Company of Galena, married Antoinette Eulberg, of Galena, and they have three children, named Stanley, Roland and Marion. Heiko B. Grimm, now a linotype operator in the office of the Galena Gazette, enlisted in Company K of the Three Hundred and Forty-second Illinois Regiment, Eighty-sixth Division, was sent for training to Camp Grant at Rockford, became a sergeant, and went overseas to France, continuing his training at Bordeaux and elsewhere, and on November 11, 1918, was on his way to the front when the armistice was signed. He was honorably discharged in 1919. The daughter Henrietta is the wife of Jacob Mueller, accountant for the Mineral Point Zinc Company of Galena, and they have three children, named Catherine, Edward and Robert. Harriett Grimm lives at home and is circulation manager of the Galena Gazette. Bertha L. is the wife of Harold C. Wiley, a farmer living at Warren, Illinois, and they have one child, Harriett Dale. Harry L. Grimm is pressman for the Galena Gazette. Raymond, the youngest of the family, is at home and working for the Mineral Point Zinc Company.

BERTIS BEE BEMIS is president of the Bemis Motor Company, Ford cars and accessories at Oregon. He was for many years a practicing dentist, and he is one of the well known members of a family which has long been prominent in this section of northern Illinois.

The Bemis family of America traces its ancestry from John Bemis, who was born at Dedham in Essex County, England, in 1550. He was the father of Joseph Bemis, Sr., and the grandfather of Joseph Bemis, Jr., who was born in England in 1619, and coming to America, settled at Watertown, Massachusetts, in 1640, when he was about twenty-one years of age. Watertown was the fifth place of settlement in Massachusetts, the four earlier towns having been Plymouth, Salem, Charlestown and Dorchester. Watertown at that time was one of the most important places in the Massachusetts Bay Colony. Many of the descendants of this early Colonial settler have been men of unusual distinction not only in Massachusetts but elsewhere. Some of them were Joseph Bemis, a soldier in King Philip's Indian war, Josuah Bemis, a soldier of the Revolution; Rev. Stephen Bemis, who was pastor of a church at Harvard for twelve years; Stephen Chapin Bemis, long prominent in western Massachusetts, who served as tax collector, member of the Legislature, and prominent leader in the democratic party, frequently nominated by that party for Congress and lieutenant governor, and mayor of Springfield in 1861-62.

Stephen Bemis was born and reared at Fitchburg, Massachusetts, married Mary Stewart, and in 1836 came to Illinois and bought a large tract of land near Oregon, adjoining what is now the Frank O. Lowden farm. Most of the Bemis landed interests are still owned by members in the family. The Bemis brothers, Judson M. and Stephen A., the founders of the Bemis Brothers Bag Company of St. Louis and other larger cities, are closely related to the Bemis family of Ogle County.

Henry H. Bemis, son of Stephen and Mary (Stewart) Bemis, was born in Nashua Township, near Oregon, was a farmer and later a painter and decorator at Oregon. Early in the Civil war he enlisted in Company E of the Forty-eighth Illinois Infantry and served in many campaigns, including Fort Donelson, Fort Henry, Shiloh, Vicksburg, Mobile, Athens, Corinth and elsewhere. He was discharged with the rank of corporal of Company E. He was for many years a member of the school board in Nashua Township, and died about 1914. He married Lucy A. Reed, and one of their children was Bertis Bee Bemis, who was born at Oregon.

Bertis Bee Bemis attended the grammar and high schools of Oregon and at the age of sixteen founded the Ogle County Local, a weekly paper, which he sold about 1889 to Seibert & Mason and which is now the Ogle County Republican. In 1890 Mr. Bemis became an employe of the Bemis Brothers Bag Company at St. Louis, remaining with that firm several years. During 1893, while the World's Fair was in progress at Chicago, he was employed by the committee on ceremonies. Following that he was in the employ of the Butler Paper Company of Chicago, and while thus employed studied dentistry, graduating from the Chicago College of Dental Surgery in 1897. Doctor Bemis practiced dentistry at Oregon for twenty-two years. During that time he was elected and served two terms as city treasurer. In 1919 he organized the Bemis Motor Company, handling the Ford agencies in Oregon and Byron. He has made this one of the largest establishments of its kind in northern Illinois, with a handsome building for sales and display rooms. He has built up an organization so complete in all departments and functioning so smoothly that Mr. Bemis spends part of each year in Florida, where he owns valuable property at Miami.

Mr. Bemis is affiliated with the Masonic Order, B. P. O. Elks and Modern Woodmen of America, belongs to the Eastern Star, is a member of the Presbyterian Church and in politics is an independent voter.

He married at Oregon, June 16, 1896, Miss Hattie E. Peck, who finished her education in the Oregon High School. Her parents were born and reared in Massachusetts and were early settlers at Oregon, where her father was in the mercantile business until his death.

HERSCHELL V. LYNN, superintendent and principal of city schools at Byron, has given most of his active career to educational work, though he has also had a rather extended business experience. His work has brought him great esteem in his section of Ogle County, where he has lived a number of years.

He was born at Salesville, Ohio, January 19, 1874. His grandparents were Francis and Nancy (Little) Lynn, his grandfather a native of Pennsylvania, who settled at Salesville, Ohio, about 1825. The Lynn family came originally from Ireland. Daniel Lynn, father of Herschell V., was born and reared at Salesville, Ohio, was a farmer and stock raiser and was widely known as a breeder of fine horses. During the Civil war he was employed as a horse buyer for the government. He died at Salesville in 1915. His wife, Sarah Jane Miller, was born and reared at Salesville, near Leatherwood Church, was educated in public schools and for a number of years taught school in Guernsey County, Ohio. She was a daughter of George Miller, an Ohio pioneer who married a Miss Law, of another early family of that state. One of their sons Abraham Miller served as a Union soldier and died a few years after the war from disabilities incurred during his service.

Herschell V. Lynn grew up in Ohio, attended public schools, graduated from the schools of Quaker City, and continued his higher education in the DeKalb State Normal School of Illinois, the University of Illinois and the University of Wisconsin. For two years he was employed as a locomotive fireman in Ohio. He spent a few months in Montana, and on returning to Ohio engaged in teaching, and for the third year was principal of the Salesville High School. In 1901 he came to Illinois and held a position with the Creston Tile Company three years. In 1905 he was made principal of the high school at Creston and served in that capacity until 1910. In that year he became principal of the high school at Forreston, and in 1912 removed to Byron as principal of the high school, and since 1921 has also been superintendent of city schools. Mr. Lynn is a high minded educator, and his aims and ideals are being written in the lives of the boys and girls of Byron, where he is loved and respected by all classes. He is a thirty-second degree Scottish Rite Mason, member of the Eastern Star, is a democrat and a Methodist, and for many years has been very active in church and Sunday School work.

He married at Quaker City, Ohio, January 30, 1897, Miss Bertha F. Gooden, of Salesville. She was educated in public schools in Ohio, and also attended school in Kansas. Her parents were George and Sarah (Ward) Gooden, of Cannonburg, Ohio. Her father was a soldier in the Union army, participating in many battles of the war. Mr. and Mrs. Lynn are the parents of two children: Miss Ardis L. and Helen, the latter a member of the junior class in the Byron High School. Ardis L. graduated from the Byron High School, from the University of Illinois in 1923, and for two years, 1923-24, was head of the English department at Herrin, Illinois, and is now teacher in the high school at Hollywood by the Sea in Florida.

Herschell V. Lynn after America entered the World war applied for enrollment in an officers training camp, but was rejected on account of age and lack of previous military training. He then applied for work with the Y. M. C. A. War Council and was assigned duty as an athletic director, being trained at Lake Geneva, Wisconsin, during May, 1918, spent one week in further training in Columbia University at New York, and went from there to Montreal, Canada, thence by transport to Liverpool, England, by rail to London, and after seven days in that city crossed the channel to LeHavre and thence to Paris. A week after his arrival he received his assignment and at his request was put in the motor transport squad, transporting supplies of the Y. M. C. A. in the fifth area. The headquarters were at Ippecourt, near Verdun, and he saw all the intensity of warfare close to the front lines in some of the busiest sectors in France. He was frequently exposed to shell fire. After the armistice he continued with the transport outfit, accompanying them to Coblenz, Germany, with the Army of Occupation, and remained there six months. He returned to New York City in July, 1919, and was honorably discharged from the New York headquarters of the Y. M. C. A. Mr. Lynn then returned to Byron, and resumed his duties as principal of the high school.

THOMAS SUTLER WILLIAMS, who has represented the Twenty-fourth Illinois District in Congress since 1915, is a resident of Louisville, Clay County, was born there, and has practiced law over thirty years.

His family has been one of note and distinction in this section of Illinois since pioneer times. His grandparents were William and Christina (Miller) Williams. William Williams was born in Durham County, North Carolina, and was of Welsh ancestry, descended from one of seven brothers who came to America in Colonial times. William Williams and two of his brothers, Jesse and James, moved from North Carolina to Indiana, and a year later, in 1831, settled in Clay County, Illinois. William Williams taught the first school in the northern part of that county. He was born in 1816 and died in 1857. He and his wife had a family of two sons and four daughters.

One of the sons was William Williams, Jr., who was born on a farm in Clay County in 1844 and lived in that one locality all his life, passing away in 1919. He was a youthful soldier of the Union army, joining Company B of the Forty-eighth Illinois Infantry soon after the outbreak of the war in 1861 and serving faithfully four and a half years, until the end of the war in 1865. His brother, Thomas Gilbert Williams, was with him as a soldier, and ties of unusual affection linked their lives. They lived on adjoining farms until death. William Williams, Jr., was a republican in politics and an active member of the Church of the Disciples. He married Nancy Freeman, who was born in Clay County, daughter of Anderson Freeman, a native of Indiana, who settled in Clay County in early times. Mrs. Nancy Williams died in 1916.

Thomas Sutler Williams, one of six children born unto William and Nancy Williams, was born on a farm in Blair Township of Clay County, February 14, 1872. The farm was his environment during his youth, and after the rural schools he attended high school at Louisville, continued his higher education in Austin College at Effingham and for five years performed the duties of a teacher, three years in country districts and two years at Edgewood. While teaching he studied law at Louisville under Judge B. D. Monroe and in 1892 was admitted to the bar and forthwith began a successful career as an attorney. In 1918 Mr. Williams bought and became publisher of the Clay County Republican.

He has served as city attorney and mayor of his home town of Louisville. In 1898 he was elected a member of the Illinois Legislature, serving one term. He was elected state's attorney in 1908, and re-elected in 1912, serving seven years. In November, 1914, he was elected to represent the Twenty-fourth Illinois District in Congress and has been one of the valuable members of the Illinois delegation in Washington for over ten years. He was in Congress throughout the World war period. During his first term he gave active consideration to and voted for the Federal Aid for road building and regards this as one of the most important episodes of his life. He was also a member of the committee on pensions which reported an important pension law. He is now a member of the committee on agriculture and for six years has given much thought and study to agricultural problems. He is also a member of the house committee on rules. Mr. Williams is a thirty-second degree Scottish Rite Mason and Shriner, member of the Independent Order of Odd Fellows, Knights of Pythias, B. P. O. Elks, and the Christian Church.

He married, June 9, 1897, at Charleston, Illinois, Miss Mabel Simpson, a native of Coles County. They have three children, Harold S., Ruth and Alice. The son Harold was in service during the World war and is now a practicing attorney.

THOMAS WASHINGTON HALL is one of the veteran bankers of southern Illinois. For over thirty years he has been active in banking at Carmi, where he is president of the First National Bank.

Mr. Hall was born on a farm in Johnson County, Illinois, November 28, 1855, son of Wiley Washington and Sarah Ann (Wise) Hall. Wiley W. Hall was born near Newport in east Tennessee, came to Illinois when a young man, and in this state met and married Sarah Ann Wise, a native of Johnson County, and daughter of William Wise, who came from North Carolina. Wiley W. Hall in 1861 removed from Johnson to Williamson County, Illinois, later to Saline County, and after two years moved to Jefferson County, where his wife died. He finally went out to Missouri and died at Liberal, that state. He was a blacksmith and wagon-maker by trade, and also a licensed physician and practiced medicine for some years. He was also a preacher in the Universalist Church, and to a limited extent farmed. During the Civil war he volunteered in the One Hundred and Twenty-eighth Illinois Infantry. Many of the recruits in the regiment, on account of their Southern sympathies, deserted, and W. W. Hall, second lieutenant, was appointed to induce these deserters to return under a promise of leniency. After the performance of this duty he resigned his commission. Wiley W. Hall and wife reared five children: Martha, Thomas W., William R., John J. and Marion M.

Thomas Washington Hall grew up on a farm. He attended country schools to the age of fourteen. When he was seventeen his mother died, and he began making his own way in the world. Three years later he had continued his education to a point where he had been granted a teacher's license, and through six winter terms following he taught school. In the years of his teaching he attended Ewing College and the Southern Illinois Normal College. During his last year in the school room he was assistant principal of the schools at Harrisburg. He was elected principal of that school for the succeeding year, but resigned to enter the Saline County Bank at Harrisburg. That was the beginning of his banking experience. He went to work for the Saline County Bank in 1887, and was subsequently with the First National Bank, which became the successor of the former bank. He resigned his position as cashier in 1893, and assisted in organizing the Carmi State Bank, which started business June 30, 1893. Mr. Hall was the first cashier. On January 1, 1894, the Carmi State Bank was reorganized as the First National Bank, Mr. Hall continuing as cashier of the new institution. On January 9, 1907, he was elected president of this bank, in active charge of which he has been since the organization of this prosperous institution. The attractive bank home was erected in 1921. Mr. Hall is a charter member of the Illinois State Bankers' Association, serving as a member of the committee on constitution and by-laws, and subsequently became one of the vice presidents of the association.

As a citizen of Carmi he has been the exemplification of public spirit and substantial generosity in promoting every matter worth while in the community. He served three terms in the City Council, and in 1919 was elected mayor, giving a splendid administration of municipal affairs. While in Saline County he served four years as deputy sheriff. Mr. Hall has always been an ardent democrat. In Masonry he is a past master of the lodges at Harrisburg and also at Carmi. Mr. Hall married, in 1881, Miss Delia Rabourn, a native of Saline County.

FRANCIS STUYVESANT PEABODY, who entered the retail coal trade in 1884, was for many years before his death one of the foremost coal operators of the middle west, founder and head of the Peabody Coal Company.

He was born in Chicago, July 24, 1859, son of Francis Bolles and Harriet Cutter (Ten Broeck) Peabody. In the paternal line he is a descendant of Francis Peabody, who came from St. Albans in Hertfordshire, England, in 1635, and settled at Ipswich, Massachusetts. Francis Bolles Peabody, who was born October 27, 1827, and died January 2, 1908, was a Chicago banker. F. S. Peabody's mother was a daughter of Rev. Petrus Stuyvesant Ten Broeck and was a direct descendant of Petrus Stuyvesant, the last Dutch governor of New York.

Francis Stuyvesant Peabody attended the Exeter Preparatory School and later the Sheffield Scientific School of Yale University, from which he graduated in 1881. In 1884 he began his business career as a retail coal merchant, but his attention was soon attracted to the operating and production side of the coal industry and he founded the Peabody Coal Company, which under his direction became one of the largest operating companies in the coal fields of Illinois and other sections of the Middle West. He was for many years president of the company and at the time of his death was chairman of its Board of Directors. He was also president of the Federal Coal Company and was chairman of the board of the Sheridan, Wyoming, Coal Company. He had many other business and financial connections.

During the World war he was made chairman of the coal production committee of the Council of National Defense and assistant to the director of the Bureau of Mines in charge of explosives. In 1920 he was decorated by the King of Italy as Knight Commander of the Crown of Italy.

Mr. Peabody died August 27, 1922. His capacity for enjoying life was not measured by his business achievements alone. He was deeply read in literature, and had many associations with literary men and organizations, being a member of the Stevenson Society, the Bibliophile Society, the Grolier Club and the Caxton Club, and he owns a notable collection of the works of Robert Louis Stevenson. He was a member of the Western Society of Engineers, the Chicago Club, Chicago Athletic Association, South Shore Club, the Links Club and Racquet-Tennis Club of New York, and the Chevy Chase Club and Metropolitan Club of Washington. He also delighted in outdoor occupation, his favorite sports being horseback riding and golf. His home was at Hinsdale, Illinois. Mr. Peabody was a democrat in politics and a member of the Episcopal Church.

He married, November 23, 1887, Miss May Henderson, of Utica, New York, and after her death he married, February 12, 1909, Mary Gertrude Sullivan. Mr. Peabody was survived by two children, Stuyvesant Peabody and Mrs. C. G. Osborne.

DONOVAN D. MCCARTY, county judge of Richland County, was admitted to the bar before he joined the colors, and after thirteen months of service in the World war he returned to Olney and engaged in a law practice which has brought him success and distinction.

He was born at Olney April 1, 1896, only son and child of C. C. and Martha V. (Davis) McCarty. His grandparents were Lafayette and Elizabeth (Sharer) McCarty, the former a native of Dayton, Ohio, and the latter of Harper's Ferry, Virginia, both of Irish ancestry. They settled in Edgar County, Illinois, and from that county Lafayette McCarty went into the Union army, serving as a commissioned officer in an Illinois regiment. Shortly after the war he removed to Colorado, where he was stricken with the fever and died. C. C. McCarty was born and reared in Edgar County, Illinois, and has been a resident of Olney for over thirty-three years. Throughout practically all that time he has been in the Railway Postal Service as a clerk. His wife, Martha V. Davis, was born in Richland County, daughter of George P. and Margaret (Maxwell) Davis, of Scotch-Irish lineage. Her father was born in Maryville, Tennessee, and her mother in Boone County, Indiana.

Donovan D. McCarty grew up at Olney, graduated from high school in 1914, and was studying law in Illinois Wesleyan University at Bloomington when America entered the war. On February 15, 1918, he was admitted to the bar, and on May 27th of the same year he enlisted, going for training to Camp Shelby, Mississippi. He was assigned to a machine gun company in the One Hundred Forty-ninth Infantry, and in September, 1918, he was sent overseas. In France he was transferred to Company D of the One Hundred Forty-fourth Infantry and was in training until after the armistice. In May, 1919, he returned to the United States and on June 13th was honorably discharged at Camp Grant at Rockford.

He then engaged in practice at Olney, and in 1922 was nominated on the republican ticket and elected county judge. In 1926 he was renominated for a second term. Judge McCarty is a member of the Masonic Order, is secretary of the Olney Lodge of B. P. O. Elks, is a member of the Richland County Bar Association, the Presbyterian Church, and in 1920 was commander of Olney Post No. 30 of the American Legion.

He married, May 7, 1924, Miss Janet E. Murray. She is a daughter of Ben S. and Grace (Van Cleve) Murray, of Olney.

E. G. ANNELL. It has been the privilege of E. G. Annell, president of the Oatman Condensed Milk Company of Dundee, to realize many of his worthy ambitions, and through the exercise of good business judgment and sagacity to wrest from his opportunities financial and general success. From the time that he left college, as a youth of nineteen years, he has been connected with his present concern, having risen from an humble capacity to the chief executive post, this achievement being solely through merit and the possession of native talent, tact and foresight.

Mr. Annell is one of the native sons of Dundee who have won success in their home community, he having been born at this place October 24, 1884, a son of Charles and Hannah (Johnson) Annell. The family has been well and favorably known in this part of Illinois for a number of years, and many of the name have occupied important positions in the business, professional and political world. E. G. Annell acquired his early educational training in the public schools of Dundee, and was graduated from the Dundee High School as a member of the class of 1903. Following

this he enrolled as a student at the Colorado School of Mines, but after one year left that institution and returned to Dundee, where he immediately entered the employ of the Oatman Condensed Milk Company in a clerical capacity. As the years passed he was advanced from position to position until in 1918 he was elected president, a post which he has since retained. He has increased the business of this large industry greatly during his administration, making it one of Dundee's important enterprises. The product of this concern has won popularity because of its purity and high quality and finds a ready market all over Illinois and in the surrounding states. While Mr. Annell's chief activities have to do with the management of this business, he has various other interests and is a director of the Dundee State Bank. He is a thirty-second degree Mason, and a member of the Consistory, as well as a Noble of the Mystic Shrine. In politics he is a supporter of the principles and candidates of the republican party. A public-spirited citizen, no list backing a worthy or constructive movement is considered complete that does not include his name.

On October 30, 1920, Mr. Annell was united in marriage with Miss Lydia Sylvester, and they are the parents of one son: Charles Sylvester.

CHESTER E. COLLINS. Never before in the history of the country have the young men been advanced to such positions of responsibility as they are being today. It is possible that the experience the majority of them secured during the World war developed them to an unusual degree, or an awakening has come as to the advisibility of having new blood and a young outlook, combined with the enthusiasm which will wear away with added years, in concerns that are forging ahead in all lines of endeavor. However, be the reason what it may, the fact remains that a large percentage of the men in positions of authority the country over are those in the late twenties or early thirties. This is the case with Chester E. Collins, general manager of the Western Gas Company of Elgin, one of the live young business men of Elgin.

Chester E. Collins was born at Elkhart, Indiana, February 2, 1895, a son of John S. and Myrtle (Taylor) Collins, natives of Delaware and Michigan, respectively. The father located at Elgin in 1895, and for twenty years thereafter was engaged in a shoe business, but is now living retired. He and his wife had two children: Chester E. and Carlton S., the latter also a resident of Elgin.

Graduated from the Elgin High School in 1913, Chester E. Collins then took three years at Northwestern University, following that event went into the coal fields of Virginia, and for six months was in the employ of the Western United Gas Company. His plans were then interrupted by his military service, as he enlisted September 17, 1917, in the artillery branch of the service, and was commissioned a second lieutenant June 1, 1918, and a first lieutenant on August 1, 1918. His honorable discharge bears the date of September 30, 1919.

Returning to Elgin, Mr. Collins entered the employ of the Western Gas Company on October 1, 1919, as chief clerk, and so rapidly did he prove his value to his company that May 1, 1920, he was advanced to district manager, which position he still holds. He is a republican, but not active in politics. He belongs to the Masonic fraternity, the Benevolent and Protective Order of Elks and the American Legion. In religious faith he is an Episcopalian. A native son of Elgin, with practically his whole life spent in its midst, it is small wonder that his interests are centered here, or that he is enthusiastic about its advancement, or willing to exert himself to further develop its manifold advantages.

ALSON W. MODERT, M. D. A young physician and surgeon of exceptionally high qualifications and standing, Doctor Modert since 1918 has had his home and professional work at Mount Vernon in Jefferson County.

He has lived in southern Illinois since he was two years of age. At that time his parents, P. M. and L. E. Modert, moved to Jefferson County from Branch County, Michigan, where Alson W. Modert was born October 23, 1890. The grandfather, Peter Modert, was born in Luxemburg, Germany, and came to America at the age of twenty-one, living for a time in New York and then going to Michigan where he reared his family. He married a native of New York of French ancestry. The maternal grandfather of Doctor Modert was Frances Rider, who was born in New York State and was also a settler in Michigan. The mother of Doctor Modert died in 1912, and the father is now living retired, for many years having been a contractor and builder. All the children except Doctor Modert were born in Jefferson County, Orley having married Ruth Wescott and has three children, and the other child is Miss Violet.

Alson W. Modert graduated from high school at Mount Vernon in 1912, and finished his literary education in the School of Medicine of Loyola University at Chicago, graduating M. D. in 1916. For one year he had the additional training and experience of an internship in the Lving-In-Hospital of Chicago, and was connected with the Detroit City Hospital at Detroit until the fall of 1918. Returning to Mount Vernon, he engaged in general practice, where his work has been such as to gain for him a reputation second to none among the younger surgeons of the county. He specializes in surgery and maternity cases and is lecturer to nurses at the Thompson Hospital at Mount Vernon. He belongs to the County, Illinois State and American Medical Associations; is a Knights Templar Mason and Shriner, a member of the Independent Order of Odd Fellows and the Phi Delta fraternity of Loyola University. He and his family are Baptists, and he is president of the School Board of Education, Mount Vernon, Illinois.

Doctor Modert married at Broughton, Illinois, December 25, 1915, Miss Eleanor Davis, daughter of Thomas and Mary (Wiggins) Davis. Her father is a farmer and is active in local democratic politics. Mrs. Modert's brothers and sisters are: Sarah, Mildred,

Leonard, Mina, Mary, Lloyd and Nell. Doctor and Mrs. Modert have four children: Jean Maxmillian, Alson W., Jr., Maxine and Rosemary.

BENJAMIN L. SMITH is a native of Carroll County and for many years has been engaged in the real estate business at Mount Carroll. Through his business spirit and his good citizenship he has done much in a far-sighted way to influence the future development and prosperity of this section.

He was born at Milledgeville in Carroll County, August 31, 1865, son of David B. and Catherine (Teitge) Smith, his mother's people being among the first settlers in Carroll County. David B. Smith was born and reared at York, Pennsylvania, attended public schools and learned the shoemaker's trade. Coming to Illinois, he settled in Milledgeville, where he followed his trade until the outbreak of the Civil war. He then joined as a private Company H of the Fifty-fifth Regular Illinois Veterans Volunteers and saw active service until wounded and incapacitated for further duty at the battle of Shiloh. He was honorably discharged and invalided home. After the war he engaged in farming, owning a farm near Mount Carroll. From the farm he came to the county seat after his election as circuit clerk and recorder, which he held for twelve years. After retiring from office he engaged in the real estate and abstract business until his death on December 5, 1889. He was one of the best known among the old time citizens of the county, was a man of probity and honor and fully earned the respect and esteem paid him. His wife, Catherine Teitge, was born and reared near Milledgeville, and she died in 1872.

Benjamin L. Smith received his public school education at Mount Carroll. After leaving high school he clerked for a time, spent two years in the service of the American Express Company, and for about seven years was in the abstract business. Since 1901 he has concentrated his attention upon a general real estate service, handling both town and country property.

Mr. Smith owns one of the most beautiful natural parks in Northern Illinois, known locally as Smith's Park. It is located two miles west of Mount Carroll, and comprises eighty-six acres of land. The principal feature of the park is Carroll Creek, also known by its Indian name of Wakarusa Creek, which in the course of ages has worn away the rocks and soil, converting it into many wonderful forms. Some of the features of this park resemble some of the scenic attractions of American parks which are annually visited by thousands, including a canyon, palisades, springs and many unique and grotesque forms of rock. With the development of hard surfaced highways in Northern Illinois this is destined to become one of the most popular places of scenic beauty in the state.

Mr. Smith is a member of the Masonic order and is a republican in politics. He married at Rushville, Illinois, May 1, 1903, Miss Anna Martin, of Rushville. She died May 15, 1904. On September 25, 1916, he married Miss Edith J. Buckwalter, of Mount Carroll. Mrs. Smith was educated in public schools, graduating from the Mount Carroll High School. She is a daughter of Rev. John L. and Clara (Gordon) Buckwalter. Rev. John L. Buckwalter was reared and educated at Mount Carroll, attended Mount Morris College, and for many years has been prominent in the ministry of the United Brethren Church, being now pastor of the church at Mount Carroll. Mr. and Mrs. Smith have two children, Gordon Benjamin and Wilda Jane.

RAY H. PETTY, M. D. A native of Mount Carroll, Doctor Petty after graduating in medicine practiced for some years in Henry County, but is now securely established in professional regard and business in his native town.

He was born at Mount Carroll February 18, 1888, and is a member of an old and well known family of this section of the state. His great-grandfather, Robert Petty, came to America from England. His grandfather, William Petty, settled at Mount Carroll about 1830, entering land from the Government. He was one of the first settlers in Carroll County and he engaged in farming in pioneer times, hauling his grain with wagons and ox teams to Chicago, later to Freeport, and finally to market at Galena. William Petty married Lydia Orcutt. Albert Petty, father of Doctor Petty, was born at Mount Carroll, was educated there and followed farming until 1925, since which date he has lived retired in Mount Carroll. He married Mary Humbert, who was born in Mount Carroll and was educated in public schools in Carroll County and in the Frances Shimer School. She taught for several years before her marriage, and she was a teacher at Milledgeville, Illinois, when the first train came through that town. Her father was Frederick Humbert, who was born and reared at Mount Carroll, son of one of the pioneer settlers of that locality. Frederick Humbert, who died about 1911, enlisted in Company C of the Ninety-second Illinois Infantry and was in active service all through the Civil war, being at Chickamauga, in many battles of the Georgia campaign and in the march to the sea. He and Otho Watson enlisted from the same town, were in the same company and were side by side in their marches and battles from the beginning to the end of the war.

Ray H. Petty was reared at Mount Carroll, graduated from the high school of that city in 1907, and for two years attended Knox College at Galesburg. He took his medical course in the University of Illinois, College of Medicine and Surgery at Chicago, graduating M. D. in 1913. Doctor Petty for twelve years was located at Hooppole in Henry County, and in 1925 returned to Mount Carroll, and has a large practice extending over the country in all directions around. He is a member of the County, State and American Medical Associations, and during the World war was a member of the Advisory Board.

Doctor Petty is a member of the Masonic fraternity and Eastern Star, is a republican and a Methodist.

He married at Chicago, June 10, 1913, Miss Mabel Poffenberger, of Mount Carroll. She grew up in Carroll County, was educated in high school there and was a clerk in the Mount Carroll post office prior to her marriage. Her parents were Daniel and Susan (Reeder) Poffenberger. Her father was born at Mount Carroll and her mother in Pennsylvania. Her father was in the general teaming business at Mount Carroll until his death. Of the six children born to Doctor and Mrs. Petty three are now living, Richard, Vivian and William, Richard and Vivian being students in the public schools at Mount Carroll.

WALTER R. WATSON, county clerk of Carroll County, has had many years of experience in the county business and is a man admirably qualified for his present post of responsibility.

Mr. Watson is a native of Carroll County and is a member of a pioneer family of this section of the state. He was born at Mount Carroll July 6, 1874, son of Frank and Nancy C. (Adair) Watson. His grandparents, Mathias and Sarah (Roulet) Watson, were born and reared in Pennsylvania, and after their marriage settled at Mount Carroll, Illinois, in 1838. They took up land from the Government, and they developed one of the early farms in this part of Western Illinois. Frank Watson, their son, was born and reared near Mount Carroll, attended public schools, and farming was his vocation through all his active years. He died in 1913. Two of his brothers, Daniel and Otho, were Union soldiers in the Civil war, members of the Ninety-second Illinois Infantry. They were in the battle of Shiloh, at Vicksburg and Chickamauga, in Sherman's Georgia campaign, and remained in the service until the war ended. After the war Otho engaged in farming near Mount Carroll, while Daniel became a railroad man for many years was in the service of the Lake Shore and Michigan Southern Railway Company. Nancy C. Adair, who became the wife of Frank Watson, was born and reared at Mount Carroll, having been educated in public schools there. She died in 1920. Her father, Hunter Adair, came from Maryland and settled at Mount Carroll in the early '40s. In 1870 he moved out to Red Oak, Iowa, and lived there until his death.

Walter R. Watson was educated in grammar and high schools in Carroll County. He was at school until 1892, and his first working experience was in the service of the Minneapolis & St. Louis Railroad Company. He was with that road for ten years. In 1902 he returned to Mount Carroll, and served as deputy circuit clerk for ten years. In 1912, on leaving that office, he became clerk in one of the mercantile establishments of Mount Carroll, and continued so until 1919, when he was made deputy county clerk. He has practically performed all the duties of county clerk since that time. In 1926 he was nominated and elected on the republican ticket to the office of county clerk.

Mr. Watson is a member of the Masonic Order and Eastern Star, the Knights of Pythias, and the D. O. K. K., belongs to the Sequoia Club and is a Baptist. He married at Clinton, Iowa, October 1, 1904, Miss Lutie K. Dresbach, of Mount Carroll. She was educated in the grammar and high schools of Mount Carroll and for a number of years was bookkeeper in one of Mount Carroll's mercantile establishments. She is a member of the Eastern Star and the Baptist Church. Her parents were Thomas E. and Susan (Sutton) Dresbach. Her father was born and reared at Mount Carroll and spent most of his life in the mercantile business there. He died July 4, 1901. Her mother was born and reared at Jacksonville, Illinois, finishing her education in the Woman's College there. She came to Mount Carroll after her marriage. Mr. and Mrs. Watson have two sons, Thomas Adair and Walter Jackson Watson, both of whom have been educated in the public schools of Mount Carroll, Thomas graduating from high school with the class of 1926, and Walter Jackson with the class of 1927.

JAMES C. WOODBURN is one of the oldest native sons of Ogle County, a member of a family that was planted in the community at Byron in pioneer times, and throughout has been identified with land, agriculture, business and public affairs. James C. Woodburn is an attorney, but is perhaps best known for his many years of successful connection with banking.

He was born at Byron, October 13, 1846, son of Allen and Mary A. (Whitney) Woodburn. His grandfather, John Woodburn, lived all his life as a farmer at Towanda, Pennsylvania. Allen Woodburn was born at Towanda, in 1809, and in 1836 came to Illinois, settling near Byron. He entered a homestead from the government four miles north of Byron, and from this original homestead he developed his landed interests until at one time he owned a thousand acres of the finest land in northern Illinois. He died in 1887. His wife, Mary A. Whitney, was born and reared in Wilkes Barre, Pennsylvania.

James C. Woodburn grew up on the home farm, attended public schools and Rockford High School, also Wheaton College for two years. In 1870 he completed his law course at the University of Michigan. He taught for one year in the public schools of Ogle County and in 1871 was admitted to the bar and began the practice of law in 1872. About the same time he organized the James C. Woodburn Bank, a private institution which was continued for many years under private management, until 1921, since which date it has been the Byron State Bank. Mr. Woodburn gave his attention to his law practice and his banking interests until 1887, when he sold his bank. The extensive farm owned by his father was divided between James C. Woodburn and his brother Fred and his sister, Mrs. Carrie Patrick, of Rockford. Mr. Woodburn still owns his share in this large estate and farm. For many years he was a director of the Rockford National Bank and has had many other interests to occupy his time and attention.

Mr. Woodburn was for twenty years secretary of the Masonic Lodge at Byron and is also a member of the Eastern Star. He is a republican and a member of the Congregational Church, and throughout his life has given generously of his efforts and means to the promotion of church work, serving as assistant superintendent of the Sunday School and as a member of various church committees.

Mr. Woodburn married at Byron, November 10, 1880, Miss Ada M. Patrick, of Byron, who was educated in the grammar and high schools of Byron and Oregon, and for several years before her marriage taught in Ogle County. She is a daughter of George T. and Martha J. (Bradstreet) Patrick. Her father was born and reared near Byron and was a well-to-do farmer and stock raiser. Mr. and Mrs. Woodburn became the parents of four children: Mary A., born in 1886; Roy M., who was born in 1890; James A., born in 1893; and Grace E., born in 1897.

Mary A. Woodburn graduated from the Byron High School in 1906, from the DeKalb State Normal in 1908, and for a number of years taught in Evanston, Maywood and Chicago Heights schools, and for several years has been principal of the Blaine School at Batavia, Illinois.

The son Roy M. Woodburn graduated from the Byron High School in 1908, attended Washington University at Seattle, Washington, two years, and for two years taught in a boys school at Faribault, Minnesota. Since 1912 he has been a resident of Chicago and connected with the Fidelity Trust & Savings Bank, of which he is assistant cashier. He married at Chicago in 1914 Miss Blanche Winterrood, of Des Moines, Iowa, and they have two children, James and Blanche.

James A. Woodburn, the second son, was educated in the Byron schools, attended the DeKalb State Normal and the Washington University at Seattle, Washington, and since 1915 has been with the Chicago Trust Company, of which he is assistant manager of the bond department. He married at Rockford in 1915, and he and his wife have one daughter, Bettie.

Grace E. Woodburn, the youngest child, attended the Byron High School, Wheaton College and Mount Carroll Seminary, and is now the wife of Ralph Winquist, of Rockford, where he is an employe of the American Express Company. They have one son, James C., now nine years old.

HON. GEORGE DANIEL CHAFEE. Of the men whose ability, industry and forethought have added to the character, wealth and good government of Shelby County, none are better known than Hon. George Daniel Chafee. Mr. Chafee is a lawyer not only by education and long practice, but by temperament and preference. He has been in active practice for approximately sixty years, the greater number at Shelbyville. Political tendencies and executive ability have added to his possibilities of professional compensation and have broadened his efforts into the channels of state representative and senator.

Senator Chafee was born July 2, 1839, at Pittsford, Rutland County, Vermont, and is a son of Benjamin and Miranda (Haven) Chafee and a grandson of Daniel Chafee and of Moses Haven. Senator Chafee's father died in 1840, and three years later his mother married William Spaulding and moved into the woods of Monroe County, Michigan, where Mr. Spaulding worked in a sawmill. On August 18, 1855, he lost his right arm in a threshing machine. George Daniel Chafee attended the district school at London, Monroe County, Michigan, for two terms, following which he received instruction at the State Normal School, Ypsilanti, Michigan, and in April, 1861, graduated with the second law class from the University of Michigan at Ann Arbor, Thomas M. Cooley being the local law professor. The securing of an education was no easy task for Senator Chafee. Funds in his household were at something more than a low ebb, and the means of advanced education were not at hand. This was an obstacle, but not one that could not be overcome, and the young aspirant taught school and went out on the highways and byways peddling "Yankee notions" in order that he secure funds. Any honorable employment that meant reimbursement found him a ready taker. Soon after locating at Shelbyville he kept books at nights and helped in the hotel of Col. Cyrus Hall, then captain of Company B, Fourteenth Volunteers, where he secured board at $2 per week, and slept on a cheap cot in his office. For three years he worked in the law office of Hon. S. W. Moulton for $300 a year, worked for the Union soldiers and widows to secure bounties and pensions, enrolled the county for the draft twice, and served as assistant assessor and collector for several years. He practiced law in justice courts, the county and circuit courts and had one important case in the United States Circuit Court at Springfield and several cases in the State Supreme Court.

In 1866 Senator Chafee formed a partnership with Hon. S. W. Moulton, and this connection continued for a period of thirty-five years, Hon. W. C. Headon being a member of the firm for many years, Hon. William H. Chew for fifteen years, and the firm later being Chafee, Chew & Baker, the other partner being J. J. Baker. He practiced with Hon. A. Thornton, once judge of the Supreme Court, the Hon. George R. Wenderling and the Hon. H. J. Hamlin, one time attorney-general. He has been local attorney for the Illinois Central Railway at Shelbyville from 1867 until the present, and has had charge of the business of that company in adjacent counties at times.

Originally Senator Chafee was an abolitionist, but joined the republican ranks, and is now a republican in a county which has a democratic majority of 1,500. In 1881 he became a member of the Lower House of the State Legislature, in which he nominated Gen. H. H. Thomas for speaker, and was chairman of the railroad and warehouse committee. In 1877 he was a Hayes elector when the President was given 185 votes. At times he was a candidate for Congress and county judge, meeting with defeat because of the strength of the democratic party in Shelby County and his congressional district, but in 1906 was elected to the State Senate. He served as chairman of two congressional conventions, and nominated Hon. William B. McKinley for Congress. Senator Chafee helped organize the Citizens Savings and Loan Association of Shelbyville, which is still a leading institution, and in 1873 assisted in the or-

ganization of the First National Bank of Shelbyville, another strong body, of which he is a charter and only surviving director. His fraternal affiliation is with the Elks, and his religious connection with the Presbyterian Church.

On May 14, 1868, at Shelbyville, Senator Chafee was united in marriage with Miss Nancy Marie "Rie" Smith, a daughter of Addison Smith, who located at Shelbyville in 1833. Addison Smith was a nephew of Sen. Dudley Chase of Vermont and of the noted Bishop Philander Chase. Her mother was Nancy Fitzgerald Hicks, of Kentucky, and one of her sisters was the wife of Col. Sheridan Reed of the Union army, who was killed at Chickamauga, and another the wife of Judge Anthony Thornton. Four children were born to Senator and Mrs. Chafee: Lucia L., who married Frank Vogel, of the Massachusetts Technical Institute; Dudley Chase, who married Spicie Belle South, of Frankfort, Kentucky; George Dexter, who married Letitia Mulholand, of Wisconsin; and Olive K., who married M. LeBosquet, of Chicago, president of the American School of Domestic Economy.

Mr. Chafee is primarily a counselor, having a keen mind, strong practical sense and ready insight into the most intricate legal complications. He is courteous and faithful to clients, retains a wholesome belief in the predominating goodness of human nature, and places dependence upon those professional and general principles which secure the greatest justice and the greatest happiness to the society of mankind.

ALFRED HANBY JONES. If, as has been asserted, individual happiness depends upon the number of contacts with life and its important interests, Alfred Hanby Jones, of Robinson, has been an exceedingly happy man as well as a very useful one to his community and state. For Mr. Jones has had contact with a great diversity of the world's important activities. He has been a farmer, business man, banker, public official, and for many years "a fighting republican," one of the most earnest and effective leaders in his party in the state. He is a lawyer by profession, and has always kept in touch with his law practice in spite of many calls to other duties. Since 1921 he has been superintendent of foods and dairies in the State Department of Agriculture.

Moses Jones, his first American ancestor, was a native of Wales and settled in Virginia. His son, Aaron Jones, was born in Virginia, in 1776, and after a period of residence in Pennsylvania moved to Ohio in 1802. In 1832, nearly a century ago, the Jones family came to Illinois and located in Crawford County. Aaron Jones married Mary Shepherd. Their son, John M. Jones, was born at Oxford, Ohio, December 25, 1815, and was a youth of about seventeen when he came to Illinois. In this state he married Elizabeth (or Betsie) Ford, a daughter of John and Hopie (Highsmith) Ford. Her mother was a daughter of Benjamin Highsmith. Benjamin Highsmith served as a soldier in the War of the Revolution, was a pioneer in Crawford County, and is one of the Revolutionary veterans buried in that county. John M. and Elizabeth (Ford) Jones after their marriage settled on a farm near Flat Rock. John M. Jones died in 1887 at the age of nearly seventy-two, and his wife passed away in 1885, aged sixty-seven. He was always a staunch republican in politics. He was reared a Methodist and his wife, a Baptist, and soon after their marriage they joined the United Brethren Church and remained in that faith, rearing their children in the same.

Alfred Hanby Jones, the son of John M. and Elizabeth (Ford) Jones, was born on the farm near Flat Rock in Crawford County, July 4, 1850. The first seventeen years of his life were spent on the farm. While there he attended country schools. Later he was a student in the United Brethren College at Westfield, Illinois, and the noted normal school and college at Lebanon, Ohio, where he obtained his Bachelor of Science degree in 1870. For about a year after leaving college he was in the West, and on his return to Robinson he began the study of law in the office of Callahan & Jones. On June 15, 1875, he was admitted to the bar, and in 1925 he celebrated his fiftieth anniversary as an Illinois attorney. He engaged in practice at Robinson and in 1876 was appointed to fill out an unexpired term as state's attorney. In 1886 he was elected on the republican ticket a member of the Lower House of the State Legislature, serving one term. In 1898 he was appointed president of the Board of Trustees of the Eastern Illinois State Normal School at Charleston, but resigned that office in 1899 to accept appointment as the first state food commissioner of Illinois. In that office he served fourteen years. It was Mr. Jones who gave efficiency to that position in the state government. In 1900 he was elected president of the Association of United States Food Officials. He became one of the five members of the association's commission to secure a national food law, and for five years he regularly attended sessions in Congress to promote that desirable object, which was finally adopted in the famous series of pure food legislation. Mr. Jones after resigning as Illinois food commissioner visited Europe and was abroad when the World war began. Returning home, after America entered the struggle he became chairman of the County Liberty Loan drives and served as county food administrator. In 1921 he was called to his present position as superintendent of foods and dairies in the Department of Agriculture.

Mr. Jones for forty-two years has served as chairman of the Crawford County Republican Committee and for eight years was a member of the state committee, and was twice selected as a delegate to the Republican National Convention, once that nominated President McKinley at St. Louis, and once that nominated President Harding at Chicago. He served three terms of two years each as a member of the State Central Committee of his Congressional District. He was the first president of the Robinson Chamber of Commerce. After oil was discovered in Crawford County, in 1905, he has taken an active part in advancing the interests of his city and county and has always been an active member of the republican party and assisted in promulgating its doctrines as expounded by its great leader Alexander Hamilton and Abraham Lincoln. He was one of the charter members of the First National Bank of Robinson, and has served since its organization as one of its directors and for a number of years was its president. Mr. Jones also served fifteen years as president of the School Board of Robinson. Mr. Jones served five years as president of the First National Bank of Robinson. He is owner of several farms, and through all the years of his life has kept in close touch with the agricultural interests of his county and state. While his success is measured in terms of several lines of business, he has always been loyal to the profession of his choice, the law. He is a Royal Arch Mason, member of the Independent Order of Odd Fellows, B. P. O. Elks and Moose, the Country Club and Chamber of Commerce, and has been affiliated with the Methodist Episcopal Church of Robinson, Illinois, for more than twenty years and has been a member of the Official Board of the church, serving as chairman of its building committee when the handsome new church was erected.

Mr. Jones on June 18, 1871, married Miss Ellen M. Thompson. She died three years later, leaving one son, Gustavus A. Jones, who is now assistant cashier of the First National Bank of Robinson. Mr. Jones on November 26, 1878, married Miss Catherine A. Beals. The only child of this marriage, a son, died in infancy.

ROBERT BLEDSOE WITCHER is one of the veteran attorneys of the bar of southern Illinois, having practiced at Olney forty-seven years. During that time he has discharged capably duties and responsibilities as a public official and as a public spirited citizen.

Judge Witcher, who came to Olney in 1877, was born on a plantation in Upshur County, Texas, April 15, 1855. His parents, Benjamin Wesley and Sarah (Bledsoe) Witcher, were born and reared in Virginia, were married in Georgia, and shortly before the birth of their son settled in Upshur County, Texas. Benjamin W. Witcher acquired a plantation of 1,280 acres in northeast Texas. In 1858, when Judge Witcher was three years old, his mother died, leaving beside him two daughters. The father married again, and he passed away when his son was seven years of age. Subsequently his widow married Dr. Frank Fisk. These were the step-parents of Robert B. Witcher, and he and his sisters grew up in their home, and owed and have given them the affection and respect due to them for the discharge of practically all the obligations of parenthood.

Robert Bledsoe Witcher first attended school in Texas. From that state the Fisk family moved to Indiana, where Doctor Fisk was born. From there another removal was made to Springfield, Missouri, where Robert B. Witcher and his sisters attended Drury College. Judge Witcher completed the scientific course in that well known institution and was graduated in 1876, at the age of twenty-one. While he was in college his step-father moved to Olney, Illinois, where the father of Doctor Fisk, also a physician, had recently died. Judge Witcher while in Springfield learned the printer's trade and on graduating from college spent a year working for a newspaper at St. Joseph, Missouri. Then, in 1877, he joined his step-parents at Olney. His step-father subsequently removed to Nashville, Tennessee, and became one of the leaders of his profession in that city, living there until his death. Judge Witcher's step-mother is now ninety years of age and resides in New York City.

On coming to Olney Mr. Witcher took up the study of law under James P. Robinson. He was admitted to the bar in 1879 and for a brief time practiced in partnership with Mr. Robinson, though the greater part of his forty-seven years as a member of the bar has been spent in practice alone. In 1884 he was elected on the democratic ticket to the office of state's attorney of Richland County and served the term of four years. In after years it was said that he showed as much ability in defending as he had in the prosecution of cases, and he was usually retained in nearly all the important criminal cases in Richland and adjoining counties. In 1914 he was elected county judge and was reelected in 1918, serving eight years. His term of county judge included the period of the World war, with many extraordinary duties imposed on all public officials, all of which he discharged with admirable patriotism.

Judge Witcher has always affiliated with the democratic party. He is a member of the Knights of Pythias, B. P. O. Elks and a charter member of the Modern Woodmen of America at Olney. Among the interests that may be classified as diversions he has been particularly fond of horses and has owned several standardbreds.

He married, September 15, 1886, at Olney, Miss Bertha Kitchell. Her father, Edward Kitchell, achieved the rank of colonel in the Union army during the Civil war and died soon after its close. Judge and Mrs. Witcher had five children: Alice, wife of Kenneth R. Elliott, a resident of Cromwell, Oklahoma; Edward K., a physician at Pawhuska, Oklahoma; Elizabeth, wife of Joseph C. Gordon, a resident of Mexia, Texas; Miss Harriet, at home; and Robert B., also a physician, now connected with the King's County Hospital at Brooklyn, New York. Both sons were with the colors during the World war, but did not get assignment to overseas duty.

NOAH M. TOHILL, whose people came to Southern Illinois in very early pioneer times, has been practicing law at Lawrenceville thirty years and is a member of one of the ablest and most successful law firms of that city, McGaughy, Tohill & McGaughy.

He was born on a farm in Crawford County, Illinois, December 10, 1864. The Irish spelling of this family name was originally O'Toole. Lawrence Tohill, a native of Ireland, was one of the pioneer settlers of Crawford County, Illinois. His son, John Tohill, was born in that county. John Tohill was the father of Lewis N. Tohill, was born in Crawford County and spent his active life there on a farm. With the outbreak of the Civil war he enlisted in the Ninety-eighth Illinois Infantry, which became part of General

Wilder's brigade, and was in the service through many battles and campaigns until the close of the war. In after years he was an active member of the Grand Army of the Republic. He was a man of industry, lived quietly and unostentiously, but was none the less a respected citizen. He and his wife were devout members of the United Brethren Church. Lewis N. Tohill died when nearly eighty years of age. His wife, who died in 1874, was Cynthia (Jones) Tohill, also a native of Crawford County. The Jones family came from Wales, first settling in Pennsylvania, and the grandfather of Cynthia Jones came from that state to Ohio, settling at Four Corners, and subsequently moved to Crawford County, Illinois. John M. Jones, father of Cynthia Jones, was ten years of age when brought to Illinois. He married Betsie Ford. Her mother's maiden name was Hopie Highsmith, daughter of Benjamin Highsmith. Benjamin Highsmith, a great-great-grandfather of Noah M. Tohill, was a soldier in the Revolutionary war. He spent his last years in Lawrence County, Illinois, and died here one of the Revolutionary veterans buried in that county.

Lewis N. Tohill and wife had six children, William L., Noah M., Ira H., Henry Grant, Mary Lillian and Martha Elizabeth, all of whom are living except Mary Lillian. Noah M. Tohill, like the other children, grew up on the farm, remaining there until nearly nineteen years of age. The country schools supplied his early advantages and subsequently he attended for one year a normal school at Bloomington, Illinois, and spent another year in the Normal College at Valparaiso, Indiana. Teaching district schools gave him the means to educate himself for the law. He read law in the office of Callahan, Jones & Lowe, able lawyers at Robinson, Illinois, and was admitted to the bar in 1895, in the month of February. In March he opened his law office at Lawrenceville, and in 1896 was nominated by the republicans and elected state's attorney of Lawrence County. He was state's attorney until 1900, but for the past quarter of a century has given his full time and energies to a growing general practice as a lawyer. However, he served several years as city attorney and one term as mayor. His administration as mayor is remembered as a very progressive one, marking the beginning of permanent street improvements.

Mr. Tohill is a member of the B. P. O. Elks and the Rotary Club, and for many years has been active in the Christian Church at Lawrenceville. He married, in 1888, Miss Rose Otey, of Robinson, Illinois. She died about a year later. In 1891 he married Miss Fannie Barnes, who died in 1893. She was survived by a daughter, Mona, who is now the wife of Fred DeTray, of Houghton Lake, Michigan. Mr. Tohill in 1899 married Miss Inez Hill.

HOWLAND JOSEPH HAMLIN for many years a resident of Shelbyville, achieved a reputation all over Central Illinois as a lawyer, philosophical thinker, in public service and as a leading citizen. In the history of the state his name is memorable as a state official with the individual ability and character to elevate a state office to one of vital importance to all the people of Illinois.

Howland Joseph Hamlin was born at Lawrence, St. Lawrence County, New York, July 13, 1850, and on both sides he was of New England Puritan stock, his paternal grandfather having been a captain in a company of Minute Men during the war of the Revolution. Many of the qualities so strongly evident in his private life and character, including generosity, loyalty, faith and fidelity to duty, might be ascribed to his ancestral inheritance. He was educated in local schools, for two years attended Lawrenceville Academy, taught a year, after which he completed his course in the academy. He was principal of a public school at Franklin, New York, and continued his education in the Normal University at Potsdam, New York, until the fall of 1870. He had first visited the West in 1868, and in the spring of 1871 he opened a select school at Windsor, Shelby County, Illinois. He introduced modern methods of teaching and manifested such magnetism and ability as a teacher that he was offered the position of superintendent of the Windsor public schools. He held this post three years and in the meantime became a law student in the office of Thornton & Wendling at Shelbyville. He utilized his leisure hours in law study, his reading being supplemented by quizzes from Judge Thornton. He was admitted to the bar by the Illinois Supreme Court at the June term of 1875. In August of the same year he opened an office at Sullivan, but after a short time returned to Shelbyville as senior member of the firm of Thornton, Wendling & Hamlin. A member of this firm was George R. Wendling. Thousands of people in Illinois and other states who never heard of George R. Wendling as a lawyer recall his wonderful eloquence as a platform lecturer, and he soon retired from law practice to give all his time to this profession. After that Mr. Hamlin and Judge Anthony Thornton were associated in practice. Judge Thornton was one of the distinguished lawyers and judges of Illinois, and his abilities brought him election to the Illinois Supreme Court. However, he voluntarily resigned from the bench because the duties of the office isolated him from the people and deprived him of the more pleasing activities of his profession.

Mr. Hamlin in a very short time achieved rank as an advocate. His commanding presence, sympathetic heart and keen intellect gave him the immediate attention, if not sympathy, of judge and jury. He was soon employed in many of the most exciting criminal and civil trials in Central Illinois, and as a trial lawyer soon had no superior. One of the early cases in which he was engaged was as one of the attorneys of the Big Four Railway Company in defending the suits brought by those injured at the Wann disaster. The general counsel of the railway company, John T. Dye, commenting on Mr. Hamlin's power and methods as an advocate in these cases, remarked that he had never witnessed such consummate skill of such complete mastery by counsel of court and jury. Mr. Hamlin became counsellor for some of the largest business interests of state and nation. The corporate properties of Central Illinois during the greater portion of his career, aside from railroads, were insignificant. His local corporate practice was consigned to the representation as local attorney of railways in his county, yet his reputation commanded some of the best railway and other corporate retainers that came to members of the profession in Central Illinois.

Mr. Hamlin was a republican in politics. Lincoln himself was not a more ardent advocate of "liberty under law" and that the Government should serve rather than master its citizens. He was a party leader whom the masses delighted to follow from the time he began to practice law until his death. For many years he served as a member of the Republican State Committee and more than once was a delegate to the party's national convention. In 1898 he was elected temporary chairman of the Republican State Convention. His keynote speech on that occasion was a masterpiece of political wisdom that became increasingly significant in subsequent years when the republican party was torn by factionalism and strife.

Mr. Hamlin in 1900 was nominated by the republicans as candidate for attorney-general and was elected, taking office in 1901. Prior to that time the office of attorney-general had been little more than that of ministerial clerk of the governor under various office departments of the state government, the actual duties having been performed by special attorneys who acted wholly independent of the attorney-general. Mr. Hamlin immediately announced that as attorney-general he was the chief law officer of the state, that no special attorney could be employed by any one without his sanction and approval, and that money could not be appropriated from the state treasury to pay the fees or salaries of such legal attorneys under the constitution and laws of the state. An opinion was given by him to the auditor of public accounts which resulted in the elimination of all special attorneys except the attorney for the insurance department, who held his office under the provisions of a special statute, which the attorney-general expressed his opinion as being unconstitutional, though he preferred to allow the decision of the question to be left to the court. This opinion is characteristic of the policy pursued by Mr. Hamlin during his entire administration. Through active personal industry, with an office force and appropriations less than one-fifth that allowed his successors, he performed the duties of the office with such distinguished ability that he commanded the approval, not only of his party and factional friends and associates, but of the lawyers and press of the entire state. A number of special achievements are credited to his administration. His vigorous measures brought into the state treasury several millions of dollars, party sums due from the national Government since the Civil war, also taxes withheld from the state, and payments held by insurance companies. He destroyed the system of paying salaries without appropriations for that purpose as required by the Constitution. He conducted the Chicago Sanitary District case, in which the State of Missouri questioned in the United States Supreme Court the right of Chicago and Illinois to discharge the waters of the sanitary district into the Mississippi River. During a coal famine in Chicago caused by congestion of loaded coal cars in the railway yards held at the request of the consignees, after a hasty investigation Mr. Hamlin went personally to Chicago, called in the presidents and general managers of the railroads, caused them to give preference to coal traffic and make immediate deliveries of coal from their yards to companies, so that within twenty-four hours after his arrival in the city the critical conditions were relieved.

No more honest, successful or universally approved administration of the office of attorney-general has been rendered during the history of Illinois. At the close of his term he was a prominent candidate for the nomination for governor. He was defeated by a combination of the state and federal political organizations, which under the convention system had the nomination of a candidate for governor completely within their control. However, his defeat caused no bitterness or regret to Mr. Hamlin. After leaving office he practiced at Springfield for a time, but the arduous duties of attorney-general and the excitement of a great political campaign were too great for a constitution that had been weakened by many years of arduous professional life. He soon withdrew to live peacefully with his family at Shelbyville until his death, which occurred December 12, 1909, at the comparatively early age of fifty-nine.

General Hamlin married Miss Mary Ella York, daughter of Dr. Eli York and niece of Dr. Jesse York of Windsor, Illinois. The five children born to their marriage were Howard Burton, Agnes York, Joseph Howland, Jack York and Mary Hal. General Hamlin was a model in the relationship of an affectionate husband and father, and was the intimate associate and companion of his wife and all his children. During the last years of his life, though not a helpless invalid, his health was so poor that he could not actively engage in any business or pursue his profession. That time was spent with his family and life-long friends at Shelbyville, esteemed and honored by all who knew him.

The players on the stage of life in competition fiercely struggle for a time; each then is succeeded by another in his turn and moves on to dark oblivion. Only those who bear a flaming torch are long remembered; and, measured by creation's time, their fame is but a fleeting thought. Yet measured by lives of men this honest, loving, faithful man gave much to those he knew and loved and left for them a heritage worthy of the life of any man. The things for which he stood and fought, to give to men of humble birth a better chance in life, the principles of justice, truth and right as ever held aloft, alone may always live.

HON. FITZ JOHN CAMPBELL, state's attorney of Jo Daviess County, and former county judge, has been one of the men of mark in northwestern Illinois for a number of years. He has come up from poverty and restricted

John Baptiste Fischer

circumstances through the exercise of a remarkable degree of persistency and energy, getting his education largely through private study and effort.

He was born at the Village of New Diggings, Lafayette County, Wisconsin, February 2, 1863, son of Thomas B. and Catherine (Gridel) Campbell, his father a native of Washington County, Pennsylvania, where he was born in 1830, and his mother was born at Cincinnati, Ohio, March 28, 1834. Both parents were probably of Scotch ancestry. Fitz John Campbell during the first twenty-two years of his life was a farm hand, and the horizon of his opportunities and experience was bounded by the farm. His only advantages up to the age of eleven were the district schools, and for several years after that he was able to attend school only during the winter season. Through the monotonous routine of farm work he made a breach into new opportunities by study at home until he had prepared himself for teaching. He taught in country districts off and on until 1892. Judge Campbell first came to Galena in 1889 as a student at the German English College. He finished his course there in 1890 and then continued in post-graduate study until he was awarded the Bachelor of Science degree in 1891. While teaching he studied law in the office of Judge William T. Hodson of Galena. He was admitted to the bar before the Appellate Court at Ottawa March 26, 1895.

Judge Campbell has had thirty years of active experience in his profession and public affairs. He practiced at Savanna until 1901, when he returned to Galena, forming a partnership with his former preceptor, Judge Hodson. They were associated in a general law practice until November 1, 1913. Judge Campbell has always taken a keen interest in politics. Soon after locating at Savanna he was nominated as a republican candidate for city attorney, being defeated by local issues. After becoming a resident of Jo Daviess County he was republican candidate for state's attorney, and on November 3, 1914, was elected judge of the County Court, taking his seat on December 7 of the same year. By reelection he served eight years, until 1922, and in all the business that came before his court he showed the qualities of an impartial judge and a careful business administrator. In 1924 he was elected state's attorney of Jo Daviess County, and in this position has again given evidence of his vigor, his integrity and fidelity to all the confidence expressed by the voters in his choice.

Several times Mr. Campbell has been called to Chicago to hold municipal court. Among his professional connections during his active law practice, he represented as attorney the Sales Mound Banking Company, the Chicago, Burlington & Quincy Railway, and Chicago, Milwaukee & St. Paul Railway, and also the Illinois Central Railroad. He has gained the reputation of being a citizen who can be relied upon for effective participation and aid in all movements for the general welfare. He is a past exalted ruler of the Lodge of Elks at Galena and a member of the Knights of Pythias, Modern Woodmen of America, Ancient Free and Accepted Masons and Independent Order of Odd Fellows.

Judge Campbell married, April 26, 1896, Miss Lizzie Oldenberg, daughter of John Oldenberg, of Galena. Judge and Mrs. Campbell were students together in college and graduated in the same class.

JOHN BAPTISTE FISCHER. In the development of architecture worthy of a city such as Chicago, John Baptiste Fischer, architect and engineer, has played an important role. This is remarkable in view of the fact that he has never enjoyed a technical training in any of the accredited institutions devoted to his specialties, his education having been virtually confined to the public schools of Chicago, yet his professional career includes a number of notable achievements and he enjoys high standing and reputation.

Mr. Fischer was born at Chicago, August 9, 1874, and is a son of John W. and Elizabeth (Lahr) Fischer, both residents of the city. His father was born in Bohemian Austria, and was an Austrian soldier in the war with Germany in 1866, soon after which he came to the United States and was married in this city. He was a pioneer in the meat packing industry in Chicago and was associated with Philip D. Armour, "Old Hutch" and other notables in the earlier years of that industry. He is now retired from active business life. Mrs. Fischer is a native of Poughkeepsie, New York.

Mr. Fischer after attending the grade and high schools took a course at the Art Institute and then interested himself in drafting and designing, for several years being head draftsman and chief designer for the famous architectural firm of Shipley, Rutan & Coolidge of Chicago. In this position he had charge of the designing and construction of several of the buildings of the University of Chicago, as well as the Borland Building, the Corn Exchange (now the National Bank of the Republic) Building and several others. After eight years of association with the above firm he joined the firm of Postle & Naylor, architects and engineers, and subsequently became a member of that firm under the style of Postle & Fischer. In 1924 he took over the business of this concern under his own name and has continued it individually, and with the success that comes from years of skilful and conscientious prosecution of his profession. In his work it has always been his first aim to combine the purely artistic with the practical or utilitarian, and plans and carries out the construction of his buildings with the idea of making them as nearly exactly appropriate to the business or industry for which they are designed as is possible.

Several years ago Mr. Fischer conceived and made tentative plans and drawings for a type of structure to be used for civic and municipal purposes, including that of a voting place for all elections. Under his plans one of these buildings would be placed in each voting section of the city, amid appropriate surroundings and would be large enough to be used as a place of public meeting. It would be embellished with inscriptions, sculptures, paintings, etc., to illustrate the progress and development of government and civilization in the United States, and one of its functions would be the holding of public meetings for instruction on the Constitution of the United States and its government, the responsibilities of citizenship, the duty to vote intelligently, and patriotic subjects of general nature. This idea Mr. Fischer would have carried out not alone at Chicago, but throughout the United States, making it a national institution for uplifting the ballot and giving to the country such laws and officials as truly represent the intelligent thought and deliberate choice of its citizens. It is a very high conception of democracy.

Mr. Fischer is a member of the Illinois Society of Architects and the Western Society of Engineers. He married Charlotte T. Olson, and they have a daughter, Helen Elizabeth. The family home is at 7322 Lafayette Street. Street.

EDGAR NELSON. To the modern generation of Chicagoans the Bush Conservatory of Music is as completely typical as any other institution representing the broad domain of art and culture, which conservatory of music has grown naturally out of the artistic impulses of the city, and perhaps for that reason it seems to have its roots in a more remote past than the actual date of its founding implies. The conservatory was founded practically at the beginning of the present century, in 1902. The founder was William Lincoln Bush, a widely known patron of music, who instituted it as a memorial to his father, William H. Bush. William L. Bush enlisted the services of Mr. Kenneth M. Bradley as director. Mr. Bradley was the director and president of the conservatory until the close of 1925. He was succeeded on January 1, 1926, by Mr. Edgar Nelson as president and director, who prior to that time had been vice president and associate director.

Mr. Nelson is a Chicago product. He was born on East Chicago Avenue, within three blocks of the present location of the Bush Conservatory. He attended the Ogden School in that community and grew up in an artistic atmosphere. His father was a director of church choirs and his mother a singer. One of his sisters is now a professional singer in New York, a younger sister is a teacher of music in Chicago public schools, and a brother is known in amateur musical circles.

Mr. Nelson finished his post-graduate studies at Bush Conservatory in 1908. He attained a creditable position in his art long before he took on the added responsibilities of executive management. He is a pianist, organist and conductor. He is conductor of the Swedish Choral Club of Chicago, and is also conductor of the Sunday Evening Club Chorus of Orchestra Hall. Practically all the eminent singers have paid high tribute to his genius as an accompanist. He is organist and director of the Oak Park Presbyterian Church, is a past president of the Illinois Music Teachers Association and the Chicago Artists Association, and has been one of the prominent members of the faculty of the Bush Conservatory. Mr. Nelson married Miss Harriet Schuettler. Her father was the late Herman Schuettler, who prior to his death had for seven years been chief of the Chicago police force and had given practically his entire life to that service, starting as a patrolman. Mrs. Nelson has long been interested in dramatic art. They have a son, Edgar Schuettler Nelson.

Mr. Nelson is a member of the B. P. O. Elks, the Lake Shore Athletic Club, the Swedish Club of Chicago and the Cliff Dwellers of Chicago. In 1920 he was decorated by the King of Sweden with the Order of Vasa. This was in the year that Mr. Nelson took his chorus through Scandinavia.

HARVEY DARLING MCCOLLUM has been for a quarter of a century a notable figure in the legal profession in Clay County, and in connection with the practice of law has looked after many other interests, including banking, farming and service in several public positions.

The McCollum family belongs to the Scotch Covenanter class, and came to America from the north of Ireland. From the eastern side of the Alleghanies they moved over into Kentucky. In Kentucky was born Alexander McCollum, great-grandfather of the Louisville attorney. Alexander McCollum in his death gained the immortality of history as being one of the seven men who fell in the battle of New Orleans, the concluding military event of the War of 1812. A son of Alexander McCollum, the soldier, was James C. McCollum, who was born near Lexington, Kentucky, in 1806, and in 1829 came from that state into Illinois, settling in Clay County, where he developed one of the first farms in the county. He lived the rest of his life in Hoosier Township.

James C. McCollum, Jr., father of Harvey D., was born on a farm in Clay County, August 9, 1844, and was in his eightieth year when he passed away January 5, 1924. James C. McCollum was a citizen of substantial prominence in Clay County. He was reared on a farm, but in early life became a merchant at Louisville and later assisted in organizing the Farmers & Merchants Bank, at first a private institution and later a state bank. He became vice president, and for several years before his death was president of that institution. James C. McCollum married, August 9, 1875, in Clay County, Mary F. Long, who is still living at Louisville at the age of seventy-two. Her father, Darling Long, was born in North Carolina and came to Illinois in 1853, first settling in Wayne County, Illinois, where his daughter Mary was born May 5, 1854, and subsequently moving to Clay County. James C. McCollum and wife became the parents of four children, three of whom died in infancy, Harvey Darling being the only survivor.

Harvey Darling McCollum was born at Louisville, March 13, 1879. He was reared and educated in his native town, and took both the literary and law courses at the University of Illinois, graduating with his law degree in 1901. He began practice with A. M. Rose, continuing until Mr. Rose was elevated to the Circuit Bench in 1906. When Judge Rose retired from the bench in 1915 the partnership was resumed and continued till the Judge's death in 1924. Mr. McCollum has had a large general practice, and has looked after the legal interests of a number of corporations, serving as local attorney for the Baltimore & Ohio and Illinois Central railroads. In September, 1926, he was appointed by the Board of Supervisors state's attorney to fill a vacancy occasioned by the resignation of the state's attorney. He has also been interested in farming. He served eight terms as master in chancery of the Clay County Circuit Court and was elected a member of the Legislature in 1908, serving in 1909-10. He was also democratic candidate for trustee of the University of Illinois in 1924.

Mr. McCollum is a member of the Masonic order, Independent Order of Odd Fellows and B. P. O. Elks. He married, in 1914, Miss Pearl Kagay, of Effingham. They have three children, Harvey Darling, Jr., James F. and Harriet.

LEO W. GOULD. After a broad experience in educational and commercial work, including public and general accounting, Mr. Gould several years ago bought out the Waukegan Business College, a school with a splendid reputation, founded in 1904, and as its proprietor he has maintained its record as an efficient school and has improved and adapted its facilities to the demands of modern commercial life.

The Waukegan Business College among other assets is fully accredited by the National Association of Accredited Commercial Schools, which is a primary test of unusually high standards of work and ideals. Under Mr. Gould the Waukegan Business College has the equipment and the teaching personnel which insure adequate opportunities and thorough and systematic training for every pupil who exercises normal diligence and application. The college offers four general courses of study, the complete business and accounting course, secretarial training course, bookkeeping course and shorthand course.

Mr. Gould was born at Nunica, Michigan in Ottawa County, March 12, 1891, son of George W. and Ellen (Wiseman) Gould. His ancestry on both sides date back in New England to the time of the Mayflower. One of his ancestors, James Wiseman, was a private soldier in the Revolutionary war. His grandparents were Lemuel and Ellen (Lilly) Gould, who lived on a farm near Hawley, Massachusetts, all their lives. George W. Gould was born at Hawley, Massachusetts, was educated in public schools and the Arms Academy, taught in his native state for several years and in 1888 moved to Michigan, locating at Nunica, where he engaged in the jewelry business. He is now a resident of Newaygo, Michigan, where he continues his business as a jeweler. For a number of years he has also been in the ministry of the Methodist Church, and at Newaygo he still fills pulpits in various charges. His wife, Ellen Wiseman, was born at Nunica, Michigan, attended school there and has always been very active in the Methodist Church. She is a daughter of George and Alethina (Lilly) Wiseman, and a granddaughter of James J. and Arville (Lawrence) Wiseman, who came from Genesee County, New York. James Wiseman was a carpenter and cabinet maker. In 1842 he came to Northern Illinois and settled at Little Fort, which some years later was changed to Waukegan. He followed his trade there. About 1850 he and one of his sons engaged in the hardware business, and continued it for many years. James Wiseman at the outbreak of the Civil war presided over the first meeting for recruiting volunteers held in Waukegan, at the Dickerson Hall, located on the second floor of the building where the Waukegan Business College is now located, on Washington Street. James Wiseman in 1866 moved to Nunica, Michigan, and continued his work as a carpenter, cabinet maker and builder until his death in 1888. His son, George Wiseman, was born in Genesee County, New York, and was five years of age when the family settled at Waukegan in 1842. He attended district and private schools in Waukegan, and while living in that city he became an employe of the Parmalee Transfer Company in Chicago. In 1866 he moved with his family to Nunica, Michigan, and there was associated with Sidney Lawrence in the lumber business, but afterwards retired to a farm and lived there until his death in 1908.

Leo W. Gould grew up at Nunica, Michigan, finished his high school course in 1907 and attended the Ottawa County Normal College, completing the work in 1909. In 1913 he was graduated from the Commercial Teachers Training School of the Ferris Institute of Big Rapids, Michigan. From 1913 to 1918 he was head of the commercial department in the high school of Granite City, Illinois. In 1918, he took his degree from the School of Commerce and Finance of St. Louis University. Mr. Gould in June, 1918, became connected with the accounting division of the Aviation Corps, and was located at St. Louis until September of that year, when he was discharged. After leaving the service Mr. Gould came to Waukegan, and was a commercial teacher in the Waukegan High School until June, 1920. He then established a public accounting office and had several years of successful experience in that line.

Mr. Gould in 1923 bought the Waukegan Business College, and has had active charge of the school since February of that year. The founder of the college in 1904 was the late B. A. Munson, a very capable educator, who gave his personal supervision to the management of the college until his death in 1922. After his death the school was continued by Mrs. Munson until she sold out to Mr. Gould.

Mr. Gould is a member of the Masonic order, the Bonnie Brook Golf Club, Waukegan Chamber of Commerce, is a republican, and has been a member of the Official Board of the First Methodist Episcopal Church at Waukegan for eight years.

He married at Nunica, Michigan, June 12, 1912 Miss Ola Parkhurst, of Nunica, where she finished her high school education and also took the Chautauqua literary course. She takes part in church affairs and Woman's Club activities at Waukegan. Her parents, William

B. and Olive (Cole) Parkhurst, were residents of Nunica, Michigan, and her father for forty-seven years was in the mercantile business in one store, and during all that time had only two brief vacations from his business, once when he attended the World's Fair at Chicago. He died in 1915, and her mother died in 1916. Mr. and Mrs. Gould have two children, Ivan Alan and Helen Margaret.

PEARL FOREST GROVE is superintendent of city schools and principal of the Mount Carroll High School, and the work he has done there has brought further reputation for his ability and skill as a teacher and educational leader.

He was born at Fisher, Illinois, June 3, 1881, son of L. M. and Lucretia (Parr) Grove, and grandson of William and Mary (Caldwell) Grove, who were born and reared in the southern part of Indiana and came to Illinois about 1855, acquiring a tract of government land and developing a farm near Fisher, where they spent the rest of their lives. L. M. Grove was born and reared near Fisher, attended public school, and after many years as a farmer located at Potomac, Illinois, where he was in the general grocery business for twelve years. Since 1912, he and his wife have lived retired. He has been affiliated with the Independent Order of Odd Fellows for over thirty-three years. His wife, Lucretia Parr, was born near Quincy, Ohio, and was brought to Illinois when twelve years of age. L. M. Grove and wife became the parents of eleven children: Oliver E., William W., George W., Frank M., Pearl Forest, Jessie C., Leonard M., James, Letha, Hazel and Reva.

Pearl Forest Grove attended public schools in Fisher, Illinois, graduated from the Potomac High School, and for six years engaged in teaching, being a teacher at Potomac from 1903 to 1907 and principal of the school at Armstrong, Illinois, from 1907 to 1909. Mr. Grove then entered the University of Illinois, in the College of Science, where he remained from 1909 to 1913, graduating with the A. B. degree in the latter year. In 1923 for additional work he was awarded the Master's degree. After graduating he was superintendent of schools at Prophetstown, Illinois, in 1913-14, and was superintendent at Sheldon from 1914 to 1916. In 1916 he returned to Urbana, Illinois, and for one year was engaged in the decorating business. In the spring of 1917 he became an assistant instructor at the University of Illinois, remaining there until June, 1918. Following that he was superintendent of schools at Kirkwood, Illinois, until June, 1922, when he came to Mount Carroll as superintendent and principal.

Mr. Grove is a Knight Templar Mason, member of the Eastern Star, the Glengary Golf Club, the Sequoia Club, and is a republican and Methodist, having given much time during the past twenty years to Sunday school and church work. He is teacher of the Men's Bible Class in the First Methodist Church.

He married, July 25, 1906, at Armstrong, Illinois, Miss Janie Hathaway Kissack, who finished her public school education at Armstrong. Her parents were William and Alice (Trotter) Kissack, natives of Illinois, her father a farmer until his death in 1905. Mrs. Kissack spent her last years with Mr. and Mrs. Grove. Mrs. Grove's grandfather was William Kissack, who was born and reared on the Isle of Man. Mr. and Mrs. Grove have four children, Alma Evelyn, Donald William, Eugene Forest and Robert Louis. Alma Evelyn graduated from the Mount Carroll High School in 1925. Donald William is a member of the high school, class of 1927, while the two younger children are in grade school.

DAVID T. WEBB, owner of the Lake County Fuel & Supply Company at Waukegan, has been the important factor in establishing and conducting several successful business enterprises in Lake County, and as a citizen has been much admired for the spirit of cooperation he has shown toward all the enterprises in his community.

Mr. Webb is member of one of the oldest of the pioneer families of Lake County and was born in the Gages Lake community of Warren Township, July 18, 1868. His paternal grandparents were Thomas P. and Margaret (Fink) Webb, who came from the vicinity of Ithaca, New York, to Lake County, Illinois, in 1846, settling near Gages Lake in Antioch Township. He took up land from the Government, and five of his brothers likewise took up land in the same vicinity. These brothers were George, Albert, Charles, Christopher and Ira, and many members of the family have lived in that community ever since. Thomas Webb was a millwright by trade. While developing his farm he worked at his trade in Chicago, and sometimes in order to spend a Sunday at home with his family would walk all the way from Chicago to Gages Lake.

His son, Chase Webb, was born in New York State in 1843, and was three years old when brought to Illinois. He attended public school in Lake County, and worked on the homestead farm until the Civil war. He enlisted in Company C of the Ninety-sixth Illinois Infantry, was in service with a supply train and participated in many battles. After the war he became a member of the Grand Army of the Republic. In 1865, soon after being mustered out, he married and took up farming and was also a stock buyer. In 1886 he was elected sheriff of Lake County and filled that office for four years. Afterwards for a number of years he was chief of police of Waukegan. Chase E. Webb died in August, 1916. His wife was Jeanette Minto, who was born at Loon Lake in Antioch Township, Lake County, in 1845. She attended the old Waukegan Academy and was a teacher before her marriage. For many years she was a devout member of the Congregational Church. Her death occurred in 1889. She was a daughter of David and Jane (Johnson) Minto, both of whom were natives of Scotland. In 1844, with their two oldest children, they came to America and settled at Loon Lake in Lake County Illinois, where they were among the first to develop land to farming purposes.

One son, David Minto, was in the Civil war, likewise in Company C of the Ninety-sixth Illinois Infantry.

David T. Webb attended public school at Avon Center in Lake County, and until 1889 was a student in the Bryant and Stratton Business College in Chicago. In the fall of 1890 he became deputy sheriff under his father, and in 1891 engaged in the ice business. Mr. Webb built up a very successful organization and service handling ice at Waukegan. He sold out in 1900, but in 1904 bought back the business and continued it until 1920. In 1923 he organized the Lake County Fuel & Supply Company, and at 126 Madison Street at Waukegan has a complete plant handling coal, masonry supplies and building materials. Mr. Webb is a business man whose abilities have brought him connections with many of Waukegan's most substantial enterprises. He is a director in the Waukegan National Bank and the capital stock of this bank was all subscribed for in Mr. Webb's office on Genesee Street. He is a director of the Pure Water Ice Company, the Advance Industrial Supply Company of Chicago, and is president of the Waukegan Building and Loan Association. David T. Webb, H. C. Burnette and A. L. Brumund are now building in Waukegan, at the corner of Genesee and Clayton streets, a new theatre building, with stores and apartments, covering a space of 171x138 square feet and costing approximately $1,000,000. It is their aim to open the theatre in September, 1927.

Mr. Webb is a trustee of the North Shore Sanitary District Board, is a Mason and Shriner, member of the Knights of Pythias and B. P. O. Elks, the Rotary Club, Hamilton Club of Chicago, was one of the first directors of the Waukegan Chamber of Commerce, and is a member of the Glen Flora Country Club. In politics he has been identified with the republican party.

Mr. Webb married at Waukegan, May 21, 1891, Miss Ida Miltimore, of Waukegan, where she finished her education. She has been a participant in the various social and civic activities of the city for many years. Her people were likewise early settlers of Lake County. Her parents, James H. and Caroline (Peck) Miltimore, were born in New York State and were children when the Miltimore and Peck families came to Illinois and settled at Miltimore Lake in Lake County. Mr. and Mrs. Webb had three children, two dying in infancy. Their daughter, Lucille J., graduated from the Waukegan High School in 1912, and is a member of the class of 1928 in Stout University at Menominee, Wisconsin.

NORMAN F. THOMPSON, JR. Rockford is recognized as the industrial center of Western Illinois, for here are centered some of the largest industries of the state outside of Chicago. They have been built up, almost without exception, by the steadfastness and ability of the men who have been, and are, heading these undertakings. One of these industries of international prestige is the Burson Knitting Company, of which the president is Norman F. Thompson, Jr., who has held the office since December 8, 1923.

Norman F. Thompson, Junior, was born at Rockford, March 14, 1884, a son of Norman F. and Adeline E. (Emerson) Thompson, natives of Georgia and Rockford, respectively. Coming to Rockford in boyhood, the elder Norman F. Thompson has risen in public esteem, and today is president of the Manufacturer's National Bank of Rockford. He and his wife were married in 1883, and they have had the following children born to them: Norman F., Junior, whose name heads this review; Ralph E., who is a resident of Boston, Massachusetts, general superintendent and member of the executive committee of the Gillette Razor Company; and Adalyn, who is deceased.

Given a careful educational training, the younger Norman F. Thompson attended the local schools and those of East Orange New Jersey, and the Hotchkiss School at Lakeville, Connecticut, being graduated from the latter in 1902. He then entered Yale University, and was graduated therefrom in 1906, with the degree of Bachelor of Arts. Returning to Rockford, July 1, 1906, he entered upon his long connection with the Burson Knitting Company, rising through successive promotions to his present high office.

On October 30, 1914, Mr. Thompson married Margaret Sheldon, a native of Rockford, and they have three children: Margaret, Norman F., III, and Adalyn. Mr. Thompson is independent in his political views. He belongs to the Masonic fraternity and to the Benevolent and Protective Order of Elks. The Second Congregational Church of Rockford holds his membership.

The Burson Knitting Company, whose immense plant employing 800 persons and occupying two city blocks and seven stores, is the outgrowth of the vision and inventive genius of William Worth Burson, and the faith in him and his inventions of the capitalist, Ralph Emerson, to whose generous financial support in the beginning the present prosperity is largely due.

William Worth Burson, a genius in mechanical research, was born on a farm, but was given the advantage of a collegiate training, for his orderly mind that was that of the well-grounded scientist. He was still a young man when he was awarded his first patent, and some fifty others followed, each one being an important contribution to perfection. The most remarkable of Mr. Burson's achievements was the automatic knitting machine which bears his name. Developed after years of the closest application, this marvelous machine actually knits stockings from toe to top to fit each curve of the leg. Until it was invented all full-fashioned hose had to be made with a seam. Just as the hand knitters use a different number of stitches at the ankle, the calf and the knee, so the Burson process shapes the stockings in the knitting with form-fitting perfection. This is the celebrated "Vee Weave" employed today in knitting Burson hosiery, probably the greatest contribution ever known to the art of knitting.

Time and the mellowing studies and labors of his calling developed Burson the boy pioneer into Burson the scientist with flowing white beard and hair. Little children called him

"Santy," and he went about with boxes of miniature stockings in his pockets to give to those who thought they recognized in him their patron saint.

To William Worth Burson fashionably gowned women owe the comfort and perfectly fitting qualities of Burson "Vee Weave" Hosiery. The admirers and wearers of these superb stockings are numbered by the hundreds of thousands. It is said, and no doubt with authority, that once a woman is accustomed to the trim fitting snugness and comfort of Burson Hosiery it is impossible to sell her any other kind. Mr. Burson no longer guides the affairs of the company he founded, but the same principles are maintained, and his successor is carrying on in a manner that retains the confidence of the public, and insures continued prosperity and further expansion of trade territory, and additional increases in annual returns.

ORION M. GROVE, county judge of Carroll County, has practiced law at Mount Carroll for thirty years. His professional career has brought him honor and distinction in the locality where he was born and grew up.

Judge Grove was born at Mount Carroll, December 16, 1870, son of John S. and Mary C. (Smith) Grove. His grandfather, George W. Grove, was one of the early settlers of Carroll County. John S. Grove was born and reared at Mount Carroll, was educated in public schools and after farming for a number of years engaged in the drug business. He was elected and served eight years as clerk of the Circuit Court of Carroll County, retiring from that office about 1898. For fifteen years he was deputy clerk in McHenry County and since then has made his home with Judge Grove at Mount Carroll. His wife, Mary C. Smith, was born and reared at Mount Carroll, daughter of John and Elizabeth (Boyer) Smith, who were early settlers and farmers in Carroll County.

Orion M. Grove acquired his early education in the grammar and high schools of Mount Carroll, graduating from high school in 1889. After that he attended Beloit College in Wisconsin, studied law a year at the University of Michigan, and finished his professional education under private lawyers, being admitted to the Illinois bar in 1896. He has had a successful and diversified general law practice in Carroll and adjoining counties. For a number of years he was city attorney, also served for a long time on the city school board, and was elected county judge in 1922.

Judge Grove is a member of the Masonic order, belongs to the Sequoia Club and the Glengary Country Club, and is active in the Baptist Church, being teacher of the boys' class in Sunday School.

He married at Oregon, Illinois, May 26, 1907, Miss Clara Diehl, of Chadwick, Illinois, where she was reared and educated. Mrs. Grove is president of the Woman's Relief Corps of Mt. Carroll. Her parents were Frederick and Elizabeth (Koehler) Diehl, of Chadwick. Her father was born in Germany, and on coming to America took up farming as an occupation. He enlisted in the Ninety-second Illinois Infantry for service in the Civil war and participated in many engagements before his return. He became one of the substantial farmers of Carroll County and died about 1916. Judge and Mrs. Grove are the parents of four children, John F., Judson J., George W. and Robert T. The sons have been given the advantages of the public schools of Mount Carroll, John having graduated from the Mount Carroll High School in 1926.

EMERY ELZA CALHOON is an attorney practicing law at Louisville, and has been a member of the bar of Clay County for over ten years.

He was born in Wright County in Southern Missouri, October 13, 1881, son of William Jasper and Elmazy Jane (Burk) Calhoon, and grandson of William Wesley Calhoon, a native of Virginia, whose father is believed to have been born in England. William Wesley Calhoon and his brother John, together with their mother, moved from Virginia to Gallia County, Ohio, where they grew up and where John spent the rest of his years. William Wesley Calhoon married Jemima Weatherholt. In 1871 they removed from Southern Ohio to Effingham County, Illinois, where he spent the rest of his life. Their family consisted of five sons and three daughters.

William Jasper Calhoon was born in Gallia County, Ohio, January 27, 1848, and after coming to Effingham County married Elmazy Jane Burk, who was born in Indiana in 1856, daughter of Gibson Burk, and she died July 4, 1908. William Jasper Calhoon spent his life as a farmer, was a democrat in politics, and died in Jefferson County, Illinois, December 20, 1919. He was the father of four children: Elmer E. and Emery E.; Wesley S., who died at the age of twenty-eight; and Welthy, who died when twenty-seven years old.

Emery Elza Calhoon was reared on a farm, had the opportunities of a country school, did some of his academic work in Austin College at Effingham, and in 1910 graduated LL. B. from the University of Chattanooga, Tennessee. Mr. Calhoon taught school through ten winter and four summer terms in country districts. In 1910 he was admitted to the Tennessee bar and was admitted to practice in Illinois in 1914. He established his office at Louisville in 1915.

Mr. Calhoon in March, 1926, was appointed master in chancery of the Clay County Circuit Court. He is a democrat in politics. In 1913 he married Miss Ethel Jennings.

REV. CHARLES ROBERT DUNLAP. Among the Protestant ministers of the City of Cairo, Rev. Charles Robert Dunlap is the dean in point of length of continuous service in any one church. Reverend Dunlap is pastor of the Lutheran Church, a very able and forceful preacher and is widely known as a public lecturer.

He was born at Barkeyville, Pennsylvania, in 1879, son of George W. and Emma (Focht) Dunlap, his father a native of York, Pennsylvania, and his mother of Harrisburg, the same state. Rev. George W. Dunlap is a Lutheran minister now located at Beloit, Kansas.

Charles Robert Dunlap was liberally educated, attending high school at Millersburg, Ohio, Wittenberg College at Springfield, Ohio, a divinity school there and did post-graduate work in a college at Richmond, Ohio. He was ordained to the Lutheran ministry at Cleveland in 1902. His service record as a minister includes a period of time as missionary pastor at Muncie, Indiana, as missionary organizer at Chicago, in a similar capacity at Pittsburgh, Pennsylvania, while in 1911 he came to Cairo as pastor of the Lutheran Church, whose activities have been greatly expanded and strengthened under his able direction.

He married in 1905 Miss Ella Phillips, who was born at Leetonia, Ohio, daughter of H. R. and Elizabeth (Nold) Phillips, her father a native of Pennsylvania and her mother of Ohio. Mr. and Mrs. Dunlap have one daughter, Lucille, now attending Wittenberg College at Springfield, Ohio.

Reverend Dunlap has taken a commendable part in community affairs of Cairo and is one of the past commissioners of that city. He is a republican, is a Scottish Rite Mason and has been chaplain of various Masonic bodies and also in the I. O. O. F. and the Encampment degree. He has acted as chaplain of the Knights of Pythias Lodge and the B. P. O. Elks. He is a member of the Lutheran Brotherhood, the Rotary Club, the Association of Commerce, the Egyptian Country Club.

EARL D. REYNOLDS came to Rockford and engaged in the practice of law in 1896. In 1923 he went on the Circuit Bench as judge of the Seventeenth Judicial District. On May 2, 1926, death overtook him at the height of his career, at the age of sixty years, just thirty of which had been spent in Winnebago County.

He was born in Van Buren Township, Hancock County, Ohio, January 17, 1866, son of Volney and Christina (Smith) Reynolds, the former a native of New York and the latter of Ohio. Of their five children all lived to grow up. Judge Reynolds was the last survivor, with the exception of his sister Fleeda, wife of Ormie Gleason, of Waldron, Michigan. When Judge Reynolds was a year old his parents moved to a farm in the vicinity of Waldron, Michigan, and he grew up in Hillsdale County, attending the country schools and working in the fields during the summer. Later he attended Hillsdale College, from which he was graduated in 1891, with the degree of Master of Arts. For several years he taught at the North Adams School in Hillsdale County, becoming its principal. Entering the law department of the University of Michigan, he was graduated LL. B. in 1896, and was valedictorian of his graduating class both at Hillsdale College and the university. In the fall of 1896 Judge Reynolds located at Rockford, and in a few years had gained practice of a large and important character.

He possessed many of the qualifications that are sought in a public official. He was a member of the Rockford Board of Education, and in 1905 became assistant attorney general under Attorney General Hamlin. In 1906 he was elected a member of the Illinois Legislature while Judge Shurtleff was speaker of the House, and in 1908 was reelected.

In 1923, while acting as chairman of the Republican County Central Committee, he was elected judge of the Seventeenth District, succeeding Judge R. K. Welsh, who had resigned. Among the many tributes to his character and service as a lawyer, judge and citizen, one of interesting significance was voiced by Lieutenant Governor Sterling in the following words: "Judge Reynolds suffered the fate of other overworked predecessors on the Circuit Bench of Winnebago County. He did the work which two men should have been doing, and paid the penalty. His untimely death is a great loss to the bench, the bar, the city and county. As a lawyer he was well read, able, resourceful and successful. As a judge he was patient, just and fair-minded, yet fearless in his rulings and decisions. As a legislator at Springfield he took first rank among House members of his time. His passing came at the very prime of his usefulness to the people of this county and is deplored by all."

Judge Reynolds was a member of Rockford Lodge No. 102, A. F. and A. M., the B. P. O. Elks, and for a number of years was head of the national law committee and local president of the Modern Woodmen of America. He was chairman of the board of the First Congregational Church while that organization was in existence, and later became identified with the Second Congregational Church.

Judge Reynolds married, December 21, 1891, Miss Florence Keith, member of a prominent Boone County family. Mrs. Reynolds and five children survive: Keith, assistant agency manager of the Rockford Life Insurance Company; Lorenzo D., a farmer in Boone County; Dorothy M., a music instructor in the Rockford High School; Lois, who graduated from Hillsdale College, Michigan, in 1925, and is now teaching English in the Roosevelt, Junior, High School; and Margaret, who graduated with the class of 1926 in the Rockford High School, and is now attending Oberlin College at Oberlin, Ohio.

JOHN E. BROWN. No suburban development around Chicago, and perhaps none anywhere, has been given so much publicity and attention as Niles Center, which only a few years ago was an isolated country village, seldom seen or heard of by Chicagoans, and now a modern suburban community of beautiful and costly homes and expanding business enterprises. The climax of this development came in the spring of 1926 with the completion of the new Skokie Valley line of the Chicago, North Shore and Milwaukee Railroad.

All of these developments have justified the declaration that Niles Center is "Chicago's Greatest Suburb." Niles Center is a village in form of government, and has undertaken the unprecedented task of carrying out improvements in street building, sewer and water installations and other improvements at a cost of $5,000,000.

The president of Niles Center village is John E. Brown. Mr. Brown has for some years been regarded as the village's natural prophet, and no one has been more active in advocacy and in practical measure for realizing the great destiny of the community. He has more than a personal interest in Niles Center. It is his birthplace, and the Brown family have been prominent there from the days when it was a cross-road village in Niles Township.

His father was the late John W. Brown, who died in 1918. John W. Brown was for many years a merchant at Niles Center, a large property owner, was president of the Niles Center State Bank, and filled practically all the offices of the village and township, including that of president of the village, supervisor of the township, trustee of the village, assessor and police magistrate. His widow still lives at Niles Center.

John E. Brown was born there in 1882, grew up and attended school in his native community, and since early manhood has been identified with its business and financial affairs. For several years he was a merchant, and is now a director of the Niles Center State Bank, of which his father was president. This is an institution which has assets of $1,750,000. He has conducted a prosperous real estate business for a number of years, handling not only his own properties but others as well.

After several years as a member of the Village Board and as village treasurer he was elected president of the village and was its official head at the culmination of the transportation development marking the completion of the electric road.

Mr. Brown married Miss Kunigunde Paroubek. They live in a home that is one of the show places of Niles Center. Their three children are Marion, John and Jane.

HENRY G. HORSTMAN, M. D. A physician and surgeon over thirty years, Doctor Horstman, of Murphysboro, has his share in the work of his profession in times and conditions not greatly removed from those of the real pioneer doctor, a character justly celebrated in history. Doctor Horstman's career has been in the period of transition. In the early years he traveled over country mud roads, and for the most part without even the aid of a telephone. In later years he has been helped by all the equipment provided by modern art and invention.

Doctor Horstman was born December 11, 1868, on a farm about eight miles north of Murphysboro, near the village of Finney. His father, John Frederick Horstman, was a native of Germany, was brought to America when ten years of age, and after a brief residence in New York went South as a civil employe of the Union army during the Civil war, being too young to enlist at a soldier. While in Mississippi he met and later married Semira Westfall. On coming to Jackson County, Illinois, he located on a farm, and died there when his son, Henry G., was only nine months old.

Henry G. Horstman had limited opportunities during his boyhood and youth. For a few months each year he attended a rural school and the rest of the time was spent in the labor of the farm. He determined when a boy to become a physician, and his subsequent efforts were directed largely with that end in view. He attended the Southern Illinois Normal at Carbondale, later studied medicine in St. Louis, and graduated M. D. March 19, 1895. Doctor Horstman for fifteen years engaged in practice at Vergennes, in Jackson County, and it was during that time that he performed the labors of an old time country doctor, riding far and near to attend his patients. In 1910 he removed to Murphysboro, and has a large city practice, though still a popular position in the rural neighborhood.

He married Luvinia Crawshaw, daughter of Samuel Crawshaw, a farmer south of Murphysboro. Her father represented an old English family and was a Union soldier in the time of the Civil war. Doctor and Mrs. Horstman have five children: Heber O. and Archaelle C., both in business in Carbondale; Mrs. R. B. Parks, of Murphysboro; Mrs. Ethel Stevenson, of Murphysboro; and Lorena E., who is a graduate of the Normal University at Carbondale and now a teacher in the public schools at Centralia.

Dr. Horstman is a member of the Masonic Order. He held a commission in the medical Reserve Corps during the World war. He is a member of the Methodist Episcopal Church. During the tornado of 1925 most of the town west and south of his home was destroyed, though his house escaped with small damage. The house of his daughter, Mrs. Stevenson, was destroyed, though none of the family injured.

MERTON R. HARNED, D. D. S. Not only is Dr. Merton R. Harned one of the most capable of the dental surgeons practicing in Winnebago County, but he is also one of the most progressive citizens and effective civic workers of Rockford and the county, and many important improvements have come about because of his energy and ability. Doctor Harned was born at Sycamore, Illinois, January 26, 1862, a son of Edmund B. and Susan (Sivright) Harned, natives of Long Island, New York, and Nova Scotia, Canada, respectively. The mother came to Illinois in 1843, and the father, in 1845, and they were married at Sycamore. For many years the father was engaged in farming. He and his wife had the following children: Eugene and Rosetta, both of whom are deceased; Arrianella, who is deceased; James E., who lives at Rockford; Susan, who is the wife of John Winchester, of Sycamore; and Doctor Harned, whose name heads this review.

Following his graduation from the Genoa High School in 1881, Doctor Harned took a short course at Bryant and Stratton's Business College. For one term thereafter he was engaged in teaching a country school, and he then entered the Philadelphia Dental College, from which he was graduated in 1884, with the degree of Doctor of Dental Surgery. Upon securing this degree Doctor Harned established himself in a general practice at Oregon, Ogle County, Illinois, and continued there for two years, leaving that city for Rockford in 1886. Here he has since remained, building up a large and lucrative practice.

On March 1, 1888, Doctor Harned married Kittie A. Sewell, youngest daughter of John M. and Mary Sewell, of Oregon, Illinois, and one daughter was born to them, namely: Lora, who is the wife of Arthur E. Sterling, son of Lieutenant Governor F. E. Sterling of Rockford. Doctor Harned is independent in his political views, and also with reference to religious matters. He belongs to the Masonic fraternity, the Modern Woodmen of America, Rockford Art Club, Kiwanis Club, University Club and Izaak Walton League. He is a charter member of the Northern Illinois Dental Society, Rockford Odontological Society, Winnebago County Dental Society, the Chicago Dental Society, Illinois State Dental Society and the National Dental Association, in all of which except the last he has been a very active and helpful member, having served as president in the first three and having written many papers and given many clinics in connection with their programs.

A close student and a man of science, Doctor Harned has always taken special interest in educational and public health movements, active in University Extension Work and president of Central Parent-Teachers Association. He called the first committee to organize the old Rockford Civic Club, and as a result of the efforts of this body the present park system was inaugurated and other civic welfare work was boosted. He served two years as president of the Rockford Club. Subsequently, after the passage of the Glaccan Act, he was appointed a committee of one to formulate plans to organize the work of combating the inroads of the "white plague." As a consequence of his wholehearted endeavor the Winnebago County Tuberculosis Association came into being, with three visiting nurses carrying on the work of prevention of infection throughout the county and nine visiting nurses giving part time in the city to tuberculosis work. Another result was the establishment of the Municipal Sanatorium for treatment of tuberculosis, with accommodations for seventy patients. Doctor Harned is president of the Board of Trustees.

Rockford is the first municipality in the state to take advantage of the Glaccan Law providing for the building and maintainance of tuberculosis sanitoria by city and county tax levy.

Doctor and Mrs. Harned were among the organizers of the Winnebago County Home for Aged, and have for nearly twenty years been active in the management of the Jennie Snow Home for Women. Mrs. Harned as president of the "Lady Board of Managers." The Doctor as one of the trustees of the estate left to endow the home.

The Harneds are real pals and recreate by travel (having visited nearly every state in the Union), by golf, photography and the management of a large farm thirty miles from Rockford, where they have a summer cottage and where they spend many happy days with friends, children and grandchildren.

JOHN F. PECK. A former president of the Illinois State Osteopathic Association, Doctor Peck is one of the best known members of his profession and for some years has enjoyed a successful practice at Kankakee, where his offices are in the Cobb Building.

Doctor Peck was born at Kankakee in 1880, son of Fayette and Clara M. (Norton) Peck, his father a native of New York State and his mother of Michigan. His father was a cattle dealer and later traveled and sold the Budlong agricultural implements. He died in 1883, while the widowed mother passed away April 15, 1907.

John F. Peck as a boy attended grammar and high schools at Kankakee, and after leaving the public schools depended upon his own initiative in determining his career. In May, 1912, he graduated from the American School of Osteopathy at Kirksville, Missouri, and since then has been engaged in practice at Kankakee. In addition to his service of one year as president of the Illinois State Osteopathic Association he has been a trustee of the association since 1920, and for four years he was a trustee of the Chicago College of Osteopathy. Doctor Peck for several years was in the furniture business at Gotebo, Oklahoma, and for three years of that time was president of the town board.

He married, April 20, 1907, Lucia DeShon Baldwin, a native of Onarga, Illinois, and daughter of James and Harriet (Babcock) Baldwin. Doctor Peck is a Presbyterian, a republican, is a Mason and member of the Eastern Star and B. P. O. Elks. He is president of the Round Table Club of Kankakee. His home is at 880 South Greenwood Avenue.

ISAAC K. LEVY is a native of southern Illinois, and for many years has been a lawyer in practice at Murphysboro. His prominence as a citizen is based on his unostentatious service and worth, rather than his own presumptions.

He was born at Murphysboro February 1, 1878. His father, Abe Levy, moved from Indiana to Murphysboro in 1875, and his home prior to living in Indiana was Ohio. He was for many years a merchant in Murphysboro.

Isaac K. Levy never had the opportunity to attend a law college. He attended the public schools of Murphysboro and depended on his own exertions and application to qualify for the profession which was his ambitious goal from boyhood. He studied law in the office of John M. Herbert, and in 1899 was admitted to the bar. He afterward became a law partner of Mr. Herbert, and for six years they practiced together under the firm name of Herbert & Levy.

Mr. Levy in 1908 was elected state's attorney of Jackson County, and served the term 1908-12. Since leaving that office he has been very actively engaged in a general law practice, a practice by no means confined to his own county. His general popularity is based on public spirit and whole hearted devotion to the welfare of his community, as well as to his success in his profession. Mr. Levy married Miss Lillian Hanks, member of a pioneer family of southern Illinois, and has two daughters, Constance and Virginia.

When the historic and very destructive tornado struck Murphysboro on March 18, 1925, Mr. Levy through his activity found himself in charge of the relief work and over night had organized his forces, which functioned very efficiently for many weeks and until relieved by the American Red Cross. In addition to being general chairman of the Citizen's Relief Committee, when the Red Cross Advisory committee was organized Mr. Levy was also unanimously elected chairman. This committee was occupied with its exacting duties for a period of one year after the disaster. It was also through his untiring efforts that the state of Illinois appropriated $275,000.00 to rebuild the public school buildings in southern Illinois that were destroyed by the tornado.

Mr. Levy is a member of the Illinois State Bar Association and also the American Bar Association, and for the term 1925-1926 was president of the Federation of Local Bar Associations for the First Supreme Judicial District of Illinois. He has a younger brother, David B. Levy, who is also a member of the bar of Jackson County. Mr. Levy socially is a Mason and also a member of the Elks Lodge.

CHARLES SAMUEL DENEEN, state's attorney of Cook County from 1896 to 1904, governor of Illinois from 1904 to 1912, and United States Senator from Illinois since February, 1925, has probably more than any of his contemporaries demonstrated consistent leadership and power in Illinois politics and public life.

Through his professional and political career his home has been in Cook County. However, he has a strong hold on the affections of the people of Southern Illinois, where he was born and reared. He is a native of Madison County, born at Edwardsville May 4, 1863, son of Samuel H. and Mary F. (Ashley) Deneen. One of his great-grandfathers was Risdon Moore, who settled in St. Clair County, Illinois, in 1812, after service as a soldier of the Revolution. He was speaker of the Illinois House in the Territorial Legislature of 1814, and subsequently was elected a member of the First General Assembly of the state and served in the Third and Fourth Assemblies. He had freed his slaves on bringing them to Illinois, and took a conspicuous part in the Legislature of 1823 in opposing a constitutional convention for the purpose of making Illinois a slave state.

Senator Deneen's grandfather, Rev. William L. Deneen, was born in Pennsylvania, October 30, 1798, came to Illinois in 1828, and spent nineteen years as a Methodist minister in the southern part of the state. On leaving that profession he became a surveyor and was county surveyor of St. Clair County from 1849 until 1855. He died in 1879. Samuel H. Deneen was born in St. Clair County in 1835, was a graduate of McKendree College, and for thirty years was professor of Latin and ancient history in that institution. He was adjutant of the One Hundred and Seventeenth Illinois Infantry during the Civil war. His wife, Mary Frances Ashley, was born at Lebanon, Illinois, December 18, 1836, daughter of Hiram K. Ashley.

Charles S. Deneen was educated in public schools at Lebanon, graduated in 1882 from McKendree College, and for several years taught school, reading law at the same time. In 1885 he came to Chicago, attended the Union College of Law, was a law office clerk, taught in the public night schools, and was admitted to the bar in 1886. His first office is said to have contained only a few worn books, a desk and two chairs, and in the absence of other clients he defended prisoners who were without counsel. In 1892 he was elected a member of the State Legislature, but it was in the office of state's attorney of Cook County that he made a reputation for forcefulness and determination and integrity, which qualities have been at the very foundation of his success as a public man.

Governor Deneen was the first governor of Illinois in thirty years reelected for a second term. His two administrations as governor constitute a notable era in Illinois public affairs, but any account of these administrations belongs to the history of the state at large. After he retired from the office of governor he resumed his law practice at Chicago. However, he remained the real leader of a large and progressive element in the republican party in the state. In November, 1924, he was elected United States senator. On February 25, 1925, he was appointed by Governor Small to serve the unexpired term of the late Senator Medill McCormick and took the oath of office as senator for the unexpired term on February 28th.

Governor Deneen married, May 10, 1891, Miss Bina Day Maloney, of Carroll County, Illinois. They have four children: Charles Ashley Deneen, of Chicago; Dorothy, Mrs. Allmand M. Blow, of Tulsa, Oklahoma; Frances, Mrs. Carl Birdsall, of Chicago; and Miss Bina D., who was born in the executive mansion at Springfield and is now a student in Bryn Mawr College.

THEODORE CHALON BURGESS was a distinguished figure in educational circles in Illinois, and gave the best years of his life to the Bradley Polytechnic Institute at Peoria, of which he was president for over twenty years.

He was born in Little Valley, New York, April 29, 1859, and was not yet sixty-six when he died in February, 1925. His parents were Rev. Chalon and Emma (Johnston) Burgess. He graduated from the State Normal School of Fredonia, New York, in 1879, and from Hamilton College with highest honors in the famous class of 1883. He married, August 17, 1887, Laura May Briggs, of Fredonia. In 1886 he took his Master's degree at Hamilton and in 1898 received his Doctor's degree at the University of Chicago. In 1923 Doctor Burgess received the honorary degree of Doctor of Laws from his alma mater.

After graduating from Hamilton, and for thirteen years thereafter, Doctor Burgess was head of the classical department of the Fredonia State Normal School, and in 1897 became head of the department of ancient languages at Bradley Polytechnic Institute. In 1899 he was appointed dean of the institute, and in 1903-4, acting director. He was managing director of the institute and president of the college from 1904 until the day of his death, at the same time maintaining his department of ancient languages.

In the summer session of the University of Chicago, 1900-1909, Doctor Burgess was professor of Greek. His literary works consist of "Epideictic Literature," published in 1902, and "Elementary Greek," published in 1907. He was president of the Classical Association of the Middle West and South, and of the Illinois Schoolmasters' Club. He was a

frequent contributor to magazines on classical subjects.

The service he gave to the Peoria institution is well expressed in an editorial that appeared at the time of his death: "It is no exaggeration to say that Doctor Burgess was the intellectual and spiritual founder of Bradley Institute and the college which succeeded it. He set the intellectual fashions and moods at Bradley, and with the aid of several men who took their Doctor's degrees at the University of Chicago —Doctors Wyckoff, Packard, Ashman and Comstock—set up educational and cultural standards which are as much parts of Bradley College as the beautiful campus upon which it is located.

"His administration was pitched on a high plane, and although Bradley had lacked needed buildings and endowments, it never has lacked the inspiration of a scholarly, judicious and modest leadership. Doctor Burgess cut his gown according to his cloth, and not only maintained the traditional Bradley morale, but held his department of ancient languages amid the ding-dong of utilitarianism, pragmatism and jazz. To a lover of the classics, this achievement alone is not the least of his accomplishments.

"Death discharges some obligations and creates others. A supreme duty devolves upon Peoria to perpetuate in brick and stone the high ideals and unflagging purposes for which Doctor Burgess gave his best efforts and finally his life. No man can be said to have died before his time if his death concentrates public attention upon his work. 'I depart from life as from an inn,' said Cicero, 'and not as from my home.' Doctor Burgess is still domiciled in the hopes and aspirations of those who survive him. Tardily the friends of Bradley will bring the brick and stone for new buildings. And when they come, we suggest that one of them is called "Burgess Hall." Such a memorial would fitly commemorate the life and unremitting zeal, the patient effort and wholesome influence as educator and citizen of Theodore Chalon Burgess."

Another view of Doctor Burgess was expressed by Frederick A. Stowe in a Peoria newspaper: "The chorus of acclaim that honors the memory of Dr. Theodore C. Burgess supplies new evidence of the advantage which serious men have over "glad-handers" and merry-makers. Dr. Burgess always was dignified, and in many respects quite unlike the typical up-to-date college executive. Yet he was always cordial, appreciative and agreeable in any company. Although a classical scholar of high attainments, he observed the rule of Apelles and never judged above the shoe-tops. He was not forward nor ostentatious. The vulgarities and banalities of others may have grieved him, but they did not incite him to attack. He was not a crusader, intellectually or socially. He did his own work thoroughly and quietly and without arousing jealousy or resentment.

"With this equipment Doctor Burgess always commanded respect and succeeded in doing without pretense what would have been impossible to many others. Doctor Burgess made a specialty of the ancient languages and maintained his department in a technical institution. Although primarily a Greek scholar, he made his cultural influence felt in an era when the public mind was farthest removed from ancient languages. Indeed, the classics have been abolished in many educational institutions."

DR. FRANK PARSONS NORBURY was born in Beardstown, Cass County, Illinois, August 5, 1863, the youngest son of Charles Joseph Norbury and Elizabeth Peters (Spence) Norbury. There were thirteen children in the family, six sons and seven daughters, of whom one son (Dr. Norbury) and four daughters survive. His parents were early settlers in the northwest portion of Morgan County at Beardstown. Later the north portion of Morgan County was detached by popular vote and by legislative action in 1837; and Cass County was thus created. The names of his father and two uncles (his mother's brothers) appear on the first poll book of election held in Cass County, August 7, 1837.

His father, born in Philadelphia, Pennsylvania, came to Illinois in 1836. His mother, born in Robertson County, Tennessee, came to Jonesboro, Union County, Illinois, about 1828, and to Morgan County in 1835, with three sisters, following the death of their parents, to make their home with their brother, Isaac Spence. Isaac and Absolom Spence were pioneers. Having intended to go "to the Galena Country," they were attracted by the fertile valley of the Sangamon, and settled in the valley east of Beardstown. Isaac Spence later took up his residence in Beardstown, where he was engaged in merchandizing. He later moved to Houston, Texas. It was in his home in Beardstown that Doctor Norbury's parents were married January 9, 1839.

Doctor Norbury is a descendant of several early Colonial families. The genealogical record of the family, compiled by his sister, Elizabeth S. Norbury, of Denver, Colorado, traces their ancestry to the Mayflower Pilgrim colony of Massachusetts; the early West Jersey Quaker colony; the Swedish colony of Delaware; the Scotch-Irish colony of New Jersey and North Carolina; the English colonies of Virginia and the Pennsylvania colony of so-called Pennsylvania Dutch, from Switzerland. The name "Norbury" is English and is one of the oldest families in England, a family closely identified with professional and political activities of that country; the church, education, law and medicine having representatives for several hundred years. The English branch of today is represented in medicine by Sir Henry Norbury, surgeon-general of the English army during the Boar war. He is living in London at the age of ninety. Although on the retired list, during the late war he took active duties in London and did valiant service, especially during the "air-raids." His two sons, both physicians, were in service during the war, one as naval surgeon in the North Sea fleet, and the other as a surgeon in special service in a base hospital in Flanders. Both English and American branches of the Norbury family are descendants of Sir John Norbury, treasurer of King Henry IV. The family in America dates from Joseph Norbury, a school-master, who came from England, in

1753, to Cape May County, New Jersey. Here, in 1758, he married Lydia Doubleday, a descendant of John Howland of the Pilgrim Mayflower colony of Massachusetts. Joseph Norbury, with his wife, later lived in Cumberland County, New Jersey, where their son, Heath Norbury, was born January 25, 1760. Joseph Norbury died in November, 1769. Heath Norbury became a "school-master" in Philadelphia, Pennsylvania. There he married, June 12, 1783, Susanna Britt, of Philadelphia of Quaker descent; also a descendant of the Swedish colony of Delaware. Heath Norbury was public spirited and interested in the social welfare of the community. During the prevalence of the cholera (1793) and later of the yellow fever (1799) epidemics in Philadelphia he was steward of the Philadelphia Hospital Lazaretto on Tinicum Island, Delaware River. He was also a member of the Board of Health of Philadelphia. The Lazaretto on Tinicum Island cared for the afflicted patients during the prevalence of these epidemics. In the epidemic of cholera in 1793 it was Stephen Girard who largely financed, individually directed, and participated in the relief activities. It is said that this was the only time that "Stephen Girard came out of his shell." He was a taciturn, recluse type of man; the wealthiest citizen of Philadelphia. He was the founder of Girard college and established the "Girard Estate," which today is the greatest financial institution in Philadelphia. The city of Philadelphia memorialized Heath Norbury by Resolutions for his unselfish devotion and fearless activity during the prevalence of these epidemics. (These resolutions are in possession of the family). He is buried in Northumberland, Pennsylvania, in the cemetery where rest the remains of Joseph Priestly, the discoverer of oxygen. Heath Norbury's wife, Susanna Britt, was a daughter of John and Mary Britt of Philadelphia, Quakers. Mary Britt was the sister of Col. Daniel Britt, of the Continental army of the Revolution, who saw service under General Wayne, principally on the western frontier.

Joseph Britt Norbury, son of Heath and Susanna Britt Norbury, was born in Philadelphia, January 25, 1788. He was educated in private schools and in Penn Charter School, Philadelphia. He became a lawyer and, later, a judge of the Court of Common Pleas. He held court in Independence Hall (then used as the Court House) in the room in which the Declaration of Independence was signed. When the public building at Broad and Market streets was completed Independence Hall was restored to its Revolutionary period. Joseph Britt Norbury married, April 23, 1809, Rebecca Minchell Frick in Northumberland, Pennsylvania. They were the parents of four sons and three daughters. The home was in Wood Street, Philadelphia, near Franklin Square. Wood Streets at that time was within a short distance of the northern limits of the city. Many of the old homes of that period, including the home of Judge Norbury, are yet to be seen in this neighborhood, which neighborhood, years ago, in the onward progress of the city, has been taken over by the incoming foreign population. Joseph Britt Norbury was active in civic and state affairs. He served as a member of the Legislative Assembly of Pennsylvania, and was in attendance in Harrisburg when the declaration of the War of 1812 was made. He was active in the preparation for war. He accepted a commission as major in the Pennsylvania troops from the governor of the state and served to the end of the war. The original commission and the sword worn, as major, are in the possession of the Norbury family. Joseph Britt Norbury's wife, Rebecca Minchell Frick, was born in Germantown, Pennsylvania, the daughter of John Frick and Anna (Witmer) Frick. She was the only daughter; there were six sons. John Frick was the grandson of Conrad Frick, who came to Philadelphia from Switzerland in 1732. His descendants have been prominent in the church, medicine, law, journalism, manufacturing, finance, banking and agriculture in Pennsylvania, Maryland and the West. Henry Clay Frick, of Pittsburgh and New York, Dr. S. Frick, of Baltimore and the Fricks of Milton, York, Lewisburg, Bethlehem, Pennsylvania, are representatives of this well-known Pennsylvania Dutch family.

Charles Joseph Norbury, the second son of Joseph Britt and Rebecca Minchell Frick Norbury, was born May 22, 1812, in Philadelphia, during the absence of his father in Harrisburg. He was educated by private teachers and later attended Penn Charter School. At the age of seventeen he entered the office of an "Importing Commission House" engaged in the West Indies trade. Later he was with a wholesale dry goods firm. It was while thus engaged he met William Bassett, of Beardstown, Illinois, who had come east to buy goods. Upon his invitation Charles Joseph Norbury came to Beardstown in 1836, and was associated with Mr. Bassett in merchandising for four years. Mr. Bassett did an extensive forwarding and common business. This was the era of settlement, growth and development of Illinois when transportation in commodities was by river and freight wagons. Charles Joseph Norbury then embarked in business for himself. He owned a wharfboat and warehouses, dealt in boat supplies and was engaged in receiving and forwarding in the shipping business. He was, also, the local express agent, being the third agent appointed in the state of Illinois. As express agent it frequently fell to his lot to transport gold, in original packages, sent from the old countries, largely Germany, to colonists, distributed from the Indiana line on the east to the Military Tract on the west and its limits on the north. This duty he performed personally, going on horseback alone over the prairies and most times unarmed. He was never molested and carried many thousands of dollars on his numerous trips. The shipping, forwarding and distribution of freight during this period was very active. The river being the main channel for transportation of merchandise and for emigrant passenger traffic in consequence the river towns became centers for distribution. Likewise centers for shipping produce originating in local and adjacent territory. Pork packing was a local industry at Beardstown, with Cincinnati, Ohio, as its only competitor in the Mississippi Valley. Charles Joseph Norbury was engaged in this industry, also as a grain dealer and in general merchandising.

When the era of railroads came there followed a revolution in business matters. Beardstown suffered and was at a disadvantage in competitive trade. When the Springfield and Illinois Southeastern Railroad was completed in 1871 Mr. Norbury became its first agent in Beardstown. This position he held until compelled to resign because of injuries received from foot-pads, who slugged and robbed him while going home from his office one evening in the fall of 1877. He never fully regained his health. He later became associated in mercantile pursuits. He lived to the age of eighty-three. His death occurred in Beardstown March 23, 1895. His wife, three sons and six daughters survived him. His wife's death occurred ten years later and two sons and two daughters have since died. The sons were over sixty-five years of age and the daughters passed seventy-five and eighty at death.

His wife, Elizabeth Peters Spence Norbury, was born September 16, 1822, in Robertson County, Tennessee (near Springfield), the daughter of Rev. Thomas Spence and Katherine Carter Spence. Katherine Carter Spence also was a descendant of a long line of Colonial ancestry. Thomas Spence was born in 1784 in Surrey County, North Carolina, the son of David Spence, born in New Jersey in 1758, and Mary McElyea (Spence), daughter of Ludovic McElyea, formerly of York, Pennsylvania. David Spence met his wife while serving in the Continental army, Pennsylvania Regiment, in the North Carolina campaign, under General Francis Marion, while the troops were marching through Surrey County. Mary McElyea was one of a group of young ladies who served buttermilk and water to the soldiers. Gourd dippers were used. The dipper with which Mary served David was kept by him. He broke it, inscribed her name on a portion of it, put it in his jacket, and said he would return after the war. This he did and claimed her as his wife. They lived for a time in Surrey County, North Carolina, where Thomas Spence was born in 1784. Later they migrated to Tennessee, locating in Robertson County. Mary McElyea Spence lived to be 104 years old. Her death occurred in 1867 in Robertson County. She was a remarkable woman, strong, active, and of unusual capabilities. She said she had lived through four wars, viz: "The Revolution, the War of 1812, the Mexican War and the Civil War." And that her family was "divided in allegiance only in the Civil war, when she saw grandsons in the Southern army and grandsons-in-law in the Northern army."

David Spence was the son of Thomas Spence and Sarah (Harriman) Spence. Thomas Spence was born in Scotland, a descendant of the Duke of Argyle. He came to New Jersey with a Scotch-Irish colony. Here he married Sarah Harriman, daughter of David Harriman, grandson of Rev. John Harriman, pastor of the First Presbyterian Church of Elizabethtown, New Jersey. John Harriman was a graduate of Yale, 1667. Memorials to Rev. John Harriman and his descendants are inscribed in the First Presbyterian Churchyard in Elizabeth, New Jersey, dating from 1664 to 1892. John Harriman's wife was Hannah Bryan, a descendant of Alexander Bryan, one of the founders in 1639 of Milford, Connecticut.

Rev. Thomas Spence and Katherine Carter were married in Robertson County, Tennessee, in 1805, by Rev. Peter Cartwright. Rev. Cartwright later migrated to the "Sangamon Country," locating at Pleasant Plaines, Sangamon County, Illinois, where he attained prominence as a minister and organizer in the Methodist Episcopal Church of Illinois. He was an opponent of Abraham Lincoln when Lincoln was elected to the U. S. Congress.

Katherine Carter was born in ·Culpeper County, Virginia, in 1790, the daughter of Daniel Carter and Anne Lemon Carter. Daniel Carter was a descendant of Capt. Thomas Carter, son of a London merchant, (Gentleman), born in 1630, who came to Lancaster County, Virginia, about 1650. He became a captain of Militia, commissioner member of the House of Burgess. He married Katherine Dale about 1670. Katherine Dale was a daughter of Major Edward Dale, member of the House of Burgess. He was from England. His wife was Diana Skipwith, a descendant of Sir William Skipwith and Alice Dymoke. The Dymoke ancestry has been traced (and certified) back to 843 A. D. The Carter family of Virginia has been from early Colonial times closely identified with the history of Virginia, the South and of our country. Present day representatives of the descendants are found principally in the South and middle west, and are especially active in professional activities—church, journalism, medicine, law and public service.

Rev. Thomas Spence and his family came to Illinois in 1830, locating at Jonesboro, Union County. Reverend Spence was sent to Illinois to organize Sunday Schools. In 1835, while engaged in this mission, riding on horse-back about the pioneer settlements, he was taken suddenly ill and died near Duquoin.

His wife Katherine, preceded him in death in 1833. Reverend Spence and his brother were very prominent in anti-slavery activities. The latter was killed while aiding slaves to escape across the Mississippi River, near Cape Girardeau. After the death of Reverend Spence four of his daughters were brought to Morgan County by their brothers, Isaac and Absolom, who had previously migrated to the "Sangamon Country" and entered land in the Sangamon Valley, east of Beardstown. The four sisters later married four young men from Philadelphia, Pennsylvania, two of whom were brothers, James and John McClure. It was Elizabeth (the third sister), who married Charles Joseph Norbury, January 9, 1839, in the home of her brother Isaac in Beardstown.

Dr. Frank Parsons Norbury, the subject of this sketch, was the sixth son and twelfth child born to this union. He was born in Beardstown, Cass County, Illinois, August 5, 1863. He began his education in the public school of Beardstown, graduating from the high school in 1881.

Mary E. Garm, who in 1890 became his wife, was also a member of the "Class of 81." Immediately after graduation he became office and field assistant to Capt. R. A. Brown, U. S. Engineer Corps, engaged in the Illinois River improvement. Here he served five years with interruptions, due to seasonal conditions when the work was "shut down" during the winter months he attended Illinois College, Jacksonville, doing special work. After taking up the study of medicine he spent his vacations in engineering work under Captain Brown. In 1885 he became a student of medicine in the office of his preceptor, Dr. George Bley, Jr., at Beardstown. In 1886 he entered the Medico-Chirurgical College, Philadelphia, Pennsylvania. Here, by intensive work he qualified to enter the senior year at Long Island College Hospital, Brooklyn, New York, from which institution he received the degree of M. D. March 9, 1888. Doctor Norbury then, by appointment, became physician on the Resident Staff of the Pennsylvania Training School for Feebleminded Children, Elwyn, Pennsylvania (near Philadelphia), of which Dr. Isaac N. Kerlin, one of the pioneer and foremost physicians engaged in this special work, was superintendent. This institution, with 800 inmates and well organized, gave Doctor Norbury an unusual opportunity to have training and experience in clinical neurology, neuropathology and the problems of mental deficiency as seen in children. A visiting staff, doing special observational work, of which Drs. William Osler, S. Weir Mitchell, George A. Oliver, John S. Stewart and others, were members contributed to create and develop clinical interest and knowledge on the part of Doctor Norbury. He was fortunate, too, in being associated daily with Dr. A. W. Wilmarth, the foremost neuropathologist in this field at that time. The proximity to Philadelphia and Doctor Norbury's previous contact with the clinics of that city enabled him to continue his special studies in neurology and internal medicine. Doctor Norbury was fortunate in coming under the instruction of Dr. S. Weir Mitchell, Charles K. Mills, William Osler, William Pepper and others.

Doctor Norbury later received the appointment on the Resident Staff of the Illinois Central Hospital for the Insane at Jacksonville. Here he served five years. He married, October 2, 1890, Mary E. Garm at Beardstown, Illinois. They made their home for three years at the State Hospital. It was here their son Garm was born January 27, 1892. In July, 1893, Doctor Norbury resigned from the state service to engage in private practice in Jacksonville. Here he aided in establishing Our Savior's Hospital and was for many years on the attending staff and is now lecturer in the Training School for Nurses. In 1893-94 he began teaching, and was professor of mental and nervous diseases, Keokuk Medical College. Later, in 1895, he moved to St. Louis, having been appointed to the chair of internal medicine in the reorganized faculty of the St. Louis College of Physicians and Surgeons, also professor of mental and nervous diseases, Woman's Medical College. He was also associate editor of the Medical Fortnightly, established by Drs. Bransford Lewis and Charles Wood Fassett. Doctor Norbury became editor later, and held this position for ten years. He, however, remained in St. Louis but one year, returning to Jacksonville to become physician to Oak Lawn Retreat, a private institution for treatment of mental and nervous disorders. He also engaged in private practice, and later was attending physician to the Illinois State School for the Blind. He was appointed lecturer on psycho-physics, Illinois College, which position he filled for eight years. He was also professor of mental and nervous diseases, Keokuk College of Physicians and Surgeons, and continued in this position until the school was absorbed by Drake University of Des Moines in 1908. In 1901, having resigned his connection with Oak Lawn Retreat, he established the Norbury Sanatorium at 806 South Diamond Street, Jacksonville. (Description and development of this institution appears elsewhere in this volume.)

Doctor Norbury having been active in social welfare work of the state, in the Illinois State Conference of Charities and Corrections for twelve years, and having served as its president and member of committees instrumental in creative interest in reorganizing state welfare work, he was invited by Governor Charles S. Deneen to help put the program, which he helped to create, into actual service. Governor Deneen in 1909 appointed him superintendent of the Kankakee State Hospital. Here he served two years, when Governor Deneen appointed him medical member (Alienist) of the Board of Administration of Illinois. This board had been in operation but two years. It was in the midst of finding itself in the varied responsibilities thrust upon it as the administrative organization having in charge the State Hospital for the Insane, the Correctional Institutions for Boys and Girls, the School for Deaf, Blind and Orphans, the Soldiers' Home. Doctor Norbury brought to this board his accumulated experience and creative interest in this specialized welfare service. He then took up his residence in Springfield, at 1133 Williams Boulevard, where he now lives. He resigned from the board in 1913 to again enter private practice. He opened an office in Springfield and later, having invited his former student and assistant, Dr. Albert H. Dollear, to be associated with him, a new company was formed and the Norbury Sanatorium, at Jacksonville, was again taken over. A complete reorganization and rehabilitation of the Sanatorium followed. Doctor Dollear became the superintendent, residing in the Sanatorium and having full charge of the managerial and resident clinical affairs of the institution.

Doctor Norbury as medical director attended to institutional duties and outside consultation field activities. He maintained an office in Springfield until 1922, since which time he has limited his work to the Sanatorium and consultations.

Doctor Norbury was president of the Board of Welfare Commissioners during the administration of Governor Frank O. Lowden. When the war came on he served as a member of the Advisory Board in Springfield until August, 1918, when he became acting medical director of the National Committee for Mental Hygiene in New York. This committee during the war acted in an advisory capacity to the Surgeon General's Office of the Army, assisting in the organization and recruiting of the Neuropsychiatric Division, also in organizing the transport service for care and treatment of mental and nervous casualties. Dr. Thomas W. Salmon, the director of the National committee, was sent in 1917 overseas to study the conditions over there leading to the organization of the Division of Neuropsychiatry of the A. E. F. Upon his return he enlisted and was attached to the Surgeon General's Office and proceeded to perfect the organization. Later, as Colonel Salmon, he went overseas as chief consultant in neuropsychiatry to the A. E. F.

Doctor Norbury became acting director of the National Committee and served during the combat period of the war and until May 1, 1919. He assisted in the organization for demobilization and was one of the group that gave aid to the U. S. Public Health Service in Washington in organizing what is now the U. S. Veterans' Bureau. In addition to directing war activities of the National Committee for Mental Hygiene, Doctor Norbury carried on the regular work of this committee. In this capacity he directed surveys in several states, the object of which was to improve the treatment and care of the insane and feeble minded, also to suggest improved legislation. He with Dr. Charles W. Pilgrim of the New York State Hospital Commission, and Dr. George W. Klein of the Massachusetts Commission, drafted the Model Commitment Law, now in force in many states of the Union. He also assisted in memoralizing the General Assembly of Missouri leading to enactment of improved laws, governing state welfare work.

Upon his return to his home in Springfield in May, 1919, Doctor Norbury was called upon to assist in organizing the work for care and treatment of mental cases occurring in the returned soldiers. This occupied some of his time for about three months. Later, by Act of Congress, this work was provided for. Doctor Norbury then returned to his regular medical duties as consulting physician and medical director of the Norbury Sanatorium, in which activities he is now engaged. In professional lines Doctor Norbury has also been active. He became a member of the Morgan County Medical Society in 1888 and of the Illinois State Medical Society in 1889. He has served as secretary and president of the County Society, as delegate and active committee worker in the State Society, and for several years was chairman of the Committee on Medical Education. He became a member of the American Medical Association in 1890 and served as delegate, also as secretary of the section on mental and nervous diseases, and as delegate to the committee on medical education. During the existence of the Mississippi Valley Medical Association he was for thirty-three years an active member. He served as vice president and later, in 1910, as president of this association. He is a fellow of the American Psychiatric Association; a fellow of the College of Physicians; a member of the Chicago Neurological Society; a member of the Central Neuropsychiatric Association; a member of the American Society for the Advancement of Science; a member of the American Eugenics Society; a member of the National Committee for Mental Hygiene; a member of the American Meterological Society; honorary member of the Colorado State Medical Society, the Chicago Medical Society and the Adams County Medical Society. Dr. Norbury has been active in social welfare work, local, state and national, having organized mental clinics in Springfield in connection with the Juvenile Court, also in mental hygiene activities in central Illinois. He is now honorary chairman of the Central Illinois Mental Hygiene Society. For many years he has been interested in propaganda work in mental hygiene, and has appeared in most of the cities of Illinois in public addressed in this service.

Doctor Norbury married, October 2, 1890, Mary E. Garm at Beardstown, Illinois. His wife and he entered the public schools together and were members of the same class throughout their school years, graduating from high school in the "Class of '81."

Mrs. Norbury is a daughter of Henry Garm and Mary D. Garm. Mr. Garm was a merchant and banker; a native of Germany and a resident of Beardstown for many years. His wife was a native of Cornwall, England, a descendant of the Dunn family and a cousin of John Gregg, who was one of the foremost organizers in the colonizing of central Illinois. He was an extensive land owner in Morgan, Menard, Sangamon, Christian and Champaign counties. Mr. Gregg is best known to older generations as a publisher of school-books in Philadelphia. He was the founder of what is now the J. B. Lippincott Publishing Company of Philadelphia. Two of Mrs. Norbury's brothers reside in Beardstown, viz: Robert H. Garm, president of the First State Bank, and John T. Garm, a clothing merchant. The other brother, Joseph E. Garm, is vice president of the Joplin National Bank, Joplin, Missouri.

Two children were born to Doctor and Mrs. Norbury. A son, Dr. Frank Garm, and Elizabeth. Dr. Frank Garm Norbury is associate physician to the Norbury Sanatorium and engaged in private practice. He is a graduate of Illinois College, A. B., and took his Masters Degree at the University of Illinois and his M. D. Degree from Harvard Medical School. He served in the Boston City Hospital and the Boston Floating Hospital. During the war he served as pathologist at Camp Devens and in overseas duty as pathologist member of the Boston City Hospital Unit. At the close of the war he came to Jacksonville to be associated with the Norbury Sanatorium. He married, in 1918, in Jacksonville, Elson Barnes, daughter of Judge and Mrs. Charles A. Barnes. They have three children, Ruth Margaret, Phyllis and Frank Barnes.

Dr. Norbury's daughter, Elizabeth, was born in Jacksonville, August 13, 1896. She attended the public school of Jacksonville, the preparatory school of Illinois Woman's College, later St. Mary's School at Knoxville and still later, after the family residence was established in Springfield, Monticello Seminary at Godfrey and the Betty Stuart School in Springfield. She is at home with her parents in Springfield.

Doctor Norbury in politics is allied with the republican party. His church affiliation has been with the Congregational Church. In fraternal affiliations he is a Mason, Knight Templar, also a member of the Knights of Pythias. Most of Doctor Norbury's activities have been professional and in social welfare work. He is fond of good books and has an extensive library, of largely scientific and professional standard publications.

THE NORBURY SANATORIUM, Jacksonville, Illinois. The Norbury Sanatorium was organized, incorporated and established in 1901, in response to a demand recognized by Dr. Frank Parsons Norbury, for more defined and individual private care for patients having mental or nervous disorders who could not, for various reasons, be received in general hospitals or could not have proper care in their homes. The natural evolution of medicine, in general, and neuro-psychiatry, in particular, emphasized the need of trained physicians and nurses and more adequate individualized service to give the care and treatment which modern medicine demanded.

In 1901 psychiatry was in the beginning of the era which has since brought it into recognition as an applied dependable science of human behavior. Neuro-psychiatry in its fundamentals (like other branches of medicine, based on the great science of biology) has been free to make use of the scientific method and in duty bound to apply it in the relief of human suffering and the promotion of human welfare.

Doctor Norbury had constantly in mind the full meaning of the trend of medical progress. He knew that the general practitioner, though daily in contact with major and minor mental disturbances, did comprehend, even if he did have aversion for, mental discordances. Further, the family physician really wanted help and sought it when it was available. Unfortunately the twenty-five years since 1901 have not entirely relieved conditions that explain the apathy and indifference manifested where mental or nervous disturbances occur. But there is an awakening, because psychiatry and general medicine are now nearer together than ever before. The importance of actual physical findings, as taught by the internist, has removed the empirical descriptive explanations of psychiatry of twenty-five years ago. Today, the laboratory, the full technic of physical examination, prolonged observation of mental symptoms, personality studies and integration of all factors concerned in clinical problems, make neuro-psychiatry a dependable science. The Norbury Sanatorium has kept step with, and contributed to, this advancement. With the facilities now offered it is able to make a complete physical, mental and social diagnosis and to outline care and treatment that will best promote adequate clinical adjustment to the factors concerned.

Organization: The present organization of the Norbury Sanatorium Company consists of Dr. Frank Parsons Norbury, president and medical director; Dr. Albert H. Dollear, vice president, treasurer and superintendent; Dr. Frank Garm Norbury, secretary and associate physician. (These three also constitute the Board of Directors.)

The Norbury Sanatorium is incorporated under the laws of Illinois. It is also licensed under the laws governing private institution and is, therefore, under the inspection of and reports to the Department of Public Welfare of Illinois. It also is in affiliation with and reports to the National Committee for Mental Hygiene in compilation of statistical data. It is a member of the American Hospital Association, and the Illinois Hospital Association. Further, every member of the medical staff is a fellow, or member, of the American Psychiatric Association.

Buildings: The Norbury Sanatorium began in a modest way, with accommodations for fifteen patients in a building at 806 South Diamond Street, formerly a residence of the Southern Colonial type, remodelled to meet the requirements of an organized hospital service, this service being patterned to meet the ways and means necessary to apply the teachings of Dr. S. Weir Mitchell, of Philadelphia, in his advocacy of "Systematized Rest." Systematized rest continues to be the leading feature of applied therapy in the Sanatorium. Today, the Sanatorium has reached a maximum capacity to care for one hundred patients and has a daily average of ninety-six patients. There are two service groups, that for men and custodial patients, being located at 806 South Diamond Street, and known as Maplewood. Four buildings comprise this group, three for patients and one the nurses' home. Thirteen acres of ground furnish necessary recreation facilities. The department for women, known as Maplecrest, is located at 1631 Mound Avenue, just outside the west limits of the city, on the hard road, Route 36. This building is modern and complete in every detail. It is located on the crest of a moraine (the highest point in Morgan County) with thirty-one acres of ground, improved and landscaped. This service offers superior classification by reason of having four independent units of ten rooms each with individual bath facilities. The physical treatment service is supplied by complete hydro-therapeutic equipment, electro-therapy, occupational therapy, diathermy, X-ray, etc., located in the sub-basement. Recreation outdoors is made available on the beautiful lawn. A concrete tennis court is a feature appreciated by many of the patients. The general offices are at Maplecrest. The Sanatorium laundry, gardens, orchard, chicken farm are on these grounds. The remodeled nurses' home completes "the lay-out" of this modern group. Fire protection and adequate water supply are dependable features of the equipment.

Nursing Service: From the beginning of the organization nursing was recognized as the imperative need if service in keeping with the practical ideals, proposed, were to be followed. It was found that nurses trained in the care and treatment of mental and nervous disorders were not available. Fortunately, with a limited number of patients and having one nurse experienced in the work, in due time others were trained. But ere long it

THE NORBURY SANATORIUM

became evident that to meet the service and growing needs of the institution better training must be supplied. To this end nurses were sent to Philadelphia, Boston and Baltimore to study the most modern technic and facilities offered in the specialized service in those medical centers. Upon their return a training school was established and was maintained for several years. It was discontinued when the new laws governing nursing in Illinois came to be effective. But the principles of nursing governing the work in the Sanatorium have always been those which meet the requirements of intensive applied methods of modern neuro-psychiatry. The nursing personnel is represented by graduate nurses, as heads of all departments, and attendants guided by the directions of the chief nurses. Night and day service is thoroughly organized.

Each patient's record is made on a twenty-four hour schedule and is complete in itself and available for a Court of Record, if necessary.

Medical Staff: The medical staff in active service now consists of four physicians: Dr. Frank Parsons Norbury, medical director; Dr. Albert H. Dollear, superintendent; Dr. Frank Garm Norbury and Dr. Samuel N. Clark, associate physicians.

Dr. Frank Parsons Norbury has been in the special work of neuro-psychiatry thirty-eight years. He is a graduate in medicine from the Long Island College Hospital, Brooklyn, New York, class of 1888. He then became resident physician on the staff of the Pennsylvania Training School for Feeble-Minded Children, at Elwyn, Pennsylvania, (near Philadelphia). At the same time he did graduate work in neuropathology and clinical neurology. He was fortunate in coming under the tutelage of Drs. S. Weir Mitchell, Charles K. Mills, William Osler and A. W. Wilmarth. Later Doctor Norbury was appointed on the resident staff of the Illinois Central Hospital for the Insane, Jacksonville, Illinois, (now Jacksonville State Hospital), where he served five years with Dr. Henry F. Carriel as superintendent. (Doctor Carriel was one of the so-called "Utica School" group of American alienists. He came from Trenton, New Jersey, Hospital, where he had served under Doctor Buttolph, one of the foremost alienists of his time.)

Doctor Norbury, with his five years' training and experience, decided in 1893 to engage in private practice. He located in Jacksonville, and soon after became attending physician to Oak Lawn Retreat, a private institution for mental and nervous diseases, established by Dr. Andrew MacFarland. Doctor Norbury served in this capacity until 1901, when he organized and established the Norbury Sanatorium. This he conducted until 1909, when, on the solicitation of Governor Charles S. Deneen, he again entered the state service. He was appointed superintendent of the Kankakee State Hospital. Here he remained two years, when Governor Deneen appointed him a member of the Board of Administration of Illinois. This board had administrative charge of the state institutions of Illinois, including state hospitals. Doctor Norbury was the medical member of the board and contributed his experience in developing the medical and nursing service in these institutions. He resigned from the board in 1913 to enter private practice. He again took over the Norbury Sanatorium, having invited Dr. Albert H. Dollear to become associated with him as a member of the company and to be superintendent. Under the able and versatile managerial abilities of Doctor Dollear the Sanatorium has been going steadily forward, fulfilling the aims and purposes of its founders.

Doctor Dollear was a student of Doctor Norbury and for two years after his graduation in 1904 from the St. Louis University, Medical Department, served as resident physician to the Norbury Sanatorium. Doctor Dollear then entered the state service on the staff of Watertown State Hospital, where he later became assistant superintendent. He was next appointed clinical assistant to the State Psychopathic Institute, of which Dr. H. Douglas Singer (now professor of psychiatry, University of Illinois, Medical School) was then director. In 1911 Doctor Dollear resigned to give his attention to a year's graduate work in neuropathology, diagnostic neurology and internal medicine under Professor Thor Rothstein, Rush Medical College, Chicago. With eight years of experience and training in varied aspects of neuro-psychiatry, including the managerial duties in hospital and organization work, Doctor Dollear was exceptionally well qualified to carry on and develop the plans for complete reorganization of Norbury Sanatorium.

Its present status as a going and growing serviceable institution, ably financed and managed, bears tribute to the versatile abilities of Doctor Dollear. As the clinical work of the Sanatorium developed, it was soon evident that additional help was needed on the medical staff. The Sanatorium had weathered the vicissitudes of the war and the influenza epidemic and demands were exacting for its services.

In April, 1919, Dr. Frank Garm Norbury, after his return from overseas medical service, joined the staff. He had seen two years of service as a member of the Medical Corps of the army. After enlistment in 1917 he served for a year at Camp Devens, in the clinical laboratory of the Base Hospital under Captain L. H. Spooner. He was a member of Base Hospital No. 7, Boston City Hospital unit, and went overseas in 1918, returning in April, 1919, having been clinical pathologist to the Base Hospital while with A. E. F. Dr. Garm Norbury is a graduate of Harvard Medical School and had training in clinical pathology in the Boston City Hospital under Prof. Frank B. Mallory and on the Children's Floating Hospital of Boston, under Dr. Carl Ten Broeck, now a professor in China. He prepared for this special work at the University of Illinois, where he took a Masters degree in physiological chemistry. Doctor Norbury has followed clinical pathology and internal medicine actively, thus contributing his experience and training to the clinical problems met with in the service of the Sanatorium. Modern psychiatry stresses the inter-relation of internal medicine with problems of mental mechanisms. As Barker says, "The internist shares with the psychiatrist the desire that knowledge of the facts regarding cause, cure and prevention of mental disorders may become widely disseminated among medical men and at least to some extent among the laity."

As the growth of the Sanatorium continued it again became necessary to have an additional dependable, trained physician on the staff. Dr. Samuel N. Clark, of Chicago, became associate physician in 1921. Doctor Clark had formerly been an assistant to Dr. Frank P. Norbury at the Kankakee State Hospital. Later, from 1913 to 1921, he was a member of the staff of the State Psychopathic Institute with Dr. H. Douglas Singer as director. For a period of eighteen months during the war Doctor Clark was loaned to the Institute for Juvenile Research in Chicago while Dr. Herman H. Adler was absent in war service. Doctor Clark was on the clinical teaching staff, first at Rush Medical College and later with his Alma Mater, the Medical Department of the University of Illinois, a period of teaching from 1914 to 1921. His exceptional training in clinical psychiatry and study of under-average and unstable children has given him qualifications to meet the varied clinical problems in human behavior from the standpoint of psychiatry.

It is with pardonable pride that the Sanatorium considers the well-rounded, well-trained qualifications of its medical staff and feels that it can offer the facilities of the institution to meet the practical problems of every-day living in which the physical, mental and social factors enter as parts of the clinical equation.

Diagnostic Clinic: To further extend its usefulness, a diagnostic clinic has been developed by the Sanatorium, and it now maintains an organized diagnostic clinic for mental and nervous disorders.

The facilities for observation, analysis and diagnosis are modern in every detail. They are offered to the family physician, the industrial surgeon, the juvenile and criminal courts, social agencies, public schools, etc., in an endeavor to aid in the solution of their varied problems. The Sanatorium is prepared to study and make recommendations in problem cases occurring in children. Carefully prepared reports and recommendations are made to physicians and authorities sending cases to the clinic. This organized service in its gradual growth has proved its value here in the middle west.

ALBERT HENRY DOLLEAR was born November 3, 1876, in Jacksonville, Morgan County, Illinois, the son of Albert N. Dollear and Annetta (Grobe) Dollear. Albert N. Dollear was a native of Sheffield, England, and came to this country when a young man and to Jacksonville in 1848. He was for many years a valued employe of the Illinois Central Hospital for the Insane, having charge of the horticultural and dairy activities of the institution. His wife, Annetta Grobe, was a native of Krinau, Canton St. Gallen, Switzerland. They were married in 1863 at Jacksonville, Illinois. Mrs. Dollear's sister was the wife of William Turner, oldest son of Jonathan B. Turner, one of the founders of Illinois College, Jacksonville.

Albert H. Dollear was the youngest son born to Albert N. and Annetta Dollear. His mother died when he was a small boy. During these early years he had a home with friends who contributed much to his education, from the fact that they spoke the German language, which became as useful to the boy as his native tongue. He attended the public schools of Jacksonville through the Junior High School grades and then entered Whipple Academy, from which he graduated in 1898. He then entered Illinois College, where he completed the four years' course in three years, graduating with B. S. degree in 1901. He then became a student of medicine in the office of Dr. Lewis A. Frost, of Jacksonville, as his preceptor. He entered the St. Louis University, Medical Department, from which he received his M. D. degree in 1904. Previous to his graduation his preceptor became an invalid and later died. During this period he became a student in the office of Dr. Frank P. Norbury, where, during his vacations, he was associated in the work of the Sanatorium. After his graduation he became resident physician to the Norbury Sanatorium, which position he held for two years. During this time he engaged, too, in general work as county physician, which gave him a varied experience in general medicine and surgery. In 1906, by Illinois Civil Service appointment, he became assistant physician to the Watertown State Hospital, and in 1907, by promotional examination, he became physician, and in 1909, by promotion, he was appointed assistant superintendent. In 1911 he again received recognition and was made clinical psychiatrist to the State Psychopathic Institute, located at the Kankakee State Hospital, of which Dr. H. Douglas Singer was director. In 1912, following a serious illness, he resigned and devoted a year to post-graduate study in neurology, clinical pathology, under Prof. Thor Rothstein, Rush Medical College, Chicago. Following this, upon invitation of Dr. Frank P. Norbury, he became a member of the reorganized Norbury Sanatorium Company of Jacksonville, where as secretary and treasurer of the company and superintendent of the Sanatorium, he gave his accumulated experience as managing officer and clinician to the reorganization, rehabilitation and rebuilding of the Sanatorium. In this work his genius as to detail and foresighted policies placed this institution as one of the most dependable of its kind in the middle west. A description of this institution appears in the sketch preceding. With the extension and growth of the clinical service, the needs for equipment and improved facilities for the Sanatorium have always been met by his wise managerial ability. In 1924, when the company was again reorganized, Doctor Dollear became vice president and Dr. Frank Garm Norbury was made secretary. Today the evenly balanced organization functions with increased efficiency, meeting all demands and sustaining its reputation for modern service and kindly consideration of the problems which it has to meet. During emergencies in managerial duties, incidental to storms, floods, etc., Doctor Dollear has shown exceptional adaptive qualifications. This was shown in the ice-storm of 1924, and the recent floods of 1926, when Jacksonville was overwhelmed by unprecedented flood experiences.

During the war, Doctor Dollear served as neurologist on the Medical Advisory Board of the district, succeeding Dr. Frank P. Norbury, who resigned to become acting medical director of the National Committee for Mental Hygiene in New York. This service Doctor Dollear gave with his usual conscientious interest.

Doctor Dollear married Pearl A. Gilbert June 19, 1907, in Jacksonville. They made their home at Watertown State Hospital, Watertown, Illinois, and later at the Kankakee State Hospital, then for a year in Chicago, where their son, Frank Gilbert, was born in 1913. In 1913, when Doctor Dollear became superintendent of the Norbury Sanatorium, they took up their residence at Maplecrest, 1631 Mound Avenue. (The woman's department of the Sanatorium), where they now reside. Here their second, Henry Albert, was born in 1916.

Doctor Dollear has professional membership in the Morgan County Medical Society, the Illinois State Medical Society, the American Medical Association, the Chicago Neurological Society and is a fellow of the American Psychiatric Association and a fellow of the American College of Physicians. Doctor Dollear has been very active in civic club affairs, especially in the Rotary Club, of which he has been president and is now a leader in the committee work of that organization, likewise an active member of the local Chamber of Commerce and is president of the Jacksonville Country Club. He is also active in other interests seeking to improvve civic affairs. His political affiliation is with the republican party. He is a Mason, Knight Templar and also a member of the Knights of Pythias. On the whole, Doctor Dollear is a useful, devoted, conscientious and public spirited citizen, as well as a well grounded physician and experienced managing officer of the Sanatorium.

JOSEPH B. STRAUSS, famous bridge designer and builder, consulting engineer and international authority on bridge design, with headquarters at Chicago, was born at Cincinnati, Ohio, January 7, 1870, a son of Raphael Strauss and his wife, Caroline. His father was an artist of note and a litterateur. His mother was a musician. The family as a whole were musically inclined, one of the daughters achieving high rank as a pianist. Mr Strauss' education was successively gained at Cincinnati's grammar schools, Hughes High School and the University of Cincinnati. He was always a leader, being class president at Hughes and for three successive years at the university. He was manager and editor of the college paper, class poet and founder of the local chapter of the Sigma Alpha Epsilon fraternity.

In spite of his artistic and literary leaning Mr. Strauss showed a strong bent for mechanics and the sciences in his youth. He was a prodigious reader and yet managed to find much time for the machine shops, the railroad yards and the laboratories, and at a very early age began to exercise inventive skill and ingenuity in devising various experimental mechanical and electrical devices.

He elected the engineering course at the University of Cincinnati, where he was graduated with distinction with the degree of Civil Engineer in 1892. In that year he began his notable career in bridge engineering as draftsman for the New Jersey Steel & Iron Company of Trenton, New Jersey. Thereafter except for one year's service as instructor in the department of engineering at his alma mater, he devoted his first ten years after graduation to acquiring practical experience, first as an engineer, detailer and estimator in the bridge shops, then as designer for the Sanitary District of Chicago and other engineering organizations in Chicago, where he gained experience in railway bridges and viaducts. It was in this latter field that he finally came in contact with the new science of bascule bridge design, being assigned to the task of revising and redesigning the early types then just introduced to a limited extent in Chicago.

In 1902 he entered private practice as a consulting engineer for the general design of bridges, viaducts and buildings. He continued in practice until 1906, and during that time he developed a type of concrete stock house built by the Universal Portland Cement Company and introduced the ribbed concrete arch bridge into the United States, designing a number of fine bridges of this then new type. He originated a plan for the erection of such bridges without false work, designing, and as a contractor, building a four-span railroad bridge in this manner for the Elgin-Belvidere Railroad at Belvidere, Illinois, which bridge because of its original and bold design, attracted attention all over the world. In 1905, with Bion J. Arnold, he acted for the City of Chicago in examining and reporting on the problem of reconstructing the Union Loop to reduce noise.

In 1904 he first developed the principle of the now well-known Strauss type of trunnion bascule bridge, and in that year became the leading designer of such structures as the founder, president and chief engineer of the Strauss Bascule Bridge Company of Chicago. The bascule bridge is the successor of the old-time swing bridge. It is a movable structure, in which one portion balances the other as it simultaneously lifts and rotates in a vertical plane, to open and close for the passage of vessels. Being both a load-carrying structure and a huge machine, it involves many problems not present in any other type of bridge structure. When Mr. Strauss' attention was directed to bridges of this type they were comparatively rare and limited in length as well as costly, largely because of the expensive cast iron counterweights employed and the complication existing in their means of operation. He took the radical step of substituting concrete counter-weights for the cast iron counter-weights. This meant counter-weights of larger bulk but of a greatly reduced cost. To permit larger bulk counter-weights to function without interference and without infringement on the supporting structure, he evolved weight system, which involved a sharp departure from customary practice. As a result the pin-connected or parallel link counter-of this and a simplified operating mechanism he effected a marked decrease in the cost of constructing bascule bridges and a corresponding expansion of their range of application and the size and weight of spans.

Following the success of the first bridge based on these principles Mr. Strauss continued the development of the bascule, producing in less than seven years four distinct types, each type having several different forms but all having the original large bulk counter-weight, the parallel link counter-weight system and the simple and direct operating mechanism.

In the development of these designs it was necessary to design entirely new forms of electrical equipment and control, compact machinery units, efficient locks, special lubricating mechanism, special devices for the trolley wire supports, automatic gates, etc. Radical departures in truss design were necessary in some instances. Existing specifications did not provide for the character of stress in these structures and threw no light on the problems encountered and it was necessary to develop such specifications. All of this creative effort Mr. Strauss carried forward with the work.

In the Strauss types of bascule new records in length and weight of span have been established, the so-called single leaf type reaching a maximum leaf length of 260 feet (the Saint Charles Air Line bridge at Chicago, built in 1919) and the double leaf simple span type reaching a length of 336 feet center to center of trunnions (the Canadian Pacific Railroad bridge at the Soo). In highway bridges the graceful double leaf deck bascule of the Burnside bridge, Portland, Oregon, is the largest to date, being 252 feet center to center 83 feet wide and the first bascule provided with a concrete deck. The Republican Bridge across the Neva at Petrograd, another magnificent bridge of the same type, leading to the former winter palace of the Czar, has a 209-foot, double leaf bascule. This bridge is 1,000 feet long over all and 90 feet wide.

These structures, all designed by Mr. Strauss, illustrate the tremendous expansion from the toy structures of Holland and the early bascule spans of Chicago that he brought about and as a result of which the bascule bridge has become an integral part of modern civilization and an essential traffic facility wherever navigable streams exist. In all Mr. Strauss has designed some 300 of these bridges, most of them distinguished by striking ingenuity. They are found in all parts of the world, introducing modern methods and American engineering triumphs to such remote parts as China, Japan and Egypt.

Turning from the bascule type to the so-called vertical lift type of movable bridge, i. e., where the bridge is raised vertically like an elevator, Mr. Strauss undertook to eliminate the cables and chains that featured these bridges. The vertical lift type is one of the oldest forms of movable bridges and up to 1910 it was considered that the vertical movement could only be effected by ropes, cables, chains, or, to a limited degree, by hydraulic rams. Mr. Strauss by an ingenious modification of the parallel link system of his bascule attained a lift of 56' 8", without either cables or chains or similar devices, either for counter-weighting or operating. In one of these bridges, that over the Rideau Canal in Ottawa, the radically new expedient was adopted of concealing the entire counter-weight and lifting mechanism in the piers, permitting a strikingly handsome structure which, when not in operation, can not be distinguished from a fixed bridge.

An equally novel design of vertical lift bridge is that furnished by Mr. Strauss for a bridge at Osaka, Japan, in which the bridge span is raised through the medium of four large pinions, whereby both the counter-balancing and operation of the bridge is effected. This structure has the added distinction of having successfully passed through the great Japanese earthquake in 1926.

A third type of lift bridge and which was the winner in a national competition is now being constructed from Mr. Strauss' designs by the State of Illinois. In this design the counter-weight cables are retained, but the operating cables are replaced by a rack and pinion drive located on the center line of the bridge, effecting a combination of economy and durability which had hitherto been unobtainable.

In 1921 Mr. Strauss was called into consultation in the solution of the problem of crossing the Golden Gate, a project which was long deemed by engineers to be an impossible one. The span necessary was 4,000 feet or more than 2½ times that of the largest span built. After a year's study Mr. Strauss developed the Cantilever-Suspension bridge, a combination of the Cantilever and Suspension which for the first time made the project possible. Following the solution Mr. Strauss' plans were approved by the War Department and form the basis for the enactment of legislature creating a bridge district to build this bridge. This bridge, which is to extend 6,700 feet, or 1.6 miles, will cost $25,000,000 and will be not only the largest bridge in the world but also the most beautiful and impressive bridge in the world.

Among other notable fixed bridges designed by Mr. Strauss is the great structure on which he is now engaged for the Montreal Harbor Commission, across the Saint Lawrence River between that city and the South Shore. This structure has some unusual features originated by Mr. Strauss, such as the Terrace-Pavilion at the juncture of the two arms of the bridge on St. Helena Island. The main span over the main channel is a 1,097-foot cantilever. The bridge will have a total length of approximately two miles; will cost $12,000,000, and will be completed in 1931. Associated with Mr. Strauss in this undertaking is the firm of Monsarrat & Pratley of Montreal, it being a requirement of the Quebec laws that a foreign engineer be associated with an engineer resident in the Province.

Mr. Strauss' inventive genius has not been confined to revolutionizing bridge engineering by new designs and bold departures from established practice in operation and structure. Among his contributions to mechanical progress in other fields is a "'Yielding Safety Barrier," the product of nine years development and a practical device adapted for modern motor traffic and the protection of life at railroad grade crossings, as well as at open ends of bridge spans. This barrier, by means of an elastic cable network (normally above the traffic clearance level and automatically brought into position across the roadway through the medium of the trains themselves), brings vehicles weighing two tons or more and traveling forty miles per hour or more to a dead stop within twenty feet of the crossing without damage to the barrier, its occupants or the vehicle. The present grade crossing toll in the United States annually is represented by 3,000 dead and 7,000 maimed. The general adoption of the barrier, now begun, means that Mr. Strauss will reclaim for mankind 10,000 useful lives every year.

A departure Mr. Strauss made from the purely utilitarian to the realm of amusement was his aeroscope, a highly popular mechanism he designed to entertain visitors at the Panama-Pacific Exposition at San Francisco in 1915. This device was a structure with a rotating arm rising to a height of 260 feet and lifting to that height a two-story car carrying 150 persons. The design was such that the car floor was horizontal in all positions of the arm while the weight was automatically balanced by every passenger passing on and off.

Mr. Strauss entered aeronautics through the application of the bascule principle to doors for hangars. This type of door is in use by the United States Navy and Post Office departments, the Mexican government, etc. He then applied the principle of bridge construction to aerial work in forming the wings of airplanes into trusses, and in the construction of the framing of lighter-than-air craft. The latter promises to effect a tremendous step forward in reducing cost of fabrication and increasing safety.

During the World war Mr. Strauss applied himself to the development of searchlight equipment. His first design in this field was a disappearing searchlight tower at Fort Hancock, New York, designed for the United States War Department in 1914. This tower, which is still in service, rises on a fixed foundation and its elevating arm raises and lowers like a bascule bridge, to a height of sixty feet. It carries a sixty-inch searchlight on a swinging platform so guided as to be level in all positions of the arm. He next developed portable outfits for searchlight work, twenty-five of which were supplied to Russia in 1916 and were in active service in the war. The United States army also used eight of these searchlight outfits.

There are other equally interesting contributions to engineering originated and carried out by Mr. Strauss, but which our limited space will not permit us to describe.

Mr. Strauss who has written several manuscripts on Bascule Bridges and other engineering subjects, has published a volume of verse of high character, entitled "By-Products of Idle Hours," and dedicated to his father, artist and scholar, which was published in 1921; and has contributed freely to the technical and general press. One of his poems, "The Optimist," is included in a notable collection of poems entitled "Facing Forward" by Joseph Morris and St. Clair Adams.

In the March issue, 1923, of the American Magazine, John Kidder Rhodes pays a remarkable tribute to Mr. Strauss in an interesting and extended article entitled "The Story of the Remarkable Career of a Great Engineer."

Those who know Mr. Strauss best are convinced that in spite of the notable advances he has been able to bring about in bridge building, his many business and professional activities, his poetical genius and his ability as a writer and speaker, nothing reveals his character so well as his founding of the American Citizenship Foundation, an organization which he continued to serve as president until he succeeded in firmly establishing it as the foremost civic movement in the country. This organization represents many years of sacrifice of time and effort and money by Mr. Strauss devoted to the reduction of an ideal to a practical entity. The American Citizenship Foundation is a program of citizenship education. Its purpose is to train America's youth of sixteen to twenty-one for effective citizenship, just as youth is trained secularly. Its tools are, first, a Citizenship Training Manual evolved by a staff of nationally known educators and civic leaders and, second, Citizenship Clubs among the boys and girls and through which the teachings of the Manual are applied.

Mr. Strauss is connected with the Chicago Division of the Boy Scouts of America, having been North Shore scout commissioner for three years. In 1924 he was appointed by Governor Small a member of the Illinois State Committee for Defense Test Day and has been appointed by Mayor Dever as a member of the Recreation Committee of Chicago. His engineering memberships are in the American Society of Testing Materials, the Engineering Institute of Canada, the American Railway Engineering Association, Western Society of Engineers, Royal Society of Arts (Great Britain), Permanent International Association of Navigation Congresses, American Association of Port Authorities and American Society of Military Engineers. Mr. Strauss is also a member of the Chicago Association of Commerce, Art Institute, Chicago Civic Opera, the Chicago Yacht Club, International Rotary, Hamilton, City Club, Chicago Motor Club, Chicago Riding Club, Ohio Society, Military Intelligence Bureau, Army Athletic Association and S. A. E. Fraternity.

As his work and his actual life abundantly reveals, Mr. Strauss' outstanding personal traits are tireless energy, forcefulness, originality, resourcefulness and versatility, motivated by idealism, vision and high ethical standards. Thus he has been enabled to produce bridges in which utility and beauty are so successfully combined with the unusual. He is essentially a founder, an originator, and both in the practical and the ideal, as an engineer, as an idealist and as a citizen has added to the world's wealth, to its efficiency and to its betterment. Perhaps the best picture of the man was painted by one of his friends, Mr. H. E. Stevens, chief engineer of the Northern Pacific Railroad, in these words:

"Mr. Strauss is at his best when engaged in the solution of a problem requiring a combination of engineering skill, inventive genius and the courage to carry out on his own responsibility plans and methods in advance of established precedents."

On June 9, 1895, Mr. Strauss married May, daughter of Charles Van, of Cincinnati, Ohio, and they have two children: Ralph Van Strauss, who entered West Point Military Academy in 1925; and Richard Kenneth Strauss, who is a student in Leland-Stanford University, California.

EDWARD P. WADE. The name Wade is closely associated with the history of Alton, through the pioneer era beginning nearly a century ago and on down to the present time.

Samuel Wade, of old New England ancestry, was born in Massachusetts, April 17, 1806, and came to Alton in 1831. He followed his trade as a carpenter and builder and subsequently was associated with Dr. Ebenezer Marsh in establishing a packing business. These two men founded the Alton Bank, which succeeded the Alton Marine & Fire Insurance Company. Dr. Marsh was president of the bank until his death in 1877, and Samuel Wade succeeded him and held the office until his death on January 1, 1885. The Alton Bank became the Alton National Bank and after the death of Samuel Wade the president was Charles A. Caldwell, who in turn was succeeded by Edward P. Wade, a son of Samuel Wade. Samuel Wade was mayor of Alton from 1849 to 1851 and again in 1855-57.

HON. CARTER H. HARRISON, who was for five terms mayor of Chicago, equaling the service of his father, Carter H. Harrison, Sr., a record unique in the history of American municipal service, was born in Chicago, April 23, 1860. He was graduated with the degree of A. B. from St. Ignatius College, now Loyola University, in 1881, and took his law degree in Yale University in 1883. Mr. Harrison practiced law in Chicago from 1883 to 1889 and then engaged in the real estate business. He was publisher and editor of the Chicago Times from 1891 to 1894.

He was first elected mayor of Chicago in 1897, about four years after his father had been assassinated. He served continuously until 1905, four terms, and in 1911 was elected for a fifth term, this time for four years. He retired from the office of mayor in 1915. During America's participation in the World war he volunteered and served with the rank of captain in the American Red Cross, spending fourteen months in the Toul sector in France, from October 1, 1918, to April 1, 1919.

Mr. Harrison is a member of the Sons of the Revolution and Sons of the American Revolution, the Society of the Cincinnati, Society of Colonial Wars, Society of the War of 1812. His ancestry includes the distinguished Harrison family of Virginia, which gave the nation two presidents and many other notable men. Mr. Harrison is a member of the University, Casino, Saddle and Cycle, Huron Mountain Clubs, and is a Knight Templar Mason.

He married at New Orleans, December 14, 1888, Miss Edith Ogden, daughter of Judge Robert N. Ogden. They have two children: Carter H., Jr., who married Lucy Cook; and Edith Ogden, who married Cyrus Edson Manierre.

FRANK H. KIMBALL, physician and surgeon, whose skilful work and kindly influence made him one of the best loved members of his profession in Rockford for forty years, was one of the founders of Rockford Hospital, and his death occurred in that institution May 8, 1926, at the age of seventy-one.

He was a native of Rockford and a grandson of Dr. George Haskell, one of the most distinguished of the early pioneer doctors of Northern Illinois. Dr. George Haskell settled in Winnebago County in 1835, and the City of Rockford retains his memory in Haskell Street and Haskell Park. Dr. George Haskell was an educator for a year after coming to Illinois, and at an earlier date in New England. He was the boyhood teacher of John Greenleaf Whittier and the original of the schoolmaster made famous in the poet's "Snow-Bound." This branch of the Kimball family goes back into the early Colonial times in Massachusetts, the first ancestors having settled in Massachusetts Bay about 1635. The ancestry of Doctor Kimball included the famous Edwards family of Massachusetts.

Dr. Frank H. Kimball was born at Rockford, July 13, 1855, son of Henry P. and Ellen (Haskell) Kimball, his father a native of Maine and his mother of Massachusetts. Henry P. Kimball was a farmer and business man and settled in Winnebago County in 1852. He and his wife had three children: Dr. Frank H., Willis M., a resident of Glendale, California, and Carlton C., a Rockford business man.

Frank H. Kimball grew up on his father's farm near Rockford, attended the district schools, and choosing as his vocation the line followed by his maternal grandfather, he continued his training in the University of Michigan, from which he graduated in 1877, and then entered the Chicago Medical College, now the medical department of Northwestern University, where he took his degree in medicine in 1880. Doctor Kimball first practiced at Rockton, and then in Rockford, where his kindly and capable ministrations were continued until abated by ill health in 1923. Doctor Kimball was a man of scientific mind, and enjoyed a reputation for exceptional skill in his work, particularly in obstetrics. His services were frequently sought as a consulting physician. He also remained a representative of the old school of doctors, his humanitarian instincts always balancing his scientific judgment. Kindness, comfort, good cheer and generosity were as much a part of his professional equipment as were his surgical instruments and his medical supplies. Much of his work was uncompensated, and he never grew wealthy in his profession except the wealth that is represented in the esteem and affection of his fellow men. He was a republican in politics, a member of the B. P. O. Elks, and

Vincent Huber,
Abbot.

was identified with the Christian Union Church at Rockford.

Doctor Kimball in January, 1881, married Miss Henrietta T. Kirk, a native of Rockford, daughter of E. A. Kirk, a pioneer of that city. She died in 1892. For three years after the death of his first wife Doctor Kimball was engaged in post-graduate work in medicine and surgery in Europe. In July, 1895, he married Miss Gudrun M. Tillisch. Mrs. Kimball and three daughters survive him, and there are also six grandchildren. The daughters are: Elizabeth, wife of Robinson Mower, of Berkeley, California; Alice, wife of Samuel Lindsay, of Rockford; and Miss Ellen.

ELLIOTT W. SPROUL, congressman from the Third Illinois District, has made a career of real distinction in the City of Chicago, particularly in business. He founded and developed the E. W. Sproul Company and for many years was president of this, one of the largest building contracting firms in the Middle West.

Mr. Sproul was born in Kings County, New Brunswick, not far from the City of St. John, on December 28, 1856, son of Elliott and Rebecca Jane (Earl) Sproul. He attended public schools to some extent, but for the most part was self-educated. As a boy he worked at the trade of brick masonry and plasterer, and in 1876 came to the United States, completing his apprenticeship at Lynn, Massachusetts. He has been a naturalized citizen of the United States since 1886.

Mr. Sproul located at Englewood in Chicago April 1, 1880, and six months later formed a partnership with Henry Holmes, under the firm name of Holmes & Sproul, contractors. The partnership was dissolved in 1883, after which Mr. Sproul engaged in business for himself, finally becoming president of the E. W. Sproul Company, until he was succeeded by his son in 1913. Mr. Sproul was contractor for the construction of probably more school buildings in the city of Chicago than any other contractor. In 1907 he built the Hammond Packing Plant at St. Joseph, Missouri, and in 1908, the plant for the same company in Chicago, and in 1909 he built the plant at St. Joseph. He was the contractor for the construction of the Medinah Temple Building. The E. W. Sproul Company was incorporated in 1908, and it continued its contracting work on an extensive scale, not only in Chicago, but in eastern cities. This company has erected a large number of the warehouses and cold storage plants, and other factories in the Central Manufacturing District of Chicago.

Along with his successful business career Mr. Sproul has been interested in public affairs, and in 1896 was elected a member of the Chicago City Council. In the council he represented the old Thirty-first Ward, which later became the Thirty-second Ward, and finally was divided into three wards, the Seventeenth, Eighteenth and Nineteenth Wards. He was for a number of years director on the public library board, resigning when elected to Congress. In 1920 he was elected to the Sixty-Seventh Congress from the Third Congressional District and was re-elected to the Sixty-eighth, Sixty-ninth and Seventieth. In 1920 he was a delegate to the Republican National Convention. Mr. Sproul is a member of the important committee on post office and post roads.

He belongs to the Building Employers Association, and the Associated Builders and Master Masons Association. He is affiliated with Englewood Lodge No. 690, A. F. and A. M., is a past high priest of Englewood Chapter No. 176, Royal Arch Masons, a member of Englewood Commandery, Knights Templar, Oriental Consistory of the Scottish Rites, the Medinah Temple of the Mystic Shrine, and also belongs to Cook County Lodge No. 204, I. O. O. F., and holds the rank of major in the Encampment, and is a member of the Rebekahs.

Mr. Sproul married, June 2, 1881, Mrs. Jessie M. (Miller) Sibbett, who was born in Illinois in 1846 and died January 11, 1920. She was a very prominent worker in Doctor Gonsalus Central Church, and had much to do with philanthropic organizations. Mr. Sproul is the father of three children: Clara J., Wilford R. and Alberta, the latter the wife of Prof. Robert Stronach.

RT. REV. VINCENT HUBER is a prominent figure among the Catholic educators of Illinois. He is a representative of the Benedictine Fathers, the oldest and greatest educational order in the Catholic Church, and since 1897 has been connected officially with St. Bede College near Peru.

St. Bede College was incorporated under the laws of Illinois, February 12, 1890, and its first scholastic year began September 7, 1891. In 1889 the chapter of St. Vincent Arch Abbey, Westmoreland County, Pennsylvania, purchased two hundred acres of land in Bureau County, Illinois, a part of the Daniel Webster farm, and on this land the original buildings were erected in 1890-91. Since its founding, St. Bede College has made a splendid record in educating and training young men for the duties and performances of Christian citizenship. The school maintains a high school and college course and there is also a seminary for theological students.

Vincent Huber was born at Carrolltown, Pennsylvania, May 10, 1855, son of Peter and Katherine (Strittmatter) Huber. His mother was born at Bellefonte, Pennsylvania, and died in 1891, at the age of seventy-five. His father, a native of Germany, was born March 6, 1818, came to the United States in 1836, and followed farming in Pennsylvania until his death on November 23, 1894, at the age of seventy-six.

Vincent Huber grew up on a Pennsylvania farm, attended public schools and at the age of fourteen, entered St. Vincent College at Beatty, Pennsylvania. In 1874 he was accepted as a novice in the Benedictine Order and was ordained July 15, 1880. He spent a period in residence and study at Rome and on returning to this country in September, 1883, took the chair of theology in St. Vincent's Seminary. In 1892 he was also made rector of the college, and remained there until 1897.

Rt. Rev. Huber on coming to St. Bede College in 1897 filled the post of rector until 1908, when he was recalled to St. Vincent's Seminary as incumbent of the chair of theology. On March 31, 1910, he was unanimously elected the first abbot of St. Bede College, which had just been elevated to the dignity of an abbey.

CLARENCE ARLINGTON PEARCE. A young man of talent, creative ability and new and unique ideas, who is making his way to the front in the specialized field of drawing in the way of commercial advertising, is Clarence Arlington Pearce, of Joliet. Since boyhood he has applied himself to a mastery of the pen, pencil and brush, and the years that he passed in preparation are now bearing fruit in the acquirement of a prosperout business and recognition of his abilities.

Mr. Pearce has spent his entire life at Joliet, where he was born February 18, 1903, a son of Charles G. and Clara Elizabeth (White) Pearce, natives of Aurora, Illinois. Charles G. Pearce has been a resident of Joliet for many years, and is well and favorably known in this city, where he is cashier of the Joliet National Bank and a citizen of substance and worth. The early education of Clarence A. Pearce was acquired in the public schools, and after leaving high school he entered the Chicago Academy of Fine Arts, where he spent two years in close study and training. Upon his return to Joliet in 1922 he opened offices at 209 D'Arcy Building, and since that time has built up a gratifying business in drawing show cards, preparing window displays, etc., and making drawings for all kinds of advertising. His refreshing ideas, his skilled technique and his grasp of his patrons' ideas have combined to make him popular, and thus have insured him a good business.

Mr. Pearce is unmarried. He is a democrat in his political views, but is so engrossed with his business that he gives only a good citizen's attention to politics. His religious connection is with the First Presbyterian Church.

FLINT BONDURANT, M. D. As a physician and surgeon Doctor Bondurant, of Cairo, has achieved a genuine distinction as a man of exceptional skill and ability, and has also been a citizen of real leadership and constructive influence in the affairs of his home community.

He was born at Charleston, Missouri, September 23, 1885, son of Alpheus Alonzo and Mary Jane (Barker) Bondurant, his father a native of Jordan, Kentucky, and his mother of Charleston, Missouri. Alpheus A. Bondurant was also a physician, and died in 1919. His widow now lives at Cairo.

Doctor Flint Bondurant was seven years of age when, in 1892, his parents moved to Cairo, where he grew up, attending grammar and high schools. He took his Bachelor of Science degree from Northwestern University at Evanston and in 1909 graduated from the Northwestern University School of Medicine. Doctor Bondurant had unusual opportunities for experience and training before engaging in private practice. For a time he was state bacteriologist under the Illinois State Board of Health and for a year and a half was resident physician at the Cook County Hospital. He also had four months of special training in New York hospitals. In 1912 he engaged in private practice at Cairo, and has had a program of varied professional activities since that time.

He married, in 1914, Miss Blanche Thistlewood, a native of Cairo and daughter of Napoleon B. Thistlewood. Doctor Bondurant is a member of the Baptist Church, was president of the Kiwanis Club in 1923 and president of the Association of Commerce for 1924-25. From 1921 to January, 1925, he was president of the Cairo Egyptian Country Club. He is a democrat, a Knights Templar Mason and Shriner and a member of the B. P. O. Elks.

In recognition of his skill as a surgeon he is a fellow of the American College of Surgeons. He also belongs to the Alexander County, Illinois State and American Medical Associations and in 1913 was president of the County Medical Society. In 1924 he was chief of staff of St. Mary's Hospital and during 1918 was on duty at an evacuation hospital as an officer of the Army Medical Corps. He is a member of the Southern Illinois Medical Society and belongs to the American Legion.

NATHANIEL GREEN was a resident of Fulton, and spent all his life of purposeful activity in that community which esteemed him no less as a public spirited citizen than as a prosperous merchant.

He was born at Fulton, August 14, 1855, and died December 16, 1922, at the age of sixty-seven. He was a son of Richard and Cornelia (Johnson) Green. Richard Green was a native of Bowling Green, Kentucky, and was a merchant for some years at Bono in Lawrence County, Indiana, and in 1849 removed to Fulton, Illinois, and was one of the pioneer merchants of that town. He continued in business, with the exception of the period of the Civil war, until his death in 1884, at the age of seventy-six. His son, William C., a child of his first marriage, and later Nathaniel Green, became associates and partners in the business, and for many years the firm of R. Green & Sons conducted a flourishing business throughout Whiteside County. It was only after the death of Nathaniel Green that the firm closed out the business.

Nathaniel Green was a democrat in politics and a member of the Presbyterian Church. He married, May 24, 1882, Miss Elizabeth Baker. She was born at Garden Plains, Illinois, and survives her husband, maintaining her home at Fulton. She is a daughter of John W. and Mary (Hall Wright) Baker. Her parents were natives of Centerville, Maryland, where her father was born in 1812 and her mother in 1813. John W. Baker was a son of Thomas and Nancy Baker and was a small boy when his father died. In December, 1836, John W. Baker arrived at Fulton, Illinois, joining his uncle, John Baker, honored as one of the founders of the Illinois community. John W. Baker had a brother, Samuel, and three sisters, named Rosina, Frances and Martha. John W. Baker was a democrat, and he and his wife were Methodists. Their children were: Anna, John T., Albert J., John W., Jr., Ellen, Thomas J., William H., Edward, Ramsey M., Mary F. and Elizabeth. Of these children the only survivor is Mrs. Green.

Surviving Nathaniel Green is one son, Dwight Phelps Green, who was born at Fulton, October 13, 1886. He was educated in public schools in his native town, attended the Morgan Park Academy of Chicago and then entered Princeton University, where he finished his literary education in 1909. In 1912 he graduated from the School of Law of the University of Chicago and has since been engaged in a successful general practice in the City of Chicago. He married Miss Ella K. Porter, of Lexington, Kentucky. They have one son, Dwight P., Jr.

As a tribute to Nathaniel Green and as a beautiful expression of appreciation of the relations of father and son, the following, which appeared in Fulton Journal January 9, 1922, written by Dwight Green, is worthy of quotation:

"Thus have we left another dear one in the quiet resting spot by the side of the road, beneath snow covered grass and the shadows of wintry boughs. The halt was but for a moment though it seemed an age. Again the march is on, the processional life, toward the end of the road that has many strange curves and beside which other tired bodies shall find resting spots and similarly they shall be laid away by devoted hands and they thus command again: March on. A strange road, the road of life. So pleasant is the journey with these loved ones, so sad the leaving; so sharp the turns; so hidden the dangers; so powerful the Hand that guides; so cruel some times seems the blow that falls; so dark the way. So might it all seem but for Faith that shines, though not all revealed yet all assuring that we have left beside the road only the burden of this dear friend, and with the lighter carriage he has gone ahead of us and will be at the end of the road to greet us.

"With this reassuring faith in the mercy and love of our Guide along this strange and uncertain road, we fall to contemplating the memory of friends, for in that we find solace also rich as that memory is in beautiful pictures of happy associations now gone.

"Early recollections flood in upon us when we were but toddlings and he in the vigor of young fatherhood; we on his knees listening to the stories of the hunting, fishing and camping he had done as a boy; tales of his boyhood with old friends that we have since learned to know and love; tales of the river that he had loved; tales of his father whom he had left beside the road much the same as we have left this dear one.

"Later those prophecies of tender age were realized and there was camping with him above town on the island and swimming and fishing that boys love and he loved. Those days that seem but yesterday, but it was much longer ago, for we were lads then and he was strong and vigorous.

"Then came days of high school years, when our appreciation of his noble qualities came to us; when his words of counsel guided rebellious youth and he pointed out to us the long way ahead and the need of preparation for more certain progress; when his example began to shine as the guiding star.

"College days quickly followed for us; self sacrificing and indulgences came for him. Days when he might have said: ''Tis too much, abide with me, I need you.' But instead he said, 'Go on.' We went on while he stayed closer to duty. These were precious days, and now is revealed to us his character. His guide and counsel we now treasure in memory.

"Through all he was faithful and encouraging, while we noticed creeping age, and noted the ebbing of middle life and during the eventide of elderly years, yet his interest in us continued on, strong and enduring. The radiance of his smile and the heartiness of his laugh and the clear vision of his blue eyes seemed as always, and deceived us that the journey of life with him was yet long for time. Then the sad news, so unexpected, of the sudden end of his journey with us, came. Did words ever burn over a wire like these? The whole world rocked and we realized a precious treasure had been lost. But this loss was not ours alone; the whole community mourned, for his daily life was a constant contact with those in all walks of life. For forty years he had been in the constant and continuous service of his business and the constant service of his fellowman; a counsellor to the troubled, a comforter to the distressed, a devoted son to his parents, a loving husband, an affectionate brother, a sacrificing father, never vexed, always kind, the soul of honor. From him the love of human kindness flowed, and in all he was modest, unpretentious, genuine, indulgent, patient and loved by all.

"His was not a public life; his reward was the gaining of the hearts of others. His was the plain and the simple life for three score and ten years, in which he loved and was loved by a host of friends."

J. B. TITTERINGTON, a retired farmer and business man, was one of the oldest living native sons of Rock Island County at the time of his death September 5, 1925, and spent all his life in that vicinity.

He was born in Rock Island Township, May 30, 1843, son of James and Eleanor (Beall) Titterington, his father a native of England and his mother of Ohio. They were married in Ohio. James Titterington, with a brother, came overland and settled in Buffalo Prairie Township of Rock Island County when all the country was new and undeveloped. His wife and daughter subsequently came by boat down the Ohio and up the Mississippi River to join him. These parents had seven children, the last survivor being J. B. Titterington.

James B. Titterington attended public and private schools at Edgington, Illinois. He never married. Up to the death of his father, in 1875, he assisted in the management of the home farm, and after that he lived with his mother until her death in 1896. At that time he bought the interests of the other heirs in the home place of 440 acres. He gave his personal attention to its management, operating half of it for general farming purposes, and the remainder for the feeding of live stock. In 1909 he became a resident of Rock Island, making his home with his sister until her death in 1921, and from 1923 was a resident of the Como Hotel. He disposed of his farm land in 1913.

Mr. Titterington was reared a Presbyterian. He served eight years as a township supervisor, and held other township offices. Mr. Titterington was one of the last surviving men who voted for Abraham Lincoln. He had just reached the age of twenty-one and was old enough to vote for Lincoln in 1864. He gave his steady support to the republican ticket all the subsequent years.

CLYDE M. ENOCH, a Doctor of Dental Surgery, has practiced both in Chicago and at Waukegan, in which latter city he has his offices at 21 N. Genesee Street.

The Enoch family records go back to the Colonial period. They were pioneers in the foothills and mountains of the Alleghany region, at first on the eastern side and later in the valleys of the rivers tributary to the great Ohio. A number of generations have lived in West Virginia, and Doctor Enoch himself is a native of that state, born at Greencastle, January 28, 1892.

He is a descendant of Henry Enoch, who served with the rank of captain in the Revolutionary forces. The records at Washington and elsewhere mention him as a captain in the Virginia Militia in 1776, while in 1777 he was for a time stationed at Fort Grave Creek, in 1778 served three months with Gaddis' command of Virginia troops in an expedition against the Indian town west of the Ohio River, and in the Virginia Revolutionary records at Richmond an entry under date of October 27, 1779, refers to a warrant issued to Captain Henry Enoch for pay of Monongalia County, Virginia. This Henry Enoch was an early settler in Hampshire County in what is now West Virginia, at the forks of the great Cacapon River, and Washington while returning from a western surveying trip stopped at his home in 1755. Henry Enoch married, in 1759, Elizabeth Pegard, a daughter of Abram Pegard, whose name subsequently came to be spelled Pygart, for whom Pygart's Valley in West Virginia was named. Henry Enoch died in May, 1812. His son, Isaac Enoch, was born January 29, 1774, at Fort Grave Creek, Virginia, and died in Wirt County, Virginia, June 9, 1852. In 1796 he settled on land at Greencastle, in what is now West Virginia. He and his wife, Amy Tracy, were the parents of Abram Enoch, who was born in 1804 and died in 1881. During the Civil war he served as a magistrate of the Western Virginia District, administering the oath of allegiance to Union men. He married, in 1830, Nancy Dent Gibbons, who was born in 1805 and died in 1887. Their son, Martin Van Buren Enoch, born at Newark, West Virginia, in 1832, and died at Greencastle, West Virginia, in 1896, was serving as a colonel in the Virginia Militia when the Civil war broke out in 1861, and while a Southerner, he did not believe in secession, and he resigned his commission and took the allegiance to support the Union. He was for two terms assessor of Wirt County, and during Cleveland's administration was in the Government service in Connecticut and Philadelphia. He married Mary Louise Bayless, who was born at Newark, West Virginia, August 18, 1836, and died at Greencastle in that state April 24, 1915.

Their son, Abram Carlyle Enoch, father of Doctor Enoch, was born at Greencastle, West Virginia, March 3, 1857, and at the age of twelve years was sent to Rochester, New York, where he completed a business college education. He returned to West Virginia about 1875, and after his marriage resided at Greencastle. For years he was manager of the D. M. Miller Lumber Company of Parkersburg, and also followed farming. He was a Methodist, a democrat, and in 1908 was elected assessor of Wirt County. He moved to Parkersburg in October, 1915, and was a deputy in the office of the internal revenue collector in that district during Wilson's administration. He died at Parkersburg in February, 1924. He married in January, 1881, Alice Sonora Marshall, of Ritchie County, West Virginia, daughter of Benjamin Marshall, a West Virginia farmer who was a Union soldier, participating in the battle of Bull Run and subsequently in the battles of Shiloh, Chickamauga and Lookout Mountain. Benjamin Marshall married Virginia Jackson, who was a second cousin of Gen. Stonewall Jackson, her father and General Jackson's father being cousins. Stonewall Jackson was himself a native of West Virginia. The children of A. C. Enoch and wife were: Lillian, wife of Ortie McCormick, who is connected with an oil well supply company at Parkersburg, West Virginia; Gardner J., of Parkersburg, field superintendent for the Sinclair Oil Company; Benjamin, who died at the age of twenty; Carl L., of Parkersburg, now of Tampico, Mexico, with the Standard Oil Company; Cecil, who was overseas and participated in the Argonne campaign and is now a shell-shocked veteran in a hospital at Marion, Virginia; Virginia, who died when twenty years old; Dr. Clyde M.; Dr. Charles C., an osteopathic physician at Brookfield, Missouri; Vivian, wife of Ernest Evans, of Parkersburg, West Virginia, in the hardware business there; Doris, wife of Erwin Withers, of Parkersburg, West Virginia, an electrical engineer; and James, connected with an oil well supply company at Parkersburg.

Clyde M. Enoch was educated in public schools in West Virginia, completed his high school course at Valparaiso University in Indiana in 1915, and in 1919 graduated Doctor of Dental Surgery from the College of Dental Surgery of Chicago. After graduating he practiced in North Chicago one year, and in 1920 passed the State Board examination in California. He soon returned to North Chicago, and practiced three years in Chicago, and in 1924 established his professional business at Waukegan.

Mr. Enoch is a member of the B. P. O. Elks, the Psi Omega dental fraternity, is a republican and a Baptist. He married at Waukegan, November 13, 1923, Miss Olive Frances McLaren, of North Chicago. She was educated in the North Chicago High School and graduated from the Waukegan Business College in 1914, and for several years before her marriage was engaged in bookkeeping and stenographic work. Her father was born and reared in Nova Scotia, and about twenty years ago moved to North Chicago, where for some years he conducted a grocery and meat market, and later took up carpentry, a business he still continues. Mrs. Enoch's father is of Scotch-Irish ancestry, and her mother, Welsh, she having been born in Wales. Doctor and Mrs. Enoch have one daughter, Patricia Lee.

EUGENE L. GATES, an engineer who has been identified with railroad and highway construction and other phases of engineering in northern Illinois for a number of years, is a resident of DuPage County, where his people were among the first settlers. Mr. Gates is the present county superintendent of highways of DuPage County, and has been responsibly connected with much of the developments and plans for modern road building through that county.

He was born at Bloomingdale Village, in Bloomingdale Township, DuPage County, in 1882, son of Robert W. and Laura A. (Landon) Gates. His mother was born in Bloomingdale Township in 1838, and at the age of eighty-eight is probably the oldest living native resident of DuPage County. Her father, Louis Landon, came to Illinois from Ithaca, New York, in 1836, and settled in Bloomingdale Township, being one of the earliest settlers there. It was at about the same time that Erastus Gary, father of Judge Gary, and Warren L. and Jesse C. Wheaton, all of Connecticut, founded the pioneer community of Wheaton.

Eugene L. Gates was reared at the old homestead in DuPage County, and after a public school education joined a surveying outfit, and actual practice and hard work brought him his knowledge of surveying and civil engineering. His experience as a civil engineer covers a period of over a quarter of a century and has involved many noteworthy undertakings, such as railroad construction, bridge construction and highway building. Mr. Gates was employed as an engineer during the construction of the Chicago, Aurora & Elgin Electric Railroad.

It was in 1925, by appointment from the governor, that Mr. Gates became superintendent of highways of DuPage County. It is a position to which his fitness and long experience make him especially valuable to his native county, and his appointment coincided with a time when road building plans and developments in the county demanded a man of his exceptional qualifications. He has carried out a policy of construction that will place DuPage County in the forefront of counties in Northern Illinois in its highway system.

A recent announcement in which Mr. Gates prominently figured, and one given a great deal of publicity by the Chicago newspapers, was the proposed plan of the Butterfield Road Super-Highway, a unit in the super-highway system being built through Cook, DuPage and Kane counties, and planned as a magnificent thoroughfare approximately 200 feet wide. When completed this will be probably the chief trunk highway in the system of highways west from Chicago. Mr. Gates is secretary of the Metropolitan Highway Association, organized for promoting the construction and maintenance of such highways, and composed of highway officials and other interested parties in the three counties named. This organization is also cooperating with village and other communities in zoning plans.

Mr. Gates is a resident of Wheaton, is married and has four children, named Charles E., Claribel, Laura May and Alice.

JOSEPH KIMBALL MONTELIUS, banker and business man of Piper City, is a member of a family that has been distinguished in the business and public life of Ford County for nearly sixty years.

His father was the late John Augustus Montelius, who died October 13, 1920. Few men of his contemporary exercised a greater influence for good or constructive effort or practical christianity than John A. Montelius. He was born in the beautiful Buffalo Valley of central Pennsylvania, in the little city of Misslinburg, May 29, 1844, and was a descendant of Marcus Montelius, who at the age of nine years was kidnapped in Holland and was brought across the ocean and sold for his passage. Marcus Montelius after his marriage settled in Buffalo Valley on August 23, 1773. He was the grandfather of John Montelius, who in turn was the grandfather of John A. Montelius. The father of John A. Montelius was Charles Montelius. John A. Montelius married, October 8, 1867, and he and his wife, Kate, came to Illinois and settled in Benton Township of Ford County just about the time Piper City was laid out. John A. Montelius was one of the pioneer business men of that community. He was also elected and served as a member of the Forty-third, Forty-sixth and Forty-seventh General Assemblies of Illinois, finally declining further honors in the political field. He and his wife were the parents of four sons and two daughters: Charles Harry, Joseph Kimball, Margaret Gast, George Dunton, John Augustus and Mary Rebecca.

Joseph Kimball Montelius was born February 17, 1870. He attended public school at Piper City, also had home instruction, continued his education in the Lake Forest Academy, and was trained for business largely in his father's office. After considerable experience in general office work he became cashier of the Piper City Bank and on April 10, 1900, was elected cashier of the First National Bank, an institution of which he is now vice president. For many years he has also been associated with the Montelius Grain Company, which was founded by his father. Mr. Montelius does a general real estate business as well.

He is a former mayor of Piper City, and since April, 1905, has served continuously on the County Board of Supervisors. He is a republican, was a member of the Chicago Board of Trade, is a Knights Templar and Scottish Rite Mason, member of the Eastern Star and Modern Woodmen of America. In the Presbyterian Church at Piper City he has served as treasurer, trustee and elder.

Mr. Montelius married, November 30, 1898, Helen B. Stadler, daughter of John and Catherine Stadler and of German ancestry. The seven children born to their marriage are Harry A., Catherine L., Alfred F., Ruth E., Helen L., Miriam G. and John A. Montelius, III.

LUIGI CARNOVALE. Peace, universal peace, is the cry of civilized mankind, and during and since the Great war, no voice in its behalf has been raised with more earnestness or greater power than that of Luigi Carnovale, now a resident of Chicago, Illinois, distinguished author, publicist and champion of the cause of universal peace. He was born at Stilo, Italy, son of Raffaele and Carmela (Morello) Carnovale, and was educated in his native land. Some years since he came to the United States, where his fame as an author had preceded him, and in 1914 he married Miss Jessie E. Shears, since deceased. He is a member of the Authors' League of America, and fellow of the American Geographical Society.

Early in his public career Luigi Carnovale won public acclaim as an apostle of patriotism and humanity, as recorded in the history of his life, published at Rome, Italy, and still further evidenced in other volumes bearing these titles: Our Contemporaries—Luigi Carnovale, by Nicola Lapegna, with preface by Andrea Vitelli, Naples, Italy; Luigi Carnovale—Apostle of Humanity—The Modern Idealist, by Ethel Torrey Hibbard, Chicago, U. S. A.; and War is Death—Peace is Life—Choose, by Ethel Torrey Beacham, Chicago.

Interesting and appreciative as these works are, it is in his own writings that the real Luigi Carnovale is most vividly made known to the public, included in these being portrayals of artistic reactions, tender sentiment, national pride, courageous criticism, and some of the most practical, carefully thought-out arguments covering the whole subject of world peace.

Thus, being temperamentally a humanitarian, and from the beginning of his intellectual life an ardent advocate of peace, Mr. Carnovale was deeply impressed with the blow brought upon civilization by the horror and devastation wrought during the earlier years of the great war in Europe. How inevitable that he should have been inspired to the composition of his Peace Plan, that remarkable document that was the first Peace Plan to be offered for the world's consideration. This Peace Plan was first presented under the title of "Human Solidarity," published in Chicago, Illinois, in July, 1917, this giving it the chronological historical priority over all others submitted during or since the great war, and inclined in its clear and logical discussions, some of the same points later included in other plans. By very many intelligent and thoughtful people in the United States this plan has been approved as the most practical solution of the most serious of world problems, the menace of war.

Ever a patron of art as well as literature, it has given Mr. Carnovale great pleasure to enrich, at times, great institutions of learning in other lands than his own with priceless Italian treasures, as, for example, when he made it possible for his countrymen in the United States, by whom he is honored and beloved, to present to leading universities a replica of the original manuscript of Dante's Divine Comedy. He greatly endeared himself to the people of his native village when he had set up in their midst the imposing monument in commemoration of the Italian hero, Tommaso Campanella.

The published works of Luigi Carnovale that are now available to American readers are: "A Visit to the Artist Andrea Cefaly"; "My Mother Carmela Morello Carnovale"; "The Dream of Francesco"; "Journalism of Italian Emigrants in America"; "Why Italy Entered into the Great War"; "Only by the Abolition of Neutrality Can Wars be Quickly and Forever Prevented"; "How America Can Easily and Quickly Prevent Wars Forever"; "The Six-hundredth Anniversary of Dante in America."

His own eloquent words seem meet with which to close this too brief sketch of Luigi Carnovale, a remarkable personality, they being the dedication of his book, "How America Can Easily and Quickly Prevent Wars Forever."

"To the American People, in whose national unity the blood, the soul, the life of all peoples of the earth omnipotently triumph, this well pondered Work, supreme expression of humanitarian love, I dedicate with fervent hope."

ORIS BARNEY HASTINGS, a native of Cairo, has for over twenty years been a prominent figure in the commercial life there. He succeeded his father as manager and proprietor of a warehouse and elevator business, which is one of the large factors in Cairo's preeminence in the grain handling industry of the Mississippi Valley.

He was born at Cairo, December 7, 1885, son of Samuel and Anise (Barney) Hastings. His parents were natives of Clay County, Illinois. His father spent all his active life as a grain merchant and in 1885 located at Cairo and was prominent in grain handling and commission circles. He was also a county commissioner and member of the Board of Trustees of the Anna State Hospital. His death occurred in 1905, while his wife passed away in 1920.

Oris Barney Hastings graduated from the Cairo High School in 1902 and also attended Northwestern University. At the death of his father he returned home to take active charge of the business, and his good judgment and energy have greatly expanded what was already a prosperous enterprise. The elevator has capacity for 250,000 bushels. This firm built the first concrete elevator of Cairo. There are also warehouses for handling hay and corn, with a capacity of three hundred cars. Mr. Hastings and his three sisters now conduct the business. They do an extensive business in buying grain in Southeastern Missouri and small grains from all over the West and northern states, and through Cairo firms ship and distribute these grains over the southeastern and southwestern quarters of the United States. There are fifty persons in the employ of the business.

Mr. Hastings married in January, 1911,

Miss Marjorie Wright, a native of Duquoin, Illinois, and daughter of J. W. C. Wright. They have one son, O. B. Hastings, born in August, 1912. Mr. Hastings is a member of the Christian Church and is one of the church trustees, is a member of the Cairo School Board and since 1923 has been a county commissioner. During the World war period he was assistant food administrator, is a republican, and in the Knight Templar Commandery of Masons has filled all the chairs except that of commander. He is also a member of the B. P. O. Elks, the Kiwanis Club, is former vice president of the Association of Commerce, and a member of the Egyptian Country Club. He is a director and first vice president of the First Bank & Trust Company. He was chairman of the building committee during the construction of the two high school buildings at Cairo and was also chairman of the finance committee that financed the construction of a Masonic Temple. He is a former president of the Cairo Board of Trade.

FRANK REICHMANN is a scion of the third generation of the Reichmann family in Chicago, where he was born and reared and where he now figures as founder and president of the Reichmann Company, one of the foremost concerns here engaged in the manufacturing of radio apparatus. In this city, in which they were born, still reside his parents, Frank J. and Josephine (Lemos) Reichmann. Frank J. Reichmann is prominently identified with manufacturing industry in Chicago, is also an artist of exceptional talent, and he has been for many years president of the Arts Club of Chicago, his wife likewise being a talented artist and her paintings having gained her high reputation in the art circles of the United States, she being a member of the Board of Directors of the Chicago Art Institute and a member of the Pennsylvania Academy of Fine Arts.

In the public schools of Chicago Frank Reichmann continued his studies until he had duly profited by the curriculum of the high school, and in 1910 he was graduated from the Michigan School of Mines at Houghton, on the upper peninsula of Michigan, from which institution he received the degrees of Bachelor of Science and Mining Engineer. After his graduation Mr. Reichmann was engaged in practice as a mining engineer about two years, and his activities in this line touched Mexico as well as the United States. Upon his return to Chicago Mr. Reichmann here turned his attention to the designing and manufacturing of loud speakers for use in radio service, and he manufactured many such devices used in baseball parks and in connection with other outdoor activities. Soon he amplified his business by adding the manufacture of other products pertaining to the radio industry, and he developed and became the executive head of the American Production Trading Company, which manufactured a very extensive line of heavy-hardware products. This concern manufactured more than 300 devices and built up a large business. After his retirement from association with this corporation Mr. Reichmann began to devote all of his time, energy and capitalistic resources to the great modern science and industry represented under the familiar name of radio, and in this connection the Reichmann Company has won recognized leadership in the designing and constructing of complete radio sets and loud speakers. It is one of the largest concerns of this kind in the United States, and in its modern factory, at 1745 West Seventy-fourth Street, are retained several hundred employes, including a large number of engineers and technical laboratory men of the first rank. Mr. Reichmann has built up the commercial business of his company until it runs into millions of dollars and constitutes an important accession to the great and varied industrial and commercial interests of Chicago. Mr. Reichmann gives his special attention to the technical and engineering departments of the great industry controlled by his company, and he is constantly carrying forward work in designing and evolving further improvements in the radio, and working out plans for the further extension of the industry. The following references to the Reichmann Company are well worthy of perpetuation in this connection:

"A trip through the modern manufacturing plant of the Reichmann Company, in the southwestern section of Chicago and in the 1700 block of West Seventy-fourth Street, is to the layman a revelation of the complexities and magnitude of the radio industry. The principal products are the Thorola Islodyne Radio Receiver and the Thorophone Loud Speaker. The Reichmann concern is not a mere assembling plant. The thousands of parts, many of them almost infinitesimal, are all manufactured here, and many of these parts are made from the finest and rarest metals and compositions, including the modern composition known as Bakelite. Even the parts made of rubber, paper and wood are all produced in this great plant. Machines for making these integral parts, some of them of most intricate workmanship, that will cut or stamp parts, down to several thousandths of an inch of accuracy, are likewise produced in this factory. Precision and accuracy in the production of these parts are insisted upon to the slightest detail—as distinctly as in the making of parts of a watch. Some of the essential units of radio and loud speaker construction, for the successful manufacture of which this plant has become famous, are the 'doughnut' coils, audo-transformers, straight-line frequency condensers, Bakelite bell horns, and sound-box reproducers. The machines here used in the manufacturing of the Bakelite horns are among the largest and most powerful in the entire United States, with a pressure capacity of 200 tons. The punch presses, die machines and other heavy mechanical equipments are of the most modern design and construction and were made especially for the Reichmann Company. At the plant are maintained three research laboratories, one of which is a chemical laboratory, and everything in connection with the designing and manufacturing of the Reichmann products is according to the best engineering and shop practice. Under the direction of Mr. Reichmann this plant has gone farther, perhaps, than any other in solving the difficult problems of radio frequency, and Mr. Reichmann's contribution to the physical sciences relating to radio manufacture, radio transmission and radio reception really place him in the ranks of the foremost industrial and technical scientists."

Mr. Reichman was one of the organizers and is an official of the Radio Manufacturers Association of America. In November, 1925, he was one of those called into conference by Secretary of Commerce Hoover, at Washington, to formulate radio regulations for the United States. He is also a member of the Municipal Radio Commission of Chicago.

Like his parents and more remote ancestors, Mr. Reichmann has artistic tastes and talents, and one of his diversions is painting in oils and water-colors, in which connection he has availed himself of the advantages of the art school of the Chicago Art Institute. Mr. Reichmann is an enthusiastic devotee of hunting, and each successive season finds him indulging in duck hunting and in deer hunting in Northern Michigan and in Canada, usually in company with his valued friend, Hon. Chase S. Osborne, former governor of the State of Michigan.

CLARENCE J. BUCKWALTER, a radio manufacturer, founder and president of the American Bureau of Engineering, has been a resident of Chicago since early boyhood.

He was born in Colorado in 1882. His father, H. H. Buckwalter, left his home state of Pennsylvania in 1868 and going West, settled in Iowa. At the time of the first great silver mining boom in the middle '70s he moved to Colorado, locating in the Leadville district. He was a pioneer silver miner and otherwise took an active part in the development of the country, being elected and serving as mayor of Silver Cliff. In 1883, with his family, he removed to Emporia, Kansas, where he lived about seven years, and then returned to Sioux City, Iowa, which had been the home of his wife. At Sioux City he engaged in business, and among other transactions he bought the last Corn Palace Building in that city. His father-in-law, H. A. Jandt, was a wholesale dry goods merchant of Sioux City. In 1893 the Buckwalter family removed to Chicago, where H. H. Buckwalter lived until his death in February, 1926.

Clarence J. Buckwalter was eleven years of age when brought to Chicago, and continued his education in the public schools. He attended the old South Division High School and was one of its most prominent athletes. In 1902 he was a member of the South Division High School team that participated in the annual relay races conducted by the University of Pennsylvania at Philadelphia, and this team won the relay that year for the South Division High. Subsequently Mr. Buckwalter attended the University of Chicago.

He has given twenty years to the engineering profession, and in 1914 founded the American Bureau of Engineering, of which he is president. He is also president of the Ambu Engineering Institute and of the Buckwalter Radio Corporation, manufacturers of six-tube and eight-tube sets, known as the Burad Supertone.

JOHN W. JARANOWSKI is serving in 1925 as mayor of Calumet City, one of the progressive and important industrial municipalities of Cook County, and he stands forth as one of the representative business men and most loyal and public-spirited citizens of the Cook County district in which he was born and reared. From the best American standard the story of the career of Calumet City's popular mayor is replete in interest and incentive, for his advancement has come entirely through his own ability and efforts, his association with the practical duties and responsibilities of life having been initiated when he was a lad of but ten years.

Mr. Jaranowski was born in a home that stood on the Illinois-Indiana state line and in the district that marks the separation of Hammond, Indiana, and the present Calumet City, Illinois, a place formerly known as West Hammond. His parents were born in Poland and were young folk when they became numbered among the Polish pioneers of the City of Hammond, Indiana, where their marriage was solemnized, they having long been highly respected citizens of West Hammond, now incorporated as Calumet City. In the public schools of West Hammond Mayor Jaranowski continued his studies up to the seventh grade, and from the age of ten years until he was sixteen years old he was employed in the Simplex industrial plant at Hammond. Thereafter he was engaged in the coffee and tea business in that city until he sold the business and turned his attention to the general teaming and transfer enterprise. His ambition for advancement was not to be denied returns, and thus he eventually engaged in the coal business, in connection with which he organized the Illinois Coal & Material Company, of which he has since continued the president and in which he is the principal stockholder. He is president also of the public Construction Company, which has developed a large and important contracting business in the construction of concrete roads and streets, as well as in the construction of sewers, waterworks, reservoirs, etc., besides doing an appreciable amount of railroad construction work and giving effective service in advancing other public improvements, especially in connection with the local district. Through this company Mr. Jaranowski had been concerned in the building of every concrete street and road pavement in Calumet City prior to his election to the office of mayor.

The first public office held by Mr. Jaranowski was that of alderman of West Hammond, a position in which he served eight years. Later he was elected highway commissioner of Thornton Township, and this office he still retains. In the spring of 1925 he was elected mayor of Calumet City, and it may well be understood that he is giving a characteristically loyal, liberal and progressive administration of the municipal government. He had previously been one of the most influential in promoting the building of the fine new city hall of Calumet City, which was dedicated in the summer of 1925 and which is one of the most substantial, attractive and well arranged municipal structures of the

Wm. A. Schwartz

SARAH SCHWARTZ

kind that can be claimed by any city of the same comparative population in the entire State of Illinois.

The Mayor is one of the most vigorous and progressive members of the Calumet City Chamber of Commerce, and is a member also of the Hammond Chamber of Commerce, the Lansing Improvement Association, the Hammond Country Club, and the Woodmar Country Club, in which he is a stockholder. He is president of the Calumet City Library Association, and is affiliated with the Benevolent and Protective Order of Elks, the Loyal Order of Moose and the Fraternal Order of Eagles. In the World war period Mayor Jaranowski served as chairman of the local committee in charge of the drives in support of the Government war bonds, was chairman of the local organization of the American Protective League, and a member of the Local Exemption Board.

Mr. Jaranowski married Miss Salome Szcypinski, of Hammond, and in her home community her popularity is on a parity with that of her husband. The Mayor and Mrs. Jaranowski have three children: Harry, Martha and John W., Jr.

CYRUS J. TUCKER, a resident of Decatur, has had a long and successful career in business, and while active as a merchant and since retiring in a large measure from his business responsibilities, has given much time to civic and political affairs. He served two terms in the Illinois Legislature, and in 1924 became democratic candidate for state senator to represent the Twenty-eighth Senatorial District.

Mr. Tucker was born at Warrensburg, Illinois, October 26, 1868, son of Joseph C. and Emma (Ferree) Tucker, his father a native of New Hampshire and his mother of Ohio. His father came to Illinois in 1861, and for many years was in business as a contractor and builder. He died in 1903 and his wife, in 1883. They had five children, Cyrus J. being the oldest; Benjamin, who is a resident of Long Beach, California; Joseph T., a farmer near Warrensburg, Illinois; and John G. and Charles, deceased.

Mr. Tucker was reared and educated on a farm and followed agriculture as his vocation for two years. He then engaged in the retail mercantile business in Warrensburg, remaining there fifteen years and moved to Decatur to engage in business as a wholesale grocer and confectioner. Several years ago he retired and his chief business activity is looking after his farming interests.

Mr. Tucker married Miss Lillian Thompson, of Warrensburg, in June, 1896. They have a son, Gerald T., who is an expert accountant living at Long Beach, California. Mr. Tucker is a Knight Templar Mason, a member of the I. O. O. F. and the Congregational Church.

His public service included two years on the County Board of Review; twelve years on the County Board of Supervisors and he was one of the representatives from the Twenty-eighth District in the Forty-seventh and Forty-eighth General Assemblies from 1910 to 1914.

WILLIAM AUGUSTUS SCHWARTZ, who since 1880 has been a lawyer and banker at Carbondale, is a member of a prominent family of Jackson County. Much of the history of the family and the dominating traits of its character and citizenship are illustrated in the life record of Mr. Schwartz's mother, the late Sarah (Kimmel) Schwartz, one of the best loved women of Jackson County, who died November 4, 1920, at the advanced age of ninety-one years and three months.

She was born in Somerset County, Pennsylvania, August 4, 1829, while Andrew Jackson was president of the United States. In 1836, when she was seven years old, her parents, Henry and Rosannah Kimmel, moved to Richland County, Ohio, and in 1840 established their home in Jackson County, Illinois, in Elk Township. Sarah Schwartz was the last survivor of the eight sons and three daughters who came with her parents to Illinois. As a girl she had a full routine of household duties and became thoroughly familiar with every phase of pioneer life, from cooking by the open fire to spinning and weaving cloth for garments. She attended a subscription school. One of the boys who grew up in the same community was William Schwartz, whose family had also come to Jackson County in pioneer times. William Schwartz after the subscription school attended McKendree College in St. Clair County and graduated. He and Sarah Kimmel were married September 26, 1850, and they then entered a tract of government land near the old Schwartz homestead in Elk Township. While developing this land the Illinois Central Railroad was in course of construction through the county, and William Schwartz hauled the material for the road while Mrs. Schwartz for a time boarded the laborers. William Schwartz in early manhood had become a member of the Christian Church and Mrs. Schwartz united with the same church at Elkville in the spring of 1851. Her daily life then and thereafter until her death was an exemplification of the duties and spirit of a true Christian. William Schwartz was a man of prominence in his community. He was deeply interested in the cause of education, not only for his own children but for others. He assisted in financing the Christian college at Carbondale and was a member of the Legislature which voted to locate the Southern Illinois Normal University there. He was a member of the Legislature when he died, September 22, 1871, when in the prime of life.

Mr. and Mrs. Schwartz had a family of eight children, Ellen, William A., Henry, Daniel, Isabel, Laura, George and Lucy. Four of the children died within two years after their father's death, and the only two who survive their mother are William A. Schwartz and George Schwartz, both of Carbondale. She was also survived by four grandchildren and five great-grandchildren.

Mrs. Schwartz after the marriage of her daughter Ellen to John D. Hayes, in September, 1880, went to live with her son William A. Schwartz at Carbondale, and she looked after the home of this son until her death. She became permanently identified with the Christian Church at Carbondale, was president of the Ladies Aid Society, a member of the loyal women's class in the Sunday school, and kept up her church work until the infirmities of advancing years compelled her to desist. Mrs. Sarah Schwartz lived a remarkable life, not only in point of time but particularly in the service she rendered those about her.

William Augustus Schwartz, now dean of the Jackson County bar, was born in Elk township, February 28, 1853, the oldest son of his parents. He attended public schools, Carthage College, the Southern Illinois Normal University, and the Union College of Law at Chicago. He was admitted to the bar in 1879, and in 1880 moved to Carbondale. In 1880 he was elected state's attorney of Jackson County, serving four years and was again elected state's attorney of that county in 1912 and served four years. Mr. Schwartz was one of the organizers of the First National Bank of Carbondale in 1892, became a director, and in 1903 took the presidency. He also helped organize in 1897, and became president of the Carbondale Trust & Savings Bank. He assisted in consolidating these two institutions in 1924, the new organization continuing under the name of the First National Bank in Carbondale, but occupying the remodeled home of the National Bank. This bank has assets of a million dollars and is the largest financial institution in Jackson County. Mr. Schwartz is its first vice president. He has been financially identified with several other industrial, public utility, and other business concerns in this section of the state.

Mr. Schwartz is a democrat, is an elder in the Christian church, has been active in Sunday school work, and is a member of the Masonic fraternity and of the Order of the Eastern Star. He has never married.

PATRICK HENRY MOYNIHAN is a native Chicagoan, and first and last in his career has been his interesting success as a coal dealer. He is an active official of the Calumet Coal Company, one of the largest organizations of its kind. Mr. Moynihan has also been prominent for a number of years in Chicago politics.

He was born in Chicago, a son of John and Cecil (O'Donnell) Moynihan, his father a native of Ireland and his mother of Salem, Massachusetts. His father was a Union soldier in the Civil war and had a family of three sons and five daughters, Patrick H. being the third child.

Patrick Henry Moynihan attended parochial schools, the public high school, and as a youth he learned the printing trade with the Calumet Publishing Company. He was active with that company for sixteen years and is now its vice president. The Calumet Coal Company, of which he is vice president, has half a dozen yards in the Calumet district of Chicago, and has become one of the largest purveyors of fuel in Chicago, and in spite of the vagaries and vicissitudes of the fuel industry this company has won high esteem for its methods. Mr. Moynihan is president of the Hiawatha Phonograph Company.

He is a member of the Illinois Commerce Commission, is president of the South Chicago Business Men's Club, and for eight years he represented the Eighth Ward in the City Council, and is now president of the republican committee of the Tenth Ward.

Mr. Moynihan married Miss Betty Jovis. They have four children, Harry, Leslie, Marie and Mildred.

HON. STANLEY H. KUNZ, congressman from the Eighth District, has lived in Chicago since infancy, was for a number of years active in business and repeatedly in the last thirty-five years has held positions of honor and trust as the gift of his fellow citizens.

Mr. Kunz was born at Wilkes Barre, Pennsylvania, September 26, 1864, and in 1867 came to Chicago with his parents. He was educated in public schools, in business college and in St. Ignatius College. For a number of years he was in the railroad service, beginning as clerk in the general passenger offices of the Chicago & Northwestern Railway in Chicago. He was also with the Chicago, Rock Island & Pacific and Chicago, Burlington & Quincy Railroads, with the latter in the freight department, and spent some time in Cincinnati with the Kanawha Dispatch Line.

On returning to Chicago Mr. Kunz engaged in business for himself at 685 Noble Street. For some years he conducted an undertaking establishment, and was also a dealer in coal and wood.

His first important position in politics came in 1888 with election to the General Assembly of Illinois, as representative of what was then the Twenty-seventh Senatorial District. In that election he received ninety-seven per cent of the total vote passed in his ward. He served a term of two years and subsequently was elected a member of Illinois Senate for four years. In the meantime he had been an alderman in the Chicago City Council, representing the old Sixteenth Ward. During his first term he voted for the thousand dollar license fee for saloons. This vote cost him reelection, but after being out of the council a year he was again elected to that party. In 1898 Mr. Kunz was again a successful candidate for the State Senate.

Mr. Kunz was first a candidate for Congress in 1902, in the old Eighth Congressional District. He ran as a democrat in what was a republican year and was defeated by Preston Harrison, though by only sixty-two votes. In 1922 Mr. Kunz was elected congressman from the Eighth District and in 1924 was reelected. He has made a good record in Congress, has been appointed member of a number of important committees, and has been particularly zealous in looking after the interests of his district and the City of Chicago generally. His district embraces many large industrial enterprises, including the Illinois Steel Company and the Peoples Gas Company.

Mr. Kunz is a member of the Cook County Democratic Central Committee, was a delegate to the National Convention that nominated Woodrow Wilson at St. Louis, and a delegate to the famous convention of 1924, where after hundreds of ballots John W. Davis was nominated. Mr. Kunz is affiliated with the Woodmen of the World, Foresters and Royal Arcanum. He married Frances Kortas and has two sons, Medard Alexander Kunz, a young lawyer in Chicago, and Stanley H. Kunz, Jr.

COL. THOMAS S. HAMMOND. In business and military circles of Illinois few men have attained to greater or more well-merited distinction within such a comparatively short period as has Col. Thomas S. Hammond, of Chicago, a resident of this city from childhood. In the capacity of president and general manager of the Whiting Corporation of Harvey, Illinois, of which he was the founder and is still the active head of the organization as chairman of the Board of Directors, one of the leading industries of the Chicago metropolitan district, while as commander of the One Hundred Twenty-fourth Field Artillery he leads one of the finest military organizations in the country.

Colonel Hammond is a native of the Empire State, born at Crown Point, New York, and was a child when brought by his parents to Chicago. His early education was acquired in the public schools of this city and he was then sent to the University of Michigan, where in addition to the regular course he studied law. He has never practiced this profession, but has found his knowledge of law greatly beneficial to him in his business affairs. For many years Colonel Hammond has been prominent in business life and has been identified with a number of Chicago's large and important industries. He is now president and general manager of the Whiting Corporation of Harvey, Illinois, manufacturers of electric traveling cranes, foundry equipment, heavy types of machinery, railway special machinery and equipment, etc., and the plant includes grey iron, steel and brass foundries, machine shops, assembly shops, structural shops, and forge shops; he is also vice president of the Grindle Fuel Equipment Company of Harvey, manufacturers of powered coal equipment; secretary of the Swenson Evaporator Company of Harvey, manufacturers of evaporators and special chemical machinery; vice president of the Joseph Harrington Company of Harvey, manufacturers of the King Cole Automatic Stoker, and vice president of the National Engineering Company of Chicago, manufacturers of sand handling and sand preparing machinery for foundries.

Colonel Hammond has had a creditable and even notable military career. He first enlisted as a private in Battery C, First Illinois Field Artillery, served with battery A of the same regiment on the Mexican border in 1916. In the World war, beginning in April, 1917, the First Illinois Field Artillery became the One Hundred Forty-ninth Field Artillery of the United States Army, which became a part of the Forty-second (Rainbow) Division, with which Colonel Hammond went overseas in October, 1917. Before leaving for France he was promoted from first lieutenant to captain, and was in command of Battery A of the old First Illinois Artillery, then the One Hundred Forty-ninth Field Artillery when this organization left for France having been promoted to a majoralty, and served throughout the war with the famous Rainbow Division, the history of which is familiar to all and the Illinois part of which appears in the historical part of this work. For bravery and distinguished service in action he was made, in France, an officer of the French Legion of Honor, and at the close of the war was advanced by his own country to the rank of lieutenant colonel. After the war closed and Colonel Hammond had returned to his home he, through the recommendation of General Reilly, was placed in command of the One Hundred Twenty-fourth Field Artillery of the Thirty-third Division. This unit had been disbanded after the war, but the War Department at Washington later decided to give a complete infantry division to Illinois, which called for two regiments of light artillery, and this in turn called for the reorganization of the One Hundred Twenty-fourth Field Artillery, which Colonel Hammond undertook. In military circles the commanding officer of the One Hundred Twenty-fourth is accorded full credit for taking this regiment, recruiting its full strength with the finest body of men obtainable, building it up into one of the best artillery regiments in the National Guard. Taking over the old Armory on Wentworth Avenue as the headquarters of the One Hundred Twenty-fourth, he has had it completely renovated and put in splendid shape.

Colonel Hammond is a member of the Flossmoor Country Club, the Olympia Fields Club, the University Club, the Racquet Club, the Industrial Club and the Chicago Club.

HON. GEORGE F. HARDING. One of Chicago's men of note is Hon. George F. Harding, prominent for years in business affairs and influential in public life. In his present responsible office of comptroller of the City of Chicago he is admirably serving the city's best interests with the same honesty and efficiency that he has displayed in other high offices to which he has been called by his fellow citizens.

George F. Harding was born at Chicago, Illinois, August 16, 1868, son of George F. and Adelaide (Mathews) Harding, grandson of Gen. Abner C. Harding, a gallant officer of the Civil war, and a great-grandson of Gen. Abner Clarke, a hero of the Revolutionary war.

Senator Harding, who served two terms in the Upper House of the Illinois State Legislature, received his early educational training in the Moseley public school, Chicago, then entered Phillips Academy, Exeter, New Hampshire, from which noted institution he was graduated in 1888, and subsequently, in 1892, was graduated from the Harvard Law School. During his four years at Harvard he was a member of the Harvard Football Varsity Team, and in 1891 went to England on the All-American team, and held the Inter-Collegiate lightweight championship 1890-91.

Upon his return to Chicago, where he has always maintained his home, Mr. Harding soon became interested in politics and also became immersed in business, taking over his late father's immense property interests, and assuming entire management of his own affairs. His wise administration proved his business capacity. He is now president of the Chicago Real Estate Loan & Trust Company, and probably is one of the largest real estate operators in this city.

Senator Harding is well known all over Northern Illinois, but to learn where he is most highly esteemed one must visit his native city, where his public spirit has so often been manifested, his earnest civic interest so often shown and his unostentatious charities have brought helpfulness and comfort. As evidence of high regard and personal confidence, he was six times elected alderman of the Second Ward, Chicago, and subsequently was elected to the State Senate, where for two terms he served his constituents with marked ability.

Senator Harding married, in 1896, Miss Ellen Davis, whose death occurred some years later. In 1914 he married Miss Catherine Fay, who is now deceased. He has one daughter, Mary Milsom Harding. His handsome private residence is on Lake Park Avenue. In political sentiment he is a republican. He is a member of such representative clubs as the Chicago Athletic, South Shore Country, Chicago Yacht, Illinois Athletic, Olympia Fields Country and the Hamilton Club.

WILLIAM J. SACKMAN, a native of Waukegan, laid the foundation of his business career as a worker in lumber and planing mills, and for a number of years has been an associate and partner of the well known lumberman and capitalist, M. H. Hussey, being secretary-treasurer and manager of the North Chicago Lumber & Coal Company.

Mr. Sackman was born at Waukegan, December 7, 1874, son of Charles F. and Louise (Spitzman) Sackman, and grandson of Joseph Sackman, who came from Buffalo, New York, to Northern Illinois in 1848 and was one of the early settlers in Lake County. He located at Little Fort, which the following year became the village of Waukegan, and was engaged in the butcher and meat business therefor many years. Not long after coming to Illinois he went across the plains in a prairie schooner as far as Colorado and Denver, but after some prospecting for precious metals returned to Waukegan and resumed his business as a meat dealer. He died in 1899. Charles F. Sackman was born at Buffalo and was a child when he came to Illinois. He attended public schools in Waukegan and was also a student in old Waukegan College, the building of which stood on the corner of where now stands the First National Bank Building. After finishing his education he took up the butcher and meat business and followed it until his death in 1918. His wife, Louise Spitzman, was born at Wheatland, Wisconsin, attended school at Racine, and died in 1880.

William J. Sackman received his early training in the grammar and high schools of Waukegan. His ambition as a boy was to become a boat builder, and he found opportunity to serve his working apprenticeship in this line with the R. J. Douglas Boat Company, builders of row boats, sail boats and pleasure craft. He was with the firm three years, until it discontinued business, and he then kept up work in the boat building line for about a year longer. In 1891 he went with the W. H. Dow Manufacturing Company, operating a mill for the manufacture of window frames and sash. After a year he took employment with the Washburn-Moen Company, in the plant that is now owned by the American Steel & Wire Company at Waukegan. Mr. Sackman left this concern in 1895, and the following year was in the Waukegan Business College under Professor Hansen, a talented teacher, a linguist who possessed the speaking and writing knowledge of seven languages. He and some of the other pupils applied themselves so industriously that their teacher found it difficult to keep pace with them. Mr. Sackman in 1896 took charge of a tobacco store in Waukegan, but in 1898 returned to the W. H. Dow Manufacturing Company as bookkeeper and later as bookkeeper and estimator. In 1903 he became manager of the Kenosha Sash & Door Company, remaining a year, and in 1904 returned to Waukegan and at that time became associated with the M. H. Hussey Lumber Company. He started as bookkeeper and estimator, and in May, 1906, joined with Mr. Hussey in the purchase of the S. E. Arnold Lumber Company at what was then South Waukegan, now North Chicago. He and Mr. Hussey organized the North Chicago Lumber & Coal Company, with Mr. Hussey as president and Mr. Sackman as secretary-treasurer and manager. This company has been in business twenty years, and from a small concern has developed one of the largest organizations of its kind along the North Shore, making good its slogan of handling everything in the building line except paint and nails. This company sells approximately 3,500,000 feet of lumber yearly and also handles gravel, sand, cement, brick, mill work and other building supplies and fuel.

Mr. Sackman is a man of well established business connections. Through all the years he has had an interesting hobby and diversion, music, and he has contributed much to the musical activities of his locality. At the age of eighteen, while an employe at the Washburn-Moen plant, he joined the local band and orchestra of Waukegan, other members of which were H. D. Orr, Charlie Alden, Fred Alden, Art Alden, John Alden (John Alden having for a number of years been a member of the Sousa Band), Robert Dow and others. Mr. Sackman for two months devoted from eight to ten hours daily in practice on the clarinet, and at the end of that time was a proficient sight reader and performer and one of the valuable members of the band and orchestra. He was with the organization in playing engagements for dances and theatres, and for several years did a great deal of this work outside of business hours, work that was well paid, though the primary object was recreation. He pursued this hobby without interfering at any time with his regular business. He was a member of the Waukegan Band when it played a performance during the World's Fair in Chicago in 1893. He kept up his orchestra work from 1892 to 1910. Mr. Sackman is a member of the Waukegan Rotary Club. During the World war he devoted a great deal of his time to democratic activities, being secretary of the Waukegan-North Chicago Chapter of the Red Cross and chairman of the Home Service Section, and member of the Executive Committee. He resigned the chairmanship of the Home Service Section in 1925, but from 1917 until that date had given it priority over other claims to his attention except his home and business. During the war he spent about four hours on the average every day in the performance of duties in connection with the various drives. Mr. Sackman is a life member of the Glen Flora Club and in politics is a republican.

He married at Waukegan, April 10, 1901, Mary E. Harbauer, who grew up at Waukegan and is a graduate of the high school there. She is active in woman's club work. Her parents were George and Barbara (Liber) Harbauer. Her father, who died in 1893, was a cabinet and furniture manufacturer. Her mother is still living at Waukegan. Mr. and Mrs. Sackman have one son, Earl W. Sackman. This son after completing his high school course attended Lake Forest University and the University of Illinois, and since his college career has been associated with his father in the North Chicago Lumber & Coal Company, of which he is now assistant manager. Earl Sackman married in May, 1924, at Waukegan, Miss Florence Porter, of that city, and they have one daughter, Dorothy Eleanor.

SAMUEL WARREN NICHOLS, veteran Illinois editor, long identified with the Jacksonville Daily Journal, has been regarded as one of the truest benefactors of that city, which has been his home since early manhood. Mr. Nichols was born near Quincy, Adams County, Illinois, February 5, 1844, son of Warren and Ann Maria (Morril) Nichols. His mother was born at Epsom, New Hampshire, was reared in Concord, that state, and in the maternal line was a descendant of the Kimball and Ayers families, both conspicuous in the early history of New England. The Nichols family came from England and were also early settlers in New England.

Warren Nichols was a pioneer minister and missionary in the West whose services should not be forgotten. Born in Reading, Massachusetts, January 25, 1803, he graduated from Williams College in 1830 and in 1833 from the Andover Theological Seminary, where he prepared for the ministry of the New School Presbyterian Church. Having decided to engage in Home Missionary work, he at once went to Missouri, spending about a year there, and while in Missouri suffered an attack of Asiatic cholera during the memorable epidemic of 1833. In 1834 he moved to Illinois, and for fifteen years labored continuously in Adams, Pike and Hancock counties. He had much to do with overcoming and counteracting the influence of the Mormon Church, then at the height of its power, with headquarters at Nauvoo in Hancock County. He was also an abolitionist and active in the underground railway through Illinois. He was associated with Dr. David Nelson in promoting educational interests in Illinois, and he served as agent for the American Tract Society and gave freely of his time and means to promote the cause of higher and religious education. He was himself a profound Hebrew, Latin and Greek scholar; also skilled in mathematics, and one of the best educated men among the pioneers in Southern Illinois at that time. In 1849 he removed to Ohio, and continued his ministry there until 1856, when failing health compelled him to abandon it. He died in June, 1862.

Samuel Warren Nichols was five years of age when his parents moved to Ohio. He attended public schools in that state and in May, 1864, at the age of twenty, enlisted in Company E of the One Hundred Fifty-first Ohio Infantry. He served four months, chiefly in defense of Washington. On November 11, 1864, he came to Illinois and entered Illinois College at Jacksonville. Though he abandoned his college course before completing it, he was voted a graduate and accorded the Bachelor's degree. In 1866 he entered the Jacksonville Business College, becoming the first graduate of that institution and for one year remained as an instructor. He resigned to become treasurer and collector for the Jacksonville Gas Company, serving three years, and in 1870 entered the First National Bank of Jacksonville as teller. A year later he became associated with Terrance Brennan and Joseph De Silva in the hardware, tinware and stove business, a firm to which he gave his time for six years. From 1877 to 1886 he operated a photographic studio, but in the meantime, in 1884, became employed as local editor of the Jacksonville Daily Journal, for about two years carrying double responsibilities. After disposing of his studio in May, 1886, he gave his time entirely to the Journal and for many years was one of its editors and proprietors, building up that paper to become one of the most powerful journals in Southern Illinois. Upon the organization of the Journal Company in November, 1886, he was elected its treasurer.

He has been secretary of the Passavant Memorial Hospital at Jacksonville since its organization in 1874, and for many years has been a member of the Prudential Committee of the Congregational Church, and he also served as superintendent of the colored Sunday School at Jacksonville. He became chairman of the Park Board upon its organization, and the city is especially indebted to him for the foundation of its park system, he having given the ground for the park southeast of the city. His benefactions have been chiefly motivated by his interest in child welfare. For many years in his travels extending all over America he was usually accompanied by two or three children, whose expenses he paid, and at the time of the Louisiana Purchase Exposition at St. Louis in 1904 he made up a special train of over 400 children from Jacksonville and gave them the opportunity of enjoying this great fair. His interest in children has continued throughout his life and has been manifested in many practical forms. For years each fall he chartered an entire railroad train to take several hundred poor children to places of interest, St. Louis several times, Springfield several times, Peoria, Bloomington, Decatur, Havana, and other places, and for years he gave all the school children, their little brothers and sisters and the poor mothers of the city a free burgoo picnic, dinner and supper at Nichols Park, and when failing health compelled him to give that up he placed several thousand dollars in the hands of trustees, the interest to be used for gifts to poor children of the city each Christmas. One year he visited the Hawaiian Islands, one year he made a tour of Egypt, Palestine, Syria, Turkey, Italy, Switzerland, Belgium, France and England, one year he visited the countries of Southern Europe and one year the lands of Northern Europe, and one year traveled around the world by way of San Francisco, Honolulu, Japan, Philippines, China, Russia and Europe, and in all he had at his expense a number of friends. For thirty years he servel as lay preacher, aiding churches temporarily without a minister. For years he was head of an amateur dramatic club, presenting a number of plays successfully and being the author of a number. Greater than all the foregoing has been his aid to young men and women getting a start in life and an education. This has been wholly quiet, without publicity or ostentation, and the names are known only to himself and the Master whom he has loved to serve.

He is a member of Matt Starr Post No. 378, Grand Army of the Republic; is affiliated with Harmony Lodge No. 3, A. F. and A. M.; Jacksonville Chapter No. 3, Royal Arch Masons; Hospitaller Commandery No. 31, Knights Templar. Mr. Nichols married, December 30, 1873, Miss Helen M. Storrs. She was born at Holliston, Massachusetts, and died January 15, 1887. On January 15, 1916, he married Mrs. Elizabeth English, who died December 11, 1920, and he is now tenderly cared for by a dutiful step-daughter, Mrs. Stanley H. Wright, and husband.

ANTRIM CAMPBELL BROWN. One of the substantial business men and representative citizens of Springfield is Antrim Campbell Brown, florist and owner of a valuable tract of land and extensive greenhouses. Mr. Brown's interest in his work, in which he is a recognized authority, is not an acquired one but a natural talent that has manifested itself since his early youth.

Antrim Campbell Brown was born June 24, 1861, in the house in which he still resides, in the City of Springfield, Illinois. His parents were James and Sarah Julia (Martin) Brown, both natives of Maryland, the latter of whom was a native of Talbot County, and died in Springfield in 1891. James Brown was born in 1805 in Queen Anne's County, Maryland, and died at Springfield in 1882. He had been a man of public importance, serving for some years as special postoffice inspector through Ohio, Indiana, Illinois and a part of Missouri. He was twice married, a surviving son of his first union being Sherman Page Brown, a leading citizen of Seattle, Washington. Nine children were born to his second marriage, the two survivors of this family being Antrim C. Brown, of Springfield, and his sister, Lida, who is the wife of George E. Copeland, of Milwaukee, Wisconsin.

Well educated in the public schools of his native city, Mr. Brown had not yet reached his twenty-first year before he took over ten acres of the home place and converted them into a small-fruit farm, and as this venture under his intelligent management proved so successful, he experimented further and for a time raised choice early lettuce for the market. By this time having decided definitely upon his future career, he applied himself to the study of greenhouse plants and in 1884 made a visit to the East and became much interested in roses grown under glass. It was just at this period that the growing of roses in a commercial way began to expand. Upon his return he built his first greenhouses. In 1887 he admitted a partner, and the business was operated under the firm name of Brown & Canfield until 1902, when Mr. Canfield withdrew and Mr. Brown continued alone. In 1904 he erected a new range of greenhouses and now has 60,000 square feet of floor space. He has always made the growing of roses a feature of his business and has been very successful in raising many choice varieties of this incomparable flower. Mr. Brown has the distinction of having been the first florist to bring the American Beauty rose to perfection in the West. His nursery plot of ten acres adjoins his greenhouses. Mr. Brown has practically devoted his life to the building up of this enterprise, and it reflects credit both upon himself and his city.

In 1915, in the Ojai Valley, California, Mr. Brown married Mrs. Frances (Brotherton) Canfield, widow of Arthur C. Canfield and mother of two children: Marian and Russell Canfield, the former of Springfield and the latter of Chicago, Illinois. Mr. and Mrs. Brown are members of the Episcopal Church, members of the Illini Country Club and he belongs to the order of Knights of Pythias, and in political life is a democrat.

CHRISTIAN V. RUHLE is a veteran business man of Kankakee, where he first located while connected with the Illinois Central Railway, but for many years past has been in business as a dealer in building supplies.

He was born in Stuttgart, Germany, August 27, 1856. He graduated from the Royal Building and Technical Institute of Stuttgart. For a number of years he acquired a thorough experience in handling cements and all practical and technical phases of building construction while employed by the German government in the construction of fortifications at and around the City of Strassburg. He had his obligatory military service with the German artillery.

In the winter of 1879-80 Mr. Ruhle came to New York and went direct to Chicago, where he was appointed foreman of bridges on the Illinois Central Railway system. He was in that service until May, 1893, his work taking him to all portions of the system, from New Orleans on the south to Sioux Falls, South Dakota, on the north. In May, 1893, Mr. Ruhle engaged in the manufacture of lime and the handling of building supplies. At 501 South West Avenue in Kankakee he owns an entire block used for business purposes.

He married, in 1884, Therese E. Radzom, a native of Germany who came to the United States with her mother and sisters, Mr. and Mrs. Ruhle's children are: William, of Springfield, Illinois; Rosa, wife of William Irwin Holcomb, manager of the Ruhle Building Supply business; Meta, a clerk in her father's business; Elsa, at home; and George C., who

is professor and a Ph. D. of chemical engineering in the University of California. Mr. Ruhle is a member of the Evangelical Church. For several terms he was an alderman from the Fourth Ward, is a republican, and has held all the principal chairs in the various Masonic bodies at Kankakee. He is a member of the Consistory Club and the Chamber of Commerce. After coming to America he had three years of experience as a member of the Illinois National Guard in the field artillery.

JESSE GRANT CHAPLINE is founder and president of La Salle Extension University at Chicago, the world's largest business training institution, an organization with facilities and personnel offering, efficient training and instruction in practically every line of modern business, including law.

Mr. Chapline was born at Waverly, Missouri, January 13, 1870, son of William Purnell and Sallie Ann Chapline. He acquired his education in public schools and in St. Louis College, and has been interested in educational work for many years.

It was under his direction and along the lines of his ideals that the La Salle Extension University has developed as the largest school devoted to higher business training. Its total enrollment is 350,000. Mr. Chapline himself is widely known for his writings on sales and business subjects. He was former manager of the John Wanamaker Century Club at Philadelphia; is a director of the Commercial Research Association, is former president of the Associated Publishing Company and is an honorary member of the Society of Applied Psychology. He belongs to the Associated Advertising Clubs, the Association of National Advertisers, the Chicago Association of Commerce and the Chicago Art Institute. He is a member of the South Shore Country Club and the Colonial Club in Chicago.

Mr. Chapline married at Chicago, May 12, 1909, Miss Ann J. Johnson. They have two children: Marjorie Anne and Dorothy Jane. His home is at 7158 Luella Avenue and his business offices are on Michigan Avenue at Forty-first Street.

CHARLES L. FISHER. A number of the veterans of the World war after returning to their own country have entered the Government service in one capacity or another, their army experience having taught them the dignity and necessity of efficiently performing the work of their country in times of peace as well as war, and these young men are proving most valuable. One of them who is worthy of all commendation is Charles L. Fisher, deputy internal revenue collector for the United States Government at Joliet. He was born in Springfield, Ohio, September 19, 1897, a son of Frederick E. and Elizabeth Mary (McMillan) Fisher, natives of Elyria, New York, and Newport, Kentucky, respectively.

Graduated from the high school course of his native city in 1916, Charles L. Fisher had hardly begun his business career when this country entered the World war, and he was one of the first to volunteer, enlisting April 14, 1917. He was first assigned to the Illinois Field Artillery at Fort Sheridan, but six weeks later was sent to Camp Mills, Long Island. On October 13, 1917, he sailed on the President Lincoln for France, and was immediately placed under intensive training. In February, 1918, he was sent to the front, and later was federalized into the One Hundred and Forty-ninth United States Field Artillery, under Col. Henry Reilly. He participated in the Champagne-Meuse defensive, and the Meuse-Marne offensive, and in the Chateau Thierry and Saint Mihiel offensives. Still later he was in the campaign in the Argonne Forest. His unit, the third complete division in France, was relieved November 9, 1918, and subsequently became the Army of Occupation in Germany, but was sent home in April, 1919, and he received his honorable discharge at Camp Grant, Illinois, May 11, 1919.

Returning to the schoolroom, Mr. Fisher took up special studies for eighteen months, and then secured a position with the traffic department of the Illinois Traction Corporation, Incorporated, which he continued to hold until December, 1921, when he was appointed deputy internal revenue collector, with headquarters at La Salle, Illinois. In July, 1922, he was transferred and made division chief of the Seventh Division, First District, at Joliet.

In April, 1922, Mr. Fisher married Adalaide G. Schuster, of Glendive, Montana. There are no children. Mr. Fisher is an Episcopalian and a Mason. In political faith he is a republican, and he is an active member of the American Legion.

WILLIAM H. HILL, president of the Hill Brick Company of East St. Louis, was the founder of the Murphysboro Paving Brick Company, and in that and in other ways has contributed to the commercial development of southern Illinois and the broader utilization of the great natural resources of this section of the state.

He was born at Summerfield, St. Clair County, Illinois, June 4, 1867. His father, William H. Hill, Sr., became a prominent building supply dealer at East St. Louis. The son has spent the greater part of his life in St. Louis, though for a few years while president of the Murphysboro Paving Brick Company he lived in that city and became highly esteemed as a business man and citizen of the locality.

Mr. Hill was educated in public schools, attended Foster Academy and completed a course in the Eastman Business College at Poughkeepsie, New York. In his father's business he received a splendid training that qualified him as his father's successor. While handling building supplies he engaged in business as a contractor in East St. Louis and vicinity.

It was in 1908 that he became interested in the brick material deposits in Jackson County. Early the following year the Murphysboro Paving Brick Company was incorporated and he served as its president until 1917, his home having been in Murphysboro from 1920 to 1923. In 1917 his son-in-law, Frank E. Robison, acquired the interests of Mr. Jenkins in the paving company and took the executive management of the business, and in 1923 when Mr. Hill retired as president and returned to East St. Louis, Mr. Robison succeeded him as president and general manager.

At that time Mr. Hill was president of the Queen City Quarry Company of East St. Louis, with plant at Alton, Illinois; director in the Southern Illinois National Bank of East St. Louis, and at the present time is the oldest director in point of years of service in that institution; and also a director in the Southern Illinois Trust Company. He was owner of the W. H. Hill Lime & Cement Company of East St. Louis. On returning to that city in 1923 he built a new plant for the manufacture of building brick, organizing the Hill Brick Company, of which he is president and H. P. Reuss vice president. Mr. Frank E. Robison, of Murphysboro, secretary and treasurer. Mr. Hill is a thirty-second degree Scottish Rite Mason and Shriner, member of the Knights of Pythias, B. P. O. Elks, and belongs to the Methodist Church.

He married November 5, 1890, Miss Jennie Thomas of East St. Louis. They have two daughters. Gertrude E. is the wife of Frank E. Robison, of Murphysboro. Ruth Jeanette married Dr. Harry P. Reuss, now practicing his profession at Granite City, Illinois.

WILLIAM SINGLETON WILSON in a career as a railroad official, banker and coal operator has long enjoyed enviable prominence in Southern Illinois. His home is at Pinckneyville, in Perry County.

He was born at Brandenburg, Kentucky, October 26, 1852, son of William S. and Letticia (Fairleigh) Wilson, his mother a daughter of William Fairleigh, of French ancestry. The Wilsons were of Scotch descent. William S. Wilson was a farmer, and served as sheriff of his home county in Kentucky. He died in 1856, shortly after leaving this office.

William Singleton Wilson was less than four years old when his father died and was reared in the home of his maternal grandfather, William Fairleigh, who for many years was county clerk of Meade County, Kentucky. Mr. Wilson as a boy of fifteen, both from necessity and a pride to be self-supporting, began learning telegraphy in the office of the Western Union Telegraph Company at Owensboro, Kentucky. That was in 1867. The war had previously interfered with some of his opportunities to attend school, and consequently his real education has been a practical product. As a telegraph operator he was employed at Evansville, Indiana, and in 1869, he got the railroad fever and was sent to Danville, Indiana, as night operator on the Indianapolis & St. Louis, now part of the Big Four system. In 1870 he located at Freeburg, Illinois, as agent and operator for the Cairo Short Line, St. Louis, Alton & Terre Haute Railroad Company, and after filling various positions on that road was appointed superintendent in January, 1886, and held that office over ten years and until the Illinois Central purchased the road. His headquarters were transferred to Pinckneyville in 1890.

Mr. Wilson in 1896 engaged in the coal business as member of the Scott-Wilson Coal Company, with plant near Carterville. He was vice president of that company, was one of the owners of the Carterville Mining Company, and also had an active part in developing the White-Walnut Coal Company, of which he was president. He disposed of these interests and organized the Bessemer Wash Coal Company, which failed during the sudden financial stringency of the panic of 1907. Mr. Wilson lost practically his entire fortune in that venture. Subsequently he and the Ritchey Brothers organized the Ritchey Coal Company, supplying coal for the Illinois Central Railway. Mr. Wilson became president of this company and continued an active coal operator until quite recently. He is gradually retiring from business. In January, 1924, he was appointed by the United States Court as associate receiver with N. C. McLean of East St. Louis for the Southern Jem Coal Corporation.

Mr. Wilson has been one of the prominent men of his community at Pinckneyville. For eighteen years he was a member and president of the Board of Education, and used all the powers of his influence and individual leadership to give the town an adequate free school system. For six years he was a member of the City Council. He became one of the organizers and the first president of the First National Bank of Pinckneyville when it was organized in 1901, retiring from the presidency in 1909. He was also president of the Pinckneyville Building & Loan Association. He is chairman of the Board of Directors of the Murphy & Wall State Bank. Mr. Wilson has for twenty years been superintendent of the Baptist Sunday School. He was an active democrat for many years and later became independent in politics.

He married at Owensboro, Kentucky, April 29, 1875, Miss Belle M. Moorman. Her father, S. M. Moorman, was a merchant at Owensboro, and a Confederate soldier. Mrs. Wilson was born December 25, 1852. In April, 1925, she and Mr. Wilson celebrated their golden wedding anniversary. The two children of their marriage are: Sarah Deane, who was married to Dr. C. H. Roe; and George Parker.

WILLISTON E. RECKHOU. Not only is Williston E. Reckhou numbered among the rising young attorneys of Rockford, but he is also in the employ of the Federal Government as a member of the internal revenue department. He was born at Rockford, March 26, 1896, a son of Judge Louis M. and Florence J. (Chapman) Reckhou, natives of Illinois and Beloit, Wisconsin, respectively. For many years Judge Reckhou was in active practice as an attorney of Winnebago County; he served as city attorney of Rockford for two years, and for twelve years was county judge of Winnebago. His death occurred July 5, 1924, and in his passing the city and county lost a distinguished citizen, and his friends a loyal and helpful associate. Two children were born to Judge Reckhou and his wife, namely: Williston E. and Eleanore, the latter being now deceased.

After being graduated from the high-school course of Rockford in 1913, Williston E. Reckhou entered Beloit College, Beloit, Wisconsin, and was graduated therefrom in 1917, with

WILLIAM H. HILL

the degree of Bachelor of Arts. The call of patriotism led him into the army, and after his honorable discharge from the service he began the study of law under the able supervision of his father, who thoroughly grounded him in the fundamentals of his learned profession. Subsequently he had as a preceptor for a period of two years Judge E. D. Reynolds. In 1920 Mr. Reckhou was admitted to the bar, and in the succeeding year was appointed a deputy collector of internal revenue. Since that date he has been rendering an efficient service to the Government.

On August 30, 1919, Mr. Reckhou married Ruth Mary Whittemore, who was born at Sycamore, Illinois, and they have two children: Robert W. and Williston E., Jr. Mr. Reckhou belongs to the Benevolent and Protective Order of Elks, the American Legion and the Kiwanis and University Clubs. In politics he is a republican. For some years he has been a consistent member of the Centennial Methodist Episcopal Church of Rockford. In every respect Mr. Reckhou measures up to the highest standards of American manhood, and his abilities and high character are recognized by his community and associates.

EDWIN S. HAMILTON, M. D., physician, a former captain in the Medical Corps with the American Expeditionary Forces, is a successful member of his profession at Kankakee, with offices in the Cobb Building.

He was born at Emington, in Livingston County, Illinois, July 30, 1890, son of Edwin C. and Emma J. (Stump) Hamilton. His father was born at Brownsville, Ohio, and his mother at Hanover in the same state, where they were married. Edwin C. Hamilton became a physician and surgeon, and in May, 1890, located at Emington, Illinois, but since 1899 has resided at 585 South Chicago Avenue in Kankakee, where he is now retired. His wife died May 20, 1919. Their children were: Miss Helen, who is her father's housekeeper; Edwin S.; Winifred L., wife of Arthur E. Gray, of Kankakee; and Marjorie Bernice, wife of Howard O. McCracken, of Kankakee.

Edwin S. Hamilton has lived at Kankakee since early boyhood. He graduated from high school there in 1907, and then took the regular academic and free medical course in the University of Illinois, where he was graduated A. B. in 1911. His professional education was acquired in Rush Medical College and the University of Chicago, graduating Bachelor of Science from the latter in 1912, and taking his medical degree at Rush in 1913. From June 1, 1913, until March 1, 1915, Doctor Hamilton was an interne in the Cook County Hospital in Chicago. He returned to Kankakee and engaged in a general practice until May 31, 1917, when he was commissioned in the Medical Reserve Corps. On April 20, 1918, he went with Base Hospital No. 14, known as St. Luke's Hospital Unit, and on July 15th sailed for overseas and was assigned duty at Beaune Cote Deor, France, from March until June 15, 1919. Returning home, he was discharged July 2, 1919, with the rank of captain in the Medical Corps.

Doctor Hamilton in September, 1919, resumed his professional work at Kankakee. He is a member of all the medical societies and organizations.

Doctor Hamilton is unmarried. He is a former commander of the Local Post of the American Legion, is a former director of the Kankakee Country Club, a member of the Kiwanis Club, is on the Official Board of the First Methodist Episcopal Church, is a trustee of the B. P. O. Elks, a republican and affiliated with the Royal Arch and Knight Templar bodies of Masonry and the Mystic Shrine. He is now chief of staff of St. Mary's Hospital in Kankakee.

EDWARD C. BLANKO is founder and president of the Northwestern Pottery Company, a new but rapidly growing and important industry in the City of Chicago. Mr. Blanko's father has been in the pottery industry all his life and the son learned the business from the ground up. In 1922 he started on a small scale the manufacture of pottery at Norwood Park Avenue and Foster Avenue. The business has increased so rapidly that additions to the equipment and facilities have been difficult to provide. The principal product of the plant is flower pots, made in different sizes ranging from one inch to twenty-four inches in diameter, the complete line embracing about 150 kinds and sizes. The product is known in the industry as red earthenware, made from scientifically blended clays, providing the exact degree of porosity required for plant growth. The kiln-burning process brings also a degree of hardness that results in a perfect flower pot, and such is the reputation of the Northwestern Pottery pots that the trade demand comes from all over the United States. The product is sold in carload lots to dealers and many individual florists, individual orders reaching from 200,000 to 1,000,000 flower pots. This plant, which now covers 40,000 square feet, has a capacity of about 30,000,000 flower pots annually. The annual volume of business is approximately $250,000. The feature leader of the manufactured articles at the plant is known as the Northwestern-Self-Watering Flower Pot, a vessel that eliminates the hazard of human judgment and neglect, and has done more to insure success in the growing of house plants by the average householder than any other single invention.

The president of the company was born in Poland, in 1879, and came to America with his parents in 1889, and has since lived in Chicago. His father is John Blanko, now seventy-four years of age, who was a potter in Poland and has given his entire active life to that industry. He is vice president of the Northwestern Pottery Company.

After finishing a public school education at Chicago, Edward C. Blanko went to work as clerk in a grocery store and learned that business thoroughly, for several years being on the road as representative for a wholesale grocery.

The success of the Northwestern Pottery Company is attributable first to the untiring energy, application and enthusiasm of Mr. Blanko, who has and still works day and night at the business, never overlooking the slightest detail. He has never hesitated to spend money liberally for improvements that will add to the efficiency and productive capacity of the plant. This plant is located on the Chicago & Northwestern Railway. Conveying machinery has been installed for loading cars in the shortest space of time and at the least expense. Mr. Blanko devised a shipping crate for pottery that makes breakage practically unknown and insures safe arrival of shipment however distant the destination. In 1925 a tunnel kiln was constructed 100 feet in length, one of the largest in the industry. All the dyes and molds are made in a machine shop connected with the plant. This business employs about fifty people. Another product of the plant is fancy and ornamental pottery, hand made by skilled craftsmen, particularly used for landscape and garden ornamentation.

FRANK H. REESE, president of the Dundee State Bank, and one of the leading citizens of Kane County, has won the confidence of his fellow citizens and established the financial prestige of his city by his sound policies and astute business methods. He was born in Lake County, Illinois, February 22, 1863, a son of Conrad H. and Sophia (Steenwart) Reese, both of whom were natives of Germany, who came to the United States in childhood. Settling in Lake County following their marriage, they became farmers, and later he was in the milling business at Dundee. Both are now deceased.

At the age of seventeen Frank H. Reese took up the burden of caring for the six brothers and sisters in the family, and went into the mercantile business with C. F. Hall. After two years he was with Norton and Bott, general merchants, and remained with that firm for two years, following which he was for a time with L. J. Schroder, the two buying a general store at Dundee and operating it under the name of Schroder & Reese for three and one-half years. This association was then dissolved, and Mr. Reese took Henry Lemke into partnership, and they remained together until 1900. In that year Mr. Reese sold his mercantile interests and specialized on buying stocks of goods and selling this merchandise at retail, with headquarters at Hampton, Iowa. Later, closing this business, he was at Waukegan in the same line until 1903, when he returned to Dundee and assisted in organizing the bank of which he is president.

On February 28, 1884, Mr. Reese married Carrie Lemke, and they had one son, who died at birth. Mr. Reese is a republican. He belongs to the Lutheran Church at Dundee.

The Dundee State Bank grew out of the persistent efforts of Charles T. Zahringer, a grocery traveling salesman, and an official of the Reuss State Bank of Naperville, Illinois, aided by Frank H. Reese and Joseph Reuss, president of the bank bearing his name at Naperville.

The first home of this bank covered a floor space 8x16 feet of the northwest corner of the Charles Daus Furniture Store, and the doors were first opened for business June 15, 1903, with Mr. Reese as cashier and bookkeeper. The first president was D. C. Haeger, who continued in office until January 1, 1912. During the life of the bank Charles S. Sinclair has been vice president, and Henry C. Wendt and Edward C. Masters, still on the board, were among the original directors.

From the beginning, aided during the first eight years by the counsel of Mr. Reuss of Naperville, this bank was a success, and a building was erected to house the bank which was opened February 12, 1904. This building covered 984 square feet of floor space, but only a portion of it was used during the following five years.

In 1912 Mr. Reese was elected president of the bank to succeed Mr. Haeger, who had moved to Aurora; and Charles C. Wolaver became cashier. The charter list of stockholders is as follows: H. H. Brey, J. C. Bohn, H. J. Baumann, James Dorsey, A. B. Eggler, Lucia A. Goram, J. C. Heidemann, D. C. Haeger, E. C. Masters, A. W. Meyer, Joseph Reuss, F. H. Reese, J. R. Smith, C. S. Sinclair, Frederick Sternberg, C. P. Todd, Emil Vette, H. C. Wendt and Charles T. Zahringer. The present officers are: Frank H. Reese, president; Charles S. Sinclair, vice president; Charles C. Wolaver, cashier; and A. E. Schuris, assistant cashier. The present Board of Directors is composed of the following: Frank H. Reese, Charles S. Sinclair, Charles C. Wolaver, E. A. Annell, Edmund H. Haeger, Louis H. Wenholz and Thomas F. Wendt.

As the business of the Dundee State Bank expanded more room was required, and finally the building erected in 1904 became too restricted. Consequently another banking home was built, and its doors were opened to the public September 11, 1919. There are 4,890 feet of floor space, and the building is of Buff Bedford stone in front, with floors and roof of solid concrete reinforced with steel, making the building fireproof. The vault is one solid mass of concrete, interwoven with steel bars every six inches in every direction, and the door is built of five layers of steel, the weight of which is nearly seven tons, and is the same size and thickness as that used by the Federal Reserve Bank of Chicago. This door was made for the bank by the Diebold Safe & Lock Company, and the vault complete, including the door and equipments, cost one-sixth of the entire cost of the building. In addition to the lobby and vestibule there are the main banking room, the ladies' retiring room, the men's room, the safe deposit booths, the safe deposit vault, the additional work room, and the community room. The entire banking home is equipped throughout with the most modern of banking furniture and appliances, and no pains or expense have been spared to make convenient and beautiful the various rooms according to the several purposes for which they are designed.

On June 15, 1903, the deposits of the Dundee State Bank were $4,327.96. At the close of the first year they were $59,216.29. On June 15, 1919, the deposits were $695,272.03. The bank maintains an investment department, which renders a service that is absolutely free, and gives advice on all kinds of investments, that oftentimes saves money for the customer, as well as averts losses. The savings department pays the usual three per cent interest on all deposits. One of the strong features of the bank since the completion of its

Andrew Courtney Campbell Jr.

new building is the safe deposit department. Valuables placed in this vault are as secure as though they were deposited with any of the large banking houses of Chicago. An inspection of the men filling the official positions in the bank, as well as those on the directorate, shows that some of the most solid financiers and business men of Kane County are connected with this institution, and headed as they are by a man of the character and sagacity of Mr. Reese, a continued prosperity is assured, which of necessity strengthens the commercial importance of Dundee and Kane County, for no section is sounder than its banks and the men who are in charge of their operation.

THEY CANNOT DIE

In loving memory of A. Courtney Campbell, Jr., Sergeant Pilot La Fayette Escadrille; killed in combat Pargny, France, October 1, 1917.

Above the strife his spirit took its flight,
  While at his feet the warring world was spread.
He died, a smiling martyr to a cause where he
  Had borne the nobler part—had led.

The starry heavens of the night were his,
  The rosy dawn, the gleaming sunset's glare,
Perhaps he seemed so near God beckoned him,
  And bade him leave the world of strife and care.

They cannot die, these men who sleep today,
  Remembered in the nation's grateful heart.
The tears and love and gratitude we give
  Are but just tributes to their larger part.

Sometimes when thoughts of other scenes and days,
  Bring back the knowledge that he is not here,
A whisper comes from out the Unseen World,
  And says, "Be comforted, my God is near."
    —*Anne Vance Mahaffey.*

ANDREW COURTNEY CAMPBELL, JR. (Sergeant Pilot Aviator, LaFayette Escadrille; Killed in combat in France over German lines, October 1, 1917.)

Three generations of the Campbell family have lived in Illinois. The first did its important work in the extreme northwestern corner of the state at the old, historic city of Galena on the Galena River, which in early days was called "Fever River."

For over half a century the Campbells have lived in Chicago and vicinity. The youngest and last of the family, Andrew Courtney Campbell, Jr., a native of Chicago, attained to immortality over the battle lines in France and is numbered among "the unreturning brave" oft h e great war.

Before coming to Illinois the Campbells were Virginians. Benjamin H. Campbell was born in King William County. Virginia, in 1814. In 1835 he came west and settled at Galena, Illinois, where he found employment in the mercantile firm of Campbell and Morehouse, the senior member of which was his brother, George W. Campbell. B. H. Campbell later became a member of the firm. In 1841 the business was sold, and B. H. Campbell then engaged in the commission business for himself and in time developed a wholesale grocery trade which extended over a wide territory as far north as Saint Paul, Minnesota. About 1850 he organized the Galena and Minnesota Packet Company to operate steamboats between Galena and Saint Paul. This line of steamboats, the first to carry United States mail, did much to extend the Campbell business and at the same time distribute it to Galena's prosperity and commercial wealth. B. H. Campbell for some years was one of the prominent men in the upper Mississippi River traffic and built and operated a number of the best boats on the river. He finally sold his boating interests to the Keokuk Packet Company.

B. H. Campbell while at Galena was a friend and neighbor of Ulysses S. Grant and his family. Soon after General Grant became president, in 1869, he appointed B. H. Campbell United States marshal for the Northern District of Illinois. To discharge the duties of this position he removed with his family to Chicago. He served as United States marshal for eight years. He was one of the organizers and became the largest stockholder of the old West Division Horse Railroad Company, which was finally sold to the Yerkes interests and later became a cable line.

Benjamin Campbell in 1837 married Eliza H. Scott. Both the Scotts and Campbells originated in Scotland. The Scotts were pioneers of Arkansas. Mrs. Eliza Campbell's father, Judge Andrew Scott, was the first United States judge of the territory of Arkansas. She was a granddaughter of John Rice Jones, a sketch of whom appears on other pages of this work. She was also a niece of Gen. George W. Jones of Iowa, who served twenty-eight years as United States senator from Iowa and was a colleague of Daniel Webster and Henry Clay. The children of Benjamin Campbell were: Annie, who married Gen. O. E. Babcock, on the staff of Gen. U. S. Grant, being his private secretary during both of his presidential administrations, and Mrs. Babcock died in Chicago; Augustus S., deceased; Benjamin H., Jr., deceased; Mary L., widow of Charles W. Ware, of Dubuque, Iowa, later of Chicago; Emily J., wife of Miles J. Nixon, of Chicago; Russella, widow of LeGrand Smith; Jessie, deceased; and A. Courtney, Sr. Campbell E. Babcock, son of Annie and Gen. O. E. Babcock, enlisted in Roosevelt's Rough Riders and served through the Spanish-American war. He subsequently joined the regular army, was appointed lieutenant and at the time of his death held a captain's commission. Benjamin H. Campbell, Jr., fought in the Civil war, enlisting at the age of seventeen. Later he was a captain on the staff of Gen. A. L. Chetlain. From this record it is evident that A. Courtney Campbell, Jr., came of fighting stock, both his uncle and cousins participating in two wars.

A. Courtney Campbell, Sr., son of Benjamin H. and Eliza (Scott) Campbell was born in Galena in 1848 and since 1869 has been a resident of Chicago. For several years he was deputy United States marshal under his father. In 1880 he removed to Wyoming and engaged in the cattle business on the open range, with headquarters near Sheridan. He divided his time between his widely extended business interests in the west and in Chicago, and for several years has been retired, though he still maintains an office in the Rookery Building. His home is in Evanston. He married Cornelia Alice Morton, a native of Chicago. Their youngest child was the late A. Courtney Campbell, Jr., and the other two, now deceased, were Morton Ben and Andrea Charity Campbell.

Mrs. Campbell is a daughter of George Clinton Morton, a native of Alexandria, New York. Mr. Morton, born in 1819, was a direct descendant on his mother's side of the Rev. John Cotton, of Derby, England. The latter, who was born in 1585, was vicar of Boston, England, from 1613 to 1633. In 1633 he came to America and later was a minister of the First Church of Boston, Massachusetts. The Morton family has been one of prominence in the history of the United States and includes famous jurists, physicians, inventors, clergymen and writers; also men who fought in the Revolutionary, Mexican and Civil wars. George C. Morton came to Chicago in 1849. He went into the lumber business and continued in that business until late in life. At one time he was president of the Chicago Lumber Exchange. His policy was to try to settle business problems by arbitration—at that time a somewhat unusual method. He died in 1887, highly respected and regretted by his many friends. George C. Morton married Charity Rathbun, of Auburn, New York. She lived a very useful life, active in church and philanthropic causes, and during the Civil war was identified with the old Marine Hospital and Camp Douglas, Chicago, and also participated in the aid and relief work following the great Chicago fire of 1871. The children of George C. Morton and his wife were: Joanna, widow of Mortimer Rathbone; Cornelia Alice, Mrs. A. Courtney Campbell; Albert Henry, deceased; Eugene Clinton, a resident of Chicago.

A. Courtney Campbell, Jr., was born in Chicago, November 19, 1891. During his boyhood he attended the Moseley School on Michigan Avenue. The family in 1905 removed to Kenilworth, Illinois, and he graduated from the Horace Mann Grammar School, Winnetka, and subsequently attended the New Trier High School. A. Courtney Campbell, Jr., after leaving high school attended Mercersburg Academy in Pennsylvania, and then entered the University of Virginia. He was one of the students at the University of Virginia who enlisted for service in France before America entered the war. Ten months before this country became involved in the great struggle A. Courtney Campbell, Jr., bade farewell to his home and parents, in June, 1916, and two weeks later enlisted in the French army and entered the Aviation Instruction School at Buc, France, and successively was a student at the aviation schools at Juvisy, Avord, Cazeaux, Pau and Plessis-Belleville, taking honors at each school. He went to the front April 17, 1917, entering the LaFayette Escadrille. Early in his flying experience he was officially credited with performing an impossible feat. While a patrol was assembling at Chaudron on the Aisne sector a lower wing of his Nieuport became detached at a height of 5,400 feet. Throwing his weight on the disabled side of the plane he came to earth smoothly. His coolness and courage enabled him to accomplish something no other aviator had ever done. This feat is described by Capt. Georges Thenault, then commander of the LaFayette Escadrille, as follows:

"During the fighting, Andrew Courtney Campbell joined the Escadrille, and some time afterwards there befell him one of the most astounding adventures that ever happened to any pilot, an adventure which made a great stir throughout the French flying world. One day flying a Nieuport at about 5,400 feet, his lower left wing broke right away, fluttered down and fell into the forest of Villers-Cotterets, where it never was found. The wing was broken off clean, just level with the body and at the points of junction with the struts. With this machine, biplane on the right and monoplane on the left, Campbell succeeded in coming down and landing intact near our aerodrome in a field of beet roots. How did he manage? It was a perfect miracle that the remaining wing did not yield in its turn, thus plunging Campbell to certain death.

"After the accident all the learned experts of Aviation came along to study such an incredible case, and prove that it was possible to fly in these conditions. None the less, it took a man like Campbell with his iron nerve to carry out this exploit which remains unique in the annals of aviation.

"For this Courtney received citation from French Minister of Aeronautiques. Mention is made of this feat by instructors at French aviation schools to emphasize what skill and coolness can achieve. It was the only time such a feat was ever known, with the aviator's life preserved."

The foregoing is quoted from Capt. Georges Thenault's book, "The Story of the Lafayette Escadrille," page 126.

During the summer of 1917 he was given official credit for bringing down four enemy planes, and had brought down several others, although too far over the lines to be observed. A. Courtney Campbell, Jr., was ideally equipped for aviation and he took the greatest pride and enthusiasm in his work. It was this enthusiasm that led him to decline transfer from the French service, in which he held the rank of sergeant in the Escadrille, to the American Air Corps, where he might on his service record have attained much higher rank. In his last letter to his parents, written only a day or two before his death, he said:

"I am asked by my own country to exchange and go under service of my own flag with higher rank than I now have, but when I signed up under the French flag it was for the duration of the war, and it was before America entered the struggle. I do not see how I can with honor make any change. France gave me my tuition and I owe them what I know. I have a sentiment, too, for the horizon blue I am wearing—I must do more for France before I can ask for a change."

The crowning day of his destiny came— October 1, 1917. On that morning Courtney Campbell was on scout duty. Suddenly three big enemy planes, each carrying two men, swooped down on another member of the Escadrille, riddling his plane and crippling the aviator. Courtney in his small plane went for them, to cover his comrade's retreat. The fight was furious. Darting in and out, looping, zooming, spinning, he engaged the three battle planes, and the fight ended when Courtney and two of the enemy planes crashed. His wounded comrade landed in his own lines, collapsed in his cock-pit and sobbed, "They got Campbell."

Sometimes an enemy honors a gallant foe. So it was in this case. The Germans buried Courtney alongside of the two he had brought down and erected a cross with name and date inscribed over the grave of each. This was north of Soissons, not far from Pargny. Then the tide of battle swept back and forth over the spot, and when the war ended the area was a vast mass of debris—not one house remained standing in the village. For two years it was not known where Courtney's body rested. Repeated efforts were made to locate the grave, but they failed. Three times Capt. Edgar Hamilton visited the approximate spot. It seemed a hopeless task. French farmers were plowing the fields. Captain Hamilton enlisted the aid of the farmers and their families and was about to enter his automobile in despair when one of the children found a cross under a mass of barbed wire fifteen feet high. Hurrying back to the spot, he found two more crosses. Underneath were three bodies. One was Courtney Campbell. There was the identification disc and in his breast pocket was his commission, photographs of his parents and their last Christmas card to him. Courtney now is buried in Belleau Wood by the side of his friend and fellow-aviator, Wallace Winter, Jr., of Chicago, who had died while in the French Air Service. Courtney was the first to go from Kenilworth and its first to die. He was the last of his line.

His military record is a part of French aviation history. He received, after a brilliant achievement, the Croix de Guerre with Palm and Gold Star. After the war General Gouraud was sent by France to Chicago to bestow in Courtney's memory upon his father the Medaille Militaire, France's highest gift. Courtney's name with those of other aviators is inscribed on a tablet in the War Museum in Les Invalides, Paris. His name (with those of other aviators) is also inscribed upon an imposing monument to the memory of the soldiers of the "Legion Etrangere" in Place des Etats Unis in Paris. His name is also one of those carved into the majestic LaFayette Escadrille memorial which is being erected in the LaFayette memorial garden at Saint Cloud near Paris.

Two tributes to his memory should here be mentioned: A bed named for him in the American Memorial Hospital at Rheims, France, and an oil portrait of him painted by Leopold Seyffert, which will shortly be unveiled and hung in the Administration Building at Mercersburg Academy, Mercersburg, Pennsylvania. Both of these memorials were endowed by the relatives, friends and parents of A. Courtney Campbell, Jr.

His name is also with those on the University of Virginia memorial tablet, beneath an inscription that is one of the most beautiful and impressive of patriotic "In memoriams."

"They shall not grow old as we that are left grow old; age shall not weary them nor the years condemn. At the going down of the sun and in the morning we shall remember them."

WILLIAM GRANT SPURGIN (1870-1926) was one of the prominent and influential members of the bar of Champaign County, and was engaged in the successful practice of his profession in the City of Urbana. Besides having built up a large and important law practice he served with characteristic loyalty and ability on the bench of the County Court of Champaign County.

Judge Spurgin was born on a farm near Beecher City, Fayette County, Illinois, on December 6, 1870, and was a son of George W. and Susanna (Riley) Spurgin, both of whom were born and reared near Mount Vernon, Knox County, Ohio, their marriage having been solemnized in their native county and they having soon afterward become pioneer settlers in Fayette County, Illinois, where they established their home about the time that Gen. John C. Fremont was made the first presidential candidate of the newly organized republican party. George W. Spurgin, who served in the Civil war under General Grant, Company K, Ninety-eighth Regiment, Illinois Volunteers, was in some of the hardest battles. He died in 1876, and his widow survived him a number of years.

Judge William Grant Spurgin was five years of age at the time of his father's death, but was able to gain excellent educational advantages, his higher education having been advanced in large measure through financial provisions that represented the results of his own efforts. He profited by the advantages of the public schools of Paxton, Ford County, Illinois, and thereafter he continued his studies in the University of Illinois until his graduation as a member of the class of 1894 and with the degree of Bachelor of Arts, the university having conferred upon him in 1898 the supplemental degree of Master of Arts, after he had completed a post-graduate course. While a student in the university Judge Spurgin gave as much time as possible to the study of law, and after his graduation he engaged in teaching in the public schools, his law studies having been carried forward in the office of the late Andrew J. Miller, who was at that time state's attorney of Champaign County, and who gave the young student opportunity to handle law cases of minor order and thus gain practical experience. His integrity of purpose and his resourcefulness as a lawyer soon brought him the confidence and respect of the court and the members of the bar. In October, 1903, he was admitted to the bar of his native state, and he continued in the active and successful practice of his profession in the City of Urbana, save for the period of his service as county judge, until the time of his death. He was known as a vigorous and successful trial lawyer and well fortified counselor, and his experience on the bench likewise worked to the expanding and solidifying of his knowledge of jurisprudence. He served on the bench of the County Court of Champaign County during the period of 1910-1914.

Judge Spurgin showed marked discernment in connection with political and local affairs, and was notably influential on the platform and in the councils and campaign activities of the republican party in Illinois, and his judgment was especially relied upon in Champaign County, where he served on the County Central Committee as a member and also as chairman 1922-1926.

In connection with the political activities that culminated in the election of Governor Deneen as chief executive of Illinois, Judge Spurgin was present at a conference in which a strong effort was made to avert the nomination of Deneen, there having been several others who sought the nomination. Judge Spurgin informed each of these aspirants that the nomination was certain to go to Deneen, and he explained with remarkable prevision that none of the other candidates could be nominated. His judgment proved correct, Deneen was nominated, and the republicans carried the state ticket. Also at a preliminary conference, incidental to the selecting of a candidate for justice of the Supreme Court of Illinois, Judge Spurgin was called into consultation, and he there predicted with a very few votes the return that would be given in his home county of Champaign. These and other instances of his keen, political judgment conspired to make him unusually influential in the councils of his party.

Judge Spurgin was a valued member of the Illinois State Chamber of Commerce, and as a member of its legislative committee was a staunch advocate of the establishing of a State Police Department, of the thorough revision of school laws, and of proper regulation of state finances, especially in requiring all state officers with monetary responsibilities to make regular monthly returns to the state treasury of all funds collected.

As a young man his first interest in his home city of Urbana was when he was elected city attorney, and from that time on he was closely identified with every public movement that he deemed beneficial to Urbana. On July 3, 1902, Attorney Spurgin was appointed public administrator by Governor Yates. He carried on this very important state office until April 21, 1911. Later he was elected a member of the school board, of which he was for fifteen consecutive years a member. He foresaw the development and growth of the city on account of the University of Illinois, and the desirability of Urbana as a residential city, and with this growth in mind he planned from the very start a system of the development of the public schools which would meet this growth and which system proved so correct that it is still, today, being followed out by the present board.

When the World war called for men Judge Spurgin was found in the forefront of national, state and city activities, supporting every move to uphold his country in her program of service to humanity. He was chairman of the Champaign County Exemption Board during the trying times of 1919. Judge Spurgin's devotion to patriotism was again shown by his membership in the "Service Veterans" and the "Civil Legion." These societies were formed from the personnel of those who contributed their time and talent to civil activities related to the war organization. His greatest community contribution was his work on the organization (1921) of the Urbana and Champaign Sanitary District. To him goes credit for the legal work associated with such an important project. He was attorney for the Sanitary District and was working on several important amendments to the State Sanitary Law at the time of his death.

Judge Spurgin was a member of the Universalist Church of Urbana, Illinois, and for the last twenty years acted as an official therein, in different capacities, at times occupying the pulpit in the absence of a regular appointed minister, and it was greatly through his efforts that the church was enabled to erect a beautiful stone structure in Urbana. He was a member of the State Board and of the Executive Committee of the state organization. A liberal contributor to all worthy civic undertakings, the Y. M. C. A., W. C. T. U., Memorial Stadium, Boy Scouts, all had his support both financially and morally.

He was a close and appreciative student of the history and teachings of the time-honored Masonic fraternity, in which he received the thirty-second degree of the Ancient Accepted Scottish Rite, his affiliation in this rite being with the Consistory at Danville, Illinois, and his Mystic Shrine affiliation being with Medinah Temple in the City of Chicago, Illinois. The Judge was a grand lecturer in the Grand Lodge, State of Illinois, master of Urbana Blue Lodge No. 157, a past commander, Knights Templar No. 16, and served as officer in several of the Masonic branches in Urbana.

July 8, 1903, recorded the marriage of William Grant Spurgin and Miss Anna McLeod, who was born and reared in Champaign County, Illinois, and who is the daughter of Norman and Mary Angeline (Tharpe Blagg) McLeod. Judge Spurgin was frank and considerate in all his dealings and was fortified in his convictions. He was respected because it was evident that in all the relationships of life his course was guided and governed by high ideals and honorable principles.

HON. G. EDWARD NELSON, assistant attorney general of Illinois, is one of the most distinguished of Menard County's citizens, and he is one of whom this region is justly proud, for he has won prestige with the bench and bar, and is filling his present high office with dignified capability. Judge Nelson was born on a farm near Cantrall, Sangamon County, Illinois, June 1, 1875, a son of the late John Nelson, an American citizen of foreign birth, as he came to this country from Smoland, Sweden, when he was twenty-two years old, and from the time of his arrival here until his death, May 7, 1897, at the age of sixty-three years, he measured up to the highest standards of Christian manhood and good citizenship.

While in his native land John Nelson acquired the equivalent of a common-school education in this country, and learned the trade of a blacksmith, but upon locating in Sangamon County, which he did upon his arrival in the United States, he began working as a farm hand, and maintained his connection with agricultural pursuits the remainder of his life. He was employed by Mr. Brittin, a farmer near Cantrall, when he enlisted in 1861 in Company C. One Hundred and Fourteenth Illinois Volunteer Infantry, under the command of Captain Mallory and Colonel Judy, and later Colonel Shoup, for service during the war between the states. His regiment was attached to the command of General Sherman, and Mr. Nelson saw most of his service in Mississippi, and participated in the siege of Vicksburg and in the engagements in its vicinity, including those at Guntown and Tupelo. Later his command was stationed in New Orleans, Louisiana, where he remained until the close of the war, and he was mustered out August 12, 1865, as a private. While he escaped being wounded or captured by the enemy, the service impaired his health, and he left the army a physical wreck. As soon as it was organized he united with the Grand Army of the Republic, and continued an enthusiast with reference to that association of old comrades as long as he lived.

Upon his return from the army he engaged in farming in the vicinity of Cantrall, and remained in that neighborhood until 1885, when he came to Menard County and settled a mile north of Athens, and there he completed his life's span. In politics he was a staunch republican, but never sought or desired office. In spite of the fact that he was working as a farm hand at the outbreak of the war he was not without means, for he owned two trading boats that plied on the Mississippi River, and these were confiscated by the Confederate government at Memphis, Tennessee, and he never realized anything from them.

When John Nelson left his far-away home he took with him the promise of Louise Larson, a girl whom he had known from childhood, to become his wife as soon as he could make a home for her, and, the war over, he sent for her, and upon her arrival in Sangamon County they were married. She died three weeks before her husband, in 1897. Their children were as follows: Charles A., who is a farmer of Percy County, Nebraska; Judge Nelson, whose name heads this review; Dora L., who is a missionary to India, representing the Woman's Foreign Missionary Society of the Methodist Episcopal Church, having served in this capacity for thirteen years; and Fred, who died unmarried in 1911.

Judge Nelson was reared on the farm in Sangamon County and at Athens, and attended the public schools. While he remained on his father's home farm until he was twenty-five years old, he did not neglect his own advancement, but read law at home, and was admitted to the bar, taking his examinations at Mount Vernon, Illinois. He opened an office at Petersburg, and for several years was associated with Walter E. Bennett, now a practicing attorney of Los Angeles, California, the two carrying on a general practice very successfully. In the meanwhile Judge Nelson was becoming a well-known figure in local politics and was recognized as one of the leading republicans of his county. He has always been a regular from the time he cast his first presidential ballot for William McKinley in 1896. Often a delegate to the local conventions of his party, he was brought before the people of Menard so favorably that when he was his party's candidate for county judge in 1910 he was elected by a gratifying majority in spite of the fact that Menard County was then democratic, and he served in that important office until 1914, succeeding Judge George B. Watkins. Upon the termination of his term he returned to private practice. In May, 1925, he was further honored by appointment as assistant attorney general of Illinois, which office he is now holding.

While his father was a Lutheran, Judge Nelson was reared in the faith of the Methodist Episcopal Church, and for years was very active in the church and Sunday School work of that denomination in Petersburg, but later became interested in Christian Science. He is a member of Abraham Lincoln Camp No. 87, Sons of Veterans, of Petersburg. In 1917 Judge Nelson organized the Old Salem Lincoln League of Petersburg and Menard County, and had much to do with the resurrection of the Old Salem Chautauqua Association that year, and has continued president of both the league and association ever since. The league took in hand the restoration of Old Salem, and his was the leading influence in securing from the state sufficient funds to preserve this historic old settlement that is replete with memories of Abraham Lincoln, and many of the pioneers of Illinois. During the late war Judge Nelson was county chairman for the Young Men's Christian Association drive; county chairman for the drives in behalf of War Savings Stamps; county chairman for the Near East Relief; a member of the Legal Advisory Board, and assisted in all of the drives, including that for the United War Chest, of which he was also county chairman.

On February 19, 1902, Judge Nelson married, in Palmyra, Illinois, Adaline Swingle, born at Athens, a daughter of William M. Swingle and his wife, Eliza F. (Graham) Swingle, the former of whom was postmaster of Athens, and died there in 1920. Mrs. Nelson is the eldest of three daughters, the other two being: Mrs. T. L. Cantrall and Mrs. Guy E. Kinner, both of whom reside at Athens. Mrs. Nelson was educated in the public schools of Athens. She is active in different organizations, was president of the Petersburg Woman's Club for several years, and is a member of the local chapter of the Daughters of the American Revolution, being descended from Capt. James Clinton of New York. Judge and Mrs. Nelson have one son, Hubert Edward, a graduate of the Petersburg High School and now attending the University of Illinois.

While Judge Nelson is now at Springfield because of his office, he belongs to Menard County. The Nelson family is a large one and has spread out into other states. An uncle of Judge Nelson, Nicholas Nelson, who died in Nebraska in the spring of 1925, in his ninetieth year, was unmarried; but Peter Nelson, another uncle, who died in Taylorsville, Illinois, in his eighty-seventh year, left a large family. Still another uncle, Adolph Nelson, a resident of Springfield, has three daughters and a son. There were two daughters in the family to which John Nelson and his brothers belonged, both of whom survive, they being: Mrs. Alfred Larson, of Roseland, Nebraska, and Mrs. David Mitts, of Spencer, Iowa. Their parents, John and Sarah (Larson) Nelson are buried in the Brittin Cemetery near Cantrall. While these sturdy pioneers have passed, the influence of their upright lives and high principles remains, and are exemplified in the work and lives of their descendants, wherever found, and is especially active through the medium of their distinguished grandson, Judge Nelson.

DR. HURCI WARWELEZ, who has prestige as a skilled and successful osteopathic practitioner in the city of Chicago, where he maintains his office and residence at 1460 Irving Park boulevard, has the distinction of being not only the only full-blood Indian engaged in professional service in Chicago but also the only one who has ever appeared as a candidate for membership in the city council. The Doctor is a full-blood Cherokee Indian and was born in a tribal camp in what is now the State of Oklahoma, in the year 1879, his parents having been prominent members of the Cherokee Nation. From an article that appeared in the Chicago Daily News in February, 1925, at the time when Doctor Warwelez appeared as a candidate for election to the city council, are taken, with minor paraphrase, the following interesting quotations, which are well worthy of preservation in this more enduring publication:

"When the new city council is inaugurated next April, sitting in the chair reserved for the alderman from the Forty-seventh ward may be seen a full-blooded Cherokee Indian with feathered headdress. In that spectacular event the name of Chicago's first Indian city father will be Alderman Hurci Warwelez, or, translated into English, Alderman Horse Warwater. The Cherokees originally dwelt in the East. The country they roamed lay in the Virginias, Maryland and the Carolinas. When their lands became valuable and were coveted by the white settlers, the tribe was removed to the Indian Territory, which is now Oklahoma. It is there that Horse War-water was born one night while his tribe was engaged in one of the numerous Indian uprisings that made the year 1879 a troublesome one in the Indian Territory. The next morning, a few hours after the birth of the infant, the tepee in which the tiny Indian papoose had first seen the darkness of this earth, was struck and the whole tribe took the warpath again. Hence the warlike name bestowed upon the smallest member of the war party.

"'After graduating from the Indian school the government maintains at Carlisle, Pennsylvania, in 1900, I spent four years in Washington University medical school and then went to California, where I built up a sanitarium,' explained Doctor Walwelez. 'I was doing very nicely when fire attacked me and everything went up in smoke. About that time I had to go back to Oklahoma, where some oil sharks were trying to hornswoggle our family out of oil rights on some land we owned on the reservation allotted to the Cherokee Nation. Ten years ago I came to Chicago, and I like this city so much that I've lived here ever since. I shall feel greatly honored if the people of my ward elect me their alderman.'

"Dr. Walwelez owns a two-story flat building on Irving Park boulevard, and there he lives with his family, and practices osteopathy. He has been active in working for clean streets and alleys in his neighborhood, and thinks his voluntary efforts to perform the duties of good citizenship have been appreciated. He says his aldermanic petitions have been signed by upward of 4,000 voters."

While Doctor Warwelez failed of election to the city council, he has in no degree abated his civic loyalty and public spirit, for which he finds many mediums of helpful expression. The Doctor was graduated in the American School of Osteopathy at Kirksville, Missouri, in 1906, this being the parent institution of this now great and important system of service to humanity. He has taken effective post-graduate course in osteopathy, and is likewise skilled as a chiropractic practitioner. In his professional stewardship he specializes in the regulation of diet and in natural methods of curing disease and the building up of both physical and mental health, with due recourse to the benefits of applied psychology. The Doctor is a constant student and reader and his scientific and general intellectual attainments are of high order. His private library is large and select and covers a wide range. Doctor Warwelez is a Republican in political allegiance and he is a popular member of the Chicago Press Club. In his profession he has built up a substantial and successful practice of representative order.

Doctor Warwelez married Miss Muriel Edith Humphreys, of Brookston, White County, Indiana, and they have a winsome little daughter, Ramona, who was born in the year 1921.

JAMES HEBER HUDSON has spent the greater part of his life at Bloomington, where his outstanding achievement was building up the Bloomington Association of Commerce into one of the most efficient organizations of the kind in the state. On September 1, 1926, after serving thirteen years as managing secretary of the Bloomington organization, he accepted the important position of secretary of the retail merchants department of the Illinois Chamber of Commerce and is making an enviable record.

Mr. Hudson was born at Milton in Rock County, Wisconsin, January 16, 1872, son of Lewis B. and Alice A. (Gilbert) Hudson. His parents and all his grandparents were born in New York State. His paternal grandparents were Daniel T. and Cynthia Hudson, while his mother was a daughter of H. W. and Alice (Slosson) Gilbert.

James Heber Hudson was a child when his parents moved to Bloomington and he attended public schools there and the Evergreen City Business College. Commercial work has been his occupation since boyhood. He started as delivery boy in a retail store and at the age of eighteen had made such progress that he was put on the staff of a wholesale house as a traveling representative. Mr. Hudson for twenty-four years represented one firm as a traveling salesman.

In 1913 he became secretary of the Bloomington Commercial Club, subsequently reorganized as the Association of Commerce. He was secretary thirteen years, and during this time he developed an organization, small in number and without particular effectiveness as a business institution, into a chamber with a membership of a thousand, annual income of $55,000, and one of the livest and most systematic working institutions of the kind in the Central West. Mr. Hudson had twelve persons on his staff, and he was the man intrusted with carrying out the extensive program of the Chamber, which involved a large number of important civic, commercial and industrial enterprises. His prominence as secretary of the Bloomington Association of Commerce brought him election as president of the Illinois Commercial Secretary's Association in 1918, and during 1924-25 he was a director of the National Association of Commercial Organization Secretaries.

On September 1, 1926, after thirteen and a half years as secretary of the Bloomington Association, Mr. Hudson accepted a position with the Illinois Chamber of Commerce in its headquarters at 10 South LaSalle Street, Chicago, as secretary of the Retail Interests Committee, and his present service is one that puts him in close touch with retail merchants all over the state. Mr. Hudson has served as a member of the Bloomington Park Board, is a republican, is secretary of Post L, Illinois Division Travelers Protective Association, member of the Bloomington Consistory of Scottish Rite Masons, the Rotary Club, Young Men's Club, Bloomington Council No. 214, United Commercial Travelers, Bloomington Club, Maplewood Country Club, and the Bloomington Y. M. C. A. He has his church membership in the Second Presbyterian Church at Bloomington.

Mr. Hudson married at Bloomington, July 2, 1894, Miss Carrie Scott, daughter of Benjamin F. and Malvina Scott. They have two children, Heber Scott Hudson, who married Edith Parker; and Nina Gladys, wife of Arthur V. Padou.

JOHN M. OLIN is one of the active younger spirits in the industrial and commercial life of Alton and vicinity. He is a son of F. W. Olin, president of the Western Cartridge Company, the Western Powder Manufacturing Company, Egyptian Powder Company, and the Equitable Powder Manufacturing Company. John M. Olin practically grew up in the powder industry, had a technical education, and since leaving University has been actively identified with his father's business. He is now vice president of the Western Cartridge Company at Alton.

He was born at Upper Alton, Illinois, November 10, 1892. The career of his father is sketched briefly on other pages of this publication. John M. Olin is the second of three sons. His older brother Franklin W., Jr., is now deceased, while the youngest is Spencer T. Olin, of Alton.

John M. Olin was educated in the public schools of Alton, and finished his higher education in his father's alma mater, Cornell University, where he graduated in 1913 with the degree Bachelor of Science in Chemical Engineering. His training as a chemical engineer fitted him for immediate duties and responsibilities in his business. He became a chemist for the Western Cartridge Company, also assistant to the president, and since about 1916 has been vice president of this corporation and is also vice president of the Equitable Powder Manufacturing Company, of the Egyptian Powder Company and of the Western Powder Manufacturing Company. He is president of the Illinois State Bank of East Alton, and of the Bethalto State Bank at Bethalto, in Madison County; is also a director of the First National Bank in St. Louis, Missouri.

Mr. Olin is affiliated with the Masonic fraternity and the Elks. He married in 1917 Miss Adele Levis, of a prominent Alton family. They had two children, Georgene and Louise.

HARRY Y. JONES. One of Grundy County's representative citizens and important public officials, is found in Harry Y. Jones, county treasurer, prominent republican political leader, and an overseas veteran of the World war. Mr. Jones is a young man to hold so responsible a public office as county treasurer, but his popularity and the confidence of the public in his ability and trustworthiness, were markedly shown in his election to this office, when he received the largest majority ever given for treasurer in this county.

Harry Y. Jones was born at Morris, Grundy County, Illinois, in 1889, and attended the public schools until he was sixteen years old, since when, through his own efforts he has advanced his fortunes, building up his substantial life structure on a foundation of industry, honesty, patriotism and efficiency. A youth of sixteen starting out in life dependent on his own resources and without technical training, finds himself today, as then, accepting the first job that comes to hand, and thus Mr. Jones, although not very well qualified physically, for a time was one of the construction force engaged in bringing the belt line of the Chicago & Rock Island Railway into Morris in 1905.

About this time Mr. Jones began to consider the acquiring of a trade and finding an opening with Frank Conden, a local cigar manufacturer, entered his factory and learned the trade of a cigarmaker, and continued work at this trade until 1917, early in which year he accepted a position with the Chicago Telephone, now the Illinois Bell Telephone Company, in which he found congenial work and associates. However well satisfied he felt, all was forgotten when the United States became involved in the World war, and he was one of the company's first employes to hasten to a recruiting office to volunteer for military service, one of several attempts, in all of which he was disappointed as his light weight prevented his acceptance. But his opportunity arrived when the draft came, of which the amusing story is told that Mr. Jones and several of his friends, anxious that the authorities should not overlook their questionnaires, took the precaution of using red ink when they wrote across their papers, "raring to go," which they considered effective as all were immediately accepted. Mr. Jones was trained at Camp Gordon and was assigned to the Twenty-sixth Division, United States Army, and with this unit landed in France in July, 1918, and during his eight months of service in that country, assisted as a brave soldier in building up the gallant record of the Twenty-sixth Division.

After his return to the United States and his honorable discharge at Camp Grant, Mr. Jones reentered the employ of the Telephone Company at Morris, where his business qualifications made him valuable and his generous spirit and genial personality made him many friends. In the meanwhile, always interested in the welfare of Morris, his native city, he continued his efforts, political and otherwise, to add to her prestige, and there are very few Illinois cities of her area and population which offer better business opportunities or more desirable home locations. In 1920 Mr. Jones was elected city treasurer of Morris, and as an evidence of the general satisfaction felt with his administration, came his election in 1922, to the office of county treasurer.

Mr. Jones was married June 19, 1920, to Miss Zena Holm, who was born at Gardner, Illinois, a member of an old pioneer family of Grundy County. Their comfortable and attractive residence is at 613 East Illinois Avenue, Mr. Jones' offices being in the handsome Grundy County Court House. At the spring primaries of 1926 Mr. Jones was nominated for sheriff of Grundy County.

GEN. GEORGE H. HARRIES, engineer and a retired brigadier general of the United States army, has since 1911 been connected with the firm of H. M. Byllesby & Company, first in consulting engineering capacity and for the past two years as an executive vice president. The H. M. Byllesby & Company was established in 1902 by the late H. M. Byllesby of Chicago and for many years has been one of the most prominent firms of its kind in America engaged in financing, designing, construction, operation and management of electric light and power, and gas companies. These public utilities now serve between eight to nine hundred communities in eighteen states of the Union.

George Herbert Harries is a native of South Wales, born September 19, 1860, in Haverford, West, a son of John and Sarah (Davies) Harries. He acquired his early education in the grammar school of his native town and came to America when a young man. He has had numerous connections with public utilities and has done a large amount of engineering work. During 1895-96 he was president of the Metropolitan Railroad Company at the City of Washington. From 1900 to 1911 he served as vice president of the Washington Railway & Electric Company and of all the companies in that corporation. During 1911-12 he was on the engineering staff of the H. M. Byllesby & Company of Chicago and since October, 1912, has been vice president of the firm. During these years he has retained his home in Washington, but his business headquarters are in Chicago and his home address in that city is the Army and Navy Club, on Lake Shore Drive.

General Harries has a notable military record. By presidential commission he served from November 30, 1897, to May 18, 1915, as brigadier general commanding the militia, both the land and naval militia of the District of Columbia. He was a colonel of the First District of Columbia infantry of the United States volunteers in 1898, serving at Santiago De Cuba during the siege of that city and also with the Cuban army of occupation. On May 18, 1915, he was promoted to major general of the militia and was retired at his own request, May 26, of the same year.

For many years he served with the war department board in the promotion of rifle practice. He was commissioned brigadier general commanding the first brigade of the Nebraska National Guard, June 25, 1917, and was brigadier general of the United States army from August 5, 1917, to September 30, 1919. During the World war period, he commanded successively the Fifty-Ninth De Paul Brigade, One Hundred Eighty-sixth Infantry Brigade in the Thirteenth Corps, Second French army, the base section No. 5 American Expeditionary forces, One Hundred Seventy-third Infantry Brigade. He was chief of the United States military mission at Berlin from December 3, 1918, to September 30, 1919. On December 28, 1920, he was made a general in the Officer's Reserve Corps. General Harries was awarded the distinguished service medal and for construction and operation of the Port of Brest was made a commander of the legion of honor by the French government and received other decorations from eight European governments.

General Harries was vice president of the Board of Education of the city of Washington from 1895 to 1903 and was president of the Washington Board of Trade in 1910-11. He is a republican, a Methodist and a member of the Army and Navy Club of Washington, the Union League and Army and Navy Clubs of Chicago, the Engineers and Bankers Clubs of New York and the Omaha Club of Omaha.

In 1912 he was honored with the office of National Commander of the Order of Indian wars in the United States. He was one of the founders in 1920 of the Military Order of the World war and has been president of that organization since its conception. It is founded upon the same principles as those of the Order of Cincinnati, made up of officers of the revolutionary army, and of the Loyal Legion, composed of officers of the Civil war. General Harries was president of the American Electric Railway Association in 1912-13; of the association of the Edison Illuminating Company in 1911-12; president of the Illuminating Engineering Society in 1920-21 and is a member of the American Institute of Electrical Engineers, the American Society of Mechanical Engineers, the National Electric Light Association, the American Gas Institute and the Western Society of Engineers. In recognition of the lectures delivered by him on colonial history, he was awarded the Master of Arts

degree by the Howard University of Washington. Kentucky State University conferred upon him the Doctor of Laws degree. General Harries married April 23, 1884, Elizabeth Langley of Washington.

C. N. PENCE, physician and surgeon, has given more than thirty-five years to the work of his profession in Madison County, Illinois. His home and office are at Wood River.

Doctor Pence is a native of Illinois, born in Adams County, January 11, 1867, son of James B. and Mary (Brown) Pence. His father was a school teacher in Adams County and from there moved across the Mississippi River to LaGrange, Lewis County, Missouri, and gave forty-four years of his life to educational work in that county. Both he and his wife died there.

Dr. C. N. Pence attended school at LaGrange, graduating from high school there and attending the Baptist College of the same town. For two years he was a student in Quincy College, and completed his medical course in the Bellevue Hospital Medical College of New York. Doctor Pence for one year practiced in his old home town of LaGrange, and in 1889 began his professional work in Madison County at Alton. He has been an able member of his profession, enjoying the confidence of a large practice, and has a splendid professional reputation in Alton, East Alton and Wood River.

Doctor Pence, who is unmarried, is a member of the Presbyterian Church, has been active in democratic politics and for many years chairman of the democratic committee. He has served a number of years as health officer of Wood River and for four terms was mayor of Alton. Doctor Pence's favorite pastime is outdoor sports, particularly hunting, and he has hunted ducks on the site of the present city of Wood River.

KIRBY B. SMITH has been established in the practice of law in the city of Mount Vernon, judicial center of Jefferson County, nearly thirty years, is one of the representative members of the bar of this county and is a scion of a sterling family that was founded in this county in the early pioneer period of its history.

Mr. Smith was born in Jefferson County, Illinois, December 12, 1860, and is a son of Jesse Hassell Smith and Eliza (Bliss) Smith, the former of whom died in 1892 and the latter of whom passed away in 1866, the children of their union having been eight in number: Harriet, eldest of the children became the wife of A. Knowles and the mother of three children; Lyman Dexter, the next in order of birth, married Mary Srivner and they had one child; Herbert is deceased; Florence married F. M. Knowles and became the mother of four children; Cora A. is the wife of William W. Rohrer and they have four children; Kirby B., of this review, was the next in order of birth; Elnora D. is the wife of Robert L. Roane and they have four children; Anson Clark wedded Anna Holder and they have four children.

Jesse H. Smith was born in Tennessee and was a youth when he accompanied his parents to Illinois, the family home having been established on a pioneer farm in Jefferson County in December, 1829, and this county having represented his home during the remainder of his long and useful life, the major part of which was given to successful farm enterprise, though as a young man he had applied himself to cutting wood on the American bottoms, for use on the river steamboats, besides which he worked in a local packing house and became an expert in the dressing of beef and hogs. He was one of the substantial agriculturists and stock-growers of the county for many years, and developed a substantial business in the buying and shipping of live stock. He was active and influential in community affairs, and served as county coroner and also as deputy sheriff.

Isaac and Millie Ann (Hassell) Smith, grandparents of him whose name initiates this review, were childhood friends in their native state of North Carolina, and after the Hassell family removed thence to Tennessee young Smith so missed the daughter Millie A. that he finally made his way to Tennessee, where their marriage was solemnized and whence they came with their family to Jefferson County, Illinois, in 1829, as previously noted in this review. The father of Isaac Smith served in the navy under Paul Jones, who was the virtual founder of the American navy. Representatives of the Hassell family were patriot soldiers in the War of the Revolution. The maternal grandfather of the subject of this review died in the state of Vermont, and his widow thereafter came with her three children Anson, George and Eliza, to Jefferson County, Illinois, where the family took up a tract of wild land and instituted the development of a pioneer farm.

Kirby B. Smith gained his preliminary education by attending the district school near the old home farm, and later he continued his studies in Ewing College until 1882. Thereafter he devoted two years to teaching in the district schools, and in the meanwhile he studied surveying and other phases of civil engineering. As a civil engineer he was for one year associated with railroad locating and construction, and he then engaged in civil engineering work at Mount Vernon, he having given eight years of service as county surveyor, and within this period having followed the course of his ambition by giving close attention to the study of law. In 1896 Mr. Smith passed the examination that gained him admission to the bar of his native state, and he has since continued to be engaged in the active practice of his profession at Mount Vernon, where he has long controlled a large and important law business that marks him as one of the leading members of the bar of his native county. He served one term as master of chancery and was for a number of years a member of the Mount Vernon board of education. Mr. Smith is a director and also the secretary of the Mount Vernon Improvement Company, an organization that is doing constructive service in advancing the civic and material interests of Mount Vernon, especially in progressive movements to obtain new industrial enterprises for the city. He is a director of the Third National Bank of Mount Vernon, this being the most substantial banking institution in southern Illinois, and he is a director also of the Davidson Company. He takes deep interest in all that concerns the well being of his home city and native county, and is one of the liberal and public-spirited citizens of Mount Vernon.

At Fairfield, Jefferson County, on the 20th of June, 1897, was solemnized the marriage of Mr. Smith to Miss Mary A. McCall, eldest of the four children born to Capt. Ridney McCall and Ophelia (Reynolds) McCall. Captain McCall served as a gallant soldier of the Union during the greater part of the Civil war, was captain of his company in an Illinois regiment, took part in many engagements, and he never recovered fully from the effects of wounds that he received in battle, his death having occurred in 1882 and his venerable widow being still a resident of Fairfield, Elizabeth, second of the McCall children, is the wife of Robert L. McKellar and they reside in the state of Montana; M. Pearl was formerly private secretary to Senator Borah, representative of Montana in the United States Senate, and while thus engaged she studied law and was admitted to the bar, she now being in charge of the postal-law department of the office of the United States attorney general, in the city of Washington, D. C., a position to which she was appointed by the late President Harding; John R., youngest of the children, married Miss Edith Dwyer and they reside in Montana, their children being two in number.

In conclusion is entered brief record concerning the children of Mr. and Mrs. Smith: Edwin Kirby is a student (1925) in the medical department of George Washington University, Washington, D. C.; Hassell Bliss is a student in the law department of the same university, was there graduated in June, 1925; and Elizabeth and Angeline, twins, are students in the Mount Vernon High School. Mr. Smith is an influential and honored member of the Jefferson County Bar Association, is a member also of the Illinois State Bar Association, and in a fraternal way he is affiliated with the Knights of Pythias.

GROVER C. PATTON is proprietor of one of the leading baking establishment in the city of Decatur, an industry he founded some years ago and has kept steadily expanding to meet the demand for the high quality of its product.

Mr. Patton was born at Moweaqua, Illinois, January 22, 1885, son of Robert A. and Minnie E. (Nims) Patton, his father a native of Pennsylvania and his mother of Missouri, both now deceased. His father was a registered pharmacist and in the drug business in Illinois during his active life, and was well known in mercantile circles in Macon County. He and his wife, Minnie Nims had three children: William R. of Lincoln, Nebraska, Grover C., and Dada E. of Decatur. There was a previous marriage of which the children were: May, wife of R. B. Sheffler of Los Angeles; Robert S.; Cora, deceased; Lula, wife of Robert Beck of Montevista, Colorado; Edith, wife of Frank Compton of Decatur; Nellie, wife of M. V. Van Horn of Bunker Hill, Illinois.

When Grover C. Patton was about a year and a half old, his father was stricken with blindness and the family then moved out to a farm ten miles from any town. They acquired a small general mercantile business, and in the atmosphere of this and the farm Grover C. Patton grew up. He had limited school advantages and when twelve years of age, he went about the country driving a huckster wagon, trading and exchanging goods with the farms. He continued this as an adjunct to farming until he was seventeen years of age. For a time he supplemented his early school advantages with a course at Charleston, and then entered the Millikin University at Decatur, paying his own way through that institution. After finishing his university career, Mr. Patton became associated with his father in the grocery business at Decatur for a year and a half, and then went on the road as a traveling salesman for the Campbell, Holton and Company, wholesale grocers of Bloomington. He had a successful traveling experience for several years, and left the road to become associated with Fred P. Dreback of Monticello, Illinois, and W. A. Fullerton of Tuscola, Illinois, establishing the Purity Baking Company at Decatur. Mr. Patton in 1922, bought out his partner and has since been president and manager of this very successful enterprise. He operates four ovens with a capacity of 16,000 loaves daily, and sells the manufactured product throughout Decatur and surrounding towns. Since the Decatur plant was purchased two other plants have been added, one in Pana, Illinois, and one in Champaign, Illinois.

Mr. Patton married October 4, 1913, Miss Fay B. Young, a native of Downs, Illinois. They have three children: Janet Lorain, Barbara Ann and Beverly Jean. Mr. Patton in politics is a democrat. He is a Knight Templar Mason and Shriner; a member of the Elks and the First Presbyterian Church at Decatur.

THE HARRIS FAMILY OF CHAMPAIGN COUNTY. Five generations of the Harris family have lived in Champaign County. The family as a group has been conspicuously identified with the land. An important distinction, however, is that they have been representative not of the older type of land holders, but rather have been users of the land for the welfare of prosperity of a large community. The head of the first generation of the Harris family in this county also became a banker. For many years the First National Bank of Champaign has been known as the Harris Bank. But at all times the Harrises have been farmers and several of them have earned national distinction as "Banker farmers," men of constructive leadership and influence in the nation's agricultural program and in agricultural finance.

Benjamin Franklin Harris, the pioneer, was born December 15, 1811, on a farm in the Shenandoah Valley of Virginia, the second of ten children of William Hickman and Elizabeth (Payne) Harris. His mother was a cousin of Dolly Payne Madison. The family was of Scotch-English extraction and Quakers and in this country became fighting Quakers, then Methodists. His great-grandfather, William Harris with two brothers from England settled on the eastern shore of Maryland in 1726. The grandfather was Benjamin Harris.

B. F. Harris, the pioneer, at the age of fifty-three nominally retired from active business responsibilities, but for over forty years after that kept in close touch with many varied interests. He died in his ninety-fourth year, in 1905. In 1916 there was held a simple ceremony at the University of Illinois, the hanging of the portrait and the name of B. F. Harris in the university Hall of Fame. At that time his grandson, the late B. F. Harris, read an address from which most of the facts of his biography are taken for this sketch.

B. F. Harris grew to manhood on his father's Virginia farm, attending the country schools until sixteen years of age. At that time President Jackson's attitude towards the United States banks so seriously affected values that wheat declined from a dollar and a half to fifty cents and Virginia lands to less than one-third of its former price. These declines so affected the father's obligations that he and his brothers each with a six horse team went into the "wagoning" or freighting business and for three years "wagoned" freight over that section and out through Pennsylvania and as far west as Zanesville, Ohio. This work they did in order to recoup their father's losses. On March 20, 1833, the Virginia farm was sold at forty per cent of its original cost. In a one-horse gig and a two-horse carry-all the Harris family set out for Ohio, arriving at Springfield, April 8th and nearby purchased and settled upon their new farm. Within the same year B. F. Harris commenced business for himself buying and driving cattle overland to Lancaster, Pennsylvania, and there disposing of them to cattle feeders.

In 1834 more than seventy years before his death, B. F. Harris started for Illinois by way of Danville, then through the present site of Sidney and Urbana (where was but one cabin) and on to what is now Monticello in Piatt County. During the ensuing year he began to accumulate farming lands in Piatt and Champaign counties and to buy cattle through all this section and as far south and west as Mount Vernon, Vandalia and Springfield. For several seasons, he bought for feeding purposes all the corn for sale in Macon, Sangamon and Champaign counties. Each year for nine years he drove these cattle overland by way of Muncie, Indiana, and Springfield and Columbus, Ohio, into Pennsylvania and then to New York and Boston, where they were sold. Subsequently St. Louis and Chicago furnished a market requiring a thirty day trip and still later the railroads broadened the outlet.

When B. F. Harris came to this section of Illinois no stream was bridged and only eleven families were on the Sangamon from its source to the limits of Piatt County. Fifteen years later, not a half dozen men had erected their cabins a mile from the timber limits; the deer and Indians were still at home there. It was the frontier, all freight carried by freight or team. In 1840 B. F. Harris visited Chicago, a town of two thousand people on stilts in a swamp. Nineteen days were required for the round trip and the corn and wheat he teamed there sold for twenty and thirty cents a bushel respectively. Fifteen years after he came not twenty-five per cent of the land in this county had passed from government ownership and the first railroad came twenty years later. The first public religious services in the western section of this county were held in his cabin, and he hewed and built the first church, 22x24 feet which was later converted into a school. When it was necessary he built the larger church, Bethel, dedicated by his brother-in-law Gen. Granville Moody. For many years his home was the shelter of all itinerant preachers through this section. He writes that the "church business was looked after as well as any other business. I never lost anything by looking after the church and school." In those years it was customary to furnish farm laborers with whiskey daily, but he always refused to do this and instead added twelve and a half cents to each man's daily pay.

B. F. Harris brought the first sawmill, mower, reaper, carriage, organ, brick and cook stove to Champaign County. He never sought public office nor did he fill such office except in pioneer days as justice of the peace and supervisor and as such helped hew the first courthouse. As justice of the peace he performed the few early marriages, dispensing simple justice on the one hand and calomel on the other. He came in the day of ox teams and lived to ride over his farm with his son, grandsons and great-grandsons in an automobile. He voted for nineteen presidential candidates beginning with Henry Clay.

For nearly three-quarters of a century he bought, fed and sold five hundred to two thousand head of cattle annually. He established the First National Bank in Champaign in 1865. B. F. Harris was one of the chief movers in the plans to raise Union troops in Champaign County, to locate railroads, to oppose bond repudiation and to induce the location of the great state university.

Personally he was a sociable man, fond of his friends and companions and was full of anecdote and reminiscence growing out of a remarkable experience. Peter Cartwright, Abraham Lincoln, David Davis, Isaac Funk, John Gillet and many other well known men were his friends and guests. He and Lincoln were long time friends and at the outset of the war he went on to Washington to encourage him in his stand. He was the guest of the president and at Lincoln's request attended a cabinet meeting and discussed the war situation with them.

For all these things the true import of his career and its lesson was that life may be what we have the courage to make it; that the will to labor with true zeal will bring results and the chiefest of these results are "the character" and "simplicities." Distinguished as he was in Champaign County, Illinois, and the nation, B. F. Harris acquired the true distinction of breadth, nobility and simplicity of character.

As a livestock man, B. F. Harris was preeminent. The Pittsburgh Livestock Journal speaking of his death referred to him as the "grand old man of the livestock trade, the oldest and most successful cattle feeder in the world." This praise was well deserved. The

New York Tribune in October, 1853, referred to his prize winning drove of cattle averaging 1,965 pounds, displayed at the New York World's Fair, then in session. His most famous herd consisted of one hundred cattle the finest and heaviest hundred cattle ever raised and fattened in one lot by one man. These were weighed on his farm by Doctor Johns the president of the State Board of Agriculture on May 23, 1856, and the average weight of a hundred was 2,378 pounds. Hundreds of visitors came from neighboring states to see these cattle. In the following February he sent twelve of these cattle to Chicago and the bunch averaged 2,786 pounds. A firm of Chicago butchers paraded the stock about Chicago's downtown streets. These were his conspicuous early achievements, but every few years his cattle topped the market, and less than a year before his death, his cattle received the highest prices for the season on the Chicago market.

Writing editorially in the Champaign Daily Gazette, May 8, 1905, J. R. Stewart said: "The death of a man devoted almost wholly to the private affairs of life will seldom attract the attention of so wide a circle of people as will that of B. F. Harris of this city. The reason is first that he lived to a remarkable age and second that he was a remarkable man. His long life journey was begun in 1811. He had few of the aids on which young men now so rely. He had to rely on himself, a resource which never seems to fail him and one in which he had unlimited personal confidence. Life for him in its early age was not an easy battle. Nature, however, had furnished him with an extraordinary physical and mental equipment.

"Everything to which Mr. Harris put his hand flourished. His judgment was so trustworthy that he made few business mistakes. He applied himself to real things and eschewed what men now call speculation. He did business on a cash basis and was never in debt. Operating on these, his chosen lines, he was a rich man long before his race was run, and he enjoyed a period of ease and entire freedom from anxiety much longer than falls to the lot of most men who are accounted fortunate in the world. An equally remarkable and gratifying thing was the retention of his wonderful faculties to the end of his life.

"Thus came to his last account a man of extraordinary qualities in whatever light we may view him. He knew this portion of the state from the period of its rude frontier aspect and he had a large share in its development into what we can see today. Every man has a niche to fill. No man could fill his better than B. F. Harris did. Measured fairly, we may say that nature does not often produce such a man. It will be long before this region sees another in all respects his equal."

Another tribute that deserves quotation was that of Andrew S. Draper, former president of the University of Illinois: "Everyone recognized the fact that he had sterling qualities of heroic mold. He did things in days and circumstances when the doing of things required stalwart men and when the doing also made men still more stalwart. In this way the fine physical frame and splendid moral character with which nature endowed him were developed and seasoned to an extent which made him a notable man in the Mississippi Valley. It was a small number of such men as he who laid the foundation of the history of the middle west, that great region of our country which is the richest in the resources and the most prolific in productivity. It is doubtless within the fact to say that no man within a hundred miles of you, if within the State of Illinois, has been so richly entitled to be so permanently and gratefully remembered. I am sure it will be so for the common feeling of the people will have it so."

The significance of his life as a farmer and its weighty contribution to the dignity of that calling were happily expressed by the Breeder's Gazette, as follows: "In literature, art, professional life, or politics, a man with a record of achievement equal to that of the late Benjamin Franklin Harris would deservedly have numerous biographers. Many a man has been made the subject of bulky biography who might not measure up to him on any score. This is not because the most inviting and interesting personalities are found outside of the farmer's calling, but largely because until recent years agriculture as a vocation had not been adequately appreciated by the public. It had not been sufficiently dignified to become the source of life histories. Other professions have furnished the candidates for the Plutarchs and contributed the heroes and heroines famous in fiction. Farming has been drawn on principally for Philistines. Its great men, geniuses, its Harrises have been overlooked by almost all writers worthy of putting their useful lives into books.

"It is gratifying to all friends of agriculture that this vital and honorable occupation at last has begun to take its rightful place in the list of man's employments. For the extremely gradual process which has wrought such a wholesome change in the popular estimate of farming, we are indebted to men of the Harris type; farmers whose lives and work are a convincing reply to all derogatory references ever made to agriculturists and their business."

B. F. Harris, the pioneer, married June 17, 1841, Elizabeth Page, daughter of Col. Harry Page of Circleville, Ohio. Their only child was Henry Hickman Harris, who followed in his father's footsteps as a farmer and cattle feeder and for forty years was active in the First National Bank of Champaign.

He was born on the Sangamon River farm of his father in Champaign County, April 27, 1844, and passed away July 15, 1914. Henry H. Harris was a stalwart citizen and under his skillful hands the fortune of his father had greatly increased and he had managed his varied interests and affairs, including the First National Bank in which he succeeded his father as president, in such a way as to justify his stewardship and all that came to him in the way of fortune and influence. His good judgment and wise administration carried the bank successfully through several financial panics. He was one of the organizing members of the Illinois Bankers Association and served as its president in 1908-09.

He was for many years a member of the city council of Champaign and to his aggressiveness and good judgment the city is indebted for many of its best improvements. He served for a number of years as president of the Champaign County Fair Association and established that organization on a sound financial basis, having taken it in a bankrupt condition. While he was a man of decided opinions and a patriot, he was of a rather retiring disposition, never accepting any political office and refused some possible opportunities to become a public servant. He was especially helpful to young men, recognizing business acumen and honesty and encouraging it in a substantial way.

Henry Hickman Harris married Melissa Megrue, who was born near Cincinnati, Ohio, April 19, 1846, and is still living at Champaign. To them were born two sons, B. F. and Newton Megrue Harris.

Benjamin Franklin Harris, grandson of the pioneer of that name, was born at the old Harris home farm September 30, 1868, and died December 19, 1920, at the age of sixty-two, yet with a record of achievement that made him one of the foremost Illinoisans of his generation.

He was graduated from the Champaign High School as class valedictorian, attended the University of Illinois for two years and was graduated in 1892 from the Columbia University in New York with a degree in law. In the fall of that year with his father, he acquired the street railway, gas and electric light property of Champaign and Urbana, disposing of them to W. B. McKinley in 1900. At that time he became vice president of the First National Bank and in 1914 succeeded his father, H. H. Harris, as the third president of that institution. In 1911 he was elected president of the Illinois Bankers' Association, an honor which previously had been bestowed upon his father. In no other instances has father and son been president of the association. He also served as chairman of the agricultural commission of the American Bankers' Association and president of the conference committee on agricultural development and education of all state bankers' associations. He inaugurated the banker-farmer movement in 1908 and as the organizer of the agricultural commission of the American Bankers' Association, he held the post of chairman for five years. The late B. F. Harris was called, "the father of the county agent movement" since it was he who definitely formulated the plan for cooperation between the state and federal government of the individual farmer in the person of the county agent.

Mr. Harris also stimulated the active interest of the bankers in the good roads movement. A third movement with which he was closely identified was a campaign to bring all Illinois banks under state or national supervision.

He served three terms as president of the Champaign Chamber of Commerce. During the World war period, Governor Lowden appointed him a member of the State Council of Defense, of which he served as vice president and as head of some of its important committees. He was a charter member of the Rotary Club of Champaign and was a member of the committee on ocean transportation of the Chamber of Commerce of the United States and a member of the Foreign Trades Council. He was a close friend of Theodore Roosevelt and was honored by the confidence of that great American.

Of the many tributes to his life, the one perhaps that expresses best his power and leadership as a farmer-banker in the nation, was that written by a fellow member of the agricultural commission of the American Bankers' Association, Mr. J. H. Wheeeler:

"He had the love, the cooperation of constructive men and he had a genius for leadership and was possessed to such remarkable ability as an organizer and executive that his work reflected great credit upon himself and brought inspiration ambition and prosperity to many. Sound thinker as he was, having a clear understanding of fundamental laws, he constantly promoted better ideas in banking, farming and good citizenship. He was preeminently a great man. In his home town the great bank founded by his grandfather has grown under his presidency to be one of the leading country banks of Illinois and a power not only in finance but in teaching thrift and developing industry. His farms are models of well managed farm plants.

"Those who have had the pleasure of visiting his great farm plant, have seen thousands of sheep, hogs and cattle, which under his supervision were being fitted for market. I remember his taking me to what he called his little farm, 320 acres, and a big enough farm plant to tax the energy and ability of most any man. Yet this farm yielded Mr. Harris $7,000 from the sale of hogs alone in one year. These great farm plants were not built in a day. They were not built because of their location or of the capital available. They were built because of the keen, skilled, honest ability of a great farmer, a great banker, a great man. But it was not the proceeds to the owner that emphasized the man. It was the influence upon the agricultural interests of the largest agricultural section of the United States. An influence which had its effect upon the great agricultural industry of the nation.

"Mr. Harris knew from experience, from study, from observation and from comparison that two blades of grass could be made to grow where one grew before and he knew how to do it. He tried and succeeded through the great banker-farmer movement in carrying the message to the small country banker throughout the United States, who again delivered it to the farmer.

"This great originator and leader of the banker-farmer work understood life. He knew that after all, good homes, good citizenship, were the prime factors and you will find in the banker-farmer platform which Mr. Harris wrote, citizenship comes first.

"Mr. Harris's constructive work and leadership in the banker-farmer movement began years ago and was a powerful influence on bringing about the organization of the agricultural commission by the American Bankers' Association.

"While chairman Mr. Harris called a convention in Chicago of the leading educators, journalists, bankers and farmers in the United States. The accomplishments of this meeting will never die. It demonstrated that the bankers were not attempting to teach agriculture but rather to cooperate and assist them to connect up with the sources of knowledge on better agriculture and better country life conditions. It indicated to the bankers what they were not to do as well as what they could do. It emphasized the necessity of greater development of the basic industry, agriculture and it stimulated an interest on the part of farmers, bankers, journalists and educators which vitalized the agricultural and educational movement."

The following sentiment which he spoke and lived can well be emulated by every one:

"The man who devotes all of his time to the accumulation of property, straddling or evading vital business and government questions, oblivious of the debt he owes society, absorbing everything he touches, giving nothing in return, is the type of citizen that is little better than the one who goes wrong, for his selfishness makes the other possible."

B. F. Harris II married December 5, 1895, Miss May Melish, daughter of William Brownell and Sallie (Gatch) Melish of Cincinnati. Mrs. Harris survives him and was the mother of four children: Henry H., William Melish, B. F. Jr. and Elizabeth Harris.

Succeeding the late B. F. Harris as president of the First National Bank of Champaign, his brother Newton M. Harris took that office. Newton M. Harris was born July 27, 1872. He graduated from Yale University in 1895 and has been closely identified with all the varied interests of the Harris family in agriculture, live stock raising, banking and community affairs.

Newton M. Harris married Mary Bruce Burnham of the well known Burnham family of Champaign County. They had three children: Bruce Burnham, who graduated from Yale University in 1923 and became vice president of the First National Bank; Barbara C., who graduated at Vassar College in 1924; and Mary Julia, a graduate of the Ogontz School for Girls at Ogontz, Pennsylvania. Mrs. N. M. Harris died January 10, 1921. She was a woman of remarkable business ability, and long prominent in charitable work, especially taking an active interest in the Burnham Hospital at Champaign.

JOHN A. CROSS, principal of the Washington School at the City of Murphysboro, has followed educational work since early manhood and has realized his ambitions for the broad valuable service open to a career as a school man.

He was born in the country, and had to work for every step of his higher education. His grandfather, Arthur Cross, moved from Virginia into Kentucky in pioneer times, and on coming to Illinois located near Shallow Hill in Randolph County, where he took up a homestead and where he followed farming the rest of his life. The father of John A. Cross, A. J. Cross, was born on May 8, 1837, on the old homestead in southern Illinois, and has likewise made agriculture his vocation. He is now in his 90th year. His home is now a farm five miles north of Murphysboro. He married Adela Gray, who died when her son John was two years old.

John A. Cross was born on his father's farm in 1877. While a boy in the country schools he determined to become a teacher. He attended high school at Murphysboro, was a student in the Southern Illinois State Normal University at Carbondale, and broadened his educational and business outlook by correspondence work with the extension department of the University of Chicago and the International Correspondence School of Scranton.

Mr. Cross, from 1897 to 1901, taught in the Wills School, in Jackson County; in 1901, for one year, he was a teacher in Vergennes, in the same county; he taught the Holiday School District No. 74 from 1902 to 1904; for one year taught at Mt. Carbon, District No. 101, and subsequently taught in District No. 77 and District No. 75. Mr. Cross has utilized his vacation and other surplus time by following the occupation of a farmer. In 1912 he bought a farm of twenty-three acres near the City of Murphysboro, and while living on the farm taught for eight years at Harrison. In 1921 he was elected principal of the Logan School at Murphysboro. He continued as principal until the school was destroyed in the tornado of March, 1925. He escaped without serious injury, though several lost their lives at the school. After the city was able to resume its school program Mr. Cross was made principal of the Washington School, taking the place of Harry Row, who had been elected superintendent of city schools.

Mr. Cross married Margaret S. Perschbacher, daughter of Frederick Perschbacher, an old soldier of the Civil war. Mrs. Cross is a descendant of the well known Patri family who came in early days from Germany and settled near Lenzburg, Illinois. Her grandmother Patri is still living there at the age of ninety-nine.

CHARLES E. HARRIS, osteopathic physician and surgeon at East St. Louis is a veteran of the World war, having served overseas with the Canadian troops. He was born at Edwardsville in Madison County, Illinois, January 2, 1887, son of John Silas and Katherine (O'Keefe) Harris. His maternal grandparents, John and Nora (Quinlan) O'Keefe, were born and married in Ireland and came to America in 1848, becoming farmers in the vicinity of St. Louis, where their daughter Katherine O'Keefe was born. The paternal grandfather, Benjamin Harris, was a native of Missouri and a merchant by occupation. He married Lucretia Messenger, also a native of Missouri. When their son John Silas was quite young, the family moved to Alton, Illinois. John Silas Harris for many years was a teacher in the schools of Madison County and died in 1894, while his widow survived until 1920. They had a family of seven children: John B., Nora, Emma, Mary, Frank, Charles E. and Loretto. The son John married Grace Grote and had seven children,

William P. Thon

while Frank married Edna Kiefer and has three children.

Dr. Charles E. Harris attended district schools in Madison County, Illinois, the Alton High school and the Alton Business College and had some years of varied employment and working experience. He took up the study of medicine and osteopathy, but before completing his course enlisted in May, 1917 with the Engineering Corps in the Canadian forces. He went into camp at St. Johns, Quebec, remaining there about six months; went overseas to England and had special training there for two months, and then went into Belgium with what was called the Fourteenth Draft Engineer's Corps. He was in Belgium during the last year of the war, and remained there until December, 1919, when he returned to England and then to Canada, receiving his honorable discharge at Valcartier, Canada, in 1920. After leaving the army he returned to Chicago and completed his course in osteopathy and since graduating has had a very successful practice in East St. Louis.

He married at Danville, Illinois, July 4, 1922, Miss Emma Streuber, daughter of Rudolph and Katherine (Schwinderman) Streuber. Her father, who died in 1896, was a miller at Greenville, Illinois. In the Streuber family were ten children: J. P., formerly State's Attorney of Madison County, who married Katherine Whorly, and had one child; Charles F., who married Annie Augustine and had three children; Fred, who died unmarried; Oscar, unmarried; Mary, wife of William R. Drummond and mother of seven children; Miss Amelia; Alvernia, wife of John Bolin and the mother of eight children; Miss Lillian, who married Edward Blacet and has seven children; Ella, wife of Joseph Cannon and the mother of two children; and Mrs. Harris.

Dr. Harris is a member of the Catholic Church; is affiliated with the Knights of Columbus; belongs to the American Legion and is a member of the American Osteopathic Association and the Illinois Osteopathic Association.

HON. WILLIAM G. THON. As a capable and honorable attorney practicing at the Chicago bar, a representative of the Twenty-third Senatorial District in the General Assembly of the State of Illinois and a citizen of the highest standing, Hon. William G. Thon is accepted as one of the most desirable of the residents of Northern Illinois. He was born at Clinton, Iowa, February 27, 1886, a son of Gustav and Louise (Krumland) Thon, the former of whom was born at Chicago in 1863, and the latter at Clinton, Iowa.

In 1888 the Thon family came to Chicago, at which time Representative Thon was two years old. Gustav Thon entered upon his long and faithful service with the Chicago & Northwestern Railroad at Clinton, Iowa, in 1882, but changes in his duties necessitated a change in residence. In July, 1925, following a period of forty-two years, Mr. Thon was placed upon the pension list of the road, and is now enjoying the leisure his many years of continuous work for this company entitled him to take. His record with the road is remarkable, not only for the length of his service, but also for the efficiency he always showed in the discharge of his duties, and his faithfulness in always being on hand. At the time of his retirement he was storekeeper of the paint department in the shops of this railroad at Chicago.

Representative Thon was reared at Chicago, and attended the public schools, the Central Young Men's Christian Association Institute, and the law school of Northwestern University, and was graduated from the latter in 1909, with the degree of Bachelor of Laws. Immediately following his graduation he entered upon the practice of his profession, and has since then carried on a general practice in all of the courts.

Since 1914 Representative Thon has been a member of the Illinois General Assembly from the Twenty-third Senatorial District, being reelected every two years including 1924. His services as a legislator have been distinctly beneficial not only directly to his constituents, but to the state at large. In the Forty-ninth General Assembly he was author of the law enacted by that Assembly, providing for the free distribution by the state of one per cent nitrate of silver solution to be used by physicians in the eyes of new-born infants so as to prevent blindness. He led the fight in the Forty-ninth, Fiftieth and Fifty-first sessions, culminating in the Fifty-first, for the enactment of a law making it unlawful for individuals to engage in the business of private banking in the State of Illinois. In the Fifty-second General Assembly he introduced and secured passage of a law providing for the establishing by the state of an institute for research into the causes of mental diseases. The most important of Representative Thon's activities in the Fifty-fourth General Assembly related to the preparation and final passage of the Thon bill, signed and approved by the governor, making it a law, under which hereafter, the nomination of judges of the Superior and Circuit courts of Cook County shall be by direct primary instead of by conventions as formerly. In the Fiftieth and Fifty-first General Assemblies he was chairman of the Committee on Charities and Corrections; in the Fifty-second he was chairman of the Committee on Uniform Laws; in the Fifty-third he was chairman of the Committee on Judicial Department and Practice. In the Fifty-fourth he was chairman of the Revenue Committee. He is one of the leading members of the Izaak Walton League of America, one of the principal objects of which is the conservation of fish and game, a matter in which he takes great interest. In the Fifty-fourth General Assembly, he introduced a bill, the object of which was to make it unlawful to cause pollution of streams and rivers, or to bring about any other condition in the waters of this state that would be harmful to fish.

Representative Thon belongs to D. C. Cregier Lodge No. 643, A. F. and A. M.; Logan Square Chapter No. 243, R. A. M.; Chicago Commandery No. 19, K. T.; Medinah Temple A. A. O. N. M. S. of Chicago; Royal League; Chicago Bar Association; Pistaqua Heights Country Club, Ferndale Rod and Gun Club,

Thirty-fourth Ward National Republican Club, of which he is president, and is a member of the Board of Trustees of Wicker Park Methodist Episcopal Church. All his life he has been a zealous republican, and has long been recognized as one of the leaders in his party. Not only is Representative Thon a well-known figure in matters above referred to, he also attained to prominence as father of a famous pair of twins: William G., Jr., and Margaret Louise, born January 24, 1922; and another son, James Glenn, born July 2, 1923. His wife, the proud mother of these interesting children, was Miss Jane Glenn of Saluda, South Carolina, prior to her marriage. The twins won second prize in the Better Babies Contest at the Central States Fair at Aurora, Illinois, in August, 1924, while at the same fair William G. Thon, Jr., individually won the highest score, 99.6. It is claimed by intimate friends that while Representative Thon takes a deep interest in his professional and political achievements, he is prouder of his twins than of anything else in the world, and those who have had the pleasure of viewing these almost perfect children do not doubt the statement, but appreciate the fact that, after all, the best service a man and his wife can render to the state is to give it children whose physical perfections make almost certain development into fine citizens and good men and women to pass on the torch of life, and continue to maintain the high ideals of this country and its government.

HARRIETT M. DANIEL-GRAVES, M. D., is one of the accomplished women of southern Illinois, a pioneer of her sex in the medical profession, and the many years she has practiced at Murphysboro have brought her success from every point of view.

She was born at Seymour, in southern Indiana, daughter of Joseph H. and Anna S. Muster, and granddaughter of John Muster, who came from France and settled in southern Indiana. He was an architect, a very skillful man in his profession, and among other works he designed the beautiful altar in the old Catholic Cathedral at Vincennes. His wife was Mary Myer, a native of Germany. Joseph H. Muster was born in Indiana, near New Alcis, was reared at Ferdinand, and became a railroad engineer, at first on the old Ohio and Mississippi and later with the Baltimore & Ohio. After forty years of continuous service for the railroad, he was killed in an accident in 1904, at the age of fifty-eight. His widow subsequently lived with her daughter, Dr. Graves, in Murphysboro, where she died in 1922 at the age of seventy-one.

Harriett M. Muster first attended school at Seymour, Indiana, and at Vincennes entered the St. Rose Academy, where she graduated. In 1893 she was married to Oliver Lincoln Daniel of New Albany, Indiana. Mr. Daniel at that time was a locomotive fireman with the Baltimore & Ohio Railroad. The young couple were very ambitious, and while he had a night run with the railroad, he enrolled as a student in the medical college at Louisville, Kentucky. After completing his medical education he located at Clay City, Illinois, remaining there a year, and in 1897 moved to Murphysboro. He engaged in practice there until his death in 1908, and acquired a large surgical and medical practice, making a reputation as a skillful surgeon.

Mrs. Daniel shared the professional enthusiasm of her husband and in 1902 she began the study of medicine in the Missouri Medical College at St. Louis. She spent two years there and in 1906 graduated from Hahnemann Medical College of Chicago. During 1907, she attended the New York Polyclinic and was given a diploma for her work. She engaged in practice at Murphysboro with her husband until his death, and since then has conducted an individual practice. She has been a very busy professional woman. In recent years she has spent her winters in California.

In January, 1925, Dr. Daniel and Willard H. Graves were united in marriage. Mr. Graves is a son of George Graves and nephew of Willard Graves, who was a prominent pioneer citizen of Mendota, Illinois. He subsequently went to Nebraska and invested in large tracts of sheep land. These lands in time made him very wealthy. To his home town of Mendota he presented a fine library and building, which bears his name. Willard H. Graves of Murphysboro was born at Wisner, Nebraska, but has lived in Jackson county, Illinois, since 1907. He acquired one of the best known farms in this section of the state, the Swallow Rock Stock farm, a property that exemplifies all that is best in equipment and management. It is located six miles southwest of Murphysboro. This combined with land owned by Mrs. Graves and under his general supervision makes 1,400 acres. Mr. and Mrs. Graves reside at Murphysboro.

FRANK J. WILLIAMS, optometrist, is a specialist with a degree from several colleges of optometry, and for several years has been engaged in successful practice at the city of Waukegan.

He was born at Adams, Massachusetts, November 5, 1895, son of Fred and Mary (Bun) Williams. His father was a native of Wales, and for many years followed the occupation of engineer.

Frank J. Williams attended grammar and high school at Wilkes Barre, Pennsylvania, later took a college course in Chicago, and in 1916 graduated from the Philadelphia Optical College. In the same year he passed the State Board examinations in Pennsylvania. In 1922 he did post-graduate work in the New Orleans College of Optometry. He was licensed by the State Board of Illinois in 1921. Doctor Williams in 1918 enlisted for service in the World war and was assigned duty as a non-commissioned officer in charge of the Thirteenth Infirmary at Camp Lee, Virginia. In October, 1918, he received an honorable discharge. Then after post-graduate work with Dr. J. J. Lewis of Chicago he spent one year with the American Optical Company and in 1920 located at Waukegan, where he opened his office and has enjoyed a very successful and prosperous business and practice. His office is at 21 North Tennessee Street.

Doctor Williams takes an earnest and public spirited part in the affairs of his community, is a republican and a member of the Baptist Church. He belongs to the Philadelphia Optometry College Alumni, the Illinois State Optometric Society and the American Optometric Association.

He married at Chicago, December 20, 1920, Miss Erma Then, who was educated in the public schools of that city. She is a daughter of Michael and Augusta (Shodiwinkle) Then. Her father was born and reared in Germany, and as a young man came to America, where he met and married his wife. He is connected with the Manz Engraving Company of Chicago. Doctor and Mrs. Williams have three daughters, Dorothy, Virginia and Margaret.

ELBRIDGE GERRY AYER was one of the most distinguished early pioneer citizens in the region along the southern boundary of Wisconsin and in McHenry County, Illinois. He was one of the earliest settlers of the present city of Kenosha, and in 1856 was one of the founders of the city of Harvard, Illinois.

He was born at Haverhill in Essex County, Massachusetts., July 25, 1813, a descendant of John Ayer, who settled in Salisbury in 1640, and is recorded as one of the free men in Haverhill in 1646. The greatgrandfather of E. G. Ayer was a soldier of the Revolution. The grandfather was Daniel Ayer and the father, Samuel Ayer. Samuel was one of the first men in America to engage in the manufacture of flannels.

Elbridge Gerry Ayer learned the wool sapling business at Lawrence, Massachusetts. For a time he was in business with his father at Albany, New York, and in 1836 came west, traveling around the Great Lakes to a hamlet then known as Southport, now the city of Kenosha, and about midway between Chicago and Milwaukee. He was a merchant there for about ten years and was also in business at Walworth, Wisconsin, until January, 1856, when he moved to a tract of four hundred acres of land in McHenry County, Illinois, and a few months later laid out the town of Harvard. Along with other business affairs he conducted a hotel, and during the Civil war he and his wife fed thousands of soldiers passing through Harvard to and from the front, never charging an ill or wounded soldier a cent. A letter from the Governor of Wisconsin at the close of the war commemorates this service and in 1886, when Judge Ayer and his wife celebrated their golden wedding anniversary, a loving cup was presented them by old soldiers thus befriended under the auspices of the Grand Army of the Republic of Wisconsin.

The title of judge was affectionately bestowed upon him because of his leadership in the community and the frequent occasions he was called upon to act as referee in neighborhood disputes. He was a whig, one of the first to join the republican party, and a member of the Masonic Order. He died at his home in Harvard in 1888, being survived by his wife until 1895. He married Mary D. Titcomb, a native of Dedham, Massachusetts. They were the parents of seven children: Mary A., the first white child born at the city of Kenosha, who married Gilbert R. Smith; Anna, who married Abner J. Burbank; Edward E.; Julia, who married Henry B. Minier; Henry C.; Harriet L., who married Marcus L. Towne; and Eva, who became the wife of Arthur G. Law.

EDWARD E. AYER, a son of Elbridge Gerry Ayer, the pioneer of northern Illinois whose career precedes this, has for over forty years been a resident of Chicago, and is best known for his deep interest in any many benefactions to the Filed Museum and other institutions of Chicago. In 1912 he was appointed a member of the United States Board of Indian Commissioners.

He was born at what is now Kenosha, Wisconsin, November 16, 1841, and was reared and educated in Walworth County, Wisconsin, and Harvard, Illinois. In 1860 he crossed the plains to the mining districts of Nevada, and to San Francisco, and in the summer of 1861 enlisted in the northern army in California, being the first man sworn in on the Pacific Coast as a member of Company E., First California Cavalry. He was in campaigns in the southwest, among the Navajo Indians of California and other tribes, and was finally promoted to second lieutenant of the First New Mexico Volunteer Infantry. He resigned his commission at Fort Craig, New Mexico, in May, 1864. On returning north he became a partner in his father's store at Harvard, but soon engaged in contracting, particularly in the supplying of ties and other timber to railroads. This developed into the chief business of his active career. He became widely known as a railroad contractor, and in 1894 joined in the founding of the notable business known as the Ayer & Lord Tie Company of Chicago, probably the largest concern of its kind in the country. Since 1900 he has been retired from active responsibilities, though he remained a director in the Ayer & Lord Tie Company.

Mr. Ayer's early experiences with the wild Indians of the West developed a study and interest in the American Aborigines that have continued through a period of more than sixty years. About 1880 he began the systematic collection of articles characteristic of the arts of the wild tribes. The Ayer collection has long been one of the most notable features of the exhibits in the Field Museum of Chicago. He also gathered probably the most extensive library of works on the American Indian, which he donated to the Newberry Library. Mr. Ayer served as president of the Field Columbian Museum from 1893 to 1898, and has since been a director of the museum, a director of the Newberry Library, of the Chicago Art Institute and is a life member of the American Historical Association. He has been an extensive traveler both at home and abroad, and from the points of contact he has maintained with the busy world of affairs and with the cultures of the past, has found the quality of never failing interest. He has offices and home in Chicago and also a country home at Lake Geneva in his native state. He married, September 7, 1865, Miss Emma Burbank, a native of Massachusetts.

JUDSON EUGENE STRONG, M.D., who died in February, 1926, had practiced medicine at Cairo for over four decades. He was more than a very skillful and able physician and surgeon. The many splendid qualities of his character adorned and exalted his professional equipment, so that he was one of the best loved and most useful citizens of Cairo and Alexander County.

He was born at Euclid, Ohio, November 27, 1854, son of A. C. and Harriet (Pelton) Strong. His father was a native of Wickliff, Ohio, and his mother of Euclid. They were farming people all their lives. Judson Eugene Strong was reared in the rural district near Cleveland, attended public schools there, afterwards the high school at Cleveland, and subsequently attended Western Reserve College, then located at Hudson, Ohio. He prepared for his profession in the Cleveland Homeopathic Medical College, graduating in 1880 with the Doctor of Medicine degree. He served as an interne in the Hahnemann Hospital at Chicago. Dr. Strong for several years practiced in Michigan, and in January, 1883, moved to Cairo, Illinois, where he carried on his work until a short time before his death. He was also an active member of the Association of Commerce, was a republican, and member of the Independent Order of Odd Fellows.

The dates and ordinary tasks of his career have been stated briefly to make room for the quotation of an editorial from the Cairo bulletin which every friend and admirer of the late Dr. Strong will recognize as a more just tribute and evaluation of his life and character than any mere statement of facts and statistics. This editorial reads as follows:

"Like news of a civic disaster, the announcement of the death of Dr. J. E. Strong will carry into countless Cairo homes its burden of sadness and sorrow and sincere grief, together with a feeling that it cannot be; that there must be some mistake. For so has Dr. Strong endeared himself to the community which he served with such tenderness and faithfulness for many years. His removal from the community life is much like the removal of an institution to which the men and women of today had become accustomed as children. His long professional activity in this section had knit him up so closely with the family life of so many of its citizens that it is impossible to realize at this moment that the gentle, kindly presence that has soothed hundreds in their pain; that has fought so many winning battles to bring back some loved one from the valley of the shadow, has indeed passed on.

"Dr. Strong was one of Cairo's oldest practitioners both in point of years and in point of practice in this city. His was a delightful personality. The doctor came more nearly approximating the older type of physician than any other in the city. He was especially beloved by the children of this city, so many of whom he had ushered into this world, and whose lasting friendship and affection naturally flowed to him as they grew into young manhood and womanhood.

"The fathers and mothers of the community were no less devoted to him, though perhaps not in such an outspoken way. This fact was proven time after time last night as the good doctor lay upon his deathbed, when hundreds of telephone calls came to the Bulletin office making inquiry as to the condition of their aged friend. Childish trebles were mixed with the resonant bass of more mature callers and the tone of anxiety and sorrow apparent in every inquiry constituted a wonderful tribute to this man who has meant so much in the life of this city.

"Dr. Strong's personality, second only to his professional skill, was most potent. All the patience, all the gentleness, all the sick room presence that a doctor should have, seemed to have been Dr. Strong's in unusual measure. His poise and balance and sympathetic understanding of both his big and little patients acted as a mild and healing balm to the minds of the suffering even before his practical helps had been applied. His was the ideal temperament for a physician, and as the years grew upon him his benevolent features seemed to take on an increased glow of kindliness, his voice a tenderer note, and his calm and unhurried gestures a more soothing influence, so that when his glance fell upon his patient it bore something of the grace and power of a benediction.

"As a citizen Dr. Strong was in all things the man he was as a professional man. He was a splendid and devoted husband and father of a fine family. His death, after these long years of close association with the public life, comes almost as an unbelievable thing, something that could not happen. And it will not all be realized at once. Full realization will not come save with the passing days, and in the years to come the memory of Dr. Strong will be held green in the hearts of scores of Cairo men and women whom he has known and served and befriended with that sweet and gentle care and tenderness which seemed peculiarly his to give."

The late Dr. Strong was twice married. At Hudson, Michigan, in 1879, he married Miss Emily Fauver, who was born at Elyria, Ohio, and died in 1882, leaving two children: Mabel of Chicago; and Florence, wife of S. S. Bayley of Los Angeles, California. Dr. Strong in 1887 married Miss Julia Ellen Nall, who survives him. Mrs. Strong is a kinswoman of General John A. Logan, and during her long residence at Cairo exemplified distinctive talents and social gifts, and is the mother of a gifted family. Her four children are: Judson Eugene Strong, Jr., of East St. Louis; Harriet Alice, wife of Dan G. Wood, of Danville, Illinois; Margaret Logan, wife of William Winter, of Cairo; and Miss Julia Ellen, an operatic singer who lives with her mother in New York City.

A. ALONZO THOMPSON. The Thompsons are one of the oldest families of Greene County. For a century their activities have been identified with farming, business and citizenship in that section of the state.

John Thompson, a Virginian, native of Botetourt County, was a soldier of the American Revolution, enlisting in 1781, the last year of the war. He served three months in Capt. Henry Hawling's company under Col. William McLelland. Later he reenlisted for six months more in Capt. David May's company and Col. Fleming's regiment. Late in life he followed his son to Greene County, Illinois, and died shortly afterward, in 1843. The body of the Revolutionary veteran rests in the Thompson grave yard at Barrow. He was the father of a large family, and his descendants are now represented not only in Greene County but in nearly every state of the west.

His son, John Thompson, moved to Illinois from Tennessee and settled in the Barrow locality after driving across the country with wagons and oxen. He died at the age of sixty years. He married Docia Bandy, and they had five sons, Israel, David, Robert, Isaac and John, while the daughters were Mrs. Matilda Baird, Mrs. Cynthia Steelman, Mrs. Jane Taylor, Mrs. Emeline Quinten, Mary Thompson and Mrs. Rachel Kidd.

David Thompson, of the third generation of the family, was born on the site of Barrow Station on the Burlington Railway in 1828, and spent all his life in that locality. He died in 1914 and is buried in the Thompson grave yard. He had such education as the local schools provided, gave all his active energies to farming, and his only public office was as school director. He was a Baptist and helped build a number of churches of worship in his locality. David Thompson married at Jacksonville, in 1849, Miss Mary Jane Cole, daughter of Robert and Rhoda (Asher) Cole. She died at the age of fifty-six. Their children were: William A., assistant cashier of the First National Bank of Roodhouse; Sarah E., widow of Thomas Conlee; Robert C. of Batesville, Arkansas; Oscar S., of Jacksonville, Illinois; A. Alonzo, of White Hall; John E., of Murrayville, Illinois; David Walter, of San Angelo, Texas; Amy J., wife of William Weller, of Carlinville, Illinois; and Ada, deceased wife of T. B. Weller.

A. Alonzo Thompson was born two and a half miles north of Roodhouse, December 8, 1864, finished the high school course in Roodhouse, and taught a term of school just east of Barrow, the old school house being now used as a dwelling on the William Wendell farm. Since this school teaching experience he has been a practical farmer. He lived at his birthplace to the age of fifty-four, then moved southeast of White Hall and subsequently bought the Ross farm, where he lives now. He has been engaged in general farming, feeding and fattening live stock for the market and also dairying, but has abandoned dairying and is now identified with a quieter routine. Mr. Thompson for the past eighteen months has rendered service to the Chicago Sanitary District in taking samples of water from the Illinois River and having the laboratory tests made. He is a democrat, and cast his first presidential vote for Grover Cleveland in 1888. He is a member of the Primitive Baptist Church and the Modern Woodmen of America.

Mr. Thompson married, July 29, 1886, Miss Sarah Edwards, daughter of Presley and Ellen (Jeffres) Edwards, the former a native of Kentucky and the latter of Virginia. Mrs. Thompson was born in Illinois, in January, 1864, and is one of five children. Her father was a Union soldier, was wounded in battle and died three years after returning from the army.

Of the children of Mr. and Mrs. Thompson the oldest is Judge Floyd E. Thompson, a conspicuous Illinoisan as a justice of the Illinois State Supreme Court. Floyd E. Thompson, whose law career has identified him with Rock Island, is a graduate of the Roodhouse High School, taught for four years, two years of that time in the Manchester High School, graduated from Law School at Chattanooga, Tennessee, was admitted to the Tennessee and Illinois bars, and located for practice at East Moline. Six months later he was elected state's attorney of Rock Island County, being the first democrat ever elected to a county office there. He was reelected, and at the age of thirty-two resigned to go on the Supreme Bench of the state, being the youngest associate justice Illinois has ever had, and at the time of his election the youngest in the United States. He was reelected to the Supreme Bench in 1921, carrying his republican district by 15,000 votes. Judge Thompson married Irene Worcester and has a daughter, Mary Ellen. The other children of A. Alonzo Thompson are: Emory A., a farmer at Fulton, Arkansas, who married Nellie Turner and has two children, Sarah Josephine and David Floyd; Mabel, wife of Allen R. McConathy, a farmer near White Hall, with two children, John and Dale; Hazel J., the wife of William J. Allen, a farmer near Roodhouse, their children being Eugenia, William Don and Carroll; David, a business man at Hollywood, California, who spent three months in an officers training school during the World war, then volunteered for the Aviation Corps and was instructor in flying at Houston, Texas, until the armistice. David married Martha A. Smith and has a son, David, Jr.

HON. WILLIAM E. HULL, for thirty-five years a resident of Peoria and closely identified with its business life, has become a prominent figure throughout the state and the middle west since his election to Congress in 1922, representing the Sixteenth Illinois District. In the Sixty-eighth Congress, beginning in 1923, he was made a member of the committee on rivers and harbors. He soon introduced the bill known as the Hull Waterway Bill, designed to carry out a plan for construction and maintenance of a nine foot waterway between Chicago and the Gulf. This bill has been one of the centers of contention and debate, not only in Congress but throughout the middle west.

Mr. Hull was one of the first to advocate hard roads in Illinois and was instrumental in the formation of the State Highway Improvement Association and served as one of its five directors. He was author of the bill passed by the Legislature to issue bonds to the amount of sixty million dollars for the building of permanent roads in Illinois. One recent recognition of his activity in behalf of good roads was his appointment in 1925 by the President as a member of a committee of seven to attend the International Good Roads Conference in Buenos Aires, South America, October, 1925.

William Edgar Hull was born at Lewiston in Fulton County, Illinois, January 13, 1866, son of William Wesley and Mary (Missplay)

Hull. His grandfather, Philip Hull, was born in Virginia in 1795, son of John and Christina (Effex) Hull. Philip Hull was very young when his parents moved to Kentucky, where he grew up and from there he went to Ohio, in which state he married Sarah McCracken. Her father, Alexander McCracken, was a native of Ireland and came to America during the Revolutionary war, fighting with the colonists for independence. Philip Hull in 1838 moved from Licking County, Ohio, to Illinois and was one of the pioneer settlers of Cass Township, Fulton County, where he remained until 1866, and then bought another farm in Lewiston Township. He was a soldier in the War of 1812 and a pensioner of that war and was a member of the Methodist Church. The family believed in the value of education, and at his own expense he erected a log schoolhouse on his land. This building is still standing and was known for many years as Hull schoolhouse, being a center of community meetings and debates.

Capt. William Wesley Hull, father of Congressman Hull, was born in Cass Township, Fulton County, and in May, 1861, enlisted for service in the Union army, receiving a commission as captain of Company H of the Seventeenth Illinois Infantry. He was with the regiment in its various campaigns and battles until June, 1864, when he was honorably discharged. Returning home, he resumed farming on a place a mile west of Lewiston and afterwards moved into Lewiston. President Arthur appointed him postmaster there and he served four years. He had various business interests and was a man of much power and influence in his community.

William Edgar Hull was the only child of his parents. He was educated at Lewiston in the public schools, also attended Illinois College at Jacksonville. At the age of eighteen, in 1884, he became assistant postmaster at Lewiston under his father and three years later became a clerk in the railway mail service. In 1889 he was appointed a gauger in the United States internal revenue department, his appointment being credited to Fulton County and his duties took him to Peoria, where he has resided since 1890. He has achieved a leading place in the business circles of Peoria. He was one of the builders of the Jefferson Hotel and of the University Building, the Palace Theatre and the Virginia Apartments. He is president of the Manito Chemical Company.

Mr. Hull, a number of years ago, was elected secretary of the Peoria County Republican Central Committee, and chairman of the Fourteenth Congressional District Committee. The Fourteenth District was a democratic stronghold, but under his guidance the district for the first time sent a republican to Congress. In 1898 Mr. Hull was appointed postmaster by President McKinley and reappointed by Roosevelt, serving two terms. He was a delegate to the National Republican Convention of 1916 and 1920 and in 1924 was reelected member of Congress from the Sixteenth District. He was a member of the Creve Coeur Club, the Country Club, the Mount Hawley Country Club, Peoria Automobile Association the Association of Commerce and is a Mason and Knight of Pythias. He married, February 25, 1888, Miss Ella Harris, of Lewiston. Her grandfather, Newton Walker, was a pioneer of Lewiston.

REV. EDWARD A. KELLY, pastor of St. Ann's Church, one of the large and flourishing parishes on the South Side of Chicago, grew up in that city, and his faithful labors as a priest have been given to that city through a period of forty-five years.

He was born at Brooklyn, New York, June 15, 1853. His parents, Charles J. and Mary (Donlin) Kelly, were natives of Ballinsloe, Roscommon County, Ireland, and came to the United States as children, being married in New York City. Charles J. Kelly for a time was a member of a militia company in New York. In June, 1854, he brought his family to Chicago and thereafter was engaged in the building contracting business. At the time of his death, which occurred at the age of seventy, he was the oldest contractor and builder in Chicago. He erected the George M. Pullman residence, one of the landmarks of the South Side, and many other fine structures. Charles J. Kelly's wife died at the age of fifty-nine. They had a family of five daughters and two sons, Edward A. being the oldest.

Edward A. Kelly was just a year old when the family settled in Chicago. He attended the Franklin School in that city, the Christian Brothers school and St. Ignacius College, and prepared for the priesthood in St. Charles Seminary and St. Mary's Seminary at Baltimore. He was ordained December 18, 1880, receiving his ecclesiastical orders from Cardinal Gibbons. His first appointment to service was in Chicago under Bishop Foley. He was at St. Bridget's Church, All Saints Church, and then was appointed to the responsibility of organizing the new parish of St. Cecilia. Upon the death of Rev. Patrick M. Flannigan he became pastor of St. Ann's Church on West Fifty-fifth Street. His labors in that parish have been abundantly prospered and he is the beloved head of one of the leading churches on the South Side.

Father Kelly has been deeply interested in many movements and undertakings for moral reform and civic advancement. A number of years ago he was associated with Father Flannigan in an effort to bring about railroad track elevation in his section of the city. For twenty-five years Father Kelly acted as a chaplain of the Seventh Regiment of the Illinois National Guard, and was with that regiment in the Spanish American war. He served on the Illinois State Board of Charities under Governor Yates, and Mayor Busse appointed him a member of the committee of fifteen to investigate crime and vice conditions.

CHARLES B. ROHLAND was a resident of Alton, where he practiced dentistry for forty years, and the profession of dentistry in Illinois will always acknowledge a debt to his leadership and personality.

Dr. Rohland was born in Lebanon, Pennsylvania, March 24, 1845, and died at Alton, June 10, 1910. He was reared in Pennsylvania, at-

tending the Lebanon High School, the New Berlin Seminary, and in Dickinson College completing the courses leading up to the Bachelor of Arts and Master of Arts degrees. He was graduated Doctor of Dental Surgery from the Philadelphia Dental College, and in 1869 moved to Alton, where he was one of the first dentists of thorough technical training to engage in practice. He enjoyed success in his individual practice, and was especially well known for the contacts he had with the profession over the state.

Dr. Rohland was the founder and first president of the Southern Illinois Dental Society. He was a life member and held all the offices of the Illinois State Dental Society. He was also a member of the Illinois State Board of Dental Examiners, the National Dental Association, and the Delta Sigma Delta fraternity.

The significance of his professional leadership is best stated in quoting from the editorial that appeared in the Dental Review in August, 1910: "The death of Dr. Rohland has removed from dentistry one of the shining lights. This is not a stereotyped phrase, but it is a literal truth. He was the very highest type of a professional gentleman, cultured, clean, capable, and above all most lovable. His wit was of the rarest, keenest, and withal the most kindly that ever fell from human lips. Whenever Dr. Rohland rose to speak in a dental gathering he at once commanded the attention of the entire assembly. This was not because he was ever in the least obtrusive—he was by nature the very opposite —but because his well-balanced brain, backed by years of study and observation, never failed to grasp the essentials of any subject which claimed his attention, and his vocabulary was so clear and incisive, his personality so attractive, that it was always a pleasure to hear him. To know such a man was an inspiration, to be his friend was a great and cherished privilege. His influence among his fellows was always for the good and he has left the world, because of his sojourn here, a better place to live."

MRS. CHARLES B. ROHLAND, who before her marriage in 1879 to Dr. C. B. Rohland was Cora Dolbee, daughter of Shadrach R. and Hannah E. (Pettingill) Dolbee, known also by that name, has had a career of genuine distinction as a musical director, composer and organizer, and her work could not pass without notice in any account of musical culture in southern Illinois.

She was born in Alton in 1856, and her musical talents were trained by a succession of teachers including Professor Floss, Froelich, Goldbeck, Robyn and Anton in St. Louis, William H. Sherwood of New York, Francon Davies and Sir H. C. Coward of England. For a number of years Mrs. Rohland was a member of the board of management of the St. Louis Symphony Orchestra and for seventeen years directed the chorus of the St. Louis Musical Club, making the club programs rare musical events in St. Louis.

Her home through all these years has been in Alton, where her chief work has been as director of the Dominant Ninth Chorus, an organization which has in reflecting her musicianship and leadership gained recognition of the best music critics of the country. It is an organization adequate to express and interpret the finest and most difficult works of musical compositions. Mrs. Rohland was founder of this chorus and for the thirty years of its existence its musical director. In connection with its festival work she directed such famous orchestras as the Chicago Symphony, St. Louis Symphony and Minneapolis Symphony. Mrs. Rohland was director of the Choral Society of Edwardsville, Illinois, and she gave many lecture recitals and has published songs and piano pieces. Mrs. Rohland is a member of the St. Louis Chapter of the Daughters of the American Revolution and the English Speaking Union.

FRANK G. TROUTNER is sheriff of Pike County. He has the distinction of being the second republican ever elected to that office in this county. He was born in the county, is member of an old and well known family there, and his personal popularity, his record as a fighting soldier with the Illinois Thirty-third Division in the World war and his exceptional qualifications earned him the office in which he is now rendering such efficient service.

His grandfather, John Troutner, was an early settler at Pittsfield. He was a machinist, and practically all the Troutners have been noted for their bent for mechanics. John Troutner was the father of nine children, and of the four living one is William D. Troutner, who was born at Pittsfield in April, 1862, and has spent his life in mechanical pursuits. He is now in the garage business at Pittsfield. He married Louise Galloway, who was born at Kansas City, Kansas, daughter of John Galloway, who moved out to Kansas from Illinois. Mrs. Louise Troutner died in 1908. She was the mother of three children: Frank Galloway; Jessie, wife of Leonard Crowder of Pittsfield; and Lindell, connected with the King Milling Company of Pittsfield.

Frank G. Troutner was born at Pittsfield December 16, 1894. After finishing a public school education he went to work in the shops of the Wabash Railway Company at Bluffs, Illinois. He was there about a year, and then became mechanic, taking care of the cars in the establishment of King and Matthews, the distributors for Dodge cars.

He left that position to volunteer for service, enlisting March 25, 1917, about two weeks before America declared war on Germany. He joined Company B, of the Fifth Illinois Infantry of the National Guard, and was put on guard duty at the Chicago & Alton Bridge over the Mississippi at Louisiana. Later he was sent to Camp Parker at Quincy, and after a month went south to Houston, Texas, where he was with the Illinois troops trained at Camp Logan, where the Thirty-third Division was organized. He was transferred from the Illinois Infantry to the One Hundred Twenty-fourth Machine Gun Battalion, and became chief machine gun mechanic for that battalion. He left Camp Logan in May, 1918, after having been in training there since the preceding September. From Camp Upton, Long Island, he went to Hoboken and sailed on the Mt. Vernon, crossing in seven days and eight hours to Brest. After three days at Brest he was sent to the British forces near the Amiens-Albert fronts, located at Molliens-Au-Bois, and was in training with the English troops until July, when he went to the French lines near Verdun, where the Thirty-third Division held the pivot on that front. He was there until October, and was then on the front near Metz until December, after which he was with the Army of Occupation in Luxemburg until March 26, 1919, when he left for home, sailing from Brest on the same vessel that took him over. He participated in three great engagements, the Somme defensive, the Meuse-Argonne offensive and the offensive in front of Metz in the final days of the war. He landed at Hoboken, went to Camp Mills and a few days later to Camp Grant at Rockford, Illinois, where he was discharged May 30, 1919. His military record really covers a period of three years, since he had joined the National Guard organization in the spring of 1916, about the time it was called into duty for Mexican border service. Mr. Troutner is a member of the Forty and Eight Military Society and helped organize the American Legion post in Pittsfield.

After the war Mr. Troutner was mechanic in charge of the trucks and cars of the M. D. King Milling Company at Pittsfield until February, 1922, when he resigned to begin his active campaign for the office of sheriff. He received the republican nomination without opposition, and in the election in the fall of that year he won by some 825 votes over his democratic opponent, in a county normally democratic by some 1,400 majority. He succeeded John Davis as sheriff. His term has been one of unusual activity in the apprehension of criminals, and his office has made three times as many arrests as is credited to the term of any previous sheriff. Sheriff Troutner has taken nine prisoners to the Southern Illinois Penitentiary at Chester, twenty-seven to the Illinois State Farm at Vandalia, six to the Pontiac State Reformatory, three to the St. Charles School for Boys and fifteen to the Illinois State School and Colony.

Mr. Troutner is affiliated with the Independent Order of Odd Fellows, Knights of Pythias and Modern Woodmen of America. He married at Pittsfield, October 10, 1922, Miss Beulah Brummell, who was born at Martinsburg in Pike County, May 28, 1902, daughter of Samuel and Lula (Petty) Brummell, now residents of Pittsfield. Mrs. Troutner has one brother, Stanley Brummell.

MARION CARNEGIE LIBRARY is an institution unusual in equipment and service facilities for a town of the size and represents the cultural spirit of the community as well as the munificence of the late Mr. Carnegie.

In 1912 the City Council of which John H. Burnett was Mayor and Eura Griggs City Clerk passed the Library Ordinance which had been prepared by W. W. Skaggs, then City Attorney. In the levy of 1912 $1,800 was levied as library tax for library purposes. The first Board of Directors appointed by Mayor Burnett was E. Longbons, G. H. Goodall, M. Woodley, John M. Dodd, W. G. Cochran, R. O. Clarida, E. B. Jackson, E. G. Lentz and Noah Payne.

March 15, 1913, the Library Board of Directors met and organized as follows: by drawing lots the term of office each should serve: One year, R. O. Clarida, Noah Payne, E. G. Lentz; two years, W. G. Cochran, J. M. Dodd, E. B. Jackson; three years, G. H. Goodall, M. Woodley, E. Longbons. Officers elected were: President, M. Woodley; Vice President, E. Longbons; Secretary, E. G. Lentz; Treasurer, J. M. Dodd.

June 24, 1913, the Library Board submitted its first annual report to the city council, telling of the progress made during the year and that there was a sum of $1,800 in the treasury.

In 1913 Mayor Burnett named E. M. Spiller, E. M. Stotlar and H. D. Norris to succeed Payne, Lentz and Cochran, the latter having died and the terms of the other two having expired. On October 11, 1913, the new Board organized with the following officers: President, M. Woodley; Vice President, R. O. Clarida; Secretary, E. B. Stotlar; Treasurer, E. B. Jackson. At this meeting a committee was appointed to seek a suitable site for the Library building and to devise means to secure the building.

At a meeting held August 22, 1914, four sites for the Library were proposed, from which the Mrs. Surilda Cline property at 206 South Market Street, at a price of $5,000 was the unanimous selection of the Board.

March 21, 1914, the Carnegie Corporation renewed an offer first made on February 13, 1909, of $18,000 for the erection of a library building only, which offer was accepted by the Library Board as quickly as all conditions contained in the offer could be met.

The architectural contract for the building was let January 5, 1915, to Grant Shopbell of Evansville, Indiana, and on May 20, 1915, the contract for the erection of the building was let to Robert Sparks of Marion, Illinois, for the sum of $15,998.15. The O'Donnell Steam Heat Co., of Evansville was awarded the heating and plumbing contract for $1,175.

The building was formally dedicated and opened to the public on the evening of February 29, 1916, at which time Dr. D. D. Hartwell was the Mayor of the city and George C. Campbell the City Clerk. The Library Board was composed of the following: President, M. Woodley; Vice President, Dr. H. D. Norris; Secretary, E. M. Stotlar; Treasurer, R. O. Clarida. Members, E. M. Spiller, G. R. Stone, P. B. Wilson, E. Longbons, F. J. McIntosh. There were then 750 volumes in the Library ready for circulation. Now, in 1926, there are ten times as many books with 38,000 circulation and 4,079 borrowers. The Library subscribes to sixty-five periodicals.

For the year ending in May, 1926, the receipts by the special library tax was $6,335.99 and the expenditures for the same period were $5,578.35. The tax is 1 8/10 mills and the value of the city property subject to tax is $2,412,748.

The personnel of the present Board is: President, M. Woodley; Vice President, E. E. Leach; Secretary, Arno Bratten; Treasurer, E. M. Stotlar. Members, Mrs. Ethel T. Holland, L. C. Campbell, Mrs. Henry Bantz, Mrs. W. S. Burkhart and E. Longbons. Mr. Woodley has served continuously since the first committee was appointed and has been the sole President of the Board. Mr. Stotlar has been a Director continuously since his appointment in 1913 and Mrs. Holland since 1916.

The first librarian was Miss Mary E. Williams who was succeeded in turn by Miss Mary Goodall, Mrs. Jennie R. Hentz, Miss Dorothy Snavlin, Miss Marie Mysche and Miss Vilda Beem, and the present efficient incumbent, Mrs. Nannie Gray Parks, who took charge in September, 1922, after having been a member of the Board of Directors for six years.

Mrs. Parks is a graduate of Christian College at Columbia, Missouri, with the class of 1900 and she did post-graduate work in music and art; later, before taking up her duties as librarian, she completed a course in library work at the University of Illinois.

Mrs. Parks was born and reared in Marion, Illinois, and is a daughter of the late Henry Gray, a native of West Virginia, who owned a large stock farm at the edge of Marion. Her mother, Mary A. Goodall, was a daughter of Joab Goodall, Sr., who laid out the town of Marion and was one of its outstanding pioneer citizens.

The assistant to Mrs. Parks as librarian is Miss Ella Pease, a graduate of the Marion Township High School and of the Library School of the University of Illinois.

JAMES WESLEY MCKINNEY. As teacher, principal and county superintendent of schools, James Wesley McKinney has given the greater part of his active life to the educational interests of Williamson County. His service as county superintendent has constituted a memorable epoch in educational history in this section of the state. Mr. McKinney is also a minister of the Gospel, and few men are more gifted intellectually.

He was born in Williamson County March 13, 1873. His father, James H. McKinney, was born in Mississippi in 1842. Left an orphan by the death of his parents at the age of twelve years, he came north to Illinois, settled in Williamson County, and at the age of nineteen enlisted in the Union army with the Eighty-first Illinois Regiment. He was in service three years and seven months, and of that time, nine months, eighteen days, was spent enduring the horrors of confinement in Andersonville Prison. After the war he achieved position and a substantial competence by his work as a farmer. He died April 11, 1914. His wife was Minerva Jane Dunn, whose father was a veteran of the Mexican war. She is now seventy-four years of age and a resident of Marion. There were ten children, eight now living. All these children were born on their father's farm, a property of a hundred and eighty acres, which has remained in the family for over half a century. Of the children, James W. is the oldest. His brothers, John R., William E. and L. Egbert, are Williamson County farmers. Another brother, Dr. Henry T. McKinney, is head of the Department of Education in Bethany College, West Virginia, having graduated from Valparaiso University of Indiana, and in 1920 received his Doctor of Philosophy degree at the University of Illinois. The three daughters are: Alice, wife of Frank Brown; Myrtle, wife of Charles Zimmerman, and Ella, wife of Orion Ice, all of whom are Williamson County farmers.

James Wesley McKinney grew up in a good home, but work was part of his training from early boyhood. He attended country schools during the winter terms. In early life he united with the Baptist Church, and at the age of eighteen was ordained and for a number of years was widely known as the "boy preacher." In the meantime he had continued his education in a select school at Marion, and in the Southern Illinois Normal University at Carbondale, and in 1903 was graduated from Valparaiso University of Indiana.

In the year 1895, he married Miss Agnes L. Neilson, daughter of W. W. Scott Neilson of Williamson County. They have four children: Harvey Lee, Robert E., Wendell H. and Ruth Afton McKinney.

Following his marriage Mr. McKinney spent twenty years as a preacher in Williamson County, and during that time was superintendent of schools at Carterville, Johnston City, Creal Springs and Golconda. In 1914 he was elected county superintendent of schools on the republican ticket and has been kept in that office by repeated reelection until the present time. He was reelected in 1918 without opposition in either party and again in 1922 by a majority of 4,500 over his democratic opponent. At the same time he has given a great deal of time and energy to the upbuilding of the church. In every community where he has been identified with the schools he has also held a local pastorate. He organized a number of churches and built new churches at Cambria, Johnston City and Marion. On taking charge of the Baptist Church at Marion he found the congregation housed in a small frame building, there being only forty members. He increased the membership to 530, and the church has a handsome new building which cost $50,000. McKinney Chapel in the south part of Williamson County which he organized and built, was named for Rev. Mr. McKinney. He is a member of the Board of Managers of the Baptist State Convention, is moderator of the Southern Illinois Baptist Association, and for the past three years has been a member of the Illinois State Examining Board for Teachers' Certificates. He is also a member of the Advisory Board of the Illinois Baptist Sanitarium at Robinson. Mr. McKinney is a member of the Masonic fraternity and Independent Order of Odd Fellows.

During his administration two Community high schools, one township high school, and one Community consolidated school have been formed. In 1923, he was given a place on the State Teachers' program at Springfield to discuss the Community Consolidated School Law. The schools of Williamson County have experienced wonderful advancement since he became county superintendent. Since that time seventy new modern school buildings have been erected and thirty buildings remodeled, and the equipment has been made to conform to the requirements of the Illinois Sanitation Law. Of the 454 teachers, ninety per cent are high school graduates, and the salaries of teachers have increased more than 200 per cent in the last twelve years. As an evidence of the estimate placed by the people of Williamson County on Mr. McKinney's administration, there is nothing better than calling attention to the fact that he has been repeatedly reelected to office.

REV. FRANCIS A. MARKS is pastor of the Catholic Church at Collinsville, and has been in the Catholic Ministry in this state for over forty years.

He was born at St. Louis, Missouri, June 28, 1859, and was about one year old when his parents moved to Breese in Clinton County, Illinois. His father Frank Parks was born in Germany, came to America in 1838, locating at St. Louis, and spent many years in the wholesale grocery business and the Steamboat transportation interests. He died in 1884. His wife Theresa Knuewer, was born in Germany and came to America in 1839 and was married at St. Louis.

Rev. Francis A. Marks is the only survivor of a family of fourteen children. He was educated in Catholic Schools in Milwaukee, and took his theological training in St. Meinrad, Indiana. He was ordained at Breese, and from 1883 to 1910, a period of nearly thirty years, he served the church at Jerseyville, Illinois. Since 1910 he has been pastor of the Catholic Church at Collinsville, and has made this a strong and cherishing church, sustaining all the activities of both church and school. His parish contains about three hundred families and the parochial school has an enrollment of about three hundred.

CHARLES CENTER CASE, lawyer, born in Flora Township, Boone County, Illinois, December 14, 1878, son of Charles Center and Charlotte (Hayden) Case, the former a descendant of James Leonard of Taunton, Massachusetts, and of Kenelm Winslow, whose brother, Edward, was first governor of Plymouth, and the latter a descendant of John and Priscilla Alden of Plymouth.

Educated in the district school; graduated from Cherry Valley (Ill.), High School, 1894; graduated from Rockford, (Ill.), High School, 1897; student of Northwestern University, 1897-99; student of Harvard University, 1899-1900; law student under personal tuition of licensed attorneys, 1900-01; student of Chicago Kent College of Law, 1901-02, and Northwestern University Law School, 1902-03; LL.B. (Northwestern) 1903; admitted to Illinois Bar, 1903.

Married Elizabeth Hodgson, of Rockford, Illinois, September 23, 1908; children; Elizabeth Center, born October 11, 1910, and Winifred Virginia, born July 1, 1914.

Associated with law firm of Heckman, Elsdon & Shaw, Chicago, 1903-06; appointed Chief Clerk of Circuit Court of Cook County, 1906, upon recommendation of judges, for purpose of reorganizing clerk's office following exposures of corruption in previous regime, and filled that office 1906-07; practiced with Gann & Peaks, and alone, 1907-12; Assistant State's Attorney 1913-19, and County Attorney (and ex-officio attorney for all county officers) three terms during that period. While Assistant State's Attorney he was successively assistant in charge of Chicago Municipal Courts, assistant in charge of Cook County Grand Juries, head of Indictment Department, assistant in charge of Criminal Court trials, and Chief Assistant, and handled police graft investigation, "million dollar burglar trust" prosecutions, "Yellow Kid" confidence game cases, Ex-Senator Lorimer-Munday-LaSalle Bank cases, and numerous other important prosecutions and cases of public interest. While County Attorney he questioned the validity of various acts of the County Board, and brought about a reformation of County governmental machinery.

Has practiced alone since 1919, general practice. Member of American and Illinois State Bar Associations, and Chicago Law Institute; member and officer of Chicago Bar Association, (Grievance Committee, 1918-20; Board of Managers, 1921-23; Committee on Administration of Criminal Justice, 1921-26, Secretary and ex-officio member of Board of Managers, 1924-25 and 1925-26). Phi Delta Theta; Phi Delta Phi; S. A. R.; Trustee North Shore Baptist Church; democrat; member Lincoln Park Lodge, A. F. & A. M.; Oriental Consistory, 32 degree; Medinah temple, A. A. O. N. M. S., and other fraternal societies, organizations and clubs. Recreations: bee-keeping and horticulture on his farm named "Intervale," at Cherry Valley, Illinois. Home, 5502 Magnolia Avenue, Chicago. Office, 160 North La Salle Street.

FRANCIS GRANT BLAIR has been state superintendent of public instruction for twenty consecutive years, and probably no individual has exercised a greater and more constructive influence on Illinois educational history than Mr. Blair, not only in his present position but throughout the service he has rendered as a teacher and school administrator.

He was born at Nashville, Illinois, October 30, 1864, son of William and Mary J. (Crane) Blair. Most of his early life was spent on a farm in Jefferson County, where he attended country schools. He also attended the Mount Vernon High School and for several years taught a rural district. In 1892 he was graduated from the Illinois State Normal University, and in 1897 received the Bachelor of Science degree from Swarthmore College in Pennsylvania. The honorary degree Doctor of Laws was conferred upon him by the Colgate University in 1912, and Illinois Wesleyan University in 1916. Mr. Blair's active educational experience covers a period of over forty years. After his work in country schools he was principal of schools in the village of Malden, in Bureau County, from 1886 to 1889, and after graduating from the Normal was principal at LeRoy, in McLean County, from 1892 to 1895. After graduating from Swarthmore College he spent two years as principal of the Franklin School at Buffalo, New York, a position that brought him in contact with some of the foremost educators of the country, including Dr. Nicholas Murray Butler, president of Columbia University. He was appointed to a fellowship in Columbia University for 1899, but about the same time was offered a position in the Eastern Illinois State Normal School at Charleston, just opened, and he became superintendent of the training department of that Normal school, serving from 1899 to 1906. The special recommendation of fitness that made him so effective a candidate for the nomination as well as for subsequent elections as State Superintendent of Public Instruction in 1906, was his seven years of work in the Normal at Charleston. Doctor Blair has been elected six consecutive times as state superintendent. At the Philadelphia meeting of the National Education Association in 1926 he was elected President of that nation wide organization.

Doctor Blair has visited probably every important community in the state in the course of his service, delivering educational addresses. A volume of these addresses have been published, and he is also author of "Schuylkill River Anthology," "Song Bird Pageant," "Wreath of Wild Flowers" and "Liberty Bell Pageant." Doctor Blair married in 1898, Miss Lillian Caton of LeRoy, Illinois.

JOHN FRANKLIN GILLHAM, Circuit Judge in the Third Judicial District, is a resident of Edwardsville, has been a member of the Illinois bar thirty years and is in his ninth year on the circuit bench.

Judge Gillham represents one of the oldest and most distinguished of Illinois pioneer names. He is a descendant of Thomas Gillham, a Scotch-Irishman who came from Ireland in 1730 and settled in Virginia, and subsequently in South Carolina. By different enlistments and in different organizations he served a total of 302 days in the war for independence. Seven of his sons and two of his sons-in-law were soldiers in the same war, five of his sons and two of his daughters with their families came to Illinois. It is probable that the ties of family relationship united a larger number of Gillhams in the early history of Southern Illinois than any other one relationship. It is stated that in 1824 the Gillhams and their kinsmen as a solid phalanx cast five hundred votes against the proposition to make Illinois a slave state.

One of the sons of the pioneer American Gillham was James Gillham, who moved out to Kentucky. The Kickapoo Indians came upon his settlement in 1790 and stole his wife and three children, taking them to Illinois. After a long search he found them in Central Illinois, and during this trip he became attracted to the new territory and in 1797 he settled with his reunited family near St. Louis. It was his accounts sent out by letters and otherwise that attracted his brothers and other members of the family. John Gillham, the fourth son of the original Thomas Gillham and the direct ancestor of Judge Gillham of Edwardsville, served with the Sixth South Carolina Regiment in the War of the Revolution, enlisting March 29, 1776, and being discharged June 1, 1777. He was also in the South Carolina Militia. In South Carolina he married Sarah Clark and they had a family of twelve children, six sons and six daughters. John Gillham with his family arrived in Illinois and settled in Monroe County in 1802, but eventually established his home near Wanda, where he died in 1832.

Ryderus C. Gillham, the third son of John Gillham, was born in South Carolina, June 18, 1773, and was twenty-nine years of age when he came with his parents to Madison County. By a land grant signed by President James Monroe, on September 29, 1817, he was given a quarter section of land that has been continuously in the possession of the Gillham family of Madison County for over a century. One of the strong reasons that impelled him to come to Illinois was his opposition to slavery. He was a pioneer in establishing the worship and organization of the Methodist Episcopal Church in Southern Illinois. He was a member of the State Militia and the territorial governor, Edwards, commissioned him a first lieutenant in the second regiment of the territorial militia. He was a juror in the first murder case tried in Madison County. The first wife of Ryderus C. Gillham was susannah Brown, who was the mother of seven children. Later he married Ruhanna (Patterson) Stockton, and to this union were born six children.

The youngest child of the second marriage was Ryderus C. Gillham, Jr., who was born July 3, 1836, and died March 23, 1910. He was educated in the public schools of the old home community, attended McKendree College one year, and as a young man he acquired from the other heirs the possession of all his father's estate except that of his brother James. He was engaged in the business of farming for over thirty years, and after 1892 lived in his new home in Edwardsville. He was present at Lincoln-Douglas debate in Alton in October, 1858, and all his life was devoted to the principles of the republican party. He became a Mason in Edwardsville Lodge in 1863, and was active in both the York and Scottish Rite bodies. He was deeply interested in local history, and particularly the annals of the Gillham family, and did much to preserve a record of their important connections with Illinois affairs.

On December 29, 1858, R. C. Gillham, Jr., married Miss Emily P. Suringer. They celebrated their golden wedding anniversary in 1908 in the presence of four children and seven grandchildren besides many other relatives.

John Franklin Gillham was the fourth son of R. C. and Emily P. (Suringer) Gillham, and was born at the old family homestead near Wanda, March 4, 1870. He was educated in his native community, spent one year in preparatory school in Evanston, and in 1892 graduated from Shurtleff College. He took the two years course in law at Washington University at St. Louis, where he was graduated in 1894. Since then he has been actively engaged in the practice of law in Madison County, and since 1896 has been a member of the Edwardsville bar. In 1904 he was elected state's attorney of Madison County and reelected in 1908, both times on the republican ticket. In June, 1915, he was elected judge of the Circuit Court. On the bench his service has been distinguished by the integrity of purpose which has been a characteristic of the Gillham family, by extensive knowledge of the law, and utmost impartiality in applying his decisions.

Judge Gillham is unmarried. He is a Scottish Rite Mason and Shriner, a member of the Knights of Pythias, Modern Woodmen of America and Moose.

OMER MURPHY WILLIS, M. D., succeeded to the large and important general practice long controlled by his honored father in the city of Metropolis, judicial center of Massac County, and, like his father before him, he has gained secure vantage ground as one of the representative physicians and surgeons of this county, with reputation for exceptional ability in his chosen profession, for his has been a varied and wide experience, besides which his postgraduate courses have kept him in the closest touch with advances made in medical and surgical science.

Doctor Willis was born December 10, 1875, in the city that is now his home, and he is a scion of sterling pioneer families of southern Illinois, where both his paternal and maternal grandfathers settled in an early day and became successful pioneer exponents of farm industry. The Doctor is a son of Dr. John Tyler Willis and Alice (Bruner) Willis, the former of whom was born in Saline County and the latter in Massac County, this state. Moses Willis, grandfather of the Doctor, was born in Kentucky and his wife, whose maiden name was Martha Davenport, was a Cherokee Indian woman of gracious personality. Moses Willis became prominently associated with the early industrial and civic development of Saline and Massac Counties, Illinois, and in the latter county he and his wife passed the closing years of their lives. The maternal grandparents of the subject of this review were Abraham and Eliza (Devers) Bruner, both natives of the State of Pennsylvania. Abraham Bruner became one of the influential pioneer citizens of Massac County, where he reclaimed and developed a productive farm and where he served two terms as county sheriff, prior to the building of any railroad line through this section of the state. As sheriff he resided at Metropolis, and it was there that his daughter Alice was born, she having been reared and educated in this county and her marriage to Dr. John T. Willis having been here solemnized.

Dr. John T. Willis received excellent educational advantages along both academic and professional lines, and he was long engaged in practice at Metropolis, as one of the leading physicians and surgeons of Massac County, besides which he owned and for many years conducted a well appointed drug store at Metropolis, his death having occurred in this city in October, 1914, and his widow being still a resident of her native city, where her circle of friends is limited only by that of her acquaintances.

After having profited by the advantages of the Metropolis public schools, including the high school, Dr. Omer M. Willis was for two years a student in the college conducted by the Christian Brothers in the city of St. Louis, Missouri. Thereafter he attended the St. Louis Medical College three years, and his technical course was then advanced by his entering the medical department of the great Johns Hopkins University, Baltimore, Maryland, where he continued his studies two years and where he received his degree of Doctor of Medicine. He has since taken various postgraduate courses, both in leading institutions of the United States and in prominent colleges and clinics of Europe, where it may be specially noted that he was for some time a student in the medical department of historic old Heidelberg University.

In 1899 Doctor Willis became associated with his father in the general practice of his profession at Metropolis, where he thus continued his services four years. Thereafter he did important post-graduate work, besides having gained valuable clinical experience in St. Louis hospitals, and he continued his residence in St. Louis until the death of his father, in 1914, when he returned to his native city and assumed the large professional business of his father. Here he is not only upholding the high professional honors of the family name but is also known for his unwavering civic loyalty and progressiveness. The Doctor's brother Albert is engaged in the successful practice of medicine at Decatur, Illinois, and his brother John Herbert is engaged in the drug business at Joppa, this state.

Doctor Willis is actively identified with the Massac County Medical Society, the Illinois State Medical Society and the American Medical Association. He is a stalwart in the local ranks of the republican party, and he has given effective service as a member of the city council of Metropolis and as justice of the peace. He and his wife are zealous members of the Methodist Episcopal Church and he is affiliated with the Benevolent and Protective Order of Elks, the Independent Order of Odd Fellows, the Improved Order of Red Men, and the Modern Woodmen of America.

In February, 1910, was solemnized the marriage of Dr. Willis to Miss Lelota Shields, who was born and reared in White County, Illinois, and who is a daughter of George and Martha (Fitzsimmons) Shields. Dr. and Mrs. Willis have two fine children—Margaret, who was born in 1911, and John T., who was born in 1917.

HENRY W. KROHN. An educator of most substantial ability, Henry W. Krohn has been for twenty years connected with the public schools of New Athens in St. Clair County.

Mr. Krohn was born in Hanover, Germany, July 8, 1873, son of John and Johanna Krohn, who spent all their years in Germany. He acquired a good education in the old country, attending the common schools and the realschule (high school) at Hagen, Germany. He pursued the regular literary course, and also had training in electrical engineering and mechanics.

Mr. Krohn came alone to America in July, 1892, and for about one year lived with some relatives on a farm. For two years he attended the Central Wesleyan College and began his teaching work in St. Clair County, Illinois. After three years of teaching, Mr.

Krohn was persuaded by his physician to get into outdoor activities, and for about three years his chief aim was to restore his health. He worked in the woods and lumber camps, and in other occupations over Arizona, Colorado and California. For some time he was employed in the car shops of the Union Pacific Railway.

Once more restored to vigorous health, Mr. Krohn returned to St. Clair County, Illinois, and engaged in school work at New Athens. He subsequently spent seven quarters in the University of Chicago and one term in Washington University in St. Louis, advancing his own studies. Mr. Krohn became principal of the high school at New Athens in 1907 and for a number of years has been superintendent of schools there, and principal of the community high school. The people of that community regard him as an ideal leader in school work, and repose in him the utmost confidence as an educator and man.

Mr. Krohn married in September, 1903, Miss Rosalie Anna Schubert, who was born in this county, daughter of Joseph and Rosalie Anna Schubert. She has two sisters, Barbara and Anna, and four brothers, Jacob, Joseph, Leo and Edward. Mr. Krohn is affiliated with the Masonic Lodge and I. O. O. F. and is a member of the Evangelical Church.

HUGH VINCENT MURRAY, state's attorney of Clinton County, Illinois, was born in Carlyle September 2, 1870. His father, Matthew Peter Murray, who died September 26, 1920, at the age of seventy-three years, was also born in Carlyle, admitted to the bar in 1870, practiced law in Clinton County, Illinois, until 1902, when he removed to St. Louis, Missouri, to take the position of general counsel for one of the largest banking trust companies of that city, and continued as the legal representative of that institution up to the time of his death. While living in Carlyle, Matthew Peter Murray held the office of state's attorney for sixteen years. His son, Hugh, is serving his eighteenth year. In his lifetime, Matthew Peter Murray was considered one of the ablest lawyers of Southern Illinois, and when he removed to St. Louis he was soon recognized as one of the leading members of the St. Louis bar. So many attorneys made a practice of consulting him over intricate questions arising in their own practice, that he became known as the lawyers' lawyer of St. Louis.

Mary Ann McGaffigan and Matthew Peter Murray were married in 1869 and the subject of this sketch is their oldest son. Altogether there were twelve children, of whom seven are still living. One of them, M. P. Murray, Jr., is commissioner of finance of the City of East St. Louis. Another, Richard L., is cashier of the State Bank of Prairie Du Rocher, Illinois. The remaining children, three sisters and a brother, reside in St. Louis, Missouri.

Hugh Vincent Murray attended the parochial school at Carlyle, Illinois, and received his higher education in St. Joseph's College, Teutopolis, Illinois, graduating there in 1889 with a degree of B. A. He taught school two years and read law in his father's office, was admitted to the bar in 1894, and spent about a year in East St. Louis, Illinois, as a member of the firm of Murray, McHale and Murray. In the fall of 1896, Mr. Murray was elected to the State Legislature, served one term, at the expiration of which he moved to Chicago, and shortly afterwards was appointed assistant prosecuting attorney under Mayor Carter H. Harrison. While holding this position he entered into a partnership with John J. Feeley, but this partnership was dissolved shortly after Mr. Feeley was elected to Congress in 1900.

When Matthew Peter Murray removed to St. Louis in 1902, his son Hugh returned to his home at Carlyle, where he has since resided. He held the office of master in chancery of Clinton County from 1903 to 1908, when he was elected state's attorney and he is now serving his fifth term in that office.

In 1905 Mr. Murray and H. J. C. Beckmeyer became law partners, but the partnership was dissolved about two years afterwards. Later Andrew O. Niehoff and Mr. Murray became law partners and now are engaged as such under the firm name of Murray and Niehoff.

Mr. Murray married Mary Ellen Hogan of St. Louis, Missouri, on February 16, 1904. They have four children, Mary Ellen, Jr., Hugh Vincent, Jr., Matthew Edward and Mary Ann. Mr. Murray is a Roman Catholic, a member of the Knights of Columbus, Catholic Order of Foresters, Modern Woodman of America, Catholic Knights of Illinois, Missouri Athletic Association, Clinton County Bar Association, Illinois State Bar Association, and the Commercial Law League of America. In politics he is a democrat.

ALBERT BAILEY GEORGE. In November, 1924, the citizens of Chicago tried out a new experiment when they elected Albert Bailey George, a well known colored lawyer, to the Municipal bench. That the experiment has turned out to be a success is evident from the fact that although at the outset he feared prejudice, he has met with little, his knowledge of law, tact, fairness and judicial bearing having gained him appreciation, as well as assisting to solve the race problem which exists in all large cities.

Judge George was born at Washington D. C., October 23, 1873, and is a son of William Marshall and Dellaphine (Brown) George, the latter of whom is deceased while the former is still a resident of Washington. William Marshall George was born in Virginia and Mrs. George in the District of Columbia and they were the parents of seven children, of whom six survive. After attending the common schools of Washington, Judge George pursued a course at the Spencerian Business College and from Washington went to Altoona, Pennsylvania, where he read law in the office of Nicholas P. Mervine, one of the foremost lawyers of that city. While at Altoona he also acted as clerk to his brother-in-law, James B. Raymond, an alderman and justice of the peace of that city. In 1896 Judge George located at Chicago and took up the study of law in the law school of Northwestern University, graduating therefrom in June, 1897, with the degree of Bachelor of

Laws. Admitted to practice at that time, on December 1st he opened a law office in the old Chicago Opera House Building, whence he removed in 1898 to the Ashland Block, 155 North Clark Street, where he has maintained an office ever since, successfully engaged in the practice of law.

In the summer of 1924 Judge George was brought forward by his friends and the republican political leaders in his ward as the republican candidate for judge of the Municipal Court, of Chicago; he was indorsed by many organizations and had the unusual distinction of united support by the colored people themselves. The Chicago Bar Association also endorsed his candidacy, saying in its report, "We deem him qualified for the office he seeks." In the November election he was elected by a large majority, receiving nearly half million votes. He was inducted into office December 1, 1924, being assigned by Chief Justice Olson to preside over a non-jury court, where for the following several months he disposed of a large number of important civil suits. He has since presided with equal satisfaction to litigants and the public in various other branches of the Municipal Court. Judge George's court, due to his thoroughly established reputation for honesty, uprightness and sense of justice, is always favored by litigants and lawyers who are in accord with and appreciate his qualities in these respects, and has received many tributes of praise from those whose court matters have come under his jurisdiction. Upon the occasion of his assuming the bench as above, Edward H. Wright, a member of the Illinois Commerce Commission presided, and addresses paying tributes to Judge George were made by Harry Olson, Chief Justice; Albert C. Barnes, Judge of the Appellate Court; Judge Samuel Trude of the Municipal Court; Roy West; Alexander W. Fyfe, President of the Hamilton Club; Anthony Czarnecki, Election Commissioner; Robert E. Crowe, State's Attorney; John Passmore, Clerk of the Criminal Court of Chicago; Joseph F. Haas, County Recorder, and others.

Judge George was for several years secretary of the board of trustees of Provident Hospital. He has been secretary of the beneficiary board of the Knights of Pythias, and has various other positions in civic and welfare organizations, among them the Chicago Urban League. He is an active member of Grace Presbyterian Church, which he joined the day after he arrived at Chicago.

Judge George married Miss Maude J. Roberts, a widely known soprano soloist and concert singer of note, who studied under the famous Herman Devries. She is chairman of the executive board of the Indiana Avenue Branch of the Young Women's Christian Association, and a member of the Metropolitan Board of Directors. Judge and Mrs. George have one son: Albert Roberts George.

GEORGE W. NIEDRINGHAUS. While the Niedringhaus family has been conspicuous in the industrial and political affairs of the City of St. Louis for seventy years, the name in Illinois especially associated with the founding and upbuilding of an industrial city that in the census of 1920 had a population of 15,000. Granite City in Madison County was established on land owned by the Niedringhaus family and around the central plant of the National Enameling & Stamping Company. Granite City is now one of the leading industrial centers of Southern Illinois, and in its growth and prosperity the Niedringhaus family has exerted a steadily progressive influence.

The founders of the town were the late William F. Niedringhaus and his brother, Frederick G. Niedringhaus. These brothers were born in Westphalia, Germany, sons of Frederick W. and Mary Niedringhaus. They were reared and educated in the old country and came to the United States about 1855. William F. Niedringhaus learned the business of manufacturing tinware and he was the first man in America to introduce enameling on sheet iron, becoming the founder of an industry which is now represented by hundreds of plants. However, the largest single industry of the kind that of Granite City, the National Enameling & Stamping Company. William F. and his brother, Fred G., established the old St. Louis Stamping Company in St. Louis, and there did some pioneer work in the manufacture of tin plate. It was in 1896 that the Niedringhaus Brothers began the building of an immense plant on land owned by them and thus established Granite City, which was laid out on modern lines of town building. Before the death of William F. Niedringhaus the National Enameling & Stamping Company was employing 4,000 people and many other interests had been grouped around this central industry. He was director-general of the National Enameling & Stamping Company, was president of the Granite City Gas Light Company, and was one of the men chiefly responsible for getting the plants of the American Steel Foundry and Commonwealth Steel Company established at Granite City. He was a director of the Granite City National Bank and the Granite City Realty Company. He was also one of the trustees of the Lindell Avenue Methodist Episcopal Church. He founded as a monument to a dead son the Niedringhaus Memorial Hospital.

George W. Niedringhaus, a son of William F. and Mary (Bittner) Niedringhaus, has for many years been identified with the industrial interests centered at Granite City. He was born in St. Louis, May 20, 1864, and was educated in the public schools, in the Smith Academy at St. Louis, and the Williston Seminary of Massachusetts.

In his nineteenth year he returned home to join his father in the manufacturing establishment, and by a thorough apprenticeship learned all details of the mechanical department as well as the executive offices. In 1889 he was made general superintendent of the old St. Louis Stamping Company. On the founding of Granite City in 1896 by his father and his uncle, F. G. Niedringhaus, the works were removed to the new location and a greatly enlarged plant established. George W. Niedringhaus was made factory manager and put in active control of the Niedringhaus real estate interests. He became vice president and a director of the National Enameling and Stamping Company, which in 1899 absorbed the old St. Louis Stamping Company. Of the corporation his uncle Frederick G. Niedringhaus is president. He was manager of the steel mills of the company at Granite City, and has been president of these mills since 1919. He was also one of the founders of the American Steel Foundry and the Commonwealth Steel Company, and is chairman of the Board of the Granite City National Bank and president of the Granite City Gas and Fuel Company.

Mr. Niedringhaus retains his residence in the City of St. Louis. He has been a conspicuous factor in republican party politics for many years, and is well known in the National councils of the party. He is a member of the St. Louis, the St. Louis Country, the Florissant Valley and Racquet Clubs, and is a member of the Methodist Church.

On November 12, 1889, he married Miss Fanita Hayward of St. Louis. Five sons were born to their marriage, Hayward, Marion, Francis, Erwin and George, Jr.

BENJAMIN E. AND JAMES W. TWITCHELL, M. D. Prominent physicians and surgeons of Belleville, Benjamin E. and James W. Twitchell are brothers who have been associated in practice there for over twenty years.

Benjamin E. Twitchell was born at Elizabethtown. Illinois, February 5, 1867, son of Capt. La Fayette and Harriet A. (Steele) Twitchell. His grandfather was a native of Maine and of the old New England Twitchell family. He was a pioneer settler of Illinois, coming West by way of Pittsburgh and the Ohio River. Doctor Twitchell's maternal grandfather, James Steele, was a native of Ireland. Capt. La Fayette Twitchell, who died in 1909, was a Union soldier with the One Hundred Thirty-first Illinois Infantry throughout the Civil war, rising to the rank of captain. After the war for many years he was permanent in the affairs of Southern Illinois, being clerk of court of Hardin County, postmaster of Elizabethtown, was a member of the Grand Army of the Republic and had fifty years of affiliation with the I. O. O. F. His wife died in 1916. They were the parents of four children: Dr. Robert A., who married Laura L. Simmons and has a daughter, Ouida; La Fayette, Jr., who married Mary Ledbetter and has one daughter, Edna; Benjamin E. and James W.

Benjamin E. Twitchell was educated in public schools at Elizabethtown, had normal school training and taught school three terms. He studied medicine in the Marion Sims Medical College of St. Louis, graduating in 1891. Soon afterwards he located at Belleville and has been engaged in general practice ever since with a reputation as one of the ablest men in his profession in St. Clair County. He has served as county coroner and county physician and during the World war was medical examiner for the county draft board.

Dr. Benjamin Twitchell married in May, 1895, at Marion, Iowa, Miss Emma Davis, daughter of James A. and Mary Davis. Her mother died in 1914 and her father in 1892. Her father was a physician, was a soldier in the Civil war and a man of prominence in his profession and in citizenship. Mrs. Twitchell's brothers and sisters were: Fred; Dr. Jacob, Mrs. Rose Sturtz, who is the mother of eleven children; Frank, now deceased; and Alice.

The five children of Doctor and Mrs. Twitchell are: Miss Angie Ruth, born in 1896; Standlee, a medical student; Helen, attending the University of Illinois; Benjamin E., Jr. who is taking his medical course at Washington University in St. Louis; and Miss Marion, a student in the Monticello Seminary at Godfrey, Illinois. Doctor Twitchell and family are Methodists. He is affiliated with the Modern Woodmen of America, the Court of Houor, Independent Order of Foresters; is a member of the County, State and American Medical Associations, and is a director of the Belleville Bank & Trust Company.

His brother, Dr. James W. Twitchell, was born June 30, 1869, and acquired his education in the same schools. He took his medical course at the Marion-Sims Medical College at St. Louis, where he was graduated in 1898. After graduating he took up hospital work at Lead, South Dakota, for the Homestead Mining Company. He remained there a year and while there, met and married Miss Bertha Pierce, member of an old family from Boston. Dr. James W. Twitchell in 1901 returned to Illinois and has since been associated in practice with his brother at Belleville.

EUGENE WILLARD MONTGOMERY is proprietor of William Hoskins and Company, wholesale and retail lumber merchants at Galena, a business that was established in 1854, when the Mississippi River was practically the only artery of commerce for heavy traffic north or south through the center of the Mississippi basin. The founder of this business, which has been in existence over seventy years, was William Hoskins, whose daughter is the wife of Eugene Willard Montgomery. Mr. Hoskins first started in the lumber business in Apple River, Illinois, in 1854, soon after the Illinois Central reached that point. He came to Galena in October, 1879, and for over thirty years he received his supply of lumber by raft from Mississippi River points.

Eugene Willard Montgomery, who came to Galena in January, 1880, was born at McCutchensville, Wyandot County, Ohio, October 24, 1853, son of Dr. John and Harriet Newell (Willard) Montgomery. Through his mother he is a direct descendant of John Alden and Priscilla Mullins, who came over in the Mayflower December 21, 1620. Mr. Montgomery's maternal grandparents were John Griswald and Melissa (Peabody) Willard. John Griswald Willard was born at Westerfield, Connecticut, February 25, 1802, being a direct descendant of Maj. Simon Willard of Colonial wars fame. John G. Willard died at West Millgrove, Ohio, February 4, 1859. He married, April 16, 1828, Melissa Peabody, who was born at North Stonington, Connecticut, November 26, 1805, and died at West Millgrove, January 5, 1893. The paternal grandfather of Eugene W. Montgomery was William Montgomery, who was born at Red Stone in Fayette County, Pennsylvania, November 21, 1791, and served as a soldier in the War of 1812 in Company A, Allen's Company of the Ohio Militia. He received an honorable discharge from that organization. He was an early settler at Mount Gilead, Ohio, where he died February 8, 1851. He married at Ross, in Jefferson County, Ohio, September 16, 1819, Elizabeth Gregg, who was born at Lancaster, Pennsylvania, February 21, 1800, and died at Mount Gilead September 1, 1883.

Dr. John Montgomery was born at Mount Gilead, Ohio, May 21, 1822, and in 1843 graduated in medicine from the Western Reserve Medical College at Cleveland, Ohio. When leaving home for college, he walked the entire distance, as there were no railroads in those days. He practiced his profession in Ohio approximately thirty-seven years and in Apple River, Illinois, over three years, 1867-70. During the Civil war for a short time in 1862-63, he was on duty guarding Confederate prisoners on Johnson's Island in Lake Erie. Dr. John Montgomery died at Adrian, in Seneca County, Ohio, January 29, 1885. On May 19, 1846, he married Harriet Newell Willard at West Millgrove in Wood County, Ohio, (a noble, Christian woman of the Presbyterian faith). She was born at Trenton, in Oneida County, New York, April 2, 1831, and died at Adrian, September 11, 1888.

Eugene Willard Montgomery attended public schools and as a youth took up telegraphy. He was the first agent and operator at Carey, Ohio, for the Hocking Valley Railroad Company, resigning December 20, 1879. Mr. Montgomery, among other telegraphers all over the country, received the final message sent out by Professor S. F. B. Morse, inventor of the telegraph, using the original instrument he had used in transmitting his first dispatch. This final message was sent in September, 1871, and read: "To all Telegraph Operators Throughout the World, Peace on Earth Good Will Toward Men. God Bless You All."

Mr. Montgomery removed from Carey, Ohio, to Galena, Illinois, in January, 1880, and since then has had an active part in the William Hoskins & Company lumber business. In October, 1912, he organized the First State and Savings Bank at Galena, and has since been its president.

Mr. Montgomery is a member of the Mayflower Society, Society of Colonial Wars, Sons of the American Revolution and of the War of 1812, the latter of which he served as a director for Illinois for several years and various other patriotic organizations. He is a member of the National Historical Society of Illinois, the New York Genealogical and Biographical Society, the New England Historical Society, being one of the vice presidents of Illinois for the Journal of American History. He is a member of the John Alden Kindred of America, of Plymouth, Massachusetts, also Midwest Chapter of the same of Chicago, Saratoga Battle Field Association of New York, Ohio Society of Chicago, and the Old Time Telegraphers Association. He is a thirty-second degree Scottish Rite Mason, member of the Mystic Shrine, and a republican in politics. He and his family are members of the Methodist Episcopal Church. He gave "The Grant" gavel to the National Republican Convention in Chicago in June, 1888. He and his late partner, T. J. Bermingham, also donated, July 4, 1890, lots 5 and 6 in token of the high esteem in which he held General Grant, which is now a part of Grant Park at Galena. They also got from the Government, April 27, 1896, General Grant's birthday, a loan for park purposes of one of the most historical souvenirs of the Civil war, a brass cannon, made in England, with the following inscription on same: "Presented to the Sovereign State of South Carolina by one of her Citizens residing abroad in commemoration of the 20th of December, 1860," they paying all the necessary expense. The cannon saw hard service judging from the dents on same, and was captured by the Union Army a short time before the close of the Civil war. It adorns Grant Park and is greatly admired by all. Mr. Montgomery was presidential elector on the McKinley and Hobart ticket in 1896 from the Ninth Illinois District. Mr. Montgomery compiled the Willard-Peabody genealogy in 1915, a copy of which is in many of the libraries throughout the United States.

He married at Apple River, Illinois, February 15, 1877, Miss Kate Clark Hoskins, born at Apple River April 11, 1856, daughter of William Hoskins. Their oldest child, Maude, was born at Carey, Ohio, November 24, 1877, and died at Galena, April 9, 1884. Their youngest child, Fannie Victoria, born at Galena May 11, 1889, died December 2, 1894. The surviving children are a son and a daughter. The son, Shelley Hoskins Montgomery, now associated with his father in William Hoskins & Company, was born at Galena, March 31, 1880, and graduated in 1898 from Shattuck School, Faribault, Minnesota. The daughter is Mrs. Harriet Montgomery Priestley, born November 8, 1883, at Galena, Illinois, and graduated in 1913 from Kemper Hall, Kenosha, Wisconsin. She married Harry Tyack Priestley at Galena, November 23, 1910. He was born at Mineral Point, Wisconsin, October 1, 1876, and died at Galena, Illinois, December 3, 1921. She has a surviving daughter, Kate Willard Priestley, born at Galena, June 21, 1914.

HAAG BROTHERS COMPANY. George A. Haag and Albert R. Haag, twin brothers, are the prosperous and reputable owners of the well known business establishment of Haag Brothers Company, Peoria. They were born at Rock Falls, Whiteside County, Illinois, on the 30th of March, 1879, and were forced to begin business before they reached their maturity. In early childhood they were sent to the public schools and there received about all the education they were permitted to secure, owing to the death of their father when they were still quite young and to the fact that they were compelled to begin business action for themselves. As the entire support of the family fell upon their mother, they were compelled to leave school and assist her to earn a living for all. They began work with different concerns at Rock Falls, and were able to assist their mother greatly, but what they earned was not sufficient to meet their growing demands. Hoping to find better and more remunerative work, they finally went to Peoria where they secured positions as assistants and helpers in the blacksmith trade of that big city. For twelve eventful years they pursued that taxing business, and greatly aided their mother in caring for her family. At the end of that period they were grown-up men with an abundance of energy and ambition and had begun action for themselves.

But they were not satisfied with mere wages or trifling profits and during the latter part of of the period began to plan for something higher and better from the business viewpoint. Both had a tendency toward invention, and at an early date realized that in the world of mechanics were abundant opportunities to invent mechanisms that might make them both rich and famous. They realized what Edison and other inventors had accomplished and were still accomplishing, so they set their wits and wisdoms at work and began to devise ingenious contrivances to save the time of purchasers and give them better results from the money standpoint. The hard work and severe and perplexing trials through which their mother had passed no doubt added to the stimulus back of their plans and efforts. Thus the minds of both were almost spontaneously directed to the task of devising mechanisms that would minimize the drudgery of the housewife.

They continued their efforts until finally, about the year 1910, they reached the conclusion that a power washing machine was the device that would give the best and most satisfactory results. By devoting all their spare time and their evenings to this task, they finally were ready to surprise and delight the mothers in thousands of homes. The first machine which they placed upon the market was operated by means of a gasoline engine and while the results were not wholly satisfactory yet they were most encouraging and promising. With the faults of the first device before them, they immediately began the construction of a new machine, with all the errors of the former device eliminated. Soon the new machine was placed upon the market with much better results.

In 1912 they came to the conclusion that they could accomplish better results both for themselves and the public by completely leaving their old business and devoting their whole time and attention to the manufacture of power washing machines. Thereupon they rented a small corner of the building at 812-16 North Commercial Street, Peoria, then occupied by the Western Stove Works, and began work in earnest along the newly determined lines. Thus far the machines which they had devised were intended almost wholly for the use of the farmwife, but now they began to direct their efforts toward a washing machine that would serve both the farmers and the city residents. Soon they realized that even better results could be accomplished with a small electric motor attached than with a big, noisy and cumbersome gasoline engine. So they redoubled their studies and efforts to attain their fresh ideals and ere long had a new machine equipped with an electric motor.

Great effort was made to secure a machine that would be practically perfect from the very start. Soon it was placed before the public, with the result that in a short time they were swamped with orders from all sections of the country. This forced them to expand or extend their business quarters and to employ additional assistance or help. They finally secured the entire main floor of the building occupied, but even that extension soon became too small for their trade. Their growth was remarkable—almost phenomenal. In a short time they took possession of the whole two-story building, and many more employes were added to their steadily and rapidly increasing force. Quickly the machines were passing out to all parts of the country.

Again it became necessary for them to consider remarkable expansion. In 1918 they saw that their quarters were becoming too small. So the following spring they purchased a site for a new and adequate building in East Peoria, and in a short time erected their present splendid $200,000 structure which bears their name and is at last the realization of their most ardent aspirations or dreams. Now they manufacture from 75 to 80 machines per day and employ about 100 workers. Still it is yet necessary for them to consider the problem of additional expansion and accordingly they have purchased adjacent tracts of land to be ready for the additional rise that is sure to come soon. Their success is both striking and extraordinary and is a surprising proof of what can be accomplished when real ability is put to the crucial test. Their building is not dingy and repulsive to the sight, but is fronted with beautiful trees and surrounded with a picturesque lawn enveloped with flowers and shrubbery that attracts the eye and kindles the outbursts of sentiment of all passers-by.

George Haag married Miss Daisy Lulay and they have one daughter, Ruth. Albert married Miss Anna Gogele and by her has one son, Albert, Jr. Both brothers are stanch republicans in politics, are much interested in local public affairs, and are prominent as superior citizens. Albert is a member of the Modern Woodmen of America.

FRANKLIN C. HAMLIN. Recognized as the leading general insurance agent of East Saint Louis, Franklin C. Hamlin has built up a very wide connection throughout this district, and at the same time has won appreciation for his civic spirit, and humanitarian principles. He was born at Newton, near Boston, Massachusetts, September 19, 1886, a son of Edward F. and Helen A. (Church) Hamlin, and grandson of Freeman Hamlin, who was a native of Plainfield, Massachusetts, as was his wife. He was clerk of his township for many years, and represented his district in the Massachusetts State Legislature. His father, great-grandfather of Franklin C. Hamlin, was a Revolutionary soldier. The maternal grandfather of Mr. Hamlin, Franklin Church, and his wife, Angeline, were also natives of Plainfield, Massachusetts.

Edward F. Hamlin, now living retired, has the honor of being a close personal friend of President Coolidge, and has filled many important offices, and been at the head of commissions the duties pertaining thereto taking him all over the country. For forty-five years he was secretary of the Governing Council of the State of Massachusetts, and was acting as such during the time that Calvin Coolidge was governor of Massachusetts. During his active years in business he was a manufacturer of shoes at Northampton, Massachusetts. When war was declared between the North and South he enlisted and was made captain of a company in the Fifty-second Massachusetts Volunteer Infantry, with which he continued to serve throughout the war. During his period of service he contracted a disability that kept him in the hospitals for some time after the close of the war. His wife died May 7, 1923, leaving one child, Mr. Hamlin of this review.

The grammar and high schools of Newton, Massachusetts grounded Franklin C. Hamlin in the fundamentals of an education, and he subsequently took a preparatory course for entrance to Harvard University, but did not matriculate, deciding upon a business career. Going to Denver, Colorado, he was in the employ of the First National Bank of that city for three years, but, meeting, and winning for his wife, a lady whose home was at East Saint Louis, he decided to locate here, so resigned from the bank, and established himself in his present business. Mr. Hamlin handles a general line of insurance, including fire, life, accident, indemnity and casualty insurance, and represents many of the leading companies of the country.

On October 9, 1901, Mr. Hamlin was married, at Denver, Colorado, to Stella M. Ernest, of East Saint Louis, a daughter of Finis P. Ernest, one of the pioneers of this city, who died in 1912. The Ernest family is one of the oldest ones of this part of Illinois, and Finis P. Ernest was a heavy landowner, owning a large amount of property at East Saint Louis, some of which he improved himself. Mr. and Mrs. Hamlin have five children: Franklin C., Jr., Helen A., Stella M., Virginia D. and Florence E. He is a Blue-Lodge Mason and a member of the Presbyterian Church. During the more than twenty years he has been in business at East Saint Louis Mr. Hamlin has shown a most commendable interest in all of the progress of his home city, and because of his integrity and honorable manner of doing business, has attained to leadership in his own line.

JOHN HRABIK, a physician and surgeon with an exceptional range of experience, training and attainments, is practicing his profession in his native City of Murphysboro, where his family has been an honored one for over forty years.

His father came from Austria at the age of seventeen, in 1870, and first located in Chicago where he was employed in a bakery on Canal Street. This bakery was destroyed in the great fire of 1871. He lost all his possessions, and leaving Chicago walked to St. Louis, where he found employment in a bakery. He had to master the English language after coming to this country. In 1880 he moved to Murphysboro, Jackson County, and was engaged in the bakery business there until he retired. His wife, Henrietta Schoch, was a daughter of Conrad Schoch, who came to America on a sailing vessel, landing at New Orleans and thence up the Mississippi River to Illinois and to Jackson County, where Henrietta Schoch was born.

Dr. John Hrabik was born at Murphysboro October 3, 1886. He attended the grade schools, one year in high school, finished a course in the Christian Brothers College of St. Louis in 1906, and subsequently studied medicine in the University of Illinois, graduating M. D. in 1912. Since then, except for the World was, he has been engaged in general practice at Murphysboro. Mr. Hrabik is unmarried. He was master of the Masonic Lodge in 1920, is a member of the Modern Woodmen of America and the Woodmen of the World and the Country Club.

In September, 1917, he was called to duty with the Army Medical Corps for service in the World war. He was first sent to Fort Benjamin Harrison at Indianapolis, then to the Rockefeller Institute of New York, also had training with the Army Medical School at Washington, and in January, 1918, went overseas to France. Doctor Hrabik was overseas nineteen months, spending most of his time in base hospitals in France. He was connected with the Three Hundred Third Motor Transport Corps in the Second Division, was assigned duty with the Third Battalion of the Ninth Infantry, and from first lieutenant was promoted to captain February 17, 1919.

LAWRENCE CHARLES JOHNSON has been a prominent member of the Henry County bar for many years, is a native of that county, and in early life was a merchant before taking up the law.

He was born at Galva, in Henry County, December 6, 1868, son of Swan P. and Mary (Swanson) Johnson. His father, a native of Sweden, came to the United States in 1857, when about eighteen years of age, locating at Galva. In April, 1861, at the outbreak of the Civil war, he enlisted in Company D of the Seventeenth Illinois Infantry, and served until taken prisoner at Holly Springs, Mississippi. Subsequently he was released on parole not to serve again. After the war he located at Galva, was a merchant and held several local offices. He was a republican in politics and a member of the Grand Army of the Republic. Swan P. Johnson died February 13, 1893, at the age of fifty-five. After coming to Henry County he married Mary Swanson, also a native of Sweden, who had come to Illinois with her parents in 1854. Her father was Olof A. Swanson. He died in 1904 when about sixty-two years of age. There are three children: Mary, who became the wife of Maurice M. Keeler, and died in 1904; Lawrence C.; and Emma A., who died at the age of eighteen. The father was reared a Lutheran, while the mother and her daughters were members of the Congregational Church.

Lawrence Charles Johnson grew up at Galva, is a graduate of the high school there, attended a business college in the mercantile business at Galva. He is a graduate of the School of Law of Northwestern University of Chicago, and since admission to the bar has earned a high place as a lawyer, commanding a general practice at Galva. He has served as township clerk, as member of the Galva City Council and Board of Education, and was a delegate from the Thirty-seventh Senatorial District in the Constitutional Convention of 1920-22. He is a republican.

Mr. Johnson, in 1895, erected the Johnson Building, one of the leading business structures in Galva. He is a member of the Henry County, Illinois State and American Bar Associations and the Commercial Law League of America. He and his family are members of the Baptist Church. He is a Knight Templar Mason and Shriner, has held offices in the local lodge and Grand Lodge of Illinois, and for two years was a member of the Board of Examiners for the state.

In 1891 Mr. Johnson married Clara Louise Seely, a native of Galva. Her father, Isaac B. Seely, was born in Orange County, New York, and was an early settler in Henry County, Illinois. Her mother, Ann Elizabeth Whittemore, was a daughter of Joel and Rachel Rebecca (Brown) Whittemore, Joel Whittemore being a son of Peter Whittemore, a soldier in the American Revolution. Mr. and Mrs. Johnson are the parents of five children. A daughter, Amy Seely, is the wife of Walter Irwin Nelson. Alice J., the second daughter, is the wife of Emerson A. Armstrong. Whitfield W. Johnson, who married Pauline Amos Skinner, is a graduate of the Liberal Arts College of Harvard University, also took his law degree there, is now engaged in practice at the City of Boston, and during the World war was in the Naval Aviation Service. The fourth child, Marian Rachel Johnson, is a graduate of Wellesley College of Massachusetts, and is now a teacher at Wilkes-Barre, Pennsylvania. Edward Lawrence Johnson, the youngest son, is a graduate of Phillips Exeter Academy of New Hampshire, and is now attending Princeton University.

WILLIAM H. SPRENGER, a veteran Peoria business man, cigar manufacturer, has an individual record that makes him a notable in the citizenship of Illinois, and has some prominent family connections, bringing into notice some of the old settlers of Peoria County.

Mr. Sprenger who is a native of Peoria, is a son of Adam Sprenger, who was born in Steinweiller, Rhein Pfaltz, Bavaria, December 4, 1829. Adam Sprenger when twelve years of age came to the United States with his widowed mother and sister, Louisa. This sister subsequently married Adam Reiser. They were on a sailing vessel that landed at New Orleans and from that city came up the Mississippi and Ohio rivers to Cincinnati. At Cincinnati, Adam Sprenger served an apprenticeship at the cooper's trade, getting only his board during his apprenticeship. About 1852 he visited Peoria, then a village along the river front, but after a short time went on to New Orleans, where he worked at his trade about two years, then back to Cincinnati, and from there again came to Peoria, acquiring land now designated as the corner of Hurlbut and Goodwin streets, but then not platted, there being a corn field including his location, while the bluffs were covered with timber. He put up a building on his land, worked at his trade and for some time traveled over Tazewell and Woodford counties, carrying a stock of general merchandise in his wagon and trading for poultry, eggs and other produce, which he ultimately marketed at Peoria. On account of the poor drainage, the land where he built his home was in a poor situation for the health of his family. Subsequently he rented his house, and spent nine months at Sheboygan, Wisconsin, working at his trade. Then for a time he lived in Cincinnati and finally resumed his residence in Peoria, where he remained until his death in May, 1913, at the age of eighty-three years.

Adam Sprenger married Mary Winkelmyer, who was born in Saxony, Germany, and was seven years of age when her mother and eight children came to the United States. She died in 1876, the mother of six children: John, Joseph, Louisa, Clara, Mary and William H. Sprenger.

William H. Sprenger was reared in the Catholic faith and as a boy attended the St. Joseph Parochial School at Peoria and also the public schools. When a youth he began an apprenticeship at the cigar maker's trade, and after completing it worked in the factory of his brothers, subsequently becoming a partner in the business. For some years the Sprenger Brothers employed the largest number of union cigar makers in any factory outside of Chicago. After the death of his brother, William H. Sprenger sold his interest in that business and established the Saratoga Cigar Factory, now located at 208 South Adams Street, and he continues this flourishing business today. He is a member of the Traveling Men's Protective Association of America, Spalding Council Knights of Columbus and he and his wife are members of the St. Bernard Catholic Church.

Mr. Sprenger married in 1896 Miss Gabriel Seiple, who was born in Peoria. Her father, John Conrad Seiple, was born in the community known as Black Partridge in Worth Township, Woodford County, Illinois, May 13, 1842. His father, John Adams Seiple, was a native of Baden, Germany, and about 1838 left that country with his family and came to the United States on a sailing vessel that landed at New Orleans. From there they came up the Mississippi and Illinois rivers to Woodford County, Illinois, where he acquired a tract of Government land at $1.25 an acre in what is now Worth Township. On this he built a log house, which was the first home of the Seiple family in America. It was a pioneer section and pioneer times when a bountiful supply of meat could be obtained from wild game. John Adams Seiple devoted his time to the farm and he met his death by accident in 1856 when his horse became frightened by a railroad train. His widow survived him some years, passing away at the age of sixty-eight. They had a family of four children: John Conrad, Adam, George and Elizabeth.

John Conrad Seiple received his early advantages in some of the pioneer schools of Woodford County, and after his father's death, put in most of his time working on the farm. In 1864 he entered the Union army as a private in Company K of the Forty-fourth Illinois Infantry and was with this regiment in its various campaigns and battles until after the close of the war. On being mustered out he returned home and farmed the old place for five years, after which he came to Peoria and followed various occupations, being for some years in the grocery business. He died in 1912.

John Conrad Seiple married in 1867, Miss Katherine Weber, who was born in Worth Township, Woodford County, September 27, 1846, daughter of Peter Weber, a native of Baden, Germany and granddaughter of Jacob Weber, who brought the family from Baden to America, landing at Baltimore. The family remained there while the son went west to select a desirable tract of land, buying such property in Worth Township, Woodford County. His father and mother and six children started to join him in Illinois. They embarked on the ill-fated steamer, Mosel, on the Ohio River. This boat when about twelve miles above Cincinnati, engaged in racing with another steamboat, and the boilers exploded, many of the crew and passengers losing their lives, including Jacob Weber and three of his children. Jacob Weber had been a distiller in Germany, had sold his business and brought his capital to America in coin, carried in a box. This box went to the bottom of the Ohio River at the time of the explosion, and the family were put on shore practically penniless. After many difficulties, the widow and her three surviving children arrived in Woodford County, Illinois, joining her son Peter, who had the task of making a home in the tract of timber, where he erected a log cabin. For some years the Weber family lived there and then Peter Weber moved to a prairie farm for five years, after which he bought land three and a half miles east of Matamora. His last years were spent in Peoria, where he died at the age of eighty-four. Peter Weber married Elizabeth Seiple, daughter of Peter Seiple, a native of Baden, but not related to John Conrad Seiple. Peter and Elizabeth Seiple reared eleven children. Mrs. Elizabeth Weber now lives with her daughter.

ELEAZER C. FINCH. One of the most reliable dealers in Ford parts and accessories and owners of a garage in Union County is Eleazer C. Finch of Anna, a man widely and favorably known all over this section, especially in connection with the automobile trade. He was born at Anna, October 1, 1868, a son of Edgar A. and Rebecca (Dresser) Finch, natives of New York and Virginia, respectively. The paternal grandparents, E. H. and Sarah (Phillips) Finch, came to Anna in 1855, and he became a grading contractor at the time the Illinois Central Railroad was built through Anna. The maternal grandparents were Nathan and Nancy (Bennett) Dresser, natives of Georgia, who moved to Petersburg, Illinois, and later to Springfield. In 1855, they, too, came to Anna, and Nathan Dresser was also connected with grading contracts in the construction of this part of the Illinois Central Railroad. Later on he became land agent for this road, express agent, and postmaster of Anna. Both he and E. H. Finch became charter members of Anna Lodge, A. F. and A. M., and Mr. Dresser was its master before the charter was granted. Edgar A. Finch was a miller by trade, and owned and operated a mill at Anna, but in 1872, sold it and moved to Columbus, Kansas, where he was engaged in farming for two years, but, selling that property, he returned to Anna, and was chief clerk at the Anna State Hospital. His father was a member of the board of governors of that institution. In 1892 Edgar A. Finch moved to Kirksville, Missouri, and there his death occurred in 1901. The mother died in 1919, at Ladells, Oregon, but both are buried at Kirksville, Missouri.

Eleazer V. Finch attended the public schools until he was sixteen years old, at which time he became an attendant and assistant baker at the Anna State Hospital. After seven years at the hospital he began working for James Norris, a hardware merchant, with whom he remained until 1898, when he established himself in a confectionery business, and continued to conduct it until the spring of 1913, when he sold it and secured the Ford Agency for Union County, having complete control of it until 1924, when he became a dealer in Ford parts and accessories, and owner of the large garage he operates in conjunction with his store, 312 and 314 South Main Street.

On February 25, 1890, Mr. Finch was married to Mary M. Steers, born at Olmstead, Illinois, a daughter of Melborne and Melissa (McIntire) Steers, natives of Springfield and Vienna, Illinois, respectively. Mr. and Mrs. Finch have no children. She is an International Bible Student. He is a republican, but not an office seeker. Fraternally he is a Royal Arch Mason and a Modern Woodman, and is active in both of his orders. He is one of the aggressive members of the Anna Chamber of Commerce and through it is accomplishing much of real value in advancing the interests of the city, and protecting it from unsound business promotors, or undue inflation of real values, both of which tend to bring about reactions and consequent depression.

CHARLES ELMER STUMBAUGH. The Stumbaugh family is one of the old and honored ones of Tazewell County, where it has long been located, the founders of it in Illinois being among the pioneers of the Prairie State. Those bearing the name have, since the earliest days been good and representative citizens, and useful workers for the good of their communities. The name has never been tarnished by disloyalty or dishonesty, and one who is sustaining its prestige is Charles Elmer Stumbaugh, a successful business man of Delavan, where he is conducting a large plumbing and heating establishment. He was born at Morton, Tazewell County, September 14, 1864, a son of the venerable Levi Stumbaugh.

Levi Stumbaugh is also a native son of Tazewell County as he was born here June 20, 1841. Reared amid strictly pioneer conditions, and educated in the little log schoolhouse of that period, he chose farming as his life work, and prospered in that calling. Beginning life with no capital except his willingness to work and save, he accumulated several valuable farms in Tazewell County, and, although long past the usual period for retirement, is still active and interested in life, and as virile mentally as one still in middle age. At present he is living at El Paso, Woodford County, where he has also farming property. Like the chief executive of the country, he has always appreciated the value of real economy, and the elimination of wastefulness, and he attributes his somewhat remarkable success in life to the fact that he has known to save a fair proportion of his income. He is a son of Samuel Stumbaugh, of Pennsylvania-Dutch stock, a native of Pennsylvania, who came to Illinois from that state, and he was first married in Woodford County, and two children were born to him and his wife, Levi, and Lizzie, now deceased, who was the wife of Hon. William A. Moore. By a second marriage, Samuel Stumbaugh had a daughter, Mrs. Phillips; and by his third marriage with Nancy Peak, he had two children: Belle, who married S. W. Myers, and Delilah, who married John W. Harber. Both these daughters of the third marriage are deceased.

Levi Stumbaugh was married in Tazewell County, to Anna Ramsey, a native of this county, and a daughter of James Ramsey, who came to Illinois from Maryland, and spent his life as a farmer. Mrs. Stumbaugh died in the '90s, having borne her husband the following children: Charles Elmer, whose name heads this review; Mollie, who married August Krider, resides at Houston, Texas; Bert Stumbaugh, who resides at El Paso, Illinois; and May, who is the wife of Frank Probasco, of Eureka, Illinois.

Growing up to a useful manhood in Tazewell and Woodford counties, Charles Elmer Stumbaugh attended the local schools, and was reared to habits of industry and thrift. He learned the plumbing trade at Bloomington, Illinois, entering his apprenticeship at the age of seventeen years, and, after completing it, worked as a journeyman plumber until 1887, when he went into business for himself at Delavan, and has built up a very fine connection, and is recognized as one of the leading men in his line in the county.

While not active in politics, he never misses an opportunity to exercise his right of suffrage, and he served Delavan as alderman for several years. For many years he was chief of the volunteer fire department, and attended the firemen's conventions, and he is a member of the Illinois Master Plumbers Association. During the late war Mr. Stumbaugh did his full duty as a good citizen with reference to the local drives for all purposes. Among other public services rendered by him is the erection of the water-works plant, one of the best and most effective of its kind in the state.

Mr. Stumbaugh was married at Delavan, in April, 1886, to Miss Sarah James, the daughter of George and Lucretia (Drake) James. Mrs. Stumbaugh was born at Delavan, and is one of four daughters and a son, namely: Lizzie, Kate, Emma, Sarah, and Walter James, the latter now a resident of San Francisco, California.

The following children have been born to Mr. and Mrs. Stumbaugh: Leo, who is in business with his father, is a graduate of the Delavan High School, married Madge Dickson, and they have two children, Shirley and Catherine; Catherine, who resides at Peoria, Illinois, is the wife of W. J. Crawford, and they have two children, William and James; Loraine, who is in business with his father, married Mrs. Mary Jost, and they have a daughter, Lillian who is a graduate of the Delavan High School, the Peoria College of Music, of the University of Illinois, and the Chicago College of Music, is one of the faculty of the last-named institution, and a musician of rare ability.

MAJ. FRANK NOLAN BUSH, who for a number of years was prominent in the Illinois National Guard, is a citizen and business man of Peoria, where he has developed a notably successful commercial printing establishment. He learned printing while a boy and is a master of that art, and an experienced executive as well.

Major Bush was born at Mount Pulaski in Logan County, Illinois, son of John C. Bush and grandson of George Bush. He was one of a large family of children, the others being: George, Anna, John, Harriet, Albert, Olive, Miles, and Walter. Frank Nolan Bush was educated in public schools at Mount Pulaski and Lincoln, and as a boy began his apprenticeship at the printer's trade in the office of the Mason City Independent. A short time later he went to Havana, Illinois, working in the plant of the Mason County Democrat, and completed his apprenticeship at Peoria in the office of the Peoria Journal. After this varied training and experience he started business for himself, his first shop being in the 700 block of South Adams Street in Peoria. His capital was small, his equipment and facilities were limited, but largely due to his personal skill and industry, he turned out exceptionally high quality of work and the demand upon his service steadily increased. After forming a partnership with his brother, Walter, they moved to the 200 block on North Adams Street, where their business has since been located. As the Bush Printing Company, the facilities and equipment have been many times increased and expanded. In 1924 the firm acquired the building in which the plant is located, having a forty-foot frontage and located only half a block from courthouse square. The mechanical facilities enabled them to handle any class of contracts for commercial and legal printing, and they also published the Peoria Labor Gazette of which Walter Bush is editor.

Major Bush married in 1902, Miss Maud M. Davis, a native of Peoria and daughter of John M. and Minnie (Krause) Davis. Her maternal grandfather, Sebastian Krause, was born in Hesse Darmstadt, Germany, January 20, 1820, son of Jacob and Katherine (Dries) Krause. When he was fourteen years of age, he began his apprenticeship to learn the blacksmith trade and completing it in 1841 he came to America, traveling on a sailing vessel. Landing at New York, he found employment for a time during the construction of the old Croton aqueduct, but subsequently moved West to Boonville, Missouri, where a brother was living. He remained there two years and in the fall of 1842 went to New Orleans, and in May, 1844, returned to Germany, where he remained two years. Again coming to America, he went to Boonville, Missouri, where he had previously acquired forty acres of land. After farming this one year he sold out, went to New Orleans, and in 1848 arrived in Peoria. For a time he followed his trade and then engaged in the mercantile business. He put most of the surplus profit from his business into real estate, improved his land with several dwellings and acquired a large amount of property. In 1864 he sold his store and after that devoted his time to the management of his real estate and his official duties. He was prominent in the democratic party in Peoria County and served as town supervisor and justice of the peace and notary public. Sebastian Krause married Margaret Shuelin, a native of Bavaria. She died in 1863, leaving two children: Charles and Minnie, the mother of Mrs. Bush.

Mr. and Mrs. Bush have two children: Janet M. and Roderic Frank. Major Bush is affiliated with Illinois Lodge No. 46, F. and A. M., Peoria Consistory of the Scottish Rite and Mohammed Temple of the Mystic Shrine; belongs to West Bluff Lodge No. 177, Knights of Pythias; El Medi Temple No. 1, D. O. K. K.; Peoria Camp No. 812, Modern Woodmen of America. Three days after Major Bush enlisted in Troop C of the First Illinois Cavalry, National Guard, he was made sergeant and had rapid promotion after that, becoming first lieutenant, captain and major, and attended every training camp in which his command took part. Soon after the breaking out of the World war he offered his services to the national Government, but they were not accepted on account of his age. However, several of his old comrades went into the war and made splendid records. Major Bush cast his first presidential vote for Mr. McKinley, and has been a staunch republican. He was elected an alderman in 1916, serving three years and in 1921 again was elected a member of the city council and reelected in 1923.

M. LINCOLN TEST. A man of the highest standing in his profession and community, M. Lincoln Test, superintendent of the Petersburg schools, brings to his important work not only a long and varied experience covering a period of thirty-five years, but also carefully trained faculties and a genuine love of teaching, without which no one ought to enter the educational field. Too much is demanded of the educator for his labors to be only regarded as mere employment. Unless he can throw his whole soul into his everyday duties, inspire others with a love of learning, and fit his pupils for what life may bring them, as well as give them a knowledge of the contents of the textbooks, then he has missed his vocation and ought to enter another calling. Mr. Test does measure up to these requirements, and his schools show the effects of his inspirational efforts.

Born in Pike County, Illinois, M. Lincoln Test is a son of Rev. O. V. Test, and grandson of Joseph Test. The family is an old one in the United States, and is of Welsh origin. It was early established in Ohio, where Joseph spent his life, being engaged in farming, and he died near Bethel, that state.

Rev. O. V. Test came to Illinois from Georgetown, Ohio, bringing his family and household possessions with him in the "covered wagon" of the period, and located near Fishhook, Pike County, but later moved to Brown County in the vicinity of Mount Sterling. In addition to being a farmer, and a successful one, he was a local Methodist preacher, and traveled about on horseback. All his life he officiated at weddings, funerals and similar gatherings where the services of a clergyman were required, and into old age he was noted for his eloquent discourses and exhortations. First a whig and later a republican, he cast his first presidential vote for William Henry Harrison, the whig candidate, in 1840.

Reverend Test was married to Lucy Snyder, a daughter of Michael Snyder, and she was born in Kentucky, and died in Illinois, February 27, 1898, surviving her husband but a few months, as he died May 12, 1897. Eleven children were born to their marriage, all of whom reached maturity, married and all save one had children. The survivors are: Nora, who is the widow of Thomas Ellege; Ella, who is Mrs. Buckley, and resides at Mount Sterling; Emma, who is Mrs. Newenham, and also resides at Mount Sterling; William F., who resides at Beverly, Illinois; and M. Lincoln Test, who was the youngest.

Reared on his father's farm in Brown County, M. L. Test, as he is familiarly known, attended the country schools during his childhood and youth. In order to further pursue his studies he taught school in the rural districts during the winter months, and attended summer schools with the funds he accumulated. His first connection with higher educational work was at Versailles, Illinois, when for a year he was principal of its high school. Matriculating at the end of that year in the University of Valparaiso, Indiana, he completed the scientific course, and was graduated therefrom in 1892, with the degree of Bachelor of Science.

For one year following his graduation Mr. Test taught in the Modern Normal School of Washington, District of Columbia, but returned to public school work as principal of the schools of Naples, Illinois, and while holding that position he began the study of law with the intention of preparing himself for the practice of that profession. After some months of study, however, he changed his mind, realizing that his talents and inclination better fitted him for the work he was so ably performing, and he remained in the calling he had already learned. Going from Naples to Chapin, Illinois, where he continued for seven years, conducting its schools with characteristic energy and capability, his next charge was at Franklin, Illinois, and from that village he went to Mount Sterling, his home city, and there remained among his friends and former associates for nine years. With the entry of this country into the World war he resigned his position, was made chairman of the local Young Men's Christian Association, put over the drive for that organization, and continued with it for a year. However, owing to the shortage of teachers, he substituted at Mount Sterling, and at the close of the war returned to educational work, being at Versailles for two years, and then came to Petersburg, succeeding J. B. Hendricks as superintendent of schools. While he was in charge of the Mount Sterling schools the housing facilities were improved by the erection of a grade building at a cost of $35,000, and since he has come to Petersburg one school building has been modernized, both grade schools have been standardized, improvements have been made on the old high school building, and the school itself has been accorded a North Central standing. A fine gymnasium has been erected at a cost of $40,000, and other improvements are contemplated. This record proves that Mr. Test is not only an able educator, but an executive of exceptional qualifications.

In addition to his public-school work Mr. Test has taught in the teachers' institutes held in Morgan, Scott and Brown counties. Of late years he has taken post-graduate work in Wesleyan University and the University of Chicago, and is thoroughly abreast of modern thought in education. Reared in the faith of the Methodist Church, he united with it, and has always been active in religious work. At Mount Sterling he served as superintendent of the Sunday School and as director of the choir. As teacher of the Men's Bible Class he is said to have but few superiors. Wherever he has lived he has been the leading spirit in religious progress. A fine and convincing speaker he is oftentimes called upon to deliver patriotic and fraternal addresses, and during the war was one of the most effective of the Four-Minute Men of the county. Fraternally he belongs to the Masonic fraternity, the Order of the Eastern Star, the Independent Order of Odd Fellows, of which he is past noble grand, the Rebekahs, and the Knights of Pythias. A zealous Rotarian he works in cooperation to that organization, and bears his share in all civic movements.

On December 24, 1902, Mr. Test was married at Chapin, Illinois, to Miss Ruth Egan, a daughter of Andrew and Elizabeth Egan. Mrs. Test was born in Chapin, where her early education was secured, but she supplemented that training with courses in the Normal University, Normal, Illinois, and she is principal of the Petersburg Ward schools. Professor and Mrs. Test have two children: Osmond V., who is a junior in Wesleyan University, specializing in mathmetics. He is an accomplished vocalist and pianist; and Mary Margaret, who is attending the grade schools.

WILLIAM VANCE RUSH, is serving as representative of his native County of Massac in the Illinois Legislature and is one of the prominent and influential citizens and business men of Metropolis, his business and industrial interests being of broad scope and much importance.

Mr. Rush was born on a farm in Massac County, July 29, 1861, and is a son of the late Dr. Charles S. and Harriet E. (Vance) Rush, the former of whom was born in New Jersey but reared and educated in the City of Philadelphia, and the latter of whom was born in Kentucky, their marriage having been solemnized at Paducah, Kentucky. Dr. Charles S. Rush effectively equipped himself for the practice of his profession and was long engaged in the practice of medicine in Massac County, besides which he was here engaged in the retail drug business for many years. Dr. Rush established his residence in Massac County in the year 1852, and here he engaged in the practice of his profession as an old-time country physician and surgeon. He became also the owner of a good farm property, and he was well advanced in years when, in 1890 he removed to the City of Metropolis, where he remained until his death, July 27, 1904, his widow having here passed away December 13, 1915, and both having been held in affectionate regard in the county that was their home for many years.

The earlier education of William V. Rush was acquired in the district schools of Massac County, and was supplemented by his attending the seminary at Metropolis. At the age of eighteen years he initiated his service as a teacher in the schools of his native county, where his pedagogic labors were continued two years. Thereafter he followed the same profession seven years in Saline County, where he then engaged in the general merchandise business in the village of New Hope, his career as a merchant at that place having covered a period of ten years. He acquired a farm in that county and while conducting his mercantile business he became also a grower of and dealer in live stock. In 1906 Mr. Rush purchased a farm in Massac County and made the same the stage of successful and progressive stock-raising enterprise, he having maintained his residence in Metropolis and having here engaged in the insurance business, the while he gave careful supervision to his fine stock farm, he being now the owner of a valuable landed estate of 287 acres in this county, and having sold thirty-six acres to the United States Government as a reservation for the Ohio River Dam No. 52. His Massac County farm estate is devoted to the raising of high-grade live stock, and he is one of the prominent exponents of this basic industry in this section of the state. He is the owner also of valuable mineral and oil land in Saline County, and at Metropolis he is one of the four principals in the Rush Lumber Company, which was organized in 1923 and in which his associates are L. M. Murrie, E. J. Cowling and C. R. Lindsey. This concern controls a large and prosperous business in the handling of all kinds of building material and has well stocked and equipped yards and office in Metropolis. Mr. Rush is a member also of the firm of Rush & Stone, which conducts a general mercantile and confectionery store in Metropolis and which maintains a dairy business with headquarters at the previously mentioned Dam No. 52.

Mr. Rush is a stalwart in the local ranks of the republican party, and has been active and influential in its councils in this section of Illinois. In Saline County he served as township clerk, and later he gave three years of effective service as a member of the board of county commissioners of Massac County. Further recognition of his ability, his civic loyalty and his progressiveness came in the autumn of 1924, when he was elected representative of Massac County in the Illinois Legislature. He is a member of the Greater Metropolis Association, and is an enthusiastic and liberal supporter of measures and enterprises that are projected for the civic and material advancement of his home city, county, and state. He has passed the various official chairs in the Independent Order of Odd Fellows, and he and his wife are members of the First Congregational Church of Metropolis, of which he is a trustee.

In the year 1883 Mr. Rush was united in marriage to Miss Ella Williams, who likewise was born and reared in Massac County, and who is a daughter of the late D. S. and Millie (Tomlinson) Williams. Mr. and Mrs. Rush became the parents of two children, the first, a daughter, having died in infancy, and Ora having died at the age of fourteen years.

HERMANN AACHTE, proprietor of one of the best groceries in Petersburg, is one of the substantial business men of Menard County, and one who has been connected with its commercial life for a long period, being an excellent representative of the American citizen of German birth. Born in Badbergen, Germany, August 7, 1868, he is a son of Gerhard and Marie (Middelkamp) Aachte, the latter a daughter of Gerhard and Catherine (Wernsing) Middelkamp. Although now eighty-seven years old Gerhard Aachte is still living, and is active in the Evangelical Church. Germany has continued his home all his life, and he served his country as government inspector for many years, forty in all, and his son, Fritz, has succeeded him in this position. His wife died in 1895, leaving five children: Henry, Hermann, William, Gretchen and Fritz, the last named having served as a lieutenant in the German army during the World war.

Hermann Aachte was reared on a farm in his native land and was educated in the military school in Quakenbrueck, from which he secured a diploma. Upon the completion of his studies he came to the United States, bringing his diploma with him. He left Germany March 15, 1885, on the steamer Main, and reached New York City April 1, fifteen days later. The voyage was an uneventful one, and he was comfortable as he was a second-class passenger, having sufficient means to avoid the steerage. With him were Mr. and Mrs. Henry Wernsing of Greenview. After landing at Hoboken they came to Greenview, Illinois, and Mr. Aachte's first employment in his new country was in the general store of Mr. Wernsing. After six years at Greenview Mr. Aachte returned to Germany, in June, 1891, and at this time was a citizen. In November, after a pleasant visit with his parents and other relatives and friends, Mr. Aachte returned to this country, and, stopping in New York City, was for two years in the employ of Henry Vehslage, a merchant of that metropolis. Once more he came to Menard County, and was employed in the rural regions where a brother, William, was also working. Within a few months, however, he located at Petersburg, and he and Mr. Behmann bought the grocery owned by Abe Golden, December 1, 1892, the firm becoming Aachte & Behmann. On May 13, 1895, Mr. Aachte bought the interest of his partner, and continued the business under his own name until January 1, 1897, when he sold to Bergen Brothers.

In 1897 Mr. Aachte once more made a trip to Germany, where he spent the summer with his family, and again returned to the land of his adoption, and resumed his residence in Petersburg. In the spring of 1898 he bought into the dry-goods firm of Bonties Brothers, which then became Bonties, Aachte & Company. This association was dissolved when he sold to his partners, March 1, 1902, and March 11, of that same year he purchased a stable at Petersburg from Terhune, Hornback & Terhune, and went into the business of handling horses and mules, and operated quite extensively, buying and shipping to St. Louis and Chicago, as well as selling locally, but finally he sold this business to Edward E. Smoot, and invested his money in the Salem, or Chautauqua as it was also called, Mining Company, together with several other partners. That summer he for the third time went back to Germany at the request of his father, and when he returned he sold his mining interests, and resumed his horse and mule business in his old quarters. On October 22, 1904, his stable was destroyed by fire and he suffered the loss of thirty head of horses, and did not resume this business, but, August 1, 1905, bought the grocery of Samuel Salveson, and has since been conducting it, in the same building he now occupies. Mr. Aachte thoroughly understands purveying to the public, and his stocks are not only large and timely, but their quality is of the best, the prices are as low as is consistent with market quotations, and the service is excellent.

Mr. Aachte has not identified himself with fraternal work, but he is active as a member of St. Paul's Evangelical Church, has been a member of its official board for many years, and is the oldest member of the church choir in point of service. During the World war he carried his burden of the work and responsibility as a patriotic citizen, and bought war securities and contributed to various organizations to the limit of his means.

On June 22, 1898, Mr. Aachte was married in Petersburg to Miss Anna Bonties, a sister of his former partners. She was born in Petersburg November 10, 1872. Mr. and Mrs. Aachte have had the following children born to them: Gerhard, who was graduated from the Petersburg High School, was a law student in New York City for a time, but is now assistant treasurer of Claflin, Incorporated, of that city; Hermann, who is a resident of Petersburg; Louise, who is a graduate of the Petersburg High School, is associated with her father in business; John, who is also a graduate of the Petersburg High School, is associated in business with his father; and Marie, who is attending the Petersburg High School.

JOHN B. MOORE, M. D., is a physician and surgeon at Benton, founder and proprietor of one of the best equipped private hospitals in Southern Illinois. His reputation as a surgeon and hospital man was acquired in Franklin County in the early years of his practice. His experience and prestige were greatly increased by his service as an army surgeon during the World war.

The professional career of Doctor Moore for the most part has been given in the county where he was born and reared. He is a son of one of Franklin County's best known citizens, John B. Moore, Sr. The parents of John B. Moore, Sr., moved from South Carolina to Indiana, where John B. was born in Posey County in 1853. In 1861 the family settled in Franklin County. Illinois. John B. Moore, Sr., was for many years a progressive farmer in Franklin County, and is now living retired at Benton. He is best known over the county on account of his two terms of capable and efficient administrations of the office of sheriff. He served as sheriff from 1888 to 1892, his first term, and his second term was from 1898 to 1902. He married Jemima Clayton of a prominent Kentucky family.

Dr. John B. Moore was born on his father's farm near Benton April 14, 1884. His resolution to become a physician was made during his boyhood. His early advantage were supplied by country schools, after which he attended Benton High School, and in 1908 he was graduated from the University of Illinois. He graduated in 1910 from Rush Medical College of Chicago and had a year and a half of experience as an interne in the Cook County Hospital. This was followed by experience as an industrial physician. For eight months he was surgeon in the United States Steel Company's Hospital at Gary, Indiana. In 1912, Doctor Moore took charge of and reopened the hospital at Ziegler, Illinois. At that time this was the only hospital in Franklin County. The successful management of that hospital for six years greatly enhanced Doctor Moore's reputation as a capable physician and surgeon.

When America entered the World war Doctor Moore was made a member of the District Medical Advisory Board for Southern Illinois. Later he himself joined the colors as a captain in the Medical Corps and was assigned to the First Army General Hospital at Baltimore, Maryland. Toward the end of the war he was assigned to surgical group No. 10 for overseas duty, but the orders were recalled on account of the signing of the armistice. He was then sent to the General Hospital No. 26 at Fort Sheridan. On leaving the service he returned to Franklin County and in January, 1920, established a private hospital at Benton, with ten beds and operating department. The facilities of this hospital were quickly outgrown and in the spring of 1921 there were provisions for twenty-five beds, and the equipment had been brought up to the standard of the most efficient hospitals in the country. In addition to the service of the hospital Doctor Moore has many other responsibilities, being chief surgeon for the Chicago, Wilmington & Franklin Coal Company, chief surgeon of the O'Gara Coal Company, and consulting surgeon for the Peabody Coal Company, Old Ben Coal Company, United States Fuel Company, Madison Coal Corporation, Franklin Coal Company and several others. He is also local examiner for the War Veteran's Bureau. He is a member of the various medical and surgical organizations, is a Knight Templar Mason, member of the Shrine at East St. Louis, the Rotary Club and Country Club. He married Miss Agnes Gloag, a daughter of Robert Gloag.

Associated with him in the hospital and practice is now his brother, Sydney C. Moore. This brother was born on the home farm August 10, 1889. After the public schools he attended Lewis Institute in Chicago, and in 1920 was graduated in medicine and surgery from Loyola University at Chicago. During the World war he spent a year with the Field Artillery Officers' Training Camp of the Three Hundred Fifty-fourth Training Battalion. Since graduating in medicine he has been with his brother, Dr. John B.

JOHN BELL HUDGENS, cashier of the First National Bank of Goreville, is one of a family whose members have been well entitled to respect and honor they enjoy in Johnson and Williamson counties.

The locality known as the Hudgens settlement in the southern part of Williamson County was established more than a century ago. The Hudgens farm, where John Bell Hudgens was born and reared, is one of the few farms in the county which have not changed ownership during the past half century. John Hudgens, grandfather of the Goreville banker, traveled by wagon from Tennessee to Williamson County in the fall of 1816. He was the founder of what afterwards became known as the Hudgens settlement, where later the town of Hudgens was started. John Hudgens was a real pioneer, coming to Illinois in the territorial period and living for many years after Illinois became a state. Like most of the other settlers who came from Tennessee, he sought not only new and undeveloped lands, but the circumstances and environment of a portion of the old Northwest territory, and he lived to see many of his hopes and expectations realized.

Zachariah Hudgens, son of John the pioneer, and father of John Bell Hudgens, was born at the old homestead April 3, 1832. He lived on the farm a number of years, later became a merchant at Marion, being associated with the firm of Campbell, Goodall & Company, which operated several merchandise stores, commission houses and warehouses, these stores being located at Creal Springs, Goreville, Pulleysville and Marion. One of the chief articles handled by the firm in former years was tobacco. With the decline of tobacco growing in this section of Southern Illinois, Zachariah Hudgens withdrew from the firm and engaged in business for himself. As a merchant and stock raiser he continued active until his death in 1903. He had been struck by an Illinois Central train and died from the injuries about a week later. In 1874 he was elected sheriff of Williamson County and held that office four years.

Zachariah Hudgens married Mary Jane Cooksey, daughter of Ephraim Cooksey, who was also one of the first settlers in Williamson County. She was born in Smith County, Middle Tennessee, in 1821, and came to Williamson County in 1848, acquiring land from the government. The Cooksey farm later came into the possession of Zachariah Hudgens and has since been known as the Hudgens homestead. Ephraim Cooksey died in 1886. His wife was Elizabeth Phillips, a native of Virginia, where her father, Thomas Phillips, died, his family shortly afterward moving to Tennessee. Zachariah and Mary Jane (Cooksey) Hudgens reared a family of fourteen children, all of whom were born at the Hudgens homestead and all of whom lived to mature years. They all married and their homes are now widely scattered, but all of them combine in pride in keeping up the old homestead, which was the scene of their early years. It is a family distinguished by a remarkable degree of loyalty to one another. The mother, Mary Jane Hudgens, died in 1888. After her death, Zachariah Hudgens married Sarah E. Todd Allen, daughter of Peter Allen.

A brief record of the children of Zachariah and Mary Jane (Cooksey) Hudgens is as follows: Emma, now deaceased, who became the wife of Doctor Hudson of Marion; John Bell; Mary E., wife of Elbert McInturff; Nancy P., wife of H. A. Nelson; Robert L.; Hiram A.; Alice N., wife of Thomas Bradley; Joshua; Zachariah; Herman; Egbert; Hugh; Lee Roy; and Arthur, all of whom are living except Mrs. Emma Hudson and Joshua.

John Bell Hudgens as the oldest son of this large family had much work and responsibility during his boyhood years. He attended the public schools near the old farm to the age of fifteen, and has always been a reader and student and has benefited from his extensive contact with men and affairs. At the age of fifteen he began work in a store at Pulleys Mill. In 1902 the mill was removed to Goreville in Johnson County, and he continued there for three years and was then elected by the directors of the First National Bank of Goreville as cashier.

The First National Bank of Goreville is the outgrowth of a private bank started at Goreville in 1903 by Dennison, Parks and H. A. Hudgens. It was reorganized in 1905 as the First National Bank, and since then Mr. T. A. Bradley has been president. A grandson of the president, Lynn Trovillion, is bookkeeper, and Val J. Hudgens, son of John Bell Hudgens, is assistant cashier.

Mr. Hudgens married Miss Anna L. McInterff, daughter of Adam McInterff, a Williamson County farmer. She died in 1892, leaving three children, Earl, Guy and Mary Ruby. In 1894, Mr. Hudgens married Bertie Fly, daughter of Doctor Fly. The six children of this marriage are Arbie F., Val J., Wilhelma, Emma, John J. and Kay Burton.

FRED B. MILLER of Centralia is a realtor, has specialized in subdivision work, and his field of operations have been by no means confined to his immediate home locality, extending over many states.

Mr. Miller was born at Washburn, Illinois, September 29, 1877, son of Demus Moses and Mary E. (Chilton) Miller, his father a native of Ohio and his mother of Indiana. The Miller family came to Illinois in the early '70s, and his father was a merchant at Washburn until his death in 1883. In 1886 the widowed mother and her children removed to Patoka, Illinois, where she died in 1908.

Fred B. Miller, second in a family of three children, secured his high school education at Patoka and attended business college at Centralia. His first active experience was in newspaper work at Patoka, following that for a year, and was in the grocery business at the same place two years. On coming to Centralia and completing his course in the business college, he was induced to remain in the school, taking charge of the bookkeeping and higher accounting department. While connected with the business college Mr. Miller decided to engage in real estate subdivision work, and his first operation in that line was at Murphysboro, Illinois. It was profitable in results, and has led to an expansion of his business organization and facilities until his operations have extended over sixteen different states. Altogether he has put on the market and sold 161 subdivisions. Besides his business headquarters at Centralia, Mr. Miller also maintains offices in Miami, Florida, and in recent years has sold large quantities of Florida real estate. He has his winter home in Miami, while his summer residence is at Centralia.

Mr. Miller in 1926 was elected president of the Merchants State Bank of Centralia. He is also manager of the M. M. & T. T. Oil Company, which operates twenty-six producing wells, and has had an important part in developing the oil industry in Southern Illinois. Mr. Miller is a republican, belongs to the Masonic Order and B. P. O. Elks, the Rotary Club, is a director of the Centralia Chamber of Commerce, member of the Daytona Beach Chamber of Commerce in Florida and the Meadow Wood Country Club of Centralia. He enjoys travel and is a baseball fan and fond of all forms of athletics.

Mr. Miller married at Vandalia, Illinois, February 8, 1898, Miss Anna Simcox, daughter of Robert A. and Hester Simcox. The Simcox family came from Kentucky and settled in Vandalia before the Civil war. Mrs. Miller is an active member of the Woman's Club and church societies. They have one daughter, Myrtle, now the wife of Dr. F. M. Phifer of Chicago.

JAMES F. OTEY. Several of the pioneer families of Williamson and Franklin counties are related through the individual record of James F. Otey.

His father, John Fraiser Otey, was born in New Kent, Virginia, February 6, 1810. He was still a young man when he came to Illinois and settled in Franklin County, acquiring land direct from the government and developing a farm after many hardships and inconveniences. John F. Otey married in 1840, Arristine L. Mitchell, daughter of Sion H. Mitchell, who was born September 19, 1797, and his wife, Betsey Mitchell, who was born in Wilson County, Tennessee, August 27, 1819. The parents of Betsey Mitchell were William and Elizabeth Mitchell. William Mitchell was born in Franklin County, North Carolina, and as a young man went to Tennessee where he married February 25, 1817, Elizabeth Cook, daughter of Jacob and Elizabeth Cook, who were natives of North Carolina. Elizabeth Cook was born in Franklin County, North Carolina, November 12, 1793.

John F. and Arristine (Mitchell) Otey were the parents of ten children: Matilda C., Marinda E., Sion M., James F., Warren N., Za-

dock G., Clinton E., Harriet A., Luella J., and Mary Arristine. Matilda, Marinda, Zadock, Warren and Harriet died in childhood.

James F. Otey was born near Corinth, in Williamson County, Illinois, July 26, 1846. His active life was devoted to farming and he was one of the prosperous and respected citizens of his county. He married Carolina Edwards.

The first member of this branch of the Edwards family to come to America was Thomas Edwards, who was born in the latter part of the seventeenth century in Wales and settled in Virginia in 1720. He married at Baltimore, Maryland. His son Cadie was born in Virginia and moved to North Carolina. William Edwards, son of Cadie, was born in 1776. John M. Edwards, son of William, was born February 13, 1799, in Orange County, North Carolina, and he married Susan Brown, who was born October 26, 1803, in Montgomery County, Maryland. John M. and Susan (Brown) Edwards were the parents of James M. Edwards, who was born April 30, 1824, and married Elizabeth Jane Hackney. One of their children was Carolina (Edwards) Otey.

James F. Otey and Caroline (Edwards) Otey had a family of seven children, six of whom are now living.

Their son Charles Otey was born December 23, 1879, on the home farm near Corinth, attended rural schools and the Crab Orchard Academy for two years, and later Valparaiso University of Indiana. He was graduated from the law department of the University of Kentucky in 1912. He was for three and a half years deputy county clerk of Marion, and in 1916 became identified with the Williamson County Loan & Improvement Company as its secretary and manager. He married Bertha Neely, daughter of Judge Rufus Neely of Marion.

The Williamson County Loan & Improvement Company was organized in 1907 by L. O. Caplinger, Judge Rufus Neely, W. O. Hartwell and others. It has exercised a tremendous power in financing and otherwise contributing to the general improvement and development of the community. Its original authorized capital was one million dollars and this was increased in 1923 to ten million dollars. The financial statement of March 31, 1926, showed assets of $831,140.23. The present officers are: L. O. Caplinger, president, Ed M. Stotlar, vice president, Charley Otey, secretary, and William Wohlwend, treasurer.

HENRY H. SCHIRDING, retired farmer and banker of Petersburg, Illinois, has spent three quarters of a century or more in that section of the state.

He was born in Hanover, Germany, October 12, 1833, son of J. Henry Schirding, who brought his family to the United States and settled near Petersburg in 1848, the first home of the family being a one-room cabin, 16 by 18 feet. J. Henry Schirding lived on his farm there until the last few months of his life. He died at Petersburg in March and his wife in May, 1893, both of them very old, he ninety-eight years and seven months, and she eighty-nine years and five months of age. They were members of the Evangelical Lutheran Church, while in politics he was a democrat. He was a plain industrious citizen, learned the English language only imperfectly, and was a good honest citizen. He and his wife had two sons, John Herman, dying in 1885 at the age of fifty-five.

Henry H. Schirding never attended school after coming to this country. He worked as a hired man on the farm and in other capacities, engaged in farming at the homestead, and remained there engaged in farming and stock raising for the greater part of his active career. The old Schirding homestead still remains in his name. He was a stock breeder, shipping his own hogs and cattle to the Chicago market, and gave his close personal supervision to the business on the farm until 1892. Since then his home has been at Petersburg.

Mr. Schirding was elected four times a commissioner of Menard County, filling that office twelve years. While he was on the Board the County Farm Home was built. He was a member of the school board of his district and for many years was a deacon in the Evangelical Church. He and his son Harry established the Schirding Bank, a private institution, which later was chartered as a state bank with capital of $100,000. Mr. Schirding was president of the bank while it was a private institution and also under the state charter, while his son Harry is vice president, with Fred T. Jurgens cashier.

Mr. Schirding married, June 26, 1864, Miss Mary Behmann, daughter of John Behmann. She was born in Hanover, Germany, March 31, 1838, and came to the United States with friends in 1860. She died March 24, 1908, and of her three children the only one now living is Harry Schirding.

JOSEPH L. GILL, a native of Chicago, born and reared in the Lake View section of the North Side, where he has always lived, has had a career of success both in business and politics.

He was born in 1885, son of Richard and Bridget (Sweeney) Gill. His parents were born in County Mayo, Ireland, but were brought to Chicago when children. Joseph L. Gill comes of a large family, having three brothers, Richard P. Gill, a captain in the Chicago Police Department, James A. Gill, assistant treasurer of the William Wrigley, Jr., Company, chewing gum manufacturers, and Frank A., and four sisters, Mary, Lauretta, Ann and Eleanor.

Joseph L. Gill was educated in public schools and the Metropolitan Business College, and for a number of years has been engaged in the general insurance business, his insurance offices being at 175 West Jackson Boulevard. Mr. Gill has filled a number of positions in county and city public life. He was for eight years chief clerk of the county treasurer's office. For six years he was comptroller of the Forest Preserve District of Cook County, and is now valuator of that commission. In his home locality he began taking an interest and influential part in democratic politics when a young man, and his leadership is now recognized throughout Cook County. He has been democratic ward committeeman for the Forty-sixth Ward since the enactment of the Direct Primary law. He is secretary of the County Central Committee of Cook County. In the general primaries of April, 1926, he was awarded the Democratic nomination for representative in the State Legislature in the Thirty-first Senatorial District.

Mr. Gill has been active in sports, being a golfer, bowler, hand-ball player and base ball fan. He is a member of DeSoto Council, Knights of Columbus, B. P. O. Elks and Lake Shore Athletic Club. He married Miss Bertha Marie Fogarty, of Springfield. Mrs. Gill is a sister of Mrs. George E. Brennan of Chicago.

CHARLES CLIFTON REID, physician and surgeon, for many years a recognized leader in his profession at Denver, Colorado, is a son of the late William Michael and Bethany Jane (Spiller) Reid, of Marion, Illinois. A full account of the family in Southern Illinois and his earlier ancestry is given elsewhere in this publication.

Doctor Reid was born at Marion, Illinois, February 28, 1873, attended country schools near Marion, spent three years in the Southern Illinois State Normal University at Carbondale, and in 1899 was one of the early graduates from the American School of Osteopathy at Kirksville, Missouri. He practiced osteopathy two years at Warren, Ohio, one year at Worcester, Massachusetts, and since then has been located at Denver. In June, 1905, he graduated M. D. from the Denver Homeopathic Medical College. He has been a deep student of his profession and has utilized his own experience for his advancement and the improvement of his skill and technique. For fifteen years he has pursued the policy of taking post-graduate work every year. He is a specialist in eye, ear, nose and throat. He has been active in the professional organizations, and during the World war, being too old for active military duty, he taught first aid classes under the supervision of the Red Cross. In 1918 he was a director in the Metropolitan State Bank of Denver.

Doctor Reid's hobby and chief financial interest outside of his profession is Black Silver Fox farming, and he has a silver fox ranch. He served as president of the Denver Lions Club in 1917-18, and was president of the International Association of Lions Clubs in 1920-21. He is a democrat in principle, though his votes have frequently disregarded party lines. He is affiliated with Temple Lodge No. 84 at Denver, Denver Chapter No. 2, Royal Arch Masons, Colorado Commandery No. 1 Knights Templar, Rocky Mountain Consistory No. 2 of the Scottish Rite, and El Jebel Temple of the Mystic Shrine. He is also a member of the Y. M. C. A., Mount Vernon Country Club and Rocky Mountain Country Club, and is active in the Central Christian Church at Denver, in which he has taught the young people's Bible class for twenty-three years.

Doctor Reid married at Denver, May 23, 1907, Miss Frances Laura Argall. Her father, Phillip Argall, who became a noted mining engineer, was born in Cornwall, England, lived for some years in Ireland, and married an Irish girl, and on coming to America was located at Leadville, Colorado, and later at Denver. His name is well known to all mining engineers as the originator of the Cyanide process of separating ores. Among his family of ten children, one is a son George O., now head of a mining industry at Leadville.

Dr. and Mrs. Reid have three children, Phillip Clifton, Homer Argall and Ellen Jane, all attending high school.

CRILLON E. WHITE is sheriff of Jackson County. As a public official he has found satisfaction in rendering good service, but has been more sensible of the esteem and confidence felt for him by his fellow citizens than by any idea of personal political power and prestige. Mr. White never sought political office. Nevertheless, he was elected sheriff of Jackson County on the democratic ticket by a majority of 1,296 when that county normally is 2,000 republican.

Mr. White is a representative of the fine American stock that came out of the upland region of the State of North Carolina. His grandfather, William White, moved from that state and settled on a farm near Salem, Illinois. His son, Daniel J. White was a year old when the family came to Illinois. Daniel J. White became a gunsmith, and in 1860 located at Carbondale, where he continued the work of his trade until his death in 1905. He married Ailsa Jane Couch, a native of Lincoln County, Tennessee, who died in 1920.

Crillon E. White was born at Carbondale March 14, 1870. His regular school advantages were continued only as far as the eighth grade. At the age of fourteen he became office boy and bookkeeper in a little grist mill, then operated by Collins Wilson. His salary was fifty cents a day. During the two years he worked there he also attended night school. Desiring to learn a good trade he apprenticed himself as a machinist in the Watson Machine Shops, where he remained a year. For two years following he was with the Graham Milling Company, beginning at fifty cents a day. At that time, as well as since, he showed his determination to master any occupation assigned him. When he decided to leave the Graham Company to join his father, he was offered the position of third miller at $2.50 per day, at that time a very generous salary. However, he was nineteen years of age, and eager to get into business for himself. He and his father and his brother Walter bought a blacksmith shop, and this business is still continued by Walter White.

Mr. Crillon White moved to Murphysboro in 1910. For four years he was deputy sheriff under C. T. Edwards. Following that he became a deputy Internal Revenue collector, and while in that service improved his opportunity to study the income tax, utilizing a correspondence course as a means thereto, and achieved more than a local reputation for his thorough knowledge of the income tax law. Mr. White resigned from the Internal Revenue service in 1920 to accept appointment as postmaster of Murphysboro. He held this office twenty-one months. In 1922 he entered the campaign as democratic candidate for sheriff, and achieved the remarkable results

Edward G Dunne

already mentioned. After his election he took a vacation of four months, the first real vacation he had had since he was fourteen years of age. Mr. White has made a splendid record as sheriff, his term closing in 1926. His name is now being urged as a candidate for county treasurer.

Mr. White married Miss Effie C. Davis, daughter of John Davis. They have two children. The daughter Ailsa Agatha White graduated from the Illinois Normal University, and for the past six years has been a teacher in the public schools of Murphysboro. The son, C. Edgar White, is a member of the class of 1927 in the law school of Northwestern University at Chicago. Mr. White's early ambition was to become a professional man. Lack of opportunity to complete a high education turned his career into other channels. However, he has seen that his son and daughter are not similarly handicapped. Mr. White generously bestows upon his wife much of the credit for his success and happiness.

ROBERT W. DOW is president of the W. H. Dow Manufacturing Company of Waukegan, an industry that was established by his father about the time of the Civil war and which for half a century or more has been one of the reliable sources of Waukegan's industrial prosperity.

His father was the late William H. Dow, who was born and reared at Rutland, Vermont. His father came from England and his maternal ancestors were Scotch. William H. Dow was left an orphan at the age of twelve years and after a brief schooling went to work for a carpenter, learning the trade. He came west in 1864 and located at Waukegan. Possessing the skill and ingenuity of a Yankee, but with limited capital, he set up a small shop operating a jig saw run by horse power. He made brackets and other scroll work used in building construction in those days. In a few years he was operating a general saw mill plant employing several men, and that became the foundation of the present W. H. Dow Manufacturing Company, now one of the largest plants of its kind in Northern Illinois. The plant now occupied by the company is the third since the founding of the business. This plant is a three story building, covering two acres of ground, and more than a hundred people are employed. The output is interior finish, sash and doors, and it is sold and distributed over a territory with a radius of a hundred miles around Waukegan. William H. Dow, the founder of the business, died in 1906. He married Amarilla M. Vose, who died in August, 1924. She was born in the state of Maine and was a child when brought to Waukegan, where she attended the public schools. Her parents were Robert E. and Relief Vose, who took up a farm from the government on coming to Lake County. Her father farmed for a number of years and later became associated with the W. H. Dow Company, working in the plant until about 1884 when he was accidentally injured. The injury resulted in blood poisoning and caused his death.

Robert W. Dow was born at Waukegan, January 4, 1874. He was educated in the grade and high schools, graduating from high school and also taking a course in the Stratton College of Chicago. For several years during vacations and holidays he had worked in his father's plant, and after leaving school he went to work there as a regular employee, at first a shipping clerk and later in various positions in the office. He became vice president, holding that office when his father died, and succeeded to the presidency of the firm, a position he has now held for twenty years. He has guided the business successfully through the changing conditions of this period, and it is more prosperous than ever.

Mr. Dow is affiliated with the B. P. O. Elks, Royal Arcanum, served one term as alderman of Waukegan, is a republican in politics and a member of the Episcopal Church.

He married February 22, 1902, Miss Cora E. Cooper of Waukegan, who was educated in the grammar and high schools of that city and in the Godschalk School of Music of New York. Mrs. Dow is active in church and club life at Waukegan. Her parents, James F. and Mary E. (Bills) Cooper, were early settlers in Lake County and farmers there. Mr. and Mrs. Dow have three children, Dorothy A., now deceased; Mary Elizabeth and William H. Mary Elizabeth graduated from the Waukegan High School in 1920, from Miss Mason's School at Tarrytown, New York, and is now secretary to her father and secretary and treasurer of the W. H. Dow Manufacturing Company. The son, William H., is a member of the high school class of 1927, and plans to continue his education in the University of Illinois.

EDWARD G. DUNNE, a native Chicagoan, whose name has frequently been associated with important real estate transactions during the past decade, is founder and active head of the Edward G. Dunne Realty Association.

Mr. Dunne was born in Chicago in 1883, son of John G. and Anna (Savage) Dunne. Since completing his education in the public schools and the Bryant & Stratton Business College, Mr. Dunne has had a business association and experience that has made him familiar with the broader activities of the Chicago District, and has brought him an extended acquaintance with men and affairs. Since 1915, he has been engaged in real estate operations, and in 1926 founded the Edward G. Dunne Realty Association. The main offices of this association are in the New Metropolitan Building at LaSalle and Randolph streets. Mr. Dunne is personally owner of subdivision property in Chicago's metropolitan area valued at over $600,000. The outstanding feature of the Edward G. Dunne Realty Association's programs is a tract of land in the famous North Shore district known as Green Bay Lawn, a tract that has been subdivided into choice home sites in a location with obvious advantages of proximity to some of the oldest and most exclusive suburban towns of the North Shore and accessible to the unrivalled transportation facilities there.

Mr. Dunne has been prominent in Catholic circles in Chicago, and was one of the originators of the idea of a great club in Chicago for Catholics exclusively. Through his activities and influence with high Catholic dignitaries and wealthy laymen of the church, he was successful in launching this notable project, which is known as the Frontenac Athletic Club, and Mr. Dunne has been head of the organized forces providing for the memberships and financing of the club, which will be one of the largest and most notable additions to Chicago's towering structures. Mr. Dunne is a parishioner of St. Gertrude's Church, and a member of the Knights of Columbus and the Columbian Country Club.

His home is at 6303 Kenmore Avenue. He married Alice L. Sweeney, daughter of former Alderman John Sweeney. They have one daughter, Virginia M. Dunne.

JAMES V. BLANEY, Chicago physician, was born at Newcastle, Maryland, in 1820, and died at Chicago in 1876. He graduated from Princeton University at the age of eighteen, and at twenty-one from Jefferson Medical College. In 1843 he accepted the chair of chemistry and materia medica in the first faculty of Rush Medical College, and that was the beginning of his long residence in Chicago. In connection with his work at the college he carried on a private practice. He was editing chief of the Illinois and Indiana Medical Journal, the first medical periodical published in this section of the West. He was one of the founders of the County Medical Society, and as one of its delegates, in 1850, helped in founding the Illinois State Medical Society, of which he was later president. During the Civil war he was medical director and medical inspector at Fortress Monroe, and in 1864 was made medical purveyor with large responsibilities at Chicago, a service which gained him the rank of lieutenant colonel. He succeeded Daniel Brainard as president of Rush Medical College. He was an active member of the Chicago Historical Society.

H. CLINTON BURNETT is president of the Waukegan National Bank. That is an institution that thoroughly reflects the growing prosperity and commercial power and strength of this industrial community in Northeastern Illinois. Mr. Burnett was one of the organizers and founders of the bank, and has been closely identified with its official management from the beginning.

He is a native of Waukegan and served his banking apprenticeship there. He was born August 31, 1874, son of George H. and Sarah A. (Seever) Burnett. His grandparents were Amzi and Johanna (Granger) Burnett, the former a native of Lyons, New York, where he was born, reared and married. In 1841, Amzi Burnett brought his family to Lake County, Illinois, and entered land from the Government in the vicinity of Wauconda, developing a farm on which he lived until his retirement. He spent his last years at Antioch, Illinois, where he died in 1885. His son, George H. Burnett, was born at Lyons, New York, but from the age of twelve was reared in Lake County, Illinois, attending the public school there and the academy at Waukegan. He learned the trade of gunsmith. When the Civil war came on he joined the Ninety-sixth Illinois Infantry and participated with his regiment in a number of campaigns and engagements, including Lookout Mountain and Chickamauga. He was once wounded in action. After the war he returned to Waukegan and followed his trade and business until retirement in 1905. He died in 1923. George H. Burnett's wife, Sarah A. Seever, was born and reared in Lake County, attending public schools there and Waukegan Academy, and for some years prior to her marriage taught in her home county. She died in 1920. Her parents were Abraham and Delilah (Marble) Seever, the former a native of New York State who came West from the Mohawk Valley about 1841, and likewise was an early settler in Lake County, Illinois. As a young man he had worked on the Erie Canal, but after coming to Illinois he followed farming until his retirement in 1880. He then moved to Waukegan and died in that city in 1897. George H. and Sarah Burnett became the parents of seven children, three of whom died in childhood, H. Clinton being the third in age. He has one brother, Seever H., and two sisters, Mrs. Josie B. Wilder and Mrs. Carolyn B. Thomas, still living. His brother Seever is in the United States Postal service at Waukegan and married Ella Denbo of Brookfield, Missouri, and has a daughter, Mary Denbo. Josie B. Wilder is the wife of Herbert G. Wilder, an electrical engineer with the Cyclone Fence Company of Waukegan, and has one child, George. Mrs. Carolyn Thomas is the wife of Harry M. Thomas, who is connected with the Johns-Manville Company at Waukegan.

H. Clinton Burnett graduated from the Waukegan High School in 1894, the following year completed a course in the Metropolitan Business College at Chicago, and since then has had thirty years in which to try out and test his qualifications for practical service. For two years, from 1895 to 1897, he was bookkeeper for a grocery at Waukegan. Since then his work and experience have been banking. He entered the First National Bank of Waukegan as messenger, was promoted to bookkeeper, assistant cashier, and continued with the bank until 1913. In that year he resigned, and became identified with a group of progressive Waukegan men in the organization of the Waukegan National Bank. Some of his associates were Willard R. Wiard, who was also an assistant cashier of the First National Bank. Others were J. W. Barwell, J. P. Arthus, F. W. Buck, C. W. Diver, N. H. Brown, F. C. Gedge, T. E. Morris, George W. Sells, D. T. Webb and L. J. Yager.

The Waukegan National Bank started with a capital of $100,000. It now has a capital of $250,000, surplus of $150,000, and its deposits are over $4,000,000. Few banks in the Middle West in thirteen years have enjoyed such notable growth and expansion. Mr. Burnett was elected vice president of the bank upon its organization in 1913, and since 1923 has been president. He is also a director of the Blatchford Calf Meal Company and the Pure Water Ice Company. During the World war he was chairman of the Lake County Liberty Loan campaign, serving the Government in all the different loan drives.

His friends and associates have much admired him for his public spirited attitude in

all matters affecting his home community. He is a member of the Masonic order, B. P. O. Elks, Modern Woodmen of America, Rotary Club, Glen Flora Country Club, Bonnie Brook Country Club, and in politics is a republican and a Baptist in religious affiliations.

He married at Waukegan, November 21, 1900, Miss Bessie Brown, who was educated in grammar and high schools at Chicago and Metropolitan Business College in that city. Mrs. Burnett takes an active part in church affairs, in the Woman's Club, in the Victory Memorial Hospital and Hattie Barwell Good Fellowship Settlement. She is a daughter of William and Mary (Robinson) Brown. Her father was an engineer in Chicago and in later life moved to Waukegan, where he died in 1922. Mrs. Burnett's mother now lives in Chicago. Mr. and Mrs. Burnett have one son, Clinton B. Burnett, who graduated from the Waukegan High School with the class of 1926, standing thirteen in a class of 161. He is now in college, and during vacations has had some working experience in his father's bank, and plans to pursue a banking career.

CARL H. WEBER was trained for the law but the greater part of his business experience has been in the field of banking. His home is in Springfield and he is now Assistant Chief Bank Examiner of State Banks. He is also a veteran of the World War.

Mr. Weber was born in Jacksonville. His father, Herman Weber, for forty-five years from 1878 was a well known grocery merchant. Born in Baden, Germany, he came to this country in 1871 at the age of sixteen and located in Jacksonville where he earned success, not only as a merchant, but as a leader in civic affairs. He was the first mayor of South Jacksonville and served several terms in that office. His death occurred at the age of sixty-seven.

Oldest in a family of four sons and two daughters, Carl H. Weber had some years working experience and training in his father's business. In the meantime he attended the Jacksonville High School from which he was graduated in 1906, and finished his law course several years later.

For nearly six years Mr. Weber was associated with F. G. Farrell and Company, Bankers of Jacksonville, serving in various clerical and executive capacities.

Upon the reorganization of the local Chamber of Commerce, Mr. Weber was chosen secretary in which capacity he served the community with credit for two years. He then became Deputy County Clerk and Probate Clerk of Morgan County.

The World War coming on, he volunteered in the Enlisted Ordnance Corps and after an intensive training at Camp Hancock, Georgia, he spent one year in France as Ordnance Sergeant in the First Army Ammunition Section, serving on the Toul Defensive Sector and in the St. Mihiel and Meuse-Argonne Offensives.

After his return from abroad he accepted a position as State Bank Examiner under Andrew Russel, Auditor of Public Accounts, and on January 1, 1921, he was commissioned Assistant Chief Bank Examiner and given joint supervision of 1186 Illinois State Banks outside of Cook County.

Mr. Weber served as Grand Patriarch of the Grand Encampment, I. O. O. F., and is Grand Representative to the Sovereign Grand Lodge of Odd Fellows. He also belongs to the Masons, Elks and American Legion.

In 1913 Mr. Weber married Miss Hattie Adams, daughter of John E. and Della (Talley) Adams. Her mother is now the widow of John Wesley Chipchase, who was a foreman in the J. Capps and Sons clothing manufacturing establishment at Jacksonville for more than twenty-five years.

Mrs. Weber is a graduate of the Jacksonville High School and attended Illinois College. For several years before her marriage she taught in the public schools.

Mr. and Mrs. Weber are active members of the Central Baptist Church in Springfield.

They have four children, Rex Adams, Virginia Adams, Marion Adams and Carl Herman, Jr.

W. HAYDEN BELL. This is a name that has become prominent in recent years in connection with Chicago real estate operations and building. Mr. Bell's experience has been always on the constructive side of real estate development. The reason for this is because he began his business career as a contractor and has to his credit a series of successful operations involving every phase of changing vacant land into home building sites and residence and business subdivisions.

Mr. Bell was born at Kansas City, Missouri, in 1890, and when six months of age was brought to Chicago by his parents, William H. and Celeste (Macmillan) Bell. His father was born in Virginia, of old Virginia ancestry. W. Hayden Bell was reared and acquired his education at Chicago. At the age of twenty-one he started out boldly in business for himself as a contractor, his first capital constituting only thirty-three dollars. Contracting naturally took him into subdivision development work. His first important achievement in this line was in the southwest Evanston district, where he bought a twenty-three acre tract on Ridge Boulevard across the street from St. Francis Hospital. It is now, thanks to Mr. Bell's initiative, one of the high class residence sections of Evanston. Following that he developed two other tracts in the same general locality.

His largest and most important development and building project, starting late in 1925, is a fifty-five acre tract at the corner of Archer and Kedzie avenues. This program involved the building of houses in units of one hundred, the total number approximating four hundred. The plan is to complete the program in 1927.

One of the most notable features of this undertaking is the surprising fact that such a tract of land, hitherto undeveloped, could be found in the Chicago district within approximately five miles of the center of the Loop, and yet immediately adjacent to the immense central manufacturing district, and only across the street from the great plant of the Crane Company. Mr. Bell had the imagination as well as the constructive business foresight to visualize the possibilities of an area that has been lacking in every attraction for residence purposes. Under his direction the underground improvements were carried out, and landscaping done involving the planting of trees and gardens, changing the scene into a beauty spot. The residences are all two-story apartment buildings of brick construction, with every equipment and facility found in modern homes. The houses also present a handsome architectural appearance and are of varied types of architecture, thus escaping the monotony usually characteristic of similar city communities.

At the same time Mr. Bell is erecting two business structures at Forty-third Street and Archer Avenue, each costing $100,000, the ground floors being used for stores and with apartments on the second floor. On January 1, 1927, Mr. Bell proposes to start in the construction of some very high class cooperative apartments and the first unit of this new departure will be the erection of a twenty-story cooperative apartment building. Having already constructed several hundred dwellings in the city, Mr. Bell is thoroughly acquainted with the housing needs of a great city and has the background of a most successful experience to work from. In conjunction with famous architects it is his purpose to provide the most modern, up to date apartments to be found in the United States and by devoting his time, energy and experience to this new departure, the ultimate success of the undertaking is assured in advance. Mr. Bell is a member of the Chicago Real Estate Board, belongs to the Illinois Athletic Club, is a York Rite Mason and Shriner and a member of the Medinah Country and Crystal Lake Country Clubs. His home is in River Forest. He married Miss Frances Marston of Chicago and they have two sons, Frank Marston Bell and James William Bell.

FRED H. LUECKE, division manager for the Central Illinois Public Service Company at Beardstown, has given most of his active life to public utility work, and is familiar with all the practical phases from construction to business management.

He was born in the village of Hustisford, Wisconsin, February 3, 1890. His grandfather, Fred Luecke, was a native of Germany, came to the United States during the '40s, and married a Miss Stocks, who followed him to this country. They were farmers in the vicinity of Sheboygan, Wisconsin. Of their eight sons and one daughter, one of the older is Christian H. Luecke, who was born in the vicinity of Sheboygan, Wisconsin, in March, 1861, and for many years has been a cheese manufacturer at Plymouth. He married Almeda Hicks, daughter of Fred and Rebecca (Putnam) Hicks, her mother being a distant relative of the Revolutionary soldier, Isaac Putnam. Almeda Hicks was born in Michigan, while her parents came from New York State. Fred H. Luecke is the oldest of his parents' children. His sister, Henrietta, lives at Plymouth, Wisconsin; Mrs. Emily Larson, also of Plymouth; and his brother Frank is associated with his father in business.

Fred H. Luecke grew up at Plymouth, attended city schools there, including high school, and completed a course in a business college at Sheboygan, Wisconsin. In the course of his practical work he also did correspondence studies in engineering at Girard, Illinois, he had his first experience in public utility work as a lineman's helper in the telegraph department of the Chicago, Burlington & Quincy Railroad. After eighteen months he returned home, worked for two years as an electrician's helper around Plymouth, and at Green Bay, Wisconsin, spent over three years with the Wisconsin Public Service Company, at first as an electrician and finally as superintendent of a transmission line. Coming back after that to Illinois he was employed as superintendent of construction for the Central Illinois Utilities Company, and when the work was completed he remained as superintendent of the electrical department, and finally as general superintendent of the company. When this company sold its property and franchises to the Central Illinois Public Service Company, the plant becoming a division of the new company, Mr. Luecke was retained as division manager, and in the fall of 1920 was transferred to Beardstown as division manager.

Mr. Luecke has taken an active and public-spirited part in the affairs of Beardstown. Upon the reorganization of the Chamber of Commerce he was elected its first president and is now serving his first term. He is a charter member and has been a director of the Rotary and Country Clubs. In Masonry he has affiliation with the Blue Lodge at Gilman, the Royal Arch Chapter at Gilman, and the Knight Templar Commandery at Paxton, and Ansar Shrine at Springfield. He was registered under the selective service act during the World war and for a brief time was connected with the fuel administration at Paxton. He cast his first presidential vote for Woodrow Wilson at Green Bay, Wisconsin, and is a member of the Congregational Church.

Mr. Luecke married at St. Louis, June 17, 1913, Miss Mabel Boylan, who was born at Allenton, Missouri, and educated in public schools there. Her father, John Boylan, was a Missouri farmer. Mr. and Mrs. Luecke have one son, John Christian, born in April, 1915.

GEORGE WASHINGTON SMITH, head of the Department of History in the State Teachers College, Carbondale, Illinois, and author of the "History of Illinois and Her People," as published in this work, is a native Illinoisan. He was born near Greenfield, Greene County, November 13, 1855.

Daniel Smith, a Virginian, of Patrick County, was born about 1740. He was the eldest of these brothers, namely: Daniel, John, Peter and Flemon. These brothers were all engaged in the battle of Cowpens, fought January 17, 1781.

During the earlier years of the Revolutionary war Daniel married a Miss Reeves, and from this marriage there were born six children, as follows: Charles, Mollie, Peter, Elizabeth, James and John M. The last named son, John, was the grandfather of Professor Smith. John M. Smith was born in Henry County, Virginia, April 23, 1781. He married Rachel Packwood in Patrick County, Virginia, about the year 1800 or 1802. The Packwoods were a numerous people in Virginia and helped to subdue the savages and the wilderness. Rachel Packwood's grandfather was captured by the Indians on Greenbrier River, a branch of the Great Kanawha, in 1710, taken to Chilicothe, Ohio, and there burned at the stake in the presence of relatives and neighbors.

From the marriage of John M. Smith and Rachel Packwood there were born twelve children—Nancy, Samuel, Daniel, Stephen, Edith, Larkin, Elizabeth, Rachel, Exoney, Polly, Lucy and John.

Stephen Smith, the fourth child of John M. Smith, was the father of Professor Smith. He was born in Patrick County, Virginia, May 23, 1809. When about two years old his parents moved to Cumberland County, Kentucky, and settled on Mud Camp Creek, a tributary of the Cumberland River. Here Stephen grew to young manhood. He worked much in the timber and in the building of flat-boats. He was an expert axeman and skilled in boat-building. He made several trips to New Orleans with flat-boats prior to 1838. On the 13th of September, 1836, he married Sallie Martin Pace, a young lady who lived in the valley of Marrowbone Creek, which flowed parallel to Mud Camp Creek. At the mouth of Marrowbone Creek was the town of Burksville, the county seat of Cumberland County.

Sallie M. Pace represented a family name which had been familiar to the people of Virginia since the days of the Virginia massacre in 1622. She was born February 22, 1816. Her grandfather, Capt. John Pace, was born in Henry County, Virginia, May 28, 1751, and died August 20, 1825. He was a captain in the Revolutionary war. His son, John Pace, was born January 1, 1787, and died October 11, 1823. He was the father of Sallie Martin Pace, the mother of Professor Smith.

John Pace married Nancy Alexander, who was born March 13, 1793, and died September 9, 1844. From this marriage there were born eight children—Milly, Lucy, Greenville, Sally, Frances, Robert, Julia and Elizabeth. Sally M. Pace married Stephen Smith, and they became the parents of nine children: Thomas, Greenville, Nancy, Edward, James, William, John, George and Mattie.

The Alexanders were prominent people in Cumberland County, Virginia. They were of Scotch descent and were from the "Campbell Clan." John Alexander married Maryart Gleason, in Glasgow, Scotland, in 1735. They came to Nottingham, Chester County, Pennsylvania, and from there to Carlisle, Pennsylvania, and then to Berkeley County, Virginia. Two nephews of John Alexander migrated to Mecklenburg County, North Carolina, and they and their descendants took part in the signing of the Mecklenburg Declaration of Independence, May, 1775, five Alexanders signing that document.

Capt. John Alexander was born in Berkeley County, Virginia, in 1741, and moved to Cumberland County, Kentucky, in 1805. His oldest son married Mollie Ramey, and their daughter, Nancy, married John Pace, the son of Capt. John Pace.

Stephen Smith and his wife and two children moved from Cumberland County, Kentucky, and settled nine miles east of White Hall in Greene County, Illinois, in 1840. The homestead was seven miles northwest of Greenfield. Here they lived a full half century and reared a large and respectable family of nine children. The three oldest sons, Thomas, Greenville and Edward, served in the Civil war. The first two served in Company D, Thirty-second Regiment, Illinois Volunteers. The colonel was Dr. John Logan, a cousin of Gen. John A. Logan. Of this large family of nine children only the four youngest are still living.

George, the subject of this sketch, was a lad of six when the Civil war began. He remembers many incidents of that conflict and often wrote letters to his older brothers who were "in the war." He attended the country schools and recalls with pleasure Miss Winnie Beason, Miss Sarah Mason, Capt. John Parks and Esquire Richard Short, his teachers. The schoolhouse was on the corner of his father's farm and was therefore easy of access.

In the fall of 1874 the subject of this sketch entered Blackburn University, Carlinville, Illinois. Here he pursued advanced studies for one year, when he was obliged to leave the college to take up teaching. After teaching for two years he again entered college for a year only. He again engaged in teaching. He never ceased studying and usually attended some good school during the summer months. As a result of this continued application to his studies he was able to pass the state examination for life certificate in the summer of 1884.

So well known was the character of the work of Professor Smith as student and as teacher that the Board of Trustees of Blackburn University, at its annual meeting in 1892, honored him by conferring on him the honorary degree of Master of Arts. This action was taken by the Board of Trustees without the knowledge of the recipient. Professor Smith has a warm place in his heart for his Alma Mater, "Old Blackburn."

Professor Smith had taught for six years in the best rural schools in the county, and in the fall of 1883 he was elected principal of the White Hall High School. In the spring of 1884 he was elected superintendent of schools of Perry, Pike County. Before taking up his duties in Perry he married Miss Nellie Adams, a popular teacher of White Hall.

Miss Adams was a direct descendant of Governor William Bradford of Plymouth, Massachusetts. She was therefore eligible to membership in the "Daughters of the Mayflower." Governor Bradford's son by his second wife was Maj. William Bradford, whose third son, Thomas, married Anne Smith. His son, James married Edith ———, and their daughter, Sarah, married Joseph Adams, the fifth in descent from Henry Adams of Devonshire, England, and the great-great-grandfather of John Adams, the second president of the United States. James Adams, the son of Joseph Adams and Sarah Bradford, married Jerusha Knight of Lisbon, Connecticut. Their son, Elisha, married Clarissa Cook, and their son, Edwin R. Adams, married Perses Ellen Parsons, of Chardon, Ohio, May 8, 1844. Three daughters were born to this union, Fannie, Nellie and Nettie. Nellie Adams was therefore the eighth in descent from Governor William Bradford and ninth in descent from Henry Adams of Braintree.

The year's work in the Perry schools was very successful and Professor Smith was re-employed at an increase in salary, but on July 24, 1885, his wife died, leaving a son, Clyde. Professor Smith resigned his position at Perry and taught in the White Hall schools for the year 1885-86. In the spring of 1886 he was elected superintendent of the White Hall schools, where he remained for the next four years.

In the summer of 1890 Professor Smith accepted a position in the faculty of the State Normal at Carbondale. In 1897 he became head of the Department of History, which position he has now held thirty years.

Professor Smith has kept in close touch with public school work. He arranged the work in history for the state course of study recently published by the State Teachers' Association. He is the author of a very popular text on Illinois history, and has prepared manuscripts for other books.

On June 16, 1888, Professor Smith was united in marriage with Miss Nettie C. Adams, the younger sister of his first wife. Clyde, the son from the first marriage, is a business man in Carbondale. He married Miss Mary Powers, of Owensboro, Kentucky. They have one daughter, Jean Catherine, who is now a student in high school. From the second marriage there are three children, Helen Christine, Eugene Russell and Frances Adams. They were all graduated from the Teachers College and have all taught.

Professor and Mrs. Smith live among a host of friends, and have always been active in all forward-looking enterprises in their home city.